The
CHELSEA HOUSE LIBRARY
_of_ LITERARY CRITICISM

_____The_____
CHELSEA HOUSE LIBRARY
of LITERARY CRITICISM

The
MAJOR AUTHORS EDITION
of the
NEW MOULTON'S LIBRARY *of* LITERARY CRITICISM

Volume 1

Medieval—Late Renaissance

General Editor
HAROLD BLOOM

1985
CHELSEA HOUSE PUBLISHERS
New York
Philadelphia

MANAGING EDITOR
Sally Stepanek

ASSOCIATE EDITORS
Brendan Bernhard
S. T. Joshi
Frank Menchaca
Patrick Nielsen Hayden
Anna Williams
Joanna Wissinger

EDITORIAL COORDINATOR
Karyn Browne

EDITORIAL STAFF
Linda Grossman
Joy Johannessen
Karin Thomsen

RESEARCH
Debbie Keates
Kevin Pask
Cornelia Pearsall
Marijke Rijsberman
Doug Smith

PICTURE RESEARCH
Juliette Dickstein

DESIGN
Susan Lusk

10 9 8 7 6 5 4 3 2

Library of Congress Cataloging in Publication
Data
The Major authors edition of the New Moulton's library of literary criticism.
(The Chelsea House library of literary criticism)
Bibliography: p.
1. English literature—History and criticism—Collected works. 2. American literature—History and criticism—Collected works. I. Bloom, Harold. II. New Moulton's library of literary criticism. III. Series.
PR85.M33   1985   820'.9
84-27426
ISBN 0-87754-815-3 (v. 1)

CONTENTS

PREFACE

The Chelsea House Library of Literary Criticism is designed to present a concise portrait of the critical heritage of every crucial British and American author. In thirty-seven volumes, the *Library* covers the entire range of British and American literature, from *Beowulf* and the earliest medieval epics to the work of such contemporary innovators as Thomas Pynchon.

For the *Major Authors Edition* (5 volumes), the editors have selected only the most widely-read British and American writers from the fourteenth to the nineteenth centuries. This first volume, *Medieval to Late Renaissance*, contains pre-twentieth-century criticism of major writers from Chaucer to Milton.

We have divided most of the chapters into two sections, extracts and essays. The extracts are grouped into *Personal*, *General*, and *Works* categories. These sections embody material such as passages from poems (a frequent pre-twentieth-century critical mode), extracts from early journals, and portions from book-length histories. The essay sections are reserved for more extensive studies of the authors and their works. Although most of the criticism is arranged chronologically, we have occasionally juxtaposed early and late reviews to highlight the critical dialogue.

Each entry contains a brief biography of the author. A list of additional reading on all authors covered concludes each volume, providing the reader with a selection of material for further research. In general, we have preserved original footnotes in the essay section and have omitted page references within the text. In honoring the style of each critic, the editors have also preserved archaic spellings and punctuation, which often vary from essay to essay, and indeed within the essays themselves. We have allowed for inconsistencies in critics' citations of original texts, and have corrected errors only for reasons of clarity. Any editorial changes or explanations appear in carets.

In determining what authors to include, the editors, in consultation with Professor Harold Bloom, have weighed each author's twentieth-century critical stature against the availability of pre-twentieth-century criticism. We have had to omit writers such as Anne Bradstreet, authors whom twentieth-century critics may regard as "major" by today's standards, but who did not receive widespread critical response before the modern era. We have, however, included such prominent writers as John Donne, whom critics have only recently come to regard as a leading Renaissance figure. Nevertheless, early critical coverage of such authors is relatively sparse.

The editors have attempted to balance in-depth coverage of major writers with a diverse representation of pre-twentieth-century criticism. As a result, the present work provides an informative survey of the development of early literary criticism and medieval and Renaissance literature in general.

The Editors

GEOFFREY CHAUCER

GEOFFREY CHAUCER

c. 1340–1400

Geoffrey Chaucer was born around 1340, the son of a prosperous vintner, probably in London. He received a good education, apparently attending the Almonry Cathedral School. In the early 1360's he studied law, perhaps at Oxford.

From 1357 to about 1360, he served as a yeoman in the court of Elizabeth, Countess of Ulster, continuing his studies when not occupied with his duties, and writing songs. In 1359, he traveled to France, the first of many journeys to the Continent in the service of the King and various noblemen.

By the mid-1360's, Chaucer had come to the attention of John of Gaunt. It is probably due to Gaunt's help that Chaucer was placed in the King's service around 1366. Gaunt, however, seems to have been not only fond of Chaucer, but also of Chaucer's wife. Between 1369 and 1372, Philippa Chaucer bore a child whose father, the evidence suggests, was John of Gaunt. It has been conjectured that Chaucer's generous portrayal of wayward women in his poetry stems from his seeming awareness and tolerance of his wife's affair with his best friend. Another reason for the magnanimity evident in his depiction of characters such as the Wife of Bath, Alisoun in the *Miller's Tale*, and "faithless Cressid" may be that Alice Perrers, King Edward's promiscuous mistress, was Chaucer's patron.

In 1372, Chaucer went to Italy on his first major diplomatic mission. This journey was a turning-point in his career, boosting his favor with the King and providing a new impetus for his poetry. For it was shortly after this journey that Chaucer began writing short tales similar to those of Petrarch and Boccaccio. The themes and techniques of his poetry also started to show the influence of Dante. By the mid-1370's, his work was receiving wide attention: in 1374 he read his poetry at court, on the festival of the Order of the Garter.

Throughout the 1370's, Chaucer served in a variety of government posts, notably as controller of customs from 1374 to 1386. However, the years of the Peasants' Revolt (1377–82) were dangerous for any government official and the constant travel throughout England and the Continent necessitated by his work made Chaucer's life very difficult.

Although he had weathered the Revolt and a term at Parliament in 1386 as the Member for Kent, the latter part of the 1380's was also trying for Chaucer. Philippa Chaucer died in 1387 and Chaucer mourned her deeply. At the height of the Duke of Gloucester's power, Chaucer's royalist sympathies caused him to fall into disfavor. In 1388 financial difficulties forced him to sell one of his annuities.

By 1391, however, Chaucer had been given a more leisurely position than that of Clerk of the King's works, an arduous post which he had held since 1389. From 1391 to 1397 he was able to concentrate on his poetry for the first time in his life. It was evidently during these years that he revised and expanded the *Canterbury Tales*. He died in London in 1400.

The establishment of a firm Chaucerian canon is comparatively recent. Works such as the *Flower and the Leaf, Chaucer's Dream*, and the *Court of Love*, which were once thought to be Chaucer's, are now no longer accepted as his. Unlike the canon, however, the dating of most of his work is still uncertain. His first completed work, the *Book of the Duchess*, was written between 1369 and 1373; during the 1370's and 1380's he composed the *House of Fame*, the *Legend of Good Women*, and *Troilus and Criseyde*. The work for which he is best known, the *Canterbury Tales*, represents the labor of a lifetime.

General

(Quod Loue) I shal tel the / this lesson to lerne myne owne trewe seruaunt / the noble philosophical poete / in Englissh / whiche euermore hym besyeth and trauayleth right sore / my name to encrease / wherefore al that wyllen me good / owe to do him worshyp & reuerence bothe / trewly his better ne his pere in schole of my rules coude I neuer fynde: he (quod she) in a treatise that he made of my seruant Troylus / hath this mater touched / and at the ful this questyon assoyled. Certaynly his noble sayenges can I not amende: In goodncs of gentyl manlyche speche / without any maner of nycite of starieres ymagynacion in wytte and in good reason of sentence he passeth al other makers. In the boke of Troylus / the answere to thy questyon mayste thou lerne. —THOMAS USK, *Testament of Love*, c. 1387, *Works*, 1532, ed. Thynne, Fol. 359b

And gret wel Chaucer whan ȝe mete,
As mi disciple and mi poete:
ffor in þe floures of his ȝouþe
In sondri wise, as he wel couþe,
Of Ditees and of songes glade,
The whiche he for mi sake made,
The lond fulfild is oueral:
Wherof to him in special
Aboue alle oþre I am most holde.
fforþi now in hise daies olde
Thou schalt him telle þis message,

1

That he vpon is latere age,
To sette an ende of alle his werk,
As he which is myn owne clerk,
Do make his testament of loue,
As þou hast do þi schrifte aboue,
So þat mi Court it mai recorde.
—JOHN GOWER, *Confessio Amantis*, c. 1390,
　Works, 1901, ed. Macaulay, p. 466

Euer as I can supprise in myn herte
Alway with feare betwyxt drede and shame
Leste oute of lose, any worde asterte
In this metre, to make it seme lame,
Chaucer is deed that had suche a name
Of fayre makyng that ⟨was⟩ without wene
Fayrest in our tonge, as the Laurer grene.

We may assay forto countrefete
His gay style but it wyl not be;
The welle is drie, with the lycoure swete
Bothe of Clye and of Caliope.
—JOHN LYDGATE, *The Flower of Courtesy*, c.
　1400, ed. Thynne, Fol. 284b

And eke my maister Chauser is ygrave
The noble Rethor, poete of Brytayne
That worthy was the laurer to haue
Of poetrye, and the palme atteyne
That made firste, to distille and rayne
The golde dewe dropes of speche and eloquence
Into our tunge, thurgh his excellence

And fonde the floures, firste of Retoryke
Our Rude speche, only to enlumyne
That in our tunge, was neuere noon hym like
For as the sonne, dothe in hevyn shyne
In mydday spere, dovne to vs by lyne
In whose presence, no ster may a pere
Right so his dytes withoutyn eny pere
Euery makyng withe his light disteyne
In sothefastnesse, who so takethe hede
Wherefore no wondre, thof my hert pleyne
Vpon his dethe, and for sorowe blede
For want of hym, nowe in my grete nede
That shulde alas, conveye and directe
And with his supporte, amende eke and corecte

The wronge traces, of my rude penne
There as I erre, and goo not lyne Right
But for that he, ne may not me kenne
I can no more, but with all my myght
With all myne hert, and myne Inwarde sight
Pray for hym, that liethe nowe in his cheste
To god above, to yeve his saule goode reste
—JOHN LYDGATE, *The Life of Our Lady*, c. 1410

To chaucer þat is floure of rethoryk
In englisshe tong & excellent poete
This wot I wel no þing may I do lyk
þogh so þat I of makynge entyrmete
And gower þat so craftily doþ trete
As in his book of moralite
þogh I to þeym in makyng am vnmete
ʒit most I schewe it forth þat is in me.

Noght lyketh me to labour ne to muse
Vppon þese olde poysees derk
ffor crystes feith suche þing schuld refuse,
Witnes vppon Ierom þe holy clerk,
Hit schold not ben a cristenmannes werk

Tho fals goddes names to renewe
ffor he þat haþ reseyued cristes merk
If he do so to crist he is vntrewe.

Of þo þar crist in heuene blis schall,
Suche manere werkes schold ben set on side,
ffor certaynly it nedeþ noght at all
To [whette] now þe dartes of cupide
Ne for to bidde þat Venus be oure gide
So þat we may oure foule lustes wynne,
On aunter lest þe same on vs betide
As dede þe same venus for hyre synne.

And certayn I haue tasted wonder lyte
As of þe welles of calliope
No wonder þough I sympilly endite
Yet will I not vnto tessiphone
Ne to allecto ne to megare
Besechin after craft of eloquence
But pray þat god of his benignyte
My spirit enspire wiþ his influence.
—JOHN WALTON, "Translator's Preface" to *De
　Consolatione Philosophiae*, 1410

What schal I calle the What is thi name?
hoccleue fadir myn men clepen me. . . .
thou were aqueynted with Caucher pardee
God haue his soule best of any Wyght. . . .

O maister deere / and fadir reuerent
Mi maister Chaucer flour of eloquence
Mirour of fructuous entendement
O vniuersal fadir in science
Allas that thou thyn excellent prudence
In thi bed mortel mightist naght by qwethe
What eiled deth / allas Whi wolde he sle the
O deth thou didest naght harme singuleer
In slaghtere of him / but al this land it smertith
But nathelees / yit hast thou no power
His name sle / his hy vertu astertith
Vnslayn fro the / Which ay vs lyfly hertyth
With bookes of his ornat endytyng
That is to al this land enlumynyng

Hast thou nat eeke my maister Gower slayn. . . .
Mi dere maistir / god his soule quyte
And fadir Chaucer fayn Wolde han me taght
But I was dul, and lerned life or naght

Allas my worthi maister honorable
This landes verray tresor and richesse
Deth by thi deth / hath harme irreparable
Vnto vs doon / hir vengeable duresse
Despoiled hath this land of the swetnesse
Of rethorik for vnto Tullius
Was neuer man so lyk amonges vs

Also who was hier in philosophie
To Aristotle / in our tonge but thow
The steppes of virgile in poesie
Thow filwedist eeke men wot wel ynow. . . .

The firste fynders of oure faire langage
Hath seyde in caas semblable & othir mo
So hyly wel that it is my dotage
For to expresse or touche any of thoo
Alasse my fadir fro the worlde is goo
My worthi maister Chaucer hym I mene
Be thou aduoket for hym heuenes quene
As thou wel knowest o blissid virgyne

With louyng hert and hye deuocioun
In thyne honour he wroot ful manye a lyne
O now thine helpe & thi promocioun
To god thi sone make a mocioun
How he thi seruaunt was mayden marie
And lat his loue floure and fructifie
Al thogh his lyfe be queynt the resemblaunce
Of him hath in me so fressh lyﬂynesse
That to putte othir men in remembraunce
Of his persone I haue heere his lyknesse
Do make to this ende in sothfastnesse
That thei that haue of him lest thought & mynde
By this peynture may ageyn him fynde
——THOMAS OCCLEVE, *The Regement of Princes*,
1412

Take þe heed sirs I prey yowe of þis compleynt of *Anelyda*
Qweene of Cartage Roote of trouthe and stedfastnesse þat
pytously compleyneþe Upon þe varyance of daun *Arcyte* lord
borne of þe blood Royal of Thebes. englisshed by Geffrey
Chaucier In the best wyse and moost Rethoricyous þe mooste
vnkou eþ metre. coloures and Rymes þᵗ euer was sayde. tofore
þis day——redeþe and preveþe þe sooþe. . . .

Loo yee louers gladeþe and comforteþe you . of þal-
lyaunce etrayted bytwene þe hardy and furyous Mars . þe
god of armes and Venus þe double goddesse of loue made by
O yee so noble and worthi pryncis and princesse, oþer estatis or
degrees, what-euer yee beo, þat haue disposicione or plesaunce
to rede or here þe stories of old tymis passed, to kepe yow frome
ydelnesse and slowthe, in escheuing oþer folies þat might be
cause of more harome filowyng, vowcheth sauf, I be-seche
yowe to fynde yowe occupacioun in þe reding here of þe tales
of Caunterburye wiche beon compilid in þis boke filowing
First foundid, ymagenid and made boþe for disporte and leorn-
yng of all þoo that beon gentile of birthe or of condicions by
þe laureal and moste famous poete þat euer was to-fore him as
in þemvelissñing of oure rude moders englisshe tonge, clepid
Chaucyer a Gaufrede of whos soule god for his mercy have
pitee of his grace. Amen.——JOHN SHIRLEY, "Introduction" to
The Knight's Tale, c. 1450

> I made the fyre and beaked me about
> Than toke A drinke my spirites to conforte
> And armed me wel fro the colde therout
> To cutte the wynter nyght and make it shorte
> I toke a queare / and left al other sporte
> Written by worthy Chaucer glorious
> Of fayre Creseyde / and lusty Troylus
>
> And there I founde. . . .
>
> ⟨Diomede's seduction of Criseyde⟩
>
> Of his distresse me nedeth nat reherse
> For worthy Chaucer in that same boke
> In goodly termes / and in ioly verse
> Compyled hath his cares who wyl loke
> To breke my slepe another queare I toke
> In whiche I founde the fatal desteny
> Of fayre Creseyde / whiche ended wretchedly
>
> Who wot if al that Chaucer wrate was trewe
> Nor I wotte nat if this narration
> Be authorysed / or forged of the newe
> Of some poete by his inuention
> Made to reporte the lamentation
> And woful ende of this lusty Creseyde
> And what distresse she was in or she deyde
> ——ROBERT HENRYSON, *Testament of Cresseid*, c.
> 1475

Thus endeth this boke whiche is named the boke of Consolacion of philosophie whiche that Boecius made for his comforte
and consolacion he beyng in exile for the comyne and publick
wele hauyng grete heuynes & thoughtes and in maner of de-
spayr / Rehercing in the sayde boke howe Philosophie appiered
to him shewyng the mutabilite of this transitorie lyfe / and also
enformyng howe fortune and happe shold bee vnderstonden /
with the predestynacion and prescience of God as moche as
maye and ys possible to bee knowen naturelly / as a fore ys sayd
in this sayd boke / Whiche Boecius was an excellente auctour
of dyuerce bookes craftely and curiously maad in prose and
metre / And also had translated dyuerce bookes oute of Greke
into latyne / and had ben senatour of that noble & famous cite
Rome. And also his two sones Senatours for their prudence &
wisedom. And for as moche as he withstode to his power the
tyrannye of theodorik thenne Emperour / & wold haue defended the sayde cite & Senate from his wicked hondes /
wherupon he was conuict & putte in prison / in whiche prisone
he made this forsaide boke of consolacion for his singular comfort, and for as moche as the stile of it / is harde & difficile to be
vnderstonde of simple persones. Therfore the worshipful fader
& first foundeur & enbelissher of ornate eloquence in our
englissh. I mene / Maister Geffrey Chaucer hath translated this
sayd werke oute of latyn in to oure vsual and moder tonge.
Folowyng the latyn as neygh as is possible to be vnderstande.
wherin in myne oppynyon he hath deservid a perpetuell lawde
and thanke of al this noble Royame of Englond / And in
especiall of them that shall rede and vnderstande it. For in the
sayd boke they may see what this transitorie & mutable worlde
is And wherto euery mann liuyng in hit / ought to entende.
Thenne for as moche as this sayd boke so translated is rare &
not spred ne knowen as it is digne and worthy. For the erudi-
cion and lernyng of suche as ben Ignoraunt & not knowyng of
it / Atte requeste of a singuler frende and gossib of myne. I
william Caxton haue done my debuoir & payne tenprynte it in
fourme as is here afore made / In hopyng that it shal prouffite
moche peple to the wele & helth of their soules / & for to lerne
to haue and kepe the better pacience in aduersitees / And
furthermore I desire & requi. re you that of your charite ye
wold praye for the soule of the sayd worshipful mann Geffrey
Chaucer / first translatour of this sayde boke into englissh &
enbelissher in making the sayd langage ornate & fayr. whiche
shal endure perpetuelly. and therfore he ought eternelly to be
remembrid. of whom the body and corps lieth buried in thab-
bay of Westmestre beside london to fore the chapele of seynte
benet. by whos sepulture is wreton on a table hongyng on a
pylere his Epitaphye maad by a poete laureat. ——WILLIAM CAX-
TON, "Epilogue" to *Chaucer's Boethius*, 1478

I fynde nomore of this werke to fore sayd / For as fer as I can
vnderstonde / This noble man Gefferey Chaucer fynysshyd at
the sayd conclusion of the metyng of lesyng and sothsawe /
where as yet they ben chekked and maye not departe / whyche
werke as me semeth is craftyly made / and dygne to be wreton
and knowen / For he towchyth in it ryght grete wysedom &
subtyll vnderstondyng / And so in alle hys werkys he excellyth
in myn oppynyon alle other wryters in our Englyssh / For he
wrytteth no voyde wordes / but alle hys mater is ful of hye and
quycke sentence / to whom ought to be gyuen laude and
preysyng for hys noble makyng and wrytyng / For of hym alle
other hauc borowed syth and taken / in alle theyr wel sayeng
and wrytyng / And I humbly beseche & praye yow / emonge
your prayers to remembre hys soule / on whyche and on alle
crysten soulis I beseche almyghty god to haue mercy Amen——
WILLIAM CAXTON, "Epilogue" to *The House of Fame*, 1483

Grete thankes lawde and honour / ought to be gyuen vnto the clerkes / poetes / and historiographs that haue wreton many noble bokes of wysedom of the lyues / passions / & myracles of holy sayntes of hystoryes / of noble and famous Actes / and faittes / And of the cronycles sith the begynnyng of the creacion of the world / vnto thys present tyme / by whyche we ben dayly enformed / and have knowleche of many thynges / of whom we shold not haue knowen / yf they had not left to vs theyr monumentis wreton / Emong whom and inespecial to fore alle other we ought to gyue a synguler laude vnto that noble & grete philosopher Gefferey chaucer the whiche for his ornate wrytyng in our tongue may wel haue the name of a laureate poete / For to fore that he by hys labour enbelysshyd / ornated / and made faire our englisshe / in thys Royame was had rude speche & Incongrue / as yet it appiereth by olde bookes / whyche at thys day ought not to haue place ne be compared emong ne to hys beauteuous volumes / and aournate writynges / of whom he made many bokes and treatyces of many a noble historye as wel in metre as in ryme and prose / and them so craftyly made / that he comprehended hys maters in short / quyck and hye sentences / eschewyng prolyxyte / castyng away the chaf of superfluyte / and shewyng the pyked grayn of sentence / vtteryd by crafty and sugred eloquence / of whom emonge all other of hys bokes / I purpose temprynte by the grace of god the book of the tales of cauntyrburye / in whiche I fynde many a noble hystorye / of euery astate and degre / Fyrst rehercyng the condicions / and tharraye of eche of them as properly as possyble is to be sayd / And after theyr tales whyche ben of noblesse / wysedom / gentylesse / Myrthe / and also of veray holynesse and vertue / wherin he fynysshyth thys sayd booke / whyche book I haue dylygently ouersen and duly examyned to thende that it be made acordyng vnto his owen makyng / For I fynde many of the sayd bookes / whyche wryters haue abrydgyd it and many thynges left out / And in somme place haue sette certayn versys / that he neuer made ne sette in hys booke / of whyche bookes so incorrecte was one brought to me vj yere passyd / whyche I supposed had ben veray true & correcte / And accordyng to the same I dyde do enprynte a certayn nombre of them / whyche anon were sold to many and dyuerse gentyl men / of whome one gentylman cam to me / and said that this book was not accordyng in many places vnto the book that Gefferey chaucer had made / To whom I answerd that I had made it accordyng to my copye / and by me was nothyng added ne mynusshyd / Thenne he sayd he knewe a book whyche hys fader had and moche louyd / that was very trewe / and accordyng vnto hys owen first book by hym made / and sayd more yf I wold enprynte it agayn he wold gete me the same book for a copye / how be it he wyst wel / that hys fader wold not gladly departe fro it / To whom I said / in caas that he coude gete me suche a book trewe and correcte / yet I wold ones endeuoyre me to enprynte it agayn / for to satysfye thauctour / where as to fore by ygnouraunce I erryd in hurtyng and dyffamyng his book in dyuerce places in settyng in somme thynges that he neuer sayd ne made / and leuyng out many thynges that he made whyche ben requysite to be sette in it / And thus we fyll at accord / And he ful gentylly gate of hys fader the said book / and delyuerd it to me / by whiche I haue corrected my book / as here after alle alonge by thayde of almyghty god shal folowe / whom I humbly beseche to gyue me grace and ayde to achyeue / and accomplysshe / to hys lawde honour and glorye / and that alle ye that shal in thys book rede or heere / wyll of your charyte emong your dedes of mercy / remembre the sowle of the sayd Gefferey chaucer first auctour / and maker of thys book / And also that alle we that shal see and rede therin / may so take and vnderstonde the good and vertuous tales / that it may so

prouffyte / vnto the helthe of our sowles / that after thys short and transitorye lyf we may come to euerlastyng lyf in heuen / Amen—WILLIAM CAXTON, "Prohemye" to *The Canterbury Tales*, 2nd ed., 1484

> O reverend Chaucere, rose of rethoris all,
> As in oure tong ane flour imperiall
> That raise in Britane ewir, quho redis rycht,
> Thou beris of makaris the tryumph riall;
> Thy fresch anamalit termes celicall
> This mater coud illumynit haue full brycht:
> Was thou noucht of oure Inglisch all the lycht,
> Surmounting ewiry tong terrestriall
> Alls fer as Mayes morow dois mydnycht?
>
> O morall Gower, and Ludgate laureate,
> Your sugurit lippis and tongis aureate,
> Bene to oure eris cause of grete delyte;
> Your angel mouthis most mellifluate
> Our rude langage has clere illumynate,
> And faire our-gilt oure speche, that imperfyte
> Stude, on your goldyn pennis schupe to wryte;
> This Ile before was bare, and desolate
> Off rethorike, or lusty fresch endyte.
>   —WILLIAM DUNBAR, *The Golden Targe*, c. 1503,
>   *Poems*, 1893, Vol. 2, ed. Small, p. 10

> Thoght venerabill Chauser, principal poet but peir,
> Hevynly trumpat, orlege and reguler,
> In eloquens balmy, cundyt and dyall,
> Mylky fontane, cleir.strand and royss ryall,
> Of fresch endyte, throu Albion iland braid,
> In hys legend of notabill ladeis said
> That he couth follow word by word Virgill,
> Wisar than I may faill in lakar stile. . . .
>
> I say nocht this of Chauser for offens,
> Bot till excuss my lewyt insufficiens,
> For as he standis beneth Virgill in gre,
> Vndir hym alsfer I grant my self to be.
> And netheless into sum place, quha kend it,
> My mastir Chauser gretly Virgill offendit.
> All thoch I be tobald hym to repreif,
> He was fer baldar, certis, by hys leif,
> Sayand he followit Virgillis lantern toforn,
> Quhou Eneas to Dydo was forsworn.
> Was he forsworn? Than Eneas was fals—
> That he admittis and callys hym traytour als.
> Thus wenyng allane Ene to haue reprevit,
> He hass gretly the prynce of poetis grevit. . . .
>
> Bot sikkyrly of resson me behufis
> Excuss Chauser fra all maner repruffis
> In lovyng of thir ladeis lylly quhite
> He set on Virgill and Eneas this wyte,
> For he was evir (God wait) all womanis frend.
>   —GAVIN DOUGLAS, "Translator's Prologue" to
>   *Aenead: Eneados, Book I*, 1513

> In this also se thou be not idle:
> Thy nece, thy cosyn, thy sister, or thy daughter,
> If she bee faire: if handsome be her middle:
> If thy better hath her loue besought her:
> Auaunce his cause, and he shall helpe thy nede,
> It is but loue, turne it to a laughter.
> But ware I say, so gold thee helpe and spede:
> That in this case thou be not so vnwise,
> As Pandar was in such a like dede.

For he the fole of conscience was so nice:
That he no gaine would haue for all his payne.
　　　—SIR THOMAS WYATT, *How to Use the Court,*
　　　c. 1540

Provided allso that all bokes in Englishe printed before the yere of our Lorde a thousande fyve hundred and fourtie intytled the Kings Hieghnes proclamacions iniunctions, translacions of the Pater noster, the Aue Maria and the Crede, the psalters prymers prayer statutes and lawes of the Realme, Cronycles Canterburye tales, Chaucers bokes Gowers bokes and stories of mennes lieues, shall not be comprehended in the prohibicion of this acte.—"An Act for Thaduancement of True Religion and for Thabbolisshment of the Contrarie," *Statute 34 and 35 Henry VIII,* 1542–43, Ch. 1, Sec. 5

The Nource of dise and cardes, is werisom Ydlenesse, enemy of vertue, ye drowner of youthe, that tarieth in it, and as Chauser doth saye verie well in the Parsons tale, the greene path waye to hel, hauinge this thing appropriat vnto it, that where as other vices haue some cloke of honestie, onely ydlenes can neyther do wel, nor yet thinke wel. . . .

　　Whose horriblenes ⟨Gaming⟩ is so large, that it passed the eloquence of our *Englishe Homer,* to compasse it: yet because I euer thought hys sayings to haue as muche authoritie, as eyther *Sophocles* or *Euripides* in Greke, therefore gladly do I remember these verses of hys. ⟨Not from Thynne's text, 1532⟩

　　Hasardry is Very mother of lesinges
　　And of deceyte and cursed sweringes
　　Blasphemie of Chist, manslaughter, and waste also,
　　Of catel of tyme, of other thynges mo.

Cursed sweryng, blasphemie of Christe, These halfe verses Chaucer in an other place, more at large doth well set out, and verye liuely expresse, sayinge.

　　Ey by goddes precious hert and his nayles
　　And by the blood of Christe, that is in Hales.
　　　—ROGER ASCHAM, *Toxophilus,* 1545

Diligence also must be vsed [by an Historian] in kepyng truly the order of tyme: and describyng lyuely, both the site of places and nature of persons not onely for the outward shape of the body: but also for the inward disposition of the mynde, as *Thucidides* doth in many places very trimly, and *Homer* euerywhere, and that always most excellently, which obseruation is chiefly to be marked in hym. And our *Chaucer* doth the same, very praise worthely: marke hym well and conferre hym with any other that writeth of in our tyme in their proudest toung, whosoeuer lyst.—ROGER ASCHAM, *A Report . . . of the Affaires and State of Germany,* 1552

Some that make *Chaucer* in Englishe and *Petrarch* in *Italian,* their Gods in verses, and yet be not able to make true difference, what is a fault, and what is a just prayse, in those two worthie wittes, will moch mislike this my writyng. But such men be euen like followers of *Chaucer* and *Petrarke* as one here in England did folow *Syr Tho. More:* who, being most vnlike vnto him, in wit and learning, neuertheles in wearing his gowne awrye vpon the one shoulder, as *Syr Tho. More* was wont to doe, would needes be counted like vnto hym.—ROGER ASCHAM, *The Scholemaster,* 1570

The first and most necessarie poynt that euer I founde meete to be considered in making of a delectable poeme is this, to grounde it vpon some fine invention. For it is not inough to roll in pleasant woordes nor yet to thunder in *Rym, Ram, Ruff,* by letter (quoth my master *Chaucer*) nor yet to abound in apt vocables, or epythetes. . . . Also our father *Chaucer* hath vsed the same libertie in feete and measures that the Latinists do vse: and who so euer do peruse and well consider his workes, he shall finde that although his lines are not alwayes of one selfe same number of Syllables, yet beyng redde by one that hath vnderstanding, the longest verse and that which hath most Syllables in it, will fall (to the eare) correspondent vnto that whiche hath fewest syllables in it: and like wise that whiche hath in it fewest syllables, shalbe founde yet to consist of woordes that haue suche naturall sounde, as may seeme equall in length to a verse which hath many moe sillables of lighter accentes. . . .

　　I had forgotten a notable kinde of ryme, called ryding rime, and that is suche as our Mayster and Father *Chaucer* vsed in his Canterburie tales, and in diuers other delectable and light enterprises.—GEORGE GASCOIGNE, "Certayne Notes of Instruction," *The Posies of George Gascoigne, Esquire,* 1575

　　The God of shepheards *Tityrus* is dead,
　　Who taught me homely, as I can, to make.
　　He, whilst he lived, was the soueraigne head
　　Of shepheards all, that bene with loue ytake:
　　Well couth he wayle his Woes, and lightly slake
　　The flames, which loue within his heart had bredd,
　　And tell vs mery tales, to keep vs wake,
　　The while our sheepe about vs safely fedde.

　　Nowe dead he is, and lyeth wrapt in lead,
　　(O why should death on hym such outrage showe?)
　　And all hys passing skil with him is fledde,
　　The fame whereof doth dayly greater growe.
　　But if on me some little drops would flowe
　　Of that the spring was in his learned hedde,
　　I soone would learne these woods, to wayle my woe,
　　And teache the trees, their trickling teares to shedde.
　　　—EDMUND SPENSER, *The Shepheardes
　　　Calendar,* 1579, Fol. 24

⟨Poets came before philosophers and historians.⟩ So among the Romans were *Liuius, Andronicus,* and *Ennius.* So in the Italian language, the first that made it aspire to be a Treasurehouse of Science, were the Poets *Dante, Boccace,* and *Petrarch.* So in our English were *Gower* and *Chaucer.*

　　After whom, encouraged and delighted with theyr excellent fore-going, others haue followed, to beautifie our mother tongue, as wel in the same kinde as in other Arts. . . .

　　See whether wisdome and temperance in *Vlisses and Diomedes,* valure in *Achilles,* friendship in *Nisus,* and *Eurialus,* euen to an ignoraunt man, carry not an apparent shyning: and contrarily, the remorse of conscience in *Oedipus,* the soone repenting pride in *Agamemnon,* the selfe-deuouring crueltie in his Father *Atreus,* the violence of ambition in the two *Theban* brothers, the sowre-sweetnes of reuenge in *Medaea,* and to fall lower, the *Terentian Gnato,* and our *Chaucer's* Pandar, so exprest, that we nowe vse their names to signifie their trades. . . .

　　Thirdly, that it ⟨Poetry⟩ is the Nurse of abuse, infecting vs with many pestilent desires: with a Syrens sweetnes, drawing the mind to the Serpents tayle of sinfull fancy. And heerein especially, Comedies giue the largest field to erre, as *Chaucer* sayth: howe both in other nations and in ours, before Poets did soften vs, we were full of courage, giuen to martiall exercises; the pillers of manlyke liberty and not lulled a sleepe in shady idlenes with Poets pastimes. . . .

　　Chaucer, vndoubtedly did excellently in hys *Troylus and Cresseid;* of whom, truly I know not, whether to meruaile more, either that he in that mistie time, could see so clearely, or that wee in this cleare age, walke so stumblingly after him.

5

Yet had he great wants, fitte to be forgiuen, in so reuerent antiquity.—SIR PHILIP SIDNEY, *An Apologie for Poetrie*, 1581

The first of our English Poets that I haue heard of was Iohn Gower . . . his freend *Chawcer* who speaketh of him oftentimes in diuers places of hys workes. *Chawcer*, who for that excellent fame which hee obtayned in his Poetry, was always accounted the God of English Poets (such a tytle for honours sake hath been giuen him), was next after if not equall in time to Gower and hath left many workes, both for delight and profitable knowledge farre exceeding any other that as yet euer since hys time directed theyr studies that way. Though the manner of hys stile may seeme blunte and course to many fine English eares at these dayes, yet in trueth, if it be equally pondered, and with good iudgment aduised, and confirmed with the time wherein he wrote, a man shall perceiue thereby euen a true picture or perfect shape of a right Poet. He by his delightsome vayne so gulled the eares of men with his deuises, that, although corruption bare such sway in most matters, that learning and truth might skant bee admitted to shewe it selfe, yet without controll-ment myght hee gyrde at the vices and abuses of all states, and gawle with very sharpe and eger inuentions, which he did so learnedly and pleasantly that none therefore would call him into question. For such was his bolde spyrit, that what enor-mities he saw in any he would not spare to pay them home, eyther in playne words, or els in some pretty and pleasant cou-ert, that the simplest might espy him. Neere in time vnto him was *Lydgate*, a Poet surely for good proportion of his verse and meetely currant style, as the time affoorded, comparable with *Chawcer*, yet more occupied in supersticious and odde matters then was requesite in so good a wytte. . . .

   Let things that are faigned for pleasures sake haue a neer resemblance of the truth. This precept may you perceiue to bee most duelie obserued of *Chawcer*: for who could with more delight prescribe such wholsome counsaile and sage aduise, where he seemeth onelie to respect the profitte of his lessons and instructions? or who coulde with greater wisedome, or more pithie skill, vnfold such pleasant and delightsome matters of mirth, as though they respected nothing but the telling of a merry tale? so that this is the very grounde of right poetrie, to give profitable counsaile, yet so as it must be mingled with delight.

   . . . For surelie I am of this opinion that the wantonest Poets of all, in their most laciuious workes wherein they busied themselues, sought rather by that meanes to withdraw mens mindes (especiallie the best natures) from such foule vices then to allure them to imbrace such beastly follies as they de-tected.—WILLIAM WEBBE, "A Discourse of English Poetrie," 1586, *Elizabethan Critical Essays*, 1904, Vol. 1, ed. Smith, pp. 241–63

Tut saies our English Italians, the finest witts our Climate sends foorth, are but drie braind doltes, in comparison of other coun-tries: whome if you interrupt with *redde rationem*, they will tell you of *Petrache*, *Tasso*, *Celiano*, with an infinite number of others; to whome if I should oppose *Chaucer, Lidgate, Gower*, with such like, that liued vnder the tirranie of ignorance, I do think their best louers, would bee much discontented, with the collation of contraries, if I should write ouer al their heads, Haile fellow well met. One thing I am sure of, that each of these three, haue vaunted their meeters, with as much admira-tion in English, as euer the proudest *Ariosto* did his verse in Italian.—THOMAS NASHE, *To the Gentlemen Students of both Universities*, 1589

And in her Maiesties time that now is are sprong vp an other crew of Courtly makers, Noble men and Gentlemen of her Maiesties owne seruauntes, who haue written excellently well. . . . But of them all particularly this is myne opinion, that *Chaucer*, with *Gower, Lidgat* and *Harding* for their antiq-uitie ought to haue the first place, and *Chaucer* as the most renowmed of them all, for the much learning appeareth to be in him aboue any of the rest. And though many of his bookes be but bare translations out of the Latin and French, yet are they wel handled, as his bookes of *Troilus* and *Cresseid*, and the Romant of the Rose, whereof he translated but one halfe, the deuice was *Iohn de Mehunes*, a French Poet, the Canterbury Tales were *Chaucers* owne inuention as I suppose, and where he sheweth more the naturall of his pleasant wit, then in any other of his workes, his similitudes comparisons, and all other descriptions are such as can not be amended. His meetre Hero-icall of *Troilus* and *Cresseid* is very graue and stately, keeping the staffe of seuen, and the verse of ten, his other verses of the Canterbury tales be but riding ryme, neuerthelesse very well becomming the matter of that pleasaunt pilgrimage in which euery mans part is played with much decency. . . .

   But our auncient rymers, as *Chaucer, Lydgate*, and oth-ers, vsed these *Cesures* either very seldome, or not at all, or else very licentiously, and many times made their meetres (they called them riding ryme) of such vnshapely wordes as would allow no conuenient *Cesure*, and therefore did let their rymes runne out at length, and neuer stayd till they came to the end.—RICHARD PUTTENHAM, *The Art of English Poesie*, 1589, pp. 49–50

> Whylome as antique stories tellen vs,
>   Those two (Cambell and Triamond) were foes the
>   fellonest on ground,
>   And battell made the draddest daungerous,
>   That euer shrilling trumpet did resound;
>   Though now their acts be no where to be found,
>   As that renowmed Poet them compiled,
>   With warlike numbers and Heroick sound,
>   Dan Chaucer, well of English vndefiled,
> On Fames eternall beadroll worthie to be filed.
>
> But wicked *Time* that all good thoughts doth waste,
>   And workes of noblest wits to nought out-weare,
>   That famous moniment hath quite defac't,
>   And robd the world of threasure endlesse deare,
>   The which mote haue enriched all vs heare.
>   O cursed Eld! the canker-worme of writs,
>   How may these rimes (so rude as doth appeare)
>   Hope to endure, sith workes of heauenly wits
> Are quite deuour'd, and brought to nought by little bits?
>
> Then pardon, O most sacred happy spirit,
>   That I thy labours lost may thus reviue,
>   And steale from thee the meed of thy due merit,
>   That none durst euer whil'st thou wast aliue,
>   And beeing dead in vaine yet many striue:
>   Ne dare I like, but through infusion sweet
>   Of thine owne spirit (which doth in me surviue)
>   I follow heere the footing of thy feet
> That with thy meaning so I may the rather meete.
>   —EDMUND SPENSER, *The Faerie Queene*,
>   1590–96, Bk. 4, Canto 2, Stanza 9

Proceede to cherish thy surpassing carminicall arte of memorie with full cuppes (as thou dost) let Chaucer *bee new scourd against the day of battaile, and* Terence *come but in nowe and then with the snuffe of a sentence, and* Dictum puta, *Weele strike it as dead as a doore naile.* . . .

   The Hexamiter verse I graunt to be a Gentleman of an auncient house (so is many an english begger), yet this Clyme of ours hee cannot thriue in; our speech is too craggy for him to set his plough in, hee goes twitching and hopping in our language like a man running vpon quagmiers, vp the hill in one Syllable and down the dale in another, retaining no part of that stately smooth gate, which he vaunts himselfe with amongst the Greeks and Latins.

Homer and Virgil, two valorous Authors, yet were they neuer knighted; they wrote in Hexameter verses: *Ergo, Chaucer,* and *Spencer* the *Homer* and *Virgil* of England, were farre ouerseene that they wrote not all their Poems in Hexamiter verses also.

In many Countries veluet and Satten is a commoner weare than cloth amongst vs, *Ergo,* wee must leaue wearing of cloth, and goe euerie one in veluet and satten, because other Countries vse so.

The Text will not beare it, good *Gilgilis Hobberdehoy.*

Our english tongue is nothing too good, but too bad *to imitate the Greeke and Latine. . . .* In a verse, when a worde of three sillables cannot thrust in but sidelings, to ioynt him euen, we are oftentimes faine to borrowe some lesser quarry of elocution from the Latine, alwaies retaining this for a principle, that a leake of indesinence as a leake in a shippe, must needly bee stopt, with what matter soeuer.

Chaucers authoritie, I am certaine shalbe alleadgd against mee for a many of these balductums. Had *Chaucer* liu'd to this age, I am verily perswaded hee would haue discarded the tone halfe of the harsher sort of them.

They were the Oouse which ouerflowing barbarisme, withdrawne to her Scottish Northren chanell, had left behind her. Art, like yong grasse in the spring of *Chaucers* florishing, was glad to peepe vp through any slime of corruption, to be beholding to she car'd not whome for apparaile, trauailing in those colde countries. There is no reason that shee a banisht Queene into this barraine soile, hauing monarchizd it so long amongst the Greeks and Romanes, should (although warres furie had humbled her to some extremitie) still be constrained when she hath recouerd her state, to weare the robes of aduersitie, iet it in her old rags, when she is wedded to new prosperitie.

Vtere moribus praeteritis, saith *Caius Caesar in Aulus Gellius, loquere verbis praesentibus.*

Thou art mine enemie, *Gabriell,* and that which is more, a contemptible vnder-foote enemie, or else I would teach thy olde *Trewantship* the true vse of words, as also how more inclinable verse is than prose to dance after the horrizonant pipe of inueterate antiquitie.

It is no matter, since thou hast brought godly instruction out of loue with thee, vse thy own destruction, raigne sole Emperour of inkehornisme, I wish vnto thee all superabundant increase of the singular gifts of absurditie, and vaineglory.—THOMAS NASHE, *Strange Newes of the Intercepting certaine Letters,* 1592

So heard it is for any liuing wight,
    All her ⟨Dame Nature's⟩ array and vestiments to tell
    That old *Dan Geffrey* (in whose gentle spright
    The pure well head of Poesie did dwell)
    In his *Foules parley* durst not with it mel,
    But it transferd to *Alane,* who he thought
    Had in his *Plaint of kindes* describ'd it well:
    Which who will read set forth so as it ought,
Go seek he out that *Alane* where he may be sought.
        —EDMUND SPENSER, "The Mutabilitie Cantos,"
        The Faerie Queene, 1599

True Poet! Who could words endue
With life, that makes the fiction true.
    All passages are seene as cleare
As if not pend, but acted here:
    Each thing so well demonstrated,
    It comes to passe, when 'tis but read.
    Here is no fault, but ours: through vs
True Poetry growes barbarous:
    While aged Language must be thought
(Because 'twas good long since) now naught.
    Thus time can silence *Chaucers* tongue
But not his witte, which now among
    The Latines hath a lowder sound;
    And what we lost, the World hath found.
    Thus the Translation will become
Th' Originall, while that growes dumbe:
    And this will crowne these labours: None
Sees *Chaucer* but in *Kinaston.*
        —EDWARD FOULIS, "Prefatory Verse" to *The*
        Loves of Troilus and Creseide, tr. into Latin
        by Sir Francis Kynaston, 1635

14 June 1663 . . . So to Sir W. Penn to visit him; and finding him alone, sent for my wife, who is in her riding-suit, to see him; which she hath not done these many months I think. By and by in comes Sir J. Mennes and Sir W. Batten, and so we sat talking; among other things, Sir J. Mennes brought many fine expressions of Chaucer, which he dotes on mightily, and without doubt is a very fine poet. . . .

8 July 1664 . . . So to Pauls churchyard about my books—and to the binders and directed the doing of my Chaucer, though they were not full neat enough for me, but pretty well it is—and thence to the clasp-makers to have it clasped and bossed. . . .

10 August 1664 . . . Up; and being ready, abroad to do several small businesses; among others, to find out one to engrave my tables upon my new sliding-Rule with silver plates, it being so small that Browne that made it cannot get one to do it. So I found out Cocker, the famous writing-master, and got him to do it; and I sat an hour by him to see him design it all, and strange it is to see him with his natural eyes to cut so small at his first designing it, and read it all over without any missing, when for my life I could not with my best skill read one word or letter of it—but it is use; but he says that the best light, for his life, to do a very small thing by (contrary to Chaucer's words to the sun: that he should lend his light to them that small seals graue), it should be by an artificiall light of a candle, set to advantage as he could do it.—SAMUEL PEPYS, *Diary,* 1663–64, pp. 184–237

    Old *Chaucer,* like the morning Star,
    To us discovers day from far,
    His light those Mists and Clouds dissolv'd,
    Which our dark Nation long involv'd;
    But he descending to the shades,
    Darkness again the Age invades.
    Next (like *Aurora*) *Spencer* rose,
    Whose purple blush the day foreshows.
        —SIR JOHN DENHAM, "On Mr. Abraham
        Cowley, His Death and Burial amongst the
        Ancient Poets," *Poems and Translations,*
        1668, p. 89

Since, dearest Harry, you will needs request
A short Account of all the Muse possest;
That, down from Chaucer's *days to* Dryden's *Times*
Have spent their noble Rage *in* British *Rhimes;*

Without more Preface, wrote in formal length,
To speak the Vndertaker's want of Strength
I'll try to make their sev'ral Beauties known,
And show their Verses worth, tho' not my own.

Long had our dull Fore-Fathers slept Supine
Nor felt the Raptures of the tuneful Nine;
'Till *Chaucer* first, a merry *Bard*, arose;
And many a Story told in Rhime and Prose.
But Age has rusted what the Poet writ,
Worn out his Language, and obscur'd his wit:
In vain he Jests in his unpolish'd Strain,
And tries to make his Readers laugh in vain.
          —JOSEPH ADDISON, "To Mr. H.
          S⟨acheverell⟩, April 3, 1694," 1694,
          Miscellany Poems, 1719, Vol. 4, ed. Dryden,
          p. 288

Short is the Date, alas, of *Modern Rhymes*;
And 'tis but just to let 'em live *betimes.*
No longer now that Golden Age appears,
When Patriarch-Wits surviv'd a *thousand* Years.
Now Length of Fame (our *second* Life) is lost,
And bare Threescore is all ev'n That can boast:
Our Sons their Father's *failing Language* see,
And such as *Chaucer* is, shall *Dryden* be.
          —ALEXANDER POPE, *An Essay on Criticism*,
          1711

Notwithstanding the Disadvantage he has mention'd, we have two Antient *English* Poets, *Chaucer* and *Spenser*, who may perhaps be reckon'd as Exceptions to this Remark. These seem to have taken deep Root, like old *British* Oaks, and to flourish in defiance of all the Injuries of Time and Weather. The former is indeed much more obsolete in his Stile than the latter; but it is owing to an extraordinary native Strength in both, that they have been able thus far to survive amidst the Changes of our Tongue, and seem rather likely, among the Curious at least, to preserve the Knowledg of our Antient Language, than to be in danger of being destroy'd with it, and bury'd under its Ruins.

Tho Spenser's Affection to his Master *Chaucer* led him in many things to copy after him, yet those who have read both will easily observe that these two Genius's were of a very different kind. *Chaucer* excell'd in his Characters; *Spenser* in his Descriptions. The first study'd Humour, was an excellent Satirist, and a lively but rough Painter of the Manners of that rude Age in which he liv'd.—JOHN HUGHES, *Essay on Allegorical Poetry*, 1715, pp. xxvi–xxvii

The inimitable brightness of ⟨Rochester's⟩ Wit has not been able to preserve ⟨his poems⟩ from being thought worthy, by wise Men, to be lost, rather than remember'd; being blacken'd and eclips'd by the Lewdness of their Stile, so as not to be made fit for Modesty to read or hear. Jeffrey Chaucer is forgotten upon the same Account; and tho' that Author is excused, by the unpoliteness of the Age he lived in, yet his Works are diligently buried, by most Readers, on that very Principle, that they are not fit for modest Persons to read.—DANIEL DEFOE, Letter to *Mist's Weekly Journal*, 1718, *Daniel Defoe: His Life and Recently Discovered Writings*, 1869, Vol. 2, ed. Lee, p. 31

I was not willing to let the present Month, the fairest in the whole Circle of the Year, pass over, without entertaining my youthful Readers of either Sex, with something suitable to the Gayety of the Season. And yet, I should have been greatly at a Loss for a proper Entertainment, had not a Gentleman, whose Knowledge of the Polite Writers in every Language is the least of his Commendations, obliged me with a Piece of fine In-

vention out of *Chaucer*, which is properly a very elegant *May-poem.* . . .

It is hard to say, whether the copiousness of *Chaucer's* Invention, or the Liveliness of his Imagination, is most to be admired through all his Writings. He flourished above Three Hundred Years ago: And yet through the Cloud of his antiquated Language, his Images still shine out with greater Brightness, than those, which appear in any of our succeeding Poets, if we except *Spencer*, and *Shakespeare*, and *Milton*. He was a great Master of Perspicuity and Simplicity in all his Narrations; and his Expression is always precise to the Justness of his Ideas. . . . *Chaucer* is, likewise, a diligent observer of Nature, whether he deals in Realities or in Fables.—AMBROSE PHILLIPS, "Introduction" to *The Cuckoo and the Nightingale* ⟨*The Boke of Cupide*⟩, *The Free-Thinker*, May 24, 1720

The Morning-Star of the *English* Poetry! was, by his own Record, in the *Testament of Love*, born in *London*; in the Reign of *Edward* the Third. His Family is suppos'd to come in with *William* the *Norman*, and, some day, his Father was a Merchant. He had his Education partly at *Oxford*, partly at *Cambridge*, and, by Circumstance, we find he was enter'd a Student of the *Inner-Temple*. He travelled in his Youth, thro' *France* and *Flanders*; and, in the Reign of *Richard* the Second, was famous for his Learning. After this he marry'd the Daughter of a Knight of *Hainault*, by which Alliance he is said to become Brother-in-Law to *John* of *Gaunt* Duke of *Lancaster*. He had several Children, a large, and ample Revenue, resided chiefly at *Woodstock*, was employ'd on several Embassies, received many great Rewards from the Crown, and was in high Esteem with the most Noble and Excellent Persons of his Time.—In the latter Part of his Life, he met with many Troubles, of which he complains, very pathetically, in some of his Pieces; yet liv'd to the Age of Seventy Two Years, and was bury'd at *Westminster*.

All agree he was the first Master of his Art among us, and that the Language, in general, is much oblig'd to him for Copiousness, Strength, and Ornament. It would be endless, almost, to enumerate the Compliments that have been paid to his Merit, by the Gratitude of those Writers, who have enrich'd themselves so much by his inestimable Legacies.—But his own Works, are his best Monument. In those appear a real Genius, as capable of inventing, as improving; equally suited to the Gay, and the Sublime; soaring in high Life, and pleasant in low: Tho' I don't find the least Authority in History to prove it. Ever both entertaining, and instructive! All which is so well known, 'tis, in a Manner, needless to repeat: But the Nature of this Work requires it, and I should not be excus'd for saying less, or omitting a Quotation; tho it is not a little difficult to chuse one that will do him Justice: Most of his principal Tales have been already exhausted by the Moderns, and, consequently, neither of them would appear to Advantage in their antiquated, original Dress; tho' the same in Complexion and Harmony of Parts.—ELIZABETH COOPER, *The Muses' Library*, 1737

All these, I say, are the Strokes of no common Genius, but of a Man perfectly conversant in the Turns and Foibles of human Nature. Observe but his Manner of Throwing Them in, and You will not think I exaggerate, if I say, these Turns of Satire, are not unworthy of PERSIUS, JUVENAL or HORACE himself. Before I cool upon this Subject, I shall venture (as far as the Ludicrous may hold Comparison with the Serious) to rank our CHAUCER with whatever We have of greatest Perfection in this Character of Painting; I shall venture to rank Him (making this Allowance) either with SALUST or CLARENDON; Who in History are allowed to have been the greatest Masters of the Picturesque; I mean the best Drawers of Characters. Even here some Criticks will not allow that the Persons, so described, are always consistent with themselves, at least that their Actions are always conformable to the Characters given of Them by their Historians; they will never be able to lay that Charge to CHAUCER. A Fault, however, more applicable to CLARENDON than to SALLUST.

For it was not to the Distinguishing of Character from Character, that the Excellence of CHAUCER was confin'd; He was equally Master of Introducing them properly on the Stage; and after having introduced them, of Supporting them agreeably to the Part They were formed to personate. In This, He claims equal Honour with the best Comedians; there is no Admirer of PLAUTUS, TERENCE, or ARISTOPHANES, that will pretend to say, CHAUCER has not equally, thro' his *Canterbury Tales*, supported his Characters. And All must allow, that the Plan, by which He connects and unites his Tales, one with another, is well designed, and well executed. You will not think it Loss of Time, if I enter into it, so far as may be requisite to our present Subject.

The Scheme of the *Canterbury Tales* is this. CHAUCER pretends, that intending to pay his Devotions to the Shrine of THOMAS A BECKET, He set up his Horse at the *Tabbard Inn* in *Southwark.*—GEORGE OGLE "Letters to a Friend," *Gaultheris and Griselda: or the Clerk of Oxford's Tale; from Boccace, Petrarch and Chaucer*, 1739, pp. vii–viii

The first of our authours, who can be properly said to have written *English*, was Sir *John Gower*, who in his *Confession of a Lover*, calls *Chaucer* his disciple, and may therefore be considered as the father of our poetry. . . .

The history of our language is now brought to the point at which the history of our poetry is generally supposed to commence, the time of the illustrious *Geoffry Chaucer*, who may perhaps, with great justice, be stiled the first of our versifiers who wrote poetically. He does not however appear to have deserved all the praise which he has received, or all the censure that he has suffered. Dryden, who mistaking genius for learning, and in confidence of his abilities, ventured to write of what he had not examined, ascribes to *Chaucer* the first refinement of our numbers, the first production of easy and natural rhymes, and the improvement of our language, by words borrowed from the more polished languages of the Continent. *Skinner* contrarily blames him in harsh terms for having vitiated his native speech by *whole cartloads of foreign words*. But he that reads the works of *Gower* will find smooth numbers and easy rhymes, of which *Chaucer* is supposed to have been the inventor, and the *French* words, whether good or bad, of which *Chaucer* is charged as the importer. Some innovations he might probably make, like others, in the infancy of our poetry, which the paucity of books does ⟨not⟩ allow us to discover with particular exactness; but the works of *Gower* and *Lydgate* sufficiently evince that his diction was in general like that of his contemporaries: and some improvements he undoubtedly made by the various dispositions of his rhymes; and by the mixture of different numbers, in which he seems to have been happy and judicious. I have selected several specimens both of his prose and verse; and among them, part of his translation of *Boetius*. . . . It would be improper to quote very sparingly an author of so much reputation, or to make very large extracts from a book so generally known.—SAMUEL JOHNSON, *Dictionary of the English Language*, 1755

On the revival of literature, the first writers seemed not to have observed any SELECTION in their thoughts and images. Dante, Petrarch, Boccace, Ariosto, make very sudden transitions from the sublime to the ridiculous. Chaucer, in his Temple of Mars, among many pathetic pictures, has brought in a strange line,

> The coke is scalded for all his long ladell.

No writer has more religiously observed the decorum here recommended than Virgil.

> This having heard and seen, some pow'r unknown,
> Strait chang'd the scene, and snatch'd me from the throne;
> Before my view appear'd a structure fair,
> Its site uncertain, if in earth or air.
> (1. 417).

The scene here changes from the TEMPLE of FAME to that of Rumour. Such a change is not methinks judicious, as it destroys the unity of the subject, and distracts the view of the reader; not to mention, that the difference between Rumour and Fame is not sufficiently distinct and perceptible. POPE has, however, the merit of compressing the sense of a great number of Chaucer's lines into a small compass. As Chaucer takes every opportunity of satyrizing the follies of his age, he has in this part introduced many circumstances, which it was prudent in POPE to omit, as they would not have been either relished or understood in the present times.

> While thus I stood intent to see and hear,
> One came, methought, and whisper'd in my ear,
> What could thus high thy rash ambition raise?
> Art thou, fond youth, a candidate for praise?
> 'Tis true, (said I,) not void of hopes I came,
> For who so fond as youthful bards, of Fame?

This conclusion is not copied from Chaucer, and is judicious. Chaucer has finished his story inartificially, by saying he was surprised at the sight of a man of great authority, and awoke in a fright. The succeeding lines give a pleasing moral to the allegory; and the two last shew the man of honour and virtue, as well as the poet:

> Unblemish'd let me live, or die unknown:
> Oh grant an honest fame, or grant me none!

In finishing this Section, we may observe, that POPE's alterations of Chaucer are introduced with judgment and art; that these alterations are more in number, and more important in conduct, than any Dryden has made of the same author. This piece was communicated to Steele, who entertained a high opinion of its beauties, and who conveyed it to Addison. POPE had ornamented the poem with the machinery of guardian angels, which he afterwards omitted. . . .

The WIFE OF BATH is the other piece of Chaucer which POPE selected to imitate. One cannot but wonder at his choice, which, perhaps, nothing but his youth could excuse. Dryden, who is known not to be nicely scrupulous, informs us, that he would not versify it on account of its indecency. POPE, however, has omitted or softened the grosser and more offensive passages. Chaucer afforded him many subjects of a more serious and sublime species; and it were to be wished, POPE had exercised his pencil on the pathetic story of the Patience of Grisilda, or Troilus and Cressida, or the Complaint of the Black Knight; or, above all, on Cambuscan and Canace. From the accidental circumstance of Dryden and POPE's having copied the gay and ludicrous parts of Chaucer, the common notion seems to have arisen, that Chaucer's vein of poetry was chiefly turned to the light and the ridiculous. But they who look into Chaucer, will soon be convinced of this prevailing prejudice; and will find his comic vein, like that of Shakespeare, to be only like one of mercury, imperceptibly mingled with a mine of gold.

CHAUCER is highly extolled by Dryden, in the spirited and pleasing preface to his fables; for his prefaces, after all, are very pleasing, notwithstanding the opposite opinions they contain, because his prose is the most numerous and sweet, the most *mellow* and *generous*, of any our language has yet produced.—Joseph Warton, *Essay on the Genius and Writings of Pope*, 1756–82

Chaucer, notwithstanding the praises bestowed on him, I think obscene and contemptible:—he owes his celebrity merely to his antiquity, which he does not deserve so well as Pierce Plowman, or Thomas of Ercildoune. English living poets I have avoided mentioning:—we have none who will survive their productions. Taste is over with us.—George Gordon, Lord Byron, "Memorandum Book, 30 November 1807," *The Life, Letters and Journals of Lord Byron*, 1830, ed. Moore, Ch. 5, p. 49

'Sweet is the holiness of Youth'—so felt
Time-honoured Chaucer when he framed the Lay
By which the Prioress beguiled the way,
And many a Pilgrim's rugged heart did melt.
Hadst thou, loved Bard! whose spirit often dwelt
In the clear land of vision, but foreseen
King, Child, and Seraph, blended in the mien
Of pious Edward kneeling as he knelt
In meek and simple Infancy, what joy
For universal Christendom had thrilled
Thy heart! what hopes inspired thy genius, skilled
(O great Precursor, genuine morning Star)
The lucid shafts of reason to employ,
Piercing the Papal darkness from afar!
   —William Wordsworth, "Sonnet XXIII:
    Edward VI," *Ecclesiastical Sonnets*, 1822,
    p. 65

It is remarkable, the character of the pleasure we derive from the best books. They impress us with the conviction, that one nature wrote and the same reads. We read the verses of one of the great English poets, of Chaucer, of Marvell, of Dryden, with the most modern joy,—with a pleasure, I mean, which is in great part caused by the abstraction of all *time* from their verses. There is some awe mixed with the joy of our surprise, when this poet, who lived in some past world, two or three hundred years ago, says that which lies close to my own soul, that which I also had well-nigh thought and said. But for the evidence thence afforded to the philosophical doctrine of the identity of all minds, we should suppose some pre-established harmony, some foresight of souls that were to be, and some preparation of stores for their future wants, like the fact observed in insects, who lay up food before death for the young grub they shall never see.—Ralph Waldo Emerson, "The American Scholar," 1837

Chaucer was a courtier, and a companion of princes; nay, a reformer also, and a stirrer out in the world. He understood that world, too, thoroughly, in the ordinary sense of such understanding; yet, as he was a true great poet in everything, so in nothing more was he so than in loving the country, and the trees and fields. It is as hard to get him out of a grove as his friend Boccaccio; and he tells us, that, in May, he would often go out into the meadows to "abide" there, solely in order to "look upon the daisy." Milton seems to have made a point of never living in a house that had not a garden to it.—Leigh Hunt, *A Jar of Honey from Mount Hybla*, 1848, p. 122

A taste for plain strong speech, what is called a biblical style, marks the English. . . . It is not less seen in poetry. Chaucer's hard painting of his Canterbury pilgrims satisfies the senses. . . . This mental materialism makes the value of English transcendental genius.

The marriage of the two qualities (materialism and intellectuality) is in their speech.—Ralph Waldo Emerson, *English Traits*, 1856, Vol. 5, Centenary ed., pp. 233–34

Chaucer, O how I wish thou wert
Alive and, as of yore, alert!
Then, after bandied tales, what fun
Would we two have with monk and nun.
Ah, surely verse was never meant
To render mortals somnolent.
In Spenser's labyrinthine rhymes
I throw my arms o'erhead at times,
Opening sonorous mouth as wide
As oystershells at ebb of tide.
Mistake me not: I honour him
Whose magic made the Muses dream
Of things they never knew before,
And scenes they never wandered o'er.
I dare not follow, nor again
Be wafted with the wizard train.
No bodyless and soulless elves
I seek, but creatures like ourselves.
If any poet now runs after
The Faeries, they will split with laughter,
Leaving him in the desert, where
Dry grass is emblematic fare.
Thou wast content to act the squire
Becomingly, and mount no higher,
Nay, at fit season to descend
Into the poet with a friend,
Then ride with him about thy land
In lithesome nutbrown boots well-tann'd,
With lordly greyhound, who would dare
Course against law the summer hare,
Nor takes to heart the frequent crack
Of whip, with curse that calls him back.
  The lesser Angels now have smiled
To see thee frolic like a child,
And hear thee, innocent as they,
Provoke them to come down and play.
  —Walter Savage Landor, "To Chaucer,"
   Heroic Idylls, 1863, pp. 142–43

The earliest poetry belongs to the same age with Wycliffe's Bible. Chaucer was possibly the friend of Wycliffe—certainly shared many of his sympathies and antipathies. He loved the priest, or, as he was called, the secular priest, who went among the people, and cared for them as his fellow countrymen; he intensely disliked the friars, who flattered them and cursed them, and in both ways governed them and degraded them. His education had been different from Wycliffe's, his early poetical powers had been called forth by the ladies and gentlemen of the court. He mingled much French with his speech, as they did; he acquired from them a kind of acquaintance with life which Wycliffe could not obtain in the Oxford schools. Had he remained under their influence he might have been merely a very musical court singer; but he entered into fellowship with common citizens. He became a keen observer of all the different forms of life and society in his time—a keen observer, and, as all such are, genial, friendly, humorous, able to understand men about him by sympathising with them, able to understand the stories of the past by his experience of the present. Without being a reformer like Wycliffe, he helped forward the Reformation by making men acquainted with themselves and their fellows, by stripping off disguises, and by teaching them to open their eyes to the beautiful world which lay about them. Chaucer is the genuine specimen of an English poet—a type of the best who were to come after him; with cordial affection for men and for nature; often tempted to coarseness, often yielding to his baser nature in his desire to enter into all the different experiences of men; apt through this desire, and through his hatred of what was insincere, to say many things of which he had need to repent, and of which he did repent; but never losing his loyalty to what was pure, his reverence for what was divine. He is an illustration of the text from which I started. The English books which live through ages are those which connect themselves with human life and action. His other poems, though graceful and harmonious, are only remembered, because in his *Canterbury Tales* he has come directly into contact with the hearts and thoughts, the sufferings and sins, of men and women, and has given the clearest pictures we possess of all the distinctions and occupations in his own day.—FREDERICK DENISON MAURICE, "On Books," 1865, *The Friendship of Books and Other Lectures*, 1874, pp. 76–77

Even if Chaucer followed invariable rules with regard to the pronouncing or suppressing of the final *e*, it cannot be expected that they should be entirely made out by examining one single text of the *Canterbury Tales*, which, though relatively a good one, is manifestly full of errors. A comparison of several of the better manuscripts would enable us to speak with much more accuracy and confidence. Tyrwhitt's arbitrary text may very frequently be used to clear up, both in this and in other particulars, the much superior manuscript published by Wright. Still the question whether an *e* was pronounced would often be one of much delicacy (as the previous question whether it actually existed is sometimes one of great difficulty), and not to be determined by counting syllables on the fingers. No supposition is indeed more absurd than that Chaucer, a master poet for any time, could write awkward, halting, or even unharmonious verses. It is to be held, therefore, that when a verse is bad, and cannot be made good anyway as it stands, then we have not the verse that Chaucer wrote. But with regard to the particular point upon which we are now engaged, it would often be indifferent, or nearly so, whether a final *e* is absolutely dropped, or lightly glided over. Then again, as not a few grammatical forms were most certainly written both with and without this termination, the fuller form would often slip in where the other would be preferable or necessary, much depending on the care, the intelligence, or the good ear of the scribe. Very often the concurrence of an initial vowel, justifying elision, with a doubtful final *e*, renders it possible to read a verse in two ways or more; and lastly, hundreds of verses are so mutilated or corrupted that no safe opinion can be based upon them. Such verses as these ought plainly not to be used either to support or impugn a conclusion; neither ought the general rules which seem to be authorized by the majority of instances be too rigorously applied to the emendation of verses that cannot be made, as they stand, to come under these rules.—FRANCIS JAMES CHILD, "Elision of Final Vowels," *Early English Pronunciation*, 1869, Pt. 1, Ch. 4, ed. Ellis, p. 360

And for the standard theological writings which are ultimately to be the foundation of this body of secular literature (the projected St. George's library), I have chosen seven authors, whose lives and works, so far as the one can be traced or the other certified, shall be, with the best help I can obtain from the good scholars of Oxford, prepared one by one in perfect editions for the St. George's schools. These seven books will

contain, in as many volumes as may be needful, the lives and writings of the men who have taught the purest theological truth hitherto known to the Jews, Greeks, Latins, Italians, and English; namely, Moses, David, Hesiod, Virgil, Dante, Chaucer, and, for seventh, summing the whole with vision of judgment, St. John the Divine.

The Hesiod I purpose, if my life is spared, to translate myself (into prose), and to give in complete form. Of Virgil I shall only take the two first Georgics, and the sixth book of the Aeneid, but with the Douglas translation; adding the two first books of Livy, for completion of the image of Roman life. Of Chaucer, I take the authentic poems, except the Canterbury Tales; together with, be they authentic or not, the Dream, and the fragment of the translation of the Romance of the Rose, adding some French chivalrous literature of the same date. I shall so order this work, that, in such measure as it may be possible to me, it shall be in a constantly progressive relation to the granted years of my life. The plan of it I give now, and will explain in full detail, that my scholars may carry it out, if I cannot.

And now let my general readers observe, finally, about all reading,—You must read, for the nourishment of your mind, precisely under the moral laws which regulate your eating for the nourishment of the body. That is to say, you must not eat for the pleasure of eating, nor read for the pleasure of reading. But, if you manage yourself rightly, you will intensely enjoy your dinner, and your book. If you have any sense, you can easily follow out this analogy: I have not time at present to do it for you; only be sure it holds, to the minutest particular, with this difference only, that the vices and virtues of reading are more harmful on the one side, and higher on the other, as the soul is more precious than the body. Gluttonous reading is a worse vice than gluttonous eating; filthy and foul reading, a much more loathsome habit than filthy eating. Epicurism in books is much more difficult of attainment than epicurism in meat, but plain and virtuous feeding the most entirely pleasurable.

And now, one step of farther thought will enable you to settle a great many questions with one answer.

As you may neither eat, nor read, for the pleasure of eating or reading, so you may do *nothing else* for the pleasure of it, but for the use. The moral difference between a man and a beast is, that the one acts primarily for use, the other for pleasure. And all acting for pleasure before use, or instead of use, is, in one word, 'Fornication.'—JOHN RUSKIN, "Letter 61," *Fors Clavigera*, 1876, pp. 21–22

I have not studied Wyatt, but Surrey I used to read: he, I think, is a greater man. He was an accomplished rhythmist, not that the experiments in couplets of long twelves and thirteens are pleasing, though this is better than couplets both twelves or both thirteens. He has a very fine style free from Euphuism. However, to speak of the sample you send, I must say that I think you have missed the clue. You take the rhythm for free triple time, iambs and anapaests say, and four feet to a line (except the refrain). But to get this you have to skip, in two lines out of these few, a whole foot as marked and stressy as any other foot. This is a licence unpardonable by the reader and incredible in the writer.

Before offering my own thoughts I must premise something. So far as I know triple time is in English verse a shy and late thing. I have not studied *Piers Ploughman* and so cannot pronounce how far triple time is boldly employed in it; at least it must have been suggested. But on the Romance side of our versification triple time appeared, I think, late. It may have been suggested by *Piers Ploughman's* rhythm, as I have said, but partly I conjecture it arose from a simple misunderstanding or misreading of Chaucer and the verse of that date and thereabouts. Chaucer and his contemporaries wrote for a pronunciation fast changing (everybody knows that final *e* for instance has often to be sounded in Chaucer, but everybody does not know that mostly it is *not* to be sounded and that the line which scans by its aid is really to be scanned another way). Their versification was popular and hit the mark in its time, but soon, as far as I can see, became obsolete, and they being much read and not rightly scanned thus came to suggest rhythms which they never thought of. The same sort of thing has, I think, happened often in the history of verse. And so far, Wyatt's piece might be scanned as you scan it—but for the two lines with a foot too much.

Now in particular I suppose that the verse called doggrel (in which the play of *Royster Doyster* is written and parts of *Love's Labour*, the *Shrew*, etc) arose in this way: I do not know how else such a shapeless thing can have arisen. If it were a spontaneous popular growth it wd. [be] simpler and stronger. It must be the corruption or degeneration of something literary misunderstood or disfigured. Its rule is: couplets, with a pause dividing each line and on either side of this either two or three (perhaps sometimes even more) stresses, so that the line may range from four to six feet, and the rhythm variable too, iambic or anapaestic.

This wretched doggrel I think Surrey was systematising and raising in that couplet of his of which I spoke above and, to come to the point, I conjecture that Wyatt is dealing with the same thing here. The main point is the pause or caesura; on that the line turns. The notion of pause or caesura had come to English versification from two different quarters; from *Piers Ploughman* and the older native poetry on the one hand, where it is marked by a sort of Greek colon or by a stroke, and from France on the other, where it is essential both to the Alexandrine and to the old ten-syllable or five-foot line of the Chansons and is marked after the fourth syllable, I find.—GERARD MANLEY HOPKINS, Letter to Robert Bridges, 1880, *The Letters of Gerard Manley Hopkins to Robert Bridges*, 1935, ed. Abbott, pp. 106–7

I have found that Chaucer's scanning, once understood, is extremely smooth and regular, much more so than is thought by Mr. Skeat and other modern Chaucerists, and they think it regularity itself compared to what Dryden and older critics thought of it.—GERARD MANLEY HOPKINS, Letter to R. W. Dixon, 1881, *The Correspondence of Gerard Manley Hopkins and R. W. Dixon*, 1935, ed. Abbott, pp. 66–67

On all other points Chaucer is of course almost immeasurably the superior of Wordsworth; in breadth of human interest, in simplicity of varied sympathies, in straightforward and superb command of his materials as an artist, the inspired man of the world as much excels the slow-thoughted and self-studious recluse as in warmth and wealth of humour, in consummate power of narrative, and in childlike manfulness of compassionate or joyous emotion; but their usual relations are reversed when the subject treated by Wordsworth exacts a deeper and intenser expression of feeling, or when his thought takes wing for higher flights of keener speculation, than the strong, elastic, equable movement of Chaucer's thought and verse could be expected to achieve or to attain. In a word, the elder singer has a thousand advantages over the later, but the one point on which the later has the advantage is worth all the rest put together: he is the sublimer poet of the two.—ALGERNON CHARLES SWINBURNE, "Chaucer Lacks Sublimity," *Miscellanies*, 1886, p. 152

The successor of the deposed king, the third Edward, ushers in the complete and central period of the Middle Ages in England. The feudal system is complete: the life and spirit of the country has developed into a condition if not quite independent, yet quite forgetful, on the one hand of the ideas and customs of the Celtic and Teutonic tribes, and on the other of the authority of the Roman Empire. The Middle Ages have grown into manhood; that manhood has an art of its own, which, though developed step by step from that of Old Rome and New Rome, and embracing the strange mysticism and dreamy beauty of the East, has forgotten both its father and its mother, and stands alone triumphant, the loveliest, brightest, and gayest of all the creations of the human mind and hand.

It has a literature of its own too, somewhat akin to its art, yet inferior to it, and lacking its unity, since there is a double stream in it. On the one hand is the court poet, the gentleman, Chaucer, with his Italianizing metres, and his formal recognition of the classical stories; on which, indeed, he builds a superstructure of the quaintest and most unadulterated mediaevalism, as gay and bright as the architecture which his eyes beheld and his pen pictured for us, so clear, defined, and elegant it is; a sunny world even amidst its violence and passing troubles, like those of a happy child, the worst of them an amusement rather than a grief to the onlookers; a world that scarcely needed hope in its eager life of adventure and love, amidst the sunlit blossoming meadows, and green woods, and white begilded manor-houses. A kindly and human muse is Chaucer's, nevertheless, interested in and amused by all life, but of her very nature devoid of strong aspirations for the future; and that all the more, since, though the strong devotion and fierce piety of the ruder Middle Ages had by this time waned, and the Church was more often lightly mocked at than either feared or loved, still the *habit* of looking on this life as part of another yet remained: the world is fair and full of adventure; kind men and true and noble are in it to make one happy; fools also to laugh at, and rascals to be resisted, yet not wholly condemned; and when this world is over we shall still go on living in another which is a part of this. Look at all the picture, note all and live in all, and be as merry as you may, never forgetting that you are alive and that it is good to live.

That is the spirit of Chaucer's poetry; but alongside of it existed yet the ballad poetry of the people, wholly untouched by courtly elegance and classical pedantry; rude in art but never coarse, true to the backbone; instinct with indignation against wrong, and thereby expressing the hope that was in it; a protest of the poor against the rich, especially in those songs of the Foresters, which have been called the mediaeval epic of revolt; no more gloomy than the gentleman's poetry, yet cheerful from courage, and not content. Half a dozen stanzas of it are worth a cartload of the whining introspective lyrics of today; and he who, when he has mastered the slight differences of language from our own daily speech, is not moved by it, does not understand what true poetry means nor what its aim is.

There is a third element in the literature of this time which you may call Lollard poetry, the great example of which is William Langland's *Piers Plowman*. It is no bad corrective to Chaucer, and in *form* at least belongs wholly to the popular side; but it seems to me to show symptoms of the spirit of the rising middle class, and casts before it the shadow of the new master that was coming forward for the workman's oppression.—WILLIAM MORRIS, "Feudal England," *Signs of Change*, 1888, pp. 73–75

We have often thought that a curiously interesting book might be written on the posthumous fortune of poets. In the case of prose writers, the verdict of the age which immediately succeeds them is, as a rule, final. Their reputation is subject to few fluctuations. Once crowned, they are seldom deposed; once deposed, they are never reinstated. Time and accident may affect their popularity, but the estimate which has been formed by competent critics of their intrinsic worth remains unmodified. How different has been the fate of poets! Take Chaucer. In 1500 his popularity was at its height. During the latter part of the sixteenth century it began to decline. From that date till the end of William III.'s reign—in spite of the influence which he undoubtedly exercised over Spenser, and in spite of the respectful allusions to him in Sidney, Puttenham, Drayton, and Milton—his fame had become rather a tradition than a reality. In the following age the good-natured tolerance of Dryden was succeeded by the contempt of Addison and the supercilious patronage of Pope. Between 1700 and 1782 nothing seemed more probable than that the writings of the first of England's narrative poets would live chiefly in the memory of antiquarians. In little more than half a century afterwards we find him placed, with Shakspeare and Milton, on the highest pinnacle of poetic renown.—JOHN CHURTON COLLINS, *Essays and Studies*, 1895, pp. 106–7

It is by no means out of accordance with the rule of things in literature and life that the English Renaissance, which was to produce by far the greatest literary results of the whole movement, had an overture, and even something much more than an overture, of portentous and almost unexampled length and dulness. . . .

The first, the most obvious, the most important, of these reasons, but perhaps still one not quite completely recognised, is the peculiar character of the English language—a character on which mere philology throws very little light, if, indeed, it does not distinctly obscure the field and distort the vision. Modern English is, of all great literary languages, the least of a natural growth or even a chemical compound, the most of a mechanical blend or adjustment. The purely English or Anglo-Saxon, the French, and the Latin elements in it, not to mention the smaller constituents, have simply taken their shapes by a secular process of rolling and jumbling together, like the pebbles on the sea-shore or the sweetmeats in a confectioner's copper basin. From this mere attrition, this mere shaking together, English grammar, English prose style, and English prosody have resulted. And this process took—could not but take—centuries before it could turn out results suitable for a Spenser or a Shakespeare, a Hooker or a Bacon. The real reason why the results of a method so apparently accomplished as Chaucer's were mere botch-work in the hands of his purely native followers, was that Chaucer came too early, and when this process of attrition had not gone on long enough. Dante, dealing with a language like Italian, homogeneous in itself, however various in dialect, was able to do his work once for all—not that Dante gives us complete modern Italian, either in grammar or even in prosody, but that there are no fundamental differences. Chaucer could do nothing of the kind. The philologers who ask "Whether Chaucer did not know his own language?" and so force on him chimerical uniformities of rhyme and syntax, may be asked in turn, "How, then, do you account for what followed?" They cannot account for it. The literary historian can.

In other words, Chaucer, by main force and gigantic dead-lift of individual genius, had got the still imperfectly adjusted materials of English into a shape sufficient for architecture of permanent and beautiful design. But when this force and this skill were taken away, the rough-edged or crumbling materials of language, the not fully organised devices of grammar and metre, were insufficient to make anything but more or less shapeless heaps. Skelton may have evaded the difficulty by adopting rococo forms; Surrey and, earlier still, Wyatt, by taking liberties with accent or quantity on the one hand, improving grammar on the other, and borrowing the constraining stay of the sonnet or the liberty of blank verse from more accomplished languages like Italian, may have made actual progress towards the true English style. But all this demanded time, experiment, unsuccessful as well as successful, and an amount of individual genius which simply did not happen to be available for the moment, or for many moments.

The prose-writers had an apparently more difficult but really easier task. They were not misled, in the very act of being assisted, by intrinsically consummate, but relatively premature and exceptional, work like Chaucer's. Chaucer's own prose, interesting and important as it is, has nothing of the exceptional and almost portentous character of his verse. It fits (with due allowance for the exceptional talent of its author) easily and naturally into the succession of its kind, from the *Ancren Riwle* and the various theological exercises of the thirteenth and early fourteenth centuries. It is itself succeeded as naturally by fresh applications and developments. The prose-writers of the fifteenth century are not, like the verse-writers of it, endeavouring to draw a bow which is not only too strong for them, but of which the yew is dry-rotted and the string frayed by time and weather. They have a great deal to do; they have not done very much as yet. But they are putting prose more and more to its naturally multifarious or rather infinite uses; they are accumulating the vocabulary; they are discovering, either by mere practice, or by borrowing, sensibly or insensibly, from the French and Latin originals, whom they almost inevitably follow, the varieties of style; they are shaping grammar by using it. In one great instance—that of Malory—they have already done a great deal more than this: they have actually made, once for all, a style that cannot be surpassed for its particular purpose. And now, in our own period, in Fisher and in Berners, we find them achieving something only less great. Berners, indeed, like Malory, "comes to the end": of the myriad purposes of prose he has found one which he can discharge excellently, but which will not need, in that particular way and style, to be discharged again. Fisher is much less positively satisfactory and interesting to us; but he is even more important to history, because he is trying the rhetorical devices, forming the tools of style, for purposes other than his own, as well as for his own itself.—GEORGE SAINTSBURY, *The Earlier Renaissance*, 1901, pp. 231–36

JOHN SKELTON
From *Phillip Sparrowe* (c. 1508)
Poetical Works of John Skelton
1843, ed. Dyce, pp. 69–75, v. 605–812

An epytaphe I wold haue
For Phyllyppes graue:
But for I am a mayde,
Tymerous, halfe afrayde,
That neuer yet asayde
Of Elyconys well,
Where the Muses dwell;
Though I can rede and spell,
Recounte, reporte, and tell
Of the Tales of Caunterbury,
Some sad storyes, some mery;
As Palamon and Arcet,
Duke Theseus, and Partelet;
And of the Wyfe of Bath,

That worketh moch scath
Whan her tale is tolde
Amonge huswyues bolde,
How she controlde
Her husbandes as she wolde,
And them to despyse
In the homylyest wyse,
Brynge other wyues in thought
Their husbandes to set at nought:
And though that rede haue I
Of Gawen and syr Guy. . . .

And though I can expounde
Of Hector of Troye,
That was all theyr ioye,
Whom Achylles slew,
Wherfore all Troy dyd rew;
And of the loue so hote
That made Troylus to dote
Vpon fayre Cressyde,
And what they wrote and sayd,
And of theyr wanton wylles
Pandaer bare the bylles
From one to the other;
His maisters loue to further,
Somtyme a presyous thyng,
An ouche, or els a ryng;
From her to hym agayn
Somtyme a prety chayn,
Or a bracelet of her here,
Prayd Troylus for to were
That token for her sake;
How hartely he dyd it take,
And moche therof dyd make;
And all that was in vayne,
For she dyd but fayne;
The story telleth playne,
He coulde not optayne,
Though his father were a kyng,
Yet there was a thyng
That made the male to wryng;
She made hym to syng
The song of louers lay;
Musyng nyght and day,
Mournyng all alone,
Comfort had he none,
For she was quyte gone;
Thus in conclusyon,
She brought him in abusyon;
In ernest and in game
She was moch to blame;
Disparaged is her fame,
And blemysshed is her name,
In maner half with shame;
Troylus also hath lost
On her moch loue and cost,
And now must kys the post;
Pandara, that went betwene,
Hath won nothing, I wene,
But lyght for somer grene;
Yet for a speciall laud
He is named Troylus baud,
Of that name he is sure
Whyles the world shall dure. . . .

I am but a yong mayd,
And cannot in effect

My style as yet direct
With Englysh wordes elect:
Our naturall tong is rude,
And hard to be enneude
With pullysshed termes lusty;
Our language is so rusty,
So cankered, and so full
Of frowardes, and so dull,
That if I wolde apply
To wryte ornatly,
I wot not where to fynd
Termes to serue my mynde.
　　　Gowers Englysh is olde,
And of no value told;
His mater is worth gold,
And worthy to be enrold.
　　　In Chauser I am sped,
His tales I haue red:
His mater is delectable,
Solacious, and commendable;
His Englysh well alowed,
So as it is enprowed,
For as it is enployd,
There is no Englysh voyd,
At those dayes moch commended,
And now men wold haue amended
His Englysh, whereat they barke,
And mar all they warke:
Chaucer, that famus clerke,
His termes were not darke,
But plesaunt, easy, and playne;
No worde he wrote in vayne.
　　　Also Johnn Lydgate
Wryteth after an hyer rate;
It is dyffuse to fynde
The sentence of his mynde,
Yet wryteth he in his kynd,
No man that can amend
Those maters that he hath pende;
Yet some men fynde a faute,
And say he wryteth to haute.

JOHN FOXE

"A Protestation to the whole Church of England"

Ecclesiasticall history contayning the Actes and Monumentes of thyngs passed in euery Kinges tyme in this Realme

1570, 2nd enlarged ed., pp. 341, 965–66

To discend now somewhat lower in drawing out the descent of the Church. What a multitude here commeth of faithful witnesses in the time of *Ioh. Wickleffe*, as *Ocliffe, Wickleffe*. an. 1376. *W. Thorpe, White, Puruey, Patshall, Payne, Gower, Chauser, Gascoyne, William Swynderby, Walter Brute, Roger Dexter, William Sautry* about the year 1400. *Iohn Badley*, an. 1410. *Nicholas Tayler, Rich. Wagstaffe, Mich. Scriuener, W. Smith, Iohn Henry, W. Parchmenar, Roger Goldsmith*, with an Ancresse called *Mathilde* in the Citie of Leicester, Lord *Cobham*, Syr *Roger Acton* Knight, *Iohn Beuerlay* preacher, *Iohn Hus, Hierome of Prage* Scholemaster, with a number of faithfull Bohemians and Thaborites not to be told with whom I might also adioyne *Laurentius Valla*, and

Ioannes Picus the learned Earle of Mirandula. But what do I stand upon recitall of names, which almost are infinite. . . .

For so much as mention is here made of these super-stitious sects of Fryers, and such other beggerly religions, it shall not seme much impartinent, being moued by the occasion hereof . . . to annexe . . . a certayne other auncient treatise compiled by Geoffray Chawcer by the way of a Dialogue or questions moued in the person of a certaine uplandish and simple ploughman of the countrey. Which treatise for the same, yᵉ autor intituled Jack vp land. . . .

Moreouer to these two ⟨Linacre and Pace⟩, I thought it not out of season to couple also some mention of Geffray Chaucer, and Iohn Gower: Whiche although beyng much discrepant from these in course of yeares, yet may seme not vnworthy to bee matched with these forenamed persons in commendation of their studie and learnyng. . . .

Likewise, as touchyng the tyme of Chaucer, by hys owne workes in the end of his first booke of Troylus and Creseide it is manifest, that he and Gower were both of one tyme, althoughe it seemeth that Gower was a great deale his auncient: both notably learned, as the barbarous rudenes of that tyme did geue: both great frendes together, and both in like kind of studie together occupied, so endeuoryng themselues, and employing their tyme, that they excelling many other in study and exercise of good letters, did passe forth their lyues here right worshipfully & godly, to the worthy fame and commendation of their name. Chaucers woorkes bee all printed in one volume, and therfore knowen to all men. This I meruell, to see the idle life of yᵉ priestes and clergy men of that tyme, seyng these lay persons shewed themselues in these kynde of liberall studies so industrious & fruitfully occupied: but muche more I meruell to consider this, how that the Bishoppes condemnyng and abolishyng al maner of Englishe bookes and treatises, which might bryng the people to any light of knowledge, did yet authorise the woorkes of Chaucer to remayne still & to be occupied: Who (no doubt) saw in Religion as much almost, as euen we do now, and vttereth in hys workes no lesse, and semeth to bee a right Wicleuian, or els was neuer any, and that all his workes almost, if they be throughly aduised, will testifie (albeit it bee done in myrth, & couertly) & especially the latter ende of his third booke of the Testament of loue: for there purely he toucheth the highest matter, that is the Communion. Wherin, excepte a man be altogether blynde, he may espye him at the full. Althoughe in the same booke (as in all other he vseth to do) vnder shadowes couertly, as vnder a visoure, he suborneth truth, in such sorte, as both priuely she may profite the godly minded, and yet not be espyed of the craftye aduersarie: And therefore the Byshops, belike, takyng hys workes but for iestes and toyes, in condemnyng other bookes, yet permitted his bookes to be read. So it pleased God to blinde then the eyes of them, for the more commoditie of his people, to the entent that through the readyng of his treatises, some fruite might redounde therof to his Churche, as no doubt, it did to many: As also I am partlye informed of certeine, whiche knewe the parties, which to them reported, that by readyng of Chausers workes, they were brought to the true knowledge of Religion. And not vnlike to be true. For to omitte other partes of his volume, whereof some are more fabulous then other, what tale can bee more playnely tolde, then the talke of the ploughman? or what finger can pointe out more directly the Pope with his Prelates to be Antichrist, then doth the poore Pellycan reasonyng agaynst the gredy Griffon? Under whiche *Hypotyposis* or Poesie, who is so blind that seeth not by the Pellicane, the doctrine of Christ, and of the Lollardes to bee defended agaynst the Churche of Rome? Or who is so impu-

dent that can denye that to be true, which the Pellicane there affirmeth in describyng the presumptuous pride of that pretensed Church? Agayne what egge can be more lyke, or figge vnto an other, then yᵉ words, properties, and conditions of that rauenyng Griphe resembleth the true Image, that is, the nature & qualities of that which we call the Churche of Rome, in euery point and degre? and therfore no great maruell, if that narration was exempted out of the copies of Chaucers workes: whiche notwithstandyng now is restored agayne, and is extant, for euery man to read that is disposed.

This Geffray Chauser being borne (as is thought) in Oxfordshire, & dwellyng in Wodstocke, lyeth buried in the Churche of the minster of S. Peter at Westminster, in an Ile on the South side of the sayd Churche, not far from the doore leading to the cloyster, and vpon his graue stone first were written these ii old verses

Galfridus Chauser vates et fama poesis
Maternae, hac sacra sum tumulatus humo.

ROBERT GREENE
From *Greene's Vision*
1592

I considered, that wee were borne to profit our countrie, not onely to pleasure our selues: then the discommodities that grew from my vaine pamphlets, began to muster in my sight: then I cald to minde, how many idle fancies I had made to passe the Presse, how I had pestred Gentlemens eyes and mindes, with the infection of many fond passions, rather infecting them with the allurements of some inchanted 'Aconiton', then tempered their thought with any honest Antidote, which consideration entered thus farre into my conscience. . . .

Being in this deepe meditation, lying contemplating vpon my bed, I fell a sleepe, where I had not lyne long in a slumber, but that me thought I was in a faire medowe, sitting vnder an Oake, viewing the beautie of the sunne which then shewed himselfe in his pride: as thus I sat gasing on so gorgeous an obiect, I spied comming downe the Meade, two ancient men, aged, for their foreheads were the Calenders of their yeares, and the whitenesse of their haires bewrayed the number of their dayes, their pace was answerable to their age, and *In diebus illis*, hung vpon their garments: their visages were wrinckled, but well featured, and their countenance conteyned much grauitie. . . .

Thou has heere two, whome experience hath taught many medicines for yong mens maladies, I am sir *Geffrey Chaucer*, this *Iohn Gower*, what we can in counsaile, shall be thy comfort, and for secrecie we are no blabs. Heering sir *Geffrey Chaucer* thus familiar, I tooke heart at grasse to my selfe, and thought nowe I might haue my doubt well debated, betweene two such excellent schollers: wherevpon putting of my hat with great reuerence, I made this replie.

Graue Lawreats, the tipes of Englands excellence for Poetry, and the worlds wonders for your wits, all haile, and happily welcome, for your presence is a salue for my passions, and the inward greefes that you perceiue by my outward lookes, are alreadie halfe eased by your comfortable promise: I cannot denie but my thoughts are discontent, and my sences in a great maze, which I haue damd vp a long while, as thinking best to smoother sorrow with silence, but now I will set fire on the straw, and lay open my secrets to your selues, that your sweet counsailes may ease my discontent. So it is, that by profession I am a scholler, and in wil do affect that which I could neuer effect in action, for faine would I haue some taste in the liberall sciences, but *Non licet cuibis adire Corinthum*, and therefore I content my selfe with a superficiall insight, and only satisfie my desire with the name of a Scholler, yet as blinde Baiard wil iumpe soonest into the mire, so haue I ventured afore many my betters, to put my selfe into the presse, and haue set foorth sundrie bookes in print of loue & such amourous fancies which some haue fauoured, as other haue misliked. But now of late there came foorth a booke called the Cobler of Canterburie, a merry worke, and made by some madde fellow, conteining plesant tales, a little tainted with scurilitie, such reuerend *Chawcer* as your selfe set foorth in your iourney to *Canterbury*. At this booke, the grauer and greater sorte repine, as thinking it not so pleasant to some, as preiudiciall to many, crossing it with such bitter inuectiues, that they condemne the Author almost for an Atheist. Now learned Lawreat, heere lyes the touch of my passions: they father the booke vppon me, whereas it is *Incerti authoris*, and suspitiouslye slaunder me with many harde reproches, for penning that which neuer came within the compasse of my Quill. . . . This father *Chawcer* hath made me enter into consideration of all my former follies, and to thinke how wantonly I haue spent my youth, in penning such fond pamphlets, that I am driuen into a dumpe whether they shall redound to my insuing credit, or my future infamie, or whether I haue doone well or ill, in setting foorth such amourous trifles, heerein resolue me, and my discontent is doone.

At this long period of mine, *Chawcer* sat downe & laught, and then rising vp and leaning his back against a Tree, he made this merry aunswer. Why *Greene* quoth he, knowest thou not, that the waters that flow from *Pernassus* Founte, are not tyed to any particular operation? that there are nine Muses, amongst whom as there is a *Clio* to write graue matters, so there is a *Thalis* to endite pleasant conceits, and that *Apollo* hath Baies for them both, aswell to crowne the one for hir wanton amours, as to honour the other for her worthy labours: the braine hath many strings, and the wit many stretches, some tragical to write, like *Euripedes*: some comicall to pen, like *Terence*: some deepely conceited to set out matters of great import: others sharpe witted to discouer pleasant fantasies: what if *Cato* set foorth seueare censures, and *Quid* amorous Axiomes, were they not both counted for their faculties excellent? yes, and *Ouid* was commended for his *Salem ingenii*, when the other was counted to haue a dull wit, & a slow memory: if learning were knit in one string, and could expresse himself but in one vaine, then should want of variety, bring all into an imperfect Chaos. But sundry men, sundry conceits, & wits are to be praised not for the grauity of the matter, but for the ripenes of the inuention: so that *Martiall*, *Horace* or any other, deserue to bee famoused for their Odes and Elegies, as wel as *Hesiode*, *Hortensius*, or any other for their deeper precepts of doctrines. Feare not then what those Morosie wil murmure, whose dead cinders brook no glowing sparkes nor care not for the opinion of such as hold none but Philosophie for a Subiect: I tell thee learning will haue his due, and let a vipers wit reach his hand to *Apollo*, and hee shall sooner haue a branch to eternize his fame, than the sowrest Satyricall Authour in the worlde. Wee haue heard of thy worke to be amorous, sententious, and well written. If thou doubtest blame for thy wantonnes, let my selfe suffice for an instaunce, whose Canter-

burie tales are broad enough before, and written homely and pleasantly: yet who hath bin more canonised for his workes, than Sir *Geffrey Chaucer*. What *Green*? Poets wits are free, and their words ought to be without checke: so it was in my time, and therfore resolue thy selfe, thou hast doone Scholler-like, in setting foorth thy pamphlets, and shalt haue perpetual fame which is learnings due for thy endeuour. This saying of *Chawcer* cheered mee vntill olde *Iohn Gower* rising vp with a sowre countenance began thus.

Iohn Gower to the Authour.

Well hath *Chawcer* said, that the braine hath sundrie strings, and the wit diuerse stretches: some bent to pen graue Poems, other to endite wanton fancies, both honoured and praised for the height of their capacitie: yet as the Diamond is more estimated in the Lapidaries shop than the Topace, and the Rose more valued in the Garden than Gillyflowers: So men that write of Morall precepts, or Philosophicall Aphorismes are more highly esteemed, than such as write Poems of loue, and conceits of fancie. . . .

Thou hast applied thy wits ill, & hast sowed chaffe & shalt reape no haruest. But my maister *Chaucer* brings in his workes for an instance, that as his, so thine shalbe famoused: no, it is not a promise to conclude vpon: for men honor his more for the antiquity of the verse, the english & prose, than for any deepe loue to the matter: for proofe marke how they weare out of vse. Therfore let me tel thee, thy books are baits that allure youth, Syrens that sing sweetly, and yet destroy with their notes, faire flowers without smel and good phrases without any profite.

Without any profite (quoth *Chawcer*) and with that hee start vp with a frown: no *Gower*, I tell thee, his labours, as they be amorous, so they be sententious: and serue as well to suppresse vanity, as they seem to import wantonnes. Is there no meanes to cure sores, but with Corasiues? no helpe for vlcers, but sharpe implasters? no salue against vice, but sowr satyres? Yes, a pleasant vaine, quips as nie the quicke as a grauer inuectiue, and vnder a merry fable can *Esope* as wel tant folly, as *Hesiode* correct manners in his Heroicks. I tell thee this man hath ioyned pleasure with profite, & though his Bee hath a sting, yet she makes sweet honny. Hath he not discouered in his workes the follies of loue, the sleights of fancy, and lightnesse of youth, to be induced to such vanities? and what more profit can there be to his countrey than manifest such open mischiefes, as grew from the conceit of beauty & deceit of women: and all this hath he painted down in his pamphlets. I grant (quoth *Gower*) the meaning is good, but the method is bad: for by aming at an inconuenience, he bringeth in a mischiefe: in seeking to suppresse fond loue, the sweetnes of his discourse allures youth to loue, like such as taking drink to cool their thirst, feele the tast so pleasant, that they drinke while they surfeit. *Ouid* drewe not so many with his remedie of Loue from loue, as his *Ars Amandi* bred amorous schollers, nor hath *Greenes* Bookes weaned so many from vanity, as they haue wedded from wantonnesse. That is the reason (quoth *Chawcer*) that youth is more prone vnto euil than to good, and with the Serpent, sucke honny from the sweetest sirops, and haue not Poets shadowed waightie precepts in slender Poems and in pleasant fancies vsed deepe perswations? who bitte the Curtizans of his time and the follies of youth more than *Horace*, and yet his Odes were wanton. Who more inuaied against the manners of men than *Martiall*, and yet his verse was lasciuious? And had hee not better (quoth *Gower*) haue discouered his principles in some graue sort as *Hesiode* did or

Pindaris, than in such amorous & wanton manner: the lightnesse of the conceit cracks halfe the credite, and the vanitie of the pen breeds the lesse beleefe. After *Ouid* had written his Art of Loue, and set the youth on fire to imbrace fancy, he could not reclaime them with

Otia si tollas periere cupidinis arcus.

The thoughts of young men are like Bauins, which once set on fire, will not out till they be ashes, and therefore doe I infer, that such Pamphlets doe rather preiudice than profite. Tush (quoth *Chawcer*) all this is but a peremptorie selfe conceit in thine owne humour. for I will shew thee for instance, such sentences as may like the grauest, please the wisest, and instruct the youngest and wantonnest, and they be these: first, of the disposition of women. . . .

Now Sir *Geffrey Chawcer* (quoth *Gower*) how like you this tale, is it not more full of humanity, then your vain and scurrulous inuention? and yet affecteth as muche in the mind of the hearers? are not graue sentences as forcible, as wanton principles? tush (quoth *Chawcer*) but these are not plesant, they breed no delight, youth wil not like of such a long circumstance. Our English Gentlemen are of the mind of the Athenians, that will sooner bee perswaded by a fable, than an Oration: and induced with a merrie tale, when they will not be brought to any compasse with serious circumstances. The more pittie (quoth *Gower*) that they should bee so fond, as to be subiect to the delight of every leud fancy, when the true badge of a Gentleman, is learning ioyned with vallour and vertue, and therefore ought they to read of Martiall Discipline, not of the slight of *Venus*: and to talke of hard labours, not to chat of foolish and effeminate amoures.

THOMAS SPEGHT
From *Scholarly Edition of Chaucer*
1598, 2nd ed. 1602

To the Readers

Some few yeers past, I was requested by certaine Gentlemen my neere friends, who loued *Chaucer*, as he well deserueth; to take a little pains in reuiuing the memorie of so rare a man, as also in doing some reparations on his works, which they iudged to be much decaied by iniurie of time, ignorance of writers, and negligence of Printers. For whose sakes thus much was then by me vndertaken, although neuer as yet fully finished. . . . As that little which then was done, was done for those priuat friends, so was it neuer my mind that it should be published. But so it fell out of late, that *Chaucers* Works being in the Presse, and three parts thereof alreadie printed, not only these friends did by their Letters sollicit me, but certaine also of the best in the Companie of Stationers hearing of these Collections, came vnto me, and for better or worse would haue something done in this Impression. Whose importunitie hath caused me to commit three faults: first in publishing that which was neuer purposed nor perfected for open view: then, in putting diuerse things in the end of the booke, which els taken in time might haue bene bestowed in more fit place: lastly, in failing in some of those eight points, which might more fully haue bene performed, if warning and conuenient leisure had bene giuen. But seeing it is as it is, I earnestly entreat all friendly Readers, that if they find anie thing amisse they would lend me their skilfull helpe against some other time, & I wil thankefully receiue their labors, assuring them that if God permit, I wil accomplish whatsoeuer may be thought vnper-

fect. And if herein I be preuented, those honest and learned Gentlemen that first set me on worke, haue promised to succeed mee in these my purposes. But howsoeuer it happen either in mine or their determination, I earnestly entreat al to accept these my endeuours in best part, as wel in regard of mine owne well meaning, as for the desert of our English Poet himselfe: who in most vnlearned times and greatest ignorance, being much esteemed, cannot in these our daies, wherein Learning and riper iudgement so much flourisheth, but be had in great reuerence, vnlesse it bee of such as for want of wit and learning, were neuer yet able to iudge what wit or Learning meaneth. And so making no doubt of the friendly acceptance of such as haue taken pains in writing themselves, and hoping wel also of all others, that meane to employ any labour in reading, I commit our Poet to your fauourable affection, and yourselues to the protection of the Almightie.

The Life of Geffrey Chaucer

This famous and learned Poet Geffrey Chaucer Esquire, was supposed by Leland to haue beene an Oxfordshire or Barkeshireman borne. . . . But as it is euident by his owne wordes in the Testament of Loue, hee was borne in the Citie of London. . . .

. . . the parents of Geffrey Chaucer were meere English, and he himselfe an Englishman borne. For els how could he haue come to that perfection in our language, as to be called, The first illuminer of the English tongue, had not both he, and his parents before him, been born & bred among vs. But what their names were or what issue they had, otherwise then by coniecture before giuen, wee can not declare.

Now whether they were Merchants, (for that in places where they haue dwelled, the Armes of the Merchants of the Staple haue been seene in the glasse windowes) or whether they were of other calling, it is not much necessary to search: but wealthy no doubt they were, and of good account in the common wealth, who brought vp their Sonne in such sort, that both he was thought fitte for the Court at home, and to be imployed for matters of state in forraine countreyes.

His Education

His bringing vp, as *Leland* saieth, was in the Vniuersitie of Oxford, as also of Cambridge, as appeareth by his owne wordes in his booke entituled 'The Court of Loue'. . . .

It seemeth that both these learned men (Chaucer and Gower) were of the inner Temple: for not many yeeres since, Master *Buckley* did see a Record in the same house, where *Geoffrey Chaucer* was fined two shillings for beating a Franciscane fryer in Fleetstreete.

Thus spending much time in the Vniuersities, Fraunce, Flaunders, and Innes of Court, he prooued a singular man in all kind of knowledge.

His Friends

Friends he had in the Court of the best sort: for besides that he alwaies held in with the Princes, in whose daies he liued, hee had of the best of the Nobility both lords and ladies, which fauoured him greatly. But chiefly Iohn of Gaunt Duke of Lancaster, at whose commandement he made the Treatise 'of the alliance betwixt Mars and Venus': and also the booke of the Duchesse. Likewise the lady Isabel daughter to King Edward the third, and wife to Ingeram De Guynes, Lord De Coucy: also the lady Margaret daughter to the same King, maried to Iohn Hastings Earle of Penbrooke, did greatly loue and fauour Geffrey Chaucer, and hee againe did as much honour them, but specially the Lady Margaret, as it may appeare in diuers Treatises by him written. Others there were of great account, wherof some for some causes tooke liking of him, and other for his rare giftes and learning did admire him. And thus hee liued in honour many yeares both at home and abroad.

Yet it seemeth that he was in some trouble in the daies of King Richard the second, as it may appeare in the Testament of Loue: where hee doth greatly complaine of his owne rashnesse in following the multitude, and of their hatred against him for bewraying their purpose. And in that complaint which he maketh to his empty purse, I do find a written copy, which I had of Iohn Stow (whose library hath helped many writers) wherein ten times more is adioined, then is in print. Where he maketh great lamentation for his wrongfull imprisonment, wishing death to end his daies: which in my iudgement doth greatly accord with that in the Testament of Loue. . . .

His Bookes

Chaucer had alwaies an earnest desire to enrich & beautifie our English tongue, which in those daies was verie rude and barren: and this he did following the example of *Dantes* and *Petrarch*, who had done the same for the Italian tongue; *Alanus* for the French; and *Iohannes Mena* for the Spanish: neither was Chaucer inferior to any of them in the performance hereof: And England in this respect is much beholden to him, as *Leland* well noteth. . . .

JOHN DRYDEN
From "Preface" to *The Fables*
1700

S*pencer* and *Fairfax* both flourish'd in the Reign of Queen *Elizabeth*: Great Masters in our Language. . . . *Milton* was the Poetical Son of *Spencer*, and Mr. *Waller* of *Fairfax*; for we have our Lineal Descents and Clans, as well as other Families: *Spencer* more than once insinuates, that the Soul of *Chaucer* was transfus'd into his Body; and that he was begotten by him Two Hundred years after his Decease. *Milton* has acknowledg'd to me that *Spencer* was his Original; . . .

But to return: Having done with *Ovid* for this time, it came into my mind, that our old *English* poet, *Chaucer*, in many Things resembled him, and that with no disadvantage on the Side of the Modern Author, as I shall endeavour to prove when I compare them: And as I am, and always have been studious to promote the Honour of my Native Country, so I soon resolv'd to put their Merits to the Trial, by turning some of the *Canterbury* Tales into our Language, as it is now refin'd: For by this Means, both the Poets being set in the same Light, and dress'd in the same *English* habit, Story to be compar'd with Story, a certain Judgment may be made betwixt them, by the Reader, without obtruding my Opinion on him: Or if I seem partial to my Country-man, and Predecessor in the Laurel, the Friends of Antiquity are not few: And, besides many of the Learn'd, *Ovid* has almost all the *Beaux*, and the whole Fair Sex his declar'd Patrons. Perhaps I have assum'd somewhat more to my self than they allow me; because I have adventur'd to sum up the Evidence; but the Readers are the Jury; and their Privilege remains entire to decide according to the Merits of the Cause: Or, if they please, to bring it to another Hearing, before some other Court. In the mean time, to follow the Thrid of my Discourse (as Thoughts, according to Mr. *Hobbs*, have always some Connexion) so from *Chaucer* I was led to think on *Boccace*, who was not only his Contemporary, but also pursu'd the same Studies; wrote Novels in Prose, and many Works in Verse; particularly is said to have invented the Octave Rhyme, or *Stanza* of Eight Lines, which ever since has been maintain'd

by the Practice of all *Italian* Writers, who are, or at least assume the title of *Heroick Poets*: He and *Chaucer*, among other Things, had this in common, that they refin'd their Mother-Tongues; but with this difference, that Dante had begun to file their Language, at least in Verse, before the time of *Boccace*, who likewise receiv'd no little Help from his Master *Petrarch*: But the Reformation of their Prose was wholly owing to *Boccace* himself; who is yet the Standard of Purity in the *Italian* Tongue; though many of his Phrases are become obsolete, as in process of Time it must needs happen. *Chaucer* (as you have formerly been told by our learn'd Mr. *Rhymer*) first adorn'd and amplified our barren Tongue from the *Provencall*, which was then the most polish'd of all the Modern Languages: But this Subject has been copiously treated by that great Critick, who deserves no little Commendation from us his Countrymen. For these Reasons of Time, and Resemblance of Genius, in *Chaucer* and *Boccace*, I resolv'd to join them in my present Work; to which I have added some Original Papers of my own; which whether they are equal or inferiour to my other Poems, an Author is the most improper Judge; and therefore I leave them wholly to the Mercy of the Reader: I will hope the best, that they will not be condemn'd; but if they should, I have the Excuse of an old Gentleman, who, mounting on Horseback before some Ladies, when I was present, got up somewhat heavily, but desir'd of the Fair Spectators, that they would count Fourscore and eight before they judg'd him. . . .

I proceed to *Ovid*, and *Chaucer*; considering the former only in relation to the latter. With *Ovid* ended the Golden Age of the *Roman* Tongue: From *Chaucer* the Purity of the *English* Tongue began. The Manners of the Poets were not unlike: Both of them were well-bred, well-natur'd, amorous, and Libertine, at least in their Writings, it may be also in their Lives. Their Studies were the same, Philosophy, and Philology. Both of them were knowing in Astronomy; of which *Ovid*'s Books of the *Roman* Feasts, and *Chaucer*'s Treatise of the *Astrolabe*, are sufficient Witnesses. But *Chaucer* was likewise an Astrologer, as were *Virgil, Horace, Persius*, and *Manilius*. Both writ with wonderful Facility and Clearness; neither were great Inventors: For *Ovid* only copied the *Grecian* Fables; and most of *Chaucer*'s Stories were taken from his *Italian* Contemporaries, or their Predecessors: *Boccace* his *Decameron* was first publish'd; and from thence our *Englishman* has borrow'd many of his *Canterbury* Tales: Yet that of *Palamon* and *Arcite* was written in all probability by some *Italian* Wit, in a former Age; as I shall prove hereafter: The tale of *Grizild* was the Invention of *Petrarch*; by him sent to *Boccace*; from whom it came to *Chaucer*: *Troilus* and *Cressida* was also written by a *Lombard* Author; but much amplified by our *English* Translatour, as well as beautified; the Genius of our Countrymen, in general, being rather to improve an Invention than to invent themselves; as is evident not only in our Poetry, but in many of our Manufactures. I find I have anticipated already, and taken up from *Boccace* before I come to him: But there is so much less behind; and I am of the Temper of most Kings, *who love to be in Debt*, are all for present Money, no matter how they pay it afterwards: Besides, the Nature of a Preface is rambling; never wholly out of the Way, nor in it. This I have learn'd from the Practice of honest *Montaign*, and return at my pleasure to *Ovid* and *Chaucer*, of whom I have little more to say. Both of them built on the Inventions of other Men; yet since *Chaucer* had something of his own, as *The Wife of Baths Tale, The Cock and the Fox*, which I have translated, and some others, I may justly give our Countryman the Precedence in that Part; since I can remember nothing of *Ovid* which was wholly his. Both of them understood the Manners; under which Name I comprehend the Passions, and, in a larger Sense, the Descriptions of Persons, and their very Habits: For an Example, I see *Baucis* and *Philemon* as perfectly before me, as if some ancient Painter had drawn them; and all the Pilgrims in the *Canterbury* Tales, their Humours, their Features, and the very Dress, as distinctly as if I had supp'd with them at the *Tabard* in *Southwark*: Yet even there, too, the Figures of *Chaucer* are much more lively, and set in a better Light: Which though I have not time to prove; yet I appeal to the Reader, and am sure he will clear me from Partiality. The Thoughts and Words remain to be consider'd, in the Comparison of the two Poets; and I have sav'd my self one half of that Labour, by owning that *Ovid* liv'd when the *Roman* Tongue was in its Meridian; *Chaucer*, in the Dawning of our Language: Therefore that Part of the Comparison stands not on an equal Foot, any more than the Diction of *Ennius* and *Ovid*; or of *Chaucer* and our present *English*. The Words are given up as a Post not to be defended in our Poet, because he wanted the Modern Art of Fortifying. The Thoughts remain to be consider'd: And they are to be measur'd only by their Propriety; that is, as they flow more or less naturally from the Persons describ'd, on such and such Occasions. The Vulgar Judges, which are Nine Parts in Ten of all Nations, who call Conceits and Jingles Wit, who see *Ovid* full of them, and *Chaucer* altogether without them, will think me little less than mad for preferring the *Englishman* to the *Roman*: Yet, with their leave, I must presume to say, that the Things they admire are only glittering Trifles, and so far from being Witty, that in a serious Poem they are nauseous, because they are unnatural. Wou'd any Man, who is ready to die for Love, describe his Passion like *Narcissus*? Wou'd he think of *inopem me copia fecit*, and a Dozen more of such Expressions, pour'd on the Neck of one another, and signifying all the same Thing? If this were Wit, was this a Time to be witty, when the poor Wretch, was in the Agony of Death? This is just *John Littlewit*, in *Bartholomew Fair*, who had a Conceit (as he tells you) left him in his Misery; a miserable Conceit. On these Occasions the Poet shou'd endeavour to raise Pity: But, instead of this, *Ovid* is tickling you to laugh. *Virgil* never made use of such Machines when he was moving you to commiserate the Death of *Dido*: He would not destroy what he was building. *Chaucer* makes *Arcite* violent in his Love, and unjust in the Pursuit of it: Yet, when he came to die, he made him think more reasonably: He repents not of his Love, for that had alter'd his Character; but acknowledges the Injustice of his Proceedings, and resigns *Emilia* to *Palamon*. What would *Ovid* have done on this Occasion? He would certainly have made *Arcite* witty on his Death-bed. He had complain'd he was further off from Possession, by being so near, and a thousand such Boyisms, which Chaucer rejected as below the Dignity of the Subject. They who think otherwise, would by the same Reason, prefer *Lucan* and *Ovid* to *Homer* and *Virgil*, and *Martial* to all Four of them. As for the Turn of Words, in which *Ovid* particularly excels all Poets; they are sometimes a Fault, and sometimes a Beauty, as they are us'd properly or improperly; but in strong Passions always to be shunn'd, because Passions are serious, and will admit no Playing. The *French* have a high Value for them; and I confess, they are often what they call Delicate, when they are introduc'd with Judgment; but *Chaucer* writ with more Simplicity, and follow'd Nature more closely, than to use them. I have thus far, to the best of my Knowledge, been an upright Judge betwixt the Parties in Competition, not medling with the Design nor the Disposition of it; because the Design was not their own; and in the disposing of it they were equal. It remains that I say somewhat of *Chaucer* in particular.

In the first place, as he is the Father of *English* Poetry, so I hold him in the same Degree of Veneration as the *Grecians* held *Homer*, or the *Romans Virgil*: He is a perpetual Fountain of good Sense; learn'd in all Sciences; and, therefore speaks properly on all Subjects: As he knew what to say, so he knows also when to leave off; a Continence which is practis'd by few Writers, and scarcely by any of the Ancients, excepting *Virgil* and *Horace*. One of our late great Poets is sunk in his Reputation, because he cou'd never forgive any Conceit which came in his way; but swept like a Drag-net, great and small. There was plenty enough, but the Dishes were ill sorted; whole Pyramids of Sweet-meats for Boys and Women; but little of solid Meat for Men: All this proceeded not from any want of Knowledge, but of Judgment; neither did he want that in discerning the Beauties and Faults of other Poets; but only indulg'd himself in the Luxury of Writing; and perhaps knew it was a Fault, but hoped the Reader would not find it. For this Reason, though he must always be thought a great Poet, he is no longer esteemed a good Writer: And for Ten Impressions, which his Works have had in so many successive Years, yet at present a hundred Books are scarcely purchased once a Twelvemonth: For, as my last Lord *Rochester* said, though somewhat profanely, *Not being of God, he could not stand.*

Chaucer follow'd Nature every where, but was never so bold to go beyond her: And there is a great Difference of being *Poeta* and *nimis Poeta*, if we may believe *Catullus*, as much as betwixt a modest Behaviour and Affectation. The Verse of *Chaucer*, I confess, is not Harmonious to us; but 'tis like the Eloquence of one whom *Tacitus* commends, it was *auribus istius temporis accommodata*: They who liv'd with him, and some time after him, thought it Musical; and it continues so even in our Judgment, if compar'd with the Numbers of *Lidgate* and *Gower*, his Contemporaries: There is the rude Sweetness of a *Scotch* Tune in it, which is natural and pleasing, though not perfect. 'Tis true, I cannot go so far as he who publish'd the last Edition of him; for he would make us believe the Fault is in our Ears, and that there were really Ten Syllables in a Verse where we find but Nine: But this Opinion is not worth confuting; 'tis so gross and obvious an Errour, that common Sense (which is a Rule in everything but Matters of Faith and Revelation) must convince the Reader, that Equality of Numbers, in every Verse which we call *Heroick*, was either not known, or not always practis'd, in *Chaucer*'s Age. It were an easie Matter to produce some thousands of his Verses, which are lame for want of half a Foot, and sometimes a whole one, and which no Pronunciation can make otherwise. We can only say, that he liv'd in the Infancy of our Poetry, and that nothing is brought to Perfection at the first. We must be Children before we grow Men. There was an *Ennius*, and in process of Time a *Lucilius*, and a *Lucretius*, before *Virgil* and *Horace*; even after *Chaucer* there was a *Spencer*, a *Harrington*, a *Fairfax*, before *Waller* and *Denham* were in being: And our Numbers were in their Nonage till these last appear'd. I need say little of his Parentage, Life, and Fortunes: They are to be found at large in all the Editions of his Works. He was employ'd abroad, and favour'd by *Edward* the Third, *Richard* the Second, and *Henry* the Fourth, and was Poet, as I suppose, to all Three of them. In *Richard*'s Time, I doubt, he was a little dipt in the Rebellion of the Commons; and being Brother-in-Law to *John of Ghant*, it was no wonder if he follow'd the Fortunes of that Family; and was well with *Henry* the Fourth when he depos'd his Predecessor. Neither is it to be admir'd, that *Henry*, who was a wise as well as a valiant Prince, who claim'd by Succession, and was sensible that his Title was not sound, but was rightfully in *Mortimer*, who had married the Heir of *York*; it was not to be admir'd, I say, if that great Politician should be pleas'd to have the greatest Wit of those Times in his Interests, and to be the Trumpet of his Praises. *Augustus* had given him the Example, by the Advice of *Mecaenas*, who recommended *Virgil* and *Horace* to him; whose Praises helped to make him Popular while he was alive, and after his Death have made him Precious to Posterity. As for the Religion of our Poet, he seems to have some little Byas towards the Opinions of *Wickliff*, after *John of Ghant* his Patron; somewhat of which appears in the Tale of *Piers Plowman*: Yet I cannot blame him for inveighing so sharply against the Vices of the Clergy in his Age: Their Pride, their Ambition, their Pomp, their Avarice, their Worldly Interest, deserv'd the Lashes which he gave them, both in that, and in most of his *Canterbury Tales*: Neither has his Contemporary *Boccace*, spar'd them. Yet both those Poets liv'd in much esteem, with good and holy Men in Orders: For the Scandal which is given by particular Priests reflects not on the Sacred Function. *Chaucer's Monk*, his *Chanon*, and his *Fryar*, took not from the Character of his *Good Parson*. A Satyrical Poet is the Check of the Laymen on bad Priests. . . .

I have followed *Chaucer*, in his Character of a Holy Man, and have enlarg'd on that Subject with some Pleasure, reserving to myself the Right, if I shall think fit hereafter, to describe another sort of Priests, such as are more easily to be found than the Good Parson; such as have given the last Blow to Christianity in this Age, by a Practice so contrary to their Doctrine. But this will keep cold till another time. In the mean while, I take up *Chaucer* where I left him. He must have been a Man of a most wonderful comprehensive Nature, because, as it has been truly observ'd of him, he has taken into the Compass of his *Canterbury Tales* the various Manners and Humours (as we now call them) of the whole *English* Nation, in his Age. Not a single Character has escap'd him. All his Pilgrims are severally distinguish'd from each other; and not only in their Inclinations, but in their very Phisiognomies and Persons. *Baptista Porta* could not have describ'd their Natures better, than by the Marks which the Poet gives them. The Matter and Manner of their Tales, and of their Telling, are so suited to their different Educations, Humours, and Callings, that each of them would be improper in any other Mouth. Even the grave and serious Characters are distinguish'd by their several sorts of Gravity: Their Discourses are such as belong to their Age, their Calling, and their Breeding; such as are becoming of them, and of them only. Some of his Persons are Vicious, and some Vertuous; some are unlearn'd, or (as *Chaucer* calls them) Lewd, and some are Learn'd. Even the Ribaldry of the Low Characters is different: the *Reeve*, the *Miller*, and the *Cook*, are several Men, and are distinguish'd from each other, as much as the mincing Lady-Prioress, and the broad-speaking, gap-tooth'd Wife of *Bathe*. But enough of this: There is such a Variety of Game springing up before me, that I am distracted in my Choice, and know not which to follow. 'Tis sufficient to say according to the Proverb, that here is God's Plenty. We have our Fore-fathers and Great Grand-dames all before us, as they were in *Chaucer's* Days; their general Characters are still remaining in Mankind, and even in *England*, though they are call'd by other Names than those of *Moncks*, and *Fryars*, and *Chanons*, and *Lady Abbesses*, and *Nuns*: For Mankind is ever the same, and nothing lost out of Nature, though every thing is alter'd. May I have leave to do myself the Justice, (since my Enemies will do me none, and are so far from granting me to be a good Poet, that they will not allow me so much as to be a Christian, or a Moral Man), may I have leave, I say, to inform my Reader, that I have confin'd my Choice to such Tales of *Chaucer* as savour nothing of Immodesty. If I had desir'd more to please than to instruct, the *Reve*, the *Miller*, the *Shipman*, the *Merchant*, the

Sumner, and above all, the *Wife of Bathe*, in the Prologue to her Tale, would have procur'd me as many Friends and Readers, as there are *Beaux* and Ladies of Pleasure in the Town. But I will no more offend against Good Manners: I am sensible as I ought to be of the Scandal I have given by my loose Writings; and make what Reparation I am able, by this Public Acknowledgment. If anything of this Nature, or of Profaneness, be crept into these Poems, I am so far from defending it, that I disown it. *Totum hoc indictum volo. Chaucer* makes another manner of Apologie for his broad-speaking, and *Boccace* makes the like; but I will follow neither of them. Our Country-man, in the end of his Characters, before the *Canterbury Tales*, thus excuses the Ribaldry, which is very gross in many of his Novels.

But first I praye you of youre curteisye
That ye n'arette it nought my vilainye
Though that I plainly speke in this matere
To telle you hir wordes and hir cheere,
Ne though I speke hir wordes proprely;
For this ye knowen also wel as I:
Who so shal telle a tale after a man
He moot reherce, as neigh as evere he can,
Everich a word, if it be in his charge;
Al speke he nevere so rudeliche and large,
Or elles he moot telle his tale untrewe,
Or feine thing, or finde wordes newe;
He may nought spare although he were his brother:
He moot as wel saye oo word as another.
Crist spak himself ful brode in Holy Writ,
And wel ye woot no vilainye is it;
Eek Plato saith, who so can him rede,
The wordes mote be cosin to the deede.

Yet if a Man should have enquir'd of *Boccace* or of *Chaucer*, what need they had of introducing such Characters, where obscene Words were proper in their Mouths, but very undecent to he heard; I know not what Answer they could have made: For that Reason, such Tales shall be left untold by me. You have here a *Specimen* of *Chaucer's* Language, which is so obsolete, that his Sense is scarce to be understood; and you have likewise more than one Example of his unequal Numbers, which were mention'd before. Yet many of his Verses consist of Ten Syllables, and the Words not much behind our present *English*: as for Example, these two Lines, in the Description of the Carpenter's Young Wife:

Wincing she was, as is a jolly Colt,
Long as a Mast, and upright as a Bolt.

I have almost done with *Chaucer*, when I have answer'd some Objections relating to my present Work. I find some People are offended that I have turn'd these Tales into modern *English*; because they think them unworthy of my Pains, and look on *Chaucer* as a dry, old-fashion'd Wit, not worth receiving. I have often heard the late Earl of *Leicester* say, that Mr. *Cowley* himself was of that opinion; who, having read him over at my Lord's Request, declared he had no Taste of him. I dare not advance my Opinion against the Judgment of so great an Author: But I think it fair, however, to leave the Decision to the Publick: Mr. *Cowley*, was too modest to set up for a Dictatour; and, being shock'd perhaps with his old Style, never examin'd into the depth of his good Sense. *Chaucer*, I confess, is a rough Diamond, and must first be polish'd, e'er he shines. I deny not likewise, that, living in our early Days of Poetry, he writes not always of a piece; but sometimes mingles trivial Things with those of greater Moment. Sometimes also, though not often, he runs riot, like *Ovid*, and knows not when he has said enough. But there are more great Wits beside *Chaucer*, whose Fault is their Excess of Conceits, and those ill sorted. An

Author is not to write all he can, but only all he ought. Having observ'd this Redundancy in *Chaucer*, (as it is an easie Matter for a Man of ordinary Parts to find a Fault in one of greater,) I have not ty'd my self to a Literal Translation; but have often omitted what I judg'd unnecessary, or not of Dignity enough to appear in the Company of better Thoughts. I have presum'd farther in some Places, and added somewhat of my own where I thought my Author was deficient, and had not given his Thoughts their true Lustre, for want of Words in the Beginning of our Language. And to this I was the more embolden'd, because, (if I may be permitted to say it of my self) I found I had a Soul congenial to his, and that I had been conversant in the same Studies. Another Poet, in another Age, may take the same Liberty with my Writings; if at least they live long enough to deserve Correction. It was also necessary sometimes to restore the Sense of *Chaucer*, which was lost or mangled in the Errors of the Press: Let this Example suffice at present in the Story of *Palamon* and *Arcite*, where the temple of *Diana* is describ'd, you find these Verses in all the Editions of our Author:

> There saw I *Dane* turned unto a Tree,
> I mean not the goddess *Diane*,
> But *Venus* Daughter, which that hight *Dane*.

Which, after a little Consideration, I knew was to be reform'd into this Sense, that *Daphne*, the daughter of *Peneus*, was turn'd into a Tree. I durst not make thus bold with *Ovid*, lest some future *Milbourn* should arise, and say, I varied from my Author, because I understood him not.

But there are other Judges, who think I ought not to have translated *Chaucer* into *English*, out of a quite contrary Notion: They suppose there is a certain Veneration due to his old Language; and that it is little less than Profanation and Sacrilege to alter it. They are farther of opinion, that somewhat of his good Sense will suffer in this Transfusion, and much of the Beauty of his Thoughts will infallibly be lost, which appear with more Grace in their old Habit. Of this Opinion was that excellent Person, whom I mention'd, the late Earl of *Leicester*, who valued *Chaucer* as much as Mr. *Cowley* despis'd him. My Lord dissuaded me from this Attempt, (for I was thinking of it some Years before his Death,) and his Authority prevail'd so far with me, as to defer my Undertaking while he liv'd, in deference to him: Yet my Reason was not convinc'd with what he urg'd against it. If the first End of a Writer be to be understood, then, as his Language grows obsolete, his Thoughts must grow obscure, *multa renascuntur, quae nunc cecidere; cadentque quae nunc sunt in honore vocabula, si volet usus, quem penes arbitrium est et jus et norma loquendi.* When an ancient Word for its Sound and Significancy, deserves to be reviv'd, I have that reasonable Veneration for Antiquity, to restore it. All beyond this is Superstition. Words are not like Land-marks, so sacred as never to be remov'd: Customs are chang'd, and even Statutes are silently repeal'd, when the Reason ceases for which they were enacted. As for the other Part of the Argument, that his Thoughts will lose of their original Beauty by the innovation of Words; in the first place, not only their Beauty, but their Being is lost, when they are no longer understood, which is the present Case. I grant, that something must be lost in all Transfusion, that is, in all Translations; but the Sense will remain, which would otherwise be lost, or at least be maim'd, when it is scarce intelligible; and that but to a few. How few are there who can read *Chaucer*, so as to understand him perfectly? And if imperfectly, then with less Profit, and no Pleasure. 'Tis not for the Use of some old *Saxon* Friends, that I have taken these Pains with him: Let them neglect my Version, because they have no need of it. I made it for their sakes who understand Sense and Poetry, as well as they; when that Poetry and Sense is put into Words which they understand. I will go farther, and dare to add, that what Beauties I lose in some Places, I give to others which had them not originally. But in this I may be partial to my self; let the Reader judge, and I submit to his Decision. Yet I think I have just Occasion to complain of them, who because they understand *Chaucer*, would deprive the greater part of their Countrymen of the same Advantage, and hoord him up, as Misers do their Grandam Gold, only to look on it themselves, and hinder others from making use of it. In sum, I seriously protest, that no Man ever had, or can have, a greater Veneration for *Chaucer* than my self. I have translated some part of his Works, only that I might perpetuate his Memory, or at least refresh it, amongst my Countrymen. If I have alter'd him any where for the better, I must at the same time acknowledge, that I could have done nothing without him: *Facile est inventis addere*, is no great Commendation; but I am not so vain to think I have deserv'd a greater. I will conclude what I have to say of him singly, with this one Remark: A Lady of my Acquaintance, who keeps a kind of Correspondence with some Authors of the Fair Sex in *France*, has been inform'd by them, that *Mademoiselle de Scudery*, who is as old as *Sibyl*, and inspir'd like her by the same God of Poetry, is at this time translating *Chaucer* into modern *French*. From which I gather, that he has been formerly translated into the old *Provencall*; (for, how she should come to understand Old *English*, I know not). But the Matter of Fact being true, it makes me think, that there is something in it like Fatality; that after certain Periods of Time, the Fame and Memory of Great Wits should be renew'd, as *Chaucer* is both in *France* and *England*. If this be wholly Chance, 'tis extraordinary; and I dare not call it more, for fear of being tax'd with Superstition.

Boccace comes last to be consider'd, who, living in the same Age with *Chaucer*, had the same Genius, and followed the same Studies: Both writ Novels, and each of them cultivated his Mother-Tongue: But the greatest Resemblance of our two Modern Authors being in their familiar Style, and pleasing way of relating Comical Adventures, I may pass it over, because I have translated nothing from *Boccace* of that Nature. In the serious part of Poetry, the Advantage is wholly on *Chaucer's* Side; for though the *Englishman* has borrow'd many Tales from the *Italian*, yet it appears, that those of *Boccace* were not generally of his own making, but taken from Authors of former ages, and by him only modell'd: So that what there was of Invention, in either of them, may be judg'd equal. But *Chaucer* has refin'd on *Boccace*, and has mended the Stories which he has borrow'd, in his way of telling; though Prose allows more Liberty of Thought, and the Expression is more easie, when unconfin'd by Numbers. Our Countryman carries Weight, and yet wins the Race at disadvantage. I desire not the Reader should take my Word; and, therefore, I will set two of their Discourses on the same Subject, in the same Light, for every Man to judge betwixt them. I translated *Chaucer* first, and amongst the rest, pitch'd on The Wife of *Bath's* Tale; not daring, as I have said, to adventure on her Prologue, because 'tis too licentious: There *Chaucer* introduces an old Woman of mean Parentage, whom a youthful Knight of Noble Blood, was forc'd to marry, and consequently loath'd her: The Crone being in bed with him on the wedding Night, and finding his Aversion, endeavours to win his Affection by Reason, and speaks a good Word for herself, (as who could blame her?) in hope to mollifie the sullen Bridegroom. She takes her Topiques from the Benefits of Poverty, the Advantages of old Age and Ugliness, the Vanity of Youth, and the silly Pride of Ancestry and Titles, without inherent Vertue, which is the true Nobility. When I had clos'd

Chaucer; I return'd to *Ovid*, and translated some more of his Fables; and, by this time, had so far forgotten The Wife of *Bath's* Tale, that when I took up *Boccace*, unawares I fell on the same Argument of preferring Virtue to Nobility of Blood, and Titles, in the Story of *Sigismonda*; which I had certainly avoided for the Resemblance of the two Discourses, if my Memory had not fail'd me. Let the Reader weigh both; and if he thinks me partial to *Chaucer*, 'tis in him to right *Boccace*.

I prefer in our Countryman, far above all his other Stories, the Noble Poem of *Palamon* and *Arcite*, which is of the *Epique* kind, and perhaps not much inferiour to the *Ilias* or the *Aeneis*: the Story is more pleasing than either of them, the Manners as perfect, the Diction as poetical, the Learning as deep and various; and the Disposition full as artful: only it includes a greater length of time; as taking up seven years at least; but *Aristotle* has left undecided the Duration of the Action; which yet is easily reduc'd into the Compass of a year, by a Narration of what preceded the Return of *Palamon* to *Athens*. I had thought for the Honour of our Nation, and more particularly for his, whose Laurel, tho' unworthy, I have worn after him, that this Story was of *English* Growth, and *Chaucer's* own: But I was undeceiv'd by *Boccace*; for casually looking on the End of his seventh *Giornata*, I found *Dioneo*, (under which name he shadows himself,) and *Fiametta*, (who represents his Mistress, the natural Daughter of *Robert*, King of *Naples*) of whom these Words are spoken. *Dioneo e Fiametta gran pezza cantarono insieme d'Arcita, e di Palemone:* by which it appears, that this Story was written before the time of *Boccace*; but the Name of its Author being wholly lost, *Chaucer* is now become an Original; and I question not but the Poem has receiv'd many Beauties, by passing through his Noble Hands. Besides this Tale, there is another of his own Invention, after the manner of the *Provencalls*, call'd *The Flower and the Leaf*; with which I was so particularly pleas'd, both for the Invention and the Moral; that I cannot hinder myself from recommending it to the Reader.

THOMAS GRAY
From *Commonplace Book*
c. 1760, Volume 2, pp. 743–57

However little ⟨Lydgate⟩ might be *acquainted* with Homer & Virgil, it is certain he was very much so with Chaucer's compositions, whom he calls his master, & who (I imagine) was so in a literal sense: certain 'tis Lydgate was full 30 years when Chaucer died. but whatever his skill were in either of the learned languages, it is sure he has not taken his 'Fall of Princes' from the original Latin prose of Boccace, but from a French Translation of it by one *Laurence*, as he tells us himself in the beginning of his work; it was indeed rather a Paraphrase than a translation, for he took the liberty of making several additions, & of reciting more at large many histories, that Boccace had slightly passed over.

And *he* saieth eke, that his entencion   Laurence
Is to amende, correcten & declare,
Not to condemne of no presumpcion,
But to support plainly & to spare
Thing touched shortly of the storie bare
Under a stile brief and compendious,
Them to prolonge when they be vertuous:
     For a storie which is not plainly tolde,
But constrained under wordes few,
For lack of truth wher they ben new or old
Men by reporte cannot the matter shewe:

These okes great be not downe yhewe
First at a stroke, but by long process,
Ner long stories a word may not expresse.

These *Long processes* indeed suited wonderfully with the attention & simple curiosity of the age, in which Lydgate lived. many a *stroke* have he & the best of his Contemporaries spent upon a sturdy old story, till they had blunted their own edge, & that of their readers. at least a modern reader will find it so; but it is a folly to judge of the understanding & of the patience of those times by our own. they loved, I will not say Tediousness, but length & a train of circumstances in a narration. the Vulgar do so still; it gives an air of reality to facts, it fixes the attention, raises and keeps in suspense their expectation, & supplies the defects of their little & lifeless imagination; it keeps pace with the slow motion of their own thoughts. tell them a story as you would tell it a Man of wit, it will appear to them as an object seen in the night by a flash of lightening; but when you have placed it in various lights & various positions, they will come at last to see & feel it, as well as others. but we need not confine ourselves to the Vulgar & to understandings beneath our own. Circumstance was ever & ever will be the Life & essence both of Oratory & Poetry. it has in some sort the same effect upon every mind, that it has on that of the populace; & I fear, the quickness & delicate impatience of these polish'd times we live in, are but forerunners of the decline of all those beautiful arts that depend upon the imagination. whether these apprehensions are well or ill grounded, it is sufficient for me, that Homer, the Father of Circumstance, has occasion for the same apology I am making for Lydgate & his Predecessors. not that I pretend to make any more comparison between his beauties & theirs, than I do between the different languages they wrote in: ours was indeed barbarous enough at that time, the Orthography unsettled, the Syntax very deficient & confused, the Metre & Number of syllables left to the ear alone, and yet with all its rudeness our Tongue had then aquired an Energy & a Plenty by the adoption of a variety of words borrow'd from the French, the Provençal, and the Italian about the middle of the 14th century, that at this day our best Writers seem to miss & to regret, for many of them have gradually drop'd into disuse, & are only now to be found in the remotest Counties of England. Another thing, which perhaps contributed something to the making our ancient Poets so voluminous, was the great facility of rhiming, which is now grown so difficult. words of two & three syllables being then newly taken from foreign languages did still retain their original accent, & that (as they were mostly derived from the French) fell according to the Genius of that tongue upon the Last Syllable, which, if it still had continued among us, had been a great advantage to our Poetry. among the Scotch this still continues in many words, for they say, Envȳ, Practīse, Pensīve, Positīve, &c: but we in process of time, have accustom'd ourselves to throw back all our accents upon the Antepenultima, in words of three or more syllables, and of our Dissyllables comparatively but a few are left, as Disdaīn, Despaīr, Repēnt, Pretēnd, &c: where the stress is not laid upon the Penultima; By this means we are almost reduced to find our Rhimes among the Monosyllables, in which our tongue too much abounds, a defect that will forever hinder it from adapting itself well to Musick, & must be no small impediment consequently to the sweetness & harmony of Versification. . . .

To return to Lydgate, I do not pretend to set him on a level with his master Chaucer, but he certainly comes the nearest to him of any contemporary writer that I am aquainted with. his choice of expression, & the smoothness of his verse far surpass both Gower & Occleve. he wanted not art in raising the more tender emotions of mind, of which I might give several examples, the first is of that sympathy which we feel for humble piety & contrition. . . .

It is observable, that in images of horrour & a certain terrible Greatness, our author comes far behind Chaucer. whether they were not suited to the Genius or the temper of Lydgate I do not determine; but it is sure that, tho' they seem'd naturally to present themselves, he has almost in general chose to avoid them. yet is there frequently a stiller kind of majesty both in his thought & expression, which makes one of his principal beauties. . . .

Lydgate seems to have been by nature of a more serious & melancholick turn of mind than Chaucer: yet one here & there meets with a stroke of Satyr and Irony that does not want humour, & it usually falls (as was the custom of those times) either upon the Women or on the Clergy. as the Religious were the principal Scholars of these ages, they probably gave the tone in writing & in wit to the rest of the nation. the celibacy imposed on them by the Church had sower'd their temper, and naturally disposed them (as it is observed of Old-Bachelors in our days) to make the Weaknesses of the other Sex their theme; & tho' every one had a profound respect for his own particular order, yet the feuds and bickerings between one Order & another were perpetual & irreconcileable: these possibly were the causes that directed the Satyr of our old Writers principally to those two objects. . . .

This kind of satyr I know, will appear to modern Men of Taste a little stale & unfashionable: but our reflections should go deeper, & lead us to consider the fading & transitory nature of Wit in general. I have attempted to shew above the source from whence the two prevailing subjects of our Ancestor's Severity were derived: let us observe their different success & duration from those times to our own. . . .

Metrum

Though I would not with Mr. Urry, the last Editor of Chaucer, insert words & syllables, unauthorized by the oldest Manuscripts, to help out what seems lame and defective in the measure of our ancient writers; yet as I see those MSS, and the first printed Editions, so extremely inconstant in their manner of spelling one & the same word, as to vary continually, often in the compass of two Lines, & seem to have no fix'd Orthography at all, I can not help thinking it probable, that many great inequalities in the metre are owing to the neglect of Transcribers, or that the manner of reading made up for the defects that appear in the writing. thus the *y* which we often see prefix'd to Participles passive, as *ycleped, yhewe,* &c: is not a mere arbitrary insertion to fill up the verse, but the old Anglo-Saxon augment, always prefix'd formerly to such Participles, as *gelufod* (loved) from *Lufian* (to love), *geraed,* from *raedan* (to read), &c. . . . This syllable, tho' (I suppose) then out of use in common speech, our Poets inserted, where it suited them, in verse. the same did they by the final syllable of verbs, as *brennin, correctin, dronkin* . . . this termination begun to be omitted, after the Danes were settled among us . . . the transition is very apparent from thence to the English, we now speak. as then our writers inserted these initial and final syllables, or omitted them; & where we see them written, we do not doubt, that they were meant to fill up the measure, it follows that these Poets had an ear not insensible to defects in metre; & where the verse seems to halt, it very probably is occasion'd by the Transcriber's neglect who seeing a word differently spelt from the manner then customary, changed or omitted a few letters without reflecting on the injury done to the measure. the case is the same with the genitive case singular, & nominative plural of

many nouns, which by the Saxon inflexion had an additional syllable, as *word,* a word, *wordes,* of a word: *smith,* a Smith, *smithes,* of a smith; *smithas,* Smiths. which (as Hickes observes) is the origin of the formation of those cases in our present tongue; but we now have reduced them by our pronunciation to an equal number of syllables with their Nominatives-singular. this was commonly done (I imagine) too in Chaucer & Lydgate's time; but in verse they took the Liberty either to follow the old language in pronouncing the final syllable; or to sink the vowel, and abridge it, as was usual; according to the necessity of their versification. for example, they would read either *vīolēttēs* with four syllables, or *violets* with three; *bánkis,* or banks, *triūmphys,* or *triūmphs,* indifferently. I have already mention'd the *e* mute & their use of it in words derived from the French and imagine, that they did the same in many of true English Origin, which the Danes had before rob'd of their final consonant, writing *bute,* for the Saxon *butan* (without) . . . here we may easily conceive, that tho' the *n* was taken away, yet the *e* continued to be pronounced faintly, and tho' in time it was quite drop'd in conversation, yet, when the Poet thought fit to make a syllable of it, it no more offended their ears, than it now does those of a Frenchman to hear it so pronounced, in verse. . . .

These reflections may serve to shew us, that Puttenham, tho' he lived within about 150 years of Chaucer's time, must be mistaken with regard to what the old Writers call'd their *riding* ryme, for the Canterbury Tales, which he gives as an example of it, are as exact in their measure & their pause as the Troilus and Creseide where he says *the meetre is very grave and stately*; and this not only in the Knight's Tale, but in the comic introduction and characters. . . .

I conclude, he was misled by the change words had undergone in their accents since the days of Chaucer, & by the seeming defects of measure that frequently occur in the printed copies.

THOMAS WARTON
From *The History of English Poetry* (1778–81)
ed. Richard Price
Volume 2, 1840, pp. 129–216

The revival of learning in most countries appears to have first owed its rise to translation. At rude periods the modes of original thinking are unknown, and the arts of original composition have not yet been studied. The writers therefore of such periods are chiefly and very usefully employed in importing the ideas of other languages into their own. They do not venture to think for themselves, nor aim at the merit of inventors, but they are laying the foundations of literature; and while they are naturalising the knowledge of more learned ages and countries by translation, they are imperceptibly improving the national language. This has been remarkably the case, not only in England, but in France and Italy. In the year 1387, John Trevisa, canon of Westbury in Gloucestershire, and a great traveller, not only finished a translation of the Old and New Testaments, at the command of his munificent patron Thomas lord Berkley, but also translated Higden's *Polychronicon,* and other Latin pieces. But these translations would have been alone insufficient to have produced or sustained any considerable revolution in our language: the great work was reserved for Gower and Chaucer. Wickliffe had also translated the Bible: and in other respects his attempts to bring about a reformation in religion at this time proved beneficial to English literature. The orthodox divines of this period generally wrote

in Latin: but Wickliffe, that his arguments might be familiarised to common readers and the bulk of the people, was
obliged to compose in English his numerous theological treatises against the papal corruptions. Edward the Third, while he
perhaps intended only to banish a badge of conquest, greatly
contributed to establish the national dialect, by abolishing the
use of the Norman tongue in the public acts and judicial
proceedings, as we have before observed, and by substituting
the natural language of the country. But Chaucer manifestly
first taught his countrymen to write English; and formed a style
by naturalising words from the Provencial, at that time the
most polished dialect of any in Europe, and the best adapted to
the purposes of poetical expression.

It is certain that Chaucer abounds in classical allusions:
but his poetry is not formed on the antient models. He appears
to have been an universal reader, and his learning is sometimes
mistaken for genius: but his chief sources were the French and
Italian poets. From these originals two of his capital poems, the
Knight's Tale, and the *Romaunt of the Rose*, are imitations or
translations. The first of these is taken from Boccacio. . . .

In passing through Chaucer's hands, this poem has received many new beauties. Not only those capital fictions and
descriptions, the temples of Mars, Venus, and Diana, with
their allegorical paintings, and the figures of Lycurgus and
Emetrius with their retinue, and so much heightened by the
bold and spirited manner of the British bard, as to strike us with
an air of originality. In the mean time it is to be remarked, that
as Chaucer in some places has thrown in strokes of his own, so
in others he has contracted the uninteresting and tedious prolixity of narrative, which he found in the Italian poet. And that
he might avoid a servile imitation, and indulge himself as he
pleased in an arbitrary departure from the original, it appears
that he neglected the embarrassment of Boccacio's stanza, and
preferred the English heroic couplet, of which this poem affords the first conspicuous example extant in our language.

The situation and structure of the temple of Mars are thus
described.

A forest
In which ther wonneth neyther man ne best:
With knotty knarry barrein trees old,
Of stubbes sharpe, and hidous to behold,
In which ther ran a romble and a swough.
As though a storme shuld bersten every bough.
And dounward from an hill, under a bent,
Ther stood the temple of Mars armipotent,
Wrought all of burned stele: of which th'entree
Was longe, and streite, and gastly for to see:
And therout came a rage and swiche a vise
That it made all the gates for to rise.
The northern light in at the dore shone,
For window on the wall ne was ther none,
Thurgh which men mighten any light discerne.
The dore was all of athamant eterne,
Yelenched overthwart and endelong,
With yren tough, and for to make it strong.
Every piler the temple to sustene
Was tonnè-grete of yren bright and shene.

The gloomy sanctuary of this tremendous fane was
adorned with these characteristical imageries.

Ther saw I first the derke imagining
Of Felonie, and alle the compassing:
The cruel Irè, red as any glede.
The Pikepurse, and eke the pale Drede;
The Smiler with the knif under the cloke:
The shepen brenning with the blakè smoke;
The Treson of the mordring in the bedde,

The open Werre with woundes all bebledde;
Conteke with bloody knif, and sharp Manace,
All full of chirking was that sory place!
The sleer of himself yet saw I there,
His herte-blood hath bathed all his here,
The naile ydriven in the shode on hight,
The colde deth, with mouth gaping upright.
Amiddes of the temple sate Mischance,
With discomfort, and sory countenance.
Yet saw I Woodnesse laughing in his rage.
Armed complaint, outhees, and fiers Outrage;
The carraine in the bush, with throte ycorven,
A thousand slain, and not of qualme ystorven.
The tirant, with the prey by force yraft,
The toun destroied, there was nothing laft,
Yet saw I brent the shippes hoppesteres,
The hunte ystrangled with the wilde beres,
The sow freting the child right in the cradel,
The cokee yscalled, for all his long ladel.
Nought was foryete by th'infortune of Marte;
The carter overridden by his carte,
Under the wheel full low he lay adoun.
Ther were also of Martes division,
The Armerer, and the Bowyer, and the Smith
That forgeth sharpè swerdes on his stith.
And all above, depeinted in a tour,
Saw I Conquest sitting in gret honour,
With thilke sharpe swerd over his hed,
Y-hanging by a subtil twined thred.

This groupe is the effort of a strong imagination, unacquainted with selection and arrangement of images. It is rudely
thrown on the canvas without order or art. In the Italian poets,
who describe every thing, and who cannot, even in the most
serious representations, easily suppress their natural predilection for burlesque and familiar imagery, nothing is more common than this mixture of sublime and comic ideas. The form
of Mars follows, touched with the impetuous dashes of a savage
and spirited pencil.

The statue of Mars upon a carte stood,
Armed, and loked grim as he were wood.
A wolf ther stood before him at his fete
With eyen red, and of a man he ete.
With subtil pensil peinted was this storie,
In redouting of Mars and of his glorie.

But the ground-work of this whole description is in the
Thebaid of Statius. . . .

Statius was a favourite writer with the poets of the middle
ages. His bloated magnificence of description, gigantic images,
and pompous diction, suited their taste, and were somewhat of
a piece with the romances they so much admired. They neglected the gentler and genuine graces of Virgil, which they
could not relish. His pictures were too correctly and chastely
drawn to take their fancies: and truth of design, elegance of
expression, and the arts of composition were not their objects.
In the mean time we must observe, that in Chaucer's Temple
of Mars many personages are added; and that those which
existed before in Statius have been retouched, enlarged, and
rendered more distinct and picturesque by Boccacio and Chaucer. Arcite's address to Mars, at entering the temple, has great
dignity, and is not copied from Statius.

O strongè god, that in the regnes cold
Of Trace honoured art, and lord yhold!
And hast in every regne, and every lond,
Of armes al the bridel in thin hond;
And hem fortunist, as thee list devise,
Accept of me my pitous sacrifise.

The following portrait of Lycurgus, an imaginary king of Thrace, is highly charged, and very great in the gothic style of painting.

Ther maist thou se, coming with Palamon,
Lycurge himself, the grete king of Trace;
Blake was his berde, and manly was his face:
The cercles of his eyen in his hed
They gloweden betwixten yalwe and red:
And like a griffon loked he about,
With kemped heres on his browes stout:
His limmes gret, his braunes hard and stronge,
His shouldres brode, his armes round and longe.
And as the guise was in his contree
Ful highe upon a char of gold stood he:
With foure white bolles in the trais.
Instead of cote-armure, on his harnais
With nayles yelwe, and bright as any gold,
He hadde a beres skin cole-blake for old.
His longe here was kempt behind his bak,
As any ravenes fetherit shone for blake,
A wreth of gold armgrete, of hugè weight,
Upon his hed sate full of stones bright,
Of fine rubins, and of diamants.
About his char ther wenten white alauns,
Twenty and mo, as gret as any stere,
To hunten at the leon or the dere;
And folwed him with mosel fast ybound,
Colered with gold and torretes filed round.
A hundred lordes had he in his route,
Armed full wel, with hertes sterne and stoute.

The figure of Emetrius king of India, who comes to the aid of Arcite, is not inferior in the same style, with a mixture of grace.

With Arcita, in stories as men find,
The gret Emetrius, the king of Inde,
Upon a stedè bay, trapped in stele,
Covered with cloth of gold diapred wele,
Came riding like the god of armes Mars:
His cote-armure was of a cloth of Tars,
Couched with perles, white, and round and grete;
His sadel was of brent gold new ybete,
A mantelet upon his shouldres hanging,
Bretfull of rubies red, as fire sparkling,
His crispè here like ringes was yronne,
And that was yelwe, and glitered as the sonne.
His nose was high, his eyen bright citrin,
His lippes round, his colour was sanguin.
And a fewe fraknes in his face ysprent,
Betwixen yelwe and blake somdele ymeint.
And as a leon he his loking caste.
Of five and twenty yere his age I caste.
His berd was well begonnen for to spring,
His vois was as a trompe thondiring.
Upon his hed he wered, of laurer grene
A gerlond freshe, and lusty for to sene.
Upon his hond he bare for his deduit
An egle tame, as any lily white.
An hundred lordes had he with him there,
All armed, save hir hedes, in all hir gere.
About this king ther ran on every part
Full many a tame leon, and leopart.

The banner of Mars displayed by Theseus, is sublimely conceived.

The red statue of Mars, with spere and targe,
So shineth in his white banner large
That al the feldes gliteren up and doun.

This poem has many strokes of pathetic description, of which these specimens may be selected.

Upon that other side Palamon
Whan that he wist Arcita was ygon,
Swiche sorwe he maketh, that the grete tour
Resouned of his yelling and clamour:
The pure fetters on his shinnes grete
Were of his bitter salte teres wete.

Arcite is thus described, after his return to Thebes, where he despairs of seeing Emilia again.

His slepe, his mete, his drinke, is him byraft;
That lene he wex, and drie as is a shaft:
His eyen holwe, and grisly to behold
His hewe falwe, and pale as ashen cold:
And solitary he was, and ever alone,
And wailing all the night, making his mone.
And if he herdè song or instrument,
Than wold he wepe, he mighte not be stent.
So feble were his spirites and so low,
And changed so, that no man coude know
His speche, ne his vois, though men it herd.

Palamon is thus introduced in the procession of his rival Arcite's funeral:

Tho came this woful Theban Palamon
With flotery berd, and ruggy ashy heres,
In clothes blake ydropped all with teres,
And, (passing over of weping Emelie,)
Was reufullest of all the compagnie.

To which may be added the surprise of Palamon, concealed in the forest, at hearing the disguised Arcite, whom he supposes to be the squire of Theseus, discover himself at the mention of the name of Emilia.

Throughout his herte
He felt a colde swerd sodenly glide:
For ire he quoke, no lenger wolde he hide,
And whan that he had herd Arcites tale,
As he were wood, with face ded and pale,
He sterte him up out of the bushes thikke, &c.

A description of the morning must not be omitted; which vies, both in sentiment and expression, with the most finished modern poetical landscape, and finely displays our author's talent at delineating the beauties of nature.

The besy larke, messager of day,
Saleweth in hire song the morwe gray;
And firy Phebus riseth up so bright,
That all the orient laugheth of the sight:
And with his stremes drieth in the greves
The silver dropes hanging on the leves.

Nor must the figure of the blooming Emilia, the most beautiful object of this vernal picture, pass unnoticed.

Emelie, that fayrer was to sene
Than is the lilie upon his stalke grene;
And fresher than the May with floures newe,
(For with the rose colour strof hire hewe).

In other parts of his works he has painted morning scenes *con amore*: and his imagination seems to have been peculiarly struck with the charms of a rural prospect at sun-rising.

We are surprised to find, in a poet of such antiquity, numbers so nervous and flowing: a circumstance which greatly contributed to render Dryden's paraphrase of this poem the most animated and harmonious piece of versification in the English language. I cannot leave the *Knight's Tale* without remarking, that the inventor of this poem appears to have possessed considerable talents for the artificial construction of a story. It exhibits unexpected and striking turns of fortune; and abounds in those incidents which are calculated to strike the fancy by opening resources to sublime description, or interest the heart by pathetic situations. On this account, even without considering the poetical and exterior ornaments of the piece, we are hardly disgusted with the mixture of manners, the confusion of times, and the like violations of propriety, which this poem, in common with all others of its age, presents in almost every page.

. . . Whatever were Chaucer's materials, he has on this subject constructed a poem of considerable merit, in which the vicissitudes of love are depicted in a strain of true poetry, with much pathos and simplicity of sentiment. He calls it, "a litill tragedie." Troilus is supposed to have seen Cresside in a temple; and retiring to his chamber, is thus naturally described, in the critical situation of a lover examining his own mind after the first impression of love.

> And whan that he in chambre was alone,
> He down upon his beddis fete him sette,
> And first he gan to sike, and efte to grone,
> And thought aie on her so withoutin lette:
> That as he satte and woke, his spirit mette
> That he her saugh, and temple, and all the wise
> Right of her loke, and gan it newe avise.

There is not so much nature in the sonnet to Love, which follows. It is translated from Petrarch; and had Chaucer followed his own genius, he would not have disgusted us with the affected gallantry and exaggerated compliments which it extends through five tedious stanzas. The doubts and delicacies of a young girl disclosing her heart to her lover, are exquisitely touched in this comparison.

> And as the newe abashid nightingale
> That stintith first, when she beginith sing,
> When that she herith any herdis tale,
> Or in the hedgis anie wight stirring,
> And after sikir doth her voice outring;
> Right so Cresseidè when that her drede stent
> Opened her herte and told him her intent.

The following pathetic scene may be selected from many others. Troilus seeing Cresside in a swoon, imagines her to be dead. He unsheaths his sword with an intent to kill himself, and utters these exclamations.

> And thou, cite, in which I live in wo,
> And thou Priam, and brethren al ifere,
> And thou, my mother, farwel, for I go:
> And, Atropos, make ready thou my bere:
> And thou Creseidè, O sweet hertè dere,
> Receive thou now my spirit, would he say,
> With swerd at hert all redy for to dey.
>
> But as god would, of swough she tho abraide,
> And gan to sighe, and TROILUS she cride:
> And he answerid, Lady mine Creseide,
> Livin ye yet? And let his sword doune glide,
> Yes, hertè mine, that thankid be Cupide,
> Quoth she: and therwithall she sorè sight
> And he began to glad her as he might.
>
> Toke her in armis two, and kist her oft,
> And her to glad he did all his entent:
> For which her ghost, that flickered aie alofte
> Into her woefull breast aien it went:
> But at the last, as that her eyin glent
> Aside, anon she gan his swerde aspie,
> As it lay bere, and gan for fere to crie:
> And askid him why he had it outdrawe?
> And Troilus anon the cause hir tolde,

> And how therwith himself he would have slawe:
> For which Creseide upon him gan behold,
> And gan him in her armis fast to fold;
> And said, O mercy, God, lo whiche a dede
> Alas! how nere we werin bothè dede!

Pathetic description is one of Chaucer's peculiar excellencies.

In this poem are various imitations from Ovid, which are of too particular and minute a nature to be pointed out here, and belong to the province of a professed and formal commentator on the piece. The Platonic notion in the third book about universal love, and the doctrine that this principle acts with equal and uniform influence both in the natural and moral world, are a translation from Boethius. And in the *Knight's Tale* he mentions, from the same favourite system of philosophy, the *Faire Chaine of Love*. It is worth observing, that the reader is referred to Dares Phrygius, instead of Homer, for a display of the achievements of Troilus.

> His worthi dedis who so list him here,
> Rede Dares, he can tel hem all ifere.

Our author, from his excessive fondness for Statius, has been guilty of a very diverting and what may be called a double anachronism. He represents Cresside, with two of her female companions, sitting in a *pavid parlour*, and reading the *Thebaid* of Statius, which is called *the Geste of the Siege of Thebes*, and *the Romance of Thebis*. In another place, Cassandra translates the Arguments of the twelve books of the *Thebaid*. In the fourth book of this poem, Pandarus endeavours to comfort Troilus with arguments concerning the doctrine of predestination, taken from Bradwardine, a learned archbishop and theologist, and nearly Chaucer's cotemporary.

This poem, although almost as long as the *Eneid*, was intended to be sung to the harp, as well as read.

> And redde where so thou be, or ellis *songe*.

. . . Nothing can be more ingeniously contrived than the occasion on which Chaucer's *Canterbury Tales* are supposed to be recited. A company of pilgrims, on their journey to visit the shrine of Thomas Becket at Canterbury, lodge at the Tabarde-inn in Southwark. Although strangers to each other, they are assembled in one room at supper, as was then the custom; and agree, not only to travel together the next morning, but to relieve the fatigue of the journey by telling each a story. Chaucer undoubtedly intended to imitate Boccacio, whose *Decameron* was then the most popular of books, in writing a set of tales. But the circumstance invented by Boccacio, as the cause which gave rise to his *Decameron*, or the relation of his hundred stories, is by no means so happily conceived as that of Chaucer for a similar purpose. Boccacio supposes, that when the plague began to abate at Florence, ten young persons of both sexes retired to a country house, two miles from the city, with a design of enjoying fresh air, and passing ten days agreeably. Their principal and established amusement, instead of playing at chess after dinner, was for each to tell a tale. One superiority, which, among others, Chaucer's plan afforded above that of Boccacio, was the opportunity of displaying a variety of striking and dramatic characters, which would not have easily met but on such an expedition;—a circumstance which also contributed to give a variety to the stories. And for a number of persons in their situation, so natural, so practicable, so pleasant, I add so rational, a mode of entertainment, could not have been imagined.

The *Canterbury Tales* are unequal, and of various merit. Few, if any, of the stories are perhaps the invention of Chaucer.

I have already spoken at large of the *Knight's Tale,* one of our author's noblest compositions. That of the *Canterbury Tales,* which deserves the next place, as written in the higher strain of poetry, and the poem by which Milton describes and characterises Chaucer, is the *Squier's Tale.* The imagination of this story consists in Arabian fiction engrafted on Gothic chivalry. Nor is this Arabian fiction purely the sport of arbitrary fancy: it is in great measure founded on Arabian learning. . . .

Every reader of taste and imagination must regret, that instead of our author's tedious detail of the quaint effects of Canace's ring, in which a falcon relates her amours, and talks familiarly of Troilus, Paris, and Jason, the notable achievements we may suppose to have been performed by the assistance of the horse of brass, are either lost, or that this part of the story, by far the most interesting, was never written. After the strange knight has explained to Cambuscan the management of this magical courser, he vanishes on a sudden, and we hear no more of him.

> At after souper goth this noble king
> To seen this Hors of Bras, with all a route
> Of lordes and of ladies him aboute:
> Swiche wondring was ther on this Hors of Bras,
> That sin the gret assege of Troyè was,
> Ther as men wondred on an hors also,
> Ne was ther swiche a wondring as was tho.
> But finally the king asketh the knight
> The vertue of his courser and the might;
> And praied him to tell his governaunce:
> The hors anon gan for to trip and daunce,
> Whan that the knight laid hond upon his reine.—
> Enfourmed whan the king was of the knight,
> And hath conceived in his wit aright,
> The maner and the forme of all this thing,
> Ful glad and blith, this noble doughty king
> Repaireth to his revel as beforne:
> The brydel is into the Toure yborne,
> And kept among his jewels lefe and dere:
> The horse vanisht: I n'ot in what manere.

By such inventions we are willing to be deceived. These are the triumphs of deception over truth.

> Magnanima mensogna, hor quando è al vero.
> Si bello, che si possa à te preporre?

The *Clerke of Oxenfordes Tale,* or the story of Patient Grisilde, is the next of Chaucer's Tales in the serious style which deserves mention. . . .

The pathos of this poem, which is indeed exquisite, chiefly consists in invention of incidents, and the contrivance of the story, which cannot conveniently be developed in this place: and it will be impossible to give any idea of its essential excellence by exhibiting detached parts. The versification is equal to the rest of our author's poetry. . . .

Dryden and Pope have modernised the two last-mentioned poems; Dryden the tale of the *Nonnes Priest,* and Pope that of *January* and *May;* intending perhaps to give patterns of the best of Chaucer's Tales in the comic species. But I am of opinion that the *Miller's Tale* has more true humour than either. Not that I mean to palliate the levity of the story, which was most probably chosen by Chaucer in compliance with the prevailing manners of an unpolished age, and agreeable to ideas of festivity not always the most delicate and refined. Chaucer abounds in liberties of this kind, and this must be his apology. So does Boccacio, and perhaps much more, but from a different cause. The licentiousness of Boccacio's tales, which he composed *per cacciar le malincolia delle femine,* to amuse the ladies, is to be vindicated, at least accounted for, on other

principles: it was not so much the consequence of popular incivility, as it was owing to a particular event of the writer's age. Just before Boccacio wrote, the plague at Florence had totally changed the customs and manners of the people. . . .

But to return to the *Miller's Tale.* The character of the Clerke of Oxford, who studied astrology, a science then in high repute, but under the specious appearance of decorum, and the mask of the serious philosopher, carried on intrigues, is painted with these lively circumstances.

> This clerk was cleped hendy Nicholas,
> Of dernè love he coude and of solas:
> And therto he was slie, and ful prive,
> And like a maiden meke for to se.
> A chambre had he in that hostelrie
> Alone, withouten any compagnie,
> Ful fetisly ydight with herbes sote;
> And he himself was swete as is the rote
> Of licoris, or any setewale.
> His almageste, and bokes grete and smale,
> His astrelabre longing for his art,
> His augrim stones layen faire apart,
> On shelves, couched at his beddes hed;
> His presse ycovered with a falding red:
> And all above there lay a gay sautrie,
> On which he made on nightes melodie
> So swetely that al the chambre rong,
> And *Angelus ad Virginem* he song.

In the description of the young wife of our philosopher's host, there is great elegance, with a mixture of burlesque allusions. Not to mention the curiosity of a female portrait, drawn with so much exactness at such a distance of time.

> Fayre was this yongè wife, and therwithal
> As any wesel hire body gent and smal.
> A seint she wered, barred all of silk,
> A barmecloth eke, as white as morwe milk,
> Upon hire lendes, ful of many a gore.
> White was hire smok, and brouded all before,
> And eke behind, on hire colere aboute,
> Of coleblak silk, within, and eke withoute.
> The tapes of hire whitè volipere
> Were of the samè suit of hire colere.
> Hire fillet brode of silk, and set full hye,
> And sikerly she had a likerous eye.
> Ful smal ypulled were hire browes two,
> And thy were bent and black as any slo.
> And she was wel more blisful on to see
> Than is the newè perienet tree;
> And softer than the wolle is of a wether:
> And by hire girdle heng a purse of lether,
> Tasseled with silk, and perlid with latoun.
> In all this world to seken up and doun,
> There nis no man so wise that coudè thenche
> So gay a popelot or swiche a wenche.
> Full brighter was the shining of hire hewe
> Than in the Tour the noble yforged newe.
> But of hire song, it was as loud and yerne,
> As any swalow sitting on a berne.
> Therto she coude skip, and make a game,
> As any kid or calf folowing his dame.
> Hire mouth was swete as braket or the meth,
> Or hord of appels laid in hay or heth.
> Winsing she was as is a joly colt,
> Long as a mast, and upright as a bolt.
> A broche she bare upon hire low colere
> As brode as is the bosse of a bokelere.
> Hire shoon were laced on hire legges hie, &c.

Nicholas, as we may suppose, was not proof against the charms of his blooming hostess. He has frequent opportunities of conversing with her; for her husband is the carpenter of Oseney Abbey near Oxford, and often absent in the woods belonging to the monastery. His rival is Absalom, a parish-clerk, the gaiest of his calling, who being amorously inclined, very naturally avails himself of a circumstance belonging to his profession: on holidays it was his business to carry the censer about the church, and he takes this opportunity of casting unlawful glances on the handsomest dames of the parish. His gallantry, agility, affectation of dress and personal elegance, skill in shaving and surgery, smattering in the law, taste for music, and many other accomplishments, are thus inimitably represented by Chaucer, who must have much relished so ridiculous a character.

> Now was ther of that chirche a parish clerke,
> The which that was ycleped Absalon,
> Crulle was his here, and as the golde it shone,
> And strouted as a fannè large and brode,
> Ful streight and even lay his joly shode.
> His rode was red, his eyen grey as goos,
> With Poules windowes corven on his shoos.
> In hosen red he went ful fetisly:
> Yclad he was ful smal and properly
> All in a kirtel of a light waget,
> Ful faire, and thickè ben the pointes set:
> And therupon he had a gay surplise
> As white as is the blosme upon the rise.
> A mery child he was, so god me save,
> Wel coud he leten blod, and clippe, and shave.
> And make a chartre of lond and a quitance;
> In twenty manere coud he trip and dance,
> After the scole of Oxenforde tho,
> And with his legges casten to and fro.
> And playen songes on a smal ribible,
> Therto he song sometime a loud quinible.

. . .⟨O⟩ur carpenter, reflecting on the danger of being wise, and exulting in the security of his own ignorance, exclaims,

> A man wote litel what shal him betide!
> This man is fallen with his astronomie
> In som woodnesse, or in som agonie.
> I thought ay wel how that it shuldè be:
> Men shuldè not know of goddes privetee.
> Ya blessed be alway the lewed-man,
> That nought but only his beleve can.
> So ferd another clerke with astronomie;
> He walked in the feldes for to prie
> Upon the sterres what there shuld befalle
> Till he was in a marlèpit yfalle;
> He saw not that. But yet, by seint Thomas,
> Me reweth sore of hendy Nicholas:
> He shall be rated for his studying.

But the scholar has ample gratification for this ridicule. The carpenter is at length admitted; and the scholar continuing the farce, gravely acquaints the former that he has been all this while making a most important discovery by means of astrological calculations. He is soon persuaded to believe the prediction: and in the sequel, which cannot be repeated here, this humorous contrivance crowns the scholar's schemes with success, and proves the cause of the carpenter's disgrace. In this piece the reader observes that the humour of the characters is made subservient to the plot.

I have before hinted, that Chaucer's obscenity is in great measure to be imputed to his age. We are apt to form romantic and exaggerated notions about the moral innocence of our ancestors. Ages of ignorance and simplicity are thought to be ages of purity. The direct contrary, I believe, is the case. Rude periods have that grossness of manners which is not less friendly to virtue than luxury itself. In the middle ages, not only the most flagrant violations of modesty were frequently practised and permitted, but the most infamous vices. Men are less ashamed as they are less polished. Great refinement multiplies criminal pleasures, but at the same time prevents the actual commission of many enormities: at least it preserves public decency, and suppresses public licentiousness.

The *Reve's Tale*, or the *Miller of Trompington*, is much in the same style, but with less humour. This story was enlarged by Chaucer from Boccacio. There is an old English poem on the same plan, entitled, *A ryght pleasant and merye history of the Mylner of Abington, with his Wife and faire Daughter, and two poore Scholars of Cambridge*. It begins with these lines.

> Faire lordinges, if you list to heere
> A mery jest your minds to cheere.

This piece is supposed by Wood to have been written by Andrew Borde, a physician, a wit, and a poet, in the reign of Henry the Eighth. It was at least evidently written after the time of Chaucer. It is the work of some tasteless imitator, who has sufficiently disguised his original, by retaining none of its spirit. I mention these circumstances, lest it should be thought that this frigid abridgement was the ground-work of Chaucer's poem on the same subject. In the class of humorous or satirical tales, the *Sompnour's Tale*, which exposes the tricks and extortions of the Mendicant friars, has also distinguished merit. This piece has incidentally been mentioned above with the *Plowman's Tale*, and Pierce Plowman.

Genuine humour, the concomitant of true taste, consists in discerning improprieties in books as well as characters. We therefore must remark under this class another tale of Chaucer, which till lately has been looked upon as a grave heroic narrative. I mean the *Rime of Sir Thopas*. Chaucer, at a period which almost realized the manners of romantic chivalry, discerned the leading absurdities of the old romances: and in this poem, which may be justly called a prelude to *Don Quixote*, has burlesqued them with exquisite ridicule. That this was the poet's aim, appears from many passages. But, to put the matter beyond a doubt, take the words of an ingenious critic. "We are to observe," says he, "that this was Chaucer's own Tale: and that, when in the progress of it, the good sense of the host is made to break in upon him, and interrupt him, Chaucer approves his disgust, and changing his note, tells the simple instructive *Tale of Meliboeus*, a *moral tale vertuous*, as he terms it; to show what sort of fictions were most expressive of real life, and most proper to be put into the hands of the people. It is further to be noted, that the *Boke* of *The Giant Olyphant, and Chylde Thopas*, was not a fiction of his own, but a story of antique fame, and very celebrated in the days of chivalry; so that nothing could better suit the poet's design of discrediting the old romances, than the choice of this venerable legend for the vehicle of his ridicule upon them." But it is to be remembered, that Chaucer's design was intended to ridicule the frivolous descriptions, and other tedious impertinencies, so common in the volumes of chivalry with which his age was overwhelmed, not to degrade in general or expose a mode of fabling, whose sublime extravagances constitute the marvellous grace of his own *Cambuscan*; a composition which at the same time abundantly demonstrates, that the manners of romance are better calculated to answer the purposes of pure poetry, to captivate the imagination, and to produce surprise, than the fictions of classical antiquity.

But Chaucer's vein of humour, although conspicuous in

the *Canterbury Tales*, is chiefly displayed in the Characters with which they are introduced. In these his knowledge of the world availed him in a peculiar degree, and enabled him to give such an accurate picture of antient manners, as no cotemporary nation has transmitted to posterity. It is here that we view the pursuits and employments, the customs and diversions, of our ancestors, copied from the life, and represented with equal truth and spirit, by a judge of mankind, whose penetration qualified him to discern their foibles or discriminating peculiarities; and by an artist, who understood that proper selection of circumstances, and those predominant characteristics, which form a finished portrait. We are surprised to find, in so gross and ignorant an age, such talents for satire, and for observation on life; qualities which usually exert themselves at more civilised periods, when the improved state of society, by subtilising our speculations, and establishing uniform modes of behaviour, disposes mankind to study themselves, and renders deviations of conduct, and singularities of character, more immediately and necessarily the objects of censure and ridicule. These curious and valuable remains are specimens of Chaucer's native genius, unassisted and unalloyed. The figures are all British, and bear no suspicious signatures of Classical, Italian, or French imitation. The characters of Theophrastus are not so lively, particular, and appropriated. A few traits from this celebrated part of our author, yet too little tasted and understood, may be sufficient to prove and illustrate what is here advanced.

The character of the Prioresse is chiefly distinguished by an excess of delicacy and decorum, and an affectation of courtly accomplishments. But we are informed, that she was educated at the school of Stratford at Bow near London, perhaps a fashionable seminary for breeding nuns.

> There was also a nonne a Prioresse
> That of hire smiling was ful simple and coy;
> Hire gretest othe n'as but by seint Eloy, &c.
> And Frenche she spake full fayre and fetisly,
> After the scole of Stratford atte Bowe,
> For Frenche of Paris was to hire unknowe,
> At metè was she wel ytaughte withalle;
> She lette no morsel from hire lippes falle,
> Ne wette hire fingres in hire saucè depe;
> Wel coude she carie a morsel, and wel kepe,
> Thatte no drope ne fell upon hire brest;
> In curtesie was sette ful moche hire lest.
> Hire overlippè wiped she so clene,
> That in hire cuppe was no ferthing sene
> Of gresè, whan she dronken hadde hire draught,
> Ful semely after hire mete she raught.—
> And peined hire to contrefeten chere
> Of court, and bene statelich of manere.

She has even the false pity and sentimentality of many modern ladies.

> She was so charitable and so pitous,
> She woldè wepe if that she saw a mous
> Caughte in a trappe, if it were ded or bledde.
> Of smalè houndes hadde she that she fed
> With rosted flesh, and milk, and wastel brede:
> But sore wept she if on of hem were dede,
> Or if men smote it with a yerdè smert:
> And all was conscience and tendre herte.

The Wife of Bath is more amiable for her plain and useful qualifications. She is a respectable dame, and her chief pride consists in being a conspicuous and significant character at church on a Sunday.

> Of clothmaking she haddè swiche an haunt
> She passed hem of Ipres and of Gaunt.

> In all the parish, wif ne was there non
> That to the offring bifore hire shulde gon;
> And if ther did, certain so wroth was she,
> That she was out of alle charite.
> Hire coverchiefs weren ful fine of ground,
> I dorste swere they weyeden a pound,
> That on the sonday were upon hire hede:
> Her hosen weren of fine scarlet rede,
> Full streite iteyed, and shoon ful moist and newe:
> Bold was hire face, and fayre and rede of hew.
> She was a worthy woman all hire live:
> Housbondes at the chirche dore had she had five.

The Frankelein is a country gentleman, whose estate consisted in free land, and was not subject to feudal services or payments. He is ambitious of showing his riches by the plenty of his table: but his hospitality, a virtue much more practicable among our ancestors than at present, often degenerates into luxurious excess. His impatience if his sauces were not sufficiently poignant, and every article of his dinner in due form and readiness, is touched with the hand of Pope or Boileau. He had been a president at the sessions, knight of the shire, a sheriff, and a coroner.

> An housholder, and that a grete, was he:
> Seint Julian he was in his contree.
> His brede, his ale, was alway after on;
> A better envyned man was no wher non.
> Withouten bake mete never was his hous
> Of fish and flesh, and that so plenteous,
> It snewed in his hous of mete and drinke,
> Of alle deintees that men coud of thinke.
> After the sondry sesons of the yere,
> So changed he his mete, and his soupere
> Ful many a fat partrich hadde he in mewe,
> And many a breme, and many a luce, in stewe.
> Wo was his coke, but if his saucè were
> Poinant and sharpe, and ready all his gere!
> His table dormant in his halle alway,
> Stole redy covered, all the longè day.

The character of the Doctor of Phisicke preserves to us the state of medical knowledge, and the course of medical erudition then in fashion. He treats his patients according to rules of astronomy: a science which the Arabians engrafted on medicine.

> For he was grounded in astronomie:
> He kept his patient a ful gret dele
> In houres by his magike naturel.

. . . The Sompnour, whose office it was to summon uncanonical offenders into the archdeacon's court, where they were very rigorously punished, is humorously drawn as counteracting his profession by his example: he is libidinous and voluptuous, and his rosy countenance belies his occupation. This is an indirect satire on the ecclesiastical proceedings of those times. His affectation of Latin terms, which he had picked up from the decrees and pleadings of the court, must have formed a character highly ridiculous.

> And whan that he wel dronken had the win,
> Than wold he speken no word but Latine.
> A fewe termes coude he two or three,
> That he had lerned out of som decree.
> No wonder is, he herd it all the day:
> And eke ye knowen wel, how that a jay
> Can clepen watte as wel as can the pope:
> But whoso wolde in other thing him grope,
> Than hadde he spent all his philosophie,
> Ay *questio quid juris* wolde he crie.

He is with great propriety made the friend and companion of the Pardonere, or dispenser of indulgences, who is just arrived from the pope, "brimful of pardons come from Rome al hote;" and who carries in his wallet, among other holy curiosities, the virgin Mary's veil, and part of the sail of Saint Peter's ship.

The Monke is represented as more attentive to horses and hounds than to the rigorous and obsolete ordinances of Saint Benedict. Such are his ideas of secular pomp and pleasure, that he is even qualified to be an abbot.

> An outrider that loved venerie,
> A manly man, to ben an abbot able:
> Ful many a deinte hors hadde he in stable.—
> This ilkè monk lette old thinges pace,
> And held after the new world the trace.
> He yave not of the text a pulled hen
> That saith, that hunters ben not holy men.

He is ambitious of appearing a conspicuous and stately figure on horseback. A circumstance represented with great elegance.

> And whan he rode, men mighte his bridel here
> Gingeling in a whistling wind, as clere
> And eke as loude, as doth the chapel bell.

The gallantry of his riding dress, and his genial aspect, is painted in lively colours.

> I saw his sleves purfiled at the hond,
> With gris, and that the finest of the lond.
> And for to fasten his hode under his chinne
> He hadde of gold ywrought a curious pinne,
> A love-knotte in the greter end ther was.
> His hed was balled, and shone as any glas,
> And eke his face as it hadde ben anoint:
> He was a lord ful fat, and in good point.
> His eyen stepe, and rolling in his hed,
> That stemed as a forneis of a led.
> His botes souple, his hors in gret estat,
> Now certainly he was a fayre prelat!
> He was not pale as a forpined gost;
> A fat swan loved he best of any rost.
> His palfrey was as broune as is a berry.

The Frere, or friar, is equally fond of diversion and good living; but the poverty of his establishment obliges him to travel about the country, and to practise various artifices to provide money for his convent, under the sacred character of a confessor.

> A frere there was, a wanton and a mery;
> A limitour, a ful solempne man:
> In all the ordres foure is non that can
> So moche of daliance, and fayre langage.—
> Ful swetely herde he confession:
> Ful plesant was his absolution.
> His tippet was ay farsed ful of knives
> And pinnes for to given fayre wives.
> And certainly he had a mery note:
> Wel coude he singe and plaien on a rote.
> Of yeddinges he bare utterly the pris.—
> Ther n'as no man no wher so vertuous;
> He was the beste begger in all his hous.—
> Somewhat he lisped for his wantonnesse,
> To make his English swete upon his tongue;
> And in his harping, whan that he hadde songe,
> His eyen twinkeled in his hed aright
> As don the sterres in a frosty night.

With these unhallowed and untrue sons of the church is contrasted the Parsoune, or parish-priest: in describing whose sanctity, simplicity, sincerity, patience, industry, courage, and

conscientious impartiality, Chaucer shows his good sense and good heart. Dryden imitated this character of the Good Parson, and is said to have applied it to bishop Ken.

The character of the Squire teaches us the education and requisite accomplishments of young gentlemen in the gallant reign of Edward the Third. But it is to be remembered, that our squire is the son of a knight, who has performed feats of chivalry in every part of the world; which the poet thus enumerates with great dignity and simplicity.

> At Alisandre' he was whan it was wonne,
> Ful often time he hadde the bord begonne,
> Aboven allè nations in Pruce.
> In Lettowe hadde he reysed and in Ruce:
> No cristen man so ofte of his degre
> In Gernade, at the siege eke hadde he be
> Of Algesir, and ridden in Belmarie.
> At Leyes was he, and at Satalie,
> Whan they were wonne: and in the gretè see:
> At many a noble armee hadde he be:
> At mortal batailles had he ben fiftene,
> And foughten for our faith at Tramissene
> In lystes thries, and ay slain his fo.
> This ilkè worthy Knight hadde ben also
> Sometime with the lord of Palatie:
> Agen another hethen in Turkie.
> And evermore he hadde a sovereine pris,
> And though that he was worthy he was wise.

. . . The character of the Reve, an officer of much greater trust and authority during the feudal constitution than at present, is happily pictured. His attention to the care and custody of the manors, the produce of which was then kept in hand for furnishing his lord's table, perpetually employs his time, preys upon his thoughts, and makes him lean and choleric. He is the terror of bailiffs and hinds; and is remarkable for his circumspection, vigilance, and subtlety. He is never in arrears, and no auditor is able to over-reach or detect him in his accounts: yet he makes more commodious purchases for himself than for his master, without forfeiting the good will or bounty of the latter. Amidst these strokes of satire, Chaucer's genius for descriptive painting breaks forth in this simple and beautiful description of the Reve's rural habitation.

> His wonning was ful fayre upon an heth,
> With grene trees yshadewed was his place.

In the Clerke of Oxenforde our author glances at the inattention paid to literature, and the unprofitableness of philosophy. He is emaciated with study, clad in a thread-bare cloak, and rides a steed lean as a rake.

> For he hadde geten him yet no benefice,
> Ne was nought worldly to have an office:
> For him was lever han at his beddes hed
> A twenty bokes, clothed in black or red,
> Of Aristotle and his philosophie,
> Then robes riche, or fidel, or sautrie:
> But allbe that he was a philosophre,
> Yet hadde he but litel gold in cofre.

His unwearied attention to logic had tinctured his conversation with much pedantic formality, and taught him to speak on all subjects in a precise and sententious style. Yet his conversation was instructive: and he was no less willing to submit than to communicate his opinion to others.

> Souning in moral vertue was his speche,
> And gladly wolde he lerne, and gladly teche.

The perpetual importance of the Serjeant of Lawe, who by habit or by affectation has the faculty of appearing busy when he has nothing to do, is sketched with the spirit and conciseness of Horace.

> No wher so besy a man as he ther n'as,
> And yet he semed besier than he was.

There is some humour in making our lawyer introduce the language of his pleadings into common conversation. He addresses the hoste,

> Hoste, quoth he, *de pardeux jeo assent.*

The affectation of talking French was indeed general, but it is here appropriated and in character.

Among the rest, the character of the Hoste, or master of the Tabarde inn where the pilgrims are assembled, is conspicuous. He has much good sense, and discovers great talents for managing and regulating a large company; and to him we are indebted for the happy proposal of obliging every pilgrim to tell a story during their journey to Canterbury. His interpositions between the tales are very useful and enlivening; and he is something like the chorus on the Grecian stage. He is of great service in encouraging each person to begin his part, in conducting the scheme with spirit, in making proper observations on the merit or tendency of the several stories, in settling disputes which must naturally arise in the course of such an entertainment, and in connecting all the narratives into one continued system. His love of good cheer, experience in marshalling guests, address, authoritative deportment, and facetious disposition, are thus expressively displayed by Chaucer.

> Gret chere made our Hoste everich on,
> And to the souper sette he us anon;
> And served us with vitaille of the beste:
> Strong was his win, and wel to drinke us leste.
> A semely man our Hostè was with alle
> For to han ben a marshal in a halle.
> A largè man he was, with eyen stepe,
> A fairer burgeis is ther non in Chepe.
> Bold of his speche, and wise, and wel ytaught,
> And of manhood him lacked righte naught.
> Eke therto was he right a mery man, &c.

Chaucer's scheme of the *Canterbury Tales* was evidently left unfinished. It was intended by our author, that every pilgrim should likewise tell a Tale on their return from Canterbury. A poet who lived soon after the *Canterbury Tales* made their appearance, seems to have designed a supplement to this deficiency, and with this view to have written a Tale called the *Marchaunt's Second Tale,* or the *History of Beryn.* It was first printed by Urry, who supposed it to be Chaucer's. In the Prologue, which is of considerable length, there is some humour and contrivance; in which the author, happily enough, continues to characterise the pilgrims, by imagining what each did, and how each behaved, when they all arrived at Canterbury. After dinner was ordered at their inn, they all proceed to the cathedral. At entering the church one of the monks sprinkles them with holy water. The Knight with the better sort of the company goes in great order to the shrine of Thomas a Becket. The Miller and his companions run staring about the church: they pretend to blazon the arms painted in the glass windows, and enter into a dispute in heraldry: but the Hoste of the Tabarde reproves them for their improper behaviour and impertinent discourse, and directs them to the martyr's shrine. When all had finished their devotions, they return to the inn. In the way thither they purchase toys for which that city was famous, called *Canterbury brochis,* and here much facetiousness passes betwixt the Frere and the Sompnour, in which the latter vows revenge on the former, for telling a Tale so palpably levelled at his profession, and protests he will retaliate on their return by a more severe story. When dinner is ended,

the Hoste of the Tabarde thanks all the company in form for their several Tales. The party then separate till supper-time by agreement. The Knight goes to survey the walls and bulwarks of the city, and explains to his son the Squier the nature and strength of them. Mention is here made of great guns. The Wife of Bath is too weary to walk far; she proposes to the Prioresse to divert themselves in the garden, which abounds with herbs proper for making salves. Others wander about the streets. The Pardoner has a low adventure, which ends much to his disgrace. The next morning they proceed on their return to Southwark: and our genial master of the Tabarde, just as they leave Canterbury, by way of putting the company into good humour, begins a panegyric on the morning and the month of April, some lines of which I shall quote, as a specimen of our author's abilities in poetical description.

> Lo! how the seson of the yere, and Averell shouris,
> Doith the bushis burgyn out blossomes and flouris.
> Lo! the prymerosys of the yere, how fresh they bene to
>   sene,
> And many othir flouris among the grassis grene.
> Lo! how they springe and sprede, and of divers hue,
> Beholdith and seith, both white, red, and blue.
> That lusty bin and comfortabyll for mannis sight,
> For I say for myself it makith my hert to light.

On casting lots, it falls to the Marchaunt to tell the first tale, which then follows. I cannot allow that this Prologue and Tale were written by Chaucer. Yet I believe them to be nearly coeval.

It is not my intention to dedicate a volume to Chaucer, how much soever he may deserve it; nor can it be expected, that, in a work of this general nature, I should enter into a critical examination of all Chaucer's pieces. Enough has been said to prove, that in elevation and elegance, in harmony and perspicuity of versification, he surpasses his predecessors in an infinite proportion; that his genius was universal, and adapted to themes of unbounded variety; that his merit was not less in painting familiar manners with humour and propriety, than in moving the passions, and in representing the beautiful or the grand objects of nature with grace and sublimity; in a word, that he appeared with all the lustre and dignity of a true poet, in an age which compelled him to struggle with a barbarous language, and a national want of taste; and when to write verses at all, was regarded as a singular qualification. It is true, indeed, that he lived at a time when the French and Italians had made considerable advances and improvements in poetry: and although proofs have already been occasionally given of his imitations from these sources, I shall close my account of him with a distinct and comprehensive view of the nature of the poetry which subsisted in France and Italy when he wrote; pointing out, in the mean time, how far and in what manner the popular models of those nations contributed to form his taste, and influence his genius. . . .

WILLIAM GODWIN

From *Life of Chaucer*
1803–4, Vol. 1, pp. i–viii, 470–85;
Vol. 2, pp. 168–84; Vol. 4, pp. 184–201

I

The two names which perhaps do the greatest honour to the annals of English literature, are those of Chaucer and of Shakespear. Shakespear we have long and justly been accustomed to regard as the first in the catalogue of poetical and creative minds; and after the dramas of Shakespear, there is no production of man that displays more various and vigorous talent than the *Canterbury Tales*. Splendour of narrative, richness of fancy, pathetic simplicity of incident and feeling, a powerful style in delineating character and manners, and an animated vein of comic humour, each takes its turn in this wonderful performance, and each in turn appears to be that in which the author was most qualified to excel.

There is one respect at least in which the works of Chaucer are better fitted to excite our astonishment than those of Shakespear. Ordinary readers are inclined to regard the times of Shakespear as barbarous, because they are remote. But in reality the age of queen Elizabeth was a period of uncommon refinement. We have since that time enlarged our theatres; we have made some improvements in the mechanism of dramatical exhibition; and we have studied, with advantage or otherwise, the laws of the Grecian stage. But we have never produced any thing that will enter into comparison with the plays of Shakespear, or even of some of his contemporaries. What age can be less barbarous than that which, beside the dramatic productions of Shakespear[1], Fletcher, Massinger and Jonson, is illustrated with the names of Raleigh, of Hooker, of Bacon, and of Spenser?

But the times of Chaucer were in a much more obvious and unquestionable sense, so far as poetry is concerned, times of barbarism. The history of the revival of literature in the twelfth and thirteenth centuries will be treated in these volumes. The sole efforts in the art of verse which had been made in Western Europe previously to Chaucer, were romances of prodigious and supernatural adventure, prolix volumes of unvaried allegory, and the rhapsodies of the vagrant minstrel. These productions, though not unrelieved by admirable flights of imagination, were for the most part rugged in versification, prosaic in language, and diffusive and rambling in their story and conduct. What had been achieved in English, was little better than a jejune table of events with the addition of rhyme. Chaucer fixed and naturalised the genuine art of poetry in our island. But what is most memorable in his eulogy, is that he is the father of our language, the idiom of which was by the Norman conquest banished from courts and civilised life, and which Chaucer was the first to restore to literature, and the muses. No one man in the history of human intellect ever did more, than was effected by the single mind of Chaucer.

These are abundant reasons why Englishmen should regard Chaucer with peculiar veneration, should cherish his memory, and eagerly desire to be acquainted with whatever may illustrate his character, or explain the wonders he performed. The first and direct object of this work, is to erect a monument to his name, and, as far as the writer was capable of doing it, to produce an interesting and amusing book in modern English, enabling the reader, who might shrink from the labour of mastering the phraseology of Chaucer, to do justice to his illustrious countryman. It seemed probable also that, if the author were successful in making a popular work, many might by its means be induced to study the language of our ancestors, and the elements and history of our vernacular speech; a study at least as improving as that of the language of Greece and Rome.

A further idea, which was continually present to the mind of the author while writing, obviously contributed to give animation to his labours, and importance to his undertaking. The full and complete life of a poet would include an extensive survey of the manners, the opinions, the arts and the literature, of the age in which the poet lived. This is the only way in which we can become truly acquainted with the history of his mind, and the causes which made him what he was. We must observe what Chaucer felt and saw, how he was educated, what

species of learning he pursued, and what were the objects, the events and the persons, successively presented to his view, before we can strictly and philosophically understand his biography. To delineate the state of England, such as Chaucer saw it, in every point of view in which it can be delineated, is the subject of this book.

But, while engaged in this study, the reader may expect to gain an additional advantage, beside that of understanding the poet. If the knowledge of contemporary objects is the biography of Chaucer, the converse of the proposition will also be true, and the biography of Chaucer will be the picture of a certain portion of the literary, political and domestic history of our country. The person of Chaucer may in this view be considered as the central figure in a miscellaneous painting, giving unity and individual application to the otherwise disjointed particulars with which the canvas is diversified. No man of moral sentiment or of taste will affirm, that a more becoming central figure to the delineation of England in the fourteenth century can be found, than the Englishman who gives name to these volumes. . . .

XV

⟨Concerning *Troilus and Creseide*⟩ . . . , it is not difficult to infer the degree of applause to which its author is entitled. It has already been observed by one of the critics upon English Poetry[2], that it is "almost as long as the *Æneid*." Considered in this point of view, the *Troilus and Creseide* will not appear to advantage. It is not an epic poem. It is not that species of composition which Milton[3] so admirably describes, as "the most consummat act of its authour's fidelity and ripeness;" the fruit of "years and industry;" the reservoir into which are poured the results of "all his considerat diligence, all his midnight watchings, and expence of Palladian oyl." The *Æneid* is a little code of politics and religion. It describes men and manners and cities and countries. It embraces an outline of the arts of peace and of war. It travels through the whole circumference of the universe; and brings together heaven and hell, and all that is natural and all that is divine, to aid the poet in the completion of his design. It is at once historical and prophetic. It comprises the sublime horrors of a great city captured and in flames, and the pathetic anguish of an ardent, disappointed and abandoned love. It comprehends a cycle of sciences and arts, as far as they could be connected with the principal subject; and if all other books were destroyed, the various elements of many sciences and arts might be drawn from an attentive perusal of this poem.

The plan of the *Æneid* in these respects, is precisely what the plan of an epic poem should be. The *Troilus and Creseide* can advance no pretensions to enter into this class of composition. It is merely a love-tale. It is not the labour of a man's life; but a poem which, with some previous knowledge of human sentiments and character, and a very slight preparation of science, the writer might perhaps be expected to complete in about as many months, as the work is divided into books. It is certainly much greater in extent of stanzas and pages, than the substratum and basis of the story can authorise.

It is also considerably barren of incident. There is not enough in it of matter generating visible images in the reader, and exciting his imagination with pictures of nature and life. There is not enough in it of vicissitudes of fortune, awakening curiosity and holding expectation in suspense.

Add to which, the catastrophe is unsatisfactory and offensive. The poet who would interest us with a love-tale, should soothe our minds with the fidelity and disinterestedness of the mutual attachment of the parties, and, if he presents us with a tragical conclusion, it should not be one which arises out of the total unworthiness of either. Creseide (as Mr. Urry, in his introduction to Henryson's epilogue to the *Troilus*, has very truly observed), however prepossessing may be the manner in which she appears in the early part of the poem, is "a false unconstant whore," and of a class which the mind of the reader almost demands to have exhibited, if not as "terminating in extream misery," at least as filled with penitence and remorse. Virgil indeed has drawn the catastrophe of his tale of Dido from the desertion of the lover. But the habits of European society teach us to apprehend less ugliness and loathsome deformity in the falshood of the lover, than of his mistress; and we repose with a tenderer and more powerful sympathy upon the abandoned and despairing state of the female. Besides, Virgil did not write a poem expressly upon the tale of Dido, but only employed it for an episode. The story of Romeo and Juliet is the most perfect model of a love-tale in the series of human invention. Dryden thoroughly felt this defect in the poem of Chaucer, and has therefore changed the catastrophe when he fitted the story for the stage, and represented the two lovers as faithful, but unfortunate.

But, when all these deductions have been made from the claims of the *Troilus and Creseide* upon our approbation, it will still remain a work interspersed with many beautiful passages, passages of exquisite tenderness, of great delicacy, and of a nice and refined observation of the workings of human sensibility. Nothing can be more beautiful, genuine, and unspoiled by the corrupt suggestions of a selfish spirit, than the sentiments of Chaucer's lovers. While conversing with them, we seem transported into ages of primeval innocence. Even Creseide is so good, so ingenuous and affectionate, that we feel ourselves as incapable as Troilus, of believing her false. Nor are the scenes of Chaucer's narrative, like the insipid tales of a pretended pastoral life, drawn with that vagueness of manner, and ignorance of the actual emotions of the heart, which, while we read them, we nauseate and despise. On the contrary, his personages always feel, and we confess the truth of their feelings; what passes in their minds, or falls from their tongues, has the clear and decisive character which proclaims it human, together with the vividness, subtleness and delicacy, which few authors in the most enlightened ages have been equally fortunate in seizing. Pandarus himself comes elevated and refined from the pen of Chaucer: his occupation loses its grossness, in the disinterestedness of his motive, and the sincerity of his friendship. In a word, such is the *Troilus and Creseide*, that no competent judge can rise from its perusal, without a strong impression of the integrity and excellence of the author's disposition, and of the natural relish he entertained for whatever is honourable, beautiful and just.

There is a great difference between the merits of any work of human genius considered abstractedly, taken as it belongs to the general stock of literary production and tried severely on its intrinsic and unchangeable pretensions, and the merits of the same work considered in the place which it occupies in the scale and series of literary history, and compared with the productions of its author's predecessors and contemporaries. In the former case the question we have to ask is, Is it good? In the latter we have to enquire, Was it good? To both these questions, when applied to Chaucer's poem of *Troilus and Creseide*, the fair answer will be an affirmative.

But it is in the latter point of view that the work we are considering shows to infinitely the greatest advantage. The poem will appear to be little less than a miracle, when we combine our examination of it, with a recollection of the times and circumstances in which it was produced. When Chaucer wrote it, the English tongue had long remained in a languid and almost perishing state, overlaid and suffocated by the insolent disdain and remorseless tyranny of the Norman ravagers and dividers of our soil. Previously to the eleventh century it had no cultivation and refinement from the cowardly and superstitious Saxons, and during that century and the following one it appeared in danger of being absolutely extinguished. With Chaucer it seemed to spring like Minerva from the head of Jove, at once accoutered and complete. Mandeville, Wicliffe and Gower, whom we may style the other three evangelists of our tongue, though all older in birth than Chaucer, did not begin too early to work upon the ore of their native language. He surprised his countrymen with a poem, eminently idiomatic, clear and perspicuous in its style, as well as rich and harmonious in its versification. His *Court of Love*, an earlier production, is not less excellent in both these respects. But it was too slight and short to awaken general attention. The *Troilus and Creseide* was of respectable magnitude, and forms an epoch in our literature.

Chaucer presented to the judgment of his countrymen a long poem, perfectly regular in its structure, and uninterrupted with episodes. It contained nothing but what was natural. Its author disdained to have recourse to what was bloated in sentiment, or romantic and miraculous in incident, for the purpose of fixing or keeping alive the attention. He presents real life and human sentiments, and suffers the reader to dwell upon and expand the operations of feeling and passion. Accordingly the love he describes is neither frantic, nor brutal, nor artificial, nor absurd. His hero conducts himself in all respects with the most perfect loyalty and honour; and his heroine, however she deserts her character in the sequel, is in the commencement modest, decorous, affectionate, and prepossessing. The loves of the *Troilus and Creseide* scarcely retain any traces of the preposterous and rude manners of the age in which they were delineated.

This poem therefore, as might have been expected, long fixed upon itself the admiration of the English nation. Chaucer, by his *Court of Love*, and the ditties and songs which had preceded it, had gratified the partiality of his friends, and given them no mean or equivocal promise of what he should hereafter be able to perform. But these, we may easily conceive, were of little general notoriety. The *Troilus and Creseide* was probably, more than any of his other works, the basis of his fame, and the foundation of his fortune. He wrote nothing very eminently superior to this, till his *Canterbury Tales*, which were the production of his declining age. Owing perhaps to the confusion and sanguinary spirit of the wars of York and Lancaster, English literature rather decayed than improved during the following century; and we had consequently no poem of magnitude, and of a compressed and continued plan, qualified to enter into competition with the *Troilus and Creseide*, from the earliest periods of our poetry to the appearance of the *Fairy Queen*. Accordingly, among many examples of its praises which might be produced, sir Philip Sidney in his *Defense of Poesy* has selected this performance, as the memorial of the talents of our poet, and the work in which he "undoubtedly did excellently well."

There are some particular defects belonging to this production beside those already mentioned, which are the more entitled to our notice, as they are adapted to characterise the stage of refinement to which our literature was advanced in the fourteenth century. In the first place, the poem is interspersed with many bases and vulgar lines, which are not only unworthy of the poet, but would be a deformity in any prose composition, and would even dishonour and debase the tone of familiar conversation. The following specimens will afford a sufficient illustration of this fact. Cupid is provoked at the ease and lightness of heart of the hero, and prepares to avenge himself of the contempt.

> —Sodainly he hitte him at the full,
> And yet as proude a pecocke can he pul.
> (B. I, ver. 210.)

> Thus wol she saine, and al the toune at ones,
> The wretch is dead, the divel have his bones.
> (ver. 806.)

> Withouten jelousie, and soche debate,
> Shall no husbonde saine unto me checkemate.
> (B. II, ver. 754.)

> For him demeth men hote, that seeth him swete.
> (ver. 1533.)

> Now loketh than, if thei be nat to blame,
> That hem avaunt of women, and by name,
> That yet behight hem never this ne that,
> Ne knowen hem more than mine oldé hat.
> (B. III, ver. 321.)

> I am, til God me better minde sende,
> At Dulcarnon, right at my wittés ende.
> (ver. 933.)

> For peril is with dretching in ydrawe,
> Nay suche abodés ben nat worthe an hawe.
> (ver. 856.)

> Soche arguments ne be nat worthe a bene.
> (ver. 1173.)

> But soche an ese therwith thei in her wrought,
> Right as a man is esed for to fele
> For ache of hedde, to clawen him on his hele.
> (B. IV, ver. 728)

> I have herd saie eke, timés twisé twelve.
> (B. V, ver. 97.)

There are also lines interspersed in the poem, which are not more degraded by the meanness of the expression, than by the rudeness, not to say the brutality, of the sentiment. We may well be surprised, after considering the delicacy and decorum with which Chaucer has drawn his heroine, to find him polluting the portrait of her virgin character in the beginning of the poem with so low and pitiful a joke as this,

> But whether that she children had or none,
> I rede it nat, therfore I let it gone.
> (B. I, ver. 132.)

The following sentiment must also be deeply disgustful to a just and well ordered mind. Calchas, the father of Creseide, languishes in the Grecian army for the restoration of his only child, and at length effects to his great joy the means of obtaining her in exchange for Antenor, a prisoner in the Grecian camp.

> The whiché tale anon right as Creseide
> Had herd, she (whiche that of her father rought,
> As in this case, right naught, ne whan he deide)
> Full busily, &c.
> (B. IV, ver. 668.)

Another defect in this poem of Chaucer, of the same nature, and that is not less conspicuous, is the tediousness into which he continually runs, seemingly without the least apprehension that any one will construe this feature of his composition as a fault. He appears to have had no idea that his readers could possibly deem it too much to peruse any number of verses which he should think proper to pour out on any branch of his subject. To judge from the poem of *Troilus and Creseide*, we should be tempted to say, that compression, the

strengthening a sentiment by brevity, and the adding to the weight and power of a work by cutting away from it all useless and cumbersome excrescences, was a means of attaining to excellence which never entered into our author's mind. A remarkable instance of this occurs in the fourth book, where upward of one hundred verses upon predestination are put into the mouth of Troilus, the materials of which are supposed to have been extracted from a treatise *De Causa Dei*, written by Thomas Bradwardine archbishop of Canterbury, a contemporary of our author. Other examples, scarcely less offensive to true taste, might be cited.

It is particularly deserving of notice that scarcely any one of the instances which might be produced under either of these heads of impropriety, has a parallel in the version made by Boccaccio of the same story, probably from the same author, and nearly at the same time. Few instances can be given in which the Italian writer has degenerated into any thing mean and vulgar, and he never suspends his narrative with idle and incoherent digressions. He seems to have been perfectly aware, that one of the methods to render a literary production commendable is to admit into it nothing which is altogether superfluous. The inference is, that, whatever may be the comparative degrees of imagination and originality between England and Italy in the fourteenth century, what is commonly called taste had made a much greater progress in the latter country than among us. . . .

XXI

The first poem which Chaucer wrote, so far as can now be ascertained, after he entered into the service of the court, is variously styled in different manuscripts, *The Assembly of Fowls*, and the *Parliament of Birds*. The subject of this poem is the suit or courtship of John of Gaunt just mentioned, and appears to have been written before the lady had accepted the addresses of her illustrious suitor. The natural construction therefore to be put upon such a performance is, that it implies a considerable degree of familiarity and confidence between the poet and the persons who are the subject of it: and indeed it is not improbable that it was penned at the request of the lover, for the purpose of softening the obduracy of his mistress's resistance. As the lady is represented in the course of the poem as deferring the suit of her admirer for a twelvemonth, a circumstance which occurs again in the Book of the Duchess above quoted, and as the marriage was solemnised in May 1359, the date of the poem obviously falls upon the year 1358.

This first courtly composition of Chaucer we may believe was written by the young poet with great care, and no ordinary degree of anxiety to produce something worthy of the masters into whose service he had entered. It was a new field that he was to occupy; and it was with very different feelings that he sat down to write. Hitherto he had been a poet in the purest and most unmingled sense of that word. He gave himself up to the impressions of nature, and to the sensations he experienced. He studied the writings of his contemporaries, and of certain of the ancients. He was learned, according to the learning of his day. He wrote, because he felt himself impelled to write. He analysed the models which were before him. He sought to please his friends and fellow-scholars in the two universities. He aspired to an extensive and lasting reputation. He formed the gigantic and arduous plan of giving poetry to a language, which could as yet scarcely be said to have any poetry to boast.

Now he was placed in a different scene. Without bearing the title of the court-poet, he was the court-poet in reality. He had no competitor. His superiority was universally acknowledged. He had been borne along on the tide of his acknowledged reputation to the eminence he at present occupied. He had the character of his country to sustain; and the literature of a nation rested upon his shoulders.

To every man a scene presented to the eye is impressive, much beyond the effect of any abstraction appealing to the understanding. This is still more the case with a poet, than with any other man. Chaucer had hitherto written for such as were lovers and discerners of true poetry, without well knowing, except perhaps within a limited circle, where they were to be found. He now wrote for the court of England, a court which at this moment was higher in lustre and character than any other in the world. He wrote for the conquerors of Cressy and Poitiers. He had before him sir John Chandos, sir Walter Manny, and the other heroes who had won immortal note on those plains. John king of France, and several of the first personages of that country, were now prisoners in London. Edward III was, it may be, no profound scholar, nor eminent judge of poetical composition. But the ardent imagination of Chaucer was not to be stopped by such impediments. He knew that a piece in which he celebrated the loves of a favourite son of the king, would be often mentioned in the highest circles, and the name of its author often repeated. He aspired, it may be, to that fame which the writer himself may hear, which brings strangers and scholars and persons of eminence to desire the happiness of knowing him, and which surrounds him with grateful whispers whenever he appears, as well as to that fame which breathes incense from the venerable tomb a thousand years after the poet is no more.

The *Parliament of Birds* is a poem marked with pregnancy of fancy and felicity of language. It is written in Rhythm Royal, the same species of stanza as that of the *Court of Love* and the *Troilus and Creseide*. It begins with an extract, beautifully expressed, of Cicero's *Somnium Scipionis* from the commentaries of Macrobius. The following stanzas will remind every reader of the manner of Spenser, mellifluous, soothing and animated.

> Then asked[4] he, if folke that here ben dede
> Have life and dwellyng in an other place?
> And[5] Affrican saied, Ye, withouten drede,
> And how our present worldly livé's space
> N'is but a maner deth, what waie we trace,
> And rightfull folke shull gon, after thei die,
> To hev'n, and shewed him the galaxie.
>
> Then shew'd he him the little yerth that here is
> To regarde of the heven's quantité,
> And after shewed he hym the nine speris,
> And after that the melodie herd he,
> That cometh of thilke sperés thrisé thre,
> That welles of musike ben and melodie
> In this worlde here, and cause of harmonie.
>
> Then saied he him, Sens that yerth was so lite,
> And full of torment, and of hardé grace,
> That he ne shuld hym in this world delite;
> Then told he him, in certain yerés space
> That ev'ry sterre should come into his place
> There it was first, and all should out of mind
> That in this worlde is doen of all mankynd.
> (ver. 50.)

The poet had spent, as he says, a whole day in the study of the *Somnium Scipionis*. He informs us that he was extremely fond of reading; and illustrates this by an apposite simile.

> For out of the olde feldés, as men saieth,
> Cometh all this newe corne fro yere to yere;
> And out of oldé bokés, in gode faieth,
> Cometh all this newe science that men lere.
> (ver. 22.)

At length the sun sets, the light by which he was reading is gone, and Chaucer betakes himself to bed. He dreams; and imagines himself, like the hero of the *Somnium Scipionis*, attended by the vanqusher of Hannibal. The passage with which he introduces his dream, forcibly brings to mind a similar passage in Shakespear, though it must be admitted in this instance that the imitator has greatly surpassed his original.

> The werie hunter sleping in his bedde,
> The wodde ayen his minde goeth anone;
> The judgé dremeth how his plees be spedde;
> The carter dremeth how his cartés gone;
> The riche of golde; the knight fight with his fone,
> The sicke ymette he drinketh of the tonne,
> The lover mette he hath his ladie wonne.[6]
> (ver. 99.)

Under the conduct of the venerable Africanus, Chaucer arrives at a park and a temple, which prove to be consecrated to the God of Love. Considerable effort and vigour of mind are employed in a description of the scenery. The principal particulars which Chaucer has introduced in his account of the temple and the grounds immediately adjacent, are to be found indeed in the seventh book of Boccaccio's *Teseide*. Chaucer's imitation however, which is by no means a close one, contains many nice and beautiful touches, as well as some trivial and mean expressions, which are not to be found in Boccaccio. Among the former may be cited his description of the breeze which blows in the Garden of Love, while the birds carol aloft.

> Therewith a winde, unneth it might be lesse,
> Made in the levés grene a noisé soft,
> Accordant to the foulés' song on loft.
> (ver. 201.)

The circumstance is also subtly imagined, and purely his own, with which he describes Venus, who had retired to an obscure corner in her temple; though it has the defect of repeating one clause of the passage last quoted.

> Darke was that place, but afterward lightnesse
> I saw a lite, unnethes it might be lesse.
> (ver. 263.)

It may be regarded as a singular circumstance, and characteristic of the imperfect refinement of the times in which Chaucer lived, that a somewhat licentious description of Priapus and Venus is introduced into a poem certainly designed for the perusal of a virgin princess, of great youth, and unimpeachable modesty. These are also among the passages which are without a counterpart in Boccaccio.

Meanwhile it is by no means clear . . . whether Chaucer took the story of Palamon and Arcite from Boccaccio, or from the Latin author from whom Boccaccio confesses that he drew his materials. From the circumstance that the description of the Garden and Temple of Love, introduced by Chaucer in this place, and which he has borrowed from the Teseide, or story of Palamon and Arcite, is not to be found in the *Knightes Tale*, the abridgment of that story in Chaucer's collections of *Canterbury Tales*, Mr. Tyrwhit thinks himself entitled to infer, "that the Poem of Palamon and Arcite must have been composed at a later period," than the *Parliament of Birds*. This proof however is by no means complete. It would follow indeed that the *Parliament of Birds* was written prior to the *Canterbury Tales*; but to establish that fact no indirect evidence is necessary. What passages might have existed in Chaucer's original unsuccessful poem of Palamon and Arcite, no trace of which is now to be discovered in his abridgment of it entitled the *Knightes Tale*, a reader of the present age is by no means competent to determine.

The most glaring fault imputable to the poem we are here considering, is that the earlier and the latter half of the composition are by no means of similar substance, or well accord with each other. The first three hundred verses are of lofty port and elevated character. Nothing can be of graver meaning, more interesting to the fancy, or more delicately expressed, than Chaucer's abstract of the *Somnium Scipionis*. To this succeed the *Garden* and *Temple of Love*, which, if they are not subjects of altogether so imposing a nature as the former, are yet fanciful, elevated, and full of poetical representation. The description of these being complete, what remains is that part of the poem which most properly answers to the title; the parliament, or assembly, of birds on St. Valentine's day to choose their mates. Chaucer here quits the Temple, and goes again into the garden, where, in a lawn, seated on a hill of flowers, and overcanopied with halls and bowers composed of the branches of trees, he finds the "quene, the noble goddesse, Nature," with the fowls of every different species assembled round her.

This part of the poem is executed with a very active fancy, and the characters of the various birds are excellently sustained. Chaucer divides his fowls into four classes; the birds of prey, the water-fowl, those which live upon insects and reptiles, and those which are nourished with seeds: and each of these classes has its representative; the falcon for the birds of prey, the goose for the water-fowl, the cuckow for the worm-eaters, and the turtle for the eaters of seed. The epithets applied to these personages are well chosen, not discovering the lazy and insignificant character often imputable to the epithets of inferior poets, but being all appropriate and expressive: and there is considerable humour in the vulgarity of the goose, the base selfishness of the cuckow, and the characteristic attributes of various other fowls which are successively introduced.

But, after all, there is something meagre and unnatural in this sort of allegory, where Chaucer introduces the lovers he means to compliment, under the personage of birds. We feel no sympathies for the amours of his male and female eagles. If the poet who attempts a plan of this sort, introduces any refined and animated sentiments, he violates the propriety of his allegory; and, if he adheres to the decorum of the fiction he has to sustain, he becomes insupportably frigid and tedious. There are indeed a ridiculous inequality and unconnectedness conspicuous through the whole of this poem. Scipio Africanus is introduced with no propriety as Chaucer's conductor to the Temple of Love; and it would have been a still greater absurdity if he had been shown among the nightingales and thrushes stung with the passion of the spring on St. Valentine's day. Accordingly he is conveniently dropped. He is just shown in the commencement of the narrative, and is heard of no more. We do not know that he even enters the Garden of Love, at the door of which he serves the poet in the capacity of a gentleman-usher.

The heroine of the poem, according to Chaucer's arrangement of it, is represented as a female eagle perched upon the hand of the goddess Nature. Three pretenders to her favour are introduced. Who these are it is impossible for us at this distance of time to determine; but it is probable that the number, and some other circumstances which are related respecting them, are founded in fact. The first is plainly the earl of Richmond, who presents himself

> With hed enclin'd, and with ful humble chere.
> (ver. 414.)

The second eagle founds his pretensions upon the length of his attachment. The third, like the first, builds his hope of success only upon the fervour of his passion. They are all treated with

considerable respect by Chaucer. They are all eagles; and he adds in summing up their addresses,

> Of al my life, syth that day I was borne,
> So gentle ple, in love or other thinge,
> Ne herden never no man me beforne.
> (ver. 484.)

The balance however is forcibly made to lean in favour of the first, or royal eagle; and his suit, though not accepted, is only deferred for a year, with every omen of final success.

This subject being dispatched, the assembly of birds, who had been exceedingly eager for their dismission, is dissolved.

> And lorde the blisse and joye which that they make!
> For ech gan other in his wingés take,
> And with her neckés eche gan other winde,
> Thankinge alway the noble' goddesse of kinde.
> (ver. 669.)

At length, the shouting that "the foules made at her flight away" rouses the poet from his dream.

> I woke, and other bokés took me to
> To rede upon, and yet I rede alway.
> (ver. 690.)

This couplet deserved to be quoted as an evidence of the poet's habits. We have here Chaucer's own testimony, that he was a man of incessant reading and literary curiosity, and that, even at thirty years of age, and amidst the allurements of a triumphant and ostentatious court, one of the first and most insatiable passions of his mind was the love of books. . . .

LV

The *Canterbury Tales* is the great basis of the fame of Chaucer, and indolent men have generally expressed themselves with contempt of the rest of his works as unworthy of attention. The enquiries in which we have been engaged have led us frequently to refer to his smaller pieces, nor has our love of poetry come away from the pursuit unrewarded. Many passages of exquisite thinking and fancy have been recited. He indeed who wishes to become personally acquainted with Chaucer, must of necessity have recourse to his minor pieces. The *Canterbury Tales* are too full of business, variety, character and action, to permit the writer in any great degree to show himself. It is in Chaucer's minor pieces that we discover his love of rural scenery, his fondness for study, the cheerfulness of his temper, his weaknesses and his strength, and the anecdotes of his life. The *Troilus and Creseide* in particular, that poem of which sir Philip Sidney speaks with so much delight, though deficient in action, cannot be too much admired for the suavity and gentleness of nature which it displays. There is nothing in it to move the rougher passions of our nature, no hatred, nor contempt, nor indignation, nor revenge. If its personages are unstudied in the refinements of artificial and systematic virtue, even their vices (if such we denominate them) are loving and gentle and undesigning and kind. All the milder and more delicate feelings of the soul are displayed in their history, and displayed in a manner which none but a poet of the purest and sweetest dispositions, and at the same time of the greatest discrimination, could have attained.

The *Canterbury Tales* is certainly one of the most extraordinary monuments of human genius. The splendour of the *Knightes Tale*, and the various fancy exhibited in that of the Squier, have never been surpassed. The history of *Patient Grisildis* is the most pathetic that ever was written; and he who compares Chaucer's manner of relating it, with that of the various authors who have treated the same materials, must be dead to all the characteristic beauties of this history, if he does not perceive how much Chaucer has outstripped all his competitors.

What infinite variety of character is presented to us in the *Prologue* to the *Canterbury Tales*! It is a copious and extensive review of the private life of the fourteenth century in England.

This has usually, and perhaps justly, been thought the most conspicuous excellence of Chaucer; his power of humour, of delineating characters, and of giving vivacity and richness to comic incidents.

Unhappily the age in which he lived was deficient in that nicety of moral apprehension and taste, upon which is built the no contemptible science of elegant manners and decorum. It has been said that men must have become debauched and consummate in their vices, before they can be masters in this science. This however is not true. There are no doubt various modes of expression, which will excite a prurient sport in the minds of the dissolute, and yet will be uttered with the most unapprehensive simplicity by the inexperienced and innocent; discrimination respecting these can only be the result of a certain familiarity with vice. But neither will these by the virtuous mind be regarded as almost any fault, even when discovered. But the licentiousness and coarseness of the tales of the twelfth and thirteenth centuries, copied by Boccaccio and Chaucer, are of a different sort; they are absolute corruption and depravity. The progress of refinement does not merely make men fastidious in their vices; it makes them in many respects more virtuous and innocent: it not only prompts us to conceal some vices, but also induces us peremptorily and resolutely to abjure many.

The *Milleres Tale* and the *Reves Tale* in Chaucer are filthy, vulgar and licentious. The *Tale of the Marchant*, and the *Wif of Bathes Prologue*, are in an eminent degree liable to the last of these accusations. Yet it has been truly observed that Chaucer never appears more natural, his style never flows more easily, and his vein is never more unaffected and copious, than on these occasions. No writer, either ancient or modern, can be cited, who excels our poet in the talent for comic narrative. The reader of the more correct taste, though offended with Chaucer for the choice of his topics, will peruse these divisions of his work again and again, for the sake of the eloquence and imagination they display. The story of the Cock and the Fox, called the *Nonnes Preestes Tale*, is the most admirable fable that ever was written, if the excellence of a fable consists in liveliness of painting, in the comic demureness with which human sentiments are made to fall from the lips of animals, or in the art of framing a consummate structure from the slightest materials. The *Sompnoures Tale*, though exceedingly offensive for the clownish joke with which it is terminated, is equal in its opening and preparatory circumstances to any satirical narrative that ever was penned. The entrance of the friar into the house of the sick man, his driving away the sleeping cat from the bench he thought proper to occupy, the manner in which he lays down his walking-stick, his scrip and his hat, and the conversation which follows, are all in the most exquisite stile of comic delineation.

To understand more precisely the degree of applause which is due to Chaucer, it is proper that we should distinguish between two principal schools in the poetry of modern European nations, the romantic, and the natural. On the first revival of poetry, the minds of men perhaps universally took a bent toward the former; we had nothing but Rowlands and Arthurs, sir Guys and sir Tristrams, and Paynim and Christian knights. There was danger that nature would be altogether cut out from the courts of Apollo. The senses of barbarians are rude, and require a strong and forcible impulse to put them in motion. The first authors of the humorous and burlesque tales of modern times were perhaps sensible of this error in the romance writers, and desirous to remedy it. But they frequently fell into an opposite extreme, and that from the same cause. They deliver us indeed from the monotony produced by the perpetual rattling of armour, the formality of processions and tapestry and cloth of gold, and the eternal straining after supernatural adventures. But they lead us into squalid scenes, the coarse buffoonery of the ale-house, and the offensive manners engendered by dishonesty and intemperance. Between the one and the other of these classes of poetry, we may find things analogous to the wild and desperate toys of Salvator Rosa, and to the boors of Teniers, but nothing that should remind us of the grace of Guido, or of the soft and simple repose of Claude Lorraine.

The *Decamerone* of Boccaccio seems to be the first work of modern times, which was written entirely on the principle of a style, simple, unaffected and pure. Chaucer, who wrote precisely at the same period, was the fellow-labourer of Boccaccio. He has declared open war against the romance manner in his *Rime of Sire Thopas*. His *Canterbury Tales* are written with an almost perpetual homage to nature. The *Troilus and Creseide*, though a tale of ancient times, treats almost solely of the simple and genuine emotions of the human heart.

Many however of the works of Chaucer must be confessed to be written in a bad taste, fashionable in the times in which he lived, but which the better judgment of later ages has rejected. The poem called *Chaucer's Dreme* is in the idlest and weakest style of Romance. Nothing can be more frivolous than the courtship of his male and female eagles in the *Parliament of Birds*. The idea of the worship of the daisy must be acknowledged to be full of affectation. A continued vein of allegory is always effeminate, strained and unnatural. This error, so far as relates to the *Romaunt of the Rose*, is only indirectly imputable to Chaucer. But, in the *Testament of Love*, and elsewhere, he has made it the express object of his choice.

Boccaccio and Chaucer, it might be supposed, would have succeeded in banishing the swelling and romantic style from the realms of poetry. We might have imagined that as knowledge and civilisation grew, the empire of nature would have continually become more firmly established. But this was not the case. These eminent writers rose too high beyond their contemporaries, and reached to refinements that their successors could not understand. . . .

What comes nearest to the preeminence of Shakespear is the Don Quixote of Cervantes, the Sir Roger de Coverley of Addison, the Lovelace of Richardson, the Parson Adams of Fielding, the Walter Shandy of Sterne, and the Hugh Strap of Smollet. Fletcher also, though perhaps his most conspicuous merits are of another sort, has great excellence in the animating of character, as will readily be discerned, particularly in his *Wit without Money*, and his *Little French Lawyer*.

The successive description of the several pilgrims in the *Prologue* to the *Canterbury Tales*, is worthy to class with these. No writer has ever exhibited so great a variety of talent in so short a compass, as Chaucer has done in this instance.

. . . His best works, his *Canterbury Tales* in particular, have an absolute merit, which stands in need of no extrinsic accident to show it to advantage, and no apology to atone for its concomitant defects. They class with whatever is best in the poetry of any country or any age. Yet when we further recollect that they were written in a remote and semi-barbarous age, that Chaucer had to a certain degree to create a language, or to restore to credit a language which had been sunk into vulgarity and contempt by being considered as a language of slaves, that history and the knowledge of past ages existed only in unconnected fragments, and that his writings, stupendous as we find them, are associated, as to the period of their production, with the first half-assured lispings of civilisation and the muse, the astonishment and awe with which we regard the great father of English poetry must be exceedingly increased, and the lover of human nature and of intellectual power will deem no time misspent that adds to his familiar acquaintance with the history of such a man, or with writings so produced.

Notes

1. A frivolous dispute has been raised respecting the proper way of spelling the name of our great dramatic poet. His own orthography in this point seems to have been unsettled. Perhaps, when the etymology of a proper name is obvious, it becomes right in us to supersede the fancy of the individual, and to follow a less capricious and more infallible guide.
2. Thomas Warton, *The History of English Poetry*, 1840, Vol. 1, Section 14.
3. *Areopagitica*; a Speech for the Liberty of Unlicenced Printing.
4. Scipio the younger, the destroyer of Numantia and Carthage.
5. Scipio the elder, the conqueror of Hannibal, whom the younger sees in his dream.
6.   She gallops night by night
     Through lovers' brains, and then they dream of love;
     O'er courtiers' knees, that dream on curtsies straight;
     O'er lawyers' fingers, who straight dream on fees;

     . . .

     Sometimes she driveth o'er a soldier's neck,
     And then dreams he of cutting foreign throats,
     Of breaches, ambuscadoes, Spanish blades,
     Of healths five fathoms deep; and then anon
     Drums in his ear; at which he starts, and wakes;
     And, being thus frighted, swears a prayer or two,
     And sleeps again.

               (*Romeo and Juliet*, act II, scene i)

WILLIAM BLAKE

From *Descriptive Catalogue* (1809)
Blake: Complete Writings, 1966, ed. Keynes, pp. 556–75

III

*Sir Jeffery Chaucer and the nine and twenty Pilgrims
on their journey to Canterbury.*

The time chosen is early morning, before sunrise, when the jolly company are just quitting the Tabarde Inn. The Knight and Squire with the Squire's Yeoman lead the Procession; next follow the youthful Abbess, her nun and three priests; her greyhounds attend her—

     Of small hounds had she, that she fed
     With roast flesh, milk and wastel bread.

Next follow the Friar and Monk; then the Tapiser, the Pardoner, and the Somner and Manciple. After these 'Our Host,' who occupies the center of the cavalcade, directs them to the Knight as the person who would be likely to commence their task of each telling a tale in their order. After the Host follows the Shipman, the Haberdasher, the Dyer, the Franklin, the Physician, the Plowman, the Lawyer, the poor Parson, the Merchant, the Wife of Bath, the Miller, the Cook, the Oxford Scholar, Chaucer himself, and the Reeve comes as Chaucer has described:

     And ever he rode hinderest of the rout.

These last are issuing from the gateway of the Inn; the Cook and the Wife of Bath are both taking their morning's draught of comfort. Spectators stand at the gateway of the Inn, and are composed of an old Man, a Woman, and Children.

The Landscape is an eastward view of the country, from the Tabarde Inn, in Southwark, as it may be supposed to have appeared in Chaucer's time, interspersed with cottages and villages; the first beams of the Sun are seen above the horizon; some buildings and spires indicate the situation of the great

City; the Inn is a gothic building, which Thynne in his Glossary says was the lodging of the Abbot of Hyde, by Winchester. On the Inn is inscribed its title, and a proper advantage is taken of this circumstance to describe the subject of the Picture. The words written over the gateway of the Inn are as follow: 'The Tabarde Inn, by Henry Baillie, the lodgynge-house for Pilgrims, who journey to Saint Thomas's Shrine at Canterbury.'

The characters of Chaucer's Pilgrims are the characters which compose all ages and nations: as one age falls, another rises, different to mortal sight, but to immortals only the same; for we see the same characters repeated again and again, in animals, vegetables, minerals, and in men; nothing new occurs in identical existence; Accident ever varies, Substance can never suffer change nor decay.

Of Chaucer's characters, as described in his *Canterbury Tales*, some of the names or titles are altered by time, but the characters themselves for ever remain unaltered, and consequently they are the physiognomies or lineaments of universal human life, beyond which Nature never steps. Names alter, things never alter. I have known multitudes of those who could have been monks in the age of monkery, who in this deistical age are deists. As Newton numbered the stars, and as Linneus numbered the plants, so Chaucer numbered the classes of men.

The Painter has consequently varied the heads and forms of his personages into all Nature's varieties; the Horses he has also varied to accord to their Riders; the costume is correct according to authentic monuments.

The Knight and Squire with the Squire's Yeoman lead the procession, as Chaucer has also placed them first in his prologue. The Knight is a true Hero, a good, great, and wise man; his whole length portrait on horseback, as written by Chaucer, cannot be surpassed. He has spent his life in the field; has ever been a conqueror, and is that species of character which in every age stands as the guardian of man against the oppressor. His son is like him with the germ of perhaps greater perfection still, as he blends literature and the arts with his warlike studies. Their dress and their horses are of the first rate, without ostentation, and with all the true grandeur that unaffected simplicity when in high rank always displays. The Squire's Yeoman is also a great character, a man perfectly knowing in his profession:

     And in his hand he bare a mighty bow.

Chaucer describes here a mighty man; one who in war is the worthy attendant on noble heroes.

The Prioress follows these with her female chaplain:

     Another Nonne also with her had she,
     That was her Chaplaine, and Priests three.

This Lady is described also as of the first rank, rich and honoured. She has certain peculiarities and little delicate affectations, not unbecoming in her, being accompanied with what is truly grand and really polite; her person and face Chaucer has described with minuteness; it is very elegant, and was the beauty of our ancestors, till after Elizabeth's time, when voluptuousness and folly began to be accounted beautiful.

Her companion and her three priests were no doubt all perfectly delineated in those parts of Chaucer's work which are now lost; we ought to suppose them suitable attendants on rank and fashion.

The Monk follows these with the Friar. The Painter has also grouped with these the Pardoner and the Sompnour and the Manciple, and has here also introduced one of the rich citizens of London: Characters likely to ride in company, all being above the common rank in life or attendants on those who were so.

For the Monk is described by Chaucer, as a man of the first rank in society, noble, rich, and expensively attended; he is a leader of the age, with certain humorous accompaniments in his character, that do not degrade, but render him an object of dignified mirth, but also with other accompaniments not so respectable.

The Friar is a character also of a mixed kind:

> A friar there was, a wanton and a merry.

but in his office he is said to be a 'full solemn man': eloquent, amorous, witty, and satyrical; young, handsome, and rich; he is a complete rogue, with constitutional gaiety enough to make him a master of all the pleasures of the world.

> His neck was white as the flour de lis,
> Thereto strong he was as a champioun.

It is necessary here to speak of Chaucer's own character, that I may set certain mistaken critics right in their conception of the humour and fun that occurs on the journey. Chaucer is himself the great poetical observer of men, who in every age is born to record and eternize its acts. This he does as a master, as a father, and superior, who looks down on their little follies from the Emperor to the Miller; sometimes with severity, oftener with joke and sport.

Accordingly Chaucer has made his Monk a great tragedian, one who studied poetical art. So much so, that the generous Knight is, in the compassionate dictates of his soul, compelled to cry out:

> 'Ho,' quoth the Knyght,—'good Sir, no more of this;
> That ye have said is right ynough I wis;
> And mokell more, for little heaviness
> Is right enough for much folk, as I guesse.
> I say, for me, it is a great disease,
> Whereas men have been in wealth and ease,
> To heare of their sudden fall, alas,
> And the contrary is joy and solas.'

The Monk's definition of tragedy in the proem to his tale is worth repeating:

> Tragedie is to tell a certain story,
> As old books us maken memory,
> Of hem that stood in great prosperity,
> And be fallen out of high degree,
> Into miserie, and ended wretchedly.

Though a man of luxury, pride and pleasure, he is a master of art and learning, though affecting to despise it. Those who can think that the proud Huntsman and Noble Housekeeper, Chaucer's Monk, is intended for a buffoon or burlesque character, know little of Chaucer.

For the Host who follows this group, and holds the center of the cavalcade, is a first rate character, and his jokes are no trifles; they are always, though uttered with audacity, and equally free with the Lord and the Peasant, they are always substantially and weightily expressive of knowledge and experience; Henry Baillie, the keeper of the greatest Inn of the greatest City; for such was the Tabarde Inn in Southwark, near London: our Host was also a leader of the age.

By way of illustration, I instance Shakspeare's Witches in *Macbeth*. Those who dress them for the stage, consider them as wretched old women, and not as Shakspeare intended, the Goddesses of Destiny; this shews how Chaucer has been misunderstood in his sublime work. Shakspeare's Fairies also are the rulers of the vegetable world, and so are Chaucer's; let them be so considered, and then the poet will be understood, and not else.

But I have omitted to speak of a very prominent character, the Pardoner, the Age's Knave, who always commands and domineers over the high and low vulgar. This man is sent in every age for a rod and scourge, and for a blight, for a trial of men, to divide the classes of men; he is in the most holy sanctuary, and he is suffered by Providence for wise ends, and has also his great use, and his grand leading destiny.

His companion, the Sompnour, is also a Devil of the first magnitude, grand, terrific, rich and honoured in the rank of which he holds the destiny. The uses to Society are perhaps equal of the Devil and of the Angel, their sublimity, who can dispute.

> In daunger had he at his own gise,
> The young girls of his diocese,
> And he knew well their counsel, &c.

The principal figure in the next groupe is the Good Parson; an Apostle, a real Messenger of Heaven, sent in every age for its light and its warmth. This man is beloved and venerated by all, and neglected by all: He serves all, and is served by none; he is, according to Christ's definition, the greatest of his age. Yet he is a Poor Parson of a town. Read Chaucer's description of the Good Parson, and bow the head and the knee to him, who, in every age, sends us such a burning and a shining light. Search, O ye rich and powerful, for these men and obey their counsel, then shall the golden age return: But alas! you will not easily distinguish him from the Friar or the Pardoner; they, also, are 'full solemn men,' and their counsel you will continue to follow.

I have placed by his side the Sergeant at Lawe, who appears delighted to ride in his company, and between him and his brother, the Plowman; as I wish men of Law would always ride with them, and take their counsel, especially in all difficult points. Chaucer's Lawyer is a character of great venerableness, a Judge, and a real master of the jurisprudence of his age.

The Doctor of Physic is in this groupe, and the Franklin, the voluptuous country gentleman, contrasted with the Physician, and on his other hand, with two Citizens of London. Chaucer's characters live age after age. Every age is a Canterbury Pilgrimage; we all pass on, each sustaining one or other of these characters; nor can a child be born, who is not one of these characters of Chaucer. The Doctor of Physic is described as the first of his profession; perfect, learned, completely Master and Doctor in his art. Thus the reader will observe, that Chaucer makes every one of his characters perfect in his kind; every one is an Antique Statue; the image of a class, and not of an imperfect individual.

This groupe also would furnish substantial matter, on which volumes might be written. The Franklin is one who keeps open table, who is the genius of eating and drinking, the Bacchus; as the Doctor of Physic is the Esculapius, the Host is the Silenus, the Squire is the Apollo, the Miller is the Hercules, &c. Chaucer's characters are a description of the eternal Principles that exist in all ages. The Franklin is voluptuousness itself, most nobly pourtrayed:

> It snewed in his house of meat and drink.

The Plowman is simplicity itself, with wisdom and strength for its stamina. Chaucer has divided the ancient character of Hercules between his Miller and his Plowman. Benevolence is the plowman's great characteristic; he is thin with excessive labour, and not with old age, as some have supposed:

> He would thresh, and thereto dike and delve
> For Christe's sake, for every poore wight,
> Withouten hire, if it lay in his might.

Visions of these eternal principles or characters of human life appear to poets, in all ages; the Grecian gods were the ancient Cherubim of Phoenicia; but the Greeks, and since them the Moderns, have neglected to subdue the gods of Priam. These gods are visions of the eternal attributes, or divine names, which, when erected into gods, become destructive to humanity. They ought to be the servants, and not the masters of man, or of society. They ought to be made to sacrifice to Man, and not man compelled to sacrifice to them; for when separated from man or humanity, who is Jesus the Saviour, the vine of eternity, they are thieves and rebels, they are destroyers.

The Plowman of Chaucer is Hercules in his supreme eternal state, divested of his spectrous shadow; which is the Miller, a terrible fellow, such as exists in all times and places for the trial of men, to astonish every neighbourhood with brutal strength and courage, to get rich and powerful to curb the pride of Man.

The Reeve and the Manciple are two characters of the most consummate worldly wisdom. The Shipman, or Sailor, is a similar genius of Ulyssean art; but with the highest courage superadded.

The Citizens and their Cook are each leaders of a class. Chaucer has been somehow made to number four citizens, which would make his whole company, himself included, thirty-one. But he says there was but nine and twenty in his company:

> Full nine and twenty in a company.

The Webbe, or Weaver, and the Tapiser, or Tapestry Weaver, appear to me to be the same person; but this is only an opinion, for full nine and twenty may signify one more or less. But I dare say that Chaucer wrote 'A Webbe Dyer,' that is, a Cloth Dyer:

> A Webbe Dyer, and a Tapiser.

The Merchant cannot be one of the Three Citizens, as his dress is different, and his character is more marked, whereas Chaucer says of his rich citizens:

> All were yclothed in o liverie.

The characters of Women Chaucer has divided into two classes, the Lady Prioress and the Wife of Bath. Are not these leaders of the ages of men? The lady prioress, in some ages, predominates; and in some the wife of Bath, in whose character Chaucer has been equally minute and exact, because she is also a scourge and a blight. I shall say no more of her, nor expose what Chaucer has left hidden; let the young reader study what he has said of her: it is useful as a scarecrow. There are of such characters born too many for the peace of the world.

I come at length to the Clerk of Oxenford. This character varies from that of Chaucer, as the contemplative philosopher varies from the poetical genius. There are always these two classes of learned sages, the poetical and the philosophical. The painter has put them side by side, as if the youthful clerk had put himself under the tuition of the mature poet. Let the Philosopher always be the servant and scholar of inspiration and all will be happy.

Such are the characters that compose this Picture, which was painted in self-defence against the insolent and envious imputation of unfitness for finished and scientific art; and this imputation, most artfully and industriously endeavoured to be propagated among the public by ignorant hirelings. The painter courts comparison with his competitors, who, having received fourteen hundred guineas and more, from the profits of his designs in that well-known work, *Designs for Blair's Grave*, have left him to shift for himself, while others, more obedient to an employer's opinions and directions, are employed, at a great expence, to produce works, in succession to

his, by which they acquired public patronage. This has hitherto been his lot—to get patronage for others and then to be left and neglected, and his work, which gained that patronage, cried down as eccentricity and madness; as unfinished and neglected by the artist's violent temper; he is sure the works now exhibited will give the lie to such aspersions.

Those who say that men are led by interest are knaves. A knavish character will often say, 'of what interest is it to me to do so and so?' I answer, 'of none at all, but the contrary, as you well know. It is of malice and envy that you have done this; hence I am aware of you, because I know that you act, not from interest, but from malice, even to your own destruction.' It is therefore become a duty which Mr. B. owes to the Public, who have always recognized him, and patronized him, however hidden by artifices, that he should not suffer such things to be done, or be hindered from the public Exhibition of his finished productions by any calumnies in future.

The character and expression in this picture could never have been produced with Rubens' light and shadow, or with Rembrandt's, or anything Venetian or Flemish. The Venetian and Flemish practice is broken lines, broken masses, and unbroken colours. Their art is to lose form; his art is to find form, and to keep it. His arts are opposite to theirs in all things.

As there is a class of men whose whole delight is the destruction of men, so there is a class of artists, whose whole art and science is fabricated for the purpose of destroying art. Who these are is soon known: 'by their works ye shall know them.' All who endeavour to raise up a style against Rafael, Mich. Angelo, and the Antique; those who separate Painting from Drawing; who look if a picture is well Drawn, and, if it is, immediately cry out, that it cannot be well Coloured—those are the men.

But to shew the stupidity of this class of men nothing need be done but to examine my rival's prospectus.

The two first characters in Chaucer, the Knight and the Squire, he has put among his rabble; and indeed his prospectus calls the Squire the fop of Chaucer's age. Now hear Chaucer:

> Of his Stature, he was of even length,
> And wonderly deliver, and of great strength;
> And he had be sometime in Chivauchy,
> In Flanders, in Artois, and in Picardy,
> And borne him well, as of so litele space.

> Was this a fop?

> Well could he sit a horse, and faire ride,
> He could songs make, and eke well indite
> Just, and eke dance, pourtray, and well write.

> Was this a fop?

> Curteis he was, and meek, and serviceable;
> And kerft before his fader at the table

> Was this a fop?

It is the same with all his characters; he has done all by chance, or perhaps his fortune,—money, money. According to his prospectus he has Three Monks; these he cannot find in Chaucer, who has only One Monk, and that no vulgar character, as he has endeavoured to make him. When men cannot read they should not pretend to paint. To be sure Chaucer is a little difficult to him who has only blundered over novels, and catchpenny trifles of booksellers. Yet a little pains ought to be taken even by the ignorant and weak. He has put The Reeve, a vulgar fellow, between his Knight and Squire, as if he was resolved to go contrary in everything to Chaucer, who says of the Reeve:

> And ever he rode hinderest of the rout.

In this manner he has jumbled his dumb dollies together and is praised by his equals for it; for both himself and his friend are equally masters of Chaucer's language. They both think that the Wife of Bath is a young, beautiful, blooming damsel, and H——— says, that she is the Fair Wife of Bath, and that the Spring appears in her Cheeks. Now hear what Chaucer has made her say of herself, who is no modest one:

> But Lord when it remembereth me
> Upon my youth and on my jollity
> It tickleth me about the heart root,
> Unto this day it doth my heart boot,
> That I have had my world as in my time;
> But age, alas, that all will envenime
> Hath bireft my beauty and my pith
> Let go; farewell: the Devil go therewith,
> The flower is gone; there is no more to tell
> The bran, as best I can, I now mote sell;
> And yet to be right merry will I fond,—
> Now forth to tell of my fourth husband.

She has had four husbands, a fit subject for this painter; yet the painter ought to be very much offended with his friend H———, who has called his 'a common scene,' 'and very ordinary forms,' which is the truest part of all, for it is so, and very wretchedly so indeed. What merit can there be in a picture of which such words are spoken with truth?

But the prospectus says that the Painter has represented Chaucer himself as a knave, who thrusts himself among honest people, to make game of and laugh at them; though I must do justice to the painter, and say that he has made him look more like a fool than a knave. But it appears in all the writings of Chaucer, and particularly in his *Canterbury Tales*, that he was very devout, and paid respect to true enthusiastic superstition. He has laughed at his knaves and fools, as I do now. But he has respected his True Pilgrims, who are a majority of his company, and are not thrown together in the random manner that Mr. S——— has done. Chaucer has no where called the Plowman old, worn out with age and labour, as the prospectus has represented him, and says that the picture has done so too. He is worn down with labour, but not with age. How spots of brown and yellow, smeared about at random, can be either young or old, I cannot see. It may be an old man; it may be a young one; it may be any thing that a prospectus pleases. But I know that where there are no lineaments there can be no character. And what connoisseurs call touch, I know by experience, must be the destruction of all character and expression, as it is of every lineament.

The scene of Mr. S———'s Picture is by Dulwich Hills, which was not the way to Canterbury; but perhaps the painter thought he would give them a ride round about, because they were a burlesque set of scare-crows, not worth any man's respect or care.

But the painter's thoughts being always upon gold, he has introduced a character that Chaucer has not; namely, a Goldsmith; for so the prospectus tells us. Why he has introduced a Goldsmith, and what is the wit of it, the prospectus does not explain. But it takes care to mention the reserve and modesty of the Painter; this makes a good epigram enough:

> The fox, the owl, the spider, and the mole,
> By sweet reserve and modesty get fat.

But the prospectus tells us, that the painter has introduced a Sea Captain; Chaucer has a Ship-man a Sailor, a Trading Master of a Vessel, called by courtesy Captain, as every master of a boat is; but this does not make him a Sea Captain. Chaucer has purposely omitted such a personage, as it only exists in certain periods: it is the soldier by sea. He who would be a

Soldier in inland nations is a sea captain in commercial nations.

All is misconceived, and its mis-execution is equal to its misconception. I have no objection to Rubens and Rembrandt being employed, or even to their living in a palace; but it shall not be at the expence of Rafael and Michael Angelo living in a cottage, and in contempt and derision. I have been scorned long enough by these fellows, who owe to me all that they have; it shall be so no longer.

> I found them blind, I taught them how to see;
> And, now, they know me not, nor yet themselves.

GEORGE CRABBE
Preface to the Canterbury Tales
1812

That the appearance of the present Volume before the Public is occasioned by a favourable reception of the former two, I hesitate not to acknowledge; because, while the confession may be regarded as some proof of gratitude, or at least of attention from an Author to his Readers, it ought not to be considered as an indication of vanity. It is unquestionably very pleasant to be assured that our labours are well received; but, nevertheless, this must not be taken for a just and full criterion of their merit: publications of great intrinsic value have been met with so much coolness, that a writer who succeeds in obtaining some degree of notice, should look upon himself rather as one favoured than meritorious, as gaining a prize from Fortune, and not a recompense for desert; and, on the contrary, as it is well known that books of very inferior kind have been at once pushed into the strong current of popularity, and are there kept buoyant by the force of the stream, the writer who acquires not this adventitious help, may be reckoned rather as unfortunate than undeserving; and from these opposite considerations it follows, that a man may speak of his success without incurring justly the odium of conceit, and may likewise acknowledge a disappointment without an adequate cause for humiliation or self-reproach.

But were it true that something of the complacency of self-approbation would insinuate itself into an author's mind with the idea of success, the sensation would not be that of unalloyed pleasure: it would perhaps assist him to bear, but it would not enable him to escape the mortification he must encounter from censures, which, though he may be unwilling to admit, yet he finds himself unable to confute; as well as from advice, which at the same time that he cannot but approve, he is compelled to reject.

Reproof and advice, it is probable, every author will receive, if we except those who merit so much of the former, that the latter is contemptuously denied them; now of these, reproof, though it may cause more temporary uneasiness, will in many cases create less difficulty, since errors may be corrected when opportunity occurs: but advice, I repeat, may be of such nature, that it will be painful to reject, and yet impossible to follow it; and in this predicament I conceive myself to be placed. There has been recommended to me, and from authority which neither inclination or prudence leads me to resist, in any new work I might undertake, an unity of subject, and that arrangement of my materials which connects the whole and gives additional interest to every part; in fact, if not an Epic Poem, strictly so denominated, yet such composition as would possess a regular succession of events, and a catastrophe to which every incident should be subservient, and which every character, in a greater or less degree, should conspire to accomplish.

In a Poem of this nature, the principal and inferior characters in some degree resemble a General and his Army, where no one pursues his peculiar objects and adventures, or pursues them in unison with the movements and grand purposes of the whole body; where there is a community of interests and a subordination of actors: and it was upon this view of the subject, and of the necessity for such distribution of persons and events, that I found myself obliged to relinquish an undertaking, for which the characters I could command, and the adventures I could describe, were altogether unfitted.

But if these characters which seemed to be at my disposal were not such as would coalesce into one body, nor were of a nature to be commanded by one mind, so neither on examination did they appear as an unconnected multitude, accidentally collected, to be suddenly dispersed; but rather beings of whom might be formed groups and smaller societies, the relations of whose adventures and pursuits might bear the kind of similitude to an Heroic Poem, which these minor associations of men (as pilgrims on the way to their saint, or parties in search of amusement, travellers excited by curiosity, or adventurers in pursuit of gain) have in points of connection and importance with a regular and disciplined Army.

Allowing this comparison, it is manifest that while much is lost for want of unity of subject and grandeur of design, something is gained by greater variety of incident and more minute display of character, by accuracy of description, and diversity of scene: in these narratives we pass from gay to grave, from lively to severe, not only without impropriety, but with manifest advantage. In one continued and connected Poem, the Reader is, in general, highly gratified or severely disappointed; by many independent narratives, he has the renovation of hope, although he has been dissatisfied, and a prospect of reiterated pleasure should he find himself entertained.

I mean not, however, to compare these different modes of writing as if I were balancing their advantages and defects before I could give preference to either; with me the way I take is not a matter of choice, but of necessity: I present not my Tales to the Reader as if I had chosen the best method of ensuring his approbation, but as using the only means I possessed of engaging his attention.

It may probably be remarked that Tales, however dissimilar, might have been connected by some associating circumstance to which the whole number might bear equal affinity, and that examples of such union are to be found in *Chaucer*, in *Boccace*, and other collectors and inventors of Tales, which considered in themselves are altogether independent; and to this idea I gave so much consideration as convinced me that I could not avail myself of the benefit of such artificial mode of affinity. To imitate the English Poet, characters must be found adapted to their several relations, and this is a point of great difficulty and hazard: much allowance seems to be required even for *Chaucer* himself, since it is difficult to conceive that on any occasion the devout and delicate *Prioress*, the courtly and valiant *Knight*, and '*the poure good Man the persone of a Towne*,' would be the voluntary companions of the drunken *Miller*, the licentious *Sompnour*, and '*the Wanton Wife of Bath*,' and enter into that colloquial and travelling intimacy which, if a common pilgrimage to the shrine of *St. Thomas* may be said to excuse, I know nothing beside (and certainly nothing in these times) that would produce such effect. *Boccace*, it is true, avoids all difficulty of this kind, by not assigning to the ten relators of his hundred Tales any marked or peculiar characters; nor, though there are male and female in company, can the sex of the narrator be distinguished in the narration. To have followed the method of *Chaucer*, might

have been of use, but could scarcely be adopted, from its difficulty; and to have taken that of the Italian writer, would have been perfectly easy, but could be of no service: the attempt at union therefore has been relinquished, and these relations are submitted to the Public, connected by no other circumstances than their being the productions of the same Author, and devoted to the same purpose, the entertainment of his Readers.

It has been already acknowledged, that these compositions have no pretensions to be estimated with the more lofty and heroic kind of Poems, but I feel great reluctance in admitting that they have not a fair and legitimate claim to the poetic character: in vulgar estimation, indeed, all that is not prose, passes for poetry; but I have not ambition of so humble a kind as to be satisfied with a concession which requires nothing in the Poet, except his ability for counting syllables; and I trust something more of the poetic character will be allowed to the succeeding pages, than what the heroes of the *Dunciad* might share with the Author: nor was I aware that by describing, as faithfully as I could, men, manners, and things, I was forfeiting a just title to a name which has been freely granted to many whom to equal and even to excel is but very stinted commendation.

In this case it appears that the usual comparison between Poetry and Painting entirely fails: the Artist who takes an accurate likeness of individuals, or a faithful representation of scenery, may not rank so high in the public estimation, as one who paints an historical event, or an heroic action; but he is nevertheless a painter, and his accuracy is so far from diminishing his reputation, that it procures for him in general both fame and emolument: nor is it perhaps with strict justice determined that the credit and reputation of those verses which strongly and faithfully delineate character and manners, should be lessened in the opinion of the Public by the very accuracy, which gives value and distinction to the productions of the pencil.

Nevertheless, it must be granted that the pretensions of any composition to be regarded as Poetry, will depend upon that definition of the poetic character which he who undertakes to determine the question has considered as decisive; and it is confessed also that one of great authority may be adopted, by which the verses now before the Reader, and many others which have probably amused, and delighted him, must be excluded: a definition like this will be found in the words which the greatest of Poets, not divinely inspired, has given to the most noble and valiant Duke of Athens—

> The Poet's eye, in a fine frenzy rolling,
> Doth glance from Heaven to Earth, from Earth to
>   Heaven;
> And, as Imagination bodies forth
> The forms of things unknown, the Poet's pen
> Turns them to shapes, and gives to airy nothing
> A local habitation, and a name.
>   (*Midsummer Night's Dream*, Act V, Scene 1.)

Hence we observe the Poet is one who, in the excursions of his fancy between heaven and earth, lights upon a kind of fairy-land in which he places a creation of his own, where he embodies shapes, and gives action and adventure to his ideal offspring; taking captive the imagination of his readers, he elevates them above the grossness of actual being, into the soothing and pleasant atmosphere of supra-mundane existence: there he obtains for his visionary inhabitants the interest that engages a reader's attention without ruffling his feelings, and excites that moderate kind of sympathy which the realities of nature oftentimes fail to produce, either because they are so familiar and insignificant that they excite no determinate emotion, or are so harsh and powerful that the feelings excited are grating and distasteful.

Be it then granted that (as *Duke Theseus* observes) '*such tricks hath strong Imagination,*' and that such Poets '*are of imagination all compact;*' let it be further conceded, that theirs is a higher and more dignified kind of composition, nay, the only kind that has pretensions to inspiration; still, that these Poets should so entirely engross the title as to exclude those who address their productions to the plain sense and sober judgment of their Readers, rather than to their fancy and imagination, I must repeat that I am unwilling to admit,—because I conceive that, by granting such right of exclusion, a vast deal of what has been hitherto received as genuine poetry would no longer be entitled to that appellation.

All that kind of satire wherein character is skilfully delineated, must (this criterion being allowed) no longer be esteemed as genuine Poetry; and for the same reason many affecting narratives which are founded on real events, and borrow no aid whatever from the imagination of the writer, must likewise be rejected: a considerable part of the Poems, as they have hitherto been denominated, of *Chaucer*, are of this naked and unveiled character; and there are in his Tales many pages of coarse, accurate, and minute, but very striking description. Many small Poems in a subsequent age of most impressive kind are adapted and addressed to the common sense of the Reader, and prevail by the strong language of truth and nature: they amused our ancestors, and they continue to engage our interest, and excite our feelings by the same powerful appeals to the heart and affections. In times less remote, *Dryden* has given us much of this Poetry, in which the force of expression and accuracy of description have neither needed nor obtained assistance from the fancy of the writer; the characters in his *Absalom and Achitophel* are instances of this, and more especially those of *Doeg* and *Ogg* in the second part: these, with all their grossness, and almost offensive accuracy, are found to possess that strength and spirit which has preserved from utter annihilation the dead bodies of *Tate* to whom they were inhumanly bound, happily with a fate the reverse of that caused by the cruelty of *Mezentius*; for there the living perished in the putrefaction of the dead, and here the dead are preserved by the vitality of the living. And, to bring forward one other example, it will be found that *Pope* himself has no small portion of this actuality of relation, this nudity of description, and poetry without an atmosphere; the lines beginning '*In the worst inn's worst room,*' are an example, and many others may be seen in his Satires, Imitations, and above all in his Dunciad: the frequent absence of those '*Sports of Fancy,*' and '*Tricks of strong Imagination,*' have been so much observed, that some have ventured to question whether even this writer were a Poet; and though, as *Dr. Johnson* has remarked, it would be difficult to form a definition of one in which *Pope* should not be admitted, yet they who doubted his claim, had, it is likely, provided for his exclusion by forming that kind of character for their Poet, in which this elegant versifier, for so he must be then named, should not be comprehended.

These things considered, an Author will find comfort in his expulsion from the rank and society of Poets, by reflecting that men much his superiors were likewise shut out, and more especially when he finds also that men not much his superiors are entitled to admission.

But in whatever degree I may venture to differ from any others in my notions of the qualifications and character of the true Poet, I most cordially assent to their opinion who assert that his principal exertions must be made to engage the attention of his Readers; and further, I must allow that the effect of Poetry should be to lift the mind from the painful realities of actual existence, from its every-day concerns, and its perpetually-occurring vexations, and to give it repose by substituting objects in their place which it may contemplate with some degree of interest and satisfaction: but what is there in all this, which may not be effected by a fair representation of existing character? nay, by a faithful delineation of those painful realities, those every-day concerns, and those perpetually-occurring vexations themselves, provided they be not (which is hardly to be supposed) the very concerns and distresses of the Reader? for when it is admitted that they have no particular relation to him, but are the troubles and anxieties of other men, they excite and interest his feelings as the imaginary exploits, adventures, and perils of romance;—they soothe his mind, and keep his curiosity pleasantly awake; they appear to have enough of reality to engage his sympathy, but possess not interest sufficient to create painful sensations. Fiction itself, we know, and every work of fancy, must for a time have the effect of realities; nay, the very enchanters, spirits, and monsters of *Ariosto* and *Spenser* must be present in the mind of the Reader while he is engaged by their operations, or they would be as the objects and incidents of a Nursery Tale to a rational understanding, altogether despised and neglected: in truth, I can but consider this pleasant effect upon the mind of a Reader, as depending neither upon the events related (whether they be actual or imaginary), nor upon the characters introduced (whether taken from life or fancy), but upon the manner in which the Poem itself is conducted; let that be judiciously managed, and the occurrences actually copied from life will have the same happy effect as the inventions of a creative fancy;—while, on the other hand, the imaginary persons and incidents to which the Poet has given '*a local habitation, and a name,*' will make upon the concurring feelings of the Reader, the same impressions with those taken from truth and nature, because they will appear to be derived from that source, and therefore of necessity will have a similar effect.

Having thus far presumed to claim for the ensuing pages the rank and title of Poetry, I attempt no more, nor venture to class or compare them with any other kinds of poetical composition; their place will doubtless be found for them.

A principal view and wish of the Poet must be to engage the mind of his Readers, as, failing in that point, he will scarcely succeed in any other: I therefore willingly confess that much of my time and assiduity has been devoted to this purpose; but, to the ambition of pleasing, no other sacrifices have, I trust, been made, than of my own labour and care. Nothing will be found that militates against the rules of propriety and good manners, nothing that offends against the more important precepts of morality and religion; and with this negative kind of merit, I commit my Book to the judgment and taste of the Reader,—not being willing to provoke his vigilance by professions of accuracy, nor to solicit his indulgence by apologies for mistakes.

WILLIAM HAZLITT
From "Troilus and Cressida"
Characters of Shakespeare's Plays
1817, pp. 89–92

In Chaucer, Cressida is represented as a grave, sober, considerate personage (a widow—he cannot tell her age, nor whether she has children or no) who has an alternate eye to her character, her interest, and her pleasure: Shakespear's Cressida is a giddy girl, an unpractised jilt, who falls in love with Troilus, as she afterwards deserts him, from mere levity and thoughtlessness of temper. She may be wooed and won to any thing and from any thing, at a moment's warning: the other knows very well what she would be at, and sticks to it, and is more governed by substantial reasons than by caprice or vanity. Pandarus again, in Chaucer's story, is a friendly sort of go-between, tolerably busy, officious, and forward in bringing matters to bear: but in Shakespear he has 'a stamp exclusive and professional:' he wears the badge of his trade; he is a regular knight of the game. The difference of the manner in which the subject is treated arises perhaps less from intention, than from the different genius of the two poets. There is no *double entendre* in the characters of Chaucer: they are either quite serious or quite comic. In Shakespear the ludicrous and ironical are constantly blended with the stately and the impassioned. We see Chaucer's characters as they saw themselves, not as they appeared to others or might have appeared to the poet. He is as deeply implicated in the affairs of his personages as they could be themselves. He had to go a long journey with each of them, and became a kind of necessary confidant. There is little relief, or light and shade in his pictures. The conscious smile is not seen lurking under the brow of grief or impatience. Every thing with him is intense and continuous—a working out of what went before.—Shakespear never committed himself to his characters. He trifled, laughed, or wept with them as he chose. He has no prejudices for or against them; and it seems a matter of perfect indifference whether he shall be in jest or earnest. According to him 'the web of our lives is of a mingled yarn, good and ill together.' His genius was dramatic, as Chaucer's was historical. He saw both sides of a question, the different views taken of it according to the different interests of the parties concerned, and he was at once an actor and spectator in the scene. If any thing, he is too various and flexible; too full of transitions, of glancing lights, of salient points. If Chaucer followed up his subject too doggedly, perhaps Shakespear was too volatile and heedless. The Muse's wing too often lifted him off his feet. He made infinite excursions to the right and the left.

> He hath done
> Mad and fantastic execution,
> Engaging and redeeming of himself
> With such a careless force and forceless care,
> As if that luck in very spite of cunning
> Bad him win all.

Chaucer attended chiefly to the real and natural, that is, to the involuntary and inevitable impressions on the mind in given circumstances: Shakespear exhibited also the possible and the fantastical,—not only what things are in themselves, but whatever they might seem to be, their different reflections, their endless combinations. He lent his fancy, wit, invention, to others, and borrowed their feelings in return. Chaucer excelled in the force of habitual sentiment; Shakespear added to it every variety of passion, every suggestion of thought or accident. Chaucer described external objects with the eye of a painter, or he might be said to have embodied them with the hand of a sculptor, every part is so thoroughly made out, and tangible:—Shakespear's imagination threw over them a lustre

> Prouder than when blue Iris bends.

We must conclude this criticism; and we will do it with a quotation or two. One of the most beautiful passages in Chaucer's tale is the description of Cresseide's first avowal of her love.

> And as the new abashed nightingale,
> That stinteth first when she beginneth sing,
> When that she heareth any herde's tale,
> Or in the hedges any wight stirring,
> And, after, sicker doth her voice outring;
> Right so Cresseide, when that her dread stent,
> Opened her heart, and told him her intent.

See also the two next stanzas, and particularly that divine one beginning

Her armes small, her back both straight and soft, &c.

Compare this with the following speech of Troilus to Cressida in the play.

> O, that I thought it could be in a woman;
> And if it can, I will presume in you,
> To feed for aye her lamp and flame of love,
> To keep her constancy in plight and youth,
> Out-living beauties out-ward, with a mind
> That doth renew swifter than blood decays.
> Or, that persuasion could but thus convince me,
> That my integrity and truth to you
> Might be affronted with the match and weight
> Of such a winnow'd purity in love;
> How were I then uplifted! But alas,
> I am as true as Truth's simplicity,
> And simpler than the infancy of Truth.

These passages may not seem very characteristic at first sight, though we think they are so. We will give two, that cannot be mistaken. Patroclus says to Achilles,

> Rouse yourself; and the weak wanton Cupid
> Shall from your neck unloose his amorous fold,
> And like a dew-drop from the lion's mane,
> Be shook to air.

Troilus, addressing the God of Day on the approach of the morning that parts him from Cressida, says with much scorn,

> What! proffer'st thou thy light here for to sell?
> Go, sell it them that smallé selés grave.

If nobody but Shakespear could have written the former, nobody but Chaucer would have thought of the latter.—Chaucer was the most literal of poets, as Richardson was of prose-writers.

Every thing in Chaucer has a downright reality. A simile or a sentiment is as if it were given in upon evidence. In Shakespear the commonest matter-of-fact has a romantic grace about it; or seems to float with the breath of imagination in a freer element. No one could have more depth of feeling or observation than Chaucer, but he wanted resources of invention to lay open the stores of nature or the human heart with the same radiant light, that Shakespear has done. However fine or profound the thought, we know what was coming, whereas the effect of reading Shakespear is 'like the eye of vassalage encountering majesty.' Chaucer's mind was consecutive, rather than discursive. He arrived at truth through a certain process; Shakespear saw every thing by intuition. Chaucer had great variety of power, but he could do only one thing at once. He set himself to work on a particular subject. His ideas were kept separate, labelled, ticketed and parcelled out in a set form, in pews and compartments by themselves. They did not play into one another's hands. They did not re-act upon one another, as the blower's breath moulds the yielding glass. There is something hard and dry in them. What is the most wonderful thing in Shakespear's faculties is their excessive sociability, and how they gossipped and compared notes together.

WILLIAM HAZLITT
"On Chaucer and Spenser" (1818)
Lectures on English Poetry
1933, pp. 30–51

Having, in the former lecture, given some account of the nature of poetry in general, I shall proceed, in the next place, to a more particular consideration of the genius and history of English poetry. I shall take, as the subject of the present lecture, Chaucer and Spenser, two out of four of the greatest names in poetry, which this country has to boast. Both of them, however, were much indebted to the early poets of Italy, and may be considered as belonging, in a certain degree, to the same school. The freedom and copiousness with which our most original writers, in former periods, availed themselves of the productions of their predecessors, frequently transcribing whole passages, without scruple or acknowledgement, may appear contrary to the etiquette of modern literature, when the whole stock of poetical common-places has become public property, and no one is compelled to trade upon any particular author. But it is not so much a subject of wonder, at a time when to read and write was of itself an honorary distinction, when learning was almost as great a rarity as genius, and when in fact those who first transplanted the beauties of other languages into their own, might be considered as public benefactors, and the founders of a national literature.—There are poets older than Chaucer, and in the interval between him and Spenser; but their genius was not such as to place them in any point of comparison with either of these celebrated men; and an inquiry into their particular merits or defects might seem rather to belong to the province of the antiquary, than be thought generally interesting to the lovers of poetry in the present day.

Chaucer (who has been very properly considered as the father of English poetry) preceded Spenser by two centuries. He is supposed to have been born in London, in the year 1328, during the reign of Edward III, and to have died in 1400, at the age of seventy-two. He received a learned education at one, or at both of the universities, and travelled early into Italy, where he became thoroughly imbued with the spirit and excellences of the great Italian poets and prose-writers, Dante, Petrarch, and Boccace; and is said to have had a personal interview with one of these, Petrarch. He was connected, by marriage, with the famous John of Gaunt, through whose interest he was introduced into several public employments. Chaucer was an active partisan, a religious reformer, and from the the share he took in some disturbances, on one occasion, he was obliged to fly the country. On his return, he was imprisoned, and made his peace with government, as it is said, by a discovery of his associates. Fortitude does not appear, at any time, to have been the distinguishing virtue of poets.—There is, however, an obvious similarity between the practical turn of Chaucer's mind and restless impatience of his character, and the tone of his writings. Yet it would be too much to attribute the one to the other as cause and effect: for Spenser, whose poetical temperament was as effeminate as Chaucer's was stern and masculine, was equally engaged in public affairs, and had mixed equally in the great world. So much does native disposition predominate over accidental circumstances, moulding them to its previous bent and purposes! For while Chaucer's intercourse with the busy world, and collision with the actual passions and conflicting interests of others, seemed to brace the sinews of his understanding, and gave to his writings the air of a man who

describes persons and things that he had known and been intimately concerned in; the same opportunities, operating on a differently constituted frame, only served to alienate Spenser's mind the more from the 'close-pent up' scenes of ordinary life, and to make him 'rive their concealing continents', to give himself up to the unrestrained indulgence of 'flowery tenderness'.

It is not possible for any two writers to be more opposite in this respect. Spenser delighted in luxurious enjoyment; Chaucer, in severe activity of mind. As Spenser was the most romantic and visionary, Chaucer was the most practical of all the great poets, the most a man of business and the world. His poetry reads like history. Everything has a downright reality; at least in the relator's mind. A simile, or a sentiment, is as if it were given in upon evidence. Thus he describes Cressid's first avowal of her love.

> And as the new abashed nightingale,
> That stinteth first when she beginneth sing,
> When that she heareth any herde's tale,
> Or in the hedges any wight stirring,
> And after, sicker, doth her voice outring;
> Right so Cresseide, when that her dread stent,
> Open'd her heart, and told him her intent.

This is so true and natural, and beautifully simple, that the two things seem identified with each other. Again, it is said in the Knight's Tale—

> Thus passeth yere by yere, and day by day,
> Till it felle ones in a morwe of May,
> That Emelie that fayrer was to sene
> Than is the lilie upon his stalke grene;
> And fresher than the May with floures newe,
> For with the rose-colour strof hire hewe;
> I n'ot which was the finer of hem two.

This scrupulousness about the literal preference, as if some question of matter of fact was at issue, is remarkable. I might mention that other, where he compares the meeting between Palamon and Arcite to a hunter waiting for a lion in a gap;—

> That stondeth at a gap with a spere,
> Whan hunted is the lion or the bere,
> And hereth him come rushing in the greves,
> And breking bothe the boughes and the leves:—

or that still finer one of Constance, when she is condemned to death:—

> Have ye not seen somtime a pale face
> (Among a prees) of him that hath been lad
> Toward his deth, wheras he geteth no grace,
> And swiche a colour in his face hath had,
> Men mighten know him that was so bestad,
> Amonges all the faces in that route;
> So stant Custance, and loketh hire aboute.

The beauty, the pathos here does not seem to be of the poet's seeking, but a part of the necessary texture of the fable. He speaks of what he wishes to describe with the accuracy, the discrimination of one who relates what has happened to himself, or has had the best information from those who have been eye-witnesses of it. The strokes of his pencil always tell. He dwells only on the essential, on that which would be interesting to the persons really concerned: yet as he never omits any material circumstance, he is prolix from the number of points on which he touches, without being diffuse on any one; and is sometimes tedious from the fidelity with which he adheres to his subject, as other writers are from the frequency of their digressions from it. The chain of his story is composed of a number of fine links, closely connected together, and rivetted by a single blow. There is an instance of the minuteness which he introduces into his most serious descriptions in his account of Palamon when left alone in his cell:

> Swiche sorrow he maketh that the grete tour
> Resouned of his yelling and clamour:
> The pure fetters on his shinnes grete
> Were of his bitter salte teres wete.

The mention of this last circumstance looks like a part of the instructions he had to follow, which he had no discretionary power to leave out or introduce at pleasure. He is contented to find grace and beauty in truth. He exhibits for the most part the naked object, with little drapery thrown over it. His metaphors, which are few, are not for ornament, but use, and as like as possible to the things themselves. He does not affect to show his power over the reader's mind, but the power which his subject has over his own. The readers of Chaucer's poetry feel more nearly what the persons he describes must have felt, than perhaps those of any other poet. His sentiments are not voluntary effusions of the poet's fancy, but founded on the natural impulses and habitual prejudices of the characters he has to represent. There is an inveteracy of purpose, a sincerity of feeling, which never relaxes or grows vapid, in whatever they do or say. There is no artificial, pompous display, but a strict parsimony of the poet's materials, like the rude simplicity of the age in which he lived. His poetry resembles the root just springing from the ground, rather than the full-blown flower. His muse is no 'babbling gossip of the air', fluent and redundant; but, like a stammerer, or a dumb person, that has just found the use of speech, crowds many things together with eager haste, with anxious pauses, and fond repetitions to prevent mistake. His words point as an index to the objects, like the eye or finger. There were none of the common-places of poetic diction in our author's time, no reflected lights of fancy, no borrowed roseate tints; he was obliged to inspect things for himself, to look narrowly, and almost to handle the object, as in the obscurity of morning we partly see and partly grope our way; so that his descriptions have a sort of tangible character belonging to them, and produce the effect of sculpture on the mind. Chaucer had an equal eye for truth of nature and discrimination of character; and his interest in what he saw gave new distinctness and force to his power of observation. The picturesque and the dramatic are in him closely blended together, and hardly distinguishable; for he principally describes external appearances as indicating character, as symbols of internal sentiment. There is a meaning in what he sees; and it is this which catches his eye by sympathy. Thus the costume and dress of the Canterbury Pilgrims—of the Knight—the Squire—the Oxford Scholar—the Gap-toothed Wife of Bath, and the rest, speak for themselves. . . .

The Serjeant at Law is the same identical individual as Lawyer Dowling in *Tom Jones*, who wished to divide himself into a hundred pieces, to be in a hundred places at once.

> No wher so besy a man as he ther n'as,
> And yet he semed besier than he was.

The Frankelein, in 'whose hous it snewed of mete and drinke'; the Shipman, 'who rode upon a rouncie, as he couthe'; the Doctour of Phisike, 'whose studie was but litel of the Bible'; the Wif of Bath, in

> All whose parish ther was non,
> That to the offring before hire shulde gon,
> And if ther did, certain so wroth was she,
> That she was out of alle charitee;

—the poure Persone of a toun, 'whose parish was wide, and houses fer asonder'; the Miller, and the Reve, 'a slendre colerike man', are all of the same stamp. They are every one samples of a kind; abstract definitions of a species. Chaucer, it has been said, numbered the classes of men, as Linnaeus numbered the plants. Most of them remain to this day: others that are obsolete, and may well be dispensed with, still live in his descriptions of them. Such is the Sompnoure:

> A Sompnoure was ther with us in that place,
> That hadde a fire-red cherubinnes face,
> For sausefleme he was, with eyen narwe,
> As hote he was, and likerous as a sparwe,
> With scalled browes blake, and pilled berd:
> Of his visage children were sore aferd.
> Ther n'as quicksilver, litarge, ne brimston,
> Boras, ceruse, ne oile of tartre non,
> Ne oinement that wolde clense or bite,
> That him might helpen of his whelkes white,
> Ne of the knobbes sitting on his chekes.
> Wel loved he garlike, onions, and lekes,
> And for to drinke strong win as rede as blood.
> Than wolde he speke, and crie as he were wood.
> And whan that he wel dronken had the win,
> Than wold he speken no word but Latin.
> A fewe termes coude he, two or three,
> That he had lerned out of som decree;
> No wonder is, he heard it all the day.—
>   In danger hadde he at his owen gise
> The yonge girles of the diocise,
> And knew hir conseil, and was of hir rede.
> A gerlond hadde he sette upon his hede
> As gret as it were for an alestake:
> A bokeler hadde he made him of a cake.
> With him ther rode a gentil Pardonere—
> That hadde a vois as smale as hath a gote.

It would be a curious speculation (at least for those who think that the characters of men never change, though manners, opinions, and institutions may) to know what has become of this character of the Sompnoure in the present day; whether or not it has any technical representative in existing professions; into what channels and conduits it has withdrawn itself, where it lurks unseen in cunning obscurity, or else shows its face boldly, pampered into all the insolence of office, in some other shape, as it is deterred or encouraged by circumstances. *Chaucer's characters modernized*, upon this principle of historic derivation, would be an useful addition to our knowledge of human nature. But who is there to undertake it?

The descriptions of the equipage, and accoutrements of the two kings of Thrace and Inde, in the Knight's Tale, are as striking and grand, as the others are lively and natural. . . .
The imagination of a poet brings such objects before us, as when we look at wild beasts in a menagerie; their claws are pared, their eyes glitter like harmless lightning; but we gaze at them with a pleasing awe, clothed in beauty, formidable in the sense of abstract power.

Chaucer's descriptions of natural scenery possess the same sort of characteristic excellence, or what might be termed *gusto*. They have a local truth and freshness, which gives the very feeling of the air, the coolness or moisture of the ground. Inanimate objects are thus made to have a fellow-feeling in the interest of the story; and render back the sentiment of the speaker's mind. One of the finest parts of Chaucer is of this mixed kind. It is the beginning of the *Flower and the Leaf*, where he describes the delight of that young beauty, shrouded in her bower, and listening, in the morning of the year, to the singing of the nightingale; while her joy rises with the rising song, and gushes out afresh at every pause, and is borne along with the full tide of pleasure, and still increases, and repeats, and prolongs itself, and knows no ebb. The coolness of the arbour, its retirement, the early time of the day, the sudden starting up of the birds in the neighbouring bushes, the eager delight with which they devour and rend the opening buds and flowers, are expressed with a truth and feeling, which make the whole appear like the recollection of an actual scene:

> Which as me thought was right a pleasing sight,
> And eke the briddes song for to here,
> Would haue rejoyced any earthly wight,
> And I that couth not yet in no manere
> Heare the nightingale of all the yeare,
> Ful busily herkened with herte and with eare,
> If I her voice perceiue coud any where.
>
> And I that all this pleasant sight sie,
> Thought sodainly I felt so sweet an aire
> Of the eglentere, that certainely
> There is no herte I deme in such dispaire,
> Ne with thoughts froward and contraire,
> So ouerlaid, but it should soone haue bote,
> If it had ones felt this savour sote.
>
> And as I stood and cast aside mine eie,
> I was ware of the fairest medler tree
> That ever yet in all my life I sie
> As full of blossomes as it might be,
> Therein a goldfinch leaping pretile
> Fro bough to bough, and as him list he eet
> Here and there of buds and floures sweet.
>
> And to the herber side was joyning
> This faire tree, of which I haue you told,
> And at the last the brid began to sing,
> Whan he had eaten what he eat wold,
> So passing sweetly, that by manifold
> It was more pleasaunt than I coud deuise,
> And whan his song was ended in this wise,
>
> The nightingale with so merry a note
> Answered him, that all the wood rong
> So sodainly, that as it were a sote,
> I stood astonied, so was I with the song
> Thorow rauished, that till late and long,
> I ne wist in what place I was, ne where,
> And ayen me thought she song euen by mine ere.
>
> Wherefore I waited about busily
> On euery side, if I her might see,
> And at the last I gan full well aspie
> Where she sat in a fresh grene laurer tree,
> On the further side euen right by me,
> That gaue so passing a delicious smell,
> According to the eglentere full well.
>
> Whereof I had so inly great pleasure,
> That as me thought I surely rauished was
> Into Paradice, where my desire
> Was for to be, and no ferther passe
> As for that day, and on the sote grasse,
> I sat me downe, for as for mine entent,
> The birds song was more conuenient,
>
> And more pleasaunt to me by manifold,
> Than meat or drinke, or any other thing,
> Thereto the herber was so fresh and cold,
> The wholesome sauours eke so comforting,
> That as I demed, sith the beginning
> Of the world was neur seene or than
> So pleasaunt a ground of none earthly man.

> And as I sat the birds harkening thus,
> Me thought that I heard voices sodainly,
> The most sweetest and most delicious
> That euer any wight I trow truly
> Heard in their life, for the armony
> And sweet accord was in so good musike,
> That the uoice to angels was most like.

There is here no affected rapture, no flowery sentiment: the whole is an ebullition of natural delight 'welling out of the heart', like water from a crystal spring. Nature is the soul of art: there is a strength as well as a simplicity in the imagination that reposes entirely on nature, that nothing else can supply. It was the same trust in nature, and reliance on his subject, which enabled Chaucer to describe the grief and patience of Griselda; the faith of Constance; and the heroic perseverance of the little child, who, going to school through the streets of Jewry,

> Oh *Alma Redemptoris mater*, loudly sung,

and who after his death still triumphed in his song. Chaucer has more of this deep, internal, sustained sentiment, than any other writer, except Boccaccio. In depth of simple pathos, and intensity of conception, never swerving from his subject, I think no other writer comes near him, not even the Greek tragedians. I wish to be allowed to give one or two instances of what I mean. I will take the following from the *Knight's Tale*. The distress of Arcite, in consequence of his banishment from his love, is thus described:

> Whan that Arcite to Thebes comen was,
> Ful oft a day he swelt and said Alas,
> For sene his lady shall he never mo.
> And shortly to concluden all his wo,
> So mochel sorwe hadde never creature,
> That is or shall be, while the world may dure.
> His slepe, his mete, his drinke is him byraft.
> That lene he wex, and drie as is a shaft.
> His eyen holwe, and grisly to behold,
> His hewe salwe, and pale as ashen cold,
> And solitary he was, and ever alone,
> And wailing all the night, making his mone.
> And if he herde song or instrument,
> Than wold he wepe, he mighte not be stent.
> So feble were his spirites, and so low,
> And changed so, that no man coude know
> His speche ne his vois, though men it herd.

This picture of the sinking of the heart, of the wasting away of the body and mind, of the gradual failure of all the faculties under the contagion of a rankling sorrow, cannot be surpassed. Of the same kind is his farewell to his mistress, after he has gained her hand and lost his life in the combat:

> 'Alas the wo! alas the peines stronge,
> That I for you have suffered, and so longe!
> Alas the deth! alas min Emilie!
> Alas departing of our compagnie;
> Alas min hertes quene! alas my wif!
> Min hertes ladie, ender of my lif!
> What is this world? what axen men to have?
> Now with his love, now in his colde grave
> Alone withouten any compagnie.'

The death of Arcite is the more affecting, as it comes after triumph and victory, after the pomp of sacrifice, the solemnities of prayer, the celebration of the gorgeous rites of chivalry. The descriptions of the three temples of Mars, of Venus, and Diana, of the ornaments and ceremonies used in each, with the reception given to the offerings of the lovers, have a beauty and grandeur, much of which is lost in Dryden's version. For instance, such lines as the following are not rendered with their true feeling:

> Why shulde I not as well eke tell you all
> The purtreiture that was upon the wall
> Within the temple of mighty Mars the rede—
> That highte the gret temple of Mars in Trace
> In thilke colde and frosty region,
> Ther as Mars hath his sovereine mansion.
> First on the wall was peinted a forest,
> In which ther wonneth neyther man ne best,
> With knotty knarry barrein trees old
> Of stubbes sharp and hidous to behold;
> In which ther ran a romble and a swough,
> As though a storme shuld bresten every bough.

And again, among innumerable terrific images of death and slaughter painted on the wall, is this one:

> The statue of Mars upon a carte stood
> Armed, and looked grim as he were wood.
> A wolf ther stood beforne him at his fete
> With eyen red, and of a man he ete.

The story of Griselda is in Boccaccio; but the Clerk of Oxenforde, who tells it, professes to have learned it from Petrarch. This story has gone all over Europe, and has passed into a proverb. In spite of the barbarity of the circumstances, which are abominable, the sentiment remains unimpaired and unalterable. It is of that kind, 'that heaves no sigh, that sheds no tear'; but it hangs upon the beatings of the heart; it is a part of the very being; it is as inseparable from it as the breath we draw. It is still and calm as the face of death. Nothing can touch it in its ethereal purity: tender as the yielding flower, it is fixed as the marble firmament. The only remonstrance she makes, the only complaint she utters against all the ill-treatment she receives, is that single line where, when turned back naked to her father's house, she says,

> Let me not like a worm go by the way.

. . . The story of the little child slain in Jewry (which is told by the Prioress, and worthy to be told by her who was 'all conscience and tender heart') is not less touching than that of Griselda. It is simple and heroic to the last degree. The poetry of Chaucer has a religious sanctity about it, connected with the manners and superstitions of the age. It has all the spirit of martyrdom.

It has also all the extravagance and the utmost licentiousness of comic humour, equally arising out of the manners of the time. In this too Chaucer resembled Boccaccio that he excelled in both styles, and could pass at will 'from grave to gay, from lively to severe'; but he never confounded the two styles together (except from that involuntary and unconscious mixture of the pathetic and humorous, which is almost always to be found in nature), and was exclusively taken up with what he set about, whether it was jest or earnest. The *Wife of Bath's Prologue* (which Pope has very admirably modernized) is, perhaps, unequalled as a comic story. The *Cock and the Fox* is also excellent for lively strokes of character and satire. *January and May* is not so good as some of the others. Chaucer's versification, considering the time at which he wrote, and that versification is a thing in a great degree mechanical, is not one of his least merits. It has considerable strength and harmony, and its apparent deficiency in the latter respect arises chiefly from the alterations which have since taken place in the pronunciation or mode of accenting the words of the language. The best general rule for reading him is to pronounce the final *e*, as in reading Italian.

It was observed in the last Lecture that painting describes what the object is in itself, poetry what it implies or suggests. Chaucer's poetry is not, in general, the best confirmation of the truth of this distinction, for his poetry is more picturesque and historical than almost any other. But there is one instance in point which I cannot help giving in this place. It is the story of the three thieves who go in search of Death to kill him, and who meeting with him, are entangled in their fate by his words, without knowing him. In the printed catalogue to Mr. West's (in some respects very admirable) picture of Death on the Pale Horse, it is observed, that 'In poetry the same effect is produced by a few abrupt and rapid gleams of description, touching, as it were with fire, the features and edges of a general mass of awful obscurity; but in painting, such indistinctness would be a defect, and imply that the artist wanted the power to portray the conceptions of his fancy. Mr. West was of opinion that to delineate a physical form, which in its moral impression would approximate to that of the visionary Death of Milton, it was necessary to endow it, if possible, with the appearance of superhuman strength and energy. He has therefore exerted the utmost force and perspicuity of his pencil on the central figure.'—One might suppose from this, that the way to represent a shadow was to make it as substantial as possible. Oh, no! Painting has its prerogatives (and high ones they are), but they lie in representing the visible, not the invisible. The moral attributes of Death are powers and effects of an infinitely wide and general description, which no individual or physical form can possibly represent, but by a courtesy of speech, or by a distant analogy. The moral impression of Death is essentially visionary; its reality is in the mind's eye. Words are here the only *things*; and things, physical forms, the mere mockeries of the understanding. The less definite, the less bodily the conception, the more vast, unformed, and unsubstantial, the nearer does it approach to some resemblance of that omnipresent, lasting, universal, irresistible principle, which everywhere, and at some time or other, exerts its power over all things. Death is a mighty abstraction, like Night, or Space, or Time. He is an ugly customer, who will not be invited to supper, or to sit for his picture. He is with us and about us, but we do not see him. He stalks on before us, and we do not mind him: he follows us close behind, and we do not turn to look back at him. We do not see him making faces at us in our lifetime, nor perceive him afterwards sitting in mock-majesty, a twin-skeleton, beside us, tickling our bare ribs, and staring into our hollow eye-balls! Chaucer knew this. He makes three riotous companions go in search of Death to kill him, they meet with an old man whom they reproach with his age, and ask why he does not die, to which he answers thus:

> Ne Deth, alas! ne will not han my lif.
> Thus walke I like a restless caitiff,
> And on the ground, which is my modres gate,
> I knocke with my staf, erlich and late,
> And say to hire, 'Leve, mother, let me in.
> Lo, how I vanish, flesh and blood and skin,
> Alas! when shall my bones ben at reste?
> Mother, with you wolde I changen my cheste,
> That in my chambre longe time hath be,
> Ye, for an heren cloute to wrap in me.'
> But yet to me she will not don that grace,
> For which ful pale and welked is my face.

They then ask the old man where they shall find out Death to kill him, and he sends them on an errand which ends in the death of all three. We hear no more of him, but it is Death that they have encountered!

ELIZABETH BARRETT BROWNING
"Mrs Browning on Chaucer" (1842)
Essays on Chaucer, ed. Frederick J. Furnivall
1868–94, pp. 157–64

But it is in Chaucer we touch the true height, and look abroad into the kingdoms and glories of our poetical literature,—it is with Chaucer that we begin our 'Books of the Poets,' our collections and selections, our pride of place and names. And the genius of the poet shares the character of his position: he was made for an early poet, and the metaphors of dawn and spring doubly become him. A morning star, a lark's exultation, cannot usher in a glory better. The 'cheerful morning face,' 'the breezy call of incense-breathing morn,' you recognise in his countenance and voice: it is a voice full of promise and prophecy. He is the good omen of our poetry, the 'good bird,' according to the Romans, 'the best good angel of the spring,' the nightingale, according to his own creed of good luck heard before the cuckoo,

Up rose the sunne, and uprose Emilie,

and uprose her poet, the first of a line of kings, conscious of futurity in his smile. He is a king, and inherits the earth, and expands his great soul smilingly to embrace his great heritage. Nothing is too high for him to touch with a thought, nothing too low to dower with an affection. As a complete creature cognate of life and death, he cries upon God,—as a sympathetic creature he singles out a daisy from the universe ('si douce est la marguerite'), to lie down by half a summer's day[1], and bless it for fellowship. His senses are open and delicate, like a young child's—his sensibilities capacious of supersensual relations, like an experienced thinker's. Child-like, too, his tears and smiles lie at the edge of his eyes, and he is one proof more among the many, that the deepest pathos and the quickest gaieties hide together in the same nature. He is too wakeful and curious to lose the stirring of a leaf, yet not too wide awake to see visions of green and white ladies[2] between the branches; and a fair House of Fame and a noble Court of Love[3] are built and holden in the winking of his eyelash. And because his imagination is neither too 'high fantastical' to refuse proudly the gravitation of the earth, nor too 'light of love' to lose it carelessly, he can create as well as dream, and work with clay as well as cloud; and when his men and women stand by the actual ones, your stop-watch shall reckon no difference in the beating of their hearts. He knew the secret of nature and art,—that truth is beauty,—and saying 'I will make "A Wife of Bath" as well as Emilie, and you shall remember her as long,' we do remember her as long. And he sent us a train of pilgrims, each with a distinct individuality apart from the pilgrimage, all the way from Southwark, and the Tabard Inn, to Canterbury and Becket's shrine: and their laughter comes never to an end, and their talk goes on with the stars, and all the railroads which may intersect the spoilt earth for ever, cannot hush the 'tramp tramp' of their horses' feet.

Controversy is provocative. We cannot help observing, because certain critics observe otherwise, that Chaucer utters as true music as ever came from poet or musician; that some of the sweetest cadences in all our English are extant in his—'swete upon his tongue' in completest modulation. Let 'Denham's strength and Waller's sweetness join' the Io pæan of a later age, the *'eurekamen'* of Pope and his generation. Not one of the 'Queen Anne's men' measuring out tuneful breath upon their fingers, like ribbons for topknots, did know the art of versification as the old rude Chaucer knew it. Call him rude for the picturesqueness of the epithet; but his verse has, at least, as much regularity in the sense of true art, and more manifestly in proportion to our increasing acquaintance with his dialect and pronunciation, as can be discovered or dreamed in the French school. Critics, indeed, have set up a system based upon the crushed atoms of first principles, maintaining that poor Chaucer wrote by accent only! Grant to them that he counted no verses on his fingers; grant that he never disciplined his highest thoughts to walk up and down in a paddock—ten paces and a turn; grant that his singing is not after the likeness of their singsong; but there end your admissions. It is our ineffaceable impression, in fact, that the whole theory of accent and quantity held in relation to ancient and modern poetry stands upon a fallacy, totters rather than stands; and that, when considered in connection with such old moderns as our Chaucer, the fallaciousness is especially apparent. Chaucer wrote by quantity, just as Homer did before him, as Goethe did after him, just as all poets must. Rules differ, principles are identical. All rhythm presupposes quantity. Organ-pipe or harp, the musician plays by time. Greek or English, Chaucer or Pope, the poet sings by time. What is this accent but a stroke, an emphasis with a successive pause to make complete the time? And what is the difference between this accent and quantity, but the difference between a harp-note and an organ-note? otherwise, quantity expressed in different ways? It is as easy for matter to subsist out of space, as music out of time.

Side by side with Chaucer comes Gower, who is ungratefully disregarded too often, because side by side with Chaucer. He who rides in the king's chariot will miss the people's 'hic est.' Could Gower be considered apart, there might be found signs in him of an independent royalty, however his fate may seem to lie in waiting for ever in his brother's ante-chamber, like Napoleon's tame kings. To speak our mind, he has been much undervalued. He is nailed to a comparative degree; and everybody seems to make it a condition of speaking of him, that something be called inferior within him, and something superior out of him. He is laid down flat, as a dark background for 'throwing out' Chaucer's light; he is used as a *pou stō* for leaping up into the empyrean of Chaucer's praise. This is not just nor worthy. His principal poem, the *Confessio Amantis*, preceded the *Canterbury Tales*, and proves an abundant fancy, a full head and full heart, and neither ineloquent.[4] We do not praise its design,—in which the father confessor is set up as a story-teller, like the bishop of Tricca, 'avec l'âme,' like the Cardinal de Retz, 'le moins ecclésiastique du monde,' —while we admit that he tells his stories as if born to the manner of it, and that they are not much the graver, nor, peradventure, the holier either, for the circumstance of the confessorship. They are, indeed, told gracefully and pleasantly enough, and if with no superfluous life and gesture, with an active sense of beauty in some sort, and as flowing a rhythm as may bear comparison with many octosyllabics of our day; Chaucer himself having done more honour to their worth as stories than we can do in our praise, by adopting and crowning several of their number for king's sons within his own palaces.[5] And this recalls that, at the opening of one glorious felony, the *Man of Lawes Tale*, he has written, a little unlawfully and ungratefully considering the connection, some lines of harsh significance upon poor Gower,[6] whence has been conjectured by the grey gossips of criticism, a literary jealousy, an unholy enmity, nothing less than a soul-chasm between the contemporary poets. We believe nothing of it; no nor of the Shakespeare and Jonson feud after it:

'To alle such cursed stories we saie fy.'

That Chaucer wrote in irritation is clear[7]: that he was angry seriously and lastingly, or beyond the pastime of passion spent in a verse as provoked by a verse, there appears to us no reason for crediting. But our idea of the nature of the irritation will expound itself in our idea of the offence, which is here in Dan Gower's proper words, as extracted from the Ladie Venus's speech in the *Confessio Amantis*:

> 'And grete well Chaucer whan ye mete,
> As my disciple and poëte!
>
> . . .
>
> Forthy now in his daies old,
> Thou shalt him tellë this message,
> That he upon his latter age,
> To sette an ende of alle his werke
> As he who is mine ownë clerke,
> Do make his testament of love.'

We would not slander Chaucer's temper,—we believe, on the contrary, that he had the sweetest temper in the world,—and still it is our conviction, none the weaker, that he was far from being entirely pleased by this 'message.' We are sure he did not like the message, and not many poets would. His 'elvish countenance' might well grow dark, and 'his sugred mouth' speak somewhat sourly, in response to such a message. Decidedly, in our own opinion, it was an impertinent message, a provocative message, a most inexcusable and odious message! Waxing hotter ourselves the longer we think of it, there is the more excuse for Chaucer. For, consider, gentle reader! this indecorous message preceded the appearance of the *Canterbury Tales*,[8] and proceeded from a rival poet in the act of completing his principal work,—its plain significance being 'I have done my poem, and you cannot do yours because you are superannuated.' And this, while the great poet addressed was looking farther forward than the visible horizon, his eyes dilated with a mighty purpose. And to be counselled by this, to shut them forsooth, and take his crook and dog and place in the valleys like a grey shepherd of the Pyrenees—he, who felt his foot strong upon the heights! he, with no wrinkle on his forehead deep enough to touch the outermost of inward smooth dreams—he, in the divine youth of his healthy soul, in the quenchless love of his embracing sympathies, in the untired working of his perpetual energies,—to 'make an ende of alle his werke' and be old, as if he were not a poet! 'Go to, O vain man,'—we do not reckon the age of the poet's soul by the shadow on the dial! Enough that it falls upon his grave.

But this Sackville stands too low for admeasurement with Spenser, and we must look back, if covetous of comparisons, to some one of a loftier and more kingly stature. We must look back far, and stop at Chaucer. Spenser and Chaucer do naturally remind us of each other, they two being the most cheerful-hearted of the poets—with whom cheerfulness, as an attribute of poetry, is scarcely a common gift.

Chaucer and Spenser fulfilled their destiny, and grew to their mutual likeness as cheerful poets, by certain of the former processes [glorifying sensual things with the inward sense, &c.]. They two are alike in their cheerfulness, yet are their cheerfulnesses most unlike. Each poet laughs: yet their laughters ring with as far a difference as the sheep-bell on the hill, and the joy-bell in the city. Each is earnest in his gladness: each active in persuading you of it. You are persuaded, and hold each for a cheerful man. The whole difference is, that Chaucer has a cheerful humanity: Spenser, a cheerful ideality. One, rejoices walking on the sunny side of the street; the other, walking out of the street in a way of his own, kept green by a blessed vision. One, uses the adroitness of his fancy by distill-

ing out of the visible universe her occult smiles; the other, by fleeing beyond the possible frown, the occasions of natural ills, to that 'cave of cloud' where he may smile safely to himself. One, holds festival with men—seldom so coarse and loud, indeed, as to startle the deer from their green covert at Woodstock[9]—or with homely Nature and her 'dame Marguerite' low in the grasses:[10] the other adopts, for his playfellows, imaginary or spiritual existences, and will not say a word to Nature herself, unless it please her to dress for his masque, and speak daintily sweet, and rare like a spirit. The human heart of one utters oracles; the imagination of the other speaks for his heart, and we miss no prophecy. For music, we praised Chaucer's, and not only as Dryden did, for 'a Scotch tune.' But never issued there from lip or instrument, or the tuned causes of nature, more lovely sound than we gather from our Spenser's Art. His rhythm is the continuity of melody. It is the singing of an angel in a dream.

Shirley is the last dramatist, *Valete et plaudite, o posteri.* Standing in his traces, and looking backward and before, we became aware of the distinct demarcations of five eras of English poetry: the first, the Chaucerian, although we might call it *Chaucer*; the second, the Elizabethan; the third, which culminates in Cowley; the fourth, in Dryden and the French school; the fifth, the return to nature of Cowper and his successors of our day. These five rings mark the age of the fair and stingless serpent we are impelled, like the Ancient Mariner, to bless—but not 'unaware.' '*Ah benedicite!*' we bless her so, out of our Chaucer's rubric, softly, but with a plaintiveness of pleasure.

Notes

1. *Prologue* to the *Legende of Good Women*, l. 179–182 of the 2nd cast of the Prologue.—Furnivall
2.   And by the hande he helde this noble quene,
        Corowned with white, and clothed al in grene.
        (*Prologue to the Legende*, 2nd cast, l. 241–2.)
   But the allusion is doubtless to the Ladies of *The Flower & Leaf*, which certainly Chaucer never wrote. It must be more than 50 years after his date.—F.
3. This poem cannot be proved to be Chaucer's.—F.
4. Apply here what Mrs Browning (that is, Miss Barrett) says at p. 163–4 on the difference between the Elizabethan period and the Cowley one. "The voices are eloquent enough, thoughtful enough, fanciful enough; but something is defective. Can any one suffer, as an experimental reader, the transition between the second and third periods, without feeling that something is defective? What is so? And who dares to guess that it may be INSPIRATION?" Gower, of course, writes most respectable verse; but he is a *bore*. It's just like him, to patronise Chaucer!—F.
5. I do not believe for a moment that Chaucer adapted his stories from Gower, as he had probably written his Constance, &c., long before Gower's *Confessio* appeared. The stories were common enough; and both writers went to the same original. But out of that they made very different poems.—F.
6. l. 78–88. Where he says that he wouldn't write of such cursed stories as Canace's (who loved her own brother sinfully), or such unnatural abominations as Tyro Apollonius, who ravisht his own daughter, and of whom Gower had written the story in his *Confessio*. Why shouldn't Chaucer have been chaffing the "moral Gower," that most respectable man, for his gross impropriety? It's just the kind of thing Chaucer would have enjoyed, especially when he had himself just finisht his free-and-easy *Miller's* and *Reeve's Tales*, and broken off the *Cook's*, because the flavour was getting a little too strong. He, in fact, said to his readers, "You may perhaps think my stories a little naughty; but really they're not half so bad as that moral and proper old gentleman's who's Poet Lawreate. Mine are only fun, whereas that old respectable's are about incest! Bad I may be; but as bad as that proper old Gower who writes about unnatural crimes!! God forbid!!!" It's something

like Swinburne reproaching Tupper for the immoral tendency of his productions. And who wouldn't enjoy that joke?—F.

7. Not to me.—F.

8. Did the *Canterbury Tales* ever appear at all, in our sense of the word? Separate Tales, or fragments or groups of them, may have been circulated during Chaucer's life; but assuredly they never "appeared" as a whole, like Gower's *Confessio* did.—F.

9. There is no foundation for the late legend that connects Chaucer with Woodstock.—F.

10. *Prologue* to the *Legende.*—F.

JAMES RUSSELL LOWELL
From *Conversations on Some of the Old Poets*
1846, pp. 16–49

P hilip: You must put no faith at all in any idea you may have got of Chaucer from Dryden or Pope. Dryden appreciated his original better than Pope; but neither of them had a particle of his humor, nor of the simplicity of his pathos. The strong point in Pope's displays of sentiment is in the graceful management of a cambric handkerchief. You do not believe a word that Heloïse says, and feel all the while that she is squeezing out her tears as if from a half-dry sponge. Pope was not a man to understand the quiet tenderness of Chaucer, where you almost seem to hear the hot tears fall, and the simple, choking words sobbed out. I know no author so tender as he; Shakspeare himself was hardly so. There is no declamation in his grief. Dante is scarcely more downright and plain. To show you how little justice Dryden has done him, I will first read you a few lines from his version of "The Knight's Tale," and then the corresponding ones of the original. It is the death-scene of Arcite.

> Conscience (that of all physic works the last)
> Caused him to send for Emily in haste;
> With her, at his desire, came Palamon.
> Then, on his pillow raised, he thus begun:
> 'No language can express the smallest part
> Of what I feel and suffer in my heart
> For you, whom best I love and value most.
> But to your service I bequeath my ghost;
> *Which, from this mortal body when untied,*
> Unseen, unheard, shall hover at your side,
> Nor fright you waking, nor your sleep offend,
> But wait officious, and your steps attend.
> *How I have loved! Excuse my faltering tongue;*
> *My spirit's feeble and my pains are strong;*
> This I may say: I only grieve to die,
> Because I lose *my charming Emily.*'

John: I am quite losing my patience. The sentiment of Giles Scroggins, and the verse of Blackmore! Surely, nothing but the meanest servility to his original could excuse such slovenly workmanship as this.

Philip: There is worse to come. Of its fidelity as a translation you can judge for yourself, when you hear Chaucer.

> 'To die when Heaven had put you in my power,
> Fate could not choose a more malicious hour!
> What greater curse could envious Fortune give
> Than just to die when I began to live?
> *Vain men, how vanishing a bliss we crave!*
> *Now warm in love, now withering in the grave!*
> *Never, O, never more to see the sun!*
> *Still dark in a damp vault, and still alone!*
> This fate is common.'

I wish you especially to bear in mind the lines I have emphasized. Notice, too, how the rhyme is impertinently

forced upon the attention throughout. We can hardly help wondering if a nuncupatory testament were ever spoken in verse before. There is none of this French-lustre in Chaucer.

> Arcite must die;
> For which he sendeth after Emily,
> And Palamon, that was his cousin dear;
> Then spake he thus, as ye shall after hear:
> 'Ne'er may the woful spirit in my heart
> Declare one point of all my sorrow's smart
> To you, my lady, that I love the most;
> But I bequeath the service of my ghost
> To you aboven any cre-a-ture,
> Since that my life may now no longer dure.
> Alas, the woe! alas, the pains so strong,
> That I for you have suffered,—and so long!
> Alas, the death! alas, mine Emily!
> Alas, the parting of our company!
> Alas, my heart's true queen! alas, my wife!
> My heart's dear lady, ender of my life!
> What is this world? What asketh man to have?
> Now with his love,—now in his cold, cold grave,
> Alone, withouten any company!
> Farewell, my sweet! farewell, mine Emily!
> And softly take me in your armes twey (two arms),
> For love of God, and hearken what I say.'

John: Perfect! I would not have a word changed, except the second "cold" before "grave." It takes away from the simplicity, and injures the effect accordingly. In the lines just before that, I could fancy that I heard the dying man gasp for breath. After hearing this, Dryden's exclamation-marks savor of the playbills, where one sees them drawn up in platoons, as a bodyguard to the name of an indifferent player,—their number being increased in proportion as the attraction diminishes. And in that seemingly redundant line,

> Alone, withouten any company,

how does the repetition and amplification give force and bitterness to the thought, as if Arcite must need dwell on his expected loneliness, in order to feel it fully! There is nothing here about "*charming* Emily," "*envious* Fortune,"—no bandying of compliments. Death shows to Arcite, as he does mostly to those who are cut off suddenly in the May-time and blossom of the senses, as a bleak, bony skeleton, and nothing more. Dryden, I remember, in his "Art of Poetry," says,

> Chaucer alone, fixed on this solid base,
> In his old style conserves a modern grace;
> Too happy, if the freedom of his rhymes
> Offended not the method of our times.

But if what you have read (unless you have softened it greatly) be a specimen of his rudeness, save us from such "method" as that of Dryden!

Philip: I hardly changed a syllable. The word to which you objected, as redundant, was an addition of my own to eke out the measure; "coldè" being pronounced as two syllables in Chaucer's time. The language of the heart never grows obsolete or antiquated, but falls as musically from the tongue now as when it was first uttered. Such lustiness and health of thought and expression seldom fail of leaving issue behind them. One may trace a family-likeness to these in many of Spenser's lines, and I please myself sometimes with imagining pencil-marks of Shakspeare's against some of my favorite passages in Chaucer. At least, the relationship may be traced through Spenser, who calls Chaucer his master, and to whom Shakspeare pays nearly as high a compliment. . . .

John: After all, your Chaucer was a satirist, and you

should, in justice, test him with the same acid which you applied so remorselessly to Pope.

Philip: Chaucer's satire is of quite another complexion. A hearty laugh and a thrust in the ribs are his weapons. He makes fun of you to your face, and, even if you wince a little, you cannot help joining in his mirth. He does not hate a vice because he has a spite against the man who is guilty of it. He does not cry, "A rat i' the arras!" and run his sword through a defenceless old man behind it. But it is not for his humor, nor, indeed, for any one quality, that our old Chaucer is dear and sacred to me. I love to call him *old* Chaucer. The farther I can throw him back into the past, the dearer he grows; so sweet is it to mark how his plainness and sincerity outlive all changes of the outward world. Antiquity has always something reverend in it. Even its most material and perishable form, which we see in pyramids, cairns, and the like, is brooded over by a mysterious presence which strangely awes us. Whatever has been hallowed by the love and pity, by the smiles and tears of men, becomes something more to us than the moss-covered epitaph of a buried age. There was a meaning in the hieroglyphics, which Champollion could not make plainer. It is only from association with Man that any thing seems old. The quarries of the Nile may be coeval with the planet itself, yet it is only the still fresh dints of the Coptic chisel that gift them with the spell of ancientness. Let but the skeleton of a man be found among the remains of those extinct antediluvian monsters, and straightway that which now claimed our homage as a triumph of comparative anatomy, shall become full of awe and mystery, and dim with the gray dawnlight of time. Once, from those shapeless holes, a human soul looked forth upon its huge empire of past and future. Once, beneath those crumbling ribs, beat a human heart, that seeming narrow isthmus between time and eternity, wherein there was yet room for hope and fear, and love and sorrow, to dwell, with all their wondrous glooms and splendors. Before, we could have gone no farther back than Cuvier. Those mighty bones of ichthyosauri and plesiosauri seemed rather a record of his energy and patience, than of a living epoch in earth's history. Now, how modern and of to-day seem Memnon and Elephanta! If there be a venerableness in any outward symbols, in which rude and dumb fashion the soul of man first strove to utter itself, how much more is there in the clearer and more inspired sentences of ancient lawgivers and poets!

John: You have contrived very adroitly to get the Deluge between us. I shall not attempt the perilous navigation to your side, and can only wish you a safe return to mine. Camoens swam ashore from a shipwreck, with the Lusiad in his teeth; and I hope you will do as much for Chaucer. I long to hear more of him.

Philip: It would be easier for me to emulate Waterton's ride on the alligator's back, and make an extempore steed of the most tractable-looking ichthyosaurus I can lay hands on. However, here I am safely back again. But before I read you any thing else from Chaucer, I must please myself by praising him a little more. His simplicity often reminds me of Homer; but, except in the single quality of *invention*, I prefer him to the Ionian. Yet we must remember that he shares this deficiency with Shakspeare, who scarcely ever scrupled to run in debt for his plots. . . .

Philip: But we must come back to Chaucer. There is in him the exuberant freshness and greenness of spring. Every thing he touches leaps into full blossom. His gladness and humor and pathos are irrepressible as a fountain. Dam them with a prosaic subject, and they overleap it in a sparkling cascade that turns even the hindrance to a beauty. Choke them

with a tedious theological disquisition, and they bubble up forthwith, all around it, with a delighted gurgle. There is no cabalistic Undine stone or seal-of-Solomon that can shut them up for ever. Reading him is like brushing through the dewy grass at sunrise. Every thing is new and sparkling and fragrant. He is of kin to Belphœbe, whose

> Birth was of the womb of morning dew,
> And her conception of the joyous prime.

I speak now of what was truly Chaucer. I strip away from him all that belonged to the time in which he lived, and judge him only by what belongs equally to all times. For it is only in as far as a poet advances into the universal, that he approaches immortality. There is no nebulosity of sentiment about him, no insipid vagueness in his sympathies. His first merit, the chief one in all art, is sincerity. He does not strive to body forth something which shall have a meaning; but, having a clear meaning in his heart, he gives it as clear a shape. Sir Philip Sydney was of his mind, when he bade poets look into their own hearts and write. He is the most unconventional of poets, and the frankest. If his story be dull, he rids his hearers of all uncomfortable qualms by being himself the first to yawn. He would have fared but ill in our day, when the naked feelings are made liable to the penalties of an act for the punishment of indecent exposure. Very little care had he for the mere decencies of life. Were he alive now, I can conceive him sending a shudder through St. James's Coffee-house, by thrusting his knife into his mouth; or making all Regent Street shriek for harts-horn, by giving a cab-driver as good as he sent, in a style that would have pleased old Burton. The highest merit of a poem is, that it reflects alike the subject and the poet. It should be neither objective nor subjective exclusively. Reason should stand at the helm, though the wayward breezes of feeling must puff the sails. Nature has hinted at this, by setting the eyes higher than the heart. Chaucer's poems can claim more of the former than of the latter of these excellencies. Observation of outward nature and life is more apparent in them than a deep inward experience, and it is the observation of a cheerful, unwearied spirit. His innocent self-forgetfulness gives us the truest glimpses into his own nature, and, at the same time, makes his pictures of outward objects wonderfully clear and vivid. Though many of his poems are written in the first person, yet there is not a shade of egoïsm in them. It is but the simple art of the story-teller, to give more reality to what he tells.

John: Yes, it was not till our own day that the poets discovered what mystical significance had been lying dormant for ages in a capital I. It seems strange that a letter of such powerful bewitchment had not made part of the juggling wares of the Cabalists and Theurgists. Yet we find no mention of it in Rabbi Akiba or Cornelius Agrippa. Byron wrought miracles with it. I fear that the noble Stylites of modern song, who, from his lonely pillar of self, drew crowds of admiring votaries to listen to the groans of his self-inflicted misery, would have been left only to feel the cold and hunger of his shelterless pinnacle in Chaucer's simpler day.

Philip: Yes, Byron always reminds me of that criminal who was shut in a dungeon, the walls of which grew every day narrower and narrower, till they crushed him at last. His selfishness walled him in, from the first; so that he was never open to the sweet influences of nature, and those sweeter ones which the true heart finds in life. The sides of his jail were semitransparent, giving him a muddy view of things immediately about him; but selfishness always builds a thick roof overhead, to cut off the heavenward gaze of the spirit. And how did it press the very life out of him, in the end!

John: Byron's spirit was more halt than his body. It had been well for him, had he been as ashamed, or at least as conscious, of one as of the other. He should have been banished, like Philoctetes, to some Isle of Lemnos, where his lameness should not have been offensive and contagious. As it was, the world fell in love with the defect. Some malicious Puck had dropped the juice of love-in-idleness upon its eyes, and limping came quite into fashion. We have never yet had a true likeness of Byron. Leigh Hunt's, I think, is more faithful than Moore's. Moore never forgot that his friend was a lord, and seemed to feel that he was paying himself a side-compliment in writing a life of him. I always imagine Moore's portrait of Byron with an "I am, my dear Moore, yours, &c." written under it, as a specimen of his autography. But to our poet. You have given me a touch of his pathos; let me hear some of the humor which you have commended so highly.

Philip: Praise beforehand deadens the flavor of the wine; so that, if you are disappointed, the blame must be laid upon me. I will read you a few passages from his "Nun's Priest's Tale." It has been modernized by Dryden, under the title of "The Cock and the Fox"; but he has lost much of the raciness of the original. I have chosen this tale, because it will, at the same time, give you an idea of his minute observation of nature. I shall modernize it as I read, preserving as much as possible the language, and, above all, the spirit of the original. But you must never forget how much our Chaucer loses by the process. The story begins with a description of the poor widow who owns the hero of the story, Sir Chaunticlere. Then we have a glimpse of the hero himself. The widow has

> A yard enclosed all about
> With sticks, and also a dry ditch without,
> In which she had a cock hight Chaunticlere;
> In all the land for voice was not his peer;
> Not merrier notes the merry organ plays
> Within the churches, upon holydays;
> And surer was his crowing in his lodge
> Than is a clock, or abbey horologe:
> He knew by nature every step to trace
> Of the equinoctial in his native place,
> And, when fifteen degrees it had ascended,
> Then crew he so as might not be amended.
> His comb was redder than the fine coràl,
> Embattled as it were a castle-wall;
> His bill was black, and like the jet it shone;
> Like azure were his legs and toes each one;
> His nails were white as lilies in the grass,
> And like the burnèd gold his color was.

John: What gusto! If he had been painting Arthur or Charlemagne, he would not have selected his colors with more care. Without pulling out a feather from his hero's cockhood, he contrives to give him a human interest. How admirable is the little humorous thrust at the astronomers, too, in restricting Sir Chaunticlere's knowledge of the heavenly motions to his own village!

Philip: Yes, Chaucer has the true poet's heart. One thing is as precious to him in point of beauty as another. He would have described his lady's cheek by the same flower to which he has here likened the nails of Chaunticlere. To go on with our story.

> This gentle cock had in his governance
> Seven wifely hens to do him all pleasaunce,
> Of whom the fairest-colored in the throat
> Was known as the fair damsel Partelote;
> Courteous she was, discreet and debonair,
> Companionable, and bore herself so fair,

> Sithence the hour she was a seven-night old,
> That truly she the royal heart did hold
> Of Chauntclere bound fast in every limb;
> He loved her so, that it was well with him.
> But such a joy it was to hear them sing,
> When that the bright sun in the east 'gan spring,
> In sweet accord!

Chaunticlere, one morning, awakens his fair wife Partelote by a dreadful groaning; and, on her asking the cause, informs her that it must have been the effect of a bad dream he had been haunted by.

> I dreamed, that, as I roamèd up and down,
> Within our yard, I there beheld a beast,
> Like to a hound, that would have made arrest
> Upon my body, and have had me dead.
> His color 'twixt a yellow was and red,
> And tippèd were his tail and both his ears
> With black, unlike the remnant of his hairs.
> His snout was small, and glowing were his eyes:
> Still, for his look, the heart within me dies.

Partelote treats his fears with scorn. She asks, indignantly,

> How durst you now for shame say to your love
> That any thing could make you feel afeard?
> Have you no manly heart, yet have a beard?

She then gives him a lecture on the physiological causes of dreams, hints at a superfluity of bile, and recommends some simple remedy which her own housewifely skill can concoct from herbs that grow within the limits of his own manor. She also quotes Cato's opinion of the small faith to be put in dreams. Her lord, who does not seem superior to the common prejudice against having his wife make too liberal a display of her learning, replies by overwhelming her with an avalanche of weighty authorities, each one of which, he tells her, is worth more than ever Cato was. He concludes with a contemptuous defiance of all manner of doses, softening it toward his lady by an adroit compliment.

> But let us speak of mirth, and stint of this:
> Dame Partelote, as I have hope of bliss,
> Of one thing God hath sent me largest grace;
> For, when I see the beauty of your face,
> You are so scarlet red about your eyes,
> That, when I look on you, my terror dies;
> For just so sure as *in principio*
> *Mulier est hominis confusio,*
> (Madam, the meaning of this Latin is,
> Woman is man's chief joy and sovereign bliss,)
> Whene'er I feel at night your downy side,
> I am so full of solace and of pride,
> That I defy the threatenings of my dream.
> And, with that word, he flew down from the
>   beam,—
> For it was day,—and eke his spouses all;
> And with a chuck he 'gan them for to call,
> For he had found a corn lay in the yard:
> Royal he was, and felt no more afeard;
> He looketh as a lion eyes his foes,
> And roameth up and down upon his toes;
> Scarcely he deigneth set his feet to ground;
> He chucketh when a kernel he hath found,
> And all his wives run to him at his call.

John: What an admirable barn-yard picture! The very chanticleer of our childhood, whose parallel Bucks county and Dorking have striven in vain to satisfy our maturer vision with! A chanticleer whose memory writes *Ichabod* upon the most populous and palatial fowl-houses of manhood! Chaucer's

Pegasus ambles along as easily, and crops the grass and daisies of the roadside as contentedly, as if he had forgotten his wings.

Philip: Yes, the work in hand is, for the time, noblest in the estimation of our poet. His eye never looks beyond it, or cheats it of its due regard by pining for something fairer and more worthy. The royalty is where he is, whether in hovel or palace. Nothing that God has not thought it beneath him to make does he deem it beneath him to study and prove worthy of all admiration. Wordsworth is like him in this. . . .

Chaucer reminds me oftenest of Crabbe, in the unstudied plainness of his sentiment, and the minuteness of his descriptions. But, in Crabbe's poetry, Tyburn-tree is seen looming up in the distance, and the bell of the parish workhouse is heard jangling. It had been better for Crabbe, if he had studied Chaucer more and Pope less. The frigid artificiality of his verse often contrasts almost ludicrously with the rudeness of his theme. It is Captain Kidd in a starched cambric neckcloth and white gloves. When Chaucer describes his Shipman, we seem to smell tar.

> There also was a shipman from far west;
> For aught I know, in Dartmouth he abode;
> Well as he could upon a hack he rode,
> All in a shirt of tow-cloth to the knee;
> A dagger hanging by a lace had he,
> About his neck, under his arm adown;
> The summer's heat had made his hue all brown.
> He was a right good fellow certainly,
> And many a cargo of good wine had he
> Run from Bordeaux while the tidewaiter slept;
> Of a nice conscience no great care he kept,
> If that he fought and had the upperhand,
> By water he sent them home to every land;
> But in his craft to reckon well the tides,
> The deep sea currents, and the shoals besides,
> The sun's height and the moon's, and pilotage,—
> There was none such from Hull unto Carthàge;
> Hardy he was and wise, I undertake;
> His beard had felt full many a tempest's shake;
> He knew well all the havens as they were
> From Gothland to the Cape de Finisterre,
> And every creek in Brittany and Spain;
> His trusty bark was named the Magdelaine.

John: The "savage Rosa" never dashed the lights and shades upon one of his bandits with more bold and picturesque effect. How that storm-grizzled beard stands out from the canvass! The effect is so real, that it seems as if the brown old sea-king had sat for his portrait, and that every stroke of the brush had been laid on within reach of the dagger hanging at his side. Witness the amiable tints thrown in here and there, to palliate a grim wrinkle or a shaggy eyebrow. The poet takes care to tell us that

He was a right good fellow certainly,

lest his sitter take umbrage at the recital of his smuggling exploits in the next verse. And then with what a rough kind of humor he lets us into the secret of his murderous propensities, by hinting that he gave a passage home by water to those of whom he got the upperhand! In spite of the would-be good-humored leer, the cut-throat look shows through. It may be very pleasant riding with him as far as Canterbury, and we might even laugh at his clumsiness in the saddle, but we feel all the while that we had rather not be overhauled by him upon the high seas. His short and easy method of sending acquaintances thus casually made to their respective homes, by water, we should not be inclined to admire so much as he himself would; especially if, as a preliminary step, he should attempt to

add to the convenience of our respiratory organs with that ugly dagger of his, by opening a larger aperture somewhere nearer to the lungs. We should be inclined to distrust those extraordinary powers of natation for which he would give us credit. Even Lord Byron, I imagine, would dislike to mount that steed that "knew its rider" so well, or even to "lay his hand upon its mane," if our friend, the Shipman, held the stirrup.

Philip: The whole prologue to the Canterbury Tales is equally admirable, but there is not time for me to read the whole. You must do that for yourself. I only give you a bunch or two of grapes. To enjoy the fruit in its perfection, you must go into the vineyard yourself, and pluck it with the bloom on, before the flavor of the sunshine has yet faded out of it; enjoying the play of light upon the leaves also, and the apt disposition of the clusters, each lending a grace to the other.

John: Your metaphor pleases me. I like the grapes better than the wine which is pressed out of them, and they seem to me a fitting emblem of Chaucer's natural innocence. Elizabeth Barrett, a woman whose genius I admire, says very beautifully of Chaucer,

> Old Chaucer, with his infantine,
> Familiar clasp of things divine,—
> *That stain upon his lips is wine.*

I had rather think it pure grape-juice. The first two lines take hold of my heart so that I believe them intuitively, and doubt not but my larger acquaintance with Chaucer will prove them to be true.

Philip: I admire them as much as you do, and to me they seem to condense all that can be said of Chaucer. But one must know him thoroughly to feel their truth and fitness fully. At the first glimpse you get of his face, you are struck with the merry twinkle of his eye, and the suppressed smile upon his lips, which betrays itself as surely as a child in playing hide-and-seek. It is hard to believe that so happy a spirit can have ever felt the galling of that

Chain wherewith we are darkly bound,

or have beaten its vain wings against the insensible gates of that awful mystery whose key can never be enticed from the hand of the warder, Death. But presently the broad, quiet forehead, the look of patient earnestness, and the benignant reverence of the slightly bowed head, make us quite forget the lightsome impression of our first look. Yet in the next moment it comes back upon us again more strongly than ever. Humor is always a main ingredient in highly poetical natures. It is almost always the superficial indication of a rich vein of pathos, nay, of tragic feeling, below. Wordsworth seems to be an exception. Yet there is a gleam of it in his sketch of that philosopher

> Who could peep and botanize
> Upon his mother's grave,

and of a grim, reluctant sort in some parts of Peter Bell and the Wagoner. But he was glad to sink a shaft beneath the surface, where he could gather the more precious ore, and dwell retired from the jeers of a boorish world. In Chaucer's poetry, the humor is playing all the time round the horizon, like heat-lightning. It is unexpected and unpredictable; but, as soon as you turn away from watching for it, behold, it flashes again as innocently and softly as ever. It mingles even with his pathos, sometimes. The laughing eyes of Thalia gleam through the tragic mask she holds before her face. In spite of your cold-water prejudices, I must confess that I like Miss Barrett's third line as well as the others. But while we are wandering so far from the poor old widow's yard, that fox, "full of iniquity,"

That new Iscariot, new Ganelon,
That false dissimulator, Greek Sinon,

as Chaucer calls him, may have made clean away with our noble friend Sir Chaunticlere.

John: Now, Esculapius defend thy bird! The Romans believed that the lion himself would strike his colors at the crowing of a cock,—a piece of natural history to which the national emblems of England and France have figuratively given the lie. But cunning is often more serviceable than bravery, and Sir Russel the fox may achieve by diplomacy the victory to which the lion was not equal.

Philip: We shall see. Diplomatists are like the two Yankees who swapped jacknives together till each had cleared five dollars. Such a Sir Philip Sydney among cocks, at least, could not fall without a burst of melodious tears from every civilized barn-yard. The poet, after lamenting that Sir Chaunticlere had not heeded better the boding of his dream, warns us of the danger of woman's counsel, from Eve's time downward; but takes care to add,

These speeches are the cock's, and none of mine;
For I no harm of woman can divine.

He then returns to his main argument; and no one, who has not had poultry for bosom-friends from childhood, can appreciate the accurate grace and pastoral humor of his descriptions. The fox, meanwhile, has crept into the yard and hidden himself.

Fair in the sand, to bathe her merrily,
Lies Partelote, and all her sisters by,
Against the sun, and Chaunticlere so free
Sang merrier than the mermaid in the sea
(For Physiologus saith certainly
How that they sing both well and merrily),
And so befell, that, as he cast his eye
Among the worts upon a butterfly,
'Ware was he of the fox that lay full low;
Nothing it lists him now to strut or crow,
But cries anon, Cuk! cuk! and up doth start,
As one that is affrayed in his heart.

The knight would have fled, as there are examples enough in Froissart to prove it would not have disgraced his spurs to do, considering the greatness of the odds against him, but the fox plies him with courteous flattery. He appeals to Sir Chaunticlere's pride of birth, pretends to have a taste in music, and is desirous of hearing him sing, hoping all the while to put his tuneful throat to quite other uses. A more bitter fate than that of Orpheus seems to be in store for our feathered son of Apollo; since his spirit, instead of hastening to join that of his Eurydice, must rake for corn in Elysian fields, with the bitter thought, that not one but seven Eurydices are cackling for him *"superis in auris."* The fox

Says, 'Gentle Sir, alas! what will you do?
Are you afraid of him that is your friend?
Now, certes, I were worse than any fiend,
If I to you wished harm or villany;
I am not come your counsel to espy,
But truly all that me did hither bring
Was only for to hearken how you sing;
For, on my word, your voice is merrier even
Than any angel hath that is in heaven,
And you beside a truer feeling show, Sir,
Than did Boece, or any great composer.
My Lord, your father (God his spirit bless!
And eke your mother, for her gentleness)
Hath honored my poor house to my great ease,
And, certes, Sir, full fain would I you please.

But, since men talk of singing, I will say
(Else may I lose my eyes this very day),
Save you, I never heard a mortal sing
As did your father at the daybreaking;
Certes, it was with all his heart he sung,
And, for to make his voice more full and strong,
He would so pain him, that with either eye
He needs must wink, so loud he strove to cry,
And stand upon his tiptoes therewithal,
And stretch his comely neck forth long and small.
Discretion, too, in him went hand in hand
With music, and no man in any land
In wisdom or in song did him surpass.'

John: I thought Chaucer's portrait of the son perfect, till Sir Russel hung up his of the father beside it. Why, Vandyke himself would look chalky beside such flesh and blood as this. Such a cock, one would think, might have served a score of Israelites for a sacrifice at their feast of atonement, or have been a sufficient thank-offering to the gods for twenty Spartan victories. Stripped of his feathers, Plato would have taken him for something more than human. It must have been such a one as this that the Stoics esteemed it as bad as parricide to slay.

Philip: The fox continues,

'Let's see, can you your father counterfeit?'
This Chaunticlere his wings began to beat,
As one that could not his foul treason spy,
So he was ravished by his flattery. . . .

Sir Chaunticlere stood high upon his toes,
Streached forth his neck and held his eyes shut close,
And gan to crow full loudly for the nonce,
When Dan Russel, the fox, sprang up at once,
And by the gorget seized Sir Chaunticlere,
And on his back toward the wood him bare.

Forthwith the seven wives begin a sorrowful ululation; Dame Partelote, in her capacity as favorite, shrieking more sovereignly than the rest. Another Andromache, she sees her Hector dragged barbarously from the walls of his native Illium, whose defence and prop he had ever been. Then follows a picture which surpasses even Hogarth.

The luckless widow and her daughters two,
Hearing the hens cry out and make their woe,
Out at the door together rushed anon,
And saw how toward the wood the fox is gone,
Bearing upon his back the cock away;
They cried 'Out, out, alas! and welaway!
Aha, the fox!' and after him they ran,
And, snatching up their staves, ran many a man;
Ran Col the dog, ran Talbot and Gerland,
And Malkin, with her distaff in her hand;
Ran cow and calf, and even the very hogs,
So frighted with the barking of the dogs,
And shouting of the men and women eke,
Ran till they thought their very hearts would break,
And yelled as never fiends in hell have done;
The dicks screamed, thinking that their sand was run;
The geese, for fear, flew cackling o'er the trees;
Out of their hive buzzed forth a swarm of bees;
So hideous was the noise, ah, *benedicite*!
Certes, not Jack Straw and his varletry
Raised ever any outcry half so shrill,
When they some Fleming were about to kill,
As that same day was made about the fox:
Vessels of brass they brought forth and of box,
And horns and bones, on which they banged and
   blew;
It seemed the very sky would split in two.

. . .

The cock, who lay upon the fox's back,
In all his dread unto his captor spake,
And said: 'Most noble Sir, if I were you,
I would (as surely as God's help I sue)
Cry, "Turn again, ye haughty villains all!
A very pestilence upon you fall!
Now I am come unto the forest's side,
Maugre your heads, the cock shall here abide;
I will him eat, i' faith, and that anon." '
Answered the fox, 'Good sooth, it shall be done!'
And, as he spake the word, all suddenly,
The cock broke from his jaws deliverly,
And high upon a tree he flew anon.
And when the fox saw that the cock was gone,
'Alas! O Chaunticlere, alas!' quoth he,
'I have, 't is true, done you some injury,
In that I made you for a while afeard,
By seizing you from forth your native yard;
But, Sir, I did it with no ill intent;
Come down, and I will tell you what I meant,
God help me as I speak the truth to you!'
'Nay,' quoth the other, 'then, beshrew us two,
But first beshrew myself both blood and bones,
If thou beguile me oftener than once;
Never again shalt thou by flattery
Make me to sing and wink the while mine eye;
For he that winketh, when he most should see,
Deserves no help from Providence, pardie.'

John: So our friend Sir Chaunticlere escapes, after all. The humorous moral of the story is heightened by the cunning Reynard's being foiled with his own weapons. The bare fact of induing animals with speech and other human properties is, in itself, highly ludicrous. Fables always inculcate magnanimity. To see our weaknesses thus palpably bodied forth in their appropriate animal costume brings them down from the false elevation to which their association with ourselves had raised them. The next time we meet them in life, their human disguise drops off, and the ape or the owl takes our own place or that of our friend. That treatise of Baptista Porta's, in which he traces the likeness between men's faces and those of animals, is painful and shocking; but when we casually note a human expression in the countenance of a brute, it is merely laughable. In the former instance, the mind is carried downward, and in the latter upward. To children there is nothing humorous in Æsop. They read his fables as soberly as they afterwards read Scott's novels. The moral is always skipped, as tedious. The honey-bag is all they seek; the sting is of no use, save to the bee. Yet, afterwards, we find that Lucian and Rabelais are dull beside Æsop; and the greater the seeming incongruity, the greater the mirth.

Philip: Chaucer was aware of this, when he put so much pedantry into the mouth of Chaunticlere; and the fox's allusion to Boethius makes me laugh in spite of myself. Chaunticlere's compliment to Dame Partelote, too, where he expresses the intense satisfaction which he feels in observing that

She is so scarlet red about her eyes,

is the keenest of satires upon those lovers who have sung the bodily perfections of their mistresses, and who have set their affections, as it were, upon this year's leaves, to fall off with them at the bidding of the first November blast of fortune. It was a Platonic notion, to which Spenser gave in his allegiance, that a fair spirit always chose a fair dwelling, and beautified it the more by its abiding. It is the sweetest apology ever invented for a physical passion. But I do not like this filching of arrows from heavenly love, to furnish forth the quiver of earthly love

withal. Love is the most hospitable of spirits, and adorns the interior of his home for the nobler welcome, not the exterior for the more lordly show. It is not the outside of his dwelling that invites, but the soft domestic murmur stealing out at the door, and the warm, homely light gushing from the windows. No matter into what hovel of clay he enters, that is straightway the palace, and beauty holds her court in vain. I doubt if Chaucer were conscious of his sarcasm, but I can conceive of no more cutting parody than a sonnet of Chaunticlere's upon his mistress's comb or beak, or other gallinaceous excellency. Imagine him enthusiastic over her sagacity in the hunting of earthworms, and her grace in scratching for them with those toes

White as lilies in the grass,

standing upon one leg as he composed a quatrain upon her tail-feathers, and finally losing himself in the melodious ecstasy of her cackle!

There is certainly, as you have said, something ludicrous in the bare idea of animals indued with human propensities and feelings, and the farther away we get from any physical resemblance, the more keenly moved is our sense of humor. That king-making jelly of the bees strips Nicholas and Victoria of their crowns and ermine, and makes them merely forked radishes, like the rest of us. And when I learned that there was domestic slavery among certain species of the ants, I could not but laugh, as I imagined some hexapodal McDuffie mounted upon a cherry-stone, and convincing a caucus of chivalrous listeners of their immense superiority to some neighbouring hill, whose inhabitants got in their own harvest of bread-crumbs and dead beetles, unaided by that patriarchal machinery.

John: The passage you first read me from the death-scene of Arcite moved me so much, that I cannot help wishing you would read me something more in the same kind.

HENRY DAVID THOREAU
From "Friday"
A Week on the Concord and Merrimack Rivers
1849

What a contrast between the stern and desolate poetry of Ossian and that of Chaucer, and even of Shakespeare and Milton, much more of Dryden, and Pope, and Gray! Our summer of English poetry, like the Greek and Latin before it, seems well advanced toward its fall, and laden with the fruit and foliage of the season, with bright autumnal tints; but soon the winter will scatter its myriad clustering and shading leaves, and leave only a few desolate and fibrous boughs to sustain the snow and rime, and creak in the blasts of ages. We cannot escape the impression that the Muse has stooped a little in her flight when we come to the literature of civilised eras. Now first we hear of various ages and styles of poetry; it is pastoral, and lyric, and narrative, and didactic; but the poetry of runic monuments is of one style, and for every age. The bard has in a great measure lost the dignity and sacredness of his office. Formerly he was called a *seer*, but now it is thought that one man sees as much as another. He has no longer the bardic rage, and only conceives the deed, which he formerly stood ready to perform. Hosts of warriors earnest for battle could not mistake nor dispense with the ancient bard. His lays were heard in the pauses of the fight. There was no danger of his being overlooked by his contemporaries. But now the hero and the bard are of different professions. When we come to the pleasant

English verse, the storms have all cleared away and it will never thunder and lighten more. The poet has come within doors, and exchanged the forest and crag for the fireside, the hut of the Gael, and Stonehenge with its circles of stones, for the house of the Englishman. No hero stands at the door prepared to break forth into song of heroic action, but a homely Englishman, who cultivates the art of poetry. We see the comfortable fireside, and hear the crackling fagots in all the verse.

Notwithstanding the broad humanity of Chaucer, and the many social and domestic comforts which we meet with in his verse, we have to narrow our vision somewhat to consider him, as if he occupied less space in the landscape, and did not stretch over hill and valley as Ossian does. Yet, seen from the side of posterity, as the father of English poetry, preceded by a long silence or confusion in history, unenlivened by any strain of pure melody, we easily come to reverence him. Passing over the earlier continental poets, since we are bound to the pleasant archipelago of English poetry, Chaucer's is the first name after that misty weather in which Ossian lived which can detain us long. Indeed, though he represents so different a culture and society, he may be regarded as in many respects the Homer of the English poets. Perhaps he is the youthfullest of them all. We return to him as to the purest well, the fountain farthest removed from the highway of desultory life. He is so natural and cheerful, compared with later poets, that we might almost regard him as a personification of spring. To the faithful reader his muse has even given an aspect to his times, and when he is fresh from perusing him they seem related to the golden age. It is still the poetry of youth and life rather than of thought; and though the moral vein is obvious and constant, it has not yet banished the sun and daylight from his verse. The loftiest strains of the muse are, for the most part, sublimely plaintive, and not a carol as free as nature's. The content which the sun shines to celebrate from morning to evening is unsung. The muse solaces herself, and is not ravished but consoled. There is a catastrophe implied, and a tragic element in all our verse, and less of the lark and morning dews than of the nightingale and evening shades. But in Homer and Chaucer there is more of the innocence and serenity of youth than in the more modern and moral poets. The *Iliad* is not Sabbath but morning reading, and men cling to this old song because they still have moments of unbaptised and uncommitted life, which give them an appetite for more. To the innocent there are neither cherubim nor angels. At rare intervals we rise above the necessity of virtue into an unchangeable morning light, in which we have only to live right on and breathe the ambrosial air. The Iliad represents no creed nor opinion, and we read it with a rare sense of freedom and irresponsibility, as if we trod on native ground and were autochthones of the soil.

Chaucer had eminently the habits of a literary man and a scholar. There were never any times so stirring that there were not to be found some sedentary still. He was surrounded by the din of arms. The battles of Hallidon Hill and Neville's Cross, and the still more memorable battles of Cressy and Poictiers, were fought in his youth; but these did not concern our poet much, Wickliffe and his reform much more. He regarded himself always as one privileged to sit and converse with books. He helped to establish the literary class. His character as one of the fathers of the English language would alone make his works important, even those which have little poetical merit. He was as simple as Wordsworth in preferring his homely but vigorous Saxon tongue when it was neglected by the court and had not yet attained to the dignity of a literature, and rendered a similar service to his country to that which Dante rendered to Italy. If Greek sufficeth for Greek, and Arabic for Arabian, and Hebrew for Jew, and Latin for Latin, then English shall suffice for him, for any of these will serve to teach truth 'right as divers pathes leaden divers folke the right waye to Rome.' In the *Testament of Love* he writes, 'Let then clerkes enditen in Latin, for they have the propertie of science, and the knowinge in that facultie, and lette Frenchmen in their Frenche also enditen their queinte termes, for it is kyndely to their mouthes, and let us shewe our fantasies in soche wordes as we lerneden of our dames tonge.'

He will know how to appreciate Chaucer best who has come down to him the natural way, through the meagre pastures of Saxon and ante-Chaucerian poetry; and yet, so human and wise he appears after such diet, that we are liable to misjudge him still. In the Saxon poetry extant, in the earliest English, and the contemporary Scottish poetry, there is less to remind the reader of the rudeness and vigour of youth than of the feebleness of a declining age. It is for the most part translation of imitation merely, with only an occasional and slight tinge of poetry, oftentimes the falsehood and exaggeration of fable without its imagination to redeem it, and we look in vain to find antiquity restored, humanised, and made blithe again by some natural sympathy between it and the present. But Chaucer is fresh and modern still, and no dust settles on his true passages. It lightens along the line, and we are reminded that flowers have bloomed, and birds sung, and hearts beaten in England. Before the earnest gaze of the reader the rust and moss of time gradually drop off, and the original green life is revealed. He was a homely and domestic man, and did breathe quite as modern men do.

There is no wisdom that can take place of humanity, and we find *that* in Chaucer. We can expand at last in his breadth, and we think that we could have been that man's acquaintance. He was worthy to be a citizen of England, while Petrarch and Boccacio lived in Italy, and Tell and Tamerlane in Switzerland and Asia, and Bruce in Scotland, and Wickliffe, and Gower, and Edward the Third, and John of Gaunt, and the Black Prince were his own countrymen as well as contemporaries; all stout and stirring names. The fame of Roger Bacon came down from the preceding century, and the name of Dante still possessed the influence of a living presence. On the whole, Chaucer impresses us as greater than his reputation, and not a little like Homer and Shakespeare, for he would have held up his head in their company. Among early English poets he is the landlord and host, and has the authority of such. The affectionate mention which succeeding early poets make of him, coupling him with Homer and Virgil, is to be taken into the account in estimating his character and influence. King James and Dunbar of Scotland speak of him with more love and reverence than any modern author of his predecessors in the last century. The same childlike relation is without a parallel now. For the most part we read him without criticism, for he does not plead his own cause, but speaks for his readers, and has that greatness of trust and reliance which compels popularity. He confides in the reader, and speaks privily with him, keeping nothing back. And in return the reader has great confidence in him, that he tells no lies, and reads his story with indulgence, as if it were the circumlocution of a child, but often discovers afterwards that he has spoken with more directness and economy of words than a sage. He is never heartless,

> For first the thing is thought within the hart,
> Er any word out from the mouth astart.

And so new was all his theme in those days, that he did not have to invent, but only to tell.

We admire Chaucer for his sturdy English wit. The easy height he speaks from in his Prologue to the *Canterbury Tales*, as if he were equal to any of the company there assembled, is as good as any particular excellence in it. But though it is full of good sense and humanity, it is not transcendent poetry. For picturesque description of persons it is, perhaps, without a parallel in English poetry; yet it is essentially humorous, as the loftiest genius never is. Humour, however broad and genial, takes a narrower view than enthusiasm. To his own finer vein he added all the common wit and wisdom of his time, and everywhere in his works his remarkable knowledge of the world, and nice perception of character, his rare common sense and proverbial wisdom, are apparent. His genius does not soar like Milton's, but is genial and familiar. It shows great tenderness and delicacy, but not the heroic sentiment. It is only a greater portion of humanity with all its weakness. He is not heroic, as Raleigh, nor pious, as Herbert, nor philosophical, as Shakespeare; but he is the child of the English muse, that child which is the father of the man. The charm of his poetry consists often only in an exceeding naturalness, perfect sincerity, with the behaviour of a child rather than of a man.

Gentleness and delicacy of character are everywhere apparent in his verse. The simplest and humblest words come readily to his lips. No one can read the Prioress's tale, understanding the spirit in which it was written, and in which the child sings *O alma redemptoris mater*, or the account of the departure of Constance with her child upon the sea, in the Man of Lawe's tale, without feeling the native innocence and refinement of the author. Nor can we be mistaken respecting the essential purity of his character, disregarding the apology of the manners of the age. A simple pathos and feminine gentleness, which Wordsworth only occasionally approaches, but does not equal, are peculiar to him. We are tempted to say that his genius was feminine not masculine. It was such a feminineness, however, as is rarest to find in woman, though not the appreciation of it; perhaps it is not to be found at all in woman, but is only the feminine in man.

Such pure and genuine and childlike love of Nature is hardly to be found in any poet.

Chaucer's remarkably trustful and affectionate character appears in his familiar, yet innocent and reverent, manner of speaking of his God. He comes into his thought without any false reverence, and with no more parade than the zephyr to his ear. If Nature is our mother, then God is our father. There is less love and simple, practical trust in Shakespeare and Milton. How rarely in our English tongue do we find expressed any affection for God! Certainly, there is no sentiment so rare, as the love of God. Herbert almost alone expresses it, 'Ah, my dear God!' Our poet uses similar words with propriety; and whenever he sees a beautiful person, or other object, prides himself on the 'maistry' of his God. He even recommends Dido to be his bride—

> if that God that heaven and yearth made,
> Would have a love for beauty and goodness,
> And womanhede, trouth, and semeliness.

But in justification of our praise, we must refer to his works themselves, to the Prologue to the *Canterbury Tales*, the account of Gentilesse, the Flower and the Leaf, the stories of Griselda, Virginia, Ariadne, and Blanche the Dutchesse, and much more of less distinguished merit. There are many poets of more taste, and better manners, who knew how to leave out their dulness; but such negative genius cannot detain us long; we shall return to Chaucer still with love. Some natures, which are really rude and ill-developed, have yet a higher standard of perfection than others which are refined and well balanced. Even the clown has taste, whose dictates, though he disregards them, are higher and purer than those which the artist obeys. If we have to wander through many dull and prosaic passages in Chaucer, we have at least the satisfaction of knowing that it is not an artificial dulness, but too easily matched by many passages in life. We confess that we feel a disposition commonly to concentrate sweets, and accumulate pleasures; but the poet may be presumed always to speak as a traveller, who leads us through a varied scenery, from one eminence to another, and it is, perhaps, more pleasing, after all, to meet with a fine thought in its natural setting. Surely fate has enshrined it in these circumstances for some end. Nature strews her nuts and flowers broadcast, and never collects them into heaps. This was the soil it grew in, and this the hour it bloomed in; if sun, wind, and rain came here to cherish and expand the flower, shall not we come here to pluck it?

A true poem is distinguished not so much by a felicitous expression, or any thought it suggests, as by the atmosphere which surrounds it. Most have beauty of outline merely, and are striking as the form and bearing of a stranger; but true verses come toward us indistinctly, as the very breath of all friendliness, and envelop us in their spirit and fragrance. Much of our poetry has the very best manners, but no character. It is only an unusual precision and elasticity of speech, as if its author had taken, not an intoxicating draught, but an electuary. It has the distinct outline of sculpture, and chronicles an early hour. Under the influence of passion all men speak thus distinctly, but wrath is not always divine.

There are two classes of men called poets. The one cultivates life, the other art—one seeks food for nutriment, the other for flavour; one satisfies hunger, the other gratifies the palate. There are two kinds of writing, both great and rare: one that of genius, or the inspired, the other of intellect and taste, in the intervals of inspiration. The former is above criticism, always correct, giving the law to criticism. It vibrates and pulsates with life for ever. It is sacred, and to be read with reverence, as the works of nature are studied. There are few instances of a sustained style of this kind; perhaps every man has spoken words, but the speaker is then careless of the record. Such a style removes us out of personal relations with its author; we do not take his words on our lips, but his sense into our hearts. It is the stream of inspiration, which bubbles out, now here, now there, now in this man, now in that. It matters not through what ice-crystals it is seen, now a fountain, now the ocean stream running under ground. It is in Shakespeare, Alpheus, in Burns, Arethuse; but ever the same. The other is self-possessed and wise. It is reverent of genius and greedy of inspiration. It is conscious in the highest and the least degree. It consists with the most perfect command of the faculties. It dwells in a repose as of the desert, and objects are as distinct in it as oases or palms in the horizon of sand. The train of thought moves with subdued and measured step, like a caravan. But the pen is only an instrument in its hand, and not instinct with life, like a longer arm. It leaves a thin varnish or glaze over all its work. The works of Goethe furnish remarkable instances of the latter.

There is no just and serene criticism as yet. Nothing is considered simply as it lies in the lap of eternal beauty, but our thoughts, as well as our bodies, must be dressed after the latest fashions. Our taste is too delicate and particular. It says nay to the poet's work, but never yea to his hope. It invites him to adorn his deformities, and not to cast them off by expansion, as the tree its bark. We are a people who live in a bright light, in houses of pearl and porcelain, and drink only light wines, whose teeth are easily set on edge by the least natural sour. If we had been consulted, the backbone of the earth would have been made, not of granite, but of Bristol spar. A modern author would have died in infancy in a ruder age. But the poet is something more than a scald, 'a smoother and polisher of language'; he is a Cincinnatus in literature, and occupies no west end of the world. Like the sun, he will indifferently select his rhymes, and with a liberal taste weave into his verse the planet and the stubble.

In these old books the stucco has long since crumbled away, and we read what was sculptured in the granite. They are rude and massive in their proportions, rather than smooth and delicate in their finish. The workers in stone polish only their chimney ornaments, but their pyramids are roughly done. There is a soberness in a rough aspect, as of unhewn granite, which addresses a depth in us, but a polished surface hits only the ball of the eye. The true finish is the work of time, and the use to which a thing is put. The elements are still polishing the pyramids. Art may varnish and gild, but it can do no more. A work of genius is rough-hewn from the first, because it anticipates the lapse of time, and has an ingrained polish, which still appears when fragments are broken off, and essential quality of its substance. Its beauty is at the same time its strength, and it breaks with a lustre.

The great poem must have the stamp of greatness as well as its essence. The reader easily goes within the shallowest contemporary poetry, and informs it with all the life and promise of the day, as the pilgrim goes within the temple, and hears the faintest strains of the worshippers; but it will have to speak to posterity, traversing these deserts, through the ruins of its outmost walls, by the grandeur and beauty of its proportions.

LEIGH HUNT
From *Stories in Verse*
1855, pp. 1–19

PREFACE, Containing Remarks on the Father of English Narrative Poetry; On the Ill-Understood Nature of Heroic Verse; On the Necessity, Equally Ill-Understood, of the Musical Element in Poetry to Poetry in General; And on the Absurdity of Confining the Name of Poetry to Any One Species of It in Particular.

As this book, in issuing from the house of Messrs. Routledge, acquires a special chance of coming under the cognizance of travellers by the railway, I have pleased myself with fancying, that it gives me a kind of new link, however remote like the rest, with my great master in the art of poetry; that is to say, with the great master of English narrative in verse, the Father of our Poetry itself, Chaucer.

Nay, it gives me two links, one general, and one particular; for as Chaucer's stories, in default of there being any printed books and travelling carriages in those days, were related by travellers to one another, and as these stories will be read, and (I hope) shown to one another, by travellers who are descendants of those travellers (see how the links thicken as we advance!), so one of Chaucer's stories concerned a wonderful Magic Horse; and now, one of the most wonderful of all such horses will be speeding my readers and me together to all parts of the kingdom, with a fire hitherto unknown to any horse whatsoever.

How would the great poet have been delighted to see the creature!—and what would he not have said of it!

I say 'creature,' because though your fiery Locomotive is a creation of man's, as that of the poet was, yet as the poet's

'wondrous Horse of Brass' was formed out of ideas furnished him by Nature, so, out of elements no less furnished by Nature, and the first secrets of which are no less amazing, has been formed this wonderful Magic Horse of Iron and Steam, which, with vitals of fire, clouds literally flowing from its nostrils, and a bulk, a rushing, and a panting like that of some huge antediluvian wild beast, is now heard and seen in all parts of the country, and in most parts of civilized Europe, breaking up the old grounds of alienation, and carrying with it the seeds of universal brotherhood.

Verily, something even of another, but most grating link, starts up out of that reflection upon the poet's miracle; for the hero who rode his horse of brass made war with Russia; and we Englishmen, the creators of the Horse of Iron, are warring with the despot of the same barbarous country, pitting the indignant genius of civilization against his ruffianly multitudes.

> At Sarra, in the land of Tartariè,
> There dwelt a king that warrièd Russiè,
> Through which there dièd many a doughty man.

Many a doughty man, many a noble heart of captain and of common soldier, has perished in this new war against the old ignorance;—an ignorance, that by its sullen persistence in rejecting the kindly advice of governments brave and great enough to be peaceful, forced the very enthusiasts of peace (myself among the number) into the conviction, that out of hatred and loathing of war itself, war must be made upon him. . . .

Let me take this opportunity of recommending such readers as are not yet acquainted with Chaucer, to make up for their lost time. The advice is not to my benefit, but it is greatly to theirs, and loyalty to him forces me to speak. The poet's 'old English' is no difficulty, if they will but believe it. A little study would soon make them understand it as easily as that of most provincial dialects. Chaucer is the greatest narrative poet in the language; that is to say, the greatest and best teller of stories, in the understood sense of that term. He is greatest in every respect, and in the most opposite qualifications; greatest in pathos, greatest in pleasantry, greatest in character, greatest in plot, greatest even in versification, if the unsettled state of the language in his time, and the want of all native precursors in the art, be considered; for his verse is anything but the rugged and formless thing it has been supposed to be; and if Dryden surpassed him in it, not only was the superiority owing to the master's help, but there were delicate and noble turns and cadences in the old poet, which the poet of the age of Charles the Second wanted spirituality enough to appreciate.

There have been several Chaucers, and Helps to Chaucer, published of late years. Mr. Moxon has printed his entire works in one double-columned large octavo volume; Messrs. Routledge have published the *Canterbury Tales* in a smaller volume, with delicate illustrations by Mr. Corbould, the best (as far as I am aware) that ever came from his pencil; and there is a set of the poet's works now going through the press, more abundant than has yet appeared in commentary and dissertation, in Robert Bell's *Annotated Edition of the English Poets*,—the only collection of the kind in the language, though it has so long been a desideratum. Chaucer's country disgraced itself for upwards of a century by considering the Father of its Poetry as nothing but an obsolete jester. Even poets thought so, in consequence of a prevailing ignorance of nine-tenths of his writings, originating in the gross tastes of the age of Charles the Second. There are passages, it is true, in Chaucer, which for the sake of all parties, persons of thorough delicacy will never read twice; for they were compliances with the licence of an age, in which the court itself, his sphere, was as clownish in some of its tastes as the unqualified admirers of Swift and Prior are now; and the great poet lamented that he had condescended to write them. But by far the greatest portion of his works is full of delicacies of every kind, of the noblest sentiment, of the purest, most various, and most profound entertainment.

Postponing, however, what I have to say further on the subject of Chaucer, it becomes, I am afraid, a little too obviously proper, as well as more politic, to return, in this Preface, to the book of the humblest of his followers. . . .

When I wrote the 'Story of Rimini' which was between the years 1812 and 1815, I was studying versification in the school of Dryden. Masterly as my teacher was, I felt, without knowing it, that there was a want in him, even in versification; and the supply of this want, later in life, I found in his far greater master, Chaucer; for though Dryden's versification is noble, beautiful, and so complete of its kind, that to an ear uninstructed in the metre of the old poet, all comparison between the two in this respect seems out of the question, and even ludicrous, yet the measure in which Dryden wrote not only originated, but attained to a considerable degree of its beauty, in Chaucer; and the old poet's immeasurable superiority in sentiment and imagination, not only to Dryden, but to all, up to a very late period, who have written in the same form of verse, left him in possession of beauties, even in versification, which it remains for some future poet to amalgamate with Dryden's in a manner worthy of both, and so carry England's noble heroic rhyme to its pitch of perfection.

Critics, and poets too, have greatly misconceived the rank and requirements of this form of verse, who have judged it from the smoothness and monotony which it died of towards the close of the last century, and from which nothing was thought necessary for its resuscitation but an opposite unsystematic extreme. A doubt, indeed, of a very curious and hitherto unsuspected, or at least unnoticed nature, may be entertained by inquirers into the musical portion of the art of poetry (for poetry is an art as well as a gift); namely, whether, since the time of Dryden, any poets whatsoever, up to the period above alluded to (and very few indeed have done otherwise since then), thought of versification as a thing necessary to be studied at all, with the exceptions of Gray and Coleridge.

The case remains the same at present; but such assuredly was not the case either with Dryden himself, or with any of the greater poets before him, the scholarly ones in particular, such as Spenser, Milton, and their father Chaucer, who was as learned as any of them for the time in which he lived, and well acquainted with metres, French, Latin, and Italian.

Poets less reverent to their art, out of a notion that the gift, in their instance, is of itself sufficient for all its purposes, (which is much as if a musician should think he could do without studying thorough-bass, or a painter without studying drawing and colours,) trust to an ear which is often not good enough to do justice to the amount of gift which they really possess; and hence comes a loss, for several generations together, of the whole musical portion of poetry, to the destruction of its beauty in tone and in movement, and the peril of much good vitality in new writers. For proportions, like all other good things, hold together; and he that is wanting in musical feeling where music is required, is in danger of being discordant and disproportionate in sentiment, of not perceiving the difference between thoughts worthy and unworthy of utterance. It is for this reason among others, that he pours forth "crotchets" in abundance, not in unison with his theme, and wanting in harmony with one another.

There is sometimes a kind of vague and (to the apprehension of the unmusical) senseless melody, which in lyrical compositions, the song in particular, really constitutes, in the genuine poetical sense of the beautiful, what the scorner of it says it falsely and foolishly constitutes—namely, a good half of its merit. It answers to variety and expression of tone in a beautiful voice, and to 'air,' grace, and freedom in the movements of a charming person. The Italians, in their various terms for the beautiful, have a word for it precisely answering to the first feeling one has in attempting to express it—*vago*,—vague; something wandering, fluctuating, undefinable, undetainable, moving hither and thither at its own sweet will and pleasure, in accordance with what it feels. It overdoes nothing and falls short of nothing; for itself is nothing but the outward expression of an inward grace. You perceive it in all genuine lyrical compositions, of whatever degree, and indeed in all compositions that sing or speak with true musical impulse, in whatsoever measure, in the effusions of Burns, of Ben Jonson, of Beaumont and Fletcher, of Allan Ramsay, of Metastasio, of Coleridge; and again in those of Dryden, of Spenser, of Chaucer, of Ariosto; in poems however long, and in passages however seemingly unlyrical; for it is one of the popular, and I am afraid, generally speaking, critical mistakes, in regard to rhymed verse, that in narrative and heroic poems there is nothing wanting to the music, provided the line or the couplet be flowing, and the general impression not rude or weak; whereas the best couplet, however admirable in itself and worthy of quotation, forms but one link in the chain of the music to which it belongs. Poems of any length must consist of whole strains of couplets, whole sections and successions of them, brief or prolonged, all as distinct from one another and complete in themselves, as the *adagios* and *andantes* of symphonies and sonatas, each commencing in the tone and obvious spirit of commencement, proceeding through as great a variety of accents, stops, and pauses, as the notes and phrases of any other musical composition, and coming at an equally fit moment to a close.

Enough stress has never yet been laid on the analogies between musical and poetical composition. All poetry used formerly to be sung; and poets still speak of 'singing' what they write. Petrarch used to 'try his sonnets on the lute'; that is to say, to examine them in their musical relations, in order to see how they and musical requirement went together; and a chapter of poetical narrative is called to this day a canto, or chant. Every distinct section or paragraph of a long poem ought to form a separate, interwoven, and varied melody; and every very short poem should, to a fine ear, be a still more obvious melody of the same sort, in order that its brevity may contain as much worth as is possible, and show that the poet never forgets the reverence due to his art.

I have sometimes thought that if Chaucer could have heard compositions like those of Coleridge's *Christabel*, he might have doubted whether theirs was not the best of all modes and measures for reducing a narrative to its most poetic element, and so producing the quintessence of a story. And for stories not very long, not very substantial in their adventures, and of a nature more imaginary than credible, so they might be. But for narrative poetry in general, for epic in particular, and for stories of any kind that are deeply to affect us as creatures of flesh and blood and human experience, there is nothing for a sustained and serious interest comparable with our old heroic measure, whether in blank verse or rhyme, in couplet or in stanza. An epic poem written in the *Christabel*, or any other brief lyrical measure, would acquire, in the course of perusal, a comparative tone of levity, an air of too great an airiness. The manner would turn to something like not being in earnest, and the matter resemble a diet made all of essences. We should miss *pièces de resistance,* and the homely, but sacred pabulum of 'our daily bread.' You could as soon fancy a guitar put in place of a church organ, as an *Iliad* or *Paradise Lost* written in that manner. You would associate with it no tone of Scripture, nothing of the religious solemnity which Chaucer has so justly been said to impart to his pathetic stories. When poor Griselda, repudiated by her husband, and about to return to her father's cottage, puts off the clothes which she had worn as the consort of a great noble, she says,—

> Thus with hir fader for a certain space
> Dwelleth this flowr of wifly pacience,
> That neither by hir wordes ne hir face,
> Biforn the folk, ne eek in hir absence,
> Ne shewed she that hire was doon offence,
> Ne of hir hye estaat no remembrance
> Ne hadde she, as by hir countenaunce.
>
> No wonder is, for in hir grete estat
> Hir gost was evere in plein humilitee:
> No tendre mouth, noon herte delicat,
> No pompe, no semblant of royaltee.

This quotation from the Bible would have been injured by a shorter measure.

Griselda, in words most proper and affecting, but which cannot so well be quoted, apart from the entire story, goes on to say, that she must not deprive of every one of its clothes the body which had been made sacred by motherhood. She tells the father of her children, that it is not fit she should be seen by the people in that condition.

> —Wherefore I you pray,
> *Let me not like a worm go by the way.*

This is one of the most imploring and affecting lines that ever were written. It is also most beautifully modulated, though not at all after the fashion of the once all in all 'smooth' couplet. But the masterly accents throughout it, particularly the emphasis on 'worm,' would have wanted room, and could have made no such earnest appeal, in a measure of less length and solemnity.

Irony itself gains by this measure. There is no sarcasm in *Hudibras,* exquisite as its sarcasm is, comparable for energy of tone and manner with Dryden's denunciation (I do not say just denunciation) of every species of priest. . . .

I have dwelt more than is customary on this musical portion of the subject of poetry, for two reasons: first, because, as I have before intimated, it has a greater connexion than is commonly thought, both with the spiritual and with the substantial portions of the art; and second, because, as I have asserted, and am prepared to show, versification, or the various mode of uttering that music, has been neglected among us to a degree which is not a little remarkable, considering what an abundance of poets this country has produced.

England, it is true, is not a musical country; at any rate not yet, whatever its new trainers may do for it. But it is a very poetical country, *minus* this requisite of poetry; and it seems strange that the deficit should be corporately, as well as nationally characteristic. It might have been imagined, that superiority in the one respect would have been accompanied by superiority in the other;—that they who excelled the majority of their countrymen in poetical perception, would have excelled them in musical. Is the want the same as that which has made us inferior to other great nations in the art of painting? Are we geographically, commercially, statistically, or how is it, that we are less gifted than other nations with those perceptions of the pleasurable, which qualify people to excel as painters

and musicians? It is observable, that our poetry, compared with that of other countries, is deficient in animal spirits.

At all events, it is this ignorance of the necessity of the whole round of the elements of poetry for the production of a perfect poetical work, and the non-perception, at the same time, of the two-fold fact, that there is no such work in existence, and that the absence of no single element of poetry hinders the other elements from compounding a work truly poetical of its kind, which at different periods of literature produce so many defective and peremptory judgments respecting the exclusive right of this or that species of poetry to be called poetry. In Chaucer's time, there were probably Chaucerophilists who would see no poetry in any other man's writing. Sir Walter Raleigh, nevertheless, who, it might be supposed, would have been an enthusiastic admirer of the Knight's and Squire's Tales, openly said, that he counted no English poetry of any value but that of Spenser. In Cowley's time, 'thinking' was held to be the all in all of poetry: poems were to be crammed full of thoughts, otherwise intellectual activity was wanting; and hence, nothing was considered poetry, in the highest sense of the term, that did not resemble the metaphysics of Cowley. His 'language of the heart,' which has survived them, went comparatively for nothing. When the Puritans brought sentiment into discredit, nothing was considered comparable, in any species of poetry, with the noble music and robust sensuous perception of Dryden. Admirable poet as he was, he was thought then, and long afterwards, to be far more admirable,—indeed, the sole

> Great high-priest of all the Nine.

Then 'sense' became the all in all; and because Pope wrote a great deal of exquisite sense, adorned with wit and fancy, he was pronounced, and long considered, literally, the greatest poet that England had seen. A healthy breeze from the unsophisticate region of the Old English Ballads suddenly roused the whole poetical elements into play, restoring a sense of the combined requisites of imagination, of passion, of simple speaking, of music, of animal spirits, &c., not omitting, of course, the true thinking which all sound feeling implies; and though, with the prevailing grave tendency of the English muse, some portions of these poetical requisites came more into play than others, and none of our poets, either since or before, have combined them all as Chaucer and Shakspeare did, yet it would as ill become poets or critics to ignore any one of them in favour of exclusive pretensions on the part of any others, as it would to say, that all the music, and animal spirits, and comprehensiveness might be taken out of those two wonderful men, and they remain just what they were.

To think that there can be no poetry, properly so called, where there is anything 'artificial,' where there are conventionalisms of style, where facts are simply related without obviously imaginative treatment, or where manner, for its own sake, is held to be a thing of any account in its presentation of matter, is showing as limited a state of critical perception as that of the opposite conventional faction, who can see no poetry out of the pale of received forms, classical associations, or total subjections of spiritual to material treatment. It is a case of imperfect sympathy on both sides;—of incompetency to discern and enjoy in another what they have no corresponding tendency to in themselves. It is often a complexional case; perhaps always so, more or less: for writers and critics, like all other human creatures, are physically as well as morally disposed to be what they become. It is the entire man that writes and thinks, and not merely the head. His leg has often as much to do with it as his head;—the state of his calves, his vitals, and his nerves.

There is a charming line in Chaucer:—
> Uprose the sun, and uprose Emily.

Now here are two simple matters of fact, which happen to occur simultaneously. The sun rises, and the lady rises at the same time. Well, what is there in that, some demanders of imaginative illustration will say? Nothing, answers one, but an hyperbole. Nothing, says another, but a conceit. It is a mere commonplace turn of gallantry, says a third. On the contrary, it is the reverse of all this. It is pure morning freshness, enthusiasm, and music. Writers, no doubt, may repeat it till it becomes a commonplace, but that is another matter. Its first sayer, the great poet, sees the brightest of material creatures, and the beautifulest of human creatures, rising at dawn at the same time. He feels the impulse strong upon him to do justice to the appearance of both; and with gladness in his face, and music on his tongue, repeating the accent on a repeated syllable, and dividing the *rhythm* into two equal parts, in order to leave nothing undone to show the merit on both sides, and the rapture of his impartiality, he utters, for all time, his enchanting record.

Now it requires animal spirits, or a thoroughly loving nature, to enjoy that line completely; and yet, on looking well into it, it will be found to contain (by implication) simile, analogy, and, indeed, every other form of imaginative expression, apart from that of direct illustrative words; which, in such cases, may be called needless commentary. The poet lets nature speak for herself. He points to the two beautiful objects before us, and is content with simply hailing them in their combination.

In all cases where Nature should thus be left to speak for herself (and they are neither mean nor few cases, but many and great) the imaginative faculty, which some think to be totally suspended at such times, is, on the contrary, in full activity, keeping aloof all irrelevancies and impertinence, and thus showing how well it understands its great mistress. When Lady Macbeth says she should have murdered Duncan herself,

> Had he not resembled
> Her father as he slept,

she said neither more nor less than what a poor criminal said long afterwards, and quite unaware of the passage, when brought before a magistrate from a midnight scuffle in a barge on the Thames;—'I should have killed him, if he had not looked so like my father while he was sleeping.' Shakspeare made poetry of the thought by putting it into verse,—into modulation; but he would not touch it otherwise. He reverenced Nature's own simple, awful, and sufficing suggestion too much, to add a syllable to it for the purpose of showing off his subtle powers of imaginative illustration. And with no want of due reverence to Shakspeare be it said, that it is a pity he did not act invariably with the like judgment;—that he suffered thought to crowd upon thought, where the first feeling was enough. So, what can possibly be imagined simpler, finer, completer, less wanting anything beyond itself, than the line in which poor old Lear, unable to relieve himself with his own trembling fingers, asks the byestander to open his waistcoat for him,—not forgetting, in the midst of his anguish, to return him thanks for so doing, like a gentleman:

> Pray you undo this button—Thank you, Sir.

The poet here presents us with two matters of fact, in their simplest and apparently most prosaical form; yet, when did ever passion or imagination speak more intensely? and this, purely because he has let them alone?

There is another line in Chaucer, which seems to be still plainer matter of fact, with no imagination in it of any kind, apart from the simple necessity of imagining the fact itself. It is in the story of the Tartar king, which Milton wished to have had completed. The king has been feasting, and is moving from the feast to a ballroom:

> Before him goeth the loud minstrelsy.

Now, what is there in this line (it might be asked) which might not have been said in plain prose? which indeed is not prose? The king is preceded by his musicians, playing loudly. What is there in that?

Well, there is something even in that, if the prosers who demand so much help to their perceptions could but see it. But verse fetches it out and puts it in its proper state of movement. The line itself, being a line of verse, and therefore a musical movement, becomes processional, and represents the royal train in action. The word 'goeth,' which a less imaginative writer would have rejected in favour of something which he took to be more spiritual and uncommon, is the soul of the continuity of the movement. It is put, accordingly, in its most emphatic place. And the word 'loud' is suggestive at once of royal power, and of the mute and dignified serenity, superior to that manifestation of it, with which the king follows.

> *Before* him goeth the loud minstrelsy.

Any reader who does not recognise the stately 'go,' and altogether noble sufficingness of that line, may rest assured that thousands of the beauties of poetry will remain for ever undiscovered by him, let him be helped by as many thoughts and images as he may.

So in a preceding passage where the same musicians are mentioned.

> And so befell, that after the third course,
> While that this King sat thus in his nobley,—
> [nobleness]
> Hearing his minstrallés their thingés play
> Before him at his board deliciously,
> In at the hallé–door all suddenly
> There came a knight upon a steed of brass,
> And in his hand a broad mirror of glass;
> Upon his thumb he had of gold a ring,
> And by his side a naked sword hanging,
> And up he rideth to the highé board.—
> In all the hallé n'as there spoke a word [*was not*]
> For marvel of this knight—Him to behold
> Full busily they waited; young and old.

In some of these lines, what would otherwise be prose, becomes, by the musical feeling, poetry. The king, 'sitting in his nobleness,' is an imaginative picture. The word 'deliciously' is a venture of animal spirits, which, in a modern writer, some critics would pronounce to be affected, or too familiar; but the enjoyment, and even incidental appropriateness and *relish* of it, will be obvious to finer senses. And in the pause in the middle of the last couplet but one, and that in the course of the first line of its successor, examples were given by this supposed unmusical old poet, of some of the highest refinements of versification.

The secret of musical, as of all other feeling, lies in the depths of the harmonious adjustments of our nature; and a chord touched in any one of them, vibrates with the rest. In the Queen's beautiful letter to Mr. Sidney Herbert, about the sufferers in the Crimea, the touching words, 'those poor noble wounded and sick men,' would easily, and with perfectly poetical sufficiency, flow into verse. Chaucer, with his old English dissyllable, *poorĕ,* (more piteous, because lingering in the sound) would have found in them a verse ready made to his hand—

Those poorĕ noble wounded and sick men.

The passage is in fact just like one of his own verses, sensitive, earnest, strong, simple, full of truth, full of harmonious sympathy. Many a manly eye will it moisten; many a poor soldier, thus acknowledged to be a 'noble,' will it pay for many a pang. What, if transferred to verse, would it need from any other kind of imaginative treatment? What, indeed, could it receive but injury? And yet, to see what is said by the demanders, on every possible poetical occasion, of perpetual commentating thoughts and imaginative analogies, one must conclude that they would pronounce it to be wholly unfit for poetry, unless something very fine were added about 'poor,' something very fine about 'noble,' something very fine about 'wounded,' and something very fine about 'sick;' a process by which our sympathy with the suffering heroes would come to nothing, in comparison with our astonishment at the rhetoric of the eulogizers,—which, indeed, is a 'consummation' that writers of this description would seem to desire.

Of all the definitions which have been given of poetry, the best is that which pronounces it to be 'geniality, singing.' I think, but am not sure, that it is Lamb's; perhaps it is Coleridge's. I had not seen it, or, if I had, had lost all recollection of it, when I wrote the book called 'Imagination and Fancy'; otherwise I would have substituted it for the definition given in that book; for it comprehends, by implication, all which is there said respecting the different classes and degrees of poetry, and excludes, at the same time, whatsoever does not properly come within the limits of the thing defined.

Geniality, thus considered, is not to be understood in its common limited acceptation of a warm and flowing spirit of companionship. It includes that and every other motive to poetic utterance, but it resumes its great primal meaning of the power of productiveness; that power from which the word Genius is derived, and which falls in so completely with the meaning of the word Poet itself, which is Maker. The poet makes, or produces, because he has a desire to do so; and what he produces is found to be worthy, in proportion as time shows a desire to retain it. As all trees are trees, whatever be the different degrees of their importance, so all poets are poets whose productions have a character of their own, and take root in the ground of national acceptance. The poet sings, because he is excited, and because whatsoever he does must be moulded into a shape of beauty. If imagination predominates in him, and it is of the true kind, and he loves the exercise of it better than the fame, he stands a chance of being a poet of the highest order, but not of the only order. If fancy predominates, and the fancy is of the true kind, he is no less a poet in kind, though inferior in degree. If thought predominate, he is a contemplative poet: if a variety of these faculties in combination, he is various accordingly; less great, perhaps, in each individually, owing to the divided interest which he takes in the claim upon his attention; but far greater, if equally great in all. Nevertheless, he does not hinder his less accomplished brethren from being poets. There is a talk of confining the appellation poet, to the inspired poet. But who and what is the inspired poet? Inspired means 'breathed into;' that is to say, by some superior influence. But how is not Dryden breathed into as well as Chaucer? Milton as well as Shakspeare? or Pope as well as Milton? The flute, though out of all comparison with the organ, is still an instrument 'breathed into.' The only question is, whether it is breathed into finely, and so as to render it a flute extraordinary; whether the player is a man of genius after his kind, not to be mechanically made. You can no more make a Burns than a Homer; no more the author of a *Rape of the Lock* than the author of *Paradise Lost*. If you could, you would have Burnses as plentiful as blackberries and as many *Rapes of the Lock* as books of mightier pretension, that are for ever coming out and going into oblivion. Meantime, the *Rape of the Lock* remains, and why? Because it is an inspired poem; a poem as truly inspired by the genius of wit and fancy, as the gravest and grandest that ever was written was inspired by passion and imagination.

This is the secret of a great, national, book-reading fact, the existence of which has long puzzled exclusives in poetry; to wit, the never-failing demand in all civilized countries for successive publications of bodies of collected verse, called English or British Poets, Italian Poets, French Poets, Spanish Poets, &c.—collections which stand upon no ceremony whatever with exclusive predilections, but tend to include every thing that has attained poetical repute, and are generally considered to be what they ought to be in proportion as they are copious. Poetasters are sometimes admitted for poets; and poets are sometimes missed, because they have been taken for poetasters. But, upon the whole, the chance of excess is preferred: and the preference is well founded; for the whole system is founded on a judicious instinct. Feelings are nature's reasons; communities often feel better than individuals reason; and they feel better in this instance.

H. SIMON
"Chaucer a Wicliffite"
Essays on Chaucer
1868–94, pp. 229–46

Notwithstanding the immense amount of work done, from the days of Caxton down to our own time, for the study of the second greatest English poet, and in spite of the meritorious publications of *Tyrwhitt, Warton, Sir Harris Nicolas, Bradshaw, Furnivall, Ten-Brink,* and others, many a problem concerning him remains still unsolved, and—considering the want of sure information about his life, and the fragmentary state in which we possess his principal work—this is not to be wondered at.

One of the questions to which no satisfactory answer has yet been given is: *What was Chaucer's relation to the Church?*

In commenting on Speght's *Life of Chaucer* Tyrwhitt (*Introd. Disc.*[1]) speaking of the preface to the *Plowman's Tale,* makes the following remark: "Though he (Chaucer) and Boccace have laughed at some of the abuses of religion and the disorders of Ecclesiastical persons, it is quite incredible that either of them, or even Wicliff himself, would have railed at the whole government of the Church, in the style of the *Plowman's Tale.* If they had been disposed to such an attempt, their times would not have borne it; but it is probable that Chaucer, though he has been pressed into the service of Protestantism by some zealous writers, was as good a Catholic as men of his understanding and rank in life have generally been. The necessity of auricular Confession, one of the great scandals of Popery, cannot be more strongly inculcated than it is in the following *Persones Tale.*" Professor *Seeley*[2] believes that the Plowman of the *Prologue* is, or is founded on, the ideal Piers Plowman; but with regard to Chaucer's relation to the Church, all the principal English Chaucerians seem to share Tyrwhitt's opinion. Of course, nobody can help perceiving the strong contrast between the *Parson's Tale* and Chaucer's well-known enmity against the clergy, as shown in many parts of the *Canterbury Tales,* but it has not, as yet, given rise to any suspicion, the generally accepted opinion being that Chaucer, bowed down by poverty, age, and infirmity, made his peace with the

Church; and Mr Furnivall suggests that he got the lease of the little house in the garden of St Mary's chapel, Westminster, as a reward for his penitence and the *Parson's Tale*. I cannot help doubting this. An engraving of the lease has been published by the Society of Antiquaries. The monk Robert Hermodesworth, who was keeper of St Mary's, and made the contract with the consent of the abbot and convent, reserved a rent of £2 13s. 4d.,—but this was, I imagine, a high rent for a little house, at that time, when money had ten times more value than now[3],—and he expressly reserved for himself, or the monastery, the ordinary power in leases, to distrain, if Chaucer should be in arrear with any part of the payment of rent for the space of 15 days[4]. Does that look like a reward?

A prominent German scholar, Professor *Pauli*, seems to hold an opinion opposed to that stated above. In his *Bilder aus Altenland* (VII. 209) he says that the great political and religious questions of his time didn't puzzle Chaucer like his friend Gower, or drive him to the opposite extreme; that, on the contrary, he saw perfectly clearly, and endeavoured to treat these questions objectively, according to his nature. The American Reed[5] says that Chaucer greeted Wicliffe's work of reform with joy; Gätschenberger[6] unconditionally calls him Wicliffe's intimate friend;—I don't know his reasons; to my direct inquiry I received no answer. Ebert, Kissner, and Hertzberg have, to my knowledge, not examined this point; Ten-Brink has not yet given his opinion; of his excellent *Chaucerstudien* only one volume is out.

To get at the truth, we must first recollect what was the public opinion in England, in the second half of the 14th century, with regard to the Pope and the Church. The reign of Edward III., in which Chaucer's youth and early manhood fell, is one of the grandest and most glorious periods in English history. During the preceding 300 years the gifted Normans had been completely amalgamated with the morally noble and bodily powerful Anglo-Saxons, and the nation thus grown into existence offered a rare image of health and strength[7]. A lively consciousness of their belonging to one another—which expressed itself in the common use of a rich and powerful, though still somewhat unwieldy, language,—had taken the place of the former hatred between the conqueror and the conquered, and, in consequence of the exercise of constitutional rights for above a hundred years, the brilliant victories in France, Spain, and Italy, the fast growing culture, the development of arts, and the increase of wealth produced by commerce, had intensified itself into a strong national feeling, into a high, but justified, self-esteem. In such times of spiritual and material progress, new ideas irresistibly make their way, overthrowing everything opposed to the general tendency—however venerable may be the traditions upon which it is founded. It was a time like that we have now in Germany; and even as the conflict with Popery has now broken out with us, so did it then rage in England; only much more furiously, because the bull *Unam sanctam* had soon been followed by the "Babylonian Exile"; the immoderate pretension of the popes, depending, as they did, on England's deadly foe, could not but be doubly felt, and the awful moral depravity of all the clergy, as well as the great Schism, must at last have filled the whole nation with contempt.

The general abhorrence vented itself in poems like the *Vision of Piers Plowman*, in the writings of Wicliffe, in Chaucer's *Canterbury Tales*. When, in this immortal work, we see Chaucer pour the biting acid of his satire on the representatives of Rome, and especially the friars, he most decidedly appears as the second and avenger of him who in his pamphlet *De otio et mendacitate*[8] had mercilessly exposed the foulest sore of the Roman Church. All the clerical and semi-clerical pilgrims are made to feel his weighty scourge; the only[9] exception—a brilliant one—is

The Parson

By the side of the repulsive characters of the friars and clergy and their officials, the Parson of the *Prologue* appears like a bright figure of sublime beauty. Nobody, perhaps, has read this delicate yet pithy picture without emotion; hundreds of times the Parson has been quoted as the ideal of Christian charity and humility, evangelical piety, unselfish resignation to the high calling of a pastor.

It cannot be that Chaucer unintentionally produced this bright image with so dark a background. Involuntarily it occurs to us, as to former critics, that a Wicliffite, perhaps the great reformer himself, sat for the picture; and the more we look at it, the more striking becomes the likeness. This observation is not new; to say nothing of English critics, *Pauli* (Bilder, VII. 202) says that the likeness of the Parson has decidedly Lollardish traces, and *Lechler* (Iohann von Wiclif, I. 408 ff.) expressly declares it to be Wicliffe's portrait, though he says, at the same time, that it is not only doubtful, but improbable, that Chaucer should have sympathized with, or really appreciated, Wicliffe's great ideas of and efforts for reform. Both scholars, however, principally refer to the description in the *General Prologue*; but the Parson is mentioned also in the *Shipman's* prologue and in that to the *Parson's Tale*; and it is exactly in the latter two that we find the most striking proofs of his unquestionably Wicliffite character.

The General Prologue

as a whole, and its description of the Parson, are the best-known parts of the *Canterbury Tales*. I can, therefore, be brief about it.

In three passages it is stated with great emphasis that the Parson took his doctrine from the gospel:

> v. 481. That Cristes gospel gladly[10] wolde preche.
> v. 498. Out of the gospel he tho wordes caughte.
> v. 527. But Cristes lore, and his apostles twelve
> He taught, and ferst he folwed it himselve.

This was a pointedly distinguishing characteristic of a Wicliffite; for the gospel was the foundation-stone of their doctrine and sermons. Wicliffe himself was indefatigable in drawing general attention to it[11]; he and his associates translated the Bible; with this sword and shield the great "Dr Evangelicus" attacked the Roman dogmas and statutes, and refuted the accusation of heresy; while the orthodox Catholic clergy never allowed the Scripture to be looked upon as the only source of Christian truth, and, especially in Chaucer's time, mostly moved on the barren sands of subtle scholastic theology. In their sermons, instead of preaching the gospel, they frequently amused their hearers by telling fables, romances, and jests.

Moreover, the Parson was a holy man; he made the gospel, as we know from v. 528, his rule of thought and life. The whole prologue proves it; I only quote two more passages:

> v. 479. But riche he was of holy thought and werk.
> v. 505. And though he holy were, and vertuous,

Wicliffe and his disciples distinguished themselves by an irreproachable life; even their worst enemies were obliged to acknowledge that. How very different were the orthodox clergy in this point! The secular clergy, indeed, were better than the monks, but it was exactly among them that Wicliffe found many most zealous followers, and out of their number he recruited his itinerant preachers[12].

v. 480 brings a new characteristic:

He was also a lerned man, a clerk.
Wicliffe and his school did not indulge in the illusion that learning was unnecessary for holy purposes; they loved and cherished it; in the ranks of their antagonists reigned incapacity and ignorance.

Finally we have a peculiar outward mark:

> v. 495. Uppon his feet, and in his hond a staf.

A chronicler of those times, Knighton, a prebendary of Leicester, says that the Wicliffite Aston "vehiculum equorum non requisivit, sed *pedestris effectus cum baculo incedens* ubique ecclesias regni—indefesse cursitando visitavit, ubique in ecclesiis regni praedicans."—*Hist. angl. Scriptores*, X. London, 1652, vol. III. col. 2658 f. (in Lechler, I. 421, Note). Th. Walsingham describes the associates of Wicliffe, "talaribus indutos vestibus de ruseto, insignum perfectionis amplioris, *incedens nudis pedibus*, qui suos errores in populo ventilarent et palam ac publice in suis sermonibus praedicarent."—*Hist. angl.*, ed. Riley, 1863, I. 324 (ibid.). And Pauli says (Bilder, VII. 243) that Archbishop *Courtenay* in 1382, after Wat Tyler's insurrection, when trying to pass the bill against heretics, expressly stated in his speech in parliament, that the Wicliffite itinerant clergy walked about in plain apparel of coarse reddish cloth, *barefoot* and *staff in hand*.

This contradicts at the same time the assumption that Wicliffe himself had been the Parson's prototype; for it was no peculiarity of his to walk about on foot and with a staff; in fact, he never was "a pore Persoun" (v. 478), for the King's favour amply provided for his wants.

The Shipman's Prologue

proves plainly that the Parson was a Wicliffite. When he earnestly, and yet mildly, rebukes the host for taking the Lord's name in vain, Henry Bailey exclaims derisively,

> v. 10. . . . . O Iankyn be ye there?
> Now, goode men, . . . herkneth me;
> I smel a *loller* in the wind,

and as the Parson makes no reply, he repeats the invective with a new oath, as if to try if he would put up with it:

> v. 13. Abideth for Goddes digne passion,
> For we schul have a predicacion;
> *This loller* heer wol[de] prechen us somwhat.

He does not "smell a loller" only, he sees him now, points him out! Even now the Parson remains silent. This silence speaks very plainly. For the nickname applied to him was in those times as generally used for "Wicliffite," as now, for instance, "quaker" is for a member of the Society of Friends[13]. The heaviest charge imaginable that could be brought against any priest had been thrown in the Parson's face: He was branded as a heretic!

For an orthodox clergyman it would have been impossible to put up with this epithet; even the most peaceful and long-suffering must have resented it, if only for the sake of the laymen who witnessed the scene, and who would, in consequence of it, have been able to cite the example of an heretical priest as an excuse for their own heresy. But the Parson remained silent. Here we may alter the proverb: *Qui tacet consentire videtur*, and say: *Qui tacet consentit*, or in ordinary English phrase, "Silence gives consent."

There can be no doubt, I think, that the Shipman was of the same opinion, as we may see by

> v. 16. 'Nay by my father soule! that schal he nat,'
> Sayde the Schipman[14]; 'heer schal he naught preche,
> He schal no gospel glosen heer ne teche.

We levyn al in the gret God,' quod he.
'He wolde sowen som difficulte,
Or springen cokkil[15] in our clene corn.'

Three times he protests energetically against the Lollard's expected sermon[16], against his 'gospel glosing,' that would only disturb the peaceful harmony of the pilgrims (or the conformity of their faith). With the skilful remark "We levyn al in the gret God," and the decided declaration that he himself is going to tell a tale now, he prevents the pending quarrel.

Who used to 'glose' on the gospel in those times? Who grounded on it a doctrine differing from that of the Church, and which was sure to produce the most violent disputes, as soon as it was pronounced before orthodox ears? Who else but the Wicliffites?

The Parson's Prologue

at last removes all doubt. The host, who only a short time before used very passionate language against the Monk, and spoke "with rude speech and bold" to the Nonne-priest, behaves very respectfully to the Parson. Not till all the other pilgrims have told their tales, and then in a conciliatory manner, does he ask him:

> v. 20. I pray to God to yeve him right good chaunce,
> That tellith us his tale lustily.

Had the quiet dignity of the Lollard made an impression upon him, or had he been struck by the idea that a religious persuasion enabling to suffer insults so quietly, could not be quite objectionable? 'Sir prest,' he says, perhaps still somewhat in doubt, owing to the Parson's peculiar dress,

> v. 22. . . . . .artow a vicory?
> Or artow a persoun[17]? say soth, by thy fay.

Perhaps he thought he might yet have done the Parson wrong, and was anxious to give him an opportunity to clear himself of the suspicion of heresy by explaining his real station. But the Parson did not avail himself of the opportunity. What could he have said? Tell an untruth he would not; and to declare himself a Wicliffite in this society would have been neither safe nor advisable. The host, however, instead of growing impatient, as was his wont, passes over this painful silence, saying: "Be what thou be, ne breke thou nought oure play" (v. 24); he even flatters him:

> v. 27. For trewely me thinketh by thy chier,
> Thou scholdist wel knyt up a gret matier.

Chaucer couldn't have paid more delicate homage to the Lollard, nor shown more forcibly the powerful influence of the Wicliffite preachers over the minds of others, than by the effect which the dignified bearing of the Parson had upon this unlicked cub of an innkeeper who had clumsily trodden on the corns of all the other tale-tellers, and even now could not quite renounce his innate coarseness. The Host asks for a fable. Now, at last, the Parson bursts out:

> v. 31. Thou getist fable noon i-told for me,
> For Poul, that writeth unto Timothé,
> Repreveth hem that weyveth sothfastnesse,
> And tellen fables, and such wrecchednesse.
>
> 35. Why schuld I sowen draf out of my fest,
> Whan I may sowe whete, if that me lest?
> For which I say, if that yow lust to hiere
> Moralité and vertuous matiere,
> And thanne that ye will yeve me audience,
>
> 40. I wot ful fayn at Cristis reverence
> Do yow plesaunce leful, as I can.
> But trusteth wel, I am a suthern man,
> I can not gestë, rum, ram, ruf, by letter,
> Ne, God wot, rym hold I but litel better.

45. And therfor, if yow lust, I wol not glose,
    I wol yow telle a mery tale in prose,
    To knyt up al this fest, and make an ende;
    And Ihesu, for his gracë, wit me sende
    To schewë yow the way, in this viage,
50. Of thilkë parfyt glorious pilgrimage
    That hatte Ierusalem celestial.

To understand the whole weight of these words, we must
read what Lechler (I. von W., I. 395 ff.) says about the
Wicliffites' manner of preaching, as opposed to that of the
Romish priests. Instead of preaching the word of God, the
latter used to tell episodes from universal, or pieces of natural,
history, the *Gesta Romanorum*, all sorts of legends, romances,
and fables, from profane sources, as Ovid's *Metamorphoses*,
sometimes even jokes, for the amusement, if not for the edification, of their hearers. The form of these sermons was as
worldly as their contents, verses in alliteration and in rhyme
alternating with each other. This sort of preaching Wicliffe
denounced with all the fervour of his pious, evangelical heart,
with all the power of his mighty word. . . .

Condemning . . . strictly the "fables and such wrecchednesse" told by the clerical pilgrims; choosing for his "meditacioun" the same subject that Wicliffe treated in his "Wicket";
following, as to form and contents, the rules given by Wicliffe
in a hundred passages of his works; and doing all this not only
in the spirit and manner, but partly with the very words, of the
great reformer[18], the Parson, in my opinion, *declares himself as
unequivocally to be à Wicliffite, as it was possible to do without
using the name.*

One essential point, however, is still to be mentioned: the
Parson's citing the epistles of St Paul to Timothy in vindication
of his refusal to tell a fable. In this condemnation, seemingly
directed only against the tales of the clerical pilgrims, he, by
this allusion, strikes the whole Roman Church a blow as with a
club. For in no other part of the Bible do we find such emphatic, nay, imploring exhortations to cling to the gospel; nowhere is the necessity of the clergy's leading a holy life so
forcibly urged; nowhere are the false doctrines and ecclesiastical statutes, as they were afterwards smuggled into Christianity from Rome, more decidedly condemned! . . . What
could be the use of all this, if he intended to follow the beaten
paths of church-doctrine? There is no sense in it, except it be
said to introduce some new doctrine; and it is perfectly in
character with a Wicliffite whose master also, at the beginning
of 1378, before the inquisition in Lambeth Hall, declared his
readiness to retract as soon as they should convince him of the
fallacy of his religious belief[19].

Not till the pilgrims consent to hear his meditacioun does
the host invite him to begin, but to be brief[20].

I have now to discuss the seeming inconsistency in the
Parson's taking part in the pilgrimage.

Canterbury had, besides the tomb of the "martyr," many
attractions, even for a Wicliffite. Beda tells us that at the time
of the Romans, one of the first, if not the first, Christian
church in Britain had been erected in Canterbury and dedicated to St Martin; there Augustin with his 40 monks had first
preached the gospel, and the first Christian King of England
had there received holy baptism; there lay, besides Becket's, the
remains of Augustin, Æthelbert, Stephen Langton (to whom
England chiefly owes her Magna Charta), and the Black
Prince, the idol of the nation, which only a short time before
had been plunged in the deepest grief by his untimely death[21].
And must not Canterbury, as a far-famed place of pilgrimage,
powerfully attract a Wicliffite preacher, whether he wished to
see with his own eyes how the "miracles" were wrought, or

hoped to find a particularly rich field of labour in a city so
much frequented from religious reasons?

One thing more. All the historians of English literature
agree in maintaining that the *Canterbury Tales* were intended
to be a great picture of the morals and customs of those times,
and by this they excuse many things that would otherwise
throw a bad light on our poet. But what should we think of this
picture, if, by the side of so many persons from all classes of
society, and of such different intellectual standing, it wanted a
representative of that prodigious world-known movement,
which the great Wicliffe, according to directions from the King
and parliament, first raised on a question of politics, but
which, with internal necessity, soon reached the department of
religion, and almost overthrew the government and doctrine of
the Established Church? Even if Chaucer himself was no
Wicliffite, such a character would have been indispensable in
his immortal picture of his times.

But we can scarcely suppose that our poet was not heartily
attached to Wicliffe's tenets. If such were the case, how could
he depict the "Lollard"[22] so ideally, and, at the same time,
display, as we have seen, such knowledge of the reformer's
writings and way of thinking? His near connection with
Wicliffe's protector, John of Gaunt, who took the learned professor as his assistant with him to Bruges, and, in 1377, delivered him, with peril to himself, from the hands of the court of
inquisition at St Paul's; the interest he took in the political
struggles of his nation; his journeys to Italy, in which he, perhaps, passed Avignon and closely saw the hierarchical Babel,
but which, at any rate, made him acquainted with the more
enlightened religious views of prominent Italians[23]; his high
sense of right and truth; lastly, the beginning of the great
Schism which deprived Popery of the last remnant of esteem;—all these tended to alienate him from the Pope and the
Church, and make him join the great reformer with whom he
was very probably personally acquainted[24].

All that his works seem to contain to the contrary, vanishes upon closer examination. Thus his *A B C* and the *Legende of Seint Cecile* are earlier productions[25]; his *Mother of God*
and the *Story of Custance* are most likely so too; and it is
doubtful whether the latter was meant to form part of the
Canterbury Tales[26]. After the pathetic, though 'bait-the-Jews,'
legend of the Prioress, Chaucer lets fly his fantastic *Sir Topas*,
as if to show that it deserves to be thrown into the same pot with
the Fabliaux; he has not a single word of praise for this nor for
the rest of the "fables and such wrecchednesse" told by the
other Romists, and the Monk's water-fall of tragedies is roughly
interrupted, while even the *Miller's* and *Reve's* tales are applauded. But the *friars* are treated more despicably than all the
others. We have only to remember the place of abode assigned
to them in hell, and the punishment they incur by their greediness (Sompnour's Prol. and Tale). A hatred so furious, a contempt passing so far beyond all bounds, are not to be explained
by the Sompnour's irritation, nor by Chaucer's dislike of the
clergy in general. They must have their peculiar cause. We
need not look long for it: the synod held at Blackfriars, which,
in May 1382, condemned Wicliffe's doctrines, consisted for
the greatest part of friars; they preached against heresy, after the
Whitsuntide procession; they published the resolutions of that
synod at Oxford; they were the beadles who executed them;
they helped to obtain Wicliffe's excommunication, and to condemn him to lose his place as professor[27].

That Chaucer himself takes part in the pilgrimage may be
accounted for by what was said about Canterbury.

The words in the General Prologue:

v. 17. The holy blisful martir for to seeke;

That hem hath holpen whan that they were seeke;

are certainly the repetition of a current phrase rather than his own sincere opinion. He knew better what to think of a pilgrimage: he makes the Parson simply call it a 'viage' (v. 49, P. Prol.), and in the Wife's Prologue he has preserved for us a proverb still applicable in our own time:

v. 655. Who that buyldith his hous al of salwes,
　　　　And pricketh his blynde hors over the falwes,
　　　　And suffrith his wyf go seken halwes,
　　　　Is worthy to ben honged on the galwes.

Nay, it is not impossible that the *Canterbury Tales* were intended to hold pilgrimage up to ridicule and contempt, by showing what loose and sinful people took part in it, and what unholy conversation used to shorten the way.

The Parson's Tale

The strictly orthodox contents of the Parson's Tale are consequently the only remaining proof that Chaucer either remained always true to the Roman creed, or at least died an orthodox Catholic. A man who could write a sermon on Penitence in which the necessity of auricular confession is so emphatically enjoined, cannot have been of Wicliffe's persuasion. True. But is it so sure that Chaucer did write it? That he wrote it as it now lies before us[28]? If it can be shown that there is a great dissimilarity between the parts, that some of them are dry, poor of thought, clumsy, yet full of paltry subtlety and hairsplitting, full of inconsistencies with the Parson's way of thinking, the Bible, common sense, and the scheme of the treatise, full of grammatical and stylistic mistakes; if the remainder can be shown to form a genuine, evangelical *De Poenitentia*—short, powerful, coming from, and going to, the heart, with a completely exhaustive and well worked-out scheme, containing nothing of auricular confession; if the probability of a falsification, and the fact that it was easy to perpetrate it, can alike be proved—will it then still be possible to adduce the Parson's Tale as a proof of Chaucer's orthodox catholicism? . . .

Conclusion

With the orthodox *Parson's Tale* falls the last and principal argument that can be adduced in favour of Chaucer's orthodoxy at his death. For the probability of his having been a Wicliffite I have given many reasons, but not all. I have yet to mention the great number and influence of the Wicliffites, according to the certainly unexceptionable testimony of *Walsingham* and *Knighton*[29]; further, the estrangement between Chaucer and his once intimate friend Gower, which has not as yet been sufficiently accounted for, but appears very natural, if we suppose Chaucer to have adopted Wicliffe's doctrines. For Gower, though a zealous advocate for the reformation of the clergy, was no friend to Wicliffe's tenets; we may see this in the second book of his *Vox Clamantis*, and in the Prologue to his *Confessio Amantis*, where he speaks contemptuously of "this new secte of Lollardie[30]." Finally, there is the beautiful poem "Fle fro the pres, and duelle with sothfastnesse," with the burden "And trouthe the schal delyver, hit ys no drede." This poem, apparently containing the gist of Chaucer's philosophy, agrees perfectly with Wicliffe's way of thinking, and does not show a trace of orthodox catholicism. That Henry IV., the persecutor of the Lollards, let fall a ray of his favour on the poet who was then on the brink of the grave, does not contradict my assumption; for Henry was the son of the Duchess Blanche, whose death-song Chaucer sang; he was, too, the son of Chaucer's protector, John of Gaunt; and, besides, it is not necessary

to suppose that the poet openly displayed his religious persuasion.

I'm perfectly aware that my solution of the problem: *What was Chaucer's relation to the Church?* is neither exhaustive nor undoubtedly correct. I did not intend it to be so; for in the present state of our knowledge of Chaucer, a thorough investigation of the question is not yet possible, since a great many other questions must first be answered, before we can be positively sure on this point. But so long as they are not answered in a sense contrary to my expectation, I think I may, without presumption, maintain, that in his heart at least

Chaucer was a Wicliffite.

Notes

1. Morris's edition, I. 249, Note 42.
2. Chaucer Soc. Rep. 1873.
3. "In 1350 the average price of a horse was 18s. 4d.; of an ox, 1l. 4s. 6d.; of a cow, 17s. 2d.; of a sheep, 2s. 6d.; of a goose, 9d.; of a hen, 2d.; of a day's labour in husbandry, 3d."—(Morris, *Introd. to Ch.*, Clar. Press Series ed., p. vii.)
4. Sir H. Nicolas, *Life of Ch.*, in Morris, I. 41.
5. *Engl. Lit.*, p. 69.
6. *History of Engl. Lit.*, I. 157.
7. See Macaulay's brilliant paragraphs on this subject in his Introduction to his *Hist. of England*, i. 16–20, ed. 1849.
8. Wycliffe.
9. The companions of the Prioress seem to make an exception also; this semblance is, however, completely destroyed by what Tyrwhitt says in his *Introd. Disc.* (Morris, I. 209 ff., with the notes).
10. Tyrwhitt and the Six-Text edition have "trewely," which is, perhaps, still more convenient for a Wicliffite.
11. *Wicliffe's Festpredigten*, No. 22, fol. 42: Idem est spiritualiter pascere auditorium *sine sententia evangelica*, ac si quis faceret *convivium sine pane* . . . . and: Quando praedicatum est ab apostolis *evangelium*, crevit ecclesia in virtute; sed modo ex defectu spiritualis seminis, continue decrescit.—*Vermischte Predigten*, No. 9, fol. 207: sacerdos Domini missus ad gignendum et nutriendum populum *verbo vitae*.—(In *Lechler*, I. v. Wiclif, I. 401.) See also p. 422.
12. *Pauli*, Bilder, VII. 202. *Lechler*, I. 417 f. and 421.
13. From Harl. Cat. 1666: "And to absteyne fro othes nedeles and unleful and repreve sinne by way of charite, is cause now why Prelates and sum Lordes sclaunderen men, and clepen hem *Lollardes*, Eretikes, etc." Tyrwhitt concludes (p. 349, note 1) that '*Lollard*' was a common invective. Common enough it was, no doubt; but to denote *a Wicliffite*! All the historical works on that time prove it. Thus Knighton says: "sicque a vulgo Wyclyf discipuli et Wicliviani sive *Lollardi* vocati sunt." (Lechler, II. 5, where some more passages to this effect are to be found, among which is one from an official document. See also p. 55!)
14. Only Arch. Seld. B. 14 has "Schipman"; 18 of the 22 MSS. of the Six-Text print have Squire, 3 Sompnour, 2 of them in opposition to the headings. It is, however, not material who spoke.
15. Lollium, in allusion to the then general derivation of "Lollard."
16. Some Protestants hate evangelical sermons as much as Papists do.
17. The Vicar took only the small tithes of his parish, while the great ones went to a Monastery or Cathedral, &c. The Parson or Rector took both the great and small tithes.
18. Concerning the expression "leful" (v. 41) see *Lechler*, II. 17 f., and especially *Knighton*, col. 2664.
19. *Pauli*, Bilder, VII. 227 ff.
20. The variations in the Six-Text print of the *Parson's Prologue* (Blank-Parson Link) are immaterial as to the sense; they all spring from mistakes of the copyists or their different orthography.
21. *Pauli*, Bilder, VII. "Canterbury."
22. I assume that the reader admits the validity of my evidence and argument.
23. *Kissner*, Ch. in seinen Beziehungen zur italienischen Literatur, p. 78.
24. What Wicliffe thought of the Schism we see in his work *De quatuor sectis novellis*, MS. 3929, fol. 225, col. 3: "Benedictus Deus, qui— divisit *caput serpentis*, movens unam partem ad aliam conteren-

dam . . . Consilium ergo sanum videtur permittere *has duas partes Antichristi* semet ipsas destruere."—(In Lechler, I. 650.) That he dared to write thus, shows plainly what was the public opinion about Popery in England.

25. *Furnivall*, Recent Work at Chaucer (in *Mac Millan's Magazine*, 1873), p. 6: B. *ten-Brink*, Chaucerstudien, p. 130, and Tyrwhitt (Morris, I. 240).
26. I only mention one reason: *Man of Law's Prol.*, v. 90, "I speke *in prose* and let him rymes make;" the Story of Custance being *in rhyme*. To solve the difficulty by supposing v. 90 to mean "I make no rhymes myself, but I will tell you a rhymed story of his," is impossible, for he *does* make rhymes in his *Prologue*; and, besides, if he was going to tell one of Chaucer's rhymed stories, he could not have said: "Though I come after him *with hawebake*" (v. 95).
27. *Pauli*, Bilder, VII. 242 ff.
28. The title it bears according to Tyrwhitt (Morris's ed., I. 251) in some MSS.: "Tractatus de Poenitentia pro fabula, ut dicitur, Rectoris," may possibly be meant to convey a doubt.
29. *Walsingham*, Hist. angl., II. 188 (ed. Riley), "1389: . . . Lollardi—in errorem suum plurimos seduxerunt."
    Knighton, V. col. 2644: "Mediam partem populi, aut majorem partem, sectae suae adquisiverunt." Ibid., col. 2666: "Secta illa in maximo honore illis diebus habebatur, et in tantum multiplicata fuit, quod vix duos videres in via, quin alter eorum discipulus Wicliffe fuerit."
30. Pauli's Introd. Essay to his edition of Gower's works. He also touches the altered relation between the two poets, but says that it was the consequence of political differences.

JAMES RUSSELL LOWELL
From "Chaucer"
Works
1870, Volume 3, pp. 298–366

The first question we put to any poet, nay, to any so-called national literature, is that which Farinata addressed to Dante, *Chi fur li maggior tui?* Here is no question of plagiarism, for poems are not made of words and thoughts and images, but of that something in the poet himself which can compel them to obey him and move to the rhythm of his nature. Thus it is that the new poet, however late he come, can never be forestalled, and the ship-builder who built the pinnace of Columbus has as much claim to the discovery of America as he who suggests a thought by which some other man opens new worlds to us has to a share in that achievement by him unconceived and inconceivable. Chaucer undoubtedly began as an imitator, perhaps as mere translator, serving the needful apprenticeship in the use of his tools. Children learn to speak by watching the lips and catching the words of those who know how already, and poets learn in the same way from their elders. They import their raw material from any and everywhere, and the question at last comes down to this,—whether an author have original force enough to assimilate all he has acquired, or that be so overmastering as to assimilate *him*. If the poet turn out the stronger, we allow him to help himself from other people with wonderful equanimity. Should a man discover the art of transmuting metals and present us with a lump of gold as large as an ostrich-egg, would it be in human nature to inquire too nicely whether he had stolen the lead?

Nothing is more certain than that great poets are not sudden prodigies, but slow results. As an oak profits by the foregone lives of immemorial vegetable races that have worked-over the juices of earth and air into organic life out of whose dissolution a soil might gather fit to maintain that nobler birth of nature, so we may be sure that the genius of every remembered poet drew the forces that built it up out of the decay of a long succession of forgotten ones. Nay, in proportion as the genius is vigorous and original will its indebtedness be greater,

will its roots strike deeper into the past and grope in remoter fields for the virtue that must sustain it. Indeed, if the works of the great poets teach anything, it is to hold mere invention somewhat cheap. It is not the finding of a thing, but the making something out of it after it is found, that is of consequence. Accordingly, Chaucer, like Shakespeare, invented almost nothing. Wherever he found anything directed to Geoffrey Chaucer, he took it and made the most of it. It was not the subject treated, but himself, that was the new thing. *Cela m'appartient de droit*, Molière is reported to have said when accused of plagiarism. Chaucer pays that "usurious interest which genius," as Coleridge says, "always pays in borrowing." The characteristic touch is his own. In the famous passage about the caged bird, copied from the *Romaunt of the Rose*, the "gon eten wormes" was added by him. We must let him, if he will, eat the heart out of the literature that had preceded him, as we sacrifice the mulberry-leaves to the silkworm, because he knows how to convert them into something richer and more lasting. The question of originality is not one of form, but of substance, not of cleverness, but of imaginative power. Given your material, in other words the life in which you live, how much can you see in it? For on that depends how much you can make of it. Is it merely an arrangement of man's contrivance, a patchwork of expediencies for temporary comfort and convenience, good enough if it last your time, or is it so much of the surface of that ever-flowing deity which we call Time, wherein we catch such fleeting reflection as is possible for us, of our relation to perdurable things? This is what makes the difference between Æschylus and Euripides, between Shakespeare and Fletcher, between Goethe and Heine, between literature and rhetoric. Something of this depth of insight, if not in the fullest, yet in no inconsiderable measure, characterizes Chaucer. We must not let his playfulness, his delight in the world as mere spectacle, mislead us into thinking that he was incapable of serious purpose or insensible to the deeper meanings of life.

There are four principal sources from which Chaucer may be presumed to have drawn for poetical suggestion or literary culture,—the Latins, the Troubadours, the Trouvères, and the Italians. It is only the two latter who can fairly claim any immediate influence in the direction of his thought or the formation of his style. The only Latin poet who can be supposed to have influenced the spirit of mediæval literature is Ovid. . . .

Chaucer, to whom French must have been almost as truly a mother tongue as English, was familiar with all that had been done by Troubadour or Trouvère. In him we see the first result of the Norman yeast upon the home-baked Saxon loaf. The flour had been honest, the paste well kneaded, but the inspiring leaven was wanting till the Norman brought it over. Chaucer works still in the solid material of his race, but with what airy lightness has he not infused it? Without ceasing to be English, he has escaped from being insular. But he was something more than this; he was a scholar, a thinker, and a critic. He had studied the *Divina Commedia* of Dante, he had read Petrarca and Boccaccio, and some of the Latin poets. He calls Dante the great poet of Italy, and Petrarch a learned clerk. It is plain that he knew very well the truer purpose of poetry, and had even arrived at the higher wisdom of comprehending the aptitudes and limitations of his own genius. He saw clearly and felt keenly what were the faults and what the wants of the prevailing literature of his country. In the *Monk's Tale* he slyly satirizes the long-winded morality of Gower, as his prose antitype, Fielding, was to satirize the prolix sentimentality of Richardson. In the rhyme of Sir Thopas he gives the *coup de grace* to the romances of Chivalry, and in his own choice of a subject he heralds that new world in which the actual and the popular were to supplant the fantastic and the heroic.

Before Chaucer, modern Europe had given birth to one great poet, Dante; and contemporary with him was one supremely elegant one, Petrarch. Dante died only seven years before Chaucer was born, and, so far as culture is derived from books, the moral and intellectual influences to which they had been subjected, the speculative stimulus that may have given an impulse to their minds,—there could have been no essential difference between them. Yet there are certain points of resemblance and of contrast, and those not entirely fanciful, which seem to me of considerable interest. Both were of mixed race, Dante certainly, Chaucer presumably so. Dante seems to have inherited on the Teutonic side the strong moral sense, the almost nervous irritability of conscience, and the tendency to mysticism which made him the first of Christian poets,—first in point of time and first in point of greatness. From the other side he seems to have received almost in overplus a feeling of order and proportion, sometimes wellnigh hardening into mathematical precision and formalism,—a tendency which at last brought the poetry of the Romanic races to a dead-lock of artifice and decorum. Chaucer, on the other hand, drew from the South a certain airiness of sentiment and expression, a felicity of phrase and an elegance of turn, hitherto unprecedented and hardly yet matched in our literature, but all the while kept firm hold of his native soundness of understanding, and that genial humor which seems to be the proper element of worldly wisdom. With Dante life represented the passage of the soul from a state of nature to a state of grace; and there would have been almost an even chance whether (as Burns says) the *Divina Commedia* had turned out a song or a sermon, but for the wonderful genius of its author, which has compelled the sermon to sing and the song to preach, whether they would or no. With Chaucer, life is a pilgrimage, but only that his eye may be delighted with the varieties of costume and character. There are good morals to be found in Chaucer, but they are always incidental. With Dante the main question is the saving of the soul, with Chaucer it is the conduct of life. The distance between them is almost that between holiness and prudence. Dante applies himself to the realities, Chaucer to the scenery of life, and the former is consequently the more universal poet, as the latter is the more truly national one. Dante represents the justice of God, and Chaucer his loving-kindness. If there is anything that may properly be called satire in the one, it is like a blast of the divine wrath, before which the wretches cower and tremble, which rends away their cloaks of hypocrisy and their masks of worldly propriety, and leaves them shivering in the cruel nakedness of their shame. The satire of the other is genial with the broad sunshine of humor, into which the victims walk forth with a delightful unconcern, laying aside of themselves the disguises that seem to make them uncomfortably warm, till they have made a thorough betrayal of themselves so unconsciously that we almost pity while we laugh. Dante shows us the punishment of sins against God and one's neighbor, in order that we may shun them, and so escape the doom that awaits them in the other world. Chaucer exposes the cheats of the transmuter of metals, of the begging friars, and of the pedlers of indulgences, in order that we may be on our guard against them in this world. If we are to judge of what is national only by the highest and most characteristic types, surely we cannot fail to see in Chaucer the true forerunner and prototype of Shakespeare, who, with an imagination of far deeper grasp, a far wider reach of thought, yet took the same delight in the pageantry of the actual world, and whose moral is the moral of worldly wisdom only heightened to the level of his wide-viewing mind, and made typical by the dramatic energy of his plastic nature.

Yet of Chaucer had little of that organic force of life which so inspires the poem of Dante that, as he himself says of the heavens, part answers to part with mutual interchange of light, he had a structural faculty which distinguishes him from all other English poets, his contemporaries, and which indeed is the primary distinction of poets properly so called. There is, to be sure, only one other English writer coeval with himself who deserves in any way to be compared with him, and that rather for contrast than for likeness.

With the single exception of Langland, the English poets, his contemporaries, were little else than bad versifiers of legends classic or mediæval, as it might happen, without selection and without art. Chaucer is the first who broke away from the dreary traditional style, and gave not merely stories, but lively *pictures* of real life as the ever-renewed substance of poetry. He was a reformer, too, not only in literature, but in morals. But as in the former his exquisite tact saved him from all eccentricity, so in the latter the pervading sweetness of his nature could never be betrayed into harshness and invective. He seems incapable of indignation. He mused good-naturedly over the vices and follies of men, and, never forgetting that he was fashioned of the same clay, is rather apt to pity than condemn. There is no touch of cynicism in all he wrote. Dante's brush seems sometimes to have been smeared with the burning pitch of his own fiery lake. Chaucer's pencil is dipped in the cheerful color-box of the old illuminators, and he has their patient delicacy of touch, with a freedom far beyond their somewhat mechanic brilliancy.

English narrative poetry, as Chaucer found it, though it had not altogether escaped from the primal curse of long-windedness so painfully characteristic of its prototype, the French Romance of Chivalry, had certainly shown a feeling for the picturesque, a sense of color, a directness of phrase, and a simplicity of treatment which give it graces of its own and a turn peculiar to itself. In the easy knack of story-telling, the popular minstrels cannot compare with Marie de France. The lightsomeness of fancy, that leaves a touch of sunshine and is gone, is painfully missed in them all. Their incidents enter dispersedly, as the old stage directions used to say, and they have not learned the art of concentrating their force on the key-point of their hearers' interest. They neither get fairly hold of their subject, nor, what is more important, does it get hold of them. But they sometimes yield to an instinctive hint of leaving-off at the right moment, and in their happy negligence achieve an effect only to be matched by the highest successes of art.

> That lady heard his mourning all
> Right under her chamber wall,
> In her oriel where she was,
> Closèd well with royal glass;
> Fulfilled it was with imagery
> Every window, by and by;
> On each side had there a gin
> Sperred with many a divers pin;
> Anon that lady fair and free
> Undid a pin of ivory
> And wide the window she open set,
> The sun shone in at her closet.

It is true the old rhymer relapses a little into the habitual drone of his class, and shows half a mind to bolt into their common inventory style when he comes to his *gins* and *pins*, but he withstands the temptation manfully, and his sunshine fills our hearts with a gush as sudden as that which illumines the lady's oriel. Coleridge and Keats have each in his way felt the charm of this winsome picture, but have hardly equalled its hearty honesty, its economy of material, the supreme test of artistic skill. I admit that the phrase *"had* there a gin" is suspicious, and suggests a French original, but I remember nothing altogether so good in the romances from the other side of the Channel. One more passage occurs to me, almost incomparable in its simple straightforward force and choice of the right word.

> Sir Graysteel to his death thus thraws,
> He welters [wallows] and the grass updraws;
>
> . . .
>
> A little while then lay he still,
> (Friends that saw him liked full ill,)
> And bled into his armor bright.

The last line, for suggestive reticence, almost deserves to be put beside the famous

> Quel giorno più non vi leggemmo avante

of the great master of laconic narration. In the same poem[1] the growing love of the lady, in its maidenliness of unconscious betrayal, is touched with a delicacy and tact as surprising as they are delightful. But such passages, which are the despair of poets who have to work in a language that has faded into diction, are exceptional. They are to be set down rather to good luck than to art. Even the stereotyped similes of these fortunate illiterates, like "weary as water in a weir," or "glad as grass is of the rain," are new, like nature, at the thousandth repetition. Perhaps our palled taste overvalues the wild flavor of these wayside treasure-troves. They are wood-strawberries, prized in proportion as we must turn over more leaves ere we find one. This popular literature is of value in helping us towards a juster estimate of Chaucer by showing what the mere language was capable of, and that all it wanted was a poet to put it through its paces. For though the poems I have quoted be, in their present form, later than he, they are, after all, but modernized versions of older copies, which they doubtless reproduce with substantial fidelity.

It is commonly assumed that Chaucer did for English what Dante is supposed to have done for Italian and Luther for German, that he, in short, in some hitherto inexplicable way, created it. But this is to speak loosely and without book. Languages are never made in any such fashion, still less are they the achievement of any single man, however great his genius, however powerful his individuality. They shape themselves by laws as definite as those which guide and limit the growth of other living organisms. Dante, indeed, has told us that he chose to write in the tongue that might be learned of nurses and chafferers in the market. His practice shows that he knew perfectly well that poetry has needs which cannot be answered by the vehicle of vulgar commerce between man and man. What he instinctively felt was, that there was the living heart of all speech, without whose help the brain were powerless to send will, motion, meaning, to the limbs and extremities. But it is true that a language, as respects the uses of literature, is liable to a kind of syncope. No matter how complete its vocabulary may be, how thorough an outfit of inflections and case-endings it may have, it is a mere dead body without a soul till some man of genius set its arrested pulses once more athrob, and show what wealth of sweetness, scorn, persuasion, and passion lay there awaiting its liberator. In this sense it is hardly too much to say that Chaucer, like Dante, found his native tongue a dialect and left it a language. But it was not what he did with deliberate purpose of reform, it was his kindly and plastic genius that wrought this magic of renewal and inspira-

tion. It was not the new words he introduced,[2] but his way of using the old ones, that surprised them into grace, ease, and dignity in their own despite. In order to feel fully how much he achieved, let any one subject himself to a penitential course of reading in his contemporary, Gower, who worked in a material to all intents and purposes the same, or listen for a moment to the barbarous jangle which Lydgate and Occleve contrive to draw from the instrument their master had tuned so deftly. Gower has positively raised tediousness to the precision of science, he has made dulness an heirloom for the students of our literary history. As you slip to and fro on the frozen levels of his verse, which give no foothold to the mind, as your nervous ear awaits the inevitable recurrence of his rhyme, regularly pertinacious as the tick of an eight-day clock and reminding you of Wordsworth's

> Once more the ass did lengthen out
> The hard, dry, seesaw of his horrible bray,

you learn to dread, almost to respect, the powers of this indefatigable man. He is the undertaker of the fair mediæval legend, and his style has the hateful gloss, the seemingly unnatural length, of a coffin. Love, beauty, passion, nature, art, life, the natural and theological virtues,—there is nothing beyond his power to disenchant, nothing out of which the tremendous hydraulic press of his allegory (or whatever it is, for I am not sure if it be not something even worse) will not squeeze all feeling and freshness and leave it a juiceless pulp. It matters not where you try him, whether his story be Christian or pagan, borrowed from history or fable, you cannot escape him. Dip in at the middle or the end, dodge back to the beginning, the patient old man is there to take you by the button and go on with his imperturbable narrative. You may have left off with Clytemnestra, and you begin again with Samson; it makes no odds, for you cannot tell one from tother. His tediousness is omnipresent, and like Dogberry he could find in his heart to bestow it all (and more if he had it) on your worship. The word *lengthy* has been charged to our American account, but it must have been invented by the first reader of Gower's works, the only inspiration of which they were ever capable. Our literature had to lie by and recruit for more than four centuries ere it could give us an equal vacuity in Tupper, so persistent a uniformity of commonplace in the "Recreations of a Country Parson." Let us be thankful that the industrious Gower never found time for recreation!

But a fairer as well as more instructive comparison lies between Chaucer and the author of *Piers Ploughman.* Langland has as much tenderness, as much interest in the varied picture of life, as hearty a contempt for hypocrisy, and almost an equal sense of fun. He has the same easy abundance of matter. But what a difference! It is the difference between the poet and the man of poetic temperament. The abundance of the one is a continual fulness within the fixed limits of good taste; that of the other is squandered in overflow. The one can be profuse on occasion; the other is diffuse whether he will or no. The one is full of talk; the other is garrulous. What in one is the refined *bonhomie* of a man of the world, is a rustic shrewdness in the other. Both are kindly in their satire, and have not (like too many reformers) that vindictive love of virtue which spreads the stool of repentance with thistle-burrs before they invite the erring to seat themselves therein. But what in *Piers Ploughman* is sly fun, has the breadth and depth of humor in Chaucer; and it is plain that while the former was taken up by his moral purpose, the main interest of the latter turned to perfecting the form of his work. In short, Chaucer had that fine literary sense which is as rare as genius, and, united with it, as it was in him, assures an immortality of fame. It is not merely what he has to say, but even more the agreeable way he has of saying it, that captivates our attention and gives him an assured place in literature. Above all, it is not in detached passages that his charm lies, but in the entirety of expression and the cumulative effect of many particulars working toward a common end. Now though *ex ungue leonem* be a good rule in comparative anatomy, its application, except in a very limited way, in criticism is sure to mislead; for we should always bear in mind that the really great writer is great in the mass, and is to be tested less by his cleverness in the elaboration of parts than by that *reach* of mind which is incapable of random effort, which selects, arranges, combines, rejects, denies itself the cheap triumph of immediate effects, because it is absorbed by the controlling charm of proportion and unity. A careless good-luck of phrase is delightful; but criticism cleaves to the teleological argument, and distinguishes the creative intellect, not so much by any happiness of natural endowment as by the marks of design. It is true that one may sometimes discover by a single verse whether an author have imagination, or may make a shrewd guess whether he have style or no, just as by a few spoken words you may judge of a man's accent; but the true artist in language is never spotty, and needs no guide-boards of admiring italics, a critical method introduced by Leigh Hunt, whose feminine temperament gave him acute perceptions at the expense of judgment. This is the Bœotian method, which offers us a brick as a sample of the house, forgetting that it is not the goodness of the separate bricks, but the way in which they are put together, that brings them within the province of art, and makes the difference between a heap and a house. A great writer does not reveal himself here and there, but everywhere. Langland's verse runs mostly like a brook, with a beguiling and wellnigh slumberous prattle, but he, more often than any writer of his class, flashes into salient lines, gets inside our guard with the homethrust of a forthright word, and he gains if taken piecemeal. His imagery is naturally and vividly picturesque, as where he says of Old Age,—

> Eld the hoar
> That was in the vauntward,
> And bare the banner before death,—

and he softens to a sweetness of sympathy beyond Chaucer when he speaks of the poor or tells us that Mercy is "sib of all sinful"; but to compare *Piers Ploughman* with the *Canterbury Tales* is to compare sermon with song.

Let us put a bit of Langland's satire beside one of Chaucer's. Some people in search of Truth meet a pilgrim and ask him whence he comes. He gives a long list of holy places, appealing for proof to the relics on his hat:—

> 'I have walked full wide in wet and in dry
> And sought saints for my soul's health.'
> 'Know'st thou ever a relic that is called Truth?
> Couldst thou show us the way where that wight
>   dwelleth?'
> 'Nay, so God help me,' said the man then,
> 'I saw never palmer with staff nor with scrip
> Ask after him ever till now in this place.'

This is a good hit, and the poet is satisfied; but, in what I am going to quote from Chaucer, everything becomes picture, over which lies broad and warm the sunshine of humorous fancy.

> In oldë dayës of the King Artour
> Of which that Britouns speken gret honour,
> All was this lond fulfilled of fayerie:
> The elf-queen with her joly compaignie
> Dancëd ful oft in many a grenë mede:
> This was the old opinion as I rede;

> I speke of many hundrid yer ago:
> But now can no man see none elvës mo,
> For now the gretë charite and prayëres
> Of lymytours and other holy freres
> That sechen every lond and every streem,
> As thick as motis in the sonnëbeam,
> Blessyng halles, chambres, kichenës, and boures,
> Citees and burghës, castels hihe and toures,
> Thorpës and bernes, shepnes and dayeries,
> This makith that ther ben no fayeries.
> For ther as wont to walken was an elf
> There walkith none but the lymytour himself,
> In undermelës and in morwenynges,
> And sayth his matyns and his holy thinges,
> As he goth in his lymytatioun.
> Wommen may now go saufly up and doun;
> In every bush or under every tre
> There is none other incubus but he,
> And he ne wol doon hem no dishonóur.

How cunningly the contrast is suggested here between the Elf-queen's jolly company and the unsocial limiters, thick as motes in the sunbeam, yet each walking by himself! And with what an air of innocent unconsciousness is the deadly thrust of the last verse given, with its contemptuous emphasis on the *he* that seems so well-meaning! Even Shakespeare, who seems to come in after everybody has done his best with a "Let me take hold a minute and show you how to do it," could not have bettered this.

Piers Ploughman is the best example I know of what is called popular poetry,—of compositions, that is, which contain all the simpler elements of poetry, but still in solution, not crystallized around any thread of artistic purpose. In it appears at her best the Anglo-Saxon Muse, a first cousin of Poor Richard, full of proverbial wisdom, who always brings her knitting in her pocket, and seems most at home in the chimney-corner. It is genial; it plants itself firmly on human nature with its rights and wrongs; it has a surly honesty, prefers the downright to the gracious, and conceives of speech as a tool rather than a musical instrument. If we should seek for a single word that would define it most precisely, we should not choose simplicity, but homeliness. There is more or less of this in all early poetry, to be sure; but I think it especially proper to English poets, and to the most English among them, like Cowper, Crabbe, and one is tempted to add Wordsworth,—where he forgets Coleridge's private lectures. In reading such poets as Langland, also, we are not to forget a certain charm of distance in the very language they use, making it unhackneyed without being alien. As it is the chief function of the poet to make the familiar novel, these fortunate early risers of literature, who gather phrases with the dew still on them, have their poetry done for them, as it were, by their vocabulary. But in Chaucer, as in all great poets, the language gets its charm from him. The force and sweetness of his genius kneaded more kindly together the Latin and Teutonic elements of our mother tongue, and made something better than either. The necessity of writing poetry, and not mere verse, made him a reformer whether he would or no; and the instinct of his finer ear was a guide such as none before him or contemporary with him, nor indeed any that came after him, till Spenser, could command. Gower had no notion of the uses of rhyme except as a kind of crease at the end of every eighth syllable, where the verse was to be folded over again into another layer. He says, for example,

> This maiden Canacee was hight,
> Both in the day and eke by night,

as if people commonly changed their names at dark. And he could not even contrive to say this without the clumsypleonasm of *both* and *eke*. Chaucer was put to no such shifts of piecing out his metre with loose-woven bits of baser stuff. He himself says, in the *Man of Law's Tale*,—

> Me lists not of the chaff nor of the straw
> To make so long a tale as of the corn.

One of the world's three or four great story-tellers, he was also one of the best versifiers that ever made English trip and sing with a gayety that seems careless, but where every foot beats time to the tune of the thought. By the skilful arrangement of his pauses he evaded the monotony of the couplet, and gave to the rhymed pentameter, which he made our heroic measure, something of the architectural repose of blank verse. He found our language lumpish, stiff, unwilling, too apt to speak Saxonly in grouty monosyllables; he left it enriched with the longer measure of the Italian and Provençal poets. He reconciled, in the harmony of his verse, the English bluntness with the dignity and elegance of the less homely Southern speech. Though he did not and could not create our language (for he who writes to be read does not write for linguisters), yet it is true that he first made it easy, and to that extent modern, so that Spenser, two hundred years later, studied his method and called him master. He first wrote *English*; and it was a feeling of this, I suspect, that made it fashionable in Elizabeth's day to "talk pure Chaucer." Already we find in his works verses that might pass without question in Milton or even Wordsworth, so mainly unchanged have the language of poetry and the movement of verse remained from his day to our own.

> Thou Polymnia
> On Pérnaso, that, with[3] thy sisters glade,
> By Helicon, not far from Cirrea,
> Singest with voice memorial in the shade,
> Under the laurel which that may not fade.
>
> And downward from a hill under a bent
> There stood the temple of Mars omnipotent
> Wrought all of burnëd steel, of which th' entrée
> Was long and strait and ghastly for to see:
> The northern light in at the doorës shone
> For window in the wall ne was there none
> Through which men mighten any light discerne;
> The dore was all of adamant eterne.

And here are some lines that would not seem out of place in the "Paradise of Dainty Devises":—

> Hide, Absolom, thy giltë [gilded] tresses clear,
> Esther lay thou thy meeknesses all adown.
>
> . . .
>
> Make of your wifehood no comparison;
> Hide ye your beauties Ysoude and Elaine,
> My lady cometh, that all this may distain.

When I remember Chaucer's malediction upon his scrivener, and consider that by far the larger proportion of his verses (allowing always for change of pronunciation) are perfectly accordant with our present accentual system, I cannot believe that he ever wrote an imperfect line. His ear would never have tolerated the verses of nine syllables, with a strong accent on the first, attributed to him by Mr. Skeat and Mr. Morris. Such verses seem to me simply impossible in the pentameter iambic as Chaucer wrote it. A great deal of misapprehension would be avoided in discussing English metres, if it were only understood that quantity in Latin and quantity in English mean very different things. Perhaps the best quantitative verses in our language (better even than Coleridge's) are to be found in Mother Goose, composed by nurses wholly by ear and beating time as they danced the baby on their knee. I suspect Chaucer and Shakespeare would be surprised into a smile by the learned arguments which supply their halting verses with every kind of

excuse except that of being readable. When verses were written to be chanted, more license could be allowed, for the ear tolerates the widest deviations from habitual accent in words that are sung. *Segnius irritant demissa per aurem.* To some extent the same thing is true of anapæstic and other tripping measures, but we cannot admit it in marching tunes like those of Chaucer. He wrote for the eye more than for the voice, as poets had begun to do long before.[4] Some loose talk of Coleridge, loose in spite of its affectation of scientific precision, about "retardations" and the like, has misled many honest persons into believing that they can make good verse out of bad prose. Coleridge himself, from natural fineness of ear, was the best metrist among modern English poets, and, read with proper allowances, his remarks upon versification are always instructive to whoever is not rhythm-deaf. But one has no patience with the dyspondæuses, the pæon primuses, and what not, with which he darkens verses that are to be explained only by the contemporary habits of pronunciation. Till after the time of Shakespeare we must always bear in mind that it is not a language of books but of living speech that we have to deal with. Of this language Coleridge had little knowledge, except what could be acquired through the ends of his fingers as they lazily turned the leaves of his haphazard reading. If his eye was caught by a single passage that gave him a chance to theorize he did not look farther. Speaking of Massinger, for example, he says, "When a speech is interrupted, or one of the characters speaks aside, the last syllable of the former speech and first of the succeeding Massinger counts for one, because both are supposed to be spoken at the same moment.

> 'And felt the sweetness *of't*
> 　　　'*How* her mouth runs over.'

Now fifty instances may be cited from Massinger which tell against this fanciful notion, for one that seems, and only seems, in its favor. Any one tolerably familiar with the dramatists knows that in the passage quoted by Coleridge, the *how* being emphatic, "*how her*" was pronounced *how'r*. He tells us that "Massinger is fond of the anapæst in the first and third foot, as:—

> Tŏ yoŭr mōre | thăn mās | cŭlĭnĕ rēa | sŏn
> 　　　thāt | cŏmmānds 'ĕm ‖ .

Likewise of the second pæon (‒ ‒ ‒ ‒) in the first foot, followed by four trochees (‒ ‒), as:—

> Sŏ grēēdĭlў | lōng fŏr, | knōw theĭr | tītĭll | ātĭons."

In truth, he was no fonder of them than his brother dramatists who, like him, wrote for the voice by the ear. "To your" is still one syllable in ordinary speech, and "masculine" and "greedily" were and are dissyllables or trisyllables according to their place in the verse. Coleridge was making pedantry of a very simple matter. Yet he has said with perfect truth of Chaucer's verse, "Let a few plain rules be given for sounding the final *è* of syllables, and for expressing the terminations of such words as *ocëan* and *natiön*, &c., as dissyllables,—or let the syllables to be sounded in such cases be marked by a competent metrist. This simple expedient would, with a very few trifling exceptions, where the errors are inveterate, enable any one to feel the perfect smoothness and harmony of Chaucer's verse." But let us keep widely clear of Latin and Greek terms of prosody! It is also more important here than even with the dramatists of Shakespeare's time to remember that we have to do with a language caught more from the ear than from books. The best school for learning to understand Chaucer's elisions, compressions, slurrings-over and runnings-together of syllables is to listen to the habitual speech of rustics with whom language is still plastic to meaning, and hurries or prolongs itself accordingly. Here is a contraction frequent in Chaucer, and still common in New England:—

> But me were lever than [lcvcr'n] all this town,
>   quod he.

Let one example suffice for many. To Coleridge's rules another should be added by a wise editor; and that is to restore the final *n* in the infinitive and third person plural of verbs, and in such other cases as can be justified by the authority of Chaucer himself. Surely his ear could never have endured the sing-song of such verses as

> I couthe telle for a gowne-cloth,

or

> Than ye to me schuld breke youre trouthe.

Chaucer's measure is so uniform (making due allowances) that words should be transposed or even omitted where the verse manifestly demands it,—and with copyists so long and dull of car this is often the case. Sometimes they leave out a needful word:—

> But er [the] thunder stynte, there cometh rain,
> When [that] we ben yflattered and ypraised,
> Tak [ye] him for the greatest gentleman.

Sometimes they thrust in a word or words that hobble the verse:—

> She trowed he were yfel in [some] maladie,
> Ye faren like a man [that] had lost his wit,
> Then have I got of you the maystrie, quod she,
> (Then have I got the maystery, quod she,)
> And quod the jugë [also] thou must lose thy head.

Sometimes they give a wrong word identical in meaning:—

> And therwithal he knew [couthë] mo proverbes.

Sometimes they change the true order of the words:—

> Therefore no woman of clerkës is [is of clerkës]
>   praised
> His felaw lo, here he stont [stont he] hool on live.
> He that covèteth is a porë wight
> For he wold have that is not in his might;
> But he that nought hath ne coveteth nought to have.

Here the "but" of the third verse belongs at the head of the first, and we get rid of the anomaly of "coveteth" differently accented within two lines. Nearly all the seemingly unmetrical verses may be righted in this way. I find a good example of this in the last stanza of *Troilus and Creseide.* As it stands, we read,—

> Thou one, two, and three, eterne on live
> That raignast aie in three, two and one.

It is plain that we should read "one *and* two" in the first verse, and "three *and* two" in the second. Remembering, then, that Chaucer was here translating Dante, I turned (after making the correction) to the original, and found as I expected

> Quell' uno *e* due e tre che sempre vive
> E regna sempre in tre *e* due ed uno.
>   (Par. xiv. 28, 29)

In the stanza before this we have,—

> To thee and to the philosophic*all* strode,
> To vouchsafe [vouchësafe] there need is, to correct;

and further on,—

> With all mine herte' of mercy ever I pray
> And to the Lord aright thus I speake and say,

where we must either strike out the second "I" or put it after "speake." . . .

I will give one more example of Chaucer's verse, again making my selection from one of his less mature works. He is speaking of Tarquin:—

> And ay the morë he was in despair
> The more he coveted and thought her fair;
> His blindë lust was all his coveting.
> On morrow when the bird began to sing
> Unto the siege he cometh full privily
> And by himself he walketh soberly
> The imáge of her recording alway new:
> Thus lay her hair, and thus fresh was her hue,
> Thus sate, thus spake, thus span, this was her cheer,
> Thus fair she was, and this was her manére.
> All this conceit his heart hath new ytake,
> And as the sea, with tempest all toshake,
> That after, when the storm is all ago,
> Yet will the water quap a day or two,
> Right so, though that her formë were absént,
> The pleasance of her forme was presént.

And this passage leads me to say a few words of Chaucer as a descriptive poet; for I think it a great mistake to attribute to him any properly dramatic power, as some have done. Even Herr Hertzberg, in his remarkably intelligent essay, is led a little astray on this point by his enthusiasm. Chaucer is a great narrative poet; and, in this species of poetry, though the author's personality should never be obtruded, it yet unconsciously pervades the whole, and communicates an individual quality,—a kind of flavor of its own. This very quality, and it is one of the highest in its way and place, would be fatal to all dramatic force. The narrative poet is occupied with his characters as picture, with their grouping, even their costume, it may be, and he feels for and with them instead of being they for the moment, as the dramatist must always be. The story-teller must possess the situation perfectly in all its details, while the imagination of the dramatist must be possessed and mastered by it. The latter puts before us the very passion or emotion itself in its utmost intensity; the former gives them, not in their primary form, but in that derivative one which they have acquired by passing through his own mind and being modified by his reflection. The deepest pathos of the drama, like the quiet "no more but so?" with which Shakespeare tells us that Ophelia's heart is bursting, is sudden as a stab, while in narrative it is more or less suffused with pity,—a feeling capable of prolonged sustention. This presence of the author's own sympathy is noticeable in all Chaucer's pathetic passages, as, for instance, in the lamentation of Constance over her child in the *Man of Law's Tale.* When he comes to the sorrow of his story, he seems to croon over his thoughts, to soothe them and dwell upon them with a kind of pleased compassion, as a child treats a wounded bird which he fears to grasp too tightly, and yet cannot make up his heart wholly to let go. It is true also of his humor that it pervades his comic tales like sunshine, and never dazzles the attention by a sudden flash. Sometimes he brings it in parenthetically, and insinuates a sarcasm so slyly as almost to slip by without our notice, as where he satirizes provincialism by the cock who

> By nature knew ech ascensioun
> Of equinoxial in thilke toun.

Sometimes he turns round upon himself and smiles at a trip he has made into fine writing:—

> Till that the brightë sun had lost his hue,
> For th' orisont had reft the sun his light,
> (This is as much to sayen as 'it was night.')

Nay, sometimes it twinkles roguishly through his very tears, as in the

> 'Why wouldest thou be dead,' these women cry,

'Thou haddest gold enough—and Emily?'
that follows so close upon the profoundly tender despair of
Arcite's farewell:—

> What is this world? What asken men to have?
> Now with his love now in the coldë grave
> Alone withouten any company!

The power of diffusion without being diffuse would seem to be
the highest merit of narration, giving it that easy flow which is
so delightful. Chaucer's descriptive style is remarkable for its
lowness of tone,—for that combination of energy with simplicity which is among the rarest gifts in literature. Perhaps all
is said in saying that he has style at all, for that consists mainly
in the absence of undue emphasis and exaggeration, in the
clear uniform pitch which penetrates our interest and retains it,
where mere loudness would only disturb and irritate.

Not that Chaucer cannot be intense, too, on occasion; but
it is with a quiet intensity of his own, that comes in as it were
by accident.

> Upon a thickë palfrey, paper-white,
> With saddle red embroidered with delight,
> Sits Dido:
> And she is fair as is the brightë morrow
> That healeth sickë folk of nightës sorrow.
> Upon a courser startling as the fire,
> Æneas sits.

Pandarus, looking at Troilus,

> Took up a light and found his countenance
> As for to look upon an old romance.

With Chaucer it is always the thing itself and not the description of it that is the main object. His picturesque bits are
incidental to the story, glimpsed in passing; they never stop the
way. His key is so low that his high lights are never obtrusive.
His imitators, like Leigh Hunt, and Keats in his *Endymion*,
missing the nice gradation with which the master toned everything down, become streaky. Hogarth, who reminds one of
him in the variety and natural action of his figures, is like him
also in the subdued brilliancy of his coloring. When Chaucer
condenses, it is because his conception is vivid. He does not
need to personify Revenge, for personification is but the subterfuge of unimaginative and professional poets; but he embodies
the very passion itself in a verse that makes us glance over our
shoulder as if we heard a stealthy tread behind us:—

> The smiler with the knife hid under the cloak.[5]

And yet how unlike is the operation of the imaginative faculty
in him and Shakespeare! When the latter describes, his epithets
imply always an impression on the moral sense (so to speak) of
the person who hears or sees. The sun "flatters the mountain-
tops with sovereign eye"; the bending "weeds lacquey the dull
stream"; the shadow of the falcon "coucheth the fowl below";
the smoke is "helpless"; when Tarquin enters the chamber of
Lucrece "the threshold grates the door to have him heard." His
outward sense is merely a window through which the metaphysical eye looks forth, and his mind passes over at once from
the simple sensation to the complex *meaning* of it,—feels *with*
the object instead of merely feeling it. His imagination is forever dramatizing. Chaucer gives only the direct impression
made on the eye or ear. He was the first great poet who really
loved outward nature as the source of conscious pleasurable
emotion. The Troubadour hailed the return of spring; but with
him it was a piece of empty ritualism. Chaucer took a true
delight in the new green of the leaves and the return of singing
birds,—a delight as simple as that of Robin Hood:—

> In summer when the shaws be sheen,
> And leaves be large and long,

> It is full merry in fair forest
> To hear the small birds' song.

He has never so much as heard of the "burthen and the mystery of all this unintelligible world." His flowers and trees and
birds have never bothered themselves with Spinoza. He himself sings more like a bird than any other poet, because it never
occurred to him, as to Goethe, that he ought to do so. He
pours himself out in sincere joy and thankfulness. When we
compare Spenser's imitations of him with the original passages,
we feel that the delight of the later poet was more in the
expression than in the thing itself. Nature with him is only
good to be transfigured by art. We walk among Chaucer's sights
and sounds; we listen to Spenser's musical reproduction of
them. In the same way, the pleasure which Chaucer takes in
telling his stories has in itself the effect of consummate skill,
and makes us follow all the windings of his fancy with sympathetic interest. His best tales run on like one of our inland
rivers, sometimes hastening a little and turning upon themselves in eddies that dimple without retarding the current;
sometimes loitering smoothly, while here and there a quiet
thought, a tender feeling, a pleasant image, a golden-hearted
verse, opens quietly as a water-lily, to float on the surface
without breaking it into ripple. The vulgar intellectual palate
hankers after the titillation of foaming phrase, and thinks nothing good for much that does not go off with a pop like a
champagne cork. The mellow suavity of more precious vin-
tages seems insipid: but the taste, in proportion as it refines,
learns to appreciate the indefinable flavor, too subtile for analysis. A manner has prevailed of late in which every other word
seems to be underscored as in a school-girl's letter. The poet
seems intent on showing his sinew, as if the power of the slim
Apollo lay in the girth of his biceps. Force for the mere sake of
force ends like Milo, caught and held mockingly fast by the
recoil of the log he undertook to rive. In the race of fame, there
are a score capable of brilliant *spurts* for one who comes in
winner after a steady pull with wind and muscle to spare.
Chaucer never shows any signs of effort, and it is a main proof
of his excellence that he can be so inadequately sampled by
detached passages,—by single lines taken away from the connection in which they contribute to the general effect. He has
that continuity of thought, that evenly prolonged power, and
that delightful equanimity, which characterize the higher orders of mind. There is something in him of the disinterestedness that made the Greeks masters in art. His phrase is never
importunate. His simplicity is that of elegance, not of poverty.
The quiet unconcern with which he says his best things is
peculiar to him among English poets, though Goldsmith, Addison, and Thackeray have approached it in prose. He prattles
inadvertently away, and all the while, like the princess in the
story, lets fall a pearl at every other word. It is such a piece of
good luck to be natural! It is the good gift which the fairy
godmother brings to her prime favorites in the cradle. If not
genius, it alone is what makes genius amiable in the arts. If a
man have it not, he will never find it, for when it is sought it is
gone.

When Chaucer describes anything, it is commonly by one
of those simple and obvious epithets or qualities that are so easy
to miss. Is it a woman? He tells us she is *fresh*; that she has *glad*
eyes; that "every day her beauty newed"; that

> Methought all fellowship as naked
> Withouten her that I saw once,
> As a coróne without the stones.

Sometimes he describes amply by the merest hint, as where the
Friar, before setting himself softly down, drives away the cat.
We know without need of more words that he has chosen the

snuggest corner. In some of his early poems he sometimes, it is true, falls into the catalogue style of his contemporaries; but after he had found his genius he never particularizes too much,— a process as deadly to all effect as an explanation to a pun. The first stanza of the *Clerk's Tale* gives us a landscape whose stately choice of objects shows a skill in composition worthy of Claude, the last artist who painted nature epically:—

> There is at the west endë of Itaile,
> Down at the foot of Vesulus the cold,
> A lusty plain abundant of vitaile,
> Where many a tower and town thou may'st behold
> That founded were in time of fathers old,
> And many another delitable sight;
> And Sàlucës this noble country hight.

The Pre-Raphaelite style of landscape entangles the eye among the obtrusive weeds and grass-blades of the foreground which, in looking at a real bit of scenery, we overlook; but what a sweep of vision is here! and what happy generalization in the sixth verse as the poet turns away to the business of his story! The whole is full of open air.

But it is in his characters, especially, that his manner is large and free; for he is painting history, though with the fidelity of portrait. He brings out strongly the essential traits, characteristic of the genus rather than of the individual. The Merchant who keeps so steady a countenance that

> There wist no wight that he was e'er in debt,

the Sergeant at Law, "who seemëd busier than he was," the Doctor of Medicine, whose "study was but little on the Bible,"— in all these cases it is the type and not the personage that fixes his attention. William Blake says truly, though he expresses his meaning somewhat clumsily, "the characters of Chaucer's Pilgrims are the characters which compose all ages and nations. Some of the names and titles are altered by time, but the characters remain forever unaltered, and consequently they are the physiognomies and lineaments of universal human life, beyond which Nature never steps. Names alter, things never alter. As Newton numbered the stars, and as Linnæus numbered the plants, so Chaucer numbered the classes of men." In his outside accessaries, it is true, he sometimes seems as minute as if he were illuminating a missal. Nothing escapes his sure eye for the picturesque,—the cut of the beard, the soil of armor on the buff jerkin, the rust on the sword, the expression of the eye. But in this he has an artistic purpose. It is here that he individualizes, and, while every touch harmonizes with and seems to complete the moral features of the character, makes us feel that we are among living men, and not the abstracted images of men. Crabbe adds particular to particular, scattering rather than deepening the impression of reality, and making us feel as if every man were a species by himself; but Chaucer, never forgetting the essential sameness of human nature, makes it possible, and even probable, that his motley characters should meet on a common footing, while he gives to each the *expression* that belongs to him, the result of special circumstance or training. Indeed, the absence of any suggestion of *caste* cannot fail to strike any reader familiar with the literature on which he is supposed to have formed himself. No characters are at once so broadly human and so definitely outlined as his. Belonging, some of them, to extinct types, they continue contemporary and familiar forever. So wide is the difference between knowing a great many men and that knowledge of human nature which comes of sympathetic insight and not of observation alone.

It is this power of sympathy which makes Chaucer's satire so kindly,—more so, one is tempted to say, than the panegyric of Pope. Intellectual satire gets its force from personal or moral antipathy, and measures offences by some rigid conventional standard. Its mouth waters over a galling word, and it loves to say *Thou*, pointing out its victim to public scorn. *Indignatio facit versus*, it boasts, though they might as often be fathered on envy or hatred. But imaginative satire, warmed through and through with the genial leaven of humor, smiles half sadly and murmurs *We*. Chaucer either makes one knave betray another, through a natural jealousy of competition, or else expose himself with a *naïveté* of good-humored cynicism which amuses rather than disgusts. In the former case the butt has a kind of claim on our sympathy; in the latter, it seems nothing strange, as I have already said, if the sunny atmosphere which floods that road to Canterbury should tempt anybody to throw off one disguise after another without suspicion. With perfect tact, too, the Host is made the *choragus* in this diverse company, and the coarse jollity of his temperament explains, if it do not excuse, much that would otherwise seem out of keeping. Surely nobody need have any scruples with *him*.

Chaucer seems to me to have been one of the most purely original of poets, as much so in respect of the world that is about us as Dante in respect of that which is within us. There had been nothing like him before, there has been nothing since. He is original, not in the sense that he thinks and says what nobody ever thought and said before, and what nobody can ever think and say again, but because he is always natural, because, if not always absolutely new, he is always delightfully fresh, because he sets before us the world as it honestly appeared to Geoffrey Chaucer, and not a world as it seemed proper to certain people that it ought to appear. He found that the poetry which had preceded him had been first the expression of individual feeling, then of class feeling as the vehicle of legend and history, and at last had wellnigh lost itself in chasing the mirage of allegory. Literature seemed to have passed through the natural stages which at regular intervals bring it to decline. Even the lyrics of the *jongleurs* were all run in one mould, and the Pastourelles of Northern France had become as artificial as the Pastorals of Pope. The Romances of chivalry had been made over into prose, and the *Melusine* of his contemporary Jehan d'Arras is the forlorn hope of the modern novel. Arrived thus far in their decrepitude, the monks endeavored to give them a religious and moral turn by allegorizing them. Their process reminds one of something Ulloa tells us of the fashion in which the Spaniards converted the Mexicans: "Here we found an old man in a cavern so extremely aged as it was wonderful, which could neither see nor go because he was so lame and crooked. The Father, Friar Raimund, said it were good (seeing he was so aged) to make him a Christian; whereupon we baptized him." The monks found the Romances in the same stage of senility, and gave them a saving sprinkle with the holy water of allegory. Perhaps they were only trying to turn the enemy's own weapons against himself, for it was the free-thinking *Romance of the Rose* that more than anything else had made allegory fashionable. Plutarch tells us that an allegory is to say one thing where another is meant, and this might have been needful for the personal security of Jean de Meung, as afterwards for that of his successor, Rabelais. But, except as a means of evading the fagot, the method has few recommendations. It reverses the true office of poetry by making the real unreal. It is imagination endeavoring to recommend itself to the understanding by means of cuts. If an author be in such deadly earnest, or if his imagination be of such creative vigor as to project real figures when it meant to cast only a shadow upon vapor; if the true spirit come, at once obsequious and terrible, when the conjurer has drawn his circle and gone through with his incantations merely to produce a proper frame of mind in his audience, as was the case with Dante, there is no longer any question of allegory as the word and thing are commonly understood. But with all secondary poets, as with Spenser for example, the allegory does not become of one substance with the poetry, but is a kind of carven frame for it, whose figures lose their meaning, as they cease to be contemporary. It was not a style that could have much attraction for a nature so sensitive to the actual, so observant of it, so interested by it, as that of Chaucer. He seems to have tried his hand at all the forms in vogue, and to have arrived in his old age at the truth, essential to all really great poetry, that his own instincts were his safest guides, that there is nothing deeper in life than life itself, and that to conjure an allegorical significance into it was to lose sight of its real meaning. He of all men could not say one thing and mean another, unless by way of humorous contrast.

In thus turning frankly and gayly to the actual world, and drinking inspiration from sources open to all; in turning away from a colorless abstraction to the solid earth and to emotions common to every pulse; in discovering that to make the best of nature, and not to grope vaguely after something better than nature, was the true office of Art; in insisting on a definite purpose, on veracity, cheerfulness, and simplicity, Chaucer shows himself the true father and founder of what is characteristically *English* literature. He has a hatred of cant as hearty as Dr. Johnson's, though he has a slier way of showing it; he has the placid common-sense of Franklin, the sweet, grave humor of Addison, the exquisite taste of Gray; but the whole texture of his mind, though its substance seem plain and grave, shows itself at every turn iridescent with poetic feeling like shot silk. Above all, he has an eye for character that seems to have caught at once not only its mental and physical features, but even its expression in variety of costume,—an eye, indeed, second only, if it should be called second in some respects, to that of Shakespeare.

I know of nothing that may be compared with the prologue to the *Canterbury Tales*, and with that to the story of the *Canon's Yeoman* before Chaucer. Characters and portraits from real life had never been drawn with such discrimination, or with such variety, never with such bold precision of outline, and with such a lively sense of the picturesque. His Parson is still unmatched, though Dryden and Goldsmith have both tried their hands in emulation of him. And the humor also in its suavity, its perpetual presence and its shy unobtrusiveness, is something wholly new in literature. For anything that deserves to be called like it in English we must wait for Henry Fielding.

Chaucer is the first great poet who has treated To-day as if it were as good as Yesterday, the first who held up a mirror to contemporary life in its infinite variety of high and low, of humor and pathos. But he reflected life in its large sense as the life of *men*, from the knight to the ploughman,—the life of every day as it is made up of that curious compound of human nature with manners. The very form of the *Canterbury Tales* was imaginative. The garden of Boccaccio, the supper-party of Grazzini, and the voyage of Giraldi make a good enough thread for their stories, but exclude all save equals and friends, exclude consequently human nature in its wider meaning. But by choosing a pilgrimage, Chaucer puts us on a plane where all men are equal, with souls to be saved, and with another world in view that abolishes all distinctions. By this choice, and by making the Host of the Tabard always the central figure, he has happily united the two most familiar emblems of life,—the short journey and the inn. We find more and more as we study him that he rises quietly from the conventional to the universal, and may fairly take his place with Homer in virtue of the breadth of his humanity.

In spite of some external stains, which those who have studied the influence of manners will easily account for without imputing them to any moral depravity, we feel that we can join the pure-minded Spenser in calling him "most sacred, happy spirit." If character may be divined from works, he was a good man, genial, sincere, hearty, temperate of mind, more wise, perhaps, for this world than the next, but thoroughly humane, and friendly with God and men. I know not how to sum up what we feel about him better than by saying (what would have pleased most one who was indifferent to fame) that we love him more even than we admire. We are sure that here was a true brotherman so kindly that, in his *House of Fame*, after naming the great poets, he throws in a pleasant word for the oaten-pipes.

> Of the little herd-grooms
> That keepen beasts among the brooms.

No better inscription can be written on the first page of his works than that which he places over the gate in his *Assembly of Fowls*, and which contrasts so sweetly with the stern lines of Dante from which they were imitated:—

> Through me men go into the blissful place
> Of the heart's heal and deadly woundës' cure;
> Through me men go unto the well of Grace,
> Where green and lusty May doth ever endure;
> This is the way to all good aventure;
> Be glad, thou Reader, and thy sorrow offcast,
> All open am I, pass in, and speed thee fast!

Notes

1. *Sir Eger and Sir Grine* in the Percy Folio. The passage quoted is from Ellis.
2. I think he tried one now and then, like "eyen *columbine*."
3. Commonly printed *hath*.
4. Froissart's description of the book of traités amoureux et de moralité, which he had had engrossed for presentation to Richard II. in 1394, is enough to bring tears to the eyes of a modern author. "Et lui plut très grandement; et plaire bien lui devoit car il était enluminé, écrit et historié et couvert de vermeil velours à dis cloux d'argent dorés d'or, et roses d'or au milieu, et à deux grands fremaulx dorés et richement ouvrés au milieu de rosiers d'or." How lovingly he lingers over it, hooking it together with *et* after *et*! But two centuries earlier, while the *jongleurs* were still in full song, poems were also read aloud.

> Pur remembrer des ancessours
> Les faits et les dits et les mours,
> Deit l'en les livres et les gestes
> Et les estoires *lire a festes*.
> (*Roman du Rou*)

But Chaucer wrote for the private reading of the closet.
5. Compare this with the Mumbo-Jumbo Revenge in Collins's Ode.

WILLIAM MINTO
From "Geoffrey Chaucer"
Characteristics of English Poets
1874, pp. 1–44

I. His Life, Character, and Works

To regard Chaucer as the first genial day in the spring of English poetry, is to take, perhaps, a somewhat insular view of his position. On a more comprehensive view, it would appear more apposite to call him a fine day, if not the last fine day, in the autumn of mediæval European poetry. He may be described as the father of English poetry—the first great poet that used the English language; but it is more instructive to look upon him as the English son and heir of a great family of French and Italian poets. He was the great English master in a poetic movement that originated in the south of Europe, among the provinces of the Langue d'Oc, which had been going on with brilliant energy for more than two centuries before his birth, and had produced among its masterpieces the *Romance of the Rose*, and the poetry of Dante and Petrarch. . . .

Chaucer was the first writer for all time that used the English language. But viewed as a figure in European literature, he must be regarded as the last of the Trouvères. His works float on the surface of the same literary wave; a deep gulf lies between them and the next, on the crest of which are the works of our great Elizabethans. Some patriotic Englishmen have strongly resented the endeavour of M. Sandras[1] to consider Chaucer as an imitator of the Trouvères. They are justified in taking offence at the word "imitator." It is too much to say that Chaucer produced nothing but imitations of G. de Lorris or other Trouvères, till he conceived the plan of the *Canterbury Tales*; and that the *Canterbury Tales*, though so far original in form, are animated throughout by the spirit of Jean de Meun. To say this is to produce a totally false impression as regards the decided individuality and pronounced English characteristics of Chaucer. He undoubtedly belongs to the line of the Trouvères. He was a disciple of theirs; he studied in the school of Guillaume de Lorris and Jean de Meun, by the side of Guillaume de Machault and Eustache Deschamps. He adopted the same poetical machinery of vision and allegory. He made the same elaborate studies of colour and form. From French predecessors he received the stimulus to his minute observation of character. It was emulation of them that kindled his happy genius for story-telling. The relation between Chaucer and the Trouvères is much closer than the relation between Shakespeare and the foreign originals that supplied him with plots, or than the relation between Mr Tennyson and the Arthurian legends. Making allowance for differences of national character, Chaucer owed as much to Guillaume de Lorris as Shakespeare to Marlowe, or Tennyson to Wordsworth; and in spite of national character, there was probably more affinity between pupil and master in the one case than in the others. At the same time, we should keep clear of such a word as imitation, which would imply that Chaucer had no character of his own. He received his impulse from the French: he made liberal use of their forms and their materials; yet his works bear the impress and breathe the spirit of a strong individuality; and this individuality, though most obvious in the *Canterbury Tales*, is throughout all his works distinctively English. Finally, to add one word on the comparative extent of Chaucer's obligations to Italian sources: while he translated largely from Boccaccio, and while it may be possible to trace an expansion of his poetic ideals coincident with the time when he may be supposed to have made his first acquaintance with Italian poetry, it is not to be questioned that he was most deeply indebted for general form, imagery, and characterization to the Trouvères, whose language and works he must have been familiar with from boyhood. . . .

It may almost be said to have been an accident that Chaucer did not write in French, as his contemporary Gower began by doing. But he had the sense to discern a capable literary instrument in the nascent English, which the king at this time was doing his utmost to encourage. A poet is not begotten by circumstances, but circumstances may do much to make or mar him, and a man of genius, able to make the new language move in verse, was sure of a warm welcome at the Court of Edward III. The atmosphere was most favourable to the development of a poet of genial pleasure-loving disposition. Edward's reign was the flowering period of chivalry in England. It was the midsummer, the July, of chivalry; the institution was

then in full blossom. All that it is customary to say about the gladness of life in the England of Chaucer's time was true of the Court; if a whole nation could be gladdened by the beautiful life of a favoured few, then all England must have been happy and merry. Pageantry was never more gorgeous or more frequent, courtesy of manner never more refined. The Court was like the Garden of Mirth in the *Romance of the Rose*; there were hideous figures on the outside of the walls, but inside all was sunshine and merry-making, and now and then the doors were thrown open and gaily attired parties issued forth to hunt or tournament. These amusements were arranged on a scale of unparalleled splendour.

It was a most gladsome and picturesque life at the Court of Edward III., and in that life Chaucer's poetry was an incident. This is a key to its joyous character. Animated playing on the surface of passion without breaking the crust, humorous pretence of incapacity when dull or difficult subjects come in the way, an eye for the picturesque, abundant supply of incident, never-failing fertility of witty suggestion—these are some of the qualities that made Chaucer's poetry acceptable to the audience for which he wrote. He never ventured on dangerous ground. He kept as far as possible from disagreeable realities. We search in vain for the most covert allusion to the painful events of the time. Devastating pestilences, disaster abroad, discontent and insurrection at home—he took for granted that his audience did not care to hear about such things, and he passed such things by. They wished to be entertained, and he entertained them charmingly, with lively adventures in high and human life, pictures of the life chivalric with its hunts and tournaments, pictures of the life vulgar with its intervals of riotous mirth, sweet love-tales, comical intrigues, graphic and humorous sketches of character. . . .

When we look closely at the construction of his poems, trying to realise how they were built up in the poet's mind, we are confirmed in our first impressions of the equability of his proceedings. We are not to suppose that he sang as the birds sing without effort—out of "the inborn kindly joyousness of his nature," as Coleridge says. His work is too solid for that. Those perfect touches of character in the Prologue to the *Canterbury Tales* were not put together with unpremeditated flow: we should as soon believe that a picture of Hogarth's was dashed off at a sitting. And, indeed, Chaucer tells us himself, in his *House of Fame*, that he wrote love-songs till his head ached, and pored over books till his eyes had a dazed look. Still, he worked equably, with patient elaboration. He is not carried away into incontinent fine frenzies of creation; his words and images do not flash together with lightning energy like the words and images of Shakespeare. His imagination is not overpowered by excited fecundity. Perhaps none of our poets combine such wealth of imagination with such perfect command over its resources: such power of expressing the incident or feeling in hand, with such ease in passing from it when it has received its just proportion; perhaps none of them can put so much into the mouth of a personage, and at the same time observe such orderly clearness, and such propriety of character. If you wish to understand his processes of construction, you cannot do better than study such passages as the elaborate self-disclosure of Januarius, when he consults with his friends about the expediency of marrying, or the imprudent candour of the Pardoner, or the talk between Chanticleer and Pertelot in the tale of the *Nun's Priest*. We are there struck by another consideration, and that is, how much he must have owed to his predecessors the garrulous inventive Fableors of northern France; and with what clearness of eye, and freedom and firmness of hand, he gathered, sifted, and recombined their opulent details of action and character. The *Canterbury Tales* could no more have grown out of the imagination and observation of one man than the *Iliad*, although one man had scope for the highest genius in adding to, taking from, kneading, and wholly recasting the materials furnished by many less distinguished labourers. . . .

II. His Language, Metres, and Imagery

Chaucer's similitudes are taken from such familiar sources, that M. Sandras charges him with giving a vulgar tone to his renderings of the chivalrous romances of Boccaccio. Whether it was that his English humour now and then broke out through his chivalrous sentiment, or whatever may be the explanation, there certainly is some ground for the charge. The comparison of Cressida to the "chief letter A," is so like our modern vulgar "A 1," that we are not perhaps unbiassed judges in that particular case. But there are a few similitudes in the *Knight's Tale* expressed with a primitive simplicity that must have drawn a smile from the poet himself. Such is the comparison of Palamon and Arcite quarrelling about Emily to two dogs fighting for a bone, while a kite comes in and carries off the object of contention. And still more amusing and unworthy of the subject is the comparison of poor humanity struggling on through the dark world with uncertain footing, to a drunk man, drunk as a mouse, who knows that he has a house, but does not know how to reach it, and finds the way very slippery. These similitudes are undeniably vivid: but unless our judgment is biassed by modern feelings, they belonged even in Chaucer's age more to the quaint monk than the chivalrous knight.

Most of Chaucer's similitudes, however—and he uses comparatively few, either as extended similes or as metaphors—are simple without being quaint or humorously inadequate to the subject. In this respect he contented himself with commonplaces, and made no effort to embellish his style with far-fetched flowers. He gives his warriors the look of griffins and lions, and makes them fight like cruel tigers and wild boars. Occasionally he expands the comparison, and gives it a certain local colour after the Italian manner, as when he introduces the Thracian hunter, or the tiger of the Galgopley, or the lion of Belmarie, or the pale face of the criminal on his way to execution. In extolling the charms of his heroines, he describes for the most part directly; and when he wants a brief illumination, makes use of the immemorial comparisons from the simple beauties of inanimate nature, the rose and the lily, sunlight and moonlight, spring-time and morning.

We are accustomed to think that Chaucer was able to dispense with a richly loaded diction, because he wrote for a primitive audience, thankful for small poetical mercies. But they were not so unsophisticated that a poet could make a reputation for colour, or as they might have called it, flowers of rhetoric, "the blossoms fresh of Tullius' garden sweet," upon the strength of comparing lovely women to roses and lilies, sunshine and spring, perennial as is the charm in thinking of such a likeness. Chaucer might have had to bestir himself for less familiar "tropes" and figures, had it not been that the structure of his poems gave him the opportunity of flooding his pages with colour in direct description. Beautiful women, heroic men, gorgeous buildings, gay processions, splendid armour, gardens and fountains, woods and rivers, birds and beasts, come in his way as the poet of fables and allegories, love, character, and romantic adventure; and he describes them enthusiastically with the utmost opulence of detail. His pictorial imagination was not called upon for many fragmentary contributions, but every now and then it received steady employment. What need had his readers for isolated touches of colour when their poet gave them such accumulations to revel

in as the Gardens of Venus, the Temple of Venus, the House of Fame, the Court of Love, the Tournament before Theseus, the rival troops of the knights and ladies of the *Flower and the Leaf?*

The *Parliament of Birds* is perhaps the richest of Chaucer's smaller poems—"imitations," as M. Sandras calls them,—but the *Book of the Duchess* is as good an example as need be of the poetical machinery that he inherited. The central aim of the poem is to commiserate the death of Blanche, Duchess of Lancaster, and to express the sorrow of her husband; but this object has grown into fold after fold of richly coloured and animated conception. . . .

III. The Chief Qualities of his Poetry

It is not unlikely that our impressions of the chief qualities of Chaucer's poetry are different in some respects from those felt by his contemporaries. In all probability we pass lightly over many things that fascinated them, and admire many things that they received with comparative indifference. Their captivating novelties have become our commonplaces, their impressive reflections have become trite; and, on the other hand, many passages that would doubtless have seemed tame and commonplace to them, strike us with all the freshness of reawakened nature, or with the strange interest of things exhumed after long ages of burial.

We cannot recover, with any assurance of certainty, the feelings of Richard II.'s courtiers when first they were charmed by the English language in the compositions of a great poet. We cannot imagine how his descriptions of fair women, fine buildings, flowers, trees, and bird-singing, were heard or read by those familiar with the *Romance of the Rose*; nor how his *Canterbury Tales* affected minds that knew such plots and incidents by the hundred. We know what a master of language can do with the most familiar materials; we know how fervently Chaucer's power was acknowledged, not only among his countrymen, but also on the other side of the Channel: but how they felt his power, which of its elements appealed to them most irresistibly, must ever remain matter for speculation.

Archaisms of word and inflection cannot but be inseparable elements in the sum total of the effects of Chaucer's poetry on us. Single words have changed their associations very materially since the days of Chaucer; and there are many that signify nothing to the present generation, many that are empty sounds, whose meaning may be attained only by dim approximation through glossarial synonyms. Words faintly picked up from a glossary have not the same power as the words of our mother-tongue. Even if we have a literary familiarity with them, the matter is not altogether mended. In all cases we may be sure that a passage with obsolete words in it does not move us as it moved contemporary readers. What may have been the effect of the passage when its words were hung about with the associations of the time, we cannot realise either by patient study or impatient flash of imagination: it is a dead thing, that no intellectual alchemy can resuscitate. We only know that it must have been different from what we experience. A phrase in a modern poem, even, does not go with equal power to the heart of every reader. Chance associations are fruitful sources of colouring peculiar to the individual. But to none of us can an obsolete word of Chaucer's have the same associations that it bore to men in whose mouths and ears it was a familiar visitor.

The natural effect of archaisms on pathetic passages is to make them sweeter and simpler by making them more childlike. Such lines as—

> The newë green, of jolif ver the prime
> And sweetë smelling flowerës white and red;

or—

And as I could this freshë flower I grette,
Kneeling alway, till it unclosed was
Upon the smallë, softë, sweetë grass,
That was with flowerës sweet embroided all—

come to us like the prattle of childhood, and fill us with the freshness of spring as no modern words could do. Even lines that are not so appropriate in the infantile mouth, are made prettier by their archaic garb. Take the following:—

She was not brown ne dun of hue,
But white as snow y-fallen new.
Her nose was wrought at point devise,
For it was gentle and tretis,
With eyen glad and browës bent;
Her hair down to her heelës went,
And she was simple as dove of tree;
Full debonaire of heart was she.

These lines, particularly the two about the lady's nose, are such as a modern reader would apply to a beautiful pet; they probably carried a more elevated sentiment when first written.

Look now at a passage that, apart from the quaintness of the language, should carry the sense of splendour—the march of Theseus upon Thebes.

The red statue of Mars with spear and targe
So shineth in his whitë banner large,
That all the fieldës glitteren up and doun:
And by his banner borne was his pennoun
Of gold full rich, in which there was y-beat
The Minotaur which that he wan in Crete.
Thus rid this duke, thus rid this conquerour,
And in his host of chivalry the flower,
Till that he came to Thebës and alight
Fair in a field there as he thought to fight.

The archaic inflections and turn of language give this a quaint unction, as if it were the imperfect utterance of an astonished child. The influence of the diction co-operates largely in reminding us that the splendour is a thing of bygone times, strange and wonderful in our imaginations. In the following astrological passage, matter and manner go together in the same way. It is the reflection of the Man of Law on the infatuated passion of the Soldan for Constance.

Paraventure, in thilkë largë book
Which that men clepe the Heaven, y-written was
With starrës, when that he his birthë took,
That he for love should have his death, alas!
For in the starrës, clearer than is glass,
Is written, God wot, whoso could it read
The death of every man withouten dread.

In starrës many a winter there beforn
Was written the death of Hector, Achilles,
Of Pompey, Julius, ere they were born;
The strife of Thebës, and of Hercules,
Of Sampson, Turnus, and of Socrates
The death; but mennës wittës been so dull
That no wight can well read it at the full.

Later on in the same tale, there is another astrological passage—an impassioned appeal to the starry destinies—when Constance is setting sail for the East to the marriage that proves so fatal.

O firstë moving cruel firmament!
With thy diurnal swough that crowdest aye
And hurlest all fro East to Occident
That naturally would hold another way!
Thy crowding set the heaven in such array
At the beginning of this fierce voyage,
That cruel Mars hath slain this marriage.

In this passage the archaic trappings, and particularly the bit of dogma about the natural course of the firmament, are rather in the way—interfering with our perception of the dignity and passion of the apostrophe.

The archaic diction makes itself felt with peculiar harmony in the narrative of supernatural manifestations, such as were ascribed to devils and magicians. Sir Walter Scott might have envied the following account of the ritual of Arcite in the temple of Mars, and the answer to his prayer:—

The prayer stint of Arcita the strong:
The ringës on the temple door that hong,
And eke the doorës clattereden full fast,
Of which Arcita somewhat him aghast.
The firës brende up on the altar bright
That it gan all the temple for to light;
A sweetë smell anon the ground up gave
And Arcita anon his hand up have,
And more incense into the fire he cast,
With other ritës mo, and at the last
The statue of Mars began his hauberk ring,
And with that sound he heard a murmuring
Full low and dim, and said thus, 'Victory!'

This is a more active and instantaneously impressive sorcery than the calm power of the stars, and the archaisms seem to go with it in readier harmony.

Take now another point. Chaucer sympathises deeply with the victims of deceitful love, and assails false lovers with cordial anger. If he were a dreamy poet like Spenser—a poet whose indignation assumed a wailful and regretful tone—the antique words and turns would be in perfect unison; they would help to translate the objects of our pity and anger farther and farther away from the living world—farther and farther back into a dim distance from indignant tears and frowns. But Chaucer is the opposite of a dreamy poet; his feelings are fresh and quick, his expression direct and demonstrative; he pities Dido, Ariadne, Phyllis, Medea, and flames out with fierce passion against Æneas, Theseus, Demophon, and Jason, as heartily as if they had all been his personal acquaintances. He cannot think of the treachery of the false lovers without getting into a passion.

But welaway! the harm, the ruth,
That hath betide for such untruth!
As men may oft in bookës read,
And all day see it yet in deed,
That for to thinken it a teen is.

He utterly repudiates the pretence of Æneas that he was urged to leave Carthage by a destiny that he could not disobey; he treats this with scorn as a shallow and commonplace excuse for leaving a love that had become stale. He travels beyond his authorities to imagine the complainings of the forsaken queen; refers his readers for the whole of the touching story to Ovid; and cries with sudden energy—

And were it not too long to endite,
By God, I would it herë write!

He is no less furious at Theseus—

How false eke was Duke Theseus,
That as the story telleth us,
How he betrayed Adriane;
The Devil be his soulës bane!

Demophon, the son of Theseus, wicked son of a wicked sire, prone to deceit as the young of the fox, is treated with contemptuous scorn for his treachery to Phyllis—

Me list not vouchësafe on him to swink,
Dispenden on him a penful of ink,

For false he was in love right as his sire;
The Devil set their soulës both on fire!

Jason is held up to especial contempt; the poet proceeds to impeach him with especial zest—

Thou root of falsë lovers, Duke Jason!
Thou sly devourer and confusion
Of gentle women, gentle crëatures!

Now there is no mistaking the genuineness of all this passion. But can we echo all these imprecations with true fervour? Do they not sound strange in our ears? Can we feel them as the poet's contemporaries did?

It was the opinion of De Quincey that, in the quality of animation, Chaucer is superior to Homer. The comparison is not, perhaps, altogether fair, because Chaucer's themes, as a rule, admit of lighter treatment than Homer's: but certainly no poet could well be more animated than Chaucer. All his works are full of bright colour, fresh feeling, and rapid ease and gaiety of movement. There is no tedious dulness in his descriptions; no lingering in the march of his narrative. With all his loquacity and vivacity, he knows when his readers have had enough of one thing, and passes easily on to something else. The ease of his transitions is very remarkable. Some writers drive so hard at the expression of what lies before them for the moment, that they cannot recover themselves quickly enough to make a graceful turn to what succeeds: they throw themselves off the track, and become confused and uncertain in their apprehension of the main subject. This Chaucer never seems to do; he always keeps his main subject clearly and firmly in view; and his well-marked digressions add to the general animation, by dispersing the feeling of rigid restraint without tending in the slightest to produce confusion.

It is in the *Knight's Tale* and the *Squire's Tale*, which deal to some extent with martial subjects, that Chaucer may most fairly be compared with Homer. The comparison is not unfavourable to our native poet. Even in conveying a vivid impression of the stir of an excited crowd, in which Homer is so excelling, we cannot allow that Chaucer is inferior. What could be more animated than Chaucer's account in the *Squire's Tale* of the bustling and buzzing multitude that assembled to stare at the magic horse, broad mirror of glass, and ring of gold, and to exchange speculations concerning the nature of these wonderful presents? Take, again, the gathering to the tournament before Theseus, in the *Knight's Tale*. What could be more inspiring, more alive with bright movement, splendid evolution, and fresh air than this? The herald has just proclaimed that the more deadly weapons are excluded from the lists; whereupon—

The voïce of the people toucheth heaven,
So loudë criedë they with merry steven:
'God savë such a lord that is so good:
He willeth no destruction of blood!'
Up goth the trumpës and the melody.
And to the listës ride the company
By ordinancë through the city large,
Hanging with cloth of gold and not with serge.
Full like a lord this noble Duke can ride;
These Two Thebanës upon either side:
And after rode the Queen, and Emily,
And of ladies another company,
And of communës after their degree.
And thus they passeden through that city,
And to the listës comen they by time.
It was not of the day yet fully prime,
When settë was Thesëus rich and high,
Hippolyta the Queen, and Emily,

And other ladies in their degrees about,
Unto the seatës presseth all the rout;
And westëward, thorough the gates of Mart,
Arcite, and eke the hundred of his part,
With banners red is entered right anon;
And in that selvë moment Palamon
Is under Venus, eastward in that place,
With banner white, and hardy cheer and face.

We should expect the courtier of Richard II., even when writing in his old age, to be more animated in his treatment of love than the blind old man of the rocky isle. And such he is. We shall see that Chaucer specially excels in depicting the tender aspects of the passion, but he was a master also of its cheering inspirations. Everybody has by heart his cheerful description of the youthful squire. That gay gentleman, however, was basking in the unbroken sunshine of love; you must take one who has known its dark eclipse, if you wish to see an example of its full power. Take Arcita of the *Knight's Tale*, who has been changed by his passion out of all recognition: he has become lean, hollow-eyed, and sallow, and his spirits have been so low that the sound of music brought tears into his eyes. Consider the change wrought on this woful lover when he has made some progress towards success, and his youthful energies return to their natural tone. Take him when he walks out of a May morning with his rising hopes, and drinks in the sympathy of nature, which also is rejoicing in its recovery from darkness and winter.

The busy larkë, messenger of day,
Salueth in her song the morrow gray;
And fiery Phœbus riseth up so bright
That all the orient laugheth of the light,
And with his streamës dryeth in the greves
The silver droppës, hanging on the leaves.
And Arcita, that is in the court royal
With Thesëus, his squiër principal,
Is risen, and looketh on the merry day.
And for to doon his observance to May,
Remembering of the point of his desire,
He on his courser, starting as the fire,
Is ridden into the fieldës him to play,
Out of the court, were it a mile or tway.
And to the grove, of which that I you told,
By aventure his way he gan to hold,
To maken him a garland of the greves,
Were it of woodëbind or hawthorn leaves,
And loud he sung against the sunnë sheen:—
'May, with all thy flowrës and thy green,
Welcome be thou, fairë freshë May!
I hope that I some greenë getten may.'
And fro his courser, with a lusty heart,
Into the grove full lustily he start,
And in a path he roamed up and down.

When we go for a feast of tender feeling to a poet possessing in large measure the quality of animation, we should not go in a languid mood. We need not, of course, follow his lead; we may choose our own pace. Instead of going with the surface of the lively brook, and seeing no more of its pebbles and the beauties of its banks and winding nooks than the rapid glance that its speed allows, we may fix on delicious spots, and feed there to our heart's content. It is this quality of animation that makes Chaucer so peculiarly the poet of outdoor summer weather, the most delightful of companions on the hillside, or by the running streams.

Chaucer's heart fitted him well to be the poet of tender sentiment. He seems to have dealt with fond observation on everything that was bright and pretty, from "the smallë fowlës that sleepen all the night with open eye," to the little herd-grooms playing on their pipes of green corn. He watched the little conies at their play, the little squirrels at their sylvan feasts; he looked into the "coldë wellë streamës, nothing dead," to admire

> The smallë fishes bright
> With finnës red, and scalës silver white.

He knew, too, the colour of every feather in Chanticleer, and had minutely studied his majesty's habits towards his subjects. But of all things of beauty in nature, the singing-birds were his most especial favourites. He often dwells on the ravishing sweetness of their melodies. His finest picture of their exuberance of joy in the spring—their tuneful defiance of the fowler, their billing and chirruping, their vows of eternal fidelity—occurs in the opening of the *Legend of Good Women*.

A man of the world himself, Chaucer still could enter into simple love-making among unsophisticated gentle creatures of a larger growth than the amorous little birds. Perhaps no passage shows the poet's exquisite tenderness better than the wooing of Thisbe by Pyramus, so well known in its ludicrous aspects from the caricature in *Midsummer Night's Dream*; and it is but an act of justice to these two faithful lovers to let them be seen as they were conceived by a sympathetic poet.

> This wall, which that betwix them bothë stood
> Was cloven atwo, right fro the top adoun,
> Of oldë time, of his foundatioun.
> But yet this clift was so narrow and lite
>
> · · ·
>
> But what is that that love cannot espy?
> Ye lovers two, if that I shall not lie,
> Ye founden first this little narrow clift!
> And with a sound as soft as any shrift,
> They let their wordës through the cliftë pace,
> And tolden while they stooden in the place,
> All their complaint of love and all their woe.
> At every timë when they durstë so,
> Upon the one side of the wall stood he,
> And on that other sidë stood Thisbe,
> The sweetë sound of other to receive.
> And thus their wardens wouldë they deceive,
> And every day this wall they wouldë threat,
> And wish to God that it were down y-beat.
>   Thus would they sayn:—'Alas, thou wicked
>   wall!
> Through thine envyë thou us lettest all!
> Why nilt thou cleave, or fallen all atwo?
> Or at the leastë, but thou wouldest so,
> Yet wouldest thou but onës let us meet,
> Or onës that we mightë kissen sweet,
> Then were we covered of our carës cold.
> But nathëless, yet be we to thee hold
> In as much as thou sufferest for to gone
> Our wordës through thy lime and eke thy stone,
> Yet oughtë we with thee been well apaid.'
>   And when these idle wordës weren said,
> The coldë wall they wouldë kissen of stone,
> And take their leave, and forth they wouldë gone.

Thoroughly as his heart seems to go with this simple, earnest passion, almost infantile in its fondness, he can strike many another key in the infinitely varied art of love. Especially is he skilled in the chivalrous profession of entire submission to his lady's will, and humble adoration of her pre-eminent excellence. Take, for example, the opening stave of his humble prayer to Pity, which, without doubt, the cruel fair was at liberty to apply to herself.

> Humblest of heart, highest of reverence,
> Benignë flower, corown of virtues allë!
> Sheweth unto your royal excellence,
> Your servant, if I durstë me so callë,
> His mortal harm, in which he is y-fallë,
> And not all only for his evil fare,
> But for your renown, as I shall declare.
>
> · · · ·
>
> What needeth to show parcel of my pain,
> Sith every wo that hartë may bethink,
> I suffer; and yet I dare not to you plain,
> For well I wot, although I wake or wink,
> Ye reckë not whether I float or sink.
> Yet nathëless my truth I shall susteen,
> Unto my death, and that shall well be seen.

All forlorn lovers have his best services at their command. We may apply to him his own favourite line, many times repeated—

> For pity runneth soon in gentle heart.

How feelingly he depicts the situation of Palamon—imprisoned and love-sick Palamon!

> In darkness and horrible and strong prison
> This seven year hath sitten Palamon,
> Forpined, what for wo and for distress.
> Who feeleth double sorrow and heaviness
> But Palamon? that love distraineth so,
> That wood out of his wit he goth for wo.

The woful pangs of sweet Aurelius too, his languor and furious torments, are followed with deep sympathy; and the heart-broken agony of forsaken Troilus is most intimately realised. In the expression of "deep heart's-sorrowing," Chaucer's words always flow with peculiar richness and intimate aptness of choice.

Naturally, however, it is womanhood in distress that enters his heart with the keenest stroke. He might well plead before the god and goddess of love that, if he had laughed at some of the foibles of the sex, he had not been indifferent to their virtues and their sufferings. His gallery of distressed heroines was as wide as the range of legend and history that was known to him: Constance, Griselda, Virginia, Cecilia, Alcyone, Alcestis, Cleopatra, Thisbe, Dido, Hypsipyle, Medea, Lucrece, Ariadne, Philomela, Phyllis, Hypermnestra. The thought of their suffering agitates him, destroys his composure; he cannot proceed without stopping to express his compassion, or to appeal to heaven against the caprice of Fortune or the wickedness of men. But he never dwells long on such scenes. It was not for him to harrow the feelings of his audience; when he has said enough to move them, he at once proceeds to effect a diversion. Lingering agonies were not to his taste. His representative the Host is almost choked with emotion at the Doctor's tale of Appius and Virginia; he relieves himself with furious denunciation of Appius, and tries to laugh the painful theme out of his memory. The legends of Constance (*Man of Law's Tale*) and Griselda (*Clerk's Tale*), have the happy termination of comedy; and the story of their prolonged sufferings is relieved by many a passing word of indignant blame against the guilty causes of their misery. Mediæval readers liked long-drawn martyrdoms, but in the hands of such an artist as Chaucer, whether he dealt with the martyrs of religion or the martyrs of love, the pathos is never hard and overbearing; our pity is kept quick and fresh, and not allowed to stagnate in oppressive anguish. Such a poem as Wordsworth's 'Margaret' was impossible for him.

One of the most delightful of the *Canterbury Tales* is the *Franklin's Tale*. The incorruptible fidelity of the beautiful Dorigen, the equanimity and magnanimity of her brave husband Arviragus, the resolution of the Squire Aurelius not to be outdone in generosity by the Knight, capped by the resolution of the Knight not to be outdone by the Squire, make this tale a unique embodiment of the highest ideals of chivalry: scrupulous adherence to a rash promise on the one hand being met by renunciation of unfair advantage on the other. The chivalry of the tale is fantastic, but the poet's art makes it credible and beautiful.

Chaucer's humour is the most universally patent and easily recognised of his gifts. The smile or laugh that he raises, by refined irony or by broad rough jest and incident, is conspicuously genial. Mephistophelian mockery and Satanic grimness are not in his way. This had nothing to do with his being the bright morning star of English poetry—writing with the buoyancy of youth at a time when the struggle for existence was less fierce, when there was no bitter feeling between high and low, no envenomed warfare of civil or religious party. There never has been age nor country in which the fierce spirit has wanted fuel for its fierceness. It was simply the nature of the man to be genial,—"attempered and soft" as the climate of his gardens of Venus. He would have been so in whatever age he had lived.

The great criterion of good-nature, the indispensable basis of humour, is the power of making or sustaining a jest at one's own expense; and none of our humorists bear this test so well as Chaucer. He often harps on his own supposed imperfections, his ignorance of love, his want of rhetorical skill, his poverty. His poverty, real or pretended—and, unfortunately, it would seem to have been real—is the subject of several jokes in his poems, as it must have been in his private talk. In the *House of Fame*, when describing how the walls, roofs, and floors of the temple were plated with gold half a foot thick "as fine as ducat of Venice," he cannot resist the temptation to add—

Of which too little in my pouch is.

His "Complaint to his Purse" is conceived in a very gay spirit:—

Now voucheth safe this day, ere it be night,
That I of you the blissful sound may hear,
Or see your colour like the sunnë bright,
That of yellowness haddë never peer.
Ye be my life! ye be mine heartës steer!
Queen of comfort and goodë company!
Beth heavy again or ellës mote I die.

We must know this hobby of his to understand the full comic force of his comparing Alison to a newly forged noble, bright from the mint.

The freedom of his humour, as one would expect, was progressive. There are unequivocal touches of humour both in *Chaucer's Dream* and in the *Court of Love*; witness the sly treatment of Morpheus, and the poet's timid entry into the sacred court; but the humour, as became the subjects, is lurking and subordinate. It is worth noting, that in the *Court of Love*, though he could not profess entire ignorance of the passion as he did so often afterwards, he professes to have kept out of the service of Venus for a most unconscionable length of time; he was actually eighteen before he went to her court, and then he had to be summoned. But the humour is much less overt in the *Court of Love*, than in the more mature *House of Fame*. In that poem, as in the *Canterbury Tales*, he treats his own personality with reckless contempt. When the poet is caught up, at first he loses consciousness; but by-and-by the eagle wakes him up with comical remonstrances at his timidity. Half reassured, he begins to wonder vaguely what all this can mean:—

O God, thought I, that madest kind,
Shall I none other wayes die?

Whe'r Jovës will me stellify,
Or what thing may this signify?
I neither am Enoch, ne Eli,
Ne Romulus, ne Ganymede,
That was y-bore up, as men read,
To heaven with Dan Jupiter,
And made the goddës botteler!
Lo, this was then my fantasy!
But he that bare me gan espy,
That I so thought, and saidë this—
'Thou deemest of thyself amiss;
For Jovës is not thereabout,
I dare will put thee out of doubt,
To make of thee as yet a star.'

The comparison between his own stout person and Ganymede, and the implied conception of himself as the butler[2] of the gods, are delicious. But, indeed, the passage throughout is so rich, that it is difficult to say which is its most comical touch.

The outcome of his broad humour is seen in the general plan of the *Canterbury Tales* as much as in some of the pronounced particulars. With the rougher sort of the pilgrims, and as we shall presently see, only with them, the pilgrimage is a tipsy revel, a hilarious holiday "outing." They are the merriest company that mine "Host of the Tabard" has had under his roof for many a day; and they are such jolly noisy good fellows that, at supper overnight, the host is tempted to propose that he should go with them and direct their merriment on the way. In the energy of his good-fellowship and confident sudden prospect of a hilarious journey, he cries for immediate decision on his plan—

Now by my father's soulë that is dead,
But ye be merry, smiteth off mine head.
Hold up your hands withouten morë speech.

They agree; and the idea thus conceived is carried out with no less spirit. The pilgrims must have made a sensation as they rode out of town. The more respectable members of the company doubtless bore themselves with becoming gravity, but the wilder spirits put no restraint upon their mirth. The Miller brought them out of town to the music of his bagpipes—and a bagpipe in the hands of a drunk man is an instrument likely to attract some attention. The harum-scarum pimpled-faced bacchanalian Summoner had put on his head a garland large enough for an alehouse sign, and flourished a cake as a buckler. His friend and compeer the Pardoner had, "for jollity," trussed up his hood in his wallet, and let his yellow flaxen hair hang in disorder on his shoulders, saying that it was the new fashion.

Full loud he sang 'Come hither, love, to me.'
This Summoner bare to him a stiff burdoun,
Was never trump of half so great a soun.

A company with spirits so uproarious in it tasked all the Host's powers of maintaining order, authoritative though he was. Of course they broke through. The Knight, who drew the lot for telling the first tale, was allowed to finish it; but as soon as he had done, the drunk Miller struck in and insisted on telling a noble tale that he knew. Though hardly able to keep his seat, he was not so drunk as not to know that he was drunk; he knew that, he said, "by his soun," and he besought them, if he said anything out of place, to lay the blame on the ale of Southwark. His tale does ample justice to his inspiration. The Host having once let the reins out of his hands was not able to resume them: the president of such a company must keep his authority by giving his subjects liberty to take their own way. The butt of the *Miller's Tale* was a carpenter; and the Reeve being a carpenter thought himself aggrieved, and wanted to return the compliment by telling an equally coarse tale about the cuckolding of a miller. The Host, with the true instinct of a ruler, at once humoured him, and asserted his own dignity by cutting short his prologue, and commanding him to tell his tale. Then the gross Cook, chuckling over the discomfiture of the Miller, wanted to tell "a little jape that fell in our city," and the judicious Host granted permission. There was more intoxicated personality, wrangling, and peace-making, as they went on. The Friar enraged the Summoner by relating an awkward adventure that happened to one of his profession; and the Summoner gave a merciless Roland for his Oliver. After a long draught of ale, the Pardoner recklessly exposed all the tricks of his trade, and had the audacious assurance, after this full confession of his roguery, to try to work upon the feelings of his brother pilgrims, and extract money from them. It is to be feared, too, that the Host required a little too much of the "corny ale" to drown his pity for poor Virginia: one cannot otherwise account for his getting into a hot quarrel with the Pardoner, which required the intervention of the Knight to smooth it over. Towards the close of the pilgrimage the Cook showed symptoms of being overcome with sleep and ale, and seemed to be in danger of falling from his horse. The Host rebuked him, and the Manciple fell out upon him with such a torrent of abuse, that poor Robin overbalanced himself and tumbled to the ground in a furious futile effort to articulate a reply, and there was much shoving to and fro before they could set him in the saddle again. A pretty pilgrimage to the shrine of a saint! There is endless food for deep animal laughter in the humours of these riotous pilgrims—particularly that madcap pair of ecclesiastics—the Summoner and the Pardoner. One is constantly finding fresh points of comical view in that precious couple. It is a mistake, I may remark, to look in the *Canterbury Tales* for satire. If there is any, it is there by failure and imperfection; it is a flaw in the poet's design, which was to provide material for disinterested laughter, zealous and profound. To suppose that there is any satire in the candid revelation of the Pardoner's gross deceptions of the credulous vulgar, is to fail to rise to the height of the humour of that great character. There is no more ill-nature in the elaboration of his reckless freaks, than in the often-quoted and justly-praised delicate irony of the opening of the *Wife of Bath's Tale*.[3]

As regards any lurking satirical purpose in the *Canterbury Tales*, if we suppose that we discern any such purpose, we may take for granted that we are still on the outside of their riotous humour. It is true that a good many of the pilgrims are men of somewhat damaged reputation, or, at least, doubtful virtue. The Merchant is not beyond suspicion; the Miller steals corn; the Reeve has secured a comfortable feathering for his own nest; the Cook is a profligate sot; all the ecclesiastics, Monk, Friar, and Pardoner, exhibit a wide difference between their practice and their doctrine; and even the respectable professional men, the Lawyer and the Doctor, have a questionable liking for large fees. But these failings are not dwelt upon from the point of view of the satirist. With all their sinful taints, the pilgrims are represented as being on the whole jovial companions, satisfied with themselves and with each other; the taints, indeed, are not shown in the aspect of sins, but rather in the aspect of ludicrous peccadilloes or foibles. The sinners are elevated by the hilarity of the occasion above the sense of sin; and the poet does not hold them up to scorn or contempt, but enters genially into the spirit of their holiday revel. He does not join them to backbite and draw out their weaknesses for the bitter amusement or sharp dislike of his readers: he joins them to enjoy their company. Chaucer's humour in the *Canterbury Tales* is not in the spirit of Jean de Meun; it comes much nearer the spirit of Burns in the "Jolly Beggars."

IV. His Delineation of Character

It is somewhat startling to put together, as I have done in the preceding section, the buffoonery that went on throughout the Canterbury pilgrimage. We remember the tales of high chivalrous sentiment and exquisite pathos, and we ask how these were compatible with such noisy ribaldry. The explanation is, that the tales are suited to the characters and manners of the different pilgrims; and that while one set of them indulge largely in ale and inebriated freaks and loud animal mirth, the more respectable sort preserve a becoming dignity.

To a certain extent Professor Lowell is right in saying that there is no caste feeling among Chaucer's pilgrims. Knight and yeoman, monk and cook, lodge all night in the same inn, set out in a company on the same errand, and contribute to a common entertainment subject to the direction of one man, and that an inn-keeper. But we should greatly misunderstand the delicacy of Chaucer's sense of manners as well as of character, if we went away with the impression that in the *Canterbury Tales* there is no trace of the distinctions of rank, and that in the pilgrimage there is no respect paid to persons.

In the *Prologue*, the poet begs pardon for not setting the pilgrims in their degree—

> Also I pray you to forgive it me
> All have I not set folk in their degree
> Here in this tale, as that they shouldë stand.
> My wit is short, ye may well understand.

He had a livelier plan in view than to make them tell off their tales in the order of their rank. But though he did not adopt this palpable and unmistakable way of indicating caste, he does really show respect of persons in several less gross and obvious ways. A line is drawn, though unobtrusively and with delicate suggested art, between "the gentles" and the other pilgrims. If this had not been done, we should have been compelled to say that our poet had inaccurately portrayed the life of the time. But he has done it, and done it not by harsh angular forced assertion, but easily and naturally in his clearsighted shaping and working out of his materials. The careful reader gets the clue from such passages as that at the end of the *Knight's Tale*, where we are told that the whole company, young and old, praised it as a noble and memorable story, "and namely," that is, particularly, "the *gentles* every one." That was the sort of tale that the gentles felt themselves at liberty to approve of. When the Pardoner took up with animation the Host's request that he should tell a merry tale, forthwith the "gentles" began to cry that they must have no ribaldry: "Tell us," they said, "some moral thing that we may learn." It is very misleading to apologise, as some writers on Chaucer do, for the gross obscenity of certain of the tales, on the ground that this was the outspoken fashion of the time—that decorum then permitted greater freedom of language. The savour of particular words may have changed since the time of Chaucer; but then, as now, people with any pretensions to refinement were bound to abstain strictly in the presence of ladies from all ribaldry of speech and manner, on pain of being classed with "churls" and "villains." In the *Court of Love*, the gentle lover is warned emphatically that he must not be

> Ribald in speech, or out of measure pass,
> Thy bound exceeding; think on this alway:
> For women been of tender heartës aye.

And in the *Canterbury Tales*, Chaucer carefully guards himself against being supposed to be ignorant of this law. The ribald tales are introduced as the humours of the lower orders, persons ignorant or defiant of the rules of refined society, and moreover, as we have seen, excited, intoxicated, out for a pilgrimage as riotous and wild as our pilgrimage to the Derby.[4]

Such riotous mirth was very far indeed from being the fashion of the time among fashionable people. Mark how careful Chaucer is to shield himself from the responsibility of it. In the *Prologue* (l. 725), he prays his readers of their courtesy not to set down his plainness of speech as his "villany": he is bound to record faithfully every word that was said, though it had been said by his own brother. He does, indeed, whether seriously or jocularly, allege the example of Christ and Plato as authorities for plainness of speech; but he does not repeat this when he returns to the matter before the first of his freespoken tales. In the prologue to the *Miller's Tale*, he is most explicit. He says that the obstinate Miller would not forbear for any man, "but told his churlish tale in his manner." And then he makes this clear and elaborate apology for rehearsing it,—

> And, therefore, every *gentle* wight I pray,
> For, Goddës love, deemeth not that I say
> Of evil intent; but for I must rehearse
> Their talës all, be they better or worse,
> *Or ellës falsen some of my matter.*
> And, therefore, whoso list it not to hear,
> Turn over the leaf and chose another tale;
> For he shall find enowë great and small,
> Of *storial thing that toucheth gentilesse,*
> And eke morality and holiness.
> Blameth not me, if that ye chose amiss.
> *The Miller is a churl, ye know well this,*
> *So was the Reeve and other many mo,*
> And harlotry they tolden bothë two.
> Aviseth you, and put me out of blame;
> And eke men shall not maken earnest of game.

Observe, accordingly, how the tales are distributed. Nothing ribald is put into the mouth of the gentles, and nothing ribald is told concerning their order. The "very perfect gentle knight," who never said any villany to any manner of man, recites the tale of Palamon and Arcite, with its chivalrous love and rivalry, its sense of high womanly beauty, its gorgeous descriptions of temple, ritual, procession, and tournament. His son, the gallant, well-mannered, well-dressed squire, embroidered like a mead, with his head full of love, romance, song, and music, gives a fragment of a romance about King Cambuscan and his daughter Canace, and the wonderful exploits of a magic horse, a magic mirror, and a magic ring. The professional men—the busy lawyer, the studious clerk, the irreligious but good-hearted doctor—give the pathetic stories of Constance, Griselda, and Virginia: the two first of which may be justly described as tales of morality. The Franklin tells the old Breton lay of Dorigen and Arviragus, models of chivalrous virtue. The Prioress and the Second Nun relate holy legends of martyrdom. These are "the gentles," and such are their tales. The tales of vulgar merriment are told by the Miller, the Reeve, the Wife of Bath, the Friar, the Summoner, the Merchant, the Shipman. And as regard is had to the condition of the narrator in the character of the tale ascribed to him, so the persons engaged in degrading adventure are below the rank of the gentles. Januarius, indeed, in the *Merchant's Tale*, is called a worthy knight; but he is a blind dotard, long past knightly exercise and knightly feeling: and his May, who is so easily won to play him false, is represented as a maiden of small degree. The rank of all the other befooled heroes is plain: they are a carpenter, a miller, a summoner, a friar, and a merchant.[5] The gentle order is respected. They join the company, and enjoy the ribald speech and behaviour of their riotous, inebriated, vulgar companions; but they do not forfeit their self-respect, by contributing a share to the noisy merriment. When they have had enough of it, or when the tales threaten to become too boisterous, they use their influence to give a more sober tone to the proceedings. They do not break rough jests on each other as the vulgar do. And mine host knows his place sufficiently well to be less familiar and imperious with them than with the Miller and the Cook; he is courteous to the Knight, and ludicrously over-polite to the Prioress.

I may seem to have insisted too much on this distinction between the "gentles" and the "roughs" in the Canterbury pilgrimage; but the truth is, that we cannot have too vivid a hold of this distinction if we wish to understand either the *Canterbury Tales*, or Chaucer's poetry generally. Unless we realise this, we cannot feel how thoroughly and intimately his poems are transfused with chivalrous sentiment. What is more, we cannot appreciate the perfect skill with which he has maintained this sentiment in the *Canterbury Tales*, and at the same time transferred to his pages a faithful representation of vulgar manners in their wildest luxuriance.

Waiving all questions as to whether Chaucer was most of Norman or of Saxon, of Celt or of Teuton, we cannot escape from admitting that he was deeply impressed with the wide difference between chivalrous sentiments and the sentiments and manners prevalent among the dependants of chivalry. The difference may not have in reality been so profound as it was in ideal; but Chaucer felt it deeply. How deeply, we see most clearly in the "Cuckoo and Nightingale," and the *Parliament of Birds*, where the antagonistic sentiments are placed in express contrast. The Cuckoo is a vulgar bird, and takes gross ridiculous views of love: the Nightingale is a gentle bird, and regards love with delicate seriousness. Similar types are represented, with greater epic variety, in the *Parliament of Birds*. There is no mistaking the contrast in these allegorical fables; the vulgar birds, the Water Fowls, the Seed Fowls, and the Worm Fowls, are sharply snubbed for their chuckling vulgarity by the haughty and refined Birds of Prey. But in the *Canterbury Tales* the poet has achieved the triumph of making the antagonistic sentiments work smoothly side by side, and that is really their main triumph as a broad picture of manners and character. There, with dignified carriage, are seen the type of men and women whose sensibilities were trained to appreciate the tender refinement of Chaucer, and who allowed themselves more boisterous entertainments only under decorous pretexts, listening without participating. Side by side, following their own humours with noisy independence, are their vulgar associates, stopping at every ale-stake to eat and drink, half choked with ribald laughter, finding in the contrast between themselves and the reserved gentles an additional incentive to their gross open mirth. The *Canterbury Tales* embody two veins of feeling that powerfully influenced the literature of the fifteenth century—the sentiment that fed on chivalrous romances, and the appetite for animal laughter that received among other gratifications the grotesque literature of miracle-plays.

If we fail to perceive this contrast between the serious and the ludicrous side of the Canterbury pilgrimage, if we miss the poet's reconciliation of the two without repression of either, Chaucer's genius, in so far as regards manners and character, has laboured for us in vain. A dead weight flattens his figures into the page. The exquisite delicacy of his delineation is confused. We drag down the Knight and the Prioress by involving them in the responsibility of the *Miller's Tale*: we crush the life out of the Miller and the Summoner, and reduce them to wretched tameness by supposing them to fraternise with the Knight in a certain amount of decorous restraint. The pilgrimage becomes a muddled, jumbled, incoherent, unintelligible thing.

We must not, however, allow our attention to two large divisions, however much that may be the key to a right understanding of the *Canterbury Tales*, to make us overlook the varied types that lie within these divisions. Every character, indeed, is typical—Knight, Squire, Yeoman, Prioress, Monk, Friar, Merchant, Clerk, Sergeant of Law, Franklin, Cheapside Burgess, Cook, Shipman, Doctor of Physic, Wife of Bath, Parson, Ploughman, Miller, Manciple, Reeve, Summoner, Pardoner: and the characteristics of their various lines of life are drawn as no other generation has been in equal space. I shall not attempt to pick out supreme examples of Chaucer's skill. The compression of masterly touches in that *Prologue* can hardly be spoken of in sane language: there is not one of the seven or eight hundred lines but contains something to admire.

Apart from the skill of the delineation, one typical individual is specially interesting from his relations to the time, and that is the poor Parson. He cannot be said to belong, in rank at least, to the gentle class: he is of poor extraction, the brother of the Ploughman. He represents the serious element among the lower classes. During the riot of the pilgrimage, he is put down and silenced. He ventures to rebuke the Host for his profane language, and is jeered at and extinguished by that worthy as a Lollard. But when the ribald intoxication of the road has exhausted itself, his grave voice is heard and respected: and he brings the pilgrims into Canterbury with a tale more in harmony with the ostensible object of their journey.

Notes

1. *Étude sur G. Chaucer, considéré comme imitateur des Trouvères*, 1859. See, in particular, Mr Furnivall's *Trial-Forewords*, *Chaucer Society*, 1871.
2. This, however, is one of those cases where Time has lent an additional touch to the humour. The butler was a higher functionary than we should understand now by the name.
3. If M. Sandras has understood English humour, which seems to baffle Frenchmen as Scotch "wut" baffles Englishmen, he would hardly have said that in the *Canterbury Tales* Chaucer's natural affinity with the spirit of Jean de Meun is made conspicuous. In the following section I shall show how Chaucer maintains his agreement with the spirit of chivalry.
4. That the behaviour of the more uproarious of Chaucer's pilgrims was based on real life we may see from one of Thorpe's indignant accounts of the actual pilgrimages to the shrine of St. Thomas (quoted in Morley's *English Writers*, 1890, ii. 291): "They will ordain with them before to have with them both men and women that can sing wanton songs, and some other pilgrims will have with them bagpipes; so that every town they come through, what with the noise of their singing, and with the sound of their piping, and with the jangling of their Canterbury bells, and with the barking out of dogs after them, that they make more noise than if the king came there away with all his clarions, and many other minstrels. And if these men and women be a month in their pilgrimage, many of them shall be a half-year after great janglers, tale-tellers, and liars." In saying that in Chaucer's company "each fellow-traveller carried his wit for bagpipe," Professor Morley seems to have overlooked the Miller's instrument, and generally he seems inclined to make the pilgrimage a much tamer affair than it would appear to have been. I have endeavoured to show how the poet's decorous self-respect is reconciled with fidelity to the manners of the time.
5. Observe, in passing, another evidence of Chaucer's sense of courtly propriety in his *Troilus and Cressida*. The knights and ladies that heard his poems read would not have tolerated Shakespeare's representation of Pandarus, one of the knights of Troy, as a gross procurer, or of Cressida, a lady of rank, as an incontinent wanton. Chaucer's Pandarus is an accomplished knight, moved to his questionable service by pity for the despair of his friend; Cressida the loveliest, most refined, and most discreet of widows, overcome by passionate love, dexterous intrigue, and favouring accidents.

FELIX LINDNER
From "The Alliteration in Chaucer's *Canterbury Tales*"
(1876)
Essays on Chaucer
1868–94, pp. 199–205

I was induced to undertake the following investigation by reading an article by Professor K. Regel, 'Die Alliteration im Layamon,' which is published in the first volume of *Germanistische Studien*, p. 171, ff. In this he shows to what a surprising extent alliteration, the original German manner of versifying, is retained in Layamon, long after the law of rhyme had been in use among the German nations. I will in this essay attempt to show that alliteration reaches to a later date,[1] that it is to be found in the poems of Chaucer, and to a greater extent than we should have expected.

I believe an investigation like this has not been undertaken till now, since the oft-quoted statement of Chaucer in the prologue to the *Persones Tale* seemed opposed to it.[2] This statement in which Chaucer says that alliterative metre was not within the range of a southern man (comp. verse 17353, ff.) runs thus:

> But trusteth wel, I am a sotherne man,
> I cannot geste rom, ram, ruf by letter,
> And God wote, rime hold I but litel better.

Now, if we did not know that Chaucer was possessed of the gift of humour, and that he was also continually chaffing his own poetry, we should plead that he, in these verses, is not speaking himself, but that these words are only the 'Persones,' who says that, being unacquainted with either alliteration or rhyme, he therefore intends to tell his tale in prose. And we should argue that if the poet said, referring to himself, that he 'holds rime but litel better,' all his poems prove the contrary; while there is no objection whatever to attributing these words to the Parson, who indeed at that time may not have been able to write verses. But knowing Chaucer's sly humour as we do, and recollecting some of the other places in which like statements are made about himself and his poetry and knowledge,[3] we cannot get out of the conclusion, that Chaucer, in the lines above, while he meant to make an excuse for giving the Parson a prose tale, also meant to chaff the old stiff alliterative poetry, as well as his own rymes (whose ease and grace were such a contrast to the former's roughness and clumsiness), just as in the *Rime of Sire Thopas*, which is intentionally so bad,[4] he was parodying the balderdash into which the minstrels and rymers of his day had degraded the old Romances, those Romances which even Shakspere praised.[5]

But because Chaucer made fun of the *rom-ram-ruf* poetry, that was no reason why he should not make use, judicious use, of the power, the gratefulness to the ear, the old-friend's-voice tones, that alliteration lends to verse. And we shall see that Chaucer has indeed made frequent use of alliterative combinations, not only of such as are found in the old English language, but also of others made up of words of French origin. In Shakspere it is the same. He endeavours to make the use of alliterative rhyme ridiculous by usually placing it in the mouths of his comic characters; for instance, *Mids. Night's Dream*, V. i.:

> Whereat with blade, with bloody blameful blade,
> He bravely broached his boiling bloody breast.

Or in *Love's L. L.*, IV. ii. 58: "I will something affect the letter, for it argues facility: The preyful princess pierced and prickt a pretty pleasing pricket."

And yet how many alliterative verses and combinations are to be found in Shakspere. See a very interesting article on this subject, 'Die Alliteration im Englischen vor und bei Shakspere,' by Rector Dr K. Seitz in the programme of the 'Marne Höheren Bürgerschule,' Easter, 1875, to whom I am indebted for most of the parallels I quote from Shakspere.

I will now endeavour to point out the reasons which made Chaucer often revert to alliteration. Our poet was a man who, from his manner of life, had sufficient opportunities of observing people of all classes. With what avidity he seized these opportunities, and borrowed from every condition its especial peculiarities, is shown in his *Canterbury Tales*. Every character of them is a type of its class. Not only does he depict their outward appearance, their thoughts and feelings, but makes them speak the language of their class. I do not mean, of course, that Chaucer produces examples of the peculiar dialects then spoken in England; only rarely do we find proofs of dialect; for example, in the *Reeves Tale*, where Chaucer puts the forms 'makes,' 'fares,' 4021; 'findes,' 'bringes,' 'says,' 'Tis,' 4084, 4200, 4237; 'thou is,' 4087, etc., into the mouths of persons from Cambridge. But the tales of the lower classes are composed in a popular tone and in the popular language, and the stories of higher situated persons are written in a loftier style and nobler language. Certainly at that time the feeling for and the pleasure in alliteration was preserved by the people to a far greater extent than at the present, when many of the old forms then in common use are lost. If Chaucer endeavoured to imitate the people's style he was almost compelled to admit into his poems alliterative forms and combinations. In the tales of persons of higher rank this was not in the same degree necessary, as they, being for the most part either of Norman descent, or brought up in the use of Norman customs and opinions, paid but little heed to the form and contents of the old English poems; while the lower classes, for the most part of Saxon descent, preserved faithfully the songs which told of the great deeds of their forefathers, and with them the tendency to alliteration. Compare Geoffrey Chaucer's *Canterbury Tales*, translated into German by Wilhelm Hertzberg, Hildburghausen, 1866, p. 45: "But just at Chaucer's time the original form of the Anglo-Saxon verse with alliteration became popular again amongst the lower classes through *Piers Ploughman's Vision*, and other similar poems of a religious tendency."

Now, Chaucer held for many years the post of Controller of the Customs in the port of London—a duty which, as his appointment testifies, he was obliged to fulfil personally, and which he might not perform by deputy. The poet was called to this office on the 8th of June, 1374, and only on the 17th of February, 1386, did he receive permission to exercise his control of customs by deputy. During this long time he certainly had daily opportunities of studying and observing the language of the people. Being a man of unusually quick observation, he made use of his varied experience. The fruit of his study of the world and of men is exhibited in his *Canterbury Tales*.

The imitation of the language of the people was therefore one reason for the poet to revive alliteration. To this may be added a second,—his sympathy with old customs and manners; this is visible in all his tales. The character of the Anglo-Saxon seems not to be quite lost in Chaucer's poems. See Hertzberg, p. 53: "It is almost as if his Anglo-Saxon nature (which we recognize in his preference for the hard-handed son of the people) wished to avenge itself on the French culture in him, by mixing blunt, peasant wit with the refined character of the court." So we may conclude, with tolerable certainty, that he had a strong natural inclination for the old alliterative forms, which was perhaps unknown to himself. We observe

how he reverts to alliteration in depicting camp scenes and strong emotions, and often produces the most glorious effects by this mixture of alliteration and rhyme.

The third reason for Chaucer's use of alliterative forms is to ornament his verses, and to make them more striking. The national character at this time was rather inclined to find peculiar pleasure in artificial verses, and therefore the poet frequently made use of alliteration for rhythmical painting, which was highly prized by the art-poets of that time. This is also shown by the many onomatopoetic verses in the *Canterbury Tales*, of which I am going to quote a few. In the verses 170 and 171 we can clearly hear the sound of the bells on the bridle of the monk's horse:

> men might his bridel here
> Gingling in a whistling wind as clere
> And eke as loud as doth a chapel belle.

The description of the sound of church bells, comp. ver. 3655:

> Till that the belles of laudes gan to ringe.

In the verses 2339–2340—

> And as it queinte it made a whisteling
> As don these brondes wet in hir brenning,

we can plainly hear the hissing of the burning wood.

Similar to the well-known onomatopoetical verse in the beginning of the *Iliad*, the rattling of the arrows in the quiver of Apollo is described, ver. 2360:

> the armes in the cas
> Of the goddesse clatteren fast and ring.

Other verses of this kind are:

> 2434: And with that sound he heard a murmuring
>   Ful low and dim
> 2602: Now ringen trompes loud and clarioun.
> 4099: With kepe kepe; stand stand; jossa warderers.
> 2607: Ther shiveren shaftes upon sheldes thicke.
> 2693: His brest tobrosten with his sadel bon.

These few hastily-selected examples are sufficient for our purpose. The two last verses are especially important, as they are both onomatopoetic and alliterative.

These are the reasons which probably induced Chaucer to employ alliterative forms and combinations. The same was the case with Chaucer's contemporaries on the continent. In Middle High German the poets also made frequent use of alliteration; compare Ignaz von Zingerle: *Die Alliteration bei mittelhochdeutschen Dichtern*, Wien, 1864; and Ferdinand Vetter: *Zum Muspilli und zur germanischen Alliterations Poesie*, Wien, 1872.

What Regel says of Layamon, that he shows his pleasure in similar sounds by his tendency to repeat several words at the beginning of successive verses, is true of Chaucer also. Here, too, I will limit myself to a few out of the great number of examples which at once strike one when reading—

> 404: His stremes and his dangers him besides
>   His herbergh and his mone, his lodemenage.
> 983: Thus ryt this duke, thus ryt this conquerour.
> 1872: Who looketh lightly now but Palamon?
>   Who springeth up for joye but Arcite?
>   Who coud it tell, or who coud it endite . . .
> 2275: Up roos the sonne and up roos Emelye.
> 2573: And after rood the queen and Emelye,
>   And after hem of ladyes another companye,
>   And after hem of comunes after her degre.
> 2775: Alas the deth! alas min Emelye!
>   Alas departing of our companye!
>   Alas min hertes quene! alas my wif!

We may compare with this vers. 590–592, 2927–60, 11458–61, etc. To the poet's lively joy in similar sounds his plays upon words also bear testimony:

7289: God *save* you alle *save* this cursed frere.
10419: Al be it that I can nat sowne his *style*,
Ne can nat clymben over so heigh a *style*.
10569: And yit is glas nought like aisshen or *ferne*
But for they han yknowen it so *ferne*.
11035: *Colours* ne know I none withouten drede
But swiche *colours* as growen in the mede.

To these may be added the repetition of certain forms of sentences which the poet frequently uses with epic skill: 'Still as eny stoon,' 3472, 7997, 10485 (compare Shakspere, *King John*, IV. i., 'I will not struggle, I will stand stone-still;' *Lucretia*: 'Stone-still astonished'); 'domb as eny stoon,' 776; ⟨and⟩ 'deed as eny stoon, 10788; 'wel I wot.'

Notes

1. It of course exists, more or less, in the whole range of English poetry, and is freely used by Gower, and Chaucer's other contemporaries and successors. "Alliteration's artful aid" has always been too great a help to the charms of poetry, to allow of its being neglected by writers of verse.
2. See an essay on alliterative poetry by the Rev. W. W. Skeat, in vol. iii. of Bishop Percy's Folio MS., Ballads and Romances.
3. Compare in the *Man of Lawes Prologue*:

I can right now no thrifty tale sain,   4466
But Chaucer (though he can but lewedly
On metres and on riming craftily)
Hath said them, in swiche English as he can
Of olde time," etc.
But natheles. . . .
I speke in prose and let him rimes make.   4516

We know that in spite of the last verse the *Man of Lawes Tale* is not told in prose, but in verse.
   In another place, ver. 11578 in the *Frankeleines Tale*, he says, as almost in the *Hous of Fame*:

I can no termes of Astrologie.

But not only this tale, but many others contain such a multitude of astrological expressions, and show such a knowledge of the science, that they prove just the contrary.
4. The host exclaims, ver. 13858:

Thy drasty riming is not worth a tord;
Thou doest nought elles but dispendest time.
Sire, at o word, thou shalt no lenger rime.

5.   (Sonnet CVI.)
When in the chronicle of wasted time
   I see descriptions of the fairest wights,
And beauty making beautiful old rhyme,
   In praise of ladies dead, and lovely knights,
Then, in the blazon of sweet beauty's best,
   Of hand, of foot, of lip, of eye, of brow,
I see their antique pen would have express'd
   Even such a beauty as you master now.
So all their praises are but prophecies
   Of this our time, all you prefiguring;
And for they look'd but with divining eyes,
   They had not skill enough your worth to sing:
For we, which now behold these present days,
Have eyes to wonder, but lack tongues to praise.

ADOLPHUS WILLIAM WARD
From "Characteristics of Chaucer and His Poetry"
Chaucer
1879, pp. 146–88

One very pleasing quality in Chaucer must have been his modesty. In the course of his life this may have helped to recommend him to patrons so many and so various, and to make him the useful and trustworthy agent that he evidently became for confidential missions abroad. Physically, as has been seen, he represents himself as prone to the habit of casting his eyes on the ground; and we may feel tolerably sure that to this external manner corresponded a quiet, observant disposition, such as that which may be held to have distinguished the greatest of Chaucer's successors among English poets. To us, of course, this quality of modesty in Chaucer makes itself principally manifest in the opinion which he incidentally shows himself to entertain concerning his own rank and claims as an author. Herein, as in many other points, a contrast is noticeable between him and the great Italian masters, who were so sensitive as to the esteem in which they and their poetry were held. Who could fancy Chaucer crowned with laurel, like Petrarch, or even, like Dante, speaking with proud humility of "the beautiful style that has done honour to him," while acknowledging his obligation for it to a great predecessor? Chaucer again and again disclaims all boasts of perfection, or pretensions to pre-eminence, as a poet. His Canterbury Pilgrims have in his name to disavow, like Persius, having slept on Mount Parnassus, or possessing "rhetoric" enough to describe a heroine's beauty; and he openly allows that his spirit grows dull as he grows older, and that he finds a difficulty as a translator in matching his rhymes to his French original. He acknowledges as incontestable the superiority of the poets of classical antiquity:—

Little book, no writing thou envý,
But subject be to all true poësy,
And kiss the steps, where'er thou seest space
Of Virgil, Ovid, Homer, Lucan, Stace.

But more than this. In the *House of Fame* he expressly disclaims having in his light and imperfect verse sought to pretend to "mastery" in the art poetical; and in a charmingly expressed passage of the *Prologue* to the *Legend of Good Women* he describes himself as merely following in the wake of those who have already reaped the harvest of amorous song, and have carried away the corn:—

And I come after, gleaning here and there,
And am full glad if I can find an ear
Of any goodly word that ye have left.

Modesty of this stamp is perfectly compatible with a certain self-consciousness which is hardly ever absent from greatness, and which at all events supplies a stimulus not easily dispensed with except by sustained effort on the part of a poet. The two qualities seem naturally to combine into that self-contained-ness (very different from self-contentedness) which distinguishes Chaucer, and which helps to give to his writings a manliness of tone, the direct opposite of the irretentive querulousness found in so great a number of poets in all times. He cannot, indeed, be said to maintain an absolute reserve concerning himself and his affairs in his writings; but as he grows older, he seems to become less and less inclined to take the public into his confidence, or to speak of himself except in a pleasantly light and incidental fashion. And in the same spirit he seems, without ever folding his hands in his lap, or ceasing to be a busy man and an assiduous author, to have grown indifferent to the lack of brilliant success in life, whether as a man of letters or otherwise. So at least one seems justified in interpreting a remarkable passage in the *House of Fame*, the poem in which, perhaps, Chaucer allows us to see more deeply into his mind than in any other. After surveying the various company of those who had come as suitors for the favours of Fame, he tells us how it seemed to him (in his long December dream) that some one spoke to him in a kindly way,

And saidë: 'Friend, what is thy name?
Art thou come hither to have fame?'
'Nay, forsoothë, friend!' quoth I;
'I came not hither (grand merci!)
For no such causë, by my head!
Sufficeth me, as I were dead,
That no wight have my name in hand.
I wot myself best how I stand;
For what I suffer, or what I think,
I will myselfë all it drink,
Or at least the greater part
As far forth as I know my art.'

With this modest but manly self-possession we shall not go far wrong in connecting what seems another very distinctly marked feature of Chaucer's inner nature. He seems to have arrived at a clear recognition of the truth with which Goethe humorously comforted Eckermann in the shape of the proverbial saying, "Care has been taken that the trees shall not grow into the sky." Chaucer's, there is every reason to believe, was a contented faith, as far removed from self-torturing unrest as from childish credulity. Hence his refusal to trouble himself, now that he has arrived at a good age, with original research as to the constellations. (The passage is all the more significant since Chaucer, as has been seen, actually possessed a very respectable knowledge of astronomy.) That winged encyclopædia, the Eagle, has just been regretting the poet's unwillingness to learn the position of the Great and the Little Bear, Castor and Pollux, and the rest, concerning which at present he does not know where they stand. But he replies, "No matter!

'. . . It is no need;
I trust as well (so God me speed!)
Them that write of this mattér,
As though I knew their places there.'

Moreover, as he says (probably without implying any special allegorical meaning), they seem so bright that it would destroy my eyes to look upon them. Personal inspection, in his opinion, was not necessary for a faith which at some times may, and at others must, take the place of knowledge; for we find him, at the opening of the *Prologue* to the *Legend of Good Women*, in a passage the tone of which should not be taken to imply less than its words express, writing as follows:—

A thousand timës I have heard men tell,
That there is joy in heaven, and pain in hell;
And I accordë well that it is so.
But nathëless, yet wot I well alsó,
That there is none doth in this country dwell
That either hath in heaven been or hell,
Or any other way could of it know,
But that he heard, or found it written so,
For by assay may no man proof receive.
    But God forbid that men should not believe
More things than they have ever seen with eye!
Men shall not fancy everything a lie
Unless themselves it see, or else it do;
For, God wot, not the less a thing is true,
Though every wight may not it chance to see.

The central thought of these lines, though it afterwards receives a narrower and more commonplace application, is no other than that which has been so splendidly expressed by Spenser in the couplet:—

Why then should witless man so much misween
That nothing is but that which he hath seen?

The *negative* result produced in Chaucer's mind by this firm but placid way of regarding matters of faith was a distrust of astrology, alchemy, and all the superstitions which in the *Parson's Tale* are noticed as condemned by the Church. This distrust on Chaucer's part requires no further illustration after what has been said elsewhere; it would have been well for his age if all its children had been as clear-sighted in these matters as he, to whom the practices connected with these delusive sciences seemed, and justly so from his point of view, not less impious than futile. His *Canon Yeoman's Tale*, a story of imposture so vividly dramatic in its catastrophe as to have suggested to Ben Jonson one of the most effective passages in his comedy *The Alchemist*, concludes with a moral of unmistakeable solemnity against the sinfulness, as well as uselessness, of "multiplying" (making gold by the arts of alchemy):—

Whoso maketh God his adversáry,
As for to work anything in contràry
Unto His will, certes ne'er shall he thrive,
Though that he multiply through all his life.

But equally unmistakeable is the *positive* side of this frame of mind in such a passage as the following—which is one of those belonging to Chaucer himself, and not taken from his French original—in *The Man of Law's Tale*. The narrator is speaking of the voyage of Constance, after her escape from the massacre in which, at a feast, all her fellow-Christians had been killed, and of how she was borne by the "wild wave" from "Surrey" (Syria) to the Northumbrian shore:—

Here men might askë, why she was not slain?
Eke at the feast who might her body save?
And I answérë that demand again:
Who savèd Daniel in th' horríble cave,
When every wight save him, master or knave,
The lion ate—before he could depart?
No wight but God, whom he bare in his heart.

"In her," he continues, "God desired to show His miraculous power, so that we should see His mighty works; for Christ, in whom we have a remedy for every ill, often by means of His own does things for ends of His own, which are obscure to the wit of man, incapable, by reason of our ignorance, of understanding His wise providence. But since Constance was not slain at the feast, it might be asked: Who kept her from drowning in the sea? Who, then, kept Jonas in the belly of the whale till he was spouted up at Ninive? Well do we know it was no one but He who kept the Hebrew people from drowning in the waters, and made them to pass through the sea with dry feet. Who bade the four spirits of the tempest, which have the power to trouble land and sea, north and south, and west and east, vex neither sea nor land nor the trees that grow on it? Truly these things were ordered by Him who kept this woman safe from the tempest, as well when she awoke as when she slept. But whence might this woman have meat and drink, and how could her sustenance last out to her for three years and more? Who, then, fed Saint Mary the Egyptian in the cavern or in the desert? Assuredly no one but Christ. It was a great miracle to feed five thousand folk with five loaves and two fishes; but God in their great need sent to them abundance."

As to the sentiments and opinions of Chaucer, then, on matters such as these, we can entertain no reasonable doubt. But we are altogether too ill acquainted with the details of his personal life, and with the motives which contributed to determine its course, to be able to arrive at any valid conclusions as to the way in which his principles affected his conduct. Enough has been already said concerning the attitude seemingly observed by him towards the great public questions, and the great historical events, of his day. If he had strong political opinions of his own, or strong personal views on questions either of ecclesiastical policy or of religious doctrine—in which assumptions there seems nothing probable—he, at all events, did not wear his heart on his sleeve, or use his poetry, allegorical or otherwise, as a vehicle of his wishes, hopes, or fears on these heads. The true breath of freedom could hardly be expected to blow through the precincts of a Plantagenet court. If Chaucer could write the pretty lines in the *Manciple's Tale* about the caged bird and its uncontrollable desire for liberty, his contemporary Barbour could apostrophise Freedom itself as a noble thing, in words the simple manliness of which stirs the blood after a very different fashion. Concerning his domestic relations, we may regard it as virtually certain that he was unhappy as a husband, though tender and affectionate as a father. Considering how vast a proportion of the satire of all times—but more especially that of the Middle Ages, and in these again pre-eminently of the period of European literature which took its tone from Jean de Meung—is directed against woman and against married life, it would be difficult to decide how much of the irony, sarcasm, and fun lavished by Chaucer on these themes is due to a fashion with which he readily fell in, and how much to the impulse of personal feeling. A perfect anthology, or perhaps one should rather say, a complete herbarium, might be collected from his works of samples of these attacks on women. He has manifestly made a careful study of their ways, with which he now and then betrays that curiously intimate acquaintance to which we are accustomed in a Richardson or a Balzac. How accurate are such incidental remarks as this, that women are "full measurable" in such matters as sleep—not caring for so much of it at a time as men do! How wonderfully natural is the description of Cressid's bevy of lady-visitors, attracted by the news that she is shortly to be surrendered to the Greeks, and of the "nice vanity"—*i. e.*, foolish emptiness—of their consolatory gossip. "As men see in town, and all about, that women are accustomed to visit their friends," so a swarm of ladies came to Cressid, "and sat themselves down, and said as I shall tell. 'I am delighted,' says one, 'that you will so soon see your father.' 'Indeed I am not so delighted,' says another, 'for we have not seen half enough of her since she has been at Troy.' 'I do hope,' quoth the third, 'that she will bring us back peace with her; in which case may Almighty God guide her on her departure.' And Cressid heard these words and womanish things as if she were far away; for she was burning all the time with another passion than any of which they knew; so that she almost felt her heart die for woe, and for weariness of that company." But his satire against women is rarely so innocent as this; and though several ladies take part in the Canterbury Pilgrimage, yet pilgrim after pilgrim has his saw or jest against their sex. The courteous *Knight* cannot refrain from the generalisation that women all follow the favour of fortune. The *Summoner*, who is of a less scrupulous sort, introduces a diatribe against women's passionate love of vengeance; and the *Shipman* seasons a story which requires no such addition by an enumeration of their favourite foibles. But the climax is reached in the confessions of the *Wife of Bath*, who quite unhesitatingly says that women are best won by flattery and busy attentions; that when won they desire to have the sovereignty over their husbands, and that they tell untruths and swear to them with twice the boldness of men; while as to the power of their tongue, she quotes the second-hand authority of her fifth husband for the saying that it is better to dwell with a lion or a foul dragon than with a woman accustomed to chide. It is true that this same *Wife of Bath* also observes with an effective *tu quoque*:—

> By God, if women had but written stories,
> As clerkës have within their oratòries,
> They would have writ of men more wickednéss
> Than all the race of Adam may redress;

and the *Legend of Good Women* seems, in point of fact, to have been intended to offer some such kind of amends as is here declared to be called for. But the balance still remains heavy against the poet's sentiments of gallantry and respect for women. It should, at the same time, be remembered that among the *Canterbury Tales* the two which are of their kind the most effective constitute tributes to the most distinctively feminine and wifely virtue of fidelity. Moreover, when coming from such personages as the pilgrims who narrate the *Tales* in question, the praise of women has special significance and value. The *Merchant* and the *Shipman* may indulge in facetious or coarse jibes against wives and their behaviour; but the *Man of Law*, full of grave experience of the world, is a witness above suspicion to the womanly virtue of which his narrative celebrates so illustrious an example, while the *Clerk of Oxford* has in his cloistered solitude, where all womanly blandishments are unknown, come to the conclusion that

> Men speak of Job, most for his humbleness,
> As clerkës, when they list, can well indite,
> Of men in special; but, in truthfulness,
> Though praise by clerks of women be but slight,
> No man in humbleness can him acquit
> As women can, nor can be half so true
> As women are, unless all things be new.

As to marriage, Chaucer may be said generally to treat it in that style of laughing with a wry mouth, which has from time immemorial been affected both in comic writing and on the comic stage, but which in the end even the most determined old bachelor feels an occasional inclination to consider monotonous.

In all this, however, it is obvious that something at least must be set down to conventionality. Yet the best part of Chaucer's nature, it is hardly necessary to say, was neither conventional nor commonplace. He was not, we may rest assured, one of that numerous class which in his days, as it does in ours, composed the population of the land of Philistia—the persons so well defined by the Scottish poet, Sir David Lyndsay (himself a courtier of the noblest type):—

> Who fixèd have their hearts and whole intents
> On sensual lust, on dignity, and rents.

Doubtless Chaucer was a man of practical good sense, desirous of suitable employment and of a sufficient income; nor can we suppose him to have been one of those who look upon social life and its enjoyments with a jaundiced eye, or who, absorbed in things which are not of this world, avert their gaze from it altogether. But it is hardly possible that rank and position should have been valued on their own account by one who so repeatedly recurs to his ideal of the true gentleman, as to a conception dissociated from mere outward circumstances, and more particularly independent of birth or inherited wealth. At times, we know, men find what they seek; and so Chaucer found in Boëthius and in Guillaume de Lorris that conception which he both translates and reproduces, besides repeating it in a little *Ballade*, probably written by him in the last *decennium* of his life. By far the best-known and the finest of these passages is that in the *Wife of Bath's Tale*, which follows the round assertion that the "arrogance" against which it protests is not worth a hen; and which is followed by an appeal to a parallel passage in Dante:—

> Look, who that is most virtuous alway
> Privy and open, and most intendeth aye
> To do the gentle deedës that he can,

Take him for the greatest gentleman.
Christ wills we claim of Him our gentleness,
Not of our elders for their old richés.
For though they give us all their heritáge
Through which we claim to be of high paráge,
Yet may they not bequeathë for no thing—
To none of us—their virtuous living,
That made them gentlemen y-callèd be,
And bade us follow them in such degree.
Well can the wisë poet of Florénce,
That Dante hightë, speak of this senténce;
Lo, in such manner of rhyme is Dante's tale:
'Seldom upriseth by its branches small
Prowess of man; for God of His prowéss
Wills that we claim of Him our gentleness;
For of our ancestors we no thing claim
But temporal thing, that men may hurt and maim.'[1]

By the still ignobler greed of money for its own sake, there is no reason whatever to suppose Chaucer to have been at any time actuated; although, under the pressure of immediate want, he devoted a *Complaint* to his empty purse, and made known, in the proper quarters, his desire to see it refilled. Finally, as to what is commonly called pleasure, he may have shared the fashions and even the vices of his age; but we know hardly anything on the subject, except that excess in wine, which is often held a pardonable peccadillo in a poet, receives his emphatic condemnation. It would be hazardous to assert of him, as Herrick asserted of himself, that though his "Muse was jocund, his life was chaste;" inasmuch as his name occurs in one unfortunate connexion full of suspiciousness. But we may at least believe him to have spoken his own sentiments in the Doctor of Physic's manly declaration that

Of all treason sovereign pestilence
Is when a man betrayeth innocence.

His true pleasures lay far away from those of vanity and dissipation. In the first place, he seems to have been a passionate reader. To his love of books he is constantly referring; indeed, this may be said to be the only kind of egotism which he seems to take a pleasure in indulging. At the opening of his earliest extant poem of consequence, the *Book of the Duchess*, he tells us how he preferred to drive away a night rendered sleepless through melancholy thoughts, by means of a book, which he thought better entertainment than a game either at chess or at "tables." This passion lasted longer with him than the other passion which it had helped to allay; for in the sequel to the well-known passage in the *House of Fame*, already cited, he gives us a glimpse of himself at home, absorbed in his favourite pursuit:—

Thou go'st home to thy house anon,
And there, as dumb as any stone,
Thou sittest at another book,
Till fully dazèd is thy look;
And liv'st thus as a hermit quite,
Although thy abstinence is slight.

And doubtless he counted the days lost in which he was prevented from following the rule of life which elsewhere he sets himself, "to study and to read alway, day by day," and pressed even the nights into his service when he was not making his head ache with writing. How eager and, considering the times in which he lived, how diverse a reader he was, has already been abundantly illustrated in the course of this volume. His knowledge of Holy Writ was considerable, though it probably, for the most part, came to him at second-hand. He seems to have had some acquaintance with patristic and homilectic literature; he produced a version of the homily on Mary Mag-

dalene, improperly attributed to Origen; and, as we have seen, emulated King Alfred in translating Boëthius's famous manual of moral philosophy. His Latin learning extended over a wide range of literature, from Virgil and Ovid down to some of the favourite Latin poets of the Middle Ages. It is to be feared that he occasionally read Latin authors with so eager a desire to arrive at the contents of their books that he at times mistook their meaning—not far otherwise, slightly to vary a happy comparison made by one of his most eminent commentators, than many people read Chaucer's own writings now-a-days. That he possessed any knowledge at all of Greek may be doubted, both on general grounds and on account of a little slip or two in quotation of a kind not unusual with those who quote what they have not previously read. His *Troilus and Cressid* has only a very distant connexion, indeed, with Homer, whose *Iliad*, before it furnished materials for the mediæval Troilus-legend, had been filtered through a brief Latin epitome, and diluted into a Latin novel, and a journal kept at the seat of war, of altogether apocryphal value. And, indeed, it must in general be conceded that, if Chaucer had read much, he lays claim to having read more; for he not only occasionally ascribes to known authors works which we can by no means feel certain as to their having written, but at times he even cites (or is made to cite, in all the editions of his works) authors who are altogether unknown to fame by the names which he gives to them. But then it must be remembered that other mediæval writers have rendered themselves liable to the same kind of charge. Quoting was one of the dominant literary fashions of the age; and just as a word without an oath went for but little in conversation, so a statement or sentiment in writing acquired a greatly enhanced value when suggested by authority, even after no more precise a fashion than the use of the phrase "as old books say." In Chaucer's days the equivalent of the modern "I have seen it said *somewhere*"—with, perhaps, the venturesome addition: "I *think*, in Horace"—had clearly not become an objectionable expletive.

Of modern literatures there can be no doubt that Chaucer had made substantially his own the two which could be of importance to him as a poet. His obligations to the French singers have probably been over-estimated—at all events, if the view adopted in this essay be the correct one, and if the charming poem of the *Flower and the Leaf*, together with the lively, but as to its meaning not very transparent, so-called *Chaucer's Dream*, be denied admission among his genuine works. At the same time, the influence of the *Roman de la Rose* and that of the courtly poets, of whom Machault was the chief in France and Froissart the representative in England, are perceptible in Chaucer almost to the last, nor is it likely that he should ever have ceased to study and assimilate them. On the other hand, the extent of his knowledge of Italian literature has probably till of late been underrated in an almost equal degree. This knowledge displays itself not only in the imitation or adaptation of particular poems, but more especially in the use made of incidental passages and details. In this way his debts to Dante were especially numerous; and it is curious to find proofs so abundant of Chaucer's relatively close study of a poet with whose genius his own had so few points in common. Notwithstanding first appearances, it is an open question whether Chaucer had ever read Boccaccio's *Decamerone*, with which he may merely have had in common the sources of several of his *Canterbury Tales*. But as he certainly took one of them from the *Teseide* (without improving it in the process), and not less certainly, and adapted the *Filostrato* in his *Troilus and Cressid*, it is strange that he should refrain from naming the author to whom he was more indebted than to any one other for poetic materials.

But wide and diverse as Chaucer's reading fairly deserves to be called, the love of nature was even stronger and more absorbing in him than the love of books. He has himself, in a very charming passage, compared the strength of the one and of the other of his predilections:—

> And as for me, though I have knowledge slight
> In bookës for to read I me delight,
> And to them give I faith and full credénce,
> And in my heart have them in reverence
> So heartily, that there is gamë none
> That from my bookës maketh me be gone,
> But it be seldom on the holiday—
> Save, certainly, when that the month of May
> Is come, and that I hear the fowlës sing,
> And see the flowers as they begin to spring,
> Farewell my book, and my devotión.

Undoubtedly the literary fashion of Chaucer's times is responsible for part of this May-morning sentiment, with which he is fond of beginning his poems (the Canterbury pilgrimage is dated towards the end of April—but is not April "messenger to May?"). It had been decreed that flowers should be the badges of nations and dynasties, and the tokens of amorous sentiment; the rose had its votaries, and the lily, lauded by Chaucer's *Prioress* as the symbol of the Blessed Virgin; while the daisy, which first sprang from the tears of a forlorn damsel, in France gave its name (*marguérite*) to an entire species of courtly verse. The enthusiastic adoration professed by Chaucer, in the *Prologue* to the *Legend of Good Women*, for the daisy, which he afterwards identifies with the good Alceste, the type of faithful wifehood, is, of course, a mere poetical figure. But there is in his use of these favourite literary devices, so to speak, a variety in sameness significant of their accordance with his own taste, and of the frank and fresh love of nature which animated him, and which seems to us as much a part of him as his love of books. It is unlikely that his personality will ever become more fully known than it is at present; nor is there anything in respect of which we seem to see so clearly into his inner nature as with regard to these twin predilections, to which he remains true in all his works and in all his moods. While the study of books was his chief passion, nature was his chief joy and solace; while his genius enabled him to transfuse what he read in the former, what came home to him in the latter was akin to that genius itself; for he at times reminds us of his own fresh Canace, whom he describes as looking so full of happiness during her walk through the wood at sunrise:—

> What for the season, what for the morning
> And for the fowlës that she heardë sing,
> For right anon she wistë what they meant
> Right by their song, and knew all their intent.

If the above view of Chaucer's character and intellectual tastes and tendencies be in the main correct, there will seem to be nothing paradoxical in describing his literary progress, so far as its *data* are ascertainable, as a most steady and regular one. Very few men awake to find themselves either famous or great of a sudden, and perhaps as few poets as other men, though it may be heresy against a venerable maxim to say so. Chaucer's works form a clearly recognisable series of steps towards the highest achievement of which, under the circumstances in which he lived and wrote, he can be held to have been capable; and his long and arduous self-training, whether consciously or not directed to a particular end, was of that sure kind from which genius itself derives strength. His beginnings as a writer were dictated, partly by the impulse of that imitative faculty which, in poetic natures, is the usual precursor of the creative, partly by the influence of prevailing tastes and the absence of native English literary predecessors whom, considering the cir-

cumstances of his life and the nature of his temperament, he could have found it a congenial task to follow. French poems were, accordingly, his earliest models; but fortunately (unlike Gower, whom it is so instructive to compare with Chaucer, precisely because the one lacked that gift of genius which the other possessed) he seems at once to have resolved to make use for his poetical writings of his native speech. In no way, therefore, could he have begun his career with so happy a promise of its future as in that which he actually chose. Nor could any course so naturally have led him to introduce into his poetic diction the French idioms and words already used in the spoken language of Englishmen, more especially in those classes for which he in the first instance wrote, and thus to confer upon our tongue the great benefit which it owes to him. Again, most fortunately, others had already pointed the way to the selection for literary use of that English dialect which was probably the most suitable for the purpose; and Chaucer, as a Southern man (like his *Parson of a Town*), belonged to a part of the country where the old alliterative verse had long since been discarded for classical and romance forms of versification. Thus the *Romaunt of the Rose* most suitably opens his literary life—a translation in which there is nothing original except an occasional turn of phrase, but in which the translator finds opportunity for exercising his powers of judgment by virtually re-editing the work before him. And already in the *Book of the Duchess*, though most unmistakeably a follower of Machault, he is also the rival of the great French *trouvère*, and has advanced in freedom of movement not less than in agreeableness of form. Then, as his travels extended his acquaintance with foreign literatures to that of Italy, he here found abundant fresh materials from which to feed his productive powers, and more elaborate forms in which to clothe their results; while at the same time comparison, the kindly nurse of originality, more and more enabled him to recast instead of imitating, or encouraged him freely to invent. In *Troilus and Cressid* he produced something very different from a mere condensed translation, and achieved a work in which he showed himself a master of poetic expression and sustained narrative; in the *House of Fame* and the *Assembly of Fowls* he moved with freedom in happily contrived allegories of his own invention; and with the *Legend of Good Women* he had already arrived at a stage when he could undertake to review, under a pleasant pretext, but with evident consciousness of work done, the list of his previous works. "He hath," he said of himself, "made many a lay and many a thing." Meanwhile the labour incidentally devoted by him to translation from the Latin, or to the composition of prose treatises in the scholastic manner of academical exercises, could but little affect his general literary progress. The mere scholarship of youth, even if it be the reverse of close and profound, is wont to cling to a man through life, and to assert its modest claims at any season; and thus Chaucer's school-learning exercised little influence either of an advancing or of a retarding kind upon the full development of his genius. Nowhere is he so truly himself as in the masterpiece of his last years. For the *Canterbury Tales*, in which he is at once greatest, most original, and most catholic in the choice of materials as well as in moral sympathies, bears the unmistakeable stamp of having formed the crowning labour of his life—a work which death alone prevented him from completing.

It may be said, without presumption, that such a general view as this leaves ample room for all reasonable theories as to the chronology and sequence, where these remain more or less unsettled, of Chaucer's indisputably genuine works. In any case, there is no poet whom, if only as an exercise in critical analysis, it is more interesting to study and re-study in connexion with the circumstances of his literary progress. He still, as has been seen, belongs to the Middle Ages, but to a period in which the noblest ideals of these Middle Ages are already beginning to pale and their mightiest institutions to quake around him; in which learning continues to be in the main scholasticism, the linking of argument with argument, and the accumulation of authority upon authority, and poetry remains to a great extent the crabbedness of clerks or the formality of courts. Again, Chaucer is mediæval in tricks of style and turns of phrase; he often contents himself with the tritest of figures and the most unrefreshing of ancient devices, and freely resorts to a mixture of names and associations belonging to his own times with others derived from other ages. This want of literary perspective is a sure sign of mediævalism, and one which has amused the world, or has jarred upon it, since the Renascence taught men to study both classical and Biblical antiquity as realities, and not merely as a succession of pictures or of tapestries on a wall. Chaucer mingles things mediæval and things classical as freely as he brackets King David with the philosopher Seneca, or Judas Iscariot with the Greek "dissimulator" Sinon. His Dido, mounted on a stout palfrey paper-white of hue, with a red-and-gold saddle embroidered and embossed, resembles Alice Perrers in all her pomp rather than the Virgilian queen. Jupiter's eagle, the poet's guide and instructor in the allegory of the *House of Fame*, invokes "Saint Mary, Saint James," and "Saint Clare" all at once; and the pair of lovers at Troy sign their letters *"la vostre T."* and *"la vostre C."* Anachronisms of this kind (of the danger of which, by the way, to judge from a passage in the *Prologue* to the *Legend of Good Women*, Chaucer would not appear to have been wholly unconscious) are intrinsically of very slight importance. But the morality of Chaucer's narratives is at times the artificial and overstrained morality of the Middle Ages, which, as it were, clutches hold of a single idea to the exclusion of all others—a morality which, when carried to its extreme consequences, makes monomaniacs as well as martyrs, in both of which species, occasionally, perhaps, combined in the same persons, the Middle Ages abound. The fidelity of Griseldis under the trials imposed upon her by her, in point of fact, brutal husband is the fidelity of a martyr to unreason. The story was afterwards put on the stage in the Elizabethan age; and though even in the play of *Patient Grissil* (by Chettle and others) it is not easy to reconcile the husband's proceedings with the promptings of common sense, yet the playwrights, with the instinct of their craft, contrived to introduce some element of humanity into his character, and of probability into his conduct. Again, the supra-chivalrous respect paid by Arviragus, the Breton knight of the *Franklin's Tale*, to the sanctity of his wife's word, seriously to the peril of his own and his wife's honour, is an effort to which probably even the Knight of La Mancha himself would have proved unequal. It is not to be expected that Chaucer should have failed to share some of the prejudices of his times as well as to fall in with their ways of thought and sentiment; and though it is the *Prioress* who tells a story against the Jews which passes the legend of Hugh of Lincoln, yet it would be very hazardous to seek any irony in this legend of bigotry. In general, much of that *naïveté* which to modern readers seems Chaucer's most obvious literary quality must be ascribed to the times in which he lived and wrote. This quality is, in truth, by no means that which most deeply impresses itself upon the observation of any one able to compare Chaucer's writings with those of his more immediate predecessors and successors. But the sense in which the term *naïf* should be understood in literary criticism is so imperfectly agreed upon among us, that we have not yet even found an English equivalent for the word.

To Chaucer's times, then, belongs much of what may at first sight seem to include itself among the characteristics of his genius; while, on the other hand, there are to be distinguished from these the influences due to his training and studies in two literatures—the French and the Italian. In the former of these he must have felt at home, if not by birth and descent, at all events by social connexion, habits of life, and ways of thought; while in the latter he, whose own country's was still a half-fledged literary life, found ready to his hand masterpieces of artistic maturity lofty in conception, broad in bearing, finished in form. There still remain, for summary review, the elements proper to his own poetic individuality—those which mark him out not only as the first great poet of his own nation, but as a great poet for all times.

The poet must please; if he wishes to be successful and popular, he must suit himself to the tastes of his public; and even if he be indifferent to immediate fame, he must, as belonging to one of the most impressionable, the most receptive species of humankind, live, in a sense, *with* and *for* his generation. To meet this demand upon his genius, Chaucer was born with many gifts which he carefully and assiduously exercised in a long series of poetical experiments, and which he was able felicitously to combine for the achievement of results unprecedented in our literature. In readiness of descriptive power, in brightness and variety of imagery, and in flow of diction, Chaucer remained unequalled by any English poet, till he was surpassed—it seems not too much to say, in all three respects—by Spenser. His verse, where it suits his purpose, glitters, to use Dunbar's expression, as with fresh enamel, and its hues are variegated like those of a Flemish tapestry. Even where his descriptive enumerations seem at first sight monotonous or perfunctory, they are, in truth, graphic and true in their details, as in the list of birds in the *Assembly of Fowls*, quoted in part on an earlier page of this essay, and in the shorter list of trees in the same poem, which is, however, in its general features, imitated from Boccaccio. Neither King James I. of Scotland, nor Spenser, who after Chaucer essayed similar *tours de force*, were happier than he had been before them. Or we may refer to the description of the preparations for the tournament and of the tournament itself in the *Knight's Tale*, or to the thoroughly Dutch picture of a disturbance in a farm-yard in the *Nun's Priest's*. The vividness with which Chaucer describes scenes and events as if he had them before his own eyes, was no doubt, in the first instance, a result of his own imaginative temperament; but one would probably not go wrong in attributing the fulness of the use which he made of this gift to the influence of his Italian studies—more especially to those which led him to Dante, whose multitudinous characters and scenes impress themselves with so singular and immediate a definiteness upon the imagination. At the same time, Chaucer's resources seem inexhaustible for filling up or rounding off his narratives with the aid of chivalrous love or religious legend, by the introduction of samples of scholastic discourse or devices of personal or general allegory. He commands, where necessary, a rhetorician's readiness of illustration, and a masque-writer's inventiveness, as to machinery; he can even (in the *House of Fame*) conjure up an elaborate but self-consistent phantasmagory of his own, and continue it with a fulness proving that his fancy would not be at a loss for supplying even more materials than he cares to employ.

But Chaucer's poetry derived its power to please from yet another quality; and in this he was the first of our English poets to emulate the poets of the two literatures to which, in the matter of his productions and in the ornaments of his diction, he owed so much. There is in his verse a music which hardly ever wholly loses itself, and which at times is as sweet as that in any English poet after him.

This assertion is not one which is likely to be gainsaid at the present day, when there is not a single lover of Chaucer who would sit down contented with Dryden's condescending mixture of censure and praise. "The verse of Chaucer," he wrote, "I confess, is not harmonious to us. They who lived with him, and some time after him, thought it musical; and it continues so, even in our judgment, if compared with the numbers of Lydgate and Gower, his contemporaries: there is a rude sweetness of a Scotch tune in it, which is natural and pleasing, though not perfect." At the same time, it is no doubt necessary, in order to verify the correctness of a less balanced judgment, to take the trouble, which, if it could but be believed, is by no means great, to master the rules and usages of Chaucerian versification. These rules and usages the present is not a fit occasion for seeking to explain.[2]

With regard to the most important of them, is it not too much to say that instinct and experience will very speedily combine to indicate to an intelligent reader where the poet has resorted to it. *Without* intelligence on the part of the reader, the beautiful harmonies of Mr. Tennyson's later verse remain obscure; so that, taken in this way, the most musical of English verse may seem as difficult to read as the most rugged; but in the former case the lesson is learnt not to be lost again; in the latter, the tumbling is ever beginning anew, as with the rock of Sisyphus. There is nothing that can fairly be called rugged in the verse of Chaucer.

And, fortunately, there are not many pages in this poet's works devoid of lines or passages the music of which cannot escape any ear, however unaccustomed it may be to his diction and versification. What is the nature of the art at whose bidding ten monosyllables arrange themselves into a line of the exquisite cadence of the following:—

> And she was fair, as is the rose in May?

Nor would it be easy to find lines surpassing in their melancholy charm Chaucer's version of the lament of Medea when deserted by Jason—a passage which makes the reader neglectful of the English poet's modest hint that the letter of the Colchian princess may be found at full length in Ovid. The lines shall be quoted *verbatim*, though not *literatim*; and perhaps no better example, and none more readily appreciable by a modern ear, could be given than the fourth of them of the harmonious effect of Chaucer's usage of *slurring*, referred to above:—

> Why likèd thee my yellow hair to see
> More than the boundès of mine honesty?
> Why likèd me thy youth and thy fairnéss
> And of thy tongue the infinite graciousness?
> O, had'st thou in thy conquest dead y-bee(n),
> Full myckle untruth had there died with thee.

Qualities and powers such as the above have belonged to poets of very various times and countries before and after Chaucer. But in addition to these he most assuredly possessed others, which are not usual among the poets of our nation, and which, whencesoever they had come to him personally, had not, before they made their appearance in him, seemed indigenous to the English soil. It would, indeed, be easy to misrepresent the history of English poetry, during the period which Chaucer's advent may be said to have closed, by ascribing to it a uniformly solemn and serious, or even dark and gloomy, character. Such a description would not apply to the poetry of

the period before the Norman Conquest, though, in truth, little room could be left for the play of fancy or wit in the hammered-out war-song, or in the long-drawn Scriptural paraphrase. Nor was it likely that a contagious gaiety should find an opportunity of manifesting itself in the course of the versification of grave historical chronicles, or in the tranquil objective reproduction of the endless traditions of British legend. Of the popular songs belonging to the period after the Norman Conquest, the remains which furnish us with direct or indirect evidence concerning them hardly enable us to form an opinion. But we know that (the cavilling spirit of Chaucer's burlesque *Rhyme of Sir Thopas* notwithstanding) the efforts of English metrical romance in the thirteenth and fourteenth centuries were neither few nor feeble, although these romances were chiefly translations, sometimes abridgments to boot— even the Arthurian cycle having been only imported across the Channel, though it may have thus come back to its original home. There is some animation in at least one famous chronicle in verse, dating from about the close of the thirteenth century; there is real spirit in the war-songs of Minot in the middle of the fourteenth; and from about its beginnings dates a satire full of broad fun concerning the jolly life led by the monks. But none of these works or of those contemporary with them show that innate lightness and buoyancy of tone which seems to add wings to the art of poetry. Nowhere had the English mind found so real an opportunity of poetic utterance in the days of Chaucer's own youth as in Langland's unique work, national in its allegorical form and in its alliterative metre; and nowhere had this utterance been more stern and severe.

No sooner, however, has Chaucer made his appearance as a poet, than he seems to show what mistress's badge he wears, which party of the two that have at most times divided among them a national literature and its representatives he intends to follow. The burden of his song is "Si douce est la marguérite:" he has learnt the ways of French gallantry as if to the manner born, and thus becomes, as it were without hesitation or effort, the first English love-poet. Nor—though in the course of his career his range of themes, his command of materials, and his choice of forms are widely enlarged—is the gay banner under which he has ranged himself ever deserted by him. With the exception of the *House of Fame*, there is not one of his longer poems of which the passion of love, under one or another of its aspects, does not either constitute the main subject or (as in the *Canterbury Tales*) furnish the greater part of the contents. It is as a love-poet that Gower thinks of Chaucer when paying a tribute to him in his own verse; it is to the attacks made upon him in his character as a love-poet, and to his consciousness of what he has achieved as such, that he gives expression in the *Prologue* to the *Legend of Good Women*, where his fair advocate tells the God of Love:—

> The man hath servèd you of his cunníng,
> And furthered well your law in his writíng,
> All be it that he cannot well indite,
> Yet hath he made unlearnèd folk delight
> To servë you in praising of your name.

And so he resumes his favourite theme once more, to tell, as the *Man of Law* says, "of lovers up and down, more than Ovid makes mention of in his old *Epistles*." This fact alone—that our first great English poet was also our first English love-poet, properly so called—would have sufficed to transform our poetic literature through his agency.

What, however, calls for special notice, in connexion with Chaucer's special poetic quality of gaiety and brightness, is the preference which he exhibits for treating the joyous aspects of this many-sided passion. Apart from the *Legend of Good Women*, which is specially designed to give brilliant examples of the faithfulness of women under circumstances of trial, pain, and grief, and from two or three of the *Canterbury Tales*, he dwells, with consistent preference, on the bright side of love, though remaining a stranger to its divine radiance, which shines forth so fully upon us out of the pages of Spenser. Thus, in the *Assembly of Fowls* all is gaiety and mirth, as indeed beseems the genial neighbourhood of Cupid's temple. Again, in *Troilus and Cressid*, the earlier and cheerful part of the love-story is that which he develops with unmistakeable sympathy and enjoyment; and in his hands this part of the poem becomes one of the most charming poetic narratives of the birth and growth of young love which our literature possesses—a soft and sweet counterpart to the consuming heat of Marlowe's unrivalled *Hero and Leander*. With Troilus it was love at first sight—with Cressid a passion of very gradual growth. But so full of nature is the narrative of this growth, that one is irresistibly reminded at more than one point of the inimitable creations of the great modern master in the description of women's love. Is there not a touch of Gretchen in Cressid, retiring into her chamber to ponder over the first revelation to her of the love of Troilus?—

> Cressid arose, no longer there she stayed,
> But straight into her closet went anon,
> And set her down, as still as any stone,
> And every word gan up and down to wind,
> That he had said, as it came to her mind.

And is there not a touch of Clärchen in her—though with a difference—when from her casement she blushingly beholds her lover riding past in triumph:

> So like a man of armës and a knight
> He was to see, filled full of high prowéss,
> For both he had a body, and a might
> To do that thing, as well as hardiness;
> And eke to see him in his gear him dress,
> So fresh, so young, so wieldly seemèd he,
> It truly was a heaven him for to see.
>
> His helm was hewn about in twenty places,
> That by a tissue hung his back behind;
> His shield was dashed with strokes of swords and
>   maces,
> In which men mightë many an arrow find
> That piercèd had the horn and nerve and rind;
> And aye the people cried: 'Here comes our joy,
> And, next his brother, holder up of Troy.'

Even in the very *Book of the Duchess*, the widowed lover describes the maiden charms of his lost wife with so lively a freshness as almost to make one forget that it is a *lost* wife whose praises are being recorded.

The vivacity and joyousness of Chaucer's poetic temperament, however, show themselves in various other ways besides his favourite manner of treating a favourite theme. They enhance the spirit of his passages of dialogue, and add force and freshness to his passages of description. They make him amusingly impatient of epical lengths, abrupt in his transitions, and anxious, with an anxiety usually manifested by readers rather than by writers, to come to the point, "to the great effect," as he is wont to call it. "Men," he says, "may overlade a ship or barge, and therefore I will skip at once to the effect, and let all the rest slip." And he unconsciously suggests a striking difference between himself and the great Elizabethan epic poet who owes so much to him, when he declines to make as long a tale of the chaff or of the straw as of the corn, and to describe all the details of a marriage-feast *seriatim*:

> The fruit of every tale is for to say:
> They eat and drink, and dance and sing and play.

This may be the fruit; but epic poets, from Homer downwards, have been generally in the habit of not neglecting the foliage. Spenser, in particular, has that impartial copiousness which we think it our duty to admire in the Ionic epos, but which, if the truth were told, has prevented generations of Englishmen from acquiring an intimate personal acquaintance with the *Fairy Queen*. With Chaucer the danger certainly rather lay in an opposite direction. Most assuredly he can tell a story with admirable point and precision, when he wishes to do so. Perhaps no better example of his skill in this respect could be cited than the *Manciple's Tale*, with its rapid narrative, its major and minor catastrophe, and its concise moral, ending thus:—

> My son, beware, and be no author new
> Of tidings, whether they be false or true;
> Whereso thou comest, among high or low,
> Keep well thy tongue, and think upon the crow.

At the same time, his frequently recurring announcements of his desire to be brief have the effect of making his narrative appear to halt, and thus, unfortunately, defeat their own purpose. An example of this may be found in the *Knight's Tale*, a narrative poem of which, in contrast with its beauties, a want of evenness is one of the chief defects. It is not that the desire to suppress redundancies is a tendency deserving anything but commendation in any writer, whether great or small; but rather, that the art of concealing art had not yet dawned upon Chaucer. And yet few writers of any time have taken a more evident pleasure in the process of literary production, and have more visibly overflowed with sympathy for, or antipathy against, the characters of their own creation. Great novelists of our own age have often told their readers, in prefaces to their fictions or in *quasi*-confidential comments upon them, of the intimacy in which they have lived with the offspring of their own brain, to them far from shadowy beings. But only the *naïveté* of Chaucer's literary age, together with the vivacity of his manner of thought and writing, could place him in so close a personal relation towards the personages and the incidents of his poems. He is overcome by "pity and ruth" as he reads of suffering, and his eyes "wax foul and sore" as he prepares to tell of its infliction. He compassionates "love's servants" as if he were their own "brother dear;" and into his adaptation of the eventful story of Constance (the *Man of Law's Tale*) he introduces apostrophe upon apostrophe, to the defenceless condition of his heroine—to her relentless enemy the Sultana, and to Satan, who ever makes his instrument of women "when he will beguile"—to the drunken messenger who allowed the letter carried by him to be stolen from him—and to the treacherous Queen-mother who caused them to be stolen. Indeed, in addressing the last-named personage, the poet seems to lose all control over himself.

> O Domegild, I have no English digne
> Unto thy malice and thy tyranny:
> And therefore to the fiend I thee resign,
> Let him at length tell of thy treachery.
> Fye, mannish, fye!—Oh nay, by God, I lie;
> Fye fiendish spirit, for I dare well tell,
> Though thou here walk, thy spirit is in hell.

At the opening of the *Legend of Ariadne* he bids Minos redden with shame; and towards its close, when narrating how Theseus sailed away, leaving his true-love behind, he expresses a hope that the wind may drive the traitor "a twenty devil way."

Nor does this vivacity find a less amusing expression in so trifling a touch as that in the *Clerk's Tale*, where the domestic sent to deprive Griseldis of her boy becomes, *eo ipso* as it were, "this ugly sergeant."

Closely allied to Chaucer's liveliness and gaiety of disposition, and in part springing from them, are his keen sense of the ridiculous and the power of satire which he has at his command. His humour has many varieties, ranging from the refined and half-melancholy irony of the *House of Fame* to the ready wit of the sagacious uncle of Cressid, the burlesque fun of the inimitable *Nun's Priest's Tale*, and the very gross salt of the *Reeve*, the *Miller*, and one or two others. The springs of humour often capriciously refuse to allow themselves to be discovered; nor is the satire of which the direct intention is transparent invariably the most effective species of satire. Concerning, however, Chaucer's use of the power which he in so large a measure possessed, viz., that of covering with ridicule the palpable vices or weaknesses of the classes or kinds of men represented by some of his character-types, one assertion may be made with tolerable safety. Whatever may have been the first stimulus and the ultimate scope of the wit and humour which he here expended, they are *not* to be explained as moral indignation in disguise. And in truth Chaucer's merriment flows spontaneously from a source very near the surface; he is so extremely diverting, because he is so extremely diverted himself.

Herein, too, lies the harmlessness of Chaucer's fun. Its harmlessness, to wit, for those who are able to read him in something like the spirit in which he wrote—never a very easy achievement with regard to any author, and one which the beginner and the young had better be advised to abstain from attempting with Chaucer in the overflow of his more or less unrestrained moods. At all events, the excuse of gaiety of heart—the plea of that *vieil esprit Gaulois* which is so often, and very rarely without need, invoked in an exculpatory capacity by modern French criticism—is the best defence ever made for Chaucer's laughable irregularities, either by his apologists or by himself. "Men should not," he says, and says very truly, "make earnest of game." But when he audaciously defends himself against the charge of impropriety by declaring that he must tell stories *in character*, and coolly requests any person who may find anything in one of his tales objectionable to turn to another:—

> For he shall find enough, both great and small,
> Of storial thing that toucheth gentleness,
> Likewise morality and holiness;
> Blame ye not me, if ye should choose amiss—

we are constrained to shake our heads at the transparent sophistry of the plea, which requires no exposure. For Chaucer knew very well how to give life and colour to his page without recklessly disregarding bounds the neglect of which was even in his day offensive to many besides the "*precious* folk" of whom he half derisively pretends to stand in awe. In one instance he defeated his own purpose; for the so-called *Cook's Tale of Gamelyn* was substituted by some earlier editor for the original *Cook's Tale*, which has thus in its completed form become a rarity removed beyond the reach of even the most ardent of curiosity hunters. Fortunately, however, Chaucer spoke the truth when he said that from this point of view he had written very differently at different times; no whiter pages remain than many of his.

But the realism of Chaucer is something more than exuberant love of fun and light-hearted gaiety. He is the first great painter of character, because he is the first great observer of it among modern European writers. His power of comic observation need not be dwelt upon again, after the illustrations of it which have been incidentally furnished in these pages. More especially with regard to the manners and ways of women, which often, while seeming so natural to women themselves, appear so odd to male observers, Chaucer's eye was ever on the alert. But his works likewise contain passages displaying a penetrating insight into the minds of men, as well as a keen eye for their manners, together with a power of generalising, which, when kept within due bounds, lies at the root of the wise knowledge of humankind so admirable to us in our great essayists, from Bacon to Addison and his modern successors. How truly, for instance, in *Troilus and Cressid*, Chaucer observes on the enthusiastic belief of converts, the "strongest-faithed" of men, as he understands! And how fine is the saying as to the suspiciousness characteristic of lewd (*i. e.*, ignorant) people, that to things which are made more subtly

> Than they can in their lewdness comprehend,

they gladly give the worst interpretation which suggests itself! How appositely the *Canon's Yeoman* describes the arrogance of those who are too clever by half; "when a man has an over-great wit," he says, "it very often chances to him to misuse it!" And with how ripe a wisdom, combined with ethics of true gentleness, the honest *Franklin*, at the opening of his *Tale*, discourses on the uses and the beauty of long-suffering:—

> For one thing, sirës, safely dare I say,
> That friends the one the other must obey,
> If they will longë holdë company.
> Love will not be constrain'd by mastery.
> When mastery comes, the god of love anon
> Beateth his wings—and, farewell! he is gone.
> Love is a thing as any spirit free.
> Women desire, by nature, liberty,
> And not to be constrainèd as a thrall;
> And so do men, if I the truth say shall.
> Look, who that is most patiént in love,
> He is at his advantage all above.
> A virtue high is patiénce, certain,
> Because it vanquisheth, as clerks explain,
> Things to which rigour never could attain.
> For every word men should not chide and plain;
> Learn ye to suffer, or else, so may I go,
> Ye shall it learn, whether ye will or no.
> For in this world certain no wight there is
> Who neither doth nor saith some time amiss.
> Sickness or ire, or constellatión,
> Wine, woe, or changing of complexión,
> Causeth full oft to do amiss or speak.
> For every wrong men may not vengeance wreak:
> After a time there must be temperance
> With every wight that knows self-governance.

It was by virtue of his power of observing and drawing character, above all, that Chaucer became the true predecessor of two several growths in our literature, in both of which characterisation forms a most important element—it might perhaps be truly said, the element which surpasses all others in importance. From this point of view the dramatic poets of the Elizabethan age remain unequalled by any other school or group of dramatists, and the English novelists of the eighteenth and nineteenth centuries by the representatives of any other development of prose-fiction. In the art of construction, in the invention and the arrangement of incident, these dramatists and novelists may have been left behind by others; in the creation of character they are, on the whole, without rivals in their respective branches of literature. To the earlier at least of these growths Chaucer may be said to have pointed the way. His personages—more especially, of course, as has been seen, those who are assembled together in the *Prologue* to the *Canterbury Tales*—are not mere phantasms of the brain, or even mere actual possibilities, but real human beings, and types true to the likeness of whole classes of men and women, or to the mould in which all human nature is cast. This is, upon the whole, the most wonderful, as it is perhaps the most generally recognised, of Chaucer's gifts. It would not of itself have sufficed to make him a great dramatist, had the drama stood ready for him as a literary form into which to pour the inspirations of his genius, as it afterwards stood ready for our great Elizabethans. But to it were added in him that perception of a strong dramatic situation, and that power of finding the right words for it, which have determined the success of many plays, and the absence of which materially detracts from the completeness of the effect of others, high as their merits may be in other respects. How thrilling, for instance, is that rapid passage across the stage, as one might almost call it, of the unhappy Dorigen in the *Franklin's Tale*! The antecedents of the situation, to be sure, are, as has been elsewhere suggested, absurd enough; but who can fail to feel that spasm of anxious sympathy with which a powerful dramatic situation in itself affects us, when the wife, whom for truth's sake her husband has bidden be untrue to him, goes forth on her unholy errand of duty? "Whither so fast?" asks the lover:

> And she made answer, half as she were mad:
> 'Unto the garden, as my husband bade,
> My promise for to keep, alas! alas!'

Nor, as the abbreviated prose version of the *Pardoner's Tale* given above will suffice to show, was Chaucer deficient in the art of dramatically arranging a story; while he is not excelled by any of our non-dramatic poets in the spirit and movement of his dialogue. The *Book of the Duchess* and the *House of Fame*, but more especially *Troilus and Cressid* and the connecting passages between some of the *Canterbury Tales*, may be referred to in various illustration of this.

The vividness of his imagination, which conjures up, so to speak, the very personality of his characters before him, and the contagious force of his pathos, which is as true and as spontaneous as his humour, complete in him the born dramatist. We can see Constance as with our own eyes, in the agony of her peril:—

> Have ye not seen some time a pallid face
> Among a press, of him that hath been led
> Towards his death, where him awaits no grace,
> And such a colour in his face hath had,
> Men mightë know his face was so bested
> 'Mong all the other faces in that rout?
> So stands Constánce, and looketh her about.

And perhaps there is no better way of studying the general character of Chaucer's pathos than a comparison of the *Monk's Tale* from which this passage is taken, and the *Clerk's Tale*, with their originals. In the former, for instance, the prayer of Constance, when condemned through Domegild's guilt to be cast adrift once more on the waters, her piteous words and tenderness to her little child as it lies weeping in her arm, and her touching leave-taking from the land of the husband who has condemned her—all these are Chaucer's own. So also are parts of one of the most affecting passages in the *Clerk's Tale*—Griseldis' farewell to her daughter. But it is as unnecessary to lay a finger upon lines and passages illustrating Chaucer's pathos as upon others illustrating his humour.

Thus, then, Chaucer was a born dramatist; but fate willed it, that the branch of our literature which might probably have

of all been the best suited to his genius was not to spring into life till he and several generations after him had passed away. To be sure, during the fourteenth century the so-called miracle-plays flourished abundantly in England, and were, as there is every reason to believe, already largely performed by the trading-companies of London and the towns. The allusions in Chaucer to these beginnings of our English drama are, however, remarkably scanty. The *Wife of Bath* mentions plays of miracles among the other occasions of religious sensation haunted by her, clad in her gay scarlet gown—including vigils, processions, preachings, pilgrimages, and marriages. And the jolly parish-clerk of the *Miller's Tale*, we are informed, at times, in order to show his lightness and his skill, played "Herod on a scaffold high"—thus, by-the-bye, emulating the parish clerks of London, who are known to have been among the performers of miracles in the Middle Ages. The allusion to Pilate's voice in the *Miller's Prologue*, and that in the *Tale* to

> The sorrow of Noah with his fellowship
> That he had ere he got his wife to ship,

seem likewise dramatic reminiscences; and the occurrence of these three allusions in a single *Tale* and its *Prologue* would incline one to think that Chaucer had recently amused himself at one of these performances. But plays are not mentioned among the entertainments enumerated at the opening of the *Pardoner's Tale*; and it would in any case have been unlikely that Chaucer should have paid much attention to diversions which were long chiefly "visited" by the classes with which he could have no personal connexion, and even at a much later date were dissociated in men's minds from poetry and literature. Had he ever written anything remotely partaking of the nature of a dramatic piece, it could at the most have been the words of the songs in some congratulatory royal pageant such as Lydgate probably wrote on the return of Henry V. after Agincourt; though there is not the least reason for supposing Chaucer to have taken so much interest in the "ridings" through the City which occupied many a morning of the idle apprentice of the *Cook's Tale*, Perkyn Revellour. It is, perhaps, more surprising to find Chaucer, who was a reader of several Latin poets, and who had heard of more, both Latin and Greek, show no knowledge whatever of the ancient classical drama, with which he may accordingly be fairly concluded to have been wholly unacquainted.

To one further aspect of Chaucer's realism as a poet reference has already been made; but a final mention of it may most appropriately conclude this sketch of his poetical characteristics. His descriptions of nature are as true as his sketches of human character; and incidental touches in him reveal his love of the one as unmistakeably as his unflagging interest in the study of the other. Even these May-morning *exordia*, in which he was but following a fashion—faithfully observed both by the French *trouvères* and by the English romances translated from their productions, and not forgotten by the author of the earlier part of the *Roman de la Rose*—always come from his hands with the freshness of natural truth. They cannot be called original in conception, and it would be difficult to point out in them anything strikingly original in execution; yet they cannot be included among those matter-of-course notices of morning and evening, sunrise and sunset, to which so many poets have accustomed us since (be it said with reverence) Homer himself. In Chaucer these passages make his page "as fresh as is the month of May." When he went forth on these April and May mornings, it was not solely with the intent of composing a roundelay or a *marguérite*; but we may be well assured he allowed the song of the little birds, the perfume of the flowers, and the fresh verdure of the English landscape, to sink into his very soul. For nowhere does he seem, and nowhere could he have been, more open to the influence which he received into himself, and which in his turn he exercised, and exercises upon others, than when he was in fresh contact with nature. In this influence lies the secret of his genius; in his poetry there is *life*.

Notes

1. The passage in Canto viii. of the *Purgatorio* is thus translated by Longfellow:

   > Not oftentimes upriseth through the branches
   > The probity of man; and this He wills
   > Who gives it, so that we may ask of Him.

   Its intention is only to show that the son is not necessarily what the father is before him; thus, Edward I. of England is a mightier man than was his father Henry III. Chaucer has ingeniously, though not altogether legitimately, pressed the passage into his service.

2. It may, however, be stated that they only partially connect themselves with Chaucer's use of forms which are now obsolete—more especially of inflexions of verbs and substantives (including several instances of the famous final *e*), and contractions with the negative *ne* and other monosyllabic words ending in a vowel, of the initial syllables of words beginning with vowels or with the letter *h*. These and other variations from later usage in spelling and pronunciation—such as the occurrence of an *e* (sometimes sounded and sometimes not) at the end of words in which it is now no longer retained, and, again, the frequent accentuation of many words of French origin in their last syllable, as in French, and of certain words of English origin analogously—are to be looked for as a matter of course in the period of our language in which Chaucer lived. He clearly foresaw the difficulties which would be caused to his readers by the variations of usage in spelling and pronunciation—variations to some extent rendered inevitable by the fact that he wrote in an English dialect which was only gradually coming to be accepted as the uniform language of English writers. Towards the close of his *Troilus and Cressid* he thus addresses his "little book," in fear of the mangling it might undergo from scriveners who might blunder in the copying of its words, or from reciters who might maltreat its verse in the distribution of the accents:—

   > And, since there is so great diversity
   > In English, and in writing of our tongue,
   > I pray to God that none may miswrite thee
   > Nor thee mismetre, for default of tongue,
   > And wheresoe'er thou mayst be read or sung,
   > That thou be understood, God I beseech.

   But in his versification he likewise adopted certain other practices which had no such origin or reason as those already referred to. Among them were the addition, at the end of a line of five accents, of an unaccented syllable; and the substitution, for the first foot of a line either of four or of five accents, of a single syllable. These deviations from a stricter system of versification he doubtless permitted to himself, partly for the sake of variety, and partly for that of convenience; but neither of them is peculiar to himself, or of supreme importance for the effect of his verse. In fact, he seems to allow as much in a passage of his *House of Fame*—a poem written, it should, however, be observed, in an easy-going form of verse (the line of four accents) which in his later period Chaucer seems, with this exception, to have invariably discarded. He here beseeches Apollo to make his rhyme

   > Somewhat agreeáble,
   > Though some verse fail in a sylláble.

   But another of his usages—the misunderstanding of which has more than anything else caused his art as a writer of verse to be misjudged—seems to have been due to a very different cause. To understand the real nature of the usage in question it is only necessary to seize the principle of Chaucer's rhythm. Of this principle it was well said many years ago by a most competent authority—Mr. R. Horne—that it is "inseparable from a full or fair exercise of the genius of our language in versification." For though this usage in its full freedom was gradually again lost to our poetry for a time, yet it

was in a large measure recovered by Shakespeare and the later dramatists of our great age, and has since been never altogether abandoned again—not even by the correct writers of the Augustan period—till by the favourites of our own times it is resorted to with a perhaps excessive liberality. It consists simply in *slurring* over certain final syllables—not eliding them or contracting them with the syllables following upon them, but passing over them lightly, so that, without being inaudible, they may at the same time not interfere with the rhythm or beat of the verse. This usage, by adding to the variety, incontestably adds to the flexibility and beauty of Chaucer's versification.

MATTHEW ARNOLD
From *Essays in Criticism*
1880, Second Series, pp. xxx–xxxvi

The predominance of French poetry in Europe, during the twelfth and thirteenth centuries, is due to its poetry of the *langue d'oil*, the poetry of northern France and of the tongue which is now the French language. In the twelfth century the bloom of this romance-poetry was earlier and stronger in England, at the court of our Anglo-Norman kings, than in France itself. But it was a bloom of French poetry; and as our native poetry formed itself, it formed itself out of this. The romance-poems which took possession of the heart and imagination of Europe in the twelfth and thirteenth centuries are French; 'they are,' as Southey justly says, 'the pride of French literature, nor have we anything which can be placed in competition with them.' Themes were supplied from all quarters; but the romance-setting which was common to them all, and which gained the ear of Europe, was French. This constituted for the French poetry, literature, and language, at the height of the Middle Ages, an unchallenged predominance. The Italian Brunetto Latini, the master of Dante, wrote his *Treasure* in French because, he says, 'la parleure en est plus delitable et plus commune a toutes gens.'. . .

Yet it is now all gone, this French romance-poetry, of which the weight of substance and the power of style are not unfairly represented by this extract from Christian of Troyes. Only by means of the historic estimate can we persuade ourselves now to think that any of it is of poetical importance.

But in the fourteenth century there comes an Englishman nourished on this poetry, taught his trade by this poetry, getting words, rhyme, metre from this poetry; for even of that stanza which the Italians used, and which Chaucer derived immediately from the Italians, the basis and suggestion was probably given in France. Chaucer (I have already named him) fascinated his contemporaries, but so too did Christian of Troyes and Wolfram of Eschenbach. Chaucer's power of fascination, however, is enduring; his poetical importance does not need the assistance of the historic estimate; it is real. He is a genuine source of joy and strength, which is flowing still for us and will flow always. He will be read, as time goes on, far more generally than he is read now. His language is a cause of difficulty for us; but so also, and I think in quite as great a degree, is the language of Burns. In Chaucer's case, as in that of Burns, it is a difficulty to be unhesitatingly accepted and overcome.

If we ask ourselves wherein consists the immense superiority of Chaucer's poetry over the romance-poetry—why it is that in passing from this to Chaucer we suddenly feel ourselves to be in another world, we shall find that his superiority is both in the substance of his poetry and in the style of his poetry. His superiority in substance is given by his large, free, simple, clear yet kindly view of human life,—so unlike the total want, in the romance-poets, of all intelligent command of it. Chaucer has not their helplessness; he has gained the power to survey the world from a central, a truly human point of view. We have only to call to mind the Prologue to 'The Canterbury Tales'. The right comment upon it is Dryden's: 'It is sufficient to say, according to the proverb, that *here is God's plenty*.' And again: 'He is a perpetual fountain of good sense.' It is by a large, free, sound representation of things, that poetry, this high criticism of life, has truth of substance; and Chaucer's poetry has truth of substance.

Of his style and manner, if we think first of the romance-poetry and then of Chaucer's divine liquidness of diction, his divine fluidity of movement, it is difficult to speak temperately. They are irresistible, and justify all the rapture with which his successors speak of his 'gold dew-drops of speech.' Johnson misses the point entirely when he finds fault with Dryden for ascribing to Chaucer the first refinement of our numbers, and says that Gower also can show smooth numbers and easy rhymes. The refinement of our numbers means something far more than this. A nation may have versifiers with smooth numbers and easy rhymes, and yet may have no real poetry at all. Chaucer is the father of our splendid English poetry; he is our 'well of English undefiled,' because by the lovely charm of his diction, the lovely charm of his movement, he makes an epoch and founds a tradition. In Spenser, Shakespeare, Milton, Keats, we can follow the tradition of the liquid diction, the fluid movement, of Chaucer; at one time it is his liquid diction of which in these poets we feel the virtue, and at another time it is his fluid movement. And the virtue is irresistible.

Bounded as is my space, I must yet find room for an example of Chaucer's virtue, as I have given examples to show the virtue of the great classics. I feel disposed to say that a single line is enough to show the charm of Chaucer's verse; that merely one line like this—

O martyr souded in virginitee!

has a virtue of manner and movement such as we shall not find in all the verse of romance-poetry;—but this is saying nothing. The virtue is such as we shall not find, perhaps, in all English poetry, outside the poets whom I have named as the special inheritors of Chaucer's tradition. A single line, however, is too little if we have not the strain of Chaucer's verse well in our memory; let us take a stanza. It is from 'The Prioress's Tale', the story of the Christian child murdered in a Jewry—

My throte is cut unto my nekke-bone
Saidè this child, and as by way of kinde
I should have deyd, yea, longè time agone;
But Jesu Christ, as ye in bookès finde,
Will that his glory last and be in minde,
And for the worship of his mother dere
Yet may I sing O *Alma* loud and clere.

Wordsworth has modernised this Tale, and to feel how delicate and evanescent is the charm of verse, we have only to read Wordsworth's first three lines of this stanza after Chaucer's—

My throat is cut unto the bone, I trow,
Said this young child, and by the law of kind
I should have died, yea, many hours ago.

The charm is departed. It is often said that the power of liquidness and fluidity in Chaucer's verse was dependent upon a free, a licentious dealing with language, such as is now impossible; upon a liberty, such as Burns too enjoyed, of making words like *neck*, *bird*, into a dissyllable by adding to them, and words like *cause*, *rhyme*, into a dissyllable by sounding the *e* mute. It is true that Chaucer's fluidity is conjoined with this liberty, and is admirably served by it; but we ought not to say that it was

dependent upon it. It was dependent upon his talent. Other poets with a like liberty do not attain to the fluidity of Chaucer; Burns himself does not attain to it. Poets, again, who have a talent akin to Chaucer's, such as Shakespeare or Keats, have known how to attain to his fluidity without the like liberty.

And yet Chaucer is not one of the great classics. His poetry transcends and effaces, easily and without effort, all the romance-poetry of Catholic Christendom; it transcends and effaces all the English poetry contemporary with it, it transcends and effaces all the English poetry subsequent to it down to the age of Elizabeth. Of such avail is poetic truth of substance, in its natural and necessary union with poetic truth of style. And yet, I say, Chaucer is not one of the great classics. He has not their accent. What is wanting to him is suggested by the mere mention of the name of the first great classic of Christendom, the immortal poet who died eighty years before Chaucer,—Dante. The accent of such verse as

In la sua volontate è nostra pace

is altogether beyond Chaucer's reach; we praise him, but we feel that this accent is out of the question for him. It may be said that it was necessarily out of the reach of any poet in the England of that stage of growth. Possibly; but we are to adopt a real, not a historic, estimate of poetry. However we may account for its absence, something is wanting, then, to the poetry of Chaucer, which poetry must have before it can be placed in the glorious class of the best. And there is no doubt what that something is. It is the *spoudaiotē*, the high and excellent seriousness, which Aristotle assigns as one of the grand virtues of poetry. The substance of Chaucer's poetry, his view of things and his criticism of life, has largeness, freedom, shrewdness, benignity; but it has not this high seriousness. Homer's criticism of life has it, Dante's has it, Shakespeare's has it. It is this chiefly which gives to our spirits what they can rest upon; and with the increasing demands of our modern ages upon poetry, this virtue of giving us what we can rest upon will be more and more highly esteemed. A voice from the slums of Paris, fifty or sixty years after Chaucer, the voice of poor Villon out of his life of riot and crime, has at its happy moments (as, for instance, in the last stanza of 'La Belle Heaulmière') more of this important poetic virtue of seriousness than all the productions of Chaucer. But its apparition in Villon, and in men like Villon, is fitful; the greatness of the great poets, the power of their criticism of life, is that their virtue is sustained.

To our praise, therefore, of Chaucer as a poet there must be this limitation; he lacks the high seriousness of the great classics, and therewith an important part of their virtue. Still, the main fact for us to bear in mind about Chaucer is his sterling value according to that real estimate which we firmly adopt for all poets. He has poetic truth of substance, though he has not high poetic seriousness, and corresponding to his truth of substance he has an exquisite virtue of style and manner. With him is born our real poetry.

ALGERNON CHARLES SWINBURNE
"Short Notes on English Poets: Chaucer; Spenser;
The Sonnets of Shakespeare; Milton" (1880)
Complete Works
1926, Volume 4, pp. 97–101

Having before this had occasion to remark in terms of somewhat strong deprecation on the principle adopted by Mr. William Rossetti in his revision and rearrangement of the text of our greatest lyric poet, I am the more desirous to bear witness to the elevation and the excellence of his critical workmanship in his *Lives of Famous Poets*. On some points I differ gravely from his estimate; once or twice I differ from it on all points; but on the whole I find it not acceptable merely but admirable as the very best and most sufficient ever yet given of some at least among the leading names of our poets.

Four of these are by him selected as composing the supreme quadrilateral of English song. It is through no lack of love and reverence for the name of Chaucer that I must question his right, though the first narrative poet of England, to stand on that account beside her first dramatic, her first epic, or her first lyric poet. But, being certainly unprepared to admit his equality with Shakespeare, with Milton, and with Shelley, I would reduce Mr. Rossetti's mystic four to the old sacred number of three. Pure or mere narrative is a form essentially and avowedly inferior to the lyrical or the dramatic form of poetry; and the finer line of distinction which marks it off from the epic marks it also thereby as inferior.

Of all whose names may claim anything like equality of rank on the roll of national poets—not even excepting Virgil—we may say that Chaucer borrowed most from abroad, and did most to improve whatever he borrowed. I believe it would be but accurate to admit that in all his poems of serious or tragic narrative we hear a French or Italian tongue speaking with a Teutonic accent through English lips. It has utterly unlearnt the native tone and cadence of its natural inflections; it has perfectly put on the native tone and cadence of a stranger's; yet is it always what it was at first—*lingua romana in bocca tedesca*. It speaks not only with more vigour but actually with more sweetness than the tongues of its teachers; but it speaks after its own fashion no other than the lesson they have taught. Chaucer was in the main a French or Italian poet, lined thoroughly and warmly throughout with the substance of an English humorist. And with this great gift of specially English humour he combined, naturally as it were and inevitably, the inseparable twin-born gift of peculiarly English pathos. In the figures of Arcite and Grisilde, he has actually outdone Boccaccio's very self for pathos: as far almost as Keats was afterwards to fall short of the same great model in the same great quality. And but for the instinctive distaste and congenital repugnance of his composed and comfortable genius from its accompanying horror, he might haply have come nearer than he has cared or dared to come even to the unapproachable pathos of Dante. But it was only in the world of one who stands far higher above Dante than even Dante can on the whole be justly held to stand above Chaucer, that figures as heavenly as the figures of Beatrice and Matilda could move unspotted and undegraded among figures as earthly as those of the Reve, the Miller, and the Wife of Bath: that a wider if not keener pathos than Ugolino's or Francesca's could alternate with a deeper if not richer humour than that of Absolon and Nicholas.

It is a notable dispensation of chance—one which a writer who might happen to be almost a theist might designate in the deliciously comical phrase of certain ambiguous pietists as 'almost providential'—that the three great typical poets of the three great representative nations of Europe during the dark and lurid lapse of the Middle Ages should each afford as complete and profound a type of a different and alien class as of a different and alien people. Vast as are the diversities of their national and personal characters, these are yet less radical than the divergences between class and class which mark off each from either of his fellows in nothing but in fame. Dante represents, as its best and highest, the upper class of the dark ages not less than he represents their Italy; Chaucer represents their middle class at its best and wisest, not less than he represents

their England; Villon represents their lower class at its worst and its best alike, even more than he represents their France. And of these three the English middle class, being incomparably the happiest and the wisest, is indisputably, considering the common circumstances of their successive times, the least likely to have left us the highest example of all poetry then possible to men. And of their three legacies, precious and wonderful as it is, the Englishman's is accordingly the least wonderful and the least precious. The poet of the sensible and prosperous middle class in England had less to suffer and to sing than the theosophic aristocrat of Italy, or the hunted and hungry vagabond who first found articulate voice for the dumb longing and the blind love as well as for the reckless appetites and riotous agonies of the miserable and terrible multitude in whose darkness lay dormant, as in a cerecloth which was also a chrysalid, the debased and disfigured god-head which was one day to exchange the degradation of the lowest populace for the revelation of the highest people—for the world-wide apocalypse of France. The golden-tongued gallows bird of Paris is distinguished from his two more dignified compeers by a deeper difference yet—a difference, we might say, of office and of mission no less than of genius and of gift. Dante and Chaucer are wholly and solely poets of the past or present—singers indeed for all time, but only singers of their own: Villon, in an equivocal and unconscious fashion, was a singer also of the future; he was the first modern and the last mediæval poet. He is of us, in a sense in which it cannot be said that either Chaucer or Dante is of us, or even could have been; a man of a changing and self-transforming time, not utterly held fast, though still sorely struggling, in the jaws of hell and the ages of faith.

But in happy perfection of manhood the great and fortunate Englishman almost more exceeds his great and unfortunate fellow-singers than he is exceeded by them in depth of passion and height of rapture, in ardour and intensity of vision or of sense. With the single and sublimer exception of Sophocles, he seems to me the happiest of all great poets on record; their standing type and sovereign example of noble and manly happiness. As prosperous indeed in their several ages and lines of life were Petrarca and Ariosto, Horace and Virgil; but one only of these impresses us in every lineament of his work with the same masculine power of enjoyment. And when Ariosto threw across the windy sea of glittering legend and fluctuant romance the broad summer lightnings of his large and jocund genius, the dark ages had already returned into the outer darkness where there is weeping and gnashing of teeth—the tears of Dante Alighieri and the laughter of François Villon. But the wide warm harvest-field of Chaucer's husbandry was all glorious with gold of ripening sunshine while all the world beside lay in blackness and in bonds, throughout all those ages of death called ages of faith by men who can believe in nothing beyond a building or a book, outside the codified creeds of a Bible or the œcumenical structures of a Church.

GEORGE DAWSON
From "Chaucer"
Biographical Lectures, ed. St. Clair
1887, pp. 205–16

If Chaucer had had the good fortune to write in Latin or Greek, the English nation would have given themselves great pains to interpret his meaning; but as he had the misfortune to write in English at an early period, there are few, even educated people, who put themselves to the trouble of comprehending his great and glorious poems.

As our time is limited, it will be very wise to confine our attention to two or three distinct points. I wish first to convince you that Chaucer was not only a great poet considering his age, but one of the five great poets the world ever produced. Then I shall have to show you that Chaucer may be read fluently in his own peculiar language, without the modernising aid of Dryden, who was unequal to the task, or of Pope, who could not do it though he tried. Afterwards I shall put before you certain passages to justify any eulogiums I may pass.

Of the man, very little is known; and though whole quartos have been written about him, like many other biographies there is very little in them. Honestly speaking, the life of Chaucer might be written in a very small compass; but it is so mixed up and involved with the political history of his noble friend and patron, John of Gaunt, that if one does not know much of the latter one cannot know much of the former; and if one does, then there is hardly any necessity to speak about Chaucer in this respect.

We will, therefore, dismiss very briefly what is acknowledged in the poet's career—his education at Cambridge and Oxford, his studies in the Temple, his admission to the splendid and brilliant court of Edward III. as a page, his there becoming a protégé of the powerful Duke of Lancaster, his rapid rise and growth in favour with the chivalrous monarch under whom he served, his successful mission as ambassador to Genoa, his subsequent rewards and pensions, his acquisition of wealth, his reduction to poverty by the death of John of Gaunt and the King, and, finally, his death in quietude and seclusion in the country. When dying, he wrote those beautiful and oft-quoted verses known as "The good counsel of Geoffrey Chaucer," which will show with what true piety and with what admirable knowledge of the world this good man went out of it.

> Fly from the press, and dwell with soothfastness;
>   Suffice unto thy good, though it be small;
> For hoard hath hate, and climbing tickleness,
>   Praise hath envy, and weal is blent owre all;
> Savour no more than thee behovë shall,
> Rede well thyself that other folk canst rede—
> And truth thee shall deliver, it is no drede.
>
> Painë thee not each crooked to redress,
>   In trust of her that turneth as a ball:
> Great rest standeth in little business,
>   Beware also to spurn against a nall,
>   Strive not as doth a crockë with a wall.
> Doomë thyself that doomest others dede,
> And truth thee shall deliver, it is no drede.
>
> That thee is sent receive in buxomness;
>   The wrestling of this world asketh a fall:
> Here is no home, here is but wilderness—
>   Forth, pilgrim, forthë beast, out of thy stall.
>   Look up on high, and thankë God for all,
> Weivë thy lusts, and let thy ghost thee lede,
> And truth thee shall deliver, it is no drede.

It is with Chaucer as a poet that we have most to do; and I do protest against an error which some people entertain relative to Chaucer. When speaking of him, they are apt to say that, "considering the circumstances of the age in which he lived, he was a great poet." Now, don't let us make any allowance or apology of this sort for Chaucer; don't say of him, as they did in the time of Pope, that considering he was "the morning star," he was a great poet. The fact is, Chaucer was absolutely one of the greatest poets the world ever brought forth; he was one of the four great English poets; and he was not merely one of the first of these, but of the universe, and one of the noblest.

Before proceeding next to notice some of the distinctive peculiarities of the ancient poet, I must pause to pay a tribute to the patriotic benefit he conferred upon the English language and the English people; and in doing so I must advert to the Norman Conquest, and the yoke put upon the bluff, hard-handed, simple Saxons by their cool, chivalrous, gentlemanly invaders. Whilst that yoke was new, and the hand of William was strong, there were two languages spoken in the country—the Saxon and the Norman French. Saxon book-making was interrupted; but the Saxon spirit remained uncontaminated and untouched: the two rivers ran side by side unmingled. The consequence was that by-and-bye the national life began to revive. Not many years after the Conquest, the Norman gentleman had to learn Saxon; and, with the resuscitation of the national spirit came the revival of the Saxon literature. Chaucer's lot was a peculiar one. He became a national poet. He was Norman by descent, a courtier by profession, a scholar by acquirement, a favourite with the learned, and the darling of the nobles; and yet he became the poet of the people. There is so much talk now-a-days about "poets of the people," that it is gratifying to find in what respect this great man was essentially worthy of that denomination. He combined the speech of the Norman gentleman with the Saxon poetry of the people; he turned himself to the people, and he did more than any other man in history in the admirable task of binding together the classes of the nation. That man does a more beautiful work who joins the hands of classes, than he who, by irate or harsh language, causes them to keep apart. Apart from being a poet, he laid his one white hand in the open, broad, brown palm of the Saxon, and the other in the fair hand of the Norman lady; he did wed together these people; and he did choose to write in the great old English tongue; he was not only England's great poet, but he was England's great patron.

Since his time the question has been settled that the man who writes a great book must write it in the popular speech, in the people's ways and manners. When Chaucer took up the people, he discovered his burgher and his miller, and so made the Canterbury Tales such a grand picture of national manners, as that Homer himself might almost "pale his ineffectual fire" before his genius. Homer lived early and sang about the early Greeks; Chaucer lived later, and he took some of the old stories of England for his themes. If we cannot give him the credit of being an inventor, yet he was the sweetest narrator of old popular legends that ever lived. But Chaucer wrote for the people in the language and spirit of a gentleman. In these days it is said you must put on fustian and go down to the people. Chaucer did not do that. His poems, to speak in a common phrase of the present day, had a "run," and he familiarised the Anglo-Norman in England. He himself said, "Let their clerks indite in Latin, for they have propriety of sense and knowledge, and let the French also in their French indite, for it is kindly in their mouths; but let us show our phantasies in such words as we have learned in our dame's tongue." To which I say a loud Amen.

Chaucer was the first author who discovered character, and drew it individually. We often hear it said of a person, "He is a character." This is no ill compliment; for it means that he is original, strong, individual, unmistakable; you cannot take him for anybody else. He is no mere John Jones, but one by himself. Look at Chaucer's works. How thoroughly individual, how truly flesh and blood his people are. There is as much difference between Chaucer and Boccaccio as there is between Homer and Virgil. Homer is grand, truthful, and life-like; Virgil is a delusion, full of magic-lantern slides and shadows. Chaucer is the Homer of England; his characters are so thoroughly real and life-like. He exercised a great influence on the drama, as he was the first of modern writers who thoroughly individualised.

As Shelley said of Shakespeare, it may well be said of Chaucer that he carries the palm over the Greek drama by the introduction of a large and genial humour into his poetry. Chaucer abounds in pathos, but it only serves to lead to his humour; and the flashes of his English humour only serve to show there are slumbrous depths of true feeling and true sympathy beneath. He was best humoured amongst men. Let him go to a dance, and all the girls wished he would dance with them first. In battle foremost, in retreat the last. In the house of God meek in his humility, great in his piety. Such was Chaucer. Shakespeare embodies the alternate play of passion, pathos, and humour; for in the case of all English humour its tears and laughter are happily intermingled: and all this is eminently displayed by Chaucer. Whilst capable of touching pathos, he had a downright hearty, genial love of fun in him.

Chaucer was the great national poet of olden time, and the best, the fairest, the truest painter of nature. He was the Adam of English poetry, and he walked in the early dew of the Paradise of poesy. He was the Homer of England. He saw things as they were, and wrote them down. He knew life well. If you wanted a courtly pageant, he could depict it; but if you wanted a portrait of a man, Montaigne could not come up to him, nor could Swift equal him. He was the type of all sorts of writers who came after him. As it is said that an overture foreshadows the best part of an opera, his was the solemn overture to English literature.

Chaucer was very unconventional; he was, moreover, frank, and if he told his hearers a dull story he gaped and told them so. It is perfect rest to get away from the laboured strains of Gray, Pope, and company, and lend oneself for a while to the freshness and sweetness of the verse of this early man. It may be said that you cannot read him; but I want to inspire you with faith enough to attempt to crack Chaucer's quaint English. There is not half the difficulty in reading Chaucer that there is in reading French; who then would be unrational enough to waste time over French and whine that Chaucer is difficult? In illustration of this, I will read you an exquisite passage from Chaucer's "Death of Emily," in the original language:

> His beard was well begunnen for to spring;
> His voice was as a trumpë thundering.

Contrast this with Dryden's reproduction of the same lines:

> Whose voice was heard around
> Loud as a trumpet with a silver sound.

. . . I place Chaucer amongst the four fine old fathers of English poesy, and I class Chaucer and Spenser, Shakespeare and Milton, in one category. He was, in fact, almost the best fruit the old English tree ever grew. Let us take his works in proof of this. His merit is that he was the first poet that drew character individually, well discriminated, and withal correct. In reading the *Canterbury Tales*, the great charm is that one can recognise every one of its people as every-day characters. One knows the features of every individual even to the cut of his nose, and can perceive all that glorious reality of life in them which only a true artist can impart. Chaucer showed Shakespeare how to depict: Shakespeare, it is true, delineated character well, as he did everything well; but Chaucer is the oldest, the truest-hearted, most deep, pathetic, and unconventional poet England ever produced. He was a new man, a first man, a fresh man, an unconventional man. He wrote down things exactly as he saw them, and as they had effect upon him—not what correct people now-a-days would say *ought* to have been the effect. Chaucer was the sincerest poet that ever

lived; and it is right pleasant to get away into his hearty, frank, jolly, jovial verses, full as they are of fine old unconventional English words. The man had a wonderful idea of satire; he was a dear lover of nature, and was, moreover, an awful "quiz." He had all the merits of Montaigne, more than the wit of Swift, and Wordsworth's love of nature as well. Whether we begin with nature or go on to character, the hand of a master is perceptible.

But he had one great misfortune to contend with—he had the bad luck to be an Englishman. If he had been a delicate Virgil, or a feeble Ennius, people in the present day might have taken the trouble perhaps to read him. But why should we not comprehend old English as well as Greek or French? Chaucer wrote in a language that is fast becoming dead to us who live in these modern times. It is true it is awkward and annoying to be obliged to turn to a dictionary in the middle of a line; but have we not often to do that with Homer? How, I will ask, do Englishmen read Burns? Many do, and do it by study. Why not with a national poet like Chaucer? The excuse that you cannot make out his language ought only to be made use of by lazy people. The proper understanding of the value of words is essential to proper speaking and proper writing; and the best study of primitive English will be found in Chaucer. Why should we mouth over a Roman pot, or go "mooning" to Kenilworth, if we neglect to familiarise ourselves with a curious and beautiful antiquity like Chaucer's poems? In a word, we ought to be acquainted with the language in which our forefathers talked, with which they rallied in the battle-field, and in which they prayed and worshipped.

To justify the view I have expressed of Chaucer's character and writings, I will give to you a series of selected and various quotations from his pages. I give them to you as a few lessons in Chaucerian reading, in the hope of convincing you of its ease and simplicity. However, I will first of all lay down a few simple rules for reading Chaucer with fluency. You must pay particular attention to the plurals and genitives, and the variation of the final syllables. You must be Teutonic in your pronunciation, and if you will call "drops" "droppës," and "streams" "streamës," &c., you will easily manage Chaucer. The language, partly Teutonic and partly Saxon as it is, may in some cases be considered vulgar; but it may be heard in use, by the country folk, in some counties, even in the present day; and it is so beautifully intermixed that each word has its full meaning, whilst the harmony of the lines,—though occasionally short of a foot, perhaps—is quite refreshing and thoroughly English.

In illustrating Chaucer's characteristics, we will commence with his love of nature, and for this we may take his exquisite lines on "The Daisy"; while quotations from the *Canterbury Tales* and *Troilus and Cresseide* will show his mastery in description of incidents in common life, and in delineating individual character. First then, about the daisy:

> And as for me, though that I can but lite,
> On bookës for to read I me delight,
> And to them give I faith and full credénce,
> And in mine heart have them in reverence
> So heartily, that there is gamë none
> That from my bookës maketh me to gone.
> But it be seldom, on the holy day,
> Save certainly when that the month of May
> Is comen, and I hear the fowlës sing
> And that the flow'rës 'ginnen for to spring,—
> Fare well my book and my devotïon.
>   Now have I then eke this conditïon
> That, above all the flow'rës in the mead,
> Then love I most those flow'rës white and red
> Such that men callen daisies in our town.

> To them have I so great affectiön,
> As I said erst, when comen is the May,
> That in my bed there daweth me no day
> That I n'am up and walking in the mead,
> To see this flow'r against the sunnë spread.
> When it upriseth early by the morrow,
> That blissful sight softeneth all my sorrow,
> So glad am I when that I have presénce
> Of it, to do it all reverence
> As she that is of all flow'rës the flow'r,
> Fulfillëd of all virtue and honóur,
> And ever alikë fair and fresh of hue
> As well in winter as in summer new,
> This love I ever, and shall until I die
> Al' swear I not of this, I will not lie.

These beautiful lines, from the prologue to the *Legend of Good Women*, may serve to illustrate Chaucer's love of nature.

[Prominent among the qualities of his poetry is the ruggedly picturesque. Short and rapid strokes of the brush are usually more powerful than they are polished: but in Chaucer the ruggedness is compensated by the concentration. He crams into a big bulging line the meaning which, in Spenser, would fill a stanza or a page. In the description of the Temple of Mars, in the *Knight's Tale*, every line is a picture, and resembles the boss upon a buckler, or the knob on a rough goblet of gold:—

> There stood the temple of Mars Armipotent,
> Wrought all of burnëd steel, of which th' entry
> Was long and strait, and ghastly for to see;
> The northern light in at the doorë shone,
> For window on the wall ne was there none,
> Through which men mighten any light-discern;
> The door was all of adamant etern.

What figures are carved there! There is

> The smiler with the knife under the cloak;

and—

> The slayer of himself yet saw I there.
> His heartë blood hath bathëd all his hair;

and—

> Woodness laughing in his rage:

and ghastlier still—

> The sow fretting the child right in the cradle;
> The cook yscalded, for all his long ladle.
> Nought was forgot by th' infortune of Martë,
> The carter overridden with his cartë,
> Under the wheel full low he lay adown.

When he follows the humourous style, Chaucer is equally sententious and striking. Thus he says of his Franklin:—

> Withouten bake-meat never was his house,
> Of fish and flesh, and that so plenteous,
> *It snowëd in his house of meat and drink.*

Of the Miller—

> His beard as any sow or fox was red,
> And thereto broad as though it were a spade,
> Upon the cop right of his nose he had
> A wart, and thereon stood a tuft of hairs,
> Red as the bristles of a sowës ears.
> His mouth widë was as a furnàce.

And of the Friar—

> Somewhat he lispëd for his wantonness,
> To make his English sweet upon his tongue,
> And in his harping, when that he had sung,
> His eyen twinkled in his head aright
> As do the starrës in a frosty night.

In this broad yet condensed style of pictorial representation Chaucer resembles Bunyan, as well as in some other qualities of his brawny genius. Bunyan, too, writes like a man of business—deals in direct strokes—puts much into few, and these simple words—has an eye for sly humour as well as for bold allegory—and with comparatively little fancy, has an immense deal of essential imagination. How different at first view the Canterbury from the Christian Pilgrims—the Friar from Evangelist—the Franklin from Great-heart—the Miller from Christian—the Sompnour from Hopeful—the Manciple from Gaius mine host—the Nun from Mercy—and the Wife of Bath from Christiana! And yet, in one very important point, they are alike; they are no cold abstractions—no stiff, formal, and half-animated figures—they are, both the pious and profane, intensely natural, and bursting at every pore with life.

Troilus and Cresseide is a lengthy poem in five books. It tells essentially the same story with the play of Shakespeare bearing the same name, but in a very different spirit. Shakespeare's great object in his drama is to laugh; and he seems for the nonce to exchange places with its real hero Thersites. Chaucer, on the other hand, extracts the pathos that is in the story, and uses it in his own fine way, "painting the afflicting circumstances slowly and assiduously, and descending exploringly into the caverns of tears." As a whole, however, the poem is tedious, although fine passages are frequent. One often quoted is that which describes Cresseide's yielding and acknowledging her love:—

> And as the now abashëd nightingale
> That stinteth first when she beginneth sing,
> When that she heareth any herdë's tale,
> Or in the hedges any wight stirring,
> And after sicker doth her voice outring:
> Right so Cresseide, when that her dreadë stent;
> Open'd her heart and told him her intent.

Let us quote, too, a passage in which we find the germ of his coming "comedy"—*The Canterbury Tales*:—

> Go, little book, go, little tragedy;
> There God my Maker yet ere that I die
> So send me might to make *some comedy*;
> But little book, make thou thee none envy,
> But subject ben unto all poesy,
> And kiss the steps where as thou seest pace
> Of Virgil, Ovid, Homer, Lucan, Stace.][1]

In conclusion, the object I have had in view has been to show the completeness and universality of the man, and also to induce you to read him for yourselves, in his own language—for no translation, however good, can do him justice. If you think well of this, you may, in the course of the ensuing winter, form a Chaucer club, and spend an evening now and then together, in reading his works, and not pass a line without thoroughly understanding every word in it.

Notes

1. The paragraphs in brackets are filled in conjecturally, from Rev. George Gillman's *Critical Dissertation*, but there can be little doubt about their identification.—GEORGE ST. CLAIR

HENRY MORLEY
From *English Writers*
1890, Volume 5, pp. 83–85, 186–282

The genius of Geoffrey Chaucer is not to be likened to a lone star glittering down on us through a rift in surrounding darkness, or to a spring-day in the midst of winter, that blossoms and fades, leaving us to wait long for its next fellow. He had in his own time for brother writers Wyclif, Langland, Gower, some of the worthiest men of our race, and the light of the English mind was not quenched when he died. Nor is it natural in any way whatever to think of Chaucer as an isolated man. No English poet equal to him had preceded him, or lived in his own day. Only one writer since his time has risen to his level, and he rose yet higher. But much of Chaucer's strength came of a genial spirit of companionship. It was his good-will to humanity, and his true sense of his own part in it, that gave him his clear insight into life. In him the simple sturdiness of the dutiful God-seeking Anglo-Saxon is blended intimately with the social joyousness of wit. Chaucer worked to the same end as Langland and Gower; not less religiously, though with much less despair over the evils that he saw. He does not see far who despairs of any part of God's creation. Having the sympathetic insight that is inseparable from genius at its best, and entering more deeply than his neighbour poets into characters of men, Chaucer could deal with them all good-humouredly; for he had the tolerance that must needs come of a large view of life, exact in its simplicity. Of Chaucer's there is not a thought coloured by prejudice or passion. He paints, in his chief work, character in all its variety, without once giving us, under some other name, a covert reproduction of himself. When he attacks hypocrisy that trades upon religion, and in so doing strips vice of its cloak, the sharpest note of his scorn has in it a rich quality of human kindliness. In perception of the ridiculous, he is beforehand with the most fastidious of his countrymen, and with his own native instinct he knows where an Englishman would turn with laughter or displeasure from words or thoughts that might seem good to any other people. Earnest as he was—disposed at times even to direct religious teaching—Chaucer was quick to see the brighter side of life, and ready to enjoy it in the flesh. When he was rich he seems to have delighted freely and naturally in whatever good things wealth would bring him; and when stripped of substance he set up no mean wailing of distress, but quietly consoling himself with a keener relish of the wealth that was within him, he dined worse and wrote his *Canterbury Tales*.

. . . His *Troylus and Criseyde* is an enlarged English version of the *Filostrato*, remarkable, as we shall find, for the illustration it affords of Chaucer's character in his treatment of the Italian original, and for its evidence of growth of the dramatic element in Chaucer's power as a writer. A tradition has come down to us on the authority of Lydgate, who was young when Chaucer died,[1] that

> In youth he made a translacion
> Of a boké whiche calléd is Trophé[2]
> In Lumbarde tonge, as men may rede and se;
> And in our vulgar, long er that he deyde,
> Gave it the name of Troylus and Creseyde.

Gower, writing between 1393 and 1398, represents it as a common pastime of young ladies "to rede and here of Troylus,"[3] and it was natural to ascribe to the young days of its writer that which became the favourite love-poem of the cultivated English youth. But comparison with its original will show in Chaucer's *Troylus and Criseyde* a ripeness, both of purpose and invention, that connects it with the work of his maturer years. I cannot think that Chaucer was of unripe age when he produced this poem. . . .

⟨The⟩ profoundly earnest close to the book is, with every touch of purity of thought contained in it, Chaucer's own, and is the final setting of the English seal to our own version of the Italian poem. Chaucer interpolates also, before the stanza tell-

ing of the death of Troilus at the hand of Achilles, his "Go, little book," his reverence for the great poets of antiquity, and his own hope that he might live to write a comedy—that is, a poem ending cheerfully. Professor ten Brink sees here a reference to the *House of Fame* as a work modelled playfully upon the *Divine Comedy* of Dante; but Chaucer may have been looking forward to some such achievement as the framework of the *Canterbury Tales*. Also he prays, that through the diversity in English and in writing of our tongue—diversity conspicuous when we compare the English of these early poems of his with the contemporary *Vision of Piers Plowman*—he might not be miswritten or have his metre spoilt by bad pronunciation. Then he tells of the death of Troilus, which he has reserved for the purpose of attaching his own English moral to the tale of fleshly passion and the sand on which it builds. Boccaccio draws no moral from his story but that (also of one of our own modern Italian songs, "La donna e mobile") woman is changeable; and he adds a dedication of it to his Fiammetta, from whom he expects faith. Chaucer follows the soul of Troilus to heaven, and shows it looking down upon the transitory passions of the flesh; then, turning from the paynim Greeks and Trojans to the Christian creed, tells of the love unchangeable that is the Christian's stay, while dedicating his book to his two earnest friends and brother poets, John Gower and Ralph Strode. . . .

⟨T⟩he original of Chaucer's *Troilus and Cressida* was written by Boccaccio, a man of thirty-four or five, when the English poet was about sixteen years old. The original, written at the court of a lascivious and fascinating murderess, and produced to please the taste of a corrupt society, was but a livelier, and, in many passages, less modest form of the conventional court poetry that rang the changes upon love. Now let us see, through alterations that he made, in what spirit the right-hearted Chaucer Englished it.

In the first place, Chaucer's version is more than half as long again as its original. The varied invocations at the opening of Chaucer's first three books, and the invocation preceding the fourth book, which is common to the fourth and fifth, are not in Boccaccio's poem. Boccaccio invokes, at the outset of the poem, Fiammetta, who is his Jove and Apollo, and whose absence caused him to write of deserted Troilus. A few details will show Chaucer's manner of enlargement. Boccaccio begins the story in the seventh and eighth stanzas of the first part of the *Filostrato*, which are expanded into three stanzas of *Troylus and Criseyde*. Two stanzas are then translated closely; then a stanza is again expanded into two; five stanzas are then translated stanza for stanza, after which three stanzas are expanded into six. Then the translation is very direct, stanza for stanza, until Chaucer digresses to the comparison, which is his own, of the prince who disdains love, with proud Bayard, first in the trace, who skips on the way until the whip reminds him that he must pull with his fellows. This stanza is interpolated, and so are the following stanzas of reflection upon love. Presently there is another incidental interpolation of what Troilus had said to lovers. The next interpolation is the sonnet of Petrarch's, translated as "the Song of Troilus," in three stanzas. But we return to Boccaccio, at the stanza beginning, "And to the God of Love, thus sayéd he." Eighteen stanzas are then closely translated, except that the Complaint of Troilus is in five stanzas instead of seven. Here ends the first part of *Il Filostrato*; the first stanza of the second part being that in which Pandarus first appears. From this stanza Chaucer has struck out the description of Pandarus as a brave young Trojan of high lineage. He brings him to Troilus as simply "a friend of his." His question, to which Boccaccio gives two lines, Chaucer expands into ten, with seven more of comments. He is to be Cressida's garrulous uncle, humorous, lachrymose, tricky, worldly wise according to the wisdom of the base; the sentimental comradeship with Troilus being an oddity which we may refer, if we please, to the fact that Troilus was a king's son, who might have any form of parasite. The next nine stanzas of dialogue are closely translated. Chaucer then interpolates the five stanzas beginning, "A whetstone is no carving instrument." The next two stanzas represent one stanza of Boccaccio's, then a stanza is translated pretty closely, and then five stanzas more are added by Chaucer to the argument of Pandarus. The next six stanzas of Boccaccio (xv.–xxii.) are expanded by Chaucer into the twenty-two beginning, "Yet Troilus, for all this, no word said," the narrative being overlaid by the garrulity of Pandarus. In Boccaccio, Griseida is represented as the cousin of Pandarus; Chaucer makes her his niece, and ascribes to him craft of age instead of the fresh valour of youth. Even when he translates closely, he gives to the dialogue a more colloquial character, although he burdens it with disquisitions, and impedes the progress of a narrative that in the verse of Boccaccio runs with a light, even, graceful step, from the first stanza to the last.

Outwardly graceful, inwardly graceless. In the next stanzas Boccaccio represents, what English Chaucer would not represent, Pandarus as a noble youth, offering help in winning his cousin's assent to dishonest love. Chaucer is not content with having taken the generosity of youth and manly dignity out of the character of Pandarus: he also modifies the character of his first offer to help Troilus. Three stanzas of Boccaccio (Bk. II. st. xxi.–xxiii.) are expanded into four, in order to secure a cleansing of the third of them. Chaucer interpolates the nine stanzas beginning, "But well is me," before he comes to the stanzas in which Pandarus proceeds with an argument concerning honour in women, better adapted to the court of Queen Giovanna of Naples than to the homes in which English-women had read to them Chaucer's *Troylus and Criseyde.* Five stanzas are here translated with omission, alteration, and interpolation. The rest of Chaucer's first book, "When Troilus heard," &c., expands and modifies five stanzas of Boccaccio (Bk. II. st. xxix.–xxxiii.), in which Pandarus laughs at modest professions made by Troilus, and Troilus embraces him as a wise friend who knows how to end his grief.

Chaucer closes his first book in the middle of the second book of *Filostrato,* and opening his own second book with an added invocation to Clio, comes altogether in his own way to the visit of Pandarus to Cressida. Boccaccio simply makes him go to her, look hard in her face, and begin offhand to call on her to forget the dead to whom her love was pledged, and think of the love torment of Troilus, to yield her love to him. Chaucer makes this part of the story, by a great deal, more dramatic as well as more honest and natural. The first thirty-two stanzas of the second book are Chaucer's own. The scene of the wily uncle's morning call upon his niece, where he

> found two other ladies set and shee
> Within a pavéd parlour, and they three
> Herden a maiden hem reden the geste
> Of the siége of Thebés, while hem leste,

the light familiar colloquy through which Pandarus makes subtle approach to his subject, the uncle's art of awakening curiosity, and the shrewd, half-comic suggestions of his worldly cunning, are all Chaucer's own, and there is nothing equal to them to be found in *Il Filostrato.* Chaucer's opening of the second book of *Troylus and Criseyde* is, indeed, evidence that—if he really wrote it in the earlier part of his life—at the time when he was bending to the fashion of the day, and writing or translating poems in the conventional way of the court, Chaucer was already a wise humourist, with a keen sense of character, and much of the original power that at last had full expression in the Prologue to the *Canterbury Tales.*

It is only in Chaucer's thirty-third stanza of the second book that Pandarus looks on Cressida "busie wise;" and we have translations again, though not close, from Boccaccio. The version is then very free till we come to the description of the grief of Troilus, "Tho (then) Pandarus a little gan to smile." Here there are several stanzas very closely followed, but there is change and amplification, and Chaucer does not represent Cressida as conquered by the description. After the departure of Pandarus, Boccaccio at once represents Cressida in love debate with herself. Chaucer prepares for this by bringing the martial figure of Troilus outside her window as he comes through the street, with broken helm and battered shield, from putting the Greeks to rout. He makes that picture of bright manliness suggestive, but even yet refuses to show Cressida as wholly won.

> For I say not that she so sodainly
> Yafe him her love, but that she gan encline
> To liken him tho, and I have told you why:
> And after that, his manhode and his pine
> Madé that love within her gan to mine.

Boccaccio made her yield at the mere hearing of "his pine." Chaucer adds the sight of him in his manhood "next his brother, holder up of Troy," before he tells somewhat of the thoughts of Cressida "as mine auctour listeth to endite." He strikes out "mine auctour's" representation of her dwelling on the beauties of Troilus, her own beauty, the fleeting of youth, the honour of secrecy. He strikes out her licentious doctrine that it is no sin to do as others do; her objection to a husband; her sense of the wisdom of preserving liberty, and of the sweetness of stolen waters. What the English poet substitutes for all this is a sense of honour and a dread of the untruth of men. Cressida's going down into the garden and hearing from Antigone the Trojan song of love, with the song itself, the coming on of night, the singing of the nightingale upon the cedar-tree, and Cressida's dream, are all added by Chaucer to the poem. The letter of Troilus to Cressida, written at the suggestion of Pandarus, is condensed, after the previous counselling of Pandarus had been amplified, and touches of humour added to the dialogue—every change being on the side of wholesomeness.

Chaucer's dealing with the next incidents is equally remarkable. Boccaccio's Cressida receives the letter of Troilus as a gallant of the court of Joan of Naples would desire a lady of the same court to receive it; and her letter in reply broadly suggests that assurance of secrecy is all her honour needs. Chaucer invents a garden dialogue, in which he adds more touches to his character of Pandarus, sets Pandarus and his niece to dine together, and by suggestions of delicate humour gives an honest picture of the slow yielding of Cressida's mind to the suit pressed on her. Again also he supplements bare imagination with a picture of Troilus riding by; this time not as a battered hero, but as a knight in all his bravery. Instead of translating the long letter of lust disguised as half refusal, Chaucer describes it in five lines, thus:

> She thonkéd him, of all that he well ment
> Towardés her, but holden him in bond
> She nolde not, ne make her selven bond
> In love, but as his suster him to please
> She wold ay faine to don his herte on ease.

And it was with modest womanly reserves that Cressida gave the letter to the go-between. After its delivery, according to Boccaccio, Pandarus again talked to his cousin, obtaining an assignation with her for Troilus by simple assurance of his secrecy. And in the next book, the fourth of Boccaccio's ten, Cressida simply rises at night after all are gone to bed, to meet Troilus with open arms in a dark, solitary place, and be with him till cockrow. After this there is nothing in the Italian poem but a continued dwelling on illicit passion, till we come presently to the claim of Calchas for the delivery of Cressida, which incident occurs at the opening of Boccaccio's fifth book. What, then, is Chaucer's story of the wiles of Pandarus, with detail of the trick of the threatened lawsuit, of the dinner at the house of Deiphobus, the feigned sickness of Troilus, the interview with him in his chamber, and the final treachery of Pandarus on occasion of the supper at his own house, and the storm? These are dramatic incidents which the English poet has invented, to the end that he may substitute as long as he can, for the base Italian ideal, a picture, suited to his own and the best English mind, of woman's grace and innocence.

But that is not all, or nearly all. When at last animal passion has its triumph, Chaucer draws upon his author for a picture of such bliss as it can give; and, as he continues to translate, still modifying, humanising, and enriching with dramatic touches, blending suggestions of womanly delicacy that yet lingers about the fallen Cressida, he proceeds with that which is for him and for his readers part of the stern moral of the story, Cressida's loss of honesty towards her lover also. In so doing, he strengthens the grace of fidelity in Troilus, to whose character he had added many a touch of manliness. For these he had no warrant in his "author Lolius," who makes Troilus fall as struck by lightning when he hears that the demand for Cressida is granted by the Trojan Senate. And, after all, he sums up with a lesson on the perishableness of earthly passion, as he points heavenward to the love that is unchanging. Religious earnestness, honour to the pure beauty of womanhood, English humour and dramatic vigour, Chaucer adds to the *Filostrato*; but in so doing, it must be granted—as a set-off to the charm of his dramatic alteration and enrichment of the character of Pandarus, wherever it touches his remodelled Cressida—that by enlargement of the dialogues between Pandarus and Troilus, equally well meant, but less interesting to himself and us, he destroys the swiftness and grace with which the original poem, immoral though it be, runs in one strain of accordant music from the opening until the close.

Chaucer's additions to the story of Cressida in the Greek camp, and her dialogue with Diomede and with her father, indicate his reading in the first romance which contained the tale of *Troilus and Cressida*, the *Geste de Troie* of Benoît de Sainte-Maure, or the Latin prose version of it by Guido Colonna. But throughout the poem the essential changes are of his own making, and directly illustrative of those qualities which we have found thus far, and shall find to the end, characteristic of the people whose best mind is expressed in the Literature whereof some part of the story is here being told. . . .

In *The House of Fame* Chaucer sustains a lofty flight of original thought with playful homeliness of speech. Throughout his verse there is the true poet's disinclination to think upon stilts. Chaucer's English is that of the cultivated townsman. His mind had a wider range of perception and expression than that of any of his contemporaries and of the greater number of his after-comers, but in his grace and tenderness and in his strongest flights of fancy or feeling, as in broadest mirth, the natural man speaks with his own unforced humour. There is no muffling of power in thick wrappers of a far-fetched phraseology; strength that lies in the thought itself wears no misfitted clothing of an artificial eloquence. The beauty and dignity of human thought moves freely in all its native grace.

As far as regards the use of words, good writing excels good speaking, because it is compelled, by a more exact fitting of the words themselves to the thought spoken, and to the energy with which it is conceived, to atone for the absence of those personal aids of eye, voice, gesture, which enforce the word of mouth. But the strength comes of making written language more not less true to the natural mind of the writer. It does not come at all of keeping a closet in one's mind for best-company words and phrases, only to be set out in impressive array on state occasions. Good written English is the home language of Englishmen intensified by the care taken to make it perfectly expressive. It should be coloured more, not less, than spoken English with that which the hearer of the spoken language also sees in trick of eye and hears in tone of voice; temper, that is, and humour of the mind which seeks to utter itself truly. All that lives in the tones and modulations of the natural voice and brightens the aspect of the speaker who is interested in his subject, the writer also, be he poet, historian, philosopher, must endeavour not to keep out of his writing in the name of a dignity that is conventional and insincere, but to keep in it, in the name of truth, which is first of the dignities of God. The true writer's question to himself is never, "Am I like all other people who look fine?" But it is, "Am I like myself when truest to a duty?" "If I have matter to sing, or to record, or reason out, is it," he asks of himself when he desires to test his work, "my own whole and exact thought that I utter, with the variations in degree of force that belong really to my own perception of the parts of it, and with the simplicity essential to that plain and full expression which begets the readiest and truest sympathy of understanding in the minds of others?"

Such doctrine may now pass unquestioned, but it is in several respects the opposite of that preached by the critics fifty or a hundred years ago. The simple directness of speech that makes Chaucer himself seem always to be walking by his reader's side, we know now for a sign of power. His fancy travels a far road, for example, in his poem of *The House of Fame*; and, in the days when periwigs were worn, readers who went to a book with their heads preoccupied by critical rules of propriety, only half saw how true to English nature was the light strain veiling depth of thought, the homely saying or good-humoured air of jest nerving the strenuous labour of an upward climb, and making the appreciation of all great thoughts that proceed out of it only the more sure and true. I say this in apt connexion with one work of Chaucer's, but it was true of his work from the first, and now, as his independent strength asserts itself more and more clearly, becomes truer and truer. . . .

The *Canterbury Tales* express the whole power of Chaucer; yet it is only by such a study as we have now made of the sequence of his other works, that we can be fairly qualified to understand the poet while we are delighting in this chief group of his poems.

There are two obstacles to a study of Chaucer himself in the *Canterbury Tales*.

One is the essentially dramatic spirit in which he occupied himself with his design, giving to his pilgrims of either sex all the variety of rank and character that he could fairly group into a single company, in order that, through them and their stories, he might reach to a broad view of life in its most typical forms, fleshly and spiritual. Had the mind of Chaucer stirred among us in the days of Queen Elizabeth, his works would have been plays, and Shakespeare might have found his match. But, except in the miracle plays and mysteries, which seldom represented ordinary human life, there was in Chaucer's time no writing formally dramatic. Dramatic genius could only speak through such poems as were acceptable to the readers of that generation; and through such poems, therefore, Chaucer poured his images of life, bright with variety of incident, and subtle in perception of all forms of character. He had that highest form of genius which can touch every part of human life, and, at the contact, be stirred to a simple sympathetic utterance. Out of a sympathy so large, good humour flows unforced, and the pathos shines upon us with a rare tranquillity. The meanness or the grandeur, fleshly grossness or ideal beauty, of each form of life, is reflected back from the unrippled mirror of Chaucer's *Canterbury Tales*, as from no other work of man, except the Plays of Shakespeare. Chaucer alone comes near to Shakespeare in that supreme quality of the dramatist which enables him to show the characters of men as they are betrayed by men themselves, wholly developed as if from within, not as described from without by an imperfect and prejudiced observer. It is a part of the same quality that makes noticeable in Chaucer, as in Shakespeare, the variety and truth of his different creations of women. As the range of Shakespeare was from Imogen to Dame Quickly and lower, so the range of Chaucer is from the ideal patience of the wife Griselda, or the girlish innocence and grace of Emelie in the *Knight's Tale*, to the Wife of Bath and lower; and in each of these great poets the predominating sense is of the beauty and honour of true womanhood.

If there were many Englishmen who read what we have of the *Canterbury Tales* straight through, it would not be necessary to say that, even in the fragment as it stands, expression of the poet's sense of the worth and beauty of womanhood very greatly predominates over his satire of the weaknesses of women. His satire, too, is genial. For the lowest he has no scorn, as he has for the hypocrisies of men who wear religion as the cloak to their offences. We have seen something of this in his transformation of Boccaccio's impure Cressida into a woman whose true dignity and perfect delicacy is slowly undermined. So, too, the transformed Pandarus jests, gossips, proses, and plots through the poem, being shown dispassionately as a character that we might see in life, and of which we are to think as we think of our living neighbours. Yet he is so shown, that, as Sir Philip Sidney said, we have "the Terentian Gnatho and our Chaucer's Pandar so exprest, that we now use their names to signify their trades."[5] And let us not forget that Boccaccio described his Pandar, unconscious of infamy in his part, as a young and honourable knight. It was only when we compared the English poem with its Italian original, and saw thereby in what spirit Chaucer had worked, that we could distinguish the mind of the English poet while we read his *Troylus and Criseyde*. And thus it is that, to a considerable extent, although not altogether, in the *Canterbury Tales*, as in the plays of Shakespeare, the dramatic genius of Chaucer has obscured his personality.

The second obstacle to a study of Chaucer himself in the *Canterbury Tales* is the fact that we have but little indication of the order in which they were written, or of the relation of any one of them to a particular time of his life. The works of his which have been hitherto discussed were usually upon themes more or less personal, and we were seldom without some indication of the time when they were written. Therefore it was possible so far to connect them with his life, as slowly, point by point, to make them furnish cumulative evidence as to a few essential features in his character. We have seen, for example, that, in a sense of his own, he takes the Daisy for his flower; and rises high above all poets of his age in honour to marriage, and praise of the purity of the wife's white daisy crown. But stories written by Chaucer at wide intervals, and very various in

merit, were, in the last years of his life, being transformed into *Canterbury Tales*. These express all his power, represent his whole mind, from the lightest jest to the profoundest earnest. They gather rays, as it were, out of all the quarters of his life; but its horizon is not to be measured in the little sun they form. . . .

Geoffrey Chaucer, who had taken delight from his youth up in the lively genius of Boccaccio, while repelled by the reflection of Italian morals in his images of life, had drawn from Boccaccio's *Decameron* the first hint of his crowning effort as a writer. He would form a collection of the stories he had rhymed or might yet rhyme, which he could leave behind him firmly bound together by a device like that which has, for all time, made one work of the hundred tales of the *Decameron*. But Chaucer's plan was better than that of the *Decameron*, and looked to a much greater result. "Forth, pilgrim, forth!" The English poet must have felt his mastery as he set his pilgrims on their way, and had every incitement to proceed with a work in which he was so perfectly achieving that which he had set himself to do. He could not have laid the *Canterbury Tales* aside for work of less account. And if he did, where is it? The last line that Chaucer wrote, when he sat for the last time at his desk as poet, pen in hand, must have been some one of the lines of the *Canterbury Tales*. Perhaps the sense of his approaching death caused him to end his labour among men with the discourse, or translation of a discourse, concerning sin, confession, and penance, which closes the work as we now have it, under the name of the "Parson's Tale." If so, the last words Chaucer wrote at his desk—certainly the last words of the *Canterbury Tales* as we now read them—look to the Heaven "ther as the body of man that whilom was seek and frel, feble and mortal, is immortal, and so strong, and so hool, that ther may no thing empeire it; ther nys neyther honger, ne thurst ne colde, but every soule replenisched with the sight of the parfyt knowyng of God. This blisful regne may men purchase by poverté espirituel, and the glorie by lowenes, the plenté of joye by hunger and thurst, and reste by travaile, and the lif by deth and mortificacioun of synne. To thilke lyf he us brynge, that boughte us with his precious blode. Amen."

Boccaccio, who died twenty-five years before Chaucer, placed the scene of his *Decameron* in a garden to which seven fashionable ladies had retired with three fashionable gentlemen, during the plague that devastated Florence in 1348.[6] The persons were all of the same class, young and rich, with no concern in life beyond the bandying of compliments. They shut themselves up in a delicious garden of the sort common in courtly inventions of the middle ages, and were occupied in sitting about idly, telling stories to each other. The tales were not seldom dissolute, often witty, sometimes exquisitely poetical, and always told in simple charming prose. The purpose of the story-tellers was to help each other to forget the duties from which they had turned aside, and stifle any sympathies they might have had for the terrible griefs of their friends and neighbours, who were dying a few miles away.

Chaucer substituted for the courtly Italian ladies and gentlemen who withdrew from fellowship with the world, as large a group as he could form of English people, of ranks widely differing, in hearty human fellowship together. Instead of setting them down to lounge in a garden, he mounted them on horseback, set them on the high road, and gave them somewhere to go and something to do. The bond of fellowship was not fashionable acquaintance and a common selfishness. It was religion; not, indeed, in a form so solemn as to make laughter and jest unseemly, yet, according to the custom of his day, a popular form of religion—the pilgrimage to the shrine of

Thomas à Becket—into which men entered with much heartiness. It happened to be a custom which had one of the best uses of religion, by serving as a bond of fellowship in which conventional divisions of rank were, for a time, disregarded; partly because of the sense, more or less joined to religious exercise of any sort, that men are equal before God, and also, in no slight degree, because men of all ranks trotting upon the high road with chance companions, whom they might never see again, have been in all generations disposed to put off restraint, and enjoy such intercourse as might relieve the tediousness of travel.

Boccaccio could produce nothing of mark in description of his ten fine ladies and gentlemen. Some of them are pleasantly discriminated: that is all. The procession of Chaucer's pilgrims is the very march of man on the high road of life. "Forth, pilgrim, forth!" There are knight and squire, sailor and merchant, parson and doctor, monk and nun, the ploughman who tills the earth, the bailiff who garners its corn and the miller who grinds it.

Finally, Chaucer's Tales, except a moral and a religious treatise each in prose, are poems, which, though they include such incidents as were thought most merry in his time, excel the tales of the *Decameron* in their prevailing tone.

Notes

1. Lydgate's Prologue to the *Fall of Princes*, st. 41.
2. Lydgate's use of "Trophe" as a name for the story of Troylus and Criseyde, points to Criseyde's perfidy, and is related to *tropē*, a turning. In modern Italian the word is *truffa*, "slight, roguery, roguish trick;" its synonyms being, according to the Della Cruscan Vocabulary, *inganno* and *furberia*.
3. Morley, *English Writers*, 1890, iv., 223.
4.   Cosi fossi io nelle sue dolce braccia
       E stretta petto a petto, e faccia a faccia,
   closes her strain of thought upon the subject.
5. Sidney's *Defence of Poesie*.
6. Morley, 1890, iv., 35, 36.

BERNHARD TEN BRINK
From "Prelude to Reformation and Renaissance"
History of English Literature
tr. William Clarke Robinson
1893, pp. 68–96

Anyone turning from the *Teseide* to the *Knight's Tale* feels that he is turning from a world of impossibilities to a world, if not of realities, at least of inner truth. The discrepancy between form and contents, between modern sentiment and ancient costume, between antique and mediæval manners, between the tone of the classical epics and the love romances, appears suppressed. Chaucer's whole story breathes the atmosphere of a romantic tale; the whole action of all the participating personages belongs to a world which is composed indeed of very different elements—antique, Byzantine, mediæval—and which is in an educational and historical sense full of gross anachronisms, but which bears, nevertheless, a uniform poetic impress—viz., the impress of a fantastic period of the Renaissance. This uniformity lies in the soul of the poet, whose many-sided and somewhat checkered education is concentrated in a living interest for what is thoroughly human, and in an increasing perception of the beautiful. Unlike Boccaccio, Chaucer makes no pretensions whatever to the epic style; yet his narrative nevertheless breathes a potent epic charm, because he does no violence to his nature, but writes just as his interest is excited, and either tarries lovingly upon details or

makes summary contractions, sometimes letting the story progress with energy, sometimes branching out loquaciously into reflections and amplifications.

The sentimental temperature of the internal action has been considerably lowered by Chaucer—his characters are more realistic, and in the way they express their feelings the poet's own sovereign humor is frequently revealed. In the conflict between friendship and love, he puts friendship entirely in the background; the love which seizes Palamon and Arcite with such violence, which dominates their entire being, separates them from their own past and strangely decides their fates; this love is Chaucer's proper theme; this he presents with keen participation, and at the same time with a roguish wink. His Palamon is much more passionate and jealous, much less magnanimous than the corresponding character in Boccaccio, and Arcite also becomes much more positive and violent in his hands. Chaucer even puts the following words in his mouth against Palamon (line 319 ff.):

> "We stryve, as dide the houndës for the boon,
> They foughte al day, and yet hir part was noon:
> There cam a kyte, whil that they were so wrothe,
> And bar away the boon betwixt hem bothe.
> And tharfore at the kyngës court, my brother,
> Eche man for himself, ther is noon other."

Chaucer succeeded, nevertheless, in bringing out with the utmost sharpness the contrast made by Boccaccio between the melancholy Arcite and the choleric Palamon; but while Boccaccio openly prefers the first, placing him always in the foreground and making him much more interesting than his rival, Chaucer strives to be equally just to both, and is able by well-timed, happy little touches to show off their characters by contrasts, and to warm the heart of the reader for each. Certain motives which are, indeed, contained in the Italian poem—as, for example, the difference in the prayers offered by the two heroes before the tournament—are first worked out with their full effect by Chaucer.

Compared with her two lovers, Emilia is kept more in the background by Chaucer than by Boccaccio. But we see enough of this lovely figure—whose heart is first inflamed by the fight of the rivals, and who nevertheless does not know her own mind, but hesitates in uncertainty between the two till the last—to appreciate the love of Palamon and Arcite.

As we have already said, Chaucer relieved his Theseus of one part of his heroic rôle. We do not see him fighting against the Amazons for power and glory for his own sake; the only fight in which we see him engaged is in the interests of humanity. He is thus so much the better suited for the impartial rôle assigned to him by Chaucer. This rôle is of a double nature—on the one side Theseus represents a sort of earthly Providence, on the other he is a sort of privileged exponent of Chaucer's humor and worldly wisdom. Nor does he stand on the conventional ideal dignity or in the narrow limits of his Italian prototype; like an English knight of the fourteenth century, he can fly into a passion with great violence. But under a somewhat rude exterior he conceals an excellent heart and sturdy manhood, sound common sense and noble humanity. He shows exquisite humor in his reflections on the fierce duel of Palamon and Arcite:

> Behold for Goddës sake that sitteth above,
> See how they bleed! be they not well arrayed?
> Thus hath their lord, the god of love, them paid
> Their wages, and their fees for their service.
> And yet they weenen for to be full wise,
> That serven love, for aught that may befall.
> And yet is this the bestë game of all,

That she for whom they have this jollity
Can them therefore as muchel thank as me.
She wot no more of all this hotë fare,
By God, than wot a cuckoo or an hare.
But all must be assayed hot or cold;
A man must be a fool either young or old.[1]

The creations of even the most objective poets do not belie their family resemblance and parentage. Shakspere's characters, with the exception of the typical clowns,—and these, also, in their way,—are all clever; and most of Chaucer's personages are inclined to philosophical reflections, in which they like to mix up scholastic arguments and learned quotations with popular phrases and old proverbs. In the *Knight's Tale* not only do Theseus and his father Ægeus philosophize in this way, but also the two lovers, and perhaps in a way not always adapted to their situation and rank. But we must not fail to mention here that, in this respect, the poet knows how to draw the light and shade, and in such things his works show a decided progress toward a greater truthfulness of characterization.

Chaucer has bestowed a great amount of care on certain descriptive portions of his poem. This is specially true of the delineation of the amphitheater built by Theseus for the tournament, with its three temples for Mars, Venus, and Diana; on this occasion the English poet differs from his predecessor in a remarkable way. The description of the three temples and the pictures or statues therein contained shows us on the one hand excellent models of characteristic amplification, and on the other hand passages which betray the influence of the Renaissance in its growing taste for plastic beauty.

The description of the tournament is given in a more general—we might almost say, in a sort of typical—style, but is nevertheless extremely vivid.

But most exquisite is the manner in which Chaucer compensates us for what was missing in his poem, viz., the enumeration and description of the heroes going to the tournament at Athens. Instead of the long and unattractive catalogue which occupies nearly the whole of the sixth book of the *Teseide*, he gives us, as it were for a symbolical characterization of both parties, two carefully executed portraits ornamented with romantic and even fabulous magnificence. Attention has been often called to the beauty of these delineations. Yet the main point seems to have been overlooked, viz., the inner relation between the appearance of King Lycurgus of Thrace and the character of Palamon, and between the character of Emetreus of India and Arcite. The appearance of Lycurgus is manly, imposing, even terrible; Emetreus unites the charm of youthful beauty with a lion-like glance and a voice of thunder.

And so everywhere there is seen a great delicacy of meaning, a conscious art, which is only fully revealed by a continued study, for it delights to hide itself under a certain gayety of tone, and in a simple though always vivid and significant diction.

By supplying so much of his own, Chaucer unavoidably sacrificed many of the beauties of his original. Whoever wishes to study Boccaccio's amiable manner, even in his imperfect creations, must read the original. But whoever wishes above all things for æsthetic pleasure, and yet still prefers the *Teseide* to the *Knight's Tale* after one or even several readings, deserves greater praise for his patience than for his literary taste. . . .

Boccaccio has created a thoroughly original and highly significant work from an episode in the Troy legend. But Chaucer succeeded in the still more astonishing performance of recreating the Italian's epic, without in any way essentially altering the story or moving the centre of interest, into a new and equally significant, perhaps a little less harmonious, but yet a deeper and richer poem ⟨*Troilus and Cryseyde*⟩.

The tragic element in Boccaccio's presentation seems to have attracted Chaucer most. The inclination to bring this element into greater prominence mainly determines the changed conception of the characters of the two lovers. In Boccaccio, Troilus is a somewhat weakly disposed young worldling, who has passed through the ordinary school of Amor. In Chaucer, he is of an equally weak disposition. But as the conception of young heroes of this stamp is generally formed in the German mind, so here, too, he is a kind of Hippolytus before the decisive moment when he perceives Cryseyde in the splendor of her beauty. Believing himself invulnerable to the tenderer passions, he amuses himself by mocking with sovereign humor the poor wretches who bear Amor's yoke. Then he is overtaken by his nemesis—with sudden violence he is smitten by the arrow of the god, who now pays him back for all the scorn he had previously heaped upon his servants. His whole being now seems changed; his mental elasticity is broken. Hope first inspires him again with new life, and the delight of love restores the young knight to his former vigor. But the sudden change of his fortunes, the pain of separation, the gnawing desire, the anxious fear, are almost more than his nature can endure. And when at last he learns that his beloved has turned out unfaithful, his first impulse is not the wish for vengeance, but the desire for death; and he seeks in battle for this delivering friend with not less ardor than for his deadly foe Diomedes.

The character of Griseida has changed more under Chaucer's hands than Troilus. As in Boccaccio, she is a widow, but this trait is brought much less into prominence than in the *Filostrato*. The English Cryseyde is more innocent, less experienced, less sensual, more modest, than her Italian prototype. What a multitude of agencies were needed to inflame her love for Troilus; what a concatenation of circumstances, what a display of trickery and intrigue, to bring her at last to his arms! We see the threads of the web in which she is entangled drawing ever closer around her; her fall appears to us excusable, indeed unavoidable. And if afterwards, after the separation, she does not resist the temptation of Diomedes—how is she accountable, if her mind is less true and deep than that of Troilus? how is she accountable, when that first fall robbed her of her moral stay? Only unwillingly, and with hesitation, does Chaucer tell of her unfaithfulness, as if he himself were not convinced of it, and only admitted the testimony of his authorities with reluctance. And he eagerly picks up points from Benoit's story which may tend to the exculpation of his heroine. She only gives her heart to Diomedes when touched with sympathy for the wounds he had received from Troilus; and her infidelity is immediately followed by repentance. She thus appears as the victim of Destiny, she, not less than Troilus; and the finger of Destiny is perceived by the poet at all the turning-points of his story. He does not go so far as to wish to deny the freedom of the human will; and yet the question, how it can exist along with the fixed and firmly locked concatenation of events and the omniscience of Providence is for him an insoluble riddle. He therefore makes his hero enunciate thoughts—in that supreme moment, when he is under the weight of his sudden misfortune and forebodes still worse disasters in the future—which Boëthius himself uses in his prison. The reply of "Philosophy," which should explain the riddle and dispel the doubt, has not been given us. It is his tragic intensiveness that leads the poet into such depths, and makes him express ideas in sonorous verses, which agitated deeply the most eminent minds of the age—ideas which touch strongly on the doctrine of predestination, such as Wyclif conceived it in following Augustine and Bradwardine. Not unworthy of notice is this coincidence between the great poet at the height of his artistic maturity and the great reformer who was then in Lutterworth closing the great life-account of his thoughts and actions.

Fortune, "who executes the ordinances of Fate, and is the shepherdess placed by God over men," finds in Chaucer's poem an appropriate instrument in Pandarus. In this character the creative power of the poet is most strongly expressed. It is a work of such intellectual boldness and assurance as can only be found equaled in the productions of the greatest masters. The more innocent Cryseyde is, the more inexperienced and helpless Troilus is, the greater grows the rôle of him who brings them together. Pandarus is here properly adapted for a pimp, and his name has remained in language as a synonym for this word. He is an elderly gentleman with great experience of life, uncle to Cryseyde, not—as in Boccaccio—her cousin. It is the poet's intention to excuse, or at least to explain, the part he plays, by the intimate friendship between him and Troilus. How far one can go out of friendship—especially to high personages—in the domain of moral concessions, how hard it is to make a halt at the right point, Chaucer himself had probably found out well enough in his relations with John of Gaunt. He presents the matter in the most objective form, but yet in such a way that the æsthetic charm given to the character of Pandarus helps us over the impression of the offense to morality in the same way as in Shakspere's Falstaff. To the insipid and somewhat cynical views of an old worldling, Pandarus unites a good dose of *naïveté*. And Chaucer makes him push his trade of pimp as naïvely as possible. When he sees Troilus, formerly the chivalrous and lusty youth, physically and morally sinking under the weight of an unexplained disease, and going actually to ruin, he feels for him the sincerest sympathy. And when, by close interrogation, he finds at length the cause of his disease, when he knows that it is solely his hopeless love for Cryseyde which is killing him, then he feels comforted and his decision is immediately made. In his opinion the whole business is not worth so much bother; but a man's mind is his kingdom; this man can be helped, and Pandarus is firmly determined to help him. Then he commences his work, and carries it triumphantly through with the greatest mastery. He has the necessary talents and the necessary liking for the play of intrigue, and knows well how to hide his roguishness under the mask of a somewhat rough good nature and a paternal recklessness.

These qualities unite excellently with the other traits lent to him by the poet. A strange combination of Polonius, Mercutio, and Sancho Panza, he is garrulous, rather vain of his homespun wisdom, but at the same time gifted richly with sound common sense and wit—he is a thoroughly humorous figure. And thus he answers the arrangement of the poem from every point of view. He is the lever that keeps the action in movement up to the climax; 'tis he who ties the tragic knot, and also he who brings the comic element into the tragedy. His practical views of life are everywhere opposed to the enthusiasm of Troilus, just as Sancho Panza forms the contrast to Don Quijote, and Jean de Meung to Guillaume de Lorris; they help us pleasantly over the onesidedness of an idealism which ignores the world, and free us from the oppressive feeling with which we are satiated by the spectacle of a self-consuming passion. It is, indeed, remarkable how this contrast is sometimes so formed that Pandarus represents the superior wisdom as opposed to the shortsightedness of Troilus when dominated by his passion. It is not difficult to prove that for some scenes between the two Chaucer had in his mind's eye the figures of "Philosophy" and the imprisoned Boëthius; for besides containing innumerable popular sayings and many tit-bits from different classical writers, the speeches of Pandarus also contain not a little from the *Consolatio*. The clever head thus knows how to take advantage of everything.

Finally, Pandarus is the figure who helps most to develop the dramatic life of the action. Just as Chaucer recognized the tragic elements in the story, so also did he perceive the dramatic possibilities which lay hidden in Boccaccio's tale. His whole genius must have forced him on to bring them to light and to make them paramount. Almost all the changes, transpositions, interpolations that he made in his original tend, if not exclusively, at least concurrently, in this direction. For, with him, all the wheels catch on to each other; one stroke strikes a thousand springs. It is mostly in the dramatic scenes, which are sometimes of a monologue sort, but are more often acted out between two or more persons, that the characters are evolved and the situations developed. The narrative portions, which serve to bind those dramatic scenes together, are of a comparatively subordinate importance. These scenes are set off with the most realistic truthfulness, even to the smallest detail, and work with the most instantaneous power; they are full of fire and force, making us shake with laughter, and rousing our interest to the highest pitch. In the fifth or last book the description falls off considerably. The situations are too unrefreshing, and partly also too undramatic. The Cryseyde-Diomedes episode gave the poet little pleasure. Troilus is condemned to passivity, and Pandarus also is *au bout de son Latin*. To make the terror of a tragic pathos die powerfully away was not Chaucer's affair. And every tragic fate is not adapted to the tragic muse. This subject was deficient in grandeur, in all that exalts. It is sufficient, therefore, if the art of the poet was able to ennoble the ambiguous or even the offensive elements of the story by the charm of a realistic, and at the same time highly poetical presentation.

How well does the poet here show himself equal to his task! If we consider the truthfulness in conception and expression, the delicacy of the motives, the well planned arrangement of the whole, and then the abundance of diversified ideas and situations, the astonishing wealth and pliancy of the language, which, in seeming to go at random, does accurate justice to every thought and situation, the broad and smoothly flowing rush of the stanza, which is responsive to every shade of feeling—then we shall thoroughly understand the wish that Chaucer sends forth along with his poem and towards its end: "And since there is so great diversity in English, and in writing of our tongue, so pray I God that none may copy thee wrongly, nor spoil the metre by false reading. And wherever thou art read or sung, God grant that thou be understood."

Troilus and Cryseyde was a book for learned and unlearned, for the poet and the philosopher, the courtier and the man of action. The "moral" Gower and the "philosophical" Strode, to whom the author addressed the work in an envoy, must have been delighted with it—each from his own point of view. But John of Gaunt was, perhaps, better able than they to appreciate the whole; and it was only natural that his family should hold the work in honor. We regard with pleasure the ornamental characters and the rich arabesques of that *Troilus* manuscript which John's grandson, the later conqueror of Agincourt, had in his possession when Prince of Wales; and, moreover, we recall with pleasure how this same poem, which delighted the hero in the time of his extravagant youth, also exercised a mighty influence on Shakspere, the great singer of this hero. Nor is it astonishing that Sidney, who pointed out with high enthusiasm the noble mission of poesie at a time when the great era of English poetry was in its morning glow, should have looked with admiration on the poet of *Troilus*, who, in such a benighted century, had followed the correct road so surely.

This developed art—compared with which the doings of most of his contemporaries appear childlike, or, indeed, childish, and even a work like *Sir Gawayne and the Green Knight* seems as the effort of a novice—enables us to appreciate how much Chaucer owes to the Italian Renaissance, of which he may be called the first English pupil—not, indeed, as scholar, but as poet.

Note

1. Tyrwhitt, *Canterbury Tales*, 1802–14, *Knight's Tale*, 942 ff.

W. P. KERR
From "The Poetry of Chaucer"
The Quarterly Review, April 1895, pp. 521–48

It is easily possible to be tired of the historical criticism that plies its formulas over the sources and origins of poetry, and attempts to work out the spiritual pedigree of a genius. It cannot, however, be seriously argued that enquiries of this sort are inept in the case of Chaucer, whose obligations to his ancestors are manifest in every page, not to speak of those debts that are less obvious. If the result, in most instances, is to bring out Chaucer's independence more in relief by the subtraction of his loans, and to prove the limitations of this historical method when it is made to confront the problems of original and underived imagination, there is no great harm done, but the contrary. It is the result to be looked for.

These volumes of Chaucer ⟨Skeat's edition⟩ present one interesting case where the enquiry into origins has scored one conspicuous success, and in an equal degree has found its limits and proved its inability, after all, to analyse the inexplicable. The *House of Fame* has been subjected to laborious study, and one important set of facts has been brought to evidence about it. The relation of the poem to the *Divine Comedy* has been considered and discussed by Sandras, Ten Brink, and other scholars, and is here explained by Mr. Skeat. The proof is decisive. There is no remnant of doubt that Chaucer had been reading Dante when he wrote the *House of Fame*; that he derived from the suggestions of Dante the images and the pageants of his dream, and many of the phrases in which it is narrated. Here, however, the proof comes to an end. The historical enquiry can do no more. And when all is said and done, the *House of Fame* still stands where it stood—a poem inexplicable by any references to the poem from which it was borrowed, a poem as different from the *Divine Comedy* as it is possible to find in any Christian tongue. The true criticism of the poem has to begin where the historical apparatus leaves off. If its quiddity is to be extracted, the *House of Fame* must be taken, first of all, as the poem it is, not as the poem from which it is derived.

It is in this way that the works of Chaucer afford the most delightful tests of ingenuity and of the validity and right use of the methods of criticism. No task is more dangerous for a critic who has his own private device for the solution of all problems. The problems in Chaucer are continually altering, and the ground is one that calls for all varieties of skill if it is to be tracked out and surveyed in all its changes of level.

The appearance of Chaucer's works at last in this satisfactory and convenient form, with the blemishes of the vulgate texts removed, and everything made easy for every one who is not too anxious about his ease, can hardly fail to call out some new devotion to the great master of stories. Chaucer is always being discovered, like Homer, Shakespeare, and the book of Baruch; and his discoverers are not to be pitied, though one may be inclined to ask them to deal gently with their ignorant friends, and not to be vexed because of the obdurate who say that Chaucer was a hack and a translator.

After the first discovery of all, there is none more pleasant

than the discovery how little Chaucer's genius is exhausted in the *Canterbury Tales*, and how far his great book is from being his greatest poem, or from representing his genius to the full. It is only by looking at the *Canterbury Tales* from the vantage-ground of the other works that the magnitude of Chaucer can be in any way estimated aright.

The *Canterbury Tales*, which include so much, do not include the whole of Chaucer. Some of his masterpieces are there, and there is nothing like the Prologue anywhere else; but outside of the group of the Tales is to be found the finest work of Chaucer in the more abstract and delicate kind of poetry 'Anelida'; the most massive and the richest of his compositions, which is *Troilus*; and the most enthralling and most musical of all his idylls, in the Prologue to the *Legend of Good Women*, with the balade of Alcestis, 'sung in carolwise':

Hyd, Absolon, thy gilte tresses clere.

The poem of 'Anelida and the false Arcite,' it may be suspected, is too often and too rashly passed over. It has a good deal of the artificial and exquisite qualities of the court poetry; it appears to be wanting in substance. Yet for that very reason the fineness of the style in this unfinished poetical essay gives it rank among the greater poems, to prove what elegance might be attained by the strong hand of the artist, when he chose to work in a small scale. Further, and apart from the elaboration of the style, the poem is Chaucer's example of the abstract way of story telling. It is the light ghost of a story, the antenatal soul of a substantial poem. The characters are merely types, the situation is a mathematical theorem; yet this abstract drama, of the faithless knight who leaves his true love for the sake of a wanton shrew, is played as admirably, in its own way, as the history of the two Noble Kinsmen, or the still nobler Troilus.

It is difficult to speak moderately of Chaucer's *Troilus*. It is the first great modern book in that kind where the most characteristic modern triumphs of the literary art have been won; in the kind to which belong the great books of Cervantes, of Fielding, and of their later pupils,—that form of story which is not restricted in its matter in any way, but is capable of taking in comprehensively all or any part of the aspects and humours of life. No other mediaeval poem is rich and full in the same way as *Troilus* is full of varieties of character and mood. It is a tragic novel, and it is also strong enough to pass the scrutiny of that Comic Muse who detects the impostures of inflated heroic and romantic poetry. More than this, it has the effective aid of the Comic Muse in that alliance of tragedy and comedy which makes an end of all the old distinctions and limitations of narrative and drama.

The original of *Troilus*, the *Filostrato* of Boccaccio, is scarcely more substantial in its dramatic part, though it is longer and has a more elaborate plot, than Chaucer's 'Anelida.' The three personages of the one poem are not more definite than the three of the other. The *Filostrato* is not merely 'done into English' in Chaucer's *Troilus and Criseyde*. Chaucer has done much more than that for the original poem; he has translated it from one form of art into another,—from the form of a light romantic melody, vague and graceful, into the form of a story of human characters, and of characters strongly contrasted and subtly understood by the author. The difference is hardly less than that between the Italian novels and the English tragedies of *Romeo* or *Othello*, as far at least as the representation of character is concerned. Chaucer learned from Boccaccio the art of construction: the design of the *Filostrato* is, in the main outline, the design of Chaucer's *Troilus and Criseyde*; but in working out his story of these 'tragic comedians,' the English poet has taken his own way, a way in which he had no forerunners that he knew of, and for successors all the dramatists and novelists of all the modern tongues.

No other work of Chaucer's has the same dignity or the same commanding beauty. It would be difficult to find in any language, in any of the thousand experiments of the modern schools of novelists, a story so perfectly proportioned and composed, a method of narrative so completely adequate. Of the dramatic capacities of the original plot, considering the use made of it in Shakespeare's *Troilus and Cressida*, there is little need to say anything. Boccaccio chose and shaped the plot of his story with absolute confidence and success; there is nothing to break the outline. The general outline is kept by Chaucer, who thus obtains for his story a plan compared with which the plan of Fielding's greatest novel is ill-devised, awkward, and irregular; while the symmetry and unity of Chaucer's story is compatible with a leisure and a profusion in the details not less than Shakespeare's, and in this case more suitably bestowed than in Shakespeare's *Troilus*. There is nothing in the art of any narrative more beautiful than Chaucer's rendering of the uncertain faltering and transient moods that go to make the graceful and mutable soul of Cressida; nothing more perfect in its conception and its style than his way of rendering the suspense of Troilus; the slowly-rising doubt and despair keeping pace in the mind of Troilus with the equally gradual and inevitable withdrawal and alteration of love in the mind of his lady, till he comes to the end of his love-story in Cressida's weak and helpless letter of defence and deprecation.

Besides the triumph of art in the representation of the characters, there are more subsidiary beauties in *Troilus* than anywhere else in Chaucer; as in the effective details of the less important scenes, the ladies reading the romance of Thebes together, the amateur medical advice for the fever of Troilus, the visit of Helen the queen, the very Helen of the *Odyssey*, to show kindness to Troilus in his sickness. There are other poems of Chaucer, the *Knight's Tale* for instance, in which Chaucer relies more consistently throughout on the spell of pure romance, without much effort at strong dramatic composition. But it is in *Troilus*, where the art of Chaucer was set to do all its utmost in the fuller dramatic form of story, that the finest passages of pure romance are also to be found; in *Troilus*, and not in the story of Palamon and Arcite, or of Constance, or of Cambuscan, or any other. At least it may be imagined that few readers who remember the most memorable passage of pure narrative in *Troilus*, his entrance into Troy from the battle without, will be inclined to dispute the place of honour given to it by Chaucer's last disciple, in his profession of allegiance in the *Life and Death of Jason*. The 'tragedie' of the lovers is embellished with single jewels more than can be easily reckoned; with scenes and pictures of pure romance; with the humours and the 'ensamples' and opinions of Pandarus; with verses of pure melody, that seem to have caught beforehand all the music of Spenser:

> And as the newe abaysshed nightingale
> That stinteth first whan she biginnith singe;

with many other passages from which the reader receives the indefinable surprise that is never exhausted by long acquaintance, and that makes the reader know he is in the presence of one of the adepts. But all these single and separable beauties are nothing in comparison with the organic and structural beauty of the poem, in the order of its story, and in the life of its personages.

Chaucer is always at his best when he is put on his mettle by Boccaccio. He is well enough content in other instances to borrow a story ready made. In his appropriation of Boccaccio he is compelled by his sense of honour to make something as

good if he can, in a way of his own. He learns from the Italian the lesson of sure and definite exposition; he does not copy the Italian details or the special rhetorical prescriptions. The story of *Palamon and Arcite*, on which Chaucer appears to have spent so much of his time, is a different sort of thing from *Troilus*; the problems are different; the result is no less fortunate in its own way. The *Teseide*, the original of the *Knight's Tale*, is reduced in compass under Chaucer's treatment, as much as the *Filostrato* is strengthened and enlarged. The *Teseide*, unlike the *Filostrato*, is an ambitious experiment, no less than the first poem in the solemn procession of modern epics according to the rules of the ancients; an epic poem written correctly, in twelve books, with epic similes. Olympian machinery, funeral games, and a catalogue of the forces sent into the field, all according to the best examples. Chaucer brings it down to the form of a romance, restoring it, no doubt, to the form of Boccaccio's lost original, whatever that may have been; at any rate to the common scale of the less involved and less extravagant among the French romances of the twelfth or thirteenth century. For Boccaccio's *Theseid*, with all its brilliance, is somewhat tedious, as an epic poem may be; it is obviously out of condition, and overburdened in its heroic accoutrements. The *Knight's Tale* is well designed, and nothing in it is superfluous. There are some well-known instances in it of the success with which Chaucer has changed the original design: reducing the pompous and unwieldy epic catalogue of heroes to the two famous contrasted pictures 'in the Gothic manner,' the descriptions of Lycurgus and Emetreus, and rejecting Boccaccio's awkward fiction in the account of the prayers of Palamon, Arcita, and Emilia. But the most significant part of Chaucer's work in this story is the deliberate evasion of anything like the drama of *Troilus and Cressida*.

The *Knight's Tale* is a romance and nothing more; a poem, a story, in which the story and the melody of the poem are more than the personages. Chaucer saw that the story would not bear a strong dramatic treatment. The Comic Muse was not to be bribed: neither then, nor later, when the rash experiment of Fletcher in the *Two Noble Kinsmen* proved how well the elder poet was justified in refusing to give this story anything like the burden of *Troilus*. The Lady Emilia, most worshipful and most shadowy lady in the romance, is too cruelly put to the ordeal of tragedy: the story is refuted as soon as it is made to bear the weight of tragic passion or thought. Chaucer, who found the story of *Troilus* capable of bearing the whole strength of his genius, deals gently with the fable of the *Theseid*; the characters are not brought forward; instead of the drama of *Troilus*, there is a sequence of pictures; the landscapes of romance, the castles and the gardens, are more than the figures that seem to move about among them. There is pathos in the *Knight's Tale*, but there is no true tragedy. How admirably Chaucer tells the pathetic story may be seen at once by comparing the meeting of Palamon and Arcita in the wood with the corresponding scene in Fletcher's play:—

> Ther nas no good day, ne no saluing;
> But streight, withouten word or rehersing,
> Everich of hem halp for to armen other,
> As freendly as he were his owne brother.

This simplicity of style is the perfection of mere narrative, as distinguished from the higher and more elaborate forms of epic poetry or prose. The situation here rendered is one that does not call for any dramatic fullness or particularity: the characters of Palamon and Arcita in any case are little qualified for impressive drama. But the pathos of the meeting, and of the courtesy rendered to one another by the two friends in their estrangement, is a pathos almost wholly independent of any delineation of their characters. The characters are nothing: it is 'any friend to any friend,' an abstract formula, used by Chaucer in this place with an art for which he found no suggestion in Boccaccio, nor obtained any recognition from Fletcher. In the *Teseide* the rivals meet and argue with one another before the duel in which they are interrupted by Theseus; in the play of the *Two Noble Kinsmen* they converse without any apparent strain. In Chaucer's poem the division between them is made deeper, and indicated with greater effect in four lines, than in the eloquence of his Italian master or his English pupil.

Such is the art of Chaucer in the *Knight's Tale*: perfect in its own kind, but that kind not the greatest. It needs the infinitely stronger fable of his *Troilus and Criseyde* to bring out the strength of his imagination. *Troilus*, to use a familiar term of Chaucer's own, cannot but 'distain' by comparison the best of the *Canterbury Tales*. *Troilus* is not a romance, but a dramatic story, in which the characters speak for themselves, in which the elements that in the *Canterbury Tales* are dissipated or distributed among a number of tales and interludes are all brought together and made to contribute in due proportion to the total effect of the poem. In the *Canterbury Tales* the comic drama is to be found at its best outside of the stories, best of all in the dramatic monologues of the 'Wife of Bath' and the 'Pardoner.' It takes nothing away from the glory of those dramatic idylls to maintain that Chaucer's Pandarus belongs to a higher and more difficult form of comic imagination. The 'Wife of Bath' and the 'Pardoner' are left to themselves as much, or very nearly as much, as the 'Northern Farmer' or 'Mr. Sludge the Medium.' Pandarus has to acquit himself as well as he may on the same stage as other and more tragic personages, in a story where there are other interests besides that of his humour and his proverbial philosophy. This is not a question of tastes and preferences; but a question of the distinction between different kinds and varieties of narrative poetry. It is open to any one to have any opinion he pleases about the value of Chaucer's poetry. But the question of value is one thing; the question of kinds is another. The value may be disputed indefinitely; the kind may be ascertained and proved. The kind of poetry to which *Troilus* belongs is manifestly different from that of each and all of the *Canterbury Tales*, and manifestly a richer and more fruitful kind; and for this reason alone the poem of *Troilus* would stand out from among all the other poems of its author.

The problems regarding Chaucer's methods of composition are inexhaustible. They are forced on the attention, naturally, by this collected edition of his writings, which makes the contradictions and paradoxes of Chaucer's life more obvious and striking than they ever were before. *Boece* and *Troilus*, which are mentioned together by Chaucer himself, are here associated in the same volume: the *Treatise on the Astrolabe* goes along with the *Legend of Good Women*. Of all the critical problems offered by this great collection of the works of a great master there is none more fascinating and none more hopeless than the task of following his changes of mood and his changes of handling. *Troilus* is followed by the *House of Fame*, a caprice, a fantasy, the poet's compensation to himself for the restraint and the application bestowed on his greater poem. 'Ne jompre eek no discordant thing yfere,' is the advice of a literary critic in the book of *Troilus* itself: the critic knew the mediaeval temptation to drag in 'termes of physik' and other natural sciences, whether they were required or not. The *House of Fame* is an indulgence, after *Troilus*, in all the mediaeval vanities that had been discouraged by the ambitious and lordly design of that poem. Allegory, description, painted walls, irrelevant sci-

ence, pageants and processions of different kinds, everything that the average mediaeval book makes play with,—these are the furniture of the *House of Fame*; and, in addition to these and through all these, there is the irony of the dream, and the humorous self-depreciation which gives to the *House of Fame* the character of a personal confession. It is one of the most intimate as well as one of the most casual of all his works; a rambling essay in which all the author's weaknesses of taste are revealed, all his fondness for conformity with his age and its manners, while at the same time there is no other poem of Chaucer's so clear and so ironical in its expression of his own view of himself. On the one hand, it is related to all the dreariest and stalest mediaeval fashions; on the other, to the liveliest moods of humorous literature. The temper of Chaucer in his tedious description of the pictures from the *Aeneid*, in the first book, is in concord with all the most monotonous and drawling poets of the mediaeval schools; his wit in the colloquy with the eagle in the second book is something hardly to be matched except in literature outside the mediaeval conventions altogether. The disillusion of the poet, when he imagines that he is going to heaven to be 'stellified,' and is undeceived by his guide, is like nothing in the world so much as the conversation with Poseidon in Heine's *Nordsee*, where the voyager has his fears removed in a manner equally patronising and uncomplimentary.

The contradictions and the problems of the *House of Fame*, in respect of its composition and its poetical elements, are merely those that are found still more profusely and more obviously in the *Canterbury Tales*. There is little need for any one to say more than Dryden has said, or to repeat what every reader can find out for himself, about the liveliness of the livelier parts of the collection. The Prologue, the Interludes of conversation and debate, the Host's too masterful good humour, the considerate and gentle demeanour of the Monk, the Shipman's defence of true religion, the confessions of the Wife of Bath and the Pardoner, the opinions of the Canon's Yeoman,—of all this, and of everything of this sort in the book, it is hopeless to look for any terms of praise that will not sound superfluous to people with eyes and wits of their own. It is not quite so irrelevant to enquire into the nature of the separate tales, and to ask how it is that so many of them have so little of the character of Chaucer, if Chaucer is to be judged by the Prologue and the Interludes.

Some of the Tales are early works, and that explains something of the mystery. Still the fact remains that those early works were adopted and ratified by Chaucer in the composition of his great work, when he made room for the Life of St. Cecilia, and expressly set himself to bespeak an audience for the gravity of *Melibeus*. Here again, though on a still larger scale, is the contradiction of the elements of the *House of Fame*, the discord between the outworn garment of the Middle Ages and the new web from which it is patched.

There is nothing in all the *Canterbury Tales* to set against the richly varied story of *Troilus and Cressida*. There are, however, certain of the *Canterbury Tales* which are not less admirable in respect of mere technical beauty of construction, though the artistic skill is not shown in the same material as in *Troilus*. The *Knight's Tale* preserves the epic, or rather the romantic unities of narrative, as admirably as the greater poem. The *Nun's Priest's Tale* is equally perfect in its own way, and that way is one in which Chaucer has no rival. The story of Virginia, the story of the fairy bride, the story of the revellers who went to look for Death, and many others, are planned without weakness or faltering in the design. There are others which have an incurable fault in the construction, a congenital weakness, utterly at variance from the habit of Chaucer as shown elsewhere, and from the critical principles which he had clearly mastered for his own guidance in his study of Boccaccio.

The *Man of Law's Tale*, the story of Constance, is a comparatively early work, which Chaucer apparently did not choose to alter as he altered his first version of *Palamon and Arcite*. At any rate, the story declares itself as part of a different literary tradition from those in which Chaucer has taken his own way with the proportions of the narrative. The story of Constance has hardly its equal anywhere for nobility of temper; but in respect of unity and harmony of design it is as weak and uncertain as the *Knight's Tale* is complete, continuous, and strong. Chaucer, whose modifications of Boccaccio are proof of intense critical study and calculation of the dimensions of his stories, here admits, to rank with his finished work, a poem beautiful for everything except those constructive excellences on which he had come to set so much account in other cases. The story of Constance follows the lines of a dull original. It has the defects, or rather the excesses, of most popular traditional fairy-tales. Chaucer, who afterwards refused to translate Boccaccio literally, here follows closely the ill-designed plot of a writer who was not in the least like Boccaccio. The story repeats twice over, with variations in detail, the adventure of the princess suffering from the treacherous malice of a wicked mother-in-law; and, also twice over, her voyage in a rudderless boat; the incident of her deliverance from a villain, the Northumbrian caitiff in the first instance, the heathen lord's steward in the second, is also repeated; while the machinery of the first false charge made against Constance by the Northumbrian adversary goes some way to spoil the effect of the subsequent false charge made by the queen-mother, Donegild. The poem has beauties enough to make any one ashamed of criticism; yet it cannot be denied that its beauties are often the exact opposite of the virtues of Chaucer's finished work, being beauties of detail and not beauties of principle and design. The *Man of Law's Tale* with all the grace of Chaucer's style has also the characteristic unwieldiness of the common mediaeval romance; while the *Knight's Tale*, which is no finer in details, is as a composition finished and coherent, with no unnecessary or irrelevant passages.

Besides the anomalies of construction in the *Canterbury Tales*, and not less remarkable than the difference between the neatness and symmetry of the *Knight's Tale* and the flaccidity of the *Man of Law's*, there is an anomaly of sentiment and of mood. *Melibeus* may be left out of account, as a portent too wonderful for mortal commentary: there are other problems and distresses in the *Canterbury Tales*, and they are singular enough, though not altogether inexplicable or 'out of all whooping,' like that insinuating 'little thing in prose' by which Sir Thopas was avenged on his detractors.

The *Knight's Tale* is an artifice, wholly successful, but not to be tampered with in any way, and above all things not to be made into a drama, except for the theatre of the mind. Chaucer refused to give to Emilie and her rival lovers one single spark of that imaginative life which makes his story of *Troilus* one of the great narrative poems of the world, without fear of comparison with the greatest stories in verse or prose. By the original conception of the *Knight's Tale*, the Lady Emilie is forbidden to take any principal part in the story. This is an initial fallacy, a want of dramatic proportion, which renders the plot impossible for the strongest forms of novel or of tragedy. But Chaucer saw that the fable, too weak, too false for the stronger kind, was exactly right when treated in the fainter kind

of narrative which may be called romance, or by any other name that will distinguish it from the order of *Troilus*, from the stronger kind of story in which the characters are true.

In some of the other Tales the experiment is more hazardous, the success not quite so admirable. What is to be said of the *Clerk's Tale*? what of the *Franklin's*? That the story of Griselda should have been chosen by the author of *Troilus* for an honourable place in his *Canterbury Tales* is almost as pleasant as the publication of *Persiles and Sigismunda* by the author of *Don Quixote*. Chaucer had good authority for the patience of Griselda; by no author has the old story been more beautifully and pathetically rendered, and his 'Envoy' saves him from the suspicion of too great solemnity: but no consideration will ever make up for the disparity between the monotonous theme and the variety of Chaucer's greater work, between this formal virtue of the pulpit and the humanities outside. In the *Franklin's Tale* again, in a different way, Chaucer has committed himself to superstitions of which there is no vestige in the more complex parts of his poetry. As Griselda represents the abstract and rectilinear virtue of mediaeval homilists, the *Franklin's Tale* revolves about the point of honour, no less gallantly than Prince Prettyman in the *Rehearsal*. The virtue of patience, the virtue of truth, are there impaled, crying out for some gentle casuist to come and put them out of their torment. Many are the similar victims, from Sir Amadace to Hernani: 'the horn of the old Gentleman' has compelled innumerable romantic heroes to take unpleasant resolutions for the sake of a theatrical effect. That the point of honour, the romantic tension between two abstract opposites, should appear in Chaucer, the first of modern poets to give a large, complete, and humorous representation of human action, is merely one of the many surprises which his readers have to accept as best they may. It is only one of his thousand and one caprices: the only dangerous mistake to which it could possibly lead, would be an assumption that the *Franklin's Tale* can stand as a sample of Chaucer's art in its fullest expression; and the danger of such an error is small. The beginning of right acquaintance with Chaucer is the conviction that nothing represents him except the whole body of his writings. So one is brought round to Dryden's comfortable and sufficient formula: 'Here is God's plenty.' From the energy and the volume of his Trojan story, as glorious as his Trojan river:

> And thou, Simoys, that as an arwe clere
> Through Troie rennest ay downward to the se;

from the passion and the music of that 'tragedie' to the doleful voices of *Melibeus*, there is no form or mood, no fashion of all the vanities, that is not in some way or other represented there. The variety of the matter of Chaucer may possibly to some extent have hindered a full and general recognition of the extraordinary variety in his poetical and imaginative art. It may be doubted whether there is any general appreciation of the height attained by Chaucer in the graver tragic form of story, or of the perfection of his style in all the manifold forms in which he made experiments. If there be any such established injustice in the common estimate of Chaucer as makes it possible for reasonable but misguided people to think of him as merely a 'great translator,' then the refutation will come best of all, without clamour or heat, from the book in which Chaucer's work is presented in the most adequate way. Mr. Skeat in his edition has excluded a number of critical questions which might be maintained to be as capable of argument as the subject of Chaucer's dialect and his practice in the composition of English verse. But although the problems of Chaucer's poetry are not exhausted, and many of them untouched, in this edition, it is still to this edition that appeal will be made for many a year to come. Its value as the first critical text of the whole of Chaucer will scarcely be much impaired by the future edition of a hundred years hence, which shall stand in the same relation to this edition as this to Tyrwhitt's, not to disparage its work, but to complement it. The spirit of the editor is fortunately such as to make him disinclined to rest on his accomplishments. It is evident from many signs that these six volumes are not yet the end of his studies, and that it will probably be something even more strongly equipped than these six volumes which will be left by him to the next age as the final version of his work.

FRANK JEWETT MATHER
From "Introduction"
*The Prologue, The Knight's Tale
and the Nun's Priest's Tale*
1899, pp. ix–xlvii

The test of style is ultimate in the determination of genius. By this we mean that there must be perfect accord between the thought in the writer's mind and the words that express that thought to the reader. Mere originality, nobility even of thought, hardly lie to their creator's credit, unless he has for them words equally novel and lofty. It is chiefly this command of style in the larger sense that gives the poet his advantage over the average fine-souled man—that makes a Burke greater than a Pitt. The first question that we ask ourselves, then, after the immediate relish of curiosity is passed, is, "Has this new writer the supreme gift of style that separates him from the writers of the day?" And this is the question we must sooner or later raise concerning Chaucer. Is his immediate and lasting charm the result of the finest genius, or, as it appears, wayward and almost accidental?

The analysis of a few passages will only confirm the feeling that Chaucer has that beauty and appropriateness of phrase which is proper to the great poets. His style bears all the traces of conscious art. Take this description of a bristling forest,—

> First on the wal was peynted a forest,
> In which ther dwelleth neither man nor best,
> With knotty, knarry, bareyn treës olde
> Of stubbes sharpe and hidous to biholde;
> In which ther ran a rumbel in a swough,
> As though a storm sholde bresten every bough.[1]

How well the harsh and angular adjectives express the gnarled trees; when Chaucer will describe the continuous roaring of the wind in the branches, how he fills the line with resonant and prolonged consonants, "m's," "n's," and "r's," and finally the crash of the "st's" in "storm," "bresten," which renders the crack of great branches torn from the parent stem! Here are the exact words to express what the eye and the ear gather from the wild scene.

I would willingly quote entire the scene of Arcite's death, the perfect sincerity and simplicity of which has touched generations of readers.[2] Note only the force of the redundant "Allone, withouten any compaignye" when put in the mouth of one upon whom had just smiled the prospect of a life in Emily's company:—

> What asketh man to have,
> Now with his love now in his colde grave
> Allone withouten any compaignye?[3]

In the following lines the very structure of the verse, the balanced participles, "giggynge," "lacynge," etc., the clause that overruns its line to end abruptly and strangely with "gnawynge," all heightens the effect of bustle and breathless preparation for the tournament:—

> Ther maystow seen . . .
> Knyghtes, of retenue, and eek squyeres
> Nailynge the speres, and helmes bokelynge,
> Giggynge of sheeldes, with layneres lacynge;
> Ther as need is, they weren nothyng ydel;
> The fomy steedes on the golden brydel
> Gnawynge, and fast the armurers also
> With fyle and hamer prikyng to and fro, *etc.*[4]

Let these few examples suffice for many.

Single lines show the same felicity. We are told of the Monk that—

> whan he rood men myghte his brydel here
> Gynglen in a whistlynge wynd as clere,
> And eek as loude as dooth the chapel belle,
> Ther as this lord was kepere of the celle;[5]

and the very whistling of the wind is in the second line with its thin "i" and "e" sounds and its resonant "n's." Or in the description of the Miller—

> He was short-sholdered, brood, a thicke knarre[6]—

the verse with its weighty compound word and its halting rhythm moves with the hulking carriage of the Miller's powerful frame.

In these instances we are dealing with no narrowly rhetorical matters; it is this mastery of his instrument that marks the great artist.

From a very early time men have noted and admired the realism of Chaucer, and probably the time will never come when lovers fail to recognize something of themselves in Troilus, and men cease to find their neighbors among the Canterbury pilgrims. Perhaps the handsomest tribute ever paid to this quality of Chaucer's is that of a very poor poet of the succeeding century, the anonymous writer of *The Book of Curtesye* (E. E. T. S., Ext. Ser. No. iii. ll. 337–343), . . .

> Our arsenal would have sounded and resounded
> With bangs and thwacks of driving bolts and nails,
> Of shaping oars and holes to put the oars in;
> With hacking, hammering, clattering, and boring;
> Words of command, whistles, and pipes and fifes.
>   (Frere's Translation.)

> Redith his bokes fulle of all pleasaunce,
>   Clere in sentence, in longage excellent,
> Brefly to write suche was his suffesaunce,
>   What-ever to sey he toke in his entent,
>   His longage was so feyre and pertinent,
> That semed unto mennys heryng
> Not only the worde, but verrely the thing.

It would be hard to better the last line. It is the complete fusion of the word in the thing that makes Chaucer not only one of the great artists, but one of the great realists.

We may well carry our analysis of this recognized quality a point further and ask, What are the methods of observation and setting-forth that make the *Prologue* and the best of the *Canterbury Tales* unique for vividness and reality? We may say at the outset that Chaucer never sought the cheaper and more obvious methods of modern realism. We never find anything like an inventory of the moral qualities of the Canterbury pilgrims; we seldom have a complete account even of their dress and physical characteristics. Of the Shipman we are told only that he rode badly, was dressed in a long coat of rough cloth, with a dagger by his side, that he was tanned and weather-beaten. The rest is description of his "easy" handling of a wine cargo, of his piratical traits, and of his seamanship, except for the single line,—

With many a tempest hadde his berd been shake. [7]

Yet what a sea-picture there is in this simple statement. I need no more than this to see the Shipman, legs wide-braced on a heaving deck, eyes, under beaten brows, strained out into the storm, while the gale sweeps a great beard back over his shoulders.

After we have learned how the Friar lived by his wits and pleased his very dupes, we part from him with the lines,—

And in his harpyng, whan that he hadde songe,
His eyen twynkled in his heed aryght
As doon the sterres in the frosty nyght. [8]

We have seen the snap of his eye and know why everybody liked him, and a poor widow would give the fellow her last farthing.

Arcite has been cruelly crushed under his horse. Chaucer says simply,—

Tho was he corven out of his harneys, [9]—

and we shudder. No surgeon's exact description of the hurt could so move us.

Two lines express the whole restless character of the Man of Law,—

Nowher so busy a man as he ther n' as,
And yet he semed bisier than he was. [10]

You cannot forget that the Reeve is "sclendre" when you have seen his legs through Chaucer's homely simile,—

Ful longe were his legges and ful lene,
Y-lyk a staf, ther was no calf y-sene. [11]

Nor will you doubt that the Prioress is sentimental and tender-hearted when you learn that a trapped mouse claimed her tears, that the death or even the chastisement of one of her lapdogs caused bitter weeping, finally that the same "smale houndes," on a diet of "rosted flessh, or milk, and wastel bred," fared better than a mistress who kept ascetic rules for herself,— not for her pets. Can you finally imagine a better simile for Chaucer's lover and soldier-squire than the almost commonplace,—

He was as fresh as is the monthe of May? [12]

It is this faculty of seizing upon the characteristic attitude or action that makes Chaucer's descriptions so vivid. He wastes no time upon the things that might be said of any lawyer or any miller, but goes straight to the traits that mark his particular lawyer and miller. We all have some way of looking or acting that reveals us; often the idiosyncrasy is so slight as to escape even our closest friends until a skilful mimic shows that this mere trick of expression marks us as our very selves. Chaucer's power lay in the unerring observation of such peculiarities. It is a method closely allied to that of caricature, and as such, much abused even by the better students of human eccentricity,— witness Dickens and Balzac. This pitfall Chaucer measurably escapes. Of course we know that the Miller's mouth was not literally "wyde . . . as a greet forneys;" the comparison none the less renders unforgettable its bigness and redness.

At the risk of repetition we must insist that Chaucer seldom tries gradually to build up a character; that he could have done so Chriseyde is abundant proof. His method then differs essentially from that of the modern novelist. His presentation of character, on the contrary, comes instantaneously through illuminating flashes, and the great masters of the short story,

such as Maupassant, are in technique his true successors. It is this power of flashing truth into a description that our poet of the *Book of Curtesye* had in mind when he spoke of Chaucer's "longage" as being so "pertinent" that it conveyed

Not only the word but verrely the thing.

The most serious passages of his poetry are seldom without a sub-quality of humor, while usually this quality is unrestrained. But Chaucer's humor rarely passes over into satire. At most he is finely ironical toward the offender against the congruous, sincerely loving and even respecting him against whom he has turned the laugh. It is this unshaken good-humor and friendliness which is most characteristic of the poet's attitude toward men. He loves to laugh at them, but he loves them too. And his humor is so fine and pervasive that it claims oftener a smile than a laugh.

Alert as this humor is, its touch is kindly. The Prioress escapes with only a fling at her airs and graces; the Monk provokes only an ironical approval of his hunting; so the Friar is commended for loving a barmaid better than a leper; the Doctor loves gold because it has medicinal value:—

For gold in physik is a cordial,
Therfore he loved gold in speciall. [13]

Sometimes this humor takes the form of burlesque. What more delicious and yet what more realistic than the description of Chaunticleer?—

His comb was redder than the fyn coral,
And batailled as it were a castel wal;
His byle was blak, and as the jeet it shoon;
Lyk asure were his legges and his toon;
His nayles whiter than the lylye flour.
And lyk the burned gold was his colour. [14]

So the old romancers loved to describe a Sir Lybeau or a Lancelot; and Chaucer must have observed the cock with a real admiration for his splendor, though seeing too the fun of cock character. Vain pedant that he is, the cock deigns to rally anxious Dame Pertelote in Latin, and to add the interpretation:—

Mulier est hominis confusio:
Madame, the sentence of this Latin is,
Woman is mannes joye, and al his blis. [15]

We can see what Mr. Robert Grant has aptly named "the furtive conjugal smile."

Few characters fail to challenge Chaucer's genial irony; and yet there are those, such as the Knight, the Parson, and the Plowman, that are treated with perfect seriousness. Souls so finely simple and genuine are impregnable even to the kindest ridicule. They disarm the humorist. "Sitting beside them the Comic Muse is grave and sisterly," is Mr. Meredith's fine word.

The frank realism of Chaucer's humor brings him at times into conflict with modern standards of the fitting, and even of the permissible. In the *Prologue* (l. 731), he has already warned us that—

Whoso shal telle a tale after a man,
He moot reherce as ny as ever he can,
Everich a word, if it be in his charge,
Al speke he never so rudeliche and large.

Consequently he lets the Miller tell on freely his "cherles tale;" nor does he hold the rein on the Miller's coarser fellows. Many of these stories, that "sownen unto" a now decorously covered sin, are quite redeemed by the brilliancy and humor of the telling. Chaucer is too much the artist to be coarse for coarseness' sake, and often lends a special refinement of manner to matter sufficiently dubious. Yet the reader of no too squeamish taste will find certain parts of these tales obtrusively nasty. Nor can he wholly excuse the poet on the ground of old-time freedom of expression; for Chaucer knew perfectly well what he was about in treating the Somnour as realistically as he did the Prioress: the choice and the responsibility were his alone. It is, however, fair to say that such work is small in amount, and to the average reader a negligible quantity. The closer student will condemn this portion of his work, or hold it justified, according to his opinion of the realistic doctrine; while those who have experienced some of life's compromises will be rather tolerant toward one whose "gipoun," unlike that of the Knight, bears stains other than those of the crusader's "habergeoun."

Supremely inventive Chaucer proved himself just once—in the *Prologue* and the plan of the *Canterbury Tales*. Elsewhere he prefers to rest upon the authority of other men, and to use his great literary powers in the re-shaping and bringing to perfection of well-known stories. He possibly never invented a plot, and when, as in the *House of Fame*, he lacked a direct model, the story quite ran away with him. Pillaging literature with a freedom that reminds us of Shakespeare digging *Macbeth* out of a chronicle, or transforming a popular novel into *As You Like It*, Chaucer now borrowed the plot of an Italian epic, now used a Latin tale of Petrarch's, now re-wrote a French *fableau*; or again a legend of Ovid, or an "example" from a monkish compilation was his theme.

But everything he borrowed became speedily his own. The *Knight's Tale* emerged a very different thing from the *Teseide*; Boccaccio would have recognized only with difficulty in *Troilus* his *Filostrato*. Even in those cases where he follows an original closely, the grace of the telling, the picturesqueness and genial humor which permeate the old material transmute it into another and far finer substance. Every one knows that inventiveness is the smallest part of the story-teller's gift. The most indifferent tale may be redeemed by the resources of the narrator's art; the most ingenious spoiled through inadequate telling. So the story-teller's business lies chiefly in presentation, very little in absolute invention. *Or dient et content et fabloient*, "Now they say and relate and tell the tale," stands at the chapter-heads of that blithest of early stories, *Aucassin and Nicolette*. Let this artless redundancy of words for telling indicate that therein lies the whole opus and labor of a difficult art. So a man tell his story supremely well, be he a Chaucer, an Ariosto, a La Fontaine, the question "Where did he get it?" troubles little the reader. He is foolish who seeks too narrowly the antecedents of bookish treasure-trove. 'T is the bookworm's, not the gentle reader's part. And be it said that such rummaging among Chaucer's "olde bokes" only illustrates his genius. Many-sided as is his genius, he must be judged, or better, enjoyed primarily, as the master of those who tell. In olden times the French trouvère of recognized preëminence received the title of king. So Adenes proudly signs himself *li rois*. Chaucer had no need to claim a title that posterity has never refused him.

We have found in Chaucer an unusual power of style, the *eloquentia* of the humanist whom Chaucer in temperament often foreshadows. And here be it said that when Matthew Arnold denied to him the possession of the "grand style," he spoke from imperfect knowledge or appreciation. As well deny this gift to Horace because he prefers the note of comedy. To style in the narrower sense Chaucer adds extraordinary descriptive power, dealing however rather in the significant line than in the elaborated study. Finally, the texture of his invention is undershot with a humor peculiarly genial and humane. The result is a style unequalled for ease and charm. This naturalness has frequently passed for *naïveté*. There could be no

greater mistake. The great poets have no "wood-notes wild," and Chaucer is of their company, *della loro schiera*.

It is, I believe, the supreme ease of his poetry that gives him his unique position among English poets. Certain it is that no other poet of the first rank gives so much, requiring of the reader so little effort in return. And this ease lies deeper than facts of style and methods of composition; it comes from a nature finely adjusted to the world in which it finds itself. When we think of the man Chaucer we are inevitably reminded of the Horace of the *Satires* and *Epistles*. We divine a man who has loved the world much, not wholly trusting it, who knows tears but prefers smiles. We recognize an experience, mellowing where embitterment were possible, which has yielded worldly wisdom of the most amiable sort. It is these qualities that make Chaucer of all our poets the friendliest.

Notes

1. *Knight's Tale*, ll. 1117ff.
2. *Knight's Tale*, ll. 1907ff.
3. "How does the repetition and amplification give force and bitterness to the thought, as if Arcite must need dwell on his expected loneliness in order to feel it fully!"—Lowell, *Conversations*, p. 17.
4. *Knight's Tale*, ll. 1644ff. My friend, Dr. M. C. Satphen, kindly supplies a parallel from Aristophanes,—the description of a busy arsenal,—which presents similar stylistic features. . . .
5. *Prologue*, ll. 174ff.
6. *Prologue*, l. 549.
7. *Prologue*, l. 406.
8. *Prologue*, ll. 266ff.
9. *Knight's Tale*, l. 1858.
10. *Prologue*, ll. 321f.
11. *Prologue*, ll. 592ff.
12. *Prologue*, l. 92.
13. *Prologue*, ll. 43f.
14. *Nun's Priest's Tale*, ll. 39ff.
15. *Nun's Priest's Tale*, ll. 343ff.

PETER BORGHESI
From *Boccaccio and Chaucer*
1903, pp. 29–69

It has been recorded by several critics and Nicolas Harris is one of these, that Chaucer did not know Italian. We think that nothing can be more absurd. The only reason they give worth considering is that he never intermingled a single Italian word in his works, whilst he used so many French and Latin words. . . .

Not only was Chaucer able to distinguish the superiority of the Italian literature over the French, but he could also choose the very best Italian books. As regards style the *Teseide* is one of Boccaccio's best works[1]. In spite of its classical imitations, the narrative is always simple and bright, the verse and the octave rhyme are generally good and this work was the forerunner of Ariosto and Tasso.

Chaucer knew at once that it was a masterpiece, although the plot in itself is not very interesting; he saw that the characters were not cold, as some are inclined to think, but passionate and full of life; he knew that it was "the first long narrative heroic poem written by a man of genius[2]". What a difference between the allegory of the *Roman de la Rose* and the human characters of the *Teseide*! It was a great step towards a better form of literature. Chaucer read this poem, he understood all its superiority, and he began to translate it. But it is most probable that he did not translate it in the form which we now possess in the *Canterbury Tales* under the title of the *Knight's*

Tale. This tale is most probably a recasting of an earlier translation, now lost, which he made before and which he mentions in his *Legend of Good Women*.

Here the usual great question arises, the question of source, as Chaucer only says that he took his work from "old stories" and from "old books", which would not be true, if, as we believe, Boccaccio's *Teseide* was his original. But was it really so?

Many eminent critics answer that it was, but a few are not of this opinion. The latter say that Boccaccio's *Teseide* and Chaucer's *Knight's Tale* have a common source. Craik is one of these and he claims to prove his assertion by saying that the *Teseide* "extends to about 12,000 octosyllabic verses" whilst Chaucer's poem extends "to not many more than 2,000 decasyllabic ones". He adds that the English work is much less detailed than the Italian and that "the two versions differ in some of the main circumstances". In another passage he says that what is thought to be translated or imitated from Boccaccio is very little and insignificant and only leads one to suppose that they were drawn from a common source. All this is absolutely denied by Furnivall, who says that the original of the *Knight's Tale* is only the Italian *Teseide*, and he adds that it is impossible to think of a French origin of the fable of the *Teseide* and therefore of the *Knight's Tale*.

Happily we are not obliged to give much weight to Craik's remarks. In the first phase we must say that he had but very little acquaintance with the Italian language. Everybody knows that Boccaccio's *Teseide* is not written in octosyllabic verses, and that it has not 12,000 verses, but only 9,896, to which we must add fifteen sonnets, and we must also add that there are 2,350 in the *Knight's Tale*.

It is also necessary to state here, that we do not say that Chaucer translated Boccaccio's *Teseide* for his *Knight's Tale*, we say that Boccaccio's *Teseide* is Chaucer's original, that therefore he knew this poem: we say that much is translated and imitated from it, and we add also that Chaucer follows the Italian poem in its general features in such a way as to show his original very clearly.

In the second place, as to the shortness of the English poem as compared with the Italian one it is necessary to know that the *Knight's Tale* is at the beginning of Chaucer's *Canterbury Tales*, which is a collection of tales told, in order to pass the time cheerfully, by at least 29 persons travelling from London to Canterbury. Now Chaucer's *Knight's Tale* is shorter than Boccaccio's *Teseide* for two reasons: first because a long tale would not amuse, secondly because the time was very limited and it was polite and necessary to leave to every member of the company sufficient time to tell two tales in going and two in returning as had been agreed upon. Therefore many secondary and even main circumstances must differ in the two versions, but it is beyond all doubt that Chaucer knew Italian, and his *Knight's Tale* has its source in the *Teseide*, as he literally translated from it about 270 verses, and either imitated or paraphrased about 500[3].

To prove this assertion we could give here a long list of many, or all the passages in the *Teseide* with Chaucer's English translations or paraphrases, but this work has already been done by Tyrwhitt, Rossetti, Skeat and others, and therefore it is unnecessary for us to do so.

After the proofs that the most learned students of Chaucer have given us, after the comparisons which have been made between the Italian and the English poems, it is impossible not to admit that Chaucer knew Italian and that the *Teseide* is the true source of the *Knight's Tale*.

If many beautiful passages in the *Teseide* are not to be found in the *Knight's Tale*, it is, as we have already pointed out, because he wanted to shorten it very much, as he often says at the beginning of his tale, and also because many passages had already been inserted in other works of his. For example, from the description of the temple of Venus Chaucer took very little for his *Knight's Tale*, as he had already inserted a very close imitation of it in his *Assembly of Fowls*[4], namely from verse 183 to verse 287, and these lines "are translated in a way that places beyond question Chaucer's knowledge of Italian. The turn of the phrase makes it quite evident that Chaucer wrote with the Italian original before him[5]". So in the same poem a list of birds and a shorter list of trees are taken or closely imitated from the *Teseide*, and many passages from this poem are to be found here and there in Chaucer's works. In the same way some of the reminiscences of the *Teseide* are also to be found in Chaucer's *Troylus and Cryseide*. The 260.th, 261.st and 262.nd stanzas of this poem are taken from the first three stanzas of the eleventh canto of the *Teseide*.

The poem of *Queen Anelida and False Arcite* bears a striking resemblance to the *Knight's Tale* and therefore to the *Teseide* "chiefly in the opening lines[6]" so that the 1.st, 2.nd and 3.rd stanzas of *Queen Anelida* correspond to the 3.rd, 2.nd and 1.st of the *Teseide*.

All this explains the gaps that are found here and there in the *Knight's Tale* and it explains also that even if Chaucer had had a mind to translate the *Teseide* literally for his *Canterbury Tales*, he could not have done so.

From all this we may infer also that Boccaccio's *Teseide* is the poem which most pleased Chaucer and from which he borrowed as much as he could.

Here another question arises: when Chaucer altered, did he alter for the worse or for the better? The answer is a very difficult one, but something also may be said on this point. There is no doubt that Boccaccio's *Teseide* has one great defect; this defect lies in the effort to remove, to keep at a distance the conclusion of the action, which is already foreseen from the middle of the poem[7]. Generally speaking, to curtail the story was to improve it, therefore many critics have praised him inasmuch as he avoided many tiresome descriptions, which, if useful or tolerable in a long poem, are not so in a short one. But in several cases, in his curtailing and in his alterations he was not guided by very good taste, as he does not avoid several of the above mentioned descriptions, he seems to delight in rhetorical tirades full of mythology and biblical quotations and expressions[8], defects which were however very common during the Middle-ages. Perhaps it was in considering these defects that Sandras was induced to say that Chaucer did not improve the *Teseide*, in fact he says that the English poet diminished its poetic merit, omitted the finest features of the fable and spoiled the truth of the story.

But, in spite of its defects, the *Knight's Tale*, which leads the series of the *Canterbury Tales*, and which in spirit as well as in language is the translation of Boccaccio's *Teseide*, had a great success in England and a great influence on English literature, as it was the basis of Fletcher's drama, of Dryden's poem, and of many other compositions.

If Chaucer took very much from the *Teseide* for his *Knight's Tale*, he certainly did not take less from the *Filostrato* for his *Troylus and Cryseide*. He did not literally translate it as he was an inventor though a disciple, an original writer though a translator[9].

Chaucer's work could not be called a translation, but it is rather a recasting of Boccaccio's *Filostrato*. . . .

Boccaccio's *Filostrato* contains 5,704 lines and Chaucer's *Troylus and Cryseide* 8,246. Chaucer adapted from the *Filostrato* 2,730 lines which he condensed into 2,583 so that only 5,663 lines belong almost exclusively to Chaucer. Therefore one third of *Troylus and Cryseide* is taken from Boccaccio and two thirds are either Chaucer's own, or taken from Boëthius, Dante and Petrarch, besides many imitations from Ovid.

It is true that many passages and episodes of Boccaccio's *Filostrato* are not to be found in the English poem, but we must always bear in mind that Chaucer was not a mere translator, and it will be easy for us to understand all the difference which exists between the two poems. We must consider that if between the two poems there are differences there are also many resemblances: so the leading incidents are the same, there are minute coincidences of expression which could not exist if Chaucer had not translated from Boccaccio, and we must not forget that Chaucer could not translate literally as he wrote poetry.

In many instances Chaucer has helped scholars to find out the sources of his works, but in the case of *Troylus and Cryseide* he rather puts them at a loss. He does not claim any merit of invention in this poem as in one passage he says that he translated it "out of Latin", but by the word Latin he might also have meant the *Latino volgare* or Italian. In other passages he incidentally refers to Homer, Dares Phrygius, Dictus Cretensis, but he certainly did not take anything from them. He states also that the author of his original was Lollius, but no one appears to recognize this as the name of a writer from whom Chaucer may have taken anything, and no one can presume to say, as Tyrwhitt does, that Lollius may be another name for Boccaccio as our great prose-writer was never so called. . . .

Now, why does not Chaucer mention Boccaccio in any place though he owes so much to him?

It was not only Chaucer's wish to be a Court poet, but he also looked to this for his means of livelihood: he was not a man of action, not a man of great courage: he was not inclined to write anything that might displease the Court. We see this in the translation of the *Roman de la Rose*, if the translation now extant is his, where he omits all passages casting reflections on Kings or other authorities. For a certain time Boccaccio was not in favour with those in authority, with the clergy and religious men in general, and this was chiefly before he expressed regret at having written the *Decameron*. Although in 1373, either just before or soon after the departure of Chaucer from Florence, Boccaccio was appointed to explain Dante to the public and his renown was reestablished, yet some rumours of his being a man of corrupt and loose habits must have reached Chaucer, who thought that these reports might get to England: he feared the King's reproaches had he mentioned that man as his master, therefore he never mentioned Boccaccio, and perhaps translated from him less than he would otherwise have done. Besides this, although it is quite certain that Chaucer knew Boccaccio's works, yet it cannot be actually proved that he knew his name, or that he knew him personally, or indeed that he ever knew he was the author of his works, as many of the manuscripts of the Middle-ages were published anonymously.

The supposition that Chaucer purposely avoided mentioning the name of Boccaccio gains strength when we remember that Chaucer's idea of decorum was superior to Boccaccio's. In Boccaccio's *Filostrato* Cryseide is a comparatively commonplace person. This rich, young, beautiful and gay widow did not wish to reject the advances of a young man of distinction: she could not live the life of a nun, and if other women amused themselves with intrigue, why should she not do the same? On being assured that her reputation would not suffer, she yields at once, and makes excuses for her reluctance. In Boccaccio's work Cryseide is bad, faithless, vicious and lustful: in Chaucer's she is not "a nun to whom earthly love is a sin", but she is rather a "victim of fate". After having read Boccaccio we despise or hate such wanton women, but Chaucer's Cryseide possesses every quality which entitles a woman to love and respect: she is won with difficulty and overcome only by surprise. The English poet rather teaches us to pity her and he endears her to his readers.

Boccaccio's Pandarus is the most despicable of men; Chaucer's is a good natured, loquacious, rather unscrupulous man, a man who knows the world and who means to enjoy life; he is quite a new creation, a good character for a good comedy, the right man in the right place.

Boccaccio's Troylus is an ordinary man, rather destitute of refined feeling, self-indulgent and practised in the art of intrigue: Chaucer's on the contrary loves with all the ardour and freshness of youth, he is the personification of what a lover ought to be.

Boccaccio does not waste words in the first part of his poem, but he loiters in the second, chiefly after the catastrophe, when all the interest of the poem has passed away. On the contrary Chaucer dwells at length on the most moral and charming part of the poem, where Cryseide is falling in love, but he so curtails the sorrowful conclusion that the fifth or last book of his poem corresponds to four of Boccaccio's cantos.

So, in justice to Chaucer, although a translation, we look upon his *Troylus and Cryseide* as a new creation, and, although Scott thought it a rather tedious work, we think it is a very good one, and we think that Rossetti is right to judge it the finest of ancient English love poems. Certainly in this work there springs up a new life, and we should say a life more moral and purer than in the Italian poem. It could not be otherwise, as Chaucer dedicates it to "the moral Gower and the philosophical Strode", and it shows also, to Chaucer's honour, that he did not require the aid of vulgarity or triviality to give expression to that vivacity and humour which are his chief characteristics.

We have pointed out that Chaucer's *Troylus and Cryseide* is more moral than Boccaccio's *Filostrato*, but it was not moral enough for the English of that time, and especially for many of the ladies of the Court. This justifies us in our supposition that Chaucer neither dared mention Boccaccio, nor admit that he was his principal master. Indeed, he knew that his poem was not well received at Court, and he wrote *The Legend of Good Women*, by the Queen's order, it is said, to remove the odium which *Troylus and Cryseide* had brought on him.

And here another question arises: is Chaucer's *Troylus and Cryseide* superior to Boccaccio's *Filostrato*?

If we consider separately the several points of Chaucer's work, perhaps, as we have already pointed out, in many passages in this poem Chaucer is superior to Boccaccio, and also, perhaps, if we consider the poem taken as a whole. In many instances Chaucer "has eminently shown his good sense and judgment in rejecting the superfluities and improving the general arrangement of the story. He frequently corrects and softens Boccaccio's manners and it is with singular address he has often abridged the Italian poet's ostentatious and pedantic parade of ancient history and mythology[10]". Perhaps this is saying too much; but at least it is partly true. On the other hand Chaucer is wanting in every respect in unity; unity of composition, unity of delineation, unity of character, unity of style;

whereas unity constitutes the peculiar attraction of Boccaccio. Chaucer is more monotonous, more diffuse, but he is "superior in depth of feeling and delineation of the passions[11]" and shows everywhere a closer knowledge of life. Boccaccio displays more "elegance of diction and ornament", and his work is and always will remain, an unrivalled master-piece.

Before speaking of the *Decameron* we think it necessary to say something about Chaucer's *Canterbury Tales*, to which we have already referred.

In Chaucer's time many persons, from all parts of England, went to Canterbury to visit the tomb of Thomas à Becket. On the sixth of May of a certain year Chaucer finds we do not know whether 29 or 30 of these pilgrims at the *Tabard*, an inn that was near London Bridge, in the South East of London, on the right bank of the Thames where in the same place, in High Street, Borough, at present stands the *Old Tabard*, a public house, but this building is very modern and there are no remains of the old one. Chaucer and the host joined the pilgrims, so that they then became either thirty-one or thirty-two and they agreed that every member of the company should tell two tales in going and two in returning from the pilgrimage. On the bright and green morning of the seventh day both journey and tales commenced.

Who does not see at once how grand is the idea, and one such as only a genius can conceive? It is not an easy task to write about 128 tales of licentious, and puts before us scenes which many would not care to see. Shall we find fault only with him, if at that time the Italian sense of delicacy was rather blunted? Shall we condemn Boccaccio if he represented society to us under the conditions that then existed and if he spoke the truth? And if we do not condemn Boccaccio, so much the less shall we rank among those who condemn Chaucer, because if the two authors wrote much which very old men might regret to have written, certainly Boccaccio had much more to regret than Chaucer. But who has not read the history of many a great man who muses sorrowfully on his best works? Chaucer's *Canterbury Tales* is his master-piece, because when he wrote it he had then become possessed of more knowledge of life, his style had improved and become firmer, clearer, more flexible, more expressive and was above all things most popular. He so excels in humour and imagination that only Shakespeare can be compared with him, only Shakespeare can pretend to rival him. He is subtle, various, sprightly; he gives gorgeous descriptions and passages with a profound and exquisite delicacy and pathos. He paints what he sees, and he knows so well how to mingle wisdom with humour that he amuses his readers, he endears them to him, and everyone feels sorry that he was able to write only so few of such tales. But, though unfinished, the work "contains about 17,000 verses, besides more than a fourth of that quantity in prose[12]". His verses are either decasyllabic or hendecasyllabic, and they are arranged either in couplets or in stanzas. Though unfinished it is the greatest of all his works and the most original, the one on which his fame stands as a rock against the ravages of time.

It can be proved, as we have seen, that Chaucer knew the *Teseide* and the *Filostrato*, but it has not yet been ascertained that he knew the *Decameron*. In all probability he did, and this is also the general opinion, but till now we have not found any material proof of it. What is certain, however, is that he did not translate from the *Decameron* as he did from the *Teseide* and the *Filostrato*, but this is no surprise to us: as Chaucer was a genius, he could not remain a translator all his life, and also because the conception of translating prose into poetry seems

rather strange or awkward. What we say, what we believe, what we should like to demonstrate clearly and beyond doubt is, that Chaucer knew the *Decameron* and that from this work he took at least the idea of his *Canterbury Tales*.

Certainly the task is not an easy one, chiefly because Chaucer disowns his obligations to Boccaccio, for not only never does he mention his name, but he often seems, in this particular, to try to lead his students and critics astray. And in this he succeeds, because as both the English and the Italian poetry of that time was, generally speaking, either a translation or an imitation of that of France, so many critics were led to believe that Boccaccio and Chaucer were not much connected with each other.

It is certain that not a single one of the *Canterbury Tales* can be ascribed to Chaucer's own imagination, and although Craik says, that the fame of Italian song could hardly have reached Chaucer's ears and although Sir Harris Nicolas is almost of the same opinion, yet Ward, who is one of the best authorities on Chaucer, admits that Chaucer's indebtedness towards Italian literature and "Boccaccio in particular is considerable" and that it seems "hardly to admit of denial". Even Craik in a passage of his history of English literature says that "it must be considered very doubtful" if any one of Chaucer's tales was really derived from Italian, and in another place he says that "this may have been the case". Therefore we see that even those who do not admit of an Italian influence on Chaucer are nevertheless in considerable doubt in making such an assertion. . . .

Let us look a little closer into the two works, and we shall find that the *Canterbury Tales* is a work of much the same kind as the *Decameron*. The *Decameron* is a species of comedy not intended for the stage and so is the *Canterbury Tales*. The subjects of the *Decameron* are of about the same kind as those of the *Canterbury Tales*, and although the framework is somewhat different, yet it has many striking resemblances.

And this resemblance not only in the general idea, but moreover several of Chaucer's tales have some resemblance to those in the *Decameron*. In fact, the pardoner in the *Canterbury Tales* is an itinerant ecclesiastic of much the same stamp as Frate Cipolla in the *Decameron*, although Chaucer may have taken the outline of the very beautiful *Pardoner's Tale* from the *Cento novelle antiche*.

The *Reeve's Tale* forms the basis of the sixth novel of the ninth day in Boccaccio's *Decameron*. The only difference is that Boccaccio's story is much more licentious than Chaucer's.

As to the *Shipman's Tale* Speght supposes that its original is the first novel of the eighth day of the *Decameron*. Although Morley frankly avows that it was taken from the *Decameron*, yet at the same time we must also record the fact that Tyrwhitt and Warton think it more probable that both Chaucer and Boccaccio derived the outline from a French *fabliau*. But, as we have said, if we believe that Chaucer had abandoned the idea of taking anything from France, it will not be difficult for us to take the side of Morley.

Chaucer asserts that he derived the *Franklin's Tale* from a Breton lay, but this lay is not known. Skeat says that "the subject seems to have survived in a popular *fabliau*, which Boccaccio has drawn upon in the *Decameron* and also introduced into the *Philocopo*", therefore also in this tale, if Chaucer did not take it from the *Decameron*, there is at least some connection with this work, namely with the fifth novel of the tenth day.

Several resemblances are also found between the *Merchant's Tale* and that of *Lidia and Nicostrato*, the seventh novel of the ninth day, and between the *Miller's Tale* and that of *Frate Puccio*, the third novel of the fourth day.

Although these resemblances are very striking, yet nothing definite can be proved, and if, for example, both Boccaccio and Chaucer find fault with the monks in similar matters, it does not of necessity follow that Chaucer borrowed from Boccaccio, but it may rather tend to show that the defects of the monks were as notorious in Italy as in England, as may be inferred from a letter written by Boniface IX in 1390, and it may be that both Boccaccio and Chaucer felt it was necessary to satirise and condemn these defects in order to put an end to them.

Furnivall says that, if Chaucer had known the *Decameron*, he would have translated and inserted some or at least one of its "racy *novelle*" in his *Canterbury Tales*. It seems to us that Furnivall and several others are inclined to wish Chaucer had translated more than he did. To some extent we have already answered this assumption when we spoke of the evolution of every author, namely when we said that almost every genius begins as a translator or as an imitator, and that it is only little by little that his own personality springs forth, but we have now another observation to make on this point. The *Canterbury Tales* is an unfinished work: there ought to be at least 120 tales, and we have only 24. Can we not suggest what Chaucer would have done if he had been allowed to finish his work? Could he not have thought of introducing some of the "racy *novelle*" into that portion of his book which he was not able to give us?

In conclusion if we look for material proofs that Chaucer knew the *Decameron*, we fail to find any as in all Chaucer's works there is no allusion to this book or to its author; neither a phrase nor a single word can be proved to have been taken from it, and the coincidences which the *Canterbury Tales* has with it are common to other books which were previously published and which Chaucer may have known. But when we consider the above coincidences, when we take into consideration Chaucer's love and enthusiasm for the Italian literature, and when we remember, as we have already pointed out, that he knew the *Teseide*, the *Filostrato* and Boccaccio's Latin works from which he took so much, we may conclude with some certainty that he knew also the *Decameron* or at least some of its tales. We can only conjecture this, but we feel that there is some ground for supposing that Morley, Mamroth and many others are right when they conclude that Chaucer owes to Boccaccio the framework of his *Canterbury Tales*.

The question has also arisen as to whether Chaucer's work is superior to Boccaccio's, and several English men of Letters have given judgment in favour of their own poet. We should like to say the contrary, but we cannot pass judgment on a question like this, because we do not feel called upon to pronounce too closely between the merits of these two geniuses, and also because it seems to us that it is very difficult to compare an unfinished work with a complete one. It has been said that in the *Canterbury Tales* there is more unity of idea, more unity of composition than in Boccaccio's *Decameron*, that the prologue is in strict accord with the following tales which are closely connected to one another. We certainly accept the suggestion that the prologue in the *Canterbury Tales* is in strict accord with the subsequent tales, and that the preface in the *Decameron* is not; but we do not see in the other portion of Chaucer's work more unity of composition than in Boccaccio's. It is so true, that Chaucer's tales are not much connected to one another that their order even is not the same in several old manuscripts. Notwithstanding this, let us grant that Chaucer's tales are a little more connected to one another than those

in the *Decameron*, let us grant that Boccaccio's work is much less moral than Chaucer's, yet we do not think that this is enough to determine Chaucer's superiority.

The *Clerk's Tale*, which is one of the best in the *Canterbury Tales*, deserves special mention. It is the matchless story of patient *Griselda and Dioneo*, the last tale in the *Decameron*, about which Petrarch said that no one could read it without shedding tears. It pleased him so much that he translated it into Latin and it is from Petrarch's Latin prose that Chaucer took it. But how did Chaucer obtain this translation? He himself says that he went to Padua to see Petrarch, whom he calls his master, and he makes his Clerk say:

> I woll you tell a tale which that I
> Learned at Padowe of a worthy clerk,
> As preved by his wordes and his werk:
> He is now dead and nailed in his chest;
> I pray to God so yeve his soule rest.
> Francis Petrarch, the laureat poet
> Highte this clerk, whose rhethoricke sweet
> Enlumined all Itaille of poetrie.

Perhaps this time Chaucer, whose statements are often doubtful or unauthorized, has spoken the truth, because if it is true that Petrarch latinised this tale in 1373, it is rather difficult for Chaucer to have got hold of the translation in Florence before his departure from the town. Perhaps he really got it in Padua from Petrarch himself.

We have said that Chaucer's statement this time is true, but still it is not quite true, as his *Clerk's Tale* cannot be a version of only what he heard from Petrarch: he follows so closely Petrarch's Latin translation that he must have had it before him when he wrote.

The fact of not having taken it from Boccaccio is considered a great argument in favour of those who affirm that Chaucer knew neither the *Decameron* nor Italian. Indeed there is not in it a single phrase which leads us to suppose that Chaucer had already read it in the *Decameron*[13]; but, if it is true that Chaucer heard this tale from Petrarch himself, can it be that Petrarch did not speak to Chaucer of the original in the *Decameron*? It may be so, but we do not believe it.

As we have already pointed out, it may be possible that although Chaucer knew several of Boccaccio's tales he may not have known this particular one. It may be that when he wrote his *Clerk's Tale*, he had not yet finished reading the *Decameron*, but it is most likely that Chaucer was more familiar with Latin than with Italian, and that therefore he preferred to take this tale from Petrarch. To this add that at that time the *Decameron* was not very much esteemed by many people, that Boccaccio had already repented of having written it, and it will not be difficult to understand why he chose Petrarch's translation, and also why he never mentioned Boccaccio in his works.

It does not matter to us whether Boccaccio was the true originator of the story, or whether the story is very old, as Petrarch himself states, or whether it was taken from life and that Griselda really existed. For us it is enough to state with certainty, that Boccaccio originated this masterpiece which gave birth to many imitations and different compositions throughout Europe, chiefly in Italy, France, Germany and England, and that, after all, Chaucer's *Clerk's Tale*, in spite of being a translation from Petrarch, is nothing else than Boccaccio's *Decameron*, which he translated. It is therefore the art of Boccaccio that he brought to England, and besides the fact of having certainly heard the *Decameron* and its author spoken about is another argument in our favour to prove that Chaucer knew this work.

Yet Chaucer did not translate this splendid tale without

curtailing much of what was of no use for his purpose and without adding something of his own. This was usual in Chaucer, who never was a "mere slavish translator[14]". Sometimes he altered for the worse and sometimes for the better. In this tale the changes he introduces really improve it: he omits a proem in which are many valuable, but, in this case, useless geographical notions, and he adds a passage on the fidelity of women, which gives so much pathos to the tale that many a critic has very much praised the English poet, and judged that the English version is perhaps superior to the Italian original. . . .

However that may be, the fact remains that he wrote this book, which does him credit, because, after Dante, Petrarch and Boccaccio, he was the first, and in England the very first, to appreciate the many good qualities of woman, and to raise her from the state of servitude and servility in which she was kept during the old and middle ages. According to him woman is a daisy in her modesty and has in her beautiful candour and sincerity the magic power of curing the wounds of the heart. If in many instances Chaucer has exposed women to derision, perhaps to correct their ridiculous habits, in this book he gives a solid proof of knowing how much a virtuous woman is deserving of praise and how superior she is to every eulogy. . . .

Our Carducci has stated that the *Decameron* is the human comedy just as Dante's work is the *Divine Comedy*. Even in this Chaucer resembles Boccaccio: if Chaucer had been born three centuries later, he would have been the English Molière just as Boccaccio would have been another Goldoni if he had lived in the XVI or XVII century.

Unhappily for us, and for the English, at that time the modern drama was not yet born, and the miracle-plays of the XIV century could not be attractive either to Boccaccio or to Chaucer. Nay, there was not yet even the embryo of the modern drama, but the vividness of the imagination of these two writers, their humour, their scorn of hypocrisy, their cleverness in seeing deeply into the heart of man, caused them to be considered as true dramatists before drama existed.

It is so true that there is dramatic power in their compositions that afterwards some subjects which are common to both Boccaccio and Chaucer were successfully brought on the stage. . . .

He died, but his works did not. Not only is it not the place here, but it is also beyond our purpose to describe the influence which they had and are still having on English literature. Up to the beginning of the Elizabethan era nothing could compare with the *Canterbury Tales*, which has till now borne fruit in a long succession of prose writers, and poets and painters. In this respect we may say that Chaucer's influence in England was superior to Boccaccio's in Italy: Chaucer had no rival in his country, whilst in Italy Dante and Petrarch were at least as famous as Boccaccio.

We do not know of any two other writers more similar, or more equal in their general characteristics than Boccaccio and Chaucer: they approach to one another closer than friends, than master and disciple, than father and son, than two brothers. Nature had given them both qualities which no one can acquire by one's self: healthy, gay, sincere and high-minded, they seem to belong to a time in which mankind had fewer cares than at present. What can we say of Boccaccio that we cannot say also of Chaucer? Either little or nothing. They are two of the most learned men of their time. As to Boccaccio, his commentary on the first sixteen cantos of the *Divine Comedy* would suffice to prove this assertion. As to Chaucer his *Astrolabe* shows that he was something of an astronomer, his *Tale of the Chanon's Yeoman* shows that he was a philosopher, his

Parson's Tale shows his knowledge of Divinity. There was no gloom in them, therefore they could easily penetrate to the heart of every man, and judge with certainty, and, as we have already pointed out, they are the true historians of their time. In their works there are pictures of public and domestic life: the clergyman is there represented in his good and his bad qualities, and so is the landlord and the poor workman, the great lady, the poor servant maid and the country-woman. On the scene of the world painted by these two authors we see in turn men and women of every social rank; now shameless vice and now modest virtue, now wickedness and deceit, now goodness, truthfulness, sincerity: all the different characters of mankind pass before our eyes as in life. And all this is brightly narrated with a freedom and vividness of imagination which our present novelists would be very proud to possess.

They were religious, but their religion, except perhaps in their later years, never approached bigotry or superstition. In any case they were always more moral than many other famous writers: indeed the only reproach which has been made to them is that in their youth they were rather unscrupulous in their love affairs. Severe critics and fearless accusers of the vices of the clergy, they were in their turn accused of having brought religion into contempt. It was not so: they reproached the vicious clergyman, but never religion itself, and if Chaucer ever espoused the cause of Wickliffe, it was certainly not for want of religion.

They both loved learning and books, but their love of nature was stronger and more absorbing, so that their works remain fresh and green, and can still be not only read, but studied with enthusiasm.

They are both the pioneers of a new language, of a new literature, we could say also of a new civilisation, and therefore they are full of natural inspirations. They copied directly from nature and put themselves between nature and the literary geniuses following them.

They were both good writers in prose and poetry, but Boccaccio wrote better prose and Chaucer better poetry. They both had great power of satire and great influence not only on literature, but also on morality and they deserve fully the monument of immortality erected to them by the generations that followed them.

Notes

1. Casini.
2. Morley.
3. Chiarini.
4. Tyrwhitt.
5. Morley.
6. Koch.
7. Casini.
8. Chiarini.
9. Taine.
10. Warton.
11. Skeat.
12. Craik.
13. Chiarini.
14. Ward.

SIR WALTER RALEIGH
From "Lecture on Chaucer"
On Writers and Writing
1926, ed. Gordon, pp. 108–19

Chaucer's strong sanity and critical commonsense, his quick power of observation, and his distaste for all extravagances and follies helped to make him a great comic poet. But he is not a railing wit, or a bitter satirist. His broad and calm philosophy of life, his delight in diversities of character, his sympathy with all kinds of people, and his zest in all varieties of experience—these are the qualities of a humorist.

Charles Lamb thought with misgiving of a heaven in which all irony and ironical modes of expression should be lacking. Certainly it would be no heaven for Chaucer. The all-pervading essence of his work is humour. Sometimes it breaks out in boisterous and rollicking laughter at the drunken and unseemly exploits of churls; sometimes it is so delicate and evanescent that you can hardly detect its existence. But it is everywhere, even in places where it has no right to be. The intellectual pleasure of standing aside and seeing things against an incongruous background was a pleasure he could not long forgo.

In this matter, and in this alone, Chaucer is sometimes guilty of what I shall call 'literary bad manners.' It is like the fault of distracted attention. Even at a funeral he must insinuate his jest. Now, it is quite excusable to jest at a funeral so long as it is regarded as a formal, official function; or if it is merely matter for thought. The suit of clay as the dwelling-house made for this creature a little lower than the angels is a jest of the Gods. But Chaucer will arouse deep feelings of pathos and sympathy, and in the atmosphere thus created, he will let off a little crackling penny jest, from pure love of mischief. This spirit of witty mischief is always breaking out.

Chaucer has the true humorist's gift—the gift of the wooden face. He utters a truism ('Honesty is the best policy') with a solemn air; and only the faintest twinkle in the eye makes one hesitate in believing him serious.

Chaucer's self-consciousness is of a piece with his critical art. Sometimes (as in *Troilus* and the *Knight's Tale*) he is fairly caught in the web of his own imagination, and forgets himself. Far more frequently he reminds you of his presence by some sly allusion to himself, or some ironical piece of self-deprecation. Then the tale becomes a mere tale again, and we come back into the company of the teller.

This is a common trait of the humorist. He sees much that is ridiculous in human life; what if he himself is ridiculous? So he anticipates criticism, and discounts the retort, by laughing at himself.

You will find this in Falstaff ('I do here walk before thee like a sow that hath overwhelmed all her litter but one.') You may find it in all the jackanapes tricks of Sterne, his posturings and grimaces. You will find it in Mr. Bernard Shaw, who cannot forget that laughter is generally a hostile weapon, and is unwilling to stand the push of it in championing his ideas. Being skilled with it, he over-values it and over-fears it. So, like Bob Acres, he stands edgeways, or turns his weapon against himself, that he may still be on the side of the laughers.

This furnishes excellent wit and comedy, but is not consistent with good epical work. The man who is afraid of being caught in a serious sentiment lest others should find it ridiculous, cannot tell a moving tale in a forthright, whole-hearted way. His mind is a kingdom divided against itself,—under two kings, a warrior and a clown. A cavalry charge cannot be led by one who is thinking of the figure he cuts in the eyes of a bystander. The professions of reformer and humorist have never been successfully combined. A reformer does not care who laughs.

The escape from this sort of self-consciousness—the besetting sin of the professed humorist—is in the drama; and all Chaucer's best and deepest humour occurs in parts of his work that are dramatic in everything but form. The dramatist stands aside and has not to defend himself. He speaks through many voices, and is himself unseen. He looks at human life and portrays it, and smiles.

All profound dramatic humour depends on sympathy and breadth of view, that keeps sight of the whole even while it spends delighted attention on a part. A wit or a satirist can be angry and laugh; he can laugh at what he misunderstands and misrepresents. The dramatic humorist laughs because he understands and enjoys. Now there never was a poet whose zest and delight in life was fuller and broader than Chaucer's. He hates nothing that he has made; in the realms of his creation the sun shines upon the evil and the good. His characters, as they come alive, almost always find in him an admirer and abetter. Pandarus, it is to be supposed, was originally designed to be a base, broken lackey, just as Falstaff may have been designed for a shallow, vainglorious, lying heartless rascal. But Pandarus, like Falstaff, comes alive, and we end by almost loving him. He has the worldly wisdom, the shrewd humour, the tender affections, and the philosophic outlook of his creator. He is a good friend, and, like Falstaff, he too is a poet.

Anything fair to see or hear awakes Chaucer's enthusiasm. Of Troilus riding into Troy he says:—

It was an hevene upon him for to see!

When the people applaud, Troilus blushes:—

That to biholde it was a noble game.

When Antigone sings in the garden:—

It an heven was hir voys to here.

Anything on a large and generous scale, such as the housekeeping of the Franklin ('It snewed in his hous of mete and drinke'), or the marriages of the Wife of Bath, arouses Chaucer's sympathy. He loves a rogue, so that the rogue be high-spirited and clever at his trade, and not a whey-faced, bloodless rascal. The Pardoner, in describing his own preaching, says:—

Myn hondes and my tonge goon so yerne,
That it is joye to see my bisiness,

and so Chaucer felt it. His joy is chronic and irrepressible.

Chaucer makes the most enormous claim on the sound sense and quick intelligence of his readers. He assumes that they are at one with him, and that it is unnecessary for him to expound his point of view. The natural form for the dramatic sense of humour is irony. Often enough Chaucer's irony is dramatic, as when the Carpenter, in the very act of being befooled by Nicholas the clerk, congratulates himself that he is a plain, unlearned man. But the best of Chaucer's irony is found in his own interpolated utterances. He seems to be telling the story simply and directly. Suspect him! He is conveying his own criticisms, expressing his own amusement, in touches—a word here and a word there—so subtle and delicate that eleven out of twelve men in any jury would acquit him of any comic intent. These quiet smiles that flicker over his face are so characteristic that I have ventured to call the passages where we can detect them *Chaucerisms*. Take the 'Shipman's Tale':—

A Marchant whylom dwelled at Seint Denys,
That riche was, for which men helde him wys,

Chaucer is at his work already.

When the merchant returns from abroad,

His wyf ful redy mette him atte gate
As she was wont of olde usage algate.

How quietly, almost inaudibly, Chaucer indicates that she had no very lively affection for her husband!

It is impossible to overpraise Chaucer's mastery of language. Here at the beginning, as it is commonly reckoned, of

Modern English literature, is a treasury of perfect speech. We can trace his themes, and tell something of the events of his life. But where did he get his style—from which it may be said that English literature has been (in some respects) a long falling away?

What is the ordinary account? I do not wish to cite individual scholars, and there is no need. Take what can be gathered from the ordinary text-books—what are the current ideas? Is not this a fair statement of them?

> English was a despised language little used by the upper classes. A certain number of dreary works written chiefly for homiletic purposes, or in order to appeal to the humble people, are to be found in the half century before Chaucer. They are poor and flat and feeble, giving no promise of the new dawn. Then arose the morning star! Chaucer adopted the despised English tongue and set himself to modify it, to shape it, to polish it, to render it fit for his purpose. He imported words from the French; he purified the English of his time from its dross; he shaped it into a fit instrument for his use.

Now I have no doubt that a competent philologist examining the facts could easily show that this account *must be* nonsense, from beginning to end. But even a literary critic can say something certain on the point—perhaps can even give aid by divination to the philologists, and tell them where it will best repay them to ply their pickaxes and spades.

No poet makes his own language. No poet introduces serious or numerous modifications into the language that he uses. Some, no doubt, coin words and revive them, like Spenser or Keats in verse, Carlyle or Sir Thomas Browne in prose. But least of all great English poets did Chaucer mould and modify the speech he found. The poets who take liberties with speech are either prophets or eccentrics. From either of these characters Chaucer was far removed. He held fast by communal and social standards for literary speech. He desired to be understood of the people. His English is plain, terse, homely, colloquial English, taken alive out of daily speech. He expresses his ideal again and again, as when the Host asks what is the use of telling a tale that sends the hearers to sleep:—

> For certeinly, as that thise clerkes seyn,
> Where-as a man may have noon audience,
> Noght helpeth it to tellen his sentence.

The same admirable literary critic repeats Chaucer's creed when he instructs the Clerk:—

> Your termes, your colours, and your figures,
> Kepe hem in stoor till so be ye endite
> Heigh style, as whan that men to kinges write,
> Speketh so pleyn at this tyme, I yow preye,
> That we may understonde what ye seye.

Chaucer has expressed his views on the model literary style so clearly and so often, and has illustrated them so well in his practice, that no mistake is possible. His style is the perfect courtly style: it has all the qualities of ease, directness, simplicity, of the best colloquial English, in short, which Chaucer recognised, three centuries before the French Academy, as the English spoken by cultivated women in society. His 'facound,' like Virginia's, 'is ful womanly and pleyn.' He avoids all 'counterfeted terms,' all subtleties of rhetoric, and addresses himself to the 'commune intente.'

Examples of his plain, terse brevity are easy to find. Take one, from the *Monk's Tale*—of Hugelin of Pisa. (The imprisoned father bites his hands for grief; his young sons think it is for hunger):

> His children wende that it for hunger was
> That he his armes gnew, and not for wo,
> And seyde, 'Fader, do not so, allas!
> But rather ete the flessh upon us two;
> Our flesh thou yaf us, take our flesh us fro,
> And ete y-nough': right thus they to him seyde,
> And after that, with-in a day or two,
> They leyde hem in his lappe adoun, and deyde.

Now a style like this, and in this perfection, implies a society at the back of it. If we are told that educated people at the Court of Edward III spoke French and that English was a despised tongue, we could deny it on the evidence of Chaucer alone. His language was shaped for him, and it cannot have been shaped by rustics. No English style draws so much as Chaucer's from the communal and colloquial elements of the language. And his poems make it certain that from his youth up he had heard much admirable, witty talk in the English tongue.

The conclusion is that Chaucer's language is the language of his own day, like Gower's, but used by a quicker intelligence, and freer from repetition, artificial tags, flatnesses, etc. It was his good fortune to live at a time when bookish learning had not yet severed classes. He broke loose from the literary fashions which at all time affect the 'educated classes,' and wrote the good English of peers and peasants. In this respect he comes near to the poets of Dryden's age.

This language was his own, not painfully acquired. Ease and skill of this kind is not attainable save in the birth tongue. Too much has been made of French; and of the dates of the 'adoption' of English for public documents, law courts, schools. The English language had throughout a healthy, full-blooded existence. Chaucer had no adequate *literary* predecessors in English. But how partial and poor a thing the manuscript literature of the time compared with the riches of spoken lore, proverb, tale and romance! As Chaucer helps us, by his portrait of the age, to correct the formal annalists, so he helps us, by his writing, to a truer appreciation of literary history.

If there is to be any profitable investigation of Chaucer's language it must be remembered that he is at the *end* of an age, not at the beginning. His pupils could make nothing of him, and the Renaissance brought in ideals which made him unintelligible. Like Burns, Chaucer is a culmination and a close. We can understand Burns only by remembering his debts to Fergusson, Ramsay, and scores of nameless poets. If we are to understand Chaucer, it must be by reference to a tribe of story-tellers, songsters, traffickers in popular lore and moral maxims who, because they did not relate themselves to paper, have almost passed, except by inference, from our ken.

123

SIR PHILIP SIDNEY

SIR PHILIP SIDNEY

1554–1586

Sir Philip Sidney, poet, statesman, and scholar, was born in 1554, at Penshurst, Kent. He attended Christ Church, Oxford, from 1568 to 1571, after which he toured the Continent from 1572 to 1575. A noted courtier, Sidney fell into disfavor in 1577 because of his outspoken opinions. While visiting his sister at Wilton, he began writing *Arcadia*, as well as pursuing such other projects as a translation of the Psalms with his sister. Eventually Sidney returned to court and in 1583 was knighted. He married Frances Walsingham in the same year. In 1586 he died from a bullet wound in his thigh while fighting the Spaniards. Sidney's major works include *Arcadia*, a pastoral prose romance written between 1580 and 1583 (published in 1590); *Astrophel and Stella*, the first sonnet sequence in English (published in 1591); and the *Apology for Poetrie*, written between 1581 and 1584 (published in 1595). Sidney was considered an ideal Renaissance man, uniting the qualities of soldier, patron, poet, and critic; his death inspired numerous elegies.

Personal

To the Noble and Vertuous Gentleman, most worthy of all titles both of Learning and Chevalrie.—EDMUND SPENSER, Title Page of *The Shepheardes Calendar*, 1579

To the right noble Gentleman, Master Philip Sidney Esquier, Stephan Gosson wisheth health of body, wealth of minde, rewarde of vertue, aduauncement of honour and good successe in godly affaires.—STEPHAN GOSSON, Dedication to *The Schoole of Abuse*, 1579

The return of the young gentleman, your sonne, whose message verie sufficientlie performed, and the relatinge thereof, is no less gratefully received and well liked of Her Majestie, than the honourable opinion he hath left behinde him with all the princes with whomme he had to negotiate, hathe left a most sweet savor and grateful remembraunce of his name in those parts. . . . There hath not been any gentleman, I am sure, these many yeres, that hathe gon through so honourable a charge with as great commendacions as he.—SIR FRANCIS WALSINGHAM, Letter to Sir Henry Sidney, 1586

Silence augmenteth griefe, writing encreaseth rage,
Staid are my thoughts, which loved and lost, the wonder of
  our age,
Yet quickened now with fire, though dead with frost ere now,
Enraged I write I know not what: dead, quick, I know not how.
Hard hearted mindes relent, and Rigor's tears abound,
And Envy strangely rues his end, in whom no fault she found;
Knowledge his light hath lost, Valor hath slaine her knight:
Sidney is dead, dead is my friend, dead is the world's
  delight.
 . . .
A spotless friend, a matchless man, whose vertue ever shined.
 . . .
He onely like himselfe, was second unto none.
 . . .
Death slue not him, but he made death his ladder
  to the skies.
     —FULKE GREVILLE (LORD BROOKE), *On Sir
     Philip Sidney*, 1586

Gentle *Sir Philip Sidney*, thou knewest what belonged to a Scholler, thou knewest what paines, what toile, what travell, conduct to perfection: wel couldst thou give every Vertue his encouragement, every Art his due, every writer his desert: cause none more vertuous, witty, or learned than thy selfe.—THOMAS NASHE, *Pierce Penilesse*, 1592

Sidney, the Syren of this latter Age;
  Sidney, the Blazing star of England's glory;
Sidney, the Wonder of the wise and sage;
  Sidney, the Subject of true Virtue's story;
    This Syren, Star, this Wonder, and this Subject,
    Is dumb, dim, gone, and marr'd by Fortune's
    Object.
    —RICHARD BARNFIELD, *The Affectionate
    Shepherd*, 1594

Still living Sidney, Cæsar of our land,
Whose never daunted valure, princely minde,
Imbellished with art and conquests hand,
Did expleiten his high aspiring kinde
(An eagles hart in crowes we cannot finde)
  If thou couldst live and purchase Orpheus quill,
  Our Monarches merits would exceed thy skill.
    —SIR WILLIAM HARBERT, *A Prophesie of
    Cadwallader*, 1604

Immortall *Sidney*, glory of the field
And glory of the Muses, and their pen
(Who equall bare the *Caduce* and the *Shield*).
    —SAMUEL DANIEL, "A Funerall Poeme upon the
    Earle of Devonshire," 1606, *Works*, Vol. 1, ed.
    Grosart, p. 176

O! but Gentry now degenerates! Nobilitie is now come to be *nuda relatio*, a meere bare relation and nothing else. How manie Players haue I seene vpon a stage, fit indeede to be Noblemen! how many that be Noblemen, fit onely to represent them.—Why, this can Fortune do, who makes some companions of her Chariot, who for desert should be lackies to her Ladiship. . . . Rise, Sidney, rise! thou England's eternall honour! Reuiue and lead the reuolting spirits of thy countreymen, against the basest foe, Ignorance. But what talke I of thee? Heauen hath not left earth thy equall: neither do I thinke that *ab orbe condito*, since Nature first was, any man hath beene in whom *Genus* and *Genius* met so right. Thou Atlas to all vertues! Thou Hercules to the Muses! Thou patron to the poor! Thou deserust a Quire of ancient *Bardi* to sing thy praises, who with their musickes melody might expresse thy soules harmonie. Were the transmigration of soules certaine—I would thy soule had flitted into my bodie or wold thou wert aliue again, that we might lead an indiuiduall life together! Thou wast not more admired at home then famous abroad; thy penne and thy sword being the Heraldes of thy Heroicke deedes.—ANTHONY STAFFORD, *Niobe*, 1611, p. 112

> Th' admired mirrour, glory of our Isle,
> Thou far-far-more than mortall man, whose stile
> Strucke more men dumbe to hearken to thy song,
> Then Orpheus Harpe, or Tullies golden tongue.
> To him (as right) for wits deepe quintessence,
> For honour, valour, virtue, excellence,
> Be all the Garlands, crowne his toombe with Ray,
> Who spake as much as eer our tongue can say.
> 　　—WILLIAM BROWNE, *Britannia's Pastorals*,
> 　　　1613, Vol. 1, Bk. 2, Song 2, ed. Hazlitt

Of whose Youth I will report no other wonder, but thus: That though I lived with him, and knew him from a child, yet I never knew him other than a man: with such staiednes of mind, lovely, and familiar gravity, as carried grace, and reverence above greater years. His talk ever of knowledge, and his very play tending to enrich his mind; So as even his teachers found something in him to observe, and learn, above that which they had usually read, or taught. Which eminence, by nature, and industry made his worthy Father stile Sir *Philip* in my hearing (though I unseen) *Lumen familiæ suæ.*—FULKE GREVILLE (LORD BROOKE), *Life of Sir Philip Sidney*, c. 1628–52

For his education, it was such as travell, and the University could afford, or his Tutours infuse; for after an incredible proficiency in all the species of Learning; he left the Academicall life, for that of the Court, whither he came by his Uncles invitation, famed afore-hand by a noble report of his accomplishments, which together with the state of his person, framed by a naturall propension to Armes, he soon attracted the good opinion of all men, and was so highly prized in the good opinion of the Queen, that she thought the Court deficient without him: And whereas (through the fame of his deserts) he was in the election for the Kingdom of *Pole*, she refused to further his advancement, not out of emulation, but out of fear to lose the jewell of her times.—SIR ROBERT NAUNTON, *Fragmenta Regalia*, c. 1630, ed. Arber, p. 34

Sir Philip Sydney, knight, was the most accomplished cavalier of his time. . . . He was not only of an excellent witt, but extremely beautifull; he much resembled his sister, but his haire was not red, but a little inclining, viz. a darke amber colour. If I were to find a fault in it, methinkes 'tis not masculine enough; yett he was a person of great courage.—JOHN AUBREY, *Brief Lives*, 1669–96, Vol. 2, ed. Clark, p. 247

No man seems to me so astonishing an object of temporary admiration as the celebrated friend of the lord Brooke, the famous Sir Philip Sidney. The learned of Europe dedicated their works to him; the republic of Poland thought him at least worthy to be in the nomination for their crown. All the muses of England wept his death. When we, at this distance of time, inquire what prodigious merits excited such admiration, what do we find? Great valour.—But it was an age of heroes.—In full of all other talents, we have a tedious, lamentable, pedantic, pastoral romance, which the patience of a young virgin in love cannot now wade through; and some absurd attempts to fetter English verse in Roman chains; a proof that this applauded author understood little of the genius of his own language. The few of his letters extant are poor matters; one to a steward of his father, an instance of unwarrantable violence. By

far the best presumption of his abilities (to us who can judge only by what we see) is a pamphlet published amongst the Sidney papers, being an answer to the famous libel called "Leicester's Commonwealth." It defends his uncle with great spirit. What had been said in derogation to their blood seems to have touched sir Philip most. He died with the rashness of a volunteer, having lived to write with the *sang-froid* and prolixity of mademoiselle Scuderi.—HORACE WALPOLE, *A Catalogue of the Royal and Noble Authors of England, Scotland, and Ireland*, 1758, Vol. 2, ed. Park, p. 230

> 　　　　　Sidney here was born;
> Sidney, than whom no gentler, braver man
> His own delightful genius ever feigned,
> Illustrating the vales of Arcady
> With courteous courage and with loyal loves.
> Upon his natal day, an acorn here
> Was planted: it grew up a stately oak,
> And in the beauty of its strength it stood
> And flourished, when his perishable part
> Had mouldered, dust to dust. That stately oak
> Itself hath mouldered now, but Sidney's fame
> Endureth in his own immortal works.
> 　　—ROBERT SOUTHEY, *For a Tablet at Penshurst*,
> 　　　1799

The life of Sir Philip Sydney was poetry put into action.— THOMAS CAMPBELL, *Essay on English Poetry*, 1819

> 　　. . . Sidney, as he fought
> And as he fell and as he lived and loved
> Sublimely mild, a Spirit without spot.
> 　　—PERCY BYSSHE SHELLEY, *Adonais*, 1821,
> 　　　Stanza 45

The noble images, passions, sentiments, and poetical delicacies of character, scattered all over the *Arcadia* (spite of some stiffness and encumberment), justify to me the character which his contemporaries have left us of the writer. I cannot think with the Critic, that Sir Philip Sydney was that *opprobrious thing* which a foolish nobleman in his insolent hostility chose to term him. I call to mind the epitaph made on him, to guide me to juster thoughts of him.—CHARLES LAMB, "Some Sonnets of Sir Philip Sydney," *London Magazine*, Sept. 1823

Was the idol of his time, and perhaps no figure reflects the age more fully and more beautifully. Fair as he was brave, quick of wit as of affection, noble and generous in temper, dear to Elizabeth as to Spenser, the darling of the Court and of the camp, his learning and his genius made him the centre of the literary world which was springing into birth on English soil. He had traveled in France and Italy, he was master alike of the older learning and of the new discoveries of astronomy. Bruno dedicated to him as to a friend his metaphysical speculations; he was familiar with the drama of Spain, the poems of Ronsard, the sonnets of Italy. He combined the wisdom of a grave councilor with the romantic chivalry of a knight-errant.— JOHN RICHARD GREEN, *A Short History of the English People*, 1874, Ch. 7

Sidney was prompt and rapid in mental movement; he formed opinions and translated them into action with great alacrity. In the very typical case of his quarrel with Lord Oxford we find him keeping his head when most men would have lost it from sheer rage; but it was all that the Queen and the Privy Council could do to prevent him from having the Earl's blood. Unquestionably he looked mild; he had a girlish face of pink and white; and Oxford, no doubt, did not know his man when he dared to bully him. But there was wiry fibre in Sidney's mind and body, and we may be sure that, in those fighting days, no mere carpet-knight would have impressed himself on the popular mind as a hero. His extraordinary ability in all the diplomatic arts is quite beyond dispute. To be a diplomatist, a man must possess sympathy, and have a rare judgment in the use of it. The ideal diplomatist, like the ideal poet, is a man in whom the masculine and feminine qualities of the intellect balance one another with absolute harmony, each supplying the wants of the other side of the character. What is related of Sidney tends to prove that he possessed this equilibrium to a very extraordinary degree, and I take it to have been the secret of his charm and of his power.—EDMUND GOSSE, "Sir Philip Sidney," *Contemporary Review*, 1886, p. 638

The real difficulty of painting an adequate portrait of Sidney at the present time is that his renown transcends his actual achievement. Neither his poetry nor his prose, nor what is known about his action, quite explains the singular celebrity which he enjoyed in his own life, and the fame which has attended his memory with almost undimmed lustre through three centuries. . . . Few spirits so blameless, few so thoroughly prepared to enter upon new spheres of activity and discipline, have left this earth. The multitudes who knew him personally, those who might have been jealous of him, and those who owed him gratitude, swelled one chorus in praise of his natural goodness, his intellectual strength and moral beauty. We who study his biography, and dwell upon their testimony to his charm, derive from Sidney the noblest lesson bequeathed by Elizabethan to Victorian England.—JOHN ADDINGTON SYMONDS, *Sir Philip Sidney (English Men of Letters)*, 1886, pp. 1, 199

Englishmen, everywhere, are proud of this fine gentleman, Sidney, who can talk in so many languages, who can turn a sonnet to a lady's eyebrow, who can fence with the best swordsmen of any court, who can play upon six instruments of music, who can outdance even his Grace of Anjou.—DONALD G. MITCHELL, *English Lands, Letters and Kings: From Celt to Tudor*, 1889, p. 239

General

Our English Petrarch.—SIR JOHN HARRINGTON, "Notes on Book XVI," *Translation of Ariosto*, 1591, p. 126

> Liberal Sidney, famous for the love
> He bare to learning and to chivalry.
> —GEORGE PEELE, "Ad Maecenatem Prologus,"
>   *The Honour of the Garter*, 1593

Oh, for some excellent pen-man to deplore their state: but he which would lively, naturally, or indeed poetically, delyneate or enumerate these occurrents, shall either lead you thereunto by a poeticall spirit, as could well, if well he might, the dead-living, life-giving Sydney, Prince of Poesie.—SIR THOMAS SMITHES, *Voiage and Entertainment in Rushia*, 1605

> That poets are far rarer births than kings,
> Your noblest father proved; like whom, before,
> Or then, or since, about our Muses' springs,
> Came not that soul exhausted so their store.
> —BEN JONSON, "To Elizabeth, Countess of
>   Rutland," 1616, *Epigrams*, No. 79

The King said Sir P. Sidney was no poet.—WILLIAM DRUMMOND, *Notes of Ben Jonson's Conversations*, 1619, ed. Laing, p. 26

> The noble Sidney . . .
> That hero for numbers, and for prose,

> That thoroughly pac'd our language, as to show
> The plenteous English hand in hand might go
> With Greek and Latin, and did first reduce
> Our tongue from Lilly's writing then in use.
> —MICHAEL DRAYTON, *Of Poets and Poesie*, c.
>   1627

The true spirit or vein of ancient poetry in this kind seems to shine most in Sir Philip Sidney, whom I esteem both the greatest poet and the noblest genius of any that have left writings behind them, and published in ours or any other modern language; a person born capable not only of forming the greatest ideas, but of leaving the noblest examples, if the length of his life had been equal to the excellence of his wit and virtues.—SIR WILLIAM TEMPLE, *Of Poetry*, 1628–98, *Works*, Vol. 3, p. 412

> Love's foe profess'd! why dost thou falsely feign
> Thyself a Sidney? from which noble strain
> He sprung, that could so far exalt the name
> Of Love, and warm a nation with his flame;
> That all we can of love or high desire
> Seems but the smoke of amorous Sidney's fire.
> —EDMUND WALLER, *At Penshurst*, c. 1636

> Sidneian showers
> Of sweet discourse, whose powers
> Can crown old winter's head with flowers.
> —RICHARD CRASHAW, "Wishes to His Supposed
>   Mistress," *The Delights of the Muses*, 1646–48

> Nor can the Muse the gallant Sidney pass,
> The plume of war! with early laurels crown'd,
> The lover's myrtle and the poet's bay.
> —JAMES THOMSON, "Summer," *The Seasons*,
>   1727

> Sidney's verse halts ill on Roman feet.
> —ALEXANDER POPE, *Imitations of Horace*, 1733,
>   Bk. 2, Epistle 1, v. 98

Had Sir Philip paid an exclusive attention to the poetical art, there is every reason to suppose that he would have occupied a master's place in this department; as it is, his poetry, though too often vitiated by an intermixture of antithesis and false wit, and by an attempt to introduce the classic metres, is still rich with frequent proofs of vigour, elegance, and harmony.—NATHAN DRAKE, *Shakspeare and His Times*, 1817, Vol. 1, p. 652

Though we cannot admit for a moment that the poetry of Sidney is debased by the vile alloy of licentiousness and pruriency, we are not blind to many other vices with which it may most justly be charged. Our author was styled, by Raleigh, the English Petrarch; and without doubt he derived many of his faults as well as excellencies from the bard of Arezzo, whom he frequently imitated both in his manner and in his exaggerated turn of expression. It was from this foreign prototype that he was probably smitten with the love of antithesis and conceit, and the other fashionable absurdities in which our best writers of sonnets then abounded.—WILLIAM GRAY, *Life of Sidney*, 1829, Boston ed., p. 36

Penshurst, when I first saw it (in 1791), was the holiest ground I had ever visited. Forty years have not abated my love and veneration for Sydney. I do not remember any character more nearly without reproach. His prose is full of poetry; and there are very fine passages among his poems,—distinguishing them from his metres, in which there is scarcely even a redeeming line, thought, or expression.—ROBERT SOUTHEY, Letter to Sir Egerton Brydges, 1830, *Brydges' Autobiography*, Vol. 2, p. 267

The truth is, that the life of Sidney is more poetical than his works; the whole tenor of his conduct is romance brought into action; and we insensibly transfer the admiration we feel for his warm humanity and his nobleness of soul, to works, which, except as they are tinged with the poetry of his character, possess little literary value.—J. H. HIPPISLEY, *Chapters on Early English Literature*, 1837, p. 250

> The silver speech
> Of Sidney's self, the starry paladin,
> Turn intense as a trumpet sounding in
> The knights to tilt,—wert thou to hear!
> —ROBERT BROWNING, *Sordello*, 1840, Bk. 1, v.
> 68–71

In the world of letters, then, Sir Philip Sidney took, for his years, rank singularly high. But we must never forget that literature was his only amusement. He knew that he had statesmanly and martial powers, which he was eager to be using. He longed, with the wild earnestness of a caged bird, for room to take his part in the great battle of freedom which was going on around him. For such work he was best fitted, and it is for the glorious beginning made by him herein that we owe him largest honour. But, knowing this we can only the more marvel that the songs with which he lightened his captivity were so eloquent, and that the truths which his youth enforced in idle moments came out of the depths of so mature a mind.—H. R. FOX BOURNE, *A Memoir of Sir Philip Sidney*, 1862, p. 419

His prose, as prose, is not equal to his friend Raleigh's, being less condensed and stately. It is too full of fancy in thought and freak in rhetoric to find now-a-days more than a very limited number of readers; and a good deal of the verse that is set in it, is obscure and uninteresting, partly from some false notions of poetic composition which he and his friend Spenser entertained when young; but there is often an exquisite art in his other poems.—GEORGE MACDONALD, *England's Antiphon*, 1868, p. 77

Sir Philip Sidney, born the year after ⟨Spenser⟩, with a keener critical instinct, and a taste earlier emancipated than his own, would have been, had he lived longer, perhaps even more directly influential in educating the taste and refining the vocabulary of his contemporaries and immediate successors. The better of his pastoral poems in the *Arcadia* are, in my judgment, more simple, natural, and, above all, more pathetic than those of Spenser, who sometimes strains the shepherd's pipe with a blast that would better suit the trumpet. Sidney had the good sense to feel that it was unsophisticated sentiment rather than rusticity of phrase that befitted such themes. He recognized the distinction between simplicity and vulgarity, which Wordsworth was so long in finding out, and seems to have divined the fact that there is but one kind of English that is always appropriate and never obsolete, namely, the very best. With the single exception of Thomas Campion, his experiments in adapting classical metres to English verse are more successful than those of his contemporaries. Some of his elegiacs are not ungrateful to the ear, and it can hardly be doubted that Coleridge borrowed from his eclogue of Strephon and Klaius the pleasing movement of his own *Catullian Hendecasyllabics*.—JAMES RUSSELL LOWELL, "Spenser," 1875, *Prose Works*, Vol. 4, Riverside ed., p. 276

Michael Drayton, in some verse complimentary to Sidney, stigmatises not much too strongly Lyly's prevailing faults, and attributes to the hero of Zutphen the purification of England from euphuism. This is hardly critical. That Sidney—a young man, and a man of fashion at the time when Lyly's oddities were fashionable—should have to a great extent resisted the temptation to imitate them (for his resistance is by no means absolute) is very creditable. But the influence of *Euphues* was at least as strong for many years as the influence of the *Arcadia* and the *Apology*; and the chief thing that can be said for Sidney is that he did not wholly follow Lyly to do evil. Nor is his positive excellence in prose to be compared for a moment with his positive excellence in poetry. His life is so universally known that nothing need be said about it beyond reminding the reader that he was born, as Lyly is supposed to have been, in 1554; that he was the son of Sir Henry Sidney, afterwards Viceroy of Ireland, and of Lady Mary, eldest daughter of the luckless Dudley, Duke of Northumberland; that he was educated at Shrewsbury and Christ Church, travelled much, acquiring the repute of one of the most accomplished cavaliers of Europe, loved without success Penelope Devereux ("Stella"), married Frances Walsingham, and died of his wounds at the battle of Zutphen, when he was not yet thirty-one years old. His prose works are the famous pastoral romance of the *Arcadia*, written to please his sister, the Countess of Pembroke, and the short *Apology for Poetrie*, a very spirited piece of work, immediately provoked by a rather silly diatribe against the theatre by one Stephan Gosson, once a playwright himself, but turned Puritan clergyman. Both appear to have been written about the same time—that is to say, between 1579 and 1581; Sidney being then in London and in the society of Spenser and other men of letters.

The amiability of Sidney's character, his romantic history, the exquisite charm of his verse at its best, and last, not least, the fact of his enthusiastic appreciation and patronage of literature at a time when literary men never failed to give aristocratic patrons somewhat more than *quid pro quo*, have perhaps caused his prose work to be traditionally a little overvalued. The *Apology for Poetry* is full of generous ardour, contains many striking and poetical expressions, and explains more than any other single book the secret of the wonderful literary production of the half-century which followed. The *Arcadia*, especially when contrasted with *Euphues*, has the great merit of abundant and stirring incident and interest, of freedom from any single affectation so pestering and continuous as Lyly's similes, and of constant purple patches of poetical description and expression, which are indeed not a little out of place in prose, but which are undeniably beautiful in themselves. But when this is said all is said. Enthusiastic as Sidney's love for poetry and for literature was, it was enthusiasm not at all according to knowledge. In the *Apology*, by his vindication of the unities, and his denunciation of the mixture of tragedy and comedy, he was (of course without knowing it) laying down exactly the two principles, a fortunate abjuration and scouting whereof gave us the greatest possession in mass and variety of merit that any literature possesses—the Elizabethan drama from Shakespere and Marlowe to Ford and Shirley. Follow Sidney, and good-bye to *Faustus*, to *Hamlet*, to *Philaster*, to *The Duchess of Malfi*, to *The Changeling*, to *The Virgin Martyr*, to *The Broken Heart*. We must content ourselves with *Gorboduc* and *Cornelia*, with *Cleopatra* and *Philotas*, at the very best with *Sejanus* and *The Silent Woman*. Again Sidney commits himself in this same piece to the pestilent heresy of prose-poetry, saying that verse is "only an ornament of poetry;" nor is there any doubt that Milton, whether he meant it or not, fixed a deserved stigma on the *Arcadia* by calling it a "vain and amatorious poem." It is a poem in prose, which is as much as to say, in other words, that it unites the faults of both kinds. Nor is Sidney less an enemy (though a "sweet enemy" in his own or Bruno's words) of the minor and more formal graces of style. If his actual vocabulary is not Latinised, or Italianised, or Lylyfied, he was one of the greatest of sinners in the special Elizabethan sin of convoluting and entangling his phrases (after the fashion best known in the mouths of Shakespere's fine gentlemen), so as to say the simplest thing in the least simple manner. Not Osric nor Iachimo detests the *mot propre* more than Sidney. Yet again, he is one of the arch offenders in the matter of spoiling the syntax of the sentence and the paragraph. As has been observed already, the unpretending writers noticed above, if they have little harmony or balance of phrase, are seldom confused or breathless. Sidney was one of the first writers of great popularity and influence (for the *Arcadia* was very widely read) to introduce what may be called the sentence-and-paragraph-heap, in which clause is linked on to clause till not merely the grammatical but the philosophical integer is hopelessly lost sight of in a tangle of jointings and appendices. It is not that he could not do better; but that he seems to have taken no trouble not to do worse. His youth, his numerous avocations, and the certainty that he never formally prepared any of his work for the press, would of course be ample excuses even if the singular and seductive beauty of many scraps throughout this work did not redeem it. But neither of the radical difference in nature and purpose between prose and verse, nor of the due discipline and management of prose itself, does Sidney seem to have had the slightest idea. Although he seldom or never reaches the beauties of the *flamboyant* period of prose, which began soon after his death and filled the middle of the seventeenth century, he contains examples of almost all its defects; and considering that he is nearly the first writer to do this, and that his writings were (and were deservedly) the favourite study of generous literary youth for more than a generation, it is scarcely uncharitable to hold him directly responsible for much mischief. The faults of *Euphues* were faults which were certain to work their own cure; those of the *Arcadia* were so engaging in themselves, and linked with so many merits and beauties, that they were sure to set a dangerous example. I believe, indeed, that if Sidney had lived he might have pruned his style not a little without weakening it, and then the richness of his imagination would probably have made him the equal of Bacon and the superior of Raleigh. But as it is, his light in English prose . . . was only too often a will-o'-the-wisp. I am aware that critics whom I respect have thought and spoken in an opposite sense, but the difference comes from a more important and radical difference of opinion as to the nature, functions, and limitations of English prose.—GEORGE SAINTSBURY, *A History of Elizabethan Literature*, 1887, pp. 40–43

Sidney, the radiant "Hesper-Phosphor" of the time of Elizabeth, fades in the brightness of that great morning, yet no radiance that follows is quite so clear and keen. He charmed by a sweet youthful gravity underlying a sweet youthful joyousness of nature. . . . He belonged heartily to the Renaissance, introducing into our prose literature the chivalric-pastoral romance, and engaging eagerly in the reform of versification and in the criticism of poetry.—EDWARD DOWDEN, *Transcripts and Studies*, 1888, pp. 282–83

Subtle, delicate, refined, with a keen and curious wit, a rare faculty of verse, a singular capacity of expression, an active but not always a true sense of form, he wrote for the few, and (it may be) the few will always love him. But his intellectual life, intense though it were, was lived among shadows and abstractions. He thought deeply, but he neither looked widely nor listened intently, and when all is said he remains no more than a brilliant amorist, too super-subtle for complete sincerity,

whose fluency and sweetness have not improved with years.—WILLIAM ERNEST HENLEY, *Views and Reviews*, 1890, p. 105

The sharper lyrical cry, the strenuous utterance of brief but deep emotion, first comes from Sidney, as in the sonnet beginning:

> Leave me, O Love, which reachest but to dust.

After this the way is open to all comers, and the full choir of song is heard in the land.—FREDERICK IVES CARPENTER, "Introduction" to *English Lyric Poetry, 1500–1700*, 1897, p. xliii

Works

ARCADIA

Read the Countesse of Pembrookes Arcadia, a gallant Legendary, full of pleasurable accidents, and profitable discourses; for three thinges especially, very notable; for amorous Courting, (he was young in yeeres;) for sage counselling, (he was ripe in judgement;) and for valorous fighting, (his soueraine profession was Armes:) and delightfull pastime by way of Pastorall exercises, may passe for the fourth. He that will Loouc, let him learn to looue of him, that will teach him to Liue; & furnish him with many pithy, and effectuall instructions, delectably interlaced by way of proper descriptions of excellent Personages, and common narrations of other notable occurrences. . . .

Liue ever sweete Booke; the siluer Image of his gentle witt, and the golden Pillar of his noble courage: and euer notify vnto the worlde, that thy Writer, was the Secretary of Eloquence; the breath of the Muses; the hooneybee of the dayntiest flowers of Witt, and Arte; the Pith of morall, & intellectuall Vertues; the arme of Bellona in the field; the toung of Suada in the chāber; the spirite of Practise in esse; and the Paragon of Excellency in Print.—GABRIEL HARVEY, *Pierces Supererogation*, 1593, *Works*, Vol. 2, ed. Grosart, pp. 100–101

Sir Philip Sidney writ his immortal poem, The Countess of Pembroke's *Arcadia*, in prose, and yet ⟨he is⟩ our rarest poet.—FRANCIS MERES, *Palladis Tamia*, 1598, p. 96

Besides its excellent language, rare contrivances, and delectable stories, ⟨Arcadia⟩ hath in it all the strains of poesy, comprehendeth the universal art of speaking, and, to them who can discern and will observe, affordeth notable rules for demeanour both private and public.—PETER HEYLIN, *Description of Arcadia in Greece*, 1622

Merely the desire of understanding so rare a book caused me to go to England, where I remained for two years in order to gain a knowledge of it.—J. BAUDOIN, *L'Arcadie de la Comtesse de Pembroke, mise en notre langue*, 1624

Those that knew him well will truly confess it to be, both in form and matter, much inferior to that unbounded spirit of his, as the industry and images of other men's works are many times raised above the writers' capacities; and besides acknowledge that however he could not choose but give them aspersions of spirit and learning from the father, yet that they were scribbled rather as pamphlets for the entertainment of time and friends than any account of himself to the world; because, if his purpose had been to leave his memory in books, I am confident, in the right use of logic, philosophy, history and poesie, nay, even in the most ingenious and mechanical arts, he would have showed such tracts of a searching and judicious spirit as the professors of every faculty would have striven no less for him than the seven cities did to have Homer of their sept; but the truth is, his end was not writing, even while he wrote, nor his knowledge moulded for tables and schools,—but both his wit and understanding bent upon his heart, to make himself and others, not in words or opinion, but in life and action, good and great.—FULKE GREVILLE (LORD BROOKE), *Life of Sir Philip Sidney*, c. 1628–52

> Sidney, warbler of poetic prose.
> —WILLIAM COWPER, *The Task*, 1785, Bk. 4

It would be an easier, though a less moral, task, to praise, than to read, four hundred and eighty-six, close printed, folio pages of such mawkish writing as this. It is singular that so gallant and distinguished a personage as sir Philip Sidney, should have written a work of these dimensions, so near to being utterly void of all genuine passion and manly spirit. To read this performance, one would think that our ancestors who admired it, had a blood that crept more feebly in their veins than we have, and that they were as yet but half awaked from the stupidity of the savage state, or, what has been called, the state of nature.— WILLIAM GODWIN, "Of English Style," *The Enquirer*, 1797

What can be more unpromising at first sight, than the idea of a young man disguising himself in woman's attire, and passing himself off for a woman among women; and that for a long space of time? Yet Sir Philip has preserved so matchless a decorum, that neither does Pyrocles' manhood suffer any stain for the effeminacy of Zelmane, nor is the respect due to the princesses at all diminished when the deception comes to be known. In the sweetly constituted mind of Sir Philip Sidney, it seems as if no ugly thought or unhandsome meditation could find a harbour. He turned all that he touched into images of honour and virtue.—CHARLES LAMB, "Specimens of Dramatic Poets," *Essays*, 1808

There are passages in this work exquisitely beautiful,—useful observations on life and manners, a variety and accurate discrimination of characters, fine sentiments, expressed in strong and adequate terms, animated descriptions, equal to any that occur in the ancient or modern poets, sage lessons of morality, and judicious reflections on government and policy. A reader who takes up the volume may be compared to a traveller who has a long and dreary road to pass. The objects that successively meet his eye may not in general be very pleasing, but occasionally he is charmed with a more beautiful prospect, with the verdure of a rich valley, with a meadow enamelled with flowers, with a murmur of a rivulet, the swelling grove, the hanging rock, the splendid villa. These charming objects abundantly compensate for the joyless regions he has traversed. They fill him with delight, exhilarate his drooping spirits, and, at the decline of day, he reposes with complacency and satisfaction.—THOMAS ZOUCH, *Memoirs of the Life and Writings of Sir Philip Sidney*, 1808

Sir Philip Sydney's *Arcadia*, the immortality of which was so fondly predicted by his admirers, and which, in truth, is full of noble thoughts, delicate images, and graceful turns of language, is now scarcely ever mentioned.—WASHINGTON IRVING, "The Mutability of Literature," *Sketch Book*, 1819–48

Enjoying for above a century a popularity which may well be compared with that of the *Diana* of Montemayor, if indeed, it did not equal it.—GEORGE TICKNOR, *History of Spanish Literature*, 1849–91, Vol. 3, p. 106

It would be mere pretence to say that the romance could be read through now by any one not absolutely Sidney-smitten in his tastes, or that, compared with the books which we do read through, it is not intolerably languid. It is even deficient in those passages of clear incisive thought which we find in the author's *Essay on Poetry*. No competent person, however, can read any considerable portion of it without finding it full of fine enthusiasm and courtesy, of high sentiment, of the breath of a gentle and heroic spirit. There are sweet descriptions in it, pictures of ideal love and friendship, dialogues of stately moral rhetoric. In style there is a finish, an attention to artifice, a musical arrangement of cadence, and occasionally a richness of phrase, for which English Prose at that time might well have been grateful. Seeing, too, that the complaints of wearisomeness which we bring against the book now, were not so likely to be made at the time of its publication, when readers had not been taught impatience by a surfeit of works of the same class—seeing, in fact, that the book was so popular as to go through ten editions in the course of fifty years—I am disposed to believe that this last merit was not the least important.—DAVID MASSON, *British Novelists and Their Styles*, 1859, p. 65

Shall I describe his pastoral epic, the *Arcadia*? It is but a recreation, a sort of poetical romance, written in the country for the amusement of his sister; a work of fashion, which, like *Cyrus* and *Clélie*, is not a monument, but a relic. This kind of book shows only the externals, the current elegance and politeness, the jargon of the world of culture,—in short, that which should be spoken before ladies; and yet we perceive from it the bent of the general spirit. In *Clélie*, oratorical development, fine and collected analysis, the flowing converse of men seated quietly on elegant arm-chairs; in the *Arcadia*, fantastic imagination, excessive sentiments, a medley of events which suited men scarcely recovered from barbarism. Indeed, in London they still used to fire pistols at each other in the streets; and under Henry VIII and his children, queens, a Protector, the highest nobles, knelt under the axe of the executioner. Armed and perilous existence long resisted in Europe the establishment of peaceful and quiet life. It was necessary to change society and the soil, in order to transform men of the sword into citizens. The high roads of Louis XIV and his regular administration, and more recently the railroads and the *sergents de ville*, came to relieve the French from habits of violence and a taste for dangerous adventure. Remember that at this period men's heads were full of tragical images. Sidney's *Arcadia* contains enough of them to supply half-a-dozen epics. 'It is a trifle,' says the author; 'my young head must be delivered.' In the first twenty-five pages you meet with a shipwreck, an account of pirates, a half-drowned prince rescued by shepherds, a voyage in Arcadia, various disguises, the retreat of a king withdrawn into solitude with his wife and children, the deliverance of a young imprisoned lord, a war against the Helots, the conclusion of peace, and many other things. Go on, and you will find princesses shut up by a wicked fairy, who beats them, and threatens them with death if they refuse to marry her son; a beautiful queen condemned to perish by fire if certain knights do not come to her succour; a treacherous prince tortured for his crimes, then cast from the top of a pyramid; fights, surprises, abductions, travels: in short, the whole programme of the most romantic tales. That is the serious element: the agreeable is of a like nature; the fantastic predominates. Improbable pastoral serves, as in Shakspeare or Lope de Vega, for an intermezzo to improbable tragedy. You are always coming upon dancing shepherds. They are very courteous, good poets, and subtle metaphysicians. There are many disguised princes who pay their court to the princesses. They sing continually, and get up allegorical dances; two bands approach, servants of Reason and Passion; their hats, ribbons, and dress are described in full. They quarrel in verse, and their hurried retorts, which follow close on one another, over-refined, keep up a tournament of wit. Who cared for what was natural or possible in this age? There were such festivals at Elizabeth's entries; and you have only to look at the engravings of Sadler, Martin de Vos, and Goltzius, to find this mixture of sensuous beauties and philosophical enigmas. The Countess of Pembroke and her ladies were delighted to picture this profusion of costumes and verses, this play beneath the trees. They had eyes in the sixteenth century, senses which sought satisfaction in poetry—the same satisfaction as in masquerading and painting. Man was not yet a pure reasoner; abstract truth was not enough for him. Rich stuffs, twisted about and folded; the sun to shine upon them, a large meadow full of white daisies; ladies in brocaded dresses, with bare arms, crowns on their heads, instruments of music behind the trees,—this is what the reader expects; he cares nothing for contrasts; he will readily provide a drawing-room in the midst of the fields.

What are they going to say there? Here comes out that restless exaltation, amidst all its folly, which is characteristic of the spirit of the age; love rises to the thirty-sixth heaven. Musidorus is the brother of Céladon; Pamela is closely related to the severe heroines of *Astrée*; all the Spanish exaggerations abound with all their faults. But in works of fashion or of the Court, primitive sentiment never retains its sincerity: wit, the necessity to please, the desire of effect, of speaking better than others, alter it, force it, confuse the embellishments and refinements, so that nothing is left but twaddle. Musidorus wished to give Pamela a kiss. She repels him. He would have died on the spot; but luckily remembers that his mistress commanded him to leave her, and finds himself still able to obey her command. He complains to the trees, weeps in verse: there are dialogues where Echo, repeating the last word, replies; double rhymes, balanced stanzas, in which the theory of love is minutely detailed; in short, all choice morsels of ornamental poetry. If they send a letter to their mistress, they speak to it, tell the ink:

> Therefore mourne boldly, my inke; for while shee lookes upon you, your blacknesse will shine: cry out boldly my lamentation; for while shee reades you, your cries will be musicke.

Again, two young princesses are going to bed:

> They impoverished their clothes to enrich their bed, which for that night might well scorne the shrine of Venus; and there cherishing one another with deare, though chaste embracements; with sweete, though cold kisses; it might seeme that love was come to play him there without dart, or that wearie of his owne fires, he was there to refresh himselfe between their sweete breathing lippes.

In excuse of these follies, remember that they have their parallels in Shakspeare. Try rather to comprehend them, to imagine them in their place, with their surroundings, such as they are; that is, as the excess of singularity and inventive fire. Even though they mar now and then the finest ideas, yet a natural freshness pierces through the disguise. Take another example:

> In the time that the morning did strew roses and violets in the heavenly floore against the coming of the sun, the nightingales (striving one with the other which could in most dainty varietie recount their wronge-caused sorrow) made them put off their sleep.—HIPPOLYTE TAINE, *The History of English Literature*, 1871, Bk. 2, tr. Van Laun, pp. 164–66

It was not a studied work, but as the story came he wrote it down on loose sheets of paper, most of it whilst his sister was beside him, and some of it as he rode or hunted over Salisbury Plain. Many of the descriptions of rural scenery he took from scenes he saw before him at Wilton. He did not finish it at Wilton, but took it up again at different times, and sent off the sheets as soon as written to his sister. The want of plan makes the story long and unartistic; perhaps Sidney was aware of this, as he never wished it to be published; but after his death, his sister thought it too rare to be lost to the world, and for some time it was a very popular book, many persons finding great delight in the complicated adventures of the various characters.—ANNA BUCKLAND, *The Story of English Literature*, 1882, p. 113

The student of English fiction would fain linger long over the pages which describe the loves of Pamela and Philoclea. For when these pages are laid aside, it is long before he may again meet with the poetry, the manly and womanly sentiment, and the pure yet stirring passion which adorn the romance of Elizabeth's Philip. Three centuries have passed away since the *Arcadia* was written, and we who live at the end of this period not unjustly congratulate ourselves on our superior civilization and refinement. And yet in all this time we have arrived of no higher conception of feminine virtue or chivalrous manhood than is to be found in this sixteenth-century romance, and during one-half of these three hundred years there was to be seen so little trace of such a conception, whether in life or in literature, that the word love seemed to have lost its nobler meaning and to stand for no more than animal desire. There is not in English fiction a more charming picture of feminine modesty than that of Pamela hiding her love for Musidorus.—BAYARD TUCKERMAN, *A History of English Prose Fiction*, 1882, p. 98

Sidney has, among several others, created one character which, forgotten as it is now, would be enough to give a permanent interest to this too much neglected romance; it is the Queen Gynecia, who is consumed by a guilty love, and who is the worthy contemporary of the strongly passionate heroes of Marlowe's plays. With her, and for the first time, the dramatic power of English genius leaves the stage and comes to light in the novel; it was destined to pass into it entirely.—J. J. JUSSERAND, *The English Novel in the Time of Shakespeare*, 1890, p. 247

ASTROPHEL AND STELLA

Sir Philip Sidney's *Astrophel and Stella* consists of a number of sonnets, which have been unaccountably passed over by Dr. Drake, and all our other critics who have written on this subject. Many of them are eminently beautiful.—HENRY KIRKE WHITE, *Melancholy Hours*, c. 1806, Vol. 2, ed. Southey, p. 247

Sidney's sonnets—I speak of the best of them—are among the very best of their sort. They fall below the plain moral dignity, the sanctity, and high yet modest spirit of self-approval, of Milton in his compositions of a similar structure. . . . They are struck full of amorous fancies—far-fetched conceits, befitting his occupation; for True Love thinks no labour to send out Thoughts upon the vast, and more than Indian voyages, to bring home rich pearls, outlandish wealth, gums, jewels, spicery, to sacrifice in self-depreciating similitudes, as shadows of true amiabilities in the Beloved. . . . I confess I can see nothing of the "jejune" or "frigid" in them; much less of the "stiff" and "cumbrous"—which I have sometimes heard objected to the *Arcadia*. The verse runs off swiftly and gallantly. It might have been tuned to the trumpet; or tempered (as himself expresses it) to "trampling horses' feet."—CHARLES LAMB,

"Some Sonnets of Sir Philip Sydney," *London Magazine*, Sept. 1823

The Stella of Sydney's poetry, and the Philoclea of his *Arcadia*, was the Lady Penelope Devereux, the elder sister of the favourite Essex. While yet in her childhood, she was the destined bride of Sidney, and for several years they were considered as almost engaged to each other: it was natural, therefore, at this time, that he should be accustomed to regard her with tenderness and unreproved admiration, and should gratify both by making her the object of his poetical raptures. She was also less openly, but even more ardently, loved by young Charles Blount, afterwards Lord Mountjoy, who seems to have disputed with Sidney the first place in her heart. She is described as a woman of exquisite beauty, on a grand and splendid scale; dark sparkling eyes; pale þrown hair; a rich vivid complexion; a regal brow and a noble figure. . . . A dark shade steals, like a mildew, over this bright picture of beauty, poetry, and love, even while we gaze upon it. The projected union between Sydney and Lady Penelope was finally broken off by their respective families, for reasons which do not appear. Sir Charles Blount offered himself, and was refused, though evidently agreeable to the lady; and she was married by her guardians to Lord Rich, a man of talents and integrity, but most disagreeable in person and manners, and her declared aversion.—ANNA BROWNELL JAMESON, *The Loves of the Poets*, 1829, Vol. 1, pp. 251–55

It is rather a singular circumstance, that, in her own and her husband's lifetime, this ardent courtship of a married woman should have been deemed fit for publication. Sidney's passion seems indeed to have been unsuccessful, but far enough from being Platonic. *Astrophel and Stella* is too much disfigured by conceits, but it is in some places very beautiful.—HENRY HALLAM, *Introduction to the Literature of Europe*, 1837–39, Pt. 2, Ch. 5, Par. 66

In a certain depth and chivalry of feeling—in the rare and noble quality of disinterestedness (to put it in one word),—he has no superior, hardly perhaps an equal, amongst our Poets; and after or beside Shakespeare's *Sonnets*, his *Astrophel and Stella* . . . offers the most intense and powerful picture of the passion of love in the whole range of our poetry.—FRANCIS TURNER PALGRAVE, *Golden Treasury of English Lyrics*, 1861–92, p. 351

Often, after reading the poets of this age, I have looked for some time at the contemporary prints, telling myself that man, body and soul, was not then such as we see him to-day. We also have our passions, but we are no longer strong enough to bear them. They distract us; we are not poets without suffering for it. Alfred de Musset, Heine, Edgar Poe, Burns, Byron, Shelley, Cowper, how many shall I instance? Disgust, mental and bodily degradation, disease, impotence, madness, suicide, at best a permanent hallucination or feverish raving,—these are now-a-days the ordinary issues of the poetic temperament. The passion of the brain gnaws our vitals, dries up the blood, eats into the marrow, shakes us like a tempest, and the skeleton man, to which civilisation has reduced us, is not substantial enough long to resist it. They, who have been more roughly trained, who are more inured to the inclemencies of climate, more hardened by bodily exercise, more firm against danger, endure and live. Is there a man living who could withstand the storm of passions and visions which swept over Shakspeare, and end, like him, as a sensible citizen and landed proprietor in his small county? The muscles were firmer, the despair less prompt. The rage of concentrated attention, the half hallucinations, the anguish and heaving of the heart, the quivering of the limbs stretching involuntarily and blindly for action, all the painful impulses which accompany large desires, exhausted them less; this is why they desired longer, and dared more. D'Aubigné, wounded with many sword-thrusts, conceiving death at hand, had himself bound on his horse that he might see his mistress once more, and rode thus several leagues, losing blood, and arriving in a swoon. Such feelings we glean still in their portraits, in the straight looks which pierce like a sword; in this strength of back, bent or twisted; in the sensuality, energy, enthusiasm, which breathe from their attitude or look. Such feelings we still discover in their poetry, in Greene, Lodge, Jonson, Spenser, Shakspeare, in Sidney, as in all the rest. We quickly forget the faults of taste which accompany it, the affectation, the uncouth jargon. Is it really so uncouth? Imagine a man who with closed eyes distinctly sees the adored countenance of his mistress, who keeps it before him all the day; who is troubled and shaken as he imagines ever and anon her brow, her lips, her eyes; who cannot and would not be separated from his vision; who sinks daily deeper in this passionate contemplation; who is every instant crushed by mortal anxieties, or transported by the raptures of bliss: he will lose the exact conception of objects. A fixed idea becomes a false idea. By dint of regarding an object under all its forms, turning it over, piercing through it, we at last deform it. When we cannot think of a thing without dimness and tears, we magnify it, and give it a nature which it has not. Then strange comparisons, over-refined ideas, excessive images, become natural. However far Sidney goes, whatever object he touches, he sees throughout the universe only the name and features of Stella. All ideas bring him back to her. He is drawn ever and invincibly by the same thought; and comparisons which seem far-fetched, only express the unfailing presence and sovereign power of the besetting image. Stella is ill; it seems to Sidney that 'Joy, which is inseparate from those eyes, Stella, now learnes (strange case) to weepe in thee.' To us, the expression is absurd. Is it for Sidney, who for hours together had dwelt on the expression of those eyes, seeing in them at last all the beauties of heaven and earth, who, compared to them, finds all light dull and all joy stale? Consider that in every extreme passion ordinary laws are reversed, that our logic cannot pass judgment on it, that we find in it affectation, childishness, fancifulness, crudity, folly, and that to us violent conditions of the nervous machine are like an unknown and marvellous land, where common sense and good language cannot penetrate. On the return of spring, when May spreads over the fields her dappled dress of new flowers, Astrophel and Stella sit in the shade of a retired grove, in the warm air, full of birds' voices and pleasant exhalations. Heaven smiles, the wind kisses the trembling leaves, the inclining trees interlace their sappy branches, amorous earth sighs greedily for the rippling water:

> In a grove most rich of shade,
> Where birds wanton musicke made,
> May, then yong, his py'd weeds showing,
> New perfum'd with flowers fresh growing,
>
> Astrophel with Stella sweet,
> Did for mutuall comfort meet,
> Both within themselves oppressed,
> But each in the other blessed. . . .
>
> Their eares hungry of each word,
> Which the deere tongue would afford,
> But their tongues restrain'd from walking,
> Till their hearts had ended talking.
>
> But when their tongues could not speake,
> Love it selfe did silence breake;
> Love did set his lips asunder,

Thus to speake in love and wonder. . . .
This small winde which so sweet is,
See how it the leaves doth kisse,
Each tree in his best attyring,
Sense of love to love inspiring.

On his knees, with beating heart, oppressed, it seems to him that his mistress is transformed:

Stella, soveraigne of my joy, . . .
Stella, starre of heavenly fire,
Stella, load-starre of desire,
Stella, in whose shining eyes
Are the lights of Cupid's skies. . . .
Stella, whose voice when it speakes
Senses all asunder breakes;
Stella, whose voice when it singeth,
Angels to acquaintance bringeth.

These cries of adoration are like a hymn. Every day he writes thoughts of love which agitate him, and in this long journal of a hundred pages we feel the inflamed breath swell each moment. A smile from his mistress, a curl lifted by the wind, a gesture,—all are events. He paints her in every attitude; he cannot see her too constantly. He talks to the birds, plants, winds, all nature. He brings the whole world to Stella's feet. At the notion of a kiss he swoons:

Thinke of that most gratefull time
When thy leaping heart will climbe,
In my lips to have his biding.
There those roses for to kisse,
Which doe breath a sugred blisse,
Opening rubies, pearles dividing.

O joy, too high for my low stile to show:
O blisse, fit for a nobler state then me:
Envie, put out thine eyes, lest thou do see
What Oceans of delight in me do flow.
My friend, that oft saw through all maskes my wo,
Come, come, and let me powre my selfe on
thee;
Gone is the winter of my miserie,
My spring appeares, O see what here doth grow,
For Stella hath with words where faith doth shine,
Of her high heart giv'n me the monarchie:
I, I, O I may say that she is mine.

There are Oriental splendours in the sparkling sonnet in which he asks why Stella's cheeks have grown pale:

Where be those Roses gone, which sweetned so our
eyes!
Where those red cheekes, which oft with faire
encrease doth frame
The height of honour in the kindly badge of shame?
Who hath the crimson weeds stolne from my
morning skies?

As he says, his 'life melts with too much thinking.' Exhausted by ecstasy, he pauses; then he flies from thought to thought, seeking a cure for his wound, like the Satyr whom he describes:

Prometheus, when first from heaven hie
He brought downe fire, ere then on earth not seene,
Fond of delight, a Satyr standing by,
Gave it a kisse, as it like sweet had beene.
Feeling forthwith the other burning power,
Wood with the smart with showts and shryking shrill,
He sought his ease in river, field, and bower,
But for the time his griefe went with him still.

At last calm returned; and whilst this calm lasts, the lively, glowing spirit plays like a flame on the surface of the deep brooding fire. His love-songs and word-portraits, delightful pagan and chivalric fancies, seem to be inspired by Petrarch or Plato. One feels the charm and liveliness under the seeming affectation:

Faire eyes, sweete lips, deare heart, that foolish I
Could hope by Cupids helpe on you to pray;
Since to himselfe he doth your gifts apply,
As his maine force, choise sport, and easefull stray.
For when he will see who dare him gainsay,
Then with those eyes he lookes, lo by and by
Each soule doth at Loves feet his weapons lay,
Glad if for her he give them leave to die.
When he will play, then in her lips he is,
Where blushing red, that Loves selfe them doth love,
With either lip he doth the other kisse:
But when he will for quiets sake remove
From all the world, her heart is then his rome,
Where well he knowes, no man to him can come.

Both heart and sense are captive here. If he finds the eyes of Stella more beautiful than anything in the world, he finds her soul more lovely than her body. He is a Platonist when he recounts how Virtue, wishing to be loved of men, took Stella's form to enchant their eyes, and make them see the heaven which the inner sense reveals to heroic souls. We recognise in him that entire submission of heart, love turned into a religion, perfect passion which asks only to grow, and which, like the piety of the mystics, finds itself too insignificant when it compares itself with the object loved:

My youth doth waste, my knowledge brings forth
toyes,
My wit doth strive those passions to defend,
Which for reward spoyle it with vaine annoyes,
I see my course to lose my selfe doth bend:
I see and yet no greater sorrow take,
Than that I lose no more for Stella's sake.

At last, like Socrates in the banquet, he turns his eyes to deathless beauty, heavenly brightness:

Leave me, O Love, which reachest but to dust,
And thou my minde aspire to higher things:
Grow rich in that which never taketh rust:
Whatever fades, but fading pleasure brings. . . .
O take fast hold, let that light be thy guide,
In this small course which birth drawes out to death.

Divine love continues the earthly love; he was imprisoned in this, and frees himself. By this nobility, these lofty aspirations, recognise one of those serious souls of which there are so many in the same climate and race. Spiritual instincts pierce through the dominant paganism, and ere they make Christians, make Platonists.—HIPPOLYTE TAINE, *The History of English Literature*, 1871, Bk. 2, tr. Van Laun, pp. 168–72

Now if you don't like these love-songs, you either have never been in love, or you don't know good writing from bad, (and likely enough both the negatives, I'm sorry to say, in modern England).—JOHN RUSKIN, "Letter XXXV," *Fors Clavigera*, 1873

"Stella" has "for all time" taken her place in the heaven of Literature beside not merely the Geraldine of Surrey earlier, or the Mary of Robert Burns later, but with the Laura of Petrarch, and Beatrice of Dante, and Rosalind and Elizabeth of Spenser, and Celia of Carew, and Castara of Habington, and Leonora of Milton, and Sacharissa of Waller.—ALEXANDER B. CROSART, "Memorial-Introduction," *Complete Poems of Sir Philip Sidney*, 1877, Vol. 1, p. lxi

As a series of sonnets the *Astrophel and Stella* poems are second only to Shakespeare's; as a series of love-poems they are perhaps unsurpassed. Other writers are sweeter, more sonorous; no other love-poet of the time is so real. The poems to Stella are steeped throughout in a certain keen and pungent individuality which leaves a haunting impression behind it. They represent, not a mere isolated mood, whether half-real like Daniel's passion for Delia, or wholly artificial like the mood of Thomas Watson's *Passions*, but a whole passage in a genuine life. . . . Not that *Astrophel and Stella* is without its make-believes. It has its "conceits," its pieces of pure word-play, in the common Elizabethan manner. No writer in the full tide of literary fashion like Sidney could afford to neglect these. But it would be scarcely fanciful to say that even in the most clearly marked of what one may call his conceited sonnets, the true Sidneian note to a reader who has learnt to catch it is almost always discernible, a note of youth and eagerness easily felt but hard to be described.—MARY A. WARD, *English Poets*, 1880, Vol. 1, ed. Ward, p. 344

The lover of Penelope Rich certainly did not find his "heart's desires" in wedlock. He chose to find his high ideal of a woman in his married sister Mary, Countess of Pembroke, and gave his romantic imagination free scope in writing her *Arcadia*. When he had been two years married, and just before he became a father, he was burning to visit the ends of the earth with Drake. Then he passed over to the Continent, and perished, the high-souled victim of his own rash enterprise—Argalus, but without a Parthenia. Dame Frances Sidney, strangely enough, married again, Robert, second Earl of Essex, the brother in arms and affection of her late husband. Their son Robert was the famous general of the Parliament, first husband of the aristocratic adulteress and murderess, Frances Howard.—HUBERT HALL, *Society in the Elizabethan Age*, 1886, p. 91

For there is no doubt that Sidney here holds the primacy, not merely in time but in value . . . putting Spenser and Shakespere aside. That thirty or forty years' diligent study of Italian models had much to do with the extraordinary advance visible in his sonnets over those of Tottel's *Miscellany* is, no doubt, undeniable. But many causes besides the inexplicable residuum of fortunate inspiration, which eludes the most careful search into literary cause and effect, had to do with the production of the "lofty, insolent, and passionate vein," which becomes noticeable in English poetry for the first time about 1580, and which dominates it, if we include the late autumn-summer of Milton's last productions, for a hundred years. Perhaps it is not too much to say that this makes its very first appearance in Sidney's verse, for *The Shepherd's Calendar*, though of an even more perfect, is of a milder strain. The inevitable tendency of criticism to gossip about poets instead of criticising poetry has usually mixed a great deal of personal matter with the accounts of *Astrophel and Stella*, the series of sonnets which is Sidney's greatest literary work, and which was first published some years after his death in an incorrect and probably pirated edition by Thomas Nash. There is no doubt that there was a real affection between Sidney (Astrophel) and Penelope Devereux (Stella), daughter of the Earl of Essex, afterwards Lady Rich, and that marriage proving unhappy, Lady Mountjoy. But the attempts which have been made to identify every hint and allusion in the series with some fact or date, though falling short of the unimaginable folly of scholastic labour-lost which has been expended on the sonnets of Shakespere, still must appear somewhat idle to those who know the usual genesis of love-poetry—how that it is of imagination all compact, and that actual occurrences are much oftener occasions and bases than causes and material of it. It is of the

smallest possible importance or interest to a rational man to discover what was the occasion of Sidney's writing these charming poems—the important point is their charm. And in this respect (giving heed to his date and his opportunities of imitation) I should put Sidney third to Shakespere and Spenser. The very first piece of the series, an oddly compounded sonnet of thirteen Alexandrines and a final heroic, strikes the note of intense and fresh poetry which is only heard afar off in Surrey and Wyatt, which is hopelessly to seek in the tentatives of Turberville and Googe, and which is smothered with jejune and merely literary ornament in the less formless work of Sidney's contemporary, Thomas Watson. The second line—

> That she, dear she, might take some pleasure of my pain,

the couplet—

> Oft turning others' leaves to see if thence would flow
> Some fresh and fruitful showers upon my sunburnt brain,

and the sudden and splendid finale—

> 'Fool!' said my muse, 'look in thy heart and write!'

are things that may be looked for in vain earlier.

A little later we meet with that towering soar of verse which is also peculiar to the period:

> When Nature made her chief work—Stella's eyes,
> In colour black, why wrapt she beams so bright?—

lines which those who deprecate insistence on the importance of form in poetry might study with advantage, for the thought is a mere commonplace conceit, and the beauty of the phrase is purely derived from the cunning arrangement and cadence of the verse. The first perfectly charming sonnet in the English language—a sonnet which holds its own after three centuries of competition—is the famous "With how sad steps, O moon, thou climbst the skies," where Lamb's stricture on the last line as obscure seems to me unreasonable. The equally famous phrase, "That sweet enemy France," which occurs a little further on is another, and whether borrowed from Giordano Bruno or not is perhaps the best example of the felicity of expression in which Sidney is surpassed by few Englishmen. Nor ought the extraordinary variety of the treatment to be missed. Often as Sidney girds at those who, like Watson, "dug their sonnets out of books," he can write in the learned literary manner with the best. The pleasant ease of his sonnet to the sparrow, "Good brother Philip," contrasts in the oddest way with his allegorical and mythological sonnets, in each of which veins he indulges hardly less often, though very much more wisely than any of his contemporaries. Nor do the other "Songs of variable verse," which follow, and in some editions are mixed up with the sonnets, display less extraordinary power.

. . . To sum up, there is no Elizabethan poet, except the two named, who is more unmistakably imbued with poetical quality than Sidney. And Hazlitt's judgment on him, that he is "jejune" and "frigid" will, as Lamb himself hinted, long remain the chiefest and most astonishing example of a great critic's aberrations when his prejudices are concerned.— GEORGE SAINTSBURY, *A History of Elizabethan Literature*, 1887, pp. 100–102

AN APOLOGY FOR POETRIE

The stormie Winter (deere Chyldren of the Muses) which hath so long held backe the glorious Sunshine of diuine Poesie, is heere by the sacred pen-breathing words of diuine Sir *Philip Sidney*, not onely chased from our fame-inuiting Clyme, but vtterly for euer banisht eternitie: then graciously regreet the perpetuall spring of euer-growing inuention, and like kinde Babes, either enabled by wit or power, help to support me poore Midwife, whose daring aduenture, hath deliuered from Obliuions wombe, this euer-to-be admired wits miracle. Those great ones, who in themselues haue interr'd this blessed innocent, wil with *Aejculapius* condemne me as a detractor from their Deities: those who Prophet-like haue but heard presage of his coming, wil (if they wil doe wel) not onely defend, but praise mee, as the first publique bewrayer of *Poesies Messias*. Those who neither haue seene, thereby to interre, nor heard, by which they might be inflamed with desire to see, let them (of duty) plead to be my Champions, sith both theyr sight and hearing, by mine incurring blame is seasoned. Excellent Poesie, (so created by this Apologie,) be thou my Defendresse; and if any wound mee, let thy beautie (my soules Adamant) recure mee: if anie commend mine endeuored hardiment, to them commend thy most diuinest fury as a winged incouragement; so shalt thou have deuoted to thee, and to them obliged.—HENRY OLNEY, "Publisher to the Reader," *An Apology for Poetry*, 1595, ed. Arber, p. 16

I have been blamed for not mentioning sir Philip's *Defence of Poetry*, which some think his best work. I had indeed forgot it when I wrote this article; a proof that I at least did not think it sufficient foundation for so high a character as he acquired. This was all my criticism pretended to say, that I could not conceive how a man, who in some respects written dully and weakly, and who, at most, was far inferior to our best authors, had obtained such immense reputation. Let his merits and his fame be weighed together, and then let it be determined whether the world has overvalued, or I undervalued, sir Philip Sidney.—HORACE WALPOLE, *A Catalogue of the Royal and Noble Authors of England, Scotland, and Ireland*, 1758, Vol. 2, ed. Park, p. 232

Sir Philip Sidney is said to have miscarried in his essays; but his miscarriage was no more than that of failing in an attempt to introduce a new fashion. The failure was not owing to any defect or imperfection in the scheme, but to the want of taste, to the irresolution and ignorance of the public.—OLIVER GOLDSMITH, *Essays*, 1773, No. 18

The *Defense of Poesy* has already been reckoned among the polite writings of the Elizabethan age, to which class it rather belongs than to that of criticism; for Sidney rarely comes to any literary censure, and is still farther removed from any profound philosophy. His sense is good, but not ingenious, and the declamatory tone weakens its effect.—HENRY HALLAM, *Introduction to the Literature of Europe*, 1837–39, Pt. 2, Ch. 7, Par. 35

It is not only an earnest and persuasive argument, but was, in style and diction, the best secular prose yet written in England, and indeed the earliest specimen of real critical talent in the literature.—GEORGE P. MARSH, *The Origin and History of the English Language*, 1862, p. 547

The elegant and too-little known treatise. . . . The only pages of his *Apologie for Poetrie* generally quoted, are those in which he laughs at the playwrights of his time for violating the unities of time and place. The drawback to this isolated quotation is that it gives the perfectly false notion of Sir Philip Sidney that he was a narrow-minded pedant, whereas, in reality, there was nowhere to be found a more liberal and delicately cultured mind than his. His criticism was founded upon the noblest philosophy of art, and amongst the numerous treatises on poetry, which form an entire and very curious branch of literature in the sixteenth century, that of Sir Philip Sidney is in every

respect the most remarkable. In addition to the learning of a Scaliger, and the enthusiasm of a Ronsard, he possessed a quality that both these men were lacking in, which, for want of a better word, I must call an *atticism*, or, more strictly speaking, an *urbanity*, taking care to retain the especial meaning of a graceful and witty raillery, which is contained in the Latin word but not to the same degree in the Greek.—PAUL STAPFER, *Shakespeare and Classical Antiquity*, 1880, tr. Carey, p. 41

The monument of the noblest phase of perhaps the noblest movement of English thought. Filled with a longing for perfection, but a perfection beyond the thought of any but a poet, Sidney gives us the poetry rather than the art or the theory of criticism.—LAURA JOHNSON WYLIE, *Evolution of English Criticism*, 1894, p. 12

SIR WALTER RALEIGH
"An Epitaph upon the Right Honorable
Sir Philip Sidney, Knight" (1586)
A Choice of Sir Walter Raleigh's Verse
1972, pp. 22–24

To praise thy life, or waile thy woorthie death,
And want thy wit, thy wit high, pure, divine,
Is far beyond the powre of mortall line,
Nor any one hath worth that draweth breath.

Yet rich in zeale, though poore in learnings lore,
And friendly care obscurde in secret brest,
And love that envie in thy life supprest,
Thy deere life donc, and death hath doubled more

And I, that in thy time and living state,
Did onely praise thy vertues in my thought,
As one that seeld the rising sunne hath sought,
With words and teares now waile thy timelesse fate.

Drawne was thy race, aright from princely line,
Nor lesse than such, (by gifts that nature gave,
The common mother that all creatures have,)
Doth vertue shew, and princely linage shine.

A king gave thee thy name, a kingly minde,
That God thee gave, who found it now too deere
For this base world, and hath resumde it neere,
To sit in skies, and sort with powres divine.

Kent thy birth daies, and Oxford held thy youth,
The heavens made haste, and staide nor yeeres, nor time,
The fruits of age grew ripe in thy first prime,
Thy will, thy words; thy words, the seales of truth.

Great gifts and wisedome rare imploide thee thence,
To treat from kings, with those more great than kings,
Such hope men had to lay the highest things,
On thy wise youth, to be transported hence.

Whence to sharpe wars sweete honor did thee call,
Thy countries love, religion, and thy friends:
Of woorthy men, the marks, the lives and ends,
And her defence, for whom we labor all.

There didst thou vanquish shame and tedious age,
Griefe, sorow, sicknes, and base fortunes might:
Thy rising day, saw never wofull night,
But past with praise, from off this worldly stage.

Backe to the campe, by thee that day was brought,
First thine owne death, and after thy long fame;
Teares to the soldiers, the proud Castilians shame;

Vertue exprest, and honor truly taught.
What hath he lost, that such great grace hath woon,
Yoong yeeres, for endles yeeres, and hope unsure,
Of fortunes gifts, for wealth that still shall dure,
Oh happie race with so great praises run.

England doth hold thy lims that bred the same,
Flaunders thy valure where it last was tried,
The Campe thy sorrow where thy bodie died,
Thy friends, thy want; the world, thy vertues fame.

Nations thy wit, our mindes lay up thy love,
Letters thy learning, thy losse, yeeres long to come,
In worthy harts sorow hath made thy tombe,
Thy soule and spright enrich the heavens above.

Thy liberall hart imbalmd in gratefull teares.
Yoong sighes, sweete sighes, sage sighes, bewaile thy fall,
Envie hir sting, and spite hath left hir gall,
Malice hir selfe, a mourning garment weares.

That day their Haniball died, our Scipio fell,
Scipio, Cicero, and Petrarch of our time,
Whose vertues wounded by my woorthles rime,
Let Angels speake, and heavens thy praises tell.

THOMAS MOFFET
"A Sorrowful Lamentation" (1589)
Lessus Lugubris
eds., trs. Virgil Heltzel, Hoyt H. Hudson
1940, pp. 99–105

Do I see you thus, O Sidney—you, a pale corpse? You, shut up in a narrow coffin, and thrust into the cold tomb? You, the poor victual of foul worms? You, whose every act had regard to eternal light and everlasting life? What plaints shall I first pour forth? Shall I lament your unmerited fate? Or rather the envious Fates? I lament the Fates envious of you as well as the fate undeserved by you.

Do I see you thus? Or do I err, seeing but your clothing, armor, and the sword by which you, the noblehearted, in times past won many victories with great renown? Indeed I err: I see naught but the clothing, armor, and sword, and those habitations of clay which that soul of yours—sent on its way to starry Olympus, free from these worldly concerns—has left behind with honor.

O dwellings rightly pleasing to me above other dwellings, habitation of the godlike mind, of virtue also the habitation! Untouched of vice, habitation free from crime! Since the guest will have deserted you and will at the same time have taken away everything of his which could be described, what now hinders me from contemplating this your outer covering and abandoned residence—mindful as I am of the master, and conversant with those labors which he undertook and completed for your enhancement?

Grant this last labor to me, O son of the Sidneys, and, if favorable spirits or stars at all prevail, if in lifeless shades any power of perception survives death unscathed and perishes not in that single stroke of destruction, grant pardon to a Muse who anatomizes all the members of her patron; let her be empowered to lift true praises, by which that man, as he withdraws from the living, first begins to live, and as one about to conquer begins to live forever.

For what rightful duty shall I perform, what due rites for Philip, what funeral obsequies of so great worth, except as I shall summon the Muses into the presence of him who was distinguished by the Muses? Or at least shall I not with my whole heart pour out upon his funeral sacrifices libations drawn from the springs of the Muses, drawn from the example of that man and from his eloquence, and drawn from labors most agreeable to him and to me?

For I do not believe that he is to be pleased by the water of any springs or by streams of snowy milk or by flood of juice flowing from the vine, or by aught else, so much as by a song of willing service and by the abundant witness of a remembering heart, by a celebration of virtues, a heralding of his achievements, and an ardent exhortation to the pursuit of glory like to his.

Therefore the head, the breast, the right hand, the left hand, and the feet let your Moffet inspect—not Phoebus, not the son of Phoebus, or the renowned Machaon, but your Moffet who comes of their family—by way of anatomizing the passages and recesses of life, from which outward beauties (playthings of the wind) did not carry off the glory—nay, those recesses of hidden life wherein lived but now the skill and the mind without flaw.

The Head

O head, beloved and worthy of reverence! Bright with starry light, and encircled with fiery beams which pious faith sent forth from the inmost secret places of the mind! For when first you entered upon the path and course of the blessed life of Christians (I recollect your deeds), your mind seemed to be kindled by fire come down from heaven and miraculously to burn—whence even now those lights, by which you appear so conspicuous, are seen to shine out and sparkle.

Perhaps the Omnipotent wishes burnt offerings to be devoted to him, wishes such offerings, and by his own fire—not by the fire which Prometheus, they say, stole from the burning wheel of Phoebus, or by that which, as feigned by the blind world, the three-headed beast dwelling on the Seven Hills has brought in, or by the fire which Aetna of the Lativi spewed out, or by any other. Thus the lamb of Abel, thus the kids of Noah and Manoah, were acceptable to Jehovah.

In no other wise did Zeal sent down from high heaven wholly kindle and inflame the mind of the son of the Sidneys, so that while alive, dying to sin, he could be called, indeed, a living sacrifice to God, to whom he consecrated himself and all he had. Yea, he embraced with his mind the faith and the faithful Christ (whose promises remain steadfast even though the world falls), and he produced and brought forth notable fruits of faith.

Complete in his obedience to divine law, and in manifesting the practice of it in his life, he watched, he sweated, he froze—not that by these high endeavors of his exalted spirit he might contrive either his own justification or sure salvation, which, having been received from Christ, he repaid (as if he owed it) to him alone; but lest he be grievous or too hostile to the Holy Spirit, by whom he was sealed throughout the everlasting cycle of the ages.

His eyes, his ears, his tongue—indeed his whole face—had nothing to do with the obscene, wrong, frivolous, or base. To have propagated these things was unlawful, to have countenanced them was heinous. Made pious by these helps he at length reaped this harvest—that, as if by a covenant and firm treaty, he ever maintained a strong and prosperous rule over himself.

What wonder, then, that his head was uniquely eminent for all liberal arts, not primarily for those arts, indeed, by which are taught speech, numbers, words, and reckoning, but for those by which one can have known even the earth and the whole of things!

Indeed, the eternal God in this one head has manifested

how far prevails a diligence adorned with steadfast devotion.

Breast

Your breast, your heart, rob me of my entire heart while I renew and gratefully call to mind their glories. How wise a heart was given to you, O wise Philip! How rare a heart was yours, beloved Philip! How clean and pure a heart was yours, Philip!

A chaste Venus, holy Graces, a Minerva born of Jove, and (as far as you were able) a gentler and nobler Cupid—these embellished that great heart and its little span of life. O breast, in which he ever loved his faithful friends! Nisus did not cherish Euryalus with more devotion; nor Damon, Pythias; nor Philemon, Baucis when both were old—than that hero Sidney cherished his companions and bosom friends in his heart, in his soul, by his words, by his vows—indeed, with all his strength.

I invoke Willoughby, honored pillar and light of the house of Silerapis and of the whole nation of England. When, attended by but a few who had fire and swords, as an impetuous warrior he would attack the Spaniards on the plains of Zutphen, and unterrified would seek a way through his enemies with their fearful din (for thus the Fates bade), after several knights had been slain here and everywhere in the fight, lo, the noble Silerapian hero, suddenly hemmed when on a charger he rushed as a leader against the endless battle line, is seized, and, his arms of no avail, is made the captive of an enemy knight. Instantly the Spaniards hastened together like a swarm and all of one accord threw their arms about the neck of the captive and, because his sword had slipped from him, seized the follower of Mars as he fought with bare fists.

When rumor had brought tidings of this to the ears of the son of Sidney, with Pegasean paces or as if carried by the bird of Jove, half-armed (for unluckily, because he was in a hurry, he had not troubled about the armor for his left thigh), he released the defenseless Willoughby—at the price of his own death, a dire, bitter, lamentable death. For while, high on his horse, eagerly he ate up the hills and the valleys and, impatient of delay, was borne against the enemy, chance or a more malign skill directed the pitiless bullet which, carrying its menace through the blue air with an ominous hiss, flew and struck and shattered the bone of the thigh—the bone of the thigh protected, as I say, with no metal.

And thus that faithful heart, that gentle heart, serene, heroic, upright, temperate, heavenly, that heart never made haughty by favorable circumstances or faltering at sudden turns of events, that holy heart, in which while yet a small and immature boy he had burned with zeal toward the heavenly ones above—nor had his zeal cooled up to this time—mounted from these hostile lands to the seats of the eternal; inclosed in a starry casket, it withdrew to the stars. From that high vault now no star shines more brightly, nor is any more gracious for its happy influence.

Right Hand

O sorrow! As I consider that right hand, sighs once more assail me and again groans and many tears burst forth. This was once the bravest hand of all. A bitter phrase indeed—"this was"; and a more bitter to come, for scarcely are we to be heartened by any hope that there will be a right hand like it!

It is a question whether that hand was more distinguished in civil employments than in vigorous warfare, nor certainly will there be anyone who can answer. For it was ever disposed to cherish the Muses and their devoted foster sons, and prompt to provide for, encourage, and support the hungry, naked, footworn, and faint. It assisted continually the widows, way-farers, and orphans, and when losses had been sustained it brought comfort. Nor less was that right hand disposed, nor less ready (the cause being just and arms supporting the cause), to come to a decision with the enemy by the sword, the dagger, the saber, the bow, the arquebus, and darts, and, opportunity being given, to thrust the weapon into the vitals of adversaries.

Come, therefore, Religion, the Prince, the Commonwealth, and mourn! Mourn all men everywhere and through all lands! Bewail the grievous overthrow of that renowned right hand. Not from him but from you, O Commonwealth, is the right hand dismembered. Not from him but from you, O Queen, has the right hand been cut off. Not from him but from you, O Religion, has the right hand been removed. Not from him but from the learned and good has the right hand been taken away.

Left Hand

As much worth or highest glory as any man can have is wholly yours by right, O bravest Sidney, if we can believe that the wisdom of the great Hebrew king saw the matter truly. For in his judgment this is the highest glory of man, this is the consummate grace of a man—to rise above passions and to hide the transgressions of brothers (in whatever way committed against you), to maintain a gentle bearing toward them and to use soft words on every occasion, so that you may make a friend out of an enemy, perchance even out of the one of deepest dye.

All ages to come will crown this worth with highest praises, and haply later times will bring you forward as an example, and with one voice will proclaim: "Oh, how excellent he was, to use the shield more often than the sword! How much better to suffer repeatedly (if injury is done repeatedly) than to inflict the least violence upon anyone!" Thus, indeed, a fame will be added to your other honors—a renown everlasting, begotten by merit, retained by valor; and, handed on, it will descend as a pattern to all of your people. Let them learn to protect with a shield whatever things are theirs.

O Sidney, let us call you Scaevola, and let this reason be given: not because the use of your right hand was deficient, but because endurance had so fortified your heart that no one can use his right hand more dexterously than you could use your left.

Feet

Nor, truly, has illustrious virtue stamped notable and clear characters upon the higher members in such fashion that it has enhanced with no honor the low and earth-pressing feet. Nay, in the hour of fateful battle the road ennobled his feet, beyond the other limbs of his body which with manifold reason I must celebrate much and often—that road, the road of valor, where glory sent down deep and living roots, when Sidney heard that his friend Willoughby was hemmed in and held by Spanish arms. Thunderstruck by such a storm of terrible things, "O Thou All-Powerful," he said, "if my vows will be of any avail, if thy heart cherishes at all thy adopted son, draw near in mercy and (I pray for nothing more) either bring back the beloved Willoughby to me or let me perish also!"

Scarcely having uttered such words, as if he found the winged sandals of Mercury, and nothing slower than the dogs of Amyclae when they chase the fleet deer with thunderous voice, he speeds, far swifter than any chariot, and with both feet so spurs the galloping steed that its wounded flanks shed bloody drops, and the blood, leaping from the throbbing viscera, dyed the soft green sod with a great stream.

The Fates favor courage, for when the enemy had seen the fleet Sidney, now ready to offer battle, headlong flight routed the Spaniards, dashed in spirit, and a feminine fear seized both the leaders and their followers. Meanwhile, the captured Silerapian hero escaped; and along the way, while he hurried to his faithful friend, he paled as he heard that that friend had been pierced through by a bullet.

Lament now, O ye Muses! Ye virtues, lament with me! Pour forth now, my Melpomene, sad-sounding plaints, and tears befitting the great Silerapian! For he did shed tears—not those white tears which drop from the trickling eyes only of frigid lovers, but red tears of a mourning heart, and, indeed, even bloody tears he shed, as if from a wound. And he wept the more for this—that the hopes and arts of the physicians were of no avail and he knew that in vain did the apothecaries sweat and Chiron, skilled in herbs, toil in vain.

Wherefore he repairs to the temples loved of the King who rules the lightning, and he prays him by his graces and by the crucified Son of God that if there could be any hope of health for his wounded comrade he might dispatch and restore it. But in vain he prays. For he saw that the heavenly assemblage had resolved to loose, first the wounded thigh and foot, and then the other members of the great Sidney, from the mortal bond, to be blessed with eternal light and heavenly peace. Nor was there delay, for instantly all warmth and color left that foot which, speedy and nimble, hastened to his comrade—yea, which, unwearied, constant, loyal, and venerable, had hastened to the Muses, the virtues, and the sacred temples.

THOMAS NASHE
"Preface" to *Astrophel and Stella* (1591)
Elizabethan Critical Essays
ed. G. Gregory Smith
1964, Vol. 2, pp. 221–28

*T*empus adest plausus; aurea pompa venit: so endes the Sceane of Idiots, and enter *Astrophel* in pompe. Gentlemen, that haue seene a thousand lines of folly, drawn forth *ex uno puncto impudentiae*, & two famous Mountaines to goe to the conception of one Mouse, that haue had your eares defned with the eccho of Fames brasen towres when only they haue been toucht with a leaden pen, that haue seene *Pan* sitting in his bower of delights & a number of *Midasses* to admire his miserable hornepipes, let not your surfeted sight, new come from such puppet play, think scorne to turn aside into this Theater of pleasure, for here you shal find a paper stage streud with pearle, an artificial heau'n to ouershadow the fair frame, & christal wals to encounter your curious eyes, while the tragicommody of loue is performed by starlight. The chiefe Actor here is *Melpomene*, whose dusky robes, dipt in the ynke of teares, as yet seeme to drop when I view them neere. The argument cruell chastitie, the Prologue hope, the Epilogue dispaire; *videte, quaeso, et linguis animisque fauete*. And here, peraduenture, my witles youth may be taxt with a margent note of presumption for offering to put vp any motion of applause in the behalfe of so excellent a Poet (the least sillable of whose name sounded in the eares of judgment is able to giue the meanest line he writes a dowry of immortality); yet those that obserue how iewels oftentimes com to their hands that know not their value, & that the cockcombes of our days, like *Esop's* Cock, had rather haue a Barly kernell wrapt vp in a Ballet then they wil dig for the welth of wit in any ground that they know not, I hope wil also hold me excused though I open the gate to his glory & inuite idle eares to the admiration of his melancholy.

Quid petitur sacris nisi tantum fama poetis?
Which although it be oftentimes imprisoned in Ladyes casks & the president bookes of such as cannot see without another man's spectacles, yet at length it breakes foorth in spight of his keepers, and vseth some priuate penne (in steed of a picklock) to procure his violent enlargement. The Sunne for a time may maske his golden head in a cloud, yet in the end the thicke vaile doth vanish, and his embellished blandishment appeares. Long hath *Astrophel* (Englands Sunne) withheld the beames of his spirite from the common view of our darke sence, and night hath houered ouer the gardens of the nine Sisters, while *Ignis fatuus* and grosse fatty flames (such as commonly arise out of Dunghilles) haue tooke occasion, in the middest eclipse of his shining perfections, to wander a broade with a wispe of paper at their tailes like Hobgoblins, and leade men vp and downe in a circle of absurditie a whole weeke, and neuer know where they are. But now that cloude of sorrow is dissolued which fierie Loue exhaled from his dewie haire, and affection hath vnburthened the labouring streames of her wombe in the lowe cesterne of his Graue; the night hath resigned her iettie throne vnto *Lucifer*, and cleere daylight possesseth the skie that was dimmed; wherfore breake off your daunce, you Fayries and Elues, and from the fieldes with the torne carcases of your Timbrils, for your kingdome is expired. Put out your rush candles, you Poets and Rimers, and bequeath your crazed quaterzayns to the Chaundlers; for loe, here he cometh that hath broke your legs. *Apollo* hath resigned his Iuory Harp vnto *Astrophel*, & he, like *Mercury*, must lull you a sleep with his musicke. Sleepe *Argus*, sleep Ignorance, sleep Impudence, for *Mercury* hath Io, & onely Io *Pæan* belongeth to *Astrophel*. Deare *Astrophel*, that in the ashes of thy Loue liuest againe like the *Phœnix*, O might thy bodie (as thy name) liue againe likewise here amongst vs! but the earth, the mother of mortalitie, hath snacht thee too soone into her chilled colde armes, and will not let thee by any meanes be drawne from her deadly imbrace; and thy diuine Soule, carried on an Angel's wings to heauen, is installed in *Hermes* place, sole *prolocutor* to the Gods. Therefore mayest thou neuer returne from the Elisian fieldes like *Orpheus*; therefore must we euer mourne for our *Orpheus*.

Fayne would a seconde spring of passion heere spend it selfe on his sweet remembrance; but Religion, that rebuketh prophane lamentation, drinkes in the riuers of those dispaireful teares which languorous ruth hath outwelled, & bids me looke back to the house of honor, where from one and the selfe same root of renowne I shal find many goodly branches deriued, & such as, with the spreading increase of their vertues, may somewhat ouershadow the Griefe of his los. Amongst the which, fayre sister of *Phœbus*, and eloquent secretary to the Muses, most rare Countesse of *Pembroke*, thou art not to be omitted, whom Artes doe adore as a second *Minerua*, and our Poets extoll as the Patronesse of their inuention; for in thee the *Lesbian Sappho* with her lirick Harpe is disgraced, and the Laurel Garlande which thy Brother so brauely aduaunst on his Launce is still kept greene in the Temple of *Pallas*. Thou only sacrificest thy soule to contemplation, thou only entertainest emptie handed *Homer*, & keepest the springs of *Castalia* from being dryed vp. Learning, wisedom, beautie, and all other ornaments of Nobilitie whatsoeuer seeke to approue themselues in thy sight and get a further seale of felicity from the smiles of thy fauour:

O Ioue digna viro ni Ioue nata fores.

I feare I shall be counted a mercenary flatterer for mixing my thoughts with such figuratiue admiration, but generall report that surpasseth my praise condemneth my rhetoricke of dulnesse for so colde a commendation. Indeede, to say the truth, my stile is somewhat heauie gated, and cannot daunce, trip, and goe so liuely, with 'oh! my loue, ah! my loue, all my loues gone,' as other Sheepheards that haue beene fooles in the Morris time cut of minde; nor hath my prose any skill to imitate the Almond leape verse, or sit tabring fiue yeres together nothing but 'to bee, to hee,' on a paper drum. Onely I can keepe pace with Grauesend barge, and care not if I haue water enough to lande my ship of fooles with the Tearme (the tyde I shoulde say). Now euery man is not of that minde; for some, to goe the lighter away, will take in their fraught of spangled feathers, golden Peebles, Straw, Reedes, Bulrushes, or anything, and then they beare out their sayles as proudly as if they were balisted with Bulbiefe. Others are so hardly bested for loading that they are faine to retaile the cinders of *Troy*, and the shiuers of broken trunchions, to fill vp their boate that else should goe empty; and if they haue but a pound weight of good Merchandise, it shall be placed at the poope, or pluckt in a thousand peeces to credit their carriage. For my part, euery man as he likes, *mens cuiusque id est quisque*. 'Tis as good to goe in cut-fingerd Pumps as corke shooes, if one were Cornish diamonds on his toes. To explain it by a more familiar example, an Asse is no great statesman in the beastes commonwealth, though he weare his eares *vpseuant muffe*, after the Muscouy fashion, & hange the lip like a Capcase halfe open, or look as demurely as a sixpenny browne loafe, for he hath some imperfections that do keepe him from the common Councel; yet of many he is deemed a very vertuous member, and one of the honestest sort of men that are. So that our opinion (as *Sextus Empiricus* affirmeth) giues the name of good or ill to euery thing. Out of whose works (latelie translated into English for the benefit of vnlearned writers) a man might collect a whole booke of this argument, which no doubt woulde proue a worthy commonwealth matter, and far better than wits waxe karnell: much good worship haue the Author.

Such is this golden age wherein we liue, and so replenisht with golden asses of all sortes, that, if learning had lost it selfe in a groue of Genealogies, wee neede doe no more but sette an olde goose ouer halfe a dozen pottle pots (which are as it were the egges of inuention), and wee shall haue such a breede of bookes within a little while after, as will fill all the world with the wilde fowle of good wits. I can tell you this is a harder thing then making golde of quick siluer, and will trouble you more then the Morrall of *Æsop's* Glow-worme hath troubled our English Apes, who, striuing to warme themselues with the flame of the Philosopher's stone, haue spent all their wealth in buying bellowes to blowe this false fyre. Gentlemen, I feare I haue too much presumed on your idle leysure, and beene too bold to stand talking all this while in an other mans doore; but now I will leaue you to suruey the pleasures of *Paphos*, and offer your smiles on the Aulters of *Venus*.

WILLIAM HAZLITT
From *Lectures on the Literature of the Age of Elizabeth*
1820, pp. 265–78

At the time that Sir Philip Sidney's *Arcadia* was written, those middle men, the critics, were not known. The author and reader came into immediate contact, and seemed never tired of each other's company. We are more fastidious and dissipated: the effeminacy of modern taste would, I am afraid, shrink back affrighted at the formidable sight of this once popular work, which is about as long (*horresco referens!*) as all Walter Scott's novels put together; but besides its size and appearance, it has, I think, other defects of a more intrinsic and insuperable nature. It is to me one of the greatest monuments of the abuse of intellectual power upon record. It puts one in mind of the court dresses and preposterous fashions of the time which are grown obsolete and disgusting. It is not romantic, but scholastic; not poetry, but casuistry; not nature, but art, and the worst sort of art, which thinks it can do better than nature. Of the number of fine things that are constantly passing through the author's mind, there is hardly one that he has not contrived to spoil, and to spoil purposely and maliciously, in order to aggrandize our idea of himself. Out of five hundred folio pages, there are hardly, I conceive, half a dozen sentences expressed simply and directly, with the sincere desire to convey the image implied, and without a systematic interpolation of the wit, learning, ingenuity, wisdom and everlasting impertinence of the writer, so as to disguise the object, instead of displaying it in its true colours and real proportions. Every page is "with centric and eccentric scribbled o'er;" his Muse is tattooed and tricked out like an Indian goddess. He writes a courthand, with flourishes like a schoolmaster; his figures are wrought in chain-stitch. All his thoughts are forced and painful births, and may be said to be delivered by the Cæsarean operation. At last, they become distorted and rickety in themselves; and before they have been cramped and twisted and swaddled into lifelessness and deformity. Imagine a writer to have great natural talents, great powers of memory and invention, an eye for nature, a knowledge of the passions, much learning and equal industry; but that he is so full of a consciousness of all this, and so determined to make the reader conscious of it at every step, that he becomes a complete intellectual coxcomb or nearly so;—that he never lets a casual observation pass without perplexing it with an endless, running commentary, that he never states a feeling without so many *circumambages*, without so many interlineations and parenthetical remarks on all that can be said for it, and anticipations of all that can be said against it, and that he never mentions a fact without giving so many circumstances and conjuring up so many things that it is like or not like, that you lose the main clue of the story in its infinite ramifications and intersections; and we may form some faint idea of the *Countess of Pembroke's Arcadia*, which is spun with great labour out of the author's brains, and hangs like a huge cobweb over the face of nature! This is not, as far as I can judge, an exaggerated description: but as near the truth as I can make it. The proofs are not far to seek. Take the first sentence, or open the volume any where and read. I will, however, take one of the most beautiful passages near the beginning, to shew how the subject-matter, of which the noblest use might have been made, is disfigured by the affectation of the style, and the importunate and vain activity of the writer's mind. The passage I allude to, is the celebrated description of Arcadia.

> So that the third day after, in the time that the morning did strew roses and violets in the heavenly floor against the coming of the sun, the nightingales (striving one with the other which could in most dainty variety recount their wrong-caused sorrow) made them put off their sleep, and rising from under a tree (which that night had been their pavilion) they went on their journey, which by and by welcomed Musidorus' eyes (wearied with the wasted soil of Laconia) with welcome prospects. There were hills which garnished their proud heights with stately trees: humble valleys whose base estate seemed com-

forted with the refreshing of silver rivers; meadows enamelled with all sorts of eye-pleasing flowers; thickets, which being lined with most pleasant shade were witnessed so to, by the cheerful disposition of many well-tuned birds; each pasture stored with sheep feeding with sober security, while the pretty lambs with bleating oratory craved the dam's comfort; here a shepherd's boy piping, as though he should never be old: there a young shepherdess knitting, and withal singing, and it seemed that her voice comforted her hands to work, and her hands kept time to her voice-music. As for the houses of the country (for many houses came under their eye) they were scattered, no two being one by the other, and yet not so far off, as that it barred mutual succour; a shew, as it were, of an accompaniable solitariness, and of a civil wildness. I pray you, said Musidorus, (then first unsealing his long-silent lips) what countries be these we pass through, which are so divers in shew, the one wanting no store, the other having no store but of want. The country, answered Claius, where you were cast ashore, and now are past through is Laconia: but this country (where you now set your foot) is Arcadia.

One would think the very name might have lulled his senses to delightful repose in some still, lonely valley, and have laid the restless spirit of Gothic quaintness, witticism, and conceit in the lap of classic elegance and pastoral simplicity. Here are images too of touching beauty and everlasting truth that needed nothing but to be simply and nakedly expressed to have made a picture equal (nay superior) to the allegorical representation of the Four Seasons of Life by Georgione. But no! He cannot let his imagination or that of the reader dwell for a moment on the beauty or power of the real object. He thinks nothing is done, unless it is his doing. He must officiously and gratuitously interpose between you and the subject as the Cicerone of Nature, distracting the eye and the mind by continual uncalled-for interruptions, analysing, dissecting, disjointing, murdering every thing, and reading a pragmatical, self-sufficient lecture over the dead body of nature. The moving spring of his mind is not sensibility or imagination, but dry, literal, unceasing craving after intellectual excitement, which is indifferent to pleasure or pain, to beauty or deformity, and likes to owe every thing to its own perverse efforts rather than the sense of power in other things. It constantly interferes to perplex and neutralise. It never leaves the mind in a wise passiveness. In the infancy of taste, the forward pupils of art took nature to pieces, as spoiled children do a watch, to see what was in it. After taking it to pieces they could not, with all their cunning, put it together again, so as to restore circulation to the heart, or its living hue to the face! The quaint and pedantic style here objected to was not however the natural growth of untutored fancy, but an artificial excrescence transferred from logic and rhetoric to poetry. It was not owing to the excess of imagination, but of the want of it, that is, to the predominance of the mere understanding or dialectic faculty over the imaginative and the sensitive. It is in fact poetry degenerating at every step into prose, sentiment entangling itself in a controversy, from the habitual leaven of polemics and casuistry in the writer's mind. The poet insists upon matters of fact from the beauty or grandeur that accompanies them; our prose-poet insists upon them because they are matters of fact, and buries the beauty and grandeur in a heap of common rubbish, "like two grains of wheat in a bushel of chaff." The true poet illustrates for ornament or use: the fantastic pretender, only because he is not easy till he can translate every thing out

of itself into something else. Imagination consists in enriching one idea by another, which has the same feeling or set of associations belonging to it in a higher or more striking degree; the quaint or scholastic style consists in comparing one thing to another by the mere process of abstraction, and the more forced and naked the comparison, the less of harmony or congruity there is in it, the more wire-drawn and ambiguous the link of generalisation by which objects are brought together, the greater is the triumph of the false and fanciful style. There was a marked instance of the difference in some lines from Ben Jonson . . . and which, as they are alternate examples of the extremes of both in the same author and in the same short poem, there can be nothing invidious in giving. In conveying an idea of female softness and sweetness, he asks—

> Have you felt the wool of the beaver,
> Or swan's down ever?
> Or smelt of the bud of the briar,
> Or the nard in the fire?

Now "the swan's down" is a striking and beautiful image of the most delicate and yielding softness; but we have no associations of a pleasing sort with the wool of the beaver. The comparison is dry, hard, and barren of effect. It may establish the matter of fact, but detracts from and impairs the sentiment. The smell of "the bud of the briar" is a double-distilled essence of sweetness: besides, there are all the other concomitant ideas of youth, beauty, and blushing modesty, which blend with and heighten the immediate feeling: but the poetical reader was not bound to know even what *nard* is (it is merely a learned substance, a non-entity to the imagination) nor whether it has a fragrant or disagreeable scent when thrown into the fire, till Ben Jonson went out of his way to give him this pedantic piece of information. It is a mere matter of fact or of experiment; and while the experiment is making in reality or fancy, the sentiment stands still; or even taking it for granted in the literal and scientific sense, we are where we were; it does not enhance the passion to be expressed: we have no love for the smell of nard in the fire, but we have an old, a long-cherished one, from infancy, for the bud of the briar. Sentiment, as Mr. Burke said of nobility, is a thing of inveterate prejudice, and cannot be created, as some people (learned and unlearned) are inclined to suppose, out of fancy or out of any thing by the wit of man. The artificial and natural style do not alternate in this way in the Arcadia: the one is but the Helot, the eyeless drudge of the other. Thus even in the above passage, which is comparatively beautiful and simple in its general structure, we have "the bleating oratory" of lambs, as if any thing could be more unlike oratory than the bleating of lambs; we have a young shepherdess knitting, whose hands keep time not to her voice, but to her "voice-music," which introduces a foreign and questionable distinction, merely to perplex the subject; we have meadows enamelled with all sorts of "eye-pleasing flowers," as if it were necessary to inform the reader that flowers pleased the eye, or as if they did not please any other sense: we have valleys refreshed "with *silver* streams," an epithet that has nothing to do with the refreshment here spoken of: we have "an accompaniable solitariness and a civil wildness," which are a pair of very laboured antitheses; in fine, we have "want of store, and store of want."

Again, the passage describing the shipwreck of Pyrochles, has been much and deservedly admired: yet it is not free from the same inherent faults.

> "But a little way off they saw the mast (of the vessel) whose proud height now lay along, like a widow having lost her mate, of whom she held her honour;"

[This needed explanation] "but upon the mast they saw a young man (at least if it were a man) bearing show of about eighteen years of age, who sat (as on horseback) having nothing upon him but his shirt, which being wrought with blue silk and gold, had a kind of resemblance to the sea" [This is a sort of alliteration in natural history] "on which the sun (then near his western home) did shoot some of his beams. His hair, (which the young men of Greece used to wear very long) was stirred up and down with the wind, which seemed to have a sport to play with it, as the sea had to kiss his feet; himself full of admirable beauty, set forth by the strangeness both of his seat and gesture; for holding his head up full of unmoved majesty, he held a sword aloft with his fair arm, which often he waved about his crown, as though he would threaten the world in that extremity."

If the original sin of alliteration, antithesis, and metaphysical conceit could be weeded out of this passage, there is hardly a more heroic one to be found in prose or poetry.

Here is one more passage marred in the making. A shepherd is supposed to say of his mistress,

Certainly, as her eyelids are more pleasant to behold, than two white kids climbing up a fair tree and browsing on his tenderest branches, and yet are nothing, compared to the day-shining stars contained in them; and as her breath is more sweet than a gentle south-west wind, which comes creeping over flowery fields and shadowed waters in the extreme heat of summer; and yet is nothing compared to the honey-flowing speech that breath doth carry; no more all that our eyes can see of her (though when they have seen her, what else they shall ever see is but dry stubble after clover grass) is to be matched with the flock of unspeakable virtues, laid up delightfully in that best-builded fold.

Now here are images of singular beauty and of Eastern originality and daring, followed up with enigmatical or unmeaning common-places, because he never knows when to leave off, and thinks he can never be too wise or too dull for his reader. He loads his prose Pegasus, like a pack-horse, with all that comes and with a number of little trifling circumstances, that fall off, and you are obliged to stop to pick them up by the way. He cannot give his imagination a moment's pause, thinks nothing done, while any thing remains to do, and exhausts nearly all that can be said upon a subject, whether good, bad, or indifferent. The above passages are taken from the beginning of the Arcadia, when the author's style was hardly yet formed. The following is a less favourable, but fairer specimen of the work. It is the model of a love-letter, and is only longer than that of Adriano de Armada, in *Love's Labour Lost.*

"Most blessed paper, which shalt kiss that hand, whereto all blessedness is in nature a servant, do not yet disdain to carry with thee the woeful words of a miser now despairing: neither be afraid to appear before her, bearing the base title of the sender. For no sooner shall that divine hand touch thee, but that thy baseness shall be turned to most high preferment. Therefore mourn boldly my ink: for while she looks upon you, your blackness will shine: cry out boldly my lamentation, for while she reads you, your cries will be music. Say then (O happy messenger of a most unhappy message) that the too soon born and too late dying creature, which dares not speak, no, not look, no, not scarcely think (as from his miserable self unto her heavenly highness), only presumes to desire thee (in the time that her eyes and voice do exalt thee) to say, and in this manner to say, not from him, oh no, that were not fit, but of him, thus much unto her sacred judgment. O you, the only honour to women, to men the only admiration, you that being armed by love, defy him that armed you, in this high estate wherein you have placed me" [*i.e.* the letter] "yet let me remember him to whom I am bound for bringing me to your presence: and let me remember him, who (since he is yours, how mean soever he be) it is reason you have an account of him. The wretch (yet your wretch) though with languishing steps runs fast to his grave; and will you suffer a temple (how poorly built soever, but yet a temple of your deity) to be rased? But he dyeth: it is most true, he dyeth: and he in whom you live, to obey you, dyeth. Whereof though he plain, he doth not complain: for it is a harm, but no wrong, which he hath received. He dies, because in woeful language all his senses tell him, that such is your pleasure: for if you will not that he live, alas, alas, what followeth, what followeth of the most ruined Dorus, but his end? End, then, evil-destined Dorus, end; and end thou woeful letter, end: for it sufficeth her wisdom to know, that her heavenly will shall be accomplished."

(Lib. ii. p.117)

This style relishes neither of the lover nor the poet. Nine-tenths of the work are written in this manner. It is in the very manner of those books of gallantry and chivalry, which, with the labyrinths of their style, and "the reason of their unreasonableness," turned the fine intellects of the Knight of La Mancha. In a word (and not to speak it profanely), the Arcadia is a riddle, a rebus, an acrostic in folio: it contains about 4000 far fetched similes, and 6000 impracticable dilemmas, about 10,000 reasons for doing nothing at all, and as many more against it; numberless alliterations, puns, questions and commands, and other figures of rhetoric; about a score good passages, that one may turn to with pleasure, and the most involved, irksome, improgressive, and heteroclite subject that ever was chosen to exercise the pen or patience of man. It no longer adorns the toilette or lies upon the pillow of Maids of Honour and Peeresses in their own right (the Pamelas and Philocleas of a later age), but remains upon the shelves of the libraries of the curious in long works and great names, a monument to shew that the author was one of the ablest men and worst writers of the age of Elizabeth.

His Sonnets, inlaid in the *Arcadia,* are jejune, far-fetched and frigid. I shall select only one that has been much commended. It is to the High Way where his mistress had passed, a strange subject, but not unsuitable to the author's genius.

High-way, since you my chief Parnassus be,
And that my Muse (to some ears not unsweet)
Tempers her words to trampling horses' feet
More oft than to a chamber melody;
Now blessed you bear onward blessed me
To her, where I my heart safe left shall meet;
My Muse, and I must you of duty greet
With thanks and wishes, wishing thankfully.
Be you still fair, honour'd by public heed,
By no encroachment wrong'd, nor time forgot;
Nor blamed for blood, nor shamed for sinful deed;
And that you know, I envy you no lot
Of highest wish, I wish you so much bliss,
Hundreds of years you Stella's feet may kiss.

The answer of the High-way has not been preserved, but the sincerity of this appeal must no doubt have moved the stocks and stones to rise and sympathise. His *Defense of Poetry* is his most readable performance; there he is quite at home, in a sort of special pleader's office, where his ingenuity, scholastic subtlety, and tenaciousness in argument stand him in good stead; and he brings off poetry with flying colours; for he was a man of wit, of sense, and learning, though not a poet of true taste or unsophisticated genius.

HENRY RICHARD FOX BOURNE
"Authorship as Courtier"
A *Memoir of Sir Philip Sidney*
1862, pp. 321–52

His leisure as a courtier Philip Sidney occupied in writing two books, not more worthy of note for the place they hold in literary history, than as illustrations of their author's character. "If his purpose had been to leave his memory in books," said the friend who knew him best, "I am confident, in the right use of logic, philosophy, history, poesy, nay even in the most ingenious of mechanical arts, he would have shown such traits of a searching and judicious spirit, as the professors of every faculty would have striven no less for him than the Seven Cities did to have Homer of their sept. But the truth is, his end was not writing, even while he wrote, but both his wit and understanding bent upon his heart to make himself and others, not in words or opinion, but in life and action, good and great."[1]

Yet, as in the world of politics, his courtly chains restrained him from attainment of the high and useful position for which he was most fit, so in the world of letters he was not yet able to do work as valuable or to exercise an influence as wholesome, as in later years. *The Countess of Pembroke's Arcadia*, albeit the offspring of strong brotherly love, shows plainly, in its style and purport, that it was the work of an Elizabethan courtier; and in *Astrophel and Stella* there is yet clearer evidence of the bondage to which the poet's noblest faculties were subject.

Sidney wrote *The Arcadia*, as we have seen, by his sister's wish. "You desired me to do it," he said in dedication, "and your desire to my heart is an absolute commandment." Perhaps the Countess of Pembroke merely urged upon him the employment of his mind in authorship; perhaps the whole first plan of the book was of her suggestion. At any rate, it was undertaken and continued not more for her brother's own pastime than for her amusement; "for severer eyes it is not, being but a trifle, and that triflingly handled." The first portion was written under her roof; the rest, penned after Sidney's return to Court, was sent down to her, piece by piece, as the sheets were written. And for even that latter part the inspiration seems to have come most freely in the neighbourhood of Wilton. "When he was writing his *Arcadia*," we learn from Aubrey, "he was wont to take his table-book out of his pocket, and write down his notions as they came into his head, as he was hunting on Sarum's pleasant plains."[2] In the elaboration of his work, however, he evidently received much influence from the Court in which he gaily moved, and the literary Areopagus to which he may still have frequently resorted.

To some extent I imagine the *Arcadia* owed its existence to John Lyly, author of *Euphues*. Lyly was a year or two older than Sidney, though not matriculated at Oxford till about the date of the other's removal from the University. He commenced systematic attendance upon Queen Elizabeth, however, in the year of Sidney's return from Germany, and then the two must often have met. But they were of different tastes in literature, and of different parties at Court. Lyly's patron was the Earl of Oxford, and he pandered too much to that nobleman's love of foreign fashions in life and speech. His lot was a hard one, for after years of humble suit for employment, the post of Master of the Revels being the object of his ambition, he thus described the issue in a letter to the Queen: "Thirteen years your Highness's servant, but yet nothing: twenty friends that, though they say they will be sure, I find them sure to be slow: a thousand hopes, but all nothing: a hundred promises, but yet nothing. Thus, casting up the inventory of my friends, hopes, promises, and times, the *summa totalis* amounteth to just nothing. My last will is shorter than mine inventory; but three legacies,—patience to my creditors, melancholy without measure to my friends, and beggary without shame to my family."[3]

Lyly's greatest work, and one far too much abused when not wholly slighted, was *Euphues: the Anatomy of Wit*. It appeared in 1579, and had for its theme the story of a young gentleman, who quitting his home in Athens to visit Naples, gave occasion for much witty and some very earnest writing concerning all that he did, and saw, and thought. But the wit was of the kind which, taking its name from this very book, is known as Euphuism, and the author often fell into the same vices of style which he essayed to ridicule. In the book there was real worth, which Sidney must have seen and acknowledged; but he could not fail also to see its weaker points. He knew that he could do better. I have no doubt that the reading of *Euphues* in 1579 led him many steps towards the writing of *The Arcadia* in 1580.

For the style and the subject of his book Sidney found in English literature no model. But in the works of some southern authors there were suggestions which he adopted. In his youth he had read diligently the Ethiopic History of Heliodorus, lately translated out of the Greek by Thomas Underdown, and he afterwards praised the old novelist for "his sugared invention of that picture of love in Theagenes and Chariclea."[4] Heliodorus doubtless inclined him to introduce a heroic element into his work; but its pastoral structure was evidently due to the recollection of Sannazzaro's Italian *Arcadia*, first printed at Milan in 1502. During the fifteenth century pastoral romances, most popular in Portugal, had been abundantly written; but Sannazzaro was the first man of real genius who adopted this mode of composition. He wrote in a style which was simple, flowing, rapid, and harmonious; often too florid and diffuse, but with honest effort to restore to Italian the polish and purity introduced by Petrarch.[5] Sidney studied this work, and probably many others which appeared in imitation of it. To George of Montemayor, the Spanish precursor of Cervantes, however, his debt was largest. Out of this writer's *Diana*, published a few years previously, he had already translated a couple of fragments in verse, and he seems to have been much pleased with its laboured beauty of style, its intricacy of plot, and its richness of imagination. Yet *The Arcadia* differed essentially from all its predecessors. In every sense an original work, the beautiful thoughts with which it was filled were altogether Sidney's own.

For heroes he painted two cousins, Musidorus, Prince of Thessalia, and Pyrocles, Prince of Macedon; between whom there was such notable friendship "as made them more like than the likeness of all other virtues, and made them more near one to the other than the nearness of their blood could aspire unto." Pyrocles, being by three or four years the younger, showed reverence, full of love, to Musidorus, and Musidorus had a delight as full of love in Pyrocles. All that the elder knew he rejoiced to teach to the younger, and the younger cared to learn of none so much as of the elder. Thus living together from childhood, they grew to be equal in everything, and superior, as it seemed, to all others in the world.

When Musidorus was about twenty years of age, it was thought right that they should travel, and with that intent they left their Thessalian home. But before very long they were shipwrecked and separated. Musidorus, by good chance, being beaten by the waves on to that edge of the Laconian shore which is opposite to the island of Cithera, was rescued by two generous shepherds, Strephon and Claius, who brought back warmth and vigour to his almost lifeless body. At his intercession they took boat and sought to recover his friend. The attempt, however, was vain, and Musidorus in his grief would have killed himself, had not the shepherds stayed his hand, and persuaded him to go with them to the residence of Kalander, a gentle and noble man, whose hospitable and upright dealing caused all to love him, and who, if any could, would be able to comfort and advise the stranger.

Ere long they set out. "The third day after, in the time that the morning did strow roses and violets in the heavenly floor against the coming of the sun, the nightingales—striving one with the other which could in most dainty variety recount their wrong-caused sorrow—made them put off their sleep, and rising from under a tree, which that night had been their pavilion, they went on their journey, which by-and-by welcomed Musidorus's eyes, wearied with the wasted soil of Laconia, with delightful prospects. There were hills, which garnished their proud heights with stately trees; humble vallies, whose base estate seemed comforted with the presence of silver rivers; meadows enamelled with all sorts of eye-pleasing flowers; thickets which, being lined with most pleasing shade, were witnessed so too by the cheerful disposition of many well-tuned birds; each pasture stored with sheep feeding with sober security, while the pretty lambs with bleating oratory craved the dam's comfort; here a shepherd's boy piping as though he should never be old; there a young shepherdess knitting, and withal singing—and it seemed that her voice comforted her hands to work, and her hands kept time to her voice-music. As for the houses of the country,—for many houses came under their eye,—they were all scattered, no two being one by the other,—yet not so far as that it barred mutual succour; a show, as it were, of an accompanible solitariness and of a civil wildness."

Such was Arcadia. Next we have a description of Kalander's abode, Sidney's ideal of a house. "The house itself was built of fair and strong stone, not affecting so much any extraordinary kind of fineness, as an honourable representing of a firm stateliness. The lights, doors, and stairs, rather directed to the use of the guest than the eye of the artificer, and yet, as the one chiefly heeded, so the other not neglected. Each place handsome without curiosity, and homely without loathsomeness, not so dainty as not to be trod on, nor yet slubbered up with good fellowship; all more lasting than beautiful, but that the consideration of the exceeding lastingness made the eye believe it was exceeding beautiful. The servants, not so many in number, as cleanly in apparel and serviceable in behaviour, testifying even in their countenances that their master took as well care to be served as of them that did serve."

In that way the story opens. Musidorus—who introduced himself as Palladius, and spoke of his friend Pyrocles as Daiphantus—became an inmate of Kalander's house, and the kind treatment of his host did much to deaden his sorrow and to fill him with hopeful, happy thoughts. The good old man, on the other hand, felt a strong fatherly love for the youth, finding in him "a mind of most excellent composition, a piercing wit quite void of ostentation, high erected thoughts seated in a heart of courtesy, an eloquence as sweet in the uttering as it was slow to come to the uttering, and a behaviour so noble as gave a majesty to adversity." Thus loved, Musidorus thought that he wanted nothing to complete his enjoyment save the presence of his friend. Soon he was to find him.

News came that Kalander's son Clitophon, joining in the Lacedemonian war against the Helots, had been made prisoner. The father was so overcome with grief that he could do nothing. But Musidorus, anxious for adventure, and anxious to make some return for his host's kindness towards him, gathered an army of Arcadians and went against the servile foes. A long and deadly battle ensued. Musidorus, brave himself to desperation, saw with astonishment the wonderful bravery of the captain of the Helots, and the captain had like wonder about Musidorus. "It was hard to say whether he more liked his doings, or misliked the effect of his doings." It could not but be that two such heroes should meet and try each other's strength. "Their courage was guided with skill, and their skill was armed with courage; neither did their hardness darken their wit, nor their wit cool their hardness; both valiant, as men despising death; both confident, as men despising to be overcome; yet doubtful by their present feeling, and respectful by what they had already seen. Their feet steady, their hands diligent, their eyes watchful, and their hearts resolute. The parts either not armed or weakly armed were well known,—and, according to the knowledge, should have been sharply visited, but that the answer was as quick as the objection. The smart bred rage, and the rage bred smart again, till both sides beginning to wax faint, and rather desirous to die accompanied, than hopeful to live victorious, the captain of the Helots, with a blow whose violence grew of fury, not of strength, or of strength proceeding of fury, struck Musidorus upon the side of the head, that he reeled astonished; and withal the helmet fell off, he remaining bareheaded." Great was the surprise of all, both friends and foes, when the captain, instead of following up his advantage, knelt down before his antagonist, saying he would rather be his prisoner than any other's general. Musidorus was lost in astonishment, until his vanquisher exclaimed, "What! hath Palladius forgotten the voice of Daiphantus?"

These, it will be remembered, were the assumed names of Musidorus and Pyrocles. The state of affairs was complicated, but not too much so for the romancer to unravel. Pyrocles explained the course of adventures by which he had become the unwilling leader of the Helots: and now after bringing them back to peace with the Spartans, he released Clitophon and repaired to the house of Kalander. Between him and Musidorus there was much loving converse with interchange of their several histories. Among the rest, Musidorus told a strange story which he had heard from Kalander, concerning Basilius, the Prince of Arcadia, and his family.

Basilius, though not a very wise, courageous, or magnificent man, was, in most particulars, meek, courteous, and merciful. His wife, Gynecia, was a woman of great wit and beauty, and displayed more princely temper than her husband. But the grace was with their daughters, Pamela and Philoclea. "When I marked them both methought there was (if, at least, such perfections may receive the word of more) more sweetness in Philoclea, but more majesty in Pamela: methought love played in Philoclea's eyes, and threatened in Pamela's: methought Philoclea's beauty only persuaded, but so persuaded as all hearts must yield; Pamela's beauty used violence, and such violence as no heart could resist. And it seems that such proportion is between their minds. Philoclea, so bashful as though her excellences had stolen into her before she was aware; so humble that she will put all pride out of countenance; in sum, such proceeding as will stir hope, but teach hope good manners: Pamela, of high thoughts, who avoids not pride by not knowing her excellences, but by making it one of her excellences to be void of pride." It was in a wild fit of jealous care for these daughters that Basilius had broken up his Court and retired into a forest hard by, and had there built two lodges. In one he now dwelt, with his wife and Philoclea; in the other he placed the elder sister, under the keeping of one Dametas, an arrant doltish clown, his ugly spouse Miso, and their horrid daughter Mopsa, inheritor of both parents' defects. To this miserable family the whole management of the maidens was assigned, the Prince maintaining his authority on one point only, that so long as he lived they should find no husbands. With that purpose he shut out all men, except a priest and some shepherds skilled in the music which he loved.

To this story Pyrocles listened with eager and retentive ears. Becoming moody and silent, he wandered often in the woods; and thereat Musidorus, though he saw not its secret, was much displeased. He urged that they should leave Arcadia, and return to the busier life of Thessalia. Pyrocles, however, would not hear of it, and spoke in eloquent tones of the sweets of a pastoral life. "I think you will make me see," said Musidorus, scoffingly, "that the vigour of your wit can show itself in any subject; or else you feed sometimes your solitariness with the conceits of the poets when they put such words in the mouths of one of these fantastical, mind-infected people, that children and musicians call lovers!" "And what, dear cousin," answered Pyrocles, "if I be not so much the poet, the freedom of whose pen can exercise itself in anything, as even that miserable subject of his cunning whereof you speak?" "Now, the eternal gods forbid," shouted Musidorus, "that ever my ears should be poisoned with so evil news of you!"

Yet it was true; and true, also, that Musidorus, like every other rash talker who runs tilt with Cupid, had very soon to make confession that he also was a willing slave to love. But this was after Pyrocles, alarmed by his harsh words, had fled from him; and after both, wandering apart, had met with many adventures which cannot here be recounted. It is enough to say that the friends, in the end, met and renewed their vows of friendship on the outskirts of the territory from which the Prince of Arcadia had banned all intruders. Pyrocles, however, calling himself Zelmane, was now dressed like a beautiful Amazon, and as such he was regarded by all save Musidorus. And Musidorus hid his real character from every eye and ear but those of Pyrocles, under the name of Dorus, and the garb of a shepherd. With the help of these disguises they were quickly able to gain entrance into the forbidden region; and their worth, being such as could nowhere and nohow be long concealed, soon became apparent, and won for them the favour of the whole company.

But their new positions were not easy ones to occupy. The perplexities of the lovers, and the perils through which they had to pass in working onward to their end, form the main subject of Sidney's romance.

Musidorus loved Pamela, but he dared not tell her so; and, that he might gain approach to her, he was forced to profess affection for her ugly keeper, Mopsa. Rightly trusting to his graceful bearing and courteous speech, however, he in time bred in Pamela such tenderness towards him, that "she could no longer keep love from looking out through her eyes or going forth in her words." He was quick in discerning this, yet it gave him little comfort. Pamela, thinking that he loved Mopsa, and blaming herself for the feelings which she could not overcome, would never listen to his suit, or allow him opportunity for telling what were his real thoughts, and what was his real station.

Of that sort were the storms of love that beat on Musidorus. With Pyrocles, for long, things fared still worse. Loving Philoclea, he was taken by her for the warlike lady whose garb he affected, and therefore she had for him only a sisterly affection; whereas, Basilius, being deceived about his sex, regarded him with a far stronger liking. Nor was this complication enough. Gynecia, also, her practised eye seeing through his Amazonian dress, cared for him more than sorted with her wifely duty. Rarely could he seek the society of Philoclea without being held back either by the ardent passion of the father, who courted him as a maiden, or by the watchful jealousy of the mother, who would win him as a man. It was hard for him to gain access to the daughter's society, even in the presence of her attendants. Yet he wooed her cunningly. After telling, as though they were another's, of the great things which he himself had done, he contrived to quicken in Philoclea a hearty admiration for the unknown knight; and at last, when once, after long waiting, he found himself alone with her, he ventured to tell her that he was not a woman, but that same knight disguised through love of her. Philoclea listened with surprise, but not with anger, and presently the surprise issued in happiness.

In Sidney's romance, the unravelling of those entanglements occupies very many pages; and some exciting interludes, adding further to the complication of the story, are inserted. At one time, the wicked lady Cecropia succeeded in a plot by which she captured Zelmane,—whose real name, it will be remembered, was Pyrocles,—Philoclea, and Pamela, and lodged them in her own castle; thinking thereby to further her ambitious schemes against Basilius, and so gratify her hatred for Gynecia. Her husband, when living, had been brother to the Prince of Arcadia, whom now she sought to depose, with the view of setting up her son Amphialus as Prince, herself being real governor. Amphialus, better than his mother, knew nothing of the capture, or of the wicked thoughts which prompted it, until it had been effected. He had long loved Philoclea, and for this the Amazonian Zelmane, in unwomanly jealousy, had lately wounded him. Now, however, though Philoclea's presence added fuel to his passions, he was not base enough to woo with violence. Cecropia, despising love and scorning chastity, condemned him for such weakness; but, rather than see him afflicted, she volunteered to urge his suit. "Therefore she went softly to Philoclea's chamber, and peeping through the side of the door, then being a little open, she saw Philoclea sitting low upon a cushion, in such a given-over manner, that one would have thought silence, solitariness, and melancholy were come there, under the ensign of mishap, to conquer delight, and drive him from his natural seat of beauty. Her tears came dropping down like rain in sunshine, and she, not taking heed to wipe the tears, they hung upon her cheeks and lips, as upon cherries which the dropping tree bedeweth. In the dressing of her hair and apparel she might see neither a careful art nor an art of carefulness, but even left to a neglected chance, which yet could no more unperfect her perfections, than a die, any way cast, could lose his squareness."

Let those descriptive sentences serve for specimens of Sidney's style at its worst; but no fault can be found with the exquisite picture of pure, noble-minded womanliness, as shown in Philoclea's resistance of all the insidious attacks, the cunning persuasions, the hard threatenings, which were directed against her. Cecropia was altogether baffled; she would willingly have revenged herself, but that she saw how, by hurting Philoclea, she would be only bringing trouble to her son. She thought, however, that one maiden would do as well as another for Amphialus, and that he would be well pleased if she could win for him some yielding mistress, instead of this disdaining beauty. Therefore, fortified with stronger arguments than ever, she betook herself to Pamela's chamber, but waited at the door, as she had done when visiting Philoclea, to see if some circumstance would arise favourable to her intended discourse. Watching thus, she saw Pamela, walking up and down like one moved by deep, though patient thoughts. "For her look and countenance was settled, her pace soft and almost still, of one measure, without any passionate gesture or violent motion, till at length, as it were awakening and strengthening herself, 'Well,' she said, 'yet this is the best; and of this I am sure, that, however they wrong me, they cannot overmaster God. No darkness blinds His eyes: no gaol bars Him out: to whom else should I fly but to Him for succour?' And therefore, kneeling down, even where she stood, she thus said, 'O All-seeing Light and Eternal Life of all things, to Whom nothing is either so great that it may resist, or so small that it is contemned; look upon my misery with Thine eye of mercy, and let Thine infinite power vouchsafe to limit out some proportion of deliverance unto me, as to Thee shall be most convenient. Let not injury, O Lord, triumph over me, and let my faults by Thy hand be corrected, and make not mine unjust enemy the minister of Thy justice. But yet, my God, if, in Thy wisdom, this be the aptest chastisement for my unexcusable folly, if this low bondage be fitted for my over high desires, if the pride of my not enough humble heart be thus to be broken, O Lord, I yield unto Thy will, and joyfully embrace what sorrow Thou wilt have me suffer. Only thus much let me crave of Thee: let my craving, O Lord, be accepted of Thee, since even that proceeds from Thee; let me crave, even by the noblest title which in my greatest affliction I may give myself, that I am Thy creature, and by Thy goodness, which is Thyself, that Thou wilt suffer some beam of Thy majesty so to shine into my mind that it may still depend constantly upon Thee. Let calamity be the exercise, but not the overthrow of my virtue; let their power prevail, but prevail not to destruction. Let my greatness be their prey; let my pain be the sweetness of their revenge; let them, if so it seem good unto Thee, vex me with more and more punishment; but, O Lord, let never their wickedness have such a hand but that I may carry a pure mind in a pure body.' And pausing awhile, 'And O most gracious Lord,' said she, 'whatever becomes of me, preserve the virtuous Musidorus.'"[6]

Such a prayer as this of Pamela's could be powerless upon none. "Even the hard-hearted wickedness of Cecropia, if it found not a love of that goodness, yet it felt an abasement at that goodness; and if she had not a kindly remorse, yet had she an irksome accusation of her own naughtiness, so that she was put from the bias of her fore-intended lesson." Something she did say at this time, and much on other days; but of course she received no answer save scornful reproof.

Virtue was a sure defence to the oppressed maidens, a truer helper than the Arcadian army, which often fought bravely for their rescue, but as often failed. Of the warfare there is lengthy description: a part of which may serve as illustration of much else of Sidney's writing, pleasant notwithstanding its extravagance of word and thought. "After the terrible salutation of warlike noise, the shaking of hands was with sharp weapons. Some lances, according to the metal they met and skill of the guider, did stain themselves in blood; some flew up in pieces, as if they would threaten heaven because they failed on earth. But their office was quickly inherited, either by the prince of weapons the sword, or by some heavy mace or biting axe, which, hunting still the weakest chase, sought ever to light there where smallest resistance might worse prevent mischief. The clashing of armour, and crushing of staves, the jostling of bodies, the resounding of blows, was the first part of that ill-

agreeing music which was beautified with the grisliness of wounds, the rising of dust, the hideous falls, and the groans of the dying. The very horses, angry in their master's anger, with love and obedience brought forth the effects of hate and resistance, and, with minds of servitude, did as if they affected glory. Some lay dead under their dead masters, whom unknightly wounds had unjustly punished for a faithful duty. Some lay upon their lords by like accidents, and in death had the honour to be borne by them whom in life they had borne. Some, having lost their commanding burthens, ran scattered about the field, abashed with the madness of mankind. The earth itself, wont to be a burial of men, was now, as it were, buried with men; so was the face thereof hidden with dead bodies, to whom death had come marked in divers manners. In one place lay disinherited heads, dispossessed of their natural seignories; in another, whole bodies to see to, but that their hearts, wont to be bound all over so close, were now with deadly violence opened; in others, fouler deaths had uglily displayed their trailing guts. There lay arms, whose fingers yet moved, as if they would feel for him that made them feel; and legs which, contrary to common reason, by being discharged of their burden were grown heavier. But no sword paid so large a tribute of souls to the eternal kingdom as that of Amphialus, who, like a tiger from whom a company of wolves did seek to ravish a new gotten prey, so he, remembering they came to take away Philoclea, did labour to make valour, strength, choler, and hatred, to answer the proportion of his love, which was infinite."

Very skilful is the rehearsal of the contest on a later day, in which Amphialus slew the famous Argalus, fair Parthenia, best and truest of wives, tending her husband in his death; of the still later contest which the same Amphialus had with one who came as a stranger knight to revenge the fate of Argalus, and who, when the death-wound had been given, proved to be none other than Parthenia; and of the deep, stern lesson which thus he learnt of the mischief that must ever come from warring in an unholy warfare. Never, he thought, would it have fallen to him blindly to have stricken down so excellent a lady, had he not been battling for a wrongful cause and in pursuance of an impure love.

But Cecropia's heart was not moved. Her son's suffering only heightened her cruelty, and added to the wickedness of the treatment she gave to her three captives, Philoclea, Pamela, and Zelmane. The story of it all is wearisome.

Sidney himself seems to have grown weary of his work. At this point there is an entire break in the narrative, and the remaining quarter of the book exists to us in a much less finished state than the three quarters from which I have drawn the preceding extracts. Indeed, we are told that the remainder was never so much as seen by its author, after he sent away the loose sheets to his sister. "Yet for that it was his," we learn, "howsoever deprived of the just grace it should have had, it was held too good to be lost, and therefore with much labour were the best coherences that could be gathered out of those scattered papers made only by her noble care to whose dear hand they were first committed, and for whose delight and entertainment only they were undertaken."

At the resuming of the story we find peace in Arcadia—Zelmane, Philoclea, and Pamela, being restored to Basilius. Yet matters were not altogether as they ought to have been. Musidorus was still suffering indignity in his disguise as a shepherd, and Pyrocles unwillingly continued to be loved, in his Amazonian dress, by the King, and, in his discovered manhood, by the Queen. Each youth had won the pure liking of the maiden whom he purely loved; but how further were they to proceed? The elder of the two solved the difficulty by persuading Pamela to flee with him to his home, and to become Duchess of Thessalia. But Pyrocles remained, "loathsomely loved and dangerously loving." He, however, found bold means for ending his perplexity. Promising gratification of their unchaste desires to both Basilius and Gynecia, he contrived lawfully to deceive them both, and to bring them to the unwitting enjoyment of each other's society; and thus he was left alone to the possession of Philoclea's love. Many perils attended the working out and the issue of this device, and they are lengthily recounted in the romance; but containing less that is either interesting or wholesome than any other part of *The Arcadia*, they need not be here repeated.

Sidney never properly completed the romance. On the last page he hastily wound up his complicated narrative. Basilius was brought back to his right mind, in respect both of his kingly office and of his domestic duty. Abandoning his unmanly seclusion, he exercised a wise rule over Arcadia, and returned to his former pure affection for his wife. Gynecia also, surrendering her evil thoughts, received and partly deserved most honourable fame throughout the world; all, save Pyrocles and Philoclea, who never betrayed her, thinking that she was the perfect mirror of wifely love, "which, though in that point undeserved, she did, in the remnant of her life, duly purchase with observing all duty and faith, to the example and glory of Greece; so uncertain are mortal judgments, the same person most infamous and most famous, and neither justly." Sidney's closing sentence indicates the matters which he doubtless originally intended to have presented with great fulness. Concerning Musidorus and Pyrocles, he said: "The solemnities of their marriages with the Arcadian pastorals, full of many comical adventures happening to those rural lovers, the strange stories of Artaxia and Plexirtus, Erona and Plangus, Hellen and Amphialus, with the wonderful chances that befel them; the shepherdish loves of Menalcas with Kalodulus's daughter; the poor hopes of the poor Philisides"—that being the name by which Sidney referred to himself—"in the pursuit of his affections; the strange continuance of Claius and Strephon's desire; lastly the son of Pyrocles, named Pyrophilus, and Melidora, the fair daughter of Pamela, by Musidorus, who even at their birth entered into admirable fortunes, may awake some other spirit to exercise his pen in that wherewith mine is already dulled."

It is not much to be wondered at that Sidney's spirit was dulled. The work was already far too long, and in it there were very many faults, by no one else so clearly seen and condemned as by the author. He thought too poorly of it to suffer it to be printed in his lifetime, and on his death-bed he desired that it might be burned. That this request was not complied with is ground for very real satisfaction. The good that was in *The Arcadia* greatly overbalanced the bad. It had some memorable lessons to teach to the world, and it taught them very effectually. But, in praising it, we must never forget that Sidney himself, in his matured years, saw reason for greatly dispraising it, and that it has lived only through the loving zeal of the sister for whom it was so lovingly prepared. Indeed we cannot fully judge of the merits of the work as left by its author. To fit it for presentment to the world, we are told that the Countess of Pembroke did much, and that "as often, repairing a ruinous house, the mending of some old part occasioneth the making of some new, so here her honourable labour began in correcting the faults, and ended in supplying the defects."[7] Many faults remain, and it is even possible that some of them were the work of the correcting hand.

One great error of *The Arcadia*, however, was in its original design. The mixing up of classical fable with chivalrous romance, and the reflection therein of many contemporary incidents, could not but produce serious confusion and contradiction. The pastoral and the heroic sort ill with one another. For combining them, Sidney had the precedent of all the Spanish and Italian romances which helped him in his work, but his own good sense and literary judgment were shown in his determination, if life and inclination had remained with him, to undo the whole story, and retain only such parts of it as would fit into a strictly historical romance with King Arthur for its hero. That was a scheme admirably suited to the full unfolding of his genius, and one upon which he could not have failed to write wonderfully well. But that design he was never able to fulfil.

In the laboured character of its details, and in its often extravagant style of thought and phrase, there is, also, ground for condemning *The Arcadia*. Overstraining, however, was a leading attribute of all studied prose writing in Sidney's day, with almost the single exception of his own *Defence of Poesie*. It makes up nearly all the substance of Lyly's *Euphues* written in 1579. In plot, of course, there is hardly room for comparison between Sidney's and Lyly's works. While *The Arcadia* was professedly an elaborate fiction, *Euphues* was designed to contain all sorts of prudent counsel and sharp satire, shaped as flesh around the dry skeleton of a tale. Lyly followed the example adopted by many of the scholastic successors of Boethius. His work was in a measure well done; there is always much good sense to be found in his quaint, extravagant sentences; but undoubtedly Sidney's mode of teaching was wiser, and his style of writing purer. Both authors wished to enforce the noblest thoughts that were in them. But *The Arcadia* contains very little of direct moralization, and, in the constant flow of description, the writer's mind is left to make an undefined yet strong impression upon the reader; whereas the thoughts of *Euphues* lose all their energy and influence in the teacher's persistent effort to present them most forcibly and discernibly. Enough has been quoted to show Sidney's method. A few sentences, neither better nor worse than the rest of the book, will suffice for illustration of Lyly's style of teaching.

> Let not gentlewomen, he says, make too much of their painted sheath, let them not be so curious in their own conceit, or so currish to their royal lovers. When the black crow's foot shall appear in their eye or the black ox tread on their foot, when their beauty shall be like the blasted rose, their wealth wasted, their bodies worn, their faces wrinkled, their fingers crooked, who will like them in their age who loved none in their youth? If you will be cherished when you be old, be courteous while you be young; if you look for comfort in your hoary hair, be not coy when you have your golden locks; if you would be embraced in the waning of your bravery, be not squeamish in the wearing of your beauty: if you desire to be kept like the roses, when they have lost their colour, smell sweet as the rose doth in the bud; if you would be tasted for old wine, be in the mouth a pleasant grape; so shall you be cherished for your courtesy, comforted for your honesty, embraced for your amity; so shall you be preserved with the sweet rose and drunk with the pleasant wine.[8]

In *The Arcadia*, as in *Euphues*, there was much sober teaching by good and bad example, and by implied satire. The book may possibly have been intended to be, as one old critic called it, "a continual grove of morality, shadowing moral and political results under the plain and easy emblems of lovers."[9] But the assertion of many others of its admirers, that it contained a complete allegorical view of the age, is certainly erroneous. It is not at all to be believed that Sidney meant to vaunt his own merits under the name of Pyrocles, or to compliment his friend Fulke Greville by presenting him as Musidorus, or to show his sister's virtue in the praise of Pamela, or to put false painting upon Lady Rich in the portrait of Philoclea, or to typify his father in Euarchus, or to defame Queen Mary of Scotland in his rehearsal of Cecropia's wickedness.

Having commenced his romance in the summer of 1580, I infer that Sidney had written about three-quarters of the whole, and all which has come down to us in a finished state, by the autumn of 1581. On the 30th of September in that year Languet died, and in the concluding eclogue of the third book of *The Arcadia* we meet with the affectionate praise of the honest Huguenot to which reference has been made. It is reasonable to suppose that the eulogy was penned soon after the event which called it forth. Indeed the entire work, though no allegory is to be found in it, gives clear evidence of the author's varying mood at the various periods of his writing. The earlier portions, composed at Wilton and in the immediate company of the Countess of Pembroke, have all the graceful flow of fancy, the fulness of pastoral imagery, the buoyancy of happy, innocent thought, which might be expected to mark the time of Sidney's retirement from Court and participation in the rich joys of true domestic life. The middle part—written, as I conclude, after his return to the world of courtly gaiety—is equally in harmony with the scenes and circumstances of its authorship. In it there is more strength of literary power, but the theme is far less inviting. Some episodes are of exquisite beauty; but the substance of the tale, including the endless description of Cecropia's abode and the things done in it, is dull and tedious. There is utterance of dainty conceits like these:

> My true love hath my heart, and I have his,
> By just exchange, one for the other given;
> I hold his dear, and mine he cannot miss;
> There never was a better bargain driven.
>
> His heart in me keeps me and him in one;
> My heart in him his thoughts and senses
> guides.
> He loves my heart, for once it was his own;
> I cherish his because in me it bides. [10]

But there is as true an echo of the writer's mind, weary of the life which he seemed forced to lead, in such mournful verse as this upon a lute:

> The world doth yield such ill consorted shows,
> With circled course, which no wise stay can
> try,
> That childish stuff, which knows not friends from
> foes,
> (Better despised) bewonders gazing eye.
> Thus noble gold down to the bottom goes,
> When worthless cork aloft doth floating lie.
> Thus in thyself least strings are loudest found,
> And lowest stops do yield the highest sound. [11]

Or this:

> Beauty hath force to catch the human sight:
> Sight doth bewitch the fancy ill awaked;
> Fancy, we feel, includes all passion's might;
> Passion, rebell'd, oft reason's strength hath
> shaked.
> No wonder then, though sight my sight did taint,
> And though thereby my fancy was infected,

> Though, yoked so, my mind, with sickness faint,
> Had reason's weight for passion's ease
> rejected.
> But now the fit is past, and time hath given
> Leisure to weigh what due desert requireth.
> All thoughts so sprung are from their dwelling
> driven,
> And wisdom to his wonted seat aspireth,
> Crying, in me, 'Eye-hopes deceitful prove;
> Things rightly prized, love is the band of love.' [12]

That cry of Wisdom we know to have been heard through many groans of passion in Sidney's own short life. In the fourth and fifth books of *The Arcadia*, brief and disjointed as we have them, we have the foretaste of many of his thoughts at a later period. His journey to Flanders, in the early spring of 1582, must have interrupted his literary work. After that there was a marked change in his temper. Honest purposes were rising in him which little accorded with many sentiments in the half-written romance. Hastily, and with not much satisfaction to himself, he finished it as briefly as he could; spoiling the perfection of the story, but very beautifully showing how his own nature was being perfected. Thus solemnly and grandly, when his tale was almost ended, did he sum up and enforce some teaching of the wisdom now fully his own, upon the deepest of all earthly mysteries:

> Since nature's works be good, and death doth serve
> As nature's work, why should we fear to die?
> Since fear is vain but when it may preserve,
> Why should we fear that which we cannot fly?
> Fear is more pain than is the pain it fears,
> Disarming human minds of native might;
> While each conceit an ugly figure bears
> Which were not ill, well viewed in reason's
> light.
> Our owly eyes, which dimmed with passions be,
> And scarce discern the dawn of coming day,
> Let them be cleared, and now begin to see
> Our life is but a step in dusty way.
> Then let us hold the bliss of peaceful mind:
> Since, feeling this, great loss we cannot find. [13]

Of sonnets, besides those scattered through *The Arcadia*, Sidney wrote a hundred and twenty-five, if not more. A hundred and eight are included in his *Astrophel and Stella*, a collection of poems, half true and half fictitious, composed during about the same period as that covered by the prose romance. . . .

He followed too much the example of his immediate predecessors, the chief of them being Wyatt and Surrey. Sir Thomas Wyatt, the elder, who died in 1540, had helped to set the fashion of travelling in Italy, and of coming back to imitate the strains of Petrarch and Ariosto. Both fashions were further enforced by the more splendid manners and the finer genius of Henry Howard, Earl of Surrey. Surrey, distantly connected by family with Sidney, showed some chance likeness to him in the brilliancy of his life and the prematureness of his death. In January, 1547, before he had ended his thirtieth year, he was executed on the foolish charge of having assumed the arms of Edward the Confessor, and thereby laid claim to royalty. Yet he lived long enough to plant firmly in England the Italian sonnet, and the still more recently invented blank verse of Italy. The Italian influence was not here first exerted upon our literature. Long before, Chaucer had borrowed much and wisely from Boccaccio, Petrarch, and Dante, and Lidgate and his companions had willingly enslaved themselves to the example of the southern poets. But this early imitation showed itself chiefly in the production of long prosaic epics, and in the repetition of short and often immoral fables; and before the dawning of the sixteenth century the epics, if not the fables, had become wearisome to English readers. There was a charm of novelty in the sonnets of Wyatt and Surrey, some of them translated, the rest closely imitated, from Petrarch and Petrarch's extravagant copyists. The great Italian had sung sweetly to his Laura; and there were numbers, both in and out of Italy, eager to outvie him in his vows and protestations. Whoever the fair Geraldine may have been, and whatever sway she may have had over Surrey, his love-poems were of the sort to take strong hold of every courtly mind. In Sidney's youth, numbers were multiplying fantastic and delicate conceits, and the fashion prevailed after he was dead. Perhaps no one so fairly illustrates it as Henry Constable, a year or two his junior. Rich in true poetry, Constable's verse abounds in evidence of the absurd style of the day. Within the limits of a single sonnet, his lady's eye is at once a glass where he beholds his heart, the keen point of a murdering dart with which she "always hits his heart, and never shoots awry," and a fire which would burn him up, were not his eye a river to prevent absolute annihilation, and to keep him in a state of boiling misery. In another, her glove gives occasion for this apostrophe:

> Sweet hand! the sweet yet cruel bow thou art,
>   From whence at me five ivory arrows fly;
>   So with five wounds at once I wounded lie,
> Bearing in breast the print of every dart.

In that school Sidney learnt to write sonnets. Often he gave full proof of having caught the infection of the time; often he wrote in far healthier way than any around him, save just one or two, could equal. To the English sonnet he imparted an energy and moral purpose never before shown, but rarely did he write with the perfect freedom of a true master of poesy.

. . . Let this sonnet . . . be read, as containing, perhaps more than any other of his composing, trace of the vicious style of his time:

> Queen Virtue's Court, which some call Stella's face,
>   Prepared by nature's choicest furniture,
>   Hath his front built of alabaster pure;
> Gold is the covering of that stately place;
> The door by which, sometimes, comes forth her
>   grace,
>   Red porphyr is, which lock of pearl makes
>   sure,
>   Whose porches rich, which name of cheeks
>   endure,
> Marble, mixed red and white, do interlace;
> The windows now, through which this heavenly
>   guest
>   Looks o'er the world and can find nothing
>   such
> Which dare claim from those lights the name of best,
>   Of touch they are that, without touch, doth
>   touch,
> Which Cupid's self, from Beauty's mind did draw;
> Of touch they are—and poor I am their straw![14]

And, on the other hand, let this be taken as one of the most poetical of Sidney's sonnets.

> Come Sleep, O Sleep! the certain knot of peace,
>   The baiting place of wit, the balm of woe,
> The poor man's wealth, the prisoner's release,

> The indifferent judge between the high and
>   low;
> With shield of proof shield me from out the press
>   Of those fierce darts Despair at me doth
>   throw;
> O make in me those civil wars to cease;
>   I will good tribute pay if thou do so.
> Take thou of me smooth pillows, sweetest bed,
>   A chamber deaf to noise and blind to light,
> A rosy garland and a weary head;
>   And if these things, as being thine by right,
> Move not thy heavy grace, thou shalt in me,
> Livelier than elsewhere, Stella's image see.[15]

Sidney was a better poet after the last sonnet in *Astrophel and Stella* had been penned. Pervading the work is an unhealthy tone, lessening the pleasure with which we regard even those passages that are really beautiful. If in reading *The Arcadia* we are sometimes reminded of the hindrance offered to Sidney's higher nature by the fascinations of Court-life, we see much more to lament in the misguided thoughts and perverted purposes of which there is evidence in his sonnets about Lady Rich. They are no whit more poetical because they tell us of a heart perplexed and tortured—because the strains with gayest sound have no echo of real happiness—because those in which he acknowledges his misery are so very full of wretchedness. Strength and honour came when that cry of wisdom, of which he sang so worthily in *The Arcadia*, was bravely listened to and obeyed; but, before reason had vanquished folly, and virtue had stifled passion, what a bitterness of grief oppressed him!

> Oft have I mused, but now at length I find,
>   Why those that die, men say 'they do depart.'
> Depart! a word so gentle to my mind,
>   Weakly did seem to paint Death's ugly dart.
> But, now the stars, with their strange course, do bind
>   Me one to leave with whom I leave my heart,
> I hear a cry of spirits, faint and blind,
>   That, parting thus, my chiefest part I part.
> Part of my life, the loathed part to me,
>   Lives to impart my weary clay some breath;
> But that good part, wherein all comforts be,
>   Now dead, doth show departure is a death;
> Yea, worse than death: death parts both woe and joy;
> From joy I part, still living in annoy.[16]

Notes

1. Fulke Greville, *Life.*
2. "My great-uncle, Mr. T. Brown, remembered him," says Aubrey in support of his gossip.
3. Lilly, *Dramatic Works*, ed. Fairholt, vol. i., p. xix.
4. *The Defence of Poesie* (ed. 1829), p. 72.
5. Salfi, cited by Hallam in his *Introduction to the Literature of Europe* (5th ed.), vol. i., pp. 265, 266.
6. This is the prayer which the author of the *Ikon Basilike* put into the mouth of King Charles the First.
7. The *Address to the Reader* prefixed to the early editions.
8. *Euphues* (ed. 1579), fo. 13.
9. *The Life and Death of Sir Philip Sidney.*
10. *Arcadia* (ed. 1655), pp. 357, 358.
11. Ibid., p. 370.
12. *Arcadia*, p. 375.
13. *Arcadia*, p. 457.
14. *Astrophel and Stella*, sonnet ix.
15. Ibid, sonnet xxxix.
16. *Miscellaneous Works*, p. 340.

HENRY MORLEY
From A *First Sketch of English Literature*
1873, pp. 391–426

At the beginning of 1580, Philip Sidney had addressed to the queen a wise and earnest written argument against the project of her marriage with the Duke of Anjou. His uncle, Leicester, whose secret marriage with Lettice, Countess of Essex, had become known, was already under the queen's displeasure; and Sidney, after writing this letter, found it best to withdraw from court. Towards the end of March, 1580, he went to stay at Wilton with his sister, the Countess of Pembroke, whom Spenser afterwards honoured as

> The greatest shepherdess that lives this day,
> And most resembling both in shape and spright
> Her brother dear;

and upon whose death, when her course was ended, Ben Jonson wrote:

> Underneath this sable herse
> Lies the subject of all verse,
> Sidney's sister, Pembroke's mother;
> Death, ere thou hast slain another
> Learn'd and fair and good as she,
> Time shall throw a dart at thee.

Sidney's sister became "Pembroke's mother" in that spring of 1580 when her brother Philip was staying at Wilton. He remained there about seven months. Brother and sister worked together at that time upon a joint translation of *The Psalms of David* into English verse. It was then also that Sidney occupied hours of his forced idleness by beginning to write for the amusement of his sister a long pastoral romance, in prose mixed with verse, according to Italian fashion, with abundance of poetical conceits—his *Arcadia*. It was done at his sister's wish, and as he wrote to her, "only for you, only to you. . . . For, indeed, for severer eyes it is not, being but a trifle, and that triflingly handled. Your dear self can best witness the manner, being done in loose sheets of paper, most of it in your presence, the rest by sheets sent unto you as fast as they were done." This romance was not published by Sidney. Not long before his death he said that he wished it to be burnt. But it belonged to his sister, who valued it, and by her it was, after his death, prepared for the press, and published in 1590. Much of it was written during the summer of 1580, and the rest chiefly, or entirely in 1581. Though long, Sidney's *Arcadia* is unfinished except by the addition of a hurried close. It is a pastoral of the school of the *Arcadia* of Sanazzaro, and the *Diana Enamorada* by George of Montemayor, but its intermixture of verse and prose develops more completely a romantic story, and it adds to the pastoral a new heroic element. This was suggested partly by the Spanish romances of "Amadis" and "Palmerin", partly by the *Æthiopian Historie* of Heliodorus, lately translated from the Greek by Thomas Underdown. Heliodorus, Bishop of Tricca, in Thessaly, who lived at the end of the fourth century, wrote, under the name of "Æthiopica," ten books of romance on the loves of Theagenes and Chariclea. Sidney had been enjoying this in Underdown's translation. In his *Defense of Poesy*, written in 1581 (although not published until 1595), after saying that Xenophon had "in his portraiture of a just empire under the name of Cyrus (as Cicero saith of him), made therein an absolute heroical poem; so," he added, "did Heliodorus in his sugared invention of that picture of love in Theagenes and Chariclea, and yet both these writ in prose:

which I speak to show that it is not rhyming and versing that maketh a poet, no more than a long gown maketh an advocate, who, though he pleaded in armour, should be an advocate and no soldier." Sidney's *Arcadia* may be, in this sense, taken as all poet's work; giving a new point of departure for heroic romance grafted upon pastoral. As he was writing for his sister a romance after the fashion of his day, Sidney, in the *Arcadia*, would amuse himself by showing how he also could be delicate and fine conceited. This is the groundwork of its story. Two cousins and close friends, Musidorus, the elder, Prince of Thessaly, and Pyrocles, the younger, Prince of Macedon, are wrecked on the Spartan coast. Musidorus is saved and taken to the delicious pastoral land of Arcadia. His friend is supposed to have been lost. Musidorus is sheltered by Kalander, an Arcadian noble. Presently he leads an Arcadian force against Helots of Sparta, who have made Kalander's son their prisoner, and at the close of combat with a mighty captain of the Helots, finds him to be his lost friend Pyrocles. Peace is made. Kalander's son is released, and the two friends begin a course of love adventures. Basilius and Gynecia, king and queen of Arcadia, have two daughters—majestic Pamela, and sweet Philoclea. To keep men away from his daughters, Basilius has built two lodges in a forest. In one he lives with his wife and his younger daughter Philoclea; in the other Pamela lives under the care of a clown Dametas, who has an ugly wife, Miso, and an ugly daughter, Mopsa. The only men who may come near are a priest and some shepherds skilled in music. Musidorus now loves Pamela; he is disguised as a shepherd, Dorus, and affects passion for Mopsa. Pyrocles loves Philoclea; he is disguised as an Amazon, Zelmane, and inspires love in King Basilius, who takes him for a woman, as well as in Queen Gynecia, who sees that he is a man. Many troubles and adventures, episodes of romance, conceited dialogues and songs, including experiments in "our English reformed versifying," are built upon this groundwork. The king's sister-in-law, Cecropia, desires to set up her son Amphialus as King of Arcadia, that she may rule through him. Cecropia carries off Pamela, Philoclea, and Zelmane. She fails to bend Philoclea to assent to the love of her son, goes to the chamber of Pamela, hoping to prevail over her, and hears her praying to heaven for succour. We shall meet again with Pamela's prayer. The Arcadian army battles for the rescue of the captives, and in the course of this contest Amphialus slays Argalus, the husband of Parthenia. She afterwards arms herself to avenge her husband, comes as a stranger knight, and is herself slain by Amphialus, who suffers grief and shame for his victory. The latter part of the *Arcadia* is less fully worked out. The princesses and Pyrocles, still as the Amazon Zelmane, are again at home. Musidorus escapes with Pamela to Thessaly. Pyrocles remains, troubled by the affections of the king and queen, but he brings both to their senses, they resume their royal duties, and the lovers are made happy.

There is much difference between the style of Sidney's *Arcadia*, and that of his *Apologie for Poetrie*, written in 1581, although not published until 1595, when Sidney was dead. This little treatise, in simple English, maintains against such attacks as Gosson's the dignity of the best literature. The *Apologie for Poetrie* is the first piece of intellectural literary criticism in our language; it springs from a noble nature feeling what is noblest in the poet's art, is clear in its plan, terse in its English, and while all that it says is well said, it is wholly free from conceits. The conceited style, indeed, it explicitly condemns, as eloquence disguised in painted affectation, "one time, with so far-fetched words, they may seem monsters, but must seem strangers to any poor Englishman; another time, with coursing of a letter, as if they were bound to follow the method of a dictionary; at another time with figures and flowers extremely winter-starved. But I would this fault were only peculiar to versifiers, and had not as large possession among prose printers; and (which is to be marvelled) among many scholars; and (which is to be pitied) among some preachers. . . . For now they cast sugar and spice upon every dish that is served to the table; like those Indians, not content to wear earrings at the fit and natural place of the ears, but they will thrust jewels through their nose and lips, because they will be sure to be fine." . . .

Philip Sidney, at court again, after the months of retirement at Wilton, during which he wrote "Arcadia," was knighted by Elizabeth in January, 1583, when his age was about twenty-eight. In the following March he was married to Frances, eldest daughter of Sir Francis Walsingham, and the next year was spent in married peace. Sidney wrote sonnets in those days—"Passions" of the old conventional type—meaning, as usual, to address them to some lady who deserved compliment, and of whom his conventional rhapsodies could not very well be taken seriously. As the Earl of Surrey addressed his love exercises to a child for whom the court felt sympathy, Sidney paid the like compliment to an unhappy wife. Penelope Devereux, daughter to his old friend the late Earl of Essex, had once been talked of as his own possible wife. Her father said that he would have been proud of Philip Sidney for a son-in-law. And if so why had the match not taken place? If Sidney had been really devoted to the lady he could have married her. He did not marry her because he did not wish to do so, and in his own day no reasonable being ever supposed that he paid suit to her except in the way of verse. Towards the close of 1580, Penelope, then about eighteen, was married by her guardian against her will to Lord Robert Rich, heir to the ill-gotten wealth of Lord Chancellor Rich. That chancellor, the grandson of two thriving London mercers, had risen by his want of principle, and had secured to himself great bargains at the suppression of the monasteries. He grasped wealth enough to endow two earldoms acquired by his descendants. The chancellor died in 1568, and his son Robert, second baron Rich, died in 1581, leaving his son and heir, another Lord Robert, the rich man to whom Penelope was sold. She protested even at the altar. The contractor for her is described as "of an uncourtly disposition, unsociable, austere, and of no very agreeable conversation to her." The unhappiness of her forced marriage made Lady Rich at this time an object of considerate attention. Philip Sidney was an old friend of her father's, and he gave her the place of honour in his sonnet-writing, wherein she was to be Stella ("the Star"), he Astrophel ("the Lover of the Star"); and certainly, as all the court knew, and as the forms of such ingenious love-poetry implied, so far as love in the material sense was concerned, with as much distance between them as if she had shone upon him from above the clouds. Sidney's *Astrophel and Stella* sonnets were being written at the time when he was about to marry Fanny Walsingham; and in those earnest Elizabethan days, at the fitfully strict court of Elizabeth, since the character of such poetical love-passions was then understood, they brought upon Sidney's credit not a breath of censure. As for Lady Rich, she gave herself to Sir Christopher Blount, who became Lord Mountjoy in 1600, and after divorce from her husband she married him. But that was a real passion, and what each felt in it was not told for the amusement of the public.

In 1584 the course of events led Sir Philip Sidney to advocate direct attack by sea upon the Spanish power. He would have Elizabeth come forward as Defendress of the Faith,

at the head of a great Protestant League. He was a member of the Parliament that met in November, 1584, and in July, 1585, he was joined with the Earl of Warwick in the Mastership of the Ordnance. His strongest desires caused him to look in two directions for his course of action: he might aid in direct attack on the Spanish possessions, which, as source of treasure, were a source of power; he might aid in the rescue from Spain of the Netherlands. During a great part of the year 1585 his mind was very much with Drake and Raleigh. . . .

In the spring of 1585, Raleigh sent a fleet of seven vessels to Virginia, in charge of his cousin, Sir Richard Grenville, with Ralph Lane, who was to be governor of the colony they went to found. Lane was left with 105 colonists on the island of Roanoake. In the same year Sir Francis Drake was sent as admiral, with a fleet of twenty-one ships, against the Spaniards in the West Indies. Sir Philip Sidney helped towards the fitting of this expedition, and was bent on taking part in it himself, sharing authority with Drake after they had put to sea. Sidney went to Plymouth; but his secret plan became known, and his sailing with Drake's fleet was stayed by the queen's absolute command. Drake, therefore, sailed without him in September; and soon afterwards a daughter was born to Sir Philip Sidney, who was baptised Elizabeth, the queen standing as a sponsor. Then he went to his death in the Low Countries.

The seven northern provinces of Holland had declared their independence on the 29th of September, 1580. In 1584, William of Orange had been assassinated. In 1585, the ten southern provinces were conquered by the Prince of Parma. Catherine de' Medici was in that year proposing to Philip of Spain invasion of England for the crushing of heresy. Philip pointed to heretics nearer home. Protestants of the Netherlands appealed to England, and on the 10th of August, 1585, a treaty was signed at Nonsuch, stipulating that England should provide 5,000 foot-soldiers and 1,000 horse to aid war in the Netherlands, while, as security for expenses, and as headquarters for troops, temporary possession was to be taken of Flushing, Brill, and the Castle of Rammekins. Then England declared war for three objects: to secure peace to all of the Reformed Faith; restoration to the Netherlands of ancient rights; and the safety of England. The English went out with the Earl of Leicester for their leader; Sir Philip Sidney as Governor of Flushing and of Rammekins; and Sir Thomas Cecil, eldest son of Lord Burghley, as Governor of Brill. Sidney went to his post in November, 1585; the earl followed in December, and spent over-much time in feasting. Sidney's heart was in his duty; he planned work in vain, and he sought in vain to protect the poor soldiers against chiefs who enriched themselves out of their pay and their supplies. In January, Leicester offended Elizabeth by accepting from the States the rank of Governor-General of the United Provinces. Sir Philip Sidney fretted at inaction. His wife joined him at Flushing. In May, 1586, Sidney received news of the death of his father. In July, he had a chief part in the capture of Axel. In August his mother died. In September he joined with Sir John Norris and Count Lewis William of Nassau, in the investment of Zutphen. On the 22nd of that month Sir Philip Sidney received his death wound in a gallant assault made by a few hundred English against a thousand cavalry, and under fire from walls and trenches. A musket-ball from one of the trenches shattered Sidney's thighbone. His horse took fright and galloped back, but the wounded man held to his seat. He was then carried to his uncle, asked for water, and when it was given, saw a dying soldier carried past, who eyed it greedily. At once he gave the water to the soldier, saying "Thy necessity is yet greater than mine." Sidney lived on, patient in suffering, until the 17th of

October. When he was speechless before death, one who stood by asked Philip Sidney for a sign of his continued trust in God. He folded his hands as in prayer over his breast, and so they were become fixed and chill when the watchers placed them by his side, and in a few minutes the stainless representative of the young manhood of Elizabethan England passed away.

JOHN ADDINGTON SYMONDS
From "The Defence of Poesy"
Sir Philip Sidney
1886, pp. 156–70

Fulke Greville, touching upon the *Arcadia*, says that Sidney "purposed no monuments of books to the world." "If his purpose had been to leave his memory in books, I am confident, in the right use of logic, philosophy, history, and poesy, nay even in the most ingenious of mechanical arts, he would have showed such tracts of a searching and judicious spirit as the professors of every faculty would have striven no less for him than the seven cities did to have Homer of their sept. But the truth is: his end was not writing, even while he wrote; nor his knowledge moulded for tables or schools; but both his wit and understanding bent upon his heart, to make himself and others, not in words or opinion, but in life and action, good and great."

"His end was not writing, even while he wrote." This is certain; the whole tenor of Sidney's career proves his determination to subordinate self-culture of every kind to the ruling purpose of useful public action. It will also be remembered that none of his compositions were printed during his lifetime or with his sanction. Yet he had received gifts from nature which placed him, as a critic, high above the average of his contemporaries. He was no mean poet when he sang as love dictated. He had acquired and assimilated various stores of knowledge. He possessed an exquisite and original taste, a notable faculty for the marshalling of arguments, and a persuasive eloquence in exposition. These qualities inevitably found their exercise in writing; and of all Sidney's writings the one with which we have to deal now, is the ripest.

Judging by the style alone, I should be inclined to place *The Defense of Poesy* among his later works. But we have no certain grounds for fixing the year of its composition. Probably the commonly accepted date of 1581 is the right one. In the year 1579 Stephen Gosson dedicated to Sidney, without asking his permission, an invective against "poets, pipers, players, and their excusers," which he called *The School of Abuse*. Spenser observes that Gosson "was for his labour scorned; if at least it lie in the goodness of that nature to scorn. Such folly is it not to regard aforehand the nature and quality of him to whom we dedicate our books." It is possible therefore that *The School of Abuse* and other treatises emanating from Puritan hostility to culture, suggested this Apology. Sidney rated poetry highest among the functions of the human intellect. His name had been used to give authority and currency to a clever attack upon poets. He felt the weight of argument to be on his side, and was conscious of his ability to conduct the cause. With what serenity of spirit, sweetness of temper, humour, and easy strength of style—at one time soaring to enthusiasm, at another playing with his subject,—he performed the task, can only be appreciated by a close perusal of the essay. It is indeed the model for such kinds of composition—a work which combines the quaintness and the blitheness of Elizabethan literature with the urbanity and reserve of a later period.

Sidney begins by numbering himself among "the paper-blurrers," "who, I know not by what mischance, in these my not old years and idlest times, having slipped into the title of a poet, am provoked to say something unto you in the defense of that my unelected vocation." Hence it is his duty "to make a pitiful defense of poor poetry, which from almost the highest estimation of learning, is fallen to be the laughing-stock of children." Underlying Sidney's main argument we find the proposition that to attack poetry is the same as attacking culture in general; therefore, at the outset, he appeals to all professors of learning: will they inveigh against the mother of arts and sciences, the "first nurse, whose milk by little and little enabled them to feed afterwards of tougher knowledge?" Musæus, Homer, and Hesiod lead the solemn pomp of the Greek writers. Dante, Petrarch, and Boccaccio in Italy, Gower and Chaucer in England came before prose-authors. The earliest philosophers, Empedocles and Parmenides, Solon and Tyrtæus, committed their metaphysical speculations, their gnomic wisdom, their marital exhortation to verse. And even Plato, if rightly considered, was a poet: "in the body of his work, though the inside and strength were philosophy, the skin as it were, and beauty, depended most of poetry." Herodotus called his books by the names of the Muses: "both he and all the rest that followed him, either stole or usurped of poetry their passionate describing of passions, the many particularities of battles which no man could affirm." They also put imaginary speeches into the mouths of kings and captains. The very names which the Greeks and Romans, "the authors of most of our sciences," gave to poets, show the estimation in which they held them. The Romans called the poet *vates*, or prophet; the Greeks *poietēs*, or maker, a word, by the way, which coincides with English custom. What can be higher in the scale of human understanding than this faculty of *making*? Sidney enlarges upon its significance, following a line of thought which Tasso summed up in one memorable sentence: "There is no Creator but God and the Poet."

He now advances a definition, which is substantially the same as Aristotle's: "Poesy is an art of imitation; that is to say, a representing, counterfeiting, or figuring forth: to speak metaphorically, a speaking picture; with this end to teach and delight." Of poets there have been three general kinds: first, "they that did imitate the inconceivable excellences of God;" secondly, "they that deal with matter philosophical, either moral or natural or astronomical or historical;" thirdly, "right poets . . . which most properly do imitate, to teach and delight; and to imitate, borrow nothing of what is, hath been, or shall be; but range only, reined with learned discretion, into the divine consideration of what may be and should be." The preference given to the third kind of poets may be thus explained: The first group are limited to setting forth fixed theological conceptions; the second have their material supplied them by the sciences; but the third are the makers and creators of ideals for warning and example.

Poets may also be classified according to the several species of verse. But this implies a formal and misleading limitation. Sidney, like Milton and like Shelley, will not have poetry confined to metre: "apparelled verse being but an ornament, and no cause to poetry; since there have been many most excellent poets that have never versified, and now swarm many versifiers that need never answer to the name of poets." Xenophon's "Cyropædia," the "Theagenes and Chariclea" of Heliodorus, are cited as true poems; "and yet both these wrote in prose." "It is not rhyming and versing that maketh a poet; but it is that feigning notable images of virtues, vices, or what else, with that delightful teaching, which must be the right describing note to know a poet by." Truly, "the senate of poets have chosen verse as their fittest raiment;" but this they did, because they meant, "as in matter they passed all in all, so in manner to go beyond them." "Speech, next to reason, is the greatest gift bestowed upon mortality;" and verse "which most doth polish that blessing of speech," is, therefore, the highest investiture of poetic thought.

Having thus defined his conception of poetry, Sidney inquires into the purpose of all learning. "This purifying of wit, this enriching of memory, enabling of judgment, and enlarging of conceit, which commonly we call learning, under what name soever it come forth, or to what immediate end soever it be directed; the final end is to lead and draw us to as high a perfection as our degenerate souls, made worse by their clay lodgings, can be capable of." All the branches of learning subserve the royal or architectonic science, "which stands, as I think, in the knowledge of a man's self in the ethic and politic consideration, with the end of well-doing, and not of well-knowing only." If then virtuous action be the ultimate object of all our intellectual endeavours, can it be shown that the poet contributes above all others to this exalted aim? Sidney thinks it can . . .

Sidney next passes the various species of poems in review: the pastoral; "the lamenting elegiac;" "the bitter but wholesome iambic;" the satiric; the comic, "whom naughty playmakers and stage-keepers have justly made odious;" "the high and excellent tragedy, that openeth the greatest wounds, and showeth forth the ulcers that are covered with tissue—that maketh kings fear to be tyrants, and tyrants to manifest their tyrannical humours—that with stirring the effects of admiration and commiseration, teacheth the uncertainty of this world, and upon how weak foundations gilded roofs are builded;" the lyric, "who with his tuned lyre and well-accorded voice giveth praise, the reward of virtue, to virtuous acts—who giveth moral precepts and natural problems—who sometimes raiseth up his voice to the height of the heavens, in singing the lauds of the immortal God;" the epic or heroic, "whose very name, I think, should daunt all backbiters . . . which is not only a kind, but the best and most accomplished kind of poetry." He calls upon the detractors of poesy to bring their complaints against these several sorts, and to indicate in each of them its errors. What they may allege in disparagement, he meets with chosen arguments, among which we can select his apology for the lyric. "Certainly, I must confess my own barbarousness: I never heard the old song of 'Percy and Douglas' that I found not my heart moved more than with a trumpet; and yet it is sung but by some blind crowder, with no rougher voice than rude style; which being so evil-apparelled in the dust and cobweb of that uncivil age, what would it work, trimmed in the gorgeous eloquence of Pindar?"

Having reached this point, partly on the way of argument, partly on the path of appeal and persuasion, Sidney halts to sum his whole position up in one condensed paragraph:

> Since, then, poetry is of all human learnings the most ancient, and of most fatherly antiquity, as from whence other learnings have taken their beginnings; since it is so universal that no learned nation doth despise it, nor barbarous nation is without it; since both Roman and Greek gave such divine names unto it, the one of prophesying, the other of making, and that indeed that name of making is fit for him, considering, that where all other arts retain themselves within their subject, and receive, as it were, their being from it, the poet only, only bringeth his own stuff, and doth not learn a conceit out of a matter, but maketh matter for a conceit; since neither his

description nor end containeth any evil, the thing described cannot be evil; since his effects be so good as to teach goodness, and delight the learners of it; since therein (namely in moral doctrine, the chief of all knowledges) he doth not only far pass the historian, but, for instructing, is well nigh comparable to the philosopher; for moving, leaveth him behind him; since the Holy Scripture (wherein there is no uncleanness) hath whole parts in it poetical, and that even our Saviour Christ vouchsafed to use the flowers of it; since all his kinds are not only in their united forms, but in their severed dissections fully commendable; I think, and think I think rightly, the laurel crown appointed for triumphant captains, doth worthily, of all other learnings, honour the poet's triumph.

Objections remain to be combated in detail. Sidney chooses one first, which offers no great difficulty. The detractors of poetry gird at "rhyming and versing." He has already laid it down that "one may be a poet without versing, and a versifier without poetry." But he has also shown why metrical language should be regarded as the choicest and most polished mode of speech. Verse, too, fits itself to music more properly than prose, and far exceeds it "in the knitting up of the memory." Nor is rhyme to be neglected, especially in modern metres; seeing that it strikes a music to the ear. But the enemy advances heavier battalions. Against poetry he alleges (1) that there are studies upon which a man may spend his time more profitably; (2) that it is the mother of lies; (3) that it is the nurse of abuse, corrupting the fancy, enfeebling manliness, and instilling pestilent desires into the soul; (4) that Plato banished poets from his commonwealth.

These four points are taken seriatim, and severally answered. The first is set aside, as involving a begging of the question at issue. To the second Sidney replies "paradoxically, but truly I think truly, that of all writers under the sun the poet is the least liar; and though he would, as a poet, can scarcely be a liar." It is possible to err, and to affirm falsehood, in all the other departments of knowledge; but "for the poet, he nothing affirmeth, and therefore nothing lieth." His sphere is not the region of ascertained fact, or of logical propositions, but of imagination and invention. He labours not "to tell you what is, or is not, but what should, or should not be." None is so foolish as to mistake the poet's world for literal fact. "What child is there, that cometh to a play, and seeing Thebes written in great letters upon an old door, doth believe that it is Thebes?" The third point is more weighty. Are poets blamable, in that they "abuse men's wit, training it to a wanton sinfulness and lustful love?" Folk say "the comedies rather teach than reprehend amorous conceits; they say the lyric is larded with passionate sonnets; the elegiac weeps the want of his mistress; and that even to the heroical Cupid hath ambitiously climbed." Here Sidney turns to Love, and, as though himself acknowledging that deity, invokes him to defend his own cause. Yet let us "grant love of beauty to be a beastly fault," let us "grant that lovely name of love to deserve all hateful reproaches," what have the adversaries gained? Surely they have not proved "that poetry abuseth man's wit, but that man's wit abuseth poetry." "But what! shall the abuse of a thing make the right odious?" Does not law, does not physic, injure man every day by the abuse of ignorant practisers? "Doth not God's Word abused breed heresy, and His name abused become blasphemy?" Yet these people contend that before poetry came to infect the English, "our nation had set their heart's delight upon action and not imagination, rather doing things worthy to be written than writing things fit to be done." But when was there that time when the Albion nation was without poetry? Of a truth, this argument is levelled against all learning and all culture. It is an attack, worthy of Goths or Vandals, upon the stronghold of the intellect. As such, we might dismiss it. Let us, however, remember that "poetry is the companion of camps: I dare undertake, Orlando Furioso or honest King Arthur will never displease a soldier; but the quiddity of *ens* and *prima materia* will hardly agree with a corselet." Alexander on his Indian campaigns left the living Aristotle behind him, but slept with the dead Homer in his tent; condemned Callisthenes to death, but yearned for a poet to commemorate his deeds. Lastly, they advance Plato's verdict against poets. Plato, says Sidney, "I have ever esteemed most worthy of reverence; and with good reason, since of all philosophers he is the most poetical." Having delivered this sly thrust, he proceeds: "first, truly, a man might maliciously object that Plato, being a philosopher, was a natural enemy of poets." Next let us look into his writings. Has any poet authorised filthiness more abominable than one can find in the "Phaedrus" and the "Symposium?" "Again, a man might ask out of what commonwealth Plato doth banish them." It is in sooth one where the community of women is permitted; and "little should poetical sonnets be hurtful, when a man might have what woman he listed." After thus trifling with the subject, Sidney points out that Plato was not offended with poetry, but with the abuse of it. He objected to the crude theology and the monstrous ethics of the myth-makers. "So as Plato, banishing the abuse not the thing, not banishing it, but giving due honour to it, shall be our patron and not our adversary."

Once again he pauses, to recapitulate:

> Since the excellencies of poesy may be so easily and so justly confirmed, and the low creeping objections so soon trodden down; it not being an art of lies, but of true doctrine; not of effeminateness, but of notable stirring of courage; not of abusing man's wit, but of strengthening man's wit; not banished, but honoured by Plato; let us rather plant more laurels for to ingarland the poets' heads (which honour of being laureate, as besides them only triumphant captains were, is a sufficient authority to show the price they ought to be held in) than suffer the ill-favoured breath of such wrong speakers once to blow upon the clear springs of poesy.

Then he turns to England. Why is it that England "the mother of excellent minds, should be grown so hard a stepmother to poets?"

> Sweet poesy, that hath anciently had kings, emperors, senators, great captains, such as, besides a thousand others, David, Adrian, Sophocles, Germanicus, not only to favour poets, but to be poets: and of our nearer times, can present for her patrons, a Robert, King of Sicily; the great King Francis of France; King James of Scotland; such cardinals as Bembus and Bibiena; such famous preachers and teachers as Beza and Melancthon; so learned philosophers as Fracastorius and Scaliger; so great orators as Pontanus and Muretus; so piercing wits as George Buchanan; so grave counsellors as, besides many, but before all, that Hospital of France; than whom, I think, that realm never brought forth a more accomplished judgment more firmly builded upon virtue; I say, these, with numbers of others, not only to read others' poesies, but to poetise for others' reading: that poesy, thus embraced in all other places, should only find, in our time, a hard welcome in England, I think the very earth laments it, and therefore decks our soil with fewer laurels than it was accustomed.

The true cause is that in England so many incapable folk write verses. With the exception of the *Mirror of Magistrates*, Lord Surrey's Lyrics, and *The Shepherd's Kalendar*, "I do not remember to have seen but few (to speak boldly) printed, that have poetical sinews in them." At this point he introduces a lengthy digression upon the stage, which, were we writing a history of the English drama, ought to be quoted in full. It is interesting because it proves how the theatre occupied Sidney's thoughts; and yet he had not perceived that from the humble plays of the people an unrivalled flower of modern art was about to emerge. *The Defence of Poesy* was written before Marlowe created the romantic drama; before Shakespeare arrived in London. It was written in all probability before its author could have attended the representation of Greene's and Peele's best plays. *Gorboduc*, which he praises moderately and censures with discrimination, seemed to him the finest product of dramatic art in England, because it approached the model of Seneca and the Italian tragedians. For the popular stage, with its chaos of tragic and comic elements, its undigested farrago of romantic incidents and involved plots, he entertained the scorn of a highly-educated scholar and a refined gentleman. Yet no one, let us be sure, would have welcomed *Othello* and *The Merchant of Venice*, *Volpone* and *A Woman Killed with Kindness*, more enthusiastically than Sidney, had his life been protracted through the natural span of mortality.

Having uttered his opinion frankly on the drama, he attacks the "courtesan-like painted affectation" of the English at his time. Far-fetched words, alliteration, euphuistic similes from stones and beasts and plants, fall under his honest censure. He mentions no man. But he is clearly aiming at the school of Lyly and the pedants; for he pertinently observes: "I have found in divers small-learned courtiers a more sound style than in some professors of learning." Language should be used, not to trick out thoughts with irrelevant ornaments or to smother them in conceits, but to make them as clear and natural as words can do. It is a sin against our mother speech to employ these meretricious arts; for whoso will look dispassionately into the matter, shall convince himself that English, both in its freedom from inflections and its flexibility of accent, is aptest of all modern tongues to be the vehicle of simple and of beautiful utterance.

The peroration to *The Defence of Poesy* is an argument addressed to the personal ambition of the reader. It somewhat falls below the best parts of the essay in style, and makes no special claim on our attention. From the foregoing analysis it will be seen that Sidney attempted to cover a wide field, combining a philosophy of art with a practical review of English literature. Much as the Italians had recently written upon the theory of poetry, I do not remember any treatise which can be said to have supplied the material or suggested the method of this apology. England, of course, at that time was destitute of all but the most meagre textbooks on the subject. Great interest therefore attaches to Sidney's discourse as the original outcome of his studies, meditations, literary experience, and converse with men of parts. Though we may not be prepared to accept each of his propositions, though some will demur to his conception of the artist's moral aim, and others to his inclusion of prose fiction in the definition of poetry, while all will agree in condemning his mistaken dramatic theory, none can dispute the ripeness, mellowness, harmony, and felicity of mental gifts displayed in work at once so concise and so compendious. It is indeed a pity that English literature then furnished but slender material for criticism. When we remember that, among the poems of the English Renaissance, only Surrey's Lyrics, *Gorboduc*, the *Mirror of Magistrates*, and *The Shepherd's Kalendar* could be praised with candour (and I think Sidney was right in this judgment), we shall be better able to estimate his own high position, and our mental senses will be dazzled by the achievements of the last three centuries. Exactly three centuries have elapsed since Sidney fell at Zutphen; and who shall count the poets of our race, stars differing indeed in glory, but stars that stream across the heavens of song from him to us in one continuous galaxy?

Sir Philip Sidney was not only eminent as pleader, critic, and poet. He also ranked as the patron and protector of men of letters. "He was of a very munificent spirit," says Aubrey, "and liberal to all lovers of learning, and to those that pretended to any acquaintance with Parnassus; insomuch that he was cloyed and surfeited with the poetasters of those days." This sentence is confirmed by the memorial verses written on his death, and by the many books which were inscribed with his name. A list of these may be read in Dr. Zouch's *Life*. It is enough for our purpose to enumerate the more distinguished. To Sidney, Spenser dedicated the first fruits of his genius, and Hakluyt the first collection of his epoch-making *Voyages*. Henri Etienne, who was proud to call himself the friend of Sidney, placed his 1576 edition of the Greek Testament and his 1581 edition of Herodian under the protection of his name. Lord Brooke, long after his friend's death, dedicated his collected works to Sidney's memory.

Of all these tributes to his love of learning the most interesting in my opinion is that of Giordano Bruno. This Titan of impassioned speculation passed two years in London between 1583 and 1585. Here he composed, and here he printed, his most important works in the Italian tongue. Two of these he presented, with pompous commendatory epistles, to Sir Philip Sidney. They were his treatise upon Ethics, styled *Lo Spaccio della Bestia Trionfante*, and his discourse upon the philosophic enthusiasm, entitled *Gli Eroici Furori*. That Bruno belonged to Sidney's circle, is evident from the graphic account he gives of a supper at Fulke Greville's house, in the dialogue called *La Cena delle Ceneri*. His appreciation of "the most illustrious and excellent knight's" character transpires in the following phrase from one of his dedications: "the natural bias of your spirit, which is truly heroical." Those who know what the word *eroica* implied for Bruno, not only of personal courage, but of sustained and burning spiritual passion, will appreciate this eulogy by one of the most penetrating and candid, as he was the most unfortunate of truth's martyrs. Had the proportions of my work justified such a digression, I would eagerly have collected from Bruno's Italian discourses those paragraphs which cast a vivid light upon literary and social life in England. But these belong rather to Bruno's than to Sidney's biography.

WALTER RALEIGH
From *The English Novel*
1894, pp. 49–64

T he most notable of the Elizabethan writers of fiction were not imitators of Lyly. With the success of *Euphues* the day of the novel was fully come, and Brian Melbancke, John Dickenson, Barnabie Rich, and many others, told their tales, and followed their progenitor to the cell of oblivion whither he retired. Of Greene and Lodge some few more words are necessary, while Nash and Sir Philip Sidney claim places by the side of Lyly as innovators in the art of prose fiction, and foreshadowers of later schools of romancers.

Yet there is much grace, wit, and vigour buried, for lack of reprint, with these almost forgotten pamphleteers; the very cheapest of them has his share of the zest and spirit of the time. "All the distinguished writers of that period," says Thoreau— and the praise might truly be extended to many of the undistinguished—"possess a greater vigour and naturalness than the more modern, . . . and when we read a quotation from one of them in the midst of a modern author, we seem to have come suddenly upon a greener ground, a greater depth and strength of soil. . . . You have constantly the warrant of life and experience in what you read. The little that is said is eked out by implication of the much that was done." And speaking in particular of Sir Walter Raleigh, he suggests an explanation of the strength and grace of his writing in words that have a wider application. "There is a natural emphasis in his style, like a man's tread, and a breathing-space between the sentences, which the best of modern writing does not furnish. . . . Every sentence is the result of a long probation. . . . The word which is best said came nearest to not being spoken at all, for it is cousin to a deed which the speaker could have better done. Nay, almost it must have taken the place of a deed by some urgent necessity, even by some misfortune, so that the truest writer will be some captive knight, after all." How true and happy a criticism this is of many writers of the time may be learnt from the annals of their lives. The monasteries were destroyed, literature as a secular profession had as yet few followers, and the adventurer was supreme there as elsewhere. Moreover, that great change in society which is called the Renaissance had convulsed the old feudal arrangements, and every man was free at last to take part in life in its fullest sense, and to store himself richly with experience. All the writers were, in one way or another, men of action, as Samuel Johnson and Thomas Carlyle never were. Lodge in the course of his life was a scholar of Oxford, a freebooting sailor, a soldier against Spain, a medical practitioner, playwright, novelist, and pamphleteer. Whetstone was courtier, soldier, farmer, and author; moreover, in the preface to his most famous work, *Promos and Cassandra*, which Shakespeare used in his *Measure for Measure*, he sets forth how his voyage with Sir Humphrey Gilbert has interfered with the correction of the "errors" in his works. Stanihurst, the translator of the *Æneid*, is spoken of thus contemptuously by Barnabie Rich: "First he was a chronicler, then a poet, after that he professed Alcumy, and now he is become a massing priest." Nor is this by any means an exhaustive account of Stanihurst's versatility, which, again, is almost equalled by Rich's own.

The emphasis and sincerity that spring from a first-hand knowledge of life are thus the great virtues of the best of Elizabethan writing. Of Sir Philip Sidney himself, whose *Arcadia* would seem but poorly to illustrate the general thesis, his friend and biographer, Lord Brooke, says, "The truth is, his end was not writing, even while he wrote, but both his wit and understanding bent upon his heart to make himself and others, not in words or opinion, but in life and action, good and great." And if the Arcadian style of writing seem to have little relation to life and action, it yet bears witness in its own way to the tumultuous activity of the time. For literature has constantly the double tendency to negative the life around it, as it were, as well as to reproduce it; the lawlessness and unrest of mediæval society are echoed, with the direction reversed, in the monkish hymns of rest and visions of the endless sabbath, while Browning's strenuous *Epilogue* and Mr. Stevenson's thrilling tales of adventure belong, it is no great cynicism to aver, to an age of sedentary occupation. Literature, that is to say, is an escape from life, its monotony or its distractions, as well as a grappling with life and its problems. And although the *Arcadia* has more in it of the first than of the second, it is nevertheless something more than

A shadowy isle of bliss
Midmost the beating of the steely sea,

and contains here and there some direct evidence of that restlessness of a high spirit which is so vividly portrayed in the *Sonnets* to Stella.

It was by his life, and not by his writings, which were published posthumously, that Sidney wielded his chief influence on the age. Even in his lifetime he was something of a romantic hero to his contemporaries, and his death added a lustre from the dazzling effect of which it is difficult even now to escape in considering his writings. He was born at Penshurst in 1554, the son of Sir Henry Sidney, afterwards Lord Deputy of Ireland and Lady Mary Dudley, the daughter of Northumberland, and sister of Leicester. He was educated at Shrewsbury, where his name was entered under the same date as the name of Fulke Greville, Lord Brooke, his lifelong friend and biographer, who, on his own death, had it inscribed on his tomb that he was "friend to Sir Philip Sidney." In 1572, in preparation for courtly employ, he began a period of three years' travel, and was sheltered during the massacre of St. Bartholomew in the house of his future father-in-law, Sir Francis Walsingham, at Paris. Thence he passed to Frankfort, where he formed another of his enduring friendships with Hubert Languet, a ripe scholar and ardent reformer of fifty-four, who did much to strengthen the lofty gravity that had always been a note of Sidney's character. Speaking of him in the *Arcadia*, Sidney says—

My skilless youth he drew
To have a feeling taste of Him that sits
Beyond the heaven, far more beyond our wits.

In the course of the next two years Sidney visited Vienna, Venice, Padua, and many other famous European cities, learning foreign languages, and everywhere winning the golden opinions of grave statesmen, until in 1575 he returned to the English court. Elizabeth called him "one of the jewels in her crown," and William the Silent, who was not prone to light eulogy, spoke of him in 1577 as one of the ripest statesmen in Europe. But before 1580 he had fallen into disfavour with the queen, and his public employ was uncertain and intermittent. Twice he sat in Parliament. In 1583 he married Frances Walsingham, and at last, having, as an outlet for his patriotic energy, accompanied Leicester to the Netherlands in the capacity of governor of Flushing, he fell at the battle of Zutphen on September 22, 1586. His body was conveyed to London, and his funeral celebrated at St. Paul's with rich ceremony. Never was poet's death so splendidly deplored; the elegies written on him are almost a literature. And the unanimity of praise is unbroken until the surly Ben Jonson, who never knew him, thought fit to censure his outward man in conversation with Drummond by the remark that "Sir P. Sidney was no pleasant man in countenance, his face being spoiled with pimples, and of high blood, and long." The letters of his friends convey a more pleasing impression.

Sidney's literary activity displays the versatility of the time. He wrote a masque for the court, a number of poetical versions of the Psalms, besides the *Arcadia* and those two other works without which his greatness could not adequately be measured, namely, the poems addressed to Stella, which constitute the first truly great sonnet sequence in the English tongue, and the *Apologie for Poetrie*, which remains to this day a piece of criticism showing enthusiasm and insight.

The *Sonnets* express the history of his passion for Penelope Devereux, sister to Essex, whom he first met at Kenilworth in 1575 when she was twelve years old. Some scheme of an alliance between the families was formed, but Sidney's loss of the queen's favour prevented it before his love was fully awake, and in 1580 Penelope, against her will, became Lady Rich.

There is a class of critics who, in view of the fact that the *Sonnets* (posthumously published) were addressed to Lady Rich after her marriage, hold the well-meaning opinion that Sidney never was in love with her, but employed her name as a peg on which to hang graceful fancies. Sidney himself, rising from the grave, could do nothing to convince the man who, having read the sonnets, clings to this belief. From first to last they are struck off at a white heat of glowing emotion, played over at times by the breath of conceit, but shaped with a vividness and minuteness that bespeak their intense sincerity. From the beginning to the end the reader is carried through the stormy vicissitudes of passion in all its phrases, until, by the time he reaches the noble lines, commonly printed at the close, in which the earthly love is renounced, he can almost feel the speed and impetuosity with which life was lived in that unexhausted time.

The very prologue to the *Sonnets* strikes their keynote—

Loving in truth, and fain in verse my love to show,
That she, dear She, might take some pleasure
of my pain. . . .
I sought fit words to paint the blackest face of woe;
Studying inventions fine, her wits to
entertain,
Oft turning other's leaves, to see if thence would flow
Some fresh and fruitful showers upon my sun-
burn'd brain. . . .
Biting my truant pen, beating myself for spite,
'Fool!' said my Muse to me, 'look in thy heart and
write!'

And before many sonnets have followed, the reader feels the truth of the poet's further declaration—

I now have learn'd love right, and learn'd even so
As they that being poisoned poison know.

The "dictionary method" of rhyming Sidney ridicules, and expressly sets aside the poetry of "graceful fancy" made to order, with no real goad in the occasion. There is a crowning sincerity and pathos in the two last sonnets—

Desire! Desire! I have too dearly bought,
With price of mangled mind, thy worthless
ware
Too long, too long, asleep thou hast me brought,
Who shouldst my mind to higher things
prepare . . .
Leave me, O Love, which reachest but to dust;
And thou, my mind, aspire to higher things;
Grow rich in that which never taketh rust;
Whatever fades, but fading pleasure
brings. . . .
Then farewell, world; thy uttermost I see.
Eternal Love, maintain thy life in me.

The contention that the "worthless ware" that Sidney purchased had no individual existence save in his own mind is at the root of a criticism that dishonours art by robbing it of its strongest inspiration, and makes of literature a bauble. It must never be forgotten that Sidney's *Sonnets* were not written originally for publication; poetry was chosen in this as in many cases at that day for the expression of the deepest personal throes and feelings, because for those feelings it was felt to be the fittest exponent. Moreover, the vindication of Sidney's sincerity is important for this reason, that his novel lacks what his poems are thus seen to contain. There can be little doubt that had Sidney chosen to write novels in the autobiographical vein of Greene and Nash, he would have produced works equal at least to the best of either. He trod a very different path in his prose, and his *Sonnets* remain to furnish another instance of how hard it was for prose fiction to maintain itself at all in that age of surpassing poetry. With the still growing drama on the one side, hungry for material, daily devouring apace the fair themes that the novelists procured, with the lighter forms of verse on the other, ready to give their highest expression to the intensest personal experience, it was no wonder that the novel did not long succeed in maintaining itself, or that where it did succeed, it maintained itself on stilts, to be out of the reach of its adversaries. Plays had large audiences, but few persons could read, and a surprisingly large number of those who could preferred reading poetry. Thus the novel held, in Elizabeth's time, very much the same place as was held by the drama at the Restoration; it was an essentially aristocratic entertainment. And the same pitfall waylaid both, the pitfall of artificiality. Dryden's audiences and the readers of the *Arcadia* both sought for better bread than is made of wheat; both were supplied with what satisfied them in an elaborate confection of husks.

The Countess of Pembroke's Arcadia, written by Sir Philip Sidney, was published in 1590, but its composition belongs chiefly to the time of retirement that Sidney passed with his sister at Wilton in 1580. It was left unfinished, and Lady Mary had even instructions to burn it. As the first example in English of a pastoral romance, it commanded an influence on later writers, both in England and France, which no other Elizabethan romance attained, so that Sidney's borrowings and lendings have a real bearing in the development of the prose story. Setting aside, then, Virgil and Longus as prototypes in the pastoral kind at too great a remove, it may be said that Sidney probably borrowed his title from the *Arcadia* (1502) of Sannazaro; his treatment and incidents in part from Montemayor's *Diana* (published in 1560), and the *Amadis of Gaul*, which he had probably read in a French translation. The admixture of adventures modelled on the later school of the Romances of Chivalry unhappily takes from the pastoral its justification, which was well enunciated by Honoré d'Urfé in his *Astrée*, a later and even more famous work than the *Arcadia*. In noticing the charge that the language of his shepherdesses was above their station, he says, "Réponds-leur, ma Bergère, que tu n'es pas, ny celles aussi qui te suivent, de ces Bergères nécessiteuses qui pour gagner leur vie conduisent les troupeaux aux pasturages; mais que vous n'avez toutes pris cette condition que pour vivre plus doucement et sans contrainte."

There is the philosophy of the pastoral romance. To devise a set of artificial conditions that shall leave the author to work out the sentimental inter-relations of his characters undisturbed by the intrusion of probability or accident, is the problem; love *in vacuo* is the beginning and end of the pastoral romance proper. And Montemayor had approached this ideal in his device of the four lovers, two nymphs and two swains, who loved each other in cyclical order. Their passion is not very passionate it is true, but it is enough to set up a rotatory action under a receiver, and the absence of any thwarting reciprocity secures the perpetual motion of the machine—under the one condition that it does no work. But the simplicity of such a design was not often unimpaired. The pastoral convention was found to afford excellent cover for wilder game than love, and political or personal satire often took shelter there. Sidney wisely avoided these, but he fell a victim to the tempta-

tion of drama and episode. The long and complicated plot of the *Arcadia* is overburdened with incident and action, which swoon into mere dream in the scented atmosphere of the style. And the author made a worse mistake when he attempted to relieve the high-strung monotony of the story by the introduction of comic characters in the clown Dametas and his wife and daughter. The Vice of the old Moralities was never naturalized in the English drama until Shakespeare's day, and Sidney had no better models than "Grim, the Collier of Croydon," who plays an irrelevant and tedious part in the *Damon and Pythias* of Richard Edwards. Thus he committed the fault that himself in the *Apologie* condemned, and "thrust in the clown by head and shoulders to play a part in majestical matters, with neither decency nor discretion." The clown is a dull clown, for his creator jokes with difficulty.

Sir Philip Sidney is one of the large body of Shakespeare's creditors. Gloucester and his sons in *Lear*, perhaps Valentine and the outlaws in the *Two Gentlemen*, were lent by him. And Day, Beaumont and Fletcher, and Shirley took from him what they could put to better use in adapting some of his incidents for the drama.

The debt of prose fiction to the *Arcadia* is not so quickly estimated. "Read the Countess of Pembroke's *Arcadia*," says Gabriel Harvey, "a gallant legendary, full of pleasurable accidents and profitable discourses; for three things especially, very notable—for amorous courting (he was young in years); for sage counselling (he was ripe in judgment); and for valourous fighting (his sovereign profession was arms); and delightful pastime by way of pastoral exercises, may pass for the fourth." Of these divisions of praise some may be discounted at once. Harvey was willing to be "epitaphed" as the "Inventor of the English Hexameter;" he was an enthusiastic supporter of the "Areopagus," or school of reformed versifying, and was delighted to find Sidney following in his steps. Hence his admiration for Sidney's "pastoral exercises," or those quaint verses, Asclepiadics, Phaleuciacs, and the like, with which the *Arcadia* is plentifully bestrewn, was no more than a commendation, to use another of his phrases, of "a pig of his own sow." Certainly the song of Dorus, in which every stanza begins—

O sweet woods, the delight of solitariness!
Oh, how much I do like your solitariness!

does not strike gratefully on a modern ear. Of the other grounds for praise, it may safely be said that the "valourous fighting" jumps better with Sidney's sovereign profession than with the artistic finish of his book, while in "sage counselling" he is no match for Lyly. There remains his greatest merit in the "amorous courting," which is his predominant theme, and which he so treated as to leave a lasting bequest to romance-writers. The lovers—and they are many—are the only interesting figures in the book. The tender love of the maiden Pamela, the servile love of the old king Basilius, and the guilty and jealous love of Queen Gynecia, are each depicted, in spite of the formal monotony lent them by the interminable "rich conceits and splendour of courtly expressions," with real differences and with real dramatic feeling. The story, with its disguisings, digressions, and cross-purposes, would furnish forth plot enough for twenty ordinary novels; but it was the sentiment of the work rather than its plot that procured its popularity and influence in the next century. The *Arcadia*, in fact, is in some sort a halfway house between the older romances of chivalry and the longwinded "heroic" romances of the seventeenth century. Action and adventure are already giving way to the description of sentiment, or are remaining merely as a frame on which the diverse-coloured flowers of sentiment may be broidered.

The characteristics of Sidney's style are in a large measure attributable to his conception of the *Arcadia* as a "prose-poem." Like almost all his contemporaries, Sidney defined poetry so as to include any literary work of the imagination, and absolutely refused to make of rhyming or versing an essential. But the instinctive craving of the imagination for some sort of definite form returns upon him, and avenges the dismissal of verse. Hence arise the formal affectations of his style, chief among which is the habit of playing with a word, or pair of words, and tossing it to and fro, until its meaning is more than exhausted. Thus the house in Arcadia to which the two ship-wrecked princes who are the heroes of the tale are welcomed is described as "all more lasting than beautiful, but that the consideration of the exceeding lastingness made the eye believe it was exceeding beautiful." One of the princes, crossed in love, finds himself "not only unhappy, but unhappy after being fallen from all happiness, and to be fallen from all happiness not by any misconceiving, but by his own fault, and his fault"—and so on, the repetition of the same word performing something of the office of the repetition of the rhyme in *terza rima*. This particular trick of style is not, of course, proper to Sidney; it is solemnly classified by his contemporary Puttenham among the figures that adorn verse, and it is common in the old romances, where it is carred to an extreme of unintelligibility—witness that "cartel of love" on the clearness and intricate argument of which Don Quixote doted, "The reason of the unreason which is done to my reason in such manner enfeebles my reason that with reason I lament your beauty."

The other marks of the style are equally poetical. The famous description of the vale of Arcadia will instance them all: "There were hills which garnished their proud heights with stately trees; humble valleys, whose base estate seemed comforted with the refreshing of silver rivers; meadows, enamelled with all sorts of eye-pleasing flowers; thickets, which, being lined with most pleasant shade, were witnessed so too by the cheerful disposition of many well-tuned birds; . . . here a shepherd's boy piping as though he should never be old; there a young shepherdess knitting, and withal singing, and it seemed that her voice comforted her hands to work, and her hands kept time to her voice-music." It is difficult not to be reminded of a fine piece of tapestry by this artificial description, which is a good instance of Sidney's love for, and frequent employment of, what Mr. Ruskin has called the "pathetic fallacy." The attributing of human emotions to all senseless things is no artistic fallacy when it is inspired by strong feeling, as in "Clorinda's" beautiful lay on the death of Sidney himself—

> Woods, hills, and rivers now are desolate,
> Sith he is gone the which them all did grace;

but when it is, as with Sidney, a constant recipe for a picturesque sentence, it is a cloying device. The remainder of the description epitomizes the author's extravagances. "As for the houses of the country, they were all scattered, no two being one by the other, and yet not so far as that it barred mutual succour; a show, as it were, of an accompanable solitariness and a civil wildness." Romeo makes use of this figure, but it is to express his love for Rosaline, not for Juliet—

> Why then, O brawling love! O loving hate!
> O anything of nothing first create!

And again, "I pray you" (said Musidorus), "what countries be these we pass through, which are so divers in show, the one wanting no store, the other having no store but of want?" Here is the favourite jingle once more, in a form that recalls more than one line of Shakespeare's. But Sidney wrote in prose, and as the poetical traits of this work passed for its chief glory in his own time, so he has had to pay for them by the neglect of

posterity. His influence reached down to the second birth of the novel in England; Pamēla, her name shortened to Pamēla, came to life again, no longer a princess, but a servant-girl; she was introduced to the public by no knight, but by a Fleet Street bookseller, whose passion was not poetry, but morality; and she has lived on to this day. Richardson is the direct inheritor of the analytic and sentimental method in romance which Sidney had developed before him.[1]

The rival tendencies of court and town which are so clearly marked in the Elizabethan drama, are no less conspicuous in the novel. Sidney and Lyly were both courtiers, and in their novels both cast in their lot with court tastes and tendencies, just as Sidney in his *Apologie* praises *Gorboduc*, which he says "climbeth to the height of Seneca his style," but has no word of praise for the new romantic drama. Indeed, it would not have gratified either author to hear his work spoken of as a "novel," for the word carried with it in those days something of evil imputation, of new-fangled Italianate proclivities, while "novellist" meant nothing but innovator, generally in religion. And the rest of the notable contributors to the prose fiction of Elizabeth's reign present a striking contrast to Sidney in the conditions of their work. On the one hand, the courtier, dreaming his valorous and amorous dreams in stately and leisured retirement, and committing them to paper for the private delight of his noble sister; on the other, a group of struggling adventurers, familiar with the scenes and shifts of penury, seeking for themselves money and notoriety by means of the stationers' shops in Paul's Churchyard, where their "novellets" and "love-pamphlets" would be ranged in heaps to tempt the young gallants who came for their daily lounge in the aisles of the church. And yet it was in the school of necessity that Greene and Nash, and, in a lesser degree, Lodge, learned to write in their happiest vein, and to shape out of their private experiences the beginnings of a true realistic romance.

Notes

1. Richardson perhaps read the *Arcadia* in Mrs. Stanley's "modernized" version (1725), where the above passage is thus rendered:— "The Shepherd-Boys were playing on their Pipes, as they were ignorant they lost the Hours they soothed: a little Distance off sat a young Shepherdess a-spinning, beguiling of her task with rural Songs and Roundelays; the Houses were scattered with a kind of pleasing Irregularity, but yet the Distance was not so great, to bar a mutual Succour, or hinder the Pleasures of Society."

DUNCAN C. TOVEY

From "England's Helicon: More Lyrics from Elizabethan Songbooks"

Reviews and Essays in English Literature
1897, pp. 177–81

Flattery of Elizabeth is not often, except in Shakespeare, so pleasingly managed, and hardly ever so temperate, as here; we cannot say, as a rule, that the courtier-poet is "happiest in fiction." Conceive that "gracious creature," Sidney, descending to this in the character of Therion, a forester, contending in song with Espilus, a shepherd, for the May-Lady:

> Two thousand deer in wildest woods I have;
> Them can I take but you I cannot hold;
> He is not poor who can his freedom save
> Bound but to you, no wealth but you I would,
> *But take this beast if beasts you fear to miss,*
> *For of his beasts the greatest beast is he.*
> (Both kneeling to her Majesty.)

Espilus: Judge you, to whom all beauty's force is lent
Therion: Judge you of Love to whom all love is bent.

This is not the Sidney whom we know; the Astrophel, the vicissitudes of whose love for Stella we can study anew in the pretty volume, so ably edited by Mr. Pollard. This "In Memoriam" of unavailing love is worthy of the man of high and chivalrous courage who wrote the letter on the French match. In Sidney's sonnets we trace the course of a passion whose only rival, whilst hope remains, is the patriotic fire that longs for active service in the field. The moral might at times be Lovelace's:

> I could not love thee, dear, so much
> Loved I not Honour more.

Nowhere has the ennobling power of a manly and worthy affection been better described than in his words—

> If that be sinne which doth the manners frame,
> Well staid with truth in word and faith of deed,
> Readie of wit, and fearing nought but shame;
> If that be sinne which on fixt hearts doth breed
> A loathing of all loose unchastitie,
> Then love is sinne, and let me sinfull be.

And, when hope is gone, the struggle is never ignoble, never undignified; the higher influences prevail, and a purer ideal at last succeeds—"*Splendidis longum valedico nugis,*" is the motto which closes the record, when he takes farewell of earthly passion:

> . . . let that light be thy guide
> In this small course which birth draws out to death,
> And think how evill becommeth him to slide,
> Who seeketh heav'n, and comes of heavenly breath.
> Then farewell, world; thy uttermost I see:
> Eternall Love, maintaine thy life in me.

Sidney is the most *dramatic* of sonneteers. In this capacity Shakespeare and he change places. Even if we suppose, with Mr. Gerald Massey, that Shakespeare only occasionally writes in his own person, he uses his art to conceal his art, to mystify rather than to embellish, and the *result* is an effect the reverse of dramatic. But Sidney is constantly revealing to us the life in which he moved, the *entourage* of that secret passion which he bore in the midst of it. He wins the prize in the tourney, in the judgment not only of his own countrymen, but of some sent, as he says in a phrase which concentrates the very spirit of chivalry, "from that sweet enemy France." Those who are skilled in horsemanship attribute his success to this; the townsfolk praise his strength; jealous rivals assign all to luck; some say that his prowess is hereditary both on the father's and the mother's side; Sidney hears it all; he alone knows the reason:

> Stella lookt on, and from her heav'nly face
> Sent forth the beames which made so faire my race.

He describes a lover's impatience in words which, with a very slight change of form, might easily pass as an excerpt from some Shakespearean scene:

> Be your words made, good sir, of Indian ware
> That you allow me them by so small a rate?
> Or do you cutted Spartanes imitate?
> Or do you meane my tender eares to spare,
> That to my questions you so totall are?
> When I demand of Phœnix Stella's state,
> You say, forsooth, you left her well of late:
> O God, thinke you that satisfies my care?
> I would know whether she did sit or walke;
> How cloth'd; how waited on; sighd she or smilde
> Whereof, with whom, how often did she talke;
> With what pastime time's journey she beguilde;

> If her lips daignd to sweeten my pore name.
> Say all: and all well-sayd, still say the same.[1]

Sometimes he moves as a knight of the rueful countenance among the bright festive gatherings of the court, and is held to be proud and reserved—

> Because he oft in darke abstracted guise
> Seemes most alone in greatest companie.

He is teased about the current questions of the day:

> How Ulster likes of that same golden bit
> Wherewith my father once made it halfe tame?
> If in the Scotch court be no weltring yet?
> These questions busie wits to me do frame:
> I, cumbred with good maners, answer do
> But know not how: for still I thinke of you.

He begs the politician who discourses to him—

>   Of courtly tides,
> Of cunning fishers in most troubled streames
> Of straying wayes, when valiant errour guides,

to take his wisdom

> To them that do such entertainment need.

His heart, he says—

>   —confers with Stella's beames
> And is even irkt that so sweet comedie
> By such unsuted speech should hindred be.

We had much more to say, if space permitted. We have taken only a partial survey of these treasures. We have wandered among the wealth which Mr. Bullen and Mr. Pollard have shown us once more, as a visitor to some noble mansion, who prefers the statuary to the Dresden china. Yet the shepherds and shepherdesses of the Elizabethan era, though they do plight their troth "before god Pan, and then to Church," are not wholly an anachronism. The city has not yet absorbed literature, its dust and dirt have not yet choked up in Euterpe's flute all the stops which echo the native sounds of the fields and woodlands. Many a reveller at the Mermaid could have held discourse with Perdita amid her flowers, and knew well, when and where to find those 'pretty daughters of the earth and sun'—

>   The daffodils
> That come before the swallow dares, and take
> The winds of March with beauty; violets dim
> But sweeter than the lids of Juno's eyes
> Or Cytherea's breath; pale primroses
> That die unmarried ere they can behold
> Bright Phœbus in his strength; bold oxlips and
> The Crown Imperial.

We are still some distance from the days once so bright and brilliant, but now like some "banquet-hall deserted" where the candles are flickering in the sockets, when dissolute beaux and frivolous women of fashion monopolized the names of pastoral song. Daphnis and Mopsus still carry with them the aroma of the country, though sometimes, alas! of the stable. Nature, with her ever-fresh sources of inspiration, is nearer to men here, even in their dreams of a life wholly fanciful and unreal, than she condescends to be to the brilliant epigrammatist of a later day, whose Daphnis has gone to the town, whence no charms can bring him back again, whose Chloe reads Rochester, whose Phyllis has taken to paint and patches, and whose Mopsus is a Mohawk.

Notes

1. Cf. Rosalind, in *As You Like It*, iii. 2, 231 *sq.*: "What did he when thou sawest him? What said he? How looked he? *Wherein went he? Did he ask for me?*" etc., etc.

JOEL E. SPINGARN
From "The General Theory of Poetry"
A History of Literary Criticism in the Renaissance
1899, pp. 34–274

The poet, so far from adding anything extraneous to the things he imitates, depicts them in their very essence; and it is because he alone finds the true beauty in things, because he attributes to them their true nobility and perfection, that he is more useful than any other writer. The poet does not, as some think, deal with the false and the unreal. He assumes nothing openly alien to truth, though he may permit himself to treat of old and obscure legends which cannot be verified, or of things which are regarded as true on account of their appearance, their allegorical signification (such as the ancient myths and fables), or their common acceptance by men. So we may conclude that not every one who uses verse is a poet, but only he who is moved by the true beauty of things—by their simple and essential beauties, not merely apparent ones. This is Fracastoro's conclusion, and it contains that mingling of Platonism and Aristotelianism which may be found somewhat later in Tasso and Sir Philip Sidney. It is the chief merit of Fracastoro's dialogue, that even while emphasizing this Platonic element, he clearly distinguishes and defines the ideal element in aesthetic imitation.

About the same time, in the public lectures of Varchi (1553), there was an attempt to formulate a more explicit definition of poetry on the basis of Aristotle's definition of tragedy. . . .

It has been seen that Varchi classed poetry with rational philosophy. The end of all arts and sciences is to make human life perfect and happy; but they differ in their modes of producing this result. Philosophy attains its end by teaching; rhetoric, by persuasion; history, by narration; poetry, by imitation or representation. The aim of the poet, therefore, is to make the human soul perfect and happy, and it is his office to imitate, that is, to invent and represent, things which render men virtuous, and consequently happy. Poetry attains this end more perfectly than any of the other arts or sciences, because it does so, not by means of precept, but by means of example. There are various ways of making men virtuous,—by teaching them what vice is and what virtue is, which is the province of ethics; by actually chastising vices and rewarding virtues, which is the province of law; or by example, that is, by the representation of virtuous men receiving suitable rewards for their virtue, and of vicious men receiving suitable punishments, which is the province of poetry. This last method is the most efficacious, because it is accompanied by delight. For men either can not or will not take the trouble to study sciences and virtues—nay, do not even like to be told what they should or should not do; but in hearing or reading poetic examples, not only is there no trouble, but there is the greatest delight, and no one can help being moved by the representation of characters who are rewarded or punished according to an ideal justice. . . .

The General Theory of Poetry in the Elizabethan Age

Those who have some aquaintance, however superficial, with the literary criticism of the Italian Renaissance will find an account of the Elizabethan theory of poetry a twice-told tale. In England, as in France, criticism during this period was of a more practical character than in Italy; but even for the technical questions discussed by the Elizabethans, some prototype, or at least some equivalent, may be found among the Italians. The first four stages of English criticism have therefore little novelty or original value; and their study is chiefly important as evidence of the gradual application of the ideas of the Renaissance to English literature.

The writers of the first stage, as might be expected, concerned themselves but little with the theory of poetry, beyond repeating here and there the commonplaces they found in the Italian rhetoricians. Yet it is interesting to note that as early as 1553, Wilson, in the third book of his *Rhetoric*, gives expression to the allegorical conception of poetry which in Italy had held sway from the time of Petrarch and Boccaccio, and which, more than anything else, colored critical theory in Elizabethan England. The ancient poets, according to Wilson, did not spend their time inventing meaningless fables, but used the story merely as a framework for contents of ethical, philosophic, scientific, or historical import; the trials of Ulysses, for example, were intended to furnish a lively picture of man's misery in this life. The poets are, in fact, wise men, spiritual legislators, reformers, who have at heart the redressing of wrongs; and in accomplishing this end,—either because they fear to rebuke these wrongs openly, or because they doubt the expediency or efficacy of such frankness with ignorant people,—they hide their true meaning under the veil of pleasant fables. This theory of poetic art, one of the commonplaces of the age, may be described as the great legacy of the Middle Ages to Renaissance criticism.

The writers of the second stage were, in many cases, too busy with questions of versification and other practical matters to find time for abstract theorizing on the art of poetry. A long period of rhetorical and metrical study had helped to formulate a rhetorical and technical conception of the poet's function, aptly exemplified in the sonnet describing the perfect poet prefixed to King James's brief treatise on Scotch poetry. The marks of a perfect poet are there given as skilfulness in the rhetorical figures, quick wit, as shown in the use of apt and pithy words, and a good memory;—a merely external view of the poet's gifts, which takes no account of such essentials as imagination, sensibility, and knowledge of nature and human life. . . .

The theory of poetry during the second stage of English criticism was in the main Horatian, with such additions and modifications as the early Renaissance had derived from the Middle Ages. The Aristotelian canons had not yet become a part of English criticism. Webbe alludes to Aristotle's dictum that Empedocles, having naught but metre in common with Homer, was in reality a natural philosopher rather than a poet; but all such allusions to Aristotle's *Poetics* were merely incidental and sporadic. The introduction of Aristotelianism into England was the direct result of the influence of the Italian critics; and the agent in bringing this new influence into English letters was Sir Philip Sidney. His *Defense of Poesy* is a veritable epitome of the literary criticism of the Italian Renaissance; and so thoroughly is it imbued with this spirit, that no other work, Italian, French, or English, can be said to give so complete and so noble a conception of the temper and the principles of Renaissance criticism. For the general theory of poetry, its sources were the critical treatises of Minturno and Scaliger. Yet without any decided novelty of ideas, or even of expression, it can lay claim to distinct originality in its unity of feeling, its ideal and noble temper, and its adaptation to circumstance. Its eloquence and dignity will hardly appear in a mere analysis, which pretends to give only the more important and fundamental of its principles; but such a summary—and this is quite as important—will at least indicate the extent of its indebtedness to Italian criticism.

In all that relates to the antiquity, universality, and preëminence of poetry, Sidney apparently follows Minturno. Poetry, as the first light-giver to ignorance, flourished before any other art or science. The first philosophers and historians were poets; and such supreme works as the *Psalms* of David and the *Dialogues* of Plato are in reality poetical. Among the Greeks and the Romans, the poet was regarded as a sage or prophet; and no nation, however primitative or barbarous, has been without poets, or has failed to receive delight and instruction from poetry.

But before proceeding to defend an art so ancient and universal, it is necessary to define it; and the definition which Sidney gives agrees substantially with what might be designated Renaissance Aristotelianism. "Poetry," says Sidney, "is an art of imitation, for so Aristotle termeth it in his word *mimesis*, that is to say, a representing, counterfeiting, or figuring forth; to speak metaphorically, a speaking picture, with this end,—to teach and delight." Poetry is, accordingly, an art of imitation, and not merely the art of versifying; for although most poets have seen fit to apparel their poetic inventions in verse, verse is but the raiment and ornament of poetry, and not one of its causes or essentials. "One may be a poet without versing," says Sidney, "and a versifier without poetry." Speech and reason are the distinguishing features between man and brute; and whatever helps to perfect and polish speech deserves high commendation. Besides its mnemonic value, verse is the most fitting raiment of poetry because it is most dignified and compact, not colloquial and slipshod. But with all its merits, it is not an essential of poetry, of which the true test is this,—feigning notable images of vices and virtues, and teaching delightfully.

In regard to the object, or function, of poetry, Sidney is at one with Scaliger. The aim of poetry is accomplished by teaching most delightfully a notable morality; or, in a word, by delightful instruction. Not instruction alone, or delight alone, as Horace had said, but instruction made delightful; and it is this dual function which serves not only as the end but as the very test of poetry. The object of all arts and sciences is to lift human life to the highest altitudes of perfection; and in this respect they are all servants of the sovereign, or architectonic, science, whose end is well-doing and not well-knowing only. Virtuous action is therefore the end of all learning; and Sidney sets out to prove that the poet, more than any one else, conduces to this end.

This is the beginning of the apologetic side of Sidney's argument. The ancient controversy—ancient even in Plato's days—between poetry and philosophy is once more reopened; and the question is the one so often debated by the Italians,— shall the palm be given to the poet, to the philosopher, or to the historian? The gist of Sidney's argument is that while the philosopher teaches by precept alone, and the historian by example alone, the poet conduces most to virtue because he employs both precept and example. The philosopher teaches virtue by showing what virtue is and what vice is, by setting down, in thorny argument, and without clarity or beauty of style, the bare rule. The historian teaches virtue by showing the experiences of past ages; but, being tied down to what actually happened, that is, to the particular truth of things and not to general reason, the example he depicts draws no necessary consequence. The poet alone accomplishes this dual task. What the philosopher says should be done is by the poet pictured most perfectly in some one by whom it has been done, thus coupling the general notion with the particular instance. The philosopher, moreover, teaches the learned only; the poet teaches all, and is, in Plutarch's phrase, "the right popular philosopher," for he seems only to promise delight, and moves men to virtue unawares. But even if the philosopher excel the poet in teaching, he cannot move his readers as the poet can, and this is of higher importance than teaching; for what is the use of teaching virtue if the pupil is not moved to act and

accomplish what he is taught? On the other hand, the historian deals with particular instances, with vices and virtues so commingled that the reader can find no pattern to imitate. The poet makes history reasonable; he gives perfect examples of vices and virtues for human imitation; he makes virtue succeed and vice fail, as history can but seldom do. Poetry, therefore, conduces to virtue, the end of all learning, better than any other art or science, and so deserves the palm as the highest and the noblest form of human wisdom.

The basis of Sidney's distinction between the poet and the historian is the famous passage in which Aristotle explains why poetry is more philosophic and of more serious value than history. The poet deals, not with the particular, but with the universal,—with what might or should be, not with what is or has been. But Sidney, in the assertion of this principle, follows Minturno and Scaliger, and goes farther than Aristotle would probably have gone. All arts have the works of nature as their principal object, and follow nature as actors follow the lines of the play. Only the poet is not tied to such subjects, but creates another nature better than ever nature itself brought forth. For, going hand in hand with nature, and being enclosed not within her limits, but only by the zodiac of his own imagination, he creates a golden world for nature's brazen; and in this sense he may be compared as a creator with God. Where shall you find in life such a friend as Pylades, such a hero as Orlando, such an excellent man as Æneas?

Sidney then proceeds to answer the various objections that have been made against poetry. These objections, partly following Gosson and Cornelius Agrippa, and partly his own inclinations, he reduces to four. In the first place, it is objected that a man might spend his time more profitably than by reading the figments of poets. But since teaching virtue is the real aim of all learning, and since poetry has been shown to accomplish this better than all other arts and sciences, this objection is easily answered. In the second place, poetry has been called the mother of lies; but Sidney shows that it is less likely to misstate facts than other sciences, for the poet does not publish his figments as facts, and, since he affirms nothing, cannot ever be said to lie. Thirdly, poetry has been called the nurse of abuse, that is to say, poetry misuses and debases the mind of man by turning it to wantonness and by making it unmartial and effeminate. But Sidney argues that it is man's wit that abuses poetry, and not poetry that abuses man's wit; and as to making men effeminate, this charge applies to all other sciences more than to poetry, which in its description of battles and praise of valiant men notably stirs courage and enthusiasm. Lastly, it is pointed out by the enemies of poetry that Plato, one of the greatest of philosophers, banished poets from his ideal commonwealth. But Plato's *Dialogues* are in reality themselves a form of poetry; and it argues ingratitude in the most poetical of philosophers, that he should defile the fountain which was his source. Yet though Sidney perceives how fundamental are Plato's objections to poetry, he is inclined to believe that it was rather against the abuse of poetry by the contemporary Greek poets that Plato was chiefly cavilling; for poets are praised in the *Ion*, and the greatest men of every age have been patrons and lovers of poetry.

ALGERNON CHARLES SWINBURNE
"Astrophel" (1894)
Works
1900, pp. 589–91

*After Reading Sir Philip Sidney's Arcadia in the
Garden of an Old English Manor House.*

O light of the land that adored thee
    And kindled thy soul with her breath,
Whose life, such as fate would afford thee,
    Was lovelier than aught but thy death,
By what name, could thy lovers but know it,
    Might love of thee hail thee afar,
Philisides, Astrophel, poet
    Whose love was thy star?

A star in the moondawn of Maytime,
    A star in the cloudland of change;
Too splendid and sad for the daytime
    To cheer or eclipse or estrange;
Too sweet for tradition or vision
    To see but through shadows of tears
Rise deathless across the division
    Of measureless years.

The twilight may deepen and harden
    As nightward the stream of it runs
Till starshine transfigure a garden
    Whose radiance responds to the sun's:
The light of the love of thee darkens
    The lights that arise and that set:
The love that forgets thee not hearkens
    If England forget.

. . .

Bright and brief in the sight of grief and love
    the light of thy lifetime shone,
Seen and felt by the gifts it dealt, the grace it
    gave, and again was gone:
Ay, but now it is death, not thou, whom time
    has conquered as years pass on.

Ay, not yet may the land forget that bore and
    loved thee and praised and wept,
Sidney, lord of the stainless sword, the name
    of names that her heart's love kept
Fast as thine did her own, a sign to light thy
    life till it sank and slept.

Bright as then for the souls of men thy brave
    Arcadia resounds and shines,
Lit with love that beholds above all joys and
    sorrows the steadfast signs,
Faith, a splendour that hope makes tender,
    and truth, whose presage the soul divines.

All the glory that girds the story of all thy life
    as with sunlight round,
All the spell that on all souls fell who saw
    thy spirit, and held them bound,
Lives for all that have heard the call and
    cadence yet of its music sound.

. . .

But England, enmeshed and benetted
    With spiritless villainies round,
With counsels of cowardice fretted,
    With trammels of treason enwound,
Is yet, though the season be other

Than wept and rejoiced over thee,
Thine England, thy lover, thy mother,
    Sublime as the sea.
Hers wast thou: if her face be now less bright,
    or seem for an hour less brave,
Let but thine on her darkness shine, thy
    saviour spirit revive and save,
Time shall see, as the shadows flee, her shame
    entombed in a shameful grave.

If death and not life were the portal
    That opens on life at the last,
If the spirit of Sidney were mortal
    And the past of it utterly past,
Fear stronger than honour was ever,
    Forgetfulness mightier than fame,
Faith knows not if England should never
    Subside into shame.

Yea, but yet is thy sun not set, thy sunbright
    spirit of trust withdrawn:
England's love of thee burns above all hopes
    that darken or fears that fawn:
Hers thou art: and the faithful heart that
    hopes begets upon darkness dawn.

The sunset that sunrise will follow
    Is less than the dream of a dream:
The starshine on height and on hollow
    Sheds promise that dawn shall redeem:
The night, if the daytime would hide it,
    Shows lovelier, aflame and afar,
Thy soul and thy Stella's beside it,
    A star by a star.

ADOLPHUS WILLIAM WARD
"Sir Philip Sidney"
English Prose, ed. Craik
1904, Volume 1, pp. 401–8

The inevitable application to Sidney of the phrase, "the Marcellus of English literature," is misleading, if not altogether meaningless. When his noble life had been sacrificed to the attractions of a futile *coup de Balaclava*, he was mourned at home in England, not only for what had been hoped from him, but for what he had already achieved. Still, it would be idle to deny that never has gallant warrior, true knight, or illustrious writer, been more fortunate than he in the opportunity of his death. To begin with, mutual sympathies were as yet stronger than antipathies in the small but expanding world of English literature; and thus, although the Queen herself had honoured the good courtier she had lost, although English nobles were his pall-bearers, while his loss was lamented by the Seven Provinces which he had helped to protect, and acknowledged even by the archfoe whose name he bore, he had no mourners more justly in earnest than the scholars and poets that claimed him as one of themselves. For the soldier who had fallen on the field of honour, the statesman whom his own Sovereign had trusted and whom the Republic of a foreign kingdom had summoned to its throne,—he too had been a citizen of that Arcadia where Imagination holds supreme sway; he too had not only taken joy in that Art of Poesy for which he had entered the lists, but had as a true student found in it compensation for the disappointments of life and love.

But if Sidney's death thus fitly called forth the tears of the Muses and of their professed votaries, among them of the poet whose praise was in itself a pledge of literary immortality, neither should its coincidence with the beginning of a new era in our literary as well as our political history be overlooked. The year following on that of Sidney's death ended the tragedy of Mary Queen of Scots; its successor in turn witnessed the catastrophe of the Spanish Armada. During these few years Spenser was already at work upon his masterpiece; in their course were published the first productions of nearly all his chief contemporaries among our epic and lyric poets; and to the same wonderful years belong the earlier plays of the most prominent among the immediate predecessors of older contemporaries of Shakespeare. How then could it have been otherwise than that the sudden extinction at such an epoch of a light which had shone forth with so brilliant a promise, should be lamented in strains appropriate to a truly national loss?

Yet, apart from all adventitious circumstances of date, who shall deny that in Sir Philip Sidney, a fit "pride of shepherds' praise" was lost to the vocal Arcady around him? Concerning his verse it must suffice to say that the lyrical form introduced into English poetry by Surrey, and domesticated in it by Sidney and Spenser, would hardly have made so speedy and so sure a settlement but for the fact that neither the one nor the other scorned to pour his own golden soul into the alien literary mould.

Nor was it far otherwise with the more imposing of the two prose works which, even more decisively than *Astrophel and Stella*, have secured to their author the unchallengeable rank of a national classic. *The Countess of Pembroke's Arcadia*, written by Sidney at his sister's house as a rough draft for her diversion, some time in the years 1580 and 1581, although not printed till after his death in 1590, forms, of course, a mere link in the connected chain of modern pastoral literature. That chain may, without injustice to Politian, be said to begin with Sannazaro's *Arcadia* (1502), and to reach down through a series of successors to and beyond the name-sake works of Sidney and Lope de Vega. In their most salient features all these productions resemble one another. They seek alike to give prominence to those emotions which humanise and soften life in the midst of the very conflicts and troubles provided in part by themselves, and thus their effect is to exalt friendship and love, but the latter most conspicuously, as absorbing the sentiments of the personages within their range, together with most of the life they lead and of the time they kill. Hence the sameness and monotony characteristic of modern in a far greater measure than of ancient pastoral. Conversely, modern pastoral almost imperceptibly substituted its own ineffable artificiality of style for the *naïveté* (conscious only to the extent in which the play of children is such) of the Sicilian Muses. Vergil is as simple and natural as it is possible for an imitator to remain. In Sannazaro there lingers at least the pretence of a rustic tone; in Tasso and Guarini simplicity has become delicacy; the Spaniards refine upon the Italians, and in Sidney the pastoral dress has become a mere accepted costume. Indeed his shepherds are in the main confessedly nothing more than courtiers in retreat—"princely shepherds," as he calls them—in their way hardly less conventional than their latest *Louis Quinze* successors. With the conventionalities of scenery and costume those of incident and character become permanently associated; we recognise as inevitable the disconsolate shepherd, the coy shepherdess, and the clown whose feats and feelings burlesque those of his superiors, although he "will stumble sometimes upon some songs that might become a better brain." Nor are we spared well-known stage tricks for setting off the stage figures, above all the familiar device of Echo repeating in moans and in puns the final syllables of lines of verse uttered among the rocks or trees.

If in these respects Sidney's *Arcadia* must perforce be pronounced the reverse of original, neither is it possible to ignore the Euphuistic element in the style of the book, or the degree in which its initial success was due to this particular cause. *Euphues*, it must be remembered, had appeared in 1579, only a year before Sir Philip Sidney temporarily withdrew from the Court where no figure had shone more conspicuously than his own; and the *Arcadia*, though not printed till eleven years afterwards, was written under the influence of an extremely fashionable and easily imitable model. Probably what seemed choicest in the style of Sidney's work to its early admirers was what most closely resembled *Euphues*. "Oh," cries Master Fastidious Brisk in *Every Man out of his Humour*, when eulogising the "harmonious and musical strain of wit" in a great lady, "it flows from her like nectar . . . as I am an honest man, would I might never stir, sir, but she does observe as pure a phrase, and use as choice figures in her ordinary conferences, as may be in the *Arcadia*." And in the same play Fungoso, who "follows the fashion afar off, like a spy," says that, while waiting for his new suit of clothes, he will "sit in his old suit, or else lie a-bed, and read the *Arcadia*." Of the significant characteristics of Euphuism hardly one, unless it be a certain monotony of cadence quite out of keeping with the superior versatility of Sidney's literary genius, is altogether missing in his book. Although he is expressly praised by Drayton for disburdening our tongue of Lyly's favourite similes from natural history, or supposed natural history, yet "this word, *Lover*, did no less pierce poor *Pyrocles*, than the right tune of music toucheth him that is sick of the *Tarantula*"; and the Forsaken Knight bears as his *impresa*, or device, "a *Catoblepas*, which so long lies dead as the moon, whereto it hath so natural a sympathy, wants her light." Nor was the author of the *Arcadia* proof against the seduction of mere tricks of sound, quite apart from the metrical experiments which furnish so moderate an enjoyment to his latter-day readers, and which need not be discussed here. Above all, full play is allowed to his intolerable fondness for puns, which a famous American historian calls "the only blemish in his character"; on the very first page of the romance, the very first Arcadian having used the adverb *last* regrets "that the word *last* should so long *last*." Nor can it be denied that notwithstanding the coherency and consequent interest as narratives of some of the interwoven episodes, such as that borrowed by Shakespeare for *King Lear*, the *Arcadia* in the general texture of its argument marks no material advance from the point of view of construction upon *Euphues* and its direct progeny of love-pamphlets.

But although as late as the days of Sir Walter Scott's *Monastery*, the conception of "perfect Arcadia" as a kind of diction cherished by the "precious," necessarily included an unmistakeable admixture of affectation, and although this affectation was mainly imitative, yet Sidney was, to begin with, as he says in one of the most charming of his Sonnets,

No pick-purse of another's wit;

Nor indeed is this, unless at a very early stage of their literary lives, a common crime with those who can boast so splendid an endowment of their own. If his *Arcadia* remains to this day interesting,—an epithet which few members of the public that reads to please itself, would be likely to apply to Lyly's *Euphues*,—the reason is not far to seek. After all, the *Arcadia* is self-confessedly a romance of chivalry in the approved pastoral form; and as such is animated with vivifying power by the spirit of Sir Calidore. This spirit is recognisable in the martial and often very sanguinary adventures which form part of the main argument, dim and discursive though this latter must be allowed to be, albeit used by one most capable dramatist (Shirley) as the plot of one of his plays. It shows itself in the love of manly exercises and diversions, of games and bouts of all kinds, and in the minute interest in the qualities and points of horses and hounds, to which divers passages of the *Arcadia* bear witness. It displays itself not less in a sincere enjoyment of well-ordered pomp and magnificence, of tournaments and pageants, of brave habiliments and gorgeous drapery. Above all it finds expression in a passionate devotion to the service of fair women, and an ecstatic enthusiasm in the detailed extolling of their charms. Philoclea is but another name for "Stella ever dear"; Pamela, if she represents any actual woman, typifies a more august, and a more self-restrained, mistress. Nor is it, in this connexion, to be overlooked that in addition to the desire for chivalrous action, whereby, as Musidorus says, man "not only betters himself but benefits others," and to the tenderness which filled Sidney's soul, the *Arcadia* reflects something of the national political sentiment of which its author was in so many ways a typical representative. This more than anything, except certain descriptive passages to which in the *Arcadia*, as in the *Faerie Queen*, our native English scenery may prefer an exclusive claim, makes Sidney's work distinctively English, and connects it organically with the great national age to which it belonged. St. Marc-Girardin has pointed out political touches, which are at the same time delicate flatteries, and which, as he says, denote the courtier. But although we may smile to find that the virtues and the beauties of Urania (Elizabeth)—in Euphuistic phrase her "sweetest fairness and fairest sweetness"—cannot be kept even out of *Arcadia*, yet we remember that the courtier who ushers them in is the good courtier of Spenser's beautiful adaptation; and that to him his sovereign is the incarnation of the purposes for which in camp and court life is worth living.

The style of such a writer can hardly lack individuality; and in Sidney's prose this master-quality has no difficulty in asserting itself in the face of more or less adventitious influences. Thus the Euphuism of the *Arcadia*, though here and there marked enough, cannot be described as a quality of the style of the book at large; as such, its place is taken by something new and individual, although perhaps something not very easy to define. In a celebrated passage extracted below, Philoclea is described as "so humble, that she would put all pride out of countenance." A page or two later, the high-minded Philanax from his sick-bed demands of his master, discouraged by an oracle, why he should "deprive himself of government, for fear of losing his government, like one that should kill himself for fear of death." In such passages as these, and in many more of the same kind, the antithesis no longer owes much of its effect to sound or cadence; and the point of their wit goes home the more truly, because it has been dipped in moral sentiment. Moreover, the effort is not, as in the master, painfully elaborated; playful touches of convincing simplicity are not uncommon, such as "No is no negative in a woman's mouth"; elsewhere the author knows how to stop short, with his Pyrocles, "like a man unsatisfied in himself, though his wit might well have served to satisfy another."

Much more might be said concerning the style of the *Arcadia* of which there is no reason for assuming that Sidney would have refused, had occasion offered, to lop many of the extravagances. Of these there is beyond doubt too luxuriant an underwood, but not enough to choke the nobler growths, or to hide the play of the sunlight between them. If Sidney's humour in the *Arcadia* must on the whole be called conventional,

while his pathos is not economised, as pathos should be if it is to become effective, he on the other hand constantly shows (the distinction will be obvious) a *feeling* which proves him an artist of a very high order. His descriptive touches, often conveyed in exquisite figures—night stretching forth her black arms to part combatants; a maiden's cheeks blushing "and withal, when she was spoken unto, a little smiling, like roses, when their leaves are with a little breath stirred"—added a fresh charm to English prose, and one which over-matched the more pretentious efforts in the same direction of earlier Elizabethan verse. Nor are such spontaneous beauties out of keeping with frequent bursts of a noble rhetoric, the result, may be, of conscious training, but not the dictation of another man's mind, and at times consecrated, as in one of the extracts given below, to the loftiest of themes. Thus the freshness, the flexibility, the essential originality and intrinsic nobility of Sidney's genius reflect themselves in the style of the most notable prose-work, taken as a whole, of an era without parallel in our literature.

The Countess of Pembroke's Arcadia resembles a beautiful and elaborate headgear such as Sidney's sister might have worn at Court while witnessing his prowess at the barriers—a product of nature interspersed with a hundred quaint artifices of wreaths and bugles and ouches and rings. The *Defence of Poesy*, which he wrote about the same time as the longer work, or but little later, is like a single gem in a simple but exquisitely appropriate setting of its own. The introduction, with Attic lightness and gracefulness, enables the author without effort or flourish to enter upon his theme, the defence of his favourite art—"having, I know not by what mischance, in these my old years and idlest times, slipped into the title of a poet." The subject is treated with both fulness and thoroughness, no care being spared in definition and classification; but even in the earlier part of the essay we are inspirited as we touch the hand of our eager guide by the contagion of his own generous enthusiasm. More especially in his review of the different kinds or species of poetry are to be found passages of inimitable freshness as well as aptitude, among them, the famous figure as to the effect of "the old song of Percy and Douglas"; although, to tell the truth, it is rather disappointing to be asked directly afterwards, what this lyric would work, were it "trimmed in the gorgeous eloquence of Pindar."

Naturally our poet-critic moves with greater freedom as he proceeds to refute the cavils of the transliterate the greek as *Misomousoi* and permits himself in the interests of the dignity of his art, to digress into a lively and combative little diatribe on the stage-plays of his day. Yet nowhere is he so perfectly felicitous as in his peroration, where he has very skilfully allowed a wave of humour to mingle in the current of his eloquence, and parts from his reader with the courteous and pleasant tone in which the essay opened.

Thus the *Defence of Poesy* is not only typical of a species of critical essays which were soon to become common in our literature, and which of course are as significant of the tastes of the public as of those of their writers. It is likewise typical, in choice of subject and in style, of the idiosyncrasy of its author, so modest in his self-estimate, so generous in his judgment of others; so bent upon fancies pure and noble, and yet in the utterance of them so pleasantly abounding in the humour proper to gentle minds.

CHRISTOPHER MARLOWE

CHRISTOPHER MARLOWE

1564–1593

Christopher Marlowe, dramatist and poet, was born at Canterbury, Kent, the son of a cobbler. He went to Corpus Christi College, Oxford, in 1581, and after intermittent attendance received his degree in 1587. In London he was a member of the "University Wits," along with Lyly, Nashe, Peele, Greene, and Lodge. A warrant was issued for Marlowe's arrest in 1593, on the charge of atheism, but he was slain soon after in a brawl at a tavern near Deptford.

Marlowe's works exerted a considerable influence over Elizabethan drama. *Tamburlaine the Great* (Part I, 1587; Part II, 1588), written in blank verse, was widely quoted and imitated by contemporaries. *The Jew of Malta* (c. 1589) and *The Tragical History of Dr. Faustus* (c. 1589–92) are marred by the rewriting of subsequent adaptations. The play *Edward the Second* (c. 1592), based on Holinshed, is considered the least violent and most mature of Marlowe's writings. Other plays include *The Massacre at Paris* and *Dido, Queen of Carthage*, the latter written in collaboration with Thomas Nashe. Marlowe also wrote the first two books of the poem *Hero and Leander* (completed by George Chapman) and "The Passionate Shepherd to His Love," to which Sir Walter Raleigh wrote "The Nymph's Reply."

I keepe my old course, to palter vp some thing in Prose, vsing mine old poesie still . . . although latelye two Gentlemen Poets, made my two mad men of Rome beate it out of their paper bucklers: & had it in derision, for that I could not make my verses iet vpon the stage in tragicall buskins, euerie worde filling the mouthe like the fuftanden of Bo-Bell, daring God out of heauen with that Atheist Tamburlan, or blaspheming with the mad priest of the sonne: but let me rather openly pocket vp the Asse at *Diogenes* hand: then wantonlye set out such impious instances of intollerable poetrie, such mad and scoffing poets, that haue propheticall spirits as bold as Merlins race, if there be anye in England that set the end of scollerisme in English blancke verse, I thinke either it is the humor of a nouice that tickles them with selfe-loue, or to much frequenting the hot house . . . hath swet out all the greatest part of their wits. —ROBERT GREENE, "To the Gentlemen Readers, Health," *Perimedes the Blacksmith*, 1538

Wonder not (for with thee wil I first begin), thou famous gracer of Tragedians, that *Greene*, who hath said with thee (like the foole in his heart), There is no God, should now giue glorie vnto his greatnes: for penetrating is his power, his hand lyes heauie vpon me, hee hath spoken vnto me with a voice of thunder, and I haue felt he is a God that can punish enemies. Why should thy excellent wit, his gift, bee so blinded, that thou shouldst giue no glorie to the giuer? Is it pestilent Machiuilian pollicy that thou hast studied? O peeuish follie! What are his rules but meere confused mockeries, able to extirpate in small time, the generation of mankind. For if *Sic volo, sic iubeo*, hold in those that are able to commaund: and if it be lawful *Fas & nefas* to doe any thing that is beneficiall, onely Tyrants should possesse the earth, and they striuing to exceed in tyrannie, should each to other be a slaughter man; till the mightiest outliuing all, one stroke were lefte for Death, that in one age mans life should end. The brocher of this Diabolicall Atheisme is dead, and in his life had neuer the felicitie hee aymed at: but as he began in craft, liued in feare, and ended in despaire. *Quam inscrutabilia sunt Dei iudicia?* This murderer of many brethren, had his conscience seared like *Caine*: this betrayer of him that gaue his life for him, inherited the portion of *Iudas*: this Apostata perished as ill as *Iulian*: and wilt thou my friend be his disciple? Looke but to me, by him perswaded to that libertie, and thou shalt find it an infernall bondage. I knowe the least of my demerits merit this miserable death, but wilfull striuing against knowne truth, exceedeth all the terrors of my soule. Defer not (with me) till this last point of extremitie; for little knowst thou how in the end thou shat be visited. —ROBERT GREENE, A *Groatsworth of Wit bought with a Million of Repentance*, 1592

Sonet

Slumbring I lay in melancholy bed,
Before the dawning of the sanguin light:
When Eccho shrill, or some Familiar Spright
Buzzed an Epitaph into my hed.

Magnifique Mindes, bred of Gargantuas race,
In grisly weedes His Obsequies raiment,
Whose Corps on Powles, whose mind triumph'd on Kent,
Scorning to bate Sir Rodomont an ace.

I mus'd awhile: and hauing mus'd awhile,
Iesu, (quoth I) is that Gargantua minde
Conquerd, and left no Scanderbeg behinde?
Vowed he not to Powles A Second bile?

What bile, or kibe? (quoth that same early Spright)
Haue you forgot the Scanderbegging wight?

Glosse

Is it a Dreame? or is the Highest minde,
That euer haunted Powles, or hunted winde,
Bereaft of that same sky-surmounting breath,
That breath, that taught the Timpany to swell?

He, and the Plague contended for the game:
The hawty man extolles his hideous thoughtes,
And gloriously insultes vpon poore soules,
That plague themselues: for faint harts plague themselues.

The tyrant Sicknesse of base-minded slaues
Or how it dominer'd in Coward Lane?
So Surquidry rang-out his larum bell,
When he had girn'd at many a dolefull knell.
The graund Disseate disdain'd his toade Conceit,
And smiling at his tamberlaine contempt,
Sternely struck-home the peremptory stroke.
He that nor feared God, nor dreaded Diu'll,
Nor ought admired, but his wondrous selfe:
Like Iunos gawdy Bird, that prowdly stares

165

On glittering fan of his triumphant taile:
Or like the vgly Bugg, that scorn'd to dy,
And mountes of Glory rear'd in towring witt:
Alas: but Babell Pride must kisse the pitt.
        —GABRIEL HARVEY, A *New Letter of Notable
        Contents,* 1593

            And after thee
Why hie they not, unhappy in thine end,
Marley, the Muses darling for thy verse;
Fitte to write passions for the soules below,
If any wretched soules in passion speake?
        —GEORGE PEELE, "Prologus," *The Honour of
        the Garter,* 1593

I present your Ladiship with the last affections of the first two Louers that euer *Muse* shrinde in the Temple of *Memorie;* being drawne by strange instigation to employ some of my serious time in so trifeling a subiect, which yet made the first Author, diuine *Musaeus,* eternall. And were it not that wee must subiect our accounts of these common receiued conceits to seruile custome; it goes much against my hand to signe that for a trifling subiect, on which more worthines of soule hath been shewed, and weight of diuine wit, than can vouchsafe residence in the leaden grauitie of any *Mony-Monger;* in whose profession all serious subiects are concluded.—GEORGE CHAP-MAN, "Dedication to Lady Walsingham," *Hero and Leander: Begun by Christopher Marlowe and finished by George Chapman,* 1598

New light gives new directions, Fortunes new
To fashion our indeuours that ensue,
More harsh (at lest more hard) more graue and hie
Our subiect runs, and our sterne *Muse* must flie,
Loues edge is taken off, and that light flame,
Those thoughts, ioyes, longings, that before became
High vnexperienst blood, and maids sharp plights
Must now grow staid, and censure the delights,
That being enioyd aske iudgement; now we praise,
As hauing parted: Euenings crowne the daies. . . .
Then thou most strangely-intellectual fire,
That proper to my soule has power t'inspire
Her burning faculties, and with the wings
Of thy vnspheared flame visitst the springs
Of spirits immortall; Now (as swift as Time
Doth follow Motion) finde th'eternall Clime
Of his free soule, whose liuing subiect stood
Vp to the chin in the Pyerean flood,
And drunke to me halfe this Musean storie,
Inscribing it to deathles Memorie;
Confer with it, and make my pledge as deepe,
That neithers draught be consecrate to sleepe.
Tell it how much his late desires I tender,
(If yet it know not) and to light surrender
My soules darke ofspring, willing it should die
To loues, to passions, and societie.
        —GEORGE CHAPMAN, "Third Sestyad," *Hero
        and Leander: Begun by Christopher Marlowe
        and finished by George Chapman,* 1598, ll.
        1–10, 183–98

As Iodelle, a French tragicall poet being an Epicure, and an Atheist, made a pitifull end: so our tragicall poet *Marlow* for his Epicurisme and Atheisme had a tragicall death; you may read of this *Marlow* more at large in the 'Theatre of God's Judgment'. . . . As the poet Lycophron was shot to death by a certain rival of his: so *Christopher Marlow* was stabbed to death

by a bawdy serving man, a rivall of his in his lewde love.—FRANCES MERES, *Palladis Tamia,* 1598

Ingenioso: Christopher Marlowe
Iudicio: Marlowe was happy in his buskind muse,
        Alas unhappy in his life and end.
        Pitty it is that wit so ill should dwell,
        Wit lent from heaven, but vices sent from hell.
Ingenioso: Our Theater hath lost, *Pluto* hath got,
        A Tragick penman for a driery plot.
        —*The Second Part of the Return from Parnassus,*
        1598–1601, *The Three Parnassus Plays,* ed.
        Leishman, 1949, pp. 242–43

Not inferiour to these was one Christopher Marlow by profession a play-maker, who, as is reported, about 7. yeeres a-goe wrote a booke against the Trinitie: but see the effects of Gods iustice; it so hapned, that at Detford, a little village about three miles distant from London, as he meant to stab with his ponyard one named Ingram, that had inuited him thither to a feast, and was then playing at tables, he quickely perceyving it, so auoyded the thrust, that withall drawing out his dagger for his defence, hee stabd this Marlow into the eye, in such sort, that his braines comming out at the daggers point, hee shortlie after dyed.—WILLIAM VAUGHAN, "Of Atheists," *The Golden Grove, moralized in three bookes,* 1600, Vol. 1, Ch. 3

Not to relate the various tragicall ends of many, who in my remembrance at London, have beene slaine in Playhouses, or upon quarrels there commenced . . . together with the *visible apparition of the Devill on the Stage at the Belsavage Playhouse, in Queene* Elizabeths *dayes, (to the great amazement both of the Actors and Spectators) whiles they were there prophanely playing the History of* Faustus (the truth of which I have heard from many now alive, who well remember it).—WILLIAM PRYNNE, *Histrio-Mastix,* 1633, Fol. 556

The true Artificer will not run away from nature, as hee were afraid of her; or depart from life, and the likenesse of Truth; but speake to the capacity of his hearers, and though his language differ from the vulgar somewhat; it shall not fly from all humanity, with the *Tamerlanes,* and Tamer-Chams of the late Age, which had nothing in them but the *scenicall* strutting, and furious vociferation, to warrant them to the ignorant gapers.—BEN JONSON, *Timber, or Discoveries,* 1640

Christopher Marlow was . . . not only contemporary with *William Shakespear,* but also, like him, rose from a Actor, to be a maker of Comedies and Tragedies, yet was he much inferior to *Shakespear,* not only in the number of his Plays, but also in the elegancy of his Style. His pen was chiefly employed in Tragedies. . . . But none made such a great noise as his Comedy of *Doctor Faustus* with his Devils, and such like tragical Sport, which pleased much the humors of the Vulgar. He also began a Poem of *Hero and Leander;* wherein he seemed to have a resemblance of that clear and unsophisticated Wit which was natural to *Musaeus* that incomparable Poet. This Poem being left unfinished by *Marlow,* who in some riotous Fray came to an untimely and violent end, was thought worthy of the finishing hand of *Chapman* . . . in the performance whereof, nevertheless he fell short of the Spirit and Invention with which it was begun.—WILLIAM WINSTANLEY, *The Lives of the Most Famous English Poets, or the Honour of Parnassus,* 1687, p. 134

But in the end, so it was, that this Marlow giving too large a swing to his own wit, and suffering his lust to have the full reins, fell to that outrage and extremity, as Jodelle a French tragical poet did, (being an epicure and an atheist,) that he denied God and his Son Christ, and not only in word blasphemed the Trinity, but also (as it was credibly reported) wrote divers discourses against it, affirming our Saviour to be a deceiver, and Moses to be a conjurer: The holy *Bible* also to contain only vain and idle stories, and all religion but a device of policy. But see the end of this person, which was noted by all, especially the precisians. For so it fell out, that he being deeply in love with a certain woman, had for his rival a bawdy serving-man, one rather fit to be a pimp, than an ingenious amoretto as Marlow conceived himself to be. Whereupon Marlo taking it to be an high affront, rush'd in upon, to stab, him, with his dagger: But the serving-man being very quick, so avoided the stroke, that withal catching hold of Marlo's wrist, he stab'd his own dagger into his own head, in such sort, that notwithstanding all the means of surgery that could be wrought, he shortly after died of his wound, before the year 1593.—ANTHONY À WOOD, *Athenae Oxonienses*, 1691

A great deal has been sayed about Marlow, his opinions and exit, from age to age; from Beard to Warton: the oldest writers ('prejudiced and peevish Puritans') directly arraigned him of atheism and blasphemy; and those of more modern times (pious and orthodox churchmen) generously labour to rescue his character; either by boldly denying, or artfully extenuating the crimes alleged against him: but not an *iota* of evidence has been produced on either side. I have a great respect for Marlow as an ingenious poet, but I have a much higher regard for truth and justice; and will therefore take the liberty to produce the strongest (if not the whole) proof that now remains of his diabolical tenets, and debauched morals; and if you, Mr. Warton, still choose to think him innocent of the charge, I shall be very glad to see him thoroughly white-washed in your next edition. The paper is transcribed from an old MS. in the Harleian library, cited in one of your notes, and was never before printed.—JOSEPH RITSON, *Observations on the Three First Volumes of the History of English Poetry in a Familiar Letter to the Author*, 1782

Christopher Marlow, a kind of second Shakesphear (whose contemporary he was) not only because like him he rose from an actor to be a maker of plays, though inferior both in fame, and merit; but also because in his begun poem of *Hero and Leander*, he seems to have a resemblance of that clean, and unsophisticated Wit, which is natural to that incomparable poet; this poem being left unfinished by Marlow, who in some riotous fray came to an untimely and violent end, was thought worthy of the finishing hand of Chapman; in the performance whereof nevertheless he fell short of the spirit and invention with which it was begun. Of all that he hath written to the stage his *Dr. Faustus* hath made the greatest noise with its Devils, and such like tragical sport, nor are his other two tragedies to be forgotten, namely his *Edward the Second* and *Massacre at Paris*, besides his *Jew of Malta*, a tragicomedy, and his tragedy of *Dido*, in which he was joined with Nash.—EDWARD PHILLIPS, *Theatrum Poetarum Anglicanorum*, first published 1675 and now enlarged, 1800, p. 113–14

The lunes of Tamburlaine are perfect 'midsummer madness.' Nebuchadnazar's are mere modest pretensions compared with the thundering vaunts of this Scythian Shepherd. He comes in (in the Second Part) drawn by conquered kings, and reproaches these *pampered jades of Asia* that they can *draw but twenty miles a day.* Till I saw this passage with my own eyes, I never believed that it was anything more than a pleasant burlesque of Mine Ancient's. But I assure my readers that it is soberly set down in a Play which their Ancestors took to be serious. I have subjoined the genuine speech for their amusement. *Enter*

Tamburlaine, drawn in his chariot by Trebizon and Soria, with bits in their mouths, reins in his left hand, in his right hand a whip, with which he scourgeth them. . . .

This tragedy is in a very different style from 'mighty Tamburlaine.' The reluctant pangs of abdicating Royalty in Edward furnished hints which Shakspeare scarce improved in his Richard the Second; and the death-scene of Marlowe's king moves pity and terror beyond any scene, ancient or modern, with which I am acquainted. . . .

Marlowe's Jew does not approach so near to Shakspeare's as his Edward II. does to Richard II. Shylock, in the midst of his savage purpose, is a man. His motives, feelings, resentments, have something human in them. 'If you wrong us, shall we not revenge?' Barabas is a mere monster, brought in with a large painted nose, to please the rabble. He kills in sport, poisons whole nunneries, invents infernal machines. He is just such an exhibition as a century or two earlier might have been played before the Londoners, *by the Royal command*, when a general pillage and massacre of the Hebrews had been previously resolved on in the cabinet. It is curious to see a superstition wearing out. The idea of a Jew (which our pious ancestors contemplated with such horror) has nothing in it now revolting. We have tamed the claws of the beast, and pared its nails, and now we take it to our arms, fondle it, write plays to flatter it: it is visited by princes, affects a taste, patronises the arts, and is the only liberal and gentleman-like thing in Christendom. . . .

The growing horrors of Faustus are awfully marked by the hours and half hours as they expire and bring him nearer and nearer to the exactment of his dire compact. It is indeed an agony and bloody sweat.

Marlowe is said to have been tainted with atheistical positions, to have denied God and the Trinity. To such a genius the history of Faustus must have been delectable food: to wander in fields where curiosity is forbidden to go, to approach the dark gulf near enough to look in, to be busied in speculations which are the rottenest part of the core of the fruit that fell from the tree of knowledge. Barabas the Jew, and Faustus the conjurer, are offsprings of a mind which at least delighted to dally with interdicted subjects. They both talk a language which a believer would have been tender of putting into the mouth of a character though but in fiction. But the holiest minds have sometimes not thought it blameable to counterfeit impiety in the person of another, to bring Vice in upon the stage speaking her own dialect, and, themselves being armed with an Unction of self-confident impunity, have not scrupled to handle and touch that familiarly, which would be death to others. Milton, in the person of Satan has started speculations hardier than any which the feeble armoury of the atheist ever furnished: and the precise strait-laced Richardson has strengthened Vice, from the mouth of Lovelace, with entangling sophistries and abstruse pleas against her adversary Virtue which Sedley, Villiers, and Rochester, wanted depth of Libertinism sufficient to have invented.—CHARLES LAMB, *Specimens of the English Dramatic Poets*, 1808

If ever there was a born poet, Marlowe was one. He perceived things in their spiritual as well as material relations, and impressed them with a corresponding felicity. Rather, he struck them as with something sweet and glowing that rushes by;— perfumes from a censer,—glances of love and beauty. And he could accumulate images into as deliberate and lofty a grandeur. Chapman said of him, that he stood

Up to the chin in the Pierian flood.

Drayton describes him as if inspired by the recollection:

Next Marlowe, bathed in the Thespian springs,
Had in him *those brave translunary things,*
That the first poets had; his raptures were
All air and fire, which made his verses clear:
For that fine madness still he did retain,
Which rightly should possess a poet's brain.

But this happy genius appears to have had as unhappy a will, which obscured his judgment. It made him condescend to write fustian for the town, in order to rule over it; subjected him to the charge of impiety, probably for nothing but too scornfully treating irreverent notions of the Deity; and brought him, in the prime of his life, to a violent end in a tavern. His plays abound in wilful and self-worshipping speeches, and every one of them turns upon some kind of ascendency at the expense of other people. He was the head of a set of young men from the university, the Peeles, Greens, and others, all more or less possessed of a true poetical vein, who, bringing scholarship to the theatre, were intoxicated with the new graces they threw on the old bombast, carried to their height the vices as well as wit of the town, and were destined to see, with indignation and astonishment, their work taken out of their hands, and done better, by the uneducated interloper from Stratford-upon-Avon.

Marlowe enjoys the singular and (so far) unaccountable honour of being the only English writer to whom Shakspeare seems to have alluded with approbation. In *As You Like It*, Phoebe says,

Dead Shepherd! now I know thy saw of might,—
'Who ever lov'd that lov'd not at first sight?'

The 'saw' is in Marlowe's *Hero and Leander*, a poem not comparable with his plays.

The ranting part of Marlowe's reputation has been chiefly owing to the tragedy of *Tamburlaine*, a passage in which is laughed at in *Henry the Fourth*, and has become famous. Tamburlaine cries out to the captive monarchs whom he has yoked to his car,—

Holla, ye pampered jades of Asia,
What! can ye draw but twenty miles a day,
And have so proud a chariot at your heels,
And such a coachman as great Tamburlaine?

Then follows a picture drawn with real poetry:

The horse that *guide the golden eye of Heaven,*
And blow the morning from their nostrils (read
    nosterils)
Making their fiery gait above the clouds,
Are not so honour'd in their governor,
As you, ye slaves, in mighty Tamburlaine.

Marlowe, like Spenser, is to be looked upon as a poet who had no native precursors. As Spenser is to be criticised with an eye to his poetic ancestors, who had nothing like the Faerie Queene, so is Marlowe with reference to the authors of *Gorboduc*. He got nothing from them; he prepared the way for the versification, the dignity, and the pathos of his successors, who have nothing finer of the kind to show than the death of Edward the Second—not Shakspeare himself:—and his imagination, like Spenser's, haunted those purely poetic regions of ancient fabling and modern rapture, of beautiful forms and passionate expressions, which they were the first to render the common property of inspiration, and whence their language drew 'empyreal air.' Marlowe and Spenser are the first of our poets who perceived the beauty of words; not as apart from their significance, nor upon occasion only, as Chaucer did (more marvellous in that than themselves, or than the originals from whom he drew), but as a habit of the poetic mood, and as

receiving and reflecting beauty through the feeling of the ideas.—LEIGH HUNT, *Imagination and Fancy*, 1844, pp. 136–41

Doctor Faustus has many magnificent passages, such as Marlowe of the 'mighty line' could not fail to write; but on the whole it is wearisome, vulgar, and ill-conceived. The lowest buffoonery, destitute of wit, fills a large portion of the scenes; and the serious parts want dramatic evolution. There is no character well drawn. The melancholy figure of Mephistophilis has a certain grandeur, but he is not the Tempter, according to the common conception, creeping to his purpose with the cunning of the serpent; nor is he the cold, ironical 'spirit that denies'; he is more like the Satan of Byron, with a touch of piety and much repentance. The language he addresses to Faustus is such as would rather frighten than seduce him.

The reader who opens *Faustus* under the impression that he is about to see a philosophical subject treated philosophically, will have mistaken both the character of Marlowe's genius and of Marlowe's epoch. *Faustus* is no more philosophical in intention than the *Jew of Malta*, or *Tamburlaine the Great*. It is simply the theatrical treatment of a popular legend,—a legend admirably characteristic of the spirit of those ages in which men, believing in the agency of the devil, would willingly have bartered their future existence for the satisfaction of present desires. Here undoubtedly is a philosophical problem, which even in the present day is constantly presenting itself to the speculative mind. Yes, even in the present day, since human nature does not change,—forms only change, the spirit remains; nothing perishes,—it only manifests itself differently. Men, it is true, no longer believe in the devil's agency; at least, they no longer believe in the power of calling up the devil and transacting business with him; otherwise there would be hundreds of such stories as that of *Faust*. But the spirit which created that story and rendered it credible to all Europe remains unchanged. The sacrifice of the future to the present is the spirit of that legend. The blindness to consequences caused by the imperiousness of desire; the recklessness with which inevitable and terrible results are braved in perfect consciousness of their being inevitable, provided that a temporary pleasure can be obtained, is the spirit which dictated Faust's barter of his soul, which daily dictates the barter of men's souls. We do not make compacts, but we throw away our lives; we have no Tempter face to face with us offering illimitable power in exchange for our futurity: but we have our own Desires, imperious, insidious, and for them we barter our existence,—for one moment's pleasure risking years of anguish.

The story of Faustus suggests many modes of philosophical treatment, but Marlowe has not availed himself of any: he has taken the popular view of the legend, and given his hero the vulgarest motives. This is not meant as a criticism, but as a statement. I am not sure that Marlowe was wrong in so treating his subject; I am only sure that he treated it so. Faustus is disappointed with logic, because it teaches him nothing but debate,—with physic, because he cannot with it bring dead men back to life,—with law, because it concerns only the 'external trash',—and with divinity, because it teaches that the reward of sin is death, and that we are all sinners. Seeing advantage in none of these studies he takes to necromancy, and there finds content; and how?

Faustus: Their conference will be a greater helpe to me,
        Then all my labours, plot I ne're so fast.

        Enter the Angell and Spirit [Bad Angel].
Good Angel: O *Faustus*, lay that damned booke aside,

And gaze not on it least it tempt thy soule,
And heape Gods heavy wrath upon thy head.

There may in this seem something trivial to modern apprehensions, yet Marlowe's audience sympathized with it, having the feelings of an age when witches were burned, when men were commonly supposed to hold communication with infernal spirits, when the price of damnation was present enjoyment.

The compact signed, Faustus makes use of his power by scampering over the world, performing practical jokes and vulgar incantations,—knocking down the Pope, making horns sprout on the heads of noblemen, cheating a jockey by selling him a horse of straw, and other equally vulgar tricks, which were just the things the audience would have done had they possessed the power. Tired of his buffooneries he calls up the vision of Helen; his rapture at the sight is a fine specimen of how Marlowe can write on a fitting occasion.

His last hour now arrives: he is smitten with remorse, like many of his modern imitators, when it is too late; sated with his power, he now shudders at the price. After some tragical raving, and powerful depicted despair, he is carried off by devils. The close is in keeping with the commencement: Faustus is damned because he made the compact. Each part of the bargain is fulfilled; it is a tale of sorcery, and Faustus meets the fate of a sorcerer.

The vulgar conception of this play is partly the fault of Marlowe, and partly of his age. It might have been treated quite in conformity with the general belief; it might have been a tale of sorcery, and yet magnificently impressive. What would not Shakespeare have made of it? Nevertheless, we must in justice to Marlowe look also to the state of opinion in his time; and we shall then admit that another and higher mode of treatment would perhaps have been less acceptable to the audience. Had it been metaphysical, they would not have understood it; had the motives of Faustus been more elevated, the audience would not have believed in them. To have saved him at last, would have been to violate the legend, and to outrage their moral sense. For, why should the black arts be unpunished? why should not the sorcerer be damned? The legend was understood in its literal sense, in perfect accordance with the credulity of the audience. The symbolical significance of the legend is entirely a modern creation.—G. H. LEWES, *The Life and Works of Goethe*, 1864, pp. 475–78

Thus was this theatre produced; a theatre unique in history, like the admirable and fleeting epoch from which it sprang, the work and the picture of this young world, as natural, as unshackled, and as tragic as itself. When an original and national drama springs up, the poets who establish it, carry in themselves the sentiments which it represents. They display better than other men the public spirit, because the public spirit is stronger in them than in other men. The passions which surround them, break forth in their heart with a harsher or a juster cry, and hence their voices become the voices of all. . . . Equally in England the poets are in harmony with their works. Almost all are Bohemians, born of the people, yet educated, and for the most part having studied at Oxford or Cambridge, but poor, so that their education contrasts with their condition. Ben Jonson is the step-son of a bricklayer, and himself a bricklayer; Marlowe is the son of a shoemaker; Shakspeare of a woollen merchant; Massinger of a servant. They live as they can, get into debt, write for their bread, go on the stage. Peele, Lodge, Marlowe, Jonson, Shakspeare, Heywood, are actors; most of the details which we have of their lives are taken from the journal of Henslowe, an old pawnbroker, later a moneylender and manager of a theatre, who gives them work, advances money to them, receives their manuscripts or their wardrobes as security. For a play he gives seven or eight pounds; after the year 1600 prices rise, and reach as high as twenty or twenty-five pounds. It is clear that, even after this increase, the trade of author scarcely brings in bread. In order to earn money, it was necessary, like Shakspeare, to become a manager, to try to have a share in the property of a theatre; but the case is rare, and the life which they lead, a life of comedians and actors, improvident, full of excess, lost amid debauchery and acts of violence, amidst women of evil fame, in contact with young profligates, in provocations and misery, imagination and licence, generally leads them to exhaustion, poverty, and death. Men received enjoyment from them, and neglected and despised them. . . .

Marlowe was an ill-regulated, dissolute, outrageously vehement and audacious spirit, but grand and sombre, with the genuine poetic frenzy; pagan moreover, and rebellious in manners and creed. In this universal return to the senses, and in this impulse of natural forces which brought on the Renaissance, the corporeal instincts and the ideas which give them their warrant, break forth impetuously. Marlowe, like Greene, like Kett, is a sceptic, denies God and Christ, blasphemes the Trinity, declares Moses 'a juggler,' Christ more worthy of death than Barabbas, says that 'yf he wer to write a new religion, he wolde undertake both a more excellent and more admirable methode,' and 'almost in every company he commeth, perswadeth men to Athiesme.' Such were the rages, the rashnesses, the excesses which liberty of thought gave rise to in these new minds, who for the first time, after so many centuries, dared to walk unfettered. From his father's shop, crowded with children, from the stirrups and awls, he found himself at Cambridge, probably through the patronage of a great man, and on his return to London, in want, amid the licence of the green-room, the low houses and taverns, his head was in a ferment, and his passions were heated. He turned actor; but having broken his leg in a scene of debauchery, he remained lame, and could no longer appear on the boards. He openly avowed his infidelity, and a prosecution was begun, which, if time had not failed, would probably have brought him to the stake. He made love to a drab, and trying to stab his rival, his hand was turned, so that his own blade entered his eye and his brain, and he died, still cursing and blaspheming. He was only thirty years old. Think what poetry could emanate from a life so passionate, and occupied in such a manner! First, exaggerated declamation, heaps of murder, atrocities, a pompous and furious display of tragedy soaked in blood, and passions raised to a pitch of madness. All the foundations of the English stage, *Ferrex and Porrex, Cambyses, Hieronymo,* even the *Pericles* of Shakspeare, reach the same height of extravagance, force, and horror. It is the first outbreak of youth. Recall Schiller's *Robbers,* and how modern democracy has recognised for the first time its picture in the metaphors and cries of Charles Moor. So here the characters struggle and jostle, stamp on the earth, gnash their teeth, shake their fists against heaven. The trumpets sound, the drums beat, coats of mail file past, armies clash together, men stab each other, or themselves; speeches are full of gigantic threats or lyrical figures; kings die, straining a bass voice; 'now doth ghastly death with greedy talons gripe my bleeding heart, and like a harpy tires on my life.' The hero in *Tamburlaine the Great* is seated on a chariot drawn by chained kings, burns towns, drowns women and children, puts men to the sword, and finally, seized with an invisible sickness, raves in monstrous outcries against the gods, whose hands afflict his soul, and whom he would fain dethrone. There already is the picture of senseless pride, of blind and murderous rage, which passing through many devastations, at last arms against heaven itself. The overflowing of savage and immoderate instinct produces this mighty sounding verse, this prodigality of carnage, this display of overloaded splendours and colours, this railing of demoniac passions, this audacity of grand impiety. If in the dramas which succeed it, *The Massacre at Paris, The Jew of Malta,* the bombast decreases, the violence remains.

There is the living, struggling, natural, personal man, not the philosophic type which Goethe has created, but a primitive and genuine man, hot-headed, fiery, the slave of his passions, the sport of his dreams, wholly engrossed in the present, moulded by his lusts, contradictions, and follies, who amidst noise and starts, cries of pleasure and anguish, rolls, knowing it and willing it, down the slope and crags of his precipice. The whole English drama is here, as a plant in its seed, and Marlowe is to Shakspeare what Perugino was to Raphael.— HIPPOLYTE TAINE, *The History of English Literature,* 1871, Bk. 1, tr. Van Laun, pp. 234–44

Marlowe's alleged writings against the Trinity have never been seen; in all probability, like some alleged infidel works of the Middle Ages, they never existed: but there seems no reason to doubt that he was, as his accusers stated, a man that neither feared God nor regarded man. Beauty, which he worshipped with passionate devotion, was the only sunshine of his life, and it shone with a burning fierceness proportioned to the violence of his tempestuous moods. The vision of Hero and Leander is a rapt surrender of the whole soul to impassioned meditation on luxurious beauty. In his life as in his plays, such intervals of delight were probably rare. Tamburlaine is a most impassioned adorer of divine Zenocrate; Faustus hangs in ecstatic worship on the lips of Helen; but these are only brief transports in lives where energy and ambition are devouringly predominant. Marlowe's genius was little adapted to sonneteering and pastoral poetry: he stigmatized the fashionable love-lyrics as 'egregious foppery,' and derided them with rough ridicule. He wrote no sonnets; only one pastoral song has been ascribed to him, and it is direct and fresh, a movement of impatient captivating sweetness, an impulsive tone of invitation that will take no denial. Marlowe was a clear and powerful genius, and we often seem to catch in his poetry an undertone of almost angry contempt for commonplace.

The most generally impressive of Marlowe's works is his fragment on the tale of Hero and Leander, and if we founded solely upon this, we should form most erroneous notions of his genius. We should suppose his worship of beauty, which was but a rare and transient passion, to have been the presiding force of his imagination. It is in his plays that we find the world of storm and strife wherein he delighted to expatiate, and a most titanic world it is, immeasurably transcending nature in breadth and height of thought, feeling, and destructive energy; a region where everything is on a gigantic scale, peopled with creatures that are monstrous in the largeness of their composition and the fierceness of their passions. . . .

Tamburlaine was Marlowe's first play, but the impetuous swell of his conceptions cannot be said to have been much moderated as he went on. His 'raptures all air and fire' were not, I believe, the extravagance of youth; still less could they have been, as Mr Collier seems to think, the result of inexperience in blank verse, and mistaken effort to make up by bombastic terms for the absence of rhyme; they were part of the constitution of this individual man. It is impossible to say what he might have done had his life been longer: he might have exhausted this high astounding vein, and proved himself capable of opening up another. But as long as he lived he found fuel for his lofty raptures. He could not repeat another conqueror of the world, but his heroes are all expanded to the utmost possible limit of their circumstances. The Jew of Malta is an incarnation of the devil himself: he is no less universal in his war against all mankind that are within reach of his power: he fights single-handed with monstrous instruments of death against a whole city, and does not scruple to poison even his own daughter. Faustus is not a malevolent being, but his ambition is even greater than Tamburlaine's; he soars beyond the petty possibilities of humanity, leagues himself with superhuman powers, and rides through space in a fiery chariot exploring the secrets of the universe. Even in his historical play of Edward II., where he is bound by the shackles of recent history more or less known to his audience, the conflict of explosive passions is superhuman in its energies; the king's court is a hell of extravagant affection and fiendish spite, wanton tyranny and mutinous unapproachable fierceness—a den of wild beasts.— WILLIAM MINTO, *Characteristics of English Poets,* 1874–75, pp. 233–37

CHRISTOPHER MARLOWE

Crowned, girdled, garbed and shod with light and fire,
    Son first-born of the morning, sovereign star!
    Soul nearest ours of all, that wert most far,
Most far off in the abysm of time, thy lyre
Hung highest above the dawn-enkindled quire
    Where all ye sang together, all that are,
    And all the starry songs behind thy car
Rang sequence, all our souls acclaim thee sire.
"If all the pens that ever poets held
    Had fed the feeling of their masters' thoughts,"
    And as with rush of hurtling chariots
The flight of all their spirits were impelled
    Toward one great end, thy glory—nay, not then,
    Not yet might'st thou be praised enough of men.
        —CHARLES ALGERNON SWINBURNE, c. 1875,
        Swinburne's Collected Works, Vol. II, 1924,
        p. 711

The dramatic merits as well as the poetic beauties of *Edward II* are extremely great. The construction is upon the whole very clear, infinitely superior *e.g.* to that of Peele's *Edward I.* The two divisions into which the reign of Edward II naturally falls, viz. the period of the ascendancy of Gaveston and that of the ascendancy of the Spensers, are skilfully interwoven; and after the catastrophe of the fourth act (the victory of the King's adversaries and his capture) the interest in what can no longer be regarded as uncertain, viz. the ultimate fate of the King, is most powerfully sustained. The characters too are mostly well drawn; there is no ignobility about the King, whose passionate love for his favourites is itself traced to a generous motive; he is not without courage and spirit in the face of danger; but his weakness is his doom. Misfortune utterly breaks him; and never have the 'drowsiness of woe' (to use Charles Lamb's expression), and, after a last struggle between pride and necessity, the lingering expectation of a certain doom, been painted with more tragic power. The scene in act iv, where the King seeks refuge among the monks of Neath Abbey, is of singular pathos; but it is perhaps even more remarkable how in the last scene of all the unutterable horror of the situation is depicted without our sense of the loathsome being aroused; and how pity and terror are mingled in a degree to which Shakspere himself only on occasion attains. For the combined power and delicacy of treatment, the murder of Edward II may be compared to the murder of Desdemona in *Othello;* for the fearful suspense in which the spectator is kept, I know no parallel except the *Agamemnon* of Aeschylus, but even here the effort is inferior, for in the English tragedy the spectator shares the suspense, and shares the certainty of its inevitable termination, with the sufferer on the stage himself. On the other characters I will not dwell; but they are not mere figures from the Chronicle. It may be worth while to note the skill with which the character of young Edward (afterward King Edward III) is drawn, and how our good-will is preserved for him, even though his name is put forward by his father's enemies. Gaveston's insolence is admirably reproduced; he is a Frenchman, and has a touch of lightheartedness to the last, when he expresses his indifference as to the precise *manner* of his death:

> I thank you all, my lords: then I perceive
> That heading's one, and hanging is the other,
> And death is all.

The imperious haughtiness of Young Mortimer is equally well depicted; in the character of the Queen alone I miss any indication of the transition from her faithful but despairing attachment to the King to a guilty love for Mortimer. The dignity of the tragedy is not marred by any comic scenes,—which is well, for humour is not Marlowe's strong point; but there is some wit in the sketch of Baldock as an unscrupulous upstart, who fawns upon the great, and gains influence by means of his ability to find for everything reasons, or, as his interlocutor terms them, *Quandoquidems.*

The play is written of course in blank verse, of a flowing as well as vigorous description; but rhymes are not unfrequent. The author's love of classical quotations finds vent on several occasions; and the number of classical allusions is extraordinary; besides Leander and Ganymede, who from different reasons were naturally in Marlowe's mind, Circe, the Cyclops, Proteus, Danaë, Helen, Atlas, Pluto, Charon, and Tisiphone, as well as Catiline and other historical parallels, are mentioned. . . .

Having dwelt at the utmost length which I could permit myself upon the several plays attributable without doubt to Marlowe, I must be brief in my concluding remarks on his position as a dramatist. His services to our dramatic literature are two-fold. As the author who first introduced blank verse to the popular stage he rendered to our drama a service which it would be difficult to over-estimate. No innovation could have done more to preserve it from the danger of artificiality of form, which so readily leads to artificiality of matter, to which the drama is at all times peculiarly exposed. It is obvious that on the stage no form of rhymed verse can, except in isolated lyrical passages, prevail except the rhymed *couplet*; and it is the couplet in particular which leads to an antithetical arrangement of thoughts, which is of its essence a constant application of rhetorical practice. Thus rhymed couplets, while their use in special cases (such as the close of a speech or even any other peculiarly emphatic passage) will always commend itself, cannot without great danger both to the continuity and the naturalness of dramatic movement be employed as the ordinary form of dramatic verse. It is not too much to say that their use in the French drama has contributed to mould the character of a whole development, which continues to this day, of French dramatic literature, while their abandonment by the English popular stage had an equally decisive effect upon our own. In substituting blank verse, Marlowe at first thought it necessary to compensate by rhetorical efforts of another kind for the loss of immediate effect entailed by the change; but already in his later plays it is perceptible how unnecessary he had come to feel the substitution of rant for antithesis; and as the metre easily adapted itself to his hand, he recognised in practice its

supreme merit of flexibility; so that whereas his earlier blank verse is monotonous, his later is varied in rhythm and cadence. The English drama never returned to rhyme, except in a phase of its history which is to be regarded as a conscious aberration from its national course; and it soon relinquished an endeavour forced upon it by the influence of foreign examples, finally renounced on this head by the most eminent of their English followers. Altogether, it may well be doubted whether any literary innovation has ever been so rapidly and so permanently successful as this, in which the critically important step is associated with the name of Marlowe.

His second service to the progress of our dramatic literature, though not perhaps admitting of so precise a statement, is even more important than the other. The genius of Marlowe, as it displays itself in the few works which have come down to us from the brief career which he ran as a dramatic author, is far from satisfying all the demands of his art. In construction, though by no means unskilful and at times eminently successful, he is careless; and it is only rarely that he applies himself to the development of character. It is not just to say of the author of *Edward II* that he never represents any dramatic conflicts except those between human impatience of all control and of all limits, and the control and the limits which the conditions of human life impose; it is not just to deny that he can move the springs of pity as well as of terror, and depict other passions besides those of ambition and defiant self-exultation. But during his brief poetic career he had not learnt the art of mingling, except very incidentally, the operation of other human motives of action with those upon which his ardent spirit more especially dwelt; and of the divine gift of humour, which lies so close to that of pathos, he at the most exhibits occasional signs. The element in which as a poet he lived was passion; and it was he and no other who first inspired with true poetic passion the form of literature to which his chief efforts were consecrated. After Marlowe had written, it was impossible for our dramatists to return to the cold horrors or tame declamation of the earlier tragic drama; the *Spanish Tragedy* and *Gorboduc* had alike been left behind. 'His raptures were all ayre and fire;' and it is this gift of passion which, together with his services to the outward form of the English drama, makes Marlowe worthy to be called not a predecessor, but the earliest in the immortal company, of our great dramatists.—ADOLPHUS WILLIAM WARD, *A History of English Dramatic Literature,* Vol. 1, 1875, pp. 196–203

But the interest of Marlowe's name has nothing to do with these obscure scandals of three hundred years ago. He is the undoubted author of some of the masterpieces of English verse; the hardly to be doubted author of others not much inferior. Except the very greatest names—Shakespeare, Milton, Spenser, Dryden, Shelley—no author can be named who has produced, when the proper historical estimate is applied to him, such work as is to be found in *Tamburlaine, Doctor Faustus, The Jew of Malta, Edward the Second,* in one department; *Hero and Leander* and the *Passionate Shepherd* in another. I have but very little doubt that the powerful, if formless, play of *Lust's Dominion* is Marlowe's, though it may have been rewritten, and the translations of Lucan and Ovid and the minor work which is, more or less probably attributed to him, swell his tale. Prose he did not write, perhaps could not have written. For the one characteristic lacking to his genius was measure, and prose without measure, as numerous examples have shown, is usually rubbish. Even his dramas show a singular defect in the architectural quality of literary genius. The vast and formless creations of the writer's boundless fancy completely master him; his aspirations after the immense too frequently leave him content with the simply unmeasured. In his best play as a play, *Edward the Second*, the limitations of a historical story impose something like a restraining form on his glowing imagination. But fine as this play is, it is noteworthy that no one of his greatest things occurs in it. *The Massacre at Paris*, where he also has the confinement of reality after a fashion, is a chaotic thing as a whole, without any great beauty in parts. The *Tragedy of Dido* (to be divided between him and Nash) is the worst thing he ever did. But in the purely romantic subjects of *Tamburlaine, Faustus*, and *The Jew of Malta*, his genius, untrammelled by any limits of story, showed itself equally unable to contrive such limits for itself, and able to develop the most marvellous beauties of detail. Shakespere himself has not surpassed, which is equivalent to saying that no other writer has equalled, the famous and wonderful passages in *Tamburlaine* and *Faustus*, which are familiar to every student of English literature as examples of the *ne plus ultra* of the poetic powers, not of the language but of language. The tragic imagination in its wildest flights has never summoned up images of pity and terror more imposing, more moving, than those excited by *The Jew of Malta*. The riot of passion and of delight in the beauty of colour and form which characterises his version of *Hero and Leander* has never been approached by any writer. But Marlowe with the fullest command of the *apeiron* had not, and as far as I can judge, never would have had, any power of introducing into it the law of the *peras*. It is usual to say that had he lived, and had his lot been happily cast, we should have had two Shakesperes. This is not wise. In the first place, Marlowe was totally destitute of humor—the characteristic which, united with his tragic and imaginative powers, makes Shakespere as, in a less degree, it makes Homer, and even, though the humour is grim and intermittent, Dante. In other words, he was absolutely destitute of the first requisite of self-criticism. In the natural course of things, as the sap of his youthful imagination ceased to mount, and as his craving for immensity hardened itself, he would probably have degenerated from bombast shot through with genius to bombast pure and 'simple, from *Faustus* to *Lust's Dominion*, and from *Lust's Dominion* to *Jeronimo* or *The Distracted Emperor*. Apart from the magnificent passages which he can show, and which are simply intoxicating to any lover of poetry, his great title to fame is the discovery of the secret of that 'mighty line' which a seldom-erring critic of his own day, not too generously given, vouchsafed to him. Up to his time the blank verse line always, and the semi-couplet in heroics, or member of the more complicated stanza usually, were either stiff or nerveless. Compared with his own work and with the work of his comtemporaries and followers who learnt from him, they are like a dried preparation, like something waiting for the infusion of blood, for the inflation of living breath. Marlowe came, and the old wooden versification, the old lay figure structure of poetic rhythm, was cast once for all into the lumber-room where only poetasters of the lowest rank went to seek it. It is impossible to call Marlowe a great dramatist, and the attempts that have been made to make him out to be such remind one of the attempts that have been made to call Molière a great poet. Marlowe was one of the greatest poets of the world whose work was cast by accident and caprice into an imperfect mould of drama; Molière was one of the greatest dramatists of the world who was obliged by fashion to use a previously perfected form of verse. The state of Molière was undoubtedly the more gracious; but the splendour of Marlowe's uncut diamonds of poetry is the more wonderful.

The characteristics of this strange and interesting school may be summed up briefly, but are of the highest importance in literary history. Unlike their nearest analogues, the French romantics of fifty years ago, they were all of academic educa-

tion, and had even a decided contempt (despite their Bohemian way of life) for unscholarly innovators. They manifested (except in Marlowe's fortuitous and purely genial discovery of the secret of blank verse) a certain contempt for form, and never, at least in drama, succeeded in mastering it. But being all, more or less, men of genius, and having the keenest sense of poetry, they supplied the dry bones of the precedent dramatic model with blood and breath, with vigour and variety, which not merely informed but transformed it. *David and Bethsaba, Doctor Faustus, Friar Bacon and Friar Bungay*, are chaotic enough, but they are of the chaos that precedes cosmic development. The almost insane bombast that marks the whole school has (as has been noticed) the character of the shrieks and gesticulations of healthy childhood, and the insensibility to the really comic which also marks them is of a similar kind. Every one knows how natural it is to childhood to appreciate bad jokes, how seldom a child sees a good one. Marlowe and his crew, too (the comparison has no doubt often been used before), were of the brook of Otus and Ephialtes, who grew so rapidly and in so disorderly a fashion that it was necessary for the gods to make an end of them. The universe probably lost little, and it certainly gained something.—GEORGE SAINTSBURY, *A History of Elizabethan Literature*, 1887, pp. 76–79

AT THE RHYMERS' CLUB

I. The Toast

Set fools untó their folly!
  Our folly is pure wit,
As 'twere the Muse turned jolly:
For poets' melancholy,—
  We will not think of it.

As once Rare Ben and Herrick
  Set older Fleet Street mad,
With wit, not esoteric,
And laughter that was lyric,
  And roystering rhymes and glad

As they, we drink defiance
  To-night to all but Rhyme,
And most of all to Science,
And all such skins of lions
  That hide the ass of time.

To-night, to rhyme as they did
  Were well,—ah, were it ours,
Who find the Muse degraded,
And changed, I fear, and faded,
  Her laurel crown and flowers.

Ah, rhymers, for that sorrow
  The more o'ertakes delight,
The more this madness borrow:—
If care be king to-morrow,
  We toast Queen Rhyme to-night.

II. Marlowe

With wine and blood and wit and deviltry,
He sped the heroic flame of English verse:
Bethink ye, rhymers, what your claim may be,
Who in smug suburbs put the Muse to nurse?
  —ERNEST RHYS, "At the Rhymer's Club,"
  A London Rose and Other Verse, 1894,
  pp. 90–91

His plays have of late years been frequently considered mainly on their technical side, and considering the vast effect produced on the English poetical drama by Marlowe's adoption of blank verse, this is not unnatural. As regards his own genius, however, it is not the right way of judging; for it is plain enough that he made his technical innovation because blank verse was the only vehicle of poetical expression adequate to the character of his thought; we see from *Tamburlaine* that he regarded eloquence as a means to a practical end; and the style of his dramas therefore cannot be fully appreciated without a full comprehension of the intellectual and imaginative motive which inspired his composition. What was this? Mr. Symonds says it may be described by the phrase *l'amour de l'impossible*. In one sense, measuring the vastness of Marlowe's conceptions and his exaggerated manner of expression by the limits of actual fact, this is true; but in another sense, looking to his philosophy, to his ideas of dramatic creation, and to his view of rhetoric, it is the exact opposite of the truth. Marlowe composed on a principle which was simple, direct, and consistent with itself, but which was distinct from every principle which had hitherto inspired tragic conception, though some approach to it had been made in the tragedies of Seneca. In Marlowe's plays there is no trace of the hereditary curse of sin, which elevates the tone of Sophocles and Aeschylus; there is no trace of the doctrine of physical Necessity, which is the ruling thought of Seneca; there is but seldom any trace of the conflict between good and evil, conscience and passion, which prevails in the Miracle Plays and Moralities. What we do find is Seneca's exaltation of the freedom of the human will, dissociated from the idea of Necessity, and joined with Machiavelli's principle of the excellence of *virtù*. This principle is represented under a great variety of aspects; sometimes in the energy of a single heroic character, as in *Tamburlaine*; sometimes in the pursuit of unlawful knowledge, as in *Faustus*; again, in *The Jew of Malta*, in the boundless hatred and revenge of Barabas; in Guise plotting the massacre of the Huguenots out of cold-blooded policy; and in Mortimer planning the murder of Edward II. from purely personal ambition. Incidentally, no doubt, in some of these instances, the indulgence of unrestrained passion brings ruin in its train; but it is not so much for the sake of the moral that Marlowe composed his tragedies, as because his imagination delighted in the exhibition of the vast and tremendous consequences produced by the determined exercise of will in pursuit of selfish objects. So far from loving grandiosity and extravagance for their own sake, the violence of his conceptions springs from a belief of what is possible to the resolved and daring soul. . . .

His dramas are very ill-constructed. He cares nothing for the development of plot and concentrates his whole attention on the exhibition of an abstract principle, embodied for the moment in a single character. When he has placed his leading personage in a situation where his ruling purpose—be it desire of conquest, as in Tamburlaine; revenge, as in Barabas; ambition, as in Mortimer or Guise—can have full play, he is satisfied. His invention occupies itself with finding means to remove the obstacles that oppose the achievement of this central purpose, and up to a certain point his method produces interesting dramatic situations: the first two acts, for example, of the *Jew of Malta* are excellent. But after a time the action drags through want of complexity; and then the exhibition of character becomes mechanical and monotonous.

Again, Marlowe's theory of dramatic action is contrary to the constitution of human nature: it eliminates the factor of Conscience. Following Machiavelli in counting 'religion but a childish toy,' and in holding that there was 'no sin but ignorance,' he exalted 'resolution' as the highest of human virtues. But this is a principle better suited for melodrama than for tragedy. If there is something fascinating in the steady purpose of even a savage like Tamburlaine, or of a villain like Barabas,

how infinitely inferior in dramatic interest is such a representation, to the portrayal of that complexity of motives and circumstance which produces the entanglements of human conduct! How ill does it compare, for example, with the situations produced by the *irresolution* of Hamlet and Macbeth, or by the senile folly of Lear? Shakespeare was not less keenly alive than Marlowe to the dramatic value of resolute will as a principle of action: he has represented it in the character of Iago, working on the credulous weakness of Othello; but he has constructed the complex action of his tragedy in such a way that the spectators are never left for a moment in doubt as to the moral judgment they ought to pass on the various characters. For the same reason *Faustus* is Marlowe's greatest and most interesting play, because in that alone does he give a sustained representation of the state of a human soul torn between the conflicting principles of good and evil.

Once more. The narrowness of Marlowe's conception of Man and Nature is seen in his representations of female character. As his tendency was to make everything in his plays bow before the march of some supreme irresistible will, the weaker feminine element in Nature was necessarily thrust by him into a subordinate position. Marlowe, like Greene, can represent only one type of woman—a being who becomes the devoted, but almost passive, instrument of masculine resolution. Zenocrate, Abigail, Isabel, and (strange to say) Catherine de Medicis, all of them cast in this mould, are the only creations he can show against the endless varieties of female character depicted in the dramas of Shakespeare.

Considering these features in Marlowe's dramas, we cannot fail to be struck with the contrast between his genius and the genius of men like Sidney and Spenser. The two latter reflect the chivalrous element that was still strong in English society, the high principle of honour, the elevation of sentiment, the sense of duty and religion. From all these restraining principles in the conscience of the nation Marlowe cut himself off; and by his exaltation of the Machiavellian principle severed his connection, not only with Puritanism, but with whatever was most lofty and noble in the history of England. On the other hand, his imagination was borne along, as Spenser's and Sidney's never was, on the full stream of a great national movement. His dramas were produced just before, and just after, the defeat of the Spanish Armada—that is to say at the moment when the people were awakening to the full consciousness of greatness in their dangers and their destinies.—W. J. COURTHOPE, A *History of English Poetry*, 1897, Vol. 2, pp. 404–21

NOTES AND DOCUMENTS (1593)
Revue Germanique, 1913, pp. 570–578

Document II.—La dénonciation de Baines
(Harl. MSS, 6848, f. 185–6)

A note [185 a] containing the opinion of on Christopher Marly concerning his damnable[1] Judgement of Religion and scorn of Godes word.

That the Indians and many authors of antiquity have assuredly writen of about 16 thousand yeares agone wheras Adam[2] is proved[3] to have lived within 6 thowsand yeares.

He affirmeth that Moyses was but a jugler & that one Heriots[4] being Sir W. Raleighs man can do more than he.

That Moyses made the Jewes to travell XL yeares in the wildernes (which Iorney might have been done in less than one yeare) ere they came to the promised land to thintent that those who were privy to most of his subtilties might perish and so an everlasting superstition remain in the hartes of the people.

That it was an easy matter for Moyses being brought up in all the artes of the Egiptians to abuse the Iewes being a rude & grosse people.

That Christ was a bastard and his mother dishonest.

That he was the sonne of a carpenter, and that if the Iewes among whome he was borne did crucify him theie best knew him and whence he came.

That Christ deserved better to dy than Barrabas and that the Iewes made a good choise, though Barrabas was both a thief and a murtherer.

That if there be any god or any good Religion, then it is in the papistes because the service of god is performed with more cerimonies, as elevation of the mass, organs, singing men, shaven crownes, etc. . that all protestantes are hypocriticall asses.

That if he were put to write a new Religion, he would undertake both a more excellent and admirable methodd and that all the new testament is filthily written.

That the woman of Samaria & her sister were whores and that Christ knew them dishonestly.

[185 b] That St Iohn the Evangelist was bedfellow to Christ[5] and leaned alwaies in his bosome, that he used him as the sinners of Sodoma.

That all they that love not Tobacco and Boies were fooles.

That all the apostles were fishermen and base fellowes neither of wit nor worth, that Paull only had wit but he was a timerous fellow in bidding men to be subiect to magistrats against his conscience.

That he had as good right to coine as the Queen of England, and that he was acquainted with one Poole a prisoner in Newgate who hath great skill in mixture of mettals and having learned some thinges of him he ment through help of a cunninge stamp maker to coin ffrench crownes pistoletes and English shillinges.

That if Christ would have instituted the Sacrament with more ceremoniall Reverence it would have bin had in more admiration, that it would have bin much better being administred in a Tobacco Pipe.

That on Ric. Cholmley[6] hath confessed that he was perswaded by Marloe's reasons to become an Atheist.

These things with many other shall by good & honest witnes be aproved to be his opinions and comon speeches and that this Marlow doth not only hould them himself, but almost into every company he cometh he perswades men to Atheism willing them not to be afeard of bugbeares and hobgoblins and utterly scorning both god and his ministers as I Richard Baines will Iustify & approve both by mine oth and the testimony of many honest men, and almost al men with whom he hath conversed any time will testify the same, and as I think all men in Christianity ought to indevor that the mouth of [186 a] so dangerous a member may be stopped, he saith likewise that he hath quoted a number of contrarieties oute of the Scripture which he hath given to some great men who in convenient time shalbe named. When these thinges shalbe called in question the witnes shalbe produced.

Richard Baines.

[186 b]   B[a]y[n]es   M[arlow]
of his blasphemyes
Bought of Mr Baker

Document II bis.—Copie du précédent envoyée a la Reine
(Harleian 6853 f. 307–8)

[307 a] A note delivered on Whitson eve last of the most horreble blasphemes and damnable opinions utteryd by Christofer Marly who within iii dayes after came to a soden & fearfull end of his life.[7]

That the Indians and many authors of Antiquitei have assuredly written of aboue 16 thowsande yeers agone, wher Adam is proved to have leyved within 6 thowsande yeers.[8]

That Moyses was but a Iuggler and that one Heriots can do more then hee.[9]

That Moyses made the Iewes to travell fortie yeers in the wilderness (which iorny might have ben don in lesse than one yeer) er they came to the promised lande, to the intente that those whoe wer privei to most of his subtilteis might perish and so an everlastinge supersticion remayne in the hartes of the people.

That the firste beginninge of Religion was only to keep men in awe.

That it was an easye matter for Moyses beinge brought up in all the artes of the Egiptians, to abvse the Iewes, beinge a rude and grosse people.

That Christ was a bastard and his mother dishonest.

That he was the sonne of a carpenter, and that yf the Iewes amonge whome he was borne did crucifye him, thei best knew him and whence he came.

[307 b] That Christ deserved better to dye than Barrabas[10] and that the Iewes made a good choyce, though Barrabas were both a theife and a murtherer.

That yf ther be any God or good Religion, then it is in the Papistes, because the service of God is performed With more ceremonyes, as elevacion of the masse, organs, singing men,[11] & c. That all protestantes ar hipocriticall Asses.

That, yf he wer put to write a new religion, he wolde undertake both a more excellent, and more admirable methode, and that all the new testament is filthely written.

That the women of Samaria wer whores and that Christ knew them dishonestlye.

That St Iohn the Evangelist was bedfellow to Christ, that he leaned alwayes in his bosome, that he vsed him as the synners of Sodoma.[12]

That all the Appostels wer fishermen and base fellowes, nether of witt nor worth, that Pawle only had witt, that he was a timerous fellow in biddinge men to be subiect to magistrates against his conscience.[13]

[308 a] That if Christ had instituted the Sacramentes with more ceremonyall reverence, it wold have ben had in more admiracion, that it wolde have been much better beinge administred in a Tobacco pype.

That the Angell Gabriell was bawde to the holy ghost because he brought the salutacion to Mary.

That one Richard Cholmelei[14] hath confessed that he was perswaded by Marloe's reason to become an Atheiste.[15]

Richard Bame[16]

[308 b] *Bought of Mr Baker.*
Copye of Marloes blasphemyes as sent to her Highness.

Document III.—Lettre de Kyd à Sir John Puckering
(Harleian 6849, f. 218–9)

[218 a] At my last being with your Lordship to entreate some speaches from you in my favour to my Lorde, whoe (though I thinke he reste not doubtfull of myne innocence) hath yet in his discreeter iudgment feared to offende in his reteyning me without your honours former pryvitie; so it is nowe Right Honourable that the denyall of that favour (to my thought resonable) hath movde me to coniecture some suspicion, that your Lordship holds me in concerning ATHEISME, a deadlie thing which I was undeserved charged withall, & therfore have I thought it requisite, as well in duetie to your Lord-

ship and the lawes, as also in the feare of god, & freedom of my conscience, therein to satisfie the world and you.

The first and most (thoughe insufficient) surmize that ever [was and][17] therein might be raisde of me, grewe thus. When I was first suspected for that libell that concern'd the state, amongst those waste and idle papers (which I carde not for) & which unaskt I did deliuer up, were founde some fragments of a disputation, toching that opinion, affirmd by Marlowe to be his, and shufled with some of myne (unknown to me) by some occasion of our wrytinge in one chamber two yeares since.

My first acquaintance with this Marlowe, rose upon his bearing name to serve my Lord: although his *Lordship* never knewe his service, but in [writing][18] for his plaiers, ffor never cold my Lord endure his name or sight [when],[18] he had heard of his conditions, nor wold indeed the forme of deuyne praiers used duelie in his *Lordships* haue quadred with such reprobates.

That I shold loue or be familer frend with one so irreligious, were verie rare, when TULLIE saith DIGNI SUNT AMITICIA QUibus IN IPSIS INEST CAUSA CUR DILIGANTUR which neither was in him for person, quallities or honestie, besides he was intemperate & of a cruel harte, the verie contraries to which, my greatest enemies will saie by me.

It is not to be nombred amongst the best conditions of men to taxe or to opbraide the deade QUIA MORTUI NON MORDENT. But thus much haue I (with your *Lordships* favour) dared in the greatest cause, which is to cleere my self of being thought an ATHEIST, which some will sweare he was.

Ffor more assurance that I was not of that vile opinion, Lett it but please your *Lordship* to enquire of such as he conversed withall, that is (as I am geven to understand) with HARRIOTT, WARNER, ROYDEN and some stationers in Paules churchyard,[19] whom I in no sort can accuse nor will excuse by reson of his companie; of whose consent if I had been, no question but I also shold have been of their consort for EX MINIMO VESTIGIO ARTIFEX AGNOSCIT ARTIFICEM.

Of my religion & life, I haue abreadie geuen some instance to the late comissioners & of my reuerend meaning to the state, although perhaps my paines and undeserved tortures felt by some, wold haue ingendred more impatience when lesse by farr hath driuen so manye IMO EXTRA CAULAS which it shall neuer do with me.

But what soeuer I have felt *Right Honourable* this is my request not for reward but in regard of my trewe inocence that it wold please your *Lordships* so t[o use the] same[20] & me, as I maic still retcyne the favours of my Lord, whom I have serud[21] almost theis iij yeres nowe, in credit untill nowe, & nowe am utterlie undon without herein be somewhat donn for my recoverie, ffor I do know his *Lordship* holdes your honours & the state in that dewe reverence, as he wold no waie moue the leste suspicion of his loues and cares both towards hir sacred Majestie your *Lordships* and the lawes where of when tyme shall serue I shall geue greater instance which I haue obserued.

As for the libel laide unto my chardg I am resoulued with receyuing of ye sacrament to satisfie your *Lordships* & the world that I was neither agent nor consenting thereunto.

[218 b] Howbeit if some outcast ISMAEL for want or of his owne dispose to lewdnes, haue with pretext of duetie or religion, or to reduce himself to that he was not borne unto by enie waie incensed your *Lordships* to suspect me, I shall besech in all humillitie & in the feare of god that it will please your *Lordships* but to censure me as I shall proue my self, and to repute them as they ar in deed CUM TOTIUS INIUSTITIAE NULLA CAPITALIOR SIT QUAM EORum, QUI TUM CUM MAXIME FALLUNT ID AGUNT UT VIRI BONI ESSE VIDEANTur? ffor doubtles

even then your *Lordships* shalbe sure to breake [in]to[22] their lewde designes and see into the truthe, when but their lyues that herein have accused me shalbe examined & rypped up effectually, soe maie I chaunce with Paul to liue & shake the vyper of my hand into the fier, for which the ignorant suspect me guiltie of the former shipwrack and thus (for nowe I feare me I growe teadious) assuring your good *Lordships* that if I knewe eny whom I cold iustlie accuse of that damnable offense to the awefull Majestie of God or of that other mutinous scdition toward the state I wold as willinglie reveale them as I wold request your *Lordships* better thoughts of me that neuer have offended you.

Your *Lordships* most humble in all duties.

Th. Kydd.[23]

[219 b]   *Bought of Mr Baker*
To the R. honorable Sr John
Puckering Knight Lord Keeper of
the great seale of Englande

Document IV.—Contre Richard Cholmeley[24]
(*Harleian 6848 f. 190*)

[190 a] Remembraunces of wordes and matter againste Ric. Cholmeley.

That he speaketh in genirall all evill of the counsell; sayenge that they are all Athistes and Machiavillians, especially my Lord Admirall.

That he made certen libellious verses in commendacion of papists & Seminary priestes very greately inveighenge againste the state, amonge which lynes this was one,

Nor may the Prince deny that Papal crowne.

That hee had a certen booke (as hee saieth) deliuered him by Sir Robert Cecill of whom he geiueth very scandalous reportes. That hee should incite him to consider there of & to frame verses & libelles in the commendacion of constant priestes & vertuous Recusantes; this book is in custodie & is called an Epistle of coumforte[25] & is printed at Paris.

That hee railes at Mr Topcliffe[26] and hath written another libell iointlye againste Sir ffranncis Drake & Justice Younge whom hee saieth hee will couple up together because hee hateth them alike.

That when the muteny happened after the Portingale voyage in the Strande[27] hee said that hee repented him of nothinge more than that hee had not killed my Lord Threasorer with his owne handes, sayenge that he could neuer haue done god better service, this was spoken in the hearinge of Frauncis Clerke and many other souldiours.

That hee saieth hee doeth entirely hate the Lord Chamberleyn & hath good cause so to doe.

That hee saieth and verely beleueth that one Marlowe is able to shewe more sounde reasons for Atheisme then any devine in Englande is able to geiue to prove devinitie and that Marloe tolde him that hee hath read the Atheist lecture to Sir Walter Raliegh & others.

That hee saieth that hee hath certen men corrupted by his persuasions who wilbee ready at all tymes & for all causes to sweare what soeuer seemeth good to him, amonge whom is one Henry Younge & Jasper Borage & others.

That hee so highly esteemeth his owne will & Judgment that he saieth that noman are sooner deceyued & abused than the counsell themselues.

That hee can goe beyonde & cossen[28] them as he liste & that if hee make any complainte in behalfe of the Queene. hee shall not onely bee presently heard & enterteyned, but hee will so vrge the counsell for money that without hee haue what hee liste hee will doe nothinge.

[190 b] That beinge imployed by some of her majesties prevy counsaile for the apprehension of Papistes & other daungerous men hee vsed as he saieth to take money of them & would lett them passe in spighte of the counsell.

That hee saieth that William Parry[29] was hanged, drawen & quartered but in leste, that he was a grosse asse. overreached by conninge, & that in trueth he neuer meant to kill the Queene more than himselfe had.

Document IV bis.—*Même sujet (Harleian 6848 f. 191)*

[191 a] Right worshipfull whereas I promised to send you worde when Cholmeley was with mee, these are to lett you understande that hee hath not yet bene with mee for he doeth partely suspect that I will bewray his villanye & his companye. But yesterday hee sente two of his companions to mee to knowe if I woulde Ioyne with him in familiaritie. & bee one of their dampnable crue. I soothed the villaynes with faire wordes in their follies because I would thereby dive into the secretes of their develishe hartes, that I might the better bewray their purposes to draw her Maiesties subiectes to be Atheistes, their practise is after her Maiesties decease to make a kinge amonge them selves & liue according to their owne lawes, & this [,] saieth Cholmeley [,] wilbee done easely, because they bee & shortely wilbe by his & his felowes persuasions as many of their opynion as of any other religion. Mr Cholmeley his manner of proceeding in seducinge the Queenes subiectes is firste to make slaunderous reportes of most noble peeres and honourable Counsailors, as the Lord Threasorer the lord Chamberleyn the Lord Admirall, Sir Robert Cecill, These saithe hee have profounde wittes, bee sounde Athiestes, & their liues & deedes shewe that they thinke their soules doe ende vanishe and perishe with their bodies.

His seconde course is to make a leste of the Scripture with these fearefull horrible & damnable speeches, that Ihesus Christe was a bastarde St Mary a whore & the Aungell Gabriell a Bawde to the holy ghoste That Christe was lustly persecuted by the lewes for his owne foolishness. That Moyses was a Iugler & Aaron a cosoner the one for his miracles to Pharao to prove there was a god, & the other for takinge the eareringes of the children of Israell to make a golden calfe with many other blasphemous speeches of the devine essence of God which I feare to rehearse.

This cursed Cholmeley hath LX of his company & hee is seldome from his felowes and therefore I beeseech your worship haue a special care of yourselfe in apprehendinge him for they bee resolute murderinge myndes.

Your worshippes

[191 b]

Ye athisme of Ch[olmley]
& others
Yong taken & made an instrument
to take ye rest
hariet[30]
borage dangerous[31]
tippinges ij[32]

Document V.—*Lettre annonçant la capture de Cholmeley (Harleian 7002 f. 10, 11)*

[10 a] Right honarabill with my umbill comendacions these ar to advartise your Lordship that yestar nyght at IV of the cloke Mr Wilbrom cam to me and brought Rich. Chamley with hym he did submet him selfe to hym ho brought a letar to me wrytton be Mr Doctar Bankero with a petesion that the said chamley had exebited to the Lord of Cantarbery his grace But

the efecte Mr Doctares Letar was that it shuld a compleche my Lords speches cometid to me that was to comet hym the sayd Chomley to preson & the reste that should be fownd of is seat [,] the wyche A haue done so that now he is to be exat by soche as it shall playse your honars to a poynt & for the reste A do not dote but the will submete themselvis now one of the prensypalle be a prehendid & fordar the sayd Chamley said unto my men as he was goying to preson that he did kno the Law that when it cam to passe he colde shefte will ynowgh [.] this desyryng the all myghty god to bless & presarve you and all youres with moche in crese of honar wrytyn this XXIX of Junii 1593.

Yours umbley to comand
Rich. Young

Notes

1. *Opynion* a été raturé.
2. *Adam* et *proved* remplacent *Moyses* et *said* barrés par l'autuer de la lettre.
3. Nous reparlerons de ce *Herriot* par la suite.
4. *The intent.*
5. Le mot a été recouvert d'un bout de papier, mais on peut encore le lire distinctement.
6. *That Cholmley* raturé.
7. Une première rédaction a été rayée en grande partie, sauf les mots *damnable opinions.* Voici ce texte original: *A note contayninge the opinion of one Christofer Marlye, concernynge his damnable opinions and judgment of relygion and scorne of gods worde.*
8. Les mots *he affyrmeth* ont été rayés.
9. Notez que l'allusion à Sir Walter Raleigh a disparu.
10. Remplace *Barabas* rayé.
11. Les mots *shaven crownes* sont barrés d'un trait.
12. Suivent les mots que voici, raturés:
That all thei that love not tobacco and Boyes are fooles.
13. Le passage suivant a été raturé:
That he had as good right to coyne as the Queen of Englande, and that he was acquainted with one Poole, a prisonner in newgate whoe hath great skill in mixture of mettals, and having learned some thinges of him, he ment, thorough help of a conninge stampe maker, to coyne french crownes, pistolettes and englishe shillings.
14. Dans la marge, on lit les mots *he is layd for* dans une écriture différente. La phrase semble indiquer qu'on a pris des dispositions pour arrêter Chomeley (voir les documents IV et suivants).
15. La fin de la lettre est barrée d'un grand trait transversal:
Theis thinges with many other shall by good and honest men be proved to be his opinions and common speeches, and that this Marloe doth not only holde them himself, but almost in every company he cometh, perswadeth men to Atheisme, willinge them not to be afrayed of bugbeares and hobgoblins, and utterly scornynge both God and his ministers as I Richard Bome (voir note suivante) will justify both by my othe and the testimony of many honest men, and almost all men with whom he hath conversed any time will testefy the same: And as I thincke all men in Christianitei ought to endevor that the mouth of so dangerous a member may be stopped.
He sayeth moreover that he hath coated [*quoted*] a number of contrarieties out of the scriptures, which he hath geeven to some great men, whoe in convenient tyme shalbe named. when theis thinges shalbe called in question, the witnesses shalbe produced.
16. Le nom de Richard Baines est mal orthographié deux fois de suite. Il est bon de dire que dans le document précédent, qui paraît être l'original, on peut très bien lire *Bame* et *Bome* au lieu de *Baines*, surtout si l'on va un peu vite en besogne.
17. Le texte est a peine lisible. M. Boas y voit [as], qui ne présente pas un sens très net et ne remplit pas tout l'espace libre.
18. Partiellement effacé.
19. Kyd désigne ici fort probablement le libraire Blount. Nous reviendrons sur tout ce passage.
20. On distingue seulement le *t* de *to*, l's de *use* et presque complètement le *the*. Notre texte est donc une conjecture pure et simple.

21. Partiellement effacé, mais lisible.
22. M. Boas lit *thro.* Cependant, on aperçoit *into* en examinant le papier par transparence.
23. Les mots en égyptienne dans notre texte sont en écriture italienne dans le document lui-même. On remarque sur la page présente que quelqu'un a écrit le mot *Kiddye.*
24. Nous essaierons de préciser la personnalité de ce Cholmeley par la suite.
25. Je n'ai pu retrouver trace de ce volume. Il existe pas mal d'opuscules du même titre, notamment une *Epistle of Comfort* contre les Anabaptistes (mais publiée à Londres en 1609).
26. Célèbre pour son hostilité contre les catholiques et la férocité avec laquelle il les martyrisait.
27. *Drake's expedition in 1589* (Boas).
28. *Cozen.*
29. On trouvera tous renseignements sur ce double traître dans le D. N. B.
30. Peut-être Herriot le mathématicien. Cela semble assez improbable.
31. Ce Borage pourrait-être un ami de Marlowe. Parmi les étudiants de Corpus Christi College, on trouve en effet un certain Borage admis en 1593. C'est probablement le même Borage que mentionnent les Actes du Conseil Privé de compagnie avec Cholmeley (voir notre discussion plus loin).
32. Est-ce un nom propre? Est-ce en livres sterling la somme payée à Yong pour trahir ses complices?
33. *Sic,* faute d'inattention au lieu de *he.*
34. Le nom a été corrigé et il est assez difficile à débrouiller. Mais la suite permet de croire qu'il s'agit de Richard Bancroft futur archevêque de Cantorbéry, alors *chaplain* du Primat Whitgift.
35. *I.*
36. Soit *examinate,* soit plutôt *examinet.*
37. *Further.*
38. *This,* comme souvent au XVI siècle, est une variante de *thus.*

THOMAS WARTON
From *The History of English Poetry*
1778–81

The *Elegies* of Ovid, which convey the obscenities of the brothel in elegant language, but are seldom tinctured with the sentiments of a serious and melancholy love, were translated by Christopher Marlowe below mentioned, and printed at Middleburgh without date. This book was ordered to be burnt at Stationers' hall, in 1599, by command of the archbishop of Canterbury and the bishop of London. . . .

Christopher Marlowe, or Marloe, educated in elegant letters at Cambridge, Shakespeare's cotemporary on the stage, often applauded both by queen Elisabeth and king James the First, as a judicious player, esteemed for his poetry by Jonson and Drayton, and one of the most distinguished tragic poets of his age, translated Coluthus's *Rape of Helen* into English rhyme, in the year 1587. I have never seen it; and I owe this information to the manuscript papers of a diligent collector of these fugacious anecdotes. But there is entered to Jones, in 1595, 'A booke entituled *Raptus Helenae,* Helens Rape, by the Athenian duke Theseus.' Coluthus's poem was probably brought into vogue, and suggested to Marlowe's notice, by being paraphrased in Latin verse the preceding year by Thomas Watson, the writer of sonnets just mentioned. Before the year 1598, appeared Marlowe's translation of the *Loves of Hero and Leander,* the elegant prolusion of an unknown sophist of Alexandria, but commonly ascribed to the antient Musaeus. It was left unfinished by Marlowe's death; but what was called a second part, which is nothing more than a continuation from the Italian, appeared by one Henry Petowe, in 1598. Another edition was published, with the first book of Lucan, translated also by Marlowe, and in blank verse, in 1600. At length George

Chapman, the translator of Homer, completed, but with a striking inequality, Marlowe's unfinished version, and printed it at London in quarto, 1606. Tanner takes this piece to be one of Marlowe's plays. It probably suggested to Shakespeare the allusion to Hero and Leander, in the *Midsummer Night's Dream,* under the player's blunder of Limander and Helen, where the interlude of Thisbe is presented. It has many nervous and polished verses. His tragedies manifest traces of a just dramatic conception, but they abound with tedious and uninteresting scenes, or with such extravagancies as proceeded from a want of judgment, and those barbarous ideas of the times, over which it was the peculiar gift of Shakespeare's genius alone to triumph and to predominate. His *Tragedy of Dido queen of Carthage* was completed and published by his friend Thomas Nashe, in 1594.

Although Jonson mentions Marlowe's MIGHTY MUSE, yet the highest testimony Marlowe has received, is from his cotemporary Drayton; who from his own feelings was well qualified to decide on the merits of a poet. It is in Drayton's Elegy, To my dearly loved friend Henry Reynolds of Poets and Poesie.

> Next Marlowe, bathed in the Thespian springes,
> Had in him those braue translunary thinges,
> That the first poets had: his raptvres were
> All air, and fire, which made his verses clear:
> For that fine madness still he did retaine
> Which rightly should possesse a poet's braine.

In the *Return from Parnassus,* a sort of critical play, acted at Cambridge in 1606, Marlowe's *buskined* MUSE is celebrated. His cotemporary Decker, Jonson's antagonist, having allotted to Chaucer and *graue* Spenser, the highest seat in the Elisian *grove of Bayes,* has thus arranged Marlowe. 'In another companie sat learned Atchlow and, (tho he had ben a player molded out of their pennes, yet because he had been their louer and register to the Muse) inimitable Bentley: these were likewise carowsing out of the holy well, &c. Whilst Marlowe, Greene, and Peele, had gott under the shadow of a large vyne, laughing to see Nashe, that was but newly come to their colledge, still haunted with the same satyricall spirit that followed him here vpon earth.'

Marlowe's wit and spriteliness of conversation had often the unhappy effect of tempting him to sport with sacred subjects; more perhaps from the preposterous ambition of courting the casual applause of profligate and unprincipled companions, than from any systematic disbelief of religion. His scepticism, whatever it might be, was construed by the prejudiced and peevish puritans into absolute atheism: and they took pains to represent the unfortunate catastrophe of his untimely death, as an immediate judgment from heaven upon his execrable impiety. He was in love, and had for his rival, to use the significant words of Wood, 'a bawdy servingman, one rather fitted to be a pimp, than an ingenious *amoretto,* as Marlowe conceived himself to be.' The consequence was, that an affray ensued; in which the antagonist having by superior agility gained an opportunity of strongly grasping Marlow's wrist, plunged his dagger with his own hand into his own head. Of this wound he died rather before the year 1593. One of Marlowe's tragedies is *The tragical history of the life and death of doctor John Faustus.* A proof of the credulous ignorance which still prevailed, and a specimen of the subjects which then were thought not improper for tragedy. A tale which at the close of the sixteenth century had the possession of the public theatres of our metropolis, now only frightens children at a puppet-show in a country-town. But that the learned John Faust continued to maintain the character of a conjuror in the sixteenth century even by authority, appears from a 'Ballad of the life and death of doctor Faustus the *great congerer*,' which in 1588 was licenced to be printed by the learned Aylmer bishop of London.

As Marlowe, being now considered as a translator, and otherwise being generally ranked only as a dramatic poet, will not occur again, I take this opportunity of remarking here, that the delicate sonnet called the Passionate Shepherd to his Love, falsely attributed to Shakespeare, and which occurs in the third act of *The Merry Wives of Windsor*, followed by the nymph's Reply, was written by Marlowe. Isaac Walton in his *Compleat Angler*, a book perhaps composed about the year 1640, although not published till 1653, has inserted this sonnet, with the reply, under the character of 'that smooth song which was made by Kit Marlowe, not at least fifty years ago: and—an Answer to it which was made by sir Walter Raleigh, in his younger days: old fashioned poetry, but choicely good.' In *England's Helicon*, a miscellany of the year 1600, it is printed with Christopher Marlowe's name, and followed by the Reply, subscribed IGNOTO, Raleigh's constant signature. A page or two afterwards, it is imitated by Raleigh. That Marlowe was admirably qualified for what Mr. Mason, with a happy and judicious propriety, calls PURE POETRY, will appear from the following passage of his forgotten tragedy of *Edward the Second*, written in the year 1590, and first printed in 1598. The highest entertainments, then in fashion, are contrived for the gratification of the infatuated Edward, by his profligate minion Piers Gaveston.

> I must have wanton Poets, pleasant wits,
> Musitians, that with touching of a string
> May draw the pliant king which way I please:
> Musicke and poetrie is his delight,
> Therefore ile have Italian maskes by night,
> Sweete speeches, comedies, and pleasing showes,
> And in the day when he shall walke abroad,
> Like *Sylvian* Nimphes my pages shall be clad,
> My men like Satyres grazing on the lawnes,
> Shall with their Goate feete daunce an antick hay.
> Sometime a lovelie boye in *Dians* shape,
> With haire that gilds the water as it glides,
> Crownets of pearle about his naked armes,
> And in his sportfull hands an Olive tree . . .
> Shall bathe him in a spring, and there hard by,
> One like *Actæon* peeping through the grove,
> Shall by the angrie goddesse be transformde,
> And running in the likenes of an Hart,
> By yelping hounds puld downe, and seeme to die.
> Such things as these best please his majestie. . . .

WILLIAM HAZLITT
From *Lectures on the Dramatic Literature of the Age of Elizabeth*
1821, pp. 55–72

Perhaps the genius of Great Britain (if I may so speak without offence or flattery), never shone out fuller or brighter, or looked more like itself, than at this period. Our writers and great men had something in them that savoured of the soil from which they grew: they were not French, they were not Dutch, or German, or Greek, or Latin; they were truly English. They did not look out of themselves to see what they should be; they sought for truth and nature, and found it in themselves. There was no tinsel, and but little art; they were not the spoiled children of affectation and refinement, but a

bold, vigorous, independent race of thinkers, with prodigious strength and energy, with none but natural grace, and heartfelt unobtrusive delicacy. They were not at all sophisticated. The mind of their country was great in them, and it prevailed. With their learning and unexampled acquirement, they did not forget that they were men: with all their endeavours after excellence, they did not lay aside the strong original bent and character of their minds. What they performed was chiefly nature's handywork; and time has claimed it for his own.—To these, however, might be added others not less learned, nor with a scarce less happy vein, but less fortunate in the event, who, though as renowned in their day, have sunk into "mere oblivion," and of whom the only record (but that the noblest) is to be found in their works. Their works and their names, "poor, poor dumb names," are all that remains of such men as Webster, Deckar, Marston, Marlow, Chapman, Heywood, Middleton, and Rowley! "How lov'd, how honour'd once, avails them not:" though they were the friends and fellow-labourers of Shakespear, sharing his fame and fortunes with him, the rivals of Jonson, and the masters of Beaumont and Fletcher's well-sung woes! They went out one by one unnoticed, like evening lights; or were swallowed up in the headlong torrent of puritanic zeal which succeeded, and swept away every thing in its unsparing course, throwing up the wrecks of taste and genius at random, and at long fitful intervals, amidst the painted gewgaws and foreign frippery of the reign of Charles II, and from which we are only now recovering the scattered fragments and broken images to erect a temple to true Fame! How long, before it will be completed? . . .

Marlowe is a name that stands high, and almost first in this list of dramatic worthies. He was a little before Shakespear's time, and has a marked character both from him and the rest. There is a lust of power in his writings, a hunger and thirst after unrighteousness, a glow of the imagination, unhallowed by any thing but its own energies. His thoughts burn within him like a furnace with bickering flames; or throwing out black smoke and mists, that hide the dawn of genius, or like a poisonous mineral, corrode the heart. His Life and Death of Doctor Faustus, though an imperfect and unequal performance, is his greatest work. Faustus himself is a rude sketch, but it is a gigantic one. This character may be considered as a personification of the pride of will and eagerness of curiosity, sublimed beyond the reach of fear and remorse. He is hurried away, and, as it were, devoured by a tormenting desire to enlarge his knowledge to the utmost bounds of nature and art, and to extend his power with his knowledge. He would realise all the fictions of a lawless imagination, would solve the most subtle speculations of abstract reason; and for this purpose, sets at defiance all mortal consequences, and leagues himself with demoniacal power, with "fate and metaphysical aid." The idea of witchcraft and necromancy, once the dread of the vulgar and the darling of the visionary recluse, seems to have had its origin in the restless tendency of the human mind, to conceive of and aspire to more than it can achieve by natural means, and in the obscure apprehension that the gratification of this extravagant and unauthorised desire, can only be attained by the sacrifice of all our ordinary hopes, and better prospects to the infernal agents that lend themselves to its accomplishment. Such is the foundation of the present story. Faustus, in his impatience to fulfil at once and for a moment, for a few short years, all the desires and conceptions of his soul, is willing to give in exchange his soul and body to the great enemy of mankind. Whatever he fancies, becomes by this means present to his sense: whatever he commands, is done. He calls back time past, and anticipates the future: the visions of antiquity pass before him, Babylon in all its glory, Paris and Œnone: all the projects of philosophers, or creations of the poet pay tribute at his feet: all the delights of fortune, of ambition, of pleasure, and of learning are centered in his person; and from a short-lived dream of supreme felicity and drunken power, he sinks into an abyss of darkness and perdition. This is the alternative to which he submits; the bond which he signs with his blood! As the outline of the character is grand and daring, the execution is abrupt and fearful. The thoughts are vast and irregular; and the style halts and staggers under them, "with uneasy steps";—"such footing found the sole of unblest feet." There is a little fustian and incongruity of metaphor now and then, which is not very injurious to the subject. It is time to give a few passages in illustration of this account. He thus opens his mind at the beginning:

> How am I glutted with conceit of this?
> Shall I make spirits fetch me what I please?
> Resolve me of all ambiguities?
> Perform what desperate enterprise I will?
> I'll have them fly to India for gold,
> Ransack the ocean for orient pearl,
> And search all corners of the new-found world,
> For pleasant fruits and princely delicates.
> I'll have them read me strange philosophy,
> And tell the secrets of all foreign kings:
> I'll have them wall all Germany with brass,
> And make swift Rhine circle fair Wittenberg;
> I'll have them fill the public schools with skill,
> Wherewith the students shall be bravely clad;
> I'll levy soldiers with the coin they bring,
> And chase the Prince of Parma from our land,
> And reign sole king of all the provinces;
> Yea, stranger engines for the brunt of war
> Than was the fiery keel at Antwerp bridge,
> I'll make my servile spirits to invent.

> *Enter* Valdes *and* Cornelius.

> Come, German Valdes, and Cornelius,
> And make me blest with your sage conference.
> Valdes, sweet Valdes, and Cornelius,
> Know that your words have won me at the last,
> To practise magic and concealed arts.
> Philosophy is odious and obscure;
> Both Law and Physic are for petty wits;
> 'Tis magic, magic, that hath ravish'd me.
> Then, gentle friends, aid me in this attempt;
> And I, that have with subtile syllogisms
> Gravell'd the pastors of the German church,
> And make the flow'ring pride of Wittenberg
> Swarm to my problems, as th' infernal spirits
> On sweet Musæus when he came to hell;
> Will be as cunning as Agrippa was,
> Whose shadow made all Europe honour him.
>   *Valdes:* These books, thy wit, and our
>   experience
> Shall make all nations to canonize us.
> As Indian Moors obey their Spanish lords,
> So shall the Spirits of every element
> Be always serviceable to us three.
> Like lions shall they guard us when we please;
> Like Almain Rutters with their horsemen's staves,
> Or Lapland giants trotting by our sides:
> Sometimes like women, or unwedded maids,
> Shadowing more beauty in their airy brows
> Than have the white breasts of the Queen of Love.
> From Venice they shall drag whole argosies,
> And from America the golden fleece,

> That yearly stuffs old Philip's treasury;
> If learned Faustus will be resolute.
>   *Faustus:* As resolute am I in this
> As thou to live, therefore object it not.

In his colloquy with the fallen angel, he shews the fixedness of his determination:—

> What is great Mephostophilis so passionate
> For being deprived of the joys of heaven?
> Learn thou of Faustus manly fortitude,
> And scorn those joys thou never shalt possess.

Yet we afterwards find him faltering in his resolution, and struggling with the extremity of his fate.

> My heart is harden'd, I cannot repent:
> Scarce can I name salvation, faith, or heaven:
> Swords, poisons, halters, and envenom'd steel
> Are laid before me to dispatch myself;
> And long ere this I should have done the deed,
> Had not sweet pleasure conquer'd deep despair.
> Have I not made blind Homer sing to me
> Of Alexander's love and Œnon's death?
> And hath not he that built the walls of Thebes
> With ravishing sounds of his melodious harp,
> Made music with my Mephostophilis?
> Why should I die then or basely despair?
> I am resolv'd, Faustus shall not repent.
> Come, Mephostophilis, let us dispute again,
> And reason of divine astrology.

There is one passage more of this kind, which is so striking and beautiful, so like a rapturous and deeply passionate dream, that I cannot help quoting it here: it is the address to the Apparition of Helen.

> *Enter* Helen *again, passing over between two Cupids.*
>   *Faustus:* Was this the face that launch'd a
>   thousand ships,
> And burnt the topless tow'rs of Ilium?
> Sweet Helen, make me immortal with a kiss.
> Her lips suck forth my soul! See where it flies.
> Come, Helen, come, give me my soul again.
> Here will I dwell, for Heav'n is in these lips,
> And all is dross that is not Helena.
> I will be Paris, and for love of thee,
> Instead of Troy shall Wittenberg be sack'd;
> And I will combat with weak Menelaus,
> And wear thy colours on my plumed crest;
> Yea, I will wound Achilles in the heel,
> And then return to Helen for a kiss.
> —Oh! thou art fairer than the evening air,
> Clad in the beauty of a thousand stars:
> Brighter art thou than flaming Jupiter,
> When he appear'd to hapless Semele;
> More lovely than the monarch of the sky
> In wanton Arethusa's azure arms;
> And none but thou shalt be my paramour.

The ending of the play is terrible, and his last exclamations betray an anguish of mind and vehemence of passion, not to be contemplated without shuddering.

> Oh, Faustus!
> Now hast thou but one bare hour to live,
> And then thou must be damn'd perpetually.
> Stand still, you ever-moving spheres of heav'n,
> That time may cease, and midnight never come.
> Fair nature's eye, rise, rise again, and make
> Perpetual day; or let this hour be but a year,
> A month, a week, a natural day,
> That Faustus may repent, and save his soul.

(*The Clock strikes Twelve.*)
It strikes, it strikes! Now, body, turn to air,
Or Lucifer will bear thee quick to hell.
Oh soul! be chang'd into small water-drops,
And fall into the ocean; ne'er be found.

(*Thunder. Enter the* Devils.)
Oh! mercy, Heav'n! Look not so fierce on me!
Adders and serpents, let me breathe awhile!—
Ugly hell, gape not! Come not, Lucifer!
I'll burn my books! Oh! Mephostophilis.

Perhaps the finest *trait* in the whole play, and that which
softens and subdues the horror of it, is the interest taken by the
two scholars in the fate of their master, and their unavailing
attempts to dissuade him from his relentless career. The regard
to learning is the ruling passion of this drama; and its indications are as mild and amiable in them as its ungoverned pursuit
has been fatal to Faustus.

Yet, for he was a scholar once admir'd
For wondrous knowledge in our German schools,
We'll give his mangled limbs due burial;
And all the students, clothed in mourning black,
Shall wait upon his heavy funeral.

So the Chorus:

Cut is the branch that might have grown full strait,
And burned is Apollo's laurel bough,
That sometime grew within this learned man.

And still more affecting are his own conflicts of mind and
agonizing doubts on this subject just before, when he exclaims
to his friends; "Oh, gentlemen! Hear me with patience, and
tremble not at my speeches. Though my heart pant and quiver
to remember that I have been a student here these thirty years;
oh! would I had never seen Wittenberg, never read book!" A
finer compliment was never paid, nor a finer lesson ever read to
the pride of learning.—The intermediate comic parts, in
which Faustus is not directly concerned, are mean and grovelling to the last degree. One of the Clowns says to another:
"Snails! what hast got there? A book? Why thou can'st not tell
ne'er a word on't." Indeed, the ignorance and barbarism of the
time, as here described, might almost justify Faustus's over-
strained admiration of learning, and turn the heads of those
who possessed it, from novelty and unaccustomed excitement,
as the Indians are made drunk with wine! Goethe, the German
poet, has written a drama on this tradition of his country,
which is considered a master-piece. I cannot find, in Marlowe's
play, any proofs of the atheism or impiety attributed to him,
unless the belief in witchcraft and the Devil can be regarded as
such; and at the time he wrote, not to have believed in both,
would have been construed into the rankest atheism and irre-
ligion. There is a delight, as Mr. Lamb says, "in dallying with
interdicted subjects;" but that does not, by any means, imply
either a practical or speculative disbelief of them.

Lust's Dominion; or, The Lascivious Queen, is referable to
the same general style of writing; and is a striking picture, or
rather caricature, of the unrestrained love of power, not as
connected with learning, but with regal ambition and external
sway. There is a good deal of the same intense passion, the
same recklessness of purpose, the same smouldering fire
within: but there is not any of the same relief to the mind in the
lofty imaginative nature of the subject; and the continual repetition of plain practical villainy and undigested horrors disgusts
the sense, and blunts the interest. The mind is hardened into
obduracy, not melted into sympathy, by such barefaced and
barbarous cruelty. Eleazar, the Moor, is such another character
as Aaron in *Titus Andronicus*, and this play might be set down

without injustice as "pue-fellow" to that. I should think Marlowe has a much fairer claim to be the author of *Titus Andronicus* than Shakespear, at least from internal evidence; and
the argument of Schlegel, that it must have been Shakespear's,
because there was no one else capable of producing either its
faults or beauties, fails in each particular. The Queen is the
same character in both these plays; and the business of the plot
is carried on in much the same revolting manner, by making
the nearest friends and relatives of the wretched victims the
instruments of their sufferings and persecution by an arch-
villain. To shew however, that the same strong-braced tone of
passionate declamation is kept up, take the speech of Eleazar
on refusing the proffered crown:

What do none rise?
No, no, for kings indeed are Deities.
And who'd not (as the sun) in brightness shine?
To be the greatest is to be divine.
Who among millions would not be the mightiest?
To sit in godlike state; to have all eyes
Dazzled with admiration, and all tongues
Shouting loud prayers; to rob every heart
Of love; to have the strength of every arm;
A sovereign's name, why 'tis a sovereign charm.
This glory round about me hath thrown beams:
I have stood upon the top of Fortune's wheel,
And backward turn'd the iron screw of fate.
The destinies have spun a silken thread
About my life; yet thus I cast aside
The shape of majesty, and on my knee
To this Imperial state lowly resign
This usurpation; wiping off your fears
Which stuck so hard upon me.

This is enough to shew the unabated vigour of the author's
style. This strain is certainly doing justice to the pride of ambition, and the imputed majesty of kings.

We have heard much of "Marlowe's mighty line," and
this play furnishes frequent instances of it. There are a number
of single lines that seem struck out in the heat of a glowing
fancy, and leave a track of golden fire behind them. The following are a few that might be given.

I know he is not dead; I know proud death
Durst not behold such sacred majesty.

Hang both your greedy ears upon my lips,
Let them devour my speech, suck in my breath.

—From discontent grows treason,
And on the stalk of treason, death.

Tyrants swim safest in a crimson flood.

The two following lines—

Oh! I grow dull, and the cold hand of sleep
Hath thrust his icy fingers in my breast—

are the same as those in *King John*—

And none of you will bid the winter come
To thrust his icy fingers in my maw.

And again the Moor's exclamation,

Now by the proud complexion of my cheeks,
Ta'en from the kisses of the amorous sun—

is the same as Cleopatra's—

But I that am with Phœbus' amorous pinches black
—&c.

Eleazar's sarcasm,

—These dignities,
Like poison, make men swell; this rat's-bane honour,
Oh, 'tis so sweet! they'll lick it till they burst—

shews the utmost virulence of smothered spleen; and his concluding strain of malignant exultation has been but tamely imitated by Young's Zanga.

> Now tragedy, thou minion of the night,
> Rhamnusia's pewfellow, to thee I'll sing,
> Upon a harp made of dead Spanish bones,
> The proudest instrument the world affords:
> To thee that never blushest, though thy cheeks
> Are full of blood, O Saint Revenge, to thee
> I consecrate my murders, all my stabs, &c.

It may be worth while to observe, for the sake of the curious, that many of Marlowe's most sounding lines consist of monosyllables, or nearly so. The repetition of Eleazar's taunt to the Cardinal, retorting his own words upon him, "Spaniard or Moor, the saucy slave shall die"—may perhaps have suggested Falconbridge's spirited reiteration of the phrase—"And hang a calve's skin on his recreant limbs."

I do not think *The Rich Jew of Malta* so characteristic a specimen of this writer's powers. It has not the same fierce glow of passion or expression. It is extreme in act, and outrageous in plot and catastrophe; but it has not the same vigorous filling up. The author seems to have relied on the horror inspired by the subject, and the national disgust excited against the principal character, to rouse the feelings of the audience: for the rest, it is a tissue of gratuitous, unprovoked, and incredible atrocities, which are committed, one upon the back of the other, by the parties concerned, without motive, passion, or object. There are, notwithstanding, some striking passages in it, as Barabbas's description of the bravo, Philia Borzo; the relation of his own unaccountable villainies to Ithamore; his rejoicing over his recovered jewels "as the morning lark sings over her young;" and the backwardness he declares in himself to forgive the Christian injuries that are offered him, which may have given the idea of one of Shylock's speeches, where he ironically disclaims any enmity to the merchants on the same account. It is perhaps hardly fair to compare the *Jew of Malta* with the *Merchant of Venice*; for it is evident, that Shakespear's genius shews to as much advantage in knowledge of character, in variety and stage-effect, as it does in point of general humanity.

Edward II. is, according to the modern standard of composition, Marlowe's best play. It is written with few offences against the common rules, and in a succession of smooth and flowing lines. The poet however succeeds less in the voluptuous and effeminate descriptions which he here attempts, than in the more dreadful and violent bursts of passion. *Edward II.* is drawn with historic truth, but without much dramatic effect. The management of the plot is feeble and desultory; little interest is excited in the various turns of fate; the characters are too worthless, have too little energy, and their punishment is, in general, too well deserved, to excite our commiseration; so that this play will bear, on the whole, but a distant comparison with Shakespear's *Richard II.* in conduct, power, or effect. But the death of Edward II. in Marlow's tragedy, is certainly superior to that of Shakespear's King; and in heart-breaking distress, and the sense of human weakness, claiming pity from utter helplessness and conscious misery, is not surpassed by any writer whatever.

> *Edward:* Weep'st thou already? List awhile to
>   me,
> And then thy heart, were it as Gurney's is,
> Or as Matrevis, hewn from the Caucasus,
> Yet will it melt ere I have done my tale.
> This dungeon, where they keep me, is the sink
> Wherein the filth of all the castle falls.
> *Lightborn:* Oh villains.

> *Edward:* And here in mire and puddle have I
>   stood
> This ten days' space; and lest that I should sleep,
> One plays continually upon a drum.
> They give me bread and water, being a king;
> So that, for want of sleep and sustenance,
> My mind's distemper'd, and my body's numb'd:
> And whether I have limbs or no, I know not.
> Oh! would my blood drop out from every vein,
> As doth this water from my tatter'd robes!
> Tell Isabel, the Queen, I look'd not thus,
> When for her sake I ran at tilt in France,
> And there unhors'd the Duke of Cleremont.

There are some excellent passages scattered up and down. The description of the King and Gaveston looking out of the palace window, and laughing at the courtiers as they pass, and that of the different spirit shewn by the lion and the forest deer, when wounded, are among the best. The Song "Come, live with me and be my love," to which Sir Walter Raleigh wrote an answer, is Marlowe's.

ALEXANDER DYCE
From "Some Account of Marlowe and His Writings"
The Works of Christopher Marlowe
1850, Volume 1, pp. xv–xlviii

With very little discrimination of character, with much extravagance of incident, with no pathos where pathos was to be expected, and with a profusion of inflated language, *Tamburlaine* is nevertheless a very impressive drama, and undoubtedly superior to all the English tragedies which preceded it;—superior to them in the effectiveness with which the events are brought out, in the poetic feeling which animates the whole, and in the nerve and variety of the versification. Marlowe was yet to shew that he could impart truthfulness to his scenes; but not a few passages might be gleaned from *Tamburlaine*, as grand in thought, as splendid in imagery, and as happy in expression, as any which his later works contain. . . .

The well-known fact, that our early dramatists usually borrowed their fables from novels or 'histories,' to which they often servilely adhered, has been thought no derogation from their merits. Yet the latest biographer of Marlowe dismisses *Faustus* as 'unworthy of his reputation,' chiefly because it 'closely follows a popular romance of the same name.' Certain it is that Marlowe has 'closely followed' the prose *History of Doctor Faustus*; but it is equally certain that he was not indebted to that *History* for the poetry and the passion which he has infused into his play, for those thoughts of surpassing beauty and grandeur with which it abounds, and for that fearful display of mental agony at the close, compared to which all attempts of the kind by preceding English dramatists are 'poor indeed.' In the opinion of Hazlitt, '*Faustus*, though an imperfect and unequal performance, is Marlowe's greatest work.' Mr. Hallam remarks, 'There is an awful melancholy about Marlowe's Mephistophiles, perhaps more impressive than the malignant mirth of that fiend in the renowned work of Goethe. But the fair form of Margaret is wanting.' In the comic scenes of *Faustus* (which are nearly all derived from the prose *History*) we have buffoonery of the worst description; and it is difficult not to believe that Marlowe is answerable for at least a portion of them, when we recollect that he had inserted similar scenes in the original copy of his *Tamburlaine*.

In what year Marlowe produced *The Jew of Malta* we are unable to determine. The words in the Prologue, 'now the

Guise is dead,' are evidence that it was composed after 23rd Dec. 1588; and Mr. Collier thinks that it was probably written about 1589 or 1590. Barabas was originally performed by Alleyn; and the aspect of the Jew was rendered as grotesque and hideous as possible by means of a false nose. In Rowley's *Search for Money*, 1609, a person is described as having 'his visage (or vizard) like the artificiall Jewe of Maltae's nose;' and a speech in the play itself, 'Oh, brave, master! I worship your nose for this,' is a proof that Marlowe intended his hero to be distinguished for the magnitude of that feature. It would seem, indeed, that on our early stage Jews were always furnished with an extra quantity of nose: it was thought that a race so universally hated could hardly be made to appear too ugly. . . .

The character of Barabas, upon which the interest of the tragedy entirely depends, is delineated with no ordinary power, and possesses a strong individuality. Unfortunately, however, it is a good deal overcharged; but I suspect, that in this instance at least, Marlowe violated the truth of nature, not so much from his love of exaggeration, as in consequences of having borrowed all the atrocities of the play from some now-unknown novel, whose author was willing to flatter the prejudices of his readers by attributing almost impossible wickedness to a son of Israel. 'The first two acts of *The Jew of Malta*,' observes Mr. Hallam, 'are more vigorously conceived, both as to character and circumstance, than any other Elizabethan play, except those of Shakespeare:' but the latter part is in every respect so inferior, that we rise from a perusal of the whole with a feeling akin to disappointment. If the dialogue has little poetry, it has often great force of expression.—That Shakespeare was well acquainted with this tragedy cannot be doubted; but that he caught from it more than a few trifling hints for *The Merchant of Venice* will be allowed by no one who has carefully compared the character of Barabas with that of Shylock.—An alteration of *The Jew of Malta* was produced at Drury-lane Theatre in 1818, when Kean was in the zenith of his fame, and, owing to his exertions in Barabas, it was very favourably received.

Warton incidentally mentions that Marlowe's *Edward the Second* was 'written in the year 1590;' and, for all we know, he may have made the assertion on sufficient grounds, though he has neglected to specify them. Mr. Collier, who regards it (and, no doubt, rightly) as one of our author's latest pieces, has not attempted to fix its date. It was entered in the Stationers' Books 6th July 1593, and first printed in 1598.

From that heaviness, which prevails more or less in all 'chronicle histories' anterior to those of Shakespeare, this tragedy is not wholly free; its crowded incidents do not always follow each other without confusion; and it has few of those 'raptures,' for which Marlowe is eulogized by one of his contemporaries. But, taken as a whole, it is the most perfect of his plays; there is no overdoing of character, no turgidity of language. On the two scenes which give the chief interest to this drama Lamb remarks: 'the reluctant pangs of abdicating royalty in *Edward* furnished hints which Shakespeare scarce improved in his *Richard the Second*; and the death-scene of Marlowe's king moves pity and terror beyond any scene ancient or modern with which I am acquainted.' The excellence of both scenes is indisputable; but a more fastidious critic than Lamb might perhaps justly object to such an exhibition of physical suffering as the latter scene affords. . . .

The Massacre at Paris was printed without date (perhaps about 1595 or 1596), either from a copy taken down, during representation, by some unskilful and ignorant short-hand-writer, or from a very imperfect transcript which had belonged to one of the theatres.

It would be rash to decide on the merits of a play which we possess only with a text both mutilated and abounding in corruptions; I strongly suspect, however, that *The Massacre at Paris*, even in its pristine state, was the very worst of Marlowe's dramas.

We must now turn from his works to the personal history of Marlowe.—It is not to be doubted that by this time he had become acquainted with most of those who, like himself, were dramatists by profession; and there can be little doubt too that beyond their circle (which, of course, included the actors) he had formed few intimacies. Though the demand for theatrical novelties was then incessant, plays were scarcely recognized as literature, and the dramatists were regarded as men who held a rather low rank in society: the authors of pieces which had delighted thousands were generally looked down upon by the grave substantial citizens, and seldom presumed to approach the mansions of the aristocracy but as clients in humble attendance on the bounty of their patrons. Unfortunately, the discredit which attached to dramatic writing as an occupation was greatly increased by the habits of those who pursued it: a few excepted, they were improvident, unprincipled, and dissolute,—now rioting in taverns and 'ordinaries' on the profits of a successful play, and now lurking in the haunts of poverty till the completion of another drama had enabled them to resume their revels.—At a somewhat later period, indeed, a decided improvement appears to have taken place in the morals of our dramatic writers: and it is by no means improbable that the high respectability of character which was maintained by Shakespeare and Jonson may have operated very beneficially, in the way of example, on the playwrights around them.—But among those of superior station there was at least one person with whom Marlowe lived on terms of intimacy: the publisher of his posthumous fragment, *Hero and Leander*, was induced to dedicate it 'to the worshipful Sir Thomas Walsingham, knight,' because he had 'bestowed upon the author many kind favours, entertaining the parts of reckoning and worth which he found in him with good countenance and *liberal affection*.' Nor is this the only proof extant that Sir Thomas Walsingham cultivated a familiarity with the dramatists of his day; for to him, as to his 'long-loved and honourable *friend*,' Chapman has inscribed by a sonnet the comedy of *Al Fooles*, 1605. . . .

This version of the *Amores*, taken altogether, does so little credit either to Marlowe's skill as a translator or to his scholarship, that one is almost tempted to believe it was never intended by him to meet the eye of the world, but was made, merely as a literary exercise, at an early period of life, when classical studies chiefly engaged his attention. We look in vain for the graces of Ovid. In many passages we should be utterly puzzled to attach a definite meaning to the words, if we had not the original at hand; and in many others the Latin is erroneously rendered, the mistranslations being sometimes extremely ludicrous. I doubt if more can be said in praise of this version than that it is occasionally spirited and flowing. Of the XVth Elegy of the First Book there are two translations,—the second, which is by B. J. (i.e. Ben Jonson) being, however, only an alteration of the first. . . .

A paraphrase on the very elegant production of the Pseudo-Musaeus had been projected and was already partly composed by Marlowe, when death put an end to his labours; and as much of *Hero and Leander* as could be discovered after his decease, having been entered in the Stationers' Books 28th September, 1593, was given to the press in 1598.—While the poem of the Greek grammarian is comprised in 341 verses, the fragment in question extends to above 800.

In this paraphrase Marlowe has somewhat impeded the

progress and weakened the interest of the story by introducing extraneous matter and by indulging in whimsical and frivolous details; he occasionally disregards costume; he is too fond of conceits, and too prodigal of 'wise saws' and moral axioms. But he has amply redeemed these faults by the exquisite perception of the beautiful which he displays throughout a large portion of the fragment, by descriptions picturesque and vivid in the extreme, by lines which glow with all the intensity of passion, by marvellous felicities of language, and by skilful modulation of the verse.—The quotation from this poem in *As You Like It* may be considered as a proof that it was admired by Shakespeare; and the words which are there applied to the author,— 'dead shepherd,'—sound not unlike an expression of pity for his sad and untimely end. Jonson, too, in *Every Man in his Humour* has cited *Hero and Leander*; and he is reported to have spoken of it often in terms of the highest praise.

ALGERNON CHARLES SWINBURNE
"Christopher Marlowe" (1883)
The Age of Shakespeare
1908, pp. 1–14

The first great English poet was the father of English tragedy and the creator of English blank verse. Chaucer and Spenser were great writers and great men: they shared between them every gift which goes to the making of a poet except the one which alone can make a poet, in the proper sense of the word, great. Neither pathos nor humour nor fancy nor invention will suffice for that: no poet is great as a poet whom no one could ever pretend to recognise as sublime. Sublimity is the test of imagination as distinguished from invention or from fancy: and the first English poet whose powers can be called sublime was Christopher Marlowe.

The majestic and exquisite excellence of various lines and passages in Marlowe's first play must be admitted to relieve, if it cannot be allowed to redeem, the stormy monotony of Titanic truculence which blusters like a simoom through the noisy course of its ten fierce acts. With many and heavy faults, there is something of genuine greatness in *Tamburlaine the Great*; and for two grave reasons it must always be remembered with distinction and mentioned with honour. It is the first poem ever written in English blank verse, as distinguished from mere rhymeless decasyllabics; and it contains one of the noblest passages, perhaps indeed the noblest in the literature of the world, ever written by one of the greatest masters of poetry in loving praise of the glorious delights and sublime submission to the everlasting limits of his art. In its highest and most distinctive qualities, in unfaltering and infallible command of the right note of music and the proper tone of colour for the finest touches of poetic execution, no poet of the most elaborate modern school, working at ease upon every consummate resource of luxurious learning and leisurely refinement, has ever excelled the best and most representative work of a man who had literally no models before him, and probably or evidently was often, if not always, compelled to write against time for his living.

The just and generous judgment passed by Goethe on the *Faustus* of his English predecessor in tragic treatment of the same subject is somewhat more than sufficient to counterbalance the slighting or the sneering references to that magnificent poem which might have been expected from the ignorance of Byron or the incompetence of Hallam. And the particular note of merit observed, the special point of the praise conferred, by the great German poet should be no less sufficient to dispose of the vulgar misconception yet lingering among sciolists and pretenders to criticism, which regards a writer than whom no man was ever born with a finer or a stronger instinct for perfection of excellence in execution as a mere noble savage of letters, a rough self-taught sketcher or scribbler of crude and rude genius, whose unhewn blocks of verse had in them some veins of rare enough metal to be quarried and polished by Shakespeare. What most impressed the author of *Faust* in the work of Marlowe was a quality the want of which in the author of *Manfred* is proof enough to consign his best work to the second or third class at most. 'How greatly it is all planned!' the first requisite of all great work, and one of which the highest genius possible to a greatly gifted barbarian could by no possibility understand the nature or conceive the existence. That Goethe 'had thought of translating it' is perhaps hardly less precious a tribute to its greatness than the fact that it has been actually and admirably translated by the matchless translator of Shakespeare—the son of Victor Hugo; whose labour of love may thus be said to have made another point in common, and forged as it were another link of union, between Shakespeare and the young master of Shakespeare's youth. Of all great poems in dramatic form it is perhaps the most remarkable for absolute singleness of aim and simplicity of construction yet is it wholly free from all possible imputation of monotony or aridity. *Tamburlaine* is monotonous in the general roll and flow of its stately and sonorous verse through a noisy wilderness of perpetual bluster and slaughter; but the unity of tone and purpose in *Doctor Faustus* is not unrelieved by change of manner and variety of incident. The comic scenes, written evidently with as little of labour as of relish, are for the most part scarcely more than transcripts, thrown into the form of dialogue, from a popular prose *History of Doctor Faustus*; and therefore should be set down as little to the discredit as to the credit of the poet. Few masterpieces of any age in any language can stand beside this tragic poem—it has hardly the structure of a play—for the qualities of terror and splendour, for intensity of purpose and sublimity of note. In the vision of Helen, for example, the intense perception of loveliness gives actual sublimity to the sweetness and radiance of mere beauty in the passionate and spontaneous selection of words the most choice and perfect; and in like manner the sublimity of simplicity in Marlowe's conception and expression of the agonies endured by Faustus under the immediate imminence of his doom gives the highest note of beauty, the quality of absolute fitness and propriety, to the sheer straightforwardness of speech in which his agonising horror finds vent ever more and more terrible from the first to the last equally beautiful and fearful verse of that tremendous monologue which has no parallel in all the range of tragedy.

It is now a commonplace of criticism to observe and regret the decline of power and interest after the opening acts of *The Jew of Malta*. This decline is undeniable, though even the latter part of the play is not wanting in rough energy and a coarse kind of interest; but the first two acts would be sufficient foundation for the durable fame of a dramatic poet. In the blank verse of Milton alone, who perhaps was hardly less indebted than Shakespeare was before him to Marlowe as the first English master of word-music in its grander forms, has the glory or the melody of passages in the opening soliloquy of Barabas been possibly surpassed. The figure of the hero before it degenerates into caricature is as finely touched as the poetic execution is excellent; and the rude and rapid sketches of the minor characters show at least some vigour and vivacity of touch.

In *Edward the Second* the interest rises and the execution

improves as visibly and as greatly with the course of the advancing story as they decline in *The Jew of Malta*. The scene of the king's deposition at Kenilworth is almost as much finer in tragic effect and poetic quality as it is shorter and less elaborate than the corresponding scene in Shakespeare's *King Richard II*. The terror of the death-scene undoubtedly rises into horror; but this horror is with skilful simplicity of treatment preserved from passing into disgust. In pure poetry, in sublime and splendid imagination, this tragedy is excelled by *Doctor Faustus*; in dramatic power and positive impression of natural effect it is as certainly the masterpiece of Marlowe. It was almost inevitable, in the hands of any poet but Shakespeare, that none of the characters represented should be capable of securing or even exciting any finer sympathy or more serious interest than attends on the mere evolution of successive events or the mere display of emotions (except always in the great scene of the deposition) rather animal than spiritual in their expression of rage or tenderness or suffering. The exact balance of mutual effect, the final note of scenic harmony between ideal conception and realistic execution, is not yet struck with perfect accuracy of touch and security of hand; but on this point also Marlowe has here come nearer by many degrees to Shakespeare than any of his other predecessors have ever come near to Marlowe.

Of *The Massacre at Paris* it is impossible to judge fairly from the garbled fragment of its genuine text which is all that has come down to us. To Mr. Collier, among numberless other obligations, we owe the discovery of a striking passage excised in the piratical edition which gives us the only version extant of this unlucky play; and which, it must be allowed, contains nothing of quite equal value. This is obviously an occasional and polemical work, and being as it is overcharged with the anti-Catholic passion of the time, has a typical quality which gives it some empirical significance and interest. That antipapal ardour is indeed the only note of unity in a rough and ragged chronicle which shambles and stumbles onward from the death of Queen Jeanne of Navarre to the murder of the last Valois. It is possible to conjecture what it would be fruitless to affirm, that it gave a hint in the next century to Nathaniel Lee for his far superior and really admirable tragedy on the same subject, issued ninety-seven years after the death of Marlowe.

The tragedy of *Dido, Queen of Carthage*, was probably completed for the stage after that irreparable and incalculable loss to English letters by Thomas Nash, the worthiest English precursor of Swift in vivid, pure, and passionate prose, embodying the most terrible and splendid qualities of a personal and social satirist; a man gifted also with some fair faculty of elegiac and even lyric verse, but in no wise qualified to put on the buskin left behind him by the 'famous gracer of tragedians,' as Marlowe had already been designated by their common friend Greene from among the worthiest of his fellows. In this somewhat thin-spun and evidently hasty play a servile fidelity to the text of Virgil's narrative has naturally resulted in the failure which might have been expected from an attempt at once to transcribe what is essentially inimitable and to reproduce it under the hopelessly alien conditions of dramatic adaptation. The one really noble passage in a generally feeble and incomposite piece of work is, however, uninspired by the unattainable model to which the dramatists have been only too obsequious in their subservience.

It is as nearly certain as anything can be which depends chiefly upon cumulative and collateral evidence that the better part of what is best in the serious scenes of *King Henry VI*. is mainly the work of Marlowe. That he is, at any rate, the principal author of the second and third plays passing under

that name among the works of Shakespeare, but first and imperfectly printed as *The Contention between the two Famous Houses of York and Lancaster*, can hardly be now a matter of debate among competent judges. The crucial difficulty of criticism in this matter is to determine, if indeed we should not rather say to conjecture, the authorship of the humorous scenes in prose, showing as they generally do a power of comparatively high and pure comic realism to which nothing in the acknowledged works of any pre-Shakespearean dramatist is even remotely comparable. Yet, especially in the original text of these scenes as they stand unpurified by the ultimate revision of Shakespeare, there are tones and touches which recall rather the clownish horseplay and homely ribaldry of his predecessors than anything in the lighter interludes of his very earliest plays. We find the same sort of thing which we find in their writings, only better done than they usually do it, rather than such work as Shakespeare's a little worse done than usual. And even in the final text of the tragic or metrical scenes the highest note struck is always, with one magnificent and unquestionable exception, rather in the key of Marlowe at his best than of Shakespeare while yet in great measure his disciple.

It is another commonplace of criticism to affirm that Marlowe had not a touch of comic genius, not a gleam of wit in him or a twinkle of humour: but it is an indisputable fact that he had. In *The Massacre at Paris*, the soliloquy of the soldier lying in wait for the minion of Henri III. has the same very rough but very real humour as a passage in the *Contention* which was cancelled by the reviser. The same hand is unmistakable in both these broad and boyish outbreaks of unseemly but undeniable fun: and if we might wish it rather less indecorous, we must admit that the tradition which denies all sense of humour and all instinct of wit to the first great poet of England is no less unworthy of serious notice or elaborate refutation than the charges and calumnies of an informer who was duly hanged the year after Marlowe's death. For if the same note of humour is struck in an undoubted play of Marlowe's and in a play of disputed authorship, it is evident that the rest of the scene in the latter play must also be Marlowe's. And in that unquestionable case the superb and savage humour of the terribly comic scenes which represent with such rough magnificence of realism the riot of Jack Cade and his ruffians through the ravaged streets of London must be recognisable as no other man's than his. It is a pity we have not before us for comparison the comic scenes or burlesque interludes of *Tamburlaine* which the printer or publisher, as he had the impudence to avow in his prefatory note, purposely omitted and left out.

The author of *A Study of Shakespeare* was therefore wrong, and utterly wrong, when in a book issued some quarter of a century ago he followed the lead of Mr. Dyce in assuming that because the author of *Doctor Faustus* and *The Jew of Malta* 'was as certainly'—and certainly it is difficult to deny that whether as a mere transcriber or as an original dealer in pleasantry he sometimes was—'one of the least and worst among jesters as he was one of the best and greatest among poets,' he could not have had a hand in the admirable comic scenes of *The Taming of a Shrew*. For it is now, I should hope, unnecessary to insist that the able and conscientious editor to whom his fame and his readers owe so great a debt was over hasty in assuming and asserting that he was a poet 'to whom, we have reason to believe, nature had denied even a moderate talent for the humorous.' The serious or would-be poetical scenes of the play are as unmistakably the work of an imitator as are most of the better passages in *Titus Andronicus* and *King Edward III*. Greene or Peele may be responsible for the bad poetry, but there is no reason to suppose that the great poet whose mannerisms he imitated with so stupid a servility was incapable of the good fun.

Had every copy of Marlowe's boyish version or perversion of Ovid's *Elegies* deservedly perished in the flames to which it was judicially condemned by the sentence of a brace of prelates it is possible that an occasional bookworm, it is certain that no poetical student, would have deplored its destruction, if its demerits—hardly relieved, as his first competent editor has happily remarked, by the occasional incidence of a fine and felicitous couplet—could in that case have been imagined. His translation of the first book of Lucan alternately rises above the original and falls short of it; often inferior to the Latin in point and weight of expressive rhetoric, now and then brightened by a clearer note of poetry and lifted into a higher mood of verse. Its terseness, vigour, and purity of style would in any case have been praiseworthy, but are nothing less than admirable, if not wonderful, when we consider how close the translator has on the whole (in spite of occasional slips into inaccuracy) kept himself to the most rigid limit of literal representation, phrase by phrase and often line by line. The really startling force and felicity of occasional verses are worthier of remark than the inevitable stiffness and heaviness of others, when the technical difficulty of such a task is duly taken into account.

One of the most faultless lyrics and one of the loveliest fragments in the whole range of descriptive and fanciful poetry would have secured a place for Marlowe among the memorable men of his epoch, even if his plays had perished with himself. His *Passionate Shepherd* remains ever since unrivalled in its way—a way of pure fancy and radiant melody without break or lapse. The untitled fragment, on the other hand, has been very closely rivalled, perhaps very happily imitated, but only by the greatest lyric poet of England—by Shelley alone. Marlowe's poem of *Hero and Leander*, closing with the sunrise which closes the night of the lovers' union, stands alone in its age, and far ahead of the work of any possible competitor between the death of Spenser and the dawn of Milton. In clear mastery of narrative and presentation, in melodious ease and simplicity of strength, it is not less pre-eminent than in the adorable beauty and impeccable perfection of separate lines or passages.

The place and the value of Christopher Marlowe as a leader among English poets it would be almost impossible for historical criticism to over-estimate. To none of them all, perhaps, have so many of the greatest among them been so deeply and so directly indebted. Nor was ever any great writer's influence upon his fellows more utterly and unmixedly an influence for good. He first, and he alone, guided Shakespeare into the right way of work; his music, in which there is no echo of any man's before him, found its own echo in the more prolonged but hardly more exalted harmony of Milton's. He is the greatest discoverer, the most daring and inspired pioneer, in all our poetic literature. Before him there was neither genuine blank verse nor genuine tragedy in our language. After his arrival the way was prepared, the paths were made straight, for Shakespeare.

ALGERNON CHARLES SWINBURNE
From *The Works of George Chapman*
1875, pp. lix–lxvi

T he name of Chapman should always be held great; yet must it always at first recall the names of greater men. For one who thinks of him as the author of his best play or his loftiest lines of gnomic verse a score will at once remember him as the translator of Homer or the continuator of Marlowe. The most daring enterprise of a life which was full of daring aspiration and arduous labour was this of resuming and completing the 'mighty line' of *Hero and Leander*. For that poem stands out alone amid all the wide and wild poetic wealth of its teeming and turbulent age, as might a small shrine of Parian sculpture amid the rank splendour of a tropic jungle. But no metaphor can aptly express the rapture of relief with which you come upon it amid the poems of Chapman, and drink once more with your whole heart of that well of sweet water after the long draughts you have taken from such brackish and turbid springs as gush up among the sands and thickets of his verse. Faultless indeed this lovely fragment is not; it also bears traces of the Elizabethan barbarism, as though the great queen's ruff and farthingale had been clapped about the neck and waist of the Medicean Venus; but for all the strange costume we can see that the limbs are perfect still. The name of Marlowe's poem has been often coupled with that of the 'first heir' of Shakespeare's 'invention;' but with all reverence to the highest name in letters be it said, the comparison is hardly less absurd than a comparison of *Tamburlaine* with *Othello*. With all its overcrowding beauties of detail, Shakespeare's first poem is on the whole a model of what a young man of genius should not write on such a subject; Marlowe's is a model of what he should. Scarcely the art of Titian at its highest, and surely not the art of Shakespeare at its dawn, could have made acceptable such an inversion of natural rule as is involved in the attempted violation by a passionate woman of a passionless boy; the part of a Joseph, as no less a moralist than Henri Beyle has observed in his great work on *Love*, has always a suspicion about it of something ridiculous and offensive: but only the wretchedest of artists could wholly fail to give charm to the picture of such a nuptial night as that of Hero and Leander. The style of Shakespeare's first essay is, to speak frankly, for the most part no less vicious than the matter: it is burdened and bedizened with all the heavy and fantastic jewellery of Gongora and Marini; it is written throughout in the style which an italian scholar knows as that of the scientist; and which the duncery of New Grubstreet in its immeasurable ignorance would probably designate as 'Della-Cruscan;' nay, there are yet, I believe, in that quarter rhymesters and libellers to be found who imagine such men as Guido Cavalanti and Dante Alighieri to have been representative members of the famous and farinaceous academy. Not one of the faults chargeable on Shakespeare's beautiful but faultful poem can justly be charged on the only not faultless poem of Marlowe. The absence of all cumbrous jewels and ponderous embroideries from the sweet and limpid loveliness of its style is not more noticeable than the absence of such other and possibly such graver flaws as deform and diminish the undeniable charms of *Venus and Adonis*. With leave or without leave of a much lauded critic who could see nothing in the glorified version or expansion by Marlowe of the little poem of Musaeus but 'a paraphrase, in every sense of the epithet, of the most licentious kind,' I must avow that I want and am well content to want the sense, whatever it be, which would enable me to discern more offence in that lovely picture of the union of two lovers in body as in soul than I can discern in the parting of Romeo and Juliet. And if it be always a pleasure to read a page of Marlowe, to read it after a page of Chapman is to the capable student of high verse 'a pleasure worthy Xerxes the great king.' Yet there is not a little to be advanced in favour of Chapman's audacious and arduous undertaking. The poet was not alive, among all the mighty men then living, who could worthily have completed the divine fragment of Marlowe. As well might we look now to find a sculptor who could worthily restore for us the arms of the Venus of Melos—'Our Lady of Beauty,' as Heine said when lying at her feet stricken to death, 'who has no hands, and cannot help us.' For of narrative poets there were none in that generation of any note but Drayton and Daniel; and though these might have more of Marlowe's limpid sweetness and purity of style they lacked the force and weight of Chapman. Nor is the continuation by any means altogether such as we might have expected it to be—a sequel by Marsyas to the song of Apollo. . . .

In Marlowe the passion of ideal love for the ultimate idea of beauty in art or nature found its perfect and supreme expression, faultless and unforced. The radiant ardour of his desire, the light and the flame of his aspiration, diffused and shed through all the forms of his thought and all the colours of his verse, gave them such shapeliness and strength of life as is given to the spirits of the greatest poets alone. He, far rather than Chaucer or Spenser, whose laurels were first fed by the dews and sunbeams of Italy and France, whose songs were full of sweet tradition from oversea, of memories and notes which 'came mended from their tongues,'—he alone was the true Apollo of our dawn, the bright and morning star of the full midsummer day of English poetry at its highest. Chaucer, Wyatt, and Spenser had left our language as melodious, as fluent, as flexible to all purposes of narrative or lyrical poetry as it could be made by the grace of genius; the supreme note of its possible music was reserved for another to strike. Of English blank verse, one of the few highest forms of verbal harmony or poetic expression, the genius of Marlowe was the absolute and divine creator. By mere dint of original and godlike instinct he discovered and called it into life; and at his untimely and unhappy death, more lamentable to us all than any other on record except Shelley's he left the marvellous instrument of his invention so nearly perfect that Shakespeare first and afterwards Milton came to learn of him before they could vary or improve on it. In the changes rung by them on the keys first tuned by Marlowe we trace a remembrance of the touches of his hand; in his own cadences we catch not a note of any other man's. This poet, a poor scholar of humblest parentage, lived to perfect the exquisite metre invented for narrative by Chaucer, giving it (to my ear at least) more of weight and depth, of force and fullness, than its founder had to give; he invented the highest and hardest form of English verse, the only instrument since found possible for our tragic or epic poetry; he created the modern tragic drama; and at the age of thirty he went

Where Orpheus and where Homer are.

Surely there are not more than two or three names in any literature which can be set above the poet's of whom this is the least that can in simple truth be said. There is no record extant of his living likeness; if his country should ever bear men worthy to raise a statue or monument to his memory, he should stand before or colour something that will not be expressed or attained, nor pass into the likeness of any perishable life; but though all were done that all poets could do,

Yet should there hover in their restless heads,
One thought, one grace, one wonder, at the least,
Which into words no virtue can digest.

No poet ever came nearer than Marlowe to the expression of this inexpressible beauty, to the incarnation in actual form of ideal perfection, to the embodiment in mortal music of immortal harmony; and he it is who has left on record and on evidence to all time the truth that no poet can ever come nearer.

A. C. BRADLEY
From "Christopher Marlowe"
The English Poets, ed. Ward
1880, Volume 1, pp. 411–17

Marlowe has one claim in our affection which everyone is ready to acknowledge; he died young. We think of him along with Chatterton and Burns, with Byron, Shelley, and Keats. And this is a fact of some importance for the estimate of his life and genius. His poetical career lasted only for six or seven years, and he did not outlive his 'hot days, when the mad blood's stirring.' An old ballad tells us that he acted at the *Curtain* theatre in Shoreditch and 'brake his leg in one rude scene, When in his early age.' If there is any truth in the last statement, we may suppose that Marlowe gave up acting and confined himself to authorship. He seems to have depended for his livelihood on his connection with the stage; and probably, like many of his fellows and friends, he lived in a free and even reckless way. A more unusual characteristic of Marlowe's was his 'atheism.' No reliance can be placed on the details recorded on this subject; but it was apparently only his death that prevented judicial proceedings being taken against him on account of his opinions. The note on which these proceedings would have been founded was the work of one Baine, who thought that 'all men in christianitei ought to endeavour that the mouth of so dangerous a member may be stopped,' and was hanged at Tyburn about eighteen months afterwards. But other testimony points in the same direction; and a celebrated passage in Greene's *Groatsworth of Wit* would lead us to suppose that Marlowe was given to blatant profanities. Whatever his offences may have been—and there is nothing to make us think he was a bad-hearted man—he had no time to make men forget them. He was not thirty when he met his death.

The plan of the present volumes excludes selections from Marlowe's plays; but as his purely poetical works give but a one-sided idea of his genius, and as his importance in the history of literature depends mainly on his dramatic writings, some general reference must be made to them. Even if they had no enduring merits of their own, their effect upon Shakespeare—an effect which, to say nothing of *Henry VI*, is most clearly visible in *Richard II*—and their influence on the drama would preserve them from neglect. The nature of this influence may be seen by a glance at Marlowe's first play. On the one hand it stands at the opposite pole to the classic form of the drama as it is found in Seneca, a form which had been adopted in *Gorboduc*, and which some of the more learned writers attempted to nationalise. There is no Chorus in *Tamburlaine* or in any of Marlowe's plays except *Dr. Faustus*; and the action takes place on the stage instead of being merely reported. On the other hand, in this, the first play in blank verse which was publicly acted, he called the audience

From jigging veins of rhyming mother-wits,
And such conceits as clownage keeps in pay,

and fixed the metre of his drama for ever as the metre of English tragedy. And, though neither here nor in *Dr. Faustus* could he yet afford to cast off all the conceits of clownage, he was in effect beginning to substitute works of art for the formless popular representations of the day. Doubtless it was only a beginning. The two parts of *Tamburlaine* are not great tragedies. They are full of mere horror and glare. Of the essence of drama, a sustained and developed action, there is as yet very little; and what action there is proceeds almost entirely from the rising passion of a single character. Nor in the conception of this character has Marlowe quite freed himself from the defect of the popular plays, in which, naturally enough, personified virtues and vices often took the place of men. Still, if there is a touch of this defect in *Tamburlaine*, as in the *Jew of Malta*, it is no more than a touch. The ruling passion is conceived with an intensity, and portrayed with a sweep of imagination unknown before; a requisite for the drama hardly less important than the faculty of construction is attained, and the way is opened for those creations which are lifted above the common and yet are living flesh and blood. It is the same with the language. For the buffoonery he partly displaced Marlowe substitutes a swelling diction, 'high astounding terms,' and some outrageous bombast, such as that which Shakespeare reproduced and put into the mouth of Pistol. But, laugh as we will, in this first of Marlowe's plays there is that incommunicable gift which means almost everything, *style*; a manner perfectly individual, and yet, at its best, free from eccentricity. The 'mighty line' of which Jonson spoke, and a pleasure, equal to Milton's, in resounding proper names, meet us in the very first scene; and in not a few passages passion, instead of vociferating, finds its natural expression, and we hear the fully-formed style, which in Marlowe's best writing is, to use his own words,

> Like his desire, lift upward and divine.

'Lift upward' Marlowe's style was at first, and so it remained. It degenerates into violence, but never into softness. If it falters, the cause is not doubt or languor, but haste and want of care. It has the energy of youth; and a living poet has described this among its other qualities when he speaks of Marlowe as singing

> With mouth of gold, and morning in his eyes.

As a dramatic instrument it developed with his growth and acquired variety. The stately monotone of *Tamburlaine*, in which the pause falls almost regularly at the end of the lines, gives place in *Edward II* to rhythms less suited to pure poetry, but far more rapid and flexible. In *Dr. Faustus* the great address to Helen is as different in metrical effect as it is in spirit from the last scene, where the words seem, like Faustus's heart, to 'pant and quiver.' . . .

The expression 'lift upward' applies also, in a sense, to most of the chief characters in the plays. Whatever else they may lack, they know nothing of half-heartedness or irresolution. A volcanic self-assertion, a complete absorption in some one desire, is their characteristic. That in creating such characters Marlowe was working in dark places, and that he develops them with all his energy, is certain. But that in so doing he shows (to refer to a current notion of him) a 'hunger and thirst after unrighteousness,' a desire, that is, which never has produced or could produce true poetry, is an idea which Hazlitt could not have really intended to convey. Marlowe's works are tragedies. Their greatness lies not merely in the conception of an unhallowed lust, however gigantic, but in an insight into its tragic significance and tragic results; and there is as little food for a hunger after unrighteousness (if there be such a thing) in the appalling final scene of *Dr. Faustus*, or, indeed, in the melancholy of Mephistopheles, so grandly touched by Marlowe, as in the catastrophe of *Richard III* or of Goethe's *Faust*. It is true, again, that in the later acts of *The Jew of Malta* Barabas has become a mere monster; but for that very reason the character ceases to show Marlowe's peculiar genius, and Shakespeare himself has not portrayed the sensual lust after gold, and the touch of imagination which redeems it from insignificance, with such splendour as the opening speech of Marlowe's play. Whatever faults however the earlier plays have, it is clear, if *Edward II* be one of his latest works, that Marlowe

was rapidly outgrowing them. For in that play, to say nothing of the two great scenes to which Lamb gave such high praise, the interest is no longer confined to a single character, and there is the most decided advance both in construction and in the dialogue.

Of the weightier qualities of Marlowe's genius the extracts from his purely poetical works give but little idea; but just for that reason they testify to the variety of his powers. Everyone knows the verses 'Come live with me, and be my love,' with their pretty mixture of gold buckles and a belt of straw. This was a very popular song; Raleigh wrote an answer to it; and its flowing music has run in many a head beside Sir Hugh Evans's. But the shepherd would hardly be called 'passionate' outside the Arcadia to which the lyric really belongs. Of the beautiful fragment in *ottava rima* nothing is known, except that it was first printed with Marlowe's name in *England's Parnassus*, 1600. The translations of Lucan and Ovid (the former in blank verse) were perhaps early studies. It is curious that Marlowe should have set himself so thankless a task as a version of Lucan which literally gives line for line; but the choice of the author is characteristic. The translation of Ovid's *Amores* was burnt on account of its indecency in 1599, and it would have been no loss to the world if all the copies had perished. The interest of these translations is mainly historical. They testify to the passion for classical poetry, and in particular to that special fondness for Ovid of which the literature of the time affords many other proofs. The study of Virgil and Ovid was a far less mixed good for poetry than that of Seneca and Plautus; and it is perhaps worth noticing that Marlowe, who felt the charm of classical amatory verse, and whose knowledge of Virgil is shown in his *Queen Dido*, should have been the man who, more than any other, secured the theatre from the dominion of inferior classical dramas.

How fully he caught the inspiration, not indeed of the best classical poetry, but of that world of beauty which ancient literature seemed to disclose to the men of the Renascence, we can see in many parts of his writings, in Faust's address to Helen, in Gaveston's description of the sports at Court, in the opening of *Queen Dido*; but the fullest proof of it is the fragment of *Hero and Leander*. Beaumont wrote a *Salmacis and Hermaphroditus*, Shakespeare a *Venus and Adonis*, but both found their true vehicle in the drama. Marlowe's poem not only stands far above one of these tales, and perhaps above both, but it stands on a level with his plays; and it is hard to say what excellence he might not have reached in the field of narrative verse. The defect of his fragment, the intrusion of ingenious reflections and of those conceits with one of which our selection unhappily terminates, was the fault of his time; its merit is Marlowe's own. It was suggested indeed by the short poem of the Pseudo-Musaeus, an Alexandrian grammarian who probably wrote about the end of the fifth century after Christ, and appears to have been translated into English shortly before 1580; but it is in essence original. Written in the so-called heroic verse, it bears no resemblance to any other poem in that metre composed before, nor, perhaps, is there any written since which decidedly recalls it, unless it be *Endymion*. 'Pagan' it is in a sense, with the Paganism of the Renascence: the more pagan the better, considering the subject. Nothing of the deeper thought of the time, no 'looking before and after,' no worship of a Gloriana or hostility to an Acrasia, interferes with its frank acceptance of sensuous beauty and joy. In this, in spite of much resemblance, it differs from *Endymion*, the spirit of which is not fruition but unsatisfied longing, and in which the vision of a vague and lovelier ideal is always turning the enjoyment of the moment into gloom. On the other hand, a further likeness to Keats may perhaps be traced in the pictorial quality of Marlowe's descriptions. His power does not lie in catching in the aspect of objects or scenes those deeper suggestions which appeal to an imagination stored with human experience as well as sensitive to colour and form; for this power does not necessarily result in what we call pictorial writing; but his soul seems to be in his eyes, and he renders the beauty which appeals directly to sense as vividly as he apprehends it. Nor is this the case with the description of objects alone. The same complete absorption of imagination in sense appears in Marlowe's account of the visit to Hero's tower. This passage is in a high degree voluptuous, but it is not prurient. For prurience is the sign of an unsatisfied imagination, which, being unable to present its object adequately, appeals to extraneous and unpoetic feelings. But Marlowe's imagination is completely satisfied; and therefore, though he has not a high theme (for it is a mere sensuous joy that is described, and there is next to no real emotion in the matter), he is able to make fine poetry of it. Of the metrical qualities of the poem there can be but one opinion. Shakespeare himself, who quoted a line of it, never reached in his own narrative verse a music so spontaneous and rich, a music to which Marlowe might have applied his own words—

> That calls my soul from forth his living seat
> To move unto the measures of delight.

Marlowe had many of the makings of a great poet: a capacity for Titanic conceptions which might with time have become Olympian; an imaginative vision which was already intense and must have deepened and widened; the gift of style and of making words sing; and a time to live in such as no other generation of English poets has known. It is easy to reckon his failings. His range of perception into life and character was contracted: of comic power he shows hardly a trace, and it is incredible that he should have written the Jack Cade scene of *Henry VI*; no humour or tenderness relieves his pathos; there is not any female character in his plays whom we remember with much interest; and it is not clear that he could have produced songs of the first order. But it is only Shakespeare who can do everything; and Shakespeare did not die at twenty-nine. That Marlowe must have stood nearer to him than any other dramatic poet of that time, or perhaps of any later time, is probably the verdict of nearly all students of the drama. His immediate successors knew well what was lost in him; and from the days of Peele, Jonson, Drayton, and Chapman, to our own, the poets have done more than common honour to his memory.

A. H. BULLEN
From "Introduction" to
The Works of Christopher Marlowe
1885, Volume 1, pp. xviii–xlv

It is difficult to over-estimate the importance of *Tamburlaine* in the history of the English drama. To appreciate how immensely Marlowe outdistanced at one bound all his predecessors, the reader must summon courage to make himself acquainted with such productions as *Gorboduc*, *The Misfortunes of Arthur*, and *Sir Clyomon and Sir Clamydes*. He will then perceive how real is Marlowe's claim to be regarded as the father of the English drama. That the play is stuffed with bombast, the exaggeration is carried sometimes to the verge of burlesque, no sensible critic will venture to deny. But the characters, with all their stiffness, have life and movement. The

Scythian conqueror, 'threatening the world in high astounding terms,' is an impressive figure. There is nothing mean or trivial in the invention. The young poet threw into his work all the energy of his passionate nature. He did not pause to polish his lines, to correct and curtail; but was borne swiftly onward by the wings of his imagination. The absence of chastening restraint is felt throughout; and, indeed, the beauty of some of the most majestic passages is seriously marred by the introduction of a weak or ill-timed verse. Take the following passage from the First Part:—

> Nature that framed us of four elements,
> Warring within our breasts for regiment,
> Doth teach us all to have aspiring minds:
> Our souls, whose faculties can comprehend
> The wondrous architecture of the world,
> And measure every wandering planet's course,
> Still climbing after knowledge infinite,
> And always moving as the restless spheres,
> Wills us to wear ourselves and never rest
> Until we reach the ripest fruit of all,
> That perfect bliss and sole felicity,
> The sweet fruition of an earthly crown.

The ear exults in the sonorous march of the stately verse as each successive line paces more majestically than the preceding; but what cruel discomfiture awaits us at the end! It seems almost inconceivable that the poet should have spoilt so magnificent a passage by the lame and impotent conclusion in the last line. For the moment we are half inclined to think that he is playing some trick upon us; that he has deliberately led up to an anti-climax in order to enjoy the malicious satisfaction of laughing at our irritation. The noble and oft-quoted passage on Beauty (1 *Tamburlaine*, v. 1) is injured considerably by the diffuseness of the context. Marlowe seems to have blotted literally nothing in this earliest play. . . .

Before leaving *Tamburlaine* a word must be said about Marlowe's introduction of blank verse. Unrhymed verse of ten syllables had been employed both for epic and dramatic purposes before Marlowe's time. The Earl of Surrey, in his translation of Books ii. and iv. of Virgil's *Aeneid*, has been the first to transplant the metre from Italy. Surrey was a charming sonneteer and graceful lyrist; but it would be absurd to claim that his translations from Virgil afford the slightest hint of the capabilities of blank verse. It is impossible to select six consecutive lines that satisfy the ear. Without freedom or swing the procession of languid lines limps feebly forward. When we come to *Gorboduc*, the first dramatic piece in which rhyme was discarded, the case is no better. Little advance, or rather none at all, has been made in rendering the verse more flexible. Misled by classical usage, all writers before Marlowe aimed at composing blank verse on the model of Greek iambics. Confusing accent with quantity, they regarded accentuated and unaccentuated syllables as respectively long and short. Hence the aim was to end each line with a strongly accentuated syllable, immediately preceded by one that was unaccentuated; in the rest of the line unaccentuated and accentuated syllables occurred alternately. Then, to complete the monotony, at the end of each verse came a pause, which effectually excluded all freedom of movement. This state of things Marlowe abolished. At a touch of the master's hand the heavy-gaited verses took symmetry and shape. That the blank verse of *Tamburlaine* left much to be desired in the way of variety is, of course, undeniable. Its sonorous music is fitted rather for epic than dramatic purposes. The swelling rotundity of the italicised lines in the following passage recalls the magnificent rhythm of Milton:—

The galleys and those pilling brigandines
That yearly sail to the Venetian Gulf,
And hover in the Straits for Christians' wreck,
Shall lie at anchor in the Isle Asant
Until the Persian fleet and men-of-war,
Sailing along the oriental sea,
Have fetched about the Indian continent
Even from Persepolis to Mexico.

Later, Marlowe learned to breathe sweetness and softness into his 'mighty line,'—to make the measure that had thundered the threats of Tamburlaine falter the sobs of a broken heart. . . .

But on the strength of internal evidence we might go further, and say that the comic scenes [in *The Jew*] are in no instance by Marlowe. As far as possible, it is well to avoid theorising, but I must state my conviction that Marlowe never attempted to write a comic scene. The Muses had dowered him with many rare qualities—nobility and tenderness and pity—but the gift of humour, the most grateful of all gifts, was withheld. To excite 'tears and laughter for all time' was given to Shakespeare alone; but all the Elizabethan dramatists, if we except Ford and Cyril Tourneur, combined to some extent humour with tragic power. The Elizabethan stage rarely tolerated any tragedy that was unrelieved by scenes of mirth. It was in vain to plead the example of classical usage, to point out that the Attic tragedians never jested. Fortunately the 'understanding' pittites were not learned in the classical tongues; they applauded when they were satisfied, and they 'mewed' when the play dragged. As the populace in Horace's time clamoured '*media inter carmina,*' for a bear or a boxer, so an Elizabethan audience, when it felt bored or scared, insisted on being enlivened by a fool or a clown. After a little fuming and fretting the poets accepted the conditions; they soon found that the demand of the audience was no outrage upon nature, and that there need be no abruptness in the passage from tears to laughter. And so was realised for the first and last time in the world's history the dream of Socrates; the theory he propounded to Agathon, who was too drunk and drowsy for argument or contradiction, as the dawn broke over that memorable symposium. But Marlowe could not don alternately the buskin and the sock. His fiery spirit walked always on the heights; no ripple of laughter reached him as he scaled the 'high pyramides' of tragic art. But while the poet was pursuing his airy path the actors at the Curtain had to look after their own interests. They knew that though they should speak with the tongues of angels yet the audience would turn a deaf ear unless some comic business were provided. Accordingly they employed some hack-writer, or perhaps a member of their own company, to furnish what was required. How execrably he performed his task is only too plain. . . .

Charles Lamb remarked that 'the reluctant pangs of abdicating royalty in *Edward* furnished hints which Shakespeare scarce improved in his *Richard the Second*; and the death-scene of Marlowe's king moves pity and terror beyond any scene, ancient or modern, with which I am acquainted.' Mr. Swinburne thinks that there is more discrimination of character in Marlowe's play than Shakespeare's; that the figures are more life-like, stand out more clearly as individual personalities. It may also be urged that there is more 'business' in Marlowe's play; that the action is never allowed to flag. The character of the gay, frank, fearless, shameless favourite, Piers Gaveston, is admirably drawn. Even in the presence of death, with the wolfish eyes of the grim nobles bent on him from every side, he loses nothing of his old jauntiness. Marlowe has thoroughly realised this character, and portrayed it in every detail with

consummate ability. Hardly less successful is the character of Young Spenser, the insolent compound of recklessness and craft, posing as the saviour of society, while he stealthily pursues his own selfish projects. In his drawing of female characters, Marlowe showed no great skill or variety. The features in some of his portraits are either so dim as to present no likeness at all, or they are excessively unlovely. Isabella is a vain, selfish woman, without any strength of character. She is hurt at finding herself neglected by the king, but the wound is only surface-deep. She acquiesces passively in her husband's death, and with equal indifference would have sacrificed her paramour. Edward, with all his weakness, is not wholly ignoble. In all literature there are few finer touches than when after recounting his fearful suffering and privations in the dungeon, he gathers his breath for one last kingly utterance:—

Tell Isabel, the queen, I looked not thus
When for her sake I ran at tilt in France,
And there unhorsed the Duke of Cleremont.

What heart-breaking pathos in those lines! For a moment, as his thoughts travel back across the years, he forgets the squalor of his dungeon and rides blithely beneath the beaming eyes of his lady. It has been objected that the representation of the king's physical suffering oversteps the limit of dramatic art. Euripides was censured by ancient critics for demeaning tragedy; but to-day the judgment of readers is on the side of Euripides, not of his critics. Besides, if Euripides erred, Sophocles erred also. The physical suffering of Philoctetes excites far more disgust than anything that we find in Euripides. There are those who think that the blinding of Gloster, in *Lear*, surpassed in horror any scene of physical agony enacted on the English stage. But criticism, which fears to raise its voice against Shakespeare, shows no mercy to Shakespeare's contemporaries.

A. W. VERITY

From *The Influence of Christopher Marlowe on Shakespere's Earlier Style*
1886, pp. 28–53

In considering Marlowe's works it is well to remember one thing, that he is the most personal of poets; it is impossible to think of him apart from his plays, and vice versâ. Usually the attempt to read between the lines, as the phrase is, and by so doing to evolve some idea of an author's personality, is not very successful: yet it is a task which some critics find extremely congenial and entertaining. Touchstone's irritating query, 'Hast any philosophy in thee?' is always on their lips when they approach a new work, the presumption in their minds being that the writer must have started with a definite purpose, 'a criticism of life' in some form or other; and this central idea once discovered ought theoretically to reveal in a measure the character of the author, and thus the true seeker is, as it were, personally conducted behind the scenes into the presence of the writer himself. Everyone remembers Schumann's indignant commentary on these acrostic-solvers, who of course almost invariably lose themselves in a maze of conflicting theories till at last 'Metaphysic calls for aid on Sense.' And so long as we deal with the Immortals of literature it must always be so, for the best work is always impersonal. The great poet is not one man, he is, in sympathy, in humanity, a dozen. It is when we come to writers of the second class that we find ourselves on firmer ground. There are some poets whose personality breathes in every line, each work being a revelation of their character, an autobiographical fragment; of such, to take the time-honoured instance, is Byron. Everything he wrote was touched with egotism, and it is this very intrusion of the personal element that lends his best work the sovereign quality of 'sincerity and strength,' which, in Mr Swinburne's words, 'covers all his offences and outweighs all his defects.' Marlowe belonged to this class of writers; for once it is safe to put a poet's work into the critical crucible. Each of his plays can be resolved into the prime conception from which the dramatist started, and each in turn brings us into close contact with the author himself. It is well to keep this in mind in looking at his dramas.

His works may be easily grouped. *Edward II.* stands by itself; it represents the highest development of the poet's genius, it represents too what was practically a new creation of Marlowe's, the genuine historical play. The tragedy of *Dido*, left unfinished at his death, is rather a love poem than a drama, and may be classed with the writer's exquisite *Hero and Leander*, both expressing in a high degree the purely sensuous Italian love of beauty for beauty's sake which was typical of the Renaissance spirit. *The Massacre at Paris* is a mere fragment; the text is so imperfect and corrupt that for purposes of criticism the play is wellnigh useless. We are left with three dramas—representing Marlowe's earlier style, the two parts of *Tamburlaine*, the *Jew of Malta*, and the *Tragical History of Dr Faustus*. They may be treated together, since each was written in conformity with a dramatic theory peculiar to Marlowe. Various writers have pointed out[1]—what indeed is sufficiently obvious—that each of these plays is a one-character drama. In *Tamburlaine* we have the great conqueror, who towers above all rivals; in the *Jew of Malta* we have Barabas, the prototype of Shylock; in *Faustus*, the magician of mediæval legend. In each case the interest centres round the one overshadowing personality; there are practically no minor characters. And if each play resolves itself into a single character, so each of these characters is the personification of a single prevailing passion. Tamburlaine represents the lust of dominion: here is the expression of his creed, given in some of the finest lines the poet ever wrote—

> The thirst of reign and sweetness of a crown
> That caused the eldest son of heavenly Ops
> To thrust his doting father from his chair,
> And place himself in the empyreal heavens,
> Moved me to manage arms against thy state.
> Nature that framed us of four elements,
> Warring within our breasts for regiment,
> Doth teach us all to have aspiring minds:
> Our souls, whose faculties can comprehend
> The wondrous architecture of the world[2],
> And measure every planet's wandering course,
> Still climbing after knowledge infinite,
> And always moving, as the restless spheres,
> Wills us to wear ourselves, and never rest,
> Until we reach the ripest fruit of all,
> That perfect bliss and sole felicity,
> The sweet fruition of an earthly crown.
>   (ii. 7, 11–29, Part 1.)

In these lines we have the gist of the whole play; and it is the same in the *Jew of Malta*. There may be a second plot—the love story of Abigail and her death—but primarily the interest centres in Barabas, and Barabas is the thirst for gold personified. Here is the outburst of his grief, when he believes that he has lost all:

> My gold! My gold! and all my wealth is gone!
> You partial heavens, have I deserved this plague?

> What! will you thus oppose me, luckless stars?
> To make me desperate in my poverty?
> And knowing me impatient in distress.
> Think me so mad as I will hang myself,
> That I may vanish o'er the earth in air
> And leave no memory that e'er I was?
> No, I will live.
>   (i. 2, 258–266.)

And so he schemes to recover his possessions, and when, in the next act, Abigail flings down the bags to him, the intensity of his passionate joy is almost fiendish and uncanny.

>   O my girl!
> My gold, my fortune, my felicity,
> Strength to my soul, death to my enemy!
> Welcome the first beginner of my bliss!
> O Abigail, Abigail, that I had thee here too!
> Then my desires were fully satisfied.
> But I will practise thy enlargement hence:
> O girl! O gold! O beauty! O my bliss!

Faustus typifies an incomparably nobler passion, the thirst for boundless knowledge. In the prologue to the *Jew of Malta* Machiavel is made to say,

> I count religion but a childish toy,
> And hold there is no sin but ignorance.

That is the philosophy of Faust. He is a very Paracelsus in ambition. Nature shall reveal her secrets to him; he will no longer be bound with the fetters imposed on other men.

In each play, then, it is this all-dominating, over-powering passion that runs like a golden thread of silk through the tangled intricacies of the parts, giving coherence to all, and ensuring harmony of effect. It is in depicting the rise and progress of this central passion that the dramatist expends all the resources of his art.[3] He shows us its beginning, a flame that slowly brightens and broadens until its fire fanned by the wind sweeps mightily onward, devastating all and at last consuming its originator. This peculiarity in Marlowe's earlier plays is undoubtedly a source of weakness. To think of one of Shakspere's greatest tragedies is not to think of a single character; if *Othello* is mentioned, our mind does not recur to Othello alone. The interest is spread over the whole. Each of the dramatis personæ contributes his share to the general effect; they are not mere ciphers moving idly about the scene, as impotent and unreal as the ghosts that gibbered round Odysseus. A great drama is complex; it flashes upon you, like the facets of a diamond, with a thousand different lights. But it is not so with Marlowe's different plays. Each emits one steady stream of scorching fire; no more. To recall to mind *The Tragical History of Dr Faustus*, is to remember the man who to win the world lost his own soul; on the other characters we bestow not a thought. And the same is true of the other plays—of *Tamburlaine*, and the *Jew of Malta*. I said above that no poet was more self-revealing than Marlowe. The impress of his personality is stamped on every page with clear, firm lines; for, although the passions which his various characters personify, seem to us at first sight to be distinct, yet if we look closer we find that in reality they are one and the same. They are but different aspects of the all-absorbing passion that burns deep down in the heart of the poet—the flame that feeds on his very soul. And that passion is desire of power. Lust of dominion—lust of wealth—lust of knowledge—they all come to that. Tamburlaine craves for kingship: like the Duke of Guise, he will weary the world with his wars—and why? To conquer is to be powerful, and it is in the exercise of power when won that he delights with a wild pagan joy.

Tamburlaine. Is it not brave to be a king, Techelles?

> Is it not passing brave to be a king,
> And ride in triumph through Persepolis?
>
> *Tech.* O, my lord, 'tis sweet and full of pomp.
>
> *Usum.* To be a king, is half to be a god.

This is the spirit of the play. Again, Barabas loves his gold as he loves his child; it is almost flesh of his flesh. But his passion is not petty; it is no sordid avarice. To Silas Marner, with no faith in man, no trust in God, with the desolation of despair in his heart, his money was the one tiny ray of light and love that shone across the gloom of his life. 'His gold as he hung over it and saw it grow, gathered his power of loving together into a hard isolation like its own.' But Barabas does not amass gold for gold's sake. It is for the power that money brings that he cares, and still more for the revenge it may give him on his enemies.

> Thus trowls our fortune in by land and sea,
> And thus are we on every side enriched.
> These are the blessings promised to the Jews
> And herein was old Abraham's happiness:
> What more may heaven do for earthly man
> Than thus to pour out plenty in their laps,
> Ripping the bowels of the earth for them,
> Making the seas their servants, and the winds
> To drive their substance with successful blasts?
> Who hateth me but for my happiness?
> Or who is honoured now but for his wealth?
> Rather had I a Jew be hated thus,
> Than pitied in a Christian poverty.
>
> (i. I, 102–115.)

This extract may give some idea of the feeling—'Money is power'—that, not perhaps formulated in any one passage, nevertheless breathes throughout the whole play[4]. And if Tamburlaine and Barabas have their conception of power and, each in his own way, strive to compass their ideal, still more is this the case with Faustus. Knowledge is his end and aim;

> But on her forehead sits a fire:
>   She sets her forward countenance
>   And leaps into the future chance
> Submitting all things to desire.
>
> Half-grown as yet, a child and vain,
>   She cannot fight the fear of death.
>   What is she, cut from love and faith,
> But some wild Pallas from the brain
>
> Of Demons? fiery hot to burst
>   All barriers in her onward race
>   For power.

These lines[5] are a perfect epitome of the Faust legend, as treated by Marlowe. It is at power that Faustus grasps, and knowledge, he thinks, can give it—but not ordinary knowledge. He has tried every science—he has exhausted them all. He passes them in review, and dismisses each with a sad, 'Why, Faustus, hast thou not attained that end?' And yet his longing has not been satisfied: he is 'but Faustus, and a man.' A man! what bitter irony for one, who has the ambition of a God. And then the thought comes that magic will put the world at his feet.—It intoxicates him. He can resist no more. He agrees to seal the compact, bids Mephistopheles return to Lucifer, and there, standing on the very brink of the precipice, is lost in one more vision of what the future will bring.

> *Faustus.* Go and return to mighty Lucifer,
>   And meet me in my study at midnight,
>   And then resolve me of thy master's mind.
>
> *Mephist.* I will, Faustus.
>
> *Faustus.* Had I as many souls as there be stars,
>   I'd give them all for Mephistophilis.

> By him I'll be great emperor of the world
> And make a bridge thorough the moving air,
> To pass the ocean with a band of men:
> I'll join the hills that bind the Afric shore
> And make that country continent to Spain,
> And both contributary to my crown.
> The emperor shall not live but by my leave,
> Nor any potentate of Germany.

'L'amour de l'impossible'—to borrow Mr Symonds' phrase—is the keynote of these three plays. It is likewise the keynote of the poet's own character. One can trace in all he wrote the presence impalpable, indefinable, of a will for ever warring with convention. He pants to be free. There is nothing petty in Marlowe's poetry. He soars aloft, 'affecting thoughts coequal with the clouds.' He reminds one of Shelley—not the 'real Shelley'—but the poet who speaks to us in some of the noblest verse and the noblest prose that our literature contains. Each was in a state of perpetual revolt against the tyranny of social custom, and each might be addressed in Shelley's own lines to William Godwin.

> Mighty eagle, thou that soarest
> O'er the misty mountain forest,
>   And amid the light of morning,
> Like a cloud of glory hiest,
> And when night descends, defiest
> The embattled tempest's warning.

We see the revolutionary bent of Marlowe's nature in the very fact that he scornfully turned aside from the path trodden by previous dramatists, and boldly struck out a new course.

> What glory is there in a common good
> That hangs for every peasant to achieve?

is the spoken thought of the Duke of Guise, and it is no less the soliloquy of the poet. He blindly stretches his hands to heaven, and clutches at something 'that flies beyond his reach.' He is like the men round him, who hardly knew what they could, and could not, do. The world had drunk too deep of the Renaissance doctrines[6]. Men were intoxicated with an unknown sensation of life, and power, and passion, pulsating in their hearts. They yearned after—they hardly knew what—and Marlowe was the incarnation of this spirit. We know very little about his life, but that little strengthens the conviction that his powers, though great, were undisciplined, uncontrolled. He has scarcely any sense of their limitation. His earlier work is lacking in proportion; it is bitter, extreme, exaggerated. Tradition accuses him of Atheism. Probably Marlowe was no more an atheist than Shelley was[7]. *Faustus* surely is a sufficient answer to this charge. The man who could paint with such terrible truth the desolation of despair, the agony of repentance, not merely fear, that sweeps over the soul of Faustus, was assuredly not devoid of religious emotion. But that Marlowe hated the Church as the Church was then constituted, that he hated its dogma, its tyranny, its system, seems to me beyond all doubt. There are passages in his plays that breathe the deepest loathing of Christianity; passages, where the bitterness of the speaker seems out of all proportion to the dramatic requirements of the context. At such times we seem to catch the ring of the poet's own voice.

To emphasize in this way the deeply personal element in Marlowe's work is not, I think, superfluous. It is surely remarkable that his first three plays should contain only three strongly-drawn characters, and that each of these should be guided by a passion, which in turn we find to have been the prevailing passion of the poet's own nature. For to say this is equivalent to saying that Tamburlaine, Barabas and Faustus are merely different aspects of the poet himself. And yet it is so. To conceive them he had to draw upon himself; he appealed to his own emotional experience. They are not the offspring of a purely creative imagination—they are rather projections from the poet's own inmost soul. Marlowe, in other words, is not in these three plays the spectator *ab extra* who conceives by the sheer force of imaginative genius a great character,—great in its goodness, or the reverse—with which he has no personal sympathy; he is the character. His passions are the passions of Faustus. There is no gulf between the poet and the beings whom he paints in his poetry; he is merged in them. Mr Furnivall in his valuable introduction to the *Leopold Shakspere* has some remarkable words on this point. He says, "As to the question how far we are justified in assuming that Shakspere put his own feelings—himself—into his own plays, some men scorn the notion; ask you triumphantly which of his characters represents him, assert that he himself is in none of them, but sits apart, serene, unruffled himself by earthly passion, making his puppets move. I believe on the contrary that all the deepest and greatest work of an artist, playwright, orator, painter, poet, is based on personal experience, on his own emotions and passions, and not merely on his observations of things or feelings outside him, on which his fancy and imagination work. . . . He himself (Shakspere), his own nature and life are in all his plays." As applied to Shakspere, this doctrine is at least unusual. If ever there was a poet with a supreme faculty for conceiving situations into which experience had never brought him—of drawing characters as unlike his own as Lear is unlike Falstaff—of being swayed, as it were, in the persons of these characters by passions which had no part or share in his own nature—that poet, one would have thought, was Shakspere. However, as far as the theory refers to Shakspere it is no task of ours to examine it. Many people would be inclined to dissent from the general proposition, that the greatest work of a great artist is based on personal experience. But so far as Marlowe is concerned, the passage quoted above admirably expresses the truth. In *Tamburlaine*, the *Jew of Malta*, and *Faustus*, Marlowe does not display the highest type of imagination. He gives us three characters; each character is, more or less, the poet himself, and each is finely drawn. But when he goes outside himself, and has recourse to the purely imaginative faculty—whatever it be—he fails completely. The other dramatis personæ are mere shadows, *simulacra modis pallentia miris*. Who, as a writer[8] on the subject fairly remarks, ever realized Cosroe, Mycetes, and the rest? To the last Marlowe never succeeded in drawing a female character. Greene was the first to give the stage women at all comparable to those of Shakspere. Again, Marlowe was deficient, I think, in the lower form of imagination. He had little inventiveness; he had none of Greene's inexhaustible fancy. Greene was never at a loss; he was full of the playwright's resource; he could always devise some ingenious scene. But Marlowe in his earlier plays shows a remarkable poverty in this respect. When he attempts a striking situation, his work is crude and rough-hewn. His effects, to vary the metaphor, are too often achieved by simple dashes of paint on the canvas.

To turn now to the first of the three works previously discussed. The two parts of *Tamburlaine*, like the two parts of *Henry IV.*, form a complete drama in ten acts, and may fairly be treated as a single play. The faults of this play are obvious; they are in the main such as would naturally spring from the peculiarities of Marlowe's dramatic method. *Tamburlaine* is not, properly speaking, a drama at all; it is rather a series of impressive scenes. We have no plot, no complexity of action, no interdependence and balance of parts. It does not begin at

any definite point, and dramatically there is no very definite reason why it should end. Tamburlaine at the outset intended to conquer the world; by the close of the tenth act he cannot, like Alexander, complain that his conquests are exhausted. Instead therefore of his death, we might have expected a third part, and so on; except indeed that of the subsidiary characters[9] few reach even the tenth act. Whereas in a play of Shakspere's we have a dozen threads that run in and out, and half tangled, half unravelled, are in the end gathered up by the dramatist and united, there is in *Tamburlaine* but a solitary streak of gold. This slender thread of interest—at times drawn perilously fine—that keeps the whole together, is of course Tamburlaine's lust of power. His passion for conquest is the *leitmotif* of the piece. There is no other continuous interest, because there are no other characters. There are indeed fine episodes, such as the death of Bajazeth (Part I. v.i.) the love scenes with Zenocrate, and the death scene of Zenocrate, Part II. ii. 3. But it is on Tamburlaine himself that the action of the whole drama turns, from the first scene where we hear him exclaim, 'I am a lord, for so my deeds shall prove'—to the last, where, tracing out 'the world of ground' that lies westward he complains that he must 'die and this unconquerèd.' The poet was determined that the central figure should arrest attention, and indisputably he has succeeded in drawing a figure of extraordinary effectiveness, the very embodiment of Titanic will and force. In the second act Tamburlaine is described.

> Of stature tall, and straightly fashioned,
> Like his desire, life upward and divine,
> So large of limbs, his joints so strongly knit,
> Such breadth of shoulders as might mainly bear
> Old Atlas' burden; twist his manly pitch,
> A pearl, more worth than all the world, is placed,
> Wherein by curious sovereignty of art
> Are fixed his piercing instruments of sight,
> Whose fiery circles bear encompassèd
> A heaven of heavenly bodies in their spheres,
> That guide his steps and actions to the throne,
> Where honour sits invested royally;
> Pale of complexion, wrought in him with passion,
> Thirsting with sovereignty and love of arms:
> His lofty brows in folds do figure death,
> And in their smoothness amity and life.
> About them hangs a knot of amber hair,
> Wrappèd in curls, as fierce Achilles' was,
> On which the breath of heaven delights to play,
> Making it dance with wanton majesty.
> His arms and fingers long and sinewy;
> Betokening valour and excess of strength,
> In every part proportioned like a man,
> Should make the world subdued to Tamburlaine.

This might be a description of some picture by Rembrandt. We seem to see the face of the great world-conqueror lit up with one of those dazzling streams of light that Rembrandt could introduce into his portraits with such infinite effect. The reader, as distinguished from the spectator, is able to realise the poet's conception of Tamburlaine in every detail, and it is this conception alone that gives coherence, or something like it, to a series of unconnected pageants. Remove Tamburlaine and the ten acts are simple chaos. That this should be so, that the play should depend entirely on the presence on the stage of one character, that there should be no balance of parts, no relief, no evolution of thought, nothing, in short, but the progress of the central figure as conqueror, is surely a great dramatic flaw. Another fault in Tamburlaine is the extravagance of style[9a], shown in two ways. In the first place there are 'the huffing braggart lines,' which 'Mine Ancient' in *Henry IV.* vainly endeavours to imitate. On this point indeed Pistol is the best critic, as he was one of the first, and really there is nothing more to be said on the subject. It would be superfluous to insist on the mere Midsummer madness of such speeches as that of Tamburlaine in the second part (iv. 4), introduced by the famous line, 'Holla, ye pampered jades of Asia.' After all Marlowe was very young when he wrote this play, and relying on the truth of a familiar epigram we may say that even the youngest poets must make mistakes. Such faults are exactly those of an unformed style. Moreover, as Collier suggests[10], Marlowe had to satisfy his audience; he could not afford at the outset to soar clean over their heads. He had taken away their rhyme, and as a substitute gave them 'high astounding terms.' The extravagance of language in *Tamburlaine* is balanced by extravagance of incident. 'Schiller,' says Coleridge, 'has the material sublime; to produce an effect he sets you a whole town on fire, and throws infants with their mothers into the flames, or locks up a father in an old tower. But Shakspere drops a handkerchief, and the same, or a greater effect, follows.' This is exactly applicable to Marlowe. When the poet would move pity, a whole troop of maidens must be put to the sword; Zenocrate dies, and the flames of Larissa can alone quench the tears of Tamburlaine.

It is this *ferocité* in tone and treatment that repels French critics of our Elizabethan literature. It is the waste of energy, the squandering of power, that a 'literature of genius' according to Mr Matthew Arnold, inevitably entails. Given a literary Court of Judgment like the French Academy, such excesses would be impossible; but then such an innovation as the introduction of blank verse would have been equally out of the question. We must balance the good with the evil. There are many faults in *Tamburlaine*, but there are also astonishing merits. To begin with—the play is full, from the first scene to the last, of the noblest poetry—poetry, that is 'simple, sensuous, impassioned,' that sweeps the reader along in its resistless course. It is verse of the kind that Wordsworth called 'inevitable;' every line fell into its place without the poet knowing how it came there. Alfred de Musset, according to tradition, would only write by fits and starts, and then with a blaze of light about him. One can imagine Marlowe working in the same way, throwing off scene after scene at white heat, never stopping to erase a single line. Hence, while much that he wrote bears the clearest marks of the author's haste and carelessness, the good—and the great body of Marlowe's poetry is supremely good—has the true ring of absolute spontaneity. The poetry comes welling up from the depths of the poet's heart—no tiny thread, whose every drop must be husbanded—but a rich, full stream. And poetry such as *Tamburlaine* contains was new to the stage. The melody was intoxicating. Putting aside for the present the question of metre, where in the contemporary drama shall we turn, with any hope of finding such lines as the following—sonorous as the notes of an organ, rhythmic as the ebb and flow of the sea-waves?

Tamburlaine.

Now walk the angels on the walls of heaven
As sentinels to warn the immortal souls,
To entertain divine Zenocrate.
Apollo, Cynthia, and the ceaseless lamps,
That gently looked upon this loathsome earth,
Shine downward now no more, but deck the
    heavens
To entertain divine Zenocrate.
The crystal springs, whose taste illuminates

Refinèd eyes with an eternal light,
Like trièd silver, run through Paradise,
To entertain divine Zenocrate.
The Cherubins and holy Seraphins,
That sing and play before the King of kings,
Use all their voices and their instruments,
To entertain divine Zenocrate.
And in the sweet and curious harmony,
The God that tunes this music to our souls,
Holds out his hands in highest majesty,
To entertain divine Zenocrate.
Then let some holy trance convey my
    thoughts
Up to the palace of the empyreal heaven
That this my life may be as short to me,
As are the days of sweet Zenocrate.
                                        (Part II. ii. 4.)

This is poetry without 'the difference.' Again, could Greene, or Peele, or Kydd, have written the dying speech of Zenocrate in the same scene? . . .

The English stage had never rung to the rhythm of such periods. Against verse like this there could be no appeal.

'His raptures were
All air and fire',

says Drayton in the oft-quoted lines on Marlowe, and these simple words exactly sum up the poetical qualities which made *Tamburlaine* at the time of its appearance unique and epoch-making. It contained more genuine poetry than all previous dramas put together, from the first Miracle-Play down to the last piece of rhymed fustian, that Nash, or Peele, or Kydd, may have brought out, while Marlowe was busy on the work which was to raise him high over their heads.

And if Marlowe rendered the stage a signal service in showing that the drama might be, and indeed thenceforth was bound to be, in the widest sense poetical, he did scarcely less good in definitely fixing the form or structure, which the drama should in the future adopt. He brings us in *Tamburlaine* straight into the presence of his characters. There are none of the ingenious contrivances of which contemporary plays are full, and which, as a rule, defeat their own end. These devices were numerous enough; to see what they were, and how supremely ridiculous, we need only turn to the works of Greene and Peele, next to Marlowe the foremost writers of the time. In Greene's *James IV.* we have a play within a play, Bohan and Oberon keeping up a running commentary on the course of the piece. The *Looking for London and England*[11], is a perfect storehouse of crude incongruities. Oseas periodically appears to point the moral; a good and an evil angel are introduced, the latter amongst other things tempting the usurer to kill himself, even 'offering the knife and rope,' as the stage-directions quaintly inform us, and yet one more absurdity from the same piece, a burning sword is let down from heaven. *The Comical History of King Alphonsus* begins and ends with an assemblage of the Muses, and throughout Venus acts as a kind of chorus; in *Friar Bacon and Friar Bungay* the introduction of the supernatural is managed rather clumsily. Peele is quite as great an offender in these matters as Greene. The *Arraignment of Paris* is confessedly classical in subject and style, but even in a classical piece the entrance of Ate ('from the lowest hell') with a prologue in her hand seems a gratuitous absurdity. In *Sir Clyomon and Clamydes*[12] there are personifications of Rumour and Providence, not indeed that anything could possibly add to the faults of a piece of which one can only say that in point of dulness it is a case of Eclipse first and the rest nowhere. The *Old Wives' Tale* deserves considerate handling as having not improbably suggested the idea of Milton's *Comus*; moreover it contains some pleasant scenes. But, like *James IV.*, it is a play within a play and the device in the hands of Peele does not succeed. In *David and Bethsabe* we have a regular chorus; in the *Battle of Alcazar* the action is eked out by the help of a Presenter, a Dumb-show, and Hercules and Jonah. Finally in *Edward I.* an earthquake takes place by special request and gets rid of the Queen for an act or two, though she subsequently reappears through a *deus ex machina*-device which the dramatist does not stop to elucidate. All these artifices were mechanical and utterly clumsy, but none the less playwrights employed them as part of their legitimate dramatic machinery. Marlowe brushed them on one side, and rightly, for such contrivances can only produce a general effect of incongruity. No doubt some of the devices were effective enough, if sparingly used. In the *Winter's Tale*, for instance, the chorus is indispensable, and the same may be said of *Henry V*. Similarly *A Midsummer Night's Dream*—not to mention *Hamlet* and the *Taming of a Shrew*—shows us what admirable effects may be attained by putting a play inside a play. But when such shifts were employed continually careless and incongruous work was the result, and everything that stands outside the main course of a play tends to create a feeling of unreality, precisely the danger against which a good dramatist guards. Hence it was an immense gain that in *Tamburlaine* the audience were brought at the outset into the presence of the dramatis personæ, that the action of the play developed naturally, that no chorus trotted in and out at odd moments, that in a word the piece possessed the primary elements of naturalness and reality.

We may say, then, that Marlowe in giving poetry a place on the stage, and in laying down sound principles of dramatic structure, did no small service to the drama. But there is another point in *Tamburlaine*. The poet was trying a great experiment, and it was essential to the success of this attempt that the material out of which his play was constructed should possess the strongest elements of popularity; he was bound to interest the spectators. His choice of a subject was admirable. The story of Tamburlaine is heroic, romantic, one that would naturally seize the attention of a large audience. The very extravagance of the piece—Tamburlaine's thirst for power—his sacrifice of all, even of his child, to the passion of his life, admitted of the sensational, melodramatic treatment that satisfied the craving for strong excitement natural to an English audience. He tells us in the prologue what we have to expect—

'We'll lead you to the stately tent of war,
Where you shall hear the Scythian Tamburlaine:
Threatening the world with high, astounding terms,
And scourging kingdoms with his conquering sword.
View but his picture in this tragic glass
And then applaud his fortune as you please.'

This is the poet's promise, and it is amply fulfilled. After *Tamburlaine* there could be no question of any continuation of the Religious, or Classical drama. Both were routed, and still more important, like 'jigging veins' and 'the conceits of clownage' were likewise swept on one side.

'Marlowe was trying a great experiment.' Like Polyphemus, who thoughtfully reserved Odysseus to the end of his banquet as a choice morsel, I have kept this point—the introduction of blank verse—to the last. Few questions in English literature are more interesting than the history of blank verse. The honour of having first employed this metre for dramatic purposes is usually given to Sackville and Norton; I think the credit belongs entirely to Marlowe.

Notes

1. No one more successfully than Professor Dowden, *Fortnightly Review*, January 1870.
2. 'The wondrous architecture of the world'—and yet Schlegel could not understand what Ben Jonson meant by 'Marlowe's mighty line'! though Marlowe might have been the 'better spirit' of whom Shakspeare himself wrote:

    'Was it the proud full sail of his great verse,

    . . .

    That did my ripe thoughts in my brain inhearse.'
3. Peele in his *Honourable Order of the Garter*, or rather in the prologue 'ad Mæcenatem', naturally alludes to Marlowe, and it is to this very capacity of the poet for depicting passion that he refers,

    Unhappy in thine end,
    Marley, the Muses' darling for thy verse,
    Fit to write passions for the souls below,
    If any wretched souls in passion speak.
4. By the 'whole play' I mean of course such parts as can be safely assigned to Marlowe. The true history of this drama we can never know; only one thing is certain, that "the first two acts of the *Jew of Malta* are more vigorously conceived both as to character and circumstance than any other Elizabethan play except those of Shakspeare"—Hallam, *Literature of Europe*, ii. 270. This is high praise, but not I think too high. The poet displays astonishing power and grasp in the first scenes; at the end of the second Act he has a noble plot in hand, and then suddenly he seems to drop the threads, and all is a hopeless maze of grotesque buffoonery. In the fifth Act there is a partial revival of power. In Acts III. and IV. we doubtless have some of Marlowe's work, but it is mixed up with the crudest clownage, the rhyme, we may note, increasing considerably. A sufficient proof of the corruptness of the text is, I think, furnished by the following passage. Ithamore is speaking to Bellamira,—iv. 4, 95–105,

    We will leave this paltry land,
    And sail from hence to Greece, to lovely Greece,
    I'll be thy Jason, thou my golden fleece,
    Where painted carpets o'er the meads are hurled,
    And Bacchus' vineyards overspread the world,
    Where woods and forests go in goodly green,
    I'll be Adonis, thou shalt be Love's queen.
    The meads, the orchards and the primrose lanes,
    Instead of sedge and reeds, bear sugar-canes:
    Thou in these groves, by Dis above,
    Shalt live with me and be my love.

    Is it credible that the poet could have written this pitiable parody of his own incomparable pastoral? Half the poets of the period attempted to imitate the inimitable 'Come live with me'. To copy it, as in the eighteenth century to write an essay on the *Spectator* model, was the Ulysses' bow which everyone tried to draw. It is scarcely probable that Marlowe himself would have dragged into his play the jingling jargon given above, ineffably worse than the worst of the avowed imitations of his lyric. The writer, I imagine, inserted them as an easy way of palming off his own 'jigging wits' as Marlowe's work. The average spectator would catch the last line and be deluded into the belief that the whole act was by Marlowe. The lyric is parodied in precisely the same way in *Lust's Dominion*, for the same reason.
5. *In Memoriam*, Canto CXIV.
6. Cf. *Shakspere's Predecessors*, p. 629.
7. Cf. Mr Bullen's *Introduction*, LXVII.–VIII. Meres, in *Palladis Tamia* says, 'As Jodelle, a French tragical poet, being an epicure and an atheist, made a pitiful end, so our tragical poet Marlowe, for his epicurism and atheism, had a tragical death.' Mr Bullen and Dyce quote similar evidence.
8. *Quarterly Review*, October, 1885.
9. The list of deaths in *Tamburlaine* is almost as formidable as the catalogue drawn up by Mr Ruskin in his criticism on *Bleak House*, e.g. Part I. ii. 7, Cosroe dies—iii. 2, Argier—v. I, Bajazeth and Zabina—Soldan of Egypt. Part II, ii. 3, Sigismund—ii. 4, Zenocrate—iii. 4, Captain of the Fort—iv. 2, Calyphas—iv. 3, Olympia—v. 1, Governor of Babylon—v. 3, Tamburlaine.

9a. If the introduction to the golden age of Elizabethan literature was marked by exaggeration of style, the silver age, the age of Tourneur and others, is open to the same charge. Cf. Mr Edmund Gosse's remarks on this point, *Shakespeare to Pope*, p. 29. The explanation is obvious. The extravagance of those who precede the great period is the extravagance of inexperience; the extravagance of those who follow a Shakspere is that of imitation. The first class of writers have no models to guide them: the second class have models, whose greatness they only parody in their attempts to reproduce it.

10. iii. 117.

11. Probably, however, Lodge was responsible for the greater part of this terrible 'Morality'. Dyce, *Greene and Peele*, p. 32.

12. Is it quite clear that this piece was by Peele? Mr Dyce says 'On the title-page of a copy of this play a MS. note in a very old hand attributes it to Peele, and I have no doubt rightly.' The evidence, as Mr Symonds says, does not seem very conclusive; there is one small point worth noticing. Some dramatists—notably Greene, as Mr Richard Grant White pointed out in discussing the *Henry VI. Parts II. and III.* question—are very fond of the peculiar idiom 'for to' with an infinitive. Peele does not often employ it: there are only scattered instances in his works, e.g. two in the *Old Wives' Tale*, three in the *Arraignment of Paris*. In *Sir Clyomon and Sir Clamydes*—a very long piece it is true—I have noted over 70 examples.

HAVELOCK ELLIS
"Christopher Marlowe"
The Best Plays of the Old Dramatists: Christopher Marlowe, ed. Havelock Ellis
1887, pp. xxix–xlviii

Early in the sixteenth century Erasmus, accompanied by Colet, visited Canterbury. Long afterwards he remembered the cathedral and its vast towers that rise into the sky "so as to strike awe even at a distant approach," the sweet music of the bells heard from afar, the "spacious majesty" of the newly completed nave. Here, fifty years later, was born Christopher, sometime called Kit, Marlowe.[1]

Meanwhile the spirit of Erasmus, and still more the ruder spirit of Colet, had heralded a revolutionary influx of new life. At the head of the movement was set by Providence, in a mood of Rabelaisian gaiety, the figure of Henry VIII. Like another Tamburlaine, Henry VIII. had carried off the rich treasures of Canterbury, the gold and the jewels, in six-and-twenty carts. The stream of pilgrims no longer passed along the familiar roads; nothing remained of the shrine of St. Thomas but the bare stones, much as we see them now, worn away by the adoration of so many ages. All that was long ago; in those days events came fast, and Elizabethan men had a trick of speaking of the near past as remote and antique. On the 26th day of February, 1564, according to the register of the parish church of St. George the Martyr, "was christened Christofer, the sonne of John Marlowe."[2]

We cannot tell the boy's dreams among the Kentish hills and fields, or beneath the jewelled windows of the great church in the city that not only still bore about it the lustre of its former sanctity, but was also the chief halting-place of princes and ambassadors who journeyed from the continent to the court of Elizabeth. Perhaps these things touched the youth little; his own life was too vivid to be concerned much with the antique sanctities at which Colet had laughed. Nor had he mixed largely with men; he rarely describes the actual external world of men and women; he had little of Ben Jonson's precise observation, and nothing of Shakespeare's gentle laughter. But every page he wrote reveals a peculiarly intense full-blooded inner life, the quintessence of youthful desires and youthful dreams. His father, it has now been ascertained, besides being "Clarke of St. Maries," was a shoemaker (Christopher appears to have been the second child and eldest son), and shoemakers have sometimes possessed and left to their children a strangely powerful endowment of idealism. He was educated at the King's School, Canterbury. In March, 1581, he matriculated as Pensioner of Benet College (now Corpus Christi), Cambridge; not having been elected, it seems, to either of the scholarships recently founded at Benet College for King's School boys. In 1583 he obtained his Bachelor's degree.[3]

How were the years after 1583 spent? There is no reliable evidence. It was asserted, on the unsupported evidence of a late and often inaccurate authority, that he became an actor. It has been conjectured,[4] as of Chapman, that he trailed a pike in the Low Countries, like Ben Jonson. The Elizabethan dramatists had the full Renaissance delight in facts and in the grasp of technical detail; they appear to have been nearly as careful about their "documents" as contemporary French novelists; the broad and genial realism of men like Ben Jonson and Middleton and Dekker, sprang from actual contact with the life around them, and young Marlowe's bold spirit may, possibly, have been touched by the impulse of adventure which at that time drew Englishmen into all parts of the world.

About the year 1588, *Tamburlaine* was acted.[5] There is no hesitation in this first work. The young "god of undaunted verse," set free

> From jigging veins of rhyming mother wits,
> And such conceits as clownage keeps in pay,

is at once a perfect master of his "great and thundering speech." *Gorboduc* had been written in blank verse twenty-five years before, and there had been other essays in the use of this new medium of expression; on the whole, however, it had remained cold and artificial and ill-received. It is an immense leap from the tame pedestrian lines of *Gorboduc* to the organised verse, with its large swelling music, of *Tamburlaine*. It was not till later, however, that Marlowe realised the full power and variety of which blank verse is capable. The strong melody of his early verse is simple and little varied; the chief variation being a kind of blank verse couplet, generally introduced near the end of a speech, in which a tumultuous *crescendo* is followed by a grave and severely iambic line:—

> And sooner shall the sun fall from his sphere,
> Than Tamburlaine be slain or overcome.

In its later more developed form, Marlowe's "mighty line" is the chief creation of English literary art; Shakespeare absorbed it, and gave it out again with its familiar cadences in *Romeo and Juliet*, and later with many broad and lovely modifications. It has become the life-blood of our literature; Marlowe's place is at the heart of English poetry, and his pulses still thrill in our verse.

He obtained his material for *Tamburlaine* chiefly from Pedro Mexia's Spanish life of Timur, which was published at Seville in 1543, and translated into Italian, French and English. The English translation, known as Fortescue's *Foreste*, appeared in 1571. Marlowe appears to have supplemented this source by the help of the *Vita Magni Tamerlanis* of Petrus Perondinus. There is abundant evidence to show the swift and extraordinary popularity of the new play, the work of the first great poet who uses our modern English speech; for Spenser was archaic even in his own day. The public were intoxicated with the high astounding terms—"the swelling bombast of a bragging blank verse," as Nash called it—of the Scythian conqueror; not less, perhaps, with the novelty of the play's scenical effects; and for many years a host of writers, including Shakespeare, laughed at those royal and pampered jades of Asia that could not draw but twenty miles a day. The new perfection, however grateful to the old, could not help treading on its heels. For us, however, the wonder of *Tamburlaine*, and of Marlowe's work generally, lies in the vivid and passionate blood, in the intensely imaginative form, with which he has clothed the dry bones of his story. He had no power of *creative* imagination; Shakespeare borrows his stories, but he freely turns them to his own ends; Marlowe nearly always clings to his story, but he makes it alive with his own soaring passion. With the exception of *Edward II.*, which stands alone, Marlowe's dramas are mostly series of scenes held together by the poetic energy of his own dominating personality. He is his own hero, and the sanguinary Scythian utters the deepest secrets of the artist's heart. "What is beauty?" he asks himself.

> If all the pens that ever poets held
> Had fed the feeling of their masters' thoughts,
> And every sweetness that inspired their hearts,
> Their minds, and muses on admirèd themes;
> If all the heavenly quintessence they still
> From their immortal flowers of poesy,
> Wherein, as in a mirror, we perceive
> The highest reaches of a human wit;
> If these had made one poem's period,
> And all combined in beauty's worthiness,
> Yet should there hover in their restless heads
> One thought, one grace, one wonder, at the least,
> Which into words no virtue can digest.

Tamburlaine is a divinely strong and eagerhearted poet, and these words are the key to his career. He sees for ever an unattainable loveliness beckoning him across the world, and how can his ardent blood rest "attemptless, faint and destitute?"

> Our souls, whose faculties can comprehend
> The wondrous architecture of the world,
> And measure every wandering planet's course,
> Still climbing after knowledge infinite,
> And always moving as the restless spheres,
> Will us to wear ourselves, and never rest,
> Until we reach the ripest fruit of all,—

the rest is Scythian bathos. Like Shelley, in some prior state of existence he had loved an Antigone, and he cannot stay. But like Keats also he has an intense feeling for the imaginative show and colour of things, of milk-white steeds laden with the heads of slain men, and

> Besmeared with blood that makes a dainty show,

of naked negroes, of bassoes clothed in crimson silk, of Turkey carpets beneath the chariot wheels, and of a hundred kings or more with "so many crowns of burnished gold." He is fascinated by the vast and mysterious charm of old-world cities, of Bagdad and Babylon and Samarcand.

> "And ride in triumph through Persepolis!"
> Is it not brave to be a king, Techelles?
> Usumcasane and Theridamas,
> Is it not passing brave to be a king,
> "And ride in triumph through Persepolis?"

With this song of radiant joy in the unattainable, young Kit Marlowe, like another Christopher, sailed to discover countries yet unknown, to attain the "sweet fruition" of his crown.

Not long after *Tamburlaine*, appeared the *Tragical History of Doctor Faustus*.[6] The legend of a man who sells his soul to the Devil seems to have appeared about the sixth century, and to have floated down the Middle Ages in many forms; in one form it was used by Calderon in *El Magico Prodigioso*. In the early part of the sixteenth century it became identified with a

Doctor Faustus, who practised necromancy, and was the friend of Paracelsus and Cornelius Agrippa. Conrad Muth the Humanist came across a magician at Erfurt called Georgius Faustus Hemitheus of Heidelberg. Trithemius, in 1506, found a Faustus junior who boasted that if all the works of Plato and Aristotle were burnt he could restore them from memory. Melanchthon knew a Johannes Faustus born at Knütlingen, in Wurtemberg, not far from his own home, who studied magic[7] at Cracow, and afterwards "roamed about, and talked of secret things." The first literary version of the story of Faust was the *Volksbuch* which, published by Spiess in 1587, at Frankfort-on-the-Main, soon after appeared in England as *The History of the Damnable Life and Deserved Death of Dr. John Faustus*. To this translation of the Faust-book Marlowe generally adhered; that is to say, in the incidents of the drama, and their sequence, he followed his authority. The wearisome comic passages, which Marlowe may or may not have written, are copied with special fidelity. Marlowe's play was probably the first dramatisation of the Faust legend; it became immediately popular, not only in England, but abroad. *Faustus*, as well as the *Jew of Malta*, was acted in German by an English company in 1608, during the Carnival, at Graetz, and remained a favourite at Vienna throughout the seventeenth and eighteenth centuries. Faustus was remodelled into a sort of Don Juan—by the Jesuits, it is said, who disliked his scepticism—and in this form he came into Goethe's hands.

Goethe's opinion of Marlowe's *Faustus* we know. He had thought of translating it; when it was mentioned he burst out with an exclamation of praise: 'How greatly it is all planned.' The three chief versions of the old legend—the *Volksbuch* with its medieval story in a Protestant garb, Marlowe's Renaissance rendering and Goethe's modern *Faust*—are all representative. The *Volksbuch* records Faust's history from his birth to his final dismemberment by the Devil, in the calmly epical fashion of a medieval legend; all his clownish tricks are narrated with great enjoyment, but the general atmosphere is moral and Protestant. Marlowe changed the point of view; Faust is no longer an unintelligible magician looked at from the outside, but a living man thirsting for the infinite; the sinner becomes a hero, a Tamburlaine, no longer eager to "ride in triumph through Persepolis," who at the thought of vaster delights has ceased to care for the finite splendours of an earthly crown.

> A god is not so glorious as a king.
> I think the pleasure they enjoy in Heaven
> Cannot compare with kingly joys in earth,

once exclaimed Tamburlaine's follower, Theridamas. Faustus, in his study, realising what magic promises, thinks otherwise:

> Emperors and kings
> Are but obeyèd in their several provinces;
> Nor can they raise the wind or rend the clouds;
> But his dominion that exceeds in this
> Stretcheth as far as doth the mind of man;
> A sound magician is a demigod.

Marlowe's Faustus is not impelled like the Faustus of the legend by the desire of "worldly pleasure," nor, like Goethe's, by the vanity of knowledge; it is power, power without bound, that he desires, all that is in the world, the lust of the flesh and the lust of the eyes and the pride of life,

> —a world of profit and delight
> Of power, of honour, and omnipotence.

This gives him a passionate energy, an emotional sensibility which Goethe's more shifting, sceptical and complex Faust lacks. For Marlowe, also, magic was a possible reality.

A very remarkable characteristic of Marlowe's *Faustus*,

and of his work generally, which has not been sufficiently emphasised,[8] is the absence of material horror. "His raptures were all air and fire." In nothing has he shown himself so much a child of the Renaissance as in this repugnance to touch images of physical ugliness. Perondinus insists on Tamburlaine's lameness, of which Marlowe says no word; the *Volksbuch* is crammed with details concerning the medieval Hell; Marlowe's conception of Hell is loftier than Dante's or Milton's. In reply to the question of Faustus: "How comes it then that thou art out of Hell?" Mephistophilis replies:

> Why this is Hell, nor am I out of it:
> Think'st thou that I who saw the face of God,
> And tasted the eternal joys of Heaven,
> Am not tormented with ten thousand Hells,
> In being deprived of everlasting bliss?

Such reticence as this was entirely out of the line of dramatic tradition, and even the able revisers of the edition of *Faustus* published in 1616, contrived to bring in a plentiful supply of horrors, not only in the account of the death of Faustus, but as a description of Hell—souls toasted on burning forks, broiling live quarters, sops of flaming fire.

I have already mentioned how closely Marlowe adhered to the incidents of the prose *History* and their sequence; such slight additions as he makes are always for the better, as the opening scene in the study, in which Goethe follows him. It is in the selection of the serious incidents from the placid prose narrative that Marlowe's genius for the tragic poetry of intense emotion is especially revealed. Perhaps the passage of Marlowe which most profoundly influenced Shakespeare and other poets is, not the awful and intense scene with which the poem closes, but the address to Helen. The scene that contains this wonderful passage, aflame with impassioned loveliness, corresponds in its bare outlines exactly to that chapter of the prose *History* in which the Doctor, after dinner one day undertakes to bring Helen of Troy before the students. "This lady appeared before them," according to the narrative, "in a most rich gown of purple velvet, costly imbroidered; her hair hanging down loose, as fair as the beaten gold, and of such length that it reached down to her hams, having most amorous cole-black eyes, a sweet and pleasant round face, with lips as red as any cherry; her cheeks of a rose-colour, her mouth small, her neck white like a swan; tall and slender of personage; in sum, there was no imperfect place in her; she looked round about her with a roling hawke's eye, a smiling and wanton countenance, which near-hand inflamed the hearts of all the students, but that they persuaded themselves she was a spirit, which made them lightly pass away such fancies: and thus fair Helena and Faustus went out again one with another." Afterwards Helena becomes his "common concubine and bed-fellow," and has a child called Justus Faustus, who, together with his mother, after the death of Faustus vanished away. That was all. It was to this material that Marlowe set his spirit. In Goethe's great and complex work the story is refined away; Goethe was compelled to treat magic and Hell with irony. Marlowe was the first to spiritualise as well as to dramatise the story; at the same time its substance has not become a symbol merely, as with Goethe, who soon flings himself free of the legend. Marlowe's *Faustus*, revealing the conflicting stress of new and old, remains a chief artistic embodiment of an intellectual attitude dominant at the Renaissance.

The vigorous design and rich free verse of the *Jew of Malta* show a technical advance on *Faustus*. Only Milton, as Mr. Swinburne has somewhere remarked, has surpassed the opening soliloquy of Barabas. But after the second act the play declines; the large conception of the Jew with his immense lust

of wealth only rivalled by his love for his daughter, topples over into harsh and extravagant caricature. Marlowe seems to have worked hastily here, and when Shakespeare, a few years later, took up the same subject, although he treated it in the same spirit, the *Merchant of Venice* by force of his sweetness, humanity and humour, easily rises to a much higher pitch of art.

The *Jew of Malta* shows the transition between Marlowe the youthful tragic poet, with his intense and fascinating personality, and Marlowe the mature dramatist. In *Edward II.* Marlowe reached the summit of his art.

There is little here of that *amour de l'impossible*, which is, as Mr. Symonds observes, his characteristic note; his passionate poetry is subdued with severe self-restraint in a supreme tragic creation. It has long been a custom among critics to compare *Edward II.* with *Richard II.* This is scarcely fair to Shakespeare; the melodramatic and careless murder of Richard cannot be mentioned in presence of the chastened tragedy and highly-wrought pathos of Edward's last days; the whole of Shakespeare's play, with its exuberant eloquence, its facile and diffuse poetry, is distinctly inferior to Marlowe's, both in organic structure and in dramatic characterisation. It was not till ten years later that Shakespeare came near to this severe reticence, these deep and solemn tragic tones.

Besides the three parts of *Henry VI.* in which Marlowe had a considerable share, two short and fragmentary plays, not included in this volume, remain to notice. The *Massacre at Paris* deals, very freely, with contemporary French history, and could not have been an early work;[9] it has come to us in a mutilated and corrupt condition. But when all allowance has been made it remains, by general consent, the very worst of Marlowe's dramas. It contains scarcely one powerful passage. The *Tragedy of Dido*, written by Marlowe and Nash, was published a year after the former's death. It is probably an early work of Marlowe's, so far as it is his at all, and it must have been elaborated and considerably enlarged by Nash in a manner that is sometimes a caricature, perhaps not quite unconsciously, of Marlowe's manner. *Dido* must be compared to *Hero and Leander* rather than to any of Marlowe's dramas. There is a certain mellifluous sweetness in the best scenes, such as that in which Dido makes love to Æneas in the cave in which they had sought shelter from the storm.

> *Dido*: Æneas!
> *Æn*: Dido!
> *Dido*: Tell me, dear love, how found you
>   out this cave?
> *Æn*: By chance, sweet queen, as Mars and
>   Venus met.
> *Dido*: Why that was in a net, where we are
>   loose;
> And yet I am not free,—O, would I were!
> *Æn*: Why, what is it that Dido may desire
> And not obtain, be it in human power?
> *Dido*: The thing that I will die before I ask,
> And yet desire to have before I die.
> *Æn*: It is not aught Æneas may achieve?
> *Dido*: Æneas! no; although his eyes do pierce.
> *Æn*: What, hath Iarbus angered her in aught?
> And will she be avengèd on his life?
> *Dido*: Not angered me, except in angering
>   thee.
> *Æn*: Who, then of all so cruel may he be
> That should detain thy eyes in his defects?
> *Dido*: The man that I do eye where'er I am;
> Whose amorous face, like Pæan, sparkles fire,
> Whenas he butts his beams on Flora's bed.
> Prometheus hath put on Cupid's shape,

And I must perish in his burning arms:
Æneas, O Æneas, quench these flames!
    Æn: What ails my queen? is she faln sick of
    late?
    Dido: Not sick, my love; but sick I must
    conceal
The torment that it boots me not reveal:
And yet I'll speak,—and yet I'll hold my peace.
Do shame her worst, I will disclose my grief:
Æneas, thou art he—what did I say?
Something it was that now I have forgot.

It seems likely that the last years of Marlowe's life grew careless and irregular; his later plays (putting aside *Edward II*.) show signs of swift and over-hasty workmanship, unlike the very careful and even work of the immature *Tamburlaine*. At the same time the thirst after the infinite and impossible dies out, and is replaced by no sane and cheerful content with earth's limits. *Edward II*. is a fiercely ironical response to Tamburlaine's supreme desire—"the sweet fruition of an earthly crown." Marlowe, like Cyril Tourneur, lacked altogether the tender humanity, the sweet and genial humour which saved the sensitive Shakespeare from the bitter pride of genius, and which marked even lesser men like Dekker and Middleton. Greene, who died just before Marlowe, reproaches him in the death-bed ravings of his *Groat's Worth of Wit* for his life and opinions. Marlowe was always outspoken, one gathers, and at this time it appears that he attracted especial attention as a freethinker. Only a few days before his death, one Richard Bame sent in a note "contayninge the opinion of one Christofer Marlye concernynge his damnable opinions and judgment of Relygion and scorne of God's worde." This informer was hanged at Tyburn next year for some degrading offence, but there seems no reason—while making judicious reservations—to doubt the substantial accuracy of his statements. It is noteworthy that Marlowe's heroes are usually heathens or infidels, and he takes every opportunity of insinuating a sceptical opinion. Probably his unorthodox views had much to do with the accusation of "vices sent from hell" in an anonymous play written shortly after his death. It is certain he had friends among the finest-natured men of his time. Walsingham was his patron; there seems a touch of tenderness in Shakespeare's apostrophe of the "dead shepherd" in *As You Like It*; Nash, who had sometimes been a jealous rival, wrote an elegy "on Marlowe's untimely death" which has not survived; an anonymous writer in 1600 speaks lovingly of "kynde Kit Marloe;" Edward Blunt, Marlowe's friend and publisher, writes, in words that have a genuine ring, of "the impression of the man that hath been dear unto us, living an after-life in our memory;" Drayton's well-inspired lines are familiar:—

    —Marlowe, bathèd in the Thespian
        springs,
Had in him those brave translunary things
That our first poets had: his raptures were
All air and fire, which made his verses clear:
For that fine madness still he did retain,
Which rightly should possess a poet's brain.

Chapman also wrote concerning
    —his free soul, whose living subject stood
Up to the chin in the Pierian flood.

There is no alloy of blame in the words of these men, Drayton and Chapman, and they were among the gravest as well as the best-loved of their time. One lingers over the faintest traces of this personality which must have been so fascinating, for we have no further trustworthy indications of the manner of man that he was in the eyes of those who knew him.

There is, at last, one previous fragment which we cannot afford to pass by, for it bears Marlowe's intensely personal impress. Without this fragment of *Hero and Leander* we should not have known the full sweetness and range of his genius. It is the brightest flower of the English Renaissance, apart from that moral energy of the Reformation of which Chapman, together with something less than usual of his elaborate obscurity, afterwards gave it some faint tincture. It is a free and fresh and eager song, "drunk with gladness,"—like Hero who "stayed not for her robes," but straight arose to open the door to her lover—full of ideal beauty that finds its expression in the form and colour of things, above all in the bodies of men and women; for the passion of love, apart from the passion of beauty, Marlowe failed to grasp. No Elizabethan had so keen a sense of physical loveliness as these lines reveal:—

    His body was as straight as Circe's wand;
    Jove might have sipped out nectar from his hand.
    Even as delicious meat is to the taste,
    So was his neck in touching, and surpassed
    The white of Pelops' shoulder: I could tell ye,
    How smooth his breast was, and how white his belly;
    And whose immortal fingers did imprint
    That heavenly path with many a curious dint
    That runs along his back.

Shakespeare could not have been younger than Marlowe when he wrote his *Venus and Adonis*, which has ever since been coupled with Marlowe's poem.[10] *Venus and Adonis* is oppressive with its unexpanded power; its workmanship is perhaps more searching and thorough, though so much less felicitous than that of *Hero and Leander*; but we turn away with delight from its massive monotonous energy, its close and sensual atmosphere, to the free and open air, the colour and light, the swift and various music of Marlowe's poem. Shelley has scarcely surpassed the sweet gravity which the verse of "our elder Shelley" here reaches:—

    It lies not in our power to love or hate,
    For will in us is over-ruled by fate.
    When two are stripped, long e'er the course begin,
    We wish that one should lose, the other win;
    And one especially do we affect
    Of two gold ingots, like in each respect:
    The reason no man knows, let it suffice,
    What we behold is censured by our eyes.
    Where both deliberate, the love is slight:
    Who ever loved, that loved not at first sight?

The peculiar beauty of these lines seems to have dwelt in Shakespeare's memory. It is little surprising that men were not easily tired of *Hero and Leander*. Taylor the water-poet tells us how his fellow scullers used to sing it as they plied their occupation on the Thames. It was these "sweet-according rimes" of Marlowe's, which, as his enthusiastic young admirer, Petowe, wrote,

        —moved such delight,
    That men would shun their sleep in still dark night
    To meditate upon his golden lines.

In the spring of 1593 the plague raged in London. The actors went into the provinces; many authors sought refuge in the country. In May we know that Marlowe was at the little village of Deptford, not many miles from London. There was turbulent blood there, and wine; there were courtesans and daggers. Here Marlowe was slain, killed by a serving-man, a rival in a quarrel over bought kisses—"a bawdy serving-man."[11] They buried him in an unknown spot, beneath the grey towers of St. Nicholas, and they wrote in the parish-book:

"Christopher Marlow, slain by ffrancis Archer, the 1 of June 1593."

Notes

1. Thomas Heywood wrote in 1635:—
   "Marlo, renowned for his rare art and wit,
   Could ne'er attain beyond the name of Kit."
2. Shakespeare was christened exactly two months later. Chapman, Green, Peele, and Lyly were all, probably, born some ten years earlier; Nash and Chettle about the same time as Marlowe; Heywood about 1570; Ben Jonson in 1573.
3. Francis Kett, a Fellow of Marlowe's college, was burnt at Norwich, in 1589, for heresy. It has been supposed that he was a freethinker, and that he may have influenced young Marlowe. He was really, however (as I am indebted to Mr. Bullen for informing me), a pious, God-fearing person, who fell a victim to the zeal with which he maintained his religious convictions.
4. By Colonel Cunningham, who points out that Marlowe's "familiarity with military terms and his fondness for using them are most remarkable," and that at "his home at Canterbury he was in the very track of the bold spirits who [in 1585] followed Leicester and Sidney to the wars of the Low Countries." It may also be pointed out, however, that Marlowe displays, especially in *Tamburlaine*, a remarkably extensive (though not always accurate) knowledge of Elizabethan geography. His interest in military affairs and in the geography of the world were both manifestations of the spirit of adventure then in the air.
5. Alleyn took the part of Tamburlaine.
6. The exact date is very doubtful. Mr. Bullen, in his generally admirable edition of Marlowe, thinks that the "Ballad of the life and death of Doctor Faustus the great Cungerer," licensed to be printed in Feb. 1589 (and supposed to be identical with the Roxburghe ballad with this title), was probably founded on the play. The ballad tells us that Faustus was educated by his uncle, who left his wealth to him, and gives details of his death. These and other points are not mentioned in the play, but they occur in the original prose *History of Dr. Faustus*, on which the ballad was certainly founded. The writer of the ballad passes by the most impressive scenes in the play, and we cannot assume that he was acquainted with it, although Professor Ward (in the full and interesting notes to his valuable edition of the play) while recognising the striking discrepancies, puts them aside with the curiously inadequate argument that ballads were often founded on plays.
7. It must be recollected that in the sixteenth century "magic" frequently included chemistry and other sciences. The services rendered to science by Paracelsus and Agrippa are scarcely yet generally recognised.
8. Professor Ward, however, points out the art with which, in *Edward II.*, Marlowe avoids exciting "the sense of the loathsome."
9. Henry III., with whose assassination the play ends, died on the 2nd August, 1589. It has been suggested that the existing version of this play is one of those short-hand piracies which seem to have been common.
10. They had a wide popular reputation, resting on their supposed licentiousness, as, at a later day, *Mademoiselle de Maupin*. "I have conveyed away all her wanton pamphlets," says Harebrain in Middleton's *A Mad World, my Masters*, "as *Hero and Leander*, *Venus and Adonis*, O two luscious marrow-bone pies for a young married wife."
11. So the brief account of Francis Meres (*Palladis Tamia*, 1598). There are other more suspected narratives, varying considerably from each other, and with a marked bias in favour of moral edification.

JAMES RUSSELL LOWELL
"Marlowe"
From *The Old English Dramatists*
1892, pp. 28–54

I shall preface what I have to say of Marlowe with a few words as to the refinement which had been going on in the lan-guage, and the greater ductility which it had been rapidly gaining, and which fitted it for the use of the remarkable group of men who made an epoch of the reign of Elizabeth. Spenser was undoubtedly the poet to whom we owe most in this respect, and the very great contrast between his *Shepherd's Calendar*, published in 1579, and his later poems awakens curiosity. In his earliest work there are glimpses, indeed, of those special qualities which have won for him the name of the poet's poet, but they are rare and fugitive, and certainly never would have warranted the prediction of such poetry as was to follow. There is nothing here to indicate that a great artist in language had been born. Two causes, I suspect, were mainly effective in this transformation, I am almost tempted to say transubstantiation, of the man. The first was his practice in translation (true also of Marlowe), than which nothing gives a greater choice and mastery of one's mother-tongue, for one must pause and weigh and judge every word with the greatest nicety, and cunningly transfuse idiom into idiom. The other, and by far the more important, was his study of the Italian poets. The *Faerie Queene* is full of loving reminiscence of them, but their happiest influence is felt in his lyrical poems. For these, I think, make it plain that Italy first taught him how much of the meaning of verse is in its music, and trained his ear to a sense of the harmony as well as the melody of which English verse was capable or might be made capable. Compare the sweetest passage in any lyric of the *Shepherd's Calendar* with the eloquent ardor of the poorest, if any be poor, in the *Epithalamion*, and we find ourselves in a new world, where music had just been invented. This we owe, beyond any doubt, to Spenser's study of the Italian canzone. Nay, the whole metrical movement of the *Epithalamion* recalls that of Petrarca's noble "*Spirito gentil.*" I repeat that melody and harmony were first naturalized in our language by Spenser. I love to recall these debts, for it is pleasant to be grateful even to the dead.

Other men had done their share towards what may be called the modernization of our English, and among these Sir Philip Sidney was conspicuous. He probably gave it greater ease of movement, and seems to have done for it very much what Dryden did a century later in establishing terms of easier intercourse between the language of literature and the language of cultivated society.

There had been good versifiers long before. Chaucer, for example, and even Gower, wearisome as he mainly is, made verses sometimes not only easy in movement, but in which the language seems strangely modern. That most dolefully dreary of books, *The Mirror for Magistrates*, and Sackville, more than any of its authors, did something towards restoring the dignity of verse, and helping it to recover its self-respect, while Spenser was still a youth. Tame as it is, the sunshine of that age here and there touches some verse that ripples in the sluggish current with a flicker of momentary illumination. But before Spenser, no English verse had ever soared and sung, or been filled with what Sidney calls "divine delightfulness." Sidney, it may be conjectured, did more by private criticism and argument than by example. Drayton says of him:

> The noble Sidney with this last arose,
> That heroë for numbers and for prose,
> That throughly paced our language as to show
> The plenteous English hand in hand might go
> With Greek and Latin, and did first reduce
> Our tongue from Lilly's writing then in use.

But even the affectations of Lilly were not without their use as helps to refinement. If, like Chaucer's frere,

> Somewhat he lisped, for his wantonness,
> it was through the desire
> To make his English sweet upon his tongue.

It was the general clownishness against which he revolted, and we owe him our thanks for it. To show of what brutalities even recent writers could be capable, it will suffice to mention that Golding, in his translation of Ovid's *Metamorphoses*, makes a witch mutter the devil's pater-noster, and Ulysses express his fears of going "to pot." I should like to read you a familiar sonnet of Sidney's for its sweetness:

> Come, Sleep: O Sleep! the certain knot of peace,
>   The baiting-place of wit, the balm of woe,
> The poor man's wealth, the prisoner's release,
>   The indifferent judge between the high and
>   low;
> With shield of proof, shield me from out the press
>   Of those fierce darts despair at me doth throw;
> O make in me those civil wars to cease:
>   I will good tribute pay if thou do so.
> Take thou of me smooth pillows, sweetest bed,
>   A chamber deaf to noise and blind to light,
> A rosy garland, and a weary head:
>   And if these things, as being thine of right,
> Move not thy heavy grace, thou shalt in me,
> Livelier than elsewhere, Stella's image see.

Here is ease and simplicity; but in such a phrase as "baiting-place of wit" there is also a want of that perfect discretion which we demand of the language of poetry, however we may be glad to miss it in the thought or emotion which that language conveys. *Baiting-place* is no more a homespun word than the word *inn*, which adds a charm to one of the sweetest verses that Spenser ever wrote; but *baiting-place* is common, it smacks of the hostler and postilion, and commonness is a very poor relation indeed of simplicity. But doubtless one main cause of the vivacity of phrase which so charms us in our earlier writers is to be found in the fact that there were not yet two languages—that of life and that of literature. The divorce between the two took place a century and a half later, and that process of breeding in and in began which at last reduced the language of verse to a kind of idiocy.

Do not consider such discussions as these otiose or nugatory. The language we are fortunate enough to share, and which, I think, Jacob Grimm was right in pronouncing, in its admirable mixture of Saxon and Latin, its strength and sonorousness, a better literary medium than any other modern tongue—this language has not been fashioned to what it is without much experiment, much failure, and infinite expenditure of pains and thought. Genius and pedantry have each done its part towards the result which seems so easy to us, and yet was so hard to win—the one by way of example, the other by way of warning. The purity, the elegance, the decorum, the chastity of our mother-tongue are a sacred trust in our hands. I am tired of hearing the foolish talk of an American variety of it, about our privilege to make it what we will because we are in a majority. A language belongs to those who know best how to use it, how to bring out all its resources, how to make it search its coffers round for the pithy or canorous phrase that suits the need, and they who can do this have been always in a pitiful minority. Let us be thankful that we too have a right to it, and have proved our right, but let us set up no claim to vulgarize it. The English of Abraham Lincoln was so good not because he learned it in Illinois, but because he learned it of Shakespeare and Milton and the Bible, the constant companions of his leisure. And how perfect it was in its homely dignity, its quiet strength, the unerring aim with which it struck once nor

needed to strike more! The language is alive here, and will grow. Let us do all we can with it but debase it. Good taste may not be necessary to salvation or to success in life, but it is one of the most powerful factors of civilization. As a people we have a larger share of it and more widely distributed than I, at least, have found elsewhere, but as a nation we seem to lack it altogether. Our coinage is ruder than that of any country of equal pretensions, our paper money is filthily infectious, and the engraving on it, mechanically perfect as it is, makes of every bank-note a missionary of barbarism. This should make us cautious of trying our hand in the same fashion on the circulating medium of thought. But it is high time that I should remember Maître Guillaume of Patelin, and come back to my sheep.

In coming to speak of Marlowe, I cannot help fearing that I may fail a little in that equanimity which is the first condition of all helpful criticism. Generosity there should be, and enthusiasm there should be, but they should stop short of extravagance. Praise should not weaken into eulogy, nor blame fritter itself away into fault-finding. Goethe tells us that the first thing needful to the critic, as indeed it is to the wise man generally, is to see the thing as it really is; this is the most precious result of all culture, the surest warrant of happiness, or at least of composure. But he also bids us, in judging any work, seek first to discover its beauties, and then its blemishes or defects. Now there are two poets whom I feel that I can never judge without a favorable bias. One is Spenser, who was the first poet I ever read as a boy, not drawn to him by any enchantment of his matter or style, but simply because the first verse of his great poem was,—

> A gentle knight was pricking on the plain,

and I followed gladly, wishful of adventure. Of course I understood nothing of the allegory, never suspected it, fortunately for me, and am surprised to think how much of the language I understood. At any rate, I grew fond of him, and whenever I see the little brown folio in which I read, my heart warms to it as to a friend of my childhood. With Marlowe it was otherwise. With him I grew acquainted during the most impressible and receptive period of my youth. He was the first man of genius I had ever really known, and he naturally bewitched me. What cared I that they said he was a deboshed fellow? nay, an atheist? To me he was the voice of one singing in the desert, of one who had found the water of life for which I was panting, and was at rest under the palms. How can he ever become to me as other poets are? But I shall try to be lenient in my admiration.

Christopher Marlowe, the son of a shoemaker, was born at Canterbury, in February, 1563, was matriculated at Benet College, Cambridge, in 1580, received his degree of bachelor there in 1583 and of master in 1587. He came early to London, and was already known as a dramatist before the end of his twenty-fourth year. There is some reason for thinking that he was at one time an actor. He was killed in a tavern brawl, by a man named Archer, in 1593, at the age of thirty. He was taxed with atheism, but on inadequate grounds, as it appears to me. That he was said to have written a tract against the Trinity, for which a license to print was refused on the ground of blasphemy, might easily have led to the greater charge. That he had some opinions of a kind unusual then may be inferred, perhaps, from a passage in his *Faust*. Faust asks Mephistopheles how, being damned, he is out of hell. And Mephistopheles answers, "Why, this is hell, nor am I out of it." And a little farther on he explains himself thus:

> Hell hath no limits, nor is circumscribed
> In one self place; for where we are is hell,
> And where hell is there must we ever be;

And, to conclude, when all the earth dissolves,
And every creature shall be purified,
All places shall be hell that are not heaven.

Milton remembered the first passage I have quoted, and puts nearly the same words into the mouth of his Lucifer. If Marlowe was a liberal thinker, it is not strange that in that intolerant age he should have incurred the stigma of general unbelief. Men are apt to blacken opinions which are distasteful to them, and along with them the character of him who holds them.

This at least may be said of him without risk of violating the rule of *ne quid nimis*, that he is one of the most masculine and fecundating natures in the long line of British poets. Perhaps his energy was even in excess. There is in him an Oriental lavishness. He will impoverish a province for a simile, and pour the revenues of a kingdom into the lap of a description. In that delightful story in the book of Esdras, King Darius, who has just dismissed all his captains and governors of cities and satraps, after a royal feast, sends couriers galloping after them to order them all back again, because he has found a riddle under his pillow, and wishes their aid in solving it. Marlowe in like manner calls in help from every remotest corner of earth and heaven for what seems to us as trivial an occasion. I will not say that he is bombastic, but he constantly pushes grandiosity to the verge of bombast. His contemporaries thought he passed it in his *Tamburlaine*. His imagination flames and flares, consuming what it should caress, as Jupiter did Semele. That exquisite phrase of Hamlet, "the modesty of nature," would never have occurred to him. Yet in the midst of the hurly-burly there will fall a sudden hush, and we come upon passages calm and pellucid as mountain tarns filled to the brim with the purest distillations of heaven. And, again, there are single verses that open silently as roses, and surprise us with that seemingly accidental perfection, which there is no use in talking about because itself says all that is to be said and more.

There is a passage in *Tamburlaine* which I remember reading in the first course of lectures I ever delivered, thirty-four years ago, as a poet's feeling of the inadequacy of the word to the idea:

> If all the pens that ever poets held
> Had fed the feeling of their masters' thoughts,
> And every sweetness that inspired their hearts,
> Their minds, and muses on admired themes;
> If all the heavenly quintessence they still
> From their immortal flowers of posey,
> Wherein, as in a mirror, we perceive
> The highest reaches of a human wit;—
> If these had made one poem's period,
> And all combined in beauty's worthiness,
> Yet should there hover in their restless heads
> One thought, one grace, one wonder, at the least,
> Which into words no virtue can digest.

Marlowe made snatches at this forbidden fruit with vigorous leaps, and not without bringing away a prize now and then such as only the fewest have been able to reach. Of fine single verses I give a few as instances of this:

> Sometimes a lovely boy in Dian's shape,
> *With hair that gilds the water as it glides,*
> Shall bathe him in a spring.

Here is a couplet notable for dignity of poise describing Tamburlaine:

> Of stature tall and straightly fashionèd,
> Like his desire, lift upward and divine.

> For every street like to a firmament
> Glistered with breathing stars.

Unwedded maids
Shadowing more beauty in their airy brows
Than have the white breasts of the queen of Love.

This from *Tamburlaine* is particularly characteristic:

> Nature
> Doth teach us all to have aspiring minds.
> Our souls, whose faculties can comprehend
> The wondrous architecture of the world,
> And measure every wandering planet's course,
> Still climbing after knowledge infinite,
> And always moving as the restless spheres,
> Will us to wear ourselves and never rest
> Until we reach the ripest fruit of all.

One of these verses reminds us of that exquisite one of Shakespeare where he says that Love is

> Still climbing trees in the Hesperides.

But Shakespeare puts a complexity of meaning into his chance sayings, and lures the fancy to excursions of which Marlowe never dreamt.

But, alas, a voice will not illustrate like a stereopticon, and this tearing away of fragments that seem to bleed with the avulsion is like breaking off a finger from a statue as a specimen.

The impression he made upon the men of his time was uniform; it was that of something new and strange; it was that of genius, in short. Drayton says of him, kindling to an unwonted warmth, as if he loosened himself for a moment from the choking coils of his *Polyolbion* for a larger breath:

> Next Marlowe bathèd in the Thespian springs
> Had in him those brave translunary things
> That the first poets had; his raptures were
> All air and fire, which made his verses clear;
> For that fine madness still he did retain
> Which rightly should possess a poet's brain.

And Chapman, taking up and continuing Marlowe's half-told story of Hero and Leander, breaks forth suddenly into this enthusiasm of invocation:

> Then, ho! most strangely intellectual fire
> That, proper to my soul, hast power to inspire
> Her burning faculties, and with the wings
> Of thy unspherèd flame visit'st the springs
> Of spirits immortal, now (as swift as Time
> Doth follow motion) find the eternal clime
> Of his free soul whose living subject stood
> Up to the chin in the Pierian flood.

Surely Chapman would have sent his soul on no such errand had he believed that the soul of Marlowe was in torment, as his accusers did not scruple to say that it was, sent thither by the manifestly Divine judgment of his violent death.

Yes, Drayton was right in classing him with "the first poets," for he was indeed such, and so continues,—that is, he was that most indefinable thing, an original man, and therefore as fresh and contemporaneous to-day as he was three hundred years ago. Most of us are more or less hampered by our own individuality, nor can shake ourselves free of that chrysalis of consciousness and give our "souls a loose," as Dryden calls it in his vigorous way. And yet it seems to me that there is something even finer than that fine madness, and I think I see it in the imperturbable sanity of Shakespeare, which made him so much an artist that his new work still bettered his old. I think I see it even in the almost irritating calm of Goethe, which, if it did not quite make him an artist, enabled him to see what an artist should be, and to come as near to being one as his nature allowed. Marlowe was certainly not an artist in the larger sense, but he was cunning in words and periods and the musical modulation of them. And even this is a very rare gift. But his mind could never submit itself to a controlling purpose, and renounce all other things for the sake of that. His plays, with the single exception of *Edward II.*, have no organic unity, and such unity as is here is more apparent than real. Passages in them stir us deeply and thrill us to the marrow, but each play as a whole is ineffectual. Even his *Edward II.* is regular only to the eye by a more orderly arrangement of scenes and acts, and Marlowe evidently felt the drag of this restraint, for we miss the uncontrollable energy, the eruptive fire, and the feeling that he was happy in his work. Yet Lamb was hardly extravagant in saying that "the death scene of Marlowe's king moves pity and terror beyond any scene, ancient or modern, with which I am acquainted." His tragedy of *Dido, Queen of Carthage*, is also regularly plotted out, and is also somewhat tedious. Yet there are many touches that betray his burning hand. There is one passage illustrating that luxury of description into which Marlowe is always glad to escape from the business in hand. Dido tells Æneas:

> Æneas, I'll repair thy Trojan ships
> Conditionally that thou wilt stay with me,
> And let Achates sail to Italy;
> I'll give thee tackling made of rivelled gold,
> Wound on the barks of odoriferous trees;
> Oars of massy ivory, full of holes
> Through which the water shall delight to play;
> Thy anchors shall be hewed from crystal rocks
> Which, if thou lose, shall shine above the waves;
> The masts whereon thy swelling sails shall hang
> Hollow pyramides of silver plate;
> The sails of folded lawn, where shall be wrought
> The wars of Troy, but not Troy's overthrow;
> For ballast, empty Dido's treasury;
> Take what ye will, but leave Æneas here.
> Achates, thou shalt be so seemly clad
> As sea-born nymphs shall swarm about thy ships
> And wanton mermaids court thee with sweet songs,
> Flinging in favors of more sovereign worth
> Than Thetis hangs about Apollo's neck,
> So that Æneas may but stay with me.

But far finer than this, in the same costly way, is the speech of Barabas in *The Jew of Malta*, ending with a line that has incorporated itself in the language with the familiarity of a proverb:

> Give me the merchants of the Indian mines
> That trade in metal of the purest mould;
> The wealthy Moor that in the Eastern rocks
> Without control can pick his riches up,
> And in his house heap pearl like pebble-stones,
> Receive them free, and sell them by the weight;
> Bags of fiery opals, sapphires, amethysts,
> Jacynths, hard topaz, grass-green emeralds,
> Beauteous rubies, sparkling diamonds,
> And seld-seen costly stones of so great price
> As one of them, indifferently rated,
> . . .
> May serve in peril of calamity
> To ransom great kings from captivity.
> This is the ware wherein consists my wealth:
> . . .
> Infinite riches in a little room.

This is the very poetry of avarice.

Let us now look a little more closely at Marlowe as a dramatist. Here also he has an importance less for what he accomplished than for what he suggested to others. Not only do

I think that Shakespeare's verse caught some hints from his, but there are certain descriptive passages and similes of the greater poet which, whenever I read them, instantly bring Marlowe to my mind. This is an impression I might find it hard to convey to another, or even to make definite to myself; but it is an old one, and constantly repeats itself, so that I put some confidence in it. Marlowe's *Edward II.* certainly served Shakespeare as a model for his earlier historical plays. Of course he surpassed his model, but Marlowe might have said of him as Oderisi, with pathetic modesty, said to Dante of his rival and surpasser, Franco of Bologna, "The praise is now all his, yet mine in part." But it is always thus. The path-finder is forgotten when the track is once blazed out. It was in Shakespeare's *Richard II.* that Lamb detected the influence of Marlowe, saying that "the reluctant pangs of abdicating royalty in Edward furnished hints which Shakespeare has scarce improved upon in Richard." In the parallel scenes of both plays the sentiment is rather elegiac than dramatic, but there is a deeper pathos, I think, in Richard, and his grief rises at times to a passion which is wholly wanting in Edward. Let me read Marlowe's abdication scene. The irresolute nature of the king is finely indicated. The Bishop of Winchester has come to demand the crown; Edward takes it off, and says:

> Here, take my crown; the life of Edward too:
> Two kings of England cannot reign at once.
> But stay awhile: let me be king till night,
> That I may gaze upon this glittering crown;
> So shall my eyes receive their last content,
> My head the latest honor due to it,
> And jointly both yield up their wishèd right.
> Continue ever, thou celestial sun;
> Let never silent night possess this clime;
> Stand still, you watches of the element;
> All times and seasons, rest you at a stay—
> That Edward may be still fair England's king!
> But day's bright beam doth vanish fast away,
> And needs I must resign my wishèd crown.
> Inhuman creatures, nursed with tiger's milk,
> Why gape you for your sovereign's overthrow?—
> My diadem, I mean, and guiltless life.
> See, monsters, see, I'll wear my crown again.
> What, fear you not the fury of the king?
> . . .
> I'll not resign, but, whilst I live, be king!

Then, after a short further parley:

>   Here, receive my crown.
> Receive it? No; these innocent hands of mine
> Shall not be guilty of so foul a crime:
> He of you all that most desires my blood,
> And will be called the murderer of a king,
> Take it. What, are you moved? Pity you me?
> Then send for unrelenting Mortimer,
> And Isabel, whose eyes, being turned to steel,
> Will sooner sparkle fire than shed a tear.
> Yet stay, for rather than I'll look on them,
> Here, here!—Now, sweet God of Heaven,
> Make me despise this transitory pomp,
> And sit for aye enthronizèd in Heaven!
> Come, Death, and with thy fingers close my eyes,
> Or, if I live, let me forget myself.

Surely one might fancy that to be from the prentice hand of Shakespeare. It is no small distinction that this can be said of Marlowe, for it can be said of no other. What follows is still finer. The ruffian who is to murder Edward, in order to evade his distrust, pretends to weep. The king exclaims:

Weep'st thou already? List awhile to me,
And then thy heart, were it as Gurney's is,
Or as Matrevis', hewn from the Caucasus,
Yet will it melt ere I have done my tale.
This dungeon where they keep me is the sink
Wherein the filth of all the castle falls,
And there in mire and puddle have I stood
This ten days' space; and, lest that I should sleep,
One plays continually upon a drum;
They give me bread and water, being a king;
So that, for want of sleep and sustenance,
My mind's distempered and my body numbed,
And whether I have limbs or no I know not.
O, would my blood dropt out from every vein,
As doth this water from my tattered robes!
Tell Isabel the queen I looked not thus,
When, for her sake, I ran at tilt in France,
And there unhorsed the Duke of Clerëmont.

This is even more in Shakespeare's early manner than the other, and it is not ungrateful to our feeling of his immeasurable supremacy to think that even he had been helped in his schooling. There is a truly royal pathos in "They give me bread and water"; and "Tell Isabel the queen," instead of "Isabel my queen," is the most vividly dramatic touch that I remember anywhere in Marlowe. And that vision of the brilliant tournament, not more natural than it is artistic, how does it not deepen by contrast the gloom of all that went before! But you will observe that the verse is rather epic than dramatic. I mean by this that its every pause and every movement are regularly cadenced. There is a kingly composure in it, perhaps, but were the passages not so finely pathetic as it is, or the diction less naturally simple, it would seem stiff. Nothing is more peculiarly characteristic of the mature Shakespeare than the way in which his verses curve and wind themselves with the fluctuating emotion or passion of the speaker and echo his mood. Let me illustrate this by a speech of Imogen when Pisanio gives her a letter from her husband bidding her meet him at Milford-Haven. The words seem to waver to and fro, or huddle together before the hurrying thought, like sheep when the collie chases them.

O, for a horse with wings!—Hear'st thou, Pisanio?
He is at Milford-Haven: read, and tell me
How far 't is thither. If one of mean affairs
May plod it in a week, why may not I
Glide thither in a day?—Then, true Pisanio—
Who long'st like me to see thy lord; who long'st
O, let me 'bate—but not like me—yet long'st—
But in a fainter kind:—O, not like me;
For mine's beyond beyond: say, and speak thick,—
Love's counsellor should fill the bores of hearing,
To the smothering of the sense,—how far it is
To this same blessed Milford: and, by the way,
Tell me how Wales was made so happy as
To inherit such a haven: but, first of all,
How we may steal from hence.

The whole speech is breathless with haste, and is in keeping not only with the feeling of the moment, but with what we already know of the impulsive character of Imogen. Marlowe did not, for he could not, teach Shakespeare this secret, nor has anybody else every learned it.

There are, properly speaking, no characters in the plays of Marlowe—but personages and interlocutors. We do not get to know them, but only to know what they do and say. The nearest approach to a character is Barabas, in *The Jew of Malta*, and he is but the incarnation of the popular hatred of the Jew.

There is really nothing human in him. He seems a bugaboo rather than a man. Here is his own account of himself:

As for myself, I walk abroad o' nights,
And kill sick people groaning under walls;
Sometimes I go about and poison wells;
And now and then, to cherish Christian thieves,
I am content to lose some of my crowns,
That I may, walking in my gallery,
See 'em go pinioned by my door along;
Being young, I studied physic, and began
To practise first upon the Italian;
There I enriched the priests with burials,
And always kept the sexton's arms in ure
With digging graves and ringing dead men's knells;
And, after that, was I an engineer,
And in the wars 'twixt France and Germany,
Under pretence of helping Charles the Fifth,
Slew friend and enemy with my stratagems.
Then, after that, was I an usurer,
And with extorting, cozening, forfeiting,
And tricks belonging unto brokery,
I filled the jails with bankrupts in a year,
And with young orphans planted hospitals;
And every moon made some or other mad,
And now and then one hang himself for grief,
Pinning upon his breast a long great scroll
How I with interest tormented him.
But mark how I am blest for plaguing them—
I have as much coin as will buy the town.

Here is nothing left for sympathy. This is the mere lunacy of distempered imagination. It is shocking, and not terrible. Shakespeare makes no such mistake with Shylock. His passions are those of a man, though of a man depraved by oppression and contumely; and he shows sentiment, as when he says of the ring that Jessica had given for a monkey: "It was my turquoise. I had it of Leah when I was a bachelor." And yet, observe the profound humor with which Shakespeare makes him think first of its dearness as a precious stone and then as a keepsake. In letting him exact his pound of flesh, he but follows the story as he found it in Giraldi Cinthio, and is careful to let us know that this Jew had good reason, or thought he had, to hate Christians. At the end, I think he meant us to pity Shylock, and we do pity him. And with what a smiling background of love and poetry does he give relief to the sombre figure of the Jew! In Marlowe's play there is no respite. And yet it comes nearer to having a connected plot, in which one event draws on another, than any other of his plays. I do not think Milman right in saying that the interest falls off after the first two acts. I find enough to carry me on to the end, where the defiant death of Barabas in a caldron of boiling oil he had arranged for another victim does something to make a man of him. But there is no controlling reason in the piece. Nothing happens because it must, but because the author wills it so. The conception of life is purely arbitrary, and as far from nature as that of an imaginative child. It is curious, however, that here, too, Marlowe should have pointed the way to Shakespeare. But there is no resemblance between the Jew of Malta and the Jew of Venice, except that both have daughters whom they love. Nor is the analogy close even here. The love which Barabas professes for his child fails to humanize him to us, because it does not prevent him from making her the abhorrent instrument of his wanton malice in the death of her lover, and because we cannot believe him capable of loving anything but gold and vengeance. There is always something extravagant in the imagination of Marlowe, but here it is the extravagance of absurdity. Generally he gives us an impression of power, of vastness, though it be the vastness of chaos, where elemental forces hurtle blindly one against the other. But they are elemental forces, and not mere stage properties. Even Tamburlaine, if we see in him—as Marlowe, I think, meant that we should see—the embodiment of brute force, without reason and without conscience, ceases to be a blusterer, and becomes, indeed, as he asserts himself, the scourge of God. There is an exultation of strength in this play that seems to add a cubit to our stature. Marlowe had found the way that leads to style, and helped others to find it, but he never arrived there. He had not self-denial enough. He can refuse nothing to his fancy. He fails of his effect by over-emphasis, heaping upon a slender thought a burthen of expression too heavy for it to carry. But it is not with fagots, but with priceless Oriental stuffs, that he breaks their backs.

Marlowe's *Dr. Faustus* interests us in another way. Here he again shows himself as a precursor. There is no attempt at profound philosophy in this play, and in the conduct of it Marlowe has followed the prose history of Dr. Faustus closely, even in its scenes of mere buffoonery. Disengaged from these, the figure of the protagonist is not without grandeur. It is not avarice or lust that tempts him at first, but power. Weary of his studies in law, medicine, and divinity, which have failed to bring him what he seeks, he turns to necromancy:

> These metaphysics of magicians
> And necromantic books are heavenly.

> . . .

> Oh, what a world of profit and delight,
> Of power, of honor, of omnipotence,
> Is promised to the studious artisan!
> All things that move between the quiet poles
> Shall be at my command. Emperors and kings
> Are but obèyed in their several provinces,
> Nor can they raise the winds or rend the clouds;
> But his dominion that exceeds in this
> Stretcheth as far as doth the mind of man;
> A sound magician is a mighty god:
> Here, Faustus, tire thy brains to gain a deity.

His good angel intervenes, but the evil spirit at the other ear tempts him with power again:

> Be thou on earth as Jove is in the sky,
> Lord and commander of these elements.

Ere long Faustus begins to think of power for baser uses:

> How am I glutted with conceit of this!
> Shall I make spirits fetch me what I please,
> Resolve me of all ambiguities,
> Perform what desperate enterprise I will?
> I'll have them fly to India for gold,
> Ransack the ocean for orient pearl,
> And search all corners of the new-found world
> For pleasant fruits and princely delicates;
> I'll have them read me strange philosophy,
> And tell the secrets of all foreign kings.

And yet it is always to the pleasures of the intellect that he returns. It is when the good and evil spirits come to him for the second time that wealth is offered as a bait, and after Faustus has signed away his soul to Lucifer, he is tempted even by more sensual allurements. I may be reading into the book what is not there, but I cannot help thinking that Marlowe intended in this to typify the inevitably continuous degradation of a soul that has renounced its ideal, and the drawing on of one vice by another, for they go hand in hand like the Hours. But even in his degradation the pleasures of Faustus are mainly of the mind, or at worst of a sensuous and not sensual kind. No doubt

in this Marlowe is unwittingly betraying his own tastes. Faustus is made to say:

> And long ere this I should have slain myself
> Had not sweet pleasure conquered deep despair.
> Have I not made blind Homer sing to me
> Of Alexander's love and Œnon's death?
> And hath not he that built the walls of Thebes
> With ravishing sound of his melodious harp
> Made music with my Mephistophilis?
> Why should I die, then? basely why despair?

This employment of the devil in a duet seems odd. I remember no other instance of his appearing as a musician except in Burn's *Tam o' Shanter.* The last wish of Faustus was Helen of Troy. Mephistophilis fetches her, and Faustus exclaims:

> Was this the face that launched a thousand ships,
> And burned the topless towers of Ilium?
> Sweet Helen, make me immortal with a kiss!

> . . .

> Here will I dwell, for Heaven is in these lips,
> And all is dross that is not Helena:

> . . .

> Oh, thou art fairer than the evening air
> Clad in the beauty of a thousand stars.

No such verses had ever been heard on the English stage before, and this was one of the great debts our language owes to Marlowe. He first taught it what passion and fire were in its veins. The last scene of the play, in which the bond with Lucifer becomes payable, is nobly conceived. Here the verse rises to the true dramatic sympathy of which I spoke. It is swept into the vortex of Faust's eddying thought, and seems to writhe and gasp in that agony of hopeless despair:

>   Ah, Faustus,
> Now hast thou but one bare hour to live,
> And then thou must be damned perpetually!
> Stand still, ye ever-moving spheres of Heaven,
> That time may cease and midnight never come;
> Fair Nature's eye, rise, rise again, and make
> Perpetual day; or let this hour be but
> A year, a month, a week, a natural day,
> That Faustus may repent and save his soul!
> The stars move still, time runs, the clock will strike,
> The devil will come, and Faustus must be damned.
> Oh, I'll leap up to my God! Who pulls me down?
> See, see, where Christ's blood streams in the
>   firmament!
> One drop would save my soul—half a drop; ah, my
>   Christ!
> Ah, rend not my heart for naming of my Christ!
> Yet will I call on Him. Oh, spare me, Lucifer!
> Where is it now? 'Tis gone; and see where God
> Stretcheth out His arm and bends His ireful brows!
> Mountains and hills, come, come and fall on me,
> And hide me from the heavy wrath of God!
> No? No?
> Then will I headlong run into the earth.
> Earth, gape! Oh no, it will not harbor me!

> . . .

> Ah! half the hour is past; 't will all be past anon.
> O God,
> If Thou wilt not have mercy on my soul,
> Yet, for Christ's sake, whose blood hath ransomed
>   me,
> Impose some end to my incessant pain;
> Let Faustus live in hell a thousand years—

A hundred thousand—and at last be saved!
Oh, no end's limited to damnèd souls.
Why wert thou not a creature wanting soul?
Or why was this immortal that thou hast?
Ah, Pythagoras' metempsychosis, were that true,
This soul should fly from me, and I be changed
Unto some brutish beast! All beasts are happy,
For when they die,
Their souls are soon dissolved in elements;
But mine must live still to be plagued in Hell!
Cursed by the parents that engendered me!
No, Faustus, curse thyself, curse Lucifer,
That hath deprived thee of the joys of Heaven.
Oh, it strikes! it strikes! Now, body, turn to air,
Or Lucifer will bear thee quick to Hell.
O soul, be changed to little waterdrops
And fall into the ocean; ne'er be found!
My God, my God, look not so fierce on me!
Adders and serpents, let me breathe awhile.
Ugly Hell, gape not. Come not, Lucifer!
I'll burn my books. Ah, Mephistophilis!

It remains to say a few words of Marlowe's poem of *Hero and Leander*, for in translating it from Musæus he made it his own. It has great ease and fluency of versification, and many lines as perfect in their concinnity as those of Pope, but infused with a warmer coloring and a more poetic fancy. Here is found the verse that Shakespeare quotes somewhere. The second verse of the following couplet has precisely Pope's cadence:—

Unto her was he led, or rather drawn,
By those white limbs that sparkled through the lawn.

It was from this poem that Keats caught the inspiration for his *Endymion*. A single passage will serve to prove this:—

So fair a church as this had Venus none:
The walls were of discolored jasper stone,
Wherein was Proteus carved; and overhead
A lively vine of green sea-agate spread,
Where by one hand light-headed Bacchus hung,
And with the other wine from grapes outwrung.

Milton, too, learned from Marlowe the charm of those long sequences of musical proper names of which he made such effective use. Here are two passages which Milton surely had read and pondered:—

So from the East unto the furthest West
Shall Tamburlaine extend his puissant arm;
The galleys and those pilling brigantines
That yearly sail to the Venetian gulf,
And hover in the straits for Christians' wreck,
Shall lie at anchor in the isle Asant,
Until the Persian fleet and men of war
Sailing along the Oriental sea
Have fetched about the Indian continent,
Even from Persepolis to Mexico,
And thence unto the straits of Jubaltar.

This is still more Miltonic:—

As when the seaman sees the Hyades
Gather an army of Cimmerian clouds,
Auster and Aquilon with wingèd steeds,
. . .
All fearful folds his sails and sounds the main.

Spenser, too, loved this luxury of sound, as he shows in such passages as this:—

Now was Aldebaran uplifted high
Above the starry Cassiopeia's chair.

And I fancy he would have put him there to make music, even had it been astronomically impossible, but he never strung such names in long necklaces, as Marlowe and Milton were fond of doing.

Was Marlowe, then, a great poet? For such a title he had hardly range enough of power, hardly reach enough of thought. But surely he had some of the finest qualities that go to the making of a great poet; and his poetic instinct, when he had time to give himself wholly over to its guidance, was unerring. I say when he had time enough, for he, too, like his fellows, was forced to make the daily task bring in the daily bread. We have seen how fruitful his influence has been, and perhaps his genius could have no surer warrant than that the charm of it lingered in the memory of poets, for theirs is the memory of mankind. If we allow him genius, what need to ask for more? And perhaps it would be only to him among the group of dramatists who surrounded Shakespeare that we should allow it. He was the herald that dropped dead in announcing the victory in whose fruits he was not to share.

JOHN CHURTON COLLINS
From "The Predecessors of Shakspeare"
Essays and Studies
1895, pp. 149–62

Of these poets the youngest in years but the first in importance was Christopher Marlowe. Born in February 1563(?), the son of a shoemaker at Canterbury, he received the rudiments of his education at the King's School in that city. He subsequently matriculated at Benet College, Cambridge, taking his degree as Bachelor of Arts in 1583, and his degree as Master of Arts four years later. Of his career at Cambridge, and of his movements between 1583 and 1587, nothing is known. It is probable that by the end of 1587 he had settled in London, having already distinguished himself by the production of *Tamburlaine*. The rest of his life is a deplorable record of misfortune, debauchery, and folly, suddenly and frightfully terminated, before he had completed his thirtieth year, by a violent death in a tavern-brawl at Deptford.

When Dryden observed of Shakspeare that he "found not, but created first the stage," he said what was certainly not true of Shakspeare, but what would, with some modification, be true of Marlowe. To no single man does our drama owe more than to this ill-starred genius. It was he who determined the form which tragedy and history were permanently to assume. It was he who first clothed both in that noble and splendid garb which was ever afterwards to distinguish them. It was he who gave the death-blow to the old rhymed plays on the one hand, and to the frigid and cumbersome unrhymed classical plays on the other. In his *Doctor Faustus* and in his *Jew of Malta* it would not be too much to say that he formulated English romantic tragedy. He cast in clay what Shakspeare recast in marble. Indeed, Marlowe was to Shakspeare in tragedy precisely what Boiardo and Berni were to Ariosto in narrative. It is certain that without the *Orlando Innámorato* we should never have had the *Orlando Furioso*. It is more than probable that without the tragedies of Marlowe we should never have had, in the form at least in which they now stand, the tragedies of Shakspeare. Of the History in the proper sense of the title, Marlowe was the creator. In his *Edward I.* Peele had, it is true, made some advance on the old Chronicles. But the difference between Peele's *Edward I.* and Marlowe's *Edward II.* is the difference between a work of art and mere botchwork. Peele's play is little better than a series of disconnected scenes loosely tagged together; superior indeed in style, but in no way superior in structure to *The Famous Victories of Henry V.* and to *The*

Troublesome Raigne of King John. In *Edward II*. Marlowe laid down, and laid down for all time, the true principles of dramatic composition as applied to history. He showed how, by a judicious process of selection and condensation, of modification and suppression, the crowded annals of many years could in effect be presented within the compass of a single play. He studied perspective and symmetry. He brought out in clear relief the central figure and the central action, grouping round each in carefully-graduated subordination the accessory characters and the accessory incidents. Chronology and tradition, when they interfered either with the harmony of his work or with dramatic effect, he never scrupled to ignore or alter, rightly discriminating between the laws imposed on the historian and the laws imposed on the dramatist. He was the first of English playwrights to discern that in dramatic composition the relative importance of events is determined, not by the space which they fill in history, but by the manner in which they impress the imagination and bear on the catastrophe. Nor are these Marlowe's only titles to the most distinguished place among the fathers of English tragedy. He was not only the first of our dramatists who, possessing a bold and vivid imagination, possessed also the faculty of adequately embodying its conceptions, but the first who, powerfully moved by strong emotion, succeeding in awakening strong emotion in others. In the hands of his predecessors tragedy had been powerless to touch the heart. As a rule, it had maintained the same dead-level of frigid and nerveless declamation. In his hands it resumed its ancient sway over the passions; it unlocked the sources of terror and pity. To compare Marlowe with the Attic dramatists would be in the highest degree absurd, and yet we must go back to the Attic dramatists to find anything equal to the concluding scenes of *Dr. Faustus* and *Edward II*.

The appearance of *Tamburlaine* has been compared to the appearance of *Hernani*. Its professed object was to revolutionise the drama. The war which Victor Hugo declared against classicism Marlowe declared against the

> jigging veins of rhyming mother wits,
> And such conceits as clownage keeps in pay.

The most remarkable of his innovations was the substitution of blank verse for rhyme and prose. It would not, of course, be true to say that Marlowe was the first of our poets to employ blank verse in dramatic composition. It had been employed in Sackville and Norton in *Gorboduc*; by Gascoigne in *Jocasta*; by Lyly in his *Woman in the Moon*; by Hughes in his *Misfortunes of Arthur*; and by the authors of other plays which in all probability preceded *Tamburlaine*. But these plays had been confined exclusively to private audiences, and had not been designed for the popular stage. Nor must we confound the blank verse of Marlowe with the blank verse of these dramas. In them it differed only from the heroic couplet in wanting rhyme. It had made no advance on Grimoald's experiments more than thirty years before. It had no variety, no incatenation, no harmony; in the contemptuous phrase of Nash, it was a drumming decasyllabon, and a drumming decasyllabon there seemed every probability of it continuing to remain. It is remarkable that, since its first introduction into our language by Surrey, though it had passed through the hands of poets whose other compositions show that they possessed no common mastery over metrical expression, its structure had never altered. The genius of Marlowe transformed it into the noblest and most flexible of English metres. If we examine the mechanism of his verse, we shall see that it differed from that of his predecessors in the resolution of the iambic into tribrachs and dactyls, in the frequent substitution of trochees and pyrrhics for

monosyllables, in the large admixture of anapests, in the interspersion of Alexandrines, in the shifting of the pauses, in the uses of hemistichs, in the interlinking of verse with verse. It was therefore no mere modification, no mere improvement on the earlier forms of blank verse; it was a new creation.

The effect of Marlowe's innovation was at once apparent. First went the old rhymed stanzas. We doubt whether it would be possible to find a single play written in stanzas subsequent to 1587. Next went the prose Histories. Then commenced the gradual disappearance of rhymed couplets. Thus plays which previous to 1587 were written in rhyme, we find after 1587 interpolated with blank verse. Such is the case with *The Three Ladies of London*; such is the case with *Selimus*; such is the case with the recast of *Tancred and Gismunda*. Before 1587 Peele habitually employed rhyme; after 1587 he discarded it entirely. Greene, who, if we interpret rightly an ambiguous passage in the Epistle prefixed to his *Perimedes*, regarded Marlowe's innovation with strong disfavour, almost immediately adopted it. In all his extant dramas blank verse is employed. By 1593 is was firmly established.

How profoundly the genius of Marlowe impressed his contemporaries is evident not only from the frequent allusions to his writings, but from the imitations, close even to servility, of his characters and his style, which abound in our dramatic literature between 1587 and 1600. Sometimes we have whole plays which are mere parodies of his; such would be Greene's *Alphonsus* and Peele's *Battle of Alcazar*; such also would be the anonymous play, *Lust's Dominion*. His Barabas and Tamburlaine took the same hold on the popular imagination as the Conrads and Laras and Harolds and Manfreds of a later age, appearing and reappearing, variously modified in numerous forms. Tamburlaine became the prototype of the stage hero. Barabas became the prototype of the stage villain. To enumerate the characters modelled on these creations of Marlowe would be to transcribe the leading *dramatis personæ* of at least two-thirds of the heroic dramas in vogue during the latter years of the sixteenth century. Indeed the influence—and we are speaking now not of the general, but of the particular influence—exercised by Marlowe over the works of his brother poets would, if traced in detail, be found to be far more extensive than is generally supposed. To go no further than Shakspeare, *Richard II*. is undoubtedly modelled on *Edward II*.; the character of Richard is the character of Edward slightly modified. In the second and third parts of *Henry VI.*, if Shakspeare did not actually work in co-operation with Marlowe, he set himself to imitate with servile fidelity Marlowe's method and Marlowe's style. Aaron in *Titus Andronicus* is Barabas in *The Jew of Malta*; so in some degree is Shylock; so in a considerable degree is *Richard III*. In the nurse who attends on Dido we have a sort of first sketch of the nurse in *Romeo and Juliet*. From *The Jew of Malta* Shakspeare derived many hints for *The Merchant of Venice*. From the concluding scene of *Dr. Faustus* he borrowed, or appears to have borrowed, one of the finest touches in *Macbeth*.

From a historical point of view it would, therefore, be scarcely possible to over-estimate the importance of Marlowe's services. Regarded as an initiator, he ranks with Æschylus. But criticism must distinguish between merit which is relative and merit which is intrinsic. It may sound paradoxical to say of the father of our Romantic drama, of the master of Shakspeare, that his genius was in essence the very reverse of dramatic, nay, that the temper of his genius was such as absolutely to disqualify him from excelling as a dramatist. And yet such is the case. In Marlowe we have the extraordinary anomaly of a man in whom the instincts of the artist and the temper of the poet met in oppugnancy. Induced partly perhaps by the exigencies of his position, partly no doubt influenced by the age in which it was his chance to live, the materials on which he worked he elected to cast in a dramatic mould. Nature had endowed him with a singular sense of fitness and harmony, with an appreciation of form Greek-like in its delicacy and subtlety. This is conspicuous in all he has left us, in his too scanty lyric poetry, in his too scanty narrative poetry. When, therefore, he applied himself to dramatic composition, the same instinct directed him unerringly to the true principles on which a drama should be constructed. It caused him to turn with disgust from the rude and chaotic style of the popular stage; it preserved him, on the other hand, from the pedantry and affectation of the classical school. In a word, what propriety of expression, what nice skill in the technique of his art, could accomplish, that Marlowe achieved, and the achievement has made his name memorable for ever in the history of the English drama.

But the moment we turn from Marlowe as an artist to Marlowe as a critic and painter of life, we feel how immeasurable is the distance which separates him, we do not say from Shakspeare, but from many of the least distinguished of his brother playwrights. His genius and temper have been admirably described by Drayton:—

> Next Marlowe, bathed in the Thespian springs,
> Had in him those brave translunary things
> That the first poets had; his raptures were
> All ayre and fire, which made his verses clear,
> For that fine madness still he did retain,
> Which rightly should possess a poet's brain.

It was in this translunary sphere that he found his characters; it was under the inspiration of this fine madness that he delineated them. Of air and fire, not flesh and blood, are the beings who people his world composed. Regarded as counterparts of mankind, as studies of humanity, they are mere absurdities. They are neither true to life nor consistent with themselves. Where they live they live by virtue of the intensity with which they embody abstract conceptions. They are delineations, not of human beings, but of superhuman passions.

The truth is that in the constitution of Marlowe's genius—and we are using the word in its widest sense—there were serious deficiencies. In the first place, he had no humour; in the second place, he had little sympathy with humanity, and with men of the common type, none—a defect which seems to us as detrimental to a dramatist as colour-blindness would be to a painter. In the faculty, again, of minute and accurate observation—a faculty which is with most dramatists an instinct—he appears to have been almost wholly lacking. Nothing is so rare in Marlowe as one of those touches which show that the poet had, as Wordsworth expresses it, "his eye on his object." His dramas teem with blunders and improprieties such as no writer who had observed mankind even with common attention could possibly have committed, and in the vagueness and conventionality of the epithets which are in almost all cases applied by him to natural objects we have conclusive evidence of the same defective vision.

The words in which Sallust describes Catiline will apply with singular propriety to Marlowe: "Vastus animus semper incredibilia, semper immoderata, nimis alta cupiebat." This is in truth Marlowe's distinguishing characteristic. It is one of the sources of his greatness as a poet; it is the main source of his weakness as a dramatist. It was to him what the less exalted egotism of a less exalted nature was to Byron. If we except Edward II., all his leading characters resolve themselves into mere incarnations of this passion. In Tamburlaine and Guise it is the illimitable lust for dominion. In Barabas it is the illimitable lust for wealth. In Faustus it is the insanity of sensual and intellectual aspiration. As impersonations of mankind neither Tamburlaine nor Guise, neither Barabas nor Faustus, will bear examination for one moment. Of Marlowe's minor characters there is not one which impresses itself with any distinctness on the memory. Indeed, they have scarcely more individuality than the "fortisque Gyas, fortisque Cloanthus" of the *Æneid,* or those heroes in the *Iliad* who are mentioned only to swell the number of the slain. Who ever realised Mycetas or Techelles, or Usumcasane or Mathias, or Ferneze or Ithamore or Lodowick? What distinguishes Amyras from Celebinus? Or Jacomo from Barnardine? Or Valdes from Cornelius? Or Calymath from Martin del Bosco? Take again his women. Where they are not mere puppets, as is the case with Zenocrate, Abigail, Bellamira, and Catharine, they are preposterously untrue to nature, as is the case with Olympia, Isabella, and Dido. In one play, and in one play only, has Marlowe displayed a power of characterisation eminently dramatic. In *Edward II.* Gaveston, Mortimer, and the King himself are as admirably drawn as they are admirably contrasted. The sculptural clearness with which the figure of Mortimer, cold, stern, remorseless, stands out from the crowded canvas; the light but firm touches which place the King's young favourite, the joyous, reckless, pleasure-loving Gaveston, vividly before us; the power and subtlety with which the quickly alternating emotions in the breast of Edward, from his first conflict with opposition to his last appalling agony, are depicted—all these combine to place this drama on a far higher level than any of Marlowe's other plays. *Edward II.* is said to have been the poet's last work. If it was so, it shows that, as his life advanced, his genius was widening and mellowing, and it increases our regret for the accident which cut short his career. But that we lost in Marlowe a possible rival of Shakspeare is an opinion in which we by no means concur. It is true that, though the two poets were born within a few weeks of each other, Marlowe was the master and Shakspeare the disciple. It is true also that the best work produced by Shakspeare at twenty-nine—to judge at least from what he gave to the world—was greatly inferior to the best work of Marlowe. But this proves little more than that the powers of Shakspeare were, up to a certain point, slow in developing, and that is almost always the case with men whose genius is of an objective cast. What we fail to see in Marlowe is any indication of power in reserve. Comparatively scanty as his work is, he is constantly repeating himself, and in the few noble and impressive scenes on which his fame as a dramatist mainly rests, we discern what is perhaps the most unpromising of all symptoms in the work of a young writer, excessive elaboration. That *Edward II.* is a considerable advance on his former plays, that it is marked throughout by greater sobriety, and that it exhibits a wider range of sympathy and insight than he has elsewhere displayed, is indisputable. But this is all, and this is not much. In a dramatic poet of the first order we look for qualities which are as conspicuously absent in Marlowe's last and maturest play as they are in the plays which preceded it.

We are not, then, inclined to assign to Marlowe that high position among dramatists which it has of late years been the fashion, and in our opinion the absurd fashion, to claim for him. But as a poet he seems to us to deserve all the praise which his admirers give him. The words "rapture" and "inspiration," which are, when applied to most poetry, little more than figurative expressions, have, when applied to his poetry, a strict propriety. Never before had passion so intense, had imagination so vivid and aspiring, had fancy so rich and graceful, co-existed in equal measure and in equal harmony.

The energy of Marlowe's genius was twofold. On the one side he is a transcendental enthusiast; on the other side he is a pagan hedonist. On the one side he reflects the intense spiritual activity, the preternatural exaltation, not merely of the emotions, but of the imagination and the intellect, which were among the most striking effects of the Renaissance in England. On the other side he reflects not less faithfully the peculiarities of that great movement as it affected academic Italy. The ardour of his passion for the ideal, and the intensity with which he has expressed that passion, are what impress us most in his dramas. In his poems, on the other hand, the predominating element is pure sensuousness. It is the poetry not of desire, but of fruition. No poem in our language is more classical, in the sense at least in which Politian and Sanazzaro would have understood the term, and assuredly no poem in our language is more sensuously lovely, than *Hero and Leander*. It reminds us in some respects of the best episodes in the *Metamorphoses*, and it reminds us still more frequently of Keats's narratives, not, indeed, of *Isabella* or of *The Eve of Saint Agnes*, but indirectly of *Endymion*, and directly of *Lamia*.

But of all Marlowe's gifts the most remarkable, perhaps, was his gift of expression. It may be said of him, with literal truth, that he "voluntary moved harmonious numbers." Of the music of his verse it is superfluous to speak. On this point we are inclined to go almost as far as Mr. Swinburne. If the melodies of Shakspeare and Milton are fuller and more complex, if the music of the poets who have during the present century revealed new capacities in our language has a subtler fascination, no clearer, no nobler, no more melodious note than the note of Marlowe vibrates in our poetry. His diction, too, when at its best—as we see it, for example, in *Hero and Leander*, in the lyric *Come Live with Me*, and in such passages in his plays as Tamburlaine's speech to Zenocrate, as Faust's apostrophe to the shade of Helen, as Edward's last speeches to Leicester, as Guise's soliloquy, as Baldwin's speech to Spenser—seems to us to approach as nearly to the style of the Greek masterpieces as anything to be found in English. It is the perfection of that diction which is at once natural and poetical, at once simple and dignified.

FREDERICK S. BOAS
From "New Light on Marlowe and Kyd"
Fortnightly Review, February 1899, pp. 212–18

There can be little doubt that 1898 will rank as a memorable year in the history of Shaksperean criticism. Seldom has the literature which gathers round the Stratford dramatist been enriched within a twelvemonth by three such important contributions as Mr. Sidney Lee's *Life*, Mr. George Wyndham's edition of the *Poems*, and the English version of Dr. Brandes' elaborate *Study*. It is just three hundred years since Mr. Francis Meres, of Cambridge, penned the first "Appreciation" of the already famous poet-playwright, and the tide of commentary and discussion is still at full flood. The old problems, viewed often in new lights, exercise their old fascination; at the close of three centuries of critical activity, Shakspere, more decisively than ever, holds the field.

But inferior in interest only to the Master, and with something of even more subtle and peculiar appeal to those who linger lovingly over "origins," are the figures of those fellow-playwrights from whom he caught "hints of the proper craft, tricks of the tool's true play." Amongst this group Marlowe stands foremost, but recent investigation more and more suggests that he must share the glory of being Shakspere's early

model in tragic art with Thomas Kyd, author of *The Spanish Tragedy*, and not improbably of the first dramatic version of the Hamlet story. The extraordinary vogue of *The Spanish Tragedy*, with its stirring plot of the revenge of Hieronimo, Marshal of Spain, for the murder of his son, is one of the most remarkable features of Elizabethan stage history. By 1633 at least twelve quarto-editions had appeared, and of eleven of these there are copies still extant. A German version of the play by Ayrer of Nuremberg soon saw the light; in Holland it was adapted by A. van den Bergh, and a later anonymous Dutch version attained such popularity that, as has been shown by Professor Schick and Herr Schönwerth of Munich, no less than nine editions of it have been preserved. The unprecedented success of the play provoked endless ridicule and parody by Kyd's rivals of some of its more high-flown passages, but it kept its hold of popular favour; and as late as 1633 the scandalised Prynne, in his *Histriomastix*, relates, on the authority of R. Brathwaite, the shocking story of an "English Gentlewoman of good ranke," who, when attended in her last moments by a "minister," made no reply at all to his exhortations, "but cried out, 'Hieronimo, Hieronimo, O let me see Hieronimo acted' (calling out for a play, instead of crying unto God for mercy), and so closed her dying eyes."

Yet, in spite of *The Spanish Tragedy's* unique "run," the life of its author was, till recently, little more than a blank. Mr. Gordon Goodwin, however, made the important discovery (*Notes and Queries*, April 21st, 1894) that the future dramatist was baptized on November 6th, 1558, in the church of St. Mary Woolnoth, Lombard Street, in the City. Of this church his father, Francis Kyd, scrivener, or "writer of the Court Letter of London," was several times churchwarden—a fact not without its bearing upon matters to be afterwards discussed, for it proves that the dramatist was reared in an orthodox atmosphere. The Christian name and occupation of Kyd's father had, however, already been made known by Mr. C. J. Robinson, who pointed out (*Academy*, xxxi., p. 346), in the Register of Merchant Taylors' School, the entry of "Thomas Kyd, son of Francis, scrivener," on October 26th, 1565—a date which marks the beginning of the dramatist's education. From this point onwards we have hitherto had no absolutely certain biographical details of his career till the early part of 1594, when, in dedicating to the Countess of Sussex his translation of Garnier's drama *Cornelie*, he alludes to "those so bitter times and priuie broken passions that I endured in the writing it." Even of this confession the precise significance has been quite obscure.

One slender piece of evidence, however, has long existed, indicating Kyd's connection with one of the most interesting episodes in Elizabethan dramatic annals, namely, the accusation of "Atheism" preferred against Marlowe just before his tragic death. Thomas Baker, the antiquarian (1656–1740), in giving a brief account of the proceedings against the author of *Tamburlaine* and *Dr. Faustus* left on record (*Harl. MSS.* 7042, Fol. 401), that "one Mr. Tho. Kydde or Kyddye had been accused to have consorted with, or to have maintained Marlowe's opinions, who seems to have been innocent, and writes a letter to the Lord Keeper, Puckering, to purge himself from these aspersions." These words of Baker were transcribed by Hunter in his MS. *Chorus Vatum* in the British Museum, and were, for the first time, given wider publicity by Mr. Sidney Lee in his article on Kyd in the *National Dictionary of Biography*. It was believed, however, that the dramatist's letter of self-defence had completely disappeared, and that there was little hope of any further clue to the proceedings being found. But I have been fortunate enough, in the course of some investigations concerning Kyd, to discover this letter, and other original documents briefly mentioned in Baker's notes. The result is to throw new and startling light upon the relations of Marlowe and Kyd, and to reveal some passages in their careers almost as sensational as any of the imaginary incidents in their plays.

It is important to remember, before beginning the examination of these documents, that during the period following the defeat of the Armada, Elizabeth's Government, relieved in part from the pressure of external enemies, was engaged in a vigorous campaign against foes of its own household. The religious settlement with which, in the opinion of the Queen's advisers, the national stability was bound up, was threatened from very diverse quarters, by Roman Catholics, Puritans, and sectaries of every shade of belief. The Privy Council, the High Commission Court, and the Ecclesiastical Courts generally took the most vigorous measures for stamping out any form of "blasphemy." One of the earlier victims was Francis Kett, a native of Norfolk, who had been a Fellow of Benet (now Corpus Christi) College, Cambridge, but who had resigned and gone down shortly before Marlowe entered the College as an undergraduate. He was burnt to death at Norwich early in 1589. From the "Articles of heretical pravity" objected against him (*Lansdowne MSS.*) by Edmund Scambler, Bishop of Norwich, and from the more detailed list of his "Blasphemous Heresyes" preserved in the Record Office we find that the creed for which he suffered was a type of Unitarianism mingled with mystical beliefs such as "that Christ is now in His human nature gathering a church here on earth in Judæa," and "that He shall come before the last daie and rayne as materiall Kynge upon Mount Zion at Jerusalem." The theory, at one time generally accepted, that Marlowe had been infected with Kett's doctrines has of late fallen into discredit on the grounds that the dramatist's revolt from orthodoxy must have been of a far more violent and "Atheistic" character. But in the light of the new documents the subject will certainly need re-examination.

The first of these documents to which I would call attention is one which, singularly enough, is not directly mentioned by Baker, though it was in his possession. It forms fols. 172–174 of *Harl. MSS.*, 6848. The first page is, apparently, complete; of the second only the lower half remains, and of the third only the upper half. This third page has the following endorsement in dark ink:

12 May 1593
Vile hereticall Conceiptes
denyinge the deity of Jhesus
Christe our Saviour fownd
emongest the papers of Thos
Kydd prisoner

and immediately below, in red ink, and evidently added later, follow the words:

which he affirmethe That he
had ffrom Marlowe.

This endorsement, therefore, informs us of the hitherto unsuspected fact that on the 12th of May, 1593, Thomas Kyd was arrested, and that amongst his papers of which the authorities took possession was a heretical production which he afterwards asserted he had got from Marlowe. A more detailed account of the matter is given in Kyd's letter to Puckering. He there states that at the time of his arrest, which, it will be afterwards seen, was on a civil not a religious charge, "amongst those waste and idle papers (which I cared not for), and which unaskt I did deliver up, were founde some fragments of a disputation toching that opinion [*i.e.*, Atheism], affirmed by Marlowe to be his, and shufled with some of myne (unknown to me), by some occasion of our wrytinge in one chamber twoe

yeares synce." There seems no reason to doubt this circumstantial story; and the words "affirmed by Marlowe to be his," if interpreted in their obvious meaning, imply that he acknowledged the authorship of the document. It is, therefore, of great importance to examine its contents, which are written in an unusually clear and elegant hand. Though Kyd's description of it as "some fragments of a disputation" is quite accurate, the extant portions are sufficient to show its character. It is far from "Atheistic" in the modern sense of the word; it is, on the contrary, a methodical defence, based on Scriptural texts, of Unitarian doctrines, akin to those of Francis Kett, though, as far as can be judged, without any admixture of his more mystical views. The following passage from fol. 172 is typical of the line of argument pursued:

> It is lawfull by many wayes to se the infirmitie of Jhesus Christ, whom Paul in the last Chapter to the Corinthians of the second Epistle denieth not to be crucified through infirmitie. And the whole course and consent of the Euangelical history doth make him subiect to the passions of man, as hunger, thirst, wearines, and fear. To the same end ar swete, anxietie, continuall praier, the consolation of the angell: again spitting, whipping, rebukes, or checks. His corps wrapped in the linnen cloth, vnburied. And to beleve, forsooth, that this nature subiect to theis infirmities and passions is God or any part of the diuine essence, what is it other but to make God mightie and of power of th[e] one part, weak and impotent of th[e] other part, which thing to think it wer madness and follie, to persuade others, impieties.

Then follows an examination of the various senses in which the word "God" is used in a number of places in the Old and New Testaments, and the assertion that, "to man it is applied but seldom, yet sometimes it is, and then we understand it as a name of mean (*i.e.*, moderate) power and not of the everlasting power." On these grounds the writer argues that even when Christ is called God as by "Paul to the Romains Ninth" or by "Thomas Didimus in the Gospel of John, Chapter twentie," yet the term does not imply divinity.

Fol. 173 develops further the thesis that "a visible God, comprehensible, and mortall," is inconsistent with "what the Scriptures do witness of God"; and fol. 174, in a more impassioned passage, emphasizes the necessity of appeal to them on all doctrinal questions:

> To which sacred fountain iust and right faith ought to cleave and lean in all controversies touching religion, chefly on this point which seemeth to be the piller and stay of our religion. Wher it is called in question concerning the inuocation of saincts or expiation of sowles, a man may err without great danger. In this point being the ground and foundation of our faith we may not err without dammage to our religion. I call that true religion which instructeth man's minde with right faith and worthy opinion of God. And I call that right faith which doth creddit and beleve that of God which the Scriptures do testify.

This passage is preceded by an autobiographical one which throws an interesting light on the circumstances under which the "disputation" was composed. It was evidently addressed to a Bishop, and was intended to sum up in a formal way views which the writer had already maintained in verbal debate:

> Albeit in this vehement and unthought on perturbation of mind, reuerend father, when labour is odious,

writing difficult, and hard commentation vnpleasant and grieuous vnto me, yet in the defence of my caus being required to write for the reuerence I owe to your Lordship above other, I have purposed brefely and compendiously to commit in writing what I think touching th[e] articles [*i.e.*, probably, articles of accusation] which mine opinion by the communication before had with your Lordship might have been evident inough and sufficiently known without writing. For first at the beginning when your Lordshipp admitted me to disputation before many witnesses, and then after to priuate and familier talk I did plainly say all that then came into my mind.

It must be frankly allowed that the treatise is not exactly of the type that we should have expected from Marlowe, and that the situation of a Bishop discussing theology in public and private with a playwright seems incongruous. But it must be remembered that Marlowe was a Master of Arts and a personage of consideration. Vaughan in *The Golden Groue*, 1600, mentions the report that "about fourteen years ago," the dramatist "wrote a booke against the Trinitie." It is, therefore, not improbable that between 1586 and 1590, he may have composed a work that brought him under the notice of the ecclesiastical authorities: that he may have had to defend his views in debate and afterwards in a written *Apologia*, fragments of which got "shufled" with Kyd's papers in 1591.

But even if Kyd's words about Marlowe affirming the fragments of the disputation "to be his" are interpreted to merely mean that he acknowledged that they belong to him, the character of the document still remains of great significance. For the dramatist would scarcely have been in possession of such a theological treatise unless he had been interested in the views it expressed, and to some extent shared them. We can imagine, for instance, such a dissertation being written by Kett to the Bishop of Norwich, and falling afterwards into the hands of one who, as a younger member of the same college, must have known him by reputation. It is most improbable that an "Atheist" would have cared to acquire a treatise of this type. Indeed, the fact that Kyd was charged with "Atheism," owing to the discovery of this Theistic pamphlet amongst his papers is the strongest possible proof of the lax way in which the term was used.

In consequence probably of Kyd's statement, during his examination, the Privy Council on the 18th of May, exactly a week after his arrest, issued a warrant to Henry Maunder, "one of the messengers of Her Majesty's Chamber, to repair to the house of Mr. T. Walsingham, in Kent or to anie other place where he shall understand Christopher Marlowe, to be remaynine and by virtue hereof to bring him to the Court in his companie, and in case of need to require ayd." We further know that Maunder was immediately successful in executing the order, for [on the 20th of May] I have found the following entry in the *MS. Register of the Privy Council*: "This day Ch. Marley of London gent. being sent for by warrant from their Lordships hath entered his appearance accordinglie for his indemnity therein, and is commanded to give his daily attendance on their Lordships till he shall be [signified?] to the contrairie." The Council meanwhile proceeded to make further inquiries about his religious views, for on May 29th they received from an informer called Richard Baines a "Note containing the opinion of one Cristofer Marley concerning his damnable Judgment of Relygion and scorn of God's word." The contents of this "Note" have long been known from *Harl. MSS.*, 6853, fol. 320. But I am now able to prove that this is only an official replica of Baines' "Note," as is indeed suggested

by the endorsement: "Copye of Marloe's blasphemyes as sent to her H" [ighness, *i.e.*, Queen Elizabeth]. I have discovered the original document which forms fol. 170–171 of *Harl. MSS.*, 6848. The endorsement is now partially illegible, but it is almost certainly to be deciphered

> Baynes Marley
> of his blasphemeyes.

The finding of this original "Note" in the informer's own hand is important, as the signature at the bottom in bold and legible characters is unquestionably Richard Baines, not Bame as the crabbed reproduction of it in the "Copye" has been generally interpreted. In the official duplicate the heading "A note contayninge the opinion of one Christofer Marlye concerning his damnable opinions and judgments of Relygion and Scorne of God's worde," has been scored out and altered into "a Note delivered on Whitson eve last of the most horrible blasphemes uttered by Christofer Marley who within iii days after came to a soden and fearfull end of his life." In Baines' paper the original heading is unaltered. The "Copye," too, makes one significant little omission. Baines' second charge against the dramatist is that he affirmeth "that Moyses was but a Juggler, and that one Heriots [*i.e.*, Harriott], being Sir Walter Raleyh's man can do more than hee." It was doubtless thought by the authorities at this stage of the inquiry that, though Raleigh at the time was in disgrace, Her Highness might not care to see her former favourite's name mixed up in such proceedings, so the words "being Sir Walter Raleyh's man," were discreetly left out in the version sent to her.

Baines, as is well known, charges Marlowe not only with the propagation of "Atheism," but of blasphemies of the most revolting nature. It is impossible to demonstrate that his accusations had absolutely no foundation. What wild and whirling words may have been spoken in London taverns, when the wine was red in the cup, no man can now tell. Robert Greene's testimony also, in his *Groatsworth of Wit* (September, 1592), that Marlowe, like himself, had said, "like the foole in his heart, there is no God," must not be overlooked. Even if we ascribe the Theistic disputation to the dramatist's pen, it is safe to assume that Marlowe, writing to a "reverend father," and Marlowe discoursing in a ribald mood to his companions, would not say exactly the same things, or in the same way. Thus it is easy to see that the passage in the *Apologia*, declaring that, "concerning the invocation of saints or expiation of sowles, a man may err without great danger," might be so put in conversation that Baines could twist it into the form, "yf there be any God or good religion it is the Papistes, and all Protestantes are hipocritical Asses." But unless we make the unwarrantable assumption that Kyd is deliberately lying when he asserts Marlowe's connection with the disputation— whether as author or owner—we now possess a new and valuable link of evidence for the conclusion, long ago shrewdly anticipated by Warton, that Marlowe's "Atheism" was his enemies' opprobrious synonym for heterodox views, often, no doubt, loosely and indiscreetly expressed.

GEORGE BERNARD SHAW
"The Spacious Times" (1896)
Dramatic Opinions and Essays
1909, pp. 36–43

M r. William Poel, in drawing up an announcement of the last exploit of the Elizabethan Stage Society, had no difficulty in citing a number of eminent authorities as to the superlative merits of Christopher Marlowe. The dotage of

Charles Lamb on the subject of the Elizabethan dramatists has found many imitators, notably Mr. Swinburne, who expresses in verse what he finds in books as passionately as a poet expresses what he finds in life. Among them, it appears, is a Mr. G. B. Shaw, in quoting whom Mr. Poel was supposed by many persons to be quoting me. But though I share the gentleman's initials, I do not share his views. He can admire a fool: I cannot, even when his folly not only expresses itself in blank verse, but actually invents that art form for the purpose. I admit that Marlowe's blank verse has charm of color and movement; and I know only too well how its romantic march caught the literary imagination and founded that barren and horrible worship of blank verse for its own sake which has since desolated and laid waste the dramatic poetry of England. But the fellow was a fool for all that. He often reminds me, in his abysmally inferior way, of Rossini. Rossini had just the same trick of beginning with a magnificently impressive exordium, apparently pregnant with the most tragic developments, and presently lapsing into arrant triviality. But Rossini lapses amusingly; writes 'Excusez du peu' at the double bar which separates the sublime from the ridiculous; and is gay, tuneful and clever in his frivolity. Marlowe, the moment the exhaustion of the imaginative fit deprives him of the power of raving, becomes childish in thought, vulgar and wooden in humor, and stupid in his attempts at invention. He is the true Elizabethan blank-verse beast, itching to frighten other people with the superstitious terrors and cruelties in which he does not himself believe, and wallowing in blood, violence, muscularity of expression and strenuous animal passion as only literary men do when they become thoroughly depraved by solitary work, sedentary cowardice, and starvation of the sympathetic centres. It is not surprising to learn that Marlowe was stabbed in a tavern brawl: what would be utterly unbelievable would be his having succeeded in stabbing any one else. On paper the whole obscene crew of these blank-verse rhetoricians could outdare Lucifer himself: Nature can produce no murderer cruel enough for Webster, nor any hero bully enough for Chapman, devout disciples, both of them, of Kit Marlowe. But you do not believe in their martial ardor as you believe in the valor of Sidney or Cervantes. One calls the Elizabethan dramatists imaginative, as one might say the same of a man in delirium tremens; but even that flatters them; for whereas the drinker can imagine rats and snakes and beetles which have some sort of resemblance to real ones, your typical Elizabethan heroes of the mighty line, having neither the eyes to see anything real nor the brains to observe it, could no more conceive a natural or convincing stage figure than a blind man can conceive a rainbow or a deaf one the sound of an orchestra. Such success as they have had is the success which any fluent braggart and liar may secure in a pothouse. Their swagger and fustian, and their scraps of Cicero and Aristotle, passed for poetry and learning in their own day because their public was Philistine and ignorant. To-day, without having by any means lost this advantage, they enjoy in addition the quaintness of their obsolescence, and, above all, the splendor of the light reflected on them from the reputation of Shakespeare. Without that light they would now be as invisible as they are insufferable. In condemning them indiscriminately, I am only doing what Time would have done if Shakespeare had not rescued them. I am quite aware that they did not get their reputations for nothing; that there were degrees of badness among them; that Greene was really amusing, Marston spirited and silly-clever, Cyril Tourneur able to string together lines of which any couple picked out and quoted separately might pass as a fragment of a real organic poem, and so on. Even the brutish pedant Jonson was not heartless, and

could turn out prettily affectionate verses and foolishly affectionate criticisms; whilst the plausible firm of Beaumont and Fletcher, humbugs as they were, could produce plays which were, all things considered, not worse than *The Lady of Lyons*. But these distinctions are not worth making now. There is much variety in a dust-heap, even when the rag-picker is done with it; but we throw it indiscriminately into the 'destructor' for all that. There is only one use left for the Elizabethan dramatists, and that is the purification of Shakespeare's reputation from its spurious elements. Just as you can cure people of talking patronizingly about 'Mozartian melody' by showing them that the tunes they imagine to be his distinctive characteristics were the commonplaces of his time, so it is possible, perhaps, to cure people of admiring, as distinctively characteristic of Shakespeare, the false, forced rhetoric, the callous sensation-mongering in murder and lust, the ghosts and combats, and the venal expenditure of all the treasures of his genius on the bedizenment of plays which are, as wholes, stupid toys. When Sir Henry Irving presently revives *Cymbeline* at the Lyceum, the numerous descendants of the learned Shakespearean enthusiast who went down on his knees and kissed the Ireland forgeries will see no difference between the great dramatist who changed Imogen from a mere name in a story to a living woman, and the manager-showman who exhibited her with the gory trunk of a newly beheaded man in her arms. But why should we, the heirs of so many greater ages, with the dramatic poems of Goethe and Ibsen in our hands, and the music of a great dynasty of musicians, from Bach to Wagner, in our ears—why should we waste our time on the rank and file of the Elizabethans, or encourage foolish modern persons to imitate them, or talk about Shakespeare as if his moral platitudes, his jingo claptraps, his tavern pleasantries, his bombast and drivel, and his incapacity for following up the scraps of philosophy he stole so aptly, were as admirable as the mastery of poetic speech, the feeling for nature, and the knack of character-drawing, fun, and hearty wisdom which he was ready, like a true son of the theatre, to prostitute to any subject, any occasion, and any theatrical employment? The fact is, we are growing out of Shakespeare. Byron declined to put up with his reputation at the beginning of the nineteenth century; and now, at the beginning of the twentieth, he is nothing but a household pet. His characters still live; his word pictures of woodland and wayside still give us a Bank-holiday breath of country air; his verse still charms us; his sublimities still stir us; the commonplaces and trumperies of the wisdom which age and experience bring to all of us are still expressed by him better than by anybody else; but we have nothing to hope from him and nothing to learn from him—not even how to write plays, though he does that so much better than most modern dramatists. And if this is true of Shakespeare, what is to be said of Kit Marlowe?

Kit Marlowe, however, did not bore me at St. George's Hall as he has always bored me when I have tried to read him without skipping. The more I see of these performances by the Elizabethan Stage Society, the more I am convinced that their method of presenting an Elizabethan play is not only the right method for that particular sort of play, but that any play performed on a platform amidst the audience gets closer home to its hearers than when it is presented as a picture framed by a proscenium. Also, that we are less conscious of the artificiality of the stage when a few well-understood conventions, adroitly handled, are substituted for attempts at an impossible scenic verisimilitude. All the old-fashioned tale-of-adventure plays, with their frequent changes of scene, and all the new problem plays, with their intense intimacies, should be done in this way.

EDMUND SPENSER

EDMUND SPENSER

1552–1599

Edmund Spenser was born in London, the son of a gentleman tradesman, and educated at the Merchant Taylors' School and Pembroke Hall, Cambridge, graduating in 1576. He became a member of Leicester's household in London. In 1579 he produced his first original work, *The Shepheards Calendar*, dedicated to Sir Philip Sidney. Becoming secretary in 1580 to Lord Grey de Wilton, the Lord Deputy in Ireland, Spenser was eventually rewarded for his services in 1586 when he was granted Kilcolman Castle in County Cork. In 1589 Spenser returned to England with Sir Walter Raleigh, who introduced the poet and the first three books of *The Faerie Queene* to Queen Elizabeth I. These three books were published in London in 1590, but, after receiving no further court favor, Spenser returned to Ireland in 1591. That same year Spenser wrote *Complaints*, *Prosopopoia*, *Teares of the Muses*, and *Daphnaida*. In 1594 Spenser married his second wife, Elizabeth Boyle. He wrote the *Amoretti*, regarding his courtship, and *Epithalamion*, commemorating the wedding. These, along with *Colin Clouts Come Home Again*, were published in 1595. In 1596 Spenser returned to London with three more books of *The Faerie Queene*, which were published that year, as were his *Fowre Hymnes*, *Prothalamion*, and the prose work, *View of the Present State of Ireland*. Spenser died in London on January 13, 1599, and his "Mutabilitie Cantos," intended as a continuation of *The Faerie Queene*, were published posthumously.

Personal

M. Digges hath the whole Aquarius of Palingenius bie hart: & takes mutch delight to repeate it often.

M. Spenser conceiues the like pleasure in the fourth day of the first Weeke of Bartas. Which he esteemes as the proper profession of *Urania*. . . .

I have often marvelled that Chaucer and Lydgate were such good astronomers in those days, while modern poets are so ignorant of astronomy—apart from Buckley, Sidney (?), Blagrave, and a very few others, sons of Urania.

Spenser himself is ashamed, though he is not completely ignorant of the globe and the astrolabe, of the difficulty he has with astronomical rules, tables, and instruments.—GABRIEL HARVEY, *Marginalia*, 1572, ed. Smith, 1913, pp. 161–62

As for Pastorall Poemes, I will not make the comparison [with the works of foreign, particularly Italian, writers], least our countrimens credit should be discountenanst by the contention, who although they cannot fare, with such inferior facilitie, yet I knowe would carrie the bucklers full easilie, from all forreine brauers, if their *subiectum circa quod*, should sauor of anything haughtie: and should the challenge of deepe conceit, be intruded by any forreiner, to bring our english wits, to the tutchstone of Arte, I would preferre, diuine Master *Spencer*, the miracle of wit to bandie line for line for my life, in the honor of *England*, against *Spaine*, *France*, *Italie*, and all the worlde. Neither is he, the only swallow of our summer.— THOMAS NASHE, *To the Gentlemen Students of both Universities*, 1589, *Works*, Vol. 3, ed. McKerrow, 1910, p. 323

In thy sweete son so blessed may'st thou bee,
For learned *Collin* laies his pipes to gage,
And is to fayrie gone a Pilgrimage:
     the more our mone.
          —MICHAEL DRAYTON, "Idea," 1593, *Works*,
          Vol. 1, ed. Hebel, 1931, p. 55

Deare *Collin*, let my Muse excused be,
Which rudely thus presumes to sing by thee,
Although her straines be harsh untun'd & ill,

Nor can attayne to thy divinest skill.
          —MICHAEL DRAYTON, "Endimion and
          Phoebe," 1595, *Works*, Vol. 1, ed. Hebel,
          p. 155

As moderne Poets shall admire the same,
I meane not you (you neuer matched men)
Who brought the Chaos of our tongue in frame,
Through these Herculean labours of your pen:
     I meane the meane, I meane no men diuine,
     But such whose fathers are but waxt like mine.

Goe weeping Truce-men in your sighing weedes,
Vnder a great *Mecaenas* I haue past you:
If so you come where learned *Colin* feedes
His louely flocke, packe thence and quickly haste
     you;
     You are but mistes before so bright a sunne,
     Who hath the Palme for deepe inuention
          wunne.
          —THOMAS LODGE, "The Induction" to
          "Phillis: Honoured with Pastorall Sonnets,"
          1593, *Complete Works*, Vol. 2, ed. Gosse, p. 6

Liue *Spenser* euer, in thy *Fairy Queene*:
Whose like (for deepe Conceit) was neuer seene.
Crownd mayst thou bee, vnto thy more renowne,
(As King of Poets) with a Lawrell crowne.
          —RICHARD BARNFIELD, *A Remembrance of some*
          English Poets, 1598, *Some Longer Elizabethan*
          Poems, ed. Bullen, p. 265

Edward [sic] Spencer of London was easily greatest among the English poets of our age, a fact which his poems, written with divine inspiration and with overwhelming genius, confirm. He died prematurely in 1598, and is buried next to Geoffrey Chaucer who was the first great English poet. These lines are written on his tomb:

Here lies Spenser next to Chaucer, next to
him in talent as next to him in death. O Spenser,
here next to Chaucer the poet, as a poet you are

buried; and in your poetry you are more permanent
than in your grave. While you were alive, English
poetry lived and approved you; now you are dead,
it too must die and fears to.
> —WILLIAM CAMDEN, *Reges, Reginae, Nobiles,*
> *& Alij in Ecclesia Collegiata B. Petri West-*
> *monasterij Sepulti,* 1600

Spenser's stanzaes pleased him not nor his matter the meaning
of which Allegorie he had delivered in papers to Sir Walter
Raughlie. . . . He Jonson hath be heart some verses of Spensers Calender, about wyne, between Soline & percye. . . .
That the Irish having robd Spensers goods, and burnt his house
and a little child new born, he and his wyfe escaped, and after,
he died for lake of bread in King Street, and refused 20 pieces
sent to him by my Lord of Essex, and said, He was sorrie he
had no time to spend them. That in that paper S. W. Raughly
had of the Allegories of his Fayrie Queen, by the Blating Beast
the Puritans were understood, by the false Duessa the Q. of
Scots.—BEN JONSON, *Conversations with William Drum-*
mond of Hawthornden, 1619, ed. Harrison, pp. 4–9

> And if ought els, great *Bards* beside,
> In sage and solemn tunes have sung,
> Of Turney's and of Trophies hung;
> Of Forests, and inchantments drear,
> Where more is meant than meets the ear.
> > —JOHN MILTON, *Il Penseroso,* 1631, Bk. 2, v.
> > 116–21

> At *Delphos* shrine, one did a doubt propound,
> Which by th'Oracle must be released,
> Whether of Poets were the best renow'nd:
> Those that survive, or they that are deceased?
> The Gods made answer by divine suggestion,
> While *Spencer* is alive, it is no question.
> > —FRANCIS BEAUMONT, "On Mr. Edm. Spenser,
> > Famous Poet," 1653, *English Poets,* Vol. 4, ed.
> > Chalmers, p. 204

Edmond Spencer born in this City, was brought up in
Pembroke-hall in Cambridge, where he became an excellent
Scholar, but especially most happy in English Poetry, as his
works do declare. In which the many *Chaucerisms* used (for I
will not say affected by him) are thought by the ignorant to be
blemishes, known by the learned to be *beauties* to this book;
which notwithstanding had been more salable, if more conformed to our modern language.

There passeth a story commonly told and believed, that
Spencer presenting his Poems to Queen *Elizabeth:* She highly
affected therewith, commanded the Lord *Cecil* Her Treasurer,
to give him an hundred pound; and when the Treasurer (a good
Steward of the Queens money) alledged that sum was too
much, then *give him* (quoth the Queen) *what is reason*; to
which the Lord consented, but was so busied, belike, about
matters of higher concernment, that *Spencer* received no reward; Whereupon he presented this petition in a small piece of
paper to the Queen in her Progress,

> I was promis'd on a time,
> To have reason for my rhyme;
> From that time unto this season,
> I receiv'd nor rhyme nor reason.

Hereupon the Queen gave strict order (not without some check
to her Treasurer) for the present payment of the hundred
pounds, the first intended unto him.

He afterwards went over into Ireland, Secretary to the
Lord *Gray,* Lord Deputy thereof; and though that his office
under his Lord was lucrative, yet he got no estate, but saith my

Author, *Peculiari Poetis fato semper cum paupertate conflic-*
tatus est. . . .

Returning into *England,* he was robb'd by the Rebels of
that little he had, and dying for grief in great want, *Anno* 1598.
was honorably buried nigh *Chaucer* in Westminster, where this
Distick concludeth his Epitaph on his Monument,

> *Anglica te vivo vixit plausitque poesis,*
> *Nunc moritura timet te moriente mori.*

Whilst thou dids't live, liv'd English poetry,
Which fears, now thou art dead, that she shall die.

Nor must we forget, that the expense of his funeral and
monument, was defrayed at the sole charge of *Robert,* first of
that name, Earl of *Essex.*—THOMAS FULLER, *The Worthies of*
England, 1662, pp. 219–20

> Old Chaucer, like the morning Star,
> To us discovers day from far,
> His light those Mists and Clouds dissolv'd,
> Which our dark Nation long involv'd;
> But he descending to the shades,
> Darkness again the Age invades.
> Next (like *Aurora*) *Spencer* rose,
> Whose purple blush the day foreshows. . . .

> Time, which made them their Fame outlive,
> To *Cowly* scarce did ripeness give.
> Old Mother Wit, and Nature gave
> *Shakespeare* and *Fletcher* all they have;
> In *Spencer,* and in *Johnson,* Art,
> Of slower Nature got the start.
> > —SIR JOHN DENHAM, "On Mr. Abraham
> > Cowley . . . ," 1668, *Poetical Works,* ed.
> > Banks, 1928, pp. 149–50

For my part, I am of opinion, that neither *Homer, Virgil,*
Statius, Ariosto, Tasso, nor our *English Spencer,* could have
form'd their Poems half so beautiful, without those Gods and
Spirits, and those Enthusiastick parts of Poetry, which compose
the most noble parts of all their writings and I will ask any man
who loves Heroick Poetry, (for I will not dispute their tastes who
do not) if the Ghost of *Polydorus* in *Virgil,* the Enchanted wood
in *Tasso,* and the Bower of bliss, in Spencer (which he borrows
from that admirable *Italian*) could have been omitted without
taking from their works some of the greatest beauties in
them.—JOHN DRYDEN, "Of Heroique Players," 1672, *Works,*
Vol. 4, eds. Scott, Saintsbury, 1882, p. 23

Edmund Spencer, the first of our *English* Poets that brought
Heroic Poesie to any perfection, his *Faery Queen* being for
great Invention and Poetic heighth judg'd little inferiour, if not
equal to the chief of the ancient Greeks and Latins or Modern
Italians, but the first Poem that brought him into Esteem was
his *Shepherds* Calendar, which so endear'd him to that Noble
Patron of all Vertue and Learning *Sir Philip Sidney,* that he
made him known to Queen Elizabeth, and by that means got
him preferr'd to be Secretary to his Brother *Sir Henry Sidney,*
who was sent deputy into *Ireland,* where he is said to have
written his *Faerie Queen,* but upon the return of *Sir Henry,* his
Employment ceasing, he also return'd into *England,* and having lost his great Friend *Sir Philip,* fell into poverty, yet made
his last Refuge to the Queens Bounty, and had 500 l. order'd
him for his Support, which nevertheless was abridg'd to 100 by
Cecil, who hearing of it, and owing him a grudge for some
reflections in Mother *Hubbards* Tale, cry'd out to the Queen,
What all this for a Song? This he is said to have taken so much
to Heart, that he contracted a deep Melancholy, which soon
after brought his life to a Period: So apt is an Ingenious Spirit to

resent a slighting, even from the greatest Persons; and thus much I must needs say of the Merit of so great a Poet from so great a Monarch, that as it is incident to the best of Poets sometimes to flatter some Royal or Noble Patron, never did any do it more to the height, or with greater Art and Elegance, if the highest of praises attributed to so Heroic a Princess can justly be term'd Flattery.—EDWARD PHILLIPS, *Theatrum Poetarum Anglicanorum*, 1675, pp. 34–36

Next to this incomparable Knight Sir *Philip Sidney*, we shall add the Life of his fellow-Poet and contemporary, Mr *Edmond Spenser*, who was born in the City of *London*, and brought up in *Pembroke-hall* in *Cambridge*, where he became a most excellent scholar, but especially very happy in English Poetry, as his Learned elaborate Works do declare. In which the many *Chaucerisms* used (for I will not say, affected by him) are thought by the ignorant to be blemishes, known by the learned to be beauties to his book: which notwithstanding (saith a learned writer) had been more Saleable, if more conformed to our modern Language.

His first flight in Poetry was that Book of his called *The Shepherds Kalendar*, applying an old name to a new work, being of Eglogues fitted to each moneth in the year: of which work hear what that worthy Knight, Sir *Philip Sidney* writes, in his *Defence of Poesy*: *The Shepherds Kalendar* (saith he) *hath much Poetry in his Eclogues, indeed worthy the reading if I be not deceived. That same framing his Stile to an old rustick Language I dare not allow, since neither* Theocritus *in Greek,* Virgil *in Latine, nor* Sanazara *in Italian did affect it.* Afterwards he translated the *Gnat*, a little fragment of *Virgils* excellency. But his main Book, and which indeed I think Envy its self cannot carp at, was his *Fairy Queen*, a Work of such an ingenious composure, as will last as long whilest times shall be no more.

Now as you have heard what esteem Sir *Philip Sidney* had of his Book, so you shall hear what esteem Mr *Spenser* had of Sir *Philip Sidney*, writing thus in his *Ruines of Time*.

> Yet will I sing; but who can better sing,
> Than thou thy selfe, thine owne selfes valiance,
> That, whilest thou livedst, madest the forrests ring,
> And fields resownd, and flockes to leap and daunce,
> And shepheards leave their lambs unto mischaunce,
> To runne thy shrill Arcadian pipe to heare:
> O happie were those dayes, thrice happie were!

There passeth a story commonly told and believed, that Mr *Spenser* presenting his Poems to Queen *Elizabeth*, she highly affected therewith, commanded the Lord Cecil, her Treasurer to give him an hundred pound; and when the Treasurer (a good Steward of the Queens money) alledged that Sum was too much for such a matter; then give him (quoth the Queen) *what is reason*; to which the Lord consented, but was so busied, belike, about matters of higher concernment, that Mr *Spenser* received no reward; whereupon he presented this Petition in a small piece of Paper to the Queen in her Progress.

> I was promis'd on a time,
> To have reason for my Ryme;
> From that time unto this season,
> I receiv'd nor Rhyme nor Reason.

Hereupon the Queen gave strict order (not without some check to her Treasurer) for the present payment of the hundred pounds she first intended unto him. . . .

He afterwards went over into *Ireland*, Secretary to the Lord Gray, Lord Deputy thereof; and though that his Office under his Lord was Lucrative, yet got he no estate; *Peculiari Poetis fato semper cum paupertate conflictatus est*, saith the reverend *Cambden*; so that it fared little better with him, than with *William Xilander* the *German*, (a most excellent Linguist, Antiquary, Philosopher, and Mathematician) who was so poor, that (as Thuanus writes) he was thought *Fami non famae scribere*.

Thriving so bad in that Boggy Country, to add to his misery, he was Rob'd by the Rebels of that little he had left; whereupon in great grief he returns into *England*, and falling into want, which to a noble Spirit is most killing, being heart broken, he died *Anno* 1598. and was honourably buried at the sole charge of *Robert*, first of that name Earl of Essex, where this Distick on his Monument.

> *Anglica te vivo, vixit plausitque Poesis;*
> *Nunc moritura, timet te moriente mori.*
> Whilest thou didst live, liv'd English Poetry,
> Which fears, now thou art dead, that she shall die.

A modern Author writes, that the Lord *Cecil* owed Mr. *Spenser* a grudge for some Reflections of his in Mother *Hubbard's Tale*, and therefore when the Queen had ordered him that money, the Lord Treasurer said, What all this for a Song? And this he is said to have taken so much to Heart, that he contracted a deep melancholy, which soon after brought his life to a period: So apt is an ingenious Spirit to resent a slighting even from the greatest persons. And thus much I must needs say of the merit of so great a Poet from so great a Monarch, that it is incident to the best of Poets sometimes to flatter some Royal or Noble Patron, never did any do it more to the height, or with greater art and elegance, if the highest of praises attributed to so Heroick a Princess can justly be termed flattery.—WILLIAM WINSTANLEY, *England's Worthies*, 1684, pp. 224–27

But *Ariosto* and Spencer, however *great Wits*, not observing this judicious Conduct of *Virgil*, nor attending to any sober Rules, are hurried on with a *boundless, impetuous* Fancy over Hill and Dale, till they are both lost in a Wood of Allegories. Allegories so *wild, unnatural*, and *extravagant*, as greatly displease the Reader. This way of writing mightily offends in this Age; and 'tis a wonder how it came to please in any.—SIR RICHARD BLACKMORE, "Preface" to *Prince Arthur*, 1695, *Critical Essays of the Seventeenth Century*, Vol. 3, ed. Spingarn, 1908, p. 238

Mr Beeston says, he was a little man, wore short haire, little band and little cuffs.

Mr Edmund Spencer was of Pembroke-hall in Cambridge; he misst the Fellowship there, which Bishop Andrewes gott. He was an acquaintance and frequenter of Sir Erasmus Dreyden: His Mistris Rosalind was a kinswoman of Sir Erasmus Ladys. The chamber there at Sir Erasmus' is still called Mr Spencers chamber. Lately, at the college takeing-downe the Wainscot of his chamber, they found an abundance of Cards, with stanzas of the *Faerie Queen* written on them.

Mr Samuel Woodford (the Poet who paraphras'd the Psalmes) lives in Hampshire neer Alton, and he told me that Mr Spenser lived sometime in these parts, in this delicate sweet ayre: where he enjoyed his Muse: and writt good part of his Verses. He had lived some time in Ireland, and made a description of it, which is printed.

I have said before that Sir Philip Sidney, and Sir Walter Ralegh were his acquaintance. Sir John Denham told me, that ABp. Usher, Lord Primate of Armagh, was acquainted with him; by this token: when Sir William Davenant's *Gondibert* came forth, Sir John askt the Lord Primate if he had seen it. Said the Primate, Out upon him, with his vaunting Preface, he speaks against my old friend Edmund Spenser.

In the South cross-aisle of Westminster abbey, next the Dore, is this Inscription:

Heare lies (expecting the second comeing of our Sav-iour Christ Jesus) the body of Edmund Spencer, the Prince of Poets of his tyme, whose divine spirit needs no other witnesse, then the workes which he left behind him. He was borne in London, in the yeare 1510, and dyed in the yeare 1596.

　　　—JOHN AUBREY, *Brief Lives*, c. 1697, ed. Dick,
　　　　　1949, pp. 282–83

The character which a living poet has given of Spenser, would be much more true of Milton:

. . . Yet not more sweet
Than pure was he, and not more pure than wise;
High Priest of all the Muses' mysteries.
　　　　　　(Southey, *Carmen Nuptiale*, Proem)

Spenser, on the contrary, is very apt to pry into mysteries which do not belong to the Muses. Milton's voluptuousness is not lascivious or sensual. He describes beautiful objects for their own sakes. Spenser has an eye to the consequences, and steeps everything in pleasure, often not of the pureset kind.—WILLIAM HAZLITT, "On the Character of Milton's Eve," *The Round Table*, 1816

Sometimes the ambitious Power of choice,
　　mistaking
Proud spring-tide swellings for a regular sea,
Will settle on some British theme, some old
Romantic tale by Milton left unsung;
More often turning to some gentle place
Within the groves of Chivalry, I pipe
To shepherd swains, or seated harp in hand,
Amid reposing knights by a river side
Or fountain, listen to the grave reports
Of dire enchantments faced and overcome
By the strong mind, and tales of warlike feats,
Where spear encountered spear, and sword with
　　sword
Fought, as if conscious of the blazonry
That the shield bore, so glorious was the strife;
Whence inspiration for a song that winds
Through ever changing scenes of votive quest
Wrongs to redress, harmonious tribute paid
To patient courage and unblemished truth,
To firm devotion, zeal unquenchable,
And Christian meekness hallowing faithful loves.

. . .

Beside the pleasant Mill of Trompington
I laughed with Chaucer in the hawthorn shade;
Heard him, while birds were warbling, tell his tales
Of amorous passion. And that gentle Bard,
Chosen by the Muses for their Page of State—
Sweet Spenser, moving through his clouded
　　heaven
With the moon's beauty and the moon's soft pace,
I called him Brother, Englishman, and Friend!
　　　—WILLIAM WORDSWORTH, *The Prelude*, 1850,
　　　　　Bk. 1, v. 166–85; Bk. 3, v. 278–85

General

The three brightest talents of Britain have been Chaucer, More, and Jewel. To those I would add three more now flour-ishing: Heywood, Sidney, and Spenser. . . .

Not manie Chawcers, or Lidgates, Gowers, or Occleues, Surries, or Heywoods, in those days: & how few Aschams, or

Phaers, Sidneys, or Spensers, Warners or Daniels, Siluesters, or Chapmans, in this pregnant age. . . .

And now translated Petrarch, Ariosto, Tasso, & Bartas himself deserue curious comparison with Chaucer, Lidgate, & owre best Inglish, aunciert and moderne. Amongst which, the Countesse of Pembroke's *Arcadia*, & the *Faerie Queene* are now freshest in request: & *Astrophil*, and *Amyntas* ar none of the idlest pastimes of sum fine humanists. . . .

Amaryllis, & Sir Walter Raleighs *Cynthia*, how fine and sweet inuentions? Excellent matter of emulation for Spencer, Constable, France, Watson, Daniel, Warner, Chapman, Sil-uester, Shakespeare, & the rest of owr florishing metricians.—GABRIEL HARVEY, *Marginalia*, 1542–98, ed. Smith, 1913, pp. 122, 231–2

Extra iocum, I like your *Dreames* passingly well and the rather, bicause they sauour of that singular extraordinarie veine and inuention, whiche I euer fancied moste, and in a manner admired onelye in *Lucian, Petrarche, Aretine, Pasquill*, and all the most delicate, and fine conceited Grecians and Italians: (for the Romanes to speake of, are but verye Ciphars in this kinde:) whose chiefest endeuour, and drifte was, to haue nothing vul-gare, but in some respecte or other, and especially in *Liuely Hyperbolicall Amplifications*, rare, queint, and odde in euery pointe, and as a man would saye, a degree or two at the leaste, aboue the reache, and compasse of a common Schollers capac-itie. In whiche respecte notwithstanding, as well for the sin-gularitie of the manner, as the Diunitie of the matter, I hearde once a Diuine, preferre *Saint Iohns Reuelation* before al the veriest *Maetaphysicall Visions*, and iollyest conceited *Dreames* or *Extasies*, that euer were diused by one or other, howe admi-rable, or superexcellent soeuer they seemed otherwise to the worlde. And truely I am so confirmed in this opinion, that when I bethinke me of the verie notablest, and most wonderful Propheticall, or Poeticall Vision, that euer I read, or hearde, me seemeth the proportion is so vnequall, that there hardly ap-peareth anye semblaunce of Comparison: no more in a manner (specially for Poets) than doth betweene the incomprehensible Wisedom of God, and the sensible Wit of Man. But what needeth this digression betweene you and me? I dare saye you wyll holde your selfe reasonably wel satisfied, if youre *Dreames* be but as well esteemed of in Englande, as *Petrarches Visions* be in Italy: whiche I assure you, is the very worst I wish you. But, see, how I haue the Arte *Memoratiue* at commaundement. In good faith I had once againe nigh forgotten your *Fairie Queene*: howbeit by good chaunce, I haue nowe sent hir home at the laste, neither in better nor worse case, than I founde hir. And must you of necessitie haue my Iudgement of hir in deede? To be plaine, I am voyde of al iudgement, if your *Nine Comoedies*, wherevnto in imitation of *Herodotus*, you giue the names of the *Nine Muses*, (and in one mans fansie not vnworthily) come not neerer *Ariostoes Comoedies*, eyther for the finenesse of plausible Elocution, or the rarenesse of Poetical Inuention, than that *Eluish Queene* doth to his *Orlando Furioso*, which notwithstanding, you wil needes seeme to emulate, and hope to ouergo, as you flatly professed your self in one of your last Letters. Besides that you know, it hath bene the vsual practise of the most exquisite and odde wittes in all nations, and spe-cially in *Italie*, rather to shewe, and aduaunce themselues that way, than any other: as namely, those three notorious dyscours-ing heads, *Bibiena, Machiauel*, and *Aretine* did, (to let *Bembo* and *Ariosto* passe) with the great admiration, and wonderment of the whole countrey: being in deede reputed matchable in all poyntes, both for conceyt of Witte, and eloquent decyphering of matters, either with *Aristophanes* and *Menander* in Greek, or with *Plautus* and *Terence* in Latin, or with any other, in any other tong. But I wil not stand greatly with you in your owne matters. If so be the *Faerye Queene* be fairer in your eie than the *Nine Muses,* and *Hobgoblin* runne away with the Garland from *Apollo:* Marke what I saye, and yet I will not say that I thought, but there an End for this once, and fare you well, till God or some good Aungell putte you in a better minde.— GABRIEL HARVEY, *Three Proper, and Wittie, Familiar Letters,* 1580

And here (heauenlie *Spencer*) I am most highly to accuse thee of forgetfulnes, that in that honourable Catalogue of our English *Heroes,* which insueth the conclusion of thy famous Fairie Queene, thou wouldest let so speciall a piller of Nobilitie [the Earl of Derby?] passe vnsaluted. The verie thought of his farre deriued discent, and extraordinarie parts wherewith hee asto[ni]eth the world, and drawes all harts to his loue, would haue inspired thy forewearied *Muse* with new furie to proceede to the next triumphs of thy statelie Goddesse, but as I in fauor of so rare a Scholer, suppose with this counsaile, he refraind his mention in this first part, that he might with full saile proceede to his due commendations in the second. Of this occasion long since I happened to frame a Sonnet, which being wholy intended to the reuerence of this renoumed Lord, (to whom I owe all the vtmost powers of my loue and deutie) I meante heere for variety of stile to insert[.]

> Perusing yesternight with idle eyes,
>   The Fairy Singers stately tuned verse:
> And viewing after Chap-mans wonted guise,
>   What strange contents the title did rehearse.
> I streight leapt ouer to the latter end,
>   Where like the queint Comaedians of our time,
> That when their Play is doone do fall to ryme,
>   I found short lines, to sundry Nobles pend.
> Whom he as speciall Mirrours singled fourth,
>   To be the Patrons of his Poetry;
> I read them all, and reuerenc't their worth,
>   Yet wondred he left out thy memory.
> But therefore gest I he supprest thy name,
>   Because few words might not comprise thy fame.

Beare with mee gentle Poet, though I conceiue not aright of thy purpose, or be too inquisitiue into the intent of thy obliuion: for how euer my coniecture may misse the cushion, yet shall my speech sauour of friendship, though it be not allied to Iudgement.—THOMAS NASHE, *Pierce Penilesse His Supplication to the Divell,* 1592, *Works,* Vol. 1, ed. McKerrow, p. 234

Petrarck was a delicate man, and with an elegant iudgement gratiously confined Loue within the limits of Honour; Witt within the boundes of Discretion; Eloquence within the termes of Ciuility: as not many yeares sithence an Inglishe Petrarck did, a singular Gentleman, and a sweete Poet, whose verse singeth, as valour might speake, and whose ditty is an image of the Sun, voutsafing to represent his glorious face in a clowde.—GABRIEL HARVEY, *Pierces Superorogation,* 1593, *Works,* Vol. 2, ed. Grosart, p. 93

> Whereby great SYDNEY & our SPENCER might,
> With those *Po*-singers beeing equalled,
> Enchaunt the world with such a sweet delight,
> That theyr eternall songs (for euer read,)
> May shew what great ELIZAS raigne hath bred.
> What musique in the kingdome of her peace,
> Hath now beene made to her, and by her might,

> Whereby her glorious fame shall neuer cease.
>   —SAMUEL DANIEL, "To the Right Honorable,
>   the Lady Marie, Countess of Pembroke,"
>   1594, *Complete Works,* Vol. 3, ed. Grosart, pp.
>   26–27

But yet so pure were Chaucers wordes in his owne daies, as *Lidgat:* that learned man calleth him *The Loadstarre of the English languagee* and so good they are in our daies, as Maister *Spencer,* following the counsaile of *Tullie* in *de Oratore,* for reuiuing of antient wordes, hath adorned his owne stile with that beauty and grauitie, which *Tully* speakes of: and his much frequenting of *Chaucers* antient speeches causeth many to allow farre better of him, than otherwise they would.—FRANCIS BEAUMONT, Letter to Thomas Speght, 1598

> *To Edmund Spenser*
> Our Virgil in Dan Chaucer dost thou see?
> Badly! if aught can badly come from thee:
> Chaucer our Ennius, thou our Virgil be!

On the same
If fertile England can number three hundred poets, why cannot she number two Spensers? That is my question. And the answer comes from our English Apollo (Spenser bids us use that honourable title): Greece, they say, bore only one Homer, nor Rome herself two Virgils.—CHARLES FITZGEOFFREY, *Affaniae: sive Epigrammatum Libri Tres,* 1601, *Poems,* ed. Grosart, p. xix

> Let This [work] prouoke our modern wits to sacre
> Their wondrous gifts to honour thee their Maker:
> That our mysterious ELFINE oracle,
> Deepe, Morall, graue, inuentions miracle:
> My deere sweet Daniel, sharpe-conceipted briefe,
> Ciuill, sententious, for pure accents chiefe:
> And our new *Naso,* that so passionates
> Th'heroicke sighes of loue-sick Potentates:
> May change their subiect, and aduance their wings
> Vp to these higher and more holy things.
>   —JOSHUA SYLVESTER, *Bartas; His Deuine
>   Weekes & Workes,* 1605, *Complete Works,* ed.
>   Grosart, p. 99

And after reu'rence done, all being set
Vpon their finny Coursers, round her throne,
And shee prepar'd to cut the watry Zone
Ingirting *Albion;* all their pipes were still,
And *Colin Clout* began to tune his quill,
With such deepe Art that euery one was giuen
To thinke *Apollo* (newly slid from Heau'n)
Had tane a humane shape to win his loue,
Or with the *Westerne Swaines* for glory stroue.
He sung th'heroicke Knights of *Faiery* land
In lines so elegant, of such command,
That had the *Thracian* plaid but halfe so well
He had not left *Eurydice* in hell.
But e're he ended his melodious song
An host of *Angels* flew the clouds among,
And rapt this Swan from his attentiue mates,
To make him one of their associates
In heauens faire Quire: Where now he sings the praise
Of him that is the *first and last of dayes.*
Diuinest *Spencer* heau'n-bred, happy Muse!
Would any power into my braine infuse
Thy worth, or all that *Poets* had before
I could not praise till thou deseru'st no more.
A dampe of wonder and amazement strooke

Thatis attendants, many a heauy looke
Follow'd sweet *Spencer*, till the thickning ayre
Sights further passage stop'd. A passionate teare
Fell from each *Nymph*, no Shepheards cheeke was dry,
A doleful *Dirge*, and mournfull *Elegie*
Flew to the shore. When mighty *Nereus* Queene
(In memory of what was heard and seene)
Imploy'd a *Factor*, (fitted well with store
Of richest Iemmes, refined *Indian Ore*)
To raise, in honour of his worthy name
A *Piramis*, whose head (like winged *Fame*)
Should pierce the clouds, yea seeme the stars to kisse,
And *Mausolus* great toombe might shrowd in *his*.
Her will had beene performance, had not *Fate*
(That neuer knew how to commiserate)
Suborn'd curs'd *Auarice* to lye in waite
For that rich prey: (*Gold is a taking baite*)
Who closely lurking like a subtile Snake
Vnder the couert of a thorny brake,
Seiz'd on the *Factor* by faire *Thetis* sent,
And rob'd our *Colin* of his Monument.
　　　　—WILLIAM BROWNE, *Britannia's Pastorals*,
　　　　　　1616, *Poems*, Vol. 1, ed. Goodwin, pp.
　　　　　　225–26

You farre-fam'd spirits of this happie Ile,
That, for your sacred songs haue gain'd the stile
Of *PHOEBVS* sons: whose notes they aire aspire
Of th'old *Ægyptian*, or the *Thracian* lyre,
That *Chaucer, Gower, Lidgate, Spencer* hight
Put on your better flames, and larger light
To waite vpon the age that shall your names new nourish
Since vertue prest shall grow, and buried arts shall flourish.
　　　　—BEN JONSON, "The Golden Age Restored,"
　　　　　　1616, *Works*, Vol. 7, eds. Herford, Simpson,
　　　　　　p. 425

Strange-headed Monsters, Painters haue described.
To which the Poets strange parts haue ascribed, . . .

On what seu'n-headed beast the Strumpet sits,
That weares the scarfe, sore troubleth many wits,
Whether seu'n sinnes be meant, or else seu'n hils,
It is a question fit for higher skils.
　　　　—SIR JOHN HARINGTON, "Of Monsters, to My
　　　　　　Lady Rogers," 1618, *Letters and Epigrams of
　　　　　　Sir John Harington*, ed. McClure, 1930, pp.
　　　　　　224–25

The word LEGEND, so called of the Latine Gerund, *Legendum*, and signifying, by the Figure *Hexoche*, things specially worthy to be read, was anciently vsed in an Ecclesiasticall sense, and restrained therein to things written in Prose, touching the Liues of Saints. Master EDMUND SPENSER was the very first among vs, who transferred the vse of the word LEGEND, from Prose to Verse: nor that vnfortunately; the Argument of his Bookes being of a kind of sacred Nature, as comprehending in them things as well Diuine as Humane. And surely, that excellent Master, knowing the weight and vse of Words, did completely answer the *Decorum* of a LEGEND, in the qualitie of his Matter, and meant to giue it a kind of Consecration in the Title. To particularize the Lawes of this Poeme, were to teach the making of a Poeme; a Worke for a Volume, not an Epistle. But the principall is, that being a *Species* of an *Epick* or Heroick Poeme, it eminently describeth the act or acts of some one or other eminent Person; not with too much labour, compasse, or extension, but roundly rather, and by way of Briefe, or *Compendium*.—MICHAEL DRAYTON, "To the Reader," *The Legends of*

Robert Duke of Normandie, 1619, *Works*, Vol. 2, ed. Hebel, p. 382

The Authors I have seen (saith he ⟨Drummond⟩) on the subject of Love, are the Earl of Surrey, Sir Thomas Wyat (whom, because of their Antiquity, I will not match with our better Times) *Sidney, Daniel, Drayton* and *Spencer*. . . . As to that which *Spencer* calleth his *Amorelli* [sic], I am not of their Opinion, who think them his; for they are so childish, that it were not well to give them so honourable a Father—WILLIAM DRUMMOND, "Heads of a Conversation betwixt the Famous Poet Ben Jonson, and William Drummond of Hawthornden," *Works*, 1619, p. 226

Graue morrall *Spencer* after these came on
Then whom I am perswaded there was none
Since the blind *Bard* his Iliads vp did make,
Fitter a taske like that to vndertake,
To set down boldly, brauely to inuent,
In all high knowledge, surely excellent.
　　　　—MICHAEL DRAYTON, "Epistle to
　　　　　　Henry Reynolds," 1627, *Works*, Vol.
　　　　　　3, ed. Hebel, p. 228

Whosoeuer will deliver a well grounded opinion and censure of any learned man, must at the least stand vpon the same leuell with him in matter of iudgement and ability: for otherwise, whiles remaining on the lower ground he looketh vp at him, he shall haue but a superficiall view of the most prominent parts, without being able to make any discouery into the large continent that lyeth behind those; wherein vsually is the richest soyle. This consideration maketh mee very vnwilling to say anything in this kind of *our* late admirable poet EDMUND SPENCER, who is seated soe high aboue the wreach of my weake eyes, as the more I looke to discerne and discry his perfections, the more faint and dazeled they grow through *the* distance and splendour of the obiect. Yet to comply *with your* desire, I will here briefly deliuer you (though *with* a hoar[s]e voyce and trembling hand) some of those rude and undigested conceptions that I haue of him; not daring to looke too farre into that sacrary of the MUSES and of learning, where to handle anything *with* boldness, were impiety. His learned workes confirme me in the beliefe *that* our NORTHEREN climate may give life to as well tempered a brain, and as rich a mind as where the sunne shineth fairest. When I read him methinks our country needth not enuy either GREECE, ROME or TUSCANY; for if affection deceiue me not very much, their POETS excell in nothing but he is admirable in the same: and in this he is the more admirable that what perfections they haue seuerally, you may find all in him alone; as though nature had striued to show in him that when she pleaseth to make a MASTER-PIECE, she can giue in one subject all those excellencies that to be in height would seeme to require euery one of them a different temper and complexion. And if at any time he pluoketh a flower out their gardens, he transplanteth it soe happily into his owne, that it groweth there fairer and sweeter then it did where first it sprang vp. his works are such, as were their true worth knowne abroad, I am perswaded *the* best witts and most learned men of other parts, would study our long neglected language, to be capable of his rich conceptions and smooth delivery of them. For certainely, weight of matter was neuer better ioyned *with* propriety of language and *with* maiestey and sweetnes of verse, then by him. And if any should except his reuiuing some obsolete words, and vsing some ancient formes of speech, in my opinion he blameth that *which* deserueth much prayse: for SPENCER doth not that out of any affectation (although his assiduity in CHAUCER might make his language familier to him) but only then when they serue to expresse more liuely and more concisely what he would say: and whensoeuer he vseth them, he doth so polish their natiue rudenes, as retaining the maiesty of antiquity the[y], want nothing of the elegancy of our freeshest speech. I hope that what he hath written will be a meanes that the english tongue will receiue no more alteration and changes, but will remaine & continue settled in that forme it now hath; for excellent authours doe draw vnto them the study of posterity, and whosoeuer is delighted *with* what he readeth in an other, feeleth in himselfe a desire to expresse like thinges in a like manner: and the more resemblance his elocutions haue to his authors *the* neerer he perswadeth himselfe he arriueth to perfection: and thus, much converstation [sic] and study in what he would imitate, begetteth a habite of doing the like. This is the cause that after the great lights of learning among the GRECIANS their language receiued no further alterations. and that the LATINE hath euer since remained in the same state whereovnto it was reduced by CICERO, VIRGILL, and the other great men of that time: and the TUSCANE tongue is at this day the same as it was left about 300 yeares agoe by DANTE PETRACHE and BOCCACE. If it is true that the vicissitudes of things (change being a necessary and inseperable condicion of all sublunary creatures) and the inundations of barbarous nations, may overgrow and ouerrune the vulgar practise of the perfectest languages, as we see of the forementioned GREEKE and LATINE; yet the vse of those tongues will flourish among learned men as long as those excellent authours remaine in the world. Which maketh me confident that noe fate nor length of time will bury SPENCERS workes and memory, nor ideed alter that language that out of his schoole we now vse vntill some general innouation happen that may shake as well the foundations of *our* nation as of our speech: from *which* hard law of stepmother Nature what Empire or kingdome hath euer yet bin free? And herein SPENCER hath bin very happy that he hath had one immediately succeeding him of partes and power to make what he planted, take deepe rootes; and to build vp that worke whose foundations he soe fairely layd; for it is beyond the compasse and reach of *our* short life and narrow power to haue the same man beginne and perfect any great thing. Noe Empire was euer settled to long continuance, but in *the* first beginnings of it there was an vninterrupted succession of heroick and braue men to defend and confirme it. A like necessity is in languages, and in cures we may promise our selues a long and flourishing age, when diuine SPENCERS sunne was noe sooner sett, but in JOHNSON a new one rose *with* as much glory and brightnes as euer shone withall; who being himself most excellent and admirable in the iudicious compositions that in seuerall kinds he hath made, thinketh no man more excellent or more admirable then this his late praedecessour in the Laurell crowne. To his wise and knowing iudgement faith may be giuen, whereas my weake one may be called in quaestion vpon any other occasion then this, where the conspicuity of truth beareth it out. SPENCER in what he saith hath a way of expression peculiar to him selfe; he bringeth downe the highest and deepest misteries that are contained in human learning, to an easy and gentle forme of deliuery: *which* sheweth he is Master of what he treateth of; he can wield it as he pleaseth: And this he hath done soe cunningly, that if one heed him not *with* great attention, rare and wonderful conceptions will vnperceiued slide by him that readeth his works, & he will thinke he hath mett *with* nothing but familiar and easy discourses but let one dwell a while vpon them and he shall feele a straunge fulnesse and roundnesse in all he saith. The most generous wines tickle the palate least; but they are noe sooner in the stomach but by their warmth and strength there, they

discouer what they are: And those streames *that* steale away *with* least noyse are vsually deepest, and most dangerous to pass ouer. His knowledge in profound learning both diuine and humane appeareth to me without controversie the greatest that any POET before him euer had, Excepting VIRGIL: Whom I dare not medle withall, otherwise then (as witty SCALIGER did) erecting an altar to him; And this his knowledge was not as many POETS are contented withall; *which* is but a meere sprinkling of seuerall superficiall notions to beautify their POEMS *with*; But he had a solide and deepe insight in THEOLOGIE, PHILOSOPHY (especially the PLATONIKE) and the MATHEMATICALL sciences, and in what others depend of these three, (as indeed all others doe). He was a Master of euery one of them: And where he maketh vse of any of them, it is not by gathering a posie out of others [sic] mens workes, but by spending of his owne stocke. And lastly where he treateth MORALL or POLITICAL learning, he giueth euidence of himself that he had a most excellently composed head to obserue and gouerne mens actions; & might haue bin eminent in the actiue part that way, if his owne choice or fortune had giuen him employment in the common wealth.—SIR KENELM DIGBY, "A Discourse concerning Edmund Spencer," Harleian MSS., 1628

Spencer, in affecting the Ancients, writ no Language: Yet I would have him read for his matter; but as *Virgil* read *Ennius*. . . .
    Words borrow'd of Antiquity, doe lend a kind of Majesty to style, and are not without their delight sometimes. For they have the Authority of yeares, and out of their intermission doe win to themselves a kind of grace-like newnesse. But the eldest of the present, and newnesse of the past Language is the best. For what was the ancient Language, which some men so doate upon, but the ancient Custome? . . . *Virgill* was most loving of Antiquity; yet how rarely doth hee insert *aquai*, and *pictai*! Lucretius is scabrous and rough in these; hee seekes 'hem: As some doe Chaucerismes with us, which were better expung'd and banish'd.—BEN JONSON, 1640, *Timber; or Discoveries* . . . , 1640, *Works*, Vol. 8, eds. Herford, Simpson, 1925, pp. 618–22

Another sort of *Poesie*, is the Delivery of necessary Truths, and wholesome Documents, couched in so significant *Parables*; and illustrated by such flowres of Rhetorick, as are helpfull to work upon the Affections, and to insinuate into Apprehensive Readers, a liking of those Truths, and Instructions, which they expresse.
    These *Inventions*, are most acceptable to those who have ascended the middle Region of *Knowledge*; For, though the wisest men make use of them in their writings; yet, they are not the wisest men for whose sake they are used. This *Poesie* is frequently varyed, according to the severall Growths, Ages, and Alterations of that *Language*, wherein it is worded: and, that, which this day is approved of as an elegancy, may seeme lesse facetious in another Age. For which cause, such *Compositions*, may be resembled to *Garments* of whole Silke, adorned with gold lace: For while the Stuffe, shape and trimming, are in fashion, they are a fit wearing for *Princes*; and (the *Materials* being unmangled) may continue useful to some purposes, for some other persons.—GEORGE WITHER, *Halelviah*, 1641

Spencer may stand here as the last of this short File of Heroick Poets; Men, whose intellectuals were of so great a making, (though some have thought them lyable to those few censures we have mention'd) as perhaps they will in worthy memory out-last even Makers of Laws, and Founders of Empire, and all but such as must therefore live equally with them, because they have recorded their Names; and consequently with their own hands led them to the Temple of Fame. And since we have dar'd to remember those exceptions which the Curious have against them; it will not be expected I should forget what is objected against *Spencer*; whose obsolete language we are constrain'd to mention, though it be grown the most vulgar accusation that is lay'd to his charge.

Language (which is the onely Creature of Man's creation) hath, like a Plant, seasons of flourishing, and decay; like Plants, it remov'd from one Soil to another, and by being so transplanted, doth often gather vigour and increase. But as it is false Husbandry to graft old Branches upon young Stocks: so we may wonder that our Language (not long before his time created out of a confusion of others, and then beginning to flourish like a new Plant) should (as helps to its increase) receive from his hand new Grafts of old wither'd Words. But this vulgar exception shall onely have the vulgar excuse; which is, That the unlucky choise of his *Stanza*, hath by repitition of Rime brought him to the necessity of many exploded words.

If we proceed from his Language to his Argument, we must observe with others, that his noble and most artfull hands deserv'd to be employ'd upon matter of a more naturall, and therefore of a more usefull kind. His Allegoricall Story (by many held defective in the Connexion) resembling (me thinks) a continuance of extraordinary Dreams; such as excellent Poets, and Painters, by being over-studious may have in the beginning of Feavers: And those morall visions are just of so much use to Humane application, as painted History, when with the cousenage of lights it is represented in Scenes, by which we are much lesse inform'd then by actions on the Stage.—WILLIAM D'AVENANT, A *Discourse upon* Gondibert . . . , 1650, *Critical Essays of the Seventeeth Century*, Vol. 2, ed. Spingarn, 1908, pp. 5–8

Thus an injudicious Poet who aims at Loftiness runs easily into the swelling puffie style, because it looks like Greatness. I remember, when I was a Boy, I thought inimitable *Spencer* a mean Poet, in comparison of *Sylvester's Dubartas.*—JOHN DRYDEN, "To the Right Honorable John, Lord Haughton," 1681, *Works*, Vol. 4, eds. Scott, Saintsbury, 1882, p. 407

Our ancient Verse, (as homely as the Times,)
Was rude, unmeasur'd, only Tagg'd with Rhymes:
Number and Cadence, that have Since been Shown,
To those unpolish'd Writers were unknown.
Fairfax was He, who, in that Darker Age,
By his just Rules restrain'd Poetic Rage;
Spencer did next in Pastorals excel,
And taught the Noble Art of Writing well:
To stricter Rules the Stanza did restrain,
And found for Poetry a richer Veine.
Then D'Avenant came.
　　　—NICOLAS BOILEAU, *The Art of Poetry*, 1683, tr.
　　　　Dryden, Soame

I believe I can tell the particular little chance that filled my head first with such Chimes of Verse, as have never since left ringing there: For I remember when I began to read, and to take some pleasure in it, there was wont to lie in my Mothers Parlour (I know not by what accident, for she her self never in her life read any Book but of Devotion) but there was wont to lie *Spencers* Works; this I happened to fall upon, and was infinitely delighted with the Stories of the Knights, and Giants, and Monsters, and brave Houses, which I found every where there: (Though my understanding had little to do with all this) and by degrees with the tinckling of the Rhyme and Dance of the Numbers, so that I think I had read him all over before I

was twelve years old, and was thus made a Poet as irremediably as a Child is made an Eunuch. With these affections of mind, and my heart set upon Letters, I went to the University.— ABRAHAM COWLEY, "Of Myself," 1688, *Essays and Other Prose Writings*, ed. Waller, 1906, pp. 457–58

The *English* have only to boast of *Spencer* and *Milton* who neither of them wanted either Genius, or Learning, to have been perfect Poets; and yet both of them are liable to many Censures. For there is no Uniformity in the Design of *Spencer*: He aims at the Accomplishment of no one Action: He raises up a Hero for every one of his Adventures; and endows each of them with some particular Moral Virtue, which renders them all equal, without Subordination of Preference. Every one is most Valiant in his own Legend; only we must do him that Justice to observe, that Magnanimity, which is the Character of Prince *Arthur*, shines throughout the whole Poem; and Succours the rest, when they are in Distress. The Original of every Knight, was then living in the Court of Queen *Elizabeth*: And he attributed to each of them that Virtue, which he thought was most conspicuous in them: An Ingenious piece of Flattery, tho' it turned not much to his Account. Had he liv'd to finish his Poem, in the six remaining Legends, it had certainly been more of a piece; but cou'd not have been perfect, because the Model was not true. But Prince *Arthur*, or his chief Patron, Sir *Philip Sidney*, whom he intended to make happy, by the Marriage of his Gloriana, dying before him, depriv'd the Poet, both of Means and Spirit, to accomplish his Design: For the rest, his Obsolete Language, and the ill choice of his Stanza, are faults but of the Second Magnitude: For notwithstanding the first he is still Intelligible, at least, after a little practice; and for the last, he is the more to be admir'd; that labouring under such a difficulty, his Verses are so Numerous, so Various, and so Harmonious, that only *Virgil*, whom he profestly imitated, has surpass'd him, among the *Romans*; and only Mr *Waller* among the *English*. . . .

[Milton's] antiquated words were his Choice, not his Necessity; for therein he imitated *Spencer*, as Spencer did *Chawcer*. . . .

In the English I remember none, which are mix'd with Prose, as *Varro's* were: But of the same kind is Mother *Hubbard's* Tale in *Spencer*. [That is, no satires.]—JOHN DRYDEN, "To the Right Honorable Charles, Earl of Dorset and Middlesex," 1693, *Works*, Vol. 13, eds. Scott, Saintsbury, 1882, pp. 17–19

SPENCER more *smooth* and *neat* than Chaucer, and none
　　than He
Could better skill of *English Quantity*;
Tho by his *Stanza* cramp'd, his *Rhimes* less chast,
And *antique* Words affected all disgrac'd;
Yet *vast* his *Genius*, *noble* were his *Thoughts*,
Whence equal Readers wink at *Lesser* faults.
　　　—SAMUEL WESLEY, "An Epistle to a Friend
　　　　concerning Poetry," 1700, p. 12

When by doing this we have laid down the Rules, we come briefly to examine, Whether those Rules are always to be kept inviolable; and if they are not, in what parts, and by whom, they may be alter'd. Then we shew how *Spencer*, by not following those Rules, fell so very far short of the Ancients: and afterwards we endeavour to make it appear, how *Milton*, by daring to break a little loose from them in some particulars, kept up in several others to the Nature of the Greater Poetry in general, and of Epick Poetry in particular, better than the best of the Ancients.—JOHN DENNIS, "The Grounds of Criticism in Poetry," 1704, *Critical Works*, Vol. 1, ed. Hooker, 1939, p. 331

My Two Great Examples, HORACE and SPENCER, in many Things resemble each other: Both have a Height of Imagination, and a Majesty of Expression in describing the *Sublime*; and both know how to temper those Talents, and sweeten the Description, so as to make it Lovely as well as Pompous: Both have equally That agreeable Manner of mixing Morality with their Story, and That *Curiosa Felicitas* in the Choice of their Diction, which every Writer aims at, and so very few have reach'd: Both are particularly Fine in their Images, and Knowing in their Numbers.—MATTHEW PRIOR, "Preface" to *An Ode, Humbly Inscribed to the Queen . . .* , 1706, *The Literary Works*, Vol. 1, eds. Wright, Spears, 1959, pp. 231–32

. . . ⟨T⟩here is another kind of Wit, which consists partly in the Resemblance of Ideas, and partly in the Resemblance of Words; which for Distinction Sake I shall call *mixt wit*. This kind of Wit is that which abounds in *Cowley*, more than in any Author that ever wrote. . . . *Milton* had a Genius much above it. *Spencer* is in the same class with *Milton*. The *Italians*, even in their Epic Poetry are full of it.—JOSEPH ADDISON, *The Spectator*, May 11, 1711

But an allegory is sometimes taken in another Sense, that is, when Vertues and Vices are represented as Persons either Humane or Divine, and proper Passions and Manners are ascrib'd to their respective Characters: Of this are several examples in *Homer's Ulysses*, and too many in the modern Epick Writers, and there is one Instance of this sort in the sixth Book of King Arthur. . . . In the second Sense, the modern Epick Poets, especially *Ariosto* and *Spencer,* have ran too far into Allegory. This sort of allegorical Imaging resembles the emblematic Draughts of great Painters, where Vertues are represented as Goddesses, and Vices as Furies; and where Liberty, Peace, Plenty, Pleasure, and various Qualities of the Mind are exhibited in Humane Forms, with peculiar Properties and Marks of Distinction. An elegant Instance of this kind of Writing is the Representation of Sin and Death in the appearance of two odious and terrible Monsters, by our celebrated *Milton* in his *Paradise Lost*; of which, I imagine, he took the Hint from the famous *Spencer*. This sort of Allegories, tho not strictly Epick, us'd with Temperance and Judgement, affect the Mind with Wonder and Delight, and enliven and beautify the Poem.— SIR RICHARD BLACKMORE, *Essays upon Several Subjects*, 1716, pp. 41–42

Where Spenser does introduce the allegories of the ancient poets, he does not always follow them so exactly as he might. And in the allegories which are purely of his own invention, though his invention is one of the richest and most beautiful that perhaps ever was, I am sorry to say that he does not only fall very short of that simplicity and propriety which is so remarkable in the works of the ancients, but runs now and then into thoughts that are quite unworthy so great a genius. I shall mark out some of these faults to you, that appear, even through all his beauties, and which may perhaps look quite gross to you when they are thus taken from them and laid together by themselves; but if they should prejudice you at all against so fine a writer, read almost any one of his entire cantos and it will reconcile you to him again. The reason of my producing these instances to you is only to show what faults the greatest allegorist may commit whilst the manner of allegorizing is left upon so unfixed and irregular a footing as it was in his time and is still among us.

The first sort of fault I shall mention to you from such allegories of Spenser as are purely of his own invention is their being sometimes too complicated or overdone. Such, for example, are his representations of Scandal, Discord and Pride. Scandal is what Spenser calls 'the Blatant Beast', and indeed, he has made a very strange beast of him. He says that his mouth was as wide as a peck (VI xii 26) and that he had a thousand tongues in it of dogs, cats, bears, tigers, men and serpents (VI vii 27). There is a duplicity in his figure of Discord which is carried on so far as to be quite preposterous. He makes her hear double and look two different ways; he splits her tongue and even her heart in two and makes her act contrarily with her two hands and walk forward with one foot and backward with the other at the same time (VI i 27–9).

There is a great deal of apparatus in Spenser's manner of introducing Pride in a personal character, and she has so many different things and attributes about her that, was this show to be represented (in the manner of our old pageants), they would rather set one aguessing what they meant themselves than serve to point out who the principal figure should be. She makes her appearance exalted in a high chariot drawn by six different creatures, every one of them carrying a Vice, as a postilion, on his back, and all drove on by Satan as charioteer (I iv 18–36). The six Vices are Idleness, on an ass; Gluttony, on a hog; Lechery, on a goat; Avarice, on a camel laden with gold; Envy, eating a toad and riding on a wolf; and Wrath, with a firebrand in his hand, on a lion. The account of each of these particular vices in Spenser is admirable; the chief fault I find with it is that it is too complex a way of characterizing Pride in general and may possibly be as improper in some few respects as it is redundant in others.

There is another particular in some of Spenser's allegories which I cannot but look upon as faulty, though it is not near so great a fault as the former. What I mean is his affixing such filthy ideas to some of his personages or characters, that it half turns one's stomach to read his account of them. Such, for example, is the description of Error in the very first canto of the poem (I i 20), of which we may very well say in the poet's own words on a like occasion,

> Such loathly matter were small lust to speake, or
> thinke.
>
> (V xi 31)

The third fault in the allegories of Spenser's own invention is that they are sometimes stretched to such a degree that they appear rather extravagant than great, and that he is sometimes so minute in pointing out every particular of its vastness to you that the object is in danger of becoming ridiculous instead of being admirable. This is not common in Spenser; the strongest instance of the few I can remember is in his description of the dragon killed by the Knight of the Red Cross in the last canto [*sic*] of his first book. The tail of this dragon, he tells you, wanted by very little of being three furlongs in length (I xi 11); the blood that gushes from his wound is enough to drive a water mill (I xi 22); and his roar is like that of a hundred hungry lions (I xi 37).

The fourth class of faults in Spenser's allegories consists of such as arise from their not being well invented. You will easily, I believe, allow me here the three following *postulata*: that in introducing allegories, one should consider whether the thing is fit to be represented as a person or not; secondly, that if you choose to represent it as a human personage, it should not be represented with anything inconsistent with the human form or nature; and thirdly, that when it is represented as a man, you should not make it perform any action which no man in his senses would do.

Spenser seems to have erred against the first of these maxims in those lines in his description of the cave of Care:

> . . . they for nought would from their worke refraine,
> Ne let his speeches come vnto their eare.
> And eke the breathfull bellowes blew amaine,
> Like to the Northren winde, that none could heare:
> Those *Pensifenesse* did moue; and *Sighes* the bellows weare.
>
> (IV v 38)

Was a poet to say that sighs are 'the bellows that blow up the fire of love', that would be only a metaphor—a poor one indeed, but not at all improper; but here they are realized, or rather metamorphized into bellows, which I could never persuade myself to think any way proper. Spenser is perhaps guilty of the same sort of fault in making Gifts, or Munera, a woman in the second canto of the fifth book (stanzas 9 ff.), though that may be only a misnomer; for if he had called her Bribery, one should not have the same objection. But the grossest instance in him of this kind is in the ninth canto of the second book, where he turns the human body into a castle, the tongue into the porter that keeps the gate, and the teeth into two and thirty warders dressed in white (stanzas 21, 25 and 26).

Spenser seems to have erred against the second of these maxims in representing the rigid execution of the laws under the character of a man all made up of iron (V i 12) and Bribery—or the lady Munera, before mentioned—as a woman with golden hands and silver feet (V ii 10); and against the third where he describes Desire as holding coals of fire in his hands and blowing them up into a flame (III xii 9)—which last particular is some degrees worse than Ariosto's bringing in Discord, in his *Orlando Furioso* (XVIII 34), with a flint and steel to strike fire in the face of Pride.

The fifth sort of faults is when the allegorical personages, though well invented, are not well marked out. There are many instances of this in Spenser which are but too apt to put one in mind of the fancifulness and whims of Ripa and Vaenius. Thus, in one canto, Doubt is represented as walking with a staff that shrinks under him (III xii 10), Hope with an aspergoire, or the instrument the Roman Catholics use for sprinkling sinners with holy water (stanza 13), Dissimulation as twisting two clews of silk together (stanza 14), Grief with a pair of pincers (stanza 16) and Pleasure with an humblebee in a phial (stanza 18). And in another—in the procession of the months and seasons—February is introduced in a wagon drawn by two fishes (VII vii 43), May as riding on Castor and Pollux (stanza 34); June is mounted on a crab (stanza 35), October on a scorpion (stanza 39); and November comes in on a centaur, all in a sweat because (as the poet observes) he had just been fatting his hogs (stanza 40).

This might full as well have been ranged under my sixth and last class of faults in Spenser's allegories, consisting of such instances as I fear can scarce be called by any softer name than that of 'ridiculous imaginations'. Such, I think, is that idea of Ignorance in the first book, where he is made to move with the back part of his head foremost (I viii 31), and that of Danger in the Fourth, with Hatred, Murder, Treason, etc., in his back (IV x 16, 17, 20). Such is the sorrowful lady with a bottle for her tears and a bag to put her repentance into and both running out almost as fast as she puts them in (VI viii 24); such the thought of a vast giant's shrinking into an empty form, like a bladder (I viii 24); the horses of Night foaming tar (I v 28); Sir Guyon putting a padlock on the tongue of Occasion (II iv 12); and Remorse nipping St George's heart (I x 27).—JOSEPH SPENCE, *Polymetis*, 1747, pp. 303–7

Imagination, in the sense of the word as giving title to a class of the following Poems, has no reference to images that are merely a faithful copy, existing in the mind, of absent external objects; but is a word of higher import, denoting operations of the mind upon those objects, and processes of creation or of composition, governed by certain fixed laws. I proceed to illustrate my meaning by instances. A parrot *hangs* from the wires of his cage by his beak or by his claws; or a monkey from the bough of a tree by his paws or his tail. Each creature does so literally and actually. In the first Eclogue of Virgil, the shepherd, thinking of the time when he is to take leave of his farm, thus addresses his goats:

> Non ego vos posthac viridi projectus in antro
> Dumosa *pendere* procul de rupe videbo.
>
> . . . half way down
> *Hangs* one who gathers samphire,
>
> (*King Lear*, IV vi 16)

is the well-known expression of Shakespeare, delineating an ordinary image upon the cliffs of Dover. In these two instances is a slight exertion of the faculty which I denominate imagination, in the use of one word: neither the goats nor the samphire-gatherer do literally hang, as does the parrot or the monkey; but, presenting to the senses something of such an appearance, the mind in its activity, for its own gratification, contemplates them as hanging.

> As when far off at sea a fleet descried
> *Hangs* in the clouds, by equinoctial winds
> Close sailing from Bengala, or the isles
> Of Ternate or Tidore, whence merchants bring
> Their spicy drugs; they on the trading flood
> Through the wide Ethiopian to the Cape
> Ply, stemming nightly toward the Pole: so seemed
> Far off the flying Fiend.
>
> (*Paradise Lost*, II 636–43)

Here is the full strength of the imagination involved in the word *hangs*, and exerted upon the whole image: first, the fleet, an aggregate of many ships, is represented as one mighty person, whose track, we know and feel, is upon the waters; but, taking advantage of its appearance to the senses, the Poet dares to represent it as *hanging in the clouds*, both for the gratification of the mind in contemplating the image itself, and in reference to the motion and appearance of the sublime objects to which it is compared. . . .

Thus far of images independent of each other, and immediately endowed by the mind with properties that do not inhere in them, upon an incitement from properties and qualities the existence of which is inherent and obvious. These processes of imagination are carried on either by conferring additional properties upon an object, or abstracting from it some of those which it actually possesses, and thus enabling it to re-act upon the mind which hath performed the process, like a new existence.

I pass from the Imagination acting upon an individual image to a consideration of the same faculty employed upon images in a conjunction by which they modify each other. The Reader has already had a fine instance before him in the passage quoted from Virgil, where apparently perilous situation of the goat, hanging upon the shaggy precipice, is contrasted with that of the shepherd contemplating it from the seclusion of the cavern in which he lies stretched at ease and in security. Take these images separately, and how unaffecting the picture compared with that produced by their being thus connected with, and opposed to, each other!

> As a huge stone is sometimes seen to lie
> Couched on the bald top of an eminence,

Wonder to all who do the same espy
By what means it could thither come, and whence,
So that it seems a thing endued with sense,
Like a sea-beast crawled forth, which on a shelf
Of rock or sand reposeth, there to sun himself.

Such seemed this Man; not all alive or dead
Nor all asleep, in his extreme old age.
. . .

Motionless as a cloud the old Man stood,
That heareth not the loud winds when they call,
And moveth altogether if it move at all.
(*Resolution and Independence*, 57–65, 75–7)

In these images, the conferring, the abstracting, and the modifying powers of the Imagination, immediately and mediately acting, are all brought into conjunction. The stone is endowed with something of the power of life to approximate it to the sea-beast; and the sea-beast stripped of some of its vital qualities to assimilate it to the stone; which intermediate image is thus treated for the purpose of bringing the original image, that of the stone, to a nearer resemblance to the figure and condition of the aged Man; who is divested of so much of the indications of life and motion as to bring him to the point where the two objects unite and coalesce in just comparison. After what has been said, the image of the cloud need not be commented upon.

Thus far of an endowing or modifying power: but the Imagination also shapes and *creates*; and how? By innumerable processes; and in none does it more delight than in that of consolidating numbers into unity, and dissolving and separating unity into number,—alternations proceeding from, and governed by, a sublime consciousness of the soul in her own mighty and almost divine powers. Recur to the passage already cited from Milton. When the compact Fleet, as one Person, has been introduced 'sailing from Bengala', 'They', *i.e.* the 'merchants', representing the fleet resolved into a multitude of ships, 'ply' their voyage towards the extremities of the earth: 'So', (referring to the word 'As' in the commencement) 'seemed the flying Fiend'; the image of his Person acting to recombine the multitude of ships into one body,—the point from which the comparison set out. 'So seemed', and to whom seemed? To the heavenly Muse who dictates the poem, to the eye of the Poet's mind, and to that of the Reader, present at one moment in the wide Ethiopian, and the next in the solitudes, then first broken in upon, of the infernal regions!

Modo me Thebis, modo ponit Athenis
(Horace, *Epistles*, II 213)

Hear again this mighty Poet,—speaking of the Messiah going forth to expel from heaven the rebellious angels,

Attended by ten thousand thousand Saints
He onward came: far off his coming shone,
(*Paradise Lost*, VI 767–8)

the retinue of Saints, and the Person of the Messiah himself, lost almost and merged in the splendour of that indefinite abstraction 'His coming!' . . .

The grand store-houses of enthusiastic and meditative Imagination, of poetical, as contra-distinguished from human and dramatic Imagination, are the prophetic and lyrical parts of the Holy Scriptures, and the works of Milton; to which I cannot forbear to add those of Spenser. I select these writers in preference to those of ancient Greece and Rome, because the anthropomorphitism of the Pagan religion subjected the minds of the greatest poets in those countries too much to the bondage of definite form; from which the Hebrews were preserved by their abhorrence of idolatry. This abhorrence was almost as strong in our great epic Poet, both from circumstances of his life, and from the constitution of his mind. However imbued the surface might be with classical literature, he was a Hebrew in soul; and all things tended in him towards the sublime. Spenser, of a gentler nature, maintained his freedom by aid of his allegorical spirit, at one time inciting him to create persons out of abstractions; and, at another, by a superior effort of genius, to give the universality and permanence of abstractions to his human beings, by means of attributes and emblems that belong to the highest moral truths and the purest sensations,—of which his character of Una is a glorious example. Of the human and dramatic Imagination the works of Shakspeare are an inexhaustible source.

I tax not you, ye Elements, with unkindness,
I never gave you kingdoms, call'd you Daughters!
(*King Lear*, III ii 16–17)
—WILLIAM WORDSWORTH, "Preface" to
Lyrical Ballads, 1815

It might appear from some passages in the former part of Mr Wordsworth's preface that he meant to confine his theory of style, and the necessity of a close accordance with the actual language of men, to those particular subjects from low and rustic life which by way of experiment he had purposed to naturalize as a new species in our English poetry. But from the train of argument that follows, from the reference to Milton and from the spirit of his critique on Gray's sonnet, those sentences appear to have been rather courtesies of modesty than actual limitations of his system. Yet so groundless does this system appear on a close examination, and so strange and overwhelming in its consequences, that I cannot, and I do not, believe that the poet did ever himself adopt it in the unqualified sense in which his expressions have been understood by others and which indeed according to all the common laws of interpretation they seem to bear. What then did he mean? I apprehend that in the clear perception, not unaccompanied with disgust or contempt, of the gaudy affectations of a style which passed too current with too many for poetic diction (though in truth it had as little pretensions to poetry as to logic or common sense), he narrowed his view for the time; and feeling a justifiable preference for the language of nature and of good sense, even in its humblest and least ornamented forms, he suffered himself to express, in terms at once too large and too exclusive, his predilection for a style the most remote possible from the false and showy splendor which he wished to explode. It is possible that this predilection, at first merely comparative, deviated for a time into direct partiality. But the real object which he had in view was, I doubt not, a species of excellence which had been long before most happily characterized by the judicious and amiable Garve, whose works are so justly beloved and esteemed by the Germans, in his remarks on Gellert, from which the following is literally translated:

> The talent that is required in order to make excellent verses is perhaps greater than the philosopher is ready to admit, or would find it in his power to acquire; the talent to seek only the apt expression of the thought, and yet to find at the same time with it the rhyme and the metre. Gellert possessed this happy gift, if ever any one of our poets possessed it; and nothing perhaps contributed more to the great and universal impression which his fables made on their first publication or conduces more to their continued popularity. It was a strange and curious phenomenon, and such as in Germany had been previously unheard of, to read verses in which every thing was expressed just as one would wish to talk, and yet all dignified, attractive and interesting; and all at the same time per-

fectly correct as to the measure of the syllables and the rhyme. It is certain that poetry when it has attained this excellence makes a far greater impression than prose. So much so indeed, that even the gratification which the very rhymes afford becomes then no longer a contemptible or trifling gratification.

However novel this phenomenon may have been in Germany at the time of Gellert, it is by no means new nor yet of recent existence in our language. Spite of the licentiousness with which Spenser occasionally compels the orthography of his words into a subservience to his rhymes, the whole *Faerie Queene* is an almost continued instance of this beauty. Waller's song *Go, lovely Rose* is doubtless familiar to most of my readers; but if I had happened to have had by me the poems of Cotton, more but far less deservedly celebrated as the author of the Virgil travestied, I should have indulged myself, and I think have gratified many who are not acquainted with his serious works, by selecting some admirable specimens of this style. There are not a few poems in that volume, replete with every excellence of thought, image and passion which we expect or desire in the poetry of the milder muse; and yet so worded that the reader sees no one reason either in the selection or the order of the words why he might not have said the very same in an appropriate conversation and cannot conceive how indeed he could have expressed such thoughts otherwise, without loss or injury to his meaning.

But in truth our language is, and from the first dawn of poetry ever has been, particularly rich in compositions distinguished by this excellence. The final *e*, which is now mute, in Chaucer's age was either sounded or dropped indifferently. We ourselves still use either *beloved* or *belov'd* according as the rhyme, or measure, or the purpose of more or less solemnity may require. Let the reader then only adopt the pronunciation of the poet and of the court at which he lived, both with respect to the final *e* and to the accentuation of the last syllable: I would then venture to ask what even in the colloquial language of elegant and unaffected women (who are the peculiar mistresses of 'pure English and undefiled'), what could we hear more natural, or seemingly more unstudied, than the following stanzas from Chaucer's *Troilus and Creseyde*: [quotes V 603–37, 645–51].

Another exquisite master of this species of style where the scholar and the poet supplies the material, but the perfect wellbred gentleman the expressions and the arrangement, is George Herbert. As from the nature of the subject and the too frequent quaintness of the thoughts, his *Temple, or Sacred Poems and Private Ejaculations* are comparatively but little known, I shall extract two poems. The first is a Sonnet [*The Bosom Sin*], equally admirable for the weight, number and expression of the thoughts, and for the simple dignity of the language (unless indeed a fastidious taste should object to the latter half of the sixth line). The second is a poem of greater length [*Love Unknown*], which I have chosen not only for the present purpose, but likewise as a striking example and illustration of an assertion hazarded in a former page of these sketches: namely that the characteristic fault of our elder poets is the reverse of that which distinguishes too many of our more recent versifiers; the one conveying the most fantastic thoughts in the most correct and natural language; the other in the most fantastic language conveying the most trivial thoughts. The latter is a riddle of words; the former an enigma of thoughts.— SAMUEL TAYLOR COLERIDGE, *Biographia Literaria*, 1817, Ch. 19

So far from the position holding true, that great wit (or genius, in our modern way of speaking), has a necessary alliance with insanity, the greatest wits, on the contrary, will ever be found to be the sanest writers. It is impossible for the mind to conceive of a mad Shakespeare. The greatness of wit, by which the poetic talent is here chiefly to be understood, manifests itself in the admirable balance of all the faculties. Madness is the disproportionate straining or excess of any one of them. 'So strong a wit,' says Cowley, speaking of a poetical friend,

> . . . did Nature to him frame,
> As all things but his judgement overcame,
> His judgement like the heavenly moon did show,
> Tempering that mighty sea below.

The ground of the mistake is, that men, finding in the raptures of the higher poetry a condition of exaltation, to which they have no parallel in their own experience, besides the spurious resemblance of it in dreams and fevers, impute a state of dreaminess and fever to the poet. But the true poet dreams being awake. He is not possessed by his subject, but has dominion over it. In the groves of Eden he walks familiar as in his native paths. He ascends the empyrean heaven, and is not intoxicated. He treads the burning marl without dismay; he wins his flight without self-loss through realms of chaos 'and old night'. Or if, abandoning himself to that severer chaos of a 'human mind untuned', he is content awhile to be mad with Lear, or to hate mankind (a sort of madness) with Timon, neither is that madness, nor this misanthropy, so unchecked, but that,—never letting the reins of reason wholly go, while most he seems to do so,—he has his better genius still whispering at his ear, with the good servant Kent suggesting saner counsels, or with the honest steward Flavius recommending kindlier resolutions. Where he seems most to recede from humanity, he will be found the truest to it. From beyond the scope of Nature if he summon possible existences, he subjugates them to the law of her consistency. He is beautifully loyal to that sovereign directress, even when he appears most to betray and desert her. His ideal tribes submit to policy; his very monsters are tamed to his hand, even as that wild sea-brood, shepherded by Proteus. He tames, and he clothes them with attributes of flesh and blood, till they wonder at themselves, like Indian Islanders forced to submit to European vesture. Caliban, the Witches, are as true to the laws of their own nature (ours with a difference), as Othello, Hamlet and Macbeth. Herein the great and the little wits are differenced; that if the latter wander ever so little from nature or actual existence, they lose themselves, and their readers. Their phantoms are lawless; their visions nightmares. They do not create, which implies shaping and consistency. Their imaginations are not active—for to be active is to call something into act and form—but passive, as men in sick dreams. For the super-natural, or something super-added to what we know of nature, they give you the plainly non-natural. And if this were all, and that these mental hallucinations were discoverable only in the treatment of subjects out of nature, or transcending it, the judgement might with some plea be pardoned if it ran riot, and a little wantonized: but even in the describing of real and every day life, that which is before their eyes, one of these lesser wits shall more deviate from nature—show more of that inconsequence, which has a natural alliance with frenzy,—than a great genius in his 'maddest fits', as Withers somewhere calls them. We appeal to any one that is acquainted with the common run of Lane's novels,—as they existed some twenty or thirty years back,—those scanty intellectual viands of the whole female reading public, till a happier genius arose, and expelled for ever the innutritious phantoms,—whether he has not found his brain more 'betossed', his memory more puzzled, his sense of when and where more confounded, among the improbable events, the incoherent incidents, the inconsistent characters, or no-characters, of some third-rate love intrigue—where the persons shall be a Lord Glendamour and a Miss Rivers, and the scene only alternate between Bath and Bond-street—a more bewildering dreaminess induced upon him, than he has felt wandering over all the fairy grounds of Spenser. In the productions we refer to, nothing but names and places is familiar; the persons are neither of this world nor of any other conceivable one; an endless string of activities without purpose, of purposes destitute of motive:—we meet phantoms in our known walks; *fantasques* only christened. In the poet we have names which announce fiction; and we have absolutely no place at all, for the things and persons of *The Faerie Queene* prate not of their 'whereabout'. But in their inner nature, and the law of their speech and actions, we are at home and upon acquainted ground. The one turns life into a dream; the other to the wildest dreams gives the sobrieties of every day occurrences. By what subtile art of tracing the mental processes it is effected, we are not philosophers enough to explain, but in that wonderful episode of the cave of Mammon, in which the Money God appears first in the lowest form of a miser, is then a worker of metals, and becomes the god of all the treasures of the world; and has a daughter, Ambition, before whom all the world kneels for favours—with the Hesperian fruit, the waters of Tantalus, with Pilate washing his hands vainly, but not impertinently, in the same stream—that we should be at one moment in the cave of an old hoarder of treasures, at the next at the forge of the Cyclops, in a palace and yet in hell, all at once, with the shifting mutations of the most rambling dream, and our judgement yet all the time awake, and neither able nor willing to detect the fallacy,—is a proof of that hidden sanity which still guides the poet in his widest seeming-aberrations.

It is not enough to say that the whole episode is a copy of the mind's conceptions in sleep; it is, in some sort—but what a copy! Let the most romantic of us, that has been entertained all night with the spectacle of some wild and magnificent vision, recombine it in the morning, and try it by his waking judgement. That which appeared so shifting, and yet so coherent, while that faculty was passive, when it comes under cool examination, shall appear so reasonless and so unlinked, that we are ashamed to have been so deluded; and to have taken, though but in sleep, a monster for a god. But the transitions in this episode are every whit as violent as in the most extravagant dream, and yet the waking judgement ratifies them.—CHARLES LAMB, "Sanity of True Genius," *New Monthly Magazine,* 1826

Works

THE SHEPHERD'S CALENDAR

Wherevnto I doubt not equally to adioyne the authoritye of our late famous English Poet, who wrote the *Shepheards Calender,* where lamenting the decay of Poetry, at these dayes, saith most sweetely to the same.

Then make thee winges of thine aspyring wytt,
And whence thou camest flye back to heauen apace.

Whose fine poeticall witt, and most exquisite learning, as he shewed aboundantly in that peace of worke, in my iudgement inferiour to the workes neither of *Theocritus* in Greeke,

nor *Virgill* in Latine, whom hee narrowly immitateth: so I nothing doubt, but if his other workes were common abroade, which are as I thinke in *the* close custodie of certaine his friends, we should haue of our own Poets, whom wee might matche in all respects with the best. And among all other his workes whatsoeuer, I would wysh to haue the sight of hys *English Poet,* which his freend E.K. did once promise to publishe, which whether he performed or not, I knowe not, if he did, my happe hath not beene so good as yet to see it. . . .

This place haue I purposely reserued for one, who if not only yet in my iudgement principally deserueth the tytle of the rightest English Poet, that euer I read: that is, the Author of the *Sheepeheardes Kalendar,* intituled to the woorthy Gentleman Master *Philip Sydney:* whether it was Master *Sp.* or what rare Scholler in Pembrooke Hall soeuer, because himself and his freendes, for what respect I knowe not, would not reueale it, I force not greatly to sette downe: sorry I am that I can not find none other with whom I might couple him in this *Catalogue,* in his rare gyft of Poetry: although one there is, though nowe long since, seriously occupied in grauer studies, (*Master Gabriell Haruey*) yet, as he was once his most special freende and fellow Poet, so because he hath taken such paynes, not onely in his Latin Poetry (for which he enjoyed great commendations of the best both in iudgement and dignity in thys Realme) but also to reforme our English verse, and to beautify the same with braue deuises, of which I thinke the cheefe lye hidde in hatefull obscurity: therefore wyll I aduenture to sette them together, as two of the rarest witts, and learnedest masters of Poetrie in England. Whose worthy and notable styl in this faculty, I would wysh if their high dignities and serious businesses would permit, they would styll graunt to bee a furtheraunce to that reformed kinde of Poetry, which Master *Haruey* did once beginne to ratify. . . .

As for the other Gentleman, if it would please him or hys freendes to let those excellent *Poemes,* whereof I know he hath plenty, come abroad, as his *Dreames,* his *Legends,* his Court of *Cupid,* his *English Poet* with other: he should not only stay the rude pens of my selfe and others, but also satisfye the thirsty desires of many which desire nothing more, then to see more of hys rare inuentions. . . .

But nowe yet at *the* last hath England hatched vppe one Poet of this sorte, in my conscience comparable with the best in any respect: euen Master *Sp.*: Author of the *Sheepeheardes Calender,* whose trauell in that peece of English Poetrie, I thinke verely is so commendable, as none of equall iudgement can yeelde him lesse prayse for his excellent skyll, and skylfull excellency shewed foorth in the same, then they would to eyther *Theocritus* or *Virgill,* who in my opinion, if the coursenes of our speeche (I meane the course of custome which he woulde not infringe) had beene no more let vnto him, then theyr pure natiue tongues were vnto them, he would haue (if it might be) surpassed them. What one thing is there in them so worthy admiration, whereunto we may not adioyne some thing of his, or equall desert? Take *Virgil* and make some little comparison betweene them, and iudge as ye shall see cause.

Virgill hath a gallant report of *Augustus* couertly comprysed in the first *Aeglogue:* the like is in him, of her Maiestie, vnder the name of *Eliza.* *Virgill* maketh a braue coloured complaint of vnstedfast freendshyppe in the person of *Corydon:* the lyke is him in his 5. *Aeglogue.* Agayne behold the pretty Pastorall contentions of *Virgill* in the third *Aeglogue:* of his in *the* eight *Eglogue.* Finally, either in comparison with them or respect of hys owne great learning, he may well were the Garlande, and steppe before ye best of all English poets that I haue seene or hearde: for I thinke no lesse deserueth (thus sayth

E.K. in hys commendations) hys wittinesse in deuising, his pithinesse in vttering, his complaintes of loue so louely, his discourses of pleasure so pleasantly, his Pastrall rudenes, his Morrall wysenesse, his due obseruing of *decorum* euery where, in personages, in season, in matter, in speeche, and generally in all seemely simplicity, of handling hys matter and framing hys wordes. The occasion of his worke is a warning to other young men, who being intangled in loue and youthful vanities, may learne to looke to themselves in time, and to auoyde inconueniences which may breede if they be not in time pre-uented. Many good Morrall lessons are therein contained, as the reuerence which young men owe to the aged in the second *Eglogue*: the caueate or warning to beware a subtill professor of freendshippe in the fift *Eglogue*: the commendation of good pastors, and shame and disprayse of idle and ambitious Goteheardes in the seauenth, the loose and retchlesse lyuing of Popish Prelates in the ninth. The learned and sweet complaynt of the contempt of learning vnder the name of Poetry in the tenth. There is also much matter vttered somewhat couertly, especially ye abuses of some whom he would not be too playne withall: in which, though it be not apparent to euery one, what hys speciall meaning was, yet so skilfully is it handled, as any man may take much delight at hys learned conueyance, and picke out much good sence in the most obscurest of it. Hys notable prayse deserued in euery parcell of that worke, because I cannot expresse as I woulde and as it should: I wyll cease to speake any more of it, the rather because I neuer hearde as yet any that hath reade it, which hath not with much admiration commended it. One only thing therin haue I hearde some curious heades call in question: *viz*: the motion of some vnsau-ery loue, such as in the sixt *Eglogue* he seemeth to deale withall, which (say they) is skant allowable to English eares, and might well haue beene left for the Italian defenders of loathsome beast-lines, of whom perhappes he learned it: to thys obiection I haue often aunswered (and I think truely) that theyr nyce opinion ouershooteth the Poets meaning, who though hee in that as in other thinges immitateth the auncient Poets, yet doth not meane, no more did they before hym, any disor-dered loue, or the filthy lust of the deuillish *Pederastice* taken in the worse sensce, but rather to shewe howe the dissolute life of young men intangled in loue of women, doo neglect the freendshyp and league with their olde freendes and familiers. Why (say they) yet he shold gyue no occasion of suspition, nor offer to the viewe of Christians, any token of such filthinesse, howe good soeuer hys meaning were: wherevnto I oppose the simple conceyte they haue of matters which concerne learning or wytt, wylling them to gyue Poets leaue to vse theyr vayne as they see good: it is their foolysh construction, not hys wryting that is blameable. Wee must prescrybe to no wryters, (much lesse to Poets) in what sorte they should vtter theyr conceyts.— WILLIAM WEBBE, A *Discourse of English Poetrie*, 1586, *Eliz-abethan Critical Essays*, Vol. 1, ed. Smith, 1904, pp. 232–65

I account the Mirrour of Magistrates, meetly furnished of bewtiful partes. And in the Earle of *Surries Lirickes*, manie thinges tasting of a Noble birth, and worthie of a Noble minde. The Sheepheards Kallender, hath much *Poetrie* in his Egloges, indeed worthie the reading, if I be not deceiued. That same framing of his style to an olde rusticke language, I dare not allow: since neither *Theocritus* in Greeke, *Virgill* in Latine, nor *Sanazara* in Italian, did affect it. Besides these, I doo not remember to haue seene but fewe (to speake bodly) printed, that haue poeticall sinnewes in them.—SIR PHILLIP SIDNEY, *An Apology For Poetrie*, 1595, ed. Shepherd, 1965, p. 133

As Sextus Propertius saide; *Nescio quid magis nascitur Iliade*: so I say of *Spencers Fairy Queene*, I knowe not what more excel-lent or exquisite Poem may be written.

As *Achilles* had the aduantage of *Hector*, because it was his fortune to be extolled and renowned by the heauenly verse of *Homer*: so *Spensers Elisa the Fairy Queen* hath the aduantage of all the Queenes in the worlde, to bee eternized by so diuine a Poet.

As *Theocritus* is famoused for his *Idyllia* in *Greeke*, and *Virgill* for his *Eclogs* in Latine: so Spencer their imitatour in his *Shepheardes Calender*, is renowned for the like argument, and honoured for fine Poeticall inuention, and most exquisit wit.— FRANCIS MERES, *Palladis Tamia*, 1598

And would at this time also gladly let thee vnderstand, what I thinke aboue the rest of the last Ode of the twelue, or if thou wilt Ballad in my Book; for both the great master of Italian rymes *Petrarch*, & our *Chawcer* & other of the vper house of the muses, haue thought their Canzons honoured in the title of a Ballade, which, for that I labour to meet truely therein with the ould English garb, I hope as able to iustifie as the learned *Colin Clout* his Roundelaye.—MICHAEL DRAYTON, "To the Reader," *Poems Lyrick and Pastorall*, 1605, *Works*, Vol. 2, ed. Hebel, p. 346

Master EDMVND SPENSER had done enough for the immor-talitie of his Name, had he only giuen vs his *Shepheards Kalender*, a Master piece if any. The *Colin Clout* of SKOGGAN, vnder King HENRY the Seuenth, is prettie: but BARKLEY's *Ship of Fooles* hath twentie wiser in it. SPENSER is the prime *Pas-toralist* of England.—MICHAEL DRAYTON, "To the Reader of His Pastorals," 1619, *Works*, Vol. 2, ed. Hebel, p. 518

Let the novice learne first to renounce the world, and so give himselfe to God, and not therefore give himselfe to God, that hee may close the better with the World, like that false Shep-herd *Palinode* in the eclogue of *May*, under whom the Poet lively personates our Prelates, whose whole life is a recantation of their pastorall vow, and whose profession to forsake the World, as they use the matter, boggs them deeper into the world: those our admired *Spencer* inveighs against, not without some presage of these reforming times.—JOHN MILTON, *Ani-madversations upon the Remonstrants Defence: against Smec-tymnuus*, 1641

Even his Dorick Dialect has an incomparable sweetness in its Clownishness, like a fair Shepherdess in her Country Russet, talking in a *Yorkshire* Tone. This was impossible for Virgil to imitate; because the severity of the *Roman* Language denied him that advantage. *Spencer* has endeavour'd it in his Shep-herds Calendar; but neither will it succeed in *English*, for which reason I forbore to attempt it.—JOHN DRYDEN, "Pref-ace" to *Sylvae*, 1685, *Works*, Vol. 12, eds. Scott, Saintsbury, 1882, p. 298

Our own Nation has produc'd a third Poet in this kind, not inferiour to the two former. For the Shepherd's Kalender of *Spencer*, is not to be match'd in any Modern Language. Not even by *Tasso's Amynta*, which infinitely transcends *Guarini's Pastor-Fido*, as having more of Nature in it, and being almost wholly clear from the wretched affectation of Learning. I will say nothing of the *Piscatory Eclogues* [of Sannazaro], because no modern *Latin* can bear Criticism. 'Tis no wonder that rolling down through so many barbarous Ages, from the Spring of *Virgil*, it bears along with it the filth and ordures of the *Goths* and *Vandals*. Neither will I mention Monsieur *Fontenelle*, the living Glory of the *French*. 'Tis enough for him to have excell'd his Master *Lucian*, without attempting to compare our miserable Age with that of *Virgil* or *Theocritus*. . . . But *Spencer* being Master of our Northern Dialect; and skill'd in *Chaucer's* English, has so exactly imitated the *Doric* of *Theocritus*, that his Love is a perfect Image of that Passion which God infus'd into both Sexes, before it was corrupted with the Knowledge of Arts, and the Ceremonies of what we call good Manners.—JOHN DRYDEN, "To the Right Honorable Hugh, Lord Clifford," 1697, *Works*, Vol. 13, eds. Scott, Saintsbury, 1882, pp. 324–25

Spenser's Calendar, in Mr Dryden's opinion, is the most complete work of this kind which any Nation has produc'd ever since the time of *Virgil*. Not but that he may be thought imperfect in some few points. His Eclogues are somewhat too long, if we compare them with the ancients. He is sometimes too allegorical, and treats of matters of religion in a pastoral style as *Mantuan* had done before him. He has employ'd the Lyric measure, which is contrary to the practice of the old Poets. His Stanza is not still the same, nor always well chosen. This last may be the reason his expression is sometimes not concise enough: for the Tetrastic has oblig'd him to extend his sense to the length of four lines, which would have been more closely confin'd in the couplet.

In the manners, thoughts, and characters, he comes near to *Theocritus* himself; tho' notwithstanding all the care he has taken, he is certainly inferior in his Dialect. For the *Doric* had its beauty and propriety in the time of *Theocritus*; it was used in part of *Greece*, and frequent in the mouths of many of the greatest persons; whereas the old *English* and country phrases of *Spenser* were entirely obsolete, or spoken only by people of the lowest condition. As there is a difference between simplicity and rusticity, so the expression of simple thoughts should be plain, but not clownish. The addition he has made of a Calendar to his Eclogues is very beautiful: since by this, besides the general moral of innocence and simplicity, which is common to other authors of pastoral, he has one peculiar to himself; he compares human Life to the several Seasons, and at once exposes to his readers a view of the great and little worlds, in their various changes and aspects. Yet the scrupulous division of his Pastorals into Months, has oblig'd him either to repeat the same description, in other words, for three months together; or when it was exhausted before, entirely to omit it: whence it comes to pass that some of his Eclogues (as the sixth, eighth, and tenth for example) have nothing but their Titles to distinguish them. The reason is evident, because the year has not that variety in it to furnish every month with a particular description, as it may every season.—ALEXANDER POPE, "A Discourse on Pastoral Poetry," 1704, *The Poems of Alexander Pope*, Vol. 1, Twickenham ed., 1961, pp. 31–33

Other writers, having the mean and despicable condition of a shepherd always before them, conceive it necessary to degrade the language of pastoral by obsolete terms and rustic words, which they very learnedly call Doric, without reflecting that they thus become authors of a mangled dialect which no human being could have spoken, that they may as well refine the speech as the sentiments of their personages, and that none of the inconsistencies which they endeavour to avoid is greater than that of joining elegance of thought with coarseness of diction. Spenser begins one of his pastorals with studied barbarity.

> Diggon Dauie, I bidde her god day:
> Or Diggon her is, or I missaye.

> DIGGON: Her was her, while it was daye light,
> But now her is a most wretched wight.
>   (*Shepheardes Calender*, 'September')

What will the reader imagine to be the subject on which speakers like these exercise their eloquence? Will he not be somewhat disappointed when he finds them met together to condemn the corruptions of the church of Rome? Surely, at the same time that a shepherd learns theology, he may gain some acquaintance with his native language.—SAMUEL JOHNSON, *The Rambler*, July 24, 1750

THE FAERIE QUEENE

Collyn I see by thy new taken taske,
  some sacred fury hath enricht thy braynes,
That leades thy muse in haughtie verse to maske,
  and loath the layes that longs to lowly swaynes.
That lifts thy notes from Shepheardes vnto kings,
So like the liuely Larke that mounting sings.

Thy louely Rosolinde seemes now forlorne,
  and all thy gentle flockes forgotten quight,
Thy chaunged hart now holdes thy pypes in scorne,
  those pretty pypes that did thy mates delight.
Those trustie mates, that loued thee so well,
Whom thou gau'st mirth: as they gaue thee the bell.

Yet as thou earst with thy sweete roundelayes,
  didst stirre to glee our laddes in homely bowers:
So moughtst thou now in these refyned layes,
  delight the dainty eares of higher powers.
And so mought they in their deepe skanning skill
Alow and grace our Collyns flowing quill.

And faire befall that *Faerie Queene* of thine,
  in whose faire eyes loue linckt with vertue sits:
Enfusing by those bewties fiers deuine,
  such high conceites into thy humble wits,
As raised hath poore pastors oaten reede,
From rusticke tunes, to chaunt heroique deedes.

So mought thy *Redcrosse* knight with happy hand
  victorious be in that faire Ilands right:
Which thou doest vaile in Type of Faery land
  Elyzas blessed field, that *Albion* hight.
That shieldes her friends, and warres her mightie foes,
Yet still with people, peace, and plentie flowes.

But (iolly Shepheard) though with pleasing style,
  thou feast the humour of the Courtly traine:
Let not conceipt thy setled sence beguile,
  ne daunted be through enuy or disdaine.
Subiect thy dome to her Empyring spright,
From whence thy Muse, and all the world takes light.
      —GABRIEL HARVEY, "To the Learned
        Shepherd," 1590

I

Me thought I saw the graue, where *Laura* lay,
Within that Temple, where the vestall flame
Was wont to burne, and passing by that way,
To see the buried dust of liuing fame,
Whose tombe faire loue, and fairer vertue kept,
All suddeinly I saw the Faery Queene:
At whose approch the soule of *Petrarke* wept,
And from thenceforth those graces were not seene.
For they this Queene attended, in whose steed
Obliuion laid him downe on *Lauras* herse:
Hereat the hardest stones were seene to bleed,

And grones of buried ghostes the heuens did perse.
Where *Homers* spright did tremble all for griefe,
And curst th'accesse of that celestiall theife.

II

The prayse of meaner wits this worke like profit brings,
As doth the Cuckoes song delight when *Philumena* sings.
If thou hast formed right true vertues face herein:
Vertue her selfe can best discerne, to whom they written bin.
If thou hast beauty praysd, let her sole lookes diuine
Iudge if ought therein be amis, and mend it by her eine.
If Chastitie want ought, or Temperaunce her dew,
Behold her Princely mind aright, and write thy Queene anew.
Meane while she shall perceiue, how far her vertues sore
Aboue the reach of all that liue, or such as wrote of yore:
And thereby will excuse and fauour thy good will:
Whose vertue can not be exprest, but by an Angels quill.
Of me no lines are lou'd, nor letters are of price,
Of all which speak our English tongue, but those of thy deuice.
—SIR WALTER RALEIGH, "Two Visions vpon this
    conceipt of the Faery Queene," 1590

The hosts tale in the xxvviij book of this worke, is a bad one: M. *Spencers* tale of the squire of Dames, in his excellent Poem of the Faery Queene, in the end of vij. Canto of the third booke, is to the like effect, sharpe and well *conceyted;* In substance thus, that his Squire of dames could in three yeares trauell, find but three women that denyed his lewd desire: of which three, one was a courtesan, that reiected him because he wanted coyne for her: the second a Nun, who refused him because he would not sweare secreacie; the third a plain countrie Gentlewoman, that of good honest simplicitie denyed him.—SIR JOHN HARINGTON, *Orlando Furioso in Heroical Verse,* 1591, p. 373

Yet let Affection interpret selfe:
Arcadia braue, and dowty *Faery Queene*
Cannot be stain'd by *Gibelin,* or *Guelph,*
Or goodliest Legend, that Witts eye hath seene.
The dainty Hand of exquisitest Art,
And nimble Head of pregnantest receit,
Neuer more finely plaid their curious part,
Then in those liuely Christals of conceit.
—GABRIEL HARVEY, "Sonnet X: A more
    particular Declaration of his Intention," 1592,
    Works, Vol. 1, ed. Grosart, p. 244

Is not the Prose of *Sir Philip Sidney* in his sweet Arcadia, the embrodery of finest *Art* and daintiest *Witt*? *Or* is not the Verse of M. *Spencer* in his braue Faery Queene, the Virginall of the diuinest Muses, and gentlest Graces? Both delicate Writers: alwaies gallant, often braue, continually delectable, sometimes admirable. What sweeter tast of Suada, than the Prose of the One: or what pleasanter relish of the Muses, then the Verse of the Other?—GABRIEL HARVEY, "A New Letter of Notable Contents," 1592, *Works,* Vol. 1, ed. Grosart, p. 266

Why do you seeke for fained *Palladins*
Out of the smoke of idle vanitie,
That maie giue glorie to the true dissignes
Of *Bourchier, Talbot, Neuile, Willoughby*?
Why should not you striue to fill vp your lines
With wonders of your owne, with veritie?
T'inflame their offspring with the loue of Good
And glorious true examples of their bloud.

O what eternall matter here is found!
Whence new immortal *Iliads* might proceed,

That those whose happie graces do abound
In blessed accents here maie haue to feed
Good thoughts, on no imaginary ground
Of hungrie shadowes which no profit breed:
Whence musicke like, instant delight may grow,
But when men all do know they nothing know.
—SAMUEL DANIEL, *The Poeticall Essayes,* 1599,
    Complete Works, Vol. 2, ed. Grosart, p. 175

Ingenioso: [Reads the names of the most famous poets, beginning with *Edmund Spencer.*] Good men and true, stand together: heare your censure, what's thy judgement of *Spencer*?

Iudicio: A sweeter swan then euer song in Poe,
              A shriller Nightingale then euer blest
              The prouder groues of selfe admiring Rome.
              Blith was each vally, and each sheapeard proud,
              While he did chaunt his rural minstralsye.
              Attentiue was full many a dainty eare.
              Nay hearers hong vpon his melting tong,
              While sweetly of his Faiery Queene he song.
              While to the waters fall he tun'd [her] fame,
              And in each barke engrau'd Elizaes name.
              And yet for all this, vnregarding soile
              Vnlac't the line of his desired life,
              Denying mayntenance for his deare reliefe,
              Carelesses [ere] to preuent his exequy,
              Scarce deigning to shut vp his dying eye.

Ingenioso: Pity it is that gentler witts should breed,
              Where thickskin chuffes laugh at a schollers need.
              But softly may our [Homer's] ashes rest,
              That lie by mery *Chaucers* noble chest.
—ANON., *The Return from Pernussus,* 1606, Vol.
    1, p. ii

Shew now faire *Muse* what afterward became
Of great *Achilles Mother;* She whose name
The *Mermaids* sing, and tell the weeping strand
A brauer Lady neuer tript on land,
Except the euer liuing *Fayerie Queene,*
Whose vertues by her *Swaine* so written beene,
That time shall call her high enchanced story
In his rare song, *The Muses chiefest Glory.*
—WILLIAM BROWNE, *Britannia's Pastorals,*
    1616, *Poems,* Vol. 1, ed. Goodwin,
    pp. 221–22

Friendship is an holy name, and a sacred communion of friends. *As the Sunne is in the Firmament, so is friendship in the world,* a most diuine and heauenly band, take this away, and take all pleasure, all ioy, all comfort, happinesse and true content out of the world, tis the greatest tye, and as the Poet decides, is much to be preferred before the rest.

Hard is the doubt, and difficult to deeme,
When all three kindes of loue together meet;
And doe dispart the heart with power extreme,
Whether shall waigh the ballance downe, to wit,
The deare affection vnto kindred sweet,
Or raging fire of loue to women kind,
Or zeale of friends combined by vertues meete.
But of them all the band of vertuous minde,
Me thinkes the gentle heart should most assured
    bind. . . .

There is no man so pusillanimous, so very dastard, whom loue would not incense, make of a divine temper, and an heroicall spirit. As hee said in like case, *Tota ruat coeli moles non terreor, &c.* Nothing can terrifie, nothing can dismay them, But as Sr *Blandamor* and *Paridell,* those two braue

Fayrye K[n]ights, fought for the loue of faire *Florimel* in presence,

> And drawing both their swords with rage anew,
> Like two mad Mastiues each on other flew,
> And shields did share, and males did rash, and
>   helmes did hew:
> So furiously each other did assaile,
> As if their soules at once they would haue rent,
> Out of their brests, that streames of blood did rayle
> Adowne, as if their springs of life were spent,
> That all the ground with purple blood was sprent,
> And all their armour stain'd with bloody gore,
> Yet scarcely once to breath would they relent.
> So mortall was their mallice and so sore,
> That both resolued (then yeeld) to dye before.

. . . And for that cause he would haue women follow the Camp, to be spectators and encouragers of noble actions: vpon such an occasion; the *Squire of Dames* himselfe, *S. Lancelot* or *Sir Tristram*, Caesar, or *Alexander* shall not be more resolute, or goe beyond them.

Gentelman hath so liuely decyphered, in his *Legend* of the *Patron of trew holinesse*, the *Knight of the Red-Crosse*; whereby, and by the rest of those his louely *Raptures*, hee hath iustly purchased the *Lawrel* of *honorable memory*, while the Pilgrimage of those his worthies are to indure.

Hee there hath brought forth our *Noble Saint George*; at the first onely in the state of a *Swayne*, before his *Glorious Queene* cast down on the ground (*Vncouth, vnkest*) *Vnacknowne, vncared off* as a dead trunke, and onely fit for the *fire* (as in our first *Period*).

But when hee had arrayed himselfe in the *Armor* of his Dying Lord, his presence is then become *Gracious*, and his person promising great things (*as one for sad incounters fit*). Which hee first *Passiuely* (as in our second *Period*), and after *Actiuely* (as in our third *Period*) doth so victoriously passe through and finish; that at the length (as in our fourth *Period*), hee is become altogether *Impassible*, whether of *Assalts* of the fraylety of *Nature* within, or *Affronts* of *Aduersaries* without, as being fully possessed of that Kingdome, against which there is none to stand vp.—ROBERT BURTON, *Anatomy of Melancholy*, 1621, pp. 519–37

I must approue the learned *Spencer*, in the rest of his Poëms, no lesse then his *Fairy Queene*, an exact body of the Ethicke doctrine: though some good iudgments haue wisht (and perhaps not without cause) that he had therein beene a little freer of his fiction, and not so close riuetted to his Morall.—HENRY REYNOLDS, "Mythomystes," 1632, *Critical Essays of the Seventeenth Century*, Vol. 1, ed. Spingarn, 1908–9, p. 147

Him our old patron St. George by his matchlesse valour slew, as the Prelat of the Garter that reads his Collect can tell. And if our Princes and Knights will imitate the fame of that old champion, as by their order of Knighthood solemnly taken, they vow, farre be it that they should uphold and side with this English Dragon; but rather to doe as indeed their oath binds them, they should make it their Knightly adventure to pursue & vanquish this mighty sailewing'd monster that menaces to swallow up the Land, unlesse her bottomlesse gorge may be satisfi'd with the blood of the Kings daughter the Church.—JOHN MILTON, *The Reason of Church-Government*, 1641

I betook me among those lofty Fables and Romances, which recount in solemne canto's the deeds of Knighthood founded by our victorious Kings; & from hence had in renowne over all Christendome. There I read it in the oath of every Knight, that he should defend to the expence of his best blood, or of his life,

if it so befell him, the honour and chastity of Virgin or Matron. From whence even then I learnt what a noble vertue chastity sure must be, to the defence of which so many worthies by such a deare adventure of themselves had sworne.—JOHN MILTON, *An Apology against a Pamphlet call'd A Modest Confutation of the Animadversations*, 1642

That vertue therefore which is but a youngling in the contemplation of evill, and knows not the utmost that vice promises to her followers, and rejects it, is but a blank vertue, not a pure; her whitenesse is but an excrementall whitenesse; Which was the reason why our sage and serious Poet *Spencer*, whom I dare be known to think a better teacher then *Scotus* or *Aquinas*, describing true temperance under the person of *Guion*, brings him in with his palmer through the cave of Mammon, and the bowr of earthly blisse that he might see and know, and yet abstain.—JOHN MILTON, *Areopagitica*, 1644

If there were a man of iron, such as *Talus*, by our Poet *Spencer*, is fain'd to be, the page of Justice, who with his iron flaile could doe all this, and expeditiously, without those deceitfull formes and circumstances of law, worse then ceremonies in religion; I say God send it don, whether by one *Talus*, or by a thousand.—JOHN MILTON, *Eikonoklastes*, 1649

> Methinks Heroick Poesie, till now
> Like some fantastick Fairy land did show;
> Gods, Devils, Nymphs, Witches, & Giants race,
> And all but man, in mans best work had place.
> Thou like some worthy Knight, with sacred Arms
> Dost drive the *Monsters* thence, and end the Charms.
>   —ABRAHAM COWLEY, "To Sir William
>   D'Avenant . . . ," 1650, *Poems*, ed. Waller,
>   1905, p. 42

Spencer, I think, may be reckon'd the first of our *Heroick Poets*; he had a large spirit, a sharp judgement, and a *Genius* for *Heroick Poesie*, perhaps above any that ever writ since *Virgil*. But our misfortune is, he wanted a true *Idea*, and lost himself, by following an unfaithful guide. Though besides *Homer* and *Virgil* he had read *Tasso*, yet he rather suffer'd himself to be misled by *Ariosto*; with whom blindly rambling on *marvellous* Adventures, he makes no Conscience of *Probability*. All is fanciful and chimerical, without any uniformity, without any foundation in truth; his Poem is perfect *Fairy-land*.

They who can love *Ariosto*, will be ravish'd with *Spencer*; whilst men of juster thoughts lament that such great Wits have miscarried in their Travels for want of direction to set them in the right way. But the truth is, in *Spencer's* time, *Italy* it self was not well satisfied with *Tasso*; and few amongst them would then allow that he had excell'd their *divine Ariosto*. And it was the vice of those Times to affect superstitiously the *Allegory*; and nothing would then be current without a mystical meaning. We must blame the Italians for debauching great *Spencer's* judgement; and they cast him on the unlucky choice of the *Stanza*, which in no wise is proper for our Language.—THOMAS RYMER, "The Preface of the Translator" to Rapin's *Reflections on Aristotle's Treatise of Poesie*, 1674

Petrarch, Ronsard, Spencer, met with much Applause upon the Subjects of Love, Praise, Grief, Reproach. *Ariosto* and *Tasso* entered boldly upon the Scene of *Heroick* Poems, but having not Wings for so high Flights, began to Learn of the old Ones, fell upon their Imitations, and chiefly of *Virgil*, as far as the Force of their Genius or Disadvantage of New Languages and Customs would allow. The Religion of the Gentiles had been woven into the Contexture of all the antient poetry, with a very agreeable mixture, which made the Moderns affect to give that of Christianity, a place also in their Poems. But the true Religion, was not found to become Fiction so well, as a false had done, and all their Attempts of this kind seemed rather to debase Religion than to heighten Poetry. *Spencer* endeavoured to Supply this, with Morality, and to make Instruction, instead of Story, the Subject of an *Epick* Poem. His Execution was Excellent, and his Flights of Fancy very Noble and High, but his Design was Poor, and his Moral lay so bare, that it lost the Effect; 'tis true, the Pill was Gilded, but so thin, that the Colour and the Taste were too easily discovered.—SIR WILLIAM TEMPLE, "Upon Poetry," *Miscellanea: The Second Part*, 1690, pp. 46–47

I consulted . . . *Milton* . . . I found in him a true sublimity, lofty thoughts, which were cloath'd with admirable *Grecisms*, and ancient words, which he had been digging from the Mines of *Chaucer*, and of *Spencer*, and which, with all their rusticity, had somewhat of Venerable in them. But I found not there neither for which I look'd. At last, I had recourse to his Master, *Spencer*, the Author of that immortal Poem call'd *Fairy Queen*; and there I met with that which I had been looking for so long in vain. *Spencer* had studi'd *Virgil* to as much advantage as *Milton* had done *Homer*. And amongst the rest of his Excellencies had Copy'd that.—JOHN DRYDEN, "Dedication to the Right Honorable Charles, Earl of Dorset and Middlesex," 1693, *Works*, Vol. 13, eds. Scott, Saintsbury, 1882, p. 117

And other Books of the like Nature, the reading of which are profitable to warm the Imagination [of the painter]: such as in *English*, are *Spencer's Fairy Queen*; The *Paradise Lost* of *Milton*; *Tasso* translated by *Fairfax*; and the History of *Polybius*, by Sir *Henry Shere*.—JOHN DRYDEN, "Observations on the Art of Painting," 1695, *Works*, Vol. 17, eds. Scott, Saintsbury, 1882, pp. 418–19

In our Language SPENSER has not contented himself with this submissive Manner of Imitation: He launches out into very flowery Paths, which still seem to conduct him into one great Road. His *Fairy Queen* (had it been finished) must have ended in the Account, which every Knight was to give of his Adventures, and in the accumulated Praises of his Heroine GLORIANA. The Whole would have been an *Heroic* Poem, but in another Cast and Figure, than any that had ever been written before. Yet it is observable, that every Hero (as far as we can judge by the Books still remaining) bears his distinguished Character, and represents some particular Virtue conducive to the whole Design.—MATTHEW PRIOR, "Preface" to *Solomon on the Vanity of the World*, 1708, *The Literary Works*, Vol. 1, eds. Wright, Spears, 1959, pp. 307–8

I was this Morning reading the Tenth Canto in the Fourth Book of *Spencer*, in which Sir *Scudamore* relates the Progress of his Courtship to *Amoret* under a very beautiful Allegory, which is one of the most natural and unmixed of any in that most excellent Author. I shall transpose it, to use Mr *Bays's* Term, for the Benefit of many *English* Lovers, who have by frequent Letters desired me to lay down some Rules for the Conduct of their virtuous Amours; and shall only premise, That by the Shield of Love, is meant a generous constant Passion for the Person beloved.

When the Fame, says he, of this celebrated Beauty first flew Abroad, I went in Pursuit of her to the *Temple of Love*. This Temple, continues he, bore the Name of the Goddess *Venus*, and was seated in a most fruitful Island, walled by Nature against all Invaders. There was a single Bridge that led into the Island, and before it a Castle garrison'd by 20 Knights. Near the Castle was an open Plain, and in the midst of it a Pillar, on which was hung the Shield of Love; and underneath it, in Letters of Gold, was this Inscription:

> Happy the Man who well can use his Bliss;
> Whose ever be the Shield, Fair Amoret be his.

My Heart panted upon reading the Inscription; I struck upon the Shield with my Spear. Immediately issued forth a Knight well mounted, and completely armed, who, without speaking, ran fiercely at me. I receiv'd him as well as I could, and by good Fortune threw him out of the Saddle. I encounter'd the whole Twenty successively, and leaving them all extended on the Plain, carried off the Shield in Token of Victory. Having thus vanquish'd my Rivals, I passed on without Impediment, till I came to the outermost Gate of the Bridge, which I found locked and barred. I knocked and called, but could get no Answer. At last I saw one on the other Side of the Gate, who stood peeping thro' a small Crevice. This was the Porter; he had a double Face resembling a *Janus*, and was continually looking about him, as if he mistrusted some sudden Danger. His Name, as I afterwards learned, was *Doubt*. Over-against him sat *Delay*, who entertain'd Passengers with some idle Story, while they lost such Opportunities as were never to be recovered. As soon as the Porter saw my Shield, he open'd the Gate; but upon my entring, *Delay* caught hold of me, and would fain have made me listen to her Fooleries. However, I shook her off, and pass'd forward, till I came to the Second Gate, *The Gate of good Desert*, which always stood wide open; but in the Porch was an hideous Giant that stopp'd the Entrance. His Name was *Danger*. Many Warriors of good Reputation, not able to bear the Sternness of his Look, went back again. Cowards fled at the first Sight of him, except some few, who watching their Opportunity, slipp'd by him unobserved. I prepared to assault him; but upon the first Sight of my Shield, he immediately gave Way. Looking back upon him, I found his hinder Parts much more deformed and terrible than his Face; *Hatred, Murther, Treason, Envy*, and *Detraction*, lying in Ambush behind him, to fall upon the Heedless and Unwary.

I now entered *The Island of Love*, which appeared in all the Beauties of Art and Nature, and feasted every Sense with the most agreeable Objects. Amidst a pleasing Variety of Walks and Allies, shady Seats, and flowry Banks, sunny Hills, and gloomy Vallies, were Thousands of Lovers sitting or walking together in Pairs, and singing Hymns to the Deity of the Place.

I could not forbear envying this happy People, who were already in Possession of all they could desire. While I went forward to the Temple, the Structure was beautiful beyond Imagination; The Gate stood open. In the Entrance sat a most amiable Woman, whose Name was *Concord*.

On either Side of her stood Two young Men, both strongly armed, as if afraid of each other. As I afterwards learn'd, they were both her Sons, but begotten of her by Two different Fathers; their Names *Love* and *Hatred*.

The Lady so well tempered and reconciled them both, that she forced them to join Hands; tho' I could not but observe, that *Hatred* turned aside his Face, as not able to endure the Sight of his younger Brother.

I at length entered the Inmost Temple, the Roof of which was raised upon an Hundred Marble Pillars, decked with Crowns, Chains, and Garlands. The Ground was strow'd with Flowers. An Hundred Altars, at each of which stood a Virgin Priestess cloathed in White, blazed all at once with the Sacrifice of Lovers, who were perpetually sending up their Vows to Heaven in Clouds of Incense.

In the Midst stood the Goddess her self upon an Altar, whose Substance was neither Gold nor Stone, but infinitely more precious than either. About her Neck flew numberless Flocks of little *Loves, Joys,* and *Graces:* and all about her Altar lay scattered Heaps of *Lovers,* complaining of the Disdain, Pride, or Treachery, of their Mistresses. One among the rest, no longer able to contain his Griefs, broke out into the following Prayer:

'*Venus,* Queen of Grace and Beauty, Joy of Gods and Men, who with a smile becalmest the Seas, and renewest all Nature, Goddess, whom all the different Species in the Universe obey with Joy and Pleasure, grant I may at last obtain the Objects of my Vows.'

The impatient Lover pronounced this with great Vehemence; but I in a soft Murmur besought the Goddess to lend me her Assistance. While I was thus praying, I chanced to cast my Eye on a Company of Ladies, who were assembled together in a Corner of the Temple waiting for the Anthem.

The foremost seemed something elder, and of a more composed Countenance, than the rest, who all appeared to be under her Direction. Her Name was *Womanhood.* On one Side of her sat *Shamefacedness,* with Blushes rising in her Cheeks, and her Eyes fixed upon the Ground. On the other was *Chearfulness,* with a smiling Look, that infused a secret Pleasure into the Hearts of all that saw her. With these sat *Modesty,* holding her Hand on her Heart; *Courtesy,* with a graceful Aspect, and obliging Behaviour; and the Two Sisters, who were always linked together, and resembled each other, *Silence* and *Obedience.*

> Thus sat they all around in seemly Rate,
> And in the Midst of them a goodly Maid,
> Ev'n in the Lap of *Womanhood* there sat,
> The which was all in Lilly white array'd;
> Where Silver Streams among the Linen stray'd;
> Like to the Morn, when first her shining Face
> Hath to the Gloomy World it self bewray'd.
> That same was fairest *Amoret* in Place,
> Shining with Beauty's Light, and Heav'nly Virtue's
>   Grace.

As soon as I beheld the charming *Amoret,* my Heart throbbed with Hopes. I stepped to her, and seized her Hand; when *Womanhood* immediately rising up, sharply rebuked me for offering in so rude a Manner to lay hold on a Virgin. I excused myself as modestly as I could, and the same Time displayed my Shield; upon which, as soon as she beheld the God emblazoned with his Bow and Shafts, she was struck mute, and instantly retired.

I still held fast the fair *Amoret,* and turning my Eyes towards the Goddess of the Place, saw that she favoured my Pretensions with a Smile, which so emboldened me, that I carried off my Prize.

The Maid, sometimes with Tears, sometimes with Smiles, entreated me to let her go: But I led her through the Temple-Gate, where the Goddess *Concord,* who had favoured my Entrance, befriended my Retreat.

This Allegory is so natural, that it explains itself. The Persons in it are very artfully described, and disposed in proper Places. The Posts assigned to *Doubt, Delay,* and *Danger,* are admirable. The Gate of *Good Desert* has something noble and instructive in it. But above all, I am most pleased with the beautiful Grouppe of Figures in the Corner of the Temple. Among these, *Womanhood* is drawn like what the Philosophers call an Universal Nature, and is attended with beautiful Representatives of all those Virtues that are the Ornaments of the Female Sex, considered in its natural Perfection and Innocence.—SIR RICHARD STEELE, *The Tatler,* July 4–6, 1710

But besides this kind of Fable there is another in which the Actors are Passions, Virtues, Vices and other imaginary Persons of the like Nature . . . The greatest Italian Wits have applied themselves to the Writing of this latter kind of Fables; as *Spencer's Fairy Queen* is one continued Series of them from the beginning to the end of that admirable Work.—JOSEPH ADDISON, *The Spectator,* Sept. 29, 1711

'After my reading a canto in Spenser two or three days ago to an old lady between seventy and eighty, she said that I had been showing her a collection of pictures,' said ⟨Spence.⟩

She said very right, and I don't know how it is but there's something in Spenser that pleases me as strongly in one's old age as it did in one's youth. I read *The Faerie Queene* when I was about twelve with a vast deal of delight, and I think it gave me as much when I read it over about a year or two ago.— ALEXANDER POPE, *Spence's Anecdotes,* 1744

> In trellised shed with clustering roses gay,
> And, Mary! oft beside our blazing fire,
> When years of wedded life were as a day
> Whose current answers to the heart's desire,
> Did we together read in Spenser's Lay
> How Una, sad of soul—in sad attire,
> The gentle Una, of celestial birth,
> To seek her Knight went wandering o'er the earth.
>
> Ah, then, Belovèd! pleasing was the smart,
> And the tear precious in compassion shed
> For Her, who, pierced by sorrow's thrilling dart,
> Did meekly bear the pang unmerited;
> Meek as that emblem of her lowly heart
> The milk-white Lamb which in a line she led,—
> And faithful, loyal in her innocence,
> Like the brave Lion slain in her defence.
>
> Notes could we hear as of a faery shell
> Attuned to words with sacred wisdom fraught;
> Free Fancy prized each specious miracle,
> And all its finer inspiration caught;
> Till in the bosom of our rustic Cell,
> We by a lamentable change were taught
> That 'bliss with mortal Man may not abide':
> How nearly joy and sorrow are allied!
>
> For us the stream of fiction ceased to flow,
> For us the voice of melody was mute.
> —But, as soft gales dissolve the dreary snow,
> And give the timid herbage leave to shoot,
> Heaven's breathing influence failed not to bestow
> A timely promise of unlooked-for fruit,
> Fair fruit of pleasure and serene content
> From blossoms wild of fancies innocent.
>
> It soothed us—it beguiled us—then, to hear
> Once more of troubles wrought by magic spell;
> And griefs whose aery motion comes not near
> The pangs that tempt the Spirit to rebel:
> Then, with mild Una in her sober cheer,
> High over hill and low adown the dell
> Again we wandered, willing to partake
> All that she suffered for her dear Lord's sake.
>
> Then, too, this Song of *mine* once more could please,
> Where anguish, strange as dreams of restless sleep,
> Is tempered and allayed by sympathies
> Aloft ascending, and descending deep,
> Even to the inferior Kinds; whom forest-trees
> Protect from beating sunbeams, and the sweep

Of the sharp winds;—fair Creatures!—to whom Heaven
A calm and sinless life, with love, hath given.

This tragic Story cheered us; for it speaks
Of female patience winning firm repose;
And, of the recompense that conscience seeks,
A bright, encouraging, example shows;
Needful when o'er wide realms the tempest breaks,
Needful amid life's ordinary woes;—
Hence, not for them unfitted who would bless
A happy hour with holier happiness.

He serves the Muses erringly and ill,
Whose aim is pleasure light and fugitive:
O, that my mind were equal to fulfil
The comprehensive mandate which they give—
Vain aspiration of an earnest will!
Yet in this moral Strain a power may live,
Belovèd Wife! such solace to impart
As it hath yielded to thy tender heart.
> —WILLIAM WORDSWORTH, Dedication to *The White Doe of Rylstone*, 1815

In after-time, a sage of mickle lore
Yclep'd Typographus, the Giant took,
And did refit his limbs as heretofore,
And made him read in many a learned book,
And into many a lively legend look;
Thereby in goodly themes so training him,
That all his brutishness he quite forsook,
When, meeting Artegall and Talus grim,
The one he struck stone-blind, the other's eyes wox dim.
> —JOHN KEATS, verses written in a copy of *The Faerie Queene*, at the end of Book 5, Canto 2, 1821.

A fine grotesque is the expression, in a moment, by a series of symbols thrown together in bold and fearless connection, of truths which it would have taken a long time to express in any verbal way, and of which the connection is left for the beholder to work out for himself; the gaps left or overleaped by the haste of the imagination, forming the grotesque character.

For instance, Spenser desires to tell us, (1) that envy is the most untamable and unappeasable of the passions, not to be soothed by any kindness; (2) that with continual labour it invents evil thoughts out of its own heart; (3) that even in this, its power of doing harm is partly hindered by the decaying and corrupting nature of the evil it lives in; (4) that it looks every way, and that whatever it sees is altered and discoloured by its own nature; (5) which discolouring, however, is to it a veil, or disgraceful dress, in the sight of others; (6) and that it never is free from the most bitter suffering, (7) which cramps all its acts and movements, enfolding and crushing it while it torments. All this it has required a somewhat long and languid sentence for me to say in unsymbolical terms,—not, by the way, that they *are* unsymbolical altogether, for I have been forced, whether I would or not, to use *some* figurative words; but even with this help the sentence is long and tiresome, and does not with any vigour represent the truth. It would take some prolonged enforcement of each sentence to make it felt, in ordinary ways of talking. But Spenser puts it all into a grotesque, and it is done shortly and at once, so that we feel it fully, and see it, and never forget it. I have numbered above the statements which had to be made. I now number them with the same numbers, as they occur in the several pieces of the grotesque:—

> And next to him malicious Envy rode
> (1) Upon a ravenous wolfe, and (2, 3) still did chaw

Between his cankred teeth a venemous tode,
That all the poison ran about his jaw.
(4, 5) All in a kirtle of discolourd say
He clothed was, y-paynted full of eies;
(6) And in his bosome secretly there lay
An hateful snake, the which his taile uptyes
(7) In many folds, and mortall sting implyes.

There is the whole thing in nine lines; or, rather in one image, which will hardly occupy any room at all on the mind's shelves, but can be lifted out, whole, whenever we want it. All noble grotesques are concentrations of this kind, and the noblest convey truths which nothing else could convey; and not only so, but convey them, in minor cases with a delightfulness,—in the higher instances with an awfulness,—which no mere utterance of the symbolised truth would have possessed, but which belongs to the effort of the mind to unweave the riddle, or to the sense it has of there being an infinite power and meaning in the thing seen, beyond all that is apparent therein, giving the highest sublimity even to the most trivial object so presented and so contemplated.

> 'Jeremiah, what seest thou?'
> 'I see a seething pot; and the face thereof is toward the north.'
> 'Out of the north an evil shall break forth upon all the inhabitants of the land.'

And thus in all ages and among all nations, grotesque idealism has been the element through which the most appalling and eventful truth has been wisely conveyed, from the most sublime words of true Revelation, to the "*all' hot' an hēmionos basileus*," etc., of the oracles, and the more or less doubtful teaching of dreams; and so down to ordinary poetry. No element of imagination has a wider range, a more magnificent use, or so colossal a grasp of sacred truth.—JOHN RUSKIN, *Modern Painters*, 1856, Vol. 3, Ch. 8

E. K.
"The Epistle" (1579)
The Poetical Works of Edmund Spenser, ed. Bagster 1807, Volume 8, pp. 7–15

Uncovthe vnkiste, Sayde the olde famous Poete Chaucer: whom for his excellencie and wonderfull skil in making, his scholler Lidgate, a worthy scholler of so excellent a maister, calleth the Loadestarre of our Language; and whom our Colin clout in his Aeglogue calleth Tityrus the God of shepheards, comparing hym to the worthiness of the Roman Tityrus Virgile. Which prouerbe, myne owne good friend Ma. Haruey, as in that good old Poete it serued well Pandares purpose, for the bolstering of his baudy brocage, so very well taketh place in this our new Poete, who for that he is vncouthe (as said Chaucer) is vnkist, and vnknown to most men, is regarded but of few. But I dout not, so soone as his name shall come into the knowledg of men, and his worthines be sounded in the tromp of fame, but that he shall be not onely kiste, but also beloued of all, embraced of the most, and wondred at of the best. No lesse I thinke, deserueth his wittinesse in deuising, his pithinesse in vttering, his complaints of loue so louely, his discourses of pleasure so pleasantly, his pastorall rudenesse, his morall wisenesse, his dewe obseruing of Decorum euerye where, in personages, in seasons, in matter, in speach, and generally in al seemely simplycitie of handeling his matter, and framing his words: the which of many thinges which in him be straunge, I know will seeme the straungest, the words them selues being so auncient, the knitting of them so short and intricate, and the whole Periode and compasse of speache so delightsome for the roundnesse, and so graue for the straungenesse. And firste of the wordes to speake, I graunt they be something hard, and of most men vnused, yet both English, and also vsed of most excellent Authors and most famous Poetes. In whom whenas this our Poet hath bene much traueiled and throughly redd, how could it be, (as that worthy Oratour sayde) but that walking in the sonne although for other cause he walked, yet needes he mought be sunburnt; and hauing the sound of those auncient Poetes still ringing in his eares, he mought needes in singing hit out some of theyr tunes. But whether he vseth them by such casualtye and custome, or of set purpose and choyse, as thinking them fittest for such rusticall rudenesse of shepheards, eyther for that theyr rough sounde would make his rymes more ragged and rustical, or els because such olde and obsolete wordes are most vsed of country folke, sure I think, and think I think not amisse, that they bring great grace and, as one would say, auctoritie to the verse. For albe amongst many other faultes it specially be obiected of Valla against Liuie, and of other against Saluste, that with ouer much studie they affect antiquitie, as coueting thereby credence and honor of elder yeeres, yet I am of opinion, and eke the best learned are of the lyke, that those auncient solemne wordes are a great ornament both in the one and in the other; the one labouring to set forth in hys worke an eternall image of antiquitie, and the other carefully discoursing matters of grauitie and importaunce. For if my memory fayle not, Tullie in that booke, wherein he endeuoureth to set forth the paterne of a perfect Oratour, sayth that ofttimes an auncient worde maketh the style seeme graue, and as it were reuerend; no otherwise then we honour and reuerence gray heares for a certein religious regard, which we haue of old age, yet nether euery where must old words be stuffed in, nor the commen Dialecte and maner of speaking so corrupted therby, that as in old buildings it seme disorderly and ruinous. But all as in most exquisite pictures they vse to blaze and portraict not onely the daintie lineaments of beautye, but also rounde about it to shadow the rude thickets and craggy clifts, that by the basenesse of such parts, more excellency may accrew to the principall; for oftimes we fynde ourselues, I knowe not how, singularly delighted with the shewe of such naturall rudenesse, and take great pleasure in that disorderly order. Euen so doe those rough and harsh termes enlumine and make more clearly to appeare the brightnesse of braue and glorious words. So oftentimes a dischorde in Musick maketh a comely concordaunce: so great delight tooke the worthy Poete Alceus to behold a blemish in the ioynt of a wel shaped body. But if any will rashly blame such his purpose in choyse of old and vnwonted words, him may I more iustly blame and condemne, or of witlesse headinesse in iudging, or of heedelesse hardinesse in condemning for not marking the compasse of hys bent, he wil iudge of the length of his cast. For in my opinion it is one special prayse, of many whych are dew to this Poete, that he hath laboured to restore, as to theyr rightfull heritage such good and naturall English words, as haue ben long time out of vse and almost cleane disherited. Which is the onely cause, that our Mother tonge, truely of it self is both ful enough for prose and stately enough for verse, hath long time ben counted most bare and barrein of both. which default when as some endeuoured to salue and recure, they patched vp the holes with peces and rags of other languages, borrowing here of the French, there of the Italian, euery where of the Latine, not weighing how il those tongues accorde with themselues, but much worse with ours: So now they haue made our English tonge, a gallimaufray or hodgepodge of al other speches.

Other some not so wel seene in the English tonge as perhaps in other languages, if them happen to here an olde word albeit very naturall and significant, crye out streight way, that we speak no English, but gibbrish, or rather such, as in old time Euanders mother spake. whose first shame is, that they are not ashamed, in their own mother tonge straungers to be counted and alienes. The second shame no lesse then the first, that what so they vnderstand not, they streight way deeme to be sencelesse, and not at al to be vnderstode. Much like to the Mole in Aesopes fable, that being blynd her selfe, would in no wise be perswaded, that any beast could see. The last more shameful then both, that of their owne country and natural speach, which together with their Nources milk they sucked, they haue so base regard and bastard iudgement, that they will not onely themselues not labor to garnish and beautifie it, but also repine, that of other it should be embellished. Like to the dogge in the maunger, that him selfe can eate no hay, and yet barketh at the hungry bullock, that so faine would feede: whose currish kind though it cannot be kept from barking, yet I conne them thanke that they refrain from byting.

Now for the knitting of sentences, whych they call the ioynts and members thereof, and for al the compasse of the speach, it is round without roughnesse, and learned wythout hardnes, such indeede as may be perceiued of the leaste, vnderstoode of the moste, but iudged onely of the learned. For what in most English wryters vseth to be loose, and as it were vngyrt, in this Authour is well grounded, finely framed, and strongly trussed vp together. In regard wherof, I scorne and spue out the rakehellye route of our ragged rymers (for so themselues vse to hunt the letter) which without learning boste, without iudgement iangle, without reason rage and fome, as if some instinct of Poeticall spirite had newly rauished them aboue the meanenesse of commen capacitie. And being in the middest of all theyr brauery, sodenly eyther for want of matter, or of ryme, or hauing forgotten theyr former conceipt, they seeme to be so pained and traueiled in theyr remembrance, as it were a woman in childebirth or as that same Pythia, when the traunce came vpon her.

Os rabidum fera corda domans &c.

Nethelesse let them a Gods name feede on theyr owne folly, so they seeke not to darken the beames of others glory. As for Colin, vnder whose person the Author selfe is shadowed, how furre he is from such vaunted titles and glorious showes, both him selfe sheweth, where he sayth.

Of Muses Hobbin. I conne no skill. And,
Enough is me to paint out my vnrest, &c.

And also appeareth by the basenesse of the name, wherein, it seemeth, he chose rather to vnfold great matter of argument couertly, then professing it, not suffice thereto accordingly. Which moued him rather in Aeglogues, then other wise to write, doubting perhaps his habilitie, which he little needed, or mynding to furnish our tongue with this kinde, wherein it faulteth, or following the example of the best and most auncient Poetes, which deuised this kind of wryting, being both so base for the matter, and homely for the manner, at the first to trye theyr habilities: and as young birdes, that be newly crept out of the nest, by little first to proue theyr tender wyngs, before they make a greater flyght. So flew Theocritus, as you may perceiue he was all ready full fledged. So flew Virgile, as not yet well feeling his winges. So flew Mantuane, as being not full somd. So Petrarque. So Boccace; So Marot, Sanazarus, and also diuaers other excellent both Italian and French Poetes, whose foting this Author euery where followeth, yet so as few, but they be wel sented can trace him out.

So finally flyeth this our new Poete, as a bird, whose principals be scarce growen out, but yet as that in time shall be hable to keepe wing with the best.

Now as touching the generall dryft and purpose of his Aeglogues, I mind not to say much, him selfe labouring to conceale it. Onely this appeareth, that his vnstayed yougth had long wandred in the common Labyrinth of Loue, in which time to mitigate and allay the heate of his passion, or els to warne (as he sayth) the young shepheards .s. his equalls and companions of his vnfortunate folly, he compiled these xij. Aeglogues, which for that they be proportioned to the state of the xij. monethes, he termeth the SHEPHEARDS CALENDAR, applying an olde name to a new worke. Hereunto haue I added a certain Glosse or scholion for the exposition of old wordes and harder phrases: which maner of glosing and commenting, well I wote, wil seeme straunge and rare in our tongue: yet for somuch as I knew many excellent and proper deuises both in wordes and matter would passe in the speedy course of reading, either as vnknowen, or as not marked, and that in this kind, as in other we might be equal to the learned of other nations, I thought good to take the paines vpon me, the rather for that by meanes of some familiar acquaintance I was made priuie to his counsell and secret meaning in them, as also in sundry other works of his. Which albeit I know he nothing so much hateth, as to promulgate, yet thus much haue I aduentured vpon his frendship, him selfe being for long time furre estraunged, hoping that this will the rather occasion him, to put forth diuers other excellent works of his, which slepe in silence, as his Dreames, his Legendes, his Court of Cupide, and sondry others; whose commendations to set out, were verye vayne; the thinges though worthy of many, yet being knowen to few. These my present paynes if to any they be pleasurable or profitable, be you iudge, mine own good Maister Haruey, to whom I have both in respect of your worthiness generally, and otherwyse vpon some particular and special considerations voued this my labour, and the maydenhead of this our commen frends Poetrie, himselfe hauing already in the beginning dedicated it to the Noble and worthy Gentleman, the right worshipfull Ma. Phi. Sidney, a special fauourer and maintainer of all kind of learning. Whose cause I pray you Sir, yf Enuie shall stur vp any wrongful accusasion, defend with your mighty Rhetorick and other your rare gifts of learning, as you can, and shield with your good wil, as you ought, against the malice and outrage of so many enemies, as I know wilbe set on fire with the sparks of his kindled glory. And thus recommending the Author vnto you, as vnto his most special good frend, and my selfe vnto you both, as one making singuler account of two so very good and so choise frends, I bid you both most hartely farwel, and commit you and your most commendable studies to the tuicion of the greatest.

Your owne assuredly to
be commaunded E. K.

E. K.
"The General Argument of the Whole Book"
The Shepheardes Calendar
1579

Little I hope, needeth me at large to discourse the first Originall of Aeglogues, hauing alreadie touched the same. But for the word Aeglogues I know is vnknown to most, and also mistaken of some the best learned (as they think) I wyll say somewhat thereof, being not at all impertinent to my present purpose.

They were first of the Greekes the inuentours or them called Aeglogaj as it were *aigon* or *aigonmōn logoi* that is Goteheards tales. For although in Virgile and others the speakers be more shepheards, then Goteheards, yet Theocritus in whom is more ground of authoritie, then in Virgile, this specially from that deriuing, as from the first head and welspring the whole Inuencion of his Aeglogues, maketh Goteheards the persons and authors of his tales. This being, who seeth not the grossenesse of such as by colour of learning would make vs beleeue that they are more rightly termed Eclogai, as they would say, extraordinary discourses of vnnecessarie matter, which difinition albe in substance and meaning it agree with the nature of the thing, yet nowhit answereth with the *analysis* and interpretation of the word. For they be not termed Eclogues, but Aeglogues. which sentence this authour very well obseruing, vpon good iudgment, though indeede few Goteheards haue to doe herein, nethelesse doubteth not to cal them by the vsed and best knowen name. Other curious discourses hereof I reserue to greater occasion. These xij. Aeclogues euery where answering to the seasons of the twelue monthes may be well deuided into three formes or ranckes. For eyther they be Plaintiue, as the first, the sixth, the eleuenth, and the twelfth, or recreatiue, such as al those be, which conceiue matter of loue, or commendation of special personages, or Moral: which for the most part be mixed with some Satyrical bitternesse, namely the second of reuerence dewe to old age, the fift of coloured deceipt, the seuenth and ninth of dissolute shepheards and pastours, the tenth of contempt of Poetrie and pleasant wits. And to this diuision may euery thing herein be reasonably applyed: a few onely except, whose speciall purpose and meaning I am not priuie to. And thus much generally of these xij. Aeclogues. Now will we speake particularly of all, and first of the first. Which he calleth by the first monethes name Ianuarie: wherin to some he may seeme fowly to haue faulted, in that he erroniously beginneth with that moneth, which beginneth not the yeare. For it is wel known, and stoutly mainteyned with stronge reasons of the learned, that the yeare beginneth in March, for then the sonne reneweth his finished course, and the seasonable spring refresheth the earth, and the pleasaunce thereof being buried in the sadnesse of the dead winter now worne away, reliueth. This opinion maynteine the olde Astrologers and Philosophers, namely the reuerend Andalo, and Macrobius in his holydayes of Saturne, which accoumpt also was generally obserued both of Grecians and Romans. But sauing the leaue of such learned heads, we mayntaine a custome of coumpting the seasons from the moneth Ianuary, vpon a more speciall cause, then the heathen Philosophers euer coulde conceiue, that is, for the incarnation of our mighty Sauiour and eternall redeemer the L. Christ, who as then renewing the state of the decayed world, and returing the compasse of expired yeres to theyr former date and first commencement, left to vs his heires a memoriall of his birth in the ende of the last yeere and beginning of the next. Which reckoning, beside that eternall monument of our saluation, leaneth also vpon good proofe of special iudgement. For albeit that in elder times, when as yet the coumpt of the yere was not perfected, as afterwarde it was by Iulius Caesar, they began to tel the monethes from Marches beginning, and according to the same God (as is sayd in Scripture) comaunded the people of the Iewes to count the moneth Abib, that which we call March, for the first moneth, in remembraunce that in that moneth he brought them out of the land of Aegipt: yet according to tradition of latter times it hath bene otherwise obserued, both in gouernment of the church, and rule of Mightiest Realmes. For from Iulius Caesar who first obserued the leape yeere which he called Bissextilem Annum, and brought in to a more certain course the odde wandring dayes which of the Greekes were called *hyperbainontes*. Of the Romanes intercalares (for in such matter of learning I am forced to vse the termes of the learned) the monethes haue bene nombred xij. which in the first ordinaunce of Romulus were but tenne, counting but CCCiiij. dayes in euery yeare, and beginning with March. But Numa Pompilius, who was the father of al the Romain ceremonies and religion, seeing that reckoning to agree neither with the course of the sonne, nor of the Moone, therevnto added two monethes, Ianuary and February: wherin it seemeth, that wise king minded vpon good reason to begin the yeare at Ianuarie, of him therefore so called *tanquam Ianua anni* the gate and entraunce of the yere, or of the name of the god Ianus, to which god for that the old Paynims attributed the byrth and beginning of all creatures new comming into the worlde, it seemeth that he therfore to him assigned the beginning and first entraunce of the yeare. Which account for the most part hath hetherto continued. Notwithstanding that the Aegiptians beginne theyr yeare at September, for that according to the opinion of the best Rabbins, and very purpose of the scripture selfe, God made the worlde in that moneth, that is called of them Tisri. And therefore he commanded them, to keepe the feast of Pauilions in the end of the yeare, in the xv. day of the seuenth moneth, which before that time was the first.

But our Authour respecting nether the subtiltie of thone parte, nor the antiquitie of thother, thinketh it fittest according to the simplicitie of commen vnderstanding, to begin with Ianuarie, wening it perhaps no decorum, that Shepheard should be seene in matter of so deepe insight, or canuase a case of so doubtful iudgement. So therefore beginneth he, and so continueth he throughout.

SIR KENELM DIGBY
Observations on the 22. Staffe in the 9th Canto of the 2d. Book of Spenser's Faery Queene
1628

My most honour'd Friend, I am too well acquainted with the weaknesses of mine abilities (far vnfit to vndergo such a Task as I have in hand) to flatter myself with the hope I may either inform your understanding, or do my self honour by what I am to write. But I am so desirous you should be possest with the true knowledge of what a bent will I have vpon all occasions to do you service, that obedience to your command weigheth much more with me, then the lawfulnesse of any excuse can, to preserve me from giving you in writing such a testimonie of my ignorance and erring Phantasie as I fear this will prove. Therefore without any more circumstance, I will, as I can, deliver to you in this paper, what th'other day I discoursed to you upon the 22. Staffe of the ninth *Canto* in the second Book of that matchlesse Poem, The Faery Queen, written by our English *Virgil*; whose words are these:

> The frame thereof seemd partly circulare,
> And part triangular, o worke diuine;
> Those two the first and last proportions are,
> The one imperfect, mortall, foeminine;
> Th'other immortall, perfect, masculine,
> And twixt them both a quadrate was the base,
> Proportioned equally by seuen and nine;
> Nine was the circle set in heauens place,
> All which compacted made a goodly *Diyapase*.

In this Staffe the Author seemes to me to proceed in a different manner from what he doth elsewhere generally though his whole Book. For in other places, although the beginning of his Allegory or mysticall sense, may be obscure, yet in the processe of it, he doth himself declare his own conceptions in such sort as they are obvious to any ordinary capacitie: But in this, he seems onely to glance at the profoundest notions that any Science can deliver us, and then on a sudden (as it were) recalling himself out of an Enthusiasme, he returns to the gentle Relation of the Allegorical History he had begun, leaving his Readers to wander up and down in much obscuritie, & to come within much danger of erring at his Intention in these lines? Which I conceive to be dictated by such a learned Spirit, and so generally a knowing Soul, that were there nothing else extant of *Spencers* writing, yet these few words would make me esteeme him no whit inferiour to the most famous men that ever have been in any age: as giving evident testimonie herein, that he was thoroughly verst in the Mathematicall Sciences, in Philosophy, and in Divinity, to which this might serve for an ample Theme to make large Commentaries upon. In my praises upon this subject, I am confident that the worth of the Author will preserve me from this Censure, that my Ignorance onely begets this Admiration, since he hath written nothing that is not admirable. But that it may appear I am guided somewhat by my own Judgement (tho' it be a meane one) and not by implicite Faith, and that I may in the best manner I can, comply with what you expect from me, I will no longer hold you in suspense, but begin immediately, (tho' abruptly) with the declaration of what I conceive to be the true sense of this place, which I shall not go about to adorne with any plausible examples drawne from other writings (since my want both of conveniency and learning would make me fall very short herein) but it shall be enough for me to intimate mine own conceptions, and offer them up to you in their own simple and naked form, leaving to your better Judgement the examination of the weight of them, and after perusall of them, beseeching you to reduce them and me if you perceive us erring.

Tis evident that the Authors intention in this *Canto* is to describe the bodie of a man inform'd with a rationall soul, and in prosecution of that designe he sets down particularly the severall parts of the one and of the other: But in this *Stanza* he comprehends the generall description of them both, as (being joyned together to frame a compleat Man) they make one perfect compound, which will the better appear by taking a survey of every severall clause thereof by it self.

> The Frame thereof seemed partly Circular,
> And part Triangular—

By these Figures, I conceive that he means the mind and body of Man; the first being by him compared to a Circle, and the latter to a Triangle. For as a Circle of all Figures is the most perfect, and includeth the greatest space, and is every way full and without Angles, made by the continuance of one onely line: so mans soul is the noblest and most beautifull Creature, that God hath created, and by it we are capable of the greatest gifts that God can bestow, which are Grace, Glory, and Hypostatically Union of the Humane nature to the Divine, and she enjoyeth perfect freedome and libertie in all her Actions, and is made without composition, which no Figures are that have Angles (for they are caus'd by the coincidence of severall lines) but of one pure substance which was by God breath'd into a Body made of such compounded earth as in the preceding *Stanza* the Author describes. And this is the exact Image of him that breathed it, representing him as fully as tis possible for any creature which is infinitely distant from a Creator. For, as God hath neither beginning nor ending: so, neither of these can be found in a Circle, although that being made of the successive motion of a line, it must be supposed to have a beginning some where, but his circumference no where: But mans soul is a Circle, whose circumference is limited by the true center of it, which is onely God. For as a circumference doth in all parts alike respect that indivisible Point, and as all lines drawn from the inner side of it, do make right Angles within it, when they meet therein: so all the interiour actions of mans soul ought to have no other respective Point to direct themselves unto, but God; and as long as they make right Angles, which is, that they keep the exact middle of virtue, and decline not to either of the sides where the contrary vices dwell, they cannot fail, but meet in their Center. By the Triangular Figure he very aptly designes the body: for as the Circle is of all other Figures the most perfect and most capacious: so the Triangle is most imperfect, and includes least space. It is the first and lowest of all Figures; for fewer than 3 right Angles cannot comprehend and inclose a superficies, having but 3 angles they are all acute (if it be equilaterall) and but equall to 2 *right*; in which respect all other regular Figures consisting of more then 3 lines, do exceed it.

(May not these be resembled to the 3 great compounded Elements in mans bodie, to wit, Salt, Sulphur and Mercurie, which mingled together make the naturall heat and radicall moysture, the 2 qualities whereby man liveth?) For the more lines that go to comprehend the Figure, the more and the greater the Angles are, and the nearer it comes to the perfection and capacitie of a Circle. A Triangle is composed of severall lines, and they of Points, which yet do not make a quantitie by being contiguous to one another: but rather the motion of them doth describe the lines. In like manner the Body of man is compounded of the foure Elements which are made of the foure primarie qualities, not compounded of them (for they are but Accidents) but by their operation upon the first matter. And as a Triangle hath three lines, so a solid Body hath three dimensions, to wit, Longitude, Latitude and Profunditie. But of all bodies, Man is of the lowest rank, (as the Triangle is among Figures) being composed of the Elements which make it liable to alteration and corruption. In which consideration of the dignitie of bodies, I divide them by a generall division, into sublunarie (which are the elementated ones) and Aethereall, which are supposed to be of their own nature, incorruptible, and peradventure there are some other *species* of corporeall substances, which is not of this place to dispute.

O work divine!

Certainly of all Gods works, the noblest and perfectest is Man, and for whom indeed all other were done. For, if we consider his *soul*, it is the very Image of God. If his *bodie*, it is adornd with the greatest beautie and most excellent symmetry of parts, of any created thing: whereby it witnesseth the perfection of the Architect, that of so drossie mold is able to make so rare a fabrick: If his *operations*, they are free: If his end, it is eternall glory. And if you take *all together*, Man is a little world, and of God himself. But in all this, me thinks, the admirablest work is the joyning together of the two *different* and indeed *opposite* substances in Man, to make one perfect compound; the *Soul* and the *Body*, which are of so contrary a nature, that their *uniting* seems to be a Miracle. For how can the one inform and work in the other, since there's no mean of operation (that we know of) between a spirituall substance and a corporeall? yet we see that it doth: as hard it is to find the true proportion betweene a Circle and a Triangle; yet, that there is a just proportion, and that they may be equall, *Archimedes* hath

left us an ingenious demonstration; but in reducing it to a Probleme, it fails in this, that because the proportion between a crooked line and a straight one, is not known, one must make use of a Mechanick way of measuring the *peripherie* of the one, to convert it to the side of the other.

These two the first and last proportions are.

What I have already said concerning a Circle and a Triangle, doth sufficiently unfold what is meant in this verse. Yet twill not be amisse to speak one word more hereof in this place. All things that have existence, may be divided into three *Classes*; which are, either what is pure and simple in it self, or what hath a nature compounded of what is simple, or what hath a nature compounded of what is compounded. In continued quantitie this may be exemplified by a Point, a line, and a superficies in Bodies: and in numbers, by an unity, a Denary, and a Centenary. The first, which is only pure & simple, like an indivisible point, or an unity, hath relation onely to the Divine nature: That point then moving in a sphericall manner (which serves to expresse the perfection of Gods actions) describes the Circles of our souls, and of Angels, and intellectual substances, which are of a pure and simple nature, but receiveth that from what is so, in a perfecter manner, and that hath his, from none else. Like lines that are made by the flowing of points; or Denaries that are composed of Unities: beyond both which there is nothing. In the last place, Bodies are to be rankt, which are composed of the Elements: and they likewise suffer composition, and may very well be compared to the lowest of the Figures which are composed of lines, that owe their being to Points (and such are Triangles) or to Centenaries that are composed of Denaries, and they of Unities. But if we will compare these together by proportion, God must be left out, since there is as infinite distance betweene the Simplicitie and Perfection of his nature, and the composition and imperfection of all created substances, as there is between an indivisible Point and a continuate quantitie, or between a simple Unitie and a compounded number. So that onely the other two kinds of substance do enter into this consideration: and of them I have already proved, that mans Soul is of the one the noblest, (being dignified by hypostaticall Union above all other intellectual substances) and his elementated Body, of the other the most low and corruptible. Whereby it is evident, that those two are the first and last Proportions, both in respect of their own Figure, and of what they expressed.

The one imperfect, Mortall, Feminine:
Th'other immortall, perfect, Masculine.

Mans Body hath all the proprieties of imperfect matter. It is but the Patient: of it self alone, it can do nothing: it is liable to corruption and dissolution if it once be deprived of the form which actuates it, and which is incorruptible and immortall. And as the feminine Sex is imperfect and receives perfection from the masculine: so doth the Body from the Soul, which to it is in lieu of a male. And as in corporall generations the female affords but grosse and passive matter, to which the Male gives active heat and prolificall vertue: so in spirituall generations (which are the operations of the minde) the body administers onely the Organs, which if they were not imployed by the Soul, would of themselves serve for nothing. And as there is a mutuall appetence between the Male and the Female, betweene matter and forme; So there is betweene the bodie and the soul of Man, but what ligament they have, our Author defineth not (and it may be Reason is not able to attaine to it) yet he tels us what is the foundation that this Machine rests on, and what keeps the parts together; in these words.

And twixt them both, a Quadrate was the Base.

By which Quadrate, I conceive, that he meaneth the foure principall humors in mans Bodie, viz. *Choler, Blood, Phleme,* and *Melancholy*: which if they be distempered and unfitly mingled, dissolution of the whole doth immediately ensue: like to a building which falls to ruine, if the foundation and Base of it be unsound or disordered. And in some of these, the vitall spirits are contained and preserved, which the other keep in convenient temper; and as long as they do so, the soul and bodie dwell together like good friends: so that these foure are the Base of the conjunction of the other two, both which he saith, are

> Proportion'd equally by seven and nine.

In which words, I understand he meanes the influences of the superior substances (which governe the inferiour) into the two differing parts of Man; to wit, of the *Starres,* the most powerfull of which, are the seven Planets, into his body: and of the Angels divided into nine Hierarchies or Orders into his soul: which in his *Astrophel,* he saith is

> By soveraigne choice from th'heavenly Quires select,
> And lineally deriv'd from Angels race.

And as much as the one governe the Body, so much the other do the Minde. Wherein is to be considered, that some are of opinion, how at the instant of a childs conception, or rather more effectually at the instant of his Birth, the conceived sperme or tender Body doth receive such influence of the Heavens as then raigne over that place, where the conception or birth is made: And all the Starres or virtuall places of the celestiall Orbes participating the qualities of the seven Planets (according to which they are distributed into so many Classes, or the compounds of them) it comes to passe, that according to the varitie of the severall Aspects of the one and of the other, there are various inclinations and qualities in mens bodies, but all reduced to seven generall heads and the compounds of them, which being to be varied innumerable wayes, cause as many different effects, yet the influence of some one Planet continually predominating. But when the matter in a womans wombe is capable of a soul to inform it, then God sendeth one from Heaven into it.

> Eternall God,
> In Paradise whilome did plant this Flower,
> Whence he it fetcht out of her native place,
> And did in Stock of earthly flesh inrace.

And this opinion the Author more plainly expresses himself to be of, in another work, where he saith:

> There she beholds with high aspiring thought
> The cradle of her own Creation;
> Emongst the seats of Angels heavenly wrought.

Which whether it have been created ever since the beginning of the world, and reserv'd in some fit place till due time, or be created on emergent occasion; no man can tell: but certain it is, that it is immortall, according to what I said before, when I spake of the Circle which hath no ending, and an uncertain beginning. The messengers to conveigh which soul into the bodie, are the Intelligences which move the Orbes of Heaven, who according to their severall natures communicate to it severall proprieties: and they most, who are Governours of those Starres at that instant, who have the superioritie in the planetary aspects. Whereby it comes to passe, that in all inclinations there's much affinitie between the Soul and the Body, being that the like is betweene the Intelligences and the Starres, both which communicate their vertues to each of them. And these Angels, being, as I said before, of nine severall Hierarchies, there are so many principle differences in humane souls, which participate most of their proprieties, with

whom in their descent they made the longest stay, and that had most active power to work on them, and accompanied them with a peculiar *Genius* (which is according to their severall Governments) like the same kind of water that running through various conduits wherein severall aromatike and odoriferous things are laid, do acquire severall kinds of tastes and smels. For it is supposed, that in their first Creation, all Souls are alike, and that their differing proprieties arive to them afterwards when they passe through the spheres of the governing Intelligences. So that by such their influence, it may be truly be said, that

> Nine was the Circle set in Heavens place.

Which verse, by assigning this office to the nine, and the proper place to the Circle, gives much light to what is said before. And for a further confirmation that this is the Authors opinion, read attentively the sixt *Canto* of the 3. Book, where most learnedly and at large he delivers the *Tenets* of this Philosophie; and for that, I commend to you to take particular notice of the 2d. and thirty two *Stanzaes*: as also the last of his *Epithalamion*: and survaying his works, you shall finde him a constant disciple of *Platoes* School.

> All which compacted, made a goodly Diapase.

In Nature there is not to be found a more compleat and more exact Concordance of all parts, then that which is betweene the compaction and conjunction of the Body and Soul of Man: Both which although they consist of many and most different faculties and parts, yet when they keepe due time with one another, they altogether make the most perfect Harmony that can be imagined. And as the nature of sounds, that consist of friendly consonancies and accords, is to mingle themselves with one another, and to slide into the eare with much sweetnesse, where by their unity they last a long time and delight it: where as contrarily, discords continually jarre, and fight together, and will not mingle with one another: but all of them striving to have the victory, their reluctation and disorder gives a speedie end to their sounds, which strike the Eare in a harsh and offensive manner, and there die in the very beginning of their Conflict: In like manner, when a mans Actions are regular, and directed towards God, they become like the lines of a Circle, which all meet in the Center, then his musick is most excellent and compleat, and all together are the Authors of that blessed harmony which maketh him happie in the glorious vision of Gods perfections, wherein the minde is filled with high knowledges and most pleasing contemplations; and the senses, as it were, drowned in eternall delight; and nothing can interrupt this Joy, this Happinesse, which is an everlasting Diapase: Whereas on the contrary, if a mans actions be disorderly, and consisting of discords, (which is, when the sensitive part rebels and wrastles with the Rationall, striving to oppresse it) then this musick is spoiled, and instead of eternall life, pleasure and joy, it causeth perpetuall death, horrour, paine, and misery. Which infortunate estate the Poet describes elsewhere; as in the conclusion of this Staffe he intimates: the other happy one, which is the never-failing Reward of such an obedient bodie, and ethereall and vertuous minde, as he makes to be the seat of the bright Virgin *Alma,* mans worthiest inhabitant, *Reason. Her* I feele to speake within me, and chide me for my bold Attempt, warning me to stray no further. For what I have said (considering how weakly it is said) your Command is all the excuse that I can pretend. But since my desire to obey that, may bee seene as well in a few lines, as in a large Discourse, it were indiscretion in me to trouble you with more, or to discover to you more of my Ignorance. I will only begge pardon of you for this blotted and interlined paper, whose Contents are so meane that it cannot deserve the paines of a Transcription, which if you make difficulty to grant it, for my sake, let it obtain it for having been yours.

And now I return to you also the Book that contains my Text, which yesterday you sent me, to fit this part of it with a Comment, which peradventure I might have performed better, if either I had afforded my selfe more time, or had had the conveniencie of some other books apt to quicken my Invention, to whom I might have been beholding for enlarging my understanding in some things that are treated here, although the Application should still have been my own: With these helps perhaps I might have dived further into the Authors Intention (the depth of which cannot be sounded by any that is lesse learned than he was). But I perswade my self very strongly, that in what I have said there's nothing contradictory to it, and that an intelligent and well learned man proceeding on my grounds might compose a worthie and true Commentarie on this Theme: Upon which I wonder how I stumbled, considering how many learned men have failed in the Interpretation of it, and have all at the first hearing, approved my opinion.

But it was Fortune that made me fall upon it, when first this Stanza was read to me for an indissoluble Riddle. And the same Discourse I made upon it, the first halfe quarter of an houre that I saw it, I send you here, without having reduced it to any better form, or added any thing at all unto it.

RICHARD HURD
"Letters 7–12"
Letters on Chivalry and Romance
1762, pp. 55–120

Letter VII

I t is not to be doubted but that each of these bards ⟨Spenser and Milton⟩ had kindled his poetic fire from classic fables. So that, of course, their prejudices would lie that way. Yet they both appear, when most inflamed, to have been more particularly wrapt with the Gothic fables of chivalry.

Spenser, though he had been long nourished with the spirit and substance of Homer and Virgil, chose the times of chivalry for his theme, and fairy land for the scene of his fictions. He could have planned, no doubt, an heroic design on the exact classic model: or, he might have trimmed between the Gothic and classic, as his contemporary Tasso did. But the charms of fairy prevailed. And if any think he was seduced by Ariosto into this choice, they should consider that it could be only for the sake of his subject; for the genius and character of these poets was widely different.

Under this idea then of a Gothic, not classical poem the FAERIE QUEENE is to be read and criticized. And on these principles, it would not be difficult to unfold its merit in another way than has been hitherto attempted.

Milton, it is true, preferred the classic model to the Gothic. But it was after long hesitation; and his favourite subject was Arthur and his knights of the round table. On this he had fixed for the greater part of his life. What led him to change his mind was, partly, as I suppose, his growing fanaticism; partly, his ambition to take a different route from Spenser; but chiefly perhaps, the discredit into which the stories of chivalry had now fallen by the immortal satire of Cervantes. Yet we see through all his poetry, where his enthusiasm flames out most, a certain predilection for the legends of chivalry before the fables of Greece.

This circumstance, you know, has given offence to the austerer and more mechanical critics. They are ready to censure his judgement, as juvenile and unformed, when they see him so delighted, on all occasions, with the Gothic romances. But do these censors imagine that Milton did not perceive the defects of these works, as well as they? No: it was not the composition of books of chivalry, but the manners described in them, that took his fancy; as appears from his *Allegro*:

> Towred cities please us then
> And the busy hum of men.
> Where throngs of knights and barons bold
> In weeds of peace high triumphs hold.
> With store of ladies, whose bright eyes
> Rain influence, and judge the prize
> Of wit, or arms, while both contend
> To win her grace, whom all commend.

And when in the *Penseroso* he draws, by a fine contrivance, the same kind of image to soothe melancholy which he had before given to excite mirth, he indeed extols an author of one of these romances, as he had before, in general, extolled the subject of them; but it is an author worthy of his praise; not the writer of *Amadis* or *Sir Launcelot of the Lake*, but Chaucer himself, who has left an unfinished story on the Gothic or feudal model:

> Or call up him that left half-told
> The story of Cambuscan bold,
> Of Cambail and of Algarsife,
> And who had Canace to wife
> That own'd the virtuous ring and glass
> And of the wondrous horse of brass,
> On which the Tartar king did ride:
> And if aught else great bards beside
> In sage and solemn tunes have sung
> Of tourneys and of trophies hung,
> Of forests and enchantments drear,
> Where more is meant than meets the ear.

The conduct then of these two poets may incline us to think with more respect than is commonly done of the Gothic manners, I mean as adapted to the uses of the greater poetry.

I say nothing of Shakespeare because the sublimity (the divinity, let it be, if nothing else will serve) of his genius kept no certain route, but rambled at hazard into all the regions of human life and manners. So that we can hardly say what he preferred or what he rejected on full deliberation. Yet one thing is clear, that even he is greater when he uses Gothic manners and machinery than when he employs classical: which brings us again to the same point, that the former have, by their nature and genius, the advantage of the latter in producing the sublime.

Letter VIII

I spoke 'of criticizing Spenser's poem, under the idea not of a classical but Gothic composition'.

It is certain much light might be thrown on that singular work, were an able critic to consider it in this view. For instance, he might go some way towards explaining, perhaps justifying, the general plan and conduct of the FAERIE QUEENE, which to classical readers has appeared indefensible.

I have taken the fancy, with your leave, to try my hand on this curious subject.

When an architect examines a Gothic structure by Grecian rules, he finds nothing but deformity. But the Gothic architecture has its own rules, by which when it comes to be examined, it is seen to have its merit, as well as the Grecian. The question is not, which of the two is conducted in the simplest or truest taste: but, whether there be not sense and design in both, when scrutinized by the laws on which each is projected.

The same observation holds of the two sorts of poetry. Judge of the FAERIE QUEENE by the classick models, and you are shocked with its disorder: consider it with an eye to its Gothick original, and you find it regular. The unity and simplicity of the former are more complete: but the latter has that sort of unity and simplicity, which results from its nature.

The FAERIE QUEENE then, as a Gothick poem, derives its *method*, as well as the other characters of its composition, from the established modes and ideas of chivalry.

It was usual, in the days of knight-errantry, at the holding of any great feast, for Knights to appear before the prince, who presided at it, and claim the privilege of being sent on any adventure, to which the solemnity might give occasion. For it was supposed that, when such *a throng of knights and barons bold*, as Milton speaks of, were got together, the distressed would flock in from all quarters, as to a place where they knew they might find and claim redress for all their grievances.

This was the real practice, in the days of pure and ancient chivalry. And an image of this practice was afterwards kept up in the castles of the great, on any extraordinary festival or solemnity: of which, if an instance be required, I refer to the description of a feast made at Lisle, in 1453, in the Court of Philip the Good, Duke of Burgundy, for a crusade against the Turks: as it is given at large in the Memoirs of *Matthieu de Conci, Olivier de la Marche*, and *Monstrelet*.

That feast was held for *twelve* days: and each day was distinguished by the claim and allowance of some adventure.

Now laying down this practice, as a foundation for the poet's design, we shall see how properly the FAERIE QUEENE is conducted. — 'I devise, says the poet himself in his Letter to Sir W. Raleigh, that the Faerie Queene kept her annual feaste xii days, upon which xii several days the occasions of the xii several adventures hapened; which being undertaken by xii several knights, are in these xii books severally handled.'

Here we have the poet delivering his own method, and the reason of it. It arose out of the order of his subject. And would we desire a better reason for his choice?

Yes; it will be said; a poet's method is not that of his subject. I grant it, as to the order of *time*, in which the recital is made; for here, as Spenser observes, (and his own practice agrees to the rule,) lies the main difference between *the poet historical*, and *the historiographer*: the reason of which is drawn from the nature of Epick composition itself, and holds equally, let the subject be what it will, and whatever the system of manners be, on which it is conducted. Gothick or Classick makes no difference in this respect.

But the case is not the same with regard to the general plan of a work, or what may be called the order of *distribution*, which is and must be governed by the subject matter itself. It was as requisite for the FAERIE QUEENE to consist of the adventures of twelve knights, as for the *Odyssey* to be confined to the adventures of one Hero: justice had otherwise not been done to his subject.

So that if we say any thing against the poet's method, we must say that he should not have chosen this subject. But this objection arises from our classick ideas of Unity, which have no place here; and are in every view foreign to the purpose, if the poet has found means to give his work, though consisting of many parts, the advantage of Unity. For in some reasonable sense or other, it is agreed, every work of art must be *one*, the very idea of a work requiring it.

If it be asked then, what is this *Unity* of Spenser's Poem? I say, it consists in the relation of its several adventures to one common *original*, the appointment of the Faerie Queene; and to one common *end*, the completion of the Faerie Queene's injunctions. The knights issued forth on their adventures on the breaking up of this annual feast; and the next annual feast, we are to suppose, is to bring them together again from the achievement of their several charges.

This, it is true, is not the classick Unity, which consists in the representation of one entire action: but it is an Unity of another sort, an unity resulting from the respect which a number of related actions have to one common purpose. In other word, It is an unity of *design*, and not of action.

This Gothick method of design in poetry may be, in some sort, illustrated by what is called the Gothick method of design in Gardening. A wood or grove cut out into many separate avenues or glades was amongst the most favourite of the works of art, which our fathers attempted in the species of cultivation. These walks were distinct from each other; had, each, their several destination; and terminated on their own proper objects. Yet the whole was brought together and considered under one view by the relation which these various openings had, not to each other, but to their common and concurrent center. Some are, perhaps, agreed that this sort of gardening is not of so true a taste as that which *Kent and Nature* have brought us acquainted with; where the supreme art of the Designer consists in disposing his ground and objects into an *entire landscape*; and grouping them, if I may use the term, in so easy a manner, that the careless observer, though he be taken with the symmetry of the whole, discovers no art in the combination:

> In lieto aspetto il bel giardin s'aperse,
> Acque stagnanti, mobili cristalli,
> Fior vari, e varie piante, herbe diverse,
> Apriche Collinette, ombrose valli,
> Selve, espelunche in *una vista* offerse:
> E quel, che'l bello, e'l caro accresce à l'opre,
> L'Arte, che tutte fà, nulla si scopre.
> (*Tasso*, C. xvi. S. ix.)

This, I say, may be the truest taste in gardening, because the simplest: yet there is a manifest regard to unity in the other method; which has had its admirers, as it may have again, and is certainly not without its *design* and beauty.

But to return to our poet. Thus far he drew from Gothick ideas; and these ideas, I think, would lead him no further. But, as Spenser knew what belonged to classick composition, he was tempted to tie his subject still closer together by *one* expedient of his own, and by *another* taken from his classick models.

His *own* was to interrupt the proper story of each book, by dispersing it into several; involving by this means, and as it were intertwisting the several actions together, in order to give something like the appearance of one action to his twelve adventures. And for this conduct, as absurd as it seems, he had some great examples in the Italian poets, though, I believe, they were led into it by different motives.

The *other* expedient which he borrowed from the classicks, was by adopting one superiour character, which should be seen throughout. Prince Arthur, who had a separate adventure of his own, was to have his part in each of the other; and thus several actions were to be embodied by the interest which one principal Hero had in them all. It is even observable, that Spenser gives this adventure of Prince Arthur in quest of Gloriana, as the proper subject of his Poem. And upon this idea the late learned editor of the FAERIE QUEENE has attempted, but I think without success, to defend the Unity and simplicity of its fable. The truth was, the violence of classick prejudices forced the poet to affect this appearance of unity, though in contradiction to his Gothick system. And, as far as we can judge of the tenour of the whole work from the finished half of it, the adventure of Prince Arthur, whatever the author pretended, and his critick too easily believed, was but an afterthought; and at least with regard to the *historical fable*, which we are now considering, was only one of the expedients by which he would conceal the disorder of his Gothick plan.

And, if this was his design, I will venture to say that both his expedients were injudicious. Their purpose was to ally two things, in nature incompatible, the Gothick, and the classick, unity: the effect of which misalliance was to discover and expose the nakedness of the Gothick.

I am of opinion then, considering the FAERIE QUEENE as an epick or *narrative* Poem constructed on Gothick ideas, that the poet had done well to affect no other unity than that of *design*, by which his subject was connected. But his Poem is not simply narrative; it is throughout *Allegorical*: he calls it *a perpetual allegory or dark conceit*: and this character, for reasons I may have occasion to observe hereafter, was even predominant in the FAERIE QUEENE. His narration is subservient to his moral, and but serves to colour it. This he tells us himself at setting out;

Fierce wars and faithful loves shall *moralize* my song.

that is, shall serve for a vehicle, or instrument, to convey the moral.

Now, under this idea, the *unity* of the FAERIE QUEENE is more apparent. His twelve knights are to exemplify as many virtues, out of which one illustrious character is to be composed. And, in this view, the part of Prince Arthur in each Book becomes *essential*, and yet not *principal*; exactly, as the poet has contrived it. They who rest in the literal story, that is, who criticise it on the footing of a narrative Poem, have constantly objected to this management. They say, it necessarily breaks the unity of design. Prince Arthur, they affirm, should either have had no part in the other adventures, or he should have had the chief part. He should either have done nothing or more. And the objection is unanswerable; at least I know of nothing that can be said to remove it but what I have supposed above might be the purpose of the poet, and which I myself have rejected as insufficient.

But how faulty soever this conduct be in the literal story, it is perfectly right in the *moral*: and that for an obvious reason, though his criticks seem not to have been aware of it. His chief hero was not to have the twelve virtues in the *degree* in which the knights had, each of them, their own; (such a character would be a monster;) but he was to have so much of each as was requisite to form his superiour character. Each virtue, in its perfection, is exemplified in its own knight: they are all, in a due degree, concentered in Prince Arthur.

This was the poet's *moral*: and what way of expressing this moral in the *history*, but by making Prince Arthur appear in each adventure, and in a manner subordinate to its proper hero? Thus, though inferiour to each in his own specifick virtue, he is superior to all by uniting the whole circle of their virtues in himself: and thus he arrives, at length, at the possession of that bright form of *Glory*, whose ravishing beauty, as seen in a dream or vision, had led him out into these miraculous adventures in the Land of Faery.

The conclusion is, that, as an *allegorical* Poem, the method of the FAERIE QUEENE is governed by the justness of the *moral*: as a *narrative* Poem, it is conducted on the ideas and usages of *chivalry*. In either view, if taken by itself, the plan is defensible. But from the union of the two designs there arises a perplexity and confusion, which is the proper, and only considerable, defect of this extraordinary Poem.

Letter IX

No doubt Spenser might have taken one single adventure, *of the Twelve*, for the subject of his Poem; or he might have given the principal part in every adventure to Prince Arthur. By this means his fable had been of the classick kind, and its unity as strict as that of Homer and Virgil.

All this the poet knew very well, but his purpose was not to write a classick poem. He chose to adorn a Gothick story; and, to be consistent throughout, he chose that the *form* of his work should be of a piece with his subject.

Did the poet do right in this? I cannot tell; but, comparing his work with that of another great poet, I see no reason to be peremptory in condemning his judgment.

The example of this poet deserves to be considered. It will afford, at least, a fresh confirmation of the point, I principally insist upon; I mean, The pre-eminence of the Gothick manners and fictions, as adapted to the ends of poetry, above the classick.

I have observed of the famous Torquato Tasso that, coming into the world a little of the latest for the success of the pure Gothick manner, he thought fit to *trim* between that and the classick model. It was lucky for his fame, perhaps, that he did so. For the Gothick fables falling every day more and more into contempt, and the learning of the times, throughout all Europe, taking a classick turn, the reputation of his work has been chiefly founded on the strong resemblance it has to the ancient epick poems. His fable is conducted in the spirit of the *Iliad*, and with a strict regard to that unity of *action* which we admire in Homer and Virgil. But this is not all; we find a studied and close imitation of those poets, in many of the smaller parts, in the minuter incidents, and even in the descriptions and similies of his poem.

The classick reader was pleased with this deference to the publick taste: he saw with delight the favourite beauties of Homer and Virgil reflected in the Italian poet: and was almost ready to excuse, for the sake of these, his magick tales and faery enchantments. I said, was *almost ready*: for the offence given by these to the more fashionable sort of criticks was so great, that nothing, I believe, could make full amends, in their judgment, for such extravagancies.

However, by this means the *Gierusalemme Liberata* made its fortune amongst the French wits, who have constantly cried it up above the *Orlando Furioso*, and principally for this reason, that Tasso was more classical in his fable, and more sparing in the wonders of Gothick fiction, than his predecessor.

The Italians have indeed a predilection for their elder bard, whether from their prejudice for antiquity; their admiration of his language; the richness of his invention; the comick air of his style and manner; or from whatever other reason.

Be this as it will, the French criticism has carried it before the Italian, with the rest of Europe. This dextrous people have found means to lead the taste, as well as set the fashions, of their neighbours: and Ariosto ranks but little higher than the rudest romancer in the opinion of those who take their notions of these things from their writers.

But the same principle, which made them give Tasso the preference to Ariosto, has led them by degrees to think very unfavourably of Tasso himself. The mixture of the Gothick manner in his work has not been forgiven. It has sunk the credit of all the rest; and some instances of false taste in the expression of his sentiments, detected, by their nicer criticks, have brought matters to that pass, that, with their good will, Tasso himself should now follow the fate of Ariosto.

I will not say, that a little national envy did not perhaps

mix itself with their other reasons for undervaluing this great poet. They aspired to a sort of supremacy in Letters; and, finding the Italian language and its best writers standing in their way, they have spared no pains to lower the estimation of both.

Whatever their inducements were, they succeeded but too well in their attempt. Our obsequious and over modest criticks were run down by their authority. Their taste of Letters, with some worse things, was brought amongst us at the Restoration. Their language, their manners, nay their very prejudices, were adopted by our Frenchified king and his Royalists. And the more fashionable wits, of course, set their fancies, as my Lord Molesworth tells us the people of Copenhagen in his time did their clocks, by the court-standard.

Sir W. Davenant opened the way to this new sort of criticism in a very elaborate preface to *Gondibert*; and his philosophick friend, Mr. Hobbes, lent his best assistance towards establishing the credit of it. These two fine Letters contain, indeed, the substance of whatever has been since written on the subject. Succeeding wits and criticks did no more than echo their language. It grew into a sort of cant, with which Rymer, and the rest of that School, filled their flimsy essays and rambling prefaces.

Our noble critick himself condescended to take up this trite theme: and it is not to be told with what alacrity and self-complacency he flourishes upon it. The *Gothick manner*, as he calls it, is the favourite object of his raillery; which is never more lively or pointed, than when exposes that 'bad taste which makes us prefer an Ariosto to a Virgil, and a Romance (without doubt he meant, of Tasso) to an Iliad.' Truly, this critical sin requires an expiation, which is easily made by subscribing to his sentence, 'That the French indeed may boast of legitimate authors of a just relish; but that the Italian are good for nothing but to corrupt the taste of those who have had no familiarity with the noble ancients.' This ingenious nobleman is, himself, one of the *gallant votaries* he sometimes makes himself so merry with. He is perfectly enamoured of his *noble ancients*, and will fight with any man who contends, not that his Lordship's mistress is not fair, but that his own is fair also.

It is certain the French wits benefited by this foible. For pretending, in great modesty, to have formed themselves on the pure taste of his noble ancients, they easily drew his Lordship over to their party: while the Italians more stubbornly pretending to a taste of their own, and choosing to *lie* for themselves, instead of adopting the authorised *lies* of Greece, were justly exposed to his resentment.

Such was the address of the French writers, and such their triumphs over the poor Italians.

It must be owned, indeed, they had every advantage on their side, in this contest with their masters. The taste and learning of Italy had been long on the decline, and the fine writers under Louis XIV. were every day advancing the French language, such as it is, (simple, clear, exact, that is, fit for business and conversation; but for that reason, besides its total want of numbers, absolutely unsuited to the genius of the greater poetry,) towards its last perfection. The purity of the ancient manner became well understood, and it was the pride of their best criticks to expose every instance of false taste in the modern writers. The Italian, it is certain, could not stand so severe a scrutiny. But they had escaped better, if the most fashionable of the French poets had not, at the same time, been their best critick.

A lucky word in a verse, which sounds well and every body gets by heart, goes further than a volume of just criticism. In short, the exact but cold Boileau happened to say something of the *clinquant* of Tasso; and the magick of this word, like the report of Astoifo's horn in Ariosto, overturned at once the solid and well-built, reputation of the Italian poetry. It is not perhaps so amazing that this potent word should do its business in France. It put us into a fright on this side the water. Mr. Addison, who gave the law in taste here, took it up and sent it about the kingdom in his polite and popular essays. It became a sort of watch-word among the criticks; and, on the sudden, nothing was heard, on all sides, but the *clinquant* of Tasso.

After all, these two respectable writers might not intend the mischief they were doing. The observation was just, but was extended much further than they meant, by their witless followers and admirers. The effect was, as I said, that the Italian poetry was rejected in the gross, by virtue of this censure; though the authors of it had said no more than this, 'That their best poet had some false thoughts, and dealt, as they supposed, too much in incredible fiction.'

I leave the reader to make his own reflexions on this short history of the Italian poetry. It is not my design to make its apology in all respects. However, with regard to the *first* of these charges, I presume to say that, as just as it is in the sense in which I persuade myself it was intended, there are more instances of natural sentiment and of that divine simplicity we admire in the ancients, even in Guarini's *Pastor Fido*, than in the best of the French poets. And, as to the *last*, I pretend to show, that it is no fault at all in the Italian poets.

Letter X

Chi non sa che cosa sia Italia?—If this question could ever be reasonably asked on any occasion, it must surely be when the wit and poetry of that people were under consideration. The enchanting sweetness of their tongue, the richness of their invention, the fire and elevation of their genius, the splendour of their expression on great subjects, and the native simplicity of their sentiments on affecting ones; all these are such manifest advantages on the side of the Italian poets, as should seem to command our highest admiration of their great and capital works.

Yet a different language has been held by our finer criticks. And in particular you hear it commonly said of the tales of Faery, which they first and principally adorned; 'That they are unnatural and absurd; that they surpass all bounds not of truth only, but of probability; and look more like the dreams of children, than the manly inventions of poets.'

All this, and more, has been said; and if truly said, who would not lament

L'arte del poëtar troppo infelice?

For they are not the cold fancies of plebeian poets, but the golden dreams of Ariosto, the celestial visions of Tasso, that are thus derided.

The only criticism, indeed, that is worth regarding, is the philosophical. But there is a sort which looks like philosophy, and is not. May not that be the case here? This criticism, whatever name it deserves, supposes that the poets, who are liars by profession, expect to have their lies believed. Surely they are not so unreasonable. They think it enough, if they can but bring you to *imagine* the possibility of them.

And how small a matter will serve for this? A legend, a tale, a tradition, a rumour, a superstition; in-short, any thing is enough to be the basis of their air-formed *visions*. Does any capable reader trouble himself about the truth, or even the credibility of their fancies? Alas, no; he is best pleased when he is made to conceive (he minds not by what magick) the existence of such things as his reason tells him did not, and were never likely to, exist.

But here, to prevent mistakes, an explanation will be necessary. We must distinguish between the *popular belief*, and *that of the reader*. The fictions of poetry do, in some degree at least, require the *first*; (they would, otherwise, deservedly pass for *dreams* indeed:) but when the poet has this advantage on his side, and his fancies have, or may be supposed to have, a countenance from the current superstitions of the age, in which he writes, he dispenses with the *last*, and gives his reader leave to be as sceptical and as incredulous, as he pleases.

An eminent French critick diverts himself with imagining 'what a person, who comes fresh from reading Mr. Addison and Mr. Locke, would be apt to think of Tasso's Enchantment.'

The English reader will, perhaps, smile at seeing these two writers so coupled together: and, with the critick's leave, we will put Mr. Locke out of the question. But if he be desirous to know what a reader of Mr. Addison would pronounce in the case, I can undertake to give him satisfaction. Speaking of what Mr. Dryden calls, *the Faery way of writing*, 'Men of cold fancies and philosophical dispositions,' says he, 'object to this kind of poetry, that it has not probability enough to affect the imagination. But—many are prepossessed with such false opinions, as dispose them to *believe* these particular delusions; at least, we have all *heard* so many pleasing relations in favour of them, that we do not care for seeing through the *falsehood*, and willingly give ourselves up to so agreeable an imposture.' *Spectator*, Vol. vi. Apply, now, this sage judgment of Mr. Addison to *Tasso's Enchantments*, and you see that a *falsehood convict* is not to be pleaded against a *supposed belief*, or even the *slightest hear-say*. So little account does this wicked Poetry make of philosophical or historical truth: all she allows us to look for, is *poetical truth*; a very slender thing indeed, and which the poet's eye, when rolling its finest frenzy, can but just lay hold of. To speak in the philosophick language of Mr. Hobbes, It is something much *beyond the actual bounds, and only within the conceived possibility, of nature.*

But the source of bad criticism, as universally of bad philosophy, is the abuse of terms. A poet, they say, must follow *Nature*; and by Nature we are to suppose can only be meant the known and experienced course of affairs in this world. Whereas the poet has a world of his own, where experience has less to do, than consistent imagination.

He has, besides, a supernatural world to range in. He has Gods, and Faeries, and Witches, at his command: and,

> O! who can tell
> The hidden *pow'r* of herbes, and might of magick spell?
>
> (*Spenser,* F. Q. B. i. C. 2.)

Thus, in the poet's world, all is marvellous and extraordinary: yet not *unnatural* in one sense, as it agrees to the conceptions that are readily entertained of these magical and wonder-working Natures.

This trite maxim of *following Nature* is further mistaken in applying it indiscriminately to all sorts of poetry.

In those species which have men and manners professedly for their theme, a strict conformity with human nature is reasonably demanded.

> Non hic Centauros, non Gorgonas, Harpyasque
> Invenies: hominem pagina nostra sapit.

is a proper motto to a book of Epigrams, but would make a poor figure at the head of an epick poem.

Still further, in those species that address themselves to the heart and would obtain their end, not through the Imagination, but through the *Passions*, there the liberty of transgressing nature, I mean the real powers and properties of human nature, is infinitely restrained; and *poetical* truth is, under these circumstances, almost as severe a thing as *histor-*

ical. The reason is, we must first *believe*, before we can be *affected*. But the case is different with the more sublime and creative poetry. This species, addressing itself solely or principally to the Imagination; a young and credulous faculty, which loves to admire and to be deceived; has no need to observe those cautious rules of credibility so necessary to be followed by him, who would touch the affections and interest the heart.

This difference, it will be said, is obvious enough. How came it then to be overlooked? From another mistake, in extending a particular precept of the drama into a general maxim.

The *incredulus odi* of Horace ran in the heads of these criticks, though his own words confine the observation singly to the stage:

> Segnius irritant animos demissa per aurem
> Quam quæ sunt oculis subjecta fidelibus, et quæ
> Ipse sibi tradit Spectator—

That, which passes in *representation*, and challenges, as it were, the scrutiny of the eye, must be truth itself, or something very nearly approaching to it. But what passes in *narration*, even on the stage, is admitted without much difficulty—

> multaque tolles
> Ex oculis, quæ mox narret facundia præsens.

In the epick narration, which may be called *absens facundia*, the reason of the thing shows this indulgence to be still greater. It appeals neither to the *eye* nor the *ear*, but simply to the *imagination*, and so allows the poet a liberty of multiplying and enlarging his impostures at pleasure, in proportion to the easiness and comprehension of that faculty.

These general reflexions hardly require an application to the present subject. The tales of Faery are exploded, as fantastick and incredible. They would merit this contempt, if presented on the stage; I mean, if they were given as the proper subject of dramatick imitation, and the interest of the poet's plot were to be wrought out of the adventures of these marvellous persons. But the epick muse runs no risque in giving way to such fanciful exhibitions.

You may call them, as one does, 'extraordinary dreams, such as excellent poets and painters, by being over studious, may have in the beginning of fevers.'

The epick poet would acknowledge the charge, and even value himself upon it. He would say, 'I leave to the sage dramatist the merit of being always broad awake, and always in his senses: the *divine dream*, and delirious fancy, are among the noblest of my prerogatives.'

But the injustice done the Italian poets does not stop here. The cry is, 'Magick and enchantments are senseless things. Therefore the Italian poets are not worth the reading.' As if, because the superstitions of Homer and Virgil are no longer believed, their poems, which abound in them, are good for nothing.

Yes, it will be said, their fine pictures of life and manners.—And may not I say the time, in behalf of Ariosto and Tasso? For it is not true that all is *unnatural* and monstrous in their poems, because of this mixture of the wonderful. Admit, for example, Armida's marvellous conveyance to the happy Island, and all the rest of the love-story is as natural, that is, as suitable to our common notions of that passion, as any thing in Virgil or (if you will) Voltaire.

Thus we see the apology of the Italian poets is easily made on every supposition. But I stick to my point, and maintain that the faery tales of Tasso do him more honour than what are called the more natural, that is, the classical parts of his poem. His imitations of the ancients have indeed their merit; for he was a genius in every thing. But they are faint and cold and almost insipid, when compared with his original fictions. We make a shift to run over the passages he has copied from Virgil. We are all on fire amidst the magical feats of Ismen, and the enchantments of Armida:

> Magnanima mensogna, hor quando è il vero
> Si bello, che si possa à te preporre?

I speak at least for myself; and must freely own; if it were not for these *lies* of Gothick invention, I should scarcely be disposed to give the *Gierusalemine Liberata* a second reading.

I readily agree to the lively observation, 'That impenetrable armour, enchanted castles, invulnerable bodies, iron men, flying horses, and other such things, are easily feigned by them that dare.' But, with the observer's leave, not so feigned as we find them in the Italian poets, unless the writer have another quality, besides that of courage.

One thing is true, that the success of these fictions will not be great, when they have no longer any footing in the popular belief: and the reason is, that readers do not usually do, as they ought; put themselves in the circumstances of the poet, or rather of those, of whom the poet writes. But this only shows, that some ages are not so fit to write epick poems in, as others; not, that they should be otherwise written. It is also true, that writers do not succeed so well in painting what they have heard, as what they believe themselves, or at least observe in others a facility of believing. And on this account I would advise no modern poet to revive these faery tales in an epick poem. But still this is nothing to the case in hand, where we are considering the merit of epick poems, written under other circumstances.

The Pagan Gods and Gothick Faeries were equally out of credit, when Milton wrote. He did well therefore to supply their room with angels and devils. If these too should wear out of the popular creed (and they seem in a hopeful way, from the liberty some late criticks have taken with them,) I know not what other expedients the epick poem might have recourse to; but this I know, the pomp of verse, the energy of description, and even the finest moral paintings, would stand him in no stead. Without *admiration* (which cannot be affected but by the marvellous of celestial intervention, I mean, the agency of superior natures really existing, or by the illusion of the fancy taken to be so,) no epick poem can be long-lived. I am not afraid to instance in the *Ilenriade* itself; which, notwithstanding the elegance of the composition, will in a short time be no more read than the *Gondibert* of Sir W. Davenant, and for the same reason.

Criticks may talk what they will of *Truth and Nature*, and abuse the Italian poets, as they will, for transgressing both in their incredible fictions. But, believe it, these fictions with which they have studied to delude the world, are of that kind of credible deceits, of which a wise ancient pronounces with assurance, '*That they, who deceive, are honester than they who do not deceive; and they, who are deceived, wiser than they who are not deceived.*'

Letter XI

But the reader may be ready to ask, if there be any truth in this representation, 'Whence it has come to pass, that the classical manners are still admired and imitated by the poets, when the Gothick have long since fallen into disuse?'

The answer to this question will furnish all that is now wanting to a proper discussion of the present subject.

One great reason of this difference certainly was; That the ablest writers of Greece ennobled the system of heroick manners, while it was fresh and flourishing; and their works, being masterpieces of composition, so fixed the credit of it in the opinion of the world, that no revolutions of time and taste could afterwards shake it. Whereas the Gothick having been disgraced in their infancy by bad writers, and a new set of manners springing up before there were any better to do them justice, they could never be brought into vogue by the attempts of later poets, who, in spite of prejudice, and for the genuine charm of these highly poetical manners, did their utmost to recommend them. But, further, the Gothick system was not only forced to wait long for real genius to do it honour; real genius was even very early employed against it.

There were two causes of this mishap. The old romancers had even outraged the truth in their extravagant pictures of chivalry: and Chivalry inself, such as it once had been, was greatly abated. So that men of sense were doubly disgusted to find a representation of things *unlike* to what they observed in real life, and *beyond* what it was ever possible should have existed. However, with these disadvantages there was still so much of the old spirit left, and the fascination of these wondrous tales was so prevalent, that a more than common degree of sagacity and good sense was required to penetrate the illusion.

It was one of this character, I suppose, that put the famous question to Ariosto, which has been so often repeated that I shall spare the reader the disgust of hearing it. Yet long before his time an immortal genius of our own (so superiour is the sense of some men to the age they live in) saw as far into this matter, as Ariosto's examiner. This sagacious person was Dan Chaucer; who, in a reign that almost realised the wonders of romantick chivalry, not only discerned the absurdity of the old romances, but has even ridiculed them with incomparable spirit.

His *Rime on Sir Topaz*, in the *Canterbury Tales*, is a manifest banter on these books, and may be considered as a sort of prelude to the adventures of Don Quixote. I call it a *manifest banter*: for we are to observe that this was Chaucer's own tale, and that, when in the progress of it the good sense of the Host is made to break in upon him, and interrupt him, Chaucer approves his disgust, and changing his note, tells the simple instructive tale of Melibœus, *a moral tale virtuous*, as he chooses to characterise it; to show, what sort of fictions were most expressive of real life, and most proper to be put into the hands of the people. One might further observe that the *Rime on Sir Topaz* itself is so managed as with infinite humour to expose the leading impertinencies of books of Chivalry, and their impertinencies only; as may be seen by the different conduct of this tale, from that of Cambuscan, which Spenser and Milton were so pleased with, and which with great propriety is put into the mouth of the Squire.

But I must not anticipate the observations which the reader will take a pleasure to make for himself on these two fine parts of the *Canterbury Tales*. Enough is said to illustrate the point, I am now upon. 'That these phantoms of chivalry had the misfortune to be laughed out of countenance by men of sense, before the substance of it had been fairly and truly represented by any capable writer.'

Still, the principal reason of all, no doubt, was, That the Gothick manners of Chivalry, as springing out of the feudal system, were as singular, as that system itself: so that, when that political constitution vanished out of Europe, the manners, that belonged to it, were no longer seen or understood. There was no example of any such manners remaining on the face of the earth: and as they never did subsist but once, and are never likely to subsist again, people would be led of course to think and speak of them, as romantick, and unnatural. The consequence of which was a total contempt and rejection of them; while the classick manners, as arising out of the customary and usual situations of humanity, would have many archetypes, and appear natural even to those who saw nothing similar to them actually subsisting before their eyes.

Thus, though the manners of Homer are perhaps as different from ours, as those of Chivalry itself, yet as we know that such manners always belong to rude and simple ages, such as Homer paints; and actually subsist at this day in countries that are under the like circumstances of barbarity, we readily agree to call them *natural*, and even take a fond pleasure in the survey of them.

The question then is easily answered, without any obligation upon me to give up the Gothick manners as visionary and fantastick. And the reason appears, why the FAERIE QUEENE, one of the noblest productions of modern poetry, is fallen into so general a neglect, that all the zeal of its commentators is esteemed officious and impertinent, and will never restore it to those honours which it has, once for all, irrecoverably lost.

In effect, what way is there of persuading the generality of readers that the romantick manners are to be accounted *natural*, when not one in ten thousand knows enough of the barbarous ages, in which they arose, to believe they ever really existed?

Poor Spenser then,

> in whose gentle spright
> The pure well-head of Poesie did dwell,

must, for ought I can see, be left to the admiration of a few lettered and curious men: while the many are sworn together to give no quarter to the *marvellous*, or, which may seem still harder, to the *moral* of his song.

However, this great revolution in modern taste was brought about by degrees; and the steps, that led to it, may be worth the tracing.

Letter XII

The wonders of Chivalry were still in the memory of men; were still existing, in some measure, in real life, when Chaucer undertook to expose the barbarous relaters of them.

This ridicule, we may suppose, hastened the fall both of Chivalry and Romance. At least from that time the spirit of both declined very fast, and at length fell into such discredit, that when now Spenser arose, and with a genius singularly fitted to immortalize the Land of Faery, he met with every difficulty and disadvantage to obstruct his design. The age would no longer bear the naked letter of these amusing stories; and the poet was so sensible of the misfortune, that we find him apologizing for it on a hundred occasions.

But apologies, in such circumstances, rarely do any good. Perhaps they only served to betray the weakness of the poet's cause, and to confirm the prejudices of his reader.

However, he did more than this. He gave an air of mystery to his subject, and pretended that his stories of knights and giants were but the cover to abundance of profound wisdom.

In short, to keep off the eyes of the prophane from prying too nearly into his subject, he threw about it the mist of allegory: he moralized his song: and the virtues and vices lay hid under his warriors and enchanters. A contrivance which he had learned indeed from his Italian masters: for Tasso had condescended to allegorize his own work; and the commentators of Ariosto had even converted the extravagances of the *Orlando Furioso*, into moral lessons.

And this, it must be owned, was a sober attempt in comparison of some projects that were made about the same time to serve the cause of the old and now expiring Romances. For it is to be observed, that the idolizers of these romances did by them, what the votaries of Homer had done by him. As the

times improved and would less bear his strange tales, they *moralized* what they could, and turned the rest into mysteries of *natural science*. And as this last contrivance was principally designed to cover the monstrous stories of the *Pagan Gods*, so it served the lovers of Romance to palliate the no less monstrous stories of *magick and enchantments*.

The editor, or translator of the 24th book of *Amadis de Gaule*, printed at Lyons in 1577, has a preface explaining the whole secret, which concludes with these words, 'Voyla, Lecteur, *le fruit*, qui se peut recueiller du sens mystique des Romans antiques par les *esprits esleus*, le commun peuple soy contentant de la *simple fleur de la lectare literale.*'

But to return to Spenser; who, as we have seen, had no better way to take in his distress, than to hide his faery fancies under the mystick cover of moral allegory. The only favourable circumstance that attended him (and this no doubt encouraged, if it did not produce, his untimely project,) was, that he was somewhat befriended in these fictions, even when interpreted according to the Letter, by the romantick Spirit of his age; much countenanced, and for a time brought into fresh credit, by the romantick Elizabeth. Her inclination for the fancies of Chivalry is well known; and obsequious wits and courtiers would not be wanting to feed and flatter it. In short, tilts and tournaments were in vogue: The ARCADIA, and The FAERIE QUEENE, were written.

With these helps the new Spirit of Chivalry made a shift to support itself for a time, when reason was but dawning, as we may say, and just about to gain the ascendant over the portentous spectres of the imagination. Its growing splendour, in the end, put them all to flight, and allowed them no quarter even amongst the poets. So that Milton, as fond as we have seen he was of the Gothick fictions, durst only admit them on the bye, and in the way of simile and illustration only.

And this, no doubt, was the main reason of his relinquishing his long-projected design of Prince Arthur, at last, for that of the *Paradise Lost*; where, instead of Giants and Magicians, he had Angels and Devils to supply him with the *marvellous*, with greater probability. Yet, though he dropped the tales, he still kept to the allegories of Spenser. And even this liberty was thought too much, as appears from the censure passed on his *Sin and Death* by the severer cricks.

Thus at length the magick of the old romances was perfectly dissolved. They began with reflecting an image indeed of the feudal manners, but an image magnified and distorted by unskilful designers. Common sense being offended with these perversions of truth and nature, (still accounted the more monstrous, as the ancient manners, they pretended to copy after, were now disused, and of most men forgotten,) the next step was to have recourse to *allegories*. Under this disguise they walked the world a while; the excellence of the moral and the ingenuity of the contrivance making some amends, and being accepted as a sort of apology, for the absurdity of the literal story.

Under this form the Tales of Faery kept their ground, and even made their fortune at court; where they became, for two or three reigns, the ordinary entertainment of our princes. But reason, in the end, (assisted however by party, and religious prejudices,) drove them off the scene, and would endure these *lying wonders*, neither in their own proper shape, nor as masked in figures.

Henceforth, the taste of wit and poetry took a new turn: and *Fancy*, that had wantoned it so long in the world of fiction, was now constrained, against her will, to ally herself with strict Truth, if she would gain admittance into reasonable company.

What we have gotten by this revolution it will be said, is a great deal of good sense. What we have lost, is a world of fine fabling; the illusion of which is so grateful to the *charmed spirit*; that, in spite of philosophy and fashion, *Faery* Spenser still ranks highest among the Poets; I mean with all those who are either come of that house, or have any kindness for it. *Earth-born* criticks may blaspheme:

> But all the *gods* are ravish'd with delight
> Of his celestial song, and musick's wondrous might.

THOMAS WARTON
From *Observations on the* Faerie Queene *of Spenser*
1762

Although Spenser formed his *Faerie Queene* upon the fanciful plan of Ariosto, yet it must be confessed, that the adventures of his knights are a more exact and immediate copy of those which we meet with in old romances, or books of chivalry, than of those which form the *Orlando Furioso*. Ariosto's knights exhibit surprising examples of their prowess, and achieve many heroick actions. But our author's knights are more professedly engaged in revenging injuries, and doing justice to the distressed; which was the proper business, and ultimate end of the ancient knight-errantry. And thus, though many of Spenser's incidents are to be found in Ariosto, such as that of blowing a horn, at the sound of which the gates of a castle fly open, of the vanishing of an enchanted palace or garden after some knight has destroyed the enchanter, and the like; yet these are not more peculiarly the property of Ariosto, than they are common to all ancient romances in general. Spenser's first Book is, indeed, a regular and precise imitation of such a series of action as we frequently find in books of chivalry. For instance; A king's daughter applies to a knight, that he would relieve her father and mother, who are closely confined to their castle, upon account of a vast and terrible dragon, that had ravaged their country, and perpetually laid wait to destroy them. The knight sets forward with the lady, encounters a monster in the way, is plotted against by an enchanter, and, after surmounting a variety of difficulties and obstacles, arrives at the country which is the scene of the dragon's devastation, kills him, and is presented to the king and queen, whom he has just delivered; marries their daughter, but is soon obliged to leave her, on account of fulfilling a former vow.

It may be moreover observed, that the circumstance of each of Spenser's twelve knights, departing from one place, by a different way, to perform a different adventure, exactly resembles that of the seven knights entering upon their several expeditions, in the well-known romance, entitled *The Seven Champions of Christendom*. In fact, these miraculous books were highly fashionable; and chivalry, which was the subject of them, was still practised and admired, in the age of queen Elizabeth. See Holinshead's *Chronicles*, vol. iii. p. 1315.

Among others, there is one romance which Spenser seems more particularly to have made use of. It is entitled, [*La*] Morte [*d'*] Arthur, *The Lyfe of King Arthur, and of his noble Knyghtes of the round table, and in thende the dolorous deth of them all*. This was translated into English from the French, by one Sir Thomas Maleory, Knight, and printed by W. Caxton, 1485. It has been reprinted twice or thrice: the last edition is dated 1634. From this fabulous history our author has borrowed many of his names, viz. Sir Tristram, Placidas, Pelleas, Pellenore, Percivall, and others. As to Sir Tristram, he has copied from this book the circumstances of his birth and edu-

cation with much exactness. Spenser informs us that Sir Tristram was born in Cornwall, &c. F. Q. vi. ii. 28.

> And Tristram is my name, the onely heire
> Of good king Meliogras, which did rayne
> In Cornewale.

And afterwards, st. 30.

> The countrie wherein I was bred,
> The which the fertile Lionesse is hight.

These particulars are drawn from the romance above mentioned. 'There was a knight Meliodas [Meliogras], and he was lord and king of the country of Lyones—and he wedded king Markes sister of Cornewale.' The issue of which marriage, as we are afterwards told, was Sir Tristram, B. ii. C. 1. Mention is then made, in our romance, of Sir Tristram's banishment from Lyons into a distant country, by the advice, and under the conduct, of a wise and learned counsellor named Governale. A circumstance alluded to by Spenser in these verse, F. Q. vi. ii. 30.

> So taking counsell of a wise man red,
> She was by him adviz'd to send me quight
> Out of the countrie, wherein I was bred,
> The which the fertile Lionesse is hight.

Sir Tristram's education is thus described in the next stanza.

> All which my daies I have not lewdly spent,
> Nor spilt the blossome of my tender yeares
> In ydlesse, but as was convenient
> Have trained bene with many noble feres
> In gentle thewes and such like semely leres;
> Mongst which my most delight hath alwaies
> been
> To hunt the salvage chace among my peres
> Of all that raungeth in the forest greene,
> Of which none is to me unknowne that e'er
> was seene.
>
> Ne is there hauke that mantleth her on pearch,
> Whether high-tow'ring, or accoasting low,
> But I the measure of her flight doe search,
> And all her pray and all her dyet knowe.

All this is agreeable to what is related in the romance. After mention being made of Tristram's having learned the language of France, courtly behaviour, and skill in chivalry, we read the following passage. 'As he growed in might and strength, he laboured ever in hunting and hawking; so that we never read of no gentleman, more, that so used himselfe therein.—And he began good measures of blowing of blasts of venery [hunting] and chase, and of all manner of vermeins; and all these termes have we yet of hawking and hunting, and therefore the booke of venery, of hawking and hunting, is called *the book of Sir Tristram*.' B. ii. C. 3. And in another place King Arthur thus addresses Sir Tristram. 'For of all manner of hunting thou bearest the prise; and of all measures of blowing thou art the beginner; and of all the termes of hunting and hawking ye are the beginner.' B. ii. C. 91.

In Tuberville's treatise *Of Falconrie*, &c. Sir Tristram is often introduced as the patron of field-sports. A huntsman thus speaks, p. 96. edit. 4to. 1611:

> Before the King I come report to make,
> Then hushe and peace for noble *Tristram's* sake.

And in another place, p. 40.

> Wherefore who lyst to learn the perfect trade
> Of venerie, &c.
> Let him give ear to skillfull *Tristram's* lore.

Many of the precepts, contained in the *Book of Sir Tristram*, are often referred to in this treatise of Tuberville.

From this romance our author also took the hint of his BLATANT BEAST; which is there called the QUESTING BEAST, B. ii. C. 53. 'Therewithall the King saw coming towards him the strangest beast that ever he saw, or heard tell of.—And the noyse was in the beasts belly like unto the *Questin* of thirtie couple of houndes.' The QUESTING BEAST is afterwards more particularly described. 'That had in shap an head like a serpent's head, and a body like a liberd, buttocks like a lyon, and footed like a hart; and in his body there was such a noyse, as it had been the noyse of thirtie couple of houndes *Questyn*, and such a noyse that beast made wheresoever he went.' He is also called the GLATISANT BEAST, ibid. B. ii. C. 98. 'Tell them that I am the knight that followeth the *Glatisant Beast*, that is to say, in English, the QUESTING BEAST, &c.' Spenser has made him a much more monstrous animal than he is here represented to be, and in general has varied from this description. But there is one circumstance in Spenser's representation, in which there is a minute resemblance, viz. speaking of his mouth, F. Q. vi. xii. 27.

> And therein were a thousand tongues empight,
> Of sundry kindes, and sundry quality;
> Some were of dogs that barked night and
> day,
> And some, &c.

By what has been hitherto said, perhaps the reader may not be persuaded, that Spenser, in his BLATANT BEAST, had the QUESTING BEAST of our romance in his eye. But the poet has himselfe taken care to inform us of this: for we learn, from the romance, that certain knights of the round table were destined to pursue the QUESTING BEAST perpetually without success: which Spenser, speaking of this BLATANT BEAST, hints at in these lines, F. Q. vi, xii. 39:

> Albe that long time after Calidore
> The good Sir Pelleas him took in hand,
> And after him Sir Lamoracke of yore,
> And all his brethren born in Britaine land;
> Yet none of them could ever bring him into band.

Sir Lamoracke and Sir Pelleas are two very valourous champions of Arthur's round table.

This romance supplied our author with the story of the mantle made of the beards of knights, and locks of ladies. The last circumstance is added by Spenser, F. Q. vi. i. 13.

> For may no knight nor lady passe along
> That way, (and yet they needs must pass that
> way
> By reason of the streight and rocks among)
> But they that Ladies lockes doe shave away,
> And that Knights berd for toll, which they for passage
> pay.

Afterwards, in st. 15.

> His name is Crudor, who through high disdaine,
> And proud despight of his selfe-pleasing
> mynd,
> Refused hath to yeeld her love againe,
> Untill a mantle she for him do fynd,
> With berds of Knights and lockes of Ladies
> lynd.

Thus in *La Morte d'Arthur*: 'Came a messenger—saying, that king Ryence had discomfited and overcomen eleaven knights, and everiche of them did him homage; and that was this; they gave him their beards cleane flayne of as much as there was: wherefore the messenger came for king Arthur's berd: for king Ryence had purfeled a mantell with king's beards, and there

lacked for one place of the mantell. Wherefore he sent for his berd; or else hee would enter into his lands, and brenn and sley, and never leave, till he have thy head and beard.' B. i. C. 24. Drayton, in his *Polyolbion*, speaks of a coat composed of the beards of kings. He is celebrating king Arthur, *Song* iv.

> As how great Rithout's self he slew in his repair,
> And ravisht Howel's niece, young Helena the fair.
> And for a trophie brought the giant's coat away,
> Made of the beards of kings.

An ancient ballad on this subject is also printed in P. Enderbie's *Cambria Triumphans*, fol. 1661, p. 197.

But Drayton, in these lines, manifestly alludes to a passage in Geoffry of Monmouth; who informs us, that a Spanish giant, named Ritho, having forcibly conveyed away, from her guard, Helena the niece of duke Hoel, possessed himself of St. Michael's Mount in Cornwall, from whence he made frequent sallies, and committed various outrages; that, at last, king Arthur conquered this giant, and took from him a certain coat, which he had been composing of the beards of kings, a vacant place being left for king Arthur's beard. See *Orig. & Gest. Reg. Brit.* B. x. 13.

And though further proofs of Spenser's copying this romance are perhaps superfluous, I shall add, that Spenser has quoted an authority for an ancient custom from *La Morte d'Arthur* in his *View of Ireland*. 'The knights in ancient times used to wear the mistresses or lover's sleeve upon their arms, as appeareth by that which is written of Sir Launcelot, that he wore the sleeve of the Faire Maid of Asteloth in a tournay: whereat queen Genever was much displeased.' This is the passage in *La Morte d'Arthur*: 'When queen Genever wist that Sir Launcelot beare the red sleeve of the Faire Maide of Astolat, she was nigh out of her minde for anger.' P. iii. Ch. 119.

There is great reason to conclude, not only from what has already been mentioned concerning Spenser's imitations from this romantick history of king Arthur and his knights, but from some circumstances which I shall now produce that it was a favourite and reigning romance about the age of queen Elizabeth; or at least one very well known and much read at that time. Spenser in the *Shepherd's Calendar* has the following passage, *Aprill*:

> And whither rennes this bevie of ladies bright
> Raunged in a row?
> They been all *Ladies of the Lake* behight,
> That unto her go.

Upon the words *Ladies of the Lake*, E. K. the old commentator on the pastorals, has left us the following remark: '*Ladies of the Lake* be nymphes: for it was an old opinion among the antient heathens, that of every spring and fountaine, was a goddesse the soveraine; which opinion stucke in the minds of men not many years since by meanes of certain fine fablers, or loose lyers; such as were the authors of *king Arthur* the great:—Who tell many an unlawfull leesing of the *Ladies of the Lake*.' These fine fablers or loose lyers, are the authors of the romance above mentioned, viz. *La Morte d'Arthur*, in which many miracles are performed, and much enchantment is conducted, by the means and interposition of the LADY OF THE LAKE. Now it should be observed, that the LADY OF THE LAKE was introduced to make part of queen Elizabeth's entertainment at Kenelworth; as evidence of which, I shall produce a passage from an ancient book, entitled A LETTER, *wherein part of the entertainment vntoo the queens majesty, at Killingworth-castl in Warwicksheer in this soomers progress, 1575, is signified.* The passage is this: 'Her highness all along this tilt-yard rode vnto the inner gate, next the base coourt of the castl: where the LADY OF THE LAKE (famous in *king Arthur's book*) with too nymphes waiting upon her, arrayed all in sylks, attended her highness comming, from the midst of the pool, whear, upon a moovabl iland, bright-blazing with torches, she, floting to land, met her majesty with a well-penned meter, and matter, after this sort; first of the auncientée of the castl; whoo had been owners of the same een till this day, most allweys in the hands of the earls of Leyceter; hoow shee had kept this lake sins king Arthurs days, and now, vnderstanding of her highness hither comming, thought it both office, and duetie, in humble wise, to discouer her, and her estate, offering up the same, her lake, and pooer therein; with promise of repayr to the coourt. It pleased her highness too thank this lady, &c.'

Gascoyne, in a little narrative, called the *Princely Pleasures of Kenelworth Castle*, gives us some of the above-mentioned metre, written by Ferrers, one of the contributors to the *Mirrour for Magistrates*, of which these may serve as a specimen:

> I am the lady of this pleasant lake,
> Who since the time of great king Arthur's
>   reigne,
> That here with royall court aboade did make,
> Have led a lowring life in restless paine;
> Till now that this your third arrival here,
> Doth cause me come abroad, and boldly thus
>   appeare.
> For after him such stormes this castle
>   shooke,
> By swarming Saxons first, who scourgde this
>   land
> As forth of this my poole I neer durst looke,
>   &c.

She is afterwards introduced complaining to the queen, that sir Bruse had insulted her for doing an injury to Merlin, an incident related in *La Morte d'Arthur*; and that he would have put her to death had not Neptune delivered her, by concealing her in that lake; from which confinement the queen is afterwards supposed to deliver her, &c.

Without expatiating upon the nature of such a royal entertainment as this, I shall observe from it, that as the LADY OF THE LAKE was a very popular character in the reign of queen Elizabeth, so consequently the romance, which supplied this fiction, was at the same time no less popular. We may add, that it is not improbable that Spenser might allude in the above-cited verses to some of the circumstances in this part of the queen's entertainment; for queen Elisabeth, the *Fayre Elisa*, is the lady whom the LADIES OF THE LAKE are represented as repairing to, in that eclogue. Nor is it improbable that this lady was often exhibited upon other occasions: nor is it improper to remark in this place, that Ben. Jonson has introduced her, together with king Arthur and Merlin, in an entertainment before the court of James I. called, *Prince Henries Barriers*.

The above ancient letter acquaints us, that the queen was entertained with a song from this romance, which is a corroborative proof of its popularity at that time. 'A minstrall came forth with a sollem song warranted for story out of *king Arthur's acts*, the first book, 24. whereof I gat a copy, and that is this:

> So it fell out on a Pentecost day
> When king Arthur, &c.'

This is the song above hinted at, where mention is made of king Ryence demanding the beard of King Arthur. In the same letter, a gentleman who shewed some particular feats of activity before the queen, is said to be 'very cunning in fens, and hardy as Gawen.' This Gawen was king Arthur's nephew,

and his achievements are highly celebrated in *La Morte d'Arthur*.

We find Spenser in another place alluding to the fable of the lady of the lake, so much spoken of in this romance, F. Q. iii. iii. 10.

> A litle whyle
> Before that Merlin dyde, he did intend
> A brasen wall in compas to compyle
> About Cairmardin, and did it commend
> Unto these sprights to bring to perfect end;
> During which time, the LADY OF THE LAKE,
> Whom long he lov'd, for him in haste did
>   send;
> Who, thereby forst his workmen to forsake,
> Them bownd, till his retourne, their labour not to
>   slake.
> In the meane time, through that false Ladies traine
> He was surpris'd and buried under beare,
> Ne ever to his worke return'd againe.

These verses are obscure, unless we consider the following relation in *La Morte d'Arthur*. 'The LADY OF THE LAKE and Merlin departed; and by the way as they went, Merlin shewed to her many wonders, and came into Cornwaile. And alwaies Merlin lay about the ladie for to have her favour; and she was ever passing wery of him, and faine would have been delivered of him; for she was afraid of him, because he was a divells son, and she could not put him away by no meanes. And so upon a time it hapned that Merlin shewed to her in a roche [rock] whereas was a great wonder, and wrought by enchauntment, which went under a stone, so by her subtile craft and working she made Merlin to go under that stone, to let him wit of the marvailes there. But she wrought so there for him, that he came never out, for all the craft that he could doe.' B. i. C. 60.

Our author has taken notice of a superstitious tradition, which is related at large in this romance, F. Q. ii. x. 53.

> Good Lucius
> That first received Christianity,
> The sacred pledge of Christs Evangely.
> Yet true it is, that long before that day
> Hither came Joseph of Arimathy,
> Who brought with him the *holy grayle*, they
>   say,
> And preacht the truth; but since it greatly did decay.

The *holy grale*, that is, the *real blood* of our blessed Saviour. What Spenser here writes *gayle*, is often written *Sangreal* or *St. grale*, in *La Morte d'Arthur*; and it is there said to have been brought into England by Joseph of Arimathea. Many of king Arthur's knights are in the same book represented as adventuring in quest, or in search of the *Sangreal*, or *sanguis realis*. This expedition was one of the first subjects of the old romance.

This romance seems to have extended its reputation beyond the reign of queen Elizabeth. Jonson, besides his allusion to it concerning the LADY OF THE LAKE, mentioned above, hints at it more than once. See his *Execration upon Vulcane*, in the *Underwoods*:

> Had I compil'd from Amadis de Gaule,
> Th' Esplandians, *Arthurs*, Palmerins, &c.

And afterwards, in the same poem,

> The whole summe
> Of errant knighthood; with the dames and dwarfes,
> The charmed boates, and the enchanted wharfes,
> The *Tristrams*, *Lanc'lotts*, &c.

And Camden refers to this history of king Arthur, as to a book familiarly known to the readers of his age. *Remains*, printed in

1604, Art. *Names*. Speaking of the Name TRISTRAM, he observes, 'I know not whether the first of his name was christned by king Arthur's fabler.' Again, of LAUNCELOT he speaks, 'Some think it to be no auncient name, but forged by the writer of king Arthur's history, for one of his douty knights.' And of GAWEN, 'A name devised by the author of king Arthur's table.'

To this we may add, that Milton manifestly hints at it in the following lines, *Par. Reg.* B. ii. 359.

> Damsels met in forests wide
> By knights of Logris, or of Lyones,
> Lancelot, or Pelleas, or Pellenore.

These are Sir Lancelot (or Sir Meliot) of Logris; Sir Tristram of Lyones, and king Pellenore, who are often mentioned in *La Morte d'Arthur*, and represented as meeting beautiful damsels in desolate forests: and probably he might have it in his eye when he wrote the following, as the Round Table is expressly hinted at, *Mansus*, v.

> Siquando indigenas revocabo in carmina reges,
> Arturumque etiam sub terris bella moventem,
> Aut dicam INVICTÆ sociali fædera MENSÆ
> Magnanimos Heroas.

To which we may subjoin, *Par. L.* B. 1. 579.

> What resounds
> In fable, or romance, or Uther's son,
> Begirt with British and Armoric knights.

Before I leave this romance, I must observe, that Ariosto has been indebted to it; I do not mean to the old translation, which Spenser made use of. He has drawn his enchanter Merlin from it, and in these verses refers to a particular story concerning him quoted above. Bradamante is supposed to visit the tomb of Merlin, C. iii. 10.

> Questa è l' antica e memorabil grotta,
> Ch' edificò Merlino, il savio mago;
> Che forse recordare odi taldotta,
> Dove ingannollo la DONNA DEL LAGO.
> Il sepolcro è qui giu, dove corrotta
> Giace la carne sua; dov' egli vago
> Di satisfare a lei, che gliel suase,
> Vivo corcossi, e morto ci rimase.

This description of Merlin's tomb, says Harington, the translator of Ariosto, in a marginal note, is out of the *book of king Arthur*. Ariosto has transferred the tomb from Wales into France. He afterwards feigns, that the prophetical sculpture in Maligigi's cave was performed by Merlin's enchantment, C. xxvi. 39.

> Merlino, il savio incantator Britanno,
> Fe' far la fonte al tempo del re Arturo,
> E di cose, ch' al mondo hanno a venire,
> La fe' da buoni artefici scolpire.

He also mentions some of the names of the knights of our romance. When Renaldo arrives in Great Britain, the poet takes occasion to celebrate that island for its singular achievements in chivalry, and for having produced many magnanimous champions; these are,

> Tristano,
> Lancillotto, Galasso, Artu, e Galuano.
> (C. iv. 52.)

Afterwards, Tristram makes a great figure, in C. xxxii.

From this romance is also borrowed Ariosto's tale of the enchanted cup, C. ii. 34; which, in Caxton's old translation, is as follows: 'By the way they met with a knight, that was sent from Morgan le Faye to king Arthur; and this knight had a faire horne all garnished with gold; and the horne had such a virtue, that there might no ladie or gentlewoman drink of that horne,

but if shee were true to her husband; and if she were false, shee should spill all the drinke; and shee were true unto her lord, shee might drinke peaceably, &c.' C. xlii. 98. Afterwards many trials are made with this cup. Ariosto's copy begins with the following verses:

> Ecco un Donzello, a chi l' ufficio tocca,
> Pon fu la mensa un bel napo d' or fino,
> Di fuor di gemme, e dentro pien di vino.

The inimitable Fontaine has new moulded this story from Ariosto, under the title of *La coupe enchantée*.

As it is manifest, from a comparison of passages, that Ariosto was intimately conversant in this romance; so I think we may fairly suppose that he drew from it the idea of his Orlando running mad with jealousy. In *La Morte d'Arthur*, Sir Lancelot, smitten with a jealous fit, is driven to madness, in which state he continues for the space of two years, performing a thousand different pranks, no less extravagant than those of Orlando; and, like him, at last he recovers his senses. A popular and ridiculous romance was a sufficient hint for what we think a fine effort of poetry.

I had forgot to remark before, that our author has borrowed the name of Materasta's [Malecasta's] castle from that of Lancelot in *La Morte d'Arthur*:

> The goodly frame
> And stately port of *Castle Joyeous*.
> (F. Q. iii. i. 31.)

Lancelot's Castle is styled, by Caxton, *Joyous gard*, or castle.

This romance, or at least the stories formed from it, sometimes furnished matter for theatrical exhibitions, as we learn form Shakspeare, II. *Part Hen.* IV. A. iii. S. iv. 'SHALLOW. I remember at Mile-end Green, when I lay at Clements-inn, I was Sir Dagonet in *Arthur's Show*.' Where Theobald remarks, 'The only intelligence I have gleaned of this worthy Wight [Sir Dagonet] is from Beaumont and Fletcher, in their *Knight of the Burning Pestle*.' Sir Dagonet is an important character in *La Morte d'Arthur*. The *magnificent* Arthur bore a considerable part in the old pageants. Thus, relating the marriage of prince Arthur, son of Henry VII. says Bacon, 'In the devices and conceits of the triumphs of this marriage—*you may be sure* that king Arthur the Briton, &c. was not forgotten.' In our author's age, we find him introduced among the entertainments exhibited at the splendid reception of lord Leicester. 'Over the entrance of the court-gate was placed aloft upon a scaffold, as it had been in a cloud or skie, *Arthur of Britaine*, whom they compared to the earl.' Holing. *Hist. Engl.* vol. iii. p. 1426. Sidney, as appears from a curious conversation between B. Jonson and Drummond of Hawthornden, recorded by the latter, intended to turn all the stories of the *Arcadia* into the admired legend of Arthur and his Knights. In his *Defence of Poesie* he plainly hints at Caxton's romance. 'I dare say, that *Orlando Furioso*, or honest king *Arthur* [his *history*] will never displease a soldier.' Ad Calc. *The Countesse of Pembroke's Arcadia*, edit. 1638, p. 558.

Caxton's recommendation of this book to the knights of England, conveys a curious picture of the times. 'O ye Knyghts of Englond! where is the custom and usage of noble chyvalry that was usid in those dayes? What do you now but go to the baynes, [baths], and play at dyse? And some not well advised, use not honest and good rule, agayn all order of knighthood. Leve this, leve it: And rede the noble volumes of *Saynt Greal* of *Lancelot*, of *Galaad*, of *Tristram*, of *Perseforest*, of *Percyval*, of *Gawayne*, and many mo: There shall ye see *manhode, curtoys* and *gentlenes*. And loke in latter dayes of the noble actes syth the conquest: as in king Richard's dayes, *Cuer de Lion*;

Edward I. and III. and his noble sones: Syr Robert Knolles, &c. Rede Froissart. Also beholde that victorious and noble king, Harry the fifthe, &c.' Ascham however tells us, 'I know when God's bible was banished the court, and *La Morte d'Arthur* received into the prince's chamber.' See his *Scholemaster*, &c. 4to. 1589. b. l. p. 25.

In the hall of the castle of Tamworth, in Warwickshire, there is an old rude painting on the wall, of Sir Lancelot du Lake, and Sir Turquin, drawn in a gigantick size, and tilting together. On Arthur's Round Table, as it is called, in the castle of Winchester, said to be founded by Arthur, are inscribed in ancient characters, the names of twenty-four of his knights, just as we find them in *La Morte d'Arthur*. This table was hanging there, in the year 1484, and was even then very old, being at that time, by tradition, called *Arthur's round table*. I presume, that in commemoration of Arthur's institution, and in direct imitation of his practice, in later ages, a round table, inscribed with his knights, was usually fixed in some publick place, wherever any magnificent tourney was held, on which probably the combatants were afterwards feasted. It is well known that tournaments were frequently celebrated in high splendor at Winchester; and this is perhaps one of those very tables. It was partly on account of a round table being thus actually exhibited, that these exercises were familiarly called by the historians of the middle age, *Tabula* or *Mensa Rotunda*. Thus Walter Hemingford, to mention no more instances: 'Eodem anno [1280] *Tabula Rotunda* tenebatur sumptuosè apud Warewyk.'

Some writers say, that king Arthur first instituted the *Round Table*, at Cairleon, in Monmouthshire; others, at Camelot in Somersetshire. Both these are mentioned in *La Morte d'Arthur*, as places where Arthur kept his court, with his knights. In the Parish of Lansannan, in Denbighshire, on the side of a stony rock is a circular area, cut out of the rock, having twenty-four seats, which they call Arthur's *Round Table*. However, its first and original establishment is generally supposed to have been at Winchester. Harding, in his *Chronicle* of English Kings from Brutus to Edward IV. in whose reign he wrote, tells us, that Uther Pendragon, Arthur's father, founded the *Round Table* at Winchester, chiefly for the recovery of *Sangreal*, but in commemoration of his marriage with Igerne. Lond. 1543. edit. Grafton. fol. 61. Joseph of Arimathea is likewise introduced on this occasion.

> And at the day he weddid her and cround,
> And she far forth with child was then begonne,
> To comfort her he set the ROUND TABLE
> At *Winchester*, of worthiest knights alone,
> Approved best in knighthood of their fone,
> Which TABLE ROUND, *Joseph of Arimathie*,
> For brother made of the *Saint Gral* only.

> In which he made the sige perilous,
> Where none should sit, without grete mischief,
> But ONE that should be *most religious*
> Of knights all, and of the *round table* CHIEF,
> The *Saint Gral* that should recover and acheve.

The ONE *most religious*, who alone was qualified to sit in the *sige perilous*, and who achieved and won the *Sangreal*, is Sir Galahad, Sir Lancelot's son.

In Caxton's romance, king Arthur's dowry with queen Guenever, is said to be the *Round Table*, made by her father Uther. Her father, king Leodegrance, says, 'I shall send him a gift that shall please him more, [than lands] for I shall give him the *Table Round*, the which *Uther Pendragon gave me*.'

There is another ancient romance, for so it may be called, though written in verse, which Spenser apparently copies, in prince Arthur's combat with the dragon, F. Q. i. xi. 29, 30, 31, 32, 33, 34, 35, 36. The miraculous manner in which the knight is healed, our author drew from this old poem, entitled, *Sir Bevis of Southampton*.

> What for weary, and what for faint,
> Sir Bevis was neere attaint:
> The dragon followed on Bevis so hard,
> That as he would have fled backward,
> There was a well as I weene,
> And he stumbled right therein.
> Then was Sir Bevis afraid and woe,
> Lest the dragon should him sloe:
> Or that he might away passe,
> When that he in the well was.
> Then was the well of such vertu
> Through the might of Christ Jesu,
> For sometime dwelled in that land
> A virgin full of Christes sand,
> That had been bathed in that well,
> That ever after, as men can tell,
> Might no venomous worme come therein,
> By the virtue of that virgin,
> Nor nigh it seven foot and more:
> Then Bevis was glad therefore,
> When he saw the Dragon fell
> Had no power to come to the well.
> Then was he glad without faile,
> And rested awhile for his availe,
> And drank of the water of his fill,
> And then he leapt out of the well,
> And with *Morglay*, his brand
> Assailed the Dragon, I understand:
> On the Dragon he strucke so fast, &c.

After which the Dragon strikes the knight with such violence, that he falls into a swoon, and tumbles as it were lifeless into the well, by whose sovereign virtue he is revived.

> When Bevis was at the ground
> The water made him whole and sound,
> And quenched all the venim away,
> This well saved Bevis that day.

And afterwards,

> But ever when Bevis was hurt sore,
> He went to the well and washed him thore;
> He was as whole as any man,
> And ever as fresh as when he began.

It may be observed, that this poem of Sir Bevis is in that short measure, which was frequently sung to the harp even in queen Elizabeth's time: a custom which probably descended from the ancient bards. The author of *The Arte of English poesie*, printed in 1589, thus speaks of it: 'So on the other side doth the overbusie and too speedy returne of one manner of tune, too much annoy, and, as it were, glut the eare, unless it be in small and popular musickes song by these cantabanqui upon benches and barrels heads, where they have none other audience than boyes, or country fellowes, that passe by them in the streete; or else by blind harpers, or such like taverne-minstrels, that give a fit of mirth for a groat; and their matters being, for the most part, stories of old time; as, the *Tale of Sir Topas*, the *Reportes of Bevis of Southampton*, *Guy of Warwicke*, *Adam Bell*, and *Clymme of the Clough*, and such other old *Romances* or *historical Rhymes*, made purposely for recreation of the common people at christmasse diners, and brideales; and in tavernes, and alehouses, and such places of base resort: also they be used in carols and rounds, and such light or lascivious poemes, which are commonly more commodiously uttered by these buffoons and VICES in plays, than by any other person:

such were the rimes of Skelton (usurping the name of a poet laureate) being in deede but a rude rayling rimer, and all his doings ridiculous; he used both short distances and short measures, pleasing only the popular eare; in our courtly MAKER we banish them utterly.' B. ii.c.9. Hence it appears, that Chaucer's pieces, or at least legends drawn from him, were, at that time, sung to the harp; for the tale, or rime, of Sir Topas is a poem of Chaucer now extant: so the Italians, at present, sing Tasso and Ariosto. Adam Bell and Clym of the Clough were two famous archers: the former of which is, on that account, alluded to by Shakspeare.

The same author, in another place, speaks of this kind of entertainment, by which we may conjecture that it was not always confined to so vulgar an audience. 'We ourselves, who compiled this treatise, have written for pleasure, a little *brief romance*, or historical ditty, in the English tong, of the isle of Great-Britaine, in short and long meeters; and by breaches or divisions to be more commodiously sung to the harpe in places of assembly, where the company shall be desirous to hear of old adventures, and valiaunces of noble knights in times past; as are those of *king Arthur, and his knights of the round table*; Sir Bevys of Southampton, Guy of Warwicke, and such other like.' B. i. c. 19.

But to return: the circumstance of the Dragon not being able to approach within seven feet of this well, is imitated by our author, where he mentions another water, which in like manner preserves the knight, F. Q. i. xi. 49.

> But nigh thereto the ever-damned beast
> Durst not approache, for he was mortal made,
> And all that life preserved did detest,
> Yet he it oft adventur'd to invade.

We feel a sort of malicious triumph in detecting the latent and obscure source, from whence an original author has drawn some celebrated description: yet this, it must be granted, soon gives way to the rapture that naturally results from contemplating the chymical energy of true genius, which can produce so noble a transmutation; and whose virtues are not less efficacious and vivifying in their nature, than those of the miraculous water here displayed by Spenser.

I take this opportunity of mentioning, by the way, that our author, in his Dragon-encounters, circumstantially adopts all the incidents which occur on this article in romances.

An ingenious correspondent has communicated to me an old ballad, or metrical romance, called *The Boy and the Mantle*, on which Spenser's conceit of *Florimel's girdle* is evidently founded. A boy brings into king Arthur's hall, at Cairleon, a magical mantle, by which trial is made of the fidelity of each of the ladies of the several knights. But this fiction is as manifestly taken from an old French piece, entitled, *Le Court Mantel*; part of which is quoted by M. de Sainte Palaye, in his learned and entertaining memoirs of ancient chivalry, and who informs us, that it is formed on the tale of the *Enchanted Cup*. Most of these old romantick stories in English, I presume, first existed in French or Italian.

Several other incidental imitations of romance, will be pointed out occasionally. As to Spenser's original and genealogy of the FAIRY NATION, I am inclined to conjecture, that part of it was supplied by his own inexhaustible imagination, and part from some fabulous history.

He tells us, that man, as first made by Prometheus, was called ELFE, who, wandering over the world, at length arrived at the gardens of Adonis, where he found a female, whom he called FAY, F. Q. ii. x. 70. *Elfe*, according to Junius, is derived from the Runick *Alfur*; who likewise endeavours to prove, that the Saxons called the *Elfes*, or spirits of the Downs, *Dunelfin*;

of the Fields, *Feldelfen*; of the Hills, *Muntelfen*; of the Woods, *Wudelfen*, &c. ELFE, signifies *quick*. FAY, or FAIRY, I shall explain hereafter. The issue of ELFE and FAY were called *Fairies*, who soon grew to be a mighty people, and conquered all nations. Their eldest son Elfin governed America, and the next to him, named Elfinan, founded the city of Cleopolis, which was enclosed with a golden wall by Elfiline. His son Elfine overcame the Gobbelines; but, of all Fairies, Elfant was most renowned, who built Panthea, of crystal. To these succeeded Elfar, who slew two brethren giants; and to him Elfinor, who built a bridge of glass over the sea, the sound of which was like thunder. At length Elficleos ruled the Fairy land with much wisdom, and highly advanced its power and honour: he left two sons, the eldest of which, fair Elferon, died a premature death, his place being supplied by the mighty Oberon; a prince, whose 'wide memorial' still remains; and who, dying, left Tanaquil to succeed him by will, she being also called *Glorian*, or GLORIANA.

In the story of Enfinel, who overcame the Gobbelines, Spenser either alludes to the fiction of the Guelfes and Gibbelines in Italy; or to another race of fairies, called *Goblins*, and commonly joined with *Elfes*. His friend and commentator, E. K., remarks, that our *Elfes* and *Goblins* were derived from the two parties Guelfes and Gibbelines. This etymology I by no means approve. The mention of it however may serve to illustrate Spenser's meaning in this passage. Elfinan perhaps is king Lud, who founded London, or Cleopolis: 'In which the fairest FAERIE queene doth well,' F. Q. i. x. 58. Elfant built her palace *Panthea*, probably Windsor-castle. The bridge of glass may mean London-bridge. But these images of the golden wall, the crystal tower, &c. seem to be all adopted from romance. At least, they all flow from a mind strongly tinctured with romantick ideas. In the latter part of this genealogy, he has manifestly adumbrated some of our English princes. Elficleos is king Henry VII., whose eldest son, prince Arthur, died at sixteen years of age, in Ludlow-castle; and whose youngest son Oberon, that is Henry VIII., succeeded to the crown, marrying his brother Arthur's widow, the princess Katherine. This Spenser particularly specifies in these verses, F. Q. ii. x. 75.

> Whose emptie place, the mightie Oberon
> Doubly supplide, in SPOUSALL and DOMINION.

And that the fame of this king was very recent in our author's age, is obvious. It is remarkable that Spenser says nothing of Edward VI. and queen Mary, who reigned between Henry VIII. and queen Elizabeth; but that he passes immediately from Oberon to Tanaquil, or GLORIANA, i. e. Elizabeth, who was excluded from her succession by those two intermediate reigns. There is much address and art in the poet's manner of making this omission.

> He dying left the fairest Tanaquill,
> Him to succeed therein by his last will;
> Fairer and nobler liveth none this howre,
> Ne like in grace, ne like in learned skill.

As to the Fairy QUEEN, considered apart from the race of fairies, the notion of such an imaginary personage was very common. Chaucer, in his *Rime of Sir Thopas*, mentions her, together with a fairy land: and Shakspeare, the poet of popular superstition, has introduced her in the *Midsummer-Night's Dream*. She was supposed to have held her court in the highest magnificence, in the reign of king Arthur; a circumstance, by which the transcendent happiness of that golden age was originally represented in its legendary chronicles. Thus Chaucer, *Wife of Bathes T.* v. 857. edit Urr.

> In the old dayis of the king Arthure,
> Of which the Britons speken great honour;

All was this lond fulfillid of fayry:
The ELF-QUENE, with her jolly company,
Daunsid full oft in many a grene mede:
This was the old opinion, as I rede.

Hence too we find, that Spenser followed the established tradition, in supposing his *Fairy Queen* to exist in the age of Arthur.

In Chaucer's *Rime of Sir Thopas*, mentioned above, the knight, like Spenser's Arthur, goes in search of a *Fairy Queen*:

An ELF-QUENE well I love, I wis,
For in this world no woman is,
    Worthy to be my make;
All othir womin I forsake,
And to an ELF-QUENE I me take
    By dale and eke by doune.
Into his saddle he clombe anone,
And pricked over style and stone
    An ELF-QUENE to espie,
Till he so long had ridden and gone,
That he fonde in a privie wone,
    The countre of FAIRIE.

He then meets a terrible giant, who threatens him with destruction, for entering that country, and tells him;

Here wonnith the QUENE OF FAIRIE,
With harpe, and pipe, and simphonie,
    Within this place and boure;
The Child said, also mote I the
To morrow woll I metin The
    Whan I have mine armoure.

In Chaucer it appears that *Fairy-land*, and *Fairies*, were sometimes used for hell, and its ideal inhabitants. Thus in the *Marchant's Tale*, v. 221.

Pluto that is king of FAYRIE.

Again,

Proserpine and all her FAYRIE.

In the same: 'And I, quoth the Quene, [*Proserpine*] am of FAYRIE.' In the *Knight's Tale*, when the brasen horse was brought into Cambuscan's hall, 'It was of FAYRIE, as the people deem'd.' That is, 'the people thought this wonderful horse was the work of the devil, and made in hell.' And in the romance of the *Seven Champions*, Proserpine is called the FAIRY *Queen*, and said 'to sit crowned amongst her FAYRIES.' P. 1 ch. 10. In *Harsenet's Declaration of Popish Imposture*, &c. 1602, pag. 57, ch. 12, Mercury is called 'Prince of the FAIRIES.'

This fiction of the *Fairies*, is supposed to have been brought, with other fantastick extravagancies of the like nature, from the Eastern nations, while the European Christians were engaged in the holy war; those expeditions being the first subjects of the elder romance. These are the words of one [Warburton] who has shown his masterly skill and penetration in every part of literature. 'Nor were the monstrous embellishments of enchantments, &c. the invention of the romancers; but formed upon Eastern tales, brought thence by travellers from their crusades and pilgrimages, which indeed have a cast peculiar to the wild imagination of the eastern people.' That the Fairies, in particular, came from the East, the testimony of M. Herbelot will more fully confirm; who tells us, that the Persians call the Fairies *Peri*; and the Arabs, *Ginn*; that they feign, there is a certain country inhabited by them, called *Ginistan*, which answers to our *Fairy-land*; and that the ancient romances of Persia are full of *Peri* or *Fairies*. See also *Ginn*, or *Gian*, in Herbelot; under the latter of which, that learned orientalist further informs us, that there is an Arabian book, entitled, 'Pieces de corail amassées sur ce qui regarde le GINNES, ou *Genies*.'

The notions however, so essential to books of chivalry, of giants, necromancers, enchantments, &c. were perhaps established, although not universally, in Europe, before the time of the Crusades. All the *Sagas*, or ancient Islandick histories, are full of them. The Fairies, in particular, held a very important rank in the old Celtick mythology. The northern nations called them *Duergar*, or *Dwarfs*. Thus the sword *Tirfing*, in the Scaldick dialogue between Hervor and Angantyr, is called *Duerga Smidi*, the work of the *Dwarfs*. This strengthens the hypothesis of the northern part of Europe, particularly Scandinavia, being peopled by colonies from the East, under the command of their general, or god, ODIN. It is well known, how strongly the superstitious belief of spirits, or invisible agents, assigned to different parts of nature, prevails even in Scotland at this day.

Our old romantick history supposes, that Arthur still reigns in Fairy-Land, from which he will one day return to Britain, and re-establish the round table in its original splendour. See Lydgate's *Fall of Princes*, b. 8, ch. 25.

He is a king ycrownid in *Fairie*,
With scepter, and sword: and with his regally
Shall resort as lord and soveraigne
Out of *Fairie*, and reigne in Britaine;
And repair again the old round table:
By prophecy Merlin set the date.

The same tradition is mentioned by Cervantes in *Don Quixote*, P. i. ch. 5.

Many other examples might be alleged, from which it would be more abundantly manifested, that our author's imagination was entirely possessed with that species of reading, which was the fashion and the delight of his age. The lovers of Spenser, I hope, will not think I have been too tedious in a disquisition, which has contributed not only to illustrate many particular passages in their favourite poet, but to display the general cast and colour of his poem. Some there are, who will censure what I have collected on this subject, as both trifling and uninteresting; but such readers can have no taste for Spenser. . . .

In reading the works of a poet who lived in a remote age, it is necessary that we should look back upon the customs and manners which prevailed in that age. We should endeavour to place ourselves in the writer's situation and circumstances. Hence we shall become better enabled to discover, how his turn of thinking, and manner of composing, were influenced by familiar appearances and established objects, which are utterly different from those with which we are at present surrounded. For want of this caution, too many readers view the knights and damsels, the tournaments and enchantments, of Spenser, with modern eyes; never considering that the encounters of chivalry subsisted in our author's age; that romances were then most eagerly and universally studied; and that consequently Spenser, from the fashion of the times, was induced to undertake a recital of chivalrous achievements, and to become, in short, a *romantick* Poet.

Spenser, in this respect, copied real manners, no less than Homer. A sensible historian observes, that 'Homer copied true natural manners, which, however rough and uncultivated, will always form an agreeable and interesting picture: but the pencil of the English poet [Spenser] was employed in drawing the affectations, and conceits, and fopperies, of chivalry.' This, however, was nothing more than an imitation of real life; as much, at least, as the plain descriptions in Homer, which corresponded to the simplicity of manners then subsisting in Greece. Spenser, in the address of the *Shepheards Calender* to Sir Philip Sidney, couples his patron's learning with his skill in chivalry; a topick of panegyrick, which would sound very odd in a modern dedication, especially before a set of pastorals. 'To the noble and virtuous gentleman, most worthy of all titles, both of Learning and *Chivalrie*, Master Philip Sydney.'

> Go, little booke; thyself present,
> As child whose parent is unkent,
> To him that is the president
> Of noblenesse and *chivalrie*.

Nor is it sufficiently considered, that a popular practice of Spenser's age, contributed, in a considerable degree, to make him an *allegorical* Poet. We should remember, that, in this age, allegory was applied as the subject and foundation of publick shows and spectacles, which were exhibited with a magnificence superiour to that of former times. The virtues and vices, distinguished by their respective emblematical types, were frequently personified, and represented by living actors. These figures bore a chief part in furnishing what they called PAGEAUNTS; which were then the principal species of entertainment, and were shown, not only in private, or upon the stage, but very often in the open streets for solemnising publick occasions, or celebrating any grand event. As a proof of what is here mentioned, I refer the reader to Holinshed's Description of the SHEW OF MANHOOD AND DESERT, exhibited at Norwich, before queen Elizabeth; and more particularly to that historian's account of a TURNEY performed by Fulke Grevile, the lords Arundell and Windsor, and Sir Philip Sidney, who are feigned to be the children of DESIRE, attempting to win the FORTRESS OF BEAUTY. In the composition of the last spectacle, no small share of poetical invention appears.

In the mean time, I do not deny that Spenser was, in great measure, tempted by the *Orlando Furioso*, to write an allegorical poem. Yet it must still be acknowledged, that Spenser's peculiar mode of allegorising seems to have been dictated by those spectacles, rather than by the fictions of Ariosto. In fact, Ariosto's species of allegory does not so properly consist in impersonating the virtues, vices, and affections of the mind, as in the adumbration of moral doctrine, under the actions of men and women. On this plan Spenser's allegories are sometimes formed: as in the first Book, where the Red-crosse Knight, or a TRUE CHRISTIAN, defeats the wiles of Archimago, or the DEVIL, &c. &c. These indeed are fictitious personages; but he proves himself a much more ingenious allegorist, where his imagination *bodies* forth unsubstantial things, *turns them to shape*, and marks out the nature, powers, and effects, of that which is ideal and abstracted, by visible and external symbols; as in his delineations of *Fear, Despair, Fancy, Envy*, and the like. Ariosto gives us but few symbolical beings of this sort; for a picturesque invention was by no means his talent: while those few, which we find in his poem, are seldom drawn with that characteristical fullness, and significant expression, so striking in the fantastick portraits of Spenser. And, that Spenser painted these figures in so distinct and animated style, may we not partly account for it from this cause; That he had been long habituated to the sight of these emblematical personages, visibly decorated with their proper attributes, and actually endued with speech, motion, and life?

As a more convincing argument in favour of this hypothesis, I shall remark, that Spenser expressly denominates his most exquisite groupe of allegorical figures, THE MASKE OF CUPID. Thus, without recurring to conjecture, his own words evidently demonstrate that he sometimes had representations of this sort in his eye. He tells us, moreover, that these figures were, (F. Q. iii. xii. 5.)

> A jolly company,
> *In a manner of a maske* enranged orderly.

In his introduction to this groupe, it is manifest that he drew from another allegorick spectacle of that age, called the *dumb shew*, which was wont to be exhibited before every act of a tragedy. See st. 3.

> And forth yssewd, as on the readie flore
> Of some theatre, a grave personage,
> Than in his hand a braunch of laurell bore,
> With comely haveour, and countnance sage,
> Yclad in costly garments, fit for tragicke stage.
>
> IV.
> Proceeding to the midst he stil did stand,
> As if in mind he somewhat had to say;
> And to the vulgar beckning with his hand,
> In sign of silence, as to heare a play,
> By lively actions he gan bewray
> Some argument of matter passioned;
> Which doen, he backe retyred soft away;
> And, passing by, his name discovered,
> *Ease*, on his robe in golden letters cyphered.

He afterwards styles these figures *Maskers*, st. 6.

> The whiles the *Maskers* marched forth in trim array.
> The first was *Fancy*, like a lovely boy, &c.

From what has been said, I would not have it objected, that I have intended to arraign the powers of our author's invention; or insinuated, that he servilely copied such representations. All I have endeavoured to prove is, that Spenser was not only better qualified to delineate fictions of this sort, because they were the real objects of his sight; but, as all men are influenced by what they see, that he was prompted and induced to delineate them, because he saw them, especially as they were so much the delight of his age.

Instead of entering into a critical examination of Spenser's manner of allegorising, and of the poetical conduct of his allegories, which has been done with an equally judicious and ingenious discernment by Mr. Spence, I shall observe, that our author frequently introduces an allegory, under which no meaning is couched; viz. *Alma* is the mind, and her *Castle* the body, F. Q. ii. ix. 21. The tongue is the porter of this castle, the nose the portcullis, and the mouth the porch, about the inside of which are placed twice sixteen warders clad in white, which are the teeth; these *Alma* passes by, who rise up, and do obeisance to her, st. 26. But how can the teeth be said to rise up and bow to the mind? Spenser here forgot, that he was allegorising, and speaks as if he was describing, without any latent meaning, a real queen, with twice sixteen real warders, who, as such, might, with no impropriety, be said to rise and bow to their queen. Many instances of his confounding allegory with reality, occur through this whole Canto, and the two next; particularly, where he is describing the kitchen of this castle, which is the belly, he gives us a formal description of such a kitchen, as was to be seen in his time in castles, and great houses, by no means expressive of the thing intended. Again, the occult meaning of his bringing Scudamore to the house of *Care*, F. Q. iv. v. 32. clashes with what he had before told us. By this allegory of Scudamore coming to *Care's* house, it should be *understood*, that 'Scudamore, from a happy, passed into a miserable state.' For we may reasonably suppose that, before he came to *Care's* house, he was unacquainted with *Care*; whereas the poet had before represented him as involved in extreme misery. It would be tedious, by an allegation of particular examples, to demonstrate how frequently his allegories are mere descriptions; and that, taken in their literal sense, they contain an improper or no signification. I shall, however, mention one. The *Blatant Beast* is said to break into the monasteries, to rob their chancels, cast down the desks of the monks, deface the altars, and destroy the images found in their churches. By the *Blatant Beast* is understood *Scandal*; and by the havock just mentioned as affected by it, is implied the suppression of religious houses and popish superstition. But how can this be properly said to have been brought about by scandal? And how could Spenser in particular, with any consistency, say this, who was, as appears by his Pastorals, a friend to the reformation, as was his heroine Elizabeth?

But there is another capital fault in our author's allegories, which does not immediately fall under the stated rules of criticism. 'Painters,' says a French writer, 'ought to employ their allegories in religious pictures, with much greater reserve than in profane pieces. They may, indeed, in such subjects as do not represent the mysteries and miracles of our religion, make use of an allegorical composition, the action whereof shall be expressive of some truth, that cannot be represented otherwise, either in painting or sculpture. I agree therefore to let them draw *Faith* and *Hope* supporting a dying person, and *Religion* in deep affliction at the feet of a deceased prelate. But I am of opinion, that artists, who treat of the miracles and dogmas of our religion, are allowed no kind of allegorical composition. The facts whereon our religion is built, and the doctrine it delivers, are subjects in which the painter's imagination has no liberty to sport.' The conduct which this author blames, is practised by Spenser, with this difference only; that the painters here condemned are supposed to adapt human allegory to divine mystery, whereas Spenser has mingled divine mystery with human allegory. Such a practice as this tends not only to confound sacred and profane subjects, but to place the licentious sallies of imagination upon a level with the dictates of divine inspiration; to debase the truth and dignity of heavenly things, by making Christian allegory subservient to the purposes of Romantick fiction.

This fault our author, through a defect of judgment rather than a contempt of religion, has most glaringly committed throughout his whole first Book, where the imaginary instruments and expedients of romance are perpetually interwoven with the mysteries contained in the BOOK OF REVELATIONS, Duessa, who is formed upon the idea of a romantick enchantress, is gorgeously arrayed in gold and purple, presented with a triple crown by the giant Orgoglio, and seated by him on a monstrous seven-headed dragon, (C. vii. st. 16.) whose tail reaches to the skies, and throws down the stars, (st. 18.) she bearing a golden cup in her hand (C. viii. st. 25.). This is the *Scarlet Whore*, and the *Red Dragon* in the REVELATIONS. 'Behold a great red dragon, having seven heads, and ten horns, and seven crowns upon his heads; and his tail drew the third part of the stars of heaven, and did cast them to earth,' Ch. xii. 3, 4. Again, 'I saw a woman sit upon a scarlet-coloured beast, full of names of blasphemy, having seven heads, and ten horns; and the woman was arrayed in purple and scarlet colour, and decked with gold, and precious stones, and pearls, having a golden cup in her hands full of abomination, and filthiness of her fornication,' Ch. xvii. 3, 4.

In Orgoglio's castle, which is described as very magnificent, Prince Arthur discovers, C. viii. st. 36,

An altare carv'd with cunning ymagery,
On which trew Christians blood was often spilt,
And holy martyres often doen to dye,
With cruell malice and strong tyranny;
Whose blessed sprites, from underneath the stone
To God for vengeance cryde continually.

The inspired author of the above-named book mentions the same of what he saw in heaven. 'I saw under the altar the souls of them that were slain for the Word of God, and for the testimony which they held; and they cried with a loud voice,

How long, O Lord, holy and true, dost thou not judge, and avenge our blood on them that dwell on earth?' Ch. vi. 9, 10.

A hermit points out to the Redcrosse Knight the New Jerusalem, (C. x. st. 53.) which an angel discovers to St. John, (Ch. xxi. 10, &c.). This prospect is taken, says the poet, from a mountain more lofty than either the mount of Olives or Parnassus. These two comparisons, thus impertinently linked together, strongly remind us of the absurdity now spoken of, the mixture of divine truth and profane invention; and naturally lead us to reflect on the difference between the oracles uttered from the former, and the fictions of those who dreamed on the latter.

Spenser, in the visionary dominions of Una's father, has planted the *Tree of Life*, and *of Knowledge*: from the first of the trees, he says, a well flowed, whose waters contained a most salutary virtue, and which the dragon could not approach. Thus, in the same scripture, Ch. xxii. 1, 2. 'He shewed me a pure river of water of life, clear as crystal, proceeding out of the throne of God, and of the Lamb. In the midst of the street of it, and on either side of the river, was there the *Tree of Life*.' The circumstance, in particular, of the dragon not being able to approach this water, is literally adopted from romance, as has been before observed. Thus also, by the steps and fictions of romance, we are conducted to the death of the dragon who besieged the parents of Una, by which is figured the destruction of the old serpent mentioned in the APOCALYPSE.

The extravagancies of Pagan mythology are not improperly introduced into a poem of this sort, as they are acknowledged falsities: or at best, if expressive of any moral truth, no more than the inventions of men. But the poet that applies the VISIONS OF GOD in such a manner is guilty of an impropriety, which, I fear, amounts to an impiety.

If we take a retrospect of English poetry from the age of Spenser, we shall find, that it principally consisted in visions and allegories. Fancy was a greater friend to the dark ages, as they are called, than is commonly supposed. Our writers caught this vein from the Provencial poets. There are indeed the writings of some English poets now remaining, who wrote before Gower or Chaucer. But these are merely chroniclers in rhyme, and seem to have left us the last dregs of that sort of composition, which was practiced by the British Bards: for instance *The Chronicle of Robert of Glocester*, who wrote, according to his account, about the year 1280. The most ancient allegorical poem, which I have seen in our language, is a manuscript Vision, in the Bodleian library, written in the reign of Edward II. by Adam Davie. It is in the short verse of the old metrical romance. However, Gower and Chaucer were justly reputed the first English poets, because they were the first, of any note at least, who introduced *invention* into our poetry; the first who *moralised their song*, and strove to render virtue more amiable by clothing her in the veil of fiction. Chaucer, it must be acknowledged, deserves to be placed the first in time of our English poets, on another account; his admirable artifice in painting the familiar manners, which none before him had ever attempted in the most imperfect degree: and it should be remembered, to his immortal honour, that he was the first writer who gave the English nation, in their own language, an idea of *humour*. About the same time flourished an allegorical satirist, the author of *Piers Plowmans Visions*. To these succeeded Lydgate; who from his principal performances, the *Fall of Princes*, and *Story of Thebes*, more properly may be classed among the legendary poets, although the first of these is in great measure a series of visions. But we have of this author two poems, viz. *The Temple of Glass*, and *The Dance of Death*, besides several other pieces, chiefly in manuscript, professedly

written in this species. Lydgate has received numberless encomiums from our old English poets, which he merited more
from his language than his imagination. Lydgate is an unani-
mated writer, yet he made considerable improvements in the
rude state of English versification; and is perhaps the first of our
poets whom common readers can peruse with little hesitation
and difficulty. He was followed by Hardyng, who wrote a
Chronicle, in verse, of all the English kings from Brutus, the
favourite subject of the British bards, or poetical genealogists,
down to the reign of Edward IV. in whose reign he lived. This
piece is often commended and quoted by our most learned
antiquaries. But the poet is lost in the historian: care in collecting, and truth in relating events, are incompatible with the
sallies of invention. So frigid and prosaick a performance, after
such promising improvements, seemed to indicate, that poetry
was relapsing into its primitive barbarism; and that the rudeness
of Robert of Glocester, would be soon reinstated in the place of
Chaucer's judgment and imagination.

However, in the reign of Henry VII. this interval of
darkness was happily removed by Stephen Hawes, a name generally unknown, and not mentioned by any compiler of the
lives of English poets. This author was at this period the re-
storer of invention, which seems to have suffered a gradual
degeneracy from the days of Chaucer. He not only revived, but
improved, the ancient allegorick vein, which Hardyng had
almost entirely banished. Instead of that dryness of description,
so remarkably disgusting in many of his predecessors, we are by
this poet often entertained with the luxuriant effusions of
Spenser. Hawes refined Lydgate's versification, and gave it sentiment and imagination; added new graces to the seven-lined
stanza which Chaucer and Gower had adopted from the Italian; and, to sum up all, was the first of our poets who decorated
invention with perspicuous and harmonious numbers. The
title of his principal performance is almost as obscure as his
name, viz. 'The historie of GRAUNDE AMOURE *and* LA BEL
PUCEL, *called the* PASTIME OF PLEASURE; *contayning the
knowledge of the seven sciences, and the course of man's life in
this worlde.* Invented by Stephen Hawes, groome of kyng
Henry the seventh his chamber.' Henry VII. is said to have
preferred Hawes to this station, chiefly on account of his extraordinary memory, for he could repeat by heart most of the
English poets, especially Lydgate. This reign produced another
allegorical poem, entitled the *Ship of Fooles.* It was translated
from the High Dutch, and professes to ridicule the vices and
absurdities of all ranks of men. The language is tolerably pure:
but it has nothing of the invention and pleasantry which the
plan seems to promise; neither of which, however, could be
expected, if we consider its original.

In the reign of Henry VIII. classical literature began to be
received and studied in England; and the writings of the ancients were cultivated, with true taste and erudition, by Sir
Thomas More, Colet, Ascham, Leland, Cheke, and other illustrious rivals in polished composition. Erasmus was entertained and patronised by the king and nobility; and the Greek
language, that inestimable repository of genuine elegance and
sublimity, was taught and admired. In this age flourished John
Skelton; who, notwithstanding the great and new lights with
which he was surrounded, contributed nothing to what his
ancestors had left him: nor do I perceive, that his versification
is, in any degree, more refined than that of one of his immediate predecessor, Hawes. Indeed, one would hardly suspect, that
he wrote in the same age with his elegant contemporaries Surrey and Wyat. His best pieces are written in the allegorical
manner, and are his *Crowne of Lawrell* and *Bowge of Court.*
But the genius of Skelton seems little better qualified for pictur-

esque than satirical poetry. In the one he wants invention,
grace, and dignity; in the other, wit and good manners.

I should be guilty of injustice to a nation, which, amid a
variety of disadvantages, has kept a constant pace with England
in the progress of literature, if I neglected to mention, in this
general review, two Scottish poets, who flourished about this
period, Sir David Lyndesay, and Sir William Dunbar; the former of which in his *Dream,* and other pieces, and the latter in
his *Golden Terge,* appear to have been animated with the noblest spirit of allegorick fiction.

Soon afterwards appeared a series of poems, entitled, the
Mirrour for Magistrates, formed upon a dramatick plan, and
capable of admitting some of the most affecting pathetical
strokes. But these pieces, however honoured with the commendation of Sidney, seem to be little better than a biographical detail. There is one poem indeed among the rest, which
exhibits a groupe of imaginary personages, so beautifully
drawn, that, in all probability, they contributed to direct, at
least to stimulate, Spenser's imagination in the construction of
the like representations. Thus much may be truly said, that
Sackville's *Induction* approaches nearer to the *Faerie Queene,*
in the richness of allegorick description, than any previous or
succeeding poem.

After the *Faerie Queene,* allegory began to decline, and by
degrees gave place to a species of poetry, whose images were of
the metaphysical and abstracted kind. This fashion evidently
took its rise from the predominant studies of the times, in
which the disquisition of school divinity, and the perplexed
subtilities of philosophick disputation, became the principal
pursuits of the learned.

Then *Una fair* gan drop her *princely mien.*

James I. is contemptuously called a *pedantick* monarch.
But, surely, nothing could be more serviceable to the interests
of learning, at its infancy, than this supposed foible. 'To stick
the doctor's chair into the throne,' was to patronise the literature of the times. In a more enlightened age, the same attention to letters, and love of scholars, might have produced
proportionable effects on sciences of real utility. This cast of
mind in the king, however indulged in some cases to an ostentatious affectation, was at least innocent.

Allegory, notwithstanding, unexpectedly rekindled some
faint sparks of its native splendour, in the *Purple Island* of
Phineas Fletcher, with whom it almost as soon disappeared:
when a poetry succeeded, in which imagination gave way to
correctness, sublimity of description to delicacy of sentiment,
and majestick imagery, to conceit and epigram. Poets began
now to be more attentive to words, than to things and objects.
The nicer beauties of happy expression were preferred to the
daring strokes of great conception. Satire, that bane of the
sublime, was imported from France. The Muses were debauched at court; and polite life, and familiar manners, became their only themes. The simple dignity of Milton was
either entirely neglected, or mistaken for bombast and insipidity, by the refined readers of a dissolute age, whose taste and
morals were equally vitiated.

From this detail it will appear, that allegorical poetry,
through many gradations, at last received its ultimate consummation in the *Faerie Queene.* Under this consideration therefore, I hope what I have here collected on this subject, will not
seem too great a deviation from the main subject of the present
remarks; which I conclude with the just and pertinent sentiments of the Abbé du Bos, on allegorical action, *Reflexions,*
tom. i. c. 25. The passage, though properly respecting dramatick poets, is equally applicable to the action of the *Faerie*

Queene. 'It is impossible for a piece, whose subject is an allegorical action, to interest us very much. Those, which writers of approved wit and talents have hazarded in this kind, have not succeeded so well as others, where they have been disposed to be less ingenious, and to treat historically in their subject.— Our heart requires truth even in fiction itself; and, when it is presented with an allegorical fiction, it cannot determine itself, if I may be allowed the expression, to enter into the *sentiments* of those chimerical personages. A theatrical piece, were it to speak only to the *mind*, would never be capable of engaging our attention through the whole performance. We may therefore apply the words of Lactantius upon this occasion. *Poetick licence has its bounds, beyond which you are not permitted to carry your fiction. A poet's art consists in making a good representation of things that might have really happened, and embellishing them with elegant images. Totum autem, quod referas, fingere, id est ineptum esse et mendacem, potius quam poetam.*'

SAMUEL TAYLOR COLERIDGE
"Spenser" (1818)
Literary Remains
1836, Volume 1, pp. 89–97

There is this difference, among many others, between Shakspeare and Spenser:—Shakspeare is never coloured by the customs of his age; what appears of contemporary character in him is merely negative; it is just not something else. He has none of the fictitious realities of the classics, none of the grotesqueness of chivalry, none of the allegory of the middle ages; there is no sectarianism either of politics or religion, no miser, no witch, no common witch,—no astrology—nothing impermanent of however long duration; but he stands like the yew tree in Lorton vale, which has known so many ages that it belongs to none in particular; a living image of endless self-reproduction, like the immortal tree of Malabar. In Spenser the spirit of chivalry is entirely predominant, although with a much greater infusion of the poet's own individual self into it than is found in any other writer. He has the wit of the southern with the deeper inwardness of the northern genius.

No one can appreciate Spenser without some reflection on the nature of allegorical writing. The mere etymological meaning of the word, allegory,—to talk of one thing and thereby convey another,—is too wide. The true sense is this,— the employment of one set of agents and images to convey in disguise a moral meaning, with a likeness to the imagination, but with a difference to the understanding,—those agents and images being so combined as to form a homogeneous whole. This distinguishes it from metaphor, which is part of an allegory. But allegory is not properly distinguishable from fable, otherwise than as the first includes the second, as a genus its species; for in a fable there must be nothing but what is universally known and acknowledged, but in an allegory there may be that which is new and not previously admitted. The pictures of the great masters, especially of the Italian schools, are genuine allegories. Amongst the classics, the multitude of their gods either precluded allegory altogether, or else made every thing allegory, as in the Hesiodic Theogonia; for you can scarcely distinguish between power and the personification of power. The Cupid and Psyche of, or found in, Apuleius, is a phenomenon. It is the Platonic mode of accounting for the fall of man. The Battle of the Soul by Prudentius is an early instance of Christian allegory.

Narrative allegory is distinguished from mythology as reality from symbol; it is, in short, the proper intermedium between person and personification. Where it is too strongly individualized, it ceases to be allegory; this is often felt in the Pilgrim's Progress where the characters are real persons with nick names. Perhaps one of the most curious warnings against another attempt to narrative allegory on a great scale, may be found in Tasso's account of what he himself intended in and by his Jerusalem Delivered.

As characteristic of Spenser, I would call your particular attention in the first place to the indescribable sweetness and fluent projection of his verse, very clearly distinguishable from the deeper and more inwoven harmonies of Shakspeare and Milton. This stanza is a good instance of what I mean:—

> Yet she, most faithfull ladie, all this while
> Forsaken, wofull, solitarie mayd,
> Far from all peoples preace, as in exile,
> In wildernesse and wastfull deserts strayd
> To seeke her knight; who, subtily betrayd
> Through that late vision which th' enchaunter
>   wrought,
> Had her abandond; she, of nought affrayd,
> Through woods and wastnes wide him daily sought,
> Yet wished tydinges none of him unto her brought.
> (*F. Qu.* B. I. c. 3. st. 3.)

2. Combined with this sweetness and fluency, the scientific construction of the metre of the Faery Queene is very noticeable. One of Spenser's arts is that of alliteration, and he uses it with great effect in doubling the impression of an image:—

> In *w*ildernesse and *w*astful deserts,—
>   . . .
> Through *w*oods and *w*astnes *w*ide,
>   . . .
> They passe the bitter *w*aves of Acheron,
> Where many soules sit *w*ailing *w*oefully,
> And come to *f*iery *f*lood of *Ph*legeton,
> Whereas the damned ghosts in torments fry,
> And with *s*harp *sh*rilling *sh*rieks doth bootlesse cry,—
>   &c.

He is particularly given to an alternate alliteration, which is, perhaps, when well used, a great secret in melody:—

> A *r*amping *l*yon *r*ushed suddenly,—
>   . . .
> And *s*ad to see her *s*orrowful constraint,—
>   . . .
> And on the grasse her *d*aintie *l*imbes *d*id *l*ay,—&c.

You cannot read a page of the Faery Queene, if you read for that purpose, without perceiving the intentional alliterativeness of the words; and yet so skilfully is this managed, that it never strikes any unwarned ear as artificial, or other than the result of the necessary movement of the verse.

3. Spenser displays great skill in harmonizing his descriptions of external nature and actual incidents with the allegorical character and epic activity of the poem. Take these two beautiful passages as illustrations of what I mean:—

> By this the northerne wagoner had set
> His sevenfold teme behind the stedfast starre
> That was in ocean waves yet never wet,
> But firme is fixt, and sendeth light from farre
> To all that in the wide deepe wandring arre;
> And chearefull chaunticlere with his note shrill
> Had warned once, that Phoebus' fiery carre
> In hast was climbing up the easterne hill,
> Full envious that Night so long his roome did fill;
> *When* those accursed messengers of hell,

That feigning dreame, and that faire-forged spright
Came, &c.—
                                        (B. I. c. 2. st. 1.)
. . .
At last, the golden orientall gate
Of greatest Heaven gan to open fayre;
And Phoebus, fresh as brydegrome to his mate,
Came dauncing forth, shaking his deawie hayre;
And hurld his glistring beams through gloomy ayre.
Which when the wakeful Elfe perceiv'd, streightway
He started up, and did him selfe prepayre
In sunbright armes and battailous array;
For with that Pagan proud he combat will that day.
                                        (Ib. c. 5. st. 2.)

Observe also the exceeding vividness of Spenser's descriptions. They are not, in the true sense of the word, picturesque; but are composed of a wondrous series of images, as in our dreams. Compare the following passage with anything you may remember in *pari materia* in Milton or Shakspeare:—

His haughtie helmet, horrid all with gold,
Both glorious brightnesse and great terrour bredd,
For all the crest a dragon did enfold
With greedie pawes, and over all did spredd
His golden winges; his dreadfull hideous hedd,
Close couched on the bever, seemed to throw
From flaming mouth bright sparkles fiery redd,
That suddeine horrour to faint hartes did show;
And scaly tayle was stretcht adowne his back full low.

Upon the top of all his loftie crest
A bounch of haires discolourd diversly,
With sprinkled pearle and gold full richly drest,
Did shake, and seemd to daunce for jollitie;
Like to an almond tree ymounted hye
On top of greene Selinis all alone,
With blossoms brave bedecked daintily,
Whose tender locks do tremble every one
At everie little breath that under heaven is blowne.
                                        (Ib. c. 7. st. 31–2.)

4. You will take especial note of the marvellous independence and true imaginative absence of all particular space or time in the Faery Queene. It is in the domains neither of history or geography; it is ignorant of all artificial boundary, all material obstacles; it is truly in land of Faery, that is, of mental space. The poet has placed you in a dream, a charmed sleep, and you neither wish, nor have the power, to inquire where you are, or how you got there. It reminds me of some lines of my own:—

Oh! would to Alla!
The raven or the sea-mew were appointed
To bring me food!—or rather that my soul
Might draw in life from the universal air!
It were a lot divine in some small skiff
Along some ocean's boundless solitude
To float for ever with a careless course,
And think myself the only being alive!
                                        (*Remorse*, Act. IV. sc. 3.)

Indeed Spenser himself, in the conduct of his great poem, may be represented under the same image, his symbolizing purpose being his mariner's compass:—

As pilot well expert in perilous wave,
That to a stedfast starre his course hath bent,
When foggy mistes or cloudy tempests have
The faithfull light of that faire lampe yblent,
And coverd Heaven with hideous dreriment;
Upon his card and compas firmes his eye,
The maysters of his long experiment,

And to them does the steddy helme apply,
Bidding his winged vessell fairely forward fly,
                                        (B. II. c. 7. st. 1.)
So the poet through the realms of allegory.

5. You should note the quintessential character of Christian chivalry in all his characters, but more especially in his women. The Greeks, except, perhaps, in Homer, seem to have had no way of making their women interesting, but by unsexing them, as in the instances of the tragic Medea, Electra, &c. Contrast such characters with Spenser's Una, who exhibits no prominent feature, has no particularization, but produces the same feeling that a statue does, when contemplated at a distance:—

From her fayre head her fillet she undight,
And layd her stole aside: her angels face,
As the great eye of Heaven, shyned bright,
And made a sunshine in the shady place;
Did never mortal eye behold such heavenly grace.
                                        (B. I. c. 3. st. 4.)

6. In Spenser we see the brightest and purest form of that nationality which was so common a characteristic of our older poets. There is nothing unamiable, nothing contemptuous of others, in it. To glorify their country—to elevate England into a queen, an empress of the heart—this was their passion and object; and how dear and important an object it was or may be, let Spain, in the recollection of her Cid, declare! There is a great magic in national names. What a damper to all interest is a list of native East Indian merchants! Unknown names are non-conductors; they stop all sympathy. No one of our poets has touched this string more exquisitely than Spenser; especially in his chronicle of the British Kings (B. II, c. 10), and the marriage of the Thames with the Medway (B. IV, c. II), in both which passages the mere names constitute half the pleasure we receive. To the same feeling we must in particular attribute Spenser's sweet reference to Ireland:—

Ne thence the Irishe rivers absent were;
Sith no lesse famous than the rest they be, &c.—Ib.
. . .
And Mulla mine, whose waves I whilom taught to
    weep.—Ib.
And there is a beautiful passage of the same sort in the Colin Clout's Come Home Again:—

"One day," quoth he, "I sat, as was my trade,
Under the foot of Mole," &c.

Lastly, the great and prevailing character of Spenser's mind is fancy under the conditions of imagination, as an ever present but not always active power. He has an imaginative fancy, but he has not imagination, in kind or degree, as Shakspeare and Milton have; the boldest effort of his powers in this way is the character of Talus. Add to this a feminine tenderness and almost maidenly purity of feeling, and above all, a deep moral earnestness which produces a believing sympathy and acquiescence in the reader, and you have a tolerably adequate view of Spenser's intellectual being.

WILLIAM HAZLITT
"On Chaucer and Spenser" (1818)
Lectures on the English Poets
1933, pp. 51–65

The interval between Chaucer and Spenser is long and dreary. There is nothing to fill up the chasm but the names of Occleve, 'ancient Gower', Lydgate, Wyatt, Surrey, and Sackville. Spenser flourished in the reign of Queen Elizabeth, and was sent with Sir John Davies into Ireland, of which he has left behind him some tender recollections in his description of the bog of Allan, and a record in an ably written paper, containing observations on the state of that country and the means of improving it, which remain in full force to the present day. Spenser died at an obscure inn in London, it is supposed in distressed circumstances. The treatment he received from Burleigh is well known. Spenser, as well as Chaucer, was engaged in active life; but the genius of his poetry was not active: it is inspired by the love of ease, and relaxation from all the cares and business of life. Of all the poets, he is the most poetical. Though much later than Chaucer, his obligations to preceding writers were less. He has in some measure borrowed the plan of his poem (as a number of distinct narratives) from Ariosto; but he has engrafted upon it an exuberance of fancy, and an endless voluptuousness of sentiment, which are not to be found in the Italian writer. Further, Spenser is even more of an inventor in the subject-matter. There is an originality, richness, and variety in his allegorical personages and fictions, which almost vies with the splendour of the ancient mythology. If Ariosto transports us into the regions of romance, Spenser's poetry is all fairy-land. In Ariosto, we walk upon the ground, in a company, gay, fantastic, and adventurous enough. In Spenser, we wander in another world, among ideal beings. The poet takes and lays us in the lap of a lovelier nature, by the sound of softer streams, among greener hills and fairer valleys. He paints nature, not as we find it, but as we expected to find it; and fulfils the delightful promise of our youth. He waves his wand of enchantment—and at once embodies airy beings, and throws a delicious veil over all actual objects. The two worlds of reality and of fiction are poised on the wings of his imagination. His ideas, indeed, seem more distinct than his perceptions. He is the painter of abstractions, and describes them with dazzling minuteness. In the Mask of Cupid he makes the God of Love 'clap on high his coloured winges *twain*': and it is said of Gluttony, in the Procession of the Passions,

> In green vine leaves he was right fitly clad.

At times he becomes picturesque from his intense love of beauty; as where he compares Prince Arthur's crest to the appearance of the almond tree:

> Upon the top of all his lofty crest,
> A bunch of hairs discolour'd diversely
> With sprinkled pearl and gold full richly
>   drest
> Did shake and seem'd to daunce for jollity:
> Like to an almond tree ymounted high
> On top of green Selenis all alone,
> With blossoms brave bedecked daintily;
> Her tender locks do tremble every one
> At every little breath that under heav'n is blown.

The love of beauty, however, and not of truth, is the moving principle of his mind; and he is guided in his fantastic delineations by no rule but the impulse of an inexhaustible imagination. He luxuriates equally in scenes of Eastern magnificence or the still solitude of a hermit's cell—in the extremes of sensuality or refinement.

In reading the *Faery Queen*, you see a little withered old man by a wood-side opening a wicket, a giant, and a dwarf lagging far behind, a damsel in a boat upon an enchanted lake,

wood-nymphs, and satyrs; and all of a sudden you are transported into a lofty palace, with tapers burning, amidst knights and ladies, with dance and revelry, and song, 'and mask, and antique pageantry'. What can be more solitary, more shut up in itself, than his description of the house of Sleep, to which Archimago sends for a dream:

> And more to lull him in his slumber soft
> A trickling stream from high rock tumbling
>   down,
> And ever-drizzling rain upon the loft,
> Mix'd with a murmuring wind, much like the
>   sound
> Of swarming Bees, did cast him in a swound.
> No other noise, nor people's troublous cries.
> That still are wont t' annoy the walled town
> Might there be heard; but careless Quiet lies
> Wrapt in eternal silence, far from enemies.

It is as if 'the honey-heavy dew of slumber' had settled on his pen in writing these lines. How different in the subject (and yet how like in beauty) is the following description of the Bower of Bliss:

> Eftsoones they heard a most melodious sound
> Of all that mote delight a dainty ear;
> Such as at once might not on living ground,
> Save in this Paradise, be heard elsewhere:
> Right hard it was for wight which did it hear,
> To tell what manner musicke that mote be;
> For all that pleasing is to living eare
> Was there consorted in one harmonee:
> Birds, voices, instruments, windes, waters, all agree.
>
> The joyous birdes shrouded in chearefull
>   shade
> Their notes unto the voice attempred sweet:
> The angelical soft trembling voices made
> To th' instruments divine respondence meet.
> The silver sounding instruments did meet
> With the base murmur of the water's fall;
> The water's fall with difference discreet,
> Now soft, now loud, unto the wind did call;
> The gentle warbling wind low answered to all.

The remainder of the passage has all that voluptuous pathos, and languid brilliancy of fancy, in which this writer excelled:

> The whiles some one did chaunt this lovely
>   lay;
> Ah! see, whoso fayre thing dost fain to see,
> In springing flower the image of thy day!
> Ah! see the virgin rose, how sweetly she
> Doth first peep forth with bashful modesty,
> That fairer seems the less ye see her may!
> Lo! see soon after, how more bold and free
> Her bared bosom she doth broad display;
> Lo! see soon after, how she fades and falls away!
>
> So passeth in the passing of a day
> Of mortal life the leaf, the bud, the flower;
> Ne more doth flourish after first decay,
> That erst was sought to deck both bed and
>   bower
> Of many a lady and many a paramour!
> Gather therefore the rose whilst yet is prime,
> For soon comes age that will her pride
>   deflower;

Gather the rose of love whilst yet is time,
Whilst loving thou mayst loved be with equal crime.
   He ceased; and then gan all the quire of birds
Their divers notes to attune unto his lay,
As in approvance of his pleasing wordes.
The constant pair heard all that he did say,
Yet swerved not, but kept their forward way
Through many covert groves and thickets close,
In which they creeping did at last display
That wanton lady with her lover loose,
Whose sleepy head she in her lap did soft dispose.

   Upon a bed of roses she was laid
As faint through heat, or dight to pleasant sin;
And was arrayed or rather disarrayed,
All in a veil of silk and silver thin,
That hid no whit her alabaster skin,
But rather shewed more white, if more might be:
More subtle web Arachne cannot spin;
Nor the fine nets, which oft we woven see
Of scorched dew, do not in the air more lightly flee.

   Her snowy breast was bare to greedy spoil
Of hungry eyes which n'ote therewith be fill'd,
And yet through languor of her late sweet toil
Few drops more clear than nectar forth distill'd,
That like pure Orient perles adown it trill'd;
And her fair eyes sweet smiling in delight
Moisten'd their fiery beams, with which she thrill'd
Frail hearts, yet quenched not; like starry light,
Which sparkling on the silent waves does seem more bright

The finest things in Spenser are, the character of Una, in the first book; the House of Pride; the Cave of Mammon, and the Cave of Despair; the account of Memory, of whom it is said, among other things,

The wars he well remember'd of King Nine,
Of old Assaracus and Inachus divine;

the description of Belphoebe; the story of Florimel and the Witch's son; the Gardens of Adonis, and the Bower of Bliss; the Mask of Cupid; and Colin Clout's vision, in the last book. But some people will say that all this may be very fine, but that they cannot understand it on account of the allegory. They are afraid of the allegory, as if they thought it would bite them: they look at it as a child looks at a painted dragon, and think it will strangle them in its shining folds. This is very idle. If they do not meddle with the allegory, the allegory will not meddle with them. Without minding it at all, the whole is as plain as a pikestaff. It might as well be pretended that we cannot see Poussin's pictures for the allegory, as that the allegory prevents us from understanding Spenser. For instance, when Britomart, seated amidst the young warriors, lets fall her hair and discovers her sex, is it necessary to know the part she plays in the allegory, to understand the beauty of the following stanza?

And eke that stranger knight amongst the rest
Was for like need enforc'd to disarray.
Tho when as vailed was her lofty crest,
Her golden locks that were in trammels gay
Upbounden, did themselves adown display,
And raught unto her heels like sunny beams
That in a cloud their light did long time stay;
Their vapour faded, shew their golden gleams,
And through the persant air shoot forth their azure streams.

Or is there any mystery in what is said of Belphoebe, that her hair was sprinkled with flowers and blossoms which had been entangled in it as she fled through the woods? Or is it necessary to have a more distinct idea of Proteus, than that which is given of him in his boat, with the frighted Florimel at his feet, while

the cold icicles from his rough beard
Dropped adown upon her snowy breast!

Or is it not a sufficient account of one of the seagods that pass by them, to say—

That was Arion crowned:—
So went he playing on the watery plain.

Or to take the Procession of the Passions that draw the coach of Pride, in which the figures of Idleness, of Gluttony, of Lechery, of Avarice, of Envy, and of Wrath speak, one should think, plain enough for themselves; such as this of Gluttony:

And by his side rode loathsome Gluttony,
Deformed creature, on a filthy swine;
His belly was up blown with luxury;
And eke with fatness swollen were his eyne;
And like a crane his neck was long and fine,
With which he swallowed up excessive feast,
For want whereof poor people oft did pine.
   In green vine leaves he was right fitly clad;
For other clothes he could not wear for heat:
And on his head an ivy garland had,
From under which fast trickled down the sweat:
Still as he rode, he somewhat still did eat.
And in his hand did bear a bouzing can,
Of which he supt so oft, that on his seat
His drunken corse he scarce upholden can;
In shape and size more like a monster than a man.

Or this of Lechery:

And next to him rode lustfull Lechery
Upon a bearded goat, whose rugged hair
And whaly eyes (the sign of jealousy)
Was like the person's self whom he did bear:
Who rough and black, and filthy did appear.
Unseemly man to please fair lady's eye:
Yet he of ladies oft was loved dear,
When fairer faces were bid standen by:
O! who does know the bent of woman's fantasy?
   In a green gown he clothed was full fair,
Which underneath did hide his filthiness;
And in his hand a burning heart he bare,
Full of vain follies and new fangleness;
For he was false and fraught with fickleness;
And learned had to love with secret looks;
And well could dance; and sing with ruefulness;
And fortunes tell; and read in loving books;
And thousand other ways to bait his fleshly hooks.
   Inconstant man that loved all he saw,
And lusted after all that he did love;
Ne would his looser life be tied to law;
But joyed weak women's hearts to tempt and prove,
If from their loyal loves he might them move.

This is pretty plain-spoken. Mr. Southey says of Spenser:

Yet not more sweet
Than pure was he, and not more pure than wise;
High priest of all the Muses' mysteries!

On the contrary, no one was more apt to pry into mysteries which do not strictly belong to the Muses.

Of the same kind with the Procession of the Passions, as little obscure, and still more beautiful, is the Mask of Cupid with his train of votaries:

> The first was Fancy, like a lovely boy
> Of rare aspect, and beauty without peer;
> His garment neither was of silk nor say,
> But painted plumes in goodly order dight,
> Like as the sun burnt Indians do array
> Their tawny bodies in their proudest plight:
> As those same plumes so seem'd he vain and light,
> That by his gait might easily appear;
> For still he far'd as dancing in delight,
> And in his hand a windy fan did bear
> That in the idle air he mov'd still here and there.

> And him beside march'd amorous Desire,
> Who seem'd of riper years than the other swain,
> Yet was that other swain this elder's sire,
> And gave him being, common to them twain:
> His garment was disguised very vain,
> And his embroidered bonnet sat awry;
> Twixt both his hands few sparks he close did strain,
> Which still he blew, and kindled busily,
> That soon they life conceiv'd and forth in flames did fly.

> Next after him went Doubt, who was yclad
> In a discolour'd coat of strange disguise,
> That at his back a broad capuccio had,
> And sleeves dependant *Albanese-wise*;
> He lookt askew with his mistrustful eyes,
> And nicely trod, as thorns lay in his way,
> Or that the floor to shrink he did avise;
> And on a broken reed he still did stay
> His feeble steps, which shrunk when hard thereon he lay.

> With him went Daunger, cloth'd in ragged weed,
> Made of bear's skin, that him more dreadful made;
> Yet his own face was dreadfull, ne did need
> Strange horror to deform his grisly shade;
> A net in th' one hand, and a rusty blade
> In th' other was; this Mischiefe, that Mishap;
> With th' one his foes he threat'ned to invade,
> With th' other he his friends meant to enwrap;
> For whom he could not kill he practiz'd to entrap.

> Next him was Fear, all arm'd from top to toe,
> Yet thought himselfe not safe enough thereby,
> But fear'd each shadow moving to and fro;
> And his own arms when glittering he did spy
> Or clashing heard, he fast away did fly,
> As ashes pale of hue, and winged-heel'd;
> And evermore on Daunger fixt his eye,
> 'Gainst whom he always bent a brazen shield,
> Which his right hand unarmed fearfully did wield.

> With him went Hope in rank, a handsome maid,
> Of chearfull look and lovely to behold;
> In silken samite she was light array'd,
> And her fair locks were woven up in gold;
> She always smil'd, and in her hand did hold
> An holy-water sprinkle dipt in dew,
> With which she sprinkled favours manifold
> On whom she list, and did great liking shew,
> Great liking unto many, but true love to few.

> Next after them, the winged God himself
> Came riding on a lion ravenous,
> Taught to obey the menage of that elfe
> That man and beast with power imperious
> Subdueth to his kingdom tyrannous:
> His blindfold eyes he bade awhile unbind,
> That his proud spoil of that same dolorous
> Fair dame he might behold in perfect kind;
> Which seen, he much rejoiced in his cruel mind.

> Of which full proud, himself uprearing high,
> He looked round about with stern disdain,
> And did survey his goodly company:
> And marshalling the evil-ordered train,
> With that the darts which his right hand did strain,
> Full dreadfully he shook, that all did quake,
> And clapt on high his colour'd winges twain,
> That all his many it afraid did make:
> Tho, blinding him again, his way he forth did take.

The description of Hope, in this series of historical portraits, is one of the most beautiful in Spenser: and the triumph of Cupid at the mischief he has made, is worthy of the malicious urchin deity. In reading these descriptions, one can hardly avoid being reminded of Rubens's allegorical pictures; but the account of Satyrane taming the lion's whelps and lugging the bear's cubs along in his arms while yet an infant, whom his mother so naturally advises to 'go seek some other playfellows', has even more of this high picturesque character. Nobody but Rubens could have painted the fancy of Spenser; and he could not have given the sentiment, the airy dream that hovers over it!

With all this, Spenser neither makes us laugh nor weep. The only jest in his poem is an allegorical play upon words, where he describes Malbecco as escaping in the herd of goats, 'by the help of his fayre horns on hight'. But he has been unjustly charged with a want of passion and of strength. He has both in an immense degree. He has not indeed the pathos of immediate action or suffering, which is more properly the dramatic; but he has all the pathos of sentiment and romance—all that belongs to distant objects of terror, and uncertain, imaginary distress. His strength, in like manner, is not strength of will or action, of bone and muscle, nor is it coarse and palpable—but it assumes a character of vastness and sublimity seen through the same visionary medium, and blended with the appalling associations of preternatural agency. We need only turn, in proof of this, to the Cave of Despair, or the Cave of Mammon, or to the account of the change of Malbecco into Jealousy. The following stanzas, in the description of the Cave of Mammon, the grisly house of Plutus, are unrivalled for the portentous massiness of the forms, the splendid chiaro-scuro, and shadowy horror.

> That house's form within was rude and strong,
> Like an huge cave hewn out of rocky clift,
> From whose rough vault the ragged breaches hung,
> Embossed with massy gold of glorious gift,
> And with rich metal loaded every rift,
> That heavy ruin they did seem to threat:
> And over them Arachne high did lift
> Her cunning web, and spread her subtle net,
> Enwrapped in foul smoke, and clouds more black than jet.

> Both roof and floor, and walls were all of gold,
> But overgrown with dust and old decay,
> And hid in darkness that none could behold

The hue thereof: for view of cheerful day
Did never in that house itself display,
But a faint shadow of uncertain light;
Such as a lamp whose life doth fade away;
Or as the moon clothed with cloudy night
Does shew to him that walks in fear and sad
   affright. . . .
    And over all sad Horror with grim hue
Did always soar, beating his iron wings;
And after him owls and night-ravens flew,
The hateful messengers of heavy things,
Of death and dolour telling sad tidings;
Whiles sad Celleno, sitting on a clift,
A song of bitter bale and sorrow sings,
That heart of flint asunder could have rift;
Which having ended, after him she flieth swift.

The Cave of Despair is described with equal gloominess and power of fancy; and the fine moral declamation of the owner of it, on the evils of life, almost makes one in love with death. In the story of Malbecco, who is haunted by jealousy, and in vain strives to run away from his own thoughts—

High over hill and over dale he flies—

the truth of human passion and the preternatural ending are equally striking,—It is not fair to compare Spenser with Shakespeare, in point of interest. A fairer comparison would be with *Comus*; and the result would not be unfavourable to Spenser. There is only one work of the same allegorical kind, which has more interest than Spenser (with scarcely less imagination): and that is the *Pilgrim's Progress*. The three first books of the *Faery Queen* are very superior to the three last. One would think that Pope, who used to ask if any one had ever read the *Faery Queen* through, had only dipped into these last. The only things in them equal to the former, are the account of Talus, the Iron Man, and the delightful episode of Pastorella.

    The language of Spenser is full, and copious, to overflowing: it is less pure and idiomatic than Chaucer's, and is enriched and adorned with phrases borrowed from the different languages of Europe, both ancient and modern. He was, probably, seduced into a certain licence of expression by the difficulty of filling up the moulds of his complicated rhymed stanza from the limited resources of his native language. This stanza, with alternate and repeatedly recurring rhymes, is borrowed from the Italians. It was peculiarly fitted to their language, which abounds in similar vowel terminations, and is as little adapted to ours, from the stubborn, unaccommodating resistance which the consonant endings of the northern languages make to this sort of endless sing-song.—Not that I would, on that account, part with the stanza of Spenser. We are, perhaps, indebted to this very necessity of finding out new forms of expression, and to the occasional faults to which it led, for a poetical language rich and varied and magnificent beyond all former, and almost all later example. His versification is, at once, the most smooth and the most sounding in the language. It is a labyrinth of sweet sounds, 'in many a winding bout of linked sweetness long drawn out'—that would cloy by their very sweetness, but that the ear is constantly relieved and enchanted by their continued variety of modulation—dwelling on the pauses of the action, or flowing on in a fuller tide of harmony with the movement of the sentiment. It has not the bold dramatic transitions of Shakespeare's blank verse, nor the high-raised tone of Milton's; but it is the perfection of melting harmony, dissolving the soul in pleasure, or holding it captive in the chains of suspense. Spenser was the poet of our waking dreams; and he has invented not only a language, but a music

of his own for them. The undulations are infinite, like those of the waves of the sea: but the effect is still the same, lulling the senses into a deep oblivion of the jarring noises of the world, from which we have no wish to be ever recalled.

LEIGH HUNT
From *The Wishing-Cap* (1833)
Leigh Hunt's Literary Criticism, ed. Houtchens
1956, pp. 446–56

I t is much to be wished (and we hereby wish it accordingly, and hope to see results from our good will) that readers who love poetry, and yet happen to be unacquainted with Spenser, should hasten to make themselves amends by getting the *Færie Queene*. If their love is of the right sort, they will rejoice in the new region thrown open to them, and wonder how they could have missed it so long. An admiration of Spenser is a test of poetical taste. Other poets may be preferred, and some few (such as Dante and Shakspeare) were greater men and profounder originals; but not to like Spenser is not to like poetry for its own sake—not to relish the beautiful and the luxurious, without the aid of other stimulants. All the poets have liked him. There has not been a more genuine favourite among them, a writer beloved more as a matter of course, or more imitated; and what is remarkable, he has been beloved by poets of all sorts, natural and artificial. To be poetical at all is to have a sympathy with him. There is a sonnet attributed of Shakspeare, in which the great dramatist says that Spenser is "dear" to him. It is of doubtful authenticity; but nobody doubts that Shakspeare must have relished him to the full. Milton avowedly regarded him as his master. Cowley was led to write verses by a copy of the *Færie Queene*, which used to lie in his mother's window. All the wits and poets of his own day, the Raleighs, Sydneys, Ben Jonsons, &c., reverenced him; and so did those of Charles the First and of Charles the Second— Dryden, in particular, who sometimes copied from him. Pope said he read him in advanced life, with as much pleasure as in youth; and Thomson eulogised him in the *Seasons*, and imitated him in his beautiful poem, the "Castle of Indolence." It would be easy to add to this list both great names and small. The most poetical poets of the last and present generation have all passionately admired him; and no stanza has been so popular as the magnificent one of his invention. Even Lord Byron wrote in it—the only poet on record who professed to have no regard for him, and whose regard was, in all probability, really less than he would have been willing to have it, at times when he spoke less under the influence of his humour. But this was the misfortune of the prose part of his life, and not the natural feeling of his poetry.

    The notion that Spenser's language is unintelligibly obsolete, vanishes on the slightest acquaintance. Ben Jonson said, that "in affecting the ancients, he wrote *no* language." Possibly the actual language of the *Færie Queene*, taken altogether, was never spoken. And the same may be said of Milton's. The English language itself, as now spoken, is a mixture of many others; and the languages of our more scholarly poets have been usually a sort of quintessence of this mixture: but they are not on that account the less intelligible; at all events not to educated readers. Spenser's was a kind of new architecture, of Gothic mould; and shedding a grace, on that very account, upon the peculiarity and remoteness of his fairy region. It is not that of passion, like Shakspeare's and Chaucer's; nor of wit and manners, like Pope's; nor of anything else which renders a common parlance essentially requisite. It is that of a fine, lazy, luxurious, far-off, majestic dream; and therefore may take all the licence of a dream, compatible with beauty and dignity. To an educated reader, Spenser very seldom, indeed, requires a glossary; there is one, however, always printed with him: it need not be often in request with any readers at all accustomed to books, or whose perceptions are of an order fit to read poetry. In fact, generally speaking, he is as easy to be comprehended, and puts his meaning as plainly on the surface, as in the first stanzas of his introduction:

> Lo! I the man whose Muse whilom did maske,
> As time her taught, in lowly shepherd's weeds;
> As now enforst, a far unfitter taske,
> For trumpets stern to change mine oaten reeds,
> And sing of knights and ladies gentle deeds;
> Whose praises have slept in silence long,
> Me, all too mean, the sacred muse areeds
> To blazon broad, amongst her learned throng:
> Fierce wars and faithful loves shall moralize my song.

Here is one word of Chaucer's (*whilom*) which was disused in the graver poetry of Spenser's days. Hundreds of his stanzas have no such old word; and if they had, who would require a better or newer style for a Gothic Romance? The word "moralize" was his own invention, and has been repeated by Pope—

> He stoop'd to truth, and moraliz'd his song.

The worst difficulties in the way of a relish of Spenser are his spelling and his diffuseness. With the rights of orthography, he certainly does take manifold and marvellous liberties; spelling, in fact, just as he pleases, with all the nonchalance of the ladies of his day; and even delighting to force his rhymes into visible harmony, where the audible harmony was sufficient; as in writing the word *sed* for *said*, in order to make it look severely of a cast with *red*; and *lam* for *lamb*, to rhyme with *dam*; carving out the very sound, as it were, with a penknife, to make it fit and tally in the nicest possible manner, and out of the sheer indulgence of his will and pleasure. And herein, we doubt not, lay the secret. Spenser pampered his imagination till it could bear no obstacles that by any possibility could be set aside. He sometimes goes so far as to coin new inflections, and consequently new words, on purpose to accommodate his rhyme, as in an instance which we shall notice presently.

The stanza invented by the poet for his long work is a remarkable and magnificent instance of this enjoyment of his will, and contempt of obstacles. It compelled him to repeat the rhyme upon one word three times, and upon another *four*. This, in English, is very difficult, and has led him, says Warton, "into many absurdities, the most striking and obvious of which are the following:

"I. It obliged him to dilate the thing to be expressed, however unimportant, with trifling and tedious circumlocution; viz. F. Q. ii. ii. 44.

> Now hath fair Phœbe, with her silver face,
> Thrice seen the shadows of this neather world,
> Sith last I left that honourable place,
> In which her roiall presence is enroll'd."

That is, it is three months since I left her palace.

"II. It necessitated him, when matter failed towards the close of a stanza, to run into a ridiculous redundancy of words; as in F. Q. ii. ix. 33.

> In which was nothing *pourtrahed nor wrought,*
> *Nor wrought nor pourtrahed,* but easy to be thought.

"III. It forced him, that he might make out his complement of rhymes, to introduce a puerile idea; as in F. Q. ii. ix. 45.

> Nor that proud towre of Troy, though richly *guilt."*

Being here laid under the compulsion of producing a consonant word to *spilt* and *built*, which are preceding rhymes, he has mechanically given us an image, at once little and improper.

"To the difficulty of a stanza so injudiciously chosen," continues Warton, "I think, we may properly impute the great number of his ellipses; and it may be easily conceived, how that constraint which occasioned superfluity, should, at the same time, be the cause of omission.

"Notwithstanding these inconveniencies flow from Spenser's measure, it must yet be owned," says the critic, "that some advantages arise from it; and we may venture to affirm, that the fulness and significancy of Spenser's descriptions, are often owing to the prolixity of his stanza, and the multitude of his rhymes. The discerning reader is desired to consider the following stanza as an instance of what is here advanced."

Warton here quotes the passage in which Sir Guyon binds Furor; and he then observes that in the subsequent stanza there are some images which perhaps were produced by a multiplicity of rhymes. F. Q. iv. v. 45.

> He all that night, that too long night, did pass;
> And now the daye, out of the ocean mayne,
> Began to peep above this earthly mass,
> With pearly due sprinkling the morning grass:
> Then up he rose, like heavy lump of lead,
> That in his face, as in a looking-glass,
> The signs of anguish one might plainly read.

This is agreeable and ingenious criticism, like all Warton's; but his general deductions are not so good as his particular instances. We cannot think Spenser's stanza is injudiciously chosen, or that he would not have been quite as luxuriant and overflowing in any other. He would only have written two stanzas for one, or twenty couplets instead of ten. He would not have been at times so weak, but probably he would have been still more diffuse. Any constrained form of verse is a restriction. It was the exuberance of Spenser's genius that made him invent the nine-lined stanza; and its popularity shows how nobly he managed it, and how suited it is to the luxuries of description and contemplation. Nor must all his weakness and diffusion be regarded in an ill light, or as being nothing but what they seem. Without the occasional superflux, we should not have been amazed with the perpetual wealth. Spenser, observe, is not to read for his story, or for any other kind of active interest, except when it pleases him to rouse himself to battle, or relate to us some astonishing marvel; at which times nobody can be more energetic than he, though it still pleases him to be stately and prince-like in his activity. He heaps his very blows with a sort of luxury, and dresses the fight with a painter's riches. As for story, we confess that with all our admiration of him, we never took any interest in his narratives; nor should we have cared to read him continuously, except that his enchantment tolls us on with the constant expectation of new and unexpected beauties. Even when we do not meet with anything very striking, still there is beauty never failing, beauty even in his languor, or, if you please, his sleep. Dryden has somewhat daringly remarked, that Milton now and then, for fifty and sixty lines together, "runs upon a flat." There are flats in Spenser, but they are only intervals between delicious places, themselves far from destitute of beauty; and the "knowing reader," to use a phrase of Milton's, "will not be unwilling to go through them, both for the sake of the neighbouring country and of their own pleasantness; just as a man of any imagination is satisfied in strolling along meadows, that seem poor enough in common eyes, but which still have grass, and trees, and wild flowers, and proofs of the same creative power that made the mountains. Spenser's world is a world to live and repose in, not to make a bustle, like others. You do not go to him for excitement before action, but for rest after it; or if you do go to him for excitement, it is for the excitement compatible with repose,—for a stimulus to the imagination, and a help to discern the riches lying about you."

> He reigns in the air from the earth to highest sky,
> He feeds on flowers, and weeds of glorious feature;
> Now this, now that, he tasteth tenderly.

An *unknowing* reader may pick a weed out of him if he chooses, and hold it up in disdain, and say, "Behold a sample of Spenser!" He might say the same of a dock-leaf in one of Titian's pictures, or of nature itself, who has given us weeds enough—the unknowing reader among them; and a great poet might shew even *him* up as something curious.

The modesty of a grateful discernment reasonably allows a fine writer to have whims and self-indulgences, that would be intolerable in one who did nothing for us. Jenkins apart—and whispering it in confidence to better readers—we own that we sometimes take the liberty of amusing ourselves at the expense of this great poet's vagaries, laughing at his superfluous rhymes and verses, and making parodies on him out of sheer love and regard, as our betters have done before us. But why do we allow ourselves to do this? Because he himself has condescended to invite us, by the pleasant extravagancies of his will, and because he can afford to let us take the liberty.

Thus, when he tells the story of Lear, after Shakspeare, and makes a dry chronicle of it without any pathos; or that of Canacé, after Chaucer, and turns it into a quaint mosaic of names, playing with his words; or gives us a sort of mathematical puzzle with a triangle; we laugh to see the mistaken humour he is in, and the solemn superfluity of his mode of impressing a poor conceit upon us: his variety is uniformity, and his "differences discreet"; but our laughter is as full of secret respect as if we beheld some demi-god condescending to mimic some piece of human state.

> Amongst these knights there were three brethren
>   bold,
>   Three bolder brethren never were yborn,
> Born of one mother in one happy mould,
>   Born at one burden, in one happy morne;
> Thrice happy mother, and thrice happy morn,
>   That bore three such, three such not to be
>   found!
> Her name was Agapè, whose children werne
>   All three as one; the first hight Priamond,
>   The second Dyamond, the youngest
>   Triamond.

The head grows dizzy with unravelling these "trinal triplicities," with bearing in mind the sympathetic discrepancies of these first, second, and third mob, as Shakspeare might have called them—these gentlemen with the singular, dual, and plural names. But he has not done yet—

> These three did love each other dearly well,
>   And with so firm affection were allyde,
> As if but one soule in them all did dwell,
>   Which did her powre into three parts divide;
>   Like three fair branches, budding far and
>   wide,
> That from one root derived their vital sap;

> And, like that root that doth her life divide,
> Their mother was; and had full blessed hap
> These three so noble babes to bring forth *at one clap*.

At one clap! "That is," quoth a grave commentator, "at once. Latin, *uno ictu*."

And another adds, "So Shakspeare, in *King Lear*, where the king's knights are discharged, A. 1, S. iv., "What! fifty of my followers at a clap! within a fortnight!"

This is one of the numerous commentating mistakes of a parallelism in letter for a parallelism in spirit and propriety. A familiar phrase, which is commendable in a moment of passion and disdain, becomes another thing in the record of a domestic event. To be sure, the phrase might have been less familiar in those days than in ours; but we are not aware of its being used in a grave way by any other writer. What renders the choice of such a rhyme the more remarkable in this instance is, that there was another word (*lap*) out of which some unobjectionable and affecting thought might have been applied by the grace and tenderness of Spenser's genius. But this true poet had always a deep and serious faith in the scenes and feelings which imagination set before him, and so far he wrote in passion upon whatever subject; and a passionate faith is grave, and does not easily take its impulses, and its mode of uttering them, for things too familiar. It is an instinctive perception to this effect, which mingles with our levity, when we venture to smile at the self-committals of a master in his art.

Spenser, it must be confessed, knows his power, and sometimes taxes our gravity to the utmost. Some of his wilful spellings involuntarily provoke a ludicrous dwelling upon them in the reader's mind; as in the following couplet:

> And of her own foule entrails makes her meat,
>   Meat fit for such a monster's monstrous dyEAT.

In reading this line, one almost sees Munden again before us, mouthing an astonishment with a visage full of grimace, and making a solemn intensity out of every syllable. The childlike propensity of the poet to make as much as he can of his wonderments (so fine in its proper place), renders this intrusion of the mock-heroical the more unavoidable.

Some of Spenser's forced rhymes would have, in modern ears, a vulgar, kitchen-like sound, if we did not know that he was one of the most unvulgar of men. Thus, in order to rhyme with *dart*, he turns the word per*vert* into per*vart*:

> Therein was writ how often thundering Jove
>   Had felt the point of his heart-piercing dart,
> And, leaving heaven's kingdom, here did rove
>   In strange disguise, to slake his scalding smart;
>   Now, like a ram, fair Hellè to per*vart*,
>   &c.

Thus, to accommodate the word *barr'd*, he writes the word *transferr'd transfarr'd*, though there is an intermediate rhyme in his stanza (*ward*) which is bound to suffer by it in a manner ludicrous to modern ears. As this last instance is in the close of the stanza following the one containing the previous extract, we will complete that one, and give the other entire, in order that the reader may have a taste of the poet's great beauties and little faults at once. He is speaking of Jupiter's transformations for love:

> Now like a ram fair Hellè to pervart;
> Now like a bull Europé to *withdraw*.

(How beautiful for the occasion is this word *withdraw*, and how well the softness and lowness of the sound comes in after the more glaring rhymes upon *dart*!)

> Ah! how the fearful lady's tender hart
> Did lively seem to tremble, when she saw

The huge seas under her, t'obey her servant's law!
Soon after that, into a golden showre,
Himself he changed, fair Danae to view;
And through the roof of her strong brazen towre,
Did raine into her lap an honey dew;
The whiles her foolish garde, that little knew
Of such deceipt, kept th' iron door fast barr'd,
And watch'd that none should enter nor issew:
Vain was the watch, and bootless all the ward,
Whenas the god to golden hew himself *transfarr'd.*

That exquisite line,

Did raine into her lap an honey dew,

in which the very gold, by whose means the god comes
through the roof of Danae's prison, is made nectareous in its
passage, and melting with the sweets of love, will remind the
traveller, who has had the luck to see it, of Titian's famous
picture on the same subject, where the bribing shower takes a
similar aspect. It has been the fashion, of late years, to draw an
extreme distinction between poetry and painting, as if they
were not only different in their means, but almost contradictory in feeling. Imagination, however, fuses the arts together,
as it does objects. Titian is often as true a poet as Spenser is a
painter.

To finish our account of these spots in a sun, the most
exquisite instance of Spenser's wilful rhyming is in the close of
the following stanza; and he must needs take a liberty as he
goes with the great name of Aacides, here called Aecidee. Why
he should have said, too, Aecidee instead of Aacidee, it is
impossible to conjecture, unless he did it to show how excessively he would have his will while he was about it, and in
order to confound, with a double perversity, the faculties of
those who would object to a single one. Yet observe what a fine
lusty picture he contrives to give us, by the way, of Jupiter
returning amorous from a feast! He is speaking of the Graces:

They are the daughters of sky-ruling Jove,
By him begot of fair Eurynome,
The Ocean's daughter, in this pleasant grove,
As he this way coming from fearful glee
Of Thetis' wedding with Aecidee.
In summer's shade, himself here rested weary.
The first of them hight mild Euphrosyne,
Next fair Aglaia, last Thalia merry;
Sweet goddesses all three, which we in mirth do
cherry.

"*Cherry* for *cherish*," quietly observes a grave commentator. Yes; a word which has no existence, but for the sake of a
rhyme!

But these licences are the result of exuberance, not of
poverty; the wantonness of sheer wealth, indolence, and enjoyment. They need not have been taken in these very places as
we have shown in one instance. But Spenser, having written
hap and *sap*, would find a rhyme for it at hand, at whatever
price, rather than baulk his humour; and so, in the present
instance, he had written *weary* and *merry*, and would not write
otherwise: he therefore takes the word "cherish" and *pares* it to
fit in.

Divine Poet! sitting in the midst of thy endless treasures,
thy luxurious landscapes, and thy descending gods! Fantastic as
Nature's self, in the growth of some few flowers of thy creation;
beauteous and perfect as herself, the rest. We have found consolation in thee at times when almost everything pained us,
and when we could find it in no other poet of thy nation,
because the world into which they took us was not equally
remote. Shakspeare, with all our love and reverence for him,
has still kept us among men and their cares, even in his en-

chanted island, and his summer-night dreams. Milton will not
let us breathe the air of his paradise, undistressed by the haunt-
ings of theology, and the shadows of what was to come. Chaucer has left his only romance unfinished, and will not relieve
us of his emotion but by mirth, and that not always such as we
can be merry with, or as he would have liked himself had he
fallen upon times worthier of him. But in coming to thee, we
have travelled in one instant thousands of miles, and to a
quarter in which no sin of reality is heard. Even its warfare is
that of poetical children; of demi-gods playing at romance.
Around us are the woods; in our distant ear is the sea; the
glimmering forms that we behold are those of nymph and
deities; or a hermit makes the loneliness more lonely; or we
hear a horn blow, and the ground trembling with the coming of
a giant; and our boyhood is again existing, full of belief, though
its hair be turning grey; because thou, a man, hast re-written its
books, and proved the surpassing riches of its wisdom.

JAMES RUSSELL LOWELL
"Spenser" (1875)
Among My Books
1876, pp. 125–200

Chaucer had been in his grave one hundred and fifty years
ere England had secreted choice material enough for the
making of another great poet. The nature of men living together in societies, as of the individual man, seems to have its
periodic ebbs and floods, its oscillations between the ideal and
the matter-of-fact, so that the doubtful boundary line of shore
between them is in one generation a hard sandy actuality
strewn only with such remembrances of beauty as a dead sea-
moss here and there, and in the next is whelmed with those
lacelike curves of ever-gaining, ever-receding foam, and that
dance of joyous spray which for a moment catches and holds
the sunshine.

From the two centuries between 1400 and 1600 the indefatigable Ritson in his *Bibliographia Poetica* has made us a
catalogue of some six hundred English poets, or, more properly, verse-makers. Ninety-nine in a hundred of them are mere
names, most of them no more than shadows of names, some of
them mere initials. Nor can it be said of them that their works
have perished because they were written in an obsolete dialect;
for it is the poem that keeps the language alive, and not the
language that buoys up the poem. The revival of letters, as it is
called, was at first the revival of *ancient* letters, which, while it
made men pedants, could do very little toward making them
poets, much less toward making them original writers. There
was nothing left of the freshness, vivacity, invention, and careless faith in the present which make many of the productions of
the Norman Trouvères delightful reading even now. The whole
of Europe during the fifteenth century produced no book
which has continued readable, or has become in any sense of
the word a classic. I do not mean that that century has left us
no illustrious names, that it was not enriched with some august
intellects who kept alive the apostolic succession of thought
and speculation, who passed along the still unextinguished
torch of intelligence, the *lampada vitæ*, to those who came
after them. But a classic is properly a book which maintains
itself by virtue of that happy coalescence of matter and style,
that innate and exquisite sympathy between the thought that
gives life and the form that consents to every mood of grace and
dignity, which can be simple without being vulgar, elevated
without being distant, and which is something neither ancient
nor modern, always new and incapable of growing old. It is not

his Latin which makes Horace cosmopolitan, nor can Béranger's French prevent his becoming so. No hedge of language however thorny, no dragon-coil of centuries, will keep men away from these true apples of the Hesperides if once they have caught sight or scent of them. If poems die, it is because there was never true life in them, that is, that true poetic vitality which no depth of thought, no airiness of fancy, no sincerity of feeling, can singly communicate, but which leaps throbbing at touch of that shaping faculty the imagination. Take Aristotle's ethics, the scholastic philosophy, the theology of Aquinas, the Ptolemaic system of astronomy, the small politics of a provincial city of the Middle Ages, mix in at will Grecian, Roman, and Christian mythology, and tell me what chance there is to make an immortal poem of such an incongruous mixture. Can these dry bones live? Yes, Dante can create such a soul under these ribs of death that one hundred and fifty editions of his poem shall be called for in these last sixty years, the first half of the sixth century since his death. Accordingly I am apt to believe that the complaints one sometimes hears of the neglect of our older literature are the regrets of archæologists rather than of critics. One does not need to advertise the squirrels where the nut-trees are, nor could any amount of lecturing persuade them to spend their teeth on a hollow nut.

On the whole, the Scottish poetry of the fifteenth century has more meat in it than the English, but this is to say very little. Where it is meant to be serious and lofty it falls into the same vices of unreality and allegory which were the fashion of the day, and which there are some patriots so fearfully and wonderfully made as to relish. Stripped of the archaisms (that turn every *y* to a meaningless *z*, spell which *quhilk*, shake *schaik*, bugle *bowgill*, powder *puldir*, and will not let us simply whistle till we have puckered our mouths to *quhissill*) in which the Scottish antiquaries love to keep it disguised,—as if it were nearer to poetry the further it got from all human recognition and sympathy,—stripped of these, there is little to distinguish it from the contemporary verse-mongering south of the Tweed. Their compositions are generally as stiff and artificial as a trellis, in striking contrast with the popular ballad-poetry of Scotland (some of which possibly falls within this period, though most of it is later), which clambers, lawlessly if you will, but at least freely and simply, twining the bare stem of old tradition with graceful sentiment and lively natural sympathies. I find a few sweet and flowing verses in Dunbar's "Merle and Nightingale,"—indeed one whole stanza that has always seemed exquisite to me. It is this:—

> Ne'er sweeter noise was heard by living man
> Than made this merry, gentle nightingale.
> Her sound went with the river as it ran
> Out through the fresh and flourished lusty vale;
> O merle, quoth she, O fool, leave off thy tale,
> For in thy song good teaching there is none,
> For both are lost,—the time and the travail
> Of every love but upon God alone.

But except this lucky poem, I find little else in the serious verses of Dunbar that does not seem to me tedious and pedantic. I dare say a few more lines might be found scattered here and there, but I hold it a sheer waste of time to hunt after these thin needles of wit buried in unwieldy haystacks of verse. If that be genius, the less we have of it the better. His *Dance of the Seven Deadly Sins*, over which the excellent Lord Hailes went into raptures, is wanting in everything but coarseness; and if his invention dance at all, it is like a galley-slave in chains under the lash. It would be well for us if the sins themselves were indeed such wretched bugaboos as he has painted for us. What

he means for humor is but the dullest vulgarity; his satire would be Billingsgate if it could, and, failing, becomes a mere offence in the nostrils, for it takes a great deal of salt to keep scurrility sweet. Mr. Sibbald, in his *Chronicle of Scottish Poetry*, has admiringly preserved more than enough of it, and seems to find a sort of national savor therein, such as delights his countrymen in a *haggis*, or the German in his *sauer-kraut*. The uninitiated foreigner puts his handkerchief to his nose, wonders, and gets out of the way as soon as he civilly can. Barbour's *Brus*, if not precisely a poem, has passages whose simple tenderness raises them to that level. That on Freedom is familiar.[1] But its highest merit is the natural and unstrained tone of manly courage in it, the easy and familiar way in which Barbour always takes chivalrous conduct as a matter of course, as if heroism were the least you could ask of any man. I modernize a few verses to show what I mean. When the King of England turns to fly from the battle of Bannockburn (and Barbour with his usual generosity tells us he has heard that Sir Aymer de Valence led him away by the bridle-rein against his will), Sir Giles d'Argente

> Saw the king thus and his menie
> Shape them to flee so speedily,
> He came right to the king in hy [hastily]
> And said, 'Sir, since that is so
> That ye thus gate your gate will go,
> Have ye good-day, for back will I:
> Yet never fled I certainly,
> And I choose here to bide and die
> Than to live shamefully and fly.'

The *Brus* is in many ways the best rhymed chronicle ever written. It is national in a high and generous way, but I confess I have little faith in that quality in literature which is commonly called nationality,—a kind of praise seldom given where there is anything better to be said. Literature that loses its meaning, or the best part of it, when it gets beyond sight of the parish steeple, is not what I understand by literature. To tell you when you cannot fully taste a book that it is because it is so thoroughly national, is to condemn the book. To say of a poem is even worse, for it is to say that what should be true of the whole compass of human nature is true only to some north-and-by-east-half-east point of it. I can understand the nationality of Firdusi when, looking sadly back to the former glories of his country, he tells us that "the nightingale still sings old Persian"; I can understand the nationality of Burns when he turns his plough aside to spare the rough burr thistle, and hopes he may write a song or two for dear auld Scotia's sake. That sort of nationality belongs to a country of which we are all citizens,—that country of the heart which has no boundaries laid down on the map. All great poetry must smack of the soil, for it must be rooted in it, must suck life and substance from it, but it must do so with the aspiring instinct of the pine that climbs forever toward diviner air, and not in the grovelling fashion of the potato. Any verse that makes you and me foreigners is not only not great poetry, but no poetry at all. Dunbar's works were disinterred and edited some thirty years ago by Mr. Laing, and whoso is national enough to like thistles may browse there to his heart's content. I am inclined for other pasture, having long ago satisfied myself by a good deal of dogged reading that every generation is sure of its own share of bores without borrowing from the past.

A little later came Gawain Douglas, whose translation of the Æneid is linguistically valuable, and whose introductions to the seventh and twelfth books—the one describing winter and the other May—have been safely praised, they are so hard to read. There is certainly some poetic feeling in them, and the welcome to the sun comes as near enthusiasm as is possible for a ploughman, with a good steady yoke of oxen, who lays over one furrow of verse, and then turns about to lay the next as cleverly alongside it as he can. But it is a wrong done to good taste to hold up this *item* kind of description any longer as deserving any other credit than that of a good memory. It is a mere bill of parcels, a *post-mortem* inventory of nature, where imagination is not merely not called for, but would be out of place. Why, a recipe in the cookery-book is as much like a good dinner as this kind of stuff is like true word-painting. The poet with a real eye in his head does not give us everything, but only the *best* of everything. He selects, he combines, or else gives what is characteristic only; while the false style of which I have been speaking seems to be as glad to get a pack of impertinences on its shoulders as Christian in the Pilgrim's Progress was to be rid of his. One strong verse that can hold itself upright (as the French critic Rivarol said of Dante) with the bare help of the substantive and verb, is worth acres of this dead cord-wood piled stick on stick, a boundless continuity of dryness. I would rather have written that half-stanza of Longfellow's, in the *Wreck of the Hesperus*, of the "billow that swept her crew like icicles from her deck," than all Gawain Douglas's tedious enumeration of meteorological phenomena put together. A real landscape is never tiresome; it never presents itself to us as a disjointed succession of isolated particulars; we take it in with one sweep of the eye,—its light, its shadow, its melting gradations of distance: we do not say it is this, it is that, and the other; and we may be sure that if a description in poetry is tiresome there is a grievous mistake somewhere. All the pictorial adjectives in the dictionary will not bring it a hair's-breadth nearer to truth and nature. The fact is that what we see is in the mind to a greater degree than we are commonly aware. As Coleridge says,

> O lady, we receive but what we give,
> And in our life alone doth Nature live!

I have made the unfortunate Dunbar the text for a diatribe on the subject of descriptive poetry, because I find that this old ghost is not laid yet, but comes back like a vampire to suck the life out of a true enjoyment of poetry,—and the medicine by which vampires were cured was to unbury them, drive a stake through them, and get them under ground again with all despatch. The first duty of the Muse is to be delightful, and it is an injury done to all of us when we are put in the wrong by a kind of statutory affirmation on the part of the critics of something to which our judgment will not consent, and from which our taste revolts. A collection of poets is commonly made up, nine parts in ten, of this perfunctory verse-making, and I never look at one without regretting that we have lost that excellent Latin phrase, *Corpus poetarum*. In fancy I always read it on the backs of the volumes,—a *body* of poets, indeed, with scarce one soul to a hundred of them.

One genuine English poet illustrated the early years of the sixteenth century,—John Skelton. He had vivacity, fancy, humor, and originality. Gleams of the truest poetical sensibility alternate in him with an almost brutal coarseness. He is truly Rabelaisian before Rabelais. But there is a freedom and hilarity in much of his writing that gives it a singular attraction. A breath of cheerfulness runs along the slender stream of his verse, under which it seems to ripple and crinkle, catching and casting back the sunshine like a stream blown on by clear western winds.

But Skelton was an exceptional blossom of autumn. A long and dreary winter follows. Surrey, who brought back with him from Italy the blank-verse not long before introduced by

Trissino, is to some extent another exception. He had the sentiment of nature and unhackneyed feeling, but he has no mastery of verse, nor any elegance of diction. We have Gascoyne, Surrey, Wyatt, stiff, pedantic, artificial, systematic as a country cemetery, and, worst of all, the whole time desperately in love. Every verse is as flat, thin, and regular as a lath, and their poems are nothing more than bundles of such tied trimly together. They are said to have refined our language. Let us devoutly hope they did, for it would be pleasant to be grateful to them for something. But I fear it was not so, for only genius can do that; and Sternhold and Hopkins are inspired men in comparison with them. For Sternhold was at least the author of two noble stanzas:

> The Lord descended from above
>   And bowed the heavens high,
> And underneath his feet he cast
>   The darkness of the sky;
> On cherubs and on cherubims
>   Full royally he rode,
> And on the wings of all the winds
>   Came flying all abroad.

But Gascoyne and the rest did nothing more than put the worst school of Italian love poetry into an awkward English dress. The Italian proverb says, "Inglese italianizzato, Diavolo incarnato," that an Englishman Italianized is the very devil incarnate, and one feels the truth of it here. The very titles of their poems set one yawning, and their wit is the cause of the dulness that is in other men. "The lover, deceived by his love, repenteth him of the true love he bare her." As thus:

> Where I sought heaven there found I hap;
>   From danger unto death,
> Much like the mouse that treads the trap
>   In hope to find her food,
> And bites the bread that stops her breath,—
>   So in like case I stood.

"The lover, accusing his love for her unfaithfulness, proposeth to live in liberty." He says:

> But I am like the beaten fowl
>   That from the net escaped,
> And thou art like the ravening owl
>   That all the night hath waked.

And yet at the very time these men were writing there were simple ballad-writers who could have set them an example of simplicity, force, and grandeur. Compare the futile efforts of these poetasters to kindle themselves by a painted flame, and to be pathetic over the lay figure of a mistress, with the wild vigor and almost fierce sincerity of the "Twa Corbies":

> As I was walking all alone
> I heard twa corbies making a moan.
> The one unto the other did say,
> Where shall we gang dine to-day?
> In beyond that old turf dyke
> I wot there lies a new-slain knight;
> And naebody kens that he lies there
> But his hawk and his hound and his lady fair.
> His hound is to the hunting gone,
> His hawk to fetch the wild fowl home,
> His lady has ta'en another mate,
> So we may make our dinner sweet.
> O'er his white bones as they lie bare
> The wind shall blow forevermair.

There was a lesson in rhetoric for our worthy friends, could they have understood it. But they were as much afraid of an attack of nature as of the plague.

Such was the poetical inheritance of style and diction into which Spenser was born, and which he did more than any one else to redeem from the leaden gripe of vulgar and pedantic conceit. Sir Philip Sidney, born the year after him, with a keener critical instinct, and a taste earlier emancipated than his own, would have been, had he lived longer, perhaps even more directly influential in educating the taste and refining the vocabulary of his contemporaries and immediate successors. The better of his pastoral poems in the *Arcadia* are, in my judgment, more simple, natural, and, above all, more pathetic than those of Spenser, who sometimes strains the shepherd's pipe with a blast that would better suit the trumpet. Sidney had the good sense to feel that it was unsophisticated sentiment rather than rusticity of phrase that befitted such themes.[2] He recognized the distinction between simplicity and vulgarity, which Wordsworth was so long in finding out, and seems to have divined the fact that there is but one kind of English that is always appropriate and never obsolete, namely, the very best.[3] With the single exception of Thomas Campion, his experiments in adapting classical metres to English verse are more successful than those of his contemporaries. Some of his elegiacs are not ungrateful to the ear, and it can hardly be doubted that Coleridge borrowed from his eclogue of Strephon and Klaius the pleasing movement of his own *Catullian Hendecasyllabics.* Spenser, perhaps out of deference to Sidney, also tried his hand at English hexameters, the introduction of which was claimed by his friend Gabriel Harvey, who thereby assured to himself an immortality of grateful remembrance. But the result was a series of jolts and jars, proving that the language had run off the track. He seems to have been half conscious of it himself, and there is a gleam of mischief in what he writes to Harvey: "I like your late English hexameter so exceedingly well that I also enure my pen sometime in that kind, which I find indeed, as I have often heard you defend in word, neither so hard nor so harsh but that it will easily yield itself to our mother-tongue. For the only or chiefest hardness, which seemeth, is in the accent, which sometime gapeth, and, as it were, yawneth ill-favoredly, coming short of that it should, and sometime exceeding the measure of the number, as in *Carpenter;* the middle syllable being used short in speech, when it shall be read long in verse, seemeth like a lame gosling that draweth one leg after her; and *Heaven* being used short as one syllable, when it is in verse stretched out with a diastole, is like a lame dog that holds up one leg."[4] It is almost inconceivable that Spenser's hexameters should have been written by the man who was so soon to teach his native language how to soar and sing, and to give a fuller sail to English verse.

One of the most striking facts in our literary history is the pre-eminence at once so frankly and unanimously conceded to Spenser by his contemporaries. At first, it is true he had not many rivals. Before the *Faery Queen* two long poems were printed and popular,—the *Mirror for Magistrates* and Warner's *Albion's England,*—and not long after it came the *Polyolbion* of Drayton and the *Civil Wars* of Daniel. This was the period of the saurians in English poetry, interminable poems, book after book and canto after canto, like far-stretching *vertebræ,* that at first sight would seem to have rendered earth unfit for the habitation of man. They most of them sleep well now, as once they made their readers sleep, and their huge remains lie embedded in the deep morasses of Chambers and Anderson. We wonder at the length of face and general atrabilious look that mark the portraits of the men of that generation, but it is no marvel when even their relaxations were such downright hard work. Fathers when their day on earth was up must have folded down the leaf and left the task to be finished by their

sons,—a dreary inheritance. Yet both Drayton and Daniel are fine poets, though both of them in their most elaborate works made shipwreck of their genius on the shoal of a bad subject. Neither of them could make poetry coalesce with gazetteering or chronicle-making. It was like trying to put a declaration of love into the forms of a declaration in trover. The *Polyolbion* is nothing less than a versified gazetteer of England and Wales,— fortunately Scotland was not yet annexed, or the poem would have been even longer, and already it is the plesiosaurus of verse. Mountains, rivers, and even marshes are personified, to narrate historical episodes, or to give us geographical lectures. There are two fine verses in the seventh book, where, speaking of the cutting down some noble woods, he says,

> Their trunks like aged folk now bare and naked stand,
> As for revenge to heaven each held a withered hand;

and there is a passage about the sea in the twentieth book that comes near being fine; but the far greater part is mere joiner-work. Consider the life of man, that we flee away as a shadow, that our days are as a post, and then think whether we can afford to honor such a draft upon our time as is implied in these thirty books all in alexandrines! Even the laborious Selden, who wrote annotations on it, sometimes more entertaining than the text, gave out at the end of the eighteenth book. Yet Drayton could write well, and had an agreeable lightsomeness of fancy, as his "Nymphidia" proves. His poem "To the Cambro-Britons on their Harp" is full of vigor; it runs, it leaps, clashing its verses like swords upon bucklers, and moves the pulse to a charge.

Daniel was in all respects a man of finer mould. He did indeed refine our tongue, and deserved the praise his contemporaries concur in giving him of being "well-languaged."[5] Writing two hundred and fifty years ago, he stands in no need of a glossary, and I have noted scarce a dozen words, and not more turns of phrase, in his works, that have become obsolete. This certainly indicates both remarkable taste and equally remarkable judgment. There is an equable dignity in his thought and sentiment such as we rarely meet. His best poems always remind me of a table-land, where, because all is so level, we are apt to forget on how lofty a plane we are standing. I think his "Musophilus" the best poem of its kind in the language. The reflections are natural, the expression condensed, the thought weighty, and the language worthy of it. But he also wasted himself on an historical poem, in which the characters were incapable of that remoteness from ordinary associations which is essential to the ideal. Not that we can escape into the ideal by *merely* emigrating into the past or the unfamiliar. As in the German legend the little black Kobold of prose that haunts us in the present will seat himself on the first load of furniture when we undertake our flitting, if the magician be not there to exorcise him. No man can jump off his own shadow, nor, for that matter, off his own age, and it is very likely that Daniel had only the thinking and languaging parts of a poet's outfit, without the higher creative gift which alone can endow his conceptions with enduring life and with an interest which transcends the parish limits of his generation. In the prologue to his *Masque at Court* he has unconsciously defined his own poetry:

> Wherein no wild, no rude, no antic sport,
> But tender passions, motions soft and grave,
> The still spectator must expect to have.

And indeed his verse does not snatch you away from ordinary associations and hurry you along with it as is the wont of the higher kinds of poetry, but leaves you, as it were, upon the bank watching the peaceful current and lulled by its somewhat monotonous murmur. His best-known poem, blunderingly misprinted in all the collections, is that addressed to the Countess of Cumberland. It is an amplification of Horace's *Integer Vitæ*, and when we compare it with the original we miss the point, the compactness, and above all the urbane tone of the original. It is very fine English, but it is the English of diplomacy somehow, and is never downright this or that, but always has the honor to be so or so, with sentiments of the highest consideration. Yet the praise of *well-languaged*, since it implies that good writing then as now demanded choice and forethought, is not without interest for those who would classify the elements of a style that will wear and hold its colors well. His diction, if wanting in the more hardy evidences of muscle, has a suppleness and spring that give proof of training and endurance. His *Defence of Rhyme*, written in prose (a more difficult test than verse), has a passionate eloquence that reminds one of Burke, and is more light-armed and modern than the prose of Milton fifty years later. For us Occidentals he has a kindly prophetic word:

> And who in time knows whither we may vent
> The treasure of our tongue? to what strange shores
> The gain of our best glory may be sent
> To enrich unknowing nations with our stores?
> What worlds in the yet unformed Occident
> May come refined with accents that are ours?

During the period when Spenser was getting his artistic training a great change was going on in our mother-tongue, and the language of literature was disengaging itself more and more from that of ordinary talk. The poets of Italy, Spain, and France began to rain influence and to modify and refine not only style but vocabulary. Men were discovering new worlds in more senses than one, and the visionary finger of expectation still pointed forward. There was, as we learn from contemporary pamphlets, very much the same demand for a national literature that we have heard in America. This demand was nobly answered in the next generation. But no man contributed so much to the transformation of style and language as Spenser; for not only did he deliberately endeavor at reform, but by the charm of his diction, the novel harmonies of his verse, his ideal method of treatment, and the splendor of his fancy, he made the new manner popular and fruitful. We can trace in Spenser's poems the gradual growth of his taste through experiment and failure to that assured self-confidence which indicates that he had at length found out the true bent of his genius,—that happiest of discoveries (and not so easy as it might seem) which puts a man in undisturbed possession of his own individuality. Before his time the boundary between poetry and prose had not been clearly defined. His great merit lies not only in the ideal treatment with which he glorified common things and gilded them with a ray of enthusiasm, but far more in the ideal point of view which he first revealed to his countrymen. He at first sought for that remoteness, which is implied in an escape from the realism of daily life, in the pastoral,—a kind of writing which, oddly enough, from its original intention as a protest in favor of naturalness, and of human as opposed to heroic sentiments, had degenerated into the most artificial of abstractions. But he was soon convinced of his error, and was not long in choosing between an unreality which pretended to be real and those everlasting realities of the mind which seem unreal only because they lie beyond the horizon of the every-day world and become visible only when the mirage of fantasy lifts them up and hangs them in an ideal atmosphere. As in the old fairy-tales, the task which the age imposes on its poet is to weave its straw into a golden tissue; and when every device has failed, in comes the witch Imagination,

and with a touch the miracle is achieved, simple as miracles always are after they are wrought.

Spenser, like Chaucer a Londoner, was born in 1553.[6] Nothing is known of his parents, except that the name of his mother was Elizabeth; but he was of gentle birth, as he more than once informs us, with the natural satisfaction of a poor man of genius at a time when the business talent of the middle class was opening to it the door of prosperous preferment. In 1569 he was entered as a sizar at Pembroke Hall, Cambridge, and in due course took his bachelor's degree in 1573, and his master's in 1576. He is supposed, on insufficient grounds, as it appears to me, to have met with some disgust or disappointment during his residence at the University.[7] Between 1576 and 1578 Spenser seems to have been with some of his kinsfolk "in the North." It was during this interval that he conceived his fruitless passion for the Rosalinde, whose jilting him for another shepherd, whom he calls Menalcas, is somewhat perfunctorily bemoaned in his pastorals.[8] Before the publication of his *Shepherd's Calendar* in 1579, he had made the acquaintance of Sir Philip Sidney, and was domiciled with him for a time at Penshurst, whether as guest or literary dependant is uncertain. In October, 1579, he is in the household of the Earl of Leicester. In July, 1580, he accompanied Lord Grey de Wilton to Ireland as Secretary, and in that country he spent the rest of his life, with occasional flying visits to England to publish poems or in search of preferment. His residence in that country has been compared to that of Ovid in Pontus. And, no doubt, there were certain outward points of likeness. The Irishry by whom he was surrounded were to the full as savage, as hostile, and as tenacious of their ancestral habitudes as the Scythians[9] who made Tomi a prison, and the descendants of the earlier English settlers had degenerated as much as the Mix-Hellenes who disgusted the Latin poet. Spenser himself looked on his life in Ireland as a banishment. In his *Colin Clout's come Home again* he tells us that Sir Walter Raleigh, who visited him in 1589, and heard what was then finished of the *Faery Queen*,

> 'Gan to cast great liking to my lore
> And great disliking to my luckless lot,
> That banisht had myself, like wight forlore,
> Into that waste, where I was quite forgot.
> The which to leave thenceforth he counselled me,
> Unmeet for man in whom was aught regardful,
> And wend with him his Cynthia to see,
> Whose grace was great and bounty most rewardful.

But Spenser was already living at Kilcolman Castle (which, with 3,028 acres of land from the forfeited estates of the Earl of Desmond, was confirmed to him by grant two years later), amid scenery at once placid and noble, whose varied charm he felt profoundly. He could not complain, with Ovid,

> Non liber hic ullus, non qui mihi commodet aurem,

for he was within reach of a cultivated society, which gave him the stimulus of hearty admiration both as poet and scholar. Above all, he was fortunate in a seclusion that prompted study and deepened meditation, while it enabled him to converse with his genius disengaged from those worldly influences which would have disenchanted it of its mystic enthusiasm, if they did not muddle it ingloriously away. Surely this sequestered nest was more congenial to the brooding of those ethereal visions of the *Faery Queen* and to giving his "soul a loose" than

> The smoke, the wealth, and noise of Rome,
>   And all the busy pageantry
> That wise men scorn and fools adore.

Yet he longed for London, if not with the homesickness of Bussy-Rabutin in exile from the Parisian sun, yet enough to make him joyfully accompany Raleigh thither in the early winter of 1589, carrying with him the first three books of the great poem begun ten years before. Horace's *nonum prematur in annum* had been more than complied with, and the success was answerable to the well seasoned material and conscientious faithfulness of the work. But Spenser did not stay long in London to enjoy his fame. Seen close at hand, with its jealousies, intrigues, and selfish basenesses, the court had lost the enchantment lent by the distance of Kilcolman. A nature so prone to ideal contemplation as Spenser's would be profoundly shocked by seeing too closely the ignoble springs of contemporaneous policy, and learning by what paltry personal motives the noble opportunities of the world are at any given moment endangered. It is a sad discovery that history is so mainly made by ignoble men.

> Vide questo globo
> Tal ch'ei sorrise del suo vil sembiante.

In his *Colin Clout*, written just after his return to Ireland, he speaks of the Court in a tone of contemptuous bitterness, in which, as it seems to me, there is more of the sorrow of disillusion than of the gall of personal disappointment. He speaks, so he tells us,

> To warn young shepherds' wandering wit
> Which, through report of that life's painted bliss,
> Abandon quiet home to seek for it
> And leave their lambs to loss misled amiss;
> For, sooth to say, it is no sort of life
> For shepherd fit to live in that same place,
> Where each one seeks with malice and with strife
> To thrust down other into foul disgrace
> Himself to raise; and he doth soonest rise
> That best can handle his deceitful wit
> In subtle shifts. . . .
> To which him needs a guileful hollow heart
> Maskèd with fair dissembling courtesy,
> A filèd tongue furnisht with terms of art,
> No art of school, but courtiers' schoolery.
> For arts of school have there small countenance,
> Counted but toys to busy idle brains,
> And there professors find small maintenance,
> But to be instruments of others' gains,
> Nor is there place for any gentle wit
> Unless to please it can itself apply.
> . . .
> Even such is all their vaunted vanity,
> Naught else but smoke that passeth soon away.
>
> So they themselves for praise of fools do sell,
> And all their wealth for painting on a wall.
> . . .
> Whiles single Truth and simple Honesty
> Do wander up and down despised of all.[10]

And again in his "Mother Hubberd's Tale," in the most pithy and masculine verses he ever wrote:

> Most miserable man, whom wicked Fate
> Hath brought to Court to sue for *Had-I-wist*
> That few have found and many one hath mist!
> Full little knowest thou that hast not tried
> What hell it is in suing long to bide;
> To lose good days that might be better spent,
> To waste long nights in pensive discontent,
> To speed to-day, to be put back to-morrow,
> To feed on hope, to pine with fear and sorrow,
> To have thy prince's grace yet want her Peers',

> To have thy asking yet wait many years,
> To fret thy soul with crosses and with cares,
> To eat thy heart through comfortless despairs,
> To fawn, to crouch, to wait, to ride, to run,
> To spend, to give, to want, to be undone.
> . . .
> Whoever leaves sweet home, where mean estate
> In safe assurance, without strife or hate,
> Finds all things needful for contentment meek,
> And will to court for shadows vain to seek,
> . . .
> That curse God send unto mine enemy![11]

When Spenser had once got safely back to the secure retreat and serene companionship of his great poem, with what profound and pathetic exultation must he have recalled the verses of Dante!

> Chi dietro a jura, e chi ad aforismi
> Sen giva, e chi seguendo sacerdozio,
> E chi regnar per forza e per solismi,
> E chi rubare, e chi civil negozio,
> Chi nei diletti della carne involto
> S' affaticava, e chi si dava all' ozio,
> Quando da tutte queste cose sciolto,
> Con Beatrice m' era suso in cielo
> Cotanto gloriosamente accolto.[12]

What Spenser says of the indifference of the court to learning and literature is the more remarkable because he himself was by no means an unsuccessful suitor. Queen Elizabeth bestowed on him a pension of fifty pounds, and shortly after he received the grant of lands already mentioned. It is said, indeed, that Lord Burleigh in some way hindered the advancement of the poet, who more than once directly alludes to him either in reproach or remonstrance. In "The Ruins of Time," after speaking of the death of Walsingham,

> Since whose decease learning lies unregarded,
> And men of armes do wander unrewarded,

he gives the following reason for their neglect:

> For he that now wields all things at his will,
> Scorns th' one and th' other in his deeper skill.
> O grief of griefs! O gall of all good hearts,
> To see that virtue should despisèd be
> Of him that first was raised for virtuous parts,
> And now, broad-spreading like an aged tree,
> Lets none shoot up that nigh him planted be:
> O let the man of whom the Muse is scorned
> Nor live nor dead be of the Muse adorned!

And in the introduction to the fourth book of the *Faery Queen*, he says again:

> The rugged forehead that with grave foresight
> Wields kingdoms' causes and affairs of state,
> My looser rhymes, I wot, doth sharply wite
> For praising Love, as I have done of late,—
> . . .
> By which frail youth is oft to folly led
> Through false allurement of that pleasing bait,
> That better were in virtues discipled
> Than with vain poems' weeds to have their fancies
>   fed.
> Such ones ill judge of love that cannot love
> Nor in their frozen hearts feel kindly flame;
> Forthy they ought not thing unknown reprove,
> Ne natural affection faultless blame
> For fault of few that have abused the same:
> For it of honor and all virtue is
> The root, and brings forth glorious flowers of fame

That crown true lovers with immortal bliss,
The meed of them that love and do not live amiss.

If Lord Burleigh could not relish such a dish of nightingales' tongues as the *Faery Queen*, he is very much more to be pitied than Spenser. The sensitive purity of the poet might indeed well be wounded when a poem in which he proposed to himself "to discourse at large" of "the ethick part of Moral Philosophy"[13] could be so misinterpreted. But Spenser speaks in the same strain and without any other than a general application in his "Tears of the Muses," and his friend Sidney undertakes the defence of poesy because it was undervalued. But undervalued by whom? By the only persons about whom he knew or cared anything, those whom we should now call Society and who were then called the Court. The inference I would draw is that, among the causes which contributed to the marvellous efflorescence of genius in the last quarter of the sixteenth century, the influence of direct patronage from above is to be reckoned at almost nothing.[14] Then, as when the same phenomenon has happened elsewhere, there must have been a sympathetic public. Literature, properly so called, draws its sap from the deep soil of human nature's common and everlasting sympathies, the gathered leaf-mould of countless generations (*hoiē per phyllōn geneē*), and not from any top-dressing capriciously scattered over the surface at some master's bidding.[15] England had long been growing more truly insular in language and political ideas when the Reformation came to precipitate her national consciousness by secluding her more completely from the rest of Europe. Hitherto there had been Englishmen of a distinct type enough, honestly hating foreigners, and reigned over by kings of whom they were proud or not as the case might be, but there was no England as a separate entity from the sovereign who embodied it for the time being.[16] But now an English people began to be dimly aware of itself. Their having got a religion to themselves must have intensified them much as the having a god of their own did the Jews. The exhilaration of relief after the long tension of anxiety, when the Spanish Armada was overwhelmed like the hosts of Pharaoh, while it confirmed their assurance of a provincial deity, must also have been like sunshine to bring into flower all that there was of imaginative or sentimental in the English nature, already just in the first flush of its spring.

(The yongë sonne
Had in *the Bull* half of his course yronne.)

And just at this moment of blossoming every breeze was dusty with the golden pollen of Greece, Rome, and Italy. If Keats could say, when he first opened Chapman's Homer,—

Then felt I like some watcher of the skies
When a new planet swims into his ken;
Or like stout Cortez when with eagle eyes
He stared at the Pacific, and all his men
Looked at each other with a wild surmise,

if Keats could say this, whose mind had been unconsciously fed with the results of this culture,—results that permeated all thought, all literature, and all talk,—fancy what must have been the awakening shock and impulse communicated to men's brains by the revelation of this new world of thought and fancy, an unveiling gradual yet sudden, like that of a great organ, which discovered to them what a wondrous instrument was in the soul of man with its epic and lyric stops, its deep thunders of tragedy, and its passionate *vox humana*! It might almost seem as if Shakespeare had typified all this in Miranda, when she cries out at first sight of the king and his courtiers,

O, wonder!
How many goodly creatures are there here!

How beauteous mankind is! O, brave new world
That hath such people in 't!

The civil wars of the Roses had been a barren period in English literature, because they had been merely dynastic squabbles, in which no great principles were involved which could shake all minds with controversy and heat them to intense conviction. A conflict of opposing ambitions wears out the moral no less than the material forces of a people, but the ferment of hostile ideas and convictions may realize resources of character which before were only potential, may transform a merely gregarious multitude into a nation proud in its strength, sensible of the dignity and duty which strength involves, and groping after a common ideal. Some such transformation had been wrought or was going on in England. For the first time a distinct image of her was disengaging itself from the tangled blur of tradition and association in the minds of her children, and it was now only that her great poet could speak exultingly to an audience that would understand him with a passionate sympathy, of

This happy breed of men, this little world,
This precious stone set in a silver sea,
This blessed plot, this earth, this realm, this
England,
This land of such dear souls, this dear, dear land,
England, bound in with the triumphant sea!

Such a period can hardly recur again, but something like it, something pointing back to similar producing causes, is observable in the revival of English imaginative literature at the close of the last and in the early years of the present century. Again, after long fermentation, there was a war of principles, again the national consciousness was heightened and stung by a danger to the national existence, and again there was a crop of great poets and heroic men.

Spenser once more visited England, bringing with him three more books of the *Faery Queen*, in 1595. He is supposed to have remained there during the two following years.[17] In 1594 he had been married to the lady celebrated in his somewhat artificial *amoretti*. By her he had four children. He was now at the height of his felicity; by universal acclaim the first poet of his age, and the one obstacle to his material advancement (if obstacle it was) had been put out of the way by the death of Lord Burleigh, August, 1598. In the next month he was recommended in a letter from Queen Elizabeth for the shrievalty of the county of Cork. But alas for Polycrates! In October the wild kerns and gallowglasses rose in no mood for sparing the house of Pindarus. They sacked and burned his castle, from which he with his wife and children barely escaped.[18] He sought shelter in London and died there on the 16th January, 1599, at a tavern in King Street, Westminster. He was buried in the neighboring Abbey next to Chaucer, at the cost of the Earl of Essex, poets bearing his pall and casting verses into his grave. He died poor, but not in want. On the whole, his life may be reckoned a happy one, as in the main the lives of the great poets must have commonly been. If they feel more passionately the pang of the moment, so also the compensations are incalculable, and not the least of them this very capacity of passionate emotion. The real good fortune is to be measured, not by more or less of outward prosperity, but by the opportunity given for the development and free play of the genius. It should be remembered that the power of expression which exaggerates their griefs is also no inconsiderable consolation for them. We should measure what Spenser says of his worldly disappointments by the bitterness of the unavailing tears he shed for Rosalind. A careful analysis of these leaves no perceptible residuum of salt, and we are tempted to believe that the passion itself was not much more real than the pastoral accessories of pipe and crook. I very much doubt whether Spenser ever felt more than one profound passion in his life, and that luckily was for his *Faery Queen*. He was fortunate in the friendship of the best men and women of his time, in the seclusion which made him free of the still better society of the past, in the loving recognition of his countrymen. All that we know of him is amiable and of good report. He was faithful to the friendships of his youth, pure in his loves, unspotted in his life. Above all, the ideal with him was not a thing apart and unattainable, but the sweetener and ennobler of the street and the fireside.

There are two ways of measuring a poet, either by an absolute æsthetic standard, or relatively to his position in the literary history of his country and the conditions of his generation. Both should be borne in mind as coefficients in a perfectly fair judgment. If his positive merit is to be settled irrevocably by the former, yet an intelligent criticism will find its advantage not only in considering what he was, but what, under the given circumstances, it was possible for him to be.

The fact that the great poem of Spenser was inspired by the Orlando of Ariosto, and written in avowed emulation of it, and that the poet almost always needs to have his fancy set agoing by the hint of some predecessor, must not lead us to overlook his manifest claim to originality. It is not what a poet takes, but what he makes out of what he has taken, that shows what native force is in him. Above all, did his mind dwell complacently in those forms and fashions which in their very birth are already obsolescent, or was it instinctively drawn to those qualities which are permanent in language and whatever is wrought in it? There is much in Spenser that is contemporary and evanescent; but the substance of him is durable, and his work was the deliberate result of intelligent purpose and ample culture. The publication of his *Shepherd's Calendar* in 1579 (though the poem itself be of little interest) is one of the epochs in our literature. Spenser had at least the originality to see clearly and to feel keenly that it was essential to bring poetry back again to some kind of understanding with nature. His immediate predecessors seem to have conceived of it as a kind of bird of paradise, born to float somewhere between heaven and earth, with no very well defined relation to either. It is true that the nearest approach they were able to make to this airy ideal was a shuttlecock, winged with a bright plume or so from Italy, but, after all, nothing but cork and feathers, which they bandied back and forth from one stanza to another, with the useful ambition of *keeping it up* as long as they could. To my mind the old comedy of *Gammer Gurton's Needle* is worth the whole of them. It may be coarse, earthy, but in reading it one feels that he is at least a man among men, and not a humbug among humbugs.

The form of Spenser's *Shepherd's Calendar*, it is true, is artificial, absurdly so if you look at it merely from the outside,—not, perhaps, the wisest way to look at anything, unless it be a jail or a volume of the *Congressional Globe*,—but the spirit of it is fresh and original. We have at last got over the superstition that shepherds and shepherdesses are any wiser or simpler than other people. We know that wisdom can be won only by wide commerce with men and books, and that simplicity, whether of manners or style, is the crowning result of the highest culture. But the pastorals of Spenser were very different things, different both in the moving spirit and the resultant form from the later ones of Browne or the *Piscatory Eclogues* of Phinehas Fletcher. And why? Browne and Fletcher wrote because Spenser had written, but Spenser wrote from a strong inward impulse—an instinct it might be called—to es-

cape at all risks into the fresh air from that horrible atmosphere into which rhymer after rhymer had been pumping carbonic-acid gas with the full force of his lungs, and in which all sincerity was on the edge of suffocation. His longing for something truer and better was as honest as that which led Tacitus so long before to idealize the Germans, and Rousseau so long after to make an angel of the savage.

Spenser himself supremely overlooks the whole chasm between himself and Chaucer, as Dante between himself and Virgil. He called Chaucer master, as Milton was afterwards to call *him*. And, even while he chose the most artificial of all forms, his aim—that of getting back to nature and life—was conscious, I have no doubt, to himself, and must be obvious to whoever reads with anything but the ends of his fingers. It is true that Sannazzaro had brought the pastoral into fashion again, and that two of Spenser's are little more than translations from Marot; but for manner he instinctively turned back to Chaucer, the first and then only great English poet. He has given common instead of classic names to his personages, for characters they can hardly be called. Above all, he has gone to the provincial dialects for words wherewith to enlarge and freshen his poetical vocabulary.[19] I look upon the *Shepherd's Calendar* as being no less a conscious and deliberate attempt at reform than Thomson's *Seasons* were in the topics, and Wordsworth's *Lyrical Ballads* in the language of poetry. But the great merit of these pastorals was not so much in their matter as their manner. They show a sense of style in its larger meaning hitherto displayed by no English poet since Chaucer. Surrey had brought back from Italy a certain inkling of it, so far as it is contained in decorum. But here was a new language, a choice and arrangement of words, a variety, elasticity, and harmony of verse most grateful to the ears of men. If not passion, there was fervor, which was perhaps as near it as the somewhat stately movement of Spenser's mind would allow him to come. Sidney had tried many experiments in versification, which are curious and interesting, especially his attempts to naturalize the *sliding* rhymes of Sannazzaro in English. But there is everywhere the uncertainty of a 'prentice hand. Spenser shows himself already a master, at least in verse, and we can trace the studies of Milton, a yet greater master, in the *Shepherd's Calendar* as well as in the *Faery Queen*. We have seen that Spenser, under the misleading influence of Sidney[20] and Harvey, tried his hand at English hexameters. But his great glory is that he taught his own language to sing and move to measures harmonious and noble. Chaucer had done much to vocalize it, as I have tried to show elsewhere,[21] but Spenser was to prove

That no tongue hath the muse's utterance heired
For verse, and that sweet music to the ear
Struck out of rhyme, so naturally as this.

The *Shepherd's Calendar* contains perhaps the most picturesquely imaginative verse which Spenser has written. It is in the eclogue for February, where he tells us of the

Faded oak
Whose body is sere, whose branches broke,
Whose naked arms stretch unto the fire.

It is one of those verses that Joseph Warton would have liked in secret, that Dr. Johnson would have proved to be untranslatable into reasonable prose, and which the imagination welcomes at once without caring whether it be exactly conformable to *barbara* or *celarent*. Another pretty verse in the same eclogue,

But gently took that ungently came,

pleased Coleridge so greatly that he thought it was his own. But in general it is not so much the sentiments and images that are new as the modulation of the verses in which they float. The cold obstruction of two centuries' thaws, and the stream of speech, once more let loose, seeks out its old windings, or overflows musically in unpractised channels. The service which Spenser did to our literature by this exquisite sense of harmony is incalculable. His fine ear, abhorrent of barbarous dissonance, his dainty tongue that loves to prolong the relish of a musical phrase, made possible the transition from the cast-iron stiffness of *Ferrex and Porrex* to the Damascus pliancy of Fletcher and Shakespeare. It was he that

> Taught the dumb on high to sing,
> And heavy ignorance aloft to fly:
> That added feathers to the learned's wing,
> And gave to grace a double majesty.

I do not mean that in the *Shepherd's Calendar* he had already achieved that transmutation of language and metre by which he was afterwards to endow English verse with the most varied and majestic of stanzas, in which the droning old alexandrine, awakened for the first time to a feeling of the poetry that was in him, was to wonder, like M. Jourdain, that he had been talking prose all his life,—but already he gave clear indications of the tendency and premonitions of the power which were to carry it forward to ultimate perfection. A harmony and alacrity of language like this were unexampled in English verse:

> Ye dainty nymphs, that in this blessed brook
>   Do bathe your breast,
> Forsake your watery bowers and hither look
>   At my request. . . . .
> And eke you virgins that on Parnass dwell,
> Whence floweth Helicon, the learned well,
>   Help me to blaze
>   Her worthy praise,
> Which in her sex doth all excel.

Here we have the natural gait of the measure, somewhat formal and slow, as befits an invocation; and now mark how the same feet shall be made to quicken their pace at the bidding of the tune:

> Bring here the pink and purple columbine,
>   With gilliflowers;
> Bring coronations and sops in wine,
>   Worne of paramours;
> Strow me the ground with daffadowndillies,
> And cowslips and kingcups and loved lilies;
>   The pretty paunce
>   And the chevisance
> Shall match with the fair flowërdelice.[22]

The argument prefixed by E. K. to the tenth Eclogue has a special interest for us as showing how high a conception Spenser had of poetry and the poet's office. By Cuddy he evidently means himself, though choosing out of modesty another name instead of the familiar Colin. "In Cuddy is set forth the perfect pattern of a Poet, which, finding no maintenance of his state and studies, complaineth of the contempt of Poetry and the causes thereof, specially having been in all ages, and even amongst the most barbarous, always of singular account and honor, *and being indeed so worthy and commendable an art, or rather no art, but a divine gift and heavenly instinct not to be gotten by labor and learning, but adorned with both, and poured into the wit by a certain Enthousiasmos and celestial inspiration*, as the author hereof elsewhere at large discourseth in his book called THE ENGLISH POET, which book being lately come into my hands, I mind also by God's grace, upon further advisement, to publish." E. K., whoever he was, never carried out his intention, and the book is no doubt lost; a loss to be borne with less equanimity than that of Cicero's treatise *De*

Gloria, once possessed by Petrarch. The passage I have italicized is most likely an extract, and reminds one of the long-breathed periods of Milton. Drummond of Hawthornden tells us, "he [Ben Jonson] hath by heart some verses of Spenser's *Calendar*, about wine, between Coline and Percye" (Cuddie and Piers).[23] These verses are in this eclogue, and are worth quoting both as having the approval of dear old Ben, the best critic of the day, and because they are a good sample of Spenser's earlier verse:

> Thou kenst not, Percie, how the rhyme should rage;
> O, if my temples were distained with wine,
> And girt in garlands of wild ivy-twine,
> How I could rear the Muse on stately stage
>   And teach her tread aloft in buskin fine
>   With quaint Bellona in her equipage!

In this eclogue he gives hints of that spacious style which was to distinguish him, and which, like his own Fame,

>   With golden wings aloft doth fly
> Above the reach of ruinous decay,
> And with brave plumes doth beat the azure sky,
> Admired of base-born men from far away.[24]

He was letting his wings grow as Milton said, and foreboding the *Faery Queen*:

> Lift thyself up out of the lowly dust
>
> . . . .
>
> To 'doubted knights whose woundless armor rusts
> And helms unbruiséd waxen daily brown:
> There may thy Muse display her fluttering wing,
> And stretch herself at large from East to West.

Verses like these, especially the last (which Dryden would have liked), were such as English ears had not yet heard and curiously prophetic of the maturer man. The language and verse of Spenser at his best have an ideal lift in them, and there is scarce any of our poets who can so hardly help being poetical.

It was this instantly felt if not easily definable charm that forthwith won for Spenser his never-disputed rank as the chief English poet of that age, and gave him a popularity which, during his life and in the following generation, was, in its select quality, without a competitor. It may be thought that I lay too much stress on this single attribute of diction. But apart from its importance in his case as showing their way to the poets who were just then learning the accidence of their art, and leaving them a material to work in already mellowed to their hands, it should be remembered that it is subtle perfection of phrase and that happy coalescence of music and meaning, where each reinforces the other, that define a man as poet and make all ears converts and partisans. Spenser was an epicure in language. He loved "seld-seen costly" words perhaps too well, and did not always distinguish between mere strangeness and that novelty which is so agreeable as to cheat us with some charm of seeming association. He had not the concentrated power which can sometimes pack infinite riches in the little room of a single epithet for his genius is rather for dilatation than compression.[25] But he was, with the exception of Milton and possibly Gray, the most learned of our poets. His familiarity with ancient and modern literature was easy and intimate, and as he perfected himself in his art, he caught the grand manner and high-bred ways of the society he frequented. But even to the last he did not quite shake off the blunt rusticity of phrase that was habitual with the generation that preceded him. In the fifth book of the *Faery Queen*, where he is describing the passion of Britomart at the supposed infidelity of Arthegall, he descends to a Teniers-like realism,[26]—he whose verses generally remind us of the dancing Hours of Guido, where we catch but a glimpse of the real earth and that far away beneath. But his habitual style is that of gracious loftiness and refined luxury.

He first shows his mature hand in the "Muiopotmos," the most airily fanciful of his poems, a marvel for delicate conception and treatment, whose breezy verse seems to float between a blue sky and golden earth in imperishable sunshine. No other English poet has found the variety and compass which enlivened the octave stanza under his sensitive touch. It can hardly be doubted that in Clarion the butterfly he has symbolized himself, and surely never was the poetic temperament so picturesquely exemplified:

> Over the fields, in his frank lustiness,
> And all the champain o'er, he soarèd light,
> And all the country wide he did possess,
> Feeding upon their pleasures bounteously,
> That none gainsaid and none did him envy.

> The woods, the rivers, and the meadows green,
> With his air-cutting wings he measured wide,
> Nor did he leave the mountains bare unseen,
> Nor the rank grassy fens' delights untried;
> But none of these, however sweet they been,
> Mote please his fancy, or him cause to abide;
> His choiceful sense with every change doth flit;
> No common things may please a wavering wit.

> To the gay gardens his unstaid desire
> Him wholly carried, to refresh his sprights;
> There lavish Nature, in her best attire,
> Pours forth sweet odors and alluring sights,
> And Art, with her contending doth aspire,
> To excel the natural with made delights;
> And all that fair or pleasant may be found,
> In riotous excess doth there abound.

> There he arriving, round about doth flie,
> From bed to bed, from one to the other border,
> And takes survey with curious busy eye,
> Of every flower and herb there set in order,
> Now this, now that, he tasteth tenderly,
> Yet none of them he rudely doth disorder,
> Ne with his feet their silken leaves displace,
> But pastures on the pleasures of each place.

> And evermore with most variety
> And change of sweetness (for all change is sweet.)
> He casts his glutton sense to satisfy,
> Now sucking of the sap of herbs most meet,
> Or of the dew which yet on them doth lie,
> Now in the same bathing his tender feet;
> And then he percheth on some branch thereby
> To weather him and his moist wings to dry.

> And then again he turneth to his play,
> To spoil [plunder] the pleasures of that paradise;
> The wholesome sage, the lavender still gray,
> Rank-smelling rue, and cummin good for eyes,
> The roses reigning in the pride of May,
> Sharp hyssop good for green wounds' remedies
> Fair marigolds, and bees-alluring thyme,
> Sweet marjoram and daisies decking prime,

> Cool violets, and orpine growing still,
> Embathèd balm, and cheerful galingale,
> Fresh costmary and breathful camomill,
> Dull poppy and drink-quickening setuale,
> Vein-healing vervain and head-purging dill,
> Sound savory, and basil hearty-hale,
> Fat coleworts and comforting perseline,
> Cold lettuce, and refreshing rosemarine.[27]

> And whatso else of virtue good or ill,
> Grew in this garden, fetched from far away,

> Of every one he takes and tastes at will,
> And on their pleasures greedily doth prey;
> Then, when he hath both played and fed his fill,
> In the warm sun he doth himself embay,
> And there him rests in riotous suffisance
> Of all his gladfulness and kingly joyance.

> What more felicity can fall to creature
> Than to enjoy delight with liberty,
> And to be lord of all the works of nature?
> To reign in the air from earth to highest sky,
> To feed on flowers and weeds of glorious feature,
> To take whatever thing doth please the eye?
> Who rests not pleasèd with such happiness,
> Well worthy he to taste of wretchedness.

The "Muiopotmos" pleases us all the more that it vibrates in us a string of classical association by adding an episode to Ovid's story of Arachne. "Talking the other day with a friend (the late Mr. Keats) about Dante, he observed that whenever so great a poet told us anything in addition or continuation of an ancient story, he had a right to be regarded as classical authority. For instance, said he, when he tells us of that characteristic death of Ulysses, . . . we ought to receive the information as authentic, and be glad that we have more news of Ulysses than we looked for."[28] We can hardly doubt that Ovid would have been glad to admit this exquisitely fantastic illumination into his margin.

No German analyzer of æsthetics has given us so convincing a definition of the artistic nature as these radiant verses. "To reign in the air" was certainly Spenser's function. And yet the commentators, who seem never willing to let their poet be a poet pure and simple, though, had he not been so, they would have lost their only hold upon life, try to make out from his "Mother Hubberd's Tale" that he might have been a very sensible matter-of-fact man if he would. For my own part, I am quite willing to confess that I like him none the worse for being *un*practical, and that my reading has convinced me that being too poetical is the rarest fault of poets. Practical men are not so scarce, one would think, and I am not sure that the tree was a gainer when the hamadryad flitted and left it nothing but ship-timber. Such men as Spenser are not sent into the world to be part of its motive power. The blind old engine would not know the difference though we got up its steam with attar of roses, nor make one revolution more to the minute for it. What practical man ever left such an heirloom to his countrymen as the *Faery Queen*?

Undoubtedly Spenser wished to be useful and in the highest vocation of all, that of teacher, and Milton calls him "our sage and serious poet, whom I dare be known to think a better teacher than Scotus or Aquinas." And good Dr. Henry More was of the same mind. I fear he makes his vices so beautiful now and then that we should not be very much afraid of them if we chanced to meet them; for he could not escape from his genius, which, if it led him as philosopher to the abstract contemplation of the beautiful, left him as poet open to every impression of sensuous delight. When he wrote the *Shepherd's Calendar* he was certainly a Puritan, and probably so by conviction rather than from any social influences or thought of personal interests. There is a verse, it is true, in the second of the two detached cantos of "Mutability,"

> Like that ungracious crew which feigns demurest
>   grace,

which is supposed to glance at the straiter religionists, and from which it has been inferred that he drew away from them as he grew older. It is very likely that years and widened experience of men may have produced in him their natural result of tolerant wisdom which revolts at the hasty destructiveness of inconsiderate zeal. But with the more generous side of Puritanism I think he sympathized to the last. His rebukes of clerical worldliness are in the Puritan tone, and as severe a one as any is in "Mother Hubberd's Tale," published in 1591.[29] There is an iconoclastic relish in his account of Sir Guyon's demolishing the Bower of Bliss that makes us think he would not have regretted the plundered abbeys as perhaps Shakespeare did when he speaks of the winter woods as "bare ruined choirs where late the sweet birds sang":

> But all those pleasant bowers and palace brave
> Guyon broke down with rigor pitiless,
> Ne ought their goodly workmanship might save
> Them from the tempest of his wrathfulness,
> But that their bliss he turned to balefulness;
> Their groves he felled, their gardens did deface,
> Their arbors spoil, their cabinets suppress,
> Their banquet-houses burn, their buildings rase,
> And of the fairest late now made the foulest place.

But whatever may have been Spenser's religious opinions (which do not nearly concern us here), the bent of his mind was toward a Platonic mysticism, a supramundane sphere where it could shape universal forms out of the primal elements of things, instead of being forced to put up with their fortuitous combinations in the unwilling material of mortal clay. He who, when his singing robes were on, could never be tempted nearer to the real world than under some subterfuge of pastoral or allegory, expatiates joyously in this untrammelled ether:

> Lifting himself out of the lowly dust
> On golden plumes up to the purest sky.

Nowhere does his genius soar and sing with such continuous aspiration, nowhere is his phrase so decorously stately, though rising to an enthusiasm which reaches intensity while it stops short of vehemence, as in his Hymns to Love and Beauty, especially the latter. There is an exulting spurn of earth in it, as of a soul just loosed from its cage. I shall make no extracts from it, for it is one of those intimately coherent and transcendentally logical poems that "moveth altogether if it move at all," the breaking off a fragment from which would maim it as it would a perfect group of crystals. Whatever there is of sentiment and passion is for the most part purely disembodied and without sex, like that of angels,—a kind of poetry which has of late gone out of fashion, whether to our gain or not may be questioned. Perhaps one may venture to hint that the animal instincts are those that stand in least need of stimulation. Spenser's notions of love were so nobly pure, so far from those of our common ancestor who could hang by his tail, as not to disqualify him for achieving the quest of the Holy Grail, and accordingly it is not uninstructive to remember that he had drunk, among others, at French sources not yet deboshed with *absinthe*.[30] Yet, with a purity like that of thrice-bolted snow, he had none of its coldness. He is, of all our poets, the most truly sensuous, using the word as Milton probably meant it when he said that poetry should be "simple, sensuous, and passionate." A poet is innocently sensuous when his mind permeates and illumines his senses; when they, on the other hand, muddy the mind, he becomes sensual. Every one of Spenser's senses was as exquisitely alive to the impressions of material, as every organ of his soul was to those of spiritual beauty. Accordingly, if he painted the weeds of sensuality at all, he could not help making them "of glorious feature." It was this, it may be suspected, rather than his "praising love," that made Lord Burleigh shake his "rugged forehead." Spenser's gamut, indeed, is

a wide one, ranging from a purely corporeal delight in "precious odors fetched from far away" upward to such refinement as

> Upon her eyelids many graces sate
> Under the shadow of her even brows,

where the eye shares its pleasure with the mind. He is courtpainter in ordinary to each of the senses in turn, and idealizes these frail favorites of his majesty King Lusty Juventus, till they half believe themselves the innocent shepherdesses into which he travesties them.[31]

In his great poem he had two objects in view: first, the ephemeral one of pleasing the court, and then that of recommending himself to the permanent approval of his own and following ages as a poet, and especially as a moral poet. To meet the first demand, he lays the scene of his poem in contemporary England, and brings in all the leading personages of the day under the thin disguise of his knights and their squires and ladyloves. He says this expressly in the prologue to the second book:

> Of Faery Land yet if he more inquire,
> By certain signs, here set in sundry place,
> He may it find; . . .
> And thou, O fairest princess under sky,
> In this fair mirror mayst behold thy face
> And thine own realms in land of Faery.

Many of his personages we can still identify, and all of them were once as easily recognizable as those of Mademoiselle de Scudéry. This, no doubt, added greatly to the immediate piquancy of the allusions. The interest they would excite may be inferred from the fact that King James, in 1596, wished to have the author prosecuted and punished for his indecent handling of his mother, Mary Queen of Scots, under the name of Duessa.[32] To suit the wider application of his plan's other and more important half, Spenser made all his characters double their parts, and appear in his allegory as the impersonations of abstract moral qualities. When the cardinal and theological virtues tell Dante,

> Noi siam qui ninfe e in ciel siamo stelle,

the sweetness of the verse enables the fancy, by a slight gulp, to swallow without solution the problem of being in two places at the same time. But there is something fairly ludicrous in such a duality as that of Prince Arthur and the Earl of Leicester, Arthegall and Lord Grey, and Belphœbe and Elizabeth.

> In this same interlude it doth befall
> That I, one Snout by name, present a wall.

The reality seems to heighten the improbability, already hard enough to manage. But Spenser had fortunately almost as little sense of humor as Wordsworth,[33] or he could never have carried his poem on with enthusiastic good faith so far as he did. It is evident that to him the Land of Faery was an unreal world of picture and illusion,

> The world's sweet inn from pain and wearisome
>   turmoil,

in which he could shut himself up from the actual, with its shortcomings and failures.

> The ways through which my weary steps I guide
>   In this delightful land of Faery
> Are so exceeding spacious and wide,
>   And sprinkled with such sweet variety
>   Of all that pleasant is to ear and eye,
> That I, nigh ravisht with rare thoughts' delight,
>   My tedious travail do forget thereby,
> And, when I 'gin to feel decay of might,

It strength to me supplies, and cheers my dullëd
  spright.

Spenser seems here to confess a little weariness; but the alacrity of his mind is so great that, even where his invention fails a little, we do not share his feeling nor suspect it, charmed as we are by the variety and sweep of his measure, the beauty or vigor of his similes, the musical felicity of his diction, and the mellow versatility of his pictures. In this last quality Ariosto, whose emulous pupil he was, is as Bologna to Venice in the comparison. That, when the personal allusions have lost their meaning and the allegory has become a burden, the book should continue to be read with delight, is proof enough, were any wanting, how full of life and light and the other-world-liness of poetry it must be. As a narrative it has, I think, every fault of which that kind of writing is capable. The characters are vague, and, even were they not, they drop out of the story so often and remain out of it so long, that we have forgotten who they are when we meet them again; the episodes hinder the advance of the action instead of relieving it with variety of incident or novelty of situation; the plot, if plot it may be called,

That shape has none
Distinguishable in member, joint, or limb,

recalls drearily our ancient enemy, the Metrical Romance; while the fighting, which, in those old poems, was tediously sincere, is between shadow and shadow, where we know that neither can harm the other, though we are tempted to wish he might. Hazlitt bids us not mind the allegory, and says that it won't bite us nor meddle with us if we do not meddle with it. But how if it bore us, which after all is the fatal question? The truth is that it is too often forced upon us against our will, as people were formerly driven to church till they began to look on a day of rest as a penal institution, and to transfer to the Scriptures that suspicion of defective inspiration which was awakened in them by the preaching. The true type of the allegory is the Odyssey, which we read without suspicion as pure poem, and then find a new pleasure in divining its double meaning, as if we somehow got a better bargain of our author than he meant to give us. But this complex feeling must not be so exacting as to prevent our lapsing into the old Arabian Nights simplicity of interest again. The moral of a poem should be suggested, as when in some mediæval church, we cast down our eyes to muse over a fresco of Giotto, and are reminded of the transitoriness of life by the mortuary tablets under our feet. The vast superiority of Bunyan over Spenser lies in the fact that we help make his allegory out of our own experience. Instead of striving to embody abstract passions and temptations, he has given us his own in all their pathetic simplicity. He is the Ulysses of his own prose-epic. This is the secret of his power and his charm, that, while the representation of what *may* happen to all men comes home to none of us in particular, the story of any one man's real experience finds its startling parallel in that of every one of us. The very home-liness of Bunyan's names and the everydayness of his scenery, too, put us off our guard, and we soon find ourselves on as easy a footing with his allegorical beings as we might be with Adam or Socrates in a dream. Indeed, he has prepared us for such incongruities by telling us at setting out that the story was of a dream. The long nights of Bedford jail had so intensified his imagination, and made the figures with which it peopled his solitude so real to him, that the creatures of his mind become *things*, as clear to the memory as if we had seen them. But Spenser's are too often mere names, with no bodies to back them, entered on the Muses' muster-roll by the specious trick of personification. There is, likewise, in Bunyan, a childlike

simplicity and taking-for-granted which win our confidence. His Giant Despair,[34] for example, is by no means the Ossianic figure into which artists who mistake the vague for the sublime have misconceived it. He is the ogre of the fairy-tales, with his malicious wife; and he comes forth to us from those regions of early faith and wonder as something beforehand accepted by the imagination. These figures of Bunyan's are already familiar inmates of the mind, and, if there be any sublimity in him, it is the daring frankness of his verisimilitude. Spenser's giants are those of the later romances, except that grand figure with the balances in the second Canto of Book V., the most original of all his conceptions, yet no real giant, but a pure eidolon of the mind. As Bunyan rises not seldom to a natural poetry, so Spenser sinks now and then, through the fault of his topics, to unmistakable prose. Take his description of the House of Alma,[35] for instance:

The master cook was cald Concoctiön,
  A careful man, and full of comely guise;
The kitchen-clerk, that hight Digestiön,
  Did order all the achates in seemly wise.

And so on through all the organs of the body. The author of Ecclesiastes understood these matters better in that last pathetic chapter of his, blunderingly translated as it apparently is. This, I admit, is the worst failure of Spenser in this kind; though, even here, when he gets on to the organs of the mind, the enchantments of his fancy and style come to the rescue and put us in good-humor again, hard as it is to conceive of armed knights entering the chamber of the mind, and talking with such visionary damsels as Ambition and Shamefastness. Nay, even in the most prosy parts, unless my partiality deceive me, there is an infantile confidence in the magical powers of Pros-opopœia which half beguiles us, as of children who *play* that everything is something else, and are quite satisfied with the transformation.

The problem for Spenser was a double one: how to com-mand poetry at all to a generation which thought it effeminate trifling,[36] and how he, Master Edmund Spenser, of imagina-tion all compact, could commend *his* poetry to Master John Bull, the most practical of mankind in his habitual mood, but at that moment in a passion of religious anxiety about his soul. *Omne tulit punctum qui miscuit utile dulci* was not only an irrefragable axiom because a Latin poet had said it, but it exactly met the case in point. He would convince the scorners that poetry might be seriously useful, and show Master Bull his new way of making fine words butter parsnips, in a rhymed moral primer. Allegory, as then practised, was imagination adapted for beginners, in words of one syllable and illustrated with cuts, and would thus serve both his ethical and pictorial purpose. Such a primer, or a first instalment of it, he proceeded to put forth; but he so bordered it with bright-colored fancies, he so often filled whole pages and crowded the text hard in others with the gay frolics of his pencil, that, as in the Grimani missal, the holy function of the book is forgotten in the ecstasy of its adornment. Worse than all, does not his brush linger more lovingly along the rosy contours of his sirens than on the modest wimples of the Wise Virgins? "The general end of the book," he tells us in his Dedication to Sir Walter Raleigh, "is to fashion a gentleman of noble person in virtuous and gentle discipline." But a little further on he evidently has a qualm, as he thinks how generously he had interpreted his promise of cuts: "To some I know this method will seem displeasant, which had rather have good discipline delivered plainly in way of precepts or sermoned at large,[37] as they use, than thus cloud-ily enwrapped in allegorical devices." Lord Burleigh was of this way of thinking, undoubtedly, but how could poor Clarion help it? Has he not said,

> And whatso else, *of virtue good or ill,*
> > Grew in that garden, fetcht from far away,
> Of every one he takes and tastes at will,
> > And on their pleasures greedily doth prey?

One sometimes feels in reading him as if he were the pure sense of the beautiful incarnated to the one end that he might interpret it to our duller perceptions. So exquisite was his sensibility,[38] that with him sensation and intellection seem identical, and we "can almost say his body thought." This subtle interfusion of sense with spirit it is that gives his poetry a crystalline purity without lack of warmth. He is full of feeling, and yet of such a kind that we can neither say it is mere intellectual perception of what is fair and good, nor yet associate it with that throbbing fervor which leads us to call sensibility by the physical name of heart.

Charles Lamb made the most pithy criticism of Spenser when he called him the poets' poet. We may fairly leave the allegory on one side, for perhaps, after all, he adopted it only for the reason that it was in fashion, and put it on as he did his ruff, not because it was becoming, but because it was the only wear. The true use of him is as a gallery of pictures which we visit as the mood takes us, and where we spend an hour or two at a time, long enough to sweeten our perceptions, not so long as to cloy them. He makes one think always of Venice; for not only is his style Venetian,[39] but as the gallery there is housed in the shell of an abandoned convent, so his in that of a deserted allegory. And again, as at Venice you swim in a gondola from Gian Bellini to Titian, and from Titian to Tintoret, so in him, where other cheer is wanting, the gentle sway of his measure, like the rhythmical impulse of the oar, floats you lullingly along from picture to picture.

> If all the pens that ever poet held
> Had fed the feeling of their master's thoughts,
> And every sweetness that inspired their hearts
> Their minds and muses on admirèd themes,
> If all the heavenly quintessence they still
> From their immortal flowers of poesy,
> If these had made one poem's period,
> And all combined in beauty's worthiness;
> Yet should there hover in their restless heads
> One thought, one grace, one wonder at the best,
> Which into words no virtue can digest.[40]

Spenser, at his best, has come as near to expressing this unattainable something as any other poet. He is so purely poet that with him the meaning does not so often modulate the music of the verse as the music makes great part of the meaning and leads the thought along its pleasant paths. No poet is so splendidly superfluous as he; none knows so well that in poetry enough is not only not so good as a feast, but is a beggarly parsimony. He spends himself in a careless abundance only to be justified by incomes of immortal youth.

> Pensier canuto nè molto nè poco
> Si può quivi albergare in alcun cuore;
> Non entra quivi disagio nè inopia,
> Ma vi sta ogn'or col corno pien la Copia.[41]

This delicious abundance and overrunning luxury of Spenser appear in the very structure of his verse. He found the *ottava rima* too monotonously iterative; so, by changing the order of his rhymes, he shifted the couplet from the end of the stave, where it always seems to put on the brakes with a jar, to the middle, where it may serve at will as a brace or a bridge; he found it not roomy enough, so first ran it over into another line, and then ran that added line over into an alexandrine, in which the melody of one stanza seems forever longing and feeling forward after that which is to follow. There is no ebb and flow in his metre more than on the shores of the Adriatic, but wave follows wave with equable gainings and recessions, the one sliding back in fluent music to be mingled with and carried forward by the next. In all this there is soothingness indeed, but no slumberous monotony; for Spenser was no mere metrist, but a great composer. By the variety of his pauses— now at the close of the first or second foot, now of the third, and again of the fourth—he gives spirit and energy to a measure whose tendency it certainly is to become languorous. He knew how to make it rapid and passionate at need, as in such verses as,

> But he, my lion, and my noble lord,
> How does he find in cruel heart to hate
> Her that him loved and ever most adored
As the God of my life? Why hath he me abhorred?[42]

or this,

> Come hither, come hither, O, come hastily![43]

Joseph Warton objects to Spenser's stanza, that its "constraint led him into many absurdities." Of these he instances three, of which I shall notice only one, since the two others (which suppose him at a loss for words and rhymes) will hardly seem valid to any one who knows the poet. It is that it "obliged him to dilate the thing to be expressed, however unimportant, with trifling and tedious circumlocutions, namely, *Faery Queen*, II. ii. 44:

> Now hath fair Phœbe with her silver face
> > Thrice seen the shadows of this nether world,
> Sith last I left that honorable place,
> > In which her royal presence is enrolled.

That is, it is three months since I left her palace.[44] But Dr. Warton should have remembered (what he too often forgets in his own verses) that, in spite of Dr. Johnson's dictum, poetry is not prose, and that verse only loses its advantage over the latter by invading its province.[45] Verse itself is an absurdity except as an expression of some higher movement of the mind, or as an expedient to lift other minds to the same ideal level. It is the cothurnus which gives language an heroic stature. I have said that one leading characteristic of Spenser's style was its spaciousness, that he habitually dilates rather than compresses. But his way of measuring time was perfectly natural in an age when everybody did not carry a dial in his poke as now. He is the last of the poets, who went (without affectation) by the great clock of the firmament. Dante, the miser of words, who goes by the same timepiece, is full of these roundabout ways of telling us the hour. It had nothing to do with Spenser's stanza, and I for one should be sorry to lose these stately revolutions of the *superne ruote*. Time itself becomes more noble when so measured; we never knew before of how precious a commodity we had the wasting. Who would prefer the plain time of day to this?

> Now when Aldebaran was mounted high
> Above the starry Cassiopeia's chair;

or this?

> By this the northern wagoner had set
> > His seven-fold team behind the steadfast star
> That was in ocean's waves yet never wet,
> > But firm is fixt and sendeth light from far
> To all that in the wide deep wandering are;

or this?

> At last the golden oriental gate
> > Of greatest heaven gan to open fair,
> And Phœbus, fresh as bridegroom to his mate,

Came dancing forth, shaking his dewy hair
And hurls his glistening beams through dewy air.

The generous indefiniteness, which treats an hour more or less
as of no account, is in keeping with that sense of endless
leisures which it is one chief merit of the poem to suggest. But
Spenser's dilatation extends to thoughts as well as to phrases
and images. He does not love the concise. Yet his dilatation is
not mere distension, but the expansion of natural growth in the
rich soil of his own mind, wherein the merest stick of a verse
puts forth leaves and blossoms. Here is one of his, suggested by
Homer:[46]

Upon the top of all his lofty crest
A bunch of hairs discolored diversly,
With sprinkled pearl and gold full richly
   drest,
Did shake, and seemed to dance for jollity;
Like to an almond-tree ymounted high
On top of green Selinus all alone
With blossoms brave bedeckèd daintily,
Whose tender locks do tremble every one
At every little breath that under heaven is blown.

And this is the way he reproduces five pregnant verses of
Dante:

Seggendo in piume
In fama non si vien, nè sotto coltre,
Senza la qual chi sua vita consuma,
Cotal vestigio in terra di se lascia
Qual fumo in aere ed in acqua la schiuma.[47]

Whoso in pomp of proud estate, quoth she,
Does swim, and bathes himself in courtly
   bliss,
Does waste his days in dark obscurity
And in oblivion ever buried is;
Where ease abounds it's eath to do amiss:
But who his limbs with labors and his mind
Behaves with cares, cannot so easy miss.
Abroad in arms, at home in studious kind,
Who seeks with painful toil shall Honor soonest
   find.

In woods, in waves, in wars, she wonts to
   dwell,
And will be found with peril and with pain,
Ne can the man that moulds in idle cell
Unto her happy mansiön attain;
Before her gate high God did Sweat ordain,
And wakeful watches ever to abide;
But easy is the way and passage plain
To pleasure's palace; it may soon be spied,
And day and night her doors to all stand open
   wide.[48]

Spenser's mind always demands this large elbow-room. His
thoughts are never pithily expressed, but with a stately and
sonorous proclamation, as if under the open sky, that seems to
me very noble. For example,

The noble heart that harbors virtuous thought
And is with child of glorious-great intent
Can never rest until it forth have brought
The eternal brood of glory excellent.[49]

One's very soul seems to dilate with that last verse. And here is
a passage which Milton had read and remembered:

And is there care in Heaven? and is there
   love
In heavenly spirits to these creatures base,
That may compassion of their evils move?

There is: else much more wretched were the
   case
Of men than beasts: but O, the exceeding
   grace
Of Highest God, that loves his creatures so,
And all his works with mercy doth embrace,
That blessed angels he sends to and fro,
To serve to wicked man, to serve his wicked foe!

How oft do they their silver bowers leave,
To come to succor us that succor want!
How oft do they with golden pinions cleave
The fleeting skies like flying pursuivant,
Against the foul fiends to aid us militant!
They for us fight, they watch and duly ward,
And their bright squadrons round about us
   plant;
And all for love and nothing for reward;
O, why should heavenly God to men have such
   regard.[50]

His natural tendency is to shun whatever is sharp and abrupt.
He loves to prolong emotion, and lingers in his honeyed sensations like a bee in the translucent cup of a lily. So entirely are
beauty and delight in it the native element of Spenser, that,
whenever in the *Faery Queen* you come suddenly on the
moral, it gives you a shock of unpleasant surprise, a kind of
grit, as when one's teeth close on a bit of gravel in a dish of
strawberries and cream. He is the most fluent of our poets.
Sensation passing through emotion into revery is a prime quality of his manner. And to read him puts one in the condition of
revery, a state of mind in which our thoughts and feelings float
motionless, as one sees fish do in a gentle stream, with just
enough vibration of their fins to keep themselves from going
down with the current, while their bodies yield indolently to all
its soothing curves. He chooses his language for its rich can-
orousness rather than for intensity of meaning. To characterize
his style in a single word, I should call it *costly*. None but the
daintiest and nicest phrases will serve him, and he allures us
from one to the other with such cunning baits of alliteration,
and such sweet lapses of verse, that never any word seems more
eminent than the rest, nor detains the feeling to eddy around it,
but you must go on to the end before you have time to stop and
muse over the wealth that has been lavished on you. But he has
characterized and exemplified his own style better than any
description could do:

For round about the walls yclothed were
With goodly arras of great majesty,
Woven with gold and silk so close and near
That the rich metal lurked privily
As faining to be hid from envious eye;
Yet here and there and everywhere, unwares
It showed itself and shone unwillingly
Like to a discolored snake whose hidden snares
Through the green grass his long bright-burnished
   back declares.[51]

And of the lulling quality of his verse take this as a sample:

And, more to lull him in his slumber soft,
A trickling stream from high rock tumbling
   down
And ever drizzling rain upon the loft,
Mixt with the murmuring wind much like the
   soun
Of swarming bees did cast him in a swoon.
No other noise, nor peoples' troublous cries,
As still are wont to annoy the wallèd town,
Might there be heard: but careless quiet lies
Wrapt in eternal silence far from enemies.[52]

In the world into which Spenser carries us there is neither time nor space, or rather it is outside of and independent of them both, and so is purely ideal, or, more truly, imaginary; yet it is full of form, color, and all earthly luxury, and so far, if not real, yet apprehensible by the senses. There are no men and women in it, yet it throngs with airy and immortal shapes that have the likeness of men and women, and hint at some kind of foregone reality. Now this place, somewhere between mind and matter, between soul and sense, between the actual and the possible, is precisely the region which Spenser assigns (if I have rightly divined him) to the poetic susceptibility of impression,

> To reign in the air from the earth to highest sky.

Underneath every one of the senses lies the soul and spirit of it, dormant till they are magnetized by some powerful emotion. Then whatever is imperishable in us recognizes for an instant and claims kindred with something outside and distinct from it, yet in some inconceivable way a part of it, that flashes back on it an ideal beauty which impoverishes all other companionship. This exaltation with which love sometimes subtilizes the nerves of coarsest men so that they feel and see, not the thing as it seems to others, but the beauty of it, the joy of it, the soul of eternal youth that is in it, would appear to have been the normal condition of Spenser. While the senses of most men live in the cellar, his " were laid in a large upper chamber which opened toward the sunrising."

> His birth was of the womb of morning dew,
> And his conception of the joyous prime.

The very greatest poets (and is there, after all, more than one of them?) have a way, I admit, of getting within our inmost consciousness and in a manner betraying us to ourselves. There is in Spenser a remoteness very different from this, but it is also a seclusion, and quite as agreeable, perhaps quite as wholesome in certain moods when we are glad to get away from ourselves and those importunate trifles which we gravely call the realities of life. In the warm Mediterranean of his mind everything

> Suffers a sea-change
> Into something rich and strange.

He lifts everything, not beyond recognition, but to an ideal distance where no mortal, I had almost said human, fleck is visible. Instead of the ordinary bridal gifts, he hallows his wife with an Epithalamion fit for a conscious goddess, and the "savage soil"[53] of Ireland becomes a turf of Arcady under her feet, where the merchants' daughters of the town are no more at home than the angels and the fair shapes of pagan mythology whom they meet there. He seems to have had a common-sense side to him, and could look at things (if we may judge by his tract on Irish affairs) in a practical and even hard way; but the moment he turned toward poetry he fulfilled the condition which his teacher Plato imposes on poets, and had not a particle of prosaic understanding left. His fancy, habitually moving about in worlds not realized, unrealizes everything at a touch. The critics blame him because in his Prothalamion the subjects of it enter on the Thames as swans and leave it at Temple Gardens as noble damsels; but to those who are grown familiar with his imaginary world such a transformation seems as natural as in the old legend of the Knight of the Swan.

> Come now ye damsels, daughters of Delight,
> Help quickly her to dight:
> But first come ye, fair Hours, which were
>   begot
> In Jove's sweet paradise of Day and
>   Night, . . .
> And ye three handmaids of the Cyprian
>   Queen,

> The which do still adorn her beauty's pride,
> Help to adorn my beautifulest bride,
> . . .
> Crown ye god Bacchus with a coronal,
> And Hymen also crown with wreaths of vine,
> And let the Graces dance unto the rest,—
>   For they can do it best.
> The whiles the maidens do their carols sing,
> To which the woods shall answer and their echo ring.

The whole Epithalamion is very noble, with an organ-like roll and majesty of numbers, while it is instinct with the same joyousness which must have been the familiar mood of Spenser. It is no superficial and tiresome merriment, but a profound delight in the beauty of the universe and in that delicately surfaced nature of his which was its mirror and counterpart. Sadness was alien to him, and at funerals he was, to be sure, a decorous mourner, as could not fail with so sympathetic a temperament; but his condolences are graduated to the unimpassioned scale of social requirement. Even for Sir Philip Sidney his sighs are regulated by the official standard. It was in an unreal world that his affections found their true object and vent, and it is in an elegy of a lady whom he had never known that he puts into the mouth of a husband whom he has evaporated into a shepherd, the two most naturally pathetic verses he ever penned:

> I hate the day because it lendeth light
> To see all things, but not my love to see.[54]

In the Epithalamion there is an epithet which has been much admired for its felicitous tenderness:

> Behold, whiles she before the altar stands,
> Hearing the holy priest that to her speakes
> And blesseth her with his two *happy* hands.

But the purely impersonal passion of the artist had already guided him to this lucky phrase. It is addressed by Holiness—a dame surely as far abstracted from the enthusiasms of love as we can readily conceive of—to Una, who, like the visionary Helen of Dr. Faustus, has every charm of womanhood, except that of being alive as Juliet and Beatrice are.

> O happy earth,
> Whereon thy innocent feet do ever tread![55]

Can we conceive of Una, the fall of whose foot would be as soft as that of a rose-leaf upon its mates already fallen,—can we conceive of her treading anything so sordid? No; it is only on some unsubstantial floor of dream that she walks securely, herself a dream. And it is only when Spenser has escaped thither, only when this glamour of fancy has rarefied his wife till she is grown almost as purely a creature of the imagination as the other ideal images with which he converses, that his feeling becomes as nearly passionate—as nearly human, I was on the point of saying—as with him is possible. I am so far from blaming this idealizing property of his mind, that I find it admirable in him. It is his quality, not his defect. Without some touch of it life would be unendurable prose. If I have called the world to which he transports us a world of unreality, I have wronged him. It is only a world of unrealism. It is from pots and pans and stocks and futile gossip and inch-long politics that he emancipates us, and makes us free of that to-morrow, always coming and never come, where ideas shall reign supreme.[56] But I am keeping my readers from the sweetest idealization that love ever wrought:

> Unto this place whenas the elfin knight
> Approachéd, him seeméd that the merry
>   sound

Of a shrill pipe, he playing heard on height,
And many feet fast thumping the hollow
  ground,
That through the woods their echo did
  rebound;
He nigher drew to wit what it mote be.
There he a troop of ladies dancing found
Full merrily and making gladful glee;
And in the midst a shepherd piping he did see.

He durst not enter into the open green
For dread of them unwares to be descried,
For breaking of their dance, if he were seen;
But in the covert of the wood did bide
Beholding all, yet of them unespied;
There he did see that pleased so much his
  sight
That even he himself his eyes envied,
A hundred naked maidens lily-white,
All rangèd in a ring and dancing in delight.

All they without were rangèd in a ring,
And dancèd round; but in the midst of them
Three other ladies did both dance and sing,
The while the rest them round about did hem,
And like a garland did in compass stem.
And in the midst of these same three was
  placed
Another damsel, as a precious gem
Amidst a ring most richly well enchased,
That with her goodly presence all the rest much
  graced.

Look how the crown which Ariadne wove
Upon her ivory forehead that same day,
That Theseus her unto his bridal bore,
(When the bold Centaurs made that bloody
  fray,
With the fierce Lapithes, that did them
  dismay)
Being now placèd in the firmament,
Through the bright heaven doth her beams
  display,
And is unto the stars an ornament,
Which round about her move in order excellent;

Such was the beauty of this goodly band,
Whose sundry parts were here too long to tell,
But she that in the midst of them did stand,
Seemed all the rest in beauty to excel,
Crowned with a rosy garland that right well
Did her beseem. And, ever as the crew
About her danced, sweet flowers that far did
  smell,
And fragrant odors they upon her threw;
But most of all those three did her with gifts endue.

Those were the graces, Daughters of Delight,
Handmaids of Venus, which are wont to
  haunt
Upon this hill and dance there, day and night;
Those three to men all gifts of grace do grant
And all that Venus in herself doth vaunt
Is borrowèd of them; but that fair one
That in the midst was placed paravant,
Was she to whom that shepherd piped alone,
That made him pipe so merrily, as never none.

She was, to weet, that jolly shepherd's lass
Which pipèd there unto that merry rout;
That jolly shepherd that there pipèd was
Poor Colin Clout; (who knows not Colin
  Clout?)

He piped apace while they him danced about;
Pipe, jolly shepherd, pipe thou now apace,
Unto thy love that made thee low to lout;
Thy love is present there with thee in place,
Thy love is there advanced to be another Grace.[57]

Is there any passage in any poet that so ripples and sparkles with simple delight as this? It is a sky of Italian April full of sunshine and the hidden ecstasy of larks. And we like it all the more that it reminds us of that passage in his friend Sidney's *Arcadia*, where the shepherd-boy pipes "as if he would never be old." If we compare it with the mystical scene in Dante,[58] of which it is a reminiscence, it will seem almost like a bit of real life; but taken by itself it floats as unconcerned in our cares and sorrows and vulgarities as a sunset cloud. The sound of that pastoral pipe seems to come from as far away as Thessaly when Apollo was keeping sheep there. Sorrow, the great idealizer, had had the portrait of Beatrice on her easel for years, and every touch of her pencil transfigured the woman more and more into the glorified saint. But Elizabeth Nagle was a solid thing of flesh and blood, who would sit down at meat with the poet on the very day when he had thus beatified her. As Dante was drawn upward from heaven to heaven by the eyes of Beatrice, so was Spenser lifted away from the actual by those of that ideal Beauty whereof his mind had conceived the lineaments in its solitary musings over Plato, but of whose haunting presence the delicacy of his senses had already premonished him. The intrusion of the real world upon this supersensual mood of his wrought an instant disenchantment:

Much wondered Calidore at this strange sight
Whose like before his eye had never seen,
And, standing long astonishèd in sprite
And rapt with pleasance, wist not what to
  ween,
Whether it were the train of Beauty's Queen,
Or Nymphs, or Fairies, or enchanted show
With which his eyes might have deluded
  been,
Therefore resolving what it was to know,
Out of the woods he rose and toward them did go.

But soon as he appearèd to their view
They vanished all away out of his sight
And clean were gone, which way he never
  knew,
All save the shepherd, who, for fell despite
Of that displeasure, broke his bagpipe quite.

Ben Jonson said that "he had consumed a whole night looking to his great toe, about which he had seen Tartars and Turks, Romans and Carthaginians, fight in his imagination"; and Coleridge has told us how his "eyes made pictures when they were shut." This is not uncommon, but I fancy that Spenser was more habitually possessed by his imagination than is usual even with poets. His visions must have accompanied him "in glory and in joy" along the common thoroughfares of life and seemed to him, it may be suspected, more real than the men and women he met there. His "most fine spirit of sense" would have tended to keep him in this exalted mood. I must give an example of the sensuousness of which I have spoken:

And in the midst of all a fountain stood
Of richest substance that on earth might be,
So pure and shiny that the crystal flood
Through every channel running one might
  see;
Most goodly it with curious imagery
Was overwrought, and shapes of naked boys,
Of which some seemed with lively jollity
To fly about, playing their wanton toys,

Whilst others did themselves embay in liquid joys.

> And over all, of purest gold was spread
> A trail of ivy in his native hue;
> For the rich metal was so colorëd
> That he who did not well avised it view
> Would surely deem it to be ivy true;
> Low his lascivious arms adown did creep
> That themselves dipping in the silver dew
> Their fleecy flowers they tenderly did steep,
> Which drops of crystal seemed for wantonness to weep.

> Infinite streams continually did well
> Out of this fountain, sweet and fair to see,
> The which into an ample laver fell,
> And shortly grew to so great quantity
> That like a little lake it seemed to be
> Whose depth exceeded not three cubits' height,
> That through the waves one might the bottom see
> All paved beneath with jasper shining bright,
> That seemed the fountain in that sea did sail upright.

> And all the margent round about was set
> With shady laurel-trees, thence to defend
> The sunny beams which on the billows bet,
> And those which therein bathëd mote offend.
> As Guyon happened by the same to wend
> Two naked Damsels he therein epsied,
> Which therein bathing seemëd to contend
> And wrestle wantonly, ne cared to hide
> Their dainty parts from view of any which them eyed.

> Sometimes the one would lift the other quite
> Above the waters, and then down again
> Her plunge, as overmasterëd by might,
> Where both awhile would coverëd remain,
> And each the other from to rise restrain;
> The whiles their snowy limbs, as through a veil,
> So through the crystal waves appeerëd plain:
> Then suddenly both would themselves unhele,
> And the amorous sweet spoils to greedy eyes reveal.

> As that fair star, the messenger of morn,
> His dewy face out of the sea doth rear;
> Or as the Cyprian goddess, newly born
> Of the ocean's fruitful froth, did first appear;
> Such seemed they, and so their yellow hear
> Crystalline humor droppëd down apace.
> Whom such when Guyon saw, he drew him near,
> And somewhat gan relent his earnest pace;
> His stubborn breast gan secret pleasance to embrace.

> The wanton Maidens him espying, stood
> Gazing awhile at his unwonted guise;
> Then the one herself low duckëd in the flood,
> Abashed that her a stranger did avise;
> But the other rather higher did arise,
> And her two lily paps aloft displayed,
> And all that might his melting heart entice
> To her delights, she unto him bewrayed;
> The rest, hid underneath, him more desirous made.

> With that the other likewise up arose,
> And her fair locks, which formerly were bound
> Up in one knot, she low adown did loose,

> Which flowing long and thick her clothed around,
> And the ivory in golden mantle gowned:
> So that fair spectacle from him was reft,
> Yet that which reft it no less fair was found;
> So hid in locks and waves from lookers' theft,
> Naught but her lovely face she for his looking left.

> Withal she laughëd, and she blushed withal,
> That blushing to her laughter gave more grace,
> And laughter to her blushing, as did fall.

. . . .

> Eftsoones they heard a most melodious sound,
> Of all that mote delight a dainty ear,
> Such as at once might not on living ground,
> Save in this paradise, be heard elsewhere:
> Right hard it was for wight which did it hear
> To read what manner music that mote be;
> For all that pleasing is to living ear
> Was there consorted in one harmony;
> Birds, voices, instruments, winds, waters, all agree.

> The joyous birds, shrouded in cheerful shade,
> Their notes unto the voice attempered sweet;
> The angelical soft trembling voices made
> To the instruments divine respondence mete;
> The silver-sounding instruments did meet
> With the base murmur of the water's fall;
> The water's fall with difference discreet,
> Now soft, now loud, unto the wind did call;
> The gentle warbling wind low answerëd to all.

Spenser, in one of his letters to Harvey, had said, "Why, a God's name, may not we, as else the Greeks, have the kingdom of our own language?" This is in the tone of Bellay, as is also a great deal of what is said in the epistle prefixed to the *Shepherd's Calendar*. He would have been wiser had he followed more closely Bellay's advice about the introduction of novel words: "Fear not, then, to innovate somewhat, particularly in a long poem, with modesty, however, with analogy, and judgment of ear; and trouble not thyself as to who may think it good or bad, hoping that posterity will approve it,—she who gives faith to doubtful, light to obscure, novelty to antique, usage to unaccustomed, and sweetness to harsh and rude things." Spenser's innovations were by no means always happy, as not always according with the genius of the language, and they have therefore not prevailed. He forms English words out of French or Italian ones, sometimes, I think, on a misapprehension of their true meaning; nay, he sometimes makes new ones by unlawfully grafting a scion of Romance on a Teutonic root. His theory, caught from Bellay, of rescuing good archaisms from unwarranted oblivion, was excellent; not so his practice of being archaic for the mere sake of escaping from the common and familiar. A permissible archaism is a word or phrase that has been supplanted by something less apt, but has not become unintelligible; and Spenser's often needed a glossary, even in his own day.[59] But he never endangers his finest passages by any experiments of this kind. There his language is living, if ever any, and of one substance with the splendor of his fancy. Like all masters of speech, he is fond of toying with and teasing it a little; and it may readily be granted that he sometimes "hunted the letter," as it was called, out of all cry. But even where his alliteration is tempted to an excess, its prolonged echoes caress the ear like the fading and gathering reverberations of an Alpine horn, and one can find in his heart to forgive even such a debauch of initial assonances as

> Eftsoones her shallow ship away did slide,
> More swift than swallow shears the liquid sky.

Generally, he scatters them at adroit intervals, reminding us of the arrangement of voices in an ancient catch, where one voice takes up the phrase another has dropped, and thus seems to give the web of harmony a firmer and more continuous texture.

Other poets have held their mirrors up to nature, mirrors that differ very widely in the truth and beauty of the images they reflect; but Spenser's is a magic glass in which we see few shadows cast back from actual life, but visionary shapes conjured up by the wizard's art from some confusedly remembered past or some impossible future; it is like one of those still pools of mediæval legend which covers some sunken city of the antique world; a reservoir in which all our dreams seem to have been gathered. As we float upon it, we see that it pictures faithfully enough the summer-clouds that drift over it, the trees that grow about its margin, but in the midst of these shadowy echoes of actuality we catch faint tones of bells that seem blown to us from beyond the horizon of time, and looking down into the clear depths, catch glimpses of towers and far-shining knights and peerless dames that waver and are gone. Is it a world that ever was, or shall be, or can be, or but a delusion? Spenser's world, real to him, is real enough for us to take a holiday in, and we may well be content with it when the earth we dwell on is so often too real to allow of such vacations. It is the same kind of world that Petrarca's Laura has walked in for five centuries with all ears listening for the music of her footfall.

The land of Spenser is the land of Dream, but it is also the land of Rest. To read him is like dreaming awake, without even the trouble of doing it yourself, but letting it be done for you by the finest dreamer that ever lived, who knows how to color his dreams like life and make them move before you in music. They seem singing to you as the sirens to Guyon, and we linger like him:

> O, thou fair son of gentle Faery
> That art in mighty arms most magnified
> Above all knights that ever battle tried,
> O, turn thy rudder hitherward awhile,
> Here may thy storm-beat vessel safely ride,
> This is the port of rest from troublous toil,
> The world's sweet inn from pain and wearisome
>   turmoil.[60]

> With that the rolling sea, resounding swift
> In his big bass, them fitly answerëd,
> And on the rock the waves, breaking aloft,
> A solemn mean unto them measurëd,
> The whiles sweet Zephyrus loud whistelëd
> His treble, a strange kind of harmony
> Which Guyon's senses softly tickelëd
> That he the boatman bade row easily
> And let him hear some part of their rare melody.

Despite Spenser's instinctive tendency to idealize, and his habit of distilling out of the actual an ethereal essence in which very little of the possible seems left, yet his mind, as is generally true of great poets, was founded on a solid basis of good-sense. I do not know where to look for a more cogent and at the same time picturesque confutation of Socialism than in the Second Canto of the Fifth Book. If I apprehend rightly his words and images, there is not only subtile but profound thinking here. The French Revolution is prefigured in the well-meaning but too theoretic giant, and Rousseau's fallacies exposed two centuries in advance. Spenser was a conscious Englishman to his inmost fibre, and did not lack the sound judgment in politics which belongs to his race. He was the

more English for living in Ireland, and there is something that moves us deeply in the exile's passionate cry:

> Dear Country! O how dearly dear
> Ought thy remembrance and perpetual band
> Be to thy foster-child that from thy hand
> Did common breath and nouriture receive!
> How brutish is it not to understand
> How much to her we owe that all us gave,
> That gave unto us all whatever good we have!

His race shows itself also where he tells us that

> chiefly skill to ride seems a science
> Proper to gentle blood,

which reminds one of Lord Herbert of Cherbury's saying that the finest sight God looked down on was a fine man on a fine horse.

Wordsworth, in the supplement to his preface, tells us that the *Faery Queen* "faded before" Sylvester's translation of Du Bartas. But Wordsworth held a brief for himself in this case, and is no exception to the proverb about men who are their own attorneys. His statement is wholly unfounded. Both poems, no doubt, so far as popularity is concerned, yielded to the graver interests of the Civil War. But there is an appreciation much weightier than any that is implied in mere popularity, and the vitality of a poem is to be measured by the kind as well as the amount of influence it exerts. Spenser has *coached* more poets and more eminent ones than any other writer of English verse. I need say nothing of Milton, nor of professed disciples like Browne, the two Fletchers, and More. Cowley tells us that he became "irrecoverably a poet" by reading the *Faery Queen* when a boy. Dryden, whose case is particularly in point because he confesses having been seduced by Du Bartas, tells us that Spenser had been his master in English. He regrets, indeed, comically enough, that Spenser could not have read the rules of Bòssu, but adds that "no man was ever born with a greater genius or more knowledge to support it." Pope says, "There is something in Spenser that pleases one as strongly in one's old age as it did in one's youth. I read the *Faery Queen* when I was about twelve with a vast deal of delight; and I think it gave me as much when I read it over about a year or two ago." Thomson wrote the most delightful of his poems in the measure of Spenser; Collins, Gray, and Akenside show traces of him; and in our own day his influence reappears in Wordsworth, Byron, Shelley, and Keats. Landor is, I believe, the only poet who ever found him tedious. Spenser's mere manner has not had so many imitators as Milton's, but no other of our poets has given an impulse, and in the right direction also, to so many and so diverse minds; above all, no other has given to so many young souls a consciousness of their wings and a delight in the use of them. He is a standing protest against the tyranny of Commonplace, and sows the seeds of a noble discontent with prosaic views of life and the dull uses to which it may be put.

Three of Spenser's own verses best characterize the feeling his poetry gives us:

> "Among wide waves set like a little nest,"
> "Wrapt in eternal silence far from enemies,"
> "The world's sweet inn from pain and wearisome
>   turmoil."

We are wont to apologize for the grossness of our favorite authors sometimes by saying that their age was to blame and not they; and the excuse is a good one, for often it is the frank word that shocks us while we tolerate the thing. Spenser needs no such extenuations. No man can read the *Faery Queen* and be anything but the better for it. Through that rude age, when Maids of Honor drank beer for breakfast and Hamlet could say a gross thing to Ophelia, he passes serenely abstracted and high, the Don Quixote of poets. Whoever can endure unmixed delight, whoever can tolerate music and painting and poetry all in one, whoever wishes to be rid of thought and to let the busy anvils of the brain be silent for a time, let him read in the *Faery Queen*. There is the land of pure heart's ease, where no ache or sorrow of spirit can enter.

Notes

1. Though always misapplied in quotation, as if he had used the word in that generalized meaning which is common now, but which could not without an impossible anachronism have been present to his mind. He meant merely freedom from prison.
2. In his *Defence of Poesy* he condemns the archaisms and provincialisms of the *Shepherd's Calendar*.
3. "There is, as you must have heard Wordsworth point out, a language of pure, intelligible English, which was spoken in Chaucer's time, and is spoken in ours; equally understood then and now; and of which the Bible is the written and permanent standard, as it has undoubtedly been the great means of preserving it." (Southey's *Life and Correspondence*, III. 193, 194.)
4. Nash, who has far better claims than Swift to be called the English Rabelais, thus at once describes and parodies Harvey's hexameters in prose, "that drunken, staggering kind of verse, which is all up hill and down hill, like the way betwixt Stamford and Beechfield, and goes like a horse plunging through the mire in the deep of winter, now soused up to the saddle, and straight aloft on his tiptoes." It was a happy thought to satirize (in this inverted way) prose written in the form of verse.
5. Edmund Bolton in his *Hypercritica* says, "The works of Sam Daniel contained somewhat a flat, but yet withal a very pure and copious English, and words as warrantable as any man's, and *fitter perhaps for prose than measure*." I have italicized his second thought, which chimes curiously with the feeling Daniel leaves in the mind. (See Haslewood's *Ancient Crit. Essays*, Vol. II.) Wordsworth, an excellent judge, much admired Daniel's poem to the Countess of Cumberland.
6. Mr. Hales, in the excellent memoir of the poet prefixed to the Globe edition of his works, puts his birth a year earlier, on the strength of a line in the sixtieth sonnet. But it is not established that this sonnet was written in 1593, and even if it were, a sonnet is not upon oath, and the poet would prefer the round number forty, which suited the measure of his verse, to thirty-nine or forty-one, which might have been truer to the measure of his days.
7. This has been inferred from a passage in one of Gabriel Harvey's letters to him. But it would seem more natural, from the many allusions in Harvey's pamphlets against Nash, that it was his own wrongs which he had in mind, and his self-absorption would take it for granted that Spenser sympathized with him in all his grudges. Harvey is a remarkable instance of the refining influence of classical studies. Amid the pedantic farrago of his omni-sufficiency (to borrow one of his own words) we come suddenly upon passages whose gravity of sentiment, stateliness of movement, and purity of diction remind us of Landor. These lucid intervals in his overweening vanity explain and justify the friendship of Spenser. Yet the reiteration of emphasis with which he insists on all the world's knowing that Nash had called him an ass, probably gave Shakespeare the hint for one of the most comic touches in the character of Dogberry.
8. The late Major C. G. Halpine, in a very interesting essay, makes it extremely probable that Rosalinde is the anagram of Rose Daniel, sister of the poet, and married to John Florio. He leaves little doubt, also, that the name of Spenser's wife (hitherto unknown) was Elizabeth Nagle. (See *Atlantic Monthly*, Vol. II. 674, November, 1858.) Mr. Halpine informed me that he found the substance of his essay among the papers of his father, the late Rev. N. J. Halpine, of Dublin. The latter published in the series of the Shakespeare Society a sprightly little tract entitled *Oberon*, which, if not quite convincing, is well worth reading for its ingenuity and research.

9. In his prose tract on Ireland, Spenser, perhaps with some memory of Ovid in his mind, derives the Irish mainly from the Scythians.
10. Compare Shakespeare's LXVI. Sonnet.
11. This poem, published in 1591, was, Spenser tells us in his dedication, "long sithens composed in the raw conceit of my youth." But he had evidently retouched it. The verses quoted show a firmer hand than is generally seen in it, and we are safe in assuming that they were added after his visit to England. Dr. Johnson epigrammatized Spenser's indictment into

    There mark what ills the scholar's life assail,
    Toil, envy, want, the patron, and the jail,

    but I think it loses in pathos more than it gains in point.
12. *Paradiso*, XI. 4–12. Spenser was familiar with the *Divina Commedia*, though I do not remember that his commentators have pointed out his chief obligations to it.
13. His own words as reported by Lodowick Bryskett. (Todd's *Spenser*, I. lx.) The whole passage is very interesting as giving us the only glimpse we get of the living Spenser in actual contact with his fellow-men. It shows him to us, as we could wish to see him, surrounded with loving respect, companionable and helpful. Bryskett tells us that he was "perfect in the Greek tongue," and "also very well read in philosophy both moral and natural." He encouraged Bryskett in the study of Greek, and offered to help him in it. Comparing the last verse of the above citation of the *Faery Queen* with other passages in Spenser, I cannot help thinking that he wrote, "do not love amiss."
14.   And know, sweet prince, when you shall come to know,
        That 't is not in the power of kings to raise
        A spirit for verse that is not born thereto;
        Nor are they born in every prince's days.
                        (Daniel's Dedic. Trag. of "Philotas.")
15. Louis XIV. is commonly supposed in some miraculous way to have created French literature. He may more truly be said to have petrified it so far as his influence went. The French *renaissance* in the preceding century was produced by causes similar in essentials to those which brought about that in England not long after. The *grand siècle* grew by natural processes of development out of that which had preceded it, and which, to the impartial foreigner at least, has more flavor, and more French flavor too, than the Gallo-Roman usurper that pushed it from its stool. The best modern French poetry has been forced to temper its verses in the colder natural springs of the ante-classic period.
16. In the Elizabethan drama the words "England" and "France" are constantly used to signify the kings of those countries.
17. I say supposed, for the names of his two sons, Sylvanus and Peregrine, indicate that they were born in Ireland, and that Spenser continued to regard it as a wilderness and his abode there as exile. The two other children are added on the authority of a pedigree drawn up by Sir W. Betham and cited in Mr. Hales's Life of Spenser prefixed to the Globe edition.
18. Ben Jonson told Drummond that one child perished in the flames. But he was speaking after an interval of twenty-one years, and, of course, from hearsay. Spenser's misery was exaggerated by succeeding poets, who used him to point a moral, and from the shelter of his tomb launched many a shaft of sarcasm at an unappreciative public. Giles Fletcher in his *Purple Island* (a poem which reminds us of the *Faery Queen* by the supreme tediousness of its allegory, but in nothing else) set the example in the best verse he ever wrote:

    Poorly, poor man, he lived; poorly, poor man, he died.

Gradually this poetical tradition established itself firmly as authentic history. Spenser could never have been poor, except by comparison. The whole story of his later days has a strong savor of legend. He must have had ample warning of Tyrone's rebellion, and would probably have sent away his wife and children to Cork, if he did not go thither himself. I am inclined to think that he did, carrying his papers with him, and among them the two cantos of Mutability, first published in 1611. These, it is most likely, were the only ones he ever completed, for, with all his abundance, he was evidently a laborious finisher. When we remember that ten years were given to the elaboration of the first three books, and that five more elapsed before the next three were ready, we shall waste no vain regrets on the six concluding books supposed to have been lost by the carelessness of an imaginary servant on their way from Ireland.

19. Sir Philip Sidney did not approve of this. "That same framing of his style to an old rustic language I dare not allow, since neither Theocritus in Greek, Virgil in Latin, nor Sannazzaro in Italian did affect it." (*Defence of Poesy.*) Ben Jonson, on the other hand, said that Guarini "kept not decorum in making shepherds speak as well as himself could." (*Conversations with Drummond.*) I think Sidney was right, for the poets' Arcadia is a purely ideal world, and should be treated accordingly. But whoever looks into the glossary appended to the *Calendar* by E. K., will be satisfied that Spenser's object was to find unhackneyed and poetical words rather than such as should seem more on a level with the speakers. See also the *Epistle Dedicatory*. I cannot help thinking that E. K. was Spenser himself, with occasional interjections of Harvey. Who else could have written such English as many passages in this Epistle?

20. It was at Penshurst that he wrote the only specimen that has come down to us, and bad enough it is. I have said that some of Sidney's are pleasing.

21. See *My Study Windows*, 264 *seqq.*

22. Of course *dillies* and *lilies* must be read with a slight accentuation of the last syllable (permissible then), in order to chime with *delice*. In the first line I have put *here* instead of *hether*, which (like other words where *th* comes between two vowels) was then very often a monosyllable, in order to throw the accent back more strongly on *bring*, where it belongs. Spenser's innovation lies in making his verses by ear instead of on the finger-tips, and in valuing the stave more than any of the single verses that compose it. This is the secret of his easy superiority to all others in the stanza which he composed, and which bears his name. Milton (who got more of his schooling in these matters from Spenser than anywhere else) gave this principle a greater range, and applied it with more various mastery. I have little doubt that the tune of the last stanza cited above was clinging in Shakespeare's ear when he wrote those exquisite verses in *Midsummer Night's Dream* ("I know a bank"), where our grave pentameter is in like manner surprised into a lyrical movement. See also the pretty song in the eclogue for August. Ben Jonson, too, evidently caught some cadences from Spenser for his lyrics. I need hardly say that in those eclogues (May, for example) where Spenser thought he was imitating what wiseacres used to call the *riding-rhyme* of Chaucer, he fails most lamentably. He had evidently learned to scan his master's verses better when he wrote his *Mother Hubberd's Tale*.

23. Drummond, it will be remarked, speaking from memory, takes Cuddy to be Colin. In Milton's *Lycidas* there are reminiscences of this eclogue as well as of that for May. The latter are the more evident, but I think that Spenser's

> Cuddie, the praise is better than the price,

suggested Milton's

> But not the praise,
> Phœbus replied, and touched my trembling ears.

Shakespeare had read and remembered this pastoral. Compare

> But, ah, Mecænas is yclad in clay,
> And great Augustus long ago is dead,
> And all the worthies liggen wrapt in lead,

with

> King Pandion, he is dead;
> All thy friends are lapt in lead.

It is odd that Shakespeare, in his "*lapt in lead,*" is more Spenserian than Spenser himself, from whom he caught this "hunting of the letter."

24. *Ruins of Time*. It is perhaps not considering too nicely to remark how often this image of *wings* recurred to Spenser's mind. A certain aerial latitude was essential to the large circlings of his style.

25. Perhaps his most striking single epithet is the "sea-shouldering whales," B. II. 12, xxiii. His ear seems to delight in prolongations. For example, he makes such words as *glorious, gratious, joyeous, havior, chapelet* dactyles, and that, not at the end of verses, where

it would not have been unusual, but in the first half of them. Milton contrives a break (a kind of heave, as it were) in the uniformity of his verse by a practice exactly the opposite of this. He also shuns a *hiatus* which does not seem to have been generally displeasing to Spenser's ear, though perhaps in the compound epithet *bees-alluring* he intentionally avoids it by the plural form.

26.
> Like as a wayward child, whose sounder sleep
> Is broken with some fearful dream's affright,
> With froward will doth set himself to weep
> Ne can be stilled for all his nurse's might,
> But kicks and squalls and shrieks for fell despight,
> Now scratching her and her loose locks misusing,
> Now seeking darkness and now seeking light,
> Then craving suck, and then the suck refusing.

He would doubtless have justified himself by the familiar example of Homer's comparing Ajax to a donkey in the eleventh book of the Iliad. So also in the *Epithalamion* it grates our nerves to hear,

> Pour not by cups, but by the bellyful,
> Pour out to all that wull.

Such examples serve to show how strong a dose of Spenser's *aurum potabile* the language needed.

27. I could not bring myself to root out this odorous herb-garden, though it make my extract too long. It is a pretty reminiscence of his master Chaucer, but is also very characteristic of Spenser himself. He could not help planting a flower or two among his serviceable plants, and after all this abundance he is not satisfied, but begins the next stanza with "And whatso *else.*"

28. Leigh Hunt's *Indicator*, XVII.

29. Ben Jonson told Drummond "that in that paper Sir W. Raleigh had of the allegories of his *Faery Queen*, by the Blatant Beast the Puritans were understood." But this is certainly wrong. There were very different shades of Puritanism, according to individual temperament. That of Winthrop and Higginson had a mellowness of which Endicott and Standish were incapable. The gradual change of Milton's opinions was similar to that which I suppose in Spenser. The passage in *Mother Hubberd* may have been aimed at the Protestant clergy of Ireland (for he says much the same thing in his *View of the State of Ireland*), but it is general in its terms.

30. Two of his eclogues, as I have said, are from Marot, and his earliest known verses are translations from Bellay, a poet who was charming whenever he had the courage to play truant from a bad school. We must not suppose that an analysis of the literature of the *demimonde* will give us all the elements of the French character. It has been both grave and profound; nay, it has even contrived to be wise and lively at the same time, a combination so incomprehensible by the Teutonic races that they have labelled it levity. It puts them out as Nature did Fuseli.

31. Taste must be partially excepted. It is remarkable how little eating and drinking there is in the *Faery Queen*. The only time he fairly sets a table is in the house of Malbecco, where it is necessary to the conduct of the story. Yet taste is not wholly forgotten:

> In her left hand a cup of gold she held,
> And with her right the riper fruit did reach,
> Whose sappy liquor, that with fulness sweld,
> Into her cup she scruzed with dainty breach
> Of her fine fingers without foul impeach,
> That so fair wine-press made the wine more sweet.
> (B. II. c. xii. 56.)

Taste can hardly complain of unhandsome treatment!

32. Had the poet lived longer, he might perhaps have verified his friend Raleigh's saying, that "whosoever in writing modern history shall follow truth too near the heels, it may haply strike out his teeth." The passage is one of the very few disgusting ones in the *Faery Queen*. Spenser was copying Ariosto; but the Italian poet, with the discreeter taste of his race, keeps to generalities. Spenser goes into particulars which can only be called nasty. He did this, no doubt, to pleasure his mistress, Mary's rival; and this gives us a measure of the brutal coarseness of contemporary manners. It becomes only the more marvellous that the fine flower of his genius could have transmuted the juices of such a soil into the purity and sweetness which are its own peculiar properties.

33. There is a gleam of humor in one of the couplets of *Mother Hubberd's Tale*, where the Fox, persuading the Ape that they should disguise themselves as discharged soldiers in order to beg the more successfully, says,

> Be you the soldier, for you likest are
> For manly semblance *and small skill in war.*

34. Bunyan probably took the hint of the Giant's suicidal offer of "knife, halter, or poison," from Spenser's "swords, ropes, poison," in *Faery Queen*, B. I. c. ix. 1.
35. Book II. c. 9.
36. See Sidney's *Defence*, and Puttenham's *Art of English Poesy*, Book I. c. 8.
37. We can fancy how we would have done this by Jeremy Taylor, who was a kind of Spenser in a cassock.
38. Of this he himself gives a striking hint, where speaking in his own person he suddenly breaks in on his narrative with the passionate cry,

> Ah, dearest God, me grant I dead be not defouled.
> (*Faery Queen*, B. I. c. x. 48.)

39. Was not this picture painted by Paul Veronese, for example?

> Arachne figured how Jove did abuse
> Europa like a bull, and on his back
> Her through the sea did bear: . . . .
> She seemed still back unto the land to look,
> And her playfellows' aid to call, and fear
> The dashing of the waves, that up she took
> Her dainty feet, and garments gathered near. . . .
> Before the bull she pictured wingèd Love,
> With his young brother Sport, . . .
> And many nymphs about them flocking round,
> And many Tritons which their horns did sound.
> (*Muiopotmos*, 281-296.)

Spenser begins a complimentary sonnet prefixed to the *Commonwealth and Government of Venice* (1599) with this beautiful verse,

> Fair Venice, flower of the last world's delight.

Perhaps we should read "lost"?
40. Marlowe's *Tamburlaine*, Part I. Act V. 2.
41.
> Grayheaded Thought, nor much nor little, may
> Take up its lodging here in any heart;
> Unease nor Lack can enter at this door;
> But here dwells full-horned Plenty evermore.
> (*Orl. Fur.*, c. vi. 73.)

42. B. I. c. iii. 7. Leigh Hunt, one of the most sympathetic of critics, has remarked the passionate change from the third to the first person in the last two verses.
43. B. II. c. viii. 3.
44. *Observations on Faery Queen*, Vol. I. pp. 158, 159. Mr. Hughes also objects to Spenser's measure, that it is "closed always by a full-stop, in the same place, by which every stanza is made as it were a distinct paragraph " (Todd's *Spenser*, II xli) But he could hardly have read the poem attentively, for there are numerous instances to the contrary. Spenser was a consummate master of versification, and not only did Marlowe and Shakespeare learn of him, but I have little doubt that, but for the *Faery Queen*, we should never have had the varied majesty of Milton's blank-verse.
45. As where Dr. Warton himself says:—

> How nearly had my spirit past,
>   Till stopt by Metcalf's skilful hand,
> To death's dark regions wide and waste
>   And the black river's mournful strand,
> Or to, etc.,

to the end of the next stanza. That is, I had died but for Dr. Metcalf's boluses.
46. *Iliad*, XVII. 55 *seqq.* Referred to in Upton's note on Faery Queen, B. I. c. vii. 32. Into what a breezy couplet trailing off with an alexandrine has Homer's *pnoiai pantoiōn anemōn* expanded! Chapman unfortunately has slurred this passage in his version, and Pope *tittivated* it more than usual in his. I have no other translation at hand. Marlowe was so taken by this passage in Spenser that he put it bodily into his *Tamburlaine*.
47. *Inferno*, XXIV. 46–52.

> For sitting upon down,
> Or under quilt, one cometh not to fame,
> Withouten which whoso his life consumeth
> Such vestige leaveth of himself on earth
> As smoke in air or in the water foam.
> (*Longfellow*.)

It shows how little Dante was read during the last century that none of the commentators on Spenser notice his most important obligations to the great Tuscan.
48. *Faery Queen*, B. II. c. iii. 40, 41.
49. Ibid., B. I. c. v. I.
50. Ibid., B. II. c. viii. 1, 2.
51. B. III. c. xi. 28.
52. B. I. c. i. 41.
53. This phrase occurs in the sonnet addressed to the Earl of Ormond and in that to Lord Grey de Wilton in the series prefixed to the *Faery Queen*. These sonnets are of a much stronger build than the *Amoretti*, and some of them (especially that to Sir John Norris) recall the firm tread of Milton's, though differing in structure.
54. *Daphnaida*, 407, 408.
55. *Faery Queen*, B. I. c. x. 9.
56. Strictly taken, perhaps his world is not *much* more imaginary than that of other epic poets, Homer (in the *Iliad*) included. He who is familiar with mediæval epics will be extremely cautious in drawing inferences as to contemporary manners from Homer. He evidently *archaizes* like the rest.
57. *Faery Queen*, B. VI. c. x. 10–16.
58. *Purgatorio*, XXIX., XXX.
59. I find a goodly number of Yankeeisms in him, such as *idee* (not as a rhyme); but the oddest is his twice spelling *dew deow*, which is just as one would spell it who wished to phonetize its sound in rural New England.
60. This song recalls that in Dante's *Purgatorio* (XIX. 19–24), in which the Italian tongue puts forth all its siren allurements. Browne's beautiful verses ("Turn, hither turn your wingèd pines") were suggested by these of Spenser. It might also seem as if Spenser had here, in his usual way, expanded the sweet old verses:

> Merry sungen the monks binnen Ely
> When Knut king rew thereby;
> 'Roweth knightés near the lond,
> That I may hear these monkés song.'

AUBREY DE VERE
"Spenser as a Philosophic Poet"
Essays
1887, Volume 1, pp. 48–100

It often happens that some eminent characteristic of a great poet has almost escaped observation owing to the degree in which other characteristics, not higher but more attractive to the many, have also belonged to him. Spenser is an instance of this. If it were asked what chiefly constitutes the merit of his poetry, the answer would commonly be, its descriptive power, or its chivalrous sentiment, or its exquisite sense of beauty; yet the quality which he himself desiderated most for his chief work was one not often found in union with these, viz. sound and true philosophic thought. This characteristic is perhaps his highest. It was the one which chiefly gained for him the praise of Shakespeare—

> Spenser to me, whose *deep conceit* is such
>   As, passing all conceit, needs no defence;

and it was doubtless the merit to which he owed the influence which Milton acknowledged that Spenser's poetry had exercised over his own. There is more of philosophy in one book of the *Faery Queen* than in all the cantos of his Italian models. In Italy the thinkers were generally astute politicians or recluse theologians; and her later poets, excepting of course Tasso, cared more to amuse a brilliant court with song and light tale than to follow the steps of Dante along the summits of serious thought. England, on the other hand, uniting both the practical and the meditative mind with the imaginative instincts of southern lands, had thereby strengthened that mind and those instincts, and thus occupied a position neither above nor beneath the region of thoughtful poetry. In the latter part of the sixteenth and earlier part of the seventeenth century, she possessed a considerable number of poets who selected, apparently without offence, very grave themes for their poetry. It will suffice to name such writers as Samuel Daniel, John Davies, George Herbert, Dr. Donne, Giles Fletcher, Habington, and, not much later, Dr. Henry More, the Platonist.

These poets, however, came later than Spenser, and were not a little indebted to him, while yet they were, in some respects, unlike him. Some of them worked on themes so abstract and metaphysical as to be almost beyond the limits of true poetic art. The difficulty was itself an attraction to them, and their ambition was more to instruct than to delight. Spenser loved philosophy as well as they, but was too truly a poet to allow of his following her when she strayed into "a barren and dry land," or of his adopting the didactic method when he illustrated philosophic themes. Truth and beauty are things correlative; and very profound truths can be elucidated in verse without the aid of such technical reasoning processes as those with which Dryden conducted his argument in the *Hind and Panther*, and Pope in his *Essays*. Spenser's imagination never forsook the region of the sympathies; but it had the special gift of drawing within their charmed circle themes which for another poet must have ever remained outside it, and of suffusing them at once with the glow of passion and with the white light of high intelligence. It is true that he dealt much in allegory; but though allegory is commonly a cold thing—always, indeed, if it be mere allegory—yet whenever Spenser's genius is true to itself, his allegory catches fire and raises to the heights of song themes which would otherwise have descended to the level of ordinary prose. Had Spenser's poetry not included this philosophic vein, it would not have been in sympathy with a time which produced a Bacon, whose prose is often the noblest poetry, as well as a Sidney, whose life was a poem. At the Merchant Taylors' Grammar School, Bishop Andrews and, as is believed, Richard Hooker, were among his companions; and when he entered Cambridge, Pembroke Hall was at least as much occupied with theological and metaphysical discussion as with classical literature.

We may go further. It was in a large measure the strength of his human sympathies which at once forced Spenser to include philosophy among the subjects of his poetry, and prevented that philosophy from becoming unfit for poetry. As he was eminently a poet of the humanities, so his philosophy was a philosophy of the humanities; he could no more have taken up a physiological theme for a poem, like Phineas Fletcher's *Purple Island*, than a geographical one, like Drayton's *Polyolbion*. The philosophy which interested him was that which "comes home to the business and bosoms of men." It was philosophy allied to life—philosophy moral, social, and political. Such philosophy is latent in all great poetry, though it is in some ages only that it becomes patent. Let us turn first to his political and social philosophy.

We know from Spenser's letter to Sir Walter Raleigh that to embody a great scheme of philosophy was the end which he proposed to himself in writing the *Faery Queen*. That poem was to consist of twelve books; and the hero of each was to impersonate one of the twelve moral virtues enumerated by Aristotle. This poem he proposed to follow up by a second, the hero of which was to have been King Arthur after he had acceded to the throne, and which was to have illustrated the political virtues. We learn from Todd's *Life of Spenser* that at a party of friends held near Dublin, in the house of Lodowick Bryskett, the poet gave the same account of his poem, then unpublished, but of which a considerable part had been written. Bryskett, on that occasion, spoke of him as "not only perfect in the Greek tongue, but also very well read in philosophy, both moral and natural."

Unhappily, only half of the earlier romance was written, or at least has reached us, and no part of the second; but much which belongs to the subject of the second poem may be found in fragments scattered over the six books of the *Faery Queen*. One of these political fragments vindicates the old claim of poets to be prophets; for the great revolutionary dogma expounded in it is one which, though its earlier mutterings may have been heard at the time of the German Anabaptists, did not "open its mouth" and "speak great things" for two centuries after Spenser had denounced the approaching imposture. That imposture is the one, now but too well known, which, in the name of justice, substitutes for it the fiction of a universal equality in the interests of which all human society hitherto known is to be levelled down and remodelled. Artegal, Spenser's emblem of Justice, rides forth on his mission accompanied by his squire Talus, the iron man, with the iron flail. On the seaside they descry "many nations" gathered together—

> There they beheld a mighty gyant stand
> Upon a rocke, and holding forth on hie
> An huge great paire of ballaunce in his hand,
> W'ith which he boasted in his surquedrie
> That all the world he would weigh equallie,
> If aught he had the same to counterpoize;
> For want whereof he weighed vanity,
> And filled his ballaunce full of idle toys;
> And was admired much of fools, women, and boys.
>
> He sayd that he would all the earth uptake
> And all the sea, divided each from either;
> So would he of the fire one ballaunce make,
> And of the ayre without or wind or weather:
> Then would he ballaunce heaven and hell together,
> And all that did within them all containe;
> Of all whose weight he would not misse a fether;
> And looke what surplus did of each remaine,
> He would to his own part restore the same againe.
>
> . . .
>
> Therefore the vulgar did about him flocke,
> And cluster thicke unto his leasings vaine,
> Like foolish flies about a hony-crocke
> In hope by him great benefit to gain.

The Knight of Justice here breaks in, and affirms that the giant ought, before restoring everything to its original condition, to ascertain exactly "What was the poyse of every part of yore." The giant knows that the best mode to meet an unanswerable reply is by reiteration—

> Therefore I will throw downe these mountains hie,
> And make them levell with the lowly plaine,
> These towring rocks which reach unto the skie,
> I will thrust down into the deepest maine,
> And as they were them equalize againe.
> Tyrants, that make men subject to their law,
> I will suppresse that they no more may raine,
> And lordlings curbe that commons overaw,

And all the wealth of rich men to the poore will draw.

Artegal retorts that what the sea devours of the land in one region it surrenders in another, and that if the field did not augment its stores by drawing decayed matter into its bosom, it could not send up the living harvest the next year. In all this interchange Nature but obeys the great Creator.

> They live, they die, like as He doth ordaine,
> Ne ever any asketh reason why;
> The hils doe not the lowly dales disdaine;
> The dales do not the lofty hils envy.
> He maketh kings to sit in sovereinty;
> He maketh subjects to their powre obey;
> He pulleth downe; He setteth up on hie;
> He gives to this; from that He takes away:
> For all we have is His: what He list doe He may.

He takes the giant at his word, and bids him test his boasted power.

> For take thy ballaunce, if thou be so wise,
> And weigh the winde that under heaven doth blow;
> Or weigh the light that in the east doth rise;
> Or weigh the thought that from man's mind doth flow.
> But if the weight of these thou canst not show,
> Weight but one word which from thy lips doth fall;
> For how canst thou those greater secrets know,
> That doest not know the least thing of them all?

Ne can he rule the great that cannot reach the small.

We have all heard of the English socialist whose triumphant appeal, "Tell me, is not one man as good as another?" was unwittingly confuted by the answer of his Irish boon-companion, "To be sure he is, *and better!*" So far as equality exists at all, it exists not by nature, but through man's law, so bitterly inveighed against by the advocates of equality; for Nature, while she is rich in compensations, makes no two things equal. Notwithstanding, the giant accepts Artegal's challenge. He places the True and the False in the opposed scales of his balance, but can get no further—

> For by no means the False will with the Truth be wayd.

He next puts Right and Wrong into his scales, but fails once more—

> Yet all the wrongs could not a little right downe-way.

The prophet thus turning out an impostor, Talus scales the rock, scourges him with his iron flail, flings him into the sea, and disperses the multitude.

Spenser, however, does not take one-sided views of things. He sees a connection between the madness of revolutionary idealisms and that tyranny which "maketh a wise man mad." Before we make acquaintance with the giant Equality, we are brought to the castle of a bandit chief, Pollente, who has grown to wealth through extortion.

> And daily he his wrongs encreaseth more;
> For never wight he lets to pass that way,
> Over his bridge, albee he rich or poore,
> But he him makes his passage-penny pay;
> Else he doth hold him backe, or beat away.
> Thereto he hath a groome of evill guize,
> Whose scalp is bare, that bondage doth bewray,
> Which pols and pils the poore in piteous wize,
> But he himself upon the rich doth tyrannize.

Pollente has a daugher, Munera; to her he brings his ill-gotten spoils, and with them she has purchased all the country round. Eventually Artegal slays the giant, and Talus, rejecting the bribes of Munera, drags her from under a heap of gold, her hiding-place, cuts off her hands, which are made of gold, and her feet, which are silver, and casts her into the flood.

Another ethical craze of our later time seems to have been anticipated by Spenser—that which claims for women all the civil and political privileges and functions which belong to men, and denounces, as the "subjection of woman," even that domestic obedience of the wife to the husband which is the noblest example of willing submission. That a wife's obedience is based neither on servile fear nor abject self-interest, but on that principle of love which is the characteristic crown of womanhood, is witnessed to in the expression, "Thy desire shall be to thy husband, and he shall have the rule over thee." The root of that claim to domestic equality which would revolutionise the whole domestic life is patent. Those who sustain it assume that obedience is, even when necessary, still essentially a degradation. This is a "vulgar error." Obedience to a spurious authority, and obedience extorted by mere force, in each of these there exists degradation; but where the obedience is paid willingly, and paid where it is due, there obedience and authority are but two converse forms of excellence, mutually supplemental. This principle of correlative though contrasted forms of excellence was appreciated by the ages of chivalry; children knelt to their parents, and the "faithful servant," who inscribed that name alone on the title-page of his story of the "knight without fear and without reproach," regarded the title "servant" as an honourable one, not less than the title master.

The "Amazon Republic" was a Greek conception, and evinced that clearness which belonged to the Greek intelligence alike in its serious and in its sportive moods. The Greek insight perceived at once that, while the equality of the sexes may substantially exist in the way of compensatory advantages and disadvantages, it could not exist in the material form of identical rights and functions. In that form, woman must have either less than equality, or more. The lady who remarked, "I do not want women to take their stand with men on the great stage of life, because unless we sat behind the scenes we could not pull the wires," understood that women possess at present a very real power of their own; and the Athenians said of old, that if Pericles governed Athens, so did his wife, since she governed him, and so did their child, since he governed her. Here is the indirect equality produced by compensation. It is in its complete Amazonian, not its incomplete, form that Spenser deals with this quaint moral problem; and there is a deep sagacity in his mode of solving it. The Knight of Justice hears that a certain Amazon Queen, Radigund, by way of righting the wrongs of her sex, has established herself in a castle, and that she defies all knights to combat, first binding them to submit to her terms. The Amazon is not actuated by zeal for her sex; next to the inspiration of pride comes that of spite; and an idle fancy has been followed up by an envenomed grudge. Neither is Artegal's resolve to do battle with the Amazon grounded merely on his sympathy with the knights thus degraded—

> "Now sure," said he, "and by the faith that I
> To maidenhead and noble knighthood owe,
> I will not rest till I her might do try!"

Her masculine claims he regards as an insult to all that is best in maidenhood and womanhood—a virtual denial alike of their true powers and dignities.

Artegal is victorious at first, and his enemy falls; admiring and compassionating, the knight throws away his sword; the Amazon revives and resumes the fight; he can only step backwards, protecting himself with his shield; she redoubles her blows; and he, by the terms of their battle, becomes her slave. But the battle has not really been fought with equal weapons; and it is owing to her beauty and his weakness that he sits ere long ranged with her other vassals, distaff in hand, and in woman's garb.

The conqueror is punished for her pride. She loses her heart to her captive in spite of her self-scorn, and she fails in her attempt to win his love. Her charm is for him gone. She has lost the power of women by claiming that which belongs to man; she has snatched at the shadow, and dropped the substance. It is woman that avenges the wrong done to womanhood. Britomart hears that her lover is in distress, and flies to his aid, though she believes that he had forgotten her. The virgin warrioress assails the castle of the Amazon, vanquishes her in single fight, and liberates the captives. Britomart is the loftiest of Spenser's heroines. Another poet would have made her turn in scorn from Artegal when she saw him among the knights plying the distaff. She does not do this. She is not woman unsexed, but woman raised above woman, and therefore woman still. The sacred obedience of love binds her to the better part. When she first saw him amid the servile crew,

> She turned her head aside as nothing glad.

But she looks on him again, and sees, not what is before her, but what she remembers. She makes him lord of the conquered city; and to it she restores peace and gladness.

Let us turn next to Spenser's philosophy considered with reference to the joys and duties of life, personal and domestic. That philosophy was a comprehensive one, and regarded human life in at least three aspects. The first is the ordinary life of men lived wisely; the second is the life spiritual founded on faith in worlds unseen; the third is life lived unwisely, and dominated either by sensual passion or by pride.

To begin with his philosophy of ordinary life when wisely led. It is set forth chiefly in the Second Book, or the Legend of Temperance. The first canto tells us of the husband under a witch's spell, of the self-slain wife, and the deserted babe—all three the victims of lawless passion in the form of corrupt pleasure. In the second canto the destructive passion is anger: two knights strive in fratricidal fury aggravated by the arts of their two lady-loves. These sirens allegorise the "Two Extremes," and are contrasted with a third sister, Medina, or the "Golden Mean," who endeavours to bring the warring knights to concord. It is not from war that she dissuades them, but from unworthy war. According to Spenser's philosophy, man's condition is by necessity "militant here on earth"; but the wars, like the loves of men, should have in them little in common with those of the inferior kinds. It was thus that Sidney wrote of "that sweet enemy, France." Rancour in the form of slander and detraction is here yet more severely judged than the most relentless war. It is the first offence punished in the temple of justice.

The secret of human happiness, according to Spenser, is self-control, especially in the use of lawful things. It is that dignity in which man was created, and that belongs not to his spirit alone, but to its earthly tabernacle also, which, far more than any servile fear, binds him over to resist whatever that dignity condemns. The mandates of conscience constitute the true glory and beauty of the world we inhabit. They are "exceedingly broad"; and only in proportion as he rejoices in them while he obeys them, does man possess the "freedom of the city" in which he dwells. Lives ruled by these radiant and benignant laws advance through boundless spaces in security as well as swiftness, like the planets which move without collision through the heavenly regions because they are faithful to their prescribed orbits; while lawless lives break themselves against

unseen obstacles, and fall helpless. This is the doctrine illustrated by the ninth canto of the second legend which describes the House of Temperance. When Guyon and Prince Arthur reach its gates, they find them barred against the attacks of a barbarous foe. Here we have one of Spenser's Irish experiences—

> As when a swarme of gnats at eventide
> Out of the fennes of Allan doe arise,
> Their murmuring small trompetts sownden wide,
> Whiles in the aire their clustring army flies,
> That as a cloud doth seeme to dim the skies,
> Ne man, nor beast may rest or take repast
> For their sharp wounds and noyous iniuries,
> Till the fierce northern wind with blustring blast
> Doth blow them quite away, and in the ocean cast.

The foes at last dispersed—the emblems of the passions that besiege the soul—the gates of the castle are thrown open, and admittance is given to the knights by the princess who keeps state within.

> Alma she called was, a virgin bright,
> That had not yet felt Cupides wanton rage;
> Yet was she woo'd of many a gentle knight,
> And many a lord of noble parentage,
> That sought with her to lincke in marriage;
> For shee was faire, as faire mote ever bee,
> And in the flowre now of her freshest age;
> Yet full of grace and goodly modestee,
> That even heven rejoicéd her sweete face to see.
>
> In robe of lilly white she was arayd,
> That from her shoulder to her heele downe raught,
> The traine whereof loose far behind her strayd,
> Branchéd with gold and perle, most richly wrought,
> And borne of two fair damsels which were taught
> That service well; her yellow golden heare
> Was trimly woven and in tresses wrought;
> No other tire she on head did weere,
> But crowned with a garland of sweet rosiere.

Alma entertains her deliverers "with gentle court and gracious delight," and, after they have rested, leads them all round her castle walls. Next she shows them the stately hall set with "tables faire," where all is bounty without excess, and the "goodly parlour" in which sit many beautiful ladies and knights who "them did in modest sort amate," and where even the son of Venus behaves with an approach to discretion—

> And eke amongst them little Cupid playd
> His wanton sportes, being retourned late
> From his fierce warres, and having from him layd
> His cruel bow, wherewith he thousands hath dismayd.

Not all of Alma's pupils are yet perfect in her lore. One of these is called "Praise-desire"; she sits "in a long purple pall" with a branch of tremulous poplar in her hand, and to Prince Arthur's demand as to the cause of her sadness she replies that it has come to her from "her great desire of glory and of fame." Another maiden has an opposite fault—an undue fear of human dispraise.

The princess leads the warriors next to a tower which commands a view of far realms. Therein three stately chambers rise one above another, each the cell of a sage. These three sages are emblems of the Future, the Present, and the Past. The walls of one chamber are painted with "infinite shapes of things dispersed there," shadows that flit through idle fantasy to charm or to scare it; devices, visions, wild opinions, and soothsayings. Here abides the sad prophet whose kingdom is the Future—a sick imagination.

> Amongst them all he sate which wonnèd there,
> That hight Phantastes by his nature true;
> A man of yeares, yet fresh as mote appere,
> Of swarth complexion, and of crabbed hew,
> That him full of meláncholy did shew;
> Bent hollow bettle brows, sharp, staring eyes,
> That mad or foolish seemed; one by his vew
> Might deeme him borne with ill-disposed skies,
> When oblique Saturne sate in th' House of Agonies.

The second chamber is painted over with the types of all that imparts dignity to state—magistracies, the tribunals of justice, the triumphs of sciences and arts. This is the kingdom of the Present; and the sage who sits in it, a strong man of "ripe and perfect age," though his wisdom has all come "through continual practise and usage," represents practical judgment, and has for his kingdom the Present. The third sage symbolises memory, and the Past is his domain.

These three sages are, we are told, severally imperfect, because they dwell apart, each in a world of his own. Each makes too much of what occupies his special field of vision. The fault is that of disproportion, one closely allied to defective self-control. Neither imagination, judgment, nor memory, is fit to rule. These are but Alma's counsellors, each ministering a knowledge which becomes wisdom only when blent with the knowledge of the other two.

Next to a temperate will, the secret of a happy life, according to Spenser's philosophy, is a contented temper and that humility from which content springs. Such is the lesson taught to Calidore, the Knight of Courtesey, by the old shepherd Melibee. Happiness, he maintains, is from within, not from without—

> It is the mind that maketh good or ill,
> That maketh wretch or happie, rich or poore;

and for this reason he affirms, that those who earn their "daily bread" are the most fortunate. That the lowly condition, when at its best, does not exclude genuine refinement, is a lesson which Calidore learns from Pastorell, the supposed daughter of old Melibee, though in reality a maiden of high degree.

The quotations made above express Spenser's estimate of human life when, with its twofold capacities, it has neither risen above ordinary humanity nor fallen below it. It is an estimate in some degree founded on the ancient philosophy, with its "mens sana in corpore sano," and yet more on that spiritual teaching which regards man's estate as at once peaceful within and militant without: peaceful, because protected from the storms of passion and lawless ambition; militant, because a ceaseless war with evil is an essential part of our earthly probation. With those two conditions of human wellbeing Spenser blended another, viz. the constant presence of that high beauty which haunted him wherever he went, alike amid the splendour of courts and in lonely vales, and which he regarded as one of God's chief gifts to man. The spirit of beauty is ever accompanied in Spenser's poetry with the kindred spirits of gladness and of love—a gladness which has nothing in common with mere pleasure, and a love which rises far above its counterfeits. With him man's nobler affections are not mere genial impulses; they are themselves virtues girdling in an outer circle those Christian virtues that stand around humanity, as, in Calidore's vision, the mountain nymphs encompassed those Three Graces who ministered to the rose-crowned maiden. The mode in which Spenser associated the virtues as well as the graces with his special idea of womanhood—an idea very remote from that common in our days—is nowhere more beautifully illustrated than in Book IV. canto x., where Scudamour describes the temple of Venus and the recovery of his lost Amoret.

> Into the inmost temple thus I came,
> Which fuming all with frankincense I found,
> And odours rising from the altars flame;
> Upon a hundred marble pillars round
> The roof up high was reerèd from the ground,
> All deck'd with crownes and chaynes and girlonds gay,
> And thousand precious gifts worth many a pound,
> The which sad lovers for their vows did pay;
> And all the ground was strewd with flowers as fresh as May.

In the midst stands on the chief altar the statue of the goddess to whom they sing a hymn. Round the steps of the altar sit many fair forms—

> The first of them did seeme of riper yeares
> And graver countenance than all the rest;
> Yet all the rest were eke her equall peares,
> And unto her obayed all the best
> Her name was Womanhood; that she exprest
> By her sad semblant, and demeanure wyse;
> For stedfast still her eyes did fixèd rest,
> Ne roved at random after gazers guyse,
> Whose luring baytes oftimes doe heedless harts entyse.

> And next to her sate goodly Shamefastness,
> Ne ever durst her eyes from ground upreare,
> Ne ever once did looke from her dais,
> As if some blame of evil she did feare,
> That in her cheek made roses oft appeare;
> And her against sweet Cherefulnesse was placed,
> Whose eyes, like twinkling stars in evening clearc,
> Were deckt with smyles that all sad humours chased,
> And darted forth delights, the which her goodly graced.

> And next to her sate sober Modestie,
> Holding her hand upon her gentle hart;
> And her against sate comely Curtesie,
> That unto every person knew her part;
> And her before was seated overthwart
> Soft Silence, and submisse Obedience,
> Both linckt together never to dispart;
> Both gifts of God not gotten but from thence,
> Both girlonds of his saints against their foes offence.

> Thus sate they all around in seemly rate;
> And in the midst of them a goodly mayd,
> Even in the lap of Womanhood there sate,
> The which was all in lilly white arrayd,
> With silver streames amongst the linnen strey'd;
> Like to the Morne when first her shining face

Hath to the gloomy world itself bewray'd,
That same was fairest Amoret in place,
Shyning with beauties light, and heavenly vertues
    grace.

Scudamour stands in doubt—

For sacrilege me seemed the church to rob.

Observing, however, a smile on the countenance of the goddess, he persists—

She often prayd, and often me besought
Sometimes with tender tears to let her goe,
Sometimes with witching smyles; but yet for nought
That ever she to me could say or doe
Could she her wishèd freedom fro me move,
But forth I led her through the temple gate.

It is easy to trace the same benignant philosophy in all these descriptions. The wisely led life is a life of truth, of simplicity, of justice, of human sympathy and mutual kindness, of reverence for humanity in all its relations, and of reverence for God. The unwise life is the opposite of these things.

But the ordinary human life, even when wisely led, constitutes in part only Spenser's ideal of human life. It includes an extraordinary portion, a mountain land ascending high above the limit of perpetual snow. This is the life which seriously aims at perfection, the life lived "from above," and of which faith and truth are not the regulative only, but the constitutive principles. It is set forth in the first Book and tenth canto of the *Faery Queen*. Una has discovered that the Red-Cross Knight, though zealous for the good, is as yet but scantly qualified by knowledge or strength for that enterprise on which he was missioned from the Faery Court. That he may learn goodly lore and goodly discipline, she brings him to "The House of Holiness." It is presided over by one who represents heavenly wisdom.

Dame Cœlia men did her call, as thought
From heaven to come, or thither to arise;
The mother of three daughters, well
    up-brought
In goodly thews and godly exercise;
The eldest two most sober, chast, and wise,
Fidelia and Speranza, virgins were,
Though spoused, yet wanting wedlock's
    solemnize;
But faire Clarissa to a lovely fere
Was linkèd, and by him had many pledges dere.

At the gateway sits a porter, "Humiltà." Entering, Una and her knight find themselves in a spacious palace court, whence "a francklin faire and free," by name Zeal, ushers them to a stately hall. There they are welcomed by "a gentle squire, hight Reverence."

We are next introduced to Cœlia's daughters, Faith and Hope. Spenser describes them as Raphael would have done, had he painted in words—

Thus as they gan of sondrie thinges devise,
Loe, two most goodly virgins came in place,
Ylinked arme in arme in lovely wise;
With countenance demure, and modest
    grace,
They numbred even steps and equally pace;
Of which the eldest, that Fidelia hight,
Like sunny beams threw from her christall
    face
That could have dazed the rash beholder's
    sight,

And round about her head did shine like heaven's
    light.
She was arayèd all in lilly white,
And in her right hand bore a cup of gold,
With wine and water fild up to the hight,
In which a serpent did himselfe enfold,
That horrour made to all that did behold;
But she no whitt did change her constant
    mood:
And in her other hand she fast did hold
A booke, that was both signd and seald with
    blood;
Wherein darke things were writt, hard to be
    understood.

Her younger sister, that Speranza hight,
Was clad in blew that her beseemèd well;
Not all so chearful seemèd she of sight,
As was her sister; whether dread did dwell
Or anguish in her hart, is herd to tell:
Upon her arme a silver anchor lay,
Whereon she leanèd ever as befell;
And ever up to heven, as she did pray,
Her stedfast eyes were bent, ne swervèd other way.

A groom, Obedience, leads the youthful knight to the guest-house; and the next day Fidelia begins to instruct him in her sacred book "with blood ywritt"—

For she was able with her wordes to kill,
And raize againe to life the hart that she did thrill.
And when she list poure out her larger spright
She would command the hasty sun to stay,
Or backward turne his course from heven's
    hight.

The knight waxes daily as in knowledge so proportionately in repentance; but Speranza teaches him to take hold of her silver anchor; and Patience, a kindly physician, pours balms into the wounds inflicted on him by Penance. He is next consigned to a holy matron, Mercy, that he may have a share in all her holy works. Mercy leads him into her great hospital—

In which seven bead-men that had vowed all
Their life to service of high heaven's king

initiate him, each into the duties which belong to his several function, the office of the first being to provide a home for the homeless, of the second to feed the hungry, of the third to provide raiment for "the images of God in earthly clay," of the fourth to release captives, of the fifth to tend the sick, of the sixth to inter the dead, of the seventh to take charge of the widow and the orphan. With all these sacred ministrations the knight is successively made acquainted, and thus fitted for a glimpse into the more exalted region of contemplation and the interior life.

Thence forward by that painful way they pass
Forth to a hill that was both steepe and hy,
On top whereof a sacred chapel was,
And eke a little hermitage thereby,
Wherein an agèd holy man did lie,
That day and night said his devotion,
Ne other worldly business did apply;
His name was hevenly Contemplation;
Of God and goodnes was his meditation.

Great grace that old man to him given had;
For God he often saw from heven's hight;
All were his earthly eyen both blunt and bad,
And through great age had lost their kindly
    sight,

> Yet wondrous quick and persuant was his
>   spright,
> As eagle's eye that can behold the sunne.

Hearing that the youth has been sent to him by Fidelia to learn "what every living wight should make his marke," the aged man shows him the Celestial City descending from heaven.

> As he thereon stood gazing, he might see
> The blessed angels to and fro descend
> From highest heaven in gladsome companee,
> And with great joy into that citty wend,
> As commonly as friend does with his friend.

The knight exclaims in ecstasy, "What need of arms since peace doth ay remain?" He is answered that his task must be accomplished before he is fit to enter into his rest; but that notwithstanding, whilst labouring on earth, he is to be a citizen of the Heavenly City as well as of God's city on earth.

Such is that supernatural life, at once active and contemplative, which, according to Spenser's philosophy, admits of being realised even upon earth by its choicer spirits. Between the two lives there is much in common as well as much diversity. In each life man's course is a warfare: in the ordinary life man has to fight against his own passions, and against all who would injure his fellow-man; in the extraordinary life the combat is chiefly one for the establishment of a divine kingdom. In each the joy of life comes largely from beauty and from love; but in the sublimer life both of these are spiritual things. In both lives fame is won, but only in the higher is it the direct voice of God. In both there is suffering, but in the higher pain works a loftier purification. Both lives have for their patrons Fidelia, Speranza, and Charissa, with whom are conjoined that other triad, Humility, Patience, and Purity; but those twelve virtues known of old are also ministering spirits to both lives, and belong to a cognate race; while that great mother-Virtue, Reverence, the mystic Cybelè of the House of Virtues, is the connecting link between the two classes of virtues. The higher life is as superior to the lower as the statue is to the pedestal; but that pedestal is yet hewn out of the same Parian marble. The ordinary human life, when wisely led, is thus the memorial of a more heroic life, once man's portion, and destined to be his again, and not the mere culmination of the life which belongs to the inferior kinds, as Epicurus esteemed it. Considered as a brief compendium of Christian teaching, at once doctrinal, practical, and contemplative, it would be difficult to excel this canto of the *Faery Queen*.

The sage tells the Red-Cross Knight that, though he knows it not, he is himself sprung from the race of England's ancient kings—

> From thence a faery thee unweeting reft,
> There as thou slep'st in tender swadling band,
> And her base elfin brood there for thee left:
> Such men to chaungelings call, so chaunged by
>   faeries' theft.

According to Spenser's estimate, humanity itself is such a changeling, and perpetually betrays its lofty origin. Spenser's philosophy, both of the humbler and the more exalted human life, will be best understood when contrasted with the two chief forms of life depraved, as illustrated by him. A large part, perhaps too large a part, of his poem is given to this subject; but it will suffice here briefly to sketch his general scheme of thought. Moral evil he contemplates in two aspects, that of the body insurgent against the soul, and that of the soul insurgent against its Maker, or passion on the one side and pride on the other. The former vice is rebuked chiefly in Book II., the Legend of Temperance, and the latter in the Legend of Holi-ness, or Book I. In the Legend of Temperance passion is exhibited in its two predominant forms of sensuality and ambition. The perils and degradations of an animalised life are shown under the allegory of Sir Guyon's sea voyage with its successive storms and whirlpools, its "rock of Reproach" strewn with wrecks and dead men's bones, its "wandering islands," its "quicksands of Unthriftihead," its "whirlpoole of Decay," its sea monsters, and lastly, its "bower of Bliss," and the doom which overtakes it, together with the deliverance of Acrasia's victims, transformed by that witch's spells into beasts. Still more powerful is the allegory of worldly ambition, illustrated under the name of "the cave of Mammon." The Legend of Holiness delineates with not less insight those enemies which wage war upon the spiritual life. As the aims of that life are the highest man proposes to himself, so its foes are the most insidious. Una, the heroine of this legend, means Truth; and the first enemy with whom her knight has to contend is Error, a serpent woman, with her monstrous brood. A craftier foe assails him soon, the magician Archimago or Hypocrisy. Separated by him from Truth, the knight becomes subjected to Falsehood and Delusion, emblemed in Duessa, by whom he is lured to the House of Pride, the great metropolis of Sin in its most exasperated form, that of a spiritual revolt. He next becomes the thrall of Orgoglio, the giant son of Earth, or Pride in its vulgarer form of vain-glorious and animal strength.

In the latter legend the vices which make up the life of Pride, in the former those which make up the life of Lawless Sense, are illustrated with a keen insight and deep moral logic. In those two forms of evil life the three pagan champions, Sans-foy, Sans-loy, and Sans-joy, have a part corresponding with that which the Christian virtues, Fidelia, Speranza, and Charissa, sustain in the spiritual life. A certain symmetry, perhaps undesigned, always makes its way into Spenser's poetry. The philosophic Poet's mind is, indeed, by nothing more marked than by this unintended and often unconscious congruity in its conceptions, and the entire coherency of part with part in its descriptions. Thence proceeds the harmony constantly found in Spenser's poetry, as long as he resists his unhappy tendency to allude covertly to the persons and events of his day, and deals in simplicity with the great ethical theme with which his genius had deliberately measured itself. Such harmony is the most conclusive proof that a poet does not write at random, but has both "a vision of his own," and a vocation to set it forth.

We have hitherto confined our attention to Spenser's philosophy of human life, first in its social and political relations, and secondly in those of a domestic or individual character. Occasionally, however, his philosophy makes excursions into regions more remote, and deals with subjects more recondite than these his favourite themes. To do justice to his genius we must note the two most remarkable of these excursions. Ten years after Spenser's death, the first six books of the *Faery Queen* were republished with a fragment of the lost second part, consisting of "two cantos of Mutabilitie." In this fragment there is a simple largeness of conception, and a stern grandeur of expression, which suggests the thought that the later half of his work would probably have surpassed the earlier in mature greatness. It belongs essentially to Spenser's philosophic vein, and embodies a train of dark and minatory thoughts, though they issue gradually into light, on the instability of all things human—thoughts such as might naturally have presented themselves to a philosopher in an age when much which had lasted a thousand years was passing away. In the remotest parts of Europe omens of change were heard, like those vague murmurs in the polar regions which announce the breaking up of the ice; and in Ireland unfriendly echoes of those voices muttered near and nearer around that ruined mansion, one of old Desmond's hundred castles, within whose halls some strange fortune had harboured the gentlest of England's singers. The "temple-haunting" bird had indeed selected a "coigne of vantage," and hung there his "pendent bed and procreant cradle"; but he had been no "guest of summer," nor at any time had "heaven's breath smelt wooingly by his loved mansionry." It was from a securer abode, in the heart of the Rydalian laurels, that musings as solemn, though less sad, drew forth the dirge of the modern poet as he looked upon England's ruined abbeys—

> From low to high doth dissolution climb,
> And sinks from high to low, along a scale
> Of awful notes whose concord shall not fail.

The poet of Faery Land sees a prophet's vision ascending out of the cloud that rests on the pagan days. A Portent, not a god, but more powerful than the gods, and boasting a lineage more ancient, a child of Titan race, one more warlike than Bellona and more terrible than Hecatè, both of them her sisters, claims a throne higher than that of those later Olympians who had cast down an earlier hierarchy of gods. Her name is Mutability. She had witnessed their victory; she had given it to them; why should they not acknowledge her as their suzeraine? On earth she had established her reign in completeness, and not over men alone. The seas had left dry their beds at her command, continents had sunk beneath the waves, mountains had fleeted like clouds, rivers had filled their mouths with desert sands, kingdoms had risen and fallen, and the languages which recorded their triumphs had died—

> That all which Nature had establisht first
> In good estate, and in meet order ranged,
> She did pervert, and all their statues burst.
> . . .
> Nor she the laws of Nature onely brake,
> But eke of justice and of policie,
> And wrong of right, and bad of good did make,
> And death for life.

It remains for her but to reign in heaven as on earth—not in the majesty of a divine law, but in lawlessness become omnipotent. This Portent scales the heavens, making way at once to the most changeful of its luminaries, Cynthia's sphere.

> Her sitting on an ivory throne she found,
> Drawn of two steeds, th' one black, the other white,
> Environed with tenne thousand starres around,
> That duly her attended day and night;
> And by her side there ran her page, that hight
> Vesper, whom we the evening starre intend;
> That with his torche, still twinkling like twylight,
> Her lightened all the way where she would wend,
> And joy to weary wandring travailers did lend.
>
> Boldly she bid the goddesse down descend,
> And let herself into that ivory throne;
> For she herselfe more worthy thereof weend,
> And better able it to guide alone;
> Whether to men, whose fall she did bemone,
> Or unto gods, whose state she did maligne,
> Or to the infernal powers.

Cynthia scorns the intruder, and "bending her hornèd brows did put her back."

The Titaness raises her hand to drag the radiant and inviolate divinity from her seat. The result is narrated in a passage of marvellous sublimity. Dimness falls at once on that glittering throne and the "fire-breathing stars" that surround it; and, at the same moment, the eclipse reaches the earth, perplexing its inhabitants with fear of change, and ascends not less to the seat of the gods. They rush simultaneously to the palace of Jove,

> Fearing least Chaos broken had his chaine.

The Father of the Gods reminds them that long since the giant-brood of earth had piled mountain upon mountain in vain hope to storm "heaven's eternal towers," and tells them that this anarch is but the last offspring of that evil blood. While the gods are still in council, the strange Visitant is in among them. For a moment she is awed by that great presence; the next, she advances her claim. Jove had dethroned his father, Saturn; her own father, Titan, was Saturn's elder brother. On earth she has hitherto abode an exile, yet there she has conquered all things to herself. She demands at last her birthright—the throne of heaven. An inferior poet would have made this portent hideous as well as terrible. Spenser knew better. He knew that revolution and destruction wear often on their countenances a baleful loveliness of their own, for which many a victim, disinterested in madness, has willingly died. The following lines are in Homer's grandest vein—

> Whil'st she thus spake, the gods that gave good ear
> To her bold words, and markèd well her grace,
> Beeing of stature tall as any there
> Of all the gods, and beautiful of face
> As any of the goddesses in place,
> Stood all astonied; like a sort of steeres,
> 'Mongst whom some beast of strange and forraine race
> Unwares is chaunced, far straying from his peeres;
> So did their ghastly gaze bewray their hidden feares.

For Jove alone the Portent has no terrors—

> "Whom what should hinder but that we likewise
> Should handle as the rest of her allies,
> And thunder-drive to hell?" With that he shooke
> His nectar-deawèd locks, with which the skyes
> And all the world beneath for terror quooke.
> And eft his burning levin-brond in hand he tooke.
>
> But when he lookèd on her lovely face,
> In which fair beams of beauty did appeare,
> That could the greatest wrath soon turn to grace
> (Such sway doth beauty, even in heaven, beare),
> He staide his hand; and having changed his cheere,
> He thus againe in milder wyse began:
> "But ah! if gods should strive with flesh yfere,
> Then shortly should the progeny of man
> Be rooted out; if Jove should do still what he can."

He bids her submit. The Titaness summons Jove to meet her before the tribunal of an impartial arbiter; and by nothing does the poet more subtly impress us with the magic power of this strange claimant, than by the Thunderer's consent to leave his Olympian throne, and stand her co-suitor before an alien potentate. That potentate is one whom our age challenges more often than Spenser's did. Her appeal is to the "God of Nature." The place of judgment is

> Upon the highest heights
> Of Arlo-Hill (who knows not Arlo-Hill?)

> That is the highest head in all men's sights
> Of my old father, Mole, whom shepherd's
>   quill
> Renownèd hath with hymnes fit for a rural skill.

"Old Mountain Mole," a name as familiar as that of the river "Mulla," his daughter, to the readers of Spenser, designates the Galtee range which rises to nearly the height of 3000 feet at the north-east of Kilcolman. Arlo-Hill is Galtymore, and overhangs the glen of Arlo, now spelt Aherlo. This mountain-range is here constituted by him a Parnassus of the north, and he tells us how that glen was long frequented by the gods, and especially by Cynthia, and how it was forsaken by the latter because she had there been betrayed by one of her nymphs, Molanna, while bathing in her favourite brook, to the gaze of "foolish god Faunus"—

> Since which, those woods and all that goodly
>   chase
> Doth to this day with wolves and thieves
>   abound;
> Which too, too true that land's indwellers since have
>   found.

Those "thieves" were the original dwellers on Desmond's confiscated lands, who had taken refuge in the forests. There is a profound pathos in the last line quoted, one which may possibly have been written but the day before those wild bands issued from the woods of Arlo, and wrapped in flame the castle of its poet, thus grimly closing the four wedded and peaceful years of his Irish life.

On the appointed day the gods assemble—the gods of heaven, of the sea, and of the land, for the infernal powers, we are told, might not appear in that sacred precinct, and not the gods alone but all other creatures. In the midst "great dame Nature" makes herself manifest. She is invested with attributes so mysterious, and tending so much towards the infinite, as to suggest the thought that Spenser, in some of his lonely musings, had occasionally advanced to the borders of a philosophy little guessed of in his own time. Some such philosophy has sometimes set up a claim like that of Spenser's Titaness, and striven to push religion from her throne. According to Spenser's teaching, those pretensions derive no countenance from Nature, though often put forward in her name. Nor was the cause of Mutability that of political revolution alone; it was also that of unbelief, of lawlessness against law, and of endless restlessness against endless peace.

> Then forth issewed (great goddess) great dame
>   Nature,
> With goodly port and gracious majesty,
> Being far greater and more tall of stature
> Than any of the gods or powers on hie;
> Yet certes by her face and physnomy,
> Whether she man or woman inly were,
> That could not any creature well descry,
> For with a veile that wimpled every where
> Her head and face was hid, that mote to none
>   appeare.

Nature, we are told, is terrible, because she devours whatever exists; and yet beautiful, for she is ever teeming with all things fair. So far she resembles the Titaness, but only so far. The glory of her face is such that the face itself is never seen by mortal eye. To each man she is but as a semblance descried in a mirror. The soul of each man is that mirror, and according to what that soul *is* she *seems*. Her veil is never withdrawn.

> That, some doe say, was so by skill devised,
> To hide the terror of her uncouth hew
> From mortall eyes that should be sore agrized,

> For that her face did like a lion shew,
> That eye of wight could not indure to view;
> But others tell that it so beauteous was,
> And round about such beams of splendour threw,
> That it the sunne a thousand times did pass,
> Ne could be seen but like an image in a glass.

She sits enthroned upon the level summit of the hill, and the earth instantaneously sends up a pavilion of mighty trees that wave above her in adoration, their branches laden with bloom and blossom; while the sod bursts into flower at her feet, and old Mole exults

> As if the love of some new nymph late seene
> Had in him kindled youthful fresh desire.

The Titaness draws near to this venerable being,

> This great grandmother of all creatures bred,
> Great Nature, ever young, yet full of eld,
> Still moving, yet unmoved from her sted;
> Unseen of any, yet of all beheld;

and appeals to her against the king of the gods,

> Since heaven and earth are both alike to thee;
> And gods no more than men thou dost esteem:
> For even the gods to thee as men to gods do seeme.

The Titaness impeaches, not Jove only, but all the gods, for having arrogated to themselves, as divinities supernatural, what belongs to Nature only, and to herself as Nature's vicegerent. She insists that she has conquered to herself all the elements, not the land and the sea only; for the fire does not belong to holy Vesta, nor the air to the queen of the gods, but both alike to her. She summons witnesses, and at the command of Nature her herald, Order, causes them to circle in long procession around the throne. First come the four Seasons, next the twelve Months. Here is one of the pictures—

> Next came fresh April, full of lustihead,
> And wanton as a kid whose horne newbuds;
> Upon a bull he rode, the same which led
> Europa floting through the Argolick fluds;
> His hornes were gilden all with golden studs,
> And garnishèd with girlonds goodly dight
> Of all the fairest flowers and freshest buds
> Which th' earth brings forth; and wet he
>   seemed in sight
> With waves through which he waded for his love's
>   delight.

The Hours follow, and the pageant is closed by Life and Death.

The Titaness next turns to Nature, and makes, in the name of all who have passed before her, their common confession; it is that all alike live but by change, and are vassals of Mutability. The Father of Gods and Men replies. His answer consists less in the denial of aught that is affirmative in her statement than in the supplying of what that statement had ignored—

> Then thus 'gan Jove: "Right truc it is that thcse
> And all things else that under heaven dwell
> Are chaunged of Time, who them doth all
>   desseize
> Of being, but who is it (to me tell)
> That Time himselfe doth move and still
>   compell
> To keepe his course? Is not that namely Wee
> Which pour that virtue from our heavenly
>   cell,
> That moves them all and makes them changèd
>   be?
> So then we gods do rule, and in them also thee."

The reply of Mutability is simply an appeal from reason, interpreting objects of sense, to the mere senses when they have discarded reason—

> But what we *see* not, who shall us persuade?

Again she enumerates her triumphs, and demands a verdict in terms which surreptitiously remove the cause from the higher courts of Nature's judicature, and confine it to one created by herself. But Nature takes counsel not with eye and ear only, but with mind and spirit also—

> So having ended, silence long ensued;
> Ne Nature to or fro spake for a space,
> But with firm eyes affixed the ground still
>   view'd.
> Meanwhile all creatures looking in her face,
> Expecting the end of this so doubtful case,
> Did hang in long suspense what would ensue,
> To whether side should fall the sovereign
>   place;
> At length she, looking up with cheerful view,
> The silence brake, and gave her doom in speeches
>   few.

> I well consider all that ye have sayd,
> And find that all things stedfastness doe hate
> And changed be: yet being rightly wayed,
> They are not changèd from their first estate;
> *But by their change their being do dilate*;
> And turning to themselves at length againe
> Doe worke their own perfection so by fate;
> Then over them Change doth not rule and
>   raigne,
> But they raigne over Change, and do their states
>   maintaine.

> Cease therefore, daughter, further to aspire,
> And thee content thus to be ruled by me;
> For thy decay thou seek'st by thy desire;
> But time shall come that all shall changèd
>   bee,
> *And from thenceforth none no more change
>   shall see.*
> So was the Titanesse put downe and whist,
> And Jove confirmed in his imperial See.
> Then was that whole assembly quite dismist,
> And Nature's selfe did vanish, whither no man wist.

According to the philosophy of Spenser it was impossible that Mutability should enjoy a final triumph, because her true function is to minister through change to that which knows no change. Revolution is but a subordinate element in a system which includes a recuperative principle, and tends ever to the stable. To the undiscerning eye things seem to pass away; to the half-discerning they seem to revolve merely in a circle; but the motion is in reality upward as well as circular; as it advances, it ascends in a spiral line; and as it ascends it ever widens. When the creation has reached the utmost amplitude of which it was originally made capable, it must then stand face to face with the Creator, and in that high solstice it must enter into the sabbath of His endless rest. Thus only could it reflect the Divine Perfection after which it was created. To understand this teaching, we must bear in mind its complement in another part of Spenser's philosophy. He held with Plato that all things great and abiding, whether in the material or the moral world, were created after the pattern of certain great ideas existing eternally in the mind of the Creator, inseparable from His essence, and in it alone perfectly realised. Creation is thus a picture of the uncreated; and the cyclical revolutions of time present an image of eternity, notwithstanding that the "opposi-

tion of matter" renders it impossible that that picture should ever be wholly faithful to its great original. Turning our eyes downward, we trace the same law in the descending grades of being. It is thus that man, himself the mirror of the Divine, is mirrored, though with a corresponding inferiority, by the inferior animals, which, not only in their chief affections, but in their intellectual processes, and often even in their social polities, rehearse, on a lower stage, parts which man is permitted to enact more nobly on a higher one. But between the creatures thus ranged on the lower and the higher stages of creation there exists one great difference: those only that occupy the highest platform possess the gift of secure progress. That progress is made through striving and pain:—the whole life of man here below, whether his individual or his social life, was regarded by Spenser as a noble warfare destined to end in victory and peace. Through such probation it becomes from age to age a vaster and a purer thing; and its mutations, notwithstanding the confusions and the sufferings they entail, are but the means through which virtue ascends, and knowledge grows wider. Spenser ends his legend with this aspiration—

> O that great Sabaoth God grant me that Sabbath's sight!

This is the voice of a spirit wearied with the storms of our lower sphere, but not daunted or weakened by them. No one can read the last verse without joining in the poet's prayer.

These remarks on Spenser's philosophy would be incomplete without a reference to a very remarkable canto of his *Faery Queen*, in which he blends his musings on humanity with others on nature, and on what is higher than nature, and thus crosses the path of the old-world philosophic poet Lucretius, who also discoursed of nature and man's life—leaving in his philosophy a very little corner for the "immortal gods," who seem, indeed, to have had little business there, and indeed to have been admitted but by courtesy. Spenser's philosophic reverie will be found in his *Garden of Adonis* (Book III. canto vi.) Human life as there described has nothing in common either with that higher, that ordinary, or that depraved form of life illustrated by him elsewhere. It is not an actual but a potential life, the conception of an existence neither fallen nor restored, and of an earth with neither benediction nor malediction resting upon it; an earth with one sorrow only—the transience of all things. The Garden is the domain of an endless productiveness, decay, and renewal. In it abide perpetually the archetypal forms of living things—

> There is the first seminary
> Of all things that are born to live and dye,
> According to their kinds.

The ever-teeming soil is encircled by two walls, one of iron and one of gold—

> And double gates it had which opened wide,
> By which both in and out men moten pas;
> Th' one faire and fresh, th' other old and
>   dried;
> Old Genius the porter of them was,
> Old Genius the which a double nature has.

> He letteth in, he letteth out to wend
> All that to come into the world desire;
> A thousand thousand naked babes attend
> About him day and night, which doe
>   require
> That he with fleshly weeds will them attire;
> Such as him list, such as eternal fate
> Ordained hath, he clothes with sinful mire,
> And sendeth forth to live in mortall state,
> Till they agayn returne, back by the hinder gate.

Their condition is an endless alternation of glad life and painless decay.

> After that they againe retourned beene
> They in that garden planted bee agayne,
> And grow afresh, as they had never seene
> Fleshly corruption, nor mortall payne:
> Some thousand yeeres so doen they there
> > remayne,
> And then of him are clad with other hew,
> Or sent into the chaungeful world agayne,
> Till thether they return, where first they grew;
> So like a wheele arowned they ronne from old to
> > new.

Countless swarms perish successively, yet the stock is never lessened—

> For in the wide wombe of the world there lyes
> In hateful darkness, and in deepe horrore
> An huge eternal Chaos, which supplies
> The substaunces of Nature's fruitful progenyes.

The substance is immortal; the successive forms "are variable and decay," for though they have but one foe, with him they cannot contend. That enemy is "wicked Time," who mows down all things with his scythe.

> Yet pitty often did the gods relent
> To see so faire things mard and spoilèd quight:
> And their great mother Venus did lament
> The losse of her deere brood, here deere delight.

Her realm has this sorrow alone. It is unshaken by jealousy or pain, doubt or shame. Over this central seat of her rolling sphere there rests "the stillness of the sleeping poles." Here the spring-tide and the harvest-tide blend, and the autumnal vine overhangs the vernal elm. Here grows

> > > every sort of flowre
> To which sad lovers were transform'd of yore.

Here Venus finds at will her lost Adonis where she laid him dead—

> And sooth it seems, they say; for he may not
> For ever dye, and ever buried bee
> In baleful night, where all things are forgot;
> All be he subject to mortalitie,
> *Yet is eterne in mutabilitie,*
> *And by succession made perpetual,*
> Transformed oft, and chaunged diverslie;
> For him the father of all formes they call;
> Therefore needs mote he live that living gives to all.

There are passages in this poem which remind the reader of Lucretius, but the contrast is greater than the resemblance. What in the Latin poet is a cynical, though imaginative, materialism becomes transfigured in the verse of one whose touch changes matter itself into spirit. The lower side of the philosophy receives its interpretation from the higher, and becomes, though not the whole truth, yet a portion of it. If the seeds of all bodies spring up spontaneously from the fruitful soil, yet souls innumerable throng the air above them, and it is their breath that imparts life to their "fleshly weeds." If no gardener is needed there "to sett or sow," yet Nature only thus exercises a sacred might bestowed on her by one who is above Nature, and has commanded her to increase. Whatever she may be in Cythera or Paphos, the goddess of love is here a true "Venus Genetrix," a Power, compassionate and benign, the mighty mother bringing forth, not in sorrow but in gladness. A healing influence works on through creation; Nature is no more suffered to prey on her own offspring; the wild boar of the forest which slew Adonis, and ever wars on youth and strength, is

"imprisoned in a strong rocky cave." In this earlier "Island Valley of Avilion," humanity heals its ancient wound, and awaits the better day. The spirit of hope here triumphs over the Lucretian spirit of despair.

The teaching of the pessimist philosopher of antiquity, whose ambition was to draw the most original of poems out of the wildest system of physics—like sunbeams extracted from cucumbers—was the opposite of this, except in points of detail. Not our world only but all worlds were fated to perish utterly, leaving behind them nothing but a whirl of atoms to fill their place; that is, they were to end like his own poem, which closes significantly with the plague at Athens. A few remarks will not here be out of place comparing the great Latin philosophical poet, as he is commonly regarded, with the English philosophic poet of the Elizabethan period. Each of them found his country passing through a momentous crisis; each must have largely affected its growing intelligence for good or for evil; each had great poetic gifts, and in some respects similar gifts, for Lucretius, like Spenser, had an ardent imagination, a descriptive power till his time unrivalled, vivid imagery, impassioned eloquence, and remarkable gifts of style, diction, and metre; and each united the courage with the perseverance needful for success in a high enterprise of song. A poet is best understood when compared with another, at once like him and unlike.

The great difference between the two philosophic poets lay in those moral and spiritual constituents of man's being by which the action of his imagination as well as of his understanding is secretly directed. In Spenser there lived an abiding spirit of reverence; and therefore for him all phenomena received their interpretation from above: for Lucretius it came from below; and his delight was to show how all great things are but small things making the most of themselves. The intellect of Spenser was a far-reaching one; it descried the remote analogy; it discerned what is lost alike upon the sensual heart and the merely logical intelligence; it accepted high thoughts as authentic if at once recommended by venerable authorities and in harmony with universal aspirations, whether or not their nature rendered them susceptible of dialectic proof. It could retain a serene faith when shrewdness winked and grimaced; and it could no less abstain from credulity when challenged by philosophic theories recommended chiefly by their strangeness and their confidence. Lucretius, on the other hand, had a vigorous but an animal intellect. He saw the wonderfulness of matter not more keenly than Spenser, who understood its witcheries perhaps but too well; but he was so dazzled by it that he could see nothing besides, and for him spirit did not exist. To him Nature was all in all; and for that reason he did not realise her highest greatness, viz. her power of leading to something higher than herself. To the Greek mythologists who had laid the basis of Greek poetry, Nature had been a divinity; to the Christian poet and philosopher she reflected a divine radiance; to Lucretius she was a Titaness slinging firebrands through the universe she had shaped, and shaping all things with no final aim but that of slaying them, and slaying herself on their pyre. For his guide he followed exclusively a single teacher of his own selection, and one even in the pagan world ill famed—Epicurus—passing by with contempt all the heads of the Greek schools during six centuries, and worshipping that one with an idolatrous but not disinterested devotion.

Seeing all things from below, Lucretius never grasps the nobler idea essentially included in each; he sees but the accidents that obscure it. In religion he sees nothing but fear; in authority but imposture; in man but animal instincts intellectualised. In woman he sees no touch of womanhood. He advises his disciples never to meddle with so noxious a toy as love; but his mode of preaching self-restraint is worthless, since it provides no substitute for troublesome pleasures, either in lofty duties or in nobler joys, for which, on his principles, there remains no place. It is not merely that the Lucretian philosophy does not encourage moral or spiritual aspirations:—it is militant against them. It commands us imperiously to tread down the very desire of immortality; and yet its denial of immortality is a wholly illogical assumption, based on another assumption wholly arbitrary: viz. that "mind" and "soul" are but material things, not less than the body, and must therefore share the body's doom. Such a philosophy, in recommending "moderation," recommends but apathy; and men not dyspeptic or exhausted do not become apathetic to please philosophers.

There is nothing positive in Lucretius's vivid appreciation of matter which does not find place equally in Spenser's philosophy. What the latter abjures is the negative part of it. In Spenser's poetry the creation is ever regarded as "the resplendent miracle," and material joys as, in their degree, objects well worthy of pursuit and gratitude; but in that poetry under material enjoyment there ever lurk the humanities, and under these something greater still. It was but the narrowness of the Lucretian philosophy which made it identify a belief in matter with a disbelief in spirit—that narrowness which so often explodes into fanaticism, with its combined characteristics of audacity and of intolerance. The Lucretian philosophy is an abject one, not because it failed to anticipate Truth then unrevealed, but because it denied and denounced truths which had been retained with more or less clearness by most of the early religions and by many philosophies, such as the spirituality of man's being, a Divine sanction to conscience, and the immortality and responsibility of the soul—beliefs which had, during sequent ages, created civilised societies with all that was best in their arts, poetry, and literature. Pagan antiquity had also retained the belief in a Providence that shaped man's life to gracious ends; and its Prometheus, a Titan though not a god, had endured as well as laboured for man. The Lucretian gods are material beings made, like the rest of the universe, by the "concurrence" of material atoms; and, like all besides, they are destined to perish. In the meantime they sit apart in festal rest, seeing in man's life, its joys, its agonies, its trials, nay, in all things external to themselves, nothing worthy of their interest. This is to make the gods not only after the image of men, but of the meanest among men. Spenser insists on a God who helps man, not because He is Himself man's image, but for an opposite reason:—on a God for whom, *since He is infinite* in all the dimensions of infinitude, it follows that as nothing is too great, so nothing is too small. There are those by whom that sublime idea is stigmatised as "anthropomorphism," while the Lucretian conception is applauded as sublime. This is not sincere thinking. It cannot be justified by the qualification "sublime *as poetry*." Low sentiment and incoherent thought are not changed into great poetry because expressed in dignified language and good metre.

The materialistic philosophy on the exposition of which the poetry of Lucretius was wrecked made a large boast. In that aspect it has an important relation with our theme; for true poetry does great things, but does not make a great boast. It was to illuminate mankind, to break down all moral and intellectual thraldom, and to kill all religion, as the easiest way of curing its corruptions—a design as philosophic as though all government were to be destroyed because it includes administrative abuses; all art, because it sometimes ministers to depraved tastes; and all science, because its professors often make mistakes. How was this wonderful work to be effected? Not by

experimental demonstrations—they are seldom appealed to by Lucretius, except in the way of demolishing counter theories—but by hardy scientific dogma, and the *pecca fortiter* of fearless assumptions. Atoms could neither be seen, felt, nor brought within the ken of scientific analysis; but it was easy to assume not only that they existed in incalculable number, but that they are of various shapes, solid, indestructible, possess weight, and even that their "uncertain sideway movement" is "the only possible origin of the free-will of living beings." So again of *Films*. These are slender veils cast, as Lucretius affirms, from the surface of all objects incessantly and into all the regions of space—a valiant assumption, but one wholly fabulous. It is amusing to observe how the same philosophic credulity which accepts all assumptions condones all incoherences. The emancipating discovery asserts that "nothing comes from nothing"; yet it affirms also that, without any creative cause, there existed a perpetual downward rain of atoms; it believes that no Divine Mind gives law to matter; yet it maintains also that Nature's course is uniform—nay, that a "concurrence of atoms" driven against each other in perpetual storm, eventually combined into all the wondrous forms on the earth—the structure of hand and eye, and brain! All that this philosophy regards as needed to justify its imperious claim on our acceptance is that its dogmas, however fantastic, should be *conceivable*, that they should be capable of being expressed in association with distinct *images*, or brain-pictures—things confounded by feeble thinkers with distinct thoughts—and that they should derive some plausible support from analogies. It asserts like one inspired: it multiplies instances, takes for granted its inferences from them—inferences which are but the preconceptions of a confident fancy—and thus eludes those troublesome questions on which the true issue of the argument depends. Drawn aside as if by an "elective affinity" towards the most materialistic views on all subjects, this philosophy hardily rejected even the material truths asserted, some five hundred years before, by Pythagoras, such as that the earth moves round the sun, as well as its sphericity and gravitation—truths probably maintained by many in the days of Lucretius, though subsequently denied by the Ptolemaic system. It affirmed, moreover, that the universe is always dropping downward, and that the real size of the heavenly bodies is little more than their apparent size to the eye. Amidst these strange aberrations of a false philosophy, the "purple patches" of real poetry survive, to vex us with the thought of the poetry Lucretius might have given to us had Plato, not Epicurus, been his master, and to remind us that high genius is seldom extinguished wholly by the most wayward abuse of the gift.

It was fortunate for England that a philosophy in essentials the opposite of Lucretius's, inspired the poetry of that great man who opened the literature of the Elizabethan age, and into whose grave the younger poets of that age flung their pens, acknowledging him as their master as he had acknowledged Chaucer to be his. His genius might otherwise have exercised that influence, stimulating indeed, but both sensualising and narrowing, on English letters which Boccaccio certainly exercised on Italy, and for which no compensation could have been adequate. Spenser's philosophy was ideal at once and traditional. It made no small points; but great ideas brooded over it. He did not boast himself as the great expositor of one self-chosen master. His humble pride was that his long-laboured work embodied the best moral teaching of the chief masters both of antiquity and of Christian times. It was not a weapon of war. It derived no stimulus from hatred. It included within itself an unpretentious yet a coherent logic; but it passed far beyond her narrow pale in its genial strength, extending itself as widely as human sympathies, and soaring as high as man's noblest aspirations. That a poet so manifold in interest, and so profound in thought, should to so many readers, though not to the best, appear simply dull, and, again, that an ancient poet the greater part of whose poetry was devoted, like that of Dr. Darwin in the last century, to the versifying of Natural Philosophy, and whose Natural Philosophy was a chimera, should yet, with many readers, take the place often claimed for Lucretius, are phenomena hard to be explained. It is true that the adage "first come, first served," applies to books, and that many an old work retains a reputation which, if new, it could never acquire. It is true also that a compliment to a classic is often a compliment to one's own scholarship; and, again, that with, not a few, the lesser qualities of poetry, possessed in eminence, are more impressive than its highest qualities less energetically exerted. We may also, perhaps, in our attempt to solve the problem, find help in one of Spenser's best known allegories—best known because it illustrates so many a strange passage in human life—the allegory of Illusion or the witch "Duessa." She represents an idea constantly in the mind of Spenser. No poet ever fixed a more reverent gaze on philosophic truth, or one more faithful to follow her "whithersoever she goeth," through the tangled labyrinths of thought or action. Yet no one felt so strongly how close beside her there treads an opposite spirit—a spirit potent alike to make the true seem false, and the false seem true, the fair seem foul, and the foul seem fair. Such is the magic power with which Duessa now reinvests her faded form with the loveliness of a youth long vanished, and now raises a mist and binds a mask of decrepitude on some beautiful rival.

It was no doubt the profound sincerity of Spenser's genius which made him muse with such a haunting sadness on that spirit of Illusion. He had had personal experience of its power. He had his own illusions, religious, political, and personal, several of which he had detected and repudiated. He had replaced the Puritanism of his early training with a form of Christianity half-Patristic and half-Platonic; although in his politics it still stretched itself, like a "bar sinister," across a shield glowing with loyalist "gules" and chivalrous devices. He had seen some of his nearest friends changeful in principle, but ever persistent in worshipping as divinities the idols of a fancy at once proud and servile. He had doubtless observed that there often exists a strange and cruel resemblance between opposites, and that the illusion is often the more complete the more absolutely they stand opposed to each other. It is thus that hypocrisy resembles virtue, and that, as a consequence, virtue may be easily mistaken for hypocrisy; that the visionary is like the "man whose eyes are open," and *vice versâ*; that bashfulness may be like guilt, and callous insensibility like innocence; that silence may betoken alike the fulness of content or an absolute despair; that, to the superficial, communism may seem the political realisation of the early Christian ethics of alms; that indifference to truth may claim to be the perfection of charity. The most fatal errors have ever been those which include in them high truths, though misapplied. Without that element they would not have proved attractive to elevated minds; and for an analogous reason the most exalted truths may long wear a form the most repulsive even to the good.

The dreadful power of illusion is a thought naturally brought home the most to minds at once reflective and imaginative. It was familiar to Shelley as well as to Spenser, unlike as were those two poets, and it is remarkably illustrated by him in the "Revolt of Islam," canto i. stanzas 25–27. In the beginning of things, as we are there told, "a blood-red comet and the morning star" hung in fight on the verge of Chaos. These two militant shapes are the rival powers of Evil and Good. Evil triumphs, and changes the morning star into a snake, which is sentenced to creep over the earth in that false semblance, abhorred by all, so long as the conqueror's reign endures. Transformations not less startling take place every day in the moral world. What is despicable when contrasted with that which is above it, may yet well appear admirable to one who can measure it only with what is below it. Shelley, who had in him much of Lucretius's poetic audacity, was himself, for a short time, the prisoner of a materialistic philosophy as wild. When he became a translator of Plato, that grim skeleton, if it ever revisited his dreams, may perhaps have reminded him of Spenser's Duessa, stripped of her glittering apparel.

R. W. CHURCH
"The *Faerie Queene*"
Spenser
1895, pp. 81–108

"Uncouth [= unknown], *unkist*," are the words from Chaucer, with which the friend, who introduced Spenser's earliest poetry to the world, bespeaks forbearance, and promises matter for admiration and delight in the *Shepherd's Calendar*. "You have to know my new poet," he says in effect: "and when you have learned his ways, you will find how much you have to honour and love him." "I doubt not," he says, with a boldness of prediction, manifestly sincere, which is remarkable about an unknown man, "that so soon as his name shall come into the knowledge of men, and his worthiness be sounded in the trump of fame, but that he shall be not only kissed, but also beloved of all, embraced of the most, and wondered at of the best." Never was prophecy more rapidly and more signally verified, probably beyond the prophet's largest expectation. But he goes on to explain and indeed apologise for certain features of the new poet's work, which even to readers of that day might seem open to exception. And to readers of to-day, the phrase, *uncouth, unkist*, certainly expresses what many have to confess, if they are honest, as to their first acquaintance with the *Faerie Queene*. Its place in literature is established beyond controversy. Yet its first and unfamiliar aspect inspires respect, perhaps interest, rather than attracts and satisfies. It is not the remoteness of the subject alone, nor the distance of three centuries which raises a bar between it and those to whom it is new. Shakespere becomes familiar to us from the first moment. The impossible legends of Arthur have been made in the language of to-day once more to touch our sympathies, and have lent themselves to express our thoughts. But at first acquaintance the *Faerie Queene* to many of us has been disappointing. It has seemed not only antique, but artificial. It has seemed fantastic. It has seemed, we cannot help avowing, tiresome. It is not till the early appearances have worn off, and we have learned to make many allowances and to surrender ourselves to the feelings and the standards by which it claims to affect and govern us, that we really find under what noble guidance we are proceeding, and what subtle and varied spells are ever round us.

1. The *Faerie Queene* is the work of an unformed literature, the product of an unperfected art. English poetry, English language, in Spenser's, nay in Shakespere's day, had much to learn, much to unlearn. They never, perhaps, have been stronger or richer, than in that marvellous burst of youth, with all its freedom of invention, of observation, of reflection. But they had not that which only the experience and practice of eventful centuries could give them. Even genius must wait for

the gifts of time. It cannot forerun the limitations of its day, nor anticipate the conquests and common possessions of the future. Things are impossible to the first great masters of art which are easy to their second-rate successors. The possibility, or the necessity of breaking through some convention, of attempting some unattempted effort, had not, among other great enterprises, occurred to them. They were laying the steps in a magnificent fashion on which those after them were to rise. But we ought not to shut our eyes to mistakes or faults to which attention had not yet been awakened, or for avoiding which no reasonable means had been found. To learn from genius, we must try to recognize both what is still imperfect and what is grandly and unwontedly successful. There is no great work of art, not excepting even the Iliad or the Parthenon, which is not open, especially in point of ornament, to the scoff or the scoffer, or to the injustice of those who do not mind being unjust. But all art belongs to man; and man, even when he is greatest, is always limited and imperfect.

The *Faerie Queene*, as a whole, bears on its face a great fault of construction. It carries with it no adequate account of its own story; it does not explain itself, or contain in its own structure what would enable a reader to understand how it arose. It has to be accounted for by a prose explanation and key outside of itself. The poet intended to reserve the central event, which was the occasion of all the adventures of the poem, till they had all been related, leaving them as it were in the air, till at the end of twelve long books the reader should at last be told how the whole thing had originated, and what it was all about. He made the mistake of confounding the answer to a riddle with the crisis which unties the tangle of a plot and satisfies the suspended interest of a tale. None of the great model poems before him, however full of digression and episode, had failed to arrange their story with clearness. They needed no commentary outside themselves to say why they began as they did, and out of what antecedents they arose. If they started at once from the middle of things, they made their story, as it unfolded itself, explain by more or less skilful devices, all that needed to be known about their beginnings. They did not think of rules of art. They did of themselves naturally what a good story-teller does, to make himself intelligible and interesting: and it is not easy to be interesting, unless the parts of the story are in their place.

The defect seems to have come upon Spenser when it was too late to remedy it in the construction of his poem; and he adopted the somewhat clumsy expedient of telling us what the poem itself ought to have told us of its general story, in a letter to Sir Walter Raleigh. Raleigh himself, indeed, suggested the letter: apparently (from the date, Jan. 23, 1590), after the first part had gone through the press. And without this afterthought, as the twelfth book was never reached, we should have been left to gather the outline and plan of the story, from imperfect glimpses and allusions, as we have to fill up from hints and assumptions the gaps of an unskilful narrator, who leaves out what is essential to the understanding of his tale.

Incidentally, however, this letter is an advantage: for we have in it the poet's own statement of his purpose in writing, as well as a necessary sketch of his story. His allegory, as he had explained to Bryskett and his friends, had a moral purpose. He meant to shadow forth, under the figures of twelve knights, and in their various exploits, the characteristics of "a gentleman or noble person," "fashioned in virtuous and gentle discipline." He took his machinery from the popular legends about King Arthur, and his heads of moral philosophy from the current Aristotelian catalogue of the Schools.

Sir, knowing how doubtfully all Allegories may be construed, and this booke of mine, which I have entituled the Faerie Queene, being a continued Allegory, or darke conceit, I haue thought good, as well for avoyding of gealous opinions and misconstructions, as also for your better light in reading thereof (being so by you commanded), to discover unto you the general intention and meaning, which in the whole course thereof I have fashioned, without expressing of any particular purposes, or by accidents, therein occasioned. The generall end therefore of all the booke is to fashion a gentleman or noble person in vertuous and gentle discipline: Which for that I conceived shoulde be most plausible and pleasing, being coloured with an historicall fiction, the which the most part of men delight to read, rather for variety of matter then for profite of the ensample, I chose the historye of King Arthure, as most fitte for the excellency of his person, being made famous by many mens former workes, and also furthest from the daunger of envy, and suspition of present time. In which I have followed all the antique Poets historicall; first Homere, who in the Persons of Agamemnon and Ulysses hath ensampled a good governour and a vertuous man, the one in his Ilias, the other in his Odysseis: then Virgil, whose like intention was to doe in the person of Aeneas; after him Ariosto comprised them both in his Orlando: and lately Tasso dissevered them againe, and formed both parts in two persons, namely that part which they in Philosophy call Ethice, or vertues of a private man, coloured in his Rinaldo; the other named Politice in his Godfredo. By ensample of which excellente Poets, I labour to pourtraict in Arthure, before he was king, the image of a brave knight, perfected in the twelve private morall vertues, as Aristotle hath devised; the which is the purpose of these first twelve bookes: which if I finde to be well accepted, I may be perhaps encoraged to frame the other part of politicke vertues in his person, after that hee came to be king.

Then, after explaining that he meant the *Faerie Queene* "for glory in general intention, but in particular" for Elizabeth, and his Faerie Land for her kingdom, he proceeds to explain, what the first three books hardly explain, what the Faerie Queene had to do with the structure of the poem.

But, because the beginning of the whole worke seemeth abrupte, and as depending upon other antecedents, it needs that ye know the occasion of these three knights seuerall adventures. For the Methode of a Poet historical is not such, as of an Historiographer. For an Historiographer discourseth of affayres orderly as they were donne, accounting as well the times as the actions; but a Poet thrusteth into the middest, even where it most concerneth him, and there recoursing to the thinges forepaste, and divining of thinges to come, maketh a pleasing Analysis of all.

The beginning therefore of my history, if it were to be told by an Historiographer should be the twelfth booke, which is the last; where I devise that the Faerie Queene kept her Annuall feaste xii. dayes; uppon which xii. severall dayes, the occasions of the xii. severall adventures hapned, which, being undertaken by xii. severall knights, are in these xii. books severally handled and discoursed. The first was this. In the beginning of the feast, there presented him selfe a tall clownishe younge man, who falling before the Queene of Faeries desired a boone (as the manner then was) which during that feast she might not refuse; which was that hee might have the atchievement of any adventure, which during that feaste should happen: that being graunted, he rested him on the floore, unfitte through his rusticity for a better place. Soone after entred a faire Ladye in mourning weedes, riding on a white Asse, with a dwarfe behinde her leading a warlike steed, that bore the Armes of a knight, and his speare in the dwarfes hand. Shee, falling before the Queene of Faeries, complayned that her father and mother, an ancient King and Queene, had beene by an huge dragon many years shut up in a brasen Castle, who thence suffred them not to yssew; and therefore besought the Faerie Queene to assygne her some one of her knights to take on him that exployt. Presently that clownish person, upstarting, desired that adventure; whereat the Queene much wondering, and the Lady much gainesaying, yet he earnestly importuned his desire. In the end that Lady told him, that unlesse that armour which she brought would serve him (that is, the armour of a Christian man specified by Saint Paul, vi. Ephes.) that he could not succeed in that enterprise; which being forthwith put upon him, with dewe furnitures thereunto, he seemed the goodliest man in al that company, and was well liked of the Lady. And eftesoones taking on him knighthood, and mounting on that straunge courser, he went forth with her on that adventure: where beginneth the first booke, viz.

A gentle knight was pricking on the playne, &c.

That it was not without reason that this explanatory key was prefixed to the work, and that either Spenser or Raleigh felt it to be almost indispensable, appears from the concluding paragraph.

Thus much, Sir, I have briefly overronne to direct your understanding to the wel-head of the History; that from thence gathering the whole intention of the conceit, ye may as in a handfull gripe al the discourse, which otherwise may happily seeme tedious and confused.

According to the plan thus sketched out, we have but a fragment of the work. It was published in two parcels, each of three books, in 1590 and 1596; and after his death two cantos, with two stray stanzas, of a seventh book were found and printed. Each perfect book consists of twelve cantos of from thirty-five to sixty of his nine-line stanzas. The books published in 1590 contain, as he states in his prefatory letter, the legends of *Holiness*, of *Temperance*, and of *Chastity*. Those published in 1596 contain the legends of *Friendship*, of *Justice* and of *Courtesy*. The posthumous cantos are entitled, *Of Mutability*, and are said to be apparently parcel of a legend of *Constancy*. The poem which was to treat of the "politic" virtues was never approached. Thus we have but a fourth part of the whole of the projected work. It is very doubtful whether the remaining six books were completed. But it is probable that a portion of them was written, which, except the cantos *On Mutability*, has perished. And the intended titles or legends of the later books have not been preserved.

Thus the poem was to be an allegorical story; a story branching out into twelve separate stories, which themselves would branch out again and involve endless other stories. It is a complex scheme to keep well in hand, and Spenser's art in doing so has been praised by some of his critics. But the art, if there is any, is so subtle that it fails to save the reader from perplexity. The truth is that the power of ordering and connecting a long and complicated plan was not one of Spenser's gifts.

In the first two books, the allegorical story proceeds from point to point with fair coherence and consecutiveness. After them the attempt to hold the scheme together, except in the loosest and most general way, is given up as too troublesome or too confined. The poet prefixes, indeed, the name of a particular virtue to each book, but with slender reference to it, he surrenders himself freely to his abundant flow of ideas, and to whatever fancy or invention tempts him, and ranges unrestrained over the whole field of knowledge and imagination. In the first two books, the allegory is transparent, and the story connected. The allegory is of the nature of the *Pilgrim's Progress*. It starts from the belief that religion, purified from falsehood, superstition, and sin, is the foundation of all nobleness in man; and it portrays, under images and with names, for the most part easily understood, and easily applied to real counterparts, the struggle which every one at that time supposed to be going on, between absolute truth and righteousness on one side, and fatal error and bottomless wickedness on the other. Una, the Truth, the one and only Bride of man's spirit, marked out by the tokens of humility and innocence, and by her power over wild and untamed natures—the single Truth, in contrast to the counterfeit Duessa, false religion, and its actual embodiment in the false rival Queen of Scots—Truth, the object of passionate homage, real with many, professed with all, which after the impostures and scandals of the preceding age, had now become characteristic of that of Elizabeth—Truth, its claims, its dangers, and its champions, are the subject of the first book: and it is represented as leading the manhood of England, in spite not only of terrible conflict, but of defeat and falls, through the discipline of repentance, to holiness and the blessedness which comes with it. The Red Cross Knight, St. George of England, whose name Georgos, the Ploughman, is dwelt upon, apparently to suggest that from the commonalty, the "tall clownish young men," were raised up the great champions of the Truth—though sorely troubled by the wiles of Duessa, by the craft of the arch-sorcerer, by the force and pride of the great powers of the Apocalyptic Beast and Dragon, finally overcomes them, and wins the deliverance of Una and her love.

The second book, *Of Temperance*, pursues the subject, and represents the internal conquests of self-mastery, the conquests of a man over his passions, his violence, his covetousness, his ambition, his despair, his sensuality. Sir Guyon, after conquering many foes of goodness, is the destroyer of the most perilous of them all, Acrasia, licentiousness, and her ensnaring Bower of Bliss. But after this, the thread at once of story and allegory, slender henceforth at the best, is neglected and often entirely lost. The third book, the *Legend of Chastity*, is a repetition of the ideas of the latter part of the second, with a heroine, Britomart, in place of the Knight of the previous book, Sir Guyon, and with a special glorification of the highflown and romantic sentiments about purity, which were the poetic creed of the courtiers of Elizabeth, in flagrant and sometimes in tragic contrast to their practical conduct of life. The loose and ill-compacted nature of the plan becomes still more evident in the second instalment of the work. Even the special note of each particular virtue becomes more faint and indistinct. The one law to which the poet feels bound is to have twelve cantos in each book; and to do this he is sometimes driven to what in later times has been called padding. One of the cantos of the third book is a genealogy of British kings from Geoffrey of Monmouth; one of the cantos of the *Legend of Friendship* is made up of an episode describing the marriage of the Thames and the Medway, with an elaborate catalogue of the English and Irish rivers, and the names of the sea-nymphs. In truth, he had exhausted his proper allegory, or he got tired of it. His poem became an elastic framework, into which he could fit whatever interested him and tempted him to composition. The gravity of the first books disappears. He passes into satire and caricature. We meet with Braggadochio and Trompart, with the discomfiture of Malecasta, with the conjugal troubles of Malbecco and Helenore, with the imitation from Ariosto of the Squire of Dames. He puts into verse a poetical physiology of the human body; he translates Lucretius, and speculates on the origin of human souls; he speculates, too, on social justice, and composes an argumentative refutation of the Anabaptist theories of right and equality among men. As the poem proceeds, he seems to feel himself more free to introduce what he pleases. Allusions to real men and events are sometimes clear, at other times evident, though they have now ceased to be intelligible to us. His disgust and resentment breaks out at the ways of the Court in sarcastic moralising, or in pictures of dark and repulsive imagery. The characters and pictures of his friends furnish material for his poem; he does not mind touching on the misadventures of Raleigh, and even of Lord Grey, with sly humour or a word of candid advice. He becomes bolder in the distinct introduction of contemporary history. The defeat of Duessa was only figuratively shown in the first portion; in the second the subject is resumed. As Elizabeth is the "one form of many names," Gloriana, Belphœbe, Britomart, Mercilla, so, "under feigned colours shading a true case," he deals with her rival. Mary seems at one time the false Florimel, the creature of enchantment, stirring up strife, and fought for by the foolish knights whom she deceives, Blandamour and Paridell, the counterparts of Norfolk and the intriguers of 1571. At another, she is the fierce Amazonian Queen, Radegund, by whom, for a moment, even Arthegal is brought into disgraceful thraldom, till Britomart, whom he has once fought against, delivers him. And, finally, the fate of the typical Duessa is that of the real Mary Queen of Scots described in great detail—a liberty in dealing with great affairs of State for which James of Scotland actually desired that he should be tried and punished. So Philip II. is at one time the Soldan, at another the Spanish monster Geryoneo, at another the fosterer of Catholic intrigues in France and Ireland, Grantorto. But real names are also introduced with scarcely any disguise; Guizor, and Burbon, the Knight who throws away his shield, Henry IV., and his Lady Flourdelis, the Lady Belge, and her seventeen sons: the Lady Irena, whom Arthegal delivers. The overthrow of the Armada, the English war in the Low Countries, the apostasy of Henry IV., the deliverance of Ireland from the "great wrong" of Desmond's rebellion, the giant Grantorto, form, under more or less transparent allegory, great part of the *Legend of Justice*. Nay, Spenser's long-fostered revenge on the lady who had once scorned him, the *Rosalind*, of the *Shepherd's Calendar*, the *Mirabella* of the *Faerie Queene*, and his own late and happy marriage in Ireland, are also brought in to supply materials for the *Legend of Courtesy*. So multifarious is the poem, full of all that he thought, or observed, or felt; a receptacle, without much care to avoid repetition, or to prune, correct, and condense, for all the abundance of his ideas, as they welled forth in his mind day by day. It is really a collection of separate tales and allegories, as much as the *Arabian Nights*, or as its counterpart and rival of our own century, the *Idylls of the King*. As a whole, it is confusing: but we need not treat it as a whole. Its continued interest soon breaks down. But it is probably best that Spenser gave his mind the vague freedom which suited it, and that he did not make efforts to tie himself down to his pre-arranged but too ambitious plan. We can hardly lose our way in it, for there is no way to lose. It is a wilderness in which we are left to wander.

But there may be interest and pleasure in a wilderness, if we are prepared for the wandering.

Still, the complexity, or, rather, the uncared-for and clumsy arrangement of the poem is a matter which disturbs a reader's satisfaction, till he gets accustomed to the poet's way, and resigns himself to it. It is a heroic poem, in which the heroine, who gives her name to it, never appears: a story, of which the basis and starting-point is whimsically withheld for disclosure in the last book, which was never written. If Ariosto's jumps and transitions are more audacious, Spenser's intricacy is more puzzling. Adventures begin which have no finish. Actors in them drop from the clouds, claim an interest, and we ask in vain what has become of them. A vein of what are manifestly contemporary allusions breaks across the moral drift of the allegory, with an apparently distinct yet obscured meaning, and one of which it is the work of dissertations to find the key. The passion of the age was for ingenious riddling in morality as in love. And in Spenser's allegories we are not seldom at a loss to make out what and how much was really intended, amid a maze of over-strained analogies and over-subtle conceits, and attempts to hinder a too close and dangerous identification.

Indeed, Spenser's mode of allegory, which was historical as well as moral, and contains a good deal of history, if we knew it, often seems devised to throw curious readers off the scent. It was purposely baffling and hazy. A characteristic trait was singled out. A name was transposed in anagram, like Irena, or distorted, as if by imperfect pronunciation, like Burbon and Arthegal, or invented to express a quality, like Una, or Gloriana, or Corceca, or Fradubio, or adopted with no particular reason from the *Morte D'Arthur*, or any other old literature. The personage is introduced with some feature, or amid circumstances which seem for a moment to fix the meaning. But when we look to the sequence of history being kept up in the sequence of the story, we find ourselves thrown out. A character which fits one person puts on the marks of another: a likeness which we identify with one real person passes into the likeness of some one else. The real, in person, incident, institution, shades off in the ideal; after showing itself by plain tokens, it turns aside out of its actual path of fact, and ends, as the poet thinks it ought to end, in victory or defeat, glory or failure. Prince Arthur passes from Leicester to Sidney, and then back again to Leicester. There are double or treble allegories; Elizabeth is Gloriana, Belphœbe, Britomart, Mercilla, perhaps Amoret; her rival is Duessa, the false Florimel, probably the fierce temptress, the Amazon Radegund. Thus, what for a moment was clear and definite, fades like the changing fringe of a dispersing cloud. The character which we identified disappears in other scenes and adventures, where we lose sight of all that identified it. A complete transformation destroys the likeness which was begun. There is an intentional dislocation of the parts of the story, when they might make it imprudently close in its reflection of facts or resemblance in portraiture. A feature is shown, a manifest allusion made, and then the poet starts off in other directions, to confuse and perplex all attempts at interpretation, which might be too particular and too certain. This was, no doubt, merely according to the fashion of the time, and the habits of mind into which the poet had grown. But there were often reasons for it, in an age so suspicious, and so dangerous to those who meddled with high matters of state.

2. Another feature which is on the surface of the *Faerie Queene*, and which will displease a reader who has been trained to value what is natural and genuine, is its affectation of the language and the customs of life belonging to an age which is not its own. It is, indeed, redolent of the present; but it is

almost avowedly an imitation of what was current in the days of Chaucer: of what were supposed to be the words, and the social ideas and conditions, of the age of chivalry. He looked back to the fashions and ideas of the Middle Ages, as Pindar sought his materials in the legends and customs of the Homeric times, and created a revival of the spirit of the age of the Heroes in an age of tyrants and incipient democracies. The age of chivalry, in Spenser's day far distant, had yet left two survivals, one real, the other formal. The real survival was the spirit of armed adventure, which was never stronger or more stirring than in the gallants and discoverers of Elizabeth's reign, the captains of the English companies in the Low Countries, the audacious sailors who explored unknown oceans and plundered the Spaniards, the scholars and gentlemen equally ready for work on sea and land, like Raleigh and Sir Richard Grenville, of the "Revenge." The formal survival was the fashion of keeping up the trappings of knightly times, as we keep up Judges' wigs, court dresses, and Lord Mayors' shows. In actual life it was seen in pageants and ceremonies, in the yet lingering parade of jousts and tournaments, in the knightly accoutrements still worn in the days of the bullet and the cannon-ball. In the apparatus of the poet, as all were shepherds when he wanted to represent the life of peace and letters, so all were knights, or the foes and victims of knights, when his theme was action and enterprise. It was the custom that the Muse masked, to use Spenser's word, under these disguises; and this conventional masquerade of pastoral poetry or knight-errantry was the form under which the poetical school that preceded the dramatists naturally expressed their ideas. It seems to us odd that peaceful sheepcots and love-sick swains should stand for the world of the Tudors and Guises, or that its cunning state-craft and relentless cruelty should be represented by the generous follies of an imaginary chivalry. But it was the fashion which Spenser found, and he accepted it. His genius was not of that sort which breaks out from trammels, but of that which makes the best of what it finds. And whatever we may think of the fashion, at least he gave it new interest and splendour by the spirit with which he threw himself into it.

The condition which he took as the groundwork of his poetical fabric suggested the character of his language. Chaucer was then the "God of English poetry;" his was the one name which filled a place apart in the history of English verse. Spenser was a student of Chaucer, and borrowed as he judged fit, not only from his vocabulary, but from his grammatical precedents and analogies, with the object of giving an appropriate colouring to what was to be raised as far as possible above familiar life. Besides this, the language was still in such an unsettled state that, from a man with resources like Spenser's, it naturally invited attempts to enrich and colour it, to increase its flexibility and power. The liberty of reviving old forms, of adopting from the language of the street and market homely but expressive words or combinations, of following in the track of convenient constructions, of venturing on new and bold phrases, was rightly greater in his time than at a later stage of the language. Many of his words, either invented or preserved, are happy additions; some which have not taken root in the language, we may regret. But it was a liberty which he abused. He was extravagant and unrestrained in his experiments on language. And they were made not merely to preserve or to invent a good expression. On his own authority he cuts down, or he alters a word, or he adopts a mere corrupt pronunciation, to suit a place in his metre, or because he wants a rime. Precedents, as Mr. Guest has said, may no doubt be found for each one of these sacrifices to the necessities of metre or rime, in some one or other living dialectic usage, or even in printed

books— "*blend*" for "*blind*," "*misleeke*" for "*mislike*," "*kest*" for "*cast*," "*cherry*" for "*cherish*," "*vilde*" for, "*vile*," or even "*wawes*" for "*waves*," because it has to rime to "*jaws*." But when they are profusely used as they are in Spenser, they argue, as critics of his own age, such as Puttenham, remarked, either want of trouble, or want of resource. In his impatience he is reckless in making a word which he wants—"fortunize," "mercified," "unblindfold," "relive"—he is reckless in making one word do the duty of another, interchanging actives and passives, transferring epithets from their proper subjects. The "humbled grass," is the grass on which a man lies humbled: the "lamentable eye" is the eye which laments. "His treatment of words," says Mr. Craik, "on such occasions"—occasions of difficulty to his verse—"is like nothing that ever was seen, unless it might be Hercules breaking the back of the Nemean lion. He gives them any sense and any shape that the case may demand. Sometimes he merely alters a letter or two; sometimes he twists off the head or the tail of the unfortunate vocable altogether. But this fearless, lordly, truly royal style makes one only feel the more how easily, if he chose, he could avoid the necessity of having recourse to such outrages."

His own generation felt his license to be extreme. "In affecting the ancients," said Ben Jonson, "he writ no language." Daniel writes sarcastically, soon after the *Faerie Queene* appeared, of those who

> Sing of knights and Palladines,
> In aged accents and untimely words.

And to us, though students of the language must always find interest in the storehouse of ancient or invented language to be found in Spenser, this mixture of what is obsolete or capriciously new is a bar, and not an unreasonable one, to a frank welcome at first acquaintance. Fuller remarks, with some slyness, that "the many Chaucerisms used (for I will not say, affected) by him are thought by the ignorant to be blemishes, known by the learned to be beauties, in his book; which notwithstanding had been more saleable, if more conformed to our modern language." The grotesque, though it has its place as one of the instruments of poetical effect, is a dangerous element to handle. Spenser's age was very insensible to the presence and the dangers of the grotesque, and he was not before his time in feeling what was unpleasing in incongruous mixtures. Strong in the abundant but unsifted learning of his day, a style of learning which in his case was strangely inaccurate, he not only mixed the past with the present, fairyland with politics, mythology with the most serious Christian ideas, but he often mixed together the very features which are most discordant, in the colours, forms, and methods by which he sought to produce the effect of his pictures.

3. Another source of annoyance and disappointment is found in the imperfections and inconsistencies of the poet's standard of what is becoming to say and to write about. Exaggeration, diffuseness, prolixity, were the literary diseases of the age; an age of great excitement and hope, which had suddenly discovered its wealth and its powers, but not the rules of true economy in using them. With the classics open before it, and alive to much of the grandeur of their teaching, it was almost blind to the spirit of self-restraint, proportion, and simplicity which governed the great models. It was left to a later age to discern these and appreciate them. This unresisted proneness to exaggeration produced the extravagance and the horrors of the Elizabethan Drama, full, as it was, nevertheless, of insight and originality. It only too naturally led the earlier Spenser astray. What Dryden, in one of his interesting critical prefaces says of himself, is true of Spenser: "Thoughts, such as they are,

come crowding in so fast upon me, that my only difficulty is to choose or to reject; to run them into verse, or to give them the other harmony of prose." There was in Spenser a facility for turning to account all material, original or borrowed, an incontinence of the descriptive faculty, which was ever ready to exercise itself on any object, the most unfitting and loathsome, as on the noblest, the purest, or the most beautiful. There are pictures in him which seem meant to turn our stomach. Worse than that, there are pictures which for a time rank the poet of *Holiness* or *Temperance* with the painters who used their great art to represent at once the most sacred and holiest forms, and also scenes which few people now like to look upon in company—scenes and descriptions which may, perhaps from the habits of the time, have been playfully and innocently produced, but which it is certainly not easy to dwell upon innocently now. And apart from these serious faults, there is continually haunting us, amid incontestable richness, vigour, and beauty, a sense that the work is overdone. Spenser certainly did not want for humour and an eye for the ridiculous. There is no want in him, either, of that power of epigrammatic terseness, which, in spite of its diffuseness, his age valued and cultivated. But when he gets on a story or a scene, he never knows where to stop. His duels go on stanza after stanza till there is no sound part left in either champion. His palaces, landscapes, pageants, feasts, are taken to pieces in all their parts, and all these parts are likened to some other things. "His abundance," says Mr. Craik, "is often oppressive; *it is like wading among unmown grass.*" And he drowns us in words. His abundant and incongruous adjectives may sometimes, perhaps, startle us unfairly, because their associations and suggestions have quite altered; but very often they are the idle outpouring of an unrestrained affluence of language. The impression remains that he wants a due perception of the absurd, the unnatural, the unnecessary; that he does not care if he makes us smile, or does not know how to help it, when he tries to make us admire or sympathise.

Under this head comes a feature which the "charity of history" may lead us to treat as simple exaggeration, but which often suggests something less pardonable, in the great characters, political or literary, of Elizabeth's reign. This was the gross, shameless, lying flattery paid to the Queen. There is really nothing like it in history. It is unique as a phenomenon that proud, able, free-spoken men, with all their high instincts of what was noble and true, with all their admiration of the Queen's high qualities, should have offered it, even as an unmeaning custom; and that a proud and free-spoken people should not, in the very genuineness of their pride in her and their loyalty, have received it with shouts of derision and disgust. The flattery of Roman emperors and Roman Popes, if as extravagant, was not so personal. Even Louis XIV. was not celebrated in his dreary old age as a model of ideal beauty and a paragon of romantic perfection. It was no worship of a secluded and distant object of loyalty: the men who thus flattered knew perfectly well, often by painful experience, what Elizabeth was: able, indeed, high-spirited, successful, but ungrateful to her servants, capricious, vain, ill-tempered, unjust, and in her old age ugly. And yet the Gloriana of the *Faerie Queene*, the Empress of all nobleness—Belphœbe, the Princess of all sweetness and beauty—Britomart, the armed votaress of all purity—Mercilla, the lady of all compassion and grace—were but the reflection of the language in which it was then agreed upon by some of the greatest of Englishmen to speak, and to be supposed to think, of the Queen.

II. But when all these faults have been admitted, faults of design and faults of execution—and when it is admitted, fur-

ther, that there is a general want of reality, substance, distinctness, and strength in the personages of the poem—that, compared with the contemporary drama, Spenser's knights and ladies and villains are thin and ghost-like, and that as Daniel says, he

Paints shadows in imaginary lines—

it yet remains that our greatest poets since the day have loved him and delighted in him. He had Shakespere's praise. Cowley was made a poet by reading him. Dryden calls Milton "the poetical son of Spenser:" "Milton," he writes, "has acknowledged to me that Spenser was his original." Dryden's own homage to him is frequent and generous. Pope found as much pleasure in the *Faerie Queene* in his later years as he had found in reading it when he was twelve years old: and what Milton, Dryden, and Pope admired, Wordsworth too found full of nobleness, purity, and sweetness. What is it that gives the *Faerie Queene* its hold upon those who appreciate the richness and music of English language, and who in temper and moral standard are quick to respond to English manliness and tenderness? The spell is to be found mainly in three things—(1) in the quaint stateliness of Spenser's imaginary world and its representatives; (2) in the beauty and melody of his numbers, the abundance and grace of his poetic ornaments, in the recurring and haunting rhythms of numberless passages, in which thought and imagery and language and melody are interwoven in one perfect and satisfying harmony; and (3) in the intrinsic nobleness of his general aim, his conception of human life, at once so exacting and so indulgent, his high ethical principles and ideals, his unfeigned honour for all that is pure and brave and unselfish and tender, his generous estimate of what is due from man to man of service, affection, and fidelity. His fictions embodied truths of character which, with all their shadowy incompleteness, were too real and too beautiful to lose their charm with time.

1. Spenser accepted from his age the quaint stateliness which is characteristic of his poem. His poetry is not simple and direct like that of the Greeks. It has not the exquisite finish and felicity of the best of the Latins. It has not the massive grandeur, the depth, the freedom, the shades and subtle complexities of feeling and motive, which the English dramatists found by going straight to nature. It has the stateliness of highly artificial conditions of society, of the Court, the pageant, the tournament, as opposed to the majority of the great events in human life and history, its vicissitudes, its catastrophes, its tradegies, its revolutions, its sins. Throughout the prolonged crisis of Elizabeth's reign, her gay and dashing courtiers, and even her serious masters of affairs, persisted in pretending to look on the world in which they lived as if through the side-scenes of a masque, and relieved against the background of a stage-curtain. Human life, in those days, counted for little; fortune, honour, national existence hung in the balance; the game was one in which the heads of kings and queens and great statesmen were the stakes—yet the players could not get out of their stiff and constrained costume, out of their artificial and fantastic figments of thought, out of their conceits and affectations of language. They carried it, with all their sagacity, with all their intensity of purpose, to the council-board and the judgment-seat. They carried it to the scaffold. The conventional supposition was that at the Court, though every one knew better, all was perpetual holiday, perpetual triumph, perpetual love-making. It was the happy reign of the good and wise and lovely. It was the discomfiture of the base, the faithless, the wicked, the traitors. This is what is reflected in Spenser's poem; at once, its stateliness, for there was no want of grandeur and

magnificence in the public scene ever before Spenser's imagination; and its quaintness, because the whole outward apparatus of representation was borrowed from what was past, or from what did not exist, and implied surrounding circumstances in ludicrous contrast with fact, and men taught themselves to speak in character, and prided themselves on keeping it up by substituting for the ordinary language of life and emotion a cumbrous and involved indirectness of speech.

And yet that quaint stateliness is not without its attractions. We have indeed to fit ourselves for it. But when we have submitted to its demands on our imagination, it carries us along as much as the fictions of the stage. The splendours of the artificial are not the splendours of the natural; yet the artificial has its splendours, which impress and captivate and repay. The grandeur of Spenser's poem is a grandeur like that of a great spectacle, a great array of the forces of a nation, a great series of military effects, a great ceremonial assemblage of all that is highest and most eminent in a country, a coronation, a royal marriage, a triumph, a funeral. So, though Spenser's knights and ladies do what no men ever could do, and speak what no man ever spoke, the procession rolls forward with a pomp which never forgets itself, and with an inexhaustible succession of circumstance, fantasy, and incident. Nor is it always solemn and high-pitched. Its gravity is relieved from time to time with the ridiculous figure of character, the ludicrous incident, the jests and antics of the buffoon. It has been said that Spenser never smiles. He not only smiles, with amusement or sly irony; he wrote what he must have laughed at as he wrote, and meant us to laugh at. He did not describe with a grave face the terrors and misadventures of the boaster Braggadochio and his Squire, whether or not a caricature of the Duke of Alençon and his "gentleman," the "petit singe," Simier. He did not write with a grave face the Irish row about the false Florimel (IV. 5):

> Then unto Satyran she was adjudged,
> Who was right glad to gaine so goodly meed:
> But Blandamour thereat full greatly grudged,
> And litle prays'd his labours evill speed,
> That for to winne the saddle lost the steed.
> Ne lesse thereat did Paridell complaine,
> And thought t' appeale from that which was decreed
> To single combat with Sir Satyrane:
> Thereto him Atè stird, new discord to maintaine.

> And eke, with these, full many other Knights
> She through her wicked working did incense
> Her to demaund and chalenge as their rights,
> Deservèd for their perilsre' compense:
> Amongst the rest, with boastfull vaine pretense,
> Stept Braggadochio forth, and as his thrall
> Her claym'd, by him in battell wonne long sense:
> Whereto her selfe he did to witnesse call:
> Who, being askt, accordingly confessed all.

> Thereat exceeding wroth was Satyran;
> And wroth with Satyran was Blandamour;
> And wroth with Blandamour was Erivan;
> And at them both Sir Paridell did loure.

Nor the behaviour of the "rascal many" at the sight of the dead Dragon (I. 12):

> And after all the raskall many ran,
> Heaped together in rude rablement,
> To see the face of that victorious man,
> Whom all admired as from heaven sent,
> And gazd upon with gaping wonderment;
> But when they came where that dead Dragon lay,
> Stretcht on the ground in monstrous large extent,

> The sight with ydle feare did them dismay,
> Ne durst approch him nigh to touch, or once assay.

> Some feard, and fledd; some feard, and well it fayned;
> One, that would wiser seeme then all the rest,
> Warnd him not touch, for yet perhaps remaynd
> Some lingring life within his hollow brest,
> Or in his wombe might lurke some hidden nest
> Of many Dragonettes, his fruitful seede:
> Another saide, that in his eyes did rest
> Yet sparckling fyre, and badd thereof, take heed;
> Another said, he saw him move his eyes indeed.

> One mother, whenas her foolehardy chyld
> Did come too neare, and with his talants play,
> Halfe dead through feare, her litle babe revyld,
> And to her gossibs gan in counsell say;
> 'How can I tell, but that his talants may
> Yet scratch my sonne, or rend his tender hand?'
> So diversly them selves in vaine they fray;
> Whiles some more bold to measure him nigh stand,
> To prove how many acres he did spred of land.

And his humour is not the less real that it affects serious argument, in the excuse which he urges for his fairy tales (II. i):

> Right well I wote, most mighty Soveraine,
> That all this famous antique history
> Of some th' aboundance of an ydle braine
> Will judged be, and painted forgery,
> Rather then matter of just memory;
> Sith none that breatheth living aire dees know
> Where is that happy land of Faery,
> Which I so much doe vaunt, yet no where show,
> But vouch antiquities, which no body can know.

> But let that man with better sence advize,
> That of the world least part to us is red;
> And daily how through hardy enterprize
> Many great Regions are discovered,
> Which to late age were never mentioned.
> Who ever heard of th' Indian Peru?
> Or who in venturous vessell measured
> The Amazon huge river, now found trew?
> Or fruitfullest Virginia who did ever vew?

> Yet all these were, when no man did them know,
> Yet have them wisest ages hidden beene;
> And later times thinges more unknowne shall show.
> Why then should witlesse man so much misweene,
> That nothing is but that which he hath seene?
> What if within the Moones fayre shining spheare,
> What if in every other starre unseene
> Of other worldes he happily should heare,
> He wonder would much more; yet such to some appeare.

The general effect is almost always lively and rich: all is buoyant and full of movement. That it is also odd, that we see strange costumes and hear a language often formal and obsolete, that we are asked to take for granted some very unaccustomed supposition and extravagant assumption, does not trouble us more than the usages and sights, so strange to ordinary civil life, of a camp, or a royal levée. All is in keeping, whatever may be the details of the pageant; they harmonise with the effect of the whole, like the gargoyles and quaint groups in a Gothic building harmonise with its general tone of majesty and subtle beauty;—nay, as ornaments, in themselves of bad taste, like much of the ornamentation of the Renaissance styles, yet find a not unpleasing place in compositions grandly and nobly designed:

So discord oft in music makes the sweeter lay.

Indeed, it is curious how much of real variety is got out of a limited number of elements and situations. The spectacle, though consisting only of knights, ladies, dwarfs, pagans, "salvage men," enchanters, and monsters, and other well-worn machinery of the books of chivalry, is ever new, full of vigour and fresh images, even if, as sometimes happens, it repeats itself. There is a majestic unconsciousness of all violations of probability, and of the strangeness of the combinations which it unrolls before us.

2. But there is not only stateliness: there is sweetness and beauty. Spenser's perception of beauty of all kinds was singularly and characteristically quick and sympathetic. It was one of his great gifts; perhaps the most special and unstinted. Except Shakespere, who had it with other and greater gifts, no one in that time approached to Spenser, in feeling the presence of that commanding and mysterious idea, compounded of so many things, yet of which the true secret escapes us still, to which we give the name of beauty. A beautiful scene, a beautiful person, a beautiful poem, a mind and character with that combination of charms, which, for want of another word, we call by that half-spiritual, half-material word "beautiful," at once set his imagination at work to respond to it and reflect it. His means of reflecting it were as abundant as his sense of it was keen. They were only too abundant. They often betrayed him by their affluence and wonderful readiness to meet his call. Say what we will, and a great deal may be said, of his lavish profusion, his heady and uncontrolled excess, in the richness of picture and imagery in which he indulges—still, there it lies before us, like the most gorgeous of summer gardens, in the glory and brilliancy of its varied blooms, in the wonder of its strange forms of life, in the changefulness of its exquisite and delicious scents. No one who cares for poetic beauty can be insensible to it. He may criticise it. He may have too much of it. He may prefer something more severe and chastened. He may observe on the waste of wealth and power. He may blame the prodigal expense of language and the long spaces which the poet takes up to produce his effect. He may often dislike or distrust the moral aspect of the poet's impartial sensitiveness to all outward beauty—the impartiality which makes him throw all his strength into his pictures of Acrasia's Bower of Bliss, the Garden of Adonis, and Busirane's Masque of Cupid. But there is no gainsaying the beauty which never fails and disappoints, open the poem where you will. There is no gainsaying its variety, often so unexpected and novel. Face to face with the Epicurean idea of beauty and pleasure is the counter-charm of purity, truth, and duty. Many poets have done justice to each one separately. Few have shown, with such equal power, why it is that both have their roots in man's divided nature, and struggle, as it were, for the mastery. Which can be said to be the most exquisite in all beauty of imagination, of refined language, of faultless and matchless melody, of these two passages, in which the same image is used for the most opposite purposes;—first, in that song of temptation, the sweetest note in that description of Acrasia's Bower of Bliss, which, as a picture of the spells of pleasure, has never been surpassed; and next, to represent that stainless and glorious purity which is the professed object of his admiration and homage. In both the beauty of the rose furnishes the theme of the poet's treatment. In the first, it is the "lovely lady" which meets the knight of Temperance amid the voluptuousness which he is come to assail and punish:

> The whiles some one did chaunt this lovely lay;
> Ah! see, whoso fayre thing doest faine to see,
> In springing flowre the image of thy day.
> Ah! see the Virgin Rose, how sweetly shee

> Doth first peepe foorth with bashfull modestee,
> That fairer seemes the lesse ye see her may.
> Lo! see soone after how more bold and free
> Her bared bosome she doth broad display;
> Lo! see soone after how she fades and falls away.
>
> So passeth, in the passing of a day,
> Of mortall life the leafe, the bud, the flowre;
> Ne more doth florish after first decay,
> That earst was sought to deck both bed and bowre
> Of many a lady, and many a Paramowre.
> Gather therefore the Rose whilest yet is prime,
> For soone comes age that will her pride deflowre;
> Gather the Rose of love whilst yet is time,
> Whilest loving thou mayst loved be with equall
>   crime.

In the other, it images the power of the will—that power over circumstance and the storms of passion, to command obedience to reason and the moral law, which Milton sung so magnificently in *Comus*:

> That daintie Rose, the daughter of her Morne,
> More deare then life she tendered, whose flowre
> The girlond of her honour did adorne:
> Ne suffred she the Middayes scorching powre,
> Ne the sharp Northerne wind thereon to showre;
> But lapped up her silken leaves most chayre,
> When so the froward skye began to lowre;
> But, soone as calmed was the christall ayre,
> She die it fayre dispred and let to florish fayre.
>
> Eternall God, in his almightie powre,
> To make ensample of his heavenly grace,
> In Paradize whylome did plant this flowre;
> Whence he it fetcht out of her native place,
> And did in stocke of earthly flesh enrace,
> That mortall men her glory should admyre.
> In gentle Ladies breste, and bounteous race
> Of woman kind, it fayrest Flowre doth spyre,
> And beareth fruit of honour and all chast desyre.
>
> Fayre ympes of beautie, whose bright shining beames
> Adorne the worlde with like to heavenly light,
> And to your willes both royalties and Reames
> Subdew, through conquest of your wondrous might,
> With this fayre flowre your goodly girlonds dight
> Of chastity and vertue virginall,
> That shall embellish more your beautie bright,
> And crowne your heades with heavenly coronall,
> Such as the Angels weare before God's tribunall!

This sense of beauty and command of beautiful expression is not seen only in the sweetness of which both these passages are examples. Its range is wide. Spenser had in his nature, besides sweetness, his full proportion of the stern and high manliness of his generation; indeed, he was not without its severity, its hardness, its unconsidering and cruel harshness, its contemptuous indifference to suffering and misery when on the wrong side. Noble and heroic ideals captivate him by their attractions. He kindles naturally and genuinely at what proves and draws out men's courage, their self-command, their self-sacrifice. He sympathizes as profoundly with the strangeness of their condition, with the sad surprises in their history and fate, as he gives himself up with little restraint to what is charming and even intoxicating in it. He can moralise with the best in terse and deep-reaching apophthegms of melancholy or even despairing experience. He can appreciate the mysterious depths and awful outlines of theology—of what our own age can see nothing in, but a dry and scholastic dogmatism. His great contemporaries were—more, perhaps, than the men of any age—many-sided. He shared their nature; and he used all that he had of sensitiveness and of imaginative and creative power, in bringing out its manifold aspects, and sometimes contradictory feelings and aims. Not that beauty, even varied beauty, is the uninterrupted attribute of his work. It alternates with much that no indulgence can call beautiful. It passes but too easily into what is commonplace, or forced, or unnatural, or extravagant, or careless and poor, or really coarse and bad. He was a negligent corrector. He only at times gave himself the trouble to condense and concentrate. But for all this, the *Faerie Queene* glows and is ablaze with beauty; and that beauty is so rich, so real, and so uncommon, that for its sake the severest readers of Spenser have pardoned much that is discordant with it—much that in the reading has wasted their time and disappointed them.

There is one portion of the beauty of the *Faerie Queene* which in its perfection and fulness had never yet been reached in English poetry. This was the music and melody of his verse. It was this wonderful, almost unfailing sweetness of numbers which probably as much as anything set the *Faerie Queene* at once above all contemporary poetry. The English language is really a musical one, and, say what people will, the English ear is very susceptible to the infinite delicacy and suggestiveness of musical rhythm and cadence. Spenser found the secret of it. The art has had many and consummate masters since, as different in their melody as in their thoughts from Spenser. And others at the time, Shakespere pre-eminently, heard, only a little later, the same grandeur and the same subtle beauty in the sounds of their mother-tongue, only waiting the artist's skill to be combined and harmonised into strains of mysterious fascination. But Spenser was the first to show that he had acquired a command over what had hitherto been heard only in exquisite fragments, passing too soon into roughness and confusion. It would be too much to say that his cunning never fails, that his ear is never dull or off its guard. But when the length and magnitude of the composition are considered, with the restraints imposed by the new nine-line stanza, however convenient it may have been, the vigour, the invention, the volume and rush of language, and the keenness and truth of ear amid its diversified tasks, are indeed admirable which could keep up so prolonged and so majestic a stream of original and varied poetical melody. If his stanzas are monotonous, it is with the grand monotony of the seashore, where billow follows billow, each swelling diversely, and broken into different curves and waves upon its mounting surface, till at last it falls over, and spreads and rushes up in a last long line of foam upon the beach.

3. But all this is but the outside shell and the fancy framework in which the substance of the poem is enclosed. Its substance is the poet's philosophy of life. It shadows forth, in type and parable, his ideal of the perfection of the human character, with its special features, its trials, its achievements. There were two accepted forms in poetry in which this had been done by poets. One was under the image of warfare; the other was under the image of a journey or voyage. Spenser chose the former, as Dante and Bunyan chose the latter. Spenser looks on the scene of the world as a continual battle-field. It was such in fact, to his experience in Ireland, testing the mettle of character, its loyalty, its sincerity, its endurance. His picture of character is by no means painted with sentimental tenderness. He portrays it in the rough work of the struggle and the toil, always hardly tested by trial, often overmatched, deceived, defeated, and even delivered by its own default to disgrace and captivity. He had full before his eyes what abounded in the society of his day, often in its noblest representatives—the strange perplexing mixture of the purer with the baser elements, in the high-

tempered and aspiring activity of his time. But it was an ideal of character which had in it high aims and serious purposes, which was armed with fortitude and strength, which could recover itself after failure and defeat.

The unity of a story, or an allegory—that chain and backbone of continuous interest, implying a progress and leading up to a climax, which holds together the great poems of the world, the *Iliad and Odyssey*, the *Æneid*, the *Commedia*, the *Paradise Lost*, the *Jerusalem Delivered*—this is wanting in the *Faerie Queene*. The unity is one of character and its ideal. That character of the completed man, raised above what is poor and low, and governed by noble tempers and pure principles, has in Spenser two conspicuous elements. In the first place, it is based on manliness. In the personages which illustrate the different virtues—Holiness, Justice, Courtesy, and the rest—the distinction is not in nicely discriminated features or shades of expression, but in the trials and the occasions which call forth a practical action or effort: yet the manliness which is at the foundation of all that is good in them is a universal quality common to them all, rooted and embedded in the governing idea or standard of moral character in the poem. It is not merely courage, it is not merely energy, it is not merely strength. It is the quality, of soul which frankly accepts the conditions in human life, of labour of obedience, of effort, of unequal success, which does not quarrel with them or evade them, but takes for granted with unquestioning alacrity that man is called—by his call to high aims and destiny—to a continual struggle with difficulty, with pain, with evil, and makes it the point of honour not to be dismayed or wearied out by them. It is a cheerful and serious willingness for hard work and endurance, as being inevitable and very bearable necessities, together with even a pleasure in encountering trials which put a man on his mettle, an enjoyment of the contest and the risk, even in play. It is the quality which seizes on the paramount idea of duty, as something which leaves a man no choice; which despises and breaks through the inferior considerations and motives—trouble, uncertainty, doubt, curiosity—which hang about and impede duty; which is impatient with the idleness and childishness of a life of mere amusement, or mere looking on, of continued and self-satisfied levity, of vacillation, of clever and ingenious trifling. Spenser's manliness is quite consistent with long pauses of rest, with intervals of change, with great craving for enjoyment—nay, with great lapses from its ideal, with great mixtures of selfishness, with coarseness, with licentiousness, with injustice and inhumanity. It may be fatally diverted into bad channels; it may degenerate into a curse and scourge to the world. But it stands essentially distinct from the nature which shrinks from difficulty, which is appalled at effort, which has no thought of making an impression on things around it, which is content with passively receiving influences and distinguishing between emotions, which feels no call to exert itself, because it recognises no aim valuable enough to rouse it, and no obligation strong enough to command it. In the character of his countrymen round him, in its highest and in its worst features, in its noble ambition, its daring enterprise, its self-devotion, as well as in its pride, its intolerance, its fierce self-will, its arrogant claims of superiority—moral, political, religious—Spenser saw the example of that strong and resolute manliness which, once set on great things, feared nothing—neither toil nor disaster nor danger—in their pursuit. Naturally and unconsciously, he laid it at the bottom of all his portraitures of noble and virtuous achievements in the *Faerie Queene*.

All Spenser's "virtues" spring from a root of manliness. Strength, simplicity of aim, elevation of spirit, courage are presupposed as their necessary conditions. But they have with him another condition as universal. They all grow and are nourished from the soil of love; the love of beauty, the love and service of fair women. This, of course, is a survival from the ages of chivalry, an inheritance bequeathed from the minstrels of France, Italy, and Germany to the rising poetry of Europe. Spenser's types of manhood are imperfect without the idea of an absorbing and overmastering passion of love; without a devotion, as to the principal and most worthy object of life, to the service of a beautiful lady, and to winning her affection and grace. The influence of this view of life comes out in numberless ways. Love comes on the scene in shapes which are exquisitely beautiful, in all its purity, its tenderness, its unselfishness. But the claims of its all-ruling and irresistible might are also only too readily verified in the passions of men; in the follies of love, its entanglements, its mischiefs, its foulness. In one shape or another it meets us at every turn; it is never absent; it is the motive and stimulant of the whole activity of the poem. The picture of life held up before us is the literal rendering of Coleridge's lines:

> All thoughts, all passions, all delights,
> Whatever stirs this mortal frame,
> Are all but ministers of Love,
>   And feed his sacred flame.

We still think with Spenser about the paramount place of manliness, as the foundation of all worth in human character. We have ceased to think with him about the rightful supremacy of love, even in the imaginative conception of human life. We have ceased to recognise in it the public claims of almost a religion, which it has in Spenser. Love will ever play a great part in human life to the end of time. It will be an immense element in its happiness, perhaps a still greater one in its sorrows, its disasters, its tragedies. It is still an immense power in shaping and colouring it, both in fiction and reality; in the family, in the romance, in the fatalities and the prosaic ruin of vulgar fact. But the place given to it by Spenser is to our thoughts and feelings even ludicrously extravagant. An enormous change has taken place in the ideas of society on this point: it is one of the things which make a wide chasm between centuries and generations which yet are of "the same passions," and have in temper, tradition, and language so much in common. The ages of the Courts of Love, whom Chaucer reflected, and whose ideas passed on through him to Spenser, are to us simply strange and abnormal states through which society has passed, to us beyond understanding and almost belief. The perpetual love-making, as one of the first duties and necessities of a noble life, the space which it must fill in the cares and thoughts of all gentle and high-reaching spirits, the unrestrained language of admiration and worship, the unrestrained yielding to the impulses, the anxieties, the pitiable despair and agonies of love, the subordination to it of all other pursuits and aims, the weeping and wailing and self-torturing which it involves, all this is so far apart from what we know of actual life, the life not merely of work and business, but the life of affection, and even of passion, that it makes the picture of which it is so necessary a part seem to us in the last degree unreal, unimaginable, grotesquely ridiculous. The quaint love sometimes found among children, so quickly kindled, so superficial, so violent in its language and absurd in its plans, is transferred with the utmost gravity to the serious proceedings of the wise and good. In the highest characters it is chastened, refined, purifed: it appropriates, indeed, language due only to the divine, it almost simulates idolatry, yet it belongs to the best part of man's nature. But in the lower and average characters it is

not so respectable; it is apt to pass into mere toying pastime and frivolous love of pleasure; it astonishes us often by the readiness with which it displays an affinity for the sensual and impure, the corrupting and debasing sides of the relations between the sexes. But however it appears, it is throughout a very great affair, not merely with certain persons, or under certain circumstances, but with every one: it obtrudes itself in public, as the natural and recognised motive of plans of life and trials of strength; it is the great spur of enterprise, and its highest and most glorious reward. A world of which this is the law is not even in fiction a world which we can conceive possible, or with which experience enables us to sympathise.

It is, of course, a purely artificial and conventional reading of the facts of human life and feeling. Such conventional readings and renderings belong in a measure to all art; but in its highest forms they are corrected, interpreted, supplemented by the presence of interspersed realities which every one recognises. But it was one of Spenser's disadvantages, that two strong influences combined to entangle him in this fantastic and grotesque way of exhibiting the play and action of the emotions of love. This all-absorbing, all-embracing passion of love, at least this way of talking about it, was the fashion of the Court. Further, it was the fashion of poetry, which he inherited; and he was not the man to break through the strong bands of custom and authority. In very much he was an imitator. He took what he found; what was his own was his treatment of it. He did not trouble himself with inconsistencies, or see absurdities and incongruities. Habit and familiar language made it not strange that in the Court of Elizabeth the most highflown sentiments should be in every one's mouth about the sublimities and refinements of love, while every one was busy with keen ambition and unscrupulous intrigue. The same blinding power kept him from seeing the monstrous contrast between the claims of the queen to be the ideal of womanly purity—claims recognised and echoed in ten thousand extravagant compliments—and the real licentiousness common all round her among her favourites. All these strange contradictions, which surprise and shock us, Spenser assumed as natural. He built up his fictions on them, as the dramatist built on a basis which, though more nearly approaching to real life, yet differed widely from it in many of its preliminary and collateral suppositions; or as the novelist builds up his on a still closer adherence to facts and experience. In this matter Spenser appears with a kind of double self. At one time he speaks as one penetrated and inspired by the highest and purest ideas of love, and filled with aversion and scorn for the coarser forms of passion—for what is ensnaring and treacherous, as well as for what is odious and foul. At another, he puts forth all his power to bring out its most dangerous and even debasing aspects in highly coloured pictures, which none could paint without keen sympathy with what he takes such pains to make vivid and fascinating. The combination is not like anything modern, for both the elements are in Spenser so unquestionably and simply genuine. Our modern poets are, with all their variations in this respect, more homogeneous; and where one conception of love and beauty has taken hold of a man, the other does not easily come in. It is impossible to imagine Wordsworth dwelling with zest on visions and imagery, on which Spenser has lavished all his riches. There can be no doubt of Byron's real habits of thought and feeling on subjects of this kind, even when his language for the occasion is the chastest; we detect in it the mood of the moment, perhaps spontaneous, perhaps put on, but in contradiction to the whole movement of the man's true nature. But Spenser's words do not ring hollow. With a kind of unconsciousness and innocence, which we now find hard to understand, and which, perhaps, belongs to the early child-hood or boyhood of a literature, he passes abruptly from one standard of thought and feeling to another; and is quite as much in earnest when he is singing the pure joys of chastened affections, as he is when he is writing with almost riotous luxuriance what we are at this day ashamed to read. Tardily, indeed, he appears to have acknowledged the contradiction. At the instance of two noble ladies of the Court, he composed two Hymns of Heavenly Love and Heavenly Beauty, to "retract" and "reform" two earlier ones composed in praise of earthly love and beauty. But, characteristically, he published the two pieces together, side by side in the same volume.

In the *Faerie Queene*, Spenser has brought out, not the image of the great Gloriana, but in its various aspects a form of character which was then just coming on the stage of the world, and which has played a great part in it since. As he has told us, he aimed at presenting before us, in the largest sense of the word, the English gentleman. It was, as a whole, a new character in the world. It had not really existed in the days of feudalism and chivalry, though features of it had appeared, and its descent was traced from those times: but they were too wild and coarse, too turbulent and disorderly, for a character which, however ready for adventure and battle, looked to peace, re-finement, order, and law as the true conditions of its perfec-tion. In the days of Elizabeth it was beginning to fill a large place in English life. It was formed amid the increasing cultiva-tion of the nation, the increasing varieties of public service, the awakening responsibilities to duty and calls to self-command. Still making much of the prerogative of noble blood and family honours, it was something independent of nobility and beyond it. A nobleman might have in him the making of a gentleman: but it was the man himself of whom the gentleman was made. Great birth, even great capacity, were not enough; there must be added a new delicacy of conscience, a new appreciation of what is beautiful and worthy of honour, a new measure of the strength and nobleness of self-control, of devotion to unselfish interests. This idea of manhood, based not only on force and courage, but on truth, on refinement, on public spirit, on soberness and modesty, on consideration for others, was taking possession of the younger generation of Elizabeth's middle years. Of course the idea was very imperfectly apprehended, still more imperfectly realised. But it was something which on the same scale had not been yet, and which was to be the seed of something greater. It was to grow into those strong, simple, noble characters, pure in aim and devoted to duty, the Falklands, the Hampdens, who amid so much evil form such a remarkable feature in the Civil Wars both on the Royalist and the Parliamentary sides. It was to grow into that high type of cultivated English nature, in the present and the last century, common both to its monarchical and its democratic embodi-ments, than which, with all its faults and defects, our western civilization has produced few things more admirable.

There were three distinguished men of that time, who one after another were Spenser's friends and patrons, and who were men in whom he saw realised his conceptions of human excel-lence and nobleness. They were Sir Philip Sidney, Lord Grey of Wilton, and Sir Walter Raleigh: and the *Faerie Queene* reflects as in a variety of separate mirrors and spiritualised forms, the characteristics of these men and of such as they. It reflects their conflicts, their temptations, their weaknesses, the evils they fought with, the superiority with which they towered over meaner and poorer natures. Sir Philip Sidney may be said to have been the first typical example in English society of the true gentleman. The charm which attracted men to him in life, the fame which he left behind him, are not to be ac-counted for simply by his accomplishments as a courtier, a poet, a lover of literature, a gallant soldier; above all this, there was something not found in the strong or brilliant men about him, a union and harmony of all high qualities differing from any of them separately, which gave a fire of its own to his literary enthusiasm, and a sweetness of its own to his courtesy. Spenser's admiration for that bright but short career was strong and lasting. Sidney was to him a verification of what he aspired to and imagined; a pledge that he was not dreaming in portray-ing Prince Arthur's greatness of soul, the religious chivalry of the Red Cross Knight of Holiness, the manly purity and self-control of Sir Guyon. It is too much to say that in Prince Arthur, the hero of the poem, he always intended Sidney. In the first place, it is clear that under that character Spenser in places pays compliments to Leicester, in whose service he be-gan life, and whose claims on his homage he ever recognised. Prince Arthur is certainly Leicester in the historical passages in the Fifth Book relating to the war in the Low Countries in 1576: and no one can be meant but Leicester, in the bold allusion in the First Book (ix. 17) to Elizabeth's supposed thoughts of marrying him. In the next place, allegory, like caricature, is not bound to make the same person and the same image always or perfectly coincide; and Spenser makes full use of this liberty. But when he was painting the picture of the Kingly Warrior, in whom was to be summed up in a magnifi-cent unity the diversified graces of other men, and who was to be ever ready to help and support his fellows in their hour of need, and in their conflict with evil, he certainly had before his mind the well-remembered lineaments of Sidney's high and generous nature. And he further dedicated a separate book, the last that he completed, to the celebration of Sidney's special "virtue" of Courtesy. The martial strain of the poem changes once more to the pastoral of the *Shepherd's Calendar* to de-scribe Sidney's wooing of Frances Walsingham, the fair Pas-torella; his conquests, by his sweetness and grace, over the churlishness of rivals; and his triumphant war against the mon-ster spirit of ignorant and loud-tongued insolence, the "Blatant Beast" of religious, political, and social slander.

Again, in Lord Grey of Wilton, gentle by nature, but so stern in the hour of trial, called reluctantly to cope not only with anarchy, but with intrigue and disloyalty, finding self-ishness and thanklessness everywhere, but facing all and doing his best with a heavy heart, ending his days prematurely under detraction and disgrace, Spenser had before him a less com-plete character than Sidney, but yet one of grand and severe manliness, in which were conspicuous a religious hatred of disorder, and an unflinching sense of public duty. Spenser's admiration of him was sincere and earnest. In his case the allegory almost becomes history. Arthur, Lord Grey, is Sir Arthegal, the Knight of Justice. The story touches, apparently, on some passages of his career, when his dislike of the French marriage placed him in opposition to the Queen, and even for a time threw him with the supporters of Mary. But the adven-tures of Arthegal mainly preserve the memory of Lord Grey's terrible exploits against wrong and rebellion in Ireland. These exploits are represented in the doings of the iron man Talus, his squire, with his destroying flail, swift, irresistible, inexorable; a figure, borrowed and altered, after Spenser's wont, from a Greek legend. His overthrow of insolent giants, his annihila-tion of swarming "rascal routs," idealise and glorify that unre-lenting policy, of which, though condemned in England, Spenser continued to be the advocate. In the story of Arthegal, long separated by undeserved misfortunes from the favour of the armed lady, Britomart, the virgin champion of right, of whom he was so worthy, doomed in spite of his honours to an early death, and assailed on his return from his victorious service by the furious insults of envy and malice, Spenser portrays, almost without a veil, the hard fate of the unpopular patron whom he to the last defended and honoured.

Raleigh, his last protector, the Shepherd of the Ocean, to whose judgment he referred the work of his life, and under whose guidance he once more tried the quicksands of the Court, belonged to a different class from Sidney or Lord Grey; but of his own class he was the consummate and matchless example. He had not Sidney's fine enthusiasm and nobleness; he had not either Sidney's affectations. He had not Lord Grey's single-minded hatred of wrong. He was a man to whom his own interests were much; he was unscrupulous; he was ostentatious; he was not above stooping to mean, unmanly compliances with the humours of the Queen. But he was a man with a higher ideal than he attempted to follow. He saw, not without cynical scorn, through the shows and hollowness of the world. His intellect was of that clear and unembarrassed power which takes in as wholes things which other man take in part by part. And he was in its highest form a representative of that spirit of adventure into the unknown and the wonderful of which Drake was the coarser and rougher example, realising in serious earnest, on the sea and in the New World, the life of knight-errantry feigned in romances. With Raleigh as with Lord Grey, Spenser comes to history; and he even seems to have been moved, as the poem went on, partly by pity, partly by amusement, to shadow forth in his imaginary world, not merely Raleigh's brilliant qualities, but also his frequent misadventures and mischances in his career at Court. Of all her favourites, Raleigh was the one whom his wayward mistress seemed to find most delight in tormenting. The offence which he gave by his secret marriage suggested the scenes describing the utter desolation of Prince Arthur's squire, Timias, at the jealous wrath of the Virgin Huntress, Belphœbe—scenes which, extravagant as they are, can hardly be called a caricature of Raleigh's real behaviour in the Tower in 1593. But Spenser is not satisfied with this one picture. In the last Book Timias appears again, the victim of slander and ill-usage, even after he had recovered Belphœbe's favour; he is baited like a wild bull by mighty powers of malice, falsehood, and calumny; he is wounded by the tooth of the Blatant Beast; and after having been cured, not without difficulty, and not without significant indications on the part of the poet that his friend had need to restrain and chasten his unruly spirit, he is again delivered over to an ignominious captivity, and the insults of Disdain and Scorn.

> Then up he made him rise, and forward fare,
> Led in a rope which both his hands did bynd;
> Ne ought that foole for pity did him spare,
> But with his whip, him following behynd,
> Him often scourg'd, and forst his feete to fynd:
> And other-whiles with bitter mockes and mowes
> He would him scorne, that to his gentle mynd
> Was much more grievous then the others blowes:
> Words sharpely wound, but greatest griefe of scorning
>   growes.

Spenser knew Raleigh only in the promise of his adventurous prime—so buoyant and fearless, so inexhaustible in project and resource, so unconquerable by checks and reverses. The gloomier portion of Raleigh's career was yet to come: its intrigues, its grand yet really gambling and unscrupulous enterprises, the long years of prison and authorship, and its not unfitting close, in the English statesman's death by the headsman—so tranquil though violent, so ceremoniously solemn,

so composed, so dignified—such a contrast to all other forms of capital punishment, then or since.

Spenser has been compared to Pindar, and contrasted with Cervantes. The contrast, in point of humour, and the truth that humour implies, is favourable to the Spaniard: in point of moral earnestness and sense of poetic beauty, to the Englishman. What Cervantes only thought ridiculous, Spenser used, and not in vain, for a high purpose. The ideas of knight-errantry were really more absurd than Spenser allowed himself to see. But that idea of the gentleman which they suggested, that picture of human life as a scene of danger, trial, effort, defeat, recovery, which they lent themselves to image forth, was more worth insisting on, than the exposure of their folly and extravagance. There was nothing to be made of them, Cervantes thought; and nothing to be done, but to laugh off what they had left, among living Spaniards, of pompous imbecility or mistaken pretensions. Spenser, knowing that they must die, yet believed that out of them might be raised something nobler and more real—enterprise, duty, resistance to evil, refinement, hatred of the mean and base. The energetic and high-reaching manhood which he saw in the remarkable personages round him he shadowed forth in the *Faerie Queene*. He idealised the excellences and the trials of this first generation of English gentlemen, as Bunyan afterwards idealised the piety, the conflicts, and the hopes of Puritan religion. Neither were universal types; neither were perfect. The manhood in which Spenser delights, with all that was admirable and attractive in it, had still much of boyish incompleteness and roughness: it had noble aims, it had generosity, it had loyalty, it had a very real reverence for purity and religion; but it was young in experience of a new world, it was wanting in self-mastery, it was often pedantic and self-conceited; it was an easier prey than it ought to have been to discreditable temptations. And there is a long interval between any of Spenser's superficial and thin conceptions of character, and such deep and subtle creations as Hamlet or Othello, just as Bunyan's strong but narrow ideals of religion, true as they are up to a certain point, fall short of the length and breadth and depth of what Christianity has made of man, and may yet make of him. But in the ways which Spenser chose, he will always delight and teach us. The spectacle of what is heroic and self-devoted, of honour for principle and truth, set before us with so much insight and sympathy, and combined with so much just and broad observation on those accidents and conditions of our mortal state which touch us all, will never appeal to English readers in vain, till we have learned a new language, and adopted new canons of art, of taste, and of morals. It is not merely that he has left imperishable images which have taken their place among the consecrated memorials of poetry and the household thoughts of all cultivated men. But he has permanently lifted the level of English poetry by a great and sustained effort of rich and varied art, in which one main purpose rules, loyalty to what is noble and pure, and in which this main purpose subordinates to itself every feature and every detail, and harmonises some that by themselves seem least in keeping with it.

R. E. NEIL DODGE
From "Spenser's Imitations from Ariosto"
PMLA, 1897, pp. 151–98

The influence of the *Orlando Furioso* on Spenser's *Faery Queen* has long been recognized. Warton, in his excellent *Observations*, devoted a section to it, and others have here and there remarked upon the affinity of the two poems. I cannot find, however, that any writer has yet given the subject more than casual attention. The reasons for this neglect are, of course, not far to seek. Men read and study the *Faery Queen*, and men read and study the *Orlando Furioso*, but few care to read and study them side by side, with the obligation of going through the *Morgante Maggiore*, the *Orlando Innamorato*, *Rinaldo*, and the *Gerusalemme Liberata*, for casual reference and general illustration. The *Faery Queen*, as it stands, is nearly twice as long as the *Odyssey*, the *Orlando Furioso* is longer than the *Faery Queen*, and the others are of varying, but always substantial bulk—a rather formidable array. Moreover, despite vast differences of spirit and method, these poems deal with the same subject-matter, romantic chivalry; and too steady converse with romantic chivalry is, to say the least, not stimulating. In view of such conditions and of the work already done by Warton, critics may very probably have felt that further labor in this field would hardly be worth while.

If one could hope for no more than to add a few parallel references to Warton's list, the labor would certainly not be worth while, for, in themselves, parallel references are mere curiosities of literature. One must classify and compare and analyze them, before the influence of one poet on another can be determined. Just this, however, Warton has not done, did not attempt to do; it was not within the scope of his plan. Yet the work would seem to be worth doing. In the following pages I have tried to cover in part the field which he very naturally neglected. I do not aim at exhaustiveness. I shall not examine how far Ariosto may have influenced the literary methods of Spenser, nor shall I attempt to analyze the *Orlando Furioso* and the *Faery Queen* as typical romance poems, to discover just what elements Spenser may have borrowed from the Ferrarese. I wish merely to discuss those specific imitations of the *Furioso* which are to be found in the *Faery Queen*, and to indicate how Spenser made direct use of his original.

I

Before taking up detail-study it may be well to give a brief preliminary glance at the beginnings of the *Faery Queen*. The earliest mention of it which has come down to us is in the two well known letters which Spenser and Harvey exchanged in the spring of 1580. Spenser writes:

> Nowe my *Dreames* and *Dying Pellicane*, being fully finished. . . . and presentlye to bee imprinted, I wil in hande forthwith with my *Faery Queene*, whyche I praye you hartily send me with al expedition: and your friendly Letters, and long expected Judgement wythal, whyche let not be shorte, but in all pointes suche, as you ordinarilye use, and I extraordinarily desire.[1]

Harvey replies, and his friendly criticism has become a classic of Spenser literature:

> To be plaine, I am voyde of al judgement, if your *Nine Comœdies*, whereunto in imitation of Herodotus, you give the names of the Nine Muses (and in one mans fansie not unworthily), come not neerer *Ariostoes Comœdies*, eyther for the finenesse of plausible Elocution, or the rarenesse of Poetical Invention, then that *Elvish Queene* doth to his *Orlando Furioso*, which notwithstanding you will needes seeme to emulate, and hope to overgo, as you flatly professed yourself in one of your last Letters.

> Besides that you know, it hath bene the usual practise of the most exquisite and odde wittes in all nations, and specially in *Italie*, rather to shewe, and advaunce themselves that way, than any other: as

namely, those three notorious dyscoursing heads, *Bibiena*, *Machiavel*, and *Aretine* did (to let *Bembo* and *Ariosto* passe) with the great admiration, and wonderment of the whole country: being in deede reputed matchable in all points, both for conceyt of Witte and eloquent decyphering of matters, either with *Aristophanes* and *Menander* in Greek, or with *Plautus* and *Terence* in Latin, or with any other, in any other tong. But I wil not stand greatly with you in your owne matters. If so be the *Faerye Queene* be fairer in your eie than the *Nine Muses*, and *Hobgoblin* runne away with the Garland from Apollo: Marke what I saye, and yet I will not say that I thought, but there an End for this once, and fare you well, till God or some good Aungell putte you in a better minde.

These passages give us one plain fact: at the very outset of his great poem Spenser is emulating the *Orlando Furioso* and hoping to surpass it. Circumstances, indeed, made the emulation almost inevitable.

In the spring of 1580, Spenser was about twenty-eight years old. He had been out of the University some three years and a half, and was then in London, the *protégé* of Leicester and the friend of Sidney, looking forward with a young man's hopefulness to a career of practical activity. The October eclogue of the *Calender*, to be sure, speaks with some bitterness of the indifference shown to poetry and true poets, and Spenser would unquestionably have liked to devote himself without check to the cultivation of his genius; but he very well understood the conditions of his day, and his lament, despite its genuine fervor, need not be taken too seriously.[2] His familiar correspondence with Harvey, of this same period, certainly shows no signs of dejection.

During these years he had been unusually active with his pen. Many of the poems which later appeared in the volume of *Complaints* had been more or less nearly completed and laid aside, and of the works in prose and verse since lost or transformed beyond certain identification we have a list of nearly two dozen numbers. He was one of the aristocratic "Areopagus," interested in classic quantities, half believing, perhaps, in the revolution to be wrought in English verse, though with a poet's inconsistency following his own irresistible bent towards the national measures and rhyme. As Immerito, or Colin Clout, or "the new poete," he was famous all over literary London. The *Calender*, indeed—in which youthful voracity of taste is so distinct—would, itself alone, indicate the varied interests and activity of his mind. None of these early works, however, was in any sense great, or opened the door to European fame, and he was of a generation which did not rest content with small things. We are, therefore, not surprised to find him already concentrating his attention on what is to be the poem of his lifetime, the *Faery Queen*.

Now, the *Orlando Furioso* was by common consent the master-piece of the century. Neither France nor England had produced anything to match it: even in Italy it was still unequalled, for the *Rinaldo*, besides being of relatively modest scope, was no more than the work of a promising youth, the *Italia Liberata* was so dull that nobody read it, and the *Gerusalemme Liberata* had not yet been published to the world. Ariosto's fame was supreme, and would be the natural mark of every ambitious young poet like Spenser. Moreover, the *Orlando Furioso* was the one long poem of Europe which, dealing with romantic chivalry, gave it accomplished artistic expression. The poetical romances of the middle ages could of course not serve him for models; the *Morte d'Arthur*, despite its fine prose dignity, could give him nothing but raw material; the *Morgante Maggiore*, which he very probably did not know, was too grotesque for his purposes; and the *Orlando Innamorato*, which also he seems not to have known, had been too thoroughly eclipsed by the *Furioso* to invite imitation. Ariosto's poem alone stood for a model to study and an achievement to emulate. We need hardly wonder, therefore, to find Spenser at the very outset of his *Faery Queen* consciously pitting himself against the great Italian.

The temper of Ariosto's mind and the main qualities of his work need not here be analyzed in detail. Essentially secular and modern in his outlook, he sees in the world of chivalry a fantastic, amusing, utterly unreal show. It stimulates his imagination; it stirs his sense of humor. He is not a strenuous poet; he has no thought for grand themes; all he cares for is complete artistic liberty. Planning to write a great poem, therefore, he looks about him for an unencumbered field, a field in which his fancy can range unrestricted, in which his wit and humor can find congenial topics and his worldly observation can be at ease, which will give him themes for varied sentiment and lively action, and satisfy his sense of beauty with landscapes and gardens and palaces and colored pageantry such as make his own Italian world so pleasant a place to live in. Just this field is open to him in romantic chivalry. It is almost infinite in extent and variety, and it has no beaten highways which a man must travel or miss his goal. Here he will be free and out of the reach of Aristotle. Furthermore, if he adopts chivalry, he can in part spare himself the labor of inventing a plot and characters. The *Orlando Innamorato* is at hand, unfinished: he can take up Bojardo's theme at the point of cessation, refine the cruder elements to meet his own more cultivated taste, and then carry it on wherever his fancy leads him. What more attractive work for a poet who, though bent on avoiding artistic constraint, has no ambition to be fundamentally creative?

The plainer qualities of Ariosto's poetry are notorious, and yet critics continue to differ about the *Orlando Furioso*. It contains passages of unquestionable irony; it contains passages of unquestionable seriousness. Is it a flippant poem, a deliberate satire on chivalry, colored here and there with rhetoric and factitious sentiment? Or is it, on the whole, a serious poem enlivened by sallies of irony and humorous extravagance? The answer seems plain: it is neither. Those critics hardly understand Ariosto who imagine that he has a set point-of-view. If ever a man was "divers et ondoyant," it is he. We find him at times playing with chivalry as Heine plays with the legend of Rhampsenit: at times we find him portraying the emotions of his characters with genuine sympathy and power. There is no inconsistency in his attitude, for he has no definite attitude, or, better, his attitude is that of the impartial artist. He is a man of the Renaissance, indifferent to moral steadfastness, alive to the beauty of the world and the interest of life, determined, above all, to have free play for his faculties. The fervor and the fine idealism of chivalry amuse him and impress him by turns, according to his mood. If a distinction were possible we might say that mere chivalry provokes him to a smile; that when he is serious he is stirred by qualities of form or feeling or thought which are not peculiar to chivalry. Or we might say that though the spirit of chivalry means nothing to him, the external forms of chivalry, in their richness and varied life, strike his imagination and rouse him to an artist's sympathy. But such distinctions are hazardous; he is too elusive to be caught by definition. We recognize, of course, that he impresses various people very distinctly. To some of us his fertility, ease, and delightful art, his humor and his sunny scepticism are a constant charm; others can see nothing but his moral indifference, his frivolity,

his licentiousness. Whether we like him or not, however, and for whatever reason, we shall certainly not understand him if we try to classify his temper as either serious or flippant. Most of us will agree that irony is the main trait of his genius, and that much of his seriousness is very conventional; but, on the other hand, we shall surely be uncritical if we deny that such passages as the crisis of Orlando's love (c. XXIII) are sincerely sympathetic. A tentative analysis might perhaps declare him to be an ironical, disillusioned courtier, gifted with the sensitive temperament of a poet. But again, he is too elusive to be caught by definition.

Looking back on Ariosto from the vantage ground of our own critical century, we can readily discriminate and weigh these elements of his genius: his contemporaries, of course, read him without need of analysis or commentary. During the sixty years, however, between the first appearance of his poem and the times of Spenser's emulation the temper of Europe changed, and in 1580 men no longer understood him as we can understand him now, or as his contemporaries understood him. If we would estimate his influence upon Spenser, therefore, even partially, we must first of all determine what Spenser really saw in him, and, to do this, we shall have to glance at the history of his reputation, that is, the development of Ariosto criticism in Italy. Certain important lines of this development do not lead us directly to Spenser's own views, but they can hardly on that account be eliminated. The movement should be taken as a whole. It is singular and interesting.

A traditional anecdote tells us that when Ariosto was planning his poem he turned to Bembo for advice, and that Bembo urged him to write it in Latin. According to another story, Bembo also urged him to cast it in regular epic form. Ariosto, whose chief desire was complete artistic liberty, would of course not listen to such suggestions as these. Yet he was far from neglecting the classics. The writing of so long a poem as the *Furioso* necessitated a careful gathering of material, and in his search for this he not only ransacked what mediaeval romances were at hand, but turned as a matter of course to the authors of antiquity. One has only to glance at some of his most effective episodes—Rodomonte within the walls of Paris, the midnight expedition of Cloridano and Medoro, Olimpia abandoned by Bireno on the desert island, Angelica exposed to the Orc and rescued by Ruggiero—to understand how freely he took from them. Nor does he, like Bojardo, utterly transform these borrowed passages in the spirit of frank and unregenerate romanticism: though accepting no limitations to his fancy, he yet has the true Renaissance taste for his originals and keeps as close to them as he fairly can. Indeed, as Professor Rajna has pointed out, the *Furioso* contains the germs of that classical movement which was to make such rapid progress in Italy during the middle of the sixteenth century. Ariosto would not hamper himself with the laws of epic construction, but he borrows from classic literature almost as freely as the pedants of later times, and seems to think with them that such imitation in itself adds beauty to a poem.

From the days of the *Furioso* onward the progress of classicism in Italy was indeed appalling. Ariosto's own comedies had already sent men back to Plautus and Terence, and in the very year in which his great poem was being prepared for the press Trissino wrote his *Sofonisba* and established the type of neoclassic tragedy. In narrative poetry the transformation came later. Before Ariosto's death, however, the *Italia Liberata* had been begun, and in 1547 Italy could at last boast of having an epic, unreadable to be sure, but rigidly classical. A little later Alamanni composed his *Avarchide*, in which Caesar's Avaricum was besieged by King Arthur exactly on the lines of the siege of Troy. Even the pure romance poem was infected. Almost within the decade of Ariosto's death Giovan Maria Verdizzotti, a lad of sixteen, divided between delight in the Ferrarese and reverence for the classics, began an *Orlando*, the style of which was to be modelled on that of the *Furioso*, while the structure was to be after Aristotle's strictest laws. In 1560 appeared Bernardo Tasso's *Amadigi*, a work of the transition, in which the attempt to cast a romance poem in Aristotelian mould was frankly made and as frankly abandoned. Two years later the attempt was at least partially successful in Torquato Tasso's *Rinaldo*. Finally, in the *Gerusalemme Liberata*, of 1581, the union of episodic romance with classic action and dignity was fully accomplished. This union, however, was but temporary. In the *Gerusalemme Conquistata* romance was at last driven out and classicism triumphed unopposed.

During this period the *Orlando Furioso* ran a singular course of celebrity and misconception. At its first appearance there were a few murmurs from the critically orthodox, but the reading public and most men of literary judgment were captivated by its charm. It took its place almost at once as the chief work of Italian literature since the days of Petrarch and Boccaccio. Then, in the course of time, as classicism more and more fully possessed the critics and men like Trissino contemptuously said that the poem was merely popular, the need was felt of defending it systematically. The chief objections of the orthodox were that it violated the laws of epic construction and that it lacked seriousness. Its champions set themselves the task of proving its artistic legitimacy.

In the matter of construction, Ariosto had worked with the freedom of the man who makes his own laws. Aiming at variety of incident and situation, he had clearly seen the need of definite action, that if his reader's attention and interest were to be held, events must move constantly forward to an avowed goal. He had accordingly laid down side by side two or three main plots, so carefully interwoven that they could be brought together in a common end, and so distinct that neither constant shifting of scene, nor continual digressions, nor the multitude of independent and active characters could obsure them. He had reduced the wilderness of romance to complete artistic order; he had brought to perfection the type created by Bojardo. It was not epic, but it was of final excellence. When, therefore, in the middle years of the century, Giraldi and Pigna came forward to defend his title, their answer to the orthodox was clear. A new type had been evolved, the romance poem, having some qualities in common with the epic and many qualities peculiar to itself. It could not be judged by the authority of Aristotle; it was its own authority. Pigna put the truth best: "Perchè d'erranti persone è tutto il poema, egli altresì errante è inquanto che piglia ed intermette infinite volte cose infinite: e sempre con arte: perciochè se bene l'ordine epico non osserva, non è che una sua regola non abbia."[2] Yet if the constructive laws of the *romanzo* differed from those laid down by Aristotle for the *poema eroico*, its higher ideals, said Pigna, were essentially the same. "Come in tutto il duello non mai da lui veduto lume ne diede esso Aristotile: così quivi ne' romanzi è stato la nostra guida: benchè egli mai non ne parlasse."[3]

These views held their own for about a generation. In 1581, however, the appearance of the *Gerusalemme Liberata* again brought the classical question to the fore.[4] The new poem was naturally compared to the *Orlando Furioso*, and as Tasso's chief boast was that he had framed it according to the strict laws of Aristotle, the argument for his admirers was evident: the *Furioso* was excellent of its kind, as good as a romance poem could ever be, but here was a poem of equal charm and of a far nobler type, for no one could deny that the romance

poem was in itself inferior to the epic. This argument, pushed by Cammillo Pellegrino in his *Caraffa*, apparently took the followers of Ariosto by surprise. So long as the issue had been between the *Furioso* and such poems as the *Avarchide*, which nobody read, they had been content with the position of Pigna and Giraldi. Now, however, with this new poem running like wild-fire among the people and through the courts, they could not listen to Pellegrino's argument with comfort. They did what most persons will do under such circumstances—they shifted ground. The quarrel which arose is one of the dreariest in literature. The Accademia della Crusca took up the cause for Ariosto, and others were drawn into the controversy, even Tasso himself. There is no need to report their bickerings: suffice it to say that the *Orlando Furioso* was now declared to be in accordance with the very letter of Aristotle, to be much more classically regular than the *Gerusalemme Liberata*. In other words Ariosto, who to an earlier generation had been the master of a wonderful new type of poetry, was now become one more humble follower of the Stagirite.

One of the few sensible opinions put forward in this controversy is that of Patrizio, that Ariosto's chief aim is to delight, not to instruct his reader. "Pellegrino ha gran torto negando che l'Ariosto mirando a solo dilettare, posposto abbia il giovamento:"[5] Others were less clairvoyant—or less frank. Even Giraldi preached the Aristotelian ideal, "indurre buoni costumi negli animi degli uomini,"[6] evidently believing that Ariosto faithfully lived up to it; and in Giolito's 1554 edition of the *Furioso* (dedicated to the Dauphin of France) we read: "non è libro nessuno dalquale e con più frutto, e con maggiore diletto imparare si possa quello, che per noi fuggire e seguitare si debba." In brief, that element of seriousness in the *Furioso* which still makes some readers uncertain how to classify the poem was being magnified and enhanced by these critics to the high seriousness of the *Iliad* and the *Aeneid*. The exaggeration was but natural, for with the progress of the classical spirit in Italy, a somewhat new conception of the dignity of literature was beginning to make itself felt: poets were at least more self-conscious. Perhaps the change was chiefly due to the times. The Renaissance was now dead; the Catholic Reaction was afoot. The cheerfulness, the freedom, the mere delight in life which the men of Ariosto's generation had felt and expressed had given way to a gayety less frank and to a sadness much more frequent. Literature, in its looser moments more abandoned than ever before, had become, in its moments of seriousness, either dull and pedantic, or plaintive, melancholy, and suspicious. Tasso is the representative of this new order, and his experience with the *Gerusalemme Liberata* is thoroughly characteristic. He wrote the romantic episodes because he delighted in romantic beauty, but when he submitted the poem to his chosen set of critics, these episodes were at once attacked. He was told that they were trivial, unworthy an epic; he was told that they might even be dangerous and that the Inquisition might feel called on to interfere; and in the end, in order to save them he had to invent an allegory which gave them a mystic meaning. Then, with the Gardens of Armida and the Enchanted Wood conveying a spiritual lesson, the romance was allowed to pass the pikes of his friends' censorship.

Among such sensitive critics the *Orlando Furioso* was strangely interpreted. We have seen how seriously Giraldi and Pigna took it: it did not have to wait till the days of Tasso to be even more gravely expouded. Ariosto, who never overlooked what might give his poem variety and richness, had here and there made use of allegory. It was purely episodic; it served an immediate purpose; that was all he cared for. Within twenty years after his death, however, Fornari and Toscanella took his poem up and systematically read allegory into its minutest episodes and details. To them it was highly serious, almost cabalistic, and called for the penetrating commentator. What more rational? There was allegory on the surface; there must, of course, be allegory below the surface; they would dig for it. This pedantry may raise a smile; yet to find an exact parallel we have only to turn to our own century and read certain commentators on Rabelais. Rabelais, like Ariosto, is at times highly serious, and at times pretty obviously allegorical: therefore, let us read high seriousness and allegory into all he says. Even Coleridge fell victim to this illusion. It is old.

We have seen what work the critics made of Ariosto: how meanwhile was he read by the public at large? Very much, I fancy, as he has always been read—for his mere delightfulness—or, unfortunately, for his casual licentiousness. The average man thought little or nothing about the meaning of the *Furioso*, not only because the average man rarely reads to think, but because the poem itself would effectively distract attention from any possible meaning. One can draw moral inspirations from Dante, even from Tasso; only a genius could draw moral inspiration from Ariosto. Even the critics of that day must have read the poem like other men—when they were not intent on professional study. However sincere their convictions, it is not probable that they all took their pleasure in it so "moult tristement" as their critical writings might imply. It had been treated contemptuously; they were moved to defend their taste for it; and their defence was necessarily governed by the recognition of certain literary axioms. That there might be a discrepancy between their critical utterances and their real enjoyment of the *Furioso* would be no stumbling-block. They would continue to read the poem for its delightfulness and to praise it for classic dignity, untroubled.

Having followed this strange history, having seen how classical prepossessions so warped men's understanding that the *Furioso* was seriously classed with the *Iliad* and the *Aeneid,* and how all manner of grave meanings were read into it, we may be reasonably sure that the Ariosto of 1516 is not quite the Ariosto whom Spenser emulated; for when an Elizabethan undertook to study Ariosto, he would naturally turn to the Italian critics for guidance, and would naturally be influenced by their formal views. How readily such an Elizabethan might thus fall into their critical dualism—read and enjoy the poem one way and interpret it another—may be judged by the case of Sir John Harington, the first English translator of the *Furioso,* a thorough man of his time.

Harington is not only translator, he is critic as well. Besides his version of the poem the volume of 1591 contains an *Apologie of Poetrie,* a *Briefe Allegorie,* a *Life of Ariosto,* and commentaries on all the cantos. He is evidently taking pains to make his opinion of the *Furioso* as distinct as possible. At times he is almost earnest—a mood which is somewhat comical when we think of his rumored point-of-departure. The story goes that in his mischievous way he Englished the notorious twenty-eighth canto of the *Furioso* and sent the manuscript round among the maids of honor, and that the Queen, irritated by this scandalous proceeding, ordered him not to show his face in court again till he had rendered the whole poem, good as well as bad. Whether apocryphal or not, this anecdote shows us how young Englishmen of that day were inclined to take Ariosto. Harington's further course is equally enlightening. He studied the poem with some care, having in mind all the while Her Majesty's rebuke, and he read the Italian commentators and their allegorical schemes, and in the end the *Furioso* stood revealed to him as a creation of high seriousness. He saw that

the allegory was "the verie kyrnell and principall part, or as the marrow, and the rest but the bone and vnprofitable shell," and he saw that, for the most part, the looser passages were but a necessity of poetical decorum, that having some faulty characters to deal with, Ariosto must at times bring his poem to their level. The poem, as a whole, was unquestionably edifying. This conversion of Harington was not consciously insincere. We find, to be sure, that his translation shows no loss of relish for the scandalous, that though throughout the poem he condenses very freely, often cuting Ariosto's narratives down by a good third, he never condenses the questionable episodes, that they are given line for line. This, however, is no more than nature asserting itself. His formal views, though he took them whole from the Italians, he held seriously, even heartily. His pleasant *Apology* is no piece of hack-work done to placate the Queen, it is manifestly genuine. He is amusingly inconsistent, but he speaks what he really thinks.

Harington's attitude toward the *Furioso* was probably that of not a few Elizabethans, since many who read the poem for mere pleasure would be only too glad to persuade themselves that they were also being edified. There must have been some of less flexible disposition, however, who would not be so readily contented, men of idealizing and thorough natures. How would they take the poem—assuming, of course, that they cared to read it at all? Perhaps no set answer is possible; yet we have the suggestion of an answer in one of those fine, self-assertive utterances of Milton, himself in so many ways but a later Elizabethan. In that passage of the *Apology for Smectymnuus* in which he speaks of the studies of his youth and early manhood, he writes:

> I betook me among those lofty fables and romances, which recount in solemn cantoes the deeds of knighthood founded by our victorious kings, and from hence had in renown over all Christendom. There I read it in the oath of every knight that he should defend to the expense of his best blood, or of his life, if it so befell him, the honor and chastity of virgin and matron; from whence even then I learned what a noble virtue chastity sure must be, to the defense of which so many worthies, by such a dear adventure of themselves, had sworn; and if I found in the story afterward, any of them, by word or deed, breaking that oath, I judged it the same fault of the poet, as that which is attributed to Homer, to have written indecent things of the gods: only this my mind gave me, that every free and gentle spirit without that oath, ought to be born a knight, nor needed to expect the gilt spur or the laying of a sword upon his shoulder, to stir him up both by counsel and his arms to secure and protect the weakness of any attempted chastity. So that even these books, which to many others have been the fuel of wantonness and loose living, I cannot think how, unless by divine indulgence, proved to me so many incitements, as you have heard, to the love and steadfast observation of that virtue which abhors the society of bordelloes.

There can be hardly a doubt, I think, that in writing these memorable words Milton was thinking chiefly of the *Orlando Furioso;* for that poem was probably the most famous romance poem of Europe, and, as we have seen, it was certainly read by young men for "the fuel of wantonness and loose living." It has always attracted curious readers, most of them only too blind to its genuinely admirable qualities. How, then, did Milton take it in the days of his early manhood? Without attempting to interpret his general statements too specifically, we can perhaps draw a reasonable inference. It is clear that he did not, like Harington, condone the looser passages. To him they were so much foulness, which could not be explained away. It is equally clear that, in despite of them, he could read his own fervent idealism into the poem, could even make them so many incentives to lofty thought. He was of the temper to mould things after his own mind. His judgment might very probably tell him that the chivalry of the *Furioso* was anything but earnest: he would read the poem with steady control of his imagination, and make it what he pleased. He would accept as much of the humor and irony as left his own ideal undisturbed; the rest he would ignore. He would exalt the serious passages to a higher seriousness. What he actually did make of Ariosto in later life we may see by comparing his Paradise of Fools (*Par. Lost*, III, 440–497) with that limbo of the moon in which Orlando's lost wit was stored (*O. F.*, XXXIV, 73–86). Ariosto's limbo is a brilliant and effective allegorical satire on the vanities of this world written by a witty courtier; Milton's is the grotesque vision of a Puritan, out of place in a great epic, perhaps, but not without impressiveness. Had Milton carried out his early plan of writing an epic on King Arthur, he might have left us imitations from Ariosto as remarkable as those by Spenser.

Harington's temper put him in sympathy with Ariosto, and he read the *Orlando* with natural delight. He took to the doctrine of its high seriousness from the need of justifying his taste. Milton's temper was the very reverse of Ariosto's, and if he read the poem with pleasure, it was because of his own transmuting idealism. He apparently felt no need of persuading himself that it had genuine moral elevation. What was Spenser's attitude?

What, in the first place, was his temper? Milton has called him "sage and serious," but had he nothing in common with Harington?

The passage from Harvey's letter of 1580 might seem significant. It tells us that Spenser had written nine comedies which, however distantly, suggested comparison with the comedies of Ariosto, Bibbiena, Macchiavelli, and Aretino. He would of course not give himself to the grosser licentiousness of those Italian plays, but we might infer that he was at least not out of sympathy with Italian comic humor. The recollection might come to us of those early drafts of the *Hymns*, written "in the greener times of my youth," which "too much pleased those of like age and disposition," and for which he was later induced to cry *peccavi*; and we might think of that golden-headed apparition in the Harvey correspondence, "altera Rosalindula, mea Domina Immerito, mea bellissima Collina Clouta." Spenser's youth was certainly not like Milton's.

It is not very likely, however, that the comedies had much Italianated humor in them. It is by their "finenesse of plausible Elocution" and "rarenesse of Poetical Invention" that they impressed Harvey, and although we really know nothing whatever about them, we might guess, without much danger of error, that they were mere closet plays, more literary than dramatic, perhaps somewhat like the comedies of Lyly. Being named after the nine Muses, they can hardly have had very much in common with the *Mandragola*. Then, as to the poet's early years, he was certainly not a Harington. An element of Puritanic coldness and strength tempered his sensuous nature, and, as he grew to maturity and his idealism more and more fully crystallized his imaginative life, merely sensuous pleasures probably appealed to him with less force. He was never austere, like Milton, for his ideals were much less inexorable and stern, but he was almost equally steadfast. Though in 1580, therefore, he may have enjoyed the looser episodes of the *Orlando Furioso* much like Harington, by 1589, when the final touches were put to the first three books of his poem, his taste must have been decidedly more sober. There are some few indications[7] that he never quite lost sympathy with Ariosto's scandalous *verve*; for instance, the tale which the Squire of Dames tells to Sir Satyrane (Bk. III, c. 7, st. 53 ff.) suggested very probably by part of mine host's tale in canto XXVIII of the *Furioso* (expecially st. 45–49), and manifestly worked up for comic effect. Such things, however, merely show that he was less rigid than Milton; they do not contradict the genuineness of his idealism.

But how did Spenser interpret Ariosto? Certainly very much like Harington. In the *Letter*, addressed to Raleigh, which prefaces the *Faery Queen*, he couples Orlando with Aeneas as being meant to "ensample" "a good governour and a vertuous man," and this of itself shows clearly that he accepted the conventional views about Ariosto's high seriousness. It was natural that he should do so; for though his temper was, in most ways, the very reverse of Ariosto's, he evidently enjoyed the *Furioso* much more than Milton did, if not so unreservedly as Harington,[8] and he would therefore be moved, like Harington, to give it the most favorable interpretation possible, without too scrupulous analysis. Since he read it in a somewhat more sober spirit, he would be less open to the feeling of inconsistency. Yet, though he might escape the grosser critical dualism of Harington—reading and enjoying the poem in the gayer spirit of Ariosto and interpreting it as though it were another *Iliad*—he could hardly avoid a certain dualism of his own. He might believe that the *Furioso* was a poem of high seriousness, but when he actually came to transfer some of its serious passages to his own lofty poem he would instinctively change and elevate them; for whatever theories he might hold, his immediate poetic sense was unerring. An example will make this clear. At the beginning of the third canto of Book III, the book of which Britomart is heroine, is an address to Love. Now, as we shall see later, the early cantos of this book are a sort of counterpart to the early cantos of the *Furioso*; they are full of the most distinct and evident imitations from the Italian. This address to Love was undoubtedly suggested to Spenser by the similar address which opens canto II of the *Furioso*. Let us compare them. Ariosto writes:

> Ingiustissimo Amor, perchè sì raro
> Corrispondent fai nostri disiri?
> Onde, perfido, avvien che t' è sì caro
> Il discorde voler ch' in dui cor miri?
> Ir non mi lasci al facil guado e chiaro,
> E nel più cieco e maggior fondo tiri:
> Da chi disìa il mio amor tu mi richiami,
> E chi m' ha in odio vuoi ch' adori ed ami.

And now Spenser:

> Most sacred fyre, that burnest mightily
> In living brests, ykindled first above
> Emongst th' eternall spheres and lamping sky,
> And thence pourd into men, which men call Love;
> Not that same which doth base affections move
> In brutish minds, and filthy lust inflame;
> But that sweete fit that doth true beautie love,
> And choseth Vertue for his dearest dame,
> Whence spring all noble deedes and never-dying fame:
> Well did antiquity a god thee deeme,
> That over mortall mindes hast so great might,
> To order them as best to thee doth seeme,
> And all their actions to direct aright:
> The fatall purpose of divine foresight

Thou doest effect in destined descents,
Through deepe impression of thy secret might,
And stirredst up th' heroës high intents,
Which the late world admyres for wondrous
    moniments.

The inference is clear. In reading Ariosto for hints Spenser was struck by the effectiveness of that opening stanza; but Ariosto's conception of Love was too radically different from his own, and, therefore, instead of directly translating the stanza, as he unquestionably would have done, had it proved adaptable, he took the theme suggested, and for the graceful, but rather conventional sentiment of the Italian substituted his own grave and lofty meditation. His general attitude, then, seems evident. Despite an instinctive sense that such passages as this were not highly serious, and despite the touches of irony and open humor with which the *Furioso* abounds, he found no difficulty in believing that Ariosto's aims were lofty and his genius eminently moral. In those days of literary dogma a man's theories and his impressions were not necessarily at one, for our modern critical analysis was then unknown.

This attitude is assuredly not that of Milton, and yet, as we can see, Spenser must constantly have studied and imitated Ariosto with the complete imaginative independence of Milton. His conception of chivalry was as noble as Milton's; indeed, it was in good part because the spirit of chivalry was so sympathetic to his own consistent idealism that he chose the deeds of Prince Arthur and the mysteries of Faery Land for the theme of his great poem; in them he could best embody his grave spiritual convictions. The chivalry of the *Furioso*, on the other hand, was anything but earnest—whatever his conception of it may have been—and it only too often provided "the fuel of wantonness and loose living." When he studied the poem, therefore, he must constantly have followed his own fervent imaginings—like Milton. When he adopted passages for imitation it was certainly with the transmuting touch of Milton. A couple of passages, which give the very essence of the two opposing views of chivalry, will make his independence clear.

In the first canto of the *Furioso* Angelica is fleeing terror-stricken from Rinaldo, the lover whom she detests and whom she will do anything to escape. He is afoot, she on her palfrey. In her headlong flight she comes upon Ferraù, another of her lovers, who, seeing her distress, rushes at Rinaldo and violently turns him off from pursuit. A furious combat is at once engaged: Angelica, not daring to await the issue, hurries on as fast as her palfrey can carry her. After some minutes of hot fighting Rinaldo, who is the cooler of the two champions, becomes aware that the lady has disappeared. He at once draws off, and with notable sense of fact suggests that it is rather foolish to be fighting for a prize which is gone. Would it not be better, he asks, to catch Angelica before we fight for her? Ferraù is rather impressed by this idea, and at once agrees. He takes up Rinaldo behind him on his horse, and the two dash off after the lady. Then Ariosto breaks out:

Oh gran bontà de' cavallieri antiqui!
Eran rivali, eran di fe diversi,
E si sentìan degli aspri colpi iniqui
Per tutta la persona anco dolersi;
E pur per selve oscure e calli obliqui
Insieme van senza sospetto aversi.
Da quattro sproni il destrier punto arriva
Dove una strada in due si dipartiva.

(st. 22.)

The effect of this serious apostrophe is evident: it heightens the comic humor of the preceding situation by a touch of unexpected irony. It is itself heightened and completed by that ludicrous image of the war-horse, bestridden by two hot champions and spurred on after the missing lady, poor beast, "da quattro sproni."

In the *Faery Queen*, in the first canto of the third book, Britomart appears on the scene unknown and runs a course with Sir Guyon. Guyon is overthrown by the power of the magic spear, and in his shame and anger would continue the combat afoot. But Prince Arthur and the Palmer interpose and by judicious words succeed in calming him. The two adversaries are reconciled, and all the party go on together in amity. Then Spenser breaks out in an apostrophe which is the exact counterpart of Ariosto's, the first line of it being a free translation from the Italian.

O goodly usage of those antique tymes,
In which the sword was servaunt unto right!
When not for malice and contentious crymes,
But all for prayse and proofe of manly might,
The martiall brood accustomed to fight:
Then honour was the meed of victory,
And yet the vanquished had no despite:
Let later age that noble use envý,
Vyle rancor to avoid and cruel surquedry!

(st. 13.)

The situation, one sees, is much the same—with a difference. Rinaldo and Ferraù are reconciled after fight, though for a comically unchivalric motive, and rush off in their wild goose chase of Angelica; Britomart and Guyon are likewise reconciled after fight, and ride on together in goodly companionship. Ariosto's apostrophe is *apropos*; Spenser adopts it. He ignores its irony, which he can hardly have failed to perceive, and accepts its literal seriousness. The conclusion is clear. When Spenser read the *Orlando Furioso* for suggestions he read it in the light of his own serene idealism.

Spenser's talent for transforming the comic into the serious may be illustrated by another example.

In the first canto[9] of the *Furioso*, Angelica, having escaped from Rinaldo and Ferraù, has put herself in the charge of Sacripante, King of Circassia, yet another of her lovers. She has persuaded him to conduct her back safely to her home in the Orient. They have hardly left the spot where she met him, however, when Rinaldo appears on the scene and loudly challenges her escort. Sacripante is not slow to defend his charge, and the two warriors rush to combat. This time Angelica waits to see the result, but before long a furious blow from Rinaldo, which partially cripples Sacripante, so alarms her that she flies the field. In her flight she meets a reverend friar, and asks the way the nearest seaport. He is surprised by her beauty and tempted to a disreputable plan; she will not stay with him, such is her fear of Rinaldo, but presses on; he conjures a demon into her palfrey, instructed to lead her a circle to a desert island, where he himself will again find her. Meanwhile, another demon sends Rinaldo and Sacripante hurrying off to Paris, by the false report that Orlando has kidnapped Angelica and is taking her thither.

These bare facts hardly render the spirit of levity in which Ariosto handles this episode. The early passages are among the most diverting in the poem, the later among the most scabrous. Such as it is, however, Spenser reproduces it in some of its main features in the sixth canto of Book I (st. 34 ff.). Una is wandering in quest of the Red Cross Knight, under conduct of Satyrane (cf. Angelica: Sacripante). They come upon Archimago in his habitual disguise of the reverend old man (cf. the reverend friar and his magic), and asking him about the Red Cross Knight, are informed that the latter has recently been slain by a Paynim champion (a lie, of course, as that with which the friar's demon troubles Rinaldo and Sacripante). Satyrane rushes ahead to find the Paynim and wreak vengeance; Una follows. When she reaches the place of the combat, which has meanwhile begun, she finds that the Paynim is Sansloy, he who formerly had her in his clutches and from whom she was rescued at the last moment by the Satyrs (in the O. F. cf. the preceding episode of Angelica rescued from Rinaldo's hot pursuit by Ferraù). When Una appears, Sansloy, recognizing her, makes at her, but is turned by Satyrane. Una in terror flics (like Angelica), and Archimago, who has been watching the affair from the bushes, hurries after her, "in hope to bring her to her last decay" (like the friar after Angelica). The champions are left fighting, and we are told nothing about the issue of their combat. In the third book Satyrane appears again; Sansloy is heard from no more. Ariosto, scrupulously careful of his plot, leaves no such loose ends: the Rinaldo-Sacripante duel is brought to a definite close.

Spenser, we see, has taken the bare facts of the episode, not necessarily humorous in themselves, and has made use of them for his own grave purposes, utterly ignoring the turn which Ariosto gave them. Yet this is one of those passages which indicate that he was not insensible to Ariosto's humor. Why did he reproduce the facts of the episode, if not because they had fixed themselves in his mind and came to him at the time he was writing this canto? And what fixed them in his mind if not an enjoyment of the humor whith which Ariosto handles them? One cannot, of course, argue from a single instance: we shall find others that are still more striking. Indeed, after surveying the whole list of Spenser's imitations from Ariosto, one can hardly resist the conviction that he enjoyed him in almost all his work, serious, humorous, even ironical— barring perhaps that variety which so particularly appealed to Harington. This makes his complete imaginative independence all the more remarkable.

II

I shall now examine more at large some of Spenser's specific imitations from the *Furioso*, with a view to indicating their character and variety. It would be tedious and unprofitable to enter into exhaustive detail, or to give a very systematic survey of the whole field. A few characteristic examples, briefly explained, will suffice.

It is well known to the readers of Ariosto that Orlando is not the hero of the poem which bears his name, and that the heroic wars of Charlemain and Agramante are not the centre of narrative interest: Ruggiero and Bradamante are the real hero and heroine, and the real centre of narrative interest is the story of their loves. This apparent inconsistency was inevitable. In continuing Bojardo's poem Ariosto found his titular hero and his main action already chosen for him, and he adopted them very willingly and made the most of them. One of his chief aims, however, being to celebrate the glories of the house of Este, and Ruggiero and Bradamante having been already set forth by Bojardo as the founders of the house, he naturally made them his chief care. They are perhaps the only prominent characters who are treated with almost uniform seriousness from beginning to end of the poem, and it is in their nuptials and Ruggiero's duel with Rodomonte that the poem comes to a triumphant close.

Now, the *Faery Queen* offers us a singular parallel to this. Prince Arthur is the nominal hero of the poem, and Gloriana the titular heroine, but by reason of the curious narrative structure which Spenser adopted, Arthur remains a mere figurehead, appearing but once in each book, and the Faery Queen

is a virtual nonentity, not appearing at all. If we seek for a real centre of interest in the poem, we shall find it only in Arthegall and Britomart and their love-story. From the beginning of the third book to the end of the fifth they are kept pretty constantly before us, and the prophecies of Merlin (Bk. III, c. 3, st. 26–29) and of the Priest of Isis (Bk. V, c. 7, st. 23) tell us enough of the future to make their story complete. How much prominence Spenser meant ultimately to give them, we have no means of telling, but, as the poem stands, their story is the only real centre of action, and they are in a way the real hero and heroine. Britomart, of course, as a "lady knight" and possessor of the magic spear, is the counterpart of Bradamante. Arthegall may stand for Ruggiero. He is certainly Spenser's ideal knight, strong, just, steadfast, much more real than the magnificent Arthur, and real because he was modelled on a real man, Arthur Lord Grey of Wilton, Spenser's chief patron. As Ariosto, therefore, made Ruggiero and Bradamante the centre of interest in his poem, to exalt the house of Este, so Spenser made Arthegall his virtual hero, in tribute to his former patron, to the man who more than any other had made a lasting mark on his imagination. He was presented as the lover of Britomart by analogy from Ariosto; to complete the analogy, the pair were made the ancestors of Elizabeth, through the genuinely British kings following Arthur.

When we come to trace the love-story we find that at almost every point it touches Ariosto. It is naturally brief, for Britomart and Arthegall, as the types of Chastity and Justice, are principally busied in allegorical action and have scant time for love. The passages which bear on the course of their love are few, and are scattered at rather wide intervals over the three books. As a centre of action the story is certainly rather slight. It is, nevertheless, the only plot of its kind in the poem. Its independence on Ariosto will be worth noting in detail.

In the first place, Britomart falls in love with Arthegall by the single glimpse which she has of his image in her father's enchanted mirror (Bk. III, c. 2, st. 22 ff.). The first account which we have of Bradamante in the *Furioso* (II, 32) tells us simply that she is in love with Ruggiero, whom she has seen but once. Now, Spenser probably did not know the *Orlando Innamorato*; he was, therefore, ignorant of the circumstances under which the two lovers first met (O. I., l. III, c. 4, st. 49 to end, c. 5, c. 6, st. 1–33), and the passage in the *Furioso*, which was intended merely to refresh the memories of Ariosto's readers, gave him no more than a bare fact. He adopted the fact and accounted for it in his own way.

In the image which Britomart sees the knight's armor is inscribed with the legend: "Achilles armes which Arthegall did win" (Bk. III, c. 2, st. 25). One of Ruggiero's greatest feats is the killing of Mandricardo in single combat, as a result of which he becomes possessed of the armor of Hector, which his antagonist had formerly borne (O. F., xxx).

The visit of Glaucè and Britomart to Merlin in his cave and the prophecy of Britomart's future line (Bk. III, c. 3) is of course taken bodily from canto III of the *Furioso*, in which Bradamante enters the cave of Merlin by chance, and is informed of her descendants by Melissa. One may note certain differences. In the *Furioso* the spirit of Merlin speaks from the tomb, and delivers a brief welcoming address of vaguely prophetic import; Bradamante's descendants are revealed to her in a series of phantoms conjured up by Melissa, like the vision of Banquo's issue in *Macbeth*. In the *Faery Queen* Merlin is sitting in his cave, alive and visible, and reveals Britomart's future line by word of mouth. In stanza 32, however, "Behold the man!" etc. would seem to indicate that Spenser had in mind the visible phantoms of the *Furioso*, and forgot himself.

Britomart wandering about Faery Land in quest of Arthegall is like Bradamante, who at the beginning of the *Furioso* is wandering about France in quest of Ruggiero (*O.F.,* II, 33). Britomart's long quest after Arthegall and the brief periods during which she enjoys his presence, periods intercalated in long months of separation, correspond very closely to the rare meetings and the long periods of separation which disturb the love-story of Ruggiero and Bradamante.

Arthegall's courtship of Britomart follows upon their very first meeting (Bk. IV, c. 6, st. 40 ff.), and her consent is given before they separate. Ruggiero and Bradamante exchange troth at their first definitive meeting in the *Furioso* (*O. F.,* XXII, 31–36). Arthegall leaving Britomart, to pursue his quest, and promising to return at the end of three months (Bk. IV, c. 6, st. 42, 43) is like Ruggiero pursuing his *affaire d' honneur* with Rodomonte and promising to rejoin Bradamante within twenty days (*O.F.,* XXX, 76–81).

Britomart waiting impatiently for the return of Arthegall, seeing the time appointed for his return slip by, tormented by fears and jealousies (Bk. V, c. 6), is the exact counterpart of the love-sick Bradamante waiting for the return of Ruggiero (*O.F.,* XXX, 84 ff.; XXXII, 10 ff.). Talus, who brings back news of Arthegall's defeat by Radegund and his captivity, thereby rousing Britomart's jealousy, corresponds to the "cavalier guascone" who brings to Bradamante the report that Ruggiero is betrothed to the warrior maiden, Marfisa. The conduct of Britomart when she receives the news is exactly like that of Bradamante: she first indulges in resentful despair, then sets out to go to her lover. The combat of Britomart with Radegund (Bk. V, c. 7, st. 26 ff.) might be likened to the combat of Bradamante with Marfisa (*O.F.,* XXXVI). As Bradamante discovers her jealousies to have been causeless, so Britomart.

Here the love-story of Britomart and Arthegall comes to an end. How Spenser would have terminated it, had he carried his poem further, we, of course, do not know. In Bk. III, c. 3, st. 28, however, we have a prophecy by Merlin of the final destiny of the pair. This destiny is almost exactly that of Bradamante and Ruggiero, as given in the *Furioso,* c. XLI, st. 60 ff.

Could any imitation be more deliberate and thorough than this? Spenser has not merely taken suggestions here and there; every point of his story has its counterpart in the *Furioso;* the correspondence from beginning to end is complete. Of course, Spenser varies the details to meet the conditions of his poem, and, of course, his story has an atmosphere of its own; but he could hardly show himself more indifferent to the merits of narrative invention. He evidently had the genuine Elizabethan instinct for saving himself the trouble of inventing a plot.

Having seen how Spenser could borrow a plot, let us see how he might take hints for a character. Perhaps the most remarkable instance of his talents for this kind of work may be found in Braggadochio, who is commonly supposed to be a satirical portrait of the Duke of Alençon.

In constructing this character Spenser determined on two main traits, inordinate boasting, and cowardice. Having chosen these he turned to his *Furioso* for suggestions.

Now there are several braggarts in the *Furioso,* but the most prominent, setting aside Marfisa, who is a woman, are Rodomonte and Mandricardo. Rodomonte is much the more celebrated of the two, as one may judge by our well-known word, "rodomontade." It would see at first sight, therefore, that Spenser would probably take him for model. But Rodomonte is something more than a braggart; there is in him a touch of the king. He is a figure of heroic size and impressiveness, hot-headed and extravagant, to be sure, but capable at times of self-

repression, even of wise counsel, and towards the close of the poem his fierceness settles into a sinister melancholy which makes him an almost sympathetic character. Mandricardo, on the other hand, though equally fearless, is merely extravagant and savage. There is no impressiveness in his truculence. His inordinate boasting is very commonly ridiculous, and leaves a mark on our memories which that of Rodomonte does not. Spenser, therefore, chose Mandricardo. As for the coward, there was no room for choice. Martano has the field to himself, and Spenser took him without question.

That Spenser had these two characters in mind when he sketched his portrait of Alençon, alias Braggadochio, may be proved by the incidents which mark the scare-crow's career. On his very first appearance (Bk. II, c. 3) he promises Archimago to go in quest of the Red Cross Knight and Guyon and kill them, and when the enchanter, perceiving him to be without a sword, suggests that on such a perilous adventure he will have need of one, he says:

> "Once did I sweare,
> When with one sword seven knightes I brought to
>   end,
> Thenceforth in battaile never sword to beare,
> But it were that which noblest knight on earth doth
>   weare."
>
> (St. 17.)

This is the vow of Mandricardo never to carry sword till he should win Orlando's famous Durindana (*O. F.,* XIV, 43). Orlando is chief of the paladins; the "noblest knight on earth" is his British peer, King Arthur. Mandricardo's vow is serious; Braggadochio's of course a mere lie, for he is a coward, which Mandricardo certainly is not.

The passages which tell of the stealing of Arthur's sword (Bk. II, c. 3, st. 18; c. 6, st. 47; c. 8, st. 19–22; c. 9, st. 2) may be compared with that which tells of the appropriation of Durindana by Mandricardo (*O.F.,* XXIV, 58, 59). Mandricardo does not win the sword in fight: he comes upon it at the time of Orlando's madness, and calmly takes possession of it, under pretext that Orlando is feigning madness to escape him. The act is virtual theft. Braggadochio, the coward, is not capable of even stealing Morddure; Archimago has to undertake that, and succeeds. The good sword does not come into Braggadochio's possession; but that is a mere variation of detail.

The next important appearance of Braggadochio is at the tournament of Satyrane (Bk. IV, c. 4 and 5). Here the knights fall out over False Florimel, and it is agreed to set her in the midst and let her choose which of them she pleases. She chooses Braggadochio, the most unworthy of them all (c. 5, st. 22 ff.).[10] This is a reminiscence of the choice given to Doralice between Rodomonte and Mandricardo, who are disputing the possession of her (*O.F.,* XXVII, 104 ff.). She chooses Mandricardo, who, as I have said, is much less worthy than his rival.

The incidents which tell us that Spenser also had Martano in mind are equally clear.

In the tournament of Satyrane Braggadochio's cowardly hesitation to joust (Bk. IV, c. 4, st. 20) is of a piece with Martano's cowardice at the tournament of Damascus (*O.F.,* XVII, 88–90).

At the tournament in honor of the spousals of Florimel (Bk. V, c. 3), Arthegall borrows Braggadochio's shield, and, riding into the *mêlée,* wins foremost honors. He then returns the shield to its owner. When the prize is to be awarded Braggadochio with his shield steps forward and claims it. Martano at the tournament of Damascus is guilty of a similar trick (*O. F.,* XVII, 108–116). While Grifone, who has won first honors, is asleep in his lodgings, Martano steals his armor and appears at court to claim the prize.

Both Braggadochio and Martano are in the end disgraced (*F. Q.*, Bk. v, c. 3, st. 37. *O.F.*, XVIII, 91–93).

In fine, in almost every incident of Braggadochio's career we find some reminiscence of either Mandricardo, the braggart, or Martano, the coward. The conclusion is plain: Spenser went to Ariosto for help in devising his character. He had already chosen the two main traits to be developed; he, therefore, selected the two characters of the *Furioso* who best embodied those traits, and drew from them. The result is his own. Braggadochio is too distinct a figure to be called a mere reproduction: for he is neither Mandricardo nor Martano, but a personality evolved from the combination of both. We shall not grudge Spenser his imitation, when the result is so original.

Turning from characters to situations[11] we find Spenser working under slightly different circumstances. No one can read the *Furioso* attentively without noticing how much of its effectiveness comes from Ariosto's unlimited genius for the handling of situation. It is just this, indeed, which perhaps more than anything else distinguishes his poem from the *Orlando Innamorato*. There are few situations in the *Innamorato* which we remember; there are scores in the *Furioso*. The twenty-seventh canto, for instance, gives us a long climax of them, which for rising brilliancy of effect is among the most remarkable passages in Italian literature. Ariosto's best situations, however, are almost exclusively comic, and were therefore ill adapted to Spenser's purposes; and yet Spenser, who must frequently have read the *Furioso* for pleasure only, could not forget them. We accordingly find him adopting them not infrequently, but giving them such a peculiar turn that they are hardly recognizable.

I have already noted the situation at the end of the sixth canto of Bk. I. It is thoroughly characteristic of Spenser's methods. He gets his external facts from Ariosto, but so renders them that the effect is not comic but highly serious. Indeed his situation, strictly speaking, is not that of Ariosto at all; for the character of a situation does not depend on mere external fact alone, but also on the qualities and the sentiments of the persons brought together. Throughout his poem Spenser works in much this same way. When he borrows the facts of a situation which in Ariosto are given a comic turn, he either treats them seriously outright, or tones down the comedy to harmonize with the general seriousness of his work. An example of such toning down will make what I mean clear.

One of the most laughable situations in the *Furioso* is that in which Marfisa and Zerbino joust together in presence of the old hag Gabrina (*O. F.*, XX, 106–129). Marfisa and Gabrina are travelling together in casual companionship, and Zerbino, meeting them, bursts out laughing at the sight of such a hideous beldam, apparently the lady of so big a knight. Marfisa resents his mirth, and challenges him to combat. Zerbino replies that he is no such fool as to fight for a hag like that. Then, says Marfisa, we will arrange matters this way: you shall joust with me, and the one who is overthrown shall be obliged to take the lady and bear her company faithfully. Zerbino confidently agrees; they come together; he is unhorsed; and Marfisa rides off laughing, calling back to him to remember his promise.

The situation is one of those which you remember: it is handled with all the liveliness and humor of which Ariosto at his best is so consummate a master. Spenser remembered it, and when he came to the hot-headed quarrels of the knights in the early cantos of Bk. IV, he made use of it. In canto 4 of this book Blandamour is riding in company with other knights,

having two ladies with him, False Florimel and the hag Atè. Braggadochio joins them, and spying False Florimel, whom he had formerly had for lady himself, claims her as his own. Blandamour refuses, of course, to part with her, but is willing to joust, and makes the following proposition (st. 9): that Florimel and Atè be made the prizes of the combat; that the winner shall have Florimel and the loser the hag, under compact to keep her company till he can win another lady. Braggadochio, as usual, avoids the combat, and the proposition is left unexecuted.

The situation, one sees, is merely suggested. Spenser could not have developed it without giving it a frankly comic turn, and that would have been incongruous to the general character of his poem. That he introduced it at all would seem to indicate that he was not insensible to Ariosto's humor.

Spenser sometimes reverses a situation.

In the seventh canto of the *Furioso* Ruggiero is brought to the palace of Alcina. His life with her is an allegory of the self-indulgence of youth. On the evening of his arrival he has secured her promise that she will come to him that very night; and when all the house is silent he awaits her with the impatience, the anxiety of expectant passion. His suspense and his final rapture are given by Ariosto with very considerable vivacity (st. 21 ff.).

In the first canto of the third book of the *Faery Queen* Britomart comes to the house of Malecasta, one of the more obvious allegories of this book. The lady of the house, naturally mistaking her sex, pays open court to her, and at night, when all is quiet, steals in timorous suspense from her chamber to that of the Britoness, and softly lays herself down beside her (st. 59–61). Britomart's rage when she becomes aware of the intruder closes the scene.

This situation is manifestly the exact reverse of Ariosto's. The spirit in which Spenser develops it, treating with moral gravity a scene which Ariosto had treated with immoral levity, is one more indication of how he could read his own steadfast idealism into the most openly licentious passages of the *Furioso*.

One has only to set these situations from the *Faery Queen* side by side with their originals to perceive that Spenser had small genius for situation. They are anything but vivid; indeed, we hardly think of them as situations at all; they are mere groups of narrative fact. It is of course evident that Spenser did not need effective situations for the *Faery Queen*. Ariosto, aiming at narrative variety and life, would find them indispensable; Spenser, in a poem chiefly reflective and picturesque, would find no use for them. Perhaps, however, this is merely another mode of saying again that he had no genius for situation.

Those who enjoy Ariosto are not likely to forget his descriptions. They have never the concise vividness of Dante's, they show no imaginative insight, they lack what we call natural magic, yet the best of them have a charm which, if somewhat external, is not the less satisfying. Ariosto's sense of beauty is not subtle; but this defect is largely compensated for by his sense of artistic balance. He never overloads his pictures; even his enumerative descriptions, which have proved so alien to our modern taste—such as the once famous portrait of Alcina—are composed with a precision and economy of effect which half reconcile us to them. Sometimes he has a distinctness which one might almost call Theocritan. The following stanzas are characteristic (*O. F.*, VIII, 19 and 20).

> Tra duri sassi e folte spine già
> Ruggiero intanto in ver la Fata saggia,
> Di balzo in balzo, e d'una in altra via,
> Aspra, solinga, inospita e selvaggia;

Tanto ch'a gran fatica riuscìa
Su la fervida nona in una spiaggia
Tra 'l mare e 'l monte, al mezodì scoperta,
Arsiccia, nuda, sterile e deserta.

Percuote il Sole ardente il vicin colle;
E del calor che si reflette adietro,
In modo l'aria e l'arena ne bolle,
Che sarìa troppo a far liquido il vetro.
Stassi cheto ogni augello all' ombra molle:
Sol la cicala col noioso metro
Fra i densi rami del fronzuto stelo
Le valli e i monti assorda, e il mare e il cielo.

Turning to the descriptive work of Spenser, we shall perhaps be surprised to find very few traces of Ariosto. The description of Belphoebe, to be sure (*F. Q.*, Bk. II, c. 3, st. 21 ff.),
might be compared for method to that of Alcina (*O.F.*, VII, 11
ff.), though it is more pompously ornamental, and the naked
beauties of Serena (*F. Q.*, Bk. VI, c. 8, st. 42, 43) might seem to
be after those of Olimpia (*O.F.*, XI, 67 ff.); but the parallel is in
neither case close, and the method is generally Italian, not
peculiar to Ariosto. The House of Morpheus (*F. Q.*, Bk. I, c. 1,
st. 39–41) was perhaps suggested[12] by the Casa del Sonno
(*O.F.*, XIV, 92–94); but one has only to set the two side by side
to see that, if so, Spenser borrowed nothing save the primal
idea. In the Gardens of Adonis (*F.Q.*, Bk. III, c. 6 and IV, c. 10)
one might see a vague similarity to certain scenes in the
Furioso—the Island of Alcina (VI, 19–22), in which the bridge
guarded by Erifila, *i.e.* Avarice (VI, 78, 79 and VII, 2–5) might
have suggested to Spenser the bridge guarded by Doubt, Delay,
Daunger, etc.; the Gardens of Logistilla (X, 61–63); the Terrestrial Paradise (XXXIV, 49–51)—but one cannot be sure that
Spenser had Ariosto in mind. Finally, such things as the tapestries of the House of Busyrane, setting forth the wars of Cupid
(Bk. III, c. 11, st. 28 ff.) are apparently borrowed from the
Furioso (cf. the pictures at the Rocca di Tristano prophesying
the wars in Italy, *O.F.*, XXXIII); but these are merely part of the
stage-setting, used indifferently, whenever convenient. In
short, Spenser could, as we have seen, take a whole plot in all
its essential details from Ariosto, he could make distinct char-
acter-studies from the figures of the *Furioso*, he could adopt
situations; but he apparently did not think it worth while to
imitate Ariosto's descriptions. His generally Italian methods of
description he might get, as I have said, from Ariosto or from
almost any sixteenth century poet.

This specific neglect of Ariosto may be ascribed to several
causes. In the first place, the *Furioso*, being essentially a poem
of plot, character, and action, Spenser would imitate it chiefly
in just these lines, the more readily in that his own genius for
plot, character, and action was not strong. In the second place,
Spenser may not have felt the charm of Ariosto's descriptions.
His own taste probably inclined towards greater richness. In the
third place, he found a much more congenial model in Tasso.
The richness which Ariosto lacked Tasso had in full measure;
indeed, to some modern critics, his descriptive beauties have
seemed rather cloying. He certainly has not the artistic balance
of Ariosto. Spenser, however, who was of Tasso's own generation, seems to have been captivated by him; at any rate, he goes
to him for descriptive work, rather than to his great predecessor.
The Bower of Bliss (Bk. II, c. 12) is taken bodily from the
Gerusalemme Liberata (c. XV, XVI), and the Retreat of
Cymochles (Bk. II, c. 5, st. 28 ff.), which gives us another
glimpse of the Bower of Bliss, is after his manner. It is possible
that the first enthusiasm roused by the appearance of the
Gerusalemme may have been an element in the eclipsing of
Ariosto.

There is one minor branch of descriptive work, however,
in which Spenser has sometimes imitated Ariosto, and that is
the comparison. The comparisons of the *Furioso*, indeed, are
often wonderfully effective, with the distinctness which comes
from clear vision and sure style. They are rarely impressive,
and almost never highly beautiful, but they generally have at
least the virtue of efficient illustration. A single example may
serve to indicate how Spenser could use them.

Ruggiero has suddenly attacked a rabble of men-at-arms,
who are conducting Ricciardetto pinioned to execution.

Come stormo d'augei, ch'in ripa a un stagno
Vola sicura e a sua pastura attende,
S' improvviso dal ciel falcon grifagno
Gli dà nel mezo, et un ne batte o prende,
Si sparge in fuga, ognun lascia il compagno,
E de lo scampo suo cura si prende:
Così veduto avreste far costoro,
Tosto che'l buon Ruggier diede fra loro.

(XXV, 12.)

Talus, the iron groom of Arthegall, is attacking a rabble
with his terrible flail. They fly from his presence and hide
themselves in holes and bushes,

As when a faulcon hath with nimble flight
Flowne at a flush of ducks foreby the brooke,
The trembling foule, dismayd with dreadfull sight
Of death, the which them almost overtooke,
Doe hide themselves from her astonying looke
Amongst the flags and covert round about.
When Talus saw they all the field forsook,
And none appear'd of all that raskall rout,
To Arthegall he turn'd, and went with him
    throughout.

(Bk. V, c. 2, st. 54.)

One cannot but note that Ariosto's version is the more
precise and effective. Indeed, the qualities of Spenser's style
hardly adapted themselves to work like this requiring point and
vivacity. He is more successful, perhaps, in his imitations of
Tasso's comparisons, which are rich, one might say Venetian,
in effect, and less strictly illustrative.

There is a field in which the dramatic and the picturesque
come together, what one might call picturesque situation. In
this field Spenser is more successful than in the field of merely
narrative or dramatic situation, and naturally, for though he is
not a poet of action, he is a descriptive poet of a very high
order. As an instance of what he could get from Ariosto in this
field one may cite the revelation of Bradamante at the Rocca di
Tristano (*O.F.*, XXXII, 79, 80). She enters the castle-hall clad in
full armor, and is of course received as a man; then, when she
takes off her helmet, her golden hair bursts from its coif and
streams down over her shoulders, revealing her a beautiful
woman. The effect is startling, and Ariosto has rendered it with
his customary brilliancy.

In the episode of Britomart at the House of Malbecco, an
episode written throughout with constant reminiscences of the
Rocca di Tristano, one might almost say distinctly modelled on
it, Spenser repeats this situation (Bk. III, c. 9, st. 20–23). In the
more dramatic quality of it one cannot say that he equals
Ariosto. The latter rests his effect on one touch, the sudden
rush of the hair when the helmet is taken off; Spenser adds a
touch by making his heroine remove the rest of her armor,
thereby revealing also her womanly form, and in so doing he
weakens his effect very badly. Yet the picturesqueness of the
situation he renders well enough; his description catches the
eye, though it is certainly not one of his more remarkable
successes.

Another category might be glanced at, in which may be grouped things rather matter-of-fact than artistic.

The famous *lancia d'oro*, for instance, reappears in the *Faery Queen* as Britomart's ebon spear (that it is of *ebony* is told us in Bk. IV, c. 5, st. 8). Its qualities are the same, and are also unknown, apparently, to its possessor.

The magic shield of Atlante reappears as the shield of Arthur (Bk. I, c. 7, st. 33–35). In the *Furioso* it has the one quality of rendering temporarily senseless those who chance to look on its dazzling surface; Spenser has added a number of qualities to this, it cannot be said felicitously. The magic horn of Astolfo, likewise, which in the *Furioso* merely serves to throw all who hear it into headlong and terrified flight, is reproduced, as the horn of Arthur's squire, with additional qualities (Bk. I, c. 8, st. 3, 4).

Rodomonte's bridge (*O.F.*, XXIX, 33–37) is made use of as the bridge of Pollentè (*F.Q.*, Bk. V, c. 2, st. 6–8), again with complicating additions, in this case, as probably in the preceding, suggested by the allegory.

In another field, Pinabello's shameful custom (*O.F.*, XXII, 48) is reproduced as the "wicked custome" of Turpine (Bk. VI, c. 6, st. 34).

There is no need to multiply instances or to attempt a detailed classification. It is evident that for such chivalric paraphernalia Spenser went to the *Furioso* with his customary freedom. Whatever caught his fancy, or would serve some immediate purpose, he adopted and transferred. He, of course, did not draw from the *Furioso* exclusively. The *Morte d'Arthur* could give him plenty of such things, or any romance of chivalry he might happen to read, and he certainly took material wherever he found what he wanted. What he borrows from the *Furioso*, however, usually has some special mark which indicates its origin, and that poem was unquestionably his chief source.

One final category may be chosen to round out this incomplete and cursory classification—the introductory stanzas with which Ariosto opens each canto and which Spenser, following him, not infrequently employs. Such stanzas in the *Furioso* are either reflective or take the form of an address to the poet's imaginary audience. Spenser's are almost always reflective—we have seen above how he could take a theme suggested by Ariosto ("Ingiustissimo Amor") and raise it to a loftier plane of meditation—but once, at least, he adopted the address, on an occasion when Ariosto's precedent seemed worth following.

By way of cautionary preface to his twenty-eighth canto—that which Harington first translated—Ariosto writes:

Donne, e voi che le donne avete in pregio,
Per Dio, non date a questa istoria orecchia,
A questa che l'ostier dire in dispregio
E in vostra infamia e biasmo s'apparecchia;
Ben che ne macchia vi può dar nè fregio
Lingua sì vile, e sia l'usanza vecchia
Che'l volgare ignorante ognun riprenda,
E parli più di quel che meno intenda.

Lasciate questo Canto; che senza esso
Può star l'istoria, e non sarà men chiara.
Mettendolo Turpino, anch' io l'ho messo,
Non per malivolenzia nè per gara.
Ch' io v'ami, oltre mia lingua che l'ha espresso,
Che mai non fu di celebrarvi avara,
N' ho fatto mille prove; e v'ho dimostro
Ch'io son, nè potrei esser se non vostro.

An apology was, without question, desirable, and Ariosto makes it in the tone of playful deprecation which he can assume so well.

When Spenser came to write of Paridell and Hellenore (Bk. III, c. 9), he seems to have thought the opportunity a good one to imitate Ariosto's apology. His own story was relatively sober, and unquestionably, had not Ariosto set the precedent, he himself would never have thought of apologizing for it; indeed, he might seem to be going somewhat out of his way to do so. Adopting the suggestion, however, he sets his own unmistakable stamp upon the stanzas. They are utterly different in tone from Ariosto's.

> Redoubted Knights, and honorable Dames,
> To whom I levell all my labours end,
> Right sore I feare least with unworthie blames
> This odious argument my rymes should shend,
> Or ought your goodly patience offend,
> Whiles of a wanton lady I doe write,
> Which with her loose incontinence doth blend
> The shyning glory of your soveraine light;
> And knighthood fowle defaced by a faithlesse knight.

> But never let th' ensample of the bad
> Offend the good: for good, by paragone
> Of evill, may more notably be rad;
> As white seemes fayrer macht with blacke attone:
> Ne all are shamed by the fault of one:
> For lo! in heven, whereas all goodnes is,
> Emongst the angels, a whole legione
> Of wicked sprightes did fall from happy blis;
> What wonder then if one, of women all, did mis?

III

To those who read the *Faery Queen* with Ariosto in mind the opening cantos of Book III are almost startling. At the very outset Britomart appears on the scene, and we at once recognize her for a copy of Bradamante. She makes her entry exactly like Bradamante, coming suddenly into view, and without pause rushing to an encounter with the knight in her path, and bearing him down (*F.Q.*, Bk. III, c. 1, st. 4 ff.; *O.F.*, I, 60 ff.). Then, a reconciliation being effected, her antagonist, Guyon, Prince Arthur, and she ride on together, till suddenly a damsel on a milk-white palfrey dashes out of the brush pursued by a lustful forester, and Arthur and Guyon immediately spur after the pair, to save the damsel from harm (c. 1, st. 15 ff.). We are reminded of Angelica in the first canto of the *Furioso*, and the sequel indicates that Spenser had her in mind (c. 4, st. 46; cf. *O.F.*, I, 21–23: c. 7, st. 1, 2; cf. *O.F.*, I, 33–35). Florimel, in fact, with her many lovers, might be taken throughout the book for the faint counterpart of Angelica. Meanwhile Britomart, continuing her course alone, comes to the House of Malecasta, where, as we have seen, her experience is an imitation of Ruggiero's experience with Alcina—just reversed. So much for the first canto. In the second and third cantos we have the beginnings of her love-story, which is continuously parallel to that of Bradamante. These main facts, and some half-dozen minor imitations bring the early cantos of Book III so close to the early cantos of the *Furioso* that Spenser might seem to have taken a fresh start in his "emulation" of Ariosto. As a whole, the third book is incomparably richer than the preceding two in reminiscences of Ariosto.

This fact is, perhaps, hardly surprising, for Britomart being heroine of the book, Spenser's mind would naturally be occupied more than ever with his original. What is much more noteworthy is that the general character of Book III differs markedly from that of the preceding books, and approximates very distinctly to the type of the *Furioso*. The phenomenon is not inexplicable.

The first two books of the *Faery Queen* are, without

doubt, the most systematic and careful of the six we now have. Each is devoted to the quest of a single knight, and each is rounded out to complete unity. In the second book, however, we can detect signs of a change. The plot of the first is rigidly concentrated; in the second—though the book can hardly be said to have a real plot, being made up of a string of unprogressive episodes—Braggadochio and Belphoebe, and the chronicle of British kings, and the combat of Arthur with Maleger mar the narrative unity, if they do not absolutely destroy it. Spenser seems to be reaching out towards a somewhat freer, more varied narrative plan.

His stricter allegorical method seems also to be giving him trouble. The career of the Red Cross Knight in its progressive vicissitudes, from the Den of Error, through the House of Pride, the Dungeon of Orgoglio, the Cave of Despair, the House of Holiness, to the final combat with the Dragon of Evil and the triumphant marriage with Una, is, on the whole, set forth with rare imaginative power. In the career of Guyon the allegory begins to lose life. The House of Golden Meane is tolerable, but Medina herself is so pale and bloodless that Spenser seems to have hardly dared make her Guyon's avowed mistress; their mutual troth is suggested only in the faintest manner (Bk. II, c. 2, st. 30, 1.5; c. 7, st. 50); and the House of Temperance with its cut and dried allegory of the human body, the house of the soul, is perilously close to a *reductio ad absurdum*. Spenser, one would think, must have felt that if his characters and scenes were to continue to be the embodiment of merely abstract qualities and conditions, or the transmogrification of things material, there would be danger of his poem becoming completely ossified. His imagination could not continue indefinitely to give life to abstractions.

We shall hardly be surprised, therefore, at the change in narration and allegory which comes with the third book.

In narration Spenser abandons unity of action. The plot of which Florimel is heroine runs side by side with the main plot, the quest of Britomart, touching it only at the outset, and other characters give other centres of interest, or incipient plots, as Timias and Belphoebe. There are frequent digressions. The scene is constantly shifting. The quest of Britomart moves towards no definite goal of action; the achievement with which she brings the book to a close is accidental and unforeseen. The end of the book, indeed, ends nothing, for all the main threads of interest are still to be spun out. In brief, the narrative character of this book is utterly different from that of the first two. For a single knight, pursuing his quest through opposing dangers, with varying vicissitudes of fortune, all accessory figures grouped about him in strict subordination, we have independent knights and ladies, whose paths cross and recross, who come and go much as fate drives them, without definite goal, all dominated by Britomart, but not controlled by her. This is manifestly the varied world of the *Furioso*.

The change in allegory is equally marked. One notices, for instance, that there are fewer allegorical sign-boards. From the "Wood of Error" to the "House of Holiness" the first book is full of them, and the second book has the "House of Golden Meane," the "Cave of Mammon," and half a dozen others: the third book has the "House of Malecasta," and that alone. One notices, too, the absence of characters labelled as mere abstractions. The first book has Despair, Orgoglio, Corceca, Sansfoy and his brethren, and others too numerous to mention; the second book has Furor, Occasion, Atin, Alma, Medina, Mammon, etc., etc.; save Malecasta and her crew—for the Masque of Cupid may fairly be set aside—the third book has hardly one. Taking the list of characters in each book at large, we discover a similar distinction. The Red Cross Knight, Una,

Duessa, Archimago are the embodiment of manifest abstractions, as also are Guyon, the Palmer, Acrasia, Cymochles; what abstractions are embodied in the characters of the third book? Britomart is nominally the embodiment of Chastity; but what abstraction does Florimel stand for? Malecasta is, of course, Unchastity incarnate; what, then, is Hellenore? If Hellenore stands for some abstraction or other, why does Spenser apologize for writing of "a wanton lady," and defend himself from the charge of aspersing womankind by saying that she is merely "one, of women all" (c. 9, st. 1 and 2)? As for Malbecco, his ultimate transformation into the abstraction, Jealousy, is described with wonderful effect: what abstraction does he represent before his transformation? Then, for the allegorical action. In the first book Holiness is shown struggling through those spiritual dangers which peculiarly beset it to the overthrow of Evil and to union with Heavenly Truth. In the second book Temperance stands firm against those passions and desires which peculiarly beset it, and in the end triumphs over Incontinence, the worst of all. In each case the allegory presents a perfectly definite succession of spiritual states considered in the abstract. What does Britomart, or Chastity, do? She reads Malecasta a lesson; she drives off Ollyphant, a type of Lust; she sets Amoret free from Busyrane—which may be taken to signify the power of Chastity freeing Womanhood from thraldom to material passion. But what is the hidden spiritual significance of her combat with Marinell, of her sojourn in the castle of Malbecco? Taking her career as a whole, one cannot but see that, whatever else the allegory may do, it certainly does not, like that of the first two books, present a succession of distinct spiritual states considered in the abstract. And turning from Britomart to Florimel, one perceives immediately that the allegory of this unfortunate lady's career is at the very antipodes to the allegory of abstractions. To sum up, the characters of Book III may fairly be regarded as men and women of certain general types engaged in actions which are typically moral. And here again we find ourselves close to the *Furioso*, which has allegorical episodes, but of general allegory only so much as one might read into almost any romance poem. Set Book III and the *Furioso* side by side, and one lends itself to allegory almost as readily as the other.

This change is certainly remarkable: it is a change of world. The world of Book I is a world of spiritual abstractions, in which the outer semblance of chivalry does not for an instant deceive the reader; the world of Book III is the world of chivalry itself, which occasional abstractions in no way perturb. Book II marks the transition. The change is lasting. In Book V we have a partial reversion to the earlier type, but Books IV and VI are distinctly of the later; Book VI, indeed, is about as purely chivalric as one could desire. Consciously or unconsciously, Spenser has drawn nearer to Ariosto. That his poem should begin in a world peculiarly his own, and then, as if irresistibly, drift into the world of the *Furioso* is perhaps not without significance.

IV

How far Ariosto influenced Spenser's literary methods and what elements in the *Faery Queen* may be traced to the *Orlando Furioso* are questions beyond the scope of the present investigation. The data we have secured, however, will afford us some general conclusions about Spenser's imaginative debt to Ariosto which will be worth a brief statement.

First, we notice that the two men are radically different in temper and views. Ariosto is humorous, ironical, worldly-wise—serious chiefly by artistic mood; Spenser is "sage and serious" by fundamental constitution. Ariosto's attitude towards chivalry is that of the urbane sceptic, or of the impressionable artist; to Spenser chivalry is an inspiring ideal, the highest expression of human nobility and earnestness. The two men, in reality, have nothing but their art in common, and even on that they are not at one. However seriously, therefore, Spenser may at times have taken Ariosto, it is manifest that the latter can have had no real influence upon his deeper imaginative life.

If any romance poet exercised such an influence on him, it was Tasso. The intense seriousness, the reverence for chivalry which pervade the *Gerusalemme Liberata* could hardly fail to attract Spenser powerfully; even its somewhat morbid sadness and *dolcezza* seem to have charmed him, for though his own temperament was serenely cheerful,[13] he certainly had a strong taste for the poetry of melancholy—witness Du Bellay, the saddest of the *Pléiade* poets and the only one of them who ever influenced him, and witness his own poetical laments. In the days when he first undertook the *Faery Queen* he was acquainted with the *Rinaldo* and borrowed from it; when the *Gerusalemme Liberata* reached him he was apparently as enthusiastic over it as the Italians themselves. If, as might very well be, he was then engaged upon his second book, the remarkable imitations of Tasso's poem of which that book is full might be taken to represent the first impulses of his enthusiasm.

How far Spenser was in sympathy with Tasso may be indicated by the character of his imitations. When he copies Ariosto it is almost always with a change. He may take the facts of a plot one by one as they stand in his original; the peculiar rendering will always be his own. He may adopt a situation—it will be with certain modifications which alter its character. He may imitate a reflective passage—the spirit of the version will be new. In other words, he is never thoroughly in touch with Ariosto. When he imitates Tasso, however, he does not feel the need of change, or if he changes, he preserves in good part the spirit of the original. The Bower of Bliss (Bk. II, c. 12) is a simple reproduction of the Gardens of Armida (*G.L.*, XV, XVI), partly by direct translation, partly by close imitation, partly by adoption of general features. The song of Phaedria (Bk. II, c. 6, st. 15–17) has not a word in common with the song of the siren (*G.L.*, XIV, 62–64); yet the spirit of the two is exactly the same; they might be transposed. In other words, Spenser finds in Tasso a kindred genius, and has no need of asserting imaginative independence.

Spenser imitated Tasso whenever he found occasion.[14] The *Gerusalemme Liberata*, however, was too little a romance poem to furnish him very much material; the epical subject-matter which Tasso had adopted was too far removed from the subject-matter of the *Faery Queen*. Having begun his poem with Ariosto in mind, therefore, he still found Ariosto his most convenient resource; indeed, as we have seen, during the very days of his early enthusiasm for the *Gerusalemme Liberata* the *Faery Queen* was drifting, as if irresistibly, towards the type of the *Furioso*, and was accumulating imitations in double volume; for Spenser was imitating, not to record his critical preferences, but to fill in the outlines of his extended poem. And, after all, it would be a grave mistake to imagine that he did not really enjoy and admire the *Orlando Furioso*. He and Ariosto were radically different in spirit, and could rarely, or never, be in complete sympathy, but we know that he thought him a grave and edifying poet, not much the worse for a strain of somewhat free humor, and it is evident to the most casual observer of his imitations that he read the *Furioso* repeatedly and assiduously. Had he undertaken to emulate it merely in the spirit of opposition, he would hardly have gone to it so fre-

quently for suggestions and direct help, he would hardly have studied it with such care. Or if we conceive of him as borrowing from it in cold blood, using it merely because it was full of convenient plots, characters, situations, etc., we must admit that his memory for things he did not really enjoy was sometimes singularly tenacious, that he has imitated passages which he could not have hunted up for the occasion and which, to the unsophisticated observer, would seem to have stuck in his mind because they pleased him. It is not necessary to assume that Ariosto fascinated him, was his favorite poet; but a careful survey of the data will convince most of us, I think, that Spenser took very genuine pleasure in the fertile and amiable Italian. He certainly did not go to him for inspiration of the higher order, but for the practical conduct of the *Faery Queen* he found him invaluable—the consummate artist of the romance poem, a poet of almost inexhaustible variety and suggestiveness. Every passage borrowed might be recast, modified, animated with another spirit—all, apparently, in repudiation of Ariosto's meaning; but that would not imply antagonism. Spenser might recognize the difference between his own poem and the *Furioso* without, therefore, disapproving of the latter—except casually; and he might read the *Furioso* like Milton without feeling any grave discrepancy between his own imaginings and the spirit of the context. He probably did not analyze his impressions like a philosopher. Ariosto had perfected the type of the romance poem; Spenser emulated and imitated him, and read him with pretty constant pleasure.

Notes

1. For this passage and the following v. Dr. Grosart's edition of Spenser, vol. IX, pp. 274 and 277.
2. It is after Mantuan.
3. G. B. Pigna: *I Romanzi*. Venice, 1554, pp. 44, 65.
4. Though not directly bearing on Spenser's early emulation of Ariosto, this phase of Ariosto criticism in Italy is too significant and important to be omitted.
5. Tasso: *Opere*. Venice, 1735, v. III, p. 155.
6. G. B. Giraldi: *De' Romanzi*; in the *Biblioteca Rara*, v. 52, p. 64.
7. v. Bk. III, c. 10, st. 48.
8. This point is discussed later.
9. The episode is strung out over three cantos: I, 72–81; II, 1–23; VIII, 29ff.
10. Braggadochio had formerly won her for his lady (Bk. III, c. 8, st. 11–14), as Mandricardo won Doralice (*O. F.*, XIV, 38ff.), but he had immediately lost her through cowardice. His exploit in winning her might be regarded as a burlesque of Mandricardo's exploit.
11. I use the term "situation" in a somewhat loose sense.
12. See, however, Chaucer: *The Book of the Duchesse*, 11. 153ff. Also Ovid: *Metam.*, XI, 591ff. Statius: *Theb.*, X, 84ff.
13. Those who read Spenser attentively will hardly be convinced, I think, that there was "a life-long vein of melancholy" in him. v. Dr. Grosart's *Spenser*, vol. I, p. 185.
14. Sometimes he superimposes Tasso upon Ariosto—not always felicitously. What Britomart says of her early training in arms (Bk. III, c. 2, st. 6, 7) is imitated from Clorinda (G. L., II, 39, 40), but is in manifest contradiction to Glaucè's words (c. 3, st. 53, 57).

GEORGE SAINTSBURY
From "Elizabethan Criticism"
A History of Literary Criticism and Literary Taste in Europe
1902, Volume 2, pp. 165–68

*F*ive Letters ("Three" and "Two")[1]—not to be confused with the *Four Letters* which Harvey issued long afterwards about Greene) are full of the subject ⟨of classical metres⟩, and of poetical criticism generally. They, together with the controversy which arose over Gosson's *School of Abuse*, and which indirectly produced Sidney's *Apology for Poetry*, make the years 1579–1580 as notable in the history of English criticism as the appearances of *Euphues* and *The Shepherd's Calendar* make them in that of creative literature.

Spenser's first letter informs Harvey that "they [Sidney and Dyer] have proclaimed in their *areiōpagō*[2] [the literary *cénacle* of Leicester House] a general surceasing and silence of bald rhymers, and also of the very best too: instead whereof they have, by the authority of their whole Senate, prescribed certain laws and rules of quantities of English syllables for English verse, having had thereof already great practice, and drawn me to their faction." And later, "I am more in love with English versifying than with rhyming, which I should have done long since if I would have followed your counsel." He hints, however, gently, that Harvey's own verses (these coterie writers always keep the name "verses" for their hybrid abortions) once or twice "make a breach in Master Drant's rules." Which was, of course, a very dreadful thing, only to be "condoned *tanto poetæ*." He requites Harvey with a few Iambics, which he "dare warrant precisely perfect for the feet, and varying not one inch from the Rule." And then follows the well-known piece beginning—

Unhappy verse, the witness of my unhappy state,

where certainly the state must have been bad if it was as infelicitous as the verse.

Not such was Gabriel Harvey that he might take even a polite correction; and his reply is a proper donnish setting-down of a clever but presumptuous youth. He respects the Areopagus—indeed they were persons of worship, and Harvey was a *roturier*—more than Spenser can or will suppose, and he likes the trimeters (indeed, though poor things, they were Spenser's own after all, and such as no man but Spenser could have written in their foolish kind) more than Spenser "can or will easily believe." But—and then follows much reviewing in the now stale hole-picking kind, which has long been abandoned, save by the descendants of Milbourne and Kenrick, and a lofty protestation that "myself never saw your gorbellied master's rules, nor heard of them before."

The Three Letters which follow[3] are distributed in subject between an Earthquake (which has long since ceased to quake for us) and the hexameters. They open with a letter from Spenser, in which he broaches the main question, "Whether our English accent will endure the Hexameter?" and doubts. Yet he has a hankering after it, encloses his own—

See ye the blindfoldèd pretty god, that feathered
archer, &c.,

and prays that Harvey would either follow the rules of the great Drant, indorsed by Sidney, or else send his own. Harvey replies in double. The first part is some very tragical mirth about the earthquake; the second, "A Gallant Familiar Letter," tackles the question of versification.

This gallant familiarity might possibly receive from harsh critics the name of uneasy coxcombry; but it is at any rate clear that the author has sent about the matter very seriously. He expresses delight that Sidney and Dyer, "the two very diamonds of her Majesty's Court," have begun to help forward "the exchange of barbarous and balductum[4] rhymes with artificial verses"; thinks their "lively example" will be much better than Ascham's "dead advertisement" in the *Schoolmaster*. He would like (as should we) to have Drant's prosody. His own Rules and Precepts will probably not be very different; but he will take time before drafting them finally. He thinks (reasonably

enough) that before framing a standard English Grammar or Rhetoric (therein including Prosody), a standard orthography must first be agreed upon. And he suggests that "we beginners" (this from the author of these truly "barbarous and balductum" antics to the author of the *Faerie Queene* is distinctly precious) have the advantage, like Homer and Ennius, of setting examples. "A New Year's Gift to M. George Bilchaunger," in very doleful hexameters, follows, and after a little gird at Spenser's "See ye the Blindfoldèd," another sprout of Harvey's brain in the same kind, which has been, perhaps, more, and more deservedly, laughed at than any of these absurdities, except the scarcely sane jargon-doggerel of Stanyhurst—

What might I call this tree? a Laurell? o bonny
Laurell!
Needs to thy boughs will I bow this knee, and veil my
bonetto;

with yet another—

Since *Galateo*[5] came in, and Tuscanism gan usurp.

He thinks that the author of this last "wanted but some delicate choice elegant poesy" of Sidney's or Dyer's for a good pattern. After some further experiments of his own, or his brother's, in hexametring some of Spenser's own "emblems" in the *Calendar*, he turns to Spenser himself, whom, it seems, he ranks next the same "incomparable and miraculous genius in the catalogue of our very principal English Aristarchi." He proceeds to speak of some of that earlier work which, as in *The Dying Pelican*, is certainly, or in the *Dreams*, possibly, lost. After which he writes himself down for all time in the famous passage about the *Faerie Queene*, which he had "once again nigh forgotten," but which he now sends home "in neither better nor worse case than he found her." "As for his judgment," he is "void of all judgment if Spenser's *Nine Comedies* [also lost] are not nearer Ariosto's than that Elvish Queene is to the *Orlando*, which" Spenser "seems to emulate, and hopes to overgo." And so he ends his paragraph with the yet more famous words, "If so be the *Faery Queene* be fairer in your eye than the Nine Muses, and Hobgoblin run away with the garland from Apollo, mark what I say, and yet I will not say what I thought, but there an end for this once, and fare you well till God or some good Angel put you in a better mind!" Which words let all who practise criticism grave in their memories, and recite them daily, adding, "Here, but for the grace of God——!" if they be modest and fear Nemesis.

After an interval, however, Harvey returns to actual criticism, and shows himself in rather better figure by protesting, in spite of "five hundred Drants," against the alternation of the quantity of English words by accenting "Majesty" and "Manfully," and "Carpenter" on the second syllable. And he falls in with Gascoigne on the subject of such words as "Heaven." Nor could he, even if he had been far less of a pedant and coxcomb, have given better or sounder doctrine than that with which he winds up. "It is the vulgar and natural mother Prosody, that alone worketh the feat, as the only supreme foundress and reformer of Position, Diphthong, Orthography, or whatsoever else; whose affirmatives are nothing worth if she once conclude the negative." And for this sound doctrine, not unsoundly enlarged upon, and tipped with a pleasant Latin farewell to "*mea domina Immerita, mea bellissima Collina Clouta*," let us leave Gabriel in charity.[6]

Notes

1. See Grosart's *Works of Gabriel Harvey*, vol. i, pp. 6–150. Parts will be found in the Globe edition of Spenser, pp. 706–710.
2. I am not responsible for the eccentricities of this form.
3. In order of composition, not of publication.

4. This word, which is certainly a cousin of "balderdash," is a good example of the slang and jargon so often mixed with their preciousness by the Elizabethans. Nash borrowed it from Harvey to use against him; and the eccentric Stanyhurst even employs it in his *Virgil*. Stanyhurst's hexameters, by the way (vide Mr Arber's Reprint in the *English Scholars Library*, No. 10, London, 1880), are, thanks partly to their astounding lingo, among the maddest things in English literature; but his prose prefatory matter, equally odd in phrase, has some method in its madness.

5. La Casa's book of etiquette and behaviour.

6. The further letters to Spenser, which Dr Grosart has borrowed from the Camden Society's *Letter-book of Gabriel Harvey*, touch literary matters not seldom, but with no new important deliverances. In the latter (1592) *Four Letters*, the embroidery of railing at the dead Greene and the living Nash has almost entirely hidden the literary canvas.

W. B. YEATS
From "Edmund Spenser"
Poems of Spenser, ed. Yeats
1902, pp. xxii–xliv

When Spenser was buried in Westminister Abbey many poets read verses in his praise, and then threw their verses and the pens that had written them into his tomb. Like him they belonged, for all the moral zeal that was gathering like a London fog, to that indolent, demonstrative Merry England that was about to pass away. Men still wept when they were moved, still dressed themselves in joyous colours, and spoke with many gestures. Thoughts and qualities sometimes come to their perfect expression when they are about to pass away, and Merry England was dying in plays, and in poems, and in strange adventurous men. . . . He had lived in the last days of what we may call the Anglo-French nation, the old feudal nation that had been established when the Norman and the Angevin made French the language of court and market. In the time of Chaucer English poets still wrote much in French, and even English labourers lilted French songs over their work; and I cannot read any Elizabethan poem or romance without feeling the pressure of habits of emotion, and of an order of life, which were conscious, for all their Latin gaiety, of a quarrel to the death with that new Anglo-Saxon nation that was arising amid Puritan sermons and Marprelate pamphlets. This nation had driven out the language of its conquerors, and now it was to overthrow their beautiful haughty imagination and their manners, full of abandon and wilfulness, and to set in their stead earnestness and logic and the timidity and reserve of a counting-house. . . .

He was, I think, by nature altogether a man of that old Catholic feudal nation, but, like Sidney, he wanted to justify himself to his new masters. He wrote of knights and ladies, wild creatures imagined by the aristocratic poets of the twelfth century, and perhaps chiefly by English poets who had still the French tongue; but he fastened them with allegorical nails to a big barn-door of common sense, of merely practical virtue. Allegory itself had risen into general importance with the rise of the merchant class in the thirteenth and fourteenth centuries; and it was natural when that class was about for the first time to shape an age in its image, that the last epic poet of the old order should mix its art with his own long-descended, irresponsible, happy art. . . .

One cannot think that he should have occupied himself with moral and religious questions at all. He should have been content to be, as Emerson thought Shakespeare was, a Master of the Revels to mankind. I am certain that he never gets that visionary air which can alone make allegory real, except when he writes out of a feeling for glory and passion. He had no deep moral or religious life. He has never a line like Dante's 'His Will is our Peace', or like Thomas à Kempis's 'The Holy Spirit has liberated me from a multitude of opinions', or even like Hamlet's objection to the bare bodkin. He had been made a poet by what he had almost learnt to call his sins. If he had not felt it necessary to justify his art to some serious friend, or perhaps even to 'that rugged forehead', he would have written all his life long, one thinks, of the loves of shepherdesses and shepherds, among whom there would have been perhaps the morals of the dovecot. One is persuaded that his morality is official and impersonal—a system of life which it was his duty to support— and it is perhaps a half understanding of this that has made so many generations believe that he was the first Poet Laureate, the first salaried moralist among the poets. His processions of deadly sins, and his houses, where the very cornices are arbitrary images of virtue, are an unconscious hypocrisy, an undelighted obedience to the 'rugged forehead', for all the while he is thinking of nothing but lovers whose bodies are quivering with the memory or the hope of long embraces. When they are not together, he will indeed embroider emblems and images much as those great ladies of the courts of love embroidered them in their castles; and when these are imagined out of a thirst for magnificence and not thought out in a mood of edification, they are beautiful enough; but they are always tapestries for corridors that lead to lovers' meetings or for the walls of marriage chambers. He was not passionate, for the passionate feed their flame in wanderings and absences, when the whole being of the beloved, every little charm of body and of soul, is always present to the mind, filling it with heroical subtleties of desire. He is a poet of the delighted senses, and his song becomes most beautiful when he writes of those islands of Phaedria and Acrasia, which angered 'that rugged forehead', as it seems, but gave to Keats his *Belle Dame sans merci* and his 'perilous seas in faery lands forlorn', and to William Morris his 'Water of the Wondrous Isles'.

The dramatists lived in a disorderly world, reproached by many, persecuted even, but following their imagination wherever it led them. Their imagination, driven hither and thither by beauty and sympathy, put on something of the nature of eternity. Their subject was always the soul, the whimsical, self-awakening, self-exciting, self-appeasing soul. They celebrated its heroical, passionate will going by its own path to immortal and invisible things. Spenser, on the other hand, except among those smooth pastoral scenes and lovely effeminate islands that have made him a great poet, tried to be of his time, or rather of the time that was all but at hand. Like Sidney, whose charm, it may be, led many into slavery, he persuaded himself that we enjoy Virgil because of the virtues of Aeneas, and so planned out his immense poem that it would set before the imagination of citizens, in whom there would soon be no great energy, innumerable blameless Aeneases. He had learned to put the State, which desires all the abundance for itself, in the place of the Church, and he found it possible to be moved by expedient emotions, merely because they were expedient, and to think serviceable thoughts with no self-contempt. . . . Spenser had learned to look to the State not only as the rewarder of virtue but as the maker of right and wrong, and had begun to love and hate as it bid him. The thoughts that we find for ourselves are timid and a little secret, but those modern thoughts that we share with large numbers are confident and very insolent. We have little else today, and when we read our newspaper and take up its cry, above all, its cry of hatred, we will not think very carefully, for we hear the marching feet. When Spenser wrote of Ireland he wrote as an official, and out of thoughts and emotions that had been organized by the State. He was the first of many Englishmen to see nothing but what he was desired to see. Could he have gone there as a poet merely, he might have found among its poets more wonderful imaginations than even those islands of Phaedria and Acrasia. He would have found among wandering story-tellers, not indeed his own power of rich, sustained description, for that belongs to lettered ease, but certainly all the kingdom of Faery, still unfaded, of which his own poetry was often but a troubled image. He would have found men doing by swift strokes of the imagination much that he was doing with painful intellect, with that imaginative reason that soon was to drive out imagination altogether and for a long time. He would have met with, at his own door, story-tellers among whom the perfection of Greek art was indeed as unknown as his own power of sustained description, but who, none the less, imagined or remembered beautiful incidents and strange, pathetic outcrying that made them of Homer's lineage. . . .

There are moments when one can read neither Milton nor Spenser, moments when one recollects nothing but that their flesh had partly been changed to stone, but there are other moments when one recollects nothing but those habits of emotion that made the lesser poet especially a man of an older, more imaginative time. One remembers that he delighted in smooth pastoral places, because men could be busy there or gather together there, after their work, that he could love handiwork and the hum of voices. One remembers that he could still rejoice in the trees, not because they were images of loneliness and mediation, but because of their serviceableness. He could praise 'the builder oake', 'the aspine, good for staves', 'the cypresse funerall', 'the eugh, obedient to the bender's will', 'the birch for shaftes', 'the sallow for the mill', 'the mirrhe sweete bleeding in the bitter wound', 'the fruitful olive', and 'the carver holme'. He was of a time before undelighted labour had made the business of men a desecration. He carries one's memory back to Virgil's and Chaucer's praise of trees, and to the sweet-sounding song made by the old Irish poet in their praise.

I got up from reading *The Faerie Queene* the other day and wandered into another room. It was in a friend's house, and I came of a sudden to the ancient poetry and to our poetry side by side—an engraving of Claude's *Mill* hung under an engraving of Turner's *Temple of Jupiter*. Those dancing countrypeople, those cowherds, resting after the day's work, and that quiet mill-race made one think of Merry England with its glad Latin heart, of a time when men in every land found poetry and imagination in one another's company and in the day's labour. Those stately goddesses, moving in slow procession towards that marble architrave among mysterious trees, belong to Shelley's thought, and to the religion of the wilderness—the only religion possible to poetry today. Certainly Colin Clout, the companionable shepherd, and Calidore, the courtly man-at-arms, are gone, and Alastor is wandering from lonely river to river finding happiness in nothing but in that Star where Spenser too had imagined the fountain of perfect things. This new beauty, in losing so much, has indeed found a new loftiness, a something of religious exaltation that the old had not. It may be that those goddesses, moving with a majesty like a procession of the stars, mean something to the soul of man that those kindly women of the old poets did not mean, for all the fullness of their breasts and the joyous gravity of their eyes. Has not the wilderness been at all times a place of prophecy?

Our poetry, though it has been a deliberate bringing back of the Latin joy and the Latin love of beauty, has had to put off the old marching rhythms, that once could give delight to more than expedient hearts, in separating itself from a life where servile hands have become powerful. It has ceased to have any burden for marching shoulders, since it learned ecstasy from Smart in his mad cell, and from Blake, who made joyous little songs out of almost unintelligible visions, and from Keats, who sang of a beauty so wholly preoccupied with itself that its contemplation is a kind of lingering trance. The poet, if he would not carry burdens that are not his and obey the orders of servile lips, must sit apart in comtemplative indolence playing with fragile things.

If one chooses at hazard a Spenserian stanza out of Shelley and compares it with any stanza by Spenser, one sees the change, though it would be still more clear if one had chosen a lyrical passage. I will take a stanza out of *Laon and Cythna*, for that is story-telling and runs nearer to Spenser than the meditative *Adonais*:

> The meteor to its far morass returned:
> The beating of our veins one interval
> Made still; and then I felt the blood that burned
> Within her frame, mingle with mine, and fall
> Around my heart like fire; and over all
> A mist was spread, the sickness of a deep
> And speechless swoon of joy, as might befall
> Two disunited spirits when they leap
> In union from this earth's obscure and fading sleep.

The rhythm is varied and troubled, and the lines, which are in Spenser like bars of gold thrown ringing one upon another, are broken capriciously. Nor is the meaning the less an inspiration of indolent Muses, for it wanders hither and thither at the beckoning of fancy. It is now busy with a meteor and now with throbbing blood that is fire, and with a mist that is a swoon and a sleep that is life. It is bound together by the vaguest suggestion, while Spenser's verse is always rushing on to some preordained thought. A 'popular poet' can still indeed write poetry of the will, just as factory girls wear the fashion of hat or dress the moneyed classes wore a year ago, but 'popular poetry' does not belong to the living imagination of the world. Old writers gave men four temperaments, and they gave the sanguineous temperament to men of active life, and it is precisely the sanguineous temperament that is fading out of poetry and most obviously out of what is most subtle and living in poetry—its pulse and breath, its rhythm. Because poetry belongs to that element in every race which is most strong, and therefore most individual, the poet is not stirred to imaginative activity by a life which is surrendering its freedom to ever new elaboration, organization, mechanism. He has no longer a poetical will, and must be content to write out of those parts of himself which are too delicate and fiery for any deadening exercise. Every generation has more and more loosened the rhythm, more and more broken up and disorganized, for the sake of subtlety of detail, those great rhythms which move, as it were, in masses of sound. Poetry has become more spiritual, for the soul is of all things the most delicately organized, but it has lost in weight and measure and in its power of telling long stories and of dealing with great and complicated events. *Laon and Cythna*, though I think it rises sometimes into loftier air than *The Faerie Queene* and *Endymion*, though its shepherds and wandering divinities have a stranger and more intense beauty than Spenser's, has need of too watchful and minute attention for such lengthy poems. In William Morris, indeed, one finds a music smooth and unexacting like that of the old story-tellers, but not their energetic pleasure, their rhythmical wills. One too often misses in his *Earthly Paradise* the minute ecstasy of modern song without finding that old happy-go-lucky tune that had kept the story marching.

Spenser's contemporaries, writing lyrics or plays full of lyrical moments, write a verse more delicately organized than his and crowd more meaning into a phrase than he, but they could not have kept one's attention through so long a poem. A friend who has a fine ear told me the other day that she had read all Spenser with delight and yet could remember only four lines. When she repeated them they were from the poem by Matthew Roydon, which is bound up with Spenser because it is a commendation of Sir Philip Sidney:

> A sweet, attractive kind of grace,
> A full assurance given by looks,
> Continual comfort in a face,
> The lineaments of Gospel books.

Yet if one were to put even these lines beside a fine modern song one would notice that they had a stronger and rougher energy, a featherweight more, if eye and ear were fine enough to notice it, of the active will, of the happiness that comes out of life itself.

SIR FRANCIS BACON

Francis Bacon

1561–1626

Francis Bacon, philosopher, statesman, and essayist, was born on January 22, 1561, at York House off the Strand, London. He was the youngest son of Sir Nicholas Bacon and Ann Cooke. Bacon studied at Trinity College from 1573 to 1575. Plagued by ill health and dissatisfaction with the Aristotelian philosophy, he left Cambridge and went to France, where he studied diplomacy until the death of his father in 1579. Bacon then entered Gray's Inn to study law, becoming a barrister in 1582. He entered Parliament in 1584, remaining a prominent member until 1614. Although he had served as sometime adviser to Elizabeth I, he fell out of favor with the Queen over his objections to a bill for royal subsidies towards expenses incurred in the war against Spain.

By 1591 Bacon had become, along with his brother Anthony, a friend and adviser to Robert Devereux, Earl of Essex, at that time a favorite of the Queen's. Essex recommended Bacon for a number of posts, including that of Solicitor General (given instead to Sir Edward Coke, a lawyer and one of Bacon's lifelong rivals), and gave Bacon a generous tract of land at Twickenham. Bacon in turn tried to protect the interests of the unstable Essex, but felt compelled to break with him after his abortive rebellion in early 1601. Bacon's tract denouncing Essex helped to secure the Earl's conviction for treason.

Having received no significant appointments during the reign of Elizabeth, Bacon did not begin to flourish until the succession of James I in 1603. At this time Bacon was knighted, and he became Solicitor General in 1607. In 1605 he published *The Advancement of Learning*, dedicated to the King, and married Alice Barnham in 1606. After Coke's dismissal in 1616, Bacon's career progressed rapidly, and he was appointed Lord Keeper in 1617, Lord Chancellor and Baron Verulam in 1618, and Viscount St. Albans in 1620–21. Bacon's advancement can be attributed to his dedication to both Parliament and the court, his own constant letters of self-recommendation, and his association with George Villiers (later the Duke of Buckingham), a favorite of the King's.

In 1621 Bacon's fortunes were suddenly reversed. Accused of accepting bribes from defendants who had cases pending, Bacon admitted the charge but claimed that the practice never influenced his decisions. He resigned from his position as Lord Chancellor, was found guilty, fined £40,000, and briefly imprisoned in the Tower of London. Disgraced, Bacon retired from public life. From 1621 until his death on April 9, 1626, he devoted much time to literary production.

In 1597 Bacon published his ten *Essayes*, the first "essays" in English; fifty-eight essays were published in 1625. These, along with *The Advancement of Learning* (1605), were written in English, although the latter was published in an expanded Latin version, *De Augmentis Scientiarum*, in 1623. Bacon's famous *Novum Organum* (literally "New Instrument") was published in Latin in 1620. This, along with the Latin version of *The Advancement of Learning* and the *Sylva Sylvarum; or A Natural History*, comprise a part of the *Instauratio Magna*, or great plan for a restoration of knowledge. In calling for a future of surer, more scientific knowledge founded upon empiricism and induction, Bacon wrote the *New Atlantis* (c. 1610), an unfinished account of an ideal commonwealth dominated by natural philosophers.

Aside from his philosophical writings, Bacon produced many legal and political works, as well as poems, apophthegms, translations of psalms into English, and a history of the reign of Henry VII.

Personal

She ⟨Queen Elizabeth⟩ did acknowledge you had a great wit and an excellent gift of speech, and much other good learning. But in the law she rather thought you could make *show* to the utmost of your knowledge than that you were *deep*.—EARL OF ESSEX, Letter to Francis Bacon

I have found an alderman's daughter, a handsome maiden to my liking.—FRANCIS BACON, Letter to Sir Robert Cecil (May 1606)

Sir Francis Bacon was married yesterday to his young wench in Maribone Chapel. He was clad from top to toe in purple, and hath made himself and his wife such store of fine raiments of cloth of silver and gold that it draws deep into her portion. The dinner was kept at his father-in-law Sir John Packington's lodging, over against the Savoy, where his chief guests were the three knights, Cope, Hicks, and Beeston; and upon this conceit (as he said himself), that since he could not have my Lord of Salisbury in person, which he wished, he would have him at least in his representative body.—SIR DUDLEY CARLETON, Letter (May 11, 1606)

Haile, happie Genius of this antient pile!
How comes it all things so about thee smile?
The fire, the wine, the men, and in the midst
Thou stand'st, as if some mystery thou did'st!
Pardon, I read it in thy face, the day
For whose returnes, and many, all these pray:
And so doe I. This is the sixtieth year,
Since Bacon, and thy Lord, was borne and here;
Son to the grave, wise Keeper of the Seale,
Fame and foundation of the English weale:
What then his father was, that since is he,

Now with a title more to the degree.
England's High Chancellor! the destined heire
In his soft cradle to his father's chair;
Whose even thred the Fates spinne round and full,
Out of their choycest and their whitest woole.
'Tis a brave cause of joy; let it be knowne,—
For 'twere a narrow gladnesse, kept thine owne.
Give me a deep-crowned bowle, that I may sing,
In raysing him, the wysdome of my King.
     —BEN JONSON, "Lord Bacons Birth-day," 1620

You found me of the Learned Counsel Extraordinary, without patent or fee—a kind of *individuum vagum*. You established me, and brought me into *Ordinary*. Soon after, you placed me *Solicitor*, where I served seven years. Then your majesty made me your *Attorney*, or *Procurator General*. Then *Privy Counselor*, while I was attorney—a kind of miracle of your favor that had not been in many ages. Thence *Keeper of your Seal*; and because that was a kind of planet and not fixed, *Chancellor*. And when your majesty could raise me no higher, it was your grace to illustrate me with beams of honor: first making me *Baron Verulam*, and now *Viscount St. Albans*. So this is the eighth rise or reach, a diapason in music, even a good number and accord for a close. And so I may without superstition be buried in St. Alban's habit or vestment.—FRANCIS BACON, Letter to King James I (1621)

The Chancellor being convicted of bribery, pretends, as if being weary of honour, he would resign his place, being much loaded with calumnies.—WILLIAM CAMDEN, *Annales Jacobi Regis*, 1603–23

There happened in my time one noble speaker, who was full of gravity in his speaking. His language (where he could spare or pass by a jest) was nobly censorious. No man ever spake more neatly, more pressly, more weightily, or suffered less emptiness, less idleness, in what he uttered. No member of his speech, but consisted of his own graces. His hearers could not cough, or look aside from him, without loss. He commanded where he spoke; and had his judges angry and pleased at his devotion. No man had their affections more in his power. The fear of every man that heard him was, lest he should make an end. . . . My conceit of his person was never increased toward him by his place, or honours: but I have and do reverence him, for the greatness that was only proper to himself, in that he seemed to me ever, by his work, one of the greatest men, and most worthy of admiration, that had been in many ages. In his adversity I ever prayed, that God would give him strength; for greatness he could not want. Neither could I condole in a word or syllabel for him, as knowing no accident could do harm to virtue, but rather help to make it manifest.—BEN JONSON, *Timber, or Discoveries*, 1641

His great spirit was brought low, and this humiliation might have raised him again, if his offences had not been so weighty as to keep him down. . . . He was a fit jewel to have beautified and adorned a flourishing kingdom, if his flaws had not disgraced the lustre that should have set him off.—ARTHUR WILSON, *The History of Great Britain; Being the Life and Reign of King James I*, 1653

None can character him to the life, save himself. He was in parts more than a man; who in any liberal profession might be whatsoever he would himself: a great honourer of ancient authors, yet a great deviser and practiser of new ways in learning: privy counsellor, as to king James, so to nature itself, diving into many of her abstruse mysteries. New conclusions he would dig out with mattocks of gold and silver; not caring what

his experience cost him, expending on the trials of nature all and more than he got by the trials at the bar; posterity being the better for his—though he the worse for his own—dear experiments. He and his servants had all in common; the men never wanting what their master had; and thus what came flowing in unto him was sent flying away from him, who, in giving of rewards, knew no bounds but the bottom of his own purse. Wherefore, when king James heard that he had given ten pounds to an under-keeper, by whom he had sent him a buck, the king said merrily, "I and he shall both die beggars;" which was condemnable prodigality in a subject. He lived many years after; and in his books will ever survive: in the reading whereof, modest men commend him in what they do—condemn themselves in what they do not—understand, as believing the fault in their own eyes, and not in the object.—THOMAS FULLER, *The Church History of Britain*, 1655

He was so excellent, so agreeable a speaker, that all who heard him were uneasy if he was interrupted, and sorry when he concluded. . . . Now this general knowledge he had in all things husbanded by his wit, and dignified by so majestical a carriage, he was known to own, struck such an awful reverence in those he questioned, that they durst not conceal the most intrinsic part of their mysteries from him, for fear of appearing ignorant or saucy: all of which rendered him no less necessary than admirable at the Council-table, where in reference to impositions, monopolies, &c., where the meanest manufactures were a usual argument; and, as I have heard, did in this baffle the Earl of Middlesex, that was born and bred a Citizen; yet without any great (if at all,) interrupting his other studies, as is not hard to be imagined of a quick apprehension, in which he was admirable.—FRANCIS OSBORNE, *Historical Memoires of the Reigns of Queen Elizabeth and King James*, 1658

Shortly after the king dissolved the Parliament, but never restored that matchless lord to his place, which made him then to wish the many years he had spent in state policy and law study had been solely devoted to true philosophy: for (said he) the one, at the best, doth but comprehend man's frailty in its greatest splendour; but the other the mysterious knowledge of all things created in the six days' work.—THOMAS BUSHELL, *Abridgment of the Lord Chancellor Bacon's Philosophical Theory in Mineral Prosecutions*, 1659

Sir Francis Bacon, knight, youngest son to Sir Nicholas Bacon, lord keeper, was born in York House, anno 1561; for, being demanded his age by Queen Elizabeth, he returned that he was two years younger than her majesty's reign. He was bred in Trinity College in Cambridge, and there first fell into a dislike of Aristotle's philosophy, as barren and jejune, enabling some to dispute, more to wrangle, few to find out truth, and none, if confining themselves to his principles.

Hence it was that afterwards he traded so largely in experiments; so that, as Socrates is said to be the first who stooped towering speculations into practical morality, Sir Francis was one of the first who reduced notional to real and scientifical philosophy.

He was afterwards bred in Gray's Inn in the study of our municipal law, attaining to great eminency, but no preferment therein, during the reign of Queen Elizabeth; imputable to the envy of a great person, who hindered his rising, for fear to be hindered by him if risen, and eclipsed in his own profession. Thus the strongest wing of merit cannot mount if a stronger weight of malice doth depress it. Yet was he even then favourite to a favourite, I mean the earl of Essex, and more true to him than the earl was to himself, for, finding him to prefer destructive before displeasing counsel, Sir Francis fairly forsook not his person (whom his pity attended to the grave) but practices; and herein was not the worse friend for being the better subject.

By King James he was made his solicitor, and afterwards his attorney (then privileged, contrary to custom, to sit a member *in Dom. Com.*) and at last lord chancellor of England. His abilities were a clear confutation of two vulgar errors, libels on learned men: first, that judgment, wit, fancy and memory cannot eminently be in conjunction in the same person; whereas our knight was a rich cabinet, filled with all four, besides a golden key to open it, elocution. Secondly, that he who is something in all, is nothing in any one art; whereas he was singular *in singulis*, and, being in-at-all, came off with credit.

Such who condemn him for pride, if in his place, with the fifth part of his parts, had been ten times prouder themselves. He had been a better master if he had been a worse, being too bountiful to his servants, and either too confident of their honesty, or too conniving at their falsehood. The story is told to his advantage, that he had two servants, one in all causes patron to the plaintiff, whom his charity presumed always injured, the other to the defendant, pitying him as compelled to law; but taking bribes of both, with this condition, to restore the money received if the cause went against them. Their lord, ignorant hereof, always did unpartial justice; whilst his men (making people pay for what was given them) by compact shared the money betwixt them, which cost their master the loss of his office.

Leading a private life, he much delighted to study in the shade of solitariness; and many useful discoveries in nature were made by him, so that he may be said to have left nothing to his executors, and all to his heirs, under which notion the learned of all ages may be beheld. His vast bounty to such who brought him presents from great persons occasioned his want afterwards, who, in rewarding them, so remembered that he had been lord chancellor, that he forgot that he was but the Lord Verulam.

He died, Anno Domini 1626, in the house of the earl of Arundel at Highgate, and was buried in Saint Michael's Church in Saint Alban's, Master Mutis his grateful servant erecting a monument for him. Since, I have read that his grave being occasionally opened, his skull (the relic of civil veneration) was by one King, a doctor of physic, made the object of scorn and contempt; but he who then derided the dead is since become the laughing-stock of the living.—THOMAS FULLER, *The Worthies of England*, 1662

Methinks in this one man I do at once find enough occasion to admire the strength of human wit, and to bewail the weakness of a mortal condition; for is it not wonderful, that he who had run through all the degrees of that profession which usually takes up men's whole time, who had studied, and practised, and governed the Common Law, who had always lived in the crowd, and borne the greatest burden of civil business, should yet find leisure enough for these retired studies, to excel all those men who separate themselves for this very purpose? He was a man of strong, clear, powerful, imagination; his genius was searching and invincible, and of this I need give no other proof than his style itself; which, as, for the most part, it describes men's minds as well as pictures do their bodies, so it did his above all men living; the course of it vigorous and majestic; the wit, bold and familiar; the comparisons, fetched out of the way, and yet the most easy; in all, expressing a soul equally skilled in men and nature.—THOMAS SPRAT, *History of the Royal Society of London*, 1667

Pity it was he was not entertained with some liberal salary, abstracted from all affairs, both of court and judicature, and

furnished with sufficiency both of means and helps for the going on of his design; which, had it been, he might have given us such a body of Natural Philosophy, and made it so subservient to the public good, that neither Aristotle nor Theophrastus amongst the Ancients nor Paracelsus, or the rest of our latest chymists, would have been considerable.—PETER HEYLYN, *Cyprianus Anglicus: or, the Life and Death of Archbishop Laud*, 1668

Who can forbear to observe and lament the weakness and infirmity of human nature? To see a man so far exalted above the common level of his fellow-creatures, to sink so far below it; to see a man who, like Seneca, gave admirable rules for the conduct of life, and condemned the avaricious pursuit after riches, and, what is unlike Seneca, condemning them in his own person, and yet be defiled thereby.—ROBERT STEPHENS, "Introduction" to *Letters of Lord Bacon*, 1702

I was infinitely pleased to find among the works of this extraordinary man a prayer of his own composing, which, for the elevation of thought, and greatness of expression, seems rather the devotion of an angel than a man. . . . In this prayer, at the same time that we find him prostrating himself before the great mercy seat, and humbled under afflictions which at that time lay heavy upon him, we see him supported by the sense of his integrity, his zeal, his devotion, and his love to mankind; which give him a much higher figure in the minds of thinking men, than that greatness had done from which he was fallen.—JOSEPH ADDISON, *The Tatler*, No. 267, Dec. 23, 1710

> If Parts allure thee, think how Bacon shined,
> The wisest, brightest, meanest of mankind!
> —ALEXANDER POPE, *An Essay on Man*, 1734,
> Epistle IV, v. 281–82

A man universally admired for the greatness of his genius, and beloved for the courteousness and humanity of his behaviour. He was the great ornament of his age and nation; and nought was wanting to render him the ornament of human nature itself, but that strength of mind which might check his intemperate desire of preferment, that could add nothing to his dignity, and might restrain his profuse inclination to expense, that could be requisite neither for his honour nor entertainment. His want of economy, and his indulgence to servants, had involved him in necessities; and, in order to supply his prodigality, he had been tempted to take bribes, by the title of presents, and that in a very open manner, from suitors in chancery. . . . The Lords insisted on a particular confession of all his corruptions. He acknowledged twenty-eight articles; and was sentenced to pay a fine of forty thousand pounds, to be imprisoned in the Tower during the King's pleasure, to be for ever incapable of any office, place, or employment, and never again to sit in Parliament, or come within the verge of the court. This dreadful sentence, dreadful to a man of nice sensibility to honour, he survived five years; and, being released in a little time from the Tower, his genius, yet unbroken, supported itself amidst involved circumstances and a depressed spirit, and shone out in literary productions, which have made his guilt or weaknesses be forgotten or overlooked by posterity.—DAVID HUME, *History of England*, 1754–62

Nature had designed him to rule a master spirit in the world of letters; but ambition led him to crouch at court in search of wealth and preferment. Neither did he fail in his object: industry and perseverance enabled him to overcome the jealousy of Elizabeth, the favouritism of James, and the intrigues of his competitors. He was not only in possession of the great seal; in addition to the rank of baron, he had recently obtained, as a new proof of the royal favour, the title of viscount St. Alban's. But, if he found the ascent to greatness slow and toilsome, his fall was sudden and instantaneous. . . . Of his guilt there was no doubt: but, had he submitted with patience to his fate, had he devoted to literary pursuits those intellectual powers which made him the prodigy of the age, he might have redeemed his character, and have conferred immortal benefits on mankind. He revised, indeed, his former works, he procured them to be translated into the Latin language, and he wrote a life of Henry VII.; but these were unwelcome tasks, suggested to him from authority, and performed with reluctance. He still looked back to the flesh pots of Egypt, the favours of the court; and in addition to the restoration to liberty, and the remission of his fine, boons which were granted, he solicited with unceasing importunity both a pension and employment. With this view he continued to harass the king, the prince, and the favourite, with letters; he pleaded his former services, he sought to move pity by prayers the most abject, and to win favour by flattery the most blasphemous. But his petitions were received with coldness, and treated with contempt; the repeated failure of his hopes soured his temper and impaired his health; and he died, the victim of mistaken and disappointed ambition, in the fifth year after his disgrace.—JOHN LINGARD, *History of England*, 1819–30, Vol. 9, pp. 183–85

A more pious mind never existed. There is scarcely a line of his works in which a deep, awful, religious feeling is not manifested. . . . He was of a temperament of the most delicate sensibility: so excitable, as to be affected by the slightest alterations in the atmosphere. It is probable that the temperament of genius may much depend upon such pressibility, and that to this cause the excellencies and failures of Bacon may frequently be traced. His health was always delicate. . . . The extent of his views was immense. He stood on a cliff, and surveyed the whole of nature. . . . His powers were varied and in great perfection. His senses were exquisitely acute. . . . His imagination was fruitful and vivid; but he understood its laws, and governed it with absolute sway. He used it as a philosopher. . . . He so mastered and subdued his mind as to counteract disinclination to study; and he prevented fatigue by stopping in due time: by a judicious intermission of studies, and by never plodding upon books; for, although he read incessantly, he winnowed quickly. . . . As a lawyer he looked with microscopic eye into its subtleties, and soon made great proficience in the science. He was active in the discharge of his professional duties: and published various works upon different parts of the law. . . . As a Judge, it has never been pretended that any decree made by him was ever reversed as unjust. . . . As a Statesman he was indefatigable in his public exertions. . . . His love of reform, his master passion, manifested itself both as a statesman and as a lawyer.—BASIL MONTAGU, "The Life of Francis Bacon," *Bacon's Complete Works*, 1834, Vol. 1

The moral qualities of Bacon were not of a high order. We do not say that he was a bad man. He was not inhuman or tyrannical. He bore with meekness his high civil honours, and the far higher honours gained by his intellect. He was very seldom, if ever, provoked into treating any person with malignity and insolence. No man more readily held up the left cheek to those who had smitten the right. No man was more expert at the soft answer which turneth away wrath. He was never accused of intemperance in his pleasures. His even temper, his flowing courtesy, the general respectability of his demeanour, made a favourable impression on those who saw him in situations which do not severally try the principles. His faults were—we write it with pain—coldness of heart and meanness of spirit. He seems to have been incapable of feeling strong affection, of facing great dangers, of making great sacrifices.—THOMAS BABINGTON MACAULAY, "Lord Bacon," *Edinburgh Review*, 1837

He idolized state and magnificence in his own person; the brilliancy of his robes and the blaze of his equipage his imagination seemed to feed on; he loved to be gazed on in the streets, and to be wondered at in the cabinet: but, with this feminine weakness, this philosopher was still so philosophic as to scorn the least prudential care of his fortune; so that, while he was enamoured of wealth, he could not bring himself down to the love of money. Participating in the corruptions of the age, he was himself incorruptible: the Lord Chancellor never gave a partial or unjust sentence; and Rushworth has told us, that not one of his decrees was ever reversed. Such a man was not made to crouch and to fawn, to breathe the infection of a corrupted court, to make himself the scapegoat in the mysterious darkness of court-intrigues; but he was this man of wretchedness!—ISAAC DISRAELI, "Bacon," *Amenities of Literature*, 1841

Bacon and Pascal appear to be men naturally very similar in their temper and powers of mind.)Bacon), born in York House, Strand, of courtly parents, educated in court atmosphere, and replying, almost as soon as he could speak, to the queen asking how old he was—"Two years younger than Your Majesty's happy reign!"—has the world's meanness and cunning engrafted into his intellect, and remains smooth, serene, unenthusiastic, and in some degree base, even with all his sincere devotion and universal wisdom; bearing, to the end of life, the likeness of a marble palace in the street of a great city, fairly furnished within, and bright in wall and battlement, yet noisome in places about the foundations.—JOHN RUSKIN, *Modern Painters*, 1843–60, Pt. 5, Ch. 20

There is in this Lord Keeper an appetite, not to say a ravenousness, for earthly promotion and the envy of surrounding flunkies, which seems to me excessive. Thou knowest him, O reader: he is that stupendous Bacon who discovered the new way of discovering truth,—as has been very copiously explained for the last half century,—and so made men of us all. Undoubtedly a most hot seething, fermenting piece of Life with liquorish viper eyes; made of the finest elements, a beautiful kind of man, if you will; but of the earth, earthy; a certain seething, ever-fermenting prurience which prodigally burns up things:—very beautiful, but very clayey and terrene every thing of them;—not a great soul, which he seemed so near being, ah no!—THOMAS CARLYLE, *Historical Sketches of Notable Persons and Events in the Reigns of James I and Charles I*, 1844–98

Among his good qualities it ought to be mentioned, that he had no mean jealousy of others, and he was always disposed to patronise merit. Feeling how long he himself had been unjustly depressed from unworthy motives, he never would inflict similar injustice on others, and he repeatedly cautions statesmen to guard against this propensity. "He that plots to be a figure among ciphers is the decay of a whole age." He retained through life his passion for planting and gardening, and, when Chancellor, he ornamented Lincoln's Inn Fields with walks and groves, and gave the first example of an umbrageous square in a great metropolis. . . . He was of a middling stature,—his limbs well formed, though not robust,—his forehead high, spacious, and open,—his eye lively and penetrating; there were deep lines of thinking in his face;—his smile was both intellectual and benevolent;—the marks of age were prematurely impressed upon him;—in advanced life, his whole appearance was venerably pleasing, so that a stranger was insensibly drawn to love before knowing how much reason there was to admire him. . . . Notwithstanding all the money he had received, duly and unduly,—such was his love of expense, and his neglect of his affairs, that upon his death his estate appears to have been found insolvent. All the six executors whom he named in his will refused to act, and on the 13th of July, 1627, administration with the will annexed was granted to Sir Thomas Meautys, and Sir Robert Rich, a Master in Chancery, as two of his creditors.—No funds were forthcoming for the foundation of his lecture-ships.—JOHN, LORD CAMPBELL, *Lives of the Lord Chancellors and Keepers of the Great Seal of England,* 1845–47, Vol. 2

No one lapse is known to have blurred the beauty of his youth. No rush of mad young blood ever drives him into brawls. To men of less temper and generosity than his own—to Devereux and Montjoy, to Percy and Vere, to Sackville and Bruce—he leaves the glory of Calais sands and Marylebone Park. If he be weak on the score of dress and pomp; if he dote like a young girl on flowers, on scents, on gay colors, on the trappings of a horse, the ins and outs of a garden, the furniture of a room; he neither drinks nor games, nor runs wild and loose in love. Armed with the most winning ways, the most glozing lip at court, he hurts no husband's peace, he drags no woman's name into the mire. He seeks no victories like those of Essex; he burns no shame like Raleigh into the cheek of one he loves. No Lady Rich, as in Sydney's immortal line, has cause

To blush when *he* is named.

When the passions fan out in most men, poetry flowers out in him. Old when a child, he seems to grow younger as he grows in years. Yet with all his wisdom he is not too wise to be a dreamer of dreams; for while busy with his books in Paris he gives ear to a ghostly intimation of his father's death. All his pores lie open to external nature. Birds and flowers delight his eye; his pulse beats quick at the sight of a fine horse, a ship in full sail, a soft sweep of country; everything holy, innocent, and gay acts on his spirits like wine on a strong man's blood. Joyous, helpful, swift to do good, slow to think evil, he leaves on every one who meets him a sense of friendliness, of peace and power.—WILLIAM HEPWORTH DIXON, *Personal History of Lord Bacon,* 1860–61, p. 14

Francis Bacon was endowed by nature with the richest gifts and most extraordinary powers. His mother was a learned woman in those days when learning for either sex implied a knowledge of the Greek and Latin classics. . . . His father was not only Lord Keeper of the Great Seal, but an eminent scholar and a patron of learning and art, who had the reputation of uniting in himself "the opposite characters of a witty and a weighty speaker." . . . An original thinker always; a curious explorer into every branch, and a master in nearly all parts, of human learning and knowledge; a brilliant essayist, an ingenious critic, a scientific inventor, a subtle, bold, and all-grasping philosopher; an accurate and profound legal writer, a leading orator and statesman, a counsellor of sovereigns and princes, a director in the affairs of nations, and, in spite of all faults, whether his own, or of his time, or of servants whose rise was his fall, "the justest Chancellor that had been in the five changes since Sir Nicholas Bacon's time."—NATHANIEL HOLMES, *The Authorship of Shakespeare,* pp. 110, 600

The meanness of Bacon, spoken of in the bitterest line of one of the bitterest poets, contrasts so strangely with the elevation of Bacon's genius, that even they who cannot get rid of the impression left upon their minds by his conduct to Essex remain perplexed by the apparent enigma. . . . That much of Bacon's advice seems, in itself, intrinsically mean, we do not for a moment deny; but what we feel very strongly is, that until we can place ourselves in the peculiar focus of his own familiar position, and of the personal relations of the great family of statesmen who then lived round the English throne, occupied by an able, crafty, and conceited—a vacillating and dangerous woman, whose word could and did decide the fate of any one or more of them, we cannot rightly judge the exact standard of Bacon's worldly wisdom.—BERNARD CRACROFT, *Essays, Political and Miscellaneous,* 1868

I am persuaded for my own part that, if he had died before Christmas 1620, his example and authority upon all questions of business, politics, administration, legislation, and morals, would have stood quite as high and been as much studied and quoted, and with quite as good reason, as it has upon questions purely intellectual. All his life he had been studying to know and to speak the truth; and I doubt whether there was ever any man whose evidence upon matters of fact may be more absolutely relied on, or who could more truly say with Kent, in *Lear,*—

> All my reports go with the modest truth;
> Nor more, nor clipp'd; but so.

. . . All the evidence shows that he was a very sensitive man, who felt acutely both kindness and unkindness, but that he was at the same time remarkably free from the ordinary defect of sensitive natures,—irritability and aptness to take offense. . . . Bacon's record is unusually full, and as his life presented to himself many doubtful problems for action, it has left to us many questionable actions for criticism; and among them not a few which he would not himself have repeated or attempted to justify. One thing, however, must be admitted to his advantage. Of the contemporaries whose opinion of him is known to us, those who saw him nearest in his private life give him the best character.—JAMES SPEDDING, *An Account of the Life and Times of Francis Bacon,* 1878, Vol. 2, pp. 521–654

He was anything rather than "mean." On the other hand, he was generous, open-hearted, affectionate, peculiarly sensitive to kindnesses, and equally forgetful of injuries. The epithet of "great," which has been so ungrudgingly accorded to him as a writer, might, without any singular impropriety, be applied to him also as a man. The story of his life, it must be confessed, is not altogether what the reader of his works would have desired, but the contrast has been so exaggerated as to amount to a serious and injurious misrepresentation.—THOMAS FOWLER, *Bacon,* 1881, p. 28

The vast intellect of "high-browed Verulam" commands our respectful admiration, but it is icy and ungenial; we cannot bring ourselves to love the man, however much we may venerate the writer.—HENRY J. NICOLL, *Landmarks of English Literature,* 1882, p. 94

If James had been capable of appreciating Bacon's genius, the name of the prophet of natural science might have come down to us as great in politics as it is in philosophy. The defects in his character would hardly have been known, or, if they had been known, they would have been lost in the greatness of his achievements.—SAMUEL RAWSON GARDINER, *History of England,* 1883, Vol. 1, p. 164

The life of Francis Bacon is one which it is a pain to write or to read. It is the life of a man endowed with as rare a combination of noble gifts as ever was bestowed on a human intellect; the life of one with whom the whole purpose of living and of every day's work was to do great things to enlighten and elevate his race, to enrich it with new powers, to lay up in store for all ages to come a source of blessings which should never fail or dry up; it was the life of a man who had high thoughts of the ends and methods of law and government, and with whom the general and public good was regarded as the standard by which the use of public power was to be measured; the life of a man who had struggled hard and successfully for the measure of prosperity and opulence which makes work easy and gives a man room and force for carrying out his purposes. All his life long his first and never-sleeping passion was the romantic and splendid ambition after knowledge, for the conquest of nature and for the service of man; gathering up in himself the spirit and longings and efforts of all discoverers and inventors of the arts, as they are symbolised in the mythical Prometheus. He rose to the highest place and honour; and yet that place and honour were but the fringe and adornment of all that made him great. It is difficult to imagine a grander and more magnificent career; and his name ranks among the few chosen examples of human achievement. And yet it was not only an unhappy life; it was a poor life. . . . When he is a lawyer, he seems only a lawyer. If he had not been the author of the *Instauratio*, his life would not have looked very different from that of any other of the shrewd and supple lawyers who hung on to the Tudor and Stuart Courts, and who unscrupulously pushed their way to preferment. . . . Both in his philosophical thinking, and in the feelings of his mind in the various accidents and occasions of life, Bacon was a religious man, with a serious and genuine religion. . . . It is not too much to say that in temper, in honesty, in labour, in humility, in reverence, he was the most perfect example that the world had yet seen of the student of nature, the enthusiast for knowledge. That such a man was tempted and fell, and suffered the Nemesis of his fall, is an instance of the awful truth embodied in the tragedy of *Faust*.— RICHARD WILLIAM CHURCH, *Bacon*, 1884, pp. 1–225

What a great failure Bacon was, whenever he was tried! Poor Essex, hunted to death merely for "getting up a row," and Bacon sacrificing him without compunction, and without seeing that he was probably made a tool of, merely to serve his personal advantage! Then the poetical justice, as they call it,— very prosaic justice,—of his own destruction, by a bolt out of a clear sky, which an enemy was adroit enough to direct to his ruin. And poor Bacon with conscience enough to feel that he deserved it, but not spirit enough to make a fight. No, if Pope's fling was undeserved, as you say, it was because of the mean and ignoble set around him. Almost as pitiable and tragic in its way, pitiable in its true sense, was the upshot of Bacon's higher and nobler life, conceiving vaguely and laboring all his days over that which he was unable and incompetent to bring to the birth. His memory reaping a great reward of fame for a century or so, and then the conclusion reluctantly reached that nothing tangible in the advancement of Natural Science can be attributed to him. Altogether, what a solemn sermon! It might be preached from the pulpit of St. Paul's.—ASA GRAY, *Letters*, 1884, Vol. 2, p. 749

Probably in consenting to contribute to the destruction of his friend ⟨Essex⟩, Bacon was acting under, what must have seemed to him, considerable pressure. If he had refused the task assigned to him by the Crown, he must have given up all chance of the Queen's favour and with it all hope of promo-

tion. Very inferior men have made as great, or greater, sacrifices; but Bacon was not the man to make such a sacrifice. . . . Bacon had a keen sense of the value of fortune, of the possibilities of a learned leisure, of the importance of his own colossal plans for the benefit of the human race; on the other hand he had a very dull sense of the claims of honour and friendship. Forced to choose between prosperity and friendship, he preferred to be prosperous even at the cost of facilitating the ruin of a friend for whom ruin, in any case, was ultimately inevitable. . . . One of the strongest helps that a man can have in the time of trouble seems to have been denied to Bacon. No record in any letter or document hitherto has attested that his wife sympathised with his pursuits, or shared any of his aspirations. Her name is scarcely mentioned in his voluminous correspondence, except in a letter indicating that her convenience, as well as his own, required that York House should be retained.—EDWIN ABBOTT ABBOTT, *Francis Bacon: An Account of His Life and Works*, 1885, pp. 81–82, 308

The great Lord Bacon, who has come down to us in Pope's epigrammatic judgment as "wisest, brightest, meanest of mankind," finds in Mr. Dixon a brilliant advocate against the charges of treachery to his patron, Essex, and receiving bribes as a judge. The sum of this defence seems to be that in Bacon's day all judges took bribes and all courtiers were ungrateful. This is equivalent to saying that Bacon was no worse than his contemporaries. The answer to this is that his contemporaries, at all events, seemed to think it wrong for a judge to take bribes, and punished Bacon for so doing. Therefore, Bacon was undeniably inferior in moral sense to his contemporaries. Indeed, he did not attempt to excuse the act except by saying that he never sold justice, that his judgments were always conscientious, although he might have received a present from one party to the suit. In respect to Essex, there can be no doubt that Bacon was disloyal to his benefactor. Bacon was a selfish man, a time-server, waiting on courts, and intent on his own fortunes. That posterity to whose judgment the great man committed his reputation has done his unparalleled genius full justice; but there are spots on the sun, and there are these distinct blemishes on Bacon's character.—IRVING BROWNE, *Iconoclasm and Whitewash*, 1885, p. 12

Bacon's conduct to Essex has been the subject of more vituperation than perhaps any other single act of any other single man. It has been denounced as mean and treacherous, dark, mournful, and shameful; it has been used to point half the morals and adorn half the tales against ingratitude for the last two centuries. Mr. Spedding has devoted a whole volume to this theme, and arranged the documents relating to the question in a manner which calls for a modification of the popular judgment similar if not equal to that achieved by Carlyle's commentary on the letters of Cromwell. In an age when a good courtier has come to be considered as the reverse of a good citizen, men will continue to wish that Bacon had acted differently; but he must be acquitted of anything like treachery.— JOHN NICOL, *Francis Bacon: His Life and Philosophy*, 1888, Pt. 1, p. 46

Here was a great mind—a wonderful intellect which everyone admired, and in which everyone of English birth, from Royalty down took—and ever will take—a national pride; but, withal, few of those amiabilities ever crop out in this great character which make men loved. He can see a poor priest culprit come to the rack without qualms; and could look stolidly on, as Essex, his special benefactor in his youth, walked to the scaffold; yet the misstatement of a truth, with respect to physics, or any matter about which truth or untruth was clearly demonstrable, affected him like a galvanic shock. His biographers, Montagu and Spedding, have padded his angularities into roundness; while Pope and Macaulay have lashed him in the grave. I think we must find the real man somewhere between them; if we credit him with a great straight-thinking, truth-seeking brain, and little or no capacity for affection, the riddle of his strange life will be more easily solved. . . . Indeed his protestations of undying friendship to all of high station, whom he addresses unctuously, are French in their amplitude, and French, too, in their vanities. He presses sharply always toward the great end of self-advancement—whether by flatteries, or cajolement, or direct entreaty. He believed in the survival of the fittest; and that the fittest should struggle to make the survival good—no matter what weak ones, or timid ones, or confiding ones, or emotional ones should go to the wall, or the bottom, in the struggle.—DONALD G. MITCHELL, *English Lands, Letters, and Kings: From Celt to Tudor*, 1889, pp. 250–53

The dispassionate mind that his philosophy required, Bacon applied somewhat too coldly to the philosophy of life. Without hatreds or warm affections, preferring always a kind course to an unkind one, but yielding easily to stubborn facts in his search for prosperity, Bacon . . . failed as a man, although he had no active evil in his character, for want of a few generous enthusiasms.—HENRY MORLEY, W. HALL GRIFFIN, *English Writers*, 1895, Vol. 11, p. 22

Bacon, with his brilliant intellectual equipment and his consciousness of his great powers, is not to be set down as simply a bad man. But his heart was cold, and he had no greatness of soul. He was absorbed, to a quite unworthy degree, in the pursuit of worldly prosperity. Always deeply in debt, he coveted above everything fine houses and gardens, massive plate, great revenues, and, as essential preliminaries, high offices and employments, titles and distinctions, which he might well have left to men of meaner worth. He passed half his life in the character of an office-seeker, met with one humiliating refusal after another, and returned humble thanks for the gracious denial. Once and once only, in his early days in Parliament, did he display some independence and rectitude; but when he saw that it gave offence in the highest places, he repented as bitterly as though he had been guilty of a sin against all political morality, and besought her Majesty's forgiveness in terms that might have befitted a detected thief.—GEORGE BRANDES, *William Shakespeare: A Critical Study*, 1898, Vol. 1, p. 309

General

Crown of all modern authors.—GEORGE SANDYS, "Notes" to *Ovid's Metamorphosis*, 1621–26

Lewis Elzevir wrote me lately from Amsterdam, that he was designed to begin shortly an edition in *quarto*, of all the works of Lord Bacon; and he desired my advice and any assistance I could give him; to the end that, as far as possible, these works might come abroad with advantage, which have been long received with the kindest eulogies, and with the most attested applause of the learned world.—ISAAC GRUTER, Letter to William Rawley (1652), *Baconiana*, ed. Tenison, 1679

Who knows not how Herbary had been improved by Theophrastus, Dioscorides, the Arabians, and other Peripatetics? who can deny that Physic, in every part of it, was improved by Galen and others, before the Lord Bacon ever sucked? and what accessionals had not Chemistry received by the cultiva-

tion of the Aristotelians, before his House of Solomon was dreamed of? Let us, therefore, not be concluded by the aphorisms of this Lord. Let his *insulse adherents* buy some salt, and make use of more than one grain when they read him; and let us believe better of the ancients, than that their methods of science were so unfruitful.—HENRY STUBBE, "Preface" to *Lord Bacon's Relation of the Sweating-Sickness Examined*, 1671, p. 5

A man who, for the greatness of genius, and compass of knowledge, did honour to his age and country; I could almost say to human nature itself. He possessed at once all these extraordinary talents which were divided amongst the greatest authors of antiquity. He had the sound, distinct, comprehensive knowledge of Aristotle, with all the beautiful lights, graces, and embellishments of Cicero. One does not know which to admire most in his writings, the strength of reason, force of style, or brightness of imagination.—JOSEPH ADDISON, *The Tatler*, No. 267, Dec. 23, 1710

Lord Bacon was the greatest genius that England (or perhaps any country) ever produced.—ALEXANDER POPE, *Spence's Anecdotes*, 1734–36, p. 128

Allowing as much sense to Sir Philip (Sidney) as his warmest admirers can demand for him, surely this country has produced many men of far greater abilities, who have by no means met with a proportionate share of applause. It were a vain parade to name them—take Lord Bacon alone, who I believe of all our writers, except Newton, is most known to foreigners, and to whom Sir Philip was a puny child in genius.—HORACE WALPOLE, Letter to David Hume (July 15, 1758), *Correspondence*, Vol. 40, ed. Lewis, p. 136

The great glory of literature in this island, during the reign of James, was Lord Bacon. . . . If we consider the variety of talents displayed by this man; as a public speaker, a man of business, a wit, a courtier, a companion, an author, a philosopher; he is justly the object of great admiration. If we consider him merely as an author and philosopher, the light in which we view him at present, though very estimable, he was yet inferior to his contemporary Galileo, perhaps even to Kepler. Bacon pointed out at a distance the road to true philosophy: Galileo both pointed it out to others, and made himself considerable advances in it. The Englishman was ignorant of geometry: the Florentine revived that science, excelled in it, and was the first that applied it, together with experiment, to natural philosophy. The former rejected, with the most positive disdain, the system of Copernicus; the latter fortified it with new proofs, derived both from reason and the senses. Bacon's style is stiff and rigid; his wit, though often brilliant, is also often unnatural and far-fetched; and he seems to be the original of those pointed smiles and long-spun allegories which so much distinguish the English authors; Galileo is a lively and agreeable, though somewhat a prolix writer. But Italy, not united in any single government, and perhaps satiated with that literary glory which it has possessed both in ancient and modern times, has too much neglected the renown which it has acquired by giving birth to so great a man. That national spirit which prevails among the English, and which forms their great happiness, is the cause why they bestow on all their eminent writers, and on Bacon among the rest, such praises and acclamations as may often appear partial and excessive.—DAVID HUME, *History of England*, 1754–62

Who is there, that, upon hearing this name, does not instantly recognise everything of genius the most profound, everything of literature the most extensive, everything of discovery the most penetrating, everything of observation on human life the most distinguishing and refined? All these must be instantly recognised, for they are all inseparably associated with the name of Lord Verulam.—EDMUND BURKE, "Speech on the Impeachment of Warren Hastings," May 28, 1794

If it be true that the compositions of Bacon are scarcely at all read in his native country, I could not devise a more effectual charm to revive a taste which ought never to have declined, than a just translation of the *Cogitata et visa.* When Hume denied this author the praise of eloquence, he must either have forgot that such a work issued from his pen; or that profound observations, clothed with enlarged sentiments and the images of a copious and exquisite fancy, will fully compensate the want of idiomatic purity, or a rhetorical structure of periods.— FRANCIS HORNER, *Journal, Memoirs and Correspondence,* 1801, Vol. 1, p. 168

That the composition of Lord Bacon, especially in his scientific works, was in general perspicuous, will not be denied; but that he reached the acme of our language, and exhibited the graces of Cicero, is surely hyperbolical praise.—NATHAN DRAKE, *Essays Illustrative of the Tatler, Spectator, and Guardian,* 1804, Vol. 2, p. 18

The vigour of his mind did not sink with his fall from power. For a while, indeed, it was broken and disturbed by the rock on which he had dashed; but soon his thoughts, bursting into a new channel, flowed onward with their accustomed, full, and majestic course.—GEORGE BURNETT, *Specimens of English Prose Writers,* 1807, Vol. 2, p. 344

It is scarcely possible to read a page of his works without seeing that the love of knowledge was his ruling passion; that his real happiness consisted in intellectual delight. How beautifully does he state this when enumerating the blessings attendant upon the pursuit and possession of knowledge.—BASIL MONTAGU, "The Life of Francis Bacon," *Bacon's Complete Works,* 1834, Vol. 1

That Shakespeare's appearance upon a soil so admirably prepared was neither marvellous nor accidental is evidenced even by the corresponding appearance of such a contemporary as Bacon. Scarcely can anything be said of Shakespeare's position generally with regard to mediæval poetry which does not also bear upon the position of the renovator Bacon with regard to mediæval philosophy. Neither knew nor mentioned the other, although Bacon was almost called upon to have done so in his remarks upon the theatre of his day. It may be presumed that Shakespeare liked Bacon but little, if he knew his writings and life, that he liked not his ostentation, which, without on the whole interfering with his modesty, recurred too often in many instances; that he liked not the fault-finding which his ill-health might have caused, nor the narrow-mindedness with which he pronounced the histrionic art to be infamous, although he allowed that the ancients regarded the drama as a school for virtue; nor the theoretic precepts of worldly wisdom which he gave forth; nor, lastly, the practical career which he lived. Before his mind, however, if he had fathomed it, he must have bent in reverence. For just as Shakespeare was an interpreter of the secrets of history and of human nature, Bacon was an interpreter of lifeless nature.—G. G. GERVINUS, *Shakespeare Commentaries,* 1849–62, tr. Bunnett, p. 884

No English writer has surpassed him in fervor and brilliancy of style, in force of expression, or in richness of magnificence of imagery. Keen in discovering analogies where no resemblance is apparent to common eyes, he has sometimes indulged, to

excess, in the exercise of this talent. But in general his comparisons are not less clear and apposite than full of imagination and meaning. He has treated of philosophy with all the splendor, yet none of the vagueness, of poetry. Sometimes, too, his style possesses a degree of conciseness very rarely to be found in the compositions of the Elizabethan age.—ABRAHAM MILLS, *The Literature and the Literary Men of Great Britain and Ireland,* 1851, Vol. 1, p. 388

If I were asked to describe Bacon as briefly as I could, I should say that he was the liberator of the hands of knowledge.— LEIGH HUNT, *Table Talk,* 1851, p. 84

I refer to him, because I fancy that many have a notion of his books on the Interpretation of Nature as very valuable for scientific men, and his books on Morals and Politics as very wise for statesmen and men of the world, but not as friends. They form this notion because they suppose, that the more we know of Bacon himself, the less sympathy we should have with him. I should be sorry to hold this opinion, because I owe him immense gratitude; and I could not cherish it if I thought of him, even as the sagest of book-makers and not as a human being. I should be sorry to hold it, because if I did not find in him a man who deserved reverence and love, I should not feel either the indignation or the sorrow which I desire to feel for his misdoings.—FREDERICK DENISON MAURICE, "On the Friendship of Books" (1856), *The Friendship of Books and Other Lectures,* 1874, ed. Hughes, p. 11

What is true of Shakespeare is true of Bacon. Bacon thought in parables. Of the astounding versatility of his thought, of the universality of its reach, the subtlety of its discrimination, the practical Machiavellian omniscience of motive good and evil, it is difficult by words to convey any adequate idea. But the plasticity of his thought is always the humble servant of his omnipresent imagination. His intellect is always at the mercy of his fancy for a clothing. All his intellectual facts are wrapt in visions of beautiful illustration.—BERNARD CRACROFT, *Essays, Political and Miscellaneous,* 1868, Vol. 2, p. 218

Except it be Milton's, there is not any prose fuller of grand poetic embodiments than Lord Bacon's.—GEORGE MACDONALD, *England's Antiphon,* 1868, p. 93

Of Bacon, more than of any other writer, it may be said that "in the very dust of his writings there is gold."—FREDERIC WILLIAM FARRAR, *Families of Speech,* 1869–73

Read a page of Macaulay, and you exhaust the thought at a single perusal. Read a page of Bacon twenty times, and at each reading you will discover new meanings, unobserved before. That haze which the naked eye could not penetrate is found by the telescope to be a nebula, composed of innumerable distinct stars. The one writer informs, the other stimulates, the mind. The one enlightens, the other inspires. The first communicates facts and opinions; the second floods and surcharges you with mental life.—WILLIAM MATHEWS, *Getting on in the World,* 1872, p. 245

Bacon's range of subjects was wide, and his command of words within that range as great as any man could have acquired. He took pains to keep his vocabulary rich. From some private notes that have been preserved, we see that he had a habit of jotting down and refreshing his memory with varieties of expression on all subjects that were likely to occur for discussion. He uses a great many more obsolete words than either Hooker or Sidney. To be sure, the language of the feelings and the language of theology have changed less than the language of science. But in his narrative and in his *Essays,* as well as in his scientific writings, Bacon shows a decided preference now and then for "inkhorn terms."—WILLIAM MINTO, *Manual of English Prose Literature*, 1872–80, p. 241

His utterances are not infrequently marked with a grandeur and solemnity of tone, a majesty of diction, which renders it impossible to forget, and difficult even to criticise them. . . . There is no author, unless it be Shakespeare, who is so easily remembered or so frequently quoted. . . . The terse and burning words, issuing, as it were, from the lips of an irresistible commander.—THOMAS FOWLER, *Francis Bacon*, 1881, p. 202

In the matter of diction he uses more obsolete words than either Hooker or Sidney, but he is immeasurably superior to them both in the perspicuity of his sentences which, though occasionally involved, as a rule allow us to see into his thoughts with great distinctness. The aphoristic style of his essays is worthy of all praise, and he may be considered the first English master of antithesis: it was perhaps his work in this direction which gave his peculiar bent to the literature of the early part of the 17th century.—C. R. L. FLETCHER, *The Development of English Prose Style*, 1881, p. 10

It is in Bacon's philosophy that the key to his political life is to be found. In its general conceptions, his statesmanship was admirable. The change which was to make religion thoughtful and tolerant, and the change which was to make England the home of peaceful industry and commercial activity, were ever present to his mind. He took no part in the wrangling disputations of contending theologians, and he turned a deaf ear to the interruptions of legal pedants.

No point of Bacon's political system has been so thoroughly discarded by later generations as that which deals with the relations between the Crown and the Houses of Parliament. Yet even here his mistake lay rather in the application of his principles than in the spirit by which they were animated. His hardest blows were directed against the error of which the French Constituent Assembly of 1789 has furnished the weightiest example; the error which regards the Executive Power and the Representative Body as capable, indeed, of treating with one another on a friendly footing, but as incapable of merging their distinct personalities in each other. It was thus that the Great Contract of 1610 was utterly distasteful to him. The King and the Lower House, he held, were not adverse parties to enter into bargains. They were members of the same commonwealth, each charged with its appropriate functions. It was not well that the King should redress grievances merely because he expected to receive something in return. It was not well that the Commons should vote supplies as the purchase-money of the redress of grievances. If the King wished to have obedient and liberal subjects, let him place himself at their head as one who knew how to lead them. Let the administration of justice be pure. Let the exercise of the prerogative be beneficent. Let Parliament be summoned frequently, to throw light upon the necessities of the country. If mutual confidence could be thus restored, everything would be gained.

In proclaiming this doctrine, Bacon showed that he had entered into the spirit of the future growth of the constitution as completely as he showed, in the *Novum Organum*, that he had entered into the spirit of the future growth of European science. That it is the business of the Government to rule, and that it is also the business of the Government to retain the confidence of the representatives of the people, are the principles which, taken together, distinguish the later English constitution from constitutions resting upon assemblies formed either after the model of the first French Empire or after the model of the Popular Assembly of Athens. Yet no man would have been more astonished than Bacon, if he had been told what changes would be required to realise the idea which he had so deeply at heart. Clinging to the old forms, he hoped against hope that James would yet win the confidence of the nation, and he shut his eyes to the defects in his character which rendered such a consummation impossible.

So far, indeed, is it from being true that the domestic policy of James must of necessity have been opposed to Bacon's views, that we have every reason to believe that in its main lines it was dictated, as far as it went, by Bacon himself. It was otherwise with James's foreign policy. For, though Bacon looked forward with hopefulness to the time when Europe should no longer be distracted by religious difficulties, he regarded Spain with the deepest distrust, and he cherished the belief that it was a national duty to prevent any further aggression of the Catholic Powers upon the Protestant States on the Continent. In this spirit he had prepared the draft of the proclamation which James had refused to use, and it was the expectation that this spirit would animate both King and Parliament which had raised his patriotic hopes more highly than they had been raised at any time since James had come to the throne.—SAMUEL RAWSON GARDINER, *History of England*, 1883, Vol. 3, pp. 396–98

Bacon was always much more careful of the value of aptness of a thought than of its appearing new and original. Of all great writers he least minds repeating himself, perhaps in the very same words; so that a simile, an illustration, a quotation pleases him, he returns to it—he is never tired of it; it obviously gives him satisfaction to introduce it again and again.—RICHARD WILLIAM CHURCH, *Bacon*, 1884, p. 29

Imagination is a compound of intellectual power and feeling. The intellectual power may be great, but if it is not accompanied with feeling, it will not minister to feeling; or it will minister to many feelings by turns, and to none in particular. As far as the intellectual power of a poet goes, few men have excelled Bacon. He had a mind stored with imagery, able to produce various and vivid illustrations of whatever thought came before him; but these illustrations touched no deep feeling; they were fresh, original, racy, fanciful, picturesque, a play of the head that never touched the heart. The man was by nature cold; he had not the emotional depth or compass of an average Englishman. Perhaps his strongest feeling of an enlarged or generous description was for human progress, but it did not rise to passion; there was no fervour, no fury in it. Compare him with Shelley on the same subject, and you will see the difference between meagreness and intensity of feeling. What intellect can be, without strong feeling, we have in Bacon; what intellect is, with strong feeling, we have in Shelley. The feeling gives the tone to the thoughts; sets the intellect at work to find language having its own intensity, to pile up lofty and impressive circumstances; and then we have the poet, the orator, the thoughts that breathe, and the words that burn. Bacon wrote on many impressive themes—on Truth, on Love, on Religion, on Death, and on the Virtues in detail; he was always original, illustrative, fanciful; if intellectual means and resources could make a man feel in these things, he would have felt deeply; yet he never did.—ALEXANDER BAIN, *Practical Essays*, 1884, p. 16

Bacon's style varied almost as much as his handwriting; but it was influenced more by the subject-matter than by youth or old age. Few men have shown equal versatility in adapting their language to the slightest shade of circumstance and purpose. His style depended upon whether he was addressing a king, or a great nobleman, or a philosopher, or a friend; whether he was composing a State paper, pleading in a State trial, magnifying the Prerogative, extolling Truth, discussing studies, exhorting a judge, sending a New Year's present, or sounding a trumpet to prepare the way for the Kingdom of Man over Nature. It is a mistake to suppose that Bacon was never florid till he grew old. On the contrary, in the early *Devices*, written during his connection with Essex, he uses a rich exuberant style and poetic rhythm; but he prefers the rhetorical question of appeal to the complex period. On the other hand, in all his formal philosophical works, even in the *Advancement of Learning*, published as early as 1605, he uses the graver periodic structure, though often illustrated with rich metaphor. . . . In his estimation, literary style was a snare quite as often as a help.—EDWIN ABBOTT ABBOTT, *Francis Bacon: An Account of His Life and Works*, 1885, pp. 447–53

In Bacon, as far as was possible in one man, the learning of the age met and mingled. All the Romance—*i.e.*, at that date all the literary—languages of Europe, were part of his province. In his pages all the classics—save Homer and the Greek dramatists—are rifled to enrich the "Globus Intellectualis." All the philosophies of the West and most of the little then known of science, come within his ken. His criticisms of history are generally sound, as are his references to the dicta and methods of previous authors, and his quotations, though somewhat overlaid, are always illuminating. He had no pretension to the minute scholarship of a Casaubon or a Scaliger; but his grasp of the Latin tongue was firm, and his use of it facile.—JOHN NICOL, *Francis Bacon: His Life and Philosophy*, 1888, Pt. 1, p. 18

The highest literary merit of Bacon's *Essays* is their combination of charm and of poetic prose with conciseness of expression and fulness of thought. But the oratorical and ideal manner in which, with his variety, he sometimes wrote, is best seen in his *New Atlantis*, that imaginary land in the unreachable seas.—STOPFORD A. BROOKE, *English Literature*, 1896, p. 109

⟨A⟩fter his fall, in May 1621, Bacon wakened afresh to the importance of his native language. In a poignant letter to the King, who was to "plough him up and sow him with anything," he promised a harvest of writings in the vernacular. In 1605 he had already made a splendid contribution to criticism in his *Advancement of Learning*; otherwise, he had mainly issued his works in Ciceronian Latin. But in 1621 he finished his *History of Henry VII.*; in 1624 he was writing the *New Atlantis*; in 1625 the *Essays* (first issued in nucleus in 1597, and meagrely enlarged in 1612) were published in full, and the *Sylva Sylvarum* was completed. These works, with his public and private letters, combine to form the English writings of Bacon. They constitute a noble mass of work, but there is no question that the reputation of Bacon dwindles if we are forced to cut away his Latin books; he no longer seems to have taken the whole world of knowledge into his province. And in his English works, considered alone, we have to confess a certain poverty. He who thought it the first distemper of learning, that men should study words and not matter, is now in the singular condition of having outlived his matter, or, at least, a great part of it, while his words are as vivid as ever. We could now wish that he could have been persuaded to "hunt more after choiceness of the phrase, and the round and clear composition of the sentence, and the sweet falling of the clauses," qualities which he had the temerity to profess to despise.

Bacon described himself as "a bell-ringer, who is up first to call others to church." The *Advancement of Learning* was

dictated by this enthusiasm. He would rise at cock-crowing to bid the whole world welcome to the intellectual feast. This is the first book in the English language which discusses the attitude of a mind seeking to consolidate and to arrange the stores of human knowledge. It was planned in two parts, the first to be a eulogy of the excellence of learning—its "proficience"—and the second to be a survey of the condition of the theme—its "advancement." Bacon had little leisure and less patience, and his zeal often outran his judgment in the act of composition. The *Advancement* is written, or finished at least, obviously in too great haste; the Second Book is sometimes almost slovenly, and the close of it leaves us nowhere. But the opening part, in which Bacon sums up first the discredits and then the dignity of learning, defending wisdom, and justifying it to its sons, remains one of the great performances of the seventeenth century. The matter of it is obsolete, human knowledge having progressed so far forwards and backwards since 1605; and something dry and unripe in Bacon's manner—which mellowed in later life—diminishes our pleasure in reading what is none the less a very noble work, and one intended to be the prologue to the author's vast edifice of philosophical inquiry. At this point, however, he unluckily determined to abandon English brick for Latin stone.

This futile disregard of his own language robs English literature of the greater part of its heritage in Bacon. He desired an immortality of readers, and fancied that to write in English would "play the bankrupt with books." Hence, even in his *Essays* we are conscious of a certain disdain. The man is not a serious composer so much as a collector of maxims and observations; he keeps his note-book and a pencil ever at his side, and jots down what occurs to him. If it should prove valuable, he will turn it out of this ragged and parochial English into the statelier and more lasting vehicle of Latin. He has no time to think about style; he will scribble for you a whole book of apophthegms in a morning. The *Essays* themselves—his "recreations," as he carelessly called them—are often mere notations or headings for chapters imperfectly enlarged, in many cases merely to receive the impressions of a Machiavellian ingenuity. They are almost all too short; the longest, those on "Friendship" and "Gardens," being really the only ones in which the author gives himself space to turn round. As a constructor of the essay considered as a department of literary art, Bacon is not to be named within hail of Montaigne.

Bacon desired that prose should be clear, masculine, and apt, and these adjectives may generally be applied to what he wrote with any care in English. He was so picturesque a genius, and so abounding in intellectual vitality, that he secured the graces without aiming at them. His *Essays* hold a certain perennial charm, artless as they are in arrangement and construction; but the student of literature will find greater instruction in examining the more sustained and uplifted paragraphs of the *Advancement*, where he can conveniently parallel Bacon with Hooker, the only earlier prose-writer who can be compared with him. He will observe with interest that the diction of Bacon is somewhat more archaic than that of Hooker.—EDMUND GOSSE, *A Short History of Modern English Literature*, 1897, pp. 130–32

The central figure in prose of the entire Jacobean period is undoubtedly Francis Bacon. He holds this position a little in spite of himself; for it was his own opinion, apparently deliberate and persistent, that English was an untrustworthy makeshift, likely to play tricks to any book written in it, and that the only secure medium for posterity was Latin. And he also holds it in spite of the fact that he had more than reached middle life at the date of the King's accession, and that his one contribution of unquestioned importance to English literature, as distinguished from English science and philosophy, was first published long before that time. For the really characteristic editions of the *Essays*—those which are not shorthand bundles of aphorisms, but works of prose art—date much later, and the whole complexion of Bacon's mind and of his matured style has the cast of Jacobean thought and manner. . . .

It is at once true of Bacon that no man has a more distinct style than he has, and that no man's style is more characteristic of its age than his. It has, indeed, been attempted to show that he had more than one style; but this does not come to much more than saying that he wrote on a considerable number of different subjects, and that, like a reasonable man, he varied his expression to suit them. Always when he is most himself—in the *Essays* as well as in the *Advancement of Learning*, in the *Henry VII.* as well as in any other English work—we come sooner or later on certain manners which are almost unmistakable, and which, though in part possessed in common with other men of the time, are in part quite idiosyncratic. All Jacobean authors, and Bacon among them, interlard their English with scraps of Latin, and constantly endeavour to play in their English context on the Latin uses of words. All aim first of all at what is called pregnancy, and attain that pregnancy by a free indulgence in conceit. Few, despite the stateliness which they affect, have any objection to those "jests and clinches" which even Jonson seems to have thought of as interfering with the "noble censoriousness" of Bacon himself. In all a certain desultoriness of detail, illustration, and the like—as if the writer had so full a mind and commonplace-book that he could not help emptying both almost at random—is combined with a pretty close faculty of argument, derived from the still prevailing familiarity with scholastic logic.

But Bacon, in addition to these characteristics, which he shares with others, has plenty of his own. His sentences, indeed, do not attain to that extraordinary music which is seen in some of Brooke and Donne, which is not wanting in Burton, which is the glory of Sir Thomas Browne, the saving grace of Milton's best prose, and the almost over-lavished and sometimes frittered away charm of Jeremy Taylor. He had begun, as we see in the earliest form of the *Essays*, with a very curt, stenographic, sharply antithetic form; and though he suppled and relaxed this afterwards, he never quite attained the full, languorous grace of Donne or Browne. But he became gorgeous enough later, the glitter of his antithesis being saved from any tinsel or "snip-snap" effect by the fulness of his thought, and his main purport being by degrees set off with elaborate paraphernalia of ornament and imagery. In the successive version of the *Essays* we see the almost skeleton forms of the earliest filling out, taking on trappings, acquiring flesh and colour and complexion in the later, while in some of the latest, the well-known ones on Building and on Gardens especially, the singular interest in all sorts of minute material facts which distinguishes him comes in with a curiously happy effect. Both the pieces just mentioned are much more like description of scenery in the most elaborate romance than like ideal suggestions for practical carrying out, drawn up by a grave lawyer, statesman, and philosopher.

No point in Bacon's literary manner is more characteristic, both of his age and of himself, than his tendency to figure. Such a sentence as this in the *Advancement*, "Nay, further, in general and in sum, certain it is that *Veritas* and *Bonitas* differ but as the seal and the print; for truth points goodness; and they be but the clouds of error which descend in the storms of passions and perturbations,"—would show itself to any person of experience as almost certainly written between 1580 and 1660 in the first place, while in the second it would at

least suggest itself to such a person as being most probably Bacon's. Although all the world in his day was searching for tropes and comparisons and conceits, the minds of few were so fertile as his; and it is not unworthy notice that even the apparently bold, even startling, change of metaphor from the "seal" to the "cloud" is in reality a much more legitimate change than it seems.

It will stand to reason that such a style is displayed to the best possible advantage by bold and richly-coloured surveys of science in general, like the *Advancement*, or by handlings of special points, like the *Essays*. Whether Bacon was really "deep," either in knowledge or in thought, has been disputed; but he was certainly one of the greatest rhetoricians, in the full and varied sense of rhetoric, that ever lived. His knowledge, deep or not, was very wide, ever ready to his hand for purposes more often perhaps of divagation than of penetration. His command of phrase was extraordinary. No one knows better than he either how to leave a single word to produce all its effect by using it in some slightly uncommon sense, and setting the wits at work to discern and adjust this; or how to unfold all manner of applications and connotations, to open all inlets of side-view and perspective. That he dazzles, amuses, half-delusively suggests, stimulates, provokes, lures on, much more than he proves, edifies, instructs, satisfies, is indeed perfectly true. But the one class of performances is at least as suitable for literary exhibition as the other, and Bacon goes through the exhibition with a gusto and an effect which can hardly be too much admired. Fertile in debate as almost all his qualities have proved, there is at least one of them about which there can be little difference of opinion, and that is his intense literary faculty. It was entirely devoted to and displayed in prose—he wrote very little verse, and that little is nothing out of the way. But in prose rhetoric—in the use, that is to say, of language to dazzle and persuade, not to convince—he has few rivals and no superiors in English. His matter is sometimes not very great, and almost always seems better than it is, but this very fact is the greatest glory of his manner.—GEORGE SAINTSBURY, *A Short History of English Literature*, 1898, pp. 369–73

In Bacon's sentences we may often find remarkable condensation of thought in few words. One does not have to search for two grains of wheat hid in two bushels of chaff. . . . His work abounds in illustrations, analogies, and striking imagery.—REUBEN POST HALLECK, *History of English Literature*, 1900, pp. 124–25

Works

ESSAYS

Sir Francis Bacon hath set out new Essays, where, in a chapter of *Deformity*, the world takes notice that he paints out his little cousin ⟨Robert Cecil, Earl of Salisbury⟩ to the life.—NICHOLAS CHAMBERLAIN, Letter to Sir Dudley Carleton (Dec. 17, 1621), *Court and Times of James I*, Vol. 1, ed. Birch, 1849, p. 214

The virtue of these *Essays* is too well allowed to require any comment. Without the elegance of Addison, or the charming egotism of Montaigne, they have acquired the widest circulation: and if Bacon had written no more, they would have bequeathed his name undying to posterity. Burke preferred them to the rest of his writings, and Dr. Johnson observed that "their excellence and value consists in their being the observations of a strong mind operating upon life, and, in consequence, you will find there what you seldom find in other books."—EDMUND MALONE, *Life of Sir Joshua Reynolds*, 1794

No book contains a greater fund of useful knowledge, or displays a more intimate acquaintance with human life and manners. The style, however, is not pleasing; it is devoid of melody and simplicity, and the sentences are too short and antithetic.—NATHAN DRAKE, *Essays Illustrative of the Tatler, Spectator, and Guardian,* 1804, Vol. 2, p. 20

The small volume to which he has given the title of *Essays,* the best known and the most popular of all his works. It is one of those where the superiority of his genius appears to the greatest advantage; the novelty and depth of his reflections often receiving a strong relief from the triteness of the subject. It may be read from beginning to end in a few hours; and yet after the twentieth perusal one seldom fails to remark in it something overlooked before. This, indeed, is a characteristic of all Bacon's writings, and is only to be accounted for by the inexhaustible aliment they furnish to our own thoughts, and the sympathetic activity they impart to our torpid faculties.—DUGALD STEWART, "First Preliminary Dissertation," *Encyclopaedia Britannica,* 1815–21

The *Essays,* which are ten in number, abound with condensed thought and practical wisdom, neatly, pressly, and weightily stated, and, like all his early works, are simple, without imagery. They are written in his favourite style of aphorisms, although each essay is apparently a continued work; and without that love of antithesis and false glitter to which truth and justness of thought is frequently sacrificed by the writers of maxims.—BASIL MONTAGU, "The Life of Francis Bacon," *Bacon's Complete Works,* 1834, Vol. 1

The transcendent strength of Bacon's mind is visible in the whole tenor of these *Essays,* unequal as they must be from the very nature of such compositions. They are deeper and more discriminating than any earlier, or almost any later, work in the English language, full of recondite observation, long matured and carefully sifted. . . . Few books are more quoted; and, what is not always the case with such books, we may add, that few are more generally read. In this respect they lead the van of our prose literature: for no gentleman is ashamed of owning that he has not read the Elizabethan writers: but it would be somewhat derogatory to a man of the slightest claim to polite letters, were he unacquainted with the *Essays* of Bacon. It is, indeed, little worth while to read this or any other book for reputation's sake; but very few in our language so well repay the pains, or afford more nourishment to the thoughts.—HENRY HALLAM, *Introduction to the Literature of Europe,* 1837–39, Pt. 3, Ch. 4, Par. 34

Bacon's *Essays* are the portrait of an ambitious and profound calculator,—a great man of the vulgar sort. Of the upper world of man's being they speak few and faint words.—RALPH WALDO EMERSON, "Milton" (1838), *Works,* Riverside ed., Vol. 12, p. 152

His English Essays and Treatises will be read and admired by the Anglo-Saxon race all over the world, to the most distant generations; while since the age which immediately succeeded his own, only a few recondite scholars have penetrated and relished the admirable good sense enveloped in his crabbed Latinity.—JOHN, LORD CAMPBELL, *Lives of the Lord Chancellors and Keepers of the Great Seal of England,* 1845–47, Vol. 2

There is scarcely a volume in the whole prose literature of England, which is, more emphatically, at once a product of the English intellect, and an agency in the history of English practical ethics. The style of the *Essays* is very attractive, though never pedantically exact, and often even negligent, in its observance of the rules of grammatical concord and regimen;

but though many Latinized words are introduced, even its solecisms are English, and it is, in all probability, a fair picture of the language used at that time by men of the highest culture, in the conversational discussion of questions of practical philosophy, or what the Germans call *world-wisdom.*—GEORGE P. MARSH, *The Origin and History of the English Language,* 1862, p. 549

Bacon's sentence bends beneath the weight of his thought, like a branch beneath the weight of its fruit. Bacon seems to have written his essays with Shakespeare's pen. . . . He writes like one on whom presses the weight of affairs; and he approaches a subject always on its serious side. He does not play with it fantastically. He lives amongst great ideas, as with great nobles, with whom he dare not be too familiar. In the tone of his mind there is ever something imperial. When he writes on building, he speaks of a palace with spacious entrances, and courts, and banqueting-halls; when he writes on gardens, he speaks of alleys and mounts, waste places and fountains, of a garden "which is indeed prince-like."—ALEXANDER SMITH, *Dreamthorp,* 1863, pp. 31–32

Stands confessedly at the head of all works of this class in English literature. It is in a sense properly taken as a model for all, and is one of the wisest and most thoughtful books for men of every condition and every age.—NOAH PORTER, *Books and Reading,* 1870, Ch. 19

The style of these brief essays, in which every sentence was compact with thought and polished in expression until it might run alone through the world as a maxim, had all the strength of euphuism and none of its weakness. The sentences were all such as it needed ingenuity to write; but this was the rare ingenuity of wisdom. Each essay, shrewdly discriminative, contained a succession of wise thoughts exactly worded.—HENRY MORLEY, *First Sketch of English Literature,* 1873, p. 465

His *Essays* are not at all sceptical, like the French essays, from which he may have borrowed this appellation: they are thoroughly dogmatic. . . . They are extremely instructive for the internal relations of English society. They show wide observation and calm wisdom, and, like his philosophical works, are a treasure for the English nation, whose views of life have been built upon them.—LEOPOLD VON RANKE, *A History of England,* 1875, Vol. 1, p. 459

In certain features they stand alone in this field of writing. There is nothing of the gay paradox of Montaigne, the sounding verbiage of Seneca, or the witty sophistry of Rochefoucauld. They express the "practical reason" of the English mind. Each sentence is beaten gold. One of his observations on men and manners is like a chalk outline by Michael Angelo. And as a model of English style, the *Essays* are unrivalled, although I think they have less of stately eloquence than the *Advancement of Learning.*—EMELYN W. WASHBURN, *Studies in Early English Literature,* 1884, p. 202

The literature of aphorism contains one English name of magnificent and immortal lustre—the name of Francis Bacon. Bacon's essays are the unique masterpiece in our literature of this oracular wisdom of life, applied to the scattered occasions of men's existence.—JOHN MORLEY, "Aphorisms" (1887), *Studies in Literature,* 1891, p. 73

Of this book Hallam said, that it "leads the van of our prose literature." In saying this, he did but formulate the impression of educated men in his day, but that was before the upper course of the stream had been adequately explored. As English prose it is indeed a very remarkable book, especially as it lets us see through the now prevailing and rampant Classicism to some select retreat where the true English tradition flourishes with its native vigour.—JOHN EARLE, *English Prose*, 1890, p. 442

This work secured for ever Bacon's fame as a writer of rare wisdom, who expressed his vigorous and original thought in a style marked by compressed fulness of meaning, calm strength, and the utmost felicity of diction. The book is a triumph of literary skill, a combination of almost perfect excellence of matter and form.—EDGAR SANDERSON, *History of England and the British Empire*, 1893, p. 511

Less than seventy years after the death of Bacon his *Essays* were so completely forgotten that when extracts from them were discovered in the common-place book of a deceased lady of quality, they were supposed to be her own, were published and praised by people as clever as Congreve, went through several editions, and were not detected until within the present century.—EDMUND GOSSE, "Tennyson—and After," *Questions at Issue*, 1894, p. 190

THE ADVANCEMENT OF LEARNING

Neither the most liberal of the professions, nor even the wider field of politics and legislation, could supply to the genius of Bacon a sufficient sphere of activity; and turning aside for a short space from the career of worldly ambition, in which he had many competitors, to that in which he marched unrivalled and alone, he completed and gave to the world in 1605 his immortal work on the *Advancement of Learning*. . . . The experience of ages has shown, that he who assumes the character of a reformer in the art of reasoning, an expositor of the errors of the schools, soars above the region of popular applause only to excite the alarms, or encounter the hostility, of the learned; whose pride, whose prejudices and whose interests he offends or threatens. Thus, whilst a few inquisitive and enlightened spirits, such as Jonson and Wotton and Raleigh, hailed with delight and saw awe the discoveries of their great contemporary, born to establish an era in the progress of the human mind, the erudite disciples of ancient error busied themselves in depreciating and decrying what they would not or could not understand.—LUCY AIKIN, *Memoirs of the Court of King James the First*, 1822, Vol. 1, pp. 193–95

The work is dedicated to King James the First, and its introduction inspires a mingled sentiment of admiration of the boldness and grandeur of the design which it announces, and of heartache at the depth of degradation to which it sinks in the servile adulation with which it besmears the king. . . . The stupendous magnitude of this undertaking, the courtly cunning, ingenuity, and meanness of suggesting it to the King as if it was an enterprise of his own, the lofty consciousness of its sublimity, and the sly implied disclaimer of it as anything more on the part of the author than a mere speculative whim to be moulded into form and substance, are all deserving of profound meditation—of more than I can give. He proceeds then to enumerate and to refute the objections against learning—of divines, of politicians, as arising from the fortunes, manners, or studies of learned men. He discusses the diseases of learning—the peccant humors which have not only given impediment to the proficiency of learning, but have given occasion to the traducement thereof. And he closes the book with a copious and cheering exhibition of the dignity of learning—a theme upon which I follow him with delight. The style is a continuous and perpetual citation of classical and scriptural quotations.—

JOHN QUINCY ADAMS, *Diary* (July 19, 1844), *Memoirs*, Vol. 12, ed. Adams, p. 72

Marked the first decisive appearance of the new philosophy. . . . He did not thoroughly understand the older philosophy which he attacked. His revolt from the waste of human intelligence which he conceived to be owing to the adoption of a false method of investigation blinded him to the real value of deduction as an instrument of discovery; and he was encouraged in his contempt for it as much by his own ignorance of mathematics as by the non-existence in his day of the great deductive sciences of physics and astronomy. Nor had he a more accurate prevision of the method of modern science.—JOHN RICHARD GREEN, *Short History of the English People*, 1874, Ch. 9

NOVUM ORGANUM

I have received three copies of that work, wherewith your Lordship hath done a great and everlasting benefit to all the children of Nature, and to Nature herself in her utmost extent and latitude, who never before had so true an Interpreter, or so inward a Secretary of her Cabinet.—SIR HENRY WOTTON, Letter to Bacon (1622), *Reliquiae Wottonianae*, 1651

He saw and taught his contemporaries and future ages, that reasoning is nothing worth, except as it is founded on facts. . . . Most valuable of all his works, and by him most highly valued. It is written in a plain unadorned style in aphorisms, invariably stated by him to be the proper style for philosophy, which, conscious of its own power, ought to go forth "naked and unarmed;" but, from the want of symmetry and ornament, from its abstruseness, from the novelty of its terms, and from the imperfect state in which it was published, it has, although the most valuable, hitherto been too much neglected; but it will not so continue. The time has arrived, or is fast approaching, when the pleasures of intellectual pursuit will have so deeply pervaded society, that they will, to a considerable extent, form the pleasures of our youth; and the lamentation in the "Advancement of Learning" will be diminished or pass away.—BASIL MONTAGU, "The Life of Francis Bacon," *Bacon's Complete Works*, 1834, Vol. 1

If Bacon constructed a method to which modern science owes its existence, we shall find its cultivators grateful for the gift, and offering the richest incense at the shrine of a benefactor whose generous labours conducted them to immortality. No such testimonies, however, are to be found. Nearly two hundred years have gone by, teeming with the richest fruits of human genius, and no grateful disciple has appeared to vindicate the rights of the alleged legislator of science. Even Newton, who was born and educated after the publication of the *Novum Organon*, never mentions the name of Bacon or his system; and the amiable and indefatigable Boyle treated him with the same disrespectful silence. When we are told, therefore, that Newton owed all his discoveries to the method of Bacon, nothing more can be meant than that he proceeded in that path of observation and experiment which had been so warmly recommended in the *Novum Organon*; but it ought to have been added, that the same method was practised by his predecessors; that Newton possessed no secret that was not used by Galileo and Copernicus; and that he would have enriched science with the same splendid discoveries if the name and the writings of Bacon had never been heard of.—SIR DAVID BREWSTER, *Memoirs of the Life, Writings, and Discoveries of Sir Isaac Newton*, 1855, Vol. 2, p. 402

There is no book which gives me such a sense of greatness; because the sayings are like keys which turn every way and *fit* whichever chamber of truth you want to turn into,—physical, mental, and moral science alike.—DORA GREENWELL, *Memoirs*, 1860, ed. Dorling, p. 47

Bacon the magnificent might be fit to lay down the chart of all knowledge; Bacon the despised seems fitter to guide patient and foot-sore pilgrims through tangled roads, amidst dangers arising from their own presumption, into a region of light. And this is, at last, the true glory of the *Novum Organum*.—FREDERICK DENISON MAURICE, *Moral and Metaphysical Philosophy*, 1862, Vol. 2, p. 233

In spite however of his inadequate appreciation either of the old philosophy or the new, the almost unanimous voice of later ages has attributed, and justly attributed, to the *Novum Organum* a decisive influence on the development of modern science.—JOHN RICHARD GREEN, *Short History of the English People*, 1874, Ch. 9

And now at last the *Novum Organum*, the fragmentary relic of that grand scheme for the restoration of the sciences which had floated before his youthful imagination in the days when he boasted that he had "taken all knowledge for his province," had passed through the press. For the reception with which it met, he cared but little: Coke might recommend him with a snarl to restore the justice and the laws of England before he meddled with the doctrines of the old philosophers; James might meet him with the silly jest that the book was like the peace of God, because it passed all understanding. It was for posterity that he worked, and for the judgment of posterity he was content to wait. . . . As a practical book addressed to practical men, it was as complete a failure as was the commercial policy of its writer. . . . That which gives to the author of the *Novum Organum* a place apart amongst "those who know," is, that being, as he was, far behind some of his contemporaries in scientific knowledge, and possessing scarcely any of the qualifications needed for scientific investigation, he was yet able, by a singular and intuitive prescience, to make the vision of the coming age his own, and not only to point out the course which would be taken by the stream even then springing into life, but to make his very errors and shortcomings replete with the highest spirit of that patient and toilsome progress from which he himself turned aside.—SAMUEL RAWSON GARDINER, *History of England*, 1883, Vol. 3, pp. 394–95

HISTORY OF HENRY VII

But this good Work was the most effectually undertaken and compleated by the Incomparable Sir Francis Bacon, who has bravely surmounted all those difficulties, and pass'd over those Rocks and Shallows, against which he took such Pains to caution other less experienc'd Historians. He has perfectly put himself into King Henry's own Garb and Livery, giving as sprightly a View of the Secrets of his Council, as if himself had been President in it. Not trivial Passages, such as are below the Notice of a Statesman, are mix'd with his Sage Remarks: Nor is any thing of Weight or Moment slubber'd over with that careless Hast and Indifferency which is too common in other Writers. No Allowances are given to the Author's own Conjecture or Invention; where a little Pains and Consideration will serve to set the Matter in its proper and true Light. No Impertinent Digressions, nor fanciful Comments, distract his Readers: But the whole is written in such a Grave and Uniform Style, as becomes both the Subject and the Artificer.—WILLIAM NICOLSON, *The English Historical Library*, 1696–1714

The only two pieces of history we have, in any respect to be compared with the ancient, are, the reign of Henry the Seventh by my lord Bacon, and the history of our civil wars in the last century by your noble ancestor my lord chancellor Clarendon.—HENRY ST. JOHN, VISCOUNT BOLINGBROKE, "Letter 6" (1735–38), *Letters on the Study and Use of History*, 1752

Sir Thomas More wrote the reign of Richard III with the inconsideration of a boy; Lord Bacon wrote an apology for a tyrant with as little regard for truth, as if nobody but a tyrant was ever to read it. The first weighed nothing he retailed; the second vended justice for wisdom, and was the more criminal of the two: for History only injures the individuals it blackens, but prejudices all mankind by palliating tyranny; and encourages it, by recommending it as policy.—HORACE WALPOLE, Letter to Robert Henry (March 28, 1783), *Correspondence*, ed. Lewis, 1951, Vol. 15, pp. 177–78

Bacon's *Henry the VIIth* betrays too much of the apologist for arbitrary power, but it is otherwise of great value; it is written from original, and now lost, materials, with vigour and philosophical acuteness.—NATHAN DRAKE, *Shakspeare and His Times*, 1817, Vol. 1, p. 476

Is in many ways a masterly work. With the true philosophic temper, he seeks, not content with a superficial narrative of events, to trace out and exhibit their causes and connections; and hence he approaches to the modern conception of history, as the record of the development of peoples, rather than of the actions of princes and other showy personages.—THOMAS ARNOLD, *Manual of English Literature*, 1862–67, p. 128

In one respect Bacon's History is in strong contrast to Macaulay's. In relating the schemes and actions of such a king as Henry, Macaulay would have overlaid the narrative with strong expressions of approval or disapproval. Bacon writes calmly, narrating facts and motives without any comment of a moral nature. Sometimes, indeed, he criticises, but it is from the point of view of a politician, not of a moralist; a piece of cruelty or perfidy is either censured only as being injudicious, or not commented upon at all. On this ground he is visited with a sonorous declamation by Sir James Mackintosh—as if his not improving the occasion were a sign that he approved of what had been done. Bacon wrote upon a principle that is beginning to be pretty widely accepted as regards personal histories claiming to be impartial—namely, that "it is the true office of history to represent the events themselves together with the counsels, and to leave the observations and conclusions thereupon to the liberty and faculty of every man's judgment." He does not seek to seal up historical facts from the useful office of "pointing a moral;" he only held that the moralising should not interfere with the narrative.—WILLIAM MINTO, *Manual of English Prose Literature*, 1872–80, p. 249

A work which, done under every advantage, would have been a rare specimen of skill, diligence, and spirit in the workman; but for which, begun as it was immediately after so tremendous an overthrow, and carried on in the middle of so many difficulties in the present and anxieties for the future, it would be hard to find a parallel. Though not one of his works which stand highest either in reputation or popularity with later times,—being neither generally read (an accident which it shares with most of the others) nor generally supposed to be of great value (in which it is more singular),—it has done its work more effectually perhaps than any of them. None of the histories which had been written before conveyed any idea either of the distinctive character of the man or the real business of his reign. Every history which has been written since has derived all its light from this, and followed its guidance in every question of importance; and the additional materials which come to light from time to time, and enable us to make many corrections in the history of the events, only serve to confirm and illustrate the truth of its interpretation of them.—JAMES SPEDDING, *An Account of the Life and Times of Francis Bacon*, 1878, Vol. 2, p. 542

The government of the first Tudor, though by no means one of the worst, was a government of usurpation. Its most efficient means of accomplishing its ends was the secret court of Star Chamber. This court kept no records, and was not responsible for its acts. Whatever was necessary for the firmer establishment of the new line was done probably without question and without scruple. Very little documentary evidence was left. But even what little existed in Bacon's time seems not to have been used by the historian. From the beginning to the end of his work, Bacon has given only one reference to an authority, and even that reference is so indefinite as almost to justify the suspicion that it was meant to mislead. The value of the history as a record of truth, therefore, rests solely upon the nature of the habits then prevailing in the investigation of knowledge, and on the character of the historian for veracity. Unfortunately, neither of these foundations is trustworthy. Bacon was not born till more than fifty years after the death of the king whose history he undertook to write. Three important and turbulent reigns had intervened. Bacon had every interest in giving to the facts, as he narrated them, a certain color. Unfortunately, we are debarred from believing that he would be overscrupulous in his searches after exact knowledge, even if exact knowledge were accessible. But it was not. It is therefore but simple truth to say that no court in any civilized community would accept of Bacon's testimony as a basis on which to build up any judicial decision whatever. Historical evidence, in order to be conclusive, must be of the same general nature as all other evidence. The conclusion to which we are brought is obvious. The book teaches us something of Bacon; it teaches us possibly something of the way in which Bacon regarded Henry VII.; it teaches us still more of the way in which Bacon desired his readers to regard his opinions of Henry VII.; but of Henry VII. himself, or of his reign, it teaches us very little indeed.—CHARLES KENDALL ADAMS, *A Manual of Historical Literature*, 1881–88, p. 8

Is a model of clear historical narration, not exactly picturesque, but never dull; and though not exactly erudite, yet by no means wanting in erudition, and exhibiting conclusions which, after two centuries and a half of record-grubbing, have not been seriously impugned or greatly altered by any modern historian. In this book, which was written late, Bacon had, of course, the advantage of his long previous training in the actual politics of a school not very greatly altered since the time he was describing, but this does not diminish the credit due to him for formal excellence.—GEORGE SAINTSBURY, *History of Elizabethan Literature*, 1887, p. 209

PHILOSOPHY

You formerly wrote me, that you knew persons who were willing to labour for the advancement of the sciences, at the cost of all sorts of observations and experiments: now, if any one who is inclined this way, could be prevailed upon to undertake a history of the appearances of the heavenly bodies, to be drawn up according to the Verulamian method, without the admixture of hypothesis; such a work as this would prove of great utility, and would save me a great deal of trouble in the prosecution of my inquiries.—RÉNÉ DESCARTES, Letter to Father Mersenne (c. 1650)

The entire logic of Lord Verulam is directed toward physics in itself, and therefore toward the truth, or genuine knowledge of things. Moreover, it consists principally in forming clear ideas since he desires foremost that all preconceived notions be wiped out, and then that new notions, or ideas inferred from new experiments properly conducted, be formed. Likewise, it consists in expressing ideas clearly, since he desires that we construct axioms from individual cases duly examined through experimentation, not by flying off the handle directly up to the highest, or most general, axioms, but by proceeding gradually in an orderly manner through intermediate steps. It consists also in making clear deductions, but only universal statements from individual cases since that is done by a legitimate induction, and not individual truths from universals, since that is done by means of the syllogism, which he does not approve of. However, since the sinew and muscle of all reasoning actually lies in the syllogism, and not even induction proves anything except by the force of a syllogism because of the general proposition clearly implied [in inductive reasoning] according to which it is claimed that everything which can be enumerated individually has been enumerated, or that not one thing can be found which does not agree with the statement, the syllogism seems to be condemned quite without reason inasmuch as he can be convicted of using it whenever he reasons at all, even though he condemns it. Accordingly, he does not seem to have rejected the syllogism totally but merely the syllogism which is founded on statements that have not been sufficiently examined and adequately confirmed; therefore, before he explains the form or uses of the syllogism, he may be expected to have estimated to what extent general propositions subject to no exceptions may exist. Meanwhile, however, just this treatise on the syllogism is lacking, and so is any general treatment of method, although he perhaps intended to furnish some such treatment when he spoke about the partition of the sciences. I shall not try to justify all those words that may be considered a trifle too affected since the founder of a new system seems to have the right to use new words or words in a new way.—PIERRE GASSENDI, *Syntagma*, 1658, tr. Brush

It is certain that Lord Bacon's way of experiment, as now prosecuted by sundry English gentlemen, affords more probabilities of glorious and profitable fruits, than the attempts of any other age or nation whatsoever.—GEORGE HAVERS, *Another Collection of Philosophical Conferences*, 1664

The Royal Society was a work well becoming the largeness of Bacon's wit to devise, and the greatness of Clarendon's prudence to establish.—THOMAS SPRAT, *History of the Royal Society of London*, 1667

> Bacon at last, a mighty man, arose, . . .
> And boldly undertook the injur'd pupil's cause.
> Bacon, like Moses, led us forth at last,
> The barren wilderness he pas'd;
>   Did on the very border stand
>   Of the bles'd promised land;
> And, from the mountain's top of his exalted wit,
>   Saw it himself, and shew'd us it.
>   —ABRAHAM COWLEY, "Ode to the Royal
>   Society," c. 1667

When our renowned Lord Bacon had demonstrated the methods for a perfect restoration of all parts of real knowledge, the success became on a sudden stupendous, and effective philosophy began to sparkle, and even to flow into beams of bright shining light all over the world.—HENRY OLDENBURG, "Preface" to *Philosophical Transactions of the Royal Society*, 1672

Though there was bred in Mr. Bacon so early a dislike of the Physiology of Aristotle, yet he did not despise him with that pride and haughtiness with which youth is wont to be puffed up. He has a just esteem of that great master of learning, greater than that which Aristotle expressed himself towards the philosophers that went before him; for he endeavoured (some say) to stifle all their labours, designing to himself an universal monarchy over opinions, as his patron Alexander did over men. Our hero owned what was excellent in him, but in his inquiries into nature he proceeded not upon his principles. He began the work anew, and laid the foundation of philosophic theory in numerous experiments.—THOMAS TENISON, *Baconiana*, 1679

The late most wise Chancellor of England was the chief writer of our age, and carried as it were the standard that we might press forward, and make greater discoveries in Philosophic matters, than any of which hitherto our schools had rung. So that if in our time any great improvements have been made in Philosophy, there has been not a little owing to that great man.—SAMUEL PUFENDORF, *Spicilegium Controversiarum*, 1680

It was owing to the sagacity and freedom of Lord Bacon that men were then pretty well enabled both to make discoveries and to remove the impediments that had hitherto kept physics from being useful.—ROBERT BOYLE, *New Experiments and Observations Touching Cold*, 1683

By standing up against the Dogmatists, he emancipated and set free philosophy, which had long been a miserable captive, and which hath ever since made conquest in the territories of Nature.—JOHN EVELYN, *Numismata*, 1697

While poorly instructed or badly intentioned adversaries made open war on it, philosophy sought refuge, so to speak, in the works of a few great men. They had not the dangerous ambition of removing the blindfolds from their contemporaries' eyes; yet silently in the shadows they prepared from afar the light which gradually, by imperceptible degrees, would illuminate the world.

The immortal Chancellor of England, Francis Bacon, ought to be placed at the head of these illustrious personages. His works, so justly esteemed (and more esteemed, indeed, than they are known), merit our reading even more than our praises. One would be tempted to regard him as the greatest, the most universal, and the most eloquent of the philosophers, considering his sound and broad views, the multitude of objects to which his mind turned itself, and the boldness of his style, which everywhere joined the most sublime images with the most rigorous precision. Born in the depths of the most profound night, Bacon was aware that philosophy did not yet exist, although many men doubtless flattered themselves that they excelled in it (for the cruder a century is, the more it believes itself to be educated in all that can be known). Therefore, he began by considering generally the various objects of all the natural sciences. He divided these sciences into different branches, of which he made the most exact enumeration that was possible for him. He examined what was already known concerning each of these objects and made the immense catalogue of what remained to be discovered. This is the aim of his admirable book *The Advancement of Learning*. In his *Novum Organum*, he perfects the views that he had presented in the first book, carries them further, and makes known the necessity of experimental physics, of which no one was yet aware. Hostile to systems, he conceives of philosophy as being only that part of our knowledge which should contribute to making us better or happier, thus apparently confining it within the limits of the science of useful things, and everywhere he recommends the study of Nature. His other writings were produced on the

same pattern. Everything, even their titles, proclaims the man of genius, the mind that sees things in the large view. He collects facts, he compares experiments and points out a large number to be made; he invites scholars to study and perfect the arts, which he regards as the most exalted and most essential part of human science; he sets forth with a noble simplicity his *Conjectures and Thoughts* on the different objects worthy of men's interest; and he would have been able to say, like that old man in Terence, that nothing which touches humanity was alien to him. Natural science, ethics, politics, economics, all seem to have been within the competence of that brilliant and profound mind. And we do not know which we ought to admire more, the riches he lavishes upon all the subjects he treats or the dignity with which he speaks of them. His writings can best be compared to those of Hippocrates on medicine; and they would be no less admired, nor less read, if the culture of the mind were as dear to mankind as the conservation of health. But in every area only the works of those who head a school of disciples make a brilliant impression. Bacon was not of that number, and the form of his philosophy prevented it; it was too wise to astonish anyone. Scholasticism, which continued to dominate, could not be overthrown except by bold and new opinions. And apparently circumstances are not such that a philosopher who is content to say to men: "Here is the little that you have learned, there is what remains for you to find," is destined to cause much stir among his contemporaries. If we did not know with what discretion, and with what superstition almost, one ought to judge a genius so sublime, we might even dare reproach Chancellor Bacon for having perhaps been too timid. He asserted that the scholastics had enervated science by their petty questions, and that the mind ought to sacrifice the study of general beings for that of individual objects; nonetheless, he seems to have shown a little too much caution or deference to the dominant taste of his century in his frequent use of the terms of the scholastics, sometimes even of scholastic principles, and in the use of divisions and subdivisions, fashionable in his time. After having burst so many irons, this great man was still held by certain chains which he could not, or dared not, break.—JEAN LE ROND D'ALEMBERT, *Preliminary Discourse to the Encyclopedia*, 1751, trs. Schwab, Rex

It has been frequently the subject of inquiry among philosophers, whether there be a first principle of human knowledge: some have supposed but one, some two, others more. Every man, I think, may by his own experience be sure of the truth of that principle on which this work is founded. Perhaps we shall even be convinced that the connexion of ideas is without comparison the simplest, the clearest, and even the most fruitful principle. At the very time when its influence was not observed, we were indebted to it for every improvement made by the human understanding.

Such were the reflexions I had made on method when I began to read my lord Bacon's works. I was afterwards as much pleased that my notions happened to coincide with this great man's on some particular points, as I was surprized that the Cartesians had borrowed nothing from him. No man was better acquainted with the cause of human error: for he perceived that there was an original defect in the framing of those ideas which are the workmanship of the mind; and consequently that to advance in the investigation of truth, new combinations are requisite. This is an advice he often repeats. But how was it possible for him to be heard? The public were so strongly prejudiced in favour of the school jargon, and of innate ideas, that they treated the regeneration of the human understanding as a chimerical project. The method proposed by his lordship was too perfect to produce a revolution; that of Descartes, by letting some errors continue, was sure of success. Farther, the English philosopher had such weighty employments as hindered him from putting his own theory in practice; consequently he was obliged to be satisfied with giving advice, which must have made but a slight impression on superficial minds. Descartes, on the contrary, delivered himself up intirely to philosophic studies, and having a more lively and more fruitful imagination, in the room of former errors he sometimes introduced others of a more imposing nature, which contributed not a little to his reputation.—ETIENNE BONNOT DE CONDILLAC, *An Essay on the Origin of Human Knowledge*, 1756, tr. Nugent, Pt. 2, Sec. 2, Ch. 3

Never did two men, gifted with such genius, recommend paths of inquiry so widely different. Descartes aspired to deduce an explanation of the whole system of things by reasoning *a priori* upon assumed principles: Bacon, on the contrary, held that it was necessary to observe Nature thoroughly before attempting to explain her ways; that we must ascend to principles through the medium of facts; and that our conclusions must be warranted by what we observe. Descartes reasoned about the World, as if the laws which govern it had not yet been established, as if every thing were still to create. Bacon considered it as a vast edifice, which it was necessary to view in all directions, to explore through all its recesses and windings, before any conjecture even could be safely formed as to the principles of its construction, or the foundations on which it rests. Thus, the philosophy of Bacon, by recommending the careful observation of Nature, still continues to be followed, whilst that of Descartes, whose essence lay in hypothesis, has wholly disappeared.—JEAN SYLVAIN BAILLY, *Histoire de l'Astronomie Moderne*, 1775–85, Vol. 2, Bk. 4

The influence of Bacon's genius on the subsequent progress of physical discovery, has been seldom duly appreciated; by some writers almost entirely overlooked, and by others considered as the sole cause of the reformation in science which has since taken place. Of these two extremes, the latter certainly is the least wide of the truth; for, in the whole history of letters, no other individual can be mentioned, whose exertions have had so indisputable an effect in forwarding the intellectual progress of mankind. On the other hand, it must be acknowledged, that before the era when Bacon appeared, various philosophers in different parts of Europe had struck into the right path; and it may perhaps be doubted, whether any one important rule with respect to the true method of investigation be contained in his works, of which no hint can be traced in those of his predecessors. His great merit lay in concentrating their feeble and scattered lights; fixing the attention of philosophers on the distinguishing characteristics of true and of false science, by a felicity of illustration peculiar to himself, seconded by the commanding powers of a bold and figurative eloquence.—DUGALD STEWART, *Account of the Life and Writings of Thomas Reid*, 1802–3, Sec. 2

This mighty genius ranks as the father of modern physics, inasmuch as he brought back the spirit of investigation from the barren verbal subtleties of the schools to nature and experience: he made and completed many important discoveries himself, and seems to have had a dim and imperfect foresight of many others. Stimulated by his capacious and stirring intellect, experimental science extended her boundaries in every direction: intellectual culture, nay, the social organization of modern Europe generally, assumed a new shape and complexion.—FREDERICK SCHLEGEL, *Lectures on the History of Literature*, 1815, p. 286

Bacon's grand distinction, considered as an improver of physics, lies in this, that he was the first who clearly and fully pointed out the rules and safeguards of right reasoning in physical inquiries. Many other philosophers, both ancient and modern, had referred to observation and experiment in a cursory way, as furnishing the materials of physical knowledge; but no one, before him, had attempted to systematize the true method of discovery; or to prove that the *inductive*, is the *only* method by which the genuine office of philosophy can be exercised, and its genuine ends accomplished. It has sometimes been stated, that Galileo was, at least in an equal degree with Bacon, the father of the Inductive Logic; but it would be more correct to say, that his discoveries furnished some fortunate illustrations of its principles. To explain these principles was no object of his; nor does he manifest any great anxiety to recommend their adoption, with a view to the general improvement of science.—MACVEY NAPIER, "Lord Bacon" (1818), *Lord Bacon and Sir Walter Raleigh*, 1853, p. 14

The opinion so prevalent during the last thirty years, that Lord Bacon introduced the art of experimental inquiry on physical subjects, and that he devised and published a method of discovering scientific truth, called the method of induction, appears to me to be without foundation, and perfectly inconsistent with the history of science. This heresy, which I consider as most injurious to the progress of scientific inquiry, seems to have been first propagated by d'Alembert, and afterwards fostered in our University by Mr. Stewart and Mr. Playfair, three men of great talent, but not one of whom ever made a single discovery in physics. . . . It has been said, however, by the admirers of Bacon, that though a few philosophers knew the secret of making advances in science, yet the great body were ignorant of it, and that Paracelsus, Van Helmont, and many others, were guided in their inquiries by very inferior methods. . . . It seems quite clear that Bacon, who knew nothing either of Mathematics or Physics, conceived the ambitious design of establishing a general method of scientific inquiry. This method, which he has explained at great length, is neither more nor less than a crusade against Aristotle, with the words *experiment and observation* emblazoned on his banner. . . . The method given by Bacon is, independent of all this, quite useless, and in point of fact has never been used in any successful inquiry. A collection of facts, however skilfully they may be conjured with, can never yield general laws unless they contain that master-fact in which the discovery resides, or upon which the law mainly depends.—SIR DAVID BREWSTER, Letter (April 26, 1824), *The Home Life of Sir David Brewster*, by Margaret Brewster, 1869, pp. 128–30

It is no proof of a solid acquaintance with Lord Bacon's philosophy, to deify his name as the ancient schools did those of their founders, or even to exaggerate the powers of his genius. Powers they were surprisingly great, yet limited in their range, and not in all respects equal; nor could they overcome every impediment of circumstance. Even of Bacon it may be said, that he attempted more than he has achieved, and perhaps more than he clearly apprehended. His objects appear sometimes indistinct, and I am not sure that they are always consistent. In the *Advancement of Learning*, he aspired to fill up, or at least to indicate, the deficiencies in every department of knowledge: he gradually confined himself to philosophy, and at length to physics. But few of his works can be deemed complete, not even the treatise *De Augmentis*, which comes nearer to this than most of the rest. Hence the study of Lord Bacon is difficult, and not, as I conceive, very well adapted to those who have made no progress whatever in the exact sciences, nor accustomed themselves to independent thinking.—HENRY HALLAM, *Introduction to the Literature of Europe*, 1837–39

It was as a philosopher that Bacon conquered immortality, and here he stands superior to all who went before and to all who have followed him. If he be not entitled to a place in the interior of the splendid temple which he imagined for those who, by inventing arts, have embellished life, his statue ought to appear in the more honourable position of the portico, as the great master who has taught how arts are to be invented . . . He accomplished more for the real advancement of knowledge than any of those who spent their lives in calm meditation under sequestered porticos or amidst academic groves.—JOHN, LORD CAMPBELL, *Lives of the Lord Chancellors and Keepers of the Great Seal of England*, 1845–47, Vol. 2

Bacon has been likened to the prophet who from Mount Pisgah surveyed the Promised Land, but left it for others to take possession of. Of this happy image perhaps part of the felicity was not perceived by its author. For though Pisgah was a place of large prospect, yet still the Promised Land was a land of definite extent and known boundaries, and moreover it was certain that after no long time the chosen people would be in possession of it all. And this agrees with what Bacon promised to himself and to mankind from the instauration of the sciences. . . . In this respect, then, as in others, the hopes of Francis Bacon were not destined to be fulfilled. It is neither to the technical part of his method nor to the details of his view of the nature and progress of science that his great fame is justly owing. His merits are of another kind. They belong to the spirit rather than to the positive precepts of his philosophy.—ROBERT LESLIE ELLIS, "General Preface" to *Bacon's Philosophical Works*, 1857, Vol. 1, pp. 63–64

With the audacity of ignorance, he presumed to criticise what he did not understand, and, with a superb conceit, disparaged the great Copernicus. . . . The more closely we examine the writings of Lord Bacon, the more unworthy does he seem to have been of the great reputation which has been awarded to him. The popular delusion to which he owes so much originated at a time when the history of science was unknown. They who first brought him into notice knew nothing of the old school of Alexandria. This boasted founder of a new philosophy could not comprehend, and would not accept, the greatest of all scientific doctrines when it was plainly set before his eyes. It has been represented that the invention of the true method of physical science was an amusement of Bacon's hours of relaxation from the more laborious studies of law and duties of a court. His chief admirers have been persons of a literary turn, who have an idea that scientific discoveries are accomplished by a mechanico-mental operation. Bacon never produced any great practical results himself, no great physicist has ever made any use of his method. He has had the same to do with the development of modern science that the inventor of the orrery has had to do with the discovery of the mechanism of the world. . . . No man can invent an organon for writing tragedies and epic poems. . . . Few scientific pretenders have made more mistakes than Lord Bacon. He rejected the Copernican system, and spoke insolently of its great author; he undertook to criticise adversely Gilbert's treatise *De Magnete*; he was occupied in the condemnation of any investigation of final causes, while Harvey was deducing the circulation of the blood from Aquapendente's discovery of the valves in the veins; he was doubtful whether instruments were of any advantage, while Galileo was investigating the heavens with the telescope. Ignorant himself of every branch of mathematics, he presumed

that they were useless in science, but a few years before Newton achieved by their aid his immortal discoveries. It is time that the sacred name of philosophy should be severed from its long connexion with that of one who was a pretender in science, a time-serving politician, an insidious lawyer, a corrupt judge, a treacherous friend, a bad man.—JOHN WILLIAM DRAPER, *History of the Intellectual Development of Europe*, 1863–76, Vol. 2, pp. 258–60

The actual and undeniable facts that when compared with the writings of the Italian natural philosophers those of Bacon breathe more of the modern spirit, and yet that he ignores the discoveries which have proved themselves to be most fruitful for subsequent times, and even their originators (Copernicus, Galileo, Gilbert, Harvey, and others), or at least is less able to appreciate them than the former,—that, further, in spite of his praise of natural science he has exerted on its development no influence worthy of the name—(facts which in recent times have led to such different verdicts on Bacon), can only be harmonised (but then easily harmonised) when we do not attribute to Bacon the position of the initiator of modern philosophy, but see in him the close of the philosophy of the Middle Ages. He has left behind him the standpoint from which natural science subjected itself to dogma and in which she contended against it. Therefore he stands higher and nearer to modern times. But this advance refers only to the relation of the doctrines of natural science to religion and the Church. . . . Measured by the standard of the Middle Ages Bacon appears modern, by that of modern times he appears mediæval. But to say this implies that his merit is no small one.—JOHANN EDWARD ERDMANN, *A History of Philosophy*, 1865–76, Vol. 1, tr. Hough, pp. 682–83

He certainly never made utility the sole object of science, or at least never restricted utility to material advantages. He asserted in the noblest language the superiority of abstract truth to all the fruits of invention, and would never have called those speculations useless which form the intellectual character of an age. Yet, on the other hand, it must be acknowledged that the general tone of his writings, the extraordinary emphasis which he laid upon the value of experiments, and above all upon the bearing of his philosophy on material comforts, represents a tendency which was very naturally developed into the narrowest utilitarianism.—W. E. H. LECKY, *Spirit of Rationalism in Europe*, 1865, Vol. 1, Ch. 4., Pt. 1

Bacon of Verulam stripped off from natural philosophy the theosophical character which it bore during the Transitional Period, and limited it in its method to experiment and induction. The fundamental traits of this method he made a part of the philosophic consciousness of mankind, as emancipated in its investigations from the restriction to any particular department of natural science. He thus became the founder—not, indeed, of the empirical method of natural investigation, but—of the empirical line of modern philosophers.—FRIEDRICH ÜBERWEG, *A History of Philosophy*, 1871–73, Vol. 2, tr. Morris, p. 33

The whole endeavor of Bacon in science is to attain the fact, and to ascend from particular facts to general. He turned away with utter dissatisfaction from the speculating *in vacuo* of the Middle Ages. His intellect demanded positive knowledge; he could not feed upon the wind. From the tradition of philosophy and from authority he reverted to nature. Between faith and reason Bacon set a great and impassable gulf. Theology is something too high for human intellect to discuss. Bacon is profoundly deferential to theology, because, as one cannot help suspecting, he was profoundly indifferent about it. The school-men for the service of faith had summoned human reason to their aid, and Reason, the ally, had in time proved a dangerous antagonist. Bacon, in the interest of science, dismissed faith to the unexceptionable province of supernatural truths. To him a dogma of theology was equally credible whether it possessed an appearance of reasonableness or appeared absurd. The total force of intellect he reserved for subjugating to the understanding the world of positive fact.—EDWARD DOWDEN, *Shakespere: A Critical Study of His Mind and Art*, 1875–80, p. 16

Certainly, more than any man of his time, Bacon seems to have realized that he was standing at the vestibule of a new age, and was charged with the mission of showing the insufficiency of the past and the bright hopes of the future.—OSCAR BROWNING, *An Introduction to the History of Educational Theories*, 1881

I get driven out of all patience by Spedding's special pleading for him. He seems to me to have done no *work*, to have shown no example of what he calls his method. But his imagination was his great faculty, and all that is most valuable in him is due to the prescient instinctive insight with which he looked on the possibilities of knowledge; the enthusiasm of a seer, not of a philosopher who had measured, and weighed, and compared, and done what Mozley calls the underground work of solid thinking. Galileo, as you say, and Pascal *did* what Bacon talked about without knowing how to do it, and they talked *after* they had touch of the realities of a hunt after physical truth.—RICHARD WILLIAM CHURCH, Letter to Asa Gray (1883), *Life and Letters of Dean Church*, 1894, p. 376

Was this not the very time when Bacon stood out before Europe the herald, if not the leader, of the great scientific movement of modern days, and to his own land set an example of sober practical thinking which the English mind has never since forgotten? If Hobbes, in the last years of Bacon's life, was gradually working his way through scholarly studies to the position of a philosophical thinker, under whose influence but Bacon's could the development proceed? From whom but the first of English modern philosophers should the second, being in actual contact with him, learn to think with the freedom of a modern, and the practical purpose of an Englishman?—GEORGE CROOM ROBERTSON, *Hobbes*, 1886, p. 18

No delusion is greater than the notion that method and industry can make up for lack of motherwit, either in science or in practical life; and it is strange that, with his knowledge of mankind, Bacon should have dreamed that his, or any other, "via inveniendi scientias" would "level men's wits" and leave little scope for that inborn capacity which is called genius. As a matter of fact, Bacon's "via" has proved hopelessly impracticable; while the "anticipation of nature" by the invention of hypotheses based on incomplete inductions, which he specially condemns, has proved itself to be a most efficient, indeed an indispensable, instrument of scientific progress. Finally, that transcendental alchemy—the superinducement of new forms on matter—which Bacon declares to be the supreme aim of science, has been wholly ignored by those who have created the physical knowledge of the present day. Even the eloquent advocacy of the Chancellor brought no unmixed good to physical science. It was natural enough that the man who, in his better moments, took "all knowledge for his patrimony," but, in his worse, sold that birthright for the mess of pottage of Court favour and professional success, for pomp and show, should be led to attach an undue value to the practical advantages which he foresaw, as Roger Bacon and, indeed, Seneca

had foreseen, long before his time, must follow in the train of the advancement of natural knowledge.—THOMAS HUMPHRY WARD, *The Reign of Queen Victoria*, 1887, Vol. 2, p. 325

Bacon is the *bête noire* and butt of Specialists, the modern Schoolmen, who resent his insufficient view of their little worlds. Mere politicians complain that he was neither a Whig nor a Tory. Mere theologians see that, with all his orthodox protestations, Religion was on the fringe of his system: Mere physicists, led by Harvey, who begins the attack in his dictum that he "wrote like a Lord Chancellor," dislike or distrust his metaphysics, and dwell, as Baron Liebig does, with acrimonious exclusiveness on his defects. Their comments are narrowly correct; but, like those of mere dryasdust philologists on the classics of literature, so one-sided as to be impertinent. The inaccuracies inevitable to universal views, must be conceded to the ingratitude of those prone to bite the hand that feeds them.—JOHN NICOL, *Francis Bacon: His Life and Philosophy*, 1889, Pt. 2, p. 242

It is an exaggeration of Bacon's merit to regard him as the creator of the experimental method and of modern science. On the contrary, Bacon was the product of the scientific revival of the sixteenth century, and his manifesto is but the conclusion, or as we might say the moral, which English common-sense draws from the scientific movement. But though he cannot be said to have originated the experimental method, we must at least concede to him the honor of having raised it from the low condition to which scholastic prejudice had consigned it, and of having insured it a legal existence, so to say, by the most eloquent plea ever made in its favor. It is no small matter to speak out what many think, and no one dares to confess even to himself. Nay, more. Though experimental *science* and its methods originated long before the time of the great chancellor, Bacon is none the less the founder of experimental *philosophy*, the father of modern positivistic philosophy, in so far as he was the first to affirm, in clear and eloquent words, that true philosophy and science have common interests, and that a *separate* metaphysics is futile.—ALFRED WEBER, *History of Philosophy*, 1892–96, tr. Thilly, p. 298

The stately tropes and metaphors; the magnificent promises and heraldings of what the new science is to give us; the cunningly adjusted scraps of classical or biblical phrase; the pithy apophthegms; the shrewd commonsense; the suggestion that seems even more pregnant than it is; the masterful employment of a learning which is perhaps more thoroughly at command than extensive or profound—all these notes of "topmost Verulam" are well known. Unjust to his predecessors, hasty and even superficial in his grasp of sciences and philosophies, rhetorical, casuistical, almost shallow, delusive in his mighty promises, hollow in his cunning schemes and methods—all these unfavorable labels have been at different times attached to Bacon, and for some at least of them the Devil's Advocate may make out a strong case. But the magnificence of his literature, and his imagination in the directions where he was imaginative, is undeniable; and he was perhaps, to those who look at literature as it affects and is affected by the social history of England, the best mouthpiece and embodiment of that side of the late Renaissance which retained the hopes of an all-embracing *philosophia prima*, supporting them on the treacherous struts and props that seemed to be lent by the new learning in physics as well as by the study of the ancients.—GEORGE SAINTSBURY, *Social England*, 1895, Vol. 4, ed. Traill, p. 105

GEORGE CHAPMAN
Dedication to *The Georgicks of Hesiod*
1618

TO THE MOST NOBLE COMBINER OF LEARNING AND
HONOUR,

SIR FRANCIS BACON, KNIGHT,

LORD HIGH CHANCELLOR OF ENGLAND, ETC.

Antient wisdom being so worthily eternized by the now-renewed instance of it in your Lordship; and this ancient Author, one of the most authentic for all wisdom crowned with justice and piety; to what sea owe these poor streams their tribute, but to your Lordship's ocean? The rather, since others of the like antiquity, in my Translation of Homer, teach these their way, and add comfort to their courses, by having received right cheerful countenance and approbation from your Lordship's most grave and honoured predecessor.

All judgments of this season (savouring anything the truth) preferring, to the wisdom of all other nations, these most wise, learned, and circularly-spoken Grecians. According to that of the poet:—

> *Graiis ingenium, Graiis dedit ore rotundo*
> *Musa loqui.*

And why may not this Roman eulogy of the *Graians* extend in praiseful intention (by way of prophetic poesy) to *Gray's-Inn* wits and orators? Or if the allusion (or petition of the principle) beg with too broad a licence in the general; yet serious truth, for the particular, may most worthily apply it to your Lordship's truly Greek inspiration, and absolutely Attic elocution. Whose all-acknowledged faculty hath banished flattery therein even from the Court; much more from my country and more-than-upland simplicity. Nor were those Greeks so circular in their elegant utterance, but their inward judgments and learnings were as round and solid; their solidity proved in their eternity; and their eternity propagated by love of all virtue and integrity;—that love being the only parent and argument of all truth, in any wisdom or learning; without which all is sophisticate and adulterate, howsoever painted and splinted with degrees and languages. Your Lordship's *Advancement of Learning*, then, well showing your love to it, and in it, being true to all true goodness, your learning, strengthening that love, must needs be solid and eternal. This *istōr phōs*, therefore, expressed in this Author, is used here as if prophesied by him then, now to take life in your Lordship, whose life is chief soul and essence to all knowledge and virtue; so few there are that live now combining honour and learning. This time resembling the terrible time whereof this poet prophesied; to which he desired he might not live, since not a Grace would then smile on any pious or worthy; all greatness much more gracing impostors than men truly desertful. The worse depraving the better; and that so frontlessly, that shame and justice should fly the earth for them. To shame which ignorant barbarism now emboldened, let your Lordship's learned humanity prove nothing the less gracious to Virtue for the community of Vice's graces; but shine much the more clear on her for those clouds that eclipse her; no lustre being so sun-like as that which passeth above all clouds unseen, over fields, turrets, and temples; and breaks out, in free beams on some humblest cottage. In whose like Jove himself hath been feasted; and wherein your Lordship may find more honour than in the fretted roofs of the mighty. To which honour, oftentimes, nothing more conduceth than noble acceptance of most humble presentments.

On this nobility in your Lordship my prostrate humility relying, I rest ever submitted, in all simple and hearty vows,
Your Honour's most truly,
And freely devoted,
GEORGE CHAPMAN.

WILLIAM RAWLEY
"The Life of Bacon"
Resuscitatio
1657–61

Francis Bacon, the glory of his age and nation, the adorner and ornament of learning, was born in York House, or York Place, in the Strand, on the two and twentieth day of January, in the year of our Lord 1560 ⟨i.e. 1561⟩. His father was that famous counsellor to Queen Elizabeth, the second prop of the kingdom in his time, Sir Nicholas Bacon, knight, lord-keeper of the great seal of England; a lord of known prudence, sufficiency, moderation, and integrity. His mother was Anne, one of the daughters of Sir Anthony Cook; unto whom the erudition of King Edward the Sixth had been committed; a choice lady, and eminent for piety, virtue, and learning; being exquisitely skilled, for a woman, in the Greek and Latin tongues. These being the parents, you may easily imagine what the issue was like to be; having had whatsoever nature or breeding could put into him.

His first and childish years were not without some mark of eminency; at which time he was endued with that pregnancy and towardness of wit, as they were presages of that deep and universal apprehension which was manifest in him afterward; and caused him to be taken notice of by several persons of worth and place, and especially by the queen; who (as I have been informed) delighted much then to confer with him, and to prove him with questions; unto whom he delivered himself with that gravity and maturity above his years, that Her Majesty would often term him, *The young Lord-keeper*. Being asked by the queen *how old he was*, he answered with much discretion, being then but a boy, *That he was two years younger than Her Majesty's happy reign*; with which answer the queen was much taken.

At the ordinary years of ripeness for the university, or rather something earlier, he was sent by his father to Trinity College, in Cambridge, to be educated and bred under the tuition of Doctor John White-gift, then master of the college; afterwards the renowned archbishop of Canterbury; a prelate of the first magnitude for sanctity, learning, patience, and humility; under whom he was observed to have been more than an ordinary proficient in the several arts and sciences. Whilst he was commorant in the university, about sixteen years of age, (as his lordship hath been pleased to impart unto myself), he first fell into the dislike of the philosophy of Aristotle; not for the worthlessness of the author, to whom he would ever ascribe all high attributes, but for the unfruitfulness of the way; being a philosophy (as his lordship used to say) only strong for disputations and contentions, but barren of the production of works for the benefit of the life of man; in which mind he continued to his dying day.

After he had passed the circle of the liberal arts, his father thought fit to frame and mould him for the arts of state; and for that end sent him over into France with Sir Amyas Paulet then employed ambassador lieger into France; by whom he was after awhile held fit to be entrusted with some message or advertisement to the queen; which having performed with great approbation, he returned back into France again, with intention to continue for some years there. In his absence in France his father the lord-keeper died, having collected (as I have heard of knowing persons) a considerable sum of money, which he had separated, with intention to have made a competent purchase of land for the livelihood of this his youngest son (who was only unprovided for; and though he was the youngest in years, yet he was not the lowest in his father's affection); but the said purchase being unaccomplished at his father's death, there came no greater share to him than his single part and portion of the money dividable amongst five brethren; by which means he lived in some straits and necessities in his younger years. For as for that pleasant site and manor of Gorhambury, he came not to it till many years after, by the death of his dearest brother, Mr. Anthony Bacon, a gentleman equal to him in height of wit, though inferior to him in the endowments of learning and knowledge; unto whom he was most nearly conjoined in affection, they two being the sole male issue of a second *venter*.

Being returned from travel, he applied himself to the study of the common law, which he took upon him to be his profession; in which he obtained to great excellency, though he made that (as himself said) but as an accessary, and not his principal study. He wrote several tractates upon that subject: wherein, though some great masters of the law did out-go him in bulk, and particularities of cases, yet in the science of the grounds and mysteries of the law he was exceeded by none. In this way he was after awhile sworn of the queen's council learned, extraordinary; a grace (if I err not) scarce known before. He seated himself, for the commodity of his studies and practice, amongst the Honourable Society of Gray's-Inn, of which house he was a member; where he erected that elegant pile or structure commonly known by the name of *The Lord Bacon's Lodgings*, which he inhabited by turns the most part of his life (some few years only excepted) unto his dying day. In which house he carried himself with such sweetness, comity, and generosity, that he was much revered and beloved by the readers and gentlemen of the house.

Notwithstanding that he professed the law for his livelihood and subsistence, yet his heart and affection was more carried after the affairs and places of estate; for which, if the majesty royal then had been pleased, he was most fit. In his younger years he studied the service and fortunes (as they call them) of that noble but unfortunate earl, the Earl of Essex; unto whom he was, in a sort, a private and free counsellor, and gave him safe and honourable advice, till in the end the earl inclined too much to the violent and precipitate counsel of others his adherents and followers; which was his fate and ruin.

His birth and other capacities qualified him above others of his profession to have ordinary accesses at court, and to come frequently into the queen's eye, who would often grace him with private and free communication, not only about matters of his profession or business in law, but also about the arduous affairs of estate; from whom she received from time to time great satisfaction. Nevertheless, though she cheered him much with the bounty of her countenance, yet she never cheered him with the bounty of her hand; having never conferred upon him any ordinary place or means of honour or profit, save only one dry reversion of the Register's Office in the Star Chamber, worth about 1600*l. per annum*, for which he waited in expectation either fully or near twenty years; of which his lordship would say in Queen Elizabeth's time, *That it was like another man's ground buttalling upon his house, which might mend his prospect, but it did not fill his barn*; (nevertheless, in the time of King James it fell unto him); which

might be imputed, not so much to Her Majesty's averseness and disaffection towards him, as to the arts and policy of a great statesman then, who laboured by all industrious and secret means to suppress and keep him down; lest, if he had risen, he might have obscured his glory.

But though he stood long at a stay in the days of his mistress Queen Elizabeth, yet after the change, and coming in of his new master King James, he made a great progress; by whom he was much comforted in places of trust, honour, and revenue. I have seen a letter of his lordship's to King James, wherein he makes acknowledgment, *That he was that master to him, that had raised and advanced him nine times; thrice in dignity, and six times in office*. His offices (as I conceive) were Counsel Learned Extraordinary to His Majesty, as he had been to Queen Elizabeth; King's Solicitor-General; His Majesty's Attorney-General; Counsellor of Estate, being yet but Attorney; Lord-Keeper of the Great Seal of England; lastly, Lord Chancellor; which two last places, though they be the same in authority and power, yet they differ in patent, height, and favour of the prince; since whose time none of his successors, until this present honourable lord ⟨Sir Edward Hyde⟩, did ever bear the title of Lord Chancellor. His dignities were first Knight, then Baron of Verulam; lastly, Viscount St. Alban; besides other good gifts and bounties of the hand which His Majesty gave him, both out of the Broad Seal and out of the Alienation Office, to the value in both of eighteen hundred pounds per annum; which, with his manor of Gorhambury, and other lands and possessions near thereunto adjoining, amounting to a third part more, he retained to his dying day.

Towards his rising years, not before, he entered into a married estate, and he took to wife Alice, one of the daughters and coheirs of Benedict Barnham, Esquire and Alderman of London; with whom he received a sufficiently ample and liberal portion in marriage. Children he had none; which, though they be the means to perpetuate our names after our deaths, yet he had other issues to perpetuate his name, the issues of his brain; in which he was ever happy and admired, as Jupiter was in the production of Pallas. Neither did the want of children detract from his good usage of his consort during the intermarriage, whom he prosecuted with much conjugal love and respect, with many rich gifts and endowments, besides a robe of honour which he invested her withal; which she wore unto her dying day, being twenty years and more after his death.

The last five years of his life, being withdrawn from civil affairs and from an active life, he employed wholly in contemplation and studies—a thing whereof his lordship would often speak during his active life, as if he affected to die in the shadow and not in the light; which also may be found in several passages of his works. In which time he composed the greatest part of his books and writings, both in English and Latin, which I will enumerate (as near as I can) in the just order wherein they were written:—*The History of the Reign of King Henry the Seventh*; *Abcedarium Naturæ*, or a Metaphysical piece which is lost; *Historia Ventorum*; *Historia Vitæ et Mortis*; *Historia Densi et Rari*, not yet printed; *Historia Gravis et Levis*, which is also lost; *a Discourse of a War with Spain*; *a Dialogue touching an Holy War*; *the Fable of the New Atlantis*; *a Preface to a Digest of the Laws of England*; *the beginning of the History of the Reign of King Henry the Eighth*; *De Augmentis Scientiarum*, or the Advancement of Learning, put into Latin, with several enrichments and enlargements; *Counsels Civil and Moral*, or his book of *Essays*, likewise enriched and enlarged; *the Conversion of certain Psalms into English Verse*; *the Translation into Latin of the History of King Henry the Seventh, of the Counsels Civil and Moral, of the Dialogue of the Holy War, of the Fable of the New Atlantis,* for the benefit of other nations; his revising of his book *De Sapientiâ Veterum; Inquisitio de Magnete; Topica Inquisitionis de Luce et Lumine;* both these not yet printed; lastly, *Sylva Sylvarum,* or *the Natural History.* These were the fruits and productions of his last five years. His lordship also designed, upon the motion and invitation of his late majesty, to have written the reign of King Henry the Eighth; but that work perished in the designation merely, God not lending him life to proceed farther upon it than only in one morning's work; whereof there is extant an *ex ungue leonem,* already printed in his lordship's *Miscellany Works.*

There is a commemoration due as well to his abilities and virtues as to the course of his life. Those abilities which commonly go single in other men, though of prime and observable parts, were all conjoined and met in him. Those are, *sharpness of wit, memory, judgment,* and *elocution.* For the former three his books do abundantly speak them; which with what sufficiency he wrote, let the world judge; but with what celerity he wrote them, I can best testify. But for the fourth, his *elocution,* I will only set down what I heard Sir Walter Raleigh once speak of him by way of comparison (whose judgment may well be trusted), *That the Earl of Salisbury was an excellent speaker, but no good penman; that the Earl of Northampton (the Lord Henry Howard) was an excellent penman, but no good speaker; but that Sir Franis Bacon was eminent in both.*

I have been induced to think, that if there were a beam of knowledge derived from God upon any man in these modern times, it was upon him. For though he was a great reader of books, yet he had not his knowledge from books, but from some grounds and notions from within himself; which, notwithstanding, he vented with great caution and circumspection. His book of *Instauratio Magna* (which in his own account was the chiefest of his works) was no slight imagination or fancy of his brain, but a settled and concocted notion, the production of many years' labour and travel. I myself have seen at the least twelve copies of the *Instauration,* revised year by year one after another, and every year altered and amended in the frame thereof, till at last it came to that model in which it was committed to the press; as many living creatures do lick their young ones, till they bring them to their strength of limbs.

In the composing of his books he did rather drive at a masculine and clear expression than at any fineness or affectation of phrases, and would often ask if the meaning were expressed plainly enough, as being one that accounted words to be but subservient or ministerial to matter, and not the principal. And if his style were polite, it was because he would do no otherwise. Neither was he given to any light conceits, or descanting upon words, but did ever purposely and industriously avoid them; for he held such things to be but digressions or diversions from the scope intended, and to derogate from the weight and dignity of the style.

He was no plodder upon books; though he read much, and that with great judgment, and rejection of impertinences incident to many authors; for he would ever interlace a moderate relaxation of his mind with his studies, as walking, or taking the air abroad in his coach, or some other befitting recreation; and yet he would lose no time, inasmuch as upon his first and immediate return he would fall to reading again, and so suffer no moment of time to slip from him without some present improvement.

His meals were refections of the ear as well as of the stomach, like the *Noctes Atticæ,* or *Convivia Deipnosophistarum,* wherein a man might be refreshed in his mind

and understanding no less than in his body. And I have known some, of no mean parts, that have professed to make use of their note-books when they have risen from his table. In which conversations, and otherwise, he was no dashing man, as some men are, but ever a countenancer and fosterer of another man's parts. Neither was he one that would appropriate the speech wholly to himself, or delight to outvie others, but leave a liberty to the co-assessors to take their turns. Wherein he would draw a man on and allure him to speak upon such a subject, as wherein he was peculiarly skilful, and would delight to speak. And for himself, he contemned no man's observations, but would light his torch at every man's candle.

His opinions and assertions were for the most part binding, and not contradicted by any; rather like oracles than discourses; which may be imputed either to the well weighing of his sentence by the scales of truth and reason, or else to the reverence and estimation wherein he was commonly had, that no man would contest with him; so that there was no argumentation, or *pro* and *con* (as they term it), at his table: or if there chanced to be any, it was carried with much submission and moderation.

I have often observed, and so have other men of great account, that if he had occasion to repeat another man's words after him, he had an use and faculty to dress them in better vestments and apparel than they had before; so that the author should find his own speech much amended, and yet the substance of it still retained; as if it had been natural to him to use good forms, as Ovid spake of his faculty of versifying,

Et quod tentabam scribere, versus erat.

When his office called him, as he was of the king's council learned, to charge any offenders, either in criminals or capitals, he was never of an insulting and domineering nature over them, but always tenderhearted, and carrying himself decently towards the parties (though it was his duty to charge them home), but yet as one that looked upon the *example* with the eye of severity, but upon the *person* with the eye of pity and compassion. And in civil business, as he was counsellor of estate, he had the best way of advising, not engaging his master in any precipitate or grievous courses, but in moderate and fair proceedings: the king whom he served giving him this testimony, *That he ever dealt in business* suavibus modis; *which was the way that was most according to his own heart.*

Neither was he in his time less gracious with the subject than with his sovereign. He was ever acceptable to the House of Commons when he was a member thereof. Being the king's attorney, and chosen to a place in parliament, he was allowed and dispensed with to sit in the House; which was not permitted to other attorneys.

And as he was a good servant to his master, being never in nineteen years' service (as himself averred) rebuked by the king for anything relating to His Majesty, so he was a good master to his servants, and rewarded their long attendance with good places freely when they fell into his power; which was the cause that so many young gentlemen of blood and quality sought to list themselves in his retinue. And if he were abused by any of them in their places, it was only the error of the goodness of his nature, but the badges of their indiscretions and intemperances.

This lord was religious: for though the world be apt to suspect and prejudge great wits and politics to have somewhat of the atheist, yet he was conversant with God, as appeareth by several passages throughout the whole current of his writings. Otherwise he should have crossed his own principles, which were, *That a little philosophy maketh men apt to forget God, as attributing too much to second causes; but depth of philosophy bringeth a man back to God again.* Now I am sure there is no man that will deny him, or account otherwise of him, but to have him been a deep philosopher. And not only so; but he was able *to render a reason of the hope which was in him,* which that writing of his of the *Confession of the Faith* doth abundantly testify. He repaired frequently, when his health would permit him, to the service of the church, to hear sermons, to the administration of the sacrament of the blessed body and blood of Christ; and died in the true faith, established in the church of England.

This is most true—he was free from malice, which (as he said himself) *he never bred nor fed.* He was no revenger of injuries; which if he had minded, he had both opportunity and place high enough to have done it. He was no heaver of men out of their places, as delighting in their ruin and undoing. He was no defamer of any man to his prince. One day, when a great statesman was newly dead, that had not been his friend, the king asked him, *What he thought of that lord which was gone?* he answered, *That he would never have made His Majesty's estate better, but he was sure he would have kept it from being worse;* which was the worst he would say of him: which I reckon not among his moral, but his Christian virtues.

His fame is greater and sounds louder in foreign parts abroad, than at home in his own nation; thereby verifying that divine sentence, *A prophet is not without honour, save in his own country, and in his own house.* Concerning which I will give you a taste only, out of a letter written from Italy (the storehouse of refined wits) to the late Earl of Devonshire, then the Lord Candish: *I will expect the new essays of my Lord Chancellor Bacon, as also his History, with a great deal of desire, and whatsoever else he shall compose: but in particular of his History I promise myself a thing perfect and singular, especially in Henry the Seventh, where he may exercise the talent of his divine understanding. This lord is more and more known, and his books here more and more delighted in; and those men that have more than ordinary knowledge in human affairs, esteem him one of the most capable spirits of this age; and he is truly such.* Now his fame doth not decrease with days since, but rather increase. Divers of his works have been anciently and yet lately translated into other tongues, both learned and modern, by foreign pens. Several persons of quality, during his lordship's life, crossed the seas on purpose to gain an opportunity of seeing him and discoursing with him; whereof one carried his lordship's picture from head to foot over with him into France, as a thing which he foresaw would be much desired there, that so they might enjoy the image of his person as well as the images of his brain, his books. Amongst the rest, Marquis Fiat, a French nobleman, who came ambassador into England, in the beginning of Queen Mary, wife to King Charles, was taken with an extraordinary desire of seeing him; for which he made way by a friend; and when he came to him, being then through weakness confined to his bed, the marquis saluted him with this high expression, *That his lordship had been ever to him like the angels; of whom he had often heard, and read much of them in books, but he never saw them.* After which they contracted an intimate acquaintance, and the marquis did so much revere him, that besides his frequent visits, they wrote letters one to the other, under the titles and appellations of father and son. As for his many salutations by letters from foreign worthies devoted to learning, I forbear to mention them, because that is a thing common to other men of learning or note, together with him.

But yet, in this matter of his fame, I speak in the comparative only, and not in the exclusive. For his reputation is great in his own nation also, especially amongst those that are of a more acute and sharper judgment; which I will exemplify but with two testimonies and no more. The former, when his *History of King Henry the Seventh* was to come forth, it was delivered to the old Lord Brook, to be perused by him; who, when he had dispatched it, returned it to the author with this eulogy, *Commend me to my lord, and bid him take care to get good paper and ink, for the work is incomparable.* The other shall be that of Doctor Samuel Collins, late provost of King's College in Cambridge, a man of no vulgar wit, who affirmed unto me, *That when he had read the book of the Advancement of Learning, he found himself in a case to begin his studies anew, and that he had lost all the time of his studying before.*

It hath been desired, that something should be signified touching his diet, and the regimen of his health, of which, in regard of his universal insight into nature, he may perhaps be to some an example. For his diet, it was rather a plentiful and liberal diet, as his stomach would bear it, than a restrained; which he also commended in his book of the *History of Life and Death.* In his younger years he was much given to the finer and lighter sort of meats, as of fowls, and such like; but afterward, when he grew more judicious, he preferred the stronger meats, such as the shambles afforded, as those meats which bred the more firm and substantial juices of the body, and less *dissipable*; upon which he would often make his meal, though he had other meats upon the table. You may be sure he would not neglect that himself, which he so much extolled in his writings, and that was the use of nitre; whereof he took in the quantity of about three grains in thin warm broth every morning, for thirty years together next before his death. And for physic, he did indeed live physically, but not miserably; for he took only a maceration of rhubarb, infused into a draught of white wine and beer mingled together for the space of half an hour, once in six or seven days, immediately before his meal (whether dinner or supper), that it might dry the body less; which (as he said) did carry away frequently the grosser humours of the body, and not diminish or carry away any of the spirits, as sweating doth. And this was no grievous thing to take. As for other physic, in an ordinary way (whatsoever hath been vulgarly spoken) he took not. His receipt for the gout, which did constantly ease him of his pain within two hours, is already set down in the end of the *Natural History.*

It may seem the moon had some principal place in the figure of his nativity: for the moon was never in her passion, or eclipsed, but he was surprised with a sudden fit of fainting; and that, though he observed not nor took any previous knowledge of the eclipse thereof; and as soon as the eclipse ceased, he was restored to his former strength again.

He died on the ninth day of April in the year 1626, in the early morning of the day then celebrated for our Saviour's resurrection, in the sixty-sixth year of his age, at the Earl of Arundel's house in Highgate, near London, to which place he casually repaired about a week before; God so ordaining that he should die there of a gentle fever, accidentally accompanied with a great cold, whereby the defluxion of rheum fell so plentifully upon his breast, that he died by suffocation; and was buried in St. Michael's church at St. Albans; being the place designed for his burial by his last will and testament, both because the body of his mother was interred there, and because it was the only church then remaining within the precincts of old Verulam: where he hath a monument erected for him in white marble (by the care and gratitude of Sir Thomas Meautys, knight, formerly his lordship's secretary, afterwards clerk of the King's Honourable Privy Council under two kings); representing his full portraiture in the posture of studying, with an inscription composed by that accomplished gentleman and rare wit, Sir Henry Wotton.

FRANCISCUS BACON, BARO DE VERULAM,
S^t. ALBANI VIC^{mes},

SEU NOTIORIBUS TITULIS

SCIENTIARUM LUMEN FACUNDIÆ LEX

SIC SEDEBAT.

QUI POSTQUAM OMNIA NATURALIS SAPIENTIÆ

ET CIVILIS ARCANA EVOLVISSET

NATURÆ DECRETUM EXPLEVIT

COMPOSITA SOLVANTUR

AN. DNI M.DC.XXVI.

ÆTAT^{is} LXVI.

TANTI VIRI

MEM.

THOMAS MEAUTUS

SUPERSTITIS CULTOR

DEFUNCTI ADMIRATOR

H. P.

But howsoever his body was mortal, yet no doubt his memory and works will live, and will in all probability last as long as the world lasteth. In order to which I have endeavoured (after my poor ability) to do this honour to his lordship, by way of conducing to the same.

FRANÇOIS MARIE AROUET DE VOLTAIRE
"Letter 12: On Chancellor Bacon" (1734)
Letters on England (Lettres Philosophiques)
tr. Tancock
1980, pp. 57–61

Not long ago, in a distinguished company, they were discussing this time-honoured and frivolous question: who was the greatest man, Caesar, Alexander, Tamburlaine, Cromwell, etc.

Somebody answered that it was unquestionable Isaac Newton. He was right, for if true greatness consists in having received from heaven a powerful genius and in having used it to enlighten himself and others, a man such as Newton, the like of whom is scarcely to be found in ten centuries, is the truly great man, and these politicians and conquerors, in which no period has been lacking, are usually nothing more than illustrious criminals. It is to the man who rules over minds by the power of truth, not to those who enslave men by violence, it is to the man who understands the universe and not to those who disfigure it, that we owe our respect.

Since you ask me to tell you about the famous men England has given birth to, I shall begin with men like Bacon, Locke, Newton, etc. The generals and ministers will come in their turn.

I must begin with the famous Earl of Verulam, known in Europe by the name of Bacon, his family name. He was the son of the Lord Keeper of the Great Seal, and for a long time was Chancellor under King James I. Yet, amid the intrigues of Court and the preoccupations of his office, enough to absorb a man completely, he found time to be a great scientific thinker, a good historian and an elegant writer, and what is even more astonishing, he lived in an age when the art of good writing was hardly known, still less scientific thought. As is customary among men, he has been more respected since his death than

in his lifetime. His enemies were at Court in London, his admirers in the whole of Europe.

When the Marquis d'Effiat conducted to England Princess Marie, daughter of Henry the Great, who was to marry the Prince of Wales, this minister went and paid a visit to Bacon who, being ill in bed, received him with the curtains drawn. 'You are like the angels,' said d'Effiat, 'one always hears about them, they are thought to be much superior to men, but one never has the consolation of seeing them.'

You know, Monsieur, how Bacon was accused of a crime ill befitting a philosopher, that of letting himself be corrupted by money, you know how he was condemned by the House of Lords to a fine of about 400,000 *livres* of our money, and to lose his rank as Chancellor and Peer.

Today the English so revere his memory that they are unwilling to admit that he may have been guilty. If you ask me what I think about it I will answer by borrowing a word I heard Lord Bolingbroke say. In his presence the conversation touched on the avarice of which the Duke of Marlborough was accused, and they gave examples of it and asked Lord Bolingbroke to bear witness because, having been his declared enemy, he could perhaps express an opinion without impropriety. 'He was such a great man,' was the answer, 'that I have forgotten his vices.'

So I will confine myself to telling you what earned for Chancellor Bacon the respect of Europe.

The best and most remarkable of his works is the one which is the least read today and the least useful: I refer to his *Novum Scientiarum Organum*. It is the scaffolding by means of which modern scientific thought has been built, and when that edifice had been raised, at least in part, the scaffolding ceased to be of any use.

Chancellor Bacon did not yet understand nature, but he knew and pointed out the roads leading to it. He had very early scorned what the Universities called Philosophy, and he did everything in his power to prevent these institutions, set up for the perfection of human reason, from continuing to spoil it with their *quiddities*, their *abhorrence of a vacuum*, their *substantial forms* and all the inappropriate expressions which not only ignorance made respectable, but which a ridiculous confusion with religion had made almost sacred.

He is the father of experimental philosophy. It is true that some amazing secrets had been discovered before his time. Men had invented the compass, printing, engraving, oil-painting, mirrors, the art of restoring to some extent sight to the aged by glasses, called spectacles, gunpowder, etc. Men had searched for, found and conquered a new world. Who would not have thought that these sublime discoveries had been made by the greatest scientists in times much more enlightened than ours? Not at all; it was in the age of the most mindless barbarism that these great changes were made on the earth. Chance alone produced almost all these inventions, and there is even every appearance that what may be called chance played a large part in the discovery of America—at all events it has always been believed that Christopher Columbus only undertook his voyage on the word of a captain who had been cast ashore by a storm on the Caribbean islands.

However that may be, men already knew how to get to the ends of the earth, how to destroy cities with an artificial thunder more terrible than the real thing, but they knew nothing about the circulation of the blood, the weight of the atmosphere, the laws of dynamics, the number of the planets, etc., and a man who upheld a thesis on the categories of Aristotle, on the universal *a parte rei* or some other such idiocy, was regarded as a prodigy.

The most wonderful and useful inventions are not those which do most honour to the human mind.

It is to a mechanical instinct, which exists in most men, that we owe all the skills, and not to a sound philosophy.

The discovery of fire, the art of making bread, of melting and forging metals, building houses, the invention of the shuttle, are of much more practical necessity than printing or the compass, yet these skills were invented by men still in a state of savagery.

Since then what prodigious use the Greeks and Romans have made of mechanical invention! Yet they thought in their time that the skies were of crystal and the stars were little lamps which sometimes fell down into the sea, and one of their great philosophers, after much research, had discovered that the heavenly bodies were pebbles that had come loose from the earth.

In a word, nobody before Chancellor Bacon had grasped experimental science, and of all the practical applications made since, scarcely one is not foreshadowed in his book. He had made several himself; he made a kind of pneumatic machine by means of which he guessed at the elasticity of the air, and he circled all round the discovery of its weight, indeed he almost had it, but the truth was seized upon by Torricelli. Not long afterwards experimental physics was suddenly taken up simultaneously in almost all parts of Europe. It was a hidden treasure the existence of which Bacon had suspected and which all the scientists, encouraged by his promise, strove to dig out.

But what has surprised me most has been to see in his book, in explicit terms, this new law of attraction for the invention of which Newton has the credit.

'We must try to discover,' says Bacon, 'whether there might not be a kind of magnetic force operating between the earth and things with weight, between the moon and the ocean, between the planets, etc.'

Elsewhere he says:

It must either be that heavy bodies are impelled towards the centre of the earth, or that they are mutually attracted by it, and in the latter case it is evident that the nearer these falling bodies get to the earth the more strongly they are attracted to each other. We must see whether the same clock with weights will go faster at the top of a mountain or at the bottom of a mine; it is probable, if the pull of the weights decreases on the mountain and increases in the mine, that the earth has a real attraction.

This precursor of science was also an elegant writer, a historian and a wit.

His *Essays* are very well thought of, but they are intended to instruct rather than to please, and being neither a satire on human nature like the *Maxims* of La Rouchefoucauld, nor a school for sceptics like Montaigne, they are less often read than those two ingenious books.

His *History of Henry VII* passed for a masterpiece, but I should be much mistaken if it could be compared with the work of our illustrious de Thou.

Speaking of the famous impostor Parkins, a Jew by birth, who so brazenly assumed the title of Richard IV, King of England, encouraged by the Duchess of Burgundy, and who laid claim to the crown of Henry VII, this is how Chancellor Bacon expresses himself:

At about this time, King Henry was haunted by evil spirits through the magic of the Duchess of Burgundy, who conjured up from the underworld the shade of Edward IV to torment King Henry. When the Duchess of Burgundy had instructed Parkins she

began to deliberate about which region of the sky she would make the comet come from, and she resolved that it would burst forth first on the horizon of Ireland.

It seems to me that our wise de Thou does not go in for all this rigmarole that was formerly taken as inspired, but is nowadays rightly called mumbo-jumbo.

THOMAS BABINGTON MACAULAY
From "Lord Bacon" (1837)
Critical, Historical, and Miscellaneous Essays
1860, Volume 3, pp. 436–95

Two words form the key of the Baconian doctrine, Utility and Progress. The ancient philosophy disdained to be useful, and was content to be stationary. It dealt largely in theories of moral perfection, which were so sublime that they never could be more than theories; in attempts to solve insoluble enigmas; in exhortations to the attainment of unattainable frames of mind. It could not condescend to the humble office of ministering to the comfort of human beings. All the schools contemned that office as degrading; some censured it as immoral. Once indeed Posidonius, a distinguished writer of the age of Cicero and Cæsar, so far forgot himself as to enumerate, among the humbler blessings which mankind owed to philosophy, the discovery of the principle of the arch, and the introduction of the use of metals. This eulogy was considered as an affront, and was taken up with proper spirit. Seneca vehemently disclaims these insulting compliments.[1] Philosophy, according to him, has nothing to do with teaching men to rear arched roofs over their heads. The true philosopher does not care whether he has an arched roof or any roof. Philosophy has nothing to do with teaching men the uses of metals. She teaches us to be independent of all material substances, of all mechanical contrivances. The wise man lives according to nature. Instead of attempting to add to the physical comforts of his species, he regrets that his lot was not cast in that golden age when the human race had no protection against the cold but the skins of wild beasts, no screen from the sun but a cavern. To impute to such a man any share in the invention or improvement of a plough, a ship, or a mill, is an insult. "In my own time," says Seneca, "there have been inventions of this sort, transparent windows, tubes for diffusing warmth equally through all parts of a building, short-hand, which has been carried to such a perfection that a writer can keep pace with the most rapid speaker. But the inventing of such things is drudgery for the lowest slaves; philosophy lies deeper. It is not her office to teach men how to use their hands. The object of her lessons is to form the soul. *Non est, inquam, instrumentorum ad usus necessarios opifex.*" If the *non* were left out, this last sentence would be no bad description of the Baconian philosophy, and would, indeed, very much resemble several expressions in the *Novum Organum.* "We shall next be told," exclaims Seneca, "that the first shoemaker was a philosopher." For our own part, if we are forced to make our choice between the first shoemaker, and the author of the three books *On Anger*, we pronounce for the shoemaker. It may be worse to be angry than to be wet. But shoes have kept millions from being wet; and we doubt whether Seneca ever kept any body from being angry. . . .

The spirit which appears in the passage of Seneca to which we have referred, tainted the whole body of the ancient philosophy from the time of Socrates downwards, and took possession of intellects with which that of Seneca cannot for a moment be compared. It pervades the dialogues of Plato. It may be distinctly traced in many parts of the works of Aristotle. Bacon has dropped hints, from which it may be inferred that, in his opinion, the prevalence of this feeling was in a great measure to be attributed to the influence of Socrates. Our great countryman evidently did not consider the revolution which Socrates effected in philosophy as a happy event, and constantly maintained that the earlier Greek speculators, Democritus in particular, were, on the whole, superior to their more celebrated successors.[2]

Assuredly if the tree which Socrates planted and Plato watered is to be judged of by its flowers and leaves, it is the noblest of trees. But if we take the homely test of Bacon, if we judge of the tree by its fruits, our opinion of it may perhaps be less favourable. When we sum up all the useful truths which we owe to that philosophy, to what do they amount? We find, indeed, abundant proofs that some of those who cultivated it were men of the first order of intellect. We find among their writings incomparable specimens both of dialectical and rhetorical art. We have no doubt that the ancient controversies were of use, in so far as they served to exercise the faculties of the disputants; for there is no controversy so idle that it may not be of use in this way. But, when we look for something more, for something which adds to the comforts or alleviates the calamities of the human race, we are forced to own ourselves disappointed. We are forced to say with Bacon that this celebrated philosophy ended in nothing but disputation, that it was neither a vineyard nor an olive-ground, but an intricate wood of briars and thistles, from which those who lost themselves in it brought back many scratches and no food.[3] . . .

At length the time arrived when the barren philosophy which had, during so many ages, employed the faculties of the ablest of men, was destined to fall. It had worn many shapes. It had mingled itself with many creeds. It had survived revolutions in which empires, religions, languages, races, had perished. Driven from its ancient haunts, it had taken sanctuary in that Church which it had persecuted, and had, like the daring fiends of the poet, placed its seat

next the seat of God,
And with its darkness dared affront his light.

Words, and more words, and nothing but words, had been all the fruit of all the toil of all the most renowned sages of sixty generations. But the days of this sterile exuberance were numbered.

Many causes predisposed the public mind to a change. The study of a great variety of ancient writers, though it did not give a right direction to philosophical research, did much towards destroying that blind reverence for authority which had prevailed when Aristotle ruled alone. The rise of the Florentine sect of Platonists, a sect to which belonged some of the finest minds of the fifteenth century, was not an unimportant event. The mere substitution of the Academic for the Peripatetic philosophy would indeed have done little good. But any thing was better than the old habit of unreasoning servility. It was something to have a choice of tyrants. "A spark of freedom," as Gibbon has justly remarked, "was produced by this collision of adverse servitude."

Other causes might be mentioned. But it is chiefly to the great reformation of religion that we owe the great reformation of philosophy. The alliance between the Schools and the Vatican had for ages been so close that those who threw off the dominion of the Vatican could not continue to recognise the authority of the Schools. Most of the chiefs of the schism treated the Peripatetic philosophy with contempt, and spoke of Aristotle as if Aristotle had been answerable for all the dogmas of Thomas Aquinas. "Nullo apud Lutheranos philosophiam esse in pretio," was a reproach which the defenders of the Church of Rome loudly repeated, and which many of the Protestant leaders considered as a compliment. Scarcely any text was more frequently cited by the reformers than that in which St. Paul cautions the Colossians not to let any man spoil them by philosophy. Luther, almost at the outset of his career, went so far as to declare that no man could be at once a proficient in the school of Aristotle and in that of Christ. Zwingle, Bucer, Peter Martyr, Calvin, held similar language. In some of the Scotch universities, the Aristotelian system was discarded for that of Ramus. Thus, before the birth of Bacon, the empire of the scholastic philosophy had been shaken to its foundations. There was in the intellectual world an anarchy resembling that which in the political world often follows the overthrow of an old and deeply rooted government. Antiquity, prescription, the sound of great names, had ceased to awe mankind. The dynasty which had reigned for ages was at an end; and the vacant throne was left to be struggled for by pretenders.

The first effect of this great revolution, was, as Bacon most justly observed,[4] to give for a time an undue importance to the mere graces of style. The new breed of scholars, the Aschams and Buchanans, nourished with the finest compositions of the Augustan age, regarded with loathing the dry, crabbed, and barbarous diction of respondents and opponents. They were far less studious about the matter of their writing than about the manner. They succeeded in reforming Latinity; but they never even aspired to effect a reform in philosophy.

At this time Bacon appeared. It is altogether incorrect to say, as has often been said, that he was the first man who rose up against the Aristotelian philosophy when in the height of its power. The authority of that philosophy had, as we have shown, received a fatal blow long before he was born. Several speculators, among whom Ramus is the best known, had recently attempted to form new sects. Bacon's own expressions about the state of public opinion in the time of Luther are clear and strong: "Accedebat," says he, "odium et contemptus, illis ipsis temporibus ortus erga Scholasticos." And again, "Scholasticorum doctrina despectui prorsus haberi cœpit tanquam aspera et barbara."[5] The part which Bacon played in this great change was the part, not of Robespierre, but of Bonaparte. The ancient order of things had been subverted. Some bigots still cherished with devoted loyalty the remembrance of the fallen monarchy and exerted themselves to effect a restoration. But the majority had no such feeling. Freed, yet not knowing how to use their freedom, they pursued no determinate course, and had found no leader capable of conducting them.

That leader at length arose. The philosophy which he taught was essentially new. It differed from that of the celebrated ancient teachers, not merely in method, but also in object. Its object was the good of mankind, in the sense in which the mass of mankind always have understood and always will understand the word good. "Meditor," said Bacon, "instaurationem philosophiæ ejusmodi quæ nihil inanis aut abstracti habeat, quæque vitæ humanæ conditiones in melius provehat."[6]

The difference between the philosophy of Bacon and that of his predecessors cannot, we think, be better illustrated than by comparing his views on some important subjects with those of Plato. We select Plato, because we conceive that he did more than any other person towards giving to the minds of speculative men that bent which they retained till they received from Bacon a new impulse in a diametrically opposite direction.

It is curious to observe how differently these great men estimated the value of every kind of knowledge. Take Arithmetic for example. Plato, after speaking slightly of the convenience of being able to reckon and compute in the ordinary transactions of life, passes to what he considers as a far more important advantage. The study of the properties of numbers, he tells us, habituates the mind to the contemplation of pure truth, and raises us above the material universe. He would have his disciples apply themselves to this study, not that they may be able to buy or sell, not that they may qualify themselves to be shopkeepers or travelling merchants, but that they may learn to withdraw their minds from the ever-shifting spectacle of this visible and tangible world, and to fix them on the immutable essences of things.[7]

Bacon, on the other hand, valued this branch of knowledge, only on account of its uses with reference to that visible and tangible world which Plato so much despised. He speaks with scorn of the mystical arithmetic of the later Platonists, and laments the propensity of mankind to employ, on mere matters of curiosity, powers the whole exertion of which is required for purposes of solid advantage. He advises arithmeticians to leave these trifles, and to employ themselves in framing convenient expressions, which may be of use in physical researches.[8]

The same reasons which led Plato to recommend the study of arithmetic led him to recommend also the study of mathematics. The vulgar crowd of geometricians, he says, will not understand him. They have practice always in view. They do not know that the real use of the science is to lead men to the knowledge of abstract, essential, eternal truth.[9] Indeed, if we are to believe Plutarch, Plato carried this feeling so far that he considered geometry as degraded by being applied to any purpose of vulgar utility. Archytas, it seems, had framed machines of extraordinary power on mathematical principles.[10] Plato remonstrated with his friend, and declared that this was to degrade a noble intellectual exercise into a low craft, fit only for carpenters and wheelwrights. The office of geometry, he said, was to discipline the mind, not to minister to the base wants of the body. His interference was successful; and from that time, according to Plutarch, the science of mechanics was considered as unworthy of the attention of a philosopher.

Archimedes in a later age imitated and surpassed Archytas. But even Archimedes was not free from the prevailing notion that geometry was degraded by being employed to produce any thing useful. It was with difficulty that he was induced to stoop from speculation to practice. He was half ashamed of those inventions which were the wonder of hostile nations, and always spoke of them slightingly as mere amusements, as trifles in which a mathematician might be suffered to relax his mind after intense application to the higher parts of his science.

The opinion of Bacon on this subject was diametrically opposed to that of the ancient philosophers. He valued geometry chiefly, if not solely, on account of those uses, which to Plato appeared so base. And it is remarkable that the longer Bacon lived the stronger this feeling became. When in 1605 he wrote the two books on the *Advancement of Learning*, he dwelt on the advantages which mankind derived from mixed mathematics; but he at the same time admitted that the beneficial effect produced by mathematical study on the intellect, though a collateral advantage, was "no less worthy than that which was principal and intended." But it is evident that his views underwent a change. When, near twenty years later, he published the *De Augmentis*, which is the Treatise on the *Advancement of Learning*, greatly expanded and carefully corrected, he made important alterations in the part which related to mathematics. He condemned with severity the high pretensions of the math-

ematicians, "delicias et fastum mathematicorum." Assuming the well-being of the human race to be the end of knowledge,[11] he pronounced that mathematical science could claim no higher rank than that of an appendage or an auxiliary to other sciences. Mathematical science, he says, is the handmaid of natural philosophy; she ought to demean herself as such; and he declares that he cannot conceive by what ill chance it has happened that she presumes to claim precedence over her mistress. He predicts—a prediction which would have made Plato shudder—that as more and more discoveries are made in physics, there will be more and more branches of mixed mathematics. Of that collateral advantage the value of which, twenty years before, he rated so highly, he says not one word. This omission cannot have been the effect of mere inadvertence. His own treatise was before him. From that treatise he deliberately expunged whatever was favourable to the study of pure mathematics, and inserted several keen reflections on the ardent votaries of that study. This fact, in our opinion, admits of only one explanation. Bacon's love of those pursuits which directly tend to improve the condition of mankind, and his jealousy of all pursuits merely curious, had grown upon him, and had, it may be, become immoderate. He was afraid of using any expression which might have the effect of inducing any man of talents to employ in speculations, useful only to the mind of the speculator, a single hour which might be employed in extending the empire of man over matter.[12] If Bacon erred here, we must acknowledge that we greatly prefer his error to the opposite error of Plato. We have no patience with a philosophy which, like those Roman matrons who swallowed abortives in order to preserve their shapes, takes pains to be barren for fear of being homely.

Let us pass to astronomy. This was one of the sciences which Plato exhorted his disciples to learn, but for reasons far removed from common habits of thinking. "Shall we set down astronomy," says Socrates, "among the subjects of study?"[13] "I think so," answers his young friend Glaucon: "to know something about the seasons, the months, and the years is of use for military purposes, as well as for agriculture and navigation." "It amuses me," says Socrates, "to see how afraid you are, lest the common herd of people should accuse you of recommending useless studies." He then proceeds, in that pure and magnificent diction which, as Cicero said, Jupiter would use if Jupiter spoke Greek, to explain that the use of astronomy is not to add to the vulgar comforts of life, but to assist in raising the mind to the contemplation of things which are to be perceived by the pure intellect alone. The knowledge of the actual motions of the heavenly bodies Socrates considers as of little value. The appearances which make the sky beautiful at night are, he tells us, like the figures which a geometrician draws on the sand, mere examples, mere helps to feeble minds. We must get beyond them; we must neglect them; we attain to an astronomy which is as independent of the actual stars as geometrical truth is independent of the lines of an ill-drawn diagram. This is, we imagine, very nearly, if not exactly, the astronomy which Bacon compared to the ox of Prometheus,[14] a sleek, well-shaped hide, stuffed with rubbish, goodly to look at, but containing nothing to eat. He complained that astronomy had, to its great injury, been separated from natural philosophy, of which it was one of the noblest provinces, and annexed to the domain of mathematics. The world stood in need, he said, of a very different astronomy, of a living astronomy,[15] of an astronomy which should set forth the nature, the motion, and the influences of the heavenly bodies, as they really are.[16]

On the greatest and most useful of all human inventions, the invention of alphabetical writing, Plato did not look with much complacency. He seems to have thought that the use of letters had operated on the human mind as the use of the go-cart in learning to walk, or of corks in learning to swim, is said to operate on the human body. It was a support which, in his opinion, soon became indispensable to those who used it, which made vigorous exertion first unnecessary and then impossible. The powers of the intellect would, he conceived, have been more fully developed without this delusive aid. Men would have been compelled to exercise the understanding and the memory, and, by deep and assiduous meditation, to make truth thoroughly their own. Now, on the contrary, much knowledge is traced on paper, but little is engraved in the soul. A man is certain that he can find information at a moment's notice when he wants it. He therefore suffers it to fade from his mind. Such a man cannot in strictness be said to know any thing. He has the show without the reality of wisdom. These opinions Plato has put into the mouth of an ancient king of Egypt.[17] But it is evident from the context that they were his own; and so they were understood to be by Quintilian.[18] Indeed they are in perfect accordance with the whole Platonic system.

Bacon's views, as may easily be supposed, were widely different.[19] The powers of the memory, he observes, without the help of writing, can do little towards the advancement of any useful sicence. He acknowledges that the memory may be disciplined to such a point as to be able to perform very extraordinary feats. But on such feats he sets little value. The habits of his mind, he tells us, are such that he is not disposed to rate highly any accomplishment, however rare, which is of no practical use to mankind. As to these prodigious achievements of the memory, he ranks them with the exhibitions of rope-dancers and tumblers. "The two performances," he says, "are of much the same sort. The one is an abuse of the powers of the body; the other is an abuse of the powers of the mind. Both may perhaps excite our wonder; but neither is entitled to our respect."

To Plato, the science of medicine appeared to be of very disputable advantage.[20] He did not indeed object to quick cures for acute disorders, or for injuries produced by accidents. But the art which resists the slow sap of a chronic disease, which repairs frames enervated by lust, swollen by gluttony, or inflamed by wine, which encourages sensuality by mitigating the natural punishment of the sensualist, and prolongs existence when the intellect has ceased to retain its entire energy, had no share of his esteem. A life protracted by medical skill he pronounced to be a long death. The existence of the art of medicine ought, he said, to be tolerated, so far as that art may serve to cure the occasional distempers of men whose constitutions are good. As to those who have bad constitutions, let them die; and the sooner the better. Such men are unfit for war, for magistracy, for the management of their domestic affairs, for severe study and speculation. If they engage in any vigorous mental exercise, they are troubled with giddiness and fulness of the head, all which they lay to the account of philosophy. The best thing that can happen to such wretches is to have done with life at once. He quotes mythical authority in support of this doctrine; and reminds his disciples that the practice of the sons of Æsculapius, as described by Homer, extended only to the cure of external injuries.

Far different was the philosophy of Bacon. Of all the sciences, that which he seems to have regarded with the greatest interest was the science which, in Plato's opinion, would not be tolerated in a well regulated community. To make men perfect was no part of Bacon's plan. His humble aim was to make imperfect men comfortable. The beneficence of his philosophy resembled the beneficence of the common Father, whose sun rises on the evil and the good, whose rain descends for the just and the unjust. In Plato's opinion man was made for philosophy; in Bacon's opinion philosophy was made for man; it was a means to an end; and that end was to increase the pleasures and to mitigate the pains of millions who are not and cannot be philosophers. That a valetudinarian who took great pleasure in being wheeled along his terrace, who relished his boiled chicken and his weak wine and water, and who enjoyed a hearty laugh over the Queen of Navarre's tales, should be treated as a *caput lupinum* because he could not read the *Timæus* without a headache, was a notion which the humane spirit of the English school of wisdom altogether rejected. Bacon would not have thought it beneath the dignity of a philosopher to contrive an improved garden chair for such a valetudinarian, to devise some way of rendering his medicines more palatable, to invent repasts which he might enjoy, and pillows on which he might sleep soundly; and this though there might not be the smallest hope that the mind of the poor invalid would ever rise to the contemplation of the ideal beautiful and the ideal good. As Plato had cited the religious legends of Greece to justify his contempt for the more recondite parts of the art of healing, Bacon vindicated the dignity of that art by appealing to the example of Christ, and reminded men that the great Physician of the soul did not disdain to be also the physician of the body.[21]

When we pass from the science of medicine to that of legislation, we find the same difference between the systems of these two great men. Plato, at the commencement of the *Dialogue on Laws*, lays it down as a fundamental principle that the end of legislation is to make men virtuous. It is unnecessary to point out the extravagant conclusions to which such a proposition leads. Bacon well knew to how great an extent the happiness of every society must depend on the virtue of its members; and he also knew what legislators can and what they cannot do for the purpose of promoting virtue. The view which he has given of the end of legislation, and of the principal means for the attainment of that end, has always seemed to us eminently happy, even among the many happy passages of the same kind with which his works abound. "Finis et scopus quem leges intueri atque ad quem jussiones et sanctiones suas dirigere debent, non alius est quam ut cives feliciter degant. Id fiet si pietate et religione recte instituti, moribus honesti, armis adversus hostes externos tuti, legum auxilio adversus seditiones et privatas injurias muniti, imperio et magistratibus obsequentes, copiis et opibus locupletes et florentes fuerint."[22] The end is the well-being of the people. The means are the imparting of moral and religious education; the providing of every thing necessary for defence against foreign enemies; the maintaining of internal order; the establishing of a judicial, financial, and commercial system, under which wealth may be rapidly accumulated and securely enjoyed.

Even with respect to the form in which laws ought to be drawn, there is a remarkable difference of opinion between the Greek and the Englishman. Plato thought a preamble essential; Bacon thought it mischievous. Each was consistent with himself. Plato, considering the moral improvement of the people as the end of legislation, justly inferred that a law which commanded and threatened, but which neither convinced the reason, nor touched the heart, must be a most imperfect law. He was not content with deterring from theft a man who still continued to be a thief at heart, with restraining a son who hated his mother from beating his mother. The only obedience on which he set much value was the obedience which an enlightened understanding yields to reason, and which a virtuous disposition yields to precepts of virtue. He really seems to have believed that, by prefixing to every law an eloquent and pathetic exhortation, he should, to a great extent, render penal enactments superfluous. Bacon entertained no such romantic hopes; and he well knew the practical inconveniences of the course which Plato recommended. "Neque nobis," says he, "prologi legum qui inepti olim habiti sunt, et leges introducunt disputantes non jubentes, utique placerent, si priscos mores ferre possemus. . . . Quantum fieri potest prologi evitentur, et lex incipiat a jussione."[23]

Each of the great men whom we have compared intended to illustrate his system by a philosophical romance; and each left his romance imperfect. Had Plato lived to finish the *Critias*, a comparison between that noble fiction and the new Atlantis would probably have furnished us with still more striking instances than any which we have given. It is amusing to think with what horror he would have seen such an institution as Solomon's House rising in his republic: with what vehemence he would have ordered the brewhouses, the perfumehouses, and the dispensatories to be pulled down; and with what inexorable rigour he would have driven beyond the frontier all the Fellows of the College, Merchants of Light and Depredators, Lamps and Pioneers.

To sum up the whole, we should say that the aim of the Platonic philosophy was to exalt man into a god. The aim of the Baconian philosophy was to provide man with what he requires while he continues to be man. The aim of the Platonic philosophy was to raise us far above vulgar wants. The aim of the Baconian philosophy was to supply our vulgar wants. The former aim was noble; but the latter was attainable. Plato drew a good bow; but, like Acestes in Virgil, he aimed at the stars; and therefore, though there was no want of strength or skill, the shot was thrown away. His arrow was indeed followed by a track of dazzling radiance, but it struck nothing.

> Volans liquidis in nubibus arsit arundo
> Signavitque viam flammis, tenuisque recessit
> Consumpta in ventos.

Bacon fixed his eye on a mark which was placed on the earth, and within bow-shot, and hit it in the white. The philosophy of Plato began in words and ended in words, noble words indeed, words such as were to be expected from the finest of human intellects exercising boundless dominion over the finest of human languages. The philosophy of Bacon began in observations and ended in arts.

The boast of the ancient philosophers was that their doctrine formed the minds of men to a high degree of wisdom and virtue. This was indeed the only practical good which the most celebrated of those teachers even pretended to effect; and undoubtedly, if they had effected this, they would have deserved far higher praise than if they had discovered the most salutary medicines or constructed the most powerful machines. But the truth is that, in those very matters in which alone they professed to do any good to mankind, in those very matters for the sake of which they neglected all the vulgar interests of mankind, they did nothing, or worse than nothing. They promised what was impracticable; they despised what was practicable; they filled the world with long words and long beards; and they left it as wicked and as ignorant as they found it.

An acre in Middlesex is better than a principality in Utopia. The smallest actual good is better than the most magnificent promises of impossibilities. The wise man of the Stoics would, no doubt, be a grander object than a steam-engine. But there are steam-engines. And the wise man of the Stoics is yet to be born. A philosophy which should enable a man to feel perfectly happy while in agonies of pain would be better than a philosophy which assuages pain. But we know that there are remedies which will assuage pain; and we know that the ancient sages liked the toothache just as little as their neighbours. A philosophy which should extinguish cupidity would be better than a philosophy which should devise laws for the security of property. But it is possible to make laws which shall, to a very great extent, secure property. And we do not understand how any motives which the ancient philosophy furnished could extinguish cupidity. We know indeed that the philosophers were no better than other men. From the testimony of friends as well as of foes, from the confessions of Epictetus and Seneca, as well as from the sneers of Lucian and the fierce invectives of Juvenal, it is plain that these teachers of virtue had all the vices of their neighbours, with the additional vice of hypocrisy. Some people may think the object of the Baconian philosophy a low object, but they cannot deny that, high or low, it has been attained. They cannot deny that every year makes an addition to what Bacon called "fruit." . . .

Bacon has been accused of overrating the importance of those sciences which minister to the physical well-being of man, and of underrating the importance of moral philosophy; and it cannot be denied that persons who read the *Novum Organum* and the *De Augmentis*, without adverting to the circumstances under which those works were written, will find much that may seem to countenance the accusation. It is certain, however, that though in practice he often went very wrong, and though, as his historical work and his essays prove, he did not hold, even in theory, very strict opinions on points of political morality, he was far too wise a man not to know how much our well-being depends on the regulation of our minds. The world for which he wished was not, as some people seem to imagine, a world of water-wheels, power looms, steam-carriages, sensualists, and knaves. He would have been as ready as Zeno himself to maintain that no bodily comforts which could be devised by the skill and labour of a hundred generations would give happiness to a man whose mind was under the tyranny of licentious appetite, of envy, of hatred, or of fear. If he sometimes appeared to ascribe importance too exclusively to the arts which increase the outward comforts of our species, the reason is plain. Those arts had been most unduly depreciated. They had been represented as unworthy the attention of a man of liberal education. "Cogitavit," says Bacon of himself, "eam esse opinionem sive æstimationem humidam et damnosam, minui nempe majestatem mentis humanæ, si in experimentis et rebus particularibus, sensui subjectis, et in materia terminatis, diu ac multum versetur: præsertim cum hujusmodi res ad inquirendum laboriosæ ad meditandum ignobiles, ad discendum asperæ, ad practicam illiberales, numero infinitæ, et subtilitate pusillæ videri soleant, et ob hujusmodi conditiones, gloriæ artium minus sint accommodatæ."[24] This opinion seemed to him "omnia in familia humana turbasse." It had undoubtedly caused many arts which were of the greatest utility, and which were susceptible of the greatest improvements, to be neglected by speculators, and abandoned to joiners, masons, smiths, weavers, apothecaries. It was necessary to assert the dignity of those arts, to bring them prominently forward, to proclaim that, as they have a most serious effect on human happiness, they are not unworthy of the attention of the highest human intellects. Again, it was by illustrations drawn from these arts that Bacon could most easily illustrate his principles. It was by improvements effected in these arts that the soundness of his principles could be most speedily and decisively brought to the test, and made manifest to common understandings. He acted like a wise commander who thins every other part of his line to strengthen a point where the enemy is attacking with peculiar fury, and on the fate of which the event of the battle seems likely to depend. In the *Novum Organum*, however, he distinctly and most truly declares that his philosophy is no less a Moral than a Natural Philosophy, that, though his illustrations are drawn from physical science, the principles which those illustrations are intended to explain are just as applicable to ethical and political inquiries as to inquiries into the nature of heat and vegetation. [25]

He frequently treated of moral subjects; and he brought to those subjects that spirit which was the essence of his whole system. He has left us many admirable practicable observations on what he somewhat quaintly called the Georgics of the mind, on the mental culture which tends to produce good dispositions. Some persons, he said, might accuse him of spending labour on a matter so simple that his predecessors had passed it by with contempt. He desired such persons to remember that he had from the first announced the objects of his search to be not the splendid and the surprising, but the useful and the true, not the deluding dreams which go forth through the shining portal of ivory, but the humbler realities of the gate of horn. [26]

True to this principle, he indulged in no rants about the fitness of things, the all-sufficiency of virtue, and the dignity of human nature. He dealt not at all in resounding nothings, such as those with which Bolingbroke pretended to comfort himself in exile, and in which Cicero vainly sought consolation after the loss of Tullia. The casuistical subtilties which occupied the attention of the keenest spirits of his age had, it should seem, no attractions for him. The doctors whom Escobar afterwards compared to the four beasts and the four-and-twenty elders in the Apocalypse Bacon dismissed with most contemptuous brevity. "Inanes plerumque evadunt et futiles." [27] Nor did he ever meddle with those enigmas which have puzzled hundreds of generations, and will puzzle hundreds more. He said nothing about the grounds of moral obligation, or the freedom of the human will. He had no inclination to employ himself in labours resembling those of the damned in the Grecian Tartarus, to spin for ever on the same wheel round the same pivot, to gape for ever after the same deluding clusters, to pour water for ever into the same bottomless buckets, to pace for ever to and fro on the same wearisome path after the same recoiling stone. He exhorted his disciples to prosecute researches of a very different description, to consider moral science as a practical science, a science of which the object was to cure the diseases and perturbations of the mind, and which could be improved only by a method analogous to that which has improved medicine and surgery. Moral philosophers ought, he said, to set themselves vigorously to work for the purpose of discovering what are the actual effects produced on the human character by particular modes of education, by the indulgence of particular habits, by the study of particular books, by society, by emulation, by imitation. Then we might hope to find out what mode of training was most likely to preserve and restore moral health. [28]

What he was as a natural philosopher and a moral philosopher, that he was also as a theologian. He was, we are convinced, a sincere believer in the divine authority of the Christian revelation. Nothing can be found in his writings, or in any other writings, more eloquent and pathetic than some passages which were apparently written under the influence of strong devotional feeling. He loved to dwell on the power of the Christian religion to effect much that the ancient philosophers could only promise. He loved to consider that religion as the bond of charity, the curb of evil passions, the consolation of the

wretched, the support of the timid, the hope of the dying. But controversies on speculative points of theology seem to have engaged scarcely any portion of his attention. In what he wrote on Church Government he showed, as far as he dared, a tolerant and charitable spirit. He troubled himself not at all about Homoousians and Homoiousians, Monothelites and Nestorians. He lived in an age in which disputes on the most subtle points of divinity excited an intense interest throughout Europe, and nowhere more than in England. He was placed in the very thick of the conflict. He was in power at the time of the Synod of Dort, and must for months have been daily deafened with talk about election, reprobation, and final perseverance. Yet we do not remember a line in his works from which it can be inferred that he was either a Calvinist or an Arminian. While the world was resounding with the noise of a disputatious philosophy and a disputatious theology, the Baconian school, like Alworthy seated between Square and Thwackum, preserved a calm neutrality, half scornful, half benevolent, and, content with adding to the sum of practical good, left the war of words to those who liked it.

We have dwelt long on the end of the Baconian philosophy, because from this peculiarity all the other peculiarities of that philosophy necessarily arose. Indeed, scarcely any person who proposed to himself the same end with Bacon could fail to hit upon the same means.

The vulgar notion about Bacon we take to be this, that he invented a new method of arriving at truth, which method is called Induction, and that he detected some fallacy in the syllogistic reasoning which had been in vogue before his time. This notion is about as well founded as that of the people who, in the middle ages, imagined that Virgil was a great conjurer. Many who are far too well informed to talk such extravagant nonsense entertain what we think incorrect notions as to what Bacon really effected in this matter.

The inductive method has been practised ever since the beginning of the world by every human being. It is constantly practised by the most ignorant clown, by the most thoughtless schoolboy, by the very child at the breast. That method leads the clown to the conclusion that if he sows barley he shall not reap wheat. By that method the schoolboy learns that a cloudy day is the best for catching trout. The very infant, we imagine, is led by induction to expect milk from his mother or nurse, and none from his father.

Not only is it not true that Bacon invented the inductive method; but it is not true that he was the first person who correctly analysed that method and explained its uses. Aristotle had long before pointed out the absurdity of supposing that syllogistic reasoning could ever conduct men to the discovery of any new principle, had shown that such discoveries must be made by induction, and by induction alone, and had given the history of the inductive process, concisely indeed, but with great perspicuity and precision.

Again, we are not inclined to ascribe much practical value to that analysis of the inductive method which Bacon has given in the second book of the *Novum Organum*. It is indeed an elaborate and correct analysis. But it is an analysis of that which we are all doing from morning to night, and which we continue to do even in our dreams. A plain man finds his stomach out of order. He never heard Lord Bacon's name. But he proceeds in the strictest conformity with the rules laid down in the second book of the *Novum Organum*, and satisfies himself that minced pies have done the mischief. "I ate minced pies on Monday and Wednesday, and I was kept awake by indigestion all night." This is the *comparentia ad intellectum instantiarum convenientium*. "I did not eat any on Tuesday and Friday, and I was quite well." This is the *comparentia instantiarum in proximo quæ natura data privantur.* "I ate very sparingly of them on Sunday, and was very slightly indisposed in the evening. But on Christmas-day I almost dined on them, and was so ill that I was in great danger." This is the *comparentia instantiarum secundum magis et minus.* "It cannot have been the brandy which I took with them. For I have drunk brandy daily for years without being the worse for it." This is the *rejectio naturarum.* Our invalid then proceeds to what is termed by Bacon the *Vindemiatio,* and pronounces that minced pies do not agree with him.

We repeat that we dispute neither the ingenuity nor the accuracy of the theory contained in the second book of the *Novum Organum;* but we think that Bacon greatly overrated its utility. We conceive that the inductive process, like many other processes, is not likely to be better performed merely because men know how they perform it. William Tell would not have been one whit more likely to cleave the apple if he had known that his arrow would describe a parabola under the influence of the attraction of the earth. Captain Barclay would not have been more likely to walk a thousand miles in a thousand hours, if he had known the place and name of every muscle in his legs. Monsieur Jourdain probably did not pronounce D and F more correctly after he had been apprised that D is pronounced by touching the teeth with the end of the tongue, and F by putting the upper teeth on the lower lip. We cannot perceive that the study of Grammar makes the smallest difference in the speech of people who have always lived in good society. Not one Londoner in ten thousand can lay down the rules for the proper use of *will* and *shall.* Yet not one Londoner in a million ever misplaces his *will* and *shall.* Doctor Robertson could, undoubtedly, have written a luminous dissertation on the use of those words. Yet, even in his latest work, he sometimes misplaced them ludicrously. No man uses figures of speech with more propriety because he knows that one figure is called a metonymy and another a synecdoche. A drayman in a passion calls out, "You are a pretty fellow," without suspecting that he is uttering irony, and that irony is one of the four primary tropes. The old systems of rhetoric were never regarded by the most experienced and discerning judges as of any use for the purpose of forming an orator. "Ego hanc vim intelligo," said Cicero, "esse in præceptis omnibus, non ut ea secuti oratores eloquentiæ laudem sint adepti, sed quæ sua sponte homines eloquentes facerent, ea quosdam observasse, atque id egisse; sic esse non eloquentiam ex artificio, sed artificium ex eloquentia natum." We must own that we entertain the same opinion concerning the study of Logic which Cicero entertained concerning the study of Rhetoric. A man of sense syllogizes in *celarent* and *sesare* all day long without suspecting it; and, though he may not know what an *ignoratio elenchi* is, has no difficulty in exposing it whenever he falls in with it; which is likely to be as often as he falls in with a Reverend Master of Arts nourished on mode and figure in the cloisters of Oxford. Considered merely as an intellectual feat, the *Organum* of Aristotle can scarcely be admired too highly. But the more we compare individual with individual, school with school, nation with nation, generation with generation, the more do we lean to the opinion that the knowledge of the theory of logic has no tendency whatever to make men good reasoners.

What Aristotle did for the syllogistic process Bacon has, in the second book of the *Novum Organum,* done for the inductive process; that is to say, he has analysed it well. His rules are quite proper; but we do not need them, because they are drawn from our own constant practice.

But, though everybody is constantly performing the process described in the second book of the *Novum Organum,* some men perform it well and some perform it ill. Some are led by it to truth, and some to error. It led Franklin to discover the nature of lightning. It led thousands, who had less brains than Franklin, to believe in animal magnetism. But this was not because Franklin went through the process described by Bacon, and the dupes of Mesmer through a different process. The *comparentiæ* and *rejectiones* of which we have given examples will be found in the most unsound inductions. We have heard that an eminent judge of the last generation was in the habit of jocosely propounding after dinner a theory, that the cause of the prevalence of Jacobinism was the practice of bearing three names. He quoted on the one side Charles James Fox, Richard Brinsley Sheridan, John Horne Tooke, John Philpot Curran, Samuel Taylor Coleridge, Theobald Wolfe Tone. These were *instantiæ convenientes.* He then proceeded to cite instances *absentiæ in proximo,* William Pitt, John Scott, William Windham, Samuel Horsley, Henry Dundas, Edmund Burke. He might have gone on to instances *secundum magis et minus.* The practice of giving children three names has been for some time a growing practice, and Jacobinism has also been growing. The practice of giving children three names is more common in America than in England. In England we still have a King and a House of Lords; but the Americans are republicans. The *rejectiones* are obvious. Burke and Theobald Wolfe Tone are both Irishmen; therefore the being an Irishman is not the cause of Jacobinism. Horsley and Horne Tooke are both clergymen; therefore the being a clergyman is not the cause of Jacobinism. Fox and Windham were both educated at Oxford; therefore the being educated at Oxford is not the cause of Jacobinism. Pitt and Horne Tooke were both educated at Cambridge; therefore the being educated at Cambridge is not the cause of Jacobinism. In this way, our inductive philosopher arrives at what Bacon calls the Vintage, and pronounces that the having three names is the cause of Jacobinism.

Here is an induction corresponding with Bacon's analysis and ending in a monstrous absurdity. In what then does this induction differ from the induction which leads us to the conclusion that the presence of the sun is the cause of our having more light by day than by night? The difference evidently is not in the kind of instances, but in the number of instances; that is to say, the difference is not in that part of the process for which Bacon has given precise rules, but in a circumstance for which no precise rule can possibly be given. If the learned author of the theory about Jacobinism had enlarged either of his tables a little, his system would have been destroyed. The names of Tom Paine and William Wyndham Grenville would have been sufficient to do the work.

It appears to us, then, that the difference between a sound and unsound induction does not lie in this, that the author of the sound induction goes through the process analysed in the second book of the *Novum Organum,* and the author of the unsound induction through a different process. They both perform the same process. But one performs it foolishly or carelessly; the other performs it with patience, attention, sagacity, and judgment. Now precepts can do little towards making men patient and attentive, and still less towards making them sagacious and judicious. It is very well to tell men to be on their guard against prejudices, not to believe facts on slight evidence, not to be content with a scanty collection of facts, to put out of their minds the *idola* which Bacon has so finely described. But these rules are too general to be of much practical use. The question is, What is a prejudice? How long does the incredulity with which I hear a new theory propounded continue to be a wise and salutary incredulity? When does it become an *idolum specus*, the unreasonable pertinacity of a too sceptical mind? What is slight evidence? What collection of facts is scanty? Will ten instances do, or fifty, or a hundred? In how many months would the first human beings who settled on the shores of the ocean have been justified in believing that the moon had an influence on the tides? After how many experiments would Jenner have been justified in believing that he had discovered a safeguard against the small-pox? These are questions to which it would be most desirable to have a precise answer; but unhappily they are questions to which no precise answer can be returned.

We think then that it is possible to lay down accurate rules, as Bacon has done, for the performing of that part of the inductive process which all men perform alike; but that these rules, though accurate, are not wanted, because in truth they only tell us to do what we are all doing. We think that it is impossible to lay down any precise rule for the performing of that part of the inductive process which a great experimental philosopher performs in one way, and a superstitious old woman in another.

On this subject, we think, Bacon was in an error. He certainly attributed to his rules a value which did not belong to them. He went so far as to say, that, if his method of making discoveries were adopted, little would depend on the degree of force or acuteness of any intellect; that all minds would be reduced to one level, that his philosophy resembled a compass or a rule which equalises all hands, and enables the most unpractised person to draw a more correct circle or line than the best draughtsmen can produce without such aid.[29] This really seems to us as extravagant as it would have been in Lindley Murray to announce that everybody who should learn his *Grammar* would write as good English as Dryden, or in that very able writer, the Archbishop of Dublin, to promise that all the readers of his *Logic* would reason like Chillingworth, and that all the readers of his *Rhetoric* would speak like Burke. That Bacon was altogether mistaken as to this point will now hardly be disputed. His philosophy has flourished during two hundred years, and has produced none of this levelling. The interval between a man of talents and a dunce is as wide as ever; and is never more clearly discernible than when they engage in researches which require the constant use of induction.

It will be seen that we do not consider Bacon's ingenious analysis of the inductive method as a very useful performance. Bacon was not, as we have already said, the inventor of the inductive method. He was not even the person who first analysed the inductive method correctly, though he undoubtedly analysed it more minutely than any who preceded him. He was not the person who first showed that by the inductive method alone new truth could be discovered. But he was the person who first turned the minds of speculative men, long occupied in verbal disputes, to the discovery of new and useful truth; and, by doing so, he at once gave to the inductive method an importance and dignity which had never before belonged to it. He was not the maker of that road; he was not the discoverer of that road; he was not the person who first surveyed and mapped that road. But he was the person who first called the public attention to an inexhaustible mine of wealth, which had been utterly neglected, and which was accessible by that road alone. By doing so, he caused that road, which had previously been trodden only by peasants and higglers, to be frequented by a higher class of travellers.

That which was eminently his own in his system was the end which he proposed to himself. The end being given, the means, as it appears to us, could not well be mistaken. If others had aimed at the same object with Bacon, we hold it to be

certain that they would have employed the same method with Bacon. It would have been hard to convince Seneca that the inventing of a safety-lamp was an employment worthy of a philosopher. It would have been hard to persuade Thomas Aquinas to descend from the making of syllogisms to the making of gunpowder. But Seneca would never have doubted for a moment that it was only by means of a series of experiments that a safety-lamp could be invented. Thomas Aquinas would never have thought that his *barbara* and *baralipton* would enable him to ascertain the proportion which charcoal ought to bear to saltpetre in a pound of gunpowder. Neither common sense nor Aristotle would have suffered him to fall into such an absurdity.

By stimulating men to the discovery of new truth, Bacon stimulated them to employ the inductive method, the only method, even the ancient philosophers and the schoolmen themselves being judges, by which new truth can be discovered. By stimulating men to the discovery of useful truth, he furnished them with a motive to perform the inductive process well and carefully. His predecessors had been, in his phrase, not interpreters, but anticipators of nature. They had been content with the first principles at which they had arrived by the most scanty and slovenly induction. And why was this? It was, we conceive, because their philosophy proposed to itself no practical end, because it was merely an exercise of the mind. A man who wants to contrive a new machine or a new medicine has a strong motive to observe accurately and patiently, and to try experiment after experiment. But a man who merely wants a theme for disputation or declamation has no such motive. He is therefore content with premises grounded on assumption, or on the most scanty and hasty induction. Thus, we conceive, the schoolmen acted. On their foolish premises they often argued with great ability; and as their object was "assensum subjugare, non res,"[30] to be victorious in controversy, not to be victorious over nature, they were consistent. For just as much logical skill could be shown in reasoning on false as on true premises. But the followers of the new philosophy, proposing to themselves the discovery of useful truth as their object, must have altogether failed of attaining that object if they had been content to build theories on superficial induction.

Bacon has remarked[31] that in ages when philosophy was stationary, the mechanical arts went on improving. Why was this? Evidently because the mechanic was not content with so careless a mode of induction as served the purpose of the philosopher. And why was the philosopher more easily satisfied than the mechanic? Evidently because the object of the mechanic was to mould things, whilst the object of the philosopher was only to mould words. Careful induction is not at all necessary to the making of a good syllogism. But it is indispensable to the making of a good shoe. Mechanics, therefore, have always been, as far as the range of their humble but useful callings extended, not anticipators but interpreters of nature. And when a philosophy arose, the object of which was to do on a large scale what the mechanic does on a small scale, to extend the power and to supply the wants of man, the truth of the premises, which logically is a matter altogether unimportant, became a matter of the highest importance; and the careless induction with which men of learning had previously been satisfied gave place, of necessity, to an induction far more accurate and satisfactory.

What Bacon did for inductive philosophy may, we think, be fairly stated thus. The objects of preceding speculators were objects which could be attained without careful induction. Those speculators, therefore, did not perform the inductive process carefully. Bacon stirred up men to pursue an object which could be attained only by induction, and by induction carefully performed; and consequently induction was more carefully performed. We do not think that the importance of what Bacon did for inductive philosophy has ever been overrated. But we think that the nature of his services is often mistaken, and was not fully understood even by himself. It was not by furnishing philosophers with rules for performing the inductive process well, but by furnishing them with a motive for performing it well, that he conferred so vast a benefit on society.

To give to the human mind a direction which it shall retain for ages is the rare prerogative of a few imperial spirits. It cannot, therefore, be uninteresting to inquire what was the moral and intellectual constitution which enabled Bacon to exercise so vast an influence on the world.

In the temper of Bacon,—we speak of Bacon the philosopher, not of Bacon the lawyer and politician,—there was a singular union of audacity and sobriety. The promises which he made to mankind might, to a superficial reader, seem to resemble the rants which a great dramatist has put into the mouth of an Oriental conqueror half-crazed by good fortune and by violent passions.

> He shall have chariots easier than air,
> Which I will have invented; and thyself
> That art the messenger shall ride before him,
> On a horse cut out of an entire diamond,
> That shall be made to go with golden wheels,
> I know not how yet.

But Bacon performed what he promised. In truth, Fletcher would not have dared to make Arbaces promise, in his wildest fits of excitement, the tithe of what the Baconian philosophy has performed.

The true philosophical temperament may, we think, be described in four words, much hope, little faith; a disposition to believe that any thing, however extraordinary, may be done; an indisposition to believe that any thing extraordinary has been done. In these points the constitution of Bacon's mind seems to us to have been absolutely perfect. He was at once the Mammon and the Surly of his friend Ben. Sir Epicure did not indulge in visions more magnificent and gigantic. Surly did not sift evidence with keener and more sagacious incredulity.

Closely connected with this peculiarity of Bacon's temper was a striking peculiarity of his understanding. With great minuteness of observation he had an amplitude of comprehension such as has never yet been vouchsafed to any other human being. The small fine mind of Labruyère had not a more delicate tact than the large intellect of Bacon. The *Essays* contain abundant proofs that no nice feature of character, no peculiarity in the ordering of a house, a garden, or a court-masque, could escape the notice of one whose mind was capable of taking in the whole world of knowledge. His understanding resembled the tent which the fairy Paribanou gave to Prince Ahmed. Fold it; and it seemed a toy for the hand of a lady. Spread it; and the armies of powerful Sultans might repose beneath its shade.

In keenness of observation he has been equalled, though perhaps never surpassed. But the largeness of his mind was all his own. The glance with which he surveyed the intellectual universe resembled that which the Archangel, from the golden threshold of heaven, darted down into the new creation.

> Round he surveyed,—and well might, where he stood
> So high above the circling canopy

> Of night's extended shade,—from eastern point
> Of Libra, to the fleecy star which bears
> Andromeda far off Atlantic seas
> Beyond the horizon.

His knowledge differed from that of other men, as a terrestrial globe differs from an Atlas which contains a different country on every leaf. The towns and roads of England, France, and Germany are better laid down in the Atlas than on the globe. But while we are looking at England we see nothing of France; and while we are looking at France we see nothing of Germany. We may go to the Atlas to learn the bearings and distances of York and Bristol, or of Dresden and Prague. But it is useless if we want to know the bearings and distances of France and Martinique, or of England and Canada. On the globe we shall not find all the market towns in our own neighbourhood; but we shall learn from it the comparative extent and the relative position of all the kingdoms of the earth. "I have taken," said Bacon, in a letter written when he was only thirty-one, to his uncle Lord Burleigh, "I have taken all knowledge to be my province." In any other young man, indeed in any other man, this would have been a ridiculous flight of presumption. There have been thousands of better mathematicians, astronomers, chemists, physicians, botanists, mineralogists, than Bacon. No man would go to Bacon's works to learn any particular science or art, any more than he would go to a twelve-inch globe in order to find his way from Kennington turnpike to Clapham Common. The art which Bacon taught was the art of inventing arts. The knowledge in which Bacon excelled all men was a knowledge of the mutual relations of all departments of knowledge.

The mode in which he communicated his thoughts was peculiar to him. He had no touch of that disputatious temper which he often censured in his predecessors. He effected a vast intellectual revolution in opposition to a vast mass of prejudices; yet he never engaged in any controversy: nay, we cannot at present recollect, in all his philosophical works, a single passage of a controversial character. All those works might with propriety have been put into the form which he adopted in the work entitled *Cogitata et visa*: "Franciscus Baconus sic cogitavit." These are thoughts which have occurred to me: weigh them well: and take them or leave them.

Borgia said of the famous expedition of Charles the Eighth, that the French had conquered Italy, not with steel, but with chalk; for that the only exploit which they had found necessary for the purpose of taking military occupation of any place had been to mark the doors of the houses where they meant to quarter. Bacon often quoted this saying, and loved to apply it to the victories of his own intellect.[32] His philosophy, he said, came as a guest, not as an enemy. She found no difficulty in gaining admittance, without a contest, in every understanding fitted, by its structure and by its capacity, to receive her. In all this we think that he acted most judiciously; first, because, as he has himself remarked, the difference between his school and other schools was a difference so fundamental that there was hardly any common ground on which a controversial battle could be fought; and, secondly, because his mind, eminently observant, preëminently discursive and capacious, was, we conceive, neither formed by nature nor disciplined by habit for dialectical combat.

Though Bacon did not arm his philosophy with the weapons of logic, he adorned her profusely with all the richest decorations of rhetoric. His eloquence, though not untainted with the vicious taste of his age, would alone have entitled him to a high rank in literature. He had a wonderful talent for packing thought close, and rendering it portable. In wit, if by wit be meant the power of perceiving analogies between things which appear to have nothing in common, he never had an equal, not even Cowley, not even the author of *Hudibras*. Indeed, he possessed this faculty, or rather this faculty possessed him, to a morbid degree. When he abandoned himself to it without reserve, as he did in the *Sapientia Veterum*, and at the end of the second book of the *De Augmentis*, the feats which he performed were not merely admirable, but portentous, and almost shocking. On these occasions we marvel at him as clowns on a fair-day marvel at a juggler, and can hardly help thinking that the devil must be in him.

These, however, were freaks in which his ingenuity now and then wantoned, with scarcely any other object than to astonish and amuse. But it occasionally happened that, when he was engaged in grave and profound investigations, his wit obtained the mastery over all his other faculties, and led him into absurdities into which no dull man could possibly have fallen. We will give the most striking instance which at present occurs to us. In the third book of the *De Augmentis* he tells us that there are some principles which are not peculiar to one science, but are common to several. That part of philosophy which concerns itself with these principles is, in his nomenclature, designated as *philosophia prima*. He then proceeds to mention some of the principles with which this *philosophia prima* is conversant. One of them is this. An infectious disease is more likely to be communicated while it is in progress than when it has reached its height. This, says he, is true in medicine. It is also true in morals; for we see that the example of very abandoned men injures public morality less than the example of men in whom vice has not yet extinguished all good qualities. Again, he tells us that in music a discord ending in a concord is agreeable, and thus the same thing may be noted in the affections. Once more, he tells us, that in physics the energy with which a principle acts is often increased by the antiperistasis of its opposite; and that it is the same in the contests of factions. If the making of ingenious and sparkling similitudes like these be indeed the *philosophia prima*, we are quite sure that the greatest philosophical work of the nineteenth century is Mr. Moore's *Lalla Rookh*. The similitudes which we have cited are very happy similitudes. But that a man like Bacon should have taken them for more, that he should have thought the discovery of such resemblances as these an important part of philosophy, has always appeared to us one of the most singular facts in the history of letters.

The truth is that his mind was wonderfully quick in perceiving analogies of all sorts. But, like several eminent men whom we could name, both living and dead, he sometimes appeared strangely deficient in the power of distinguishing rational from fanciful analogies, analogies which are arguments from analogies which are mere illustrations, analogies like that which Bishop Butler so ably pointed out, between natural and revealed religion, from analogies like that which Addison discovered, between the series of Grecian gods carved by Phidias and the series of English kings painted by Kneller. This want of discrimination has led to many strange political speculations. Sir William Temple deduced a theory of government from the properties of the pyramid. Mr. Southey's whole system of finance is grounded on the phænomena of evaporation and rain. In theology, this perverted ingenuity has made still wilder work. From the time of Irenæus and Origen down to the present day, there has not been a single generation in which great divines have not been led into the most absurd expositions of Scripture, by mere incapacity to distinguish analogies proper, to use the scholastic phrase, from analogies metaphorical.[33] It is curious that Bacon has himself mentioned this very kind of delusion among the *idola specus*; and has mentioned in language which, we are inclined to think, shows that he knew himself to be subject to it. It is the vice, he tells us, of subtle minds to attach too much importance to slight distinctions; it is the vice, on the other hand, of high and discursive intellects to attach too much importance to slight resemblances; and he adds that, when this last propensity is indulged to excess, it leads men to catch at shadows instead of substances.[34]

Yet we cannot wish that Bacon's wit had been less luxuriant. For, to say nothing of the pleasure which it affords, it was in the vast majority of cases employed for the purpose of making obscure truth plain, of making repulsive truth attractive, of fixing in the mind forever truth which might otherwise have left but a transient impression.

The poetical faculty was powerful in Bacon's mind, but not, like his wit, so powerful as occasionally to usurp the place of his reason, and to tyrannize over the whole man. No imagination was ever at once so strong and so thoroughly subjugated. It never stirred but at a signal from good sense. It stopped at the first check from good sense. Yet, though disciplined to such obedience, it gave noble proofs of its vigour. In truth, much of Bacon's life was passed in a visionary world, amidst things as strange as any that are described in the *Arabian Tales*, or in those romances on which the curate and barber of Don Quixote's village performed so cruel an *auto-da-fé*, amidst buildings more sumptuous than the palace of Aladdin, fountains more wonderful than the golden water of Parizade, conveyances more rapid than the hippogryph of Ruggiero, arms more formidable than the lance of Astolfo, remedies more efficacious than the balsam of Fierabras. Yet in his magnificent day-dreams there was nothing wild, nothing but what sober reason sanctioned. He knew that all the secrets feigned by poets to have been written in the books of enchanters are worthless when compared with the mighty secrets which are really written in the book of nature, and which, with time and patience, will be read there. He knew that all the wonders wrought by all the talismans in fable were trifles when compared to the wonders which might reasonably be expected from the philosophy of fruit, and that, if his words sank deep into the minds of men, they would produce effects such as superstition had never ascribed to the incantations of Merlin and Michael Scot. It was here that he loved to let his imagination loose. He loved to picture to himself the world as it would be when his philosophy should, in his own noble phrase, "have enlarged the bounds of human empire."[35] We might refer to many instances. But we will content ourselves with the strongest, the description of the House of Solomon in the *New Atlantis*. By most of Bacon's contemporaries, and by some people of our time, this remarkable passage would, we doubt not, be considered as an ingenious rodomontade, a counterpart to the adventures of Sinbad or Baron Munchausen. The truth is, that there is not to be found in any human composition a passage more eminently distinguished by profound and serene wisdom. The boldness and originality of the fiction is far less wonderful than the nice discernment which carefully excluded from that long list of prodigies every thing that can be pronounced impossible, every thing that can be proved to lie beyond the mighty magic of induction and of time. Already some parts, and not the least startling parts, of this glorious prophecy have been accomplished, even according to the letter; and the whole, construed according to the spirit, is daily accomplishing all around us.

One of the most remarkable circumstances in the history of Bacon's mind is the order in which its powers expanded themselves. With him the fruit came first and remained till the last; the blossoms did not appear till late. In general, the development of the fancy is to the development of the judgment what the growth of a girl is to the growth of a boy. The fancy attains at an earlier period to the perfection of its beauty, its power, and its fruitfulness; and, as it is first to ripen, it is also first to fade. It has generally lost something of its bloom and freshness before the sterner faculties have reached maturity; and is commonly withered and barren while those faculties still retain all their energy. It rarely happens that the fancy and the judgment grow together. It happens still more rarely that the judgment grows faster than the fancy. This seems, however, to have been the case with Bacon. His boyhood and youth appear to have been singularly sedate. His gigantic scheme of philosophical reform is said by some writers to have been planned before he was fifteen, and was undoubtedly planned while he was still young. He observed as vigilantly, meditated as deeply, and judged as temperately when he gave his first work to the world as at the close of his long career. But in eloquence, in sweetness and variety of expression, and in richness of illustration, his later writings are far superior to those of his youth. In this respect the history of his mind bears some resemblance to the history of the mind of Burke. The *Treatise on the Sublime and Beautiful*, though written on a subject which the coldest metaphysician could hardly treat without being occasionally betrayed into florid writing, is the most unadorned of all Burke's works. It appeared when he was twenty-five or twenty-six. When, at forty, he wrote the *Thoughts on the Causes of the existing Discontents*, his reason and his judgment had reached their full maturity; but his eloquence was still in its splendid dawn. At fifty, his rhetoric was quite as rich as good taste would permit; and when he died, at almost seventy, it had become ungracefully gorgeous. In his youth he wrote on the emotions produced by mountains and cascades, by the master-pieces of painting and sculpture, by the faces and necks of beautiful women, in the style of a Parliamentary report. In his old age he discussed treaties and tariffs in the most fervid and brilliant language of romance. It is strange that the *Essay on the Sublime and Beautiful*, and the *Letter to a Noble Lord*, should be the productions of one man. But it is far more strange that the *Essay* should have been a production of his youth, and the *Letter* of his old age.

We will give very short specimens of Bacon's two styles. In 1597, he wrote thus: "Crafty men contemn studies; simple men admire them; and wise men use them; for they teach not their own use: that is a wisdom without them, and won by observation. Read not to contradict, nor to believe, but to weigh and consider. Some books are to be tasted, others to be swallowed, and some few to be chewed and digested. Reading maketh a full man, conference a ready man, and writing an exact man. And therefore if a man write little, he had need have a great memory; if he confer little, have a present wit; and if he read little, have much cunning to seem to know that he doth not. Histories make men wise, poets witty, the mathematics subtle, natural philosophy deep, morals grave, logic and rhetoric able to contend." It will hardly be disputed that this is a passage to be "chewed and digested." We do not believe that Thucydides himself has anywhere compressed so much thought into so small a space.

In the additions which Bacon afterwards made to the *Essays*, there is nothing superior in truth or weight to what we have quoted. But his style was constantly becoming richer and softer. The following passage, first published in 1625, will show the extent of the change: "Prosperity is the blessing of the Old Testament; adversity is the blessing of the New, which carrieth the greater benediction and the clearer evidence of God's favour. Yet, even in the Old Testament, if you listen to David's harp you shall hear as many hearse-like airs as carols; and the pencil of the Holy Ghost hath laboured more in describing the afflictions of Job than the felicities of Solomon. Prosperity is not without many fears and distastes; and adversity is not without comforts and hopes. We see in needleworks and embroideries it is more pleasing to have a lively work upon a sad and solemn ground, than to have a dark and melancholy work upon a lightsome ground. Judge therefore of the pleasure of the heart by the pleasure of the eye. Certainly virtue is like precious odours, most fragrant when they are incensed or crushed; for prosperity doth best discover vice, but adversity doth best discover virtue."

It is by the *Essays* that Bacon is best known to the multitude. The *Novum Organum* and the *De Augmentis* are much talked of, but little read. They have produced indeed a vast effect on the opinions of mankind; but they have produced it through the operation of intermediate agents. They have moved the intellects which have moved the world. It is in the *Essays* alone that the mind of Bacon is brought into immediate contact with the minds of ordinary readers. There he opens an exoteric school, and talks to plain men, in language which everybody understands, about things in which everybody is interested. He has thus enabled those who must otherwise have taken his merits on trust to judge for themselves; and the great body of readers have, during several generations, acknowledged that the man who has treated with such consummate ability questions with which they are familiar may well be supposed to deserve all the praise bestowed on him by those who have sat in his inner school.

Without any disparagement to the admirable treatise *De Augmentis*, we must say that, in our judgment, Bacon's greatest performance is the first book of the *Novum Organum*. All the peculiarities of his extraordinary mind are found there in the highest perfection. Many of the aphorisms, but particularly those in which he gives examples of the influence of the *idola*, show a nicety of observation that has never been surpassed. Every part of the book blazes with wit, but with wit which is employed only to illustrate and decorate truth. No book ever made so great a revolution in the mode of thinking, overthrew so many prejudices, introduced so many new opinions. Yet no book was ever written in a less contentious spirit. It truly conquers with chalk and not with steel. Proposition after proposition enters into the mind, is received not as an invader, but as a welcome friend, and though previously unknown, becomes at once domesticated. But what we most admire is the vast capacity of that intellect which, without effort, takes in at once all the domains of science, all the past, the present, and the future, all the errors of two thousand years, all the encouraging signs of the passing times, all the bright hopes of the coming age. Cowley, who was among the most ardent, and not among the least discerning followers of the new philosophy, has, in one of his finest poems, compared Bacon to Moses standing on Mount Pisgah. It is to Bacon, we think, as he appears in the first book of the *Novum Organum*, that the comparison applies with peculiar felicity. There we see the great Lawgiver looking round from his lonely elevation on an infinite expanse; behind him a wilderness of dreary sands and bitter waters, in which successive generations have sojourned, always moving, yet never advancing, reaping no harvest, and building no abiding city; before him a goodly land, a land of promise, a land flowing with milk and honey. While the multitude below saw only the flat sterile desert in which they had so long wandered, bounded on every side by a near horizon, or diversified only by some deceitful mirage, he was gazing from a far higher stand on a far lovelier country, following with his eye the long course of fertilising rivers, through ample pastures, and under the bridges of great capitals, measuring the distances of marts and havens, and portioning out all those wealthy regions from Dan to Beersheba.

It is painful to turn back from contemplating Bacon's philosophy to contemplate his life. Yet without so turning back it is impossible fairly to estimate his powers. He left the University at an earlier age than that at which most people repair thither. While yet a boy he was plunged into the midst of diplomatic business. Thence he passed to the study of a vast technical system of law, and worked his way up through a succession of laborious offices, to the highest post in his profession. In the mean time he took an active part in every Parliament; he was an adviser of the Crown: he paid court with the greatest assiduity and address to all whose favour was likely to be of use to him; he lived much in society; he noted the slightest peculiarities of character, and the slightest changes of fashion. Scarcely any man has led a more stirring life than that which Bacon led from sixteen to sixty. Scarcely any man has been better entitled to be called a thorough man of the world. The founding of a new philosophy, the imparting of a new direction to the mind of speculators, this was the amusement of his leisure, the work of hours occasionally stolen from the Woolsack and the Council Board. This consideration, while it increases the admiration with which we regard his intellect, increases also our regret that such an intellect should so often have been unworthily employed. He well knew the better course, and had, at one time, resolved to pursue it. "I confess," said he in a letter written when he was still young, "that I have as vast contemplative ends as I have moderate civil ends." Had his civil ends continued to be moderate, he would have been, not only the Moses, but the Joshua of philosophy. He would have fulfilled a large part of his own magnificent predictions. He would have led his followers, not only to the verge, but into the heart of the promised land. He would not merely have pointed out, but would have divided the spoil. Above all, he would have left, not only a great, but a spotless name. Mankind would then have been able to esteem their illustrious benefactor. We should not then be compelled to regard his character with mingled contempt and admiration, with mingled aversion and gratitude. We should not then regret that there should be so many proofs of the narrowness and selfishness of a heart, the benevolence of which was yet large enough to take in all races and all ages. We should not then have to blush for the disingenuousness of the most devoted worshipper of speculative truth, for the servility of the boldest champion of intellectual freedom. We should not then have seen the same man at one time far in the van, at another time far in the rear of his generation. We should not then be forced to own that he who first treated legislation as a science was among the last Englishmen who used the rack, that he who first summoned philosophers to the great work of interpreting nature, was among the last Englishmen who sold justice. And we should conclude our survey of a life placidly, honourably, beneficently passed, "in industrious observations, grounded conclusions, and profitable inventions and discoveries,"[36] with feelings very different from those with which we now turn away from the checkered spectacle of so much glory and so much shame.

Notes

1. Seneca, *Epist.* 90.
2. *Novum Organum*, Lib. 1. Aph. 71, 79. *De Augmentis*, Lib. 3. Cap. 4. *De Principiis atque originibus. Cogitata et visa. Redargutio philosophiarum.*
3. *Novum Organum*, Lib. 1. Aph. 73.
4. *De Augmentis*, Lib. 1.
5. Both these passages are in the first book of the *De Augmentis.*
6. *Redargutio Philosophiarum.*
7. Plato's *Republic*, Book 7.
8. *De Augmentis*, Lib. 3. Cap. 6.
9. Plato's *Republic*, Book 7.
10. Plutarch, *Sympos.* viii. and *Life of Marcellus.* The machines of Archytas are also mentioned by Aulus Gellius and Diogenes Laertius.
11. Usui et commodis hominum consulimus.
12. Compare the passage relating to mathematics in the Second Book of the *Advancement of Learning*, with the *De Augmentis*, Lib. 3. Cap. 6.
13. Plato's *Republic*, Book 7.
14. *De Augmentis*, Lib. 3. Cap. 4.
15. *Astronomia viva.*
16. "Quae substantiam et motum et influxum coelestium, prout re vera sunt proponat." Compare this language with Plato's "*ta d'en tō ouranō iasomen.*"
17. Plato's *Phaedrus.*
18. Quinctilian, XI.
19. *De Augmentis*, Lib. 5. Cap. 5.
20. Plato's *Republic*, Book 3.
21. *De Augmentis*, Lib. 4. Cap. 2.
22. *De Augmentis*, Lib. 8. Cap. 3. Aph. 5.
23. *De Augmentis*, Lib. 8. Cap. 3. Aph. 69.
24. *Cogitata et visa.* The expression *opinio humida* may surprise a reader not accustomed to Bacon's style. The allusion is to the maxium of Heraclitus the obscure: "Dry light is the best." By dry light, Bacon understood the light of the intellect, not obscured by the mists of passion, interest, or prejudice.
25. *Novum Organum*, Lib. 1. Aph. 127.
26. *De Augmentis*, Lib. 7. Cap. 3.
27. *Ib.*, Lib. 7. Cap. 2.
28. *De Augmentis*, Lib. 7. Cap. 3.
29. *Novum Organum*, Praef. and Lib. 1. Aph. 122.
30. *Novum Organum*, Lib. 1. Aph. 29.
31. *De Augmentis*, Lib. 1.
32. *Novum Organum*, Lib. 1. Aph. 35 and elsewhere.
33. See some interesting remarks on this subject in Bishop Berkeley's *Minute Philosopher*, Dialogue IV.
34. *Novum Organum*, Lib. 1. Aph. 55.
35. *New Atlantis.*
36. From a letter of Bacon to Lord Burleigh.

JOHN CAIRD
From "The Scientific Character of Bacon" (1880)
University Addresses
1898, pp. 128–56

Bacon the philosopher of science, the author of the *De Augmentis* and *Novum Organum*, and Bacon the lawyer, politician, courtier; Bacon the high priest of nature, the herald of the new era of knowledge, inspired with a noble intellectual ardour, leading mankind back from the paths of error, and pointing the way to the kingdom of light and truth, and Bacon the subtle courtier, the ambitious, eager place-hunter, stooping to be jostled among the herd of time-servers and political lackeys in the courts of Elizabeth and James I.—seem to be not one man but two. In the one aspect of him we behold an intelligence of the highest order, conceiving and steadily pursuing all through life a project far in advance of his time, for the reorganization of the whole field of human knowledge; in the other aspect we seem to see the same intelligence busying itself with the petty aims and struggles of the pushing political adventurer, restlessly contriving how to supplant rivals, to curry favour with the dispensers of patronage, to secure a place if even in the very outskirts of the sphere of office and court favour, rejoicing in the faintest recognition of royalty—of royalty in the person of a vain pedant, "the wisest fool in Christendom," and of a woman who combined, in advanced years, the watchful jealousy of a despot with the waywardness of a youthful coquette. View him only as a thinker, and all the qualities that attract reverence for intellectual greatness—enthusiastic ardour in the pursuit of truth, penetrating and prophetic insight, grasp and comprehensiveness of mind, and a certain noble audacity of speculation and irrepressible confidence in human progress—meet the eye. View him only as an actor on the stage of public life, at one of the most corrupt periods of England's political history, and it is possible to see in him only a clever, pliant man of the world, inspired with a somewhat vulgar ambition for the good things of life, yielding to the contaminating influences of the time, cold and somewhat faithless in his friendships, identifying himself with the measures of rulers conspicuous for their meanness, duplicity, and cruelty, and sacrificing his own self-respect, if not for worldly gain, at least to serve the ends of people who were not worthy, and whom he must have known not to be worthy, to untie his shoe-latchet.

Such, or something like this, are the materials from which it has been possible to produce the picture, full of coarsely-drawn contrasts, of glaring lights and ink-black shadows, Hyperion and Satyr combined, which popular writers have offered to us as the faithful representation of the character of Bacon. Even were it nearer the truth than it is, it is difficult to understand the strange zest which these writers seem to feel in exposing the weaknesses and inconsistencies of a great nature, and in ferreting out every obscure and doubtful detail by which the proof of his supposed infamy can be strengthened. There are those, indeed, who can find consolation for their own littleness in the failings of an exalted mind, and whose delight in this sort of morbid anatomy is not to be wondered at; but surely for those who, by their own acknowledgment, find in Bacon "the most exquisitely constructed intellect that has ever been bestowed on any of the children of men," the worthier attitude would be, instead of airing one's wit and fancy and fine-writing over the inconsistencies of greatness, if possible, to ignore and forget them, if not, to speak of them with a regret too profound for flippancy. . . .

In reflecting on the bearing of Bacon's life on his philosophy, the question naturally suggests itself, whether his achievements as a philosopher would have been greater had his life been wholly devoted to philosophy. He was anything but a secluded thinker with no vocation but that of scientific investigation. If science, as he himself asserts, was his mistress, at first sight he seems to have been but an inconstant lover—content, at least, with but brief and infrequent interviews with the object of his adoration. His whole life, with but occasional intervals, was spent in the thick and throng of the world, amidst the exigencies of professional and public duty. He was a hardworking lawyer, first working his way by incessant study and application into practice; then acting as professional adviser of the crown, and finally, as Keeper of the Seals and Lord Chancellor, getting through an amount of business, and with an exactness and despatch which were in his day unprecedented. He was a leading Member of Parliament, taking an active share in the discussion of all important public measures. He was a courtier whose time and thought were at the disposal of officials and of a royal master and mistress whose caprices and humours made the pursuit of court favour and preferment anything but a sinecure. From all these vocations and the various social demands involved in them, it was but fragments

of his time and fag-ends of his thought which he could secure for literature and science. And yet in literature and science he worked harder and produced more than most men who have nothing else to do. Whatever the final verdict of criticism on the value of his philosophical and scientific labours, there can be no question that his productiveness as a writer was incessant and far beyond that of most men whose sole vocation was study, and that, whether his fame be justly earned or no, he achieved, and has long retained, the splendid reputation of the founder of the inductive philosophy, and as such, of the greatest contributor to the intellectual progress of mankind in modern times.

Regarding him, then, as a thinker and writer, was all this professional and public work sheer waste or malversation of intellectual power? Must we regret that so fine an instrument was set to do work so coarse and unsuitable? Would he have done more and to more purpose in his proper calling of thinker and writer, if he had had nothing to do but think and write? Now there can be no doubt that for most minds of average, or even more than average ability, it is a wise advice to say, Find out your work and stick to it. There are many whose career has been marred or frustrated either by missing their true vocation, or by scattering their energies so as to achieve poor and partial success in several lines, rather than much or great success in one. The old story of the dilettante peer who was, at best, only a philosopher among lords and a lord among philosophers is often repeated. Was Bacon, then, one of these instances of misdirected energy?

If we are to take his own word for it, the answer would undoubtedly be that he was. "Many errors," says he, "I do willingly acknowledge, and amongst the rest this great one that led the rest: that knowing myself by inward calling to be better fitted to hold a book than to play a part, I have led my life in civil causes for which I was not very fit by nature, and more unfit by preoccupation of mind." And again, in a prayer which he composed towards the close of his life, he confesses that "the talent of gifts and graces" which he had received he had "not put where it might have made best profit," but had "misspent in things for which he was least fit, so that he might truly say, 'My soul hath been a stranger in the course of my pilgrimage.'"

Yet, it may be questioned whether in so writing Bacon judged himself truly or from a correct estimate of his own special aptitudes. At first sight it seems to go without saying that undivided application to study is most favourable to production. But, on the other hand, there are men whose temperament is such that activity of mind grows with the demands made upon it. Within certain limits, the mental stimulation of multifarious employments more than makes up for the loss of time they involve; and they do their very best in one particular line, not when they can give their whole time to it, but when they have many other things to do. Moreover, for some minds at least, the whet of society is indispensable in order to the attainment of the right temper and use of their powers. Men dream of the great things they would do if they could only command unbroken leisure for thought and study, but when the leisure comes the dream is seldom realized. And this, if we have regard to Bacon's special genius and capacities, would not unlikely have been the result in his case, had his longing, real or feigned, for escape from the toils of business and society been gratified. For, as we shall immediately attempt to show, his great strength as a thinker lay, not in the region of philosophy and speculation, but in that of practical ethics, and the wisdom that is the outcome of much and varied experience and contact with the world. It may seem almost a heresy to say it, but I venture to affirm that Bacon's greatest and most characteristic work is not the *De Augmentis*, or the *Novum Organum*, or any of his purely scientific writings, but the *Essays*, and that even of his more ambitious works the most valuable element is the many incidental remarks and suggestions which constitute a kind of practical worldly wisdom or philosophy of common life.

Whatever may be said of Bacon's capacity to be the prophet of science, there can be but one opinion of his genius for the office of practical philosopher and professor of worldly wisdom. Nowhere perhaps in all literature ancient or modern can we find any other book which can be compared with Bacon's *Essays* as a manual of that wisdom which consists of the knowledge, not of man but of men—their tendencies, passions, prejudices, weaknesses; nowhere at any rate a book in which the whole experience of a most sagacious observer of human life is reproduced in such brief compass, expressed in language so packed with meaning, yet so sparkling with wit and fancy, grave humour, picturesque metaphor, and felicitous illustration. The *Essays* betray no talent for abstract speculation. There is no attempt in them at the exhaustive analysis of principles. The movement of thought is analogical rather than logical. They consist, for the most part, of miscellaneous remarks on human conduct, on the motives, illusions, self-deceptions, jealousies, ambitions, failures, successes, of men in the various relations of life, of prudential maxims, hints for the dexterous management of individuals and classes, counsels for youth and age, for the married and single, for parents and children, suggestions for the attainment of success in life, and consolations for the lack of it—advices to all sorts of people, sometimes profound, always sagacious and sensible, set off by striking illustrations and apt historic allusions, and couched in a form of expression, quaint, pointed, picturesque, and in almost every sentence having the stamp of a strong and original nature upon it.

Now this obviously is a kind of philosophy which is not to be learnt in lettered retirement, but only through much converse with the world. If Bacon had fled, as he often threatened to do, from the distractions of public life to the seclusion of a college cloister, or to the solitude of his study and gardens at Gorhambury, we might have gained more cumbrous treatises on scientific method, and a fuller elaboration of his vast yet impracticable scheme for the reorganization of human knowledge; but we should never have possessed the less pretentious but, in its own way, more genuine philosophy, the distilled essence of worldly wisdom and practical common sense which is preserved for us in the pages of the *Essays*. . . .

The splendour of Bacon's fame as a philosophical thinker and writer is due, in some measure at least, to the fact that he reflects and represents the intellectual spirit of his time. To say this is not to detract from his just claim to honour, though it may abate somewhat the exaggerated reverence which the popular mind has long rendered to him as the originator of the inductive method, and the founder of experimental science. Even if the speculative value of his exposition of the method of the sciences had been greater than can now be conceded to it, to ascribe to him the origination of that method and the impulse from which the vast and brilliant results of scientific investigation during the last two centuries have emanated, is altogether to misconceive the nature of the relation between science and what may be called the philosophy of science. Philosophy is a later birth of time than action, philosophical method is not the parent but child of practical experience. The analysis of an art, the unveiling of the intellectual process which runs through and unconsciously regulates it, is no mean achievement, nor one which is barren of practical results. But it is absurd to regard philosophical method as the creator of the

art itself, or the guide to the right practice of it. Grammar comes after speech, logic after reasoning, prosody after poetry. Grammatical principles and rules may help children to correct blunders of speech, rules of logic may sometimes assist us to detect, or at least to give formal reasons for the exposure of paralogisms and fallacious arguments; rules of prosody may enable a boy to put the proper number of syllables into a hexameter line or to produce a technically correct copy of verses; but it would be ridiculous to say that the first philosophic grammarian founded the art of correct speaking and writing, that men first learnt from Aristotle how to reason, or that the treasures of poetic genius which the world possesses owe their origin to the man who first elaborated the principles and rules of versification. In all these cases men have acted before they began to philosophize on their acting. It is as certain that the power to practise an art and the actual experimental exercise of that power must precede the investigating and formulating of the principles that underlie it, as that eating, drinking and digesting must precede physiology, or that the exercise of the bodily functions must precede anatomy. In point of fact (as has been remarked), the age of the grammarians of classic literature was long subsequent to the time of its greatest writers, nor can we suppose that Homer, or Sophocles, or Aeschylus ever formally studied Greek grammar or prosody, or that if they had done so, all their poetical triumphs must be traced back, if such a man had existed, to an early writer on the structure and grammar of the Greek language and the formal rules of fine writing.

And the same thing is true, *mutatis mutandis*, of the relation between science and the philosophy of science, between discovery and the reduction to rules of the method of scientific investigation. It is the scientific discoverer who comes first, and it is only later, and following in the wake of his movements, that the philosopher and logician gives speculative development to those methods of investigation which, by a kind of tact or instinct, the former has already pursued. It is not Bacon, but Copernicus, Galileo, Kepler, Gilbert, and others of that galaxy of experimental investigators, who, in obedience to a common impulse, had already, before Bacon took pen in hand, practised with splendid success what he preached,—it is they who must be regarded as the true originators of the great scientific revolution of the sixteenth century, and the forerunners of Newton and Leibnitz and Laplace, of Herschel and Faraday and Thomson, of that great intellectual host who in modern times have been the true interpreters of nature, and the practical asserters of man's dominion over her. To expound the philosophy of nature and the principles of scientific method is, as I have said, no mean achievement, and it betrays prejudice and narrowness of mind in any man of science if he slights or contemns it; but the province to which this achievement belongs is speculative, not practical, and its influence on scientific investigation and discovery is, at best, only indirect. Even, therefore, if Bacon's attempt to methodize science, and to unfold the principles and laws of scientific investigation, had been perfectly successful, his claim to be the creator and guide of scientific enquiry is of precisely the same sort as would be the claim of a writer on logic and rhetoric to be the inspirer and guide of all the thinkers and orators whose writings have not sinned against the laws of reason, or whose eloquence has ever carried conviction to human minds.

But we must now go on to remark that Bacon's attempt to methodize science, judged by its own merits, was far from successful. The *Novum Organum* is, in many respects, a marvellous work to be produced by a man whose own scientific knowledge was very meagre, who was absolutely ignorant of mathematics and of the principles and methods of the mathematical sciences, and who never was at the pains to acquaint himself with the labours of the great natural philosophers of Italy and of his own country, and with the results in the domain of mechanics and physical science already attained by them. What a powerful and comprehensive mind, fired with a genuine enthusiasm for knowledge, and a general conception of the right direction in which knowledge was to be sought, could achieve from materials so inadequate, Bacon has here accomplished. It was impossible for such a man to write so largely, on whatever subject, and with whatever design, without writing much that is instructive and interesting. And this great work is full of sage remarks, of knowledge of the human mind both in its weakness and its strength, and of acute incidental observations on all sorts of subjects; and it is pervaded by a noble ardour and loftiness of spirit, a grave yet intense enthusiasm for science, and a certain prophetic faith in the intellectual future of humanity.

But, estimated from a strictly scientific point of view, it has all the imperfection from which even the greatest mind, working with inadequate preparation, cannot escape. The method of scientific investigation which it propounds is one which no man of science has ever followed or could follow, the rules deduced from it are impracticable, and the ends at which it aims by the application of that method are chimerical and illusory. Let me try very briefly to show that it is so. Bacon's avowed aim, which in the *Novum Organum* he supposed himself to have realized, was to furnish mankind with a new and infallible method of discovery, by which the difficulties of scientific investigation should be, in a great measure, overcome, and the whole field of knowledge at no distant day explored. But the most striking advantage of this supposed method or instrument of discovery was, as its author conceived, that it would supersede inventive genius in science, and, in the work of investigation, confer on the most ordinary the same power with the highest minds. When we attempt to draw a circle with the unaided hand, the diversities of manual skill come out in the result, but with a pair of compasses all men can describe circles with equal exactitude, and the skilled draftsman has no advantage over others. So for his *Novum Organum* Bacon claimed the extraordinary merit of endowing all men of ordinary attention and industry with a capacity of penetrating into nature's secrets which should leave no room for disparities of intelligence.

It is needless to say that the history of scientific discovery since his day has proved the futility of any such notion as this levelling up or down of intellectual differences in the domain of physical enquiry. Great discoverers can no more be artificially manufactured than great poets or historians or philosophers. In science, as in other departments of human activity, there is room for the useful functions of the hewers of wood and drawers of water, as well as for that of the higher and more gifted intelligences; but the distinction in the kind and value of their work between these two classes still remains, and if the last two centuries have been signalized by the splendid advances which have been made in all departments of physical enquiry, that result is due mainly to the vast amount of intellectual ability and application which science has called forth.

But when we go on to consider what was Bacon's conception of the nature of science and of the problems which it seeks to solve, we are no longer surprised at the artificial character of his method and the exaggerated anticipations he entertained of its success. If the system of nature were what Bacon supposed it to be, it would be a comparatively easy thing for the dullest mind, once possessed of the key which his method supplies, to read off her most hidden secrets. The whole physical world, with all the infinite variety of objects it contains, he conceived to consist of a limited number of simple elements or qualities variously combined, just as, according to his own comparison, the countless multiplicity of words in a language are only various combinations of the small number of letters which compose its alphabet. And as the knowledge of the alphabet enables us to understand the composition of every word, so all that was necessary in order to the complete knowledge of all concrete objects in nature was simply to get hold of her simple elementary qualities; nay, as he who knows the alphabet and the laws of spelling and syntax, can not only read, but reproduce the words and sentences, so he seems to have supposed that the grammar of nature thus learned would make a man master of nature, and enable him to reproduce and modify her substances at will. "The forms" (or immanent causes), says he, "of motion, of vegetation, of gravity and levity, of density and tenuity, of heat, of cold, and all other natures and qualities, like an alphabet, are not many; and of these the essences upheld by matter of all creatures do consist." "The simple forms or differences of things are few in number, and the degrees and co-ordinations thereof make all this variety." "Gold," for example, he says, "has these natures, greatness of weight, closeness of parts, fixation, pliantness or softness, immunity from rust, colour or tincture of yellow. Therefore the sure way to make gold is to know the causes of the several natures before rehearsed. For if a man can make a metal that hath all these properties, let men dispute whether it be gold or no."

This, then, being his conception of nature, the problem of science became a comparatively simple one, and the solution of it, in every case, a purely mechanical or artificial process. The rules of investigation and discovery are as capable of being formulated and preached as the rule of three or the method of extracting the square root, or the way in which an apothecary mixes up the ingredients of a doctor's prescription. What you have to do in order to discover the cause of a given phenomenon is, first, to make a collection of facts or instances in which the phenomenon in question is present, then another collection of instances in which it is absent, and finally one in which it is present in various degrees of intensity; and then, by careful elimination or exclusion of irrelevant causes, you will necessarily come to detect in the residuum, in the cause or element which is left, that cause of which you are in quest. With all its vast parade of terms and distinctions, Bacon's method of finding out the causes of phenomena comes to little more than such a direction as this for discovering the author, say, of a disturbance at a public meeting. First, find out a number of instances in which this fellow along with others was present at public meetings when a row took place; secondly, find out a number of other instances of meetings in which all these other people were present, but not he, and no row took place; then by the method of exclusion or elimination it is quite clear that he must have been the creator of the row.

It is impossible in this brief sketch to give a more detailed account of Bacon's method, or even to notice the objections which have been urged against it in recent times. I must content myself with this single remark, that the problem which meets the scientific enquirer is a very different one from that which Bacon conceived it to be, and one to which his short and easy method is, in the great majority of cases, inapplicable. In a scientific investigation the desired result is seldom, if ever, one which can be reached merely by a process of elimination or exclusion. It can only be so reached in those cases in which a concrete or complex phenomenon is the combined result of a number of *known* agents, and in which, in order to ascertain what part of that result is due to any one of these agents, it is possible to deduct the known effects of all the rest. But not only are there innumerable cases in which a particular effect is due, not to a single cause, but to the concurrent action of a plurality of causes; but, in general, it is to be considered that Bacon's method presupposes that all the agents to which a given result is due are known, and what we do is simply to ascribe the residuary part of the result, by elimination, to one of these agents; and he takes no account of the fact that the process of discovery, where its results are most valuable, does not consist in rejecting from a number of known causes all but one, but in rising by the penetrative insight or divination of the scientific mind from a multiplicity of apparently discordant facts and phenomena to the idea of a hitherto *unknown* law or relation which harmonizes and explains them—a process which implies an attitude of mind quite beyond the compass of the ordinary observer.

When once the unknown element, the law or relation, has been discovered, it is a very easy matter to pronounce, among the complex phenomena before us, how much is due to it and how much to other concurrent conditions; but the latter operation, which is all that Bacon's method includes, presupposes the former; that is, presupposes that the discovery to which it is to lead us is already made. Even if there were any truth in Bacon's notion of an alphabet of nature, it would no more furnish its possessor with inventive power, or the capacity of attaining scientific knowledge, than the ability to repeat the A, B, C of a language gives a child the capacity to understand the profoundest works which its literature contains, or qualifies him, by dexterous manipulation and combination of the letters, to reproduce these works. When we have mastered the orthography or even the grammar of a language in which a great book is written, we are a long way from an intelligent appreciation of its contents, a much longer way from the capacity to write such a book. And as it is not the collocation of letters or words, but the ideas, the hidden element of thought that expresses itself through the verbal symbols and links them together in a spiritual order, which is the true key to the significance of a book; so, in deciphering the volume of nature, that which is the main function of the scientific discoverer, that which made Kepler and Galileo and Newton masters in scientific research, was not the mere capacity to observe and manipulate facts according to a cut-and-dry system of rules, but the capacity, along with accurate and comprehensive powers of observation, to grasp the hidden conception which the facts had never hinted to other eyes, to make the dumb, disjointed symbols articulate with the living rhythm of law, and over the hitherto obscure or meaningless page of the book of nature to shed the light of intelligible order and system. In one word, not only do we know, in point of fact, that neither Bacon himself nor any other man ever made a single scientific discovery, great or little, by means of his so-called new organon of science, but we know that from the very nature of the case they never could. Neither this nor any other machinery of technical rules could have enabled Newton to write the *Principia* any more than it could have qualified Homer to write the *Iliad*, or Plato the *Republic*, or Milton the *Paradise Lost*. Whatever incidental merit it possesses, the *Novum Organum*, so far as science is concerned, is but the record of vast yet misdirected and abortive labour—a *splendid* failure, it may be, but still a failure.

And now, lastly, if Bacon's greatness was not that either of the man of science or of the philosopher of science, what, we are led to ask, in relation to science and scientific investigation, is his true title to fame? One answer which has been given to this question by a very popular writer . . . , is that the special and characteristic merit of Bacon's philosophy is that in all his speculations he aimed at practical *utility*. He sought to bring science down from the clouds, and to make it useful to man. Insight into nature has, as its sole and supreme end, command over nature for the service of man. Knowledge is to be sought after because it enables man to turn physical forces into agents for human uses. His imagination had been kindled by those inventions, such as the art of printing, gunpowder, the mariner's compass, which had already so wonderfully contributed to the extension of man's power and dignity, and the convenience and comfort of human life; and his supreme endeavour was, by a new and infallible method, to enable inventors to do systematically what they had hitherto accomplished by happy accidents. Instead of lighting occasionally on ingenious contrivances, with this instrument in hand they would go forth with a kind of mechanical certainty to turn the knowledge of nature into command over nature, and to render all the forces and laws of the physical world subservient to the satisfaction of man's wants, the multiplying of his pleasures, and even the prolongation of his life. And this practical aim, in contrast with the merely theoretic and therefore useless character of the philosophy of preceding ages, constitutes the great and imperishable title of its author to human reverence and gratitude.

Nor can we wonder that this should, in Macaulay's view, be the main excellence of Bacon's philosophy, seeing his criterion of philosophical merit leads him to regard the first shoemaker as a greater benefactor of mankind than Seneca. "If," says he, "we are to make our choice between the first shoemaker and the author of the three Books On Anger, we pronounce for the shoemaker. It may be worse to be angry than wet. But shoes have kept millions from being wet, and we doubt whether Seneca ever kept any one from being angry,"— an illustration which tempts us to enquire whether, on the same principle, Macaulay would have regarded the maker of shoes as a greater man and of juster title to human reverence than the writer of sparkling review articles and popular books of history.

But even if this account of Bacon's philosophy were more accurate than we believe it to be, it is not in regarding utility as the supreme end of science that we can find his highest claim to honour. To set up practical utility as the aim and criterion of science would be a more misleading idol than any of those against which Bacon warns us. If knowledge is valuable only in so far as it can be shown to contribute to the material uses and advantages of life, half at least of the intellectual possessions of mankind, including the greatest, or what men have consented to regard as the greatest, books in ancient and modern literature, must be consigned to the waste-basket. By an unconscious, but wise and rational instinct, men in all ages have exalted knowledge to a higher place in the scale of excellence than any material pleasures or advantages to which knowledge can contribute. They have regarded the scientific impulse, the desire to know, to bring human intelligence into converse with truth, as that which is noblest in our nature, as the very image of God impressed upon it. In art, in science, in religion, the highest minds have ever regarded the communion of thought with what is true and fair and good, as precious in itself, and not in order to any ulterior advantages, least of all to the gratification of bodily appetites and the securing of physical comfort. It has been their profound belief, that if the whole world were made materially comfortable, if everybody were secure of three meals a day, and of food, clothing, and all sorts of sensuous enjoyments, there would still be a part of man's nature, a capacity or desire more essential to its completeness, left unappeased, and whose unsatisfied cravings would leave him miserable as well as contemptible amidst all his comforts. It is no paradox to say that, even in the proper domain of science, to know nature and her laws is a nobler thing than to extract physical gain or enjoyment out of them; and in another and higher province inspired lips have taught us not that we must know and believe in order to be safe and happy, but that "*this is life eternal, to know Thee the true God.*"

But if not to the utilitarian aim of his philosophy, to what else can Bacon's world-wide fame be justly ascribed? I answer that, though we cannot acknowledge him as the founder or the philosopher of experimental science, he may, at least, be designated the greatest of its prophets. "It is not," says Sir John Herschel, "the introduction of inductive reasoning, as a new and hitherto untried process, which characterizes the Baconian philosophy, but his keen perception, and his broad, spirit-stirring, almost enthusiastic announcement of its paramount importance, as the alpha and omega of science." And this is, perhaps, the view to which all competent judges would now be disposed to assent.

In all great revolutions—social, scientific, religious—there is need, not only for the profound intelligence which grasps the new principles and laboriously works out their results, but also for the inspired mind that can apprehend their general significance, and the eloquent tongue that can proclaim and popularize them. His is no mean office, but rather a function second only to that of the creator of a new era, who can comprehend its magnitude, and with lofty eloquence rouse the world to the appreciation of it. In our day, the freedom of science, like the freedom of the press or the liberty of the subject, has become a theme only for schoolboy rhetoric; but in the time of Bacon, science was only beginning to realize and rejoice in its emancipation, at once from the authority of Aristotle and from the more oppressive and deadening authority of the traditions and dogmas of the Church; and it was a task worthy of the best intellects of the day to give articulate expression to the new-born sense of liberty, and to warn men against the idols which had hitherto enslaved them. To the modern mind, again, it seems a mere truism to say that, for the knowledge of nature, we must look to nature herself, that observation and experiment, and not *a priori* reasonings, are the true instruments of investigation, and that it is by careful inductions from observed facts, and not by deduction from principles arbitrarily assumed or based on slight and inadequate observation, that we can frame our theories as to the laws of the natural world.

But what are truisms to us were the startling novelties of the time of which we write, or, at most, ideas which had only recently dawned upon the most advanced minds, of the truth of which even the educated world was only half-convinced, and the significance and fruitfulness of which only a few had been able to appreciate. Of these few, and of the thoughts and anticipations with which they were inspired, Bacon was the greatest representative and exponent. Like them he saw the ancient reign of night and darkness passing away, he perceived, in the morning light of a new day, a world boundless and inexhaustible in its yet unexplored resources stretching away before him; and of the joyous awakening, the sanguine hopes, the intellectual ardour of conquest, with which these sons of the light were filled, no voice was found to give more expressive and jubilant utterance than the voice of Bacon. It is no slight honour to ascribe to the great prophet of the new time, that in his own day he arrested by his commanding eloquence the attention of multitudes who knew not, or took little note, of the intellectual revolution that was taking place around them, and that in our own time, with all the immense advancement which scientific knowledge and scientific method have gained from centuries of experience, there are many of the stirring utterances of that long-silent voice to which mankind have not ceased to listen.

In conclusion, let me say in a single sentence, that for all educated men (and especially for those whose work in life is implicated with the advancement of knowledge and the intellectual progress of the world), there is one reflection which, perhaps more emphatically than any other, the life of Bacon suggests. It is easy to say that science should purify and ennoble the life, that intellectual pursuits should raise us above vulgar aims and mean ambitions, make us no longer the slaves of our own senses or of the opinions of men, and by supplying us with resources which custom cannot stale nor age wither, nor the changes and troubles of life affect, should communicate to us a noble independence of spirit. This, however, is a philosophy which it is easier to preach than to practise, and the contemplation of one living example of it is more persuasive than a thousand homilies. The admirer of Bacon's genius must sadly acknowledge that in him that example loses something of its ideal clearness and force. But though we cannot aver that in his case science and philosophy lent uniform dignity and elevation to life, this at least we can say, that in him we have an example of the happiness which intellectual pursuits can diffuse through a life otherwise chequered and troubled. Never has there lived a human soul in which the love of knowledge glowed with a purer and more inextinguishable ardour; never another human life in which science proved more signally its power to satisfy, to support, to console, to dull the sting of care, to make the heart serene amidst outward disasters and misfortunes, and even to render social infamy and dishonour not intolerable. Simulation, policy, ambiguity, were but too familiar to his lips, but *then* at least there is ever the unmistakable ring of sincerity in his words, when he celebrates the glories of science and the triumphs it is destined to achieve. In that placid nature, that cold and unimpassioned heart, a stranger to human tenderness, and in which even religion woke no sentiment but that of a rational conviction, there was one emotion—the love of knowledge—which kindled into a fervour more intense than love or patriotism or devotion in other men. Wealth, place, preferment, the gauds and shows of the world, he had sought; but the deepest place in his heart after all was not for these. And when these failed him, when the edifice of worldly greatness he had laboriously reared lay crumbling around his feet, when, in age and sickness and disappointment, all the joy seemed gone from life, he turned with an almost new-born youthful avidity, to find in study and investigation a still unfailing source of interest and delight. As we close our review of a career, lofty and splendid indeed, but whose splendour is shadowed and softened by an almost pathetic human interest, may I venture to express the hope that, though remote from the experience of any of us may be either the perilous greatness of the path he trod, or the temptations to which even his great spirit succumbed, we may at least catch some spark of intellectual ardour from the inspiration of his genius, some touch of sympathy with that indomitable devotion to truth and knowledge which, despite of all anomalies and imperfections, has made his an immortal name.

RICHARD WILLIAM CHURCH
"Bacon as a Writer"
Bacon
1884, pp. 209–27

Bacon's name belongs to letters as well as to philosophy. In his own day, whatever his contemporaries thought of his *Instauration of Knowledge*, he was in the first rank as a speaker and a writer. Sir Walter Raleigh, contrasting him with Salisbury, who could speak but not write, and Northampton, who could write but not speak, thought Bacon eminent both as a speaker and a writer. Ben Jonson, passing in review the more famous names of his own and the preceding age, from Sir Thomas More to Sir Philip Sidney, Hooker, Essex and Raleigh, places Bacon without a rival at the head of the company as the man who had "fulfilled all numbers," and "stood as the mark and *akmè* of our language." And he also records Bacon's power as a speaker. "No man," he says, "ever spoke more neatly, more pressly, or suffered less emptiness, less idleness, in what he uttered." . . . "His hearers could not cough or look aside from him without loss. He commanded when he spoke, and had his judges angry and pleased at his devotion . . . the fear of every man that heard him was that he should make an end." He notices one feature for which we are less prepared, though we know that the edge of Bacon's sarcastic tongue was felt and resented in James's Court. "His speech," says Ben Jonson, "was nobly censorious when he could *spare and pass by a jest.*" The unpopularity which certainly seems to have gathered round his name may have had something to do with this reputation.

Yet as an English writer Bacon did not expect to be remembered, and he hardly cared to be. He wrote much in Latin, and his first care was to have his books put into a Latin dress. "For these modern languages," he wrote to Toby Matthew towards the close of his life, "will at one time or another play the bank-rowte with books, and since I have lost much time with this age, I would be glad if God would give me leave to recover it with posterity." He wanted to be read by the learned out of England, who were supposed to appreciate his philosophical ideas better than his own countrymen, and the only way to this was to have his books translated into the "general language." He sends Prince Charles the *Advancement* in its new Latin dress. "It is a book," he says, "that will live, and be a citizen of the world, as English books are not." And he fitted it for continental reading by carefully weeding it of all passages that might give offence to the censors at Rome or Paris. "I have been," he writes to the King, "mine own *Index Expurgatorius*, that it may be read in all places. For since my end of putting it in Latin was to have it read everywhere, it had been an absurd contradiction to free it in the language and to pen it up in the matter." Even the *Essays* and the *History of Henry VII.* he had put into Latin "by some good pens that do not forsake me." Among these translators are said to have been George Herbert and Hobbes, and on more doubtful authority, Ben Jonson and Selden. The *Essays* were also translated into Latin and Italian with Bacon's sanction.

Bacon's contemptuous and hopeless estimate of "these modern languages," forty years after Spenser had proclaimed and justified his faith in his own language, is only one of the proofs of the short-sightedness of the wisest and the limitations of the largest-minded. Perhaps we ought not to wonder at his silence about Shakespeare. It was the fashion, except among a set of clever but not always very reputable people, to think the stage, as it was, below the notice of scholars and statesmen; and Shakespeare took no trouble to save his works from neglect. Yet it is a curious defect in Bacon that he should not have been more alive to the powers and future of his own language. He early and all along was profoundly impressed with the contrast, which the scholarship of the age so abundantly presented, of words to things. He dwells in the *Advancement* on that "first distemper of learning, when men study words and not matter." He illustrates it at large from the reaction of the new learning and of the popular teaching of the Reformation against the utilitarian and unclassical terminology of the schoolmen; a

reaction which soon grew to excess and made men "hunt more after choiceness of the phrase, and the round and clean composition of the sentence, and the sweet falling of the clauses," than after worth of subject, soundness of argument, "life of invention or depth of judgment." "I have represented this," he says, "in an example of late times, but it hath been and will be *secundum majus et minus* in all times;" and he likens this "vanity" to "Pygmalion's frenzy,"—"for to fall in love with words which are but the images of matter, is all one as to fall in love with a picture." He was dissatisfied with the first attempt at translation into Latin of the *Advancement* by Dr. Playfer of Cambridge, because he "desired not so much neat and polite, as clear, masculine, and apt expression." Yet, with this hatred of circumlocution and prettiness, of the cloudy amplifications, and pompous flourishings, and "the flowing and watery vein," which the scholars of his time affected, it is strange that he should not have seen that the new ideas and widening thoughts of which he was the herald would want a much more elastic and more freely-working instrument than Latin could ever become. It is wonderful indeed what can be done with Latin. It was long after his day to be the language of the exact sciences. In his *History of the Winds*, which is full of his irrepressible fancy and picturesqueness, Bacon describes in clear and intelligible Latin the details of the rigging of a modern man-of-war, and the mode of sailing her. But such tasks impose a yoke, sometimes a rough one, on a language which has "taken its ply" in very different conditions, and of which the genius is that of indirect and circuitous expression, "full of majesty and circumstance." But it never, even in those days of scholarship, could lend itself to the frankness, the straightforwardness, the fullness and shades of suggestion and association, with which, in handling ideas of subtlety and difficulty, a writer would wish to speak to his reader, and which he could find only in his mother tongue. It might have been thought that with Bacon's contempt of form and ceremony in these matters, his consciousness of the powers of English in his hands might have led him to anticipate that a flexible, and rich, and strong language might create a literature, and that a literature, if worth studying, would be studied in its own language. But so great a change was beyond even his daring thoughts. To him, as to his age, the only safe language was the Latin. For familiar use English was well enough. But it could not be trusted; "it would play the bankrupt with books." And yet Galileo was writing in Italian as well as in Latin; only within twenty-five years later, Descartes was writing *De la Méthode*, and Pascal was writing in the same French in which he wrote the *Provincial Letters*, his *Nouvelles Expériences touchant le Vide*, and the controversial pamphlets which followed it; showing how in that interval of five-and-twenty years an instrument had been fashioned out of a modern language such as for lucid expression and clear reasoning, Bacon had not yet dreamed of. From Bacon to Pascal is the change from the old scientific way of writing to the modern; from a modern language as learned and used in the 16th century, to one learned in the 17th.

But the language of the age of Elizabeth was a rich and noble one, and it reached a high point in the hands of Bacon. In his hands it lent itself to many uses, and assumed many forms, and he valued it, not because he thought highly of its qualities as a language, but because it enabled him with least trouble "to speak as he would," in throwing off the abundant thoughts that rose within his mind, and in going through the variety of business which could not be done in Latin. But in all his writing it is the matter, the real thing that he wanted to say, which was uppermost. He cared how it was said, not for the sake of form or ornament, but because the force and clearness of what was said depended so much on how it was said. Of course, what he wanted to say varied indefinitely with the various occasions of his life. His business may merely be to write "a device" or panegyric for a pageant in the Queen's honour, or for the revels of Gray's Inn. But even these trifles are the result of real thought, and are full of ideas, ideas about the hopes of knowledge or about the policy of the State; and though, of course, they have plenty of the flourishes and quaint absurdities indispensable on such occasions, yet the "rhetorical affectation" is in the thing itself, and not in the way it is handled: he had an opportunity of saying some of the things which were to him of deep and perpetual interest, and he used it to say them, as forcibly, as strikingly, as attractively as he could. His manner of writing depends, not on a style, or a studied or acquired habit but on the nature of the task which he has in hand. Everywhere his matter is close to his words, and governs, animates, informs his words. No one in England before had so much as he had the power to say what he wanted to say, and exactly as he wanted to say it. No one was so little at the mercy of conventional language or customary rhetoric, except when he persuaded himself that he had to submit to those necessities of flattery, which cost him at last so dear.

The book by which English readers, from his own time to ours, have known him best, better than by the originality and the eloquence of the *Advancement*, or than by the political weight and historical imagination of the *History of Henry VII.*, is the first book which he published, the volume of *Essays*. It is an instance of his self-willed but most skilful use of the freedom and ease which the "modern language," which he despised, gave him. It is obvious that he might have expanded these "Counsels, moral and political," to the size which such essays used to swell to after his time. Many people would have thanked him for doing so; and some have thought it a good book on which to hang their own reflections and illustrations. But he saw how much could be done by leaving the beaten track of set treatise and discourse, and setting down unceremoniously the observations which he had made and the real rules which he had felt to be true, on various practical matters which come home to men's "business and bosoms." He was very fond of these moral and political generalisations, both of his own collecting and as found in writers who, he thought, had the right to make them, like the Latins of the Empire and the Italians and Spaniards of the Renaissance. But a mere string of maxims and quotations would have been a poor thing and not new; and he cast what he had to say into connected wholes. But nothing can be more loose than the structure of the essays. There is no art, no style, almost, except in a few, the political ones, no order: thoughts are put down and left unsupported, unproved, undeveloped. In the first form of the ten, which composed the first edition of 1597, they are more like notes of analysis or tables of contents; they are austere even to meagreness. But the general character continues in the enlarged and expanded ones of Bacon's later years. They are like chapters in Aristotle's *Ethics* and *Rhetoric* on virtues and characters; only Bacon's takes Aristotle's broad marking lines as drawn, and proceeds with the subtler and more refined observations of a much longer and wider experience. But these short papers say what they have to say without preface, and in literary undress, without a superfluous word, without the joints and bands of structure: they say it in brief, rapid sentences, which come down, sentence after sentence, like the strokes of a great hammer. No wonder that in their disdainful brevity they seem rugged and abrupt, "and do not seem to end, but fall." But with their truth and piercingness and delicacy of observation, their roughness gives a kind of flavour which no elaboration

could give. It is none the less that their wisdom is of a somewhat cynical kind, fully alive to the slipperiness and self-deceits and faithlessness which are in the world and rather inclined to be amused at them. In some we can see distinct records of the writer's own experience: one contains the substance of a charge delivered to Judge Hutton on his appointment; another of them is a sketch drawn from life of a character which had crossed Bacon's path, and in the essay on *Seeming Wise* we can trace from the impatient notes put down in his *Commentarius Solutus*, the picture of the man who stood in his way, the Attorney-General Hobart. Some of them are memorable oracular utterances not inadequate to the subject, on *Truth*, or *Death*, or *Unity*. Others reveal an utter incapacity to come near a subject, except as a strange external phenomena, like the essay on *Love*. There is a distinct tendency in them to the Italian school of political and moral wisdom, the wisdom of distrust and of reliance on indirect and roundabout ways. There is a group of them, "of *Delays*," "of *Cunning*," "of *Wisdom for a Man's Self*," "of *Despatch*," which show how vigilantly and to what purpose he had watched the treasurers and secretaries and intriguers of Elizabeth's and James's Courts; and there are curious self-revelations, as in the essay on *Friendship*. But there are also currents of better and larger feeling, such as those which show his own ideal of "Great Place," and what he felt of its dangers and duties. And mixed with the fantastic taste and conceits of the time, there is evidence in them of Bacon's keen delight in nature, in the beauty and scents of flowers, in the charm of open air life, as in the essay on *Gardens*, "The purest of human pleasures, the greatest refreshment to the spirits of man."

But he had another manner of writing for what he held to be his more serious work. In the philosophical and historical works there is no want of attention to the flow and order and ornament of composition. When we come to the *Advancement of Learning*, we come to a book which is one of the landmarks of what high thought and rich imagination have made of the English language. It is the first great book in English prose of secular interest; the first book which can claim a place beside the *Laws of Ecclesiastical Polity*. As regards its subject-matter, it has been partly thrown into the shade by the greatly enlarged and elaborate form in which it ultimately appeared, in a Latin dress, as the first portion of the scheme of the *Instauratio*, the *De Augmentis Scientiarum*. Bacon looked on it as a first effort, a kind of call-bell to awaken and attract the interest of others in the thoughts and hopes which so interested himself. But it contains some of his finest writing. In the *Essays* he writes as a looker-on at the game of human affairs, who, according to his frequent illustration, sees more of it than the gamesters themselves, and is able to give wiser and faithful counsel, not without a touch of kindly irony at the mistakes which he observes. In the *Advancement* he is the enthusiast for a great cause and a great hope, and all that he has of passion and power is enlisted in the effort to advance it. The *Advancement* is far from being a perfect book. As a survey of the actual state of knowledge in his day, of its deficiencies and what was wanted to supply them, it is not even up to the materials of the time. Even the improved *De Augmentis* is inadequate; and there is reason to think the *Advancement* was a hurried book, at least in the later part, and it is defective in arrangement and proportion of parts. Two of the great divisions of knowledge—history and poetry—are despatched in comparatively short chapters; while in the division on "Civil Knowledge," human knowledge as it respects society, he inserts a long essay, obviously complete in itself and clumsily thrust in here, on the ways of getting on in the world, the means by which a man may be "*Faber fortunæ suæ*"—the architect of his own success; too lively a picture to be pleasant of the arts with which he had become acquainted in the process of rising. The book, too, has the blemishes of its own time; its want of simplicity, its inevitable though very often amusing and curious pedantries. But the *Advancement* was the first of a long line of books which have attempted to teach English readers how to think of knowledge; to make it really and intelligently the interest, not of the school or the study or the laboratory only, but of society at large. It was a book with a purpose, new then, but of which we have seen the fulfilment. He wanted to impress on his generation, as a very practical matter, all that knowledge might do in wise hands, all that knowledge had lost by the faults and errors of men and the misfortunes of time, all that knowledge might be pushed to in all directions by faithful and patient industry and well-planned methods for the elevation and benefit of man in his highest capacities as well as in his humblest. And he further sought to teach them *how* to know; to make them understand that difficult achievement of self-knowledge, to know *what it is* to know; to give the first attempted chart to guide them among the shallows and rocks and whirlpools which beset the course and action of thought and inquiry; to reveal to them the "idols" which unconsciously haunt the minds of the strongest as well as the weakest, and interpose their delusions when we are least aware,—"the fallacies and false appearances inseparable from our nature and our condition of life." To induce men to believe not only that there was much to know that was not yet dreamed of, but that the way of knowing needed real and thorough improvement, that the knowing mind bore along with it all kinds of snares and disqualifications of which it is unconscious, and that it needed training quite as much as materials to work on, was the object of the *Advancement*. It was but a sketch; but it was a sketch so truly and forcibly drawn, that it made an impression which has never been weakened. To us its use and almost its interest is passed. But it is a book which we can never open without coming on some noble interpretation of the realities of nature or the mind; some unexpected discovery of that quick and keen eye which arrests us by its truth; some felicitous and unthought-of illustration, yet so natural as almost to be doomed to become a commonplace; some bright touch of his incorrigible imaginativeness, ever ready to force itself in amid the driest details of his argument.

The *Advancement* was only one shape out of many into which he cast his thoughts. Bacon was not easily satisfied with his work; even when he published he did so, not because he had brought his work to the desired point, but lest anything should happen to him and it should "perish." Easy and unstudied as his writing seems, it was, as we have seen, the result of unintermitted trouble and varied modes of working. He was quite as much a talker as a writer, and beat out his thoughts into shape in talking. In the essay on *Friendship* he describes the process with a vividness which tells of his own experience:

> But before you come to that [the faithful counsel that a man receiveth from his friend], certain it is that whosoever hath his mind fraught with many thoughts, his wits and understanding do clarify and break up in the communicating and discoursing with another. He tosseth his thoughts more easily; he marshalleth them more orderly; he seeth how they look when they are turned into words; finally, he waxeth wiser than himself, and that more by an hour's discourse than by a day's meditation. It was well said by Themistocles to the King of Persia, "That speech was like cloth of arras opened and put abroad, whereby the imagery doth appear in figure; whereas in thought, they lie in packs." Neither is this second

fruit of friendship, in opening the understanding, restrained only to such friends as are able to give a man counsel. (They are, indeed, best.) But even without that, a man learneth of himself, and bringeth his own thoughts to light, and whetteth his wits against a stone which itself cuts not. In a word, a man were better to relate himself to a *statua* or a picture, than to suffer his thoughts to pass in smother.

Bacon . . . was a great maker of notes and note-books: he was careful not of the thought only but of the very words in which it presented itself; everything was collected that might turn out useful in his writing or speaking, down to alternative modes of beginning or connecting or ending a sentence. He watched over his intellectual appliances and resources much more strictly than over his money concerns. He never threw away and never forgot what could be turned to account. He was never afraid of repeating himself, if he thought he had something apt to say. He was never tired of re-casting and re-writing, from a mere fragment or preface to a finished paper. He has favourite images, favourite maxims, favourite texts, which he cannot do without. "*Da Fidei quæ sunt Fidei,*" comes in from his first book to his last. The illustrations which he gets from the myth of Scylla, from Atalanta's ball, from Borgia's saying about the French marking their lodgings with chalk, the saying that God takes delight, like the "innocent play of children," "to hide his works in order to have them found out," and to have kings as "his playfellows in that game," these, with many others, reappear, however varied the context, from the first to the last of his compositions. An edition of Bacon with marginal references and parallel passages would show a more persistent recurrence of characteristic illustrations and sentences than perhaps any other writer.

The *Advancement* was followed by attempts to give serious effect to its lesson. This was nearly all done in Latin. He did so, because in these works he spoke to a larger and, as he thought, more interested audience; the use of Latin marked the gravity of his subject as one that touched all mankind; and the majesty of Latin suited his taste and his thoughts. Bacon spoke, indeed, impressively on the necessity of entering into the realm of knowledge in the spirit of a little child. He dwelt on the paramount importance of beginning from the very bottom of the scale of fact, of understanding the commonplace things at our feet, so full of wonder and mystery and instruction, before venturing on theories. The sun is not polluted by shining on a dunghill, and no facts were too ignoble to be beneath the notice of the true student of nature. But his own genius was for the grandeur and pomp of general views. The practical details of experimental science were, except in partial instances, yet a great way off; and what there was, he either did not care about or really understand, and had no aptitude for handling. He knew enough to give reality to his argument; he knew, and insisted on it, that the labour of observation and experiment would have to be very heavy and quite indispensable. But his own business was with great principles and new truths; these were what had the real attraction for him; it was the magnificent thoughts and boundless hopes of the approaching "kingdom of man" which kindled his imagination and fired his ambition. "He writes philosophy," said Harvey, who had come to his own great discovery through patient and obscure experiments on frogs and monkeys, "he writes philosophy like a Lord Chancellor." And for this part of the work, the stateliness and dignity of the Latin corresponded to the proud claims which he made for his conception of the knowledge which was to be. English seemed to him too homely to express the hopes of the world, too unstable to be trusted with them. Latin was the language of command and law. His Latin, without enslaving itself to Ciceronian types, and with a free infusion of barbarous but most convenient words from the vast and ingenious terminology of the schoolmen, is singularly forcible and expressive. It is almost always easy and clear; it can be vague and general, and it can be very precise where precision is wanted. It can, on occasion, be magnificent, and its gravity is continually enlivened by the play upon it, as upon a background, of his picturesque and unexpected fancies. The exposition of his philosophical principles was attempted in two forms. He began in English. He began, in the shape of a personal account, a statement of a series of conclusions to which his thinking had brought him, which he called the "Clue of the Labyrinth," *Filum Labyrinthi*. But he laid this aside unfinished, and rewrote and completed it in Latin, with the title *Cogitata et visa*. It gains by being in Latin; as Mr. Spedding says, "it must certainly be reckoned among the most perfect of Bacon's productions." The personal form with each paragraph begins and ends. "*Franciscus Bacon sic cogitavit . . . itaque visum est ei*," gives to it a special tone of serious conviction, and brings the interest of the subject more keenly to the reader. It has the same kind of personal interest, only more solemn and commanding, which there is in Descartes's *Discours de la Méthode*. In this form Bacon meant at first to publish. He sent it to his usual critics, Sir Thomas Bodley, Toby Matthew, and Bishop Andrewes. And he meant to follow it up with a practical exemplification of his method. But he changed his plan. He had more than once expressed his preference for the form of *aphorisms* over the argumentative and didactic continuity of a set discourse. He had, indeed, already twice begun a series of aphorisms on the true methods of interpreting nature, and directing the mind in the true path of knowledge, and had begun them with the same famous aphorism with which the *Novum Organum* opens. He now reverted to the form of the aphorism, and resolved to throw the materials of the *Cogitata et visa* into this shape. The result is the *Novum Organum*. It contains, with large additions, the substance of the treatise, but broken up and re-arranged in the new form of separate impersonal generalised observations. The points and assertions and issues which, in a continuous discourse, careful readers mark and careless ones miss, are one by one picked out and brought separately to the light. It begins with brief, oracular, unproved maxims and propositions, and goes on gradually into larger developments and explanations. The aphorisms are meant to strike, to awaken questions, to disturb prejudices, to let in light into a nest of unsuspected intellectual confusions and self-misunderstandings, to be the mottoes and watchwords of many a laborious and difficult inquiry. They form a connected and ordered chain, though the ties between each link are not given. In this way Bacon put forth his proclamation of war on all that then called itself science; his announcement that the whole work of solid knowledge must be begun afresh, and by a new, and, as he thought, infallible method. On this work Bacon concentrated all his care. It was twelve years in hand, and twelve times underwent his revision. "In the first book especially," says Mr. Ellis, "every word seems to have been carefully weighed; and it would be hard to omit or change anything without injuring the meaning which Bacon intended to convey." Severe as it is, it is instinct with enthusiasm, sometimes with passion. The Latin in which it is written answers to it; it has the conciseness, the breadth, the lordliness of a great piece of philosophical legislation.

The world has agreed to date from Bacon the systematic reform of natural philosophy, the beginning of an intelligent attempt, which has been crowned by such signal success, to place the investigation of nature on a solid foundation. On purely scientific grounds his title to this great honour may require considerable qualification. What one thing, it is asked, would not have been discovered in the age of Galileo and Harvey, if Bacon had never written? What one scientific discovery can be traced to him, or to the observance of his peculiar rules? It was something, indeed, to have conceived, as clearly as he conceived it, the large and comprehensive idea of what natural knowledge must be, and must rest upon, even if he were not able to realise his idea, and were mistaken in his practical methods of reform. But great ideas and great principles need their adequate interpreter, their *vates sacer*, if they are to influence the history of mankind. This was what Bacon was to science, to that great change in the thoughts and activity of men in relation to the world of nature around them: and this is his title to the great place assigned to him. He not only understood and felt what science might be, but he was able to make others—and it was no easy task beforehand, while the wonders of discovery were yet in the future—understand and feel it too. And he was able to do this because he was one of the most wonderful of thinkers and one of the greatest of writers. The disclosure, the interpretation, the development of that great intellectual revolution which was in the air, and which was practically carried forward in obscurity, day by day, by the fathers of modern astronomy and chemistry and physiology, had fallen to the task of a genius, second only to Shakespeare. He had the power to tell the story of what they were doing and were to do with a force of imaginative reason of which they were utterly incapable. He was able to justify their attempts and their hopes as they themselves could not. He was able to interest the world in the great prospects opening on it, but to which none but a few students had the key. The calculations of the astronomer, the investigations of the physician, were more or less a subject of talk, as curious or possibly useful employments. But that which bound them together in the unity of science, which gave them their meaning beyond themselves, which raised them to a higher level and gave them their real dignity among the pursuits of men, which forced all thinking men to see what new and unsuspected possibilities in the knowledge and in the condition of mankind were opened before them, was not Bacon's own attempts at science, not even his collections of facts and his rules of method, but that great idea of the reality and boundless worth of knowledge which Bacon's penetrating and sure intuition had discerned, and which had taken possession of his whole nature. The impulse which he gave to the progress of science came from his magnificent and varied exposition of this idea; from his series of grand and memorable generalisations on the habits and faults of the human mind—on the difficult and yet so obvious and so natural precautions necessary to guide it in the true and hopeful track. It came from the attractiveness, the enthusiasm, and the persuasiveness of the pleading; from the clear and forcible statements, the sustained eloquence, the generous hopes, the deep and earnest purpose of the *Advancement* and the *De Augmentis*; from the nobleness, the originality, the picturesqueness, the impressive and irresistible truth of the great aphorisms of the *Novum Organum*.

C. STOPES

From "The History of the Heresy"

The Bacon-Shakspere Question Answered
1889, pp. 185–99

Farmer, in 1789, was the first real anti-Shaksperean; and Horace Walpole's *Historic Doubts* have been ranked in the list. But this present contest was really first broached in *The*

Romance of Yachting, a novel written in 1848 by Hart, New York.

On August 7, 1852, in *Chambers's Edinburgh Journal*, Mr. Jamieson wrote the anonymous article, "Who wrote Shakespeare?" and suggested that he "kept a poet."[1]

Miss Delia Bacon's article on the *Philosophy of Shakespeare's Plays Unfolded* appeared in *Putnam's Magazine* for January 1856, and was afterwards reprinted. She held that the poet Shakspere kept was "Bacon," and that he had used these plays to unfold his new philosophy. She was nevertheless so inconsistent as to dwell over every souvenir of Shakspere; to haunt the places where he had lived; to spend even a night in Stratford Church by his tomb; and to lose her reason in her perplexity. But she suggested the idea in America, where many subsequent writers took it up. Meanwhile in England Mr. William Henry Smith was working at it, and in 1857 he published his book *Bacon and Shakespeare, an Inquiry touching Players, Playhouses, and Playwriters in the days of Elizabeth*. This was said to have convinced Lord Palmerston.

Mr. William D. O'Connor, in a novel entitled *Harrington, a Story of True Love*, published in Boston, U.S., gave his strong support to Miss Delia Bacon's views, 1860.

The Hon. Nathaniel Holmes, called by Mr. Wyman, the bibliographer, "the apostle of Baconianism," in 1866 wrote a substantial book to prove that Bacon wrote the plays, and that he was known to be the author by some of his contemporaries. His *Authorship of Shakespeare*, written in two volumes, has reached the third edition. This is really the text-book of the Baconians proper, and gives all their strong "points." It sifts out a chronological order of production of the plays, and of the several writings of Bacon, and shows there can be no possibility of borrowing; and that the parallel or identical passages are incontestable proofs of Bacon's authorship, especially those in science and philosophy.

It represents much good work with a mistaken idea. It is much the best book on that side, and is certainly interesting to read as a psychological development.

The Australians next became interested in the question; and Dr. William Thompson of Melbourne in 1878 wrote a pamphlet entitled *The Political Purpose of the Renascence Drama: The Key of the Argument*; another in 1880, *Our Renascence Drama, or History made Visible*; in 1881 he added a continuation, *William Shakespeare in Romance and Reality*; in the same year *Bacon and Shakespeare*; and another pamphlet, *Bacon, not Shakespeare, on Vivisection*. In 1882 he published still another pamphlet, *The Political Allegories in the Renascence Drama of Francis Bacon*. In 1883 appeared *A Minute among the Amenities*, which he puts forth as answer to some Shaksperean critics, whom he thought had been severe on him.

Dr. Thompson, in *Bacon, not Shakespeare, on Vivisection*, says that Bacon was a vivisector; that Harvey caught his idea from him; and that the medicine in the plays agrees with Bacon's views; and that the examination of the murderers of Sir Thomas Overbury had taught Bacon the powers of poison, as shown in *Hamlet* and *King Lear*. He also in *The Renascence Drama* says that the division into five acts and many scenes was an alteration in the plays; that they were all originally written in trilogy, as may be seen by intelligent comparison; that W. H. of the sonnets is William Herbert, afterwards Earl of Pembroke, who supported Bacon twenty years after against the bitter attacks of Southampton in the House of Lords. There is no authority for Shakspere knowing Chapman, though *Troilus and Cressida* is taken from his *Homer*.

"Camden never mentioned Shakespeare in his Annals; neither did Bacon." But Camden did mention Shakespeare.

Bacon also forgot to mention Ben Jonson, Beaumont, Fletcher, and many others.

Meanwhile many short articles appeared on either side; but in his *Shakespearean Myth*, 1881, Mr. Appleton Morgan slightly varied the ground. He says in it that there are three Anti-Shakespearean Theories:—

1. The Delia Bacon, or Junta Theory.
2. The Baconian or Unitary Theory.
3. The New Theory.

It is a little difficult at first to grasp the distinction of the New Theory. He says that "experts have proved that the styles of Bacon and Shakespeare are as far apart as the poles. Yet that internal evidence preponderates in favour of the Baconians. The New Theory is, that all the learned parts are by a learned hand, but that Shakespeare put in all the clown business. The New Theory and the Delia Bacon Theory agree in this, that William Shakespeare was fortunate in the manuscripts brought to him, and grew rich in making plays out of them. A modern manager does the same. Our gratitude is due to W. Shakespeare as editor, though not as author of the plays. *The plays could not have been popular then*; therefore his own plays were of a different and popular class, but his name was at every one's service, and his own real plays are apparently lost. Among all the stage managers, only one, William Shakespeare, was able to retire as a landed gentleman, and purchase an Esquire." Mr. Morgan has forgotten Alleyn, and the property Burbage at one time owned, and that without the help of *writing* plays. "Bacon was daily writing under other names, and much of his handwriting is preserved. None of Shakespeare's is left. The 'unblotted' copies could only have been the stage parts. The literature of the country had, up to the date of their appearance, failed to furnish, and has been utterly powerless since to produce, any type, likeness, or formative[2] trace of them. The history for a century on either side of their era discloses no resources upon which levy could have been made for their creation. The death of the author attracted no contemporary attention, and for many years afterwards the dramas remained unnoticed. Mr. Manager Shakespeare produced them, but nobody cared to know the author. To suppose he *wrote* the plays, was to suppose a miracle in London. Is a Jack-of-all-trades about a theatre the ideal poet, philosopher, and seer? There is no record of his plays in his will. Grant that the circulation of the blood was a familiar fact in the days of Shakespeare, that the *Menæchmus* of Plautus was translated; that Iago's speech in *Othello* and the stanza of Berni's *Orlando Innamorato* were mere coincidences; or better still, admit that there was an English version of the poem in Shakespeare's day; admit if required that the *Hamlet* of Saxo-Grammaticus had been translated. The Stationers' Company records bear no trace of any such claimant as William Shakespeare."

It is wise occasionally to quote a few passages *in extenso*. Mr. Morgan is fairer than most anti-Shakespeareans. He does grant that though Harvey's "circulation of the blood was discovered in 1619, published 1628, that Servetus had taught it in 1553; Walter Warner spoke of it; Ricardus Columbus and Cisalpinus believed in it many years before Harvey wrote on it." But he does not seem aware that the *Menæchmus* of Plautus *was* translated at least before the play of the *Comedy of Errors*;[3] that the particular idea of Berni's, upon which Iago's speech must have been founded, *was* rendered in Thomas Wilson's *Art of Rhetoric*, which Shakspere more than likely studied at school; that Saxo-Grammaticus[4] *was* translated not only into Danish but into French, and through that into English; and that the Stationers' Company records *do* bear several traces of William Shakspere as a claimant at his own date.

This shows that reasoning upon negatives is not so strong as on affirmatives, at it leaves more room for changing views with extending knowledge.

He says further that "Gravitation is mentioned in *Troilus and Cressida*, though Newton's book came out in 1642, and that in *Hamlet* the philosophy of Giordano Bruno (then Professor of Philosophy in Wittenberg) was taught." But Mr. Morgan forgets that Giordano Bruno was in Oxford, 1583–86, publicly lecturing against Aristotle and in support of the Copernican theory of the earth, which *Bacon disbelieved.*

He asserts that there is "*no proof* that Shakespeare knew Southampton;" yet further on he quotes a letter from Roland White to Sir Robert Sydney, October 11, 1599, saying, "My Lord Southampton and Lord Rutland come not to the Court, the one but very seldom; they pass away the time merely in going to plays every day;" therefore Southampton *must*, at least, have known Shakspere from afar on one side; as the dedications show, Shakspere must have known Southampton to a certain degree on the other. He also reminds us that Wotton, in a letter to Bacon, says that "the burning of the Globe destroyed only a little wood and straw, and a few forsaken cloaks." This, opposed to De Witt's evidence, makes one suspicious of Wotton, whose authority has more than once been proved insufficient. "The gaining arms to Shakespeare involved venality and falsehood in father, son, and two kings-at-arms, and did not escape protest." If this were true, it would not be to the point; but it is not true, and three kings-at-arms would have been involved.

He repeats again, "The New Theory, that *various noblemen* wrote these plays, and that they used Shakespeare's name as a *nom de plume*, and that the printed plays are totally different from those acted and popular as his. Hemmings and Condoll only selected 25 out of the 42 plays credited to Shakespeare in life, and added nine *never before heard of.*" "The Shakespeareans take Jonson's verses, but are marvellously afraid to take his prose. Ben does not put Shakespeare among the wits, but among his personal acquaintance. Yet on Jonson's uncorroborated lines they build his fame. Bacon, Raleigh, Matthew never heard of Shakespeare, or would have spoken of him." As Morgan does not confess to be a Baconian, it may be hoped that further reading may induce him to return to the "faith of his fathers."

In 1883 Mrs. Pott published a large volume called *Bacon's Promus of Formularies and Elegancies*, which she edited with voluminous notes, and parallel passages from various authors of the period, chiefly Shakspere, asserting that Bacon wrote his plays at least, if not those of several other dramatists.

The *Promus* had been noticed and condensed in Spedding's edition of Bacon's Life and Works, but Mrs. Pott thought it worthy of being printed *in extenso*, as a specimen of Bacon's literary workshop. It commences in 1594, and goes on for two or three years.

I do not think it proves much. The quotations were evidently not original; indeed most of them can be traced to older dates; and those that cannot, probably arose from remembrance of conversations.

In 1884 Mrs. Pott published a pamphlet called *Thirty-two Reasons for Believing that Bacon wrote Shakspere*. As these contain the "reasons" of Judge Holmes and other Baconians in a condensed form, I treat them here as illustrating the general question.

I condense her statements:—

I. "That nothing in his life makes it impossible for Bacon to have written the plays."

II. "That chronological order, dates, and other particulars coincide with facts in the life of Bacon."

III. "The hints given by the author's experiences applicable to Bacon and not to Shakspere."

IV. "That Bacon was a poet."

V. "That Bacon was addicted to the theatre, got up masques, and wrote *The Conference of Pleasure, The Gesta Grayorum, Masque of an Indian Prince*." No person who *could* write the plays *would* have written these. . . .

VI. "The Earls of Southampton and Pembroke are not shown to have any intimacy with Shakspere, but they had with Bacon." The "dedications" would have been all the more impossible to Bacon had they been written to an intimate.

The Baconians make so much use of tradition, that they also should remember the very persistent one that Southampton *gave* Shakspere the money to buy New Place as a present from himself for dedicating his poems to him.

VII. "Many of the wits and poets acknowledged Bacon their chief. For example—

The Great Assises of Parnassus." We have shown in Chap. v. how entirely the interior of this pamphlet, of which the title-page is quoted here, supports Shakspere in his true position as actor and dramatic poet, and leaves Bacon merely as scientist and Lord Chancellor.

VIII. "That Ben Jonson used the same words in addressing both." Only one similar phrase, and I show elsewhere how that might arise. "Ben Jonson does not put Shakspere among the sixteen greatest *wits* of the day." That has been accounted for. "Sir Henry Wotton does not mention him at all." As, however, he also omitted Spenser and other great poets, this is not so surprising.

IX. "That in the time of Bacon's poverty, 1623, Ben Jonson tried to push the sale of Shakspere's works." The conclusion desired does not follow. These were printed by Isaac Jaggard and Edward Blount, at the charges of W. Jaggard, Ed. Blount, J. Smithweeke, and W. Apsley, and all profits were shared by these, with probably a commission to Ben Jonson, and no share to Bacon.

X. "That Bacon had some connexion with Shakspere." This is, however, only shown by the same clerk scribbling their names on the same sheet of paper in the Northumberland MS., explained in Chap. iv.

XI. "That he uses 'the alphabet,'" and that this means a secret cipher, whereas it really means the "Alphabet of the Sciences." See Chap. vii., and Spedding's *Bacon*.

XII. "That Sir Toby Matthew's letter from abroad adds: P.S.—The most prodigious wit that ever I knew of my nation *on this side of the sea* is of your Lordship's name, though he be known by another." This of course refers to his brother, Anthony Bacon; when on his secret-service missions abroad he used an alias. "This side of the sea" excludes the possibility of his meaning Francis Bacon, as Matthew did not meet him there, when in his extreme youth he was abroad. "That Bacon speaks of his inventions, meaning poems." "Invention" he repeatedly uses as the application of imagination to experiment so as to make discoveries.

XIII. "That he called himself a 'concealed poet' to Sir John Davies." Unless it implied that Bacon had written Davies' *Nosce Teipsum* for him, how was Davies to know what he meant? If Bacon wrote Shakspere's plays and spoke of it, he would not be a 'concealed poet.' It really however refers to his parabolical writings. See his definitions of poetry referred to in Chapter iv.

XIV. and XV. "The knowledge in the plays is that of Bacon, as, for instance, in Law and Classics," &c. As Shakspere had a cousin and many friends lawyers; as he lived near the law courts, frequenting the same taverns; as his father had been in an office that required some legal knowledge; as all people of the period seemed to go through numerous petty litigations; and as most dramatic writers of the time used law phrases freely, it is not unnatural Shakspere should have done so. Shakspere for his classical stories used the translations then so abundant—North's rendering of *Plutarch's Lives*, published by Vautrollier; translations of Ovid and Cicero by the same; *Diana of Montemayor*, translated by Thomas Wilson; *The Menæchmi* of Plautus, translated earlier, and published in 1595; Montaigne's *Essays*, translated by Florio; Baudwin's *Collection of the Sayings of all the Wise*, 1547. Then there were Lyly's *Euphues*, Sidney's *Arcadia*, Greene's plays and novels, with those of Marlowe and others; histories, travels, essays, probably Bacon's among the number.

"Shakspere's library," or the books he has referred to, has been collected by Collier and Hazlitt. But Bacon's *knowledge* is much more extensive and thorough than that of the plays, and of a different nature.

The general science of the plays comes not from Bacon's mind. The flowers of Shakspere are those naturally observed by a poet born amid rich woodland and river scenery, and transported to the suburbs of a large city, where woods were still within walking distance, and where some plants not very common were found by Gerard in the very theatre-field. (See Gerard's *Historie of Plants*, 1597.)

XVI. "That the subjects which engross them are the same."

XVII. "That the observations on character are the same."

XVIII. "That the scientific *errors* are the same." That is very natural, and depends on the advancement of the times; the scientific *knowledge*, however, is different both in kind and in degree.

XIX. "Bacon's studies of any time introduced into plays of the same date;" and

XX. "In several editions of a play, Bacon's increased knowledge shown in the later editions." There are different means of accounting for the element of truth that lies in these; as well as in the fact that

XXI. "The vocabulary is very much the same."

XXIII. "Baconian ideas and groups of ideas appear in the plays." I have shown elsewhere, however, that Bacon, no less than Shakspere, read much and borrowed much.

XXIV. "Mrs. Cowden Clarke's ninety-five points of Shakspere's style common to Bacon."

XXV. "Shakspere's grammar of Dr. Abbott serves for Bacon."

XXVI. "Figures of speech frequently the same."

XXVII. "The *Promus* notes do not appear in Bacon's works, but in Shakspere's plays." Very probably they were taken from them, or from common sources. None of them were original; but we see that many of the proverbs and headings *do* appear in Bacon's works and not in Shakspere's: for instance, phrases regarding wine.

XXVIII. "Superstitious and religious belief the same."

XXIX. "Bacon's favourite authors Shakspere's also." But we must remember Bacon's age was nearly the same as Shakspere's, his period, his place of residence, his public, his sovereign, some of his friends, and many of his circumstances. Is there no resemblance between other two writers in the same period, or of Dryden's period, or Wordsworth's period of a similar nature?

XXX. "Striking *omissions* from the plays fit the character and circumstances of Bacon. No village experiences, no brewing, cider-making, or baking." We have shown that just in these points Bacon was more interested than Shakspere, and more likely to mention them.

"No children are mentioned, therefore the childless Bacon wrote them." I think Mrs. Pott trips here. Macduff's feeling for his children could only be portrayed by a father. Constance and Arthur, and other parents and children appear, and boys are always called "sweet." But the interests of the times were more centred in plays on adult life, and Shakspere supplied the demand; and though they enjoyed "children players," these generally performed plays suitable for adults.

XXXI. "That the folio of 1623 included plays never before heard of." That is to say, it included plays of which the criticism by name has not come down to us in some way or other. But these were very few, only two or three. And they were preserved and collected by the proprietors of the theatre to which he sold them; who had no interest in publishing the plays beyond their loving desire to "keep the memory of their worthy fellow alive," even at the cost of their copyright. "The folio was published two years after Bacon's fall, when he was trying to publish everything on account of poverty and failing health." But how, without a free confession, could he get his hands into the manuscript chest of the theatre, so as to select and reconstruct and cipher the number he wished printed? How did he bribe so many concerned—proprietors, printers, publishers, poets—Ben Jonson in particular—not only to tell such wholesale lies, but to stick to them? What profit could come to him, as his proportion of the reprint, done at "the charges" of other men? What cause, other than profit or honour, could have tempted him so to spend his failing health in toils that kept him away from the great work of his life?

XXXII. "That the difficulties which have to be explained away are much less in the case of Bacon than of Shakspere." I do not agree with this statement, or with any of the above, or I should not have taken the trouble to write these pages; and I think careful comparison would convince any one that any appearance of truth they have is only superficial.

Mrs. Pott's other pamphlet, published in 1885, *Did Francis Bacon write Shakspeare?* treats the same ideas in a different way. But I cannot see how any one could consider them either proofs or reasonings. The first PROOF brought forward is, "Bacon's mother was a lady; Shakspere's mother, of a peasant family." Though this constrast is quite irrelevant to the subject in hand, genius being of a different sphere from social distinction, one cannot accept it. The family of the Ardens was very far above the rank of peasants; a comfortable well-to-do, well-connected family, farming their own lands, and living in houses very much above the average of the times, having a memory of a higher past, and aspirations towards a higher future, *that could not have entered a peasant's brain*. It is very evident that Mary Arden was at once possessed of powers and charms. She was her father's favourite daughter, and his executor, and was most probably a methodical help-meet for her ambitious but unpractical husband. She lived long, had a handsome family; and if we judge by the traces of her in the female characters of the plays, must have been tender, pure, and noble. A happier and more healthy-minded mother was she certainly, in any case, for a great man, than the learned, ambitious, narrow, masterful Lady Bacon, whose mind preyed on itself until it went crazy.

"It will tax ingenuity to invent any satisfactory explanation of the facts that some of Shakspere's plays appeared during his lifetime without his name, and some did not appear till after his death, supposing William Shakspere to have been the author." The very simple and satisfactory explanation is, that the habits of these days in regard to publication were perfectly different from ours; that it was perfectly common for writers to publish even their own writings without name or signature, and to do so in some editions and not in others; that Shakspere wrote *for the stage*, and therefore for the proprietors, and it was not to their interest to publish; and his later plays, when his name had been famous some time, were more likely to be more jealously guarded than the earlier. But the pirates were always about, and either put on names or no names on the title-page, to suit their own convenience. Printing and publishing was a difficult business in these days, as we can see in the Stationers' records. "After his retirement," the Rev. John Ward, Vicar of Stratford-on-Avon, in 1663 writes that "Shakspere wrote two plays every year for the stage, for which he was so well paid, he could spend at the rate of a thousand a year;" and the Rev. J. Ward knew Shakspere's daughter Judith.

I believe it was a sense that, being removed from the sphere of pure poetry by the mercantile impulse towards them, they fell so far short of his ideas of what they should be, which prevented his caring to publish them. Yet his brain may have been full of plans of correction and publication when he died. Various other queries and difficulties are brought forward, all the *important* points of which have been answered. The parallelisms only show how well the industry of Shakspere kept him abreast of the literature of the time. But we could not go through each trifling dispute in detail without writing a mighty volume. Our ignorance of many facts is to be deplored; but research daily reduces our ignorance.

The revolt against authority and custom of our awakened and intelligent period, good to a certain degree, sometimes goes too far. It often deems the reasons it brings stronger than the reasons it finds, merely because of bringing them. It would destroy the carefully guarded, to replace it with new forms, whose only value lies in novelty. It should base itself on Bacon's laws regarding antiquity and novelty, and it would be at once more valuable and more practical.

Much has been said and proved, contested and disproved, regarding the authorship of the fourth Gospel. This attempt at disproving our *fifth* Gospel is another outcome of the same destructive creed, but I consider that the laws regarding the authenticity of testimony and credibility of witnesses can be fully satisfied in this case, and the attack resisted. The *Daily Telegraph* committed a fallacy in using the question-begging epithet, *"Dethroning Shakspere,"* in the correspondence on this subject, reproduced in book-form. Without doubt, it was an *attempt* to do so. Success requires greater strength than that. The "attempt and not the deed confounds it."

Yet some good comes out of all evil. The good for us in this discussion is, that it sends us back from second-hand traditions and repeated errors, forgeries, misstatements, and misconstructions, to read anew the real authors, and their real friends and foes, in the living reality of time and space contemporary with them. The more one reads of them, the less it seems necessary to answer the Baconian statements; the answers seem so simple and self-evident.

Notes

1. "Who wrote Shakespeare?"—*Chambers's Edinburgh Journal*, Saturday, August 7, 1852. "Thus asks Mrs. Kitty in *High Life Below Stairs*; to which his Grace, my lord Duke, gravely replies, 'Ben Jonson.' 'Oh, no,' quoth my Lady Bab; 'Shakespeare was written by one Mr. Finis, for I saw his name at the end of the book.'" Though the author of this article laughs at these errors, he goes hastily through the subject, suggesting that Shakspere *kept a poet*; that when the poet died, the plays ceased to appear; but Shakspere, as manager, retired rich.
2. See Mr. Symonds' antecedent dramatic literature.
3. June 10, 1594, Thomas Creede entered for his "booke entituled *Menæchmi*, beinge a pleasant and fine conceyted Comedye taken out of the most excellent wittie Poet Plautus, chosen purposely from out the rest as being least harmful and most delightful."—*The Stationers' Registers*.

   The Comedy of Errors was not played until the end of December same year.
4. Saxo-Grammaticus in the twelfth century wrote the *History of Denmark*, and in it of Hamblet. Bellforest, a French author, translates the tale, slightly altering it. On an English translation of this romance, called *The History of Hamblet*, Shakspere based his play. It is in black-letter, printed by Richard Bradocke for Thomas Pavier, 1560. Some suppose the modern story satirised modern characters. Burleigh, as old Polonius, gave his son similar advice before he set out on his travels in 1598. Sir Philip Sydney was supposed to be the real Hamlet.

JOHN DONNE

John Donne

1572–1631

John Donne was born in London in 1572. His father was a prosperous merchant; his mother (the daughter of the epigrammatist John Heywood) was a devout Catholic whose family had suffered religious persecution and exile. Donne matriculated from Oxford in 1584, and although he did not receive a degree, the university would later award him an honorary M. A. Donne also trained as a lawyer—his entrance in 1591 to Thavies Inn was followed by admittance to Lincoln's in 1592—and some critics have remarked upon the traces of legal training evident in the conceits and tight reasoning of his verse. Donne appears to have remained at Lincoln's until 1596, when he joined the English expedition to Cadiz. On his return to England in 1597, he spent several years in the service of Sir Thomas Egerton, staying with Egerton while he entered Parliament as the Member for Brackley. One of the decisive turning points of his life occurred in December 1601, when he secretly married Ann More, Lady Egerton's niece. The confession of his marriage to his father-in-law in February 1602 resulted in imprisonment and dismissal from Egerton's service. His marriage was subsequently to cause Donne so much difficulty that he would write in a letter to his wife in 1602, "John Donne, Ann Donne, Un-done."

Donne was unsuccessful in his application for employment in the Queen's household, and for secretaryships in Ireland and with the Virginia Company. In 1614, he served as Member of Parliament for Taunton and sat on several select committees; he was, however, still unable to find state employment. In 1615, he took orders in the Church of England, a step which had been urged on him by the Dean of Gloucester eight years before. From this time on, he served in various ecclesiastical functions: as Royal Chaplain, rector and vicar of several parishes, Reader in Divinity at Lincoln's Inn, and as a Justice in the Court of Delegates. The crowning achievement of his career came in 1621, when he was elected Dean of St. Paul's. He preached widely, both at Court and abroad, and his sermons were received with acclaim and published in 1622, 1625, and 1626. He was a strong candidate for a bishopric in 1630, but fell seriously ill late that year. He died in 1631 and is buried in St. Paul's. Although he is best known today for his poems, few of them were published in his lifetime: the First and Second Anniversaries came out in 1612, as did "Break of Day," and "Elegy upon Prince Henry" was published the following year. The first collected edition of the poetry appeared in 1633.

Personal

JOHANNES DONNE,
Sac. Theol. Profess.
Poet Varia Studia, Quibus Ab Annis
Tenerrimis Fideliter, Nec Infeliciter
Incubuit;
Instinctu Et Impulsu Sp. Sancti, Monitu
Et Hortatu
Regis Jacobi, Ordines Sacros Amplexus,
Anno Sui Jesu, MDCXIV. Et Suæ Ætatis
XLII.
Decanatu Hujus Ecclesiæ Indutus,
XXVII. Novembris, MDCXXI
Exutus Morte Ultimo Die Martii,
MDCXXXI.
Hic Licet In Occiduo Cinere, Aspicit Eum
Cujus Nomen Est Oriens.
—Inscription on Monument

To have liv'd eminent, in a degree
Beyond our lofti'st flights, that is, like Thee
Or t' have had too much merit, is not safe;
For such excesses find no Epitaph.
At common graves we have Poetic eyes
Can melt themselves in easy Elegies. . . .
But at Thine, Poem, or Inscription
(Rich soul of wit, and language) we have none.
Indeed, a silence does that tomb befit,

Where is no Herald left to blazon it.
—HENRY KING, "To the Memory of My Ever Desired Friend Doctor Donne," c. 1631

He was of stature moderately tall; of a straight and equally-proportioned body, to which all his words and actions gave an unexpressible addition of comeliness. The melancholy and pleasant humour were in him so contempered, that each gave advantage to the other, and made his company one of the delights of mankind. His fancy was unimitably high, equalled only by his great wit; both being made useful by a commanding judgment. His aspect was cheerful, and such as gave a silent testimony of a clear knowing soul, and of a conscience at peace with itself. His melting eye shewed that he had a soft heart, full of noble compassion; of too brave a soul to offer injuries, and too much a Christian not to pardon them in others. . . . He was by nature highly passionate, but more apt to reluct at the excesses of it. A great lover of the offices of humanity, and of so merciful a spirit, that he never beheld the miseries of mankind without pity and relief.—IZAAK WALTON, *The Life of Dr. John Donne*, 1639

Mr. John Dunne, who leaving Oxford, lived at the Innes of Court, not dissolute, but very neat; a great Visitor of Ladies, a great frequenter of Playes, a great writer of conceited Verses; until such times as King James taking notice of the pregnancy of his Wit, was a means that he betook him to the study of Divinity, and thereupon proceeding Doctor, was made Dean of Pauls; and became so rare a Preacher, that he was not only

commended, but even admired by all who heard him.—SIR
RICHARD BAKER, *A Chronicle of the Kings of England*, 1641

Dr. Donne, . . . a laureate wit; neither was it impossible that a
vulgar soul should dwell in such promising features.—JOHN
HACKET, *Life of Archbishop Williams*, 1693, Par. 74

The life of Donne is more interesting than his poetry.—
THOMAS CAMPBELL, *Specimens of the British Poets*, 1819

Dr. Donne, once so celebrated as a writer, now so neglected, is
more interesting for his matrimonial history, and for one little
poem addressed to his wife, than for all his learned, metaphysical, and theological productions.—ANNA BROWNELL
JAMESON, *The Loves of the Poets*, 1829, Vol. 2, p. 94

The knowledge of Donne's immense learning, the subtlety and
capacity of his intellect, the intense depth and wide scope of his
thought, the charm of his conversation, the sadness of his life,
gave a vivid meaning and interest to his poems . . . circulated
among his acquaintances, which at this distance of time we
cannot reach without a certain effort of imagination. . . . Dr.
Donne is one of the most interesting personalities among our
men of letters. The superficial facts of his life are so incongruous as to be an irresistible provocation to inquiry. What
are we to make of the fact that the founder of a licentious
school of erotic poetry, a man acknowledged to be the greatest
wit in a licentious Court, with an early bias in matters of
religion towards Roman Catholicism, entered the Church of
England when he was past middle age and is now numbered
among its greatest divines? Was he a convert like St. Augustine,
or an indifferent worldling like Talleyrand? Superficial appearances are rather in favour of the latter supposition.—
WILLIAM MINTO, "John Donne," *The Nineteenth Century*,
1880, p. 849

Against the wall of the south choir aisle in the Cathedral of St.
Paul is a monument which very few of the thousands who visit
the church daily observe, or have an opportunity of observing,
but which, once seen, is not easily forgotten. It is the long,
gaunt, upright figure of a man, wrapped close in a shroud,
which is knotted at the head and feet, and leaves only the face
exposed—a face wan, worn, almost ghastly, with eyes closed as
in death. This figure is executed in white marble, and stands
on an urn of the same, as if it had just arisen therefrom. The
whole is placed in a black niche, which, by its contrast, en-
hances the death-like paleness of the shrouded figure. Above
the canopy is an inscription recording that the man whose
effigy stands beneath, though his ashes are mingled with western dust, looks towards Him whose name is the Orient. . . . It
was not such a memorial as Donne's surviving friends might
think suitable to commemorate the deceased, but it was the
very monument which Donne himself designed as a true emblem of his past life and his future hopes.—J. B. LIGHTFOOT,
Historical Essays, 1895, pp. 221–223

His graceful person, vivacity of conversation, and many accomplishments secured for him the *entrée* at the houses of the
nobility and a recognised position among the celebrities of
Queen Elizabeth's court. He was conspicuous as a young man
of fortune who spent his money freely, and mixed on equal
terms with the courtiers, and probably had the character of
being richer than he was. . . . The young man, among his
other gifts, had the great advantage of being able to do with
very little sleep. He could read all night and be gay and wakeful
and alert all day. He threw himself into the amusements and
frivolities of the court with all the glee of youth, but never so as
to interfere with his duties. The favourite of fortune, he was too
the favourite of the fortunate—the envy of some, he was the

darling of more. Those of his contemporaries who knew him
intimately speak of him at all times as if there was none like
him; the charm of his person and manners were irresistible. He
must have had much love to give, or he could never had so
much bestowed upon him.—AUGUSTUS JESSOPP, *John
Donne, Sometime Dean of St. Paul's*, 1897, pp. 13, 18

History presents us with no instance of a man of letters more
obviously led up to by the experience and character of his
ancestors than was John Donne. As we have him revealed to
us, he is what a genealogist might wish him to be. Every salient
feature in his mind and temperament is foreshadowed by the
general trend of his family, or by the idiosyncrasy of some
individual member of it. . . . The greatest preacher of his
age. . . . No one, in the history of English literature, as it
seems to me, is so difficult to realise, so impossible to measure,
in the vast curves of his extraordinary and contradictory features. Of his life, of his experiences, of his opinions, we know
more now than it has been vouchsafed to us to know of any
other of the great Elizabethan and Jacobean galaxy of writers,
and yet how little we fathom his contradictions, how little we
can account for his impulses and his limitations. Even those of
us who have for years made his least adventures the subject of
close and eager investigation must admit at last that he eludes
us. He was not the crystal-hearted saint that Walton adored and
exalted. He was not the crafty and redoubtable courtier whom
the recusants suspected. He was not the prophet of the intricacies of fleshly feeling whom the young poets looked up to and
worshipped. He was none of these, or all of these, or more.
What was he? It is impossible to say, for, with all his superficial
expansion, his secret died with him. We are tempted to declare
that of all great men he is the one of whom least is essentially
known. Is not this, perhaps, the secret of his perennial fascination?—EDMUND GOSSE, *The Life and Letters of John Donne*,
1899, Vol. 1, pp. 3, 11, Vol. 2, p. 290

Sermons

A preacher in earnest; weeping sometimes for his auditory,
sometimes with them; always preaching to himself, like an
angel from a cloud, but in none; carrying some, as St. Paul
was, to heaven in holy raptures; and enticing others by a sacred
art and courtship to amend their lives: here picturing a Vice so
as to make it ugly to those that practised it; and a Virtue so as to
make it beloved, even by those who loved it not; and all this
with a most particular grace and an unexpressible addition of
comeliness.—IZAAK WALTON, *The Life of Dr. John Donne*,
1639

The sermons of Donne have sometimes been praised in late
times. They are undoubtedly the productions of a very ingenious and a very learned man; and two folio volumes by such
a person may be expected to supply favorable specimens. In
their general character, they will not appear, I think, much
worthy of being rescued from oblivion. The subtilty of Donne,
and his fondness for such inconclusive reasoning as a subtle
disputant is apt to fall into, runs through all of these sermons at
which I have looked. His learning he seems to have perverted
in order to cull every impertinence of the fathers and schoolmen, their remote analogies, their strained allegories, their
technical distinctions; and to these he has added much of a
similar kind from his own fanciful understanding.—HENRY
HALLAM, *Introduction to the Literature of Europe*, 1837–39,
Pt. 3, Ch. 2, Par. 70

Donne's published sermons are in form nearly as grotesque as
his poems, though they are characterized by profounder

qualities of heart and mind. It was his misfortune to know thoroughly the works of fourteen hundred writers, most of them necessarily worthless; and he could not help displaying his erudition in his discourses. Of what is now called taste he was absolutely destitute. His sermons are a curious mosaic of quaintness, quotation, wisdom, puerility, subtilty, and ecstasy. The pedant and the seer possess him by turns, and in reading no other divine are our transitions from yawning to rapture so swift and unexpected. He has passages of transcendent merit, passages which evince a spiritual vision so piercing, and a feeling of divine things so intense, that for the time we seem to be communing with a religious genius of the most exalted and exalting order; but soon he involves us in a maze of quotations and references, and our minds are hustled by what Hallam calls "the rabble of bad authors" that this saint and sage has always at his skirts, even when he ascends to the highest heaven of contemplation.—EDWIN P. WHIPPLE, *The Literature of the Age of Elizabeth*, 1859–68, p. 237

The sermons of Donne, while they are superior in style, are sometimes fantastic, like his poetry, but they are never coarse, and they derive a touching interest from his history.—ANNE C. LYNCH BOTTA, *Hand-Book of Universal Literature*, 1860, p. 476

In Donne's sermons, an intellectual epicure not too fastidious to read sermons will find a delicious feast. Whether these sermons can be taken as patterns by the modern preacher is another affair. It will not be contended that any congregation is equal to the effort of following his subtleties. In short, as exercises in abstract subtlety, fanciful ingenuity, and scholarship, the sermons are admirable. Judged by the first rule of popular exposition, the style is bad—a bewildering maze to the ordinary reader, much more to the ordinary hearer.—WILLIAM MINTO, *Manual of English Prose Literature*, 1872–80, p. 253

During this year, 1622, Donne's first printed sermon appeared. It was delivered at Paul's Cross on 15 Sept. to an enormous congregation, in obedience to the king's commands, who had just issued his "Directions to Preachers," and had made choice of the dean of St. Paul's to explain his reasons for issuing the injunctions. The sermon was at once printed; copies of the original edition are rarely met with. Two months later Donne preached his glorious sermon before the Virginian Company. . . . Donne's sermon struck a note in full sympathy with the larger views and nobler aims of the minority. His sermon may be truly described as the first missionary sermon printed in the English language. The original edition was at once absorbed. The same is true of every other sermon printed during Donne's lifetime; in their original shape they are extremely scarce. The truth is that as a preacher at this time Donne stood almost alone. Andrewes's preaching days were over (he died in September 1626), Hall never carried with him the conviction of being much more than a consummate gladiator, and was rarely heard in London; of the rest there was hardly one who was not either ponderously learned like Sanderson, or a mere performer like the rank and file of rhetoricians who came up to London to air their eloquences at Paul's Cross. The result was that Donne's popularity was always on the increase, he rose to every occasion, and surprised his friends, as Walton tells us, by the growth of his genius and earnestness even to the end.—AUGUSTUS JESSOPP, *Dictionary of National Biography*, 1888, Vol. 15, p. 229

General

One thing more I must tell you; but so softly, that I am loth to hear myself: and so softly, that if that good lady were in the room, with you and this letter, she might not hear. It is, that I am brought to a necessity of printing my poems, and addressing them to my Lord Chamberlain. This I mean to do forthwith: not for much public view, but at mine own cost, a few copies. I apprehend some incongruities in the resolution; and I know what I shall suffer from many interpretations; but I am at an end, of much considering that; and, if I were as startling in that kind, as I ever was, yet in this particular, I am under an unescapable necessity, as I shall let you perceive when I see you. By this occasion I am made a rhapsodist of mine own rags, and that cost me more diligence, to seek them, than it did to make them. This made me ask to borrow that old book of you, which it will be too late to see, for that use, when I see you; for I must do this as a valediction to the world, before I take orders. But this is it, I am to ask you: whether you ever made any such use of the letter in verse, *à notre comtesse chez vous*, as that I may not put it in, amongst the rest to persons of that rank; for I desire it very much, that something should bear her name in the book, and I would be just to my written words to my Lord Harrington to write nothing after that. I pray tell me as soon as you can, if I be at liberty to insert that: for if you have by any occasion applied any pieces to it, I see not, that it will be discerned, when it appears in the whole piece. Though this be a little matter, I would be sorry not to have an account of it, within as little after New Year's-tide, as you could.—JOHN DONNE, letter to Sir Henry Goodyere, Dec. 20, 1614, *The Works of John Donne*, ed. Henry Alford, Vol. 6, 1839, p. 367

Donne, the delight of Phœbus and each Muse,
Who, to thy one, all other brains refuse;
Whose every work of thy most early wit
Came forth example, and remains so yet;
Longer a-knowing than most wits do live,
And which no affection praise enough can give!
To it, thy language, letters, arts, best life,
Which might with half mankind maintain a strife;
All which I meant to praise, and yet I would;
But leave, because I cannot as I should!
    —BEN JONSON, "To John Donne," 1616

That Done's Anniversarie was profane and full of blasphemies: that he told Mr. Done, if it had been written of the Virgin Marie it had been something; to which he answered, that he described the Idea of a Woman, and not as she was. That Done, for not keeping of accent, deserved hanging. . . . He esteemeth John Done the first poet in the world in some things: his verses of the "Lost Chaine" he heth by heart; and that passage of the "Calme," *That dust and feathers doe not stirr, all was so quiet*. Affirmeth Done to have written all his best pieces ere he was 25 years old.—WILLIAM DRUMMOND, *Notes on Ben Jonson's Conversations*, 1619

The Muses' garden, with pedantic weeds
O'erspread, was purg'd by thee, the lazie seeds
Of servile imitation throwne away,
And fresh invention planted; thou didst pay
The debts of our penurious bankerout age:
. . . . . whatsoever wrong
By ours was done the Greek or Latin tongue,
Thou hast redeem'd, and opened as a mine
Of rich and pregnant fancie . . .
    . . . to the awe of thy imperious wit
Our troublesome language bends, made only fit,
With her tough thick-rib'd hoopes, to gird about
Thy gyant fancy.
    —THOMAS CAREW, "An Elegie upon the Death of Doctor Donne," *Works*, c. 1631, ed. Hazlitt, pp. 93–94

. . . all the softnesses,
The Shadow, Light, the Air, and Life, of Love;
The Sharpness of all Wit; ev'n bitterness
Makes Satire Sweet; all wit did God improve,
'Twas flamed in him, 'Twas but warm upon
His Embers; He was more; and it is Donne.
—GEORGE DANIEL, "A Vindication of Poesy,"
1647

Would not Donne's satires, which abound with so much wit, appear more charming, if he had taken care of his words, and of his numbers? But he followed Horace so very close, that of necessity he must fall with him; and I may safely say it of this present age, that if we are not so great wits as Donne, yet, certainly, we are better poets.—JOHN DRYDEN, "Essay on Satire," *Works*, 1692, Vol. 13, eds. Scott, Saintsbury, p. 109

If it be true that the purport of poetry should be to please, no author has written with such utter neglect of the rule. It is scarce possible for a human ear to endure the dissonance and discord of his couplets, and even when his thoughts are clothed in the melody of Pope, they appear to me hardly worth the decoration.—NATHAN DRAKE, *Literary Hours*, 1798, No. 28

Donne had not music enough to render his broken rhyming couplets sufferable, and neither his wit, nor his pointed satire, were sufficient to rescue him from that neglect which his uncouth and rugged versification speedily superinduced.—HENRY KIRKE WHITE, "Melancholy Hours," *Remains*, 1806, Vol. 2, ed. Southey

Since Dryden, the metre of our poets leads to the sense: in our elder and more genuine bards, the sense, including the passion, leads to the metre. Read even Donne's satires as he meant them to be read, and as the sense and passion demand, and you will find in the lines a manly harmony.—SAMUEL TAYLOR COLERIDGE, *Notes on Beaumont and Fletcher*, 1818, ed. Ashe, p. 427

Nothing could have made Donne a poet, unless as great a change had been worked in the internal structure of his ears, as was wrought in elongating those of Midas.—ROBERT SOUTHEY, *Specimens of the Later English Poets*, 1807, Vol. 1, p. xxiv

Donne was the "best good-natured man, with the worst natured Muse." A romantic and uxorious lover, he addresses the object of his real tenderness with ideas that outrage decorum. He begins his own epithalamium with most indelicate invocation to his bride. His ruggedness and whim are almost proverbially known. Yet there is a beauty of thought which at intervals rises from his chaotic imagination, like the form of Venus smiling on the waters.—THOMAS CAMPBELL, *An Essay on English Poetry*, 1819

Donne is the most inharmonious of our versifiers, if he can be said to have deserved such a name by lines too rugged to seem metre. Of his earlier poems, many are very licentious; the later are chiefly devout. Few are good for much; the conceits have not even the merit of being intelligible: it would perhaps be difficult to select three passages that we should care to read again.—HENRY HALLAM, *Introduction to the Literature of Europe*, 1837–39, Pt. 3, Ch. 5, Par. 39

Having a dumb angel, and knowing more noble poetry than he articulates.—ELIZABETH BARRETT BROWNING, *The Book of Poets*, 1842–63, Vol. 2, p. 50

Of stubborn thoughts a garland thought to twine;
To his fair Maid brought cabalistic posies,

And sung quaint ditties of metempsychosis;
"Twists iron pokers into true love-knots,"
Coining hard words, not found in polyglots.
—HARTLEY COLERIDGE, "Donne," *Sketches of the English Poets, Poems*, 1849, Vol. 2, p. 295

With vast learning, with subtile and penetrating intellect, with a fancy singularly fruitful and ingenious, he still contrived to disconnect, more or less, his learning from what was worth learning, his intellect from what was reasonable, his fancy from what was beautiful. His poems, or rather his metrical problems, are obscure in thought, rugged in versification, and full of conceits which are intended to surprise rather than to please; but they still exhibit a power of intellect, both analytical and analogical, competent at once to separate the minutest and connect the remotest ideas. This power, while it might not have given his poems grace, sweetness, freshness, and melody, would still, if properly directed, have made them valuable for their thoughts; but in the case of Donne it is perverted to the production of what is *bizarre* or unnatural, and his muse is thus as hostile to use as to beauty. The intention is, not to idealize what is true, but to display the writer's skill and wit in giving a show of reason to what is false. The effect of this on the moral character of Donne was pernicious. A subtile intellectual scepticism, which weakened will, divorced thought from action and literature from life, and made existence a puzzle and a dream, resulted from this perversion of his intellect. He found that he could wittily justify what was vicious as well as what was unnatural; and his amatory poems, accordingly, are characterized by a cold, hard, labored, intellectualized sensuality, worse than the worst impurity of his contemporaries, because it has no excuse of passion for its violations of decency.—EDWIN P. WHIPPLE, *The Literature of the Age of Elizabeth*, 1859–68, p. 231

Donne, altogether, gives us the impression of a great genius ruined by a false system. He is a charioteer run away with by his own pampered steeds. He begins generally well, but long ere the close, quibbles, conceits, and the temptation of shewing off recondite learning, prove too strong for him, and he who commenced following a serene star, ends pursuing a will-o'-wisp into a bottomless morass. Compare, for instance, the ingenious nonsense which abounds in the middle and the close of his "Progress of the Soul" with the dark, but magnificent stanzas which are the first in the poem. In no writings in the language is there more spilt treasure—a more lavish loss of beautiful, original, and striking things than in the poems of Donne.—GEORGE GILFILLAN, *Specimens with Memoirs of the Less-Known British Poets*, 1860, Vol. 1, p. 203

On a superficial inspection, Donne's verses look like so many riddles. They seem to be written upon the principle of making the meaning as difficult to be found out as possible,—of using all the resources of language, not to express thought, but to conceal it. Nothing is said in a direct, natural manner; conceit follows conceit without intermission; the most remote analogies, the most farfetched images, the most unexpected turns, one after another, surprise and often puzzle the understanding; while things of the most opposite kinds—the harsh and the harmonious, the graceful and the grotesque, the grave and the gay, the pious and the profane—meet and mingle in the strangest of dances. But, running through all this bewilderment, a deeper insight detects not only a vein of the most exuberant wit, but often the sunniest and most delicate fancy, and the truest tenderness and depth of feeling.—GEORGE L. CRAIK, *A Compendious History of English Literature and of the English Language*, 1861, Vol. 1, p. 579

There is indeed much in Donne, in the unfolding of his moral and spiritual life, which often reminds us of St. Augustine. I do not mean that, noteworthy as on many accounts he was, and in the language of Carew, one of his contemporaries,

> A king who ruled as he thought fit
> The universal monarchy of wit.

he at all approached in intellectual or spiritual stature to the great Doctor of the Western Church. But still there was in Donne the same tumultuous youth, the same final deliverance from them; and then the same passionate and personal grasp of the central truths of Christianity, linking itself as this did with all that he had suffered, and all that he had sinned, and all through which by God's grace he had victoriously struggled.— RICHARD CHENEVIX TRENCH, *A Household Book of English Poetry*, 1868, p. 403

A pungent satirist, of terrible crudeness, a powerful poet, of a precise and intense imagination, who still preserves something of the energy and thrill of the original inspiration. But he deliberately abuses all these gifts, and succeeds with great difficulty in concocting a piece of nonsense. . . . Twenty times while reading him we rub our brow, and ask with astonishment, how a man could so have tormented and contorted himself, strained his style, refined on his refinement, hit upon such absurd comparisons?—H. A. TAINE, *History of English Literature*, 1871, Vol. 1, tr. Van Laun, Bk. 2, Ch. 1, pp. 203–4

His reputation as a poet, great in his own day, low during the latter part of the seventeenth and the whole of the eighteenth centuries, has latterly revived. In its days of abasement, critics spoke of his harsh and rugged versification, and his leaving nature for conceit. It seems to be now acknowledged that, amidst much bad taste, there is much real poetry, and that of a high order, in Donne.—ROBERT CHAMBERS, *Cyclopædia of English Literature*, 1876, ed. Carruthers

> Better and truer verse none ever wrote . . .
> Than thou, revered and magisterial Donne!
> —ROBERT BROWNING, *The Two Poets of Croisic*, 1878

We find little to admire, and nothing to love. We see that farfetched similes, extravagant metaphors, are not here occasional blemishes, but the substance. He should have given us simple images, simply expressed; for he loved and suffered much: but fashion was stronger than nature.—ALFRED WELSH, *Development of English Literature and Language*, 1882, Vol. 1, p. 413

Donne's poems were first collected in 1633: they cover an extraordinary range in subject, and are throughout marked with a strange originality almost equally fascinating and repellent. It is possible that his familiarity with Italian and Spanish literatures, both at that time deeply coloured by fantastic and far-fetched thought, may have in some degree influenced him in that direction. His poems were probably written mainly during youth. There is a strange solemn passionate earnestness about them, a quality which underlies the fanciful "conceits" of all his work.—FRANCIS T. PALGRAVE, *The Treasury of Sacred Song*, 1889, note, p. 333

In him the Jacobean spirit, as opposed to the Elizabethan, is paramount. His were the first poems which protested, in their form alike and their tendency, against the pastoral sweetness of the Spenserians. Something new in English literature begins in Donne, something which proceeded, under his potent influence, to colour poetry for nearly a hundred years. The exact mode in which that influence was immediately distributed is unknown to us, or very dimly perceived. To know more about it is one of the great desiderata of literary history. The imitation of Donne's style begins so early, and becomes so general, that several critics have taken for granted that there must have been editions of his writings which have disappeared. . . . The style of Donne, like a very odd perfume, was found to cling to every one who touched it, and we observe the remarkable phenomenon of poems which had not passed through a printer's hands exercising the influence of a body of accepted classical work. In estimating the poetry of the Jacobean age, therefore, there is no writer who demands more careful study than this enigmatical and subterranean master, this veiled Isis whose utterances outweigh the oracles of all the visible gods.—EDMUND GOSSE, *The Jacobean Poets*, 1894, pp. 47–48

After he had taken holy orders Donne seldom threw his passions into verse; even his "Divine Poems" are, with few exceptions, of early date; the poet in Donne did not cease to exist, but his ardour, his imagination, his delight in what is strange and wonderful, his tenderness, his tears, his smiles, his erudition, his intellectual ingenuities, were all placed at the service of one whose desire was that he might die in the pulpit, or if not die, that he might take his death in the pulpit, a desire which was in fact fulfilled. . . . Donne as a poet is certainly difficult of access. . . . He sometimes wrote best, or thought he wrote best, when his themes were wholly of the imagination. Still it is evident that Donne, the student, the recluse, the speculator on recondite problems, was also a man who adventured in pursuit of violent delights which had violent ends. . . . In whatever sunny garden, and at whatever banquet Donne sits, he discerns in air the dark Scythesman of that great picture attributed to Orcagna. An entire section of his poetry is assigned to death.—EDWARD DOWDEN, *New Studies in Literature*, 1895, pp. 90–91, 107–17

"The Will of John Donne" is probably the wittiest and the bitterest lyric in our language. Donne's love passages and their record in verse were over before the author was of age. His wit then turned into metaphysical sermon-writing and theological polemics, and his bitterness into a despairing austerity.— OSWALD CRAWFORD, *Lyrical Verse from Elizabeth to Victoria*, 1896, p. 426

Donne is a thoroughly original spirit and a great innovator; he is thoughtful, indirect, and strange; he nurses his fancies, lives with them, and broods over them so much that they are still modern in all their distinction and ardour, in spite of the strangeness of their apparel—a strangeness no greater perhaps than that of some modern poets, like Browning, as the apparel of their verse will appear two hundred years hence. Ingenuity, allusiveness, the evocation of remote images and of analogies that startle the mind into a more than half acquiescence, phantoms of deep thoughts, and emotions half-sophisticated and wholly intense: these things mark the poetry of Donne. His lyric is original and taking, but it lacks simple thoughts; it does not sing. It is ascetic and sometimes austere; the sense of sin, the staple of contemporary tragedy, enters the lyric with Donne. He is all for terseness and meaning; and his versification accords with his thought and is equally elliptical.— FREDERIC IVES CARPENTER, "Introduction" to *English Lyric Poetry*, *1500–1700*, 1897, p. lviii

One of the most enigmatical and debated, alternately one of the most attractive and most repellent, figures in English literature.—DAVID HANNAY, *The Later Renaissance*, 1898, p. 220

In one way he has partly become obsolete because he belonged so completely to the dying epoch. The scholasticism in which his mind was steeped was to become hateful and then contemptible to the rising philosophy; the literature which he had assimilated went to the dust-heaps; preachers condescended to drop their doctorial robes; downright common-sense came in with Tillotson and South in the next generation; and not only the learning but the congenial habit of thought became unintelligible. Donne's poetical creed went the same way, and if Pope and Parnell perceived that there was some genuine ore in his verses and tried to beat it into the coinage of their own day, they only spoilt it in trying to polish it. But on the other side, Donne's depth of feeling, whether tortured into short lyrics or expanding into voluble rhetoric, has a charm which perhaps gains a new charm from modern sentimentalists. His morbid or "neurotic" constitution has a real affinity for latter-day pessimists. If they talk philosophy where he had to be content with scholastic theology the substance is pretty much the same. He has the characteristic love for getting pungency at any price; for dwelling upon the horrible till we cannot say whether it attracts or repels him; and can love the "intense" and supersublimated as much as if he were skilled in all the latest æsthetic canons.—LESLIE STEPHEN, "John Donne," *The National Review*, 1899, p. 613

Was the mind of the dialectician, of the intellectual adventurer; he is a poet almost by accident, or at least for reasons with which art in the abstract has but little to do. He writes verse, first of all, because he has observed keenly, and because it pleases the pride of his intellect to satirise the pretensions of humanity. Then it is the flesh which speaks in his verse, the curiosity of woman, which he has explored in the same spirit of adventure; then passion, making a slave of him for love's sake, and turning at last to the slave's hatred; finally, religion, taken up with the same intellectual interest, the same subtle indifference, and, in its turn, passing also into passionate reality. A few poems are inspired in him by what he has seen in remote countries; some are marriage songs and funeral elegies, written for friendship or for money. But he writes nothing "out of his own head," as we say; nothing lightly, or, it would seem, easily; nothing for the song's sake. He speaks, in a letter, of "descending to print anything in verse"; and it is certain that he was never completely absorbed by his own poetry, or at all careful to measure his achievements against those of others. He took his own poems very seriously, he worked upon them with the whole force of his intellect; but to himself, even before he became a divine, he was something more than a poet. Poetry was but one means of expressing the many-sided activity of his mind and temperament. Prose was another, preaching another; travel and contact with great events and persons scarcely less important to him, in the building up of himself.—ARTHUR SYMONS, "John Donne," *Fortnightly Review*, 1899, p. 735

John Donne is of interest to the student of literature chiefly because of the influence which he exerted on the poetry of the age. His verse teems with forced comparisons and analogies between things remarkable for their dissimilarity. An obscure likeness and a worthless conceit were as important to him as was the problem of existence to Hamlet.—REUBEN POST HALLECK, *History of English Literature*, 1900, p. 186

WILLIAM HAZLITT
From "On Cowley, Butler, Suckling, etc."
Lectures on the English Comic Writers (1819)
The Collected Works of William Hazlitt,
eds., A. R. Walker and Arnold Gower
1903, Vol. 8, pp. 51–53

Donne, who was considerably before Cowley, is without his fancy, but was more recondite in his logic, and rigid in his descriptions. He is hence led, particularly in his satires, to tell disagreeable truths in as disagreeable a way as possible, or to convey a pleasing and affecting thought (of which there are many to be found in his other writings) by the harshest means, and with the most painful effort. His Muse suffers continual pangs and throes. His thoughts are delivered by the Cæsarean operation. The sentiments, profound and tender as they often are, are stifled in the expression; and 'heaved pantingly forth,' are 'buried quick again' under the ruins and rubbish of analytical distinctions. It is like poetry waking from a trance: with an eye bent idly on the outward world, and half-forgotten feelings crowding about the heart; with vivid impressions, dim notions, and disjointed words. The following may serve as instances of beautiful or impassioned reflections losing themselves in obscure and difficult applications. He has some lines to a Blossom, which begin thus:

> Little think'st thou, poor flow'r,
> Whom I have watched six or seven days,
> And seen thy birth, and seen what every hour
> Gave to thy growth, thee to this height to raise,
> And now dost laugh and triumph on this bough.
> > Little think'st thou
> That it will freeze anon, and that I shall
> To-morrow find thee fall'n, or not at all.

This simple and delicate description is only introduced as a foundation for an elaborate metaphysical conceit as a parallel to it, in the next stanza.

> Little think'st thou (poor heart
> That labour'st yet to nestle thee,
> And think'st by hovering here to get a part
> In a forbidden or forbidding tree,
> And hop'st her stiffness by long siege to bow:)
> > Little think'st thou,
> That thou to-morrow, ere the sun doth wake,
> Must with this sun and me a journey take.

This is but a lame and impotent conclusion from so delightful a beginning.—He thus notices the circumstance of his wearing his late wife's hair about his arm, in a little poem which is called the Funeral.

> Whoever comes to shroud me, do not harm
> > Nor question much
> That subtle wreath of hair, about mine arm;
> The mystery, the sign you must not touch.

The scholastic reason he gives quite dissolves the charm of tender and touching grace in the sentiment itself—

> For 'tis my outward soul,
> Viceroy to that, which unto heaven being gone,
> > Will leave this to control,
> And keep these limbs, her provinces, from
> dissolution.

Again, the following lines, the title of which is Love's Deity, are highly characteristic of this author's manner, in which the thoughts are inlaid in a costly but imperfect mosaic-work.

> *I long to talk with some old lover's ghost,*
> *Who died before the God of Love was born:*
> *I cannot think that he, who then lov'd most,*
> *Sunk so low, as to love one which did scorn.*
> *But since this God produc'd a destiny,*
> *And that vice-nature, custom, lets it be;*
> *I must love her that loves not me.*

The stanza in the Epithalamion on a Count Palatine of the Rhine, has been often quoted against him, and is an almost irresistible illustration of the extravagances to which this kind of writing, which turns upon a pivot of words and possible allusions, is liable. Speaking of the bride and bridegroom he says, by way of serious compliment—

> Here lies a she-Sun, and a he-Moon there,
> She gives the best light to his sphere;
> Or each is both and all, and so
> They unto one another nothing owe.

His love-verses and epistles to his friends give the most favourable idea of Donne. His satires are too clerical. He shews, if I may so speak, too much disgust, and, at the same time, too much contempt for vice. His dogmatical invectives hardly redeem the nauseousness of his descriptions, and compromise the imagination of his readers more than they assist their reason. The satirist does not write with the same authority as the divine, and should use his poetical privileges more sparingly. 'To the pure all things are pure,' is a maxim which a man like Dr. Donne may be justified in applying to himself; but he might have recollected that it could not be construed to extend to the generality of his readers, *without benefit of clergy.*

<h3 style="text-align:center">UNSIGNED</h3>

Retrospective Review, 1823, pp. 31–35

Theobald, in his egregious preface to Shakspeare, calls Donne's Poems "nothing but a continued heap of riddles."—We shall presently shew that he knew as little about Donne as he himself has shewn that he knew about Shakspeare. If *he* could have written such "riddles," or even expounded them, Pope might have put him into the *Dunciad* in vain.

Donne was contemporary with Shakspeare, and was not unworthy to be so. He may fairly be placed, in point of talent, at the head of the minor poets of that day. Imbued, to saturation, with all the learning of his age—with a most active and piercing intellect—an imagination, if not grasping and comprehensive, most subtle and far-darting—a fancy rich, vivid, picturesque, and, at the same time, highly *fantastical*,—if we may so apply the term—a mode of expression singularly terse, simple, and condensed—an exquisite ear for the melody of versification— and a wit, admirable as well for its caustic severity as its playful quickness; all he wanted to make him an accomplished poet of the second order was, sensibility and taste: and both of these he possessed in a certain degree; but neither in a sufficient degree to keep them from yielding to the circumstances in which he was placed. His sensibility was by nature strong, but sluggish and deep-seated. It required to be roused and awakened by the imagination, before it would act; and this process seldom failed to communicate to the action which it created, an appearance of affectation (for it was nothing more than the appearance), which is more destructive to the effect of sentimental poetry than any thing else. We do not mind the images and illustrations of a sentiment being recondite and far-fetched; and, indeed, this has frequently a good effect; but if the sentiment itself has any appearance of being so, we doubt the truth of it immediately; and if we doubt its truth, we are disposed to give it any reception rather than a sympathetic one. The scholastic habits of Donne's intellect also, without weakening his sensibility, contributed greatly to deform and denaturalize its outward manifestations. It was not the fashion of his time for a scholar and a poet to express himself as other people would; for if he had done so, what advantage would he or the world have derived from his poetry or his scholarship? Accordingly, however intense a feeling might be, or however noble a thought, it was to be heightened and illustrated, in the expression of it, by clustering about it a host of images and associations (congruous or not, as it might happen), which memory or imagination, assisted by the most quick-eyed wit, or the most subtle ingenuity, could in any way contrive to link to it: thus pressing the original thought or

sentiment to death, and hiding even the form of it, beneath a profusion of superfluous dress. This was the crying fault of all the minor poets of the Elizabethan age; and of Donne more than of any other: though *his* thoughts and feelings would, generally speaking, bear this treatment better than those of any of his rivals in the same class. These persons never acted avowedly, (though they sometimes did unconsciously) on the principle that an idea or a sentiment may be poetical *per se*; for they had no notion whatever of the fact. They considered that *man* was the creator of poetry, not Nature; and that any thing might be made poetical, by connecting it, in a certain manner, with something else. A thought or a feeling was, to them, not a thing *to express*, but a theme to write *variations* upon—a nucleus, about which other thoughts and feelings were to be made to crystallize. A star was not bright to *their* eyes till it had been set in a constellation; a rose was not sweet till it had been gathered into a bouquet, and its hue and odour contrasted and blended with a thousand others. In fact, they had little simplicity of feeling, and still less of taste. They did not know the real and intrinsic value of any object, whether moral or physical; but only in what manner it might be connected with any other object, in so as to be made subservient to their particular views at the moment. They saw at once how far it was available *to them*, but nothing whatever of the impression it was calculated to make for itself.

We are speaking, now, of a particular class or school of poets of that day; for they differed as much from all others, and were as much allied by a general resemblance of style among themselves, as the Della Cruscan school in our own day. Indeed, in some particulars, there is no slight resemblance between the two styles; inasmuch, as both are purely artificial, and are dependent for their effect on a particular *manner* of treating their subject: at least, their intended effect is dependent on this—for the school to which Donne belongs often delights us in the highest degree, not in consequence of this manner, but in spite of it. There is also this other grand difference in favour of the latter,—that, whereas the Della Cruscans tried to make things poetical by means of *words* alone, *they* did it by means of thoughts and images;—the one considered poetry to consist in a certain mode of expression; the other, in a certain mode of seeing, thinking, and feeling. This is nearly all the difference between them; but this is a vast difference indeed: for the one supposes the necessity of, and in fact uses, a vast fund of thoughts and images; while the other can execute all its purposes nearly as well without any of these. In short, the one kind of writing requires very considerable talent to produce it, and its results are very often highly poetical; whereas the other requires no talent at all, and can in no case produce poetry, but very frequently covers and conceals it where it is.

But it is not at present our intention to go into a general discussion of that particular school of poetry to which Donne belongs; but merely to bring to light some of the exquisite beauties which have hitherto lain concealed from the present age, among the learned as well as unlearned lumber which he has so unaccountably mixed up with them. We say unaccountably—for it is impossible to give a reasonable account of any poetical theory, the perpetual results of which are the most pure and perfect beauties of every kind—of thought, of sentiment, of imagery, of expression, and of versification—lying in immediate contact with the basest deformities, equally of every kind; each given forth alternately in almost equal proportions, and in the most unconscious manner on the part of the writer as to either being entitled to the preference; and indeed without one's being able to discover that he saw any difference between them, even in kind.

Before doing this, however, it may be well to let the reader know what was thought of Donne in his own day, lest he should suppose that we are introducing him to a person little known at that time, or lightly valued.

If a prophet has little honour in his own time and country, the same can seldom be said of a poet; though *he*, too, is in some sort a prophet. The day in which Donne lived was the most poetical the world ever knew, and yet there can be little doubt, from the evidence of the fugitive literature of the time, that Donne was, upon the whole, more highly esteemed than any other of his contemporaries. We do not, however, mean to attribute all his fame to his published poetry. He was undoubtedly a very extraordinary person in many other respects. He possessed vast knowledge and erudition, and was highly distinguished for the eloquence of his public preaching. But the greater part of the admiration bestowed on him, was avowedly directed to the poetical writings. . . .

It is remarkable that the writer, of whom this could be said by persons of repute, (whether truly or not is no matter) in an age which produced Shakspeare and the elder dramatists—besides Spenser, Syndey, Herbert, Raleigh, and a host of minor names—should so long have remained unknown in an after age, one of the distinguishing boasts of which is, that it has revived a knowledge of, and a love for its great predecessor, at the same time that it has almost rivalled it.

In pieces that can be read with unmingled pleasure, and admired as perfect wholes, the poetry of Donne is almost entirely deficient. This may serve, in some degree, to account for the total neglect which has so long attended him. Almost every beauty we meet with, goes hand in hand with some striking deformity, of one kind or another; and the effect of this is, at first, so completely *irritating* to the imagination, as well as to the taste, that, after we have experienced it a few times, we hastily determine to be without the one, rather than purchase it at the price of the other. But the reader who is disposed, by these remarks, and the extracts that will accompany them, to a perusal of the whole of this poet's works, may be assured that this unpleasant effect will very soon wear off, and he will soon find great amusement and great exercise for his *thinking* faculties, (if nothing else) even in the objectionable parts of Donne; for he is always, when indulging in his very worst vein, filled to overflowing with thoughts, and materials for engendering thought.

The following short pieces are beautiful exceptions to the remark made just above, as to the mixed character of this poet's writings. The first is a farewell from a lover to his mistress, on leaving her for a time. For clearness and smoothness of construction, and a passionate sweetness and softness in the music of the versification, it might have been written in the present day, and may satisfy the ear of the most fastidious of modern readers; and for thought, sentiment, and imagery, it might *not* have been written in the present day;—for, much as we hold in honour our living poets, we doubt if any one among them is capable of it. In fact, it is one of those pieces which immediately strike us as being purely and exclusively attributable to the writer of them—which satisfy us, that, *but for him*, we never could have become possessed of them—which bear a mark that we cannot very well expound, even to ourselves, but which we know no one could have placed on them but him; and this, by-the-bye, is one of the most unequivocal criterions of a true poet. Perhaps the piece itself will explain better what we mean, than any thing we could say of it.

As virtuous men pass mildly away

The simile of the compasses, notwithstanding its quaintness, is more perfect in its kind, and more beautiful, than any thing we are acquainted with. Perhaps the above is the only poem we could extract, that is not disfigured by *any* of the characteristic faults of Donne. Several of them have, however, very few. The following is one of these. It has an air of serious gaiety about it, as if it had been composed in the very bosom of bliss. The versification too, is perfect. It is called, "The Good-Morrow."

I wonder by my troth, what thou and I
Did till we lov'd

The following, though not entirely without the faults of his style, is exceedingly graceful and elegant:

The Dream
Dear love, for nothing less than thee

What follows is extremely solemn and fine, and scarcely at all disfigured by the author's characteristic faults:

The Apparition
When by thy scorn, O murderess, I am dead

The next specimens that we shall give of this singular writer will be taken from among those of his poems which unite, in a nearly equal proportion, his characteristic faults and beauties; and which may be considered as scarcely less worthy of attention than the foregoing, partly on account of that very union of opposite qualities, but chiefly on account of their remarkable fullness of thought and imagery; in which, indeed, his very worst pieces abound to overflowing.

Notwithstanding the extravagance, as well as the ingenuity, which characterize the two following pieces, there is an air of sincerity about them, which renders their general effect impressive, and even solemn; to say nothing of their individual beauties, both of thought and expression.

The Anniversary
All kings, and all their favourites
Love's Growth
I scarce believe my love to be so pure

The reader will not fail to observe the occasional obscurities which arise out of the extreme condensation of expression in the foregoing pieces, and in most of those which follow. These passages may always be unravelled by a little attention, and they seldom fail to repay the trouble bestowed upon them. But they must be regarded as unequivocal faults nevertheless.

The following is, doubtless, "high-fantastical," in the last degree; but it is fine notwithstanding, and an evidence of something more than mere ingenuity.

Let me pour forth

The feelings which dictated such poetry as this, (for it is poetry, and nothing but real feelings *could* dictate it,) must have pierced deeper than the surface of both the heart and the imagination. In fact, they wanted nothing but to have been excited under more favourable circumstances, to have made them well-springs of the richest poetry uttering itself in the rarest words.

For clearness of expression, melody of versification, and a certain wayward simplicity of thought peculiarly appropriate to such compositions as these, the most successful of our modern lyrists might envy the following trifle:

The Message
Send home my long stray'd eyes to me

Perhaps the two short pieces which follow, include all the characteristics of Donne's style—beauties as well as faults.

A Lecture [upon the Shadow]
Stand still, and I will read to thee
The Expiration
So, so,—break off this last lamenting kiss

The following piece, entitled "The Funeral," is fantastical and far-fetched to be sure; but it is very fine nevertheless. The comparison of the nerves and the braid of hair, and anticipating similar effects from each, could never have entered the thoughts of any one but Donne; still less could any one have made it *tell* as he has done. The piece is altogether an admirable and most interesting example of his style.

Whoever comes to shroud me, do not harm

As a specimen of Donne's infinite fullness of meaning, take a little poem, called "The Will"; almost every line of which would furnish matter for a whole treatise in modern times.

Before I sigh my last gasp, let me breathe

The following (particularly the first stanza) seems to us to express even more than it is intended to express; which is very rarely the case with the productions of this writer. The love expressed by it is a love for the passion excited, rather than for the object exciting it; it is a love that lives by *"chewing the cud of sweet and bitter fancy,"* rather than by hungering after fresh food—that broods, like the stock dove, over its own voice, and listens for no other—that is all sufficient to itself, and (like virtue) its own reward.

I never stooped as low as they

What follows is in a different style, and it offers a singular specimen of the perverse ingenuity with which Donne sometimes bandies a thought about (like a shuttle-cock) from one hand to the other, only to let it fall to the ground at last.

THE PROHIBITION
Take heed of loving me

The following, in common with many other whole pieces and detached thoughts of this writer, has been imitated by other love-poets in proportion as it has not been read.

SONG
Go and catch a falling star

The following is to the same purpose, but more imbued with the writer's subtlety of thought and far-fetched ingenuity of illustration.

WOMAN'S CONSTANCY
Now thou hast loved me one whole day

The whole of the foregoing extracts are taken from the first department of Donne's poetry—the Love-verses. The only others that we shall choose from these, will be a few specimens of the truth and beauty that are frequently to be met with in Donne, in the shape of detached thoughts, images, &c. Nothing was every more exquisitely felt or expressed, than this opening stanza of a little poem, entitled "The Blossom."

Little thinkest thou, poor flower

The admirer of Wordsworth's style of language and versification will see, at once, that it is, at its best, nothing more than a *return* to this.

How beautiful is the following bit of description!

When I behold a stream, which from the spring
Doth with doubtful melodious murmuring,
Or in a speechless slumber calmly ride
Her wedded channel's bosom, and there chide,
And bend her brows, and swell, if any bough
Do but stoop down to kiss her utmost brow, &c.

The following is exquisite in its way. It is part of an epithalamion.

—and night is come; and yet we see
Formalities retarding thee.
What mean these ladies, which (as though
They were to take a clock to pieces) go

So nicely about the bride?
A bride, before a good-night could be said,
Should vanish from her cloathes into her bed,
As souls from bodies steal, and are not spy'd.

The simile of the clock is an example (not an offensive one) of Donne's peculiar mode of illustration. He scarcely writes a stanza without some ingenious simile of this kind.

The two first lines of the following are very solemn and far-thoughted. There is nothing of the kind in poetry superior to them. I add the lines which succeed them, merely to shew the manner in which the thought is applied.

I long to talk with some old lover's ghost
Who died before the God of Love was born

Of Donne's other poems, the Funeral Elegies, Epistles, Satires, and what he calls his "Divine Poems," particularly the last named, we have little to say in the way of general praise, and but few extracts to offer. We shall, however, notice and illustrate each class briefly, in order that the reader may have a fair impression of the whole body of this writer's poetical works.

The Epistles of Donne we like less than any of his other poems, always excepting the religious ones. Not that they are without his usual proportion of subtle thinking, felicitous illustration, and skilful versification; but they are disfigured by more than his usual obscurity—by a harshness of style, that is to be found in few of his other poems, except the satires—by an extravagance of hyperbole in the way of compliment, that often amounts to the ridiculous—and by an evident want of sincerity, that is worse than all. To whomever they are addressed, all are couched in the same style of expression, and reach the same pitch of praise. Every one of his correspondents is, without exception, "wisest, virtuousest, discreetest, best." It is as if his letters had been composed at leisure, and kept ready *cut and dried* till wanted.

Though it will not exactly bear quotation, perhaps the most poetical, as well as the most characteristic of the Epistles is the imaginary one (the only one of that description) from Sappho to Philaenis.

The following is finely thought and happily expressed. It is part of an Epistle to Sir Henry Wotton.

Be then thine own home, and in thyself dwell;
Inn anywhere, continuance maketh hell.
And seeing the snail, which everywhere doth roam,
Carrying his own house still, still is at home,
Follow (for he is easy paced) this snail,
Be thine own palace, or the world's thy goal.
And in the world's sea, do not like cork sleep
Upon the water's face; nor in the deep
Sink like a lead without a line: but as
Fishes glide, leaving no print where they pass,
Nor making sound, so closely thy course go,
Let men dispute, whether thou breathe, or no.

We can afford no other extract from the Epistles, although many most curious ones might be found; but pass on to the Funeral Elegies. All Donne's poems, even his best, with one or two exceptions, are laboured in the highest degree; and the Funeral Elegies are still more so than any of the others. They have all the faults of his style, and this one above all. Still they abound in passages of great force, depth, and beauty; but none of them will bear extracting entire—at least, none which are properly included in this class. But there is one poem printed among these, which we shall extract the greater portion of, and which the reader will find to be written in a somewhat different style from that of almost all the others that we have quoted. There is a solemn and sincere earnestness about it, which will cause it to be read with great interest, even by those who may not be capable of appreciating, in detail, the rich and pompous flow of the verse, and the fine harmony of its music; the elegant simplicity of the language; and the extreme beauty of some of the thoughts and images.

The poem seems to have been addressed to his mistress, on the occasion of his taking leave of her, after her having offered to attend him on his journey in the disguise of a page. It is headed strangely enough. ·

ELEGY ON HIS MISTRESS
By our first strange and fatal interview

It only remains to speak of Donne's Satires; for his Divine Poems must be left to speak for themselves. General readers are probably acquainted with Donne chiefly as a writer of satires; and, in this character, they know him only through the medium of Pope; which is equivalent to knowing Homer only through the same medium. The brilliant and refined modern attempted to give his readers an idea of Donne, by changing his roughness into smoothness, and polishing down his force into point. In fact, he altered Donne into Pope—which was a mere impertinence. Each is admirable in his way—quite enough so to make it impossible to change either, with advantage, into a likeness of any other.

Donne's Satires are as rough and rugged as the unhewn stones that have just been blasted from their native quarry; and they must have come upon the readers at whom they were levelled, with the force and effect of the same stones flung from the hand of a giant. The following detached character is the only specimen we have left ourselves room to give of them. It strikes us as being nearly the perfection of this kind of writing.

Therefore I suffered this; towards me did run
A thing more strange than on Nile's slime the sun
E'er bred, or all which into Noah's Ark came:
A thing, which would have posed Adam to name:
Stranger than seven antiquaries' studies,
Than Afric's monsters, Guiana's rarities,
Stranger than strangers; one, who for a Dane,
In the Danes' Massacre had sure been slain,
If he had lived then; and without help dies,
When next the 'prentices 'gainst strangers rise.
One, whom the watch at noon lets scarce go by,
One, to whom, the examining Justice sure would
    cry,
'Sir, by your priesthood tell me what you are.'
His clothes were strange, though coarse; and black,
    though bare;
Sleeveless his jerkin was, and it had been
Velvet, but 'twas now (so much ground was seen)
Become tufftaffaty; and our children shall
See it plain rash awhile, then naught at all.
This thing hath travelled, and saith, speaks all
    tongues
And only knoweth what to all states belongs,
Made of th' accents, and best phrase of all these,
He speaks one language; if strange meats displease,
Art can deceive, or hunger force my taste,
But pedant's motley tongue, soldier's bombast,
Mountebank's drugtongue, nor the terms of law
Are strong enough perparatives, to draw
Me to bear this, yet I must be content
With his tongue: in his tongue, called compliment:
. . .
He names me, and comes to me; I whisper, 'God!
How have I sinned, that thy wrath's furious rod,
This fellow, chooseth me?' He sayeth, 'Sir,
I love your judgement; whom do you prefer,
For the best linguist?' And I sillily

Said, that I thought Calepine's Dictionary;
'Nay but of men, most sweet Sir'. Beza then,
Some Jesuits, and two reverend men
Of our two Academies, I named. There
He stopped me, and said; 'Nay, your Apostles were
Good pretty linguists, and so Panurge was;
Yet a poor gentleman, all these may pass
By travail.' Then, as if he would have sold
His tongue, he praised it, and such wonders told
That I was fain to say, 'If you had lived, Sir,
Time enough to have been interpreter
To Babel's bricklayers, sure the Tower had stood.'
He adds, 'If of Court life you knew the good,
You would leave loneness.' I said, 'Not alone
My loneness is; but Spartan's fashion,
To teach by painting drunkards, doth not last
Now; Aretine's pictures have made few chaste;
No more can princes' Courts, though there be few
Better pictures of vice, teach me virtue';
He, like to a high stretched lute string squeaked, 'O
    Sir,
'Tis sweet to talk of kings.' 'At Westminster,'
Said I, 'the man that keeps the Abbey tombs,
And for his price doth with whoever comes,
Of all our Harrys, and our Edwards talk,
From king to king and all their kin can walk:
Your ears shall hear naught, but kings; your eyes
    meet
Kings only; The way to it, is King Street.'
He smacked, and cried, 'He's base, mechanic,
    coarse,
So are all your Englishmen in their discourse.
Are not your Frenchmen neat?' 'Mine? as you see,
I have but one Frenchman, look, he follows me.'
'Certes they are neatly clothed. I of this mind am,
Your only wearing is your grogaram.'
'Not so Sir, I have more.' Under this pitch
He would not fly; I chaffed him; but as itch
Scratched into smart, and as blunt iron ground
Into an edge, hurts worse: so, I (fool) found,
Crossing hurt me; to fit my sullenness,
He to another key his style doth dress,
And asks, 'What news?' I tell him of new plays.
He takes my hand, and as a still, which stays
A semi-breve 'twixt each drop, he niggardly,
As loth to enrich me, so tells many a lie,
More than ten Holinsheds, or Halls, or Stows,
Of trivial household trash he knows; he knows
When the Queen frowned, or smiled, and he knows
    what
A subtle statesman may gather of that;
He knows who loves; whom; and who by poison
Hastes to an office's reversion;
He knows who hath sold his land, and now doth beg
A licence, old iron, boots, shoes, and egg-
Shells to transport; shortly boys shall not play
At span-counter, or blow-point, but they pay
Toll to some courtier; and wiser than all us,
He knows what lady is not painted; thus

We had intended to close this paper with a few examples of the most glaring faults of Donne's style; but the reader will probably think that we have made better use of our space. We have endeavoured to describe those faults, and the causes of them; and not a few of them—or of those parts which should perhaps be regarded as *characteristics*, rather than absolute faults—will be found among the extracts now given. Those who wish for more may find them in almost every page of the writer's works. They may find the most far-fetched and fantastical allusions and illustrations brought to bear upon the thought or feeling in question, sometimes by the most quick-eyed and subtle ingenuity, but oftener in a manner altogether forced and arbitrary; turns of thought that are utterly at variance with the sentiment and with each other; philosophical and scholastic differences and distinctions, that no sentiment could have suggested, and that nothing but *searching for* could have found; and, above all, paradoxical plays of words, antitheses of thought and expression, and purposed involutions of phrase, that nothing but the most painful attention can untwist. All this they may find, and more. But, in the midst of all, they not only may, but must find an unceasing activity and an overflowing fullness of mind, which seem never to fail or flag, and which would more than half redeem the worst faults (of mere style) that could be allied to them.

HENRY ALFORD
From "Life of Dr. Donne"
The Works of John Donne
1839, Vol. 1, pp. xvii–xxvi

As a preacher . . . he was most highly valued by his illustrious contemporaries. It was an age of flattery; but the encomiums which I have collected below[1] will bear with them the evidence of genuineness and real feeling. His royal master, no mean judge of ability, except in his own case, first foresaw his eminence in preaching, and ever afterwards valued himself on that discernment.

Donne is a rare instance of powers first tried, and then consecrated. Having studied, not by compulsion, but by choice, the whole body of divinity, and matured his judgment on controverted points, in the fulness of age and mental strength he commenced his clerical labours. Hence we never find in him poverty of thought, but are rather sensible (as generally in reading the most eminent of human writings, and always in the Scriptures) that the store has been but sparingly dealt out, and that much more remained, if he would have said it. Having shone as a wit in an age of wit, and an age when wit was not confined to ludicrous associations, but extended to a higher skill of point and antithesis, and cunning interweaving of choice words, he gained his hearers by flattering their discernment; and served up to the English Solomon and his court, dark sentences, which, in these days, when we have levelled our diction for convenience, and use language as a mere machine, require some thoughtful unravelling before their meaning is detected. That he should have gained among the moderns the reputation of obscurity is no wonder; for, on the one hand, the language of one age will always be strange to those who live in, and are entirely of, another of a totally different character; and again, this intricacy of words frequently accompanies subtle trains of thoughts and argument, which it requires some exertion to follow. But it must be remembered that obscurity is a subjective term, that is, having its place in the estimation of him who judges, and not necessarily in the language judged of; and is therefore never to be imputed to an author without personal examination of his writings. And I am satisfied that such an examination of the sermons of Donne would result in his being cleared from this charge. A man is obscure, either from his thoughts being confused and ill-arranged; or from his language being inadequate to express his meaning; or because he affects obscurity. Neither of these three was the fault of Donne. Precision and definiteness of thought, and studied arrangement of the steps of an argument, are to be found in all his sermons; and it is always more evident what he is proving, than whether his premises legitimately belong to that conclusion. "Whereunto all this tendeth" is a note which never need be placed in his margin, as far as the immediate subject is concerned. Again, his power over the English language, one rarely surpassed in its capabilities of ministering to thought, was only equalled by one or two of his great contemporaries. And the affectation of obscurity, (the resource of weakness and ignorance, and the greatest of crimes in a literary, much more in an ecclesiastical writer,) can hardly be laid to the charge of one so single-hearted in his zeal, and so far above such a meanness, both from his learning and genius. His faults in this matter are the faults of his time, somewhat increased by a mind naturally fond of subtilty and laborious thought. And even the real difficulties of his style will soon give way and become familiar to the reader, who is capable of discovering and appreciating the treasures which it contains.

But it is not in diction, or genius, or power of thought, that we must look for the crowning excellence of these Sermons. We find in them, what we feel to be wanting in most of the great preachers of that and the succeeding age, a distinct and clear exposition of the doctrines of redemption, as declared in the Scriptures, and believed by the Church in England. This too is set forth, without any dread of that poisonous maxim, "the further from Rome, the nearer the truth;" to the working of which we owe most of the dissent from, and the ignorance in, the present English church. That these remarks are not to be taken without exception; that Donne does fall, upon comparatively minor points, into very many puerilities and superstitions; that the implicit following of the Fathers is, in divinity, his besetting fault, and often interferes with his lucid declarations of the truth, no impartial reader of his sermons can deny.[2] Still when all these have been amply allowed for—all the obnoxious or trifling passages struck out—I think every reader will be equally convinced, that there is left unimpaired a genuine body of orthodox divinity (in the best sense of the words) not to be found, perhaps, in any other English theologian.

In his expositions of Scripture he follows chiefly the close and verbal method of the day: which though it frequently leads him to make too much of an indifferent word, never allows the passing over of an important one; and the want of which is, perhaps, more to be regretted in modern divinity, than its use despised in ancient. His arrangements are often artificial and fanciful; but always easily retained, and instructive to the Scripture student. It has been observed of him, that he has the faculty of making whatever he touches upon to appear important. It should, perhaps, rather have been said, that he resolves all minor matters into more important ones, and by constantly fixing the attention of his hearer on the great objects of Christian faith, and bringing every doctrine and opinion to bear upon them in greater or less degree, invests every subject with a dignity which does not belong to it, considered apart.

In illustration by simile or allusion, Donne shows the true marks of great genius. The reader of the following Sermons will find sentences and passages which he will be surprised he never before had read, and will think of ever after. In depth and grandeur these far surpass (in my judgment) the strings of beautiful expressions to be found in Jeremy Taylor; they are the recreations of a loftier mind; and while Taylor's similes are exquisite in their melody of sound, and happy in external description, Donne enters into the inner soul of art, and gives his reader more satisfactory and permanent delight.[3] Sir Thomas Browne is, perhaps, the writer whose style will be most forcibly recalled to the mind of the reader by many parts of these Sermons; but here again Donne has immeasurably the advantage. While the one is ever guessing at truth, the other is pouring it forth from the fulness of his heart. While the one in his personal confessions keeps aloof and pities mankind, the other is of them, and feels with them.

Donne's epistolary writings are models in their kind. Laboured compliments, and studied antitheses have seldom been so ably or pleasingly strung together; or playfulness and earnest, pathos and humour, more happily blended.

His poems were mostly written in his youth; his satires, according to one of the panegyrics on him, before he was twenty. It has been remarked, that the juvenile poems of truly great men are generally distinguished by laborious condensation of thought; and the remark is amply borne out in this instance. This labour of compression on his part has tended to make his lines harsh and unpleasing; and the corresponding effort required on the reader's part to follow him, renders most persons insensible to his real merits. That he had and could turn to account a fine musical ear, is amply proved by some of his remaining pieces.[4] Why Dr. Johnson should have called him a metaphysical poet, is difficult to conceive. What "wittily associating the most discordant images" has to do with metaphysics is not very clear; and Johnson, perhaps, little thought that the title which he was giving to one of the most apparently laboured of poets, belonged of all others to his immortal contemporary, who is recorded "never to have blotted a line". A greater man that Dr. Johnson, even Dryden, has said in his dedication of Juvenal to the Earl of Dorset, that Donne "affects the metaphysics;" probably meaning no more than that scholastic learning and divinity are constantly to be found showing themselves in his poems.

The personal character of Donne is generally represented to us to have undergone a great change, between his youth and the time when he entered holy orders. This representation is countenanced by the uniform tenor of deep penitence with which he speaks in his Sermons of his former life; and by the licentiousness of some of his poetical pieces. It would be wrong, however, to infer moral depravity solely from the latter circumstance, as this strain was in keeping with the prevalent taste of the times; and the object addressed in the Love-poems of the day, and the circumstances introduced, were often both equally imaginary. That his manners were the manners of the court and the society in which he lived, is the most reasonable and the most charitable sentence; and the reader who values what is truly valuable, will rather consider the holiness and purity of his more mature years, than any reproach which report or his writings may have fixed on his youth; and with the charity which "rejoiceth not in iniquity, but rejoiceth in the truth," will look rather on these Sermons and Devotions, in which he has built himself and the church a lasting memorial, than on the few scattered leaves, which betray after all, perhaps, no more than simplicity and fearlessness of natural disposition; and that he showed what others have concealed. Mankind are always more apt to judge mildly of one whose heart is open; and to sympathise where confidence is given. And we find, I think, that those writers with whose lives, and trials, and changes of opinion we are acquainted, and who speak to us not from the forbidding height of apathy, but as men giving and requiring sympathy, have always stood, other things being equal, highest in the public esteem. With no writer is this more the case than with Donne. Every Sermon is the voice of the same man; in every solemn appeal, every serious direction for self-searching and reflection, we see the footsteps of the same Providence, whose ways having been manifested to the preacher in his own experience, are by him

imparted to the hearer. Egotism is a word which has obtained a bad name; but it must not be forgotten that it has a good sense; and that in this sense every truly great man is an egotist. For it is by intimate moral and critical acquaintance with himself that he becomes powerful over the thoughts and feelings of our kind in general; and, as the greatest of public speakers says in his Funeral Oration, That the praises of others are only tolerable up to a point of excellence, which the hearer thinks he could have equalled[5], so it may be generally said of the productions of the greatest minds, that they are most valued, and take most hold of the universal heart of mankind, when the man uttering them is shown to have been what all might have been, and to have felt what all have felt.[6]

I own I have indulged a hope, that these Sermons will become standard volumes in the English Divinity Library. For myself, what I have acquired from them has been invaluable; and I can only wish that they may give as much instruction and delight to the reader, as I have received in editing them.

Notes

1. Walton, a frequent hearer of Donne, thus characterises his preaching:—"A preacher in earnest, weeping sometimes for his auditory, sometimes with them; always preaching to himself like an angel from a cloud, but in none; carrying some, as St. Paul was, to heaven in holy raptures, and enticing others by a sacred art and courtship to amend their lives; here picturing a vice so as to make it ugly to those that practised it; and a virtue, so as to make it beloved even by those that loved it not; and all this with a most particular grace and an inexpressible addition of comeliness."—*Life of Donne.* Ed. Zouch.

   Mr. Chudleigh, one of the contributors of Elegies on Donne's death, has the following lines:—

   > He kept his love, but not his object. Wit
   > He did not banish, but transplanted it;
   > Taught it both time and place, and brought it home
   > To piety, which it doth best become.
   > For say, had ever pleasure such a dress?
   > Have you seen crimes so shaped, or loveliness
   > Such as his lips did clothe religion in?
   > Had not reproof a beauty passing sin?
   > —Id. ibid.

   In a Latin Poem, by Darnelly, the following description of his eloquence occurs:—

   >   vidi
   > Audivi, et stupui, quoties orator in æde
   > Paulinâ stetit, et nurâ gravitate levantes
   > Corda oculosque viros tenuit: dum Nestoris ille
   > Fudit verba; omni quanto mage dulcia melle!
   > Nunc habet attonitos, pandit mysteria plebi
   > Non concessa prius, nondum intellecta; revolvunt
   > Mirantes, tacitique arrectis auribus astant.
   >   Mutatis mox ille modo formaque loquendi
   > Tristia pertractat; fatumque, et flebile mortis
   > Tempus, et in cineres redeunt quod corpora primos.
   > Tum gemitum cunctos dare, tunc lugere videres,
   > Forsitan a lacrimis aliquis non temperat, atque
   > Ex oculis largum stillat rorem.

   In an Elegy by Mr. R. B.—

   > Methinks I see him in the pulpit standing,
   > Not ears, nor eyes, but all men's hearts commanding,
   > When we that heard him, to ourselves did feign
   > Golden Chrysostom was alive again;
   > And never were we wearied, till we saw
   > His hour (and but an hour) to end did draw.

   In another by Mr. Mayne of Christ Church:—

   > Thou with thy words could'st charm thine audience,
   > That at thy sermons, ear was all our sense;
   > Yet have I seen thee in the pulpit stand,
   > Where we might take notes, from thy look, and hand;
   > And from thy speaking action bear away

More sermon, than some teachers use to say.
Such was thy carriage, and thy gesture such,
As could divide the heart, and conscience touch.
Thy motion did confute, and we might see
An error vanquished by delivery.
Not like our sons of zeal, who to reform
Their hearers, fiercely at the pulpit storm,
And beat the cushion into worse estate
Than if they did conclude it reprobate,
Who can out-pray the glass, then lay about
Till all predestination be run out;
And from the point such tedious uses draw,
Their repetitions would make Gospel, law.
No, in such temper would thy sermons flow,
So well did doctrine, and thy language show,
And had that holy fear, as, hearing thee,
The court would mend, and a good Christian be.

2. I have selected a few passages which may enable the reader shortly to exemplify the above remarks:—

For an exposition of the doctrine of redemption free and universal, by the assumption of the human nature by Christ, see vol. I., p. 566, line 36.

On the Church, and the Scripture, see vol. I., p. 418, l. 33; vol. IV., p. 176, l. 20.

On the Sacraments—Baptism, see vol. I., p. 583, l. 12. Baptism and the Lord's Supper, see the whole of Ser. 78, vol. III., p. 414. The sacrificial nature of the Lord's Supper, vol. VI., p. 39, l. 21, seq. The real presence, in ditto, vol. III., p. 327, l. 13–22; vol. I., p. 479, l. 5–10.

Prayer for the dead entered into, Ser. 77, vol. III.

His judgment of the Roman Church, Ser. 99, vol. IV., p. 295, l. 4.

Confession to the priest, Ser. 66, vol. III., p. 563, l. 22, seq.

Estimation of the fathers by the Roman Church, vol. III., p. 309, l. 18, seq.

Prayer to saints; vol. III., p. 320, l. 7.

For an instance of puerility and superstition, see vol. I., p. 456, l. 12.

3. I have subjoined one or two specimens as a foretaste to the reader. Speaking of eternity, he says:—"A day that hath no *pridie*, nor *postridie*; yesterday doth not usher it in, nor to-morrow shall not drive it out. Methusalem, with all his hundreds of years, was but a mushroom of a night's growth, to this day; all the four monarchies, with all their thousands of years, and all the powerful kings, and all the beautiful queens of this world, were but as a bed of flowers, some gathered at six, some at seven, some at eight, all in one morning, in respect of this day." Vol. III., p. 326.

"Our flesh, though glorified, cannot make us see God better, nor clearer, than the soul above hath done, all the time, from our death to our resurrection. But as an indulgent father, or a tender mother, when they go to see the king in any solemnity, or any other thing of observation and curiosity, delights to carry their child, which is flesh of their flesh, and bone of their bone, with them, and though the child cannot comprehend it as well as they, they are as glad that the child sees it, as that they see it themselves;—such a gladness shall my soul have, that this flesh (which she will no longer call her prison, nor her tempter, but her friend, her companion, her wife), that this flesh, that is, I, in the re-union and redintegration of both parts, shall see God: for then one principal clause in her rejoicing, and acclamation, shall be, that this flesh is her flesh; *in my flesh shall I see God.*" Vol. IV., p. 239.

"O what a Leviathan is sin, how vast, how immense a body! and then what a spawner, how numerous! Between these two, the denying of sins which we have done, and the bragging of sins which we have not done, what a space, what a compass is there, for millions of millions of sins!" Vol. IV., p. 370.

4. See especially the piece, "Come live with me and be my love;" that written to his wife on parting from her to go into France, (vol. VI., p. 554,) and the opening of his Epithalamion on the marriage of the Princess Elizabeth.

5. Thucydides, book II., chap. 35.

6. It may be interesting to the reader to know that the marble figure of Donne in his shroud, which formed part of his monument in old St. Paul's, is the only relic which has been preserved whole from the ravages of the fire, and is now to be seen in the crypt.

UNSIGNED
Lowe's Edinburgh Magazine, 1846, pp. 228–236

For every individual reader of the poems of John Donne, there have probably been a hundred readers of the exquisite "Life" of him, by Izaak Walton. Unprefaced by this "Life," no edition of Donne's poems ought ever to have appeared. Not only is the memoir itself in every respect worthy of its subject—executed *con amore*—coming, paragraph after paragraph, like a succession of "meadow-gales in spring," over the heart of the habitual wanderer in the arid wastes of modern biographical literature; touching the souls of men with a tender sorrow for the noble days gone by—a sorrow which hardly subsides at thought of the nobler, but far different days to come; not only has it all these and many similar merits, but it moreover supplies a commentary upon the writings of our poet which could ill have been dispensed with. To the fact that "his father was masculinely and lineally descended from a very ancient family in Wales," and that "by his mother he was descended of the family of the famous and learned Sir Thomas More, some time Lord Chancellor of England," we may trace the lofty self-possession which breathes through all his writings, and which, in literature as in manners, is almost invariably the result of lofty extraction. In the circumstances, that although "his friends were of the Romish persuasion," young Donne would not receive their, or any creed implicitly; but "about the nineteenth year of his age, he being then unresolved what religion to adhere to, and considering how much it concerned his soul to choose the most orthodox, did therefore (though his youth and health promised him a long life), to rectify all scruples that might concern that, presently lay aside all study of the law, and of all other sciences that might give him a denomination, and began seriously to survey and consider the body of divinity, as it was controverted betwixt the Reformed and the Roman Church," we find an explanation of the peculiar vent of thought and imagination which characterizes all his writings, but particularly the first, namely the "Satires," and "Funeral Elegies." In his deep and various acquaintance with the physical, mathematical, and metaphysical sciences, as they then existed, we discover the origin of many of his far-fetched, and often painfully-ingenious illustrations. In his travels and his troubles, we find him undergoing the true poet-education, an experimental knowledge of men and sorrows. Finally, in his latterly blameless and holy life, we behold his defence against those who might otherwise have been inclined to infer, from the wonderful subtlety of his religion, an absence of a great sincerity in its pursuit.

Though too often neglected, it is one of the first duties of the critic, in his estimation of the merits and demerits of a literary production, to point out, as far as may be in his power, what of those merits and demerits belong to the author, and what to the time he wrote in. An endeavour to do this in a general manner shall be our first step in criticizing the poems of Donne.

His death occurred in 1631, when he was 58 years old. Shakespeare died in 1616. Therefore English intellect was at its height in the age Donne wrote. Mental philosophy was profounder and purer than it had ever been before; but it was occasionally wronged by an attempt to wed it with physical science: a marriage of which the times forbade the bans, because the latter was as yet unripe. Philosophy being profound and pure, so was religion; and in the midst of a vigorous and flourishing philosophy, and of a true religion, what could poetry be but vigorous, flourishing, and true?

Religion, also, in various ways, enhanced the poetic liberty of the time: especially it extinguished that false shame which Romanism had attached to the contemplation of the sexual relations. The purity of these relations had been for long ages lied away by the enforcement, *as a permanent doctrine,* of what St. Paul had advised merely as *"good for the present distress,"* (I Cor. vii. 26) caused by the persecutions in his day. But the Reformation had arisen, and commanded, that what God had declared to be clean, no man should call common. The command had been received with an obedience which had not, in Donne's time, been deadened or destroyed by the poisonous taint of Romanism, which yet lurked in the doctrine, and afterwards developed itself in the life-blood of the new era. The consequence was, that the sphere of nature was yet widened to the rejoicing poet, who now revered true chastity all the more that he was no longer obliged to bow down to the really unchaste mockeries of her "unblemished form," which had been set up for his worship by the harlot, Rome.

Again, a true philosophy gave birth to powers of the subtlest perception; which it did by inducing a faith in those powers. A good, perhaps the best, test of the subtlety of a poet's perception, is his appreciation of the female character; which, presenting, as it does, an endless series of contradictions to the understanding, thus declares itself to be the subject of a wholly different tribunal. Poets, whose powers of perception have fallen short of the highest, have made endless unavailing attempts to *solve* the character of woman. The subtle singers of Donne's time knew that they might as well endeavour to solve an irrational equation, or to express, in terminated decimals, a "surd quantity." But they knew that a comprehension of her character was no indispensable qualification for depicting it; and accordingly, and *therefore,* they have depicted it, as no poets had ever done before, or have done since.

In Donne's day, the faith in instinctive immediate perception was not a thing merely to talk about and admire, or to act upon within due and decent limitation, as it is with our living poets; it was a thing to possess and act upon unconsciously, and without limits imposed by the logical faculty, or by the hyperbole-hating decencies of flat conventionality. Our modern carpet-poets tread their way upon hyperbole as nicely as they would do over ice of an uncertain strength, dreading every moment to be drowned by ridicule, or sucked into some bottomless abyss, by an "Edinburgh" or "Quarterly" "Attack." Not so in Shakespeare's time:—

> Tempests themselves, high seas, and howling winds,
> The gutter'd rocks, and congregated sands,—
> Traitors ensteep'd to clog the guiltless keel,
> As having sense of beauty, did omit
> Their mortal natures, letting go safely by
> The divine Desdemona.

So much then, for the qualities of the period; qualities which Donne, as a poet, must necessarily participate in, and represent. We now proceed to name and illustrate some of his peculiarities. To begin with censure, and to prepare our readers for the quotations we shall make, let us state our conviction, that Donne's ordinary *versification* is about the very ruggedest that ever has been written. We shall not extract any particular lines to prove this assertion, since we shall make few quotations which will *not* prove it. This defect will always prevent Donne from becoming popular: fit and few will be his audience as long as poetry is read.

Another quality, equally against his popularity, is his profundity of thought, and the constant attention which is therefore required in order to understand him. Though his poems may be read once through, as a kind of disagreeable duty, by the professed student of English literature, they will be pored over, again and again, as true poetry should be, only by the most faithful and disciplined lovers of the muse. With these latter, however, Donne will always be a peculiar favourite. By them his poems will be valued as lumps of precious golden ore, touched, here and there, with specks of richest gold, and almost everywhere productive of the shining treasure, when submitted to the operation of affectionate reflection. By such readers even his worst versification will be pardoned, since no sacrifice of meaning is ever made to it,—it thus becoming so much more palatable to the truly cultivated taste than the expensive melody of some modern versifiers.

Donne's Poems seem to divide themselves naturally into three classes:—I. His early "Songs and Sonnets" and "Elegies," chiefly love-poems, and his "Epithalamions." II. His "Satires," "Letters," and "Funeral Elegies." III. His "Divine Poems." We will notice the contents of each class in its order.

The love-poems seem rather to be inspired by a *love of love,* than by any very powerful passion for the object of whom they chiefly discourse. Most lovers love their object because they confound her with their ideal of excellence. Donne seems ever aware that his is the mere suggestion of that ideal which he truly loves. His love is a lofty and passionate, but voluntary, contemplation, deriving its nourishment mainly from the intellect, and not a fiery atmosphere, in which he lives and moves always, and whether he will or no.

On the whole, this class of his poems is greatly inferior to the second order. It is much more deformed by the intrusion of "conceits" and its general lack of spontaneous feeling is compensated by no general profundity of thought. Here and there, however, we find gems of admirable and various lustre, though no one, of any magnitude, without defect. We give the following noble poem entire. It is, perhaps, the most perfect thing of its length in Donne's whole volume. Its versification is generally good, and, sometimes, exquisite.

> As virtuous men pass mildly away,
>   And whisper to their souls, to go,
> Whilst some of their sad friends do say,
>   The breath goes now, and some say, no:
>
> So let us melt, and make no noise,
>   No tear-floods, nor sigh-tempests move,
> 'Twere profanation of our joys
>   To tell the laity our love.
>
> Moving of th'earth brings harms and fears,
>   Men reckon what it did and meant,
> But trepidation of the spheres,
>   Though greater far, is innocent.
>
> Dull sublunary lovers' love
>   (Whose soul is sense) cannot admit
> Absence, because it doth remove
>   Those things which elemented it.
>
> But we by a love, so much refined,
>   That our selves know not what it is,
> Inter-assured of the mind,
>   Care less, eyes, lips, and hands to miss.
>
> Our two souls therefore, which are one,
>   Though I must go, endure not yet
> A breach, but an expansion,
>   Like gold to aery thinness beat.
>
> If they be two, they are two so
>   As stiff twin compasses are two,
> Thy soul the fixed foot, makes no show
>   To move, but doth, if th'other do.
>
> And though it in the centre sit,
>   Yet when the other far doth roam,

> It leans, and hearkens after it,
> And grows erect, as that comes home.
> Such wilt thou be to me, who must
> Like th' other foot, obliquely run;
> Thy firmness makes my circle just,
> And makes me end, where I begun.

Old Izaak Walton mentions this poem in his "Life,"—"a copy of verses given by Mr. Donne to his wife at the time he then parted from her (to spend some months in France). And I beg leave to tell, that I have heard some critics, learned both in languages and poetry, say, that none of the Greek or Latin poets did ever equal them."

The above is the only entire poem, and indeed the only considerable passage of continuous beauty in the love-poems. There are indeed little exquisite touches without number, starting up here and there, like violets in the rough, and, as yet, leafless woods. Of these we will give only as many as we think may be sufficient to sharpen the appetite of the lover of poetry, and send him to their source for more. . . .

Unfortunately, (or shall we say, fortunately?) the best thing in a true poet is that which it is impossible to convey any fit notion of, by a few and limited extracts. "Every great poet has, in a measure, to create the taste by which he is to be enjoyed." ⟨Wordsworth⟩ The divine *aura* that breathes about his works, is not to be found by the chance reader in any particular passage or poem. This only reveals itself to the loving student of the Muses, and departs from him who departs from them, or endeavours to a-muse himself by carelessly attending to their songs. The longest and most famous of these "Epithalamions," has scarcely a quotable passage. Its whole merit lies in this inexplicable, incommunicable *aura*.

The "Elegies," which we have classed with the early poems, and "Epithalamions," form rather, indeed, a link between these and the second class. We give the following passage, which seems to illustrate our assertion, combining, as it does, the fantastic beauty of the former, the maturer thought of the latter, and the faults of both.

Donne's "Satires,"—to speak of which we now come—are, to our mind, the best in the English language. A satirist should never get into a passion with that which he is satirizing, and call names, as Dryden and Pope do; it is totally inconsistent with the dignity of the judicial position he assumes. To be sure, a lofty indignation may sometimes be allowed, but only on great occasions, and not against such petty-larceny practices and people as are, for the most part, the objects of satire. This was fully felt by the gentlemanly Donne, who, in his satires, resorts more often to the simple and the crushing strength of truth, than to the "cat-o'-nine-tails" of invective. We quote largely from Satire III.; it is upon the adoption of a religion—a subject which, as we have seen, had engaged our author's deepest thoughts.

Throughout all our former quotations, there was a tolerable smoothness of versification: sometimes there was the sweetest music; but they were, in this, exceptions to the rule. The above passage is a good specimen of the average flow (!) of Donne's verses. But who, that, loving best of course the marriage of sound and meaning, would not yet prefer climbing, with Donne, these crags, where all the air is fresh and wholesome, to gliding with Thomas Moore, over flats, from beneath the rank verdure of which arises malaria and invisible disease?

Pope took it upon himself to "improve" some of Donne's satires; and he did it, but in much the same style as the sailor who, having obtained a curiosity in the form of the weapon of a sword-fish, "improved" it by scraping off, and rubbing down, all the protuberances by which it was distinguishable from any

other bone. Fortunately, however, in most editions of Pope's writings, the original crudities are printed side by side with the polished improvement upon them; as sometimes we see, uphung in triumph at the doors of writing-masters, pairs of documents to some such effect as this:—I. "This is my handwriting before taking lessons of Mr. Pope. Signed. John Donne." II. "This is my handwriting after taking lessons of Mr. Pope. Signed. John Donne." Let us, however, give specimens of those so-different handwritings. The theme is the appearance of a reduced courtier.

I. This is Donne, before being improved by Pope:—

> T'wards me did run
> A thing more strange than on Nile's slime the sun
> E'er bred, or all which into Noah's ark came;
> A thing which would have posed Adam to name:
> Stranger than seven antiquaries' studies,
> Than Afric monsters, Guiana's rarities,
> Stranger than strangers: one who for a Dane
> In the Dane's massacre had sure been slain,
> If he had lived then; and without help dies,
> When next the 'prentices 'gainst strangers rise;
> One, whom the watch at noon scarce lets go by—
> One, to whom th' examining justice sure would cry,
> "Sir, by your priesthood, tell me what you are!"

II. This is Donne, after being improved by Pope:—

> Behold! there came
> A thing which Adam had been posed to name;
> Noah had refused it lodging in his ark,
> Where all the race of reptiles might embark:
> A verier monster than on Afric's shore
> The sun e'er got, or slimy Nilus bore;
> Or Sloan or Woodward's wondrous shelves
> contain,—
> Nay, all that lying travellers can feign.
> The watch would scarcely let him pass at noon,
> At night would swear him dropp'd out of the moon;
> One whom the mob, when next we find or make
> A popish plot, shall for a Jesuit take;
> And the wise justice, starting from his chair,
> Cry, "By your priesthood, tell me what you are!"

Oh, wonderful Mr. Pope! powerful to knock off such excrescences as,

> Stranger than seven antiquaries' studies.

and, "Stranger than strangers"; powerful to introduce such improvements as,

> Nay, all that lying travellers can feign!

We had marked many more passages for quotation from the "Satires," but we must, for want of space, hurry on, skipping the "Letters," which are crowded with gems of purest ray serene, and give a sweet word or two from the "Funeral Elegies," which contain more wisdom and poetry in the same space, than almost anything out of Shakespeare. We will take only one of the Elegies and string some of its gems together without remark,—

> Her pure and eloquent soul
> Spoke in her cheeks, and so distinctly wrought,
> That one might almost say, her body thought.
> They who did labour Babel's tower to erect,
> Might have consider'd that, for that effect,
> All His whole solid earth would not allow
> Nor furnish forth materials enow;
> And that his centre, to raise such a place,
> Was far too little to have been the base;
> No more affords this world foundation
> To erect true joy.

> In all she did
> Some figure of the golden times was hid.
> She is in Heaven; whither who doth not strive
> The more because she's there, he doth not know
> That accidental joys in Heaven do grow.

(Speaking of closing the eyes of the dead)

> O, they confess much in the world amiss,
> Who dare not trust a dead man's eyes with that,
> Which they from God and angels cover not.

The "Divine Poems" are, for the most part, very poor, compared to these "Elegies"; but here, as everywhere, splendid thoughts and splendid words abound. One instance or two is all we can give. Here is a description of Leviathan in the style of Milton, who made him "swim the ocean stream."

> At every stroke his brazen fins do take,
> More circles in the broken sea they make
> Than cannons voices, when the air they tear;
> His ribs are pillars and his high-arch'd roof
> Of bark that blunts best steel, is thunder-proof.

To his soul—

> O make thyself with holy mourning black,
> And red with blushing as thou art with sin.

Of a repentant sinner,—

> Tears in his eyes quench the amazing light.

With these extracts we conclude, hoping that we shall have introduced many of our readers to hundreds more like them, by having sent them to the volume out of which we have copied.

JOHN ALFRED LANGFORD
From "An Evening with Donne"
The Working Man's Friend
December 1850, pp. 18–21

A mong the many glories of English literature, not the least is her possession of so long a list of truly religious poets. In this, the highest order of poetry, we have names unsurpassed by those of any nation, or of any time. Setting aside the matchless glory of Milton, we have the quaint song of the pious old George Herbert; the epigrammatic force of the "Night Thoughts" of Young; the genial, warm-hearted homeliness of the strains of Cowper; the childlike lyrics of the ever-loved Watts; the smooth, stream-like flow of Montgomery; the soul-raising thought of the nature-loving Wordsworth; and not to mention others of high and lofty fame, whose works the world will not willingly let die, we have him with whom we propose to spend the present evening—the old, antiquated, and venerable DONNE.

Dr. Johnson has offered some very curious reasons why religious poetry has not been successful in attaining a very high state of excellence. We venture to opine that in this respect the Doctor has committed himself, by giving a verdict which posterity will not confirm. We could select from our religious writers passages unequalled, in all that constitutes high poetry, by any equal number of passages from the greatest bards who have not especially devoted their talents to religion, such as Byron and Shelley, for instance. It is curious to think that the Doctor should fall into such a mistake; and it is still more curious to think of the numbers who have since re-echoed the opinion, considering that all the facts are against them. Why, the greatest of every land, and of every faith, are the religious ones, whether we look at the sublime old Hebrew bards, with "the fires of Sinai, and the thunders of the Lord!" or at the poets of classic Greece, or at their numerous successors, who have drawn their inspiration from the Christian faith, the fact is the same. Well has a modern poet said,

> The high and holy works, mid lesser lays,
> Stand up like churches among village cots:
> And it is joy to think that in every age,
> However much the world was wrong therein,
> The greatest works of mind or hand have been
> Done unto God. So may they ever be!
> It shows the strength of wish we have to be great,
> And the sublime humility of might.
>
> —Festus.

But now to Donne. He was born in London in the year 1573. His parents were of the Roman Catholic faith, but their son, convinced of the truth of Protestantism, early declared himself a proselyte to the doctrines of the Reformation. He studied, and successfully, at both the Universities, and became, as one of the critics well observes, "completely *saturated* with the learning of his times." His works are rather voluminous, filling six goodly sized volumes, and consist of satires, ejaculations, occasional poems, elegies, and devotional pieces.

There is a class of poets known as the metaphysical. Of these Donne is perhaps the first in point of time, though some give "rare old Ben," the precedence. Their chief characteristic is their intellectualism. Forsaking the pure and genial naturalness of the Elizabethan poets, they seek by strange and far-fetched allusions, similes, and figures, to clothe a simple thought in party-coloured garments; and to offer it to the reader in as many varied aspects as the most violent twistings and torturings of this brave English language would allow. Extremely learned, in whatever was considered learning in their day, they ransacked all their store in the search for refined, *recherché*, and difficult analogies. Physics, metaphysics, scholastic literature, were made to bear tribute to their love of "the blue-eyed maid" chimera. "The metaphysical poets," says Dr. Johnson, "were men of learning; and to show their whole endeavour, but, unluckily, resolving to show it in rhyme, instead of writing poetry, they only wrote verses, and very often such verses as stood the trial of the finger better than of the ear, for the modulation was so imperfect, that they were only found to be verses by counting the syllables." Such is sure to be the case, when men sit down to put thoughts into verse, instead of waiting till the divine afflatus compels them to utter their feelings, which necessarily take the form of song; as different a thing from verse as light is from darkness. Goethe has well said in one of those world-famous *Xenien* of his,

> What many sing and say,
> Must still by us be borne!
> Ye worthy—great and small—
> Tired you sing yourselves and lorn;
> And yet let no one tune his lay
> Except for what he has to say.

But of these poets, if we except Cowley, Donne holds the highest place. He had much wit, in which gift Dryden confesses himself and his contemporaries to be inferior. He had, as we have seen, a vast erudition, some fancy and elegance, together with strong piety. These combined must surely make a poet of no ordinary power. His satires are strong, vigorous, and masculine. Compared with Pope his verses would certainly want smoothness, but Pope himself would have been a much greater poet, had he possessed some of the wholesome roughness, and known that amidst a profusion of sweets that a bitter is often welcome and good. It is true that Donne is very capricious about the place of accent; but few readers would have to count the fingers to tell whether it were verse or no. Certain we are, if much of his writing be not verse, there is much of it that is poetry. Take the following lines on the "Last Night of the Year":—

> This twilight of two years, not past nor next,
> Some emblem is of me, or I of this,
> Who meteor-like, of stuff and form perplext,
> Whose what and where in disputation is,
> If I should call me anything, should miss.
> I sum the years and me, and find me not,
> Debtor to th' old, nor creditor to th' new.
> That cannot say, my thanks I have forgot,
> Nor trust I this with hopes, and yet scarce
> true
> This bravery is, since these times showed me
> you.

The critic we have quoted above as saying that Donne was saturated with all the learning of his times, also says of him "That he was endowed with a most active and piercing intellect—an imagination, if not grasping and comprehensive, most subtle and far-darting—a fancy rich, vivid, and picturesque—and a wit admirable as well for its caustic severity as for its playful quickness." This is particularly applicable to his satires, which are the precursors of Dryden and Pope's. It would be useless to select from these, as it is but by examination of them as a whole that their force, their truthfulness, and their caustic severity and playful quickness can be felt. To take a passage from any at all adapted to the limits of this paper, in order to show their quality, would be about as wise as the man who having a house to sell, carried a brick with him as a specimen. We may say of them, what can be said of but few satires, that they possess more than a temporary interest, and may be read with profit and advantage at the present time.

The following piece illustrates pretty well the best and worst qualities of Donne.

> As virtuous men pass mildly away,
> And whisper to their souls, to go,
> Whilst some of their sad friends do say,
> The breath goes now, and some say, no:
>
> So let us melt, and make no noise,
> No tear-floods, nor sigh-tempests move,
> 'Twere profanation of our joys
> To tell the laity our love.
>
> Moving of th' earth brings harms and fears,
> Men reckon what it did and meant,
> But trepidation of the spheres,
> Though greater far, is innocent.
>
> Dull sublunary lovers' love
> (Whose soul is sense) cannot admit
> Absence, because it doth remove
> Those things which elemented it.
>
> But we by a love, so much refined,
> That our selves know not what it is,
> Inter-assured of the mind,
> Care less, eyes, lips, and hands to miss.
>
> Our two souls therefore, which are one,
> Though I must go, endure not yet
> A breach, but an expansion,
> Like gold to aery thinness beat.
>
> If they be two, they are two so
> As stiff twin compasses are two,
> Thy soul the fixed foot, makes no show
> To move, but doth, if th'other do.
>
> And though it in the centre sit,
> Yet when the other far doth roam,
> It leans, and hearkens after it,

> And grows erect, as that comes home.
> Such wilt thou be to me, who must
> Like th' other foot, obliquely run;
> Thy firmness makes my circle just,
> And makes me end, where I begun.

A strange analogy this; but yet not so absurd as at first reading it may appear. It is true it may need reading over more than once clearly to seize its hidden meaning; but what then, shall we turn aside from every one "who does not wear his heart upon his sleeve for daws to peck at"?

One more extract, and we bid our poet good night. It is on the littleness of temporal existence, compared with the great, solemn eternity beyond. The lines are quaint, but their spirit fine.

> Think in how poor a prison thou didst lie
> After, enabled but to suck and cry.
> Think, when 'twas grown to most, 'twas a poor inn,
> A province packed up in two yards of skin,
> And that usurped or threatened with the rage
> Of sicknesses, or their true mother, age.
> But think that death hath now enfranchised thee,
> Thou hast thy expansion now, and liberty;
> Think that a rusty piece, discharged, is flown
> In pieces, and the bullet is his own,
> And freely flies; this to thy soul allow,
> Think thy shell broke, think thy soul hatched but
> now.

GEORGE MACDONALD
From "Dr. Donne: His Mode and Style"
England's Antiphon
1868–69, pp. 114–24

He (Donne) is represented by Dr. Johnson as one of the chief examples of that school of poets called by himself the *metaphysical*, an epithet which, as a definition, is almost false. True it is that Donne and his followers were always ready to deal with metaphysical subjects, but it was from their mode, and not their subjects, that Dr. Johnson classed them. What this mode was we shall see presently, for I shall be justified in setting forth its strangeness, even absurdity, by the fact that Dr. Donne was the dear friend of George Herbert, and had much to do with the formation of his poetic habits. Just twenty years older than Herbert, and the valued and intimate friend of his mother, Donne was in precisely that relation of age and circumstance to influence the other in the highest degree.

The central thought of Dr. Donne is nearly sure to be just: the subordinate thoughts by means of which he unfolds it are often grotesque, and so wildly associated as to remind one of the lawlessness of a dream, wherein mere suggestion without choice or fitness rules the sequence. As some of the writers of whom I have last spoken would play with words, Dr. Donne would sport with ideas, and with the visual images or embodiments of them. Certainly in his case much knowledge reveals itself in the association of his ideas, and great facility in the management and utterance of them. True likewise, he says nothing unrelated to the main idea of the poem; but not the less certainly does the whole resemble the speech of a child of active imagination, to whom judgment as to the character of his suggestions is impossible, his taste being equally gratified with a lovely image and a brilliant absurdity: a butterfly and a shining potsherd are to him similarly desirable. Whatever wild thing starts from the thicket of thought, all is worthy game to the hunting intellect of Dr. Donne, and is followed without question of tone, keeping, or harmony. In his play with words, Sir Philip Sidney kept good heed that even that should serve the end in view; in his play with ideas, Dr. John Donne, so far from serving the end, sometimes obscures it almost hopelessly: the hart escapes while he follows the squirrels and weasels and bats. It is not surprising that, their author being so inartistic with regard to their object, his verses themselves should be harsh and unmusical beyond the worst that one would imagine fit to be called verse. He enjoys the unenviable distinction of having no rival in ruggedness of metric movement and associated sounds. This is clearly the result of indifference; an indifference, however, which grows very strange to us when we find that he *can* write a lovely verse and even an exquisite stanza.

Greatly for its own sake, partly for the sake of illustration, I quote a poem containing at once his best and his worst, the result being such an incongruity that we wonder whether it might not be called his best *and* his worst, because we cannot determine which. He calls it *Hymn to God, my God, in my Sickness*. The first stanza is worthy of George Herbert in his best mood.

> Since I am coming to that holy room,
>> Where with the choir of saints for evermore
> I shall be made thy music, as I come
>> I tune the instrument here at the door,
>> And what I must do then, think here before.

To recognize its beauty, leaving aside the depth and truth of the phrase, "Where I shall be made thy music," we must recall the custom of those days to send out for "a noise of musicians." Hence he imagines that he has been summoned as one of a band already gone in to play before the king of "The High Countries:" he is now at the door, where he is listening to catch the tone, that he may have his instrument tuned and ready before he enters. But with what a jar the next stanza breaks on heart, mind, and ear!

> Whilst my physicians by their love are grown
>> Cosmographers, and I their map, who lie
> Flat on this bed, that by them may be shown
>> That this is my south-west discovery,
>> *Per fretum febris*—by these straits to die;—

Here, in the midst of comparing himself to a map, and his physicians to cosmographers consulting the map, he changes without warning into a navigator whom they are trying to follow upon the map as he passes through certain straits— namely, those of the fever—towards his south-west discovery, Death. Grotesque as this is, the absurdity deepens in the end of the next stanza by a return to the former idea. He is alternately a map and a man sailing on the map of himself. But the first half of the stanza is lovely: my reader must remember that the region of the West was at that time the Land of Promise to England.

> I joy that in these straits I see my West;
>> For though those currents yield return to
>> none,
> What shall my West hurt me? As west and east
>> In all flat maps (and I am one) are one,
>> So death doth touch the resurrection.

It is hardly worth while, except for the strangeness of the phenomenon, to spend any time in elucidating this. Once more a map, he is that of the two hemispheres, in which the east of the one touches the west of the other. Could anything be much more unmusical than the line, "In all flat maps (and I am one) are one"? But the next stanza is worse.

> Is the Pacific sea my home? Or are
>> The eastern riches? Is Jerusalem?

> Anvan, and Magellan, and Gibraltar?
>> All straits, and none but straits are ways to
>> them,
>> Whether where Japhet dwelt, or Cham, or
>> Sem.

The meaning of the stanza is this: there is no earthly home: all these places are only straits that lead home, just as they themselves cannot be reached but through straits.

Let my reader now forget all but the first stanza, and take it along with the following, the last two:

> We think that Paradise and Calvary,
>> Christ's cross and Adam's tree, stood in one
>> place:
> Look, Lord, and find both Adams met in me;
>> As the first Adam's sweat surrounds my face,
>> May the last Adam's blood my soul embrace.

> So, in his purple wrapped, receive me, Lord;
>> By these his thorns give me his other crown;
> And as to others' souls I preached thy word,
>> Be this my text, my sermon to mine own:
>> *Therefore, that he may raise, the Lord throws
>> down.*

Surely these are very fine, especially the middle verse of the former and the first verse of the latter stanza. The three stanzas together make us lovingly regret that Dr. Donne should have ridden his Pegasus over quarry and housetop, instead of teaching him his paces.

The next I quote is artistic throughout. Perhaps the fact, of which we are informed by Izaak Walton, "that he caused it to be set to a grave and solemn tune, and to be often sung to the organ by the choristers of St. Paul's church in his own hearing, especially at the evening service," may have something to do with its degree of perfection. There is no sign of his usual haste about it. It is even elaborately rhymed after Norman fashion, the rhymes in each stanza being consonant with the rhymes in every stanza.

A Hymn to God the Father.

> Wilt thou forgive that sin where I begun,
>> Which was my sin, though it were done before?
> Wilt thou forgive that sin, through which I run,
>> And do run still, though still I do deplore?—
>> When thou hast done, thou hast not done;
>> For I have more.

> Wilt thou forgive that sin which I have won
>> Others to sin, and made my sins their door?
> Wilt thou forgive that sin which I did shun
>> A year or two, but wallowed in a score?—
>> When thou hast done, thou hast not done;
>> For I have more.

> I have a sin of fear, that when I've spun
>> My last thread, I shall perish on the shore;
> But swear by thyself, that at my death thy Son
>> Shall shine, as he shines now and heretofore;
>> And having done that, thou hast done:
>> I fear no more.

In those days even a pun might be a serious thing: witness the play in the last stanza on the words *son* and *sun*—not a mere pun, for the Son of the Father is the Sun of Righteousness: he is Life *and* Light.

What the Doctor himself says concerning the hymn, appears to me not only interesting but of practical value. He "did occasionally say to a friend, 'The words of this hymn have restored to me the same thoughts of joy that possessed my soul in my sickness, when I composed it.'" What a help it would be to many, if in their more gloomy times they would but recall the visions of truth they had, and were assured of, in better moments!

Here is a somewhat strange hymn, which yet possesses, rightly understood, a real grandeur:

A HYMN TO CHRIST
At the Author's last going into Germany.[1]

In what torn ship soever I embark,
That ship shall be my emblem of thy ark;
What sea soever swallow me, that flood
Shall be to me an emblem of thy blood.
Though thou with clouds of anger do disguise
Thy face, yet through that mask I know those eyes,
  Which, though they turn away sometimes—
    They never will despise.

I sacrifice this island unto thee,
And all whom I love here and who love me:
When I have put this flood 'twixt them and me,
Put thou thy blood betwixt my sins and thee.
As the tree's sap doth seek the root below
In winter, in my winter[2] now I go
  Where none but thee, the eternal root
    Of true love, I may know.

Nor thou, nor thy religion, dost control
The amorousness of an harmonious soul;
But thou wouldst have that love thyself: as thou
Art jealous, Lord, so I am jealous now.
Thou lov'st not, till from loving more thou free
My soul: who ever gives, takes liberty:
  Oh, if thou car'st not whom I love,
    Alas, thou lov'st not me!

Seal then this bill of my divorce to all
On whom those fainter beams of love did fall;
Marry those loves, which in youth scattered be
On face, wit, hopes, (false mistresses), to thee.
Churches are best for prayer that have least light:
To see God only, I go out of sight;
  And, to 'scape stormy days, I choose
    An everlasting night.

To do justice to this poem, the reader must take some trouble to enter into the poet's mood.

It is in a measure distressing that, while I grant with all my heart the claim of his "Muse's white sincerity," the taste in—I do not say *of*—some of his best poems should be such that I will not present them.

Out of twenty-three *Holy Sonnets*, every one of which, I should almost say, possesses something remarkable, I choose three. Rhymed after the true Petrarchian fashion, their rhythm is often as bad as it can be to be called rhythm at all. Yet these are very fine.

Thou hast made me, and shall thy work decay?
  Repair me now, for now mine end doth haste;
  I run to death, and death meets me as fast,
And all my pleasures are like yesterday.
I dare not move my dim eyes any way,
  Despair behind, and death before doth cast
  Such terror; and my feeble flesh doth waste
By sin in it, which it towards hell doth weigh.
Only thou art above, and when towards thee
  By thy leave I can look, I rise again;
But our old subtle foe so tempteth me,
  That not one hour myself I can sustain:
Thy grace may wing me to prevent his art,
And thou like adamant draw mine iron heart.

If faithful souls be alike glorified
  As angels, then my father's soul doth see,
  And adds this even to full felicity,
That valiantly I hell's wide mouth o'erstride:
But if our minds to these souls be descried
  By circumstances and by signs that be
  Apparent in us—not immediately—
How shall my mind's white truth by them be tried?
  They see idolatrous lovers weep and mourn,
And, style blasphemous, conjurors to call
On Jesu's name, and pharisaical
  Dissemblers feign devotïon. Then turn,
O pensive soul, to God; for he knows best
Thy grief, for he put it into my breast.

Death, be not proud, though some have callèd thee
  Mighty and dreadful, for thou art not so;
  For those whom thou think'st thou dost
    overthrow,
Die not, poor Death; nor yet canst thou kill me.
From rest and sleep, which but thy picture be,
  Much pleasure, then from thee much more
    must flow;
  And soonest our best men with thee do go,
Rest of their bones, and soul's delivery!
  Thou'rt slave to fate, chance, kings, and
    desperate men,
And dost with poison, war, and sickness dwell;
And poppy or charms can make us sleep as well,
  And better than thy stroke. Why swell'st thou
    then?
One short sleep past, we wake eternally,
And death shall be no more: Death, thou shalt die.

In a poem called *The Cross*, full of fantastic conceits, we find the following remarkable lines, embodying the profoundest truth.

As perchance carvers do not faces make,
But that away, which hid them there, do take:
Let crosses so take what hid Christ in thee,
And be his image, or not his, but he.

One more, and we shall take our leave of Dr. Donne. It is called a fragment; but it seems to me complete. It will serve as a specimen of his best and at the same time of his most characteristic mode of presenting fine thoughts grotesquely attired.

RESURRECTION

Sleep, sleep, old sun; thou canst not have
  re-past
As yet the wound thou took'st on Friday last.
Sleep then, and rest: the world may bear thy stay;
A better sun rose before thee to-day;
Who, not content to enlighten all that dwell
On the earth's face as thou, enlightened hell,
And made the dark fires languish in that vale,
As at thy presence here our fires grow pale;
Whose body, having walked on earth and now
Hastening to heaven, would, that he might allow
Himself unto all stations and fill all,
For these three days become a mineral.
He was all gold when he lay down, but rose
All tincture; and doth not alone dispose
Leaden and iron wills to good, but is
Of power to make even sinful flesh like his.
Had one of those, whose credulous piety
Thought that a soul one might discern and see
Go from a body, at this sepulchre been,
And issuing from the sheet this body seen,

He would have justly thought this body a soul,
If not of any man, yet of the whole.

What a strange mode of saying that he is our head, the captain of our salvation, the perfect humanity in which our life is hid! Yet it has its dignity. When one has got over the oddity of these last six lines, the figure contained in them shows itself almost grand.

As an individual specimen of the grotesque form holding a fine sense, regard for a moment the words,

He was all gold when he lay down, but rose
All tincture;

which means, that, entirely good when he died, he was something yet greater when he rose, for he had gained the power of making others good: the *tincture* intended here was a substance whose touch would turn the basest metal into gold.

Through his poems are scattered many fine passages; but not even his large influence on the better poets who followed is sufficient to justify our listening to him longer now.

Notes

1. He was sent by James I. to assist an embassy to the Elector Palatine, who had married his daughter Elizabeth.
2. He has lately lost his wife, for whom he had a rare love.

EDMUND GOSSE
"John Donne"
The Jacobean Poets
1894, pp. 51–67

The poems of Donne were not published until after his death. The first edition, the quarto of 1633, is very inaccurate and ill-arranged; the octavos of 1635 and 1639 are much fuller and more exact. Donne, however, still lacks a competent editor. We have no direct knowledge of the poet's own wish as to the arrangement of his poems, nor any safe conjecture as to the date of more than a few pieces. The best lyrics, however, appear to belong to the first decade of James I.'s reign, if they are not even of earlier composition. There seems to be no doubt that the *Satires*, an imperfect manuscript of which bears the date 1593, are wholly Elizabethan. These are seven in number, and belong to the same general category as those of Hall, Lodge, and Guilpin. Neither in date nor in style do they belong to the period treated of in this volume, and it is therefore not necessary to dwell on them at great length here. They are brilliant and picturesque beyond any of their particular compeers, even beyond the best of Hall's satires. But they have the terrible faults which marked all our Elizabethan satirists, a crabbed violence alike of manner and matter, a fierce voluble conventionality, a tortured and often absolutely licentious and erroneous conception of the use of language. The fourth is, doubtless, the best written, and may be taken as the best essay in this class of poetry existing in English literature before the middle-life of Dryden; its attraction for Pope is well known.

"The Progress of the Soul," as named by its author "Poema Satyricon," takes its natural place after the satires, but is conjectured to have been written not earlier than 1610. De Quincey, with unwonted warmth, declared that "massy diamonds compose the very substance of this poem, thoughts and descriptions which have the fervent and gloomy sublimity of Ezekiel or Æschylus." It is written in a variant of the Spenserian stanza, and is a hyperbolical history of the development of the human soul, extended to more than five hundred lines, and not ended, but abruptly closed. It is one of the most difficult of Donne's writings, and started a kind of psychologi-

cal poetry of which, as the century progressed, many more examples were seen, none, perhaps, of a wholly felicitous character. It has the poet's characteristics, however, to the full. The verse marches with a virile tread, the epithets are daring, the thoughts always curious and occasionally sublime, the imagination odd and scholastic, with recurring gleams of passion.

Here is a fragment of this strange production—

Into an embryon fish our soul is thrown,
And in due time thrown out again, and grown
To such vastness, as if, unmanacled
From Greece, Morea were, and that, by some
Earthquake unrooted, loose Morea swum,
Or seas from Afric's body had severèd
And torn the hopeful promontory's head;
This fish would seem these, and, when all hopes fail,
A great ship overset, or without sail
    Hulling, might (when this was a whelp) be like
        this whale.

At every stroke his brazen fins do take
More circles in the broken sea they make
Then cannons' voices, when the air they tear;
His ribs are pillars, and his high-arch'd roof,
Of bark that blunts best steel, is thunder-proof;
Swim in him, swallow'd dolphins, without fear,
And feel no sides, as if his vast womb were
Some inland sea, and ever as he went
He spouted rivers up, as if he meant
    To join our seas with seas above the
        firmament.

. . .

Now drinks he up seas, and he eats up flocks;
He jostles islands and he shakes firm rocks;
Now in a roomful house this soul doth float,
And like a prince she sends her faculties
To all her limbs, distant as provinces.
The Sun hath twenty times both crab and goat
Parchèd, since first launch'd forth this living boat;
'Tis greatest now and to destruction
Nearest; there's no pause at perfection,
    Greatness a period hath, but hath no station.

Far less extraordinary are the Epistles, which form a large section of Donne's poetical works. All through life he was wont to address letters, chiefly in the heroic couplet, to the most intimate of his friends. These epistles are conceived in a lighter vein than his other writings, and have less of his characteristic vehemence. The earliest, however, "The Storm," which he addressed from the Azores, possesses his Elizabethan mannerism; it is crudely picturesque and licentious, essentially unpoetical. "The Calm," which is the parallel piece, is far better, and partly deserves Ben Jonson's high commendation of it to Drummond. The epistle to Sir Henry Goodyer is noticeable for the dignified and stately manner in which the four-line stanza, afterwards adopted by Gray for his *Elegy*, is employed; this poem is exceedingly like the early pieces written by Dryden some fifty years later. The school of the Restoration is plainly foreshadowed in it.

Many of these epistles are stuffed hard with thoughts, but poetry is rarely to be found in them; the style is not lucid, the construction is desperately parenthetical. It is not often that the weary reader is rewarded by such a polished piece of versification as is presented by this passage about love in the "Letter to the Countess of Huntingdon."

It is not love that sueth, or doth contend;
Love either conquers, or but meets a friend.
Man's better part consists of purer fire,
And finds itself allowed, ere it desire.

Love is wise here, keeps home, gives reason sway,
And journeys not till it find summer-way.
A weather-beaten lover, but once known,
Is sport for every girl to practise on.
Who strives, through woman's scorns, woman to
        know,
Is lost, and seeks his shadow to outgo;
It must be sickness, after one disdain,
Though he be called aloud, to look again;
Let others sin and grieve; one cunning slight
Shall freeze my love to crystal in a night.
I can love first, and, if I win, love still,
And cannot be removed, unless she will;
It is her fault if I unsure remain;
She only can untie, I bind again;
The honesties of love with ease I do,
But am no porter for a tedious woe.

Most of these epistles are New Year's greetings, and many are addressed to the noble and devout ladies with whom he held spiritual converse in advancing years. The poet superbly aggrandizes the moral qualities of these women, paying to their souls the court that younger and flightier cavaliers reserved for the physical beauty of their daughters.

The Epithalamia of Donne form that section of his work in which, alone, he seems to follow in due succession after Spenser. These marriage-songs are elegant and glowing, though not without the harshness which Donne could not for any length of time forego. That composed for the wedding of Frederick Count Palatine and the Lady Elizabeth, in 1613, is perhaps the most popular of all Donne's writings, and opens with a delicious vivacity.

Hail, Bishop Valentine, whose day this is!
        All the air is thy diocese,
        And all the chirping choristers
And other birds are thy parishioners;
        Thou marryest every year
The lyric lark and the grave whispering dove,
The sparrow that neglects his life for love,
The household bird with the red stomacher;
Thou mak'st the blackbird speed as soon
As doth the goldfinch or the halcyon;
The husband cock looks out, and straight is sped,
And meets his wife, which brings her feather-bed.
This day more cheerfully than ever shine,—
This day, which might enflame thyself, old
        Valentine.

The ode within the rather stiff setting of the Allophanes and Idios eclogue is scarcely less felicitous.

The miscellaneous secular poems of Donne are generically classed under the heading of "Elegies." We have here some of the most extraordinary aberrations of fancy, some of the wildest contrasts of character and style, to be observed in literature. They are mainly Ovidian or Tibullan studies of the progress of the passion of love, written by one who proclaims himself an ardent, but no longer an illusioned lover,—hot, still, but violent and scandalous. The youth of the author is disclosed in them, but it is not the callous youth of first inexperience. He is already a past master in the subtle sophistry of love, and knows by rote "the mystic language of the eye and hand." Weary with the beauty of spring and summer, he has learned to find fascination in an autumnal face. The voluptuous character of these elegies has scandalized successive critics. Several of them, to be plain, were indeed too outspoken for the poet's own, or for any decent age. Throughout it is seldom so much what the unbridled lover says, as his utter intemperance in saying it, that surprises, especially in one who, by

the time the poems were given to the public, had come to be regarded as the holiest of men. Even saints, however, were coarse in the age of James, and the most beautiful of all Donne's elegies, the exquisite "Refusal to Allow His Young Wife to Accompany Him Abroad as a Page," which belongs to his mature life and treats of a very creditable passion, is marred by almost inconceivable offences against good taste.

Another section of Donne's poems is composed of funeral elegies or requiems, in which he allowed the sombre part of his fancy to run riot. In these curious entombments we read nothing that seems personal or pathetic, but much about "the magnetic force" of the deceased, her spiritual anatomy, and her soul's "meridians and parallels." Amid these pedantries, we light now and then upon extraordinary bursts of poetic observation, as when the eminence of the spirit of Mistress Drury reminds the poet of a vision, seen years before in sailing past the Canaries, and he cries out—

Doth not a Teneriffe or higher hill,
Rise so high like a rock, that one might think
The floating moon would shipwreck there, and sink,

or as when one of his trances comes upon him, and he sighs—

        when thou know'st this,
Thou know'st how wan a ghost this our world is.

These lovely sudden bursts of pure poetry are more frequent in the "Funeral Elegies" than in any section of Donne's poetry which we have mentioned, and approach those, to be presently noted, in the Lyrics. The spirit of this strange writer loved to dwell on the majestic and gorgeous aspects of death, to wave his torch within the charnel-house and to show that its walls are set with jewels.

This may be taken as an example of his obscure mortuary imagination—

As men of China, after an age's stay,
Do take up porcelain where they buried clay,
So at this grave, her limbeck (which refines
The diamonds, rubies, sapphires, pearls and mines
Of which this flesh was), her soul shall inspire
Flesh of such stuff, as God, when his last fire
Annuls this world, to recompense it, shall
Make and name them the elixir of this All.
They say, the sea, when it gains, loseth too,
If carnal Death (the younger brother) do
Usurp the body; our soul, which subject is
To the elder Death, by sin, is freed by this;
They perish both, when they attempt the just,
For graves our trophies are, and both death's dust.

The presence of the emblems of mortality rouses Donne to an unusual intellectual ecstasy. The latest of these elegies is dated 1625, and shows that the poet retained his art in this kind of writing to the very end of his career, adding polish to his style, without any perceptible falling off in power.

A large number of "Holy Sonnets," which Izaak Walton thought had perished, were published in 1669, and several remain still unprinted. They are more properly quatorzains than sonnets, more correct in form than the usual English sonnet of the age—for the octett is properly arranged and rhymed—but closing in the sestett with a couplet. These sonnets are very interesting from the light they throw on Donne's prolonged sympathy with the Roman Church, over which his biographers have been wont to slur. All these "Holy Sonnets" probably belong to 1617, or the period immediately following the death of Donne's wife. In the light of certain examples in the possession of the present writer, which have not yet appeared in print, they seem to confirm Walton's remark that

though Donne inquired early in life into the differences between Protestantism and Catholicism, yet that he lived until
the death of his wife without religion.

A pathetic sonnet from the Westmoreland manuscript,
here printed for the first time, shows the effect of that bereave-
ment upon him—

> Since she whom I loved hath paid her last debt,
>   To Nature, and to hers and my good is dead,
>   And her soul early into heaven vanished.—
> Wholly on heavenly things my mind is set.
> Here the admiring her my mind did whet
>   To seek thee, God; so streams do show their
>   head,
>   But tho' I have found thee, and thou my thirst
>   has fed,
> A holy thirsty dropsy melts me yet.
> But why should I beg more love, when as thou
>   Does woo my soul for hers, off'ring all thine:
> And dost not only fear lest I allow
>   My love to Saints and Angels, things divine,
> But in thy tender jealousy dost doubt
> Lest this World, Flesh, yea Devil put thee out?

The sonnet on the Blessed Virgin Mary, however, has
probably been attributed to Donne by error; the more likely
name of Constable has been suggested as that of its author.

In his other divine poems, also, the Roman element is
often very strong, and the theology of a cast which is far removed from that of Puritanism. In the very curious piece
called "The Cross," he seems to confess to the use of a material
crucifix, and in "A Litany" he distinctly recommends prayer to
the Virgin Mary,

> That she-cherubim which unlocked Paradise.

All these are matters which must be left to the future
biographers of Donne, but which are worthy of their closest
attention in developing the intricate anomalies of his character.

We have now, by a process of exhaustion, arrived at what
is the most interesting of the sections of Donne's poetry, his
amatory lyrics. These are about seventy in number, and so far
as the scanty evidence can be depended upon, belong to various periods from his twentieth to his thirty-fifth year. The
series, as we now hold it, begins with the gross and offensive
piece of extravagance called, "The Flea," but is followed by
"The Good-Morrow," which strikes a very different note. As a
rule, these poems are extremely personal, confidential, and
vivid; the stamp of life is on them. None the less, while confessing with extraordinary frankness and clearness the passion
of the writer, they are so reserved in detail, so immersed and
engulphed in secrecy, that no definite conjecture can be hazarded as to the person, or persons, or the class of persons, to
whom they were addressed. One or two were evidently inspired
by Donne's wife, others most emphatically were not, and in
their lawless, though not gross, sensuality, remind us of the still
more outspoken "Elegies." In spite of the alembicated verbiage, the tortuousness and artificiality of the thought, sincerity burns in every stanza, and the most exquisite images lie
side by side with monstrous conceits and ugly pedantries.

A peculiarity of the lyrics is that scarcely two of the seventy are written in the same verse-form. Donne evidently laid
himself out to invent elaborate and farfetched metres. He was
imitated in this down to the Restoration, when all metrical
effects tended to merge in the heroic couplet. But of the innumerable form-inventions of Donne and of his disciples scarcely
one has been adopted into the language, although more than
one, by their elegance and melody, deserve to be resumed.
This exemplifies one of the prettiest of his stanza-forms—

> If thou be'st born to strange sights,
>   Things invisible to see,
> Ride ten thousand days and nights,
>   Till age snow white hairs on thee;
> Thou, when thou return'st, wilt tell me
> All strange wonders that befell thee,
>   And swear
>   Nowhere
> Lives a woman true and fair.
> If thou find'st one, let me know;
>   Such a pilgrimage were sweet.
> Yet do not,—I would not go
>   Though at next door we might meet,
> Though she were true when you met her,
> And last till you write your letter,
>   Yet she
>   Will be
> False, ere I come, with two or three.

It now remains to examine this body of poetry in general
terms, and, first of all, it is necessary to make some remarks
with regard to Donne's whole system of prosody. The terms
"irregular," "unintelligible," and "viciously rugged," are commonly used in describing it, and it seems even to be supposed
by some critics that Donne did not know how to scan. This last
supposition may be rejected at once; what there was to know
about poetry was known to Donne. But it seems certain that he
intentionally introduced a revolution into English versification. It was doubtless as a rebellion against the smooth and
somewhat nerveless iambic flow of Spenser and the earliest
contemporaries of Shakespeare, that Donne invented his violent mode of breaking up the line into quick and slow beats.
The best critic of his own generation, Ben Jonson, hated the
innovation, and told Drummond "that Donne, for not keeping
of accent, deserved hanging." It is difficult to stem a current of
censure which has set without intermission since the very days
of Donne itself, but I may be permitted to point out what I
imagine was the poet's own view of the matter.

He found, as I have said, the verse of his youth, say of
1590, exceedingly mellifluous, sinuous, and inclining to flaccidity. A five-syllabled iambic line of Spenser or of Daniel trots
along with the gentlest amble of inevitable shorts and longs. It
seems to have vexed the ear of Donne by its tendency to
feebleness, and it doubtless appeared to him that the very gifted
writers who immediately preceded him had carried the softness
of it as far as it would go. He desired new and more varied
effects. To see what he aimed at doing, we have, I believe, to
turn to what has been attempted in our own time, by Mr.
Robert Bridges, in some of his early experiments, and by the
Symbolists in France. The iambic rhymed line of Donne has
audacities such as are permitted to his blank verse by Milton,
and although the felicities are rare in the older poet, instead of
being almost incessant, as in the later, Donne at his best is not
less melodious than Milton. When he writes—

> Blasted with sighs and surrounded with tears,

we must not dismiss this as not being iambic verse at all, nor,—
much less,—attempt to read it—

> Blastéd with síghs, and surroundéd with teárs,

but recognize in it the poet's attempt to identify the beat of his
verse with his bewildered and dejected condition, reading it
somewhat in this notation:—

> Blasted | with sighs || and surrounded | with tears.

The violence of Donne's transposition of accent is most curiously to be observed in his earliest satires, and in some of his
later poems is almost entirely absent. Doubtless his theory

became modified with advancing years. No poet is more diffi-cult to read aloud. Such a passage as the following may excus-ably defy a novice:

> No token of worth but Queen's man and fine
> Living barrels of beef and flagons of wine.
> I shook like a spied spy. Preachers which are
> Seas of wit and arts, you can then dare
> Drown the sins of this place, for, for me,
> Which am but a scant brook, it enough shall be
> To wash the stains away.

But treat the five-foot verse not as a fixed and unalterable sequence of cadences, but as a norm around which a musician weaves his variations, and the riddle is soon read—

> No token | of worth | but Queen's | man | and fine
> Living | barrels of | beef and | flagons of | wine.
> I shook | like a spied | spy. | Preachers | which are
> Seas | of wit | and arts, | you can then | dare
> Drown | the sins | of this place, | for, | for me,
> Which am | but a scant | brook, | it enough | shall be
> To wash | the stains | away.

The poetry of Donne possesses in no small degree that "unusual and indefinable witchery" which Dr. Jessopp has noted as characteristic of the man himself. But our enjoyment of it is marred by the violence of the writer, by his want of what seems to us to be good taste, and by a quality which has been overlooked by those who have written about him, but which seems to provide the key to the mystery of his position. Donne was, I would venture to suggest, by far the most modern and contemporaneous of the writers of his time. He rejected all the classical tags and imagery of the Elizabethans, he borrowed nothing from French or Italian tradition. He arrived at an excess of actuality in style, and it was because he struck them as so novel and so completely in touch with his own age that his immediate coevals were so much fascinated with him. His poems are full of images taken from the life and habits of the time. Where earlier poets had summoned the myths of Greece to adorn their verse, Donne weaves in, instead, the false zool-ogy, the crude physics and philosophy, of his own fermenting epoch. The poem called "Love's Exchange," is worthy of care-ful examination in this respect. Each stanza is crowded with conceits, each one of which is taken from the practical or professional life of the moment in which the poet wrote. This extreme modernness, however, is one potent source of our lack of sympathy with the poetry so inspired. In the long run, it is the broader suggestion, the wider if more conventional range of classic imagery, which may hope to hold without fatigue the interest of successive generations.

For us the charm of Donne continues to rest in his occa-sional felicities, his burst of melodious passion. If his song were not so tantalizingly fragmentary, we should call him the unques-tioned nightingale of the Jacobean choir. No other poet of that time, few poets of any time, have equalled the concentrated passion, the delicate, long-drawn musical effects, the bold and ecstatic rapture of Donne at his best. In such a poem as "The Dream," he realizes the very paroxysm of amatory song. In his own generation, no one approached the purity of his cascades of ringing monosyllables, his

> For God's sake, hold your tongue and let me love,

or,

> I long to talk with some old lover's ghost
> Who died before the God of Love was born,

or,

> Oh more than moon,

> Draw not thy seas to drown me in thy sphere.

or,

> A bracelet of bright hair about the bone.

In these and similar passages, of which a not very slender florilegium might be gathered from his voluminous produc-tions, Donne reminds us that Ben Jonson esteemed him "the first poet in the world in some things." But this quality of passionate music is not the only one discernible, nor often to be discerned. The more obvious characteristic was summed up by Coleridge in a droll quatrain—

> With Donne, whose Muse on dromedary trots,
> Wreathe iron pokers into true-love-knots;
> Rhyme's sturdy cripple, Fancy's maze and clue,
> Wit's forge and fire-blast, Meaning's press and screw.

In the use of these ingenuities, which it was once the fashion to call "metaphysical," Donne shows an amazing per-tinacity. He is never daunted by the feeling that his wit is exercised "on subjects where we have no right to expect it," and where it is impossible for us to relish it. He pushes on with relentless logic,—sometimes, indeed, past chains of images that are lovely and appropriate; but, oftener, through briars and lianas that rend his garments and trip up his feet. He is not affected by the ruggedness of his road, nor by our unwillingness to follow him. He stumbles doggedly on until he has reached his singular goal. In all this intellectual obstinacy he has a certain kinship to Browning, but his obscurity is more dense. It is to be hoped that the contemporary maligned him who re-ported Donne to have written one of his elegies in an inten-tional obscureness, but that he delighted in putting his readers out of their depth can scarcely be doubted. It is against this lurid background, which in itself and unrelieved would possess a very slight attraction to modern readers, that the electrical flashes of Donne's lyrical intuition make their appearance, al-most blinding us by their brilliancy, and fading into the dark tissue of conceits before we have time to appreciate them.

The prominence here given to Donne will be challenged by no one who considers what his influence was on the poetical taste of the time. It is true that among his immediate contem-poraries the following of Spenser did not absolutely cease at once. But if a study on the poets of Charles I. were to succeed the present volume, the name of Donne would have to be constantly prominent. On almost everything nondramatic published in the succeeding generation, from Crashaw to Davenant, from Carew to Cowley, the stamp of Donne is set. Dryden owed not a little to him, although, as time went on, he purged himself more and more fully of the taint of meta-physical conceit. So late as 1692, in the preface to *Eleanora*, Dryden still held up Donne as "the greatest wit, though not the best poet of our nation." His poems were among the few non-dramatic works of the Jacobean period which continued to be read and reprinted in the age of Anne, and Pope both borrowed from and imitated Donne.

So far as we trace this far-sweeping influence exercised on the poets of a hundred years, we have difficulty in applauding its effects. The empassioned sincerity, the intuitions, the clar-ion note of Donne were individual to himself and could not be transmitted. It was far otherwise with the jargon of "meta-physical" wit, the trick of strained and inappropriate imagery. These could be adopted by almost any clever person, and were, in fact, employed with fluent effect by people in whom the poetical quality was of the slightest. Writers like Mildmay Fane, Earl of Westmoreland, or like Owen Feltham (in his verse), show what it was that Donne's seed produced when it fell upon stony ground.

FELIX E. SCHELLING
From "Introduction"
A Book of Elizabethan Lyrics
1895, pp. xxi–lxix

The most important poetical influence of this decade ⟨1590–1600⟩ is that of that grave and marvelous man, Dr. John Donne. I would respectfully invite the attention of those who still persist with Dr. Johnson in regarding this great poet as the founder of a certain "Metaphysical School of Poetry,"[1] a man all but contemporary with Cowley, and a writer harsh, obscure, and incomprehensible in his diction, first to an examination of facts which are within the reach of all, and, secondly, to an honest study of his works. Ben Jonson told Drummond[2] that "Donne's best poems were written before he was twenty-five years old," *i.e.*, before 1598, and Francis Davison, apparently when collecting material for his *Poetical Rhapsody* in 1600, includes in a memorandum of "M.S.S. to get," certain poems of Donne.[3] The Carews, Crashaws, and Cowleys begin at least thirty years later, and, be their imitations of Donne's characteristics what they may, Donne himself is an Elizabethan in the strictest possible acceptation of that term, and far in fact as in time from the representative of a degenerate and false taste. It is somewhat disconcerting to find an author whom, like Savage Landor in our own century, the critic cannot glibly classify as the founder of a school or the product of a perfectly obvious series of literary influences. Donne is a man of this difficult type. For, just as Shakespeare touched life and man at all points, and, absorbing the light of his time, gave it forth a hundredfold, so Donne, withdrawn almost wholly from the influences affecting his contemporaries, shone and glowed with a strange light all his own.

Few lyrical poets have ever rivaled Donne in contemporary popularity. Mr. Edmund Gosse has recently given a reason for this, which seems worthy of attention, while by no means explaining everything. "Donne was, I would venture to suggest, by far the most modern and contemporaneous of the writers of his time. . . . He arrived at an excess of actuality of style, and it was because he struck them as so novel, and so completely in touch with his age, that his immediate coevals were so much fascinated with him."[4] A much bequoted passage of the *Conversations with Drummond* informs us that Ben Jonson "esteemeth Donne the first poet in the world in some things."[5] An analysis of these "some things," which space here forbids, will, I think, show them to depend, to a large degree, upon that deeper element of the modern lyric, poetic insight; the power which, proceeding by means of the clash of ideas familiar with ideas remote, flashes light and meaning into what has hitherto appeared mere commonplace. This, mainly, though with much else, is the positive originality of Donne. A quality no less remarkable is to be found in what may be called his negative originality, by which I mean that trait which caused Donne absolutely to give over the current mannerisms of his time; to write neither in the usual Italian manner, nor in borrowed lyrical forms; indeed, to be at times wantonly careless of mere expression, and, above all, to throw away every trace of the conventional classic imagery and mannerisms which infected and conventionalized the poetry of so many of his contemporaries. It seems to me that no one, excepting Shakespeare, with Sidney, Greville, and Jonson in lesser measure, has done so much to develop intellectualized emotion in the Elizabethan lyric as John Donne. But Donne is the last poet to demand a proselyting zeal of his devotees, and all those who have learned to love his witching personality will agree to the charming sentiment of his faithful adorer, Izaak Walton, when he says: "Though I must omit to mention divers persons, . . . friends of Sir Henry Wotton; yet I must not omit to mention of a love that was there begun betwixt him and Dr. Donne, sometime Dean of Saint Paul's; a man of whose abilities I shall forbear to say anything, because he who is of this nation, and pretends to learning or ingenuity, and is ignorant of Dr. Donne, deserves not to know him."[6]

But in the great age of Elizabeth, miracles were not the monopoly of the immortals. Strenuous Titans, such as those that wrought poetical cosmos out of the chaos of *Barons' Wars* or *Civil Wars*, out of disquisitions on statecraft and ponderous imitations of Senecan rhetoric, could also work dainty marvels in song. The lyrics of that most interesting and "difficult" of poets, Fulke Greville, have already been noticed, and are the more remarkable in their frequent grace of fancy, uncommon wit, originality, and real music of expression in that they are the sister products of the obscure and intricate musings and the often eccentric didacticism of *Mustapha* and *Alaham*. Of Daniel, a conscientious artist as he was a sensible theorist in verse, we might expect less masterly restraint; whilst Donne displayed the daring of an individualism that enabled him, while his poems were yet in manuscript, to exercise upon his contemporaries the effect of an accepted classic.

The story of Shakespeare's gradual enfranchisement from the trammels of imitation and the adherence to ephemeral rules of art has been often told, and is as true of his work, considered metrically, as from any other point of view. With increasing grasp of mind came increasing power and abandon in style and versification; and this applies to the incidental lyrics of his plays (as far as the data enables us to judge), as it applies to the sweep and cadence of his blank verse.[7]

On the other hand, Jonson, despite his unusual versatility in the invention and practice of new and successful lyrical forms, displays the conservative temper throughout, in avoiding mixed meters, stanzas of irregular structure or of differing lengths, and in such small matters as his careful indication of elision where the syllable exceeds the strict number demanded by the verse-scheme. Many of Jonson's utterances, too, attest his detestation of license (*e.g.*, "that Donne, for not keeping of accent, deserved hanging"); his esteem of the formal element in literature (*e.g.*, "that Shakespeare wanted art"); or his dislike to innovation.[8] Towards the close of his life, Jonson grew increasingly fond of the decasyllabic rimed couplet, the meter which was to become the maid of all work in the next generation. This meter it was that he defended in theory against the heresies of Campion and Daniel,[9] and it was in this meter that he wrote, at times with a regularity of accent and antithetical form that reminds us of the great hand of Dryden in the next age.[10] Jonson's tightening of the reins of regularity in the couplet and in lyric forms—in which latter, despite his inspiration, Herrick followed his master with loving observance of the law—is greatly in contrast with the course of dramatic blank verse, which, beginning in the legitimate freedom of Shakespeare, descended, through the looseness of Fletcher and Massinger, to the license of Davenant and Crowne.

By far the most independent lyrical metrist of this age was John Donne, who has been, it seems to me, quite as much misunderstood on this side as on the side of his eccentricities of thought and expression. In a recent chapter on Donne, in several other respects far from satisfactory, Mr. Edmund Gosse has treated this particular topic very justly. Speaking of Donne's "system of prosody," he says: "The terms 'irregular,' 'unintelligible' and 'viciously rugged,' are commonly used in describing it, and it seems even to be supposed by some critics that Donne did not know how to scan. This last supposition may be rejected at once; what there was to know about poetry was known to Donne. But it seems certain that he intentionally introduced a revolution into English versification. It was doubtless a rebellion against the smooth and somewhat nervous iambic flow of Spenser and the earliest contemporaries of Shakespeare, that Donne invented his violent mode of breaking up the line into quick and slow beats." Mr. Gosse finds this innovation the result of a desire for "new and more varied effects," adding: "The iambic rimed line of Donne has audacities such as are permitted to his blank verse by Milton, and although the felicities are rare in the older poet instead of being almost incessant, as in the later, Donne at his best is not less melodious than Milton."[11] We need not be detained by the query, whether it was not the strange personality of the poet rather than any unusual desire for "new and more varied effects" which produced a result so unusual. It is certain, that for inventive variety, fitness, and success, the lyrical stanzas of Donne are surpassed by scarcely any Elizabethan poet. In short, Donne seems to have applied to the lyric the freedom of the best dramatic verse of his age, and stood as the exponent of novelty and individualism in form precisely as Jonson stood for classic conservatism.

We have thus seen how in form as well as in thought the governing influence upon the English Elizabethan lyric was the influence of Italy, the Italy of the Renaissance; how, organically considered, there was a steady advance towards greater variety of measure and inventiveness in stanzaic form, and a general growth of taste in such matters as alliteration, the distribution of pauses, and the management of rime. As might be expected, the analogies of certain forms of verse to certain forms of thought were far less rigidly preserved in the English literature of this day than in that of Italy; and there is scarcely a form of English verse, of which it can be said that it was restricted to a given species of poetry. Spenser less completely than Sidney is the exponent of the Italianate school of poetry in England; for in Sidney is to be found not only its pastoral presentation, but the sonnet sequence and the madrigal, both long to remain the favorite utterance of contemporary lyrists. But even if Sidney was the representative of the Italianate school, the lyric took almost at once in his hands, and in those of Spenser and Shakespeare, the characteristics of a genuine vernacular utterance which it afterwards maintained, adapting itself in the minutiæ of style and versification as in the character of thought and theme. The Italian influence, although completely assimilated especially among dramatists like Dekker, Fletcher, and Beaumont, and in Browne and the later poetry of Drayton, still continued dominant in poets such as Davison, Drummond, and the writers of madrigals; but failed, as the classic influence too failed, to reach Donne. It was here that the new classic influence arose with Ben Jonson, an assimilated classicism—as far as possible removed from the imitative classicism of Harvey and Spenser in the days of the Areopagus; and it was this spirit that came finally to prevail—not that of Donne which substituted one kind of radicalism for another;—it was this spirit of conservative nicety of style and regularity of versification that led on through Herrick and Sandys to the classicism of Dryden and Pope.

Notes

1. *Lives of the English Poets*, ed. Tauchnitz, I,11.
2. *Conversations*, Shakespeare Society, p. 8.
3. *Poetical Rhapsody*, ed. Nicolas, p. xlv.
4. Edmund Gosse, *The Jacobean Poets*, 1894, p. 64.
5. *Conversations*, as above, p. 8.

6. *Life of Wotton, Lives*, etc., Amer. ed., 1846, p. 136.
7. There is a wide step in versification between *Silvia* or the *Song* from the *Merchant of Venice*, and the free cadenced songs of the *Tempest*.
8. See *Jonson's Conversations, Sh. Soc. Pub.*, p. 3.
9. See, especially, the opening passage of the *Conversations* concerning his Epic, "all in couplets, for he detesteth all other rimes. Said he had written a Discourse of Poesie, both against Campion and Daniel, . . . where he proves couplets to be the bravest sort of verse, especially when they are broken like hexameters," i.e., exhibit a strong medial cæsura.
10. See, especially, the later epistles and occasional verses, such as the *Epigrams* to the Lord Treasurer of England, *To my Muse*, etc.
11. *The Jacobean Poets*, p. 61 f.

J. B. LIGHTFOOT
"Donne, the Poet-Preacher"
Historical Essays
1896, pp. 232–45

As a layman he had been notably a poet; as a clergyman he was before all things a preacher. He had remarkable gifts as an orator, and he used them well. Henceforward preaching was the main business of his life. After he had preached a sermon, "he never gave his eyes rest," we are told, "till he had chosen out a new text, and that night cast his sermon into a form, and his text into divisions, and the next day he took himself to consult the fathers, and so commit his meditations to his memory, which was excellent."[1] On the Saturday he gave himself an entire holiday, so as to refresh body and mind, "that he might be enabled to do the work of the day following not faintly, but with courage and cheerfulness." When first ordained he shunned preaching before town congregations. He would retire to some country church with a single friend, and so try his wings. His first sermon was preached in the quiet village of Paddington. But his fame grew rapidly; and he soon took his rank as the most powerful preacher of his day in the English Church. Others envied him and murmured, says an admirer, that, having been called to the vineyard late in the day, he received his penny with the first.[2]

More than a hundred and fifty of his sermons are published. Some of them were preached at Lincoln's Inn, where he held the Lectureship; others at St. Dunstan's-in-the-West, of which church he was vicar; others at Whitehall, in his turn as Royal Chaplain, or before the Court on special occasions; others, and these the most numerous, at St. Paul's. Of this last class a few were delivered at the Cross, by special appointment, but the majority within the Cathedral, when year after year, according to the rule which is still in force at St. Paul's, he preached as Dean at the great festivals of the Church—Christmas and Easter and Whitsunday—or when he expounded the Psalms assigned to his prebendal stall, or on various incidental occasions.

An eminent successor of Donne, the late Dean Milman, finds it difficult to "imagine, when he surveys the massy folios of Donne's sermons—each sermon spreads out over many pages—a vast congregation in the Cathedral or at Paul's Cross listening not only with patience, but with absorbed interest, with unflagging attention, even with delight and rapture, to those interminable disquisitions. . . ." "It is astonishing to us," he adds, "that he should hold a London congregation enthralled, unwearied, unsatiated."[3]

And yet I do not think that the secret of his domination is far to seek.

Fervet immensusque ruit.

There is throughout an energy, a glow, an impetuosity, a force as of a torrent, which must have swept his hearers onward despite themselves. This rapidity of movement is his characteristic feature. There are faults in abundance, but there is no flagging from beginning to end. Even the least manageable subjects yield to his untiring energy. Thus he occupies himself largely with the minute interpretation of scriptural passages. This exegesis is very difficult of treatment before a large and miscellaneous congregation. But with Donne it is always interesting. It may be subtle, wire-drawn, fanciful at times, but it is keen, eager, lively, never pedantic or dull. So, again, his sermons abound in quotations from the fathers; and this burden of patristic reference would have crushed any common man. But here the quotations are epigrammatic in themselves; they are tersely rendered, they are vigorously applied, and the reader is never wearied by them. Donne is, I think, the most animated of the great Anglican preachers.

I select two or three examples out of hundreds which might be chosen, as exhibiting this eagerness of style, lit up by the genius of a poet, and heated by the zeal of an evangelist. Hear this, for instance:—

"God's house is the house of prayer. It is His court of requests. There he receives petitions; there He gives orders upon them. And you come to God in His house as though you came to keep Him company, to sit down and talk with Him half an hour; or you come as ambassadors, covered in His presence, as though ye came from as great a prince as He. You meet below, and there make your bargains for biting, for devouring usury, and then you come up hither to prayers, and so make God your broker. You rob and spoil and eat His people as bread by extortion and bribery, and deceitful weights and measures, and deluding oaths in buying and selling, and then come hither, and so make God your receiver, and His house a den of thieves. . . . As if the Son of God were but the son of some lord that had been your schoolfellow in your youth, and so you continue a boldness to him ever after; so because you have been brought up with Christ from your cradle, and catechised in His name, His name becomes reverend unto you; and *sanctum et terribile*, holy and reverend, holy and terrible, should His name be.". . .[4]

Listen to such words as I have read; and to complete the effect summon up in imagination the appearance and manner of the preacher. Recall him as he is seen in the portrait attributed to Vandyck—the keen, importuning "melting eye,"[5] the thin, worn features, the poetic cast of expression, half pensive, half gracious. Add to this the sweet tones of his voice and the "speaking action,"[6] which is described by eye-witnesses as more eloquent than the words of others, and you will cease to wonder at the thraldom in which he held his audience. "A preacher in earnest," writes Walton, "weeping sometimes *for* his auditory, sometimes *with* them; always preaching to himself; like an angel *from* a cloud but *in* none; carrying some, as St. Paul was, to heaven in holy raptures and enticing others by a sacred art and courtship to amend their lives; here picturing a vice so as to make it ugly to those who practised it, and a virtue so as to make it beloved even by those that loved it not. . . ."[7] Indeed we cannot doubt that he himself was alive to that feeling which he ascribes to the "blessed fathers" when preaching, "a holy delight to be heard and to be heard with delight."[8]

Donne's sermons are not faultless models of pulpit oratory. From this point of view they cannot be studied as the sermons of the great French preachers may be studied. Under the circumstances this was almost an impossibility. Preaching his hour's sermon once or twice weekly, he had not time to

arrange and rearrange, to prune, to polish, to elaborate. As it is, we marvel at the profusion of learning, the richness of ideas and imagery, the abundance in all kinds, poured out by a preacher who thus lived, as it were, from hand to mouth.

Moreover, the taste of the age for fantastic imagery, for subtle disquisition, for affectations of language and of thought, exercised a fascination over him. Yet even here he is elevated above himself and his time by his subject. There is still far too much of that conceit of language, of that subtlety of association, of that "sport with ideas," which has been condemned in his verse compositions; but, compared with his poems, his sermons are freedom and simplicity itself. And, whenever his theme rises, he rises too; and then in the giant strength of an earnest conviction he bursts these green withes which a fantastic age has bound about him, as the thread of tow snaps at the touch of fire. Nothing can be more direct or more real than his eager impetuous eloquence, when he speaks of God, of redemption, of heaven, of the sinfulness of human sin, of the bountifulness of Divine Love.

At such moments he is quite the most modern of our older Anglican divines. He speaks directly to our time, because he speaks to all times. If it be the special aim of the preacher to convince of sin and of righteousness and of judgment, then Donne deserves to be reckoned the first of our classic preachers. We may find elsewhere more skilful arrangement, more careful oratory, more accurate exegesis, more profuse illustration; but here is the light which flashes and the fire which burns.

Donne's learning was enormous; and yet his sermons probably owe more to his knowledge of men than to his knowledge of books. The penitent is too apt to shrink into the recluse. Donne never yielded to this temptation. He himself thus rebukes the mistaken extravagance of penitence: "When men have lived long from God, they never think they come near enough to Him, except they go beyond Him."[9] No contrition was more intense than his; but he did not think to prove its reality by cutting himself off from the former interests and associations of his life. He had been a man of the world before; and he did not cease to be a man in the world now. "Beloved"—he says this term "beloved" is his favourite mode of address—"Beloved, salvation itself being so often presented to us in the names of glory and of joy, we cannot think that the way to that glory is a sordid life affected here, an obscure, a beggarly, a negligent abandoning of all ways of preferment or riches or estimation in this world, for the glory of heaven shines down, in those beams hither. . . . As God loves a cheerful giver, so He loves a cheerful taker that takes hold of His mercies and His comforts with a cheerful heart."[10] This healthy, vigorous good sense is the more admirable in Donne, because it is wedded to an intense and passionate devotion.

I wish that time would allow me to multiply examples of his lively imagination flashing out in practical maxims and lighting up the common things of life; as, for instance, where he pictures the general sense of insecurity on the death of Elizabeth: "Every one of you in the city were running up and down like ants with their eggs bigger than themselves, every man with his bags, to seek where to hide them safely."[11] Or where he enforces the necessity of watchfulness against minor temptations: "As men that rob houses thrust in a child at the window, and he opens greater doors for them, so lesser sins make way for greater."[12] Or when he describes the little effect of preaching on the heartless listener: "He hears but the logic or the rhetoric or the ethic or the poetry of the sermon, but the sermon of the sermon he hears not."[13] Of such pithy sayings

Donne's sermons are an inexhaustible storehouse, in which I would gladly linger; but I must hasten on to speak of one other feature before drawing to a close. Irony is a powerful instrument in the preacher's hands, if he knows how to wield it; otherwise it were better left alone. The irony of Donne is piercing. Hear the withering scorn which he pours on those who think to condone sinful living by a posthumous bequest: "We hide our sins in His house by hypocrisy all our lives, and we hide them at our deaths, perchance, with an hospital. And truly we had need do so; when we have impoverished God in His children by our extortions, and wounded Him and lamed Him in them by our oppressions, we had need to provide God an hospital."[14] Or hear this again, on the criticism of sermons: "Because God calls preaching foolishness, you take God at His word and think preaching a thing under you. Hence it is that you take so much liberty in censuring and comparing preacher and preacher."[15] And lastly, observe the profound pathos and awe which are veiled under the apparent recklessness of these daring words: "At how cheap a price was Christ tumbled up and down in this world! It does almost take off our pious scorn of the low price at which Judas sold Him, to consider that His Father sold Him to the world for nothing."[16]

For preaching Donne lived; and in preaching he died. He rose from a sick-bed and came to London to take his customary sermon at Whitehall on the first Friday in Lent. Those who saw him in the pulpit, says Walton quaintly, must "have asked that question in Ezekiel, 'Do these bones live?'" The sermon was felt to be the swan's dying strain. Death was written in his wan and wasted features, and spoke through his faint and hollow voice.

The subject was in harmony with the circumstances. He took as his text[17] the passage in the Psalms, "Unto God the Lord belong the issues of death." His hearers said at the time that "Dr. Donne had preached his own funeral sermon."

The sermon was published. It betrays in part a diminution of his wonted fire and animation. We seem to see the preacher struggling painfully with his malady. But yet it is remarkable. The theme and the circumstances alike invest it with a peculiar solemnity; and there are flashes of the true-preacher still.

"This whole world," he says, "is but a universal church-yard, but one common grave: and the life and motion that the greatest persons have in it is but as the shaking of buried bodies in their graves by an earthquake."[18]

"The worm is spread under thee, and the worm covers thee. *There* is the mats and carpet that lie under, and *there* is the state and the canopy that hangs over the greatest of the sons of men."[19]

"The tree lies as it falls, it is true, but yet it is not the last stroke that fells the tree, nor the last word nor the last gasp that qualifies the man."[20]

Hear now the closing words, and you will not be at a loss to conceive the profound impression which they must have left on his hearers, as the dying utterance of a dying man:—

"There we leave you in that blessed dependency, to hang upon Him that hangs upon the Cross. There bathe in His tears, there suck at His wounds, and lie down in peace in His grave, till He vouchsafes you a resurrection and an ascension into that kingdom which He hath purchased for you with the inestimable price of His incorruptible blood. Amen."

Amen it was. He had prayed that he might die in the pulpit, or (if not this) that he might die of the pulpit; and his prayer was granted. From this sickness he never recovered; the effort hastened his dissolution; and, after lingering on a few weeks, he died on the last day of March 1631.

This study of Donne as a preacher will be fitly closed with the last stanza from his poem entitled, "Hymn to God, my God, in my sickness," which sums up the broad lesson of his life and teaching:—

> So in *His* purple wrapped, receive me, Lord;
> By these *His* thorns give me His other crown;
> And as to others' souls I preached Thy Word,
> Be this my text, my sermon to mine own:
> *Therefore, that He may raise, the Lord throws down.*[21]

Notes

1. Walton's *Life*, p. 119.
2. Elegy by Mr. R. B., attached to *Poems* by John Donne (1669), p. 393.
3. *Annals of St. Paul's Cathedral*, p. 328.
4. *Works*, vol. iii. p. 217 sq.
5. Walton's *Life*, p. 150.
6. Elegy by Mr. Mayne, attached to *Poems* by John Donne (1669), p. 387.
7. *Life*, p. 69.
8. *Works*, vol. i. p. 98.
9. *Works*, vol. ii. p. 31.
10. *Works*, vol. ii. p. 142.
11. Ibid. vol. vi. p. 137.
12. Ibid. vol. ii. p. 556.
13. Ibid. vol. i. p. 72.
14. Ibid. vol. ii. p. 555.
15. Ibid. vol. ii. p. 219.
16. Ibid. vol. i. p. 61.
17. *Life*, p. 135 sq.
18. *Works*, vol. vi. p. 283.
19. Ibid. p. 288.
20. Ibid. p. 290.
21. *Poems*, vol. ii. p. 340.

GEORGE SAINTSBURY
From "Introduction"
Poems of John Donne, ed. E. K. Chambers
1896, Vol. 1, pp. xi–xxxiii

There is hardly any, perhaps indeed there is not any, English author on whom it is so hard to keep the just mixture of personal appreciation and critical measure as it is on John Donne. It is almost necessary that those who do not like him should not like him at all; should be scarcely able to see how any decent and intelligent human creature can like him. It is almost as necessary that those who do like him should either like him so much as to speak unadvisedly with their lips, or else curb and restrain the expression of their love for fear that it should seem on that side idolatry. But these are not the only dangers. Donne is eminently of that kind which lends itself to sham liking, to coterie worship, to a false enthusiasm; and here is another weapon in the hands of the infidels, and another stumbling-block for the feet of the true believers. Yet there is always something stimulating in a subject of this kind, and a sort of temptation to attempt it.

To write anything about Donne's life, after Walton, is an attempt which should make even hardened *écrivailleurs* and *écrivassiers* nervous. That the good Izaak knew his subject and its atmosphere thoroughly; that he wrote but a very few years after Donne's own death; and that he was a writer of distinct charm, are discouraging things, but not the most discouraging. It is perhaps only those who after being familiar for years with Donne's poems, of which Walton says very little, make subsequent acquaintance with Walton's presentment of the man, who can appreciate the full awkwardness of the situation. It is the worst possible case of *pereant qui ante nos*. The human Donne whom Walton depicts is so exactly the poetical Donne whom we knew, that the effect is uncanny. Generally, or at least very frequently, we find the poet other than his form of verse: here we find him quite astoundingly akin to it.

. . . ⟨T⟩here is a strange, though by no means unexampled, division between the two periods of his life and the two classes of his work. Roughly speaking, almost the whole of at least the secular verse belongs to the first division of the life, almost the whole of the prose to the second. Again, by far the greater part of the verse is animated by what may be called a spiritualized worldliness and sensuality, the whole of the prose by a spiritualism which has left worldliness far behind. The conjunction is, I say, not unknown: it was specially prevalent in the age of Donne's birth and early life. It has even passed into something of a commonplace in reference to that Renaissance of which, as it slowly passed from south to north, Donne was one of the latest and yet one of the most perfect exponents. The strange story which Brantôme tells of Margaret of Navarre summoning a lover to the church under whose flags his mistress lay buried, and talking with him of her, shows, a generation before Donne's birth, the influence which in his day had made its way across the narrow seas as it had earlier across the Alps, and had at each crossing gathered gloom and force if it had lost lightness and colour. Always in him are the two conflicting forces of intense enjoyment of the present, and intense feeling of the contrast of the present with the future. He has at once the transcendentalism which saves sensuality and the passion which saves mysticism. Indeed the two currents run so full and strong in him, they clash and churn their waves so boisterously, that this is of itself sufficient to account for the obscurity, the extravagance, the undue quaintness which have been charged against him. He was "of the first order of poets"; but he was not of the first amongst the first. Only Dante perhaps among these greatest of all had such a conflict and ebullition of feeling to express. For, as far as we can judge, in Shakespeare, even in the Sonnets, the poetical power mastered to some extent at the very first the rough material of the poetic instinct, and prepared before expression the things to be expressed. In Dante we can trace something of the presence of slag and dross in the ore; and even in Dante we can perhaps trace faintly also the difficulty of smelting it. Donne, being a lesser poet than Dante, shows it everywhere. It is seldom that even for a few lines, seldomer that for a few stanzas, the power of the furnace is equal to the volumes of ore and fuel that are thrust into it. But the fire is always there—over-tasked, over-mastered for a time, but never choked or extinguished; and ever and anon from gaps in the smouldering mass there breaks forth such a sudden flow of pure molten metal, such a flower of incandescence, as not even in the very greatest poets of all can be ever surpassed or often rivalled.

For critical, and indeed for general purposes, the poetical works of Donne may be divided into three parts, separated from each other by a considerable difference of character and, in one case at least, of time. These are the Satires, which are beyond all doubt very early; the Elegies and other amatory poems, most of which are certainly, and all probably, early likewise; and the Divine and Miscellaneous Poems, some of which may not be late, but most of which certainly are. All three divisions have certain characteristics in common; but the best of these characteristics, and some which are not common to the three, belong to the second and third only.

It was the opinion of the late seventeenth and of the whole of the eighteenth century that Donne, though a clever man, had no ear. Chalmers, a very industrious student, and not such a bad critic, says so in so many words; Johnson undoubtedly thought so; Pope demonstrated his belief by his fresh "tagging" of the Satires. They all to some extent no doubt really believed what they said; their ears had fallen deaf to that particular concord. But they all also no doubt founded their belief to a certain extent on certain words of Dryden's which did not exactly import or comport what Mr. Pope and the rest took them to mean. Dryden had the knack, a knack of great value to a critic, but sometimes productive of sore misguiding to a critic's readers—of adjusting his comments solely to one point of view, to a single scheme in metric and other things. Now, from the point of view of the scheme which both his authority and his example made popular, Donne *was* rather formless. But nearly all the eighteenth-century critics and criticasters concentrated their attention on the Satires; and in the Satires Donne certainly takes singular liberties, no matter what scheme be preferred. It is now, I believe, pretty well admitted by all competent judges that the astonishing roughness of the Satirists of the late sixteenth century was not due to any general ignoring of the principles of melodious English verse, but to a deliberate intention arising from the same sort of imperfect erudition which had in other ways so much effect on the men of the Renaissance generally. Satiric verse among the ancients allowed itself, and even went out of its way to take, licences which no poet in other styles would have dreamt of taking. The Horace of the impeccable odes writes such a hideous hexameter as—

> Non ego, namque parabilem amo Venerem
> facilemque,

and one of the Roman satirists who was then very popular, Persius, though he could rise to splendid style on occasion, is habitually as harsh, as obscure, and as wooden as a Latin poet well can be. It is not probable, it is certain, that Donne and the rest imitated these licences of malice prepense.

But it must be remembered that at the time when they assumed this greater licence, the normal structure of English verse was anything but fixed. Horace had in his contemporaries, Persius and Juvenal had still more in their forerunners, examples of versification than which Mr. Pope himself could do nothing more "correct"; and their licences could therefore be kept within measure, and still be licentious enough to suit any preconceived idea of the ungirt character of the Satiric muse. In Donne's time the very precisians took a good deal of licence: the very Virgils and even Ovids were not apt to concern themselves very greatly about a short vowel before *s* with a consonant, or a trisyllable at the end of a pentameter. If therefore you meant to show that you were *sans gêne*, you had to make demonstrations of the most unequivocal character. Even with all this explanation and allowance it may still seem probable that Donne's Satires never received any formal preparation for the press, and are in the state of rough copy. Without this allowance, which the eighteenth century either did not care or did not know how to give, it is not surprising that they should have seemed mere monstrosities.

The satiric pieces in which these peculiarities are chiefly shown, which attracted the attention of Pope, and which, through his recension, became known to a much larger number of persons than the work of any other Elizabethan Satirist, have the least share of Donne's poetical interest. But they display to the full his manly strength and shrewd sense, and they are especially noticeable in one point. They exhibit much less of that extravagant exaggeration of contemporary vice and folly which makes one of their chief contemporaries, Marston's *Scourge of Villainy*, almost an absurd thing, while it is by no means absent from Hall's *Virgidemiarum*. We cannot indeed suppose that Donne's satire was wholly and entirely sincere, but a good deal in it clearly was. Thus his handling of the perennial subjects of satire is far more fresh, serious, and direct than is usual with Satirists, and it was no doubt this judicious and direct quality which commended it to Pope. Moreover, these poems abound in fine touches. The Captain in the first Satire—

> Bright parcel-gilt with forty dead men's pay—

the ingenious evildoers in the second—

> for whose sinful sake,
> Schoolmen new tenements in hell must make—

the charming touch at once so literary and so natural in the fifth—

> so controverted lands
> 'Scape, like Angelica, the striver's hands,

are only a few of the jewels five words long that might be produced as specimens. But it is not here that we find the true Donne: it was not this province of the universal monarchy of wit that he ruled with the most unshackled sway. The provinces that he did so rule were quite other: strange frontier regions; uttermost isles where sensuality, philosophy, and devotion meet, or where separately dwelling they rejoice or mourn over the conquests of each other. I am not so sure of the *Progress of the Soul* as some writers have been—interesting as it is, and curious as is the comparison with Prior's *Alma*, which it of necessity suggests, and probably suggested. As a whole it seems to me uncertain in aim, unaccomplished in execution. But what things there are in it! What a line is—

> Great Destiny, the Commissary of God!

What a lift and sweep in the fifth stanza—

> To my six lustres almost now outwore!

What a thought that—

> This soul, to whom Luther and Mahomet were
> Prisons of flesh!

And the same miraculous pregnancy of thought and expression runs through the whole, even though it seems never to have found full and complete delivery in artistic form. How far this curious piece is connected with the still more famous 'Anniversaries,' in which so different a stage of "progress" is reached, and which ostensibly connect themselves with the life and death of Mrs. Elizabeth Drury, is a question which it would be tedious to argue out in any case, and impossible to argue out here. But the successive stages of the 'Anatomy of the World' present us with the most marvellous poetical exposition of a certain kind of devotional thought yet given. It is indeed possible that the union of the sensual, intellectual, poetical, and religious temperaments is not so very rare; but it is very rarely voiceful. That it existed in Donne's pre-eminently, and that it found voice in him as it never has done before or since, no one who knows his life and works can doubt. That the greatest of this singular group of poems is the 'Second Anniversary,' will hardly, I think, be contested. Here is the famous passage—

> Her pure and eloquent blood
> Spoke in her cheeks and so distinctly wrought,
> That one might almost say her body thought—

which has been constantly quoted, praised, and imitated. Here, earlier, is what I should choose if I undertook the perilous task of singling out the finest line in English sacred poetry—

> so long
> As till God's great *Venite* change the song—

a *Dies Iræ* and a *Venite* itself combined in ten English syllables.

Here is that most vivid and original of Donne's many prose and verse meditations on death, as—

> A groom
> That brings a taper to the outward room.

Here too is the singular undernote of "she" repeated constantly in different places of the verse, with the effect of a sort of musical accompaniment or refrain, which Dryden (a great student of Donne) afterwards imitated on the note "you" in *Astræa Recluse*, and the *Coronation*. But these, and many other separate verbal or musical beauties, perhaps yield to the wonder of the strange, dreamy atmosphere of moonlight thought and feeling which is shed over the whole piece. Nowhere is Donne, one of the most full-blooded and yet one of the least earthly of English poets, quite so unearthly.

The Elegies, perhaps better known than any of his poems, contain the least of this unearthliness. The famous 'Refusal to Allow His Young Wife to Accompany Him as His Page,' though a very charming poem, is, I think, one of the few pieces of his which have been praised enough, if not even a little overpraised. As a matter of taste it seems to me indeed more open to exception than the equally famous and much more "fie-fied" 'To His Mistress Going to Bed,' a piece of frank naturalism redeemed from coarseness by passion and poetic completeness. The Elegies again are the most varied of the divisions of Donne's works, and contain next to the Satires his liveliest touches, such as—

> The grim, eight-foot-high, iron-bound,
> serving-man,
> That oft names God in oaths, and only than

or as the stroke—

> Lank as an unthrift's purse.

In Epithalamia Donne was good, but not consummate, falling far short of his master, Spenser, in this branch. No part of his work was more famous in his own day than his 'Epistles' which are headed by the 'Storm' and 'Calm,' that so did please Ben Jonson. But in these and other pieces of the same division, the misplaced ingenuity which is the staple of the general indictment against Donne, appears, to my taste, less excusably than anywhere else. Great passion of love, of grief, of philosophic meditation, of religious awe, had the power to master the fantastic hippogriff of Donne's imagination, and make it wholly serviceable; but in his less intense works it was rather unmanageable. Yet there are very fine things here also; especially in the Epistle to Sir Henry Goodyere, and those to Lucy Countess of Bedford, and Elizabeth Countess of Huntingdon. The best of the 'Funeral Elegies' are those of Mrs. Boulstred. In the Divine Poems there is nothing so really divine as the astonishing verse from the 'Second Anniversary' quoted above. It must always however seem odd that such a poet as Donne should have taken the trouble to tag the Lamentations of Jeremiah into verse, which is sometimes much more lamentable in form than even in matter. The epigram as to Le Franc de Pompignan's French version, and its connection, by dint of Jeremiah's prophetic power, with the fact of his having lamented, might almost, if any Englishman had had the wit to think of it, have been applied a century earlier to parts of this of Donne. The 'Litany' is far better, though it naturally suggests Herrick's masterpiece in divine song-writing; and even the 'Jeremiah' ought not perhaps to be indiscriminately disapproved. The opening stanzas especially have a fine melancholy clang not unknown, I think, as a model to Mr. Swinburne.

But to my fancy no division of Donne's poems—the 'Second Anniversary' always excepted—shows him in his quiddity and essence as do the Lyrics. Some of these are to a certain extent doubtful. One of the very finest of the whole, 'Absence, hear thou my protestation,' with its unapproached fourth stanza, appeared first in Davison's *Poetical Rhapsody* unsigned. But all the best authorities agree (and for my part I would almost go to the stake on it) that the piece is Donne's. In those which are undoubtedly genuine the peculiar quality of Donne flames through and perfumes the dusky air which is his native atmosphere in a way which, though I do not suppose that the French poet had ever heard of Donne, has always seemed to me the true antitype and fulfilment by anticipation of Baudelaire's

> Encensoir oublié qui fume
> En silence à travers la nuit.

Everybody knows the

> Bracelet of bright hair about the bone

of the late discovered skeleton, identifying the lover: everybody the perfect fancy and phrase of the exordium—

> I long to talk with some old lover's ghost
> Who died before the god of Love was born.

But similar touches are almost everywhere. The enshrining once for all in the simplest words of a universal thought—

> I wonder by my troth what thou and I
> Did till we loved?

The selection of single adjectives to do the duty of a whole train of surplusage—

> Where can we find two better hemispheres
> Without *sharp* north, without *declining* west?—

meet us, and tell us what we have to expect in all but the earliest. In comparison with these things, such a poem as 'Go and catch a falling star,' delightful as it is, is perhaps only a delightful quaintness, and 'The Indifferent' only a pleasant quip consummately turned. In these perversities Donne is but playing *tours de force*. His natural and genuine work re-appears in such poems as 'Canonizations,' or as 'The Legacy.' It is the fashion sometimes, and that not always with the worst critics, to dismiss this kind of heroic rapture as an agreeable but conscious exaggeration, partly betrayed and partly condoned by flouting-pieces like those just mentioned. The gloss does not do the critic's knowledge of human nature or his honesty in acknowledging his knowledge much credit. Both moods and both expressions are true; but the rapture is the truer. No one who sees in these mere literary or fashionable exercises, can ever appreciate such an *aubade* as 'Stay, O Sweet, and Do Not Rise,' or such a midnight piece as 'The Dream,' with its never-to-be-forgotten couplet—

> I must confess, it could not choose but be
> Profane to think thee anything but thee.

If there is less quintessence in 'The Message,' for all its beauty, it is only because no one can stay long at the point of rapture which characterizes Donne at his most characteristic, and the relaxation is natural—as natural as is the pretty fancy about St. Lucy—

> Who but seven hours herself unmasks—

the day under her invocation being in the depths of December. But the passionate mood, or that of mystical reflection, soon returns, and in the one Donne shall sing with another of the wondrous phrases where simplicity and perfection meet—

> So to engraft our hands as yet
> Was all our means to make us one,

> And pictures in our eyes to get
> Was all our propagation.

Or in the other dwell on the hope of buried lovers—

> To make their souls at the last busy day,
> Meet at this grave, and make a little stay.

I am not without some apprehension that I shall be judged to have fallen a victim to my own distinction, drawn at the beginning of this paper, and shown myself an unreasonable lover of this astonishing poet. Yet I think I could make good my appeal in any competent critical court. For in Donne's case the yea-nay fashion of censorship which is necessary and desirable in the case of others is quite superfluous. His faults are so gross, so open, so palpable, that they hardly require the usual amount of critical comment and condemnation. But this very peculiarity of theirs constantly obscures his beauties even to not unfit readers. They open him; they are shocked, or bored, or irritated, or puzzled by his occasional nastiness (for he is now and then simply and inexcusably nasty), his frequent involution and eccentricity, his not quite rare indulgence in extravagances which go near to silliness; and so they lose the extraordinary beauties which lie beyond or among these faults. It is true that, as was said above, there are those, and many of them, who can never and will never like Donne. No one who thinks *Don Quixote* a merely funny book, no one who sees in Aristophanes a dirty-minded fellow with a knack of Greek versification, no one who thinks it impossible not to wish that Shakespeare had not written the Sonnets, no one who wonders what on earth Giordano Bruno meant by *Gli eroici Furori*, need trouble himself even to attempt to like Donne. "He will never *have done* with that attempt," as our Dean himself would have unblushingly observed, for he was never weary of punning on his name.

But for those who have experienced, or who at least understand, the ups-and-downs, the ins-and-outs of human temperament, the alternations not merely of passion and satiety, but of passion and laughter, of passion and melancholy reflection, of passion earthly enough and spiritual rapture almost heavenly, there is no poet and hardly any writer like Donne. They may even be tempted to see in the strangely mixed and flawed character of his style, an index and reflection of the variety and the rapid changes of his thought and feeling. To the praise of the highest poetical art he cannot indeed lay claim. He is of course entitled to the benefit of the pleas that it is uncertain whether he ever prepared definitely for the press a single poetical work of his; that it is certain that his age regarded his youth with too much disapproval to bestow any critical care on his youthful poems. But it may be retorted that no one with the finest sense of poetry as an art, could have left things so formless as he has left, that it would have been intolerable pain and grief to any such till he had got them, even in MS., into shape. The retort is valid. But if Donne cannot receive the praise due to the accomplished poetical artist, he has that not perhaps higher but certainly rarer, of the inspired poetical creator. No study could have bettered—I hardly know whether any study could have produced—such touches as the best of those which have been quoted, and as many which perforce have been left out. And no study could have given him the idiosyncrasy which he has. *Nos passions*, says Bossuet, *ont quelque chose d'infini*. To express infinity no doubt is a contradiction in terms. But no poet has gone nearer to the hinting and adumbration of this infinite quality of passion, and of the relapses and reactions from passion, than the author of 'The Second Anniversary' and 'The Dream,' of 'The Relique' and 'The Ecstasy.'

EDMUND GOSSE
From *The Life and Letters of John Donne*
1899, Vol. I pp. 61–77, 263–69, Vol. II p. 329–44

The Lyrical Poems

When we come to consider the relation of the early poetry of Donne to that which was being produced elsewhere in England, so abundantly, during the closing years of the sixteenth century, we shall have to dwell on its curious divergence from all the established literary traditions of the time. Among these traditions, that of taking an imaginary episode in love and embroidering fancies upon it was one of the most accepted. In the more favourable instances of a pretended revelation of amatory adventure in verse, such as the *Idea* of Drayton in 1593 and 1594, or the *Amoretti* of Spenser in 1595, it is almost impossible for the most ingenious reader to build on the shadowy and nebulous basis any superstructure of conjectural biography. At first sight it may seem that Donne offers the same intangibility; but there is this difference, that, after twenty readings, the story indicated by Spenser or Drayton in his sonnets continues as vague as ever, whereas the careful study of Donne, when the first obscure crust is broken, reveals a condition of mind and even a sequence of events so personal, that we hardly dare to take our legitimate advantage from it.

We read Donne, however, to little purpose if we do not perceive that he was, above all things, sincere. His writings, like his actions, were faulty, violent, a little morbid even, and abnormal. He was not, and did not attempt to be, an average man. But actions and writings alike, in their strangeness, their aloofness, were unadulterated by a tinge of affectation. Donne was Elizabethan in his absolute straightforwardness of character; it was left to his Caroline disciples to introduce into a mode of expression founded upon his a trick of pastiche, an alloy of literary pretence. Donne, in turbid and violent language—for, with all his genius, he lacked the last ornament of a perfect style, lucidity—expressed what he himself perceived, suffered, and desired. If, therefore, we can but comprehend what Donne is saying, and realise what his character is, if we can but appreciate the curious alternations of cautious reserve and bold confession in which he indulges, if we can but discover how to stand on his own level, there is hardly a piece of his genuine verse which, cryptic though it may seem, cannot be prevailed upon to deliver up some secret of his life and character.

The dangers of such a conjectural reconstruction of biography are obvious, yet I believe that in few cases in literary history is that method more legitimate than here. When Donne speaks of his personal experience, there is something so convincing in his accent, poignant and rude at once, that it is impossible not to believe it the accurate record of a genuine emotional event. I am not unaware that, in 1625, writing to Sir Robert Ker, he said, "You know my uttermost [in verse] when it was best, and even then I did best when I had least truth for my subjects." By truth he means here what, in the evolution of his taste, he had come to regard as an excess of realism; and beyond question, what he here describes as his "best" were those pieces of metaphysical extravagance, where he had "least truth for his subjects," but embroidered conceit after conceit upon a false or trivial first idea. The Second Elegy, with its extravagant ingenuity about the elements of a fair face, the "anagram" of beauty, is a capital example of what we now have come to detest as thoroughly bad art, but of what particularly dazzled the followers of Donne, and laid the foundation of his excessive

fame as a wit. These are what Donne regarded with complacency as his "best," but to us they are little else than grotesque, the symptoms of a malady of the mind.

Very different, however, from these chains of "enormous and disgusting hyperboles," as Dr. Johnson called them, are the numerous poems in which Donne, retaining of course the tortured manner natural to him, recounted the adventures of his body and his soul. In their consideration of these poems the biographers of Donne, misled by an amiable fallacy, have not chosen to give their true weight and meaning to words about the scope of which there can be no honest question. Walton, in his exquisite portrait of his friend, has nothing at all to say of the stormy and profane youth which led up to that holy maturity of faith and unction. He chose to ignore or to forget anything which might seem to dim the sacred lustre of the exemplary Dean of St. Paul's. Yet even Walton admitted that Donne "was by nature highly passionate," and doubtless he was well aware that below the sanctity of his age lay a youth scored with frailty and the injuries of instinct. Later biographers have had less excuse for attempting to conceal those tenebrous and fiery evidences, which but add a more splendid majesty to the career rising out of them into peace and light. To pretend that Donne was a saint in his youth is to nullify the very process of divine grace in the evolution of a complex soul, in the reduction of a magnificent rebel to a still more brilliant and powerful servant. . . .

In ⟨the⟩ earliest series of his poems we find him a mere butterfly of the court, ostentatiously flitting from flower to flower, indulging his curiosity and his sensuousness wherever satisfaction is offered to him. "Women's Constancy" is the complete expression of his unattached condition of mind and body. In "Love's Usury," with the impertinence of the successful gallant, he promises to turn monogamous when he is old. In these early days his experiences are all sensation and superficial emotion. He wanders wherever his desires attract him, rifles all blossoms for their honey, boasts—in the manner of impudent youth—his detachment from all chains of duty or reflection. He is the ideal light o' love; he will pluck the rose wherever he finds it, and he is confident that for the wise youth who knows how to nip the flower discreetly there can be no thorns. The tone of these earliest lyrics is one of sceptical, even contemptuous, arrogance. In "A Fever" the mistress of the moment is ill, but it only amuses the lover. The malady is an excuse for a *feu de joie* of conceits; she may die of it, for all he really cares. In these foppish, heartless lyrics Donne is most interesting when most frankly sensual. "The Good Morrow" is the perfectly contented and serene record of an illicit, and doubtless of an ephemeral, adventure. "The Sun Rising," perhaps the strongest of the early lyrics, gives no evidence of soul, but is a fine hymn of sturdy, virile satisfaction. What could be more spirited, in its boyish way, than the opening stanza—

> Busy old fool, unruly Sun,
>   Why dost thou thus,
> Thro' windows and thro' curtains, call on us?
> Must to thy motions lovers' seasons run?
>   Saucy pedantic wretch, go chide
>   Late schoolboys and sour prentices;
> Go tell court-huntsmen that the king will ride,
>   Call country ants to harvest offices;
> Love, all alike, no season knows nor clime,[1]
> Nor hours, days, months, which are the rags of time.

From a young lover in this mood we need not be scandalised to receive such a poem as "The Flea," that extremely clever piece of impudent ribaldry, nor expect a deeper sense of the dignity of womanhood than is found in "The Indifferent," that uproarious claim to absolute freedom in love. Here Donne reminds us of a very different poet, of the nomadic Verlaine, with his "Es tu brune ou es tu blonde?—Je ne sais!" In "The Legacy," more seriously, and with an intuition of deeper feeling, Donne playfully upbraids his heart for its own too-flagrant infidelities. When he rips up his bosom to send his heart to the woman of the moment he is alarmed at first to find none there, and he suffers his first shudder, his earliest movement of conscience, in this instant, when the threatened impotency of genuine feeling suddenly chills the light tumult of his love. But in another moment he recovers his composure: all is not lost—

> Yet I found something like a heart,
> But colours it, and corners had;
> It was not good, it was not bad,
> It was entire to none, and few had part;
> As good as could be made by art
> It seemed, and therefore for our loss be sad.
> I meant to send that heart instead of mine,
> But O! no man could hold it, for 'twas thine.

Serious for a moment, with a presage of better things, the mood has changed before the stanza was over, and the lash of satire at feminine frailty leaps out. Of this arrogance of juvenile cynicism the mandrake song remains the most poetical expression—

> If thou be'st born to strange sights,
>   Things invisible to see,
> Ride ten thousand days and nights
>   Till age snow white hairs on thee,
> Thou, when thou return'st, wilt tell me
> All strange wonders that befell thee,
>   And swear
>   Nowhere
> Lives a woman true and fair.
>
> If thou find'st one, let me know;
>   Such a pilgrimage were sweet.
> Yet do not, I would not go,
>   Though at next door we might meet.
> Tho' she were true when you met her,
> And last till you write your letter,
>   Yet she
>   Will be
> False, ere I come, to two or three.

. . . His life since manhood had been haunted by all the phantoms of infidelity. He had been pursuing with frenzy an illusive chimera of pleasure. But in spite of all his impudent protests, the strong heart of John Donne could not be satisfied by these ephemeral captures. His passions were now dominant and his blood imperious. The instinct that drives vehement young men to acts of madness was violent in him. He had been looking around him for an adventure, for some liaison which could give him the measure of his own vital intensity. If the moralists will allow us to say so, his ethical ambition had risen a grade, from the pursuit of woman as a species to the selection of one who should present herself to his imagination as a symbol of the Feminine. We must remember, to comprehend the conditions depicted in the "Songs and Sonnets" and the "Elegies," that we have to do with no simple pastoral swain, but with one of the most headstrong and ingenious intellects of the century, now, for the time being, concentrating itself on the evolution of its own *vita sexualis*. And we must remember, too, that it was from these agonies and errors, bleeding as from rods with the wounds of passion, that Donne rose slowly to those spiritual heights in which he so glorified the grace of God.

But to such a nature, so roused even in the storm of illicit passion, there was but a short space for complete satisfaction. At first the crushing of "joy's grape," as Keats puts it, excluded every other sentiment, and Donne composed—we dare not allow ourselves to overlook the fact—some of the most sensual poetry written in the history of English literature by any poet of eminence. It was, perhaps, needful that he should go off to the Islands, since the liaison was carried on in the first instance with astonishing effrontery. The husband was a deformed man, and was stationary all day in a basket-chair. This gave the lovers confidence, but the lady, as Donne tells her in one of the later denunciatory pieces, was dull in speech and unready in mind. Their secret meetings, stolen correspondence, and artificial language were, no doubt, thoroughly after Donne's own ingenious heart, but they distracted and alarmed the lady. With singular complacency, alluding to her original want of cleverness, he says that he has "refined her into a blissful paradise." "The Apparition" shows that Donne did too well his work of awakening those slumbering faculties which the roughness and jealousy of her husband had crushed so long. On this subject the Seventh Elegy throws a curious light.

But when he returned from the Azores, and took up once more those vows of constancy which had been sealed during his absence by stealthy means—"we can love by letters still, and gifts"—there seems evidence of a change in the poet's sentiments. By a perverse ingenuity very characteristic of him, he reversed the process which had made the easy seduction of the lady grateful to his vanity, and in that very fact, no longer flattering to him, he sees a proof of her lack of stability and value. He discovers her to be less youthful than he thought her, and, in the reflex of his passion, her autumnal sensuality exasperates him. She overdoes the mysteries of their meetings, the alphabet of flowers, the secret messengers, the elaborate and needless subterfuges. The Thirteenth Elegy is, doubtless, the expression of this turn of the tide. She is still his "dove-like friend," still in profuse and burning couplets his love rages when he thinks upon her. Yet he upbraids the passion which he cannot resist, and even the lady he still worships—

> Was't not enough that thou didst hazard us
> To paths in love so dark and dangerous,
> And those so ambush'd round with household spies,
> And over all thy husband's towering eyes?

He begins to feel the horror and the ridicule of the intimate feast under the light of the family candlesticks, where the afflicted and jealous husband, daring not to complain openly in words, yet

> Swollen and pamper'd with great fare,
> Sits down and snorts, caged in his basket-chair.

The poet's first revolt is a refusal to meet in the lady's own house—

> Now I see many dangers; for it is
> His realm, his castle, and his diocese.

As yet, Donne still exults in the betrayal, but the Nemesis of his sin is falling upon him. They must part, make fewer meetings, run less risk; "she must go, and I must mourn." He permits the symptoms of a growing lassitude in himself to be perceived; there follow angry words, and those recriminations that are so surely the death of love. The Third Elegy marks a sense of her declining devotion to him, and characteristically, although he cools to her, his pride is exquisitely wounded at her becoming less ardent to him. In a note of mingled mockery and trepidation he recommends to her an "apostasy" that may confirm her love, and in a brilliant flash of caprice informs her that

> Change is the nursery
> Of music, joy, life and eternity.

Does she take him at his word, or does he mistake her timorous withdrawal for the heart's act of treason? We cannot tell, but the sources of his forbidden joy are poisoned, and jealousy stings him at last to vehement and gross attack. There are no hate-poems in the language finer of their kind, filled with a stronger wind of vindictive passion, than those which now close this incident.

To distribute these lyrics according to the order of their composition would be preposterous. They possess a close similarity of style; they were probably written at short intervals, all possibly in the summer of 1597. "The Curse" is an expression of the angry lover's first rage; but he comforts himself that his mistress has been extremely discreet and secret, and that the open ridicule of defeat may be spared him. "The Message" breathes the same egotistical spirit, and denounces the forced fashions and false passions which have fooled him and destroyed him. He perversely parodies Marlowe's beautiful pastoral song to satirise those hands and eyes that, as he believes, have been his ruin—

> Let others freeze with angling reeds,
> And cut their legs with shells and weeds,
> Or treach'rously poor fish beset,
> With strangling snare or windowy net.
>
> Let coarse bold hands from slimy nest
> The bedded fish in banks out-wrest;
> Or curious traitors, sleeve-silk flies,
> Bewitch poor fishes' wandering eyes.

With all his rage, he feels himself still drawn to the false one, with agonising threads of desire; and "Love's Deity," with the enchanting melody of its opening couplet, gives expression to his torture—

> I long to talk with some old lover's ghost,
> Who died before the God of Love was born;
> I cannot think that he who, then, loved most,
> Sunk so low as to love one which did scorn.
> But since this God produced a destiny,
> And that vice-nature, custom, lets it be,
> I must love her that loves not me.

Here the note is as the note of Catullus—

> Odi et amo. Quare id faciam fortasse requiris.
> Nescio, sed fieri sentio et excrucior.

To this period also we may assign the passionate wilfulness of "The Prohibition"—

> Take heed of loving me;
> At least remember, I forbade it thee.
> Not that I shall repair my unthrifty waste
> Of breath and blood upon thy sighs and tears,
> By being to me then what to me thou wast;
> But so great joy our life at once outwears.
> Then, lest that love by my dearth frustrate be,
> If thou love me,—take heed of loving me.

"The Will" carries us on a further step to acrid scorn and contemptuous satire. He will die, smitten by great Love, to whom, however, he prays for a moment's respite, that he may make some legacies. His codicils are burning ironies; he gives—

> My tongue to Fame; to ambassadors mine ears;
> To women—or the sea—my tears.

Jealousy has now taken possession of him. He fancies that his mistress has had twenty lovers before him, that she entertains younger lovers now. In the midst of the boisterous cynicism of this poem there are touches which we like to note—

> My constancy I to the planets give;
> My truth to them who at the court do live;
> Mine ingenuity and openness
> To Jesuits; to buffoons my pensiveness;
> My silence to any, who abroad have been;
> My money to a Capuchin;

and this—

> To him for whom the passing-bell next tolls,
> I give my physic-books; my written rolls
> Of moral counsels I to Bedlam give;
> My brazen medals unto them which live
> In want of bread; to them which pass among
> All foreigners, my English tongue.

Much more serious, indeed of a noble and resigned melancholy, is "The Funeral," in which he announces that he is "Love's martyr," and, by an image which had impressed his fancy so much that he repeats it in several poems, announces that when they come to enshroud his body, they will find

> That subtle wreath of hair, which crowns my arm,
> The mystery, the sign you must not touch,

all that remains to him now of one loved so passionately and proved to be so false. Since she will now have none of him, he will at least bury some of her, and at the Last Day, when the bodies stir, his arm will be seen to wave with "a bracelet of bright hair about the bone."

But all these poems of hatred and enforced resignation pale before "The Apparition," in which, as he tosses between sleep and waking, the horror of his situation, the vileness of the woman he has loved, and the whole squalor of the outworn liaison come upon him and overwhelm him. The fierce passion in this brief lyric, a "hate-poem" of the very first class, is closely akin to those flashes of lurid light in which the contemporary tragedians excelled, "steeping us," as Charles Lamb says, "in agonies infernal." Such error, however, as Donne had indulged in could be washed out in no less bitter waters. "The Apparition" is brief, and must be read complete to produce the terrific effect of its reluctant malediction—

> When by thy scorn, O murderess, I am dead,
> And that thou think'st thee free
> From all solicitation from me,
> Then shall my ghost come to thy bed,
> And thee, feign'd vestal, in worse arms shall see;
> Then thy sick taper will begin to wink,
> And he, whose thou art then, being tired before,
> Will, if thou stir, or pinch to wake him, think
> Thou call'st for more,
> And, in false sleep, will from thee shrink:
> And then, poor aspen wretch, neglected thou,
> Bathed in a cold quicksilver sweat wilt lie
> A verier ghost than I.
> *What I will say, I will not tell thee now,*
> Lest that preserve thee; and since my love is spent,
> I'd rather thou should'st painfully repent,
> Than by my threatenings rest still innocent.

This is the culmination of the incident, the flames of hatred now quickly subsiding into a heap of the ashes of indifference and satiety. This exhausted cynicism is interpreted by "Love's Alchemy," where the poet protests that all women are alike vile, and the elixir of happiness an imposture not to be discovered by any alchemist who "glorifies his pregnant pot," only to be fooled and disenchanted. So, also, in a most curious ode, the "Nocturnal upon St. Lucy's Day," amid fireworks of conceit, he calls his mistress dead, and protests that his hatred has grown calm at last. So this volcanic passion sinks back into its crater at length, leaving this series of astonishing poems to illustrate it, poems which, as Donne himself says, are "as all-confessing and through-shine" as glass itself. When he grew supine once more, he reflected, rather splenetically, on his want of common prudence in this revelation of the adventures of the soul. As he said to Rowland Woodward, he had shown these "love-song weeds and satiric thorns" to too many of his friends to be able to quench the incident in oblivion, and too many copies of them had been made by his private admirers to preclude their circulation.

Donne, in his own words, had "stained" his soul's "first white," but his conduct from this time forth seems to have given no scandal. One or two love-passages appear to have ruffled the tenour of the wave of life which was carrying him towards the bourne of matrimony. He sees and is the sudden victim of beauty again and again.

His sensitive heart is ingenious in self-torture, and to what extremities it still can fling him we read in "The Blossom." The lady of the moment has left him a week ago, and in three weeks more he is to meet her in London. In subtle, modulated verse his heart taunts and plagues him, for he no longer knows what he desires nor what he is. His previous adventures have made him cautious, even sceptical, and he will not frankly give way to this sweet, insidious hope. He apostrophises his own trembling heart, which knows not whether to bide with him or to follow the new and desired mistress—

> Well then, stay here; but know,
> When thou hast stay'd and done thy most,
> A *naked thinking heart, that makes no show,*
> *Is to a woman but a kind of ghost;*
> How shall she know my heart?

To the same vague category of emotions which faintly stirred the poet between his great criminal liaison and his ultimate betrothal, I am inclined also to attribute, on internal and structural evidence, the Tenth Elegy, as well as, perhaps, the extremely fantastic lyric called "The Ecstasy," with its obsession on the word "violet"; this had, unquestionably, at the time of its composition an illuminating meaning which time has completely obscured. A few of the Epistles, too, may belong to this early period, and one of the most important of these, the second to Sir Henry Wotton, I am able for the first time to date. This poem is given in the Westmoreland MS., in my possession, with the heading, "To Mr. H. W. 20 July 1598. At Court." But the majority of the Letters in Verse, and probably all the Divine Poems, belong to a period subsequent to the poet's marriage.

To any date earlier than that of his own marriage may be assigned a poem which holds a somewhat unique position in the rolls of Donne's undoubted writings. In the "Epithalamion made at Lincoln's Inn" he drops his accustomed manner and closely imitates the imagery, the prosody, and the tone of Spenser. His own peculiar individuality lies below the rich Spenserian embroidery, and the result has a mellifluous glow which we could wish to see more frequent in Donne. The occasion of this stately, sensuous ode is uncertain; all we know is that the bridegroom was one who was a member of the Inn, and not an assiduous one, for he combined "study" with "play" in it. So impersonal is the poem, so made to order, that we know not whether to indulge a guess that the nuptials of Christopher Brooke form its theme. If it were suggested that Donne's own secret marriage was here celebrated, we should be unable to reject the idea on any internal evidence. In this class of Elizabethan poem the best of men permitted themselves so fescennine a liberty, that it is difficult to give a spec-

imen to modern readers; this stanza, however, represents the poem not unfairly—

> Daughters of London, you which be
> Our golden mines and furnish'd treasury,
> You which are angels, yet still bring with you
> Thousands of angels on your marriage days,
> Help with your presence, and devise to praise
> These rites, which also unto you grow due;
> Conceitedly dress her, and be assign'd
> By you fit place for every flower and jewel;
> Make her for love fit fuel,
> As gay as Flora and as rich as Ind;
> So may she, fair and rich, in nothing lame,
> To-day put on perfection and a woman's name.

The pun about "angels"—the divine ministrants and the earthly coin—was a favourite one with Donne. In the Eleventh Elegy he plays upon it until we lose all patience with so much self-satisfied ingenuity—

> *Angels,* which heaven commanded to provide
> All things to me, and be my faithful guide,
> To gain new friends, to appease great enemies,
> To comfort my soul, when I lie or rise;

or—

> Twelve righteous *angels,* which as yet
> No leaven of vile solder did admit;

or—

> Pity these *angels* yet; their dignities
> Pass Virtues, Powers, and Principalities.

The extravagance might be pardoned once, but its recurrence is more and more intolerable. Yet it was precisely this dross and slag of his genius which endeared Donne as a poet to his immediate followers. . . .

Divine Poems

The Divine Poems of Donne offer considerable difficulty to his biographer. A few of them already are, or can approximately be, dated, but the majority are subject to conjecture founded upon internal evidence. They are of two orders; there are hymns and spiritual poems of Donne's which, however rugged their form, breathe a fervid spirit of faith and a genuine humility. In others the intellectual element outweighs the religious. These verses are rather extremely ingenious exercises in metrical theology than bursts of impulsive piety. It may be broadly suggested that the latter belong to the second, and the former to the third or final, division of Donne's career. That is to say, the more metaphysical pieces are the outcome of the years when religious inquiry formed one of his prominent studies, but when no exclusive call had summoned him to the ministry. In form all the sacred poetry of Donne suffers from his determination to introduce Spanish effects into English prosody, and Spanish ingenuities into the expression of English thought. If Donne's early hymns and litanies do not move us, it is largely due to the fact that they did not move himself. They are frigid, they are stiffened with legal and medical phraseology, the heart of a sinner saved does not beat beneath their "cross and correct concupiscence of wit."

An excess of ingenuity is peculiarly fatal to the unction of religious poetry. Unless it is spontaneous, unless it palpitates with ecstasy or moans with aspiration, unless it is the outpouring of a contrite spirit, it leaves upon the listener a sense of painful artificiality. The dogmatic verses of Donne do not escape from this disability. We admit their cleverness, and are sure that it is misplaced. The solemn mystery of Christ's three days' sojourn in the tomb is not, for instance, illuminated when Donne speaks of Him as one

> Whose body, having walk'd on earth, and now
> Hasting to heaven, would—that He might allow
> Himself unto all stations and fill all—
> For those three days become a mineral.
> He was all gold when He lay down, but rose
> All tincture, and doth not alone dispose
> Leaden and iron wills to good, but is
> Of power to make e'en sinful flesh like His.

Here Donne's intellectual arrogance stood him in evil stead. He would not continue and intensify the tradition of such gentle Catholic singers of the Elizabethan age as Southwell and Constable; the hymns of Wither he had probably never seen, and would have despised; he shows not the slightest sign of having read the noblest religious poem written between the *Vision of Piers Plowman* and *Paradise Lost*, that *Christ's Victory and Triumph* which Giles Fletcher published just when Donne was moving into Drury House in 1610. He had doubtless read, without advantage to his style, Sylvester's popular version of the *Divine Weeks and Works*. But he disdained all that was purely English. His sympathy with Elizabethan verse, good or bad, was a negative quality, and we can scarcely trace that he allowed himself to be even conscious of the existence of Spenser or Shakespeare. Among his English contemporaries he admired but one poet, Ben Jonson, and to him he was attracted by the very qualities which we now recognise as being anti-Elizabethan. Hence, in the history of literature, the sacred poetry of Donne is interesting mainly for its resolute independence of all existing English types, and for its effect in starting a new and efficient school of religious verse in which many of the disciples far exceeded the master. Donne prophesied, while those poets were not born or were but children, of George Herbert, of Crashaw, of the Vaughans, of Herrick in the *Noble Numbers*, of Cowley in the *Davideis*; and when we come to consider his posthumous glory we shall have to return to his crabbed and litigious early sacred poetry.

Of Donne's spiritual poems the most important, if we omit the two cycles of "Holy Sonnets," which belong to a later period, is that which he called "A Litany." He composed it in his bed, during his tedious illness at Mitcham in 1609, and he sent it to Sir Henry Goodyer with a learned note on the Litaneia, or public form of chanted prayer to God, and on its use in the Primitive Church. His own specimen is composed in a curious measure of his invention, in grave lines with an odd singing break in the middle of each stanza, an artifice from which, it is only fair to say, he rarely extracts so much charm as we might reasonably expect. The "Litany" is burdened with ingenuity. From a dogmatic point of view it shows Donne still imperfectly divorced from the tenets of Rome. He still proclaims the efficacy of the Virgin Mary's prayers to God the Father for souls on earth. Donne, who was much occupied at this time with the principle of martyrdom, dedicates these stanzas to the martyrs and confessors—

> And since Thou so desirously
> Didst long to die, that long before thou could'st
> And long since Thou no more could'st die,
> Thou in thy scatter'd mystic body would'st
> In Abel die; and ever since
> In Thine; let their blood come
> To beg for us a discreet patiënce
> Of death, or of worse life; for O, to some
> Not to be martyrs is a martyrdom.
>
> Therefore with thee triumpheth there

> A virgin squadron of white cónfessors,
> Whose bloods betroth'd, not married, were,
> Tender'd, not taken, by those ravishers.
> They know, and pray that we may know,
> In every Christian
> Hourly tempestuous persecutions grow;
> Temptations martyr us alive; a man
> Is to himself a Diocletian.

The ingenious darkness of Donne's poetical expression never went further or achieved a richer gloom than it does in some of his Sacred Poems. The "Litany" is certainly not for use by the poor of the flock. The intellectual dangers so strangely petitioned against in the following stanza do not certainly afflict many humble-minded Christians, although they were real enough to Donne—

> That learning, Thine ambassador,
> From Thine allegiänce we never tempt;
> That beauty, paradise's flower,—
> For physic made,—from poison be exempt;
> That wit,—born apt high good to do—
> By dwelling lazily
> On Nature's nothing be not nothing too;
> That our affections kill us not, nor die;
> Hear us, weak echoes, O Thou Ear and Eye.

One more stanza may be given from this highly metaphysical poem, in which a considerable flower of beauty is choked by the weeds of pedantry and misplaced intelligence—

> From being anxious, or secure,
> Dead clods of sadness, or light squibs of mirth,
> From thinking that great courts immure
> All, or no happiness, or that this earth
> Is only for our prison fram'd;
> Or that Thou'rt covetous
> To them whom Thou lovest, or that they are maim'd
> From reaching this world's sweet who seek Thee thus,
> With all Thy might, Good Lord, deliver us.

A poem which we can exactly date is that written for Good Friday 1613. Donne had been staying at Polesworth, in Warwickshire, with Sir Henry Goodyer, and he set forth on horseback to visit Magdalen Herbert and her son, Sir Edward, at Montgomery Castle. Six years earlier he had sent to this beloved lady "holy hymns and sonnets," of which but one survives, the quatorzain beginning—

> Her of your name, whose fair inheritance
> Bethina was, and jointure Magdalo.

He now, looking forward to the joys of high spiritual converse with these elected friends, sends to him whom he leaves at Polesworth a meditation on the day. He is more direct and less tortured than usual—

> I am carried towards the west,
> This day, when my soul's form bows to the East;
> There I should see a Sun by rising set,
> And by that setting endless day beget;
> But that Christ on His cross did rise and fall,
> Sin had eternally benighted all.
> Yet dare I almost be glad, I do not see
> That spectacle of too much weight for me;
> Who sees God's face, that is self-life, must die,—
> What a death were it then to see God die!

That is impressive, and comparatively simple; but a spasm of his disease of style catches him, and he proceeds—

> It made His own lieutenant, Nature, shrink,
> It made His footstool crack, and the sun wink.

> Could I behold those hands, which span the poles
> And tune all spheres at once, pierced with those holes?
> Could I behold that endless height, which is
> Zenith to us and our antipodes,
> Humbled below us?

Nothing could be more odious; yet, such was the taste of the day that, no doubt, when he read these verses that evening in Montgomery Castle, the noble Herberts were not merely astonished, but charmed and edified.

We may confidently attribute "The Cross" to the Mitcham period. It shows Donne still more indignant at the obstinacy of political recusants than convinced with regard to the dogmas which separate Rome from the Reformed Churches. He writes here precisely as any fervent Italian or Spanish monk might do—

> From me no pulpit, nor misgrounded law,
> Nor scandal taken, shall this cross withdraw,

and he rejoices to see its emblem in every manifestation of natural force—

> Look down, thou spiest out crosses in small things;
> Look up, thou seest birds rais'd on cross'd wings;
> All the globe's frame, and spheres, is nothing else
> But the meridian's crossing parallels.

In composing these early sacred poems, although he was at the very time fighting with Morton for the Anglicans, he could not but look back to Rome as the real arbiter, and he had no warmer excuse to make for his odes and litanies than that the Roman Church herself need not call them defective.

It is to be observed that the early and amatory writings of Donne contain no single example of the sonnet, and that with the exception of one or two unimportant epistles in the quatorzain form, all his work in this class is to be found among his divine poems. He disdained the softness and vagueness of the Petrarchists, and had no ambition to compete with Drayton or Daniel in their addresses to a dimly-outlined Idea or Delia. The form he ultimately adopted for his sonnets is neither purely Italian, nor purely Elizabethan. He had not Milton's courage in recurring to the splendid fulness of the sonnet of Petrarch, but he eschewed the laxity of the English writers of his age; and though we have to regret that he adopted the final couplet, his octett is of perfect arrangement, and boasts but two rhymes. It is strange that he did not perceive how much his sonnets lose in grandeur by this concession to triviality in the sestett. It is part, however, of Donne's irremediable imperfection as an artist, that he has produced much noble poetry in his divine sonnets, and yet not one sonnet that can be considered faultless.

The style of this section of his poetry is extremely characteristic of himself and of certain exotic influences of his time. When he was in Italy, he must have been familiar with Tansillo and Molza, the polished Petrarchists of the age, who celebrated love and religion with an equal refinement. But he is not more touched by their manner of writing than by that of Spenser. Underneath the graceful accomplishment of the Cinque Cento, however, there ran hidden the vehement stream of speculative philosophic style, rugged and bold, and it was this which attracted Donne. With Galileo we know that he had a close sympathy. Did he dip with curiosity into the forbidden writings of Galileo's fellow-martyr, Giordano Bruno? We know not; yet here at least was an Italian with whom Donne had not a little fellowship in the construction of his mind. He had still more with that of a Dominican monk who was more exactly his contemporary, and of whose misfortunes he cannot fail to have heard. The Sonnets of Campanella have more kinship with "La Corona" and the Ecclesiastical Sonnets of Donne than with any other English writings. Yet neither poet can well have read the work of the other, and it is even a stretch of probability to hope that Donne may have seen the obscure volume of Campanella's poems which the German, Tobias Adami, published in 1622. The similarity is accidental, and is founded upon a certain double sympathy with the obscurity and with the heterodoxy of the strange Italian pantheists of the age. Had Donne been born south of the Alps, his work might probably have taken a less tormented form than it actually adopted, but his body would almost certainly have been tortured with Campanella's, if by a happy fate it escaped the stake with Vanini's. . . .

The Influence of Donne

In examining the remarkable wide and deep, though almost entirely malign, influence of Donne upon the poetry of this country, it is necessary first of all to dwell on the complete intellectual isolation of his youth and middle age. The Elizabethan poets were, as a rule, a sociable and sympathetic body of men. They acted and interacted upon one another with vivacity; they met at frequent intervals to encourage themselves in the art they exercised and to read each other's verses. The habit which sprang up of contributing strings of complimentary effusions to accompany the published efforts of a friend was symptomatic of the gregarious tendency of the age. So, even, were the fierce feuds and noisy, rather than envenomed, encounters which periodically thrilled the poetic world. It was not hatred, so much, or even jealousy, which inspired these famous battles, as the inevitability that in a society, the atoms of which hustled about so rapidly in the immediate neighbourhood of the rest, collisions should occasionally occur. In the last years of Elizabeth and the first years of James, London swarmed with poets and poeticules, and each of these was, more or less, in personal relation with the others.

Herein lies the first peculiarity of Donne. After the juvenile concession to the taste of the hour, implied in his *Satires* of 1593 and onward, he gave no further hostages to the fashion. Nor do we find that he paid any attention to the leaders of literature whom it was inevitable that he should meet at Court or in the taverns. At no period even of his youth does he seem to have been impressed by the fame of his English compeers, to have felt admiration or even curiosity in their work. One is left with the impression that Donne would not have turned to see Edmund Spenser go by, nor have passed into an inner room at the Mermaid to listen to the talk of Shakespeare. His was the scornful indifference of the innovator, the temperament of the man born to inaugurate a new order of taste. . . .

It is a curious fact that Jonson alone, of those who in the first half of the seventeenth century discussed the characteristics of Donne's style, commented on the peculiarities of his metre. This would seem to have filled even his fondest disciples with horror, and it is much to be doubted whether they understood the principle upon which he worked. On this point, successive critics have agreed in finding Donne an unpardonable sinner. It seems even to be supposed by some writers that the curious condition of his early verse is due to ignorance, and that Donne did not know how to scan. As to this, I can but repeat, what I have said before,[2] that what there was to know about prosody was, we may be sure, perfectly known by Donne. But it is evident that he intentionally essayed to introduce a revolution into English versification. One of the main objections he took to the verse of his youth was that it was so mellifluous, sinuous, and soft. A five-syllabled iambic line of Spenser or of Daniel trots along with the gentlest amble of inevitable shorts and longs. Donne thought that the line should be broken up into successive quick and slow beats. The conventional line vexed his ear with its insipidity, and it doubtless appeared to him that his great predecessors had never completely shaken off a timidity and monotony which had come down to them from Surrey and Gascoigne. It is possible that he wished to improve on the rhymed verse of Spenser, as Shakespeare had improved on the blank verse of Sackville.

The curious ruggedness of the *Satires* and *Elegies* becomes comprehensible only when we adopt some such theory I have suggested. Part of Donne's iconoclasm consisted in his scorn of the flaccid beat of the verse of the sonnetteers. He desired greatly to develop the orchestral possibilities of English verse, and I have remarked that the irregular lyrics of Mr. Robert Bridges and the endless experiments of the Symbolists in France are likely to be far more fruitful to us in trying to understand Donne's object, than any conventional repetition of the accepted rules of prosody. The iambic rhymed line of Donne has audacities such as are permitted to his blank verse by Milton; and although the felicities are rare in the older poet, instead of being almost incessant as in the younger, Donne at his best is not less melodious than Milton. One of his most famous traps for the ear, is the opening line of "Twickenham Garden," which the ordinary reader is ever tempted to dismiss as not being iambic verse at all. We have to recognise in it the poet's attempt to identify the beat of his verse with his bewildered and dejected state, reading it somewhat in this notation:—

Blásted | with sighs || and | surroúnded | with teárs.

It is almost certain that this intrepid shifting about at will of the accent is a symptom of youth in the poem, that we can almost, that is to say, approximately, date any given piece of his by the degree in which this prosodical violence is sustained.[3] After middle-life, Donne dropped the experiment more and more completely, having found, no doubt, that his closest friends were by no means certain to comprehend what he meant by the rapid changes of the instrument; nor, in reading to themselves, could produce the effect which he had intended. These variations of cadence, then, must be looked upon as a peculiarity not essential to Donne's style, nor persistent in it, but as a studied eccentricity of his youth. At his very best, as in

> I long to talk with some old lover's ghost,
> Who died before the God of Love was born,

or as in

> A naked, thinking heart, that makes no show,
> Is to a woman but a kind of ghost,

there is no trace of this "not keeping of accent," which puzzled and enraged Ben Jonson.

His conscious isolation, no doubt, made Donne hesitate to press his poetry upon his own generation. He found its flavour, the strong herbal perfume of it, not agreeable in the nostrils of the latest Elizabethans. Neither the verse, nor the imagination, nor the attitude of soul were what people in 1600 were ready to welcome, or even to apprehend. We can imagine Donne rather wistfully saying—

> Ho io appreso quel che, s'io ridico,
> A molti fia savor di forte agrume,[4]

and this may have been a main reason why he refrained from publication. He kept his rosemary and his marjoram, his rough odorous herbs, to himself. . . .

What these young poets (who emulated Donne between 1620 and 1650) saw in Donne, and what attracted them so passionately to him, was the concentration of his intellectual personality. He broke through the tradition; he began as if poetry had never been written before; he, as Carew says—

> open'd us a mine
> Of rich and pregnant fancy.

He banished the gods and goddesses from his verse, not a Roundhead fiercer than he in his scorn of "those old idols." He wiped away "the wrong" which the English language in its neopagan raptures had "done the Greek or Latin tongue." His gigantic fancy put such a strain upon the resources of the English language, that its "tough, thick-ribb'd hoops" almost burst beneath the pressure. The earlier Elizabethan writers had been "libertines in poetry"; Donne recalled them to law and order. This is how Carew describes the extraordinary emotion caused by the first reading of Donne's poems—

> the flame
> Of thy brave soul, that shot such heat and light
> As burned our earth and made our darkness bright,
> Committed holy rapes upon the will,
> Did through the eye the melting heart distil,
> And the deep knowledge of dark truths did teach.

Once again, Donne has

> open'd us a mine
> Of rich and pregnant fancy, drawn a line
> Of masculine expression . . .
> Thou shalt yield no precedence, but of time,—

that is to say, the ancient poets have no advantage of originality over thee, save the purely accidental one of having been born in an earlier age.

When we turn to Donne's poems, but in particular to his lyrics, and endeavour to find out what it was which excited these raptures of appreciation, we are at first unable to accept the seventeenth-century point of vision. Nothing is more difficult than to be certain that we value in the old poets what their contemporaries valued. Those pieces of Shakespeare which are on every tongue to-day, and excite our unbounded admiration, are not alluded to by any of his contemporaries. We have no evidence that a single friend of Milton saw what we all see in the central part of "L'Allegro" or in "At a Solemn Music." What contemporary criticism found in Herrick was "a pretty flowery and pastoral gale of fancy, in a vernal prospect of some hill, cave, rock, or fountain." We ask ourselves, in despair, what can the people who wrote such words have seen in "Gather the Rosebuds While Ye May," or in "Bid Me to Live"? In the same way, we have the greatest difficulty in constraining ourselves to regard Donne's verse from the point of view and in the light of its early, enthusiastic readers of 1620.

Perhaps we cannot do better than read over again an entirely typical poem, written towards the middle of his career, and illustrating, without extravagance, the very peculiarities which Donne's disciples admired. For this purpose, "Twickenham Garden" may serve as well as any:—

> Blasted with sighs, and surrounded with tears,
>   Hither I come to seek the spring,
> And at mine eyes, and at mine ears,
>   Receive such balms as else cure every thing.
>   But O! self-traitor, I do bring
> The spider Love, which transubstantiates all,
>   And can convert manna to gall;
> And that this place may thoroughly be thought
> True paradise, I have the serpent brought.
>
> 'Twere wholesomer for me that winter did
>   Benight the glory of this place,
> And that a grave frost did forbid
>   These trees to laugh and mock me to my face;
>   But that I may not this disgrace
> Endure, nor yet leave loving, Love, let me
>   Some senseless piece of this place be;
> Make me a mandrake, so I may grow here,
> Or a stone fountain weeping out my year.

Hither with crystal phials, lovers, come,
    And take my tears, which are love's wine,
And try your mistress' tears at home,
    For all are false, that taste not just like mine.
    Alas! hearts do not in eyes shine,
Nor can you more judge woman's thoughts by tears
    Than, by her shadow, what she wears.
O perverse sex, where none is true but she
Who's therefore true, because her truth kills me.

If we compare this with an analogous piece of ordinary Elizabethan or early Jacobean poetry, we observe, first of all, that it is tightly packed with thought. As to the value of the thought, opinions may differ, but of the subtlety, the variety, and the abundance of mental movement in this piece there can be no question. The Elizabethan poet had held a mirror up to nature; Donne (the illustration is almost his own) shivered the glass, and preserved a reflection from every several fragment. This redundancy of intellectual suggestion was one of Donne's principal innovations.

In the second place, we notice an absence of all conventional or historical ornament. There is no mention here of "cruel Amaryllis," or "great Pan," or "the wanton shears of Destiny." A rigid adherence to topics and to objects familiar to the non-poetical reader of the moment is strictly observed. This, as I suppose, was another of the main sources of Donne's fascination; he was, in a totally new and unprecedented sense, a realist. In this he revolted with success against all the procedure of the Renaissance, and is, in his turbid and unskilful way, the forerunner of modern Naturalism in English poetry. This is an aspect of his influence which has been strangely overlooked, and, no doubt, for this reason, that what was realistic in the reign of James I. seems utterly old-fangled and antiquarian in that of Victoria; so that the poetry of Donne, instead of striking us—as it did his contemporaries—as amazingly fresh and new in its illustrations, strikes us as unspeakably moth-eaten and decrepid. In this poem of "Twickenham Hill" there is even an innovation in naming, topographically, a place by its existing, modern name; and this prepares us for all the allusions to habits, superstitions, rites, occasions of the moment which occur to the rapid brain of the author.

If the poems of Donne are examined, we shall find that it is only on the rarest occasions that he draws his imagery from mythology or romantic history. He has no interest in Greek or Latin legend. He neither translates nor paraphrases the poets of antiquity. For the conventional elements of beauty, as it was understood in that age, for roses, that is to say, and shepherds, lutes, zephyrs, "Thetis' crystal floods," and "flower-enamelled meadows," Donne has a perfect contempt. He endeavours to extract intellectual beauty from purely subjective sources, by the concentration of intensity and passion upon modern thought. Accordingly, he draws his illustrations, not from asphodel or from the moon, but from the humdrum professional employments of his own age, from chemistry, medicine, law, mechanics, astrology, religious ritual, daily human business of every sort. The decency of reticence between lovers reminds him of a sacerdotal mystery, and he cries—

'Twere profanation of our joys
    To tell the laity our love.

Love is a spider dropped into the luscious chalice of life and "transubstantiating" it to poison. The sun is no more Phœbus, or the golden-haired son of Hyperion, but a pedantic lackey, whose duty is to "tell court-huntsmen that the king will ride." If the poet abuses his mistress for her want of faith, he does it in the language of an attorney, and his curses are "annexed in

schedules" to the document. A woman's tear, on which her lover's tear falls, is like a round ball, on which a skilled workman paints the countries of the world.

From the days of Dr. Johnson downwards, the nature of these images has been not a little misunderstood. They have two characteristics, which have been unduly identified—they are sometimes realistic, and they are sometimes inappropriate. To us to-day they are almost all grotesque, because they are fetched from a scheme of things now utterly obsolete; but we must endeavour to recollect that such phrases as—

    no chemic yet the elixir got
But glorifies his pregnant pot,
If by the way to him befall
Some odoriferous thing, or medicinal,

or,

As he that sees a star fall, runs apace,
    And finds a jelly in the place,

phrases which now call for a commentary, and disturb our appreciation of the poet's fancy, were references to the science or half-science of the Jacobean age as modern and "topical" as allusions to the Röntgen rays would be today.

. . . We must, at length, give to Donne such credit as is due to complete originality in working out and forcing upon English taste a style in which affectation and wilful obscurity took a part so prominent that by ordinary readers no other qualities are nowadays perceived.

Notes

1. If, as I think likely, this was written about 1595, the "clime" was probably France, and "the king" Henry IV., a mighty hunter, our ally, and very popular in England. But there is no need to press a poet to this extremity of exact allusion.
2. *The Jacobean Poets*, 1894, pp. 60–63; from which a few lines are here reproduced.
3. In the interesting notes scribbled in 1811 by Coleridge, in Lamb's copy of Donne's *Poems*, S.T.C. remarks on the judicious use Donne makes of the anapaest in iambic measures where he wishes, in the eagerness of haste, to confirm or to exaggerate emotion. This valuable copy is now in the possession of Mr. W. H. Arnold, of New York.
4. *Paradiso*, xvii. 116, 117.

W. J. COURTHOPE
From "The School of Metaphysical Wit: John Donne"
A History of English Poetry
1903, Vol. 3, pp. 147–168

Beyond the sphere of theological allegory, in which the traditions of the schools were still preserved, lay the region of pure thought; and here the contradiction between mediæval and modern ideas furnished ample materials for the exercise of "wit." Assailed at once by the forces of the new faith, the new science, and the growing spirit of civic liberty, the ancient fabric of Catholicism and Feudalism fell more and more into ruin, but the innovating philosophy was yet far from having established a system of order and authority. The reasoning of Copernicus and Galileo shook men's belief in the truth of the Ptolemaic astronomy: the discoveries of Columbus extended their ideas of the terrestrial globe: the study of Greek and Hebrew literature in the original disturbed the symmetrical methods of scholastic logic: the investigations of the Arabian chemists produced havoc in the realm of encyclopædic science. Still, the old learning had rooted itself too firmly in the convictions of society to be easily abandoned, and the first effect of the collision between the opposing principles was to propagate a feeling of philosophic doubt. In the sphere of reason a new kind of Pyrrhonism sprang up, which expressed itself in Montaigne's motto, *Que sçay je?* and this disposition of mind naturally exerted another kind of influence on the men of creative imagination. In active life the confusion of the times was the opportunity of the buccaneer and the soldier of fortune, who hoped to advance themselves by their swords; and like these, many poets, in their ideal representations of Nature, seized upon the rich materials of the old and ruined philosophy to decorate the structures which they built out of their lawless fancy. On such foundations rose the school of metaphysical wit, of which the earliest and most remarkable example is furnished in the poetry of John Donne. . . .

The character of Donne's poetry reflects very exactly the changes in his life and opinions. Most of his compositions in verse are said to have been written while he was still a young man. To this class belong his *Satires*, his *Songs and Sonnets*, his *Elegies*, and *The Progress of the Soul*. A graver and more philosophic period follows, in which were produced most of the *Verse Epistles*, his *Epicedes and Obsequies*, and *The Anatomy of the World*; while the *Divine Poems* and the paraphrase of the *Lamentations of Jeremiah* are the work of the time when he was about to be, or had been, ordained.

Ben Jonson said to Drummond, speaking of *The Progress of the Soul*: "Of this he (Donne) never wrote but one sheet, and now, since he was made Doctor, repenteth highly, and seeketh to destroy all his poems." The thing is probable enough. Donne was educated as a Roman Catholic. His love-poems are those of a man who has assimilated, with thorough appreciation, all the learning and intellectual methods of the schoolmen—their fine distinctions, their subtle refinement, their metaphysical renderings of the text of Scripture. We know that, at some uncertain date, he abandoned the Roman Catholic faith, but his scholastic education had grounded in his mind a doctrine which, to the close of his life, continued to lie at the root of all his convictions, and to give form and colour to his poetical style, namely, the belief in the indestructible character of the soul. He constantly alludes to the old theory of the schoolmen respecting the triple nature of the soul, as in the lines:—

> We first have souls of growth and sense; and those,
> When our last soul, our soul immortal, came,
> Were swallowed into it, and have no name.[1]

In the middle period of his life, when his opinions were becoming more settled and religious, he writes of this individual soul:—

> Our soul, whose country's heaven, and God her
>   father,
>   Into this world, corruption's sink, is sent;
> Yet so much in her travel she doth gather,
>   That she returns home wiser than she went.[2]

This mixture of strong religious instinct and philosophic scepticism appears in its simplest form in his third *Satire*, which we know to have been among the earliest of his works. What interest is there, the poet asks, which can compare with religion? Why, then, are men prepared to risk their lives for the smallest material stake—money, adventure, honour—while at the same time they give no thought to their spiritual foes—the world, the flesh, and the devil?—

> Flesh itself's death; and joys which flesh can taste
> Thou lovest; and thy fair goodly soul, which doth
> Give this flesh power to taste joy, thou dost loathe.

But then he goes on: "Seek true religion, O where?" Some, he says, seek her in the ancient, decayed authority of Rome; others

in the sullen Protestantism of Geneva; some put up with Erastianism; others abhor all forms of religion, just because all cannot be good; others, on the contrary, think all are equally good. He concludes:—

> Doubt wisely; in strange way
> To stand inquiring right, is not to stray;
> To sleep or run wrong is. On a huge hill,
> Cragged and steep, Truth stands, and he that will
> Reach her, about must and about must go,
> And what th' hill's suddenness resists win so.
> Yet strive so, that before age, death's twilight,
> Thy soul rest, for none can work in that night.

On this principle he himself seems to have proceeded. Certain it is that, in his poem called *The Progress of the Soul*, he had reached a stage of contemplative scepticism. To this composition, which bears the following title and date: "Infinitati sacrum, 16 August 1601. Metempsychosis. Poema Satyricon," is prefixed a highly characteristic epistle, in which the author says:—

> I forbid no reprehender, but him that like the Trent Council forbids not books but authors, damning whatever such a name hath or shall write. None writes so ill, that he gives not something exemplary to follow or fly. Now when I begin this book I have no purpose to come into any man's debt; how my stock will hold out I know not; perchance waste, perchance increase in use. If I do borrow anything of antiquity, besides that I make account that I pay it with as much and as good, you shall still find me to acknowledge it, and to thank not only him that hath digged out treasure for me, but that hath lighted me a candle to the place, all which I will bid you remember (for I will have no such readers as I can teach) is, that the Pythagorean doctrine doth not only carry one soul from man to man, nor man to beast, but indifferently to plants also; and therefore you must not grudge to find the same soul in an Emperor, in a Posthorse, and in a Macaron, since no unreadiness in the soul, but an indisposition in the organs, works this.

In the poem itself Donne feigns that the soul, which moves all things—plants and beasts, as well as men—entered into the world by the plucking of an apple from the Tree of Life. The subtle and searching analysis of the poet's imagination may be illustrated by the following stanza:—

> For the great soul which here amongst us now
> Doth dwell, and moves that hand, and tongue, and
>   brow,
> Which, as the moon the sea, moves us; to hear
> Whose story with long patience you will long,
> —For 'tis the crown and last strain of my song—
> This soul to whom Luther and Mahomet were
> Prisons of flesh; this soul which oft did tear
> And mend the wracks of th' Empire, and late Rome,
> And lived when every great change did come,
>   Had first in Paradise a low but fatal room.

By the woman eating the apple, corruption passed by transmission through the whole race of mankind; and Donne's "wit" settles on each detail of the metaphysical conception, thus:—

> Prince of the orchard, fair as dawning morn,
> Fenced with the law, and ripe as soon as born,
> That apple grew, which this soul did enlive,
> Till the then climbing serpent, that now creeps
> For that offence, for which all mankind weeps,
> Took it, and to her whom the first man did wive
> —Whom and her race only forbiddings drive—

He gave it, she to her husband; both did eat:
So perished the eaters and the meat;
     And we—for treason taints the blood—thence
         die and sweat.
Man all at once was thus by woman slain,
And one by one we're here slain o'er again
By them. The mother poisoned the well-head,
The daughters here corrupt us, rivulets;
No smallness scapes, no greatness breaks their nets;
She thrust us out, and by them we are led
Astray, from turning to whence we are fled.
Were prisoners judges, 'twould seem rigorous:
She sinned, we bear; part of our pain is thus
     To love them whose fault to this painful love
         yoked us.
So fast in us did this corruption grow,
That now we dare ask why we should be so.
Would God—disputes the curious rebel—make
A law, and would not have it kept? Or can
His creature's will cross His? Of every man
For one will God (and be just) vengeance take?
Who sinned? 'twas not forbidden to the snake,
Nor her, who was not then made; nor is't writ
That Adam cropp'd, or knew, the apple; yet
     The worm, and he, and she, and we endure
         for it.

The apple once plucked, the soul flies from the Tree through the aperture, and enters successively into a plant (the mandrake), the egg of a bird (sparrow, symbol of lechery), a fish, a sea-osprey, a whale, a mouse, an elephant, a wolf, an ape, and a woman. All these are described, with various allegorical and satirical reflections by the way upon the manners and morals of mankind, especially at Court. The poem has no conclusion. Ben Jonson told Drummond: "The conceit of Done's transformation or Metempsychōsis was that he sought the soul of that apple which Eve pulled, and thereafter made it the soul of a bitch, then of a she-wolf, and so of a woman: his general purpose was to have brought in all the bodies of the heretics from the soul of Cain, and at last left it in the body of Calvin." Though this description of the poem is inaccurate in detail, it may well be that Donne originally designed some satiric stroke against Calvin; for his conclusion is steeped in the merest Pyrrhonism:—

Whoe'er thou beest that read'st this sullen writ,
Which just so much courts thee as thou dost it,
Let me arrest thy thoughts; wonder with me,
Why ploughing, building, ruling, and the rest
Or most of these arts, whence our lives are blest,
By cursed Caïn's race invented be,
And blest Seth vex'd us with astronomy.
There's nothing simply good or ill alone;
Of every quality Comparison
The only measure is, and judge, Opinion.

Here we have plainly the utterance of a sceptic in religion, who, having thrown off the forms of authoritative belief, indulges his imagination with a reconstruction of the ruins of Pythagorean and Rabbinical philosophy. Many allusions to natural history and theological dogma are scattered through Donne's *Songs and Sonnets*, and all are couched in the same reckless spirit.

And as Donne was at this stage a sceptic in religion, so was he a revolutionist in love. We have seen that, for many centuries, the law of chivalrous love had been rigorously defined. The Provençal poets and the female presidents of the *Cours d'Amours* had revised and extended the ancient canons of the art as expounded by Ovid; and, while they tacitly recognised

the physical basis of the passion, they disguised it by the elaborate character of the imaginative superstructure they raised upon it. In the delicacy of their observation, the nicety of their distinctions, and the keenness of their logic, they rivalled the theological science of the schoolmen; and by allying the phenomena of love with the loftier virtues of constancy, patience, loyalty, and self-surrender, they so spiritualised the former that, under the *régime* of chivalry—to use the words of Burke,—"vice itself lost half its evil by losing all its grossness."[3]

This fine Platonic edifice is ruthlessly demolished in the poetry of Donne. To him love, in its infinite variety and inconsistency, represented the principle of perpetual flux in Nature. At the same time, his imagination was stimulated by the multitude of paradoxes and metaphors which were suggested to him by the varying aspects of the passion. He pushed to extremes the scholastic analysis and conventional symbolism of the Provençals; but he applied them within the sphere of vulgar *bourgeois* intrigue, as may be inferred from the following characteristic lines:—

Nature's lay idiot, I taught thee to love,
And in that sophistry, O! thou dost prove
Too subtle; fool, thou didst not understand
The mystic language of the eye nor hand;
Nor couldst thou judge the difference of the air
Of sighs, and say, "This lies, this sounds despair";
Nor by th' eye's water cast a malady,
Desperately hot, or changing feverously.
I had not taught thee then the alphabet
Of flowers, how they, devisefully being set
And bound up, might, with speechless secrecy,
Deliver errands mutely and mutually.
Remember since all thy words used to be
To every suitor, "Ay, if my friends agree";
Since household charms thy husband's name to
    teach,
Were all the love-tricks that thy wit could reach;
And since an hour's discourse could scarce have
    made
An answer in thee, and that ill-arrayed
In broken proverbs and short sentences.[4]

The law of love in the *Cours d'Amours* required unfailing constancy in both lovers: in the philosophy of Donne this law is contrary to Nature, and is therefore heresy:—

Venus heard me sigh this song,
And by love's sweetest part, variety, she swore
She heard not this till now; it should be so no more.
She went, examined, and returned ere long,
And said, "Alas! some two or three
Poor heretics in love there be,
Which think to 'stablish dangerous constancy.
But I have told them, 'Since you will be true,
You shall be true to them who're false to you.'"[5]

Over and over again he insists on the essential falsehood and fickleness of women. He asks, for instance, "where lives a woman true and fair," and proceeds:—

If thou find'st one let me know;
    Such a pilgrimage were sweet.
Yet do not, I would not go,
    Though at next door we might meet.
Though she were true when you met her,
And last till you write your letter,
    Yet she
    Will be
False, ere I come, to two or three.[6]

This is the spirit of Ariosto's story of Giocondo. But Donne goes further, and cynically erects this observed habit of fickleness into a rule for constant, but discriminating, change:—

> By Nature, which gave it, this liberty
> Thou lovest, but O! canst thou love it and me?
> Likeness glues love; and if that thou so do,
> To make us like and love, must I change too?
> More than thy hate I hate it; rather let me
> Allow her change, then change as oft as she;
> And so not teach, but force, my opinion
> To love not any one, nor every one.
> To live in one land is captivity,
> To run all countries a wild roguery.
> Waters stink soon, if in one place they bide,
> And in that vast sea are more putrified;
> But when they kiss one bank, and leaving this
> Never look back, but the next bank do kiss,
> There are they purest; change is the nursery
> Of music, joy, life, and eternity.[7]

From this spirit of cynical lawlessness he was perhaps reclaimed by genuine love. To his wife he seems to have been devotedly attached, and in the poems written after his marriage in 1601 we find a complete change of sentiment and style. The old underlying conviction of the indestructible nature of the soul and of the corruption of the material world remains, but it is now made the starting-point for a graver philosophy of conduct. The *Verse Letters* written to the Countesses of Bedford, Huntingdon, and Salisbury, though all are couched in a vein of metaphysical compliment, are decorous in tone; in *The Anatomy of the World* Donne seems to have intended to embody his serious thoughts about the meaning and duties of human life. Whether there was any real ground for the hyperbolical praise with which he exalts the memory of Elizabeth Drury, we have no means of knowing. It is said, indeed, that she was betrothed to Henry, Prince of Wales; but Ben Jonson probably expressed a general opinion when he said to Drummond that "Done's 'Anniversarie' was profane and full of blasphemies: that he told Mr. Done, if it had been written of the Virgin Marie it had been something; to which he answered that it described the Idea of a Woman, and not as she was."

Viewed literally, *The Anatomy of the World* fully deserves the sentence passed upon it by Jonson. The poet asserts that after the death of Elizabeth Drury the whole mortal universe lost its vitality; that nothing but the shadow of life remained in it; that the disorder in the constitution of things, the decay and weakness of mankind, and the failure of the influence of the heavenly bodies, are all due to her removal from the earthly sphere. It is no wonder that such absurdities should have provoked matter-of-fact criticism. They are, however, not of the essence of the composition. "I hear from England," writes Donne in Paris to a correspondent with the initials Sir G. F., "of many censures of my book of Mrs. Drury; if any of these censures do but pardon me my descent in printing anything in verse (which if they do they are more charitable than myself; for I do not pardon myself, but confess that I did it against my conscience, that is against my own opinion, that I should not have done so), I doubt not that they will soon give over that other part of the indictment, which is that I have said so much; for nobody can imagine that I, who never saw her, could have purpose in that, than that when I had received so very good testimony of her worthiness, and was gone down to print verses, it became me to say, not what I was sure was just truth, but the best that I could conceive; for that would have been a new weakness in me to have praised anybody in printed verse, that had not been capable of the best verse that I could give."

The true character of *The Anatomy of the World* is indicated in the respective titles of the two Anniversaries. That of the first runs: "Wherein, *by occasion of the untimely death of Mistress Elizabeth Drury*, the frailty and decay of this whole world is represented." The subject of the second is defined thus: "Wherein, *by occasion of the religious death of Mistress Elizabeth Drury*, the incommodities of the soul in this life, and her exaltation in the next, are contemplated." In other words, the early death and religious character of Elizabeth Drury are merely the text justifying an elaborate exposition of Donne's philosophy of life. The girl stood to Donne, for his poetical purpose, in the same relation as Beatrice stood to Dante in the *Vita Nuova* and the *Divine Comedy*, being the incarnate symbol of the spiritual perfection—the Idea of Woman, as he put it to Ben Jonson—which he sought to express. When he says that her death was the cause of all the imperfections of the material world, he intended, in the first place, to pay a hyperbolical compliment to the daughter of his patron, and in the second, to express the theological doctrine of the corruption of Nature after the fall of man from his original state of perfection.

On the whole, it seems to me probable that the publication of *The Anatomy of the World* was part of a deliberate literary design on Donne's part. His affected depreciation of verse-writing is not to be taken seriously. His views of life were changing with his years: he was anxious for either secular or sacred employment: he regretted the evidences of a dissipated past which existed in his youthful poems: he hoped to attain the object of his ambition by giving public proof of the present gravity of his mind, and by securing the special favour of the most influential patrons of literature, such as the famous ladies of the Court, to whom so many of his *Verse Letters* are addressed. He writes to a correspondent in 1614: "This made me ask to borrow that old book" (*i.e.* an MS. collection of his poems), "which it will be too late to see, for that use, when I see you: for I must do this as a valediction to the world before I take orders. But this it is I am to ask of you: whether you ever made any such use of the letter in verse *à nostre comtesse chez vous*, as that I may put it in among the rest to persons of rank; for I desire it very much that something should bear her name in the book, and I would be just to my written words to my Lord Harrington, to write nothing after that." To Lady Bedford herself he writes, in a *Verse Letter*, perhaps the one above referred to:—

> So whether my hymns you admit or choose,
> In me you've hallowèd a pagan muse,
> And denizened a stranger who, mistaught
> By blamers of the times they've marred, hath sought
> Virtues in corners, which now bravely do
> Shine in the world's best part, or all it,—you.

As to the poems being a "valediction to the world," Donne kept his promise. His letter to Sir H. Goodyere was written within a year of his taking orders, and henceforth all his publications in prose and verse were of a religious and theological cast. The last period of his poetical genius contains the *Divine Poems*, comprising meditations on the various mysteries of the Christian faith, a version of Tremellius' *Lamentations of Jeremiah*, written after the death of his much-loved wife, and other religious topics. As John Chudleigh, one of his panegyrists, said in the edition of his poems published after his death in 1650:—

> Long since this task of tears from you was due,
> Long since, O poets, he did die to you,
> Or left you dead, when wit and he took flight
> On divine wings, and soared out of your sight.

In close friendship with George Herbert and other divines of the period, he helped during the remainder of his life to swell the volume of Anglican ascetic thought which, under the direction of Laud, formed, in the reign of Charles I., the counterbalancing force to the movement of iconoclastic Puritanism.

But though his view of life and his object in art were thus completely altered, his poetical method remained consistently the same. As his admirer, Chudleigh, again remarks:—

> He kept his loves, but not his objects: Wit
> He did not banish, but transplanted it;
> Taught it his place and use, and brought it home
> To piety which it doth best become;
> He showed us how for sins we ought to sigh,
> And how to sing Christ's epithalamy.

How just this criticism is may be seen from Donne's *Hymn to Christ at the Author's last going into Germany*:—

> Nor Thou, nor Thy religion, dost control
> The amorousness of an harmonious soul;
> But Thou wouldst have that love Thyself; as Thou
> Art jealous, Lord, so am I jealous now;
> Thou lovest not, till from loving more Thou free
> My soul; whoever gives takes liberty;
>   Oh, if Thou carest not whom I love,
>   Alas! Thou lovest not me.
>
> Seal then this bill of my divorce to all
> On whom those fainter beams of love did fall;
> Marry those loves, which in youth scattered be
> On fame, wit, hopes—false mistresses—to Thee.
> Churches are best for prayer that have least light;
> To see God only I go out of sight;
>   And to escape stormy days, I choose
>   An everlasting night.

Here we have precisely the same kind of paradoxical logic, the same subtlety of thought and imagery, as we find in the *Elegy on Change*, and though the imagination is now fixed on an unchangeable object, it plays round it precisely in the same way. The essence of Donne's wit is abstraction. Whether he is writing on the theme of sacred or profane love, his method lies in separating the perceptions of the soul from the entanglements of sense, and after isolating a thought, a passion, or a quality, in the world of pure ideas, to make it visible to the fancy by means of metaphorical images and scholastic allusions. The most characteristic specimens of his wit are to be found in his *Songs and Sonnets*, where he is dealing with the metaphysics of love, for here his imagination is at liberty to move whithersoever it chooses; and the extraordinary ingenuity with which he masters and reduces to epigrammatic form the most minute distinctions of thought, as well as the facility with which he combines contrary ideas and images, are well exemplified in a poem called *The Primrose Hill*:—

> Upon this Primrose Hill,
>   Where, if heaven would distill
> A shower of rain, each several drop might go
> To his own primrose, and grow manna so;
> And where their form and their infinity
>   Make a terrestrial galaxy,
>   As the small stars do in the sky,
> I walk to find a true-love, and I see
> That 'tis not a mere woman that is she,
> But must or more or less than woman be. [8]
>
>   Yet know I not which flower
>   I wish, a six or four:
> For should my true love less than woman be,
> She were scarce anything; and then should she
> Be more than woman, she would get above
>   All thought of sex, and think to move
>   My heart to study her, and not to love.

Both these were monsters; since there must reside
Falsehood in woman, I could more abide
She were by art than nature falsified.

>   Live, primrose, then, and thrive
>   With thy true number five;
> And, woman, whom this flower doth represent,
> With this mysterious number be content;
> Ten is the farthest number; if half ten
>   Belongs unto each woman, then
>   Each woman may take half us men:
> Or—if this will not serve their turn—since all
> Numbers are odd or even, and they fall
> First into five, women may take us all. [9]

But for the purposes of great and true art the flight of metaphysical wit soon reveals the limitations of its powers. Sceptic as he was, Donne never formed any organic idea of Nature as a whole, and his sole aim, as a poet, was to associate the isolated details of his accumulations of learning with paradoxes and conceits, which are of no permanent value. For example, he was acquainted with the Copernican theory, but he is only interested in it as far as it helps to supply him with a poetical illustration:—

> As new philosophy arrests the sun,
> And bids the passive earth about it run,
> So we have dulled our mind; it hath no ends,
> Only the body's busy, and pretends. [10]

The theory that the earth was gradually approaching the sun suggests to him the following reflection:—

> If the world's age and death be argued well
>   By the sun's fall, which now towards earth
>   doth bend,
> Then we might fear that virtue, since she fell
>   So low as woman, should be near her end.

But he at once corrects this conclusion into an extravagant compliment:—

> But she's not stooped but raised; exiled by men,
>   She fled to heaven, that's heavenly things,
>   that's you. [11]

The general scepticism, produced in his mind by the collision between the new philosophy and the old theology, is forcibly expressed in his first Anniversary:—

> The new philosophy calls all in doubt;
> The element of fire is quite put out;
> The sun is lost, and th' earth, and no man's wit
> Can well direct him where to look for it.
> And freely men confess that the world's spent,
> When in the planets and the firmament
> They seek so many new; they see that this
> Is crumbled out again to his atomies.
> 'Tis all in pieces, all coherence gone,
> All just supply and all relation.
> Prince, subject, father, son, are things forgot,
> For every man alone thinks he hath got
> To be a phœnix, and that there can be
> None of that kind of which he is, but he. [12]

The conclusion at which he finally arrived was the one to which all such souls, who have in them the element of religion, must be brought:—

> In this low form, poor soul, what wilt thou do?
> When wilt thou shake off this pedantry
> Of being taught by sense and fantasy?
> Thou look'st through spectacles; small things seem
>   great
> Below; but up into thy watch-tower get,
> And see all things despoiled of fallacies;

Thou shalt not peep through lattices of eyes,
Nor hear through labyrinths of ears, nor learn
By circuit or collections to discern.
In heaven thou straight know'st all concerning it,
And what concerns it not shalt straight forget.

But before he arrives at this intelligible goal, his soul, wandering through an infinite maze of metaphysical ideas, has made shift to embody its transitory perceptions in the forms of poetical art; and, while he is engaged in a business which he acknowledges to be vain, he delights in involving himself and his readers in inextricable labyrinths of paradox. One of his favourite ideas is that Love is Death, and this thought he divides and subdivides by means of an endless variety of images. Thus he finds an opportunity of associating it with the reflections aroused by the shortest day, sacred to St. Lucy. All Nature, he says, seems to have shrivelled into nothing:—

The world's whole sap is sunk;
The general balm th' hydroptic earth hath drunk,
Whither, as to the bed's feet, life is shrunk,
Dead and interr'd; yet all these seem to laugh,
Compared to me, who am their epitaph.

He then calls on all lovers to come and study him as a "very dead thing,"

For whom Love wrought new alchemy;
    For his art did express
A quintessence even from nothingness,
From dull privations, and lean emptiness;
He ruin'd me, and I am rebegot
Of absence, darkness, death—things which are not.

He goes on to intensify the idea of annihilation, by saying that he is "the grave of all that's nothing"; that he is

Of the first nothing the elixir grown;

nay, he is something less than nothing:

If I an ordinary nothing were,
As shadow, a light and body must be here,
But I am none.[13]

In a poem called *The Paradox* he indulges in still more intricate logic on the same subject:—

No lover saith I love, nor any other
    Can judge a perfect lover;
He thinks that else none can nor will agree
    That any loves but he:
I cannot say I loved, for who can say
    He was killed yesterday?
Love with excess of heat, more young than old,
    Death kills with too much cold.
We die but once, and who loved best did die,
    He that saith twice did lie;
For though he seem to move and stir awhile,
    He doth the sense beguile.
Such life is like the light which bideth yet,
    When the life's light is set,
Or like the heat which fire in solid matter
    Leaves behind two hours after.
Once I loved and died; and am now become
    Mine epitaph and tomb;
Here dead men speak their last, and so do I;
    Love slain, lo! here I lie.

This perpetual endeavour to push poetical conception beyond the limits of sense and Nature produced its necessary effect on the character of Donne's metrical expression. When he seeks to embody a comparatively simple and natural thought, he can write with admirable harmony, as in the following lines, describing love in the Golden Age:—

What pretty innocence in those days moved!
Man ignorantly walked by her he loved;
Both sigh'd and interchang'd a speaking eye;
Both trembled and were sick; both knew not why.
That natural fearfulness, that struck man dumb,
Might well—those times considered—man become.
As all discoverers, whose first essay
Finds but the place, after, the nearest way,
So passion is to woman's love, about,
Nay, farther off, than when we first set out.
It is not love that sueth or doth contend;
Love either conquers or but meets a friend;
Man's better part consists of purer fire,
And finds itself allowed ere it desire.[14]

Here, too, is an excellent compliment in a *Verse Letter* to the Countess of Salisbury, grounded on the idea that chivalrous love is a liberal education:—

So, though I'm born without those eyes to live,
Which Fortune, who hath none herself, doth give,
Which are fit means to see bright courts and you,
Yet, may I see you thus, as now I do:
I shall by that all goodness have discern'd,
And, though I burn my library, be learn'd.

His whole philosophy of life, in his early days, is condensed in the following couplet:—

Be then thine own home, and in thyself dwell;
Inn anywhere: continuance maketh hell.[15]

And he is most vivid in the presentation of abstract ideas, as in the famous lines:—

Her pure and eloquent blood
Spoke in her cheeks, and so distinctly wrought
That one might almost say her body thought.[16]

The abrupt and forcible openings of his poems often strike a key-note of thought which promises completeness of treatment, but his metaphysical wit and his love of endless distinctions generally cause the composition to end nowhere. He begins a poem called *Love's Deity* thus:—

I long to talk with some old lover's ghost,
    Who died before the God of Love was born.

The object of the discourse is to be the mystery why love should be forced from one lover where there is no return from the other. This is a subject of universal interest, and the poet, on the assumption that Love, after being made into a deity, has abused his power, conducts a striking thought, by means of an appropriate image, to an intelligible conclusion:—

O were we wakened by this tyranny
To ungod this child again, it could not be
    I should love her who loves not me.

But such straightforward logic would not have suited the supersubtle character of Donne's intellect; and he proceeds to invert his reasoning, and to close his poem with a stanza of pure paradox, leaving the mind without that sense of repose which art requires:—

Rebel and atheist, why murmur I,
    As though I felt the worst that love could do?
Love may make me leave loving, or might try
    A deeper plague, to make her love me too;
Which, since she loves before, I'm loth to see.
Falsehood is worse than hate; and that must be,
    If she whom I love should love me.

Where he thinks simply the reader perceives that his thoughts are really common enough. He begins a *Verse Letter* to Sir H. Goodyere on his favourite subject of the necessity of change:—

> Who makes the last a pattern for next year,
>> Turns no new leaf, but still the same thing
>>> reads;
> Seen things he sees again, heard things doth hear,
>> And makes his life but like a pair of beads.

This has the simplicity and directness of Sir John Davies in his *Nosce Teipsum*. But we soon come to a quatrain in which the poet is anxious to show his wit:—

> To be a stranger hath that benefit,
>> We can beginnings, but not habits choke.
> Go—whither? hence. You get, if you forget;
>> New faults, till they prescribe to us, are
>>> smoke.

We certainly do *not* get anything by the mere negative act of forgetting; and nobody could gather from the last line that the meaning was, "new faults, till they become our masters, are *merely* smoke." Eagerness for novelty and paradox leads the poet to obscurity of expression; and the reader is justly incensed when he finds that the labour required to arrive at the meaning, hidden behind involved syntax and unmeasured verse, has been expended in vain. Ben Jonson does not express this feeling too strongly when he says, "That Done for not keeping of accent deserved hanging." It is superfluous to justify this verdict by examples. The reader, in the numerous extracts I have given from Donne's poems, will have observed for himself how deliberately he seeks to attract attention to the extravagance of his thought, by the difficulty of his grammatical constructions, and by the dislocation of his accents.

All these things must be taken into account in deciding the place to be assigned to this acute and powerful intellect in the history of English poetry. Donne's qualities were essentially those of his age. His influence on his contemporaries and on the generation that succeeded him was great. They had all been educated under the same scholastic conditions as himself; they were all in touch with his theological starting-point, and set a value on the subtlety of his metaphysical distinctions. In Dryden's time, when the prestige of "wit," still represented by the genius of Cowley, was weakening before the poetical school which aimed first at correctness of expression, men continued to speak with reverence of Donne's genius. But as the philosophy of Bacon, Newton, and Locke gradually established itself, the traditions of the schoolmen fell into discredit, so that, in the days of Johnson and Burke, the practice of the metaphysical wits had come to be regarded in the light of an obsolete curiosity. The revival of mediæval sentiment, which has coloured English taste during the last three generations, has naturally awakened fresh interest in the poems of Donne, and there is perhaps in our own day a tendency to exaggerate his merits. "If Donne," writes a learned and judicious critic, "cannot receive the praise due to the accomplished poetical artist, he has that not perhaps higher, but certainly rarer, of the inspired poetical creator."[17] Poetical creation implies that organic conception of Nature, and that insight into universal human emotions, which make the classical poets of the world—Homer and Dante, and Chaucer and Milton; and to this universality of thought, as I have endeavoured to show, Donne has no claim. Nor can he be reckoned among the poets who, by their sense of harmony and proportion, have helped to carry forward the refinement of our language from one social stage to another. The praise which Johnson bestows upon his learning adds little to his fame, for the science contained in his verse is mostly derived from those encyclopædic sources of knowledge which, even in his own time, were being recognised as the fountains of "Vulgar Error." On the other hand, to those who see in poetry a mirror of the national life, and who desire to amplify and

enrich their own imagination by a sympathetic study of the spiritual existence of their ancestors, the work of Donne will always be profoundly interesting. No more lively or characteristic representative can be found of the thought of an age when the traditions of the ancient faith met in full encounter with the forces of the new philosophy. The shock of that collision is far from having spent its effect, even in our own day; and he who examines historically the movements of imagination will find in Donne's subtle analysis and refined paradoxes much that helps to throw light on the contradictions of human nature.

Notes

1. *Verse Letter* to the Countess of Bedford.
2. *Verse Letter* to Sir H. Goodyere.
3. *Reflections on the French Revolution.*
4. Elegy vii.
5. *The Indifferent.*
6. Song, "Go and catch a falling star."
7. Elegy iii.
8. The conceit of the poem turns on the two facts that the normally constituted primrose has five segments in its corolla, and that the token of true love among the country folk of Donne's time was the exceptional primrose, with either four or six segments.
9. The argument in this stanza is drawn from the science of numbers. Five being half of ten, the farthest number (i.e. the first double number, and the basis of the whole metric system), women may claim to represent half of what is in human nature; or, if this be not enough for their ambition, then (numbers being either odd or even, and falling first into five, i.e. 2 + 3) since five is woman's number, women may have the whole of human nature given over to them.
10. *Verse Letter* to Countess of Bedford.
11. *Verse Letter* to Countess of Huntingdon.
12. *Anatomy of the World*, first Anniversary, 205–218.
13. *A Nocturnal upon St. Lucy's Day.*
14. *Verse Letter* to the Countess of Huntingdon.
15. *Verse Letter* to Sir H. Wotton.
16. *Anatomy of the World*, second Anniversary, 244–246.
17. Professor Saintsbury, *Preface to Poems of John Donne.* Edited by E. K. Chambers.

JOHN W. HALES
"John Donne"
The English Poets, ed. Thomas Humphrey Ward
1903, Vol. 1, pp. 558–60

Donne's contemporary reputation as a poet, and still more as a preacher, was immense; and a glance at his works would suffice to show that he did not deserve the contempt with which he was subsequently treated. But yet his chief interest is that he was the principal founder of a school which especially expressed and represented a certain bad taste of his day. Of his genius there can be no question; but it was perversely directed. One may almost invert Jonson's famous panegyric on Shakespeare, and say that Donne was not for all time but for an age.

To this school Dr. Johnson has given the title of the Metaphysical; and for this title there is something to be said. 'Donne,' says Dryden, 'affects the metaphysics not only in his Satires, but in his amorous verses where Nature only should reign, and perplexes the minds of the fair sex with nice speculations of philosophy when he should engage their hearts and entertain them with the softnesses of love.' Thus he often ponders over the mystery of love, and is exercised by subtle questions as to its nature, origin, endurance. But a yet more notable distinction of this school than its philosophising, shallow or deep, is what may be called its fantasticality, its quaint wit, elaborate ingenuity, far-fetched allusiveness; and it might better be called the Ingenious, or Fantastic School. Various and out-of-the-way information and learning is a necessary qualification for membership. Donne in one of his letters speaks of his 'embracing the worst voluptuousness, an hydroptic immoderate desire of human learning and languages.' Eminence is attained by using such stores in the way to be least expected. The thing to be illustrated becomes of secondary importance by the side of the illustration. The more unlikely and surprising and preposterous this is, the greater the success. This is wit of a kind. From one point of view, wit, as Dr. Johnson says, 'may be considered as a kind of *discordia concors*; a combination of dissimilar images or discovery of occult resemblances in things apparently unlike. Of wit thus defined they [Donne and his followers] have more than enough. The most heterogeneous ideas are yoked by violence together; nature and art are ransacked for illustrations, comparisons, and allusions; their learning instructs, and their subtility surprises; but the reader commonly thinks his improvement dearly bought, and though he sometimes admires is seldom pleased.'

And so in the following curious passage from Donne's Dedication of certain poems to Lord Craven it should be observed how 'wit' and 'poetry' are made to correspond: 'Amongst all the monsters this unlucky age has teemed with, I find none so prodigious as the poets of these late times [this is very much what Donne's own critics must say], wherein men, as if they would level undertakings too as well as estates, acknowledging no inequality of parts and judgments, pretend as indifferently to the chair of wit as to the pulpit, and conceive themselves no less inspired with the spirit of poetry than with that of religion.' Dryden styles Donne 'the greatest wit though not the best poet of our nation.'

The taste which this school represents marks other literatures besides our own at this time. It was 'in the air' of that age; and so was not originated by Donne. But it was he who in England first gave it full expression—who was its first vigorous and effective and devoted spokesman. And this secures him a conspicuous position in the history of our literature when we remember how prevalent was the fashion of 'conceits' during the first half of the seventeenth century, and that amongst those who followed it more or less are to be mentioned, to say nothing of the earlier poems of Milton and Waller and Dryden, Suckling, Denham, Herbert, Crashaw, Cleveland, Cowley.

This misspent learning, this excessive ingenuity, this laborious wit seriously mars almost the whole of Donne's work. For the most part we look on it with amazement rather than with pleasure. It reminds us rather of a 'pyrotechnic display,' with its unexpected flashes and explosions, than of a sure and constant light (compare the *Valediction* given in our selections). We weary of such unmitigated cleverness—such ceaseless straining after novelty and surprise. We long for something simply thought, and simply said.

His natural gifts were certainly great. He possesses a real energy and fervour. He loved, and he suffered much, and he writes with a passion which is perceptible through all his artificialities. Such a poem as *The Will* is evidence of the astonishing rapidity and brightness of his fancy.

He also claims notice as one of our earliest formal satirists. Though not published till much later, there is proof that some at least of his satires were written three or four years before those of Hall. Two of them (ii. and iv.) were reproduced—'versified'—in the last century by Pope, acting on a suggestion by Dryden; No. iii. was similarly treated by Parnell. In these versions, along with the roughness of the metre, disappears much of the general vigour; and it should be remembered that the metrical roughness was no result of incapacity, but was designed. Thus the charge of metrical uncouthness so often brought against Donne on the ground of his satires is altogether mistaken. How fluently and smoothly he could write if he pleased, is attested over and over again by his lyrical pieces.

GEORGE HERBERT

GEORGE HERBERT

1593–1633

George Herbert, devotional poet and miscellaneous writer, was born at Montgomery Castle, on the Welsh border. A member of a noble family, George Herbert was the brother of Edward Herbert, first Baron Herbert of Cherbury, and the son of Magdalen Herbert, a friend and patron of John Donne. Educated at Westminster School, Herbert acquired a reputation for being a brilliant scholar. He was elected a member of Trinity College, Cambridge, in 1614, a reader in rhetoric in 1618, and public orator of the University, from 1620 to 1627. Although serving in 1624 and 1625 as M.P. for Montgomery, Herbert relinquished his ambitions for a secular career after the death of his royal patron James I. Ordained a deacon in 1625, Herbert resigned from his Public Oratorship in 1628. His mother died in 1627. He became an ordained priest in 1630. Until his death in 1633, Herbert lived and worked as a rural parish priest at Bemerton in Wiltshire, with Jane Danvers, whom he had married in 1629.

George Herbert is most widely known for his devotional poems, which are largely influenced by the metaphysical school of John Donne. His earliest known poems consist of two sonnets, sent to his mother on New Year's Day, in 1610. In these, the young Herbert declares that the subject of verse should concern the poet's love of God, rather than of woman. This theme of complete religious devotion was to preoccupy Herbert throughout his life, as manifested in his works, which are exclusively devotional.

It is believed that Herbert wrote the majority of his extant poems at Bemerton, as well as revising earlier poems, writing a prose treatise on the duties of a country priest, *A Priest to the Temple, or the Country Parson* (published 1652), a translation of Luigi Cornaro's *Treatise on Temperance* (published 1558), and annotations of Juan de Valdes' *Considerations* (published Italian translation, 1550). As Herbert had a reputation during his lifetime, some of his poems doubtless circulated in manuscript form. Before he died, Herbert sent a manuscript of his collected verses to Nicholas Ferrar, leader of a religious community at Little Gidding, with the request that Ferrar either burn or publish them. Ferrar published the volume under the title *The Temple: Sacred Poems and Private Ejaculations* (1633). Immensely popular in the seventeenth century, Herbert's poems combine metaphysical conceits, precise craftsmanship (with as much attention to the visual impression of his poems), with what appears to be a profound religious sincerity.

Personal

My brother George was so excellent a scholar, that he was made the public orator of the University in Cambridge; some of whose English works are extant; which, though they be rare in their kind, yet are far short of expressing those perfections he had in the Greek and Latin tongue, and all divine and human literature; his life was most holy and exemplary; insomuch, that about Salisbury, where he lived, beneficed for many years, he was little less than sainted. He was not exempt from passion and choler, being infirmities to which all our race is subject, but that excepted, without reproach in his action.—EDWARD, LORD HERBERT OF CHERBURY, *The Autobiography of Edward Lord Herbert of Cherbury*, 1643, ed. Lee, rev. ed. 1906, pp. 11–13

So pious his life, that, as he was a copy of primitive, he might be a pattern of Sanctity to posterity. To testifie his independency on all others, he never mentioned the name of Jesus Christ, but with this addition, "My Master." Next God the Word, he loved the Word of God; being heard often to protest, "That he would not part with one leaf thereof for the whole world."—THOMAS FULLER, *The Worthies of England*, 1662, Vol. 2, ed. Nichols, p. 601

He was buryed (according to his owne desire) with the singing service for the buriall of dead, by the singing men of Sarum. Fr(ancis) Sambroke (attorney) then assisted as a chorister boy; my uncle, Thomas Danvers, was at the funerall. Vide in the Register booke at the office when he dyed, for the parish regis-

ter is lost. Memorandum: in the chancell are many apt sentences of the Scripture. . . . When he was first maried he lived a yeare or better at Dantesey house. H. Allen, of Dantesey, was well acquainted with him, who has told me that he had a very good hand on the lute, and that he sett his own lyricks or sacred poems. 'Tis an honour to the place, to have had the heavenly and ingeniose contemplation of this good man, who was pious even to prophesie; e.g.

> Religion now on tip-toe stands,
> Ready to goe to the American strands.

—JOHN AUBREY, *Brief Lives*, 1669–96, Vol. 1, ed. Clark, pp. 309–10

He was for his person of a stature inclining towards tallness; his body was very straight, and so far from being cumbered with too much flesh, that he was lean to an extremity. His aspect was cheerful, and his speech and motion did both declare him a gentleman; for they were all so meek and obliging, that they purchased love and respect from all that knew him. . . . Brought most of his parishioners, and many gentlemen in the neighbourhood, constantly to make a part of his congregation twice a day: and some of the meaner sort of his parish did so love and reverence Mr. Herbert, that they would let their plough rest when Mr. Herbert's Saint's-bell rung to prayers, that they might also offer their devotions to God with him; and would then return back to their plough. And his most holy life was such, that it begot such reverence to God, and to him, that they thought themselves the happier, when they carried Mr. Herbert's blessing back with them to their labour. Thus power-

ful was his reason and example to persuade others to a practical
piety and devotion.—IZAAC WALTON, *The Life of Mr. George
Herbert*, 1670

> . . .*Herbert*: he, whose education,
> Manners, and parts, by high applauses blown,
> Was deeply tainted with Ambition;
> And fitted for a Court, made that his aim:
> At last, without regard to Birth or Name,
> For a poor Country-Cure, does all disclaim.
> Where, with a soul compos'd of Harmonies,
> Like a sweet *Swan*, he warbles, as he dies
> His makers praise, and, his own obsequies.
>
> —CHARLES COTTON, "To My Old, and Most
> Worthy Friend Mr. Isaac Walton," *The Life of
> Mr. George Herbert*, 1670, p. 10

Mr. *Herbert*'s Reputation is so firmly and so justly establish'd
among all Persons of *Piety* and *Ingenuity*, his Sense so good,
and most of his Poetry so fine, that those who Censure him will
be in more danger of having their Judgments question'd, than
such as with good reason Admire him. Nor can the Time he
writ in, when Poetry was not near so refin'd as 'tis now, be justly
objected against him, so as to make his Works of small or no
Value, any more than the *oddness* or *flatness* of some Expressions and Phrases, since something of these are to be found
in all other Compositions that have yet appear'd in our Language; and besides this, they were probably many of 'em made
to Tunes, Mr. *Herbert* being so great a Musitian, which every
one knows will often weaken the Sense. For *The Synagogue*, all
know 'tis none of his, tho' there are many fine Thoughts, and
not a few good Lines in't, carrying all thro' in an Air and Spirit
of great *Sense*, *Piety* and *Devotion*, much more Valuable than
all the foolish Wit that has so often directed the World at so
dear a Rate.—JOHN DUNTON, *Athenian Mercury*, Jan. 6,
1694

> Seraphic Singer! where's the fire
> That did these lines and lays inspire?
> B'ing dropt from heav'n, it scorn'd to dwell
> Long upon earth, and near to hell!
> The heart it purg'd, it did consume,
> Exhal'd the sacrifice in fume,
> And with it mounted, as of old
> The angel, in the smoke enroll'd;
> Return'd in haste, like thine own *Star*,
> Pleas'd with its prize, to native sphere.
> But blest perfume, that here I find,
> The sacrifice has left behind!
> Strange! how each fellow-saint's surpris'd
> To see himself anatomiz'd!
> The *Sion*'s mourner breathes thy strains,
> Sighs thee, and in thy notes complains;
> Amaz'd, and yet refresh'd to see
> His wounds, drawn to the life, in thee!
> The warrior, just resolv'd to quit
> The field, and all the toils of it,
> Returns with vigour, will renew
> The fight, with victory in view;
> He stabs his foes, and conquers harms,
> With spear, and nails, and *Herbert*'s arms.
> The racer, almost out of breath,
> Marching through shades and vale of death,
> Recruits, when he to thee is come,
> And sighs for heav'n, and sings thy *Home*;
> The tempted soul, whose thoughts are whirl'd,
> About th' inchantments of the world,

> Can o'er the snares and scandals skip,
> Born up by *Frailty*, and the *Quip*;
> The victor has reward paid down,
> Has earnest here of life and crown;
> The conscious priest is well releas'd
> Of pain and fear, in *Aaron* drest;
> The preaching envoy can proclaim
> His pleasure in his *Master*'s name;
> A name, that like the grace in him,
> Sends life and ease to ev'ry limb;
> Rich magazine of health! where's found
> Specific balm for ev'ry wound!
> Hail rev'rend bard! hail thou, th' elected shrine
> Of the great Sp'rit, and Shecinah divine!
> Who may speak thee! or aim at thy renown,
> In lines less venerable than thy own!
> Silent we must admire! upon no head
> Has, since thy flight, been half thy unction shed.
> What wit and grace thy lyric strains command!
> Hail, great apostle of the muses land!
> Scarce can I pardon the great *Cowley*'s claim,
> He seems t' usurp the glories of thy fame;
> 'Tis *Herbert*'s charms must chase (whate'er he boasts)
> The fiends and idols from poetic coasts;
> The *Mistress*, the *Anacreontic* lays,
> More demons will, and more disorders raise,
> Than his fam'd hero's lyre, in modern play,
> Or tun'd by Cowley's self, I fear, can lay;
> 'Tis *Herbert*'s notes must un-inchant the ear,
> Make the deaf adder, and th' old serpent hear.
>
> Soon had religion, with a gracious smile,
> Vouchsaf'd to visit this selected isle;
> The *British* emp'ror first her liv'ry wore,
> And sacred cross with *Roman* eagles bore;
> The sev'ral states, at last, her empire own,
> And swear allegiance to her rightful throne;
> Only the muses lands abjure her sway,
> They heathen still, and unconverted lay.
> Loth was the prince of darkness to resign
> Such fertiliz'd dominions, and so fine,
> *Herbert* arose! and sounds the trumpet there,
> He makes the muses land the seat of war,
> The forts he takes, the squadrons does pursue,
> And with rich spoils erects a *Temple* too;
> A structure, that shall roofs of gold survive,
> Shall *Solomonic* and *Mosaic* work out-live,
> Shall stay to see the universal fire,
> And only, with the temple of the world, expire.
>
> Strange, the late bard should his devotion rear
> At *Synagogue*, when, lo! the *Temple*'s near!
> Such sacrilege it were of old, t' espouse
> The wandring tent, before the wondrous house;
> The house, in which a southern queen might be
> A sacrifice to art and ecstasie.
> Poor poets thus ingeniously can prove
> Their sacred zeal misguided as their love!
>
> Go forth, saint-bard! exert thy conqu'ring hand!
> Set up thy Temple through the muses land!
> Down with the stage, its wanton scenes cashier,
> And all the demons wont to revel there!
> Great *Pan* must dy, his oracles be dumb,
> Where'er thy temple and its flames shall come;
> Convert the *Muses*, teach them how to be
> Ambitious of the *Graces* companie;
> Purge *Helicon*, and make *Parnassus* still

To send his vicious streams to *Sion's* hill!
Thence banish all th' unhallow'd, tuneful men,
From *Homer*, down to the phantastic *Ben*!
Baptize the future poets, and infuse
A sacred flame in all belov'd by muse!
Teach them the efforts of great *Shiloh's* love,
The anthems, and the melodies above!
Tell them what matter, and what theam's in store,
For sacred past'ral, and divine amour;
Shiloh himself would condescend so low,
To be a shepherd, and a bridegroom too.
What myst'ries in church militant there to,
Teach them to look, and soar, and sing like thee.
Here poesy's high birth, and glory shine,
'Tis here, that it, like other grace, we see
From glory differs only in degree!

    Whilst to thy temple proselytes repair,
And offer, and inflame devotion there.
Whilst, on its pillars deep inscrib'd, thy name
Stands consecrated to immortal fame,
Do thou enjoy the rich resolves of *Love*,
The pleasures, the society above!
No more thou'lt tune thy lute unto a strain
That may with thee all day complain;
No more shall sense of ill, and *Griefs* of time
Dis-tune thy viol, and disturb thy rhyme;
No more shall *Sion's* wrongs and sorrows sharp,
Upon the willows hang thy trembling harp;
The wish'd-for sight, the dear perfection's gain'd
The *Longing*, and the *Search*, have now obtain'd;
On Sion's mount, join thou the blisful throng,
That here were skill'd in sacred love and song;
Consort with *Heman*, *Asaph*, and the rest,
Akin to thee, in Temple-service blest;
Who all rejoyce thy lov'd access to see,
And ply their harps, no doubt, to welcome thee;
Music and Love triumph! and *Herbert's* lyre,
Serenely sounds amidst th' harmonious quire!
There still, on *Love* in his own person, gaze,
Drink in the beams flow from his radiant face,
Still to thy harp chant forth th' immortal verse
Does *Love's* exploits in foreign land rehearse,
Move him to hasten his return below,
That church, now mil'tant, may triumphant grow,
And all thy pros'lyte-bands may mount, and see
The Temple there, and all the scenes of joy, with thee.
    —JOHN REYNOLDS, "To the Memory of the
        Divine Mr. Herbert," A *View of Death*, 1725,
        pp. 110–18

What was said of the late venerable Dr. John Brown, of Edinburgh, that "his face was a sermon for Christ," holds of the thought-lined, burdened-eyed, translucent as if transfigured face of Herbert. There is a noble "ivory palace" for the meek and holy soul there; brow steep rather than wide; lips tremulous as with music; nose pronounced as Richard Baxter's; cheeks worn and thin; hair full and flowing as in younger days: altogether a face which one could scarcely pass without note—all the more that there are lines in it which inevitably suggest that if George Herbert mellowed into the sweet lovingness and gentleness of John "whom Jesus loved," it was of grace, and through masterdom of a naturally lofty, fiery spirit. After all, these are the men of God who leave the deepest mark on their generation.—ALEXANDER GROSART, "George Herbert," *Leisure Hour*, 1873, p. 455

He was buried at Bemerton, where a new church has been built in his honor. It may be found on the high-road leading west from Salisbury, and only a mile and a half away; and at Wilton—the carpet town—which is only a fifteen minutes' walk beyond, may be found that gorgeous church, built not long ago by another son of the Pembroke stock (the late Lord Herbert of Lea), who perhaps may have had in mind the churchly honors due to his poetic kinsman; and yet all the marbles which are lavished upon this Wilton shrine are poorer, and will sooner fade than the mosaic of verse builded into *The Temple* of George Herbert.—DONALD G. MITCHELL, *English Lands, Letters, and Kings from Elizabeth to Anne*, 1890, p. 119

At Bemerton he lived, as he wrote, the ideal life of "A Priest to the Temple." While his simple sermons and his life of goodness won his people to a good life, he was writing poems which should catch the hearts of the next generation and enlist men's sentiment and sympathy in the restoration of the Church. Herbert's life was itself the noblest of his poems, and while it had the beauty of his verses it had their quaintnesses as well. Those exquisite lines of his, so characteristic of his age and his style, give a picture suggestive of his own character:

    Sweet day, so cool, so calm, so bright,
    The bridal of the earth and sky.
    —WILLIAM HOLDEN HUTTON, *Social England*,
      1895, Vol. 4, ed. Traill, p. 34

General

View a true Poet, whose bare lines
Include more goodnesse then some shrines.
Wee'le canonize him, and what er
Befalls, style him heauens Chorister.
No Muse inspird his quill, the three
Graces, faith, Hope, and Charitie
Inflamd that breast, whose heat farre higher. . . .
    —ROBERT CODRINGTON, "On Herbert's
        Poem," 1638

The first, that with an effectual success attempted a diversion of this foul and overflowing stream, was the blessed man, Mr. George Herbert, whose holy life and verse gained many pious converts—of whom I am the least—and gave the first check to a most flourishing and admired wit of his time.—HENRY VAUGHAN, "Preface" to *Silex Scintillans*, 1650

But I must confess, after all, that, next the Scripture Poems, there are none so savoury to me as Mr. George Herbert's and Mr. George Sandys'. I know that Cowley and others far exceed Herbert in wit and accurate composure; but as Seneca takes with me above all his contemporaries, because he speaketh things by words, feelingly and seriously, like a man that is past jest; so Herbert speaks to God like one that really believeth a God, and whose business in the world is most with God. Heart-work and Heaven-work make up his books.—RICHARD BAXTER, "Prefatory Address" to *Poetical Fragments*, 1681

Mr. Herbert's *Poems* have met with so general and deserv'd Acceptance, that they have undergone Eleven Impressions near Twenty Years ago: He hath obtain'd by way of Eminency, the Name of *Our Divine Poet*, and his Verses have been frequently quoted in Sermons and other Discourses; yet, I fear, few of them have been Sung since his Death, the Tunes not being at the Command of ordinary Readers.
    This attempt therefore, (such as it is) is to bring so many of them as I well could, which I judg'd suited to the Capacity and Devotion of Private Christians, into the *Common Metre* to be Sung in their Closets or Families. . . .

How much more fit is Herbert's *Temple* to be set to the Lute, than Cowley's *Mistress*! It is hard that no one can be taught Musick, but in such wanton Songs as fill the Hearts of many Learners with Lust and Vanity all their Days. Why should it be thought a greater Prophaning of Spiritual Songs to use them in a Musick-Scool, than it is of the New Testament, to teach Children to spell; yet what Christian would not rather have his Child taught to read in a Bible than in a Play-Book? Especially, when they who learn Musick are generally more apt to receive Impressions from the Matter of the Song, than Children are from the Books in which they first learn to Spell. My attempt hath been easie, only to alter the measures of some Hymns, keeping strictly to the Sence of the Author; But how noble an undertaking were it, if any one could and would rescue the high flights, and lofty strains found in the most Celebrated Poets, from their sacrilegious Applications to *Carnal Love*, and restore them to the *Divine Love*! When the Devil drew off the Nations from the True God, He caus'd the same Institutions with which God was honoured, to be used in the Idol Service, *Temple, Priests, Sacrifices,* &c. and amongst the rest *Psalmody*: And it is strange, that when we have so long been emerg'd out of Heathenism, that such a Remnant of it should be amongst us, wherein the most devotional Part of Religion doth consist.

Almost all Phrases and Expressions of Worship due only to God, are continu'd in these artificial Composures in the Heathenish use of them even from the *inspirations* that they invoke in their beginning, to the *Raptures, Flames, Adorations,* &c. That they pretend to in the Progress: Nor are these meer empty Names with them, but their Hearts are more fervently carried out in the musical use of them, than they would be if their Knees were bow'd to *Baal* and *Astaroth*: Few Holy Souls are more affected with the Praises of a Redeemer, than they are of the wanton Object that they profess to adore. Oh for some to write *Parodies*, by which Name I find one Poem in *Herbert* call'd, which begins, *Souls Joy, where art thou gone,* and was, I doubt not, a light Love-song turn'd into a Spiritual Hymn. Parōdia, *Est quum alterius Poetae Versus in aliud Argumentum transferuntur.* I do not find it hath been made a Matter of scruple to turn the Temples built for Idols into Churches: And as to this Case, it is to be consider'd that the Musick and Poetry was an excellent Gift of God, which ought to have been us'd for Him; and that their high strains of Love, Joy, &c. Suit none but the adorable Saviour; and all their most warm and affecting Expressions are stollen from the Churches Adoration of Christ; and who can doubt but the Church may take her own, whereever she finds it, whether in an Idolatrous Mass-Book or Prophane Love-song? It was a noble Resolution of him that said,

> I'll Consecrate my Magdalene to Thee

The *Eyes, Mouth, Hair,* which had been abus'd to Lust and Vanity were us'd to *Wash, Kiss, Wipe* the feet of a Saviour: May Man and Angels Praise him for ever and ever! *Amen.*— UNSIGNED, "Preface" to *Select Hymns, Taken out of Mr. Herbert's Temple,* 1697

A writer of the same class, though infinitely inferior to both Quarles and Crashaw. His poetry is a compound of enthusiasm without sublimity, and conceit without either ingenuity or imagination. . . . When a man is once reduced to the impartial test of time,—when partiality, friendship, fashion, and party, have withdrawn their influence,—our surprise is frequently excited by past subjects of admiration that now cease to strike. He who takes up the poems of Herbert would little suspect that he had been public orator of an university, and a favourite of his sovereign; that he had received flattery and praise from Donne and from Bacon; and that the biographers of the day had enrolled his name among the first names of his country.—HENRY HEADLEY, *Select Beauties of Ancient Poetry,* 1787

His beauties of thought and diction are so overloaded with farfetched conceits and quaintnesses; low, and vulgar, and even indelicate imagery; and a pertinacious appropriation of Scripture language and figure, in situations where they make a most unseemly exhibition, that there is now very little probability of his ever regaining the popularity which he has lost. That there was much, however, of the real Poetical temperament in the composition of his mind, the following lines, although not free from his characteristic blemishes, will abundantly prove:

> Sweet Day! so cool, so calm, so bright,
> —HENRY NEELE, *Lectures on English Poetry,*
> 1827

Another poet in that age was George Herbert, the author of *The Temple*, a little book of Divine songs and poems which ought to be on the shelf of every lover of religion and poetry. It is a book which is apt to repel the reader on his first acquaintance. It is written in the quaint epigrammatic style which was for a short time in vogue in England, a style chiefly marked by the elaborate decomposition to which every object is subjected. The writer is not content with the obvious properties of natural objects but delights in discovering abstruser relations between them and the subject of his thought. This both by Cowley and Donne is pushed to affectation. By Herbert it is used with greater temperance and to such excellent ends that it is easily forgiven if indeed it do not come to be loved.

It has been justly said of Herbert that if his thought is often recondite and far fetched yet the language is always simple and chaste. I should cite Herbert as a striking example of the power of exalted thought to melt and bend language to its fit expression. Language is an organ on which men play with unequal skill and each man with different skill at different hours. The man who stammers when he is afraid or when he is indifferent, will be fluent when he is angry, and eloquent when his intellect is active. Some writers are of that frigid temperament that their sentences always seem to be made with grammar and dictionary. To such the easy structure of prose is laborious, and metre and rhyme, and especially any difficult metre is an insurmountable bar to the expression of their meaning. Of these Byron says,

> Prose poets like blank verse
> Good workmen never quarrel with their tools.
> (*Don Juan*, I, 201)

Those on the contrary who were born to write, have a self-enkindling power of thought which never knows this obstruction but find words so rapidly that they seem coeval with the thought. And in general according to the elevation of the soul will be the power over language and lively thoughts will break out into spritely verse. No metre so difficult but will be tractable so that you only raise the temperature of the thought.

'For my part,' says Montaigne, 'I hold and Socrates is positive in it, that whoever has in his mind a lively and clear imagination, he will express it well enough in one kind or another and though he were dumb by signs.'

Every reader is struck in George Herbert with the inimitable felicity of the diction. The thought has so much heat as actually to fuse the words, so that language is wholly flexible in his hands, and his rhyme never stops the progress of the sense. . . .

What Herbert most excels in is in exciting that feeling which we call the moral sublime. The highest affections are touched by his muse. I know nothing finer than the turn with which his poem on affliction concludes. After complaining to his maker as if too much suffering had been put upon him he threatens that he will quit God's service for the world's:

Well, I will change the service and go seek
    Some other master out
Ah, my dear God, though I be clean forgot
Let me not love thee if I love thee not.
            (*Affliction* (I), 11. 63–6)

Herbert's Poems are the breathings of a devout soul reading the riddle of the world with a poet's eye but with a saint's affections. Here poetry is turned to its noblest use. The sentiments are so exalted, the thought so wise, the piety so sincere that we cannot read this book without joy that our nature is capable of such emotions and criticism is silent in the exercise of higher faculties.

It is pleasant to reflect that a book that seemed formed for the devotion of angels, attained, immediately on its publication, great popularity. Isaac Walton informs us that 20,000 copies had been sold before 1670, within forty years. After being neglected for a long period several new editions of it have appeared in England and one recently in America.—RALPH WALDO EMERSON, Lecture on Ben Jonson, Herrick, Herbert, Walton, delivered Dec. 31, 1835, *The Early Lectures of Ralph Waldo Emerson*, 1959, Vol. 1, eds. Wicher, Spiller, pp. 349–53

Now the imagination of George Herbert is just as vigourous [as Bunyan's] and his communings with God as immediate, but they are the imagination & the communings of a well bridled & disciplined mind, and therefore though he feels himself to have sold Christ over & over again for definite pieces of silver, for pleasures or promises of this world, he repents and does penance for such actual sin—he does not plague himself about a singing in his ears. There is as much difference between the writings & feelings of the two men as between the high bred, keen, severe, thoughtful countenance of the one—and the fat, vacant, vulgar, boy's *face* of the other. Both are equally Christians, equally taught of God, but taught through different channels, Herbert through his brains, Bunyan through his liver. . . .

I have been more and more struck on rethinking and rereading with the singular differences between Bunyan & Herbert. Bunyan humble & contrite enough, but always dwelling painfully & exclusively on the relations of the deity to his own little self—not contemplating God as the God of all the earth, nor loving him as such, nor so occupied with the consideration of his attributes as to forget himself in an extended gratitude, but always looking to his own interests & his own state—loving or fearing or doubting, just as *he* happened to fancy God was dealing with him. Herbert on the contrary, full of faith & love, regardless of himself, outpouring his affection in all circumstances & at all times, and never *fearing*, though often weeping. Hear him speaking of such changes of feeling as Bunyan complains of:

Whether I fly with angels, fall with dust,
Thy hands made both, & I am there.
Thy power & love, my love & trust
Make one place everywhere,
            (*The Temper* (I), 11. 25–8)

Vide the three last lovely stanzas of *The Temper.* I think Bunyan's a most dangerous book, in many ways—first because to people who do not allow for his ignorance, low birth, & sinful & idle youth, the workings of his diseased mind would give a most false impression of God's dealings—secondly be-

cause it encourages in ill taught religious people, such idle, fanciful, selfish, profitless modes of employing the mind as not only bring discredit on religion generally, but give rise to all sorts of schisms, heresies, insanities and animosities—and again, because to people of a turn of mind like mine, but who have [no] less stability of opinion, it would at once suggest the idea of all religion being nothing more than a particular phase of indigestion coupled with a good imagination & bad conscience.—JOHN RUSKIN, Letters to His Mother, April 13 and 20, 1845, *Ruskin in Italy: Letters to His Parents 1845*, 1872, ed. Shapiro, pp. 17–18

Even the friendly taste of Mr. Keble was offended by the constant flutter of his fancy, forever hovering round and round the theme. But this was a peculiarity which the most gifted writers admired. Dryden openly avowed that nothing appeared more beautiful to him than the imagery in Cowley, which some readers condemned. It must, at least, be said, in praise of this creative playfulness, that it is a quality of the intellect singularly sprightly and buoyant; it ranges over a boundless landscape, pierces into every corner, and by the light of its own fire—to adopt a phrase of Temple—discovers a thousand little bodies, or images in the world, unseen by common eyes, and only manifested by the rays of that poetic sun.—ROBERT ARIS WILLMOTT, "Introduction" to *The Works of George Herbert*, 1854

Herbert was an intimate friend of Donne, and no doubt a great admirer of his poetry but his own has been to a great extent preserved from the imitation of Donne's peculiar style, into which it might in other circumstances have fallen, in all probability by its having been composed with little effort or elaboration, and chiefly to relieve and amuse his own mind by the melodious expression of his favorite fancies and contemplations. His quaintness lies in his thoughts rather than in their expression, which is in general sufficiently simple and luminous.—GEORGE L. CRAIK, A *Compendious History of English Literature and of the English Language*, 1861, Vol. 2, p. 19

Here comes a poet indeed! and how am I to show him due honour? With his book humbly, doubtfully offered, with the ashes of the poems of his youth fluttering in the wind of his priestly garments, he crosses the threshold. Or rather, for I had forgotten the symbol of my book, let us all go from our chapel to the choir, and humbly ask him to sing that he may make us worthy of his song. In George Herbert there is poetry enough and to spare: it is the household bread of his being. . . . With a conscience tender as a child's, almost diseased in its tenderness, and a heart loving as a woman's, his intellect is none the less powerful. Its movements are as the sword-play of an alert, poised, well-knit, strong-wristed fencer with the rapier, in which the skill impresses one more than the force, while without the force the skill would be valueless, even hurtful, to its possessor. There is a graceful humour with it occasionally, even in his most serious poems adding much to their charm.—GEORGE MACDONALD, *England's Antiphon*, 1886, pp. 174–76

Although later generations have moderated the lavish praise bestowed upon Herbert by his contemporaries, the final judgment seems strongly in favor of the poet's claims to lasting recognition. His poems are at times overloaded with conceits and quaint imagery—the great fault of that age—but this cannot destroy the vein of true, devotional poetry running through them all.—JOHN S. HART, A *Manual of English Literature*, 1872, p. 76

The place of George Herbert among the sacred poets of England may be safely pronounced as secure as that of the greatest of his contemporaries. By this we do not at all mean to claim for him such quality or quantity of genius as belongs to these "greatest;" nor indeed would we even put him on a level with Henry Vaughan the Silurist, or Richard Crashaw. But we do mean that his fame is as true and catholic, and covetable and imperishable, as that of any. We could as soon conceive of the skylark's singing dying out of our love, or the daisy of the "grene grasse" ceasing to be "a thing of beauty," as of the verse-Temple built fully two centuries and a half ago being now suffered to go to ruin or to take stain. Myriads treasure in their heart of hearts the poems of George Herbert who know little and do not care to know more of the mighty sons of song.—ALEXANDER B. GROSART, "George Herbert," *Leisure Hour*, 1873, Vol. 22, p. 325

Herbert is the psalmist dear to all who love religious poetry with exquisite refinement of thought. So much piety was never married to so much wit. Herbert identifies himself with Jewish genius, as Michael Angelo did when carving or painting prophets and patriarchs, not merely old men in robes and beards, but with the sanctity and the character of the Pentateuch and the prophecy conspicuous in them. His wit and his piety are genuine, and are sure to make a lifelong friend of a good reader.— RALPH WALDO EMERSON, "Preface" to *Parnassus*, 1875, p. vi

It is to another literature that we must look for much that is peculiar to George Herbert; and this will not only account for many of his faults, but will explain by what side of his character this scholar and gentleman was attracted to country life, and could find contentment in the talk and ways of villagers. The writings to which we allude are those of the moralists of the silver age or later, pagans of the decline, or, at best, but demi-Christians, whose works seem to us so trite and dull, but on which our forefathers, unspoiled by excitement, and not yet exigent in literary style, ruminated with a quiet delight such as we seldom feel. It is from the writings of these authors in many cases that they formed the proverbs which they esteemed as the highest axioms of practical wisdom, and which George Herbert has treasured so fondly in his "Jacula Prudentum."— WENTWORTH WEBSTER, *The Academy*, 1882, p. 22

It may be confessed without shame and without innuendo that Herbert has been on the whole a greater favourite with readers than with critics, and the reason is obvious. He is not prodigal of the finest strokes of poetry. To take only his own contemporaries, and undoubtedly pupils, his gentle moralising and devotion are tame and cold beside the burning glow of Crashaw, commonplace and popular beside the intellectual subtlety and, now and then, the inspired touch of Vaughan. But he never drops into the flatness and the extravagance of both these writers, and his beauties, assuredly not mean in themselves, and very constantly present, are both in kind and in arrangement admirably suited to the average comprehension. He is quaint and conceited; but his quaintnesses and conceits are never beyond the reach of any tolerably intelligent understanding. He is devout, but his devotion does not transgress into the more fantastic regions of piety. He is a mystic, but of the more exoteric school of mysticism. Thus he is among sacred poets very much (though relatively he occupies a higher place) what the late Mr. Longfellow was among profane poets. He expresses common needs, common thoughts, the everyday emotions of the Christian, just sublimated sufficiently to make them attractive. The fashion and his own taste gave him a pleasing quaintness, which his good sense kept from being ever obscure or offensive or extravagant.—GEORGE SAINTSBURY, *A History of Elizabethan Literature*, 1887, p. 372

Herbert's imagery shows much overelaboration, after the manner of Donne, who had been a close friend of his mother, and of his own youth: but his verses are free from the dulness of most of Vaughan's poems and the extravagance of many of Crashaw's. He is the poet of a meditative and sober piety that is catholic alike in the wideness of its appeal and in its love of symbol and imagery.—J. HOWARD B. MASTERMAN, *The Age of Milton*, 1897, p. 108

Vaughan's intellectual debt to Herbert revolves itself into somewhat less than nothing; for in following him with zeal to the Missionary College of the Muses, he lost rather than gained, and he is altogether delightful and persuasive only where he is altogether himself. Nevertheless, a certain spirit of conformity and filial piety towards Herbert has betrayed Vaughan into frequent and flagrant imitations.—LOUISE IMOGEN GUINEY, "Henry Vaughan," *A Little English Gallery*, 1894, p. 95

Herbert has an extraordinary tenderness, and it is his singular privilege to have been able to clothe the common aspirations, fears, and needs of the religious mind in language more truly poetical than any other Englishman. He is often extravagant, but rarely dull or flat; his greatest fault lay in an excessive pseudo-psychological ingenuity, which was a snare to all these lyrists, and in a tasteless delight in metrical innovations, often as ugly as they were unprecedented. He sank to writing in the shape of wings and pillars and altars. On this side, in spite of the beauty of their isolated songs and passages, the general decadence of the age was apparent in the lyrical writers. There was no principle of poetic style recognised, and when the spasm of creative passion was over, the dullest mechanism seemed good enough to be adopted.—EDMUND GOSSE, *A Short History of Modern English Literature*, 1897, p. 147

Works

Sir, I pray deliver this little book to my dear brother Farrer, and tell him, he shall find in it a picture of the many spiritual conflicts that have passed betwixt God and my soul, before I could subject mine to the will of Jesus my Master: in whose service I have now found perfect freedom. Desire him to read it; and then, if he can think it may turn to the advantage of any dejected poor soul: let it be made public; if not let him burn it; for I and it are less than the least of God's mercies.—GEORGE HERBERT, "To Mr. Duncan," *The Life of George Herbert*, 1632

The dedication of this work having been made by the Authour to the *Divine Majestie* onely, how should we now presume to interest any mortall man in the patronage of it? Much lesse think we it meet to seek the recommendation of the Muses, for that which himself was confident to have been inspired by a diviner breath then flows from *Helicon*. The world therefore shall receive it in that naked simplicitie, with which he left it, without any addition either of support or ornament, more than is included in it self. We leave it free and unforestalled to every mans judgement, and to the benefit that he shall finde by perusall. Onely for the clearing of some passages, we have thought it not unfit to make the common Reader privie to some few particularities of the condition and disposition of the Person;

Being nobly born, and as eminently endued with gifts of the minde, and having by industrie and happy education perfected them to that great height of excellencie, whereof his fellowship of Trinitie Colledge in Cambridge, and his Oratorship in the Universitie, together with that knowledge which the Kings Court had taken of him, could make relation farre above ordinarie. Quitting both his deserts and all the opportunities that he had for wordly prefermen, he betook himself to the Sanctuarie and Temple of God, choosing rather to serve at Gods Altar, then to seek the honour of State-employments. As for those inward enforcements to this course (for outward there was none) which many of these ensuing verses bear witnesse of, they detract not from the freedome, but adde to the honour of this resolution in him. As God had enabled him, so he accounted him meet not onely to be called, but to be compelled to this service: Wherein his faithfull discharge was such, as may make him justly a companion to the primitive Saints, and a pattern or more for the age he lived in.

To testifie his independencie upon all others, and to quicken his diligence in this kinde, he used in his ordinarie speech, when he made mention of the blessed name of our Lord and Saviour Jesus Christ, to adde, *My Master.*

Next God, he loved that which God himself hath magnified above all things, that is, his Word: so as he hath been heard to make solemne protestation, that he would not part with one leaf thereof for the whole world, if it were offered him in exchange.

His obedience and conformitie to the Church and the discipline thereof was singularly remarkable. Though he abounded in private devotions, yet went he every morning and evening with his familie to the Church; and by his example, exhortations, and encouragements drew the greater part of his parishioners to accompanie him dayly in the publick celebration of Divine Service.

As for worldly matters, his love and esteem to them was so little, as no man can more ambitiously seek, then he did earnestly endeavour the resignation of an Ecclesiasticall dignitie, which he was possessour of. But God permitted not the accomplishment of this desire, having ordained him his instrument for reedifying of the Church belonging thereunto, that had layen ruinated almost twenty yeares. The reparation whereof, having been uneffectually attempted by publick collections, was in the end by his own and some few others private free-will-offerings successfully effected. With the remembrance whereof, as of an especiall good work, when a friend went about to comfort him on his death-bed, he made answer, *It is a good work, if it be sprinkled with the bloud of Christ:* otherwise then in this respect he could finde nothing to glorie or comfort himself with, neither in this, nor in any other thing.

And these are but a few of many that might be said, which we have chosen to premise as a glance to some parts of the ensuing book, and for an example to the Reader. We conclude all with his own Motto, with which he used to conclude all things that might seem to tend any way to his own honour;

> Lesse then the least of Gods mercies.
> —Nicholas Farrer, "Preface" to *The Temple,* 1633

Haile Sacred Architect
Thou doest a glorious Temple raise
    stil ecchoinge his praise.
who taught thy genius thus to florish it
with curious gravings of a Peircinge witt.
    Statelye thy Pillers bee,
    Westwards the Crosse, the Quier, and
        thine Alter Eastward stande,
    where Is most Catholique Conformitie
with out a nose-twange spoylinge harmonie.
    Resolve to Sinne noe more,
    from hence a penitent sigh, and groane
        cann flintye heartes unstone;

and blowe them to their happye porte heaven's
    doore,
where Herberts Angell's flowen awaye before.
    —John Polwhele, "On Mr. Herberts Devine
    Poeme *The Church*," c. 1633

A book, in which by declaring his own spiritual conflicts, he hath comforted and raised many a dejected and discomposed soul, and charmed them into sweet and quiet thoughts: a book, by the frequent reading whereof, and the assistance of that Spirit that seemed to inspire the Author, the Reader may attain habits of Peace and Piety, and all the gifts of the Holy Ghost and Heaven: and may, by still reading, still keep those sacred fires burning upon the altar of so pure a heart, as shall free it from the anxieties of this world, and keep it fixed upon things that are above.—Isaac Walton, *Life of Dr. John Donne,* 1639, p. 37

What Church is this? Christs Church. Who builds it?
Mr. *George Herbert.* Who assisted it?
Many assisted: who, I may not say,
So much contention might arise that way.
If I say Grace gave all, Wit straight doth thwart,
And sayes all that is there is mine: but Art
Denies and sayes ther's nothing there but's mine:
Nor can I easily the right define.
Divide: say, Grace the matter gave, and Wit
Did polish it, Art measured and made fit
Each severall piece, and fram'd it all together.
No, by no means: this may not please them neither.
None's well contented with a part alone,
When each doth challenge all to be his owne:
The matter, the expressions, and the measures,
Are eqyally Arts, Wits, and Graces treasures.
Then he that would impartially discusse
This doubtfull question, must answer thus:
In building of this temple Mr. *Herbert*
Is equally all Grace, all Wit, all Art.
    Roman and *Grecian* Muses all give way:
    One *English* Poem darkens all your day.
    —Christopher Harvey, "The Synagogue,"
    1640

Know you faire, on what you looke;
Divinest love lyes in this booke:
Expecting fire from your eyes,
To kindle this his sacrifice.
When your hands unty these strings,
Thinke you have an Angell by th' wings.
One that gladly will bee nigh,
To wait upon each morning sigh.
To flutter in the balmy aire,
Of your well perfumed prayer.
These white plumes of his heele lend you,
Which every day to heaven will send you:
To take acquaintance of the spheare,
And all the smooth faced kindred there.
And though *Herbert's* name doe owe
These devotions, fairest; know
That while I lay them on the shrine
Of your white hand, they are mine.
    —Richard Crashaw, "On Mr. G. Herbert's
    Booke intituled *The Temple*," *Steps to the
    Temple*, 1646

Lord! yet how dull am I?
    When I would flye!

Up to the Region, of thy Glories where
    Onlie true formes appeare;
My long brail'd Pineons, (clumsye, and unapt)
    I cannot Spread;
    I am all dullnes; I was Shap't
Only to flutter, in the lower Shrubbs
    Of Earth-borne-follies. Out alas!
        When I would treade
A higher Step, ten thousand, thousand Rubbs
    Prevent my Pace.

This Glorious Larke; with humble Honour, I
    Admire and praise;
        But when I raise
My Selfe, I fall asham'd, to see him flye:
The Royall Prophet, in his Extasie,
        First trod this path;
Hee followes neare; (I will not Say, how nigh)
    In flight, as well as faith.
Let me asham'd creepe backe into my Shell;
    And humbly Listen to his Layes:
Tis prejudice, what I intended Praise;
As where they fall soe Lowe, all Words are Still.
    Our Untun'd Liricks, onlie fitt
        To Sing, our Selfe-borne-Cares,
    Dare not, of Him. Or had wee Witt,
        Where might wee find out Ears
Worthy his Character? if wee may bring
    Our Accent to his Name?
This Stand, of Lirick's, Hee the utmost Fame
Has gain'd; and now they vaile, to heare Him Sing
Horace in voice; and Casimire in winge.
    —GEORGE DANIEL, "An Ode upon the
        Incomparable Liricke Poesie written by Mr.
        George Herbert; entituled: *The Temple*" (1648),
        *The Selected Poems of George Daniel of
        Beswick 1616–1657*, 1959, ed. Stroup, pp.
        66–67

If zeal and genius, Piety and wit in like
    Pre-em'nence in one Book have ever joined,
'Tis, Herbert, this of thine: thou'st borne off every prize,
    Who melody so sweet canst sanctify.
No Lyre sang sacred hymns so graciously as thine,
    Save David's only—his, or none's.
What profit, then, to bid my Muses hither come
    To lessen thy great Songs with measures slight?
For I in vain should try to sing such lofty praise,
    Or in thy *Temple*'s feet my measures write,
Unless thy holy Dove's own wing provide my pen,
    Or coal from off thine altar touch my lips;
Unless, in fine, my heart should feel those holy flames
    Through which I too might have that sacred vein.
Permit me then thy proper phrases to return
    And mine own gardens water from thy fount.
For better, god-like Poet, I cannot praise thy work
    Than thou the Noble Royal Book didst laud:
'Why mention "Vatican" and "Bodleian", O friend?
    One single book a library is to us'.
For my part this I'll add: to me no other Book,
    God's Word apart, so sacred is or good.
Since, then, on earth no Hymn is so divine, nor like
    And equal to thy *Temple* any Song,
This yet remains for thee: in heaven eternal poems

To sound, and verses fit for angels' Choirs.
    —JAMES DUPORT, "In Divinum Poema (Cui
        Titulus Templum) Georgii Herberti," *Musae
        subsecivae, sev Poetica Stromata*, 1676, pp.
        357–58

I find more substantial comfort now in pious George Herbert's *Temple*, which I used to read to amuse myself with his quaintness, in short, only to laugh at, than in all the poetry since the poems of Milton.—SAMUEL TAYLOR COLERIDGE, *Lectures and Notes on Shakespere*, 1818

Another exquisite master of this species of style where the scholar and the poet supplies the material, but the perfect well-bred gentleman the expressions and the arrangement, is George Herbert. As from the nature of the subject and the too frequent quaintness of the thoughts, his *Temple, or Sacred Poems and Private Ejaculations* are comparatively but little known, I shall extract two poems. The first is a Sonnet, equally admirable for the weight, number and expression of the thoughts, and for the simple dignity of the language (unless indeed a fastidious taste should object to the latter half of the sixth line). The second is a poem of greater length, which I have chosen not only for the present purpose, but likewise as a striking example and illustration of an assertion hazarded in a former page of these sketches: namely that the characteristic fault of our elder poets is the reverse of that which distinguishes too many of our more recent versifiers; the one conveying the most fantastic thoughts in the most correct and natural language; the other in the most fantastic language conveying the most trivial thoughts. The latter is a riddle of words; the former an enigma of thoughts. The one reminds me of an odd passage in Drayton's *Ideas*:

    As other men, so I myself do muse,
    Why in this sort I wrest invention so;
    And why these giddy metaphors I use,
    Leaving the path the greater part do go;
    I will resolve you: I am lunatic!
        ⟨"Sonnet IX"⟩

    The other recalls a still odder passage in the 'Synagogue, or the Shadow of the Temple,' a connected series of poems in imitation of Herbert's *Temple* and in some editions annexed to it:

        O how my mind
            Is gravell'd!
                Not a thought,
      That I can find,
            But's ravell'd
                All to nought.
      Short ends of threds,
            And narrow shreds
                Of lists,
      Knot's snarled ruffs,
            Loose broken tufts
                Of twists,
Are my torn meditation's ragged cloathing.
Which, wound and woven, shape a sute for nothing:
One while I think, and then I am in pain
To think how to unthink that thought again.

Immediately after these burlesque passages I cannot proceed to the extracts promised without changing the ludicrous tone of feeling by the interposition of the three following stanzas of Herbert's:

    Sweet day, so cool, so calm, so bright,
    The bridal of the earth and sky:

The dew shall weep thy fall to-night,
    For thou must die!
Sweet rose, whose hue angry and brave
Bids the rash gazer wipe his eye:
Thy root is ever in its grave,
    And thou must die!

Sweet spring, full of sweet days and rose
A nest where sweets compacted lie:
My musick shows ye have your closes,
    And all must die!

⟨ "Virtue"⟩

Lord, with what care hast thou begirt us round!
Parents first season us; then schoolmasters
Deliver us to laws: they send us bound
To rules of reason, holy messengers,
Pulpits and Sundays, sorrow dogging sin,
Afflictions sorted, anguish of all sizes,
Fine nets and stratagems to catch us in,
Bibles laid open, millions of surprizes;
Blessings beforehand, ties of gratefulness,
The sound of glory ringing in our ears:
Without, our shame; within, our consciences;
Angels and grace, eternal hopes and fears!

    Yet all these fences, and their whole array
    One cunning bosom-sin blows quite away.

⟨ "The Bosom Sin"⟩

Dear friend, sit down, the tale is long and sad:
And in my faintings, I presume, your love
Will more comply than help. A Lord I had,
And have, of whom some grounds, which may
    improve,
I hold for two lives, and both lives in me.
To him I brought a dish of fruit one day
And in the middle placed my heart. But he
            (I sigh to say)
Lookt on a servant who did know his eye
Better than you know me, or (which is one)
Than I myself. The servant instantly
Quitting the fruit, seiz'd on my heart alone,
And threw it in a font, wherein did fall
A stream of blood, which issued from the side
Of a great rock: I well remember all,
And have good cause: there it was dipt and dy'd,
And washt, and wrung! the very wringing yet
Enforceth tears. *Your heart was foul, I fear.*
Indeed 'tis true. I did and do commit
Many a fault, more than my lease will bear;
Yet still ask'd pardon, and was not deny'd.
But you shall hear. After my heart was well,
And clean and fair, as I one eventide
            (I sigh to tell)
Walkt by myself abroad, I saw a large
And spacious furnace flaming, and thereon
A boiling caldron, round about whose verge
Was in great letters set AFFLICTION.
The greatness shew'd the owner. So I went
To fetch a sacrifice out of my fold,
Thinking with that which I did thus present,
To warm his love which, I did fear, grew cold.
But as my heart did tender it, the man
Who was to take it from me, slipt his hand,
And threw my heart into the scalding pan;
My heart that brought it (do you understand?)
The offerer's heart. *Your heart was hard, I fear.*
Indeed 'tis true. I found a callous matter
Began to spread and to expatiate there:

But with a richer drug than scalding water
I bath'd it often, ev'n with holy blood,
Which at a board, while many drank bare wine,
A friend did steal into my cup for good,
Ev'n taken inwardly, and most divine
To supple hardnesses. But at the length
Out of the caldron getting, soon I fled
Unto my house, where to repair the strength
Which I had lost, I hasted to my bed;
But when I thought to sleep out all these faults
            (I sigh to speak)
I found that some had stuff'd the bed with
    thoughts,
I would say *thorns.* Dear, could my heart not break
When with my pleasures ev'n my rest was gone?
Full well I understood who had been there:
For I had given the key to none but one:
It must be he. *Your heart was dull, I fear.*
Indeed a slack and sleepy state of mind
Did oft possess me, so that when I pray'd,
Though my lips went, my heart did stay behind.
But all my scores were by another paid,
Who took the debt upon him. *Truly friend,*
For ought I hear, your master shows to you
More favour than you wot of. Mark the end!
The font did only what was old renew:
The caldron suppled what was grown too hard:
The thorns did quicken what was grown too dull:
All did but strive to mend what you had marr'd.
Wherefore be cheer'd, and praise him to the full
Each day, each hour, each moment of the week,
Who fain would have you be new, tender, quick!

⟨ "Love Unknown"⟩

—SAMUEL TAYLOR COLERIDGE, *Biographia*
    Literaria, 1818, ed. George Watson

Its poetical merit is of a very rare, lofty, and original order. It is full of that subtle perception of analogies which is competent only of high poetical genius. . . . Altogether, there are few places on earth nearer Heaven, filled with a richer and holier light, adorned with chaster and nobler ornaments, or where our souls can worship with a more entire forgetfulness of self, and a more thorough realisation of the things unseen and eternal, than in *The Temple* of George Herbert.—GEORGE GIFILLAN, *The Poetical Works of George Herbert,* 1853, pp. xxi–xxvi

His poetry is the *bizarre* expression of a deeply religious and intensely thoughtful nature, sincere at heart, but strange, far-fetched, and serenely crotchety in utterance. Nothing can be more frigid than the conceits in which he clothes the great majority of his pious ejaculations and heavenly ecstasies. Yet every reader feels that his fancy, quaint as it often is, is a part of the organism of his character; and that his quaintness, his uncouth metaphors and comparisons, his squalid phraseology, his holy charades and pious riddles, his inspirations crystallized into ingenuities, and his general disposition to represent the divine through the exterior guise of the odd, are vitally connected with that essential beauty and sweetness of soul which give his poems their wild flavor and fragrance. Amateurs in sanctity, and men of fine religious taste, will tell you that genuine emotion can never find an outlet in such an elaborately fantastic form; and the proposition, according, as it does, with the rules of Blair and Kames and Whately, commands your immediate assent; but still you feel that genuine emotion is there, and, if you watch sharply, you will find that Taste, entering holy George Herbert's *Temple*, after a preliminary sniff of imbecile contempt, somehow slinks away abashed after the first verse at the "Church-porch." . . . One of the profoundest utterances of the Elizabethan age, George Herbert's lines on Man.—EDWIN P. WHIPPLE, *The Literature of the Age of Elizabeth*, 1859–68, pp. 247–48

The Temple is the enigmatical history of a difficult resignation; it is full of the author's baffled ambition and his distress, now at the want of a sphere for his energies, now at the fluctuations of spirit, the ebb and flow of intellectual activity, natural to a temperament as frail as it was eager. There is something a little feverish and disproportioned in his passionate heart-searchings. The facts of the case lie in a nutshell. Herbert was a younger son of a large family; he lost his father early, and his mother, a devout, tender, imperious woman, decided, partly out of piety and partly out of distrust of his power to make his own way in the world, that he should be provided for in the Church. When he was twenty-six he was appointed Public Orator at Cambridge, and hoped to make this position a stepping-stone to employment at court. After eight years his patrons and his mother were dead, and he made up his mind to settle down with a wife on the living of Bemerton, where he died after a short but memorable incumbency of three years. The flower of his poetry seems to belong to the two years of acute crisis which preceded his installation at Bemerton or to the Indian summer of content when he imagined that his failure as a courtier was a prelude to his success in the higher character of a country parson.—GEORGE AUGUSTUS SIMCOX, *English Poets*, 1880, Vol. 2, ed. Ward, p. 193

It is a book to be taken as a friend to be loved, rather than as a performance to be criticised. As a manual of devotion it is as though a seraph covered his face with his wings in rapturous adoration; as a poem it is full of that subtle perception of analogies to be found only in works of genius; while the passage on "Man" shows how the poets in their loftiest moods may sometimes anticipate some of the most wonderful discoveries of science and some of the sublimest speculations of philosophy.—JOHN BROWN, "The Parson of Bemerton," *Good Words*, 1890, p. 697

ISAAK WALTON
From "The Life of Mr. George Herbert" (1670)
The Lives of Dr. John Donne, Sir Henry Wotton,
Richard Hooker, George Herbert,
and Dr. Robert Sanderson
1860, pp. 257–308

George Herbert spent much of his childhood in a sweet content under the eye and care of his prudent Mother, and the tuition of a Chaplain, or tutor to him and two of his brothers, in her own family,—for she was then a widow,—where he continued till about the age of twelve years; and being at that time well instructed in the rules of Grammar, he was not long after commended to the care of Dr. Neale, who was then Dean of Westminster; and by him to the care of Mr. Ireland, who was then Chief Master of that School; where the beauties of his pretty behaviour and wit shined and became so eminent and lovely in this his innocent age, that he seemed to be marked out for piety, and to become the care of Heaven, and of a particular good angel to guard and guide him. And thus he continued in that School, till he came to be perfect in the learned languages, and especially in the Greek tongue, in which he after proved an excellent critic.

About the age of fifteen—he being then a King's Scholar—he was elected out of that School for Trinity College in Cambridge, to which place he was transplanted about the year 1608; and his prudent Mother, well knowing that he might easily lose or lessen that virtue and innocence, which her advice and example had planted in his mind, did therefore procure the generous and liberal Dr. Nevil, who was then Dean of Canterbury, and Master of that College, to take him into his particular care, and provide him a Tutor; which he did most gladly undertake, for he knew the excellencies of his mother, and how to value such a friendship. . . .

And in Cambridge we may find our George Herbert's behaviour to be such, that we may conclude he consecrated the first-fruits of his early age to virtue, and a serious study of learning. And that he did so, this following Letter and Sonnet, which were, in the first year of his going to Cambridge, sent his dear Mother for a New-year's gift, may appear to be some testimony.

—"But I fear the heat of my late ague hath dried up those springs, by which scholars say the Muses use to take up their habitations. However, I need not their help to reprove the vanity of those many love-poems, that are daily writ, and consecrated to Venus; nor to bewail that so few are writ, that look towards God and Heaven. For my own part, my meaning—dear Mother—is, in these Sonnets, to declare my resolution to be, that my poor abilities in Poetry, shall be all and ever consecrated to God's glory: and I beg you to receive this as one testimony."

My God, where is that ancient heat towards thee,
    Wherewith whole shoals of Martyrs once did burn,
      Besides their other flames? Doth Poetry
Wear Venus' livery? only serve her turn?
Why are not Sonnets made of thee? and lays
    Upon thine altar burnt? Cannot thy love
    Heighten a spirit to sound out thy praise
As well as any she? Cannot thy Dove
Outstrip their Cupid easily in flight?
    Or, since thy ways are deep, and still the same,
      Will not a verse run smooth that bears thy name?
Why doth that fire, which by the power and might
    Each breast does feel, no braver fuel choose
    Than that, which one day, worms may chance refuse?
Sure, Lord, there is enough in thee to dry
    Oceans of ink; for as the Deluge did
    Cover the Earth, so doth thy Majesty;
Each cloud distils thy praise, and doth forbid
Poets to turn it to another use.
    Roses and lilies speak Thee; and to make
    A pair of cheeks of them, is thy abuse.
Why should I women's eyes for crystal take?
Such poor invention burns in their low mind
    Whose fire is wild, and doth not upward go
    To praise, and on thee, Lord, some ink bestow.
Open the bones, and you shall nothing find
    In the best face but filth; when, Lord, in Thee
    The beauty lies, in the discovery.

This was his resolution at the sending this letter to his dear Mother, about which time he was in the seventeenth year of his age; and as he grew older, so he grew in learning, and more and more in favour both with God and man; insomuch that, in this morning of that short day of his life, he seemed to be marked out for virtue, and to become the care of Heaven; for God still kept his soul in so holy a frame, that he may and ought to be a pattern of virtue to all posterity, and especially to his brethren of the Clergy, of which the Reader may expect a more exact account in what will follow.

I need not declare that he was a strict student, because, that he was so, there will be many testimonies in the future part of his life. I shall therefore only tell, that he was made Bachelor of Arts in the year 1611; Major Fellow of the College, March 15th, 1615: and, that in that year he was also made Master of Arts, he being then in the 22d year of his age; during all which time, all, or the greatest diversion from his study, was the practice of Music, in which he became a great master; and of which he would say, "That it did relieve his drooping spirits, compose his distracted thoughts, and raised his weary soul so far above earth, that it gave him an earnest of the joys of Heaven, before he possessed them." And it may be noted, that from his first entrance into the College, the generous Dr. Nevil was a cherisher of his studies, and such a lover of his person, his behaviour, and the excellent endowments of his mind, that he took him often into his own company; by which he confirmed his native gentleness: and if during his time he expressed any error, it was, that he kept himself too much retired, and at too great a distance with all his inferiors; and his clothes seemed to prove, that he put too great a value on his parts and parentage. . . .

I may not omit to tell, that he had often designed to leave the University, and decline all study, which he thought did impair his health; for he had a body apt to a consumption, and to fevers, and other infirmities, which he judged were increased by his studies; for he would often say, "He had too thoughtful a wit; a wit like a penknife in too narrow a sheath, too sharp for his body." But his Mother would by no means allow him to leave the University, or to travel; and though he inclined very much to both, yet he would by no means satisfy his own desires at so dear a rate, as to prove an undutiful son to so affectionate a Mother; but did always submit to her wisdom. And what I have now said may partly appear in a copy of verses in his printed poems; 'tis one of those that bear the title of Affliction; and it appears to be a pious reflection on God's providence, and some passages of his life, in which he says,

Whereas my birth and spirit rather took
    The way that takes the town;
Thou didst betray me to a lingering book,
    And wrapt me in a gown:
I was entangled in a world of strife,
Before I had the power to change my life.

Yet, for I threaten'd oft the siege to raise,
    Not simpering all mine age;
Thou often didst with academic praise
    Melt and dissolve my rage;
I took the sweeten'd pill, till I came where
I could not go away, nor persevere.

Yet, lest perchance I should too happy be
    In my unhappiness,
Turning my purge to food, thou throwest me
    Into more sicknesses.
Thus doth thy power cross-bias me, not making
Thine own gifts good, yet me from my ways taking.

Now I am here, what thou wilt do with me
    None of my books will show.
I read, and sigh, and I wish I were a tree,
    For then sure I should grow
To fruit or shade, at least some bird would trust
Her household with me, and I would be just.

Yet, though thou troublest me, I must be meek,
    In weakness must be stout,

Well, I will change my service, and go seek
    Some other master out;
Ah, my dear God! though I am clean forgot,
Let me not love thee, if I love thee not.

In this time of Mr. Herbert's attendance and expectation of some good occasion to remove from Cambridge to Court, God, in whom there is an unseen chain of causes, did in a short time put an end to the lives of two of his most obliging and most powerful friends, Lodowick Duke of Richmond, and James Marquis of Hamilton; and not long after him King James died also, and with them, all Mr. Herbert's Court-hopes: so that he presently betook himself to a retreat from London, to a friend in Kent, where he lived very privately, and was such a lover of solitariness, as was judged to impair his health, more than his study had done. In this time of retirement, he had many conflicts with himself, whether he should return to the painted pleasures of a Court-life, or betake himself to a study of Divinity, and enter into Sacred Orders, to which his dear mother had often persuaded him. These were such conflicts, as they only can know, that have endured them; for ambitious desires, and the outward glory of this world, are not easily laid aside: but at last God inclined him to put on a resolution to serve at his altar.

He did, at his return to London, acquaint a Court-friend with his resolution to enter into Sacred Orders, who persuaded him to alter it, as too mean an employment, and too much below his birth, and the excellent abilities and endowments of his mind. To whom he replied, "It hath been formerly judged that the domestic servants of the King of Heaven should be of the noblest families on earth. And though the iniquity of the late times have made clergymen meanly valued, and the sacred name of priest contemptible; yet I will labour to make it honourable, by consecrating all my learning, and all my poor abilities to advance the glory of that God that gave them; knowing that I can never do too much for him, that hath done so much for me, as to make me a christian. And I will labour to be like my Saviour, by making humility lovely in the eyes of all men, and by following the merciful and meek example of my dear Jesus."

This was then his resolution; and the God of constancy, who intended him for a great example of virtue, continued him in it, for within that year he was made Deacon, but the day when, or by whom, I cannot learn; but that he was about that time made Deacon, is most certain; for I find by the Records of Lincoln, that he was made Prebend of Layton Ecclesia, in the diocese of Lincoln, July 15th, 1626, and that this Prebend was given him by John, then Lord Bishop of that See. And now he had a fit occasion to shew that piety and bounty that was derived from his generous mother, and his other memorable ancestors, and the occasion was this. . . .

I have now brought him to the Parsonage of Bemerton, and to the thirty-sixth year of his age, and must stop here, and bespeak the Reader to prepare for an almost incredible story, of the great sanctity of the short remainder of his holy life; a life so full of charity, humility, and all Christian virtues, that it deserves the eloquence of St. Chrysostom to commend and declare it: a life: that if it were related by a pen like his, there would then be no need for this age to look back into times past for the examples of primitive piety: for they might be all found in the life of George Herbert. But now, alas! who is fit to undertake it? I confess I am not; and am not pleased with myself that I must; and profess myself amazed, when I consider how few of the Clergy lived like him then, and how many live so unlike him now. But it becomes not me to censure: my design is rather to assure the Reader, that I have used very great diligence to inform myself, that I might inform him of the truth of what follows; and though I cannot adorn it with eloquence, yet I will do it with sincerity.

When at his induction he was shut into Bemerton Church, being left there alone to toll the bell,—as the Law requires him,—he staid so much longer than an ordinary time, before he returned to those friends that staid expecting him at the Church-door, that his friend Mr. Woodnot looked in at the Church-window, and saw him lie prostrate on the ground before the Altar; at which time and place—as he after told Mr. Woodnot—he set some rules to himself, for the future manage of his life; and then and there made a vow to labour to keep them.

And the same night that he had his induction, he said to Mr. Woodnot, "I now look back upon my aspiring thoughts, and think myself more happy than if I had attained what then I so ambitiously thirsted for. And I now can behold the Court with an impartial eye, and see plainly that it is made up of fraud and titles, and flattery, and many other such empty, imaginary, painted pleasures; pleasures that are so empty, as not to satisfy when they are enjoyed. But in God, and his service, is a fulness of all joy and pleasure, and no satiety. And I will now use all my endeavours to bring my relations and dependents to a love and reliance on Him, who never fails those that trust him. But above all, I will be sure to live well, because the virtuous life of a Clergyman is the most powerful eloquence to persuade all that see it to reverence and love, and at least to desire to live like him. And this I will do, because I know we live in an age that hath more need of good examples than precepts. And I beseech that God, who hath honoured me so much as to call me to serve him at his altar, that as by his special grace he hath put into my heart these good desires and resolutions; so he will, by his assisting grace, give me ghostly strength to bring the same to good effect. And I beseech him, that my humble and charitable life may so win upon others, as to bring glory to my Jesus, whom I have this day taken to be my Master and Governor; and I am so proud of his service, that I will always observe, and obey, and do his will; and always call him Jesus my Master; and I will always contemn my birth, or any title or dignity that can be conferred upon me, when I shall compare them with my title of being a Priest, and serving at the Altar of Jesus my Master."

And that he did so, may appear in many parts of his book of Sacred Poems: especially in that which he calls "The Odour." In which he seems to rejoice in the thoughts of that word Jesus, and say, that the adding these words, my Master, to it, and the often repetition of them, seemed to perfume his mind, and leave an oriental fragrance in his very breath. And for his unforced choice to serve at God's altar, he seems in another place of his poems, "The Pearl," (Matth. xiii. 45, 46,) to rejoice and say—"He knew the ways of learning; knew what nature does willingly, and what, when it is forced by fire; knew the ways of honour, and when glory inclines the soul to noble expressions: knew the Court; knew the ways of pleasure, of love, of wit, of music, and upon what terms he declined all these for the service of his Master Jesus;" and then concludes, saying,

> That, through these labyrinths, not my grovelling wit,
>   But thy silk twist, let down from Heaven to
>   me,
> Did both conduct, and teach me, how by it
>   To climb to thee.

The third day after he was made Rector of Bemerton, and had changed his sword and silk clothes into a canonical coat,

he returned so habited with his friend Mr. Woodnot to Bainton; and immediately after he had seen and saluted his wife, he said to her—"You are now a Minister's wife, and must now so far forget your father's house, as not to claim a precedence of any of your parishioners; for you are to know, that a Priest's wife can challenge no precedence or place, but that which she purchases by her obliging humility; and I am sure, places so purchased do best become them. And let me tell you, that I am so good a Herald, as to assure you that this is truth." And she was so meek a wife, as to assure him, "it was no vexing news to her, and that he should see her observe it with a cheerful willingness." And, indeed, her unforced humility, that humility that was in her so original, as to be born with her, made her so happy as to do so; and her doing so begot her an unfeigned love, and a serviceable respect from all that conversed with her; and this love followed her in all places, as inseparably as shadows follow substances in sunshine.

It was not many days before he returned back to Bemerton, to view the Church, and repair the Chancel: and indeed to rebuild almost three parts of his house, which was fallen down, or decayed by reason of his predecessor's living at a better Parsonage-house; namely, at Minal, sixteen or twenty miles from this place. At which time of Mr. Herbert's coming alone to Bemerton, there came to him a poor old woman, with an intent to acquaint him with her necessitous condition, as also with some troubles of her mind: but after she had spoke some few words to him, she was surprised with a fear, and that begot a shortness of breath, so that her spirits and speech failed her; which he perceiving, did so compassionate her, and was so humble, that he took her by the hand, and said, "Speak, good mother; be not afraid to speak to me; for I am a man that will hear you with patience; and will relieve your necessities too, if I be able: and this I will do willingly; and therefore, mother, be not afraid to acquaint me with what you desire." After which comfortable speech, he again took her by the hand, made her sit down by him, and understanding she was of his parish, he told her "He would be acquainted with her, and take her into his care." And having with patience heard and understood her wants,—and it is some relief for a poor body to be but heard with patience,—he, like a Christian Clergyman, comforted her by his meek behaviour and counsel; but because that cost him nothing, he relieved her with money too, and so sent her home with a cheerful heart, praising God, and praying for him. Thus worthy, and—like David's blessed man—thus lowly, was Mr. George Herbert in his own eyes, and thus lovely in the eyes of others.

At his return that night to his wife at Bainton, he gave her an account of the passages betwixt him and the poor woman; with which she was so affected, that she went next day to Salisbury, and there bought a pair of blankets, and sent them as a token of her love to the poor woman: and with them a message, "That she would see and be acquainted with her, when her house was built at Bemerton. . . ."

The texts for all his future sermons—which God knows, were not many—were constantly taken out of the Gospel for the day; and he did as constantly declare why the Church did appoint that portion of Scripture to be that day read; and in what manner the Collect for every Sunday does refer to the Gospel, or to the Epistle then read to them; and, that they might pray with understanding, he did usually take occasion to explain, not only the Collect for every particular Sunday, but the reasons of all the other Collects and Responses in our Church-service; and made it appear to them, that the whole service of the Church was a reasonable, and therefore an acceptable sacrifice to God: as namely, that we begin with "Confession of ourselves to be vile, miserable sinners;" and that we begin so, because, till we have confessed ourselves to be such, we are not capable of that mercy which we acknowledge we need, and pray for: but having, in the prayer of our Lord, begged pardon for those sins which we have confessed; and hoping, that as the Priest hath declared our absolution, so by our public confession, and real repentance, we have obtained that pardon; then we dare and do proceed to beg of the Lord, "to open our lips, that our mouth may shew forth his praise;" for till then we are neither able nor worthy to praise him. But this being supposed, we are then fit to say, "Glory be to the Father, and to the Son, and to the Holy Ghost;" and fit to proceed to a further service of our God, in the Collects, and Psalms, and Lauds, that follow in the service.

And as to these Psalms and Lauds, he proceeded to inform them why they were so often, and some of them daily, repeated in our Church-service; namely, the Psalms every month, because they be an historical and thankful repetition of mercies past, and such a composition of prayers and praises, as ought to be repeated often, and publicly; for with such sacrifice God is honoured and well-pleased. This for the Psalms.

And for the Hymns and Lauds appointed to be daily repeated or sung after the first and second Lessons are read to the congregation; he proceeded to inform them, that it was most reasonable, after they have heard the will and goodness of God declared or preached by the Priest in his reading the two chapters, that it was then a seasonable duty to rise up, and express their gratitude to Almighty God, for those his mercies to them, and to all mankind; and then to say with the Blessed Virgin, "that their souls do magnify the Lord, and that their spirits do also rejoice in God their Saviour:" and that it was their duty also to rejoice with Simeon in his song, and say with him, "That their eyes have" also "seen their salvation;" for they have seen that salvation which was but prophesied till his time: and he then broke out into those expressions of joy that he did see it; but they live to see it daily in the history of it, and therefore ought daily to rejoice, and daily to offer up their sacrifices of praise to their God, for that particular mercy. A service, which is now the constant employment of that Blessed Virgin and Simeon, and all those blessed Saints that are possessed of Heaven: and where they are at this time interchangeably and constantly singing, "Holy, holy, holy, Lord God; glory be to God on high, and on earth peace." And he taught them, that to do this was an acceptable service to God, because the Prophet David says in his Psalms, "He that praiseth the Lord honoureth him."

He made them to understand how happy they be that are freed from the incumbrances of that law which our forefathers groaned under: namely, from the legal sacrifices, and from the many ceremonies of the Levitical law; freed from Circumcision, and from the strict observation of the Jewish Sabbath, and the like. And he made them know, that having received so many and so great blessings, by being born since the days of our Saviour, it must be an acceptable sacrifice to Almighty God, for them to acknowledge those blessings daily, and stand up and worship, and say as Zacharias did, "Blessed be the Lord God of Israel, for he hath—in our days—visited and redeemed his people; and—he hath in our days—remembered, and shewed that mercy, which by the mouth of the Prophets, he promised to our forefathers; and this he hath done according to his holy covenant made with them." And he made them to understand that we live to see and enjoy the benefit of it, in his Birth, in his Life, his Passion, his Resurrection, and Ascension into Heaven, where he now sits sensible of all our temptations and infirmities; and where he is at this present time making inter-

cession for us, to his and our Father: and therefore they ought daily to express their public gratulations, and say daily with Zacharias, "Blessed be the Lord God of Israel, that hath thus visited and thus redeemed his people."—These were some of the reasons, by which Mr. Herbert instructed his congregation for the use of the Psalms and Hymns appointed to be daily sung or said in the Church-service.

He informed them also, when the Priest did pray only for the congregation, and not for himself; and when they did only pray for him; as namely, after the repetition of the Creed before he proceeds to pray the Lord's Prayer, or any of the appointed Collects, the Priest is directed to kneel down, and pray for them, saying, "The Lord be with you;" and when they pray for him, saying, "And with thy spirit;" and then they join together in the following Collects: and he assured them, that when there is such mutual love, and such joint prayers offered for each other, then the holy Angels look down from Heaven, and are ready to carry such charitable desires to God Almighty, and he as ready to receive them; and that a Christian congregation calling thus upon God with one heart, and one voice, and in one reverent and humble posture, looks as beautifully as Jerusalem, that is at peace with itself.

He instructed them also why the prayer of our Lord was prayed often in every full service of the Church; namely, at the conclusion of the several parts of that service; and prayed then, not only because it was composed and commanded by our Jesus that made it, but as a perfect pattern for our less perfect forms of prayer, and therefore fittest to sum up and conclude all our imperfect petitions.

He instructed them also, that as by the second Commandment we are required not to bow down, or worship an idol, or false God; so, by the contrary rule, we are to bow down and kneel, or stand up and worship the true God. And he instructed them why the Church required the congregation to stand up at the repetition of the Creeds; namely, because they thereby declare both their obedience to the Church, and an assent to that faith into which they had been baptized. And he taught them, that in that shorter Creed or Doxology, so often repeated daily, they also stood up to testify their belief to be, that "the God that they trusted in was one God, and three persons; the Father, the Son and the Holy Ghost; to whom they and the Priest gave glory." And because there had been heretics that had denied some of those three persons to be God, therefore the congregation stood up and honoured him, by confessing and saying, "It was so in the beginning, is now so, and shall ever be so world without end." And all gave their assent to this belief, by standing up and saying, Amen.

He instructed them also what benefit they had by the Church's appointing the celebration of holidays and the excellent use of them, namely, that they were set apart for particular commemorations of particular mercies received from Almighty God; and—as reverend Mr. Hooker says—to be the landmarks to distinguish times; for by them we are taught to take notice how time passes by us, and that we ought not to let the years pass without a celebration of praise for those mercies which those days give us occasion to remember, and therefore they were to note that the year is appointed to begin the 25th day of March; a day in which we commemorate the Angel's appearing to the Blessed Virgin, with the joyful tidings that "she should conceive and bear a son, that should be the Redeemer of mankind." And she did so forty weeks after this joyful salutation; namely, at our Christmas; a day in which we commemorate his Birth with joy and praise; and that eight days after this happy birth we celebrate his Circumcision; namely in that which we call New-year's day. And that, upon that day which we call

Twelfth-day, we commemorate the manifestation of the unsearchable riches of Jesus to the Gentiles: and that that day we also celebrate the memory of his goodness in sending a star to guide the three Wise Men from the East to Bethlehem, that they might there worship, and present him with their oblations of gold, frankincense, and myrrh. And he—Mr. Herbert—instructed them, that Jesus was forty days after his birth presented by his blessed Mother in the Temple; namely, on that day which we call, "The Purification of the Blessed Virgin, Saint Mary." And he instructed them, that by the Lent-fast we imitate and commemorate our Saviour's humiliation in fasting forty days; and that we ought to endeavour to be like him in purity: and that on Good Friday we commemorate and condole his Crucifixion; and at Easter commemorate his glorious Resurrection. And he taught them, that after Jesus had manifested himself to his Disciples to be "that Christ that was crucified, dead and buried;" and by his appearing and conversing with his Disciples for the space of forty days after his Resurrection, he then, and not till then, ascended into Heaven in the sight of those Disciples; namely, on that day which we call the Ascension, or Holy Thursday. And that we then celebrate the performance of the promise which he made to his Disciples at or before his Ascension; namely, "that though he left them, yet he would send them the Holy Ghost to be their Comforter;" and that he did so on that day which the Church calls Whitsunday.—Thus the Church keeps an historical and circular commemoration of times, as they pass by us; of such times as ought to incline us to occasional praises, for the particular blessings which we do, or might receive, by those holy commemorations.

He made them know also why the Church hath appointed Ember-weeks; and to know the reasons why the Commandments, and the Epistles and Gospels, were to be read at the Altar, or Communion Table: why the Priest was to pray the Litany kneeling; and why to pray some Collects standing: and he gave them many other observations, fit for his plain congregation, but not fit for me now to mention; for I must set limits to my pen, and not make that a treatise, which I intended to be a much shorter account than I have made it: but I have done, when I have told the Reader, that he was constant in catechising every Sunday in the afternoon, and that his catechising was after his Second Lesson, and in the pulpit; and that he never exceeded his half hour, and was always so happy as to have an obedient and a full congregation.

And to this I must add, that if he were at any time too zealous in his Sermons, it was in reproving the indecencies of the people's behaviour in the time of divine service; and of those Ministers that huddle up the Church-prayers, without a visible reverence and affection; namely, such as seemed to say the Lord's prayer, or a Collect, in a breath. But for himself, his custom was, to stop betwixt every Collect, and give the people time to consider what they had prayed, and to force their desires affectionately to God, before he engaged them into new petitions.

And by this account of his diligence to make his parishioners understand what they prayed, and why they praised and adored their Creator, I hope I shall the more easily obtain the Reader's belief to the following account of Mr. Herbert's own practice; which was to appear constantly with his wife and three nieces—the daughters of a deceased sister—and his whole family, twice every day at the Church-prayers, in the Chapel, which does almost join to his Parsonage-house. And for the time of his appearing, it was strictly at the canonical hours of ten and four: and then and there he lifted up pure and charitable hands to God in the midst of the congregation. And he would joy to have spent that time in that place, where the honour of his Master Jesus dwelleth; and there, by that inward devotion which he testified constantly by an humble behaviour and visible adoration, he, like Joshua, brought not only "his own household thus to serve the Lord;" but brought most of his parishioners, and many gentlemen in the neighbourhood, constantly to make a part of his congregation twice a day: and some of the meaner sort of his parish did so love and reverence Mr. Herbert, that they would let their plough rest when Mr. Herbert's Saint's-bell rung to prayers, that they might also offer their devotions to God with him; and would then return back to their plough. And his most holy life was such, that it begot such reverence to God, and to him, that they thought themselves the happier, when they carried Mr. Herbert's blessing back with them to their labour. Thus powerful was his reason and example to persuade others to a practical piety and devotion. . . .

In this time of his decay, he was often visited and prayed for by all the Clergy that lived near to him, especially by his friends the Bishop and Prebends of the Cathedral Church in Salisbury; but by none more devoutly than his wife, his three nieces,—then a part of his family,—and Mr. Woodnot, who were the sad witnesses of his daily decay; to whom he would often speak to this purpose: "I now look back upon the pleasures of my life past, and see the content I have taken in beauty, in wit, in music, and pleasant conversation, are now all past by me like a dream, or as a shadow that returns not, and are now all become dead to me, or I to them; and I see, that as my father and generation hath done before me, so I also shall now suddenly (with Job) make my bed also in the dark; and I praise God I am prepared for it; and I praise him that I am not to learn patience now I stand in such need of it; and that I have practised mortification, and endeavoured to die daily, that I might not die eternally; and my hope is, that I shall shortly leave this valley of tears, and be free from all fevers and pain; and, which will be a more happy condition, I shall be free from sin, and all the temptations and anxieties that attend it: and this being past, I shall dwell in the New Jerusalem; dwell there with men made perfect; dwell where these eyes shall see my Master and Saviour Jesus; and with him see my dear Mother, and all my relations and friends. But I must die, or not come to that happy place. And this is my content, that I am going daily towards it: and that every day which I have lived, hath taken a part of my appointed time from me; and that I shall live the less time, for having lived this and the day past." These, and the like expressions, which he uttered often, may be said to be his enjoyment of Heaven before he enjoyed it. The Sunday before his death, he rose suddenly from his bed or couch, called for one of his instruments, took it into his hand and said,

> My God, my God,
> My music shall find thee,
>   And every string
> Shall have his attribute to sing.

And having tuned it, he played and sung

>   The Sundays of man's life,
> Threaded together on time's string,
> Make bracelets to adorn the wife
>   Of the eternal glorious King:
> On Sundays Heaven's door stands ope;
> Blessings are plentiful and rife,
>   More plentiful than hope.

Thus he sung on earth such Hymns and Anthems, as the Angels, and he, and Mr. Farrer, now sing in Heaven.

Thus he continued meditating, and praying, and rejoicing, till the day of his death; and on that day said to Mr. Woodnot, "My dear friend, I am sorry I have nothing to present to my merciful God but sin and misery; but the first is pardoned, and a few hours will now put a period to the latter; for I shall suddenly go hence, and be no more seen." Upon which expression Mr. Woodnot took occasion to remember him of the re-edifying Layton Church, and his many acts of mercy. To which he made answer, saying, "They be good works, if they be sprinkled with the blood of Christ, and not otherwise." After this discourse he became more restless, and his soul seemed to be weary of her earthly tabernacle: and this uneasiness became so visible, that his wife, his three nieces, and Mr. Woodnot, stood constantly about his bed, beholding him with sorrow, and an unwillingness to lose the sight of him, whom they could not hope to see much longer. As they stood thus beholding him, his wife observed him to breathe faintly, and with much trouble, and observed him to fall into a sudden agony; which so surprised her, that she fell into a sudden passion, and required of him to know how he did. To which his answer was, "that he had passed a conflict with his last enemy, and had overcome him by the merits of his Master Jesus." After which answer, he looked up, and saw his wife and nieces weeping to an extremity, and charged them, if they loved him to withdraw into the next room, and there pray every one alone for him; for nothing but their lamentations could make his death uncomfortable. To which request their sighs and tears would not suffer them to make any reply; but they yielded him a sad obedience, leaving only with him Mr. Woodnot and Mr. Bostock. Immediately after they had left him, he said to Mr. Bostock, "Pray, Sir, open that door, then look into that cabinet, in which you may easily find my last Will, and give it into my hand:" which being done, Mr. Herbert delivered it into the hand of Mr. Woodnot, and said, "My old friend, I here deliver you my last Will, in which you will find that I have made you my sole Executor for the good of my wife and nieces, and I desire you to shew kindness to them, as they shall need it: I do not desire you to be just; for I know you will be so for your own sake; but I charge you, by the religion of our friendship, to be careful of them." And having obtained Mr. Woodnot's promise to be so, he said, "I am now ready to die." After which words, he said, "Lord, forsake me not now my strength faileth me: but grant me mercy for the merits of my Jesus. And now, Lord— Lord, now receive my soul." And with those words he breathed forth his divine soul, without any apparent disturbance, Mr. Woodnot and Mr. Bostock attending his last breath, and closing his eyes.

Thus he lived and thus he died, like a Saint, unspotted of the world, full of alms-deeds, full of humility, and all the examples of a virtuous life; which I cannot conclude better, than with this borrowed observation:

> —All must to their cold graves:
> But the religious actions of the just
> Smell sweet in death, and blossom in the dust.

Mr. George Herbert's have done so to this, and will doubtless do so to succeeding generations.—I have but this to say more of him; that if Andrew Melvin died before him, then George Herbert died without an enemy, I wish—if God shall be so pleased—that I may be so happy as to die like him.

DANIEL BAKER

"On Mr. George Herbert's Sacred Poems, Called, *The Temple*"

Poems upon Several Occasions
1697, pp. 83–89

I.

S o long had Poetry possessed been
   By Pagans, that a Right in her they claim'd,
Pleaded Prescription for their Sin,
And Laws they made, and Arguments they fram'd,
Nor thought it Wit, if God therein was nam'd:
The true GOD; for of false ones they had store,
   Whom Devils we may better call,
   And ev'ry thing they deifi'd,
And to a Stone, Arise and help they cri'd.
   And Woman-kind they fell before;
Ev'n Woman-kind, which caus'd at first their Fall,
Were almost the sole Subject of their Pen,
And the chief Deities ador'd by fond and sottish Men.

II.

   Herbert at last arose,
   Herbert inspir'd with holy Zeal,
Their Arguments he solv'd, their Laws he did repeal,
   And Spight of all th'enraged Foes
That with their utmost Malice did oppose,
He rescu'd the poor Captive, Poetry,
Whole her vile Masters had before decreed
All her immortal Spirit to employ
   In painting out the Lip or Eye
Of some fantastick Dame, whose Pride Incentives did not need.
This mighty *Herbert* could not brook;
It griev'd his pious Soul to see
   The best and noblest Gift,
   That God to Man has left,
Abus'd to serve vile Lust, and sordid Flattery:
So, glorious Arms in her Defence he took;
And when with great Success he'd set her free,
He rais'd her fancy on a stronger Wing,
Taught her of God above, and Things Divine to sing.

III.

Th' infernal Powers that held her fast before
And great Advantage of their Pris'ner made,
   And drove of Souls a gainful Trade,
   Began to mutiny and roar.
So when *Demetrius* and his Partners[1] view'd
Their Goddess, and with her, their dearer Gains to fall,
They draw together a confus'd Multitude,
   And into th' Theater they crowd,
And great *Diana*, great, they loudly call.
   Up into th' Air their Voices flie,
   Some one thing, some another crie,
   And most of them they know not why.
They crie aloud, 'till the Earth ring again,
   Aloud they crie; but all in vain.
Diana down must go; They can no more
Their sinking Idol help, than she could them before.
Down she must go with all her Pomp and Train:
The glorious Gospel-Sun her horned Pride doth stain,
No more to be renew'd, but ever in the Wane;
And Poetry, now grown Divine above must ever reign.

IV.

   A Mon'ment of this Victory
Our *David*, our Sweet Psalmist, rais'd on high,
When he this Giant under foot did tread,
And with Verse, his own Sword, cut off the Monster's Head.
For as a Sling and Heav'n-directed Stone
Laid flat the *Gathite* Champion, who alone
Made Thousands tremble, while he proudly stood
Bidding Defiance to the Hosts of God:
So fell th' infernal Pow'rs before the Face
Of mighty *Herbert*, who upon the Place
   A Temple built, that does outdo

Both *Solomon's*, and *Herod's* too,
And all the Temples of the Gods by far;
So costly the Materials, and the Workmanship so rare
A Temple built, as God did once ordain
   Without the Saw's harsh Noise
Or the untuneful Hammer's Voice,[2]
But built with sacred Musick's sweetest strain,
Like *Theban* Walls of old, as witty Poets feign.

V.

Hail, heav'nly Bard, to whom great LOVE has giv'n
   (His mighty Kindness to express)
To bear his Three mysterious Offices;
Prophet, and Priest on Earth thou wast, and now a King in
   Heav'n.
     There thou dost reign, and there
     Thy Bus'ness is the same 'twas here,
And thine old Songs thou singest o'er agen:
     The Angels and the Heav'nly Quire
      Gaze on thee, and admire
To hear such Anthems from an earthly Lyre,
Their own Hymns almost equall'd by an human Pen.
     We foolish Poets hope in vain
     Our Works Eternity shall gain:
     But sure those Poems needs must die
     Whose Theme is but Mortality.
Thy wiser and more noble Muse
     The best, the only way did chuse
To grow Immortal: For what Chance can wrong,
     What Teeth of Time devour that Song
Which to a Heav'nly Tune is set for glorifi'd Saints to use?
O may some Portion of thy Spirit on me
(Thy poor Admirer) light, whose Breast
By wretched mortal Loves hath been too long
   possest!
When, Oh! when will the joyful Day arise
     That rescu'd from these Vanities,
     These painted Follies I shall be,
If not an inspir'd Poet, yet an holy Priest like thee.

Notes

1. 'Acts 19.24 ff.' (author's marginal note).
2. 'I Kings 6.7' (author's marginal note).

S. MARGARET FULLER
From "The Two Herberts"
Papers on Art and Literature
1846, pp. 15–34

The following sketch is meant merely to mark some prominent features in the minds of the two Herberts, under a form less elaborate and more reverent than that of criticism.

A mind of penetrating and creative power could not find a better subject for a masterly picture. The two figures stand as representatives of natural religion, and of that of the Son of Man, of the life of the philosophical man of the world, and the secluded, contemplative, though beneficent existence.

The present slight effort is not made with a view to the great and dramatic results so possible to the plan. It is intended chiefly as a setting to the Latin poems of Lord Herbert, which are known to few,—a year ago, seemingly, were so to none in this part of the world. The only desire in translating them has been to do so literally, as any paraphrase, or addition of words impairs their profound meaning. It is hoped that, even in their present repulsive garb, without rhyme or rhythm, stripped, too,

of the majestic Roman mantle, the greatness of the thoughts, and the large lines of spiritual experience, will attract readers, who will not find time misspent in reading them many times.

George Herbert's heavenly strain is better, though far from generally, known.

There has been no attempt really to represent these persons speaking their own dialect, or in their own individual manners. The writer loves too well to hope to imitate the sprightly, fresh, and varied style of Lord Herbert, or the quaintness and keen sweets of his brother's. Neither have accessories been given, such as might easily have been taken from their works. But the thoughts imputed to them they might have spoken, only in better and more concise terms, and the facts—are facts. So let this be gently received with the rest of the modern tapestries. We can no longer weave them of the precious materials princes once furnished, but we can give, in our way, some notion of the original design.

It was an afternoon of one of the longest summer days. The sun had showered down his amplest bounties, the earth put on her richest garment to receive them. The clear heavens seemed to open themselves to the desire of mortals; the day had been long enough and bright enough to satisfy an immortal.

In a green lane leading from the town of Salisbury, in England, the noble stranger was reclining beneath a tree. His eye was bent in the direction of the town, as if upon some figure approaching or receding; but its inward turned expression showed that he was, in fact, no longer looking, but lost in thought.

"Happiness!" thus said his musing mind, "it would seem at such hours and in such places as if it not merely hovered over the earth, a poetic presence to animate our pulses and give us courage for what must be, but sometimes alighted. Such fulness of expression pervades these fields, these trees, that it excites, not rapture, but a blissful sense of peace. Yet, even were this permanent in the secluded lot, would I accept it in exchange for the bitter sweet of a wider, freer life? I could not if I would; yet, methinks, I would not if I could. But here comes George, I will argue the point with him." . . .

"Let us not return at once," said Lord Herbert. "I had already waited for you long, and have seen all the beauties of the parsonage and church."

"Not many, I think, in the eyes of such a critic," said George, as they seated themselves in the spot his brother had before chosen for the extent and loveliness of prospect.

"Enough to make me envious of you, if I had not early seen enough to be envious of none. Indeed, I know not if such a feeling can gain admittance to your little paradise, for I never heard such love and reverence expressed as by your people for you."

George looked upon his brother with a pleased and open sweetness. Lord Herbert continued, with a little hesitation—"To tell the truth, I wondered a little at the boundless affection they declared. Our mother has long and often told me of your pure and beneficent life, and I know what you have done for this place and people, but, as I remember, you were of a choleric temper."

"And am so still!"

"Well, and do you not sometimes, by flashes of that, lose all you may have gained?"

"It does not often now," he replied, "find open way. My Master has been very good to me in suggestions of restraining prayer, which come into my mind at the hour of temptation."

Lord H: Why do you not say, rather, that your own discerning mind and maturer will show you more and more the folly and wrong of such outbreaks.

George H: Because that would not be saying all that I think. At such times I feel a higher power interposed, as much as I see that yonder tree is distinct from myself. Shall I repeat to you some poor verses in which I have told, by means of various likenesses, in an imperfect fashion, how it is with me in this matter?

Lord H: Do so! I shall hear them gladly; for I, like you, though with less time and learning to perfect it, love the deliberate composition of the closet, and believe we can better understand one another by thoughts expressed so, than in the more glowing but hasty words of the moment.

George H:

Prayer—the church's banquet; angel's age;
    God's breath in man returning to his birth;
The soul in paraphrase; heart in pilgrimage;
    The Christian plummet, sounding heaven
        and earth.

Engine against th' Almighty; sinner's tower;
    Reversed thunder; Christ's side-piercing spear;
The six-days' world transposing in an hour;
    A kind of tune, which all things hear and fear.

Softness, and peace, and joy, and love, and bliss;
    Exalted manna; gladness of the best;
Heaven in ordinary; man well drest;
    The milky way; the bird of paradise;
Church bells beyond the stars heard; the soul's blood;
The land of spices; something understood.

Lord H: (who has listened attentively, after a moment's thought.)—There is something in the spirit of your lines which pleases me, and, in general, I know not that I should differ; yet you have expressed yourself nearest to mine own knowledge and feeling, where you have left more room to consider our prayers as aspirations, rather than the gifts of grace; as—

"Heart in pilgrimage;"
"A kind of tune, which all things hear and fear."
"Something understood."

In your likenesses, you sometimes appear to quibble in a way unworthy the subject.

George H: It is the nature of some minds, brother, to play with what they love best. Yours is of a grander and severer cast; it can only grasp and survey steadily what interests it. My walk is different, and I have always admired you in yours without expecting to keep pace with you.

Lord H: I hear your sweet words with the more pleasure, George, that I had supposed you were now too much of the churchman to value the fruits of my thought.

George H: God forbid that I should ever cease to reverence the mind that was, to my own, so truly that of an elder brother! I do lament that you will not accept the banner of my Master, and drink at what I have found the fountain of pure wisdom. But as I would not blot from the book of life the prophets and priests that came before Him, nor those antique sages who knew all

That Reason hath from Nature borrowed,
Or of itself, like a good housewife spun,
In laws and policy: what the stars conspire:
What willing Nature speaks; what, freed by fire:
Both th' old discoveries, and the new found seas:
The stock and surplus, cause and history,—

As I cannot resign and disparage these, because they have not what I conceive to be the pearl of all knowledge, how could I you?

Lord H: You speak wisely, George, and, let me add, religiously. Were all churchmen as tolerant, I had never assailed the basis of their belief. Did they not insist and urge upon us

their way as the one only way, not for them alone, but for all, none would wish to put stumbling-blocks before their feet.

George H: Nay, my brother, do not misunderstand me. None, more than I, can think there is but one way to arrive finally at truth.

Lord H: I do not misunderstand you; but, feeling that you are one who accept what you do from love of the best, and not from fear of the worst, I am as much inclined to tolerate your conclusions as you to tolerate mine.

George H: I do not consider yours as conclusions, but only as steps to such. The progress of the mind should be from natural to revealed religion, as there must be a sky for the sun to give light through its expanse.

Lord H: The sky is—nothing!

George H: Except room for a sun, and such there is in you. Of your own need of such, did you not give convincing proof, when you prayed for a revelation to direct whether you should publish a book against revelation?[1]

Lord H: You borrow that objection from the crowd, George; but I wonder you have not looked into the matter more deeply. Is there any thing inconsistent with disbelief in a partial plan of salvation for the nations, which, by its necessarily limited working, excludes the majority of men up to our day, with belief that each individual soul, wherever born, however nurtured, may receive immediate response, in an earnest hour, from the source of truth.

George H: But you believed the customary order of nature to be deranged in your behalf. What miraculous record does more?

Lord H: It was at the expense of none other. A spirit asked, a spirit answered, and its voice was thunder; but, in this, there was nothing special, nothing partial wrought in my behalf, more than if I had arrived at the same conclusion by a process of reasoning.

George H: I cannot but think, that if your mind were allowed, by the nature of your life, its free force to search, it would survey the subject in a different way, and draw inferences more legitimate from a comparison of its own experience with the gospel.

Lord H: My brother does not think the mind is free to act in courts and camps. To me it seems that the mind takes its own course everywhere, and that, if men cannot have outward, they can always mental seclusion. None is so profoundly lonely, none so in need of constant self-support, as he who, living in the crowd, thinks an inch aside from, or in advance of it. The hermitage of such an one is still and cold; its silence unbroken to a degree of which these beautiful and fragrant solitudes give no hint. These sunny sights and sounds, promoting reverie rather than thought, are scarce more favourable to a great advance in the intellect, than the distractions of the busy street. Beside, we need the assaults of other minds to quicken our powers, so easily hushed to sleep, and call it peace. The mind takes a bias too easily, and does not examine whether from tradition or a native growth intended by the heavens.

George H: But you are no common man. You shine, you charm, you win, and the world presses too eagerly on you to leave many hours for meditation.

Lord H: It is a common error to believe that the most prosperous men love the world best. It may be hardest for them to leave it, because they have been made effeminate and slothful by want of that exercise which difficulty brings. But this is not the case with me; for, while the common boons of life's game have been too easily attained, to hold high value in my eyes, the goal which my secret mind, from earliest infancy, prescribed, has been high enough to task all my energies. Every year has helped to make that, and that alone, of value in my eyes; and did I believe that life, in scenes like this, would lead me to it more speedily than in my accustomed broader way, I would seek it to-morrow—nay, to-day. But is it worthy of a man to make him a cell, in which alone he can worship? Give me rather the always open temple of the universe! To me, it seems that the only course for a man is that pointed out by birth and fortune. Let him take that and pursue it with clear eyes and head erect, secure that it must point at last to those truths which are central to us, wherever we stand; and if my road, leading through the busy crowd of men, amid the clang and bustle of conflicting interests and passions, detain me longer than would the still path through the groves, the chosen haunt of contemplation, yet I incline to think that progress so, though slower, is surer. Owing no safety, no clearness to my position, but so far as it is attained to mine own effort, encountering what temptations, doubts and lures may beset a man, what I do possess is more surely mine, and less a prey to contingencies. It is a well-tempered wine that has been carried over many seas, and escaped many shipwrecks.

George H: I can the less gainsay you, my lord and brother, that your course would have been mine could I have chosen.

Lord H: Yes; I remember thy verse:—

> Whereas my birth and spirits rather took
> The way that takes the town;
> Thou didst betray me to a lingering book,
> And wrap me in a gown.

It was not my fault, George, that it so chanced.

George H: I have long learnt to feel that it noway chanced; that thus, and no other, was it well for me. But how I view these matters you are, or may be well aware, through a little book I have writ. . . .

Have you never faltered till you felt the need of a friend? strong in this clear vision, have you never sighed for a more homefelt assurance to your faith? steady in your demand of what the soul requires, have you never known fear lest you want purity to receive the boon if granted?

Lord H: I do not count those weak moments, George; they are not my true life.

George H: It suffices that you know them, for, in time, I doubt not that every conviction which a human being needs, to be reconciled to the Parent of all, will be granted to a nature so ample, so open, and so aspiring. Let me answer in a strain which bespeaks my heart as truly, if not as nobly as yours answers to your great mind,—

> My joy, my life, my crown!
> My heart was meaning all the day
> Somewhat it fain would say;
> And still it runneth, muttering, up and down,
> With only this—*my joy, my life, my crown*.
>
> Yet slight not these few words;
> If truly said, they may take part
> Among the best in art.
> The fineness which a hymn or psalm affords,
> Is, when the soul unto the lines accords.
>
> He who craves all the mind
> And all the soul, and strength and time;
> If the words only rhyme,
> Justly complains, that somewhat is behind
> To make his verse or write a hymn in kind.
>
> Whereas, if the heart be moved,
> Although the verse be somewhat scant,
> God doth supply the want—
> As when the heart says, sighing to be approved,
> "Oh, could I love!" and stops; God writeth, *loved*.

Lord H: I cannot say to you truly that my mind replies to this, although I discern a beauty in it. You will say I lack humility to understand yours.

George H: I will say nothing, but leave you to time and the care of a greater than I. We have exchanged our verse, let us now change our subject too, and walk homeward; for I trust you, this night, intend to make my roof happy in your presence, and the sun is sinking.

Lord H: Yes, you know I am there to be introduced to my new sister, whom I hope to love, and win from her a sisterly regard in turn.

George H: You, none can fail to regard; and for her, even as you love me, you must her, for we are one.

Lord H: (smiling)—Indeed; two years wed, and say that.

George H: Will your lordship doubt it? From your muse I took my first lesson.

> With a look, it seem'd denied
> All earthly powers but hers, yet so
> As if to her breath he did owe
> This borrow'd life, he thus replied—
> And shall our love, so far beyond
> That low and dying appetite,
> And which so chaste desires unite,
> Not hold in an eternal bond?
> O no, belov'd! I am most sure
> Those virtuous habits we acquire,
> As being with the soul entire,
> Must with it evermore endure.
> Else should our souls in vain elect;
> And vainer yet were heaven's laws
> When to an everlasting cause
> They gave a perishing effect.

Lord H: (sighing) You recall a happy season, when my thoughts were as delicate of hue, and of as heavenly a perfume as the flowers of May.

George H: Have those flowers borne no fruit?

Lord H: My experience of the world and men had made me believe that they did not indeed bloom in vain, but that the fruit would be ripened in some future sphere of our existence. What my own marriage was you know,—a family arrangement made for me in my childhood. Such obligations as such a marriage could imply, I have fulfilled, and it has not failed to bring me some benefits of good-will and esteem, and far more, in the happiness of being a parent. But my observation of the ties formed, by those whose choice was left free, has not taught me that a higher happiness than mine was the destined portion of men. They are too immature to form permanent relations; all that they do seems experiment, and mostly fails for the present. Thus I had postponed all hopes except of fleeting joys or ideal pictures. Will you tell me that you are possessed already of so much more?

George H: I am indeed united in a bond, whose reality I cannot doubt, with one whose thoughts, affections, and objects every way correspond with mine, and in whose life I see a purpose so pure that, if we are ever separated, the fault must be mine. I believe God, in his exceeding grace, gave us to one another, for we met almost at a glance, without doubt before, jar or repentance after, the vow which bound our lives together.

Lord H: Then there is indeed one circumstance of your lot I could wish to share with you. (After some moments' silence on both sides)—They told me at the house, that, with all your engagements, you go twice a-week to Salisbury. How is that? How can you leave your business and your happy home, so much and often?

George H: I go to hear the music; the great solemn church music. This is, at once, the luxury and the necessity of my life. I know not how it is with others, but, with me, there is a frequent drooping of the wings, a smouldering of the inward fires, a languor, almost a loathing of corporeal existence. Of this visible diurnal sphere I am, by turns, the master, the interpreter, and the victim; an ever burning lamp, to warm again the embers of the altar; a skiff, that cannot be becalmed, to bear me again on the ocean of hope; an elixir, that fills the dullest fibre with ethereal energy; such, music is to me. It stands in relation to speech, even to the speech of poets, as the angelic choir, who, in their subtler being, may inform the space around us, unseen but felt, do to men, even to prophetic men. It answers to the soul's presage, and, in its fluent life, embodies all I yet know how to desire. As all the thoughts and hopes of human souls are blended by the organ to a stream of prayer and praise, I tune at it my separate breast, and return to my little home, cheered and ready for my day's work, as the lark does to her nest after her morning visit to the sun.

Lord H: The ancients held that the spheres made music to those who had risen into a state which enabled them to hear it. Pythagoras, who prepared different kinds of melody to guide and expand the differing natures of his pupils, needed himself to hear none on instruments made by human art, for the universal harmony which comprehends all these was audible to him. Man feels in all his higher moments, the need of traversing a subtler element, of a winged existence. Artists have recognised wings as the symbol of the state next above ours; but they have not been able so to attach them to the forms of gods and angels as to make them agree with the anatomy of the human frame. Perhaps music gives this instruction, and supplies the deficiency. Although I see that I do not feel it as habitually or as profoundly as you do, I have experienced such impressions from it.

George H: That is truly what I mean. It introduces me into that winged nature, and not as by way of supplement, but of inevitable transition. All that has budded in me, bursts into bloom, under this influence. As I sit in our noble cathedral, in itself one of the holiest thoughts ever embodied by the power of man, the great tides of song come rushing through its aisles; they pervade all the space, and my soul within it, perfuming me like incense, bearing me on like the wind, and on and on to regions of unutterable joy, and freedom, and certainty. As their triumph rises, I rise with them, and learn to comprehend by living them, till at last a calm rapture seizes me, and holds me poised. The same life you have attained in your description of the celestial choirs. It is the music of the soul, when centred in the will of God, thrilled by the love, expanded by the energy, with which it is fulfilled through all the ranges of active life. From such hours, I return through these green lanes, to hear the same tones from the slightest flower, to long for a life of purity and praise, such as is manifested by the flowers.

At this moment they reached the door, and there paused to look back. George Herbert bent upon the scene a half-abstracted look, yet which had a celestial tearfulness in it, a pensiveness beyond joy. His brother looked on *him*, and, beneath that fading twilight, it seemed to him a farewell look. It was so. Soon George Herbert soared into the purer state, for which his soul had long been ready, though not impatient.

The brothers met no more; but they had enjoyed together one hour of true friendship, when mind drew near to mind by the light of faith, and heart mingled with heart in the atmosphere of Divine love. It was a great boon to be granted two mortals.

ROBERT ARIS WILMOTT
From "Introduction" to *The Works of George Herbert*
1854, pp. xxi–xxx

Life, it has been said, is a Poem. This is true, probably, of the life of the human race as a whole, if we could see its beginning and end, as well as its middle. But it is not true of all lives. It is only a life here and there, which equals the dignity and aspires to the completeness of a genuine and great Poem. Most lives are fragmentary, even when they are not foul—they disappoint, even when they do not disgust—they are volumes without a preface, an index, or a moral. It is delightful to turn from such apologies for life to the rare but real lives which God-gifted men, like Milton or Herbert, have been enabled to spend even on this dark and melancholy foot-breadth for immortal spirits, called the earth.

We class Milton and Herbert together, for this, among other reasons, that in both, the life and the poems were thoroughly correspondent and commensurate with each other. Milton lived the *Paradise Lost* and the *Paradise Regained*, as well as wrote them. Herbert was, as well as built, *The Temple*. Not only did the intellectual archetype of its structure exist in his mind, but he had been able, in a great measure, to realise it in life, before expressing it in poetry. . . .

We come not to criticise *The Temple*, although the term criticism applied to what is a bosom companion rather than a book may seem cold and out of place. We come, then, we shall rather say, to announce our profound love for the work, and to assign certain reasons for that love. We may first, however, allude to the faults with which it has been justly charged. These are, however, venial, and are those not of the author so much as of his day. He is often quaint, and has not a few conceits, which are rather ingenious than tasteful. Anagrams, acrostics, verbal quibbles, and a hundred other formulae, cold in themselves, although indigenous to the age, and greatly redeemed by the fervour his genius throws into them, abound in *The Temple*, and so far suit the theme, that they remind us of the curious figures and devices which add their Arabesque border to the grandeur of old Abbeys and Cathedrals. It was the wild, crude rhythm of the period, and had Herbert not conformed himself to it, he had either been a far less or a far greater poet than he was. Yet, though bound in chains, he became even in durance an alchymist, and turned his chains into gold.

Herbert has, besides, what may be considered more formidable faults than these. He is often obscure, and his allegorising vein is opened too often, and explored too far; so much so, that had we added a commentary or extended notes on *The Temple*, it would have necessarily filled another volume nearly as large as the present. This the plan of our publication, of course, entirely forbids. We may merely premise these advices to those who would care to understand as well as read the succeeding poem: 1*st*, Let them regard it as in many portions a piece of picture-writing; 2*dly*, Let them seek the secret of this, partly by a careful study of the book itself, and partly by reading the similar works of Donne, Quarles, Giles Fletcher, and John Bunyan; 3*dly*, Let them believe in Herbert, even when they do not understand him; and 4*thly*, Let them rejoice that the great proportion of the book is perfectly clear and plain, to Christians by experience, to poets by imaginative sympathy, to all men in general by the power of conscience, the sense of guilt, and that fear of the terrors and that hope of the joys of a future state of being, by which all hearts at times are moved. . . .

The Temple, looking at it more narrowly, may be viewed in its devotional, in its poetical, and in its philosophical aspects, which we may figure as its altar, its painted window, and its floor and foundation. First, as a piece of devotion it is a Prayer-book in verse. We find in it all the various parts of prayer. Now like a seraph he casts his crown at God's feet, and covers his face with his wings, in awful adoration. Now he looks up in His face, with the happy gratitude of a child, and murmurs out his thanksgiving. Now he seems David the penitent, although fallen from an inferior height, and into pits not nearly so deep and darksome, confessing his sins and shortcomings to his Heavenly Father. And now he asks, and prays, and besieges heaven for mercy, pardon, peace, grace, and joy, as with "groanings that cannot be uttered." We find in it, too, a perpetual undersong of praise. It is a Psalter, no less than a Prayer-book. And how different its bright sparks of worship going up without effort, without noise, by mere necessity of nature, to heaven, from the majority of hymns which have since appeared! No namby-pambyism, no false unction, no nonsensical raptures, are to be found in them; their very faults and mannerisms serve to attest their sincerity, and to shew that the whole man is reflected in them. Even although the poem had possessed far less poetic merit, its mere devotion, in its depth and truth, would have commended it to Christians, as, next to the Psalms, the finest collection of ardent and holy breathings to be found in the world.

But its poetical merit is of a very rare, lofty, and original order. It is full of that subtle perception of analogies which is competent only to high poetical genius. All things, to Herbert, appear marvellously alike to each other. The differences, small or great, whether they be the interspaces between leaves, or the gulfs between galaxies, shrivel up and disappear. The ALL becomes one vast congeries of mirrors—of similitudes—of duplicates—

> Star nods to star, each system has its brother,
> And half the universe reflects the other.[1]

This principle, or perception, which is the real spring of all fancy and imagination, was very strong in Herbert's mind, and hence the marvellous richness, freedom, and variety of his images. He hangs upon his *Temple* now flowers and now stars, now blossoms and now full-grown fruit. He gathers glories from all regions of thought—from all gardens of beauty—from all the history, and art, and science then accessible to him,— and he wreathes them in a garland around the bleeding brow of Immanuel. Sometimes his style exhibits a clear massiveness like one of the Temple pillars, sometimes a dim richness like one of the Temple windows; and never is there wanting the Temple music, now wailing melodiously, now moving in brisk, lively, and bird-like measures, and now uttering loud paeans and crashes of victorious sound. It has been truly said of him, that he is "inspired by the Bible, as its vaticinators were inspired by God." It is to him not only the "Book of God, but the God of Books." He has hung and brooded over its pages, like a bird for ever dipping her wing in the sea; he has imbibed its inmost spirit—he has made its divine words "the men of his counsel, and his song in the house of his pilgrimage," till they are in his verse less imitated than reproduced. In this, as in other qualities, such as high imagination, burning zeal, quaint fancy, and deep simplicity of character he resembles that "Child-Angel," John Bunyan, who was proud to be a babe of the Bible, although his genius might have made him without it a gigantic original.

We might have quoted many passages corroborating our impressions of the surpassing artistic merit of George Herbert's poem. But the book, as well as the criticism, is now in the reader's hands, and he is called upon to judge for himself. We may merely recommend to his attention, as especially beautiful and rich, "The Church-Porch," "The Agony," "Redemption," "Easter," "Sin," "Prayer," "Whitsunday," "Affliction," "Humility," "To all Angels and Saints," "Vanity," "Virtue" (which contains the stanza so often quoted, "Sweet Day," &c.), "The British Church," "The Quip," and "Peace." Many more will detain and fascinate him as he goes along,—some by their ingenious oddity, some by their tremulous pathos, some by the peculiar profundity of their devotional spirit; and the rest by the sincerity and truth which burn in every line.

We have spoken of the philosophy of *The Temple*. We do not mean by this, that it contains any elaborately constructed, distinctly defined, or logically defended system, but simply that it abounds in glimpses of philosophic thought of a very profound and searching cast. The singular earnestness of Herbert's temperament was connected with—perhaps we should rather say *created* in him—an eye which penetrated below the surface, and looked right into the secrets of things. In his peculiarly happy and blessed constitution, piety and the philosophic genius were united and reconciled; and from those awful depths of man's mysterious nature, which few have more thoroughly, although incidentally, explored than he, he lifts up, not a howl of despair, nor a curse of misanthropy, nor a cry of mere astonishment, but a hymn of worship. We refer especially to those two striking portions of the poem entitled "Man" and "Providence." The first is a fine comment on the Psalmist's words, "I am fearfully and wonderfully made." Herbert first saw, or at least first expressed in poetry, the central position of man to the universe—the fact that all its various lines find a focus in him—that he is a microcosm to the All, and that every part of man is, in its turn, a little microcosm of him. The germ of some of the abstruse theories propounded by Swedenborg, and since enlarged and illustrated by the author of *The Human Body, Considered in its Relation to Man* (a treatise written with a true Elizabethan richness of style and thought, and which often seems to approach, at least, great abysses of discovery), may be found in Herbert's verses. "Man," Herbert says, "is everything and more." He is "a beast, yet is or should be more." He is "all symmetry—full of *proportions, one limb to another, and all to all the world besides.*"

> Head with foot hath private amity,
> And both with moons and tides.
>
> His eyes dismount the highest star:
> He is in little all the sphere.
> Herbs gladly cure our flesh, because that they
> Find their acquaintance there.
>
> Each thing is full of duty.
>
> More servants wait on Man,
> Than he'll take notice of: in every path
> He treads down that which doth befriend him,
> When sickness makes him pale and wan.
> Oh, mighty love! Man is one world, and hath
> Another to attend him.

How strikingly do these words bring before us the thought of Man the Mystery! "What a piece of workmanship" verily he is! He is formed as of a thousand lights and shadows. He is compacted out of all contradictions. While his feet touch the dust, and are of miry clay, his head is of gold, and strikes the Empyrean. . . . Altogether, there are few places on earth nearer Heaven, filled with a richer and holier light, adorned with chaster and nobler ornaments, or where our souls can worship with a more entire forgetfulness of self, and a more thorough realisation of the things unseen and eternal, than in

The Temple of George Herbert. You say, as you stand breathless below its solemn arches, "This is none other than the house of God, it is the gate of Heaven. How dreadful, yet how dear is this place!"

Notes

1. Adapted from Pope's "Epistle to Burlington", ll. 117–18: 'Grove nods at grove, each Alley has a brother, / And half the platform just reflects the other'. The allusion was identified by Mr Anthony W. Shipps.

JOHN NICHOL
From "Introduction" to
The Poetical Works of George Herbert
1863, pp. vi–vii, xix–xxvi

The collection of poems entitled *The Temple*, which, with the prose treatise, "A Country Parson," "The Church Militant," and a few minor verses in English and Latin, completes the list of our author's works, embraces an almost indefinite variety of theme and measure, from the slender notes of the flute to the full tones of the organ bass; yet it is pervaded by a unity of thought and purpose which justifies the single name. Those poems are a series of hymns and meditations within the walls of an English church. They are Church music crystallised. There is a speciality about them which continually recalls the circumstances of the writer. *The Temple*, as Coleridge remarked, will always be read with fullest appreciation by those who share the poet's devotion to the Dear Mother whose praises he has undertaken to celebrate. The verses on "Easter" and "Lent," on "Baptism" and "Communion," on "Church Monuments" and "Music," seem most directly to address the worshippers in that flock of which he was so good a shepherd, whose affections are entwined around his Church, who love to linger on the associations of her festivals, the rubrics of her creed, and the formularies of her service—to feel themselves under the shadow of the old cathedrals—to draw allegories from the fantasies of their fretted stone—to watch the light flicker through the painted glass on marble tombs, and listen to the anthems throbbing through the choir. Yet there is in the author and in his work catholicity enough to give his volume a universal interest, and make his prayer and praise a fit expression of Christian faith under all varieties of form. The defects of the book—those which remove it, as a whole, from the first class of poetry—are those which are peculiar to the writer and his Church and time; its excellences, which raise it to the front of the second rank result from an exercise of those qualities which Herbert shares with all great religious poets. Those defects are serious, and have emboldened depreciatory critics to say that the author of *The Temple* has been handed down to us more by his life than his work. Foremost among them is a want of condensation, which has led the poet into frequent repetition of the same ideas under slightly altered phraseology. Sometimes, even within the limits of the same poem, he turns a thought over till we are tired of it; and to read through his book continuously is no easy task. It has been said correctly that Herbert has more genius than taste; and his deficiency in the latter quality, combined with a grotesque vein of allegory which belonged to the time, has not unfrequently, as in the verse entitled "Jesu," led the most reverent of men into conceits which seem to approach irreverence. The extremes of levity and pious word-worship meet now and then in a devout pun. There are many instances in which we cannot help complaining that too much is made of little things, as in a pre-Raphaelite picture the whole effect is apt to be sacrificed to microscopic detail; so that we think of *The Temple* rather in connexion with the mosaic-work of Wilton Chapel, than the neighbouring and more stately grandeur of the severe majestic Salisbury. Herbert is prone, by his own admission, to overlay his matter with far-fetched, and sometimes incongruous imagery. . . .

The best poems in the volume, as "The Church Porch," "The Agony," "Sin," "Faith," "Love," "The Temper," "Employments," "Church Music," "Sunday," "The World," "Lent," "Virtue," "The Pearl," "Man," "Mortification," "The British Church," "The Quip," "The Size," and many more, in themselves make up a treasury of sacred song whose price is beyond rubies. They are more like modern psalms than any other poems we know. Like those older and grander voices, they, too, have their place by the wayside of the Christian life—rousing, warning; cheering, comforting, sorrowing and rejoicing with us as we go. Like church windows they have a double aspect; we may look in through them from without on the writer's heart, and see him as a priest and man struggling like ourselves with doubts and fears, but with "a face not fearing light," and a will well bent to do his Master's work; we may look out through them from within on the world as seen with the poet's eye—a fair round world of light and shade, overarched by clouds and stars. . . .

Herbert's poem on "Man" is his masterpiece. The most philosophic as well as the most comprehensive of his writings, it stands by itself, and has enlisted the admiration even of those furthest removed from him in creed, and cast, and time. Embodying his recognition of the mysterious relationship of the chief of created beings to his Creator and to the universe, it seems to anticipate centuries of discovery. The faculty which can range from heaven to earth, from earth to heaven, discerns the hidden links by which the world is woven together, and poetry prophesies what science proves. In the microcosm of man—

> East and west touch,—the poles do kiss,
>   And parallels meet.
>   ("The Search", ll. 43–4)

Man, with Herbert, is everything, "a tree," "a beast, yet is, is, or should be more;" he is

> all symmetry,
> Full of proportions, one limb to another,
>   And all to all the world besides.
>   ("Man", ll. 13–15)

This, which was the prayer and effort of his life, was surely in full measure granted to George Herbert. Nothing arrests us more than his perfect honesty. There is no writing for effect in his pages; as we turn them we feel ourselves in the presence of a man speaking out of the fulness of his heart and carried away into a higher air by the sustaining power of his own incessant aspirations.

Herbert can scarcely be called a lesser Milton. His Gothic temple has nothing of the classic grace and grandeur of the hand that reared the great dome of our English Epic on smooth pillars of everlasting verse. He breathes rather the spirit of the author of the *Olney Hymns*, but Herbert's was a more cheerful faith than Cowper's and the brightness of God's countenance seemed ever to shine upon him as he went on his way singing to the gates of the celestial city.

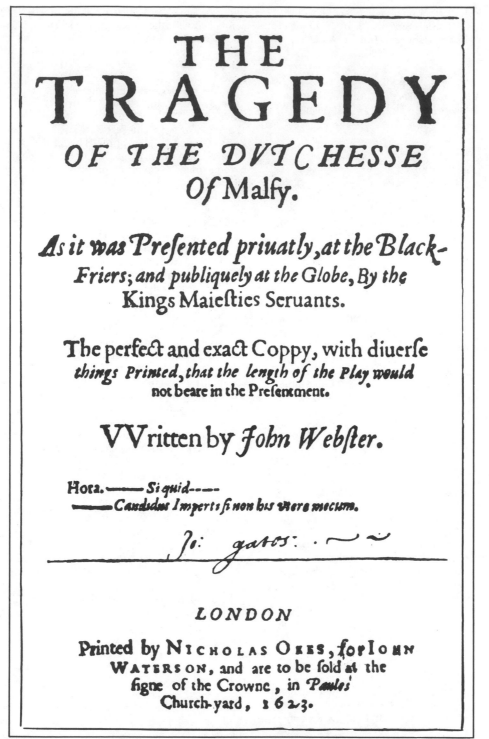

THE
TRAGEDY
OF THE DVTCHESSE
Of Malfy.

As it was Presented priuatly, at the Black-Friers; and publiquely at the Globe, By the Kings Maiesties Seruants.

The perfect and exact Coppy, with diuerse *things Printed, that the length of the Play would not beare in the Presentment.*

VVritten by *John Webster.*

Hora. —— *Si quid* ——
—— *Candidus Imperti si non his vtere mecum.*

Ji: gatos:

LONDON

Printed by N I C H O L A S O K E S, for I O H N W A T E R S O N, and are to be sold at the signe of the Crowne, in *Paules* Church-yard, 1 6 2 3.

Title page of *The Duchess of Malfi*

JOHN WEBSTER

c. 1570–c. 1634

Little is known of the life of John Webster. In a preface to his Lord Mayor's show for 1624, *Monuments of Honor*, Webster describes himself "born free" of the Merchant Taylor's Company, the son of another freeman, John Webster. A John Webster was a member of the English Comedians under Robert Brown, in the service of the German count Maurice of Hesse-Kessel in 1595, and another John Webster entered the Middle Temple in 1598 or still another John Webster, "clothworker," who died in September, 1625. Certainly, John Webster the playwright was dead by 1634, as in that year he was referred to in the past tense by a contemporary.

John Webster collaborated on plays with leading dramatists, including Dekker, Middleton, Drayton, Ford and perhaps Massinger, Chettle, Chapman, Heywood, and Rowley. Many of these plays, or rumored plays are lost. However, some eight plays are extant. In 1604, Webster wrote the introduction to Marston's *The Malcontent*. Collaborating chiefly with Thomas Dekker, Webster contributed to *The Famous History of Sir Thomas Wyatt* (with Dekker, published 1607) and wrote *Northward Hoe* and *Westward Hoe*, also with Dekker (both published in 1607). Plays which are attributed to Webster by most include *Appius and Virginia* (published in 1654), *A Cure for a Cuckold* (published 1661), *The Devil's Law-Case* (published 1623). It seems certain that Webster wrote *Monuments of Honour* (1624), a City pageant, as well as some non-dramatic verse, including an elegy on the death of Henry, Prince of Wales, titled A *Monumental Columne* (1613). In addition, Webster contributed prefatory verses to Munday's translation of *Palmerin of England* (1602), Harrison's *Arches of Triumph* (1604), and Heywood's *Apology for Actors* (1612).

Webster's fame rests chiefly on two plays which he himself wrote: *The White Devil: Or the Tragedy of Paolo Giordana Ursini, Duke of Brachiano, with the Life and Death of Vittoria Corombona the famous Venetian Curtizan* (first produced in 1608) known to most audiences simply as *The White Devil*, and *The Duchess of Malfi*, first produced between 1608 and 1614. These plays, particularly *The Duchess of Malfi*, are examples of the villain play, a type that developed out of the earlier revenge tragedy. In them, dark imagery and naturalistic (albeit brooding and violent) characters predominate over the interests of plot development, affording an atmosphere which combines scathing satire with a sense of overwhelming despair.

General

But hist! with him, crabbed Websterio,
The playwright-cartwright (whether either!). Ho!
No further. Look as you'd be looked into;
Sit as ye would be read. Lord! who would know him?
Was ever man so mangled with a poem?
See how he draws his mouth awry of late,
How he scrubs, wrings his wrists, scratches his pate.
A midwife, help! By his brain's coitus
Some centaur strange, some huge Bucephalus,
Or Pallas, sure, engendered in his brain,
Strike Vulcan, with thy hammer once again.
This is the critic that of all the rest
I'd not have view me, yet I fear him least.
Here's not a word cursively I have writ
But he'll industriously examine it,
And in some twelve months hence, or thereabout,
Set in a shameful sheet my errors out.
But what care I? It will be so obscure
That none shall understand him I am sure.
 —HENRY FITZJEFFREY, "Notes from
  Blackfriars," *Certain Elegies by Sundry
  Excellent Wits*, 1617

Webster the next, though not so much of note
Nor's name attended with such noise and crowd,
Yet by the Nine and by Apollo's vote,
Whose groves of bay are for his head allowed—
Most sacred spirit (some may say I dote),

Of thy three noble tragedies be as proud
As great voluminous Jonson; thou shalt be
Read longer and with more applause than he.
 —SAMUEL SHEPPARD, "The Fairy King," 1651

An Author that liv'd in the Reign of King *James* the First: and was in those Days accounted an Excellent Poet. He joyn'd with *Decker, Marston,* and *Rowley,* in several Plays; and was likewise Author of others, which have even in our Age gain'd Applause. . . . Mr. *Philips* has committed a great Mistake, in ascribing several Plays to our Author, and his Associate Mr. *Decker;* One of which belong to another Writer, whose Name is annexed, and the rest are Anonymous.—GERARD LANGBAINE, *An Account of the English Dramatick Poets*, 1691, pp. 508–10

In his pictures of wretchedness and despair, he has introduced touches of expression which curdle the very blood with terror, and make the hair stand erect. Of this, the death of The Dutchesse of Malfy, with all its preparatory horrors, is a most distinguishing proof. The fifth act of his *Vittoria Corombona* shows, also, with what occasional skill he could imbibe the imagination of Shakspeare, particularly where its features seem to breathe a more than earthly wildness.—NATHAN DRAKE, *Shakspere and his Times*, 1817, Vol. 2, p. 565

Some single scenes are to be found in ⟨Webster's⟩ works, inferior in power of passion to nothing in the whole range of the drama. He was a man of a truly original genius, and seems to have felt strong pleasure in the strange and fantastic horrors that rose up from the dark abyss of his imagination. The vices and the crimes which he delights to paint, all partake of an extravagance which, nevertheless, makes them impressive and terrible, and in the retribution and the punishment there is a character of corresponding wildness. But our sympathies, suddenly awakened, are allowed as suddenly to subside. There is nothing of what Wordsworth calls "a mighty stream of tendency" in the events of his dramas, nor, in our opinion, is there a single character that clearly and boldly stands out before us, like a picture.—JOHN WILSON (as "H.M."), *Blackwood's Edinburgh Magazine*, March 1818, pp. 657–58

Webster has a gloomy force of imagination, not unmixed with the beautiful and pathetic. But it is "beauty in the lap of horror:" he caricatures the shapes of terror, and his Pegasus is like a nightmare.—THOMAS CAMPBELL, *An Essay on English Poetry*, 1819

His *White Devil* and *Dutchess of Malfi*, upon the whole, perhaps, come the nearest to Shakspeare of any thing we have upon record: the only drawback to them, the only shade of imputation that can be thrown upon them, "by which they lose some colour," is, that they are too like Shakspeare, and often direct imitations of him, both in general conception and individual expression.—WILLIAM HAZLITT, "Lecture 3," *Lectures on the Literature of the Age of Elizabeth*, 1820

Webster was formed upon Shakspere. He had no pretensions to the inexhaustible wit, the all-penetrating humour, of his master; but he had the power of approaching the terrible energy of his passion, and the profoundness of his pathos, in characters which he took out of the great muster-roll of humanity and placed in fearful situations and sometimes with revolting imaginings almost beyond humanity. . . . It is clear what dramatic writers were the objects of Webster's love. He did not aspire to the "full and heightened style of Master Chapman," nor would his genius be shackled by the examples of "the laboured and understanding works of Master Jonson." He belonged to the school of the romantic dramatists.—CHARLES KNIGHT, *William Shakspere: A Biography*, 1842

John Webster, a mighty and funereal genius, is the next author we shall mention. We can compare his mind to nothing so well as to some old Gothic cathedral, with its arches soaring heavenward, but carved with monsters and angels, with saints and fiends, in grotesque confusion. Gleams of sunlight fall here and there, it is true, through the huge window, but they are coloured with the sombre dies of painted glass, bearing records of human pride and human nothingness, and they fall in long slanting columns, twinkling silently with motes and dusty splendour, upon the tombs of the mighty; lighting dimly up now the armour of a recumbent Templar or the ruff of some dead beauty, and now feebly losing themselves amid the ragged coffins and scutcheons in the vaults below. His fancy was wild and powerful, but gloomy and monstrous, dwelling ever on the vanities of earthly glory, on the nothingness of pomp, not without many terrible hints at the emptiness of our trust, and many bold questionings of human hopes of a hereafter.—THOMAS B. SHAW, *Outlines of English Literature*, 1847, p. 130

Webster's most famous works are *The Duchess of Malfy* and *Vittoria Corombona*, but we are strongly inclined to call *The Devil's Law-Case* his best play. The two former are in a great measure answerable for the "spasmodic" school of poets, since the extravagances of a man of genius are as sure of imitation as the equable self-possession of his higher moments is incapable of it. Webster had, no doubt, the primal requisite of a poet, imagination, but in him it was truly untamed, and Aristotle's admirable distinction between the *Horrible* and the *Terrible* in

tragedy was never better illustrated and confirmed than in the *Duchess* and *Vittoria*. His nature had something of the sleuthhound quality in it, and a plot, to keep his mind eager on the trail, must be sprinkled with fresh blood at every turn. . . . He has not the condensing power of Shakespeare, who squeezed meaning into a phrase with an hydraulic press, but he could carve a cherry-stone with any of the *concettisti*, and abounds in imaginative quaintnesses that are worthy of Donne, and epigrammatic tersenesses that reminds us of Fuller. Nor is he wanting in poetic phrases of the purest crystallization.—JAMES RUSSELL LOWELL, "Prose Works," *Library of Old Authors*, 1858, Vol. 1, p. 279–81

Webster was one of those writers whose genius consists in the expression of special moods, and who, outside of those moods, cannot force their creative faculties into vigorous action. His mind by instinctive sentiment was directed to the contemplation of the darker aspects of life. He brooded over crime and misery until his imagination was enveloped in their atmosphere, found a fearful joy in probing their sources and tracing their consequences, became strangely familiar with their physiognomy and psychology, and felt a shuddering sympathy with their "deep groans and terrible ghastly looks." There was hardly a remote corner of the soul, which hid a feeling capable of giving mental pain, into which this artist in agony had not curiously peered. . . . He is such a spendthrift of his stimulants, and accumulates horror on horror, and crime on crime, with such fatal facility, that he would render the mind callous to his terrors, were it not that what is acted is still less than what is suggested, and that the souls of his characters are greater than their sufferings or more terrible than their deeds. The crimes and the criminals belong to Italy as it was in the sixteenth century, when poisoning and assassination were almost in the fashion; the feelings with which they are regarded are English; and the result of the combination is to make the poisoners and assassins more fiendishly malignant in spirit than they actually were. . . .

Of all the contemporaries of Shakespeare, Webster is the most Shakespearian. His genius was not only influenced by its contact with one side of Shakespeare's many-sided mind, but the tragedies . . . abound in expressions and situations either suggested by or directly copied from the tragedies of him he took for his model. . . . —EDWIN P. WHIPPLE, *The Literature of the Age of Elizabeth*, 1859, pp. 139–41

Webster's characters could not have been drawn nor his scenes constructed in a hurry. Appius and Romelio are unsurpassed as broad and elaborate studies, filled in with indefatigable detail and accommodated with subtle art to a profound conception. In following these masterpieces the student of character is kept in an ecstasy of delight by stroke after stroke of the most unerring art. In every other scene their replies and ways of taking things surprise us, yet every such paradox on reflection is seen to accord with the central conception of their character, and increases our admiration of the dramatist's deep insight and steady grasp. And these plays are not merely closet-plays, whose excellences can be picked out and admired only at leisure. The characters have not the simplicity and popular intelligibility of Shakespeare's Richard or Iago. The plots, too, except in *Appius and Virginia*, where all the incidents lie in the direct line of the catastrophe, are involved with obscure windings and turnings. Yet all the scenes are carefully constructed for dramatic effect. Mark how studious Webster has been that his actors shall never go lamely off the stage: they make their exit at happily chosen moments, and with some remark calculated to leave a buzz of interest behind them. When we look closely into Webster's plays we become aware that no dramatist loses more in closet perusal: all his dialogues were written with a careful eye to the stage. Everywhere throughout his plays we meet with marks of deep meditation and just design. It is not with his plays as with Fletcher's. The more we study Webster, the more we find to admire. His characters approach nearer to the many-sidedness of real men and women than those of any dramatist except Shakespeare; and his exhibition of the changes of feeling wrought in them by the changing progress of events, though characterised by less of revealing instinct and more of penetrating effort than appear in Shakespeare, is hardly less powerful and true.

Webster did not attempt comedy, unless in conjunction with Dekker, and before he had felt where his strength lay. The moral saws wrought into his dialogues show that his meditations held chiefly to the dark side of the world. In forming our impression of the man, we are perhaps unduly dominated by the concluding scenes of *Vittoria Corombona* and *The Duchess of Malfi*: it is from these scenes that he has received the name of "the terrible Webster." It showed a strange ignorance of his own power that in the preface to *Vittoria* he regretted that the nature of the English stage would not permit him to write sententious tragedy after the model of the ancients, "observing all the critical laws, as height of style and gravity of person, enriching it with the sententious chorus, and, as it were, *enlivening death in the passionate and weighty* NUNTIUS." He does undoubtedly observe height of style, and his persons are exempt from meanness and ignobility. Uncontrollable passionate love, and a temporary insanity of avarice pursued with subtle policy and bitterly repented of, are the chief impelling forces of his four great plays; and even inferior instruments of villany, such as Ludowick, Flamineo, and Bosola, are invested with a certain dignity. But that Webster should have desired to relate those terrific death-scenes instead of exhibiting them as he has done, showed a strange obliviousness of the basis of his own fame and the excellence of modern tragedy.—WILLIAM MINTO, *Characteristics of English Poets*, 1874

In passing onward to John Webster, we come into the presence of a poet to whom a foremost place has been rarely denied among the later writers of the great age of our drama, and in whom it is impossible not to recognise a genius of commanding originality, though apparently of not very versatile powers. It is most unfortunate that but few plays should have been preserved of which he was the sole author; for it is in these that his most distinctive gifts stand forth with incomparably the greatest clearness, and, as is pointed out by the most adequate of his modern critics, he seems, like Shakspere and Jonson, to have preferred to work alone.

. . . Webster loves to accumulate the favourite furniture of theatrical terror—murders and executions, the dagger and the pistol, the cord and the coffin, together with skulls and ghosts, and whatever horrors attend or are suggested by the central horror of them all. Herein he is not exceptional among the Elisabethans, of whom, from Kyd to Tourneur, so many were alike addicted to the employment of the whole apparatus of death. What is distinctive in Webster, is in the first place the extraordinary intensity of his imagination in this sphere of ideas, and again the elaborateness of his workmanship, which enabled him to surpass—it may fairly be said—all our old dramatists in a field which a large proportion were at all times ready to cultivate. As for later endeavours in our literature to rival this familiarity with death and its ghastly associations, they have rarely escaped the danger of artificiality or succeeded in stimulating the imaginative powers of any generation but their own. Among all these poets of the grave and its terrors we meet with but few whose very soul seems, like Webster's, a denizen of the gloom by which their creations are overspread.

But Webster's most powerful plays and scenes are characterised by something besides their effective appeal to the emotion of terror. He has a true insight into human nature, and is capable of exhibiting the operation of powerful influences upon it with marvellous directness. He is aware that men and women will lay open the inmost recesses of their souls in moments of deep or sudden agitation; he has learnt that on such occasions unexpected contrasts—an impulse of genuine compassion in an assassin, a movement of true dignity in a harlot—are wont to offer themselves to the surprised observer; he is acquainted with the fury and the bitterness, the goad and the after-sting of passion, and with the broken vocabulary of grief. All these he knows and understands, and is able to reproduce, not continually or wearisomely, but with that unerring recognition of supremely fitting occasions which is one of the highest, as it is beyond all doubt one of the rarest, gifts of true dramatic genius.

. . . What Webster in general reproduces with inimitable force, is a succession of situations of overpowering effect; in construction he is far from strong, and in characterisation he only exceptionally passes beyond the range of ordinary types. There seems little moral purpose at work in his most imposing efforts; and his imagination, instead of dwelling by preference on the associations of the law-court and the charnel-house, would have had to sustain itself on nutriment more diverse and more spiritual, in order to wing his mighty genius to freer and loftier flights.—ADOLPHUS WILLIAM WARD, *A History of English Dramatic Literature*, 1875, Vol. 3, pp. 51–65

> Thunder: the flesh quails, and the soul bows down.
>   Night: east, west, south, and northward, very night.
>   Star upon struggling star strives into sight,
> Star after shuddering star the deep storms drown.
> The very throne of night, her very crown,
>   A man lays hand on, and usurps her right.
>   Song from the highest of heaven's imperious height
> Shoots, as a fire to smite some towering town.
> Rage, anguish, harrowing fear, heart-crazing crime,
> Make monstrous all the murderous face of Time
>   Shown in the spheral orbit of a glass
> Revolving. Earth cries out from all her graves,
> Frail, on frail rafts, across wide-wallowing waves,
>   Shapes here and there of child and mother pass.
>   —ALGERNON CHARLES SWINBURNE, "John
>   Webster," 1882

John Webster excelled in the delineation of strange and fantastic horrors. He was pre-eminently the dramatist of Death. But his works abound in passages of surprising tenderness and beauty. The vices and crimes which he delighted to paint have, notwithstanding their extravagance, an appearance of terrible reality; and he had the wonderful faculty of surmising and looking into the inmost thoughts and springs of action in the human mind. He was an artist of the highest type.—JAMES BALDWIN, "English Poetry," *English Literature and Literary Criticism*, 1882, p. 238

Of *Appius and Virginia* the best thing to be said is to borrow Sainte-Beuve's happy description of Molière's *Don Garcie de Navarre*, and to call it an *essai pale et noble*. Webster is sometimes very close to Shakspere; but to read *Appius and Virginia*, and then to read *Julius Cæsar* or *Coriolanus*, is to appreciate, in perhaps the most striking way possible, the universality which all good judges from Dryden downwards have recognised in the prince of literature. Webster, though he was evidently a good scholar, and even makes some parade of scholarship, was a Romantic to the core, and was all abroad in these classical measures. *The Devil's Law Case* sins in the opposite way, being hopelessly undigested, destitute of any central interest, and, despite fine passages, a mere "salmagundi." There remain the two famous plays of *The White Devil* or *Vittoria Corombona* and *The Duchess of Malfi*—plays which have not, I think, been acted since their author's days, and of which the earlier and, to my judgment, better was not a success even then, but which the judgment of three generations has placed at the very head of all their class, and which contain magnificent poety.—GEORGE SAINTSBURY, A *History of Elizabethan Literature*, 1887, p. 274

Webster, as man and artist, never descends to Tourneur's level. He selects his two great subjects from Italian story, deriving thence the pith and marrow of veracity. These subjects he treats carefully and conscientiously, according to his own conception of the dreadful depths in human nature revealed to us by sixteenth century Italy. He does not use the vulgar machinery of revenge and ghosts in order to evolve an action. In so far as this goes, he may even be said to have advanced a step beyond *Hamlet* in the evolution of the Tragedy of Blood. His dramatic issues are worked out, without much alteration, from the matter given in the two Italian tales he used. Only he claims the right to view human fates and fortunes with despair, to paint a broad black background for his figures, to detach them sharply in sinister or pathetic relief, and to leave us at the last without a prospect over hopeful things. "One great Charybdis swallows all," said the Greek Simonides; and this motto might be chosen for the work of Shakespeare's greatest pupil in the art of tragedy. Yet Webster never fails to touch our hearts, and makes us remember a riper utterance upon the piteousness of man's ephemeral existence:—

Sunt lacrimæ rerum, et mentem mortalia tangunt.

It is just this power of blending tenderness and pity with the exhibition of acute moral anguish by which Webster is so superior to Tourneur as a dramatist.

. . . No dramatist showed more consummate ability in heightening terrific effects, in laying bare the inner mysteries of crime, remorse, and pain combined to make men miserable. He seems to have had a natural bias toward the dreadful stuff with which he deals so powerfully. He was drawn to comprehend and reproduce abnormal elements of spiritual anguish. The materials with which he builds are sought for in the ruined places of abandoned lives, in the agonies of madness and despair, in the sarcasms of reckless atheism, in slow tortures, griefs beyond endurance, the tempests of sin-haunted conscience, the spasms of fratricidal bloodshed, the deaths of frantic hope-deserted criminals. He is often melodramatic in the means employed to bring these psychological elements of tragedy home to our imagination. He makes free use of poisoned engines, daggers, pistols, disguised murderers, masques, and nightmares. Yet his firm grasp upon the essential qualities of diseased and guilty human nature, his profound pity for the innocent who suffer shipwreck in the storm of evil passions not their own, save him, even at his gloomiest and wildest, from the unrealities and extravagances into which less potent artists—Tourneur, for example—blundered.—JOHN ADDINGTON SYMONDS, "Introduction" to *Webster and Tourneur*, 1888, pp. xi–xxii

There are, indeed, wondrous flashes of dramatic power; by whiles, too, there are refreshing openings-out to the light or sinlessness of common day—a lifting of thought and consciousness up from the great welter of crime and crime's en-

tanglements; but there is little brightness, sparse sunshine, rare panoply of green or blooming things; even the flowers are put to sad offices, and

do cover
The friendless bodies of unburied men.

When a man's flower culture gets reduced to such narrow margin as this it does not carry exhilarating odors with it.—DONALD G. MITCHELL, *English Lands, Letters, and Kings, From Elizabeth to Anne*, 1890, p. 90

Nothing so much as a close and careful study of his imagery can bring home to one the extraordinary originality and power of Webster in his particular sphere. Webster worked consciously, deliberately, and with a thorough command of his materials. His pages are strewn with tropes, and, in spite of their profusion, such is the keenness of his marvelous "analogical instinct" and the dramatic force of his imagination that scarcely ever do they seem forced or out of keeping. Language here seems to reach the extreme of ruthless and biting intensity. There is scarcely any faded imagery, and there are very few conventional tags; everything stands out in sharp lines, as if etched. The characteristic fault of Webster's imagery, the defect of his peculiar quality, is that he errs if anything on the side of the bizarre, or even of the grotesque. This criticism could be enforced by many citations. . . . The acrid nature of Webster's genius is everywhere felt in his pungent use of similitudes. The sardonic character of Flamineo in *The White Devil* is heightened by the irony of his incessant similes. So in *The Duchess of Malfi* Antonio's rather colorless virtues are artfully depicted through his fondness for sententious comparisons.—FREDERIC IVES CARPENTER, *Metaphor and Simile in the Minor Elizabethan Drama*, 1895, pp. 75–77

Greater in some respects than any but Shakespeare, is John Webster, who requires but a closer grasp of style and a happier architecture to rank among the leading English poets. The *Duchess of Malfy*, which is believed to have been produced in 1612, has finer elements of tragedy than exist elsewhere outside the works of Shakespeare. In a ruder form, we find the same distinguished intensity of passion in the earlier *White Devil*. Webster has so splendid a sense of the majesty of death, of the mutability of human pleasures, and of the velocity and weight of destiny, that he rises to conceptions which have an Æschylean dignity; but, unhappily, he grows weary of sustaining them, his ideas of stage-craft are rudimentary and spectacular, and his single well-constructed play, *Appius and Virginia*, has a certain disappointing tameness. Most of the Elizabethan and Jacobean dramatists are now read only in extracts, and this test is highly favourable to Webster, who strikes us as a very noble poet driven by the exigencies of fashion to write for a stage, the business of which he had not studied and in which he took no great interest.—EDMUND GOSSE, *Modern English Literature*, 1897, pp. 118–19

Works

THE WHITE DEVIL
(VITTORIA COROMBONA)

To those who report I was a long time in finishing this tragedy, I confess I do not write with a goose-quill winged with two feathers; and, if they will needs make it my fault, I must answer them with that of Euripides to Alcestides, a tragick writer: Alcestides objecting that Euripides had only in three daies composed three verses, whereas himself had written three hundredth; Thou telst truthe (quoth he), but heres the difference, thine shall only be read for three daies, whereas mine shall continue three ages.—JOHN WEBSTER, "Preface," *The White Devil*, 1612

I never saw anything like the funeral dirge in this play, for the death of Marcello, except the ditty which reminds Ferdinand of his drowned father in the *Tempest*. As that is of the water, watery; so this is of the earth, earthy. Both have that intenseness of feeling, which seems to resolve itself into the element which it contemplates.—CHARLES LAMB, *Specimens of English Dramatic Poets Who Lived About the Time of Shakspeare*, 1808

⟨*The White Devil*⟩ is so disjointed in its action,—the incidents are so capricious and so involved,—and there is, throughout, such a mixture of the horrible and the absurd—the comic and the tragic—the pathetic and the ludicrous,—that we find it impossible, within our narrow limits, to give any thing like a complete and consistent analysis of it. . . .

There is great power in this drama, and even much fine poetry,—but, on the whole, it shocks rather than agitates, and the passion is rather painful than tragical. There are, in truth, some scenes that altogether revolt and disgust,—and mean, abandoned, and unprincipled characters occupy too much of our attention throughout the action of the play. There is but little imagination breathed over the passions of the prime agents, who exhibit themselves in the bare deformity of evil,—and scene follows scene of shameless profligacy, unredeemed either by great intellectual energy, or occasional burstings of moral sensibilities. The character of Vittoria Corombona, on which the chief interest of the drama depends, is sketched with great spirit and freedom,—but though true enough to nature, and startling by her beauty and her wickedness, we feel that she is not fit to be the chief personage of tragedy, which ought ever to deal only with great passions, and with great events. There is, however, a sort of fascination about this "White Devil of Venice," which accompanies her to the fatal end of her career,—and something like admiration towards her is awakened by the dauntless intrepidity of her death.—JOHN WILSON (as "H.M."), *Blackwood's Edinburgh Magazine*, Aug. 1818, pp. 556–62

Of the two plays of Webster in which his tragic genius has produced its most potent effects, *The White Devil, or The Tragedy of Paulo Giordano Vrsini, Duke of Brachiano, with the Life and Death of Vittoria Corombona, the famous Venetian Curtizan*, first printed in 1612 and perhaps acted 1607–8, is the earlier. Although I cannot agree with those who regard this tragedy as the masterpiece of its author, it is beyond all doubt a most remarkable work. Its plot as well as its characters appears to have been borrowed directly from an Italian source, inasmuch as the history of the Duke of Brachiano and his two wives, of whom the second bore the name of Vittoria Accorambuoni and was the widow of the nephew of Cardinal Montalto, afterwards Pope Sixtus V, does not appear to have been reproduced in any English or French version.

This extraordinary tragedy, whose finest scenes and passages have, in the judgment of Mr. Swinburne, been never surpassed or equalled except by Shakspere 'in the crowning qualities of tragic or dramatic poetry,' must be described as at once highly elaborated and essentially imperfect. In the address *To the Reader* already referred to, Webster confesses with conscious pride that this play was the fruit of protracted labour; but his efforts appear to have been directed rather to accumulating and elaborating effective touches of detail than to producing a well-proportioned whole. The catastrophe seems to lag too far after the climax; and in spite of the mighty impression created by the genius of the author, it is difficult to resist a sense of weariness in the progress of the later part of the action. But a

yet more serious defect appears to me to attach to *Vittoria Corombona*. The personages of this tragedy—above all that of the heroine—are conceived with the most striking original power and carried out with unerring consistency; but we crave—and crave in vain—some relief to the almost sickening combination of awe and loathing created by such characters and motives as this drama presents.

The character of Vittoria herself—the White Devil—is not easily to be put into words. Hot passion covering itself by an assumption of cool outward self-control and of contemptuous superiority to the ordinary fears or scruples of women,—this is a conception which we instinctively feel to be true to nature—to nature, that is, in one of her abnormal moods. In the first scene in which Vittoria appears she reveals the deadliness of her passionate resolution, when relating to her paramour the dream which is to urge him on to the murder of his duchess and her own husband. The ghastliness of the imagery of the vision is indescribably effective, together with the horrible scornfulness of the closing phrase:

> When to my rescue there arose, methought,
> A whirlwind, which let fall a massy arm
> From that strong plant;
> And both were struck dead by that sacred yew,
> *In that base shallow grave that was their due.*

The scene in which Vittoria is tried for the murder of her husband has attracted the comment of several critics—among others of Charles Lamb, who strangely enough speaks of her 'innocence-resembling boldness.' Dyce demurs to this view, which appears to me utterly erroneous, and destructive of the consistency which the character throughout maintains. Not 'sweetness' and 'loveliness' but a species of strange fascination, such as is only too often exercised by heartless pride, seems to pervade the figure and the speech of the defiant sinner who refuses to withdraw an inch from the position which she has assumed, and meets her judges with a front of withering scorn. Almost equally effective are the burst of passion with which she turns upon the jealous Brachiano, and the gradual subsiding of her wrath, as of a fire, under his caresses. The terrible energy of the last act is almost unparalleled; but the character of Vittoria remains true to itself, except perhaps in the last—rather trivial—reflexion with which she dies.

The remaining characters of the tragedy are drawn with varying degrees of force; but they all seem to stand forth as real human figures under the lurid glare of a storm-laden sky: nor is it easy to analyse the impression created by so dense a mixture of unwholesome humours, wild passions, and fearful sorrows. The total effect is unspeakably ghastly—though in one of the most elaborately terrible scenes the intention becomes too obvious, and 'several forms of distraction' exhibited by the mad Cornelia strike one as in some degree conventional, as they are to some extent plagiarised.

It must however be observed that in this play, as in *The Duchess of Malfi*, Webster creates some of his most powerful effects by single touches—flashes of genius which seem to light up of a sudden a wide horizon of emotions. It is in these flashes, so vivid as to illumine the dullest perception, so subtle as to search the closest heart, that Webster alone among our dramatists can be said at times to equal Shakspere.—ADOLPHUS WILLIAM WARD, *A History of English Dramatic Literature*, 1875, Vol. 3, pp. 56–59

One of the most glorious works of the period. Vittoria is perfect throughout, and in the justly-lauded trial scene she has no superior on any stage. Brachiano is a thoroughly life-like portrait of the man who is completely besotted with an evil woman. Flamineo I have spoken of, and not favourably; yet in literature, if not in life, he is a triumph; and above all the absorbing tragic interest of the play, which it is impossible to take up without finishing, has to be counted in. But the real charm of *The White Devil* is the wholly miraculous poetry in phrases and short passages which it contains. Vittoria's dream of the yew-tree, almost all the speeches of the unfortunate Isabella, and most of her rival's, have this merit. But the most wonderful flashes of poetry are put in the mouth of the scoundrel Flamineo, where they have a singular effect.—GEORGE SAINTSBURY, A *History of Elizabethan Literature*, 1887, p. 275

In 1612 John Webster stood revealed to the then somewhat narrow world of readers as a tragic poet and dramatist of the very foremost rank in the very highest class. *The White Devil*, also known as *Vittoria Corombona*, is a tragedy based on events then comparatively recent—on a chronicle of crime and retribution in which the leading circumstances were altered and adapted with the most delicate art and the most consummate judgment from the incompleteness of incomposite reality to the requisites of the stage of Shakespeare. By him alone among English poets have the finest scenes and passages of this tragedy been ever surpassed or equalled in the crowning qualities of tragic or dramatic poetry—in pathos and passion, in subtlety and strength, in harmonious variety of art and infallible fidelity to nature.—ALGERNON CHARLES SWINBURNE, *Studies in Prose and Poetry*, 1894, p. 50

THE DUCHESS OF MALFI

Crown him a poet, whom nor Rome nor Greece
Transcend in all their's for a masterpiece;
In which, whiles words and matter change, and men
Act one another, he, from whose clear pen,
They all took life, to memory hath lent
A lasting fame to raise his monument.
     —JOHN FORD, "To the Reader of the Author, and His 'Dutchess of Malfi'," 1623

I never saw thy Duchess till the day
That she was lively bodied in thy play:
How'er she answer'd her low-rated love
Her brother's anger did so fatal prove,
Yet my opinion is, she might speak more,
But never in her life so well before.
     —WILLIAM ROWLEY, "To His Friend, Mr. John Webster, Upon His 'Dutchess of Malfi'," 1623

All the several parts of the dreadful apparatus with which the death of the Duchess is ushered in, the waxen images which counterfeit death, the wild masque of madmen, the tombmaker, the bellman, the living person's dirge, the mortification by degrees,—are not more remote from the conceptions of ordinary vengeance, than the strange character of suffering which they seem to bring upon their victim is out of the imagination of ordinary poets. As they are not like inflictions of this life, so her language seems not of this world. She has lived among horrors till she is become "native and endowed unto that element." She speaks the dialect of despair; her tongue has a smatch of Tartarus and the souls in bale. To move a horror skilfully, to touch a soul to the quick, to lay upon fear as much as it can bear, to wean and weary a life till it is ready to drop, and then step in with mortal instruments to take its last forfeit: this only a Webster can do. Inferior geniuses may "upon horror's head horrors accumulate" but they cannot do this. They mistake quantity for quality; they "terrify babes with painted devils;" but they know not how a soul is to be moved. Their terrors want dignity, their affrightments are without decorum.—CHARLES LAMB, *Specimens of English Dramatic Poets Who Lived About the Time of Shakspeare*, 1808

The *Duchess of Malfy* is not, in my judgment, quite so spirited or effectual a performance as the *White Devil*. But it is distinguished by the same kind of beauties, clad in the same terrors. I do not know but the occasional strokes of passion are even profounder and more Shakespearian; but the story is more laboured, and the horror is accumulated to an overpowering and insupportable height. However appalling to the imagination and finely done, the scenes of the madhouse to which the *Duchess* is condemned with a view to unsettle her reason, and the interview between her and her brother, where he gives her the supposed dead hand of her husband, exceed, to my thinking, the just bounds of poetry and of tragedy. At least, the merit is of a kind, which, however great, we wish to be rare.—WILLIAM HAZLITT, "Lecture 3," *Lectures on the Literature of the Age of Elizabeth*, 1820

The *Duchess of Malfy* abounds more in the terrible than *The White Devil*. It turns on the mortal offence which the lady gives to her two proud brothers, Ferdinand, Duke of Calabria, and a cardinal, by indulging in a generous, though infatuated passion, for Antonio, her steward. This passion, a subject always most difficult to treat, is managed in this case with infinite delicacy; and, in a situation of great peril for the author, she condescends, without being degraded, and declares the affection with which her dependant has inspired her, without losing anything of dignity and respect.—ABRAHAM MILLS, *The Literature and the Literary Men of Great Britain and Ireland*, 1851, Vol. 1, p. 345

Webster's *Duchess of Malfi* teaches both the triumphs and the dangers of the dramatic fury. The construction runs riot; certain characters are powerfully conceived, others are wild figments of the brain. It is full of most fantastic speech and action; yet the tragedy, the passion, the felicitious language and imagery of various scenes, are nothing less than Shakespearean. To comprehend rightly the good and bad qualities of this play is to have gained a liberal education in poetic criticism.—EDMUND CLARENCE STEDMAN, *The Nature and Elements of Poetry*, 1892, p. 249

Was first printed in the memorable year which witnessed the first publication of his collected plays. This tragedy stands out among its compeers as one of the imperishable and ineradicable landmarks of literature. All the great qualities apparent in *The White Devil* reappear in *The Duchess of Malfy*, combined with a yet more perfect execution, and utilized with a yet more consummate skill. No poet has ever so long and so successfully sustained at their utmost heighth and intensity the expressed emotions and the united effects of terror and pity. The transcendent imagination and the impassioned sympathy which inspire this most tragic of all tragedies save *King Lear* are fused together in the fourth act into a creation which has hardly been excelled for unflagging energy of impression and of pathos in all the dramatic or poetic literature of the world.—ALGERNON CHARLES SWINBURNE, *Studies in Prose and Poetry*, 1894, p. 51

APPIUS AND VIRGINIA

In *Appius and Virginia*, printed in 1654, probably after its author's death, we may consider ourselves justified in recognising a work of his later manhood, if not of his old age. The theme is indeed one which might readily be supposed to have commended itself to Webster's love of the terrible; but he has treated it without adding fresh effects of his own invention to those which he found ready to his hand. Yet the play has genuine power; and were it not that the action seems to continue too long after the death of Virginia, this tragedy might be described as one of the most commendable efforts of its class. The evenness, however, of its execution, and the absence (except in the central situation) of any passages of a peculiarly striking or startling character, exclude *Appius and Virginia* from the brief list of Webster's most characteristic productions.—ADOLPHUS WILLIAM WARD, *A History of English Dramatic Literature*, 1875, Vol. 3, p. 62

. . . ⟨W⟩ithout a study of his Roman play, justice can hardly be done to the scope and breadth of Webster's genius. Of *Appius and Virginia* Mr. Dyce observed with excellent judgment: "this drama is so remarkable for its simplicity, its deep pathos, it unobtrusive beauties, its singleness of plot, and the easy, unimpeded march of its story, that perhaps there are readers who will prefer it to any other of our author's productions." Webster, who was a Latin scholar, probably studied the fable in Livy; but its outlines were familiar to English people through Painter's "Palace of Pleasure." He has drawn the mutinous camp before Algidum, the discontented city ruled by a licentious noble, the stern virtues of Icilius and Virginius, and the innocent girlhood of Virginia with a quiet mastery and self-restraint which prove that the violent contrasts of his Italian plays were calculated for a peculiar effect of romance. When treating a classical subject, he aimed at classical severity of form. The chief interest of the drama centres in Appius. This character suited Webster's vein. He delighted in the delineation of a bold, imperious tyrant, marching through crimes to the attainment of his lawless ends, yet never wholly despicable. He also loved to analyse the subtleties of a deep-brained intriguer, changing from open force to covert guile, fawning and trampling on the objects of his hate by turns, assuming the tone of diplomacy and the truculence of autocratic will at pleasure, on one occasion making the worse appear the better cause by rhetoric, on another espousing evil with reckless cynicism. The variations of such a character are presented with force and lucidity in *Appius*. Yet the whole play lacks those sudden flashes of illuminative beauty, those profound and searching glimpses into the bottomless abyss of human misery, which render Webster's two Italian tragedies unique. He seems to have been writing under self-imposed limitations, in order to obtain a certain desired effect—much in the same way as Ford did when he composed the irreproachable but somewhat chilling history of *Perkin Warbeck*.—JOHN ADDINGTON SYMONDS, "Introduction" to *Webster and Tourneur*, 1888, pp. xvii–xix

Appius and Virginia differs largely from the other plays in diction and figure. It is more rhetorical and declamatory, it contains fewer striking and original similitudes; and with a sort of dramatic propriety its language is more latinized and conventional. The attempt is obviously in another vein than the Italianate tragedies of *The White Devil* and *The Duchess of Malfi*.—FREDERIC IVES CARPENTER, *Metaphor and Simile in the Minor Elizabethan Drama*, 1895, p. 80

ALEXANDER DYCE
From "Some Account of John Webster and His Writings"
The Works of John Webster, Vol. 1
ed. Alexander Dyce
1830, pp. v–xiv

Seldom has the biographer greater cause to lament the deficiency of materials for his task than when engaged on the life of any of our early dramatists. Among that illustrious band JOHN WEBSTER occupies a distinguished place; and yet so little do we know concerning him, that the present essay must consist almost entirely of an account of his different productions, and of an attempt to show that he was not the author of certain prose pieces which have been attributed to his pen.

It is said that he was clerk of St. Andrew's, Holborn, and a Member of the Merchant Tailors' Company.

Like some other of his contemporaries, he was perhaps an actor as well as a dramatist; but, when in a tract (hereafter to be mentioned) called *Histriomastrix*, &c. Hall and his coadjutor term him "the quondam *player*," they appear only to have meant "writer of plays."

The earliest notice of Webster yet discovered, occurs in the papers of Henslowe:

"May
"1602 Two Harpies, by Dekker, Drayton, Middleton, Webster, and Mundy.
"Nov.
"1602 Lady Jane, by Henry Chettle, Thomas Dekker, Thomas Heywood, Wentworth Smith, and John Webster.
"The Second Part of Lady Jane, by Thomas Heywood, John Webster, Henry Chettle and Thomas Dekker."
(Malone's *Shakespeare*, (by Boswell), vol. iii. p. 327).

The *Two Harpies* and *Lady Jane* are among the lost dramas of our ancestors.

In 1604 Webster made some additions to the *Malcontent* of Marston. This was a work for which he was not ill fitted. The masculine character of his mind and style would very aptly harmonize with the characteristics of his predecessor; with whom, indeed, he has many qualities in common, and from the study of whose writings he perhaps in no slight degree modelled his own.

In 1607 were given to the press *The History of Sir Thomas Wyatt*, *Westward Ho*, and *Northward Ho*,—all which were composed by Webster, in alliance with Dekker.

That the authors did not superintend the printing of *Sir Thomas Wyatt* there can be no doubt, as the text is miserably corrupt; and I am inclined to believe that it is merely made up from fragments of the drama called *Lady Jane*, already mentioned in the quotation from Henslowe's papers.

Westward Ho, and *Northward Ho*, (the former of which was on the stage in 1605) are full of life and bustle, and exhibit as curious a picture of the manners and customs of the time as we shall anywhere find. Though by no means pure, they are comparatively little stained by that grossness from which none of our old comedies are entirely free. In them the worst things are always called by the worst names: the licentious and the debauched always speak most strictly in character; and the rake, the bawd, and the courtezan, are as odious in representation as they would be if actually present. But the public taste has now reached the highest pitch of refinement, and such coarseness is tolerated in our theatres no more. Perhaps, however, the language of the stage is purified in proportion as our morals have deteriorated, and we dread the mention of the vices which we are not ashamed to practise; while our forefathers, under the sway of a less fastidious but a more energetic principle of virtue, were careless of words and only considerate of actions.

In 1612, the *White Devil* was printed, a play of extraordinary power. The plot, though somewhat confused, is eminently interesting; and the action though abounding, perhaps a little overcharged, with fearful circumstances, is such as the imagination willingly receives as credible. What genius was required to conceive, what skill to embody, so forcible, so various, and so consistent a character as Vittoria! We shall not easily find, in the whole range of our ancient drama, a more effective scene than that in which she is arraigned for the murder of her husband. It is truth itself. Brachiano's throwing down his gown for his seat, and then, with impatient ostentation, leaving it behind him on his departure; the pleader's Latin exordium; the jesting interruption of the culprit; the overbearing intemperance of the Cardinal; the prompt and unconquerable spirit of Vittoria—altogether unite in impressing the mind with a picture as strong and diversified as any which could be received from an actual transaction of real life. Mr. Lamb, in his *Specimens of English Dramatic Poets*, (the most tasteful selection ever made from any set of writers) speaks of the "innocence-resembling boldness of Vittoria." For my own part, I admire the dexterity with which Webster has discriminated between that simple confidence in their own integrity which characterises the innocent under the imputation of any great offence, and that forced and practised presence of mind which the hardened criminal may bring to the place of accusation. Vittoria stands before her judges, alive to all the terrors of her situation, relying on the quickness of her wit, conscious of the influence of her beauty, and not without a certain sense of protection, in case of extreme need, from the interposition of Brachiano. She surprises by the readiness of her replies, but never, in a single instance, has the author ascribed to her one word which was likely to have fallen from an innocent person under similar circumstances. Vittoria is undaunted, but it is by effort. Her intrepidity has none of the calmness which naturally attends the person who knows that his own plain tale can set down his adversary; but it is the high-wrought and exaggerated boldness of a resolute spirit,—a determination to outface facts, to brave the evidence she cannot refute, and to act the martyr though convicted as a culprit. Scattered throughout the play are passages of exquisite poetic beauty, which, once read by any person of taste and feeling, can never be forgotten.

Three Elegies on the most lamented death of Prince Henry appeared in 1613: the part of this tract written by Webster, entitled *A Monumental Column*, &c. contains some striking lines, but nothing very characteristic of its author.

In 1623 were published *The Dutchess of Malfi* (which must have been acted as early as 1619) and *The Devil's Law-case*. Of the latter of these plays the plot is disagreeable, and not a little improbable, but portions of the serious scenes are certainly not unworthy of Webster. Few dramas possess a deeper interest in their progress, or are more affecting in their conclusion, than *The Dutchess of Malfi*. The passion of the Dutchess for Antonio, a subject most difficult to treat, is managed with infinite delicacy; and, in a situation of great peril for the author, she condescends without being degraded, and declares the affection with which her dependant had inspired her without losing anything of dignity and respect. Her attachment is justified by the excellence of its object; and she seems only to exercise the privilege of exalted rank in raising merit from obscurity. We sympathise from the first moment in the loves of the Dutchess and Antonio, as we would in a long standing domestic affection, and we mourn the more over the misery that attends them because we feel that happiness was the natural and legitimate fruit of so pure and rational an attachment. It is the wedded friendship of middle life transplanted to cheer the cold and glittering solitude of a court: it flourishes but for a short space in that unaccustomed sphere, and is then violently rooted out. How pathetic is the scene where they part never

to meet again! And how beautiful and touching is her exclamation!

> "the birds that live i' th' field,
> On the wild benefit of nature, live
> Happier than we; for they may choose their mates,
> And carol their sweet pleasures to the spring!"

The sufferings and death of the imprisoned Dutchess haunt the mind like painful realities; but it is the less necessary to dwell on them here, as no part of our author's writings is so well known to the generality of readers as the extraordinary scenes where they are depicted. In such scenes Webster was on his own ground. His imagination had a fond familiarity with objects of awe and fear. The silence of the sepulchre, the sculptures of marble monuments, the knolling of church bells, the cearments of the corpse, the yew that roots itself in dead men's graves, are the illustrations that most readily present themselves to his imagination. If he speaks of love, and of the force of human passion, his language is,—

> "This is flesh and blood, sir;
> 'Tis not the figure cut in alabaster,
> Kneels at my husband's tomb"—

and when we are told that

> "Glories, like glow-worms, afar off shine bright,
> But look'd to near, have neither heat nor light,"

we almost feel satisfied that the glow-worm which Webster saw, and which suggested the reflection, was sparkling on the green sod of some lowly grave.

Of the piece next to be mentioned I have spared no pains in endeavouring to procure a copy, but unfortunately I have not succeeded. It is a small pamphlet, entitled *The Monument of Honour, at the confirmation of the right worthy brother John Goare in his high office of his Majesty's lieutenant over his royal chamber, at the charge and expense of the right worthy and worshipfull fraternity of eminent Merchant-Taylors. Invented and written by John Webster, Taylor. 1624. 4to.*

Appius and Virginia was printed in 1654. When I consider its simplicity, its deep pathos, its unobtrusive beauties, its singleness of plot, and the easy unimpeded march of its story, I cannot but suspect that there are readers who will prefer this drama to any other of our author's productions.

Before the time that *Appius and Virginia* was given to the press, Webster was, in all probability, dead.

In 1661, Kirkman, the bookseller, published from manuscripts in his possession, A *Cure for a Cuckold* and *The Thracian Wonder*, asserting that these were written by our author, in conjunction with William Rowley. Webster's hand may, I think, be traced in parts of the former play. Of any share in the concoction of the latter, he certainly was guiltless.

Webster composed several dramas of which only the names remain; and others, doubtless, of which there is no memorial. Henslowe's notice of the *Two Harpies* and *Lady Jane* has been already cited, at p. v. Among the extracts from Sir Henry Herbert's official register, given by G. Chalmers, (*Supplemental Apology*, p. 219,) we find "A new Tragedy called A *Late Murther of the sonn upon the Mother*, written by Forde and Webster;" of which, when we consider how well the terrible subject was fitted to the powers of the two writers, we cannot fail to regret the loss. Webster himself, in the dedication to *The Devil's Law-case*, mentions *The Guise* as one of his dramatic performances.

CHARLES KINGSLEY
From "Plays and Puritans" (1859)
*Plays and Puritans and Other
Historical Essays*
1889, pp. 50–56

The whole story of 'Vittoria Corrombona' is one of sin and horror. The subject-matter of the play is altogether made up of the fiercest and the basest passions. But the play is not a study of those passions from which we may gain a great insight into human nature. There is no trace—nor is there, again, in the *Duchess of Malfi*—of that development of human souls for good or evil which is Shakspeare's especial power—the power which, far more than any accidental 'beauties,' makes his plays, to this day, the delight alike of the simple and the wise, while his contemporaries are all but forgotten. The highest aim of dramatic art is to exhibit the development of the human soul; to construct dramas in which the conclusion shall depend, not on the events, but on the characters; and in which the characters shall not be mere embodiments of a certain passion, or a certain 'humour': but persons, each unlike all others; each having a destiny of his own by virtue of his own peculiarities, and of his own will; and each proceeding toward that destiny as he shall conquer, or yield to, circumstances; unfolding his own strength and weakness before the eyes of the audience; and that in such a way that, after his first introduction, they should be able (in proportion to their knowledge of human nature) to predict his conduct under those circumstances. This is indeed 'high art': but we find no more of it in Webster than in the rest. His characters, be they old or young, come on the stage ready-made, full grown, and stereotyped; and therefore, in general, they are not characters at all, but mere passions or humours in human form. Now and then he essays to draw a character: but it is analytically, by description, not synthetically and dramatically, by letting the man exhibit himself in action; and in the *Duchess of Malfi* he falls into the great mistake of telling, by Antonio's mouth, more about the Duke and the Cardinal than he afterwards makes them act. Very different is Shakspeare's method of giving, at the outset, some single delicate hint about his personages which will serve as a clue to their whole future conduct; thus 'showing the whole in each part,' and stamping each man with a personality, to a degree which no other dramatist has ever approached.

But the truth is, the study of human nature is not Webster's aim. He has to arouse terror and pity, not thought, and he does it in his own way, by blood and fury, madmen and screech-owls, not without a rugged power. There are scenes of his, certainly, like that of Vittoria's trial, which have been praised for their delineation of character: but it is one thing to solve the problem, which Shakspeare has so handled in *Lear*, *Othello*, and *Richard the Third*,—'Given a mixed character, to show how he may become criminal,' and to solve Webster's 'Given a ready-made criminal, to show how he commits his crimes.' To us the knowledge of character shown in Vittoria's trial scene is not an insight into Vittoria's essential heart and brain, but a general acquaintance with the conduct of all bold bad women when brought to bay. Poor Elia, who knew the world from books, and human nature principally from his own loving and gentle heart, talks of Vittoria's 'innocence-resembling boldness'[1]—and 'seeming to see that matchless beauty of her face, which inspires such gay confidence in her,' and so forth.

Perfectly just and true, not of Vittoria merely, but of the average of bad young women in the presence of a police magistrate: yet amounting in all merely to this, that the strength of Webster's confest master-scene lies simply in intimate acquaintance with vicious nature in general. We will say no more on this matter, save to ask, *Cui bono?* Was the art of which this was the highest manifestation likely to be of much use to mankind, much less able to excuse its palpably disgusting and injurious accompaniments?

The *Duchess of Malfi* is certainly in a purer and loftier strain: but in spite of the praise which has been lavished on her, we must take the liberty to doubt whether the poor Duchess is a 'person' at all. General goodness and beauty, intense though pure affection for a man below her in rank, and a will to carry out her purpose at all hazards, are not enough to distinguish her from thousands of other women: but Webster has no such purpose. What he was thinking and writing of was not truth, but effect; not the Duchess, but her story; not her brothers, but their rage; not Antonio, her major-domo and husband, but his good and bad fortunes; and thus he has made Antonio merely insipid, the brothers merely unnatural, and the Duchess (in the critical moment of the play) merely forward. That curious scene, in which she acquaints Antonio with her love for him and makes him marry her, is, on the whole, painful. Webster himself seems to have felt that it was so; and, dreading lest he had gone too far, to have tried to redeem the Duchess at the end by making her break down in two exquisite lines of loving shame: but he has utterly forgotten to explain or justify her love by giving to Antonio (as Shakspeare would probably have done) such strong specialties of character as would compel, and therefore excuse, his mistress's affection. He has plenty of time to do this in the first scenes,—time which he wastes on irrelevant matter; and all that we gather from them is that Antonio is a worthy and thoughtful person. If he gives promise of being more, he utterly disappoints that promise afterwards. In the scene in which the Duchess tells her love, he is far smaller, rather than greater, than the Antonio of the opening scene: though (as there) altogether passive. He hears his mistress's declaration just as any other respectable youth might; is exceedingly astonished, and a good deal frightened; has to be talked out of his fears till one naturally expects a revulsion on the Duchess's part into something like scorn or shame (which might have given a good opportunity for calling out sudden strength in Antonio): but so busy is Webster with his business of drawing mere blind love, that he leaves Antonio to be a mere puppet, whose worthiness we are to believe in only from the Duchess's assurance to him that he is the perfection of all that a man should be; which, as all lovers are of the same opinion the day before the wedding, is not of much importance.

Neither in his subsequent misfortunes does Antonio make the least struggle to prove himself worthy of his mistress's affection. He is very resigned and loving, and so forth. To win renown by great deeds, and so prove his wife in the right to her brothers and all the world, never crosses his imagination. His highest aim (and that only at last) is slavishly to entreat pardon from his brothers-in-law for the mere offence of marrying their sister; and he dies by an improbable accident, the same pious and respectable insipidity which he has lived,—'*ne valant pas la peine qui se donne pour lui.*' The prison-scenes between the Duchess and her tormentors are painful enough, if to give pain be a dramatic virtue; and she appears in them really noble; and might have appeared far more so, had Webster taken half as much pains with her as he has with the madmen, ruffians, ghosts, and screech-owls in which his heart really delights. The only character really worked out so as to live and grow under his hand is Bosola, who, of course, is the villain of the piece, and being a rough fabric, is easily manufactured with rough tools. Still, Webster has his wonderful touches here and there—

Cariola: Hence, villains, tyrants, murderers! Alas!
    What will you do with my lady? Call for help!
Duchess: To whom? to our next neighbours? they are mad folk.
    Farewell, Cariola.
    I pray thee look thou giv'st my little boy
    Some syrup for his cold; and let the girl
    Say her prayers ere she sleep.—Now, what you please;
    What death?

And so the play ends, as does *Vittoria Corrombona*, with half a dozen murders *coram populo*, howls, despair, bedlam, and the shambles; putting the reader marvellously in mind of that well-known old book of the same era, *Reynolds's God's Revenge*, in which, with all due pious horror and bombastic sermonising, the national appetite for abominations is duly fed with some fifty unreadable Spanish histories, French histories, Italian histories, and so forth, one or two of which, of course, are known to have furnished subjects for the playwrights of the day.

Note
1. C. Lamb, *Specimens of English Dramatic Poets*, p. 229. From which specimens, be it remembered, he has had to expunge not only all the comic scenes, but generally the greater part of the plot itself, to make the book at all tolerable.

ALGERNON CHARLES SWINBURNE
"John Webster" (1886)
The Age of Shakespeare
1908, pp. 15–59

There were many poets in the age of Shakespeare who make us think, as we read them, that the characters in their plays could not have spoken more beautifully, more powerfully, more effectively, under the circumstances imagined for the occasion of their utterance: there are only two who make us feel that the words assigned to the creatures of their genius are the very words they must have said, the only words they could have said, the actual words they assuredly did say. Mere literary power, mere poetic beauty, mere charm of passionate or pathetic fancy, we find in varying degrees dispersed among them all alike; but the crowning gift of imagination, the power to make us realise that thus and not otherwise it was, that thus and not otherwise it must have been, was given—except by exceptional fits and starts—to none of the poets of their time but only to Shakespeare and to Webster.

Webster, it may be said, was but as it were a limb of Shakespeare: but that limb, it might be replied, was the right arm. 'The kingly-crownèd head, the vigilant eye,' whose empire of thought and whose reach of vision no other man's faculty has ever been found competent to match, are Shakespeare's alone for ever: but the force of hand, the fire of heart, the fervour of pity, the sympathy of passion, not poetic or theatric merely, but actual and immediate, are qualities in which the lesser poet is not less certainly or less unmistakably pre-eminent than the greater. And there is no third to be set beside them: not even if we turn from their contemporaries to Shelley himself. All that Beatrice says in *The Cenci* is beautiful and conceivable and admirable: but unless we except her exquisite last words—and even they are more beautiful than inevitable—we shall hardly find what we find in *King Lear* and *The White Devil*, *Othello* and *The Duchess of Malfy*; the tone

of convincing reality; the note, as a critic of our own day might call it, of certitude.

There are poets—in our own age, as in all past ages—from whose best work it might be difficult to choose at a glance some verse sufficient to establish their claim—great as their claim may be—to be remembered for ever; and who yet may be worthy of remembrance among all but the highest. Webster is not one of these: though his fame assuredly does not depend upon the merit of a casual passage here or there, it would be easy to select from any one of his representative plays such examples of the highest, the purest, the most perfect power, as can be found only in the works of the greatest among poets. There is not, as far as my studies have ever extended, a third English poet to whom these words might rationally be attributed by the conjecture of a competent reader.

We cease to grieve, cease to be fortune's slaves,
    Nay, cease to die, by dying.

There is a depth of severe sense in them, a height of heroic scorn, or a dignity of quiet cynicism, which can scarcely be paralleled in the bitterest or the fiercest effusions of John Marston or Cyril Tourneur or Jonathan Swift. Nay, were they not put into the mouth of a criminal cynic, they would not seem unworthy of Epictetus. There is nothing so grand in the part of Edmund; the one figure in Shakespeare whose aim in life, whose centre of character, is one with the view or the instinct of Webster's two typical villains. Some touches in the part of Flamineo suggest, if not a conscious imitation, an unconscious reminiscence of that prototype: but the essential and radical originality of Webster's genius is shown in the difference of accent with which the same savage and sarcastic philosophy of self-interest finds expression through the snarl and sneer of his ambitious cynic. Monsters as they may seem of unnatural egotism and unallayed ferocity, the one who dies penitent, though his repentance be as sudden if not as suspicious as any ever wrought by miraculous conversion, dies as thoroughly in character as the one who takes leave of life in a passion of scorn and defiant irony which hardly passes off at last into a mood of mocking and triumphant resignation. There is a cross of heroism in almost all Webster's characters which preserves the worst of them from such hatefulness as disgusts us in certain of Fletcher's or of Ford's: they have in them some salt of manhood, some savour of venturesome and humorous resolution, which reminds us of the heroic age in which the genius that begot them was born and reared—the age of Richard Grenville and Francis Drake, Philip Sidney and William Shakespeare.

The earliest play of Webster's now surviving—if a work so piteously mutilated and defaced can properly be said to survive—is a curious example of the combined freedom and realism with which recent or even contemporary history was habitually treated on the stage during the last years of the reign of Queen Elizabeth. The noblest poem known to me of this peculiar kind is the play of *Sir Thomas More*, first printed by Mr. Dyce in 1844 for the Shakespeare Society: the worst must almost certainly be that 'Chronicle History of Thomas Lord Cromwell' which the infallible verdict of German intuition has discovered to be 'not only unquestionably Shakespeare's, but worthy to be classed among his best and maturest works.' About midway between these two I should be inclined to rank *The Famous History of Sir Thomas Wyatt*, a mangled and deformed abridgment of a tragedy by Dekker and Webster on the story of Lady Jane Grey. In this tragedy, as in the two comedies due to the collaboration of the same poets, it appears to me more than probable that Dekker took decidedly the greater part. The shambling and slipshod metre, which seems now and then to hit by mere chance on some pure and tender note of simple and exquisite melody—the lazy vivacity and impulsive inconsequence of style—the fitful sort of slovenly inspiration, with interludes of absolute and headlong collapse—are qualities by which a very novice in the study of dramatic form may recognise the reckless and unmistakable presence of Dekker. The curt and grim precision of Webster's tone, his terse and pungent force of compressed rhetoric, will be found equally difficult to trace in any of these three plays. *Northward Ho*, a clever, coarse, and vigorous study of the realistic sort, has not a note of poetry in it, but is more coherent, more sensibly conceived and more ably constructed, than the rambling history of Wyatt or the hybrid amalgam of prosaic and romantic elements in the compound comedy of *Westward Ho*. All that is of any great value in this amorphous and incongruous product of inventive impatience and impetuous idleness can be as distinctly traced to the hand of Dekker as the crowning glories of *The Two Noble Kinsmen* can be traced to the hand of Shakespeare. Any poet, even of his time, might have been proud of these verses, but the accent of them is unmistakable as that of Dekker.

> Go, let music
> Charm with her excellent voice an awful silence
> Through all this building, that her sphery soul
> May, on the wings of air, in thousand forms
> Invisibly fly, yet be enjoyed.

This delicate fluency and distilled refinement of expression ought properly, one would say, to have belonged to a poet of such careful and self-respectful genius as Tennyson's: whereas in the very next speech of the same speaker we stumble over such a phrase as that which closes the following sentence:—

> We feed, wear rich attires, and strive to cleave
> The stars with marble towers, fight battles, spend
> Our blood to buy us names, *and, in iron hold,*
> *Will we eat roots, to imprison fugitive gold.*

Which he who can parse, let him scan, and he who can scan, let him construe. It is alike incredible and certain that the writer of such exquisite and blameless verse as that in which the finer scenes of *Old Fortunatus* and *The Honest Whore* are so smoothly and simply and naturally written should have been capable of writing whole plays in this headlong and halting fashion, as helpless and graceless as the action of a spavined horse, or a cripple who should attempt to run.

It is difficult to say what part of these plays should be assigned to Webster. Their rough realistic humour, with its tone of somewhat coarse-grained good-nature, strikes the habitual note of Dekker's comic style: there is nothing of the fierce and scornful intensity, the ardour of passionate and compressed contempt, which distinguishes the savagely humorous satire of Webster and of Marston, and makes it hopeless to determine by intrinsic evidence how little or how much was added by Webster in the second edition to the original text of Marston's *Malcontent*: unless—which appears to me not unreasonable—we assume that the printer of that edition lied or blundered after the manner of his contemporary kind in attributing on the title-page—as apparently he meant to attribute—any share in the additional scenes or speeches to the original author of the play. In any case, the passages thus added to that grimmest and most sombre of tragicomedies are in such exact keeping with the previous text that the keenest scent of the veriest bloodhound among critics could not detect a shade of difference in the savour.

The text of either comedy is generally very fair—as free from corruption as could reasonably be expected. The text of *Sir Thomas Wyatt* is corrupt as well as mutilated. Even in Mr.

Dyce's second edition I have noted, not without astonishment, the following flagrant errors left still to glare on us from the distorted and disfigured page. In the sixth scene a single speech of Arundel's contains two of the most palpably preposterous:—

> The obligation wherein we all stood bound
>
> . .
> Cannot be concealed without great reproach
> To us and to our issue.

We should of course read 'cancelled' for 'concealed': the sense of the context and the exigence of the verse cry alike aloud for the correction. In the sixteenth line from this we come upon an equally obvious error:—

> Advice in this I hold it better far,
> To keep the course we run, than, seeking change,
> Hazard our lives, our honours, and the realm.

It seems hardly credible to those who are aware how much they owe to the excellent scholarship and editorial faculty of Mr. Dyce, that he should have allowed such a misprint as 'heirs' for 'honours' to stand in this last unlucky line. Again, in the next scene, when the popular leader Captain Brett attempts to reassure the country folk who are startled at the sight of his insurgent array, he is made to utter (in reply to the exclamation, 'What's here? soldiers!') the perfectly fatuous phrase, 'Fear not good speech.' Of course—once more—we should read, 'Fear not, good people'; a correction which rectifies the metre as well as the sense.

The play attributed to Webster and Rowley by a publisher of the next generation has been carefully and delicately analysed by a critic of our own time, who naturally finds it easy to distinguish the finer from the homelier part of the compound weft, and to assign what is rough and crude to the inferior, what is interesting and graceful to the superior poet. The authority of the rogue Kirkman may be likened to the outline or profile of Mr. Mantalini's early loves: it is either no authority at all, or at best it is a 'demd' authority. The same swindler who assigned to Webster and Rowley the authorship of *A Cure for a Cuckold* assigned to Shakespeare and Rowley the authorship of an infinitely inferior play—a play of which German sagacity has discovered that 'none of Rowley's other works are equal to this.' Assuredly they are not—in utter stolidity of platitude and absolute impotence of drivel. Rowley was a vigorous artist in comedy and an original master of tragedy: he may have written the lighter or broader parts of the play which rather unluckily took its name from these, and Webster may have written the more serious or sentimental parts: but there is not the slightest shadow of a reason to suppose it. An obviously apocryphal abortion of the same date, attributed to the same poets by the same knave, has long since been struck off the roll of Webster's works.

The few occasional poems of this great poet are worth study by those who are capable of feeling interest in the comparison of slighter with sublimer things, and the detection in minor works of the same style, here revealed by fitful hints in casual phrases, as that which animates and distinguishes even a work so insufficient and incompetent as Webster's 'tragecomedy' of *The Devil's Law-case*. The noble and impressive extracts from this most incoherent and chaotic of all plays which must be familiar to all students of Charles Lamb are but patches of imperial purple sewn on with the roughest of needles to a garment of the raggedest and coarsest kind of literary serge. Hardly any praise can be too high for their dignity and beauty, their lofty loyalty and simplicity of chivalrous manhood or their deep sincerity of cynic meditation and self-contemptuous mournfulness: and the reader who turns from these magnificent samples to the complete play must expect to find yet another and a yet unknown masterpiece of English tragedy. He will find a crowning example of the famous theorem, that 'the plot is of no use except to bring in the fine things.' The plot is in this instance absurd to a degree so far beyond the most preposterous conception of confused and distracting extravagance that the reader's attention may at times be withdrawn from the all but unqualified ugliness of its ethical tone or tendency. Two of Webster's favourite types, the meditative murderer or philosophic ruffian, and the impulsive impostor who is liable to collapse into the likeness of a passionate penitent, will remind the reader how much better they appear in tragedies which are carried through to their natural tragic end. But here, where the story is admirably opened and the characters as skilfully introduced, the strong interest thus excited at starting is scattered or broken or trifled away before the action is half-way through: and at its close the awkward violence or irregularity of moral and scenical effect comes to a crowning crisis in the general and mutual condonation of unnatural perjury and attempted murder with which the victims and the criminals agree to hush up all grudges, shake hands all round, and live happy ever after. There is at least one point of somewhat repulsive resemblance between the story of this play and that of Fletcher's 'Fair Maid of the Inn': but Fletcher's play, with none of the tragic touches or interludes of superb and sombre poetry which relieve the incoherence of Webster's, is better laid out and constructed, more amusing if not more interesting and more intelligent if not more imaginative.

A far more creditable and workmanlike piece of work, though glorified by no flashes of such sudden and singular beauty, is the tragedy of *Appius and Virginia*. The almost infinite superiority of Webster to Fletcher as a poet of pure tragedy and a painter of masculine character is in this play as obvious as the inferiority in construction and conduct of romantic story displayed in his attempt at a tragicomedy. From the evidence of style I should judge this play to have been written at an earlier date than *The Devil's Law-case*: it is, I repeat, far better composed; better, perhaps, than any other play of the author's: but it has none of his more distinctive qualities; intensity of idea, concentration of utterance, pungency of expression and ardour of pathos. It is written with noble and equable power of hand, with force and purity and fluency of apt and simple eloquence: there is nothing in it unworthy of the writer: but it is the only one of his unassisted works in which we do not find that especial note of tragic style, concise and pointed and tipped as it were with fire, which usually makes it impossible for the dullest reader to mistake the peculiar presence, the original tone or accent, of John Webster. If the epithet unique had not such a tang of German affectation in it, it would be perhaps the aptest of all adjectives to denote the genius or define the manner of this great poet. But in this tragedy, though whatever is said is well said and whatever is done well done, we miss that sense of positive and inevitable conviction, that instant and profound perception or impression as of immediate and indisputable truth, which is burnt in upon us as we read the more Websterian scenes of Webster's writing. We feel, in short, that thus it may have been: not, as I observed at the opening of these notes, that thus it must have been. The poem does him no discredit; nay, it does him additional honour, as an evidence of powers more various and many-sided than we should otherwise have known or supposed in him. Indeed, the figure of Virginius is one of the finest types of soldierly and fatherly heroism ever presented on the stage: there is equal force of dramatic effect, equal fervour of eloquent passion, in the scene of his pleading before the senate on behalf

of the claims of his suffering and struggling fellow-soldiers, and in the scene of his return to the camp after the immolation of his daughter. The mere theatric effect of this latter scene is at once so triumphant and so dignified, so noble in its presentation and so passionate in its restraint, that we feel the high justice and sound reason of the instinct which inspired the poet to prolong the action of his play so far beyond the sacrifice of his heroine. A comparison of Webster's Virginius with any of Fletcher's wordy warriors will suffice to show how much nearer to Shakespeare than to Fletcher stands Webster as a tragic or a serious dramatist. Coleridge, not always just to Fletcher, was not unjust in his remark 'what strange self-trumpeters and tongue-bullies all the brave soldiers of Beaumont and Fletcher are'; and again almost immediately—'all B. and F.'s generals are pugilists, or cudgel-fighters, that boast of their bottom and of the "claret" they have shed.' There is nothing of this in Virginius; Shakespeare himself has not represented with a more lofty fidelity, in the person of Coriolanus or of Brutus, 'the high Roman fashion' of austere and heroic self-respect. In the other leading or dominant figure of this tragedy there is certainly discernible a genuine and thoughtful originality or freshness of conception; but perhaps there is also recognisable a certain inconsistency of touch. It was well thought of to mingle some alloy of goodness with the wickedness of Appius Claudius, to represent the treacherous and lecherous decemvir as neither kindless nor remorseless, but capable of penitence and courage in his last hour. But Shakespeare, I cannot but think, would have prepared us with more care and more dexterity for the revelation of some such redeeming quality in a character which in the act immediately preceding Webster has represented as utterly heartless and shameless, brutal in its hypocrisy and impudent in its brutality.

If the works already discussed were their author's only claims to remembrance and honour, they might not suffice to place him on a higher level among our tragic poets than that occupied by Marston and Dekker and Middleton on the one hand, by Fletcher and Massinger and Shirley on the other. *Antonio and Mellida*, *Old Fortunatus*, or *The Changeling*— *The Maid's Tragedy*, *The Duke of Milan*, or *The Traitor*— would suffice to counterweigh (if not, in some cases, to outbalance) the merit of the best among these: the fitful and futile inspiration of *The Devil's Law-case*, and the stately but subdued inspiration of *Appius and Virginia*. That his place was with no subordinate poet—that his station is at Shakespeare's right hand—the evidence supplied by his two great tragedies is disputable by no one who has an inkling of the qualities which confer a right to be named in the same day with the greatest writer of all time.

Æschylus is above all things the poet of righteousness. 'But in any wise, I say unto thee, revere thou the altar of righteousness': this is the crowning admonition of his doctrine, as its crowning prospect is the reconciliation or atonement of the principle of retribution with the principle of redemption, of the powers of the mystery of darkness with the coeternal forces of the spirit of wisdom, of the lord of inspiration and of light. The doctrine of Shakespeare, where it is not vaguer, is darker in its implication of injustice, in its acceptance of accident, than the impression of the doctrine of Æschylus. Fate, irreversible and inscrutable, is the only force of which we feel the impact, of which we trace the sign, in the upshot of *Othello* or *King Lear*. The last step into the darkness remained to be taken by 'the most tragic' of all English poets. With Shakespeare—and assuredly not with Æschylus—righteousness itself seems subject and subordinate to the masterdom of fate: but fate itself, in the tragic world of Webster, seems merely the servant or the synonym of chance. The two chief agents in his two great tragedies pass away—the phrase was, perhaps, unconsciously repeated—'in a mist': perplexed, indomitable, defiant of hope and fear; bitter and sceptical and bloody in penitence or impenitence alike. And the mist which encompasses the departing spirits of these moody and mocking men of blood seems equally to involve the lives of their chastisers and their victims. Blind accident and blundering mishap—'such a mistake,' says one of the criminals, 'as I have often seen in a play'—are the steersmen of their fortunes and the doomsmen of their deeds. The effect of this method or the result of this view, whether adopted for dramatic objects or ingrained in the writer's temperament, is equally fit for pure tragedy and unfit for any form of drama not purely tragic in evolution and event. In *The Devil's Law-case* it is offensive, because the upshot is incongruous and insufficient: in *The White Devil* and *The Duchess of Malfy* it is admirable, because the results are adequate and coherent. But in all these three plays alike, and in these three plays only, the peculiar tone of Webster's genius, the peculiar force of his imagination, is distinct and absolute in its fullness of effect. The author of *Appius and Virginia* would have earned an honourable and enduring place in the history of English letters as a worthy member—one among many—of a great school in poetry, a deserving representative of a great epoch in literature: but the author of these three plays has a solitary station, an indisputable distinction of his own. The greatest poets of all time are not more mutually independent than this one—a lesser poet only than those greatest—is essentially independent of them all.

The first quality which all readers recognise, and which may strike a superficial reader as the exclusive or excessive note of his genius and his work, is of course his command of terror. Except in Æschylus, in Dante, and in Shakespeare, I at least know not where to seek for passages which in sheer force of tragic and noble horror—to the vulgar shock of ignoble or brutal horror he never condescends to submit his reader or subdue his inspiration—may be set against the subtlest, the deepest, the sublimest passages of Webster. Other gifts he had as great in themselves, as precious and as necessary to the poet: but on this side he is incomparable and unique. Neither Marlowe nor Shakespeare had so fine, so accurate, so infallible a sense of the delicate line of demarcation which divides the impressive and the terrible from the horrible and the loathsome—Victor Hugo and Honoré de Balzac from Eugène Sue and Émile Zola. On his theatre we find no presentation of old men with their beards torn off and their eyes gouged out, of young men imprisoned in reeking cesspools and impaled with red-hot spits. Again and again his passionate and daring genius attains the utmost limit and rounds the final goal of tragedy; never once does it break the bounds of pure poetic instinct. If ever for a moment it may seem to graze that goal too closely, to brush too sharply by those bounds, the very next moment finds it clear of any such risk and remote from any such temptation as sometimes entrapped or seduced the foremost of its forerunners in the field. And yet this is the field in which its paces are most superbly shown. No name among all the names of great poets will recur so soon as Webster's to the reader who knows what it signifies, as he reads or repeats the verses in which a greater than this great poet—a greater than all since Shakespeare—has expressed the latent mystery of terror which lurks in all the highest poetry or beauty, and distinguishes it inexplicably and inevitably from all that is but a little lower than the highest.

> Les aigles sur les bords du Gange et du Caÿstre
> 　　　Sont effrayants;

> Rien de grand qui ne soit confusément sinistre;
> 　　　Les noirs pæans,
> Les psaumes, la chanson monstrueuse du mage
> 　　　Ézéchiel,
> Font devant notre œil fixe errer la vague image
> 　　　D'un affreux ciel.
> L'empyrée est l'abîme, on y plonge, on y reste
> 　　　Avec terreur.
> Car planer, c'est trembler; si l'azur est céleste,
> 　　　C'est par l'horreur.
> L'épouvante est au fond des choses les plus belles;
> 　　　Les bleus vallons
> Font parfois reculer d'effroi les fauves ailes
> 　　　Des aquilons.

And even in comedy as in tragedy, in prosaic even as in prophetic inspiration, in imitative as in imaginative works of genius, the sovereign of modern poets has detected the same touch of terror wherever the deepest note possible has been struck, the fullest sense possible of genuine and peculiar power conveyed to the student of lyric or dramatic, epic or elegiac masters.

> De là tant de beautés difformes dans leurs œuvres;
> 　　　Le vers charmant
> Est par la torsion subite des couleuvres
> 　　　Pris brusquement;
> A de certains moments toutes les jeunes flores
> 　　　Dans la forêt
> Ont peur, et sur le front des blanches métaphores
> 　　　L'ombre apparaît;
> C'est qu'Horace ou Virgile ont vu soudain le spectre
> 　　　Noir se dresser;
> C'est que là-bas, derrière Amaryllis, Électre
> 　　　Vient de passer.

Nor was it the Electra of Sophocles, the calm and impassive accomplice of an untroubled and unhesitating matricide, who showed herself ever in passing to the intent and serious vision of Webster. By those candid and sensible judges to whom the praise of Marlowe seems to imply a reflection on the fame of Shakespeare, I may be accused—and by such critics I am content to be accused—of a fatuous design to set Webster beside Sophocles, or Sophocles—for aught I know—beneath Webster, if I venture to indicate the superiority in truth of natural passion— and, I must add, of moral instinct—which distinguishes the modern from the ancient. It is not, it never will be, and it never can have been natural for noble and civilised creatures to accept with spontaneous complacency, to discharge with unforced equanimity, such offices or such duties as weigh so lightly on the spirit of the Sophoclean Orestes that the slaughter of a mother seems to be a less serious undertaking for his unreluctant hand than the subsequent execution of her paramour. The immeasurable superiority of Æschylus to his successors in this quality of instinctive righteousness—if a word long vulgarised by theology may yet be used in its just and natural sense—is shared no less by Webster than by Shakespeare. The grave and deep truth of natural impulse is never ignored by these poets when dealing either with innocent or with criminal passion: but it surely is now and then ignored by the artistic quietism of Sophocles—as surely as it is outraged and degraded by the vulgar theatricalities of Euripides. Thomas Campbell was amused and scandalised by the fact that Webster (as he is pleased to express it) modestly compares himself to the playwright last mentioned; being apparently of opinion that *Hippolytus* and *Medea* may be reckoned equal or superior, as works of tragic art or examples of ethical elevation, to *The White Devil* and *The Duchess of Malfy*; and being no less apparently ignorant, and incapable of understanding, that as there is no poet morally nobler than Webster so is there no poet ignobler in the moral sense than Euripides: while as a dramatic artist—an artist in character, action, and emotion—the degenerate tragedian of Athens, compared to the second tragic dramatist of England, is as a mutilated monkey to a well-made man. No better test of critical faculty could be required by the most exacting scrutiny of probation than is afforded by the critic's professed or professional estimate of those great poets whose names are not consecrated—or desecrated—by the conventional applause, the factitious adoration, of a tribunal whose judgments are dictated by obsequious superstition and unanimous incompetence. When certain critics inform a listening world that they do not admire Marlowe and Webster— they admire Shakespeare and Milton, we know at once that it is not the genius of Shakespeare—it is the reputation of Shakespeare that they admire. It is not the man that they bow down to: it is the bust that they crouch down before. They would worship Shirley as soon as Shakespeare—Glover as soon as Milton—Byron as soon as Shelley—Ponsard as soon as Hugo—Longfellow as soon as Tennyson—if the tablet were as showily emblazoned, the inscription as pretentiously engraved.

The nobility of spirit and motive which is so distinguishing a mark of Webster's instinctive genius or natural disposition of mind is proved by his treatment of facts placed on record by contemporary annalists in the tragic story of Vittoria Accorambuoni, Duchess of Bracciano. That story would have been suggestive, if not tempting, to any dramatic poet: and almost any poet but Shakespeare or Webster would have been content to accept the characters and circumstances as they stood nakedly on record, and adapt them to the contemporary stage of England with such dexterity and intelligence as he might be able to command. But, as Shakespeare took the savage legend of Hamlet, the brutal story of Othello, and raised them from the respective levels of the Heimskringla and the Newgate Calendar to the very highest 'heaven of invention,' so has Webster transmuted the impressive but repulsive record of villainies and atrocities, in which he discovered the motive for a magnificent poem, into the majestic and pathetic masterpiece which is one of the most triumphant and the most memorable achievements of English poetry. If, in his play, as in the legal or historic account of the affair, the whole family of the heroine had appeared unanimous and eager in complicity with her sins and competition for a share in the profits of her dishonour, the tragedy might still have been as effective as it is now from the theatrical or sensational point of view; it might have thrilled the reader's nerves as keenly, have excited and stimulated his curiosity, have whetted and satiated his appetite for transient emotion, as thoroughly and triumphantly as now. But it would have been merely a criminal melodrama, compiled by the labour and vivified by the talent of an able theatrical journeyman. The one great follower of Shakespeare—'haud passibus æquis' at all points; 'longo sed proximus intervallo'—has recognised, with Shakespearean accuracy and delicacy and elevation of instinct, the necessity of ennobling and transfiguring his characters if their story was to be made acceptable to the sympathies of any but an idle or an ignoble audience. And he has done so after the very manner and in the very spirit of Shakespeare. The noble creatures of his invention give to the story that dignity and variety of interest without which the most powerful romance or drama can be but an example of vigorous vulgarity. The upright and high-minded mother and brother of the shameless Flamineo and the shame-stricken Vittoria refresh and purify the tragic atmosphere of the poem by the passing presence of their virtues. The shallow and fiery nature

of the fair White Devil herself is a notable example of the difference so accurately distinguished by Charlotte Brontë between an impressionable and an impressible character. Ambition, self-interest, passion, remorse and hardihood alternate and contend in her impetuous and wayward spirit. The one distinct and trustworthy quality which may always be reckoned on is the indomitable courage underlying her easily irritable emotions. Her bearing at the trial for her husband's murder is as dexterous and dauntless as the demeanour of Mary Stuart before her judges. To Charles Lamb it seemed 'an innocence-resembling boldness'; to Mr. Dyce and Canon Kingsley the innocence displayed in Lamb's estimate seemed almost ludicrous in its misconception of Webster's text. I should hesitate to agree with them that he has never once made his accused heroine speak in the natural key of innocence unjustly impeached: Mary's pleading for her life is not at all points incompatible in tone with the innocence which it certainly fails to establish—except in minds already made up to accept any plea as valid which may plausibly or possibly be advanced on her behalf; and the arguments advanced by Vittoria are not more evasive and equivocal, in face of the patent and flagrant prepossession of her judges, than those put forward by the Queen of Scots. It is impossible not to wonder whether the poet had not in his mind the actual tragedy which had taken place just twenty-five years before the publication of this play: if not, the coincidence is something more than singular. The fierce profligacy and savage egotism of Brachiano have a certain energy and activity in the display and the development of their motives and effects which suggest rather such a character as Bothwell's than such a character as that of the bloated and stolid sensualist who stands or grovels before us in the historic record of his life. As presented by Webster, he is doubtless an execrable ruffian: as presented by history, he would be intolerable by any but such readers or spectators as those on whom the figments or the photographs of self-styled naturalism produce other than emetic emotions. Here again the noble instinct of the English poet has rectified the æsthetic unseemliness of an ignoble reality. This 'Brachiano' is a far more living figure than the porcine paramour of the historic Accorambuoni. I am not prepared to maintain that in one scene too much has not been sacrificed to immediate vehemence of effect. The devotion of the discarded wife, who to shelter her Antony from the vengeance of Octavius assumes the mask of raging jealousy, thus taking upon herself the blame and responsibility of their final separation, is expressed with such consummate and artistic simplicity of power that on a first reading the genius of the dramatist may well blind us to the violent unlikelihood of the action. But this very extravagance of self-sacrifice may be thought by some to add a crowning touch of pathos to the unsurpassable beauty of the scene in which her child, after the murder of his mother, relates her past sufferings to his uncle. Those to whom the great name of Webster represents merely an artist in horrors, a ruffian of genius, may be recommended to study every line and syllable of this brief dialogue.

> *Francisco*: How now, my noble cousin? what, in
>   black?
> *Giovanni*: Yes, uncle, I was taught to imitate you
>   In virtue, and you [?now] must imitate me
>   In colours of your garments. My sweet mother
>   Is—
> *Francisco*: How! where?
> *Giovanni*: Is there; no, yonder: indeed, sir, I'll not
>   tell you,
>   For I shall make you weep.
> *Francisco*: Is dead?

Giovanni: Do not blame me now, I did not tell you
    so.
Lodovico: She's dead, my lord.
Francisco: Dead!
Monticelso: Blest lady, thou art now above thy woes!

  . . . .

Giovanni: What do the dead do, uncle? do they eat,
    Hear music, go a hunting, and be merry,
    As we that live?
Francisco: No, coz; they sleep.
Giovanni: Lord, Lord, that I were dead!
    I have not slept these six nights.—When do
    they wake?
Francisco: When God shall please.
Giovanni: Good God, let her sleep ever!
    For I have known her wake an hundred nights
    When all the pillow where she laid her head
    Was brine-wet with her tears. I am to complain
    to me, sir;
    I'll tell you how they have used her now she's
    dead:
    They wrapped her in a cruel fold of lead,
    And would not let me kiss her.
Francisco: Thou didst love her.
Giovanni: I have often heard her say she gave me
    suck,
    And it should seem by that she dearly loved
    me,
    Since princes seldom do it.
Francisco: O, all of my poor sister that remains!—
    Take him away, for God's sake!

I must admit that I do not see how Shakespeare could have improved upon that. It seems to me that in any one of even his greatest tragedies this scene would have been remarkable among its most beautiful and perfect passages; nor, upon the whole, do I remember a third English poet who could be imagined capable of having written it. And it affords, I think, very clear and sufficient evidence that Webster could not have handled so pathetic and suggestive a subject as the execution of Lady Jane Grey and her young husband in a style so thin and feeble, so shallow in expression of pathos and so empty of suggestion or of passion, as that in which it is presented at the close of *Sir Thomas Wyatt*.

There is a perfect harmony of contrast between this and the death-scene of the boy's father: the agony of the murdered murderer is as superb in effect of terror as the sorrow of his son is exquisite in effect of pathos. Again we are reminded of Shakespeare, by no touch of imitation but simply by a note of kinship in genius and in style, at the cry of Brachiano under the first sharp workings of the poison:

          O thou strong heart!
There's such a covenant 'tween the world and it,
They're loth to break.

Another stroke well worthy of Shakespeare is the redeeming touch of grace in this brutal and cold-blooded ruffian which gives him in his agony a thought of tender care for the accomplice of his atrocities:

    Do not kiss me, for I shall poison thee.

Few instances of Webster's genius are so well known as the brief but magnificent passage which follows; yet it may not be impertinent to cite it once again.

Brachiano: O thou soft natural death, that art joint
    twin
    To sweetest slumber! no rough-bearded comet
    Stares on thy mild departure; the dull owl
    Beats not against thy casement; the hoarse wolf

    Scents not thy carrion; pity winds thy corpse,
    Whilst horror waits on princes.
Vittoria: I am lost for ever.
Brachiano: How miserable a thing it is to die
    'Mongst women howling!—What are those?
Flamineo: Franciscans:
    They have brought the extreme unction.
Brachiano: On pain of death, let no man name death
    to me;
    It is a word [? most] infinitely terrible.

The very tremor of moral and physical abjection from nervous defiance into prostrate fear which seems to pant and bluster and quail and subside in the natural cadence of these lines would suffice to prove the greatness of the artist who could express it with such terrible perfection: but when we compare it, by collation of the two scenes, with the deep simplicity of tenderness, the childlike accuracy of innocent emotion, in the passage previously cited, it seems to me that we must admit, as an unquestionable truth, that in the deepest and highest and purest qualities of tragic poetry Webster stands nearer to Shakespeare than any other English poet stands to Webster; and so much nearer as to be a good second; while it is at least questionable whether even Shelley can reasonably be accepted as a good third. Not one among the predecessors, contemporaries, or successors of Shakespeare and Webster has given proof of this double faculty—this coequal mastery of terror and pity, undiscoloured and undistorted, but vivified and glorified, by the splendour of immediate and infallible imagination. The most grovelling realism could scarcely be so impudent in stupidity as to pretend an aim at more perfect presentation of truth: the most fervent fancy, the most sensitive taste, could hardly dream of a desire for more exquisite expression of natural passion in a form of utterance more naturally exalted and refined.

In all the vast and voluminous records of critical error there can be discovered no falsehood more foolish or more flagrant than the vulgar tradition which represents this high-souled and gentle-hearted poet as one morbidly fascinated by a fantastic attraction towards the 'violent delights' of horror and the nervous or sensational excitements of criminal detail; nor can there be conceived a more perverse or futile misapprehension than that which represents John Webster as one whose instinct led him by some obscure and oblique propensity to darken the darkness of southern crime or vice by an infusion of northern seriousness, of introspective cynicism and reflective intensity in wrongdoing, into the easy levity and infantile simplicity of spontaneous wickedness which distinguished the moral and social corruption of renascent Italy. Proof enough of this has already been adduced to make any protestation or appeal against such an estimate as preposterous in its superfluity as the misconception just mentioned is preposterous in its perversity. The great if not incomparable power displayed in Webster's delineation of such criminals as Flamineo and Bosola—Bonapartes in the bud, Napoleons in a nutshell, Cæsars who have missed their Rubicon and collapse into the likeness of a Catiline—is a sign rather of his noble English loathing for the traditions associated with such names as Cæsar and Medici and Borgia, Catiline and Iscariot and Napoleon, than of any sympathetic interest in such incarnations of historic crime. Flamineo especially, the ardent pimp, the enthusiastic pandar, who prostitutes his sister and assassinates his brother with such earnest and single-hearted devotion to his own straightforward self-interest, has in him a sublime fervour of rascality which recalls rather the man of Brumaire and of Waterloo than the man of December and of Sedan. He has something too of Napoleon's ruffianly good-humour—the frankness of a thieves' kitchen or an imperial court, when the last thin figleaf of pretence has been plucked off and crumpled up and flung away. We can imagine him pinching his favourites by the ear and dictating memorials of mendacity with the self-possession of a self-made monarch. As it is, we see him only in the stage of parasite and pimp—more like the hired husband of a cast-off Creole than the resplendent rogue who fascinated even history for a time by the clamour and glitter of his triumphs. But the fellow is unmistakably an emperor in the egg—so dauntless and frontless in the very abjection of his villainy that we feel him to have been defrauded by mischance of the only two destinations appropriate for the close of his career—a gibbet or a throne.

This imperial quality of ultimate perfection in egotism and crowning complacency in crime is wanting to his brother in atrocity, the most notable villain who figures on the stage of Webster's latest masterpiece. Bosola is not quite a possible Bonaparte; he is not even on a level with the bloody hirelings who execute the orders of tyranny and treason with the perfunctory atrocity of Anicetus or Saint-Arnaud. There is not, or I am much mistaken, a touch of imaginative poetry in the part of Flamineo: his passion, excitable on occasion and vehement enough, is as prosaic in its homely and cynical eloquence as the most fervent emotions of a Napoleon or an Iago when warmed or goaded into elocution. The one is a human snake, the other is a human wolf. Webster could not with equal propriety have put into the mouth of Flamineo such magnificent lyric poetry as seems to fall naturally, however suddenly and strangely, from the bitter and bloodthirsty tongue of Bosola. To him, as to the baffled and incoherent ruffian Romelio in the contemporary play of *The Devil's Law-case*, his creator has assigned the utterance of such verse as can only be compared to that uttered by Cornelia over the body of her murdered son in the tragedy to which I have just given so feeble and inadequate a word of tribute. In his command and in his use of the metre first made fashionable by the graceful improvisations of Greene, Webster seems to me as original and as peculiar as in his grasp and manipulation of character and event. All other poets, Shakespeare no less than Barnfield and Milton no less than Wither, have used this lyric instrument for none but gentle or gracious ends: Webster has breathed into it the power to express a sublimer and a profounder tone of emotion; he has given it the cadence and the colour of tragedy; he has touched and transfigured its note of meditative music into a chord of passionate austerity and prophetic awe. This was the key in which all previous poets had played upon the metre which Webster was to put to so deeply different an use.

> Walking in a valley greene,
> Spred with Flora summer queene:
> Where shee heaping all hir graces,
> Niggard seem'd in other places:
> Spring it was, and here did spring
> All that nature forth can bring.
> > (*Tullies Loue*, p. 53, ed. 1589.)
>
> Nights were short, and daies were long;
> Blossoms on the Hauthorns hung:
> Philomele (Night-Musiques King)
> Tolde the comming of the spring.
> > (*Grosart's Barnfield* [1876], p. 97.)
>
> On a day (alack the day!)
> Love, whose month is ever May,
> Spied a blossom passing fair
> Playing in the wanton air.
> > (*Love's Labour's Lost*, Act iv.
> > Sc. iii.)

And now let us hear Webster.

> Hearke, now every thing is still,
> The Scritch-Owle, and the whistler shrill,
> Call upon our Dame, aloud,
> And bid her quickly don her shrowd:
> Much you had of Land and rent,
> Your length in clay's now competent.
> A long war disturb'd your minde,
> Here your perfect peace is sign'd.
> Of what is 't, fooles make such vaine keeping?
> Sin their conception, their birth, weeping:
> Their life, a generall mist of error,
> Their death, a hideous storme of terror.
> Strew your haire with powders sweete:
> Don cleane linnen, bath[e] your feete,
> And (the foule feend more to checke)
> A crucifixe let blesse your necke:
> 'Tis now full tide 'tweene night and day,
> End your groane, and come away.
> > (*The Tragedy of the Dutchesse of Malfy*: 1623:
> > sig. K, K 2.)

The toll of the funereal rhythm, the heavy chime of the solemn and simple verse, the mournful menace and the brooding presage of its note, are but the covering, as it were, or the outer expression, of the tragic significance which deepens and quickens and kindles to its close. Æschylus and Dante have never excelled, nor perhaps have Sophocles and Shakespeare ever equalled in impression of terrible effect, the fancy of bidding a live woman array herself in the raiment of the grave, and do for her own living body the offices done for a corpse by the ministers attendant on the dead.

The murderous humourist whose cynical inspiration gives life to these deadly lines is at first sight a less plausible, but on second thoughts may perhaps seem no less possible a character than Flamineo. Pure and simple ambition of the Napoleonic order is the motive which impels into infamy the aspiring parasite of Brachiano: a savage melancholy inflames the baffled greed of Bosola to a pitch of wickedness not unqualified by relenting touches of profitless remorse, which come always either too early or too late to bear any serviceable fruit of compassion or redemption. There is no deeper or more Shakespearean stroke of tragic humour in all Webster's writings than that conveyed in the scornful and acute reply—almost too acute perhaps for the character—of Bosola's remorseless patron to the remonstrance or appeal of his instrument against the insatiable excess and persistence of his cruelty: 'Thy pity is nothing akin to thee.' He has more in common with Romelio in *The Devil's Law-case*, an assassin who misses his aim and flounders into penitence much as that discomfortable drama misses its point and stumbles into vacuity: and whose unsatisfactory figure looks either like a crude and unsuccessful study for that of Bosola, or a disproportioned and emasculated copy from it. But to him too Webster has given the fitful force of fancy or inspiration which finds expression in such sudden snatches of funereal verse as this:

> How then can any monument say
> 'Here rest these bones till the last day,'
> When Time, swift both of foot and feather,
> May bear them the sexton kens not whither?
> What care I, then, though my last sleep
> Be in the desert or the deep,
> No lamp nor taper, day and night,
> To give my charnel chargeable light?
> I have there like quantity of ground,
> And at the last day I shall be found.

The villainous laxity of versification which deforms the grim and sardonic beauty of these occasionally rough and halting lines is perceptible here and there in *The Duchess of Malfy*, but comes to its head in *The Devil's Law-case*. It cannot, I fear, be denied that Webster was the first to relax those natural bonds of noble metre 'whose service is perfect freedom'—as Shakespeare found it, and combined with perfect loyalty to its law the most perfect liberty of living and sublime and spontaneous and accurate expression. I can only conjecture that this greatest of the Shakespeareans was misguided out of his natural line of writing as exemplified and perfected in the tragedy of Vittoria, and lured into this cross and crooked byway of immetrical experiment, by the temptation of some theory or crotchet on the score of what is now called naturalism or realism; which, if there were any real or natural weight in the reasoning that seeks to support it, would of course do away, and of course ought to do away, with dramatic poetry altogether: for if it is certain that real persons do not actually converse in good metre, it is happily no less certain that they do not actually converse in bad metre. In the hands of so great a tragic poet as Webster a peculiar and impressive effect may now and then be produced by this anomalous and illegitimate way of writing; it certainly suits well with the thoughtful and fantastic truculence of Bosola's reflections on death and dissolution and decay—his 'talk fit for a charnel,' which halts and hovers between things hideous and things sublime. But it is a step on the downward way that leads to the negation or the confusion of all distinctions between poetry and prose; a result to which it would be grievous to think that the example of Shakespeare's greatest contemporary should in any way appear to conduce.

The doctrine or the motive of chance (whichever we may prefer to call it) is seen in its fullest workings and felt in its furthest bearings by the student of Webster's masterpiece. The fifth act of *The Duchess of Malfy* has been assailed on the very ground which it should have been evident to a thoughtful and capable reader that the writer must have intended to take up—on the ground that the whole upshot of the story is dominated by sheer chance, arranged by mere error, and guided by pure accident. No formal scheme or religious principle of retribution would have been so strangely or so thoroughly in keeping with the whole scheme and principle of the tragedy. After the overwhelming terrors and the overpowering beauties of that unique and marvellous fourth act, in which the genius of this poet spreads its fullest and its darkest wing for the longest and the strongest of its flights, it could not but be that the subsequent action and passion of the drama should appear by comparison unimpressive or ineffectual; but all the effect or impression possible of attainment under the inevitable burden of this difficulty is achieved by natural and simple and straightforward means. If Webster has not made the part of Antonio dramatically striking and attractive—as he probably found it impossible to do—he has at least bestowed on the fugitive and unconscious widower of his murdered heroine a pensive and manly grace of deliberate resignation which is not without pathetic as well as poetical effect. In the beautiful and well-known scene where the echo from his wife's unknown and new-made grave seems to respond to his meditative mockery and forewarn him of his impending death, Webster has given such reality and seriousness to an old commonplace of contemporary fancy or previous fashion in poetry that we are fain to forget the fantastic side of the conception and see only the tragic aspect of its meaning. A weightier objection than any which can be brought against the conduct of the play might be suggested to the minds of some readers—and these, perhaps, not too exacting or too captious readers—by the sudden vehemence of transformation which in the great preceding act

seems to fall like fire from heaven upon the two chief criminals who figure on the stage of murder. It seems rather a miraculous retribution, a judicial violation of the laws of nature, than a reasonably credible consequence or evolution of those laws, which strikes Ferdinand with madness and Bosola with repentance. But the whole atmosphere of the action is so charged with thunder that this double and simultaneous shock of moral electricity rather thrills us with admiration and faith than chills us with repulsion or distrust. The passionate intensity and moral ardour of imagination which we feel to vibrate and penetrate through every turn and every phrase of the dialogue would suffice to enforce upon our belief a more nearly incredible revolution of nature or revulsion of the soul.

It is so difficult for even the very greatest poets to give any vivid force of living interest to a figure of passive endurance that perhaps the only instance of perfect triumph over this difficulty is to be found in the character of Desdemona. Shakespeare alone could have made her as interesting as Imogen or Cordelia; though these have so much to do and dare, and she after her first appearance has simply to suffer: even Webster could not give such individual vigour of characteristic life to the figure of his martyr as to the figure of his criminal heroine. Her courage and sweetness, her delicacy and sincerity, her patience and her passion, are painted with equal power and tenderness of touch: yet she hardly stands before us as distinct from others of her half angelic sisterhood as does the White Devil from the fellowship of her comrades in perdition. But if, as we may assuredly assume, it was on the twenty-third 'nouell' of William Painter's *Palace of Pleasure* that Webster's crowning masterpiece was founded, the poet's moral and spiritual power of transfiguration is here even more admirable than in the previous case of his other and wellnigh coequally consummate poem. The narrative degrades and brutalises the widowed heroine's affection for her second husband to the actual level of the vile conception which the poet attributes and confines to the foul imagination of her envious and murderous brothers. Here again, and finally and supremely here, the purifying and exalting power of Webster's noble and magnanimous imagination is gloriously unmistakable by all and any who have eyes to read and hearts to recognise.

For it is only with Shakespeare that Webster can ever be compared in any way to his disadvantage as a tragic poet: above all others of his country he stands indisputably supreme. The place of Marlowe indeed is higher among our poets by right of his primacy as a founder and a pioneer: but of course his work has not—as of course it could not have—that plenitude and perfection of dramatic power in construction and dramatic subtlety in detail which the tragedies of Webster share in so large a measure with the tragedies of Shakespeare. Marston, the poet with whom he has most in common, might almost be said to stand in the same relation to Webster as Webster to Shakespeare. In single lines and phrases, in a few detached passages and a very few distinguishable scenes, he is worthy to be compared with the greater poet; he suddenly rises and dilates to the stature and the strength of a model whom usually he can but follow afar off. Marston, as a tragic poet, is not quite what Webster would be if his fame depended simply on such scenes as those in which the noble mother of Vittoria breaks off her daughter's first interview with Brachiano—spares, and commends to God's forgiveness, the son who has murdered his brother before her eyes—and lastly appears 'in several forms of distraction,' 'grown a very old woman in two hours,' and singing that most pathetic and imaginative of all funereal invocations which the finest critic of all time so justly and so delicately compared to the watery dirge of Ariel. There is less refinement, less exaltation and perfection of feeling, less tenderness of emotion and less nobility of passion, but hardly less force and fervour, less weighty and sonorous ardour of expression, in the very best and loftiest passages of Marston: but his genius is more uncertain, more fitful and intermittent, less harmonious, coherent, and trustworthy than Webster's. And Webster, notwithstanding an occasional outbreak into Aristophanic license of momentary sarcasm through the sardonic lips of such a cynical ruffian as Ferdinand or Flamineo, is without exception the cleanliest, as Marston is beyond comparison the coarsest writer of his time. In this as in other matters of possible comparison that 'vessel of deathless wrath,' the implacable and inconsolable poet of sympathy half maddened into rage and aspiration goaded backwards to despair—it should be needless to add the name of Cyril Tourneur—stands midway between these two more conspicuous figures of their age. But neither the father and master of poetic pessimists, the splendid and sombre creator of Vindice and his victims, nor any other third whom our admiration may discern among all the greatest of their fellows, can be compared with Webster on terms more nearly equal than those on which Webster stands in relation to the sovereign of them all.

EDMUND GOSSE
From *The Jacobean Poets*
1894, pp. 166–73

Webster's masterpiece is *The Duchess of Malfy*, of which it may confidently be alleged that it is the finest tragedy in the English language outside the works of Shakespeare. The poet found his story in that storehouse of plots, the *Novelle* of Bandello, but it had been told in English by others before him. It was one pre-eminently suited to inflame the sombre and enthusiastic imagination of Webster, and to inspire this great, irregular and sublime poem. Dramatic, in the accepted sense, it may scarcely be called. In the nice conduct of a reasonable and interesting plot to a satisfactory conclusion, Webster is not the equal of Fletcher or of Massinger; some still smaller writers may be considered to surpass him on this particular ground. But he aimed at something more, or at least, something other, than the mere entertainment of the groundlings. With unusual solemnity he dedicates his tragedy to his patron as a "poem," and his contemporaries perceived that this was a stronger and more elaborate piece of dramatic architecture than the eye was accustomed to see built for half a dozen nights, and then disappear. Ford, when he read *The Duchess of Malfy*, exclaimed—

> Crown him a poet, whom nor Rome nor Greece
> Transcend in all theirs for a masterpiece,

and Middleton described it as Webster's own monument, fashioned by himself in marble. He had the reputation of being a slow and punctilious writer, among a set of poets, with whom a ready pen was more commonly in fashion. We look to Webster for work designed at leisure, and executed with critical and scrupulous attention. This carefulness, however, was unfavourable to a well-balanced composition, the movement of the whole being sacrificed to an extraordinary brilliancy in detailed passages, and though *The Duchess of Malfy* has again and again been attempted on the modern stage, each experiment has but emphasized the fact that it is pre-eminently a tragic poem to be enjoyed in the study.

It is curious that in a writer so distinguished by care in the working out of detail, we should find so lax a metrical system as marks *The Duchess of Malfy*. Here, again, Webster seems to be content to leave the general surface dull, while burnishing his own favourite passages to a high lustre. He has lavished the beauties both of his imagination and of his verse on what Mr. Swinburne eloquently calls "the overwhelming terrors and the overpowering beauties of that unique and marvellous fourth act, in which the genius of the poet spreads its fullest and darkest wing for the longest and the strongest of its flights."

This is what Bosola ejaculates when the Duchess dies—

> O, she's gone again! There the cords of life broke.
> O sacred innocence, that sweetly sleeps
> On turtle's feathers, whilst a guilty conscience
> Is a black register wherein is writ
> All our good deeds and bad, a perspective
> That shows us hell! that we can not be suffer'd
> To do good when we have a mind to it!
> This is manly sorrow;
> These tears, I am very certain, never grew
> In my mother's milk: my estate is sunk
> Below the degree of fear: where were
> These penitent fountains while she was living?
> O, they were frozen up! Here is a sight
> As direful to my soul as is the sword
> Unto a wretch hath slain his father. Come,
> I'll bear thee hence,
> And execute thy last will; that's deliver
> Thy body to the reverent dispose
> Of some good women; that the cruel tyrant
> Shall not deny me. Then I'll post to Milan,
> Where somewhat I will speedily enact
> Worth my dejection.

The characterization of the Duchess, with her independence, her integrity, and her noble and yet sprightly dignity, gradually gaining refinement as the joy of life is crushed out of her, is one calculated to inspire pity to a degree very rare indeed in any tragical poetry. The figure of Antonio, the subject whom she secretly raises to a morganatic alliance with her, is simply and wholesomely drawn. All is original, all touching and moving, while the spirit of beauty, that rare and intangible element, throws its charm like a tinge of rose-colour over all that might otherwise seem to a modern reader harsh or crude.

On one point, however, with great diffidence, the present writer must confess that he cannot agree with those great authorities, Lamb and Mr. Swinburne, who have asserted, in their admiration for Webster, that he was always skilful in the introduction of horror. In his own mind, as a poet, Webster doubtless was aware of the procession of a majestic and solemn spectacle, but when he endeavours to present that conception on the boards of the theatre, his "terrors want dignity, his affrightments want decorum." The horrible dumb shows of *The Duchess of Malfy*—the strangled children, the chorus of maniacs, the murder of Cariola, as she bites and scratches, the scuffling and stabbing in the fifth act, are, it appears to me—with all deference to the eminent critics, who have applauded them—blots on what is notwithstanding a truly noble poem, and what, with more reserve in this respect, would have been one of the first tragedies of the world.

Similar characteristics present themselves to us in *The White Devil*, but in a much rougher form. The sketchiness of this play, which is not divided into acts and scenes, and progresses with unaccountable gaps in the story, and perfunctory makeshifts of dumb show, has been the wonder of critics. But Webster was particularly interested in his own work as a romantic rather than a theatrical poet, and it must be remembered that after a long apprenticeship in collaboration, *The White Devil* was his first independent play. It reads as though the writer had put in only what interested him, and had left the rest for a coadjutor, who did not happen to present himself, to fill up. The central figure of Vittoria, the subtle, masterful, and exquisite she-devil, is filled up very minutely and vividly in the otherwise hastily painted canvas; and in the trial-scene, which is perhaps the most perfectly sustained which Webster has left us, we are so much captivated by the beauty and ingenuity of the murderess that, as Lamb says in a famous passage, we are ready to expect that "all the court will rise and make proffer to defend her in spite of the utmost conviction of her guilt." The fascination of Vittoria, like an exquisite poisonous perfume, pervades the play, and Brachiano strikes a note, which is the central one of the romance, when he says to her—

> Thou hast led me like a heathen sacrifice,
> With music and with fatal yokes of flowers,
> To my eternal ruin.

The White Devil is not less full than the *Duchess of Malfy* of short lines and phrases full of a surprising melody. In the fabrication of these jewels, Webster is surpassed only by Shakespeare.

If, as is now supposed, the composition of *Appius and Virginia* followed closely upon that of *The White Devil*, it is plain that the reception of the latter play must have drawn Webster's attention to the necessity of paying more attention to theatrical requirements. While the romantic and literary glow of language is severely restrained, there is here a very noticeable advance in every species of dramatic propriety, and *Appius and Virginia* is by far the best constructed of Webster's plays. The Jacobean dramatists were constantly attempting to compose Roman tragedies, in which they vaguely saw the possibility of reaching the classic perfection of form at which they aimed in their less agitated moments. Ben Jonson's plays of this class have been already mentioned, and these, to his own contemporaries, seemed to be by far the most coherent and satisfactory. Posterity, however, has placed *Julius Cæsar* high above *Sejanus* and *Catiline*, and without seeking to put Webster by the side of Shakespeare, his Roman tragedy must be admitted to be more graceful, pathetic, and vigorous than Jonson's.

A speech of Virginius in the fourth act will give an idea of the high Roman tone of the play—

> Have I, in all this populous assembly
> Of soldiers that have proved Virginius' valour,
> One friend? Let him come thrill his partizan
> Against this breast, that thro' a large wide wound
> My mighty soul might rush out of this prison,
> To fly more freely to yon crystal palace,
> Where honour sits enthronized. What, no friend?
> Can this great multitude, then, yield an enemy
> That hates my life? Here let him seize it freely.
> What, no man strike? am I so well belov'd?—
> Minertius, then to thee; if in this camp
> There lives one man so just to punish sin,
> So charitable to redeem from torments

> A ready soldier, at his worthy hand
> I beg a death.

The scenes are largely set, the characters, especially those of Virginius and of Appius, justly designed and well contrasted, while the stiffness of Roman manners, as seen through a Jacobean medium, is not in this case sufficient to destroy the suppleness of the movement nor the pathos of the situation. *Appius and Virginia*, as a poem, will never possess the attractiveness of the two great Italian romances, but it is the best-executed of Webster's dramas.

If the playwright took a step forwards in his Roman play, he took several backwards in his incoherent tragicomedy of *The Devil's Law-Case*. Here no charm attaches to the characters; the plot moves around no central interest; the structure of the piece, from a stage point of view, is utterly at fault. None the less, this strange play will always have its readers, for Webster's literary faculty is nowhere exhibited to greater perfection, and the poetry of the text abounds in verbal felicities. Unfortunately, the special attention of the poet seems to have been concentrated on the unravelling of a most fantastic skein of legal intrigues. In listening to the quibbles and the serpentining subtleties of Ariosto and Crispiano the reader loses not merely his interest, but his intelligence; he is not amused, but merely bewildered. Leonora, who, to avenge the wrongs of her lover, charges her own son with illegitimacy, is a being outside the pale of sympathy.

The abrupt withdrawal of Webster from writing for the stage—a step which he seems to have taken when he was little over thirty years of age—points to a sense of want of harmony between his genius and the theatre. In fact, none of the leading dramatists of our great period seems to have so little native instinct for stage-craft as Webster, and it is natural to suppose that in another age, and in other conditions, he would have directed his noble gifts of romantic poetry to other provinces of the art. If it were not absolutely certain that he flourished between 1602 and 1612, we should be inclined to place the period of his activity at least ten years earlier. Although in fact an exact contemporary of Beaumont and Fletcher, and evidently much Shakespeare's junior, a place between Marlowe and those dramatists seems appropriate to him, so primitive is his theatrical art, so ingenuous and inexperienced his notion of the stage. That he preferred the more stilted and buskined utterances of drama to grace and suppleness may be gathered from Webster's own critical distinctions; he has no words of admiration too high for Chapman and Jonson; Shakespeare he commends, with a touch of patronage, on a level with Dekker and Heywood, for his "right happy and copious industry," placing the romantic Beaumont and Fletcher above him. This points to a somewhat academic temper of mind, and to a tendency to look rather at the splendid raiment of drama than at the proficiency and variety of those who wear it. Webster is an impressive rather than a dexterous playwright; but as a romantic poet of passion he takes a position in the very first rank of his contemporaries.

BEN JONSON

BEN JONSON

c. 1573–1637

Ben Jonson, dramatist, poet and critic, was probably born in Westminster, near London, the posthumous son of a clergyman. Jonson himself claimed to be of Scottish ancestry. He attended a school in St. Martin's Lane, then the Westminster School, where the kindness of the headmaster, the antiquary William Camden, later inspired Jonson to dedicate plays to him. His mother remarried a bricklayer, to whom Jonson was apprenticed after graduating from the Westminster School. Little is known of the next five years, except that Jonson volunteered for military service in Flanders, and married in 1594.

By 1597, Jonson was a member of Philip Henslowe's company, serving as an actor and as a playwright. That year, Jonson was arrested, along with the author and others, for acting in Nashe's *Isle of Dogs*. During these early years with Henslowe, Jonson collaborated with Dekker, Marston, Chapman, Chettle and others. In 1598 he was arrested again, this time for killing the actor Gabriel Spenser. Jonson escaped capital punishment by pleading "benefit of clergy," based on his ability to read the Bible in Latin, although his thumb was branded. While in prison, Jonson became a Roman Catholic, a faith he was to hold for twelve years. Also in 1598, Jonson's play *Every Man in his Humour* was produced, followed by *Every Man Out of his Humour* (1599), *Cynthia's Revels, or The Fountain of Self-love* (1600) and *Poetaster, or The Arraignment* (1601), the latter of which lampooned Marston and Dekker and contributed to the "war of the theatres." One of the two extant classical tragedies Jonson wrote, *Sejanus, His Fall* (1603), included Shakespeare in its cast. Shakespeare was to remain a close colleague. Jonson's next play, *Eastward Hoe* (1604), was written in collaboration with Marston and Chapman, which led to a brief imprisonment for all three, because of allegedly treasonous statements regarding the Scots.

The subsequent period constitutes Jonson's most successful one, in which he wrote the comedies *Volpone, or The Fox* (1606), *Epicoene, or The Silent Woman* (1609), *The Alchemist* (1610) and *Bartholomew Fair* (1614). During this time, Jonson also wrote his second tragedy, *Catiline, His Conspiracy* (1611). His later plays, which include *The Devil is an Asse* (1616), *The Staple of News* (1625), *The New Inne* (1629), and others, were not widely admired, and were later labelled by Dryden "mere dotages."

In 1605, Jonson's quasi-drama *The Masque of Blackness* was presented to the court of James I, and with it Jonson embarked on a fairly lengthy career of court entertainment. In all, Jonson was to write over twenty-five masques, including *Hymenaei* (1606), commemorating the marriage of the Earl of Essex and Francis Howard, *The Masque of the Queens* (1609), in which Jonson introduces the "antimasque," and numerous others. These masques were generally staged—and upstaged—by the architect and designer Inigo Jones, with whom Jonson engaged in fierce rivalry. During these years, Jonson also spent a year in Europe acting as tutor to Sir Walter Raleigh's son (1612–13) and travelled to Scotland (1618–19), making what became a famous visit to William Drummond of Hawthornden, who kept a detailed record of their conversation. He was honored by the city of Edinburgh and claimed to have received honorary degrees from both Oxford and Cambridge, although records survive of the Oxford induction only. In 1621, James I offered him a knighthood, which he did not take; he was relatively secure in a small pension he received from the king. In 1623 Jonson's personal library was burned in a fire, an event commemorated in his poem "An Execration upon Vulcan."

After the death of James I in 1625, Jonson was not asked to write masques for the new court of Charles I until 1628. Meanwhile, he served as official Chronologer of London in 1628, until he suffered from a stroke in that same year. Although weakened, Jonson continued to lead the life of a London wit, acting as unofficial Poet Laureate (receiving the pay, although not the title, of the position). Widely admired in his time, Jonson headed a generation of authors known as "the tribe of Ben," and held court first in the Mermaid Tavern, then in the Devil. After Jonson's death, a collection of elegies from thirty-three admirers, *Jonsonus Virbius* (1638), was published.

Jonson's own poems, most of which adhered to classical forms, were collected in *Epigrams* and *The Forrest* (both 1616), as well as *Underwoods* (1640). The best known of Jonson's prose works remains *Timber; or Discourses made upon Men and Matters*, a series of notes and essays on life and letters (1640). Jonson's only pastoral, *The Sad Shepherd*, was left unfinished. The first folio edition of his works was published in 1616; a second, in 1640. The playwright died on August 6, 1637, and is buried in Westminster Abbey, under the inscription "O rare Ben Jonson."

Personal

His Grandfather came from Carlisle, and, he thought, from Anandale to it: he served King Henry 8, and was a gentleman.

His Father lost all his estate under Queen Marie, having been cast in prisson and forfaitted; at last turn'd Minister: so he was a minister's son. He himself was posthumous born, a moneth after his father's decease; brought up poorly, putt to school by a friend (his master Cambden): after taken from it, and put to ane other craft (*I think was to be a wright or bricklayer*), which he could not endure; then went he to the Low Countries: but returning soone he betook himself to his wonted studies. In his service in the Low Countries, he had, in the face of both the campes, killed ane enemie and taken *opima spolia* from him; and since his comming to England, being appealed to the fields, he had killed his adversarie, which had hurt him in the arme, and whose sword was 10 inches longer than his; for the which he was emprissoned, and almost at the gallowes. Then took he his religion by trust, of a priest who visited him in prisson. Thereafter he was 12 yeares a Papist.

He was Master of Arts in both the Universities, by their favour, not his studie.

He maried a wyfe who was a shrew, yet honest: 5 yeers he had not bedded with her, but remayned with my Lord Aulbanie.

In the tyme of his close imprisonment, under Queen Elizabeth, his judges could get nothing of him to all their demands but I and No. They placed two damn'd villains to catch advantage of him, with him, but he was advertised by his keeper: of the Spies he hath ane epigrame.

When the King came in England at that tyme the pest was in London, he being in the country at Sir Robert Cotton's house with old Cambden, he saw in a vision his eldest sone, then a child and at London, appear unto him with the mark of a bloodie crosse on his forehead, as if it had been cutted with a suord, at which amazed he prayed unto God, and in the morning he came to Mr. Cambden's chamber to tell him; who persuaded him it was but ane apprehension of his fantasie, at which he sould not be disjected: in the mean tyme comes there letters from his wife of the death of that boy in the plague. He appeared to him (he said) of a manlie shape, and of that grouth that he thinks he shall be at the resurrection.

He was delated by Sir James Murray to the King, for writting something against the Scots, in a play Eastward Hoe, and voluntarily imprissonned himself with Chapman and Marston, who had written it amongst them. The report was, that they should then [have] had their ears cut and noses. After their delivery, he banqueted all his friends; there was Camden, Selden, and others: at the midst of the feast his old Mother dranke to him, and shew him a paper which she had (if the sentence had taken execution) to have mixed in the prisson among his drinke, which was full of lustie strong poison, and that she was no churle, she told, she minded first to have drunk of it herself.

He had many quarrells with Marston, beat him, and took his pistol from him, wrote his Poetaster on him; the beginning of them were, that Marston represented him in the stage, in his youth given to venerie. He thought the use of a maide nothing in comparison to the wantoness of a wyfe, and would never have ane other mistress. He said two accidents strange befell him: one, that a man made his own wyfe to court him, whom he enjoyed two yeares ere he knew of it, and one day finding them by chance, was passingly delighted with it: ane other, lay divers tymes with a woman, who shew him all that he wished, except the last act, which she would never agree unto.

S. W. Raulighe sent him governour with his Son, anno 1613, to France. This youth being knavishly inclyned, among other pastimes (as the setting of the favour of damosells on a cwdpiece), caused him to be drunken, and dead drunk, so that he knew not wher he was, therafter laid him on a carr, which he made to be drawen by pioners through the streets, at every corner showing his governour stretched out, and telling them, that was a more lively image of the Crucifix then any they had:

at which sport young Raughlie's mother delyghted much (saying, his father young was so inclyned), though the Father abhorred it.

He can set horoscopes, but trusts not in them. He with the consent of a friend cousened a lady, with whom he had made ane appointment to meet ane old Astrologer, in the suburbs, which she keeped; and it was himself disguysed in a longe gowne and a whyte beard at the light of dimm burning candles, up in a little cabinet reached unto by a ledder.

Every first day of the new year he had 20 lb. sent him from the Earl of Pembrok to buy bookes.

After he was reconciled with the Church, and left of to be a recusant, at his first communion, in token of true reconciliation, he drank out all the full cup of wyne.

Being at the end of my Lord Salisburie's table with Inigo Jones, and demanded by my Lord, Why he was not glad? My Lord, said he, yow promised I should dine with yow, bot I doe not, for he had none of his meate; he esteemed only that his meate which was of his own dish.

He heth consumed a whole night in lying looking to his great toe, about which he hath seen Tartars and Turks, Romans and Carthaginians, feight in his imagination.

Northampton was his mortall enimie for beating, on a St. George's day, one of his attenders: He was called before the Councell for his Sejanus, and accused both of poperie and treason by him.

Sundry tymes he hath devoured his bookes, i.[e.] *sold them all for necessity*.

He heth a minde to be a churchman, and so he might have favour to make one sermon to the King, he careth not what therafter sould befall him: for he would not flatter though he saw Death.

At his hither comming, Sʳ Francis Bacon said to him, He loved not to sie Poesy goe on other feet than poeticall Dactylus and Spondaeus. . . .

He is a great lover and praiser of himself; a contemner and scorner of others; given rather to losse a friend than a jest; jealous of every word and action of those about him (especiallie after drink, which is one of the elements in which he liveth); a dissembler of ill parts which raigne in him, a bragger of some good that he wanteth; thinketh nothing well bot what either he himself or some of his friends and countrymen hath said or done; he is passionately kynde and angry; careless either to gaine or keep; vindicative, but, if he be well answered, at himself.

For any religion, as being versed in both. Interpreteth best sayings and deeds often to the worst. Oppressed with fantasie, which hath ever mastered his reason, a generall disease in many Poets. His inventions are smooth and easie; but above all he excelleth in a Translation. —WILLIAM DRUMMOND, *Notes on Ben Jonson's Conversations*, 1619

A session was held the other day,
And Apollo himself was at it, they say,
The laurel that had been so long reserv'd,
Was now to be given to him best deserv'd.

                       And

Therefore the wits of the town came thither,
'Twas strange to see how they flocked together.
Each strongly confident of his own way,
Thought to gain the laurel away that day.

. . . .

The first that broke silence was good old Ben,
Prepared before with canary wine,

And he told them plainly he deserved the bays,
For his were called works, where others were but plays.

And

Bid them remember how he had purg'd the stage
Of errors, that had lasted many an age,
And he hoped they did not think the *Silent Woman*,
The *Fox* and the *Alchemist*, outdone by no man.

Apollo stopt him there, and bade him not go on,
'Twas merit, he said, and not presumption
Must carry't, at which Ben turned about.
And in great choler offer'd to go out:

But

Those that were there thought it not fit
To discontent so ancient a wit;
And therefore Apollo call'd him back again,
And made him mine host of his own New Inn.
—Sir John Suckling, "A Session of the Poets"
(c. 1637), *Fragmenta Aurea*, 1646

Though I cannot with all my industrious inquiry find him in his cradle, I can fetch him from his long coats. When a little child, he lived in Harts-horn-lane near Charing-cross, where his Mother married a Bricklayer for her second husband. . . . He help'd in the building of the new structure of Lincoln's Inn, when, having a trowell in his hand, he had a book in his pocket. Some gentlemen, pitying that his parts should be buried under the rubbish of so mean a calling, did by their bounty manumise him freely to follow his own ingenious inclinations. Indeed his parts were not so ready to run of themselves, as able to answer the spur; so that it may be truly said of him, that he had an elaborate wit wrought out by his own industry. He would sit silent in learned company, and suck in (besides wine) their several humors into his observation. What was ore in others, he was able to refine to himself. . . .

Many were the wit-combates betwixt ⟨Shakespeare⟩ and *Ben Johnson*; which two I behold like a Spanish Great Gallion and an English man-of-War: Master *Johnson* (like the former) was built far higher in Learning; Solid, but Slow in his performances. *Shakespear*, with the English man-of-War, lesser in bulk, but lighter in sailing, could turn with all tides, tack about, and take advantage of all winds, by the quickness of his Wit and invention.—Thomas Fuller, *The History of the Worthies of England*, 1662

His mother, after his father's death, married a bricklayer; and 'tis generally sayd that he wrought sometime with his father-in-lawe (and particularly on the gardenwall of Lincoln's Inne next to Chancery-lane—from old parson ⟨Richard⟩ Hill, of Stretton, Hereff., 1646), and that . . . , a knight, a bencher, walking thro' and hearing him repeat some Greeke verses out of Homer, discoursing with him, and finding him to have a witt extraordinary, gave him some exhibition to maintaine him at Trinity college in Cambridge, where he was. . . . (quaere). Then he went into the Lowe-countreys, and spent some time (not very long) in the armie, not to the disgrace of . . . , as you may find in his Epigrammes. Then he came over into England, and acted and wrote, but both ill, at the Green Curtaine, a kind of nursery or obscure playhouse, somewhere in the suburbes (I thinke towards Shoreditch or Clarkenwell)—from J. Greenhill. Then he undertooke againe to write a playe, and did hitt it admirably well, viz. "Every man. . . ." which was his first good one. . . . He was (or rather had been) of a clear and faire skin; his habit was very plaine. I have heard Mr. Lacy, the player, say that he was wont to weare a coate like a coachman's coate, with slitts under the arme-pitts. He would many times exceed in drinke (Canarie was his beloved liquour):

then he would tumble home to bed, and, when he had thoroughly perspired, then to studie. I have seen his studyeing chaire, which was of strawe, such as old woemen used, and as Aulus Gellius is drawn in. . . . He lies buryed in the north aisle in the path of square stone (the rest is lozenge), opposite to the scutcheon of Robertus de Ros, with this inscription only on him, in a pavement square, of blew marble, about 14 inches square,

O RARE BENN IOHNSON

which was donne at the chardge of Jack Young (afterwards knighted) who, walking there when the grave was covering, gave the fellow eighteen pence to cutt it.—John Aubrey, *Brief Lives*, 1696, Vol. 2, ed. Clark, pp. 11–13

Jonson hath been often represented as of an envious, arrogant, overbearing temper, and insolent and haughty in his converse; but these ungracious drawings were the performance of his enemies; who certainly were not solicitous to give a flattering likeness of the original. But considering the provocations he received, with the mean and contemptible talents of those who opposed him, what we condemn as vanity or conceit, might be only the exertions of conscious and insulted merit. . . . In his studies Jonson was laborious and indefatigable: his reading was copious and extensive; his memory so tenacious and strong that, when turned of forty, he could have repeated all that he ever wrote: his judgment was accurate and solid; and often consulted by those who knew him well, in branches of very curious learning, and far remote from the flowery paths loved and frequented by the muses.—Peter Whalley, "Life of Jonson," *Jonson's Works*, 1756, ed. Peter Whalley, p. lv

How Decker's hearers must have appreciated every allusion to the arrogant Ben the Poet; with the fierce mouth and small beard; his face marked with small pox; his hollow cheeks; his speaking through his nose; his sour face when he reads his own songs; his stamping on the stage as if he was treading mortar. The audience all knew Master Jonson had once killed a man in a duel, and had left brick-making to make rails; they knew he took months writing a play, and that he despised the opinion of his audience, and they laughed accordingly.—George Walter Thornbury, *Shakspere's England*, 1856, Vol. 2, p. 13

This man, Ben Jonson, commonly stands next to Shakespeare in a consideration of the dramatic literature of the age of Elizabeth; and certainly if the "thousand-souled" Shakespeare may be said to represent mankind, Ben as unmistakably stands for English-kind. He is "Saxon" England in epitome,—John Bull passing from a name into a man,—a proud, strong, tough, solid, domineering individual, whose intellect and personality cannot be severed, even in thought, from his body and personal appearance. Ben's mind, indeed, was rooted in Ben's character; and his character took symbolic form in his physical frame. He seemed built up, mentally as well as bodily, out of beef and sack, mutton and Canary; or, to say the least, was a joint product of the English mind and the English larder, of the fat as well as the thought of the land, of the soil as well as the soul of England. The moment we attempt to estimate his eminence as a dramatist, he disturbs the equanimity of our judgment by tumbling head-foremost into the imagination as a big, bluff, burly, and quarrelsome man, with "a mountain belly and a rocky face." He is a very pleasant boon companion as long as we make our idea of his importance agree with his own; but the instant we attempt to dissect his intellectual pretensions, the living animal becomes a dangerous subject,—his countenance flames, his great hands double up, his thick lips begin to twitch with impending invective, and, while the critic's impression of him is thus all the more vivid, he is checked in its expression by a very natural fear of the consequences. There is no safety but in taking this rowdy leviathan of letters at his own valuation; and the relation of critics towards him is as perilous as that of the jurymen towards the Irish advocate, who had an unpleasant habit of sending them the challenge of the duellist whenever they brought in a verdict against any of his clients. There is, in fact, such a vast animal force in old Ben's self-assertion, that he bullies posterity as he bullied his contemporaries; and, while we admit his claim to rank next to Shakespeare among the dramatists of his age, we beg our readers to understand that we do it under intimidation.—EDWIN P. WHIPPLE, *The Literature of the Age of Elizabeth*, 1868, p. 85

According to the local tradition, he asked the King (Charles I.) to grant him a favour. "What is it?" said the King.—"Give me eighteen inches of square ground." "Where?" asked the King.—"In Westminster Abbey." This is one explanation given of the story that he was buried standing upright. Another is that it was in view to his readiness for the Resurrection. . . . This stone ⟨covering his grave⟩ was taken up when, in 1821, the Nave was repaved, and was brought back from the stoneyard of the clerk of the works, in the time of Dean Buckland, by whose order it was fitted into its present place in the north wall of the Nave. Meanwhile, the original spot had been marked by a small triangular lozenge, with a copy of the old inscription. When, in 1849, Sir Robert Wilson was buried close by, the loose sand of Jonson's grave (to use the expression of the clerk of the works who superintended the operation) "rippled in like a quicksand," and the clerk "saw the two leg-bones of Jonson, fixed bolt upright in the sand, as though the body had been buried in the upright position; and the skull came rolling down among the sand, from a position above the leg-bones, to the bottom of the newly-made grave. There was still hair upon it, and it was of a red colour." It was seen once more on the digging of John Hunter's grave; and "it had still traces of red hair upon it. The world long wondered that he should lie buried from the rest of the poets and want a tomb." This monument, in fact, was to have been erected by subscription soon after his death, but was delayed by the breaking-out of the Civil War. The present medallion in Poets' Corner was set up in the middle of the last century by "a person of quality, whose name was desired to be concealed." By a mistake of the sculptor, the buttons were set on the left side of the coat. Hence this epigram—

> O rare Ben Jonsøn—what a turncoat grown!
> Thou ne'er wast such, till clad in stone:
> Then let not this disturb thy sprite,
> Another age shall set thy buttons right.
> —ARTHUR PENRHYN STANLEY, *Historical
> Memorials of Westminster Abbey*,
> 1896, pp. 288–89

Jonson's person was not built on the classical type of graceful or dignified symmetry: he had the large and rugged dimensions of a strong Borderland river, swollen by a sedentary life into huge corpulence. Although in his later days he jested at his own "mountain belly and his rocky face," he probably bore his unwieldy figure with a more athletic carriage than his namesake the lexicographer. Bodily as well as mentally he belonged to the race of Anak. His position among his contemporaries was very much what Samuel Johnson's might have been had he been contradicted, and fought against by independent rivals, jealous and resentful of his dictatorial manner. Ben Jonson's large and irascible personality could not have failed to command respect; but his rivals had too much respect for

themselves to give way absolutely to his authority. They refused to be as grasshoppers in his sight. We should do wrong, however, to suppose that this disturbed the giant's peace of mind.—WILLIAM MINTO, *Characteristics of English Poets*, 1874–85, p. 338

Besides being a born critic, Jonson was possessed of both a generous heart and a robust intellect; and there is a ludicrous incongruity with the transparent nature of the man in the supposition that it was poisoned by a malignant hatred of Shakspere and his fame. The difference between the two poets was indeed extremely great, and reflects itself in almost everything left to us from their respective hands. But it is not a whit less absurd to look upon Jonson and Shakspere as the heads of opposite schools or tendencies in literature, than to suppose the one writer to have personally regarded the other with a jealous feeling of rivalry. . . . Ben Jonson was a genuine scholar, whose chief pride was his library, afterwards destroyed by a fire which inflicted an irreparable loss upon our literature. His love of reading must have been insatiable; of his book-learning numberless illustrations are furnished by his plays, in one of which he bears testimony to it with pardonable self-sufficiency. But to the canary-sack must be ascribed part of the boastfulness which made him tell Drummond that "he was better versed, and knew more in Greek and Latin, than all the Poets in England, and"—here Drummond appears to have imperfectly understood the author of the "English Grammar"—"quintessence their brains."—ADOLPHUS WILLIAM WARD, *A History of English Dramatic Literature*, 1875–99, Vol. 2, pp. 297–314

A man of extreme convivial and decidedly undomestic turn, he was accessible to everyone at the taverns he frequented, and besides the group of "Sons," which is famous, and included all the more noted men of letters of the second half of our period, he seems to have had a wide circle of *protégés* and clients extending, as later traditions more or less dimly indicate, all over the kingdom. This semi-Falstaffian gift of tavern-kingship, however, could not have availed of itself to give Jonson the postion he held. But his more solid claims to literary respect were usually great. Although it is very doubtful whether he belonged to either University in any but an honorary capacity, scholars of the strictest academic sufficiency like Selden, Farnaby, and others, admitted his scholarship; he was the honoured friend of Raleigh and Bacon; and it is impossible for any reader, himself possessing the slightest tincture of classical learning, not to recognise in every work of Jonson's—be it play, poem, or prose—the presence of reading which never obscured, though it sometimes stiffened and hardened, the creative faculties of the author.—GEORGE SAINTSBURY, *Social England*, 1895, Vol. 4, ed. Traill, p. 113

He was strong and massive in body, racy and coarse, full of self-esteem, and combative instincts, saturated with the conviction of the scholar's high rank and the poet's exalted vocation, full of contempt for ignorance, frivolity, and lowness, classic in his tastes, with a bent towards careful structure and leisurely development of thought in all that he wrote, and yet a true poet in so far as he was not only irregular in his life and quite incapable of saving any of the money he now and then earned, but was, moreover, subject to hallucinations: once saw Carthaginians and Romans fighting on his great toe, and, on another occasion, had a vision of his son with a bloody cross on his brow, which was supposed to forbode his death. . . . With all his weaknesses, however, he was a sturdy, energetic, and high-minded man, a commanding, independent, and very comprehensive intelligence, and from 1598, when he makes his first appearance on Shakespeare's horizon, throughout the rest of his life, he was, so far as we can see, the man of all his contemporaries whose name was oftenest mentioned along with Shakespeare's. . . . Though his society may have been somewhat fatiguing, it must nevertheless have been both instructive and stimulating to Shakespeare, since Ben was greatly his superior in historical and linguistic knowledge, while as a poet he pursued a totally different ideal.—GEORGE BRANDES, *William Shakespeare, A Critical Study*, 1898, Vol. 1, pp. 385–88

General

Our English Horace.—CHETTLE HENRY, *England's Mourning Garment*, 1603

> Johnson, whose full of merit to reherse
> Too copious is to be confined in verse;
> Yet therein only fittest to be known,
> Could any write a line which he might own.
> One, so judicious; so well-knowing; and
> A man whose least worth is to understand;
> One so exact in all he doth prefer
> To able censure; for the theatre
> Not Seneca transcends his worth of praise;
> Who writes him well shall well deserve the bays.
> —WILLIAM BROWNE, *Britannia's Pastorals*,
> 1613, Bk. 2, Song 2

If I should declare mine own rudeness rudely, I should then confess, that I never tasted English more to my liking, nor more smart, and put to the height of use in poetry, than in that vital, judicious, and most practicable language of Benjamin Jonson's poems.—EDMUND BOLTON, *Hypercritica*, 1624

> He better loves Ben Jonson's book of plays,
> But that therein of wit he finds such plenty
> That he scarce understands a jest of twenty.
> —FRANCIS LENTON, *The Young Gallant's
> Whirligig*, 1629

> What are his faults (O Envy!) that you speake
> English at Court, the learned Stage acts Greeke?
> That Latine Hee reduc'd, and could command
> That which your *Shakespeare* scarce could understand?
> —H. RAMSAY, *Upon the Death of Benjamin
> Jonson*, 1638

> And now, since Jonson's gone, we well may say,
> The stage hath seen her glory and decay.
> Whose judgment was't refined it? or who
> Gave laws, by which hereafter all must go,
> But solid Jonson? from whose full strong quill,
> Each line did like a diamond drop distil,
> Though hard, yet clear.
> —OWEN FELTHAM, *To the Memory of Immortal
> Ben*, 1638

> Had this been for some meaner poet's herse,
> I might have then observ'd the laws of verse:
> But here they fail, nor can I hope to express
> In numbers, what the world grants numberless:
> Such are the truths, we ought to speak of thee,
> Thou great refiner of our poesy,
> Who turn'st to gold that which before was lead;
> Then with that pure elixir rais'd the dead!
> Nine sisters who (for all the poets lies),
> Had been deem'd mortal, did not Jonson rise,
> And with celestial sparks (not stoln) revive
> Those who could erst keep winged fame alive:

> 'Twas he that found (plac'd) in the seat of wit,
> Dull grinning ignorance, and banish'd it;
> He on the prostituted stage appears
> To make men hear not by their eyes, but ears;
> Who painted virtues, that each one might know,
> And point the man, that did such treasure owe:
> So that who could in Jonson's lines be high,
> Needed not honors, or a riband buy;
> But vice he only shewed us in a glass,
> Which by reflection of those rays that pass,
> Retains the figure lively, set before.
> And that withdrawn, reflects at us no more;
> So, he observ'd the like decorum, when
> He whipt the vices, and yet spar'd the men:
> When heretofore, the Vice's only note,
> And sign from virtue was his party-coat;
> When devils were the last men on the stage,
> And pray'd for plenty, and the present age.
>   Nor was our English language only bound
> To thank him, for he Latin Horace found
> (Who so inspired Rome, with his lyric song)
> Translated in the macaronic tongue;
> Cloth'd in such rags, as one might safely vow,
> That his Mæcenas would not own him now:
> On him he took this pity, as to clothe
> In words, and such expression, as for both,
> There's none but judgeth the exchange will come
> To twenty more, than when he sold at Rome.
> Since then, he made our language pure and good,
> And us to speak, but what we understood,
> We owe this praise to him, that should we join
> To pay him, he were paid but with the coin
> Himself hath minted, which we know by this,
> That no words pass for current now, but his.
> And though he in a blinder age could change
> Faults to perfections, yet 'twas far more strange
> To see (however times and fashions frame)
> His wit and language still remain the same
> In all men's mouths; grave preachers did it use
> As golden pills, by which they might infuse
> Their heavenly physic; ministers of state
> Their grave dispatches in his language wrate;
> Ladies made curt'sies in them, courtiers, legs,
> Physicians bills;—perhaps, some pedant begs
> He may not use it, for he hears 'tis such,
> As in few words a man may utter much.
> Could I have spoken in his language too,
> I had not said so much, as now I do,
> To whose clear memory I this tribute send,
> Who dead's my Wonder, living was my Friend.
> —SIR JOHN BEAUMONT, *To the Memory of him
> who can never be Forgotten, Master Benjamin
> Jonson*, 1638

To compare our English Dramatick Poets together (without taxing them) *Shakespear* excelled in a natural Vein, *Fletcher* in Wit, and *Johnson* in Gravity and ponderousness of Style; whose onely fault was, he was too elaborate; and had he mixt less erudition with his Playes, they had been more pleasant and delightful than they are. Comparing him with *Shakespear*, you shall see the difference betwixt Nature and Art; and with *Fletcher*, the difference between Wit and Judgement: Wit being an exuberant thing, like *Nilus*, never more commendable then when it overflowes; but Judgement a stayed and reposed thing, always containing it self within its bounds and limits.—RICH-

ARD FLECKNOE, *A Short Discourse of the English Stage*, c. 1660–64

He was paramount in the Dramatique part of Poetry, and taught the Stage an exact conformity to the laws of Comedians. His Comedies were above the Volge (which are only tickled with downright obscenity), and took not so well at the first stroke as at the rebound, when beheld the second time; yea they will endure reading, and that with due commendation, so long as either ingenuity or learning are fashionable in our Nation. If his later be not so spriteful and vigorous as his first pieces, all that are old will, and all that desire to be old should, excuse him therein.—THOMAS FULLER, *The Worthies of England*, 1662, Vol. 2, ed. Nichols, p. 112

. . . Ben Jonson is to be admired for many excellencies; and can be taxed with fewer failings than any English poet. I know I have been accused as an enemy of his writings; but without any other reason, than that I do not admire him blindly, and without looking into his imperfections. For why should there be any *ipse dixit* in our poetry, any more than there is in our philosophy? I admire and applaud him where I ought: Those, who do more, do but value themselves in their admiration of him; and, by telling you they extol Ben Jonson's way, would insinuate to you that they can practise it. For my part, I declare that I want judgment to imitate him; and should think it a great impudence in myself to attempt it. To make men appear pleasantly ridiculous on the stage, was, as I have said, his talent; and in this he needed not the acumen of wit but that of judgment. For the characters and representations of folly are only the effects of observation; and observation is an effect of judgment. Some ingenious men, for whom I have a particular esteem, have thought I have much injured Ben Jonson, when I have not allowed his wit to be extraordinary: But they confound the notion of what is witty, with what is pleasant. That Ben Jonson's plays were pleasant, he must want reason who denies: But that pleasantness was not properly wit, or the sharpness of conceit; but the natural imitation of folly: Which I confess to be excellent in its kind, but not to be of that kind which they pretend. . . .—JOHN DRYDEN, "Preface" to *An Evening's Love, or the Mock Astrologer*, 1671

I cannot be of their Opinion, who think he wanted Wit: I am sure, if he did, he was so far from being the most faultless, that he was the most faulty Poet of his Time. But it may be answered, that his Writings were correct, though he wanted Fire; but I think flat and dull Things are as incorrect, and shew as little Judgment in the Author, nay less, than sprightly and mettled Nonsense does. But I think he had more true Wit than any of his Contemporaries: that other Men had sometimes Things, that seem'd more Fiery than his, was because they were placed with so many sordid and mean Things about them, that they made a greater Show. . . .

Nor can I think, to the writing of his Humours (which were not only the Follies, but the Vices and Subtilties of Men) that Wit was not required, but Judgment; where, by the way, they speak as if Judgment were a less thing than Wit. But certainly it was meant otherwise by Nature, who subjected Wit to the Government of Judgment, which is the noblest Faculty of the Mind. Fancy rough-draws, but Judgment smooths and finishes: nay, Judgment does not comprehend Wit; for no Man can have that, who has not Wit. In Fancy Mad-men equal, if not excell, all others; and one may as well say, that one of those Mad-men is as good a Man, as temperate a Wise-man, as that one of the very fanciful Plays (admir'd most by Women) can be so good a Play, as one of *Johnson's* Correct and Well-govern'd Comedies.

The Reason given by some, why *Johnson* needed not Wit in writing Humour, is, because Humour is the effect of Observation, and Observation the effect of Judgment; but Observation is as much Necessary in all other Plays, as in Comedies of Humour. . . .

The most Excellent *Johnson* put Wit into the Mouths of the meanest of his People, and, which is infinitely Difficult, made it proper for 'em. And I once heard a Person of the greatest Wit and Judgment of the Age say, That *Bartholomew-Fair*, (which consists most of low Persons) is one of the wittiest Plays in the World. If there be no Wit required, in the rendring Folly ridiculous, or Vice odious, we must accuse *Juvenal*, the best Satyrist and wittiest Man of all the *Latin* Writers, for want of it.—THOMAS SHADWELL, "Preface" to *The Humorists*, 1671

Benjamin Johnson, the most learned, judicious and correct, generally so accounted, of our *English* Comedians, and the more to be admired for being so, for that neither the height of natural parts, for he was no *Shakespear*, nor the cost of Extraordinary Education; for he is reported but a Bricklayers Son, but his own proper Industry and Addiction to Books advance him to this perfection: In three of his Comedies, namely the *Fox*, *Alchymist* and *Silent Woman*, he may be compared, in the Judgment of Learned Men, for Decorum, Language, and well Humouring of the Parts, as well with the chief of the Ancient Greec and Latin Comedians as the prime of Modern *Italians*, who have been judg'd the best of *Europe* for a happy Vein in Comedies, nor is his *Bartholomew-Fair* much short of them; as for his other Comedies *Cinthia's Revells*, *Poetaster*, and the rest, let the name of *Ben Johnson* protect them against whoever shall think fit to be severe in censure against them: The Truth is, his Tragedies *Sejanus* and *Catiline* seem to have in them more of an artificial and inflate than of a pathetical and naturally Tragic height: In the rest of his Poetry, for he is not wholly Dramatic, as his Underwoods, Epigrams, &c. he is sometimes bold and strenuous, sometimes Magisterial, sometimes Lepid and full enough of conceit, and sometimes a Man as other Men are.—EDWARD PHILLIPS, *Theatrum Poetarum*, 1675

Men of the quickest apprehensions, and aptest Geniuses to anything they undertake, do not always prove the greatest Masters in it. For there is more Patience and Flegme required in those that attaine to any Degree of Perfection, then is commonly found in the Temper of active, and ready wits, that soone tire and will not hold out; as the swiftest Race-horse will not perform a longe Jorney so well as a sturdy dull Jade. Hence it is that Virgil who wanted much of that Natural easines of wit that Ovid had, did nevertheless with hard Labour and long Study in the end, arrive at a higher perfection then the other with all his Dexterity of wit, but less Industry could attaine to: The same we may observe of Johnson, and Shakespeare. *For he that is able to thinke long and study well*, will be sure to finde out better things then another man can hit upon suddenly, though of more quick and ready Parts, *which is commonly but chance, and the other Art and Judgment.*—SAMUEL BUTLER, *Characters and Passages from Note-books*, c. 1680

To come lastly to *Ben Johnson*, who (as Mr. *Dryden* affirms) has borrow'd more from the Ancients than any: I crave leave to say in his behalf, that our late *Laureat* ⟨Dryden⟩ has far outdone him in Thefts, proportionable to his Writings: and therefore he is guilty of the highest Arrogance, to accuse another of a Crime, for which he is most of all men liable to be arraign'd.

Quis tulerit Gracchos de seditione querentes?

I must further alledge that Mr. *Johnson* in borrowing from the Ancients, has only follow'd the Pattern of the great Men of former Ages, *Homer, Virgil, Ovid, Horace, Plautus, Terence, Seneca, &c.* all which have imitated the Example of the industrious Bee, which sucks Honey from all sorts of Flowers, and lays it up in a general Repository. 'Twould be *actum agere* to repeat what is known to all Learned Men; that there was an *Illiad* written before that of *Homer*, which *Aristotle* mentions; and from which . . . *Homer* is supposed to have borrow'd his Design. . . . I could enumerate more Instances, but these are sufficient Precedents to excuse Mr. *Johnson*.

Permit me to say farther in his behalf, That if in imitation of these illustrious Examples, and Models of Antiquity, he has borrow'd from them, as they from each other; yet that he attempted, and as some think, happily succeeded in his Endeavours of Surpassing them: insomuch that a certain Person of Quality makes a Question, "Whether any of the Wit of the *Latine* Poets be more Terse and Eloquent in their Tongue, than this Great and Learned Poet appears in ours."

Whether Mr. *Dryden*, who has likewise succeeded to admiration in this way, or Mr. *Johnson* have most improv'd, and best advanc'd what they have borrow'd from the Ancients, I shall leave to the decision of the abler Criticks: only this I must say, in behalf of the later, that he has no ways endeavour'd to conceal what he has borrow'd, as the former has generally done. Nay, in his Play called *Sejanus* he has printed in the Margent throughout, the places from whence he borrow'd: the same he has practic'd in several of his Masques, (as the Reader may find in his Works;) a Pattern, which Mr. *Dryden* would have done well to have copied, and had thereby sav'd me the trouble of the following Annotations.

There is this difference between the Proceedings of these Poets, that Mr. *Johnson* has by Mr. *Dryden's* Confession *Design'd his Plots himself*; whereas I know not any One Play, whose Plot may be said to be the Product of Mr. *Dryden's* own Brain. When Mr. *Johnson* borrow'd, 'twas from the Treasury of the Ancients, which is so far from any diminution of his Worth, that I think it is to his Honor; at least-wise I am sure he is justified by his Son *Carthwright*, in the following Lines:

What tho' thy searching Muse did rake the dust . . .

Give me leave to say a word, or two, in Defence of Mr. *Johnson's* way of Wit, which Mr. *Dryden* calls *Clenches.*

There have been few great Poets which have not propos'd some Eminent Author for their Pattern. . . . Mr. *Johnson* propos'd *Plautus* for his Model, and not only borrow'd from him, but imitated his way of Wit in English. There are none who have read him, but are acquainted with his way of playing with Words. . . . Nor might this be the sole Reason for Mr. *Johnson's* Imitation, for possibly 'twas his Compliance with the Age that induc'd him to this way of writing, it being then as Mr. *Dryden* observes the Mode of Wit, the Vice of the Age, and not *Ben Johnson's*: and besides Mr. *Dryden's* taxing Sir *Philip Sidney* for playing with his Words, I may add that I find it practis'd by several Dramatick Poets, who were Mr. *Johnson's* Cotemporaries. . . .

As to his Reflections on this Triumvirate in general: I might easily prove, that his Improprieties in Grammar, are equal to theirs: and that He himself has been guilty of Solecisms in Speech, and Flaws in Sence, as well as *Shakespear, Fletcher,* and *Johnson.*—GERARD LANGBAINE, *An Account of the English Dramatick Poets,* 1691, pp. 145–50

Sometimes *Personal Defects* are misrepresented for *Humours.*

I mean, sometimes Characters are barbarously exposed on the Stage, ridiculing Natural Deformities, Casual Defects in the Senses, and Infirmities of Age. . . . But much need not be said upon this Head to any body, especially to you, who, in one

of your Letters to me concerning Mr. *Johnson's Fox,* have justly excepted against this Immoral part of *Ridicule* in *Corbaccio's* Character; and there I must agree with you to blame him whom otherwise I cannot enough admire for his great Mastery of true Humour in Comedy. . . .

The Character of *Morose* in the *Silent Woman* I take to be a Character of Humour. And I choose to instance this Character to you from many others of the same Author, because I know it has been Condemn'd by many as Unnatural and Farce: And you have your self hinted some dislike of it for the same Reason, in a Letter to me concerning some of *Johnson's* Plays.

Let us suppose *Morose* to be a Man Naturally Splenetick and Melancholly; is there any thing more offensive to one of such a Disposition than Noise and Clamour? Let any Man that has the Spleen . . . be Judge. . . . Well, but *Morose,* you will say, is so Extravagant, he cannot bear any Discourse or Conversation above a Whisper. Why, It is his excess of this Humour that makes him become Ridiculous, and qualifies his Character for Comedy. If the Poet had given him but a Moderate proportion of that Humour, 'tis odds but half the Audience would have sided with the Character and have Condemn'd the Author for Exposing a Humour, which was neither Remarkable nor Ridiculous. Besides, the distance of the Stage requires the Figure represented to be something larger than the Life; and sure a Picture may have Features larger in Proportion, and yet be very like the Original. . . .

The Character of Sir *John Daw* in the same Play is a Character of Affectation. He every where discovers an Affectation of Learning, when he is not only Conscious to himself, but the Audience also plainly perceives that he is Ignorant. . . .

The Character of *Cob* in *Every Man in his Humour* and most of the under Characters in *Bartholomew-Fair* discover only a Singularity of Manners, appropriated to the several Educations and Professions of the Persons represented. They are not Humours but Habits contracted by Custom.—WILLIAM CONGREVE, "Mr. Congreve to Mr. Dennis, Concerning Humour in Comedy," *Letters upon Several Occasions,* 1696, pp. 80–96

Too nicely Jonson knew the critic's part;
Nature in him was almost lost in art.
—WILLIAM COLLINS, *Epistle to Sir Thomas Hammer,* 1743

Ben Johnson has *Humour* in his *Characters,* drawn with the most masterly Skill and Judgement; In Accuracy, Depth, Propriety, and Truth, he has no *Superior* or *Equal* amongst Ancients or *Moderns;* But the *Characters* he exhibits are of a *satirical,* and *deceitful,* or of a *peevish,* or *despicable* Species; as *Volpone, Subtle, Morose,* and *Abel Drugger;* In all of which there is something very justly to be *hated* or *despised;* And you feel the same Sentiments of *dislike* for every other *Character* of *Johnson's;* so that after you have been *gratify'd* with their *Detection* and *Punishment,* you are quite tired and disgusted with their Company. . . .

Johnson in his COMIC Scenes has expos'd and ridicul'd *Folly* and *Vice; Shakespear* has usher'd in *Joy, Frolic,* and *Happiness.*—The *Alchymist, Volpone,* and *Silent Woman* of *Johnson,* are most exquisite *Satires.* The *comic* Entertainments of *Shakespear* are the highest Compositions of *Raillery, Wit,* and *Humour. Johnson* conveys some Lesson in every Character. *Shakespear* some new Species of Foible and Oddity. The one pointed his Satire with masterly Skill; the other was inimitable in touching the Strings of Delight. With *Johnson* you are confin'd and instructed, with *Shakespear* unbent and dissolv'd in

Joy. *Johnson* excellently concerts his Plots, and all his Characters unite in the one Design. *Shakespear* is superior to such Aid or Restraint; His Characters continually sallying from one independent Scene to another, and charming you in each with fresh Wit and Humour.

It may be further remark'd, that *Johnson* by pursuing the most useful Intention of *Comedy*, is in Justice oblig'd to *hunt down* and *demolish* his own *Characters*. Upon this Plan he must necessarily expose them to your *Hatred*, and of course can never bring out an amiable Person. His *Subtle*, and *Face* are detected at last, and become mean and despicable. Sir *Epicure Mammon* is properly trick'd, and goes off ridiculous and detestable. The *Puritan Elders* suffer for their Lust of Money, and are quite nauseous and abominable; And his *Morose* meets with a severe Punishment, after having sufficiently tired you with his Peevishness.—But *Shakespear*, with happier Insight, always supports his Characters in your *Favour*. His Justice *Shallow* withdraws before he is tedious; The *French Doctor*, and *Welch* Parson, go off in full Vigour and Spirit; Ancient *Pistoll* indeed is scurvily treated; however, he keeps up his Spirits; and continues to threaten to do well, that you are still desirous of his Company; and it is impossible to be tir'd or dull with the gay unfading Evergreen *Falstaff*.

But in remarking upon the Characters of *Johnson*, it would be unjust to pass *Abel Drugger* without notice; This is a little, mean, sneaking, sordid Citizen, hearkening to a Couple of Sharpers, who promise to make him rich; they can scarcely prevail upon him to resign the least Title he possesses, though he is assur'd, it is in order to get more; and your Diversion arises, from seeing him *wrung* between *Greediness* to *get* Money, and *Reluctance* to *part* with any for that Purpose. His Covetousness continually prompts him to follow the Conjurer, and puts him at the same Time upon endeavouring to stop his Fees. All the while he is excellently managed, and spirited on by *Face*. However, this Character upon the whole is *mean* and *despicable*, without any of that free spiritous jocund Humour abounding in *Shakespear*. But having been strangely exhibited upon the Theatre, a few Years ago, with odd Grimaces and extravagant Gestures, it has been raised into more Attention than it justly deserved; It is however to be acknowledg'd, that *Abel* has no Hatred, Malice, or Immorality, nor any assuming Arrogance, Pertness or Peevishness; And his eager Desire of getting and saving Money, by Methods he thinks lawful, are excusable in a Person of his Business; He is therefore not odious or detestable, but harmless and inoffensive in private Life; and from thence, correspondent with the Rule already laid down, he is the most capable of any of *Johnson's* Characters, of being a Favourite on the Theatre.

It appears, that in Imagination, Invention, Jollity, and gay Humour, *Johnson* had little *Power*; But *Shakespear* unlimited Dominion. The first was cautious and strict, not daring to sally beyond the Bounds of Regularity. The other bold and impetuous, rejoicing like a Giant to run his Course, through all the Mountains and Wilds of Nature and Fancy.

It requires an almost painful Attention to mark the Propriety and Accuracy of *Johnson*, and your Satisfaction arises from Reflection and Comparison; But the Fire and Invention of *Shakespear* in an instant are shot into your Soul, and enlighten and chear the most indolent Mind with their own Spirit and Lustre.—Upon the whole, *Johnson's* Compositions are like finished Cabinets, where every Part is wrought up with the most excellent Skill and Exactness;—*Shakespear's* like magnificent Castles, not perfectly finished or regular, but adorn'd with such bold and magnificent Designs, as at once delight and astonish you with their Beauty and Grandeur.—CORBYN

MORRIS, *An Essay towards Fixing the True Standards of Wit, Humour, Raillery, Satire, and Ridicule*, 1744, pp. 29–36

Then Jonson came, instructed from the school,
To please in method, and invent by rule;
His studious patience and laborious art,
By regular approach assail'd the heart:
Cold approbation gave the lingering bays,
For those, who durst not censure, scarce could praise.
A mortal born, he met the general doom,
But left, like Egypt's kings, a lasting tomb.
> —SAMUEL JOHNSON, *Prologue, spoken by Mr. Garrick at the opening of the Theatre Royal, Drury Lane*, 1747

Jonson possessed all the learning which was wanting to Shakspeare, and wanted all the genius of which the other was possessed. Both of them were equally deficient in taste and elegance, in harmony and correctness. A servile copyist of the ancients, Jonson translated into bad English the beautiful passages of the Greek and Roman authors, without accommodating them to the manners of his age and country. His merit has been totally eclipsed by that of Shakspeare, whose rude genius prevailed over the rude art of his contemporary.—DAVID HUME, *The History of England*, 1754–62

Jonson, in the serious drama, is as much an imitator as Shakespeare is an original. He was very learned, as Samson was very strong, to his own hurt: blind to the nature of tragedy, he pulled down all antiquity on his head, and buried himself under it; we see nothing of Jonson, nor indeed of his admired (but also murdered) ancients; for what shone in the historian is a cloud on the poet; and *Catiline* might have been a good play, if Sallust had never written.

Who knows whether Shakespeare might not have thought less, if he had read more? Who knows, if he might not have laboured under the load of Jonson's learning, as Enceladus under Etna?—EDWARD YOUNG, "Conjectures on Original Composition, in a Letter to the Author of *Sir Charles Grandison*," 1759

The book of man he read with nicest art,
And ransack'd all the secrets of the heart;
Exerted penetration's utmost force,
And traced each passion to its proper source;
Then, strongly mark'd, in liveliest colours drew
And brought each foible forth to public view:
The coxcomb felt a lash in every word,
And fools, hung out, their brother fools deterr'd.
His comic humour kept the world in awe,
And laughter frighten'd Folly more than Law.
> —CHARLES CHURCHILL, *The Rosciad*, 1761

He was as defective in tragedy, as he was excellent in comedy; and that excellence is confined to a few of his works. In Shakspeare, we see the force of genius; in Jonson, the power of industry. He is frequently deficient in the harmony, and sometimes even in the measure, of his verses. What appears to be facility in his compositions is generally the effect of uncommon labour.—JAMES GRANGER, *Biographical History of England*, 1769–1824, Vol. 2, p. 125

Jonson gave an early example of metaphysical poetry; indeed, it was the natural resource of a mind amply stored with learning, gifted with a tenacious memory and the power of constant labour, but to which was denied that vivid perception of what is naturally beautiful, and that happiness of expression, which at once conveys to the reader the idea of the poet. . . . In reading

Shakspeare, we often meet passages so congenial to our nature and feelings, that, beautiful as they are, we can hardly help wondering they did not occur to ourselves; in studying Jonson, we have often to marvel how his conceptions could have occurred to any human being. The one is like an ancient statue, the beauty of which, springing from the exactness of proportion, does not always strike at first sight, but rises upon us as we bestow time in considering it; the other is the representation of a monster, which is at first only surprising, and ludicrous or disgusting ever after.—SIR WALTER SCOTT, *Life of John Dryden*, 1805

He endeavoured to form an exact estimate of what he had on every occasion to perform; hence he succeeded best in that species of the drama which makes the principal demand on the understanding and with little call on the imagination and feeling,—the comedy of character. He introduced nothing into his works which critical dissection should not be able to extract again, as his confidence in it was such, that he conceived it exhausted everything which pleases and charms us in poetry. He was not aware that in the chemical retort of the critic what is most valuable, the volatile living spirit of a poem, evaporates. His pieces are in general deficient in soul, in that nameless something which never ceases to attract and enchant us even because it is indefinable. In the lyrical pieces, his Masques, we feel the want of a certain mental music of imagery and intonation, which the most accurate observation of difficult measures cannot give. He is everywhere deficient in those excellencies which, unsought, flow from the poet's pen, and which no artist who purposely hunts for them can ever hope to find. We must not quarrel with him, however, for entertaining a high opinion of his own works, since whatever merits they have he owed, like acquired moral properties, altogether to himself. The production of them was attended with labour, and unfortunately it is also a labour to read them. They resemble solid and regular edifices, before which, however, the clumsy scaffolding still remains, to interrupt and prevent us from viewing the architecture with ease and receiving from it a harmonious impression.—AUGUSTUS WILLIAM SCHLEGEL, *Dramatic Art and Literature*, 1809

Ben Jonson is original; he is, indeed, the only one of the great dramatists of that day who was not either directly produced, or very greatly modified, by Shakspere. In truth, he differs from our great master in everything—in form and in substance—and betrays no tokens of his proximity. He is not original in the same way as Shakspere is original; but after a fashion of his own, Ben Jonson is most truly original. . . . Ben Jonson exhibits a sterling English diction, and he has with great skill contrived varieties of construction; but his style is rarely sweet or harmonious, in consequence of his labour at point and strength being so evident. In all his works, in verse or prose, there is an extraordinary opulence of thought; but it is the produce of an amassing power in the author, and not of a growth from within. Indeed a large proportion of Ben Jonson's thoughts may be traced to classic or obscure modern writers, by those who are learned and curious enough to follow the steps of this robust, surly, and observing dramatist.—SAMUEL TAYLOR COLERIDGE, *Notes on Jonson, Beaumont, Fletcher, and Massinger*, 1818, ed. Ashe, pp. 396–97

In the regular drama he certainly holds up no romantic mirror to nature. His object was to exhibit human characters at once strongly comic and severely and instructively true; to nourish the understanding, while he feasted the sense of ridicule. He is more anxious for verisimilitude than even for comic effect. He

understood the humors and peculiarities of his species scientifically, and brought them forward in their greatest contrasts and subtlest modifications. If Shakspeare carelessly scattered illusion, Jonson skillfully prepared it. This is speaking of Jonson in his happiest manner. There is a great deal of harsh and sour fruit in his miscellaneous poetry. It is acknowledged that in the drama he frequently overlabours his delineation of character, and wastes it tediously upon uninteresting humours and peculiarities. He is a moral painter, who delights overmuch to show his knowledge of moral anatomy.— THOMAS CAMPBELL, *An Essay on English Poetry*, 1819

I do not think that his Poetical merits are yet properly appreciated. I cannot consent that the palm of humour alone shall be given to him; while in wit, feeling, pathos, and Poetical diction, he is to be sunk fathoms below Fletcher and Massinger. In the last particular, I think that he excels them both, and, indeed, all his contemporaries, excepting Shakspeare.— HENRY NEELE, *Lectures on English Poetry*, 1828

Ben Jonson was a man of the *new* age, and the *new* direction of mind; he was that half of Shakspeare which reached forward into the future, but in a more eminent degree. His chief strength was in the very excess of his one-sidedness. With the immense force of his intellectual, reflective, and critical powers, he knocked down everything in his own way—but overthrew the good together with the bad. His first principle was, to have definite palpable reasons for everything: he wished at every point *to know* what ought to be done or left undone. The clearness of the reflecting *consciousness* was the standard to which he referred everything; but of that immediate creative faculty of fancy and feeling which is properly artistic, he possessed scarcely a germ. On this account the other half of Shakspeare's character, which, like the whole of the English national theatre, belonged to the romantic middle ages, was to him hateful, inconceivable, and worthless.—HERMANN ULRICI, *Shakspeare's Dramatic Art*, 1839, pp. 81–82

Jonson's intense observation was microscopical when turned to the minute evolutions of society, while his diversified learning at all times bore him into a nobler sphere of comprehension. This taste for reality, and this fullness of knowledge on whatever theme he chose, had a reciprocal action; and the one could not go without the other. Our poet doggedly set to "a humour" through its slightest anomalies, and, in the pride of his comic art, expanded his prototype. Yet this was but half the labor which he loved: his mind was stored with the most burdensome knowledge; and to the scholar the various erudition which he had so diligently acquired threw a more permanent light over those transient scenes which the painter of manners had so carefully copied.—ISAAC DISRAELI, "The 'Humours' of Jonson," *Amenities of Literature*, 1841

O rare Ben Jonson, let us have thy songs, rounded each with a spherical thought, and the lyrics from thy masques alive with learned fantasy, and thine epigrams keen and quaint, and thy noble epitaphs, under which the dead seem stirring! . . . At Jonson's name we stop perforce, and do salutation in the dust to the impress of that "learned sock." He was a learned man, as everybody knows; and as everybody does not believe, not the worse for his learning. His material, brought laboriously from East and West, is wrapt in a flame of his own. If the elasticity and abandonment of Shakespeare and of certain of Shakespeare's brothers, are not found in his writings, the reason of the defects need not be sought out in his readings. His genius, high and verdant as it grew, yet belonged to the hard woods: it was lance-wood rather than bow-wood—a genius rather noble than graceful—eloquent, with a certain severity and emphasis of enunciation.—ELIZABETH BARRETT BROWNING, *The Book of the Poets*, 1842–63

With this basis of sound English sense, Jonson has fancy, humor, satire, learning, a large knowledge of men and motives, and a remarkable command of language, sportive, scornful, fanciful, and impassioned. One of the fixed facts in English literature, he is too strongly rooted ever to be upset. He stands out from all his contemporaries, original, peculiar, leaning on none for aid, and to be tried by his own merits alone. Had his imagination been as sensitive as that of many of his contemporaries, or his self-love less, he would probably have fallen into their conscious or unconscious imitation of Shakespeare; but, as it was, he remained satisfied with himself to the last, delving in his own mine.—EDWIN P. WHIPPLE, "Old English Dramatists," *Essays and Reviews*, 1846, Vol. 2, p. 26

Shakespeare had permanently near him one envious person, Ben Jonson, an indifferent comic poet, whose *début* he assisted.—VICTOR HUGO, *William Shakespeare*, 1864, tr. Baillot, p. 23

Ben Jonson has been regarded as the first person who has done much in settling the *"grammar* of the English language." This merit is duly awarded to him, and Pope gives him the credit of having brought critical learning into vogue; also of having instructed both actors and spectators in what was the proper province of the dramatic Muse. His prose style, however, is a transcript of his laborious and painstaking mind, ostentatiously correct, and frequently forcible, with commonly a satisfactory felicity of epithet; but his sentences never appear to be extemporaneous, but always studied, and as being one result of the primæval curse, for he seems to have produced both his thoughts and his language "by the sweat of his brow."—CHARLES COWDEN CLARKE, "On the Comic Writers of England," 1871, *Gentleman's Magazine*, N.S., Vol. 6, p. 633

Ben Jonson had a mind of immense force and pertinacious grasp; but nothing could be wider of the truth than the notion maintained with such ferocity by Gifford, that he was the father of regular comedy, the pioneer of severe and correct taste. Jonson's domineering scholarship must not be taken for more than it was worth: it was a large and gratifying possession in itself, but he would probably have written better plays and more poetry without it. It is a sad application of the mathematical method to the history of our literature to argue that the most learned playwright of his time superseded the rude efforts of such untaught mother-wits as Shakespeare with compositions based on classical models. What Jonson really did was to work out his own ideas of comedy and tragedy, and he expressly claimed the right to do so. The most scrupulous adherence to the unity of time, and the most rigid exclusion of tragic elements from comedy, do not make a play classical. Ben Jonson conformed to these externals; but there was not a more violently unclassical spirit than his among all the writers for the stage in that generation.—WILLIAM MINTO, *Characteristics of English Poets*, 1874–85, p. 337

To the modern reader, Ben Jonson's plays have lost their old attraction; but his occasional poems are full of heroic thought, and his songs are among the best in the language.— RALPH WALDO EMERSON, "Preface" to *Parnassus*, 1875, p. 6

By literary comedies, I mean comedies of classic inspiration, drawn chiefly from Menander and the Greek New Comedy through Terence; or else comedies of the poet's personal conception, that have had no model in life, and are humorous exaggerations, happy or otherwise. These are the Comedies of

Ben Jonson, Massinger, and Fletcher. Massinger's Justice Greedy we can all of us refer to a type, 'with fat capon lined' that has been and will be; and he would be comic, as Panurge is comic, but only a Rabelais could set him moving with real animation. Probably Justice Greedy would be comic to the audience of a country booth and to some of our friends. If we have lost our youthful relish for the presentation of characters put together to fit a type, we find it hard to put together the mechanism of a civil smile at his enumeration of his dishes. Something of the same is to be said of Bobadil, swearing 'by the foot of Pharaoh'; with a reservation, for he is made to move faster, and to act. The comic of Jonson is a scholar's excogitation of the comic; that of Massinger a moralist's.—GEORGE MEREDITH, "On the Idea of Comedy and of the Uses of the Comic Spirit" (1877), *Miscellaneous Prose*, 1910, pp. 10–11

Broad-absed, broad-fronted, bounteous, multiform,
With many a valley impleached with ivy and vine,
Wherein the springs of all the streams run wine,
And many a crag full-faced against the storm,
The mountain where thy Muse's feet made warm
Those lawns that revelled with her dance divine,
Shines yet with fire as it was wont to shine
From tossing torches round the dance aswarm.
Nor less, high-stationed on the gray grave heights,
High-thoughted seers with heaven's heart-kindling lights
Hold converse: and the herd of meaner things
Knows or by fiery scourge or fiery shaft
When wrath on thy broad brows has risen, and laughed,
Darkening thy soul with shadow of thunderous wings.
—ALGERNON CHARLES SWINBURNE, *Ben Jonson*, 1882

Ben Jonson stands at the head of that school of dramatists who take for their *Dramatis Personæ* not individuals but conventional types, and who somewhat ignore the complexities of human nature. No argument is wanted to show that Shakspere's method of truly holding the mirror up to nature is the higher, the greater, and the truer method, but Jonson has ancient tradition in favour of his view of the dramatic art. . . . Seldom departs from the strict tradition: his cowardly braggarts are most inveterate cowards and braggarts, his knaves most arrant knaves, his fools have no redeeming touch of good sense, and his misers are grasping and avaricious beyond all human precedent and possibility. Nevertheless, the magnificent genius of the man—chiefly a literary genius—takes the reader's judgment by storm; and if the reader's, how much more would the hearer be captivated by the broad persistent humor of Bobadill and the mordant cynicism of Mosca and Volpone!—OSWALD CRAWFORD, *English Comic Dramatists*, 1883, p. 12

The more I read of the literary history of those days the more impressed I am by the predominance of Ben Jonson;—a great, careless, hard-living, hard-drinking, not ill-natured literary monarch. His strength is evidenced by the deference shown him—by his versatility; now some musical masque sparkling with little dainty bits which a sentimental miss might copy in her album or chant in her boudoir; and this, matched or followed by some labored drama full of classic knowledge, full of largest wordcraft, snapping with fire-crackers of wit, loaded with ponderous nuggets of strong sense, and the whole capped and booted with prologue and epilogue where poetic graces shine through proudest averments of indifference—of scorn of applause—of audacious self-sufficiency.—DONALD G. MITCHELL, *English Lands Letters and Kings, From Elizabeth to Anne*, 1890, p. 26

He repels his admirers, he holds readers at arm's length. He is the least sympathetic of all the great English poets, and to appreciate him the rarest of literary tastes is required,—an appetite for dry intellectual beauty, for austerity of thought, for poetry that is logical, and hard, and lusty. Yet he did a mighty work for the English language. At a time when it threatened to sink into mere prettiness or oddity, and to substitute what was non-essential for what was definite and durable, Jonson threw his massive learning and logic into the scale, and forbade Jacobean poetry to kick the beam. He was rewarded by the passionate devotion of a tribe of wits and scholars; he made a deep mark on our literature for several generations subsequent to his own, and he enjoys the perennial respect of all close students of poetry.—EDMUND GOSSE, *The Jacobean Poets*, 1894, pp. 37–38

Jonson, whose splendid scorn took to itself lyric wings in the two great Odes to Himself, sang high and aloof for a while, then the frenzy caught him, and he flung away his lyre to gird himself for deeds of mischief among nameless and noteless antagonists. . . . He lost the calm of his temper and the clearness of his singing voice, he degraded his magnanimity by allowing it to engage in street-brawls, and he endangered the sanctuary of the inviolable soul.—WALTER RALEIGH, *Style*, 1897, pp. 68–71

It was Jonson who first revealed to the age the literary possibilities of the masque, and lesser men were not slow to follow in the path which he had marked out. Had it not been for Jonson, it is hardly too much to say that the masque would today be the exclusive property of the Court chronicler and the antiquarian, and of no more significance to literature than a tilting match or a Christmas gambol.—HERBERT ARTHUR EVANS, "Introduction" to *English Masques*, 1897, p. xi

Works

EVERY MAN IN HIS HUMOUR

In . . . low characters of vice and folly, lay the excellency of ⟨Jonson,⟩ that inimitable writer; who, when at any time he aimed at wit in the stricter sense, that is, sharpness of conceit, was forced either to borrow from the ancients, as to my knowledge he did very much from Plautus; or, when he trusted himself alone, often fell into meanness of expression. Nay, he was not free from the lowest and most grovelling kind of wit, which we call clenches, of which *Every Man in his Humour* is infinitely full; and, which is worse, the wittiest persons in the drama speak them.—JOHN DRYDEN, "Defence of the Epilogue," *Almanzor and Almahide, or the Conquest of Granada*, 1671

Every Man in his Humour is founded on such follies and passions as are perpetually incident to, and connected with, man's nature; such as do not depend upon local custom or change of fashion; and, for that reason, will bid fair to last as long as many of our old comedies. The language of Jonson is very peculiar; in perspicuity and elegance he is inferior to Beaumont and Fletcher, and very unlike the masculine dialogue of Massinger. It is almost needless to observe that he comes far short of the variety, strength, and natural flow, of Shakspeare. To avoid the common idiom, he plunges into stiff, quaint, and harsh, phraseology: he has borrowed more words, from the Latin tongue, than all the other authors of his time. However, the style of this play, as well as that of *The Alchemist* and *Silent Woman*, is more disentangled and free from foreign auxiliaries than the greatest part of his works. Most of the

characters are truly dramatic.—THOMAS DAVIES, *Dramatic Miscellanies*, 1783, Vol. 2, p. 53

Every Man in his Humour is perhaps the earliest of European domestic comedies that deserves to be remembered; for even the Mandragora of Machiavel shrinks to a mere farce in comparison. A much greater master of comic powers than Jonson was indeed his contemporary, and, as he perhaps fancied, his rival; but, for some reason Shakspeare had never yet drawn his story from the domestic life of his countrymen. Jonson avoided the common defect of the Italian and Spanish theatre, the sacrifice of all other dramatic objects to one only, a rapid and amusing succession of incidents: his plot is slight and of no great complexity; but his excellence is to be found in the variety of his characters, and in their individuality, very clearly defined, with little extravagance.—HENRY HALLAM, *Introduction to the Literature of Europe*, 1839, Pt. 2, Ch. 6, Par. 53

EVERY MAN OUT OF HIS HUMOUR

If the reader would see the extravagance of building dramatic manners on abstract ideas, in its full light, he needs only turn to B. Johnson's *Every Man out of his Humour*; which under the name of a *play of character* is in fact, an unnatural, and, as the painters call it, *hard* delination of a group of simply existing passions, wholly chimerical, and unlike to anything we observe in the commerce of real life. Yet this comedy has always had its admirers. And *Randolph* in particular, was so taken with the design, that he seems to have formed his *muse's looking-glass* in express imitation of it.—RICHARD HURD, *A Dissertation on the Several Provinces of the Drama*, 1757, Vol. 1, p. 266

He is above everything a satirist of vice: he hates it, and he lashes it with a whip of scorpions. Listen to Asper—clearly Jonson himself—in the introduction to *Every Man Out of His Humour*. It is very scathing; but it is very splendid. As a mere question, of language, how nervous it is, how like the very best and strongest utterings of our own time! Contempt is the most frequent note; but sometimes it swells to defiance, and becomes gratuitously, recklessly insulting.—T. E. BROWNE, "Ben Jonson," *The New Review*, 1896, Vol. 14, p. 522

CYNTHIA'S REVELS

However we may respect Jonson's sterling qualities as man and poet, we cannot read the prologue and epilogue to *Cynthia's Revels* without resenting its strain of self-laudation. The three characters, used by him as masks in the three "Comical Satires," namely, Asper, Crites, Horace, make us justly angry. We cannot stomach the writer who thus dared to praise and puff himself.—JOHN ADDINGTON SYMONDS, *Ben Jonson*, 1886, p. 35

THE POETASTER

This Roman play ⟨*The Poetaster*⟩ seems written to confute those enemies of Ben in his own days and ours, who have said that he made a pedantical use of his learning. He has here revived the whole Court of Augustus, by a learned spell. We are admitted to the society of the illustrious dead. Virgil, Horace, Ovid, Tibullus, converse in our own tongue more finely and poetically than they were used to express themselves in their native Latin. Nothing can be imagined more elegant, refined, and court-like, than the scenes between this Louis the Fourteenth of antiquity and his literati. The whole essence and secret of that kind of intercourse is contained therein. The economical liberality by which greatness, seeming to waive some part of its prerogative, takes care to lose none of the essentials; the prudential liberties of an inferior, which flatter by commanded boldness and soothe with complimentary sincerity. These, and a thousand beautiful passages from his *New Inn*, his *Cynthia's Revels*, and from those numerous court-masques and entertainments which he was in the daily habit of furnishing, might be adduced to show the poetical fancy and elegance of mind of the supposed rugged old bard. —CHARLES LAMB, *Specimens of English Dramatic Poets*, 1808

Poetaster is Jonson's acknowledged reply to the numerous attacks that had been made upon him during a period of three years. . . . So far as Jonson was concerned "The War of the Theatres" was ended, although peace was not declared. —JOSIAH H. PENNIMAN, *The War of the Theatres*, 1897, p. 118

SEJANUS

Act I.—
　　Arruntius: The name Tiberius,
　　　　I hope, will keep, howe'er he hath foregone
　　　　The dignity and power.
　　Silius: Sure, while he lives.
　　Arr: And dead, it comes to Drusus. Should he fail,
　　　　To the brave issue of Germanicus;
　　　　And they are three: too many (ha?) for him
　　　　To have a plot upon?
　　Sil: I do not know
　　　　The heart of his designs; but, sure, their face
　　　　Looks farther than the present.
　　Arr: By the gods,
　　　　If I could guess he had but such a thought,
　　　　My sword should cleave him down . . .

The anachronic mixture in this Arruntius of the Roman republican, to whom Tiberius must have appeared as much a tyrant as Sejanus, with his James-and-Charles-the-First zeal for legitimacy of descent in this passage, is amusing. Of our great names Milton was, I think, the first who could properly be called a republican. My recollections of Buchanan's works are too faint to enable me to judge whether the historian is not a fair exception.
　　Act ii. Speech of Sejanus:
　　　　Adultery! it is the lightest ill
　　　　I will commit. A race of wicked acts
　　　　Shall flow out of my anger, and o'erspread
　　　　The world's wide face, which no posterity
　　　　Shall e'er approve, nor yet keep silent . . .

The more we reflect and examine, examine and reflect, the more astonished shall we be at the immense superiority of Shakespeare over his contemporaries;—and yet what contemporaries!—giant minds indeed! Think of Jonson's erudition, and the force of learned authority in that age; and yet, in no genuine part of Shakespeare's works is there to be found such an absurd rant and ventriloquism as this, and too, too many other passages ferruminated by Jonson from Seneca's tragedies, and the writings of the later Romans. I call it ventriloquism, because Sejanus is a puppet, out of which the poet makes his own voice appear to come.
　　Act v. Scene of the sacrifice to Fortune.
　　This scene is unspeakably irrational. To believe, and yet to scoff at, a present miracle is little less than impossible. Sejanus should have been made to suspect priestcraft and a secret conspiracy against him. —SAMUEL TAYLOR COLERIDGE, *Notes on Ben Jonson*, 1818

In 1603, he produced his weighty tragedy of *Sejanus*, at Shakespeare's theatre, The Globe,—Shakespeare himself acting one of the inferior parts. Think of Shakespeare laboriously committing to memory the blank verse of Jonson! Though *Sejanus* failed of theatrical success, its wealth of knowledge and solid thought made it the best of all answers to his opponents. It was as if they had questioned his capacity to build a ship, and he had confuted them with a man-of-war. —EDWIN P. WHIPPLE, *The Literature of the Age of Elizabeth*, 1868, p. 102

⟨*Sejanus* was⟩ not very successful, but it succeeded better after he had recast it in part and made it all his own. It was printed in 1605, and the small criticisms of a pedantic age Ben Jonson forestalled by footnotes citing the authority for all that he had worked into harmonious and very noble play. Because the footnotes were there, and looked erudite, the superficial thing to do was to pronounce the play pedantic. But it is not pedantic. Jonson was no pedant. He had carried on for himself the education received at Westminster School, was a good scholar, delighted in his studies, and accumulated a large library, which, in or about the year 1622, was burnt. But he was true poet and true artist. —HENRY MORLEY, and W. HALL GRIFFIN, *English Writers*, 1895, Vol. 11, p. 219

VOLPONE, OR THE FOX

　　. . .the art which thou alone
　Hast taught our tongue, the rules of time, of place,
　And other rites, delivered with the grace
　Of comic style, which only, is far more
　Than any English stage hath known before.
　　　　—FRANCIS BEAUMONT, "To My Dear Friend,
　　　　　Master Ben Jonson, upon his 'Fox,'," 1607?

In the comedy of *The Fox*, there is not much to be censured, except the language, which is so pedantic and struck so full of Latinity, that few, except the learned, can perfectly understand it. "Jonson," says Dr. Young, "brought all the antients upon his head: by studying to speak like a Roman, he forgot the language of his country." —THOMAS DAVIES, *Dramatic Miscellanies*, 1783, Vol. 2, p. 97

This admirable, indeed, but yet more wonderful than admirable, play is, from the fertility and vigour of invention, character, language, and sentiment, the strongest proof how impossible it is to keep up any pleasurable interest in a tale, in which there is no goodness of heart in any of the prominent characters. After the third act, this play becomes not a dead, but a painful, weight on the feelings. *Zeluco* is an instance of the same truth. Bonario and Celia should have been made in some way or other principals in the plot; which they might have been, and the objects of interest, without having been made characters. In novels, the person in whose fate you are most interested, is often the least marked character of the whole. If it were possible to lessen the paramountcy of Volpone himself, a most delightful comedy might be produced, by making Celia the ward or niece of Corvino, instead of his wife, and Bonario her lover. —SAMUEL TAYLOR COLERIDGE, *Notes on Ben Jonson*, 1818

The revolting aspects of life exhibited in ⟨*Volpone*⟩ are likely to prevent full justice being rendered its merits by most modern readers. Yet it long retained its hold over the national stage, while—which is less to be wondered at—the central character continued for generations to express to the popular mind the incarnation of a most loathsome variety of the vast *genus* hypocrite. Everybody knows how, at a critical stage of events in the reign of Queen Anne, Dr. Sacheverell in his notorious sermon pointed an attack upon the Whig leaders as representatives of revolution principles, by alluding to the Lord Treasurer Godolphin under the nickname of the Old Fox or Volpone.—

ADOLPHUS WILLIAM WARD, *A History of English Dramatic Literature*, 1899, Vol. 2, p. 363

EPICOENE, OR THE SILENT WOMAN

When his play of a *Silent Woman* was first acted, ther was found verses after on the stage against him, concluding that that play was well named the *Silent Woman*, ther was never one man to say Plaudite to it.—WILLIAM DRUMMOND, *Notes on Ben Jonson's Conversations*, 1619

⟨*Epicoene*⟩ is to my feelings the most entertaining of old Ben's comedies, and more than any other, would admit of being brought out anew, if under the management of a judicious and stage-understanding play-wright; and an actor, who had studied Morose, might make his fortune.—SAMUEL TAYLOR COLERIDGE, *Notes on Ben Jonson*, 1818

The plot is a distasteful one to my own feelings: it is coarse in design, coarse in its improbability, and, in short, is a direct contradiction of the author's own theory as to that which should characterise *legitimate* comedy; for the play of *Epicene* is little better than a hoydening farce. The character of Morose himself is certainly well sustained, although in it an extreme case is put throughout; and enormous demands are made upon the credulity of the audience that such a man could be supposed to exist at all, with so morbid a sensitiveness to noise as to poison his whole existence.—CHARLES COWDEN CLARKE, "On the Comic Writers of England," 1871, *Gentleman's Magazine*, N.S., Vol. 6, p. 643

THE ALCHEMIST

To say, this comedy pleased long ago,
Is not enough to make it past you now.
Yet, gentlemen, your ancestors had wit;
When few men censured, and when fewer writ.
And Jonson, of those few the best, chose this,
As the best model of his masterpiece.
Subtle was got by our Albumazar,
That Alchymist by this Astrologer;
Here he was fashion'd, and we may suppose
He liked the fashion well, who wore the clothes.
But Ben made nobly his what he did mould;
What was another's lead becomes his gold:
Like an unrighteous conqueror he reigns,
Yet rules that well, which he unjustly gains.
                    —JOHN DRYDEN, "Prologue," *Albumazar*, 1668

This comedy, which was laudably written to ridicule a prevailing folly, must, no doubt, have been greatly successful originally, since we have seen it very much followed and admired during the time Garrick ornamented the stage. His incomparable performance, however, of Abel Drugger was a considerable drawback from the proper reputation of the author, and in great measure the cause of the successs of the play; at the same time it must be confessed that the best acting can do nothing without good materials, with which certainly the *Alchymist* abounds.—CHARLES DIBDIN, *A Complete History of the Stage*, 1795, Vol. 3, p. 295

The judgment is perfectly overwhelmed by the torment of images, words, and book-knowledge, with which Epicure Mammon (Act 2, Scene 2) confounds and stunts his incredulous hearer. They come pouring out like the successive falls of Nilus. They "doubly redouble strokes upon the foe." Description outstrides proof. We are made to believe effects before we have testimony for their causes. If there is no one image which

attains the height of the sublime, yet the confluence and assemblage of them all produces a result equal to the grandest poetry. The huge Xerxean army contervails against single Achilles. Epicure Mammon is the most determined offspring of its author. It has the whole "matter and copy of the father—eye, nose, lip, the trick of his frown." It is just such a swaggerer as contemporaries have described old Ben to be. Meercraft, Bobadil, the Host of the New Inn, have all his image and superscription. But Mammon is arrogant pretension personified. Sir Samson Legend, in "Love for Love," is such another lying, overbearing character, but he does not come up to Epicure Mammon. What a "towering bravery" there is in his sensuality! he affects no pleasure under a Sultan. It is as if "Egypt with Assyria strove in luxury."—CHARLES LAMB, *Specimens of English Dramatic Poets*, 1808

⟨*The Alchemist*⟩ remains, in spite of its proved unfittedness for the stage, and its antiquated interests, one of the most splendid compositions written by an English hand. Lamb, with unerring instinct, hit upon the central jewel of the whole splendid fabric when he selected for special praise the long scene in Subtle's house, where Epicure Mammon boasts what rare things he will do when he obtains the philosopher's stone. Here Jonson, running and leaping under the tremendous weight of his own equipment, perfectly overwhelms the judgment "by the torrent of images, words, and book-knowledge with which Mammon confounds and stuns" us.—EDMUND GOSSE, *The Jacobean Poets*, 1894, p. 28

CATILINE

With strenuous, sinewy words that Catiline swells,
I reckon it not among men—miracles.
How could that poem well a vigour lack,
When each line oft cost Ben a cup of sack.
                    —R. BARON, *Pocula Castalia*, 1650, p. 113

Catiline is only less interesting than *Sejanus*, because it presents no such difficult problem of characterisation as Tiberius. Within the limits of his subject, however, Jonson has fully availed himself of his opportunities. Each of the characters, notably those of the conspirators, stands out distinctly from the rest; perhaps in his effort to draw distinctly, the dramatist has, after his manner, rather overdrawn the humours, thereby impairing the humanity, of his personages,—the visionary imbecility of Lentulus, the braggadocio of Cethegus, the savage ferocity of Catiline. On the other hand, the oratorical expansiveness of Cicero is delicately, though copiously illustrated; the danger is avoided of rendering him ridiculous, although both his love of speech and his respect for his own achievements are allowed ample expression. Of Cæsar and of Cato enough is hardly made; the key to the double-handed policy of the former is not clearly revealed, while the latter appears too generally as the mere echo of Cicero. The female characters of the play are drawn with a humour nothing less than exuberant.—ADOLPHUS WILLIAM WARD, *A History of English Dramatic Literature*, 1899, Vol. 2, p. 341

BARTHOLOMEW FAIR

In *Bartholomew Fair*, or the lowest kind of comedy, that degree of heightening is used, which is proper to set off that subject: It is true the author was not there to go out of prose, as he does in his higher arguments of comedy, *The Fox* and *Alchemist*; yet he does so raise his matter in that prose, as to render it delightful; which he could never had performed, had he only said or done those very things, that are daily spoken or practised in the fair:

for then the fair itself would be as full of pleasure to an in-genious person as the play, which we manifestly see it is not. But he hath made an excellent lazar of it; the copy is of price, though the original be vile. You see in *Catiline* and *Sejanus* where the argument is great, he sometimes ascends to verse, which shows he thought it not unnatural in serious plays; and had his genius been as proper for rhyme as it was for honour, or had the age in which he lived attained to as much knowledge in verse as ours, it is probable he would have adorned those sub-jects with that kind of writing.—JOHN DRYDEN, *A Defence of an Essay of Dramatic Poesy; being an answer to the Preface of the Great Favorite, or The Duke of Lerma*, 1668, p. 296

This strange play, out of which might be framed the humour of half a dozen farces, is fuller, perhaps, of comic characters than any thing that ever appeared on the stage. We are given to understand that Jonson wrote it purposely to ridicule the age in which he lived, for the prevalent preference given to low wit, instead of polished and refined writing. If this was his motive he has outwitted himself, for there is more nature in *Bar-tholomew Fair* than in any one of his other works; but yet, being as it is, crammed full of extraneous and heterogeneous incidents, he has as much overshot the mark as he had come short of it in his *Catiline*, which this play was written purposely to defend; that tragedy having nothing interesting in it, on account of its dullness and declamation; and this comedy, on account of its wildness and extravagance.—CHARLES DIBDIN, *A Complete History of the Stage*, 1795, Vol. 3, p. 297

Absolutely original, so far as is known, in both conception and construction, it abounds with the most direct kind of satire and with the broadest fun.—ADOLPHUS WILLIAM WARD, *A His-tory of English Dramatic Literature*, 1899, Vol. 2, p. 37

There is no dramatic work in English at all comparable in its own kind with this brilliant and bewildering presentment of a comic turmoil, and, by a curious chance, it is exactly here, where it might be expected that the dramatist would be pecu-liarly tempted to subordinate all attempt at character-painting to the mere embodiment of humours, that one of Ben Jonson's few really living and breathing creatures is found in the person of the Puritan, Rabbi Zeal-of-the-Land.—EDMUND GOSSE, *The Jacobean Poets*, 1894, p. 32

THE SAD SHEPHERD

Fletcher's pastoral, blasted as it is in some parts by fire not from heaven, is still a green and leafy wilderness of poetical beauty; Jonson's, deformed also by some brutality more elaborate than anything of the same sort in Fletcher, is at the best but a trim garden, and, had it been ever so happily finished, would have been nothing more.—GEORGE L. CRAIK, *A Compendious History of English Literature and of the English Language*, 1861, Vol. 1, p. 605

A very charming fragment; so sweet and gentle, that it stands alone in conspicuous beauty amidst the rough and stalwart productions of his dramatic Muse.—CHARLES COWDEN CLARKE, "On the Comic Writers of England," 1871, *Gen-tleman's Magazine*, N.S., Vol. 6, p. 649

The *Sad Shepherd* is not quite complete; but, though not with-out a few blots and stains, it contains some of Jonson's finest poetry. The shepherdess Amie is such a sweet creation that one is indignant at the dramatist for the vulgar and wholly super-fluous immodesty of one of her expressions in her first confes-sion of unrest: to the pure all things are pure, but it exposes the simple shepherdess to unnecessary ridicule from the ordinary reader. One is surprised to find such sympathy with simple

innocence in rare but rough Ben—all the more that the *Sad Shepherd* was written in his later years, when he was exacer-bated by failure and poverty.—WILLIAM MINTO, *Charac-teristics of English Poets*, 1885, p. 343

JOHN DRYDEN
From "An Essay of Dramatick Poesie" (1668)
The Works of John Dryden, Volume 17
ed. Samuel Holt Monk
1971, pp. 57–64

As for *Johnson*, to whose Character I am now arriv'd, if we look upon him while he was himself, (for his last Playes were but his dotages) I think him the most learned and judi-cious Writer which any Theater ever had. He was a most severe Judge of himself as well as others. One cannot say he wanted wit, but rather that he was frugal of it. In his works you find little to retrench or alter. Wit and Language, and Humour also in some measure we had before him; but something of Art was wanting to the *Drama* till he came. He manag'd his strength to more advantage then any who preceded him. You seldome find him making Love in any of his Scenes, or endeavouring to move the Passions; his genius was too sullen and saturnine to do it gracefully, especially when he knew he came after those who had performed both to such an height. Humour was his proper Sphere, and in that he delighted most to represent Me-chanick people. He was deeply conversant in the Ancients, both *Greek* and *Latine*, and he borrow'd boldly from them: there is scarce a Poet or Historian among the *Roman* Authours of those times whom he has not translated in *Sejanus* and *Catiline*. But he has done his Robberies so openly, that one may see he fears not to be taxed by any Law. He invades Authours like a Monarch, and what would be theft in other Poets, is onely victory in him. With the spoils of these Writers he so represents old *Rome* to us, in its Rites, Ceremonies and Customs, that if one of their Poets had written either of his Tragedies, we had seen less of it then in him. If there was any fault in his Language, 'twas that he weav'd it too closely and laboriously, in his Comedies especially: perhaps too, he did a little too much Romanize our Tongue, leaving the words which he translated almost as much *Latine* as he found them: wherein though he learnedly followed their language, he did not enough comply with the Idiom of ours. If I would compare him with *Shakespeare*, I must acknowledge him the more cor-rect Poet, but *Shakespeare* the greater wit. *Shakespeare* was the *Homer*, or Father of our Dramatick Poets; *Johnson* was the *Virgil*, the pattern of elaborate writing; I admire him, but I love *Shakespeare*. To conclude of him, as he has given us the most correct Playes, so in the precepts which he has laid down in his *Discoveries*, we have as many and profitable Rules for perfect-ing the Stage as any wherewith the *French* can furnish us.

Having thus spoken of the Authour, I proceed to the ex-amination of his Comedy, *The Silent Woman*.

Examen of the Silent Woman

To begin first with the length of the Action, it is so far from exceeding the compass of a Natural day, that it takes not up an Artificial one. 'Tis all included in the limits of three hours and an half, which is no more than is requir'd for the presentment on the Stage. A beauty perhaps not much ob-serv'd; if it had, we should not have look'd on the *Spanish* Translation of *Five Hours* with so much wonder. The Scene of it is laid in *London*; the latitude of place is almost as little as you can imagine: for it lies all within the compass of two Houses, and after the first Act, in one. The continuity of Scenes is observ'd more than in any of our Playes, except his own *Fox* and *Alchymist*. They are not broken above twice or thrice at most in the whole Comedy, and in the two best of *Corneille's* Playes, the *Cid* and *Cinna*, they are interrupted once. The action of the Play is intirely one; the end or aim of which is the setling *Morose's* Estate on *Dauphine*. The Intrigue of it is the greatest and most noble of any pure unmix'd Comedy in any Language: you see in it many persons of various characters and humours, and all delightful: As first, *Morose*, or an old Man, to whom all noise but his own talking is offensive. Some who would be thought Criticks, say this humour of his is forc'd: but to remove that objection, we may consider him first to be naturally of a delicate hearing, as many are to whom all sharp sounds are unpleasant; and secondly, we may attribute much of it to the peevishness of his Age, or the wayward authority of an old man in his own house, where he may make himself obeyed; and to this the Poet seems to allude in his name *Morose*. Beside this, I am assur'd from divers persons, that *Ben. Johnson* was actually acquainted with such a man, one altogether as ridiculous as he is here represented. Others say it is not enough to find one man of such an humour; it must be common to more, and the more common the more natural. To prove this, they instance in the best of Comical Characters, *Falstaffe*: There are many men resembling him; Old, Fat, Merry, Cowardly, Drunken, Amorous, Vain, and Lying: But to convince these people, I need but tell them, that humour is the ridiculous extravagance of conversation, wherein one man differs from all others. If then it be common, or communicated to many, how differs it from other mens? or what indeed causes it to be ridiculous so much as the singularity of it? As for *Falstaffe*, he is not properly one humour, but a Miscellany of Humours or Images, drawn from so many several men; that wherein he is singular is his wit, or those things he sayes, *præter expectatum*, unexpected by the Audience; his quick evasions when you imagine him surpriz'd, which as they are extreamly diverting of themselves, so receive a great addition from his person; for the very sight of such an unwieldy old debauch'd fellow is a Comedy alone. And here having a place so proper for it I cannot but enlarge somewhat upon this subject of humour into which I am fallen. The Ancients had little of it in their Comedies; for the *to geloin* of the old Comedy, of which *Aristophanes* was chief, was not so much to imitate a man, as to make the people laugh at some odd conceit, which had commonly somewhat of unnatural or obscene in it. Thus when you see *Socrates* brought upon the Stage, you are not to imagine him made ridiculous by the imitation of his actions, but rather by making him perform something very unlike himself: something so childish and absurd, as by comparing it with the gravity of the true *Socrates*, makes a ridiculous object for the Spectators. In their new Comedy which succeeded, the Poets sought indeed to express the *emos* as in their Tragedies the *pathos* of Mankind. But this *emos* contain'd onely the general Characters of men and manners; as old men, Lovers, Servingmen, Courtizans, Parasites, and such other persons as we see in their Comedies; all which they made alike: that is, one old man or Father; one Lover, one Courtizan so like another, as if the first of them had begot the rest of every sort: *Ex homine hunc natum dicas*. The same custome they observ'd likewise in their Tragedies. As for the *French*, though they have the word *humeur* among them, yet they have small use of it in their Comedies, or Farces; they being but ill imitations of the *ridiculum*, or that which stirr'd up laughter in the old Comedy. But among the *English* 'tis otherwise: where by humour is

meant some extravagant habit, passion, or affection; particular (as I said before) to some one person: by the oddness of which, he is immediately distinguish'd from the rest of men; which being lively and naturally represented, most frequently begets that malicious pleasure in the Audience which is testified by laughter: as all things which are deviations from customes are ever the aptest to produce it: though by the way this laughter is onely accidental, as the person represented is Fantastick or Bizarre; but pleasure is essential to it, as the imitation of what is natural. The description of these humours, drawn from the knowledge and observation of particular persons, was the peculiar genius and talent of *Ben. Johnson*; To whose Play I now return.

Besides *Morose*, there are at least 9 or 10 different Characters and humours in the *Silent Woman*, all which persons have several concernments of their own, yet are all us'd by the Poet, to the conducting of the main design to perfection. I shall not waste time in commending the writing of this Play, but I will give you my opinion, that there is more wit and acuteness of Fancy in it then in any of *Ben. Johnson's*. Besides that, he has here describ'd the conversation of Gentlemen in the persons of *True-Wit*, and his Friends, with more gayety, ayre and freedom, then in the rest of his Comedies. For the contrivance of the Plot 'tis extream elaborate, and yet withal easie; for the *lysis*, or untying of it, 'tis so admirable, that when it is done, no one of the Audience would think the Poet could have miss'd it; and yet it was conceald so much before the last Scene, that any other way would sooner have enter'd into your thoughts. But I dare not take upon me to commend the Fabrick of it, because it is altogether so full of Art, that I must unravel every Scene in it to commend it as I ought. And this excellent contrivance is still the more to be admir'd, because 'tis Comedy where the persons are onely of common rank, and their business private, not elevated by passions or high concernments as in serious Playes. Here every one is a proper Judge of all he sees; nothing is represented but that with which he daily converses: so that by consequence all faults lie open to discovery, and few are pardonable. 'Tis this which *Horace* has judiciously observ'd:

> *Creditur ex medio quia res arcessit habere*
> *Sudoris minimum, sed habet Comedia tanto*
> *Plus oneris, quanto veniæ minus.* ──

But our Poet, who was not ignorant of these difficulties, has made use of all advantages; as he who designes a large leap takes his rise from the highest ground. One of these advantages is that which *Corneille* has laid down as the greatest which can arrive to any Poem, and which he himself could never compass above thrice in all this Playes, *viz.* the making choice of some signal and long-expected day, whereon the action of the Play is to depend. This day was that design'd by *Dauphine* for the setling of his Uncles Estate upon him; which to compass he contrives to marry him: that the marriage had been plotted by him long beforehand is made evident by what he tells *True-Wit* in the second Act, that in one moment he had destroy'd what he had been raising many months.

There is another artifice of the Poet, which I cannot here omit, because by the frequent practice of it in his Comedies, he has left it to us almost as a Rule, that is, when he has any Character or humour wherein he would show a *Coup de Maistre*, or his highest skill; he recommends it to your observation by a pleasant description of it before the person first appears. Thus, in *Bartholomew Fair* he gives you the Pictures of *Numps* and *Cokes*, and in this those of *Daw, Lafoole, Morose*, and the *Collegiate Ladies*; all which you hear describ'd before you see them. So that before they come upon the Stage you have a longing expectation of them, which prepares you to receive them favourably; and when they are there, even from their first appearance you are so far acquainted with them, that nothing of their humour is lost to you.

I will observe yet one thing further of this admirable Plot; the business of it rises in every Act. The second is greater then the first; the third then the second, and so forward to the fifth. There too you see, till the very last Scene, new difficulties arising to obstruct the action of the Play; and when the Audience is brought into despair that the business can naturally be effected, then, and not before, the discovery is made. But that the Poet might entertain you with more variety all this while, he reserves some new Characters to show you, which he opens not till the second and third Act. In the second, *Morose, Daw,* the *Barber* and *Otter;* in the third the *Collegiat Ladies:* All which he moves afterwards in by-walks, or under-Plots, as diversions to the main design, least it should grow tedious, though they are still naturally joyn'd with it, and somewhere or other subservient to it. Thus, like a skilful Chest-player, by little and little he draws out his men, and makes his pawns of use to his greater persons.

If this Comedy, and some others of his, were translated into *French* Prose (which would now be no wonder to them, since *Moliere* has lately given them Playes out of Verse which have not displeas'd them) I believe the controversie would soon be decided betwixt the two Nations, even making them the Judges. But we need not call our Hero's to our ayde; Be it spoken to the honour of the *English,* our Nation can never want in any Age such who are able to dispute the Empire of Wit with any people in the Universe. And though the fury of a Civil War, and Power, for twenty years together, abandon'd to a barbarous race of men, Enemies of all good Learning, had buried the Muses under the ruines of Monarchy; yet with the restoration of our happiness, we see reviv'd Poesie lifting up its head, & already shaking off the rubbish which lay so heavy on it. We have seen since His Majesties return, many Dramatick Poems which yield not to those of any forreign Nation, and which deserve all Lawrels but the *English.* I will set aside Flattery and Envy: it cannot be deny'd but we have had some little blemish either in the Plot or writing of all those Playes which have been made within these seven years: (and perhaps there is no Nation in the world so quick to discern them, or so difficult to pardon them, as ours:) yet if we can perswade our selves to use the candour of that Poet, who (though the most severe of Criticks) has left us this caution by which to moderate our censures;

Ubi plura nitent in carmine non ego paucis
offendar maculis.

If in consideration of their many and great beauties, we can wink at some slight, and little imperfections; if we, I say, can be thus equal to our selves, I ask no favour from the *French.* And if I do not venture upon any particular judgment of our late Playes, 'tis out of the consideration which an Ancient Writer gives me; *Vivorum, ut magna admiratio ita censura difficilis:* betwixt the extreams of admiration and malice, 'tis hard to judge uprightly of the living. Onely I think it may be permitted me to say, that as it is no less'ning to us to yield to some Playes, and those not many of our own Nation in the last Age, so can it be no addition to pronounce of our present Poets that they have far surpass'd all the Ancients, and the Modern Writers of other Countreys.

WILLIAM HAZLITT
From *Lectures on the Dramatic Literature of the Age of Elizabeth* (1820)
The Complete Works of William Hazlitt,
ed. P. P. Howe
1931, pp. 262–307

Lecture 4
On Beaumont and Fletcher, Ben Jonson, Ford, and Massinger

Ben Jonson's serious productions are, in my opinion, superior to his comic ones. What he does, is the result of strong sense and painful industry; but sense and industry agree better with the grave and severe, than with the light and gay productions of the muse. "His plays were works," as some one said of them, "while others' works were plays." The observation had less of compliment than of truth in it. He may be said to mine his way into a subject, like a mole, and throws up a prodigious quantity of matter on the surface, so that the richer the soil in which he labours, the less dross and rubbish we have. His fault is, that he sets himself too much to his subject, and cannot let go his hold of an idea, after the insisting on it becomes tiresome or painful to others. But his tenaciousness of what is grand and lofty, is more praiseworthy than his delight in what is low and disagreeable. His pedantry accords better with didactic pomp than with illiterate and vulgar gabble; his learning, engrafted on romantic tradition or classical history, looks like genius.

Miraturque novas frondes et non sua poma.

He was equal, by an effort, to the highest things, and took the same, and even more successful pains to grovel to the lowest. He raised himself up or let himself down to the level of his subject, by ponderous machinery. By dint of application, and a certain strength of nerve, he could do justice to Tacitus and Sallust no less than to mine host of the New Inn. His tragedy of 'The Fall of Sejanus,' in particular, is an admirable piece of ancient mosaic. The principal character gives one the idea of a lofty column of solid granite, nodding to its base from its pernicious height, and dashed in pieces by a breath of air, a word of its creator—feared, not pitied, scorned, unwept, and forgotten. The depth of knowledge and gravity of expression sustain one another throughout: the poet has worked out the historian's outline, so that the vices and passions, the ambition and servility of public men, in the heated and poisoned atmosphere of a luxurious and despotic court, were never described in fuller or more glowing colours. I am half afraid to give any extracts, lest they should be tortured into an application to other times and characters than those referred to by the poet. Some of the sounds, indeed, may bear (for what I know) an awkward construction: some of the objects may look double to squint-eyed suspicion. But that is not my fault. It only proves that the characters of prophet and poet are implied in each other; that he who describes human nature well once, describes it for good and all, as it was, is, and, I begin to fear, will ever be. Truth always was, and must always remain, a libel to the tyrant and the slave. Thus Satrius Secundus and Pinnarius Natta, two public informers in those days, are described as

Two of Sejanus' blood-hounds, whom he breeds
With human flesh, to bay at citizens.

But Rufus, another of the same well-bred gang, debating the point of his own character with two senators whom he has entrapped, boldly asserts, in a more courtly strain,

. . . To be a spy on traitors
Is honourable vigilance.

This sentiment of the respectability of the employment of a government spy, which had slept in Tacitus for near two thousand years, has not been without its modern patrons. The effects of such "honourable vigilance" are very finely exposed in the following high-spirited dialogue between Lepidus and Arruntius, two noble Romans, who loved their country, but were not unfashionable enough to confound their country with its oppressors, and the extinguishers of its liberty.

Arr.: What are thy arts (good patriot, teach them me)
That have preserv'd thy hairs to this white dye,
And kept so reverend and so dear a head
Safe on his comely shoulders?
Lep.: Arts, Arruntius!
None but the plain and passive fortitude
To suffer and be silent; never stretch
These arms against the torrent; live at home
With my own thoughts and innocence about me,
Not tempting the wolves' jaws: these are my arts.
Arr.: I would begin to study 'em, if I thought
They would secure me. May I pray to Jove
In secret, and be safe? ay, or aloud?
With open wishes? so I do not mention
Tiberius or Sejanus! Yes, I must,
If I speak out. 'Tis hard, that. May I think,
And not be rack'd? What danger is't to dream?
Talk in one's sleep, or cough? Who knows the law?
May I shake my head without a comment? Say
It rains, or it holds up, and not be thrown
Upon the Gemonies? These now are things
Whereon men's fortunes, yea, their fate depends;
Nothing hath privilege 'gainst the violent ear.
No place, no day, no hour (we see) is free
(Not our religious and most sacred times)
From some one kind of cruelty; all matter,
Nay, all occasion pleaseth. Madman's rage,
The idleness of drunkards, women's nothing,
Jesters' simplicity, all, all is good
That can be catch'd at.

'Tis a pretty picture; and the duplicates of it, though multiplied without end, are seldom out of request.

The following portrait of a prince besieged by flatterers (taken from 'Tiberius') has unrivalled force and beauty, with historic truth:

. . . If this man
Had but a mind allied unto his words,
How blest a fate were it to us, and Rome?
Men are deceived, who think there can be thrall
Under a virtuous prince. Wish'd liberty
Ne'er lovelier looks than under such a crown.
But when his grace is merely but lip-good,
And that, no longer than he airs himself
Abroad in public, there to seem to shun
The strokes and stripes of flatterers, which within
Are lechery unto him, and so feed
His brutish sense with their afflicting sound,
As (dead to virtue) he permits himself
Be carried like a pitcher by the ears
To every act of vice; this is a case
Deserves our fear, and doth presage the nigh
And close approach of bloody tyranny.
Flattery is midwife unto princes' rage:
And nothing sooner doth help forth a tyrant

Than that, and whisperers' grace, that have the time,
The place, the power, to make all men offenders!

The only part of this play in which Ben Jonson has completely forgotten himself (or rather seems not to have done so) is in the conversations between Livia and Eudemus, about a wash for her face, here called a *fucus*, to appear before Sejanus. 'Catiline's Conspiracy' does not furnish by any means an equal number of striking passages, and is spun out to an excessive length with Cicero's artificial and affected orations against Catiline, and in praise of himself. His apologies for his own eloquence, and declarations that in all his art he uses no art at all, put one in mind of Polonius's circuitous way of coming to the point. Both these tragedies, it might be observed, are constructed on the exact principles of a French historical picture, where every head and figure is borrowed from the antique; but, somehow, the precious materials of old Roman history and character are better preserved in Jonson's page than on David's canvas.

Two of the most poetical passages in Ben Jonson are the description of Echo in 'Cynthia's Revels,' and the fine comparison of the mind to a temple, in the 'New Inn;' a play which, on the whole, however, I can read with no patience. . . .

Lecture 6
On Miscellaneous Poems; F. Beaumont,
P. Fletcher, Drayton, Daniel, etc.;
Sir P. Sidney's 'Arcadia,' and other works

. . . Ben Jonson's detached poetry I like much, as indeed I do all about him, except when he degraded himself by "the laborious foolery" of some of his farcical characters, which he could not deal with sportively, and only made stupid and pedantic. I have been blamed for what I have said, more than once, in disparagement of Ben Jonson's comic humour; but I think he was himself aware of his infirmity, and has (not improbably) alluded to it in the following speech of Crites in 'Cynthia's Revels:'

Oh, how despised and base a thing is man,
If he not strive to erect his groveling thoughts
Above the strain of flesh! But how more cheap,
When even his best and understanding part
(The crown and strength of all his faculties)
Floats like a dead-drown'd body, on the stream
Of vulgar humour, mix'd with common'st dregs:
I suffer for their guilt now; and my soul
(Like one that looks on ill-affected eyes)
Is hurt with mere intention on their follies.
Why will I view them then? my sense might ask me:
Or is't a rarity or some new object
That strains my strict observance to this point:
But such is the perverseness of our nature,
That if we once but fancy levity,
(How antic and ridiculous soever
It suit with us) yet will our muffled thought
Chuse rather not to see it than avoid it . . .

Ben Jonson had self-knowledge and self-reflection enough to apply this to himself. His tenaciousness on the score of critical objections does not prove that he was not conscious of them himself, but the contrary. The greatest egotists are those whom it is impossible to offend, because they are wholly and incurably blind to their own defects; or if they could be made to see them, would instantly convert them into so many beauty-spots and ornamental graces. Ben Jonson's fugitive and lighter pieces are not devoid of the characteristic merits of that class of composition; but still often in the happiest of them, there is a specific gravity in the author's pen, that sinks him to the bottom of his subject, though buoyed up for a time with art and painted plumes, and produces a strange mixture of the mechanical and fanciful, of poetry and prose, in his songs and odes. For instance, one of his most airy effusions is the 'Triumph of his Mistress:' yet there are some lines in it that seem inserted almost by way of burlesque. It is, however, well worth repeating.

> See the chariot at hand here of love
> Wherin my lady rideth!
> Each that draws it is a swan or a dove;
> And well the car love guideth!
> As she goes all hearts do duty
>   Unto her beauty:
> And enamour'd, do wish so they might
>   But enjoy such a sight,
> That they still were to run by her side,
> Through swords, through seas, whither she would
>   ride.
> Do but look on her eyes, they do light
>   All that love's world compriseth!
> Do but look on her hair, it is bright
>   As love's star when it riseth!
> Do but mark, her forehead's smoother
>   Than words that soothe her:
> And from her arch'd brows, such a grace
>   Sheds itself through the face,
> As alone their triumphs to the life
> All the gain, all the good of the elements' strife.
> Have you seen but a bright lily glow,
> Before rude hands have touch'd it?
> Ha' you mark'd but the fall of the snow
> Before the soil hath smutch'd it?
> Ha' yu felt *the wool of beaver?*
> Or swan's down ever?
> Or have smelt o' the bud o' the briar?
> Or *the nard in the fire?*
> Or have tasted the bag of the bee?
> Oh, so white! Oh, so soft! Oh, so sweet is she!

His 'Discourse with Cupid,' which follows, is infinitely delicate and *piquant*, and without one single blemish. It is a perfect "nest of spicery."

> Noblest Charis, you that are
> Both my fortune and my star!
> And do govern more my blood,
> Than the various moon the flood!
> Hear, what late discourse of you,
> Love and I have had; and true.
> 'Mongst my Muses finding me,
> Where he chanc'd your name to see
> Set, and to this softer strain;
> 'Sure,' said he, 'If I have brain,
> This here sung can be no other,
> By description, but my mother!
> So hath Homer prais'd her hair;
> So Anacreon drawn the air
> Of her face, and made to rise,
> Just about her sparkling eyes,
> Both her brows bent like my bow.
> By her looks I do her know,
> Which you call my shafts. And see!
> Such my mother's blushes be,
> As the bath your verse discloses
> In her cheeks, of milk and roses;
> Such as oft I wanton in.

> And, above her even chin,
> Have you plac'd the bank of kisses,
> Where you say, men gather blisses,
> Ripen'd with a breath more sweet,
> Than when flowers and west-winds meet,
> Nay, her white and polish'd neck,
> With the lace that doth it deck,
> Is my mother's! hearts of slain
> Lovers, made into a chain!
> And between each rising breast
> Lies the valley, call'd my nest,
> Where I sit and proyne my wings
> After flight; and put new stings
> To my shafts! Her very name
> With my mother's is the same.'—
> 'I confess all,' I replied,
> 'And the glass hangs by her side,
> And the girdle 'bout her waist,
> All is Venus: save unchaste.
> But, alas! thou seest the least
> Of her good, who is the best
> Of her sex; but could'st thou, Love,
> Call to mind the forms that strove
> For the apple, and those three
> Make in one, the same were she.
> For this beauty yet doth hide
> Something more than thou hast spied.
> Outward grace weak love beguiles:
> She is Venus when she smiles,
> But she's Juno when she walks,
> And Minerva when she talks.'

In one of the songs in 'Cynthia's Revels,' we find, amidst some very pleasing imagery, the origin of a celebrated line in modern poetry—

> Drip, drip, drip, drip, drip . . .

This has not even the merit of originality, which is hard upon it. Ben Jonson had said two hundred years before,

> Oh, I could still
> (Like melting snow upon some craggy hill)
> Drop, drop, drop, drop,
> Since nature's pride is now a wither'd daffodil.

His 'Ode to the Memory of Sir Lucius Cary and Sir H. Morrison' has been much admired, but I cannot but think it one of his most fantastical and perverse performances.

I cannot, for instance, reconcile myself to such stanzas as these:

> Of which we priests and poets say
> Such truths as we expect for happy men,
> And there he lives with memory; and Ben

> *The Stand.*
> Jonson, who sung this of him, ere he went
> Himself to rest,
> Or taste a part of that full joy he meant
> To have exprest,
> In this bright asterism;
> Where it were friendship's schism
> (Were not his Lucius long with us to tarry)
> To separate these twi-
> Lights, the Dioscori;
> And keep the one half from his Harry.
> But fate doth so alternate the design,
> While that in Heaven, this light on earth doth shine.

This seems as if because he cannot without difficulty write smoothly, he becomes rough and crabbed in a spirit of defiance, like those persons who cannot behave well in company, and affect rudeness to show their contempt for the opinions of others.

His 'Epistles' are particularly good, equally full of strong sense and sound feeling. They show that he was not without friends, whom he esteemed, and by whom he was deservedly esteemed in return. The controversy started about his character is an idle one, carried on in the mere spirit of contradiction, as if he were either made up entirely of gall, or dipped in "the milk of human kindness." There is no necessity or ground to suppose either. He was no doubt a sturdy, plain-spoken, honest, well-disposed man, inclining more to the severe than the amiable side of things; but his good qualities, learning, talents, and convivial habits preponderated over his defects of temper or manners; and in a course of friendship some difference of character, even a little roughness or acidity, may relish to the palate; and olives may be served up with effect as well as sweetmeats. Ben Jonson, even by his quarrels and jealousies, does not seem to have been curst with the last and damning disqualification for friendship,—heartless indifference. He was also what is understood by a *good fellow*, fond of good cheer and good company: and the first step for others to enjoy your society, is for you to enjoy theirs. If any one can do without the world, it is certain that the world can do quite as well without him. His 'Verses Inviting a Friend to Supper' give us as familiar an idea of his private habits and character, as his 'Epistle to Michael Drayton,' that to Selden, &c.; his 'Lines to the Memory of Shakspeare,' and his noble prose 'Eulogy on Lord Bacon,' in his disgrace, do a favourable one.

JOHN ADDINGTON SYMONDS
From *Ben Jonson*
1886, pp. 50–121

Chapter 3
Jonson's Dramatic Style

Those who have made a special study of Ben Jonson will agree, I think, in judging that his fame must ultimately rest upon four comedies—*Volpone*, *The Alchemist*, *The Silent Woman*, and *Bartholomew Fair*. If a fifth be added to this number, they will unanimously vote for *Every Man in his Humour*. Should such critics differ, the points at issue will probably concern the order of these plays in merit, and the question whether *Every Man in his Humour* is not superior to *The Silent Woman*. At the point we have reached in Jonson's biography, I propose to pause and analyse these four plays in detail. This appears to me the best way of introducing Jonson in his character of playwright to the modern public; even though the minute dissection of comedies and the criticism of characters must involve of necessity some tedious passages. But before proceeding to examine the plays themselves in chronological order, I shall preface this inquiry with remarks on Jonson's style in general.

When our author in his *Poetaster* made Dekker twit him with being 'a mere sponge, nothing but humours and observation,' when Marston in the same play taxed him for 'filching by translation,' Jonson struck the key-note of his own dramatic style. What first strikes us in studying one of his plays is the extraordinary combination of accurately imitated manners with voluminous erudition. The common people of Elizabethan London, frequenters of the aisles of St. Paul's, danglers about the theatres, haunters of taverns and worse places of amusement, sharpers and their dupes, actors and their cronies, bad poets and cowardly captains, country gentlemen and Puritans from Amsterdam, vulgar city knights, poor squires, spendthrift heirs, madams who wear acres in pounced velvet on their backs, miserly old men, pedlars, bear-leaders, watercarriers, Thames watermen, all the motley crowd of street and fair and market-place and river, jostle together, each with wellseized peculiarities, like the puppets of a marionette show. The fund of humours is inexhaustible; the observation with which they have been caught and made fit subjects for the comic muse is penetrative. But they are set for us in a quaint framework of elaborate learning. All the classics have been ransacked to point their foibles and exhibit their absurdities. The literature of the Renaissance, Erasmus and Rabelais, the literature of the Middle Ages, books on sports and hunting, books on alchemy, books on natural history, books on Rosicrucian mysticism, furnish unexpected illustrations of the commonest, most vulgar incidents. Beneath the cumbersome panoply of close translations from Greek and Latin authors, ponderous quotations and barbarous jargon out of dusty libraries, these puppets of the moment skip and jump and play their pranks with strange mechanic nimbleness. This combination of the pithiest realism with encyclopædic erudition is the first thing to notice about Jonson; and for modern readers it forms a serious obstacle to the enjoyment of his art. We have to learn, as it were, a new language before we can enter into the spirit of his comedy.

It has been well said that his dramas are like solidly built houses from which the scaffolding has not been removed. We recognise the skill of their construction and the substantial strength of the edifice; but we never fail to be too conscious of the means employed for a desired result. Admirably as the plots of his best pieces are put together, so admirably that they have wrung enthusiastic applause from brother craftsmen, yet they strike us as Titanic timber-work. Jonson piqued himself on making his own plots, not dramatising a novel or a history, as was the fashion of that day. Consequently, his plays are all of one piece: the whole and the parts of each bespeak the man from whose strong brain they issued. Without predecessor and without legitimate successor, he stands alone, colossal, ironjointed, the Behemoth of the drama.

Jonson's style is vigorous, robustly English, rarely condescending to the graces of melodious diction. Yet when we analyse his language, we shall find that it is frequently a cento of translations from the classics. This wholesale and indiscriminate translation is managed with admirable freedom. He held the prose writers and poets of antiquity in solution in his spacious memory. He did not need to dovetail or weld his borrowings into one another; but rather, having fused them in his own mind, poured them plastically forth into the mould of thought. Therefore, unless we happen to recognise the originals on whom he has been drawing, we shall fancy that he is speaking from his own stores. This kind of looting from classical treasuries of wit and wisdom was accounted no robbery in that age; and Jonson's panegyrists praised him as a conqueror who spoiled the empires of the past like Alexander. 'The greatest man of the last age, Ben Jonson,' says Dryden, 'was willing to give place to the classics in all things: he was not only a professed imitator of Horace, but a learned plagiary of all the others; you track him everywhere in their snow. If Horace, Lucan, Petronius Arbiter, Seneca, and Juvenal had their own from him, there are few serious thoughts which are new in him. But he has done his robberies so openly, that one may see he fears not to be taxed by any law. He invades authors like a monarch; and what would be theft in other poets is only victory in him.'[1]

Another general point to notice is that, though a careful

observer and minute recorder, Jonson rarely touched more than the outside of character. Not penetrating with the clairvoyance of imagination into the groundwork of personality, but constructing individuals from what appears of them upon the surface, he was too apt to present one glaring quality to the exclusion of all others. Thus his men and women are the incarnations of abstract properties rather than living human beings. We obtain a clear conception of them, and remember each apart from his neighbour. But the rigid maintenance of their master-passion, the strict definition of their leading humour, gives them an air of mechanism. In this respect the feeblest of the romantic dramatists excelled him. While Jonson made masks, the despised Dekker and Heywood created souls. Their persons move before us with the reality of life; we become familiar with them as entire men and women.

The critical distinction here indicated is so important in its bearings on Jonson's relation to the drama of his day that I must take leave to enlarge on it. The comedy of character and manners, which was derived from antique models, brought types rather than individuals into play. Its *dramatis personæ* were the jealous man, the avaricious man, the misanthrope, the wanton woman: who are always jealous, always avaricious, always misanthropical, always wanton. Romantic art, whether tragic or comic, the English art which rebelled against classical precedent and gave Shakespeare to the world, has never pursued this course. It aims at the creation of personalities, in whom such qualities, though predominant and determinative of the dramatic action, shall yet be blended with a multiplicity of other moral motives, as they usually are in life. We find this tendency even in the allegories of the Moral Plays, where men like Hick Scorner, women like Delilah, speedily supplant the personified abstractions of Juventus or Abominable Living. When the romantic style obtained its victory in England, the licences of time and place involved in the dramatisation of a novel favoured this truer and more vital character-drawing. It enabled great artists to exhibit the development of a quality which shall tyrannise over the whole nature of the man. In Othello we witness the growth of jealousy, in Macbeth the growth of ambition, in Timon the growth of misanthropy, in Coriolanus the growth of pride, in Antony the growth of amorous dotage, to such a degree of predominance that their destinies are irretrievably determined by the mastery which one moral element has gained over the whole complex of their nature. To use German phrases, the romantic sphere of art is *das Werdende*, not *das Bestimmte*: character in process of formation, not fixed types. It is just here that Jonson diverged most radically from the spirit of the English drama in his age. He starts with character, set, formed, fully defined; a master passion in complete empire; the man absorbed in his specific humour. This he unfolds with inexhaustible variety and brilliant wit before our eyes. He creates as many situations and occasions as he can for its display. But it never alters. The strict logic of his powerful understanding, his grasp of common circumstance, the immense resources of his thought and language, enabled him to flash rays of light on each facet of the chosen humour. Yet we always know what to expect in every conceivable situation where his persons shall be placed. Asper is sure to utter a censure; Macilente, a reflection on the unmerited good fortune of his neighbours; Sir Epicure Mammon disappoints us if he opens his mouth without indulging in some gorgeous dream of far-fetched luxury, or some vast speculation on his future wealth; Morose must always shut his ears from noise, and bawl out for tranquillity. All the persons of Jonson's comedies are thus like masqueraders, with whom it is a point of honour to maintain a certain assumed character; and the index

to their maker's notion of their duties may be aptly studied in his list of persons prefixed to *Every Man out of his Humour*. I have already remarked that the romantic licence as to time and place favoured the Shakespearian grasp of character in evolution. Macbeth could not grow from a bluff general into a world-wearied tyrant, Timon from a generous spendthrift into a cynical man-hater, Antony from a bold politician into a woman's plaything, in a single day. Given but twenty-four hours for the dramatic action, and fixed types of character, which do not grow, but are analysed, become inevitable. Now Jonson was so far a classic by culture and instinct that he adhered to the unities; and comedy, in which he principally dealt, has ever observed them. His mechanical handling of character belonged, therefore, in a measure to his ideal of art. Still this consideration will not suffice to excuse him altogether. He fails in so far as he does not analyse the type presented, as Molière does, but is contented with displaying and illustrating its outer form.

It is possible that the woodenness which fatigues the reader of all but Jonson's five best comedies may not have struck spectators of the same plays on the stage. Perpetual movement, bright costume, and the vivacity of actors can touch a stiff mechanic thing with liveliness. None of Jonson's pieces suffer from deficiency of business; and his personages are so sharply defined that they offer opportunities to able players. Regarded as forms to be filled with the actor's own breath of life and individuality, even these mechanic puppets may have moved mirth.

Lest I should overstate the case against Jonson for mechanical hardness of delineation, I ought to remark that this defect is closely allied to one of his chief qualities. No playwright of that age, if we except Shakespeare, had so eminent a power of characterisation. The truth of this will be apparent in the next chapter, where I propose to examine his four greatest comedies. It is mainly in the minor personages of his drama that the author's method tends to rigidity. We are too much aware of his intention, and of the means he uses to attain certain effects. To borrow a phrase from painting, there is a want of atmosphere in his elaborated pictures. And here, since no better opportunity will present itself, I may introduce what I have to say about his two tragedies, 'the flat sanity and smoke-dried sobriety' of which have been alluded to by Mr. Swinburne. *Sejanus* and *Catiline* are Roman history done into robust blank verse—Tacitus, Cicero, and Sallust not always bettered by translation. Coleridge wished that we had more of these ponderous studies. He must surely have forgotten the tedium of the minor characters; the long soliloquies; the interminable orations; the heavy choruses in Seneca's manner. And yet these plays are distinguished by two eminent qualities: sustained dignity of language, and trenchant character-drawing. In *Sejanus*, both Tiberius and his favourite are portrayed with masterly force. A tyrant advancing to his ends by dissimulation, and a vulgar upstart calling down upon his head the vengeance of the gods by arrogant self-confidence, could not be more vigorously contrasted. The moral atmosphere of imperial Rome, clogged with suspicion and heavy with dread, as

> when Jove
> Will o'er some high-viced city hang his poison
> In the sick air,

weighs upon us while we thread the laboriously developed intricacies of the plot. That *Sejanus* could not have been a good acting play is certain; and the same may be said about *Catiline*, which its author preferred, and I think rightly. This tragedy well repays careful perusal, however. It compels our interest and our admiration by its rugged Roman strength. The first act, which is wholly devoted to the conspirators, might be quoted as a magnificent study in the sombre manner of a literary Salvator Rosa. Wily and plausible Catiline sets off the vain and superstitious Lentulus; vehement Cethegus, blinded by his blood-lust, finds a foil in the twice-dyed traitor Curius; cautious Cæsar presents a striking contrast to lukewarm, egotistical Antonius. Cicero, always over-voluble of speech, yet dignified by patriotism and rendered amiable by a kind of personal grace, shines with benign radiance by the side of downright, hot-headed Cato, and vindictive Catulus. The two female characters are no less effectively presented. Fulvia, a voluptuous Roman wanton of Messalina's type; Sempronia, who dabbles in politics, reads Greek, and thinks herself the match of Cicero in eloquence, of Cæsar in statecraft. Both are treacherous: Sempronia to the State, Fulvia to the conspiracy. From these two tragedies passages of great poetic beauty, noble images, and weighty maxims might be culled. Jonson made no idle boast when he called attention to his 'height of elocution' and to the 'fullness and frequency of sentence,' in which, with Milton, he recognised 'the offices of a tragic writer.'

When we inquire into the causes which breed satiety in the readers of Jonson's plays, we shall find that a fatal inability to stop at the right moment is a principal. He never knew when his audience might fairly be supposed to have enough of the substantial diet set before them; but went on heaping period on period, and turning a brace of thoughts in a score of fashions. Whether the character on which he is engaged be Horace or Tucca matters little. He employs the same labour in developing his protagonists and his supernumeraries. Nor does he spare rhetoric when dealing with repulsive themes. It has, therefore, well been said of him that 'his tenaciousness of what is grand and lofty is more praiseworthy than his delight in what is low and disagreeable.' But we have no right to assert that he took pleasure in the vulgar for its own sake. If he had that on hand, he worked it out as fully as the nobler elements of art. All the authors of the English Renaissance erred on the side of redundancy. But while Shakespeare and Fletcher were carried away by a luxuriant fancy, Jonson yielded to prodigious memory and a scholar's conscientiousness. He tells us that he wrote in prose first, and then versified. This probably accounts for the long-winded paragraphs of frigidly expanded oratory which surfeit our attention. Like a mole, as it has been well put, he burrowed into his material, and threw up the soil upon the surface. If, then, he chanced on rich and generous veins, his readers had the benefit; no substance is more marrowy or charged with mental stuff. If not, he still performed the delver's toil, turning the last clod of a clayey earth with satisfaction to himself.[2]

I have touched upon his vast and indiscriminate learning. In the employment of this he neglected the Greek rule of 'Nothing overmuch,' no less than in his rhetorical expansion of given themes. We gasp astounded at the wealth of erudition he possessed. Not only the choicer authors of antiquity, on whom a humanistic education is built up; but the sophists, compilers, grammarians, and historical epitomists of the decadence—men like Athenæus, Libanius, Philostratus, the writers of Augustan histories, scholiasts, Strabo, Photins—obey his bidding. The fragments of Greek tragic and comic poets, then embedded in the prose of obscure essayists: the fragments of Ennius and Lucilius; the fragments of Æolic lyrists and Ionian sages; the fragments of Roman inscriptions, imperfectly distributed through treatises of dull Italian scholars: all had been appropriated by his indefatigable industry. Not a jot or tittle of this curious learning does he spare us in his comedies. The same is true of even more recondite subjects. Subtle delivers exact lectures upon alchemy. The *Masque of Queens* supplies an encyclopædia of witchcraft. The foresters of masque and pastoral expound venery. In one laborious scene he teaches the science of cosmetics; in another the mysteries of the Rosicrucian order. He cannot call upon Arcadian nymphs to scatter flowers without reciting a list of twenty-seven species, in which the pride of Elizabethan horticulture seems to be epitomised. This determination to be exhaustive belonged to some essentially scientific quality of Jonson's mind. Order, classification, rule, measure, governed his conception of the literary builder's art; and he was not satisfied unless he had accumulated on each given point the whole mass of its learning; yet his robust shoulders were scarcely burdened with the weight they bore. Like Atlas, he supported a world of knowledge. But, all the while, he moved beneath that load with no more effort than war-elephants who carry garrisons upon their backs. It is the mark of insolently virile intellects to sustain the bulk of erudition with facility, and to sport beneath a camel's pack in wantonness. Lord Macaulay, in his comparatively smaller way, came near to Jonson; but no one who has not read and re-read *Volpone* or *The Alchemist* has formed a true conception of elephantine sprightliness.

Jonson paid the penalty of these extraordinary qualities. It follows from what I have said of his work that he put nothing into his plays which patient criticism may not extract: the wand of the enchanter has not passed over them. There is no music which we hear but shall not capture; no aërial hues that elude description; no 'scent of violets hidden in the grass'; no 'light that never was on sea or land'; no 'casements opening on the foam of perilous seas in faery lands forlorn.' These higher gifts of poetry, with which Shakespeare—'nature's child'—was so richly endowed, are almost absolutely wanting in Ben Jonson. Perhaps the names of Earine and Aeglamour in the *Sad Shepherd*, and a few of this shepherd's speeches, have just a touch of the enchantment. On its rare occurrence in Jonson's masques and lyrics I shall dwell when my argument brings me to that part of the inquiry.

In Jonson's qualities of style we discern the same robust virtues and the same limitations. For his prose I must confess a deep and reverent partiality. Its massive periods are moulded with a force anticipating Milton at his best; and at times he sparkles into epigrams and fiery fits of passion, emitted in single sentences, beyond which it were impossible for our speech to travel. His blank verse is always manly, always individual;—unlike that of any of his contemporaries;—but grace, subtlety, emotion, suggestiveness, are wanting, sacrificed to scholarly solidity and even strength. I cannot but think that it suffered greatly from the poet's habit of converting prose into verse, whereby the thews of prose were wasted on a tolerable mediocrity of metre. It never falls very low; but it rarely rises to imaginative or impassioned heights. It is rough-hewn with the sinews of a Cyclops; but no Praxitelean finish has been bestowed upon this brawny chisel-work; no Ariel of the spirit has blown the poet's feeling into the fine stuff of thought, to float and shine with permanent or passing iridescence: such exquisite tenuity of verse, in short, as we rejoice in when we find it in the work of men like Fletcher or like humble Dekker. It wants lightness and the charm of chance. Indeed, when we compare Ben Jonson's blank verse style with that of the least of his contemporaries, we seem to be contemplating a sound substantial edifice of the Palladian manner—the front of Whitehall for example. Whereas Massinger reminds us of the intricacies of Sansovino, Shakespeare of Gothic aisles or heaven's cathedral, Fletcher of the sylvan architecture of wild green-woods, Ford of glittering Corinthian colonnades, Webster of vaulted crypts, Heywood of homely manor-houses on our English country-side, Marlowe of masoned clouds, and Marston, in his better moments, of the fragmentary vigour of a Roman ruin.

Jonson's art of translation, so highly prized by him, so envied by his rivals, was of a like texture; fabric, not of fancy or imagination, but of understanding. It would be easy to cite examples. They may be culled in both his tragedies by handfuls; but I would not call him to the bar of criticism there. I prefer to go further afield, and invite my readers to study the lines from the fourth Æneid which he placed on Virgil's lips in the *Poetaster* (act v. sc. 1); or to indicate the version from a passage of Catullus on the cropped flower in his *Barriers*. These show that the exquisite sensibility to perfume in an antique author's style failed Jonson. And yet, when I have said so much, I must face round, and add that lyric visitings were not unfrequent to his muse. In other words, he was at times felicitous. He found for a fragment of Sappho,

Lēros angelos himerophōnos aēdōn

this phrase:

The dear good angel of the spring,
The nightingale.

He turned a score of scattered sentences from the prose of Philostratus into that deathless song, 'Drink to me only with thine eyes.' Like many poets whom the muses love, Jonson uttered his best things by accident, and what weighed heavily upon his genius was the fixed idea that scholarship and sturdy labour could supply the place of inspiration.

Before concluding these remarks upon the general features of Jonson's dramatic style, I must point out the fact that he failed to create a single female character of excellence. We do not expect from him an Imogen, a Duchess of Malfi, or even an Aspasia. Such women belong essentially to the romantic species, and it is only in *The Case is Altered* and *The New Inn* that Jonson tried to assume the tone of romantic art. Yet it might have been thought that he would have produced something in the same kind as Dame Quickly. This, however, is not the case. With the exception of Widow Purecraft and her daughter, in *Bartholomew Fair*, and Mrs. Fitz Dottrel in *The Devil is an Ass*, and Lady Frampul in *The New Inn*, all Jonson's women are mere pieces of machinery—more wooden than his men.

This defect is remarkable, because he possessed one virtue which was rare in that century, and which showed a delicacy of feeling that ought to have made him appreciative of feminine excellence. His plays, though often coarse and nasty, are never licentious. To the public taste for filthy jests he refused to pander, nor would he allow his art to palliate immorality by adding the charm of pathos, wit, or poetic beauty to vice. Indeed, he treated wickedness of every kind so sternly that even his best plays fail to win our sympathy from the utter atrocity of their characters and the nakedness with which Jonson has unmasked them. Hallam says justly of *Volpone* that 'five of the principal characters are wicked beyond any retribution that comedy can dispense;' while Coleridge remarks that the extreme badness of the personages destroys the interest of this stupendous play. The spectacle of their unmitigated evil presented to our gaze affects us much in the same way as the perusal of a treatise on ethics. Instead of regarding these monsters as men with passions like our own, we recognise the abstractions which a powerful rhetorician has gifted with mechanical vitality.

At the end of this inquiry into the general characteristics

of Jonson's style, it will be useful to survey the whole course of his development as a playwright, and to classify the various species of his dramas which have survived. The first period of his activity was occupied in romantic journey-work. Of the fruits of these earliest labours, if we except *The Case is Altered*, we possess nothing. To ascribe the fragment of *Mortimer* to that epoch of his life would be dangerous, in the absence of any direct evidence; though it may be mentioned that a play bearing that title was being acted in 1602. The additions to *The Spanish Tragedy* were written three years after he had formed his own peculiar style. *Every Man in his Humour* (1598) marks the emergence of this original manner, formed upon observation of contemporary life and exact study of the ancients. It also opens the cycle of his comedies of humours, which he closed, in his old age, with *The Magnetic Lady*. But after arriving at self-consciousness, and creating his own art in this epoch-making play, Jonson swerved aside and abandoned the comic drama, properly so called, for what he termed comical satire, in *Every Man out of his Humour* and *Cynthia's Revels* (1599 and 1600). These two pieces are rather puppet-shows of character, affording scope for satirical caricatures, analytical descriptions of contemporary affectations, humorous dialogues, and witty personifications of abstract qualities, than comedies. They cannot properly be said to have an action or a plot. The one reminds us of a morality, the other of a masque. We notice, moreover, that the influence of the Latin drama is now exchanged for that of the *Plutus* of Aristophanes, which henceforth exercised a somewhat baneful power over Jonson's method. The tendency to general and personal satire, which had already been perceptible in *The Case is Altered*, was now freely indulged. The playwright, posing as an Aristarchus and a Juvenal, made bitter enemies, not only among men of letters, but also among players and playgoers, courtiers and soldiers. The quarrels in which he became involved led to the production of the *Poetaster* (1601). This was no puppet-show of humours, but a play, in which living characters contributed by their action to the development of a plot. After the *Poetaster*, Jonson abandoned comedy for tragedy, producing *Sejanus* (1603) in a style to some extent modelled upon that of Seneca. It was followed by a second tragic play called *Catiline* (1611). These two plays achieved, and deserved, only a cold success of esteem. But before the latter date he had resumed his 'learned sock.' *Volpone* (1605), *The Silent Woman* (1609), *The Alchemist* (1610), and *Bartholomew Fair* (1614), followed each other within the space of nine industrious years. Four true comedies, excellent in plot, masterly in character-drawing, vigorous in style, were added to the treasures of English literature. The manner, which was first formed in *Every Man in his Humour*, reached its full expansion in these masterpieces. On the accession of James I., Jonson opened a new vein by the production of his masques and entertainments. Here he found scope for the lyrical faculty and capricious inventiveness which lurked beneath the rugged exterior of his dramatic muse. But though he showed a decided preference for this sort of composition, he did not abandon the comedy of humours. *The Devil is an Ass* (1616) may be reckoned a satisfactory piece of workmanship in the manner specific to Ben Jonson. But *The Staple of News* (1625), founded upon the *Plutus* of Aristophanes; *The New Inn* (1629), an attempt to break ground in romantic comedy too late; *The Magnetic Lady* (1632), which closes the cycle of humours, and *A Tale of a Tub* (1633), which feebly echoes the Rabelaisian laughter of *Bartholomew Fair*: all of these five latest products of Jonson's pen deserve the hard sentence which was passed on them by Dryden. They are works of his decadence. In this brief bird's-eye view of his dramatic industry, it only remains to mention the fragment of a tragedy called *Mortimer*, which was found among his papers after his death, and an imperfect pastoral entitled *The Sad Shepherd*. I shall have to enter at some length into questions relating to the date of this pastoral. Here they would be out of place. It is enough to say that this rustic play combines Jonson's regularity of structure with the fancy which had sported so freely in the best of his masques. The prologue, as we have it, was written about 1637 in the last months of the poet's life. But it is scarcely credible that the still extant portion of the drama can have been composed at that epoch. We have at any rate to deplore the accident—whether of Jonson's death before the piece was finished, or of the carelessness with which his MSS. were handled after his decease—whereby English dramatic literature has been defrauded of what would otherwise have been its most ingeniously constructed and firmly executed pastoral play.

After this summary review of Jonson's dramatic works, it will be possible to arrange them in the following groups. First of all we may place the two tragedies, *Sejanus* and *Catiline*, with the fragment of *Mortimer*. The masques, triumphs, entertainments, barriers, form a second class. The unfinished *Sad Shepherd* has to stand alone, touching the masques on one side and the comedies upon the other. I am inclined to place *The Case is Altered*, *The New Inn*, and the additions to the *Spanish Tragedy* in a fourth group, since these illustrate Jonson's essays in romantic art. *The Silent Woman*, *Bartholomew Fair*, and *A Tale of a Tub* may be described as farces. To comedies of humour we can assign *Every Man in his Humour*, *Every Man out of his Humour*, *Cynthia's Revels*, *The Devil is an Ass*, *The Staple of News*, and *The Magnetic Lady*. It is true that these plays differ much in their construction; two following the model of Aristophanic allegory, one moulding itself upon the type of Latin comedy, and one borrowing suggestions from the masque. Yet all are marked by the same observation of humours, as the phrase was understood by Jonson. *The Poetaster*, on account of its avowed satiric intention and the peculiarity of its Roman fable, must stand alone, though Jonson would probably have classed it with *Every Man out of his Humour* and *Cynthia's Revels* under the name of comical satire. The two masterpieces of Jonson's dramatic art, *Volpone* and *The Alchemist*, cannot be grouped with comedies of humour. *Volpone* is a deeply reaching dramatic satire on the vice of covetousness. *The Alchemist* is a comedy of character and manners, indulging a lighter vein of satire upon human foibles. In form, it leans more to the farcical type than its sombre predecessor.

Chapter 4
The Masterpieces
Volpone

Volpone is no mere comedy of humours or comical satire. It is a sinister and remorseless analysis of avarice in its corrosive influence on human character. Nowhere else has Jonson with so firm a touch bared one master vice, absorbing and perverting all the virtues, passions, and rational faculties of man. 'The accursed thirst for gold' is here displayed as a fell tyrant, swaying the love of kindred and of honour; before which lust, jealousy, and fear of shame are forced to bow; which compels an Italian husband to prostitute his wife, an advocate to perjure himself twice in open court, a gentleman to disinherit and disown his son, an English lady to risk her reputation, and all these dupes to hazard fame and fortune blindly on a cast of chance.

The play takes its title from the hero, Volpone, or the Old Fox. He is a Venetian nobleman, childless, without heirs: who, at the time when the first act opens, has been feigning the last diseases of decrepitude through three years, in order to delude the folk around him. It amuses the subtle voluptuary to study various and well-developed forms of covetousness in his friends and neighbours. His palace has become the haunt of *captatores*, legacy-hunters, each one of whom believes that his name will be found alone inscribed upon Volpone's testament. Yet none are quite secure and easy in their expectation. So long as the Fox is above ground, he may always change his dispositions. Therefore the birds of prey, scenting his carcass while he yet lives, keep hovering about his pretended sick-bed. There he lies, smeared with chalk and oils, coughing and drivelling, simulating blindness, deafness, palsy. From time to time they bring rich presents, regarding these as good investments for the future, competing one with another for Volpone's favour. But of them enough has now been said. On three carefully selected specimens of the tribe, Voltore, Corbaccio, and Corvino (Italian for vulture, old raven, and spruce young crow), the action of the drama turns; and in my analysis of the play we shall hear more about them.

Right instinct led Jonson to lay the scene in Venice, and to make his hero a Magnifico of the Republic. He has conceived Volpone as a man in green old age, sound still of constitution, enjoying the possession of his senses and his intellect. Craft and extravagant voluptuousness form the main-springs of his character. He has grown hoary in vice, and nothing now delights him more than the spectacle of human baseness. Therefore he expends his more than ordinary mental powers and ill-acquired knowledge of the world on subtle schemes for making life a comedy, and proving all the men around him knaves and fools. He is avaricious but not blinded by the love of gold. Wealth he values chiefly as the means for tempting and corrupting others, after he has surfeited himself with every pleasure it can purchase. Fantastic in his sensuality, he lives like a Roman of the Empire or an Oriental, secluded from the world among his creatures—the parasite, the pigmy, the eunuch, and the page. To this curious company Jonson has given descriptive names—Mosca, the fly; Nano, the dwarf; Castrone, the wether; Androgyno, the hermaphrodite. Mosca is the Fox's right hand. Without him Volpone's schemes would be impracticable; and the ruin, which comes upon him in the end, is due to his habit of regarding this devil of roguery as a second self. In Mosca Jonson paints a monumental portrait of the parasite, as he may possibly have existed at the worst courts in the most debased epochs of civilisation. Plausible, ingenious, pliant to his master's whims, loving evil for its own sake, Mosca glides through the dangerous and complicated circumstances of their common plots with the suppleness and quickness of a serpent. But when he sees the way to build up his own fortunes on Volpone's downfall, he turns round suddenly, implacably, upon his patron. With the same cold cynicism which he had used against Corbaccio to tickle the Fox's fancy, he now lays his fox-trap. How both fall eventually into it together we shall see.

I have said that Jonson obeyed a right instinct when he laid the scene of this comedy in Venice. The exorbitances and eccentricities of evil he has chosen to depict, would have gained but little credence if the action had taken place in London. But the sensualities of Aretino, the craft of Machiavelli, the diabolical ingenuity of Italian despots, lent veri similitude to his picture—'that most vivid picture,' in Taine's absurd enthusiastic language, 'of the manners of the century, where wicked covetousnesses display themselves in their full beauty, where sensuality, cruelty, lust for gold, and the impudicity of vice develop a sinister and splendid poetry, worthy of some Bacchanalian piece by Titian.'

The key-note of the drama is struck in the first lines. Volpone and Mosca are discovered in a room of the Venetian palace, standing before a curtain which veils the treasury. Volpone speaks:

> Good morning to the day; and next, my gold!
> Open the shrine, that I may see my saint.
> Hail the world's soul and mine! More glad than is
> The teeming earth to see the longed-for sun
> Peep through the horns of the celestial ram,
> Am I, to view thy splendour darkening his;
> That lying here, amongst my other hoards,
> Shew'st like a flame by night, or like the day
> Struck out of chaos, when all darkness fled
> Unto the centre. O thou sun of Sol,
> But brighter than thy father, let me kiss,
> With adoration, thee, and every relic
> Of sacred treasure in this blessed room.
> Well did wise poets, by thy glorious name,
> Title that age which they would have the best;
> Thou being the best of things, and far transcending
> All style of joy in children, parents, friends,
> Or any other waking dream on earth.
> Thy looks when they to Venus did ascribe,
> They should have given her twenty thousand
>   Cupids;
> Such are thy beauties and our loves! Dear saint,
> Riches, the dumb god, that giv'st all men tongues,
> That canst do naught, and yet mak'st men do all
>   things;
> The price of souls; even hell, with thee to boot,
> Is made worth heaven. Thou art virtue, fame,
> Honour and all things else. Who can get thee,
> He shall be noble, valiant, honest, wise.

Critics have judged that this opening invocation to the presiding deity of the drama rises to tragic sublimity. The playwright must indeed have had full confidence in his power to sustain the action upon a corresponding note of passionate intensity, when he composed it. Nor was he mistaken; for Volpone's rhetoric of adoration lives again in every word and deed of all the characters. True to his habit of firmly expounding the main situation and the leading motives of his personages in the first scene, Jonson next makes Volpone reflect with satisfaction on the acquisition of his treasure:

> Yet I glory
> More in the cunning purchase of my wealth,
> Than in the glad possession, since I gain
> No common way.

It is not by trade, industry, agriculture, usury, hoarding, that he has brought together 'the price of souls.' And he can afford to spend it freely. Mosca begs for a trifle, and Volpone gives him gold:

> What should I do,
> But cocker up my genius, and live free
> To all delights my fortune calls me to?
> I have no wife, no parent, child, ally,
> To give my substance to: but whom I make,
> Must be my heir; and this makes men observe me:
> This draws new clients daily to my house,
> Women and men of every sex and age,
> That bring me presents, send me plate, coin, jewels,
> With hope that when I die (which they expect
> Each greedy minute) it shall then return
> Ten-fold upon them.

While he is thus soliloquising, the dwarf, page, and eunuch enter, fantastically attired, and play a comic farce with songs to entertain him; in the middle of which show his clients begin to gather.

> Fetch me my gown,
> My furs and night-caps; say, my couch is changing:
> And let him entertain himself awhile
> Without i' the gallery. Now, now my clients
> Begin their visitation! Vulture, kite,
> Raven and gorcrow, all my birds of prey,
> That think me turning carcase, now they come;
> I am not for them yet!

The first to appear is Voltore, the advocate. He has brought a massive piece of plate, which he thrusts into Volpone's trembling hands, feebly lifted from the counterpane to clutch it. Voltore gloats over the thin and quavering accents of thanks, which come, half-smothered in choking coughs, from beneath the bed-clothes; and then, without taking the trouble to withdraw from the sick man's chamber, he turns to Mosca:

> *Volt.*:   Pray thee, hear me:
>   Am I inscribed his heir for certain?
> *Mos.*:   Are you?
>   I do beseech you, sir, you will vouchsafe
>   To write me in your family. All my hopes
>   Depend upon your worship; I am lost,
>   Except the rising sun do shine on me.
> *Volt.*: It shall both shine and warm thee, Mosca.
> *Mos.*:   Sir,
>   I am a man, that hath not done your love
>   All the worst offices: here I wear your keys,
>   See all your coffers and your caskets lock'd
>   Keep the poor inventory of your jewels,
>   Your plate and monies; am your steward, sir,
>   Husband your goods here.
> *Volt.*:   But am I sole heir?
> *Mos.*: Without a partner, sir; confirm'd this morning:
>   The wax is warm yet, and the ink scarce dry
>   Upon the parchment.
> *Volt.*:   Happy, happy me!
>   By what good chance, sweet Mosca?
> *Mos.*:   Your desert, sir.

They are yet talking, when a second knock is heard upon the door without. Voltore has but just time to creep away, and Volpone to jump up and kiss Mosca for the excellent sport, before Corbaccio appears. The Old Raven is a masterpiece of Jonson's dreadful art. Deaf, worn out with the diseases of extreme old age, he yet clings sordidly to the miserable shreds of life, and burdens his last days with detestable crimes for the sake of the gold he cannot carry with him beyond the tomb. He has brought an opiate:

> *Mos.*: He will not hear of drugs.
> *Corb.*:   Why! I myself
>   Stood by while it was made, saw all the ingredients;
>   And know, it cannot but most gently work:
>   My life for his, 'tis but to make him sleep.
> *Volp.*: Ay, his last sleep, if he would take it.   [*Aside.*

The reader must remember that these scenes are enacted in the presence of Volpone, who is supposed to be stone-deaf and blind, but who hears and sees everything with lynx eyes and fox's ears from behind his bed-curtains. The situation lends itself to accumulated touches of saturnine humour. Mosca paints a fancy picture of his master's disorders—apoplexy, palsy, vertigo, loathsome affections of the mucous membrane. Old Corbaccio recognises and ticks off the symptoms. They are familiar to himself:

Yet I am better, ha!
Excellent, excellent! Sure I shall outlast him:
This makes me young again, a score of years.

Being far more deaf than Volpone, he stumbles into ludicrous mistakes of Mosca's meaning, each of which is so contrived as to reveal his one absorbing preoccupation with the Fox's inheritance. It is only by stimulating his jealousy of Voltore that the parasite brings him to lay down a heavy bag of cash as goodwill offering. Then Mosca undertakes to induce Volpone to execute a will in his favour; but in order to ensure success, would it not be well if Corbaccio should also make a will in favour of Volpone? So signal a mark of devotion is certain to clinch the dying man's gratitude. Corbaccio doubts for a moment whether he can disinherit his son; but Mosca urges that Volpone is sure to die first. That argument cannot be resisted, and Corbaccio adopts the plan as though he had invented it:

Corb.: He must pronounce me his?
Mos.: 'Tis true.
Corb.: This plot
      Did I think on before.
Mos.: I do believe it.
Corb.: Do you not believe it?
Mos.: Yes, sir.
Corb.: Mine own project.
Mos.: Which, when he hath done, sir—
Corb.: Published me his heir?
Mos.: And you so certain to survive him—
Corb.: Ay.
Mos.: Being so lusty a man—
Corb.: 'Tis true.
Mos.: Yes, sir—
Corb.: I thought on that too. See how he should be
      The very organ to express my thoughts!
Mos.: You have not only done yourself a good—
Corb.: But multiplied it on my son.
Mos.: 'Tis right, sir.
Corb.: Still, my invention.

Corbaccio departs to execute the unnatural will, no less gulled than Voltore before him. Then, while Mosca and his patron are performing an interlude of mutual flattery and joy at their successful villainy, a third harpy interrupts them. This time it is the spruce young merchant Corvino. He is the most contemptible and reckless of the set, swallowing any bait, committing himself to plans for Volpone's murder more openly than Corbaccio, ready, as we shall see, to merge his ruling passion of jealousy and to drown his honour in the madness of his gold-lust. Corvino has brought a fine pearl for his present. Volpone faintly murmurs *Signor Corvino!* while his fingers shut upon the jewel. This raises Corvino's suspicion. Can he talk freely in the bedchamber?

Corv.:   Does he not perceive us?
Mos.: No more than a blind harper. He knows no man,
    No face of friend, nor name of any servant;
    Who 'twas that fed him last or gave him drink.

Corvino, whom Jonson has made a gross and brutal fellow in the prime of vulgar manhood, in order to contrast him with the lean greediness of Voltore and Corbaccio's senile delirium of covetousness, now pours loathsome invectives into Volpone's ears. Mosca flatters this humour to the bent, heaping hideous imprecations on the prostrate man. Yet, when Corvino departs, Volpone's cynicism is so marble-hard that he only applauds the gruesome comedy which should have made him tremble. He leaps from his bed, tired, but satisfied with his morning's imposture.

My divine Mosca!
Thou hast to-day outgone thyself. [*Knocking within.*]
  Who's there?
I will be troubled with no more. Prepare
Me music, dances, banquets, all delights;
The Turk is not more sensual in his pleasures
Than will Volpone.

Mosca goes out and returns with the news that Lady Would-be, wife to an English knight, seeks an interview. This time she must content herself with being Lady Cannot-be; for Volpone will have none of her, though it is hinted that she is ready to give him everything. He spends an hour more agreeably by listening to Mosca's glowing description of Celia—the young, beautiful, and virtuous wife of Corvino. And thus the first act closes.

In this act Jonson has introduced us to the chief personages of the drama. They are drawn with grim precision, in bold lines, as ugly and as natural as the dwarfs and monarchs of Velasquez. Also, their work has been cut out for them; and the mention of Celia in the last scene prepares us for what follows in the second act.

The tying and unloosing of the plot in this misnomered comedy shall be related more briefly. Volpone, obeying his humour for fantastic pleasure and extravagant disguises, goes forth to win a sight of Celia. He attires himself in the costume of a quack doctor, Mosca in that of the charlatan's drudge. They set up their platform under Corvino's windows. Volpone acts the mountebank with such spirit that Celia is drawn to the balcony, and while she takes her pastime of the crowd, her husband rushes in and drags her to a back room with brutal insults. The man is here revealed under the violent pressure of coarse jealousy, just at the very moment when he will be made to sacrifice his honour to his avarice. Mosca is sent to work upon his master-passion; for the sight of Celia has persuaded Volpone that she and none but she can satisfy his appetite. Corvino then is told by Mosca that the mountebank's powders have revived the Fox, and that nothing is wanting to his cure but the warmth of an Abishag to comfort his decrepitude. The doctors and the legacy-hunters are vying with each other in offering their nearest relatives.

Mos.:   They are all
    Now striving who shall first present him; therefore—
    . . . . . Have you no kinswoman!
    Odso! Think, think, think, think, think, think, sir,
    One of the doctors offered there his daughter.
Corv.: . . . . . . I will prevent him. Wretch!
    Covetous wretch! Mosca, I have determined.
Mos.:   How, sir?
Corv.: We'll make all sure. The party you wot of
    Shall be mine own wife, Mosca.

After this master-stroke of villainy, we do not wonder at Mosca's breaking into a soliloquy upon his superiority to common city-parasites and trencher-scrapers.

Meanwhile the plot is now in full swing. Corvino drags his outraged wife with blows and gross taunts to Volpone's bedside. When he has withdrawn, the Fox throws off his mask and falls at Celia's feet:

Nay, fly me not,
Nor let thy false imagination
That I was bed-rid make thee think I am so;
Thou shalt not find it. I am now as fresh,
As hot, as high, and in as jovial plight
As when, in that so celebrated scene,
At recitation of our comedy,

> For entertainment of the great Valois,
> I acted young Antinous.

This introduces a scene, in which Jonson has given rein to his peculiar fancy. Every word used by Volpone to ply Celia, every voluptuous image he suggests, is drawn from some repository of antique conceits; but these are so fused and interwoven that they appear to be the natural utterance of a hoary sybarite's desire. She, who had shrunk with horror from the bed of a diseased and drivelling old man, sees before her an eloquent and insidious seducer. She shrieks for succour; and at her cries Bonario, Corbaccio's son, appears to rescue her. This young man had been hidden in a gallery by Mosca, in order that he might be witness to the act whereby his father meant to disavow and disinherit him. The parasite, it seems, had hoped to work upon his natural resentment so that he should commit some act of violence—either murder Corbaccio or compromise himself by yielding to his own fury. I shall take occasion, later on, to criticise this motive on its artistic merits; for the present, it is enough to point out that it brings about the first catastrophe in the drama.

Volpone stands unmasked. Bonario carries off the rescued lady. And at this juncture Voltore appears, while Corbaccio comes hobbling in with his will signed and attested. It looks as though the Fox were at his last gasp. But Mosca rises to the occasion. He has been wounded in the scuffle with Bonario. Now he takes both victims of gold-lust in hand. Voltore is persuaded that Corbaccio's will was meant to swell Volpone's fortune in the lawyer's interest. Corbaccio is made to believe that his son has been lurking in the palace to take his father's life before it was too late to save his own estate. Corvino has also to be settled: but Mosca works with ease upon the grossness of his avaricious appetite. The three legacy-hunters, hating each other as they do, yet severally blinded by their covetousness, are combined into one band to extricate Volpone from his difficulties. They have to swear that Celia and Bonario have been guilty lovers, and that each was practising against the Fox in his own palace. These parts they play in open court, the one vying against the other in false-swearing and in ventilating his own shame. Lady Would-be is dragged opportunely into the same meshes of intrigue, and gives suspicious testimony to Celia's public wantonness. Mosca drives the discordant team with consummate skill and audacity. They perjure themselves, repudiate their kindred, stamp the brand of dishonour on their foreheads, labouring with avidity to win Volpone and secure his fortune, in their blindness, each for his own self. The fixed idea of wealth to be inherited has taken hold upon their brains, and, like clockwork, they strike true to the machinery invented for them.

Justice is baffled for the moment. Under the deluge of adroitly prepared false witness, the judges, who were favourable to Bonario and Celia, admit that a monstrous case has been made out against them. Volpone, who appeared in court bedridden, is carried home to his palace, and there he hugs Mosca for the success of their deeply laid plots. This opens the fifth act; and here, in a sense, the drama is concluded. But it was required by Jonson's plan that poetical justice should be done, and that the Fox should finally be caught. The poet has heaped ignominy on the legacy-hunters. But he leaves two innocent persons, Bonario and Celia, under unmerited disgrace. His work will not be finished until Volpone and the parasite have been taken in their own toils. At this juncture he calls the Até of the gods, the insolence of guilty creatures swollen with their own conceit, to the aid of his languishing intrigue. Volpone is so intoxicated with the triumph of his craft, so contemptuous of human nature, that he resolves to indulge his cynicism with

a new trick. He feigns death, and gives to Mosca a will in which the parasite's name is inserted as sole heir. The *captatores* scent the carcass. First comes Voltore; then Corbaccio, carried in a chair; next Corvino; lastly, Lady Would-be. Mosca receives them in the palace, allowing them to dangle at his heels. He holds an inventory in his hands, which he checks by items in the several apartments. They raise a fugue of clamorous entreaties to see the will, each firmly believing that his name will be written there, to the exclusion of the rest. Mosca, at last, flings the deed over his shoulder, and the fugue becomes a chorus in unison of indignant objurgation. Mosca, meanwhile, goes on with his inventory: 'Two cabinets, one of ebony, the other mother-of-pearl—I am very busy; good faith, it is a fortune thrown on me—Item, one salt of onyx—not of my seeking.' One after the other they pounce down upon him. But he has the sting of the epigram for each. To Lady Would-be:

> Remember what your ladyship offered me,
> To be his heir!

To Corvino:

>   You are
> A declared cuckold . . . .
> Go home, be melancholy too, or mad.

To Corbaccio:

> Are you not he, that filthy, covetous wretch,
> With the three legs, that here, in hope of prey,
> Have any time this three years snuffed about
> With your most grovelling nose, and would have lured
> Me to the poisoning of my patron, sir.

All shrink away except Voltore, who has not yet received his answer. He still clings with the tenacity of a rapacious bird of prey to his imagined quarry. Mosca affects to ignore him:

> Why, who are you?
> What! who did send for you? O, cry you mercy,
> Reverend sir! Good faith, I am grieved for you,
> That any chance of mine should thus defeat
> Your (I must needs say) most deserving travails.

At last he beats him off with insolence; but the heavy-pinioned Vulture is sent flying on an errand which shall break the overstrained meshes of the close net woven round him.

Volpone, as usual, has witnessed this comedy of thwarted passions from his hiding-place. He now concerts new schemes with Mosca for the bantering of his victims, yielding yet once again to the intoxication of self-conceit. Mosca is to assume the robes of a Magnifico; his master the dress of a common sheriff's officer. Thus attired, they roam the streets of Venice, jeering at the disappointed *captatores*. The game, however, has been carried too far. It is the hour at which Bonario and Celia have to receive sentence from the judges. All the actors of the drama assemble in court, led by various curiosities. Then, to the surprise of every one, Voltore, who has been maddened by disappointment and envenomed against his rivals, declares the stratagem by which the guiltless pair have been drawn to the verge of ruin. Still, the intrigue is not ripe for its catastrophe. Volpone, beginning to suspect that Mosca may play him false, whispers to the advocate that he is yet alive. Voltore, responding to his dominant motive, upon this hint that he may still inherit, repudiates what he has just delivered, and pretends that witchcraft has deprived him of his reason. The judges know not what course to take. The accused stand waiting for their sentence. It seems as though no issue from the deadlock could be found. But at this moment Mosca, who has hitherto been absent, enters the court. Volpone runs to him, as to his last resource of safety. He is met with boxes on the ears:

What busy knave is this?. . . .
Whose drunkard is this same? speak, some that know
    him:
I never saw his face.

Mosca is playing now at high stakes. Of course he recognises his patron, and he offers, in asides, to compound with him for half of Volpone's estate. But the tension is too great for compromise. Fox and parasite are equally whirled away upon the tide of the moment. The judges take the dispute into their own hands, and order Volpone to be whipped, that he may bear himself discreetly to a gentleman in Mosca's position. Up to the last, thus Jonson scourged society's adulation of wealth; for here are the Venetian officers of justice bending before an enriched parasite. The insult rouses one hot drop of noble blood in Volpone's veins. Rather than tolerate such indignity, he will declare all. It is only the affair of throwing off his disguise. This he does, and in one moment the whole plot is dissolved.

I am Volpone, and this is my knave.
                  [*Pointing to Mosca.*

Nothing more remains but the vindication of the innocent, and a proper apportionment of punishments to the guilty.

What most excites admiration in *Volpone* is the sustained vigour of the action, and the ingenuity of the fable. Few extant plays exhibit so closely connected an intrigue. The mechanic force and versatility of invention which are lavished on the framework of this comedy suffice to carry the reader or spectator onward to its unforeseen conclusion. Yet some objections may be taken to the plot. As Dryden first pointed out, the unity of action is not well preserved; one motive being exhausted at the end of act iv., 'the second forced from it in act v.' The slight and meagre under-plot of Sir Policy Would-be and his wife (which I have omitted in my analysis, except in so far as Lady Would-be affects Volpone) is superfluous and tolerably tedious. But the heaviest blot upon Jonson's construction remains to be noted. He has suggested no adequate motive for Mosca's introduction of Bonario into Volpone's palace, at the moment when Corbaccio is coming to execute his will, and Celia is being brought by her unworthy husband. Bonario's presence there was necessary for the conduct of the intrigue. But this circumstance hangs upon so fine a thread of calculation in Mosca's brain, that we must regard it as not sufficiently accounted for. In all other respects, the use which Jonson has made of base passions as the cords of human conduct in this drama may be looked upon as masterly; and the skill with which he has woven them into a comic net of serried strength is indubitable. The spectacle, alas! is too grisly. Nature rebels against it. We do not easily or willingly believe that men and women are such as Jonson painted them. We rise from the study of *Volpone*, as we do from that of some of Balzac's masterpieces, with the sense that all these human reptiles, true enough in their main points to life, yet over-fattened in the vast slime of the poet's brain, represent actual humanity less than they personate ideals, which the potent intellect, brooding upon one vice of man's frail being, has diversified into a score of splendidly imagined specimens. . . .

Bartholomew Fair

Bartholomew Fair is a pure farce, conceived in the spirit of rollicking mirth, and executed with colossal energy. It is no satire either of manners or of individuals, but a broad Dutch painting of the humours of a London Carnival, such as only a man bred from boyhood to the town could have produced. The personages are admirably studied and grouped together with consummate insight into dramatic effect. The proctor, with his pretty wife and puritanical mother-in-law; the sleek minister from Banbury, who woos the widow; the squire from Harrow, and his watchful attendant; the justice of the peace, for ever blundering in his preposterous disguises; the ginger-bread women and toyshop people; the greasy cook, who sells roast pig and carries on more questionable business; the bailiffs, watchmen, sharpers, and bullies, who abound in every booth; the puppet-show, the ballad singer, the madman, and the miscellaneous crowd of costermongers, porters, pickpockets, and passengers, compose one varied ever-moving kaleidoscope of human beings.

We are introduced into this motley crowd by a device which enables the playwright to contrast the coarse diversions of Smithfield with the canting squeamishness of the vulgar Puritans, who supply his scenes with their most lively humours. Dame Purecraft's daughter, Win-the-fight, married to doltish John Littlewit the proctor, is in an interesting situation, and manifests caprices pardonable in her state of health. She has conceived an irresistible longing to eat roast pig at Bartholomew Fair. This, like the wrath of Achilles in the Iliad, is the motive-passion of the comedy. Roast pig at home will not content her. The pig on which her heart is set must be cooked and eaten in a booth at Smithfield. A matron like Dame Purecraft found herself thus placed in a position involving casuistry. On the one hand she dared not contradict her daughter's longings, however unreasonable they might be, and however unlawful this particular longing was according to her creed. She attempts at first the way of admonition and discouragement:

Look up, sweet Win-the-fight, and suffer not the enemy to enter you at this door; remember that your education has been with the purest. What polluted one was it that named first the unclean beast, pig, to you, child?

When Mrs. Littlewit has reluctantly admitted how the longing came upon her, Dame Purecraft resumes her godly exhortations:

O, resist it, Win-the-fight! It is the tempter, the wicked tempter, you may know it by the fleshly motion of the pig; be strong against it and its foul temptations, in these assaults, whereby it broacheth flesh and blood, as it were on the weaker side; and pray against its carnal provocations; good child, sweet child, pray.

Such pleading is, however, all to no purpose. Mrs. Littlewit is resolved to eat pig in a booth, or to ruin the hopes of her husband's posterity. In this difficulty her mother bethinks her of the godly man from Banbury, Brother Zeal-of-the-land Busy, who is sure to be equal to the problem:

What shall we do? Call our zealous brother Busy hither, for his faithful fortification in this charge of the adversary. Child, my dear child, you shall eat pig; be comforted, my sweet child.

At this point the audience are pretty well informed that Dame Purecraft herself has no insurmountable objection to pig in the abstract. But Win-the-fight will not ratify a bargain on these terms. Her longing is for pig at Smithfield; so she answers:

Mrs. Lit.: Ay, but in the Fair, mother!
Pure.: I mean in the Fair, if it can be any way made or found lawful.

Meanwhile, Zeal-of-the-land Busy, one of the most unctuous creations of a comic poet's brain, has been discovered in the pantry, comforting himself with a glass of malmsey and a cut of cold turkey-pie. The pious man appears, wiping his lips, and is immediately appealed to by the widow:

> O, brother Busy! your help here, to edify and raise us up in a scruple; my daughter Win-the-fight is visited with a natural disease of women, called a longing to eat pig.

Mr. Littlewit, who has no less longing for Smithfield than his spouse, here puts in a word:

> Ay, sir, a Bartholomew pig; and in the Fair.

His mother-in-law takes him up:

> And I would be satisfied from you, religiously-wise, whether a widow of the sanctified assembly, or a widow's daughter, may commit the act without offence to the weaker sisters.

Thus appealed to, the answer of the Rabbi, delivered doubtless in a rich baritone snuffle, is highly edifying, but hardly satisfactory to the persons concerned. Zeal-of-the-land has no objection to the eating of roast pig in itself. He sticks at the place where it must be eaten:

> Verily, for the disease of longing, it is a disease, a carnal disease, or appetite, incident to women; and as it is carnal and incident, it is natural, very natural. Now pig, it is a meat, and a meat that is nourishing and may be longed for, and so consequently eaten; it may be eaten; very exceedingly well eaten: but in the Fair, and as a Bartholomew pig, it cannot be eaten; for the very calling it a Bartholomew pig, and to eat it so, is a spice of idolatry, and you make the Fair no better than one of the high-places. This, I take it, is the state of the question: a high-place.

True to her name, Win-the-fight persists in her determination: and Dame Purecraft is forced to consult the oracle once more for casuistical easements:

> Good brother Zeal-of-the-land, think to make it as lawful as you can.

This time, the oracle itself is smitten with the savoury temptation of pig at the Fair. He then replies with the same fulsome reiteration of phrases which marks the canting hypocrite:

> Surely, it may be otherwise, but it is subject to construction, subject, and hath a face of offence with the weak, a great face, a foul face: but that face may have a veil put over it, and be shadowed as it were; it may be eaten, and in the Fair, I take it, in a booth, the tents of the wicked: the place is not much, not very much, we may be religious in the midst of the profane, so it be eaten with a reformed mouth, with sobriety and humbleness; not gorged in with gluttony or greediness, there's the fear: for should she go there, as taking pride in the place, or delight in the unclean dressing, to feed the vanity of the eye, or lust of the palate, it were not well, it were not fit, it were abominable, and not good.

Having delivered himself of this convenient sophistry, Brother Busy invokes the spirit of zeal, and rhapsodises as follows:

> In the way of comfort to the weak, I will go and eat. I will eat exceedingly, and prophesy. There may be a good use made of it too now I think on't. By the public eating of swine's flesh, to profess our hate and loathing of Judaism, whereof the brethren stand taxed. I will therefore eat, yea, I will eat exceedingly.

It was Jonson's invariable practice to introduce the main personages of his drama in the first act, and to set forth the leading comic motive with such clearness that the future conduct of the plot should involve no difficulties for the understanding.

We are therefore now prepared, upon the opening of the second act, to find ourselves among the booth of Bartholomew Fair; and here we witness a series of diverting incidents in the expectation of soon returning to the company of our Puritan friends. This expectation is not frustrated; for in due time, though we have to wait for them until the first scene of the third act, Dame Purecraft and Mr. and Mrs. Littlewit, led by Rabbi Busy, are seen advancing with set faces through the booths:

> *Busy*: So, walk on in the middle way, foreright, turn neither to the right hand nor to the left; let not your eyes be drawn aside with vanity, nor your ears with noises.

The toy-sellers and apple-women gather round them; but the pious man continues his nasal exhortation:

> Look not toward them, hearken not; the place is Smithfield, or the field of smiths, the grove of hobby-horses and trinkets; the wares are the wares of devils, and the whole Fair is the shop of Satan. They are hooks and baits, very baits, that are hung out on every side to catch you, and to hold you as it were by the gills and by the nostrils, as the fisher doth. Therefore you must not look nor turn toward them. The heathen man could stop his ears with wax against the harlot of the sea; do you the like with your fingers against the bells of the beast.

But their object at the Fair is to eat pig; and how are they to find it if they do not use their eyes? The proctor, who is a weak brother, takes this view, and stands stock still before Ursula's booth:

> *Lit.*: [*Gazing at the inscription.*] This is fine verily! HERE BE THE BEST PIGS; AND SHE DOES ROAST THEM AS WELL AS EVER SHE DID, the pig's head says!
>
> *Pure.*: Son, were you not warned of the vanity of the eye? Have you forgot the wholesome admonition so soon?
>
> *Lit.*: Good mother, how shall we find a pig, if we do not look about for 't? Will it run off o' the spit into our mouths, think you, as in Lubber land, and cry *wee wee.*'

Busy's casuistry is equal to the occasion. He had warned his flock to close their ears and shut their eyes; but another sense might lead them no less surely to the object of their quest.

> *Busy*: No, but your mother, religiously-wise, conceiveth it may offer itself by other means to the sense, as by way of steam, which I think it doth here in this place,—huh, huh—yes, it doth. [*He scents after it like a hound.*] And it were a sin of obstinacy, great obstinacy, high and horrible obstinacy, to decline or resist the good titillation of the famelic sense, which is the smell. Therefore be bold—huh, huh, huh—follow the scent: enter the tents of the unclean, for once, and satisfy your wife's frailty. Let your frail wife be satisfied; your zealous mother and my suffering self will also be satisfied.

To this admirable exposition he adds the further casuistical reflection, that 'we scape so much of the other vanities by our early entering'; and Dame Purecraft assents: 'It is an edifying consideration.' Mrs. Littlewit grumbles: 'This is scurvy, that we must come to the Fair, and not look on 't.' However, the whole party enters Ursula's booth; and the voice of the Rabbi is heard within its curtains, sonorously declaiming: 'A pig prepare presently, let a pig be prepared to us.' There we leave him for awhile to the gratification of his sanctified appetite. The plot calls our attention to other persons of the comedy. These I must omit, being unable to set so miscellaneous a crowd of characters adequately before my readers, and wishing to concentrate attention upon Jonson's full-length portrait of the Puritan minister.

When Busy has eaten to his heart's content, and drunk no little too it may be guessed, he sallies forth, inspired with zeal against the profanities of the Fair:

> Thou art the seat of the beast, O Smithfield, and I will leave thee! Idolatry peepeth out on every side of thee.

His eyes light upon a toyshop, and the toy-man presses 'rattles, drums, babies' on his devout attention:

> Peace, with thy apocryphal wares, thou profane publican; thy bells, thy dragons, and thy Tobie's dogs. Thy hobby-horse is an idol, a very idol, a fierce and rank idol; and thou, the Nebuchadnezzar, the proud Nebuchadnezzar of the Fair, that sett'st it up for children to fall down to and worship.

The toy-man thrusts a drum into his face:

> It is the broken belly of the beast, and thy bellows there are his lungs, and these pipes are his throat, those feathers are of his tail, and thy rattles the gnashing of his teeth.

Would he like gingerbread perhaps?

> The provender that pricks him up. Hence with thy basket of popery, thy nest of images, and whole legend of ginger-work.

Dame Purecraft, seeing that he is about to fall upon the gingerbread basket and send it flying in the fervour of his indignation, attempts to calm him down with 'Good brother Zeal'; but he will hear no reason:

> Hinder me not, woman! I was moved in spirit to be here this day, in this Fair, this wicked and foul Fair; and fitter may it be called a Foul than a Fair: to protest against the abuses of it, the foul abuses of it, in regard of the afflicted saints, that are troubled, very much troubled, exceedingly troubled, with the opening of the merchandize of Babylon again, and the peeping of popery upon the stalls here, here, in the high-places. See you not Goldylocks, the purple strumpet there, in her yellow gown and green sleeves? the profane pipes? the tinkling timbrels? A shop of relicks!

> *(Attempts to seize the toys.)*

Then, having lashed himself into a fury, he bears down upon the gingerbread:

> And this idolatrous grove of images, this flasket of idols, which I will pull down [*overthrows the gingerbread basket*] in my zeal, and glory to be thus exercised.

The ensuing commotion brings a brace of watchmen on the scene, who take hold of Busy, and carry him off to the stocks, saying they will stop his noise:

> Thou canst not; 'tis a sanctified noise: I will make a loud and most strong noise, till I have daunted the profane enemy. And for this cause I will thrust myself into the stocks, upon the pikes of the land.

We next behold him in the stocks, roaring and testifying, but displaying withal that obstinate courage and unconcern for what the world might think which gave force to the Puritans in the succeeding age. When a bystander jeeringly asks what he is, he answers:

> One that rejoiceth in his affliction, and sitteth here to prophesy the destruction of fairs and May-games, wakes and Whitson-ales, and doth sigh and groan for the reformation of these abuses.

We may wonder whether Jonson, when he put these words into the mouth of Busy, surmised the probability of his prophecy being shortly realised in dismal fact throughout England. A fellow-prisoner, the unfortunate justice of the peace, Adam Overdo, quotes stoical phrases from Horace and Persius to keep his courage up. The Rabbi overhears him, and delivers a cutting rubuke:

> Friend, I will leave to communicate my spirit with you, if I hear any more of those superstitious relics, those lists of Latin, the very rags of Rome, and patches of Popery.

With his wonted skill in throwing side lights upon all points of a favourite character, Jonson here exhibits the Puritan dislike of culture and the gross ignorance of the sect. But when Dame Purecraft comes up, and condoles with him on his misfortune, the valiant spirit of the martyr (as stout in tragic as it here appears in comic difficulty) breaks forth:

> Peace, religious sister, it is my calling; comfort yourself: an extraordinary calling, and done for my better standing, my surer standing, hereafter.

Notwithstanding this enthusiasm, he is glad enough to escape when the stocks are opened by accident. His Quixotic zeal soon plunges him into other comical adventures. A farcical puppet-show on the pathetic story of Hero and Leander, which might serve as an excellent illustration of English mock-heroic parody, if we had space to dwell on it, is being acted in a booth. The dialogue, of the lowest description, is moving briskly, when a sudden snort and trampling announces the advent of the Rabbi:

> Down with Dagon! down with Dagon! 'tis I; I will no longer endure your profanations. I will remove Dagon there, I say, that idol, that heathenish idol, that remains, as I may say, a beam, a very beam not a beam of the sun, nor a beam of the moon, nor a beam of a balance, neither a house-beam, nor a weaver's beam, but a beam in the eye, in the eye of the brethren; a very great beam, an exceeding great beam: such as are your stage-players, rimers, and morrice-dancers, who have walked hand in hand, in contempt of the brethren and the cause; and been borne out by instruments of no mean countenance.

His zeal overvaults itself, and leaves him out of breath; whereupon the showman quietly observes:

> Sir, I present nothing but what is licensed by authority.

This sets Busy off again upon the word licence:

> *Busy*: Thou art all licence, even licentiousness itself, Shimei.
> *Leath*: I have the Master of the Revels' hand for 't, sir.
> *Busy*: The Master of the Rebels' hand thou hast, Satan's! hold thy peace, thy scurrility, shut up thy mouth, thy profession is damnable, and in pleading for it thou dost plead for Baal. I have long opened my mouth wide, and gaped; I have gaped as the oyster for the tide, after thy destruction: but cannot compass it by suit or dispute; so that I look for a bickering, ere long, and then a battle.

Eventually, Rabbi Zeal-of-the-land is drawn into a controversy upon theatrical ethics with the showman, which gives Jonson an opportunity for marshalling the arguments advanced by Puritans against play-acting. His own counter-arguments he puts into the mouth of Busy's antagonist, who in the end confutes and silences the man of Banbury.

Such is the best portrait of a Puritan which remains for us upon the pages of our dramatists. After studying its powerful outlines, we feel the truth of Gifford's observation: 'All this proves how profoundly Jonson had entered into the views and expectations of this turbulent and aspiring race.' Whether he is right in adding: 'Had his royal master understood them half so well, long years of calamity and disgrace might have been averted,' is open to more doubt. It was not Charles' misconception of the Puritans which moved John Hampden and Pym to their resistance of royal tyranny. Yet the fact remains that the playwright, while caricaturing the fanatics who subsequently formed the Rump Parliament, painted them in their day of comparative obscurity just as they afterwards displayed themselves in the day of their triumph.

Notes

1. Malone's *Prose Works of Dryden*, vol. iii, pp. 51, 103.
2. For example, the interlude of the parasites, and the scene of the mountebank, in *Volpone*.

ALGERNON CHARLES SWINBURNE
From A *Study of Ben Jonson*
1889, pp. 9–89

There is nothing accidental in the work of Ben Jonson: no casual inspiration, no fortuitous impulse, ever guides or misguides his genius aright or astray. And this crowning and damning defect of a tedious and intolerable realism was even exceptionally wilful and premeditated. There is little if anything of it in the earliest comedy admitted into the magnificent edition which was compiled and published by himself in the year of the death of Shakespeare. And the humours of a still earlier comedy attributed to his hand, and printed apparently without his sanction just seven years before, are not worked out with such wearisome patience nor exhibited with such scientific persistency as afterwards distinguished the anatomical lecturer on vice and folly whose ideal of comic art was a combination of sarcasm and sermon in alternately epigrammatic and declamatory dialogue. I am by no means disposed to question the authenticity of this play, an excellent example of romantic comedy dashed with farce and flavoured with poetry: but, as far as I am aware, no notice has yet been taken of a noticeable coincidence between the manner or the circumstances of its publication and that of a spurious play which had nine years previously been attributed to Shakespeare. Some copies only of *The Case is Altered* bear on the title-page the name of Jonson, as some copies only of *Sir John Oldcastle* bear on the title-page the name of Shakespeare. In the earlier case, there can of course be no reasonable doubt that Shakespeare on his side, or the four actual authors of the gallimaufry on theirs, or perhaps all five together in the common though diverse interest of their respective credits, must have interfered to put a stop to the piratical profits of a lying and thieving publisher by compelling him to cancel the impudently mendacious title-page which imputed to Shakespeare the authorship of a play announced in its very prologue as the work of a writer or writers whose intention was to counteract the false impression given by Shakespeare's caricature, and to represent Prince Hal's old lad of the castle in his proper character of hero and martyr. In the later case, there can be little if any doubt that Jonson, then at the height of his fame and influence, must have taken measures to preclude the circulation under his name of a play which he would not or could not honestly acknowledge. So far, then, as external evidence goes, there is no ground whatever for a decision as to whether *The Case is Altered* may be wholly or partially or not at all assignable to the hand of Jonson. My own conviction is that he certainly had a hand in it, and was not

improbably its sole author: but that on the other hand it may not impossibly be one of the compound works on which he was engaged as a dramatic apprentice with other and less energetic playwrights in the dim back workshop of the slave-dealer and slave-driver whose diary records the grinding toil and the scanty wages of his lean and laborious bondsmen. Justice, at least since the days of Gifford, has generally been done to the bright and pleasant quality of this equally romantic and classical comedy; in which the passionate humour of the miser is handled with more freshness and freedom than we find in most of Jonson's later studies, while the figure of his putative daughter has more of grace and interest than he usually vouchsafed to be at the pains of bestowing on his official heroines. It is to be regretted, it is even to be deplored, that the influence of Plautus on the style and the method of Jonson was not more permanent and more profound. Had he been but content to follow his first impulse, to work after his earliest model—had he happily preferred those 'Plautinos et numeros et sales' for which his courtly friend Horace expressed so courtierly a contempt to the heavier numbers and the more laborious humours which he set himself to elaborate and to cultivate instead, we might not have had to applaud a more wonderful and admirable result, we should unquestionably have enjoyed a harvest more spontaneous and more gracious, more generous and more delightful. Something of the charm of Fletcher, his sweet straightforward fluency and instinctive lightness of touch, would have tempered the severity and solidity of his deliberate satire and his heavy-handed realism.

And the noble work of comic art which followed on this first attempt gave even fuller evidence in its earlier than its later form of the author's capacity for poetic as well as realistic success. The defence of poetry which appears only in the first edition of *Every Man in his Humour* is worth all Sidney's and all Shelley's treatises thrown together. A stern and austere devotion to the principle which prohibits all indulgence in poetry, precludes all exuberance of expression, and immolates on the altar of accuracy all eloquence, all passion, and all inspiration incompatible with direct and prosaic reproduction of probable or plausible dialogue, induced its author to cancel this noble and majestic rhapsody; and in so doing gave fair and full forewarning of the danger which was to beset this too rigid and conscientious artist through the whole of his magnificent career. But in all other points the process of transformation to which its author saw fit to subject this comedy was unquestionably a process of improvement. Transplanted from the imaginary or fantastic Italy in which at first they lived and moved and had their being to the actual and immediate atmosphere of contemporary London, the characters gain even more in life-like and interesting veracity or verisimilitude than in familiar attraction and homely association. Not only do we feel that we know them better, but we perceive that they are actually more real and cognisable creatures than they were under their former conditions of dramatic existence. But it must be with regret as well as with wonder that we find ourselves constrained to recognize the indisputable truth that this first acknowledged work of so great a writer is as certainly his best as it certainly is not his greatest. Never again did his genius, his industry, his conscience and his taste unite in the triumphant presentation of a work so faultless, so satisfactory, so absolute in achievement and so free from blemish or defect. The only three others among all his plays which are not unworthy to be ranked beside it are in many ways more wonderful, more splendid, more incomparable with any other product of human intelligence or genius: but neither *The Fox*, *The Alchemist*, nor *The Staple of News*, is altogether so blameless and flawless a piece of work; so free from anything that might as well or better be dispensed with, so simply and thoroughly compact and complete in workmanship and in result. Molière himself has no character more exquisitely and spontaneously successful in presentation and evolution than the immortal and inimitable Bobadil: and even Bobadil is not unworthily surrounded and supported by the many other graver or lighter characters of this magnificent and perfect comedy.

It is difficult to attempt an estimate of the next endeavours or enterprises of Ben Jonson without incurring either the risk of impatient and uncritical injustice, if rein be given to the natural irritation and vexation of a disappointed and bewildered reader, or the no less imminent risk of one-sided and one-eyed partiality, if the superb literary quality, the elaborate intellectual excellence, of these undramatic if not inartistic satires in dialogue be duly taken into account. From their author's point of view, they are worthy of all the applause he claimed for them; and to say this is to say much; but if the author's point of view was radically wrong, was fundamentally unsound, we can but be divided between condemnation and applause, admiration and regret. No student of our glorious language, no lover of our glorious literature, can leave these miscalled comedies unread without foregoing an experience which he should be reluctant to forego: but no reader who has any sense or any conception of comic art or of dramatic harmony will be surprised to find that the author's experience of their reception on the stage should have driven him by steady gradations of fury and consecutive degrees of arrogance into a state of mind and a style of work which must have seemed even to his well-wishers most unpromising for his future and final triumph. Little if anything can be added to the excellent critical remarks of Gifford on *Every Man out of his Humour, Cynthia's Revels,* and *Poetaster, or his Arraignment.* The first of these magnificent mistakes would be enough to ensure immortality to the genius of the poet capable of so superb and elaborate an error. The fervour and intensity of the verse which expresses his loftier mood of intolerant indignation, the studious and implacable versatility of scorn which animates the expression of his disgust at the viler or crueller examples of social villainy then open to his contemptuous or furious observation, though they certainly cannot suffice to make a play, suffice to make a living and imperishable work of the dramatic satire which passes so rapidly from one phase to another of folly, fraud, or vice. And if it were not an inadmissible theory that the action or the structure of a play might be utterly disjointed and dislocated in order to ensure the complete presentation or development, the alternate exhibition or exposure, of each figure in the revolving gallery of a satirical series, we could hardly fear that our admiration of the component parts which fail to compose a coherent or harmonious work of art could possibly carry us too far into extravagance of applause. The noble rage which inspires the overture is not more absolute or perfect than the majestic structure of the verse: and the best comic or realistic scenes of the ensuing play are worthy to be compared—though it may not be altogether to their advantage—with the similar work of the greatest succeeding artists in narrative or dramatic satire. Too much of the studious humour, too much of the versatile and laborious realism, displayed in the conduct and evolution of this satirical drama, may have been lavished and misused in the reproduction of ephemeral affectations and accidental forms of folly: but whenever the dramatic satirist, on purpose or by accident, strikes home to some deeper and more durable subject of satire, we feel the presence and the power of a poet and a thinker whose genius was not born to deal merely with ephemeral or casual matters. The small patrician fop and his smaller plebeian ape, though even now not undiverting figures, are inevitably less diverting to us, as they must have been even to the next generation from Jonson's, than to the audience for whom they were created: but the humour of the scene in which the highly intelligent and intellectual lady, who regards herself as the pattern at once of social culture and of personal refinement, is duped and disgraced by an equally simple and ingenious trick played off on her overweening and contemptuous vanity, might have been applauded by Shakespeare or by Vanbrugh, approved by Congreve or Molière. Here, among too many sketches of a kind which can lay claim to no merit beyond that of an unlovely photograph, we find a really humorous conception embodied in a really amusing type of vanity and folly; and are all the more astonished to find a writer capable of such excellence and such error as every competent reader must recognize in the conception and execution of this rather admirable than delightful play. For Molière himself could hardly have improved on the scene in which a lady who is confident of her intuitive capacity to distinguish a gentleman from a pretender with no claim to that title is confronted with a vulgar clown, whose introducers have assured her that he is a high-bred gentleman masquerading for a wager under that repulsive likeness. She wonders that they can have imagined her so obtuse, so ignorant, so insensible to the difference between gentleman and clown: she finds that he plays his part as a boor very badly and transparently; and on discovering that he is in fact the boor she would not recognize, is driven to vanish in a passion of disgust. This is good comedy: but we can hardly say as much for the scene in which a speculator who has been trading on the starvation or destitution of his neighbours and tenants is driven to hang himself in despair at the tidings of a better market for the poor, is cut down by the hands of peasants who have not recognized him, and on hearing their loudly expressed regrets for this act of inadvertent philanthropy becomes at once a beneficent and penitent philanthropist. Extravagant and exceptional as is this instance of Jonson's capacity for dramatic error—for the sacrifice at once of comic art and of common sense on the altar of moral or satirical purpose, it is but an extreme example of the result to which his theory must have carried his genius, gagged and handcuffed and drugged and blindfolded, had not his genius been too strong even for the force and the persistence of his theory. No reader and no spectator of his next comedy can have been inclined to believe or encouraged in believing that it was. The famous final verse of the epilogue to *Cynthia's Revels* can hardly sound otherwise to modern ears than as an expression of blustering diffidence—of blatant self-distrust. That any audience should have sat out the five undramatic acts of this 'dramatic satire' is as inconceivable as that any reader, however exasperated and exhausted by its voluminous perversities, should fail to do justice to its literary merits; to the vigour and purity of its English, to the masculine refinement and the classic straightforwardness of its general style. There is an exquisite song in it, and there are passages—nay, there are scenes—of excellent prose: but the intolerable elaboration of pretentious dullness and ostentatious ineptitude for which the author claims not merely the tolerance or the condonation which gratitude or charity might accord to the misuse or abuse of genius, but the acclamation due to its exercise and the applause demanded by its triumph—the heavy-headed perversity which ignores all the duties and reclaims all the privileges of a dramatic poet—the Cyclopean ponderosity of perseverance which hammers through scene after scene at the task of ridicule by anatomy of tedious and preposterous futilities—all these too conscientious outrages offered to the very principle of comedy, of poetry, or of drama, make us wonder that we have no record of a retort from the exhausted audience—if haply there were any auditors left—to the dogged defiance of the epilogue:

> By God 'tis good, and if you like 't you may.
> —By God 'tis bad, and worse than tongue can say.

For the most noticeable point in this studiously wayward and laboriously erratic design is that the principle of composition is as conspicuous by its absence as the breath of inspiration: that the artist, the scholar, the disciple, the student of classic models, is as indiscoverable as the spontaneous humourist or poet. The wildest, the roughest, the crudest offspring of literary impulse working blindly on the passionate elements of excitable ignorance was never more formless, more incoherent, more defective in structure, than this voluminous abortion of deliberate intelligence and conscientious culture.

There is a curious monotony in the variety—if there be not rather a curious variety in the monotony—of character and of style which makes it even more difficult to resume the study of *Cynthia's Revels* when once broken off than even to read through its burdensome and bulky five acts at a sitting; but the reader who lays siege to it with a sufficient supply of patience will find that the latter is the surer if not the only way to appreciate the genuine literary value of its better portions. Most of the figures presented are less than sketches and little more than outlines of inexpert and intolerant caricature: but the 'half-saved' or (as Carlyle has it) 'insalvable' coxcomb and parasite Asotus, who puts himself under the tuition of Amorphus and the patronage of Anaides, is a creature with something of real comic life in him. By what process of induction or deduction the wisdom of critical interpreters should have discerned in the figure of his patron, a fashionable ruffler and ruffian, the likeness of Thomas Dekker, a humble, hard-working, and highly-gifted hack of letters, may be explicable by those who can explain how the character of Hedon, a courtly and voluptuous coxcomb, can have been designed to cast ridicule on John Marston, a rude and rough-hewn man of genius, the fellow-craftsman of Ben Jonson as satirist and as playwright. But such absurdities of misapplication and misconstruction, once set afloat on the Lethean waters of stagnating tradition, will float for ever by grace of the very rottenness which prevents them from sinking. Ignorance assumes and idleness repeats what sciolism ends by accepting as a truth no less indisputable than undisputed. To any rational and careful student it must be obvious that until the publication of Jonson's *Poetaster* we cannot trace, I do not say with any certainty of evidence, but with any plausibility of conjecture, the identity of the principal persons attacked or derided by the satirist. And to identify the originals of such figures as Clove and Orange in *Every Man out of his Humour* can hardly, as Carlyle might have expressed it, be matter of serious interest to any son of Adam. But the famous polemical comedy which appeared a year later than the appearance of *Cynthia's Revels* bore evidence about it, unmistakable by reader or spectator, alike to the general design of the poet and to the particular direction of his personalities. Jonson of course asserted and of course believed that he had undergone gross and incessant provocation for years past from the 'petulant' onslaughts of Marston and Dekker: but what were his grounds for this assertion and this belief we have no means whatever of deciding—we have no ground whatever for conjecture. What we cannot but perceive is the possibly more important fact that indignation and ingenuity, pugnacity and self-esteem, combined to produce and succeeded in producing an incomparably better comedy than the author's last and a considerably better composition than the

author's penultimate attempt. Even the 'apologetical dialogue' appended for the benefit of the reader, fierce and arrogant as it seems to us in its bellicose ambition and its quarrelsome self-assertion, is less violent and overweening in its tone than the furious eloquence of the prelude to *Every Man out of his Humour*. The purity of passion, the sincerity of emotion, which inspires and inflames that singular and splendid substitute for an ordinary prologue, never found again an expression so fervent and so full in the many and various appeals of its author to his audience, immediate or imaginary, against the malevolence of enemies or of critics. But in this Augustan satire his rage and scorn are tempered and adapted to something of dramatic purpose; their expression is more coherent, if not less truculent,—their effect is more harmonious, if not more genuine,—than in the two preceding plays.

There is much in the work of Ben Jonson which may seem strange and perplexing to the most devout and rapturous admirer of his genius: there is nothing so singular, so quaint, so inexplicable, as his selection of Horace for a sponsor or a patron saint. The affinity between Virgil and Tennyson, between Shelley and Lucretius, is patent and palpable: but when Jonson assumes the mask of Horace we can only wonder what would have been the sensation on Olympus if Pluto had suddenly proposed to play the part of Cupid, or if Vulcan had obligingly offered to run on the errands of Mercury. This eccentricity of egoism is only less remarkable than the mixture of care and recklessness in the composition of a play which presents us at its opening with an apparent hero in the person, not of Horace, but of Ovid; and after following his fortunes through four-fifths of the action, drops him into exile at the close of the fourth act, and proceeds with the business of the fifth as though no such figure had ever taken part in the conduct of the play. Shakespeare, who in Jonson's opinion 'wanted art,' assuredly never showed himself so insensible to the natural rules of art as his censor has shown himself here. Apart from the incoherence of construction which was perhaps inevitable in such a complication of serious with satirical design, there is more of artistic merit in this composite work of art than in any play produced by its author since the memorable date of *Every Man in his Humour*. The character of Captain Pantilius Tucca, which seems to have brought down on its creator such a boiling shower-bath or torrent of professional indignation from quarters in which his own distinguished service as a soldier and a representative champion of English military hardihood would seem to have been unaccountably if not scandalously forgotten, is beyond comparison the brightest and the best of his inventions since the date of the creation of Bobadil. But the decrease in humanity of humour, in cordial and genial sympathy or tolerance of imagination, which marks the advance of his genius towards its culmination of scenical and satirical success in *The Alchemist* must be obvious at this stage of his work to those who will compare the delightful cowardice and the inoffensive pretention of Bobadil with the blatant vulgarity and the flagrant rascality of Tucca.

In the memorable year which brought into England her first king of Scottish birth, and made inevitable the future conflict between the revolutionary principle of monarchy by divine right and the conservative principle of self-government by deputy for the commonweal of England, the first great writer who thought fit to throw in his lot with the advocates of the royalist revolution produced on the boards a tragedy of which the moral, despite his conscious or unconscious efforts to disguise or to distort it, is as thoroughly republican and as tragically satirical of despotism as is that of Shakespeare's *Julius Cæsar*. It would be well for the fame of Jonson if the parallel could be carried further: but, although *Sejanus his Fall* may not have received on its appearance the credit or the homage due to the serious and solid merit of its composition and its execution, it must be granted that the author has once more fallen into the excusable but nevertheless unpardonable error of the too studious and industrious Martha. He was careful and troubled about many things absolutely superfluous and super-erogatory; matters of no value or concern whatever for the purpose or the import of a dramatic poem: but the one thing needful, the very condition of poetic life and dramatic interest, he utterly and persistently overlooked. Tiberius, the central character of the action—for the eponymous hero or protagonist of the play is but a crude study of covetous and lecherous ambition,—has not life enough in the presentation of him to inform the part with interest. No praise—of the sort which is due to such labours—can be too high for the strenuous and fervid conscience which inspires every line of the laborious delineation: the recorded words of the tyrant are wrought into the text, his traditional characteristics are welded into the ac-tion, with a patient and earnest fidelity which demands ap-plause no less than recognition: but when we turn from this elaborate statue—from this exquisitely articulated skeleton—to the living figure of Octavius or of Antony, we feel and understand more than ever that Shakespeare 'hath chosen the good part, which shall not be taken away from him.'

Coleridge has very justly animadverted on 'the ana-chronic mixture' of Anglican or Caledonian royalism with the conservatism of an old Roman republican in the character of Arruntius: but we may trace something of the same in-congruous combination in the character of a poet who was at once the sturdiest in aggressive eagerness of self-assertion, and the most copious in courtly effusion of panegyric, among all the distinguished writers of his day. The power of his verse and the purity of his English are nowhere more remarkable than in his two Roman tragedies: on the other hand, his great fault or defect as a dramatist is nowhere more perceptible. This general if not universal infirmity is one which never seems to have occurred to him, careful and studious though he was always of his own powers and performances, as anything of a fault at all. It is one indeed which no writer afflicted with it could reasona-bly be expected to recognize or to repair. Of all purely negative faults, all sins of intellectual omission, it is perhaps the most serious and the most irremediable. It is want of sympathy; a lack of cordial interest, not in his own work or in his own genius,—no one will assert that Jonson was deficient on that score,—but in the individual persons, the men and women represented on the stage. He took so much interest in the creations that he had none left for the creatures of his intellect or art. This fault is not more obvious in the works of his disciples Cartwright and Randolph than in the works of their master. The whole interest is concentrated on the intellectual composition and the intellectual development of the characters and the scheme. Love and hatred, sympathy and antipathy, are superseded and supplanted by pure scientific curiosity: the clear glow of serious or humorous emotion is replaced by the dry light of analytical investigation. *Si vis me flere*—the proverb is something musty. Neither can we laugh heartily or long where all chance of sympathy or cordiality is absolutely inconceivable. The loving laughter which salutes the names of Dogberry and Touchstone, Mrs. Quickly and Falstaff, is never evoked by the most gorgeous opulence of humour, the most glorious audacity of intrigue, which dazzles and delights our understanding in the parts of Sir Epicure Mammon, Rabbi Zeal-of-the-Land Busy, Morose and Fitzdottrel and Mosca: even Bobadil, the most comically attractive of all cowards and

braggarts on record, has no such hold on our regard as many a knave and many a fool of Shakespeare's comic progeny. The triumph of 'Don Face' over his confederates, though we may not be so virtuous as to grudge it him, puts something of a strain upon our conscience if it is heartily to be applauded and enjoyed. One figure, indeed, among all the multitude of Jon-son's invention, is so magnificent in the spiritual stature of his wickedness, in the still dilating verge and expanding proportion of his energies, that admiration in this single case may possibly if not properly overflow into something of intellectual if not moral sympathy. The genius and the courage of Volpone, his sublimity of cynic scorn and his intensity of contemptuous enjoyment,—his limitless capacity for pleasure and his dauntless contemplation of his crimes,—make of this superb sinner a figure which we can hardly realize without some sense of imperious fascination. His views of humanity are those of Swift and of Carlyle: but in him their fruit is not bitterness of sorrow and anger, but rapture of satisfaction and of scorn. His English kinsman, Sir Epicure Mammon, for all his wealth of sensual imagination and voluptuous eloquence, for all his liv-ing play of humour and glowing force of faith, is essentially but a poor creature when set beside the great Venetian. Had the study of Tiberius been informed and vivified by something of the same fervour, the tragedy of *Sejanus* might have had in it some heat of more than merely literary life. But this lesser excellence, the merit of vigorous and vigilant devotion or ap-plication to a high and serious object of literary labour, is apparent in every scene of the tragedy. That the subject is one absolutely devoid of all but historical and literary interest—that not one of these scenes can excite for one instant the least tough, the least phantom, the least shadow of pity or terror—would apparently have seemed to its author no argument against its claim to greatness as a tragic poem. But if it could be admitted, as it will never be by any unperverted judgment, that this eternal canon of tragic art, the law which defines terror and pity as its only proper objects, the alpha and omega of its aim and its design, may ever be disregarded or ignored, we should likewise have to admit that Jonson had in this instance achieved a success as notable as we must otherwise consider his failure. For the accusation of weakness in moral design, of feeble or unnatural treatment of character, cannot with any show of justice be brought against him. Coleridge, whose judg-ment on a question of ethics will scarcely be allowed to carry as much weight as his authority on matters of imagination, ob-jects with some vehemence to the incredible inconsistency of Sejanus in appealing for a sign to the divinity whose altar he proceeds to overthrow, whose power he proceeds to defy, on the appearance of an unfavourable presage. This doubtless is not the conduct of a strong man or a rational thinker: but the great minister of Tiberius is never for an instant throughout the whole course of the action represented as a man of any genuine strength or any solid intelligence. He is shown to us as merely a cunning, daring, unscrupulous and imperious upstart, whose greed and craft, impudence and audacity, intoxicate while they incite and undermine while they uplift him.

The year which witnessed the appearance of *Sejanus* on the stage—acclaimed by Chapman at greater length if not with greater fervour than by any other of Jonson's friends or satel-lites—witnessed also the first appearance of its author in a character which undoubtedly gave free play to some of his most remarkable abilities, but which unquestionably diverted and distorted and absorbed his genius as a dramatist and his talent as a poet after a fashion which no capable student can contem-plate without admiration or consider without regret. The few readers whose patient energy and conscientious curiosity may have led them to traverse—a pilgrimage more painful than Dante's or than Bunyan's—the entire record of the 'Entertainment' which escorted and delayed, at so many successive stations, the progress through London and Westminster of the long-suffering son of Mary Queen of Scots, will probably agree that of the two poetic dialogues or eclogues contributed by Jonson to the metrical part of the ceremony, the dialogue of the Genius and the Flamen is better than that of the Genius and Thamesis; more smooth, more vigorous, and more original. The subsequent prophecy of Electra is at all points unlike the prophecies of a Cassandra: there is something doubly tragic in the irony of chance which put into the mouth of Agamemnon's daughter a prophecy of good fortune to the royal house of Stuart on its first entrance into the capital and ascension to the throne of England. The subsequent *Panegyre* is justly praised by Gifford for its manly and dignified style of official compliment—courtliness untainted by servility: but the style is rather that of fine prose, sedately and sedulously measured and modulated, than that of even ceremonial poetry.

In the same energetic year of his literary life the Laureate produced one of his best minor works—*The Satyr*, a little lyric drama so bright and light and sweet in fancy and in finish of execution that we cannot grudge the expenditure of time and genius on so slight a subject. *The Penates*, which appeared in the following year, gave evidence again of the strong and lively fancy which was to be but too often exercised in the same field of ingenious and pliant invention. The metre is well conceived and gracefully arranged, worthy indeed of nobler words than those which it clothes with light and pleasant melody. The octosyllabics, it will be observed by metrical students, are certainly good, but decidedly not faultless: the burlesque part sustained by Pan is equally dexterous and brilliant in execution.

In 1605 the singular and magnificent coalition of powers which served to build up the composite genius of Jonson displayed in a single masterpiece the consummate and crowning result of its marvellous energies. No other of even his very greatest works is at once so admirable and so enjoyable. The construction or composition of *The Alchemist* is perhaps more wonderful in the perfection and combination of cumulative detail, in triumphant simplicity of process and impeccable felicity of result: but there is in *Volpone* a touch of something like imagination, a savour of something like romance, which gives a higher tone to the style and a deeper interest to the action. The chief agents are indeed what Mr. Carlyle would have called 'unspeakably unexemplary mortals': but the serious fervour and passionate intensity of their resolute and resourceful wickedness give somewhat of a lurid and distorted dignity to the display of their doings and sufferings, which is wanting to the less gigantic and heroic villainies of Subtle, Dol, and Face. The absolutely unqualified and unrelieved rascality of every agent in the later comedy—unless an exception should be made in favour of the unfortunate though enterprising Surly—is another note of inferiority; a mark of comparative baseness in the dramatic metal. In *Volpone* the tone of villainy and the tone of virtue are alike higher. Celia is a harmless lady, if a too submissive consort; Bonario is an honourable gentleman, if too dutiful a son. The Puritan and shopkeeping scoundrels who are swindled by Face and plundered by Lovewit are viler if less villainous figures than the rapacious victims of Volpone.

As to the respective rank or comparative excellence of these two triumphant and transcendent masterpieces, the critic who should take upon himself to pass sentence or pronounce judgment would in my opinion display more audacity than discretion. The steadfast and imperturbable skill of hand which

has woven so many threads of incident, so many shades of character, so many changes of intrigue, into so perfect and superb a pattern of incomparable art as dazzles and delights the reader of *The Alchemist* is unquestionably unique—above comparison with any later or earlier example of kindred genius in the whole range of comedy, if not in the whole world of fiction. The manifold harmony of inventive combination and imaginative contrast—the multitudinous unity of various and concordant effects—the complexity and the simplicity of action and impression, which hardly allow the reader's mind to hesitate between enjoyment and astonishment, laughter and wonder, admiration and diversion—all the distinctive qualities which the alchemic cunning of the poet has fused together in the crucible of dramatic satire for the production of a flawless work of art, have given us the most perfect model of imaginative realism and satirical comedy that the world has ever seen; the most wonderful work of its kind that can ever be run upon the same lines. Nor is it possible to resist a certain sense of immoral sympathy and humorous congratulation, more keen than any Scapin or Mascarille can awake in the mind of a virtuous reader, when Face dismisses Surly with a promise to bring him word to his lodging if he can hear of 'that Face' whom Surly has sworn to mark for his if ever he meets him. From the date of Plautus to the date of Sheridan it would surely be difficult to find in any comedy a touch of glorious impudence which might reasonably be set against this. And the whole part is so full of brilliant and effective and harmonious touches or strokes of character or of humour that even this crowning instance of serene inspiration in the line of superhuman audacity seems merely right and simply natural.

And yet, even while possessed and overmastered by the sense of the incomparable energy, the impeccable skill, and the indefatigable craftsmanship, which combined and conspired together to produce this æsthetically blameless masterpiece, the reader whose instinct requires something more than merely intellectual or æsthetic satisfaction must recognize even here the quality which distinguishes the genius of Ben Jonson from that of the very greatest imaginative humourists—Aristophanes or Rabelais, Shakespeare or Sterne, Vanbrugh or Dickens, Congreve or Thackeray. Each of these was evidently capable of falling in love with his own fancy—of rejoicing in his own imaginative humour as a swimmer in the waves he plays with: but this buoyant and passionate rapture was controlled by an instinctive sense which forbade them to strike out too far or follow the tide too long. However quaint or queer, however typical or exceptional, the figure presented may be—Olivia's or Tristram Shandy's uncle Toby, Sir John Brute or Mr. Peggotty, Lady Wishfort or Lady Kew,—we recognize and accept them as lifelike and actual intimates whose acquaintance has been made for life. Sir Sampson Legend might undoubtedly find himself as much out of place in the drawing-room of the Countess Dowager of Kew as did Sir Wilful Witwoud, on a memorable occasion, in the saloon of his aunt Lady Wishfort: Captain Toby Shandy could hardly have been expected to tolerate the Rabelaisian effervescences of Sir Toby Belch: and Vanbrugh's typical ruffians of rank have little apparently in common with Dickens's representative heroes of the poor. But in all these immortal figures there is the lifeblood of eternal life which can only be infused by the sympathetic faith of the creator in his creature—the breath which animates every word, even if the word be not the very best word that might have been found, with the vital impulse of infallible imagination. But it is difficult to believe that Ben Jonson can have believed, even with some half sympathetic and half sardonic belief, in all the leading figures of his invention. Scorn and indignation are but too often the motives or the mainsprings of his comic art; and when dramatic poetry can exist on the sterile and fiery diet of scorn and indignation, we may hope to find life sustained in happiness and health on a diet of aperients and emetics. The one great modern master of analytic art is somewhat humaner than Jonson in the application of his scientific method to the purpose of dramatic satire. The study of Sludge is finer and subtler by far than the study of Subtle: though undoubtedly it is, in consequence of that very perfection and sublimation of exhaustive analysis, less available for any but a monodramatic purpose. No excuse, no plea, no pretext beyond the fact of esurience and the sense of ability, is suggested for the villainy of Subtle, Dol, and Face. But if we were to see what might possibly be said in extenuation of their rogueries, to hear what might possibly be pleaded in explanation or condonation of their lives, the comedy would fall through and go to pieces: the dramatic effect would collapse and be dissolved. And to this great, single, æsthetic end of art the consummate and conscientious artist who created these immortal figures was content to subdue or to sacrifice all other and subordinate considerations. Coleridge, as no reader will probably need to be reminded, 'thought the Œdipus Tyrannus, The Alchemist, and Tom Jones; the three most perfect plots ever planned.' With the warmest admiration and appreciation of Fielding's noble and immortal masterpiece, I cannot think it at all worthy of comparison, for blameless ingenuity of composition and absolute impeccability of design, with the greatest of tragic and the greatest of comic triumphs in construction ever accomplished by the most consummate and the most conscientious among ancient and modern artists. And when we remember that this perfection of triumphant art is exhibited, not on the scale of an ordinary comedy, whether classic or romantic, comprising a few definite types and a few impressive situations, but on a scale of invention so vast and so various as to comprise in the course of a single play as many characters and as many incidents, all perfectly adjusted and naturally developed out of each other, as would amply suffice for the entire dramatic furniture, for the entire poetic equipment, of a great dramatic poet, we feel that Gifford's expression, a 'prodigy of human intellect,' is equally applicable to *The Fox* and to *The Alchemist*, and is not a whit too strong a term for either. Nor can I admit, as I cannot discern, the blemish or imperfection which others have alleged that they descry in the composition of *Volpone*—the unlikelihood of the device by which retribution is brought down in the fifth act on the criminals who were left at the close of the fourth act in impregnable security and triumph. So far from regarding the comic Nemesis or rather Ate which infatuates and impels Volpone to his doom as a sacrifice of art to morality, an immolation of probability and consistency on the altar of poetic justice, I admire as a master-stroke of character the haughty audacity of caprice which produces or evolves his ruin out of his own hardihood and insolence of exulting and daring enjoyment. For there is something throughout of the lion as well as of the fox in this original and incomparable figure. I know not where to find a third instance of catastrophe comparable with that of either *The Fox* or *The Alchemist* in the whole range of the highest comedy; whether for completeness, for propriety, for interest, for ingenious felicity of event or for perfect combination and exposition of all the leading characters at once in supreme simplicity, unity, and fullness of culminating effect.

And only in the author's two great farces shall we find so vast a range and variety of characters. The foolish and famous couplet of doggrel rhyme which brackets *The Silent Woman* with *The Fox* and *The Alchemist* is liable to prejudice the reader against a work which if compared with those marvellous masterpieces must needs seem to lose its natural rights to notice, to forfeit its actual claim on our rational admiration. Its proper place is not with these, but beside its fellow example of exuberant, elaborate, and deliberately farcical realism—*Bartholomew Fair*. And the two are not less wonderful in their own way, less triumphant on their own lines, than those two crowning examples of comedy. Farcical in construction and in action, they belong to the province of the higher form of art by virtue of their leading characters. Morose indeed, as a victimized monomaniac, is rather a figure of farce than of comedy: Captain Otter and his termagant are characters of comedy rather broad than high: but the collegiate ladies, in their matchless mixture of pretention and profligacy, hypocrisy and pedantry, recall rather the comedies than the farces of Molière by the elaborate and vivid precision of portraiture which presents them in such perfect finish, with such vigour and veracity of effect. Again, if *Bartholomew Fair* is mere farce in many of its minor characters and in some of its grosser episodes and details, the immortal figure of Rabbi Busy belongs to the highest order of comedy. In that absolute and complete incarnation of Puritanism full justice is done to the merits while full justice is done upon the demerits of the barbarian sect from whose inherited and infectious tyranny this nation is as yet but imperfectly delivered. Brother Zeal-of-the-Land is no vulgar impostor, no mere religious quacksalver of such a kind as supplies the common food for satire, the common fuel of ridicule: he is a hypocrite of the earnest kind, an Ironside among civilians; and the very abstinence of his creator from Hudibrastic misrepresentation and caricature makes the satire more thoroughly effective than all that Butler's exuberance of wit and prodigality of intellect could accomplish. The snuffling glutton who begins by exciting our laughter ends by displaying a comic perversity of stoicism in the stocks which is at least more respectable if not less laughable than the complacency of Justice Overdo, the fatuity of poor Cokes, the humble jocosity of a Littlewit, or the intemperate devotion of a Waspe. Hypocrisy streaked with sincerity, greed with a cross of earnestness and craft with a dash of fortitude, combine to make of the Rabbi at once the funniest, the fairest, and the faithfullest study ever taken of a less despicable than detestable type of fanatic.

Not only was the genius of Jonson too great, but his character was too radically noble for a realist or naturalist of the meaner sort. It is only in the minor parts of his gigantic work, only in its insignificant or superfluous components or details, that we find a tedious insistence on wearisome or offensive topics of inartistic satire or ineffectual display. Nor is it upon the ignoble sides of character that this great satiric dramatist prefers to concentrate his attention. As even in the most terrible masterpieces of Balzac, it is not the wickedness of the vicious or criminal agents, it is their energy of intellect, their dauntless versatility of daring, their invincible fertility of resource, for which our interest is claimed or by which our admiration is aroused. In Face as in Subtle, in Volpone as in Mosca, the qualities which delight us are virtues misapplied: it is not their cunning, their avarice, or their lust, it is their courage, their genius, and their wit in which we take no ignoble or irrational pleasure. And indeed it would be strange and incongruous if a great satirist who was also a great poet had erred so grossly as not to aim at this result, or had fallen so grievously short of his aim as not to vindicate the dignity of his design. The same year in which the stage first echoed the majestic accents of Volpone's opening speech was distinguished by the appearance of the *Masque of Blackness*: a work eminent even among its author's in splendour of fancy, invention, and flowing eloquence. Its companion or counterpart, the *Masque of Beauty*, a poem even more notable for these qualities than its precursor, did not appear till three years later. Its brilliant and picturesque variations on the previous theme afford a perfect example of poetic as distinct from prosaic ingenuity.

Between the dates of these two masques, which were first printed and published together, three other entertainments had employed the energetic genius of the Laureate on the double task of scenical invention and literary decoration. The first occasion was that famous visit of King Christian and his hard-drinking Danes which is patriotically supposed to have done so much harm to the proverbially sober and abstemious nation whose temperance is so vividly depicted by the enthusiastic cordiality of Iago. The *Entertainment of Two Kings at Theobalds* opens well, with two vigorous and sonorous couplets of welcome: but the Latin verses are hardly worthy of Gifford's too fervid commendation. The mock marriage of the boyish Earl of Essex and the girl afterwards known to ill fame as Countess of Somerset gave occasion of which Jonson availed himself to the full for massive display of antiquarian magnificence and indefatigable prodigality of inexhaustible detail. The epithalamium of these quasi-nuptials is fine—when it is not coarse (we cannot away, for instance, with the comparison, in serious poetry, of kisses to—cockles!): but the exuberant enthusiasm of Gifford for 'this chaste and beautiful gem' is liable to provoke in the reader's mind a comparison 'with the divine original': and among the very few poets who could sustain a comparison with Catullus no man capable of learning the merest rudiments of poetry will affirm that Ben Jonson can be ranked. His verses are smooth and strong, 'well-torned and true-filed': but the matchless magic, the impeccable inspiration, the grace, the music, the simple and spontaneous perfection of the Latin poem, he could pretend neither to rival nor to reproduce. 'What was my part,' says Jonson in a note, 'the faults here, as well as the virtues, must speak.' These are the concluding words of a most generous and cordial tribute to the merits of the mechanist or stage-carpenter, the musician, and the dancing-master—Inigo Jones, Alfonso Ferrabosco, and Thomas Giles—who were employed on the composition of this magnificent if ill-omened pageant: and they may very reasonably be applied to the two translations from Catullus which the poet—certainly no prophet on this particular occasion—thought fit to introduce into the ceremonial verse of the masques held on the first and second nights of these star-crossed festivities. The faults and the virtues, the vigour of phrase and the accuracy of rendering, the stiffness of expression and the slowness of movement, are unmistakably characteristic of the workman. But in the second night's masque it must be noted that the original verse is distinctly better than the translated stanzas: the dispute of Truth and Opinion is a singularly spirited and vigorous example of amœbæan allegory. In the next year's *Entertainment* of the king and queen at Theobalds, then ceded by its owner to the king, the happy simplicity of invention and arrangement is worthily seconded or supported by the grave and dignified music of the elegiac verse which welcomes the coming and speeds the parting master. Next year *The Masque of Beauty* and the masque at Lord Haddington's marriage, each containing some of Jonson's finest and most flowing verse, bore equal witness to the energy and to the elasticity of his genius for apt and varied invention. The amœbæan stanzas in the later of these two masques have more freedom of movement and spontaneity of music than will perhaps be found in any other poem of equal length from the same indefatigable hand. The fourth of these stanzas is simply magnificent: the loveliness of the next is impaired by that anatomical particu-

larity which too often defaces the serious verse of Jonson with grotesque if not gross deformity of detail. No other poet, except possibly one of his spiritual sons, too surely 'sealed of the tribe of Ben,' would have introduced 'liver' and 'lights' into a sweet and graceful effusion of lyric fancy, good alike in form and sound; a commendation not always nor indeed very frequently deserved by the verse of its author. The variations in the burden of 'Hymen's war' are singularly delicate and happy.

The next was a memorable year in the literary life of Ben Jonson: it witnessed the appearance both of the magnificent *Masque of Queens* and of the famous comedy or farce of *The Silent Woman*. The marvellously vivid and dexterous application of marvellous learning and labour which distinguishes the most splendid of all masques as one of the typically splendid monuments or trophies of English literature has apparently eclipsed, in the appreciation of the general student, that equally admirable fervour of commanding fancy which informs the whole design and gives life to every detail. The interlude of the witches is so royally lavish in its wealth and variety of fertile and lively horror that on a first reading the student may probably do less than justice to the lofty and temperate eloquence of the noble verse and the noble prose which follow.

Of *The Silent Woman* it is not easy to say anything new and true. Its merits are salient and superb: the combination of parts and the accumulation of incidents are so skilfully arranged and so powerfully designed that the result is in its own way incomparable—or comparable only with other works of the master's hand while yet in the fullness of its cunning and the freshness of its strength. But a play of this kind must inevitably challenge a comparison, in the judgment of modern readers, between its author and Molière: and Jonson can hardly, on the whole, sustain that most perilous comparison. It is true that there is matter enough in Jonson's play to have furnished forth two or three of Molière's: and that on that ground—on the score of industrious intelligence and laborious versatility of humour—*The Silent Woman* is as superior to the *Misanthrope* and the *Bourgeois Gentilhomme* as to *Twelfth Night* and *Much Ado about Nothing*. But even when most dazzled by the splendour of studied wit and the felicity of deliberate humour which may even yet explain the extraordinary popularity or reputation of this most imperial and elaborate of all farces, we feel that the author could no more have rivalled the author of *Twelfth Night* than he could have rivalled the author of *Othello*. The Nemesis of the satirist is upon him: he cannot be simply at ease: he cannot be happy in his work without some undertone of sarcasm, some afterthought of allusion, aimed at matters which Molière would have reserved for a slighter style of satire, and which Shakespeare would scarcely have condescended to recognise as possible objects of even momentary attention. His wit is wonderful—admirable, laughable, laudable—it is not in the fullest and the deepest sense delightful. It is radically cruel, contemptuous, intolerant: the sneer of the superior person—Dauphine or Clerimont—is always ready to pass into a snarl: there is something in this great classic writer of the bull-baiting or bear-baiting brutality of his age. We put down *The Fox* or *The Alchemist* with a sense of wondering admiration, hardly affected by the impression of some occasional superfluity or excess: we lay aside *The Silent Woman*, not indeed without grateful recollection of much cordial enjoyment, but with distinct if reluctant conviction that the generous table at which we have been so prodigally entertained was more than a little crowded and overloaded with multifarious if savoury encumbrance of dishes. And if, as was Gifford's opinion, Shakespeare took a hint from the mock duellists in this comedy for the mock duellists in *Twelfth Night*, how wonderfully has he improved on his model! The broad rude humour of Jonson's practical joke is boyishly brutal in the horseplay of its violence: the sweet bright fun of Shakespeare's is in perfect keeping with the purer air of the sunnier climate it thrives in. The divine good-nature, the godlike good-humour of Shakespeare can never be quite perfectly appreciated till we compare his playfulness or his merriment with other men's. Even that of Aristophanes seems to smack of the barbarian beside it.

I cannot but fear that to thorough-going Jonsonians my remarks on the great comedy in which Dryden found the highest perfection of dramatic art on record may seem inadequate if not inappreciative. But to do it anything like justice would take up more space than I can spare: it would indeed, like most of Jonson's other successful plays, demand a separate study of some length and elaboration. The high comedy of the collegiate ladies, the low comedy of Captain and Mrs. Otter, the braggart knights and the Latinist barber, are all as masterly as the versions of Ovid's elegiacs into prose dialogue are tedious in their ingenuity and profitless in their skill. As to the chief character—who must evidently have been a native of Ecclefechan—he is as superior to the *malade imaginaire*, or to any of the Sganarelles of Molière, as is Molière himself to Jonson in lightness of spontaneous movement and easy grace of inspiration. And this is perhaps the only play of Jonson's which will keep the reader or spectator for whole scenes together in an inward riot or an open passion of subdued or unrepressed laughter.

The speeches at Prince Henry's Barriers, written by the Laureate for the occasion of the heir apparent's investiture as Prince of Wales, are noticeable for their fine and dexterous fusion of legend with history in eloquent and weighty verse. But the *Masque of Oberon*, presented the day before the tournament in which the prince bore himself so gallantly as to excite 'the great wonder of the beholders,' is memorable for a quality far higher than this: it is unsurpassed if not unequalled by any other work of its author for brightness and lightness and grace of fancy, for lyric movement and happy simplicity of expression.

Such work, however, was but the byplay in which the genius of this indefatigable poet found its natural relaxation during the year which gave to the world for all time a gift so munificent as that of *The Alchemist*. This 'unequalled play,' as it was called by contemporary admirers, was not miscalled by their enthusiasm; it is in some respects unparalleled among all the existing masterpieces of comedy. No student worthy of the name who may agree with me in preferring *The Fox* to *The Alchemist* will wish to enforce his preference upon others. Such perfection of plot, with such multiplicity of characters—such ingenuity of incident, with such harmony of construction—can be matched, we may surely venture to say, nowhere in the whole vast range of comic invention—nowhere in the whole wide world of dramatic fiction. If the interest is less poignant than in *Volpone*, the fun less continuous than in *The Silent Woman*, the action less simple and spontaneous than that of *Every Man in his Humour*, the vein of comedy is even richer than in any of these other masterpieces. The great Sir Epicure is enough in himself to immortalize the glory of the great artist who conceived and achieved a design so fresh, so daring, so colossal in its humour as that of this magnificent character. And there are at least nine others in the play as perfect in drawing, as vivid in outline, as living in every limb and every feature, as even his whose poetic stature overtops them all. The deathless three confederates, Kastrill and Surly,

Dapper and Drugger, the too perennial Puritans whose villainous whine of purity and hypocrisy has its living echoes even now—not a figure among them could have been carved or coloured by any other hand.

Nor is the list even yet complete of Jonson's poetic work during this truly wonderful year of his literary life. At Christmas he produced 'the Queen's Majesty's masque' of *Love freed from Ignorance and Folly*; a little dramatic poem composed in his lightest and softest vein of fancy, brilliant and melodious throughout. The mighty and majestic Poet Laureate would hardly, I fear, have accepted with benignity the tribute of a compliment to the effect that his use of the sweet and simple heptasyllabic metre was worthy of Richard Barnfield or George Wither: but it is certain that in purity and fluency of music his verse can seldom be compared, as here it justly may, with the clear flutelike notes of *Cynthia* and *The Shepherd's Hunting*. An absurd misprint in the last line but three has afflicted all Jonson's editors with unaccountable perplexity. 'Then, then, angry music sound,' sings the chorus at the close of a song in honour of 'gentle Love and Beauty.' It is inconceivable that no one should yet have discovered the obvious solution of so slight but unfortunate an error in the type as the substitution of 'angry' for 'airy.'

The tragedy of *Catiline his Conspiracy* gave evidence in the following year that the author of *Sejanus* could do better, but could not do much better, on the same rigid lines of rhetorical and studious work which he had followed in the earlier play. Fine as is the opening of this too laborious tragedy, the stately verse has less of dramatic movement than of such as might be proper—if such a thing could be—for epic satire cast into the form of dialogue. Catiline is so mere a monster of ravenous malignity and irrational atrocity that he simply impresses us as an irresponsible though criminal lunatic: and there is something so preposterous, so abnormal, in the conduct and language of all concerned in his conspiracy, that nothing attributed to them seems either rationally credible or logically incredible. Coleridge, in his notes on the first act of this play, expresses his conviction that one passage must surely have fallen into the wrong place—such action at such a moment being impossible for any human creature. But the whole atmosphere is unreal, the whole action unnatural: no one thing said or done is less unlike the truth of life than any other: the writing is immeasurably better than the style of the ranting tragedian Seneca, but the treatment of character is hardly more serious as a study of humanity than his. In fact, what we find here is exactly what we find in the least successful of Jonson's comedies: a study, not of humanity, but of humours. The bloody humour of Cethegus, the braggart humour of Curius, the sluggish humour of Lentulus, the swaggering humour of Catiline himself—a huffcap hero as ever mouthed and strutted out his hour on the stage—all these alike fall under the famous definition of his favourite phrase which the poet had given twelve years before in the induction to the second of his acknowledged comedies. And a tragedy of humours is hardly less than a monster in nature—or rather in that art which 'itself is nature.' Otherwise the second act must be pronounced excellent: the humours of the rival harlots, the masculine ambition of Sempronia, the caprices and cajoleries of Fulvia, are drawn with Jonson's most self-conscious care and skill. But the part of Cicero is burden enough to stifle any play: and some even of the finest passages, such as the much-praised description of the dying Catiline, fine though they be, are not good in the stricter sense of the word; the rhetorical sublimity of their diction comes most perilously near the verge of bombast. Altogether, the play is another magnificent mistake: and each time we open or close it we find it more difficult to believe that the additions made by its author some ten years before to *The Spanish Tragedy* can possibly have been those printed in the later issues of that famous play.[1] Their subtle and spontaneous notes of nature, their profound and searching pathos, their strange and thrilling tone of reality, the beauty and the terror and the truth of every touch, are the signs of a great, a very great tragic poet: and it is all but unimaginable that such an one could have been, but a year or so afterwards, the author of *Sejanus*—and again, eight years later, the author of *Catiline*. There is fine occasional writing in each, but it is not dramatic: and there is good dramatic work in each, but it is not tragic.

For two years after the appearance of *Catiline* there is an interval of silence and inaction in the literary life of its author; an intermission of labour which we cannot pretend to explain in the case of this Herculean workman, who seems usually to have taken an austere and strenuous delight in the employment and exhibition of his colossal energies. His next work is one of which it seems all but impossible for criticism to speak with neither more nor less than justice. Gifford himself, the most devoted of editors and of partisans, to whom all serious students of Jonson owe a tribute of gratitude and respect, seems to have wavered in his judgment on this point to a quite unaccountable degree. In his memoirs of Ben Jonson *Bartholomew Fair* is described as 'a popular piece, but chiefly remarkable for the obloquy to which it has given birth.' In his final note on the play, he expresses an opinion that it has 'not unjustly' been considered as 'nearly on a level with those exquisite dramas, *The Fox* and *The Alchemist*.' Who shall decide when not only do doctors disagree, but the most self-confident of doctors in criticism disagrees with himself to so singular an extent? The dainty palate of Leigh Hunt was naturally nauseated by the undoubtedly greasy flavour of the dramatic viands here served up in such prodigality of profusion: and it must be confessed that some of the meat is too high and some of the sauces are too rank for any but a very strong digestion. But those who turn away from the table in sheer disgust at the coarseness of the fare will lose the enjoyment of some of the richest and strongest humour, some of the most brilliant and varied realism, that ever claimed the attention or excited the admiration of the study or the stage. That 'superlunatical hypocrite,' the immortal and only too immortal Rabbi Busy, towers above the minor characters of the play as the execrable fanaticism which he typifies and embodies was destined to tower above reason and humanity, charity and common sense, in its future influence on the social life of England. But in sheer force and fidelity of presentation this wonderful study from nature can hardly be said to exceed the others which surround and set it off; the dotard Littlewit, the booby Cokes, the petulant fidelity and pig-headed self-confidence of Waspe, the various humours and more various villainies of the multitudinous and riotous subordinates; above all, that enterprising and intelligent champion of social purity, the conscientious and clear-sighted Justice Adam Overdo. When all is said that can reasonably be said against the too accurate reproduction and the too voluminous exposition of vulgar and vicious nature in this enormous and multitudinous pageant—too serious in its satire and too various in its movement for a farce, too farcical in its incidents and too violent in its horseplay for a comedy—the delightful humour of its finer scenes, the wonderful vigour and veracity of the whole, the unsurpassed ingenuity and dexterity of the composition, the energy, harmony, and versatility of the action, must be admitted to ensure its place for ever among the minor and coarser masterpieces of comic art.

The masque of *Love Restored*, to which no date is assigned by the author or his editors, has some noticeable qualities in common with the play which has just been considered, and ought perhaps to have taken precedence of it in our descriptive catalogue. Robin Goodfellow's adventures at court are described with such realistic as well as fantastic humour that his narrative might have made part of the incidents or episodes of the Fair without any impropriety or incongruity; but the lyric fancy and the spirited allegory which enliven this delightful little miniature of a play make it more heartily and more simply enjoyable than many or indeed than most of its author's works. Three other masques were certainly produced during the course of the year 1614. *A Challenge at Tilt at a Marriage*, which was produced eight years after the *Masque of Hymen*, opened the new year with a superb display in honour of the second nuptials of the lady whose previous marriage, now cancelled as a nullity, had been acclaimed by the poet with such superfluous munificence of congratulation and of augury as might have made him hesitate, or at least might make us wish that he had seen fit to hesitate, before undertaking the celebration of the bride's remarriage—even had it not been made infamously memorable by association with matters less familiar to England at any time than to Rome under Pope Alexander VI. or to Paris under Queen Catherine de' Medici. But from the literary point of view, as distinguished from the ethical or the historical, we have less reason to regret than to rejoice in so graceful an example of the poet's abilities as a writer of bright, facile, ingenious and exquisite prose. *The Irish Masque*, presented four days later, may doubtless have been written with no sarcastic intention; but if there was really no such under-current of suggestion or intimation designed or imagined by the writer, we can only find a still keener savour of satire, a still clearer indication of insight, in the characteristic representation of a province whose typical champions fall to wrangling and exchange of reciprocal insults over the display of their ruffianly devotion: while there is not merely a tone of official rebuke or courtly compliment, but a note of genuine good feeling and serious good sense, in the fine solid blank verse delivered by 'a civil gentleman of the nation.' On Twelfth Night the comic masque of *Mercury Vindicated from the Alchemists* gave evidence that the creator of Subtle had not exhausted his arsenal of ridicule, but had yet some shafts of satire left for the professors of Subtle's art or mystery. The humour here is somewhat elaborate, though unquestionably spirited and ingenious.

The next year's is again a blank record; but the year 1616, though to us more mournfully memorable for the timeless death of Shakespeare, is also for the student of Ben Jonson a date of exceptional importance and interest. The production of two masques and a comedy in verse, with the publication of the magnificent first edition of his collected plays and poems, must have kept his name more continuously if not more vividly before the world than in any preceding year of his literary life. The masque of *The Golden Age Restored*, presented on New Year's Night and again on Twelfth Night, is equally ingenious and equally spirited in its happy simplicity of construction and in the vigorous fluency of its versification; which is generally smooth, and in the lyrical dialogue from after the first dance to the close may fairly be called sweet; an epithet very seldom applicable to the solid and polished verse of Jonson. And if *The Devil is an Ass* cannot be ranked among the crowning masterpieces of its author, it is not because the play shows any sign of decadence in literary power or in humorous invention: the writing is admirable, the wealth of comic matter is only too copious, the characters are as firm in outline and as rich in colour as any but the most triumphant examples of his satirical or sympathetic skill in finished delineation and demarcation of humours. On the other hand, it is of all Ben Jonson's comedies since the date of *Cynthia's Revels* the most obsolete in subject of satire, the most temporary in its allusions and applications: the want of fusion or even connection (except of the most mechanical or casual kind) between the various parts of its structure and the alternate topics of its ridicule makes the action more difficult to follow than that of many more complicated plots: and, finally, the admixture of serious sentiment and noble emotion is not so skilfully managed as to evade the imputation of incongruity. Nevertheless, there are touches in the dialogue between Lady Tailbush and Lady Eitherside in the first scene of the fourth act which are worthy of Molière himself, and suggestive of the method and the genius to which we owe the immortal enjoyment derived from the society of Cathos and Madelon—I should say, Polixène and Aminte, of Célimène and Arsinoé, and of Philaminte and Bélise. The third scene of the same act is so nobly written that the reader may feel half inclined to condone or to forget the previous humiliation of the too compliant heroine—her servile and undignified submission to the infamous imbecility of her husband—in admiration of the noble and natural eloquence with which the poet has here endowed her. But this husband, comical as are the scenes in which he develops and dilates from the part of a dupe to the part of an impostor, is a figure almost too loathsome to be ludicrous—or at least, however ludicrous, to be fit for the leading part in a comedy of ethics as well as of manners. And the prodigality of elaboration lavished on such a multitude of subordinate characters, at the expense of all continuous interest and to the sacrifice of all dramatic harmony, may tempt the reader to apostrophize the poet in his own words:

> You are so covetous still to embrace
> More than you can, that you lose all.

Yet a word of parting praise must be given to Satan: a small part as far as extent goes, but a splendid example of high comic imagination after the order of Aristophanes, admirably relieved by the low comedy of the asinine Pug and the voluble doggrel of the antiquated Vice.

Not till nine years after the appearance of this play, in which the genius of the author may be said—in familiar phraseology—to have fallen between two stools, carrying either too much suggestion of human interest for a half allegorical satire, or not enough to give actual interest to the process of the satirical allegory, did Ben Jonson produce on the stage a masterpiece of comedy in which this danger was avoided, this difficulty overcome, with absolute and triumphant facility of execution. In the meantime, however, he had produced nine masques—or ten, counting that which appeared in the same year with his last great work of comic art. The *Masque of Christmas*, which belongs to the same year as the two works last mentioned, is a comfortable little piece of genial comic realism; pleasant, quaint, and homely: the good-humoured humour of little Robin Cupid and his honest old mother 'Venus, a deaf tirewoman,' is more agreeable than many more studious and elaborate examples of the author's fidelity as a painter or photographer of humble life. Next year, in the masque of *Lovers made Men*, called by Gifford *The Masque of Lethe*, he gave full play to his lighter genius and lyric humour: it is a work of exceptionally simple, natural, and graceful fancy. In the following year he brought out the much-admired *Vision of Delight*; a very fair example of his capacities and incapacities. The fanciful, smooth, and flowing verse of its graver parts would be worthy of Fletcher, were it not that the music is less fresh and pure in melody, and that among the finest and sweetest passages there are interspersed such lamentably flat and stiff couplets as would have been impossible to any other poet of equal rank. If justice has not been done in modern times to Ben Jonson as one of the greatest of dramatists and humourists, much more than justice has been done to him as a lyric poet. The famous song of Night in this masque opens and closes most beautifully and most sweetly: but two out of the eleven lines which compose it, the fifth and the sixth, are positively and intolerably bad. The barbarous and pedantic license of inversion which disfigures his best lyrics with such verses as these—'Create of airy forms a stream,' 'But might I of Jove's nectar sup'—is not a fault of the age but a vice of the poet. Marlowe and Lyly, Shakespeare and Webster, Fletcher and Dekker, could write songs as free from this blemish as Tennyson's or Shelley's. There is no surer test of the born lyric poet than the presence or absence of an instinctive sense which assures him when and how and where to use or to abstain from inversion. And in Jonson it was utterly wanting.

The next year's masque, *Pleasure Reconciled to Virtue*, would be very graceful in composition if it were not rather awkward in construction. The verses in praise of dancing are very pretty, sedate, and polished: and the burlesque part (spoken by 'Messer Gaster' in person) has more than usual of Rabelaisian freedom and energy. The antimasque afterwards prefixed to it, *For the Honour of Wales*, is somewhat ponderous in its jocularity, but has genuine touches of humour and serious notes of character in its 'tedious and brief' display of the poet's incomparable industry and devotion to the study of dialects and details: and the close is noble and simple in its patriotic or provincial eloquence. But in the year 1620 the comic genius of Jonson shone out once more in all the splendour of its strength. The only masque of that year, *News from the New World discovered in the Moon*, is worthy of a prose Aristophanes: in other words, it is a satire such as Aristophanes might have written, if that greater poet had ever condescended to write prose. Here for once the generous words of Jonson's noble panegyric on Shakespeare may justly be applied to himself: in his own immortal phrase, the humour of this little comedy is 'not of an age, but for all time.' At the very opening we find ourselves on but too familiar ground, and feel that the poet must have shot himself forward by sheer inspiration into our own enlightened age, when we hear 'a printer of news' avowing the notable fact that 'I do hearken after them, wherever they be, at any rates; I'll give anything for a good copy now, be it true or false, so it be news.' Are not these, the reader must ask himself, the accents of some gutter gaolbird—some dunghill gazetteer of this very present day? Or is the avowal too honest in its impudence for such lips as these? After this, the anticipation of something like railways ('coaches' that 'go only with wind')—if not also of something like balloons ('a castle in the air that runs upon wheels, with a winged lanthorn')—seems but a commonplace example of prophetic instinct.

The longest of Ben Jonson's masques was expanded to its present bulk by the additions made at each successive representation before the king; to whose not over delicate or fastidious taste this *Masque of the Metamorphosed Gipsies* would seem to have given incomparable if not inexhaustible delight. And even those readers who may least enjoy the decidedly greasy wit or humour of some among its once most popular lyrical parts must admire and cannot but enjoy the rare and even refined loveliness of others. The fortune most unfortunately told of his future life and death to the future King Charles I. is told in the very best lyric verse that the poet could command: a strain of quite exceptional sweetness, simplicity, and purity of music: to which, as we read it now, the record of history seems to play a most tragically ironical accompaniment, in a minor key of subdued and sardonic presage. And besides these graver and lovelier interludes of poetry which relieve the somewhat obtrusive realism of the broader comic parts, this masque has other claims on our notice and remembrance; the ingenuity and dexterity, the richness of resource and the pliability of humour, which inform and animate all its lyric prophecies or compliments.

The masque which appeared in the following year is a monument of learning and labour such as no other poet could have dreamed of lavishing on a ceremonial or official piece of work, and which can only be appreciated by careful reading and thorough study of the copious notes and references appended to the text. But the writer's fancy was at a low ebb when it could devise nothing better than is to be found in this *Masque of Augurs*: the humour is coarse and clumsy, the verses are flat and stiff. In the next year's Twelfth-Night masque, *Time vindicated to himself and to his honours*, the vigorous and vicious personalities of the attack on George Wither give some life to the part in which the author of *Abuses Stript and Whipt* is brought in under the name of Chronomastix to make mirth for the groundlings of the Court. The feeble and facile fluency of his pedestrian Muse in the least fortunate hours of her too voluble and voluminous improvisation is not unfairly caricatured; but the Laureate's malevolence is something too obvious in his ridicule of the 'soft ambling verse' whose 'rapture' at its highest has the quality denied by nature to Jonson's—the divine gift of melodious and passionate simplicity. A better and happier use for his yet unimpaired faculty of humour was found in the following year's masque of *Neptune's Triumph for the Return of Albion*; which contains the most famous and eloquent panegyric on the art of cookery that ever anticipated the ardours of Thackeray and the enthusiasm of Dumas. The passage is a really superb example of tragicomic or mock-heroic blank verse; and in the closing lyrics of the masque there is no lack of graceful fancy and harmonious elegance. For the next year's masque of *Pan's Anniversary, or The Shepherd's Holiday*, not quite so much can reasonably be said. It is a typical and a flagrant instance of the poet's proverbial and incurable tendency to overdo everything: there is but artificial smoothness in the verse, and but clownish ingenuity in the prose of it.

But the year 1625 is memorable to the students and admirers of Ben Jonson for the appearance of a work worth almost all his masques together; a work in which the author of *The Fox* and *The Alchemist* once more reasserted his claim to a seat which no other poet and no other dramatist could dispute. The last complete and finished masterpiece of his genius is the splendid comedy of *The Staple of News*. This, rather than *The Silent Woman*, is the play which should be considered as the third—or perhaps we should say the fourth—of the crowning works which represent the consummate and incomparable powers of its author. No man can know anything worth knowing of Ben Jonson who has not studied and digested the text of *Every Man in his Humour*, *The Fox*, *The Alchemist*, and *The Staple of News*: but any man who has may be said to know him well. To a cursory or an incompetent reader it may appear at first sight that the damning fault of *The Devil is an Ass* is also the fault of this later comedy: that we have here again an infelicitous and an incongruous combination of realistic satire with Aristophanic allegory, and that the harmony of the different parts, the unity of the composite action, which a pupil of Aristophanes should at least have striven to attain—or, if he could not, at least to imitate and to respect—can here be considered as conspicuous only by their absence. But no care-

ful and candid critic will retain such an impression after due study has been given to the third poetic comedy which reveals to us the genius of Jonson, not merely as a realistic artist in prose or a master of magnificent farce, but as a great comic poet. The scheme of his last preceding comedy had been vitiated by a want of coherence between the actual and the allegorical, the fantastic and the literal point of view; and the result was confusion without fusion of parts: here, on the other hand, we have fusion without confusion between the dramatic allegory suggested by Aristophanes, the admirably fresh and living presentation of the three Pennyboys, and the prophetic satire of the newsmarket or Stock Exchange of journalism. The competent reader will be divided between surprise at the possibility and delight in the perfection of the success achieved by a poet who has actually endowed with sufficiency of comic life and humorous reality a whole group of symbolic personifications; from the magnificent Infanta herself, Aurelia Clara Pecunia, most gracious and generous yet most sensitive and discreet of imperial damsels, even down to little 'blushet' Rose Wax the chambermaid. Her young suitor is at least as good a picture of a generous light-headed prodigal as ever was shown on any stage: as much of a man as Charles Surface, and very much more of a gentleman. The miserly uncle, though very well drawn, is less exceptionally well drawn: but Pennyboy Canter, the disguised father, is equally delightful from the moment of his entrance with an extempore carol of salutation on his lips to those in which he appears to rescue the misused Infanta from the neglectful favourite of her choice, and reappears at the close of the play to rescue his son, redeem his brother, and scatter the community of jeerers: to whose humour Gifford is somewhat less than just when he compares it with 'the *vapouring* in *Bartholomew Fair*': for it is neither coarse nor tedious, and takes up but very little space; and that not unamusingly. As for the great scene of the Staple, it is one of the most masterly in ancient or modern comedy of the typical or satirical kind. The central 'Office' here opened, to the great offence (it should seem) of 'most of the spectators'—a fact which, as Gifford justly remarks, 'argues very little for the good sense of the audience,'—may be regarded by a modern student as representing the narrow little nest in which was laid the modest little egg of modern journalism—that bird of many notes and many feathers, now so like an eagle and now so like a vulture: now soaring as a falcon or sailing as a pigeon over continents and battle-fields, now grovelling and groping as a dunghill kite, with its beak in a very middenstead of falsehood and of filth. The vast range of Ben Jonson's interest and observation is here as manifest as the wide scope and infinite variety of his humour. Science and warfare, Spinoza and Galileo, come alike within reach of its notice, and serve alike for the material of its merriment. The invention of torpedos is anticipated by two centuries and a half; while in the assiduity of the newsmongers who traffic in eavesdropping detail we acknowledge a resemblance to that estimable race of tradesmen known to Parisian accuracy as interwieveurs. And the lunacy of apocalyptic interpreters or prophets is gibbeted side by side with the fanatical ignorance of missionary enthusiasm, with impostures of professional quackery and speculations in personal libel. Certainly, if ever Ben deserved the prophetic title of Vates, it was in this last magnificent work of his maturest genius. Never had his style or his verse been riper or richer, more vigorous or more pure. And even the interludes in which we hear the commentary and gather the verdict of 'these ridiculous gossips' (as their creator calls them) 'who tattle between the acts' are incomparably superior to his earlier efforts or excursions in the same field of humorous invention. The intrusive commentators on *Every Man out of his Humour*, for instance, are mere nullities—the awkward and abortive issue of unconscious uneasiness and inartistic egoism. But Expectation, Mirth, Tattle, and Censure, are genuine and living sketches of natural and amusing figures: and their dialogues, for appropriate and spirited simplicity, are worthy of comparison with even those of a similar nature which we owe not more to the genius than to the assailants of Molière.

In 1625 Ben Jonson had brought out his last great comedy: in 1626 he brought out the last of his finer sort of masques. The little so-called *Masque of Owls*, which precedes it in the table of contents, is (as Gifford points out) no masque at all: it is a quaint effusion of doggrel dashed with wit and streaked with satire. But in *The Fortunate Isles, and their Union*, the humour and the verse are alike excellent: the jest on Plato's ideas would have delighted Landor, and the wish of Merefool to 'see a Brahman or a Gymnosophist' is worthy of a modern believer in esoteric Buddhism. Few if any of the masques have in them lyrics of smoother and clearer flow; and the construction is no less graceful than ingenious. The next reappearance of the poet, after a silence during three years of broken or breaking health, was so memorably unfortunate in its issue that the name and the fate of a play which was only too naturally and deservedly hooted off the stage are probably familiar to many who know nothing of the masterpiece which had last preceded it. Ever since Lamb gathered some excerpts from the more high-toned and elaborate passages of *The New Inn, or The Light Heart*, and commended in them 'the poetical fancy and elegance of mind of the supposed rugged old bard,' it has been the fashion to do justice if not something more than justice to the literary qualities of this play; which no doubt contains much vigorous and some graceful writing, and may now and then amuse a tolerant reader by its accumulating and culminating absurdities of action and catastrophe, character and event. But that the work shows portentous signs of mental decay, or at all events of temporary collapse in judgment and in sense, can be questioned by no sane reader of so much as the argument. To rank any preceding play of Jonson's among those dismissed by Dryden as his 'dotages' would be to attribute to Dryden a verdict displaying the veriest imbecility of impudence: but to *The New Inn* that rough and somewhat brutal phrase is on the whole but too plausibly applicable.

At the beginning of the next year Jonson came forward in his official capacity as court poet or laureate, and produced 'the Queen's Masque,' *Love's Triumph through Callipolis*, and again, at Shrovetide, 'the King's Masque,' *Chloridia*. A few good verses, faint echoes of a former song, redeem the first of these from the condemnation of compassion or contempt: and there is still some evidence in its composition of conscientious energy and of capacity not yet reduced from the stage of decadence to the stage of collapse. But the hymn which begins fairly enough with imitation of an earlier and nobler strain of verse at once subsides into commonplace, and closes in doggrel which would have disgraced a Sylvester or a Quarles. It is impossible to read *Chloridia* without a regretful reflection on the lapse of time which prevented it from being a beautiful and typical instance of the author's lyric power: but, however inferior it may be to what he would have made of so beautiful a subject in the freshness and fullness of his inventive and fanciful genius, it is still ingenious and effective after a fashion; and the first song is so genuinely graceful and simple as to remind us of Wordsworth in his more pedestrian but not uninspired moods or measures of lyrical or elegiac verse.

The higher genius of Ben Jonson as a comic poet was yet once more to show itself in one brilliant flash of parting splendour before its approaching sunset. No other of his works would seem to have met with such all but universal neglect as *The Magnetic Lady*; I do not remember to have ever seen it quoted or referred to, except once by Dryden, who in his *Essay of Dramatic Poesy* cites from it an example of narrative substituted for action, 'where one comes out from dinner, and relates the quarrels and disorders of it, to save the undecent appearance of them on the stage, and to abbreviate the story.' And yet any competent spectator of its opening scenes must have felt a keen satisfaction at the apparent revival of the comic power and renewal of the dramatic instinct so lamentably enfeebled and eclipsed on the last occasion of a new play from the same hand. The first act is full of brilliant satirical description and humorous analysis of humours: the commentator Compass, to whom we owe these masterly summaries of character, is an excellent counterpart of that 'reasonable man' who so constantly reappears on the stage of Molière to correct with his ridicule or control by his influence the extravagant or erratic tendencies of his associates. Very few examples of Jonson's grave and deliberate humour are finer than the ironical counsel given by Compass to the courtly fop whom he dissuades from challenging the soldier who has insulted him, on the ground that the soldier

> has killed so many
> As it is ten to one his turn is next:
> You never fought with any, less, slew any;
> And therefore have the [fairer] hopes before you.

The rest of the speech, with all that follows to the close of the scene, is no less ripe and rich in sedate and ingenious irony. There is no less admirable humour in the previous discourse of the usurer in praise of wealth—especially as being the only real test of a man's character:

> For, be he rich, he straight with evidence knows
> Whether he have any compassion
> Or inclination unto virtue, or no:
> Where the poor knave erroneously believes
> If he were rich he would build churches, or
> Do such mad things.

Most of the characters are naturally and vigorously drawn in outline or in profile: Dame Polish is a figure well worthy the cordial and lavish commendation of Gifford: and the action is not only original and ingenious, but during the first four acts at any rate harmonious and amusing. The fifth act seems to me somewhat weaker; but the interludes are full of spirit, good humour, and good sense.

A Tale of a Tub, which appeared in the following year, is a singular sample of farce elaborated and exalted into comedy. This rustic study, though 'not liked' by the king and queen when acted before them at court, has very real merits in a homely way. The list of characters looks unpromising, and reminds us to regret that the old poet could not be induced to profit by Feltham's very just and reasonable animadversions on 'all your jests so nominal'; which deface this play no less than *The New Inn*, and repel the most tolerant reader by their formal and laborious puerility. But the action opens brightly and briskly: the dispute about 'Zin Valentine' is only less good in its way than one of George Eliot's exquisite minor touches—Mr. Dempster's derivation of the word Presbyterian from one Jack Presbyter of historic infamy: the young squire's careful and testy 'man and governor' is no unworthy younger brother of Numps in *Bartholomew Fair*: and the rustic heroine, a figure sketched with rough realistic humour, is hardly less than delightful when she remarks, after witnessing the arrest of her intended bridegroom on a charge of highway robbery, 'He might have married one first, and have been hanged after, if he had had a mind to 't;' a reflection worthy of Congreve or Vanbrugh, Miss Hoyden or Miss Prue. But Jonson had never laid to heart the wisdom expressed in the admirable proverb—'Qui trop embrasse mal étreint;' the simple subject of the play and the homely motive of the action are overlaid and overloaded by the multiplicity of minor characters and episodical superfluities, and the upshot of all the poet's really ingenious contrivances is pointless as well as farcical and flat as well as trivial. But there is certainly no sign of dotage in any work of Ben Jonson's produced before or after the lamentable date of *The New Inn*. The author apologizes for the homely and rustic quality of his uncourtly play; but if it be a failure, it is not on account of its plebeian humility, but through the writer's want of any real sympathy with his characters, any hearty relish of his subject: because throughout the whole conduct of a complicated intrigue he shows himself ungenially observant and contemptuously studious of his models: because the qualities most needed for such work, transparent lucidity and straightforward simplicity of exposition, are not to be found in these last comedies: because, for instance, as much attention is needed to appreciate the ingenious process of 'humours reconciled' in *The Magnetic Lady*, or to follow the no less ingenious evolution of boorish rivalries and clownish intrigues in the play just noticed, as to follow the action and appreciate the design of *The Fox* or *The Alchemist*.

The masque of this year, *Love's Welcome at Welbeck*, is a thing of very slight pretentions, but not unsuccessful or undiverting after its homely fashion. In the next year's companion masque, *Love's Welcome at Bolsover*, the verse, though not wanting in grace or ease, is less remarkable than the rough personal satire on Inigo Jones; who, it may be observed, is as ready with a quotation from Chaucer as Goody Polish in *The Magnetic Lady* or Lovel in *The New Inn*.

Of this great dramatist's other than dramatic work in poetry or in prose this is not the place to speak: and his two posthumous fragments of dramatic poetry, interesting and characteristic as they are, can hardly affect for the better or for the worse our estimate of his powers. Had *Mortimer his Fall* been completed, we should undoubtedly have had a third example of rhetorical drama, careful, conscientious, energetic, impassive and impressive; worthy to stand beside the author's two Roman tragedies: and Mortimer might have confronted and outfaced Sejanus and Catiline in sonorous audacity of rhythmic self-assertion and triumphant ostentation of magnificent vacuity. In *The Sad Shepherd* we find the faults and the merits of his best and his worst masques so blended and confounded that we cannot but perceive the injurious effect on the Laureate's genius or instinct of intelligence produced by the habit of conventional invention which the writing of verse to order and the arrangement of effects for a pageant had now made inevitable and incurable. A masque including an antimasque, in which the serious part is relieved and set off by the introduction of parody or burlesque, was a form of art or artificial fashion in which incongruity was a merit; the grosser the burlesque, the broader the parody, the greater was the success and the more effective was the result: but in a dramatic attempt of higher pretention than such as might be looked for in the literary groundwork or raw material for a pageant, this intrusion of incongruous contrast is a pure barbarism—a positive solecism in composition. The collocation of such names and such figures as those of Æglamour and Earine with such others as Much and Maudlin, Scathlock and Scarlet, is no whit less preposterous or less ridiculous, less inartistic or less irritating, than the conjunction in Dekker's *Satiromastix* of Peter Flash and Sir Quintilian, Sir Adam Prickshaft and Sir Vaughan ap

Rees, with Crispinus and Demetrius, Asinius and Horace: and the offence is graver, more inexcusable and more inexplicable, in a work of pure fancy or imagination, than in a work of poetic invention crossed and chequered with controversial satire. Yet Gifford, who can hardly find words or occasions sufficient to express his sense of Dekker's 'inconceivable folly,' or his contempt for 'a plot that can scarcely be equalled in absurdity by the worst of the plays which Dekker was ever employed to "dress,"' has not a syllable of reprehension for the portentous incongruities of this mature and elaborate poem. On the other hand, even Gifford's editorial enthusiasm could not overestimate the ingenious excellence of construction, the masterly harmony of composition, which every reader of the argument must have observed with such admiration as can but intensify his regret that scarcely half of the projected poem has come down to us. No work of Ben Jonson's is more amusing and agreeable to read, as none is more nobly graceful in expression or more excellent in simplicity of style.

The immense influence of this great writer on his own generation is not more evident or more memorable than is the refraction or reverberation of that influence on the next. This 'sovereign sway and masterdom,' this overpowering preponderance of reputation, could not but be and could not but pass away. No giant had ever the divine versatility of a Shakespeare: but of all the giant brood none ever showed so much diversity of power as Jonson. In no single work has he displayed such masterly variety of style as has Byron in his two great poems, *Don Juan* and *The Vision of Judgment*: the results of his attempts at mixture or fusion of poetry with farce will stand exposed in all their deformity and discrepancy if we set them beside the triumphant results of Shakespeare's. That faultless felicity of divine caprice which harmonizes into such absolute congruity all the outwardly incompatible elements of such works as *Twelfth Night* and *The Tempest*, the *Winter's Tale* and *A Midsummer Night's Dream*, is perhaps of all Shakespeare's incomparable gifts the one most utterly beyond reach of other poets. But when we consider the various faculties and powers of Jonson's genius and intelligence, when we examine severally the divers forces and capacities enjoyed and exercised by this giant workman in the performance of his work, we are amazed into admiration only less in its degree than we feel for the greatest among poets. It is not admiration of the same kind: there is less in it of love and worship than we give to the gods of song; but it is with deep reverence and with glowing gratitude that we salute in this Titan of the English stage 'il maestro di color che sanno.'

Notes

1. No student will need to be reminded of what is apparently unknown to some writers who have thought fit to offer an opinion on this subject—that different additions were made at different dates, and by different hands, to certain popular plays of the time. The original *Faustus* of Marlowe was altered and re-altered, at least three times, by three if not more purveyors of interpolated and incongruous matter: and even that superb masterpiece would hardly seem to have rivalled the popularity of Kyd's tragedy—a popularity by no means unmerited.

ELISABETH WOODBRIDGE
From *Studies in Jonson's Comedy*
1898, pp. 28–79

Chapter 3
Character Treatment in Jonson's Typical Comedy

Accepting . . . Jonson's work as of the judicial type, consider in detail his treatment of character. And first, it does not do to rest upon his own assertions with regard to his writing. For, with the best intentions, one seldom tells the exact truth about oneself, and though what a man says of himself is always significant and worth regarding, it is often to be taken as indirectly indicative of his real nature and purpose rather than as directly descriptive of them. Jonson, moreover, was sometimes singularly infelicitous in speaking of himself, and the mere culling from prologue and epilogue of all the lines in which he expresses his dramatic theory will not give quite an adequate conception of his actual work. Especially is this true of his comedies, where his artistic sense sometimes led him to depart as a playwright from some of his theories as a thinker. It was not that his utterances were insincere, but that his theory was not quite complete enough to cover all of his practice.

This method of collecting his statements and adding them together to stand for his art is perhaps responsible for the assumption generally made that Jonson's comedies always enforce a moral lesson. This is simply not true, although he himself does with great emphasis and entire sincerity assert that the duty of the comedian is to punish vice. Thus here:

> But with an armed and resolved hand,
> I'll strip the ragged follies of the time
> Naked as at their birth . . . .
>   . . . . and with a whip of steel,
> Print wounding lashes in their iron-ribs.
>   . . . . my strict hand
> Was made to seize on vice, and with a gripe
> Squeeze out the humor of such spongy souls,
> As lick up every idle vanity.[1]

This is well enough for a part of his work. It applies to *Volpone*; it applies also to *The Poetaster* and to *Cynthia's Revels*, though not in the same sense, for the genuine morality of *Volpone* is as diverse as possible from the pharisaic, egotistic superiority of the last two plays. It applies also to Jonson's two tragedies, and to parts of his other comedies. On the other hand, the moral of *The Alchemist* or of *Bartholomew Fair* would be hard to find. For Jonson did indeed teach and scourge, but not always did his teaching inculcate morality or his scourging lash the scoundrel as such. On the whole, his efforts are directed quite as much against intellectual weakness as against moral, and he preached quite as emphatically from the text "don't be a fool" as from the text "don't be a knave," while if we except his tragedies, the weight of emphasis is rather on the first than on the second. Run rapidly through the important plays with this in view:

In *Every Man in His Humour* there are a number of rogues and a few honest men, but the line of division is drawn, not on a basis of honesty, but on a basis of wit. The three witty rogues, Wellbred, Young Knowell, and Brainworm, are successful in discomfiting not only the other rogues, but also the honest men, and Brainworm is at the end pardoned for his offenses because he has shown such ability in committing them. Such a play can scarcely be called moral, though no one would call it immoral either, unless it were some zealot such as Zeal-of-the-land Busy. If it teaches anything, it teaches that it is convenient to have a quick brain, a ready tongue, and an elastic conscience.

In *Every Man out of His Humour* the tone is more severe, and the author, speaking through Macilente, does indeed lash vice as well as folly. Every person is in turn exposed and censured, but the moral tone is spoiled by the fact that Macilente himself, through whose malignant activity these exposures are brought about, is left untouched. He is rather the most disagreeable scoundrel of them all, yet he goes free, and leaves the

stage at the end licking his chops over the discomfiture he has occasioned.

In *Cynthia's Revels* and *The Poetaster* the pharisaic tone already alluded to may be called moral, but it seems more truly immoral than the most direct praise of vice could be.

Sejanus and *Volpone*, which follow, may be taken together, though one is called tragedy and one comedy. In these the tone, for the first and almost the last time, is that of a firm and strenuous morality. Both plays show stupendous vice bringing upon itself its own ruin—a negative kind of morality, to be sure, but genuine and consistent.

In *Epicoene*, however, we have pure farce, without a trace of moral tone, and all the better for its freedom from it, and in *The Alchemist* we have the very apotheosis of roguery. Three people conspire to cheat the world. Their success is complete and they outwit the vicious, the hypocritical, the simple; but they also bring about the discomfiture of the only honest man in the play. When at last they are brought to bay, one of the three saves himself by deserting the other two, and purchases his master's forgiveness by making over to him their ill-gotten gains.

Finally, in the coarse but good-natured laughter of *Bartholomew Fair*, even the fools are let off easily, while the knaves find the mad, merry rascality of the fair a very Elysium. One might go on through the rest of the plays, but the great ones end here, and the rest would not furnish anything new.

Jonson's comedy, then, is judicial but not always moral, that is, it always subjects its persons to a judgment according to some standard, but this standard is quite as apt to be an intellectual one as a moral one. Among those which apply an intellectual standard, *The Alchemist* and *Bartholomew Fair* are preëminent; among those which apply the moral standard, *Volpone* stands alone among the comedies, but in this as in other respects it may be classed with the tragedies *Sejanus* and *Catiline*.

Thus far we have been considering the general tone and purpose of the comedies in their treatment of character. The next question is as to the method of treatment. Satire, Moulton remarks, may accomplish its end in one of two ways; "the one declares a thing ridiculous, the other exhibits it in a ridiculous disguise. Reducing the two to their lowest terms, in the one you call a man a fool, in the other you disguise yourself in his likeness and then play the fool"—he illustrates by citing the *Saturday Review* and *Punch*, "the first alleges folly, the latter presents it."[2]

In the case of the dramatist, one would suppose that only the second method would be employed. As a matter of fact the temptation to "allege" folly as well to "present" it is usually too great to be resisted. Even Molière sometimes has a wise Dorine or a Cléante to explain or expose the follies of the other characters, while Jonson almost always has some such character to stand, as it were, with pointer in hand, as demonstrator of the action. Once one begins to watch for this feature it is really remarkable how constant it is. Sometimes there is one demonstrator for the entire play, sometimes there are several who take turns. Thus, in *Every Man out of His Humour* Macilente is demonstrator in chief; for the scenes where he is absent, Carlo Buffone acts as understudy.[3] In *Cynthia's Revels*, Crites holds the pointer;[4] in *The Poetaster*, it is Horace; in *The Silent Woman*, it is any one of the three friends: Truewit, Dauphine, or Clerimont; in *Volpone*, it is, for the main action, Mosca and Volpone themselves, who both egg on their victims and comment on their folly, while for the subinterest of Sir Politick Would-be, the demonstrator or showman is Peregrine. Even Jonson's tragedy is not free from this peculiarity, for in *Sejanus* the function of Arruntius in the play is only as a commenter on the other characters.

Such an expedient seems essentially undramatic. When used to excess, as Jonson often used it, it is so. To be constantly explaining the nature of the characters implies either that the dramatist does not trust the cogency of his presentation, or that he does not trust the perceptive powers of the audience. The latter alternative is in Jonson's case not unlikely, but it is also true that, save when he was at his very best, his genius was more expository than dramatic; his mind was more akin to Bacon's than to Shakespeare's, and it was possibly a little easier for him to explain in crisp phrase exactly how a man was a fool, than for him to give the man free scope to act according to his folly.[5] Some of the best things in his dramas are found in these non-dramatic lapses. In *Every Man out of His Humour*, for instance, in the scene where the scented courtier, Fastidious Brisk, meets the court lady, Saviolina, Macilente stands by watching, and one of his comments is worth all the rest of the scene put together. Fastidious, knowing the lady is about to enter, says, "A kind of affectionate reverence strikes me with a cold shivering, methinks." Macilente mutters sardonically: "I like such tempers well, as stand before their mistresses with fear and trembling; and before their Maker, like impudent mountains!"[6]

When the practise is not carried to excess, however; it is not out of place, but is entirely consistent with the spirit of this kind of comedy. For, as will more clearly appear in the discussion of plots, the characters in any such play may always be divided into two groups, a large group of victims, a small group of victimizers or intriguers who control events and search out ways to "gull" the victims. Such being the case, it is quite natural that they should at the same time laugh at and discuss their folly. Thus in *Volpone*, the comments of Mosca and his master on the stupid greed of the legacy-hunters are dramatically proper, whereas those of Peregrine on Sir Politick are doubtful. In *Epicoene* the gleeful asides of the three young men as they work up the two fools, Daw and La-Foole, are as legitimate as are the whispered gibes of Sir Toby, Sir Andrew and Maria as they watch Malvolio from their ambush.

In his treatment of character, there are two dangers liable to beset the satiric dramatist. His material being human infirmity, his tone judicial and didactic, his temper a little superior if not scornful, he is apt to do one of two things:—if he is not broad-minded enough and impersonal enough he will be too particular, and fall into personal invective; if he has not a firm grasp of the concrete or artistic he will be too general, and will trench upon allegory.

The tendency toward personalities is easy to comprehend. It characterized the beginnings of comedy, and Aristophanes boldly and deliberately gave way to it. Menander appears to have broken away from it,—partly probably for political reasons,—and the Roman comedy is to some extent free from it, but it has always been one of the pitfalls of satire. Jonson certainly fell into it in two plays, *Cynthia's Revels* and *The Poetaster*, and probably in some parts of many of his other plays, and though he is vehement in defending himself from the charge of personality, his very defences, like his repeated assertions that he was above feeling the abuse of his enemies, do not leave upon us quite the impression he intended. Yet if this was his besetting sin, he knew it for a fault, knew that

> poet never credit gain'd
> By writing truths, but things, like truths, well
>   feign'd.[7]

And doubtless he was often enough misunderstood and wilfully misinterpreted. There were plenty of "small fry" about town,

ready to "make a libel which he meant a play,"[8] and he has us heartily on his side when he scores the "State-decypher, or politick picklock of the scene," who is "so solemnly ridiculous as to search out, who was meant by the gingerbread-woman, who by the hobby-horse man, who by the costard-monger, nay, who by their wares. Or that will pretend to affirm on his own inspired ignorance, what Mirror of Magistrate is meant by the justice, what great lady by the pig-woman, what concealed statesman by the seller of mouse-traps, and so of the rest."[9]

Compare with this an interesting parallel in Molière:

> Et voilà de quoi j'ouïs l'autre jour se plaindre Molière, parlant à des personnes qui le chargeoient de même chose que vous. Il disoit que rien ne lui donnoit du déplaisir comme d'être accusé de regarder quelqu'un dans les portraits qu'il fait; que son dessein est de peindre les moeurs sans vouloir toucher aux personnes . . . . et que si quelque-chose étoit capable de le dégoûter de faire des comédies, c'étoit les ressemblances qu'on y vouloit toujours trouver, etc.[10]

While, for an agreement which was perhaps even deliberately verbal, note Congreve's:

> Others there are, whose malice we'd prevent:
> Such, who watch plays, with scurrilous intent
> To mark out who by characters are meant:
> And though no perfect likeness they can trace,
> Yet each pretends to know the copied face.
> These, with false glosses, feed their own ill-nature,
> And turn to libel what was meant a satire.[11]

The opposite tendency, that towards allegory, is a natural result of the comic point of view. For since the comedian regards defects, oddities of character, he is usually led to the study of temperaments in their extreme development, and his treatment is necessarily bound to emphasize the eccentricities in the temperament, leaving the rest of the personality somewhat shadowy. Indeed, it was a part of Jonson's theory that if eccentricity is anything more than external, it will effect the entire personality. To any such case he applies the term "humour," defining the term thus:

> As when some one peculiar quality
> Doth so possess a man, that it doth draw
> All his affects, his spirits, and his powers,
> In their confluctions, all to run one way,
> This may be truly said to be a humor.[12]

The theory is psychologically perfectly sound, but it, as well as Jonson's practice, has met with rather harsh treatment at the hands of critics. Thus Hazlitt:

> His imagination fastens instinctively on some one mark or sign by which he designates the individual, and never lets it go, for fear of not meeting with any other means to express himself by. A cant phrase, an odd gesture, an old-fashioned regimental uniform, a wooden leg, a tobacco-box, or a hacked sword, are the standing topics by which he embodies his characters to the imagination.[13]

Such a statement simply showed that Hazlitt entirely missed the point of Jonson's work. Curiously enough, too, his criticism may be answered out of Jonson's own mouth, if we simply go on quoting the passage from *Every Man out of His Humour* begun above. The speaker, Asper, who represents Jonson, continues—give ear, Hazlitt—

> But that a rook, by wearing a pyed feather,
> The cable hatband, or the three piled ruff,
> A yard of shoe-tye, or the Switzer's knot
> On his French garters, should affect a humor!
> O, it is more than most ridiculous.[14]

In other words, Jonson emphasizes the fact that it is inner and spiritual eccentricity with which he has to do, not accidents of external appearance.

Coleridge's censure touches him nearer, because it involves a truth, being scarcely more than a burlesque restatement of the above lines:

> Jonson's [characters] are either a man with a huge wen, having a circulation of its own, and which we might conceive amputated, and the patient thereby losing all his character; or they are mere wens themselves instead of men—wens personified, or with eyes, nose, and mouth cut out, mandrake fashion.[15]

Under the fantastic figure, Coleridge does here touch upon a real danger which besets all such writing—the danger of emphasizing a single odd trait to such an extent that the individual is lost sight of, or—which amounts to nearly the same thing—choosing as a subject for treatment some odd trait which is of so narrow a reach that it does not mold the rest of the character, but rather obscures it, and has the force of monomania, or "obsession." This is in fact a fault which Jonson's inferior work shows. Thus, the plot of *The Silent Woman* is based on a single characteristic of Morose, his hatred of noise. The play is, however, pure farce throughout, and as such the character of Morose is legitimate enough. If the play needed defense, however, the argument Gifford has chosen, if it were true, is the right one. He says:

> Both Upton and Whalley have mistaken the character of Morose, they suppose it to be a dislike of noise; whereas this is an accidental quality altogether dependent upon the master-passion, or 'humour,' a most inveterate and odious self love.[16]

Even an admirer of Jonson may not quite agree with Gifford in this instance, but it is usually true that of Jonson's mature work Coleridge's criticism does not hold. In his three greatest plays, *The Alchemist*, *Volpone*, and *Bartholomew Fair*, he never passes the bounds of the dramatic. *Bartholomew Fair* is the most concretely realistic piece of portraiture he ever did, *Volpone* deals more with generalized types, while *The Alchemist* stands between the two, but all keep within artistic limits.

In his less great work, however, the tendency to personification of single qualities is very clear. In *The Magnetic Lady*, for example, Lady Loadstone's powers of attraction are continually alluded to, though with no apparent reason unless it be perhaps the sound of her name, and at the end she is married to Captain Ironside, presumably because magnet attracts iron. In *The Staple of News* the symbolism is more than verbal, but is puzzlingly capricious. Pecunia is apparently an ordinary young lady, but occasionally she is made to stand for money or wealth taken allegorically, and though young Pennyboy assures us that "she kisses like a mortal creature" the reader is never quite clear in his mind as to whether she is a girl or a money-bag.[17]

These are extreme cases, but it would be possible to choose out characters from the plays so as to make a series illustrating steps in the process all the way from vivid artistic portraiture like that of the Puritan zealot in *Bartholomew Fair* to personification like that of Lady Pecunia, with her attendant maids, Mortgage, Statute, Band and Wax, and her gentleman-usher, Broker. Finally, it is interesting to note that the lapses into personification occur more frequently in his late plays, as his powers waned, while his over-personal invective appears to have come early, before he was inclined to control his resentments.

Another objection, most comprehensive of all, is made to comedy of the class to which Jonson's belongs. It is of Molière's plays, but it might as well be of Jonson's, that Freytag says:

> The highest dramatic life is lacking to them—the processes of coming into being, the growth of character. We prefer to recognize on the stage how one *becomes* a miser, rather than how he *is* one.[18]

But this ⟨is⟩ an indictment, not of Molière's or Jonson's comedy, but of all comedy. What we must look for in Jonson's comedies, as in Molière's, is a study not of character development but of characters which are already formed, or which are treated as if they were already formed. For, "how a man becomes a miser" is not a comic but a tragic spectacle. The essentially tragic in Browning's *A Soul's Tragedy* is the spectacle of Chiappino's degeneration; but a comedian might take up Chiappino where Browning left him, and make him the hero of a comedy like *Tartuffe*. He could not take the period of his life that Browning takes—the period of his "becoming" and treat it deeply or truly, without making it tragic.[19] Again, the history of Lydgate in *Middlemarch*, is, as it stands, a "soul's tragedy"; but the final Lydgate, the conventional, prosperous physician, specialist in gout, would furnish good material for the satiro-comic artist. And Tartuffe himself—would it have been comic to watch how he *became* Tartuffe? It is indeed true, as Hegel suggests, that to preserve the comic in a comedy we must drop the curtain in time. But it is perhaps equally true that we must, at its beginning, not raise the curtain too soon.

Of Jonson's five great plays the earliest has been called, perhaps rightly, his most perfect.[20] *Bartholomew Fair* is certainly the most recklessly, riotously funny, while *The Alchemist* and *Volpone* contend for the position of the greatest. *The Alchemist*, is, indeed, structurally the most marvelous of plays, but there are some readers at least with whom no comedy leaves the impression that *Volpone* does,—an impression comparable in intensity with that made by a tragedy, though the effect here is mainly intellectual rather than emotional. It is the effect of the double character, Volpone-Mosca, which impresses us with a kind of hugeness, a diabolical fertility of power almost too great for comedy, and one cannot help wishing that Jonson had honored these two with opponents as worthy of their genius as those Shakespeare gave Iago.

Finally, to say that Jonson does not appeal to the imagination[21] is to forget Volpone, and Sir Epicure Mammon. What is true, is, that he appeals wholly to the intellect. Any one who expects to be emotionally touched will be disappointed, but if one is satisfied with the stimulus that comes of contact with a master mind, he will not seek in vain. Indeed one sometimes feels that, in coming from the sunny hedonism of some among the Elizabethans, there is a kind of pleasure, bracing while it chills, in getting into touch with this man, who stands apart from the rest, among them and not of them, whose "light" had not their "sweetness" and whose savage judgments never grew thoroughly humane, yet who had the nobleness that comes of power and sincerity and seriousness. . . .

Chapter 5
Jonson's Romantic Comedy

That Jonson had ever written any but satiric humor-comedy is hard to realize, for we are accustomed to thinking of him as one whose powers, like those of his own humor-ridden creations, "ran all one way." And indeed, the mature Jonson is singularly unvarying in point of view and in practice. We might apply to him Aurelia's mocking reproach to her sister:

> What, true-stitch, sister! Both your sides alike![22]

But unvarying as he seems, Jonson had his romantic period. A few years younger than Shakespeare, he was still doing hackwork of the stage, recasting old plays, and acting, while the elder poet was producing his early comedies—*Love's Labour's Lost*, *The Comedy of Errors*, *The Two Gentlemen of Verona*, *A Midsummer Night's Dream*, and *The Merchant of Venice*. It is difficult to suppose that Jonson should have been uninfluenced by this wonderful series of plays, even if we imagine him, according to the conventional picture, with his eyes glued to the page of Plautus and Terence and Seneca. Of such influence we find few traces in his typical work and his expressed theory, but that it was for a time strong, parts of some of his plays and the whole of one give evidence.

This one is *The Case Is Altered*, produced apparently at the end of 1598, a few months after *Every Man in His Humour*. So different is this from his usual work, that it has been questioned whether the play really is Jonson's. The earliest printed form known to us is a quarto of 1609, of which some copies give Jonson's name, others do not, and we may take our choice of two hypotheses: either Jonson's name was unwarrantably inserted by the printers, and taken out of some copies by the writer's own orders: or it was printed without credit to him, and his name afterwards inserted.[23] Thus far no other evidence is forthcoming. Gifford and Cunningham both accept the play as Jonson's, as do all his critics, except C. H. Herford who, in his introduction to the 'Mermaid' edition of Jonson, writes: "The same year [1599!] probably produced a fourth [play], still extant, in which it seems equally clear that Jonson wrote a part, and that he did not write the whole—*The Case Is Altered*."[24] Mr. Herford gives no hint of his reasons either for dating the play a year later, or for denying its accepted authorship. The "part" written by Jonson is, we presume, Valentine's satirical description of the "Utopian" (English) stage, the hit at Anthony Munday, and the Jaques incident. But this last, which is unquestionably Jonson's, is so intimately bound in with the Rachel-plot that to accept it as Jonson's almost involves accepting work as unlike his usual manner as any in the play.

Assuming, then, that the play is Jonson's, we have the interesting case of a purely "Romantic" comedy written by the greatest of the opposed school. It might almost be interpolated into the series of Shakespeare's comedies just mentioned—it would certainly be no more puzzling there than is *All's Well that Ends Well* in a later group. Structurally it is far above *Love's Labour's Lost*, though it has nothing so masterly as the great exposure scene of that play. If we had to place the play we should put it about with *The Two Gentlemen of Verona*, when Shakespeare's comedy was passing out of its stage of farce and situation, into its distinctive early form.

It may be worth while to pause a moment over these early plays. *Love's Labour's Lost* consists of one situation, the exposure of the four "forsworn" youths,—a scene worked out with a cleanness of stroke worthy of Molière. Indeed the motive of the play and its attitude strongly suggest Molière. Armado might be a study of a humor, and the catastrophe, where the four gentlemen are by the loving discipline of their ladies brought 'out of their humours' is Jonsonesque. Biron's recantation:

> Taffeta phrases, silken terms precise,
> I do forswear them, and I here protest,
> . . .
> Henceforth my wooing mind shall be express'd
> In russet yeas and honest Kersey noes.[25]

finds a parallel—somewhat extravagant, indeed—in the litany of the reformed revellers in *Cynthia's Revels*:

> From Spanish shrugs, French faces, smirks, irpes,
>   and all affected humors,
>   Good Mercury defend us, etc.[26]

The Comedy of Errors, largely farcical, adds nothing, except perhaps a firmer grasp of the laws of structure and plot. But in *The Two Gentlemen of Verona* the note of "Romantic Comedy" is clear. The interwoven love-plots give the delicate but firm setting, while Launce with his foil and victim Speed, serve as the most good natured of burlesques on the lofty raptures of the lovers.

The likeness between this play and *The Case Is Altered* is rather interesting. In part it can be reduced to details, in part it is a case of "atmosphere," or of the writer's attitude. One of the most striking points is the fact that the humor is the same. Onion and Juniper are, to be sure, not so bright as Launce and Speed, their humor is at once less funny and more coarse—there is no surer way of appreciating Shakespeare's delicate-mindedness than to compare his humorous scenes with those of his contemporaries—but it is the same in kind, it is the comedy of sympathy. We laugh at Juniper, "sweet youth, whose tongue has a happy turn when he sleeps," and at Onion, the ardent lover of Rachel, but we are fond of the fellows, and our laugh is very different from that provoked by "Master Stephen," or by any of the rest of the "gulls" and fools of Jonson's world. Moreover, the use of the comic element is somewhat the same in both. In *The Two Gentlemen of Verona*, following immediately on the farewell of Julia and Proteus, comes Launce's version of his own heartrending parting from his family—depicted the more graphically with the aid of his slippers and his stony-hearted dog. Again, hard upon Valentine, steeped in "endless dolor" at his banishment from Silvia, comes Launce again with the announcement that he too is in love:

> He lives not now that knows me to be in love; yet I am in love; but a team of horse shall not pluck that from me; nor who 'tis I love; and yet 'tis a woman; but what woman I will not tell myself; and yet 'tis a milkmaid.[27]

The parody in *The Case Is Altered* is not so consistent nor so pointed, yet we can hardly miss the kindly satire implied in Onion's wooing of Rachel, even though it is separated by a whole act from the ardent pursuit of her by the various gentlemen of rank.

> *Onion*: O brave! she's yonder: O terrible!
>   she's gone.
> *Juniper*: Yea, so nimble in your dilemmas, and
>   your hyperboles! *Hey my love! O my love!* at
>   the first sight, by the mass.
> *Onion*: O how she scudded! O sweet scud, how
>   she tripped! O delicate trip and go![28]

In the serious parts of the play the intermingling of jest and earnest suggests Shakespeare. The two young girls, introducing themselves through Aurelia's mock-solemn announcement:

> Room for a case of matrons, colored black.

enter the scene almost like another Rosalind and Celia—at least they might have been first studies for them. Paulo, the ardent young lover, and Angelo, his faithless friend, remind us of Valentine and Proteus; indeed in V, 3 the exposure of Angelo's treachery by his friend and their instantaneous reconciliation is a situation identical with the conclusion of *The Two Gentlemen of Verona*.

Only the character of Jaques is out of keeping with the rest. He is distinctly Jonsonesque,[29] and in his addresses to his gold we feel the power of the author of *Volpone*, though even here there is a reminiscence of Shakespeare in his cry:

"Thou hast made away my child, thou hast my gold:

. . .

The thief is gone, my gold's gone, Rachel's gone."[30]

Another point is the presence of sub-plots, or at least sub-interests. It is hard to decide what we can call the principal plot, but perhaps the Camillo-Gasper interest may serve as well as any. Besides this, we have: (1) the interests centering directly about Rachel, Paulo's love and Angelo's treachery being the central issues, while the infatuation of Ferneze, of Christophero and of Onion (!) are side interests; (2) the interest centering round Jaques, his gold, and his secret; this shades into (3) the Juniper and Onion interests, while (4) Aurelia and Chamont form a very slight fourth interest. All these threads are dexterously interwoven to a loose but fairly even tissue,—too even, perhaps, for the lack of a predominating group of characters is a fault.[31]

Finally, it will be noted that the comic element is found not in any of the more important plots, but in the under-issues or asides. This is a trait of the "Romantic" comedy; in Jonson's typical plays, the comic element is bound up with—is contained in—the main action.

The play, then, is distinctly romantic, and if we accept it as Jonson's it acquires peculiar significance as an indication of the kind of work he might have done in this field if he had chosen it for his mature activity.[32] That it was possibly written after his first play in his later manner need not be a difficulty.[33] With a poet who worked as consciously and deliberately as Jonson it would have been quite possible to write a play in the accepted manner, even while he was in the act of breaking away from that manner.[34]

It is interesting to note that in this, his one "Romantic" comedy, Jonson follows the Roman comedians more closely than anywhere else. In the Jaques incidents the *Aulularia* was his model, in the Camillo-Gasper plot he was adapting from the *Captivi*. This would seem to bear out what was said in a preceding chapter as to the romantic possibilities of the Roman plots. The fact that Jonson so easily gave to his material the treatment needed to make these possibilities actual, is, moreover, an indication of his native power in other fields than those wherein he chose to excel. For this play, while not without faults, has in its manner a lightness of touch, in its humor a humaneness that is not equalled in the early work—scarcely in the mature work—of any contemporary save Shakespeare. That he turned aside to follow other courses we must, in the case of so conscious and conscientious an artist, attribute to deliberate choice; and in making an estimate of him we ought not to ignore, as critics have sometimes done, these two of his works wherein he showed other powers than those which he ordinarily allowed free play. Lightly to set aside *The Case Is Altered* and *The Sad Shepherd* as exceptions which need not be considered "in making up the main account" is only to justify the poet's slurs on "the world's coarse thumb and finger." Exceptional they are, but not accidental or unimportant.

Perhaps Jonson was right in choosing as he did, since in the work which he made characteristically his own he had no equal, whereas in the realms that he abandoned he would have had one superior. Yet the lover of Jonson cannot but find something pathetic in this self-imposed narrowing of his mighty powers,—cannot but wish that in determining the direction of

his artistic genius, in pruning its growth, he had been a little less severe, less ruthless.

Notes

1. Induction, *Every Man out of His Humour*, *Works*, II, 12, 18.
2. Moulton, *The Ancient Classical Drama*, p. 256.
3. Cf. infra, pp. 58–60.
4. Mercury & Cupid are assistant-demonstrators, cf. infra, p. 83.
5. Extreme instances of this are *Every Man out of His Humour* and *Cynthia's Revels*. Cf. infra, pp. 57–60, 82, 83.
6. *Every Man out of His Humour*, Act III, Sc. 3; *Works*, II, 118.
7. Prologue, *The Silent Woman*; *Works*, III, 332.
8. Ibid. Cf. also in the Dedicatory Letter to *Volpone*: "I know that nothing can be so innocently writ or carried, but may be made obnoxious to construction," etc. *Works*, III, 158.
9. Induction, *Bartholomew Fair*; *Works*, IV, 353.
10. Moliere: *L'Impromptu de Versailles: Oeuvres*, III, 413.
11. Congreve: Epilogue, *The Way of the World*.
12. Induction, *Every Man out of His Humour*; *Works*, II, 16.
13. Hazlitt: *English Comic Writers*, 77.
14. Ibid., p. 17.
15. Coleridge: *Literary Remains*, II, 279.
16. Gifford's note, *The Silent Woman*, III, 399.
17. Cf. infra, pp. 90–92.
18. Freytag: *Technique of the Drama*, pp. 250–251.
19. Cf. Supra, pp. 17, 18. Note, however, that the process of reasoning does not imply any assertion that the converse is true; namely, that tragedy *must* involve character development. Few great tragedies have such a basis.
20. Swinburne: *A Study of Ben Jonson*, pp. 3, 14.
21. Aronstein: *Ben Jonson's Theorie des Lustspiels: Anglia*, XVII, 477.
22. *The Case Is Altered*, Act II. Sc. 3; *Works*, VI, 331.
23. Cf. Fleay: *A Chronicle of the English Drama*; I, 357–358.
24. Herford: Introduction to *The Best Plays of Ben Jonson*, p. xxv.
25. *Love's Labour's Lost*, V, 2.
26. Palinode, *Cynthia's Revels*, V, 3; *Works*, III, 337, 359.
27. *The Two Gentlemen of Verona*, III, 1.
28. *The Case Is Altered*, IV, 4; *Works*, VI, 364.
29. That he was modeled on Plautus is only another indication of this—such work was characteristic of Jonson.
30. *The Case Is Altered*, V, 1; *Works* VI, 380.
31. Nor is the texture without flaw; the two characters, Balladino and Francisco Colonia, are hangers-on in the play. The first was evidently inserted as a "local hit." The presence of the second seems unmotived.
32. *The New Inn* is sometimes called a romantic comedy, and with a degree of reason . . . On the other hand, the romantic fragment, *The Sad Shepherd*, ought to be classed with Theocritus and Spenser, as romantic pastoral, rather than with romantic comedy.
33. Koeppel, however, thinks it was his first work. Cf. his *Quellen-Studien zu den Dramen Ben Jonson's, John Marston's und Beaumont's und Fletcher's*, pp. 1, 19.
34. The hit at Anthony Munday, Act I, sc. 1, may, indeed, be also a comment on some of the criticism to which the new play, *Every Man in His Humour*, must certainly have given rise.

GEORGE SAINTSBURY
From "Elizabethan Criticism" (1900)
A History of English Criticism
1911, pp. 80–92

Save perhaps in one single respect (where the defect was not wholly his fault), Ben Jonson might be described as a critic armed at all points. His knowledge of literature was extremely wide, being at the same time solid and thorough. While he had an understanding above all things strong and masculine, he was particularly addicted, though in no dilettante fashion, to points of form. His whole energies, and they were little short of

Titanic, were given to literature. And, lastly, if he had not the supremest poetic genius, he had such a talent that only the neighbourhood of supremacy dwarfs it. Where he came short was not in a certain hardness of temper and scholasticism of attitude: for these, if kept within bounds, and tempered by that enthusiasm for letters which he possessed, are not bad equipments for the critic. It was rather in the fact that he still came too early for it to be possible for him, except by the help of a miracle, to understand the achievements and value of the vernaculars. By his latest days, indeed,[1] the positive performance of these was already very great. Spain has hardly added anything since, and Italy not very much, to her share of European literature; France was already in the first flush of her "classical" period, after a long and glorious earlier history: and what Ben's own contemporaries in England had done, all men know. But mediæval literature was shut from him, as from all, till far later; he does not seem to have been much drawn to Continental letters, and, perhaps in their case, as certainly in English, he was too near—too much a part of the movement—to get it into firm perspective.

In a sense the critical temper in Jonson is all-pervading. It breaks out side by side with, and sometimes even within, his sweetest lyrics; it interposes what may be called *parabases* in the most unexpected passages[2] of his plays. *The Poetaster* is almost as much criticism dramatised as *The Frogs*. But there are three "places," or groups of places, which it inspires, not in mere suggestion, but with propriety—the occasional Prefaces, or observations, to and on the plays themselves, the *Conversations with Drummond*, and, above all, the at last fairly (though not yet sufficiently) known *Discoveries* or *Timber*.

To piece together, with any elaboration, the more scattered critical passages would be fitter for a monograph on Jonson than for a History of Criticism. The "Address to the Readers" of *Sejanus*, which contains a reference to the author's lost *Observations on Horace, his Art of Poetry* (not the least of such losses) is a fair specimen of them: the dedication of *Volpone* to "the most noble and most equal sisters, Oxford and Cambridge," a better. In both, and in numerous other passages of prose and verse, we find the real and solid, though somewhat partial, knowledge, the strong sense, the methodic scholarship of Ben, side by side with his stately, not Euphuistic, but rather too close-packed style, his not ill-founded, but slightly excessive, self-confidence, and that rough knock-down manner of assertion and characterisation which reappeared in its most unguarded form in the *Conversations* with Drummond.

The critical utterances of these *Conversations* are far too interesting to be passed over here, though we cannot discuss them in full. They tell us that Ben thought all (other) rhymes inferior to couplets, and had written a treatise (which, again, would we had!) against both Campion and Daniel (see *ante*). His objection to "stanzas and cross rhymes" was that "as the purpose might lead beyond them, they were all forced." Sidney "made every one speak as well as himself," and so did not keep "decorum" (cf. Puttenham above). Spenser's stanzas and language did not please him. Daniel was no poet. He did not like Drayton's "long verses," nor Sylvester's and Fairfax's translations. He thought the translations of Homer (Chapman's) and Virgil (Phaer's) into "long Alexandrines" (*i.e.*, fourteeners) were but prose: yet elsewhere we hear that he "had some of Chapman by heart." Harington's *Ariosto* was the worst of all translations. Donne was sometimes "profane," and "for not keeping of accent deserved hanging"; but elsewhere he was "the first poet of the world in some things," though, "through not being understood, he would perish."[3] Shakespeare "wanted art": and "Abram Francis (Abraham Fraunce) in his English

Hexameters was a fool." "Bartas was not a poet, but a verser, because he wrote not fiction." He cursed Petrarch for reducing verses to sonnets, "which were like Procrustes' bed." Guarini incurred the same blame as Sir Philip: and Lucan was good in parts only. "The best pieces of Ronsard were his Odes." Drummond's own verses "were all good, but smelled too much of the schools." The "silver" Latins, as we should expect, pleased him best. "To have written Southwell's 'Burning Babe,' he would have been content to destroy many of his."

These are the chief really critical items, though there are others (putting personal gossip aside) of interest; but it may be added, as a curiosity, that he told Drummond that he himself "writ all first in prose" at Camden's suggestion, and held that "verses stood all by sense, without colours or accent" (poetic diction or metre), "which yet at other times he denied," says the reporter, a sentence ever to be remembered in connection with these jottings. Remembering it, there is nothing shocking in any of these observations, nor anything really inconsistent. A true critic never holds the neat, positive, "reduced-to-its-lowest-terms" estimate of authors, in which a criticaster delights. His view is always facetted, conditioned. But he may, in a friendly chat, or a conversation for victory, exaggerate this facet or condition, while altogether suppressing others; and this clearly is what Ben did.

For gloss on the *Conversations*, for reduction to something like system of the critical remarks scattered through the works, and for the nearest approach we can have to a formal presentment of Ben's critical views, we must go to the *Discoveries*.

The fact that we find no less than four titles for the book—*Timber, Explorata, Discoveries*, and *Sylva*—with others of its peculiarities, is explained by the second fact that Jonson never published it. It never appeared in print till the folio of 1641, years after its author's death. The *Discoveries* are described as being made "upon men and matter as they have flowed out of his daily reading, or had their reflux to his peculiar notions of the times." They are, in fact, notes unnumbered and unclassified (though batches of more or fewer sometimes run on the same subject), each with its Latin heading, and varying in length from a few lines to that of his friend (and partly master) Bacon's shorter *Essays*. The influence of those "silver" Latins whom he loved so much is prominent: large passages are simply translated from Quintilian, and for some time[4] the tenor is ethical rather than literary. A note on *Perspicuitas—elegantia* breaks these, but has nothing noteworthy about it, and *Bellum scribentium* is only a satiric exclamation on the folly of "writers committed together by the ears for ceremonies, syllables, points," &c. The longer *Nil gratius protervo libro* seems a retort for some personal injury, combined with the old complaint of the decadence and degradation of poetry.[5] There is just but rather general stricture in *Eloquentia* on the difference between the arguments of the study and of the world. "I would no more choose a rhetorician for reigning in a school," says Ben, "than I would choose a pilot for rowing in a pond."[6] *Memoria* includes a gird at Euphuism. At last we come to business. *Censura de poetis*, introduced by a fresh fling at Euphuism, in *De vere argutis*, opens with a tolerably confident note, "Nothing in our age is more preposterous than the running judgments upon poetry and poets," with much more to the same effect, the whole being pointed by the fling, "If it were a question of the water-rhymer's[7] works against Spenser's, I doubt not but they would find more suffrages." The famous passage on Shakespeare follows: and the development of Ben's view, "would he had blotted a thousand," leads to a more general disquisition on the differences of wits, which includes the sentence already referred to. "Such [i.e., haphazard and inconsistent] are all the Essayists, even their master Montaigne." The notes now keep close to literature throughout in substance, though their titles (*e.g., Ignorantia animæ*), and so forth, may seem wider. A heading, *De Claris Oratoribus*, leads to yet another of the purple passages of the book—that on Bacon, in which is intercalated a curious *Scriptorum catalogus*, limited, for the most part, though Surrey and Wyatt are mentioned, to prose writers. And then for some time ethics, politics, and other subjects, again have Ben's chief attention.[8]

We return to literature, after some interval (but with a parenthetic glance at the *poesis et pictura* notion three pages earlier), with a curious unheaded letter to an unnamed Lordship on Education, much of which is translated directly from Ben Jonson's favourite Quintilian; and then directly accost it again with a tractatule *De stilo et optimo scribendi genere*, hardly parting company thereafter. Ben's prescription is threefold: read the best authors, observe the best speakers, and exercise your own style much. But he is well aware that no "precepts will profit a fool," and he adapts old advice to English ingeniously, in bidding men read, not only Livy before Sallust, but also Sidney before Donne, and to beware of Chaucer or Gower at first. Here occurs the well-known *dictum*, that Spenser "in affecting the ancients writ no language; yet I would have him read for his matter." A fine general head opens with the excellent version of Quintilian, "We should not protect our sloth with the patronage of Difficulty," and this is followed by some shrewd remarks on diction—the shrewdest being that, after all, the best custom makes, and ever will continue to make, the best speech—with a sharp stroke at Lucretius for "scabrousness," and at Chaucerisms. Brevity of style, Tacitean and other, is cautiously commended. In the phrase (*Oratio imago animi*), "language most shows a man," Ben seems to anticipate Buffon, as he later does Wordsworth and Coleridge, by insisting that style is not merely the dress, but the body of thought.[9] All this discussion, which enters into considerable detail, is of the first importance, and it occupies nearly a quarter of the whole book. It is continued, the continuation reaching till the end, by a separate discussion of poetry.

It is interesting, but less so than what comes before. A somewhat acid, though personally guarded, description of the present state of the Art introduces the stock definition of "making," and its corollary that a poet is not one who writes in measure, but one who feigns—all as we have found it before, but (as we should expect of Ben) in succincter and more scholarly form. Yet the first requisite of the poet is *ingenium*—goodness of natural wit; the next exercise of his parts— "bringing all to the forge and file" (*sculpte, lime, cisèle!*); the third Imitation—to which Ben gives a turn (not exactly new, for we have met it from Vida downwards), which is not an improvement, by keeping its modern meaning, and understanding by it the following of the classics. "But that which we especially require in him is an exactness of study and multiplicity of reading." Yet his liberty is not to be so narrowly circumscribed as some would have it. This leads to some interesting remarks on the ancient critics, which the author had evidently meant to extend: as it is, they break off short.[10] We turn to the Parts of comedy and tragedy, where Ben is strictly regular—the fable is the imitation of one entire and perfect action, &c. But this also breaks off, after a discussion of fable itself and episode, with an evidently quite disconnected fling at "hobbling poems which run like a brewer's cart on the stones."

These *Discoveries* have to be considered with a little general care before we examine them more particularly. They were, it has been said, never issued by the author himself, and we do not know whether he ever would have issued them in their present form. On the other hand, they are very carefully written, and not mere jottings. In form (though more modern in style) they resemble the earlier essays of that Bacon whom they so magnificently celebrate, in their deliberate conciseness and pregnancy. On the other hand, it is almost impossible to doubt that some at least were intended for expansion; it is difficult not to think that there was plenty more stuff of the same kind in the solidly constructed and well-stored treasuries of Ben's intelligence and erudition. It is most difficult of all not to see that, in some cases, the thoughts are coordinated into regular tractates, in others left loose, as if for future treatment of the same kind.

Secondly, we should like to know rather more than we do of the *time* of their composition. Some of them—such as the retrospect of Bacon, and to a less degree that of Shakespeare—*must* be late; there is a strong probability that all date from the period between the fire in Ben's study, which destroyed so much, and his death—say between 1620 and 1637. But at the same time there is nothing to prevent his having remembered and recopied observations of earlier date.

Thirdly, it is most important that we rightly understand the composition of the book. It has sometimes been discovered[11] in these *Discoveries*, with pride, or surprise, or even scorn, that Ben borrowed in them very largely from the ancients. Of course he did, as well as something, though less, from the Italian critics of the age immediately before his own.[12] But in neither case could he have hoped for a moment—and in neither is there the slightest reason to suppose that he would have wished if he could have hoped—to disguise his borrowings from a learned age. When a man—such as, for instance, Sterne—wishes to steal and escape, he goes to what nobody reads, not to what everybody is reading. And the Latins of the Silver Age, the two Senecas, Petronius, Quintilian, Pliny, were specially favourites with the Jacobean time. In what is going to be said no difference will be made between Ben's borrowings and his original remarks: nor will the fact of the borrowing be referred to unless there is some special critical reason. Even the literal translations, which are not uncommon, are made his own by the nervous idiosyncrasy of the phrase, and its thorough adjustment to the context and to his own vigorous and massive temperament.

Of real "book-criticism" there are four chief passages, the brief flings at Montaigne and at "*Tamerlanes* and *Tamerchams*," and the longer notices of Shakespeare and Bacon.

The flirt at "all the Essayists, even their master Montaigne," is especially interesting, because of the high opinion which Jonson elsewhere expresses of Bacon, the chief, if not the first, English Essayist of his time, and because of the fact that not a few of these very *Discoveries* are "Essays," if any things ever were. Nor would it be very easy to make out a clear distinction, in anything but name, between some of Ben's most favourite ancient writers and these despised persons. It is, however, somewhat easier to understand the reason of the condemnation. Jonson's classically ordered mind probably disliked the ostentatious desultoriness and incompleteness of the Essay, the refusal, as it were out of mere insolence, to undertake an orderly treatise. Nor is it quite impossible that he failed fully to understand Montaigne, and was to some extent the dupe of that great writer's fanfaronade of promiscuousness.

The "*Tamerlane* and *Tamercham*"[13] fling is not even at first sight surprising. It was quite certain that Ben would seriously despise what Shakespeare only laughed at—the confusion, the bombast, the want of order and scheme in the "University Wits"—and it is not probable that he was well enough acquainted with the even now obscure development of the earliest Elizabethan drama to appreciate the enormous improvement which they wrought. Nay, the nearer approach even of such a dull thing as *Gorboduc* to "the height of Seneca his style," might have a little bribed him as it bribed Sidney. He is true to his side—to his division of the critical creed—in this also.

The train of thought—censure of the vulgar preference—runs clear from this to the best known passage of the whole, the section *De Shakespeare Nostrat*. It cannot be necessary to quote it, or to point out that Ben's eulogy, splendid as it is, acquires tenfold force from the fact that it is avowedly given by a man whose general literary theory is different from that of the subject, while the censure accompanying it loses force in exactly the same proportion. What Ben here blames, any ancient critic (perhaps even Longinus) would have blamed too: what Ben praises, it is not certain that any ancient critic, except Longinus, would have seen. Nor is the captious censure of "Cæsar did never wrong but with just cause" the least interesting part of the whole. The paradox is not in our present texts: and there have, of course, not been wanting commentators to accuse Jonson of garbling or of forgetfulness. This is quite commentatorially gratuitous and puerile. It is very like Shakespeare to have written what Ben says: very like Ben to object to the paradox (which, *pace tanti viri*, is not "ridiculous" at all, but a deliberate and effective hyperbole); very like the players to have changed the text; and most of all like the commentators to make a fuss about the matter.

What may seem the more unstinted eulogy of Bacon is not less interesting. For here it is obvious that Ben is speaking with fullest sympathy, and with all but a full acknowledgment of having met an ideal. Except the slight stroke, "when he could spare or pass by a jest," and the gentle insinuation that *Strength*, the gift of God, was what Bacon's friends had to implore for him, there is no admixture whatever in the eulogy of "him who hath filled up all numbers,[14] and performed that in our tongue which may be compared or preferred to insolent Greece or haughty Rome." Indeed it could not have been—even if Ben Jonson had not been a friend, and, in a way, follower of Bacon—but that he should regard the Chancellor as his chief of literary men. Bacon, unluckily for himself, lacked the "unwedgeable and gnarled" strength of the dramatist, and also was without his poetic fire, just as Ben could never have soared to the vast, if vague, conceptions of Bacon's materialist-Idealism. But they were both soaked in "literature," as then understood; they were the two greatest masters of the closely packed style that says twenty things in ten words: and yet both could, on occasion, be almost as rhetorically imaginative as Donne or Greville. It is doubtful whether Bacon's own scientific scorn for words without matter surpassed Jonson's more literary contempt of the same phenomenon. Everywhere, or almost everywhere, there was between them the *idem velle et idem nolle*.

A limited précis, however, and a few remarks on special points, cannot do the *Discoveries* justice. The fragmentary character of the notes that compose it, the pregnant and deliberately "astringed" style in which these notes are written, so that they are themselves the bones, as it were, of a much larger treatise, defy such treatment. Yet it is full of value, as it gives us more than glimpses

> Of what a critic was in Jonson lost

or but piecemeal shown. We shall return, in the next chapter, to his relative position; but something should be said here of his intrinsic character.

He does not, as must have been clearly seen, escape the "classical" limitation. With some ignorance, doubtless, and doubtless also some contempt, of the actual achievements of prose romance, and with that stubborn distrust of the modern tongues for miscellaneous prose purposes, which lasted till far into the seventeenth century, if it did not actually survive into the eighteenth, he still clings to the old mistakes about the identity of poetry and "fiction," about the supremacy of oratory in prose. We hear nothing about the "new versifying," though no doubt this would have been fully treated in his handling of Campion and Daniel: but had he had any approval for it, that approval must have been glanced at. His preference for the (stopped) couplet[15] foreshadowed that which, with beneficial effects in some ways, if by no means in all, was to influence the whole of English poetry, with the rarest exceptions, for nearly two centuries. The personal arrogance which, as in Wordsworth's case, affected all Ben's judgment of contemporaries, and which is almost too fully reflected in the Drummond Conversations, would probably have made even his more deliberate judgments of these—his judgments "for publication"—inadequate. But it is fair to remember that Ben's theory (if not entirely his practice, especially in his exquisite lyrics and almost equally exquisite masques) constrained him to be severe to those contemporaries, from Spenser, Shakespeare, and Donne downwards. The mission of the generation may be summed up in the three words, Liberty, Variety, Romance. Jonson's tastes were for Order, Uniformity, Classicism.

He is thus doubly interesting—interesting as putting both with sounder scholarship and more original wit what men from Ascham to Puttenham, and later, had been trying to say before him, in the sense of adapting classical precepts to English: and far more interesting as adumbrating, beforehand, the creed of Dryden, and Pope, and Samuel Johnson. Many of his individual judgments are as shrewd as they are one-sided; they are always well, and sometimes admirably, expressed, in a style which unites something of Elizabethan colour, and much of Jacobean weight, with not a little of Augustan simplicity and proportion. He does not head the line of English critics: but he heads, and worthily, that of English critics who have been great both in criticism and in creation.[16]

Notes

1. These days carried him far beyond the 16th century. His solidarity with the Elizabethans proper, however, makes his inclusion here imperative. It may be added that since this book was first written, the classical strain of the Discoveries has been indicated with much learning, but with excessive strain of unfavorable reference, by a French critic, M. Castellain.

2. Take this interesting passage in the masque of *The New World Discovered in the Moon*—

   Chro.: Is he a man's poet or a woman's poet, I pray you?
   2nd Her.: Is there any such difference?
   Fact.: Many, as betwixt your man's tailor and your woman's tailor.
   1st Her.: How, may we beseech you?
   Fact.: I'll show you: your man's poet may break out strong and deep i' the mouth, . . . but your woman's poet must flow, and stroke the ear, and as one of them said of himself sweetly—

   > Must write a verse as smooth and calm as cream
   > In which there is no torrent, nor scarce stream.

   On this Gifford discovered in Theobald's copy the note: *"Woman's Poet, his soft versification—Mr P——."*

   The Introduction to *Every Man out of His Humour*, a very large part of *Cynthia's Revels*, not a little of *The Silent Woman*, and scores of other places, might be added. (Since this was written Dr David Klein has made a good collection, *Literary Criticism from the Elizabethan Dramatists* (New York, 1910), including Ben and drawing on others.)

3. These dicta, thus juxtaposed, should make all argument about apparently one-sided judgements superfluous. If Drummond had omitted almost any single one, we should have been utterly wrong in arguing from the remainder.

4. It may be observed that the shorter aphorisms rise to the top—at least the beginning.

5. "He is upbraidingly called a poet. . . . The professors, indeed, have made the learning cheap."

6. It is here that Ben borrows from Petronius not merely the sentiment but the phrase, "umbratical doctor."

7. "Taylor the Water-Poet," certainly bad enough as a poet—though not as a man. But the selection of Spenser as the other pole is an invaluable correction to the sweeping attack in the *Conversations*.

8. Perhaps, indeed, an exception should be made in favour of the section *De malignitate Studentium*, which reiterates the necessity of "the exact knowledge of all virtues and their contraries" on the part of the poet.

9. He may have taken this from the Italians.

10. This is one of the most lacrimable of the gaps. Ben must have known other authorities besides Quintilian well; he even quotes, though only in part, the great passage of Simylus.

11. Not by Dr Schelling, whose own indagations of Ben's debts are most interesting, and always made in the right spirit, while, like a good farmer and sportsman, he has left plenty for those who come after him to glean and bag. For instance, the very curious passage, taken verbatim from the elder Seneca, about the Platonic *Apology*. As for M. Castellain, he does, I think, exaggerate the want of originality.

12. Yet in re-reading Jonson, just after a pretty elaborate overhauling of the Italians, I find very little certain indebtedness of detail. Mr Spingarn seems to me to go too far in tracing "small Latin and less Greek" to Miturno's "small Latin and *very* small Greek," and the distinction of *poeta, poema, poesis* to Scaliger or Maggi. Fifty

people might have independently thought of the first; and the second is an application of a "common form" nearly as old as rhetoric. Ben, however, owes a good deal to Heinsius.

13. "The *Tamerlanes* and *Tamerchams* of the late age, which had nothing in them but the scenical strutting and furious vociferation to warrant them." It is just worth noting that Jonson thought there was more than this in Marlowe; and that the early edd. of *Tamburlaine* are anonymous.

14. One cannot but remember—with pity or glee, according to mood or temperament—how the Bacon-Shakespeare-maniacs have actually taken this in the sense of *poetic* "numbers". But in truth their study is not likely to be much in haughty Rome and its language, or to have led them either to Petronius and his *omnium nume[ro]rum*, or to Seneca and his insolenti Græciæ.

15. Daniel had frankly defended *enjambement*.

16. It seemed unnecessary to enlarge the space given to the men of Eliza and our James, by including the merer grammarians and pedagogues, from Mulcaster to that fervid Scot, Mr Hume, who, in 1617, extolled the "Orthography and Congruity" of his native speech (1865). Of Mulcaster, however, it deserves to be mentioned that, not so much in his *Positions* (1581), which have been, as in his *Elementarie*, which should be, reprinted, he displays a more than Pléiade enthusiasm for the vernacular. Unluckily this last is not easy of access, even the B.M. copy being a "Grenville" book, and hedged around with forms and fears. As to Ben himself, it is perhaps desirable to repeat that, in the opinion of the present writer, far too much stress has been laid (even by Mr Spingarn in *Camb. Hist of Eng. Lit.*) on the recent exhibition by a French critic (. . . named *supra*) of his indebtedness to the ancients, Heinsius, &c. This indebtedness ought always to have been known to all and was known to some: nor does it in any material degree interfere with Jonson's position. His selection and arrangement is something: his application to Shakespeare, Bacon, Spenser, more: and after all, in the vulgar sense of "originality," how much original criticism is there in the world?

Title page of *Steps to the Temple*

RICHARD CRASHAW

c. 1613-1649

Richard Crashaw was born in London, the only son of William Crashaw, a Puritan divine noted for the vigor of his anti-Papist views. Crashaw attended the Charterhouse School and Pembroke College, Cambridge. He became a Fellow of Peterhouse in 1634 and remained there after receiving an M.A. in 1638. While at Cambridge, Crashaw held a minor post at the church of Little St Mary's and may have been ordained. He became interested in the quasi-monastic Anglican community of Little Gidding and was a frequent visitor there. The advent of the Civil War, however, changed Crashaw's life. Both Peterhouse and Pembroke had been influenced by Archbishop Laud and had espoused his High Church ideals. When the Puritan Parliamentary Commission arrived in Cambridge, it stripped the chapel of Peterhouse and the church of Little St Mary's. Crashaw decided it was time to leave. Subsequently, he seems to have spent some time at Oxford and Leyden; by 1646, he had converted to Roman Catholicism and was living in Paris. A recommendation to the Pope by Queen Henrietta Maria sent him to Rome, where he eventually became a minor canon at the Cathedral of Loreto, in 1649. He died four months after his appointment.

Crashaw first published poems in 1634, the year of his graduation from Pembroke. The first edition of *Steps to the Temple* was prepared for publication in 1646, with a revised and enlarged edition following in 1648. In 1652, the final edition of Crashaw's English sacred poems was published posthumously under the title *Carmen Deo Nostro*.

Personal

His faith perhaps in some nice tenets might
Be wrong; his life, I'm sure, was in the right.
And I myself a Catholic will be,
So far at least, great Saint, to pray to thee.
Hail bard triumphant! and some care bestow
On us, the poets militant below!

. . .

And when my Muse soars with so strong a wing,
'Twill learn of things divine, and first of thee, to sing.
—ABRAHAM COWLEY, "On the Death of Crashaw," 1650

If Crashaw was not generally popular, and if his detractors malignantly defamed him as a "small poet," a "slip of the times," and as a "peevish, silly seeker, who glided away from his principles in a poetical vein of fancy and an impertinent curiosity," he enjoyed, on the other hand, the praise of some applauded men, and a general "sweet savour" of renown in his day and generation. He is said to have been a universal scholar—versed in the Hebrew, Greek, Latin, Spanish, and Italian languages—to have made the Grecian and Roman poets his study—and to have possessed, besides, the accomplishments of music, drawing, engraving, and painting. In his habits, too, he was temperate to severity; indeed, had he not been so, his poetry would have sunk from a panegyric on God into a bitter, unintentional satire on himself.—GEORGE GILFILLAN, "The Life and Poetry of Richard Crashaw," *The Poetical Works of Richard Crashaw*, 1857, p. vii

General

Learned Reader,
The Authors friend, will not usurpe much upon thy eye: This in onely for those, whom the name of our Divine Poet hath not yet siezed into admiration, I dare undertake, that what *Jamblicus (in vita Pythagoræ)* affirmeth of his Master, at his Contemplations, these Poems can, *viz.* They shal lift thee Reader, some yards above the ground: and, as in *Pythagoras* Schoole,

every temper was first tuned into a height by severall proportions of Musick; and spiritualiz'd for one of his weighty Lectures; So maist thou take a Poem hence, and tune thy soule by it, into a heavenly pitch; and thus refined and borne up upon the wings of meditation. In these Poems thou maist talke freely of God, and of that other state.

Here's *Herbert*'s second, but equall, who hath retriv'd Poetry of late, and return'd it up to its Primitive use; Let it bound back to heaven gates, whence it came. Thinke yee, St. *Augustine* would have steyned his graver Learning with a booke of Poetry, had he fancied their dearest end to be the vanity of Love-Sonnets, and Epithalamiums? No, no, he thought with this, our Poet, that every foot in a high-borne verse, might helpe to measure the soule into that better world: *Divine Poetry*; I dare hold it, in position against *Suarez* on the subject, to be the Language of the Angels; it is the Quintessence of Phantasie and discourse center'd in Heaven; 'tis the very Outgoings of the soule; 'tis what alone our Author is able to tell you, and that in his owne verse.

It were prophane but to mention here in the Preface those under-headed Poets, Retainers to seven shares and a halfe; Madrigall fellowes, whose onely businesse in verse, is to rime a poore six-penny soule, a Subburd sinner into hell;—May such arrogant pretenders to Poetry vanish, with their prodigious issue of tumorous heats and flashes of their adulterate braines, and for ever after, may this our Poet fill up the better roome of man. Oh! when the generall arraignment of Poets shall be, to give an accompt of their higher soules, with what a triumphant brow, shall our divine Poet sit above, and looke downe upon poore *Homer*, *Virgil*, *Horace*, *Claudian*? &c. who had amongst them the ill lucke to talke out a great part of their gallant Genius, upon Bees, Dung, froggs, and Gnats, &c. and not as himselfe here, upon Scriptures, divine Graces, Martyrs and Angels.

Reader, we stile his Sacred Poems, *Stepps to the Temple*, and aptly, for in the Temple of God, under his wing, he led his life in St. *Maries* Church neere St. *Peters* Colledge: There he lodged under *Tertullian*'s roofe of Angels: There he made his nest more gladly than *David*'s Swallow neere the house of God:

where like a primitive Saint, he offered more prayers in the night, then others usually offer in the day; There, he penned these Poems, *Stepps* for happy soules to climbe heaven by.

And those other of his pieces intituled, *The Delights of the Muses*, (though of a more humane mixture) are as sweet as they are innocent.

The praises that follow are but few of many that might be conferr'd on him, hee was excellent in five Languages (besides his Mother tongue) *vid.* Hebrew, Greek, Latine, Italian, Spanish, the two last whereof hee had little helpe in, they were of his owne acquisition.

Amongst his other accomplishments in Accademick (as well pious as harmlesse arts) hee made his skill in Poetry, Musicke, Drawing, Limming, graving, (exercises of his curious invention and sudden fancy) to bee but his subservient recreations for vacant houres, not the grand businesse of his soule.

To the former Qualifications I might adde that which would crowne them all, his rare moderation in diet (almost Lessian temperance) hee never created a Muse out of distempers, nor with our Canary scribblers cast any strange mists of surfets before the Intelectuall beames of his mind or memory, the latter of which, hee was so much a master of, that hee had there under locke and key in readinesse, the richest treasures of the best Greeke and Latine Poets, some of which Authors hee had more at his command by heart, then others that onely read their workes, to retaine little, and understand lesse.

Enough Reader, I intend not a volume of praises, larger then his booke, nor need I longer transport thee to thinke over his vast perfections, I will conclude all that I have impartially writ of this Learned young Gent. (now dead to us) as hee himselfe doth, with the last line of his Poem upon Bishop *Andrews* Picture his Sermons

> *Verto paginas.*
> —*Look on his following leaves, and see him breath.*
> —UNSIGNED, "The Preface to the Reader," *The Delights of the Muses*, 1648

I take this poet to have writ like a gentleman, that is, at leisure hours, and more to keep out of idleness than to establish a reputation, so that nothing regular or just can be expected from him.—ALEXANDER POPE, Letter to H. Cromwell, Dec. 17, 1710, *Pope's Works*, Vol. 6, eds. Courthope, Elwin

Crashawe possessed the requisites of a genuine poet, enthusiasm and sublimity; but he never undertook any grand or original work.—NATHAN DRAKE, *Literary Hours*, 1798, No. 28

Crashaw formed his style on the most quaint and conceited school of Italian poetry, that of Marino; and there is a prevalent harshness and strained expression in his verses; but there are also many touches of beauty and solemnity, and the strength of his thoughts sometimes appears even in their distortion.
—THOMAS CAMPBELL, "Richard Crashaw," *Specimens of the British Poets*, 1819, p. 357

Crashaw was a hectic enthusiast in religion and in poetry, and erroneous in both.—WILLIAM HAZLITT, "On Miscellaneous Poems," *Lectures on the Literature of the Age of Elizabeth*, 1820, p. 192

These verses were ever present to my mind whilst writing the second part of "Christabel"; if indeed, by some subtle process of the mind, they did not suggest the first thought of the whole poem.—SAMUEL TAYLOR COLERIDGE, cited in Thomas Allsop, *Letters, Conversations and Recollections of S. T. Coleridge*, 1836, p. 606

I can only mention to you Quarles, a great favorite with my uncle Southey, and Crashaw, whose sacred poetry I think more truly poetical than any other, except Milton and Dante. I asked Mr. Wordsworth what he thought of it, and whether he did not admire it; to which he responded very warmly. My father, I recollect, admired Crashaw; but then neither Quarles nor Crashaw would be much liked by the modern general reader. They would be thought queer and extravagant.—SARA COLERIDGE, Letter to Mrs. Richard Townsend, Sept. 1847, *Memoir and Letters*, 1874, pp. 320–21

Had Milton, before leaving Christ's College, become acquainted with the younger versifier of Pembroke, and read his "Music's Duel," his "Elegies on the Death of Mr. Herrys," and such other pieces of verse, original or translated, as he then had to show, he would have found in them a sensuous beauty of style and sweetness of rhythm quite to his taste.

. . . On the whole, there was a richer vein of poetical genius in Crashaw than in Herbert. . . . Apart from the modified intellectual assent expressly accorded by Donne, by Ferrar, and by others, to some of the Catholic doctrines which Crashaw seems to have made his spiritual diet, we trace a more occult effect of the same influence in a rhetorical peculiarity common to many of the writers of this theological school. We cannot define the peculiarity better than by saying that it consists in a certain flowing effeminacy of expression, a certain languid sensualism of fancy, or, to be still more particular, an almost cloying use of the words, "sweet," "dear," and their cognates, in reference to all kinds of objects.—DAVID MASSON, *The Life of John Milton*, 1858, Vol. 1, Ch. 6

As a poet, his works have ever been appreciated by those most qualified to decide upon their sterling beauties, and have suggested to others (too frequently without acknowledgment) some of their finest imageries. In every volume of any pretensions to taste, designed to offer specimens of English poetry, extracts are to be found; yet, with the exception of being partially, and by no means accurately, printed in the bulky and inconvenient collections of Chalmers and Anderson, it is somewhat remarkable that, in an age when familiarity with our Old English Authors is so eagerly sought, a full reprint should have been deferred till now.—WILLIAM B. TURNBULL, "Preliminary Observations," *Complete Works of Richard Crashaw*, 1858, p. x

Having said so much on this subject, I fear I cannot point out as much in detail as I would wish, a very striking peculiarity in Crashaw's lyrical poems which seems deserving of special attention. I refer to the extraordinary resemblance both in structure, sentiment, and occasionally in expression, which many passages (that are comparatively less spoiled than others by the prevailing bad taste of Crashaw's time) bear to the lyrics of that first of England's *poet*-lyrists,—I of course mean Shelley. Strange as it may appear, there are many things in common between them. They both, at great personal sacrifices, and with equal disinterestedness, embraced what they conceived to be the truth. Fortunately, in Crashaw's case, Truth and Faith were synonymous; unhappily with Shelley the Abnegation of Faith seemed to be of more importance than the reception of any tangible or intelligible substitute. Both were persecuted, neglected, and misunderstood; and both terminated their brief lives, at about the same age, on opposite shores of the same beautiful country, whither even at that early period "The Swans of Albion" had begun to resort, there perchance in a moment of peace to sing one immortal death-song, and so die.—D. F. M'CARTHY, "Crashaw and Shelley," *Notes and Queries*, June 5, 1858, p. 419

He is perhaps, after Donne, the greatest of these religious poets of the early part of the seventeenth century. He belongs in manner to the same school with Donne and Herrick, and in his lighter pieces he has much of their lyrical sweetness and delicacy; but there is often a force and even occasionally what may be called a grandeur of imagination in his more solemn poetry which Herrick never either reaches or aspires to.—GEORGE L. CRAIK, *A Compendious History of English Literature and of the English Language*, 1861, Vol. 2, p. 20

If Richard Crashaw, a poet who, by reason of his entire devotion to his faith and his absolute purity, belongs to this group ⟨Southwell, Habington, Crashaw⟩, had written nothing except the final of "The Flaming Heart," he would deserve more fame than at present distinguishes his name. "The Flaming Heart," marred as it is by those exasperating conceits which Crashaw never seemed tired of indulging in, is full of the intense fervor which the subject—"the picture of the seraphical Saint Teresa, as she is usually expressed with seraphim beside her"—would naturally suggest to a religious and poetic mind. After what Mr. Simcox very justly calls "an atrocious and prolonged conceit," ⟨*The English Poets*⟩ this poem beautifully closes:

O thou undaunted daughter of desires!
By all thy dower of lights and fires;
By all the eagle in thee, all the dove;
By all thy lives and deaths of love;
By thy large draughts of intellectual day,
And by thy thirsts of love more large than they;
By all thy brim-fill'd bowls of fierce desire,
By thy last morning's draught of liquid fire,
By the full kingdom of that final kiss
That seized thy parting soul and sealed thee His;
By all the heav'n thou hast in him,
(Fair sister of the seraphim!)
By all of him we have in thee,
Leave nothing of myself in me.
Let me so read thy life that I
Unto all life of mine may die.

The mystical fire which lights this poem is a characteristic of all Crashaw's religious verses. "Intellectual day" is a favorite expression of his; "the brim-fill'd bowls of fierce desire" is one of those lowering conceits that occur so jarringly in Habington's poetry and that are intolerably frequent in Crashaw. Born about 1615, he began to write at a time when a poem lacking in quaint conceits was scarcely a poem, and his verse, delicate, tender, original, and singularly fluent in diction, lost much strength from this circumstance and from his habit of diluting a thought or a line until all its force was lost. No poet since his time has been given so greatly to dilution and repetition, except Swinburne. In the famous "Wishes," written to a mythical mistress,

Whoe'er she be,
That not impossible she
That shall command my heart and me,

he plays with one idea, fantastically twisting it and repeating it until the reader grows weary.

In 1646, four years before his death, Richard Crashaw published "Steps to the Temple." Reading it, one may well exclaim, with Cowley:

Poet and saint to thee alone are given,
The two most sacred names in earth and heaven!

It glows with an impetuous devotion which is like the rush of a fiery chariot. It carries the soul upward, although an occasional earthly conceit clogs its ascending rush. And yet it is evident that the devotion of the poet was so genuine that he did not think of his mode of expression. He tore out the words that came nearest to him, in order to build a visible thought. Pope did not hesitate to borrow the finest passages in "Eloise and Abelard" from Crashaw, and there are many lines in Crashaw's

poems which unite the perfect finish of Pope to a spontaneity and poetic warmth which the "great classic" never attained.

Crashaw was born in an "intellectual day" tempered by a dim religious light. His father, like Habington's, was an author, a preacher in the Temple Church, London, near which the poet was born. He took his degree at Cambridge. He entered the Anglican Church as a minister. But his views were not orthodox; he was expelled from his living, and soon after he became a Catholic. From his poems it is plain that Crashaw was always a Catholic at heart. He entered the church as one who, having lived in a half-forgotten place in dreams, enters it without surprise. Crashaw went to court, but gained no preferment. The "not impossible she" whose courtly opposites suggested the portrait never "materialized" herself. He became a priest, and died in 1650, canon of Loretto—an office which he obtained, it is said, through the influence of the exiled Queen Henrietta Maria. Crashaw's poems are better known than Habington's, though, with the exception of "Wishes," which, like Herrick's "To Daffodils," is quoted in almost every reader, and the lovely poem beginning,

Lo! here a little volume but large book,
(Fear it not, sweet,
It is no hypocrite,)
Much larger in itself than in its look,

they are read only in odd lines or striking couplets. Crashaw had the softened fire of Southwell with the placid sweetness of Habington. He possessed a wider range than either of them; the fact that he was at his best in paraphrases shows that he did not own the force and power which Habington had in less degree than Southwell, or that his fluency of diction and copiousness of imagery easily led him to ornament the work of others rather than to carve out his own. As he stands, any country—even that which boasts of a Shakspere—may be proud to claim him. For the fame of our three Catholic poets it is unfortunate that they wrote in the great shade of Shakspere; but in the presence of great intellectual giants they are by no means dwarfs. Flawless as men, unique and genuine as poets, they cannot die as long as the world honors goodness and that divine spark which men call poetry. They were Catholic; true alike to their faith and their inspiration; faithful, and, being faithful, pure as poets or men are seldom pure.—MAURICE F. EGAN, "Three Catholic Poets," *Catholic World*, Oct. 1880, pp. 138-40

Crashaw is full of diffuseness and repetition; in the "Wishes for his Mistress" he puts in every fantastic way possible the hope that she will not paint; often the variations are so insignificant that he can hardly have read the poem through before sending it to press. . . . He spins the 23rd psalm into three dozen couplets. The Stabat Mater is very far from being the severest of mediæval hymns, but there is no appropriateness in Crashaw's own title for his paraphrase "A Pathetical descant on the devout Plain Song of the Church," as though he were a pianist performing variations upon a classical air. He extemporises at ease in his rooms at Peterhouse, then the ritualistic college of Cambridge. Like Herbert he was a piece of a courtier, but he did not go to court to seek his fortune, he found nothing there but materials for a sketch of the supposed mistress who never disturbed his pious vigils.—G. A. SIMCOX, *English Poets*, 1880, ed. Ward, pp. 195–96

Crashaw's verse is marked by some of the highest qualities of poetry. He has strong affinities to two of our great nineteenth-century poets; he has the rich imagination and sensuousness of Keats, and the subtlety of thought and exquisite lyrical flow of Shelley. Crashaw is essentially a sacred poet, and, compared with George Herbert, is his superior, judged from the purely poetic standpoint. Herbert is, in a limited degree, a popular poet; Crashaw is not, and has never been so. One of the reasons for this is (probably) the taste for artificial poetry of the school of Waller, Dryden, Pope, &c., during the seventeenth and eighteenth centuries. The fact of his being a Catholic would also deter many readers from studying his works; but, poetical thought now being wider, and religious intolerance almost a thing of the past, it may be hoped that Crashaw will soon receive the recognition which is his due.—J. R. TUTIN, "Preface" to *Poems of Richard Crashaw*, 1887, p. viii

Crashaw's sacred poems breathe a passionate fervour of devotion, which finds its outlet in imagery of a richness seldom surpassed in our language. . . . Diffuseness and intricate conceit, which at times become grotesque, are the defects of Crashaw's poetry. His metrical effects, often magnificent, are very unequal. He has little of the simple tenderness of Herbert, whom he admired, and to whom he acknowledged his indebtedness.—SIDNEY LEE, *Dictionary of National Biography*, 1888, Vol. 13, pp. 35–36

Crashaw represents sensuous Mysticism. . . . Like Quarles, (though not to the same degree), he quits the ideal point of view, the high Platonic aether. We cannot say of him, as has been said of that "Son of Light," Origen, the great founder of Christian Mysticism, that he "is never betrayed into the imagery of earthly passion used by the monastic writers," and which also marked the style of the Italian Marino, from whose "Herod" Crashaw has left a brilliant paraphrase. Yet this mode of feeling has its place; it also demands and deserves its compartment in a Sacred Anthology. Crashaw's work in poetry, as a whole, is incomplete and irregular; Pope, whilst praising him, was correct in recognizing that he was an amateur rather than an artist. It was the same with Marvell:—neither, one would say, did justice to his fine natural gift. But Crashaw has a charm so unique, an imagination so nimble and subtle, phrases of such sweet and passionate felicity, that readers who . . . turn to his little book, will find themselves surprised and delighted, in proportion to their sympathetic sense of Poetry, when touched to its rarer and finer issues.—FRANCIS TURNER PALGRAVE, *The Treasury of Sacred Song*, 1889, Note, p. 342

Crashaw is remarkable among poets for the extraordinary inequality of his work. It is impossible to open a page of his poems without being rewarded by some charming novelty of metre or language, some sudden turn of expression of melodious cadence of rhythm. But the music flags, and the moment or inspiration passes, and Crashaw sinks to earth, the child of Marini and Gongora, the weaver of trivial conceits and overelaborate fancies. It is this inequality that has made his poetry less read than it deserves to be. Poets of as widely different schools as Pope, Coleridge, and Shelley—have each acknowledged their indebtedness to him; and Mr. Swinburne has in our own day restored some of his lyrical measures to English verse.—J. HOWARD B. MASTERMAN, *The Age of Milton*, 1897

Crashaw is in poetry as in religion an emotional ritualist; a rich and sensuous pathos characterizes his diction and his rhythms, and redeems from tastelessness conceits over-subtle and symbolical, and marked by all the extravagance of the rococo vein.—FREDERIC IVES CARPENTER, "Introduction" to *English Lyric Poetry, 1500–1700*, 1897, p. lix

His age gave the preference to Cowley, in whose odes there is unlimited ostentation of dominating ardour without the reality, the result being mere capricious and unmeaning dislocation of form. Too much of the like is there in Crashaw; but every now and again he ascends into real fervour, such as makes metre and diction plastic to its own shaping spirit of inevitable rightness. This is the eminent praise of Crashaw, that he marks an epoch, a turn of the tide in English lyric, though the crest of the tide was not to come till long after, though—like all first innovators—he not only suffered present neglect, but has been overshadowed by those who came a century after him. He is fraught with suggestion—infinite suggestion. More than one poet has drawn much from him, yet much remains to be drawn. But it is not only for poets he exists. Those who read for enjoyment can find in him abundant delight, if they will be content (as they are content with Wordsworth) to grope through his plenteous infelicity. He is no poet of the human and household emotions; he has not pathos, or warm love, or any of the qualities which come home to the natural kindly race of men. But how fecund is his brilliant imagery, rapturous ethereality. He has, at his best, an extraordinary cunning of diction, cleaving like gold-leaf to its object. In such a poem as "The Musician and the Nightingale" the marvel of diction becomes even too conscious; in the moment of wondering at the miracle, we feel that the miracle is too researched: it is the feat of an amazing gymnast in words rather than of an unpremeditating angel. Yet this poem is an extraordinary verbal achievement, and there are numerous other examples in which the miracle seems as unconscious as admirable.—FRANCIS THOMPSON, "Excursions in Criticism," *The Academy*, 1897, p. 427

A more ardent temperament than either Herbert's or Vaughan's, a more soaring and glowing lyrical genius, belonged to Richard Crashaw (1613–1649). The son of a Puritan preacher who denounced the Pope as Antichrist, Crashaw at Cambridge came under the influence of that powerful wave of reaction of which the Laudian movement was only a symptom. His artistic temperament felt the charm of church music and architecture, and his ardent disposition responded, like the Dutch Vondel's, to the Catholic glorification of love as well as faith, the devotion to Christ and the Virgin of the martyr and the saint. He read Italian and Spanish, and was infected by the taste for what one might call the religious confectionery of which Marino's poems are full. His *Epigrammata Sacra* (1634) elaborate with great cleverness and point tender and pious conceits. Of his English poems, the secular *Delights of the Muses* (1648) include experiments in conceit and metrical effect such as *Love's Duel* and *Wishes*, and eulogies in the highly abstract style of Donne's, with less of thought and more of sentiment. But his most characteristic and individual work is the religious poetry contained in the *Steps to the Temple* (1646) written before, and the *Carmen Deo Nostro* (1652) published in Paris after his ardent nature and the failure of Laud's endeavour had driven him to seek shelter in the bosom of the Roman Church, poems on all the favourite subjects of Catholic devotion—the Name of Christ, the Virgin, Mary Magdalene weeping, martyrs, saints, and festivals.

Crashaw's style may have been influenced by Marino as well as Donne. His conceits are frequently of the physical and luscious character, to which the Italian tended always, the English poet never. He translated the first canto of the *Strage degli Innocenti*, frequently intensifying the imaginative effect, at other times making the conceit more pointed and witty, occasionally going further in the direction of confectionery even than Marino. The latter does not describe hell as a "shop of woes," nor say that the Wise Men went—

Westward to find the world's true Orient

nor would Marino, I think, speak of the Magdalen's tears as flowing upward to become the cream upon the Milky Way.

Marino's early and purer style in religious poetry is better represented by Drummond's sacred sonnets.

But if Crashaw's taste in conceits is at times worse than Marino's, his lyrical inspiration is stronger, his spiritual ecstasies more ardent. There is more of Vondel than Marino in the atmosphere of his religious poetry. The northern temperament vibrates with a fuller music. His hymn, *On the Glorious Assumption*, is written in the same exalted strain as Vondel's dedication of the *Brieven der Heilige Maeghden*, but Vondel's style is simpler and more masculine. Crashaw's fire is too often coloured—"happy fireworks" is the epithet he applies to his beloved Saint Theresa's writings—but its glow is unmistakable, and occasionally, as in the closing lines of *The Flaming Heart*, it is purified by its own ardour.—HERBERT J. C. GRIERSON, "English Poetry," *The First Half of the Seventeenth Century*, 1906, pp. 169-71

GEORGE GILFILLAN
From "The Life and Poetry of Richard Crashaw"
Poetical Works of Richard Crashaw
1857, pp. viii–xviii

From the beginning of his being, Crashaw was a Catholic; and in saying so, we deem that we have stated at once the source of his poetic weakness and strength, as well as that of all men of genius similarly situated. Roman Catholicism, in our judgment, is not Christianity; but, by dwelling in its neighbourhood, and trying to mimic its marvellous results, it has imbibed a portion of its spirit, and bears nearly that relation to it which Judaism would have done, had it been contemporaneous with, instead of prior to the Christian scheme. Besides, the admixture of fiction, the amount of ceremony, the quantity to be *supposed*, to be implicitly believed, to be loved without reason, and admitted without proof,—all this renders Popery favourable to the exercise of the poetic imagination; while, on the other hand, the false and useless mystery, the tame subjection it requires of soul and heart and intellect, its "proud limitary spirit," the routine of idle monotonous rite,— stamp a certain vulgarity upon it, against which the wings of lofty genius have to struggle, and often to struggle in vain. In Crashaw, the struggle is generally successful. He looks at Popery, not as Dryden does, through the cold medium of the intellect, but through the burning haze of the imagination. His spirit is generally that of a true Christian poet, although considerably perverted by a false and bad form of the religion. In soaring imagination, in gorgeous language, in ardent enthusiasm, and in ecstasy of lyrical movement, Crashaw very much resembles Shelley, and may be called indeed the Christian Shelley.

His raptures are,
All air and fire.

His verse is pervaded everywhere by that fine madness, characteristic of the higher order of bards.

There can, we think, be little doubt that a great deal of Popish, and not a little of Protestant piety, is animalism inverted and transfigured. The saying of Pope about lust, "through certain strainers well-refined," becoming "gentle love," admits of another application. Desire, thrown into a new channel, becomes devotion—devotion sincere and strong, although assuming a spurious and exaggerated form. Hence in some writers, the same epithets are applied to the Saviour and to God, which in others are used to the objects of earthly tenderness, and we are disgusted with a profusion of "sweet Saviour," "dear lovely Jesus," &c. In the writings of the mystics, in the poems for instance of Madame Guion, you see a

temperament of the warmest kind turned into the channel of a high-soaring and rather superstitious piety. Conceive of Anacreon converted, and beginning to sing of celestial love, in the same numbers with which he had previously chanted the praises of women and wine! Nay, we need not make any such supposition. Moore—the modern Anacreon—has written Hebrew melodies, in which you find something of the same lusciousness of tone as in Tom Little's poems; the *nature* coming out irresistibly in both. We are far from questioning the sincerity of these writers, and far from denying that they are better employed when singing of Divine things, than when fanning the flames of earthly passion; but we should ever be ready, while reading their strains, to *subtract* a good deal on account of their temperament. Such writers too frequently become mawkish, and loathsomely sweet, and thus at once repel the tasteful and gratify the profane. Croly says, somewhere, "our religion is a *manly* religion," but we would not refer those who wished a proof of this to the love-sick and sentimental class in question, who seem to prefer Solomon's Song to every other book of the Bible, and without the excuse of oriental day, discover all the languor and voluptuousness of the oriental bosom. There is, too, considerable danger of a reaction on their part—that the fire, after turning up its crest for a season toward heaven, should sink into its old furnace again, and that then their "last state should be worse than the first."

These remarks apply in some measure to Crashaw, although the strength of his genius in a measure counteracts the impression. Yet, often you hear the language of earthly instead of celestial love, and discover a certain swooning, languishing voluptuousness of feeling, as when in his lines on Teresa, he says:

> Oh, what delight when she shall stand,
> And teach *thy lips Heaven* with her hand,
> On which thou now may'st to thy wishes
> Heap up thy *consecrated kisses*.
> What joy shall seize thy soul when she,
> Bending her blessed eyes on thee,
> Those second smiles of Heaven, shall dart
> Her mild rays through thy *melting* heart.

More offensive are the following lines on "The Wounds of our Crucified Lord:"

> O thou, that on this foot hast laid,
> Many a kiss, and many a tear,
> Now thou shalt have all repaid,
> Whatsoe'er thy charges were.
> This foot hath got a mouth and lips,
> To pay the *sweet sum of thy kisses*;
> To pay thy tears, an eye that weeps,
> Instead of tears, such gems as this is.

We may remark, in passing, how different and how far superior is Milton's language in reference to women to that of the Crashaw school! How respectful, dignified, admiring, yet modest and delicate, all Milton's allusions to female beauty! How different from the tone of languishment, the everlasting talk about "sighs," and "kisses," and "bosoms," found in some parts of our poet! Milton seems as much struck with woman's resemblance to, as with her difference from man, and regards her as a fainter stamp of the same Divine image—fainter but more exquisitely finished: her smile that of man, dying away in a dimple of loveliness, the lovelier for the dissolution; her eye his, less, but seeming sometimes larger from the tenderness with which it is filled; her brow his, in minia-desire, and shedding a mild steadfast moonlight on the whole picture and scheme of things;—all this, and much more than all this, to be found in Roman Catholicism, is calculated to please the fancy or delight the taste, or to rouse and rivet the imagination. All this Milton, as well as Crashaw, understood and felt; but he had the intellectual strength and moral hardihood to resist their fascination. He entered the splendid Catholic temple, and he did not refuse his admiration, he bathed his brow in the "dim religious light," he praised the pictures, he was ravished with the music, but he did not remain to worship; he turned away in sorrow and in anger, saying, "It is iniquity, even the solemn meeting: your new moons and your appointed feasts my soul hateth: they are a trouble unto me; I am weary to bear them." Crashaw, on the other hand, seems, without a struggle, to have yielded to the soft seductions of the system, and was soon sighingly but luxuriously lost.

He is a strong man, but no Milton—nay, rather a strong man unnerved by perfumes and lulled with unhealthy opiates—who writes the following lines "in a prayer-book:"

> Am'rous languishments, luminous trances,
>   Sights which are not seen with eyes,
> Spiritual and soul-piercing glances,
>   Whose pure and subtle lightning flies
> Home to the heart, and sets the house on fire,
> And melts it down in sweet desire,
>   Yet doth not stay
> To ask the windows' leave to pass that way.
> Delicious deaths, soft exhalations
> Of soul! dear, and divine annihilations!
>   A thousand unknown rites
>   Of joys, and rarefied delights;
> An hundred thousand loves and graces,
>   And many a mystic thing,
>   Which the divine embraces
> Of th' dear spouse of spirits with them will bring.

If our readers will turn to Shelley, and read his "Lines addressed to the noble and unfortunate Lady Emilia V—," they will find extremes meeting, and that the sceptical Shelley, and the Roman Catholic Crashaw, write, the one of earthly, nay, illicit love, and the other of spiritual communion, in language marvellously similar both in beauty and extravagance. These two poets resembled each other in the weakness that was bound up with their strength. Their fault was an excess of the emotional—a morbid excitability and enthusiasm, which in Shelley, and probably in Crashaw too, sprung from a scrofulous habit and a consumptive tendency. Shelley's conception of love, however, is in general purer and more ideal than that of the other poet.

Crashaw's volume is a small one, and yet small as it is, it contains a good deal of that quaint and tricky conceit, which Johnson has called, by a signal misnomer, "metaphysic." Crashaw, at least, has never mingled metaphysics with his poetry, although here and there he is as fantastic as Donne or Cowley, or any of the class. For instance, he writes thus on the text—"And he answered them nothing:"

> O mighty Nothing! unto thee,
> Nothing, we owe all things that be;
> God spake once when he all things made,
> He saved all when he nothing said.
> The world was made by Nothing then;
> 'Tis made by Nothing now again.

Johnson valued himself on his brief but vigorous account of the "Metaphysical Poets," in his *Life of Cowley.* We think, however, with all deference to his high critical authority, that not only has he used the word "metaphysical" in an arbitrary and inapposite sense, but that he has besides confounded wit with perverted ingenuity, and very much under-rated the genius of the men. He calls them, after Dryden, "wits, not poets," but if

wit is almost always held to signify a *sudden perception of analogies more or less recondite*, along with a TENDENCY *to the ludicrous*, then these writers have very little of the quality indeed. They see and shew remote analogies, but the analogies are too remote or too grave to excite any laughable emotion. Coming from far—coming as captives—and coming violently chained together in pairs, they produce rather wonder, tinctured with melancholy, than that vivid delight which creates smiles, if it does not explode into laughter. Sometimes, indeed, the conceits produce a ridiculous effect, but this arises rather from their absurdity than their wit. Who can laugh, however, at such lines as these describing God harmonising the chaos?

> Water and air he for the *Tenor* chose,
> Earth made the *Base*—the *Treble* flame arose.

But apart from their perverted ingenuity, their straining after effect, their profusion of small and often crooked points, and their desire to shew their learning, these writers had undoubtedly high imagination. Cowley, in his poetry and in his prose, has given undeniable evidences of a genius at once versatile, elegant, and powerful—nay, we venture to uphold the great poetical merit of some of the lines Johnson quotes from him to condemn—of the following for example:

> His bloody eyes he *hurls* round; his sharp paws
> Tear up the ground—then runs he wild about,
> Lashing his angry tail, and roaring out;
> Beasts creep into their dens, and tremble there.
> Trees, though no wind is stirring, shake for fear;
> Silence and horror fill the place around,
> *Echo itself dares scarce repeat the sound.*

These are bold metaphors, but they are not conceits. We feel them to rise naturally out of, and exactly to measure the majesty of the theme, not like conceits, to be *arbitrarily embossed* upon the shield of a subject, without any regard to its size, proportions, or general effect. We are happy to find De Quincy coinciding in part with our opinion of Johnson's criticism. Let us hear him speaking with a special reference to Donne: "Dr Johnson inconsiderately calls him and Cowley, &c., metaphysical poets, but rhetorical would have been a more accurate designation. In saying that, however, we revert to the original use of the word rhetoric, as laying the principal stress upon the management of the thoughts, and only a secondary one upon the ornaments of style. Few writers have shewn a more extraordinary compass of powers than Donne, for he combined the last sublimation of dialectical subtlety and address with the most impassioned majesty. Many diamonds compose the very substance of his poem on the Metempsychosis, thoughts and descriptions which have the fervent and gloomy sublimity of Ezekiel or Eschylus, whilst a diamond dust of rhetorical brilliance is strewed over the whole of his occasional verses and his prose. No criticism was ever more unhappy than that of Dr Johnson, which denounces all this artificial display as so much perversion of taste. There cannot be a falser thought than this, for upon that principle a whole class of compositions might be vicious by conforming to its own ideal. The artifice and machinery of rhetoric furnishes in its degree as legitimate a basis for intellectual pleasure as any other—that the pleasure is of an inferior order can no more attaint the idea or model of the composition, than it can impeach the excellence of an epigram that it is not a tragedy. Every species of composition is to be tried by its own laws."

Here it will be noticed that De Quincy takes somewhat different ground from what we would take in reply to Johnson. He seems to think that Johnson principally objected to the *manner* of these writers, and he argues, very justly, that as professed rhetoricians they had a right to use the artifices of rhetoric, and none the less that they wrote in metre; and he might have maintained, besides, that finding a peculiar mode of writing in fashion, they were quite as justifiable in using it, IF they did not caricature it, as in wearing the bag, sword, and ruffles of their day. But Johnson, besides, denied that these men were poets; he objected to the *matter* as well as the manner of their song; and here we join issue with him, nay, are ready to admit that they were often rhetorically faulty, even by their own standard, if it be granted that they possessed a real and sublime poetic genius. That De Quincy agrees with us in this belief, we are certain, but it was his part to defend them upon another and a lower basis of assault. The most powerful passage in Johnson's account of the Metaphysical Poets is that in which he denies their claims to sublimity. He says with great eloquence—"The sublime was not within their reach—they never attempted that comprehension and expanse of mind, which at once filled the whole mind, and of which the first effect is sudden astonishment, and the second rational admiration. Sublimity is produced by aggregation, and littleness by dispersion. Great thoughts are always general, and consist in positions not limited by exceptions, and in descriptions not descending to minuteness. It is with great propriety that subtlety, which in its original import means exility of particles, is taken, in its metaphorical meaning, for nicety of distinction. Those writers who lay on the watch for novelty could have little hope of greatness; for great things cannot have escaped former observation. Their attempts were always analytic; they broke every image into fragments, and could no more represent, by their slender conceits and laboured particularities, the prospects of nature or the scenes of life, than he who dissects a sunbeam with a prism can exhibit the wide effulgence of a summer's noon."

In these remarks there is much truth as well as splendour; but Dr Johnson seems to forget that with all the elaborate pettiness of much in their writings—Cowley in portions of his "Davideis;" Donne in his "Metempsychosis;" Crashaw in his "Sospetto d'Herode;" Quarles in a few of his "Emblems;" and Herbert in certain parts of his *Temple*, have, perhaps *in spite of* their own system, attained a rare grandeur of thought and language. He might have remembered, too, that in prose Jeremy Taylor and Sir Thomas Browne, who both sinned in over-subtlety and subdivision of thinking, and were "Metaphysical Prose Poets," have both produced passages surpassed by nothing, even in Milton, for sublimity of imagination. He says "Great things cannot have escaped former observation;" but surely, although all men in all ages have seen the sun, the ocean, the earth, and the stars, new aspects of them are often presenting themselves to the poetic eye: all men in all ages have seen the sun, but did all men from the beginning see him eclipsed at noonday in May 1836? all men have seen the stars, but have all looked through a Rossian telescope at the Moon, Mars, or Saturn? The truth is, Dr Johnson had great sympathy with the broad—the materially sublime and the colossally great; but, from a defect in eyesight and in mind, had little or none with either the beautiful or the subtle, and did not perceive the exquisite effects which a minute use of the knowledge of both these often produces. Of the great passages of Milton he had much admiration, but could not understand such lines as—

> Many a winding bout
> Of linked sweetness long drawn out,—

as what a poet calls it—"a charming embodiment of thin air and sound in something palpable, tangible, malleable;" nor that other wondrous line of "imaginative incarnation"—

> Rose like a steam of rich, distill'd perfumes;

nor would he have, we fear, admired Crashaw's "Music's Duel," which, altogether, we think, is not only his finest effort, but accomplishes with magical ease one of the most difficult of poetic tasks, and seems almost higher than nature. Like an Arabian sorcerer, the soul of the poet leaps back and forward, from the musician to the bird, entering into the very heart, and living in the very voice of each. Let our readers read the whole, and they will agree with us that they have read the most deliciously-true and incredibly-sustained piece of poetry in probably the whole compass of the language.

Just think of this; could Shakspeare have surpassed it?—

> Her supple breast thrills out
> Sharp airs, and *staggers in a warbling doubt*
> Of dallying sweetness, hovers o'er her skill,
> And *folds in wav'd notes with a trembling bill*
> The *pliant series of her slipp'ry song*;
> Then starts she suddenly into a throng
> Of short, thick sobs,

We may close by strongly recommending to our readers the "Sospetto d'Herode," that fine transfusion of Crashaw's—a poem from which Milton, in his "Hymn on the Nativity," has derived a good deal; and by expressing the peculiar satisfaction with which we present the public with a handsome edition of the too little known productions of this exquisite poet.

GEORGE MACDONALD
From "Crashaw and Marvell"
England's Antiphon
1868, pp. 238–46

I come now to one of the loveliest of our angel-birds, Richard Crashaw. Indeed he was like a bird in more senses than one; for he belongs to that class of men who seem hardly ever to get foot-hold of this world, but are ever floating in the upper air of it.

What I said of a peculiar Æolian word-music in William Drummond applies with equal truth to Crashaw; while of our own poets, somehow or other, he reminds me of Shelley, in the silvery shine and bell-like melody both of his verse and his imagery; and in one of his poems, *Music's Duel*, the fineness of his phrase reminds me of Keats. But I must not forget that it is only with his sacred, his best poems too, that I am now concerned.

The date of his birth is not known with certainty, but it is judged about 1616, the year of Shakspere's death. He was the son of a Protestant clergyman zealous even to controversy. By a not unnatural reaction Crashaw, by that time, it is said, a popular preacher, when expelled from Oxford in 1644 by the Puritan Parliament because of his refusal to sign their Covenant, became a Roman Catholic. He died about the age of thirty-four, a canon of the Church of Loretto. There is much in his verses of that sentimentalism which, I have already said in speaking of Southwell, is rife in modern Catholic poetry. I will give from Crashaw a specimen of the kind of it. Avoiding a more sacred object, one stanza from a poem of thirty-one, most musical, and full of lovely speech concerning the tears of Mary Magdalen, will suit my purpose.

> Hail, sister springs,
> Parents of silver-footed rills!
> Ever-bubbling things!
> Thawing crystal! Snowy hills,
> Still spending, never spent!—I mean
> Thy fair eyes, sweet Magdalene!

The poem is called *The Weeper*, and is radiant of delicate fancy. But surely such tones are not worthy of fitting moth-like about the holy sorrow of a repentant woman! Fantastically beautiful, they but play with her grief. Sorrow herself would put her shoes off her feet in approaching the weeping Magdalene. They make much of her indeed, but they show her little reverence. There is in them, notwithstanding their fervour of amorous words, a coldness like that which dwells in the ghostly beauty of icicles shining in the moon.

But I almost reproach myself for introducing Crashaw thus. I had to point out the fact, and now having done with it, I could heartily wish I had room to expatiate on his loveliness even in such poems as *The Weeper*.

His *Divine Epigrams* are not the most beautiful, but they are to me the most valuable of his verses, inasmuch as they make us feel afresh the truth which he sets forth anew. In them some of the facts of our Lord's life and teaching look out upon us as from clear windows of the past. As epigrams, too, they are excellent—pointed as a lance.

UPON THE SEPULCHRE OF OUR LORD

Here, where our Lord once laid his head,
Now the grave lies burïed.

THE WIDOW'S MITES

Two mites, two drops, yet all her house and land,
Fall from a steady heart, though trembling hand;
The other's wanton wealth foams high and brave:
The other cast away—she only gave.

ON THE PRODIGAL

Tell me, bright boy! tell me, my golden lad!
Whither away so frolic? Why so glad?
What! *all* thy wealth in council? *all* thy state?
Are husks so dear? Troth, 'tis a mighty rate!

I value the following as a lovely parable. Mary is not contented: to see the place is little comfort. The church itself, with all its memories of the Lord, the gospel-story, and all theory about him, is but his tomb until we find himself.

COME, SEE THE PLACE WHERE THE LORD LAY

Show me himself, himself, bright sir! Oh show
Which way my poor tears to himself may go.
Were it enough to show the place, and say,
"Look, Mary; here see where thy Lord once lay;"
Then could I show these arms of mine, and say,
"Look, Mary; here see where thy Lord once lay."

From one of eight lines, on the Mother Mary looking on her child in her lap, I take the last two, complete in themselves, and I think best alone.

This new guest to her eyes new laws hath given:
'Twas once *look up*, 'tis now *look down to heaven*.

And there is perhaps his best.

TWO WENT UP INTO THE TEMPLE TO PRAY

Two went to pray? Oh rather say,
One went to brag, the other to pray.

One stands up close, and treads on high,
Where the other dares not lend his eye.

One nearer to God's altar trod;
The other to the altar's God.

This appears to me perfect. Here is the true relation between the forms and the end of religion. The priesthood, the altar and all its ceremonies, must vanish from between the sinner and his God. When the priest forgets his mediation of a servant, his duty of a door-keeper to the temple of truth, and takes upon him the office of an intercessor, he stands between

man and God, and is a Satan, an adversary. Artistically considered, the poem could hardly be improved.

Here is another containing a similar lesson.

I AM NOT WORTHY THAT THOU SHOULDST COME UNDER MY ROOF

Thy God was making haste into thy roof;
Thy humble faith and fear keeps him aloof.
He'll be thy guest: because he may not be,
He'll come—into thy house? No; into thee.

The following is a world-wide intercession for them that know not what they do. Of those that reject the truth, who can be said ever to have *truly* seen it? A man must be good to see truth. It is a thought suggested by our Lord's words, not an irreverent opposition to the truth of *them*.

BUT NOW THEY HAVE SEEN AND HATED

Seen? and yet *hated thee?* They did not see—
They saw thee not, that saw and hated thee!
No, no; they saw thee not, O Life! O Love!
Who saw aught in thee that their hate could move.

We must not be too ready to quarrel with every oddity: an oddity will sometimes just give the start to an outbreak of song. The strangeness of the following hymn rises almost into grandeur.

EASTER DAY.

Rise, heir of fresh eternity,
From thy virgin-tomb;
Rise, mighty man of wonders, and thy world with
thee;
Thy tomb, the universal East—
Nature's new womb;
Thy tomb—fair Immortality's perfuméd nest.
Of all the glories make noon gay
This is the morn;
This rock buds forth the fountain of the streams of
day;
In joy's white annals lives this hour,
When life was born,
No cloud-scowl on his radiant lids, no tempest-
lower.
Life, by this light's nativity,
All creatures have;
Death only by this day's just doom is forced to die.
Nor is death forced; for, may he lie
Throned in thy grave,
Death will on this condition be content to die.

When we come, in the writings of one who has revealed masterdom, upon any passage that seems commonplace, or any figure that suggests nothing true, the part of wisdom is to brood over that point; for the probability is that the barrenness lies in us, two factors being necessary for the result of sight—the thing to be seen and the eye to see it. No doubt the expression may be inadequate, but if we can compensate the deficiency by adding more vision, so much the better for us.

In the second stanza there is a strange combination of images: the rock buds; and buds a fountain; the fountain is light. But the images are so much one at the root, that they slide gracefully into each other, and there is no confusion or incongruity: the result is an inclined plane of development.

I now come to the most musical and most graceful, therefore most lyrical, of his poems. I have left out just three stanzas, because of the sentimentalism of which I have spoken: I would have left out more if I could have done so without spoiling the symmetry of the poem. My reader must be friendly enough to one who is so friendly to him, to let his peculiarities pass unquestioned—amongst the rest his conceits, as well as the trifling discord that the shepherds should be called, after the classical fashion—ill agreeing, from its associations, with Christian song—Tityrus and Thyrsis.

A HYMN OF THE NATIVITY SUNG BY THE SHEPHERDS.

Chorus: Come, we shepherds, whose blest sight
　　Hath met love's noon in nature's night;
　　Come, lift we up our loftier song,
　　And wake the sun that lies too long.

　　To all our world of well-stolen[1] joy
　　　　He slept, and dreamed of no such thing,
　　While we found out heaven's fairer eye,
　　　　And kissed the cradle of our king:
　　Tell him he rises now too late
　　To show us aught worth looking at.

　　Tell him we now can show him more
　　　　Than he e'er showed to mortal sight—
　　Than he himself e'er saw before,
　　　　Which to be seen needs not his light:
　　Tell him, Tityrus, where thou hast been;
　　Tell him, Thyrsis, what thou hast seen.

Tityrus: Gloomy night embraced the place
　　　　Where the noble infant lay:
　　The babe looked up and showed his face:
　　　　In spite of darkness it was day.
　　It was thy day, sweet, and did rise
　　Not from the east, but from thy eyes.

Chorus: It was thy day, sweet, &c.

Thyrsis: Winter chid aloud, and sent
　　　　The angry north to wage his wars:
　　The north forgot his fierce intent,
　　　　And left perfumes instead of scars.
　　By those sweet eyes' persuasive powers,
　　Where he meant frosts, he scattered flowers.

Chorus: By those sweet eyes', &c.

Both: We saw thee in thy balmy nest,
　　　　Young dawn of our eternal day;
　　We saw thine eyes break from the east,
　　　　And chase the trembling shades away.
　　We saw thee, and we blessed the sight;
　　We saw thee by thine own sweet light.

Chorus: We saw thee, &c.

Tityrus: "Poor world," said I, "what wilt thou do
　　　　To entertain this starry stranger?
　　Is this the best thou canst bestow—
　　　　A cold and not too cleanly manger?
　　Contend, the powers of heaven and earth,
　　To fit a bed for this huge birth."

Chorus: Contend, the powers, &c.

Thyrsis: "Proud world," said I, "cease your contest,
　　　　And let the mighty babe alone:
　　The phœnix builds the phœnix' nest—
　　　　Love's architecture is his own.
　　The babe, whose birth embraves this morn,
　　Made his own bed ere he was born."

Chorus: The babe, whose birth, &c.

Tityrus: I saw the curl'd drops, soft and slow,
　　　　Come hovering o'er the place's head,
　　Offering their whitest sheets of snow
　　　　To furnish the fair infant's bed:
　　"Forbear," said I; "be not too bold:
　　Your fleece is white, but 'tis too cold."

Chorus: "Forbear," said I, &c.

Thyrsis: I saw the obsequious seraphim
　　　　Their rosy fleece of fire bestow;
　　For well they now can spare their wings,
　　　　Since heaven itself lies here below.
　　"Well done," said I; "but are you sure
　　Your down, so warm, will pass for pure?"

Chorus: "Well done," said I, &c.

Full Chorus: Welcome all wonders in one sight!
　　　　Eternity shut in a span!
　　Summer in winter! day in night!
　　　　Heaven in earth, and God in man!
　　Great little one, whose all-embracing birth
　　Lifts earth to heaven, stoops heaven to earth!

　　Welcome—though not to those gay flies
　　　　Gilded i' th' beams of earthly kings—
　　Slippery souls in smiling eyes—
　　　　But to poor shepherds, homespun things,
　　Whose wealth's their flocks, whose wit's to be
　　Well read in their simplicity.

　　Yet when young April's husband showers
　　　　Shall bless the fruitful Maia's bed,
　　We'll bring the firstborn of her flowers
　　　　To kiss thy feet, and crown thy head:
　　To thee, dear Lamb! whose love must keep
　　The shepherds while they feed their sheep.

　　To thee, meek Majesty, soft king
　　　　Of simple graces and sweet loves,
　　Each of us his lamb will bring,
　　　　Each his pair of silver doves.
　　At last, in fire of thy fair eyes,
　　Ourselves become our own best sacrifice.

A splendid line to end with! too good for the preceding one. All temples and altars, all priesthoods and prayers, must vanish in this one and only sacrifice. Exquisite, however, as the poem is, we cannot help wishing it looked less heathenish. Its decorations are certainly meretricious.

Notes

1. How unpleasant conceit can become. The joy of seeing the Saviour was *stolen* because they gained it in the absence of the sun!

ALEXANDER B. GROSART

From "Essay on the Life and Poetry of Crashaw"

Complete Works of Richard Crashaw

Volume 2, 1873, pp. lxii–lxxv

Four things appear to me to call for examination, in order to give the essentials of Crashaw as a Poet, and to gather his main characteristics: (*a*) Imaginative-sensuousness; (*b*) Subtlety of emotion; (*c*) Epigrams; (*d*) Translations and (briefly) Latin and Greek Poetry. I would say a little on each.

(*a*) *Imaginative-sensuousness*. Like 'charity' for 'love,' the word 'sensuous' has deteriorated in our day. It is, I fear, more than in sound and root confused with 'sensual,' in its base application. I use it as Milton did, in the well-known passage when he defined Poetry to be 'simple, *sensuous*, and passionate;' and I qualify 'sensuousness' with 'imaginative,' that I may express our Poet's peculiar gift of looking at everything with a full, open, penetrative eye, yet through his imagination; his imagination not being as spectacles (coloured) astride the nose, but as a light of white glory all over his intellect and entire faculties. Only Wordsworth and Shelley, and recently Rossetti and Jean Ingelow, are comparable with him in this. You can scarcely err in opening on any page in your out-look for it. The very first poem, 'The Weeper,' is lustrous with it. For example, what a grand reach of 'imaginative' comprehensiveness have we so early as in the second stanza, where from the swimming eyes of his 'Magdalene' he was, as it were, swept upward to the broad transfigured sky in its wild ever-varying beauty of the glittering silver rain!

> Heauns thy fair eyes be;
> > Heauens of ever-falling starres.
> 'Tis seed-time still with thee;
> > And starres thou sow'st whose haruest dares
> Promise the Earth to counter-shine
> Whateuer makes heaun's forehead fine.

How grandly vague is that 'counter-shine *whatever*,' as it leads upwards to the 'forehead'—superb, awful, Godcrowned—of the 'heauns'! Of the same in kind, but unutterably sweet and dainty also in its exquisiteness, is stanza vii.:

> > The deaw no more will weap
> > The primrose's pale cheek to deck:
> > The deaw no more will sleep
> > Nuzzel'd in the lily's neck:
> > Much rather would it be thy tear,
> > And leaue them both to tremble there.

Wordsworth's vision of the 'flashing daffodils' is not finer than this. A merely realistic Poet (as John Clare or Bloomfield) would never have used the glorious singular, 'thy tear,' with its marvellous suggestiveness of the multitudinous dew regarding itself as outweighed in everything by one 'tear' of such eyes. Every stanza gives a text for commentary; and the rapid, crowding questions and replies of the Tears culminate in the splendid homage to the Saviour in the conclusion, touched with a gentle scorn:

> We goe not to seek
> > The darlings of Aurora's bed,
> > The rose's modest cheek,
> > Nor the violet's humble head,
> Though the feild's eyes too Weepers be,
> Because they want such teares as we.
> > Much lesse mean to trace
> > The fortune of inferior gemmes,
> > Preferr'd to some proud face,
> > Or pertch't vpon fear'd diadems:
> *Crown'd heads are toyes. We goe to meet*
> A worthy object, our *Lord's feet*.

'Feet' at highest; mark the humbleness, and the fitness too. Even more truly than of Donne (in Arthur Wilson's 'Elegy') may it be said of Crashaw, here and elsewhere, thou 'Couldst give both life and sense unto a flower,'—faint prelude of Wordsworth's 'meanest flower.'

Dr. Macdonald (in *Antiphon*) is perplexingly unsympathetic, or, if I may dare to say it, wooden, in his criticism on 'The Weeper;' for while he characterises it generally as 'radiant of delicate fancy,' he goes on: 'but surely such tones are not worthy of flitting moth-like about the holy sorrow of a repentant woman! Fantastically beautiful, they but play with her grief. Sorrow herself would put her shoes off her feet in approaching the weeping Magdalene. They make much of her indeed, but they show her little reverence. There is in them, notwithstanding their fervour of amorous words, a coldness, like that which dwells in the ghostly beauty of icicles shining in the moon' (p. 239). Fundamentally blundering is all this: for the Critic ought to have marked how the Poet's 'shoes' are put off his feet in approaching the weeping Magdalene; but that *she* is approached as far-back in the Past or in a Present wherein her

tears have been 'wiped away,' so that the poem is dedicate not so much to The Weeper as to her Tears, as things of beauty and pricelessness. Mary, 'blessed among women,' is remembered all through; and just as with her Divine Son we must 'sorrow' in the vision of His sorrows, we yet have the remembrance that they are all done, 'finished;' and thus we can expatiate on them not with grief so much as joy. The prolongation of 'The Weeper' is no 'moth-like flitting about the holy sorrow of a repentant woman,' but the never-to-be-satisfied rapture over the evidence of a 'godly sorrow' that has worked to repentance, and in its reward given loveliness and consecration to the tears shed. The moon 'shining on icicles' is the antithesis of the truth. Thus is it throughout, as in the backgrounds of the great Portrait-painters as distinguished from Land-scapists and Sea-scapists and Sky-scapists—Crashaw inevitably works out his thoughts through something he has looked at as transfigured by his imagination, so that you find his most mystical thinking and feeling framed (so to say) with images drawn from Nature. That he did look not at but into Nature, let 'On a foule Morning, being then to take a Journey,' and 'To the Morning; Satisfaction for Sleepe,' bear witness. In these there are penetrative 'looks' that Wordsworth never has surpassed, and a richness almost Shakesperean. Milton must have studied them keenly. There is this characteristic also in the 'sensuousness' of Crashaw, that while the Painter glorifies the ignoble and the coarse (as Hobbima's Asses and red-cloaked Old Women) in introducing it into a scene of Wood, or Wayside, or Sea-shore, his outward images and symbolism are worthy in themselves, and stainless as worthy (passing exceptions only establishing the rule). His epithets are never superfluous, and are, even to surprising nicety, true. Thus he calls Egypt '*white* Egypt' (vol. i. p. 81); and occurring as this does 'In the glorious Epiphanie of ovr Lord God,' we are reminded again how the youthful Milton must have had this extraordinary composition in his recollection when he composed his immortal Ode.[1] Similarly we have '*hir'd* mist' (vol. i. p. 84); '*pretious* losse' (ib.); '*fair-ey'd* fallacy of Day' (ib. p. 85); '*black* but faithfull perspectiue of Thee' (ib. p. 86); '*abasèd* liddes' (ib. p. 88); '*gratious* robbery' (ib. p. 156); 'thirsts of loue' (ib.); '*timerous* light of starres' (ib. p. 172); '*rebellious* eye of Sorrow' (ib. p. 112); and so in hundreds of parallels. Take this from 'To the Name above every Name' (ib. p. 60):

> O come away . . .
> O, see the weary liddes of wakefull Hope—
> Love's eastern windowes—all wide ope
> > With curtains drawn,
> To catch the day-break of Thy dawn.
> O, dawn at last, long-lookt-for Day,
> Take thine own wings, and come away.

Comparing Cowley's and Crashaw's 'Hope,' Coleridge thus pronounces on them: 'Crashaw seems in his poems to have given the first ebullience of his imagination, unshapen into form, or much of what we now term sweetness. In the poem Hope, by way of question and answer, his superiority to Cowley is self-evident;' and he continues, 'In that on the Name of Jesus, equally so; but his lines on St. Teresa are the finest.' 'Where he does combine richness of thought and diction, nothing can excel, as in the lines you so much admire,

> Since 'tis not to be had at home
> . . . .
> She'l to the Moores and martyrdom.[2]

And then as never-to-be-forgotten 'glory' of the Hymn to Teresa, he adds: 'these verses were ever present to my mind whilst writing the second part of Christabel; if indeed, by some subtle process of the mind, they did not suggest the first thought of the whole poem' (*Letters and Conversations*, 1836, i. 196). Coleridge makes another critical remark which it may be worth while to adduce and perhaps qualify. 'Poetry as regards small Poets may be said to be, in a certain sense, conventional in its accidents and in its illustrations. Thus [even] Crashaw uses an image "as sugar melts in tea away;" which although *proper then* and *true now*, was in bad taste at that time equally with the present. In Shakespeare, in Chaucer, there was nothing of this' (as before). The great Critic forgot that 'sugar' and 'tea' were not vulgarised by familiarity when Crashaw wrote, that the wonder and romance of their gift from the East still lay around them, and that their use was select, not common. Thus later I explain Milton's homeliness of allusion, as in the word 'breakfast,' and 'fell to,' and the like; words and places and things that have long been not prosaic simply, but demeaned and for ever unpoetised. I am not at all careful to defend the 'sugar' and 'tea' metaphor; but it, I think, belongs also to his imaginative-sensuousness, whereby orient awfulness almost, magnified and dignified it to him.

Moreover the canon in *Antiphon* is sound: 'When we come, in the writings of one who has revealed masterdom, upon any passage that seems commonplace, or any figure that suggests nothing true, the part of wisdom is to brood over that point; for the probability is that the barrenness lies in us, two factors being necessary for the result of sight—the thing to be seen, and the eye to see it. No doubt the expression may be inadequate; but if we can compensate the deficiency by adding more vision, so much the better for us' (p. 243).

I thank Dr. George Macdonald[3] (in *Antiphon*) for his quaint opening words on our Crashaw, and forgive him, for their sake, his blind reading of 'The Weeper.' 'I come now to one of the loveliest of our angel-birds, Richard Crashaw. Indeed, he was like a bird in more senses than one; for he belongs to that class of men who seem hardly ever to get foot-hold of this world, but are ever floating in the upper air of it' (p. 238). True, and yet not wholly; or rather, if our Poet ascends to 'the upper air,' and sings there with all the divineness of the skylark, like the skylark his eyes fail not to over-watch the nest among the grain beneath, nor his wings to be folded over it at the shut of eve. Infinitely more, then, is to be found in Crashaw than Pope (in his Letter to his friend Henry Cromwell) found: 'I take this poet to have writ like a gentleman; that is, at leisure hours, and more to keep out of idleness than to establish a reputation: so that nothing regular or just can be expected of him. All that regards design, form, fable (which is the soul of poetry), all that concerns exactness, or consent of parts (which is the body), will probably be wanting; only pretty conceptions, fine metaphors, glittering expressions, and something of a neat cast of verse (which are properly the dress, gems, or loose ornaments of poetry), may be found in these verses.' Nay verily, the form is often exquisite; but 'neat' and 'pretty conceptions' applied to such verse is as 'pretty' applied to Niagara—so full, strong, deep, thought-laden is it. I have no wish to charge plagiarism on Pope from Crashaw, as Peregrine Phillips did (see onward); but neither is the contemptuous as ignorant answer by a metaphor of Hayley to be received. The two minds were essentially different: Pope was talented, and used his talents to the utmost; Crashaw had absolute as unique genius.[4]

(*b*) *Subtlety of emotion.* Dr. Donne, in a memorable passage, with daring originality, sings of Mrs. Drury rapturously:

> Her pure and eloquent soul
> Spoke in her cheeks, and so distinctly wrought,
> That one might almost say her body thought.

I have much the same conception of Crashaw's thinking. It was so emotional as almost always to tremble into feeling. Bare intellect, 'pure' (= naked) thought, you rarely come on in his Poems. The thought issues forth from (in old-fashioned phrase) the heart, and its subtlety is something unearthly even to awfulness. Let the reader give hours to the study of the composition entitled 'In the glorious Epiphanie of ovr Lord God, a Hymn svng as by the three Kings,' and 'In the holy Nativity of ovr Lord God.' Their depth combined with elevation, their grandeur softening into loveliness, their power with pathos, their awe bursting into rapture, their graciousness and lyrical music, their variety and yet unity, will grow in their study. As always, there is a solid substratum of original thought in them; and the thinking, as so often in Crashaw, is surcharged with emotion. If the thought may be likened to fire, the praise, the rapture, the yearning may be likened to flame leaping up from it. Granted that, as in fire and flame, there are coruscations and jets of smoke, yet is the smoke that 'smoak' of which Chudleigh in his 'Elegy for Donne' sings:

> Incense of love's and fancie's *holy smoak*;

or, rather, that 'smoke' which filled the House to the vision of Isaiah (vi. 4). The hymn 'To the admirable Sainte Teresa,' and the 'Apologie' for it, and related 'Flaming Heart,' and 'In the glorious Assvmption of our Blessed Lady,' are of the same type. Take this from the 'Flaming Heart' (vol. i. p. 155):

> Leaue her . . . the flaming heart:
> Leaue her that, and thou shalt leaue her
> Not one loose shaft, but Loue's whole quiver.
> *For in Loue's feild was neuer found*
> *A nobler weapon than a wovnd.*
> Loue's passiues are his actiu'st part,
> The wounded is the wounding heart.
>   . . .
> Liue here, great heart; and loue and dy and kill,
> And bleed and wound; and yeild and conquer still.

His homage to the Virgin is put into words that pass the bounds which we Protestants set to the 'blessed among women' in her great renown, and even while a Protestant Crashaw fell into what we must regard as the strange as inexplicable forgetfulness that it is The *Man*, not The Child, who is our ever-living High-Priest 'within the veil,' and that not in His mother's bosom, but on the Throne of sculptured light, is His place. Still, you recognise that the homage to the Virgin-mother is to the Divine Son through her, and through her in fine if also mistaken humility. 'Mary' is the Muse of Crashaw; the Lord Jesus his 'Lord' and hers. I would have the reader spend willing time, in slowly, meditatively reading the whole of our Poet's sacred Verse, to note how the thinking thus thrills into feeling, and feeling into rapture—the rapture of adoration. It is miraculous how he finds words wherewith to utter his most subtle and vanishing emotion. Sometimes there is a daintiness and antique richness of wording that you can scarcely equal out of the highest of our Poets, or only in them. Some of his images from Nature are scarcely found anywhere else. For example, take this very difficult one of ice, in the 'Verse-Letter to the Countess of Denbigh' (vol. i. p. 298, ll. 21–26), 'persuading' her no longer to be the victim of her doubts:

> So, when the Year takes cold, we see
> Poor waters *their own prisoners be*;
> *Fetter'd and lock'd-up fast they lie*
> *In a cold self-captivity.*
> Th' astonish'd Nymphs their Floud's strange fate deplore,
> To find themselves their own severer shoar.

Young is striking in his use of the ice-metaphor:

> in Passion's flame
> Hearts melt; but *melt like ice, soon harder froze.*
> (Night-Thoughts, N. II. 1. 522–3.)

But how strangely original is the earlier Poet in so cunningly working it into the very matter of his persuasion! Our quotation from Young recalls that in the 'Night-Thoughts' there are evident reminiscences of Crashaw: *e.g.*

> Midnight veil'd his face:
> Not such as this, not such as Nature makes;
> A midnight Nature shudder'd to behold;
> A midnight new; a dread eclipse, without
> Opposing spheres, from her Creator's frown.
> (Night IV. ll. 246–250.)

So in 'Gilt was Hell's gloom' (N. VII. l. 1041), and in this portrait of Satan:

> Like meteors in a stormy sky, how roll
> His baleful eyes!
> (N. IX. ll. 280–1.)

and

> the fiery gulf,
> That flaming bound of wrath omnipotent;
> (Ib. ll. 473–4)

and

> Banners streaming as the comet's blaze;
> (Ib. l. 323)

and

> Which makes a hell of hell,
> (Ib. l. 340)

we have the impress and inspiration of our Poet.

How infinitely soft and tender and Shakesperean is the 'Epitaph vpon a yovng Married Covple dead and bvryed together' (with its now restored lines), thus!—

> Peace, good Reader, doe not weep;
> Peace, the louers are asleep.
> They, sweet turtles, folded ly
> In the last knott that Loue could ty.
> And though they ly as they were dead,
> Their pillow stone, their sheetes of lead
> (Pillow hard, and sheetes not warm),
> Loue made the bed; they'l take no harm:
> Let them sleep; let them sleep on,
> Till this stormy night be gone,
> And the æternall morrow dawn;
> Then . . . .
> (vol. i. pp. 230–1.)

The hush, the tranquil stillness of a church-aisle, within which 'sleep' old recumbent figures, comes over one in reading these most pathetically beautiful words. Of the whole poem, Dodd in his 'Epigrammatists' (as onward) remarks, 'after reading this Epitaph, all others on the same subject must suffer by comparison. Yet there is much to be admired in the following by Bishop Hall, on Sir Edward and Lady Lewkenor. It is translated from the Latin by the Bishop's descendant and editor, the Rev. Peter Hall (Bp. Hall's Works, 1837–9, xii. 331):

> In bonds of love united, man and wife,
> Long, yet too short, they spent a happy life;
> United still, too soon, however late,
> Both man and wife receiv'd the stroke of fate:
> And now in glory clad, enraptur'd pair,
> The same bright cup, the same sweet draught they
>   share.
> Thus, first and last, a married couple see,
> In life, in death, in immortality.

There is much beauty also in an anonymous epitaph in the 'Festoon' 143, 'On a Man and his Wife:'

> Here sleep, whom neither life nor love,
>   Nor friendship's strictest tie,
> Could in such close embrace as thou,
>   Their faithful grave, ally;
> Preserve them, each dissolv'd in each,
>   For bands of love divine,
> For union only more complete,
>   Thou faithful grave, than thine.
> (p. 253.)

His 'Wishes to his (supposed) Mistresse' has things in it vivid and subtle as anything in Shelley at his best; and I affirm this deliberately. His little snatch on 'Easter Day,' with some peculiarities, culminates in a grandeur Milton might bow before. The version of 'Dies Irae' is wonderfully severe and solemn and intense. Roscommon undoubtedly knew it. And so we might go on endlessly. His melody—with exceptional discords—is as the music of a Master, not mere versification. Once read receptively, and the words haunt almost awfully, and, I must again use the word, unearthily. Summarily—as in our claim for Vaughan, as against the preposterous traditional assertions of his indebtedness to Herbert poetically, while really it was for spiritual benefits he was obligated—we cannot for an instant rank George Herbert as a Poet with Crashaw. Their piety is alike, or the 'Priest' of Bemerton is more definite, and clear of the 'fine mist' of mysticism of the recluse of 'Little St. Mary's;' but only very rarely have you in *The Temple* that light of genius which shines as a very Shekinah-glory in the *Steps to the Temple*. These 'Steps' have been spoken of as 'Steps' designed to lead into Herbert's *Temple*, whereas they were 'Steps' to the 'Temple' or Church of the Living God. Crashaw 'sang' sweetly and generously of Herbert (vol. i. pp. 139–140); but the two Poets are profoundly distinct and independent. Clement Barksdale, probably, must bear the blame of foolishly subordinating Crashaw to Herbert, in his Lines in 'Nympha Libethris' (1651):

HERBERT AND CRASHAW

> When unto Herbert's Temple I ascend
> By Crashaw's Steps, I do resolve to mend
> My lighter verse, and my low notes to raise,
> And in high accent sing my Maker's praise.
> Meanwhile these sacred poems in my sight
> I place, that I may learn to write.

Notes

1. The 'Epiphanie' has some of the grandest things of Crashaw, and things so original in the thought and wording as not easily to be paralleled in other Poets: *e.g.* '*Dread* Sweet' (l. 236), and the superb 'Something a *brighter shadow*, Sweet, of thee' (l. 250). The most Crashaw-like of early 'Epiphany' or Christmas Hymns is that of Bishop Jeremy Taylor, from which I take these lines:

> Awake, my soul, and come away!
>   Put on thy best array;
>   Least if thou longer stay,
> Thou lose some minitts of so blest a day,
>   Goe run,
> And bid good-morrow to the sun;
> Welcome his safe return
>   To Capricorn;
> And that great Morne
> Wherein a God was borne,
> Whose story none can tell,
> But He whose every word's a miracle.
> (Our ed. of Bp. Taylor's *Poems*, pp. 22–3.)

En Passant, since our edition of Bishop Taylor's *Poems* was issued we have discovered that a 'Christmas Anthem or Carol by T.P.,' which appeared in James Clifford's 'Divine Services and Anthems' (1663), is Bishop Taylor's Hymn. This we learn from *The Musical Times*, Feb. 1st, 1871, in a paper on Clifford's book. Criticising the words as by an unknown T. P.—ignorant that he was really criticising Bp. Jeremy Taylor—the (I suppose) learned Writer thus appreciatively writes of the grand Hymn and these passionate yearning words: 'Who, for instance, could seriously sing in church such stuff as the following Christmas Anthem or Carol, by T. P.? which Mr. William Childe (not yet made Doctor) had set to music.' Ahem! And so on, in stone-eyed, stone-eared stupidity.—Of modern celebrations I name as worthy of higher recognition than it has received the following 'Hymn to the Week above every Week,' by Thomas II. Gill; Lon., Mudie, 1844 (pp. 24). There is no little of the rich quaint matter and manner of our elder Singers in this fine Poem.

2. Cf. vol. i. p. 143.

3. Like Macaulay in his *History of England* (1st edition), Dr. Macdonald by an oversight speaks of Crashaw as 'expelled from *Oxford*,' instead of Cambridge (cf. our vol. i. p. 32).

4. The Letter of Pope to Mr. Henry Cromwell is in all the editions of his Correspondence. Willmott (as before) also gives it *in extenso*. Of 'The Weeper' Pope says: 'To confirm what I have said, you need but look into his first poem of 'The Weeper,' where the 2d, 4th, 6th, 14th, 21st stanzas are as sublimely dull as the 7th, 8th, 9th, 16th, 17th, 20th, and 23d stanzas of the same copy are soft and pleasing. And if these last want anything, it is an easier and more unaffected expression. The remaining thoughts in that poem might have been spared, being either but repetitions, or very trivial and mean. And by this example one may guess at all the rest to be like this; a mixture of tender gentle thoughts and suitable expressions, of forced and inextricable conceits, and of needless fillers-up of the rest,' &c. &c. 'Sweet' is the loftiest epithet Pope uses for Crashaw, and that in the knowledge of the 'Suspicion of Herod.' In 'The Weeper' he passes some of the very finest things. In his 'Abelard and Eloisa' he incorporates felicities from Crashaw's 'Alexias' within inverted commas; but elsewhere is not very careful to mark indebtedness.

EDMUND GOSSE
From "Richard Crashaw" (1882/1913)
Seventeenth Century Studies
Volume 1, 1913, pp. 157–182

No sketch of the English literature of the middle of the seventeenth century can pretend to be complete if it does not tell us something of that serried throng of poets militant who gave in their allegiance to Laud, and became ornaments and then martyrs of the High Church party. Their piety was much more articulate and objective than that which had inspired the hymn-writers and various divine songsters of an earlier age; an element of political conviction, of anger and apprehension, gave ardour and tension to their song. They were conservative and passive, but not oblivious to the tendencies of the time, and the gathering flood of Puritanism forced them, to use an image that they would not themselves have disdained, to climb on to the very altar-step of ritualism, or even in extreme instances to take wing for the mystic heights of Rome itself.

It is from such extreme instances as the latter that we learn to gauge their emotion and their desperation, and it is therefore Crashaw rather than Herbert whom we select for the consideration of a typical specimen of the High Church poets. Nor is it only the hysterical intensity of Crashaw's convictions which marks him out for our present purpose; his position in history, his manhood spent in the last years of the reign of "Thorough," and in the very forefront of the crisis, give him a greater claim

upon us than Herbert, who died before Laud succeeded to the Primacy, or Vaughan, who was still a boy when Strafford was executed. There are many other points of view from which Crashaw is of special interest; his works present the only important contribution to English literature made by a pronounced Catholic, embodying Catholic doctrine, during the whole of the seventeenth century, while as a poet, although extremely unequal, he rises, at his best, to a mounting fervour which is quite electrical, and hardly rivalled in its kind before or since. . . .

Crashaw's English poems were first published in 1646, soon after his arrival in Paris. He was at that time in his thirty-fourth year, and the volume contains his best and most mature as well as his crudest pieces. It is, indeed, a collection of juvenile and manly verses thrown together with scarcely a hint of arrangement, the uncriticised labour of fifteen years. The title is *Steps to the Temple, Sacred Poems, with other delights of the Muses*. The sacred poems are so styled by his anonymous editor because they are "steps for happy souls to climb heaven by;" the *Delights of the Muses* are entirely secular, and the two divisions of the book, therefore, reverse the order of Herrick's similarly edited *Hesperides* and *Noble Numbers*. The *Steps to the Temple* are distinguished at once from the collection with which it is most natural to compare them, the *Temple* of Herbert, to which their title refers with a characteristic touch of modesty, by the fact that they are not poems of experience, but of ecstasy—not of meditation, but of devotion. Herbert, and with him most of the sacred poets of the age, are autobiographical; they analyse their emotions, they take themselves to task, they record their struggles, their defeats, their consolation.

But if the azure cherubim of introspection are the dominant muses of English sacred verse, the flame-coloured seraph of worship reigns in that of Crashaw. He has made himself familiar with all the amorous phraseology of the Catholic metaphysicians; he has read the passionate canticles of St. John of the Cross, the books of the Carmelite nun, St. Teresa, and all the other rosy and fiery contributions to ecclesiastical literature laid by Spain at the feet of the Pope during the closing decades of the sixteenth century. The virginal courage and ardour of St. Teresa inspire Crashaw with his loveliest and most faultless verses. We need not share nor even sympathise with the sentiment of such lines as these to acknowledge that they belong to the highest order of lyric writing:

> Thou art Love's victim, and must die
> A death more mystical and high;
> Into Love's arms thou shalt let fall
> A still-surviving funeral.
> His is the dart must make thy death,
> Whose stroke will taste thy hallowed breath—
> A dart thrice dipped in that rich flame
> Which writes thy spouse's radiant name
> Upon the roof of heaven, where aye
> It shines and with a sovereign ray
> Beats bright upon the burning faces
> Of souls which in that name's sweet graces
> Find everlasting smiles. So rare,
> So spiritual, pure, and fair,
> Must be the immortal instrument
> Upon whose choice point shall be spent
> A life so loved; and that there be
> Fit executioners for thee,
> The fairest first-born sons of fire,
> Blest seraphim, shall leave their choir,
> And turn Love's soldiers, upon thee
> To exercise their archery.

Nor in the poem from which these lines are quoted does this melodious rapture flag during nearly two hundred verses. But such a sustained flight is rare, as in the similar poem of "The Flaming Heart," also addressed to St. Teresa, where, after a long prelude of frigid and tuneless conceits, it is only at the very close that the poet suddenly strikes upon this golden chord of ecstasy:

Let all thy scattered shafts of light, that play
Among the leaves of thy large books of day,
Combined against this breast at once break in,
And take away from me myself and sin;
This gracious robbery shall thy bounty be,
And my best fortunes such fair spoils of me.
O thou undaunted daughter of desires!
        By all thy dower of lights and fires,
        By all the eagle in thee, all the dove,
        By all thy lives and deaths of love.
By thy large draughts of intellectual day,
And by thy thirsts of love more large than they,
By all thy brim-filled bowls of fierce desire,
By thy last morning's draught of liquid fire,
By the full kingdom of that final kiss
That seized thy parting soul and sealed thee His;
By all the heaven thou hast in Him,
Fair sister of the seraphim!
By all of thine we have in thee—
Leave nothing of myself in me;
Let me so read thy life that I
Unto all life of mine may die.

If Crashaw had left us nothing more than these two fragments, we should be able to distinguish him by them among English poets. He is the solitary representative of the poetry of Catholic psychology which England possessed until our own days; and Germany has one no less unique in Friedrich Spe. I do not know that any critic has compared Spe and Crashaw, but they throw lights upon the genius of one another which may seasonably detain us for a while. The great Catholic poet of Germany during the seventeenth century was born in 1591. Like Crashaw, he was set in motion by the Spanish Mystics; like him, he stood on the verge of a great poetical revolution without being in the least affected by it. To Waller and to Opitz, with their new dry systems of precise prosody, Crashaw and Spe owed nothing; they were purely romantic and emotional in style. Spe was born a Catholic, spent all his life among the Jesuits, and died, worn out with good works and immortalised by an heroic struggle against the system of persecution for witchcraft, in the hospital of Trèves in 1635, just when Crashaw was becoming enthralled by the delicious mysteries of Little Gidding. Both of them wrote Jesuit eclogues. In Spe the shepherd winds his five best roses into a garland for the infant Jesus; in Crashaw he entertains the "starry stranger" with conceits about his diamond eyes and the red leaves of his lips. In each poet there is an hysterical delight in blood and in the details of martyrdom, in each a shrill and frantic falsetto that jars on the modern ear, in each a sweetness of diction and purity of fancy that redeem a hundred faults.[1] The poems of Spe, entitled *Trutz-Nachtigal*, were first printed in 1649, the year that Crashaw died.

The chief distinction between Spe and Crashaw is, in the first place, that Crashaw is by far the greater and more varied of the two as regards poetical gifts, and, secondly, that while Spe was inspired by the national *Volkslied*, and introduced its effects into his song, Crashaw was an adept in every refinement of metrical structure which had been invented by the poet-artists of England, Spain, and Italy. The progress of our poetical literature in the seventeenth century will never be thoroughly explained until some competent scholar shall examine the influence of Spanish poetry upon our own. This influence seems to be particularly strong in the case of Donne, and in the next generation in that of Crashaw. I am not sufficiently familiar with Spanish poetry to give an opinion on this subject which is of much value; but as I write I have open before me the works of Gongora, and I find in the general disposition of his *Octavas Sacras* and in the style of his *Canciones* resemblances to the staves introduced to us by Crashaw which can scarcely be accidental.

Mr. Shorthouse reminds me that Ferrar was much in Spain; we know that Crashaw "was excellent in Italian and Spanish," and we are thus led on to consider the more obvious debt which he owed to the contemporary poetry of Italy. One of the largest pieces of work which he undertook was the translation of the first canto of the *Strage degli Innocenti*, or *Massacre of the Innocents*, a famous poem by the Neapolitan Cavaliere Marini, who had died in 1625. Crashaw has thrown a great deal of dignity and fancy into this version, which, however, outdoes the original in ingenious illustration, as the true Marinists, such as Achillini, outdid Marini in their conceited sonnets. Crashaw, in fact, is a genuine Marinist, the happiest specimen which we possess in English, for he preserves a high level of fantastic foppery, and seldom, at his worst, sinks to those crude animal imagings—illustrations from food, for instance—which occasionally make such writers as Habington and Carew not merely ridiculous but repulsive.

In criticising with severity the piece on Mary Magdalene which stands in the forefront of Crashaw's poems, and bears the title of "The Weeper," I have the misfortune to find myself at variance with most of his admirers. I cannot, however, avoid the conviction that the obtrusion of this eccentric piece on the threshold of his shrine has driven away from it many a would-be worshipper. If language be ever liable to abuse in the hands of a clever poet, it is surely outraged here. Every extravagant and inappropriate image is dragged to do service to this small idea—namely, that the Magdalen is for ever weeping. Her eyes, therefore, are sister springs, parents of rills, thawing crystal, hills of snow, heavens of ever-falling stars, eternal breakfasts for brisk cherubs, sweating boughs of balsam, nests of milky doves, a voluntary mint of silver, and Heaven knows how many more incongruous objects, from one to another of which the labouring fancy flits in despair and bewilderment. In this poem all is resigned to ingenuity; we are not moved or softened, we are merely startled, and the irritated reader is at last appeased for the fatigues he has endured by a frank guffaw, when he sees the poet, at his wits' end for a simile, plunge into the abyss of absurdity, and style the eyes of the Magdalen

Two walking baths, two weeping motions,
Portable and compendious oceans.

These are the worst lines in Crashaw. They are perhaps the worst in all English poetry, but they must not be omitted here, since they indicate to us the principal danger to which not he only but most of his compeers were liable. It was from the tendency to call a pair of eyes "portable and compendious oceans" that Waller and Dryden, after both of them stumbling on the same stone in their youth, finally delivered us. It is useless to linger with indulgence over the stanzas of a poem like "The Weeper," simply because many of the images are in themselves pretty. The system upon which these juvenile pieces of Crashaw are written is in itself indefensible, and is founded upon what Mr. Matthew Arnold calls an "incurable defect of style."

Crashaw, however, possesses style, or he would not deserve the eminent place he holds among our poets. The ode in praise of Teresa, written while the author was still among the Protestants, and therefore probably about 1642, has already been cited here. It is an exquisite composition, full of real vision, music of the most delicate order, and imagery which, although very profuse and ornate, is always subordinated to the moral meaning and to the progress of the poem. The "Shepherd's Hymn," too, is truly ingenious and graceful, with its pretty pastoral tenderness. "On Mr. G. Herbert's Book sent to a Gentleman" evidently belongs to the St. Teresa period, and contains the same charm. The lyrical epistle persuading the Countess of Denbigh to join the Roman communion contains extraordinary felicities, and seems throbbing with tenderness and passion. We have already drawn attention to the splendid close of "The Flaming Heart." There is perhaps no other of the sacred poems in the volume of 1646 which can be commended in its entirety. Hardly one but contains felicities; the dullest is brightened by such flashes of genius as—

> Lo, how the thirsty lands
> Gasp for the golden showers with long-stretch'd
> hands!

But the poems are hard, dull, and laborious, the exercises of a saint indeed, but untouched by inspiration, human or divine. We have to return to the incomparable "Hymn to St. Teresa" to remind ourselves of what heights this poet was capable.

There can be very little doubt that Crashaw regarded the second section of his book, the secular *Delights of the Muses*, as far inferior in value and importance to the *Steps to the Temple*. That is not, however, a view in which the modern reader can coincide, and it is rather the ingenuity of his human poems than the passion of his divine which has given him a prominent place among poets. The *Delights* open with the celebrated piece called the "Muse's Duel," paraphrased from the Latin of Strada. As one frequently sees a reference to the "Latin poet Strada," it may be worth while to remark that Famianus Strada was not a poet at all, but a lecturer in the Jesuit colleges. He belonged to Crashaw's own age, having been born in 1572, and dying in the year of the English poet's death, 1649. The piece on the rivalry of the musician and the nightingale was published first at Rome in 1617, in a volume of *Prolusiones* on rhetoric and poetry, and occurs in the sixth lecture of the second course on poetic style. The Jesuit rhetorician has been trying to familiarise his pupils with the style of the great classic poets by reciting to them passages in imitation of Ovid, Lucretius, Lucan, and the rest, and at last he comes to Claudian. This, he says, is an imitation of the style of Claudian, and so he gives us the lines which have become so famous. That a single fragment in a school-book should suddenly take root and blossom in European literature, when all else that its voluminous author wrote and said was promptly forgotten, is very curious, but not unprecedented.

In England the first person who adopted or adapted Strada's exercise was John Ford, in his play of *The Lover's Melancholy*, in 1629. Dr. Grosart found another early version among the Lansdowne MSS., and Ambrose Phillips a century later essayed it. There are numerous references to it in other literatures than ours, and in the present age M. François Coppée has introduced it with charming effect into his pretty comedy of *Le Luthier de Crémone*. Thus the schoolmaster's task, set as a guide to the manner of Claudian, has achieved, by an odd irony of fortune, a far more general and lasting success than any of the actual verses of that elegant writer. With regard to the comparative merits of Ford's version, which is in blank verse, and of Crashaw's, which is in rhyme, a confident opinion has generally been expressed in favour of the particular poet under consideration at the moment; nor is Lamb himself superior to this amiable partiality. He denies that Crashaw's version "can at all compare for harmony and grace with this blank verse of Ford's." But my own view coincides much rather with that of Mr. Swinburne, who says that "between the two beautiful versions of Strada's pretty fable by Ford and Crashaw, there will always be a diversity of judgment among readers; some must naturally prefer the tender fluency and limpid sweetness of Ford, others the dazzling intricacy and affluence in refinements, the supple and cunning implication, the choiceness and subtlety of Crashaw." Mr. Shorthouse, on the other hand, suggests to me that "Crashaw's poem is surely so much more full and elaborate, that it must be acknowledged to be the more important effort." There can be no doubt that it presents us with the most brilliant and unique attempt which has been made in our language to express the very quality and variety of musical notation in words. It may be added that the only reference made by Crashaw in any part of his writings to any of the dramatists his contemporaries is found in a couplet addressed to Ford:

> Thou cheat'st us, Ford, mak'st one seem two by art;
> What is *love's sacrifice* but *the broken heart?*

After "Music's Duel," the best-known poem of Crashaw's is his "Wishes to his Supposed Mistress," a piece in forty-two stanzas, which Mr. Palgrave reduced to twenty-one in his *Golden Treasury*. He neglected to mention the "sweet theft," and accordingly most readers know the poem only as he reduced and rearranged it. The act was bold, perhaps, but I think that it was judicious. As Crashaw left it, the poem extends beyond the limits of a lyric, tediously repeats its sentiments and gains neither in force nor charm by its extreme length. In Mr. Palgrave's selection it challenges comparison with the loveliest and most original pieces of the century. It never, I think, rises to the thrilling tenderness which Donne is capable of on similar occasions. Crashaw never pants out a line and a half which leave us faint and throbbing, as if the heart of humanity itself had been revealed to us for a moment; with all his flying colour and lambent flame, Crashaw is not Donne. But the "Wishes" is more than a charming, it is a fascinating poem, the pure dream of the visionary poet, who liked to reflect that he too might marry if he would, and choose a godly bride. He calls upon her—

> Whoe'er she be
> That not impossible She
> That shall command my heart and me;
> Where'er she lie
> Locked up from mortal eye
> In shady leaves of destiny—

to receive the embassy of his wishes, bound to instruct her in that higher beauty of the spirit which his soul demands—

> Something more than
> Taffata or tissue can,
> Or rampant feather, or rich fan.

But what he requires is not spiritual adornment alone; he will have her courteous and accomplished in the world's ways also, the possessor of

> Sydneian showers
> Of sweet discourse, whose powers
> Can crown old Winter's head with flowers;

and finally,

> Life, that dares send
> A challenge to his end,
> And when it comes say, 'Welcome, friend.'

I wish her store
Of worth may leave her poor
Of wishes; and I wish—no more.

The same refined and tender spirit animates the "Epitaph upon Husband and Wife, who died and were buried together." The lovely rambling verses of "To the Morning, in satisfaction for Sleep," are perhaps more in the early manner of Keats than any other English lines. In some of those sacred poems which we have lately been considering, he reminds us no less vividly of Shelley, and there are not a few passages of Crashaw which it would require a very quick ear to distinguish from Mr. Swinburne. We may safely conjecture that the latter poet's "Song in Season" was written in deliberate rivalry of that song of Crashaw's which runs—

O deliver
Love his quiver;
From thine eyes he shoots his arrows,
Where Apollo
Cannot follow,
Feathered with his mother's sparrows.

But perhaps the sweetest and most modern of all Crashaw's secular lyrics is that entitled *Love's Horoscope*. The phraseology of the black art was never used with so sweet and picturesque an ingenuity, and the piece contains some of the most delicately musical cadences to be found in the poetry of the age:

Thou know'st a face in whose each look
Beauty lays ope Love's fortune-book,
On whose fair revolutions wait
The obsequious motions of Love's fate.
Ah! my heart! her eyes and she
Have taught thee new astrology.
Howe'er Love's native hours were set,
Whatever starry synod met,
'Tis in the mercy of her eye
If poor Love shall live or die.

It is probable from internal and from external evidence also that all these secular poems belong to Crashaw's early years at Cambridge. The pretty lines "On Two Green Apricocks sent to Cowley by Sir Crashaw" evidently date from 1633; the various elegies and poems of compliment can be traced to years ranging from 1631 to 1634. It is doubtful whether the "Wishes" themselves are at all later than this. Even regarding him as a finished poet ten years before the publication of his book, however, he comes late in the list of seventeenth century lyrists, and has no claims to be considered as an innovator. He owed all the basis of his style, as has been already hinted, to Donne and to Ben Jonson. His originality was one of treatment and technique; he forged a more rapid and brilliant short line than any of his predecessors had done, and for brief intervals and along sudden paths of his own he carried English prosody to a higher refinement, a more glittering felicity, than it had ever achieved. Thus, in spite of his conceits and his romantic colouring, he points the way for Pope, who did not disdain to borrow from him freely.

It is unfortunate that Crashaw is so unequal as to be positively delusive; he baffles analysis by his uncertain hold upon style, and in spite of his charm and his genius is perhaps most interesting to us because of the faults he shares with purely modern poets. It would scarcely be unjust to say that Crashaw was the first real poet who allowed himself to use a splendid phrase when a simple one would have better expressed his meaning; and in an age when all but the best poetry was apt to be obscure, crabbed, and rugged, he introduces a new fault, that of being visionary and diffuse, with a deliberate intention not only, as the others did, to deck Nature out in false ornament, but to represent her actual condition as being something more "starry" and "seraphical" than it really is. His style has hectic beauties that delight us, but evade us also, and colours that fade as promptly as the scarlet and the amber in a sunset sky. We can describe him best in negatives; his is not so warm and real as Herrick, nor so drily intellectual as the other hymnists, nor coldly and respectably virile like Cowley. To use an odd simile of Shelley's, he sells us gin when the other poets offer us legs of mutton, or at all events baskets of bread and vegetables. . . .

Too often it is with regret, or with a grudged esteem, that we hail newly-discovered works by standard authors. The best writing generally takes care of itself, and is remembered and preserved, whatever may be lost. The first sprightly running is commonly the best, and editors scarcely earn our thanks by troubling the lees for us. For once we have an exception before us. The pamphlet of newly-discovered poems by Crashaw which Dr. Grosart forwarded to his subscribers in 1888 contains some things which, even in the congested condition of our national literature, are never likely to be obscured again. The British Museum bought from a bookseller, who had picked it up as an odd lot at Sotheby's or Puttick & Simpson's, a MS. volume of Crashaw's poems, indubitably, as would appear, in his own, previously untraced, handwriting. Dr. Grosart gives us an example of the latter in facsimile, selecting the page which contains the well-known epigram on "The Water being made Wine."

We turn at once to the poems which are entirely new. Here is one apparently intended to form the dedication to a gift-volume of the poet's *Steps to the Temple*:

At the ivory tribunal of your hand,
Fair one, these tender leaves do trembling stand,
Knowing 'tis in the doom of your sweet eye
Whether the Muse they clothe shall live or die;
Live she or die to Fame, each leaf you meet
Is her life's wing, or else her winding-sheet.

We could swear this was Crashaw if we picked it up anonymous on Pitcairn's Island. Moreover, something very like the second couplet is to be found already in *Love's Horoscope*:

'Tis in the mercy of her eye
If poor Love shall live or die.

It is very pretty. But this, a nameless lyric, is more than pretty; it is exquisite, and in Crashaw's most transcendental manner:

Though now 'tis neither May nor June,
And nightingales are out of tune,
Yet in these leaves, fair One, there lies
(Sworn servant to your sweetest eyes)
A nightingale, who, may she spread
In your white bosom her chaste bed,
Spite of all the maiden snow
Those pure untrodden paths can show,
You straight shall see her wake and rise,
Taking fresh life from your fair eyes,
And with claspt wings proclaim a spring,
Where Love and she shall sit and sing;
For lodged so near your sweetest throat
What nightingale can lose her note?
Nor let her kindred birds complain
Because she breaks the year's old reign;
For let them know she's none of those
Hedge-quiristers whose music owes
Only such strains as serve to keep

Sad shades, and sing dull night asleep.
No, she's a priestess of that grove,
The holy chapel of chaste love,
Your virgin bosom. Then whate'er
Poor laws divide the public year,
Whose revolutions wait upon
The wild turns of the wanton sun,
Be you the Lady of Love's year,
Where your eyes shine his suns appear,
There all the year is Love's long Spring,
There all the year
Love's nightingales shall sit and sing.

The break in the penultimate verse is a charming addition to the melody, and I am very much mistaken if this lyric does not take its place among the best of Charles I.'s reign.

The remainder of the new poems are religious, and they are not in Crashaw's very finest manner. "To Pontius, Washing his Blood-stained Hands," is a typical example of the monstrous chains of conceits which these most unequal poets were at any moment liable to produce. The face of Pilate was originally a nymph—

The daughter of a fair and well-famed fountain
As ever silver-tipped the side of shady mountain,—

(in itself a charming image); this nymph has suffered the fate of Philomela from this new Tereus, the hand of Pilate, and "appears nothing but tears." A paraphrase of Grotius gives us a first version of the well-known verse on the Eucharist:

The water blushed and started into wine.

We trace the great Crashaw of the fiery surprises but seldom in this long, tame, and somewhat crabbed poem; but he asserts himself in a few such phrases as this:

Before the infant shrine
Of my weak feet, the Persian Magi lay,
And left their mithra for my star;

and this, which well describes the condition of Crashaw's muse:

A sweet inebriated ecstasy.

The new readings of old poems which the MS. gives are neither, it would seem, very numerous nor very important. "The Weeper" is such a distressing, indeed such a humiliating poem, that we receive a new stanza of it with indifference; we may note one novelty,—this string of preposterous conceits on the tears of the Magdalen must in future close with a conceit that swallows up all the rest:

Of such fair floods as this
Heaven the crystal ocean is.

Dr. Grosart takes this opportunity of recording an interesting little discovery. Crashaw's important Latin poem "Bulla" is found to have made its first appearance in a very rare Cambridge volume, the *Crepundia Siliana* of Heynsius, in 1646, two years after the poet's ejection from his Fellowship. It appeared the same year in the *Delights of the Muses*, with a considerable number of variations of the text. It is a pity that Crashaw did not write "Bulla" in English, for it is full of the characteristics of his style.

Notes

1. As an illustration of almost all these qualities, and as a specimen of Spe's metrical gifts, I give one stanza from the *Trutz-Nachtigal*:

Aus der Seiten
Lan sich leiten
    Rote Strahlen wie Korall;
Aus der Seiten
Lan sich leiten
    Weisse Wässer wie Krystal!

O du reines,
Hübsch und feines
    Bächlein von Korall und Glas,
Nit noch weiche,
Nit entschleiche,
    O Rubin und Perlengass!

GEORGE SAINTSBURY
From "Caroline Poetry"
History of Elizabethan Literature
1887, pp. 364–69

The third of this great trio of poets ⟨Carew, Herrick and Crashaw⟩, and with them the most remarkable of our whole group, was Richard Crashaw. He completes Carew and Herrick both in his qualities and (if a kind of bull may be permitted) in his defects, after a fashion almost unexampled elsewhere and supremely interesting. Hardly any one of the three could have appeared at any other time, and not one but is distinguished from the others in the most marked way. Herrick, despite his sometimes rather obtrusive learning, is emphatically the natural man. He does not show much sign of the influence of good society, his merits as well as his faults have a singular unpersonal and, if I may so say, *terræfilian* connotation. Carew is a gentleman before all; but a rather profane gentleman. Crashaw is religious everywhere. Again, Herrick and Carew, despite their strong savour of the fashion of the time, are eminently critics as well as poets. Carew has not let one piece critically unworthy of him pass his censorship: Herrick (if we exclude the filthy and foolish epigrams into which he was led by corrupt following of Ben) has been equally careful. These two bards may have trouble with the *censor morum*,—the *censor literarum* they can brave with perfect confidence. It is otherwise with Crashaw. That he never, as far as can be seen, edited the bulk of his work for press at all matters little or nothing. But there is not in his work the slightest sign of the exercise of any critical faculty before, during, or after production. His masterpiece, one of the most astonishing things in English or any other literature, comes without warning at the end of "The Flaming Heart." For page after page the poet has been poorly playing on some trifling conceits suggested by the picture of Saint Theresa and a seraph. First he thinks the painter ought to have changed the attributes; then he doubts whether a lesser change will not do; and always he treats his subject in a vein of grovelling and grotesque conceit which the boy Dryden in the stage of his elegy on Lord Hastings would have disdained. And then in a moment, in the twinkling of an eye, without warning of any sort, the metre changes, the poet's inspiration catches fire, and there rushes up into the heaven of poetry this marvellous rocket of song:

Live in these conquering leaves: live all the same;
And walk through all tongues one triumphant flame;
Live here, great heart; and love, and die, and kill;
And bleed, and wound, and yield, and conquer still.
Let this immortal life where'er it comes
Walk in a crowd of loves and martyrdoms.
Let mystic deaths wait on't; and wise souls be
The love-slain witnesses of this life of thee.
O sweet incendiary! show here thy art,
Upon this carcase of a hard cold heart;
Let all thy scatter'd shafts of light, that play
Among the leaves of thy large books of day,
Combin'd against this breast at once break in,
And take away from me myself and sin;
This gracious robbery shall thy bounty be
And my best fortunes such fair spoils of me.

O thou undaunted daughter of desires!
By all thy pow'r of lights and fires;
By all the eagle in thee, all the dove;
By all thy lives and deaths of love;
By thy large draughts of intellectual day;
And by thy thirsts of love more large than they;
By all thy brim-fill'd bowls of fierce desire;
By thy last morning's draught of liquid fire;
By the full kingdom of that final kiss
That 'sayed thy parting soul, and seal'd thee his;
By all the heavens thou hast in him,
(Fair sister of the seraphim)
By all of him we have in thee;
Leave nothing of myself in me.
Let me so read thy life, that I
Unto all life of mine may die.

The contrast is perhaps unique as regards the dead col-ourlessness of the beginning, and the splendid colour of the end. But contrasts like it occur all over Crashaw's work. . . .

Our chief subject . . . is the English poems proper, sacred and profane. In almost all of these there is noticeable an ex-traordinary inequality, the same in kind, if not in degree, as that on which we have commented in the case of "The Flam-ing Heart." Crashaw is never quite so great as there; but he is often quite as small. His exasperating lack of self-criticism has sometimes led selectors to make a cento out of his poems—notably in the case of the exceedingly pretty "Wishes to His Unknown Mistress," beginning, "Whoe'er she be, That not impossible she, That shall command my heart and me"—a poem, let it be added, which excuses this dubious process much less than most, inasmuch as nothing in it is positively bad, though it is rather too long. Here is the opening, preceded by a piece from another poem, "A Hymn to Saint Theresa":

Those rare works, where thou shalt leave writ
Love's noble history, with wit
Taught thee by none but him, while here
They feed our souls, shall clothe thine there.
Each heavenly word by whose hid flame
Our hard hearts shall strike fire, the same
Shall flourish on thy brows and be
Both fire to us and flame to thee:
Whose light shall live bright, in thy face
By glory, in our hearts by grace.

Thou shalt look round about, and see
Thousands of crown'd souls throng to be
Themselves thy crown, sons of thy vows:
The virgin births with which thy spouse
Made fruitful thy fair soul; go now
And with them all about thee, bow
To Him, 'Put on' (He'll say) 'put on,
My rosy love, that thy rich zone,
Sparkling with the sacred flames,
Of thousand souls whose happy names
Heaven heaps upon thy score, thy bright
Life brought them first to kiss the light
That kindled them to stars.' And so
Thou with the Lamb thy Lord shall go,
And whereso'er He sets His white
Steps, walk with Him those ways of light.
Which who in death would live to see
Must learn in life to die like thee."

Whoe'er she be,
That not impossible she,
That shall command my heart and me;

Where'er she lie,
Lock'd up from mortal eye,
In shady leaves of destiny;

Till that ripe birth
Of studied Fate stand forth,
And teach her fair steps to our earth:
Till that divine
Idea take a shrine
Of crystal flesh, through which to shine:
Meet you her, my wishes
Bespeak her to my blisses,
And be ye call'd, my absent kisses.

The first hymn to Saint Theresa, to which "The Flaming Heart" is a kind of appendix, was written when Crashaw was still an Anglican (for which he did not fail, later, to make a characteristic and very pretty, though quite unnecessary, apol-ogy). It has no passage quite up to the Invocation—Epi-phonema, to give it the technical term—of the later poem. But it is, on the contrary, good almost throughout, and is, for uniform exaltation, far the best of Crashaw's poems. Yet such uniform exaltation must be seldom sought in him. It is in his little bursts, such as that in the stanza beginning, "O mother turtle dove," that his charm consists. Often, as in verse after verse of "The Weeper," it has an unearthly delicacy and witch-ery which only Blake, in a few snatches, has ever equalled; while at other times the poet seems to invent, in the most casual and unthinking fashion, new metrical effects and new jewelries of diction which the greatest lyric poets since—Coleridge, Shelley, Lord Tennyson, Mr. Swinburne—have rather deliberately imitated than spontaneously recovered. Yet to all this charm there is no small drawback. The very maddest and most methodless of the "Metaphysicals" cannot touch Crashaw in his tasteless use of conceits. When he, in "The Weeper" just above referred to, calls the tears of Magdalene "Wat'ry brothers," and "Simpering sons of those fair eyes," and when, in the most intolerable of all the poet's excesses, the same eyes are called "Two waking baths, two weeping motions, Portable and compendious oceans," which follow our Lord about the hills of Galilee, it is almost difficult to know whether to feel most contempt or indignation for a man who could so write. It is fair to say that there are various readings and omis-sions in the different editions which affect both these passages. Yet the offence is that Crashaw should ever have written them at all. Amends, however, are sure to be made before the reader has read much farther. Crashaw's longest poems—a version of Marini's *Sospetto d'Herode*, and one of the rather overpraised "Lover and Nightingale" story of Strada—are not his best; the metre in which both are written, though the poet manages it well, lacks the extraordinary charm of his lyric measures. It does not appear that the "Not impossible she" ever made her appearance, and probably for a full half of his short life Crashaw burnt only with religious fire. But no Englishman has expressed that fire as he has, and none in his expression of any sentiment, sacred and profane, has dropped such notes of ethe-real music. At his best he is far above singing, at his worst he is below a very childish prattle. But even then he is never coarse, never offensive, not very often actually dull; and everywhere he makes amends by flowers of the divinest poetry.

FRANCIS THOMPSON
From "Excursions in Criticism: VI.—Crashaw"
The Academy and Literature, November 20,
1897, pp. 27–28

Strange are both the commissions and omissions of this day, in which an uncritical zeal for the poets of the sixteenth and seventeenth centuries has stimulated reprint upon reprint.

It seems to be enough for editorial zeal that a poet should have been born in one of those privileged centuries; and he shall find republication. Not alone Campion and other minor lyrists of merit, but even a wielder of frigid conceits like Henry Constable finds his editor—nay, is issued with all the pomp of sumptuous decorative *ensemble*. Yet, while editors search among the dross of these ages for poets to revive, they neglect the gold. Else how comes it that while Henry Vaughan finds reprint, his worthy yokefellow, Crashaw, is passed by? How comes it that Cowley is inaccessible yet to modern readers? Eminent modern poets have singled Crashaw as a man of genius and a source of inspiration. Coleridge declared that Crashaw's "Hymn to St. Teresa" was present to his mind while he was writing the second part of "Christabel"; "if, indeed, by some subtle process of the mind, they did not suggest the first thought of the whole poem." The influence of Crashaw is to be traced in the "Unknown Eros": notably and conspicuously in the "Sponsa Dei."

. . .

Lyric poetry is a very inclusive term. It includes Milton and Herrick, Burns and Shelley, "Tintern Abbey" and "The Grecian Urn," the odes of Coventry Patmore and the songs of Tennyson. But its highest form—that which is to other lyric forms what the epic is to the narrative poem or the ballad—is the form typically represented by the ode. This order of lyric may again be divided into such lyrics as are distinguished by stately structure, and such as are distinguished by ardorous abandonment. In the former kind ardour *may* be present, though under the continual curb of the structure; and this is the highest species of the lyric. In the latter kind the ardour is naked and predominant: it is to the former kind what the flight of the skylark is to the flight of the eagle. The conspicuous first appearance of the former kind in English poetry was the monumental *Epithalamion* of Spenser. Ardour cannot, as a rule, be predicated of Spenser; but *there* is ardour of the most ethereal impulse, equipoised throughout with the most imperial and imperious structure. For the development of the latter kind English poetry had to await the poet of *Prometheus Unbound*. But its first, almost unnoticed and unperfected appearance, was in the work of Richard Crashaw. His age gave the preference to Cowley, in whose odes there is unlimited ostentation of dominating ardour without the reality, the result being mere capricious and unmeaning dislocation of form. Too much of the like is there in Crashaw; but every now and again he ascends into real fervour, such as makes metre and diction plastic to its own shaping spirit of inevitable rightness. This is the eminent praise of Crashaw, that he marks an epoch, a turn of the tide in English lyric, though the crest of the tide was not to come till long after, though—like all first innovators—he not only suffered present neglect, but has been overshadowed by those who came a century after him.

He is fraught with suggestion—infinite suggestion. More than one poet has drawn much from him, yet much remains to be drawn. But it is not only for poets he exists. Those who read for enjoyment can find in him abundant delight, if they will be content (as they are content with Wordsworth) to grope through his plenteous infelicity. He is no poet of the human and household emotions; he has not pathos, or warm love, or any of the qualities which come home to the natural kindly race of men. But how fecund is his brilliant imagery, rapturous ethereality. He has, at his best, an extraordinary cunning of diction, cleaving like gold-leaf to its object. In such a poem as "The Musician and the Nightingale" (not in this volume included) the marvel of diction becomes even too conscious; in the moment of wondering at the miracle, we feel that the miracle is too researched: it is the feat of an amazing gymnast in words rather than of an unpremeditating angel. Yet this poem is an extraor-dinary verbal achievement, and there are numerous other examples in which the miracle seems as unconscious as admirable.

For an example of his sacred poems, take the "Nativity," which has less deforming conceit than most. Very different from Milton's great Ode, which followed it, yet it has its own characteristic beauty. The shepherds sing it turn by turn—as thus:

> Gloomy night embraced the place
>> Where the noble Infant lay.
> The Babe looked up and showed His face;
>> In spite of darkness, it was day.
> It was Thy day, Sweet! and did rise,
>> Not from the East, but from Thine eyes.

Here is seen one note of Crashaw—the human and lover-like tenderness which informs his sacred poems, differentiating them from the conventional style of English sacred poetry, with its solemn aloofness from celestial things.

> I saw the curled drops, soft and slow
>> Come hovering o'er the place's head;
> Offering their whitest sheets of snow
>> To furnish the fair Infant's bed:
> Forbear, said I,; be not too bold,
>> Your fleece is white, but 'tis too cold.
>
> I saw the obsequious Seraphim
>> Their rosy fleece of fire bestow,
> For well they now can spare their wing,
>> Since heaven itself lies here below.
> Well done, said I; but are you sure
>> Your down so warm will pass for pure?

In the second stanza is shown the fire of his fancy; in "The curled drops," &c., the happiness of his diction. In "The Weeper" (a poem on the Magdalen), amid stanzas of the most frigid conceit, are others of the loveliest art in conception and expression:

> The dew no more will weep
>> The primrose's pale cheek to deck:
> The dew no more will sleep
>> Nuzzled in the Lily's neck;
> Much rather would it be thy tear,
> And leave them both to tremble here.
>
> . . .
>
> Not in the Evening's eyes
>> When they red with weeping are
> For the Sun that dies,
>> Sits Sorrow with a face so fair.
> Nowhere but here did ever meet
> Sweetness so sad, sadness so sweet.

Two more alien poets could not be conceived than Crashaw and Browning. Yet in the last couplet of these most exquisite stanzas we have a direct coincidence with Browning's line—

> Its sad in sweet, its sweet in sad.

In the "Hymn to St. Teresa" are to be found the most beautiful delicacies of language and metre. Listen to this (*apropos* of Teresa's childish attempt to run away and become a martyr among the Moors):

> She never undertook to know
> What Death with Love should have to do;
> Nor has she e'er yet understood
> Why to slow love she should shed blood,
> Yet though she cannot tell you why,
> She can love, and she can die.

Among the poems not contained in this volume ⟨J.R. Tutin, *Poems of Richard Crashaw*, 1905⟩, the wonderfully dainty "Wishes to a Supposed Mistress" shows what Crashaw might have been as an amative poet:

> Whoe'er she be,
> That not impossible She,
> That shall command my heart and me;
> Where'er she lie,
> Shut up from mortal eye
> In shady leaves of Destiny.

And so on through a series of unequal but often lovely stanzas. So, too, does "Love's Horoscope." His epitaphs are among the sweetest and most artistic even of that age, so cunning in such kind of verse. For instance, that on a young gentleman:

> Eyes are vocal, tears have tongues,
> And there be words not made with lungs—
> Sententious showers; O let them fall!
> Their cadence is rhetorical!

But, to come back to the peoms contained in Mr. Tutin's book, with what finer example can I end than the close of "The Flaming Heart," Crashaw's second hymn to St. Teresa?—

> Oh, thou undaunted daughter of desires!
> By all thy dower of lights and fires;
> By all the eagle in thee, all the dove;
> By all thy lives and deaths of love;
> By thy large draughts of intellectual day,
> And by thy thirsts of love more large than they;
> By all thy brim-filled bowls of fierce desire,
> By thy last morning's draught of liquid fire;
> By the full kingdom of that final kiss,
> That seized thy parting soul, and sealed thee His;
> By all the Heaven thou hast in Him
> (Fair Sister of the seraphim!)
> By all of Him we have in thee;
> Leave nothing of myself in me.
> Let me so read thy life, that I
> Unto all life of mine may die.

It has all the ardour and brave-soaring transport of the highest lyrical inspiration.

FELIX E. SCHELLING
From "Introduction"
A Book of Seventeenth Century Lyrics
1899, pp. xxx–xxxiii, li–liii

It is an error to regard the Caroline conceit as wholly referable to Donne's irresponsible use of figure. It is neither so limited and abstract in the range of phenomena chosen for figurative illustration, so unconcerned with the recognition of the outward world, nor so completely referable to the intellectualization of emotion. Let us take a typical passage of Donne:

> But, O, alas! so long, so far
> Our bodies why do we forbear?
> They are ours, though not we; we are
> The intelligences, they the spheres;
> We owe them thanks, because they thus
> Did us to us at first convey,
> Yielded their senses' force to us,
> Nor are dross to us but alloy.
> On man heaven's influence works not so,
> But that it first imprints the air;
> For soul into the soul may flow
> Though it to body first repair. [1]

This passage is subtle, almost dialectic. A keen, sinuous, reasoning mind is playing with its powers. Except for the implied personification of the body regarded apart from the soul,

the language is free from figure; there is no confusion of thought. There is the distinctively Donnian employment of ideas derived from physical and speculative science: the body is the 'sphere' or superficies which includes within it the soul, a term of the old astro-philosophy; the body is not 'dross' but an 'alloy,' alchemical terms; the 'influence' of heaven is the use of that word in an astrological sense, meaning "the radiation of power from the stars in certain positions or collections affecting human actions and destinies"; and lastly, the phrase "imprints the air" involves an idea of the old philosophy, by which "sensuous perception is explained by effluxes of atoms from the things perceived whereby images are produced ('imprinted') which strike our senses." Donne subtly transfers this purely physical conception to the transference of divine influences. [2]

On the other hand, take this, the one flagging stanza of Crashaw's otherwise noble "Hymn of the Nativity." The Virgin is spoken of, and represented with the Child, who is addressed by the poet:

> She sings thy tears asleep, and dips
> Her kisses in thy weeping eye;
> She spreads the red leaves of thy lips,
> That in their buds yet blushing lie.
> She 'gainst those mother diamonds tries
> The points of her young eagle's eyes. [3]

This difficult passage may perhaps be thus explained: the Virgin sings to her babe until, falling asleep, his tears cease to flow. "And dips her kisses in thy weeping eye," she kisses lightly his eyes, suffused with tears. Here the lightness of the kiss and the over-brimming fullness of the eyes suggest the hyperbole and the implied metaphor, which likens the kiss to something lightly dipped into a stream. "She spreads the red leaves of thy lips," i.e., kisses the child's lips, which lie lightly apart in infantile sleep, and which are like *rosebuds* in their color and in their childish undevelopment. "Mother diamonds" are the eyes of the Virgin, bright as diamonds and resembling those of the child. "Points" are the rays or beams of the eye, which, according to the old physics, passed, in vision, from one eye to another. Lastly, the eyes of the child are likened to those of a young eagle, and the Virgin tests them against her own as the mother eagle is supposed to test her nestling's eyes against the sun.

Leaving out the figure involved in 'points,' which is Donnian and probably wholly due to the fashion set by him, this passage of Crashaw is inspired, not by the intellect, which clears and distinguishes objects, but by passion, which blends and confuses them. The language is one mass of involved and tangled figure, in which similarity suggests similarity in objects contemplated and intensely visualized—not in abstractions incapable of visualization. Donne fetches his images from the byways of mediæval science and metaphysic and intellectualizes them in the process. Crashaw derives his imagery from the impetus of his feelings and from an intense visualization of the outer world, which causes him to revel in light, color, motion, and space. He at times confuses his images in a pregnancy of thought that involves a partial obscuration of the thing to be figured. These two methods are at the very poles from each other, and incapable of derivation, the one from the other. But if the difficulties of Donne are largely due to subtlety of thought, and those of Crashaw to impetus of feeling, the figures of the lesser poets may often be referred to a striving after original effect, an ingenious pursuit of similitudes in things repugnant, that amounts to a notorious vice of style. The books are full of illustrations of this false taste, and it is easy to find them in the verse of Quarles, Cartwright, Crashaw,

Lovelace, and Davenant; even in Carew, Herbert, and Vaughan. . . .

In 1646 appeared *Steps to the Temple*, with a few secular poems under the sub-title, *The Delights of the Muses*, by Richard Crashaw. The *Steps* was so named in modest reference and relation to Herbert's *Temple*, which was Crashaw's immediate inspiration. Crashaw while a student at Cambridge came under influences which, considering the difference in the two ages, are not incomparable to the Oxford or Tractarian Movement of our own century. In the fervent and pious life of Nicholas Ferrar, into whose hands we have already seen the dying Herbert confiding his poetry, Crashaw found much to emulate and admire. Ferrar, notable in science, and a successful man of affairs, forsook the world and formed, with his kinfolk about him, a small religious community at Little Giddings in Huntingdonshire, where he sought to lead a spiritual life in accord with the principles of the Anglican Church. Predisposed as was Crashaw to that intense and sensuous visualization of spiritual emotion which has characterized the saints and fathers of the Roman Church in many ages, in the life of Saint Theresa the poet found his ideal and his hope. His artistic temperament had led him early "to denounce those who disassociate art from religious worship"; the charity and benignity of his temper caused him equally to oppose those who made an attack upon the papacy an article of faith. It is easy to see how this attitude, under the spiritual influence of such men as Herbert, Robert Shelford, and Ferrar, should gradually have led Crashaw, with the help of some added political impetus, over to the old faith. This impetus came in the form of the parliamentary act by which it was provided that all monuments of superstition be removed from the churches and that the fellows of the universities be required to take the oath of the Solemn League and Covenant. On the enforcement of this act against Peterhouse, Crashaw's own college, and the consequent desecration of its beautiful chapel, Crashaw indignantly refused the League and Covenant, and was expelled from his fellowship. Before long he withdrew to Paris, where he met Cowley. Crashaw died in Italy a few years later, a priest of the Church of Rome. The picture of Cowley, the fair-minded, meditative Epicurean, befriending the young enthusiast, when both were in exile, is pleasant to dwell upon.

The relation of Crashaw to Herbert, save for his discipleship, which changed very little Crashaw's distinctive traits, is much that of Herrick and Carew. Herbert and Crashaw were both good scholars; Herbert knew the world and put it aside as vanity; Crashaw could never have been of the world; his was a nature alien to it, and yet there is a greater warmth in Crashaw than in Herbert. Crashaw turns the passions of earth to worship and identifies the spiritual and the material in his devotion; Herbert has the Puritan spirit within him, which is troubled in the contemplation of earthly vanities, and struggles to rise above and beyond them. It is the antithesis of Protestantism and Roman Catholicism, an antithesis which we can understand better if we can bring ourselves to sympathize with each than if we seek to throw ourselves into an attitude of attack or defense of either.

In matter of poetic style, too, despite his quips and conceits, and despite the fact that with him, as with many devotional poets, execution waits upon the thought and often comes limpingly after, Herbert is far more self-restrained, and his poetry of more uniform workmanship and excellence. But if Herbert has never fallen into Crashaw's extravagances, he is equally incapable of his inspired, rhapsodic flights. Herbert felt the beauties of this visible world and has some delicate touches of appreciation, as where he says:

> I wish I were a tree
> For sure then I should grow
> To fruit or shade; at least some bird would trust
> Her household to me, and I should be just.[4]

Crashaw knows less of the concrete objects of the world, but is a creature of light and atmosphere, and revels in color and the gorgeousness thereof. Crashaw often rhapsodizes without bridle, and is open at times to grave criticism on the score of taste. It is for these shortcomings that he has been, time out of mind, the stock example of the dreadful things into which the ill-regulated poetical fancy may fall. The "sister baths" and "portable oceans" of *Magdalene* are easily ridiculed, but it is almost as easy, while ridiculing these distortions of fancy, to forget the luminousness and radiance, the uncommon imaginative power and volatility of mind—if I may venture the term—of this devout Shelley of the reign of Charles I.

Notes
1. "The Ecstasy," ed. 1650, p. 43.
2. See Ueberweg's *History of Philosophy*, I, 71.
3. See Felix Schelling, *A Book of Seventeenth Century Lyrics*, 1899, p. 113.
4. Herbert, ed. Grosart, p. 40.

H. C. BEECHING
From "Introduction"
Poems of Richard Crashaw, ed. Tutin
1905, pp. xxxvi–lv

The most interesting feature of ⟨*Steps to the Temple*⟩ . . . is the dedicatory poem to the Countess of Denbigh "against irresolution in religion" and still more interesting is the fact that a revised and enlarged version of this exists in a single copy in the British Museum, bearing the imprint "London," but with no publisher's name, and with a manuscript note in a contemporary hand, marking the date of publication as 23 Sext. (*i.e.* August) 1653. It may have been that Crashaw revised the poem after leaving Paris, and sent his corrected MS. to the Countess or to Cowley, without sending a copy to his editor; or it may have been that Car mislaid the revised copy, and recovered it too late for publication in the volume. But it is idle to conjecture. Turnbull noted the existence of this second version, but it was not reprinted until Dr Grosart included it in his private issue (1874). . . . It is in Crashaw's happiest vein. The suggestion that the lady addressed is sure to come over to the writer's side by-and-bye, and so is guilty now of the sin of delay, is a sufficiently subtle weapon in controversy; but how poetically subtle is the expression Crashaw gives it:

> Who grants at last, a great while tried,—
> And did his best,—to have denied.

Having assumed that Rome is her destined haven, he chides her for not emulating the urgency of all natural things, which, as Bacon says, "move violently to their place." But the climax of the poem is the ironical suggestion of reasons for man's reluctance to be saved, passing into a passionate enunciation of the great Christian dogma of the love which prompted the Incarnation.

> All things swear friends to Fair and Good,
> Yea suitours; man alone is woo'd,
> Tediously woo'd and hardly won,
> Only not slow to be undone.
> As if the bargain had been driven
> So hardly betwixt Earth and Heaven;
> Our God would thrive too fast, and be

> Too much a gainer by't, should we
> Our purchas'd selves too soon bestow.
> On Him, who has not lov'd us so.
> When love of us called Him to see
> If we'd vouchsafe His company,
> He left His father's court, and came
> Lightly as a lambent flame,
> Leaping upon the hills, to be
> The humble king of you and me.

I know nothing in devotional poetry finer than this. The best known of the religious poems is the "Hymn to St. Teresa," which has been praised by every critic—by Coleridge amongst the number; and praise can hardly be too high for it. From first to last the inspiration does not flag, but passes with sure success from the tender humour and pathos in which the child's ardour for martyrdom is told, to the ecstatic picture of the mystical martrydom that does await her, followed by the calm bliss of the beatific vision. This poem is succeeded by an Apology for its being written "when the author was among the Protestants," but Protestantism is not referred to in it. Rather it is an apology to Englishmen for praising a Spaniard, and to Spaniards for writing in English. In the second edition (1648), the Apology embraces both the Hymn and a poem called "The Flaming Heart," which was added to that volume and needs more than all the apology that can be made for it. For seventy lines the writer discourses with a pitiful want of taste upon a picture of Saint Teresa, "with a seraphim beside her," to the general effect that the saint is the better seraph of the two. But in the edition of 1652 twenty-four lines are added, which have nothing to do with the picture, but are a passionate invocation of the saint herself. The first eight of these seem to have been written in order to connect the new with the old, but they barely serve their purpose; for the purple passage beginning, "O thou undaunted daughter of desires," is as far superior to them as they are to the old poem. In fact, these glowing verses may well be recognised as the highest achievement of the Muse of religious ecstasy.[1]

The most ambitious of the religious poems, and the one which the poet himself probably ranked highest, for with it he opened his final selection, is the hymn "To the Name above every Name"— an appeal to all the voices of Nature and Art to join with him in the great celebration. It is full of good things. The passages about music are especially beautiful:

> O you, my soul's most certain wings,
> 　Complaining pipes and prattling strings;
> 　　　Bring all the store
> Of sweets you have, and murmur that you have no
> 　more.

And a little below wood and stringed instruments are described as

> 　　　Such
> As sigh with supple wind
> Or answer artful touch.

Again how noble is the opening of the final invocation (ll. 114–133), and the passage towards the close about the martyrs, beginning, "O that it were as it was wont to be" (l. 190). But with all its merits, the poem cannot, as a whole, be reckoned a success. It is too fluent; there are repetitions both as to sentiments and phrases—*e.g.* the word *nest* occurs no fewer than five times and always as a rhyme; and there is not enough substance in the thought to bear being spun into two hundred and forty verses. Moreover, Crashaw indulges himself now and then in a "conceit" which leaves the modern reader gasping (*e.g.* ll. 132–5). To be successful he needed a subject less vague in definition, and a metre constraining to conciseness. One

cannot help wishing that Crashaw had been born a few years earlier, so that at Cambridge he might have formed a friendship with Milton instead of with Cowley. He would have been attracted, we cannot doubt, to "the Lady of Christ's"; and Milton's jealous care that the word, the phrase, the paragraph should be as perfect as choice could make them, would have been invaluable to Crashaw, if he could have learned it. There might also have been some reciprocal influence in matters of temperament which was as sorely needed. But *dis aliter visum*, and we could not have afforded the loss of Cowley's noble elegy on the "Martyr and Saint," even at the price of "Lycidas" purged of its venomous onslaught on the clergy.

"Charitas Nimia" is one of the few religious poems of Crashaw in which no critic could wish for an excision; it is perhaps also the only one that shows any influence of George Herbert. The Hymns upon Christmas and Epiphany, which in form resemble one another, are of curiously different merit. One might have anticipated that such a subject as the visit of the Magi would have set Crashaw's imagination on fire, but it did not do so. The poem is turgid and full of dull "conceits." The Christmas poem, on the contrary, is as full of happy expressions and ideas, such as the line about the snow, the description of courtiers as "slippery souls in smiling eyes," and the stanza on the Mother and Child. Many of the religious poems are elaborate versions of the old Church hymns, best perhaps described in the poet's own phrase as "a descant upon plain song." Nothing could be more unlike the simple directness of the Latin than Crashaw's flamboyant paraphrases; at the same time it must be admitted that he always keeps to his subject and in his wildest excursion never loses the key. The most admired of these has been the "Dies Iræ"; the closest version is the *Laudes Sion Salvatorem*, which nevertheless succeeds in breathing poetry into a piece of mediæval scholasticism; the most elaborate is the *Office of the Holy Crosse*. To show Crashaw's method, it will be sufficient to put one stanza of his by a stanza of the original. The hymn in the Office for the third hour runs:

> *Crucifige* clamitant hora tertiarum:
> Illusus induitur veste purpurarum:
> Caput ejus pungitur corona spinarum:
> Crucem portat humeris ad locum pœnarum.

This becomes in Crashaw's rendering:

> The third hour's deafened with the cry
> Of *Crucify Him, crucify.*
> So goes the vote (nor ask them why!)
> 'Live Barabas, and let God die.'
> But there is wit in wrath, and they will try
> A 'Hail' more cruel than their 'crucify.'
> For while in sport He wears a spiteful crown,
> The serious showers along His decent face run sadly
> 　down.

The antiphons in the Office deserve particular notice; in the original they are, of course, in prose. Among the translations are included characteristic versions of two Psalms. No one but Crashaw would have rendered "He leadeth me in the paths of righteousness," etc., by

> He expounds the weary wonder
> Of my giddy steps, and under
> Spreads a path, clear as day,
> Where no churlish rub says *nay*
> To my joy-conducted feet,
> Whilst they gladly go to meet
> Grace and Peace to learn new lays
> Tun'd to my great Shepherd's praise.

The longest of all the translations is the *Suspicion of Herod*, a canto of sixty-six stanzas done, with Crashaw's usual licence, out of the Italian of Marini. As a piece of writing it is excellent, the stanza with its triple rhyme is well managed, and there are not a few passages which for dignity of style recall Milton, who had undoubtedly profited by its perusal. Take, for example, this verse from the speech of Satan:

> He has my heaven (what would He more?) whose bright
> And radiant sceptre this bold hand should bear:
> And for the never-fading fields of light,
> My fair inheritance, he confines me here
> To this dark house of shades, horror, and night,
> To draw a long-liv'd death, where all my cheer
>   Is the solemnity my sorrow wears
>   That mankind's torment waits upon my tears.

Among the religious poems are usually included two about which a word must be added—the amœbean stanzas upon Hope between Crashaw and Cowley, and "The Weeper." Coleridge, referring to the former in a letter to a friend, remarks that "Crashaw's superiority to Cowley is self-evident." I must confess, temerarious as it is to differ from Coleridge on a point of literary criticism, that even though I am at the moment holding a brief for Crashaw the superiority seems to me altogether on the other side. There is undoubtedly great cleverness in the way Cowley's points are taken up one by one and turned against him; but there is nothing in Crashaw's verse that finds a lodging in the memory, as do Cowley's fine lines about the cloud:

> Thin empty cloud which th' eye deceives
> With shapes that our own fancy gives.
> A cloud which gilt and painted now appears
> But must drop presently in tears;

or these in the last stanza:

> Brother of Fear, more gaily clad,
> The merrier fool o' th' two, yet quite as mad.
> Sire of repentance, child of fond desire
> That blow'st the chymick's and the lover's fire
>   Still leading them insensibly on
>   With the strong witchcraft of anon.

"The Weeper" is the poem that in most editions opens the *Steps to the Temple*, and it has proved a stumblingblock to many would-be worshippers; amongst others, to that very appreciative critic Mr Edmund Gosse, who in an essay included in his *Seventeenth Century Studies* speaks of it as "distressing" and "humiliating" and "a string of preposterous conceits." Undoubtedly it is a poem that requires us at the outset not to be entirely out of sympathy with our author's subject. If we start by calling the theme "a very small" one, we shall inevitably be more and more provoked as the poem draws out its length. But it is the first duty of a critic to renounce prejudice, and one would imagine that in reading the works of a Roman Catholic poet for æsthetic purposes it might be pardonable to abate something from the rigour of our Protestantism. It may be granted that there are stanzas in the poem—most of them added in the second edition—which ought never to have been written, and need not be read; such as the 4th to 6th, 19th to 22nd, 27th, and 29th.[2] But when these nine stanzas have been excised from the thirty-three, there remains a poem which, if its topic be once allowed—it is a rosary of devotion to St Mary Magdalene—should give nothing but delight to the lover of poetry. To begin with, the stanza is admirably fashioned for a "rosary" (by which I mean a string of stanzas the thought in each of which is complete in itself), because it opens with a shortened trochaic[3] line, which emphasises each new begin-

ning, and concludes in a couplet which emphasises the close. The only other poem in English that for a similar contemplative effect can be compared with it, is Rossetti's "Staff and Scrip," but in that case the separate roundness of each stanza is not so completely an advantage, as the poem tells a continuous tale. It will be observed how much variety of rhythm Crashaw obtains within each stanza, without violating the metre, by merely shifting the pause.

> Th' dew no more will weep
>   The primrose's pale cheek to deck:
> Th' dew no more will sleep
>   Nuzzel'd in the lily's neck;
> Much rather would it be thy tear,
> And leave them both to tremble here
> Not the soft gold which
>   Steals from the amber-weeping tree,
> Makes sorrow half so rich
>   As the drops distill'd from thee,
> Sorrow's best jewels lie in these
> Caskets, of which heaven keeps the keys.
> Not in th' Evening's eyes
>   When they red with weeping are
> For the sun that dies,
>   Sits sorrow with a face so fair,
> Nowhere but here did ever meet
> Sweetness so sad, sadness so sweet.

But, says Mr. Gosse, these are "preposterous conceits." What is a "conceit?" How does it differ from the legitimate poetical image, the offspring of that imaginative power which illuminates one object by the light reflected on it from another? According to Dr Johnson, the difference is that the latter, though not obvious, is upon its first production acknowledged to be just, whereas, in the case of conceits, "the reader, far from wondering that he missed them, wonders more frequently by what perverseness of industry they were ever found." This distinction, stated in the straightforward commonsense manner of the great eigthteenth-century critic, seems to be a true one, and indeed seems to be the grain of truth at the bottom of the more pretentious distinction between the images of the "fancy" and the "imagination," of which Coleridge, and after him Ruskin, have made so much. Accordingly we may expect to find that, although the greater poet is, the more natural and satisfying will be the general run of his images, yet even among those of the greatest poets some will strike us by their cleverness rather than their truth, and even in times when the rage for novelty is paramount, some will charm by their truth as much as their novelty. The seventeenth-century writers, coming in the ebb of the great Elizabethan wave, were certainly tempted to depend too much upon ingenuity, too little upon the freshness of natural suggestion; and Cowley's writings afforded Dr Johnson an inexhaustible storehouse of the wrong sort of "wit"; but then Cowley is no less full of metaphors that are as just as they are striking. The lines quoted above are an instance. And so it is with Crashaw. It cannot be denied that when the bright heaven of invention is overcast, he can be beyond measure dull and tedious with his hackneyed conceits of "nests" and "fires" and "eyes," but what ample amends he makes by-and-by whether in single epithets like the "*weary* lids of Hope" or in such splendid images as that in the Description of a Religious House, "still rolling a round sphere of still returning pain." Our modern taste may be jarred by the arrogance of poets who set out with the deliberate intention of saying as many fine things as they can upon Hope or a Saint's tears, instead of "waiting for the spark from heaven to fall"; but for all that we have no right to condemn the result *en bloc*: we must take each several trope upon its merits. Of course it is never the mere intellectual element in the figure that constitutes the poetry, apart from the emotion that has suggested it, or at any rate prompted the search for it, and it is the intellectual element that is predominant in the Caroline poets, but Crashaw's verses do not lack passion. And besides all this, there is the actual writing; and those who refuse to find the conceits other than ingenious, and the passion other than preposterous, cannot be deaf to the exquisite music of the verse.

> There's no need at all
> That the balsam-sweating bough
> So coyly should let fall
> Her med'cinable tears; for now
> Nature hath learnt to extract a dew
> More sovereign and sweet from you.
>
> Yet let the poor drops weep—
> Weeping is the ease of woe—
> Softly let them creep,
> Sad that they are vanquisht so,
> They, though to others no relief,
> Balsam may be for their own grief.
>
> Golden though he be,
> Golden Tagus murmurs though;
> Were his way by thee,
> Content and quiet he would go,
> So much more rich would he esteem
> Thy silver, than his golden stream.
>
> Well does the May, that lies
> Smiling in thy cheeks, confess
> The April in thine eyes;
> Mutual sweetness they express.
> No April ere lent kinder showers
> Nor May returned more faithful flowers.

To pass now from the *Steps to the Temple* to the "other delights of the Muses," Crashaw's temperament was so eminently devotional that it is not surprising to find but few of his secular pieces of any high merit. The best, and the best known through its inclusion in the *Golden Treasury* (though in a too curtailed form, and from an inferior text) is the "Wishes to his (supposed) Mistress," a poem written in an original and effective metre of three lines of four, six, and eight syllables. It is full of fine thoughts and phrases, some in Crashaw's own superlative manner, as when he speaks of "tresses"

> Whose native ray
> Can tame the wanton day
> Of gems that in their bright shades play.
>
> Each ruby there
> Or pearl, that dare appear
> Be its own blush, be its own tear;

Others in a direct style of high and simple dignity, that might belong to any of the greater masters; as when he wishes for his mistress

> Whate'er delight
> Can make day's forehead bright
> Or give down to the wings of night.
>
> Days that need borrow
> No part of their good morrow
> From a fore-spent night of sorrow.
>
> Life that dares send
> A challenge to his end,
> And when it comes, say, 'Welcome, friend.'

The version of Strada's contest between the lutanist and the nightingale, called "Music's duel," is rather a *tour de force* than a very successful or pleasing poem, inasmuch as vocabulary, though necessary to poetry, is not so necessary as feeling.

The reader is amazed more than he is delighted. But an amazing poem it is, and the merit is Crashaw's; for though the story and the plan of the poem are taken from Strada, most of the description of the nightingale's song is Crashaw's own. To even describe the description would task a poet. Mr Swinburne speaks of "its dazzling intricacy and affluence in refinements, its supple and cunning implications, its choiceness and subtlety." But it must be confessed that a part, as often with Crashaw, would have been more than the whole. The "Epitaph on a young Married Couple" is written in the octosyllables that hardly any seventeenth-century poet could handle without some success, and Crashaw is always happy in them.

> Peace, good reader, do not weep.
> Peace, the lovers are asleep.
> They, sweet turtles, folded lie
> In the last knot that love could tie.
> And though they lie as they were dead,
> Their pillow stone, their sheets of lead,
> (Pillow hard, and sheets not warm)
> Love made the bed; they'll take no harm.

"Love's Horoscope," in octosyllabic stanzas, is an even finer piece of writing, curiously perfect in its balanced structure, and the astrological idea is fully worked out, but without over-elaboration. A "song out of the Italian," in a metre copied by Mr Swinburne, equally fantastic in idea, is equally perfect in execution. The decasyllabic poems are not so completely successful, though occasionally they admit of effects in Crashaw's peculiar style, as in the close of "Satisfaction for Sleep":

> Why threatst thou so?
> Why dost thou shake thy leaden sceptre? Go
> Bestow thy poppy upon wakeful Woe,
> Sickness, and Sorrow, whose pale lids ne'er know
> Thy downy finger; dwell upon their eyes,
> Shut in their tears, shut out their miseries.

The history of the development of the heroic couplet is too large a subject to discuss at the end of an Introduction. It happens, however, that Pope in one of his letters to Henry Cromwell has given a criticism upon Crashaw, interesting in itself and for the light it throws upon the eighteenth-century standards of taste. The following extract gives the substance of the criticism

> I take this poet to have writ like a gentleman, that is at leisure hours, and more to keep out of idleness than to establish a reputation; so that nothing regular or just can be expected from him. All that regards design, form, fable (which is the soul of poetry), all that concerns exactness, or consent of parts (which is the body) will probably be wanting; only pretty conceptions, fine metaphors, glittering expressions, and something of a neat cast of verse (which are properly the dress, gems, or loose ornaments of poetry) may be found in these verses. . . . To speak of his numbers is a little difficult, they are so various and irregular, and mostly Pindarick: 'tis evident his heroic verse (the best example of which is his 'Music's Duel') is carelessly made up; but one may imagine, from what it now is, that had he taken more care, it had been musical and pleasing enough, not extremely majestic, but sweet. And the time considered, of his writing, he was (even as incorrect as he is) none of the worse versificators.[4]

There is justice in some of these strictures. Crashaw was certainly wanting in the architectonics of poetry, and never attempted an epic or a drama. As certainly he was given to vain repetitions. But he had imagination and he had passion, neither of which qualities has a place in Mr Pope's Anatomy of Poetry. But to speak only of the heroic couplet; let the reader turn to Crashaw's "Description of a Religious House," and then to Pope's "Eloisa and Abelard" and say whether he can fail to adjudge the meed to Crashaw.[5] Pope's couplet, excellent for satiric verse and epigram, is too frail a vehicle for passion. The recurring cæsura in the third foot, often followed by a conjunction or preposition, and the inevitable epithet in every line make a thin and artificial instrument which soon disgusts. Crashaw's verses have far greater variety and far greater robustness, and his epithets, while perhaps they are over-plentiful, all add something to the conception.

Another poet who headed the reaction from the school of Pope agrees with him generally both in his praise and blame of Crashaw. "Crashaw," says Coleridge, "seems in his poems to have given the first ebullience of his imagination, unshapen into form, or much of what we now term sweetness." He goes on to say that certain verses from the Hymn to St Teresa (ll. 43–64) "were ever present to my mind whilst writing the second part of Christabel; if, indeed by some subtle process of the mind they did not suggest the first thought of the whole poem." The student who turns to the second part of Christabel will be puzzled to trace any direct influence of Crashaw upon the poem. Coleridge's versification, with its abundance of extra syllables is jerky by comparison, and suggests hasty workmanship far more than Crashaw's. But perhaps Coleridge is referring to that portion of the second part of Christabel which was never written.[6] Coleridge, however, sometimes recalls Crashaw by the richness of his lines, as Shelley does by his smooth and limpid flow; but at his best Crashaw has more radiance than either.

There is a further respect in which Crashaw and Coleridge are alike: they both belong to that body of poets between whose best and worst there seems no recognisable relation. At worst they are both singularly flat and unprofitable and sometimes ludicrous; at best their verse supplies a meaning to the term commonly used of poets, the word "inspiration"; it suggests a theory that the poet is only a medium for supernatural powers to play upon, an Æolian harp for the spirit which blows as it lists; for their best writing seems as far as possible removed from any result that Art alone could compass. Jonson tells us that "a good poet's made as well as born," and in reading Jonson, and indeed in reading his greater disciple Milton, we assent to the theory, for the conscious artist reveals himself in every line. But when we turn to Crashaw we revert to the older theory of the poet as a paradisal creature, "born not made," a "winged and holy being,"[7] whose poems are not the work of man, but divine, and though we may readily admit that Prospero would be a more useful member of human society than Ariel, we cannot but regard Ariel with the more wonder for his gift of ethereal music. But besides this inexplicable charm of music, when inspired, Crashaw was gifted with the fervour of a devout enthusiast; and so it comes about that although he has occasionally fine poetry which is not religious, and too often ardent religious verse which is not poetry, yet his most exalted verse is that in which both influences meet. Then the whole man is sublimed and becomes, "all air and fire."

Notes

1. Crashaw's critics usually speak as if the concluding lines of "The Flaming Heart" had formed part of the original poem. Thus Mr Saintsbury: "And then in a moment, in the twinkling of an eye, without warning of any sort, the metre changes, the poet's inspiration catches fire, and there rushes up into the heaven of poetry this marvellous rocket of song" (*Elizabethan Literature*, p. 365).

2. The numeration follows the 1652 edition adopted in J.R. Tutin, *Poems of Richard Crashaw*, 1905.

3. That the effect of the line is meant to be generally trochaic seems certain from the fact that it is so in most of the early stanzas which fix the mould of the metre; also the twelfth stanza opens "There's no need at all," where otherwise it would have been as simple to write "There is no need at all." Even in the lines having six syllables, which are the majority, it will be observed that the dissyllabic words are trochees.

4. Correspondence, Croker and Elwin, vi. 116. The letter contains also a fairly just criticism of "The Weeper."

5. Pope in this psuedo-Gothic poem borrows a verse from Crashaw's "Description," which, alas, will not fit its new context:

   > How happy is the blameless vestal's lot,
   > The world forgetting, by the world forgot:
   > Eternal sunshine of the spotless mind!
   > Each pray'r accepted and each wish resign'd
   > Labour and rest that equal periods keep,
   > 'Obedient slumbers that can wake and weep.'
   >
   > (ll. 201–12)

   It is plain that if labour and rest keep equal periods, the slumbers must be such as do *not* wake and weep. But it is easy to sympathise with Pope's admiration for Crashaw's line. In its own place it is admirable:

   > A hasty portion of prescribed sleep;
   > Obedient slumbers, that can wake and weep,
   > And sing, and sigh, and work, and sleep again;
   > Still rolling a round sphere of still-returning pain.

6. *Letters, Conversations, and Recollections of Samuel Taylor Coleridge*, 1836. Coleridge repeatedly spoke of the poem as containing 1400 lines, but the editions know only of less than half this number. See note to Dykes Campbell's edition, p. 602.

7. Plato, *Ion*, 534.

ROBERT HERRICK

ROBERT HERRICK

1591–1674

Robert Herrick, cleric and poet, was born in Goldsmith's Row, Cheapside, London, the son of a goldsmith. His father died when Herrick was very young (perhaps by suicide), and Herrick and his siblings were raised by their uncle, the king's jeweler. Herrick graduated from Westminster School in 1607 and began a ten-year apprenticeship in the family business.

Herrick entered St. John's College, Cambridge, in 1613, transferring to Trinity Hall, Cambridge in 1616 to study law. Herrick received a B.A. in 1617 and an M.A. in 1620, although he never pursued a legal career. In 1623 he was ordained a deacon and accompanied the Duke of Buckingham on his expedition to Île de Rhé in 1627 as a military chaplain. Herrick returned to London to begin the life of a literary man-about-town.

Joining the poets and musicians of Ben Jonson's circle, Herrick was a poet of high reputation. In 1629, however, Charles II appointed Herrick to the parish of Dean Prior, Devonshire, in the West Country. Initially Herrick lamented the cessation of his London life and despaired of his churlish congregation. Nevertheless, it was in the quiet of the countryside that Herrick wrote most of his poems. In 1647 Herrick was asked to leave because of his refusal to subscribe to the Solemn League and Covenant, which supported further church reform. Herrick was reinstated by the restored king, Charles II, in 1662. He remained in Devonshire until he died in 1674.

Many of Herrick's poems were included in manuscript commonplace books, including the anthologies *A Description of the King and Queen of Fayres* (1635), *Lachrymae Musarum* (1649), and *Witts Recreation* (1650), which carried sixty-two of Herrick's poems. Herrick himself only published one book of poetry in his lifetime, *Hesperides, or the Works, both Humane and Divine of Robert Herrick, Esq.* (1648), which included religious verse under the title *His Noble Numbers*, dated 1647. The book consisted of some 1,400 poems, varying from elegies, satires, epigrams, marriage songs, ecclesiastical and festival songs, and complimentary verse. Herrick never married, but a number of his poems are addressed to imaginary mistresses. Herrick's *Hebrides* was not reprinted until 1823.

Personal

Being in Devonshire during the last summer, we took an opportunity of visiting Dean Prior, for the purpose of making some inquiries concerning Herrick, who, from the circumstance of having been vicar of that parish (where he is still talked of as a poet, a wit, and a hater of the county), for twenty years, might be supposed to have left some unrecorded memorials of his existence behind him. We found many persons in the village who could repeat some of his lines. . . . The person, however, who knows more of Herrick than all the rest of the neighbourhood, we found to be a poor woman in the ninety-ninth year of her age, named Dorothy King. She repeated to us, with great exactness, five of his *Noble Numbers*, among which was the beautiful Litany. These she had learned from her mother, who was apprenticed to Herrick's successor in the vicarage. She called them her prayers, which, she said, she was in the habit of putting up in bed, whenever she could not sleep: and she therefore began the Litany at the second stanza,

> When I lie within my bed, &c.

Another of her midnight orisons was the poem beginning

> Every night thou dost me fright,
> And keep mine eyes from sleeping, &c.

She had no idea that these poems had ever been printed, and could not have read them if she had seen them. She is in possession of few traditions as to the person, manners, and habits of life of the poet; but in return, she has a whole budget of anecdotes respecting his ghost; and these she details with a careless but serene gravity, which one would not willingly discompose by any hints at a remote possibility of their not being exactly true. Herrick, she says, was a bachelor, and kept a maid-servant, as his poems, indeed, discover; but she adds, what they do not discover, that he also kept a pet-pig, which he taught to drink out of a tankard. And this important circumstance, together with a tradition that he one day threw his sermon at the congregation, with a curse for their inattention, forms almost the sum total of what we could collect of the poet's life.—BARRON FIELD, *The Quarterly Review*, 1810, pp. 171–72

This fine old fellow, this joyous heart, who lived to be eighty-three, in spite of "dull Devonshire" and the bad times, wrote almost as much as Carew, Lovelace, and Suckling united, and how much there is in his weed-choked garden, which is comparable with their best compositions! How little we know of him! how scantily he has been realized to us! Could we but raise up for a summer afternoon the Devonshire which he lived in, and the people with whom he mixed or summon the ghost of faithful Prudence Baldwin, we might be furnished with inspiration to do something better than the bare sketch which follows.—WILLIAM CAREW HAZLITT, "Preface" to *Hesperides*, 1869, Vol. 1, p. viii

Being ejected by Cromwell from his church living in 1648, he dropped his title of "Reverend" to assume that of "Esquire," and published a volume to which he gave the title of *Hesperides; or, the Works both Humane and Divine, of Robert Herrick, Esq.* Doubtless the "Esquire" was accepted by the public, as well as by himself, as more appropriate than "Reverend" would have been to the character of the lyrics, some part of which he yet seems rather arrogantly to call "Divine."—JUSTIN S. MORRILL, *Self-Consciousness of Noted Persons*, 1887, p. 90

This Robert Herrick was a ponderous, earthy-looking man, with huge double chin, drooping cheeks, a great Roman nose, prominent glassy eyes, that showed around them the red lines begotten of strong potions of Canary, and the whole set upon a massive neck which might have been that of Heliogabalus. It was such a figure as the artist would make typical of a man who loves the grossest pleasures.—DONALD G. MITCHELL, *English Lands, Letters, and Kings: Elizabeth to Anne*, 1890, p. 124

Mr. Gosse, for example, assures us that Julia really walked the earth, and even gives us some details of her mundane pilgrimage; other critics smile, and shake their heads, and doubt. It matters not; she lives and she will continue to live when we who dispute the matter lie voiceless in our graves. The essence of her personality lingers on every page where Herrick sings of her. His verse is heavy with her spicy perfumes, glittering with her many-colored jewels, lustrous with the shimmer of her silken petticoats. Her very shadow, her sighs, distills sweet odors on the air, and draws him after her, faint with their amorous languor. How lavish she is with her charms, this woman who neither thinks nor suffers; who prays, indeed, sometimes, with great serenity, and dips her snowy finger in the font of blessed water, but whose spiritual humors pale before the calm vigor of her earthly nature! How kindly, how tranquil, how unmoved, she is; listening with the same slow smile to her lover's fantastic word-play, to the fervid conceits with which he beguiles the summer idleness, and to the frank and sudden passion with which he conjures her, "dearest of thousands," to close his eyes when death shall summon him, to shed some true tears above the sod, to clasp forever the book in which he writes her name! How gently she would have fulfilled these last sad duties had the discriminating fates called her to his bier; how fragrant the sighs she would have wafted in that darkened chamber; how sincere the temperate sorrow for a remediable loss! And then, out into the glowing sunlight, where life is sweet, and the world exults, and the warm blood tingles in our veins, and, underneath the scattered primrose blossoms, the frozen dead lie forgotten in their graves.—AGNES REPPLIER, "English Love-Songs," *Points of View*, 1891, p. 33

It seems likely that Perilla and her fair companions were actually known to Herrick in London, and were then made the topic of many a gallant verse; and that after he sailed away to the West he continued to write to their memory as though they were actually present; that, in fact, the goddesses he was never weary of worshipping were, to a large extent, abstractions and ideals. And when in the quiet of his little parsonage, or in a sunny Devonshire meadow bright with wild flowers, his fancy coined some musical verse in honour of his ideal love, his memory would glide quickly back and dwell longingly on her prototype of flesh and blood whom he had known and loved in former years; and, cut off from all the noises and all the rivalries of the town, it must have seemed to him that he was thinking of another Robert Herrick who had lived long ago.—H.M. SANDERS, "Robert Herrick," *The Gentleman's Magazine*, 1896, p. 604

Whether or not the bovine features in Marshall's engraving are a libel on the poet, it is to be regretted that oblivion has not laid its erasing finger on that singularly unpleasant counterfeit presentment. . . . The aggressive face bestowed upon him by the artist lends an air of veracity to the tradition that the vicar occasionally hurled the manuscript of his sermon at the heads of his drowsy parishioners, accompanying the missive with pregnant remarks. He has the aspect of one meditating assault and battery. To offset the picture there is much indirect testimony to the amiability of the man, aside from the evidence

furnished by his own writings. . . . I picture him as a sort of Samuel Pepys, with perhaps less quaintness, and the poetical temperament added. Like the prince of gossips, too, he somehow gets at your affections.—THOMAS BAILEY ALDRICH, "Introduction" to *Poems of Robert Herrick*, 1900, pp. xxvi–xxx

General

Robert Herric, a writer of poems of much about the same standing and the same rank in fame with the last mentioned ⟨Robert Heath⟩, though not particularly influenced by any nymph or goddess except his *Maid Pru*. That which is chiefly pleasant in these poems, is now and then a pretty flowery and pastoral gale of fancy; a vernal prospect of some hill, cave, rock, or fountain; which but for the interruption of other trivial passages, might have made up none of the worst poetic landscapes.—EDWARD PHILLIPS, *Theatrum Poetarum Anglicanorum*, 1675

Robert Herric one of the Scholars of *Apollo* of the middle Form, yet something above *George Withers*, in a pretty Flowry and Pastoral Gale of Fancy, in a vernal Prospect of some Hill, Cave, Rock, or Fountain; which but for the Interruption of other trivial Passages, might have made up none of the worst Poetick Landskips. Take a view of his Poetry in his Errata to the Reader in these lines.

> For these Errata's, Reader thou do'st see,
> Blame thou the Printer for them, and not me:
> Who gave him forth good Grain, tho he mistook,
> And so did sow these Tares throughout my Book.

I account him in Fame much of the same rank, as he was of the same Standing, with one *Robert Heath*, the Author of a Poem, Entituled, *Clarastella*, the ascribed Title of that Celebrated Lady, who is supposed to have been both the Inspirer and chief Subject of them.—WILLIAM WINSTANLEY, *The Lives of the Most Famous English Poets*, 1687

Robert Heyrick was a Londoner born, but descended from those of his name (which are antient and genteel) in Leicestershire, was elected fellow of Alls. coll. from that of S. John's as it seems, in the year 1628, but took no degree, as I can yet find. Afterwards being patroniz'd by the earl of Exeter, lived near the river Dean-Bourne in Devonshire, where he exercis'd his muse as well in poetry as other learning, and became much beloved by the gentry in those parts for his florid and witty discourse: but being forced to leave that place, he retired to London, where he published

Hesperides: or, Works both humane and divine. Lond. 1648, in a thick oct. with his picture (a shoulder-piece) before it.

His noble Numbers: or, his Pieces. Wherein (among other things) he sings the Birth of Christ, and Sighs for his Saviour's Sufferings on the Cross—printed with *Hesperides*. These two books of poetry made him much admired in the time when they were published, especially by the generous and boon loyalists, among whom he was numbered as a sufferer. Afterwards he had a benefice conferr'd on him (in Devonsh. I think) by the said E. of Essex, and was living in S. Ann's parish in Westminster, after his majesty's restoration. He had a brother or near kinsman named Rich. Heyrick a divine, whom I have elsewhere mention'd.—ANTHONY À WOOD, *Athenae Oxonienses*, 1691–1721

It appears from the effects of her inspiration, that Prue was but indifferently qualified for a tenth muse.—JAMES GRANGER, *Biographical History of England*, 1769–76, Vol. 3, p. 136

One chief cause of the neglect into which the poetry of Herrick has fallen, is its extreme inequality. It would appear he thought it necessary to publish every thing he composed, however trivial, however ridiculous or indecorous. The consequence has been, that productions, which Marlowe or Milton might have owned with pleasure, have been concealed, and nearly buried, in a crude and undigested mass. Had he shewn any taste in selection, I have no doubt the fate of his volume, though reduced two-thirds of its present size, had been widely different. Perhaps there is no collection of poetry in our language, which, in some respects, more nearly resembles the *Carmina* of Catullus. It abounds in Epigrams disgusting and indecent, in satirical delineations of personal defects, in frequent apologies for the levity of his Muse, and repeated declarations of the chastity of his life; it is interspersed, also, with several exquisite pieces of the amatory and descriptive kind, and with numerous addresses to his friends and relations, by whom he appears to have been greatly beloved. The variety of metre he has used in this work is truly astonishing; he has almost exhausted every form of rhymed versification, and in many he moves with singular ease and felicity.

It has been observed by Mr. Headley, that "Waller is too exclusively considered as the first man who brought versification to any thing like its present standard. Carew's pretensions to the same merit are seldom sufficiently either considered or allowed." I may venture, I think, to introduce Herrick to my reader, as having greatly contributed toward this mechanical perfection. Many of his best effusions have the sweetness, the melody, and elegance of modern compositions. He was nearly, if not altogether, contemporary with Carew; for, if the account of Clarendon, who had been intimate with him, be correct, Carew lived fifty years, and as we know that he died in 1639, he must have been born only a year or two anterior to Herrick. It is true Carew's Poems were published earlier, being given to the world shortly after his death, probably in the year 1640 or 1641, for the second edition of his works bears date 1642; but as Herrick's productions were all written before 1648, and many of them twenty, or, perhaps, thirty years previous to this period, it is obvious he could have been no imitator of the friend of Clarendon, but must have been indebted merely to his own exertions and genius, for the grace and polish of his versification. I consider, likewise, the two little Poems, entitled the "Primrose" and the "Inquiry," which were first published in Carew's works, and afterwards appeared among the Poems of Herrick, to have certainly belonged to the latter, and to have been attributed to Carew by the Editor's mistake. In the first place it is not probable that Herrick, who certainly superintended and arranged his own productions, and who must have been familiar with the volume of his ingenious rival, would have republished these pieces as his own, if he had not possessed a prior claim to them; and, secondly, the Poem termed the "Inquiry," by the Editor of Carew, is, in Herrick, addressed to a beloved Mistress, to "Mrs. Eliz. Wheeler," under the name of the lost Shepherdess; and by the nature of its variations from the copy in Carew, bears indubitable marks of being the original from whence those lines were taken; and which, being probably written early, and circulated in manuscript by Herrick's friends, might easily, from a general resemblance of style and manner, be mistaken, by the Editor, for a genuine production of Carew.

If, in point of versification, Herrick may enter into competition with either Carew or Waller, he will be found still more competent to contend with them as to sentiment and imagery. It has been justly observed, that "Carew has the ease, without the pedantry, of Waller;" the remark will apply with equal propriety to Herrick. His amatory poems unite the playful gaiety of Anacreon with the tender sweetness of Catullus, and are altogether devoid of that mythological allusion and cold conceit, which, in the pages of Waller, so frequently disgust the reader. There is a vein also of rich description in the poetry of Herrick, undiscoverable in the productions of the two other poets, and which resembles the best manner of Milton's Minora, and Marlowe's Passionate Shepherd. Nor has he been unsuccessful in imitating the Horatian style and imagery, of which I shall give a specimen, while, at the same time, the morality of another portion of his lyrics breathes an air of the most pleasing melancholy. I hesitate not, therefore, to consider him in the same degree superior to Carew, as Carew most assuredly is to Waller, whose versification, as I have elsewhere observed, has alone embalmed his memory.—NATHAN DRAKE, "On the Life, Writings and Genius of Robert Herrick," *Literary Hours*, 1804, Vol. 2, pp. 368–71

Herrick is a writer who does not answer the expectations I had formed of him. He is in a manner a modern discovery, and so far has the freshness of antiquity about him. He is not trite and thread bare. But neither is he likely to become so. He is a writer of epigrams, not of lyrics. He has point and ingenuity, but I think little of the spirit of love or wine. From his frequent allusion to pearls and rubies, one might take him for a lapidary instead of a poet.—WILLIAM HAZLITT, *Lectures on the Literature of the Age of Elizabeth*, 1820

A coarse-minded and beastly writer, whose dunghill, when the few flowers that grew therein had been transplanted, ought never to have been disturbed. Those flowers indeed are beautiful and perennial; but they should have been removed from the filth and ordure in which they are embedded.—ROBERT SOUTHEY, *Lives of Uneducated Poets*, 1831, p. 85

A contemporary and friend of Ben Jonson was Robert Herrick, the author of the *Hesperides* and *Noble Numbers*, a genuine English Poet. His verse is exclusively lyric, composed [of] short fugitive compositions upon all topics grave and gay, dainty and coarse, upon the objects of common life. . . . The man of poetic temperament never feels his privilege more proudly than among common and mean objects. The drudge is exalted by the sight of a volcano, an eclipse, or a conflagration but the poet's eye gilds the dullest common or street, his kitchen or hen coop with light and grace. He delights in this victory of genius over custom. He delights to show the muse is not nice or squeamish, but can tread with firm and elastic step in sordid places and take no more pollution then the sun-beam which shines alike on the carrion and the violet. Herrick by the choice often of base and even disgusting themes, has pushed this privilege too far, rather I think out of the very wantonness of poetic power, than as has been said by his biographers, to make his book sell, by feeding the grosser palates of his public.

His talent lies in his mastery of all the strength and lighter graces of the language so that his verse is all music, and, what he writes in the indulgence of the most exquisite fancy is at the same time expressed with as perfect simplicity as the language of conversation. . . .

A beautiful example of the delicacy of his poetic vision is in the little stanza "To Silvia":

> I am holy while I stand
> Circumcrost by thy pure hand
> But when that is gone again
> I like others am profane.

Many of his poems are mere couplets or stanzas of four lines like his "Clothes for Continuance,"

> The garments lasting evermore
> Are works of mercy to the poor
> And neither tettar time or moth
> Shall fray that silk or fret this cloth,

or his definition of Beauty,

> Beauty no other thing is than a beam
> Flashed out between the middle and extreme,

which may serve as a counterpart to Winkelmann's fine criticism upon the antique: "Beauty with the ancients was the tongue on the balance of expression." There is an air of magnanimity in the confidence with which the poet gives us on many grave topics his sense in so little compass as a stanza of two, four, or six lines. It evinces his belief in what I take to be an admitted fact in Criticism, that there may be as unquestionable evidence of wit in a sentence as in a treatise, or that whosoever has written one good sentence has given proof of his ability to write a book. For a good sentence is not merely a proposition grammatically stated but one which contains in itself its own apology, or the reason why it was said. A proposition set down in words is not therefore affirmed. It must affirm itself or no propriety and no vehemence of language will give it evidence.—RALPH WALDO EMERSON, "Ben Jonson, Herrick, Herbert, Wotton" (1835), *The Early Lectures of Ralph Waldo Emerson*, 1959, Vol. 1, eds. Whicher, Spiller, pp. 346–49

Without the exuberant gayety of Suckling, or perhaps the delicacy of Carew, he is sportive, fanciful, and generally of polished language. The faults of his age are sometimes apparent: though he is not often obscure, he runs, more perhaps for the sake of variety than any other cause, into occasional pedantry. He has his conceits and false thoughts; but these are more than redeemed by the numerous very little poems (for those of Herrick are frequently not longer than epigrams), which may be praised without much more qualification than belongs to such poetry.—HENRY HALLAM, *Introduction to the Literature of Europe*, 1837–39, Pt. 3, Ch. 5

As a loyalist and sufferer in the cause, there can be no doubt that Herrick was popular with the Cavalier party, and that his poems were received with the favour they deserved by his contemporaries, for that they were popular must be inferred from the number of them which were set to music by Henry Lawes, Laniere, Wilson, and Ramsay; it is somewhat difficult to account for the seeming neglect which they experienced in after times.—S. W. SINGER, "Biographical Notice" to *Hesperides*, 1846, Vol. 1, p. xxv

More than any eminent writer of that day, Herrick's collection requires careful sifting; but there is so much fancy, so much delicacy, so much grace, that a good selection would well repay the publisher. Bits there are that are exquisite. . . . But his real delight was among flowers and bees, and nymphs and cupids; and certainly these graceful subjects were never handled more gracefully.—MARY RUSSELL MITFORD, *Recollections of a Literary Life*, 1851, pp. 143–44

He was an Anacreon or Catullus in holy orders, whiling away, at the ripe age of forty, the dulness of his Devonshire parsonage in such ditties as these:

> Much I know, of time is spent, &c., &c.

. . . And so, in every other poem, he sings or sips his wine, with his arm round a Julia! What eyes, what lips, what a neck! and so on amorously, beyond all clerical limits. Like Anacreon, he is sweet, too, in light sensuous descriptions of physical nature. . . . There was, moreover, a tinge of amiable melancholy in his genius—the melancholy on which the Epi-

curean philosophy itself rests.—DAVID MASSON, *The Life of John Milton*, 1858, Vol. 1, Ch. 6

It is an especial pleasure to write the name of Robert Herrick amongst the poets of religion, for the very act records that the jolly, careless Anacreon of the church, with his head and heart crowded with pleasures, threw down at length his wine-cup, tore the roses from his head, and knelt in the dust.—GEORGE MACDONALD, *England's Antiphon*, 1868, p. 163

Making due allowance of the time when Herrick's verses were written, his temptation to suit the taste of courtiers and kings, his volumes contain much admirable poetry, tempered with religious devotion. He wrote sweet and virtuous verse, with lines here and there that should not have been written. But he is an antedote to the vice in his lines, and may well have place in the scholar's library with Donne, Daniel, Cowley, Shakespeare, and contemporaries.—A. BRONSON ALCOTT, *Concord Days*, 1872, p. 136

Many of his compositions are, in the fullest sense of the term, trifles; others are at least exquisite trifles; some are not trifles, and are exquisite. After more than a century of neglect, ensuing upon their first ample popularity, Herrick's writings have for years been kept freshened with a steady current of literary laudation—certainly not unjustified, so far as their finer qualities go, but tending a little to the indiscriminate.—WILLIAM MICHAEL ROSSETTI, Note to *Humorous Poems*, 1872, p. 98

Beyond all dispute, the best of the early lyric poets is Robert Herrick, whose verses are flushed with a joyous and tender spirit. He may be styled the Burns of his time, and was imbued with something of the reckless soul of the great north-countryman. . . . Flowers, music, woman, all these had their intense and several charms for him, and, strangely enough for a middle-aged clergyman, he was clearly an amorous and erotic poet.—GEORGE BARNETT SMITH, "English Fugitive Poets," *Poets and Novelists*, 1875, pp. 381–82

Among the English pastoral poets, Herrick takes an undisputed precedence, and as a lyrist generally he is scarcely excelled, except by Shelley. No other writer of the seventeenth century approached him in abundance of song, in sustained exercise of the purely musical and intuitive gifts of poetry. Shakspeare, Milton, and perhaps Fletcher, surpassed him in the passion and elevated harmony of their best lyrical pieces, as they easily excelled him in the wider range of their genius and the breadth of their accomplishment. But while these men exercised their art in all its branches, Herrick confined himself very narrowly to one or two, and the unflagging freshness of his inspiration, flowing through a long life in so straitened a channel, enabled him to amass such a wealth of purely lyrical poetry as no other Englishman has produced. His level of performance was very high; he seems to have preserved all that he wrote, and the result is that we possess more than twelve hundred of his little poems, in at least one out of every three of which we may find something charming or characteristic. Of all the Cavalier lyrists Herrick is the only one that followed the bent of his genius undisturbed, and lived a genuine artist's life.—EDMUND GOSSE, "Robert Herrick," *English Poets*, 1880, Vol. 2, ed. Ward, p. 124

By a strange irony of fortune the only letters we possess from the genial and glowing pen of the great poet of the *Hesperides* are a series of plaintive notes to his rich uncle, Sir William Herrick; and we may gather from them that this amiable relative's money paid for the piping of some of the most graceful lyrics in the English language.—W. BAPTISTE SCOONES, *Four Centuries of English Letters*, 1880, p. 67

He sings well chiefly when he sings of love, but this love is not of the kind which inspires our greatest poets. He is enamoured with the accessories of a woman's beauty—the colour of a ribbon, the flaunting of a ringlet, with "a careless shoe-string," or the wave of a petticoat. The charms he sees in his mistress are likened to precious stones, and all the treasures of the lapidary are represented in his verse. There are few traces of tenderness in Herrick and none of passion; it is probable that every pretty girl he saw suggested a pretty fancy. To judge from his own saying, "no man at one time can be wise and love." Herrick was not wise. If we may trust his verses, the poet was perennially in love, chiefly with Julia, "prime of all," but warmly too with Anthea, Lucia, Corinna, and Perilla. Making love is in Herrick's eyes a charming amusement, and the more love-making the more poetry. If Julia prove unkind, he can solace himself with Sappho; and if Sappho be perverse, some other mistress will charm him with her "pretty witchcrafts."—JOHN DENNIS, *Heroes of Literature*, 1883, p. 97

None of our English lyric poets has shown a more perfect sense of words and of their musical efficiency, none has united so exquisitely a classic sense of form to that impulsive tunefulness which we have come to consider as essentially English. In his earlier lyrics Herrick has perhaps more of this impulse, but it served him with the same youthful freshness to the last. . . . It is the way in which Herrick adds to and completes this natural lyrical impulse by the further grace of verse taught by the Latin verse-writers and their English disciples, that makes him so consummate an artist within his range. . . . There is magic in these lyrics, that indefinable quality, born of the spirit, which can alone avail in the end to make poetry live.—ERNEST RHYS, "Introduction" to *Hesperides: Poems by Robert Herrick*, 1887, pp. xxxi–xxxiii

> Many suns have set and shone,
> Many springs have come and gone,
> *Herrick*, since thou sang'st of Wake,
> Morris-dance, and Barley-break;
> Many men have ceased from care,
> Many maidens have been fair,
> Since thou sang'st of *Julia's* eyes,
> *Julia's* lawns and tiffanies;
> Many things are past—but thou,
> *Golden-Mouth*, art singing now,
> Singing clearly as of old,
> And thy numbers are of gold.
> —AUSTIN DOBSON, "In a Copy of the Lyrical Poems of Robert Herrick," *Scribner's Magazine*, Jan. 1887, p. 66

Divided, in the published form, into two classes: they may be divided, for purposes of poetical criticism, into three. The *Hesperides* (they are dated 1648, and the *Noble Numbers* or sacred poems 1647; but both appeared together) consist in the first place of occasional poems, sometimes amatory, sometimes not; in the second, of personal epigrams. Of this second class no human being who has any faculty of criticism can say any good. They are supposed by tradition to have been composed on parishioners: they may be hoped by charity (which has in this case the support of literary criticism) to be merely literary exercises—bad imitations of Martial, through Ben Jonson. They are nastier than the nastiest work of Swift; they are stupider than the stupidest attempts of Davies of Hereford; they are

farther from the author's best than the worst parts of Young's *Odes* are from the best part of the *Night Thoughts*. It is impossible without producing specimens (which God forbid that any one who has a respect for Herrick, for literature, and for decency, should do) to show how bad they are. Let it only be said that if the worst epigram of Martial were stripped of Martial's wit, sense, and literary form, it would be a kind of example of Herrick in this vein. In his two other veins, but for certain tricks of speech, it is almost impossible to recognise him for the same man. The secular vigour of the *Hesperides*, the spiritual vigour of the *Noble Numbers*, has rarely been equalled and never surpassed by any other writer.—GEORGE SAINTSBURY, *A History of Elizabethan Literature*, 1887, p. 355

Herrick the inexhaustible in dainties; Herrick, that parson-pagan, with the soul of a Greek of the Anthology, and a cure of souls (Heaven help them!) in Devonshire. His Julia is the least mortal of these "daughters of dreams and of stories," whom poets celebrate; she has a certain opulence of flesh and blood, a cheek like a damask rose, and "rich eyes," like Keats' lady; no vaporous Beatrice, she; but a handsome English wench, with

> A cuff neglectful and thereby
> Ribbons to flow confusedly;
> A winning wave, deserving note
> In the tempestuous petticoat.
> —ANDREW LANG, *Letters on Literature*, 1889, p. 149

There were those critics and admirers who saw in Herrick an allegiance to the methods of Catullus; others who smacked in his epigrams the verbal felicities of Martial; but surely there is no need, in that fresh spontaneity of the Devon poet, to hunt for classic parallels, nature made him one of her own singers, and by instincts born with him he fashioned words and fancies into jewelled shapes. The "more's the pity" for those gross indelicacies which smirch so many pages; things unreadable, things which should have been unthinkable and unwritable by a clergyman of the Church of England.—DONALD G. MITCHELL, *English Lands, Letters, and Kings: From Elizabeth to Anne*, 1890, p. 125

In Herrick the air is fragrant with new-mown hay; there is a morning light upon all things; long shadows streak the grass, and on the eglantine swinging in the hedge the dew lies white and brilliant. Out of the happy distance comes a shrill and silvery sound of whetting scythes; and from the near brook-side rings the laughter of merry maids in circle to make cowslipballs and babble of their bachelors. As you walk you are conscious of 'the grace that morning meadows wear,' and mayhap you meet Amaryllis going home to the farm with an apronful of flowers. Rounded is she and buxom, cool-cheeked and vigorous and trim, smelling of rosemary and thyme, with an appetite for curds and cream and a tongue of 'cleanly wantonness.' For her singer has an eye in his head, and exquisite as are his fancies he dwells in no land of shadows. The more clearly he sees a thing the better he sings it; and provided that he do see it nothing is beneath the caress of his muse. The bays and rosemary that wreath the hall at Yule, the log itself, the Candlemas box, the hock-cart and the maypole, nay,

> See'st thou that cloud as silver clear,
> Plump, soft, and swelling everywhere?
> 'Tis Julia's bed!—

And not only does he listen to the 'clecking' of his hen and know what it means: he knows too that the egg she has laid is long and white; so that ere he enclose it in his verse, you can see him take it in his hand, and look at it with a sort of boyish wonder and delight. This freshness of spirit, this charming and innocent curiosity, he carries into all he does. He can turn a sugared compliment with the best, but when Amaryllis passes him by he is yet so eager and unsophisticate that he can note that 'winning wave in the tempestuous petticoat' which has rippled to such good purpose through so many graceful speeches since. So that though Julia and Dianeme and Anthea have passed away, though Corinna herself is merely 'a fable, song, a fleeting shade,' he has saved enough of them from the ravin of Time for us to love and be grateful for eternally. Their gracious ghosts abide in a peculiar nook of the Elysium of Poesy. There 'in their habit as they lived' they dance in round, they fill their laps with flowers, they frolic and junket sweetly, they go for ever maying. Soft winds blow round them, and in their clear young voices they sing the verse of the rare artist who called them from the multitude and set them for ever where they are.

And Amaryllis herself will not, mayhap, be found so fair as those younglings of the year she bears with her in 'wicker ark' or 'lawny continent.' Herrick is pre-eminently the poet of flowers. He alone were capable of bringing back

Le bouquet d'Ophélie
De la rive inconnue où les flots l'ont laissé.

He knows and loves the dear blossoms all. He considers them with tender and shining eyes, he calls them his sweetest fancies and his fondest metaphors. Their idea is inseparable from that of his girls themselves, and it is by the means of the one set of mistresses that he is able so well to understand the other. The flowers are maids to him, and the maids are flowers. In an ecstasy of tender contemplation he turns from those to these, exampling Julia from the rose and pitying the hapless violets as though they were indeed not blooms insensitive but actually 'poor girls neglected.' His pages breathe their clean and innocent perfumes, and are beautiful with the chaste beauty of their colour, just as they carry with them something of the sweetness and simplicity of maidenhood itself. And from both he extracts the same pathetic little moral: both are lovely and both must die. And so, between his virgins that are for love indeed and those that sit silent and delicious in the 'flowery nunnery,' the old singer finds life so good a thing that he dreads to lose it, and not all his piety can remove the passionate regret with which he sees things hastening to their end.

That piety is equally removed from the erotic mysticism of Richard Crashaw and from the adoration, chastened and awful and pure, of Cowper. To find an analogue, you have to cross the borders of English into Spain. In his *Noble Numbers* Herrick shows himself to be a near kinsman of such men as Valdivielso, Ocaña, Lope de Ubeda; and there are versicles of his that in their homely mixture of the sacred and the profane, in their reverent familiarity with things divine, their pious and simple gallantry, may well be likened to the graceful and charming romances and villancicos of these strangers. Their spirit is less Protestant than Catholic, and is hardly English at all, so that it is scarce to be wondered at if they have remained unpopular. But their sincerity and earnestness are as far beyond doubt as their grace of line and inimitable daintiness of surface.—WILLIAM ERNEST HENLEY, "Herrick," *Views and Reviews*, 1890

Not Shakespeare himself had more confidence in the immortality of his verse than Robert Herrick. He was well content to let 'his poetry' be 'his pillar.'

Behold this living stone
I rear for me,
Ne'er to be thrown
Down, envious Time, by thee.

Pillars let some set up,
If so they please:
Here is my hope
And my Pyramides.

He is constantly giving expression to this comfortable attitude; not even 'The Nipples of Julia's Breast'—each as 'a strawberry, half-drown'd in cream'—or her 'tempestuous petticoat,' are more frequent themes. 'To his Book,' 'To his Muse,' are constantly recurring titles, bearing witness to that more than maternal delight which every devoted artist finds in his work. True, that when Charles I. gave him the living of Dean Prior, in Devonshire, he wrote: 'Mr. Robert Herick: his farewell unto Poetrie,' and bade a no less bitter 'Farewell to Sack,' probably at the same time, yet we all know when the poet is sick, how the poet (like another personage) a saint will be; and Herrick loved both sack and poetry too well to really forsake them. No doubt he was far more glad than sorry to be ejected from his living in 1648—on the charge of disloyalty—and be once more free to join his chums in merry London, for it goes without saying that he was hail-fellow with all who loved a song and a glass—and a petticoat. Not that Herrick never wrote what we somewhat absurdly distinguish as serious verse. His poem, 'To his Dying Brother, Master William Herrick,' shows that he knew the tragic as well as the pathetic note of life—though there was probably little of tragic feeling in the comfortable relationship of the two brothers. A poet always thus outsoars his theme:

Life of my life, take not so soon thy flight,
But stay the time till we have bade good-night.
Thou hast both wind and tide with thee; thy way
As soon despatch'd is by the night as day. . . .
There's pain in parting, and a kind of hell,
When once true lovers take their last farewell.

And in regard to pathos, is it not really that tender, tearful quality that has made famous the best known of Herrick's verse—the Horatian sigh for youth going and gone, for the beauty that is so fair, and yet so soon past? His cry is continually 'To the Virgins, to make much of Time,' to the daffodils to

Stay, stay,
Until the hasting day
Has run
But to the evensong.

The passing of the glory of the world is continually filling his eyes with tears, which overflow in pearls that drop within his book. There are people—surely they must have lived in a monastery or a vacuum—who are always puzzled that the men who do these exquisite things in poetry should be sensuous, let us say sensual, in their lives; but apart from the many-sidedness of man, it is surely the sensuous man alone who is capable of these rich tearful moments. One must have lived to have lost, and Herrick lived as generously as Solomon, and his poems are a sort of Restoration Ecclesiastes, with less of the whine and a kinder heart. Yet his *Noble Numbers*, or his *Pious Pieces*, though at first they strike one somewhat ludicrously as coming from him, are no mere 'making it right' with the powers above—they are the result of the real religious devotion which was at the bottom of Herrick's, as of every other poet's, heart.— RICHARD LE GALLIENNE, "Robert Herrick" (1891), *Retrospective Reviews*, 1896, pp. 1–3

Herrick is distinctively a poet from whom to receive pleasure. He is not necessarily to be studied; he is to be enjoyed. Doubtless many who love his verses will be led on by an honorable curiosity to desire to know this and that concerning the man and his work. But the poetic enjoyment is the main thing.

Herrick is a very individual poet. He has something about him which lifts him out of the crowd of Jacobean and Caroline lyrists, such as Carew and Suckling, nor do we think of him as on precisely the same level as his predecessors the Elizabethans. His poems have a certain air of distinction. Many of them are trivial enough, doubtless, but they are never quite commonplace.—EDWARD EVERETT HALE, JR., "Introduction" to *Selections from the Poetry of Robert Herrick*, 1895, p. lxiii

Herrick is indeed the last expression of the pagan Renaissance, prolonged into the quiddities of the metaphysics, the self-reproaches of the mystics and the devotees, and the darkness of Puritanism. Herrick rises to no spiritual heights nor does he sink into spiritual glooms. He is frankly for this world while it lasts, piously content with its good gifts. His naïveté is partly art, partly nature, or rather it is nature refined by art; for he is out and out an artist—the most perfect specimen of the minor poet that England has ever known. He is purely a lyrist, and in his own vein he is really unsurpassed, whether in the English lyric or any other.—FREDERIC IVES CARPENTER, "Introduction" to *English Lyric Poetry, 1500–1700*, 1897, p. liii

Our own age has awarded the foremost place among Caroline lyrical poets to Robert Herrick, whose verses, after having been unaccountably neglected throughout the eighteenth century, are now represented in all selections of English poetry. . . . "Corinna going a-Maying," perhaps the best known of all Herrick's country poems, is one of the most perfect studies of idealized village life in the language.—J. HOWARD B. MASTERMAN, *The Age of Milton*, 1897, pp. 101–5

Works

HESPERIDES

I sing of *Brooks*, of *Blossomes*, *Birds*, and *Bowers*:
Of *April*, *May*, of *June*, and *July*-Flowers.
I sing of *May-poles*, *Hock-carts*, *Wassails*, *Wakes*,
Of *Bride-grooms*, *Brides*, and of their *Bridall-cakes*.
I write of *Youth*, of *Love*, and have Accesse
By these, to sing of cleanly-*Wantonnesse*.
I sing of *Dewes*, of *Raines*, and piece by piece
Of *Balme*, of *Oyle*, of *Spice*, and *Amber-Greece*.
I sing of *Times trans-shifting*; and I write
How *Roses* first came *Red*, and *Lillies White*.
I write of *Groves*, of *Twilights*, and I sing
The Court of *Mab*, and of the *Fairie-King*.
I write of *Hell*; I sing (and ever shall)
Of *Heaven*, and hope to have it after all.
　　—ROBERT HERRICK, "The Argument of his Book," *Hesperides*, 1648

Ships lately from the islands came,
With wines, thou never heard'st by name.
Montefiasco, Frontiniac,
Vernaccio, and that old sack
Young Herric took to entertaine
The muses in a sprightly vein.
　　—UNSIGNED, "To Parson Weeks, an Invitation to London," *Musarum Deliciae*, 1656

An then *Flaccus Horace*,
　He was but a sowr-ass,
And good for nothing but *Lyricks*,
　There's but One to be found
　In all English ground
Writes as well;—who is hight Robert Herick.
　　—UNSIGNED, *Naps upon Parnassus*, 1658

Herrick published his poems at an age when youth and inexperience could not be urged in extenuation of the blemishes which they presented. The author was fifty-seven years old when the *Hesperides* issued from the press, replete with beauties and excellencies, and at the same time abounding in passages of outrageous grossness. The title was perhaps rather apt to mislead, for besides golden apples, this garden assuredly contained many rank tares and poisonous roots. It would scarcely suffice to plead the freedom and breadth of speech customary among all classes and with both sexes at that period. Some share of the blame must, beyond question, be laid to Herrick's voluptuousness of temperament, and not very cleanly ardour of imagination; yet, after all deductions which it is possible to make, what a noble salvage remains! Enough beauty, wit, nay piety, to convert even the prudish to an admiration of the genius which shines transparent through all.—WILLIAM CAREW HAZLITT, "Preface" to *Hesperides*, 1869, Vol. 1, p. viii

The *Hesperides* is so rich in jewelry, that the most careless selection can hardly be unsatisfactory. Yet being so rich, there might have been more independent taste. One is led to ask how much of popular favouritism even in literature is, like fashion in clothes, due to dictation of the purveyors.—W.J. LINTON, *Rare Poems of the Sixteenth and Seventeenth Centuries*, 1882, p. 242

In the quiet of his parsonage, the music of his life found utterance in every mood. His whole mind expressed itself, animal and spiritual. In the texture of his book he evidently meant to show the warp and woof of life. He aimed at effects of contrast that belonged to the true nature of man, in whom, as in the world at large, "the strawberry grows underneath the nettle," and side by side with promptings of the flesh, spring up the aspirations of the spirit. Even the dainty fairy pieces written under influence of the same fashion that caused Shakespeare to describe Queen Mab and Drayton to write his Nymphidia, even such pieces of his, written in earlier days, Herrick sprinkled about his volume in fragments. He would not make his nosegay with the flowers of each sort bunched together in so many lumps. There is truth in the close contact of a playful sense of ugliness with the most delicate perception of all forms of beauty. Herrick's "epigrams", on running eyes and rotten teeth, and the like, are such exaggerations as may often have tumbled out spontaneously, in the course of playful talk, and if they pleased him well enough were duly entered in his book. In a healthy mind, this whimsical sense of deformity may be but the other side of a fine sense of beauty.—HENRY MORLEY, "Introduction" to *Hesperides*, 1884, p. 7

That the *Hesperides* is the most typical single book of the class and kind there can be little doubt, though there may be higher and rarer touches in others. Its bulk, its general excellence in its own kind, make it exhibit the combined influences of Donne and Jonson (which, as was pointed out earlier, tell upon, and to some extent account for, this lyrical outburst) better than any other single volume. And long as Herrick had to wait for his public (it must be confessed that, though the times do not seem to have in the least chained the poet's tongue, they did much to block his hearers' ears), there is now not much difference of opinion in general points, however much there may be in particulars, about the poetical value of "The Mad Maid's Song" and "To Daffodils," of the "Night Piece to Julia" and "To the Virgins," of the "Litany" and "The White Island." Yet this book is only the most popular and coherent collection among an immense mass of verse, all informed by the most singular and attractive quality.—GEORGE SAINTSBURY, *Social England*, 1895, Vol. 4, ed. Traill, p. 300

NOBLE NUMBERS

Herrick's sacred poems . . . have often much merit. We cannot doubt their sincerity. But they are mostly strained, and show Herrick ill at ease. They are strangely disfigured with conceits, and the best of them are half secular.—T. ASHE, "Robert Herrick," *Temple Bar*, May 1883, p. 132

Of the religious poems the already-mentioned "Litany," while much the most familiar, is also far the best. There is nothing in English verse to equal it as an expression of religious fear; while there is also nothing in English verse to equal the "Thanksgiving," also well known, as an expression of religious trust.—GEORGE SAINTSBURY, *A History of Elizabethan Literature*, 1887, p. 356

The religious pieces grouped under the title of *Noble Numbers* distinctly associate themselves with Dean Prior, and have little other interest. Very few of them are "born of the royal blood." They lack the inspiration and magic of his secular poetry, and are frequently so fantastical and grotesque as to stir a suspicion touching the absolute soundness of Herrick's mind at all times. The lines in which the Supreme Being is assured that he may read Herrick's poems without taking any tincture from their sinfulness might have been written in a retreat for the unbalanced.—THOMAS BAILEY ALDRICH, "Introduction" to *Poems of Robert Herrick*, 1900, p. xxv

---

EDMUND GOSSE
"Robert Herrick" (1875)
Seventeenth Century Studies
1883, pp. 125–56

It is told of Mahommed that when the political economists of the day provoked him by the narrowness of their utilitarian schemes, he was wont to silence them with these words: "If a man has two loaves of bread, let him exchange one for some flowers of the narcissus; for bread only nourishes the body, but to look on the narcissus feeds the soul." Robert Herrick was one of the few who have been content to carry out this precept, and to walk through life with a little bread in the one hand, and in the other a bunch of golden flowers. With an old serving-woman in a tumble-down country parsonage, his life passed merrily among such dreams as Oriental sultans wear themselves out to realise, and his figure stands out in front of the shining ranks of his contemporaries as that around which most vividly of all there flashes the peculiar light of imagination. He may be well contrasted with a man whose native genius was probably exceedingly like his own, but whose life was as brilliant and eventful as Herrick's was retired, namely, Sir John Suckling. The wit, fire, and exuberant imagination that interpenetrated both found scope in the life of one and in the works of the other. Suckling's poems are strangely inadequate to represent his genius and fame; Herrick, on the other hand, may be taken almost as the typical poet, the man who, if not a lyrist, would be nothing—the birdlike creature whose only function was to sing in a cage of trammelling flesh.

There are many features in his career, besides the actual excellence of his verse, which make him an object of peculiar interest. Among the pure poets he occupies the most prominent position in the school that flourished after Ben Jonson and before Milton, and though his life was of immense duration—

he was born before Marlowe died, and died after the birth of Addison—his actual period of production covers the comparatively small space occupied by the reign of Charles I. This period was one of great lyrical ability; the drama was declining under Cartwright and Shirley, and all the young generation of poets, brought up at the feet of Jonson and Fletcher, were much more capable of writing songs than plays. Indeed, no one can at this time determine what degree of technical perfection English literature might not have attained if the Royalist lyrists had been allowed to sun themselves unmolested about the fountains of Whitehall, and, untroubled by the grave questions of national welfare, had been able to give their whole attention to the polishing of their verses. In fact, however, it will be noticed that only one of the whole school was undisturbed by the political crisis. The weaker ones, like Lovelace, were completely broken by it; the stronger, like Suckling, threw themselves into public affairs with a zeal and intensity that supplied the place of the artificial excitements of poetry so completely as to put a stop to their writing altogether. Herrick alone, with imperturbable serenity, continued to pipe out his pastoral ditties, and crown his head with daffodils, when England was torn to pieces with the most momentous struggle for liberty in her annals. To the poetic student he is, therefore, of especial interest, as a genuine specimen of an artist pure and simple. Herrick brought out the *Hesperides* a few months before the King was beheaded, and people were invited to listen to little madrigals upon Julia's stomacher at the singularly inopportune moment when the eyes of the whole nation were bent on the unprecedented phenomenon of the proclamation of an English republic. To find a parallel to such unconsciousness we must come down to our own time, and recollect that Théophile Gautier took occasion of the siege of Paris to revise and republish his *Emaux et Camées*.

Herrick was born in London, in "the golden Cheapside," and bapized on the 23rd of August 1591. His father died in the course of the next year, from a fall from an upper window, which was attributed to suicide. All we can guess about the poet's childhood is to be picked up in one of his own confidential pieces about himself, where he speaks with intense delight of his early life by the river-side, going to bathe in the "summer's sweeter evenings" with crowds of other youths, or gliding with pomp in a barge, with the young ladies of the period, "soft-smooth virgins," up as far as Richmond, Kingston, and Hampton Court. In the same poem he speaks of his "beloved Westminster," from which allusion it has been illogically imagined that he was at school there. The first certain fact in his life is that in 1607 he was apprenticed to his uncle, the rich goldsmith of Wood Street, with whom one may presume that he remained until 1615, when we find him entered as fellowcommoner of St. John's College, Cambridge. His London life, therefore, closed when his age was twenty-four, and his acquaintance with literary life in the metropolis must have come to rapid development within the eight years of his apprenticeship. Speculation in this case is not so vain as usual. If any fact about Herrick be certain, it is that he sat at the feet of Ben Jonson; the poems of rapturous admiration and reverence that abound in the *Hesperides* set this beyond question. In one piece, it will be remembered, he speaks, with passion unusual to him, of the old days when Ben Jonson's plays were brought out at the London theatres, and gives us an important date by describing the unfavourable reception of the *Alchemist*, much as a poet of the Romanticism would have described the reception of *Hernani* for the first time at the Théâtre *Français*. But the *Alchemist* was brought out in 1610, when our poet was nineteen years old, and it was received with great excitement as an innovation. We may well believe that the young apprentice, fired with enthusiasm for the great poet, distinguished himself by the loudness and truculence of his applause, and claimed the privilege of laying his homage afterwards at the author's feet. Nineteen years later exactly the same thing was done by a younger generation, when Carew, Randolph, and Cleaveland made a riot at the damning of the *New Inn*, and then laid their lyric worship at the grand old poet's feet.

Jonson loved to receive such homage, and to pose as the poet of the age; in fact, we cannot be too often reminded that to the intellectual public of that day he took exactly the same regal position among his contemporaries that we now unanimously accord to Shakespeare. Taking for granted that Herrick became a familiar member of Jonson's circle about 1610, we must suppose him to have witnessed in succession the first performances of *Catiline* and of *Bartholomew Fair*, and to have known the poet of the "mountain belly and the rocky face" at the very height of his creative power. More important for us, however, as being far more in unison with the tastes and genius of Herrick, are the masques upon which Jonson was engaged at this time. It is very strange that no writer upon the poetry of that age has noticed what an extraordinary influence the masques of Ben Jonson had upon Herrick. We have seen that he must have become acquainted with that poet in 1610. It is more than remarkable to notice that it was in this year that Jonson produced *Oberon the Fairy Prince*, a beautiful masque that contains the germs of many of Herrick's most fantastic fairy-fancies. *The Masque of Queens*, brought out some months earlier, is full of Herrick-like passages about hags and witches; and we might pursue the parallel much further, did space permit, showing how largely Jonson, on the milder and more lyrical side of his genius, inspired the young enthusiast and pointed out to him the poetic path that he should take.

We cannot with equal certainty say that Herrick was acquainted with any other of the great poets. Shakespeare was settled at Stratford, and in London only briefly and at distant intervals; he died at the end of Herrick's first year at Cambridge. Herrick writes of Fletcher thirty years later as though he had known him slightly, and speaks of the power of the *Maid's Tragedy* to make "young men swoon," as though he had seen it at the first performance in 1611. He must have known Jonson's jolly friend Bishop Corbet, who was also a lover of fairy-lore, and he may have known Browne, whose poetry Jonson approved of, and who was then studying in the Inner Temple, and beginning to publish *Britannia's Pastorals*. It was probably at this time, and through Ben Jonson, that he became acquainted with Selden, for whose prodigious learning and wit he preserved an extravagant admiration through life. This is as far as we dare to go in speculation. If Herrick, so fond of writing about himself, had found time for a few more words about his contemporaries, we might discover that he had dealings with other interesting men during this period of apprenticeship, but probably his circle was pretty much limited to the personal and intimate friends of Jonson.

In 1615, as we have said, he took up his abode at Cambridge as a fellow-commoner of St. John's, and here and at Trinity Hall he seems to have remained till 1629, when his mother died. How these fourteen years of early manhood were spent it is now impossible to conjecture. That he became Master of Arts in 1620 is not so important an item of history as that he was certainly very poor, and in the habit of making a piteous annual appeal to his rich uncle for ten pounds to buy books with. Fourteen of these appeals exist, written in a florid, excited style, with a good many Latin quotations and old-fashioned references to "Apelles ye painter," in the manner of *Euphues*. It

is amusing to note that he manages to spell his own surname in six different ways, and not one of them that which is now adopted on the authority of the title-page of the *Hesperides*. There can be no doubt that he began writing in London; it is certain that he was known as a poet at Cambridge. One of the few dates in the *Hesperides* in 1627, two years before the exodus into Devonshire, and in "Lacrime" he says that before he went into exile into the loathed west

> He could rehearse
> A lyric verse,
> And speak it with the best.

The *Hesperides*, in its present state, offers no assistance to us in trying to discover what was written early or late, for nothing is more obvious than that the verses were thrown together without the slightest regard to the chronology of their composition. However, on the 2nd of October 1629, he succeeded Potter, Bishop of Carlisle, in the living of Dean Prior, under Dartmoor, in South Devon, and there he remained in quiet retirement until 1648, when he was ejected by the Puritans.

Such is the modest biography of this poet up to the time of the publication of the two books which caused and have retained his great reputation. Fortunately he has himself left copious materials for autobiography in the gossipy pages of his own confidential poems. Glancing down the index to the *Hesperides*, one is constantly struck by such titles as "On Himself," "To His Muse," and "His Farewell to Sack," and one is not disappointed in turning to these to collect an impression of the author's individuality. Indeed, few writers of that age appear more vividly in relief than Herrick; the careful student of his poems learns to know him at last as a familiar friend, and every feature of body and mind stands out clearly before the eye of the imagination. He was physically a somewhat gross person, as far as his portrait will enable one to judge, with great quantities of waving or curling black hair, and a slight black moustache; the eyebrows distinct and well arched, the upper lip short, the nose massive and Roman. In the weighty points of the face, especially in the square and massive under-jaw, there is much of the voluptuous force of the best type among the Roman emperors; and bearing these features well in mind, it becomes easy to understand how it was that Herrick came to write so much that an English gentleman, not to say clergyman, had better have left unsaid. His temperament was scarcely clerical:—

> I fear no earthly powers,
> But care for crowns of flowers;
> And love to have my beard
> With wine and oil besmeared.
> This day I'll drown all sorrow;
> Who knows to live to-morrow?

This was his philosophy, and it is not to be distinguished from that of Anacreon or Horace. One knows not how the old pagan dared to be so outspoken in his dreary Devonshire vicarage, with no wild friends to egg him on or to applaud his fine frenzy.

His Epicureanism was plainly a matter of conviction, and though he wrote *Noble Numbers*, preached sermons, and went through all the perfunctory duties of his office, it is not in these that he lives and has his pleasure, but in half-classical dreams about Favonius and Isis, and in flowery mazes of sweet thoughts about fair, half-imaginary women. It matters little to him what divinity he worships, if he may wind daffodils into the god's bright hair. In one hand he brings a garland of yellow flowers for the amorous head of Bacchus, with the other he decks the osier-cradle of Jesus with roses and Lent-lilies. He has no sense of irreverence in this rococo devotion. It is the attribute, and not the deity he worships. There is an airy frivolity, an easy-going callousness of soul, that makes it impossible for him to feel very deeply.

There is a total want of passion in Herrick's language about women. The nearest approach to it, perhaps, is in the wonderful song "To Anthea," where the lark-like freshness of the ascending melody closely simulates intense emotion. With all his warmth of fancy and luxurious animalism, he thinks more of the pretty eccentricities of dress than of the charms the garments contain. He is enraptured with the way in which the Countess of Carlisle wears a riband of black silk twisted round her arm; he palpitates with pleasure when Mistress Katherine Bradshaw puts a crown of laurel on his head, falling on one knee, we may believe, and clasping his hands as he receives it. He sees his loves through the medium of shoe-strings and pomander bracelets, and is alive, as no poet has been before or since, to the picturesqueness of dress. Everybody knows his exquisite lines about the "tempestuous petticoat," and his poems are full of little touches no less delicate than this.

Only two things make him really serious: one is his desire of poetic fame. Every lyric he writes he considers valuable enough to be left as a special legacy to some prime friend. He is eager to die before the world; to pass away, like Pindar, garlanded, and clasped in the arms of love, while the theatre resounds with plaudits. His thirst for fame is insatiable, and his confidence of gaining it intense. His poesy is "his hope and his pyramides," a living pillar "ne'er to be thrown down by envious Time," and it shall be the honour of great musicians to set his pieces to music when he is dead. When he is dead! That has a saddening sound! Life was meant to last for ever, and it makes him angry to think of death. He rings his head about with roses, clasps Julia to his arms, and will defy death. Yet, if death should come, as he sometimes feels it must, he is not unmindful of what his end should be. No thoughts of a sad funeral or the effrontery of a Christian burial oppress him; he cannot even think of dismal plumes or of a hearse. He will be wound in one white robe, and borne to a quiet garden-corner, where the overblown roses may shower petals on his head, and where, when the first primrose blossoms, Perilla may remember him, and come to weep over his dust:—

> Then shall my ghost not walk about, but keep
> Still in the cool and silent shades of sleep.

He was never married; he explains over and over again that he values his liberty far too highly to give it into any woman's hands, and lived in the country, as it would seem, with no company save that of an excellent old servant, Prudence Baldwin.

In many sweet and sincere verses he gives us a charming picture of the quiet life he led in the Devonshire parsonage that he affected to loathe so much. The village had its rural and semi-pagan customs, that pleased him thoroughly. He loved to see the brown lads and lovely girls, crowned with daffodils and daisies, dancing in the summer evenings in a comely country round; he delighted in the maypole, ribanded and garlanded like a thyrsus, reminding his florid fancy of Bacchus and the garden god. There were morris dances at Dean Prior, wakes and quintels; mummers, too, at Christmas, and quaint revellings on Twelfth Night, with wassail bowls and nut-brown mirth; and we can imagine with what zeal the good old pagan would encourage these rites against the objections of any roundhead Puritan who might come down with his newfangled Methodistical notions to trouble the sylvan quiet of Dean Prior. For Herrick the dignity of episcopal authorship had no charm, and the thunders of Nonconformity no terror. Graver minds were at this moment occupied with *Holy Living and Holy Dying*, and thrilled with the Sermons of Calamy. It is delightful to think of Herrick, blissfully unconscious of the tumult of tongues and all the windy war, more occupied with morris dances and barley-breaks than with prayer-book or psalter. The Revolution must indeed have come upon him unaware.

Herrick allowed himself to write a great deal of nonsense about his many mistresses. It was the false Anacreontic spirit of the day; and a worse offender was in the field, even Abraham Cowley, who, never having had the courage to speak of love to a single woman, was about to publish, in 1648, a circumstantial account of his affairs with more than one-and-twenty mistresses. It is not easy to determine how much of Herrick's gallantry is as imaginary as this. We may dismiss Perilla, Silvia, Anthea, and the rest at once, as airy nothings, whom the poet created for the sake of hanging pretty amorous fancies on their names; but Julia is not so ephemeral or so easily disposed of. She may well be supposed to have died or passed away before Herrick left Cambridge. All the poet's commentators seem to have forgotten how old he was before he retired to that country vicarage where they rightly enough perceive that the presence of a Julia was impossible. When we recollect that he did not enter holy orders till he was thirty-eight, we may well believe that Julia ruled his youth, and yet admit his distinct statement with regard to his clerical life, that

> Jocund his muse was, but his life was chaste.

We have a minute chronicle of Julia's looks and ways in the *Hesperides*, and they bear a remarkable air of truth about them. She is presented to us as a buxom person, with black eyes, a double chin, and a strawberry-cream complexion. Her attire, as described by our milliner-poet, is in strict accordance with the natural tastes of a woman of this physical nature. She delights in rich silks and deep-coloured satins; on one occasion she wears a dark blue petticoat, starred with gold, on other she ravishes her poet-lover by the glitter and vibration of her silks as she takes her stately walks abroad. Her hair, despite her dark eyes, is bright and dewy, and the poet takes a fantastic pleasure in tiring and braiding it. An easy, kindly woman, we picture her ready to submit to the fancies of her lyric lover; pleased to have roses on her head, still more pleased to perfume herself with storax, spikenard, galbanum, and all the other rich gums he loved to smell; dowered with so much refinement of mind as was required to play fairly on the lute, and to govern a wayward poet with tact; not so modest or so sensitive as to resent the grossness of his fancy, yet respectable enough and determined enough to curb his license at times. She bore him one daughter, it seems, to whom he addressed one of his latest poems and one of his tamest.

But it is time to turn from the poet to his work, from Julia to the *Hesperides* that she inspired. They are songs, children of the West, brought forth, if not conceived, in the soft, sweet air of Devonshire. And the poet strikes a keynote with wonderful sureness in the opening couplets of the opening poem:—

> I sing of brooks, of blossoms, birds and bowers,
> Of April, May, of June and July flowers;
> I sing of maypoles, hock-carts, wassails, wakes,
> Of bridegrooms, brides, and of their bridal-cakes.

It would not have been easy to describe more correctly what he does sing of. The book is full of all those pleasant things of spring and summer, full of young love, happy nature, and the joy of mere existence. As far as flowers are concerned, the atmosphere is full of them. We are pelted with roses and daffodils from every page, and no one dares enter the sacred precincts without a crown of blossoms on his hair. Herrick's muse might be that Venus of Botticelli who rises, pale and dewy, from a sparkling sea, blown at by the little laughing winds, and showered upon with violets and lilies of no earthly growth. He tells us that for years and years his muse was content to stay at home, or straying from village to village, to pipe to handsome young shepherds and girls of flower-sweet breath, but that at last she became ambitious to try her skill at Court, and so came into print in London. In other words, these little poems circulated widely in manuscript long before they were published. They are not all of the bird and blossom kind, unhappily; the book is fashioned, as we shall presently see, closely upon the model of the *Epigrams* of Martial; and as there the most delicate and jewel-like piece of sentiment rubs shoulders with a coarse and acrid quatrain of satire, so has Herrick shuffled up odes, epithalamia, epigrams, occasional verses and canzonets, in glorious confusion, without the slightest regard to subject, form, or propriety. There are no less than one thousand two hundred and thirty-one distinct poems in the book, many of them, of course, only two lines long. There are too many "epigrams," as he called them, scraps of impersonal satire, in the composition of which he followed Ben Jonson, who had followed Martial. These little couplets and quatrains are generally very gross, very ugly, and very pointless; they have, sometimes, a kind of broad Pantagruelist humour about them which has its merit, but it must be confessed even of these that they greatly spoil the general complexion of the book.

More worthy of attention in every way are the erotic lyrical pieces, which fortunately abound, and which are unrivalled in our literature for their freshness and tender beauty. They are interpenetrated with strong neo-pagan emotion; had they been written a century earlier, they would be called the truest English expression of the passion of the Renaissance. This is, however, what they really are. Late in the day as they made their appearance, they were as truly an expression of the delirious return to the freedom of classical life and enjoyment as the Italian paintings of the fifteenth or the French poetry of the sixteenth century. The tone of the best things in the *Hesperides* is precisely the same as that which permeates the wonderful designs of the *Hypnerotomachia*. In Herrick's poems, as in that mysterious and beautiful romance, the sun shines on a world re-arisen to the duty of pleasure; Bacchus rides through the valleys, with his leopards and his maidens and his ivy-rods; loose-draped nymphs, playing on the lyre, bound about their foreheads with vervain and the cool stalks of parsley, fill the silent woods with their melodies and dances; this poet sings of a land where all the men are young and strong, and all the women lovely, where life is only a dream of sweet delights of the bodily senses. The *Hesperides* is an astounding production when one considers when it was written, and how intensely grave the temper of the age had become. But Herrick hated sobriety and gravity, and distinguished very keenly between the earnestness of art and the austerity of religion. Here he lays down his own canons:—

> In sober mornings, do not thou rehearse
> The holy incantation of a verse;
> But when that men have both well drunk and fed,
> Let my enchantments then be sung or read.
> When laurel spirts in the fire, and when the hearth
> Smiles to itself, and gilds the roof with mirth,
> When up the thyrse is raised, and when the sound
> Of sacred orgies flies around, around,
> When the rose reigns, and locks with ointment
>   shine,
> Let rigid Cato read these lines of mine.

At such moments as these Herrick is inspired above a mortal pitch, and listens to the great lyre of Apollo with the rapture of a prophet. From a very interesting poem, called "The Apparition of his Mistress calling him to Elysium," we quote a few lines that exemplify at the same moment his most ideal condition of fancy and the habitual oddities of his style. This is the landscape of the Hesperides, the golden isles of Herrick's imagination:—

> Here in green meadows sits eternal May,
> Purpling the margents, while perpetual day
> So doubly gilds the air, as that no night
> Can ever rust the enamel of the light.
> Here naked younglings, handsome striplings, run
> Their goals for maidens' kisses, which when done,
> Then unto dancing forth the learned round
> Commixt they meet, with endless roses crowned;
> And here we'll sit on primrose-banks, and see
> Love's chorus led by Cupid.

But although he lived in this ideal scenery, he was not entirely unconscious of what actually lay around him. He was the earliest English poet to see the picturesqueness of homely country life, and all his little landscapes are exquisitely delicate. No one has ever known better than Herrick how to seize, without effort and yet to absolute perfection, the pretty points of modern pastoral life. Of all these poems of his, none surpasses "Corinna's going a-Maying," which has something of Wordsworth's faultless instinct and clear perception. The picture given here of the slim boys and the girls in green gowns going out singing into the corridors of blossoming whitethorn, when the morning sun is radiant in all its "fresh-quilted colours," is ravishing, and can only be compared for its peculiar charm with that other where the maidens are seen at sunset, with silvery naked feet and dishevelled hair crowned with honeysuckle, bearing cowslips home in wicker-baskets. Whoever will cast his eye over the pages of the *Hesperides*, will meet with myriads of original and charming passages of this kind:—

> Like to a solemn sober stream
> Bankt all with lilies, and the cream
> Of sweetest cowslips filling them,

the "cream of cowslips" being the rich yellow anthers of the water-lilies. Or this, comparing a bride's breath to the faint, sweet odour of the earth:—

> A savour like unto a blessed field,
>   When the bedabbled morn
> Washes the golden ears of corn.

Or this, a sketched interior:—

> Yet can thy humble roof maintain a choir
>   Of singing crickets by the fire,
> And the brisk mouse may feed herself with crumbs,
>   Till that the green-eyed kitling comes.

Nor did the homeliest details of the household escape him. At Dean Prior his clerical establishment consisted of Prudence Baldwin, his ancient maid, of a cock and hen, a goose, a tame lamb, a cat, a spaniel, and a pet pig, learned enough to drink out of a tankard; and not only did the genial vicar divide his loving attention between the various members of this happy family, but he was wont, a little wantonly, one fears, to gad about to wakes and wassailings and to increase his popular reputation by showing off his marvellous learning in old rites and ceremonies. These he has described with loving minuteness, and not these only, but even the little arts of cookery do not escape him. Of all his household poems, not one is more characteristic and complete than the "Bride-cake," which we remember having had recited to us years ago with immense gusto, at the making of a great pound-cake, by a friend since widely known as a charming follower of Herrick's poetic craft:—

> This day, my Julia, thou must make
> For Mistress Bride the wedding-cake:
> Knead but the dough, and it will be
> To paste of almonds turned by thee,
> Or kiss it, thou, but once or twice,
> And for the bride-cake there'll be spice.

There is one very curious omission in all his descriptions of nature, in that his landscapes are without background; he is photographically minute in giving us the features of the brook at our feet, the farmyard and its inmates, the open fireplace and the chimney corner, but there is no trace of anything beyond, and the beautiful distances of Devonshire, the rocky tors, the rugged line of Dartmoor, the glens in the hills—of all these there is not a trace. In this he contrasts curiously with his contemporary William Browne, another Devonshire poet, whose pictures are infinitely vaguer and poorer than Herrick's, but who has more distance, and who succeeds in giving a real notion of Devonian rock and moor, which Herrick never so much as suggests. In short, it may be said that Herrick made for himself an Arcadian world, in the centre of which the ordinary daily life of a country parish went contentedly on, surrounded by an imaginary land of pastoral peace and plenty, such as England can hardly have been then in the eyes of any other mortal, unless in those of the French poet St. Amant, who came over to the court at Whitehall just before the Rebellion broke out, while Herrick was piping at Dean Prior, and who on his return wrote a wonderfully fulsome ode to their serenest majesties Charles and Mary, in which he took precisely the same view of our island as Herrick did:—

> Oui, c'est ce pays bienheureux
> Qu'avec des regards amoureux
> Le reste du monde contemple;
> C'est cette île fameuse où tant d'aventuriers
> Et tant de beautés sans exemple
> Joignirent autrefois les myrtes aux lauriers!

St. Amant lived to alter his opinion, and hurl curses at the unconscious Albion; but to Herrick the change came too late, and when the sunshine ceased to warm him, he simply ceased to sing, as we shall see.

The personal epithalamium is a form of verse which had a very brief period of existence in England, and which has long been completely extinct. Its theme and manner gave too much opportunity to lavish adulation on the one hand, and unseemly innuendo on the other, to suit the preciser manners of our more reticent age; but it flourished for the brief period contained between 1600 and 1650, and produced some exquisite masterpieces. The *Epithalamion* and *Prothalamion* of Spenser struck the keynote of a fashion that Drayton, Ben Jonson, and others adorned, and of which Herrick was the last and far from the least ardent votary. His confidential muse was delighted at being asked in to arrange the ceremonies of a nuptial feast, and described the bride and her surroundings with a world of pretty extravagance. Every admirer of Herrick should read the "Nuptial Ode on Sir Clipseby Crew and his Lady." It is admirably fanciful, and put together with consummate skill. It opens with a choral outburst of greeting to the bride:—

> What's that we see from far? the spring of day
> Bloom'd from the east, or fair enjewelled May
> Blown out of April? or some new
> Star filled with glory to our view
> Reaching at Heaven,
> To add a nobler planet to the seven?

Less and less dazzled, he declares her to be some goddess floating out of Elysium in a cloud of tiffany. She leaves the church treading upon scarlet and amber, and spicing the chafed air with fumes of paradise. Then they watch her coming towards them down the shining street, whose very pavement breathes out spikenard. But who is this that meets her? Hymen, with his fair white feet, and head with marjoram crowned, who lifts his torch, and, behold, by his side the bridegroom stands, flushed and ardent. Then the maids shower them with shamrock and roses, and so the dreamy verses totter under their load of perfumed words, till they close with a benediction over the new-married couple, and a peal of maiden laughter over love and its flower-like mysteries.

Once more, before we turn to more general matters, there is one section of the *Hesperides* that demands a moment's attention—that, namely, devoted to descriptions of Fairyland and its inhabitants. We have seen that it was probably the performance of Ben Jonson's pretty masque of *Oberon* that set Herrick dreaming about that misty land where elves sit eating butterflies' horns round little mushroom tables, or quaff draughts

> Of pure seed-pearl of morning dew,
> Brought and besweetened in a blue
> And pregnant violet.

And with him the poetic literature of Fairyland ended. He was its last laureate, for the Puritans thought its rites, though so shadowy, superstitious, and frowned upon their celebration, while the whole temper of the Restoration, gross and dandified at the same time, was foreign to such pure play of the imagination. But some of the greatest names of the great period had entered its sacred bounds and sung its praises. Shakespeare had done it eternal honour in A *Midsummer-Night's Dream*, and Drayton had written an elaborate romance, *The Court of Faerie*. Jonson's friend Bishop Corbet had composed fairy ballads that had much of Herrick's lightness about them. It was these literary traditions that Herrick carried with him into the west; it does not seem that he collected any fresh information about the mushroom world in Devonshire; we read nothing of river-wraiths or pixies in his poems. He adds, however, a great deal of ingenious fancy to the stores he received from his elders; and his fairy-poems, all written in octosyllabic verse, as though forming parts of one projected work, may be read with great interest as a kind of final compendium of all that the poets of the seventeenth century imagined about fairies.

Appended to the *Hesperides*, but bearing date one year earlier, is a little book of poems, similar to these in outward form, but dealing with sacred subjects. Here our pagan priest is seen, despoiled of his vine-wreath and his thyrsus, doing penance in a white sheet and with a candle in his hand. That rubicund visage, with its sly eye and prodigious jowl, looks ludicrously out of place in the penitential surplice; but he is evidently sincere, though not very deep, in his repentance, and sings hymns of faultless orthodoxy, with a loud and lusty voice to the old pagan airs. Yet they are not inspiriting reading, save where they are least Christian; there is none of the religious passion of Crashaw, burning the weak heart away in a flame of adoration, none of the sweet and sober devotion of Herbert—nothing, indeed, from an ecclesiastical point of view, so good as the best of Vaughan, the Silurist. Where the *Noble Numbers* are most readable is where they are most secular. One sees the same spirit here as throughout the worldly poems. In a charming little "Ode to Jesus" he wishes the Saviour to be crowned with roses and daffodils, and laid in a neat white osier cradle; in "The Present," he will take a rose to Christ and, sticking it in His stomacher, beg for one mellifluous kiss. The epigrams of the earlier volume are replaced in the *Noble Numbers* by a series of couplets, attempting to define the nature of God, of which none equals in neatness this, which is the last:—

> Of all the good things whatsoe'er we do,
> God is the *Archē* and the *Telos* too.

As might be expected, his religion is as grossly anthropomorphic as it is possible to be. He almost surpasses in indiscretion those mediæval priests of Picardy who brought such waxen images to the Madonna's shrine as no altar had seen since pagan days; and certain verses on the circumcision are more revolting in their grossness than any of those erotic poems—

> unbaptized rhymes
> Writ in my wild unhallowed times—

for which he so ostentatiously demands absolution.

It is pleasant to turn from these to the three or four pieces that are in every way worthy of his genius. Of these, the tenderest is the "Thanksgiving," where he is delightfully confidential about his food, thus:—

> Lord, I confess, too, when I dine
> The pulse is Thine,
> And all those other bits that be
> Placed there by Thee,—
> The worts, the purslain, and the mess
> Of water-cress.
>
> . . .
>
> 'Tis Thou that crown'st my glittering hearth
> With guiltless mirth,
> And giv'st me wassail-bowls to drink,
> Spiced to the brink.

And about his house:—

> Like as my parlour, so my hall
> And kitchen's small,
> A little buttery, and therein
> A little bin.

The wild and spirited "Litany" is too well known to be quoted here, but there are two very fine odes in the *Noble Numbers* that are hardly so familiar. One is the "Dirge of Jephthah's Daughter," written in a wonderfully musical and pathetic measure, and full of fine passages, of which this is a fair sample:—

> May no wolf howl, or screech-owl stir
> A wing about thy sepulchre!
> No boisterous winds or storms come hither
> To starve or wither
> Thy soft sweet earth, but, like a spring,
> Love keep it ever flourishing.

But beyond question the cleverest and at the same time the most odd poem in the *Noble Numbers* is "The Widows' Tears; or, Dirge of Dorcas," a lyrical chorus supposed to be wailed out by the widows over the death-bed of Tabitha. The bereaved ladies disgrace themselves, unfortunately, by the greediness of their regrets, dwelling on the loss to them of the bread—"ay! and the flesh and the fish"—that Dorcas was wont to give them; but the poem has stanzas of marvellous grace and delicacy, and the metre in which it is written is peculiarly sweet. But truly Herrick's forte did not lie in hymn-writing, nor was he able to refrain from egregious errors of taste, whenever he attempted to reduce his laughing features to a proper clerical gravity. Of all his solecisms, however, none is no monstrous as one almost incredible poem "To God," in which he gravely encourages the Divine Being to read his secular poems, assuring Him that—

> Thou, my God, may'st on this impure look,
> Yet take no tincture from my sinful book.

For unconscious impiety this rivals the famous passage in which Robert Montgomery exhorted God to "pause and think."

We have now rapidly considered the two volumes on which Herrick claims his place among the best English lyrical poets. Had he written twenty instead of two, he could not have impressed his strong poetic individuality more powerfully on our literature than he has done in the *Hesperides*. It is a storehouse of lovely things, full of tiny beauties of varied kind and workmanship; like a box full of all sorts of jewels—ropes of seed-pearl, opals set in old-fashioned shifting settings, antique gilt trifles sadly tarnished by time; here a ruby, here an amethyst, and there a stray diamond, priceless and luminous, flashing light from all its facets, and dulling the faded jewellery with which it is so promiscuously huddled. What gives a special value to the book is the originality and versatility of the versification. There is nothing too fantastic for the author to attempt, at least; there is one poem written in rhyming triplet, each line having only *two* syllables. There are clear little trills of sudden song, like the lines to the "Lark;" there are chance melodies that seem like mere wantonings of the air upon a wind-harp; there are such harmonious endings as this, "To Music":—

> Fall on me like a silent dew,
> Or like those maiden showers
> Which by the peep of day do strew
> A baptism o'er the flowers.
> Melt, melt my pains
> With thy soft strains,
> That, having ease me given,
> With full delight
> I leave this light
> And take my flight
> For heaven.

With such poems as these, and with the delicious songs of so many of Herrick's predecessors and compeers before them, it is inexplicable upon what possible grounds the critics of the eighteenth century can have founded their astonishing dogma that the first master of English versification was Edmund Waller, whose poems, appearing some fifteen years after the *Hesperides*, are chiefly remarkable for their stiff and pedantic movement, and the brazen clang, as of stage armour, of the dreary heroic couplets in which they strut. Where Waller is not stilted, he owes his excellence to the very source from which the earlier lyrists took theirs—a study of nature and a free but not licentious use of pure English. But not one of his songs, except "Go, Lovely Rose," is worth the slightest of those delicate warbles that Herrick piped out when the sun shone on him and the flowers were fresh.

It is an interesting speculation to consider from what antique sources Herrick, athirst for the pure springs of pagan beauty, drank the deep draughts of his inspiration. Ben Jonson it was, beyond doubt, who first introduced him to the classics, but his mode of accepting the ideas he found there was wholly his own. In the first place, one must contradict a statement that all the editors of Herrick have repeated, sheep-like, from one another, namely, that Catullus was his great example and model. In all the editions of the *Hesperides* we find the same old blunder: "There is no collection of poetry in our language which more nearly resembles the *Carmina* of Catullus." In reality, it would be difficult to name a lyric poet with whom he has less in common than with the Veronese, whose eagle-flights into the very noonday depths of passion, swifter than

Shelley's, as flaming as Sappho's, have no sort of fellowship with the pipings of our gentle and luxurious babbler by the flowery brooks. In one of his poems, "To Live Merrily," where he addresses the various classical poets, and where, by the way, he tries to work himself into a great exaltation about Catullus, he does not even mention the one from whom he really took most of form and colour. No one carefully reading the *Hesperides* can fail to be struck with the extraordinary similarity they bear to the *Epigrams* of Martial; and the parallel will be found to run throughout the writings of the two poets, for good and for bad, the difference being that Herrick is much the more religious pagan of the two, and that he is as much a rural as Martial an urban poet. But in the incessant references to himself and his book, the fondness for gums and spices, the delight in the picturesqueness of private life, the art of making a complete and gemlike poem in the fewest possible lines, the curious mixture of sensitiveness and utter want of sensibility, the trick of writing confidential little poems to all sorts of friends, the tastelessness that mixes up obscene couplets with delicate odes "De Hortis Martialis" or "To Anthea"—in all these and many more qualities one can hardly tell where to look for a literary parallel more complete. As far as I know, Herrick mentions Martial but once, and then very slightly. He was fond of talking about the old poets in his verse, but never with any critical cleverness. The best thing he says about any of them is said of Ovid in a pretty couplet. In a dream he sees Ovid lying at the feet of Corinna, who presses

> With ivory wrists his laureat head, and steeps
> His eyes in dew of kisses while he sleeps.

How much further Herrick's learning proceeded it is difficult to tell. Doubtless he knew some Greek; he mentions Homer and translates from the spurious Anacreon. The English poets of that age, learned as many of them were, do not seem to have gone much further than Rome for their inspiration. Chapman is, of course, a great exception. But none of them, as all the great French poets of the Renaissance did, went directly to the Anthology, Theocritus and Anacreon. Perhaps Herrick had read the Planudian Anthology; the little piece called "Leander's Obsequies" seems as though it must be a translation of the epigram of Antipater of Thessalonica.

It is curious to reflect that at the very time that the *Hesperides* was printed, Salmasius, soon to be hunted to death by the implacable hatred of Milton, was carrying about with him in his restless wanderings the manuscript of his great discovery, the inestimable Anthology of Constantine Cephalas. One imagines with what sympathetic brotherliness the Vicar of Dean Prior would have gossiped and glowed over the new storehouse of Greek song. That the French poets of the century before were known to Herrick is to me extremely doubtful. One feels how much there was in such a book as *La Bergerie* of Remy Belleau, in which our poet would have felt the most unfeigned delight, but I find no distinct traces of their style in his; and unless the Parisian editions of the classics influenced him, I cannot think that he brought any honey, poisonous or other, from France. His inspiration was Latin; that of Ronsard and Jodelle essentially Greek. It was the publication of the Anthology in 1531, and of Henri Estienne's *Anacreon* in 1554, that really set the Pleiad in movement, and founded *l'école gallo-grecque.* It was rather the translation of Ovid, Lucan, Seneca, and Virgil that gave English Elizabethan poetry the start-word.

To return to Herrick, there is not much more to say. He had sung all the songs he had to sing in 1648, being then fifty-seven years of age. He came up to London when the Puritans

ejected him from his living, and seems to have been sprightly enough at first over the pleasant change to London life. Soon, however, bad times came. So many friends were gone; Jonson was dead, and Fletcher; Selden was very old and in disgrace. It was poor work solacing himself with Sir John Denham, and patronising that precocious lad Charles Cotton; and by-and-by the Puritans cut off his fifths, and poor old Herrick is vaguely visible to us in poor lodgings somewhere in Westminster, supported by the charity of relations. In August 1662, some one or other graciously recollected him, and he was sent back in his seventy-second year to that once detested vicarage in "rocky Devonshire," which must now have seemed a kind asylum for his old age.

The latest verses of his which seem to have been preserved are these, carved on the tomb of two of his parishioners in the south aisle of Dean Prior Church—

> No trust to metals nor to marbles, when
> These have their fate and wear away as men;
> Times, titles, trophies may be lost and spent,
> But virtue rears the eternal monument.
> What more than these can tombs or tombstones pay?
> But here's the sunset of a tedious day:
> These two asleep are: I'll but be undress'd
> And so to bed: pray wish us all good rest.

There is something extremely pathetic in the complete obscurity of the poet's last days. In those troublesome times his poetry, after a slight success, passed completely out of all men's minds. The idiotic Winstanley, in his *Lives of the Most Famous English Poets*, written shortly after Herrick's death, says that "but for the interruption of trivial passages, he might have made up none of the worst poetic landscapes." This is the last word spoken, as I think, on Herrick, till Mr. Nichols revived his fame in 1796. All we know of his latest years is summed up in one short extract from the church register of Dean Prior: "Robert Herrick, vicker, was buried ye 15th day of October 1674." By that time a whole new world was formed in poetry. Milton was dead; Wycherley and Dryden were the fashionable poets; Addison and Swift were lately born; next year the *Pilgrim's Progress* was to appear; all things were preparing for that bewigged and bepowdered eighteenth century, with its mob of gentlemen who wrote with ease, its Augustan self-sufficiency, and its horror of nature; and what wonder that no one cared whether Herrick were alive or dead?

F. T. PALGRAVE
"Robert Herrick"
Macmillan's Magazine, April 1877, pp. 475–81

Robert Herrick's personal fate is in one point like Shakespeare's. We know or seem to know them both, through their works, with singular intimacy. But with this our knowledge substantially ends. No private letter of Shakespeare, no record of his conversation, no account of the circumstances in which his writings were published, remains: hardly any statement how his greatest contemporaries ranked him. A group of Herrick's youthful letters on business has, indeed, been preserved; of his life and studies, of his reputation during his own time, almost nothing. For whatever facts affectionate diligence could now gather, readers are referred to Mr. Grosart's "Introduction."[1] But if, to supplement the picture, inevitably imperfect, which this gives, we turn to Herrick's own book, we learn little, biographically, except the names of a few friends,—that his general sympathies were with the Royal cause,—and that he wearied in Devonshire for London. So far as is known, he published but this one volume, and that, when not far from his sixtieth year. Some pieces may be traced in earlier collections; some few carry ascertainable dates; the rest lie over a period of near forty years, during a great portion of which we have no distinct account where Herrick lived, or what were his employments. We know that he shone with Ben Jonson and the wits at the nights and suppers of those gods of our glorious early literature: we may fancy him at Beaumanor, or Houghton, with his uncle and cousins, keeping a Leicestershire Christmas in the Manor-house: or, again, in some sweet southern county with Julia and Anthea, Corinna and Dianeme by his side (familiar then by other names now never to be remembered), sitting merry, but with just the sadness of one who hears sweet music, in some meadow among his favourite flowers of spring-time;— there, or "where the rose lingers latest.". . . . But "the dream, the fancy," is all that Time has spared us. And if it be curious that his contemporaries should have left so little record of this delightful poet and (as we should infer from the book) genial-hearted man, it is not less so that the single first edition should have satisfied the seventeenth century, and that, before the present, notices of Herrick should be of the rarest occurrence.

The artist's "claim to exist" is, however, always far less to be looked for in his life, than in his art, upon the secret of which the fullest biography can tell us little—as little, perhaps, as criticism can analyse its charm. But there are few of our poets who stand less in need than Herrick of commentaries of this description,—in which too often we find little more than a dull or florid prose version of what the author has given us admirably in verse. Apart from obsolete words or allusions, Herrick is the best commentator upon Herrick. A few lines only need therefore be added, aiming rather to set forth his place in the sequence of English poets, and especially in regard to those near his own time, than to point out in detail beauties which he unveils in his own way, and so most durably and delightfully.

When our Muses, silent or sick for a century and more after Chaucer's death, during the years of war and revolution, reappeared, they brought with them foreign modes of art, ancient and contemporary, within the forms of which they began to set to music the new material which the age supplied. At the very outset, indeed, the moralising philosophy which has characterised the English from the beginning of our national history, appears in the writers of the troubled times lying between the last regnal years of Henry VIII. and the first of his great daughter. But with the happier hopes of Elizabeth's accession, poetry was once more distinctly followed, not only as a means of conveying thought, but as a Fine Art. And hence something constrained and artificial blends with the freshness of the Elizabethan literature. For its great underlying elements it necessarily reverts to those embodied in our own earlier poets, Chaucer above all, to whom, after barely one hundred and fifty years, men looked up as a father of song: but in points of style and treatment, the poets of the sixteenth century lie under a double external influence—that of the poets of Greece and Rome (known either in their own tongues or by translation), and that of the modern literatures which had themselves undergone the same classical impulse. Italy was the source most regarded during the more strictly Elizabethan period; whence its lyrical poetry, and the dramatic in a less degree, are coloured much less by pure and severe classicalism with its closeness to reality, than by the allegorical and elaborate style, fancy, and fact curiously blended, which had been generated in Italy under the peculiar and local circumstances of her pilgrimage in literature and art from the age of Dante onwards. Whilst that influence lasted, such brilliant pictures of actual life, such

directness, movement, and simplicity in style, as Chaucer often shows, were not yet again attainable: and although satire, narrative, the poetry of reflection, were meanwhile not wholly unknown, yet they only appear in force at the close of this period. And then also the pressure of political and religious strife, veiled in poetry during the greater part of Elizabeth's actual reign under the forms of pastoral and allegory, again imperiously breaks in upon the gracious but somewhat slender and artificial fashions of England's Helicon: the

Divom numen, sedesque quietae

which, in some degree the Elizabethan poets offer, disappear; until filling the central years of the seventeenth century we reach an age as barren for inspiration of new song as the Wars of the Roses; although the great survivors from earlier years mask this sterility;—masking also the revolution in poetical manner and matter which we can see secretly preparing in the later "Cavalier" poets, but which was not clearly recognized before the time of Dryden's culmination.

In the period here briefly sketched, what is Herrick's portion? His verse is eminent for sweet and gracious fluency; this is a real note of the "Elizabethan" poets. His subjects are frequently pastoral, with a classical tinge, more or less slight, infused; his language, though not free from exaggeration, is generally free from intellectual conceits and distortion, and is eminent throughout for a youthful *naïveté*. Such, also, are qualities of the latter sixteenth century literature. But if these characteristics might lead us to call Herrick "the last of the Elizabethans," born out of due time, the differences between him and them are not less marked. Herrick's directness of speech is accompanied by an equally clear and simple present-ment of his thought; we have, perhaps, no poet who writes more consistently and earnestly with his eye upon his subject. An allegorical or mystical treatment is alien from him: he handles awkwardly the few traditional fables which he introduces. He is also wholly free from Italianizing tendencies: his classicalism even is that of an English student,—of a school-boy, indeed, if he be compared with a Jonson or a Milton. Herrick's personal eulogies on his friends and others, further, witness to the extension of the field of poetry after Elizabeth's age;—in which his enthusiastic geniality, his quick and easy transitions of subject, have also little precedent.

If, again, we compare Herrick's book with those of his fellow-poets for a hundred years before, very few are the traces which he gives of imitation, or even of study. During the long interval between Herrick's entrance on his Cambridge and his clerical careers (an interval all but wholly obscure to us), it is natural to suppose that he read, at any rate, his Elizabethan predecessors: yet (beyond those general similarities already noticed) the Editor can find no positive proof of familiarity. Compare Herrick with Marlowe, Greene, Breton, Drayton, or other pretty pastoralists of the *Helicon*—his general and radical unlikeness is what strikes us; whilst he is even more remote from the passionate intensity of Sidney and Shakespeare, the Italian graces of Spenser, the pensive beauty of *Parthenophil*, of *Diella*, of *Fidessa*, of the *Hecatomapathia* and the *Tears of Fancy*.

Nor is Herrick's resemblance nearer to many of the contemporaries who have been often grouped with him. He has little in common with the courtly elegance, the learned polish, which too rarely redeem commonplace and conceits in Carew, Habington, Lovelace, Cowley, or Waller. Herrick has his *concetti* also; but they are in him generally true plays of fancy; he writes throughout far more naturally than these lyrists, who, on the other hand, in their unfrequent successes reach a more complete and classical form of expression. Thus, when Carew speaks of an aged fair one

> When beauty, youth, and all sweets leave her,
> Love may return, but loves never!

Cowley, of his mistress—

> Love in her sunny eyes does basking play,
> Love walks the pleasant mazes of her hair:

or take Lovelace, "To Lucasta," Waller, in his "Go, lovely rose,"—we have a finish and condensation which Herrick hardly attains; a literary quality alien from his "woodnotes wild," which may help us to understand the very small appreciation he met from his age. He had "a pretty pastoral gale of fancy," said Phillips, cursorily dismissing Herrick in his *Theatrum*: not suspecting how inevitably artifice and mannerism, if fashionable for a while, pass into forgetfulness, whilst the simple cry of Nature partakes in her permanence.

Donne and Marvell, stronger men, leave also no mark on our poet. The elaborate thought, the metrical harshness of the first, could find no counterpart in Herrick; whilst Marvell, beyond him in imaginative power, though twisting it too often into contortion and excess, appears to have been little known as a lyrist then:—as, indeed, his great merits have never reached anything like due popular recognition. Yet Marvell's natural description is nearer Herrick's in felicity and insight than any of the poets named above. Nor, again, do we trace anything of Herbert or Vaughan in Herrick's *Noble Numbers*, which, though unfairly judged if held insincere, are obviously far distant from the intense conviction, the depth and inner fervour of his high-toned contemporaries.

It is among the great dramatists of this age that we find the only English influences palpably operative on this singularly original writer. The greatest, in truth, is wholly absent: and it is remarkable that although Herrick may have joined in the wit-contests and genialities of the literary clubs in London soon after Shakespeare's death, and certainly lived in friendship with some who had known him, yet his name is never mentioned in the poetical commemorations of the *Hesperides*. In Herrick, echoes from Fletcher's idyllic pieces in the *Faithful Shepherdess* are faintly traceable; from his songs, "Hear what love can do," and "The lusty Spring," more distinctly. But to Ben Jonson, whom Herrick addresses as his patron saint in song, and ranks on the highest list of his friends, his obligations are much more perceptible. In fact, Jonson's non-dramatic poetry,—the *Epigrams* and *Forest* of 1616, the *Underwoods* of 1641, (he died in 1637),—supply models, generally admirable in point of art, though of very unequal merit in their execution and contents, of the principal forms under which we may range Herrick's *Hesperides*. The graceful love-song, the celebration of feasts and wit, the encomia of friends, the epigram as then understood, are all here represented: even Herrick's vein in natural description is prefigured in the odes to Penshurst and Sir Robert Wroth, of 1616. And it is in the religious pieces of the *Noble Numbers*, for which Jonson afforded the least copious precedents, that, as a rule, Herrick is least successful.

Even if we had not the verses on his own book, in proof that Herrick was no careless singer, but a true artist, working with conscious knowledge of his art, we might have inferred the fact from the choice of Jonson as his model. That great poet, as Clarendon justly remarked, had "judgment to order and govern fancy, rather than excess of fancy: his productions being slow and upon deliberation." No writer could be better fitted for the guidance of one so fancy-free as Herrick; to whom the curb, in the old phrase, was more needful than the spur, and whose invention, more fertile and varied than Jonson's, was ready at once to fill up the moulds of form provided. He

does this with a lively facility, contrasting much with the evidence of labour in his master's work. Slowness and deliberation are the last qualities suggested by Herrick. Yet it may be doubted whether the volatile ease, the effortless grace, the wild bird-like fluency with which he

> Scatters his loose notes in the waste of air

are not, in truth, the results of exquisite art working in co-operation with the gifts of nature. The various readings which our few remaining manuscripts or printed versions have supplied to Mr. Grosart's "Introduction," attest the minute and curious care with which Herrick polished and strengthened his own work: his airy facility, his seemingly spontaneous melodies, as with Shelley—his counterpart in pure lyrical art within this century—were earned by conscious labour; perfect freedom was begotten of perfect art;—nor, indeed, have excellence and permanence any other parent.

With the error that regards Herrick as a careless singer is closely twined that which ranks him in the school of that master of elegant pettiness who has usurped and abused the name Anacreon; as a mere light-hearted writer of pastorals, a gay and frivolous Renaissance amourist. He has indeed those elements: but with them is joined the seriousness of an age which knew that the light mask of classicalism and bucolic allegory could be worn only as an ornament, and that life held much deeper and further-reaching issues than were visible to the narrow horizons within which Horace or Martial circumscribed the range of their art. Between the most intensely poetical, and so, greatest, among the French poets of this century, and Herrick, are many points of likeness. He too, with Alfred de Musset, might have said

> Quoi que nous puissions faire,
> Je souffre; il est trop tard; le monde s'est fait vieux.
> Une immense espérance a traversé la terre;
> Malgré nous vers le ciel il faut lever les yeux.

Indeed, Herrick's deepest debt to ancient literature lies not in the models which he directly imitated, nor in the Anacreontic tone which with singular felicity he has often taken. These are common to many writers with him:—nor will he who cannot learn more from the great ancient world ever rank among poets of high order, or enter the innermost sanctuary of art. But, the power to describe men and things as the poet sees them with simple sincerity, insight, and grace: to paint scenes and imaginations as perfect organic wholes;—carrying with it the gift to clothe each picture, as if by unerring instinct, in fit metrical form, giving to each its own music; beginning without affectation, and rounding off without effort;—the power, in a word, to leave simplicity, sanity, and beauty as the last impressions lingering on our minds, these gifts are at once the true bequest of classicalism, and the reason why (until modern effort equals them) the study of that Hellenic and Latin poetry in which these gifts are eminent above all other literatures yet created, must be essential. And it is success in precisely these excellences which is here claimed for Herrick. He is classical in the great and eternal sense of the phrase: and much more so, probably, than he was himself aware of. No poet in fact is so far from dwelling in a past or foreign world; it is the England, if not of 1648, at least of his youth, in which he lives and moves and loves: his Bucolics shows no trace of Sicily; his Anthea and Julia were no "buckles of the purest gold," nor have anything about them foreign to Middlesex or Devon. Herrick's imagination has no far horizons; like Burns and Crabbe fifty years since, or Barnes (that exquisite and neglected pastoralist of fair Dorset, perfect within his narrower range as Herrick) to-day it is his own native land only which he sees and paints: even the fairy world in which, at whatever inevitable interval, he is second to Shakespeare, is pure English; or rather, his elves live in an elfin county of their own, and are all but severed from humanity. Within that greater circle of Shakespeare, where Oberon and Ariel and their fellows move, aiding or injuring mankind, and reflecting human life in a kind of unconscious parody, Herrick cannot walk: and it may have been due to his good sense and true feeling for art, that here, where resemblance might have seemed probable, he borrows nothing from *Midsummer-Night's Dream* or *Tempest*. If we are moved by the wider range of Byron's or Shelley's sympathies, there is a charm, also, in this sweet insularity of Herrick; a narrowness perhaps, yet carrying with it a healthful reality absent from the vapid and artificial "cosmopolitanism" that did such wrong on Goethe's genius. If he has not the exotic blooms and strange odours which poets who derive from literature show in their conservatories, Herrick has the fresh breeze and thyme-bed fragrance of open moorland, the grace and greenery of English meadows; with Homer and Dante, he too shares the strength and inspiration which come from touch of man's native soil.

What has been here sketched is not planned so much as a criticism in form on Herrick's poetry as an attempt to seize his relations to his predecessors and contemporaries. If we now tentatively inquire what place may be assigned to him in our literature at large, Herrick has no single lyric to show equal in pomp of music, brilliancy of diction, or elevation of sentiment to some which Spenser before, Milton in his own time, Dryden and Gray, Wordsworth and Shelley, since have given us. Nor has he, as already noticed, the peculiar finish and reserve (if the phrase may be allowed) traceable, though rarely, in Ben Jonson and others of the seventeenth century. He does not want passion; yet his passion wants concentration: it is too ready, also, to dwell on externals: imagination with him generally appears clothed in forms of fancy. Among his contemporaries, take Crashaw's "Wishes:" Sir J. Beaumont's elegy on his child Gervase: take Bishop King's "Surrender":

My once-dear Love! Hapless, that I no more
Must call thee so. . . . The rich affection's store
That fed our hopes, lies now exhaust and spent,
Like sums of treasure unto bankrupts lent:—
We that did nothing study but the way
To love each other, with which thoughts the day
Rose with delight to us, and with them set,
Must learn the hateful art, how to forget!
—Fold back our arms, take home our fruitless
        loves,
That must new fortunes try, like turtle doves
Dislodgéd from their haunts. We must in tears
Unwind a love knit up in many years.
In this one kiss I here surrender thee
Back to thyself: so thou again art free:—

take eight lines by some old unknown Northern singer:

When I think on the happy days
    I spent wi' you, my dearie,
And now what lands between us lie,
    How can I be but eerie!

How slow ye move, ye heavy hours,
    As ye were wae and weary!
It was na sae ye glinted by
    When I was wi' my dearie:—

—O! there is an intensity here, a note of passion beyond the deepest of Herrick's. This tone (whether from temperament or circumstance or scheme of art) is wanting to the *Hesperides* and *Noble Numbers*: nor does Herrick's lyre, sweet and varied as it is, own that purple chord, that more inwoven harmony, possessed by poets of greater depth and splendour,—by Shake-

speare and Milton often, by Spenser more rarely. But if we put aside these "greater gods" of song, with Sidney,—in the Editor's judgment Herrick's mastery (to use a brief expression), both over Nature and over Art, clearly assigns to him the first place as lyrical poet, in the strict and pure sense of the phrase, among all who flourished during the interval between Henry V. and a hundred years since. Single pieces of equal or higher quality we have, indeed, meanwhile received, not only from the master-singers who did not confine themselves to the lyric, but from many poets—some the unknown contributors to our early anthologies, then Jonson, Marvell, Waller, Collins, and others, with whom we reach the beginning of the wider sweep which lyrical poetry has since taken. Yet, looking at the whole work, not at the selected jewels, of this great and noble multitude, Herrick, as lyrical poet strictly, offers us by far the most homogeneous, attractive, and varied treasury. No one else among lyrists, within the period defined, has such unfailing freshness: so much variety within the sphere prescribed to himself; such closeness to nature, whether in description or in feeling; such easy fitness in language: melody so unforced and delightful. His dull pages are much less frequent: he has more lines, in his own phrase, "born of the royal blood": the

Inflata rore non Achaico verba

are rarer with him: although superficially mannered, nature is so much nearer to him, that far fewer of his pieces have lost vitality and interest through adherence to forms of feeling or fashions of thought now obsolete. A Roman contemporary is described by the younger Pliny in words very appropriate to Herrick: who in fact, if Greek in respect of his method and style, in the contents of his poetry displays the "frankness of nature and vivid sense of life" which criticism assigns as marks of the great Roman poets. *Facit versus, quales Catullus aut Calvus. Quantum illis leporis, dulcedinis, amaritudinis, amoris! Inserit sane, sed data opera, mollibus lenibusque duriusculos quosdam: et hoc, quasi Catullus aut Calvus.* Many pieces have been refused admittance, whether from coarseness of phrase or inferior value: yet these are rarely defective in the lyrical art, which, throughout the writer's work, is so simple and easy as almost to escape notice through its very excellence. In one word, Herrick, in a rare and special sense, is unique.

To these qualities we may, perhaps, ascribe the singular neglect which, so far as we may infer, he met with in his own age, and certainly in the century following. For the men of the Restoration period he was too natural, too purely poetical: he had not the learned polish, the political allusion, the tone of the city, the didactic turn, which were then and onwards demanded from poetry. In the next age, no tradition consecrated his name; whilst writers of a hundred years before were then too remote for familiarity, and not remote enough for reverence. Moving on to our own time, when some justice has at length been conceded to him, Herrick has to meet the great rivalry of the poets who, from Burns and Cowper to Tennyson, have widened and deepened the lyrical sphere, making it at once on the one hand more intensely personal, on the other, more free and picturesque in the range of problems dealt with: whilst at the same time new and richer lyrical forms, harmonies more intricate and seven-fold, have been created by them, as in Hellas during her golden age of song, to embody ideas and emotions unknown or unexpressed under Tudors and Stuarts. To this latter superiority Herrick would, doubtless, have bowed, as he bowed before Ben Jonson's genius. "Rural ditties," and "oaten flute" cannot bear the competition of the full modern orchestra. Yet this author need not fear! That exquisite and lofty pleasure which it is the first and the last aim of all true art to give, must, by its own nature, be lasting also. As the eyesight fluctuates, and gives the advantage to different colours in turn, so to the varying moods of the mind the same beauty does not always seem equally beautiful. Thus from the "purple light" of our later poetry there are hours in which we may look to the daffodil and rose-tints of Herrick's old Arcadia, for refreshment and delight. And the pleasure which he gives is as eminently wholesome as pleasurable. Like the holy river of Virgil, to the souls who drink of him, Herrick offers "securos latices." He is conspicuously free from many of the maladies incident to his art. Here is no overstrain, no spasmodic cry, no wire-drawn analysis or sensational rhetoric, no music without sense, no mere second-hand literary inspiration, no mannered archaism:—above all, no sickly sweetness, no subtle, unhealthy affectation. Throughout his work, whether when it is strong, or in the less worthy portions, sanity, sincerity, simplicity, lucidity, are everywhere the characteristics of Herrick: in these, not in his pretty Pagan masquerade, he shows the note,—the only genuine note,—of Hellenic descent. Hence, through whatever changes and fashions poetry may pass, her true lovers he is likely to "please now, and please for long." His verse, in the words of a poet greater than himself, is of that quality which "adds sunlight to daylight"; which is able to "make the happy happier." He will, it may be hoped, carry to the many Englands across the seas, east and west, pictures of English life exquisite in truth and grace:—to the more fortunate inhabitants (as they must perforce hold themselves!) of the old country, her image, as she was two centuries since, will live in the "golden apples" of the West, offered to us by this sweet singer of Devonshire. We have greater poets, not a few; none more faithful to nature as he saw her, none more perfect in his art:—none, more companionable.

Notes

1. See the Herrick edited by this gentleman, and lately published by Messrs. Chatto and Windus. Looking to the care taken to collect all facts bearing on the poet's life and book, to the critical correctness of the text, and the fulness of annotation, it is not too high praise to say that these volumes for the first time give Herrick a place among books not printed only, but edited.

ALGERNON CHARLES SWINBURNE
"Robert Herrick" (1891)
Studies in Prose and Poetry
1894

It is singular that the first great age of English lyric poetry should have been also the one great age of English dramatic poetry; but it is hardly less singular that the lyric school should have advanced as steadily as the dramatic school declined from the promise of its dawn. Born with Marlowe, it rose at once with Shakespeare to heights inaccessible before and since and for ever, to sink through bright gradations of glorious decline to its final and beautiful sunset in Shirley; but the lyrical record that begins with the author of *Euphues* and *Eudymion* grows fuller if not brighter through a whole chain of constellations, till it culminates in the crowning star of Herrick. Shakespeare's last song, the exquisite and magnificent overture to *The Two Noble Kinsmen*, is hardly so limpid in its flow, so liquid in its melody, as the two great songs in *Valentinian*; but Herrick, our last poet of that incomparable age or generation, has matched them again and again. As a creative and inventive singer he surpasses all his rivals in quantity of good work; in quality of spontaneous instinct and melodious inspiration he reminds us, by frequent and flawless evidence, who, above all others, must beyond all doubt have been his first master and his first model

in lyric poetry—the author of 'The Passionate Shepherd to his Love'.

The last of his line, he is and will probably be always the first in rank and station of English song-writers. We have only to remember how rare it is to find a perfect song, good to read and good to sing, combining the merits of Coleridge and Shelley with the capabilities of Tommy Moore and Haynes Bayly, to appreciate the unique and unapproachable excellence of Herrick. The lyrist who wished to be a butterfly, the lyrist who fled or flew to a lone vale at the hour (whatever hour it may be) 'when stars are weeping', have left behind them such stuff as may be sung, but certainly cannot be read and endured by any one with an ear for verse. The author of the Ode on France and the author of the Ode to the West Wind have left us hardly more than a song apiece which has been found fit for setting to music; and, lovely as they are, the fame of their authors does not mainly depend on the song of Glycine or the song of which Leigh Hunt so justly and so critically said that Beaumont and Fletcher never wrote anything of the kind more lovely. Herrick, of course, lives simply by virtue of his songs; his more ambitious or pretentious lyrics are merely magnified and prolonged and elaborated songs. Elegy or litany, epicede or epithalamium, his work is always a song-writer's; nothing more, but nothing less, than the work of the greatest song-writer—as surely as Shakespeare is the greatest dramatist—ever born of English race. The apparent or external variety of his versification is, I should suppose, incomparable; but by some happy tact or instinct he was too naturally unambitious to attempt, like Jonson, a flight in the wake of Pindar. He knew what he could not do: a rare and invaluable gift. Born a blackbird or a thrush, he did not take himself (or try) to be a nightingale.

It has often been objected that he did mistake himself for a sacred poet; and it cannot be denied that his sacred verse at its worst is as offensive as his secular verse at its worst; nor can it be denied that no severer sentence of condemnation can be passed upon any poet's work. But neither Herbert nor Crashaw could have bettered such a divinely beautiful triplet as this:—

> We see Him come, and know Him ours,
> Who with His sunshine and His showers
> Turns all the patient ground to flowers.

That is worthy of Miss Rossetti herself; and praise of such work can go no higher.

But even such exquisite touches or tones of colour may be too often repeated in fainter shades or more glaring notes of assiduous and facile reiteration. The sturdy student who tackles his Herrick as a schoolboy is expected to tackle his Horace, in a spirit of pertinacious and stolid straightforwardness, will probably find himself before long so nauseated by the incessant inhalation of spices and flowers, condiments and kisses, that if a musk-rat had run over the page it could hardly be less endurable to the physical than it is to the spiritual stomach. The fantastic and the brutal blemishes which deform and deface the loveliness of his incomparable genius are hardly so damaging to his fame as his general monotony of matter and of manner. It was doubtless in order to relieve this saccharine and 'mellisonant' monotony that he thought fit to intersperse these interminable droppings of natural or artificial perfume with others of the rankest and most intolerable odour; but a diet of alternate sweetmeats and emetics is for the average of eaters and drinkers no less unpalatable than unwholesome. It is useless and thankless to enlarge on such faults or such defects as it would be useless and senseless to ignore. But how to enlarge, to expatiate, to insist on the charm of Herrick at his best—a charm so incomparable and so inimitable that even English poetry can boast of nothing quite like it or worthy to be named after it—the most appreciative reader will be the slowest to affirm or imagine that he can conjecture. This, however, he will hardly fail to remark: that Herrick, like most if not all other lyric poets, is not best known by his best work. If we may judge by frequency of quotation or of reference, the ballad of the ride from Ghent to Aix is a far more popular, more generally admired and accredited specimen of Mr. Browning's work than 'The Last Ride Together', and 'The Lost Leader' than 'The Lost Mistress'. Yet the superiority of the less popular poem is in either case beyond all question or comparison: in depth and in glow in spirit and of harmony, in truth and charm of thought and word, undeniable and indescribable. No two men of genius were ever more unlike than the authors of *Paracelsus* and *Hesperides*; and yet it is as true of Herrick as of Browning that his best is not always his best-known work. Everyone knows the song, 'Gather ye rosebuds while ye may'; few, I fear, by comparison, know the yet sweeter and better song, 'Ye have been fresh and green'. The general monotony of style and motive which fatigues and irritates his too persevering reader is here and there relieved by a change of key which anticipates the note of a later and very different lyric school. The brilliant simplicity and pointed grace of the three stanzas to Œnone ('What conscience, say, is it in thee') recall the lyrists of the Restoration in their cleanlier and happier mood. And in the very fine epigram headed by the words, 'Devotion makes the Deity', he has expressed for once a really high and deep thought in words of really noble and severe propriety. His 'Mad Maid's Song', again, can only be compared with Blake's, which has more of passionate imagination if less of pathetic sincerity.

ALFRED W. POLLARD
"Herrick and His Friends"
Macmillan's Magazine, December 1892, pp. 142–48

To all but his professed admirers Herrick is chiefly known by a little handful of lyrics, which appear with great regularity in the anthologies, but bring with them a very incomplete impression of their author's personality and life. In the case of Herrick this is no great wonder. The same sensuous feeling which made him invest his friends with the perfume of Juno or Isis, sing of their complexions as roses overspread with lawn, compare their lips to cherries, and praise their silver feet, had also its other side. The unlucky wights who incurred the poet's wrath were treated in a fashion equally offensive to good taste and good manners. Nor are these gruesome epigrams the only apples in the garden of Herrick's *Hesperides* which have affronted the taste of modern readers. The epigrams indeed, if apples at all, are rather the dusty apples of the Dead Sea than the pleasant fruit of the Western Isles; but Herrick's *Epithalamia*, odes whose sustained splendour gives them a high rank among his poems, because they sing of other marriage-rites than those of rice and slipper, have also tended to restrict the circle of his readers in an age which prides itself on its modesty. Hence it has come about that while the names of the lovely ladies of the poet's imagination,—Julia, Dianeme, Electra, Perilla—are widely known, those of the men and women whom Herrick treasured as his friends are all but forgotten, and the materials for constructing a picture of the society amid which the poet moved have been neglected and thrown aside.

Like most bachelors Herrick set a high value upon friendship, and in his sedater middle age, when his poetry had lost something of its fire, he set himself to construct a poetic temple to commemorate the virtues of the men and women whom he most loved or honoured. Sometimes instead of a temple he speaks of a book, sometimes his friends are his "elect," his "righteous tribe," language which recalls the "sealed of the tribe of Ben" of his favourite Jonson. Inclusion among them was clearly reckoned as an honour, and many of the poems in which it is conferred were evidently written in response to solicitation, sportive or earnest as we may choose to think. These friends of his later days are not always very interesting. Many of them are of his relations, Herricks, or some of the innumerable Stones and Soames, well-to-do folk with whom the poet claimed cousinship through his mother, Julia Stone. Some of the outsiders are more to our purpose—John Selden the antiquary, for instance, whose intimacy was no small honour, and Dr. Alabaster, who in his young days had become a convert to Catholicism while serving with Essex in Spain, but whose apocalyptic writings brought him into trouble with the Inquisition, from whose clutches he was glad to find refuge in a return to Protestantism and an English living. Mr. John Crofts, cup-bearer to the King, is another friend who brings with him a distinct sense of reality. Herrick calls him his "faithful friend," and their acquaintance was probably of long standing, for we hear of Crofts as in the King's service a year or two before the poet buried himself in his Devonshire living, and on the other hand all these "Temple" poems impress us as having been written late in Herrick's life. In his younger days Crofts himself may have been a rhymester, for in the State Papers there is a letter from Lord Conway thanking William Weld for some verses, and expressing a hope that the lines may be "strong enough to bind Robert Maule and Jack Crofts" from evermore using some phrase unknown. Mr. Crofts seems to have had worse faults than this of using incorrect phrases, for a year or two later (1634) there is a record of a petition from George, Lord Digby, praying to be released from an imprisonment incurred for assaulting Herrick's friend under very irritating provocation. Jack had passed some insult on a lady under Lord Digby's escort, had apologised, had boasted of the original offence, and when finally brought to book had interspersed remarks such as "Well!" and "What then?" in a manner which made caning seem too good for him. But this is the petitioner's account, and Jack himself might have given a different version.

Others of Herrick's friends seem occasionally to have got themselves into trouble. Dr. John Parry, for instance, Chancellor of the Diocese of Exeter, when first appointed was accused of having oppressed divers people with excommunications for the sake of fees; but we hear of him afterwards as highly recommended by the Deputy-Lieutenants, and his early exactions must have been atoned to the King's satisfaction, since the chancellor was thought worthy to be made a judge-marshal, and to receive the honour of knighthood.

Many of Herrick's poems bear reference, direct or indirect, to the Civil War. He bewailed the separation of the King and Queen, welcomed Charles to the West in verse which sang the "white omens" of his coming, congratulated him on his taking of Leicester in May, 1645, and composed an ode, "To the King upon his welcome to Hampton Court," in which he took all too cheerful a view of the royal prospects. His book is dedicated to Charles II., and it contains also an address "To Prince Charlie upon his coming to Exeter," which probably refers to a visit in 1645. Years before he had sung the Prince's birth in a pretty choral ode, taking note of the star which appeared at noontide when the King his father went to make thanksgiving at St. Paul's Cathedral. Two other incidents in the west-country campaign inspired his muse, the taking and holding of Exeter by Sir John Berkeley, and the gallant victories won in Cornwall by Lord Hopton over very superior numbers.

For the rest there is nothing in the *Hesperides* to show that Herrick was a bigoted royalist. Utterances in favour of the divine right of kings and the duty of implicit obedience are not hard to find; but they are balanced by epigrams which show a much more Parliamentary spirit, and it is often difficult to tell where Herrick is expressing his own sentiments and where he is simply running into verse some sentence or phrase which happened to catch his attention.

When the end came, Herrick, like many another country priest, was turned out of his living, shook the dust of Dean Prior off his feet, and returned contentedly to London, there to take his place in a little band of wits who were able to endure the gloom of the Presbyterian rule which then held the city in its grasp. He passed his *Hesperides* and *Noble Numbers* through the press, made friends with young John Hall, then fresh from Cambridge but with a European reputation for cleverness; addressed his "honoured friend" Mr. Charles Cotton, probably the friend of Izaak Walton and translator of Montaigne; overpraised Leonard Willan, a wretched poet and dramatist, and contributed a curious poem to the *Lachrymæ Musarum*, in which, under the editorship of Richard Brome, all the wits of the day poured forth their lament for the death of Lord Hastings in 1649. Then Herrick vanishes from our sight, and save that he returned to his living after the Restoration and died there at Dean Prior in 1674 we know no more of him.

The mention of Herrick's "Temple" or "Book" of his heroes has led us to gossip first of the less interesting half of his life which followed on his acceptance of a country living. The nine or ten years which passed between his leaving Cambridge and his retirement to Devonshire were probably the most poetically productive in all his career, and, from the glimpses which his poems give us, were certainly the gayest and most amusing.

He had gone to the University unusually late in life, in 1613 when he was already in his twenty-first year, that is to say, five or six years senior to the average freshman of those days. After his father's suicide (for the fall from a window following immediately on making his will can hardly have been accidental, and was not so regarded at the time) the care of the poet and his brothers had devolved on their uncles Robert and William, and the latter, who was jeweller, goldsmith, and banker to James I., shortly after receiving the honour of knighthood from the King, on September 25, 1607, accepted his nephew as an apprentice for ten years. Herrick's appreciation of material beauty was so keen that the absence from his poems (so far as all memory serves me) of any striking allusions to goldsmiths' work may perhaps be taken as evidence that during his apprenticeship with his uncle he did not make any great progress in the craft. At all events he persuaded Sir William to excuse him the last four years of his time, and betook himself to Cambridge, the poet's University.

Fourteen letters which he wrote to his uncle from his college still survive, all written in a high-flown rhetorical style, sometimes lapsing into blank verse, and with one unvarying theme,—the need of a prompt remittance. His allowance was £40 a year (some £200 present value), probably paid out of the remnant of the £600 odd which came to him from his father's estate. This of itself was no bad "stipend," to use the poet's word, and from the tone of the letters we may guess that it was also supplemented by occasional gifts from his uncle and aunt. But it was apparently not paid regularly; Herrick was frequently in pecuniary straits, and about 1616 he migrated from St. John's to Trinity Hall in order to curtail his expenses, taking his bachelor's degree from the latter college in 1617.

It would be placing too touching a faith in undergraduate nature to attach much importance to the fact that the payments which Herrick requests were mostly to be made through booksellers, and that (save once when he confesses to having "run somewhat deep into my tailor's debt") the need of books or the advancement of his studies are the pretexts mostly given for his requests for speedy payment. But there is no reason to imagine that Herrick's university career was an idle one. His poems show considerable traces of a knowledge and love of the classics. He translates from Virgil that charming passage which describes the meeting of Æneas with Venus clad as a simple huntress, is full of Horatian reminiscences, borrows a few couplets from Ovid, adapts quite a number of epigrams from Martial, makes so much use of his Catullus that we may guess he knew a fair number of his odes by heart, quotes Cicero, turns a tag or two from Sallust and Tacitus, and had a very extensive acquaintance with Seneca. In Greek he takes a couplet from Hesiod as a motto for his *Noble Numbers*, alludes to Homer, though his reference to Helen at the Scæan Gate is perhaps rather from the *Love Letters* of Aristænetus than the Iliad, translates some twenty lines of Theocritus into the pretty poem entitled *The Cruel Maid*, knew something of the Planudean Anthology, and knew, loved, translated, and imitated the pseudo-Anacreon.

This brief survey of Herrick's classical studies may suffice to prove that he was no idler, and when he left the university and returned to town he must have been well able to hold his own with the best wits of the day. The well-known poem on "His Age," "dedicated to his peculiar friend, Mr. John Weekes under the name of Posthumus," contains in the printed version some vague reminiscences of their sportive days. In Egerton MS. 2725 at the British Museum one verse of this poem assumes a much more specific form:

> Then the next health to friends of mine
> In oysters and Burgundian wine,
> Hind, Goderiske, Smith,
> And Nansagge, sons of clune and pith,
>   Such who know well
> To board the magic bowl, and spill
> Almighty blood, and can do more
> Than Jove and Chaos them before.

The identity of these heroes is not every easily determined. A friend suggests that Hind may have been John Hind, an Anacreontic poet and friend of Greene, and has found references to a Goderiske (Goodrich) and a Nansagge, of whom, however, only the names are known. Smith, despite the commonness of the name, may almost certainly be identified with James Smith, a poet whose few verses sometimes strike a curiously modern note. Like Herrick he acted at one time as chaplain to a squadron sent to the relief of the Isle of Rhé, and like Herrick also became a Devonshire parson. He was, too, one of the editors and writers of the Anthology known as *Musarum Deliciæ*, and his colleague in that task, the gallant royalist sailor, Sir John Mennis, was also a friend of Herrick, who addressed a poem to him. John Wicks, or Weekes, the "Posthumus" of Herrick's verses, was another friend of Mennis and Smith, and also a country clergyman. The first poem in the *Musarum Deliciæ* is addressed "To Parson Weeks; an invitation to London." "One friend?" he is told—

> Why thou hast thousands here
> Will strive to make thee better cheer.
> Ships lately from the islands came
> With wines, thou never heard'st their name—
> Montefiasco, Frontiniac,
> Viatico and that old Sack
> Young Herrick took to entertain
> The Muses in a sprightly vein—

an invitation which links together the names of all these topers. Weekes, however, so Antony Wood tells us, was a good preacher as well as a merry fellow. His living was in Cornwall, but he added to it a canonry at Bristol. Herrick addresses two other poems to him; one "a paræneticall or advisive verse," beginning,

> Is this a life to break thy sleep,
> To rise as soon as day doth peep?
> To tire thy patient ox or ass
> By noon and let thy good days pass,
> Not knowing this, that Jove decrees
> Some mirth to adulce man's miseries?

lines which seem to show that Parson Weekes took the cultivation of his glebe somewhat too seriously. In the third poem he is again addressed as Herrick's "peculiar friend," and having apparently come off better than most royalist parsons under the Commonwealth, is exhorted to hospitality:

> Since shed or cottage I have none,
> I sing the more than thou hast one,
> To whose glad threshold and free door
> I may a poet come, though poor,
> And eat with thee a savoury bit,
> Paying but common thanks for it.

If Herrick made some friends among members of his own profession, his love of music probably procured him many more. He addresses poems to William and Henry Lawes, both of whom set verses of his to music; he alludes also to Dr. John Wilson, to Gaulthier, to Lanière, and to Robert Ramsay, in terms of familiarity. The last named, who "set" his version of the dialogue between Horace and Lydia, may have been a Cambridge friend, as he was organist of Trinity College (1628–1634). With another organist, John Parsons of Westminster Abbey, who died in 1623, Herrick must have been acquainted very shortly after his return from Cambridge. Evidence of the friendship remains in two charming little poems addressed to the musician's daughters, Dorothy and Thomasine:

> If thou ask me, dear, wherefore
> I do write of thee no more,
> I must answer, sweet, thy part
> Less is here than in my heart,

are the lines which have given the elder sister immortality, while the attractions of the second are for ever celebrated in the couplet,—

> Grow up in beauty, as thou dost begin
> And be of all admired, Thomasine.

Another family into which Herrick's love of music was probably the key which gained him admission, was that of the Norgates. According to the *Calendars of State Papers*, Edward Norgate the elder was in 1611 appointed, in conjunction with Andrea Bassano, to the office of tuner of the King's virginals, organs, and other instruments; and six-and-twenty years later we find him superintending the repair of the organ in the chapel at Hampton Court. His son, another Edward, was originally a scrivener in the King's service, and was employed "to write, limn and garnish with gold and colours" the royal letters to a picturesque list of foreign potentates, including the Grand Signior, the King of Persia, the Emperor of Russia, the Great Mogul and other remote princes, such as the Kings of Bantam, Macassar, Barbary, Siam, Achee, Fez, and Sus. From scrivener he was raised to be Clerk of the Signet Extraordinary, and thence to be Windsor Herald, and to fill a variety of small offices of profit. Herrick addresses him as "the most accom-

plished gentleman, Master Edward Norgate, Clerk of the Signet to his Majesty," and remarks that

> For one so rarely tun'd to fit all parts,
> For one to whom espoused are all the arts,
> Long have I sought for, but could never see
> Them all concentered in one man but thee—

a flattering tribute to the universality of Norgate's talents.

We may pass now to some of Herrick's patrons. His relations with the royal family we have already touched on, so nothing more need be said about them here. After the King, the Duke of Buckingham, whom he accompanied as chaplain to the Isle of Rhé, was probably the most influential of the poet's protectors, and Herrick addresses an effusive poem to him, and a prettier one to his sister, Lady Mary Villiers. With the Earl of Westmoreland, himself the author of a volume of verse (*Otia Sacra*), Herrick was probably on rather more intimate terms. He addresses poems also to the Duke of Richmond and Lennox, the Earl of Pembroke (Massinger's patron), Edward Earl of Dorset, Viscount Newark, and also to the Viscount's son, whom he calls "*Ultimus Heroum*, or the most learned and the Right Honourable Henry Marquis of Dorchester." Joseph Hall, Bishop of Exeter (his diocesan), and Williams, Bishop of Lincoln, are the only episcopal recipients of his verses. He bespeaks the favour of the former for his book, while to the latter he addresses a carol and a congratulation on his release from imprisonment, in which he speaks obscurely of some ill-turn which Williams had done him. The list of lesser men of rank, knights and baronets, among Herrick's friends is of about the same length. Sir Simeon Steward, who competed with him in writing fairy poems, is still remembered by literary antiquaries, and Sir John Denham, whom he congratulated on his "prospective poem" (*Cooper's Hill*), is, of course, well known. But Sir Clipsby Crew, Sir Lewis Pemberton, Sir Edward Fish, Sir Thomas Heale, Sir Thomas Southwell, and other worthy magnates of the day, now only survive in Herrick's verse and the indices to County Histories. Sir Clipsby Crew, to whom he addresses five poems (besides two to his lady), was probably the most intimate of these friends, as Herrick speaks of him as "My Crew," "My Clipsby," and after telling him how he and his friends "securely live and eat the cream of meat," quoting Anacreon and Horace the while, bids the "brave knight" come to visit his cell, an invitation which implies familiarity. Yet it is to be feared that with all these good knights Herrick held the Elizabethan relation of poet to patron rather than a purely equal friendship. Various verses to Sir Clipsby Crew, Sir Lewis Pemberton, Mr. Kellan and others, show that Herrick loved to frequent a rich man's table, and that when his own cellar was empty he was not slow to remind his friends that without Bacchus song is impossible. Herrick's ducal patrons probably repaid his compliments in broad pieces, and even a plain commoner, Master Endymion Porter, is commended for his liberality to poets, in that he "not only praised but paid them too."

This Endymion Porter is the last of Herrick's friends with whom we shall concern ourselves, and in many respects the most interesting of them all. Originally in the service of Buckingham, he accompanied the Duke and Prince Charles on their visit to Spain, and passed into the latter's service some time in the year 1624 as a groom of the chamber. He made himself useful to the King in many ways, and as early as May, 1625, was granted a pension of £500 a year for life, and three years later was assigned the invidious office of Collector of Fines to the Star Chamber, "with a moiety of the fines he shall bring in." Porter was as full also of projects as Steele himself, and turned them, it would seem, to much better account. Thus we hear of ventures of his in ships called the *Samaritan* and the *Roebuck*, the latter of which proved so remunerative that the common sailors took £20 apiece as their share. He contracted to drain Somercoates Marsh in Lincolnshire, and complained to the Privy Council when his workmen were interfered with. In 1635 he joined with Lord Conway in petitioning the King for a grant of a kind of inspectorship of silks, for which dues were to be levied and £100 a year paid to the Treasury, the balance passing to the inspectors. Two years later Porter and his son George became deputies in the management of His Majesty's Posts. Then we hear of him as an assistant in the Corporation of Saltmakers of Yarmouth, and a little later he is concerned in the erection of a lighthouse and harbour at Filey, near Flamborough Head. An invention for perfecting bar-iron without the use of Scotch coal was his next venture, and, having apparently obtained a patent for this, he prays the King for a grant of the forest of Exmoor in fee-farm with a tenure in socage and the liberty of disafforestation. Next year (1638) he was given the reversion of the Surveyorship of Petty Customs in the Port of London (Chaucer's old post), and a little later on, with the Marquis of Hamilton, obtained leave from the King to examine all accounts made to his Majesty, and when they found any accountants to have deceived the King, to make what advantage they could, either by compounding with delinquents of that kind or by prosecuting them, the King to have one half the profit, and Porter and the Marquis the other. Many accountants, we are told, came in and offered very considerable compositions, so much more grist to Porter's ever busy mill. These grants and petitions, it must be confessed, shed but a sorry light on the way affairs were managed during the eleven years of Charles's personal government, but Porter knew how to make himself a favourite with the King by purchasing him works of art, conducting negotiations with Rubens and other painters, and many similar services. The State Papers which give us all these details of his business life tell us also some interesting scraps as to his taste in dress and at the table. He orders wine from abroad, and apparently uses his influence to get it in duty free, while a friend gratefully informs him that he has tried the largest soles he ever saw, fried them and pickled them according to Endymion's directions, and found them excellent. A husband who knows much about cookery does not always contribute to the easy digestion of family meals. If Endymion interfered much in this or other respects, he may probably have repented of it, for his wife, Olive, was plainly a little hot-tempered. While Endymion was absent in Spain the letters of husband and wife are full of pretty quarrels and reconciliations. "Her will," he writes once, "must be done, or else there will be but little quiet;" and again,—"I wish no more wrangling till we meet, absence being punishment enough. I beg you not to beat George (their eldest son) so much, unless he be very like me. I will never beat Charles for being like you." But Mrs. Porter could be submissive as well as provoking. Her brother tells her that Endymion is very angry, and she writes that—"She did not think he could have been so cruel to have stayed so long away, and not to forgive that which he knows was spoken in passion. She knows not how to beg his pardon, because she has broken word with him before, but she hopes his good nature will forgive her, and that he will come home." Some day the temptation to piece together these married love-letters, with a sketch of what can be found out as to this interesting man, will become irresistible. Here I must hasten to justify Porter's appearance on the present occasion. Five of Herrick's poems are addressed to him, all in the vein of a poet to a patron with whom he was on familiar terms. One I take to

be an answer to a letter of condolence on the death of one of Herrick's own brothers, though it is usually maintained that the death alluded to is that of a brother of Porter himself. The others are all sportive; a letter in praise of a country life, a dialogue in which Herrick and Porter sing in turns the charms of country and court, and two encomiums on Porter's liberality.

> Let there be patrons, patrons like to thee,
> Brave Porter! poets ne'er will wanting be;
> Fabius and Cotta, Lentulus all live
> In thee, thou man of men! who here dost give
> Not only subject-matter for our wit
> But likewise oil of maintenance for it.

And again this quatrain, which calls up an amusing picture:

> When to thy porch I come and ravish'd see
> The state of poets there attending thee,
> Those bards and I all in a chorus sing
> We are thy prophets, Porter, thou our King.

As these verses remind us, Porter was a patron of many other poets besides Herrick, and by them also was duly besung. He was a patron, too (the trait is too delightful to be omitted), of the redoubtable Captain Dover, and in his capacity of Groom of the Bed-chamber, gave that worthy a suit of the King's clothes to lend more grace to the celebration of the Cotswold Games. But here, alas, we must bid farewell to him. There are yet others of Herrick's friends of whom we would fain write, notably a group of charming ladies: Mistress Bridget Lowman, to whom he wrote his "Meadow Verse;" Mrs. Dorothy Kennedy, from whom he parted with so much sorrow; the "most comely and proper Mistress Elizabeth Finch;" "Mrs. Catherine Bradshaw, the lovely, that crowned him with laurels;" and last, but certainly not least, that "Pearl of Putney, the mistress of all singular manners, Mistress Portman." But these, alas, are as mysterious to us as Julia and Dianeme themselves. The gossip that has here been set down has been gleaned, painfully enough, from old records and registers, and even these seemingly inexhaustible treasures will not always yield the information we desire.

GEORGE SAINTSBURY
From "Introduction"
The Poetical Works of Robert Herrick
Volume 1, 1893, pp. xxv–liii

Few poets have had, so far as their poetical reputation is concerned, a more curious history than Robert Herrick. He had, at his death, outlived his own generation, but this has sometimes been almost of itself a passport to immortality. Campbell, for instance, and some others found in the fact the securest assurance of continued popularity. But in Herrick's case things went differently. He published very late; and he did not publish at all till the taste for his style was waning. After he published that taste waned still more and more; and it was nearly a century and a half before it revived. Hence it happened that the *Hesperides* occupies, almost alone, the position of a collection of the truest poetry which never had, either in its own day or in any day at all near to its own, any popularity at all. Some two centuries and a quarter after his own birth Herrick met in Hazlitt a critic of the first class, and one who was well disposed to his own style of poetry, who could yet put him by as something newly discovered and hardly worth the discovering. Even a century after the "discovery" his place can hardly be said to be fixed. Part of his work disgusts those who are most prepared to be delighted with other parts of it. Part of the rest finds, in persons quite prepared to appreciate the remainder, critics ill-equipped for its enjoyment. He is described in almost directly contradictory terms by his own admirers. His qualities and his defects by turns attract and repel the very same adherents. Even Mr. Swinburne finds him at times "monotonous" and "nauseating." He less than almost any writer known to me wrote for "Prince Posterity;" and it was left for Prince Posterity almost entirely to do him honour, yet to do it with the uncertain touch which comes from late and literary appreciation. . . .

⟨*Hesperides*⟩ contains, counting "Humane" and Divine poems together, almost exactly fourteen hundred pieces, the longest of them not extending to very many pages, the great majority not consisting of more than a very few lines. The division of the poems into divine and human is common enough: but there is another division in the human poems themselves which must have very often suggested itself to readers, and which has since been carried out in the excellent and elegant edition of Mr. Pollard. This is the separation of a certain class of epigrams which Herrick, either by accident or purposely, included among his non-divine poems, and which are regarded with exceedingly scant affection even by his greatest admirers. The majority of these epigrams consists of brief, excessively foul-mouthed, and for the most part very defectively witty lampoons on persons who are asserted by tradition or guesswork to have been, sometimes at least, parishioners of Dean Prior. They do not as a rule sin very grossly in what is commonly and exclusively called indecency; they cannot for a moment be compared in this respect to the epigrammatic work of the two authors who would seem to have suggested them, Martial and Ben Jonson. They are even more destitute of the poisoned wit of the Roman satirist, and the bludgeonly strength which frequently characterizes Ben's performances in this kind. But most of all are they destitute of the literary merit which always distinguishes Martial, and which very commonly distinguishes Jonson. Herrick's epigrammatic work is incomparably the worst, in a literary point of view, that he has left; and it is, even among the mass of dull, coarse epigram which the late sixteenth and early seventeenth century has left us, exceptionally coarse and dull. It chiefly contents itself with alleging and upbraiding physical weaknesses and defects, common to or exceptional in humanity, in the plainest and foulest terms. It is not much, if at all, above the scribblings on the wall of the lowest kind of schoolboy or popular wit. So astonishingly does it contrast with the main tenor of the work with which it is associated, that some ingenious paradoxers have wondered whether it was not introduced as an intentional foil to the too soft and luscious graces of the rest. It is not necessary to give an opinion on this point. Even elsewhere it is sufficiently evident that Herrick's taste was not impeccable; he nowhere shows much real wit; and the abusive epigram was a favourite form of his master Ben's. It is probably not needful to look further in order to account for the presence of these loathsome weeds in an otherwise charming, if somewhat "careless-ordered" garden.

On a second, a larger, and a much more respectable division of Herrick's verse, the *Divine Poems*, or *Noble Numbers*, somewhat diverse opinions and many not particularly necessary theories have been uttered. By the admirers of his best productions they have, with a few exceptions, been somewhat disdained; either on that falsest of all grounds, "I must take pleasure in the thing represented before I can take pleasure in the representation," or for other reasons. A collection of poems which contains the "Litany to the Holy Spirit," and "The

White Island," to name no others, could not, as it seems to me, be spoken of with anything but respect by any true and catholic lover of poetry. But as a matter of fact we should have to mention much else. What may be called the Divine Epigrams—though they may sometimes stand, for purely poetic worth, in not so very different a relation to the masterpieces as the epigrams of the other division do to the masterpieces there—have at any rate a vast advantage of subject, and an advantage, not so very much less, of form. Herrick had little or no wit: but he had a fair allowance of sententious aphoristic faculty. And many of these pious pieces, even if they attain not to the first two, are splendid verse: "To find God," "The Thanksgiving," "To his Conscience," a score or two more might be instanced. However, the positive or comparative merit of these exercises seems to have employed the critics less than the temper which they may be supposed to express. Were they palinodes, expressions of repentance for earlier license, and attempts to consecrate the hitherto profaned fire? Some would fain think and have us think so. Were they merely professional exercitations, not necessarily the outcome of a deliberate hypocrisy, but "duty work" of a piece with the Sunday sermon, official, not personal, dramatic, not authentic? Some would incline more or less strongly to this hypothesis. Or were they, without being either of these, poetical studies of a not necessarily feigned but somewhat unreal kind, resembling the studies which, beyond all doubt, make up the greater sum of amatory verse? Was Herrick a "Pagan" who simply saw in the religion of his time a suitable subject for verse, likely to be popular and not unlikely to be good, and who, though by no means singing with tongue in cheek, was least of all things singing from or with his heart? None of these theories has wanted defenders.

I have elsewhere expressed my inability to adopt any of these explanations, or even to think that any very elaborate explanation is necessary: and subsequent study of the matter has only confirmed me in this disinclination. I take Herrick to have been not in the least a "Pagan," but very much of a "natural man." Had he been born in the first three centuries or so I do not think he would have become a Christian; I think he would have been quite simply and sincerely contented with whatsoever religion he was educated in. But I think Christianity on more than one of its sides—especially on that side of emotional and almost sensual devotion in which the English agrees with the Roman branch of the Church (though it does not go quite so far), and also in those points of theology which concern the fatherhood of God, the mediatorship of Christ, and so forth—had a strong appeal to Herrick's kindly and fanciful, if not daringly intellectual, soul. I think that his devotion was as sincere, as kindly, though perhaps nearly as little high-flying or metaphysical as his more earthly passions. If (which is probable, but by no means certain) he had led a somewhat loose life in his time, I think that the crime of sense never with him became a crime of malice, and that if his repentances in their turn were not the repentances of saints and martyrs they were genuine enough in their way.

This combination of genuineness with absence of depth is the key-note of all Herrick's work; it at once imparts and interprets the peculiar character of the third, the largest, the most famous, and by far the most brilliant division of his poems. It is obvious enough, yet it seems to have escaped or puzzled some, and few have kept it quite so steadily before them as might have been desirable. It is a combination eminently suited to produce a man skilled at catching, and contented to catch, the thoughts, the impressions, the joys, the sorrows of the present minute. Whatever matters, trivial or otherwise, Herrick is meditating he is always *totus in illis*. They do not interfere with each other; and I no more believe that the "Litany" is insincere because it occurs in the same volume with the "Vine," than I believe that Herrick was insincere in his praises of Julia because we find them side by side with raptures about Electra or Dianeme.

Indeed, his numerous actual or pretended loves are hardly more characteristic of, and hardly more beneficial to his verse than the still more numerous subjects of interest of a non-amatory character which he found to sing of. Except the scenery of Devonshire (which he regarded with a Philistinism greater than his century can excuse), and his early troubles for lack of money, whereof he sang not, most of the accidents of life seem to have found in Herrick a sympathetic spectator, sharer, chronicler. Not only his own "girls," but the loves and the weddings (not by any means forgetting the wedding-feasts) of other people, sack in Fleet Street, as well as the hock-cart in the country, funerals not much less than weddings or christenings—all such things attracted the musings and the muse of this singular parson. Nor were his interests limited to occasions of festivity or of sensual pleasure. He was not, as has been said (being a man very much of his age, and not troubled with any excessive originality), gratified with the "warty incivility" of that fringe of Dartmoor towards the South Hams in which his beneficed life was cast. He professed, and very likely felt, a vivid preference for the attractions of the town. Yet not Wordsworth himself, in his very different way, has shown himself more penetrated with appreciation of the joys and beauties of the country than Herrick. It may have been accident, or it may have been intention, that made the later poet, or the later poet's sister, meet the earlier full tilt on the subject of daffodils. But to any impartial judge it is to this day difficult to award the crown—time allowance being given according to the proper rules of such contests—between them. And the daffodils are not alone in having received from Herrick a poetical celebration that in its own way can not be surpassed. Primroses, violets, the very "meads" themselves, owe him to all time a royalty of honour for the magnificent countenance that he has bestowed on them. A contemporary and fellow "son" of his in Ben's family had anticipated him by saying the last word on "Red and White Roses" with a touch of quintessential elegance which even Herrick rarely reached; but Herrick has, on the other hand, the advantage of Carew in a wider range, in a more genuine and unforced inspiration, and in a certain *bonhomie* which is rare in poets. The moderns are, as a rule, wont to deny him the higher extravagances of passion, and the denial may be justified by a sufficient number of documents; but "The Mad Maid's Song," "The Litany," "The White Island," and not a few others are there to show what he could have attained an he would, and what he did sometimes attain when he would. He had two gifts which are in the very rarest instances found together. The one was an original and unique gift of style; the other was a range—low, perhaps, if any one chooses to insist on that point, but wide—of interest which supplied him with the subjects on which he exercised that style. I am not quite sure that there is any English poet who unites these two gifts in quite the same degree except one or two of the very greatest.

The range of Herrick's subjects is wont, I think, to be a little underrated. One or two English critics, followed by such few foreigners as have taken note of him at all, have treated him as a mere "folk-lorist" in verse, busied about old and decaying ceremonies. Hazlitt, in almost the most memorable of his memorable injustices, thought him best as a translator,

and rather a lapidary than a poet. Not a few others, while not wholly denying his merits, treat him as an artificial amorist who is sometimes very coarse, and never thoroughly genuine. Now—as I have already endeavoured to make out, and as I hope many readers of this edition who take it as it comes, and are not, as Hazlitt rather strangely says, "dazzled by the motes" of Herrick's poetry, will perceive—he *is* these things, at least on the good side of them; but he is also something more. He is what may be called a common enjoyer, a person who, just as some other persons constantly select the evil, troublesome, and uncomfortable sides of life for their special attention, selects its joyous, pleasing, and gay sides for his special province. Secondly, he is one who is capable of manifold observation; who is not limited to one or two sides of life any more than he is limited to one or two loves. He describes one of the latter in a delightful poem as

> Sappho next, a principal.

The truth is that the girl or the thing which or who happened to be uppermost in his thoughts for the moment was always the "principal" to Herrick. It was sack or it was beer; it was Prue or it was Perilla; it was Sir Clipseby Crewe or no matter what neighbour, or parishioner, or friend; it was King Charles or King Oberon; it was witchcraft or religion; it was the vision of Julia's petticoat or the vision of himself on his deathbed. He might be thinking of his own ill-fortune in being exiled to "this dull Devonshire," or of his good fortune in possessing a competence, of his father, Ben Jonson, or his friend that singular courtier Endymion Porter, who affected in his life and after it the imagination of so many men of letters. He might be meditating unworthy vengeance on any churl or slut in his parish. But he took up all these subjects—so many and so various— with an equal and an almost indescribable zest and relish. Although a good deal in his style is strongly artificial, nothing is more rare in Herrick than the taint of the exercise, nothing more absolutely unknown in him than the mark of the collar. He writes, if not exactly because he must, at any rate because he chooses and feels i' the vein. He has the quality which a superannuated school of criticism in another art used to call *gusto*. There is no subject attacked by him that he does not in this way or that touch and transform with the peculiar transfiguration of art, effected partly by his interest in the subject itself, and partly by the idiosyncrasy of his wonderful style.

This style has some of the most singular combinations of quality that can be found anywhere. It is prim and it is easy; it is intensely charged with classical reminiscence and even classical quotation, and it is as racy of the soil of England as any style of any English poet; it is extremely artificial, and it has a dewy freshness not easy to parallel elsewhere. Its most obvious and easily characterized characteristics are, as usual, far from being its best. Herrick's diminutives have attracted, and it is impossible that they should not attract, a great deal of attention. They strongly recall, and may not impossibly have been suggested by, the similar indulgences of the French Pléiade school, which (though *Zepheria* and a few other things are its chief actual analogues and descendants in Elizabethan English) certainly had some influence on our shores. But to me, at least, they seem to be caricatures by the author of his own genuine spirit—mistaken attempts to emphasize, for the sake of the vulgar, faculties which he could display in a far better and more legitimate manner. "Rubelet," "Compartlement," "Shephardling," always make me think of Bacon's celebrated denunciation of carpet bedding two centuries before it came into fashion. You may oft-times see things as good in tarts.

They are all the more unfortunate that what they do emphasize, at least to the taste of the present age, is rather the mechanical and artificial side of Herrick's genius than the natural and poetic.

Yet this latter side is of such rarity and charm as need no garish artificialities to set them off. It reminds us at once in likeness and difference of the most magnificent stanza of Herrick's younger contemporary Marvell:—

> My love is of a birth as rare
> As 'tis for object strange and high,
> For 'tis begotten of Despair
> Upon Impossibility.

Very different indeed was the actual parentage of Herrick's muse. It was begotten apparently of easy Confidence upon facile Possibility, and its objects were rarely high or strange. But yet it was of a birth as rare as might be found in a month's journey through libraries. It has in the most eminent degree that peculiar quality—a great constituent of style but not to be identified with it, and though never subsisting without it sometimes missing where style is—the quality which can be only called Phrase. There are some, though few, great masters of style who have no very distinct phrase; there are not a few writers cunning in phrase who are too much its servants to be masters of style. But Herrick's phrase though intensely individual was well under his control, and seldom or never got the better of him. In generic character it was not very different from the other great phrases and styles, even from some phrases and styles not exactly great, of his day—the day of what may be called the second Elizabethan period, which comprehends in itself in sub-varieties the Jacobean and the Caroline. The writers of this stage, under the general influence of Jonson, aped, to an extent from which their predecessors were free, classical form in grammar, vocabulary, and order. Mr. Pollard has specified, more fully I think than any precedent editor, the exact and literal transcripts in English from Catullus, Martial, Ovid, Horace, Virgil, and the rest, which Herrick introduces into his verse. I am not sure that there is not something a little profane in thus betraying to the unlearned the coincidences and echoes which have always been an additional, perhaps a main, ingredient in the pleasure with which scholars read the *Hesperides*. But the facts are indisputable enough, and the classicality thus introduced into English is one of the main differentiæ of the poet's species.

What is less easy to define is the native and individual quality with which he blends and subdues this almost excessive classicality, so as to make it an English style of the simplest and the most original, hardly smelling at all of the lamp or the lexicon. Here we seem to come at once, as with others we come later and after preliminary analyses, to the ultimate quality of style. It is comparatively easy to say that the sententious perfection of his phrase, possessed in lesser degree by persons like Cotton and Sherburne, in equal or greater by persons like Crashaw and Carew, and exhibited in different material by others like Herbert and Vaughan, was endemic—that it was the mere trick of the time, easy then, unattainable afterwards or before. It is tolerably safe to go a little further, and to assign the influences which produced it to the sinking but still powerful tide of Elizabethan passion and ardour meeting and mixed with the rising tide of classical imitation. Whether such a confluence or conflict would be thought likely to produce such an effect, if we had not the effect before us, is a question which it is unnecessary to discuss. It must be sufficient to say here that there is some such idiosyncrasy in Herrick and (which is extremely interesting) that by the time his book appeared it was an idiosyncrasy which had somehow or other lost its relish for the public taste. For those of Herrick's generation who had sunk a little farther—the Cottons, the Davenants, and so forth—there was still a public. But for Herrick, as far as we can tell, there was none. It is seldom safe to boast ourselves over our fathers, but we may here at least be thankful if not boastful.

On the separate divisions of his subjects it is probably not necessary to say much here. The "folk-lorist" section has been already glanced at, and is at this time of day rather in danger of over- than of under-valuation. It was certainly fortunate that at a critical time we had such a poet as this to record for us the fleeting accidents of an earlier, and as some irreconcilables still think a better, state of society. Another division, that of the fairy poems, seems to me, though charming, less charming than it has seemed to some others. Herrick simply continued Drayton with a less masculine though perhaps a more delicate conception of the fairy theory of their day. Bishop Corbet in his well-known lament has given a version of the same view which, if it is inferior in grace and in strictly poetical expression both to *Nymphidia* and to Herrick's pieces, seems to me to go more to the root of the matter. And in the true envisagement of fairy subjects Scott and Keats, those strangely different and complementary contemporaries, have said the last word. "La Belle Dame sans Merci" sums the matter up once for all on one side, as Scott's various pieces, connected or not with Thomas the Rhymer, do on the other. In what may be called his "various" moods—complimentary, satirical, commemorative and other—Herrick does but example his time in his own inimitable and charming way. We would not lose these pieces, but we do not attach to them any special or extraordinary value. His sacred work has been already discussed, and this again could not be spared; but with one or two famous and already noted exceptions it has been better done by others. The chief attraction of it is the fact of its having been done at all, and having been in these one or two instances done supremely, by the author of the other work which also stands to the name of Herrick, and especially to that of the author of the convivial and amatory poems.

The value of these last seems to me not merely exceptional, but even unique. It is, of course, to a certain extent the value of the whole period; but it is specially presented and differentiated. Donne is a far "greater" poet than Herrick, and moves in a far higher sphere, both of poetry and passion. But he had not Herrick's mastery of expression, and he gave at least some countenance to the theory that his later life had become ashamed of its earlier scenes. Herrick is "smooth and round;" there is nothing that jars with any part of his work in any other part of it. In the very long period which passed between the publication of the *Hesperides* and his death he may have fallen into a different vein of thought or sentiment from that which announces itself even in the *Noble Numbers*, even in the apologetic couplet which closes the *Hesperides* themselves. But we have absolutely no evidence of the fact. He is, if not exactly passionate—I should hold that he sometimes is, and that such pieces as the famous "Bid me to live," and "I dare not ask" have a thrill and a quiver inseparable from sincere passion—eminently simple, and all of a piece. It only remains to examine what this simplicity shows us.

It shows us, as I think, a nature curiously sound and healthy, with no bad blood in it, if with a slight deficiency of some of the nobler spirits which transcend the blood. It has been urged that Herrick has "too many kisses" in him, that he is too luscious. Such a point is impossible to argue, for it is a pure matter of taste. Catullus would not have agreed with these censors: nor do I. But what does seem to me worth noting is that Herrick is entirely free from the chief vice of most amatory poets. It may be the consequence of a defect in sentiment of him, of an insufficient power of feeling

> Le regret pensif et confus
> D'avoir été et n'être plus,

which makes him so destitute of bitterness towards old loves. But of that vice we find nothing at all in him. To Herrick, as to too few poetical lovers, though perhaps to all good lovers, poetical or not, to love once is to love always, however slight and temporary be the bonds. You may add, however wide the range, new loves to the list; but you must never strike out the old.

In the service of Bacchus, as distinguished from that of Venus, Herrick is meretricious rather than absolutely accomplished. His taste seems to me to have been wanting in quality. He anticipated, however, the taste of the next generation in detecting the excellence of Burgundy, and we are still, despite all that has been written on the subject, too uncertain as to what sack really was to appreciate his devotion in that direction. I should conjecture that just as Herrick shows a certain lack of discrimination in his love, so his taste in wine was something promiscuous, and disposed to admit whatsoever, without nastiness or bad after effects, would produce the requisite exaltation.

And these are things infinitely unimportant. The important thing is that we have in Herrick a poet who was able, by the kindness of the Upper Powers, to give a distinct and extraordinary form to his impressions, who was also able, again by the kindness of the Upper Powers, to secure for poetical representation a most unusual number of interesting subjects, and who combined the two gifts in a manner which if not unequalled is equalled by very few persons in poetical history. Indeed, it is not easy to find a poet who is in his own way so *complete* as Herrick. The sole blot of his verse, the dull and dirty epigram section, is rather an excrescence than a fault in grain; his deficiencies, as they have been and may be called, are connected in a singular and intimate manner with his excellences, and his charm is of the very first and greatest. Much of it is quite unaccountable; you may reduce it to its very lowest terms, and the irreducible personal element remains. Some of it only appeals, no doubt, to certain persons, though I cannot help thinking that this appeal is made to all the more fortunately and happily constituted of the sons of men. A little of Herrick calls for the broom and the dust-pan, but taking him altogether, he is one of the English poets who deserve most love from lovers of English poetry, who have most idiosyncrasy, and with it most charm.

THOMAS BAILEY ALDRICH
From "Introduction"
Poems of Robert Herrick
1900, pp. xxxviii–l

The details that have come down to us touching Herrick's private life are as meager as if he had been a Marlowe or a Shakespere. But were they as ample as could be desired they would still be unimportant compared with the single fact that in 1648 he gave to the world his *Hesperides*. The environments of the man were accidental and transitory. The significant part of him we have, and that is enduring so long as wit, fancy, and melodious numbers hold a charm for mankind.

A fine thing incomparably said instantly becomes familiar, and has henceforth a sort of dateless excellence. Though it may have been said three hundred years ago, it is as modern as yesterday; though it may have been said yesterday, it has the trick of seeming to have been always in our keeping. This quality of remoteness and nearness belongs, in a striking degree, to Herrick's poems. They are as novel to-day as they were on the lips of a choice few of his contemporaries, who, in reading them in their freshness, must surely have been aware here and there of the ageless grace of old idyllic poets dead and gone.

Herrick was the bearer of no heavy message to the world, and such message as he had he was apparently in no hurry to deliver. On this point he somewhere says:

> Let others to the printing-presse run fast;
> Since after death comes glory, I 'll not haste.

He had need of his patience, for he was long detained on the road by many of those obstacles that waylay poets on their journeys to the printer. Herrick was nearly sixty years old when he published the *Hesperides*. It was, I repeat, no heavy message, and the bearer was left an unconscionable time to cool his heels in the antechamber. Though his pieces had been set to music by such composers as Lawes, Ramsay, and Laniere, and his court poems had naturally won favor with the Cavalier party, Herrick cut but a small figure at the side of several of his rhyming contemporaries who are now forgotten. It sometimes happens that the light love-song, reaching few or no ears at its first singing, outlasts the seemingly more prosperous ode which, dealing with some passing phase of thought, social or political, gains the instant applause of the multitude. In most cases the timely ode is somehow apt to fade with the circumstance that inspired it, and becomes the yesterday's editorial of literature. Oblivion likes especially to get hold of occasional poems. That makes it hard for feeble poets laureate.

Mr. Henry James once characterized Alphonse Daudet as "a great little novelist." Robert Herrick is a great little poet. The brevity of his poems—for he wrote nothing *de longue haleine*—would place him among the minor singers; his workmanship places him among the masters. The Herricks were not a family of goldsmiths and lapidaries for nothing. The accurate touch of the artificer in jewels and costly metals was one of the gifts transmitted to Robert Herrick. Much of his work is as exquisite and precise as the chasing on a dagger-hilt by Cellini; the line has nearly always that vine-like fluency which seems impromptu, and is never the result of anything but austere labor. The critic who called these carefully wrought poems "wood-notes wild" mistook his vocation. They are full of subtle simplicity. Here we come across a stanza as severely cut as an antique cameo,—the stanza, for instance, in which the poet speaks of his lady-love's "winter face,"—and there a couplet that breaks into unfading daffodils and violets. The art, though invisible, is always there. His amatory songs and catches are such poetry as Orlando would have liked to hang on the boughs in the forest of Arden. None of the work is hastily done, not even that portion of it we could wish had not been done at all. Be the motive grave or gay, it is given that faultlessness of form which distinguishes everything in literature that has survived its own period. There is no such thing as "form" alone; it is only the close-grained material that takes the highest finish. The structure of Herrick's verse, like that of Blake, is simple to the verge of innocence. Such rhythmic intricacies as those of Shelley, Tennyson, and Swinburne he never dreamed of. But his manner has this perfection: it fits his matter as the cup of the acorn fits its meat.

Of passion, in the deeper sense, Herrick has little or none.

Here are no "tears from the depth of some divine despair," no probings into the tragic heart of man, no insight that goes much farther than the pathos of a cowslip on a maiden's grave. The tendrils of his verse reach up to the light, and love the warmer side of the garden wall. But the reader who does not detect the seriousness under the lightness misreads Herrick. Nearly all true poets have been wholesome and joyous singers. A pessimistic poet, like the poisonous ivy, is one of nature's sarcasms. In his own bright pastoral way Herrick must always remain unexcelled. His limitations are certainly narrow, but they leave him in the sunshine. Neither in his thought nor in his utterance is there any complexity; both are as pellucid as a woodland pond, content to duplicate the osiers and ferns, and, by chance, the face of a girl straying near its crystal. His is no troubled stream in which large trout are caught. He must be accepted on his own terms.

The greatest poets have, with rare exceptions, been the most indebted to their predecessors or to their contemporaries. It has wittily been remarked that only mediocrity is ever wholly original. Impressionability is one of the conditions of the creative faculty: the sensitive mind is the only mind that invents. What the poet reads, sees, and feels, goes into his blood, and becomes an ingredient of his originality. The color of his thought instinctively blends itself with the color of its affinities. A writer's style, if it have distinction, is the outcome of a hundred styles. Though a generous borrower of the ancients, Herrick appears to have been exceptionally free from the influence of contemporary minds. Here and there in his work are traces of his beloved Ben Jonson, or fleeting impressions of Fletcher, and in one instance a direct infringement on Suckling; but the sum of Herrick's obligations in this sort is inconsiderable. This indifference to other writers of his time, this insularity, was doubtless his loss. The more exalted imagination of Vaughan or Marvell or Herbert might have taught him a deeper note than he sounded in his purely devotional poems. Milton, of course, moved in a sphere apart. Shakspere, whose personality still haunted the clubs and taverns which Herrick frequented on his first going up to London, failed to lay any appreciable spell upon him. That great name, moreover, is a jewel which finds no setting in Herrick's rhyme. His general reticence relative to brother poets is extremely curious when we reflect on his penchant for addressing four-line epics to this or that individual. They were, in the main, obscure individuals, whose identity is scarcely worth establishing. His London life, at two different periods, brought him into contact with many of the celebrities of the day; but his verse has helped to confer immortality on very few of them. That his verse had the secret of conferring immortality was one of his unshaken convictions. Shakspere had not a finer confidence when he wrote:

> Not marble nor the gilded monuments
> Of princes shall outlive this powerful rhyme,

than has Herrick whenever he speaks of his own poetry, and he is not by any means backward in speaking of it. It was the breath of his nostrils. Without his Muse those nineteen years in that dull, secluded Devonshire village would have been unendurable.

His poetry has the value and the defect of that seclusion. In spite, however, of his contracted horizon there is great variety in Herrick's themes. Their scope cannot be stated so happily as he has stated it:

> I sing of brooks, of blossoms, birds and bowers,
> Of April, May, of June, and July-flowers;
> I sing of May-poles, hock-carts, wassails, wakes,
> Of bridegrooms, brides, and of their bridal cakes;
> I write of Youth, of Love, and have access

> By these to sing of cleanly wantonness;
> I sing of dews, of rains, and piece by piece
> Of balm, of oil, of spice and ambergris;
> I sing of times trans-shifting, and I write
> How roses first came red and lilies white;
> I write of groves, of twilights, and I sing
> The Court of Mab, and of the Fairy King;
> I write of Hell; I sing (and ever shall)
> Of Heaven, and hope to have it after all.

Never was there so pretty a table of contents! When you open his book the breath of the English rural year fans your cheek; the pages seem to exhale wildwood and meadow smells, as if sprigs of tansy and lavender had been shut up in the volume and forgotten. One has a sense of hawthorn hedges and wide-spreading oaks, of open lead-set lattices half hidden with honeysuckle; and distant voices of the hay-makers, returning home in the rosy afterglow, fall dreamily on one's ear, as sounds should fall when fancy listens. There is no English poet so thoroughly English as Herrick. He painted the country life of his own time as no other has painted it at any time. It is to be remarked that the majority of English poets regarded as national have sought their chief inspiration in almost every land and period excepting their own. Shakspere went to Italy, Denmark, Greece, Egypt, and to many a hitherto unfooted region of the imagination, for plot and character. It was not Whitehall Garden, but the Garden of Eden and the celestial spaces, that lured Milton. It is the "Ode on a Grecian Urn," "The Eve of St. Agnes," and the noble fragment of "Hyperion" that have given Keats his spacious niche in the gallery of England's poets. Shelley's two masterpieces, *Prometheus Unbound* and *The Cenci*, belong respectively to Greece and Italy. Browning's *The Ring and the Book* is Italian; Tennyson wandered to the land of myth for the *Idylls of the King*; and Matthew Arnold's "Sohrab and Rustum"—a narrative poem second in dignity to none produced in the nineteenth century—is a Persian story. But Herrick's "golden apples" sprang from the soil in his own day, and reddened in the mist and sunshine of his native island.

Even the fairy poems, which must be classed by themselves, are not wanting in local flavor. Herrick's fairy world is an immeasurable distance from that of *A Midsummer Night's Dream*. Puck and Titania are of finer breath than Herrick's little folk, who may be said to have Devonshire manners and to live in a miniature England of their own. Like the magician who summons them from nowhere, they are fond of color and perfume and substantial feasts, and indulge in heavy draughts —from the cups of morning-glories. In the tiny sphere they inhabit everything is marvelously adapted to their requirement; nothing is out of proportion or out of perspective. The elves are a strictly religious people in their winsome way, "part pagan, part papistical"; they have their pardons and indulgences, their psalters and chapels, and

> An apple's core is hung up dried,
> With rattling kernels, which is rung
> To call to morn- and even-song;

and very conveniently,

> Hard by, i' th' shell of half a nut,
> The holy water there is put.

It is all delightfully naïve and fanciful, this elfin-world, where the impossible does not strike one as incongruous, and the England of 1648 seems never very far away.

It is only among the apparently unpremeditated lyrical flights of the Elizabethan dramatists that one meets with anything like the lilt and liquid flow of Herrick's songs. While in no degree Shaksperian echoes, there are epithalamia and dirges of his that might properly have fallen from the lips of Posthumus in *Cymbeline*. This delicate epicede would have fitted Imogen:

> Here a solemne fast we keepe
> While all beauty lyes asleepe;
> Husht be all things; *no noyse here*
> *But the toning of a teare,*
> *Or a sigh of such as bring*
> *Cowslips for her covering.*

Many of the pieces are purely dramatic in essence; the "Mad Maid's Song," for example. The lyrist may speak in character, like the dramatist. A poet's lyrics may be, as most of Browning's are, just so many *dramatis personæ.* "Enter a Song singing" is the stage-direction in a seventeenth-century play whose name escapes me. The sentiment dramatized in a lyric is not necessarily a personal expression. In one of his couplets Herrick neatly denies that his more mercurial utterances are intended presentations of himself:

> To his Book's end this last line he'd have placed—
> Jocund his Muse was, but his Life was chaste.

In point of fact he was a whole group of imaginary lovers in one. Silvia, Anthea, Electra, Perilla, Perenna, and the rest of those lively ladies ending in *a,* were doubtless, for the most part, but airy phantoms dancing—as they should not have danced—through the brain of a sentimental old bachelor who happened to be a vicar of the Church of England. Even with his over-plus of heart it would have been quite impossible for him to have had enough to go round had there been so numerous actual demands upon it.

Thus much may be conceded to Herrick's verse: at its best it has wings that carry it nearly as close to heaven's gate as any of Shakspere's lark-like interludes. The brevity of the poems and their uniform smoothness sometimes produce the effect of monotony. The crowded richness of the line advises a desultory reading. But one must go back to them again and again. They bewitch the memory, having once caught it, and insist on saying themselves over and over. Among the poets of England the author of the *Hesperides* remains, and is likely to remain, unique. As Shakspere stands alone in his vast domain, so Herrick stands alone in his scanty plot of ground.

Shine, Poet! in thy place, and be content.

F. CORNISH WARRE
From "Robert Herrick"
The Edinburgh Review, January 1904, pp. 109–27

The risings and settings of poets on the horizon of fame cannot be calculated. In the long night of the Middle Ages the star of Virgil alone shone undimmed. The great names of antiquity were obscured, some for a time, some for ever, unless the sands of Egypt or the ashes of Herculaneum bring back to light some fragments of the lost treasures. And what the barbarian and Mohammedan cataclysms did on a grand scale has been repeated by the petty neglect of great authors and petty inflation of small authors since the time when the printing press supplied to all classes of writings the prospect of a cheap immortality, and the stream was choked by its own fulness. Shakespeare's fame was obscured for a time; Milton slept on the shelf for a hundred years; Dante had a great reputation, but no readers, in the time when *Pastor Fido* and *L'Adone* were admired. And Johnson, in his *Lives of the Poets,* which canonise Christopher Pitt, Thomas Yalden, and Elijah Fenton, has no place for Herrick. Herrick is of his own time,

one of the poets who continued Elizabethan tradition into the Caroline age and who went out of fashion with the Restoration—not that the Restoration had much to do with the change of fashion; if one generation is classical the next shall be romantic or call it what you will; change of fashion has often little to recommend it but the pleasure of change—anyhow, the Elizabethan lyric, of which Herrick was the latest inheritor, gave place to Pindarics and heroics, and Herrick ceased to please; and for a hundred and fifty years no one cared for his memory. 'He was practically forgotten' till Nichols fished him up in the *Gentleman's Magazine,* 1796–7, since[1] which time his reputation has risen with some critics to such a height that there may be danger of its becoming overblown. Yet we doubt whether he is even now commonly estimated at his true value.

We said above that Herrick was of his own time, and that he continued Elizabethan traditions. This may seem a contradiction: but it need not be so. It is easy to under-estimate or to over-estimate the extent of a poet's obligation to the fashion of his day: some lead, some follow a lead, and a poet may be consciously or unconsciously one of a group or a school of innovators or of conservatives, or may by date and temperament belong both to the incoming and the outgoing fashion. Crabbe and Cowper, for instance, whilst undermining the conventions in which they were brought up and levelling the way to be trodden by Wordsworth and the Lakers, who seemed to themselves pioneers—we do not dispute the claim—obeyed the Augustan rule of verse as conscientiously as Gray or Thomson, though they allowed themselves to be 'licentious' in choice of language. No one ever succeeded in defining the terms 'romantic' and 'classical,' which in their day stood to represent the eternal dualism of art which takes new forms as the spirit breathes; and many good poets—as Byron, who maintained the authority of Pope and wrote the *Giaour* were at once Classicists and Romanticists, or neither. There have been moments when a choice had to be made, as when the *Lyrical Ballads* were issued, or when the Preraphaelite brethren attacked established conventions; but for the most part poets write what it is given them to write, without much thought of movements and schools, and little comes of this classifying and docketing of poets and thinkers like specimens in a museum. The 'school' is formed by the imitators, not the inventor, who thinks more of what he has to say than of the dialect in which his followers will repeat it after him. . . .

Herrick, then, owed some of his lyrical mastery to the models of the preceding age. He knew how to play on an instrument the practice of which had been brought to perfection; he used also the exquisiteness of language studied by the framers of conceits, the neatness and quaintness of which George Herbert sets the pattern; but besides this he had his own note and his own methods.

It is sometimes assumed that because Herrick wrote the most delightful country verse that has ever been written since the *Idyls,* the *Eclogues,* and the *Georgics,* he was just a linnet who sang as the linnets do, 'native woodnotes wild.' So he did; but he was also a finished artist, well read in ancient and modern poetry, a man of letters and a man of the world, one who understood the value of perfection as well as Ben Jonson himself.

The gentleman in Horace who could reel you off two hundred verses at a standing was very proud of his fluency; but fluency is not the same thing as fulness; you may have either without the other. Morris is fluent, Browning full, Byron, Shelley, and Scott are both full and fluent. Fulness is a gift of Nature, but fluency may be acquired; and it is the height of wit to give the appearance of ease to the fruit of effort. Readiness is a convenient quality, but not in any way indispensable, nor even a guarantee of good work. The four qualities or capacities of readiness, freshness, fluency, fulness, are not the same thing, though easily confused. Readiness is rather a thing to wonder at than to admire; it is not even essential to wit, though without it wit may often lose its occasion; it is invaluable to the orator, talker, and letter-writer, not so much to the poet. Freshness is inseparable from all good work, whether produced rapidly or slowly; the smell of the lamp is odious, though you burn perfumed oils, and over-elaboration is as fatal to effort as Sheridan's remark upon easy and hard in reading and writing. We know how Macaulay wrote and rewrote, and was content with two pages a day. We know also that *Alexander's Feast* was written in one evening. . . .

To apply this to Herrick. It is no compliment to him to think that he wrote poetry by accident and God's grace, and no disparagement to him if he laboured to attain perfection as other poets have laboured. The appearance of fluency and readiness may be an indication of freshness, not of carelessness; the poet himself would not desire to offer to the Muses that which cost him nothing; his own inclination would rather be to think little of that which came to him easily; he might even take a secret pleasure in counting the cost, known to himself alone, of that which seemed to be so lightly won. If we object to Herrick that he is superficial and immature, we mean that we do not care for his thought and his subjects, not that we comdemn his method; for it is beyond all question that he struck the note which he meant to strike, and with no uncertain finger. His volant touch never failed him when he was poetical, though when he was witty he went sometimes miserably astray.

What his own judgment was he has told us in his 'Request to Julia':

> Julia, if I chance to die
> Ere I print my poetry,
> I must humbly thee desire
> To commit it to the fire;
> *Better 'twere my book were dead,*
> *Than to live not perfected.*

In considering the position of a poet among other poets—a barren comparison, but one cannot altogether avoid it—something must be set down on the score of quantity. A poet must bring his sheaves with him; armfuls, not handfuls, or chosen samples of grain more golden than gold, but full measure, running over. The actual bulk of Herrick's work is not great—one small volume contained all that he chose to print; but he has the quality of fulness; there is no poverty of ideas nor any sense that he has said all he had to say within the circle of which he chose to limit himself; the 'monotony of style and motive,' of which Swinburne complains, is only due to that limitation; and if we turn the pages of *Hesperides* to see what poems are to be cherished and set among the masterpieces, we shall find more such there than in the works of poets who wrote twice and three times as much. He is not at his best in long poems; the *Epithalamies* are the best of them; he is, like Schubert and Burns, a singer, and for poems a few stanzas long, faultless in sentiment, diction, and workmanship, he must be put in the very first rank. If we were making an English lyrical Anthology, two or three poems each would be all that we should take from Lovelace, Suckling, Vaughan, Crashaw, Donne, Denham, or the moderns such as Moore, Campbell, Leigh Hunt, Coleridge, or the more modern still, Arnold, Clough, Browning; to find an equal number of indispensable poems we must go to the masters of lyric verse, Shakespeare,

Milton, Scott, Wordsworth, Tennyson, and Shelley. But when we come to Herrick, we could not do without the 'Daffodils,' nor all the Julia poems—'Cherry Ripe,' 'Whennas in Silks,' the 'Night-piece,' 'Delight in Disorder,' 'Julia's Churching'—nor 'Corinna's Maying,' Sappho's 'Apron of Flowers,' 'To Blossoms,' 'Gather ye Rosebuds,' 'To Anthea,' the 'Ode for Saint Ben,' the 'Mad Maid,' and more still, till the bunch of flowers would seem almost too big for the garden in which they grew. For these poems have all of them the quality of perfection. They have not the heat and passion of Catullus and Burns, nor the sustained sweetness and strength of Horace, but they bear comparison with Horace better than with any other poet; and where Horace reaches perfection, he is most like Herrick. This is high praise; but in freshness and sureness of effect, in choice of words, in colour, form, and rhythm, Herrick is to be placed among the highest poets, quite above the region of Donne or Herbert; and Mr. Swinburne's praise is not exaggerated when he says of Herrick[2]:—

> As a creative and inventive singer he surpasses all his rivals in quantity of good work. In quality of spontaneous inspiration he reminds us, by frequent and flawless evidence, who above all others must beyond all doubt have been his first master and his first model in lyric poetry—the author of 'The Passionate Shepherd to his Love.'

It is also not to be forgotten, as Mr. Swinburne goes on to say, that Herrick is a song-writer, 'first in rank and station of English song-writers,' one whose songs are 'good to read and good to sing,' musical as well as poetical in intention. In more sustained flights music may give a fresh meaning and power to words, translating them to a new atmosphere, as in Stanford's 'Revenge,' for instance; or the words may be little more than a vehicle for the music, as in Handel's metrical oratorios. When Heine combines with Schumann we have the perfection of song-writing, and the advance of music from Lawes and his contemporaries to the present day has not altered the relation of the song to its setting; the same tunefulness and neatness are still required, and a song must not be burdened with thought, which must always be subordinate to feeling, nor obscure in language. If Herrick asks and solves no riddles for a painful world, this is in part because his thought is musical, not metaphysical.

Why, then, has he not a greater fame, and why is he disparaged by some critics as a trifler? Principally because his range of subjects is small—

> I sing of brooks, of blossoms, birds, and bowers,
> Of April, May, of June, and July flowers;
>
> I sing of Maypoles, hock-carts, wassails, wakes,
> Of bridegrooms, brides, and of their bridal cakes.
> I write of Youth, of Love, and have access,
> By these, to sing of cleanly wantonness.

Here was his domain—no Urania visited him darkling; he did not sound the depths and climb the heights like the greatest poets; no indignation stings him to write like Juvenal and 'snaky Persius,' His love is no vampire, like Catullus's Lesbia, to lacerate his heart. He could not write sonnets on slaughtered saints or martyred kings, though the 'untuneable times' unstrung his harp, and the tone of his later poems, when he suffered for his opinions, is more serious than his pastoral vein. Nor is there any philosophy in his poetry, except the everyday philosophy of contentment with life and love of beauty; there are no problems or lofty musings and aspirations, no high flights of religion or patriotism. All these abatements detract from his claim to be set among great poets; but a poet he approves himself as truly as any son of Apollo, if you seek what you shall find, and is in his own region unsurpassed. That region is what he has himself defined in the lines just quoted. His country is true England, not Arcadia, and so far more genuine than that of Theocritus and Virgil, if less divinely tuneful; and he paints youth and beauty without description and detail so deliciously that we must go to Shakespeare himself to better him, for no one else can do it, unless it be Tennyson, some of whose creations are perhaps worthy to sit by the side of Julia.

It may be said that his stock-in-trade is small, and that shared with other contemporary poets. The trivial round of quarrelets of pearl, rubies and corals, roses and cherries, cream and lilies comes in all the stylists of the time; but somehow Herrick's cream is whiter and his cherries riper than the others, and the roses and lilies grow in his Devonshire garden, not in the inkstand, where perchance Saint Ben the scholar found some of his. Herrick, to be sure, swore in his 'Farewell to Sack'—

> What's done by me
> Hereafter shall smell of the lamp, not thee.

But we feel sure that his study was not indoors, but under the apple trees in the Rectory orchard.

So well-read and so sensitive a poet could not but have some echoes from other poets. We are reminded not only of Marlowe, but of Shakespeare, of Herbert, and other sixteenth and seventeenth century writers. But Herrick owed most to his beloved 'Ben,' whose full melodiousness emboldened his follower to rise above conceits and niceties and pour himself out in round English words. He comes so near sometimes that one wonders whether it is Herrick or Jonson that is the imitator:

> Give me a look, give me a face
> That makes simplicity a grace;
> Robes loosely flowing, hair as free,
> Such sweet neglect more taketh me
> Than all the adulteries of art;
> They strike my eyes but not my heart:

says one; and the other, as if continuing the thought—

> A sweet disorder in the dress
> Kindles in clothes a wantonness.
>
>   . . .
>
> A winning wave, deserving note,
> In the tempestuous petticoat;
> A careless shoe-string, in whose tie
> I see a wild civility:
> Do more bewitch me, than when art
> Is too precise in every part.

Herrick might have written 'Drink to me only with thine eyes' without departing from his natural manner; and Jonson the verses dedicated to Posthumus. Jonson's bowl is deeper and filled with more generous wine; but Herrick's liquor, too, is *merus Thyonianus.*

Of the ancient poets—and he knew them all—he owes most to Horace. Horace, it is true, was a moralist and philosopher, and Herrick was neither. Like Horace, he has the security of touch, which is the earnest of success, and the workmanlike feeling that will not leave a poem till it is complete and finished. Horace has, beyond other poets, the gift of unity, at least in the shorter odes which we love better than his Pindarics; Herrick has it too, if in a less degree. 'No Luck in Love' is purely Horatian, both in execution and in sentiment:

> I do love, I know not what;
> Sometimes this and sometimes that:
> All conditions I aim at.

> But, as luckless, I have yet
> Many shrewd disasters met,
> To gain her whom I would get.
> Therefore, now I'll love no more,
> As I've doted heretofore.
> He who must be, shall be poor.

The idea and its expression count for more than the personal feeling. Poets have said it a hundred times and not meant it. There is a like unreality of feeling joined with consummate expression in 'Quis multa gracilis,' which so caught the ear of Milton; more, we may be sure, by its manner than its matter. Horace's Phidyle, Pyrrha, Neæra, Glycera, like Tennyson's Adeline, Lilian, Dora, are visions of womanhood and phases of sentiment, not transcripts of passion; and this is partly true of Herrick, as we shall see.

Compare, not with Horace's 'Quo me, Bacche, rapis,' of which he translates the opening words, but with any of his shorter poems, the 'Canticle to Bacchus'—

> Whither dost thou hurry me,
> Bacchus, being full of thee?
> This way, that way; that way, this,
> Here and there a fresh love is;
> That doth like me, this doth please:
> Thus a thousand mistresses
> I have now; yet I alone
> Having all, enjoy not one.

The following poem, though not specially Horatian, resembles Horace in dignity and the art of saying much in a few lines. It might have been lifted a little higher, and found a place in *Comus*; it might have come as a song in a play of Shakespeare. There is little novelty in thought or diction, nothing to stir the pulses, its echoes of Latin poetry are trite; yet it is perfect—

> Music, thou queen of heaven, care-charming spell,
>   That strik'st a stillness into hell;
> Thou that tam'st tigers, and fierce storms that rise,
>   With thy soul-melting lullabies:
> Fall down, down, down, from those thy chiming spheres,
> To charm our souls, as thou enchant'st our ears.

His 'Protestation to Julia' is Horatian, again because the pleasure which it gives us is rather from the expression than the depth of feeling. Once for all let it be said that Herrick is not one of those poets who write with their heart's blood. Without being insincere, Herrick, like other poets, sometimes writes more for the sake of his verse, or for a turn of expression, than because he must sing just so, or break his heart like the nightingale; that is not our jolly Herrick's way. He laughed, and may have wept; but he seldom sighed—

> Why dost thou wound and break my heart,
> As if we should for ever part?
> Hast thou not heard an oath from me,
> After a day, or two, or three,
> I would come back and live with thee?
> Take, if thou dost distrust that vow,
> This second protestation now:
> Upon thy cheek that spangled tear
> Which sits as dew of roses there,
> That tear shall scarce be dried before
> I'll kiss the threshold of thy door.
> Then weep not, sweet, but thus much know,
> I'm half returned before I go.

The words may be too strong for the occasion, which is apparently the same as that of his 'Sailing from Julia;' but the tender feeling is as genuine as the expression is faultless.

We like these better than such direct imitations of Horace as the poem to Posthumus, or the 'Country Life,' which are as much dilutions as imitations, and show to disadvantage, inasmuch as the English language has not the marble smoothness of the Latin, and cannot be cut to such fineness. In the former, however, he gets clear away from Horace, and gives us himself—

> To thee, and then again, to thee
> We'll drink, my Wickes, until we be
>   Plump as the cherry,
> Though not so fresh, yet full as merry
>   As the cricket,
> The untamed heifer, or the pricket,
> Until our tongues shall tell our ears
> We're younger by a score of years.

'His Poetry his Pillar' is inspired by Horace's 'Exegi momumentum,' but is not an imitation. It is not pitched in so high a strain, nor is it so elaborate; but it is not every poet who could say without fear of envious laughter—

> Pillars let some set up
>   If so they please:
>   Here is my hope
> And my pyramides.

Horace was Herrick's model, so far as he had a model. He knew the Latin poets so well that echoes of others reach our ear—in particular he was beholden to Martial, whose terse and neat versification, as well as his unrestrained wit, attracted him. The Latin poets taught him the value of good workmanship. We may be sure that Herrick's verse was pruned down, not built up. The rich substance came first, the shaping and polishing later.

What are we to say of Herrick's mistresses, Anthea, Corinna, Sappho, Perilla, Lucia, Lalage, Biancha, Myrrha, Silvia, Electra, Dianeme, and 'stately Julia, prime of all'? Are they fancies or realities? Did they live in Devonshire or in London? Did Herrick leave them, or they him?

> . . . all are gone,
> Only Herrick's left alone,
> For to number sorrow by
> Their departures hence, and die.

Did he love them all? and all at once, or singly, or are they but names? There is no external evidence, such as identifies Catullus's Lesbia and Ovid's Corinna, nor any personal certainty, as in the case of the Cynthia whose love was the bane of Propertius. We can only judge from the poems themselves. The dilemma is this: either Herrick wrote these poems in praise of town-bred maidens whom he loved in his early London days, the 'soft, smooth virgins,' with whom he used to glide 'in barge with boughs and rushes beautified' to Richmond and Hampton Court, amongst the swans and the 'pure and silver-wristed Naiades;' or they are addressed to country girls by a middle-aged or elderly country parson, for Herrick was well past thirty-five, the age fixed by Byron as the period of love-making, before he left the 'smoother sphere' and 'most civil government' of London, and migrated to the farmhouses and granges of 'dull Devonshire.'

If we compare 'Discontents in Devon' with another poem on his 'banishment' to the West, we find him saying—

> Justly, too, I must confess,
> I ne'er invented such
> Ennobled numbers for the press
>   As where I loath'd so much;

which seems to give the *Noble Numbers* to the nineteen years of exile; whilst

> Before I went
> To banishment
>   Into the loathèd West,
> I could rehearse
> A lyric verse,
>   And speak it with the best,

would give the poems of the true Herrick note to his earlier life in London. There remains the suggestion that he, too, like Milton, did not care for 'the tangles of Neæra's hair,' and that his many-named love was but a symbol of incarnate virgin youth. But the mere mention of Milton's chaste severity in the same sentence with Herrick's warmth and merrier art disposes of this at once.

If we knew the dates of Herrick's poems, we should know more about his loves. Probably many of his love-poems are youthful fancies, partly real, partly fictitious, the English temperament inspired by classical poetry—poems preserved by him, not as the story of his life, but for their own beauty, for so great an artist must have known the worth of what he wrote. He gave to these visions of beauty, as he would, sweet names from Rome or Greece, whatever suited the line—

> Call me Sappho, call me Chloris,
> Call me Lalage, or Doris.

Some of them no doubt belong to his earlier life; but Julia and Anthea are with him to the last. Corinna, the 'sweet slug-a-bed,' may have gone a-Maying to Kensington or Chelsea, for the poem speaks of streets, and there was whitethorn then within reach of Londoners; as she is named 'for her wit, and the graceful use of it,' she is not an abstraction. 'Smooth Anthea' of the white skin and 'heaven-like crystalline' eyes, smells of the country, for she is invited to go to the wake:

> Come, Anthea, let us two
> Go to feast, as others do.

The Devonshire 'revel' is described with just a touch of contempt. Maybe, in this poem, 'Anthea' is merely a vocative, not the name of a woman; and, in spite of all its fervour and passionate protesting, we doubt whether 'to Anthea, who may command him anything' is much more than a beautiful piece of music. The relation of a poet to love is not that of a mere lover. He is in love with love itself, not with a woman only, and his inspiration comes from art as well as nature. We have no right to call him insincere because he dramatises. But Anthea is addressed again in a more serious vein, when he couples her name with thoughts of his own death:—

> Now is the time, when all the lights wax dim;
> And, thou, Anthea, must withdraw from him
> Who was thy servant. Dearest, bury me
> Under that holy oak or Gospel tree,
> Where, though thou seest not, thou mayst think
>   upon
> Me, when thou yearly go'st procession;
> Or, for mine honour, lay me in that tomb
> In which thy sacred relics shall have room.
> For my embalming, sweetest, there will be
> No spices wanting when I'm laid by thee;

and again:—

> So three in one small plot of ground shall lie,
> Anthea, Herrick, and his poetry.

There is tenderness and friendship in these lines, if no passion.

What shall we say of Sappho?[3] The exquisite poem which begins—

> To gather flowers Sappho went,
>   And homeward she did bring

> Within her lawny continent
>   The treasure of the spring,

need not have a personal reference; but Sappho is put by him as 'next' (to Julia) 'a principal.'

Electra is a more sensuous creation; her rising out of bed brings back the day a-kindling. Hers is the image of his 'Vision,' and of the 'Semele' poem; but these lines redeem his innocence and her chaste coldness:

> I dare not ask a kiss,
>   I dare not beg a smile;
> Lest having that, or this,
>   I might grow proud the while.
> No, no, the utmost share
>   Of my desire shall be
> Only to kiss that air
>   That lately kissèd thee.

Myrrha, too, is hard-hearted, and so is Dianeme:

> If thou, composed of gentle mould,
>   Art so unkind to me,
> What dismal stories will be told
>   Of those that cruel be?

So the sweet procession goes by, a dream of fair women. They are neither real nor unreal; they warmed the poet's fancy, but did not possess his heart. They came across his way, some in youth, some in riper years, when like Herbert he was vowed to the book and the gown in his Devonshire banishment, rustic maids, daughters of yeomen from the upland farms among the sycamores and ashes, who talked the country dialect, wore rough country shoes and stockings, rode to market on Dartmoor ponies, and made butter of clotted cream in a lime-wood bowl. We can imagine the merry Rector living among his simple flock, winning the hearts of young and old and breaking none but his own, not straitlaced enough to please Puritan parishioners whose fathers had been out against Spain in 1588, but welcome in all companies, from the Hoptons and Grenvilles to the freeholders who rode with them to Stratton Down to fight for the King, in those primitive regions where lack of society smoothes distinctions of rank, and the parson has a right of entry everywhere.

But Julia was a lady born, and married in her own condition. Julia alone of all has colour and outline and substance. Though she does not speak, and is only 'briefly' described, she is as real as one of Shakespeare's heroines; and we must go to Shakespeare for her paragon, or to the creators of the most lovely visions of womankind in painting or poetry. Herrick's book is full of Julia from end to end. Her lips are redder than rubies and cherries; 'rubies, corals, scarlets, all' wonder at them. Her teeth are 'quarrelets of pearl.' Her eyes are 'life-begetting,' her breath is 'all the spices of the East,' her voice is 'smooth, sweet, and silvern.' Her raiment becomes part of herself:

> Whenas in silks my Julia goes,
> Then, then, methinks, how sweetly flows
> The liquefaction of her clothes.
>
> Next, when I cast my eyes and see
> That brave vibration each way free,
> O, how that glittering taketh me!

—a poem which for sweetness and daring is unsurpassed. Only Herrick, again, could have spoken of Julia's azure robe as—

> Erring here, and wandering there,
> Pleased with transgression everywhere;

or, again, for it must be Julia, though she is not named:

> A sweet disorder in the dress
> Kindles in clothes a wantonness;

and the rest of that lovely poem. The riband about her waist is a 'zonulet of love.' Were ever clothes so glorified, unless it were to do honour to Clarissa?

Perhaps all these things have been said before; but Herrick says them as new, and with a directness of feeling which makes them different. He leaves to her the burning of his poetry if he dies before it is printed; he asks her to take in his last breath:

> My fates are ended—when thy Herrick dies,
> Clasp thou his book, then close thou up his eyes.

When he must leave her, he takes his leave in these exquisitely tender lines:

> When that day comes, whose evening says I'm gone
> Into that wat'ry desolation,
> Devoutly to thy closet gods then pray
> That my wing'd ship may meet no Remora.
>   . . .
> Mercy and Truth live with thee! and forbear,
> In my short absence, to unsluice a tear;
> But yet, for Love's sake, let thy lips do this,
> Give my dead picture one engend'ring kiss;
> Work that to life, and let me ever dwell
> In thy remembrance, Julia. So farewell

—lines which would not be out of place in one of Shakespeare's sonnets. . . .

It was the custom of that time to circulate poetry in manuscript, and Herrick's poems, like Donne's, were widely read before they were printed. It was thus possible for a writer to have a reputation before he had published a verse; and it was also less easy for him to suppress what had already been seen abroad than never to break privacy at all. The word sent out was not irrevocable, but it was hard to recall. This has been alleged as a reason why Donne's poems were published without expurgation; and if that excuse is accepted, it may serve for Herrick too. His youthful poems were already to some extent published before they were printed, and he had lost the control of them. He alludes to this in a poem entitled 'To His Books,' in which, with a reminiscence of Horace, he says:

> While thou did'st keep thy candour undefil'd,
> Dearly I lov'd thee as my first-born child;
> But when I saw thee wantonly to roam
> From house to house, and never stay at home:
> I broke my bonds of love and bade thee go,
> Regardless whether well thou sped'st or no.
> On with thy fortunes then, whate'er they be:
> If good, I'll smile; if bad, I'll sigh for thee.

There is no certainty to be had with regard to the date of any given poem; and the poems as published in the *Hesperides* are without any arrangement whether of date or subject. There are but three dates in Herrick's life—his appointment to the living of Dean Bourn, his ejection, and his return: which poems preceded or followed any of these must be a matter of guess. The *Noble Numbers* are presumably later than the frolicsome ditties addressed to his loves; and the more sober-suited poems, those that talk of monuments, winding-sheets, and funeral odours, have a waft of death in them; but his style was formed early; and though there may be 'a change from Herrick's early poems, with their supreme daintiness and touch of Elizabethan conceit, to his later work, with its almost classical severity,' this criticism,[4] sound though it may be in the main, must not be pressed too closely. Such a theory holds good if we compare the well-known poem on 'His Return to London' with 'Cherry Ripe' or the 'Maids of Honour;' but it is shaken by these lines, certainly among the latest of all, and yet closely resembling his earlier vein:

I will no longer kiss,
     I can no longer stay;
The way of all flesh is
     That I must go this day.
Since longer I can't live,
     My frolic youths, adieu!
My lamp to you I'll give,
     And all my troubles too.

We take it that the content and discontent in Devonshire had more to do with what Herrick wrote, than youth or age, secular or clerical estate. When he was merry, he could be old Anacreon; when he was sad, he thought of his grave, and Julia or Anthea must bury him. The most probable conclusion is that the greater part of Herrick's poetry was written when he was young, that his vein flowed, less freely, but in a more stately manner, in maturer age, and that the *Noble Numbers* were written late.

Lovers of Herrick will always care more for the *Hesperides* than the *Noble Numbers*. They are more fresh and genial, and in that part of his work Herrick has no rival, whereas in this he must be compared at a disadvantage with Herbert, Crashaw, Vaughan, and others. He was a Christian, a clergyman, and a poet, and therefore he wrote sacred verses. Like Herbert, though without Herbert's emotion, in his 'Farewell to Poetry' he exchanged secular poetry for religious, parting from his Muse 'with a kiss of warmth and love.' There is genuine feeling in 'His Prayer for Absolution':

For these my unbaptisèd rhymes,
Writ in my wild unhallow'd times;
For ev'ry sentence, clause, and word
That's not inlaid with Thee, my Lord,
Forgive me, God, and blot each line
Out of my book that is not Thine.

But this is a higher flight than is common with him; his religion was contemplative, not emotional, his piety aimed at no visions of glory, no blissful union of the soul with its Lord; it was fuller of charity and hope than faith. His faith is thus expressed:

God is above the sphere of our esteem,
And is the best known, not defining him.

His description of 'a true Lent' is—

To fast from strife,
     From old debate,
     And hate;
To circumcise thy life.

He is thankful and merciful; and for Heaven he says—

I sing and ever shall
Of Heaven, and hope to have it when I die.

But he also says:

Weep for the dead, for they have lost their light;
And weep for me, lost in an endless night;
Or mourn or make a marble verse for me,
Who writ for many—*Benedicite*—

a thought as far removed from the spirit of Herbert, Keble, Cowper, or Charles Wesley as it is possible to conceive, but not from that of Falkland or Browne; a spirit in which faith is mingled with doubt, and there is more of resignation than of aspiration, of contemplation than of devotion; neither pagan nor devout, but thankful for life and the lives of others, and content to praise God for the past and present, and leave the future in His hands. This spirit will not raise men to be saints, and Herrick was not a saint, but it is not an unchristian spirit.

There are indeed some poems, like the 'Litany to the Holy Spirit,' which speak the language of true devotion; and as Herrick was certainly not a hypocrite, it is reasonable as well as charitable to take him at his best.

We cannot leave our subject without touching on a part of Herrick's work which has much impaired his reputation, and not unjustly: the gross and licentious poems which are found scattered up and down the *Hesperides*. They are not numerous, but we wish them away. Most of them were probably written in his youthful London days, when he was living with the wits, and living as they did, and we do not reckon among them the 'Epithalamies,' which nowhere go beyond the freedom common to such poems and have no taint of licentiousness. Men and women spoke more openly in those days than they do now; and Herrick need not be ashamed to have written—

To read my book the virgin shy
May blush while Brutus standeth by;
But when he's gone, read through what's writ,
And never stain a cheek for it.

Shakespeare must nowadays be expurgated for the London stage, but Julia saw him acted, and only blushed behind her fan to hear what Imogen, Beatrice, and Rosalind said openly. Not a few are satirical descriptions of his Devonshire neighbours, and can only be explained by a wish to meet Catullus and Martial on their own ground, and their wit does not redeem their scurrility and ugliness. Satire was never more foulmouthed than in Herrick's age, and other poets of the time sin more than Herrick; but they were laymen, and we cannot grant a priest the license of a layman. But when all is said, we accept his own apology:

Peruse my measures thoroughly, and where
Your judgement finds a guilty poem, there
Be you a judge, but not a judge severe.

Though we do not approve, we do not feel called upon to judge him by the rule of 'rigid Cato,' still less to class him with Swift and Sterne. He is as far from the dirtiness of the one as the lubricity of the other, and it is not often that he goes beyond the limit set by himself:

I write of Youth, of Love, and have access,
By these, to sing of *cleanly wantonness*.

Leave out a few, and Cato may read Herrick in his sober hours, not only

When the rose reigns, and locks with ointments shine.

Our conclusion is, that whereas all the world knows Herrick as the author of a few exquisite poems, the amount of his contribution has been commonly underrated; that he is not only a natural singer, but a finished artist and a student of perfection, learned and choice as well as spontaneous; that he is not an immoral writer, though there are blots on his page; and that finally in richness of fancy, fulness of diction, and pure melody of cadence he is worthy to be placed in the highest ring of English poets—

Whose thoughts make rich the blood of the world;

and one of his highest merits is that his lovers are never tired of him, but go back to him with fresh pleasure again and again.

Notes

1. A. H. Bullen in *Dict. of Nat. Biography* [Herrick, Robert].
2. Preface to Alfred Pollard's edition, 1898.
3. The first edition and Mr. Pollard's read 'Sappha' here, but 'Sappho' in other places.
4. Herbert Horne, xxxvii., in Mr. Earnest Rhys's Preface to his selection.

JOHN MILTON

JOHN MILTON

1608–1674

John Milton was born in Cheapside, London, on December 9, 1608, the son of a scrivener and moneylender who had been disinherited for converting to Protestantism. Milton probably entered St. Paul's School in 1620, although he may have begun as early as 1615. In addition, he had a private tutor. His earliest known poems were rhymed paraphrases of Psalms 114 and 136, probably written when he was fifteen.

In 1625 Milton entered Christ's College, Cambridge, receiving the B.A. in 1629 and the M.A. in 1632. Because of his delicate appearance and abstemious behavior, Milton was called "The Lady" at college. There, however, Milton wrote six Italian sonnets and his Christmas ode, "On the Morning of Christ's Nativity" (1629). It is believed that Milton wrote the companion poems "L'Allegro" and "Il Penseroso" during a long vacation in 1631. He also wrote many Latin poems while at college.

After leaving Cambridge in 1632, Milton settled into a five-year-long retirement in his father's household, first at Hammersmith and then at Horton, Buckinghamshire. He continued his studies and his writing. Probably in 1632 he wrote a short masque, *Arcades*, at the request of a friend, the composer Henry Lawes. This was followed by a longer masque, also written at Lawes' request, *A Maske Presented at Ludlow Castle 1634: on Michaelmasse Night*. Now known as *Comus*, this pastoral was first performed on September 29, 1634, before John Egerton, Earl of Bridgwater. In 1637 Milton contributed the elegy "Lycidas" to a volume of elegies regarding the drowning of a college friend, Edward King.

Milton spent the next few years abroad, chiefly in Italy. He wrote a number of Latin poems, including "Mansus," an epistle. Soon after his return to England in 1639, he wrote the Latin pastoral elegy "Epitaphium Damonis," in honor of Charles Diodati, who had been his friend since childhood.

Having returned to England because of the increasing political tensions there, Milton settled in London. He initially took in pupils, but became more and more dedicated to the causes of civil and religious liberty, convictions which were to dominate his life and writings from 1641 to 1660. During these years he wrote numerous tracts and pamphlets on a wide range of topics. A collection of his early poems was published in 1645.

His early pamphlets concerned freedom of religion, and included such works as *Of Reformation Touching Church-Discipline in England* (1641) and *Reason of Church-Government* (1642). He also wrote four tracts between 1643 and 1645 advocating the right to divorce. In 1642 Milton himself had married Mary Powell, who left him after one month; she returned two years later. Mary Milton bore four children, of whom three, all daughters, survived. She herself died in childbirth in 1652. Milton married twice again, first to Catherine Woodcocke, who with her infant daughter died in childbirth, and then to Elizabeth Minshull, who survived her husband.

Milton's tract writing continued through the years of the Civil War and the Commonwealth. *Of Education* was published in 1644, as was the celebrated *Areopagitica*, which advocated freedom of the press. The political tract *The Tenure of Kings and Magistrates* (1649), Milton's first, appeared two weeks after the execution of Charles I. Soon afterwards Milton was asked to be Latin, or foreign, secretary to Cromwell. Milton also edited the Commonwealth newspaper *Mercurius Politicus*, and continued writing numerous tracts, including *Eikonoklastes* (1649), the two *Defences of the English People* (1649, 1654) against the Royalist claims of Salmasius and Alexander More, *A Treatise of Civil Power in Ecclesiastical Causes* (1659), and his last political pamphlet, *The Readie and Easie Way to Establish a Free Commonwealth* (1660).

Milton went blind in the winter of 1651–52, while still Latin secretary. He wrote a sonnet on his blindness; this, along with some seventeen other sonnets and versifications of various psalms, comprises the poetry he wrote while otherwise engaged in twenty years of public service. In the months following Restoration, Milton was in serious danger of being hanged for treason. He was initially hidden and protected by friends. Although arrested and briefly imprisoned in 1660, he was released and pardoned, perhaps with the help of his friends Andrew Marvell and William Davenant.

It is believed that *Paradise Lost* was begun while Milton was still Latin secretary, perhaps between 1655 and 1658. His work was dictated—to assistants, relatives, including his younger daughters, and friends—in a daily routine which Milton likened to being "milked." The first edition, consisting of ten books, was finished in 1665 and published in 1667. The second and final edition was published in 1674, and it contained, along with minor revisions, twelve books, as books VII and X were each divided in half. The sequel, *Paradise Regained*, concerns Christ in the wilderness, overcoming Satan's temptations, and was published in 1671. In that same year Milton published *Samson Agonistes*, which chronicles the triumph of the blind Samson and is modeled on the principles of Greek drama.

For most of the remainder of his life Milton lived at Cripplegate, enjoying a peaceful life in the company of his third wife, whom he married in 1663. Milton died on November 8, 1674, "of the gout struck in," and is buried along with his father in St. Giles-in-the-Fields.

Personal

I was born in London, of an honorable family. My father was a man of supreme integrity, my mother a woman of purest reputation, celebrated throughout the neighborhood for her acts of charity. My father destined me in early childhood for the study of literature, for which I had so keen an appetite that from my twelfth year scarcely ever did I leave my studies for my bed before the hour of midnight. This was the first cause of injury to my eyes, whose natural weakness was augmented by frequent headaches. Since none of these defects slackened my assault upon knowledge, my father took care that I should be instructed daily both in school and under other masters at home. When I had thus become proficient in various languages and had tasted by no means superficially the sweetness of philosophy, he sent me to Cambridge, one of our two universities. There, untouched by any reproach, in the good graces of all upright men, for seven years I devoted myself to the traditional disciplines and liberal arts, until I had attained the degree of Master, as it is called, *cum laude*. Then, far from fleeing to Italy, as that filthy rascal alleges, of my own free will I returned home, to the regret of most of the fellows of the college, who bestowed on me no little honor. At my father's country place, whither he had retired to spend his declining years, I devoted myself entirely to the study of Greek and Latin writers, completely at leisure, not, however, without sometimes exchanging the country for the city, either to purchase books or to become acquainted with some new discovery in mathematics or music, in which I then took the keenest pleasure.—JOHN MILTON, *A Second Defence of the English People*, 1654, tr. North

> On evil days though fallen, and evil tongues;
> In darkness, and with dangers compassed round,
> And solitude; yet not alone. . . .
> —JOHN MILTON, *Paradise Lost*, 1667, Bk. 7

An Author that liv'd in the Reign of King *Charles* the Martyr. Had his Principles been as good as his Parts, he had been an Excellent Person; but his demerits towards his Sovereign, has very much sullied his Reputation.—GERARD LANGBAINE, *An Account of the English Dramatick Poets*, 1691, p. 375

He had three Daughters who surviv'd him many years (and a Son) all by his first Wife . . . : *Anne* his Eldest as abovesaid, and *Mary* his Second, who were both born at his House in *Barbican*; and *Debora* the youngest, who is yet living, born at his House in *Petty-France*, between whom and his Second Daughter, the Son, named *John*, was born as above-mention'd, at his Apartment in *Scotland Yard*. By his Second Wife, *Catharine* the Daughter of Captain *Woodcock* of *Hackney*, he had only one Daughter, of which the Mother the first year after her Marriage died in Child bed, and the Child also within a Month after. By his Third Wife *Elizabeth* the daughter of one Mr. *Minshal* of *Cheshire* (and Kinswoman to Dr. *Paget*), who surviv'd him, and is said to be yet living, he never had any Child; and those he had by the First he made serviceable to him in that very particular in which he most wanted their Service, and supplied his want of Eye-sight by their Eyes and Tongue; for though he had daily about him one or other to Read to him, some persons of Man's Estate, who of their own accord greedily catch'd at the opportunity of being his Readers, that they might as well reap the benefit of what they Read to him, as oblige him by the benefit of their reading; others of younger years sent by their Parents to the same end; yet excusing only the Eldest Daughter by reason of her bodily Infirmity, and difficult utterance of Speech, (which to say truth I doubt was the Principal cause of excusing her), the other two were Condemn'd to the performance of Reading, and exactly pronouncing of all the Languages of whatever Book he should at one time or other think fit to peruse; *Viz.* The *Hebrew* (and I think the *Syriac*), the *Greek*, the *Latin*, the *Italian*, *Spanish* and *French*. All which sorts of Books to be confined to Read, without understanding one word, must needs be a Tryal of Patience, almost beyond endurance; yet it was endured by both for a long time; yet the irksomeness of this imployment could not always be concealed, but broke out more and more into expressions of uneasiness; so that at length they were all (even the Eldest also) sent out to learn some Curious and Ingenious sorts of Manufacture, that are proper for Women to learn, particularly Imbroideries in Gold or Silver. It had been happy indeed if the Daughters of such a Person had been made in some measure Inheritrixes of their Father's Learning; but since Fate otherwise decreed, the greatest Honour that can be ascribed to this now living (and so would have been to the others, had they lived) is to be Daughter to a man of his extraordinary Character.—EDWARD PHILLIPS, "The Life of Mr. John Milton," *Letters of State*, English ed., 1694

⟨Isaac Penington⟩ had an intimate acquaintance with Dr. Paget, a physician of note in London, and he with John Milton, a gentleman of great note for learning throughout the learned world, for the accurate pieces he had written on various subjects and occasions.

This person, having filled a public station in the former times, lived now a private and retired life in London, and having wholly lost his sight, kept always a man to read to him, which usually was the son of some gentleman of his acquaintance, whom in kindness he took to improve in his learning.

Thus, by the mediation of my friend Isaac Penington with Dr. Paget, and of Dr. Paget with John Milton, was I admitted to come to him, not as a servant to him (which at that time he needed not), nor to be in the house with him, but only to have the liberty of coming to his house at certain hours when I would, and to read to him what books he should appoint me, which was all the favour I desired.

But this being a matter which would require some time to bring about, I in the meanwhile returned to my father's house in Oxfordshire.

. . . I committed the care of the house to a tenant of my father's who lived in the town, and taking my leave of Crowell, went up to my sure friend Isaac Penington again; where understanding that the mediation used for my admittance to John Milton had succeeded so well that I might come when I would, I hastened to London, and in the first place went to wait upon him.

He received me courteously, as well for the sake of Dr. Paget, who introduced me, as of Isaac Penington, who recommended me; to both whom he bore a good respect. And having inquired divers things of me with respect to my former progression in learning, he dismissed me, to provide myself with such accommodation as might be most suitable to my future studies.

I went therefore and took myself a lodging as near to his house (which was then in Jewyn Street) as conveniently as I could, and from thenceforward went every day in the afternoon, except on the first days of the week, and sitting by him in his dining-room read to him in such books in the Latin tongue as he pleased to hear me read.

At my first sitting to read to him, observing that I used the English pronunciation, he told me, if I would have the benefit of the Latin tongue, not only to read and understand Latin authors, but to converse with foreigners, either abroad or at home, I must learn the foreign pronunciation. To this I consenting, he instructed me how to sound the vowels; so different from the common pronunciation used by the English, who speak Anglice their Latin, that—with some few other variations in sounding some consonants in particular cases, as *c* before *e* or *i* like *ch*, *sc* before *i* like *sh*, etc.—the Latin thus spoken seemed as different from that which was delivered, as the English generally speak it, as if it were another language.

I had before, during my retired life at my father's, by unwearied diligence and industry, so far recovered the rules of grammar, in which I had once been very ready, that I could both read a Latin author and after a sort hammer out his meaning. But this change of pronunciation proved a new difficulty to me. It was now harder to me to read than it was before to understand when read. But

Labor omnia vincit
Improbus.
Incessant pains,
The end obtains.

And so did I. Which made my reading the more acceptable to my master. He, on the other hand, perceiving with what earnest desire I pursued learning, gave me not only all the encouragement but all the help he could; for, having a curious ear, he understood by my tone when I understood what I read and when I did not; and accordingly would stop me, examine me, and open the most difficult passages to me.

Thus went I on for about six weeks' time, reading to him in the afternoons; and exercising myself with my own books in my chamber in the forenoons, I was sensible of an improvement.—THOMAS ELLWOOD, *The History of the Life of Thomas Ellwood*, 1714, ed. Crump, pp. 88–90

One that had Often seen him, told me he us'd to come to a House where He Liv'd, and he has also Met him in the Street, Led by *Millington*, the same who was so Famous an Auctioneer of Books about the time of the Revolution, and Since. This Man was then a Seller of Old Books in *Little Britain*, and *Milton* lodg'd at his house. This was 3 or 4 Years before he Dy'd. he then wore no Sword that My Informer remembers, though Probably he did, at least 'twas his Custom not long before to wear one with a Small Silver-Hilt, and in Cold Weather a Grey Camblet Coat. his Band was Usually not of the Sort as That in the Print I have given, That is, as my Original is, but like What are in the Common Prints of him, the Band usually wore at That time; to have a more Exact Idea of his Figure, let it be remembered that the Fashion of the Coat Then was not Much Unlike what the Quakers Wear Now.

I have heard many Years Since that he Us'd to Sit in a Grey Coarse Cloath Coat at the Door of his House, near *Bunhill* Fields Without *Moor-gate*, in Warm Sunny Weather to Enjoy the Fresh Air, and So, as well as in his Room, received the Visits of People of Distinguish'd Parts, as well as Quality. and very Lately I had the Good Fortune to have Another Picture of him from an Ancient Clergy-man in *Dorsetshire*, Dr. *Wright*; He found him in a Small House, he thinks but One Room on a Floor; in That, up One pair of Stairs, which was hung with a Rusty Green, he found *John Milton*, Sitting in an Elbow Chair, Black Cloaths, and Neat enough, Pale, but not Cadaverous, his Hands and Fingers Gouty, and with Chalk Stones. among Other Discourse He exprest Himself to This Purpose; that was he Free from the Pain This gave him, his Blindness would be Tolerable.

Sufficient Care had not been taken of This Body, he had a Partiality for his Mind; but All that Temperance, Chastity, and every Wholesom Vertue could do, was done; Nor did he forbear Sometimes to Walk and Use Exercise, as himself says, *Eleg* I. 50. VII. 51. and in a Passage in his *Apol.* for *Smectymnuus* which will be Quoted Anon on Another Occasion. but This was not Enough to Support him Under that Intense Study and Application which he took to be his Portion *in This* Life. He lov'd the Country, but was little There. nor do we hear any thing of his Riding, Hunting, Dancing, &c. When he was Young he learnt to Fence, probably as a Gentlemanly Accomplishment, and that he might be Able to do Himself Right in Case of an Affront, which he wanted not Courage nor Will for, as Himself intimates, though it does not appear he ever made This Use of his Skill. after he was Blind he us'd a Swing for Exercise.

Musick he Lov'd Extreamly, and Understood Well. 'tis said he Compos'd, though nothing of That has been brought down to Us. he diverted Himself with Performing, which they say he did Well on the Organ and Bas-Viol. and This was a great Relief to him after he had lost his Sight.

in relation to his Love of Musick, and the Effect it had upon his Mind, I remember a Story I had from a Friend I was Happy in for many Years, and who lov'd to talk of *Milton*, as he Often Did. *Milton* hearing a Lady Sing Finely, *now will I Swear*" (says he) *This Lady is Handsom.*" his Ears Now were Eyes to Him.—JONATHAN RICHARDSON, *Explanatory Notes and Remarks on Milton's Paradise Lost*, 1734

In his way of living he was an example of sobriety and temperance. He was very sparing in the use of wine or strong liquors of any kind. . . . He was likewise very abstemious in his diet, not fastidiously nice or delicate in his choice of dishes, but content with anything that was most in season, or easiest to be procured; eating and drinking (according to the distinction of the philosopher) that he might live, and not living that he might eat or drink. So that probably his gout descended by inheritance from one or other of his parents; or, if it was of his own acquiring, it must have been owing to his studious and sedentary life.—THOMAS NEWTON, "Life of Milton," *Milton's Poetical Works*, 1749–59, ed. Newton

In his youth he is said to have been extremely handsome, and while he was a student at Cambridge, he was called "the Lady of Christ's-College," and he took notice of this himself in one of his Public Prolusions before that university; "A *quibusdam audivi nuper domina*." The colour of his hair was a light brown; the symmetry of his features exact; enlivened with an agreeable air, and a beautiful mixture of fair and ruddy. . . . Mr. Wood observes, that "his eyes were none of the quickest." His stature, as we find it measured by himself, did not exceed the middle-size; he was neither too lean, nor too corpulent; his limbs well proportioned, nervous, and active, serviceable in all respects to his exercising the sword, in which he much delighted, and wanted neither skill, nor courage, to resent an affront from men of the most athletic constitutions. In his diet he was abstemious; not delicate in the choice of his dishes; and strong liquors of all kinds were his aversion. Being too sadly convinced how much his health had suffered by night-studies in his younger years, he used to go early (seldom later than nine) to rest; and rose commonly in the summer at four, and in the winter at five in the morning; but when he was not disposed to rise at his usual hours, he always had one to read to him by his bed-side. At his first rising he had usually a chapter read to him out of the Hebrew bible; and he commonly studied all the morning till twelve, then used some exercise for an hour, afterwards dined, and after dinner played on the organ, and either sung himself, or made his wife sing, who, he said, had a good voice, but no ear, and then he went up to study again till six, when his friends came to visit him, and sat with him till eight. Then he went down to supper, which was usually olives and some light thing; and after supper he smoked his pipe, and drank a glass of water, and went to bed. When his blindness restrained him from other exercises, he had a machine to swing in for the preservation of his health; and diverted himself in his chamber with playing on an organ. He had a delicate ear and excellent voice, and great skill in vocal and instrumental music. His deportment was erect, open and affable; and his conversation easy, cheerful, and instructive.—THOMAS BIRCH, *An Historical and Critical Account of the Life and Writings of Mr. John Milton*, 1753

His literature was unquestionably great. He read all the languages which are considered either as learned or polite: Hebrew, with its two dialects, Greek, Latin, Italian, French, and Spanish. In Latin his skill was such as places him in the first rank of writers and critics; and he appears to have cultivated Italian with uncommon diligence. The books in which his daughter, who used to read to him, represented him as most delighting, after Homer, which he could almost repeat, were Ovid's *Metamorphoses* and Euripides. His Euripides is, by Mr. Cradock's kindness, now in my hands: the margin is sometimes noted; but I have found nothing remarkable.

Of the English poets he set most value upon Spenser, Shakespeare, and Cowley. Spenser was apparently his favourite: Shakespeare he may easily be supposed to like, with every skilful reader; but I should not have expected that Cowley, whose ideas of excellence were different from his own, would have had much of his approbation. His character of Dryden, who sometimes visited him, was, that he was a good rhymist, but no poet.

His theological opinions are said to have been first Calvinistical; and afterwards, perhaps when he began to hate the Presbyterians, to have tended towards Arminianism. In the mixed questions of theology and government he never thinks that he can recede far enough from popery or prelacy; but what Baudius says of Erasmus seems applicable to him—*magis habuit quod fugeret, quam quod sequeretur*. He had determined rather what to condemn, than what to approve. He has not associated himself with any denomination of Protestants: we know rather what he was not than what he was. He was not of the Church of Rome; he was not of the Church of England.

To be of no Church is dangerous. Religion, of which the rewards are distant, and which is animated only by faith and hope, will glide by degrees out of the mind, unless it be invigorated and reimpressed by external ordinances, by stated calls to worship, and the salutary influence of example. Milton, who appears to have had a full conviction of the truth of Christianity, and to have regarded the Holy Scriptures with the profoundest veneration, to have been untainted by any heretical

peculiarity of opinion, and to have lived in a confirmed belief of the immediate and occasional agency of Providence, yet grew old without any visible worship. In the distribution of his hours there was no hour of prayer, either solitary or with his household; omitting public prayers, he omitted all.

Of this omission the reason has been sought upon a supposition, which ought never to be made, that men live with their own approbation, and justify their conduct to themselves. Prayer certainly was not thought superfluous by him who represents our first parents as praying acceptably in the state of innocence, and efficaciously after their fall. That he lived without prayer can hardly be affirmed; his studies and meditations were an habitual prayer. The neglect of it in his family was probably a fault for which he condemned himself, and which he intended to correct, but that death, as too often happens, intercepted his reformation.

His political notions were those of an acrimonious and surly republican, for which it is not known that he gave any better reason than that *a popular government was the most frugal; for the trappings of a monarchy would set up an ordinary commonwealth.* It is surely very shallow policy that supposes money to be the chief good; and even this, without considering that the support and expense of a Court is, for the most part, only a particular kind of traffic, for which money is circulated without any national impoverishment.

Milton's republicanism was, I am afraid, founded in an envious hatred of greatness, and a sullen desire of independence; in petulance impatient of control, and pride disdainful of superiority. He hated monarchs in the State, and prelates in the Church; for he hated all whom he was required to obey. It is to be suspected that his predominant desire was to destroy rather than establish, and that he felt not so much the love of liberty as repugnance to authority.

It has been observed that they who most loudly clamour for liberty do not most liberally grant it. What we know of Milton's character in domestic relations is that he was severe and arbitrary. His family consisted of women; and there appears in his books something like a Turkish contempt of females, as subordinate and inferior beings. That his own daughters might not break the ranks, he suffered them to be depressed by a mean and penurious education. He thought woman made only for obedience, and man only for rebellion.—SAMUEL JOHNSON, "John Milton," *Lives of the Poets*, 1779

Yea, our blind Poet, who in his later day,
Stood almost single; uttering odious truths—
Darkness before, and danger's voice behind,
Soul awful—if the earth has ever lodged
An awful soul—I seemed to see him here
Familiarly, and in his scholar's dress
Bounding before me, yet a stripling youth—
A boy, no better, with his rosy cheeks
Angelical, keen eye, courageous look,
And conscious step of purity and pride.
    —WILLIAM WORDSWORTH, *The Prelude*,
    1799–1805, Bk. 2

Milton alone remained faithful to the memory of Cromwell. While minor authors, vile, perjured, bought by restored power, insulted the ashes of a great man at whose feet they had grovelled, Milton gave him an asylum in his genius, as in an inviolable temple. Milton might have been reinstated in office. His third wife (for he espoused two after the death of Mary Powell) beseeching him to accept his former place as Secretary, he replied, "You are a woman, and would like to keep your carriage; but I will die an honest man." Remaining a Republican, he wrapped himself in his principles, with his Muse and his poverty. He said to those who reproached him with having served a tyrant, "He delivered us from kings." Milton affirmed that he had only fought for the cause of God and of his country. One day, walking in St. James's Park, he suddenly heard repeated near him, "The king! the king!" "Let us withdraw," he said to his guide, "I never loved kings." Charles II. accosted the blind man. "Thus, Sir, has Heaven punished you for having conspired against my father." "Sire," he replied, "if the ills that afflict us in this world be the chastisements for our faults, your father must have been very guilty."—FRANÇOIS RENÉ, VICOMTE DE CHATEAUBRIAND, *Sketches of English Literature*, 1837, Vol. 2, p. 80

Indignant at every effort to crush the spirit, and to cheat it, in his own words, "of that liberty which rarefies and enlightens it like the influence of heaven," he proclaimed the rights of man as a rational immortal being, undismayed by menace and obloquy, amid a generation of servile and unprincipled sycophants. The blindness which excluded him from the things of earth opened to him more glorious and spiritualized conceptions of heaven, and aided him in exhibiting the full influence of those sublime truths which the privilege of free inquiry in religious matters had poured upon the mind.—WILLIAM H. PRESCOTT, "Chateaubriand's English Literature" (1839), *Biographical and Critical Miscellanies*, 1845

Perhaps no man ever inhabited more houses than our great epic poet, yet scarcely one of these now remains. . . . We come now to Milton's last house, the narrow house appointed for all living, in which he laid his bones beside those of his father. This was in the church of St. Giles, Cripplegate. He died on Sunday, the 8th of November, 1674, and was buried on the 12th. His funeral is stated to have been very splendidly and numerously attended. By the parish registry we find that he was buried in the chancel: "John Milton, gentleman. Consumption. Chancell. 12. Nov., 1674." Dr. Johnson supposed that he had no inscription, but Aubrey distinctly states that "when the two steppes to the communion-table were raysed in 1690, his stone was removed." Milton's grave remained a whole century without a mark to point out where the great poet lay, till in 1793 Mr. Whitbread erected a bust and an inscription to his memory. What is more, there is every reason to believe that his remains were, on this occasion of raising the chancel and removing the stone, disturbed. The coffin was disinterred and opened, and numbers of relic-hunters were eager to seize and convey off fragments of his bones. The matter at the time occasioned a sharp controversy, and the public were at length persuaded to believe that they were not the remains of Milton, but of a female, that by mistake had been thus treated. But when the workmen had the inscribed stone before them, and dug down directly below it, what doubt can there be that the remains were those of the poet? By an alteration in the church when it was repaired in 1682, that which was the old chancel ceased to be the present one, and the remains of Milton thus came to lie in the great central aisle. The monument erected by Whitbread marks, as near as possible, the place. The bust is by Bacon. It is attached to a pillar, and beneath it is this inscription:

JOHN MILTON,
AUTHOR OF PARADISE LOST,
BORN DEC^R. 1608
DIED NOV^R. 1674.
His father, John Milton, died March, 1646.
They were both interred in this church.

Samuel Whitbread posuit, 1793.
—WILLIAM HOWITT, *Homes and Haunts of the Most Eminent British Poets*, 1847, Vol. 1, pp. 75–115

The best portraits of Milton represent him seated at the foot of an oak at sunset, his face turned towards the beams of the departing luminary, and dictating his verses to his well-beloved Deborah, listening attentively to the voice of her father; while his wife Elizabeth looks on him as Eve regarded her husband after her fault and punishment. His two younger daughters meanwhile gather flowers from the meadows, that he may inhale some of the odors of Eden which perfumed his dreams. Our thoughts turn involuntarily to the lot of that wife and daughters, after the death of the illustrious old man on whom they were attending; and the poet, thus brought back to our eyes again, becomes more interesting than the poem. Happy are they whose glory is watered with tears! Such reputation penetrates to the heart, and in the heart alone the poet's name becomes immortal.—ALPHONSE DE LAMARTINE, "Milton," *Memoirs of Celebrated Characters*, 1854

With respect to the worldly circumstances of this great man, little is known with certainty. It is evident that during his travels, and after his return, the allowance made him by his father was liberal. It was adequate, we may see, to the support of himself and his two nephews, for it is not likely that his sister paid him anything for them. He must also have considered himself able to support a family, without keeping school, when he married Miss Powell. He of course inherited the bulk of his father's property, but of the amount of it we are ignorant; all we know is that it included the interest in his house in Bread-street. His losses were not inconsiderable. A sum of £2000, which he had invested in the Excise Office, was lost at the Restoration, as the Government refused to recognize the obligations of the Commonwealth; according to the account of his granddaughter, he lost another sum of £2000, by placing it in the hands of a money-scrivener; and he also lost at the Restoration a property of £60 a year out of the lands of the Dean and Chapter of Westminster, which he very probably had purchased. His house in Bread-street was destroyed by the Great Fire. The whole property which he left behind him, exclusive of his claim on the Powell family for his wife's fortune, and of his household goods, did not exceed £1500, including the produce of his library, a great part of which he is said to have disposed of before his death.—THOMAS KEIGHTLEY, *An Account of the Life, Opinions, and Writings of John Milton*, 1855, p. 75

He attends no church, belongs to no communion, and has no form of worship in his family; notable circumstances, which we may refer, in part at least, to his blindness, but significant of more than that. His religion was of the spirit, and did not take kindly to any form. Though the most Puritan of the Puritans, he had never stopped long in the ranks of any Puritan party, or given satisfaction to Puritan ecclesiastics and theologians. In his youth he had loved the night; in his old age he loves the pure sunlight of early morning as it glimmers on his sightless eyes. The music which had been his delight since childhood has still its charm, and he either sings or plays on the organ or bass violin every day. In his grey coat, at the door of his house in Bunhill Fields, he sits on clear afternoons; a proud, ruggedly genial old man, with sharp satiric touches in his talk, the untunable fibre in him to the last. Eminent foreigners come to see him; friends approach reverently, drawn by the splendour of his discourse. It would range, one can well imagine, in glittering freedom, like "arabesques of lightning," over all ages and all literatures. He was the prince of scholars; a memory of superlative power waiting as handmaid on the queenliest imagination. The whole spectacle of ancient civilisation, its cities, its camps, its landscapes, was before him. There he sat in his grey coat, like a statue cut in granite. He recanted nothing, repented of nothing. England had made a sordid failure, but he had not failed. His soul's fellowship was with the great Republicans of Greece and Rome, and with the Psalmist and Isaiah and Oliver Cromwell.—PETER BAYNE, *The Chief Actors in the Puritan Revolution*, 1878, p. 345

I do not find that Milton, though he wrote against paid ministers as hirelings, ever expressly formulated an opinion against ministers as such. But as has already been hinted, there grew up in him, in the last period of his life, a secret sympathy with the mode of thinking which came to characterise the Quaker sect. Not that Milton adopted any of their peculiar fancies. He affirms categorically the permissibility of oaths, of military service, and requires that women should keep silence in the congregation. But in negativing all means of arriving at truth except the letter of Scripture interpreted by the inner light, he stood upon the same platform as the followers of George Fox.—MARK PATTISON, *Milton*, 1879, p. 148

As a man, too, not less than as a poet, Milton has a side of unsurpassable grandeur. A master's touch is the gift of nature. Moral qualities, it is commonly thought, are in our own power. Perhaps the germs of such qualities are in their greater or less strength as much a part of our natural constitution as the sense for style. The range open to our own will and power, however, in developing and establishing them, is evidently much larger. Certain high moral dispositions Milton had from nature, and he sedulously trained and developed them until they became habits of great power.—MATTHEW ARNOLD, "A French Critic on Milton," *Mixed Essays*, 1879, p. 269

On the 4th of August, 1790, according to a small volume written by Philip Neve, Esq. (of which two editions were published in the same year), Milton's coffin was removed and his remains exhibited to the public on the 4th and 5th of that month. Mr. George Stevens, the great editor of Shakspere, who justly denounced the indignity intended, not offered, to the great Puritan poet's remains by Royalist Land-sharks, satisfied himself that the corpse was that of a woman of fewer years than Milton. . . . Mr. Stevens's assurance gives us good reason for believing that Mr. Philip Neve's indignant protest is only good in general, and that Milton's hallowed reliques still rest undisturbed within their peaceful shrine.—C. M. INGLEBY, *Shakespeare's Bones*, 1883

On the whole, Milton's character was not an amiable one, nor even wholly estimable. It is probable that he never in the course of his whole life did anything that he considered wrong; but unfortunately, examples are not far to seek of the facility with which desire can be made to confound itself with deliberate approval. That he was an exacting, if not a tyrannical husband and father, that he held in the most peremptory and exaggerated fashion the doctrine of the superiority of man to woman, that his egotism in a man who had actually accomplished less would be held ludicrous and half disgusting, that his faculty of appreciation beyond his own immediate tastes and interests was small, that his intolerance surpassed that of an inquisitor, and that his controversial habits and manners outdid the license even of that period of controversial abuse,—these are propositions which I cannot conceive to be disputed by any

competent critic aware of the facts. If they have ever been denied, it is merely from the amiable but uncritical point of view which blinks all a man's personal defects in consideration of his literary genius. That we cannot afford to do here, especially as Milton's personal defects had no small influence on his literary character.—GEORGE SAINTSBURY, *A History of Elizabethan Literature*, 1887, p. 317

There is something very fascinating in the records we have of Milton's one visit to the Continent. A more impressive Englishman never left our shores. Sir Philip Sidney perhaps approaches him nearest. Beautiful beyond praise, and just sufficiently conscious of it to be careful never to appear at a disadvantage, dignified in manners, versed in foreign tongues, yet full of the ancient learning,—a gentleman, a scholar, a poet, a musician, and a Christian,—he moved about in a leisurely manner from city to city, writing Latin verses for his hosts and Italian sonnets in their ladies' albums, buying books and music, and creating, one cannot doubt, an all too flattering impression of an English Protestant.—AUGUSTINE BIRRELL, "John Milton," *Obiter Dicta, Second Series*, 1887, p. 14

Milton was nicknamed the "lady" at college, from his delicate complexion and slight make. He was, however, a good fencer, and thought himself a "match for any one." Although respected by the authorities, his proud and austere character probably kept him aloof from much of the coarser society of the place. He shared the growing aversion to the scholasticism against which one of his exercises is directed. Like Henry More, who entered Christ's in Milton's last year, he was strongly attracted by Plato, although he was never so much a philosopher as a poet. He already considered himself as dedicated to the utterance of great thoughts, and to the strictest chastity and self-respect, on the ground that he who would "write well hereafter in laudable things ought himself to be a true poem."—LESLIE STEPHEN, *Dictionary of National Biography*, 1894, Vol. 38, p. 25

In Milton's life, as in Milton's prose writings, occur passages which are not admirable, which are indeed the reverse of admirable. The student of literature, we may presume, is a lover of beauty, and the temptation with him to shirk the ugly passages of a life is a temptation easily understood. Here he may say, as Mr. Matthew Arnold has said of Shelley, here, in *Comus* and *Samson*, here in the Council Chamber sheltering Davenant from dangers incurred through his Royalist ardours, here, in company with Lawrence, listening to the lute well touched, is the Milton we desire to know, the Milton who delights. Let us, at least as long as we are able, avert our eyes from the Milton who disgusts, from the unamiable Milton, the Milton who calls his opponent "an idiot by breeding and a solicitor by presumption," the Milton who helped to embitter his daughters' lives, and remembered them as "unkind children" in his will. What is gained by forcing this disgusting Milton on our attention? We choose, if we can, to retain a charming picture of the great poet. The delightful Milton is the true Milton after all. Ah, give us back the delightful Milton!—EDWARD DOWDEN, "The Teaching of English Literature," *New Studies in Literature*, 1895, p. 442

It was fortunate for the harmonious development of Milton's genius that during the critical years between youth and manhood, years which in most men's lives are fullest of turmoil and dubiety, he was enabled to live a life of quiet contemplation. His nature was fiercely polemical, and without this period of calm set between his college life and his life as a public disputant, the sweeter saps of his mind would never have come to flower and fruitage. It was particularly fortunate, too, that this interim should be passed in the country, where the lyric influences were softest, where all that was pastoral and genial in his imagination was provoked. The special danger of men of his stamp, in whom will and doctrine are constantly president over impulse, is the loss of plasticity, the stiffening of imagination in its bonds.—WILLIAM VAUGHN MOODY, "Life of Milton," *Poetical Works of Milton*, 1899, Cambridge ed., p. xiii

But he is more than idealist or artist—he was a superlatively noble, brave, truly conscientious man, who could never have intentionally done a mean thing; who was pure and clean in thought, speech, and action; who was patriotic to the point of sublime self-sacrifice; who loved his neighbor to the point of risking his life for republican principles of liberty; who, finally, spent his every moment as in the sight of the God he both worshiped and loved. Possessed of sublime powers, his thought was to make the best use of them to the glory of God and the good of his fellow-man. We may not think that he always succeeded; but who among the men of our race save Washington is such an exemplar of high and holy and effective purpose? Beside his white and splendid flame nearly all the other great spirits of earth burn yellow, if not low. Truly, as Wordsworth said, his soul was like a star; and, if it dwelt apart, should we therefore love it the less? It is more difficult to love the sublime than to love the approximately human, but the necessity for such love is the essence of the first and greatest commandment.—WILLIAM P. TRENT, *John Milton: A Short Study of His Life and Works*, 1899, p. 55

General

It is not any private respect of gain, Gentle Reader (for the slightest Pamphlet is nowadays more vendible than the works of learnedest men), but it is the love I have to our own Language that hath made me diligent to collect and set forth such Pieces, both in Prose and Verse, as may renew the wonted honour and esteem of our English tongue; and it's the worth of these both English and Latin Poems, not the flourish of any prefixed encomions, that can invite thee to buy them—though these are not without the highest commendations and applause of the learnedest Academicks, both domestic and foreign, and, amongst those of our own country, the unparalleled attestation of that renowned Provost of Eton, Sir Henry Wotton. . . . The author's more peculiar excellency in those studies was too well known to conceal his papers, or to keep me from attempting to solicit them from him. Let the event guide itself which way it will, I shall deserve of the age by bringing into the light as true a birth as the Muses have brought forth since our famous Spenser wrote; whose Poems in these English ones are as rarely imitated as sweetly excelled. Reader, if thou art eagle-eyed to censure their worth, I am not fearful to expose them to thy exactest perusal.—HUMPHREY MOSELEY, "The Stationer to the Reader," *Milton's Poems*, 1645

John Milton was one, whose natural parts might deservedly give him a place amongst the principal of our English Poets, having written two Heroick Poems and a Tragedy; namely, *Paradice Lost, Paradice Regain'd*, and *Sampson Agonista*. But his Fame is gone out like a Candle in a Snuff, and his Memory will always stink, which might have ever lived in honourable Repute, had not he been a notorious Traytor, and most impiously and villainously bely'd that blessed Martyr King *Charles* the First.—WILLIAM WINSTANLEY, *The Lives of the Most Famous English Poets*, 1687

Three *Poets*, in three distant *Ages* born,
Greece, Italy, and *England* did adorn.
The *First* in loftiness of thought Surpass'd;
The *Next* in Majesty; in both the *Last*.
The force of *Nature* cou'd no farther goe:
To make a *Third* she joynd the former two.
　　—JOHN DRYDEN, "Lines on Milton," 1688

　　But Milton, next, with high and haughty stalks,
Unfetter'd in majestick numbers walks;
No vulgar hero can his muse ingage;
Nor earth's wide scene confine his hallow'd rage.
See! see, he upward springs, and tow'ring high
Spurns the dull province of mortality,
Shakes heaven's eternal throne with dire alarms,
And sets the Almighty thunderer in arms.
What-e'er his pen describes I more than see,
Whilst ev'ry verse arrayed in majesty,
Bold, and sublime, my whole attention draws,
And seems above the critick's nicer laws.
How are you struck with terror and delight,
When angel with arch-angel copes in fight!
When great Messiah's out-spread banner shines,
How does the chariot rattle in his lines!
What sounds of brazen wheels, what thunder, scare,
And stun the reader with the din of war!
With fear my spirits and my blood retire,
To see the seraphs sunk in clouds of fire;
But when, with eager steps, from hence I rise,
And view the first gay scenes of Paradise;
What tongue, what words of rapture can express
A vision so profuse of pleasantness.
Oh had the poet ne'er profan'd his pen,
To varnish o'er the guilt of faithless men;
His other works might have deserv'd applause!
But now the language can't support the cause;
While the clean current, tho' serene and bright,
Betrays a bottom odious to the sight.
　　—JOSEPH ADDISON, "An Account of the Greatest
　　　English Poets," 1694

Had his education, and first display'd his Parts in *Christ-Colledge* in *Cambridge*, which he improv'd by his Travels and his indefatigable industry to that Degree, that he became the Wonder of the Age, tho' always affecting uncommon and heterodoxical Opinions. He was made *Latine* Secretary to the long Parliament, and afterwards to *Cromwell* Himself; in which Stations he shew'd himself a most inveterate and unexampled Enemy to the Memory of the Murder'd and Martyr'd King; insomuch that at the Restoration some of his Books were order'd to be burnt, and he himself was in great Danger. He was certainly a Man of prodigious Parts, and wrot many Books; but what did most, and most justly distinguish him was his Poetry, particularly his *Paradise lost*, in which he manifested such a wonderful sublime Genius, as perhaps was never exceeded in any Age or Nation in the World.—LAURENCE ECHARD, *The History of England*, 1718, Vol. 3, p. 369

　　Is not each great, each amiable Muse
Of classic ages in thy Milton met?
A genius universal as his theme,
Astonishing as Chaos, as the bloom
Of blowing Eden fair, as Heaven sublime!
　　—JAMES THOMSON, "Summer," *The Seasons*,
　　　1727

I have nothing to say for rhyme, but that I doubt whether a poem can support itself without it, in our language; unless it be stiffened with such strange words, as are likely to destroy our language itself. The high style, that is affected so much in blank verse, would not have been borne, even in Milton, had not his subject turned so much on such strange out-of-the-world things as it does.—ALEXANDER POPE, *Spence's Anecdotes*, 1737–39

The best example of an exquisite ear that I can produce. . . . The more we attend to the composition of Milton's harmony, the more we shall be sensible how he loved to vary his pauses, his measures, and his feet, which gives that enchanting air of freedom and wildness to his versification, unconfined by any rules but those which his own feeling and the nature of his subject demanded. Thus he mixes the line of eight syllables with that of seven, the Trochee and the Spondee with the Iambic foot, and the single rhyme with the double.—THOMAS GRAY, "Observations on English Metre" (c. 1761), *Works*, Vol. 1, pp. 332–33

It is, however, remarkable, that the greatest genius by far that shone out in England during this period was deeply engaged with these fanatics, and even prostituted his pen in theological controversy in factious disputes, and in justifying the most violent measures of the party. This was John Milton, whose poems are admirable, though liable to some objections; his prose writings disagreeable, though not altogether defective in genius. Nor are all his poems equal; his *Paradise Lost*, his *Comus*, and a few others, shine out amidst some flat and insipid compositions; even in the *Paradise Lost*, his capital performance, there are very long passages, amounting to near a third of the work, almost wholly destitute of harmony and elegance, nay of all vigour of imagination. This natural inequality in Milton's genius was much increased by the inequalities in his subject; of which some parts are of themselves the most lofty that can enter into human conception, others would have required the most laboured elegance of composition to support them. It is certain, that this author, when in a happy mood, and employed on a noble subject, is the most wonderfully sublime of any poet in any language, Homer and Lucretius and Tasso not excepted. More concise than Homer, more simple than Tasso, more nervous than Lucretius; had he lived in a later age, and learned to polish some rudeness in his verses; had he enjoyed better fortune, and possessed leisure to watch the returns of genius in himself, he had attained the pinnacle of perfection, and borne away the palm of epic poetry.—DAVID HUME, *History of England*, 1762

Milton had such superior merit, that I will only say, that if his angels, his Satan, and his Adam, have as much dignity as the Apollo Belvedere, his Eve has all the delicacy and graces of the Venus of Medici, as his description of Eden has the colouring of Albano. Milton's tenderness imprints ideas as graceful as Guido's Madonnas: and the *Allegro*, *Penseroso*, and *Comus* might be denominated from the Three Graces, as the Italians gave singular titles to two or three of Petrarch's best sonnets.—HORACE WALPOLE, Letter to John Pinkerton (June 26, 1785), *Correspondence*, Vol. 16, ed. Lewis, p. 270

> In Homer's craft Jock Milton thrives.
> —ROBERT BURNS, "Poem on Pastoral Poetry," c. 1796

The reader of Milton must be always on his duty: he is surrounded with sense; it rises in every line; every word is to the purpose. There are no lazy intervals; all has been considered, and demands and merits observation. If this be called obscu-

rity, let it be remembered that it is such an obscurity as is a compliment to the reader; not that vicious obscurity, which proceeds from a muddled head.—SAMUEL TAYLOR COLERIDGE, "Notes on Milton" (1796), *Literary Remains*, Vol. 1, ed. Coleridge, p. 184

The fact seems to be, that Milton was dissatisfied with the shapeless chaos in which our language appeared in former writers and set himself, with that ardour which always distinguished him, to reform it. His success indeed is not entitled to unlimited encomium. The gigantic structure of his genius perhaps somewhat misled him. He endeavoured to form a language of too lofty and uniform a port. The exuberance of his mind led him to pour out his thoughts with an impetuosity, that often swept away with it the laws of simplicity and even the rules of grammatical propriety. His attempt however to give system to the lawless dialect of our ancestors, was the mark of a generous spirit, and entitles him to our applause. If we compare the style of Milton to that of later writers, and particularly to that of our own days, undoubtedly nothing but a very corrupt taste can commend it. But the case is altered, if we compare it with the writings of his predecessors. An impartial critic would perhaps find no language in any writer that went before Milton, of so much merit as that of Milton himself.—WILLIAM GODWIN, "Milton and Clarendon," *The Enquirer*, 1797, p. 405

> Milton! thou shouldst be living at this hour:
> England hath need of thee: she is a fen
> Of stagnant waters: altar, sword, and pen,
> Fireside, the heroic wealth of hall and bower,
> Have forfeited their ancient English dower
> Of inward happiness. We are selfish men;
> Oh! raise us up, return to us again;
> And give us manners, virtue, freedom, power.
> Thy soul was like a Star, and dwelt apart:
> Thou hadst a voice whose sound was like the sea:
> Pure as the naked heavens, majestic, free,
> So didst thou travel on life's common way,
> In cheerful godliness; and yet thy heart
> The lowliest duties on herself did lay.
> —WILLIAM WORDSWORTH, "London, 1802," 1802

> If, fallen in evil days on evil tongues,
>   Milton appeal'd to the Avenger, Time,
> If Time, the Avenger, execrates his wrongs,
>   And makes the word "Miltonic" mean "*sublime*,"
> *He* deign'd not to belie his soul in songs,
>   Nor turn his very talent to a crime;
> *He* did not loathe the Sire to laud the Son,
>   But closed the tyrant-hater he begun.
> —GEORGE GORDON, LORD BYRON, "Dedication" to *Don Juan*, 1818, St. 10

> Chief of organic numbers!
> Old Scholar of the Spheres!
> Thy spirit never slumbers,
> But rolls about our ears
> For ever and for ever!
> O what a mad endeavour
>   Worketh He,
> Who to thy sacred and ennobled hearse
> Would offer a burnt sacrifice of verse
>   And melody.
>
> How heavenward thou soundest!
> Live Temple of sweet noise,

And Discord unconfoundest,
Giving Delight new joys,
And Pleasure nobler pinions
O where are thy dominions?
          Lend thine ear
To a young Delian oath—ay, by thy soul,
By all that from thy mortal lips did roll,
And by the kernel of thy earthly love,
Beauty in things on earth and things above.
          I swear!

     When every childish fashion
     Has vanished from my rhyme,
     Will I, grey gone in passion,
     Leave to an after-time
     Hymning and Harmony
Of thee and of thy works, and of thy life;
But vain is now the burning and the strife;
Pangs are in vain, until I grow high-rife
          With old Philosophy,
And mad with glimpses of futurity.

For many years my offerings must be hush'd;
When I do speak, I'll think upon this hour,
Because I feel my forehead hot and flushed,
Even at the simplest vassal of thy power.
          A lock of thy bright hair,—
          Sudden it came,
And I was startled when I caught thy name
          Coupled so unaware;
Yet at the moment temperate was my blood—
I thought I had beheld it from the flood!
          —JOHN KEATS, "On a Lock of Milton's Hair,"
          1818

He stood alone and aloof above his times, the bard of immortal subjects, and, as far as there is perpetuity in language, of immortal fame. The very choice of those subjects bespoke a contempt for any species of excellence that was attainable by other men. There is something that overawes the mind in conceiving his long deliberated selection of that theme—his attempting it when his eyes were shut upon the face of nature—his dependence, we might almost say, on supernatural inspiration, and in the calm air of strength with which he opens *Paradise Lost*, beginning a mighty performance without the appearance of an effort. Taking the subject all in all, his powers could nowhere else have enjoyed the same scope. It was only from the height of this great argument that he could look back upon eternity past, and forward upon eternity to come; that he could survey the abyss of infernal darkness, open visions of Paradise, or ascend to heaven and breathe empyreal air.—THOMAS CAMPBELL, *An Essay on English Poetry*, 1819

     Most musical of mourners, weep again!
     Lament anew, Urania!—He died,
     Who was the Sire of an immortal strain,
     Blind, old, and lonely, when his country's pride,
     The priest, the slave, and the liberticide,
     Trampled and mocked with many a loathèd rite
     Of lust and blood; he went, unterrified,
     Into the gulf of death; but his clear Sprite
Yet reigns o'er earth; the third among the sons of light.
     —PERCY BYSSHE SHELLEY, *Adonais*, 1821, St. 4

               With other emotion
Milton's severer shade I saw and, in reverence humbled
Gazed on that soul sublime: of passion now as of blindness
Heal'd, and no longer here to Kings and to Hierarchs hostile,

He was assoil'd from taint of the fatal fruit; and in Eden
Not again to be lost, consorted an equal with Angels.
          —ROBERT SOUTHEY, A *Vision of Judgment*,
          1821, Sec. 9

This character of power runs through all Milton's works. His descriptions of nature show a free and bold hand. He has no need of the minute, graphic skill which we prize in Cowper or Crabbe. With a few strong or delicate touches, he impresses, as it were, his own mind on the scenes which he would describe, and kindles the imagination of the gifted reader to clothe them with the same radiant hues under which they appeared to his own. This attribute of power is universally felt to characterize Milton. His sublimity is in every man's mouth. Is it felt that his poetry breathes a sensibility and tenderness hardly surpassed by its sublimity? We apprehend that the grandeur of Milton's mind has thrown some shade over his milder beauties; and this it has done, not only by being more striking and imposing, but by the tendency of vast mental energy to give a certain calmness to the expression of tenderness and deep feeling.— WILLIAM ELLERY CHANNING, *Remarks on the Character and Writings of John Milton*, 1826

Milton was abundantly skilled in the dialectic art; he had a divine intuition into the logic of poetry; but he was not particularly remarkable, among men of genius, for penetrating and comprehensive intellect. This is very clear from his political and theological writings. His scheme of Government is that of a purely ideal commonwealth, and has the fault common to the greater number of such conceptions, that it never could be practised, except among beings for whom no government at all would be necessary. His opinions as to a Church Establishment are of an exactly similar description; and no imagination less powerful than his could have realized such visions to any mind. Nor could these phantom plans have obtained, in the thoughts of a nation, the living force necessary to their action, unless every man had been able to breathe into them from himself a breath of existence as powerful as that with which they were imbued by their creator.—JOHN STERLING, "Shades of the Dead" (1829), *Essays and Tales*, 1848, Vol. 1, ed. Hare, p. 76

Milton frequently innovates upon the high harmonies of his *accented* verse with the substitution of *quantities*; sometimes difficult at first sight to master, but generally admirable in effect, and heightening,—even when harshest, the majesty of his strains like a momentary crash of discord, thrown by the skilful organist, into the full tide of instrumental music, which gives intenser sweetness to what follows.—JAMES MONTGOMERY, *Lectures on General Literature*, 1833, p. 92

Milton was not an extensive or discursive thinker, as Shakspeare was; for the motions of his mind were slow, solemn, sequacious, like those of the planets; not agile and assimilative; not attracting all things within its own sphere; not multiform: repulsion was the law of his intellect—he moved in solitary grandeur. Yet, merely from this quality of grandeur, unapproachable grandeur, his intellect demanded a larger infusion of Latinity into his diction. For the same reason (and without such aids he would have had no proper element in which to move his wings) he enriched his diction with Hellenisms and with Hebraisms; but never, as could be easy to show, without a full justification in the result. Two things may be asserted of all his exotic idioms—1st, That they express what could not have been expressed by any native idiom; 2nd, That they harmonize with the English language, and give a colouring of the antique, but not any sense of strangeness, to the diction.—THOMAS DE QUINCEY, *Autobiography*, 1835

It will not be easy to acquit Milton, altogether, of injustice towards his countryman; but if he disdained to mention Surrey, he also disdained to copy from him—both the merits and the faults of Milton's versification are *his own!* . . . Perhaps no man ever paid the same attention to the quality of his rhythm as Milton. What other poets affect, as it were, by chance, Milton achieved by the aid of science and of art; he *studied* the aptness of his numbers, and diligently tutored an ear, which nature had gifted with the most delicate sensibility. In the flow of his rhythm, in the quality of his letter-sounds, in the disposition of his pauses, his verse almost ever *fits* the subject; and so insensibly does poetry blend with this—the last beauty of exquisite versification, that the reader may sometimes doubt whether it be the thought itself, or merely the happiness of its expression, which is the source of a gratification so deeply felt.—EDWIN GUEST, *A History of English Rhythms*, 1838, Vol. 2, pp. 240–42

He must not be ranked with Shakespeare. He stands relative to Shakespeare as Tasso or Ariosto does to Dante, as Virgil to Homer. He is conscious of writing an epic, and of being the great man he is. No great man ever felt so great a consciousness as Milton. That consciousness was the measure of his greatness; he was not one of those who reach into actual contact with the deep fountain of greatness. His *Paradise Lost* is not an epic in its composition as Shakespeare's utterances are epic. It does not come out of the heart of things; he hadn't it lying there to pour it out in one gush; it seems rather to have been welded together afterward. His sympathies with things are much narrower than Shakespeare's—too sectarian. In universality of mind there is no hatred; it doubtless rejects what is displeasing, but not in hatred for it. Everything has a right to exist. Shakespeare was not polemical: Milton was polemical altogether.— THOMAS CARLYLE, *Lectures on the History of Literature*, 1838, p. 165

The invectives of this great poet against prelates and Presbyterians will perfectly astonish those, who as yet are conversant only with his immortal work, his descriptions of the Garden of Eden, and the piety and innocence of our first parents.—WILLIAM SMYTH, *Lectures on Modern History*, 1840

Milton was a very great poet, second only (if second) to the very greatest, such as Dante and Shakspeare; and, like all great poets, equal to them in particular instances. He had no pretensions to Shakspeare's universality; his wit is dreary; and (in general) he had not the faith in things that Homer and Dante had, apart from the intervention of words. He could not let them speak for themselves without helping them with his learning. In all he did, after a certain period of youth (not to speak it irreverently), something of the schoolmaster is visible; and a gloomy religious creed removes him still farther from the universal gratitude and delight of mankind. He is understood, however, . . . to have given this up before he died. He had then run the circle of his knowledge, and probably come round to the wiser, more cheerful, and more poetical beliefs of his childhood.

In this respect, "Allegro" and "Penseroso" are the happiest of his productions; and in none is the poetical habit of mind more abundantly visible. They ought to precede the "Lycidas" (not unhurt with theology) in the modern editions of his works, as they did in the collection of minor poems made by himself. *Paradise Lost* is a study for imagination and elaborate musical

structure. Take almost any passage, and a lecture might be read from it on contrasts and pauses, and other parts of metrical harmony; while almost every word has its higher poetical meaning and intensity; but all is accompanied with a certain oppressiveness of ambitious and conscious power. In the "Allegro" and "Penseroso," &c., he is in better spirits with all about him; his eyes had not grown dim, nor his soul been forced inwards by disappointment into a proud self-esteem, which he narrowly escaped erecting into self-worship. He loves nature, not for the power he can get out of it, but for the pleasure it affords him; he is at peace with town as well as country, with courts and cathedral-windows; goes to the play and laughs; to the village-green and dances; and his study is placed, not in the Old Jewry, but in an airy tower, from whence he good-naturedly hopes that his candle—I beg pardon, his "lamp" (for he was a scholar from the first, though not a Puritan)—may be "seen" by others. His mirth, it is true, is not excessively merry. It is, as Warton says, the "dignity of mirth;" but it is happy, and that is all that is to be desired. The mode is not to be dictated by the mode of others; nor would it be so interesting if it were. The more a man is himself the better, provided he add a variation to the stock of comfort, and not of sullenness. Milton was born in a time of great changes; he was bred to be one of the changers; and in the order of events, and the working of good out of ill, we are bound to be grateful to what was of a mixed nature in himself, without arrogating for him that exemption from the mixture which belongs to no man. But upon the same principle on which nature herself loves joy better than grief, health than disease, and a general amount of welfare than the reverse (urging men towards it where it does not prevail, and making many a form of discontent itself but a mode of pleasure and self-esteem), so Milton's great poem never has been, and never can be popular (sectarianism apart) compared with his minor ones; nor does it, in the very highest sense of popularity, deserve to be. It does not work out the very piety it proposes; and the piety which it does propose wants the highest piety of an intelligible charity and reliance. Hence a secret preference for his minor poems among many of the truest and selectest admirers of *Paradise Lost*,—perhaps with all who do not admire power in any shape above truth in the best; hence Warton's found edition of them, delightful for its luxurious heap of notes and parallel passages.—LEIGH HUNT, "Milton," *Imagination and Fancy*, 1844

No species of literature, no language, no book, no art or science seems to have escaped his curiosity, or resisted the combined ardour and patience of his industry. His works may be considered as a vast arsenal of ideas drawn from every region of human speculation, and either themselves the condensed quintessence of knowledge and wisdom, or dressing and adoring the fairest and most majestic conceptions.—THOMAS B. SHAW, *Outlines of English Literature*, 1847, p. 162

No one can fitly reverence Milton who has not studied the character of the age of Charles II., in which his later fortunes were cast. He was Dryden's contemporary in time, but not his master or disciple in slavishness. He was under the anathema of power; a republican, in days of abject servility; a Christian, among men whom it would be charity to call infidels; a man of pure life and high principle, among sensualists and renegades. On nothing external could he lean for support. In his own domain of imagination perhaps the greatest poet that ever lived, he was still doomed to see such pitiful and stupid poetasters as Shadwell and Settle bear away the shining rewards of letters. Well might he declare that he had fallen on evil times! . . . The genius of Milton is indeed worthy all the admiration we award marvellous intellectual endowment; but how much more do we venerate the whole man, when we find it riveted to that high and hardy moral courage which makes his name thunder rebuke to all power that betrays freedom, to all genius that is false to virtue!—EDWIN P. WHIPPLE, "Authors in Their Relations to Life," *Lectures on Subjects Connected with Literature and Life*, 1850, pp. 24–25

> Like to some deep-chested organ whose grand
>   inspiration,
> Serenely majestic in utterance, lofty and calm,
> Interprets to mortals with melody great as its burthens,
> The mystical harmonies chiming for ever throughout the
>   bright spheres.
>   —GEORGE MEREDITH, "The Poetry of Milton,"
>   1851, *Works*, Vol. 31, p. 139

He was the most learned of all our poets, the one who from his childhood upwards was a devourer of Greek and Latin books, of the romances of the Middle Ages, of French and Italian poetry, above all of the Hebrew Scriptures. All these became his friends; for all of them connected themselves with the thoughts that occupied men in his own time, with the deep religious and political controversies which were about to bring on a civil war. Many persons think that the side which he took in that war must hinder us from making his books our friends; that we may esteem him as a great poet, but that we cannot meet him cordially as a man. No one is more likely to entertain that opinion than an English clergyman, for Milton dealt his blow unsparingly enough, and we come in for at least our full share of them. I know all that, and yet I must confess that I have found him a friend, and a very valuable friend, even when I have differed from him most and he has made me smart most.—FREDERICK DENISON MAURICE, "The Friendship of Books" (1856), *The Friendship of Books and Other Lectures*, 1874, ed. Hughes, p. 14

Graced with every intellectual gift, he was personally so comely that the romantic woods of Vallambrosa are lovelier from their association with his youthful figure sleeping in their shade. He had all the technical excellences of the scholar. At eighteen he wrote better Latin verses than have been written in England. He replied to the Italian poets who complimented him in Italian pure as their own. He was profoundly skilled in theology, in science, and in the literature of all languages. These were his accomplishments, but his genius was vast and vigorous. While yet a youth he wrote those minor poems which have the simple perfection of productions of nature; and in the ripeness of his wisdom and power he turned his blind eyes to heaven, and sang the lofty song which has given him a twin glory with Shakespeare in English renown. It is much for one man to have exhausted the literature of other nations and to have enriched his own. But other men have done this in various degrees. Milton went beyond it to complete the circle of his character as the scholar. You know the culmination of his life. The first scholar in England and in the world at that time fulfilled his office. His vocation making him especially the representative of liberty, he accepted the part to which he was naturally called, and turning away from all the blandishments of ease and fame, he gave himself to liberty and immortality.— GEORGE WILLIAM CURTIS, "The Duty of the American Scholar" (1856), *Orations and Addresses*, 1893, Vol. 1, p. 12

Take any,—the most hackneyed passage of *Comus*, the "L'Allegro," the "Penseroso," the *Paradise Lost*, and see the freshness, the sweetness, and the simplicity, which is strangely combined with the pomp, the self-restraint, the earnestness of every word;

take him even, as an *experimentum crucis*, when he trenches upon ground heathen and questionable, and tries the court poets at their own weapons,—

> Or whether (as some sages sing),
> The frolic wind that breathes the spring,
> Zephyr with Aurora playing,
> As he met her once a-maying,
> There on beds of violets blue,
> And fresh-blown roses washed in dew.

but why quote what all the world knows?—Where shall we find such real mirth, ease, sweetness, dance and song of words in any thing written for five-and-twenty years before him? True, he was no great dramatist. He never tried to be one: but there was no one in his generation who could have written either *Comus* or *Samson Agonistes*. And if, as is commonly believed, and as his countenance seems to indicate, he was deficient in humour, so were his contemporaries, with the sole exception of Cartwright. Witty he would be, and bitter: but he did not live in a really humorous age; and if he has none of the rollicking fun of the fox-hound puppy, at least he has none of the obscene gibber of the ape.—CHARLES KINGSLEY, "Plays and Puritans" (1859), *Plays and Puritans and Other Historical Essays*, 1873

Milton does not appear to have derived any pecuniary advantage from his labours as a Poet. His juvenile productions, and a few other minor pieces, were published for the first time in 1645. His Poems were evidently at that period not more esteemed than many of the contemporaneous poetical volumes of similar character. If we may judge from the fact of those poems being issued without any of those commendatory verses,—the tribute of praise so generally accorded by way of introduction to the effusions of a brother poet,—we may fairly come to the conclusion that Milton was, at that period, comparatively little known in the poetical world. Unlike also the works of other poets of the day, those of Milton are not inscribed to any patron, but are merely introduced to the public by an address from Humphrey Moseley the publisher. The volume bears no indication that it had been even published under the superintendence of the author. The Poems are arranged without much attention to their chronological order; and some of the Sonnets are without the headings that occur in the originals in the Trinity College Manuscript. Besides this, several of the Sonnets written before 1645, are omitted, as also other of his early poetical productions.—SAMUEL LEIGH SOTHEBY, *Ramblings in the Elucidation of the Autograph of Milton*, 1861, p. 12

> O mighty-mouth'd inventor of harmonies,
> O skill'd to sing of Time or Eternity,
>   God-gifted organ-voice of England,
>   Milton, a name to resound for ages;
> Whose Titan angels, Gabriel, Abdiel,
> Starr'd from Jehovah's gorgeous armouries,
>   Tower, as the deep-domed empyrëan
>   Rings to the roar of an angel onset—
> Me rather all that bowery loneliness,
> The brooks of Eden mazily murmuring,
>   And bloom profuse and cedar arches
>   Charm, as a wanderer out in ocean,
> Where some refulgent sunset of India
> Streams o'er a rich ambrosial ocean isle,
>   And crimson-hued the stately palm-woods
>   Whisper in odorous heights of even.
>   —ALFRED, LORD TENNYSON, "Milton," 1863

Milton put off his singing robes to labour for the State, and between the springtime of his genius and the glorious harvest of its autumn, gave the summer of his life to direct service of the country. He was then the pen of the Commonwealth, the voice of England to the outer world. And in his earlier and later verse, not less than in the middle period of his prose writing, Milton's genius was rich with the life of his own time, although he thought apart from the crowd, and spoke for himself, royally, with independent power. No poet is for all time who is not also for his age, reflecting little or much of its outward manner, but a part of its best mind.—HENRY MORLEY, "Introduction" to *The King and the Commons*, 1868, p. xx

If George Herbert's utterance is like the sword-play of one skilful with the rapier, that of Milton is like the sword-play of an old knight, flashing his huge but keen-cutting blade in lightnings about his head. Compared with Herbert, Milton was a man in health. He never *shows*, at least, any diseased regard of himself. His eye is fixed on the truth, and he knows of no ill-faring. While a man looks thitherward, all the movements of his spirit reveal themselves only in peace. . . . The unity of his being is the strength of Milton. He is harmony, sweet and bold, throughout. Not Philip Sidney, not George Herbert loved words and their melodies more than he; while in their use he is more serious than either, and harder to please, uttering a music they have rarely approached.—GEORGE MACDONALD, *England's Antiphon*, 1868, pp. 194–95

Milton was a pamphleteer, only a pamphleteer of original genius. Had he less originality, with the same power of language, he would probably have figured more in the history of the time, because he would have become more distinctly the mouthpiece of a party. But because the weight of his mind always carries him below the surface of the subject, because in these pamphlets he appeals constantly to first principles, opens the largest questions, propounds the most general maxims, we are not therefore unfairly to compare them with complete treatises on politics, or to forget that they are essentially pamphlets still.—JOHN ROBERT SEELEY, "Milton's Political Opinions," *Macmillan's Magazine*, 1868, p. 302

John Milton was not one of those fevered souls, void of self-command, whose rapture takes them by fits, whom a sickly sensibility drives for ever to the extreme of sorrow or joy, whose pliability prepares them to produce a variety of characters, whose inquietude condemns them to paint the insanity and contradictions of passion. Vast knowledge, close logic, and grand passion: these were his marks. His mind was lucid, his imagination limited. He was incapable of disturbed emotion or of transformation. He conceived the loftiest of ideal beauties, but he conceived only one. He was not born for the drama, but for the ode. He does not create souls, but constructs arguments and experiences emotions. Emotions and arguments, all the forces and actions of his soul, assemble and are arranged beneath a unique sentiment, that of the sublime; and the broad river of lyric poetry streams from him, impetuous, with even flow, splendid as a cloth of gold. . . . He was speculative and chimerical. Locked up in his own ideas, he sees but them, is attracted but by them. . . . He lived complete and untainted to the end, without loss of heart or weakness; experience could not instruct nor misfortune depress him; he endured all, and repented of nothing. . . . When Milton wishes to joke, he looks like one of Cromwell's pikemen, who, entering a room to dance, should fall upon the floor, and that with the extra momentum of his armour.—HIPPOLYTE TAINE, *History of English Literature*, 1871, Vol. 1, tr. Van Laun, Bk. 2, Ch. 6

I pace the sounding sea-beach and behold,
   How the voluminous billows roll and run,
   Upheaving and subsiding, while the sun
Shines through their sheeted emerald far unrolled,
And the ninth wave, slow gathering fold by fold
   All its loose-folding garments into one,
   Plunges upon the shore, and floods the dun
Pale reach of sands, and changes them to gold.
So in majestic cadence rise and fall
   The mighty undulations of thy song,
   O sightless bard, England's Mæonides!
And ever and anon, high over all
   Uplifted, a ninth wave superb and strong,
   Floods all the soul with its melodious seas.
   —HENRY WADSWORTH LONGFELLOW,
    "Milton," *A Book of Sonnets*, 1873

With Milton, Nature was not his first love, but held only a secondary place in his affections. He was in the first place a scholar, a man of letters, with the theologian and polemic latent in him. A lover of all artistic beauty he was, no doubt, and of Nature mainly as it lends itself to this perception. And as is his mode of apprehending Nature, such is the language in which he describes her.—JOHN CAMPBELL SHAIRP, *On Poetic Interpretation of Nature*, 1877, p. 186

An ordinary mind contemplating Milton can realize to itself the feeling of the Athenian who resented hearing Aristides for ever styled "the Just." Such a mind feels a little and excusably provoked at the serene and severe loftiness of a Milton, and casts about to find him blame-worthy in his very superiority—an exacting husband and father, an over-learned writer, cumbrous or stilted in prose and scholastically accoutred in verse, a political and religious extremist. There may be something in these objections, or the smaller kind of souls will please themselves by supposing there is something in them. Honour is the predominant emotion naturally felt towards Milton—hardly enthusiasm—certainly not sympathy. Perhaps a decided feeling of unsympathy would affect many of us, were it not for the one great misfortune of the poet. Nature has forbidden him to be infirm in himself, but gave him a crown of accidental or physical infirmity, and bowed him somewhat—a little lower than the angels—towards sympathy.—WILLIAM MICHAEL ROSSETTI, *Lives of Famous Poets*, 1878, p. 76

Admire as we may *Paradise Lost*; try as we may to admire *Paradise Regained*; acknowledge as we must the splendour of the imagery and the stately march of the verse—there comes upon us irresistibly a sense of the unfitness of the subject for Milton's treatment of it. If the story which he tells us is true, it is too momentous to be played with in poetry. We prefer to hear it in plain prose, with a minimum of ornament and the utmost possible precision of statement. Milton himself had not arrived at thinking it to be a legend, a picture, like a Greek Mythology. His poem falls between two modes of treatment and two conceptions of truth; we wonder, we recite, we applaud, but something comes in between our minds and a full enjoyment, and it will not satisfy us better as time goes on.—JAMES ANTHONY FROUDE, *Bunyan*, 1880, p. 116

Milton is the most sublime of our poets, and next to Wordsworth, he is perhaps the most intense. I mean that every line he utters, every scene he describes, is felt and seen by the writer; that his poetry is the expression of his innermost life, and that his individuality pervades it. Unlike Spenser and Shakespeare, Milton can seldom escape from himself, but his egotism is of the noblest order. We see this egotism in the earliest poems, in the sonnets written in middle age, and again in his latest work, the *Samson Agonistes*, in which, as in a mirror, may be witnessed the struggles of his soul and the sorrows of his life.—JOHN DENNIS, *Heroes of Literature*, 1883, p. 127

The greatness of the man was conspicuous in his blindness, for though he was fallen on evil days and evil tongues, he was unchanged, and though he was in solitude he was not alone. Urania visited his slumbers nightly, and governed his song, and found an audience—fit audience though few. The Spirit of Heavenly Song attained its greatest height with *Paradise Lost* in 1667, and, slowly wheeling through the firmament of English Verse, began to descend in 1671 with *Paradise Regained* and *Samson Agonistes*. It reached the lowest deep in the next half century in the Psalms and Hymns of Watts.—RICHARD HENRY STODDARD, "Introduction" to *English Verse: Chaucer to Burns*, 1883, p. xxxviii

The essence of the Greek pastoral elegy is the contrast of man's individual life with Nature's apparent eternity—a melancholy sentiment becoming the lisp of a modern materialist, but in the author of "Lycidas," the poetical champion of a faith before which the material universe is but dust and ashes compared with the soul of the veriest wretch who wears the form of man, almost grotesquely out of place. Why should Nature lament the escape of a divinity greater than herself from its clay prison? The Greek chorus in the social life of the Hebrews speaking the Puritanism of England in *Samson Agonistes* is not a stranger union of incongruities than the poet of individual immortality repeating the materialism of the Greek in lamentations for Edward King. Plainly the individualism of the sixteenth and seventeenth centuries did not know whether it was of earth or the infinite; and this confused judgment made it willing to look on Nature partially as a beautiful machine, its exquisite mechanism worthy of such word-pictures as "L'Allegro" and "Il Penseroso" contain, partially as a pagan god to be duly invoked only in good old pagan fashion, and partially as a perishable nullity destined to be "rolled together as a scroll"—in any case connected by no profoundly real links with man's social and individual life.—HUTCHESON MACAULAY POSNETT, *Comparative Literature*, 1886, p. 384

> O Milton, thou hast only half thy praise
> In having lowered the heavens within man's ken;
> Thine other, equal labor was to raise
> The human spirit up to heaven again;
> So, underneath thy forehead's aureole blaze,
> Thine awful eyes are mild with love to men.
> —HARRY LYMAN KOOPMAN, "Milton," *Orestes and Other Poems*, 1888, p. 148

If we were to discuss the influence of Milton in the English poetry of the nineteenth century, we should have to analyse large portions of the works of recent and living English poets. Wordsworth's blank verse, when it is truly verse, is at times almost an echo of Milton; and Lord Tennyson, far too exquisite an artist to be ever a mere imitator, has in his perfection of form been a true follower of Milton's spirit. Neither has Milton's prose been fruitless in the latter days; for something of its majestic reverberations may be heard in Landor, a master of English prose if ever there was one, from whom Milton received most loyal and yet unconstrained homage. Johnson's rooted loyalty to letters had constrained him, too, to do homage; the last paragraph of his life of Milton redeems all the rest, effacing mistakes and prejudices in the fellow-feeling of a true scholar. He must be an exceedingly bold or an exceedingly

fastidious Englishman who does not worship where Johnson and Landor have alike bowed the knee.—FREDERICK POLLOCK, "John Milton," *Fortnightly Review*, 1890, p. 519

Our amiable Dr. Channing, with excellent data before him, demonstrated his good Unitarian faith; but though Milton might have approved his nice reasonings, I doubt if he would have gone to church with him. He loved liberty; he could not travel well in double harness, not even in his household or with the elders. His exalted range of vision made light of the little aids and lorgnettes which the conventional teachers held out to him. Creeds and dogmas and vestments and canons, and all humanly consecrated helps, were but Jack-o'-lanterns to him, who was swathed all about with the glowing clouds of glory that rolled in upon his soul from the infinite depths.—DONALD G. MITCHELL, *English Lands, Letters, and Kings: From Elizabeth to Anne*, 1890, p. 179

Where Milton's style is fine it is *very* fine, but it is always liable to the danger of degenerating into mannerism. Nay, where the imagination is absent and the artifice remains, as in some of the theological discussions in *Paradise Lost*, it becomes mannerism of the most wearisome kind. Accordingly, he is easily parodied and easily imitated. Philips, in his "Splendid Shilling," has caught the trick exactly. . . . Philips has caught, I say, Milton's trick; his real secret he could never divine, for where Milton is best, he is incomparable. But all authors in whom imagination is a secondary quality, and whose merit lies less in what they say than in the way they say it, are apt to become mannerists, and to have imitators, because manner can be easily imitated. Milton has more or less colored all blank verse since his time, and, as those who imitate never fail to exaggerate, his influence has in some respects been mischievous. Thomson was well-nigh ruined by him. In him a leaf cannot fall without a Latinism, and there is circumlocution in the crow of a cock. Cowper was only saved by mixing equal proportions of Dryden in his verse, thus hitting upon a kind of cross between prose and poetry. In judging Milton, however, we should not forget that in verse the music makes a part of the meaning, and that no one before or since has been able to give to simple pentameters the majesty and compass of the organ. He was as much composer as poet.—JAMES RUSSELL LOWELL, "Fragments," *The Century*, 1891, pp. 24–25

The truth is, that in our literary history both Shakespeare and Milton stand apart by themselves, too inimitable and too spontaneous either to found a critical school or to carry with them any long train of followers. And as regards Milton, he may be viewed as a gigantic survival of the Elizabethan period, more Italianised than Spenser, more of the Puritan Englishman than was Shakespeare. "His soul was like a star, and dwelt apart."—JOHN AMPHLETT EVANS, "Dryden and Ben Jonson," *Temple Bar*, 1892, p. 109

Admittedly and indisputably our highest summit in Style. . . . He best proves the truth that in poetry Style is the paramount and invincible force. What else is the secret of his supremacy among our poets—a supremacy which no poet can doubt, and no true critic of poetry? For pure poetic endowment he sits unapproached on England's Helicon; yet, in comparison with Shakespeare, it cannot be said that his is a very rich or large nature uttering itself through literature. He has no geniality, he has no humour; he is often pedantic, sometimes pedagogic. Although his Invention was stupendous, in the quite distinct and finer quality of Imagination, or contagious spiritual vision, he has superiors; his human sympathies were neither warm nor broad; Shakespeare's contempt for the mass of mankind may be hesitatingly inferred from casual evidences, but Milton's is everywhere manifest.—WILLIAM WATSON, "The Mystery of Style," *Excursions in Criticism*, 1893, pp. 105–10

In one respect Milton stands alone in his management of a great poetic medium. Shakespeare, because of the vast license of the English stage and its mixture of verse and prose, here stands out of the comparison, and we know nothing of Homer's predecessors. But no one, not Sophocles with the iambic trimeter, not even Virgil with the Latin hexameter, hardly even Dante with the Italian hendecasyllabic, has achieved such marvellous variety of harmony independent of meaning as Milton has with the English blank verse. All three, perhaps, had a better lexicon—it is permissible to think Milton's choice of words anything but infallible. But no one with his lexicon did such astonishing feats.—GEORGE SAINTSBURY, *Social England*, 1895, Vol. 4, ed. Traill, p. 425

"L'Allegro" and "Il Penseroso," the earliest great lyrics of the landscape in our language, despite all later competition still remain supreme for range, variety, lucidity, and melodious charm within their style. And this style is essentially that of the Greek and the earlier English poets, but enlarged to the conception of whole scenes from Nature; occasionally even panoramic. . . . What we gain from Milton, as these specimens in his very purest vein—his essence of landscape—illustrate, is the immense enlargement, the finer proportions, the greater scope, of his scenes from Nature. And with this we have that exquisite style, always noble, always music itself—Mozart without notes—in which Milton is one of the few very greatest masters in all literature: in company—at least it pleases me to fancy—with Homer and Sophocles, with Vergil, with Dante, with Tennyson.—FRANCIS TURNER PALGRAVE, *Landscape in Poetry*, 1896, pp. 158–59

It is certain that Milton deals with the invisible more than any other poet that ever lived. . . . Milton has not the spontaneity of imagination that distinguishes Shakespeare, nor has he so large a nature, but his sense of form is more unfailing, and in loftiness of character he towers far above the bard of Avon. Puritan as he is, he is more of an aristocrat, and more of a man, than is Shakespeare. His nobility of poetic form is but the expression of a lofty soul, thrilled to the center of its being with the greatest of possible themes—the struggle of good and evil, of God and Satan, and the triumph of the Almighty in the redemption of man. When this theme grows old, then will *Paradise Lost* and *Paradise Regained* grow old. But so long as man recognizes and values his own immortality, so long will the poetry of Milton vindicate its claim to be immortal.—AUGUSTUS HOPKINS STRONG, *The Great Poets and Their Theology*, 1897, pp. 246–56

Milton's lyric style is not so purely lyrical and personal; it is rather idyllic and objective. In this he is in a measure the poetic son of Spenser; and he, too, last of the Elizabethans, has a certain turn of lyric rhythm and phrase never afterwards recaptured. "L'Allegro" and "Il Penseroso" are the objective and idyllic presentations of the two fundamental subjective states of the human soul. In these poems all the rhythmical witchery and the subtle beauty of symbolism developed or suggested in the lyrics of Spenser, Shakespeare, Campion, Fletcher, Drummond, and Browne, is taken up and carried into the last perfection of English idyllic metre and fancy. And the "Lycidas" carries on the vein of earlier Ode and Elegy to a like perfection. Through all the concrete symbolism of these poems, however, we read the suggestion of the new ethical and subjective mood of the time, saturated with and subdued to the genius of the

man Milton.—FREDERIC IVES CARPENTER, "Introduction" to *English Lyric Poetry 1500–1700*, 1897, p. liv

Every page of the works of that great exemplar of diction, Milton, is crowded with examples of felicitous and exquisite meaning given to the infallible word. Sometimes he accepts the secondary and more usual meaning of a word only to enrich it by the interweaving of the primary and etymological meaning.—WALTER RALEIGH, *Style*, 1897, p. 35

That the influence of Milton, in the romantic revival of the eighteenth century, should have been hardly second in importance to Spenser's is a confirmation of our remark that Augustan literature was "classical" in a way of its own. . . . Milton is the most truly classical of English poets; and yet, from the angle of observation at which the eighteenth century viewed him, he appeared a romantic. It was upon his romantic side, at all events, that the new school of poets apprehended and appropriated him.—HENRY A. BEERS, A *History of English Romanticism*, 1898, p. 146

Milton is one of the world's great minds. It is elevating to have intercourse with him and to follow his thought. Even in his partisanship—if to such independent and positive convictions as his that term can be applied—he is great. In carefulness and self-consistency he can give lessons to every living writer. He appears to best advantage when compared with other men of admitted power. Alongside of Homer he seems a kindred spirit. Bacon's interpretation of the ancient myths is puerile in comparison with his. His insight into the Sacred Scriptures often shames trained theologians. That his celebrated epic, the *Paradise Lost*, is even now but poorly understood is evidence of his superiority.—JOHN A. HINES, "Preface" to *Paradise Lost*, 1898, p. iii

Milton is the great idealist of our Anglo-Saxon race. In him there was no shadow of turning from the lines of thought and action marked out for him by his presiding genius. His lines may not be our lines; but if we cannot admire to the full his ideal steadfastness of purpose and his masterful accomplishment, it is because our own capacity for the comprehension and pursuit of the ideal is in so far weak and vacillating. And it is this pure idealism of his that makes him by far the most important figure, from a moral point of view, among all Anglo-Saxons.—WILLIAM P. TRENT, *John Milton: A Short Study of His Life and Works*, 1899, p. 53

Works

COMUS

MY LORD: This poem, which received its first occasion of birth from your self and others of your noble family, and much honour from your own person in the performance, now returns again to make a finall dedication of itself to you. Although not openly acknowledged by the author, yet it is a legitimate offspring, so lovely, and so much desired, that the often copying of it hath tired my pen to give my severall friends satisfaction, and brought me to a necessity of producing it to the publike view, and now to offer it up in all rightful devotion to those fair hopes and rare endowments of your much-promising youth, which gave a full assurance, to all that knew you, of a future excellence.—HENRY LAWES, "To Lord-Viscount Brackly," *Comus*, 1637

Since your going, you have charged me with new obligations, both for a very kinde letter from you, dated the sixth of this month, and for a charity piece of entertainment which came therewith,—wherein I should much commend the tragical part if the lyrical did not ravish me with a certain Dorique delicacy in your songs and odes; whereunto I must plainly confess to have seen nothing parallel in our language.—SIR HENRY WOTTON, Letter to John Milton, April 13, 1638

On the whole, whether *Comus* be or be not deficient as a drama, whether it is considered as an epic drama, a series of lines, a mask, or a poem, I am of opinion that Milton is here only inferior to his own *Paradise Lost*.—THOMAS WARTON, *Milton's Poems on Several Occasions*, 1785, p. 263

Even Milton deigned to contribute one of his most fascinating poems to the service of the drama; and, notwithstanding the severity of his puritanic tenets, *Comus* could only have been composed by one who felt the full enchantment of the theatre.—SIR WALTER SCOTT, *The Life of John Dryden*, 1805

Can there be a test of merit more indisputable than this?—for *Comus*, though by no means faultless as a Masque, has to boast of a poetry more rich and imaginative than is to be found in any other composition save *The Tempest* of Shakspeare.—NATHAN DRAKE, *Shakspeare and His Times*, 1817, Vol. 2, p. 579

A young girl and her brothers are benighted and separated as they pass through a forest in Herefordshire. How meagre is this solitary fact! how barren a paragraph would it have made for the Herefordshire journal,—had such a journal been then in existence! Submit it to Milton, and beautiful is the form which it assumes. Then rings that wood with the jocund revelry of Comus and his company; and the maiden draws near, in the strength of unblemished chastity, and her courage waxes strong as she sees

> A sable cloud
> Turn forth her silver lining on the night—

and she calls upon Echo to tell her of the flowery cave which hides her brothers, and Echo betrays her to the enchanter. Then comes the spirit from the "starry threshold of Jove's court," and in shepherd-weeds leads on the brothers to her rescue; and the necromancer is put to flight, but not till he has bound up the lady in fetters of stone; and Sabrina hastens from under her "translucent wave" to dissolve the spell—and again they all three bend their happy steps back to the roof of their fathers. This is not extravagant rhapsody—the tale is still actually preserved; but it is preserved like a fly in amber. The image is a mere thing of wood, but Milton enshrines it, and it becomes an object of worship.—ROBERT SOUTHEY, "Todd's Edition of Milton," *Quarterly Review*, 1827, p. 45

The great force derivable from repetition of particular vowel sounds in verse, is little understood, or quite overlooked, even by those versifiers who dwell most upon what is commonly called "alliteration." How richly melodious are these lines of Milton's *Comus*!

> May thy *brimm*ed waves for *this*
> Their full *tribute* never *miss*—
> May thy *billows* roll ashore
> The beryl and the *golden ore!*

—and yet it seems especially singular that, with the full and noble volume of the long ō resounding in his ears, the poet should have written, in the last line, "beryl," when he might so well have written "onyx."—EDGAR ALLAN POE, *Marginalia*, 1844, *Complete Works*, Vol. 16, ed. Harrison, pp. 26–27

One of the last and loveliest radiations of the dramatic spirit, which seemed almost to live its life out in about half a century of English literature, beginning in the times of Queen Eliz-

abeth, and ending in those of Charles the First. . . . Of *Comus*, I think, it might be said, as truly as of any poem in the language, that it is admirably adapted to inspire a real feeling for poetry. It abounds with so much of true imagination, such attractiveness of fancy, such grace of language and of metre, and withal contains so much thought and wisdom wherewith to win a mind unused to the poetic processes, that were I asked what poem might best be chosen to awaken the imagination to a healthful activity, I would point to Milton's *Comus*, as better fitted than almost any other for the purpose.—HENRY REED, *Lectures on English Literature, from Chaucer to Tennyson*, 1855, pp. 189–90

With these sounds left on the ear, and a final glow of angelic light on the eye, the performance ends, and the audience rises and disperses through the castle. The castle is now a crumbling ruin, along the ivy-clad walls and through the dark passages of which the visitor clambers or gropes his way, disturbing the crows and the martlets in their recesses; but one can stand yet in the doorway through which the parting guests of that night descended into the inner court; and one can see where the stage was, on which the sister was lost by her brothers, and Comus revelled with his crew, and the lady was fixed as marble by enchantment, and Sabrina arose with her water-nymphs, and the swains danced in welcome of the earl, and the Spirit gloriously ascended to its native heaven. More mystic it is to leave the ruins, and, descending one of the winding streets that lead from the castle into the valley of the Teme, to look upwards to castle and town seen as one picture, and, marking more expressly the three long pointed windows that gracefully slit the chief face of the wall towards the north to realize that it was from that ruin, and from those windows in the ruin, that the verse of *Comus* was first shook into the air of England. Much as Milton wrote afterwards, he never wrote anything more beautiful, more perfect than *Comus*.—DAVID MASSON, *The Life of John Milton*, 1858, Vol. 1, Ch. 7

The sublimity of Milton's genius—the quality which, in the literature of his own country at all events, so pre-eminently distinguishes him as a poet—shines forth with marvellous fulness in this glorious work of his youth. The execution falls but little short of the conception. The lyric portions, although perhaps Macaulay goes too far in describing them as completely overshadowing the dramatic, are among the poet's noblest verse; and the dialogue, though its versification is less stately and its diction less ample than that of *Paradise Lost*, which indeed almost precludes dramatic declamation, rises at the climax of the moral interest—in the argument between Comus and the Lady—to almost matchless beauty. Indeed there may be those who cannot suppress a wish that Milton had always adhered to this earlier and easier treatment of his favourite metre—easier I mean to hands under which language passed into combinations "musical, as is Apollo's lute."—ADOLPHUS WILLIAM WARD, A *History of English Dramatic Literature*, 1875–99, Vol. 3, p. 200

The tale is told beautifully, simply; without plot or any artifice; and with no regard to superficial probabilities. Frankly discarding everything of the drama, except its form, the poet does not stoop, as, within certain limits, the successful dramatist must, to be a literary mocking-bird. Aloft on his perch, like a nightingale, he fills the grove with his music, varying his note as the subject varies, but always with the same volume of sound and the same rich and mellow tone. None of the masters of English poetry, Milton's predecessors, not Chaucer, not Spenser, not Shakespeare even, had done much to detract from the originality, or to herald the perfection of *Comus*. Chaucer's blank verse is not to be mentioned with that of Milton.—PETER BAYNE, *The Chief Actors in the Puritan Revolution*, 1878, p. 309

It is moreover raised above an ethical poem by its imaginative form and power; and its literary worth enables us to consider it, if we choose, apart from its dramatic form. Its imagination, however, sinks at times, and one can scarcely explain this otherwise than by saying that the Elizabethan habit of fantastic metaphor clung to Milton at this time. When he does fall, the fall is made more remarkable by the soaring strength of his loftier flight and by the majesty of the verse. Nothing can be worse in conception than the comparison of night to a thief who shuts up, for the sake of his felony, the stars whose lamps burn everlasting oil in his dark lantern. The better it is carried out and the finer the verse, the worse it is. And yet it is instantly followed by the great passage about the fears of night, the fantasies and airy tongues that syllable men's names, and by the glorious appeal to conscience, faith, and God, followed in its turn by the fantastic conceit of the cloud that turns out its silver lining on the night. This is the Elizabethan weakness and strength, the mixture of gold and clay, the want of that art-sensitiveness which feels the absurd: and Milton, even in *Paradise Lost*, when he had got further from his originals, falls into it not unfrequently. It is a fault which runs through a good deal of his earlier work, it is more seen in *Comus* than elsewhere; but it was the fault of that poetic age.—STOPFORD A. BROOKE, *Milton*, 1879, p. 24

The beautiful soul makes beautiful the outward form; the base act debases the soul of him who commits it. This was Milton's highest message to the world. This was the witness of Puritanism at its best. This was "the sage and serious doctrine of virginity," of that singleness of heart and spirit which is the safeguard of purity in marriage or out of marriage. Between the ideal of womanhood formed by Milton in his youth and that of even such a man as Massinger there is a great gulf. To Milton the world is a place in which the lady can break the spells of Comus by the very force of innocence. To Massinger it is a place to be shunned and avoided as altogether evil. His Camiola can only find rest by its renunciation.—SAMUEL R. GARDINER, *History of England*, 1883, Vol. 7, p. 337

His greatest work, if scale and merit are considered. . . . The versification, as even Johnson saw, is the versification of *Paradise Lost*, and to my fancy at any rate it has a spring, a variety, a sweep and rush of genius, which are but rarely present later. As for its beauty in parts, *quis vituperavit?* It is impossible to single out passages, for the whole is golden. The entering address of Comus, the song "Sweet Echo," the descriptive speech of the Spirit, and the magnificent eulogy of the "sun-clad power of chastity," would be the most beautiful things where all is beautiful, if the unapproachable "Sabrina fair" did not come later, and were not sustained before and after, for nearly two hundred lines of pure nectar. If poetry could be taught by the reading of it, then indeed the critic's advice to a poet might be limited to this: "Give your days and nights to the reading of *Comus*."— GEORGE SAINTSBURY, A *History of Elizabethan Literature*, 1887, pp. 318–21

Judged simply as a masque, *Comus* is perhaps inferior to some of Ben Jonson's. It is overweighted with moral teaching and lacks the lightening influence of humour. But Milton's genius overflowed the limits of its appointed task, and *Comus* remains a splendid protest, at an hour when such a protest was needed the most, on behalf of a reasonable life. For if *Comus* is the

expression of the distaste with which Milton regarded the growing licence of Cavalier society, its production is no less clearly a repudiation of the doctrines of Prynne and the moroser Puritans, to whom the drama was an unholy thing.—J. HOWARD B. MASTERMAN, *The Age of Milton*, 1897, p. 16

LYCIDAS

In "Lycidas" there is perhaps more poetry than sorrow. But let us read it for its poetry. It is true that passion plucks no berries from the myrtle and ivy, nor calls upon Arethus and Mincius, nor tells of rough satyrs with cloven heel. But poetry does this; and in the hands of Milton does it with a peculiar and irresistible charm.—THOMAS WARTON, *Milton's Poems on Several Occasions*, 1785, p. 36

"Lycidas,"—though highly poetical,—I agree, with Johnson, breathes little sincere sorrow, and is therefore essentially defective as a Monody.—THOMAS GREEN, *Extracts from the Diary of a Lover of Literature*, 1810

It has been said that this is not the natural mode of expressing passion—that where it is real, its language is less figurative and that "where there is leisure for fiction there is little grief." In general this may be true; in the case of Milton its truth may be doubted. . . . The mind of Milton was perfect fairy-land; and every thought which entered it, whether grave or gay, magnificent or mean, quickly partook of a fairy form.—ROBERT SOUTHEY, "Todd's Edition of Milton," *Quarterly Review*, 1827, p. 46

The common *metre* of six accents, which spread so widely during the sixteenth century, seldom tolerated a verse with a compound section. The reluctance to admit these verses was strengthened by the example of Drayton, who rigidly excluded them from the *Polyolbion*. There are, however, a few poems, in which they are admitted freely enough to give a peculiar character to the rhythm. One of these poems is the "Elegy" written by Brysket, (though generally ascribed to Spenser), on the death of Sir Philip Sidney. It has very little poetical merit, but deserves attention, as having undoubtedly been in Milton's eye, when he wrote his "Lycidas." From it Milton borrowed his irregular rhimes, and that strange mixture of Christianity and Heathenism, which shocked the feelings and roused the indignation of Johnson. It may be questioned, if the peculiarity in the meter can fairly be considered as a blemish. Like endings, recurring at uncertain distances, impart a wildness and an appearance of negligence to the verse, which suits well with the character of elegy. But to bring in St. Peter hand in hand with a pagan deity is merely ludicrous; it was the taste of the age, and that is all that can be urged in its excuse. Still, however, the beauties of this singular poem may well make us tolerant of even greater absurdity. No work of Milton has excited warmer admiration, or called forth more strongly the zeal of the partizan.—EDWIN GUEST, A *History of English Rhythms*, 1838, *Vol. 1, p. 274*

"Lycidas" appeals not only to the imagination, but to the educated imagination. There is no ebb and flow of poetical power as in *Comus*; it is an advance on all his previous work, and it fitly closes the poetic labour of his youth. It is needless to analyse it, and all criticism is weaker than the poem itself. Yet we may say that one of its strange charms is its solemn undertone rising like a religious chaunt through the elegiac musick; the sense of a stern national crisis in the midst of its pastoral mourning; the sense of Milton's grave force of character among the flowers and fancies of the poem; the sense of the Christian religion pervading the classical imagery. We might say that these things are ill-fitted to each other. So they would be, were not the art so fine and the poetry so over-mastering; were they not fused together by genius into a whole so that the unfitness itself becomes fascination.—STOPFORD A. BROOKE, *Milton*, 1879, p. 26

In "Lycidas" (1637) we have reached the high-water mark of English poesy and of Milton's own production. A period of a century and a half was to elapse before poetry in England seemed, in Wordsworth's *Ode on Immortality* (1807), to be rising again toward the level of inspiration which it had once attained in "Lycidas." . . . "Lycidas" opens up a deeper vein of feeling, a patriot passion so vehement and dangerous that, like that which stirred the Hebrew prophet, it is compelled to veil itself from power, or from sympathy, in utterance made purposely enigmatical.—MARK PATTISON, *Milton*, 1879, pp. 27–28

Mr. Arnold, like everyone else who speaks with authority on such matters, is horrified when Dr. Johnson bluntly condemns "Lycidas." Now I could read over the "Allegro" and "Penseroso" a thousand times without tiring of them. *Comus, Paradise Regained*, the other secondary poems, all of them, give me great pleasure, though in different degrees; but as for "Lycidas," well, I say ditto to old Sam. In the first place the kind of idyll is not to my taste. If a poet really sorrows over the death of a friend to that degree that he cannot, as a relief to the soul, refrain from pouring out his sorrow in song, I think his utterance should be natural and straightforward; he should not speak in a falsetto tone, or overlay his theme with classical affectations. On the other hand, if the grief is only a half grief, conjured up by the imagination to play with like a toy, then, in my opinion, the bard had better hold his tongue. In the second place, the jumbling together of Christian and heathen traditions jars upon me just as it jarred upon the tough old dictionary-maker. Nay, besides all this, "Lycidas" appears to me not so much a spontaneous outburst as a self-appointed task. One of Milton's editors tells us that Mr. King's friends—Milton being one of those friends—agreed to write, and bind up together, a lot of verses on his death, but that when "Lycidas" made its appearance, it proved so much more important than all the other poems put together, that it was withdrawn from the book, to be afterwards separately published; and even now, I think, traces of the original business-like arrangement are to be found in the elegy as we have it.—SIR FRANCIS HASTINGS DOYLE, *Reminiscences and Opinions*, 1886, p. 184

There are indeed blotches in it. The speech of Peter, magnificently as it is introduced, and strangely as it has captivated some critics, who seem to think that anything attacking the Church of England must be poetry, is out of place, and in itself is obscure, pedantic, and grotesque. There is some over-classicism, and the scale of the piece does not admit the display of quite such sustained and varied power as in *Comus*. But what there is, is so exquisite that hardly can we find fault with Mr. Pattison's hyperbole when he called "Lycidas" the "high-water mark of English poetry." High-water mark even in the physical world is a variable limit. Shakespere constantly, and some other poets here and there in short passages go beyond Milton. But in the same space we shall nowhere find anything that can outgo the passage beginning "Alas what boots it," down to "head of thine," and the whole conclusion from "Return Alpheus." For melody of versification, for richness of images, for curious felicity of expression, these cannot be surpassed.—GEORGE SAINTSBURY, *A History of Elizabethan Literature*, 1887, p. 322

The flowers that we lay upon a tomb
Are withered by the morrow,—ere the crowd

Which for a moment ceased its hum, and bowed
Its head, as Death flew by and made a gloom,
Resumes its whirl. And scarcely longer bloom
The sculptured wreathes with which a tomb more proud,
In some pale minster, may have been endowed;
For marble petals share the common doom.
But thou canst twine the wreaths that never die;
And something tells me thou wilt stay behind
When I am gone; I know it, I know not why.
The sea-gull's scream, the wailing of the wind,
The ocean's roar, sound like Death's prophecy:
I fain would have a garland thou hadst twined.
　　　　—EUGENE LEE-HAMILTON, "Lycidas to Milton
　　　　　　(1637)," *Imaginary Sonnets*, 1888

"Lycidas" is the elegy of much more than Edward King; it is the last note of the inspiration of an age that was passing away. It is redolent of the "sweet mournfulness of the Spenserian time, upon whose joys Death is the only intruder." No such elegy was to adorn our English literature until "two hundred years after." Shelley and Matthew Arnold produced the two elegiac poems which alone in our language deserve to rank with Milton's—for the wider scope of *In Memoriam* removes it from this category. "Thyrsis" excels "Lycidas" in the expression of chastened sorrow and tender recollection, but Matthew Arnold loved Clough and Oxford as Milton never loved King of Cambridge. *Adonais* is charged with deeper thought and more harmonious passion; but both owe to "Lycidas" a debt which "Lycidas" owes to no other poem.—J. HOWARD B. MASTERMAN, *The Age of Milton*, 1897, p. 24

"Lycidas" has a beauty and passion unknown to its Alexandrian predecessors, and it has not a touch of their oriental effeminacy and licentiousness. . . . The rhythm is varied, and flows now in leaping waves, now in long rolling billows that carry all before them, like the surging periods of *Paradise Lost*. There is probably no short poem in the language the rhythm of which has been more deservedly praised and studied, or more despaired of by other poets. Milton's mastery of rhythm, remarkable from the first, almost culminated in "Lycidas," in spite of the fact that he was there subjected (practically for the last time) to what he afterward called "the troublesome and modern boundage of riming."—WILLIAM P. TRENT, *John Milton: A Short Study of His Life and Works*, 1899, p. 140

PARADISE LOST

When I beheld the Poet blind, yet bold,
In slender Book his vast Design unfold,
Messiah Crown'd, *Gods* Reconcil'd Decree,
Rebelling *Angels*, the Forbidden Tree,
Heav'n, Hell, Earth, Chaos, All; the Argument
Held me a while misdoubting his Intent,
That he would ruine (for I saw him strong)
The sacred Truths to Fable and old Song,
(So *Sampson* groap'd the Temples Posts in spight)
The World o'rewhelming to revenge his Sight.
　　　Yet as I read, soon growing less severe,
I lik'd his Project, the success did fear;
Through that wide Field how he his way should find
O're which lame Faith leads Understanding blind;
Lest he perplext the things he would explain,
And what was easie he should render vain.
　　　Or if a Work so infinite he spann'd,
Jealous I was that some less skilful hand
(Such as disquiet always what is well,
And by ill imitating would excell)

Might hence presume the whole Creations day
To change in Scenes, and show it in a Play.
　　　Pardon me, *mighty Poet*, nor despise
My causeless, yet not impious, surmise.
But I am now convinc'd, and none will dare
Within thy Labours to pretend a Share.
Thou hast not miss'd one thought that could be fit,
And all that was improper dost omit:
So that no room is here for Writers left,
But to detect their Ignorance or Theft.
　　　That Majesty which through thy Work doth Reign
Draws the Devout, deterring the Profane.
And things divine thou treatst of in such state
As them preserves, and Thee inviolate.
At once delight and horrour on us seize,
Thou singst with so much gravity and ease;
And above humane flight dost soar aloft,
With Plume so strong, so equal, and so soft.
The *Bird* nam'd from that *Paradise* you sing
So never Flags, but alwaies keeps on Wing.
　　　Where couldst thou Words of such a compass find?
Whence furnish such a vast expense of Mind?
Just Heav'n Thee, like *Tiresias*, to requite,
Rewards with *Prophesie* thy loss of Sight.
　　　Well mightst thou scorn thy Readers to allure
With tinkling Rhime, of thy own Sense secure;
While the *Town-Bays* writes all the while and spells,
And like a Pack-Horse tires without his Bells.
Their Fancies like our bushy Points appear,
The Poets tag them; we for fashion wear.
I too transported by the *Mode* offend,
And while I meant to *Praise* thee, must Commend.
Thy verse created like thy *Theme* sublime,
In Number, Weight, and Measure, needs not *Rhime*.
　　　—ANDREW MARVELL, "On Mr. *Milton's*
　　　　　　　Paradise lost," 1674

That *Paradise lost* of *Miltons*, which some are pleas'd to call a Poem.—THOMAS RYMER, *The Tragedies of the Last Age*, 1678

Milton, whose Muse with such a daring Flight,
Led out the warring Saraphims to fight.
　　　—JOHN OLDHAM, "A Pastoral on the Death of
　　　　　　　the Earl of Rochester," 1680

Imitation is a nice point, and there are few Poets who deserve to be Models in all they write. *Miltons Paradice Lost* is admirable; but am I therefore bound to maintain, that there are no flats amongst his Elevations, when 'tis evident he creeps along sometimes, for above an Hundred lines together? cannot I admire the height of his Invention, and the strength of his expression, without defending his antiquated words, and the perpetual harshness of their sound? 'Tis as much commendation as a Man can bear, to own him excellent; all beyond it is Idolatry.—JOHN DRYDEN, "Preface" to *Sylvae*, 1685

As for Mr. *Milton*, whom we all admire with so much Justice, his Subject is not that of an Heroique Poem; properly so call'd: His Design is the Losing of our Happiness; his Event is not prosperous, like that of all other Epique Works: His Heavenly Machines are many, and his Humane Persons are but two. But I will not take Mr. *Rymer's* Work out of his Hands. He has promis'd the World a Critique on that Author; wherein, tho' he will not allow his Poem for Heroick, I hope he will grant us, that his Thoughts are elevated, his Words Sounding, and that no Man has so happily Copy'd the Manner of *Homer*; or so copiously translated his *Grecisms*, and the *Latin* Elegancies of

Virgil. 'Tis true, he runs into a flat of Thought, sometimes for a Hundred Lines together, but 'tis when he is got into a Track of Scripture: His Antiquated words were his Choice, not his Necessity; for therein he imitated *Spencer*, as *Spencer* did *Chawcer*. And tho', perhaps, the love of their Masters, may have transported both too far, in the frequent use of them; yet in my Opinion, Obsolete Words may then be laudably reviv'd, when either they are more Sounding, or more Signifcant than those in practice: And when their Obscurity is taken away, by joining other Words to them which clear the Sense; according to the Rule of *Horace*, for the admission of new Words. But in both cases, a Moderation is to be observ'd, in the use of them: For unnecessary Coynage, as well as unnecessary Revival, runs into Affectation; a fault to be avoided on either hand. Neither will I Justifie *Milton* for his Blank Verse, tho' I may excuse him, by the Example of *Hannibal Caro*, and other *Italians*, who have us'd it: For whatever Causes he alledges for the abolishing of Rhyme (which I have not now the leisure to examine) his own particular Reason is plainly this, that Rhyme was not his Talent; he had neither the Ease of doing it, nor the Graces of it; which is manifest in his *Juvenilia*, or Verses written in his Youth: Where his Rhyme is always constrain'd and forc'd, and comes hardly from him at an Age when the Soul is most pliant; and the Passion of Love, makes almost every Man a Rhymer, tho' not a Poet.—JOHN DRYDEN, *Discourse concerning the Original and Progress of Satire*, 1692

It must be acknowledged that till about forty years ago Great Britain was barren of critical learning, though fertile in excellent writers; and in particular had so little taste for epic poetry, and was so unacquainted with the essential properties and peculiar beauties of it, that *Paradise Lost*, an admirable work of that kind, published by Mr. Milton, the great ornament of his age and country, lay many years unspoken of and entirely disregarded, till at length it happened that some persons of great delicacy and judgment found out the merit of that excellent poem, and, by communicating their sentiments to their friends, propagated the esteem of the author, who soon acquired universal applause.—SIR RICHARD BLACKMORE, *Essays on Several Subjects*, 1716

When Milton first published his famous poem, the first edition was very long going off; few either read, liked, or understood it; and it gained ground merely by its merit.—JONATHAN SWIFT, Letter to Charles Wogan, Aug. 2, 1732

Milton's style, in his *Paradise Lost*, is not natural; 'tis an exotic style.—As his subject lies a good deal out of our world, it has a particular propriety in those parts of the poem: and, when he is on earth, wherever he is describing our parents in Paradise, you see he uses a more easy and natural way of writing.—Though his formal style may fit the higher parts of his own poem, it does very ill for others who write on natural and pastoral subjects.—ALEXANDER POPE, *Spence's Anecdotes*, 1734–36, p. 131

The British nation, which has produced the greatest men in every profession, before the appearance of Milton could not enter into any competition with antiquity, with regard to the sublime excellencies of poetry. Greece could boast an Euripides, Eschylus, Sophocles and Sappho; England was proud of her Shakespeare, Spenser, Johnson and Fletcher; but their then ancients had still a poet in reserve superior to the rest, who stood unrivalled by all succeeding times, and in epic poetry, which is justly esteemed the highest effort of genius, Homer had no rival. When Milton appeared, the pride of Greece was humbled, the competition became more equal, and since *Par-*

adise Lost is ours; it would, perhaps, be an injury to our national fame to yield the palm to any state, whether ancient or modern.—THEOPHILUS CIBBER, *Lives of the Poets*, 1753, Vol. 2, p. 108

> Nor second He, that rode sublime
> Upon the seraph-wings of Extasy,
> The secrets of th' Abyss to spy.
> He pass'd the flaming bounds of Place and Time:
> The living Throne, the sapphire-blaze,
> Where Angels tremble, while they gaze,
> He saw; but blasted with excess of light,
> Closed his eyes in endless night.
> —THOMAS GRAY, *The Progress of Poesy*, 1757

"What? the barbarian who constructed a long commentary on the first chapter of Genesis in ten books of harsh verse? The clumsy imitator of the Greeks who caricatures creation and who, while Moses represents the Eternal Being as creating the world by his word, makes the Messiah take a big compass out of a cupboard in heaven to trace out the work? What? I admire the man who has spoilt Tasso's hell and Tasso's devil; who makes Lucifer masquerade, now as a toad, now as a pigmy; who puts the same speech in his mouth a hundred times over; who represents him as arguing on divinity; who, in attempting a serious imitation of Ariosto's comic invention of fire-arms, makes the devils fire cannon in heaven? Neither I, nor anybody in Italy, has ever been able to take pleasure in all these dismal extravagances. His marriage of Sin and Death, and the snakes of which Sin is delivered, make any man of tolerably delicate taste sick, and his long description of a hospital is only good for a grave-digger. This obscure, eccentric, and disgusting poem was despised at its birth: and I treat it to-day as it was treated in its own country by its own contemporaries. Anyhow, I say what I think, and I really care very little whether others agree with me or not."—FRANÇOIS MARIE AROUET DE VOLTAIRE, *Candide*, 1759, Ch. 25

Adam and Eve, in the state of innocence, are well imagined, and admirably supported; and the different sentiments arising from difference of sex, are traced out with inimitable delicacy, and philosophical propriety. After the fall, he makes them retain the same characters, without any other change than what the transition from innocence to guilt might be supposed to produce: Adam has still that preeminence in dignity, and Eve in loveliness, which we should naturally look for in the father and mother of mankind.—Of the blessed spirits, Raphael and Michael are well distinguished; the one for affability, and peculiar good-will to the human race; the other for majesty, but such as commands veneration, rather than fear.—We are sorry to add, that Milton's attempt to soar still higher, only shows, that he had already soared as high, as, without being "blasted with excess of light," it is possible for the human imagination to rise.—JAMES BEATTIE, *An Essay on Poetry and Music*, 1776

Was there ever any thing so delightfull as the Music of the *Paradise Lost*? It is like that of a fine Organ; has the fullest & the deepest Tones of Majesty, with all the Softness & Elegance of the Dorian Flute. Variety without End! & never equal'd unless perhaps by Virgil. Yet the Doctor has little or nothing to say upon this copious Theme, but talks something about the unfitness of the English Language for Blank Verse, & how apt it is, in the Mouth of some Readers to degenerate into Declamation. Oh! I could thresh his old Jacket 'till I made his Pension Jingle in his Pocket.—WILLIAM COWPER, Letter to William Unwin, Oct. 31, 1779

Milton has written a sublime poem upon a ridiculous story of eating an apple, and of the eternal vengeance decreed by the Almighty against the whole human race, because their progenitor was guilty of this black and detestable offence.—WILLIAM GODWIN, "Of Choice in Reading," *The Enquirer*, 1797, p. 135

His epic is, at the very outset, exposed to the difficulties which beset all Christian poems that celebrate the holy mysteries of religion. It is strange that he failed to discover the incompleteness of *Paradise Lost* as a unique whole, and that it could only appear, as it really is, the first act of a great Christian drama, of which the Creation, the Fall, and Redemption, are so many successive acts, closely linked together. He eventually perceived the defect, it is true, and appended *Paradise Regained*: but the proportions of this latter to the first performance were not in keeping, and much too slight to admit of its constituting an efficient key-stone. When compared with Dante and Tasso, who were his models, Milton, as a Protestant, laboured under considerable disadvantages, since he was deprived of a vast storehouse of emblematical representation, tales, and traditions, which considerably enriched their verse. Accordingly, he sought to supply the deficiency by means of fables and allegories selected from the Koran and the Talmud, a remedy not at all in harmonious unison with the general complexion of a serious Christian poem. The merits of his epic do not, accordingly, consist in regularity of plan so much as in scattered passages of independent beauty, and in the perfection of his poetic diction. The universal admiration of Milton in the eighteenth century is based on his isolated descriptions of paradisaic innocence and beauty, his awful picture of Hell, with the character of its inhabitants, whom he sketched, after the antique, as giants of the Abyss. It is questionable if any real benefit accrued to the language of English poetry from its increased leaning to the Latinism of Milton rather than to the Germanism of Spenser: but this tendency being a fact, Milton must be regarded as the greatest master of style, and in many respects the standard of dignified poetic expression. It is not, however, easy to propose any fixed normal standard for a language composed, as the English is, of mixed ingredients: suspended between two extremes, it cannot but be subject to occasional oscillation to and fro. Shakspere alone exhibits the varied elements of copiousness, power, and brilliancy inherent in it.—FRIEDRICH SCHLEGEL, *Lectures on the History of Literature*, 1815

The Genius of Milton, more particularly in respect to its span in immensity, calculated him, by a sort of birth-right, for such an "argument" as the *Paradise Lost*: he had an exquisite passion for what is properly, in the sense of ease and pleasure, poetical Luxury; and with that, it appears to me, he would fain have been content, if he could, so doing, have preserved his self-respect and feel[ing] of duty performed; but there was working in him, as it were, that same sort of thing as operates in the great world to the end of a Prophecy's being accomplish'd: therefore he devoted himself rather to the ardours than the pleasures of song, solacing himself at intervals with cups of old wine; and those are, with some exceptions the finest parts of the poem.—JOHN KEATS, "Notes on Milton's *Paradise Lost*," 1818

I am not persuaded that the *Paradise Lost* would not have been more nobly conveyed to posterity, not perhaps in heroic couplets, although even *they* could sustain the subject if well balanced, but in the stanza of Spenser or of Tasso, or in the terza rima of Dante, which the powers of Milton could easily have grafted on our language.—GEORGE GORDON, LORD BYRON, "Some Observations upon an Article in *Blackwood's Magazine*," 1820

The poetry of Dante may be considered as the bridge thrown over the stream of time, which unites the modern and antient World. The distorted notions of invisible things which Dante and his rival Milton have idealised, are merely the mask and the mantle in which these great poets walk through eternity enveloped and disguised. It is a difficult question to determine how far they were conscious of the distinction which must have subsisted in their minds between their own creeds and that of the people. Dante at least appears to wish to mark the full extent of it by placing Riphæus, whom Virgil calls *justissimus unus*, in Paradise, and observing a most heretical caprice in his distribution of rewards and punishments. And Milton's poem contains within itself a philosophical refutation of that system, of which, by a strange and natural antithesis, it has been a chief popular support. Nothing can exceed the energy and magnificence of the character of Satan as expressed in *Paradise Lost*. It is a mistake to suppose that he could ever have been intended for the popular personification of evil. Implacable hate, patient cunning and a sleepless refinement of device to inflict the extremest anguish on an enemy, these things are evil; and, although venial in a slave, are not to be forgiven in a tyrant; although redeemed by much that ennobles his defeat in one subdued, are marked by all that dishonours his conquest in the victor. Miltons' Devil as a moral being is as far superior to his God, as One who perseveres in some purpose which he has conceived to be excellent in spite of adversity and torture, is to One who in the cold security of undoubted triumph inflicts the most horrible revenge upon his enemy, not from any mistaken notion of inducing him to repent of a perseverance in enmity, but with the alleged design of exasperating him to deserve new torments. Milton has so far violated the popular creed (if this shall be judged to be a violation) as to have alleged no superiority of moral virtue to his God over his Devil. And this bold neglect of a direct moral purpose is the most decisive proof of the supremacy of Milton's genius. He mingled as it were the elements of human nature as colours upon a single pallet, and arranged them in the composition of his great picture according to the laws of epic truth; that is, according to the laws of that principle by which a series of actions of the external universe and of intelligent and ethical beings is calculated to excite the sympathy of succeeding generations of mankind. The *Divina Commedia* and *Paradise Lost* have conferred upon modern mythology a systematic form; and when change and time shall have added one more superstition to the mass of those which have arisen and decayed upon the earth, commentators will be learnedly employed in elucidating the religion of ancestral Europe, only not utterly forgotten because it will have been stamped with the eternity of genius.—PERCY BYSSHE SHELLEY, *A Defence of Poetry*, 1821

The Second great name in the annals of English poetry is Milton: which is the First, of course, I need not say. Many other Poets have excelled him in variety and versatility; but none ever approached him in intensity of style and thought, in unity of purpose and in the power and grandeur with which he piles up the single monument of Genius, to which his mind is for the time devoted. His Harp may have but one string, but that is such an one, as none but his own finger knows how to touch. *Paradise Lost* has few inequalities; few feeblenesses. It seems not like a work taken up and continued at intervals; but one continuing effort; lasting, perhaps, for years, yet never remitted: elaborated with the highest polish, yet all the marks of

ease and simplicity in it's composition.—HENRY NEELE, *Lectures on English Poetry*, 1827–29, Lecture 2

In the *Paradise Lost*—indeed in everyone of his poems—it is Milton himself whom you see; his Satan, his Adam, his Raphael, almost his Eve—are all John Milton; and it is a sense of this intense egotism that gives me the greatest pleasure in reading Milton's works. The egotism of such a man is a revelation of spirit.—SAMUEL TAYLOR COLERIDGE, *Table Talk*, Aug. 18, 1833

If the poet sometimes betrays fatigue, if the lyre drops from his wearied hand, he rests, and I rest along with him. . . . Who ever wrote like this? What poet ever spoke such language? How miserable seem all modern compositions beside these strong and magnificent conceptions.—FRANÇOIS RENÉ, VICOMTE DE CHATEAUBRIAND, *Sketches of English Literature*, 1837, Vol. 2, pp. 118–30

The slowness of Milton's advance to glory is now generally owned to have been much exaggerated: we might say that the reverse was nearer the truth. . . . It would hardly, however, be said, even in this age, of a poem 3,000 copies of which had been sold in eleven years, that its success had been small; and some, perhaps, might doubt whether *Paradise Lost*, published eleven years since, would have met with a greater demand. There is sometimes a want of congeniality in public taste which no power of genius will overcome. For Milton it must be said by every one conversant with the literature of the age that preceded Addison's famous criticism, from which some have dated the reputation of *Paradise Lost*, that he took his place among great poets from the beginning.—HENRY HALLAM, *Introduction to the Literature of Europe*, 1837–39, Pt. 4, Ch. 5, Par. 34

Adam and Eve are beautiful, graceful objects, but no one has breathed the Pygmalion life into them; they remain cold statues. Milton's sympathies were with things rather than with men, the scenery and phenomena of nature, the trim gardens, the burning lake; but as for the phenomena of the mind, he was not able to see them. He has no delineations of mind except Satan, of which we may say that Satan was his own character, the black side of it. I wish however, to be understood not to speak at all in disparagement of Milton; far from that.—THOMAS CARLYLE, *Lectures on the History of Literature*, 1838, p. 166

Its sale was no evidence that its merits were comprehended, and may be referred to the general reputation of its author; for we find so accomplished a critic as Sir William Temple, some years later, omitting the name of Milton in his roll of writers who have done honour to modern literature, a circumstance which may, perhaps, be imputed to that reverence for the ancients which blinded Sir William to the merits of their successors. How could Milton be understood in his own generation, in the grovelling, sensual court of Charles the Second? How could the dull eyes, so long fastened on the earth, endure the blaze of his inspired genius? It was not till time had removed him to a distance that he could be calmly gazed on and his merits fairly contemplated. Addison, as is well known, was the first to bring them into popular view, by a beautiful specimen of criticism that has permanently connected his name with that of his illustrious subject. More than half a century later, another great name in English criticism, perhaps the greatest in general reputation, Johnson, passed sentence of a very different kind on the pretensions of the poet. A production more discreditable to the author is not to be found in the whole of his voluminous works; equally discreditable, whether regarded in an historical light or as a sample of literary criticism.—WILLIAM H. PRESCOTT, "Chateaubriand's English Literature" (1839), *Biographical and Critical Miscellanies*, 1845

In *Paradise Lost* we feel as if we were admitted to the outer courts of the Infinite. In that all-glorious temple of genius inspired by truth, we catch the full diapason of the heavenly organ. With its first choral swell the soul is lifted from the earth. In the *Divina Commedia* the man, the Florentine, the exiled Ghibelline, stands out, from first to last, breathing defiance and revenge. Milton, in some of his prose works, betrays the partisan also; but in his poetry we see him in the white robes of the minstrel, with upturned though sightless eyes, rapt in meditation at the feet of the heavenly muse. Dante, in his dark vision, descends to the depths of the world of perdition, and, homeless fugitive as he is, drags his proud and prosperous enemies down with him, and buries them, doubly destroyed, in the flaming sepulchres of the lowest hell. Milton, on the other hand, seems almost to have purged off the dross of humanity. Blind, poor, friendless, in solitude and sorrow, with quite as much reason as his Italian rival to repine at his fortune and war against mankind, how calm and unimpassioned is he in all that concerns his own personality! He deemed too highly of his divine gift, to make it the instrument of immortalizing his hatreds. One cry, alone, of sorrow at his blindness, one pathetic lamentation over the evil days on which he had fallen, bursts from his full heart. There is not a flash of human wrath in all his pictures of woe. Hating nothing but evil spirits, in the childlike simplicity of his heart, his pure hands undefiled with the pitch of the political intrigues in which he had lived, he breathes forth his inexpressibly majestic strains,—the poetry not so much of earth as of heaven.—EDWARD EVERETT, *Orations and Speeches*, 1850, Vol. 2, p. 222

Milton is one of the three great Christian poets who were to the theogony of the Middle Ages what Homer was to the Olympus of paganism. The triumvirate consists of Dante, Tasso, and Milton. The *Divine Comedy* of Dante, the *Jerusalem Delivered* of Tasso, the *Paradise Lost* of Milton, are the *Iliads* and *Odysseys* of our theological system. . . . Milton is the least original of the three great Christian poets. At first he imitates Homer, then Virgil, and lastly Dante and Tasso; but his real model is Dante. He impresses the same supernatural subject on the Christian theogony; he sings to England what Italy has already heard—the strife of created angels in revolt against their Maker—the blissful loves of Eden—the seduction of woman —the fall of man—the intercession of the Son of God with the Father—the mercy obtained by his own sacrifice, and the redemption partially gleaming through the distance, as the *dénouement* of this sublime tragedy. Finally, he embraces the entire series of mysteries which the philosopher penetrates with his conjectures, the theologian explains, and the poet describes, without demanding of them other components than miracles, images, and emotions. Why, then, did Milton select this overpowering theological subject, and transplant it to England, so rich in Saxon and Celtic traditions, already popular, and admirably adapted for the text of a grand national and original northern epic? The answer is to be found in his character and his life. By nature he was theological, and the youngest half of his existence had been passed in Italy. The first voyage of a youth is a second birth; from it he imbibes new sensations and ideas, which produce a species of personal transformation. The phenomenon of petrification is not confined to the effect of water upon a plant; it operates upon man through

the air that he breathes.—ALPHONSE DE LAMARTINE, *Memoirs of Celebrated Characters*, 1854

How noble this metre is in Milton's hands, how completely it shows itself capable of the grand, nay of the grandest, style, I need not say. To this metre, as used in the *Paradise Lost*, our country owes the glory of having produced one of the only two poetical works in the grand style which are to be found in the modern languages; the *Divine Comedy* of Dante is the other. England and Italy here stand alone; Spain, France and Germany have produced great poets, but neither Calderón, nor Corneille, nor Schiller, nor even Goethe, has produced a body of poetry in the true grand style, in the sense in which the style of the body of Homer's poetry, or Pindar's, or Sophocles's, is grand. But Dante has, and so has Milton; and in this respect Milton possesses a distinction which even Shakespeare, undoubtedly the supreme poetical power in our literature, does not share with him. Not a tragedy of Shakespeare but contains passages in the worst of all styles, the affected style; and the grand style, although it may be harsh, or obscure, or cumbrous, or over-laboured, is never affected. In spite, therefore, of objections which may justly be urged against the plan and treatment of the *Paradise Lost*, in spite of its possessing, certainly, a far less enthralling force of interest to attract and to carry forward the reader than the *Iliad* or the *Divine Comedy*, it fully deserves, it can never lose, its immense reputation; for, like the *Iliad* and the *Divine Comedy*, nay in some respects to a higher degree than either of them, it is in the grand style.— MATTHEW ARNOLD, *On Translating Homer*, 1861

In *Samson* he finds a cold and lofty tragedy, in *Paradise Regained* a cold and noble epic; he composes an imperfect and sublime poem in *Paradise Lost*. . . . Adam and Eve, the first pair! I approach, and it seems as though I discovered the Adam and Eve of Raphael Sanzio, imitated by Milton, so his biographers tell us, glorious, strong, voluptuous children, naked in the light of heaven, motionless and absorbed before grand landscapes, with bright vacant eyes, with no more thought than the bull or the horse on the grass beside them. I listen, and I hear an English household, two reasoners of the period— Colonel Hutchinson and his wife. Heavens! dress them at once. Folk so cultivated should have invented before all a pair of trousers and modesty. What dialogues! Dissertations capped by politeness, mutual sermons concluded by bows. . . . This Adam entered Paradise *via* England. There he learned respectability, and there he studied moral speechifying.—HIPPOLYTE TAINE, *History of English Literature*, 1871, Vol. 1, tr. Van Laun, Bk. 2, Ch. 6

Let *Paradise Lost*, then, be called a *Vorstellung*. But what a *Vorstellung* it is! That World of Man, the world of all our stars and starry transparencies, hung but drop-like after all from an Empyrean; the great Empyrean itself, "undetermined square or round," so that, though we do diagram it for form's sake, it is beyond all power of diagram; A Hell, far beneath, but still measurably far, with its outcast infernal Powers tending disastrously upwards or tugging all downwards; finally, between the Empyrean and Hell, a blustering blackness of unimaginable Chaos, roaring around the Mundane Sphere and assaulting everlastingly its outermost bosses, but unable to break through, or to disturb the serenity of the golden poise that steadies it from the zenith—what phantasmagory more truly all-significant than this has the imagination of poet ever conceived? What expense of space comparable to this for vastness has any other poet presumed to fill with visual symbolisms, or to occupy with a coherent story? The physical universe of Dante's great poem would go into a nutshell as compared with that to which the imagination must stretch itself out in *Paradise Lost*. In this respect—in respect of the extent of physical immensity through which the poem ranges, and which it orbs forth with soul-dilating clearness and maps out with never-to-be-oblit- erated accuracy before the eye—no possible poem can ever overpass it. And then the story itself! What story mightier or more full of meaning can there ever be than that of the Arch- angel rebelling in Heaven, degraded from Heaven into Hell, reascending from Hell to the Human Universe, winging through the starry spaces of that Universe, and at last possess- ing himself of our central Earth, and impregnating its incipient history with the spirit of Evil? Vastness of scene and power of story together, little wonder that the poem should have so impressed the world. Little wonder that it should now be Milton's Satan, and Milton's narrative of the Creation in its various transcendental connexions, that are in possession of the British imagination, rather than the strict Biblical accounts from which Milton so scrupulously derived the hints to which he gave such marvellous expansion.—DAVID MASSON, *The Poetical Works of John Milton*, 1874, Vol. 1, p. 101

I don't think I've read him these forty years; the whole Scheme of the Poem, and certain Parts of it, looming as grand as any- thing in my Memory; but I never could read ten lines together without stumbling at some Pedantry that tipped me at once out of Paradise, or even Hell, into the Schoolroom, worse than either.—EDWARD FITZGERALD, Letter to C. E. Norton, Feb. 7, 1876, *Letters*, Vol. 3, eds. Terhune, Terhune, p. 655

The cosmogony of the universe as conceived by Milton in *Paradise Lost*, though very simple, is very little understood. Nobody confesses to not reading the poem. Many do read it; many more to their own loss, begin and do not finish it; all attempt it. And yet how few know the simple plan of creation which it presupposes, and without a just conception of which it is totally impossible to understand the poem. Indeed, it is no doubt in large part the want of this conception which induces many readers to forego the further perusal of the work after having reached the third book. They are wearied by the very peculiar and incomprehensible movements of Satan on his journey earthward. In what kind of a world is it that Satan, Raphael, Michael, Uriel, and the rest move about? How does it happen that Satan, in going from Hell to Earth, flies down- ward? and how is it that in the journey he is compelled to pass by the gate of Heaven? Where is the Paradise of Fools through which the poet, in one of the most scornful and extraordinary passages in the book, makes him wander? Where is the throne of Chaos and old Night? There is little use in attempting to read the poem without understanding these things. They are very simple. A diagram or two will be sufficient to explain them.—E. S. NADEL, "The Cosmogony of *Paradise Lost*," *Harper's*, Dec. 1877, p. 137

The triumph of the Puritan poet was as signal as the triumph of the Puritan king. No Anglican minstrel is nearly equal to Milton; neither the Temple nor the Christian Year will com- pare with *Paradise Lost*. We naturally place it side by side with the poem in which Dante enshrined Catholicism. Dante excels Milton in tenderness; in intimate knowledge of the human heart; in the delineation of all passions, except revenge and ambition, pride and hatred. Dante has the infallible Shake- spearian touch whenever his theme is love; Milton in the like case paints with great literary dexterity and with a frank audac- ity of sensuous colour which would fain be passionate and tender; but he never gets beyond painted love. . . . For Eve's

face he has not a word; not one syllable for the crimson of the lip, for the ravishment of the smile. Conventional golden tresses, slender waist, and ringlets "wanton," which surely they had no call to be in Eden;—this is what we find in Milton's first woman, whom Charlotte Brontë says he never saw. Against Dante, on the other hand, and in favour of Milton, we have to put the traces of Middle-age childishness, the nursery goblinism, grotesquerie, and allegorical wire-drawing, which are present in the *Divine Comedy*. The sustained grandeur which has made "Miltonic" a convertible term with "sublime" is far above all that.—PETER BAYNE, *The Chief Actors in the Puritan Revolution*, 1878, pp. 335–36

The style is always great. On the whole it is the greatest in the whole range of English poetry, so great that when once we have come to know and honour and love it, it so subdues the judg- ment that the judgment can with difficulty do its work with temperance. It lifts the low, gives life to the commonplace, dignifies even the vulgar, and makes us endure that which is heavy and dull. We catch ourselves admiring things not al- together worthy of admiration, because the robe they wear is so royal. No style, when one has lived in it, is so spacious and so majestic a place to walk in. . . . Fulness of sound, weight of march, compactness of finish, fitness of words to things, fitness of pauses to thought, a strong grasp of the main idea while other ideas play round it, power of digression without loss of the power to return, equality of power over vast spaces of imag- ination, sustained splendour when he soars

> With plume so strong, so equal and so soft,

a majesty in the conduct of thought, and a music in the maj- esty which fills it with solemn beauty, belong one and all to the style; and it gains its highest influence on us, and fulfils the ultimate need of a grand style in being the easy and necessary expression of the very character and nature of the man. It reveals Milton, as much, sometimes even more than his thought.—STOPFORD A. BROOKE, *Milton*, 1879, p. 83

Whatever conclusion may be the true one from the amount of the public demand, we cannot be wrong in asserting that from the first, and now as then, *Paradise Lost* has been more ad- mired than read. The poet's wish and expectation that he should find "fit audience, though few," has been fulfilled. Partly this has been due to his limitation, his unsympathetic disposition, the deficiency of the human element in his imag- ination, and his presentation of mythical instead of real beings. But it is also in part a tribute to his excellence, and is to be ascribed to the lofty strain, which requires more effort to ac- company than an average reader is able to make, a majestic demeanour which no parodist has been able to degrade, and a wealth of allusion demanding more literature than is possessed by any but the few whose life is lived with the poets. An appreciation of Milton is the last reward of consummated scholarship; and we may apply to him what Quintilian has said of Cicero, "Ille se profecisse sciat, cui Cicero valde place- bit."—MARK PATTISON, *Milton*, 1879, p. 210

Who now reads the ancient writers? Who systematically reads the great writers, be they ancient or modern, whom the con- sent of ages has marked out as classics: typical, immortal, pecu- liar teachers of our race? Alas! the *Paradise Lost* is lost again to us beneath an inundation of graceful academic verse, sugary stanzas of ladylike prettiness, and ceaseless explanations in more or less readable prose of what John Milton meant or did not mean, or what he saw or did not see, who married his great aunt, and why Adam or Satan is like that, or unlike the other. We read a perfect library about the *Paradise Lost*, but the

Paradise Lost itself we do not read.—FREDERIC HARRISON, "The Choice of Books" (1879), *The Choice of Books and Other Literary Pieces*, 1886, p. 13

Klopstock made up his mind to fulfil the prophecy in himself. When he left school in 1745, he had already conceived the plan of the *Messias*, and in his farewell speech on the nature and office of the epic poet, he distinctly alludes to the great work which he contemplated. . . . It was the most popular subject that he could choose, and as yet no poet had exhausted it or brought it once and for all into definite shape, as Milton had the history of the Fall, to the exclusion of all possible rivals on the same ground. It was the vision of Milton that floated before the poet's eyes, and indeed he could not have had a better model, for Milton had achieved the highest that could be done for the Biblical tradition. Milton's *Paradise Lost* stood unrivalled in grandeur of conception and effective development of the theme. Amid Klopstock's many debts to Milton, the following may be mentioned: the detailed description of hell, the council of the devils, the differences of opinion amongst them, their punishment by metamorphosis, the paths through the universe along which devils and angels wander and fly, and the vision of the Last Judgment at the close of the poem. But Klopstock did not profit half enough by Milton's example. While Milton leads us from hell into paradise, and thus relieves a gloomy scene by a bright one, Klopstock, on the contrary, begins with the glories of heaven, and then keeps us in his irksome limbo of disembodied spirits till we long for a change out of very weariness. Milton exerts himself to the utmost not to let the interest flag, and pays particular attention to unity of composition, steady unfolding of the plot, and graphic narration; Klopstock, on the other hand, lets the thread of his narrative decidedly drag, and accompanies each step of the gradual *dénouement* with the sentiments of all the spectators. . . . His poetry is full of the very faults which Milton condemned, and, however much Milton may have been his model, yet his *Messias* is more closely related to the religious oratorios than to *Paradise Lost.*—WILHELM SCHERER, *A History of German Literature*, 1883–86, tr. Conybeare, Vol. 2, pp. 31–33

The dust of the conflict had fallen; and the mountain heights shone out once more from the serene distance: once more he confronted the mighty works of ancient genius. They pleased him still, from their severity and their simplicity; but they did not satisfy him—because they wanted elevation. In his *Paradise Lost* he raised and endeavoured to spiritualise the antique epic. There are many who will always regard St. Peter's temple in the air as the first of architectural monuments. The admirers of the classic will, however, feel that the amplitude and height of the wondrous dome are no sufficient substitute for that massive simplicity and breadth of effect which belong to the Parthenon; while those who revere our cathedrals will maintain that it lacks the variety, the mystery, the aspiration, and the infinitude which characterise the Christian architecture of the North. On analogous grounds the more devoted admirers of Homer and of Shakespeare will ever be dissatisfied with Milton's work, however they may venerate his genius. It is obviously composite in its character—the necessary result of its uniting a Hebraic spirit with a classic form. Dante, like Milton, uses the Greek mythology freely; considering it, no doubt, as part of that "inheritance of the Heathen," into possession of which Christendom had a right to enter; but he uses it as a subordinate ornament, and in matters of mere detail. His poem is a Vision, not an Epic, that vision of supernatural truth, of Hell, Purgatory, and Paradise, which passed before the eyes of

the mediæval Church as she looked up in nocturnal vigil; not the mundane circle of life and experience, of action and of passion, exhibited in its completeness, and contemplated with calm satisfaction by a Muse that looks down from heaven.—AUBREY DE VERE, *Essays, Chiefly on Poetry*, 1887, Vol. 2, p. 112

I cannot stay to characterize his great poem; nor is there need; immortal in more senses than one; humanity counts for little in it; one pair of human creatures only, and these looked at, as it were, through the big end of the telescope; with gigantic, Godlike figures around one, or colossal demons prone on fiery floods. It is not a child's book; to place it in schools as a parsing-book is an atrocity that I hope is ended. Not, I think, till we have had some fifty years to view the everlasting fight between good and evil in this world, can we see in proper perspective the vaster battle which, under Milton's imagination, was pictured in Paradise between the same foes. Years only can so widen one's horizon as to give room for the reverberations of that mighty combat of the powers of light and darkness.—DONALD G. MITCHELL, *English Lands, Letters, and Kings: From Elizabeth to Anne*, 1890, p. 171

I have said that the grandest of English supernatural creations is Milton's Satan. No other personage has at once such magnitude and definiteness of outline as that sublime, defiant archangel, whether in action or in repose. Milton, like Dante, has to do with the unknown world. The Florentine bard soars at last within the effulgence of "the eternal, coeternal beam." Milton's imagination broods "in the wide womb of uncreated night." We enter that "palpable obscure," where there is "no light, but rather darkness visible," and where lurk many a "grisly terror and execrable shape."—EDMUND CLARENCE STEDMAN, *The Nature and Elements of Poetry*, 1892, p. 245

Long after I had thought never to read it—in fact when I was *nel mezzo del cammin di nostra vita*—I read Milton's *Paradise Lost*, and found in it a splendor and majestic beauty that justified to me the fame it wears, and eclipsed the worth of those lesser poems which I had stupidly and ignorantly accounted his worthiest.—WILLIAM DEAN HOWELLS, *My Literary Passions*, 1895, p. 239

What a magnificent opportunity for describing the gradual dawn of living beauty was in the hands of the man who did not hesitate to write poetry about the creation! Does he avail himself of it? Does he give us any suggestion of the tender grace of the young, wondering world, the slow awakening and unfolding of all fair things till they reach the perfection of their loveliness? Oh no! There is chaos, void, abyss, emptiness. We wait and watch. Suddenly—hey! presto! The world is made. There it whirls,—round, smooth, neatly finished. There are the oceans with the fishes, the mountains, the trees, yes, and the flowers and beasts.—VIDA M. SCUDDER, *The Life of the Spirit in the Modern English Poets*, 1895, p. 19

Paradise Lost is the product of two great movements—Puritanism and the Renaissance. Or, to put the same thought in another way, the conception of the poem is Hebraic, its form and imagery are classical. Within the limits of the sacred narrative, from which Milton would not allow himself to deviate, his luxuriant imagination found ample scope for all its stored wealth of learning; and the issue is something far different from the Hebrew original. Few of us, probably, realize how often we unconsciously read into the Scriptural narrative of the Creation and the Fall ideas instilled by Milton's splendid poem.—J. HOWARD B. MASTERMAN, *The Age of Milton*, 1897, p. 54

PARADISE REGAINED

Some little time before I went to Aylesbury prison I was desired by my quondam master, Milton, to take a house for him in the neighbourhood where I dwelt, that he might go out of the city, for the safety of himself and his family, the pestilence then growing hot in London. I took a pretty box for him in Giles Chalfont, a mile from me, of which I gave him notice, and intended to have waited on him, and seen him sell settled in it, but was prevented by that imprisonment.

But now being released and returned home, I soon made a visit to him, to welcome him into the country.

After some common discourses had passed between us, he called for a manuscript of his; which being brought he delivered to me, bidding me take it home with me, and read it at my leisure; and when I had so done, return it to him with my judgment thereupon.

When I came home, and had set myself to read it, I found it was that excellent poem which he entituled *Paradise Lost.* After I had, with the best attention, read it through, I made him another visit, and returned him his book, with due acknowledgment of the favour he had done me in communicating it to me. He asked me how I liked it and what I thought of it, which I modestly but freely told him, and after some further discourse about it, I pleasantly said to him, "Thou hast said much here of *Paradise Lost,* but what hast thou to say of *Paradise Found?*" He made me no answer, but sat some time in a muse; then brake off that discourse, and fell upon another subject.

After the sickness was over, and the city well cleansed and become safely habitable again, he returned thither.

And when afterwards I went to wait on him there, which I seldom failed of doing whenever my occasions drew me to London, he showed me his second poem, called *Paradise Regained,* and in a pleasant tone said to me, "This is owing to you, for you put it into my head by the question you put to me at Chalfont, which before I had not thought of".—THOMAS ELLWOOD, *The History of the Life of Thomas Ellwood,* 1714, ed. Crump, pp. 144–45

Readers would not be disappointed in this latter poem, if they proceeded to a perusal of it with a proper preconception of the kind of interest intended to be excited in that admirable work. In its kind it is the most perfect poem extant, though its kind may be inferior in interest—being in its essence didactic— to that other sort, in which instruction is conveyed more effectively, because less directly, in connection with stronger and more pleasurable emotions, and thereby in a closer affinity with action. But might we not as rationally object to an accomplished woman's conversing, however agreeably, because it has happened that we have received a keener pleasure from her singing to the harp?—SAMUEL TAYLOR COLERIDGE, "Notes on Milton," 1807, *Literary Remains,* Vol. 1, ed. Coleridge, p. 179

Milton has no idealism,—not even in the *Paradise Regained,* where there was most scope for it. His poetry is for the most part quite literal; and the objects he describes have all a certain definiteness and individuality which separates them from the infinite. He has often endeavoured to present images where every thing should have been lost in sentiment.—JOHN WILSON, "Wordsworth" (c. 1826), *Essays Critical and Imaginary,* 1856

The neglect which *Paradise Lost* never experienced seems to have been long the lot of *Paradise Regained.* It was not popular with the world: it was long believed to manifest a decay of the poet's genius; and, in spite of all that the critics have written, it is still but the favorite of some whose predilections for the Miltonic sytle are very strong. The subject is so much less capable of calling forth the vast powers of his mind, that we should be unfair in comparing it throughout with the greater poem: it has been called a model of the shorter epic, an action comprehending few characters and a brief space of time. The love of Milton for dramatic dialogue, imbibed from Greece, is still more apparent than in *Paradise Lost:* the whole poem, in fact, may almost be accounted a drama of primal simplicity; the narrative and descriptive part serving rather to diversify and relieve the speeches of the actors, than their speeches, as in the legitimate epic, to enliven the narration. *Paradise Regained* abounds with passages equal to any of the same nature in *Paradise Lost;* but the argumentative tone is kept up till it produces some tediousness; and perhaps, on the whole, less pains have been exerted to adorn and elevate that which appeals to the imagination.—HENRY HALLAM, *Introduction to the Literature of Europe,* 1837–39, Pt. 4, Ch. 5, Par. 35

In this poem he has not only curbed his imagination, but has almost suppressed it. He has amplified, but has hardly introduced any circumstance which is not in the original. *Paradise Regained* is little more than a paraphrase of the Temptation as found in the synoptical gospels. It is a marvel of ingenuity that more than two thousand lines of blank verse can have been constructed out of some twenty lines of prose, without the addition of any invented incident, or the insertion of any irrelevant digression. In the first three books of *Paradise Regained* there is not a single simile. Nor yet can it be said that the version of the gospel narrative has the fault of most paraphrases, viz., that of weakening the effect, and obliterating the chiselled features of the original.—MARK PATTISON, *Milton,* 1879, p. 187

As he grew older the taste of Milton grew more austere. The change in the character of his ornament is deeply marked when we ascend from the alpine meadows of *Paradise Lost* to the peaks of *Paradise Regained,* where the imaginative air is so highly rarefied that many readers find it difficult to breathe.— EDMUND GOSSE, *Short History of Modern English Literature,* 1897, p. 167

The latter epic indubitably shows some falling off in the poet's powers; the supernatural vein has already yielded the best of its ore; earth must now be the main scene of the drama; the piercing splendors of the poet's earlier verse give place to something more like grand and sonorous prose. Yet now and then the old inspiration seems to seize him.—AUGUSTUS HOPKINS STRONG, *The Great Poets and Their Theology,* 1897, p. 252

In this poem there is noticeable a distinct change from Milton's earlier manner,—a sudden purging away of ornament, a falling back on the naked concept, a preference for language as slightly as possible tinctured with metaphoric suggestion. A portion of this change may be due to failing vividness of imagination; certainly the abandonment of rapid narrative for tedious argumentation marks the increasing garrulity of age. Christ and Satan in the wilderness dispute with studied casuistry, until the sense of the spiritual drama in which they are protagonists is almost lost. As this same weakness is apparent also in the later books of *Paradise Lost,* we must lay it largely to the score of flagging creative energy. But in still greater measure the change seems to be a deliberate experiment in style, or perhaps more truly a conscious reproduction, in language, of that rarefied mental atmosphere to which the author had climbed from the rich valley mists of his youth.—WILLIAM

MOODY, "Life of Milton," *Poetical Works of Milton*, 1899, Cambridge ed., p. xxxi

SAMSON AGONISTES

I have lately read his *Samson*, which has more of the antique spirit than any production of any other modern poet. He is very great, and his own blindness enabled him to describe with so much truth the situation of Samson. Milton was really a poet; one to whom wc owe all possible respect.—JOHANN WOLFGANG VON GOETHE, *Conversations with Eckermann*, 1830, Vol. 2, tr. Oxenford, p. 220

The tragedy of *Samson* breathes all the energy and simplicity of the antique. The poet himself is depicted in the person of the Israelite, blind, a prisoner, and unfortunate. A noble way of revenging himself on his age.—FRANÇOIS RENÉ, VICOMTE DE CHATEAUBRIAND, *Sketches of English Literature*, 1837, Vol. 2, p. 106

Johnson considered the versification of these choruses "so harsh and dissonant, as scarce to preserve (whether the lines end with or without rhyme) any appearance of metrical regularity;" and it must be confessed there are lines which almost seem to merit a censure thus severe. But modern pronunciation is *not* the pronunciation of Milton. Many verses, as they are now read by some of Milton's admirers, would disgust the poet, full as much as his critic.—EDWIN GUEST, A *History of English Rhythms*, 1838, Vol. 2, p. 259

The most successful attempt at reproducing the Greek tragedy, both in theme and treatment, is the *Samson Agonistes*, as it is also the most masterly piece of English versification. Goethe admits that it alone, among modern works, has caught life from the breath of the antique spirit.—JAMES RUSSELL LOWELL, "Swinburne's Tragedies," *My Study Windows*, 1871, p. 220

From a purely literary point of view the tragedy of *Samson Agonistes*, which, as the Preface needlessly states, was "never intended to the stage," cannot be said to possess merits commensurate with its historical and biographical value. That it has escaped representation under conditions wholly uncongenial to it, may be due not only to the sacred character of the source of the subject, but also to the circumstance that by composing music to it as an oratorio Handel has removed it for ever from possible contact with the play-house.—ADOLPHUS WILLIAM WARD, A *History of English Dramatic Literature*, 1875–99, Vol. 3, p. 204

We have now shown that the two most noticeable characteristics of the *Samson Agonistes*, the personal element which runs through it and its dramatic form, modelled upon that of the ancient Greek tragedy; are even more markedly the special features of the *Samson* of Vondel. We know, further, that the Dutch play preceded the English one by at least five years. It only remains for us to show from internal evidence that Milton was acquainted with the language of Vondel's play in order to complete the chain of evidence, and make it more than probable that the one is the direct descendant of the other.—GEORGE EDMUNDSON, *Milton and Vondel*, 1885, p. 170

The *Samson Agonistes*, the most Greek-like drama ever written since the death of Euripides, gives us some insight into the passion-seething abysses of his soul, whose swelling turbulence was only kept down by a sovereign faith. Professor Scclcy finely calls it "the thundering reverberation of a mighty spirit struck by the plectrum of disappointment;" but though that plectrum struck the reverberant chords into thunder, it was the last sob of

the retiring storm beyond which we already see the gleam of blue.—FREDERICK WILLIAM FARRAR, "Three Portraits of Milton," *The English Illustrated Magazine*, 1891, p. 120

The opinions which critics have ventured on the versification of the choruses in *Samson Agonistes* would be sufficient proof that they had met with something not well understood, even if they had never misinterpreted the rhythm. It is not less than an absurdity to suppose that Milton's carefully-made verse could be unmusical: on the other hand it is easy to see how the farsought effects of the greatest master in any art may lie beyond the general taste.—ROBERT BRIDGES, *Milton's Prosody*, 1893, p. 32

SONNETS

The sonnets of Milton, like those of Danté, are frequently deficient in sweetness of diction and harmony of versification, yet they possess, what seldom is discernible in compositions of this kind, energy and sublimity of sentiment. The sonnets to Cyriac Skinner, to Fairfax, Cromwell, and Vane, are remarkable for these qualities, and for vigour of expression, whilst those addressed to the Nightingale and to Mr. Laurence, can boast, I may venture to assert, both of melody in language and elegance in thought. It should also be observed, that Milton has altogethcr avoided the quaint and metaphysic concetti of Petrarch.—NATHAN DRAKE, *Literary Hours*, 1798–1820, Vol. 1, p. 80

> Scorn not the Sonnet; . . .
>   . . . when a damp
> Fell round the path of Milton, in his hand
> The thing became a trumpet; whence he blew
> Soul animating strains—alas, too few!
>   —WILLIAM WORDSWORTH, "Sonnet," 1827

> 'Twas not unseemly in the bravest bard
> From Paradise and angels to descend,
> And crown his country's saviour with a wreath
> Above the regal: Few his words, but strong,
> And sounding through all ages and all climes.
> He caught the sonnet from the dainty hand
> Of Love, who cried to lose it; and he gave
> The notes to Glory.
>   —WALTER SAVAGE LANDOR, "To the President
>   of the French Republic," 1848

Even when Milton's matter repels or fails to interest, there is always something in his manner which compels an attentive and fascinated hearing. The personal quality, which was of pure and high self-containedness all compact, informs the language and gives it a magical power. He on his mountain-top had learned from the silent stars and voiceful winds a speech which was not the dialect of the crowd, and, whatever be the burden of the saying, there is a spell in the mere intonation. We feel the spell sometimes almost humorously, as in the rough-hewn sonnet with its harsh, unpoetic, bald, monosyllabic rhymes—"clogs," "dogs," "frogs," "hogs,"—which leaves almost the same sense of weight and mass that we derive from his nobler and more delightful utterances. Among these, it is needless to say, one stands apart in unapproached and unapproachable majesty. The great sonnet "On the late Massacres in Piedmont" is one of those achievements in which matter of the noblest order moulds for itself a form of the highest excellence, matter and form being, as in music and in all supreme art, so bound up and interfused that, though we know both of them to be there, we cannot know them or think of them apart. Much has been said in eulogy of this sonnet, and said worthily and well; but there is a perfection which mocks praise, and it is this perfection that is here attained; not the perfection which consists in this quality or in that, but which comes when all qualities which may be displayed, all potentialities which can be exerted, meet in triumphant, satisfying, utter accomplishment.—JAMES ASHCROFT NOBLE, "The Sonnet in England" (1880), *The Sonnet in England and Other Essays*, 1893, p. 33

They differ from all the sonnets of the time, in that they are simple in thought and unstudied in expression, and that they convince us of the entire sincerity of the singer. We feel that they were not written because other poets had made a reputation by such compositions, but because their writer had something to say, and knew that the best way for him to say it was in this form. If he had read Shakspere and Drummond, or Drayton and Daniel, he forgot them in his remembrance of Petrarch, whose form he mastered, at the age of twenty-three, as no English poet since Sidney had done. They do not read like the productions of a young man, for they are mature in conception and severe in execution—demanding our deepest respect as well as our highest admiration. The credentials of a strong intellect, which knows itself and the work it has to do, their gravity is Shaksperean. They bear a weight of thought which had never before laid upon the English sonnet, and they bear it lightly as a flower.—RICHARD HENRY STODDARD, "The Sonnet in English Poetry," *Scribner's Monthly*, 1881, p. 915

Hallam and certain other writers have declared themselves unable to reconcile their judgment to the frequent violation of the legitimate structure in Milton's sonnets. It is true that the pause between the major and minor portions of the sonnet (so uniformly observed in the best Italian examples) is not to be found in Milton, but the rhyme-scheme is always faultlessly in conformity with the most rigid rule, and the sonnets, even where they link themselves together—as in the cases of the two divorce sonnets and the two sonnets on his blindness—stand alone in self-centered unity, and never become sonnet stanzas. The serious divergence favoured by Milton in his practice of running octave into sestet was clearly the result of a deliberate conviction that the sonnet in his hands was too short a poem to be broken into halves, and hence his sonnets, each done in a breath as to metrical flow, possess the intellectual unity of oneness of conception, at the same time that they are devoid of the twofold metrical and intellectual unity which comes of the rounded perfectness of linked and contrasted parts. Much may be said for the beauty of the sonnet structure adopted by Milton, and indeed the model has been so much in requisition in recent years, that it appears to merit the distinct nomenclature which, in the index of metrical groups, I have ventured to give it.—HALL CAINE, *Sonnets of Three Centuries*, 1882, p. 280

Some of Milton's most famous sonnets were never published in his lifetime. They were not even printed until 1694, and then from copies which had been circulating from hand to hand in manuscript. It was not until 1753 that the text was published from the originals. These at once made it plain that the variations which had crept in were, with one possible exception, variations for the worse, and, in some instances, grossly for the worse.—THOMAS R. LOUNSBURY, *Studies in Chaucer*, 1892, Vol. 1, p. 232

His sonnets were no chamber exercises: each owed its inspiration to a real occasion, and that inspiration of reality lifted it high above mere simulation of the Horatian mode.—A. T. QUILLER-COUCH, "Introduction" to *English Sonnets*, 1897, p. xvi

ON THE MORNING OF CHRIST'S NATIVITY

The "Ode on the Nativity," far less popular than most of the poetry of Milton, is perhaps the finest in the English language. A grandeur, a simplicity, a breadth of manner, an imagination at once elevated and restrained by the subject, reign throughout it. If Pindar is a model of lyric poetry, it would be hard to name any other ode so truly Pindaric; but more has naturally been derived from the Scriptures. Of the other short poems, that on the death of the Marchioness of Westminister deserves particular mention.—HENRY HALLAM, *Introduction to the Literature of Europe*, 1837–39, Pt. 3, Ch. 5, Par. 63

The most distinct foreshadowing of Milton's great epic poem, and of his own independent genius, is an earlier poem—"The Hymn of the Nativity"—which gives the poet the fame of having composed almost in his youth the earliest of the great English odes, the like of which had not, I believe, been heard, since Pindar, two thousand years before, had struck the lyre for assembled Greece. It is a lyric that might have burst from that religious bard of paganism, could he have had prophetic vision of the Advent. It is a poem that revealed a new mastery of English versification, disciplined afterward to such power in the blank verse of *Paradise Lost*. Nothing in the way of meter can be grander than some of the transitions from the gentle music of the quiet passages to the passionate parts, and their deep reverberating lines that seem to go echoing on, spiritually sounding, long after they are heard no more.—HENRY REED, *Lectures on English Literature, from Chaucer to Tennyson*, 1855, p. 193

Show me one who delights in the "Hymn on the Nativity," and I will show you one who may never indeed be a singer in this world, but who is already a listener to the best.—GEORGE MACDONALD, *England's Antiphon*, 1868, p. 200

When, at the close of 1629, Milton began his "Ode on the Morning of Christ's Nativity," he was still closely imitating the form of these favourites of his, the Fletchers, until the fifth stanza was reached, and then he burst away in a magnificent measure of his own, pouring forth that hymn which carried elaborate lyrical writing higher than it had ever been taken before in England.—EDMUND GOSSE, *Short History of Modern English Literature*, 1897, p. 143

The "Hymn" may be reckoned the first fully opened flower of Milton's poetic springtime. . . . It would be difficult to find a poem that would better exemplify certain of the characteristics of a lyric poem than does the "Hymn on the Nativity." The religious fervor of the young poet informs every stanza of the poem; the pictures are painted for their dynamic emotional value only; the language is adorned with "rich and various gems" of expression; the sentiment is elevated; the metrical form is graceful and harmonious with the thought.—ALBERT PERRY WALKER, *Selections from the Poetical Works of John Milton*, 1900, p. 257

L'ALLEGRO AND IL PENSEROSO

I have heard a very judicious critic say, that he had an higher idea of Milton's style in poetry from the two following poems, than from his *Paradise Lost*. It is certain the imagination shewn in them is correct and strong. The introduction to both in irregular measure is borrowed from the Italians, and hurts an

English ear.—OLIVER GOLDSMITH, "Introductory Criticism" to *The Beauties of English Poetry*, 1767

Of all the English poems in the descriptive style, the richest and most remarkable are, Milton's "Allegro" and "Penseroso." The collection of gay images on the one hand, and of melancholy ones on the other, exhibited in these to small, but inimitably fine poems, are as exquisite as can be conceived. They are, indeed, the storehouse whence many succeeding poets have enriched their descriptions of similar subjects; and they alone are sufficient for illustrating the observations which I made, concerning the proper selection of circumstances in descriptive writing.—HUGH BLAIR, *Lectures on Rhetoric and Belles-Lettres*, 1783, ed. Mills, Lecture 40

We find nowhere in his writings that whining sensibility and exaggeration of morbid feeling, which makes so much of modern poetry effeminating. If he is not gay, he is not spirit-broken. His "L'Allegro" proves, that he understood thoroughly the bright and joyous aspects of nature; and in his "Penseroso," where he was tempted to accumulate images of gloom, we learn, that the saddest views which he took of creation, are such as inspire only pensive musing or lofty contemplation.— WILLIAM ELLERY CHANNING, *Remarks on the Character and Writings of John Milton*, 1826

There can be little doubt as to which of the two characters he portrays was after Milton's own heart. He portrays "L'Allegro" with much skill and excellence; but he cannot feign with him the sympathy he genuinely feels with the other; into his portrait of "Il Penseroso" he throws himself, so as to speak, with all his soul.—JOHN W. HALES, *Longer English Poems*, 1872, p. 231

As for "L'Allegro" and "Il Penseroso," who shall praise them fitly? They are among the few things about which there is no difference of opinion, which are as delightful to childhood as to criticism, to youth as to age. To dwell on their technical excellences (the chief of which is the unerring precision with which the catalectic and acatalectic lines are arranged and interchanged) has a certain air of impertinence about it. Even a critical King Alfonso El Sabio could hardly think it possible that Milton might have taken a hint here, although some persons have, it seems, been disturbed because skylarks do not come to the window, just as others are troubled because the flowers in "Lycidas" do not grow at the same time, and because they think they could see stars through the "star-proof" trees of the "Arcades."—GEORGE SAINTSBURY, *A History of Elizabethan Literature*, 1887, p. 320

Of course Milton's "Il Penseroso" and "L'Allegro" have far more value even as country poems than hundreds of more literal transcripts. From a literary point of view indeed the juxtapositions of half a dozen epithets alone would prove the genius of the writer. But there are no sharp outlines; the scholar pauses in his walk to peer across the watered flat, or raises his eyes from his book to see the quiver of leaves upon the sunlit wall; he notes an effect it may be; but his images do not come like treasures lavished from a secret storehouse of memory.— A. C. BENSON, "Andrew Marvell," *Essays*, 1896, p. 71

The language of these two little masterpieces has been the despair of poets. It is not that it is so beautiful, for others have equaled or excelled it in the mere conjuring power of suggestion; but that it is, as a French critic has finely said, so *just* in its beauty. The means are exquisitely proportioned to the end. The speech incarnates the thought as easily, as satisfyingly, as the muscles of a Phidian youth incarnate the motor-impulse of his brain. Always fruition is just gently touched. To

the connoisseur in language there is a sensation of almost physical soothing in its perfect poise and play.—WILLIAM VAUGHN MOODY, *Poetical Works of Milton*, 1899, Cambridge ed., p. 26

LATIN POEMS

Milton, like most of the learned men of the age, wrote in Latin both in prose and verse. The former will, we believe, bear a comparison with any Latin prose of the time, unless we should think that of the natives of the countries which speak languages derived from the Latin to be excepted; as a modern Latin poet, critics are disposed to assign him a place in the first rank. It is not unworthy of notice, that while in English prose he delighted in long and involving sentences, his Latin periods are not very long nor much involved.—THOMAS KEIGHTLEY, *An Account of the Life, Opinions, and Writings of John Milton*, 1855, p. 388

It is perhaps sufficient to say that critics of such different times, tempers, and attitude towards their subject as Johnson and the late Rector of Lincoln,—critics who agree in nothing except literary competence,—are practically at one as to the remarkable excellence of Milton's Latin verse at its best. It is little read now, but it is a pity that any one who can read Latin should allow himself to be ignorant of at least the beautiful "Epitaphium Damonis" on the poet's friend, Charles Diodati.— GEORGE SAINTSBURY, *A History of Elizabethan Literature*, 1887, p. 318

The "Epitaphium Damonis" is the best, and—except for a few fragments—the last of Milton's Latin poems. His Latin verse surpassed that of his contemporaries, not so much in scholarly elegance as in force of expression. To him Latin is almost a living language.—J. HOWARD B. MASTERMAN, *The Age of Milton*, 1897, p. 28

As to the artistic qualities of this poetry, it would not be profitable to speak here at length. In the main they are qualities of delicacy and felicitousness rather than of strength. They bear a relation to Milton's later English poetry roughly analogous to that which Tennyson's early lyrical experiments bear to his adult work. In them Milton learned his trade of poet, at least on its technical and imitative side. The habit of assimilation, the power to freight his lines with the accumulated riches of past thought, we see here in the making, and we see also how the habit of conveying commonplace thought in a sonorous and magniloquent medium fostered that large Miltonic diction, which was so noble in Milton's own hands, and so intolerably hollow in the hands of his eighteenth century imitators. It would be wrong, however, to think of these poems as consciously disciplinary. When they were written, the chances seemed even that Milton's main work as a poet would be in Latin rather than in English; they represent sincere creative effort, and offer many rare intrinsic beauties in spite of their immaturity.—WILLIAM VAUGHN MOODY, *Poetical Works of Milton*, 1899, Cambridge ed., p. 320

PROSE WORKS

His prose writings disagreeable, though not altogether defective in genius.—DAVID HUME, *History of England*, 1762

Dr. Johnson endeavoured to give an air of dignity and novelty to his diction by affecting the order of words usual in poetry. Milton's prose has not only this drawback, but it has also the disadvantage of being formed on a classical model. It is like a fine translation from the Latin; and, indeed, he wrote originally in Latin. . . . Milton's prose-style savours too much of poetry, and, as I have already hinted, of an imitation of the Latin.—WILLIAM HAZLITT, "On the Prose Style of Poets," *The Plain Speaker*, 1826

In many passages of his polemics there is an intensity of eloquence that seems to fuse the multitude of his thoughts, and send them glowing white, from the crucible of his mind into the mind of the reader, scarcely able to contain them in the mould of his narrower conception. We find also an impetuosity and impatience in Milton's prose which never occurs in his verse. The vehemence of his argument, whether as an advocate or an accuser, carries him out of himself, in acrimonious invective or rapturous panegyric.—JAMES MONTGOMERY, "Memoir," *The Poetical Works of John Milton*, 1843, Vol. 1, p. xv

Independently of the subject-matter, his treatises are among the most remarkable ever written. Their mere style (we use the word in its widest sense) is absolutely unrivalled. It is a very difficult thing, indeed, to decide properly on the style of a period so remote as that of Milton; we are perpetually misled in our judgment, by the impossibility of identifying ourselves with the writers—of inducing a full sympathy with the circumstances which impelled them, and thus with the objects for which they wrote—the ends proposed in composition. In fact, it is only by *the degree of its adjustment* to the result intended, that any style can be justly commended as good or condemned as bad. But, holding in view this adjustment, and making the necessary allowances for lapses, effected through Time, in the language, we feel ourselves fully warranted in saying, that no man has ever surpassed, if, indeed, any man has ever equalled the author of the *Areopagitica* in purity—in force—in copiousness—in majesty—or, in what may be termed without the least exaggeration, a gorgeous magnificence of style. Some of his more directly controversial works rise at times into a species of lyrical rhapsody—divinely energetic—constituting for itself a department of composition which is neither prose nor poetry, but something with all the best qualities of each, and upon the whole superior to either.—EDGAR ALLAN POE, Review of *The Prose Works of John Milton*, 1845, *Complete Works*, Vol. 12, ed. Harrison, p. 245

The expression is not too strong. There are moments when, shaking from him the dust of his arguments, the poet bursts suddenly forth, and bears us away in a torrent of incomparable eloquence. We get, not the phrase of the orator, but the glow of the poet, a flood of images poured around his arid theme, a rushing flight carrying us above his paltry controversies. The polemical writings of Milton are filled with such beauties. The prayer which concludes the treatise on Reformation in England, the praise of zeal in the *Apology for Smectymnus*, the portrait of Cromwell in the Second Defense of the English People, and, finally, the whole tract on the *Liberty of Unlicensed Printing* from beginning to end, are some of the most memorable pages in English literature, and some of the most characteristic products of the genius of Milton.—EDMOND SCHERER, "Milton," *Essays on English Literature*, 1868, tr. Arnold

Concerning Milton's style the most diverse opinions have been pronounced. Everything depends upon the point of view. Rich and powerful it is undeniably, coming from such a master of words, and yields in the highest degree the pleasure of luxurious expression. But the student need hardly be warned that Milton's prose is to be enjoyed without being imitated: for modern purposes the language and idiom are too stiffly Latinised, and the imagery too fantastic. Further, for a work of

controversy the style is too ornate, too unmethodical, and too coarsely vituperative to have much convincing or converting power. In Milton still more than in Taylor the application is lost in the gorgeous splendour of words and imagery, and all but decided adherents are repelled by the unmeasured discharge of abuse and ridicule.—WILLIAM MINTO, *Manual of English Prose Literature*, 1872–80, p. 308

Jeremy Taylor's prose is poetical prose. Milton's prose is not poetical prose, but a different thing, the prose of a poet; not like Taylor's, loaded with imagery on the outside; but coloured by imagination from within. Milton is the first English writer who, possessing in the ancient models a standard of the effect which could be produced by choice of words, set himself to the conscious study of our native tongue with a firm faith in its as yet undeveloped powers as an instrument of thought.—MARK PATTISON, *Milton*, 1879, p. 68

Milton, when, as he said, he wished "to soar a little," had a magnificent abundance of words at his command, and at times he broke out into rich poetical prose. But when he had to write some plain description, his prose lumbered as clumsily as a heavy cart over rough paving-stones.—THOMAS SERGEANT PERRY, *English Literature in the Eighteenth Century*, 1883, p. 7

The passages which diversify and relieve his prose works are far more beautiful in their kind than anything to be found elsewhere in English prose. . . . There is no English prose author whose prose is so constantly racy with such a distinct and varied savour as Milton's. It is hardly possible to open him anywhere after the fashion of the *Sortes Virgilianæ* without lighting on a line or a couple of lines, which for the special purpose it is impossible to improve. And it might be contended with some plausibility that this abundance of jewels, or purple patches, brings into rather unfair prominence the slips of grammar and taste, the inequalities of thought, the deplorable attempts to be funny, the rude outbursts of bargee invective, which also occur so numerously. One other peculiarity, or rather one result of these peculiarities, remains to be noticed; and that is that Milton's prose is essentially inimitable. It would be difficult even to caricature or to parody it; and to imitate it as his verse, at least his later verse, has been so often imitated, is simply impossible.—GEORGE SAINTSBURY, *A History of Elizabethan Literature*, 1887, p. 325

The incoherence and awkwardness of humanistic prose in England reach their climax in some of Milton's cumbrous periods. Sentence, sub-sentence, parenthesis, qualifying clause, are only kept together by a liberal expenditure of what may be described as verbal hooks and eyes.—JOHN ADDINGTON SYMONDS, "Notes on Style," *Essays Speculative and Suggestive*, 1890, Vol. 1, p. 324

To Milton prose was an unnatural medium, which he never subdued to his purposes. As a prose writer he commands admiration only where he enlists sympathy. He used the weapon provided for him by his age with consummate power; but it was a weapon which he seized as he found it, which owed its force to the arm that wielded it, and which he left with no sharpness added to its temper, no new polish to its surface, no new facility in its contrivance.—HENRY CRAIK, "Introduction" to *English Prose*, 1893, Vol. 2, p. 6

Milton's colloquial sallies are at times such as might be expected from an excessive familiarity with epistolary Latin, at other times they are the efforts of a forced sportiveness too grim to be altogether agreeable. But even in these, and how infinitely more in the wealth of illustrations, images, and ideas lavished upon any subject which he is fain to treat, do we recognise the wealth of an imagination which seems at times, within the limits of a single sentence, to master diction and syntax and all the conditions of written speech! To decry such a style as composite is to revive the short-sighted captiousness of an obsolete method of criticism, which was capable of analysing materials, but not of apprehending the power which transfuses what it has appropriated. Milton's prose, all exceptions taken, and all cavils allowed their force, remains the most extraordinary literary prose, and the most wonderful poet's prose, embodied in English literature.—ADOLPHUS WILLIAM WARD, *English Prose*, 1893, Vol. 2, ed. Craik, p. 462

In truth, the influence of Milton's English prose writings seems to have been very slight. In his attacks upon prelacy he went with the stream, and his voice mingled with the universal shout. When he took an independent line, when he pleaded for liberty of divorce, or, with a heroism of which even he might not have been capable if his infirmity had not severed him from the world, launched pamphlets against monarchy on the very vigil of the Restoration, he produced absolutely no effect whatever. Nor can we perceive that his *Areopagitica* hastened the liberty of the press by a day, though, when this had come about by wholly different agencies, it was rightly adopted as the gospel of the new dispensation: as the newly-discovered Venus of Milo might be made the goddess of a classical revival inaugurated while she yet slept under the sod. The only prose production of Milton to which a considerable contemporary effect can be justly ascribed is not an English but a Latin one, his defence of the English people against Salmasius.—RICHARD GARNETT, "Introduction" to *Prose of Milton*, 1894, p. viii

Milton's prose works are perhaps not read, at the present day, to the extent demanded by their great and varied merits, among which may be named their uncompromising advocacy of whatsoever things are true, honest, just, pure, lovely, and of good report; their eloquent assertion of the inalienable rights of men to a wholesome exercise of their intellectual faculties, the right to determine for themselves, with all the aids they can command, what is truth and what is error; the right freely to communicate their honest thoughts from one to another,—rights which constitute the only sure and lasting foundation of individual, civil, political, and religious liberty; the ever-conscious sentiment which they exhibit, on the part of the poet, of an entire dependence upon "that Eternal Spirit, who can enrich with all utterance and knowledge, and sends out his Seraphim with the hallowed fire of his altar, to touch and purify the lips of whom he pleases;" the ever-present consciousness they exhibit of that stewardship which every man as a probationer of immortality must render an account, according to the full measure of the talents with which he has been intrusted—of the sacred obligation, incumbent upon every one, of acting throughout the details of life, private or public, trivial or momentous, "as ever in his great Task-Master's eye."—HIRAM CORSON, *An Introduction to the Prose and Poetical Works of John Milton*, 1899, p. xiii

DOCTRINE AND DISCIPLINE OF DIVORCE

If the early date of the pamphlet be the true date; if the *Doctrine and Discipline* was in the hands of the public on August 1; if Milton was brooding over this seething agony of passion all through July, with the young bride, to whom he had been barely wedded a month, in the house where he was writing, then the only apology for this outrage upon the charities, not to say decencies, of home is that which is suggested by the passage

referred to. Then the pamphlet, however imprudent, becomes pardonable. It is a passionate cry from the depths of a great despair; another evidence of the noble purity of a nature which refused to console itself as other men would have consoled themselves; a nature which, instead of an egotistical whine for its own deliverance, sets itself to plead the common cause of man and of society. He gives no intimation of any individual interest, but his argument throughout glows with a white heat of concealed emotion, such as could only be stirred by the sting of some personal and present misery.—MARK PATTISON, *Milton*, 1879, p. 55

Of Milton's pamphlet it is everyone's duty to speak with profound respect. It is a noble and passionate cry for a high ideal of married life, which, so he argued, had by inflexible laws been changed into a drooping and disconsolate household captivity, without refuge or redemption. . . . This pamphlet on divorce marks the beginning of Milton's mental isolation. Nobody had a word to say for it. Episcopalian, Presbyterian, and Independent held his doctrine in as much abhorrence as did the Catholic, and all alike regarded its author as either an impracticable dreamer or worse.—AUGUSTINE BIRRELL, "John Milton," *Obiter Dicta, Second Series*, 1887, pp. 22–23

What gross injustice the world has done him on this point! Married at an age when a man who has preserved the lofty ideals and personal purity of youth is peculiarly liable to deception, to a woman far below him in character and intellect, a pretty fool utterly unfitted to take a sincere and earnest view of life or to sympathize with him in his studies; deserted by her a few weeks after the wedding-day; met by stubborn refusal and unjust reproaches in every attempt to reclaim and reconcile her; accused by her family of disloyalty in politics, and treated as if he were unworthy of honourable consideration; what wonder that his heart experienced a great revulsion, that he began to doubt the reality of such womanhood as he had described and immortalized in *Comus*, that he sought relief in elaborating a doctrine of divorce which should free him from the unworthy and irksome tie of a marriage which was in truth but an empty mockery? That divorce doctrine which he propounded in the heat of personal indignation, disguised even from himself beneath a mask of professedly calm philosophy, was surely false, and we cannot but condemn it. But can we condemn his actual conduct, so nobly inconsistent with his own theory?—HENRY VAN DYKE, "Milton and Tennyson," *The Poetry of Tennyson*, 1889–98, p. 80

AREOPAGITICA

It would not be easy to discover, in the whole stream and succession of literary productions any thing more cogent and forcible than this tract.—WILLIAM GODWIN, *History of the Commonwealth of England*, 1824, Vol. 1, p. 352

The *Paradise Lost* is, indeed, scarcely a more glorious monument of the genius of Milton than that *Areopagitica*. If, even at the present day, when the cause for which it was written has long since triumphed, it is impossible to read it without emotion, we can hardly doubt that when it first appeared it exercised a mighty influence over the awakening movement of liberty.—W. E. H. LECKY, *Spirit of Rationalism in Europe*, 1865

All who care for English literature have read the *Areopagitica*. It is the most literary of Milton's pamphlets, eloquent, to the point, and full of noble images splendidly wrought and fitted to their place. Its defence of books and the freedom of books will last as long as there are writers and readers of books. Its scorn of—

the censorship of writing is only excelled by its uplifted praise of true writing.—STOPFORD A. BROOKE, *Milton*, 1879, p. 45

The right of the *Areopagitica* to rank as best, as it is clearly the most popular, of Milton's prose works, has been disputed by the jealous admirers of others. The popularity, no doubt due in part to the subject, is also to be ascribed to the greater equability and clearness of style. If he does not soar to quite such heights, there are fewer descents and contortions, and it remains at a high level of lofty eloquence.—LESLIE STEPHEN, *Dictionary of National Biography*, 1894, Vol. 38, p. 29

DEFENCES OF THE ENGLISH PEOPLE

That Mr. Milton doe prepare something in answer to the book of Salmasius, and when he hath done itt bring itt to the Councill.—*Order-Book of the Council of State*, Jan. 8, 1649/50

I did not satisfie my self in the Account I gave you, of presenting your Book to my Lord, although it seemed to me that I writ to you all which the Messengers speedy Returne the same night from Eaton would permit me. . . . I shall now studie it even to the getting of it by Heart: esteeming it according to my poor Judgement (which yet I wish it were so right in all Things else) as the most compendious Scale, for so much, to the Height of the Roman eloquence. When I consider how equally it turnes and rises with so many figures, it seems to me a Trajans columne in whose winding ascent we see imboss'd the severall Monuments of your learned victoryes. And Salmatius and Morus make up as great a Triumph as That of Decebalus, whom too for ought I know you shall have forced as Trajan the other, to make themselves away out of a just Desperation.—ANDREW MARVELL, Letter to John Milton, June 2, 1654

A. About this time 1649 came out two books, one written by Salmasius, a Presbyterian, against the murder of the King; another written by Milton, an English Independent, in answer to it.

   B. I have seen them both. They are very good Latin both, and hardly to be judged which is better; and both very ill reasoning, hardly to be judged which is worse; like two declamations, *pro* and *con*, made for exercise only in a rhetoric school by one and the same man. So like is a Presbyterian to an Independent.—THOMAS HOBBES, *Behemoth*, 1660, Pt. 4

Perhaps the King could have wrote better, but I think no man else in the three Kingdoms. What a venomous spirit is in that serpent Milton, that black-mouthed Zoilus, that blows his viper's breath upon those immortal devotions, from the beginning to the end! This is he that wrote with all irreverence against the Fathers of our Church, and showed as little duty to his father that begat him. The same that wrote for the Pharisees, that it was lawful for a man to put away his wife for every cause; and against Christ, for not allowing divorces. The same, O horrid! that defended the lawfulness of the greatest crime that was ever committed, to put our thrice-excellent King to death. A pretty schoolboy scribbler, that durst grapple in such a cause with the prince of the learned men of his age—Salmasius—"the delight, the musick of all knowledge," who would have scorned to drop a pen full of ink against so base an adversary, but to maintain the honour of so good a King, whose merits he adorns with this praise—*De quo si quis dixerit omnia bona, vix pro suis meritis, satis illum, ornaret* (Contr. Milton, p. 237). Get thee behind me, Milton, thou savourest not the things that be of truth and loyalty, but of pride, bitterness and falsehood.—JOHN HACKETT, *The Life of Archbishop Williams*, 1693

And now we com to his Master-piece, his chief and favorit Work in Prose, for Argument the noblest, as being the Defence of a whole free Nation, the People of *England*; for stile and disposition the most eloquent and elaborat, equalling the old *Romans* in the purity of their own Language, and their highest Notions of Liberty; as universally spread over the learned World as any of their Compositions; and certain to endure while Oratory, Politics, or History, bear any esteem among Men. *It cannot be deny'd*, says that excellent Critic *Monsieur Baile*, that Milton's *Latin stile is easy, brisk and elegant; nor that he defended the Republican Cause with a world of Address and Wit*: Agreable to which Judgment is the unanimous Suffrage of Foreners, not excepting the most zealous Assertors of Monarchy.—JOHN TOLAND, *The Life of John Milton*, 1698

King Charles II., being now sheltered in Holland, employed Salmasius, professor of polite learning at Leyden, to write a *Defence* of his father and of monarchy; and, to excite his industry, gave him, as was reported, a hundred jacobuses. Salmasius was a man of skill in languages, knowledge of antiquity, and sagacity of emendatory criticism, almost exceeding all hope of human attainment; and having, by excessive praises, been confirmed in great confidence of himself, though he probably had not much considered the principles of society or the rights of government, undertook the employment without distrust of his own qualifications; and, as his expedition in writing was wonderful, in 1649 published *Defensio Regis*.

   To this Milton was required to write a sufficient answer, which he performed (1650) in such a manner, that Hobbes declared himself unable to decide whose language was best, or whose arguments were worst. In my opinion, Milton's periods are smoother, neater, and more pointed; but he delights himself with teasing his adversary as much as with confuting him. He makes a foolish allusion of Salmasius, whose doctrine he considers as servile and unmanly, to the stream of *Salmacis*, which whoever entered left half his virility behind him. Salmasius was a Frenchman, and was unhappily married to a scold. *Tu es Gallus*, says Milton, *et, ut aiunt, nimium gallinaceus*. But his supreme pleasure is to tax his adversary, so renowned for criticism, with vicious Latin. He opens his book with telling that he has used *persona*, which, according to Milton, signifies only a *mask*, in a sense not known to the Romans, by applying it as we apply *person*. But as Nemesis is always on the watch, it is memorable that he has enforced the charge of a solecism by an expression in itself grossly solecistical, when for one of those supposed blunders, he says, as Ker, and I think some one before him, has remarked, *propino te grammatistis tuis* vapulandum. From *vapulo*, which has a passive sense, *vapulandus* can never be derived. No man forgets his original trade: the rights of nations, and of kings, sink into questions of grammar, if grammarians discuss them.

   Milton, when he undertook this answer, was weak of body and dim of sight; but his will was forwarded, and what was wanting of health was supplied by zeal. He was rewarded with a thousand pounds, and his book was much read—for paradox, recommended by spirit and elegance, easily gains attention; and he who told every man that he was equal to his King, could hardly want an audience.

   That the performance of Salmasius was not dispersed with equal rapidity, or read with equal eagerness, is very credible. He taught only the stale doctrine of authority, and the unpleasing duty of submission; and he had been so long not only the monarch but the tyrant of literature, that almost all mankind was delighted to find him defied and insulted by a new name, not yet considered as any one's rival. If Christina, as is said, commended the *Defence of the People*, her purpose must be to torment Salmasius, who was then at her court; for neither her civil station nor her natural character could dispose them to favour the doctrine, who was by birth a queen, and by temper despotic.

That Salmasius was, from the appearance of Milton's book, treated with neglect, there is not much proof; but to a man so long accustomed to admiration, a little praise of his antagonist would be sufficiently offensive, and might incline him to leave Sweden, from which however he was dismissed, not with any mark of contempt, but with a train of attendance scarcely less than regal.

He prepared a reply, which, left as it was imperfect, was published by his son in the year of the Restoration. In the beginning, being probably most in pain for his Latinity, he endeavours to defend his use of the word *persona*; but, if I remember right, he misses a better authority than any that he has found, that of Juvenal in his fourth satire:

—Quid agas cum dira et fœdior omni
Crimine *persona* est?

As Salmasius reproached Milton with losing his eyes in the quarrel, Milton delighted himself with the belief that he had shortened Salmasius's life; and both, perhaps, with more malignity than reason. Salmasius died at the Spa, September 3, 1653; and, as controvertists are commonly said to be killed by their last dispute, Milton was flattered with the credit of destroying him.—SAMUEL JOHNSON, "John Milton," *Lives of the English Poets*, 1779

The celebrated controversy of *Salmasius*, continued by Morus with *Milton*—the first the pleader of King Charles, the latter the advocate of the people—was of that magnitude, that all Europe took a part in the paper-war of these two great men. The answer of Milton, who perfectly massacred Salmasius, is now read but by the few. Whatever is addressed to the times, however great may be its merits, is doomed to perish with the times; yet on these pages the philosopher will not contemplate in vain.—ISAAC DISRAELI, "Milton," *Curiosities of Literature*, 1791

Controversies like these are pitiful sights. It is sad to see a magnificent genius like Milton stooping to fling those paving-stones of abuse—"rogue, puppy, foul-mouthed wretch"—which come ready to the hand of every sot and shrew in England.—WILLIAM FRANCIS COLLIER, A *History of English Literature*, 1861, p. 201

Milton's *Defences of the English People* are rendered provoking by his extraordinary language concerning his opponents. "Numskull," "beast," "fool," "puppy," "knave," "ass," "mongrel-cur," are but a few of the epithets that may be selected for this descriptive catalogue. This is doubtless mere matter of pleading, a rule of the forum where controversies between scholars are conducted; but for that very reason it makes the pamphlets as provoking to an ordinary reader as an old bill of complaint in Chancery must have been to an impatient suitor who wanted his money.—AUGUSTINE BIRRELL, "John Milton," *Obiter Dicta, Second Series*, 1887, p. 34

The *Defence* is not wanting in powerful expression, as indeed, being Milton's, it could hardly be; but it bears on the face of it the obvious signs of a work written to order. It has no complete study of government or scheme of political philosophy. It is a robust, but not profound or convincing, answer to a powerful attack. Politics were merged in personalities, and most men must needs admit that it was an ill cause that was driven to accuse Charles I. of poisoning his father, and to twit Salmasius with being governed by his wife.—WILLIAM HOLDEN HUTTON, *Social England*, 1895, Vol. 4, ed. Traill, p. 289

JOHN AUBREY
"John Milton"
Brief Lives
1669–96

Mr. John Milton was of an Oxfordshire familie. His Grandfather was a Roman Catholic of Holton, in Oxfordshire, near Shotover.

His father was brought-up in the University of Oxon, at Christ Church, and his grandfather disinherited him because he kept not to the Catholique Religion (he found a Bible in English, in his Chamber). So therupon he came to London, and became a Scrivener (brought up by a friend of his; was not an Apprentice) and gott a plentifull estate by it, and left it off many yeares before he dyed. He was an ingeniose man; delighted in musique; composed many Songs now in print, especially that of *Oriana*. I have been told that the Father composed a Song of fourscore parts for the Lantgrave of Hess, for which his Highnesse sent a meddall of gold, or a noble present. He dyed about 1647; buried in Cripple-gate-church, from his house in the Barbican.

His son John was borne the 9th of December, 1608, *die Veneris*, half an hour after 6 in the morning, in Bread Street, in London, at the Spread Eagle, which was his house (he had also in that street another howse, the Rose; and other houses in other places). Anno Domini 1619, he was ten yeares old; and was then a Poet. His school-master then was a Puritan, in Essex, who cutt his haire short.

He went to Schoole to old Mr. Gill, at Paule's Schoole. Went at his owne Chardge only, to Christ's College in Cambridge at fifteen, where he stayed eight yeares at least. Then he travelled into France and Italie (had Sir H. Wotton's commendatory letters). At Geneva he contracted a great friendship with the learned Dr. Deodati of Geneva. He was acquainted with Sir Henry Wotton, Ambassador at Venice, who delighted in his company. He was severall yeares beyond Sea, and returned to England just upon the breaking-out of the Civill Warres.

From his brother, Christopher Milton:—when he went to Schoole, when he was very young, he studied very hard, and sate-up very late, commonly till twelve or one a clock at night, and his father ordered the mayde to sitt-up for him, and in those yeares (10) composed many Copies of Verses which might well become a riper age. And was a very hard student in the University, and performed all his exercises there with very good Applause. His first Tutor there was Mr. Chapell; from whom receiving some unkindnesse (whipt him) he was afterwards (though it seemed contrary to the Rules of the College) transferred to the Tuition of one Mr. Tovell, who dyed Parson of Lutterworth. He went to travell about the year 1638 and was abroad about a year's space, chiefly in Italy.

Immediately after his return he took a lodging at Mr. Russell's, a Taylour, in St. Bride's Churchyard, and took into his tuition his sister's two sons, Edward and John Philips, the first 10, the other 9 years of age; and in a yeare's time made them capable of interpreting a Latin authour at sight. And within three years they went through the best of Latin and Greek Poetts—Lucretius and Manilius, of the Latins (and with him the use of the Clobes, and some rudiments of Arithmetic and Geometry.) Hesiod, Aratus, Dionysius Afer, Oppian, Apollonii *Argonautica*, and Quintus Calaber. Cato, Varro and Columella *De re rustica* were the very first Authors they learn't. As he was severe on the one hand, so he was most familiar and free in his conversation to those to whome most sowre in his way of education. N.B. he mad his Nephews Songsters, and sing, from the time they were with him.

His first wife (Mrs. Powell, a Royalist) was brought up and lived where there was a great deale of company and merriment, dancing, etc. And when she came to live with her husband, at Mr. Russell's, in St. Bride's Churchyard, she found it very solitary; no company came to her; oftimes heard his Nephews beaten and cry. This life was irkesome to her, and so she went to her Parents at Fost-hill. He sent for her, after some time; and I thinke his servant was evilly entreated: but as for matter of wronging his bed, I never heard the least suspicions; nor had he, of that, any Jealousie.

Two opinions doe not well on the same Boulster; she was a Royalist, and went to her mother to the King's quarters, neer Oxford. I have perhaps so much charity to her that she might not wrong his bed: but what man, especially contemplative, would like to have a young wife environ'd and storm'd by the Sons of Mars, and those of the enemi partie? He parted from her, and wrote the Triplechord about divorce.

He had a middle wife, whose name was Katharin Wood-cock. No child living by her.

He maried his third wife, Elizabeth Minshull, the year before the Sicknesse: a gent. person, a peacefull and agreable humour.

Hath two daughters living: Deborah was his amanuensis (he taught her Latin, and to reade Greeke to him when he had lost his eie-sight).

His sight began to faile him at first upon his writing against Salmasius, and before 'twas full compleated one eie absolutely faild. Upon the writing of other bookes, after that, his other eie decayed. His eie-sight was decaying about 20 yeares before his death. His father read without spectacles at 84. His mother had very weake eies, and used spectacles presently after she was thirty yeares old.

His harmonicall and ingeniose Soul did lodge in a beautifull and well proportioned body. He was a spare man. He was scarce so tall as I am (*quaere*, quot feet I am high: *resp.*, of middle stature).

He had abroun hayre. His complexion exceeding faire—he was so faire that they called him *the Lady of Christ's College.* Ovall face. His eie a darke gray.

He was very healthy and free from all diseases: seldome tooke any physique (only sometimes he tooke manna): only towards his latter end he was visited with the Gowte, Spring and Fall.

He had a delicate tuneable Voice, and had good skill. His father instructed him. He had an Organ in his howse; he played on that most. Of a very cheerfull humour. He would be chearfull even in his Gowte-fitts, and sing.

He had a very good Memorie; but I believe that his excellent Method of thinking and disposing did much to helpe his Memorie.

His widowe haz his picture, drawne very well and like, when a Cambridge-schollar, which ought to be engraven; for the Pictures before his bookes are not at all like him.

His exercise was chiefly walking. He was an early riser (*scil.* at 4 a clock *manè*) yea, after he lost his sight. He had a man to read to him. The first thing he read was the Hebrew bible, and that was at 4 h. *manè*, ½ h. plus. Then he contemplated.

At 7 his man came to him again, and then read to him again, and wrote till dinner; the writing was as much as the reading. His daughter, Deborah, could read to him in Latin, Italian and French, and Greeke. Maried in Dublin to one Mr.

Clarke (sells silke, etc.) very like her father. The other sister is Mary, more like her mother.

After dinner he used to walke 3 or four houres at a time (he always had a Garden where he lived) went to bed about 9.

Temperate man, rarely dranke between meales. Extreme pleasant in his conversation, and at dinner, supper, etc.; but Satyricall. (He pronounced the letter R (*littera canina*) very hard—a certaine signe of a Satyricall Witt—*from John Dreyden*.)

All the time of writing his *Paradise Lost*, his veine began at the Autumnall Aequinoctiall, and ceased at the Vernall or thereabouts (I believe about May) and this was 4 or 5 yeares of his doeing it. He began about 2 yeares before the King came-in, and finished about three yeares after the King's restauracion.

In the 4th booke of *Paradise Lost* there are about six verses of Satan's Exclamation to the Sun, which Mr. E. Philips remembers about 15 or 16 yeares before ever his Poem was thought of, which verses were intended for the Beginning of a Tragoedie which he had designed, but was diverted from it by other businesse.

He was visited much by the learned; more then he did desire. He was mightily importuned to goe into France and Italie. Foraigners came much to see him, and much admired him, and offer'd to him great preferments to come over to them; and the only inducement of severall foreigners that came over into England, was chiefly to see Oliver Protector, and Mr. John Milton; and would see the hous and chamber wher he was borne. He was much more admired abrode then at home.

His familiar learned Acquaintance were Mr. Andrew Marvell, Mr. Skinner, Dr. Pagett, M.D.

John Dreyden, Esq., Poet Laureate, who very much admires him, went to him to have leave to putt his *Paradise Lost* into a Drame in rythme. Mr. Milton recieved him civilly, and told him *he would give him leave to tagge his Verses.*

His widowe assures me that Mr. T. Hobbs was not one of his acquaintance, that her husband did not like him at all, but he would acknowledge him to be a man of great parts, and a learned man. Their Interests and Tenets did run counter to each other.

Whatever he wrote against Monarchie was out of no animosity to the King's person, or owt of any faction or interest, but out of a pure Zeale to the Liberty of Mankind, which he thought would be greater under a fre state than under a Monarchiall government. His being so conversant in Livy and the Roman authors, and the greatness he saw donne by the Roman commonwealth, and the vertue of their great Commanders induc't him to.

Mr. John Milton made two admirable Panegyricks, as to Sublimitie of Witt, one on Oliver Cromwel, and the other on Thomas, Lord Fairfax, both which his nephew Mr. Philip hath. But he hath hung back these two yeares, as to imparting copies to me for the Collection of mine. Were they made in commendation of the Devill, 'twere all one to me: 'tis the *hypsos* that I looke after. I have been told that 'tis beyond Waller's or anything in that kind.

ANTHONY À WOOD
From *Fasti Oxonienses*
1691

T his year ⟨1635⟩ was incorporated Master of Arts *John Milton*, not that it appears so in the Register, for the reason I have told you in the Incorporations 1629, but from his own mouth to my friend, who was well acquainted with, and had from him, and from his Relations after his death, most of this account of his life and writings following. (1) That he was born in *Breadstreet* within the City of *London*, between 6 and 7 a clock in the morning of the ninth of *Decemb.* an. 1608. (2) That his father *Joh. Milton* who was a Scrivner living at the *Spread Eagle*[1] in the said street, was a Native of *Halton* in *Oxfordshire*, and his mother named *Sarah* was of the antient family of the *Bradshaws*. (3) That his Grandfather *Milton* whose Christian name was *John*, as he thinks, was an Under-Ranger or Keeper of the Forest of *Shotover* near to the said town of *Halton*, but descended from those of his name who had lived beyond all record at *Milton* near *Halton* and *Thame* in *Oxfordshire*. Which Grandfather being a zealous Papist, did put away, or, as some say, disinherit, his Son, because he was a Protestant, which made him retire to *London*, to seek, in a manner, his fortune. (4) That he the said *John Milton* the Author, was educated mostly in *Pauls* school under *Alex. Gill* senior, and thence at 15 years of age was sent to *Christs* Coll. in *Cambridge*, where he was put under the tuition of *Will. Chappell*, afterwards Bishop of *Ross* in *Ireland*, and there, as at School for 3 years before, 'twas usual with him to sit up till midnight at his book, which was the first thing that brought his eyes into the danger of blindness. By this his indefatigable study he profited exceedingly, wrot then several Poems, paraphras'd some of *David's Psalms*, performed the collegiate and academical exercise to the admiration of all, and was esteemed to be a vertuous and sober person, yet not to be ignorant of his own parts. (5) That after he had taken the degrees in Arts, he left the University of his own accord, and was not expelled for misdemeanors, as his Adversaries have said. Whereupon retiring to his Fathers house in the Country, he spent some time in turning over Latin and Greek Authors, and now and then made[2] excursions into the great City to buy books, to the end that he might be instructed in Mathematicks and Musick, in which last he became excellent, and by the help of his Mathematicks could compose a Song or Lesson. (6) That after five years being thus spent, and his Mother (who was very charitable to the poor) dead, he did design to travel, so that obtaining the rudiments of the Ital. Tongue, and Instructions how to demean himself from Sir *Hen. Wotton*, who delighted in his company, and gave him Letters of commendation to certain persons living at *Venice*, he travelled into *Italy*, an. 1638. (7) That in his way thither, he touched at *Paris*, where *Joh. Scudamoure*, Vicount *Slego*, Embassador from K. *Ch.* I. to the French king, received him kindly, and by his means became known to *Hugo Grotius*, then and there Embassador from the Qu. of *Sweden*; but the manners and genius of that place being not agreeable to his mind, he soon left it. (8) That thence by *Geneva* and other places of note, he went into *Italy*, and thro *Legorne*, *Pisa*, &c. he went to *Florence*, where continuing two months, he became acquainted with several learned men, and familiar with the choicest Wits of that great City, who introduced and admitted him into their private Academies, whereby he saw and learn'd their fashions of literature. (9) That from thence he went to *Sena* and *Rome*, in both which places he spent his time among the most learned there, *Lucas Holsteinius* being one; and from thence he journied to *Naples*, where he was introduced into the acquaintance of *Joh. Bapt. Mansus* an Italian Marquess (to whom *Torquatus Tassus* an Italian poet wrot his book *De Amicitia*) who shewed great civilities to him, accompanied him to see the rarieties of that place, visited him at his Lodgings, and sent to, the testimony of his great esteem for, him, in this Distich,

Ut mens, forma, decor, mos, si pietas sic,
   Non Anglus, verum herculè Angelus ipse fores.

And excus'd himself at parting for not having been able to do him more honour, by reason of his resolute owning his (Protestant) religion: which resoluteness he using at *Rome*, many there were that dared not to express their civilities towards him, which otherwise they would have done: And I have heard it confidently related, that for his said Resolutions, which out of policy, and for his own safety, might have been then spared, the English Priests at *Rome* were highly disgusted, and it was question'd whether the Jesuits his Countrymen there, did not design to do him mischief. Before he left *Naples* he return'd the Marquess an acknowledgment of his great favours in an elegant copy of verses entit. *Mansus*, which is among the Latin poems. (10) That from thence (*Naples*) he thought to have gone into *Sicily* and *Greece*, but upon second thoughts he continued in *Italy*, and went to *Luca, Bononia, Ferrara*, and at length to *Venice*; where continuing a month, he went and visited *Verona* and *Millan*. (11) That after he had ship'd the books and other goods which he had bought in his travels, he returned thro *Lombardy*, and over the *Alpes* to *Geneva*, where spending some time, he became familiar with the famous *Joh. Deodate* D.D. Thence, going thro *France*, he returned home, well fraught with Knowledge and Manners, after he had been absent one year and three months. (12) That soon after he setled in an house in *S. Bride's* Churchyard, near *Fleetstreet*, in *London*, where he instructed in the Lat. Tongue two Youths named *John* and *Edw. Philips*, the Sons of his Sister *Anne* by her Husband *Edward Philips*: both which were afterwards Writers, and the eldest principl'd as his Uncle. But the times soon after changing, and the Rebellion thereupon breaking forth, *Milton* sided with the Faction, and being a man of parts, was therefore more capable than another of doing mischief, especially by his pen, as by those books which I shall anon mention, will appear. (13) That at first we find him a Presbyterian and a most sharp and violent opposer of Prelacy, the established ecclesiastical Discipline and the orthodox Clergy. (14) That shortly after he did set on foot and maintained very odd and novel Positions concerning Divorce, and then taking part with the Independents, he became a great Antimonarchist, a bitter Enemy to K. *Ch.* I. and at length arrived to that monstrous and unparallel'd height of profligate impudence, as in print to justify the most execrable Murder of him the best of Kings, as I shall anon tell you. Afterwards being made Latin Secretary to the Parliament, we find him a Commonwealths man, a hater of all things that looked towards a single person, a great reproacher of the Universities, scholastical degrees, decency and uniformity in the Church. (15) That when *Oliver* ascended the Throne, he became the Latin Secretary, and proved to him very serviceable when employed in business of weight and moment, and did great matters to obtain a name and wealth. To conclude, he was a person of wonderful parts, of a very sharp, biting and satyrical wit. He was a good Philosopher and Historian, an excellent Poet, Latinist, Grecian and Hebritian, a good Mathematician and Musitian, and so rarely endowed by nature, that had he been but honestly principled, he might have been highly useful to that party, against which he all along appeared with much malice and bitterness.

Notes

1. The arms that *Joh. Milton* did use and seal his letters with, were, *Argent a spread eagle with two heads gules, legg'd and beak'd sable.*
2. See in Joh. Milton's book intit. *Defensio secunda*: edit. *Hag. Com.* 1654, p. 61, &c.

JOSEPH ADDISON
From *The Spectator*
1712

No. 267. January 5, 1712
Cedite Romani Scriptores, cedite Graii.
(Propert.)

There is nothing in Nature more irksom than general Discourses, especially when they turn chiefly upon Words. For this Reason I shall wave the Discussion of that Point which was started some Years since, Whether *Milton's Paradise Lost* may be called an *Heroick Poem?* Those who will not give it that Title, may call it (if they please) a *Divine Poem.* It will be sufficient to its Perfection, if it has in it all the Beauties of the highest kind of Poetry; and as for those who alledge it is not an Heroick Poem, they advance no more to the Diminution of it, than if they should say *Adam* is not *Æneas,* nor *Eve Helen.*

I shall therefore examine it by the Rules of Epic Poetry, and see whether it falls short of the *Iliad* or *Æneid* in the Beauties which are essential to that kind of Writing. The first thing to be considered in an Epic Poem, is the Fable, which is perfect or imperfect, according as the Action which it relates is more or less so. This Action should have three Qualifications in it. First, It should be but one Action. Secondly, It should be an entire Action; and Thirdly, It should be a great Action. To consider the Action of the *Iliad,* *Æneid,* and *Paradise Lost* in these three several Lights. *Homer* to preserve the Unity of his Action hastens into the midst of things, as *Horace* has observed: Had he gone up to *Leda's* Egg, or begun much later, even at the Rape of *Helen,* or the Investing of *Troy,* it is manifest that the Story of the Poem would have been a Series of several Actions. He therefore opens his Poem with the Discord of his Princes, and artfully interweaves in the several succeeding parts of it, an account of every thing material which relates to them, and had passed before this fatal Dissension. After the same manner *Æneas* makes his first appearance in the *Tyrrhene* Seas, and within sight of *Italy,* because the Action proposed to be celebrated was that of his Settling himself in *Latium.* But because it was necessary for the Reader to know what had happened to him in the taking of *Troy,* and in the preceding parts of his Voyage, *Virgil* makes his Hero relate it by way of Episode in the second and third Books of the *Æneid.* The Contents of both which Books come before those of the first Book in the Thread of the Story, tho' for preserving of this Unity of Action, they follow it in the Disposition of the Poem. *Milton,* in Imitation of these two great Poets, opens his *Paradise Lost* with an Infernal Council plotting the Fall of Man, which is the Action he proposed to celebrate; and as for those great Actions, the Battel of the Angels, and the Creation of the World, (which preceded in point of time, and which, in my Opinion, would have entirely destroyed the Unity of his Principal Action, had he related them in the same Order that they happened) he cast them into the fifth, sixth and seventh Books, by way of Episode to this noble Poem.

Aristotle himself allows, that *Homer* has nothing to boast of as to the Unity of his Fable, tho' at the same time that great Critick and Philosopher endeavours to palliate this Imperfection in the *Greek* Poet, by imputing it in some Measure to the very Nature of an Epic Poem. Some have been of Opinion, that the *Æneid* also labours in this particular, and his Episodes which may be looked upon as Excrescencies rather than as Parts of the Action. On the contrary, the Poem which we have now under our Consideration, hath no other Episodes than such as naturally arise from the Subject, and yet is filled with such a multitude of astonishing Incidents, that it gives us at the same time a Pleasure of the greatest Variety, and of the greatest Simplicity; uniform in its Nature, tho' diversified in the Execution.

I must observe also, that as *Virgil* in the Poem which was designed to celebrate the Original of the *Roman* Empire, has described the Birth of its great Rival, the *Carthaginian* Commonwealth: *Milton* with the like Art in his Poem on the Fall of Man, has related the Fall of those Angels who are his professed Enemies. Besides the many other Beauties in such an Episode, it's running Parallel with the great Action of the Poem, hinders it from breaking the Unity so much as another Episode would have done, that had not so great an Affinity with the principal Subject. In short, this is the same kind of Beauty which the Criticks admire in the *Spanish Fryar,* or the *Double Discovery,* where the two different Plots look like Counterparts and Copies of one another.

The second Qualification required in the Action of an Epic Poem is, that it should be an *entire* Action: An Action is entire when it is compleat in all its Parts; or as *Aristotle* describes it, when it consists of a Beginning, a Middle, and an End. Nothing should go before it, be intermix'd with it, or follow after it, that is not related to it. As on the contrary, no single Step should be omitted in that just and regular Progress which it must be supposed to take from its Original to its Consummation. Thus we see the Anger of *Achilles* in its Birth, its Continuance and Effects; and *Æneas's* Settlement in *Italy,* carried on through all the Oppositions in his way to it both by Sea and Land. The Action in *Milton* excels (I think) both the former in this particular; we see it contrived in Hell, executed upon Earth, and punished by Heaven. The parts of it are told in the most distinct manner, and grow out of one another in the most natural Order.

The third Qualification of an Epic Poem is its *Greatness.* The Anger of *Achilles* was of such Consequence, that it embroiled the Kings of *Greece,* destroy'd the Heroes of *Asia,* and engaged all the Gods in Factions. *Æneas's* Settlement in *Italy* produced the *Cæsars,* and gave Birth to the *Roman* Empire. *Milton's* Subject was still greater than either of the former; it does not determine the Fate of single Persons or Nations, but of a whole Species. The united Powers of Hell are joyned together for the Destruction of Mankind, which they effected in part, and would have completed, had not Omnipotence it self interposed. The principal Actors are Man in his greatest Perfection, and Woman in her highest Beauty. Their Enemies are the fallen Angels: The Messiah their Friend, and the Almighty their Protector. In short, every thing that is great in the whole Circle of Being, whether within the Verge of Nature, or out of it, has a proper Part assigned it in this admirable Poem.

In Poetry, as in Architecture, not only the whole, but the principal Members, and every part of them, should be Great. I will not presume to say, that the Book of Games in the *Æneid,* or that in the *Iliad,* are not of this nature, nor to reprehend *Virgil's* Simile of the Top, and many other of the same Kind in the *Iliad,* as liable to any Censure in this Particular; but I think we may say, without derogating from those wonderful Performances, that there is an Indisputable and Unquestioned Magnificence in every Part of *Paradise Lost,* and indeed a much greater than could have been formed upon any Pagan System.

But *Aristotle,* by the Greatness of the Action, does not only mean that it should be great in its Nature, but also in its Duration, or in other Words, that it should have a due length in it, as well as what we properly call Greatness. The just Measure of this kind of Magnitude, he explains by the following Similitude. An Animal, no bigger than a Mite, cannot appear perfect to the Eye, because the Sight takes it in at once, and has only a confused Idea of the whole, and not a distinct Idea of all its Parts; If on the contrary you should suppose an Animal of ten thousand Furlongs in length, the Eye would be so filled with a single Part of it, that it could not give the Mind an Idea of the whole. What these Animals are to the Eye, a very short or a very long Action would be to the Memory. The first would be, as it were, lost and swallowed up by it, and the other difficult to be contained in it. *Homer* and *Virgil* have shewn their principal Art in this Particular; the Action of the *Iliad*, and that of the *Æneid*, were in themselves exceeding short, but are so beautifully extended and diversified by the Invention of *Episodes*, and the Machinery of Gods, with the like Poetical Ornaments, that they make up an agreeable Story sufficient to employ the Memory without overcharging it. *Milton's* Action is enriched with such a variety of Circumstances, that I have taken as much Pleasure in reading the Contents of his Books, as in the best invented Story I ever met with. It is possible, that the Traditions on which the *Iliad* and *Æneid* were built, had more Circumstances in them than the History of *the Fall of Man*, as it is related in Scripture. Besides it was easier for *Homer* and *Virgil* to dash the Truth with Fiction, as they were in no danger of offending the Religion of their Country by it. But as for *Milton*, he had not only a very few Circumstances upon which to raise his Poem, but was also obliged to proceed with the greatest Caution in every thing that he added out of his own Invention. And, indeed, notwithstanding all the Restraints he was under, he has filled his Story with so many surprising Incidents, which bear so close Analogy with what is delivered in Holy Writ, that it is capable of pleasing the most delicate Reader, without giving Offence to the most scrupulous.

The Modern Criticks have collected from several Hints in the *Iliad* and *Æneid* the Space of Time, which is taken up by the Action of each of those Poems; but as a great part of *Milton's* Story was transacted in Regions that lie out of the reach of the Sun and the Sphere of Day, it is impossible to gratifie the Reader with such a Calculation, which indeed would be more curious than instructive; none of the Criticks, either Ancient or Modern, having laid down Rules to circumscribe the Action of an Epic Poem with any determined number of Years, Days or Hours.

But of this more particularly hereafter.

No. 273. January 12, 1712

. . . Notandi sunt tibi Mores.

(Hor.)

Having examined the Action of *Paradise Lost*, let us in the next place consider the Actors. This is *Aristotle's* Method of considering; first the Fable, and secondly the Manners, or, as we generally call them in *English*, the Fable and the Characters.

Homer has excelled all the Heroic Poets that ever wrote, in the multitude and variety of his Characters. Every God that is admitted into his poem, acts a Part which would have been suitable to no other Deity. His Princes are as much distinguished by their Manners as by their Dominions; and even those among them, whose Characters seem wholly made up of Courage, differ from one another as to the particular kinds of Courage in which they excell. In short, there is scarce a Speech or Action in the *Iliad*, which the Reader may not ascribe to the Person that speaks or acts, without seeing his Name at the Head of it.

Homer does not only out-shine all other Poets in the Variety, but also in the Novelty of his Characters. He has introduced among his *Græcian* Princes a Person, who had lived in three Ages of Men, and conversed with *Theseus, Hercules, Polyphemus*, and the first Race of Heroes. His principal Actor is the Son of a Goddess, not to mention the Off-spring of other Deities, who have likewise a Place in his Poem, and the venerable *Trojan* Prince, who was the Father of so many Kings and Heroes. There is in these several Characters of *Homer*, a certain Dignity as well as Novelty, which adapts them in a more peculiar manner to the Nature of an Heroic Poem. Tho', at the same time, to give them the greater variety, he has described a *Vulcan*, that is, a Buffoon among his Gods, and a *Thersites* among his Mortals.

Virgil falls infinitely short of *Homer* in the Characters of his Poem, both as to their Variety and Novelty. *Æneas* is indeed a perfect Character, but as for *Achates*, tho' he is stiled the Hero's Friend, he does nothing in the whole Poem which may deserve that Title. *Gyas, Mnestheus, Sergestus*, and *Cloanthus*, are all of them Men of the same Stamp and Character,

> . . . *Fortemque Gyan, fortemque Cloanthum:* Virg.

There are indeed several very natural Incidents in the Part of *Ascanius*; as that of *Dido* cannot be sufficiently admired. I do not see any thing new or particular in *Turnus*. *Pallas* and *Evander* are remote Copies of *Hector* and *Priam*, as *Lausus* and *Mezentius* are almost Parallels to *Pallas* and *Evander*. The Characters of *Nisus* and *Eurialus* are beautiful, but common. We must not forget the Parts of *Sinon, Camilla*, and some few others, which are fine Improvements on the *Greek* Poet. In short, there is neither that Variety nor Novelty in the Persons of the *Æneid*, which we meet with in those of the *Iliad*.

If we look into the Characters of *Milton*, we shall find that he has introduced all the Variety his Fable was capable of receiving. The whole Species of Mankind was in two Persons at the time to which the Subject of his Poem is confined. We have, however, four distinct Characters in these two Persons. We see Man and Woman in the highest Innocence and Perfection, and in the most abject State of Guilt and Infirmity. The two last Characters are, indeed, very common and obvious, but the two first are not only more magnificent, but more new than any Characters either in *Virgil*, or *Homer*, or indeed in the whole Circle of Nature.

Milton was so sensible of this Defect in the Subject of his Poem, and of the few Characters it would afford him, that he has brought into it two Actors of a Shadowy and Fictitious Nature, in the Persons of Sin and Death, by which means he has wrought into the Body of his Fable a very beautiful and well invented Allegory. But not withstanding the Fineness of this Allegory may attone for it in some measure; I cannot think that Persons of such a Chymerical Existence are proper Actors in an Epic Poem; because there is not that measure of Probability annexed to them, which is requisite in Writings of this kind, as I shall shew more at large hereafter.

Virgil has, indeed, admitted *Fame* as an Actress in the *Æneid*, but the Part she acts is very short, and none of the most admired Circumstances in that Divine Work. We find in Mock-Heroic Poems, particularly in the *Dispensary* and the *Lutrin*, several Allegorical Persons of this Nature, which are very beautiful in those Compositions, and may, perhaps, be used as an Argument, that the Authors of them were of Opinion, such Characters might have a Place in an Epic Work. For my own part, I should be glad the Reader would think so, for the sake of the Poem I am now examining, and must further add, that if such empty unsubstantial Beings may be ever made use of on this occasion, never were any more nicely imagined, and employed in more proper Actions, than those of which I am now speaking.

Another Principal Actor in this Poem is the great Enemy of Mankind. The part of *Ulysses* in *Homer's Odissey* is very much admired by *Aristotle*, as perplexing that Fable with very agreeable Plots and Intricacies, not only by the many Adventures in his Voyage, and the Subtilty of his Behaviour, but by the various Concealments and Discoveries of his Person in several parts of that Poem. But the Crafty Being I have now mentioned, makes a much longer Voyage than *Ulysses*, puts in practice many more Wiles and Stratagems, and hides himself under a greater variety of Shapes and Appearances, all of which are severally detected, to the great Delight and Surprize of the Reader.

We may likewise observe with how much Art the Poet has varied several Characters of the Persons that speak in his infernal Assembly. On the contrary, how has he represented the whole Godhead exerting it self towards Man in its full Benevolence under the Three-fold Distinction of a Creator, a Redeemer and a Comforter!

Nor must we omit the Person of *Raphael*, who amidst his Tenderness and Friendship for Man, shews such a Dignity and Condescention in all his Speech and Behaviour, as are suitable to a Superior Nature. The Angels are indeed as much diversified in *Milton*, and distinguished by their proper Parts, as the Gods are in *Homer* or *Virgil*. The Reader will find nothing ascribed to *Uriel*, *Gabriel*, *Michael*, or *Raphael*, which is not in a particular manner suitable to their respective Characters.

There is another Circumstance in the principal Actors of the *Iliad* and *Æneid*, which gives a peculiar Beauty to those two Poems, and was therefore contrived with very great Judgment. I mean the Authors having chosen for their Heroes Persons who were so nearly related to the People for whom they wrote. *Achilles* was a *Greek*, and *Æneas* the remote Founder of *Rome*. By this means their Countrymen (whom they principally proposed to themselves for their Readers) were particularly attentive to all the parts of their Story, and sympathized with their Heroes in all their Adventures. A *Roman* could not but rejoice in the Escapes, Successes and Victories of *Æneas*, and be grieved at any Defeats, Misfortunes or Disappointments that befel him; as a *Greek* must have had the same regard for *Achilles*. And it is plain, that each of those Poems have lost this great Advantage, among those Readers to whom their Heroes are as Strangers, or indifferent Persons.

Milton's Poem is admirable in this respect, since it is impossible for any of its Readers, whatever Nation, Country or People he may belong to, not to be related to the persons who are the principal Actors in it; but what is still infinitely more to its Advantage, the principal Actors in this Poem are not only our Progenitors, but our Representatives. We have an actual Interest in every thing they do, and no less than our utmost Happiness is concerned, and lies at Stake in all their Behaviour.

I shall subjoyn as a Corollary to the foregoing Remark, an admirable Observation out of *Aristotle*, which hath been very much misrepresented in the Quotations of some Modern Criticks. 'If a Man of perfect and consummate Virtue falls into a Misfortune, it raises our Pity, but not our Terror, because we do not fear that it may be our own Case, who do not resemble the Suffering Person. But as that great Philosopher adds, 'If we see a Man of Virtue mixt with Infirmities, fall into any Misfortune, it does not only raise our Pity but our Terror; because we are afraid that the like Misfortunes may happen to our selves, who resemble the Character of the Suffering Person.'

I shall only remark in this Place, that the foregoing Observation of *Aristotle*, tho' it may be true in other Occasions, does not hold in this; because in the present Case, though the Persons who fall into Misfortune are of the most perfect and consummate Virtue, it is not to be considered as what may possibly be, but what actually is our own Case; since we are embark'd with them on the same Bottom, and must be partakers of their Happiness or Misery.

In this, and some other very few Instances, *Aristotle's* Rules for Epic Poetry (which he had drawn from his Reflections upon *Homer*) cannot be supposed to square exactly with the Heroic Poems which have been made since his Time; since it is evident to every impartial Judge his Rules would still have been more perfect, cou'd he have perused the *Æneid* which was made some hundred Years after his Death.

In my next I shall go through other parts of *Milton's* Poem; and hope that what I shall there advance, as well as what I have already written, will not only serve as a Comment upon *Milton*, but upon *Aristotle*.

No. 279. January 19, 1712

Reddere personæ scit convenientia cuique.

(Hor.)

We have already taken a general Survey of the Fable and Characters in *Milton's Paradise Lost*: The Parts which remain to be consider'd, according to *Aristotle's* Method, are the *Sentiments* and the Language. Before I enter upon the first of these, I must advertise my Reader, that it is my Design as soon as I have finished my general Reflections on these four several Heads, to give particular Instances out of the poem now before us of Beauties and Imperfections which may be observed under each of them, as also of such other Particulars as may not properly fall under any of them. This I thought fit to premise, that the Reader may not judge too hastily of this Piece of Criticism, or look upon it as Imperfect, before he has seen the whole Extent of it.

The Sentiments in an Epic Poem are the Thoughts and Behaviour which the Author ascribes to the Persons whom he introduces, and are *just* when they are comformable to the Characters of the several Persons. The Sentiments have likewise a relation to *Things* as well as *Persons*, and are then perfect when they are such as are adapted to the Subject. If in either of these Cases the Poet endeavours to argue or explain, to magnifie or diminish, to raise Love or Hatred, Pity or Terror, or any other Passion, we ought to consider whether the Sentiments he makes use of are proper for those Ends. *Homer* is censured by the Criticks for his Defect as to this Particular in several parts of the *Iliad* and *Odyssey*, tho' at the same time those who have treated this great Poet with Candour, have attributed this Defect to the Times in which he lived. It was the fault of the Age, and not of *Homer*, if there wants that Delicacy in some of his Sentiments, which now appears in the Works of Men of a much inferior Genius. Besides, if there are Blemishes in any particular Thoughts, there is an infinite Beauty in the greatest part of them. In short, if there are many Poets who wou'd not have fallen into the meanness of some of his Sentiments, there are none who cou'd have risen up to the Greatness of others. *Virgil* has excelled all others in the Propriety of his Sentiments. *Milton* shines likewise very much in this Particular: Nor must we omit one Consideration which adds to his Honour and Reputation. *Homer* and *Virgil* introduced Persons whose Characters are commonly known among Men, and such as are to be met with either in History, or in ordinary Conversation. *Milton's* Characters, most of them, lie out of Nature, and were to be formed purely by his own Invention. It shews a greater Genius in *Shakespear* to have drawn his *Calyban*, than his *Hotspur* or *Julius Cæsar*: The one was to be supplied out of his own Imagination, whereas the other might have been formed upon Tradition, History and Observation. It was much easier therefore for *Homer* to find proper Sentiments for an Assembly of *Grecian* Generals, than for *Milton* to diversifie his Infernal Council with proper Characters, and inspire them with a variety of Sentiments. The Loves of *Dido* and *Æneas* are only Copies of what has passed between other Persons. *Adam* and *Eve*, before the Fall, are a different Species from that of Mankind, who are descended from them; and none but a Poet of the most unbounded Invention, and the most exquisite Judgment, cou'd have filled their Conversation and Behaviour with so many apt Circumstances during their State of Innocence.

Nor is it sufficient for an Epic Poem to be filled with such Thoughts as are *Natural*, unless it abound also with such as are *Sublime*. *Virgil* in this Particular falls short of *Homer*. He has not indeed so many Thoughts that are Low and Vulgar; but at the same time has not so many Thoughts that are Sublime and Noble. The truth of it is, *Virgil* seldom rises into very astonishing Sentiments, where he is not fired by the *Iliad*. He every where charms and pleases us by the force of his own Genius; but seldom elevates and transports us where he does not fetch his Hints from *Homer*.

Milton's chief Talent, and indeed his distinguishing Excellence, lies in the Sublimity of his Thoughts. There are others of the Moderns who rival him in every other part of Poetry; but in the greatness of his Sentiments he triumphs over all the Poets both Modern and Ancient, *Homer* only excepted. It is impossible for the Imagination of Man to distend it self with greater Ideas, than those which he has laid together in his first, second and sixth Books. The Seventh, which describes the Creation of the World, is likewise wonderfully Sublime, tho' not so apt to stir up Emotion in the Mind of the Reader, nor consequently so perfect in the Epic way of Writing, because it is filled with less Action. Let the judicious Reader compare what *Longinus* has observed on several Passages in *Homer*, and he will find Parallels for most of them in the *Paradise Lost*.

From what has been said we may infer, that as there are two kinds of Sentiments, the Natural and the Sublime, which are always to be pursued in an Heroic Poem, there are also two kinds of Thoughts which are carefully to be avoided. The first are such as are affected and unnatural; the second such as are mean and vulgar. As for the first kind of Thoughts we meet with little or nothing that is like them in *Virgil*: He has none of those trifling Points and Puerilities that are so often to be met with in *Ovid*, none of the Epigrammatick Turns of *Lucan*, none of those swelling Sentiments which are so frequent in *Statius* and *Claudian*, none of those mixed Embellishments of *Tasso*. Every thing is just and natural. His Sentiments shew that he had a perfect Insight into Human Nature, and that he knew every thing which was the most proper to affect it.

Mr. *Dryden* has in some Places, which I may hereafter take notice of, misrepresented *Virgil's* way of thinking as to this Particular, in the Translation he has given us of the *Æneid*. I do not remember that *Homer* any where falls into the Faults above mentioned, which were indeed the false Refinements of later Ages. *Milton*, it must be confest, has sometimes erred in this Respect, as I shall shew more at large in another Paper; tho' considering all the Poets of the Age in which he writ, were infected with this wrong way of thinking, he is rather to be admired that he did not give more into it, than that he did sometimes comply with the vicious Taste which prevails so much among Modern Writers.

But since several Thoughts may be natural which are low and groveling, an Epic Poet should not only avoid such Sentiments as are unnatural or affected, but also such as are mean

and vulgar. *Homer* has opened a great Field of Raillery to Men of more Delicacy than Greatness of Genius, by the Homeliness of some of his Sentiments. But, as I have before said, these are rather to be imputed to the Simplicity of the Age in which he lived, to which I may also add, of that which he described, than to any Imperfection in that Divine Poet. *Zoilus*, among the Ancients, and Monsieur *Perrault*, among the Moderns, pushed their Ridicule very far upon him, on account of some such Sentiments. There is no Blemish to be observed in *Virgil* under this Head, and but a very few in *Milton*.

I shall give but one Instance of this Impropriety of Thought in *Homer*, and at the same time compare it with an Instance of the same nature, both in *Virgil* and *Milton*. Sentiments which raise Laughter, can very seldom be admitted with any decency into an Heroic Poem, whose Business is to excite Passions of a much nobler Nature. *Homer*, however, in his Characters of *Vulcan* and *Thersites*, in his Story of *Mars* and *Venus*, in his Behaviour of *Irus*, and in other Passages, has been observed to have lapsed into the Burlesque Character, and to have departed from that serious Air which seems essential to the Magnificence of an Epic Poem. I remember but one Laugh in the whole *Æneid*, which rises in the Fifth Book upon *Monœtes*, where he is represented as thrown overboard, and drying himself upon a Rock. But this Piece of Mirth is so well timed, that the severest Critick can have nothing to say against it, for it is in the Book of Games and Diversions, where the Reader's Mind may be supposed to be sufficiently relaxed for such an Entertainment. The only Piece of Pleasantry in *Paradise Lost*, is where the Evil Spirits are described as rallying the Angels upon the Success of their new invented Artillery. This Passage I look upon to be the most exceptionable in the whole Poem, as being nothing else but a String of Punns, and those too very indifferent.

. . . *Satan* beheld their Plight,
And to his Mates thus in derision call'd.
          O Friends, why come not on these Victors
              proud!
E'er while they fierce were coming, and when we,
To entertain them fair with *open Front*,
And Breast, (what could we more) propounded terms
Of Composition, strait they chang'd their Minds,
Flew off, and into strange Vagaries fell,
As they would dance, yet for a Dance they seem'd
Somewhat extravagant, and wild, perhaps
For Joy of offer'd Peace: but I suppose
If our Proposals once again were *heard*,
We should compel them to a quick *Result*.
          To whom thus *Belial* in like gamesome mood.
Leader, the Terms we sent, were Terms *of weight*,
Of *hard Contents*, and full of force urg'd home,
Such as we might perceive amus'd them all,
And *stumbled* many; who receives them right,
Had need, from Head to Foot, well *understand*;
Not *understood*, this Gift they have besides,
They shew us when our Foes *walk not upright*.
          Thus they among themselves in pleasant vein
Stood scoffing . . .

No. 285. January 26, 1712

Ne quicunque Deus, quicunque adhibebitur heros,
Regali conspectus in auro nuper & ostro,
Migret in Obscuras humili sermone tabernas:
Aut dum vitat humum, nubes & inania captet.

                                              (Hor.)

Having already treated of the Fable, the Characters, and Sentiments in the *Paradise Lost*, we are in the last place to consider the *Language*; and as the learned World is very much divided upon *Milton* as to this Point, I hope they will excuse me if I appear particular in any of my Opinions, and encline to those who judge the most advantagiously of the Author.

It is requisite that the Language of an Heroic Poem should be both Perspicuous and Sublime. In proportion as either of these two Qualities are wanting, the Language is imperfect. Perspicuity is the first and most necessary Qualification; insomuch, that a good-natured Reader sometimes overlooks a little Slip even in the Grammar or Syntax, where it is impossible for him to mistake the Poet's Sense. Of this kind is that Passage in *Milton*, wherein he speaks of *Satan*.

> . . . God and his Son except,
> Created thing nought valu'd be nor shunn'd.

And that in which he describes *Adam* and *Eve*.

> *Adam* the goodliest Man of Men since born
> His Sons, the fairest of her Daughters *Eve*.

It is plain, that in the former of these Passages, according to the natural Syntax, the Divine Persons mentioned in the first Line are represented as created Beings; and that in the other, *Adam* and *Eve* are confounded with their Sons and Daughters. Such little Blemishes as these, when the Thought is great and natural, we should, with *Horace*, impute to a pardonable Inadvertency, or to the Weakness of Human Nature, which cannot attend to each minute Particular, and give the last finishing to every Circumstance in so long a Work. The Ancient Criticks therefore, who were acted by a Spirit of Candour, rather than that of Cavilling, invented certain figures of Speech, on purpose to palliate little Errors of this nature in the Writings of those Authors, who had so many greater Beauties to attone for them.

If Clearness and Perspicuity were only to be consulted, the Poet would have nothing else to do but to cloath his Thoughts in the most plain and natural Expressions. But, since it often happens, that the most obvious Phrases, and those which are used in ordinary Conversation, become too familiar to the Ear, and contract a kind of Meanness by passing through the Mouths of the Vulgar, a Poet should take particular care to guard himself against Idiomatick ways of speaking. *Ovid* and *Lucan* have many Poornesses of Expression upon this account, as taking up with the first Phrases that offered, without putting themselves to the trouble of looking after such as would not only be natural, but also elevated and sublime. *Milton* has but a few Failings in this kind, of which, however, you may meet with some Instances, as in the following Passages.

> *Embrio's* and Idiots, Eremites and Fryars
> *White*, *Black* and *Grey*, with all their *Trumpery*,
> Here Pilgrims roam . . .
> . . . A while Discourse they hold,
> *No fear lest Dinner cool*; when thus began
> Our Author . . .
> Who of all Ages to succeed, but feeling
> The Evil on him brought by me, will curse
> My Head, ill fare our Ancestor impure,
> *For this we may thank* Adam . . .

The great Masters in Composition know very well that many an elegant Phrase becomes improper for a Poet or an Orator, when it has been debased by common use. For this reason the Works of Ancient Authors, which are written in dead Languages, have a great Advantage over those which are written in Languages that are now spoken. Were there any mean Phrases or Idioms in *Virgil* and *Homer*, they would not shock the Ear of the most delicate Modern Reader, so much as they would have done that of an old *Greek* or *Roman*, because we never hear them pronounced in our Streets, or in ordinary Conversation.

It is not therefore sufficient, that the Language of an Epic Poem be Perspicuous, unless it be also Sublime. To this end it ought to deviate from the common Forms and ordinary Phrases of Speech. The Judgment of a Poet very much discovers it self in shunning the common Roads of Expression, without falling into such ways of Speech as may seem stiff and unnatural; he must not swell into a false Sublime, by endeavouring to avoid the other Extream. Among the *Greeks*, *Eschylus*, and sometimes *Sophocles*, were guilty of this Fault; among the *Latins*, *Claudian* and *Statius*; and among our own Countrymen, *Shakespear* and *Lee*. In these Authors the Affectation of Greatness often hurts the Perspicuity of the Stile, as in many others the Endeavour after Perspicuity prejudices its Greatness.

Aristotle has observed, that the Idiomatick Stile may be avoided, and the Sublime formed, by the following Methods. First, by the use of Metaphors: such are those in *Milton*.

> *Imparadis'd* in one anothers Arms,
> . . . And in his Hand a Reed
> Stood waving *tipt* with Fire; . . .
> The grassie Clods now *calv'd*. . . .
> *Spangled* with Eyes . . .

In these and innumerable other Instances, the Metaphors are very bold but just; I must however observe, that the Metaphors are not thick sown in *Milton*, which always savours too much of Wit; that they never clash with one another, which as *Aristotle* observes, turns a Sentence into a kind of an Enigma or Riddle; and that he seldom has Recourse to them where the proper and natural Words will do as well.

Another way of raising the Language, and giving it a Poetical Turn, is to make use of the Idioms of other Tongues. *Virgil* is full of the *Greek* Forms of Speech, which the Criticks call *Hellenisms*, as *Horace* in his Odes abounds with them much more than *Virgil*. I need not mention the several Dialects which *Homer* has made use of for this end. *Milton*, in conformity with the Practice of the Ancient Poets, and with *Aristotle's* Rule has infused a great many *Latinisms*, as well as *Græcisms*, and sometimes *Hebraisms*, into the Language of his Poem, as towards the Beginning of it.

> *Nor* did they *not* perceive the evil plight
> In which they were, *or* the fierce Pains *not* feel.
> Yet *to* their Gen'ral's Voice they soon obey'd.
> . . . Who shall tempt with wandring Feet
> The dark unbottom'd Infinite Abyss,
> And through the *palpable Obscure* find out
> His uncouth way, or spread his airy Flight
> Upborn with indefatigable Wings
> Over the *vast Abrupt!*
> . . . So both ascend
> In the Visions of God . . .
>
> (B. II.)

Under this Head may be reckoned the placing the Adjective after the Substantive, the transposition of Words, the turning the Adjective into a Substantive, with several other Foreign Modes of Speech, which this Poet has naturalized to give his Verse the greater Sound, and throw it out of Prose.

The third Method mentioned by *Aristotle*, is what agrees with the Genius of the *Greek* Language more than with that of any other Tongue, and is therefore more used by *Homer* than by any other Poet. I mean the lengthning of a Phrase by the Addition of Words, which may either be inserted or omitted, as also by the extending or contracting of particular Words by the Insertion or Omission of certain Syllables. *Milton* has put in practice this Method of raising his Language, as far as the nature of our Tongue will permit, as in the Passage above-mentioned, *Eremite*, for what is Hermit, in common Discourse. If you observe the Measure of his Verse, he has with great Judgment suppressed a Syllable in several Words, and shortned those of two Syllables into one, by which Method, besides the above-mentioned Advantage, he has given a greater Variety to his Numbers. But this Practice is more particularly remarkable in the Names of Persons and of Countries, as *Beëlzebub*, *Hessebon*, and in many other Particulars, wherein he has either changed the Name, or made use of that which is not the most commonly known, that he might the better depart from the Language of the Vulgar.

The same Reason recommended to him several old Words, which also makes his Poem appear the more venerable, and gives it a greater Air of Antiquity.

I must likewise take notice, that there are in *Milton* several Words of his own Coining, as *Cerberean*, *miscreated*, *Helldoom'd*, *Embryon* Atoms, and many others. If the Reader is offended at this Liberty in our *English* Poet, I would recommend him to a Discourse in *Plutarch*, which shews us how frequently *Homer* has made use of the same Liberty.

Milton, by the above-mentioned Helps, and by the choice of the noblest Words and Phrases which our Tongue wou'd afford him, has carried our Language to a greater height than any of the *English* Poets have ever done before or after him, and made the Sublimity of his Stile equal to that of his Sentiments.

I have been the more particular in these Observations on *Milton*'s Stile, because it is that part of him in which he appears the most singular. The Remarks I have here made upon the Practice of other Poets, with my Observations out of *Aristotle*, will perhaps alleviate the Prejudice which some have taken to his Poem upon this Account; tho' after all, I must confess, that I think his Stile, tho' admirable in general, is in some places too much stiffened and obscured by the frequent use of those Methods, which *Aristotle* has prescribed for the raising of it.

This Redundancy of those several ways of Speech which *Aristotle* calls *foreign Language*, and with which *Milton* has so very much enriched, and in some places darkned the Language of his Poem, was the more proper for his use, because his Poem is written in Blank Verse. Rhyme, without any other Assistance, throws the Language off from Prose, and very often makes an indifferent Phrase pass unregarded; but where the Verse is not built upon Rhymes, there Pomp of Sound, and Energy of Expression, are indispensably necessary to support the Stile, and keep it from falling into the Flatness of Prose.

Those who have not a Taste for this Elevation of Stile, and are apt to ridicule a Poet when he goes out of the common Forms of Expression, would do well to see how *Aristotle* has treated an Ancient Author, called *Euclid*, for his insipid Mirth upon this Occasion. Mr. *Dryden* used to call this sort of Men his Prose-Criticks.

I should, under this Head of the Language, consider *Milton*'s Numbers, in which he has made use of several Elisions, that are not customary among other *English* Poets, as may be particularly observed in his cutting off the Letter Y. when it precedes a Vowel. This, and some other Innovations in the Measure of his Verse, has varied his Numbers in such a manner, as makes them incapable of satiating the Ear and cloying the Reader, which the same uniform Measure would certainly have done, and which the perpetual Returns of Rhime never fail to do in long Narrative Poems. I shall close these Reflections upon the Language of *Paradise Lost*, with

observing that *Milton* has copied after *Homer*, rather than *Virgil*, in the length of his Periods, the Copiousness of his Phrases, and the running of his Verses into one another.

FRANÇOIS MARIE AROUET DE VOLTAIRE
From *An Essay upon Epick Poetry*
1727

*M*ilton is the last in *Europe* who wrote an *Epick* Poem, for I wave all those whose Attempts have been unsuccessful, my Intention being not to descant on the many who have contended for the Prize, but to speak only of the very few who have gain'd it in their respective Countries.

Milton, as he was travelling through *Italy* in his Youth, saw at *Florence* a Comedy call'd *Adamo*, writ by one *Andreino* a Player, and dedicated to *Mary de Medicis* Queen of *France*. The Subject of the Play was the *Fall of Man*; the Actors, God, the Devils, the Angels, *Adam*, *Eve*, the Serpent, Death, and the Seven Mortal Sins. That Topick so improper for a Drama, but so suitable to the absurd Genius of the *Italian* Stage, (as it was at that Time) was handled in a Manner intirely conformable to the Extravagance of the Design. The Scene opens with a Chorus of Angels, and a Cherubim thus speaks for the Rest: "Let the Rainbow be the Fiddlestick of the Fiddle of the Heavens, let the Planets be the Notes of our Musick, let Time beat carefully the Measure, and the Winds make the Sharps, &c." Thus the Play begins, and every Scene rises above the last in Profusion of Impertinence.

Milton pierc'd through the Absurdity of that Performance to the hidden Majesty of the Subject, which being altogether unfit for the Stage, yet might be (for the Genius of *Milton*, and for his only) the Foundation of an *Epick* Poem.

He took from that ridiculous Trifle the first Hint of the noblest Work, which human Imagination hath ever attempted, and which he executed more than twenty Years after.

In the like Manner, *Pythagoras* ow'd the Invention of Musick to the Noise of the Hammer of a Blacksmith. And thus in our Days Sir *Isaak Newton* walking in his Gardens had the first Thought of his System of Gravitation, upon seeing an Apple falling from a Tree.

If the Difference of Genius between Nation and Nation, ever appear'd in its full Light, 'tis in *Milton's* Paradise lost.

The *French* answer with a scornful Smile, when they are told there is in *England* an *Epick* Poem, the Subject whereof is the Devil fighting against God, and *Adam* and *Eve* eating an Apple at the Persuasion of a Snake. As that Topick hath afforded nothing among them, but some lively Lampoons, for which that Nation is so famous; they cannot imagine it possible to build an *Epick* Poem upon the subject of their Ballads. And indeed such an Error ought to be excused; for if we consider with what Freedom the politest Part of Mankind throughout all *Europe*, both Catholicks and Protestants, are wont to ridicule in Conversation those consecrated Histories; nay, if those who have the highest Respect for the Mysteries of the Christian Religion, and who are struck with Awe at some Parts of it, yet cannot forbear now and then making free with the *Devil*, the *Serpent*, the Frailty of our first Parents, the Rib which *Adam* was robb'd of, and the like; it seems a very hard Task for a profane Poet to endeavour to remove those Shadows of Ridicule, to reconcile together what is Divine and what looks absurd, and to command a Respect that the sacred Writers could hardly obtain from our frivolous Minds.

What *Milton* so boldly undertook, he perform'd with a superior Strength of Judgement, and with an Imagination productive of Beauties not dream'd of before him. The *Meaness* (if there is any) of some Parts of the Subject is lost in the Immensity of the Poetical Invention. There is something above the reach of human Forces to have attempted the Creation without Bombast, to have describ'd the Gluttony and Curiosity of a Woman without Flatness, to have brought Probability and Reason amidst the Hurry of imaginary Things belonging to another World, and as far remote from the Limits of our Notions as they are from our Earth; in short to force the Reader to say, "If God, if the Angels, if Satan would speak, I believe they would speak as they do in *Milton*."

I have often admir'd how barren the Subject appears, and how fruitful it grows under his Hands.

The *Paradise Lost* is the only Poem wherein are to be found in a perfect Degree that Uniformity which satisfies the Mind and that Variety which pleases the Imagination. All its Episodes being necessary Lines which aim at the Centre of a perfect Circle. Where is the Nation who would not be pleas'd with the Interview of *Adam* and the *Angel*? With the Mountain of Vision, with the bold Strokes which make up the Relentless, undaunted, and sly Character of Satan? But above all with that sublime Wisdom which *Milton* exerts, whenever he dares to describe God, and to make him speak? He seems indeed to draw the Picture of the Almighty, as like as human Nature can reach to, through the mortal Dust in which we are clouded.

The *Heathens* always, the *Jews* often, and our Christian Priests sometimes, represent God as a Tyrant infinitely powerful. But the God of *Milton* is always a Creator, a Father, and a Judge, nor is his Vengeance jarring with his Mercy, nor his Predeterminations repugnant to the Liberty of Man. These are the Pictures which lift up indeed the Soul of the Reader. *Milton* in that Point as well as in many others is as far above the ancient Poets as the Christian Religion is above the *Heathen* Fables.

But he hath especially an indisputable Claim to the unanimous Admiration of Mankind, when he descends from those high Flights to the natural Description of human Things. It is observable that in all other Poems Love is represented as a Vice, in *Milton* only 'tis a Virtue. The Pictures he draws of it, are naked as the Persons he speaks of, and as venerable. He removes with a chaste Hand the Veil which covers everywhere else the enjoyments of that Passion. There is Softness, Tenderness and Warmth without Lasciviousness; the Poet transports himself and us, into that State of innocent Happiness in which *Adam* and *Eve* continued for a short Time: He soars not above human, but above corrupt Nature, and as there is no Instance of such Love, there is none of such Poetry.

How then it came to pass that the *Paradise Lost* had been so long neglected, (nay almost unknown) in *England*, (till the Lord *Sommers* in some Measure *taught Mankind to admire it,*) is a Thing which I cannot reconcile, *neither* with the Temper, *nor* with the Genius of the *English* Nation.

The Duke of *Buckingham* in his Art of Poetry gives the Preference to *Spencer*. It is reported in the Life of the Lord *Rochester*, that he had no Notion of a better Poet than *Cowley*.

Mr. *Dryden's* Judgement on *Milton* is still more unaccountable. He hath bestow'd some Verses upon him, in which he puts him upon a Level with, nay above *Virgil* and *Homer*;

> The Force of Nature could not further go,
> To make a third she join'd the former two.

The same Mr. *Dryden* in his Preface upon his Translation of the *Æneid*, ranks *Milton* with *Chapellain* and *Lemoine* the most impertinent Poets who ever scribbled. How he could extol him so much in his Verses, and debase him so low in his Prose, is a Riddle which, being a Foreigner, I cannot understand.

In short one would be apt to think that Milton has not obtained his true Reputation till Mr. *Adisson*, the best Critick as well as the best Writer of his Age, pointed out the most hidden Beauties of the *Paradise Lost*, and settled forever its Reputation.

It is an easy and a pleasant Task to take Notice of the many Beauties of *Milton* which I call universal: But 'tis a ticklish Undertaking to point out what would be reputed a Fault in any other Country.

I am very far from thinking that one Nation ought to judge of its Productions by the Standard of another, nor do I presume that the *French* (for Example) who have no *Epick* Poets, have any Right to give Laws on *Epick* Poetry.

But I fancy many *English* Readers, who are acquainted with the *French* language, will not be displeas'd to have some Notion of the Taste of that Country: And I hope they are too just either to submit to it, or despise it barely upon the Score of its being foreign to them.

Would each Nation attend a little more than they do, to the Taste and the Manners of their respective Neighbours, perhaps a general good Taste might diffuse itself through all *Europe* from such an intercourse of Learning, and from that useful Exchange of Observations. The *English* Stage, for Example, might be clear'd of mangled Carcasses, and the Style of their tragick Authors, come down from their forced Metaphorical Bombast to a nearer Imitation of Nature. The *French* would learn from the *English* to animate their Tragedies with more Action, and would contract now and then their long Speeches into shorter and warmer Sentiments.

The *Spaniards* would introduce in their Plays more Pictures of human Life, more Characters and Manners, and not puzzle themselves always in the Entanglements of confus'd Adventures, more romantick than natural. The *Italian* in Point of Tragedy would catch the Flame from the *English*, and all the Rest from the *French*. In Point of Comedy, they would learn from Mr. *Congreve* and some other Authors, to prefer Wit and Humour to Buffoonery.

To proceed in that View, I'll venture to say that none of the *French* Criticks could like the Excursions which *Milton* makes sometimes beyond the strict Limits of his Subject. They lay down for a Rule that an Author himself ought never to appear in his Poem; and his own Thoughts, his own Sentiments must be spoken by the Actors he introduces. Many judicious Men in *England* comply with that Opinion, and Mr. *Adisson* favours it. I beg Leave in this place to hazard a Reflection of my own, which I submit to the Reader's Judgement.

Milton breaks the Thread of his Narration in two Manners. The first consists of two or three kinds of prologues, which he premises at the Beginning of some Books. In one Place he expatiates upon his own Blindness; in another he compares his Subject and prefers it to that of the *Iliad*, and to the common Topicks of War, which were thought before him the only Subject fit for *Epick* Poetry; and he adds that he hopes to soar as high as all his Predecessors, unless the cold Climate of *England* damps his Wings.

His other Way of interrupting his Narration, is by some Observations which he intersperses now and then upon some great Incident, or some interesting Circumstance. Of that Kind is his Digression on Love in the fourth Book;

> Whatever *Hippocrites* austerely talk
> Defaming as impure, what God declares
> Pure, and commands to some, leaves free to all.
> Our Maker bids increase, who bids abstain
> But our Destroyer foe to God and Men?
> Hail wedded Love, &c.

As to the first of these two Heads, I cannot but own that an Author is generally guilty of an impardonable Self-love, when he lays aside his Subject to descant on his own Person; but that human Frailty is to be forgiven in *Milton*; nay, I am pleas'd with it. He gratifies the Curiosity, it raises in me about his Person, when I admire the Author, I desire to know something of the Man, and he whom all Readers would be glad to know, is allow'd to speak of himself. But this however is a very dangerous Example for a Genius of an inferior Order, and is only to be justified by Success.

As to the second Point I am so far from looking on that Liberty as a Fault, that I think it to be a great Beauty. For if Morality is the aim of Poetry, I do not apprehend why the Poet should be forbidden to intersperse his Descriptions with moral Sentences and useful Reflexions, provided he scatters them with a sparing Hand, and in proper Places either when he wants Personages to utter those Thoughts, or when their Character does not permit them to speak in the Behalf of Virtue.

'Tis strange that *Homer* is commended by the Criticks for his comparing *Ajax* to an Ass pelted away with Stones by some Children, *Ulysses* to a Pudding, the Council-board of *Priam* to Grashoppers. 'Tis strange, I say, that they defend so clamorously those Similes tho' never so foreign to the Purpose, and will not allow the natural Reflexions, the noble Digressions of *Milton* tho' never so closely link'd to the Subject.

I will not dwell upon some small Errors of *Milton*, which are obvious to every Reader, I mean some few Contradictions and those frequent Glances at the *Heathen* Mythology, which Fault by the by is so much the more unexcusable in him, by his having premis'd in his first Book that those Divinities were but Devils worship'd under different Names, which ought to have been a sufficient Caution to him not to speak of the Rape of *Proserpine*, of the Wedding of *Juno* and *Jupiter*, &c. as Matters of Fact.

I lay aside likewise his preposterous and aukward Jests, his Puns, his too familiar Expressions so inconsistent with the Elevation of his Genius, and of his Subject.

To come to more essential Points and more *liable* to be debated. I dare affirm that the Contrivance of the *Pandaemonium* would have been entirely disapprov'd of by Criticks like *Boyleau, Racine*, &c.

That Seat built for the Parliament of the Devils, seems very preposterous: Since Satan hath summon'd them altogether, and harangu'd them just before in an ample Field. The Council was necessary; but where it was to be held, 'twas very indifferent. The Poet seems to delight in building his *Pandaemonium* in *Doric* Order with Freeze and Cornice, and a Roof of Gold. Such a Contrivance savours more of the wild Fancy of our Father *le Moine*, then of the serious spirit of *Milton*. But when afterwards the Devils turn dwarfs to fill their Places in the House, as if it was impracticable to build a Room large enough to contain them in their natural Size; it is an idle Story which would match the most extravagant Tales. And to crown all, Satan and the chief Lords preserving their own monstrous Forms, while the rabble of the Devils shrink into Pigmees, heightens the Ridicule of the whole Contrivance to an unexpressible Degree. Methinks the true Criterion for discerning what is really ridiculous in an *Epick* Poem, is to examine if the same Thing would not fit exactly the Mock heroick. Then I dare say that no-thing is so adapted to that ludicrous way of Writing as the Metamorphosis of the Devils into Dwarfs.

The Fiction of *Death* and *Sin* seems to have in it some great Beauties and many gross Defects. In order to canvass this Matter with Order. We must first lay down that such shadowy Beings, as *Death, Sin, Chaos*, are intolerable when they are not allegorical. For Fiction is nothing but Truth in Disguise. It must be granted too, that an Allegory must be short, decent and noble. For an Allegory carried too far or too low, is like a beautiful Woman who wears always a Mask. An Allegory is a long Metaphor; and to speak too long in metaphor's must be tiresom, because unnatural. This being premis'd, I must say that in general those Fictions, those imaginary beings, are more agreeable to the Nature of *Milton*'s Poem, than to any other; because he hath but two natural Persons for his Actors, I mean *Adam* and *Eve*. A great Part of the Action lies in imaginary Worlds, and must *of course* admit of imaginary Beings.

Then *Sin* springing out of the Head of Satan, seems a beautiful Allegory of Pride, which is look'd upon as the first Offence committed against God. But I question if *Satan*, getting his Daughter with Child, is an Invention to be approv'd off. I am afraid that Fiction is but a meer Quibble; for if Sin was of a masculine Gender in *English, as it is in all the other Languages*, that whole Affair Drops, and the Fiction vanishes away. But suppose we are not so nice, and we allow Satan to be in Love with *Sin, because this Word is made feminine in* English (as Death passes also for masculine) what a horrid and loathsome Idea does *Milton* present to the Mind, in this Fiction? *Sin* brings forth Death, this Monster inflam'd with Lust and Rage, lies with his Mother, as she had done with her Father. From that new Commerce, springs a Swarm of Serpents, which creep in and out of their Mother's Womb, and gnaw and tear the Bowels they are born from.

Let such a Picture be never so beautifully drawn, let the Allegory be never so obvious, and so clear, still it will be intolerable, on the Account of its Foulness. That Complication of Horrors, that Mixture of Incest, that Heap of Monsters, that Loathsomeness so far fetch'd, cannot but shock a Reader of delicate Taste.

But what is more intolerable, there are Parts in that Fiction, which bearing no Allegory at all, have no Manner of Excuse. There is no Meaning in the Communication between Death and Sin, 'tis distasteful without any Purpose; or if any Allegory lies under it, the filthy Abomination of the Thing is certainly more obvious than the Allegory.

I see with Admiration, *Sin*, the *Portress* of Hell, opening the Gates of the Abiss, but unable to shut them again; that is really beautiful, because 'tis true. But what signifies Satan and Death quarrelling together, grinning at one another, and ready to fight?

The Fiction of *Chaos, Night*, and *Discord*, is rather a Picture, than an Allegory; and for ought I know, deserves to be approv'd, because it strikes the Reader with Awe, not with Horror.

I know the Bridge built by Death and Sin, would be dislik'd in *France*. The nice Criticks of that Country would urge against that Fiction, that it seems too common, and that it is useless; for Men's Souls want no paved Way, to be thrown into Hell, after their Separation from the Body.

They would laugh justly at the Paradise of Fools, at the Hermits, Fryars, Cowles, Beads, Indulgences, Bulls, Reliques, toss'd by the Winds, at *St. Peter*'s waiting with his Keys at the Wicket of Heaven. And surely the most passionate Admirers of *Milton*, could not vindicate those low comical Imaginations, which belong by Right to *Ariosto*.

Now the sublimest of all the Fictions calls me to examine it. I mean the War in Heaven. The Earl of *Roscommon*, and Mr. *Addison* (whose Judgement seems either to guide, or to justify the Opinion of his Countrymen) admire chiefly that Part of the Poem. They bestow all the Skill of their Criticism and the Strength of their Eloquence, to set off that favourite Part. I may affirm, that the very Things they admire, would not be tolerated by the *French* Criticks. The Reader will perhaps see with Pleasure, *in what consists so strange a Difference*, and what may be the Ground of it.

First, they would assert, that a War in Heaven being an imaginary Thing, which lies out of the Reach of our Nature, should be contracted in two or three Pages, rather than lengthen'd out into two Books; because we are naturally impatient of removing from us the Objects which are not adapted to our Senses.

According to that Rule, they would maintain that 'tis an idle Task to give the Reader the full Character of the Leaders of that War, and to describe *Raphael, Michael, Abdiel, Moloch*, and *Nisroth*, as *Homer* paints *Ajax, Diomede*, and *Hector*.

For what avails it to draw at length the Picture of these Beings, so utterly Strangers to the Reader, that he cannot be affected any Way towards them; by the same Reason, the long Speeches of these imaginary Warriors, either before the Battle or in the Middle of the Action, their mutual Insults, seem an injudicious Imitation of *Homer*.

The aforesaid Criticks would not bear with the Angels plucking up the Mountains, with their Woods, their Waters, and their Rocks, and flinging them on the Heads of their Enemies. Such a Contrivance (they would say) is the more puerile, the more it aims at Greatness. Angels arm'd with Mountains in Heaven, resemble too much the Dipsodes in *Rabelais*, who wore an Armour of *Portland* Stone six Foot thick.

The Artillery seems of the same Kind, yet more trifling, because more useless.

To what Purpose are these Engines brought in? Since they cannot wound the Enemies, but only remove them from their Places, and make them tumble down: Indeed (if the Expression may be forgiven) 'tis to play at Nine-Pins. And the very Thing which is so dreadfully great on Earth, becomes very low and ridiculous in Heaven.

I cannot omit here, the visible Contradiction which reigns in that Episode. God sends his faithful Angels to fight, to conquer and to punish the Rebels. *Go* (says He, to *Michael* and *Gabriel*)

> . . . And to the Brow of Heaven
> Pursuing, drive them out from God and Bliss,
> Into their Place of Punishment, the Gulph
> Of *Tartarus*, which ready opens wide
> His fiery Chaos to receive their Fall.

How does it come to pass, after such a positive Order, that the Battle hangs doubtful? And why did God the Father command *Gabriel* and *Raphael*, to do what He executes afterwards by his Son only.

I leave it to the Readers, to pronounce, if these Observations are right, or ill-grounded, and if they are carried to far. But in case these Exceptions are just, the severest Critick must however confess there are Perfections enough in *Milton*, to attone for all his Defects.

I must beg leave to conclude this Article on Milton with two Observations.

His Hero (I mean *Adam*, his first Personage) is unhappy. That demonstrates against all the Criticks, that a very good Poem may end unfortunately, in Spight of all their pretended Rules. Secondly, the *Paradise Lost* ends compleatly. The Thread of the Fable is spun out to the last. *Milton* and *Tasso* have been careful of not stopping short and abruptly. The one does not abandon *Adam* and *Eve*, till they are driven out of *Eden*. The other does not conclude, before *Jerusalem* is taken. *Homer* and *Virgil* took a contrary Way, the *Iliad* ends with the Death of *Hector*, the *Æneid*, with that of *Turnus*: The Tribe of Commentators have upon that enacted a Law, that a House

ought never to be finish'd, because *Homer* and *Virgil* did not compleat their own; but if *Homer* had taken *Troy*, and *Virgil* married *Lavinia* to *Æneas*, the Criticks would have laid down a Rule just the contrary.

SAMUEL JOHNSON
From "John Milton"
Lives of the English Poets
1779

In the examination of Milton's poetical works I shall pay so much regard to time as to begin with his juvenile productions. For his early pieces he seems to have had a degree of fondness not very laudable; what he has once written he resolves to preserve, and gives to the public an unfinished poem, which he broke off because he was *nothing satisfied with what he had done*, supposing his readers less nice than himself. These preludes to his future labours are in Italian, Latin, and English. Of the Italian I cannot pretend to speak as a critic; but I have heard them commended by a man well qualified to decide their merit. The Latin pieces are lusciously elegant; but the delight which they afford is rather by the exquisite imitation of the ancient writers, by the purity of the diction, and the harmony of the numbers, than by any power of invention, or vigour of sentiment. They are not all of equal value; the elegies excel the odes; and some of the exercises on *Gunpowder Treason* might have been spared.

The English poems, though they make no promises of *Paradise Lost*, have this evidence of genius, that they have a cast original and unborrowed. But their peculiarity is not excellence: if they differ from verses of others, they differ for the worse; for they are too often distinguished by repulsive harshness; the combinations of words are new, but they are not pleasing; the rhymes and epithets seem to be laboriously sought, and violently applied.

That in the early parts of his life he wrote with much care appears from his manuscripts, happily preserved at Cambridge, in which many of his smaller works are found as they were first written, with the subsequent corrections. Such relics show how excellence is acquired; what we hope ever to do with ease we must learn first to do with diligence.

Those who admire the beauties of this great poet sometimes force their own judgment into false approbation of his little pieces, and prevail upon themselves to think that admirable which is only singular. All that short compositions can commonly attain is neatness and elegance. Milton never learned the art of doing little things with grace; he overlooked the milder excellence of suavity and softness; he was a *lion* that had no skill *in dandling the kid*.

One of the poems on which much praise has been bestowed is "Lycidas," of which the diction is harsh, the rhymes uncertain, and the numbers unpleasing. What beauty there is we must therefore seek in the sentiments and images. It is not to be considered as the effusion of real passion; for passion runs not after remote allusions and obscure opinions. Passion plucks no berries from the myrtle and ivy, nor calls upon Arethuse and Mincius, nor tells of rough *satyrs* and *fauns with cloven heel*. Where there is leisure for fiction there is little grief.

In this poem there is no nature, for there is nothing new. Its form is that of a pastoral, easy, vulgar, and therefore disgusting; whatever images it can supply are long ago exhausted, and its inherent improbability always forces dissatisfaction on the mind. When Cowley tells of Hervey, that they studied together, it is easy to suppose how much he must miss the companion of his labours, and the partner of his discoveries; but what image of tenderness can be excited by these lines?—

> We drove a field, and both together heard
> What time the grey fly winds her sultry horn,
> Battening our flocks with the fresh dews of night.

We know that they never drove a field, and that they had no flocks to batten; and though it be allowed that the representation may be allegorical, the true meaning is so uncertain and remote that it is never sought because it cannot be known when it is found.

Among the flocks, and copses, and flowers, appear the heathen deities—Jove and Phœbus, Neptune and Æolus, with a long train of mythological imagery, such as a college easily supplies. Nothing can less display knowledge, or less exercise invention, than to tell how a shepherd has lost his companion, and must now feed his flocks alone, without any judge of his skill in piping; and how one god asks another god what is become of Lycidas, and how neither god can tell. He who thus grieves will excite no sympathy; he who thus praises will confer no honour.

This poem has yet a grosser fault. With these trifling fictions are mingled the most awful and sacred truths, such as ought never to be polluted with such irreverend combinations. The shepherd likewise is now a feeder of sheep, and afterwards an ecclesiastical pastor, a superintendent of a Christian flock. Such equivocations are always unskilful; but here they are indecent, and at least approach to impiety, of which, however, I believe the writer not to have been conscious.

Such is the power of reputation justly acquired, that its blaze drives away the eye from nice examination. Surely no man could have fancied that he read "Lycidas" with pleasure had he not known its author.

Of the two pieces, "L'Allegro" and "Il Penseroso," I believe opinion is uniform; every man that reads them reads them with pleasure. The author's design is not, what Theobald has remarked, merely to show how objects derive their colours from the mind, by representing the operation of the same things upon the gay and the melancholy temper, or upon the same man as he is differently disposed; but rather how, among the successive variety of appearances, every disposition of mind takes hold on those by which it may be gratified.

The *cheerful* man hears the lark in the morning; the *pensive* man hears the nightingale in the evening. The *cheerful* man sees the cock strut, and hears the horn and hounds echo in the wood; then walks, *not unseen*, to observe the glory of the rising sun, or listen to the singing milkmaid, and view the labours of the ploughman and the mower; then casts his eyes about him over scenes of smiling plenty, and looks up to the distant tower, the residence of some fair inhabitant; thus he pursues rural gaiety through a day of labour or of play, and delights himself at night with the fanciful narratives of superstitious ignorance.

The *pensive* man, at one time, walks *unseen* to muse at midnight; and at another hears the sullen curfew. If the weather drives him home, he sits in a room lighted only by *glowing embers*, or by a lonely lamp outwatches the north star, to discover the habitation of separate souls, and varies the shades of meditation by contemplating the magnificent or pathetic scenes of tragic and epic poetry. When the morning comes, a morning gloomy with rain and wind, he walks into the dark trackless woods, falls asleep by some murmuring water, and with melancholy enthusiasm expects some dream of prognostication, or some music played by aerial performers.

Both Mirth and Melancholy are solitary, silent inhabitants of the breast, that neither receive nor transmit communication;

no mention is therefore made of a philosophical friend, or a pleasant companion. The seriousness does not arise from any participation of calamity, nor the gaiety from the pleasures of the bottle.

The man of *cheerfulness*, having exhausted the country, tries what *towered cities* will afford, and mingles with scenes of splendour gay assemblies and nuptial festivities; but he mingles a mere spectator, as, when the learned comedies of Jonson or the wild dramas of Shakespeare are exhibited, he attends the theatre.

The *pensive* man never loses himself in crowds, but walks the cloister, or frequents the cathedral. Milton probably had not yet forsaken the Church.

Both his characters delight in music; but he seems to think that cheerful notes would have obtained from Pluto a complete dismission of Eurydice, of whom solemn sounds only procured a conditional release.

For the old age of Cheerfulness he makes no provision; but Melancholy he conducts with great dignity to the close of life. His cheerfulness is without levity, and his pensiveness without asperity.

Through these two poems the images are properly selected, and nicely distinguished; but the colours of the diction seem not sufficiently discriminated. I know not whether the characters are kept sufficiently apart. No mirth can indeed be found in his melancholy; but I am afraid that I always meet some melancholy in his mirth. They are two noble efforts of imagination.

The greatest of his juvenile performances is the *Masque of Comus*, in which may very plainly be discovered the dawn or twilight of *Paradise Lost*. Milton appears to have formed very early that system of diction, and mode of verse, which his maturer judgment approved, and from which he never endeavoured nor desired to deviate.

Nor does *Comus* afford only a specimen of his language; it exhibits likewise his power of description and his vigour of sentiment employed in the praise and defence of virtue. A work more truly poetical is rarely found; allusions, images, and descriptive epithets, embellish almost every period with lavish decoration. As a series of lines, therefore, it may be considered as worthy of all the admiration with which the votaries have received it.

As a drama it is deficient. The action is not probable. A masque, in those parts where supernatural intervention is admitted, must indeed be given up to all the freaks of imagination; but, so far as the action is merely human, it ought to be reasonable, which can hardly be said of the conduct of the two brothers, who, when their sister sinks with fatigue in a pathless wilderness, wander both away together in search of berries too far to find their way back, and leave a helpless Lady to all the sadness and danger of solitude. This, however, is a defect overbalanced by its convenience.

What deserves more reprehension is, that the prologue spoken in the wild wood by the attendant Spirit is addressed to the audience; a mode of communication so contrary to the nature of dramatic representation, that no precedents can support it.

The discourse of the Spirit is too long—an objection that may be made to almost all the following speeches; they have not the sprightliness of a dialogue animated by reciprocal contention, but seem rather declamations deliberately composed, and formally repeated, on a moral question. The auditor therefore listens as to a lecture, without passion, without anxiety.

The song of Comus has airiness and jollity; but, what may recommend Milton's morals as well as his poetry, the invitations to pleasure are so general, that they excite no distinct images of corrupt enjoyment, and take no dangerous hold on the fancy.

The following soliloquies of Comus and the Lady are elegant, but tedious. The song must owe much to the voice, if it ever can delight. At last the Brothers enter, with too much tranquillity; and when they have feared lest their sister should be in danger, and hoped that she is not in danger, the Elder makes a speech in praise of chastity, and the Younger finds how fine it is to be a philosopher.

Then descends the Spirit in form of a shepherd, and the Brother, instead of being in haste to ask his help, praises his singing, and inquires his business in that place. It is remarkable, that at this interview the Brother is taken with a short fit of rhyming. The Spirit relates that the Lady is in the power of Comus; the Brother moralises again; and the Spirit makes a long narration, of no use because it is false, and therefore unsuitable to a good being.

In all these parts the language is poetical, and the sentiments are generous; but there is something wanting to allure attention.

The dispute between the Lady and Comus is the most animated and affecting scene of the drama, and wants nothing but a brisker reciprocation of objections and replies to invite attention and detain it.

The songs are vigorous, and full of imagery; but they are harsh in their diction, and not very musical in their numbers.

Throughout the whole the figures are too bold, and the language too luxuriant for dialogue. It is a drama in the epic style, inelegantly splendid, and tediously instructive.

The *Sonnets* were written in different parts of Milton's life, upon different occasions. They deserve not any particular criticism; for of the best it can only be said, that they are not bad; and perhaps only the eighth and twenty-first are truly entitled to this slender commendation. The fabric of a sonnet, however adapted to the Italian language, has never succeeded in ours, which, having greater variety of termination, requires the rhymes to be often changed.

Those little pieces may be despatched without much anxiety; a greater work calls for greater care. I am now to examine *Paradise Lost*; a poem which, considered with respect to design, may claim the first place, and with respect to performance, the second, among the production of the human mind.

By the general consent of critics the first praise of genius is due to the writer of an epic poem, as it requires an assemblage of all the powers which are singly sufficient for other compositions. Poetry is the art of uniting pleasure with truth, by calling imagination to the help of reason. Epic poetry undertakes to teach the most important truths by the most pleasing precepts, and therefore relates some great event in the most affecting manner. History must supply the writer with the rudiments of narration, which he must improve and exalt by a nobler art, must animate by dramatic energy, and diversify by retrospection and anticipation; morality must teach him the exact bounds, and different shades, of vice and virtue; from policy, and the practice of life, he has to learn the discriminations of character, and the tendency of the passions, either single or combined; and physiology must supply him with illustrations and images. To put these materials to poetical use, is required an imagination capable of painting nature and realising fiction. Nor is he yet a poet till he has attained the whole extension of his language, distinguished all the delicacies of phrase, and all the colours of words, and learned to adjust their different sounds to all the varieties of metrical modulation.

Bossu is of opinion that the poet's first work is to find a *moral*, which his fable is afterwards to illustrate and establish.

This seems to have been the process only of Milton; the moral of other poems is incidental and consequent; in Milton's only it is essential and intrinsic. His purpose was the most useful and the most arduous; *to vindicate the ways of God to man*; to show the reasonableness of religion, and the necessity of obedience to the Divine Law.

To convey this moral, there must be a *fable*, a narration artfully constructed, so as to excite curiosity, and surprise expectation. In this part of his work Milton must be confessed to have equalled every other poet. He has involved in his account of the Fall of Man the events which preceded, and those that were to follow it: he has interwoven the whole system of theology with such propriety, that every part appears to be necessary; and scarcely any recital is wished shorter for the sake of quickening the progress of the main action.

The subject of an epic poem is naturally an event of great importance. That of Milton is not the destruction of a city, the conduct of a colony, or the foundation of an empire. His subject is the fate of worlds, the revolutions of heaven and of earth; rebellion against the Supreme King, raised by the highest order of created beings; the overthrow of their host, and the punishment of their crime; the creation of a new race of reasonable creatures; their original happiness and innocence, their forfeiture of immortality, and their restoration to hope and peace.

Great events can be hastened or retarded only by persons of elevated dignity. Before the greatness displayed in Milton's poem, all other greatness shrinks away. The weakest of his agents are the highest and noblest of human beings, the original parents of mankind; with whose actions the elements consented; on whose rectitude, or deviation of will, depended the state of terrestrial nature, and the condition of all the future inhabitants of the globe.

Of the other agents in the poem, the chief are such as it is irreverence to name on slight occasions. The rest were lower powers;

> —of which the least could wield
> Those elements, and arm him with the force
> Of all their regions;

powers which only the control of Omnipotence restrains from laying creation waste, and filling the vast expanse of space with ruin and confusion. To display the motives and actions of beings thus superior, so far as human reason can examine them, or human imagination represent them, is the task which this mighty poet has undertaken and performed.

In the examination of epic poems much speculation is commonly employed upon the *characters*. The characters in the *Paradise Lost*, which admit of examination, are those of angels and of man; of angels good and evil; of man in his innocent and sinful state.

Among the angels, the virtue of Raphael is mild and placid, of easy condescension and free communication; that of Michael is regal and lofty, and, as may seem, attentive to the dignity of his own nature. Abdiel and Gabriel appear occasionally, and act as every incident requires; the solitary fidelity of Abdiel is very amiably painted.

Of the evil angels the characters are more diversified. To Satan, as Addison observes, such sentiments are given as suit *the most exalted and most depraved being*. Milton has been censured by Clarke for the impiety which sometimes breaks from Satan's mouth. For there are thoughts, as he justly remarks, which no observation of character can justify, because no good man would willingly permit them to pass, however transiently, through his own mind. To make Satan speak as a rebel, without any such expressions as might taint the reader's imagination, was indeed one of the greatest difficulties in Milton's undertaking, and I cannot but think that he has extricated himself with great happiness. There is in Satan's speeches little that can give pain to a pious ear. The language of rebellion cannot be the same with that of obedience. The malignity of Satan foams in haughtiness and obstinacy; but his expressions are commonly general, and no otherwise offensive than as they are wicked.

The other chiefs of the celestial rebellion are very judiciously discriminated in the first and second books; and the ferocious character of Moloch appears, both in the battle and the council, with exact consistency.

To Adam and to Eve are given, during their innocence, such sentiments as innocence can generate and utter. Their love is pure benevolence and mutual veneration; their repasts are without luxury, and their diligence without toil. Their addresses to their Maker have little more than the voice of admiration and gratitude. Fruition left them nothing to ask; and Innocence left them nothing to fear.

But with guilt enter distrust and discord, mutual accusation and stubborn self-defence; they regard each other with alienated minds, and dread their Creator as the avenger of their transgression. At last they seek shelter in his mercy, soften to repentance, and melt in supplication. Both before and after the Fall the superiority of Adam is diligently sustained.

Of the *probable* and the *marvellous*, two parts of a vulgar epic poem which immerge the critic in deep consideration, the *Paradise Lost* requires little to be said. It contains the history of a miracle, of Creation and Redemption; it displays the power and the mercy of the Supreme Being; the probable therefore is marvellous, and the marvellous is probable. The substance of the narrative is truth; and as truth allows no choice, it is, like necessity, superior to rule. To the accidental or adventitious parts, as to everything human, some slight exceptions may be made. But the main fabric is immoveably supported.

It is justly remarked by Addison, that this poem has, by the nature of its subject, the advantage above all others, that it is universally and perpetually interesting. All mankind will, through all ages, bear the same relation to Adam and to Eve, and must partake of that good and evil which extend to themselves.

Of the *machinery*, so called from *Theos apo mēchanēs* by which is meant the occasional interposition of supernatural power, another fertile topic of critical remarks, here is no room to speak, because everything is done under the immediate and visible direction of Heaven; but the rule is so far observed, that no part of the action could have been accomplished by any other means.

Of *episodes*, I think there are only two, contained in Raphael's relation of the war in heaven, and Michael's prophetic account of the changes to happen in this world. Both are closely connected with the great action; one was necessary to Adam as a warning, the other as a consolation.

To the completeness or *integrity* of the design nothing can be objected; it has distinctly and clearly what Aristotle requires, a beginning, a middle, and an end. There is perhaps no poem, of the same length, from which so little can be taken without apparent mutilation. Here are no funeral games, nor is there any long description of a shield. The short digressions at the beginning of the third, seventh, and ninth books might doubtless be spared; but superfluities so beautiful, who would take away? or who does not wish that the author of the *Iliad* had gratified succeeding ages with a little knowledge of himself? Perhaps no passages are more frequently or more attentively

read than those extrinsic paragraphs; and, since the end of poetry is pleasure, that cannot be unpoetical with which all are pleased.

The questions, whether the action of the poem be strictly *one*, whether the poem can be properly termed *heroic*, and who is the hero, are raised by such readers as draw their principles of judgment rather from books than from reason. Milton, though he entitled *Paradise Lost* only a *poem*, yet calls it himself *heroic song*. Dryden, petulantly and indecently, denies the heroism of Adam, because he was overcome; but there is no reason why the hero should not be unfortunate, except established practice, since success and virtue do not go necessarily together. Cato is the hero of Lucan; but Lucan's authority will not be suffered by Quintilian to decide. However, if success be necessary, Adam's deceiver was at last crushed; Adam was restored to his Maker's favour, and therefore may securely resume his human rank.

After the scheme and fabric of the poem, must be considered its component parts, the sentiments and the diction.

The *sentiments*, as expressive of manners, or appropriated to characters, are for the greater part unexceptionally just.

Splendid passages, containing lessons of morality, or precepts of prudence, occur seldom. Such is the original formation of this poem, that as it admits no human manners till the Fall, it can give little assistance to human conduct. Its end is to raise the thoughts above sublunary cares or pleasures. Yet the praise of that fortitude with which Abdiel maintained his singularity of virtue against the scorn of multitudes, may be accommodated to all times; and Raphael's reproof of Adam's curiosity after the planetary motions, with the answer returned by Adam, may be confidently opposed to any rule of life which any poet has delivered.

The thoughts which are occasionally called forth in the progress are such as could only be produced by an imagination in the highest degree fervid and active, to which materials were supplied by incessant study and unlimited curiosity. The heat of Milton's mind might be said to sublimate his learning, to throw off into his work the spirit of science, unmingled with its grosser parts.

He had considered creation in its whole extent, and his descriptions are therefore learned. He had accustomed his imagination to unrestrained indulgence, and his conceptions therefore were extensive. The characteristic quality of his poem is sublimity. He sometimes descends to the elegant, but his element is the great. He can occasionally invest himself with grace; but his natural port is gigantic loftiness. He can please when pleasure is required; but it is his peculiar power to astonish.

He seems to have been well acquainted with his own genius, and to know what it was that nature had bestowed upon him more bountifully than upon others; the power of displaying the vast, illuminating the splendid, enforcing the awful, darkening the gloomy, and aggravating the dreadful; he therefore chose a subject on which too much could not be said, on which he might tire his fancy without the censure of extravagance.

The appearances of nature, and the occurrences of life, did not satiate his appetite of greatness. To paint things as they are requires a minute attention, and employs the memory rather than the fancy. Milton's delight was to sport in the wide regions of possibility; reality was a scene too narrow for his mind. He sent his faculties out upon discovery, into worlds where only imagination can travel, and delighted to form new modes of existence, and furnish sentiment and action to superior beings, to trace the counsels of hell, or accompany the choirs of heaven.

But he could not be always in other worlds; he must sometimes revisit earth, and tell of things visible and known. When he cannot raise wonder by the sublimity of his mind, he gives delight by its fertility.

Whatever be his subject, he never fails to fill the imagination. But his images and descriptions of the scenes or operations of nature do not seem to be always copied from original form, nor to have the freshness, raciness, and energy of immediate observation. He saw nature, as Dryden expresses it, *through the spectacles of books*; and on most occasions calls learning to his assistance. The garden of Eden brings to his mind the vale of Enna, where Proserpine was gathering flowers. Satan makes his way through fighting elements, like Argo between the Cyanean rocks, or Ulysses between the two Sicilian whirlpools, when he shunned Charybdis on the *larboard*. The mythological allusions have been justly censured, as not being always used with notice of their vanity; but they contribute variety to the narration, and produce an alternate exercise of the memory and the fancy.

His similes are less numerous and more various than those of his predecessors. But he does not confine himself within the limits of rigorous comparison: his great excellence is amplitude, and he expands the adventitious image beyond the dimensions which the occasion required. Thus, comparing the shield of Satan to the orb of the moon, he crowds the imagination with the discovery of the telescope, and all the wonders which the telescope discovers.

Of his moral sentiments it is hardly praise to affirm that they excel those of all other poets; for this superiority he was indebted to his acquaintance with the sacred writings. The ancient epic poets, wanting the light of revelation, were very unskilful teachers of virtue: their principal characters may be great, but they are not amiable. The reader may rise from their works with a greater degree of active or passive fortitude, and sometimes of prudence; but he will be able to carry away few precepts of justice, and none of mercy.

From the Italian writers it appears that the advantages of even Christian knowledge may be possessed in vain. Ariosto's pravity is generally known; and though the *Deliverance of Jerusalem* may be considered as a sacred subject, the poet has been very sparing of moral instruction.

In Milton every line breathes sanctity of thought and purity of manners, except when the train of the narration requires the introduction of the rebellious spirits; and even they are compelled to acknowledge their subjection to God, in such a manner as excites reverence and confirms piety.

Of human beings there are but two; but those two are the parents of mankind, venerable before their fall for dignity and innocence, and amiable after it for repentance and submission. In their first state their affection is tender without weakness, and their piety sublime without presumption. When they have sinned, they show how discord begins in mutual frailty, and how it ought to cease in mutual forbearance, how confidence of the Divine favour is forfeited by sin, and how hope of pardon may be obtained by penitence and prayer. A state of innocence we can only conceive, if indeed in our present misery it be possible to conceive it; but the sentiments and worship proper to a fallen and offending being we have all to learn, as we have all to practise.

The poet, whatever be done, is always great. Our progenitors in their first state conversed with angels; even when folly and sin had degraded them, they had not in their humiliation *the port of mean suitors*; and they rise again to reverential regard when we find that their prayers were heard.

As human passions did not enter the world before the Fall, there is in the *Paradise Lost* little opportunity for the pathetic; but what little there is has not been lost. That passion which is peculiar to rational nature, the anguish arising from the consciousness of transgression, and the horrors attending the sense of the Divine displeasure, are very justly described and forcibly impressed. But the passions are moved only on one occasion; sublimity is the general and prevailing quality of this poem; sublimity variously modified, sometimes descriptive, sometimes argumentative.

The defects and faults of *Paradise Lost*—for faults and defects every work of man must have—it is the business of impartial criticism to discover. As, in displaying the excellence of Milton, I have not made long quotations, because of selecting beauties there had been no end, I shall in the same general manner mention that which seems to deserve censure; for what Englishman can take delight in transcribing passages which, if they lessen the reputation of Milton, diminish in some degree the honour of our country?

The generality of my scheme does not admit the frequent notice of verbal inaccuracies; which Bentley, perhaps better skilled in grammar than poetry, has often found, though he sometimes made them, and which he imputed to the obtrusions of a reviser, whom the author's blindness obliged him to employ; a supposition rash and groundless if he thought it true, and vile and pernicious if, as is said, he in private allowed it to be false.

The plan of *Paradise Lost* has this inconvenience, that it comprises neither human actions nor human manners. The man and woman who act and suffer are in a state which no other man or woman can ever know. The reader finds no transaction in which he can by any effort of imagination place himself; he has therefore little natural curiosity or sympathy.

We all, indeed, feel the effects of Adam's disobedience; we all sin like Adam, and like him must all bewail our offences: we have restless and insidious enemies in the fallen angels, and in the blessed spirits we have guardians and friends; in the redemption of mankind we hope to be included; in the description of heaven and hell we are surely interested, as we are all to reside hereafter either in the regions of horror or bliss.

But these truths are too important to be new; they have been taught to our infancy; they have mingled with our solitary thoughts and familiar conversation, and are habitually interwoven with the whole texture of life. Being therefore not new, they raise no unaccustomed emotion in the mind; what we knew before, we cannot learn; what is not unexpected, cannot surprise.

Of the idea suggested by these awful scenes, from some we recede with reverence, except when stated hours require their association; and from others we shrink with horror, or admit them only as salutary inflictions, as counterpoises to our interests and passions. Such images rather obstruct the career of fancy than incite it.

Pleasure and terror are indeed the genuine sources of poetry; but poetical pleasure must be such as human imagination can at least conceive, and poetical terrors such as human strength and fortitude may combat. The good and evil of eternity are too ponderous for the wings of wit; the mind sinks under them in passive helplessness, content with calm belief and humble adoration.

Known truths, however, may take a different appearance, and be conveyed to the mind by a new train of intermediate images. This Milton has undertaken, and performed with pregnancy and vigour of mind peculiar to himself. Whoever considers the few radical positions which the Scriptures afforded him, will wonder by what energetic operation he expanded them to such extent, and ramified them to so much variety, restrained as he was by religious reverence from licentiousness of fiction.

Here is a full display of the united force of study and genius; of a great accumulation of materials, with judgment to digest, and fancy to combine them: Milton was able to select from nature, or from story, from an ancient fable, or from modern science, whatever could illustrate or adorn his thoughts. An accumulation of knowledge impregnated his mind, fermented by study, and exalted by imagination.

It has been therefore said, without an indecent hyperbole, by one of his encomiasts, that in reading *Paradise Lost* we read a book of universal knowledge.

But original deficience cannot be supplied. The want of human interest is always felt. *Paradise Lost* is one of the books which the reader admires and lays down, and forgets to take up again. None ever wished it longer than it is. Its perusal is a duty rather than a pleasure. We read Milton for instruction, retire harassed and overburdened, and look elsewhere for recreation; we desert our master and seek for companions.

Another inconvenience of Milton's design is, that it requires the description of what cannot be described, the agency of spirits. He saw that immateriality supplied no images, and that he could not show angels acting but by instruments of action; he therefore invested them with form and matter. This, being necessary, was therefore defensible; and he should have secured the consistency of his system, by keeping immateriality out of sight, and enticing his reader to drop it from his thoughts. But he has unhappily perplexed his poetry with his philosophy. His infernal and celestial powers are sometimes pure spirit, and sometimes animated body. When Satan walks with his lance upon the *burning marle*, he has a body; when, in his passage between hell and the new world, he is in danger of sinking in the vacuity, and is supported by a gust of rising vapours, he has a body; when he animates the toad, he seems to be mere spirit, that can penetrate matter at pleasure; when he *starts up in his own shape*, he has at least a determined form; and when he is brought before Gabriel, he has *a spear and a shield*, which he had the power of hiding in the toad, though the arms of the contending angels are evidently material.

The vulgar inhabitants of Pandæmonium, being *incorporeal spirits*, are *at large, though without number*, in a limited space: yet in the battle, when they were overwhelmed by mountains, their armour hurt them, *crushed in upon their substance, now grown gross by sinning*. This likewise happened to the uncorrupted angels, who were overthrown the *sooner for their arms, for unarmed they might easily as spirits have evaded by contraction or remove.* Even as spirits they are hardly spiritual; for *contraction* and *remove* are images of matter; but if they could have escaped without their armour, they might have escaped from it, and left only the empty cover to be battered. Uriel, when he rides on a sunbeam, is material; Satan is material when he is afraid of the prowess of Adam.

The confusion of spirit and matter which pervades the whole narration of the war of heaven fills it with incongruity; and the book in which it is related is, I believe, the favourite of children, and gradually neglected as knowledge is increased.

After the operation of immaterial agents, which cannot be explained, may be considered that of allegorical persons, which have no real existence. To exalt causes into agents, to invest abstract ideas with form, and animate them with activity, has always been the right of poetry. But such airy beings are, for the most part, suffered only to do their natural office, and retire. Thus Fame tells a tale, and Victory hovers over a general, or perches on a standard; but Fame and Victory can do more. To give them any real employment, or ascribe to them any material agency, is to make them allegorical no longer, but to shock the mind by ascribing effects to non-entity. In the *Prometheus* of Æschylus we see Violence and Strength, and in the *Alcestis* of Euripides we see Death brought upon the stage, all as active persons of the drama; but no precedents can justify absurdity.

Milton's allegory of Sin and Death is undoubtedly faulty. Sin is indeed the mother of Death, and may be allowed to be the portress of hell; but when they stop the journey of Satan, a journey described as real, and when Death offers him battle, the allegory is broken. That Sin and Death should have shown the way to hell, might have been allowed; but they cannot facilitate the passage by building a bridge, because the difficulty of Satan's passage is described as real and sensible, and the bridge ought to be only figurative. The hell assigned to the rebellious spirits is described as not less local than the residence of man. It is placed in some distant part of space, separated from the regions of harmony and order by a chaotic waste and an unoccupied vacuity; but Sin and Death worked up a *mole of aggravated soil*, cemented with *asphaltus*; a work too bulky for ideal architects.

This unskilful allegory appears to me one of the greatest faults of the poem; and to this there was no temptation but the author's opinion of its beauty.

To the conduct of the narrative some objection may be made. Satan is with great expectation brought before Gabriel in Paradise, and is suffered to go away unmolested. The creation of man is represented as the consequence of the vacuity left in heaven by the expulsion of the rebels; yet Satan mentions it as a report *rife in heaven* before his departure.

To find sentiments for the state of innocence was very difficult, and something of anticipation perhaps is now and then discovered. Adam's discourse of dreams seems not to be the speculation of a new-created being. I know not whether his answer to the angel's reproof for curiosity does not want something of propriety; it is the speech of a man acquainted with many other men. Some philosophical notions, especially when the philosophy is false, might have been better omitted. The angel, in a comparison, speaks of *timorous deer* before deer were yet timorous, and before Adam could understand the comparison.

Dryden remarks, that Milton has some flats among his elevations. This is only to say that all the parts are not equal. In every work one part must be for the sake of others; a palace must have passages; a poem must have transitions. It is no more to be required that wit should always be blazing than that the sun should always stand at noon. In a great work there is a vicissitude of luminous and opaque parts, as there is in the world a succession of day and night. Milton, when he has expatiated in the sky, may be allowed sometimes to revisit earth; for what other author ever soared so high, or sustained his flight so long?

Milton, being well versed in the Italian poets, appears to have borrowed often from them; and as every man catches something from his companions, his desire of imitating Ariosto's levity has disgraced his work with the "Paradise of Fools"—a fiction not in itself ill-imagined, but too ludicrous for its place.

His play on words, in which he delights too often; his equivocations, which Bentley endeavours to defend by the example of the ancients; his unnecessary and ungraceful use of terms of art, it is not necessary to mention, because they are easily remarked, and generally censured, and at last bear so little proportion to the whole that they scarcely deserve the attention of a critic.

Such are the faults of that wonderful performance *Paradise Lost*, which he who can put in balance with its beauties must be considered not as nice but as dull, as less to be censured for want of candour, than pitied for want of sensibility.

Of *Paradise Regained*, the general judgment seems now to be right, that it is in many parts elegant, and everywhere instructive. It was not to be supposed that the writer of *Paradise Lost* could ever write without great effusions of fancy, and exalted precepts of wisdom. The basis of *Paradise Regained* is narrow: a dialogue without action can never please like an union of the narrative and dramatic powers. Had this poem been written not by Milton, but by some imitator, it would have claimed and received universal praise.

If *Paradise Regained* has been too much depreciated, *Samson Agonistes* has in requital been too much admired. It could only be by long prejudice, and the bigotry of learning, that Milton could prefer the ancient tragedies, with their encumbrance of a chorus, to the exhibitions of the French and English stages; and it is only by a blind confidence in the reputation of Milton that a drama can be praised in which the intermediate parts have neither cause nor consequence, neither hasten nor retard the catastrophe.

In this tragedy are however many particular beauties, many just sentiments and striking lines; but it wants that power of attracting the attention which a well-connected plan produces.

Milton would not have excelled in dramatic writing; he knew human nature only in the gross, and had never studied the shades of character, nor the combinations of concurring, or the perplexity of contending, passions. He had read much, and knew what books could teach, but had mingled little in the world, and was deficient in the knowledge which experience must confer.

Through all his greater works there prevails an uniform peculiarity of *diction*, a mode and cast of expression which bears little resemblance to that of any former writer, and which is so far removed from common use that an unlearned reader, when he first opens his book, finds himself surprised by a new language.

This novelty has been, by those who can find nothing wrong in Milton, imputed to his laborious endeavours after words suitable to the grandeur of his ideas. *Our language*, says Addison, *sunk under him*. But the truth is that, both in prose and verse, he had formed his style by a perverse and pedantic principle. He was desirous to use English words with a foreign idiom. This in all his prose is discovered and condemned; for there judgment operates freely, neither softened by the beauty nor awed by the dignity of his thoughts; but such is the power of his poetry, that his call is obeyed without resistance, the reader feels himself in captivity to a higher and nobler mind, and criticism sinks in admiration.

Milton's style was not modified by his subject; what is shown with greater extent in *Paradise Lost* may be found in *Comus*. One source of his peculiarity was his familiarity with the Tuscan poets; the disposition of his words is, I think, frequently Italian, perhaps sometimes combined with other tongues. Of him, at last may be said what Jonson says of Spenser, that *he wrote no language*, but has formed what Butler calls a *Babylonish dialect*, in itself harsh and barbarous, but made, by exalted genius and extensive learning, the vehicle of so much instruction and so much pleasure that, like other lovers, we find grace in its deformity.

Whatever be the faults of his diction, he cannot want the praise of copiousness and variety: he was master of his language in its full extent; and has selected the melodious words with such diligence, that from his book alone the Art of English Poetry might be learned.

After his diction, something must be said of his *versification*. The *measure*, he says, *is the English heroic verse without rhyme*. Of this mode he had many examples among the Italians, and some in his own country. The Earl of Surrey is said to have translated one of Virgil's books without rhyme; and, besides our tragedies, a few short poems had appeared in blank verse, particularly one tending to reconcile the nation to Raleigh's wild attempt upon Guiana, and probably written by Raleigh himself. These petty performances cannot be supposed to have much influenced Milton, who more probably took his hint from Trissino's *Italia Liberata*; and, finding blank verse easier than rhyme, was desirous of persuading himself that it is better.

Rhyme, he says, and says truly, *is no necessary adjunct of true poetry*. But, perhaps, of poetry as a mental operation, metre or music is no necessary adjunct: it is, however, by the music of metre that poetry has been discriminated in all languages; and, in languages melodiously constructed with a due proportion of long and short syllables, metre is sufficient. But one language cannot communicate its rules to another: where metre is scanty and imperfect, some help is necessary. The music of the English heroic line strikes the ear so faintly, that it is easily lost, unless all the syllables of every line co-operate together; this co-operation can be only obtained by the preservation of every verse unmingled with another as a distinct system of sounds; and this distinctness is obtained and preserved by the artifice of rhyme. The variety of pauses, so much boasted by the lovers of blank verse, changes the measures of an English poet to the periods of a declaimer; and there are only a few happy readers of Milton who enable their audience to perceive where the lines end or begin. *Blank verse*, said an ingenious critic, *seems to be verse only to the eye*.

Poetry may subsist without rhyme, but English poetry will not often please; nor can rhyme ever be safely spared but where the subject is able to support itself. Blank verse makes some approach to that which is called the *lapidary style*; has neither the easiness of prose, nor the melody of numbers, and therefore tires by long continuance. Of the Italian writers without rhyme, whom Milton alleges as precedents, not one is popular; what reason could urge in its defence has been confuted by the ear.

But, whatever be the advantage of rhyme, I cannot prevail on myself to wish that Milton had been a rhymer; for I cannot wish his work to be other than it is; yet, like other heroes, he is to be admired rather than imitated. He that thinks himself capable of astonishing may write blank verse; but those that hope only to please must condescend to rhyme.

The highest praise of genius is original invention. Milton cannot be said to have contrived the structure of an epic poem, and therefore owes reverence to that vigour and amplitude of mind to which all generations must be indebted for the art of poetical narration, for the texture of the fable, the variation of incidents, the interposition of dialogue, and all the stratagems that surprise and enchain attention. But, of all the borrowers from Homer, Milton is perhaps the least indebted. He was naturally a thinker for himself, confident of his own abilities, and disdainful of help or hindrance: he did not refuse admission to the thoughts or images of his predecessors, but he did not seek them. From his contemporaries he neither courted nor received support; there is in his writings nothing by which the pride of other authors might be gratified, or favour gained: no exchange of praise, nor solicitation of support. His great works were performed under discountenance, and in blindness, but difficulties vanished at his touch; he was born for whatever is arduous; and his work is not the greatest of heroic poems, only because it is not the first.

SAMUEL TAYLOR COLERIDGE
"Milton" (1818)
Literary Remains, ed. Coleridge
Volume 1, 1836, pp. 166–78

If we divide the period from the accession of Elizabeth to the Protectorate of Cromwell into two unequal portions, the first ending with the death of James I. the other comprehending the reign of Charles and the brief glories of the Republic, we are forcibly struck with a difference in the character of the illustrious actors, by whom each period is rendered severally memorable. Or rather, the difference in the characters of the great men in each period, leads us to make this division. Eminent as the intellectual powers were that were displayed in both; yet in the number of great men, in the various sorts of excellence, and not merely in the variety but almost diversity of talents united in the same individual, the age of Charles falls short of its predecessor; and the stars of the Parliament, keen as their radiance was, in fulness and richness of lustre, yield to the constellation at the court of Elizabeth;—which can only be paralleled by Greece in her brightest moment, when the titles of the poet, the philosopher, the historian, the statesman and the general not seldom formed a garland round the same head, as in the instances of our Sidneys and Raleighs. But then, on the other hand, there was a vehemence of will, an enthusiasm of principle, a depth and an earnestness of spirit, which the charms of individual fame and personal aggrandisement could not pacify,—an aspiration after reality, permanence, and general good,—in short, a moral grandeur in the latter period, with which the low intrigues, Machiavellic maxims, and selfish and servile ambition of the former, stand in painful contrast.

The causes of this it belongs not to the present occasion to detail at length; but a mere allusion to the quick succession of revolutions in religion, breeding a political indifference in the mass of men to religion itself, the enormous increase of the royal power in consequence of the humiliation of the nobility and the clergy—the transference of the papal authority to the crown,—the unfixed state of Elizabeth's own opinions, whose inclinations were as popish as her interests were protestant—the controversial extravagance and practical imbecility of her successor—will help to explain the former period; and the persecutions that had given a life and soul-interest to the disputes so imprudently fostered by James,—the ardour of a conscious increase of power in the commons, and the greater austerity of manners and maxims, the natural product and most formidable weapon of religious disputation, not merely in conjunction, but in closest combination, with newly awakened political and republican zeal, these perhaps account for the character of the latter æra.

In the close of the former period, and during the bloom of the latter, the poet Milton was educated and formed; and he survived the latter, and all the fond hopes and aspirations which had been its life; and so in evil days, standing as the representative of the combined excellence of both periods, he produced the *Paradise Lost* as by an after-throe of nature. "There are some persons (observes a divine, a contemporary of Milton's) of whom the grace of God takes early hold, and the good spirit inhabiting them, carries them on in an even constancy through innocence into virtue, their Christianity bearing equal date with their manhood, and reason and religion, like warp and woof, running together, make up one web of a wise and exemplary life. This (he adds) is a most happy case, wherever it happens; for, besides that there is no sweeter or more lovely thing on earth than the early buds of piety, which drew from our Saviour signal affection to the beloved disciple, it is better to have no wound than to experience the most sovereign balsam, which, if it work a cure, yet usually leaves a scar behind." Although it was and is my intention to defer the consideration of Milton's own character to the conclusion of this Lecture, yet I could not prevail on myself to approach the *Paradise Lost* without impressing on your minds the conditions under which such a work was in fact producible at all, the original genius having been assumed as the immediate agent and efficient cause; and these conditions I find in the character of the times and in his own character. The age in which the foundations of his mind were laid, was congenial to it as one golden æra of profound erudition and individual genius;—that in which the superstructure was carried up, was no less favourable to it by a sternness of discipline and a show of self-control, highly flattering to the imaginative dignity of an heir of fame, and which won Milton over from the dear-loved delights of academic groves and cathedral aisles to the anti-prelatic party. It acted on him, too, no doubt, and modified his studies by a characteristic controversial spirit, (his presentation of God is tinted with it)—a spirit not less busy indeed in political than in theological and ecclesiastical dispute, but carrying on the former almost always, more or less, in the guise of the latter. And so far as Pope's censure of our poet,—that he makes God the Father a school divine—is just, we must attribute it to the character of his age, from which the men of genius, who escaped, escaped by a worse disease, the licentious indifference of a Frenchified court.

Such was the *nidus* or soil, which constituted, in the strict sense of the word, the circumstances of Milton's mind. In his mind itself there were purity and piety absolute; an imagination to which neither the past nor the present were interesting, except as far as they called forth and enlivened the great ideal, in which and for which he lived; a keen love of truth, which, after many weary pursuits, found a harbour in a sublime listening to the still voice in his own spirit, and as keen a love of his country, which, after a disappointment still more depressive, expanded and soared into a love of man as a probationer of immortality. These were, these alone could be, the conditions under which such a work as the *Paradise Lost* could be conceived and accomplished. By a life-long study Milton had known—

> What was of use to know,
> What best to say could say, to do had done.
> His actions to his words agreed, his words
> To his large heart gave utterance due, his heart
> Contain'd of good, wise, fair, the perfect shape;

and he left the imperishable total, as a bequest to the ages coming, in the Paradise Lost.

Difficult as I shall find it to turn over these leaves without catching some passage, which would tempt me to stop, I propose to consider, 1st, the general plan and arrangement of the work;—2ndly, the subject with its difficulties and advantages;—3rdly, the poet's object, the spirit in the letter, the *enthymion en mytho*, the true school-divinity; and lastly, the characteristic excellencies of the poem, in what they consist, and by what means they were produced.

1. As to the plan and ordonnance of the Poem.

Compare it with the *Iliad*, many of the books of which might change places without any injury to the thread of the story. Indeed, I doubt the original existence of the *Iliad* as one poem; it seems more probable that it was put together about the time of the Pisistratidæ. The *Iliad*—and, more or less, all epic poems, the subjects of which are taken from history—have no rounded conclusion; they remain, after all, but single chapters from the volume of history, although they are ornamental chapters. Consider the exquisite simplicity of the *Paradise Lost*. It and it alone really possesses a beginning, a middle, and an end; it has the totality of the poem as distinguished from the *ab ovo* birth and parentage, or straight line, of history.

2. As to the subject.

In Homer, the supposed importance of the subject, as the first effort of confederated Greece, is an after-thought of the critics; and the interest, such as it is, derived from the events themselves, as distinguished from the manner of representing them, is very languid to all but Greeks. It is a Greek poem. The superiority of the *Paradise Lost* is obvious in this respect, that the interest transcends the limits of a nation. But we do not generally dwell on this excellence of the *Paradise Lost*, because it seems attributable to Christianity itself;—yet in fact the interest is wider than Christendom, and comprehends the Jewish and Mohammedan worlds;— nay, still further, inasmuch as it represents the origin of evil, and the combat of evil and good, it contains matter of deep interest to all mankind, as forming the basis of all religion, and the true occasion of all philosophy whatsoever.

The FALL of Man is the subject; Satan is the cause; man's blissful state the immediate object of his enmity and attack; man is warned by an angel who gives him an account of all that was requisite to be known, to make the warning at once intelligible and awful; then the temptation ensues, and the Fall; then the immediate sensible consequence; then the consolation, wherein an angel presents a vision of the history of men with the ultimate triumph of the Redeemer. Nothing is touched in this vision but what is of general interest in religion; any thing else would have been improper.

The inferiority of Klopstock's *Messiah* is inexpressible. I admit the prerogative of poetic feeling, and poetic faith; but I cannot suspend the judgment even for a moment. A poem may in one sense be a dream, but it must be a waking dream. In Milton you have a religious faith combined with the moral nature; it is an efflux; you go along with it. In Klopstock there is a wilfulness; he makes things so and so. The feigned speeches and events in the *Messiah* shock us like falsehoods; but nothing of that sort is felt in the *Paradise Lost*, in which no particulars, at least very few indeed, are touched which can come into collision or juxta-position with recorded matter.

But notwithstanding the advantages in Milton's subject, there were concomitant insuperable difficulties, and Milton has exhibited marvellous skill in keeping most of them out of sight. High poetry is the translation of reality into the ideal under the predicament of succession of time only. The poet is an historian, upon condition of moral power being the only force in the universe. The very grandeur of his subject ministered a difficulty to Milton. The statement of a being of high intellect, warring against the supreme Being, seems to contradict the idea of a supreme Being. Milton precludes our feeling this, as much as possible, by keeping the peculiar attributes of divinity less in sight, making them to a certain extent allegorical only. Again, poetry implies the language of excitement; yet how to reconcile such language with God? Hence Milton confines the poetic passion in God's speeches to the language of scripture; and once only allows the *passio vera*, or *quasi-*

humana to appear, in the passage, where the Father contemplates his own likeness in the Son before the battle:—

> Go then, thou Mightiest, in thy Father's might,
> Ascend my chariot, guide the rapid wheels
> That shake Heaven's basis, bring forth all my war,
> My bow and thunder; my almighty arms
> Gird on, and sword upon thy puissant thigh;
> Pursue these sons of darkness, drive them out
> From all Heaven's bounds into the utter deep:
> There let them learn, as likes them, to despise
> God and Messiah his anointed king.
>
> (B. VI. v. 710.)

3. As to Milton's object:—

It was to justify the ways of God to man! The controversial spirit observable in many parts of the poem, especially in God's speeches, is immediately attributable to the great controversy of that age, the origination of evil. The Arminians considered it a mere calamity. The Calvinists took away all human will. Milton asserted the will, but declared for the enslavement of the will out of an act of the will itself. There are three powers in us, which distinguish us from the beasts that perish;—1, reason; 2, the power of viewing universal truth; and 3, the power of contracting universal truth into particulars. Religion is the will in the reason, and love in the will.

The character of Satan is pride and sensual indulgence, finding in self the sole motive of action. It is the character so often seen *in little* on the political stage. It exhibits all the restlessness, temerity, and cunning which have marked the mighty hunters of mankind from Nimrod to Napoleon. The common fascination of men is, that these great men, as they are called, must act from some great motive. Milton has carefully marked in his Satan the intense selfishness, the alcohol of egotism, which would rather reign in hell than serve in heaven. To place this lust of self in opposition to denial of self or duty, and to show what exertions it would make, and what pains endure to accomplish its end, is Milton's particular object in the character of Satan. But around this character he has thrown a singularity of daring, a grandeur of sufferance, and a ruined splendour, which constitute the very height of poetic sublimity.

Lastly, as to the execution:—

The language and versification of the *Paradise Lost* are peculiar in being so much more necessarily correspondent to each than those in any other poem or poet. The connexion of the sentences and the position of the words are exquisitely artificial; but the position is rather according to the logic of passion or universal logic, than to the logic of grammar. Milton attempted to make the English language obey the logic of passion as perfectly as the Greek and Latin. Hence the occasional harshness in the construction.

Sublimity is the pre-eminent characteristic of the *Paradise Lost*. It is not an arithmetical sublime like Klopstock's, whose rule always is to treat what we might think large as contemptibly small. Klopstock mistakes bigness for greatness. There is a greatness arising from images of effort and daring, and also from those of moral endurance; in Milton both are united. The fallen angels are human passions, invested with a dramatic reality.

The apostrophe to light at the commencement of the third book is particularly beautiful as an intermediate link between Hell and Heaven; and observe, how the second and third book support the subjective character of the poem. In all modern poetry in Christendom there is an under consciousness of a sinful nature, a fleeting away of external things, the mind or subject greater than the object, the reflective character predominant. In the *Paradise Lost*, the sublimest parts are the revelations of Milton's own mind, producing itself and evolving its own greatness; and this is so truly so, that when that which is merely entertaining for its objective beauty is introduced, it at first seems a discord.

In the description of Paradise itself you have Milton's sunny side as a man; here his descriptive powers are exercised to the utmost, and he draws deep upon his Italian resources. In the description of Eve, and throughout this part of the poem, the poet is predominant over the theologian. Dress is the symbol of the Fall, but the mark of intellect; and the metaphysics of dress are, the hiding what is not symbolic and displaying by discrimination what is. The love of Adam and Eve in Paradise is of the highest merit—not phantomatic, and yet removed from every thing degrading. It is the sentiment of one rational being towards another made tender by a specific difference in that which is essentially the same in both; it is a union of opposites, a giving and receiving mutually of the permanent in either, a completion of each in the other.

Milton is not a picturesque, but a musical, poet; although he has this merit that the object chosen by him for any particular foreground always remains prominent to the end, enriched, but not incumbered, by the opulence of descriptive details furnished by an exhaustless imagination. I wish the *Paradise Lost* were more carefully read and studied than I can see any ground for believing it is, especially those parts which, from the habit of always looking for a story in poetry, are scarcely read at all,—as for example, Adam's vision of future events in the 11th and 12th books. No one can rise from the perusal of this immortal poem without a deep sense of the grandeur and the purity of Milton's soul, or without feeling how susceptible of domestic enjoyments he really was, notwithstanding the discomforts which actually resulted from an apparently unhappy choice in marriage. He was, as every truly great poet has ever been, a good man; but finding it impossible to realize his own aspirations, either in religion, or politics, or society, he gave up his heart to the living spirit and light within him, and avenged himself on the world by enriching it with this record of his own transcendant ideal.

WILLIAM HAZLITT
From "On Shakspeare and Milton"
Lectures on the English Poets
1818

Milton has borrowed more than any other writer, and exhausted every source of imitation, sacred or profane; yet he is perfectly distinct from every other writer. He is a writer of centos, and yet in originality scarcely inferior to Homer. The power of his mind is stamped on every line. The fervour of his imagination melts down and renders malleable, as in a furnace, the most contradictory materials. In reading his works, we feel ourselves under the influence of a mighty intellect, that the nearer it approaches to others, becomes more distinct from them. The quantity of art in him shews the strength of his genius: the weight of his intellectual obligations would have oppressed any other writer. Milton's learning has the effect of intuition. He describes objects, of which he could only have read in books, with the vividness of actual observation. His imagination has the force of nature. He makes words tell as pictures.

> Him followed Rimmon, whose delightful seat
> Was fair Damascus, on the fertile banks
> Of Abbana and Pharphar, lucid streams.

The word *lucid* here gives to the idea all the sparkling effect of the most perfect landscape.

And again:

> As when a vulture on Imaus bred,
> Whose snowy ridge the roving Tartar bounds,
> Dislodging from a region scarce of prey,
> To gorge the flesh of lambs and yeanling kids
> On hills where flocks are fed, flies towards the springs
> Of Ganges or Hydaspes, Indian streams;
> But in his way lights on the barren plains
> Of Sericana, where Chineses drive
> With sails and wind their cany waggons light.

If Milton had taken a journey for the express purpose, he could not have described this scenery and mode of life better. Such passages are like demonstrations of natural history. Instances might be multiplied without end.

We might be tempted to suppose that the vividness with which he describes visible objects, was owing to their having acquired an unusual degree of strength in his mind, after the privation of his sight; but we find the same palpableness and truth in the descriptions which occur in his early poems. In 'Lycidas' he speaks of 'the great vision of the guarded mount,' with that preternatural weight of impression with which it would present itself suddenly to 'the pilot of some small night-foundered skiff': and the lines in the 'Penseroso,' describing 'the wandering moon,'

> Riding near her highest noon,
> Like one that had been led astray
> Through the heaven's wide pathless way,

are as if he had gazed himself blind in looking at her. There is also the same depth of impression in his descriptions of the objects of all the different senses, whether colours, or sounds, or smells—the same absorption of his mind in whatever engaged his attention at the time. It has been indeed objected to Milton, by a common perversity of criticism, that his ideas were musical rather than picturesque, as if because they were in the highest degree musical, they must be (to keep the sage critical balance even, and to allow no one man to possess two qualities at the same time) proportionably deficient in other respects. But Milton's poetry is not cast in any such narrow, common-place mould; it is not so barren of resources. His worship of the Muse was not so simple or confined. A sound arises 'like a stream of rich distilled perfumes'; we hear the pealing organ, but the incense on the altars is also there, and the statues of the gods are ranged around! The ear indeed predominates over the eye, because it is more immediately affected, and because the language of music blends more immediately with, and forms a more natural accompaniment to, the variable and indefinite associations of ideas conveyed by words. But where the associations of the imagination are not the principal thing, the individual object is given by Milton with equal force and beauty. The strongest and best proof of this, as a characteristic power of his mind, is, that the persons of Adam and Eve, of Satan, &c. are always accompanied, in our imagination, with the grandeur of the naked figure; they convey to us the ideas of sculpture. As an instance, take the following

> He soon
> Saw within ken a glorious Angel stand,
> The same whom John saw also in the sun:
> His back was turned, but not his brightness hid;
> Of beaming sunny rays a golden tiar
> Circled his head, nor less his locks behind
> Illustrious on his shoulders fledge with wings

Lay waving round; on some great charge employ'd
He seem'd, or fix'd in cogitation deep.
Glad was the spirit impure, as now in hope
To find who might direct his wand'ring flight
To Paradise, the happy seat of man,
His journey's end, and our beginning woe.
But first he casts to change his proper shape,
Which else might work him danger or delay
And now a stripling cherub he appears,
Not of the prime, yet such as in his face
Youth smiled celestial, and to every limb
Suitable grace diffus'd, so well he feign'd:
Under a coronet his flowing hair
In curls on either cheek play'd; wings he wore
Of many a colour'd plume sprinkled with gold,
His habit fit for speed succinct, and held
Before his decent steps a silver wand.

The figures introduced here have all the elegance and precision of a Greek statue; glossy and impurpled, tinged with golden light, and musical as the strings of Memnon's harp!

Again, nothing can be more magnificent than the portrait of Beelzebub:

With Atlantean shoulders fit to bear
The weight of mightiest monarchies:

Or the comparison of Satan, as he 'lay floating many a rood,' to 'that sea beast,'

Leviathan, which God of all his works
Created hugest that swim the ocean-stream!

What a force of imagination is there in this last expression! What an idea it conveys of the size of that hugest of created beings, as if it shrunk up the ocean to a stream, and took up the sea in its nostrils as a very little thing? Force of style is one of Milton's greatest excellences. Hence, perhaps, he stimulates us more in the reading, and less afterwards. The way to defend Milton against all impugners, is to take down the book and read it.

Milton's blank verse is the only blank verse in the language (except Shakspeare's) that deserves the name of verse. Dr. Johnson, who had modelled his ideas of versification on the regular sing-song of Pope, condemns the *Paradise Lost* as harsh and unequal. I shall not pretend to say that this is not sometimes the case; for where a degree of excellence beyond the mechanical rules of art is attempted, the poet must sometimes fail. But I imagine that there are more perfect examples in Milton of musical expression, or of an adaptation of the sound and movement of the verse to the meaning of the passage, than in all our other writers, whether of rhyme or blank verse, put together, (with the exception already mentioned). Spenser is the most harmonious of our stanza writers, as Dryden is the most sounding and varied of our rhymists. But in neither is there any thing like the same ear for music, the same power of approximating the varieties of poetical to those of musical rhythm, as there is in our great epic poet. The sound of his lines is moulded into the expression of the sentiment, almost of the very image. They rise or fall, pause or hurry rapidly on, with exquisite art, but without the least trick or affectation, as the occasion seems to require. . . .

Dr. Johnson and Pope would have converted his vaulting Pegasus into a rocking-horse. Read any other blank verse but Milton's,—Thomson's, Young's, Cowper's, Wordsworth's,—and it will be found, from the want of the same insight into 'the hidden soul of harmony,' to be mere lumbering prose.

To proceed to a consideration of the merits of *Paradise Lost*, in the most essential point of view, I mean as to the poetry of character and passion. I shall say nothing of the fable, or of

other technical objections or excellences; but I shall try to explain at once the foundation of the interest belonging to the poem. I am ready to give up the dialogues in Heaven, where, as Pope justly observes, 'God the Father turns a school-divine'; nor do I consider the battle of the angels as the climax of sublimity, or the most successful effort of Milton's pen. In a word, the interest of the poem arises from the daring ambition and fierce passions of Satan, and from the account of the paradisaical happiness, and the loss of it by our first parents. Three-fourths of the work are taken up with these characters, and nearly all that relates to them is unmixed sublimity and beauty. The two first books alone are like two massy pillars of solid gold.

Satan is the most heroic subject that ever was chosen for a poem; and the execution is as perfect as the design is lofty. He was the first of created beings, who, for endeavouring to be equal with the highest, and to divide the empire of heaven with the Almighty, was hurled down to hell. His aim was no less than the throne of the universe; his means, myriads of angelic armies bright, the third part of the heavens, whom he lured after him with his countenance, and who durst defy the Omnipotent in arms. His ambition was the greatest, and his punishment was the greatest; but not so his despair, for his fortitude was as great as his sufferings. His strength of mind was matchless as his strength of body; the vastness of his designs did not surpass the firm, inflexible determination with which he submitted to his irreversible doom, and final loss of all good. His power of action and of suffering was equal. He was the greatest power that was ever overthrown, with the strongest will left to resist or to endure. He was baffled, not confounded. He stood like a tower; or

As when Heaven's fire
Hath scathed the forest oaks or mountain pines.

He was still surrounded with hosts of rebel angels, armed warriors, who own him as their sovereign leader, and with whose fate he sympathises as he views them round, far as the eye can reach; though he keeps aloof from them in his own mind, and holds supreme counsel only with his own breast. An outcast from Heaven, Hell trembles beneath his feet, Sin and Death are at his heels, and mankind are his easy prey.

All is not lost; th' unconquerable will,
And study of revenge, immortal hate,
And courage never to submit or yield,
And what else is not to be overcome,

are still his. The sense of his punishment seems lost in the magnitude of it; the fierceness of tormenting flames is qualified and made innoxious by the greater fierceness of his pride; the loss of infinite happiness to himself is compensated in thought, by the power of inflicting infinite misery on others. Yet Satan is not the principle of malignity, or of the abstract love of evil—but of the abstract love of power, of pride, of self-will personified, to which last principle all other good and evil, and even his own, are subordinate. From this principle he never once flinches. His love of power and contempt for suffering are never once relaxed from the highest pitch of intensity. His thoughts burn like a hell within him; but the power of thought holds dominion in his mind over every other consideration. The consciousness of a determined purpose, of 'that intellectual being, those thoughts that wander through eternity,' though accompanied with endless pain, he prefers to nonentity, to 'being swallowed up and lost in the wide womb of uncreated night.' He expresses the sum and substance of all ambition in one line. 'Fallen cherub, to be weak is miserable, doing or suffering!' After such a conflict as his, and such a defeat, to retreat in order, to rally, to make terms, to exist at all, is something; but he does more than this—he founds a new empire in hell, and from it conquers this new world, whither he bends his undaunted flight, forcing his way through nether and surrounding fires. The poet has not in all this given us a mere shadowy outline; the strength is equal to the magnitude of the conception. The Achilles of Homer is not more distinct; the Titans were not more vast; Prometheus chained to his rock was not a more terrific example of suffering and of crime. Wherever the figure of Satan is introduced, whether he walks or flies, 'rising aloft incumbent on the dusky air,' it is illustrated with the most striking and appropriate images: so that we see it always before us, gigantic, irregular, portentous, uneasy, and disturbed—but dazzling in its faded splendour, the clouded ruins of a god. The deformity of Satan is only in the depravity of his will; he has no bodily deformity to excite our loathing or disgust. The horns and tail are not there, poor emblems of the unbending, unconquered spirit, of the writhing agonies within. Milton was too magnanimous and open an antagonist to support his argument by the bye-tricks of a hump and cloven foot; to bring into the fair field of controversy the good old catholic prejudices of which Tasso and Dante have availed themselves, and which the mystic German critics would restore. He relied on the justice of his cause, and did not scruple to give the devil his due. Some persons may think that he has carried his liberality too far, and injured the cause he professed to espouse by making him the chief person in his poem. Considering the nature of his subject, he would be equally in danger of running into this fault, from his faith in religion, and his love of rebellion; and perhaps each of these motives had its full share in determining the choice of his subject.

Not only the figure of Satan, but his speeches in council, his soliloquies, his address to Eve, his share in the war in heaven, or in the fall of man, shew the same decided superiority of character. To give only one instance, almost the first speech he makes:

> Is this the region, this the soil, the clime,
> Said then the lost archangel, this the seat
> That we must change for Heaven; this mournful
> gloom
> For that celestial light? Be it so, since he
> Who now is sov'rain can dispose and bid
> What shall be right: farthest from him is best,
> Whom reason hath equal'd, force hath made
> supreme
> Above his equals. Farewel happy fields,
> Where joy for ever dwells: Hail horrors, hail
> Infernal world, and thou profoundest Hell,
> Receive thy new possessor: one who brings
> A mind not to be chang'd by place or time.
> The mind is its own place, and in itself
> Can make a Heav'n of Hell, a Hell of Heav'n.
> What matter where, if I be still the same,
> And what I should be, all but less than he
> Whom thunder hath made greater? Here at least
> We shall be free; th' Almighty hath not built
> Here for his envy, will not drive us hence:
> Here we may reign secure, and in my choice
> To reign is worth ambition, though in Hell:
> Better to reign in Hell, than serve in Heaven.

The whole of the speeches and debates in Pandemonium are well worthy of the place and the occasion—with Gods for speakers, and angels and archangels for hearers. There is a decided manly tone in the arguments and sentiments, an eloquent dogmatism, as if each person spoke from thorough conviction; an excellence which Milton probably borrowed from his spirit of partisanship, or else his spirit of partisanship from the natural firmness and vigour of his mind. In this respect Milton resembles Dante, (the only modern writer with whom he has any thing in common) and it is remarkable that Dante, as well as Milton, was a political partisan. That approximation to the severity of impassioned prose which has been made an objection to Milton's poetry, and which is chiefly to be met with in these bitter invectives, is one of its great excellences. The author might here turn his philippics against Salmasius to good account. The rout in Heaven is like the fall of some mighty structure, nodding to its base, 'with hideous ruin and combustion down.' But, perhaps, of all the passages in *Paradise Lost*, the description of the employments of the angels during the absence of Satan, some of whom 'retreated in a silent valley, sing with notes angelical to many a harp their own heroic deeds and hapless fall by doom of battle,' is the most perfect example of mingled pathos and sublimity.—What proves the truth of this noble picture in every part, and that the frequent complaint of want of interest in it is the fault of the reader, not of the poet, is that when any interest of a practical kind takes a shape that can be at all turned into this, (and there is little doubt that Milton had some such in his eye in writing it,) each party converts it to its own purposes, feels the absolute identity of these abstracted and high speculations; and that, in fact, a noted political writer of the present day has exhausted nearly the whole account of Satan in the *Paradise Lost*, by applying it to a character whom he considered as after the devil, (though I do not know whether he would make even that exception) the greatest enemy of the human race. This may serve to shew that Milton's Satan is not a very insipid personage.

Of Adam and Eve it has been said, that the ordinary reader can feel little interest in them, because they have none of the passions, pursuits, or even relations of human life, except that of man and wife, the least interesting of all others, if not to the parties concerned, at least to the by-standers. The preference has on this account been given to Homer, who, it is said, has left very vivid and infinitely diversified pictures of all the passions and affections, public and private, incident to human nature—the relations of son, of brother, parent, friend, citizen, and many others. Longinus preferred the *Iliad* to the *Odyssey*, on account of the greater number of battles it contains; but I can neither agree to his criticism, nor assent to the present objection. It is true, there is little action in this part of Milton's poem; but there is much repose, and more enjoyment. There are none of the every-day occurrences, contentions, disputes, wars, fightings, feuds, jealousies, trades, professions, liveries, and common handicrafts of life; 'no kind of traffic; letters are not known; no use of service, of riches, poverty, contract, succession, bourne, bound of land, tilth, vineyard none; no occupation, no treason, felony, sword, pike, knife, gun, nor need of any engine.' So much the better; thank Heaven, all these were yet to come. But still the die was cast, and in them our doom was sealed. In them

> The generations were prepared; the pangs,
> The internal pangs, were ready, the dread strife
> Of poor humanity's afflicted will,
> Struggling in vain with ruthless destiny.

In their first false step we trace all our future woe, with loss of Eden. But there was a short and precious interval between, like the first blush of morning before the day is overcast with tempest, the dawn of the world, the birth of nature from 'the unapparent deep,' with its first dews and freshness on its cheek, breathing odours. Theirs was the first delicious taste of life, and on them depended all that was to come of it. In them hung trembling all our hopes and fears. They were as yet alone in the world, in the eye of nature, wondering at their new being, full of enjoyment and enraptured with one another, with the voice of their Maker walking in the garden, and ministering angels attendant on their steps, winged messengers from heaven like rosy clouds descending in their sight. Nature played around them her virgin fancies wild; and spread for them a repast where no crude surfeit reigned. Was there nothing in this scene, which God and nature alone witnessed, to interest a modern critic? What need was there of action, where the heart was full of bliss and innocence without it! They had nothing to do but feel their own happiness, and 'know to know no more.' 'They toiled not, neither did they spin; yet Solomon in all his glory was not arrayed like one of these.' All things seem to acquire fresh sweetness, and to be clothed with fresh beauty in their sight. They tasted as it were for themselves and us, of all that there ever was pure in human bliss. 'In them the burthen of the mystery, the heavy and the weary weight of all this unintelligible world, is lightened.' They stood awhile perfect, but they afterwards fell, and were driven out of Paradise, tasting the first fruits of bitterness as they had done of bliss. But their pangs were such as a pure spirit might feel at the sight—their tears 'such as angels weep.' The pathos is of that mild contemplative kind which arises from regret for the loss of unspeakable happiness, and resignation to inevitable fate. There is none of the fierceness of intemperate passion, none of the agony of mind and turbulence of action, which is the result of the habitual struggles of the will with circumstances, irritated by repeated disappointment, and constantly setting its desires most eagerly on that which there is an impossibility of attaining. This would have destroyed the beauty of the whole picture. They had received their unlooked-for happiness as a free gift from their Creator's hands, and they submitted to its loss, not without sorrow, but without impious and stubborn repining.

> In either hand the hast'ning angel caught
> Our ling'ring parents, and to th' eastern gate
> Led them direct, and down the cliff as fast
> To the subjected plain; then disappear'd.
> They looking back, all th' eastern side beheld
> Of Paradise, so late their happy seat,
> Wav'd over by that flaming brand, the gate
> With dreadful faces throng'd, and fiery arms:
> Some natural tears they dropt, but wip'd them soon;
> The world was all before them, where to choose
> Their place of rest, and Providence their guide.

WILLIAM HAZLITT
From "On Milton's Sonnets"
Table-Talk
1821–22

The great object of the Sonnet seems to be, to express in musical numbers, and as it were with undivided breath, some occasional thought or personal feeling, 'some fee-grief due to the poet's breast.' It is a sigh uttered from the fulness of the heart, an involuntary aspiration born and dying in the same moment. I have always been fond of Milton's *Sonnets* for this reason, that they have more of this personal and internal character than any others; and they acquire a double value when we consider that they come from the pen of the loftiest of our poets. Compared with *Paradise Lost*, they are like tender

flowers that adorn the base of some proud column or stately temple. The author in the one could work himself up with unabated fortitude 'to the height of his great argument;' but in the other he has shewn that he could condescend to men of low estate, and after the lightning and the thunder-bolt of his pen, lets fall some drops of 'natural pity' over hapless infirmity, mingling strains with the nightingale's, 'most musical, most melancholy.' The immortal poet pours his mortal sorrows into our breasts, and a tear falls from his sightless orbs on the friendly hand he presses. The *Sonnets* are a kind of pensive record of past achievements, loves, and friendships, and a noble exhortation to himself to bear up with cheerful hope and confidence to the last. Some of them are of a more quaint and humorous character; but I speak of those only, which are intended to be serious and pathetical.—I do not know indeed but they may be said to be almost the first effusions of this sort of natural and personal sentiment in the language. Drummond's ought perhaps to be excepted, were they formed less closely on the model of Petrarch's, so as to be often little more than translations of the Italian poet. But Milton's *Sonnets* are truly his own in allusion, thought, and versification. Those of Sir Philip Sidney, who was a great transgressor in this way, turn sufficiently on himself and his own adventures; but they are elaborately quaint and intricate, and more like riddles than sonnets. They are 'very tolerable and not to be endured.' Shakespear's, which some persons better-informed in such matters than I can pretend to be, profess to cry up as 'the divine, the matchless, what you will,'—to say nothing of the want of point or a leading, prominent idea in most of them, are I think overcharged and monotonous, and as to their ultimate drift, as for myself, I can make neither head nor tail of it. Yet some of them, I own, are sweet even to a sense of faintness, luscious as the woodbine, and graceful and luxuriant like it. Here is one.

> From you have I been absent in the spring,
> When proud-pied April, dress'd in all his trim,
> Hath put a spirit of youth in every thing;
> That heavy Saturn laugh'd and leap'd with him.
> Yet nor the lays of birds, nor the sweet smell
> Of different flowers in odour and in hue,
> Could make me any summer's story tell,
> Or from their proud lap pluck them where they grew:
> Nor did I wonder at the lilies white,
> Nor praise the deep vermilion in the rose;
> They were but sweet, but figures of delight,
> Drawn after you, you pattern of all those.
> Yet seem'd it winter still; and you away,
> As with your shadow, I with these did play.

I am not aware of any writer of Sonnets worth mentioning here till long after Milton, that is, till the time of Warton and the revival of a taste for Italian and for our own early literature. During the rage for French models, the Sonnet had not been much studied. It is a mode of composition that depends entirely on *expression*; and this the French and artificial style gladly dispenses with, as it lays no particular stress on any thing—except vague, general common-places. Warton's *Sonnets* are undoubtedly exquisite, both in style and matter: they are poetical and philosophical effusions of very delightful sentiment; but the thoughts, though fine and deeply felt, are not, like Milton's subjects, identified completely with the writer, and so far want a more individual interest. Mr. Wordsworth's are also finely conceived and high-sounding Sonnets. They mouth it well, and are said to be sacred to Liberty. Brutus's exclamation, 'Oh Virtue, I thought thee a substance, but I find thee a shadow,' was not considered as a compliment, but as a bitter sarcasm. The beauty of Milton's *Sonnets* is their sincerity, the spirit of poetical patriotism which they breathe. Either Milton's or the living bard's are defective in this respect. There is no Sonnet of Milton's on the Restoration of Charles II. There is no Sonnet of Mr. Wordsworth's corresponding to that of 'the poet blind and bold,' 'On the late Massacre in Piedmont.' It would be no niggard praise to Mr. Wordsworth to grant that he was either half the man or half the poet that Milton was. He has not his high and various imagination, nor his deep and fixed principle. Milton did not worship the rising sun, nor turn his back on a losing and fallen cause.

> Such recantation had no charms for him!

Mr. Southey has thought proper to put the author of *Paradise Lost* into his late Heaven, on the understood condition that he is 'no longer to kings and to hierarchs hostile.' In his life-time, he gave no sign of such an alteration; and it is rather presumptuous in the poet-laureate to pursue the deceased antagonist of Salmasius into the other world to compliment him with his own infirmity of purpose. It is a wonder he did not add in a note that Milton called him aside to whisper in his ear that he preferred the new English hexameters to his own blank verse!

Our first of poets was one of our first of men. He was an eminent instance to prove that a poet is not another name for the slave of power and fashion; as is the case with painters and musicians—things without an opinion—and who merely aspire to make up the pageant and shew of the day. There are persons in common life who have that eager curiosity and restless admiration of bustle and splendour, that sooner than not be admitted on great occasions of feasting and luxurious display, they will go in the character of livery-servants to stand behind the chairs of the great. There are others who can so little bear to be left for any length of time out of the grand carnival and masquerade of pride and folly, that they will gain admittance to it at the expense of their characters as well as of a change of dress. Milton was not one of these. He had too much of the *ideal* faculty in his composition, a lofty contemplative principle, and consciousness of inward power and worth, to be tempted by such idle baits. We have plenty of chaunting and chiming in among some modern writers with the triumphs over their own views and principles; but none of a patient resignation to defeat, sustaining and nourishing itself with the thought of the justice of their cause, and with firm-fixed rectitude. I do not pretend to defend the tone of Milton's political writings (which was borrowed from the style of controversial divinity) or to say that he was right in the part he took:—I say that he was consistent in it, and did not convict himself of error: he was consistent in it in spite of danger and obloquy, 'on evil days though fallen, and evil tongues,' and therefore his character has the salt of honesty about it. It does not offend in the nostrils of posterity. He had taken his part boldly and stood to it manfully, and submitted to the change of times with pious fortitude, building his consolations on the resources of his own mind and the recollection of the past, instead of endeavouring to make himself a retreat for the time to come. As an instance of this, we may take one of the best and most admired of these Sonnets, that addressed to Cyriac Skinner, on his own blindness.

> Cyriac, this three years' day, these eyes, though clear,
> To outward view, of blemish or of spot,
> Bereft of light their seeing have forgot,
> Nor to their idle orbs doth sight appear
> Of sun or moon or star throughout the year,
> Or man or woman. Yet I argue not

> Against Heav'n's hand or will, nor bate a jot
> Of heart or hope; but still bear up and steer
> Right onward. What supports me, dost thou ask?
> The conscience, Friend, to have lost them overply'd
> In liberty's defence, my noble task,
> Of which all Europe talks from side to side.
> This thought might lead me through the world's vain
>   mask,
> Content though blind, had I no better guide.

Nothing can exceed the mild, subdued tone of this Sonnet, nor the striking grandeur of the concluding thought. It is curious to remark what seems to be a trait of character in the two first lines. From Milton's care to inform the reader that 'his eyes were still clear to outward view of spot or blemish,' it would be thought that he had not yet given up all regard to personal appearance; a feeling to which his singular beauty at an earlier age might be supposed naturally enough to lead.— Of the political or (what may be called) his *State-Sonnets*, those to Cromwell, to Fairfax, and to the younger Vane, are full of exalted praise and dignified advice. They are neither familiar nor servile. The writer knows what is due to power and to fame. He feels the true, unassumed equality of greatness. He pays the full tribute of admiration for great acts atchieved, and suggests becoming occasion to deserve higher praise. That to Cromwell is a proof how completely our poet maintained the erectness of his understanding and spirit in his intercourse with men in power. It is such a compliment as a poet might pay to a conqueror and head of the state, without the possibility of self-degradation. . . .

There could not have been a greater mistake or a more unjust piece of criticism than to suppose that Milton only shone on great subjects; and that on ordinary occasions and in familiar life, his mind was unwieldy, averse to the cultivation of grace and elegance, and unsusceptible of harmless pleasures. The whole tenour of his smaller compositions contradicts this opinion, which however they have been cited to confirm. The notion first got abroad from the bitterness (or vehemence) of his controversial writings, and has been kept up since with little meaning and with less truth. His *Letters to Donatus* and others are not more remarkable for the display of a scholastic enthusiasm, than for that of the most amiable dispositions. They are 'severe in youthful virtue unreproved.' There is a passage in his prose-works (the *Treatise on Education*) which shews, I think, his extreme openness and proneness to pleasing outward impressions in a striking point of view. 'But to return to our own institute,' he says, 'besides these constant exercises at home, there is another opportunity of gaining experience to be won from pleasure itself abroad. *In those vernal seasons of the year, when the air is calm and pleasant, it were an injury and sullenness against nature, not to go out and see her riches, and partake in her rejoicing with Heaven and earth. I should not therefore be a persuader to them of studying much then, but to ride out in companies with prudent and well staid guides, to all quarters of the land,*' &c. Many other passages might be quoted, in which the poet breaks through the ground-work of prose, as it were, by natural fecundity and a genial, unrestrained sense of delight. To suppose that a poet is not easily accessible to pleasure, or that he does not take an interest in individual objects and feelings, is to suppose that he is no poet; and proceeds on the false theory, which has been so often applied to poetry and the Fine Arts, that the whole is not made up of the particulars. If our author, according to Dr. Johnson's account of him, could only have treated epic, high-sounding subjects, he would not have been what he was, but another Sir Richard Blackmore.—I may conclude with observing, that I have often wished that Milton had lived to see the Revolution of 1688. This would have been a triumph worthy of him, and which he would have earned by faith and hope. He would then have been old, but would not have lived in vain to see it, and might have celebrated the event in one more undying strain!

THOMAS BABINGTON MACAULAY
From "Milton" (1825)
Critical, and Historical, and Miscellaneous Essays
Volume 1, 1860, pp. 204–66

I t is by his poetry that Milton is best known; and it is of his poetry that we wish first to speak. By the general suffrage of the civilised world, his place has been assigned among the greatest masters of the art. His detractors, however, though outvoted, have not been silenced. There are many critics, and some of great name, who contrive in the same breath to extol the poems and to decry the poet. The works they acknowledge, considered in themselves, may be classed among the noblest productions of the human mind. But they will not allow the author to rank with those great men who, born in the infancy of civilisation, supplied, by their own powers, the want of instruction, and, though destitute of models themselves, bequeathed to posterity models which defy imitation. Milton, it is said, inherited what his predecessors created; he lived in an enlightened age; he received a finished education; and we must therefore, if we would form a just estimate of his powers, make large deductions in consideration of these advantages.

We venture to say, on the contrary, paradoxical as the remark may appear, that no poet has ever had to struggle with more unfavourable circumstances than Milton. He doubted, as he has himself owned, whether he had not been born "an age too late." For this notion Johnson has thought fit to make him the butt of much clumsy ridicule. The poet, we believe, understood the nature of his art better than the critic. He knew that his poetical genius derived no advantage from the civilisation which surrounded him, or from the learning which he had acquired; and he looked back with something like regret to the ruder age of simple words and vivid impressions.

We think that, as civilisation advances, poetry almost necessarily declines. Therefore, though we fervently admire those great works of imagination which have appeared in dark ages, we do not admire them the more because they have appeared in dark ages. On the contrary, we hold that the most wonderful and splendid proof of genius is a great poem produced in a civilised age. We cannot understand why those who believe in that most orthodox article of literary faith, that the earliest poets are generally the best, should wonder at the rule as if it were the exception. Surely the uniformity of the phænomenon indicates a corresponding uniformity in the cause. . . .

He who, in an enlightened and literary society, aspires to be a great poet, must first become a little child. He must take to pieces the whole web of his mind. He must unlearn much of that knowledge which has perhaps constituted hitherto his chief title to superiority. His very talents will be a hindrance to him. His difficulties will be proportioned to his proficiency in the pursuits which are fashionable among his contemporaries; and that proficiency will in general be proportioned to the vigour and activity of his mind. And it is well if, after all his sacrifices and exertions, his works do not resemble a lisping man or a modern ruin. We have seen in our own time great talents, intense labour, and long meditation, employed in this struggle against the spirit of the age, and employed, we will not

say absolutely in vain, but with dubious success and feeble applause.

If these reasonings be just, no poet has ever triumphed over greater difficulties than Milton. He received a learned education: he was a profound and elegant classical scholar: he had studied all the mysteries of Rabbinical literature: he was intimately acquainted with every language of modern Europe, from which either pleasure or information was then to be derived. He was perhaps the only great poet of later times who has been distinguished by the excellence of his Latin verse. The genius of Petrarch was scarcely of the first order; and his poems in the ancient language, though much praised by those who have never read them, are wretched compositions. Cowley, with all his admirable wit and ingenuity, had little imagination: nor indeed do we think his classical diction comparable to that of Milton. The authority of Johnson is against us on this point. But Johnson had studied the bad writers of the middle ages till he had become utterly insensible to the Augustan elegance, and was as ill qualified to judge between two Latin styles as a habitual drunkard to set up for a wine-taster.

Versification in a dead language is an exotic, a far-fetched, costly, sickly, imitation of that which elsewhere may be found in healthful and spontaneous perfection. The soils on which this rarity flourishes are in general as ill suited to the production of vigorous native poetry as the flower-pots of a hot-house to the growth of oaks. That the author of the *Paradise Lost* should have written the *Epistle to Manso* was truly wonderful. Never before were such marked originality and such exquisite mimicry found together. Indeed in all the Latin poems of Milton the artificial manner indispensable to such works is admirably preserved, while, at the same time, his genius gives to them a peculiar charm, an air of nobleness and freedom, which distinguishes them from all other writings of the same class. They remind us of the amusements of those angelic warriors who composed the cohort of Gabriel:

> About him exercised heroic games
> The unarmed youth of heaven. But o'er their heads
> Celestial armoury, shield, helm, and spear,
> Hung high, with diamond flaming and with gold.

We cannot look upon the sportive exercises for which the genius of Milton ungirds itself, without catching a glimpse of the gorgeous and terrible panoply which it is accustomed to wear. The strength of his imagination triumphed over every obstacle. So intense and ardent was the fire of his mind, that it not only was not suffocated beneath the weight of fuel, but penetrated the whole superincumbent mass with its own heat and radiance.

It is not our intention to attempt any thing like a complete examination of the poetry of Milton. The public has long been agreed as to the merit of the most remarkable passages, the incomparable harmony of the numbers, and the excellence of that style, which no rival has been able to equal, and no parodist to degrade, which displays in their highest perfection the idiomatic powers of the English tongue, and to which every ancient and every modern language has contributed something of grace, of energy, or of music. In the vast field of criticism on which we are entering, innumerable reapers have already put their sickles. Yet the harvest is so abundant that the negligent search of a straggling gleaner may be rewarded with a sheaf.

The most striking characteristic of the poetry of Milton is the extreme remoteness of the associations by means of which it acts on the reader. Its effect is produced, not so much by what it expresses, as by what it suggests; not so much by the ideas which it directly conveys, as by other ideas which are connected with them. He electrifies the mind through conductors. The most unimaginative man must understand the *Iliad*. Homer gives him no choice, and requires from him no exertion, but takes the whole upon himself, and sets the images in so clear a light, that it is impossible to be blind to them. The works of Milton cannot be comprehended or enjoyed, unless the mind of the reader co-operate with that of the writer. He does not paint a finished picture, or play for a mere passive listener. He sketches, and leaves others to fill up the outline. He strikes the key-note, and expects his hearer to make out the melody.

We often hear of the magical influence of poetry. The expression in general means nothing: but, applied to the writings of Milton, it is most appropriate. His poetry acts like an incantation. Its merit lies less in its obvious meaning than in its occult power. There would seem, at first sight, to be no more in his words than in other words. But they are words of enchantment. No sooner are they pronounced, than the past is present and the distant near. New forms of beauty start at once into existence, and all the burial-places of the memory give up their dead. Change the structure of the sentence; substitute one synonyme for another, and the whole effect is destroyed. The spell loses its power; and he who should then hope to conjure with it would find himself as much mistaken as Cassim in the Arabian tale, when he stood crying, "Open Wheat," "Open Barley," to the door which obeyed no sound but "Open Sesame." The miserable failure of Dryden in his attempt to translate into his own diction some parts of the *Paradise Lost*, is a remarkable instance of this.

In support of these observations we may remark, that scarcely any passages in the poems of Milton are more generally known or more frequently repeated than those which are little more than muster-rolls of names. They are not always more appropriate or more melodious than other names. But they are charmed names. Every one of them is the first link in a long chain of associated ideas. Like the dwelling-place of our infancy revisited in manhood, like the song of our country heard in a strange land, they produce upon us an effect wholly independent of their intrinsic value. One transports us back to a remote period of history. Another places us among the novel scenes and manners of a distant region. A third evokes all the dear classical recollections of childhood, the school-room, the dog-eared Virgil, the holiday, and the prize. A fourth brings before us the splendid phantoms of chivalrous romance, the trophied lists, the embroidered housings, the quaint devices, the haunted forests, the enchanted gardens, the achievements of enamoured knights, and the smiles of rescued princesses.

In none of the works of Milton is his peculiar manner more happily displayed than in the "Allegro" and the "Penseroso." It is impossible to conceive that the mechanism of language can be brought to a more exquisite degree of perfection. These poems differ from others, as atar of roses differs from ordinary rose water, the close packed essence from the thin diluted mixture. They are indeed not so much poems, as collections of hints, from each of which the reader is to make out a poem for himself. Every epithet is a text for a stanza.

The *Comus* and the *Samson Agonistes* are works which, though of very different merit, offer some marked points of resemblance. Both are lyric poems in the form of plays. There are perhaps no two kinds of composition so essentially dissimilar as the drama and the ode. The business of the dramatist is to keep himself out of sight, and to let nothing appear but his characters. As soon as he attracts notice to his personal feelings, the illusion is broken. The effect is as unpleasant as that which is produced on the stage by the voice of a prompter or the entrance of a scene-shifter. Hence it was, that the tragedies of Byron were his least successful performances. They resemble those pasteboard pictures invented by the friend of children, Mr. Newbery, in which a single moveable head goes round twenty different bodies, so that the same face looks out upon us successively, from the uniform of a hussar, the furs of a judge, and the rags of a beggar. In all the characters, patriots and tyrants, haters and lovers, the frown and sneer of Harold were discernible in an instant. But this species of egotism, though fatal to the drama, is the inspiration of the ode. It is the part of the lyric poet to abandon himself, without reserve, to his own emotions.

Between these hostile elements many great men have endeavoured to effect an amalgamation, but never with complete success. The Greek Drama, on the model of which the *Samson* was written, sprang from the Ode. The dialogue was ingrafted on the chorus, and naturally partook of its character. The genius of the greatest of the Athenian dramatists co-operated with the circumstances under which tragedy made its first appearance. Æschylus was, head and heart, a lyric poet. In his time, the Greeks had far more intercourse with the East than in the days of Homer; and they had not yet acquired that immense superiority in war, in science, and in the arts, which, in the following generation, led them to treat the Asiatics with contempt. From the narrative of Herodotus it should seem that they still looked up, with the veneration of disciples, to Egypt and Assyria. At this period, accordingly, it was natural that the literature of Greece should be tinctured with the Oriental style. And that style, we think, is discernible in the works of Pindar and Æschylus. The latter often reminds us of the Hebrew writers. The book of Job, indeed, in conduct and diction, bears a considerable resemblance to some of his dramas. Considered as plays, his works are absurd; considered as choruses, they are above all praise. If, for instance, we examine the address of Clytemnestra to Agamemnon on his return, or the description of the seven Argive chiefs, by the principles of dramatic writing, we shall instantly condemn them as monstrous. But if we forget the characters, and think only of the poetry, we shall admit that it has never been surpassed in energy and magnificence. Sophocles made the Greek drama as dramatic as was consistent with its original form. His portraits of men have a sort of similarity; but it is the similarity not of a painting, but of a bas-relief. It suggests a resemblance; but it does not produce an illusion. Euripides attempted to carry the reform further. But it was a task far beyond his powers, perhaps beyond any powers. Instead of correcting what was bad, he destroyed what was excellent. He substituted crutches for stilts, bad sermons for good odes.

Milton, it is well known, admired Euripides highly, much more highly than, in our opinion, Euripides deserved. Indeed the caresses which this partiality leads our countryman to bestow on "sad Electra's poet," sometimes remind us of the beautiful Queen of Fairy-land kissing the long ears of Bottom. At all events, there can be no doubt that this veneration for the Athenian, whether just or not, was injurious to the *Samson Agonistes*. Had Milton taken Æschylus for his model, he would have given himself up to the lyric inspiration, and poured out profusely all the treasures of his mind, without bestowing a thought on those dramatic proprieties which the nature of the work rendered it impossible to preserve. In the attempt to reconcile things in their own nature inconsistent, he has failed, as every one else must have failed. We cannot identify ourselves with the characters, as in a good play. We cannot identify ourselves with the poet, as in a good ode. The conflicting ingredients, like an acid and an alkali mixed, neutralise each other. We are by no means insensible to the merits of this celebrated piece, to the severe dignity of the style, the graceful and pathetic solemnity of the opening speech, or the wild and barbaric melody which gives so striking an effect to the choral passages. But we think it, we confess, the least successful effort of the genius of Milton.

The *Comus* is framed on the model of the Italian Masque, as the *Samson* is framed on the model of the Greek Tragedy. It is certainly the noblest performance of the kind which exists in any language. It is as far superior to the *Faithful Shepherdess*, as the *Faithful Shepherdess* is to the *Aminta*, or the *Aminta* to the *Pastor Fido*. It was well for Milton that he had here no Euripides to mislead him. He understood and loved the literature of modern Italy. But he did not feel for it the same veneration which he entertained for the remains of Athenian and Roman poetry, consecrated by so many lofty and endearing recollections. The faults, moreover, of his Italian predecessors were of a kind to which his mind had a deadly antipathy. He could stoop to a plain style, sometimes even to a bald style; but false brilliancy was his utter aversion. His muse had no objection to a russet attire; but she turned with disgust from the finery of Guarini, as tawdry and as paltry as the rags of a chimney-sweeper on May-day. Whatever ornaments she wears are of massive gold, not only dazzling to the sight, but capable of standing the severest test of the crucible.

Milton attended in the *Comus* to the distinction which he afterwards neglected in the *Samson*. He made his Masque what it ought to be, essentially lyrical, and dramatic only in semblance. He has not attempted a fruitless struggle against a defect inherent in the nature of that species of composition; and he has therefore succeeded, wherever success was not impossible. The speeches must be read as majestic soliloquies; and he who so reads them will be enraptured with their eloquence, their sublimity, and their music. The interruptions of the dialogue, however, impose a constraint upon the writer, and break the illusion of the reader. The finest passages are those which are lyric in form as well as in spirit. "I should much commend," says the excellent Sir Henry Wotton in a letter to Milton, "the tragical part if the lyrical did not ravish me with a certain Dorique delicacy in your songs and odes, whereunto, I must plainly confess to you, I have seen yet nothing parallel in our language." The criticism was just. It is when Milton escapes from the shackles of the dialogue, when he is discharged from the labour of uniting two incongruous styles, when he is at liberty to indulge his choral raptures without reserve, that he rises even above himself. Then, like his own good Genius bursting from the earthly form and weeds of Thyrsis, he stands forth in celestial freedom and beauty; he seems to cry exultingly,

> Now my task is smoothly done,
> I can fly or I can run,

to skim the earth, to soar above the clouds, to bathe in the Elysian dew of the rainbow, and to inhale the balmy smells of nard and cassia, which the musky winds of the zephyr scatter through the cedared alleys of the Hesperides.

There are several of the minor poems of Milton on which we would willingly make a few remarks. Still more willingly would we enter into a detailed examination of that admirable poem, the *Paradise Regained*, which, strangely enough, is scarcely ever mentioned except as an instance of the blindness of the parental affection which men of letters bear towards the offspring of their intellects. That Milton was mistaken in preferring this work, excellent as it is, to the *Paradise Lost*, we readily admit. But we are sure that the superiority of the *Paradise Lost* to the *Paradise Regained* is not more decided, than

the superiority of the *Paradise Regained* to every poem which has since made its appearance. Our limits, however, prevent us from discussing the point at length. We hasten on to that extraordinary production which the general suffrage of critics has placed in the highest class of human compositions.

The only poem of modern times which can be compared with the *Paradise Lost* is the *Divine Comedy*. The subject of Milton, in some points, resembled that of Dante; but he has treated it in a widely different manner. We cannot, we think, better illustrate our opinion respecting our own great poet, than by contrasting him with the father of Tuscan literature.

The poetry of Milton differs from that of Dante, as the hieroglyphics of Egypt differed from the picture-writing of Mexico. The images which Dante employs speak for themselves; they stand simply for what they are. Those of Milton have a signification which is often discernible only to the initiated. Their value depends less on what they directly represent than on what they remotely suggest. However strange, however grotesque, may be the appearance which Dante undertakes to describe, he never shrinks from describing it. He gives us the shape, the colour, the sound, the smell, the taste; he counts the numbers; he measures the size. His similes are the illustrations of a traveller. Unlike those of other poets, and especially of Milton, they are introduced in a plain, business-like manner; not for the sake of any beauty in the objects from which they are drawn; not for the sake of any ornament which they may impart to the poem; but simply in order to make the meaning of the writer as clear to the reader as it is to himself. The ruins of the precipice which led from the sixth to the seventh circle of hell were like those of the rock which fell into the Adige on the south of Trent. The cataract of Phlegethon was like that of Aqua Cheta at the monastery of St. Benedict. The place where the heretics were confined in burning tombs resembled the vast cemetery of Arles.

Now let us compare with the exact details of Dante the dim intimations of Milton. We will cite a few examples. The English poet has never thought of taking the measure of Satan. He gives us merely a vague idea of vast bulk. In one passage the fiend lies stretched out huge in length, floating many a rood, equal in size to the earth-born enemies of Jove, or to the sea-monster which the mariner mistakes for an island. When he addresses himself to battle against the guardian angels, he stands like Teneriffe or Atlas: his stature reaches the sky. Contrast with these descriptions the lines in which Dante has described the gigantic spectre of Nimrod. "His face seemed to me as long and as broad as the ball of St. Peter's at Rome; and his other limbs were in proportion; so that the bank, which concealed him from the waist downwards, nevertheless showed so much of him that three tall Germans would in vain have attempted to reach to his hair." We are sensible that we do no justice to the admirable style of the Florentine poet. But Mr. Cary's translation is not at hand; and our version, however rude, is sufficient to illustrate our meaning.

Once more, compare the lazar-house in the eleventh book of the *Paradise Lost* with the last ward of Malebolge in Dante. Milton avoids the loathsome details, and takes refuge in indistinct but solemn and tremendous imagery, Despair hurrying from couch to couch to mock the wretches with his attendance, Death shaking his dart over them, but, in spite of supplications, delaying to strike. What says Dante? "There was such a moan there as there would be if all the sick who, between July and September, are in the hospitals of Valdichiana, and of the Tuscan swamps, and of Sardinia, were in one pit together; and such a stench was issuing forth as is wont to issue from decayed limbs."

We will not take upon ourselves the invidious office of

settling precedency between two such writers. Each in his own department is incomparable; and each, we may remark, has wisely, or fortunately, taken a subject adapted to exhibit his peculiar talent to the greatest advantage. The *Divine Comedy* is a personal narrative. Dante is the eye-witness and ear-witness of that which he relates. He is the very man who has heard the tormented spirits crying out for the second death, who has read the dusky characters on the portal within which there is no hope, who has hidden his face from the terrors of the Gorgon, who has fled from the hooks and the seething pitch of Barbariccia and Draghignazzo. His own hands have grasped the shaggy sides of Lucifer. His own feet have climbed the mountain of expiation. His own brow has been marked by the purifying angel. The reader would throw aside such a tale in incredulous disgust, unless it were told with the strongest air of veracity, with a sobriety even in its horrors, with the greatest precision and multiplicity in its details. The narrative of Milton in this respect differs from that of Dante, as the adventures of Amadis differ from those of Gulliver. The author of *Amadis* would have made his book ridiculous if he had introduced those minute particulars which give such a charm to the work of Swift, the nautical observations, the affected delicacy about names, the official documents transcribed at full length, and all the unmeaning gossip and scandal of the court, springing out of nothing, and tending to nothing. We are not shocked at being told that a man who lived, nobody knows when, saw many very strange sights, and we can easily abandon ourselves to the illusion of the romance. But when Lemuel Gulliver, surgeon, resident at Rotherhithe, tells us of pygmies and giants, dying islands, and philosophising horses, nothing but such circumstantial touches could produce for a single moment a deception on the imagination.

Of all the poets who have introduced into their works the agency of supernatural beings, Milton has succeeded best. Here Dante decidedly yields to him: and as this is a point on which many rash and ill-considered judgments have been pronounced, we feel inclined to dwell on it a little longer. The most fatal error which a poet can possibly commit in the management of his machinery, is that of attempting to philosophise too much. Milton has been often censured for ascribing to spirits many functions of which spirits must be incapable. But these objections, though sanctioned by eminent names, originate, we venture to say, in profound ignorance of the art of poetry.

What is spirit? What are our own minds, the portion of spirit with which we are best acquainted? We observe certain phænomena. We cannot explain them into material causes. We therefore infer that there exists something which is not material. But of this something we have no idea. We can define it only by negatives. We can reason about it only by symbols. We use the word; but we have no image of the thing; and the business of poetry is with images, and not with words. The poet uses words indeed; but they are merely the instruments of his art, not its objects. They are the materials which he is to dispose in such a manner as to present a picture to the mental eye. And if they are not so disposed, they are no more entitled to be called poetry than a bale of canvas and a box of colours to be called a painting.

Logicians may reason about abstractions. But the great mass of men must have images. The strong tendency of the multitude in all ages and nations to idolatry can be explained on no other principle. The first inhabitants of Greece, there is reason to believe, worshipped one invisible Deity. But the necessity of having something more definite to adore produced, in a few centuries, the innumerable crowd of Gods and Goddesses. In like manner the ancient Persians thought it impious

to exhibit the Creator under a human form. Yet even these transferred to the Sun the worship which, in speculation, they considered due only to the Supreme Mind. The History of the Jews is the record of a continued struggle between pure Theism, supported by the most terrible sanctions, and the strangely fascinating desire of having some visible and tangible object of adoration. Perhaps none of the secondary causes which Gibbon has assigned for the rapidity with which Christianity spread over the world, while Judaism scarcely ever acquired a proselyte, operated more powerfully than this feeling. God, the uncreated, the incomprehensible, the invisible, attracted few worshippers. A philosopher might admire so noble a conception: but the crowd turned away in disgust from words which presented no image to their minds. It was before Deity embodied in a human form, walking among men, partaking of their infirmities, leaning on their bosoms, weeping over their graves, slumbering in the manger, bleeding on the cross, that the prejudices of the Synagogue, and the doubts of the Academy, and the pride of the portico, and the fasces of the Lictor, and the swords of thirty legions, were humbled in the dust. Soon after Christianity had achieved its triumph, the principle which had assisted it began to corrupt it. It became a new Paganism. Patron saints assumed the offices of household gods. St. George took the place of Mars. St. Elmo consoled the mariner for the loss of Castor and Pollux. The Virgin Mother and Cecilia succeeded to Venus and the Muses. The fascination of sex and loveliness was again joined to that of celestial dignity; and the homage of chivalry was blended with that of religion. Reformers have often made a stand against these feelings; but never with more than apparent and partial success. The men who demolished the images in Cathedrals have not always been able to demolish those which were enshrined in their minds. It would not be difficult to show that in politics the same rule holds good. Doctrines, we are afraid, must generally be embodied before they can excite a strong public feeling. The multitude is more easily interested for the most unmeaning badge, or the most insignificant name, than for the most important principle.

From these considerations, we infer that no poet, who should affect that metaphysical accuracy for the want of which Milton has been blamed, would escape a disgraceful failure. Still, however, there was another extreme, which, though far less dangerous, was also to be avoided. The imaginations of men are in a great measure under the control of their opinions. The most exquisite art of poetical colouring can produce no illusion, when it is employed to represent that which is at once perceived to be incongruous and absurd. Milton wrote in an age of philosophers and theologians. It was necessary, therefore, for him to abstain from giving such a shock to their understandings as might break the charm which it was his object to throw over their imaginations. This is the real explanation of the indistinctness and inconsistency with which he has often been reproached. Dr. Johnson acknowledges that it was absolutely necessary that the spirit should be clothed with material forms. "But," says he, "the poet should have secured the consistency of his system by keeping immateriality out of sight, and seducing the reader to drop it from his thoughts." This is easily said; but what if Milton could not seduce his readers to drop immateriality from their thoughts? What if the contrary opinion had taken so full a possession of the minds of men as to leave no room even for the half belief which poetry requires? Such we suspect to have been the case. It was impossible for the poet to adopt altogether the material or the immaterial system. He therefore took his stand on the debatable ground. He left the whole in ambiguity. He has, doubtless, by so doing, laid himself open to the charge of inconsistency. But, though philosophically in the wrong, we cannot but believe that he was poetically in the right. This task, which almost any other writer would have found impracticable, was easy to him. The peculiar art which he possessed of communicating his meaning circuitously through a long succession of associated ideas, and of intimating more than he expressed, enabled him to disguise those incongruities which he could not avoid.

Poetry which relates to the beings of another world ought to be at once mysterious and picturesque. That of Milton is so. That of Dante is picturesque indeed beyond any that ever was written. Its effect approaches to that produced by the pencil or the chisel. But it is picturesque to the exclusion of all mystery. This is a fault on the right side, a fault inseparable from the plan of Dante's poem, which, as we have already observed, rendered the utmost accuracy of description necessary. Still it is a fault. The supernatural agents excite an interest; but it is not the interest which is proper to supernatural agents. We feel that we could talk to the ghosts and dæmons without any emotion of unearthly awe. We could, like Don Juan, ask them to supper, and eat heartily in their company. Dante's angels are good men with wings. His devils are spiteful ugly executioners. His dead men are merely living men in strange situations. The scene which passes between the poet and Farinata is justly celebrated. Still, Farinata in the burning tomb is exactly what Farinata would have been at an *auto da fe*. Nothing can be more touching than the first interview of Dante and Beatrice. Yet what is it, but a lovely woman chiding, with sweet austere composure, the lover for whose affection she is grateful, but whose vices she reprobates? The feelings which give the passage its charm would suit the streets of Florence as well as the summit of the Mount of Purgatory.

The spirits of Milton are unlike those of almost all other writers. His fiends, in particular, are wonderful creations. They are not metaphysical abstractions. They are not wicked men. They are not ugly beasts. They have no horns, no tails, none of the fee-faw-fum of Tasso and Klopstock. They have just enough in common with human nature to be intelligible to human beings. Their characters are, like their forms, marked by a certain dim resemblance to those of men, but exaggerated to gigantic dimensions, and veiled in mysterious gloom.

Perhaps the gods and dæmons of Æschylus may best bear a comparison with the angels and devils of Milton. The style of the Athenian had, as we have remarked, something of the Oriental character; and the same peculiarity may be traced in his mythology. It has nothing of the amenity and elegance which we generally find in the superstitions of Greece. All is rugged, barbaric, and colossal. The legends of Æschylus seem to harmonize less with the fragrant groves and graceful porticoes in which his countrymen paid their vows to the God of Light and Goddess of Desire, than with those huge and grotesque labyrinths of eternal granite in which Egypt enshrined her mystic Osiris, or in which Hindostan still bows down to her seven-headed idols. His favourite gods are those of the elder generation, the sons of heaven and earth, compared with whom Jupiter himself was a stripling and an upstart, the gigantic Titans, and the inexorable Furies. Foremost among his creations of this class stands Prometheus, half fiend, half redeemer, the friend of man, the sullen and implacable enemy of heaven. Prometheus bears undoubtedly a considerable resemblance to the Satan of Milton. In both we find the same impatience of control, the same ferocity, the same unconquerable pride. In both characters also are mingled, though in very different proportions, some kind and generous feelings. Prometheus, however, is hardly superhuman enough. He talks too much of his chains and his uneasy posture: he is rather too much depressed and agitated. His resolution seems to depend on the knowledge which he possesses that he holds the fate of his torturer in his hands, and that the hour of his release will surely come. But Satan is a creature of another sphere. The might of his intellectual nature is victorious over the extremity of pain. Amidst agonies which cannot be conceived without horror, he deliberates, resolves, and even exults. Against the sword of Michael, against the thunder of Jehovah, against the flaming lake, and the marl burning with solid fire, against the prospect of an eternity of unintermitted misery, his spirit bears up unbroken, resting on its own innate energies, requiring no support from any thing external, nor even from hope itself.

To return for a moment to the parallel which we have been attempting to draw between Milton and Dante, we would add that the poetry of these great men has in a considerable degree taken its character from their moral qualities. They are not egotists. They rarely obtrude their idiosyncrasies on their readers. They have nothing in common with those modern beggars for fame, who extort a pittance from the compassion of the inexperienced by exposing the nakedness and sores of their minds. Yet it would be difficult to name two writers whose works have been more completely, though undesignedly, coloured by their personal feelings.

The character of Milton was peculiarly distinguished by loftiness of spirit; that of Dante by intensity of feeling. In every line of the *Divine Comedy* we discern the asperity which is produced by pride struggling with misery. There is perhaps no work in the world so deeply and uniformly sorrowful. The melancholy of Dante was no fantastic caprice. It was not, as far as at this distance of time can be judged, the effect of external circumstances. It was from within. Neither love nor glory, neither the conflicts of earth nor the hope of heaven could dispel it. It turned every consolation and every pleasure into its own nature. It resembled that noxious Sardinian soil of which the intense bitterness is said to have been perceptible even in its honey. His mind was, in the noble language of the Hebrew poet, "a land of darkness, as darkness itself, and where the light was as darkness." The gloom of his character discolours all the passions of men, and all the face of nature, and tinges with its own livid hue the flowers of Paradise and the glories of the eternal throne. All the portraits of him are singularly characteristic. No person can look on the features, noble even to ruggedness, the dark furrows of the cheek, the haggard and woful stare of the eye, the sullen and contemptuous curve of the lip, and doubt that they belong to a man too proud and too sensitive to be happy.

Milton was, like Dante, a statesman and a lover; and, like Dante, he had been unfortunate in ambition and in love. He had survived his health and his sight, the comforts of his home, and the prosperity of his party. Of the great men by whom he had been distinguished at his entrance into life, some had been taken away from the evil to come; some had carried into foreign climates their unconquerable hatred of oppression; some were pining in dungeons; and some had poured forth their blood on scaffolds. Venal and licentious scribblers, with just sufficient talent to clothe the thoughts of a pandar in the style of a bellman, were now the favourite writers of the Sovereign and of the public. It was a loathsome herd, which could be compared to nothing so fitly as to the rabble of *Comus*, grotesque monsters, half bestial half human, dropping with wine, bloated with gluttony, and reeling in obscene dances. Amidst these that fair Muse was placed, like the chaste lady of the Masque, lofty, spotless, and serene, to be chattered at, and pointed at, and grinned at, by the whole rout of Satyrs and Goblins. If ever despondency and asperity could be excused in any man, they might have been excused in Milton. But the strength of his mind overcame every calamity. Neither blindness, nor gout, nor age, nor penury, nor domestic afflictions, nor political disappointments, nor abuse, nor proscription, nor neglect, had power to disturb his sedate and majestic patience. His spirits do not seem to have been high, but they were singularly equable. His temper was serious, perhaps stern; but it was a temper which no sufferings could render sullen or fretful. Such as it was when, on the eve of great events, he returned from his travels, in the prime of health and manly beauty, loaded with literary distinctions, and glowing with patriotic hopes, such it continued to be when, after having experienced every calamity which is incident to our nature, old, poor, sightless and disgraced, he retired to his hovel to die.

Hence it was that, though he wrote the *Paradise Lost* at a time of life when images of beauty and tenderness are in general beginning to fade, even from those minds in which they have not been effaced by anxiety and disappointment, he adorned it with all that is most lovely and delightful in the physical and in the moral world. Neither Theocritus nor Ariosto had a finer or a more healthful sense of the pleasantness of external objects, or loved better to luxuriate amidst sunbeams and flowers, the songs of nightingales, the juice of summer fruits, and the coolness of shady fountains. His conception of love unites all the voluptuousness of the Oriental harem, and all the gallantry of the chivalric tournament, with all the pure and quiet affection of an English fireside. His poetry reminds us of the miracles of Alpine scenery. Nooks and dells, beautiful as fairy land, are embosomed in its most rugged and gigantic elevations. The roses and myrtles bloom unchilled on the verge of the avalanche.

Traces, indeed, of the peculiar character of Milton may be found in all his works; but it is most strongly displayed in the *Sonnets*. Those remarkable poems have been undervalued by critics who have not understood their nature. They have no epigrammatic point. There is none of the ingenuity of Filicaja in the thought, none of the hard and brilliant enamel of Petrarch in the style. They are simple but majestic records of the feelings of the poet; as little tricked out for the public eye as his diary would have been. A victory, an expected attack upon the city, a momentary fit of depression or exultation, a jest thrown out against one of his books, a dream which for a short time restored to him that beautiful face over which the grave had closed for ever, led him to musings, which, without effort, shaped themselves into verse. The unity of sentiment and severity of style which characterise these little pieces remind us of the *Greek Anthology*, or perhaps still more of the *Collects of the English Liturgy*. The noble poem on the Massacres of Piedmont is strictly a *Collect* in verse.

The *Sonnets* are more or less striking, according as the occasions which gave birth to them are more or less interesting. But they are, almost without exception, dignified by a sobriety and greatness of mind to which we know not where to look for a parallel. It would, indeed, be scarcely safe to draw any decided inferences as to the character of a writer from passages directly egotistical. But the qualities which we have ascribed to Milton, though perhaps most strongly marked in those parts of his works which treat of his personal feelings, are distinguishable in every page, and impart to all his writings, prose and poetry, English, Latin, and Italian, a strong family likeness.

His public conduct was such as was to be expected from a man of a spirit so high and of an intellect so powerful. He lived at one of the most memorable eras in the history of mankind, at the very crisis of the great conflict between Oromasdes and Arimanes, liberty and despotism, reason and prejudice. That great battle was fought for no single generation, for no single land. The destinies of the human race were staked on the same

cast with the freedom of the English people. Then were first proclaimed those mighty principles which have since worked their way into the depths of the American forests, which have roused Greece from the slavery and degradation of two thousand years, and which, from one end of Europe to the other, have kindled an unquenchable fire in the hearts of the oppressed, and loosed the knees of the oppressors with an unwonted fear.

Of those principles, then struggling for their infant existence, Milton was the most devoted and eloquent literary champion. We need not say how much we admire his public conduct. But we cannot disguise from ourselves that a large portion of his countrymen still think it unjustifiable. The civil war, indeed, has been more discussed, and is less understood, than any event in English history. The friends of liberty laboured under the disadvantage of which the lion in the fable complained so bitterly. Though they were the conquerors, their enemies were the painters. As a body, the Roundheads had done their utmost to decry and ruin literature; and literature was even with them, as, in the long run, it always is with its enemies. The best book on their side of the question is the charming narrative of Mrs. Hutchinson. May's *History of the Parliament* is good; but it breaks off at the most interesting crisis of the struggle. The performance of Ludlow is foolish and violent; and most of the later writers who have espoused the same cause, Oldmixon for instance, and Catherine Macaulay, have, to say the least, been more distinguished by zeal than either by candour or by skill. On the other side are the most authoritative and the most popular historical works in our language, that of Clarendon, and that of Hume. The former is not only ably written and full of valuable information, but has also an air of dignity and sincerity which makes even the prejudices and errors with which it abounds respectable. Hume, from whose fascinating narrative the great mass of the reading public are still contented to take their opinions, hated religion so much that he hated liberty for having been allied with religion, and has pleaded the cause of tyranny with the dexterity of an advocate while affecting the impartiality of a judge. . . .

That from which the public character of Milton derives its great and peculiar splendour, still remains to be mentioned. If he exerted himself to overthrow a forsworn king and a persecuting hierarchy, he exerted himself in conjunction with others. But the glory of the battle which he fought for the species of freedom which is the most valuable, and which was then the least understood, the freedom of the human mind, is all his own. Thousands and tens of thousands among his contemporaries raised their voices against Ship-money and the Starchamber. But there were few indeed who discerned the more fearful evils of moral and intellectual slavery, and the benefits which would result from the liberty of the press and the unfettered exercise of private judgment. These were the objects which Milton justly conceived to be the most important. He was desirous that the people should think for themselves as well as tax themselves, and should be emancipated from the dominion of prejudice as well as from that of Charles. He knew that those who, with the best intentions, overlooked these schemes of reform, and contented themselves with pulling down the King and imprisoning the malignants, acted like the heedless brothers in his own poem, who, in their eagerness to disperse the train of the sorcerer, neglected the means of liberating the captive. They thought only of conquering when they should have thought of disenchanting.

> Oh, ye mistook! Ye should have snatched his wand
> And bound him fast. Without the rod reversed,
> And backward mutters of dissevering power,
> We cannot free the lady that sits here

Bound in strong fetters fixed and motionless.

To reverse the rod, to spell the charm backward, to break the ties which bound a stupefied people to the seat of enchantment, was the noble aim of Milton. To this all his public conduct was directed. For this he joined the Presbyterians; for this he forsook them. He fought their perilous battle; but he turned away with disdain from their insolent triumph. He saw that they, like those whom they had vanquished, were hostile to the liberty of thought. He therefore joined the Independents, and called upon Cromwell to break the secular chain, and to save free conscience from the paw of the Presbyterian wolf. With a view to the same great object, he attacked the licensing system, in that sublime treatise which every statesman should wear as a sign upon his hand and as frontlets between his eyes. His attacks were, in general, directed less against particular abuses than against those deeply-seated errors on which almost all abuses are founded, the servile worship of eminent men and the irrational dread of innovation.

That he might shake the foundations of these debasing sentiments more effectually, he always selected for himself the boldest literary services. He never came up in the rear, when the outworks had been carried and the breach entered. He pressed into the forlorn hope. At the beginning of the changes, he wrote with incomparable energy and eloquence against the bishops. But, when his opinion seemed likely to prevail, he passed on to other subjects, and abandoned prelacy to the crowd of writers who now hastened to insult a falling party. There is no more hazardous enterprise than that of bearing the torch of truth into those dark and infected recesses in which no light has ever shone. But it was the choice and the pleasure of Milton to penetrate the noisome vapours, and to brave the terrible explosion. Those who most disapprove of his opinions must respect the hardihood with which he maintained them. He, in general, left to others the credit of expounding and defending the popular parts of his religious and political creed. He took his own stand upon those which the great body of his countrymen reprobated as criminal, or derided as paradoxical. He stood up for divorce and regicide. He attacked the prevailing systems of education. His radiant and beneficent career resembled that of the god of light and fertility.

> Nitor in adversum; nec me, qui cætera, vincit
> Impetus, et rapido contrarius evehor orbi.

It is to be regretted that the prose writings of Milton should, in our time, be so little read. As compositions, they deserve the attention of every man who wishes to become acquainted with the full power of the English language. They abound with passages compared with which the finest declamations of Burke sink into insignificance. They are a perfect field of cloth of gold. The style is stiff with gorgeous embroidery. Not even in the earlier books of the *Paradise Lost* has the great poet ever risen higher than in those parts of his controversial works in which his feelings, excited by conflict, find a vent in bursts of devotional and lyric rapture. It is, to borrow his own majestic language, "a sevenfold chorus of hallelujahs and harping symphonies."

We had intended to look more closely at these performances, to analyse the peculiarities of the diction, to dwell at some length on the sublime wisdom of the *Areopagitica* and the nervous rhetoric of the *Iconoclast*, and to point out some of those magnificent passages which occur in the *Treatise of Reformation*, and the *Animadversions on the Remonstrant*. But the length to which our remarks have already extended renders this impossible.

We must conclude. And yet we can scarcely tear ourselves away from the subject. The days immediately following the publication of this relic of Milton appear to be peculiarly set apart, and consecrated to his memory. And we shall scarcely be censured if, on this his festival, we be found lingering near his shrine, how worthless soever may be the offering which we bring to it. While this book lies on our table, we seem to be contemporaries of the writer. We are transported a hundred and fifty years back. We can almost fancy that we are visiting him in his small lodging; that we see him sitting at the old organ beneath the faded green hangings; that we can catch the quick twinkle of his eyes, rolling in vain to find the day, that we are reading in the lines of his noble countenance the proud and mournful history of his glory and his affliction. We image to ourselves the breathless silence in which we should listen to his slightest word, the passionate veneration with which we should kneel to kiss his hand and weep upon it, the earnestness with which we should endeavour to console him, if indeed such a spirit could need consolation, for the neglect of an age unworthy of his talents and his virtues, the eagerness with which we should contest with his daughters, or with his Quaker friend Elwood, the privilege of reading Homer to him, or of taking down the immortal accents which flowed from his lips.

These are perhaps foolish feelings. Yet we cannot be ashamed of them; nor shall we be sorry if what we have written shall in any degree excite them in other minds. We are not much in the habit of idolizing either the living or the dead. And we think that there is no more certain indication of a weak and ill-regulated intellect than that propensity which, for want of a better name, we will venture to christen Boswellism. But there are a few characters which have stood the closest scrutiny and the severest tests, which have been tried in the furnace and have proved pure, which have been weighed in the balance and have not been found wanting, which have been declared sterling by the general consent of mankind, and which are visibly stamped with the image and superscription of the Most High. These great men we trust that we know how to prize; and of these was Milton. The sight of his books, the sound of his name, are pleasant to us. His thoughts resemble those celestial fruits and flowers which the Virgin Martyr of Massinger sent down from the gardens of Paradise to the earth, and which were distinguished from the productions of other soils, not only by superior bloom and sweetness, but by miraculous efficacy to invigorate and to heal. They are powerful, not only to delight, but to elevate and purify. Nor do we envy the man who can study either the life or the writings of the great poet and patriot, without aspiring to emulate, not indeed the sublime works with which his genius has enriched our literature, but the zeal with which he laboured for the public good, the fortitude with which he endured every private calamity, the lofty disdain with which he looked down on temptations and dangers, the deadly hatred which he bore to bigots and tyrants, and the faith which he so sternly kept with his country and with his fame.

FRANÇOIS RENÉ, VICOMTE DE CHATEAUBRIAND
"Milton in *Paradise Lost*"
Sketches of English Literature
Volume 2, 1837, pp. 145–54

The republican is conspicuous in every verse of *Paradise Lost*: the speeches of Satan breathe a hatred of subjection. Milton, however, who, although an enthusiast of liberty, had nevertheless served Cromwell, reveals the kind of republic which accorded with his ideas: it is not a republic of equality, a plebeian republic; he desired an aristocratic republic, in which gradations of rank are admitted. Satan says:—

if not equal all, yet free,
Equally free; for orders and degrees
Jar not with liberty, but well consist.
Who can in reason then, or right, assume
Monarchy over such as live by right
His equals, if in power or splendour less,
In freedom equal? or can introduce
Law and edict on us, who without law
Err not? much less for this to be our Lord,
And look for adoration, to the abuse
Of those imperial titles, which assert
Our being ordained to govern, not to serve.
(Paradise Lost, Book V.)

If there could remain any doubt on this subject, Milton, in his tract entitled *The Ready and Easy Way to Establish a Free Commonwealth*, speaks a language calculated to dispel all uncertainty; he therein avows that the republic should be governed *by a grand or general perpetual council*; he rejects the *popular remedy* adopted to check the ambition of this permanent council, as the people would plunge headlong into a *licentious and unbridled democracy*. Milton, the proud republican, had a coat of arms: he bore on a field sable, an eagle argent, double-headed gules, beak and legs sable. An eagle was, for the poet at least, a speaking escutcheon. The Americans have escutcheons of a more feudal character than those of the knights of the fourteenth century; such fancies are altogether harmless.

The speeches which constitute the greater part of *Paradise Lost*, have acquired new interest since we have had a representative government. The poet has introduced into his work the political forms of the government of his native land. Satan convokes in hell a real parliament; he divides it into two chambers; Tartarus rejoices in a chamber of peers. Eloquence is one of the essential qualities of the author's talent; the speeches delivered by his personages are frequently models of skill and energy. Abdiel, when parting from the rebel angels, addresses Satan in these words:—

O alienate from God, O spirit accurs'd,
Forsaken of all good! I see thy fall
Determined, and thy hapless crew involv'd
In this perfidious fraud, contagion spread
Both of thy crime and punishment: henceforth
No more be troubled how to quit the yoke
Of God's Messiah; those indulgent laws
Will not be now vouchsaf'd; other decrees
Against thee are gone forth without recall;
That golden sceptre, which thou didst reject,
Is now an iron rod to bruise and break
Thy disobedience. Well thou didst advise;
Yet not for thy advice and threats I fly
These wicked tents devoted, lest the wrath
Impendent, raging into sudden flame,
Distinguish not: for soon expect to feel
His thunder on thy head, devouring fire.
Then who created thee lamenting learn,
When who can uncreate thee thou shalt know.

There is, in the poem, something which at first sight appears unaccountable: the infernal republic attempts to overthrow the celestial monarchy; Milton, though his sentiments are wholly republican, invariably ascribes justice and victory to the Almighty! The reason of this is that the poet was swayed by his religious opinions. In accordance with the Independents, he desired a theocratic republic, a hierarchical liberty, subject only to the dominion of Heaven; he had represented Cromwell as the lieutenant-general of God and the protector of the republic:—

Cromwell, our chief of men, who, through a
cloud
Not of war only, but detractions rude,
Guided by faith and matchless fortitude,
To peace and truth thy glorious way hast
plough'd,
And on the neck of crowned fortune proud
Hast rear'd God's trophies, and his works
pursued,
While Darwen stream, with blood of Scots
imbrued,
And Dunbar field resounds thy praises loud,
And Worcester's laureat wreath. Yet much remains
To conquer still; peace hath her victories
No less renown'd than war: new foes arise
Threat'ning to bind our souls with secular chains:
Help us to save free conscience from the paw
Of hireling wolves, whose gospel is their maw.

Satan and his angels were pictured to Milton's imagination by the proud Presbyterians, who refused to submit to the *Saints*, Milton's own faction, of which he hailed the inspired Cromwell as the godly leader.

We discern in Milton a man of troubled spirit; still under the influence of revolutionary scenes and passions, he stood erect after the downfall of the revolution which had fled to him for shelter, and palpitated in his bosom. But the earnestness of that revolution overpowers him; religious gravity forms the counterpoise to his political agitations. Stunned, however, at the overthrow of his fondest illusions, at the dissipation of his dreams of liberty, he knows not which way to turn, but remains in a state of perplexity, even respecting religious truth.

An attentive perusal of *Paradise Lost* fixes on the mind the impression that Milton fluctuated between a variety of systems. In the very opening of his poem, he avows himself a Socinian by the celebrated expression "one greater man;" he is silent respecting the Holy Ghost, never names the Trinity, nowhere states the Son to be equal to the Father. The Son is not begotten of all eternity; the poet even places his creation after that of the angels. Milton is, if anything, an Arian; he does not admit what is properly called the *creation*, but supposes a pre-existing matter, co-eternal with the spirit. The particular creation of the universe is no more, in his opinion, than the arrangement of a little corner of chaos, which is ever threatening to return to its previous state of confusion. All the known philosophical theories of the poet have more or less taken root amongst his beliefs; at one time, Plato with the exemplars of ideas, or Pythagoras with the harmony of the spheres; at another, Epicurus, or Lucretius, with his materialism, as when he exhibits to view the half-formed animals issuing from the earth. He is a fatalist when making the rebel angel say of himself and his companions:—

We know no time when we were not as now;
Know none before us, self-begot, self-rais'd
By our own quick'ning power, when fatal course
Had circled his full orb.

Milton is, moreover, a pantheist or Spinozist, but his pantheism is of an extraordinary kind.

The poet first appears to admit of the known pantheism, a medley of matter and mind; but, if man had not sinned, Adam would have gradually extricated himself from matter, and acquired the nature of angels. Adam falls into sin. With a view to redeem the spiritual part of man, the Son of God, who is all spirit, assumes a material substance, descends upon earth, dies, and re-ascends into heaven, after passing through matter. Christ thus becomes the vehicle by means of which matter, brought into contact with intelligence, becomes spiritualised. At length, the due time having elapsed, matter or the material world is at an end, and merges into the other principle. "The Son," says Milton, "shall be absorbed in the bosom of the Father, with the rest of the creatures; God shall be all in all." This is a spiritual pantheism, succeeding the pantheism of the two principles.

Thus our soul will be absorbed in the source of spirituality. What is that sea of intelligence, a single drop of which, contained within matter, is sufficiently powerful to comprehend the motion of the spheres and to investigate the nature of God? What is the Infinite? What! still worlds after worlds! Imagination is bewildered in its endeavours to penetrate those abysses, and Milton is wrecked in the attempt. Nevertheless, amidst this chaos of principles, the poet remains biblical and a Christian; he rehearses the fall and the redemption. A Puritan at first, then an Independent and an Anabaptist, he becomes a *saint*, a quietist, and an enthusiast; it is at length but a voice that sings the praises of the Almighty. Milton had forsaken the house of God; he no longer gave any external signs of religion; in *Paradise Lost* he declares that prayer is the only worship acceptable to God.

This poem, which opens in hell, and, passing over the earth, terminates in heaven, exhibits only two human beings in the vast wilderness of the new creation; the rest are the supernatural inhabitants of the abyss of endless felicity, or of the gulf of everlasting misery. Well, then, the poet has dared to penetrate this solitude, where he presents himself as the child of Adam, a deputy of the human race, fallen through disobedience. He there appears as the hierophant, the prophet, commissioned to learn the history of man's fall, and to sing it on the harp devoted to the penances of David. He is so full of genius, holiness, and grandeur, that his noble head is not misplaced near that of our first parent, in the presence of God and of his angels. Issuing forth from the abyss of darkness, he hails that holy light which is denied to his eyes.

> Hail, holy light, offspring of heaven first-born,
> Or of the Eternal co-eternal beam,
> May I express thee unblam'd? since God is light,
> And never but in unapproached light
> Dwelt from eternity, dwelt there in thee,
> Bright effluence of bright essence increate!
> Or hear'st thou rather, pure ethereal stream,
> Whose fountain who shall tell? Before the sun,
> Before the heavens, thou wert, and, at the voice
> Of God, as with a mantle, didst invest
> The rising world of waters, dark and deep,
> Won from the void and formless infinite.
> Thee I revisit now with bolder wing,
> Escap'd the Stygian pool. . . .
> And feel thy sovran, vital lamp; but thou
> Revisit'st not these eyes, that roll in vain
> To find thy piercing ray, and find no dawn;
> So thick a drop serene hath quench'd their orbs,
> Or dim suffusion veil'd. Yet not the more
> Cease I to wander where the muses haunt
> Clear spring or shady grove. . . .
>   . . . nor sometimes forget
> Those other two equall'd with me in fate.
> So were I equall'd with them in renown,
> Blind Thamyris, and blind Mæonides,
> And Tiresias and Phineus, prophets old;
> There feed on thoughts, that voluntary move
> Harmonious numbers; as the wakeful bird
> Sings darkling, and in shadiest covert hid
> Tunes her nocturnal note. Thus with the year

> Seasons return; but not to me returns
> Day, or the sweet approach of even or morn,
> Or sight of vernal bloom, or summer's rose,
> Or flocks, or herds, or human face divine;
> But clouds instead, and ever-during dark
> Surrounds me, from the cheerful ways of men
> Cut off, and for the book of knowledge fair
> Presented with a universal blank
> Of Nature's works, to me expung'd and ras'd,
> And wisdom at one entrance quite shut out.
> So much the rather thou, celestial light,
> Shine inward, and the mind through all her powers
> Irradiate; there plant eyes, all mist from thence
> Purge and disperse; that I may see and tell
> Of things invisible to mortal sight.

Elsewhere he exclaims in not less pathetic strains:

> If answerable style I can obtain
> Of my celestial patroness, who deigns
> Her nightly visitation unimplor'd,
>   . . . higher argument
> Remains; sufficient of itself to raise
> That name, unless an age too late, or cold
> Climate, or years, damp my intended wing
> Depress'd.

How lofty must have been the intelligence of Milton, which could sustain this intercourse face to face with God, and the wonderful beings he has created! No man ever displayed a more sober and at the same time a more delicate genius. "It was," says Hume, "during a state of poverty, blindness, disgrace, danger, and old age, that Milton composed his wonderful poem, which not only surpassed all the performances of his cotemporaries, but all the compositions which had flowed from his pen during the vigour of his age and the height of his prosperity." We actually distinguish in this poem, through the ardour of youthful years, the maturity of age and the gravity of misfortune; this imparts to *Paradise Lost* an extraordinary fascination of old age and youth, of restlessness and peace, of sadness and joy, of reason and love.

RALPH WALDO EMERSON
"Milton" (1838)
Complete Works
Volume 12, 1904, pp. 247–79

The discovery of the lost work of Milton, the treatise *Of the Christian Doctrine*, in 1823, drew a sudden attention to his name. For a short time the literary journals were filled with disquisitions on his genius; new editions of his works, and new compilations of his life, were published. But the new-found book having in itself less attraction than any other work of Milton, the curiosity of the public as quickly subsided, and left the poet to the enjoyment of his permanent fame, or to such increase or abatement of it only as is incidental to a sublime genius, quite independent of the momentary challenge of universal attention to his claims.

But if the new and temporary renown of the poet is silent again, it is nevertheless true that he has gained, in this age, some increase of permanent praise. The fame of a great man is not rigid and stony like his bust. It changes with time. It needs time to give it due perspective. It was very easy to remark an altered tone in the criticism when Milton reappeared as an author, fifteen years ago, from any that had been bestowed on the same subject before. It implied merit indisputable and illustrious; yet so near to the modern mind as to be still alive and life-giving. The aspect of Milton, to this generation, will be part of the history of the nineteenth century. There is no name in English literature between his age and ours that rises into any approach to his own. And as a man's fame, of course, characterizes those who give it, as much as him who receives it, the new criticism indicated a change in the public taste, and a change which the poet himself might claim to have wrought.

The reputation of Milton had already undergone one or two revolutions long anterior to its recent aspects. In his lifetime, he was little or not at all known as a poet, but obtained great respect from his contemporaries as an accomplished scholar and a formidable pamphleteer. His poem fell unregarded among his countrymen. His prose writings, especially the *Defence of the English People*, seem to have been read with avidity. These tracts are remarkable compositions. They are earnest, spiritual, rich with allusion, sparkling with innumerable ornaments; but as writings designed to gain a practical point, they fail. They are not effective, like similar productions of Swift and Burke; or, like what became also controversial tracts, several masterly speeches in the history of the American Congress. Milton seldom deigns a glance at the obstacles that are to be overcome before that which he proposes can be done. There is no attempt to conciliate,—no mediate, no preparatory course suggested,—but, peremptory and impassioned, he demands, on the instant, an ideal justice. Therein they are discriminated from modern writings, in which a regard to the actual is all but universal.

Their rhetorical excellence must also suffer some deduction. They have no perfectness. These writings are wonderful for the truth, the learning, the subtility and pomp of the language; but the whole is sacrificed to the particular. Eager to do fit justice to each thought, he does not subordinate it so as to project the main argument. He writes whilst he is heated; the piece shows all the rambles and resources of indignation, but he has never *integrated* the parts of the argument in his mind. The reader is fatigued with admiration, but is not yet master of the subject.

Two of his pieces may be excepted from this description, one for its faults, the other for its excellence. The *Defence of the People of England*, on which his contemporary fame was founded, is, when divested of its pure Latinity, the worst of his works. Only its general aim, and a few elevated passages, can save it. We could be well content if the flames to which it was condemned at Paris, at Toulouse, and at London, had utterly consumed it. The lover of his genius will always regret that he should not have taken counsel of his own lofty heart at this, as at other times, and have written from the deep convictions of love and right, which are the foundations of civil liberty. There is little poetry or prophecy in this mean and ribald scolding. To insult Salmasius, not to acquit England, is the main design. What under heaven had Madame de Saumaise, or the manner of living of Saumaise, or Salmasius, or his blunders of grammar, or his niceties of diction, to do with the solemn question whether Charles Stuart had been rightly slain? Though it evinces learning and critical skill, yet, as an historical argument, it cannot be valued with similar disquisitions of Robertson and Hallam, and even less celebrated scholars. But when he comes to speak of the reason of the thing, then he always recovers himself. The voice of the mob is silent, and Milton speaks. And the peroration, in which he implores his countrymen to refute this adversary by their great deeds, is in a just spirit. The other piece is his *Areopagitica*, the discourse, addressed to the Parliament, in favor of removing the censorship of the press; the most splendid of his prose works. It is, as Luther said of one of Melancthon's writings, "alive, hath

hands and feet,—and not like Erasmus's sentences, which were made, not grown." The weight of the thought is equalled by the vivacity of the expression, and it cheers as well as teaches. This tract is far the best known and the most read of all, and is still a magazine of reasons for the freedom of the press. It is valuable in history as an argument addressed to a government to produce a practical end, and plainly presupposes a very peculiar state of society.

But deeply as that peculiar state of society, in which and for which Milton wrote, has engraved itself in the remembrance of the world, it shares the destiny which overtakes everything local and personal in Nature; and the accidental facts on which a battle of principles was fought have already passed, or are fast passing, into oblivion. We have lost all interest in Milton as the redoubted disputant of a sect; but by his own innate worth this man has steadily risen in the world's reverence, and occupies a more imposing place in the mind of men at this hour than ever before.

It is the aspect which he presents to this generation, that alone concerns us. Milton the polemic has lost his popularity long ago; and if we skip the pages of *Paradise Lost* where "God the Father argues like a school divine," so did the next age to his own. But, we are persuaded, he kindles a love and emulation in us which he did not in foregoing generations. We think we have seen and heard criticism upon the poems, which the bard himself would have more valued than the recorded praise of Dryden, Addison and Johnson, because it came nearer to the mark; was finer and closer appreciation; the praise of intimate knowledge and delight; and, of course, more welcome to the poet than the general and vague acknowledgment of his genius by those able but unsympathizing critics. We think we have heard the recitation of his verses by genius which found in them that which itself would say; recitation which told, in the diamond sharpness of every articulation, that now first was such perception and enjoyment possible; the perception and enjoyment of all his varied rhythm, and his perfect fusion of the classic and the English styles. This is a poet's right; for every masterpiece of art goes on for some ages reconciling the world unto itself, and despotically fashioning the public ear. The opposition to it, always greatest at first, continually decreases and at last ends; and a new race grows up in the taste and spirit of the work, with the utmost advantage for seeing intimately its power and beauty.

But it would be great injustice to Milton to consider him as enjoying merely a critical reputation. It is the prerogative of this great man to stand at this hour foremost of all men in literary history, and so (shall we not say?) of all men, in the power *to inspire*. Virtue goes out of him into others. Leaving out of view the pretensions of our contemporaries (always an incalculable influence), we think no man can be named whose mind still acts on the cultivated intellect of England and America with an energy comparable to that of Milton. As a poet, Shakspeare undoubtedly transcends, and far surpasses him in his popularity with foreign nations; but Shakspeare is a voice merely; who and what he was that sang, that sings, we know not. Milton stands erect, commanding, still visible as a man among men, and reads the laws of the moral sentiment to the new-born race. There is something pleasing in the affection with which we can regard a man who died a hundred and sixty years ago in the other hemisphere, who, in respect to personal relations, is to us as the wind, yet by an influence purely spiritual makes us jealous for his fame as for that of a near friend. He is identified in the mind with all select and holy images, with the supreme interests of the human race. If hereby we attain any more precision, we proceed to say that we think no man in these later ages, and few men ever, possessed so great a conception of the manly character. Better than any other he has discharged the office of every great man, namely, to raise the idea of Man in the minds of his contemporaries and of posterity,—to draw after Nature a life of man, exhibiting such a composition of grace, of strength and of virtue, as poet had not described nor hero lived. Human nature in these ages is indebted to him for its best portrait. Many philosophers in England, France and Germany have formally dedicated their study to this problem; and we think it impossible to recall one in those countries who communicates the same vibration of hope, of self-reverence, of piety, of delight in beauty, which the name of Milton awakens. Lord Bacon, who has written much and with prodigious ability on this science, shrinks and falters before the absolute and uncourtly Puritan. Bacon's *Essays* are the portrait of an ambitious and profound calculator,—a great man of the vulgar sort. Of the upper world of man's being they speak few and faint words. The man of Locke is virtuous without enthusiasm, and intelligent without poetry. Addison, Pope, Hume and Johnson, students, with very unlike temper and success, of the same subject, cannot, taken together, make any pretension to the amount or the quality of Milton's inspirations. The man of Lord Chesterfield is unworthy to touch his garment's hem. Franklin's man is a frugal, inoffensive, thrifty citizen, but savors of nothing heroic. The genius of France has not, even in her best days, yet culminated in any one head— not in Rousseau, not in Pascal, not in Fénelon—into such perception of all the attributes of humanity as to entitle it to any rivalry in these lists. In Germany, the greatest writers are still too recent to institute a comparison; and yet we are tempted to say that art and not life seems to be the end of their effort. But the idea of a purer existence than any he saw around him, to be realized in the life and conversation of men, inspired every act and every writing of John Milton. He defined the object of education to be, "to fit a man to perform justly, skilfully and magnanimously all the offices, both private and public, of peace and war." He declared that "he who would aspire to write well hereafter in laudable things, ought himself to be a true poem; that is, a composition and pattern of the best and honorablest things, not presuming to sing high praises of heroic men or famous cities, unless he have in himself the experience and the practice of all that which is praiseworthy." Nor is there in literature a more noble outline of a wise external education than that which he drew up, at the age of thirty-six, in his Letter to Samuel Hartlib. The muscles, the nerves and the flesh with which this skeleton is to be filled up and covered exist in his works and must be sought there.

For the delineation of this heroic image of man, Milton enjoyed singular advantages. Perfections of body and of mind are attributed to him by his biographers, that, if the anecdotes had come down from a greater distance of time, or had not been in part furnished or corroborated by political enemies, would lead us to suspect the portraits were ideal, like the Cyrus of Xenophon, the Telemachus of Fénelon, or the popular traditions of Alfred the Great.

Handsome to a proverb, he was called the lady of his college. Aubrey says, "This harmonical and ingenuous soul dwelt in a beautiful, well-proportioned body." His manners and his carriage did him no injustice. Wood, his political opponent, relates that "his deportment was affable, his gait erect and manly, bespeaking courage and undauntedness." Aubrey adds a sharp trait, that "he pronounced the letter R very hard, a certain sign of satirical genius." He had the senses of a Greek. His eye was quick, and he was accounted an excellent master of his rapier. His ear for music was so acute that he was not only

enthusiastic in his love, but a skilful performer himself; and his voice, we are told, was delicately sweet and harmonious. He insists that music shall make a part of a generous education.

With these keen perceptions, he naturally received a love of Nature and a rare susceptibility to impressions from external beauty. In the midst of London, he seems, like the creatures of the field and the forest, to have been tuned in concord with the order of the world; for, he believed, his poetic vein only flowed from the autumnal to the vernal equinox; and in his essay on Education, he doubts whether, in the fine days of spring, any study can be accomplished by young men. "In those vernal seasons of the year, when the air is calm and pleasant, it were an injury and sullenness against Nature not to go out and see her riches and partake in her rejoicing with heaven and earth." His sensibility to impressions from beauty needs no proof from his history; it shines through every page. The form and the voice of Leonora Baroni seemed to have captivated him in Rome, and to her he addressed his Italian sonnets and Latin epigrams.

To these endowments it must be added that his address and his conversation were worthy of his fame. His house was resorted to by men of wit, and foreigners came to England, we are told, "to see the Lord Protector and Mr. Milton." In a letter to one of his foreign correspondents, Emeric Bigot, and in reply apparently to some compliment on his powers of conversation, he writes: "Many have been celebrated for their compositions, whose common conversation and intercourse have betrayed no marks of sublimity or genius. But as far as possible, I aim to show myself equal in thought and speech to what I have written, if I have written anything well."

These endowments received the benefit of a careful and happy discipline. His father's care, seconded by his own endeavor, introduced him to a profound skill in all the treasures of Latin, Greek, Hebrew and Italian tongues; and, to enlarge and enliven his elegant learning, he was sent into Italy, where he beheld the remains of ancient art, and the rival works of Raphael, Michael Angelo and Correggio; where, also, he received social and academical honors from the learned and the great. In Paris, he became acquainted with Grotius; in Florence or Rome, with Galileo; and probably no traveller ever entered that country of history with better right to its hospitality, none upon whom its influences could have fallen more congenially.

Among the advantages of his foreign travel, Milton certainly did not count it the least that it contributed to forge and polish that great weapon of which he acquired such extraordinary mastery,—his power of language. His lore of foreign tongues added daily to his consummate skill in the use of his own. He was a benefactor of the English tongue by showing its capabilities. Very early in life he became conscious that he had more to say to his fellow men than they had fit words to embody. At nineteen years, in a college exercise, he addresses his native language, saying to it that it would be his choice to leave trifles for a grave argument,—

> Such as may make thee search thy coffers round,
> Before thou clothe my fancy in fit sound;
> Such where the deep transported mind may soar
> Above the wheeling poles, and at Heaven's door
> Look in, and see each blissful deity,
> How he before the thunderous throne doth lie.

Michael Angelo calls "him alone an artist, whose hands can execute what his mind has conceived." The world, no doubt, contains many of that class of men whom Wordsworth denominates *silent poets*, whose minds teem with images which they want words to clothe. But Milton's mind seems to have no thought or emotion which refused to be recorded. His mastery of his native tongue was more than to use it as well as any other; he cast it into new forms. He uttered in it things unheard before. Not imitating but rivalling Shakspeare, he scattered, in tones of prolonged and delicate melody, his pastoral and romantic fancies; then, soaring into unattempted strains, he made it capable of an unknown majesty, and bent it to express every trait of beauty, every shade of thought; and searched the kennel and jakes as well as the palaces of sound for the harsh discords of his polemic wrath. We may even apply to his performance on the instrument of language, his own description of music:—

> Notes, with many a winding bout
> Of linkèd sweetness long drawn out,
> With wanton heed and giddy cunning,
> The melting voice through mazes running,
> Untwisting all the chains that tie
> The hidden soul of harmony.

But whilst Milton was conscious of possessing this intellectual voice, penetrating through ages and propelling its melodious undulations forward through the coming world, he knew that this mastery of language was a secondary power, and he respected the mysterious source whence it had its spring; namely, clear conceptions and a devoted heart. "For me," he said, in his *Apology for Smectymnuus,* "although I cannot say that I am utterly untrained in those rules which best rhetoricians have given, or unacquainted with those examples which the prime authors of eloquence have written in any learned tongue, yet true eloquence I find to be none but the serious and hearty love of truth; and that whose mind soever is fully possessed with a fervent desire to know good things, and with the dearest charity to infuse the knowledge of them into others, when such a man would speak, his words, by what I can express, like so many nimble and airy servitors, trip about him at command, and in well-ordered files, as he would wish, fall aptly into their own places."

But as basis or fountain of his rare physical and intellectual accomplishments, the man Milton was just and devout. He is rightly dear to mankind, because in him, among so many perverse and partial men of genius,—in him humanity rights itself; the old eternal goodness finds a home in his breast, and for once shows itself beautiful. His gifts are subordinated to his moral sentiments; and his virtues are so graceful that they seem rather talents than labors. Among so many contrivances as the world has seen to make holiness ugly, in Milton at least it was so pure a flame that the foremost impression his character makes is that of elegance. The victories of the conscience in him are gained by the commanding charm which all the severe and restrictive virtues have for him. His virtues remind us of what Plutarch said of Timoleon's victories, that they resembled Homer's verses, they ran so easy and natural. His habits of living were austere. He was abstemious in diet, chaste, an early riser, and industrious. He tell us, in a Latin poem, that the lyrist may indulge in wine and in a freer life; but that he who would write an epic to the nations must eat beans and drink water. Yet in his severity is no grimace or effort. He serves from love, not from fear. He is innocent and exact, because his taste was so pure and delicate. He acknowledges to his friend Diodati, at the age of twenty one, that he is enamoured, if ever any was, of moral perfection: "For whatever the Deity may have bestowed upon me in other respects, he has certainly inspired me, if any ever were inspired, with a passion for the good and fair. Nor did Ceres, according to the fable, ever seek

her daughter Proserpine with such unceasing solicitude as I have sought this *tou kalou idean,* this perfect model of the beautiful in all forms and appearances of things."

When he was charged with loose habits of living, he declares that "a certain niceness of nature, an honest haughtiness and self-esteem either of what I was or what I might be, and a modesty, kept me still above those low descents of mind beneath which he must deject and plunge himself that can agree" to such degradation. "His mind gave him," he said, "that every free and gentle spirit, without that oath of chastity, ought to be born a knight; nor needed to expect the gilt spur, or the laying of a sword upon his shoulder, to stir him up, by his counsel and his arm, to secure and protect" attempted innocence.

He states these things, he says, "to show that though Christianity had been but slightly taught him, yet a certain reservedness of natural disposition and moral discipline, learned out of the noblest philosophy, was enough to keep him in disdain of far less incontinences than these" that had been charged on him. In like spirit, he replies to the suspicious calumny respecting his morning haunts. "Those morning haunts are where they should be, at home; not sleeping, or concocting the surfeits of an irregular feast, but up and stirring, in winter, often ere the sound of any bell awake men to labor or devotion; in summer, as oft with the bird that first rouses, or not much tardier, to read good authors, or cause them to be read, till the attention be weary, or memory have its perfect fraught; then with useful and generous labors preserving the body's health and hardiness, to render lightsome, clear and not lumpish obedience to the mind, to the cause of religion and our country's liberty, when it shall require firm hearts in sound bodies to stand and cover their stations. These are the morning practices." This native honor never forsook him. It is the spirit of *Comus,* the loftiest song in the praise of chastity that is in any language. It always sparkles in his eyes. It breathed itself over his decent form. It refined his amusements, which consisted in gardening, in exercise with the sword and in playing on the organ. It engaged his interest in chivalry, in courtesy, in whatsoever savored of generosity and nobleness. This magnanimity shines in all his life. He accepts a high impulse at every risk, and deliberately undertakes the defence of the English people, when advised by his physicians that he does it at the cost of sight. There is a forbearance even in his polemics. He opens the war and strikes the first blow. When he had cut down his opponents, he left the details of death and plunder to meaner partisans. He said, "he had learned the prudence of the Roman soldier, not to stand breaking of legs, when the breath was quite out of the body."

To this antique heroism, Milton added the genius of the Christian sanctity. Few men could be cited who have so well understood what is peculiar in the Christian ethics, and the precise aid it has brought to men, in being an emphatic affirmation of the omnipotence of spiritual laws, and, by way of marking the contrast to vulgar opinions, laying its chief stress on humility. The indifferency of a wise mind to what is called high and low, and the fact that true greatness is a perfect humility, are revelations of Christianity which Milton well understood. They give an inexhaustible truth to all his compositions. His firm grasp of this truth is his weapon against the prelates. He celebrates in the martyrs "the unresistible might of weakness." He told the bishops that "instead of showing the reason of their lowly condition from divine example and command, they seek to prove their high preëminence from human consent and authority." He advises that in country places, rather than to trudge many miles to a church, public worship be maintained nearer home, as in a house or barn. "For notwithstanding the gaudy superstition of some still devoted ignorantly to temples, we may be well assured that he who disdained not to be born in a manger disdains not to be preached in a barn." And the following passage, in the *Reason of Church Government*, indicates his own perception of the doctrine of humility. "Albeit I must confess to be half in doubt whether I should bring it forth or no, it being so contrary to the eye of the world, that I shall endanger either not to be regarded, or not to be understood. For who is there, almost, that measures wisdom by simplicity, strength by suffering, dignity by lowliness?" Obeying this sentiment, Milton deserved the apostrophe of Wordsworth:—

> Pure as the naked heavens, majestic, free,
> So didst thou travel on life's common way
> In cheerful godliness; and yet thy heart
> The lowliest duties on itself did lay.

He laid on himself the lowliest duties. Johnson petulantly taunts Milton with "great promise and small performance," in returning from Italy because his country was in danger, and then opening a private school. Milton, wiser, felt no absurdity in this conduct. He returned into his revolutionized country, and assumed an honest and useful task, by which he might serve the state daily, whilst he launched from time to time his formidable bolts against the enemies of liberty. He felt the heats of that "love" which "esteems no office mean." He compiled a logic for boys; he wrote a grammar; and devoted much of his time to the preparing of a Latin dictionary. But the religious sentiment warmed his writings and conduct with the highest affection of faith. The memorable covenant, which in his youth, in the second book of the *Reason of Church Government*, he makes with God and his reader, expressed the faith of his old age. For the first time since many ages, the invocations of the Eternal Spirit in the commencement of his books are not poetic forms, but are thoughts, and so are still read with delight. His views of choice of profession, and choice in marriage, equally expect a divine leading.

Thus chosen, by the felicity of his nature and his breeding, for the clear perception of all that is graceful and all that is great in man, Milton was not less happy in his times. His birth fell upon the agitated years when the discontents of the English Puritans were fast drawing to a head against the tyranny of the Stuarts. No period has surpassed that in the general activity of mind. It is said that no opinion, no civil, religious, moral dogma can be produced that was not broached in the fertile brain of that age. Questions that involve all social and personal rights were hasting to be decided by the sword, and were searched by eyes to which the love of freedom, civil and religious, lent new illumination. Milton, gentle, learned, delicately bred in all the elegancy of art and learning, was set down in England in the stern, almost fanatic society of the Puritans. The part he took, the zeal of his fellowship, make us acquainted with the greatness of his spirit as in tranquil times we could not have known it. Susceptible as Burke to the attractions of historical prescription, of royalty, of chivalry, of an ancient church illustrated by old martyrdoms and installed in cathedrals,—he threw himself, the flower of elegancy, on the side of the reeking conventicle; the side of humanity, but unlearned and unadorned. His muse was brave and humane, as well as sweet. He felt the dear love of native land and native language. The humanity which warms his pages begins, as it should, at home. He preferred his own English, so manlike he was, to the Latin, which contained all the treasures of his memory. "My mother bore me," he said, "a speaker of what God made mine own, and not a translator." He told the Parliament that "the imprimaturs of Lambeth House had been writ in Latin; for that

our English, the language of men ever famous and foremost in the achievements of liberty, will not easily find servile letters enow to spell such a dictatory presumption." At one time he meditated writing a poem on the settlement of Britain, and a history of England was one of the three main tasks which he proposed to himself. He proceeded in it no further than to the Conquest. He studied with care the character of his countrymen, and once in the *History*, and once again in the *Reason of Church Government*, he has recorded his judgment of the English genius.

Thus drawn into the great controversies of the times, in them he is never lost in a party. His private opinions and private conscience always distinguish him. That which drew him to the party was his love of liberty, ideal liberty; this therefore he could not sacrifice to any party. Toland tells us, "As he looked upon true and absolute freedom to be the greatest happiness of this life, whether to societies or single persons, so he thought constraint of any sort to be the utmost misery; for which reason he used to tell those about him the entire satisfaction of his mind that he had constantly employed his strength and faculties in the defence of liberty, and in direct opposition to slavery." Truly he was an apostle of freedom; of freedom in the house, in the state, in the church; freedom of speech, freedom of the press; yet in his own mind discriminated from savage license, because that which he desired was the liberty of the wise man, containing itself in the limits of virtue. He pushed, as far as any in that democratic age, his ideas of *civil* liberty. He proposed to establish a republic, of which the federal power was weak and loosely defined, and the substantial power should remain with primary assemblies. He maintained that a nation may try, judge and slay their king, if he be a tyrant. He pushed as far his views of *ecclesiastical* liberty. He taught the doctrine of unlimited toleration. One of his tracts is writ to prove that no power on earth can compel in matters of religion. He maintained the doctrine of *literary* liberty, denouncing the censorship of the press, and insisting that a book shall come into the world as freely as a man, so only it bear the name of author or printer, and be responsible for itself like a man. He maintained the doctrine of *domestic* liberty, or the liberty of divorce, on the ground that unfit disposition of mind was a better reason for the act of divorce than infirmity of body, which was good ground in law. The tracts he wrote on these topics are, for the most part, as fresh and pertinent to-day as they were then. The events which produced them, the practical issues to which they tend, are mere occasions for this philanthropist to blow his trumpet for human rights. They are all varied applications of one principle, the liberty of the wise man. He sought absolute truth, not accommodating truth. His opinions on all subjects are formed for man as he ought to be, for a nation of Miltons. He would be divorced when he finds in his consort unfit disposition; knowing that he should not abuse that liberty, because with his whole heart he abhors licentiousness and loves chastity. He defends the slaying of the king, because a king is a king no longer than he governs by the laws; "it would be right to kill Philip of Spain making an inroad into England, and what right the king of Spain hath to govern us at all, the same hath the king Charles to govern tyrannically." He would remove hirelings out of the church, and support preachers by voluntary contributions; requiring that such only should preach as have faith enough to accept so self-denying and precarious a mode of life, scorning to take thought for the aspects of prudence and expediency. The most devout man of his time, he frequented no church; probably from a disgust at the fierce spirit of the pulpits. And so, throughout all his actions and opinions, is he a consistent spiritualist, or believer in the omnipotence of spiritual laws. He wished that his writings should be communicated only to those who desired to see them. He thought nothing honest was low. He thought he could be famous only in proportion as he enjoyed the approbation of the good. He admonished his friend "not to admire military prowess, or things in which force is of most avail. For it would not be matter of rational wonder, if the wethers of our country should be born with horns that could batter down cities and towns. Learn to estimate great characters, not by the amount of animal strength, but by the habitual justice and temperance of their conduct."

Was there not a fitness in the undertaking of such a person to write a poem on the subject of Adam, the first man? By his sympathy with all Nature; by the proportion of his powers; by great knowledge, and by religion, he would reascend to the height from which our nature is supposed to have descended. From a just knowledge of what man should be, he described what he was. He beholds him as he walked in Eden:—

> His fair large front and eye sublime declared
> Absolute rule; and hyacinthine locks
> Round from his parted forelock manly hung
> Clustering, but not beneath his shoulders broad.

And the soul of this divine creature is excellent as his form. The tone of his thought and passion is as healthful, as even and as vigorous as befits the new and perfect model of a race of gods.

The perception we have attributed to Milton, of a purer ideal of humanity, modifies his poetic genius. The man is paramount to the poet. His fancy is never transcendent, extravagant; but as Bacon's imagination was said to be "the noblest that ever contented itself to minister to the understanding," so Milton's ministers to the character. Milton's sublimest song, bursting into heaven with its peals of melodious thunder, is the voice of Milton still. Indeed, throughout his poems, one may see, under a thin veil, the opinions, the feelings, even the incidents of the poet's life, still reappearing. The sonnets are all occasional poems. "L'Allegro" and "Il Penseroso" are but a finer autobiography of his youthful fancies at Harefield; the *Comus* a transcript, in charming numbers, of that philosophy of chastity, which, in the *Apology for Smectymnuus*, and in the *Reason of Church Government*, he declares to be his defence and religion. The *Samson Agonistes* is too broad an expression of his private griefs to be mistaken, and is a version of the *Doctrine and Discipline of Divorce*. The most affecting passages in *Paradise Lost* are personal allusions; and when we are fairly in Eden, Adam and Milton are often difficult to be separated. Again, in *Paradise Regained*, we have the most distinct marks of the progress of the poet's mind, in the revision and enlargement of his religious opinions. This may be thought to abridge his praise as a poet. It is true of Homer and Shakspeare that they do not appear in their poems; that those prodigious geniuses did cast themselves so totally into their song that their individuality vanishes, and the poet towers to the sky, whilst the man quite disappears. The fact is memorable. Shall we say that in our admiration and joy in these wonderful poems we have even a feeling of regret that the men knew not what they did; that they were too passive in their great service; were channels through which streams of thought flowed from a higher source, which they did not appropriate, did not blend with their own being? Like prophets, they seem but imperfectly aware of the import of their own utterances. We hesitate to say such things, and say them only to the unpleasing dualism, when the man and the poet show like a double consciousness. Perhaps we speak to no fact, but to mere fables, of an idle mendicant Homer, and of a Shakspeare content with a mean and jocular way of life. Be it how it may, the genius and office of Milton

were different, namely, to ascend by the aids of his learning and his religion—by an equal perception, that is, of the past and the future—to a higher insight and more lively delineation of the heroic life of man. This was his poem; wherof all his indignant pamphlets and all his soaring verses are only single cantos or detached stanzas. It was plainly needful that his poetry should be a version of his own life, in order to give weight and solemnity to his thoughts; by which they might penetrate and possess the imagination and the will of mankind. The creations of Shakspeare are cast into the world of thought to no further end than to delight. Their intrinsic beauty is their excuse for being. Milton, fired "with dearest charity to infuse the knowledge of good things into others," tasked his giant imagination and exhausted the stores of his intellect for an end beyond, namely, to teach. His own conviction it is which gives such authority to his strain. Its reality is its force. If out of the heart it came, to the heart it must go. What schools and epochs of common rhymers would it need to make a counterbalance to the severe oracles of his muse:—

> In them is plainest taught and easiest learnt,
> What makes a nation happy, and keeps it so.

The lover of Milton reads one sense in his prose and in his metrical compositions; and sometimes the muse soars highest in the former, because the thought is more sincere. Of his prose in general, not the style alone but the argument also is poetic; according to Lord Bacon's definition of poetry, following that of Aristotle, "Poetry, not finding the actual world exactly conformed to its idea of good and fair, seeks to accommodate the shows of things to the desires of the mind, and to create an ideal world better than the world of experience." Such certainly is the explanation of Milton's tracts. Such is the apology to be entered for the plea for freedom of divorce; an essay, which, from the first, until now, has brought a degree of obloquy on his name. It was a sally of the extravagant spirit of the time, overjoyed, as in the French Revolution, with the sudden victories it had gained, and eager to carry on the standard of truth to new heights. It is to be regarded as a poem on one of the griefs of man's condition, namely, unfit marriage. And as many poems have been written upon unfit society, commending solitude, yet have not been proceeded against, though their end was hostile to the state; so should this receive that charity which an angelic soul, suffering more keenly than others from the unavoidable evils of human life, is entitled to.

We have offered no apology for expanding to such length our commentary on the character of John Milton; who, in old age, in solitude, in neglect, and blind, wrote the *Paradise Lost*; a man whom labor or danger never deterred from whatever efforts a love of the supreme interests of man prompted. For are we not the better; are not all men fortified by the remembrance of the bravery, the purity, the temperance, the toil, the independence and the angelic devotion of this man, who, in a revolutionary age, taking counsel only of himself, endeavored, in his writings and in his life, to carry out the life of man to new heights of spiritual grace and dignity, without any abatement of its strength?

THOMAS DE QUINCEY
From "On Milton" (1839)
Collected Writings, ed. Masson
Volume 10, 1890, pp. 398–406

Who and what *is* Milton? Dr. Johnson was furiously incensed with a certain man, by trade an author and manufacturer of books, wholesale and retail, for introducing Milton's name into a certain index under the letter M thus—"Milton, Mr. John." That *Mister*, undoubtedly, was hard to digest. Yet very often it happens to the best of us—to men who are far enough from "thinking small beer of themselves"—that about ten o'clock A.M. an official big-wig, sitting at Bow Street, calls upon the man to account for his *sprees* of the last night, for his feats in knocking down lamp-posts, and extinguishing watchmen, by this ugly demand of—"Who and what are you, sir?" And perhaps the poor man, sick and penitential for want of soda-water, really finds a considerable difficulty in replying satisfactorily to the worthy *beak's* apostrophe, although, at five o'clock in the evening, should the culprit be returning into the country in the same coach as his awful interrogator, he might be very apt to look fierce and retort this amiable inquiry, and with equal thirst for knowledge to demand, "Now, sir, if you come to *that*, who and what are *you*?" And the *beak* in *his* turn, though so apt to indulge his own curiosity at the expense of the public, might find it very difficult to satisfy that of others.

The same thing happens to authors; and to great authors beyond all others. So accustomed are we to survey a great man through the cloud of years that has gathered round him—so impossible is it to detach him from the pomp and equipage of all who have quoted him, copied him, echoed him, lectured about him, disputed about him, quarrelled about him, that in the case of any Anacharsis the Scythian coming amongst us—any savage, that is to say, uninstructed in our literature, but speaking our language, and feeling an intelligent interest in our great men—a man could hardly believe at first how perplexed he would feel, how utterly at a loss for any *adequate* answer to this question, suddenly proposed—"*Who and what was Milton?*" That is to say, what is the place which he fills in his own vernacular literature? what station does he hold in universal literature?

I, if abruptly called upon in that summary fashion to convey a *commensurate* idea of Milton, one which might at once correspond to his pretensions, and yet be readily intelligible to the savage, should answer perhaps thus:—Milton is not an author amongst authors, not a poet amongst poets, but a power amongst powers; and the *Paradise Lost* is not a book amongst books, not a poem amongst poems, but a central force amongst forces. Let me explain:—There is this great distinction amongst books: some, though possibly the best in their class, are still no more than books—not indispensable, not incapable of supplementary representation by other books. If they had never been, if their place had continued for ages unfilled, not the less, upon a sufficient excitement arising, there would always have been found the ability either directly to fill up the vacancy, or at least to meet the same passion virtually, though by a work differing in form. Thus, supposing Butler to have died in youth, and the *Hudibras* to have been intercepted by his premature death, still the ludicrous aspects of the Parliamentary War and its fighting saints were too striking to have perished. If not in a narrative form, the case would have come forward in the drama. Puritanical sanctity, in collision with the ordinary interests of life and with its militant propensities, offered too striking a field for the Satiric Muse, in any case, to have passed in total neglect. The impulse was too strong for repression—it was a volcanic agency, that, by some opening or other, must have worked a way for itself to the upper air. Yet Butler was a most original poet, and a creator within his own province. But, like many another original mind, there is little doubt that he quelled and repressed, by his own excellence, other minds of the same cast. Mere despair of excelling

him, so far as not, after all, to seem imitators, drove back others who would have pressed into that arena, if not already brilliantly filled. Butler failing, there would have been another Butler, either in the same, or in some analogous form.

But with regard to Milton and the Miltonic power the case is far otherwise. If the man had failed, the power would have failed. In that mode of power which he wielded the function was exhausted in the man, the species was identified with the individual, the poetry was incarnated in the poet.

Let it be remembered that, of all powers which act upon man through his intellectual nature, the very rarest is that which we moderns call the *sublime*. The Grecians had apparently no word for it, unless it were that which they mean by *to semnon*: for *hypsos* was a comprehensive expression for all qualities which gave a character of life or animation to the composition,—such even as were philosophically opposed to the sublime. In the Roman poetry, and especially in Lucan, at times also in Juvenal, there is an exhibition of a moral sublime, perfectly distinct from anything known to the Greek poetry. The delineations of republican grandeur, as expressing itself through the principal leaders in the Roman camps, or the trampling under foot of ordinary superstitions, as given in the reasons assigned to Labienus for passing the oracle of the Libyan Jupiter unconsulted, are in a style to which there is nothing corresponding in the whole Grecian literature; nor would they have been comprehensible to an Athenian. The famous line "Jupiter est quodcunque vides, quocunque moveris," and the brief review of such questions as might be worthy of an oracular god, with the summary declaration that every one of those points we know already by the light of nature, and could not know them better though Jupiter Ammon himself were to impress them on our attention—

> Scimus, et hæc nobis non altius inseret
> Ammon:
> We know it, and no Ammon will ever sink it deeper
> into our hearts:

all this is truly Roman in its sublimity, and so exclusively Roman that there, and not in poets like the Augustan, expressly modelling their poems on Grecian types, ought the Roman mind to be studied.

On the other hand, for that species of the sublime which does not rest purely and merely on moral energies, but on a synthesis between man and nature—for what may properly be called the ethico-physical sublime—there is but one great model surviving in the Greek poetry: viz. the gigantic drama of the Prometheus crucified on Mount Elborus. And this drama differs so much from everything else even in the poetry of Æschylus,—as the mythus itself differs so much from all the rest of the Grecian mythology (belonging apparently to an age and a people more gloomy, austere, and nearer to the *incunabula mundi* than those which bred the gay and sunny superstitions of Greece),—that much curiosity and speculation have naturally gathered round the subject of late years. Laying this one insulted case apart, and considering that the Hebrew poetry of Isaiah and Ezekiel, as having the benefit of inspiration, does not lie within the just limits of competition, we may affirm that there is no human composition which can be challenged as constitutionally sublime,—sublime equally by its conception and by its execution, or as uniformly sublime from first to last,—excepting the *Paradise Lost*. In Milton only, first and last, is the power of the sublime revealed. In Milton only does this great agency blaze and glow as a furnace kept up to a white heat, without suspicion of collapse.

If, therefore, Milton occupies this unique position—and

let the reader question himself closely whether he can cite any other book than the *Paradise Lost* as continuously sublime, or sublime even by its prevailing character—in that case there is a peculiarity of importance investing that one book which belongs to no other; and it must be important to dissipate any erroneous notions which affect the integrity of that book's estimation. Now, there are two notions, countenanced by Addison and by Dr. Johnson, which tend greatly to disparage the character of its composition. If the two critics, one friendly, the other very malignant, but both endeavouring to be just, have in reality built upon sound principles, or at least upon a sound appreciation of Milton's principles, in that case there is a mortal taint diffused over the whole of the *Paradise Lost*: for not a single book is clear of one or other of the two errors which they charge upon him. We will briefly state the objections, and then as briefly reply to them, by exposing the true philosophy of Milton's practice. For we are very sure that, in doing as he did, this mighty poet was governed by no carelessness or oversight (as is imagined), far less by affectation or ostentation, but by a most refined theory of poetic effects.

1. The first of these two charges respects a supposed pedantry, or too ambitious a display of erudition. It is surprising to us that such an objection should have occurred to any man: both because, after all, the quantity of learning cannot be great for which any poem can find an opening; and because, in any poem burning with concentrated fire, like the Miltonic, the passion becomes a law to itself, and will not receive into connexion with itself any parts so deficient in harmony as a cold ostentation of learned illustrations must always have been found. Still, it is alleged that such words as *frieze, architrave, cornice, zenith, &c.*, arc words of art, out of place amongst the primitive simplicities of Paradise, and at war with Milton's purpose of exhibiting the paradisaical state.

Now, here is displayed broadly the very perfection of ignorance, as measured against the very perfection of what may be called poetic science. We will lay open the true purpose of Milton by a single illustration. In describing impressive scenery as occurring in a hilly or a woody country, everybody must have noticed the habit which young ladies have of using the word *amphitheatre*: "amphitheatre of woods," "amphitheatre of hills"—these are their constant expression. Why? Is it because the word *amphitheatre* is a Grecian word? We question if one young lady in twenty knows that it is; and very certain we are that no word would recommend itself to her use by that origin, if she happened to be aware of it. The reason lurks here:—In the word *theatre* is contained an evanescent image of a great audience, of a populous multitude. Now, this image—half-withdrawn, half-flashed upon the eye, and combined with the word *hills* or *forests*—is thrown into powerful collision with the silence of hills, with the solitude of forests; each image, from reciprocal contradiction, brightens and vivifies the other. The two images act, and react, by strong repulsion and antagonism.

This principle I might exemplify and explain at great length; but I impose a law of severe brevity upon myself. And I have said enough. Out of this one principle of subtle and lurking antagonism may be explained everything which has been denounced under the idea of pedantry in Milton. It is the key to all that lavish pomp of art and knowledge which is sometimes put forward by Milton in situations of intense solitude, and in the bosom of primitive nature—as, for example, in the Eden of his great poem, and in the Wilderness of his *Paradise Regained*. The shadowy exhibition of a regal banquet in the desert draws out and stimulates the sense of its utter solitude and remotion from men or cities. The images of archi-

tectural splendour suddenly raised in the very centre of Paradise, as vanishing shows by the wand of a magician, bring into powerful relief the depth of silence and the unpopulous solitude which possess this sanctuary of man whilst yet happy and innocent Paradise could not in any other way, or by any artifice less profound, have been made to give up its essential and differential characteristics in a form palpable to the imagination. As a place of rest, it was necessary that it should be placed in close collision with the unresting strife of cities; as a place of solitude, with the image of tumultuous crowds; as the centre of mere natural beauty in its gorgeous prime, with the images of elaborate architecture and of human workmanship; as a place of perfect innocence in seclusion, that it should be exhibited as the antagonist pole to the sin and misery of social man.

Such is the covert philosophy which governs Milton's practice, and which might be illustrated by many scores of passages from both the *Paradise Lost* and the *Paradise Regained*.[1] In fact, a volume might be composed on this one chapter. And yet, from the blindness or inconsiderate examination of his critics, this latent wisdom, this cryptical science of poetic effects, in the mighty poet has been misinterpreted, and set down to the effect of defective skill, or even of puerile ostentation.

2. The second great charge against Milton is, *prima facie*, even more difficult to meet. It is the charge of having blended the Pagan and Christian forms. The great realities of Angels and Archangels are continually combined into the same groups with the fabulous impersonations of the Greek Mythology. Eve is interlinked in comparisons with Pandora, with Aurora, with Proserpine. Those impersonations, however, may be thought to have something of allegoric meaning in their conceptions which in a measure corrects this paganism of the idea. But Eve is also compared with Ceres, with Hebe, and other fixed forms of pagan superstition. Other allusions to the Greek mythologic forms, or direct combination of them with the real existences of the Christian heavens, might be produced by scores, were it not that we decline to swell our paper beyond the necessity of the case. Now, surely this at least is an error. Can there be any answer to this?

At one time we were ourselves inclined to fear that Milton had been here caught tripping. In this instance, at least, he seems to be in error. But there is no trusting to appearances. In meditating upon the question, we happened to remember that the most colossal and Miltonic of painters had fallen into the very same fault, if fault it were. In his *Last Judgment* Michael Angelo has introduced the pagan deities in connexion with the hierarchy of the Christian Heavens. Now, it is very true that one great man cannot palliate the error of another great man by repeating the same error himself. But, though it cannot avail as an excuse, such a conformity of ideas serves as a summons to a much more vigilant examination of the case than might else be instituted. One man might err from inadvertency; but that two, and both men trained to habits of constant meditation, should fall into the same error, makes the marvel tenfold greater.

Now we confess that, as to Michael Angelo, we do not pretend to assign the precise key to the practice which he adopted. And to our feelings, after all that might be said in apology, there still remains an impression of incongruity in the visual exhibition and direct juxtaposition of the two orders of supernatural existence so potently repelling each other. But, as regards Milton, the justification is complete. It rests upon the following principle:—

In all other parts of Christianity the two orders of superior beings, the Christian Heaven and the Pagan Pantheon, are felt to be incongruous—not as the pure opposed to the impure (for, if that were the reason, then the Christian fiends should be incongruous with the angels, which they are not), but as the unreal opposed to the real. In all the hands of other poets we feel that Jupiter, Mercury, Apollo, Diana, are not merely impure conceptions, but that they are baseless conceptions, phantoms of air, nonentities; there is much the same objection, in point of just taste, to the combination of such fabulous beings in the same groups with glorified saints and angels as there is to the combination by a painter or a sculptor of real flesh-and-blood creatures with allegoric abstractions.

This is the objection to such combination in all other poets. But this objection does not apply to Milton; it glances past him, and for the following reason:—Milton has himself laid an early foundation for his introduction of the Pagan Pantheon into Christian groups: *the false gods of the heathen world were, according to Milton, the fallen Angels.* See his inimitable account of the fallen angels—who and what they subsequently became. In itself, and even if detached from the rest of the *Paradise Lost*, this catalogue is an *ultra*-magnificent poem. They are not false, therefore, in the sense of being unreal, baseless, and having a merely fantastical existence, like our European Fairies, but as having drawn aside mankind from a pure worship. As ruined angels under other names, they are no less real than the faithful and loyal angels of the Christian heavens. And in that one difference of the Miltonic creed, which the poet has brought pointedly and elaborately under his reader's notice by his matchless roll-call of the rebellious angels, and of *their pagan transformations*, in the very first book of the *Paradise Lost*, is laid beforehand[2] the amplest foundation for his subsequent practice, and at the same time, therefore, the amplest answer to the charge preferred against him by Dr. Johnson, and by so many other critics, who had not sufficiently penetrated the latent theory on which he acted.

Notes

1. For instance, this is the key to that image in the *Paradise Regained* where Satan, on first emerging into sight, is compared to an old man gathering sticks, "to warm him on a winter's day." This image, at first sight, seems little in harmony with the wild and awful character of the supreme fiend. No; it is *not in* harmony, nor is it meant to be in harmony. On the contrary, it is meant to be in antagonism and intense repulsion. The household image of old age, of human infirmity, and of domestic hearths, are all meant as a machinery for provoking and soliciting the fearful idea to which they are placed in collision, and as so many repelling poles.

2. Other celebrated poets have laid no such preparatory foundations for their intermixture of heathen gods with the heavenly host of the Christian revelation; for example, amongst thousands of others, Tasso, and still more flagrantly Camoens, who is not content with allusions or references that suppose the Pagan Mythology still substantially existing, but absolutely introduces them as potent agencies amongst superstitious and bigoted worshippers of papal saints. Consequently, they, beyond all apology, are open to the censure which for Milton is subtly evaded.

DAVID MASSON

From "The Three Devils:
Luther's, Milton's, and Goethe's" (1844)
The Three Devils
1874, pp. 9–32

The difficulties which Milton had to overcome in writing his *Paradise Lost* were immense. The gist of those difficulties may be defined as consisting in this, that the poet had at once to represent a supernatural condition of being and to construct a story. He had to describe the ongoings of Angels, and at the same time to make one event follow another. It is comparatively easy for Milton to sustain his conception of those superhuman beings as mere objects or phenomena—to represent them flying singly through space like huge black shadows, or standing opposite to each other in hostile battalions; but to construct a story in which these beings should be the agents, to exhibit these beings thinking, scheming, blundering, in such a way as to produce a likely succession of events, was enormously difficult. The difficulty was to make the course of events correspond with the reputation of the objects. To do this perfectly was literally impossible. It is possible for the human mind to conceive twenty-four great supernatural beings existing together at any given moment in space; but it is utterly impossible to conceive what would occur among those twenty-four beings during twenty-four hours. The value of time, the amount of history that can be transacted in a given period, depends on the nature and prowess of the beings whose volitions make the chain of events; and so a lower order of beings can have no idea at what rate things happen in a higher. The mode of causation will be different from that with which they are acquainted.

This is the difficulty with which Milton had to struggle; or, rather, this is the difficulty with which he did not struggle. He had to construct a narrative; and so, while he represents to us the full stature of his superhuman beings as mere objects or phenomena, he does not attempt to make events follow each other at a higher rate among those beings than they do amongst ourselves, except in the single respect of their being infinitely more powerful physical agents than we are. Whatever feeling of inconsistency is experienced in reading the *Paradise Lost* may be traced, perhaps, to the fact that the necessities of the story obliged the poet not to attempt to make the rate of causation among those beings as extraordinary as his description of them as phenomena. Such a feeling of inconsistency there is; and yet Milton sustains his flight as nobly as mortal could have done. Throughout the whole poem we see him recollecting his original conception of Satan as an object:

> Thus Satan, talking to his nearest mate,
> With head uplift above the waves, and eyes
> That sparkling blazed; his other parts besides,
> Prone on the flood, extended long and large,
> Lay floating many a rood.

And this is a great thing to have done. If the poet ever flags in his conception of those superhuman beings as objects, it is when he finds it necessary to describe a multitude of them assembled together in some *place*; and his usual device then is to reduce the bulk of the greatest number. This, too, is for the behoof of the story. If it is necessary, for instance, to assemble the Angels to deliberate, this must be done in an audience-hall, and the human mind refuses to go beyond certain limits in its conception of what an audience-hall is. Again the gate of Hell is described, although the Hell of Milton is a mere vague extent of fiery element, which, in strict keeping, could not be described as having a gate. The narrative, however, requires the conception. And so in other cases. Still, consistency of description is well sustained.

Nor is it merely as objects or phenomena that Milton sustains throughout his whole poem a consistent conception of the Angels. He is likewise consistent in his description of them as physical agents. Lofty stature and appearance carry with them a promise of so much physical power; and hence, in Milton's case, the necessity of finding words and figures capable of expressing modes and powers of mechanical action, on the part of the Angels, as superhuman as the stature and appearance he has given to them. This complicated his difficulties very much. It is quite conceivable that a man should be able to describe the mere appearance of a gigantic being standing up, as it were, with his back to a wall, and yet utterly break down, and not be able to find words, when he tried to describe this gigantic being stepping forth into colossal activity and doing some characteristic thing. Milton has overcome the difficulty. His conception of the Angels as physical agents does not fall beneath his conception of them as mere objects. In his description, for instance, in the sixth book, of the Angels tearing up mountains by the roots and flinging them upon each other, we have strength suggested corresponding to the reputed stature of the beings. In extension of the same remark, we may observe how skilfully Milton has aggrandized and eked out his conception of the superhuman beings he is describing by endowing them with the power of infinitely swift motion through space. On this point we offer our readers an observation which they may verify for themselves:—Milton, we are persuaded, had it vaguely in his mind, throughout *Paradise Lost*, that the bounding peculiarity between the human condition of being and the angelic one he is describing is the law of gravitation. We, and all that is cognisable by us, are subject to this law; but Creation may be peopled with beings who are not subject to it, and to us these beings are as if they were not. But, whenever one of those beings becomes cognisable by us, he instantly becomes subject to gravitation; and he must resume his own mode of being ere he can be free from its consequences. The Angels were not subject to gravitation; that is to say, they had the means of moving in any direction at will. When they rebelled, and were punished by expulsion from Heaven, they did not *fall* out; for, in fact, so far as the description intimates, there existed no planet, no distinct material element, towards which they could gravitate. They were *driven* out by a pursuing fire. Then, after their fall, they had the power of rising upward, of navigating space, of quitting Hell, directing their flight to one glittering planet, alighting on its rotund surface, and then bounding off again, and away to another. A corollary of this fundamental difference between the human condition of being and the angelic would be that angels are capable of direct vertical action, whereas men are capable mainly of horizontal. An army of men can exist only as a square, or other plane figure, whereas an army of angels can exist as a cube or parallelopiped.

Now, in everything relating to the physical action of the Angels, even in carrying out this notion of their mode of being, Milton is most consistent. But it was impossible to follow out the superiority of these beings to its whole length. The attempt to do so would have made a narrative impossible. Exalting our conception of these beings as mere objects, or as mere physical agents, as much as he could, it would have been suicidal in the poet to attempt to realize history as it must be among such beings. No human mind could do it. He had, therefore, except where the notion of physical superiority assisted him, to make events follow each other just as they would in a human narrative. The motives, the reasonings, the misconceptions of those beings, all that determined the succession of events, he had to make substantially human. The whole narrative, for instance, proceeds on the supposition that those supernatural beings had no higher degree of knowledge than human beings, with equal physical advantages, would have had under similar circumstances. Credit the spirits with a greater degree of insight—credit them even with such a strong conviction of the Divine omnipotence as, in their reputed condition of being, we can hardly conceive them not attaining—and the whole of Milton's story is rendered impossible. The crushing conviction of the Divine omnipotence would have prevented them from rebelling with the alleged motive; or, after they had rebelled, it would have prevented them from struggling with the alleged hope. In *Paradise Lost* the working notion which the devils have about God is exactly that which human beings have when they hope to succeed in a bad enterprise. Otherwise the poem could not have been written. Suppose the fallen Angels to have had a working notion of the Deity as superhuman as their reputed appearance and physical greatness: then the events of the *Paradise Lost* might have happened nevertheless, but the chain of volitions would not have been the same, and it would have been impossible for any human poet to realize the narrative.

These remarks are necessary to prepare us for conceiving the Satan of Milton. Except, as we have said, for an occasional feeling during a perusal of the poem that the style of thinking and speculating about the issue of their enterprise is too meagre and human for a race of beings physically so superhuman, one's astonishment at the consistency of the poet's conceptions is unmitigated throughout. Such keeping is there between one conception and another, such a distinct material grasp had the poet of his whole subject, so little is there of the mystic or the hazy in his descriptions from beginning to end, that it would be quite possible to prefix to the *Paradise Lost* an illustrative diagram exhibiting the universal space in which Milton conceived his beings moving to and fro, divided, as he conceived it, at first into two or three, and afterwards into four tropics or regions. Then his narrative is so clear that a brief prose version of it would be a history of Satan in the interval between his own fall and the fall of Man.

It is to be noted that Milton as a poet proceeds on the Homeric method, and not on the Shakespearian, devoting the whole strength of his genius to the object, not of being discursive and original, not of making profound remarks on everything as he goes along, but of carrying on a sublime and stately narrative. We should hardly be led to assert, however, that the difference between the epic and the drama lies in this, that the latter may be discursive and reflective while the former cannot. We can conceive an epic written after the Shakespearian method; that is, one which, while strictly sustaining a narrative, should be profoundly expository in its spirit. Certain it is, however, that Milton wrote after the Homeric method, and did not exert himself chiefly in strewing his text with luminous propositions. One consequence of this is that the way to obtain an idea of Milton's Satan is not to lay hold of specific sayings that fall from his mouth, but to go through his history. Goethe's Mephistopheles, we shall find, on the other hand, reveals himself in the characteristic propositions which he utters. Satan is to be studied by following his progress; Mephistopheles by attending to his remarks.

In the history of Milton's Satan it is important to begin at the time of his being an Archangel. Before the creation of our World, there existed, according to Milton, a grand race of beings altogether different from what we are. Those beings were Spirits. They did not lead a planetary existence; they tenanted space in some strange, and, to us, inconceivable way. Or, rather, they did not tenant all space, but only that upper and illuminated part of infinity called Heaven. For Heaven, in Milton, is not to be considered as a locality, but as a region stretching infinitely out on all sides—an immense extent of continent and kingdom. The infinite darkness, howling and blustering underneath Heaven, was Chaos or Night. What was the exact mode of being of the Spirits who lived in dispersion through Heaven is unknown to us; but it was social. Moreover, there subsisted between the multitudinous far-extending population of Spirits and the Almighty Creator a relation closer, or at least more sensible and immediate, than that which exists between human beings and Him. The best way of expressing this relation in human language is by the idea of physical nearness. They were God's Angels. Pursuing, each individual among them, a life of his own, agreeable to his wishes and his character, yet they all recognised themselves as the Almighty's ministering spirits. At times they were summoned, from following their different occupations in all the ends of Heaven, to assemble near the Divine presence. Among these Angels there were degrees and differences. Some were, in their very essence and constitution, grander and more sublime intelligences than the rest; others, in the course of their long existence, had become noted for their zeal and assiduity. Thus, although really a race of beings living on their own account as men do, they constituted a hierarchy, and were called Angels.

Among all the vast angelic population three or four individuals stood pre-eminent and unapproachable. These were the Archangels. Satan was one of these: if not the highest Archangel in Heaven, he was one of the four highest. After God, he could feel conscious of being the greatest being in the Universe. But, although the relation between the Deity and the angelic population was so close that we can only express it by having recourse to the conception of physical nearness, yet even to the Angels the Deity was so shrouded in clouds and mystery that the highest Archangel might proceed on a wrong notion of his character, and, just as human beings do, might believe the Divine omnipotence as a theological proposition, and yet, in going about his enterprises, might not carry a working consciousness of it along with him. There is something in the exercise of power, in the mere feeling of existence, in the stretching out of a limb, in the resisting of an obstacle, in being active in any way, which generates a conviction that our powers are self-contained, hostile to the recollection of inferiority or accountability. A messenger, employed in his master's business, becomes, in the very act of serving him, forgetful of him. As the feeling of enjoyment in action grows strong, the feeling of a dependent state of being, the feeling of being a messenger, grows weak. Repose and physical weakness are favourable to the recognition of a derived existence: hence the beauty of the feebleness of old age preceding the approach of death. The feebleness of the body weakens the self-sufficient feeling, and disposes to piety. The young man, rejoicing in his strength, cannot believe that his breath is in his nostrils. In some such way the Archangel fell. Rejoicing in his strength, walking colossal through Heaven, gigantic in his conceptions, incessant in his working, ever scheming, ever imagining new enterprises, Satan was in his very nature the most active of God's Archangels. He was ever doing some great thing, and ever thirsting for some greater thing to do. And, alas! his very wisdom became his folly. His notion of the Deity was higher and grander than that of any other Angel: but, then, he was not a contemplative spirit; and his feeling of derived existence grew weak in the glow and excitement of constant occupation. As the feeling of enjoyment in action grew strong, the feeling of being an Angel grew weak. Thus the mere duration of his existence had undermined his strength and prepared him for sin. Although the greatest Angel in Heaven—nay, just because he was such—he was the readiest to fall.

At last an occasion came. When the intimation was made by the Almighty in the Congregation of the Angels that he had anointed his only-begotten Son King on the holy hill of Zion, the Archangel frowned and became a rebel: not because he had weighed the enterprise to which he was committing himself, but because he was hurried on by the impetus of an over-

wrought nature. Even had he weighed the enterprise, and found it wanting, he would have been a rebel nevertheless; he would have rushed into ruin on the wheels of his old impulses. He could not have said to himself "It is useless to rebel, and I will not;" and, if he could, what a hypocrite to have remained in Heaven! His revolt was the natural issue of the thoughts to which he had accustomed himself; and his crime lay in having acquired a rebellious constitution, in having pursued action too much, and spurned worship and contemplation. Herein lay the difference between him and the other Archangels, Raphael, Gabriel, and Michael.

Satan in his revolt carried a third part of the Angels with him. He had accustomed many of the Angels to his mode of thinking. One of the ways in which he gratified his desire for activity had been that of exerting a moral and intellectual influence over the inferior Angels. A few of these he had liked to associate with, discoursing with them, and observing how they imbibed his ideas. His chief associate, almost his bosom-companion, had been Beelzebub, a princely Angel. Moloch, Belial, and Mammon, had likewise been admitted to his confidence. These five had constituted a kind of clique in Heaven, giving the word to a whole multitude of inferior Angels, all of them resembling their leader in being fonder of action than of contemplation. Thus, in addition to the mere hankering after action, there had grown up in Satan's mind a love of power. This feeling that it was a glorious thing to be a leader seems to have had much to do with his voluntary sacrifice of happiness. We may conceive it to have been voluntary. Foreseeing never so much misery would not have prevented such a spirit from rebelling. Having a third of the Angels away with him in some dark, howling region, where he might rule over them alone, would have seemed, even if he had foreseen it, infinitely preferable to the puny sovereignty of an Archangel in that world of gold and emerald: "better to reign in Hell than serve in Heaven." Thus we conceive him to have faced the anticipation of the future. It required little persuasion to gain over the kindred spirit of Beelzebub. These two appear to have conceived the enterprise from the beginning in a different light from that in which they represented it to their followers. Happiness with the inferior Spirits was a more important consideration than with such Spirits as Satan and Beelzebub; and to have hinted the possibility of losing happiness in the enterprise would have been to terrify them away. Satan and Beelzebub were losing happiness to gain something which they thought better; to the inferior Angels nothing could be mentioned that would appear better. Again, the inferior Angels, judging from narrower premises, might indulge in enthusiastic expectations which the greater knowledge of the leaders would prevent them from entertaining. At all events, the effect of the intercourse with the Angels was that a third of their number joined the standard of Satan. Then began the wars in Heaven, related in the poem.

It may be remarked that the carrying on those wars by Satan with the hope of victory is not inconsistent with what has been said as to the possibility of his not having proceeded on a false calculation. We are apt to imagine those wars as wars between the rebel Angels and the armies of God. Now this is true; but it is scarcely the proper idea in the circumstances. How could Satan have hoped for victory in that case? You can only suppose that he did so by lessening his intellect, by making him a mere blundering Fury, and not a keen, far-seeing Intelligence. But in warring with Michael and his followers he was, until the contrary should be proved, warring merely against his fellow-beings of the same Heaven, whose strength he knew and feared not. The idea of physical nearness between the Almighty and the Angels confuses us here. Satan had heard the threat which had accompanied the proclamation of the Messiah's sovereignty; but it may have been problematical in his mind whether the way in which God would fulfil the threat would be to make Michael conquer him. So he made war against Michael and his Angels. At last, when all Heaven was in confusion, the Divine omnipotence interfered. On the third day the Messiah rode forth in his strength, to end the wars and expel the rebel host from Heaven. They fled, driven before his thunder. The crystal wall of Heaven opened wide, and the two lips, rolling inward, disclosed a spacious gap yawning into the wasteful Deep. The reeling Angels saw down, and hung back affrighted; but the terror of the Lord was behind them: headlong they threw themselves from the verge of Heaven into the fathomless abyss, eternal wrath burning after them down through the blackness like a hissing fiery funnel.

And now the Almighty determined to create a new kind of World, and to people it with a race of beings different from that already existing, inferior in the meantime to the Angels, but with the power of working themselves up into the Angelic mode of being. The Messiah, girt with omnipotence, rode out on this creating errand. Heaven opened her everlasting gates, moving on their golden hinges, and the King of Glory, uplifted on the wings of Cherubim, rode on and on into Chaos. At last he stayed his fervid wheels and took the golden compasses in his hand. Centering one point where he stood, he turned the other silently and slowly round through the profound obscurity. Thus were the limits of *our* Universe marked out—that azure region in which the stars were to shine, and the planets were to wheel. On the huge fragment of Chaos thus marked out the Creating Spirit brooded, and the light gushed down. In six days the work of creation was completed. In the centre of the new Universe hung a silvery star. That was the Earth. Thereon, in a paradise of trees and flowers, walked Adam and Eve, the last and the fairest of all God's creatures.

Meanwhile the rebel host lay rolling in the fiery gulf underneath Chaos. The bottom of Chaos was Hell. Above it was Chaos proper, a thick, black, sweltering confusion. Above it again was the new experimental World, cut out of it like a mine, and brilliant with stars and galaxies. And high over all, behind the stars and galaxies, was Heaven itself. Satan and his crew lay rolling in Hell, the fiery element underneath Chaos. Chaos lay between them and the new World. Satan was the first to awake out of stupor and realize the whole state of the case—what had occurred, what was to be their future condition of being, and what remained to be attempted. In the first dialogue between him and Beelzebub we see that, even thus early, he had ascertained what his function was to be for the future, and decided in what precise mode of being he could make his existence most pungent and perceptible.

> Of this be sure,
> To do aught good never will be our task,
> But ever to do evil our sole delight,
> As being the contrary to His high will
> Whom we resist.

Here the ruined Archangel first strikes out the idea of existing for ever after as the Devil. It is important to observe that his becoming a Devil was not the mere inevitable consequence of his being a ruined Archangel. Beelzebub, for instance, could see in the future nothing but a prospect of continued suffering, until Satan communicated to him his conception of a way of enjoying action in the midst of suffering. Again, some of the Angels appear to have been ruminating the possibility of retrieving their former condition by patient enduring. The gigan-

tic scheme of becoming a Devil was Satan's. At first it existed in his mind only as a vague perception that the way in which he would be most likely to get the full worth of his existence was to employ himself thenceforward in doing evil. The idea afterwards became more definite. After glancing round their new domain, Beelzebub and he aroused their abject followers. In the speech which Satan addresses to them after they had all mustered in order we find him hint an opening into a new career, as if the idea had just occurred to him:—

> Space may produce new worlds; whereof so rife
> There went a fame in Heaven that He ere long
> Intended to create, and therein plant
> A generation whom His choice regard
> Should favour equal to the sons of Heaven:
> Thither, if but to pry, shall be perhaps
> Our first eruption.

Here is an advance in definiteness upon the first proposal—that, namely, of determining to spend the rest of existence in doing evil. Casting about in his mind for some specific opening, Satan had recollected the talk they used to have in Heaven about the new World that was to be cut out of Chaos, and the new race of beings that was to be created to inhabit it; and it instantly struck his scheming fancy that *this* would be the weak point of the Universe. If he could but insert the wedge here! He did not, however, announce the scheme fully at the moment, but went on thinking. In the council of gods which was summoned some advised one thing, some another. Moloch was for open war; Belial had great faith in the force of circumstances; and Mammon was for organizing their new kingdom so as to make it as comfortable as possible. No one, however, could say the exact thing that was wanted. At last Beelzebub, prompted by Satan, rose and detailed the project of their great leader:—

> There is a place
> (If ancient and prophetic fame in Heaven
> Err not), another world, the happy seat
> Of some new race called Man, about this time
> To be created, like to us, though less
> In power and excellence, but favoured more
> Of Him who rules above. So was His will
> Pronounced among the gods, and by an oath
> That shook Heaven's whole circumference
> confirmed.
> Thither let us bend all our thoughts, and learn
> What creatures there inhabit, of what mould
> Or substance, how endued, and what their power
> And where their weakness: how attempted best;
> By force or subtlety.

This was Satan's scheme. The more he had thought on it the more did it recommend itself to him. It was more feasible than any other. It held out an indefinite prospect of action. Success in it would be the addition of another fragment of the Universe to Satan's kingdom, mingling and confounding the new World with Hell, and dragging down the new race of beings to share the perdition of the old. The scheme was universally applauded by the Angels; who seem to have differed from their leaders in this, that they were sanguine of being able to better their condition, whereas their leaders sought only the gratification of their desire of action.

The question next was, Who would venture out of Hell to explore the way to the new World? Satan volunteered the perilous excursion. Immediately, putting on his swiftest wings, he directs his solitary flight towards Hell-gate, where sat Sin and Death. When, at length, the gate was opened to give him exit, it was like a huge furnace-mouth, vomiting forth smoke and flames into the womb of Chaos. Issuing thence, Satan spread his sail-broad wings for flight, and began his toilsome way upward, half on foot, half on wing, swimming, sinking, wading, climbing, flying, through the thick and turbid element. At last he emerged out of Chaos into the glimmer surrounding the new Universe. Winging at leisure now through the balmier ether, and still ascending, he could discern at last the whole empyrean Heaven, his former home, with its opal towers and sapphire battlements, and, depending thence by a golden chain, our little World or Universe, like a star of smallest magnitude on the full moon's edge. At the point of suspension of this World from Heaven was an opening, and by that opening Satan entered.

When Satan thus arrived in the new Creation the whole phenomenon was strange to him, and he had no idea what kind of a being Man was. He asked Uriel, whom he found on the sun fulfilling some Divine errand, in which of all the shining orbs round him Man had fixed his seat, or whether he had a fixed seat at all, and was not at liberty to shift his residence, and dwell now in one star, now in another. Uriel, deceived by the appearance which Satan had assumed, pointed out the way to Paradise.

Alighting on the surface of the Earth, Satan walks about immersed in thought. Heaven's gate was in view. Overhead and round him were the quiet hills and the green fields. Oh, what an errand he had come upon! His thoughts were sad and noble. Fallen as he was, all the Archangel stirred within him. Oh, had he not been made so high, should he ever have fallen so low? Is there no hope even now, no room for repentance? Such were his first thoughts. But he roused himself and shook them off. "The past is gone and away; it is to the future that I must look. Perish the days of my Archangelship! perish the name of Archangel! Such is my name no longer. My future, if less happy, shall be more glorious. Ah, and this is the World I have singled out for my experiment! Formerly, in the days of my Archangelship, I ranged at will through infinity, doing one thing here and another there. Now I must contract the sphere of my activity, and labour nowhere but here. But it is better to apply myself to the task of thoroughly impregnating one point of space with my presence than henceforth to beat my wings vaguely all through infinitude. Ah, but may not my nature suffer by the change? In thus selecting a specific aim, in thus concerning myself exclusively with one point of space, and forswearing all interest in the innumerable glorious things that may be happening out of it, shall I not run the risk of degenerating into a smaller and meaner being? In the course of ages of dealing with the puny offspring of these new beings, may I not dwindle into a mere pungent, pettifogging Spirit? What would Raphael, Gabriel, and Michael say, were they to see their old co-mate changed into such a being? But be it so. If I cannot cope with the Almighty on the grand scale of infinitude, I shall at least make my existence felt by opposing His plans respecting this new race of beings. Besides, by beginning with this, may I not worm my way to a more effective position even in infinitude? At all events, I shall have a scheme on hand, and be incessantly occupied. And, as time makes the occupation more congenial, if I do become less magnanimous, I shall, at the same time, become happier. And, whether my fears on this point are visionary or not, it will, at least, be a noble thing to be able to say that I have caused a whirlpool that shall suck down generation after generation of these new beings, before their Maker's eyes, into the same wretched condition of being to which He has doomed us. It will be something so to vitiate the Universe that, let Him create, create on, as He chooses, it will be like pouring water into a broken vessel."

In the very course of this train of thinking Satan begins to degenerate into a meaner being. He is on the very threshold of that career in which he will cease for ever to be the Archangel and become irrevocably the Devil. The very manner in which he tempts the first pair is devil-like. It is in the shape of a cormorant on a tree that he sits watching his victims. He sat at the ear of Eve "squat like a toad." It was in the shape of a serpent that he tempted her. And, when the evil was done, he slunk away through the brush wood. In the very act of ruining Man he committed himself to a life of ignominious activity: he was to go on his belly and eat dust all his days.

WALTER BAGEHOT
From "John Milton" (1859)
Collected Works, ed. St. John-Stevas
Volume 2, 1965, pp. 134–48

If from the man we turn to his works, we are struck at once with two singular contrasts. The first of them is this. The distinction between ancient and modern art is sometimes said, and perhaps truly, to consist in the simple bareness of the imaginative conceptions which we find in ancient art, and the comparatively complex clothing in which all modern creations are embodied. If we adopt this distinction, Milton seems in some sort ancient, and in some sort modern. Nothing is so simple as the subject-matter of his works. The two greatest of his creations—the character of Satan and the character of Eve—are two of the simplest—the latter probably the very simplest—in the whole field of literature. On this side Milton's art is classical. On the other hand, in no writer is the imagery more profuse, the illustrations more various, the dress altogether more splendid. And in this respect the style of his art seems romantic and modern. In real truth, however, it is only ancient art in a modern disguise. The dress is a mere dress, and can be stripped off when we will. We all of us do perhaps in memory strip it off for ourselves. Notwithstanding the lavish adornments with which her image is presented, the character of Eve is still the simplest sort of feminine essence,—the pure embodiment of that inner nature which we believe and hope that women have. The character of Satan, though it is not so easily described, has nearly as few elements in it. The most purely modern conceptions will not bear to be unclothed in this manner. Their romantic garment clings inseparably to them. Hamlet or Lear are not to be thought of except as complex characters, with very involved and complicated embodiments. They are as difficult to draw out in words as the common characters of life are; that of Hamlet, perhaps, is more so. If we make it, as perhaps we should, the characteristic of modern and romantic art that it presents us with creations which we cannot think of or delineate except as very varied, and, so to say, circumstantial, we must not rank Milton among the masters of romantic art. And without involving the subject in the troubled sea of an old controversy, we may say that the most striking of the poetical peculiarities of Milton is the bare simplicity of his ideas, and the rich abundance of his illustrations.

Another of his peculiarities is equally striking. There seems to be such a thing as second-hand poetry. Some poets, musing on the poetry of other men, have unconsciously shaped it into something of their own: the new conception is like the original, it would never probably have existed had not the original existed previously; still it is sufficiently different from the original to be a new thing, not a copy or a plagiarism; it is a creation, though, so to say, a suggested creation. Gray is as good an example as can be found of a poet whose works abound in this species of semi-original conceptions. Industrious critics track his best lines back, and find others like them which doubtless lingered near his fancy while he was writing them. The same critics have been equally busy with the works of Milton, and equally successful. They find traces of his reading in half his works; not, which any reader could do, in overt similes and distinct illustrations, but also in the very texture of the thought and the expression. In many cases, doubtless, they discover more than he himself knew. A mind like his, which has an immense store of imaginative recollections, can never know which of his own imaginations is exactly suggested by which recollection. Men awake with their best ideas; it is seldom worth while to investigate very curiously whence they came. Our proper business is to adapt, and mould, and act upon them. Of poets perhaps this is true even more remarkably than of other men; their ideas are suggested in modes, and according to laws, even more impossible to specify than the ideas of the rest of the world. Second-hand poetry, so to say, often seems quite original to the poet himself; he frequently does not know that he derived it from an old memory; years afterwards it may strike him as it does others. Still, in general, such inferior species of creation is not so likely to be found in minds of singular originality as in those of less. A brooding, placid, cultivated mind, like that of Gray, is the place where we should expect to meet with it. Great originality disturbs the adaptive process, removes the mind of the poet from the thoughts of other men, and occupies it with its own heated and flashing thoughts. Poetry of the second degree is like the secondary rocks of modern geology,—a still, gentle, alluvial formation; the igneous glow of primary genius brings forth ideas like the primeval granite, simple, astounding, and alone. Milton's case is an exception to this rule. His mind has marked originality, probably as much of it as any in literature; but it has as much of moulded recollection as any mind too. His poetry in consequence is like an artificial park, green, and soft, and beautiful, yet with outlines bold, distinct, and firm, and the eternal rock ever jutting out; or, better still, it is like our own lake scenery, where nature has herself the same combination—where we have Rydal Water side by side with the everlasting upheaved mountain. Milton has the same union of softened beauty with unimpaired grandeur; and it is his peculiarity.

These are the two contrasts which puzzle us at first in Milton, and which distinguish him from other poets in our remembrance afterwards. We have a superficial complexity in illustration, and imagery, and metaphor; and in contrast with it we observe a latent simplicity of idea, an almost rude strength of conception. The underlying thoughts are few, though the flowers on the surface are so many. We have likewise the perpetual contrast of the soft poetry of the memory, and the firm, as it were fused, and glowing poetry of the imagination. His words, we may half fancifully say, are like his character. There is the same austerity in the real essence, the same exquisiteness of sense, the same delicacy of form which we know that he had, the same music which we imagine there was in his voice. In both his character and his poetry there was an ascetic nature in a sheath of beauty.

No book, perhaps, which has ever been written is more difficult to criticise than *Paradise Lost*. The only way to criticise a work of the imagination, is to describe its effect upon the mind of the reader,—at any rate, of the critic; and this can only be adequately delineated by strong illustrations, apt similies, and perhaps a little exaggeration. The task is in its very nature not an easy one; the poet paints a picture on the fancy of the critic, and the critic has in some sort to copy it on the paper. He must say what it is before he can make remarks upon it. But in the case of *Paradise Lost* we hardly like to use illustrations. The subject is one which the imagination rather shrinks from. At any rate, it requires courage, and an effort to compel the mind to view such a subject as distinctly and vividly as it views other subjects. Another peculiarity of *Paradise Lost* makes the difficulty even greater. It does not profess to be a mere work of art; or rather, it claims to be by no means that, and that only. It starts with a dogmatic aim; it avowedly intends to

> assert eternal Providence,
> And justify the ways of God to men.

In this point of view we have always had a sympathy with the Cambridge mathematician who has been so much abused. He said, 'After all, *Paradise Lost* proves nothing;' and various persons of poetical tastes and temperament have been very severe on the prosaic observation. Yet, 'after all,' he was right. Milton professed to prove something. He was too profound a critic,—rather, he had too profound an instinct of those eternal principles of art which criticism tries to state,—not to know that on such a subject he must prove something. He professed to deal with the great problem of human destiny; to show why man was created, in what kind of universe he lives, whence he came, and whither he goes. He dealt of necessity with the greatest of subjects. He had to sketch the greatest of objects. He was concerned with infinity and eternity even more than with time and sense; he undertook to delineate the ways, and consequently the character, of Providence, as well as the conduct and the tendencies of man. The essence of success in such an attempt is to satisfy the religious sense of man; to bring home to our hearts what we know to be true; to teach us what we have not seen; to awaken us to what we have forgotten; to remove the 'covering' from all people, and 'the veil' that is spread over all nations; to give us, in a word, such a conception of things, divine and human, as we can accept, believe, and trust. The true doctrine of criticism demands what Milton invites—an examination of the degree in which the great epic attains this aim. And if, in examining it, we find it necessary to use unusual illustrations, and plainer words than are customary, it must be our excuse that we do not think the subject can be made clear without them.

The defect of *Paradise Lost* is that, after all, it is founded on a *political* transaction. The scene is in heaven very early in the history of the universe, before the creation of man or the fall of Satan. We have a description of a court. The angels,

> By imperial summons called,

appear

> Under their hierarchs in orders bright.
> Ten thousand thousand ensigns high advanced,
> Standards and gonfalons, 'twixt van and rear,
> Stream in the air, and for distinction serve
> Of hierarchies, of orders, and degrees.

To this assemblage 'th' Omnipotent' speaks:

> Hear, all ye Angels, progeny of light,
> Thrones, Dominations, Princedoms, Virtues, Powers,
> Hear my decree, which unrevoked shall stand!
> This day I have begot whom I declare
> My only Son, and on this holy hill
> Him have anointed, whom ye now behold
> At my right hand. Your head I him appoint;
> And by myself have sworn to him shall bow
> All knees in Heaven, and shall confess him Lord.
> Under his great vicegerent reign abide,
> United as one individual soul,
> For ever happy. Him who disobeys

Me disobeys, breaks union, and, that day,
Cast out from God and blessed vision, falls
Into utter darkness deep engulfed, his place
Ordained without redemption, without end.

This act of patronage was not popular at court; and why should it have been? The religious sense is against it. The worship which sinful men owe to God is not transferable to lieutenants and vicegerents. The whole scene of the court jars upon a true feeling. We seem to be reading about some emperor of history, who admits his son to a share in the empire, who confers on him a considerable jurisdiction, and requires officials, with 'standards and gonfalons,' to bow before him. The orthodoxy of Milton is quite as questionable as his accuracy. The old Athanasian creed was not made by persons who would allow such a picture as that of Milton to stand before their imaginations. The generation of the Son was to them a fact 'before all time,' an eternal fact. There was no question in their minds of patronage or promotion. The Son was the Son before all time, just as the Father was the Father before all time. Milton had in such matters a bold but not very sensitive imagination. He accepted the inevitable materialism of biblical, and, to some extent, of all religious language as distinct revelation. He certainly believed, in contradiction to the old creed, that God had both 'parts and passions.' He imagined that earth

Is but the shadow of Heaven, and, things therein
Each to other like, more than on Earth is thought!

From some passages it would seem that he actually thought of God as having 'the members and form' of a man. Naturally, therefore, he would have no toleration for the mysterious notions of time and eternity which are involved in the traditional doctrine. We are not, however, now concerned with Milton's belief, but with his representation of his creed—his picture, so to say, of it in *Paradise Lost*; still, as we cannot but think, that picture is almost irreligious, and certainly different from that which has been generally accepted in Christendom. Such phrases as 'before all time,' 'eternal generation,' are doubtless very vaguely interpreted by the mass of men; nevertheless, no sensitively orthodox man *could* have drawn the picture of a generation, not to say an exaltation, *in* time.

We shall see this more clearly by reading what follows in the poem:

All seemed well pleased; all seemed, but were not all.

One of the archangels, whose name can be guessed, decidedly disapproved, and calls a meeting, at which he explains that

orders and degrees
Jar not with liberty, but well consist;

but still, that the promotion of a new person, on grounds of relationship merely, above, even infinitely above, the old angels with imperial titles, was 'a new law,' and rather tyrannical. Abdiel,

than whom none with more zeal adored
The Deity, and divine commands obeyed,

attempts a defence:

Grant it thee unjust
That equal over equals monarch reign—
Thyself, though great and glorious, dost thou count,
Or all angelic nature join'd in one,
Equal to him, begotten Son, by whom?
As by his Word, the mighty Father made
All things, even thee, and all the Spirits of Heaven
By him created in their bright degrees,
Crowned them with glory, and to their glory named

Thrones, Dominations, Princedoms, Virtues,
Powers?—
Essential Powers; nor by his reign obscured,
But more illustrious made; since he, the head,
One of our number thus reduced becomes;
His laws our laws; all honour to him done
Returns our own. Cease then this impious rage,
And tempt not these; but hasten to appease
The incensed Father and the incensed Son,
While pardon may be found, in time besought.

Yet though Abdiel's intentions were undeniably good, his argument is rather specious. Acting as an instrument in the process of creation would scarcely give a valid claim to the obedience of the created being. Power may be shown in the act, no doubt; but mere power gives no true claim to the obedience of moral beings. It is a kind of principle of all manner of idolatries and false religions to believe that it does so. Satan, besides, takes issue on the fact:

That we were formed then, say'st thou? and the work
Of secondary hands, by task transferred
From Father to his Son? Strange point and new!
Doctrine which we would know whence learned!

And we must say that the speech in which the new ruler is introduced to the 'thrones, dominations, princedoms, virtues, powers,' is hard to reconcile with Abdiel's exposition. 'This day' he seems to have come into existence, and could hardly have assisted at the creation of the angels, who are not young, and who converse with one another like old acquaintances.

We have gone into this part of the subject at length, because it is the source of the great error which pervades *Paradise Lost*. Satan is made *interesting*. This has been the charge of a thousand orthodox and even heterodox writers against Milton. Shelley, on the other hand, has gloried in it; and fancied, if we remember rightly, that Milton intentionally ranged himself on the Satanic side of the universe, just as Shelley himself would have done, and that he wished to show the falsity of the ordinary theology. But Milton was born an age too early for such aims, and was far too sincere to have advocated any doctrine in a form so indirect. He believed every word he said. He was not conscious of the effect his teaching would produce in an age like this, when scepticism is in the air, and when it is not possible to help looking coolly on his delineations. Probably in our boyhood we can recollect a period when any solemn description of celestial events would have commanded our respect; we should not have dared to read it intelligently, to canvass its details and see what it meant: it was a religious book; it sounded reverential, and that would have sufficed. Something like this was the state of mind of the seventeenth century. Even Milton probably shared in a vague reverence for religious language. He hardly felt the moral effect of the pictures he was drawing. His artistic instinct, too, often hurries him away. His Satan was to him, as to us, the hero of his poem. Having commenced by making him resist on an occasion which in an earthly kingdom would have been excusable and proper, he probably a little sympathised with him, just as his readers do.

The interest of Satan's character is at its height in the first two books. Coleridge justly compared it to that of Napoleon. There is the same pride, the same satanic ability, the same will, the same egotism. His character seems to grow with his position. He is far finer after his fall, in misery and suffering, with scarcely any resource except in himself, than he was originally in heaven; at least if Raphael's description of him can be trusted. No portrait which imagination or history has drawn of a revolutionary anarch is nearly so perfect; there is all the grandeur of the greatest human mind, and a certain infinitude in his circumstances which humanity must ever want. Few Englishmen feel a profound reverence for Napoleon I. There was no French alliance in *his* time; we have most of us some tradition of antipathy to him. Yet hardly any Englishman can read the account of the campaign of 1814 without feeling his interest for the Emperor to be strong, and without perhaps being conscious of a latent wish that he may succeed. Our opinion is against him, our serious wish is of course for England; but the imagination has a sympathy of its own, and will not give place. We read about the great general—never greater than in that last emergency—showing resources of genius that seem almost infinite, and that assuredly have never been surpassed, yet vanquished, yielding to the power of circumstances, to the combined force of adversaries, each of whom singly he outmatches in strength, and all of whom together he surpasses in majesty and in mind. Something of the same sort of interest belongs to the Satan of the first two books of *Paradise Lost*. We know that he will be vanquished; his name is not a recommendation. Still we do not imagine distinctly the minds by which he is to be vanquished; we do not take the same interest in them that we do in him; our sympathies, our fancy, are on his side.

Perhaps much of this was inevitable; yet what a defect it is! Especially what a defect in Milton's own view, and looked at with the stern realism with which he regarded it! Suppose that the author of evil in the universe were the most attractive being in it; suppose that the source of all sin were the origin of all interest to us! We need not dwell upon this.

As we have said, much of this was difficult to avoid, if indeed it could be avoided, in dealing with such a theme. Even Milton shrank, in some measure, from delineating the divine character. His imagination evidently halts when it is required to perform that task. The more delicate imagination of our modern world would shrink still more. Any person who will consider what such an attempt must end in will find his nerves quiver. But by a curiously fatal error, Milton has selected for delineation exactly that part of the divine nature which is most beyond the reach of the human faculties, and which is also, when we try to describe our fancy of it, the least effective to our minds. He has made God *argue*. Now, the procedure of the divine mind from truth to truth must ever be incomprehensible to us; the notion, indeed, of his proceeding at all, is a contradiction: to some extent, at least, it is inevitable that we should use such language, but we know it is in reality inapplicable. A long train of reasoning in such a connection is so out of place as to be painful; and yet Milton has many. He relates a series of family prayers in heaven, with sermons afterwards, which are very tedious. Even Pope was shocked at the notion of Providence talking like 'a school-divine.' And there is the still worse error, that if you once attribute reasoning to Him, subsequent logicians may discover that He does not reason very well.

Another way in which Milton has contrived to strengthen our interest in Satan is the number and insipidity of his good angels. There are old rules as to the necessity of a supernatural machinery for an epic poem, worth some fraction of the paper on which they are written, and derived from the practice of Homer, who believed his gods and goddesses to be real beings, and would have been rather harsh with a critic who called them machinery. These rules had probably an influence with Milton, and induced him to manipulate these serious angels more than he would have done otherwise. They appear to be excellent administrators with very little to do; a kind of grand chamberlains with wings, who fly down to earth and communicate information to Adam and Eve. They have no character; they are essentially messengers, merely conductors, so to say, of the providential will: no one fancies that they have an independent power of action; they seem scarcely to have minds of their own. No effect can be more unfortunate. If the struggle of Satan had been with Deity directly, the natural instincts of religion would have been awakened; but when an angel with mind is only contrasted to angels with wings, we sympathise with the former.

In the first two books, therefore, our sympathy with Milton's Satan is great; we had almost said unqualified. The speeches he delivers are of well-known excellence. Lord Brougham, no contemptible judge of emphatic oratory, has laid down that if a person had not an opportunity of access to the great Attic masterpieces, he had better choose these for a model. What is to be regretted about the orator is that he scarcely acts up to his sentiments. 'Better to reign in hell than serve in heaven' is, at any rate, an audacious declaration. But he has no room for exhibiting similar audacity in action. His offensive career is limited. In the nature of the subject there was scarcely the possibility for the fallen archangel to display in the detail of his operations the surpassing intellect with which Milton has endowed him. He goes across chaos, gets into a few physical difficulties; but these are not much. His grand aim is the conquest of our first parents; and we are at once struck with the enormous inequality of the conflict. Two beings just created, without experience, without guile, without knowledge of good and evil, are expected to contend with a being on the delineation of whose powers every resource of art and imagination, every subtle suggestion, every emphatic simile, has been lavished. The idea in every reader's mind is, and must be, not surprise that our first parents should yield, but wonder that Satan should not think it beneath him to attack them. It is as if an army should invest a cottage.

We have spoken more of theology than we intended; and we need not say how much the monstrous inequalities attributed to the combatants affect our estimate of the results of the conflict. The state of man is what it is, because the defenceless Adam and Eve of Milton's imagination yielded to the nearly all-powerful Satan whom he has delineated. Milton has in some sense invented this difficulty; for in the book of Genesis there is no such inequality. The serpent may be subtler than any beast of the field; but he is not necessarily subtler or cleverer than man. So far from Milton having justified the ways of God to man, he has loaded the common theology with a new encumbrance.

We may need refreshment after this discussion; and we cannot find it better than in reading a few remarks of Eve.

> That day I oft remember, when from sleep,
> I first awaked, and found myself reposed,
> Under a shade, on flow'rs, much wond'ring where
> And what I was, whence thither brought, and how.
> Not distant far from thence a murm'ring sound
> Of waters issued from a cave, and spread
> Into a liquid plain; then stood unmoved,
> Pure as the expanse of Heav'n. I thither went
> With unexperienced thought, and laid me down
> On the green bank, to look into the clear
> Smooth lake, that to me seem'd another sky.
> As I bent down to look, just opposite
> A shape within the watery gleam appear'd,
> Bending to look on me. I started back;
> It started back: but pleased I soon returned;
> Pleased it returned as soon with answering looks
> Of sympathy and love. There I had fix'd
> Mine eyes till now, and pined with vain desire,
> Had not a voice thus warned me: 'What thou seest,
> What there thou seest, fair creature, is thyself;

With thee it came and goes: but follow me,
And I will bring thee where no shadow stays
Thy coming, and thy soft embraces—he
Whose image thou art; him thou shalt enjoy
Inseparably thine; to him shalt bear
Multitudes like thyself, and thence be call'd
Mother of Human Race.' What could I do
But follow straight, invisibly thus led?
Till I espied thee, fair, indeed, and tall,
Under a platan; yet methought less fair,
Less winning soft, less amiably mild,
Than that smooth watery image. Back I turn'd:
Thou, following, cry'dst aloud, 'Return, fair Eve;
Whom fly'st thou?'

Eve's character, indeed, is one of the most wonderful efforts of the human imagination. She is a kind of abstract woman; essentially a typical being; an official 'mother of all living.' Yet she is a real interesting woman, not only full of delicacy and sweetness, but with all the undefinable fascination, the charm of personality, which such typical characters hardly ever have. By what consummate miracle of wit this charm of individuality is preserved, without impairing the general idea which is ever present to us, we cannot explain, for we do not know.

Adam is far less successful. He has good hair,—'hyacinthine locks' that 'from his parted forelock manly hung;' a 'fair large front' and 'eye sublime;' but he has little else that we care for. There is, in truth, no opportunity of displaying manly virtues, even if he possessed them. He has only to yield to his wife's solicitations, which he does. Nor are we sure that he does it well. He is very tedious; he indulges in sermons which are good; but most men cannot but fear that so delightful a being as Eve must have found him tiresome. She steps away, however, and goes to sleep at some of the worst points.

Dr. Johnson remarked, that, after all, *Paradise Lost* was one of the books which no one wished longer: we fear, in this irreverent generation, some wish it shorter. Hardly any reader would be sorry if some portions of the later books had been spared him. Coleridge, indeed, discovered profound mysteries in the last; but in what could not Coleridge find a mystery if he wished? Dryden more wisely remarked, that Milton became tedious when he entered upon a 'tract of Scripture.' Nor is it surprising that such is the case. They style of many parts of Scripture is such that it will not bear addition or subtraction. A word less, or an idea more, and the effect upon the mind is the same no longer. Nothing can be more tiresome than a sermonic amplification of such passages. It is almost too much when, as from the pulpit, a paraphrastic commentary is prepared for our spiritual improvement. In deference to the intention we bear it, but we bear it unwillingly; and we cannot endure it at all when, as in poems, the object is to awaken our fancy rather than to improve our conduct. The account of the creation in the book of Genesis is one of the compositions from which no sensitive imagination would subtract an iota, to which it could not bear to add a word. Milton's paraphrase is alike copious and ineffective. The universe is, in railway phrase, 'opened,' but not created; no green earth springs in a moment from the indefinite void. Instead, too, of the simple loneliness of the Old Testament, several angelic officials are in attendance, who help in nothing, but indicate that heaven must be plentifully supplied with tame creatures.

There is no difficulty in writing such criticisms, and, indeed, other unfavourable criticisms, on *Paradise Lost*. There is scarcely any book in the world which is open to a greater number, or which a reader who allows plain words to produce a due effect will be less satisfied with. Yet what book is really

greater? In the best parts the words have a magic in them; even in the inferior passages you are hardly sensible of their inferiority till you translate them into your own language. Perhaps no style ever written by man expressed so adequately the conceptions of a mind so strong and so peculiar; a manly strength, a haunting atmosphere of enhancing suggestions, a firm continuous music, are only some of its excellencies. To comprehend the whole of the others, you must take the volume down and read it,—the best defence of Milton, as has been said most truly, against all objections.

Probably no book shows the transition which our theology has made, since the middle of the seventeenth century, at once so plainly and so fully. We do not now compose long narratives to 'justify the ways of God to men.' The more orthodox we are, the more we shrink from it; the more we hesitate at such a task, the more we allege that we have no powers for it. Our most celebrated defences of established tenets are in the style of Butler, not in that of Milton. They do not profess to show a satisfactory explanation of human destiny; on the contrary, they hint that probably we could not understand such an explanation if it were given us; at any rate, they allow that it is not given us. Their course is palliative. They suggest an 'analogy of difficulties.' If our minds were greater, so they reason, we should comprehend these doctrines: now we cannot explain analogous facts which we see and know. No style can be more opposite to the bold argument, the boastful exposition of Milton. The teaching of the eighteenth century is in the very atmosphere we breathe. We read it in the teachings of Oxford; we hear it from the missionaries of the Vatican. The air of the theology is clarified. We know our difficulties, at least; we are rather prone to exaggerate the weight of some than to deny the reality of any.

We cannot continue a line of thought which would draw us on too far for the patience of our readers. We must, however, make one more remark, and we shall have finished our criticism on *Paradise Lost*. It is analogous to that which we have just made. The scheme of the poem is based on an offence against positive morality. The offence of Adam was not against nature or conscience, not against anything of which we can see the reason, or conceive the obligation, but against an unexplained injunction of the Supreme Will. The rebellion in heaven, as Milton describes it, was a rebellion, not against known ethics, or immutable spiritual laws, but against an arbitrary selection and an unexplained edict. We do not say that there is no such thing as positive morality; we do not think so; even if we did, we should not insert a proposition so startling at the conclusion of a literary criticism. But we are sure that wherever a positive moral edict is promulgated, it is no subject, except perhaps under a very peculiar treatment, for literary art. By the very nature of it, it cannot satisfy the heart and conscience. It is a difficulty; we need not attempt to explain it away. There are mysteries enough which will never be explained away. But it is contrary to every principle of criticism to state the difficulty as if it were not one; to bring forward the puzzle, yet leave it to yourself; to publish so strange a problem, and give only an untrue solution of it: and yet such, in its bare statement, is all which Milton has done.

Of Milton's other writings we have left ourselves no room to speak; and though every one of them, or almost every one of them, would well repay a careful criticism, yet few of them seem to throw much additional light on his character, or add much to our essential notion of his genius, though they may exemplify and enhance it. *Comus* is the poem which does so the most. Literature has become so much lighter than it used to be, that we can scarcely realise the position it occupied in the light literature of our forefathers. We have now in our own language many poems that are pleasanter in their subject, more graceful in their execution, more flowing in their outline, more easy to read. Dr. Johnson, though perhaps no very excellent authority on the more intangible graces of literature, was disposed to deny to Milton the capacity of creating the lighter literature: 'Milton, madam, was a genius that could cut a colossus from a rock, but could not carve heads upon cherry-stones.' And it would not be surprising if this generation, which has access to the almost indefinite quantity of lighter compositions which have been produced since Johnson's time, were to echo his sentence. In some degree, perhaps, the popular taste does so. *Comus* has no longer the peculiar exceptional popularity which it used to have. We can talk without general odium of its defects. Its characters are nothing, its sentiments are tedious, its story is not interesting. But it is only when we have realised the magnitude of its deficiences that we comprehend the peculiarity of its greatness. Its power is in its style. A grave and firm music pervades it: it is soft, without a thought of weakness; harmonious and yet strong; impressive, as few such poems are, yet covered with a bloom of beauty and a complexity of charm that few poems have either. We have, perhaps, light literature in itself better, that we read oftener and more easily, that lingers more in our memories; but we have not any, we question if there ever will be any, which gives so true a conception of the capacity and the dignity of the mind by which it was produced. The breath of solemnity which hovers round the music attaches us to the writer. Every line, here as elsewhere in Milton, excites the idea of indefinite power.

And so we must draw to a close. The subject is an infinite one, and if we pursued it, we should lose ourselves in miscellaneous commentary, and run on far beyond the patience of our readers. What we have said has at least a defined intention. We have wished to state the impression which the character of Milton and the greatest of Milton's works are likely to produce on readers of the present generation,—a generation, almost more than any other, different from his own.

EDMOND SCHERER

From "Milton and *Paradise Lost*" (1868)
Essays on English Literature, tr. Saintsbury
1891, pp. 134–49

VI

*P*aradise Lost is a work of the Renaissance, full of imitation of the ancients. The plan is modelled upon the consecrated patterns, especially on that of the *Æneid*. There is an exposition, there is an invocation; after which the author plunges *in medias res*. Satan and his accomplices are discovered stranded on the floor of hell, like Æneas on the coast of Carthage. At this point the action begins. It is and will be very simple throughout. As Æneas triumphs over Turnus, so Satan will ruin humanity in the person of our first parents. This unity of action is demanded by the rules; but it is necessary, on the other hand, that the poet should tell us what has gone before, and what will come after, otherwise there would not be material enough. So resource is had to narratives. Æneas tells Dido of the Fall of Troy: Raphael narrates to Adam the revolt of the angels and the creation of the world. Thus we are posted up as to the past: but the future remains. The poet cannot leave us with the death of Turnus or the Fall of the first human beings, because the true interest of the two poems lies in the relations of Æneas with the destinies of the Roman

people and in the relations of Adam's sin with the lot of all mankind. Patience! a new device will get us out of the difficulty. Æneas descends to Hades, and there finds Anchises, who shows him the procession of his posterity. The archangel Michael leads Adam to a hill and delivers a complete course of lectures to him on sacred history, from the death of Abel to the coming of Christ, and even to the Last Judgment.

Such is the plan of *Paradise Lost*: there is nothing more regular or more classical. We recognize the superstitions of the Renaissance in this faithfulness to models. But the result is that Milton's poem presents a sort of tertiary formation, the copy of a copy. It is to the Latin epics what these are to Homer. We shall see presently what Milton has succeeded in throwing into the traditional mould; but as for the form of his poem he did not create it for himself, he received it. It is a legacy of antiquity.

VII

If the form of *Paradise Lost* was supplied by the Renaissance the substance was furnished by Puritanism. *Paradise Lost* is an epic, but it is a theological epic, and the theology of the poem is made up of the favorite dogmas of the Puritans—the Fall, Justification, the sovereign laws of God. Moreover, Milton makes no secret of the fact that he is defending a thesis: his end, he says in the first lines, is to "assert eternal providence And justify the ways of God to man."

There are, therefore, in *Paradise Lost* two things which must be kept distinct: an epic poem and a theodicy. Unluckily, these two elements—answering to the two men of which Milton was himself made up, and to the two tendencies which his age obeyed—these two elements, I say, were incapable of thorough fusion. Nay, they are at complete variance, and from their juxtaposition there results an undertone of contradiction which runs through the whole work, affects its solidity, and endangers its value. It would be vain to plead the example of the classical epic. The Gods no doubt hold a great place both in the *Iliad* and the *Æneid*; but Christianity is in this respect very differently situated from Paganism. Christianity is a religion which has been formally "redacted" and settled; and it is impossible, without doing it violence, to add anything to it or subtract anything from it. Moreover, Christianity is a religion serious in itself and insisting upon being taken seriously, devoted to ideas the gravest, not to say the saddest, that imagination can form: those of sin, redemption, self-denial, good works—all of them things which, as Boileau says, are not fitted for being smartened up by ornament.

> L'évangile à l'esprit n'offre de tous côtés
> Que pénitence à faire et tourments mérités,
> Et de vos fictions le mélange coupable
> Même à ses vérités donne l'air de la fable.[1]

But this is not all. Christianity is a religion of dogma: in place of the fantastic and intangible myths of which the Aryan religions were made up, it has abstruse distinctions, paradoxical mysteries, subtle teachings. In short, it amounts to a metaphysic, or, to return to the expression I used at first, a theology. And theology has never had the reputation of being favorable to poetry. Lastly, and as a climax, this theology is still alive. It is for thousands an object of faith and hope: it is not "to let," if I may so speak, there is no vacancy in it; and the poet who carries into it the creations of his fantasy has all the appearance of committing sacrilege.

This, as it is, looks ill for Milton's poem; but we have not yet said all. *Paradise Lost* is not only a theological poem—two words which cry out at finding themselves united—but it is at the same time a commentary on texts of Scripture. The author

655

has chosen for his subject the first chapters of Genesis, that is to say a story, which the stoutest or the simplest faith hesitates to take quite literally, a story in which serpents are heard speaking, and the ruin of the human race is seen to be bound up with a fault merely childish in appearance. In fixing on such a subject, Milton was obliged to treat the whole story as a literal and authentic history; and, worse still, to take a side on the questions which it starts. Now, these questions are the very thorniest in theology: and so it comes about that Milton, who intended to instruct us, merely launches us on a sea of difficulties. What are we to understand by the Son of the Most High, who, one fine day, is begotten and raised to the rank of viceroy of creation? How are we to comprehend an angel who enters on a conflict with God, that is to say, with a being whom he knows to be omnipotent? What kind of innocence is it which does not prevent a man from eating forbidden fruit? How, again, can this fault extend its effects to ourselves? By what effort of imagination or of faith can we regard the history of Adam as part of our own history, and acknowledge solidarity with his crime in ourselves? And if Milton does not succeed in arousing this feeling in us, what becomes of his poem? What is its value, what its interest? It becomes equally impossible to take it seriously as a profession of faith (since this faith escapes us) and even to regard it as the poetical expression of a theodicy which is out of date, because that theodicy could only become poetic on the terms of being intelligible.

Paradise Lost has shared the fate of its hero, that is to say, of the devil. The idea of Satan is a contradictory idea: for it is contradictory to know God and yet attempt rivalry with Him. Accordingly, the flourishing time of belief in the devil was a time of logical impotence. The devil at this time of day has been riddled through and through, he has become a comic character, he supplies us with our little jokes.[2] As for *Paradise Lost* it lives still, but it is none the less true that its fundamental conceptions have become strange to us, and that if the work survives, it is in spite of the subject which it celebrates.

VIII

Nor is this the only trick which Milton's theology has played upon his poetry. The marvellous is an essential part of classical poetry, and this is intelligible enough. In a certain sense Paganism is more religious than Christianity, and associates the Deity with every act of human life more naturally and more of necessity. From the very fact that it has Gods for everything—for the domestic hearth, for love, for marriage, for fighting—there is not a circumstance in which these Gods have not a *locus standi*. Much more is this so when the subject is a hero whose valor is inconceivable without divine protection, or a great historical event, whereof the decrees of Zeus supply the sovereign explanation. It is by no means the same with the moderns, in whom the much more exalted, but much vaguer idea of divine Providence, has replaced the crowd of special deities. If there is in this a metaphysical progress, there is at the same time a poetical impoverishment. It is not that Christianity also has not produced its own mythology: we have a whole Catholic Olympus, pretty well populated. But the attributes are uncertain, the parts ill distributed: and, in spite of everything, there clings to these creations a sort of inborn spiritualism, which is proof against the materialism of popular beliefs. Christianity, I have said, is a religion wanting in ductility. Since it damns those who do not believe it, it perceives the necessity of offering them clearly defined doctrines. Everything in it is more or less settled and agreed upon. Imagination, therefore, can only assign very narrow limits, or, so to say, a circle drawn beforehand, to the utterances of God or the ac-

tions of angels. Hence the awkwardness of poets who have tried to draw from the Christian theology the marvels of which they had need. They satisfy the demands neither of piety nor of poetry. They are hampered by the fear of going too far; and, however timid they show themselves, they still have an air of temerity. The *Gerusalemme Liberata*, the *Henriade*, the *Messiade, Les Martyrs*, show the faults of the kind palpably. Dante alone escapes, because with admirable tact or, if anyone pleases, art, he has brought into play only the sinners and the saved.

Yet Milton has been more fortunate than most of the epic poets of the Christian period. Indeed, there was no necessity for him to make a shift to supply his epic with the element of the marvellous, since the whole was already placed straight off in the region of the supernatural. God and his Son, the devils and the angels, were not kept in the background and reserved for the denouement. They themselves filled the principal parts. Even our first parents, placed as they were in the garden of Eden and in a state of innocence, shared in a kind of superior existence. Thus there was from the first no need to introduce the divinity arbitrarily. The author of *Paradise Lost* had but to remain within the conditions of his subject and to extend a little the outlines of the sacred history.

But if Milton avoided factitious marvels it was at the cost of inconvenience elsewhere, of baldness in story, of poverty in ethical quality. Not only is the reader lifted into the sphere of religious abstractions, where the eye of man cannot see or his breast draw breath; but the whole action and actors alike are too destitute of complexity. In strictness there is but one personage in possession of the stage—God the Father; since God cannot show Himself without eclipsing all the rest, nor speak without His will being done. The Son is but a double of the Father. The angels and archangels are but his messengers; nay, they are even less—personifications of his decrees, supers in a drama which would have gone on equally well without them.

Milton did not yield without a struggle to the conditions of his chosen subject. He tried to evade them, and only made the defect more sensible. The long discourses with which he fills the gaps between the action are only sermons, and do but make evident the absence of dramatic matter. Then, since after all some sort of action, some sort of contest was necessary, the poet had recourse to the revolt of the angels. But, unluckily, the fundamental defects of the subject were such that this expedient turned in a fashion against him. What the drama gains in movement, it loses in verisimilitude. We see a battle, but we cannot take either the fight or the fighters seriously. A God who can be resisted is not a God. A struggle with Omnipotence is not only rash, but silly. Belial saw that very well when, in the Infernal Council, he rejected the idea of a contest, either open or concealed, with Him who is all-seeing and all-powerful. Nor can one, indeed, comprehend how his colleagues did not at once give way to so self-evident a consideration. But, I repeat, the poem only became possible at the cost of this impossibility; and so Milton bravely made up his mind to it. He urged to the last, he accepted, even in its uttermost consequences, the most inadmissible of fictions. He presents to us Jehovah anxious for His omnipotence, afraid of seeing His position turned, His palace surprised, His throne usurped.[3] He sketches for us angels throwing mountains, and firing cannon, at each other's heads. He shows us victory evenly balanced till the Son arrives armed with thunder and mounted on a car with four cherubs harnessed to it.

We have still to inquire whether Milton had an epic imagination, or whether his subject did not do him good service by dispensing him from drawing more largely on his own resources. As a matter of fact, he scarcely ever strays from this subject without falling into burlesque. His prince of the rebel angels, who changes himself into a toad and a cormorant; his demons, who become dwarfs in order to be less crowded in their Parliament house; the punishment inflicted on them, which consists of being changed once a year into serpents; the Paradise of Fools; the famous, but extravagant allegory of Sin and Death—all these fictions give us but a feeble notion of Milton's inventive genius, and make it permissible to think that he would not have succeeded in a subject where he had to create his heroes and imagine his situations.

IX

Let me not be misunderstood. I do not reproach Milton, because, with his sixteenth century Calvinism, he is found out of harmony with nineteenth century thought. I care very little about his believing in witches and in astrology. Where would Homer be, where Dante, if, refusing to place ourselves at their point of view, we judged them from the level of our modern criticism? Not a single work of art could support such a trial. But the position of Milton is not exactly this. Milton wants to prove something, he is sustaining a thesis, he means to do the work of a theologian as well as of a poet. In a word, whether intentionally or merely as a fact, *Paradise Lost* is a didactic work, and, as a consequence, its form cannot be separated from its matter. Now, it so happens that the idea of the poem does not bear examination; that its explanation of the problem of evil verges on the burlesque; that the characters of its heroes, Jehovah and Satan, are incoherent; that the fate of Adam touches us little; and finally, that the action passes in regions where the interests and the passions of our common humanity have nothing to do. I have already pointed out this contradiction in Milton's epic. The story on which it rests has neither meaning nor value unless it retains its dogmatic import, and at the same time it cannot retain this import without falling into theology, that is to say, into a domain foreign to art. The subject of the poem is nothing unless it is real, unless it touches us as the secret of our destinies; and the more the poet tries to grasp this reality the more it escapes him.

So intangible in character are these conceptions, that Milton knew not even where to pitch the scene of his drama. He is obliged to forge a system of the world on purpose, a system in which he himself only half believes. He is hampered by the science of his time. Men are no longer in the fourteenth century, when Dante could image hell as a great hole burrowing beneath the surface of our globe. Copernicus and Galileo have intervened. So the cosmology of the Scriptures must be modified and accommodated to the enlightenment of the day. There is nothing more curious than to read *Paradise Lost* from this point of view, and to note the modifications imposed by science on tradition. Milton regards space as infinite, but divided into two regions, that of light or creation, and that of darkness or of chaos. On earth, in the country of Eden, is the Earthly Paradise, communicating by a staircase with the abode of the Most High. Chaos surrounds the whole of this created world, but on the edge of chaos, in the twilight, is the Limbo of vanity, and beyond chaos, in the depths of uncreated space, is found Hell, with a gate and a bridge constructed by Sin and Death, over which is the road from earth to the abyss.[4]

A vague conception, half literal, half symbolic, whereof the author had need as a scene for his personages, but in which he himself has no entire confidence—a striking example of the kind of antinomy with which I charge the whole poem, of the combined necessity, and impossibility of taking things at the foot of the letter.

X

Let us sum up. *Paradise Lost* is an unreal poem, a grotesque poem, a tiresome poem. There is not one reader in a hundred who can read Books Nine and Ten without a smile, or Books Eleven and Twelve without a yawn. The thing does not hold together: it is a pyramid balanced on its apex, the most terrible of problems solved by the most childish of means. And yet *Paradise Lost* is immortal. It lives by virtue of some episodes which will be for ever famous. In contrast with Dante, who must be read as a whole if we wish really to grasp his beauties, Milton ought not to be read except in fragments; but these fragments form a part of the poetic patrimony of the human race. The invocation to Light, the character of Eve, the description of the earthly Paradise, of the morning of the world, of its first love, are all masterpieces. The discourses of the Prince of Hell are incomparably eloquent. Lord Brougham used to cite them as worthy to be set side by side with the greatest models of antiquity, and another orator of our time, Mr. Bright, is said to be a constant reader of Milton. *Paradise Lost* is, moreover, strewn with incomparable lines. The poetry of Milton is the very essence of poetry. The author seems to think but in images, and these images are grand and proud as his own soul—a marvellous mingling of the sublime and the picturesque. Every word of his vocabulary of expression is a discovery and unique. "Darkness visible" is well known. If he would paint night he shows us the fairies dancing by the woodside:

> while overhead the moon
> Sits arbitress, and nearer to the earth
> Wheels her pale course.

The sun shines on the expanse of the deluge waters and begins to evaporate them:

> And the clear sun on his wide watery glass
> Gaz'd hot, and of the fresh wave largely drew,
> As after thirst.

Peace follows fighting:

> The brazen throat of war had ceased to roar.

The chaste happiness of the wedded pair is drawn in a word:

> Imparadised in one another's arms.

Verses of this kind, always as exact as they are beautiful, are innumerable in Milton, and one is almost ashamed to cite them, so capricious does choice seem in the midst of such riches.

Besides, all is not said when some verses of Milton have been quoted. He has not only imagery and vocabulary, but the period, the great musical phrase, a little long, a little loaded with ornament and convolved with inversions, but swaying all with it in its superb undulation. After all, and above all, he has an indefinable serenity and victoriousness, a sustained equality, an indomitable power; one might almost say that he wraps us in the skirt of his robe and wafts us with him to the eternal regions where he himself dwells.[5]

Notes

1.   [In Gospel truth nought's by the mind discerned
       But penance due and punishments well-earned;
       And when your art a blameful blend supplies
       You give its very truths the air of lies.—*Trans.*]
2. [There is, however, a proverb in M. Scherer's language, *Rira bien qui rira le dernier*; and one may also think of Sandy Mackaye's very pregnant and luminous protest against the premature interment of this personage.—*Trans.*]
3. *Paradise Lost*, v. 719, *et seq.* In fact and in fine Satan *has* won something, and *has* succeeded. His own lot is made no worse, and, on the other hand, a great many men will be damned, x. 375. It is

useless, therefore, to represent Evil as merely passing, or even as a means to good, x. 629.
4. Milton introduced not merely his cosmology but also his politics into his poem. See his republicanism and tyranny, xii. 64–101.
5. Milton himself has given the rule of poetry. According to him, it must be "simple, sensuous, and impassioned," which comes to the three conditions of simplicity, fulness of imagery, and movement.

MATTHEW ARNOLD
"Milton"
Essays in Criticism, Second Series
1888

The most eloquent voice of our century uttered, shortly before leaving the world, a warning cry against 'the Anglo-Saxon contagion.' The tendencies and aims, the view of life and the social economy of the ever-multiplying and spreading Anglo-Saxon race, would be found congenial, this prophet feared, by all the prose, all the vulgarity amongst mankind, and would invade and overpower all nations. The true ideal would be lost, a general sterility of mind and heart would set in.

The prophet had in view, no doubt, in the warning thus given, us and our colonies, but the United States still more. There the Anglo-Saxon race is already most numerous, there it increases fastest; there material interests are most absorbing and pursued with most energy; there the ideal, the saving ideal, of a high and rare excellence, seems perhaps to suffer most danger of being obscured and lost. Whatever one may think of the general danger to thc world from the Anglo-Saxon contagion, it appears to me difficult to deny that the growing greatness and influence of the United States does bring with it some danger to the ideal of a high and rare excellence. The *average man* is too much a religion there; his performance is unduly magnified, his shortcomings are not duly seen and admitted. A lady in the State of Ohio sent to me only the other day a volume on American authors; the praise given throughout was of such high pitch that in thanking her I could not forbear saying that for only one or two of the authors named was such a strain of praise admissible, and that we lost all real standard of excellence by praising so uniformly and immoderately. She answered me with charming good temper, that very likely I was quite right, but it was pleasant to her to think that excellence was common and abundant. But excellence is not common and abundant; on the contrary, as the Greek poet long ago said, excellence dwells among rocks hardly accessible, and a man must almost wear his heart out before he can reach her. Whoever talks of excellence as common and abundant, is on the way to lose all right standard of excellence. And when the right standard of excellence is lost, it is not likely that much which is excellent will be produced.

To habituate ourselves, therefore, to approve, as the Bible says, things that are really excellent, is of the highest importance. And some apprehension may justly be caused by a tendency in Americans to take, or, at any rate, attempt to take, profess to take, the average man and his performances too seriously, to overrate and overpraise what is not really superior.

But we have met here to-day to witness the unveiling of a gift in Milton's honour, and a gift bestowed by an American, Mr. Childs of Philadelphia; whose cordial hospitality so many Englishmen, I myself among the number, have experienced in America. It was only last autumn that Stratford-upon-Avon celebrated the reception of a gift from the same generous donor in honour of Shakspeare. Shakspeare and Milton—he who wishes to keep his standard of excellence high, cannot choose two better objects of regard and honour. And it is an American who has chosen them, and whose beautiful gift in honour of one of them, Milton, with Mr. Whittier's simple and true lines inscribed upon it, is unveiled to-day. Perhaps this gift in honour of Milton, of which I am asked to speak, is, even more than the gift in honour of Shakspeare, one to suggest edifying reflections to us.

Like Mr. Whittier, I treat the gift of Mr. Childs as a gift in honour of Milton, although the window given is in memory of his second wife, Catherine Woodcock, the 'late espoused saint' of the famous sonnet, who died in childbed at the end of the first year of her marriage with Milton, and who lies buried here with her infant. Milton is buried in Cripplegate, but he lived for a good while in this parish of St. Margaret's, Westminster, and here he composed part of *Paradise Lost*, and the whole of *Paradise Regained* and *Samson Agonistes*. When death deprived him of the Catherine whom the new window commemorates, Milton had still some eighteen years to live, and Cromwell, his 'chief of men,' was yet ruling England. But the Restoration, with its 'Sons of Belial,' was not far off; and in the meantime Milton's heavy affliction had laid fast hold upon him, his eyesight had failed totally, and he was blind. In what remained to him of life he had the consolation of producing the *Paradise Lost* and the *Samson Agonistes*, and such a consolation we may indeed count as no slight one. But the daily life of happiness in common things and in domestic affections—a life of which, to Milton as to Dante, too small a share was given—he seems to have known most, if not only, in his one married year with the wife who is here buried. Her form 'vested all in white,' as in his sonnet he relates that after her death she appeared to him, her face veiled, but with 'love, sweetness, and goodness' shining in her person,—this fair and gentle daughter of the rigid sectarist of Hackney, this lovable companion with whom Milton had rest and happiness one year, is a part of Milton indeed, and in calling up her memory, we call up his.

And in calling up Milton's memory we call up, let me say, a memory upon which, in prospect of the Anglo-Saxon contagion and of its dangers supposed and real, it may be well to lay stress even more than upon Shakspeare's. If to our English race an inadequate sense for perfection of work is a real danger, if the discipline of respect for a high and flawless excellence is peculiarly needed by us, Milton is of all our gifted men the best lesson, the most salutary influence. In the sure and flawless perfection of his rhythm and diction he is as admirable as Virgil or Dante, and in this respect he is unique amongst us. No one else in English literature and art possesses the like distinction.

Thomson, Cowper, Wordsworth, all of them good poets who have studied Milton, followed Milton, adopted his form, fail in their diction and rhythm if we try them by that high standard of excellence maintained by Milton constantly. From style really high and pure Milton never departs; their departures from it are frequent.

Shakspeare is divinely strong, rich, and attractive. But sureness of perfect style Shakspeare himself does not possess. I have heard a politician express wonder at the treasures of political wisdom in a certain celebrated scene of *Troilus and Cressida*; for my part I am at least equally moved to wonder at the fantastic and false diction in which Shakspeare has in that scene clothed them. Milton, from one end of *Paradise Lost* to the other, is in his diction and rhythm constantly a great artist in the great style. Whatever may be said as to the subject of his poem, as to the conditions under which he received his subject and treated it, that praise, at any rate, is assured to him.

For the rest, justice is not at present done, in my opinion, to Milton's management of the inevitable matter of a Puritan epic, a matter full of difficulties, for a poet. Justice is not done to the *architectonics*, as Goethe would have called them, of *Paradise Lost*; in these, too, the power of Milton's art is remarkable. But this may be a proposition which requires discussion and development for establishing it, and they are impossible on an occasion like the present.

That Milton, of all our English race, is by his diction and rhythm the one artist of the highest rank in the great style whom we have; this I take as requiring no discussion, this I take as certain.

The mighty power of poetry and art is generally admitted. But where the soul of this power, of this power at its best, chiefly resides, very many of us fail to see. It resides chiefly in the refining and elevation wrought in us by the high and rare excellence of the great style. We may feel the effect without being able to give ourselves clear account of its cause, but the thing is so. Now, no race needs the influences mentioned, the influences of refining and elevation, more than ours; and in poetry and art our grand source for them is Milton.

To what does he owe this supreme distinction? To nature first and foremost, to that bent of nature for inequality which to the worshippers of the average man is so unacceptable; to a gift, a divine favour. 'The older one grows,' says Goethe, 'the more one prizes natural gifts, because by no possibility can they be procured and stuck on.' Nature formed Milton to be a great poet. But what other poet has shown so sincere a sense of the grandeur of his vocation, and a moral effort so constant and sublime to make and keep himself worthy of it? The Milton of religious and political controversy, and perhaps of domestic life also, is not seldom disfigured by want of amenity, by acerbity. The Milton of poetry, on the other hand, is one of those great men 'who are modest'—to quote a fine remark of Leopardi, that gifted and stricken young Italian, who in his sense for poetic style is worthy to be named with Dante and Milton— 'who are modest, because they continually compare themselves, not with other men, but with that idea of the perfect which they have before their mind.' The Milton of poetry is the man, in his own magnificent phrase, of 'devout prayer to that Eternal Spirit that can enrich with all utterance and knowledge, and sends out his Seraphim with the hallowed fire of his altar, to touch and purify the lips of whom he pleases.' And finally, the Milton of poetry is, in his own words again, the man of 'industrious and select reading.' Continually he lived in companionship with high and rare excellence, with the great Hebrew poets and prophets, with the great poets of Greece and Rome. The Hebrew compositions were not in verse, and can be not inadequately represented by the grand, measured prose of our English Bible. The verse of the poets of Greece and Rome no translation can adequately reproduce. Prose cannot have the power of verse; verse-translation may give whatever of charm is in the soul and talent of the translator himself, but never the specific charm of the verse and poet translated. In our race are thousands of readers, presently there will be millions, who know not a word of Greek and Latin, and will never learn those languages. If this host of readers are ever to gain any sense of the power and charm of the great poets of antiquity, their way to gain it is not through translations of the ancients, but through the original poetry of Milton, who has the like power and charm, because he has the like great style.

Through Milton they may gain it, for, in conclusion, Milton is English; this master in the great style of the ancients is English. Virgil, whom Milton loved and honoured, has at the end of the *Æneid* a noble passage, where Juno, seeing the defeat of Turnus and the Italians imminent, the victory of the Trojan invaders assured, entreats Jupiter that Italy may nev-

ertheless survive and be herself still, may retain her own mind, manners, and language, and not adopt those of the conqueror.

Sit Latium, sint Albani per secula reges!

Jupiter grants the prayer; he promises perpetuity and the future to Italy—Italy reinforced by whatever virtue the Trojan race has, but Italy, not Troy. This we may take as a sort of parable suiting ourselves. All the Anglo-Saxon contagion, all the flood of Anglo-Saxon commonness, beats vainly against the great style but cannot shake it, and has to accept its triumph. But it triumphs in Milton, in one of our own race, tongue, faith, and morals. Milton has made the great style no longer an exotic here; he has made it an inmate amongst us, a leaven, and a power. Nevertheless he, and his hearers on both sides of the Atlantic, are English, and will remain English—

Sermonem Ausonii patrium moresque tenebunt.

The English race overspreads the world, and at the same time the ideal of an excellence the most high and the most rare abides a possession with it for ever.

EDWARD DOWDEN
"The Idealism of Milton"
Transcripts and Studies
1888, pp. 454–73

The critic who would find some single expression which resumes the tendency of each of an artist's works, or an expression which resumes the tendency of all his works taken together, is commonly engaged in falsifying the truth of criticism, and in all cases runs a risk of losing the faithfulness of sympathy, the disengagedness of intelligence, the capacity for assuming various spiritual attitudes which should belong to him. A man will not be comprehended in a formula, nor will the work of a man. But in the case of Milton, and those who resemble him in his method as an artist, this doctrinaire style of criticism is at least not illegitimate. No poem, of course, is reducible to an abstract statement or idea; yet the statement, the idea, may be the germ from which the poem has sprung. A tree glorious with all its leaves and blossoming is much more than the seed in which it lay concealed; yet from the seed, with favourable earth and skies, it grew. Milton never sang as the bird sings, with spontaneous pleasure, through an impulse unobserved and unmodified by the intellect. The intention of each poem is clearly conceived by himself; the form is elaborated with a conscious study of effects. There is in him none of the delicious *imprévu* of Shakspere. Milton's nature never reacted simply and directly, finding utterance in a lyrical cry, when impressions from the world of nature or of society aroused the faculty of song. The reaction was checked, and did not find expression until he had considered his own feelings, and modified or altered them upon the suggestions of his intellect. Milton's passion is great, but deliberate, approved by his judgment, and he never repents, feeling that repentance would be a confession, not only of sin, but of extreme weakness and fatuity. He is not imaginative in the highest—in Shakspere's— manner. Each character of his masque, his drama, his epics, is an ideal character—a Miltonic abstraction incarnated. He himself is, as much as may be, an ideal personage: his life does not grow in large, vital unconsciousness, but is modelled, sometimes laboriously, after an idea. And consequently his life, like his writings, lacks the *imprévu*. He resolves in early youth that it shall be a great life, and he carries out his resolution unfalteringly from first to last. He tends his own genius, and observes it. He waits for its maturity, and watches. He accepts his powers as trusts from God, and will neither go beyond nor fall short of them. He is noble, but we are sometimes painfully aware that it is a nobleness prepense. He loves to imagine himself in heroic attitudes—as defender of England and of liberty, as the afflicted champion of his people, fallen on evil days. His very recreation is pre-arranged—Mild heaven ordains a time for pleasure.[1]

In all this Milton was unlike Shakspere; and as the men differed, so did the times. During the brighter years of the Elizabethan period, when life—life of the intellect, life of the imagination, religious life, life of the nation, and life of the individual—with one great bound had broken through and over the mediæval dykes and dams, and was rushing onwards, somewhat turbid, somewhat violent, yet gaining a law and a majestic order from the mere weight of the advancing mass of waters—at that fortunate time to live was the chief thing, not to adopt and adhere to a theory of living.

> Bliss was it in that dawn to be alive,
> But to be young was very heaven!

At the time when Milton reached manhood, the unity of this new life of England was broken, and there were two conspicuous theories of life, to one of which each man was compelled to attach himself; two experiments of living, of which each person must assay one; two doctrines in religion, two tendencies in politics, two systems of social conduct and of manners. The large *insouciance* of the earlier fashion of living was gone; everyone could tell why he was what he was.

Thus the character of the period fell in with Milton's natural tendency towards the conscious modelling of his life as a man, and of his works as an artist after certain ideals, types, abstractions. It is not a little remarkable that we have the authority and example of Milton himself for applying to his writings that criticism which looks for an intention or express purpose as the germinal centre of each, and which attempts to discover an unity in them all, resulting from the constant presence of one dominant idea. In the *Defensio Secunda* Milton looks back over his more important prose works, and he finds that they all move in a harmonious system around a central conception of liberty. An ideal of liberty was that which presided over his public life, his life in the world of action, and the books which were meant to bear upon the world of action refer to that ideal. There are three forms or species of liberty, Milton tells us, which are essential to the happiness of man as a member of society—religious liberty, domestic, civil. From an early period the first of these had occupied his thoughts. "What he had in view when he hesitated to become a clergyman," Professor Masson remarks, "was, in all probability, less the letter of the articles to be subscribed, and of the oaths to be taken, than the general condition of the Church at that particular time." Prelatical tyranny, and the theories by which it was justified, inspired the indignant pamphlets to write which Milton resolutely put poetry aside. Domestic liberty "involves three material questions—the conditions of the conjugal tie, the education of children, and the free publication of one's thoughts."[2] Each of these was made a subject of distinct consideration—in *Tetrachordon* and other writings on the question of divorce, in the Letter addressed to Samuel Hartlib on education, and in the Speech for the liberty of unlicensed printing. Were it one of Milton's critics, and not Milton himself, who had thus classed the *Areopagitica* amongst the treatises in defence of domestic liberty, or who had represented the letter to Hartlib as concerned with liberty in any of its forms, should we not be ready to declare that he had departed from the sincerity of criticism, and was forcing the author's works at any cost to

accord with a theory of his own? Yet there is no forcing here; there is only the compulsion put upon Milton himself by his dominant idea. Civil liberty occupied him last. He thought at an earlier season that it might be left to the magistrates. It was not until events had proved that his pen might be wielded as a powerful weapon in its defence, that the *Iconoclastes*, the *Pro Populo Anglicano Defensio*, and the *Defensio Secunda* were produced.

Thus we are directed by Milton himself to observe how the great cycle of his prose works revolves around this controlling idea of liberty. One is tempted to go on, and endeavour to apply this authorised kind of criticism to Milton's poetry. Would it be surprising, or not rather a thing to be expected, if a certain unity of idea became apparent in the work of the poet as in that of the pamphleteer? Milton being what he was, a man governed by ideas, and those ideas being persistent and few—Milton's poetry at the same time dealing with moral truth, and the abiding meanings of things—might we not naturally look for a single chief tendency, a permanent presence of one dominant conception in all his poetical self-utterance, epic and dramatic?

Milton's inner life, of which his poetry is an expression, as his prose is an expression of his outer, public life, was an unceasing tending from evil to good, from base or common to noble, a perpetual aspiration to moral greatness. Not less than Goethe he studied self-culture. But while Goethe, with his deliberate Hellenism, made man an end to himself, Milton, over whom the Hebrew spirit kept jealous guard, considered man at his highest as the creature of God. And in the hierarchy of human faculties Milton assigned the place of supreme authority, as Goethe never did, to those powers which lie upon the Godward side of our humanity, to those perceptions and volitions which are concerned with moral good and evil. The impartiality of Goethe's self-culture was undisturbed by any vivid sense of sin. No part of his being seemed to him in extreme peril from spiritual foes, no part appeared the object of a fierce assault; it was easy for him to transfer his attention serenely from this side of his nature to that, while with resolute and calm persistence he strove to attain completeness of self-development. To Goethe the world was a gymnasium or academy, and life a period of higher education. The peculiarity of Milton's view was, that before him the world lay as a battle-field, life was a warfare against principalities and powers, and the good man a champion of God. The sense of sin never forsook him, nor that of a glorious possibility of virtue. To Goethe nature presented itself as a harmonious group of influences favourable, upon the whole, towards man; what he chiefly feared was a mistake in his plan of culture, the substituting in his lifelong education of a subordinate power or faculty of his nature for the master power. What Milton feared before all else was disloyalty to God, and a consequent hell; and to him nature, in its most significant aspect, was the scene of an indefatigable antagonism between good and evil. In other words, Milton was essentially a Puritan. In spite of his classical culture, and his Renaissance sense of beauty, he not less than Bunyan saw, as the prime fact of the world, Diabolus at odds with Immanuel. He, as well as Bunyan, beheld a Celestial City and a City of Destruction, standing remote from each other, with hostile rulers. Milton added, as Bunyan also added, that final victory must lie on the side of good. That is, he asserted eternal Providence. There is a victory, which is God's, not ours; it is our part to cleave to the Eternal One, his part to achieve the triumph on our behalf.

Here we possess the dominant idea which governed the inner life of Milton, and the dominant idea around which revolves the cycle of his poetical works, as that of his prose works revolves around the idea of liberty. There is a mortal battle waged between the powers of good and evil. Therefore in each of Milton's greater poems there are two parties, opposed as light and darkness are opposed, there are hostile forces arrayed for strife on this side and on that. But God is omnipotent, the everlasting Jehovah. There is, therefore, in every instance a victory of the righteous, wrought out for them by Divine help.

In addition to this, let it be borne in mind that Milton, as an artist, works in the manner of an idealist. His starting-point is ordinarily an abstraction. Whereas with Bunyan abstract virtues and vices are perpetually tending to become real persons, with Milton each real person tends to become the representative of an idea or a group, more or less complex, of ideas. Hopeful, and old Honest, and Mr Feeble-Mind, as we read, grow by degrees into actual human beings, who, had we lived two centuries ago, might have been known to us as respected Puritan neighbours. Samson and Dalila, and not along these persons of remote Eastern tradition, but Lady Alice Egerton and her brothers,[3] veritably alive and breathing, are, as Milton shows them, objects (to borrow a phrase of Cardinal Newman) rather of notional than real apprehension.

Comus is the work of a youthful spirit, enamoured of its ideals of beauty and of virtue, zealous to exhibit the identity of moral loveliness with moral severity. The real incident from which the mask is said to have originated disengages itself, in the imagination of Milton, from the world of actual occurrences, and becomes an occasion for the dramatic play of his own poetical abstractions. The young English gentlemen cast off their identity and individuality, and appear in the elementary shapes of "First Brother" and "Second Brother." The Lady Alice rises into an ideal impersonation of virgin strength and virtue. The scene is earth, a wild wood; but earth, as in all the poems of Milton, with the heavens arching over it—a dim spot, in which men "strive to keep up a frail and feverish being" set below the "starry threshold of Jove's Court,"

> Where those immortal shapes
> Of bright aerial spirits live inspher'd
> In regions mild of calm and serene air.

From its first scene to the last the drama is a representation of the trials, difficulties, and dangers to which moral purity is exposed in this world, and of the victory of the better principle in the soul, gained by strenuous human endeavour aided by the grace of God. In this spiritual warfare the powers of good and evil are arrayed against one another; upon this side the Lady, her brothers (types of human helpfulness weak in itself, and liable to go astray), and the supernatural powers auxiliar to virtue in heaven and in earth—the Attendant Spirit and the nymph Sabrina.

The enchanter Comus is son of Bacchus and Circe, and inheritor of twofold vice. If Milton had pictured the life of innocent mirth in "L'Allegro," here was a picture to set beside the other, a vision of the genius of sensual indulgence. Yet Comus is inwardly, not outwardly foul; no grim monster like that which the mediæval imagination conjured up to terrify the spirit and disgust the senses. The attempt of sin upon the soul as conceived by Milton is not the open and violent obsession of a brute power, but involves a cheat, an imposture. The soul is put upon its trial through the seduction of the senses and the lower parts of our nature. Flattering lies entice the ears of Eve; Christ is tried by false visions of power and glory, and beneficent rule; Samson is defrauded of his strength by deceitful blandishment. And in like manner Comus must needs possess a beauty of his own, such beauty as ensnares the eye untrained

in the severe school of moral perfection. Correggio sought him as a favourite model, but not Michael Angelo. He is sensitive to rich forms and sweet sounds, graceful in oratory, possessed, like Satan, of high intellect, but intellect in the service of the senses; he surrounds himself with a world of art which lulls the soul into forgetfulness of its higher instincts and of duty; his palace is stately, and "set out with all manner of deliciousness."

Over against this potent enchanter stands the virginal figure of the Lady, who is stronger than he. Young men, themselves conscious of high powers, and who are more truly acquainted with admiration than with love, find the presence of strength in woman invincibly attractive. Shakspere, in his earlier dramatic period, delighted to represent such characters as Rosalind, and Beatrice, and Portia; characters at once stronger and weaker than his Imogens and Desdemonas,—stronger because more intellectual, weaker because less harmoniously feminine. Shelley, who was never other than young, exhibited different types of heroic womanly nature, as conceived by him, in Cyntha of *The Revolt of Islam*, and in Bearice Cenci. Something of weakness belongs to the Lady of Milton's poem, because she is a woman, accustomed to the protection of others, tenderly nurtured, with a fair and gentle body; but when the hour of trial comes she shows herself strong in powers of judgment and of reasoning, strong in her spiritual nature, in her tenacity of moral truth, in her indignation against sin. Although alone, and encompassed by evil and danger, she is fearless, and so clear-sighted that the juggling practice of her antagonist is wholly ineffectual against her. There is much in the Lady which resembles the youthful Milton himself—he, the Lady of his college—and we may well believe that the great debate concerning temperance was not altogether dramatic (where, indeed, is Milton truly dramatic?), but was in part a record of passages in the poet's own spiritual history. Milton admired the Lady as he admired the ideal which he projected before him of himself. She is, indeed, too admirable to be an object of cherishing love. We could almost prolong her sufferings to draw a more complete enthusiasm from the sight of her heroic attitude.

The Lady is unsubdued, and indeed unsubduable, because her will remains her own, a citadel without a breach; but "her corporal rind" is manacled, she is set in the enchanted chair and cannot leave it. Richardson, an artist who like Milton wrought in the manner of the idealists, conceived a similar situation in his Clarissa. To subdue the will of the noble and beautiful woman against whom he has set himself is as much the object of Lovelace as to gain possession of her person. His mastery over her outward fate grows steadily from less to more, until at length it is absolute; but her true personality (and Richardson never lets us forget this) remains remote, untouched, victorious, and her death itself is not defeat, but a well-conducted retreat from this life to a position of greater security and freedom. Meanwhile,—to return to *Comus*—the brothers wander in the wood. They are alike in being aimless and helpless; if they are distinguished from each other, it is only as "First Brother" and "Second Brother," and by one of the simple devices common to ideal artists—first brother is a philosopher and full of hope and faith; second brother is more apprehensive, and less thoroughly grounded in ethics and metaphysics. The deliverance of their sister would be impossible but for supernatural interposition, the aid afforded by the Attendant Spirit from Jove's court. In other words, Divine Providence is asserted. Not without higher than human aid is the Lady rescued, and through the weakness of the mortal instruments of divine grace but half the intended work is accomplished. Comus escapes bearing his magic wand, to deceive other strayers in the wood, to work new enchantments, and swell his rout of ugly-headed followers.

Little need be said of *Paradise Lost*; the central idea is obvious. There is again a great contention, Heaven and Hell striving for the mastery. Satan and his angels are warring, first tumultuously and afterwards by crafty ways, against God and Messiah, and the executors of God's purposes. Each of the infernal Thrones and Dominations is an ideal conception, the representative of a single living lust. Satan himself is *the spirit of disobedience*, that supreme sin of which all sins are but modes; he is a will alienated from God, and proudly accepting such alienation as the law of his nature. Man's virtue is placed upon its trial. Paradise, so far from being the peaceful garden, is the central battle-field of the whole universe. Adam falls, and evil for a time appears to have gained the day; but such an appearance must needs be fallacious—the woman contains within her the seed of promise, the great Deliverer who shall bruise the serpent's head. To "assert eternal Providence" is the declared intention of the whole work. It closes, if in no triumphant strain, yet in a spirit of serious confidence concerning the future:—

> Some natural tears they dropp'd, but wiped them
>   soon;
> The world was all before them, where to choose
> Their place of rest, and Providence their guide:
> They hand in hand, with wand'ring steps and slow,
> Through Eden took their solitary way.

By the time *Paradise Lost* was written, Milton had known love as distinct from admiration, the attraction not of identical but of complementary qualities. The novel delight of surrender to a charm, the charm of a being weaker and fairer than himself, had been enough, and he had not provided for the difficulties of accommodating this new self-surrender to the self-maintenance which was his natural and his habitual temper. Ere long the discovery was made of feminine frailty. The Lady of *Comus* had been created out of elements which belonged to his own character. Eve was created out of all that he was not and could not be. The Lady is admirable; Eve is supremely desirable. If the Lady had been seduced by the fraud of Comus, and had fallen, we should leave her among the monsters, and despair of goodness; but Eve, when she has eaten the apple, is hardly less lovable than before, and we know that hardly any fall is fatal to a character like hers, which has no inexorable virtue; it bends, but is not broken. "Eve is a kind of abstract woman; essentially a typical being; an official mother of all living." She is the Miltonic conception of the "eternal feminine" (*das Ewig-Weibliche*) in nature.

What passage in the life of Christ would Milton select for treatment as the subject of his second epic? Paradise had been forfeited by the disobedience of Adam; by the perfect obedience of the Son of God it was recovered. The supreme act of submission to his Father's will was surely his obedience unto death, "even the death of the cross." "O my Father, if this cup may not pass away from me except I drink it, Thy will be done." The contrast is absolute between such obedient fidelity as this, and the wilfulness and disloyalty of the first Adam. And when Christ had suffered death, and despoiled hell, and risen again, then Paradise was truly and completely regained. Yet it is not the passion, the death, and the triumphant resurrection of the Saviour which Milton determined to render into song. Does the reader not feel a certain incongruity in the appropriating of this name *Paradise Regained* to a poem which leaves Christ at the outset of his early career, with his crown of thorns yet to wear, and his cross to be borne to Calvary? Not so did Milton feel. To him the first complete victory over Satan was equiv-

alent to the final overthrow of the kingdom of darkness, and the restoration of the reign of all goodness. The great warfare was then brought to an issue—then, for the first time—and that issue was decisive. Satan had found one mightier than he in the Divine Man. Now, obviously, no passage in the life of Christ illustrates in such naked contrast the struggle between the powers of good and of evil as the assault made upon the virtue of Christ himself by the arch-enemy. Victory in such a contest must be ultimate victory. This, therefore, naturally from Milton's point of view became the subject of *Paradise Regained*.

In treating the history of the temptation in the wilderness, the genius of the poet moved under peculiar advantages. Milton was never dramatic in the high sense of that word. Varying, vital movement of thought and passion he was unable to exhibit. The mystery and obscurity of life do not belong to the characters created by him. Each of them is perfectly intelligible. But Milton excelled in the representation of characters *in position*, and more particularly in the discussion of a "topic" by two characters who occupy fixed and opposing points of view. This was not dialogue; there is no giving and taking of ideas, no shifting of positions, no fluctuant moods, no mobility of thought. It was rather debate, a forensic pleading, with counsel on this side and on that. It was a duel, not with rapiers gleaming under and over each other, and in a moment's irregular strife changing hands—not such a duel, but one much more deliberate, the antagonists alternately letting off their heavy charges of argument, and alternately awaiting the formidable reply. *Paradise Regained* is a series of such debates, which remind us of the scene between Comus and the Lady in Milton's early poem, where already the Miltonic manner appears fully formed.

By obedience Christ regains paradise. Loyalty to God, fidelity to the righteous father, is the supreme excellence of his character; its strength is not Pagan self-dependence, but Hebrew self-devotion to the Eternal One. The consciousness of filial virtue, of the union of his will with that of the Father, supports him through every trial. At the same time this obedience, unlike that claimed from Adam, does not lie in the passive accepting of an arbitrary rule. The Saviour is a champion of God. He is filled, like the ancient heroes of the Jewish race, with active zeal for the glory of God, and his people's service:—

> Virtuous deeds
> Flamed in my heart, heroic acts; one while
> To rescue Israel from the Roman yoke;
> Then to subdue and quell, o'er all the earth,
> Brute violence and proud tyrannic pow'r,
> Till truth were freed, and equity restored.

He is a worthy leader of mankind in the great warfare against sin and death, greater in his virtue than Adam could possibly have been, because the virtue of Christ is generous and aspiring, not mere obedience for obedience' sake. Such an antagonist, no power of evil could withstand. Satan is not only foiled, but crushingly defeated. The purpose and the promise of God are fulfilled. As the poem closes, we hear the anthems of angelic quires sung for the victory of the righteous cause.

Samson Agonistes remains to be briefly studied. Once again there is the antagonism of good and evil. God, the people of God, and their afflicted chieftain are set over against Dagon, his impious crew of worshippers, the enchantress Dalila, and the champion of the Philistines, the giant Harapha. It is apparently an unequal warfare. Samson is blind—

> Ask for this great deliverer now, and find him
> Eyeless in Gaza at the mill with slaves—

and his nation is likewise in bondage. God's order seems to be reversed. It is the hour of Dagon's triumph. Worst of all, it was by the moral weakness of their leader that the people of Israel had fallen. But Adam had sinned and was an exile from Paradise, and yet God's order stood. Christ was in the wilderness in his humiliation, cold and hungry, drenched with rain, environed by the powers of hell. The Lady sat enthralled by the spells of her deadly enemy, alone in the midst of a rout of unclean creatures, and yet deliverance had been wrought. And now the chosen nation, God's representative among the peoples, was but tried and afflicted for a time. A sudden and awful victory is achieved on their behalf. And once again the choral song which ends the tragedy is a confession of a divine order of things, an assertion of eternal Providence:—

> All is best, though we oft doubt
> What th' unsearchable dispose
> Of highest Wisdom brings about,
> And ever best found in the close.

What is Samson? He is the man gifted with divine strength; one who is great by the grace of God, yet a mortal, and therefore liable to fall. As Milton's first important dramatic conception, the Lady, is wrought out of materials supplied from his own character and inner experience, so is this, the last. But as the beautiful youth, a poet more than a fighter, full of noble hopes and unrealized aspirations, differed from the aged man who had warred a good warfare, who had known disappointment and defeat, and now was fallen on evil days, so widely does Samson differ from Milton's first glad ideal. The transformation is a strange one, and yet we recognise the one same personality. Samson's manner of self-contemplation is precisely that of Milton. He loves to present to his own imagination the glory of his strength, the greatness of his past achievements, and his present afflicted state. This strength which he possesses he looks upon as Milton from his early years was accustomed to look upon his own extraordinary powers—as something entrusted to him, of which he must render an account. It is his sorrow that such a noble gift should be compelled to base uses, and be made the gaze and scorn of his enemies. But no suffering is so cruel as the memory of his folly. Had Milton ever been betrayed into such weakness as that of Samson he would have felt precisely as Samson feels. The single fall is fatal and irrecoverable. He is not one of those who, under the influence of time, and the world, and changing action, can slip back into his self-respect. Being despicable once, he must be always despicable. The thought of an honourable death, self-inflicted, yet not criminal nor weakly sought, must have been the one partial assuagement of his grief that ever came to him. In this death which befalls Samson there is something deeper than poetical justice. It brings peace and consolation, and "calm of mind, all passion spent," as nothing else could. It is the witness of God to the faithfulness, through all weakness and folly, of his champion.

Harapha, the Philistine giant, is so unmistakably contrasted with Samson, that it is impossible to miss Milton's intention. Samson is the man gifted with divine strength; Harapha is the type of the fleshly strength of this world, insolent and brutal. He is the force which Christ in his ardent youth burned to subdue over all the earth,—

Brute violence and proud tyrannic power. It was Harapha after the restoration of Charles who insulted the bodies of Cromwell and Ireton and Bradshaw. It is Harapha who still rules wherever material power is dissociated from moral and spiritual. He is boastful, pitiless, vulgar, and, with all his insolence, in the presence of divine strength he is a coward. Let the Chorus interpret for us the significance of the meeting of the two champions:—

> Oh, how comely it is and how reviving
> To the spirits of just men long opprest!
> When God into the hands of their deliverer
> Puts invincible might
> To quell the mighty of the earth, th' oppressor,
> The brute and boist'rous force of violent men
> Hardy and industrious to support
> Tyrannic power, but raging to pursue
> The righteous and all such as honour truth;
> He all their ammunition
> And feats of war defeats,
> With plain heroic magnitude of mind
> And celestial vigour arm'd.

The brute violence of the flesh has for its appropriate ally the deceitful beauty of the flesh, full of vanity, and lust, and cruelty. Such beauty has now lost all its fascination for Samson. Even Harapha is less intolerable than Dalila—"Out, out, hyæna!" The Lady of *Comus* was created out of all that Milton conceived as admirable; Eve out of all in woman that is desirable; Dalila out of all that is detestable. Her feminine curiosity, her feminine love of dress—she comes towards the blind prisoner "with all her bravery on"—her fleshly desire, her incapacity for any noble thought, her feigned religion, her honeyed words implying the weakness and fatuity of him whom she addresses, her wifely treachery and hard-heartedness, make up a personality which, above all others, must have been hateful to Milton. Shakspere would have smiled, and secretly accepted the enchantress as a fruitful subject of study. Milton brings her upon the scene only to expose her, and drive her away with most genuine indignation. The Lady, Eve, Dalila—these are the women of Milton; each a great ideal figure, one dedicated to admiration, one to love, and the last to loathing.

We have now gone the round of Milton's poetical works. A line will recapitulate the substance of this essay. Milton works from the starting-point of an idea, and two such ideas brought into being what he accomplished as a man and as an artist. His prose works, the outcome of his life of public action, have for their ideal centre a conception of human liberty. His poetical works, the outcome of his inner life, his life of artistic contemplation, are various renderings of one dominant idea—that the struggle for mastery between good and evil is the prime fact of life; and that a final victory of the righteous cause is assured by the existence of a divine order of the universe, which Milton knew by the name of "Providence."

Notes

1. Sonnet to Cyriac Skinner.
2. *Defensio Secunda*.
3. If, indeed, they be presented in *Comus*.

ADDITIONAL READING

GEOFFREY CHAUCER

Ainger, A. "Women of Chaucer." *English Illustrated Magazine* 1 (1884): 733. *Anniversary Papers by Colleagues and Pupils of George Lyman Kittredge*. Boston: Ginn, 1913. See articles by J. L. Lowes, J. M. Manly, J. S. P. Tatlock, K. Young.

Bailey, John Cann. *Poets and Poetry*. Oxford: Oxford University Press, 1911.

Brooke, S.A. "The Descriptive Poetry of Chaucer." *Macmillan's Magazine* 24 (1871): 268.

Case, M.P. "Chaucer and His Times." *Bibliotheca Sacra* 11 (1854): 394.

Clerke, E.M. "Chaucer and Boccaccio." *National Review* 8 (1886): 379.

Egan, M.F. "Chaucer and His Circle." *Catholic World* 31 (1880): 695.

Francis, H.T. "The Buddhist Birth Story in Chaucer." *Academy* 24 (1883): 416.

Furnivall, F. J. "Recent Work at Chaucer." *Macmillan's Magazine* 27 (1873): 383.

Gwynn, Stephen Lucius. *Masters of English Literature*. New York: Macmillan, 1904.

Holmes, J. B. "The Humor of Chaucer." *Harvard Monthly* 17 (1893): 175.

Lowell, James Russell. "The Sources and Genius of Chaucer." *North American Review* 111 (1870): 155.

MacCunn, Florence. "A Study of the Women of Chaucer." *Good Words* 34 (1893): 205.

Maunder, E.W. "The Astronomy of the *Canterbury Tales*." *Knowledge* 21 (1893): 205.

Norton, G. "Chaucer and Balzac." *Nation* 40 (1884): 417.

Palgrave, R.T. "Chaucer and the Italian Renaissance." *Century* 24 (1893): 340.

Peacock, E. "The *Miller's Tale*." *Athenaeum* 2 (1887): 54, 84.

Ransome, C. "The *Prologue*." *Macmillan's Magazine* 63 (1890): 23.

Scott, Mary A. "Chaucer and Italy." *Nation* 63 (1896): 309, 365, 385.

Wilson, J. "Dryden on Chaucer." *Blackwood's Magazine* 57 (1843): 617, 771; 58(1843): 114.

SIR PHILIP SIDNEY

Brie, Friedrich. *Sidneys Arcadia: Ein Studie zur Englischen Renaissance*. Strassburg: 1918.

Collins, Arthur, ed. *Letters and Memorials of State Written and Collected by Sir Henry Sydney*. London: T. Osborne, 1746.

Greenlaw, Edwin. "Sidney's *Arcadia* as an Example of Elizabethan Allegory." *Kittridge Anniversary Papers*. Boston: Ginn, 1913.

Tannenbaun, Samuel. *Sir Philip Sidney: A Concise Bibliography*. New York: S. A. Tannenbaun, 1941.

CHRISTOPHER MARLOWE

Carpenter, Frederic Ives. "Christopher Marlowe." In *Metaphor and Simile in the Minor Elizabethan Drama*. Chicago: University of Chicago Press, 1895, pp. 35–48.

Chan, Lois Mai. *Marlowe Criticism: A Bibliography*. Boston: G. K. Hall, 1978.

Collier, M. Payne. "Christopher Marlowe, and the Employment of Blank Verse Upon the Public Stage." In *The History of English Dramatic Poetry to the Time of Shakespeare: and Annals of the Stage to the Restoration*, Volume III. London: J. Murray, 1831, pp. 107–46.

Courtney, W. L. "Kit Marlowe's Death." *The Universal Review* 6 (1890): 356–72.

Crofts, Ellen. "Marlowe." In *Chapters in the History of English Literature: From 1509 to the Close of the Elizabethan Period*. London: Rivingston, 1884, pp. 171–94.

Deighton, K. "Marlowe." In *The Old Dramatists: Conjectural Readings*. Westminster: Archibald Constable & C., 1896, pp. 116–26.

Elze, Karl. "Marlowe." In *Notes on Elizabethan Dramatists with Conjectural Emendations of the Text*. Halle: Max Niemeyer, 1880, pp. 28–31.

Fleay, Frederick Gard. "On the Marlowe Group of Plays." In *A Chronicle History of the Life and Works of William Shakespeare*. London: J. C. Nimmo, 1886, pp. 255–83.

Horne, R. H. *The Death of Marlowe: A Tragedy; In One Act*. London: Saunders and Otley, 1837, pp. 6–23.

Logeman, Henri. "The Name of Christopher Marlowe's Murderer." *Anglia* 38 (1914): 374–76.

Mitford, J. "Retrospective Review: The Works of Christopher Marlowe." *Gentleman's Magazine*, January 1841, pp. 45–48.

Phelps, William Lyon. "Christopher Marlowe." In *Masterpieces of the English Drama*. New York: American Book Co., 1912, pp. 1–26.

Smith, G. C. Moore. "Marlowe at Cambridge." *The Modern Language Review* 6 (1908–09): 167–77.

Swinburne, Algernon Charles. "In the Bay." In *The Complete Works of Algernon Charles Swinburne*, Vol. III. London: William Heinemann Ltd.; New York: Gabriel Wells, 1925, pp. 7–17.

EDMUND SPENSER

Carpenter, W. Boyd. "Edmund Spenser." In *The Religious Spirit in the Poets*. New York: T. Y. Crowell, 1901.

Craik, George L. *Spenser and His Poetry*. London: C. Knight, 1845. 3 vols.

Dowden, Edward. *Transcripts and Studies*. London: K. Paul, Trench, Trübner & Co., 1887.

Dunham, S. A. *Eminent Literary and Scientific Men of Great Britain and Ireland*. London: Longman, Rees, Orme, Brown, Green, & Longman, 1836, Volume 1, pp. 213–51.

Hunt, Theodore W. "The Lyrics of Edmund Spenser." In *English Meditative Lyrics*. New York: Eaton & Mains, 1899, pp. 26–33.

Keightley, Thomas. "Edmund Spenser: His Life and Poetry." *British Quarterly Review* 22 (1855): 368–412.

Mayer, Carl. "Edmond Spenser et la critique de M. Taine." *Le Correspondant* 42 (1869): 1124–50.

Pancoast, Henry S. "One Aspect of Spenser's *Faerie Queene*." *Andover Review* 12 (1889): 372–85.

Reed, Henry. *Lectures on the British Poets*. Philadelphia: Parry & McMillan, 1857. 2 vols.

Scudder, Vida D. *The Life of the Spirit in the Modern English Poets*. Boston: Houghton Mifflin, 1895, pp. 96–144.

Wendell, Barrett. *The Temper of the Seventeenth Century in English Literature*. New York: Scribner's, 1904.

Whipple, Edwin P. *The Literature of the Age of Elizabeth*. Boston: Fields, Osgood, 1891, pp. 189–220.

FRANCIS BACON

Barthélemy-St. Hilaire, Jules. *Étude sur François Bacon.* Paris: Alcan, 1890.

Calvert, Albert F. *Bacon and Shakespeare.* London: Dean & Son, 1902.

Deleyre, Alexandre. *Analyse de la philosophie du chancelier François Bacon.* Amsterdam: Artskée, 1755. 2 vols.

Finch, A. Ellery. *On the Inductive Philosophy, Including a Parallel between Lord Bacon and A. Comte as Philosophers.* London: Longmans, 1872.

Fischer, Kuno. *Francis Bacon of Verulam.* Tr. John Oxenford. London: Longmans, 1857.

Gibson, R. W. *Francis Bacon: A Bibliography of His Works and Baconiana to the Year 1750.* Oxford: Scrivener Press, 1950.

Gordon, Thomas. *Francis, Lord Bacon.* London: J. Roberts, 1721.

Mallet, David. *The Life of Francis Bacon.* London: A. Millar, 1740.

Pott, Constance. *Francis Bacon and His Secret Society.* Chicago: F. J. Shulte, 1891.

Tyler, Samuel. *A Discourse of the Baconian Philosophy.* Frederick City, MD: D. Schley & T. Haller, 1846.

Wyman, W. H. *Bibliography of the Bacon-Shakespeare Controversy.* Cincinnati: P. G. Thomson, 1884.

JOHN DONNE

Bradford, G. "The Poetry of Donne." *Andover Review* 18 (1892): 350.

Dowden, E. "The Poetry of John Donne." *Fortnightly Review* 53 (1889): 809.

Furst, C.B. "The Life and Poetry of Donne." *Citizen* 2 (1897): 229.

Minto, W. *Nineteenth Century* 7 (1879): 845.

Wendell, Barrett. *The Temper of the Seventeenth Century in English Literature.* New York; Scribner's, 1904.

Unsigned. "Donne the Metaphysician." *Temple Bar* 3 (1861): 78.

Unsigned. "Donne: First of the English Satirists." *Temple Bar* 47 (1876): 337.

GEORGE HERBERT

Addison, Joseph. *Spectator,* 7 May 1711, p. 14.

Buchanan, E. S. *George Herbert, Melodist,* London: Eliot Stock, 1910.

Daniell, John J. *The Life of George Herbert of Bemerton.* London: Society for Promoting Christian Knowledge, 1902.

Hyde, A. G. *George Herbert and His Times.* New York: G. P. Putnam, 1906.

Unsigned. *British Quarterly Review* 19 (1854): pp. 393–98.

Unsigned. "George Herbert and His Times." *Christian Remembrancer,* July 1862, pp. 133–37.

JOHN WEBSTER

Archer, William. "Webster, Lamb, and Swinburne." *The New Review* VIII (1893): 96–106.

Poel, William. "A New Criticism of Webster's *The Duchess of Malfi.*" *Library Review* II (1893): 21–24.

Symonds, John Addington. "The English Drama During the Reigns of Elizabeth and James." *Cornhill Magazine* XI (1865): 604-18.

Wang, Tao-Liang. *The Literary Reputation of John Webster to 1830.* Salzburg: Institut für Englische Sprache and Literatur, Universität Salzburg, 1975.

BEN JONSON

Alden, Raymond MacDonald. "Ben Jonson." In *The Rise of Formal Satire in England.* Philadelphia: University of Pennsylvania Press, 1899, pp. 192–98.

Anderson, Robert. "The Life of Jonson." In *The Poetical Works of Benjamin Jonson.* Edinburgh: Mundell & Son, 1793, pp. 523–30.

Austin, Wiltshire Stanton and John Ralph. "Ben Jonson." In *Lives of the Poets-Laureate.* London: R. Bentley, 1853, pp. 49–108.

Disraeli, Isaac. "Ben Jonson and Thomas Decker." In *Quarrels of Authors.* Vol. 3. New York: John Murray, 1814, pp. 123–70.

Duppa, Brian, ed. *Jonsonus Virbius; or the Memoire of B. J. Revived.* London: Printed by E. P. for Henry Seile, 1638.

Gifford, William, ed. *The Works of Ben Jonson, With Notes, Critical and Explanatory, and a Biographical Memoir.* 9 vols. London: G. & W. Nicol, 1816.

Kingsley, Henry. "Ben Jonson." *Temple Bar* 42 (1874): 35–50.

Parrott, Katherine. "Ben Jonson." *Radcliffe Magazine* 2 (1900): 115–28.

Sanders, H. M. "The Poems of Ben Jonson." *Temple Bar* 121 (1900): 213–29.

Schelling, Felix E. "Ben Jonson and the Classical School." *PMLA* 13 (1898): 221–49.

Symonds, John Addington. "Ben Jonson's 'To Celia'." *Academy* 26 (1884): 377–78.

Taine, Hippolyte. "Ben Jonson." In *The History of English Literature.* Vol. 3. Philadelphia: Gebbie, 1883, pp. 1–49.

RICHARD CRASHAW

Anderson, Robert. "Life of Richard Crashaw." In *A Complete Edition of the Poets of Great Britain.* Volume 4. London: J. & A. Arch, 1793.

Clutton-Brock, Arthur. "Crashaw's Christmas Poems." *More Essays on Religion.* London: Methuen, 1927.

Holliday, Carl. "Richard Crashaw." In *The Cavalier Poets.* New York: Neale, 1911.

O'Brien, Edward J. "The Inspiration of Crashaw." *Poet-Lore* 21 (1910): 397–400.

Phillips, Peregrine, ed. *Poetry by Richard with some Account of the Author.* London: Rickaby, 1785.

Quiller-Couch, Sir A. T. "Traherne, Crashaw and Others." In *Studies in Literature First Series.* New York: Putnam's, 1918.

Tutin, J. R. *Notes and Illustrations to Crashaw's* The Delights of the Muses, Steps to the Temple, *and* Carmen Deo Nostro. Yorkshire, 1901.

Unsigned. "Particulars of Crashaw's Early Life and Writings." *Gentlemen's Magazine* 63(1793): 1001–3.

ROBERT HERRICK

Beeching, H. C. "The Poetry of Herrick." *National Review* 40 (1902–03): 788–99.

Choate, Isaac Bassett. "Robert Herrick." In *Wells of English.* Boston: Roberts Brothers, 1892, pp. 211–16.

Deshler, Charles D. *Afternoons with the Poets.* New York: Harper, 1879, pp. 133–37.

Gilson, Mary. "The Inspiration of the Pastoral Element in Robert Herrick." *Wellesley Magazine,* 8 October 1898, pp. 21–27.

[King, Richard John]. "Robert Herrick and His Vicarage." *Fraser's Magazine* 47 (1853): 103–9.

Mills, Abraham. "Robert Herrick." In *The Literature and the*

Literary Men of Great Britain and Ireland. Volume 1. New York: Harper, 1851, pp. 212–18.

Palmer, F. S. "Herrick and His Verse." *Harvard Monthly* 3 (1886): 8–13.

Weatherly, Cecil. "Robert Herrick." *Spirit Lamp*, 10 March 1893, pp. 67–71.

JOHN MILTON

Carpenter, William. *The Life and Times of John Milton*. London: Wakelin, 1836.

Darbishire, Helen, ed. *The Early Lives of Milton*. London: Constable, 1932.

Edmunds, Cyrus R. *John Milton: A Biography*. London: Cockshaw, 1851.

Garnett, Richard. *Life of John Milton*. London: W. Scott, 1890.

Hood, E. P. *John Milton: The Patriot and Poet*. London: Partridge & Oakey, 1852.

Ivimey, Joseph. *John Milton: His Life and Times, Religious and Political Opinions*. London: Wilson, 1833.

Masson, David. *The Life of John Milton Narrated in Connexion with the History of His Time*. London: Macmillan, 1859–94. 7 vols.

Raleigh, Walter. *Milton*. London: E. Arnold, 1900.

Shawcross, John T. *Milton: A Bibliography for the Years 1624–1700*. Birmingham, NY: Medieval and Renaissance Texts and Studies, 1984.

Stephen, Leslie. "New Light on Milton." In *Studies of a Biographer*. Volume 4. New York: Putnam's, 1902, pp. 86–129.

Stevens, David Harrison. *Reference Guide to Milton: From 1800 to the Present Day*. Chicago: University of Chicago Press, 1930.

Symmons, Charles. *The Life of John Milton*. London: T. Bensley, 1806.

Todd, Henry John. *Some Account of the Life and Writings of John Milton*. London: Law & Gilbert, 1809.